INTRODUCTION & CONTENTS

■ "What's New Pussycat?", as Tom Jones would holler. Well, quite a lot in this, the 16th edition of British Hit Singles. For starters, there are 20 "stories behind the songs" articles which pick the bones out of some of the most intriguing songs ever created. Also, having celebrated the 50th anniversary of the singles chart in 2002, we celebrate the 40th and 20th anniversaries of the British Invasions of the American chart with an in-depth feature. The transatlantic theme in this book goes further with statistics and graphs exploring the success of US and UK acts in each other's charts down the years.

There's more. In addition to the most up-to-date gossip and facts from the past 12 months in pop, we look back to the biggest hits from the early post-war period, enabling some of our older readers, at long last, to find the No.1 songs from their youth.

Controversially, we also take a look at all those Record Mirror, Disc and other charts from the 1950s and 60s for all of you who recall 'Please, Please Me' by The Beatles topping other charts which are not used by this book.

And what about those classic No.2 hits that never made the top spot which fail to make an appearance in our annual run-down of all the No.1s? This year we list a selection of the likes of T. Rex, David Bowie, Ultravox and Oasis suffering at the hands of Clive Dunn, Little Jimmy Osmond, Joe Dolce and Robson and Jerome.

So how can we accommodate the largest number of facts, features and charts the book has ever included? Simple: by making one major change to the main listing of hits included in the book. For the first time, we have removed all those chart re-entry lines and saved a ton of space. And that doesn't mean you have lost any vital information. Each time a single re-enters the chart it is logged and, to use the example of 'My Way' by Frank Sinatra, it carries the note (8re) which indicates that the record has re-entered the chart eight times. If they are re-entries worthy of note, we do just that with a footnote.

Still, the most important additions to this edition are the 901 new singles that entered the chart over the past 12 months. So spare a thought for UK vocalist Rick Guard's 'Stop It (I Like It)' which failed to make the Top 75 (stumbling at 76) and the pages of this book. Better luck next time, Rick.

David Roberts Editor, British Hit Singles

CHART MILESTONES

■ The 50 years of UK charts used to compile British Hit Singles have seen many transformations. Here we list some of the significant changes in chart history and events, inventions and TV and radio programmes that helped to generate so much interest in what is now the most respected pop chart in the world

The BBC Juke Box Jury panel deliberates over the next hit or miss

1952 The first UK singles chart was launched by New Musical Express. No.1 in this first Top 12 (dated 14 November) was 'Here in My Heart' by Al Martino

1953 Seven-inch vinyl 45 rpm pop singles introduced

1954 The chart became a Top 20 on 1 October

1955 BBC radio's 'Pick of the Pops', presented by Franklin Engelmann, appeared for the first time on 4 October.

Lonnie Donegan holds court on TV's '6.5 Special'

Ruby Murray became the first act to have five singles simultaneously in the Top 20. 'Rock Around the Clock' by Bill Haley and His Comets was the first rock No.1

1956 Elvis Presley began a record-breaking run of hits covering six decades and 46 years. A Top 30 was established on 13 April

1957 The first live TV show to feature rock 'n' roll acts regularly was '6.5 Special', launched on 16 February with Pete Murray and Josephine Douglas presenting

1958 Cliff Richard began a chart career that will span six decades. 'Oh Boy!' on TV and 'Saturday Club' on radio were broadcast for the first time. 'Jailhouse Rock' by Elvis was the first record to enter the singles chart at No.1

1959 Sales of vinyl 45s overtook those of 78s and David Jacobs presented the

first edition of the popular TV hit-or-miss singles review show 'Juke Box Jury' on 1 June

1960 In March the last NME Top 30 was used to compile this book when, in the week ending 5 March, data from the Record Retailer Top 50 chart replaced it

1961 'Thank Your Lucky Stars!' was launched in April with Brian Matthew, Keith Fordyce, Jimmy Savile, Pete Murray, Barry Aldis, Kent Walton, Sam Costa, Jimmy Young, Don Moss and Alan Dell among the presenters

1962 'The Young Ones' by Cliff Richard and the Shadows was the first single by a UK act to enter the chart at No.1

1963 The Beatles began a run of 11 consecutive UK chart-toppers of which five will sell more than a million copies. Chart was independently audited for

'Ready Steady Go!' presenter Cathy McGowan interviews Mick Jagger

Record Retailer. 'Ready Steady Go!' launched on 9 August with presenters Cathy McGowan and Keith Fordyce

1964 Jimmy Savile presented the first edition of BBC TV's Top of the Pops on 1 January, Beatles hold top five places on US chart

1965 British invasion of the US singles chart reached its peak when nine of the top 10 records were UK recordings

1967 BBC launched Radio 1, formerly the Light Programme

1968 Louis Armstrong, at 66 years and 187 days, became the oldest chart-topper

1969 'Je t'aime ... moi non plus' was banned by the BBC. Top 50 now compiled for Record Retailer and the BBC by the British Market Research Bureau

1970 The early period of the new decade saw singles sales dip as albums became increasingly popular. Top-earning acts such as Led Zeppelin and Pink Floyd avoided releasing singles

1973 The first year in which BPI trade delivery figures were announced saw a year's sales of singles total 54.6 million units

1975 'Bohemian Rhapsody' began a record-breaking first of four appearances at the top of the charts in a calendar year. Mike Mansfield's 'Supersonic!' TV show launched on 6 September

1977 The first 12-inch singles released in January. 'Mull of Kintyre' / 'Girls' School' became the first single to sell more than two million copies in the UK. Total sales for the year rose to 62.1 million. The first edition of The Guinness Book of British Hit Singles published

1978 Official chart expanded to a Top 75

1979 Sales of singles continued to rise with 88.1 million in 1978 and an all-time high of 89.1 million in 1979 boosted by the popularity of new wave and disco releases

1980 The new decade started with a 10 million drop in singles sales in its first year

1982 'A Little Peace' by Nicole was the UK's 500th No.1 and Channel 4 launched 'The Tube', presented by Jools Holland and Paula Yates, on 5 November

Mike Mansfield directs operations on 'Supersonic!'

Tony Blackburn 'spins' 'Flowers in the Rain' by The Move: the very first record played on BBC Radio 1

1983 Chart compilation taken over by Gallup, with 500 record outlets used

1984 A record-breaking six singles sold in excess of a million copies each, with 'Do They Know It's Christmas?' bagging 3.55 million sales to become the UK's best-selling single

1986 Jackie Wilson's 'Reet Petite' hit the top posthumously 29 years after his chart debut. Sales of singles dropped to 67.4 million, the first dip below 70 million in nine years

1987 Cassette singles introduced for the first time. The chart announcement changed from Tuesday lunchtime to Sunday evening on 4 October. MTV Europe launched on 1 August

1988 First CD singles released

1991 '(Everything I Do) I Do It For You' by Bryan Adams smashed the record for the

longest stay at No.1 with 16 consecutive weeks at the top

1992 For the first time, the CD format outsold vinyl and cassette singles in a year of change that saw an all-time sales low of 52.9 million units. The chart produced in association with the BPI and Bard became the copyright of Chart Information Network Co Ltd or CIN for short

1994 Whigfield became the first debut act to enter the chart at No.1. Millward Brown took over the chart compilation from Gallup, using a sample of 1,000 record outlets

1995 The new CD format began to boost sales, and media interest in a Blur vs Oasis chart battle for No.1 soared as sales for the year passed the 70 million mark again

1997 World and UK sales records were shattered as Elton John's 'Candle in the Wind 1997' / 'Something

The Peter Blake-designed Band Aid single sleeve

About the Way You Look Tonight' registered the biggest ever sale for a single. This increased the total singles sales figure to 87 million for the year

2000 Total sales for the year stood at 66.1 million, a drop of 14 million compared to 1999

2001 CIN changed its name to The Official UK Charts Company and the downward sales trend continued with 59.5 million singles sold in the year

2002 The UK singles chart celebrated its 50th anniversary and 'Top of the Pops' its 2,000th show. Will Young beat Hear'Say's 2001 record as the fastest-selling debut act and Elvis Presley made No.1 again 46 years after his first hit and a quarter of a century after his death

Will Young makes chart history with his first single release

Today's chart ...

The Official UK Charts Company is responsible for the commissioning, marketing, distribution and management of the UK's Official music charts. Sales information is supplied by over 5,600 retailers including all the major high street music retail chains, supermarkets, a number of internet retailers and approximately 600 independent record stores. This market research sample equates to 99% of the total UK singles market. The week's sales that contribute to the official charts are collated after the close of business on Saturday for release from noon the following day. The chart rundown at 4pm on Sundays is still the most listened-to programme on BBC Radio 1.

POP REVIEW OF THE YEAR

■ Bruno MacDonald and Sarah Brooks leave no stone unturned in their search for the juiciest of pop news stories from 2002

JANUARY

Still reeling from the demise of **Steps**, Britain extends the mourning period with the chart's first back-to-back posthumous No.1s since **John Lennon**'s twosome in 1981: **Aaliyah**'s 'More Than a Woman' and **George Harrison**'s 'My Sweet Lord'. The latter is performed in tribute by **Luther Vandross** at the American Music Awards, where **Destiny's Child**, **Alicia Keys**, **Faith Hill** and **Aaliyah** clean up and **Michael Jackson** receives his first artist-of-the-century award of the year.

*N Sync, however, endure jeers when they beat **U2** to Best Group. "Quit booing," counters **Justin Timberlake**. "**U2**'s going to get Grammys." Meanwhile, Star Wars spokes people confirm Justin and co are to appear in Attack of the Clones (they don't)... "The whole thing's a conspiracy and they are out to get me," claims **Adam Ant** after attracting the long arm of the law by brandishing a replica gun. The dandy highwayman winds up in what he brands "the Alice in Wonderland ward" of a

7,294 new singles released in 2002
7,242 in 2001

hospital... "You don't have to be mad to work here" might not be EMI's motto but **Mariah Carey**'s not looking too loopy with a reported £19m payoff. In happier news for the embattled record

company, it begins the year as it'll end it: with **Robbie** atop the album chart... **Christina Milian**, reportedly popstress of choice at Beckingham Palace, has her first hit of the year with 'AM to PM', while 'Get the Party Started' is the apposite curtain-raiser to **Pink**'s amazing year... **Hear'Say** admit **Kym Marsh** has quit... Rock fans may be unmoved by the passing of the **Black Crowes** but surely shed a tear with the engagement of **Bush**'s **Gavin Rossdale** to **No Doubt**'s **Gwen Stefani**... Mate of the **Strokes** and **Courtney**, ex of **Soul Asylum**'s **Dave Pirner** and occasional actress **Winona Ryder** begins a year as the **Ol' Dirty Bastard** of Hollywood, appearing in court on prescription drug and shoplifting charges. "She should hit Bloomingdales," advises rapper **Sticky Fingaz**...

Sugababes: 'Freak Like Me', best single of the year according to the Q awards

Boy George's semi-autobiographical show Taboo opens in London... **Nick Carter** is arrested at a Florida strip joint. The **Backstreet Boy** – whose nicknames are "Chaos" and "Mr Hyper Man" – promptly bursts into tears in front of surprised onlookers... **Cameron Crowe**'s Vanilla Sky has a fab soundtrack boasting **REM**, **Radiohead** and, as usual, the director's other half, **Heart**'s **Nancy Wilson**... Avowed vegan **Moby** threatens to eat a cat that bit him... **Brian Wilson** plays in London as the **Beach Boys**' 'Pet Sounds' enjoys a renaissance... After knocking about for years Down Under, **Puretone**'s 'Addicted to Bass' is a hit up here... **J.Lo** inspires Death Row daddy **Suge Knight** to revive his feud with **P Diddy**: "She turns around and drops you for a dancer?"... **Ronan Keating** and **S Club 7** guest as **Bryan Westlife** marries **Kerry Ex-Kitten**... **Kurrent Kitten Liz** is rumoured to be dating **Lee** of **Blue**. The latter later tells Channel 4's PopWorld, "We wuz only wiv each ovver for a short while"... 'Always on Time' and, it seems, always on the chart, **Ja Rule** and **Ashanti** begin an enviably successful year. At one point, **Ashanti** has three hits in the US Top 10 simultaneously: 'Always on Time', her own 'Foolish' and the **Fat Joe** hook-up 'What's Luv?', all of which subsequently score over here too.

The White Stripes as Lego people, in their spring 2002 'Fell in Love with a Girl' video

happened to the guys in The Clash?"... Also representing the Latin quarter is **Enrique Iglesias**: Julio Junior makes the No.1 spot his own with 'Hero', whose video stars **Jennifer Love Hewitt** and the missing-presumed-unemployed **Mickey Rourke**... Holby City star **Jeremy Edwards** proposes to **S Club** pin-up **Rachel** on Valentine's Day... 'Fell in Love with a Girl' is a hit for the **White Stripes**, who turn into Lego people for the video... **Oasis** live? "The Americans don't want it,

Pretty cool"... In a jelly-shaking month for **Nirvana**, 'Smells Like Teen Spirit' is blended with '**Bootylicious**' by **Destiny's Child**. The much MP3'd bootleg is a headline-grabbing example of the mash-up mixing that will reap dividends for the **Sugababes** and, this month, sees **Kylie** showcasing 'Can't Get Blue Monday Out of My Head' at the Brits... The Brits are otherwise notable for **Westlife**'s **Bryan** taking on **So Solid Crew**. "Very stupid" is the verdict of bandmate **Shane**. An Outstanding Achievement accolade goes to a shirtless **Sting** – but only **Robbie** really livens things up. Winning his third Best British Male award, he declares: "I'd just like to say to **Will** from Popstars: I'm too strong, buddy! I'm too big! I've got too much time under my belt! Three times! Three! And you wanna come and take this?! You wanna come and take food off my table?! That's gonna put my kids through college?! I don't think so! **Craig David** couldn't do it – what makes you think you can do it?!" **Kylie** collects a handful, while 'Can't Get You Out of My Head' finally makes her a star Stateside too... Flushed with the news that their tour was 2001's biggest, **U2** provide half-time entertainment at Stateside football fest

Single with most weeks on chart – 'Unchained Melody' Gareth Gates 27

the Super Bowl. **Bono** and the boys also win four Grammys, while **Alicia Keys** collects five... One of Brit rock's best-kept secrets, **A**, hit with 'Nothing'. Also keeping air guitarists in business are everyone's favourite new band the **Hives**, whose signature song 'Hate to Say I Told You So' is finally released as a single... **Destiny's Child** are hit by lawsuits from former members claiming the 'Survivor' lyrics violated an "anti-dissing" agreement... Still sadly missing, **Manic Street Preachers**' **Richey Edwards** is officially deceased as of 1 February 2002. What would he have made of the millions tuning in to see **Will Young** beat **Gareth Gates** in ITV's search-for-a-star Pop Idol? **Darius Danesh**, back from post-Popstars oblivion, lets slip: "I feel so sorry for whoever wins this. It's a poisoned chalice."

FEBRUARY

Gwen's back back back with **No Doubt**'s 'Hey Baby', as are fellow feisty femmes **Alanis Morissette** ('Hands Clean') and **Beverley Knight** ('Shoulda Woulda Coulda'). Trumping them all for naughtiness yet enjoying the endorsement of **Jarvis Cocker**, 'Bad Babysitter' makes **Princess Superstar** a short-lived sensation... Destined for greater things is **Shakira**, whose 'Whenever, Wherever' becomes one of the year's biggest sellers. "Hey," **Ms Mebarak Ripoll** quizzes Blender magazine (apropos of nothing as usual), "what

man," **Liam** tells Mojo. "We've been slogging the arse off it for years and I don't want it no more." Instead, **Oasis** are among the stars of a week of cancer charity gigs at London's Royal Albert Hall. Other headliners include **The Who**, whose troubled year begins with **Pete Townshend** falling off stage during the encore... "Big shout out to **Paul McCartney**," beams **Knoc-Turn'Al** after **Sir Thumbs Aloft** approves the rapper's sampling of his 'Old Siam, Sir' for the forthcoming Stateside summer release 'Muzik'... Meanwhile, **Macca** picks **John Lennon** as his hero in Mojo: "Did he ever disappoint me? Yeah, from time to time... but only infrequently." **Ash**'s **Tim Wheeler**, picking **Kurt Cobain**, remembers a pivotal **Nirvana** gig: "They came on bellydancing to **Tori Amos**'s version of 'Smells Like Teen Spirit'.

MARCH

First to taste the poison are **Westlife** whose 'World of our Own' is toppled from the chart peak by **Will**'s double A-side 'Evergreen'/'Anything Is Possible'. That's followed by **Gareth**'s 'Unchained Melody' – the song's eighth incarnation to make the UK chart, and one which replicates the chart-topping achievements of the **Righteous Brothers** and **Robson and Jerome**. But **Noel Gallagher** isn't impressed: "If some kid's working at Tesco's and he starts to make a million quid by doing all this malarkey... I'd do it. It's better than working at Tesco's. But don't call it music." He won't be buying **Rik Waller**'s 'I Will Always Love You' then... After objections from an 80s funk group of the same name, **Liberty** announce their new name: **Liberty X**... Rock rocking rock is bolstered by **Nickelback**'s chart limpet 'How You Remind Me' and **Marilyn Manson**'s contender for video of the year, 'Tainted Love'... **The Osbournes** becomes MTV's most successful premiere to date. "Oh my God, my language!" **Sharon Osbourne** tells Rolling Stone. "We were all kind of silent for a couple of days"... **Megadeth** split up, but fear not metal fans, **Paul Cattermole** is leaving S Club 7 to join nu-metal band **Skua**. "I want a change musically," he tells The Sun. The surviving sextet continue as S Club... Never much of a presence singles-wise, **Norah Jones** nonetheless begins a

successful run with the release of her 'Come Away with Me' album... **J.Lo** and **Ja Rule** hit with 'Ain't It Funny'. "I can't say I've never seen her be nasty," says **Ja** (Jeffrey Atkins to his mom) of **La Lopez**, "but we got along great"... **Hear'Say** cancel their forthcoming tour so new

Alicia Keys at the keys, in a year which saw her grab five Grammys

member **Johnny Shentall** can "settle in". **Kym**'s replacement has allegedly been chosen at a public audition but turns out to have been in minor hitsters Boom! and is engaged to Stepstress **Lisa Scott-Lee**... **Bono** appears in court to testify on behalf of **Peter Buck**. By April, the **REM**

guitarist will be acquitted of alleged airborne antics in 2001... Fancy something rude and ridiculous? Take your pick from **Ali G**'s **Shaggy**-starring 'Me Julie' or **George Michael**'s 'Freeek'... **Tiffany** poses for Playboy, which is, the 80s popstress tells MTV, "frankly just a way to slap that mall-girl stigma in the face"... **Robert De Niro** appears in London to launch the musical We Will Rock You, which he helped to produce despite being unable to name a favourite **Queen** song... In a troubled month for **Nirvana**, a mooted box set remains entwined in legal tussles between **Dave Grohl**, **Krist Novoselic** and **Courtney Love**. The last spins the unreleased 'You Know I'm Right' when she DJs at **Alan McGee**'s London club Death Disco, before diving on to the dancefloor... **Cher** says her forthcoming tour will be her last... **Leftfield** split up but dance fans are consoled by Belgian duo **Soulwax**, whose '2 Many DJs' album finishes on everyone's best-of-the-year list and introduces the **Jack White** (Stripe)-fronted 'Danger! High Voltage' by **Electric Six**... Shortly to take their place on every dance compilation are the hits 'Shake Ur Body' by **Shy FX and T-Power** and 'Lazy' by **X-Press 2**. Warbling on the latter is **David Byrne**, whose acrimony with his fellow **Talking Heads** is suspended to celebrate their induction into the Rock and Roll Hall of Fame in New York. Also in are the **Ramones** – inducted by **Eddie Vedder** and commemorated by **Green Day** – and

CHART WATCHING
Dave McAleer runs his expert eye over the 2002 chart ups and downs

■ Without a doubt, 2002 was the year of the Pop Idol. As the show neared its climax, anyone of us would have bet on Will Young, Gareth Gates and Darius being hitmakers. Will proved that anything is possible by smashing Popstar winners Hear'Say's debut single sales record, and Gareth too sold in excess of a million with his first single. Picked-by-the-public performers sold 6.5 million singles and topped the chart for 18 weeks, and the year ended with a trio of acts from Popstars: the Rivals hogging the top three positions.

The "made-in-Britain" Pop Idol/ Popstars phenomenon was also similarly successful internationally, though, oddly, winning seemed to harm rather than help an act's chances elsewhere. It appeared that you had to have been there to

appreciate the artist or record. Interestingly, Popstars runners-up Liberty X were the UK's most successful reality TV act internationally in 2002.

As prophesied in the 15th edition of British Hit Singles, 2002 was great for solo males with Enrique, Ronan Keating, Eminem and Daniel Bedingfield joining the aforementioned three Pop Idols at the top, while George Harrison and Elvis claimed two of the year's record three posthumous No.1s.

Other leading lads included Blue, Oasis, new teen team Blazin' Squad and Westlife, who set more unbreakable records. Holly Valance, Pink, Christina Aguilera and the late Aaliyah flew the flag for female soloists, while on the girl-group front Sugababes got stronger and Las Ketchup, Atomic Kitten and Girls Aloud were also

represented in the year's 30 No.1s – just one fewer than the previous year.

Single sales were down nearly 15 per cent, but revenue from their parent albums was up and all-hits compilation albums still sold in vast quantities, proving there was no drop in interest. Indeed, when you consider the record number of internet downloads and the staggering sales of blank CDRs, we can probably assume that hit singles found their way into more homes than ever before.

Free downloads are, of course, welcome, but it's obvious that the amount of new tracks available would decrease drastically if money did not find its way to the music's suppliers. The record industry pointed out that the public doesn't expect to be entertained in cinemas, theatres or

Isaac Hayes, who warns, "It's not all about bling bling"... Not so much bling bling as clang clang, one-time British Hit Singles pop review staple Ol' Dirty Bastard suffers career-worst reviews for his inconvenienced-by-incarceration album 'The Trials and Tribulations of Russell Jones'... Britney's Crossroads opens over here. "If she had a clue," opines Justin Timberlake of his ex's endeavours, "she wouldn't have made that movie, don't you think?"

APRIL

The kids are united – well, sort of. GMTV has its "Totstars" slot; Kaci and Alizee are rocking the Lolita vote and Mad Donna mix 'The Wheels on the Bus' with 'Ray of Light'. Towering over all – not literally, obviously – are S Club Juniors, who debut with 'One Step Closer'. "I quite like 'em actually," Liam Gallagher tells

CD:UK. He can afford to be generous as Oasis return to rocking form with the No.1 'The Hindu Times'... The Gallaghers' old mate Robbie duets with Faithless figurehead Maxi Jazz on

Total No.1 hits in 2002 30

1 Giant Leap's 'My Culture'... Doves launch a chart conquest with the deleted-in-a-day 'There Goes the Fear'; the Streets hit with 'Let's Push Things Forward' and Moby's back with 'We Are All Made of Stars'... For the first time since 1963, the Billboard Hot 100 features not one UK act... Norah Jones meets Keith Richards at Willie Nelson's tribute shows. "He was awesome," she tells Q. "I fell in love"... Reheated Prince tunes? Production whizzkids The Neptunes can't stop turning 'em into hits. This month's is *N Sync's Nelly-

featuring 'Girlfriend'... Blessed with a Badly Drawn Boy soundtrack, About a Boy opens in cinemas, as do 24 Hour Party People, the film of the Factory Records saga, Bend It Like Beckham, featuring ex-All Saint Shaznay Lewis, and Queen of the Damned, starring Aaliyah.... Sade collects an OBE for services to music. It is, she says, "a great gesture to me and all black women in England". Also picking up honours is Serge Gainsbourg's panting pal Jane 'Je t'aime' Birkin... This month's Next Big Thing is Michelle Branch with 'Everywhere'. "I'm not a big fan of Madonna's music," Mich says of her Maverick label boss. "I'd much rather listen to the Beatles"... Paul McCartney is made an honorary detective by the NYPD. "So," Macca reports for Q, "when I smelt some weed in the crowd... I was able to announce that I would shortly be

at live concerts for free, so why should recorded entertainment be different? When you consider that reportedly two out of every five records sold worldwide are illegal, and that the music business lost around $4.2bn in 2001 alone, you can understand why the industry is investing so heavily in trying to get people back into the buying habit.

The sales of British acts are improving internationally, although Robbie Williams was the only UK representative in either of the year's European Top 10 singles or albums lists. The media made much of the fact that, for the first time since 1963, there were no British acts in the US Hot 100 for a few weeks in 2002. They forgot to mention, or were unaware, that US record sales are at their lowest since the Great Depression of the 1930s (they dropped another 61.5 per cent this year) and all the average

single needed to sell to reach No.1 was 10,000. In the UK it was nearer 100,000. It's the US album chart that counts and, although this wasn't a great British year, UK acts were never absent.

What does the future hold in store? Obviously the three Rs – rap, R&B and rock – will still thrive, and maybe we'll see the return of the singer/ songwriter. The interest in Asian beats should grow and it could be the year of the "The" groups or skater punk. The early years of a decade often find a new "sound of the underground" surfacing, so this next 12 months might give us the "Sound of the Noughties". And who's to say it won't emanate, as before, from the UK? Perhaps next year's Chart Watching will be all about the third British Invasion of America.

Boasting the most implausible ingredients for a smash since the heyday of **Flat Eric**, the **Sugababes** blend a minor 1995 **Adina Howard** hit and **Tubeway Army**'s 1979 No.1 'Are 'Friends' Electric?' to produce arguably the year's finest chart-topper, 'Freak Like Me'. "**The Sugababes** were great to work with," producer **Richard X** tells worldpop.com. "And, beautifully, had no idea who **Gary Numan** is"... With equal success, albeit slightly less invention and far fewer clothes, **Holly Valance** kangaroos from Neighbours to No.1 with 'Kiss Kiss' (descendant of a song that's gone round the world in various guises)...

coming into the audience and busting some people"... **Kid Rock** proposes to **Pamela Anderson**... Jay-Z and R Kelly almost top the US album chart with 'The Best of Both Worlds' but alleged sexploits

request for psychiatry made by her **Nirvana** enemies would "serve no purpose other than to contribute a circus-like atmosphere"...

New chart entries in 2002 **901**

by **Kelly** mean he spends more time in court than in the charts. **Jay** promptly seeks solace in the arms of **Beyoncé**... **Chris Martin** headlines an Oxfam-backed campaign to promote fair trade. He's also rumoured to believe **Coldplay**'s forthcoming album is so good that they should quit while they're ahead ("**S Club Juniors** – they produced most of it"). Indulging no such silliness, Parlophone points out the group has signed a five-album deal and is staying put... In a medical month for **Nirvana**, **Courtney** is spared a sanity test. A judge rules the

US cult phenomenon **Phish** star on **The Simpsons**... **Kylie** kicks off her European tour in Wales. Meanwhile, organisers of a London charity auction withdraw a pair of hotpants from sale after failing to confirm they'd ever been worn by **Her Minogueness**. "We can't verify whether these pants are authentic or not," admits a spokeswoman.

Holly Valance: from Neighbours to No.1

Pink damns Britney in the lyrics to her No.6 smash hit single, 'Don't Let Me Get Me'

Andrea Corr (79th), Alicia Keys (80th), Myleene Hear'Say (84th), Dido (87th), So Solid's Lisa Maffia (91st), Pink (95th) and Mis-Teeq's Alesha (98th); the last, rues FHM, "sadly already bagged by Harvey from those naughty boys So Solid Crew"... Fleeing the troubled So Solid circle, Ms Dynamite bids for fabdom with 'It Takes More'... Marilyn Manson's bassist Twiggy Ramirez bids adieu to his boss... At the dangerously junior end of the spectrum, Charlotte Church is voted "Rear of the Year"... At the veteran end, Bob Dylan tours the UK... Ozzy hosts the rainsoaked Ozzfest and enjoys dinner at the White House. "Ozzy," announces President Bush, "Mom loves your stuff"... The Sex Pistols cash in on the Jubilee with a re-released 'God Save the Queen'... The Queen of Pop, Madonna, begins her West End stage run in Up for Grabs... Speaking of Queen, British Hit Singles readers voted 'Bohemian Rhapsody' their favourite single of all time, and BHS editor David Roberts presented Brian May and fellow Rhapper Roger Taylor with an award to mark the achievement... Cher guests in Will and Grace and the Samantha Mumba-starring The Time Machine opens at cinemas, as does Nick Broomfield's provocative Biggie and Tupac... Sir Elton brands Hear'Say "the ugliest band in

Ex-Stepstress Faye Tozer, tracked by a fluffy mic at the 2002 British Hit Singles book launch

Rounding off a busy month atop the chart, Ronan warbles 'If Tomorrow Never Comes' and Liberty X slink to success with 'Just a Little'... 'Can't Get You Out of My Head' wins three Ivor Novello awards. "I needed to pay the bills," explains co-writer Cathy Dennis. Meanwhile, Kylie splits from James Gooding. "Contrary to media reports," says a stern statement, "there is and never has been any truth to marriage, pregnancy or infidelity stories"... "Now is the time," announces Alanis, "to be experimenting with sexuality." Allegedly experimenting with Enrique Iglesias, Anna Kournikova tops FHM's 100 Sexiest Women in the World poll. The top pop babes on the list are S Club's Rachel (2nd), Hannah (17th) and Tina (56th), Britney (3rd), J.Lo (4th), Kylie (6th) and Dannii (29th), Holly Valance (8th), Shakira (9th), Louise (22nd), Beyoncé (26th), ex-Stepstresses Lisa (57th), Claire (55th) and Faye (62nd), Sophie Ellis Bextor (60th), Anastacia (65th), Christina Aguilera (67th), Jenny Kitten (68th), Christina Milian (77th),

Total singles sales in 2002 **44 million**

51.2 million in 2001

pop"... Mark Westlife is reported to have stopped swooning over Mariah long enough to woo Cathy from Bellefire. Curiously, Bellefire's cover of U2's 'All I Want Is You' is out the same week... Westlife help to make Lulu's 'Reload'-style 'Together' the most successful album of her career, but, for only the second time in their catalogue to date, 'Bop Bop Baby' fails to top the chart (despite Vinnie Jones in the video)... An "incredibly happy" Mariah signs to Island/Def Jam... Alien Ant Farm's tour bus crashes in Spain, killing their driver... The month's most-discussed lyric is Pink's reference to "Damn Britney

Spears" in 'Don't Let Me Get Me'. "She's completely terrified," suggests the Pinkstress, "or she just gets it"... Hit hip hop comes courtesy of Missy Elliott's protégée Tweet, with 'Oops (Oh My)', and this month's Neptunes number: the Busta Rhymes/P Diddy showdown 'Pass the Courvoisier Part II'... "Pass the ice" is what Jay of Jamiroquai might be saying after a scuffle with a photographer outside a London hotel leaves him with a bloody nose... Widespread bootlegging obliges the release of Eminem's 'The Eminem Show' album to be brought forward... In a jubilant month for Nirvana, Hole split up.

JUNE

An unlikely trio tops the chart. Eminem's first with 'Without Me', whose video boasts porn star Jenna Jameson, Dr Dre as Batman, himself as Osama bin Laden and, fuelling one of the year's more pathetic feuds, a dig at Moby... Will

Young's next, returning his Pop Idol showstopper 'Light My Fire' to the UK chart for the first time since the Mike Flowers Pops scraped the Top 40 in 1996... Showing these whippersnappers how to do it properly, Elvis begins a month at the summit with his 18th UK No.1 'A Little Less Conversation', albeit with a little help from remixer JXL (tactfully abbreviated from his customary tag Junkie XL). It's the first time Elvis has been remixed since 1985's 'The Elvis Medley' which was, Presley archivist Ernst Jorgensen tells Blender, "in the tradition of 'Stars on 45'. It was a terrible idea"... Brian May opens the Party at the Palace, playing 'God Save the Queen' atop Buck House. Usual suspects from Will Young to Sir Paul are wheeled out, with Ozzy striking the oddest note. On being invited, Sharon O wonders, "What can we nick?" then rues Kermit's

intrusion into a royal photo op with her hubbie: "He gets to meet the Queen of England with a ******* frog on his shoulder"... As the world goes footie mad, 'On the Ball' by Ant and Dec and a re-mixed 'Hey Baby' by DJ Otzi prove even the charts aren't immune... As the world goes Spider-Man mad, Nickelback's Chad Kroeger hits with

2002 biggest seller: 'Anything Is Possible' / 'Evergreen'

'Hero' (no relation to Enrique's). More radio-friendly rock comes courtesy of The Calling's 'Wherever You Will Go'... With an acting CV consisting of an Emmerdale cameo last Christmas, Wet Wet Wet's Marti Pellow joins the cast of West End musical Chicago... LL Cool J stars in the remake of Rollerball... Scooter deliver terrifying Teutonic techno with 'The Logical Song'... Michael Jackson visits Britain, airing his woes with Sony and appearing at Exeter City

Football Club – sadly, in an honorary rather than sporting capacity... Michael's mucker Diana Ross plays London's Hyde Park with Ronan and Rod Stewart... Rod reappears at the Glastonbury festival, while Robbie cavorts with his ex, Rachel Hunter. (The pair are soon splashed over tabloid front pages.) Other Glasto headliners include Stereophonics and Coldplay. The latter's Chris Martin is promptly linked to backstage ligger Natalie Imbruglia. "Coldplay have got a big heart," she tells Q. Elsewhere on the bill, Queens of the Stone Age boast the drumming of one D Grohl, who's also guitaring on Bowie's best received album for yonks, 'Heathen'... In a paternal month for Nirvana, their legacy is invested in New Zealand newcomers The Vines, who hit with 'Get Free'... Noel Gallagher brands Kylie "a demonic little idiot" in an OK! magazine interview.

1,783,919

Brian May gets the Queen's jubilee pop concert under way on top of Buckingham Palace

2002 BEST SELLERS

Figures supplied by the The Official UK Charts Company

1. **EVERGREEN/ ANYTHING IS POSSIBLE**
   Will Young   1,783,919

2. **UNCHAINED MELODY**
   Gareth Gates   1,329,740

3. **HERO**
   Enrique Iglesias   689,279

4. **DILEMMA**
   Nelly featuring
   Kelly Rowland   659,662

5. **A LITTLE LESS CONVERSATION**
   Elvis vs JXL   634,364

6. **ANYONE OF US (STUPID MISTAKE)**
   Gareth Gates   573,125

7. **WHENEVER, WHEREVER**
   Shakira   554,756

8. **THE KETCHUP SONG (ASEREJE)**
   Las Ketchup   538,591

9. **JUST A LITTLE**
   Liberty X   487,037

10. **WITHOUT ME**
    Eminem   486,138

Meanwhile, **Oasis** object to the British Army's use of 'Wonderwall' and 'Hello' on a recruitment video. A Ministry of Defence spokesman says, "We didn't realise we needed permission to use the songs."... **Atomic Kitten** film a Home and Away cameo... At a New York gig that **Rolling Stone** votes 2002's Best Moment in Music, **The Hives** perform in front of a black and white Stars and Stripes and **Howlin' Pelle Almqvist** announces he'll be the next president... **Posh** parts company with Virgin... **Macca** marries **Heather Mills**; **Peter Gabriel** is reported to have married his girlfriend **Meah Flynn** and **Morleigh Steinberg** becomes Mrs **The Edge** after bellydancing into the guitarist's affections on **U2**'s Zoo TV tour a decade ago... **Weezer** enlist the **Muppets** for a video shoot... This month's **Neptunes** hits are **No Doubt**'s 'Hella Good' and **Nelly**'s 'Hot in Herre', whose superfluous consonant strrikes a chorrd with **Christina Aguilera**. "She's talented though," concedes **Nelly**. "The girl can blow"... While her '**Full Moon**' hits the UK chart, **Brandy**'s Special Delivery airs on Stateside TV. "Who wants to see her weird ass giving birth?" demands **Kelly Osbourne**... **Love**'s **Arthur Lee** is invited to **Parliament** when MP **Peter Bradley** motions to have 'Forever Changes' declared "the greatest rock album of all time"... '**Britney**'s Dance Beat' hits computer game consoles... "She doesn't really have it all together," **Eminem** reportedly says of alleged ex-squeeze **Mariah**. **Ms Carey** later ripostes, "I did not date him. Is that clear enough?"... The newly knighted

Atomic Kitten's September release was 10th in the 2002 Chart Stayers list

2002 CHART STAYERS

By weeks on chart and peak positions. 75 points for a week at No.1, 74 for a week at No.2 and so on, down to one point for one week at the bottom chart position of No.75

1. **HOW YOU REMIND ME**
   Nickelback   1,138

2. **HERO**
   Enrique Iglesias   1,087

3. **WHENEVER, WHEREVER**
   Shakira   1,068

4. **UNCHAINED MELODY**
   Gareth Gates   991

5. **JUST A LITTLE**
   Liberty X   914

6. **WITHOUT ME**
   Eminem   899

7. **THE LOGICAL SONG**
   Scooter   876

8. **IF TOMORROW NEVER COMES**
   Ronan Keating   860

9. **EVERGREEN/ANYTHING IS POSSIBLE**
   Will Young   849

10. **THE TIDE IS HIGH (GET THE FEELING)**
    Atomic Kitten   841

Sir Mick Jagger admits, "I've been teased. I've had people on their knees, and I've even had plastic swords waved at me."

JULY

Finally displacing **Elvis**, **Gareth Gates** scores his second No.1 of the year with 'Anyone of Us (Stupid Mistake)'... Madame Tussaud's third and raunchiest re-creation of **Kylie** is unveiled in London: the waxwork is posing on all fours... "I know about **Kylie** and **Robbie** and Pop Idol and stuff like that," announces **David Bowie**. "You can't get away from that when you hit the shore, so I know all about the cruise ship entertainment aspect of British pop"... Back back back but briefly, **Prodigy** reheat 'Firestarter' for 'Baby's Got a Temper', although the Rohypnol lyric and revolting video attract more attention than the music... Marijuana shares plummet as **Snoop Dogg** cleans up his act. "I've smoked enough sticky-icky-icky," he claims, "to keep me high for three lifetimes"... Reportedly getting jiggy are **Janet Jackson** and **Justin Timberlake**. Or are they drumming up drama for their duet on **Just**'s forthcoming album? By next month he'll be dating actress **Alyssa Milano**... Meanwhile, **Britney** cuts short the final show of her world tour. "I'm human too," she wails. "I get mad like everyone else"... "I would never have dreamed," admits **Darius**, "when I did a godawful cover of a Britney Spears song, two years later I'd be head to head with **Britney** in the charts." But that's what's what when his 'Colourblind' is released on the same day as her 'Boys'. The latter is one of this month's **Neptunes** hits, the others being **Beyoncé**'s 'Work It Out' – like 'Boys', from the **Beyoncé**-starring Austin Powers in Goldmember – and **N*E*R*D**'s 'Rock Star'... This month's **Human League** hit is 'Love Action', aka **George Michael**'s controversy-courting 'Shoot the Dog'. Meanwhile, Heat moots a **Wham!** reunion... This year's **Gay Dad** are **Fischerspooner**. **Bowie** puts them on at his **Meltdown** festival; **Kylie** works with them and enough people believe the hype for 'Emerge' to scrape the chart... **Red Hot Chili Peppers** score their biggest UK hit with the title track to one of 2002's finest albums, 'By the Way'... After making the US chart her own, **Vanessa Carlton** tinkles 'A Thousand Miles' into our Top 40... **P Diddy** and **Usher** team up for 'I Need a Girl' and **Primal Scream** are back with 'Miss Lucifer'... **Mick Taylor** and **Bill Wyman** are rumoured to be guesting on the **Stones**' forthcoming tour. "Who said that?" demands **Ron Wood**. "**Mick Taylor and Bill Wyman**," wheezes Keef. And why are they charging more than **Macca**? **Keef** again: "There's more of us"... Fousands of **Fatboy Slim** fans lay waste to Brighton at Captain Cook's second Big Beach Boutique. "I've created a monster," he admits... Meanwhile, Ibiza has a quiet year. Top choon? **Tim Deluxe**

(ex **Double 99**) featuring **Sam Obernik**, say many, with 'It Just Won't Do'... "Why'd they have to find it in my bum, of all places?" grimaces **Sharon Osbourne** when she's diagnosed with cancer. "It's

Most weeks at No.1 in 2002 4

'Hero' – Enrique Iglesias
'Unchained Melody' – Gareth Gates
'A Little Less Conversation' – Elvis vs JXL

embarrassing"... A car crash puts a dent in **Oasis**'s US tour. "If this was 1995 and I was selling lots of records, then I'd be getting loads of good wishes," grumbles **Noel**. Their UK tour stops off in Scotland for the T in the Park festival, where **Starsailor**'s **James Walsh** recklessly incurs the irritation of both brothers... **Hear'Say** flee a service station on the M1 after a man brandishes a fake gun... **Dolly Parton**'s 'Halos and Horns' album includes a cover of 'Stairway to Heaven'... One month after **John Entwistle** dies on the eve of **The Who**'s latest US tour, **Pete Townshend** stops dedicating shows to the bassist: "It's not working, he hasn't shown up."

AUGUST

Darius makes a good start on fulfilling his platinum predictions by knocking **Gareth** off No.1. "I always knew he was gonna be the geezer," **Liam Gallagher** tells CD:UK. "I was like, that guy, man – he's 'avin' it." Among those **Darius** beats to the top are his idols **Coldplay** with 'In My Place'. "He deserves to be No.1," admits **Chris Martin**, "cos I acted like a **** when I met him"... Next up at No.1 are the **Sugababes** with 'Round Round',

before **Blazin' Squad** – a sort of **So Solid Crew** meets **S Club Juniors** – take their version of **Bone Thugs-N-Harmony**'s 'Tha Crossroads' to the top... **Abs** revisits **Althia and Donna**'s 'Uptown Top Ranking' to hitmaking effect on 'What You Got' and spills the beans on his former bandmates from **Five**. "**Sean**'s got a newsagent," he tells Popworld. "**Rich** is training to become a Kwik-Fit man and **J** I believe, is selling flowers, 10 for three pound." He also denies

Red Hot Chili Peppers enjoy their biggest UK hit, taken from the album of the same name

romance with both **Suzanne Hear'Say** ("It's nuttin' deep") and **Heidi Sugababe** ("We're not looking for a house together yet or anything")... **Kym Marsh** marries EastEnders bod **Jack Ryder**, but invites Liberty X rather than **Hear'Say** to the wedding... **Paul Oakenfold** hits with the love-it-or-hate-it 'Starry Eyed Surprise' featuring **Shifty Shellshock** of **Crazy Town**, and **Romeo** scores with

Look wot they dun. The University of Wolverhampton honours Slade

'Romeo Dunn'. The **So Solid** star shares a name with the forthcoming baby Beckham, who debuts in September... **Stereophonics** headline the V festival, as they always do. Elsewhere on the bill are **N*E*R*D**, aka – ta da! – the **Neptunes**. This month's **Neptunes** hit – Stateside anyway – is 'Grindin'' by **Clipse**... In a mixed month for **Nirvana**, the **Foos** headline the Leeds and Reading weekenders (alongside the **Strokes**, **Prodigy** and **Guns N' Roses**). **Krist** reports there is "goodwill" with **Courtney** and **Dave** declines an interview with a BBC reporter at the Kerrang! awards because "I just want to hang out with my girlfriend and my mom" ... Hard-of-hearing people turn up to a Hull club playback of the **Queens of the Stone Age** album 'Songs for the Deaf'. "They didn't see the funny side and left straight away," reports the Spiders venue... A belated UK release for the 'Melody AM' album makes **Röyksopp** this year's **Air**... **Robbie** evicts a cybersquatter from a contested website after complaining to the UN. The culprit was using the address to point people towards an **Oasis** site. Meanwhile, **Robbie** and **Bob the Builder** are reported to be joining forces for the Jeans for Genes appeal organised by the Great Ormond Street Children's

Hospital... Amid predictions of **Pulp**'s demise, **Jarvis** wins Celebrity Stars in Their Eyes with a **Rolf Harris** impersonation... **Will Smith**'s back on the big screen in Men in Black II, while Disney moots a remake of Freaky Friday starring **Kelly Osbourne**... **Will Young** performs at the Commonwealth Games' closing ceremony in Manchester, as do **Dave Stewart**, **Jimmy Cliff**, **Heather Small** of **M People**, **Ms Dynamite**, **Toploader** and, doubtless much to Her Majesty's pleasure, hip hop god **Grandmaster Flash**... **Slipknot**'s **Corey Taylor** – last heard on the Spider-Man soundtrack – and **Joey Jordison** launch side projects **Stone Sour** and **Murderdolls**, and finish the year predicting the demise of the 'knot... A mix-up at the MTV Video Music Awards makes **Michael Jackson** think that a birthday cake from **Britney** is actually another artist-of-the-millennium award. Accepting three awards, **Eminem** is greeted by jeers, which he attributes to **Moby**: "Keep booing, little girl. I will hit a man with glasses"... **Bowling for Soup** hit with 'Girl All the Bad Guys Want', largely due to a video which spoofs nu-metallers and features a girl bending down a lot... While **Oasis**'s UK tour sells out in hours, their US jaunt is

jeopardised when **Noel** forgets his passport. The American embassy saves the day... Single of the month for many is **Truth Hurts**' 'Addictive' – featuring **Rakim** and masterminded by **Dr Dre** – although its sample of the 20-year-old song 'Thoda Resham Lagta Hai' by Indian artist **Lata Mangeshkar** will later provoke a multi-million-dollar lawsuit.

SEPTEMBER

Looking oddly venerable next to **Blazin' Squad**, **Atomic Kitten** knock the east London urchins off No.1 with their **Blondie**-lite bonanza 'The Tide Is High (Get the Feeling)'... Rather more robustly, **Pink** challenges **Oasis** for the year's rockingest No.1 with the boss bitchfest 'Just Like a Pill'. With parent album 'M!ssundaztood' rarely far from the upper reaches of the chart, the former **Alecia Moore** becomes the biggest-selling woman of the year, if not the happiest. "I'm grumpy, all right," she tells Blender. "I'm Grumpy Smurf..." Also heading pop off at the pass are **Black Rebel**

Quomen Parfitt and Rossi returned to the Top 20 for the first time since 1990

Motorcycle Club, who hit with 'Whatever Happened to My Rock 'n' Roll (Punk Song)', Bon Jovi, who bounce back with 'Everyday', and Feeder, who 'Come Back Around' after the suicide of drummer Jon Lee... Straddling the rock/pop divide are Appleton with 'Fantasy', Kelly Osbourne with 'Papa Don't Preach', Alanis's spiritual heir Avril Lavigne with 'Complicated' and Blink 182's grandchildren Busted with 'What I Go to School For'... Slade go to school for fellowships when they're honoured by the University of Wolverhampton... While the Stones set off on a Stateside tour, Madonna's mate Mirwais covers their 1978 smash 'Miss You'. It's the song's second revamp of the year, following Dr Dre's makeover for the Goldmember soundtrack... Moby plays the Ramones' 'Blitzkrieg Bop' at a gig for Radio 1... The astronautical aspirations of *N Sync's Lance Bass are dashed by a dispute over the spaceflight fee... Marilyn Manson exhibits his paintings in LA. "I'm afraid," art critic Matthew Collings tells Q, "this art stuff he's doing is a total waste of everyone's time"... Marc Bolan is immortalised in a bronze bust, unveiled in London to mark the 25th anniversary of his death... Status Quo launch their 'Heavy Traffic' album with a gig on HMS Ark Royal. "We've got the spark back," Francis Rossi tells Mojo... "Norm is on board," reports Alex James of Blur's Fatboy-enhanced new album. Not on board is going-going-gone guitarist Graham Coxon. Meanwhile, dust off the handbags: Liam is mocking

Damon Albarn's anti-war efforts. "Ridiculous," ripostes the Blurster... Liam proposes to Nicole Appleton while Gwen Stefani marries Gavin Rossdale in London and LA. "We didn't want to impose on anyone," explains Gav...

Damon Albarn laughs off Liam Gallagher's jibes about his anti-war activities

"What, would you go a year without washing?" is among the teasers on The Strokes' spoofing 'Someday' video which pits them against Guided By Voices on a game show. The Strokes join Courtney as she fronts MTV2 for 24 hours, while also on a screen near you – if, that is, you live in Wales – is Stereophonics drummer Stuart Cable's show Cable

Shakira 790,000

Best-selling female singles act in 2002

TV... Cartoon Network creates an animated video for the Sugababes after the trio provides the Powerpuff Girls movie theme. "The Powerpuff Girls are

really wicked," says Keisha. "We might even get them to do security for us"... Ms Dynamite enjoys success with the irresistible 'Dy-Na-Mi-Tee'... Coldplay's 'A Rush of Blood to the Head' tops the UK album chart and is a smash Stateside too. "No words can express the joy of being in Coldplay," Chris Martin tells Radio 1. "Let me just translate it by this sound: wheeeeeeee"... Kelly Clarkson, winner of the Stateside version of Pop Idol, conquers the US singles chart with 'A Moment Like This'. American Idol judge Paula Abdul remains at war with co-panellist Simon Cowell: "The only sexual tension is the fact that his pants are so tight." Meanwhile, Popstars: the Rivals kicks off over here. The aim? To staff a girl group and boy band. The judges? Pete Waterman, Westlife's manager Louis Walsh and, to the incredulity of Liam Gallagher, Geri Halliwell: "How can Geri Halliwell ever turn round and say, 'You're rubbish'?"

OCTOBER

October kicks off with Will 'n' Gareth's 'The Long and Winding Road'/ 'Suspicious Minds' and Las Ketchup's 'The Ketchup Song (Asereje)' so let us merely record that they topped the chart and proceed quickly to Nelly and Kelly Rowland's divine 'Dilemma' which sees the St Louis star unite with the Destiny's Child dame for a No.1 on both sides of the Atlantic... Hear'Say split up, blaming abuse from "people in the street"... Having finally persuaded Larry Mullen to take a lead role in a video, **U2** return with 'Electrical Storm'. **Mullen**'s co-star is **Samantha Morton**, who's also spotted at a gig by plucky punksters **The Libertines**... **Madge 'n' Guy**'s movie Swept Away opens Stateside to, reports Rolling Stone, "tears of joy from grateful cinéastes who had run out of Glitter jokes"... This month's **Neptunes** hits are **Justin Timberlake**'s 'Like I Love You' and **LL Cool J**'s 'Luv U Better'. LL also co-hosts, with **Mis-Teeq**'s **Alesha**, the Mobo awards, where **Ms Dynamite** cleans up... UK hip hop hopes are invested in **Big Brovaz**, who score with '**Nu Flow**'... **Britney** is caught with **Nick Carter**; **Kelly Osbourne** hooks up with **The Used**'s **Bert McCracken** and **Beyoncé** is reportedly now engaged to **Jay-Z**... **Pete Waterman** admits in BBC Music magazine that many of his hits came from classical works. The Guardian promptly devotes inches to **Johann Pachelbel**, whose 'Canon in D' inspired 'I Should Be So Lucky'... Lucky-lucky-lucky is **John Otway**, who spurs his fanbase to make '**Bunsen Burner**' a Top 10 smash. It's originally scheduled to compete with **Elvis's** 'Burning Love' but, reports **Otway**,

"Elvis's record company chickened out. It's a bit of a shame as I was looking forward to that battle"... While **The Strokes** support the **Stones**, **Celine Dion**'s plan to call her Las Vegas show "Muse" is scuppered by the band of the same name... **Prince** plays rare UK shows... **John Lennon**'s assassin **Mark Chapman** is refused release for the second time... Soldiering on despite locking his keys in the car, **Gary Numan** graces the Q awards to present Best Single to the **Sugababes**. "We're not **Atomic Kitten**," announces **Keisha**. More metal goes to **Echo and**

the **Bunnymen**, **The Hives**, **Tom Jones**, **Electric Soft Parade**, **Jimmy Cliff**, **Moby**, **Depeche Mode**, **Radiohead**, **Pink** and **Coldplay**... In a star-studded month for **Coldplay**, **Ms Dynamite** and **Noel Gallagher** join **Chris Martin** at a London gig for Oxfam, while **Gwyneth Paltrow** turns up at Wembley and gets 'In My Place' dedicated to her... The **So Solid**-sized **Polyphonic Spree** are this month's **Fischerspooner**, collecting more column inches than cash for their '**Hanging Around**'... **Ryan Adams** stops a show in Nashville when a fan shouts out for **Bryan Adams**' 'Summer of 69'... **The Manics** return with 'There By the Grace of God' and **David Gray**'s 'A New Day at Midnight' beats **Gareth Gates** to the top of the album chart... **Eve** plays a "sexy tomboy, a tough chick" in xXx... A mooted movie of The Magic Roundabout is to feature **Kylie** as Florence and, as **Dougal**, **Robbie Williams**... Meanwhile, **Robbie** signs a new deal with EMI reported to be worth up to £80m. "I wanna continue to break records and make records with EMI!" says **the Robster**. "I thought of that all by myself"... In a similarly money-making month for **Nirvana**, their best-of is finally released and **Foo Fighters**' 'All My Life' is a hit trailer for the chart-topping album 'One By One'. "These kids today," **Mr Grohl** mourns. "They look at me like I'm Neil Young. **Nirvana** is the band their parents listen to."

NOVEMBER

A house cover of **Bryan Adams**' hit 'Heaven', you say? By an act calling itself **DJ Sammy and Yanou featuring Do**? Excellent! Please proceed straight to No.1... Sanity of sorts is restored by **Westlife** with 'Unbreakable', then **Christina Aguilera** with **Redman**, ace arseless chaps and 'Dirrty'. **Aguilera**'s banned-in-Thailand video is promptly spoofed by Buffy's **Sarah Michelle Gellar** on Saturday Night Live: "When people see this video, they gonna stop thinking of me as some blonde-haired, bubblegum music industry ho and start thinking of me as an actual ho." The Official UK

Chart Company hosts a shindig at the British Library to celebrate the golden anniversary of the hit parade. MC for the evening, former British Hit Singles co-author **Paul Gambaccini** sees at least one-fifth of a way towards the next half-century: "Five years from now we should have a chart that incorporates – and indeed is downloaded by – internet hits from around the world."... Celebrating the 10th anniversary of a riot-torn Canadian gig, chaos greets the cancellation of a **Guns N' Roses** show in Vancouver. Still no sign of their album though. "Try holding your breath for Jesus," advises **Axl**. "I hear the pay-off may be that much greater"... **Take That** heart-throb **Mark Owen** wins Channel 4's Celebrity Big

Brother, while **Myleene Hear'Say** breaks down on The **Frank Skinner** Show... **Missy Elliott**'s back with 'Work It', as are **Shania Twain** with 'I'm Gonna Getcha Good!' and **Soundgarden** screecher **Chris Cornell** plus **Rage Against the Machine**'s ones who aren't the singer as **Audioslave**... "Absolute and total shock" is **Victoria Beckham**'s reaction to the arrest of nine people for allegedly conspiring to kidnap her... In a mad month for **Nirvana**, the Dave Grohl-drummed 'No One Knows' is a hit for

Queens of the Stone Age; **Tenacious D** tell Q that "in another world **Dave Grohl** would probably be an actor"; **TD**'s video director **Liam Lynch** strikes out with 'United States of Whatever' and **Kurt Cobain**'s journals are published... In a madder month for **Robbie**, he talks to Radio 1 about his ex **Nicole Appleton**'s abortion revelation ("I was completely behind her because secrets can make you sick"), beats **Oasis**'s record for Knebworth ticket sales and sees 'Escapology' become 2002's fastest selling album... "I got caught up in the excitement of the moment," apologises **Michael Jackson** after dangling his baby son from a Berlin hotel window. Adding to his woes, an unflatteringly close-up photograph from a California courtroom becomes a mucho-downloaded internet image... One-time Jacksons teenybop rival **Donny Osmond** rises from the ashes with an ITV1 An Audience with..., a cover of 'Puppy Love' by **S Club Juniors**, 'One Bad Apple' on the Anita and Me soundtrack and his own hit album

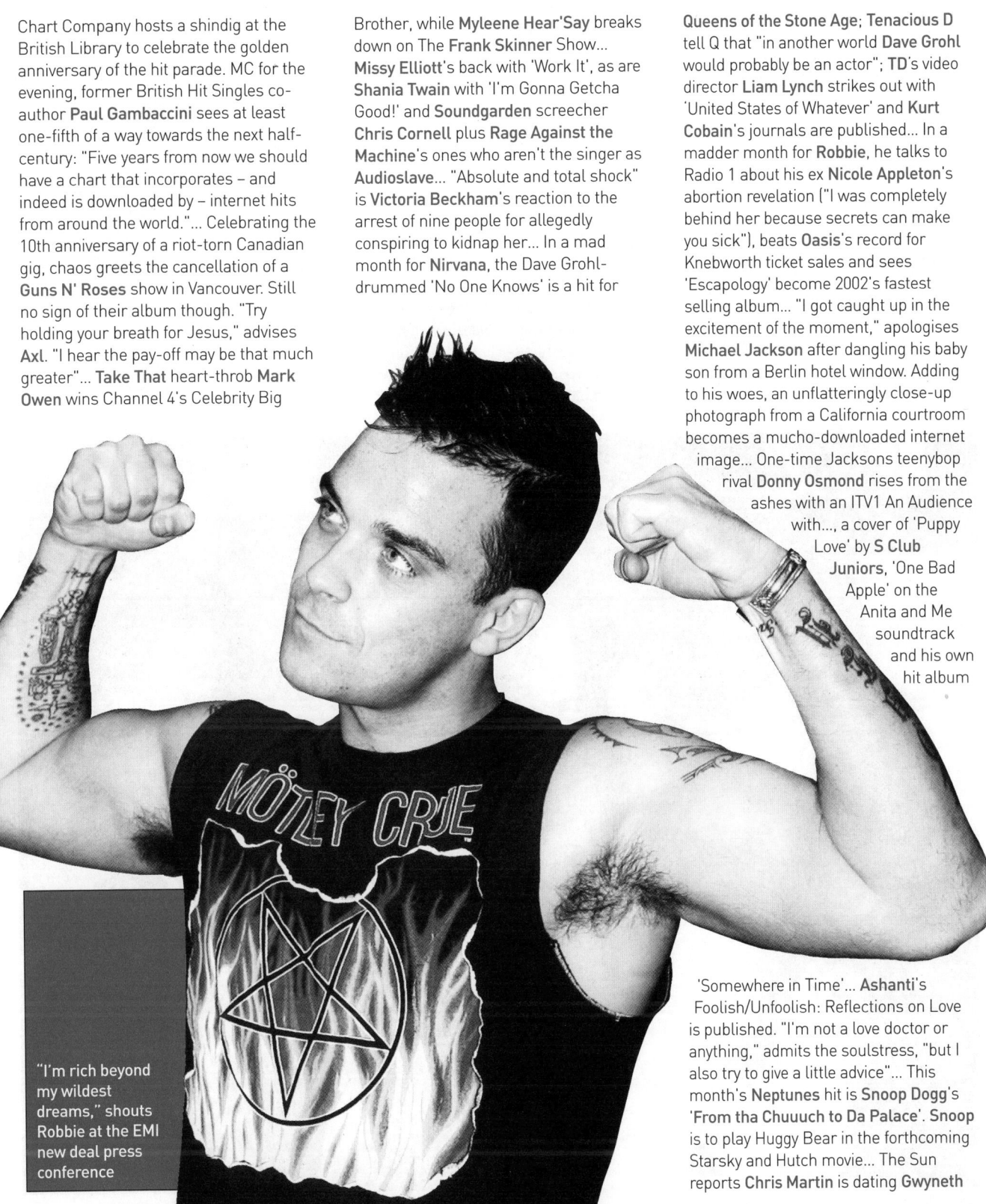

"I'm rich beyond my wildest dreams," shouts Robbie at the EMI new deal press conference

'Somewhere in Time'... **Ashanti**'s Foolish/Unfoolish: Reflections on Love is published. "I'm not a love doctor or anything," admits the soulstress, "but I also try to give a little advice"... This month's **Neptunes** hit is **Snoop Dogg**'s 'From tha Chuuuch to Da Palace'. Snoop is to play Huggy Bear in the forthcoming Starsky and Hutch movie... The Sun reports **Chris Martin** is dating **Gwyneth**

Paltrow. "This is all very weird," he says, "because she's a big Hollywood star and I'm just the bloke from **Coldplay**." Meanwhile, **J.Lo**'s flashing her engagement ring from **Ben Affleck**... **Heidi Sugababe** reportedly collapses at a nightclub. "**Heidi** hadn't had a square meal all day," insists a Sugababes spokesperson, "and was feeling very faint"... Music lovers feel very faint when **Britney** takes on 'I Love Rock 'n' Roll'... **a1** are alleged to have split... **Mick Jones** joins **Joe Strummer** to play **Clash** classics at a London charity gig. Sadly, despite a mooted reunion for their 2003 induction into the Rock and Roll Hall of Fame, this will be the duo's last ever performance together... **Eminem**'s movie

8 Mile attracts Oscar nomination nods. "Which would be cool," quips Rolling Stone, "solely for the sight of **D12** getting into a backstage scuffle with **Dame Judi Dench**'s posse." **Em** also wins big at the MTV Europe Music Awards. Fellow winner **Moby** says, "I have nothing but peace and respect for **Eminem**." The show's hosted by **P Diddy**, wearing a tribute T-shirt to **Run DMC**'s slain DJ **Jam Master Jay**... "We're retired," announces **Reverend Run** in the wake of **Jay**'s killing in October. "Does anybody have a job out there?" Meanwhile, Adidas announces a highly sought after limited-edition JMJ trainer... **Marilyn Manson** appears in **Michael Moore**'s movie Bowling for

Columbine... **Elvis Costello**, **Lenny Kravitz**, **Tom Petty**, **Mick 'n' Keef** and **Brian Setzer** go to rock 'n' roll fantasy camp courtesy of **The Simpsons**... **Sir Elton** is inducted into the Top of the Pops Hall of Fame at the show's awards in Manchester. "We had this huge fight," says **Moby** of **Elt**. "We were beating each other with cricket bats." **Will Young, Kylie** and **Ms Dynamite** don't go home empty-handed... **Madge** meets Her Maj at the royal premiere of Die Another Day, the Bond movie for which she appears uncredited and provides the No.3 hit, 'Die Another Day'. Playing a fencer means **Madonna** gets to tell the current 007, **Pierce Brosnan**, "You handle your weapon well..."

Girls Aloud come over all emotional when presented with their No.1 award by Davina McCall

DECEMBER

A year after 'Gotta Get Thru This' busted from his bedroom to the top of the chart, **Daniel Bedingfield** returns to No.1 with 'If You're Not the One' and is rumoured to be appearing in Sabrina the Teenage Witch... **Eminem** follows him with 'Lose Yourself', then **Blue** celebrate a chart-topping version of **Elton John**'s 'Sorry Seems to Be the Hardest Word', featuring the Piano Player himself. **Elton**'s 'Don't Let the Sun Go Down on Me' helps **David Sneddon** to win the BBC's search for a star, Fame Academy. He and runner-up **Sinead Quinn** also duet on 'I Guess That's Why They Call it the Blues'... In more 70s-style shenanigans, **Atomic Kitten** adapt ELO's 'Last Train to London' for 'Be with You'... Triumph and tragedy for **Girls Aloud**: the Popstars: the Rivals victors beat the boys ("**One True Voice**? Who came up with that name? It's awful. It sounds like a church choir or something" – **Jenny Kitten**) to Christmas No.1 with 'Sound of the Underground' and even enjoy the endorsement of wicked website popbitch.com. British Hit Singles presents the fresh-faced five-piece with an official BHS award to recognise their

Elton and Blue's fruitful recording partnership looks unlikely to last beyond their Christmas No.1 smash, 'Sorry Seems to Be the Hardest Word'

Kylie, **Will** and **Gareth** top the bill at the Royal Variety Performance in London. The **Prince of Wales** tells **Kylie** they "must stop meeting like this" after she had, at his behest, graced the Morecambe and Wise tribute The Play What I Wrote a few days before... **Charlie** of **Busted** admits texting **Heidi Sugababe** with an appreciative message about her rear... "This next one is for my teeth," announces **Liam** as the **Oasis** tour kicks off in Cardiff. He's recently undergone surgery to replace two front teeth lost in a Munich barney...

Will Young 2,520,000

Best-selling male singles act in 2002

chart-smashing achievement. But their tour manager **John McMahon** is tragically killed in a car crash on Christmas Day... Beatle bother: "This is very petty," grumbles **Yoko Ono** via her lawyer when **Paul McCartney** reverses the traditional "**Lennon/McCartney**" writing credit for **Beatles** tracks on his 'Back in the US' live album... In a triumphant month for **Nirvana**, 'Nevermind' tops Q readers' 100 Greatest Albums Ever poll... **Duran Duran** fans are accused of hijacking a Virgin Radio poll of the best British acts of all time... Twig-thin Transylvanian twins the **Cheeky Girls** strike terror into the heart of the chart with 'The Cheeky Song (Touch My Bum)'...

Myleene Hear'Say is to record a classical solo album: "It will just be me and a piano"... Mucho-hyped metallers **The Datsuns** crashland in the UK... **Liberty X** head for Bosnia to entertain the troops... Runaway winners of the VH1 "You Kiss Your Mother With That Mouth?" and "Strange But True" awards, honouring best swearing and best reality show, respectively, are **the Osbournes**. **Sharon**'s attempt at thanks is derailed when she inadvertently gets rid of her gum on her speech. **Mrs O** does, however, make an alternative Queen's speech for Channel 4. "2002 has been a very weird year," she concludes. "I wish the English many sunny days."

BRIT HITS IN THE USA

The British Invasion and the pre-Fab Four years

■ UK acts may be having a thin time in the US charts currently but here chart consultant Dave McAleer reports on the acts that first made an impression Stateside and two periods in pop history when British pop crossed the Atlantic to dominate the Billboard charts.

In the Victorian era, British entertainers were held in high esteem in the US. In fact, many Americans considered that performers from "The Old Country" had more "class" than their own home-grown talent. Even then, it was not unusual for British singers, tempted by the big money, to take the long voyage across the Atlantic to entertain their "colonial cousins".

In the 1890s, the first decade of recorded music, no artist outsold Belfast-born George J Gaskin, who gave the world such favourites as 'After the Ball' and 'When You Were Sweet Sixteen'. Similarly, Oldham's own Ada Jones (who relocated to Philadelphia at the age of six) was the most popular female singer in the US in the first 20 years of the 20th century. Her name may not ring too many bells but some of her hits might: 'By the Light of the Silvery Moon', 'What Do You Want to Make Those Eyes at Me For' and 'Shine on Harvest Moon'.

Music hall's most celebrated Scotsman, Sir Harry Lauder, who was famous for top tunes such as 'Stop Your Ticklin' Jock' and 'Roamin' in the Gloamin', also sold a lot of cylinders in the pre-First World War years. Nonetheless, by the early 20th century, Americans were

EARLY UK HITS IN THE US

DATE OF CHART ENTRY – PEAK POSITION – SONG – ACT

Best-sellers

15/02/47	2	LINDA – Ray Noble and His Orchestra with Buddy Clark
06/12/47	3	I'LL DANCE AT YOUR WEDDING – Ray Noble and His Orchestra with Buddy Clark
31/01/48	4	NOW IS THE HOUR – Gracie Fields
22/05/48	14	YOU CAN'T BE TRUE DEAR – Vera Lynn
03/07/48	19	YOU CAN'T BE TRUE DEAR – Dick James
14/08/48	6	UNDERNEATH THE ARCHES – Primo Scala
28/01/50	16	WEDDING SAMBA – Edmundo Ros
01/12/51	10	CHARMAINE – Mantovani and His Orchestra
21/06/52	1	AUF WIEDERSEH'N SWEETHEART – Vera Lynn and Chorus
25/10/52	9	YOURS – Vera Lynn
23/05/53	13	THE SONG FROM THE MOULIN ROUGE (WHERE IS YOUR HEART) – Mantovani and His Orchestra
30/05/53	6	(TERRY'S THEME FROM) 'LIMELIGHT' – Frank Chacksfield and His Orchestra
05/09/53	2	EBB TIDE – Frank Chacksfield and His Orchestra
05/12/53	9	OH, MEIN PAPA – Eddie Calvert
01/05/54	4	THE HAPPY WANDERER – Frank Weir with His Saxophone, Chorus and Orchestra
18/09/54	10	CARA MIA – David Whitfield with Mantovani, His Orchestra and Chorus
07/04/56	8	ROCK ISLAND LINE – Lonnie Donegan
12/08/57	7	RAINBOW – Russ Hamilton
31/03/58	2	HE'S GOT THE WHOLE WORLD (IN HIS HANDS) – Laurie London

Hot 100

12/01/59	10	MANHATTAN SPIRITUAL – Reg Owen
02/02/59	13	THE CHILDREN'S MARCHING SONG (NICK NACK PADDY WACK) – Cyril Stapleton
16/02/59	5	PETITE FLEUR (LITTLE FLOWER) – Chris Barber Jazz Band
31/07/61	18	MY KIND OF GIRL – Matt Monro
28/08/61	5	DOES YOUR CHEWING GUM LOSE ITS FLAVOUR (ON THE BEDPOST OVERNIGHT) – Lonnie Donegan
02/10/61	8	LET'S GET TOGETHER – Hayley Mills
24/02/62	2	MIDNIGHT IN MOSCOW – Kenny Ball
14/04/62	1	STRANGER ON THE SHORE – Mr Acker Bilk
22/09/62	20	SILVER THREADS AND GOLDEN NEEDLES – Springfields
29/09/62	5	I REMEMBER YOU – Frank Ifield
24/11/62	1	TELSTAR – Tornados
30/11/63	3	YOU DON'T HAVE TO BE A BABY TO CRY – Caravelles

providing most of the world's popular music with UK acts taking a back seat on the pop music bandwagon – a place they held until the Beatles-led British Invasion. It wasn't all doom and gloom for Brit hits in the first half of the century. Between the wars sophisticated British orchestras such as those of Ray Noble, Ambrose, Henry Hall, and the up-and-coming Mantovani had successful singles.

The first official US Best Selling Singles chart was launched in July 1940, but it was not until London-born LA resident Ray Noble clicked with a couple of Top 10 entries in 1947 that any British act made a mark – and then they both featured US vocalist Buddy Clark. A good year for UK acts was 1948, with Top 20 entries by Gracie Fields, Primo Scala, Vera Lynn and Dick James (yes, The Beatles' and Elton John's music publisher). However, don't get the impression that this was an early British invasion. In 1948 a US musicians' union strike meant that no recordings could be made there and, therefore, record companies had little choice but to promote records from the most commercial of the other English-speaking countries. When the strike ended, interest in British vocalists waned and the only Top 20 entries over the next three years came from the orchestras of (Trinidad-born British citizen) Edmundo Ros and (Italian-born British citizen) Mantovani.

In 1952, just months before the NME launched the first UK Hit Parade, Vera Lynn became the first UK artist to top the US chart, when 'Auf Wiederseh'n Sweetheart' held the No.1 slot for nine weeks – a record no UK act bettered until 1981. All of the British entries in the US Top 20 between the launch of the UK chart (14 Nov 1952) to the first Beatles chart entry (18 Jan 1964) are included in this list. It shows that, apart from Dame Vera and Hull's big-voiced

The aptly named British export Laurie London, who as a 13-year-old reached No.2 in the US chart

David Whitfield (assisted by Mantovani), the only other big UK hits in America in the pre rock 'n' roll years were from instrumental acts: Frank Chacksfield, Eddie Calvert and Frank Weir – the last with a record that failed to chart in his homeland.

Lonnie Donegan was one of the first rock-orientated acts to score Stateside; he and fellow newcomer Elvis Presley were simultaneously in the Top 10 in 1956. British vocalists managed only one Top 10 single in 1957 and 1958. Interestingly, the former, 'Rainbow', which made a pot of gold for the Liverpool singer/songwriter Russ Hamilton, was the overlooked B-side of his No.2 hit 'We Will Make Love' in his homeland. The UK's 1958 winner, 13-year-old Laurie London's 'He's Got the Whole World in His Hands', which topped the US Cash Box chart, stalled outside the UK Top 10. The last year of

the decade was also the best for British records in the US, with three singles sitting simultaneously in the US Top 20 in February. Yet again they were all by instrumental outfits.

In 1961 three British vocal singles reached the US Top 20, two of which (Hayley Mills and Lonnie Donegan) could be categorised as novelty recordings. The following year, two of Britain's leading trad jazz acts Acker Bilk and Kenny Ball had huge hits there, but they did not herald the start of any similar craze in the land where that style of music had originated. That same year also saw the first Top 20 hit by a UK vocal group, The Springfields, and the first No.1 by a group, The Tornadoes (another instrumental). In

THE AMERICAN PERSPECTIVE from Fred Bronson

■ The first hint of the British Invasion came in the summer of 1963. Los Angeles Top 40 station KRLA had hired a new DJ named Casey Kasem. The station was playing the Vee Jay single 'From Me to You' by The Beatles, and Kasem explained they were as popular in England as The Four Seasons were in America. "Wow," I thought, "that big?" Six months later, 'I Want to Hold Your Hand' became the first song to debut at No.1 on the KRLA Tune-Dex. Soon the station was playing singles by Dave Clark Five, The Searchers and The Hollies. As 1964 rolled on, Americans couldn't get enough of the British. We dressed like the Brits and wore our hair longer and went around saying words like "fab" and "gear".

As a budding journalist, I started writing for the station's newspaper, the KRLA Beat, and also got a job in my local record store in Culver City, California. We had another store next to a hotel at LA airport, and one day in 1965 the manager called and told me Herman's Hermits were at the pool in the hotel and I should rush over and interview them. I grabbed a tape recorder and introduced myself to the five long-haired guys sitting around the pool. I asked if I could interview them, and they said yes. A few minutes into the interview, I realised that Peter Noone was not present, and it started to dawn on me I was NOT interviewing Herman's Hermits. But whom was I talking to? I hadn't asked any questions that gave my ignorance away, but I knew I had to get them to mention the name of one of their songs so I would know who they were. Finally, in response to one query, one of the guys

Fred Bronson is the author of 'The Billboard Book of Number One Hits' and 'Billboard's Hottest Hot 100 Hits' and writes the Chart Beat column in Billboard

mentioned 'Heart Full of Soul', and I realised I was in the middle of an interview with the Yardbirds, including Keith Relf and Jeff Beck.

the year leading up to the first real British Invasion, eight UK singles cracked the US Top 100 but only one of them reached the Top 20: 'You Don't Have to Be a Baby to Cry' by girl duo The Caravelles. It exited the Top 20 as 'I Want to Hold Your Hand' by The Beatles rocketed into the Top 100 on 18 Jan 1964.

Statistically speaking, in the first nine years of rock music (1955-1963), of the 1,187 singles to reach the US Top 20 only 1.25 per cent originated in Britain (a figure that increased to 26 per cent in 1964). In truth, British acts at that time did not seriously consider the possibility that they might have a US hit when they

recorded, as a British entry in the Top 100 was so rare at that time that the UK music media handed out plaudits to any act that could manage to reach even the lower rungs. Among the acts to achieve that lesser feat were Cliff Richard, Marty Wilde, Anthony Newley, Helen Shapiro, Charlie Drake and Hogmanay hero Andy

Chart-toppers by UK-born acts in the US 1952-2002

■ Here are the US chart-topping singles by UK-born acts for each year starting from 14 November 1952. Any act bigger than solo is included if half or more of its members are UK born

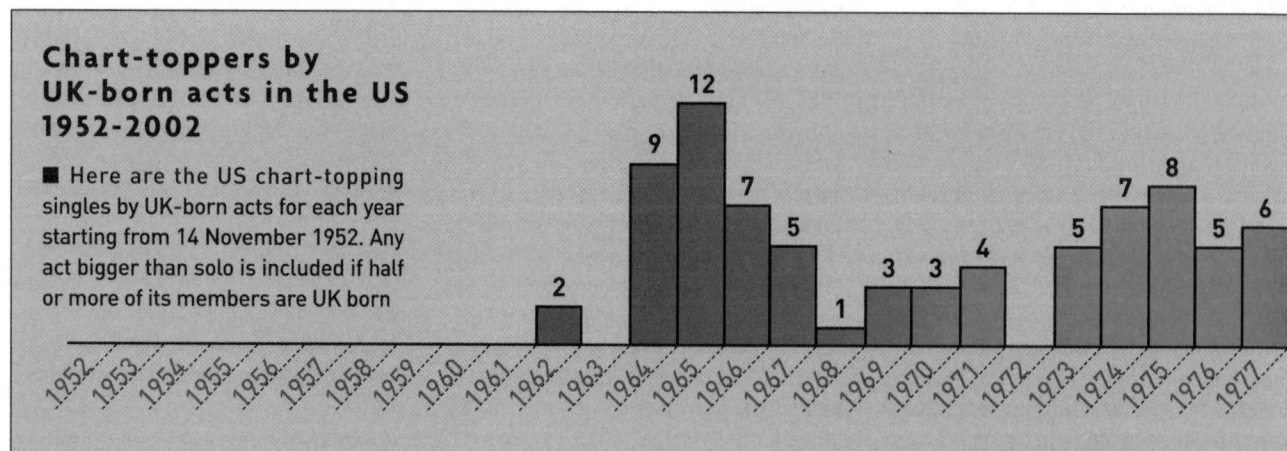

The Beatles: the most important factor in the mid-60s British music invasion of the US

IN MARCH 1964, THE BEATLES HAD THE US TOP 3 SINGLES; IN APRIL THEY HOGGED THE WHOLE TOP 5 AND HAD 14 TRACKS IN THE TOP 100 AND IN MAY HAD THREE OF THE TOP 4 ALBUMS AS WELL

Stewart. Interestingly Frankie Vaughan, The Beverley Sisters, Bob Sharples, Ron Goodwin, Lord Rockingham's XI, Mike Preston, Betty Smith and Knightsbridge Strings all managed Top 100 placings with songs that failed to click in the UK.

Forty years ago, it was by no means a foregone conclusion that The Beatles, or any of the British "beat boom" brigade, would be successful in the US; history showed quite the opposite. Merseybeat (a term which encompassed all the groups coming out of the lively Liverpool music scene) was a huge musical craze in the UK, as had trad jazz and skiffle been previously – and there was no reason to think that its impact overseas would be any stronger. UK acts might have had the odd hit in the US, but a long-term career there was considered completely out of the question. Among the British records that fell by the wayside in America in 1963 were three singles and an album by The Beatles.

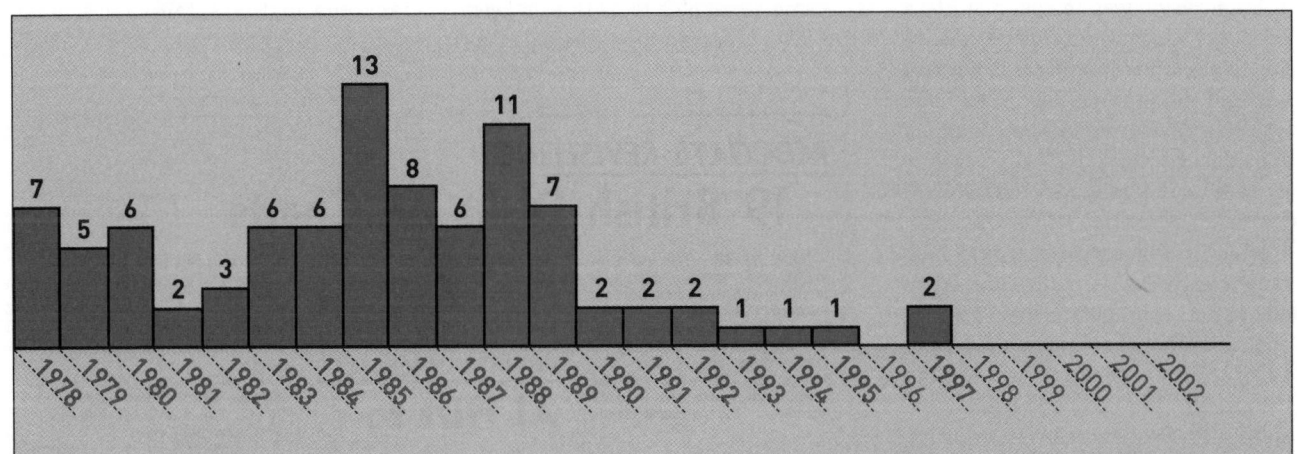

'Please Please Me' had received some radio support but sales there were minimal, and The Beatles' UK chart-topper 'From Me to You' came a poor second in the US to a cover version by Del Shannon, the two reaching positions 116 and 77 respectively.

The British music industry did not expect Beatlemania to be repeated in the US. However, EMI and the group's manager Brian Epstein had confidence in their charges. They invested an astonishing $50,000 (around $1m in today's money) into the promotion of 'I Want to Hold Your Hand'. The first battle of the invasion was to convince EMI's US outlet, Capitol Records, to release the single in the first place. (They had rejected the previous four.) The hope was that the American media would consider the story of Beatlemania in Britain to be newsworthy, and of interest to a normally insular US public. This all-or-nothing publicity attack on America was as carefully planned as any battle. Even before their first US chart entry the group received saturation coverage in top-selling magazines Time, Life and Newsweek, and British Beatlemania was shown on

the CBS and NBC TV news as well as the top-rated Jack Paar TV show. Added to this, unprecedented double-page adverts were taken in most music magazines. This media onslaught helped to convince the celebrated TV show host Ed Sullivan to book them for two consecutive shows, despite the fact that he did not think they had the potential to break in the US, and wondered if his $3,000 payment to them had been well spent.

The hype not only worked, but it was also far more successful than anyone could have anticipated. 'I Want to Hold Your Hand' entered the Hot 100 at No.45 on 18 Jan 1964 and was topping the charts when a record-shattering 73 million Americans watched The Beatles on their first Ed Sullivan TV show appearance on 9 February. This single was replaced at the top by a re-issued 'She Loves You' and then by 'Can't Buy Me Love', whose 1.7 million advance orders broke the US record. In March 1964, the Beatles had the US Top 3 singles; in April they hogged the whole Top 5 and had 14 tracks in the Top 100 and in May had three of the Top 4 albums as well.

The barriers that previously prevented British acts from progressing in the US were instantly broken down and it became a real plus to be British. Every US label searched their catalogues for

previously overlooked UK records, and fought each other over the rights to current UK hits. Battalions of Brits followed The Beatles into charts that year including No.1 hitmakers Peter and Gordon, The Animals and Manfred Mann. In 1964, UK records spent 24 weeks at the top and 49 singles reached the Top 20 – compared to a grand total of 31 in the previous 24 years of the charts (1940-1963). Many British bands even shot up the charts with "friendly fire" – songs written and originally recorded by Americans. In the past, British cover versions would not even merit a release, but now they were outselling the original recordings. You could say that the battle was well and truly over by Independence Day when UK acts held five of the Top 10 chart placings. Billboard summed the year up by saying: "This was undoubtedly the greatest year in the history of the UK record industry ... Great Britain has not been as influential in American affairs since before the American revolution in 1775!"

British artists continued to rule the airwaves in the US in 1965, with chart-toppers from The Beatles, Petula Clark, Rolling Stones, Dave Clark Five and Manchester bands Freddie and the Dreamers, Wayne Fontana and the Mindbenders and Herman's Hermits. In fact, the last was the year's most successful band Stateside, even

THE 1980s INVASION INCLUDED FAR MORE ORIGINAL SONGS THAN ITS 1960s EQUIVALENT AND, UNLIKE THE EARLIER INVASION, IT DID NOT SLOW DOWN AFTER A COUPLE OF YEARS ■

Chartbeat

U.K. Toppers Swarm Over U.S. Chart

By PAUL GREIN

(Continued on page 57)

The increasing interaction between British and American pop singles charts is dramatized this week, with each of the top five singles spots the States occupied by an act that's hit No. 1 in the U.K. within the past year.

Irene Cara ("Flashdance") topped the British chart last July with "Fame"; Cul...

googoo's "Too Shy," which hit No. 1 in Britain in February, is up to 15; **Duran Duran's** "Is There Something I Should Know," No. 1 in the U.K. in March, is up to 32; **New Edition's** "Candy Girl," No. 1 in Britain in May, climbs to 48; **Michael Jackson's** "Billie Jean," No. 1 in both countries in March, dips to 70; and **Dexy's Midnight Runners'** "Com..." also No. 1 in bo... co...

man League hit No. 1 in both co... tries last year with "Don't You V Me."

★ ★ ★

Motown Surge: Several Mot albums are streaking up the chart the wake of the surprisingly st ratings racked up by the labe cent 25th anniversary special "... #1 Hits From 25 Years"...

claiming two US No.1s that were considered "too British" to be released in their homeland: 'Mrs Brown You've Got a Lovely Daughter' (with a staggering 600,000 advance orders it entered the Hot 100 at a record-breaking No.12 position) and 'I'm Henry the VIII, I Am'. Arguably, the invasion reached its peak on 8 May when nine of the Top 10 US singles were "made in Britain". However, by the end of the summer of 1965, American acts were fighting back. British acts still continued to rack up hit after hit over the next 18 months, with more than 300 UK singles reaching the US Top 100 between 1964 and 1966. As the NME's Derek Johnson put it: "Rest assured we shall never return to the dark days of not long ago when the appearance of a British disc on the American charts was regarded as a fluke."

The Second Invasion

Although British acts had less chart presence between 1967 and 1982 there was never a year in which fewer than a dozen UK singles climbed into the Top 10. It was therefore understandable that the media considered the "second British invasion" to be relatively less newsworthy, and the public was under the impression that it was less successful than the first one 20 years

earlier. Nothing could be further from the truth. In May 1982, "First British Invasion" veteran Paul McCartney (with Stevie Wonder) had topped the chart, but it was not until electro pop pioneers Human League headed the lists in July that the "second invasion" really got under way. Once their new synth-led sound was accepted by Americans, it quickly opened the doors for such similar programmed-pop bands as ABC, A Flock of Seagulls and Soft Cell, whose debut hit 'Tainted Love' broke the longevity record on the Hit 100 with a vast 43-week run.

MTV and American record buyers were looking for exciting new sounds presented by video-genic artists. British bands such as The Fixx, Naked Eyes, Spandau Ballet, Culture Club and Duran Duran fitted the bill perfectly, and were among the UK artists that put 34 singles into the Top 10 in 1983.

There was also room at the top end of the US charts for Adam Ant, Madness and Kajagoogoo. Add to this No.1 hits by Dexy's Midnight Runners, David Bowie, Police, Eurythmics, Bonnie Tyler and Paul McCartney (this time with Michael Jackson). Unlike the first invasion, this time there were also troops from other parts of Europe and Australia in action on the charts. In June 1983, for the first

time more than half of the entries in the US Hot 100 (including 60 per cent of the Top 40) were by acts from outside America, and in August a record 37 per cent of the Top 100 records were by British artists. Yet again, being a British act was a real plus and American rock fans could not get enough of the sounds from this side of the Atlantic. A UK record company head happily noted: "US companies are now actively chasing UK acts, and we are back again to the days of big advances."

Although the number of UK records to crack the US Top 10 dropped slightly in 1984, Culture Club, Phil Collins, a revitalised Yes, Duran Duran and newcomers John Waite (whose earlier band The Babys had also been far more successful Stateside than in their homeland) and Wham! achieved chart toppers, while first-time Top 20 entrants included Wang Chung, Thompson Twins, Billy Idol and the successful comedian and TV star and singer Tracey Ullman.

It should be noted that the 1980s invasion included far more original songs than its 1960s equivalent and that, unlike the earlier invasion, it did not slow down after a couple of years. In fact, 1985 and 1986 were almost as successful as 1983. An American record company head bemoaned: "US radio and MTV are to blame for playing UK music in preference to our home-grown artists and the success of British bands is detrimental to local acts."

The phenomenally successful Phil Collins added a further three US No.1s to his tally in 1985, as did Wham!, while Tears for Fears and Duran Duran scored two apiece and Dire Straits and Anglo-American outfit Foreigner scored their first chart-toppers. In addition, Top 20 British newcomers Simple Minds, Paul Young and John Parr also contributed to the 25 weeks which UK acts spent in the top spot. Among the other notable UK chart newcomers in 1985 were Frankie Goes To Hollywood, Julian Lennon (a second-generation British invader) and Duran Duran off-shoots Arcadia and Power Station.

Never shy about self-promotion, Culture Club spearheaded the second British invasion in 1983 with the transatlantic No.1 'Karma Chameleon'

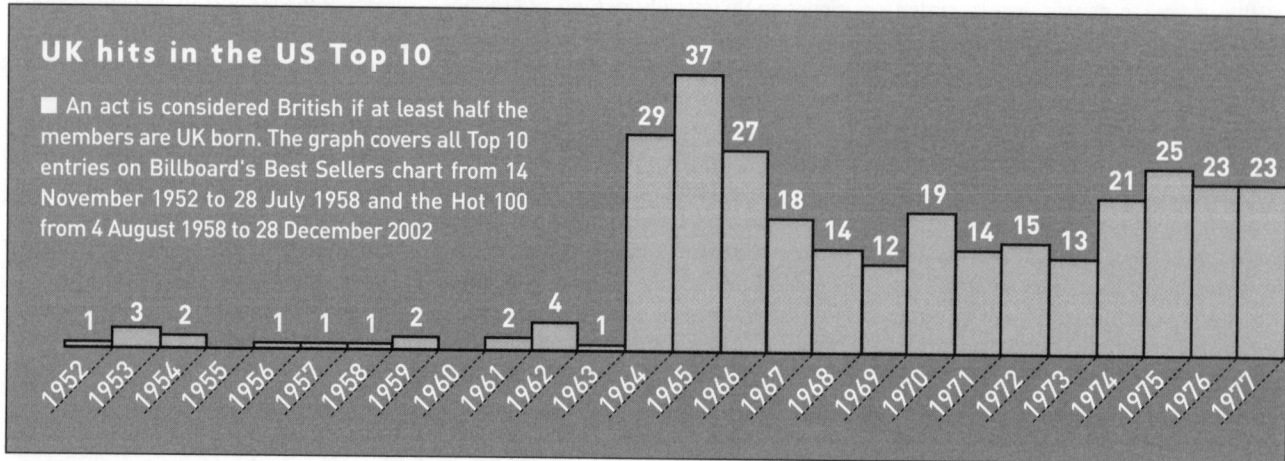

UK hits in the US Top 10

■ An act is considered British if at least half the members are UK born. The graph covers all Top 10 entries on Billboard's Best Sellers chart from 14 November 1952 to 28 July 1958 and the Hot 100 from 4 August 1958 to 28 December 2002

Year	Value
1952	1
1953	3
1954	2
1955	
1956	1
1957	1
1958	1
1959	2
1960	
1961	2
1962	4
1963	1
1964	29
1965	37
1966	27
1967	18
1968	14
1969	12
1970	19
1971	14
1972	15
1973	13
1974	21
1975	25
1976	23
1977	23

Only four times in history have British acts amassed 30 or more US Top 10 entries in a year and three of those occurred between 1983 and 1986. The eight UK acts that held the top position in 1986 included such diverse Top 10 debutants as Robert Palmer, Pet Shop Boys, Simply Red and Peter Gabriel, while Genesis, Bananarama and Steve Winwood all clocked up their first chart-toppers, with the last British No.1 of the year Stateside aptly coming from the act that kickstarted the invasion, Human League.

It should be noted that 1987 and 1988 were also excellent years for the Brits, with another 17 No.1s being added to the country's total. You will see from the graph below that in 1990 the number of UK entrants to reach the US Top 10 in the year dropped below 20, and since 1992 no one year has had as many as 10 entries. Understandably, there was a lot of media attention given to the state of British records in the US in 2002 since this millennium has seen the worst performances since the late 1950s. However, who would bet against the Brits coming back with a bang? And if our British influence goes in 20-year cycles then we are just about due the third invasion.

TOP UK ACTS IN THE US

■ Here is a run-down of the best of British exports since the UK chart began in 1952. This Top 20 is calculated by the number of US chart-toppers, then No.2 peak positions and No.3s to separate any ties

Pos / Act	No.1 Hits	Weeks at top	No.2 Hits	No.3 Hits
1. BEATLES	20	59	4	2
2. PAUL McCARTNEY	9	30	2	2
3. BEE GEES	9	27	0	2
4. ELTON JOHN*	8	30	4	1
5. GEORGE MICHAEL**	8	18	1	0
6. ROLLING STONES	8	17	2	2
7. PHIL COLLINS	7	15	1	1
8. OLIVIA NEWTON-JOHN	5	18	0	4
9. ROD STEWART***	4	20	0	1
10. ANDY GIBB	3	13	0	0
11. WHAM!	3	8	0	2
12. GEORGE HARRISON	3	6	1	0
13. UB40	2	8	0	0
14. QUEEN	2	7	1	0
15. JOHN LENNON	2	6	1	2
16. TEARS FOR FEARS	2	5	1	1
17. STEVE WINWOOD	2	5	0	0
18. DURAN DURAN	2	4	2	3
19. HERMAN'S HERMITS	2	4	1	1
20. PETULA CLARK	2	4	0	2

Just failing to make the Top 20, here are the only other UK acts to have secured two US chart-toppers: Human League, David Bowie, Rick Astley, Leo Sayer, Ringo Starr, Simply Red and Fine Young Cannibals

* Not including No.1 as a quarter of Dionne Warwick and Friends
** Including one Wham! No.1 where he got label billing
*** Includes No.1 as part of the trio Bryan Adams, Rod Stewart and Sting

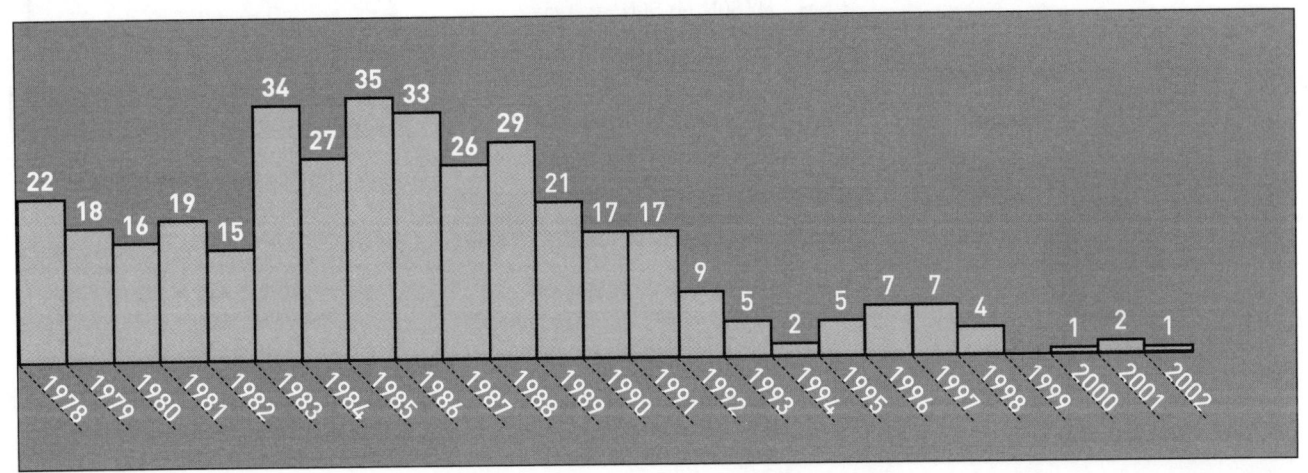

THE 946 NO.1 HITS

■ Fifty years of UK No.1 singles are listed here, in chronological order with the song title, name and the weeks it spent at the top. Readers wishing to pinpoint what was No.1 on a particular day should note that the dates listed below are the end of a particular song's first week at the top spot, as chart tradition decrees. Therefore, if the date which interests you is 20 Jan 1953, 'Comes A-Long A-Love' by Kay Starr would have been No.1. For more help, visit our website at www.britishhitsingles.com which lets registered users search for the No.1 on any particular date. The Christmas No.1 is the last single listed each year.

1952

14 Nov **HERE IN MY HEART** Al Martino **9**

1953

16 Jan **YOU BELONG TO ME** Jo Stafford **1**
23 Jan **COMES A-LONG A-LOVE** Kay Starr **1**
30 Jan **OUTSIDE OF HEAVEN** Eddie Fisher **1**
6 Feb **DON'T LET THE STARS
        GET IN YOUR EYES** Perry Como **5**

■ 1952: Here in My Heart

13 Mar **SHE WEARS RED FEATHERS**
        Guy Mitchell **4**
10 Apr **BROKEN WINGS** Stargazers **1**
17 Apr **(HOW MUCH IS) THAT DOGGIE IN
        THE WINDOW** Lita Roza **1**
24 Apr **I BELIEVE** Frankie Laine **9**
26 Jun **I'M WALKING BEHIND YOU** Eddie
        Fisher featuring Sally Sweetland **1**
3 Jul **I BELIEVE** Frankie Laine **6**
14 Aug **SONG FROM THE MOULIN ROUGE**
        Mantovani and His Orchestra **1**
21 Aug **I BELIEVE** Frankie Laine **3**
11 Sep **LOOK AT THAT GIRL**
        Guy Mitchell **6**
23 Oct **HEY JOE!** Frankie Laine **2**
6 Nov **ANSWER ME** David Whitfield **1**
13 Nov **ANSWER ME** Frankie Laine **8**
11 Dec (equal top for one week)
        ANSWER ME David Whitfield **1**

1954

8 Jan **OH, MEIN PAPA** Eddie Calvert **9**
12 Mar **I SEE THE MOON** Stargazers **5**
16 Apr **SECRET LOVE** Doris Day **1**
23 Apr **I SEE THE MOON** Stargazers **1**
30 Apr **SUCH A NIGHT** Johnnie Ray **1**
7 May **SECRET LOVE** Doris Day **8**
2 Jul **CARA MIA** David Whitfield
        with Chorus and Mantovani
        and His Orchestra **10**
10 Sep **LITTLE THINGS MEAN A LOT**
        Kitty Kallen **1**
17 Sep **THREE COINS IN THE FOUNTAIN**
        Frank Sinatra **3**
8 Oct **HOLD MY HAND** Don Cornell **4**
5 Nov **MY SON, MY SON** Vera Lynn **2**
19 Nov **HOLD MY HAND** Don Cornell **1**
26 Nov **THIS OLE HOUSE**
        Rosemary Clooney **1**
3 Dec **LET'S HAVE ANOTHER PARTY**
        Winifred Atwell **5**

1955

7 Jan **THE FINGER OF SUSPICION**
        Dickie Valentine **1**
14 Jan **MAMBO ITALIANO**
        Rosemary Clooney **1**
21 Jan **THE FINGER OF SUSPICION**
        Dickie Valentine **2**
4 Feb **MAMBO ITALIANO** Rosemary Clooney **2**

18 Feb **SOFTLY, SOFTLY** Ruby Murray **3**
11 Mar **GIVE ME YOUR WORD**
        Tennessee Ernie Ford **7**
29 Apr **CHERRY PINK AND APPLE
        BLOSSOM WHITE** Perez Prado **2**
13 May **STRANGER IN PARADISE**
        Tony Bennett **2**
27 May **CHERRY PINK AND APPLE
        BLOSSOM WHITE** Eddie Calvert **4**
24 Jun **UNCHAINED MELODY**
        Jimmy Young **3**
15 Jul **DREAMBOAT** Alma Cogan **2**
29 Jul **ROSE MARIE** Slim Whitman **11**
14 Oct **THE MAN FROM LARAMIE**
        Jimmy Young **4**
11 Nov **HERNANDO'S HIDEAWAY**
        Johnston Brothers **2**
25 Nov **ROCK AROUND THE CLOCK**
        Bill Haley and His Comets **3**
16 Dec **CHRISTMAS ALPHABET**
        Dickie Valentine **3**

■ 1955: Softly, Softly

1956

6 Jan **ROCK AROUND THE CLOCK**
        Bill Haley and His Comets **2**
20 Jan **SIXTEEN TONS**
        Tennessee Ernie Ford **4**
17 Feb **MEMORIES ARE MADE OF THIS**
        Dean Martin **4**
16 Mar **IT'S ALMOST TOMORROW**
        Dreamweavers **2**
30 Mar **ROCK AND ROLL WALTZ**
        Kay Starr with the Hugo
        Winterhalter Orchestra **1**

■ 1956: Why Do Fools Fall in Love?

1956

6 Apr **IT'S ALMOST TOMORROW**
Dreamweavers **1**
13 Apr **THE POOR PEOPLE OF PARIS**
Winifred Atwell **3**
4 May **NO OTHER LOVE** Ronnie Hilton **6**
15 Jun **I'LL BE HOME** Pat Boone **5**
20 Jul **WHY DO FOOLS FALL IN LOVE?**
Teenagers featuring
Frankie Lymon **3**
10 Aug **WHATEVER WILL BE WILL BE**
Doris Day **6**
21 Sep **LAY DOWN YOUR ARMS**
Anne Shelton **4**
19 Oct **A WOMAN IN LOVE** Frankie Laine **4**
16 Nov **JUST WALKIN' IN THE RAIN**
Johnnie Ray **7**

1957

4 Jan **SINGING THE BLUES** Guy Mitchell **1**
11 Jan **SINGING THE BLUES**
Tommy Steele and The Steelmen **1**
18 Jan **SINGING THE BLUES** Guy Mitchell **1**
25 Jan **THE GARDEN OF EDEN**
Frankie Vaughan **4**
1 Feb (top equal for one week)
SINGING THE BLUES Guy Mitchell **1**
22 Feb **YOUNG LOVE** Tab Hunter **7**
12 Apr **CUMBERLAND GAP**
Lonnie Donegan **5**
17 May **ROCK-A-BILLY** Guy Mitchell **1**
24 May **BUTTERFLY** Andy Williams **2**
7 Jun **YES TONIGHT, JOSEPHINE**
Johnnie Ray **3**
28 Jun **GAMBLIN' MAN / PUTTING ON
THE STYLE** Lonnie Donegan **2**
12 Jul **ALL SHOOK UP** Elvis Presley **7**
30 Aug **DIANA** Paul Anka **9**
1 Nov **THAT'LL BE THE DAY** Crickets **3**

22 Nov **MARY'S BOY CHILD** Harry Belafonte **7**

1958

10 Jan **GREAT BALLS OF FIRE**
Jerry Lee Lewis **2**
24 Jan **JAILHOUSE ROCK** Elvis Presley **3**
14 Feb **THE STORY OF MY LIFE**
Michael Holliday **2**
28 Feb **MAGIC MOMENTS** Perry Como **8**
25 Apr **WHOLE LOTTA WOMAN**
Marvin Rainwater **3**
16 May **WHO'S SORRY NOW?**
Connie Francis **6**
27 Jun **ON THE STREET WHERE YOU LIVE**
Vic Damone **2**
4 Jul (equal top for one week)
**ALL I HAVE TO DO IS DREAM /
CLAUDETTE** Everly Brothers **1**
11 Jul **ALL I HAVE TO DO IS DREAM /
CLAUDETTE** Everly Brothers **6**
22 Aug **WHEN** Kalin Twins **5**
26 Sep **CAROLINA MOON / STUPID CUPID**
Connie Francis **6**
7 Nov **IT'S ALL IN THE GAME**
Tommy Edwards **3**
28 Nov **HOOTS MON**
Lord Rockingham's XI **3**
19 Dec **IT'S ONLY MAKE BELIEVE**
Conway Twitty **5**

1959

23 Jan **THE DAY THE RAINS CAME**
Jane Morgan **1**
30 Jan **ONE NIGHT / I GOT STUNG**
Elvis Presley **3**
20 Feb **AS I LOVE YOU** Shirley Bassey **4**
20 Mar **SMOKE GETS IN YOUR EYES**
Platters **1**
27 Mar **SIDE SADDLE** Russ Conway **4**
24 Apr **IT DOESN'T MATTER ANYMORE**
Buddy Holly **3**
15 May **A FOOL SUCH AS I / I NEED YOUR
LOVE TONIGHT** Elvis Presley **5**
19 Jun **ROULETTE** Russ Conway **2**
3 Jul **DREAM LOVER** Bobby Darin **4**
31 Jul **LIVING DOLL**
Cliff Richard and The Drifters **6**
11 Sep **ONLY SIXTEEN** Craig Douglas **4**
9 Oct **HERE COMES SUMMER**
Jerry Keller **1**
16 Oct **MACK THE KNIFE** Bobby Darin **2**
30 Oct **TRAVELLIN' LIGHT**
Cliff Richard and The Shadows **5**

4 Dec (one week equal)
WHAT DO YOU WANT Adam Faith **3**
18 Dec (one week equal)
**WHAT DO YOU WANT TO MAKE
THOSE EYES AT ME FOR**
Emile Ford and The Checkmates **6**

1960

29 Jan **STARRY EYED** Michael Holliday **1**
5 Feb **WHY** Anthony Newley **4**
10 Mar **POOR ME** Adam Faith **1**
17 Mar **RUNNING BEAR** Johnny Preston **2**
31 Mar **MY OLD MAN'S A DUSTMAN**
Lonnie Donegan **4**
28 Apr **DO YOU MIND** Anthony Newley **1**
5 May **CATHY'S CLOWN** Everly Brothers **7**
23 Jun **THREE STEPS TO HEAVEN**
Eddie Cochran **2**
7 Jul **GOOD TIMIN'** Jimmy Jones **3**
28 Jul **PLEASE DON'T TEASE**
Cliff Richard and The Shadows **1**
4 Aug **SHAKIN' ALL OVER**
Johnny Kidd and The Pirates **1**
11 Aug **PLEASE DON'T TEASE**
Cliff Richard and The Shadows **2**
25 Aug **APACHE** Shadows **5**
29 Sep **TELL LAURA I LOVE HER**
Ricky Valance **3**
20 Oct **ONLY THE LONELY** Roy Orbison **2**
3 Nov **IT'S NOW OR NEVER** Elvis Presley **8**
29 Dec **I LOVE YOU**
Cliff Richard and the Shadows **2**

1961

12 Jan **POETRY IN MOTION**
Johnny Tillotson **2**

■ 1960: Tell Laura I Love Her

■ 1961: On the Rebound

26 Jan **ARE YOU LONESOME TONIGHT?**
Elvis Presley **4**
23 Feb **SAILOR** Petula Clark **1**
2 Mar **WALK RIGHT BACK / EBONY EYES**
Everly Brothers **3**
23 Mar **WOODEN HEART** Elvis Presley **6**
4 May **BLUE MOON** Marcels **2**
18 May **ON THE REBOUND** Floyd Cramer **1**
25 May **YOU'RE DRIVING ME CRAZY**
Temperance Seven **1**
1 Jun **SURRENDER** Elvis Presley **4**
29 Jun **RUNAWAY** Del Shannon **3**
20 Jul **TEMPTATION** Everly Brothers **2**
3 Aug **WELL I ASK YOU** Eden Kane **1**
10 Aug **YOU DON'T KNOW** Helen Shapiro **3**
31 Aug **JOHNNY REMEMBER ME**
John Leyton **3**
21 Sep **REACH FOR THE STARS / CLIMB
EV'RY MOUNTAIN** Shirley Bassey **1**
28 Sep **JOHNNY REMEMBER ME**
John Leyton **1**
5 Oct **KON-TIKI** Shadows **1**
12 Oct **MICHAEL** Highwaymen **1**
19 Oct **WALKIN' BACK TO HAPPINESS**
Helen Shapiro **3**
9 Nov **LITTLE SISTER /
HIS LATEST FLAME** Elvis Presley **4**
7 Dec **TOWER OF STRENGTH**
Frankie Vaughan **3**
28 Dec **MOON RIVER** Danny Williams **2**

1962

11 Jan **THE YOUNG ONES**
Cliff Richard and The Shadows **6**
22 Feb **ROCK-A-HULA BABY / CAN'T HELP
FALLING IN LOVE** Elvis Presley **4**
22 Mar **WONDERFUL LAND** Shadows **8**

17 May **NUT ROCKER**
B Bumble and The Stingers **1**
24 May **GOOD LUCK CHARM** Elvis Presley **5**
28 Jun **COME OUTSIDE**
Mike Sarne with Wendy Richard **2**
12 Jul **I CAN'T STOP LOVING YOU**
Ray Charles **2**
26 Jul **I REMEMBER YOU** Frank Ifield **7**
13 Sep **SHE'S NOT YOU** Elvis Presley **3**
4 Oct **TELSTAR** Tornados **5**
8 Nov **LOVESICK BLUES** Frank Ifield **5**
13 Dec **RETURN TO SENDER** Elvis Presley **3**

1963

3 Jan **THE NEXT TIME / BACHELOR BOY**
(second track listed from 10 Jan only)
Cliff Richard and The Shadows **3**
24 Jan **DANCE ON** Shadows **1**
31 Jan **DIAMONDS**
Jet Harris and Tony Meehan **3**
21 Feb **THE WAYWARD WIND** Frank Ifield **3**
14 Mar **SUMMER HOLIDAY**
Cliff Richard and The Shadows **2**
28 Mar **FOOT TAPPER** Shadows **1**
4 Apr **SUMMER HOLIDAY**
Cliff Richard and The Shadows **1**
11 Apr **HOW DO YOU DO IT?**
Gerry and The Pacemakers **3**
2 May **FROM ME TO YOU** Beatles **7**
20 Jun **I LIKE IT** Gerry and The
Pacemakers **4**
18 Jul **CONFESSIN'** Frank Ifield **2**
1 Aug **(YOU'RE THE) DEVIL IN DISGUISE**
Elvis Presley **1**
8 Aug **SWEETS FOR MY SWEET**
Searchers **2**

■ 1961: Reach for the Stars /
Climb Ev'ry Mountain

22 Aug **BAD TO ME**
Billy J Kramer and The Dakotas **3**
12 Sep **SHE LOVES YOU** Beatles **4**
10 Oct **DO YOU LOVE ME**
Brian Poole and The Tremeloes **3**
31 Oct **YOU'LL NEVER WALK ALONE**
Gerry and The Pacemakers **4**
28 Nov **SHE LOVES YOU** Beatles **2**
12 Dec **I WANT TO HOLD YOUR HAND**
Beatles **5**

1964

16 Jan **GLAD ALL OVER** Dave Clark Five **2**
30 Jan **NEEDLES AND PINS** Searchers **3**
20 Feb **DIANE** Bachelors **1**
27 Feb **ANYONE WHO HAD A HEART**
Cilla Black **3**
19 Mar **LITTLE CHILDREN**
Billy J Kramer and The Dakotas **2**
2 Apr **CAN'T BUY ME LOVE** Beatles **3**
23 Apr **A WORLD WITHOUT LOVE**
Peter and Gordon **2**
7 May **DON'T THROW YOUR LOVE AWAY**
Searchers **2**
21 May **JULIET** Four Pennies **1**
28 May **YOU'RE MY WORLD** Cilla Black **4**
25 Jun **IT'S OVER** Roy Orbison **2**
9 Jul **THE HOUSE OF THE RISING SUN**
Animals **1**
16 Jul **IT'S ALL OVER NOW**
Rolling Stones **1**
23 Jul **A HARD DAY'S NIGHT** Beatles **3**
13 Aug **DO WAH DIDDY DIDDY**
Manfred Mann **2**
27 Aug **HAVE I THE RIGHT?** Honeycombs **2**
10 Sep **YOU REALLY GOT ME** Kinks **2**
24 Sep **I'M INTO SOMETHING GOOD**
Herman's Hermits **2**
8 Oct **OH, PRETTY WOMAN** Roy Orbison **2**
22 Oct **(THERE'S) ALWAYS SOMETHING
THERE TO REMIND ME** Sandie Shaw **3**
12 Nov **OH, PRETTY WOMAN** Roy Orbison **1**
19 Nov **BABY LOVE** Supremes **2**
3 Dec **LITTLE RED ROOSTER**
Rolling Stones **1**
10 Dec **I FEEL FINE** Beatles **5**

1965

14 Jan **YEH, YEH** Georgie Fame
and The Blue Flames **2**
28 Jan **GO NOW!** Moody Blues **1**
4 Feb **YOU'VE LOST THAT LOVIN' FEELIN'**
Righteous Brothers **2**

18 Feb **TIRED OF WAITING FOR YOU** Kinks **1**
25 Feb **I'LL NEVER FIND ANOTHER YOU**
Seekers **2**
11 Mar **IT'S NOT UNUSUAL** Tom Jones **1**
18 Mar **THE LAST TIME** Rolling Stones **3**
8 Apr **CONCRETE AND CLAY** Unit 4 Plus 2 **1**
15 Apr **THE MINUTE YOU'RE GONE**
Cliff Richard **1**
22 Apr **TICKET TO RIDE** Beatles **3**
13 May **KING OF THE ROAD** Roger Miller **1**
20 May **WHERE ARE YOU NOW (MY LOVE)**
Jackie Trent **1**
27 May **LONG LIVE LOVE** Sandie Shaw **3**
17 Jun **CRYING IN THE CHAPEL**
Elvis Presley **1**
24 Jun **I'M ALIVE** Hollies **1**
1 Jul **CRYING IN THE CHAPEL**
Elvis Presley **1**
8 Jul **I'M ALIVE** Hollies **2**
22 Jul **MR TAMBOURINE MAN** Byrds **2**
5 Aug **HELP!** Beatles **3**
26 Aug **I GOT YOU BABE** Sonny and Cher **2**
9 Sep **(I CAN'T GET NO) SATISFACTION**
Rolling Stones **2**
23 Sep **MAKE IT EASY ON YOURSELF**
Walker Brothers **1**
30 Sep **TEARS** Ken Dodd **5**
4 Nov **GET OFF OF MY CLOUD**
Rolling Stones **3**
25 Nov **THE CARNIVAL IS OVER** Seekers **3**
16 Dec **DAY TRIPPER /**
WE CAN WORK IT OUT Beatles **5**

1966

20 Jan **KEEP ON RUNNIN'**
Spencer Davis Group **1**
27 Jan **MICHELLE** Overlanders **3**
17 Feb **THESE BOOTS ARE MADE FOR**
WALKIN' Nancy Sinatra **4**
17 Mar **THE SUN AIN'T GONNA SHINE**
ANYMORE Walker Brothers **4**
14 Apr **SOMEBODY HELP ME**
Spencer Davis Group **2**
28 Apr **YOU DON'T HAVE TO SAY**
YOU LOVE ME Dusty Springfield **1**
5 May **PRETTY FLAMINGO** Manfred Mann **3**
26 May **PAINT IT BLACK** Rolling Stones **1**
2 Jun **STRANGERS IN THE NIGHT**
Frank Sinatra **3**
23 Jun **PAPERBACK WRITER** Beatles **2**
7 Jul **SUNNY AFTERNOON** Kinks **2**
21 Jul **GET AWAY** Georgie Fame
and The Blue Flames **1**
28 Jul **OUT OF TIME** Chris Farlowe
and The Thunderbirds **1**

4 Aug **WITH A GIRL LIKE YOU** Troggs **2**
18 Aug **YELLOW SUBMARINE / ELEANOR**
RIGBY Beatles **4**
15 Sep **ALL OR NOTHING** Small Faces **1**
22 Sep **DISTANT DRUMS** Jim Reeves **5**
27 Oct **REACH OUT I'LL BE THERE**
Four Tops **3**
17 Nov **GOOD VIBRATIONS** Beach Boys **2**
1 Dec **GREEN GREEN GRASS OF HOME**
Tom Jones **7**

1967

19 Jan **I'M A BELIEVER** Monkees **4**
16 Feb **THIS IS MY SONG** Petula Clark **2**
2 Mar **RELEASE ME (AND LET ME LOVE**
AGAIN) Engelbert Humperdinck **6**
13 Apr **SOMETHIN' STUPID**
Nancy and Frank Sinatra **2**
27 Apr **PUPPET ON A STRING**
Sandie Shaw **3**
18 May **SILENCE IS GOLDEN** Tremeloes **3**
8 Jun **A WHITER SHADE OF PALE**
Procol Harum **6**
19 Jul **ALL YOU NEED IS LOVE** Beatles **3**
9 Aug **SAN FRANCISCO (BE SURE**
TO WEAR SOME FLOWERS IN
YOUR HAIR) Scott McKenzie **4**
6 Sep **THE LAST WALTZ**
Engelbert Humperdinck **5**
11 Oct **MASSACHUSETTS** Bee Gees **4**
8 Nov **BABY, NOW THAT I FOUND YOU**
Foundations **2**
22 Nov **LET THE HEARTACHES BEGIN**
Long John Baldry **2**
6 Dec **HELLO, GOODBYE** Beatles **7**

1968

24 Jan **THE BALLAD OF BONNIE**
AND CLYDE Georgie Fame **1**
31 Jan **EVERLASTING LOVE** Love Affair **2**
14 Feb **MIGHTY QUINN** Manfred Mann **2**
28 Feb **CINDERELLA ROCKAFELLA**
Esther and Abi Ofarim **3**
20 Mar **THE LEGEND OF XANADU** Dave
Dee, Dozy, Beaky, Mick and Tich **1**
27 Mar **LADY MADONNA** Beatles **2**
10 Apr **CONGRATULATIONS** Cliff Richard **2**
24 Apr **WHAT A WONDERFUL WORLD /**
CABARET Louis Armstrong **4**
22 May **YOUNG GIRL**
Gary Puckett and The Union Gap **4**
19 Jun **JUMPIN' JACK FLASH**
Rolling Stones **2**

■ 1966: Keep on Runnin'

3 Jul **BABY COME BACK** Equals **3**
24 Jul **I PRETEND** Des O'Connor **1**
31 Jul **MONY MONY**
Tommy James and The Shondells **2**
14 Aug **FIRE** Crazy World of Arthur Brown **1**
21 Aug **MONY MONY**
Tommy James and The Shondells **1**
28 Aug **DO IT AGAIN** Beach Boys **1**
4 Sep **I'VE GOTTA GET A MESSAGE TO**
YOU Bee Gees **1**
11 Sep **HEY JUDE** Beatles **2**
25 Sep **THOSE WERE THE DAYS**
Mary Hopkin **6**
6 Nov **WITH A LITTLE HELP FROM MY**
FRIENDS Joe Cocker **1**
13 Nov **THE GOOD, THE BAD AND**
THE UGLY Hugo Montenegro
and His Orchestra **4**
11 Dec **LILY THE PINK** Scaffold **3**

1969

1 Jan **OB-LA-DI, OB-LA-DA** Marmalade **1**
8 Jan **LILY THE PINK** Scaffold **1**
15 Jan **OB-LA-DI, OB-LA-DA** Marmalade **2**
29 Jan **ALBATROSS** Fleetwood Mac **1**
5 Feb **BLACKBERRY WAY** Move **1**
12 Feb **(IF PARADISE IS) HALF AS NICE**
Amen Corner **2**
26 Feb **WHERE DO YOU GO TO MY LOVELY**
Peter Sarstedt **4**
26 Mar **I HEARD IT THROUGH**
THE GRAPEVINE Marvin Gaye **3**
16 Apr **ISRAELITES**
Desmond Dekker and The Aces **1**
23 Apr **GET BACK**
Beatles with Billy Preston **6**
4 Jun **DIZZY** Tommy Roe **1**

■ 1970: Voodoo Chile

11 Jun **BALLAD OF JOHN AND YOKO**
Beatles **3**
2 Jul **SOMETHING IN THE AIR**
Thunderclap Newman **3**
23 Jul **HONKY TONK WOMEN**
Rolling Stones **5**
30 Aug **IN THE YEAR 2525 (EXORDIUM &
TERMINUS)** Zager and Evans **3**
20 Sep **BAD MOON RISING**
Creedence Clearwater Revival **3**
11 Oct **JE T'AIME … MOI NON PLUS**
Jane Birkin and Serge Gainsbourg **1**
18 Oct **I'LL NEVER FALL IN LOVE AGAIN**
Bobbie Gentry **1**
25 Oct **SUGAR SUGAR** Archies **8**
20 Dec **TWO LITTLE BOYS** Rolf Harris **6**

1970

31 Jan **LOVE GROWS (WHERE MY
ROSEMARY GOES)**
Edison Lighthouse **5**
7 Mar **WAND'RIN' STAR** Lee Marvin **3**
28 Mar **BRIDGE OVER TROUBLED WATER**
Simon and Garfunkel **3**
18 Apr **ALL KINDS OF EVERYTHING** Dana **2**
2 May **SPIRIT IN THE SKY**
Norman Greenbaum **2**
16 May **BACK HOME**
England World Cup Squad **3**
6 Jun **YELLOW RIVER** Christie **1**
13 Jun **IN THE SUMMERTIME**
Mungo Jerry **7**
1 Aug **THE WONDER OF YOU**
Elvis Presley **6**
12 Sep **THE TEARS OF A CLOWN**
Smokey Robinson and The Miracles **1**
19 Sep **BAND OF GOLD** Freda Payne **6**

31 Oct **WOODSTOCK**
Matthews' Southern Comfort **3**
21 Nov **VOODOO CHILE**
Jimi Hendrix Experience **1**
28 Nov **I HEAR YOU KNOCKING**
Dave Edmunds **6**

1971

9 Jan **GRANDAD** Clive Dunn **3**
30 Jan **MY SWEET LORD** George Harrison **5**
6 Mar **BABY JUMP** Mungo Jerry **2**
20 Mar **HOT LOVE** T. Rex **6**
1 May **DOUBLE BARREL**
Dave and Ansil Collins **2**
15 May **KNOCK THREE TIMES** Dawn **5**
19 Jun **CHIRPY CHIRPY CHEEP CHEEP**
Middle of the Road **5**
24 Jul **GET IT ON** T. Rex **4**
21 Aug **I'M STILL WAITING** Diana Ross **4**
18 Sep **HEY GIRL DON'T BOTHER ME**
Tams **3**
9 Oct **MAGGIE MAY** Rod Stewart **5**
13 Nov **COZ I LUV YOU** Slade **4**
11 Dec **ERNIE (THE FASTEST MILK MAN
IN THE WEST)** Benny Hill **4**

1972

8 Jan **I'D LIKE TO TEACH THE
WORLD TO SING** New Seekers **4**
5 Feb **TELEGRAM SAM** T. Rex **2**
19 Feb **SON OF MY FATHER** Chicory Tip **3**
11 Mar **WITHOUT YOU** Nilsson **5**
15 Apr **AMAZING GRACE** Pipes and
Drums and Military Band of the
Royal Scots Dragoon Guards **5**

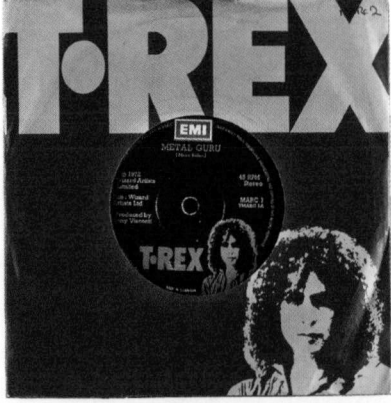

■ 1972: Metal Guru

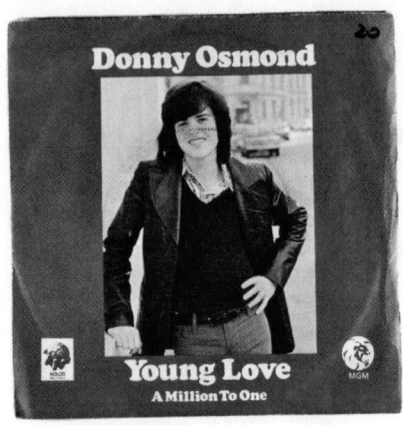

■ 1973: Young Love

20 May **METAL GURU** T. Rex **4**
17 Jun **VINCENT** Don McLean **2**
1 Jul **TAKE ME BAK 'OME** Slade **1**
8 Jul **PUPPY LOVE** Donny Osmond **5**
12 Aug **SCHOOL'S OUT** Alice Cooper **3**
2 Sep **YOU WEAR IT WELL** Rod Stewart **1**
9 Sep **MAMA WEER ALL CRAZEE NOW**
Slade **3**
30 Sep **HOW CAN I BE SURE** David Cassidy **2**
14 Oct **MOULDY OLD DOUGH**
Lieutenant Pigeon **4**
11 Nov **CLAIR** Gilbert O'Sullivan **2**
25 Nov **MY DING-A-LING** Chuck Berry **4**
23 Dec **LONG HAIRED LOVER FROM
LIVERPOOL** Little Jimmy Osmond **5**

1973

27 Jan **BLOCKBUSTER!** Sweet **5**
3 Mar **CUM ON FEEL THE NOIZE** Slade **4**
31 Mar **THE TWELFTH OF NEVER**
Donny Osmond **1**
7 Apr **GET DOWN** Gilbert O'Sullivan **2**
21 Apr **TIE A YELLOW RIBBON ROUND THE
OLE OAK TREE** Dawn **4**
19 May **SEE MY BABY JIVE** Wizzard **4**
16 Jun **CAN THE CAN** Suzi Quatro **1**
23 Jun **RUBBER BULLETS** 10cc **1**
30 Jun **SKWEEZE ME PLEEZE ME** Slade **3**
21 Jul **WELCOME HOME** Peters and Lee **1**
28 Jul **I'M THE LEADER OF THE GANG
(I AM!)** Gary Glitter **4**
25 Aug **YOUNG LOVE** Donny Osmond **4**
22 Sep **ANGEL FINGERS (A TEEN BALLAD)**
Wizzard **1**
29 Sep **EYE LEVEL** Simon Park Orchestra **4**
27 Oct **DAYDREAMER / THE PUPPY SONG**
David Cassidy **3**

■ 1974: Everything I Own

17 Nov **I LOVE YOU LOVE ME LOVE**
Gary Glitter **4**

15 Dec **MERRY XMAS EVERYBODY**
Slade **5**

1974

19 Jan **YOU WON'T FIND ANOTHER FOOL LIKE ME** New Seekers **1**

26 Jan **TIGER FEET** Mud **4**

23 Feb **DEVIL GATE DRIVE** Suzi Quatro **2**

9 Mar **JEALOUS MIND** Alvin Stardust **1**

16 Mar **BILLY, DON'T BE A HERO**
Paper Lace **3**

6 Apr **SEASONS IN THE SUN**
Terry Jacks **4**

4 May **WATERLOO** Abba **2**

18 May **SUGAR BABY LOVE** Rubettes **4**

15 Jun **THE STREAK** Ray Stevens **1**

22 Jun **ALWAYS YOURS** Gary Glitter **1**

29 Jun **SHE** Charles Aznavour **4**

27 Jul **ROCK YOUR BABY**
George McCrae **3**

17 Aug **WHEN WILL I SEE YOU AGAIN**
Three Degrees **2**

31 Aug **LOVE ME FOR A REASON**
Osmonds **3**

21 Sep **KUNG FU FIGHTING**
Carl Douglas **3**

12 Oct **ANNIE'S SONG** John Denver **1**

19 Oct **SAD SWEET DREAMER**
Sweet Sensation **1**

26 Oct **EVERYTHING I OWN** Ken Boothe **3**

16 Nov **GONNA MAKE YOU A STAR**
David Essex **3**

7 Dec **YOU'RE THE FIRST, THE LAST, MY EVERYTHING** Barry White **2**

21 Dec **LONELY THIS CHRISTMAS** Mud **4**

1975

18 Jan **DOWN DOWN** Status Quo **1**

25 Jan **MS GRACE** Tymes **1**

1 Feb **JANUARY** Pilot **3**

22 Feb **MAKE ME SMILE (COME UP AND SEE ME)**
Steve Harley and Cockney Rebel **2**

8 Mar **IF** Telly Savalas **2**

22 Mar **BYE BYE BABY** Bay City Rollers **6**

3 May **OH BOY** Mud **2**

17 May **STAND BY YOUR MAN**
Tammy Wynette **3**

7 Jun **WHISPERING GRASS**
Windsor Davies and Don Estelle **3**

28 Jun **I'M NOT IN LOVE** 10cc **2**

12 Jul **TEARS ON MY PILLOW**
Johnny Nash **1**

19 Jul **GIVE A LITTLE LOVE**
Bay City Rollers **3**

9 Aug **BARBADOS** Typically Tropical **1**

16 Aug **CAN'T GIVE YOU ANYTHING (BUT MY LOVE)** Stylistics **3**

6 Sep **SAILING** Rod Stewart **4**

4 Oct **HOLD ME CLOSE** David Essex **3**

25 Oct **I ONLY HAVE EYES FOR YOU**
Art Garfunkel **2**

8 Nov **SPACE ODDITY** David Bowie **2**

22 Nov **D.I.V.O.R.C.E.** Billy Connolly **1**

29 Nov **BOHEMIAN RHAPSODY** Queen **9**

1976

31 Jan **MAMMA MIA** Abba **2**

14 Feb **FOREVER AND EVER** Slik **1**

21 Feb **DECEMBER '63 (OH WHAT A NIGHT)** Four Seasons **2**

■ 1975: Sailing

■ 1977: Mull of Kintyre / Girls' School

6 Mar **I LOVE TO LOVE (BUT MY BABY LOVES TO DANCE)** Tina Charles **3**

27 Mar **SAVE YOUR KISSES FOR ME**
Brotherhood of Man **6**

8 May **FERNANDO** Abba **4**

5 Jun **NO CHARGE** J J Barrie **1**

12 Jun **COMBINE HARVESTER (BRAND NEW KEY)** Wurzels **2**

26 Jun **YOU TO ME ARE EVERYTHING**
Real Thing **3**

17 Jul **THE ROUSSOS PHENOMENON EP**
Demis Roussos **1**

24 Jul **DON'T GO BREAKING MY HEART**
Elton John and Kiki Dee **6**

4 Sep **DANCING QUEEN** Abba **6**

16 Oct **MISSISSIPPI** Pussycat **4**

13 Nov **IF YOU LEAVE ME NOW** Chicago **3**

4 Dec **UNDER THE MOON OF LOVE**
Showaddywaddy **3**

25 Dec **WHEN A CHILD IS BORN (SOLEADO)** Johnny Mathis **3**

1977

15 Jan **DON'T GIVE UP ON US** David Soul **4**

12 Feb **DON'T CRY FOR ME ARGENTINA**
Julie Covington **1**

19 Feb **WHEN I NEED YOU** Leo Sayer **3**

12 Mar **CHANSON D'AMOUR**
Manhattan Transfer **3**

2 Apr **KNOWING ME, KNOWING YOU** Abba **5**

7 May **FREE** Deniece Williams **2**

21 May **I DON'T WANT TO TALK ABOUT IT / FIRST CUT IS THE DEEPEST**
Rod Stewart **4**

18 Jun **LUCILLE** Kenny Rogers **1**

25 Jun **SHOW YOU THE WAY TO GO**
Jacksons **1**

2 Jul **SO YOU WIN AGAIN** Hot Chocolate **3**
23 Jul **I FEEL LOVE** Donna Summer **4**
20 Aug **ANGELO** Brotherhood of Man **1**
27 Aug **FLOAT ON** Floaters **1**
3 Sep **WAY DOWN** Elvis Presley **5**
8 Oct **SILVER LADY** David Soul **3**
29 Oct **YES SIR, I CAN BOOGIE** Baccara **1**
5 Nov **THE NAME OF THE GAME** Abba **4**
3 Dec **MULL OF KINTYRE / GIRLS' SCHOOL** Wings **9**

1978

4 Feb **UPTOWN TOP RANKING** Althia And Donna **1**
11 Feb **FIGARO** Brotherhood of Man **1**
18 Feb **TAKE A CHANCE ON ME** Abba **3**
11 Mar **WUTHERING HEIGHTS** Kate Bush **4**
8 Apr **MATCHSTALK MEN AND MATCHSTALK CATS AND DOGS (LOWRY'S SONG)** Brian and Michael **3**
29 Apr **NIGHT FEVER** Bee Gees **2**
13 May **RIVERS OF BABYLON / BROWN GIRL IN THE RING** Boney M **5**
17 Jun **YOU'RE THE ONE THAT I WANT** John Travolta and Olivia Newton-John **9**
19 Aug **THREE TIMES A LADY** Commodores **5**
23 Sep **DREADLOCK HOLIDAY** 10cc **1**
30 Sep **SUMMER NIGHTS** John Travolta and Olivia Newton-John **7**
18 Nov **RAT TRAP** Boomtown Rats **2**
2 Dec **DA' YA' THINK I'M SEXY** Rod Stewart **1**
9 Dec **MARY'S BOY CHILD – OH MY LORD** Boney M **4**

■ 1979: Cars

1979

6 Jan **Y.M.C.A.** Village People **3**
27 Jan **HIT ME WITH YOUR RHYTHM STICK** Ian and The Blockheads **1**
3 Feb **HEART OF GLASS** Blondie **4**
3 Mar **TRAGEDY** Bee Gees **2**
17 Mar **I WILL SURVIVE** Gloria Gaynor **4**
14 Apr **BRIGHT EYES** Art Garfunkel **6**
26 May **SUNDAY GIRL** Blondie **3**
16 Jun **RING MY BELL** Anita Ward **2**
30 Jun **ARE 'FRIENDS' ELECTRIC?** Tubeway Army **4**
28 Jul **I DON'T LIKE MONDAYS** Boomtown Rats **4**
25 Aug **WE DON'T TALK ANYMORE** Cliff Richard **4**
22 Sep **CARS** Gary Numan **1**
29 Sep **MESSAGE IN A BOTTLE** Police **3**
20 Oct **VIDEO KILLED THE RADIO STAR** Buggles **1**
27 Oct **ONE DAY AT A TIME** Lena Martell **3**
17 Nov **WHEN YOU'RE IN LOVE WITH A BEAUTIFUL WOMAN** Dr Hook **3**
8 Dec **WALKING ON THE MOON** Police **1**
15 Dec **ANOTHER BRICK IN THE WALL (PART 2)** Pink Floyd **5**

1980

19 Jan **BRASS IN POCKET** Pretenders **2**
2 Feb **THE SPECIAL A.K.A. LIVE EP** Specials **2**
16 Feb **COWARD OF THE COUNTY** Kenny Rogers **2**
1 Mar **ATOMIC** Blondie **2**
15 Mar **TOGETHER WE ARE BEAUTIFUL** Fern Kinney **1**
22 Mar **GOING UNDERGROUND / DREAMS OF CHILDREN** Jam **3**
12 Apr **WORKING MY WAY BACK TO YOU – FORGIVE ME GIRL** Detroit Spinners **2**
26 Apr **CALL ME** Blondie **1**
3 May **GENO** Dexy's Midnight Runners **2**
17 May **WHAT'S ANOTHER YEAR** Johnny Logan **2**
31 May **THEME FROM M*A*S*H (SUICIDE IS PAINLESS)** Mash **3**
21 Jun **CRYING** Don McLean **3**
12 Jul **XANADU** Olivia Newton-John and Electric Light Orchestra **2**
26 Jul **USE IT UP AND WEAR IT OUT** Odyssey **2**

■ 1980: The Special A.K.A. Live EP

9 Aug **THE WINNER TAKES IT ALL** Abba **2**
23 Aug **ASHES TO ASHES** David Bowie **2**
6 Sep **START** Jam **1**
13 Sep **FEELS LIKE I'M IN LOVE** Kelly Marie **2**
27 Sep **DON'T STAND SO CLOSE TO ME** Police **4**
25 Oct **WOMAN IN LOVE** Barbra Streisand **3**
15 Nov **THE TIDE IS HIGH** Blondie **2**
29 Nov **SUPER TROUPER** Abba **3**
20 Dec **(JUST LIKE) STARTING OVER** John Lennon **1**
27 Dec **THERE'S NO ONE QUITE LIKE GRANDMA** St Winifred's School Choir **2**

1981

10 Jan **IMAGINE** John Lennon **4**
7 Feb **WOMAN** John Lennon **2**

■ 1980: There's No One Quite Like Grandma

■ 1982: Computer Love / The Model

21 Feb **SHADDAP YOU FACE**
Joe Dolce Music Theatre **3**

14 Mar **JEALOUS GUY** Roxy Music **2**

28 Mar **THIS OLE HOUSE** Shakin' Stevens **3**

18 Apr **MAKING YOUR MIND UP**
Bucks Fizz **3**

9 May **STAND AND DELIVER**
Adam and The Ants **5**

13 Jun **BEING WITH YOU**
Smokey Robinson **2**

27 Jun **ONE DAY IN YOUR LIFE**
Michael Jackson **2**

11 Jul **GHOST TOWN** Specials **3**

1 Aug **GREEN DOOR** Shakin' Stevens **4**

29 Aug **JAPANESE BOY** Aneka **1**

5 Sep **TAINTED LOVE** Soft Cell **2**

19 Sep **PRINCE CHARMING**
Adam and The Ants **4**

17 Oct **IT'S MY PARTY**
Dave Stewart with Barbara Gaskin **4**

14 Nov **EVERY LITTLE THING SHE
DOES IS MAGIC** Police **1**

21 Nov **UNDER PRESSURE**
Queen and David Bowie **2**

5 Dec **BEGIN THE BEGUINE (VOLVER
A EMPEZAR)** Julio Iglesias **1**

12 Dec **DON'T YOU WANT ME**
Human League **5**

1982

16 Jan **LAND OF MAKE BELIEVE**
Bucks Fizz **2**

30 Jan **OH JULIE** Shakin' Stevens **1**

6 Feb **COMPUTER LOVE / THE MODEL**
Kraftwerk **1**

13 Feb **A TOWN CALLED MALICE /
PRECIOUS** Jam **3**

6 Mar **THE LION SLEEPS TONIGHT**
Tight Fit **3**

27 Mar **SEVEN TEARS**
Goombay Dance Band **3**

17 Apr **MY CAMERA NEVER LIES**
Bucks Fizz **1**

24 Apr **EBONY AND IVORY**
Paul McCartney with
Stevie Wonder **3**

15 May **A LITTLE PEACE** Nicole **2**

29 May **HOUSE OF FUN** Madness **2**

12 Jun **GOODY TWO SHOES** Adam Ant **2**

26 Jun **I'VE NEVER BEEN TO ME**
Charlene **1**

3 Jul **HAPPY TALK** Captain Sensible **2**

17 Jul **FAME** Irene Cara **3**

7 Aug **COME ON EILEEN**
Dexys Midnight Runners
and The Emerald Express **4**

4 Sep **EYE OF THE TIGER** Survivor **4**

2 Oct **PASS THE DUTCHIE**
Musical Youth **3**

23 Oct **DO YOU REALLY WANT TO HURT ME**
Culture Club **3**

13 Nov **I DON'T WANT TO DANCE**
Eddy Grant **3**

4 Dec **BEAT SURRENDER** Jam **2**

18 Dec **SAVE YOUR LOVE**
Renée and Renato **4**

1983

15 Jan **YOU CAN'T HURRY LOVE**
Phil Collins **2**

29 Jan **DOWN UNDER** Men at Work **3**

19 Feb **TOO SHY** Kajagoogoo **2**

5 Mar **BILLIE JEAN** Michael Jackson **1**

12 Mar **TOTAL ECLIPSE OF THE HEART**
Bonnie Tyler **2**

26 Mar **IS THERE SOMETHING
I SHOULD KNOW** Duran Duran **2**

9 Apr **LET'S DANCE** David Bowie **3**

30 Apr **TRUE** Spandau Ballet **4**

28 May **CANDY GIRL** New Edition **1**

4 Jun **EVERY BREATH YOU TAKE**
Police **4**

2 Jul **BABY JANE** Rod Stewart **3**

23 Jul **WHEREVER I LAY MY HAT (THAT'S
MY HOME)** Paul Young **3**

13 Aug **GIVE IT UP**
KC and The Sunshine Band **3**

3 Sep **RED RED WINE** UB40 **3**

24 Sep **KARMA CHAMELEON**
Culture Club **6**

5 Nov **UPTOWN GIRL** Billy Joel **5**

10 Dec **ONLY YOU** Flying Pickets **5**

1984

14 Jan **PIPES OF PEACE** Paul McCartney **2**

28 Jan **RELAX** Frankie Goes To Hollywood **5**

3 Mar **99 RED BALLOONS** Nena **3**

24 Mar **HELLO** Lionel Richie **6**

5 May **THE REFLEX** Duran Duran **4**

2 Jun **WAKE ME UP BEFORE YOU GO-GO**
Wham! **2**

16 Jun **TWO TRIBES**
Frankie Goes To Hollywood **9**

18 Aug **CARELESS WHISPER**
George Michael **3**

8 Sep **I JUST CALLED TO SAY I LOVE YOU**
Stevie Wonder **6**

20 Oct **FREEDOM** Wham! **3**

10 Nov **I FEEL FOR YOU** Chaka Khan **3**

1 Dec **I SHOULD HAVE KNOWN BETTER**
Jim Diamond **1**

8 Dec **THE POWER OF LOVE**
Frankie Goes To Hollywood **1**

15 Dec **DO THEY KNOW IT'S CHRISTMAS?**
Band Aid **5**

1985

19 Jan **I WANT TO KNOW WHAT LOVE IS**
Foreigner **3**

9 Feb **I KNOW HIM SO WELL**
Elaine Paige and Barbara Dickson **4**

9 Mar **YOU SPIN ME RIGHT ROUND
(LIKE A RECORD)** Dead or Alive **2**

23 Mar **EASY LOVER**
Philip Bailey (duet with Phil Collins) **4**

20 Apr **WE ARE THE WORLD**
USA for Africa **2**

4 May **MOVE CLOSER** Phyllis Nelson **1**

11 May **19** Paul Hardcastle **5**

15 Jun **YOU'LL NEVER WALK ALONE**
Crowd **2**

29 Jun **FRANKIE** Sister Sledge **4**

27 Jul **THERE MUST BE AN ANGEL
(PLAYING WITH MY HEART)**
Eurythmics **1**

3 Aug **INTO THE GROOVE** Madonna **4**

31 Aug **I GOT YOU BABE** UB40,
guest vocals by Chrissie Hynde **1**

7 Sep **DANCING IN THE STREET**
David Bowie and Mick Jagger **4**

5 Oct **IF I WAS** Midge Ure **1**

12 Oct **THE POWER OF LOVE** Jennifer Rush **5**

16 Nov **A GOOD HEART** Feargal Sharkey **2**

30 Nov **I'M YOUR MAN** Wham! **2**

14 Dec **SAVING ALL MY LOVE FOR YOU**
Whitney Houston **2**

CHRIS DE BURGH
THE LADY IN RED

■ 1986: The Lady in Red

28 Dec   MERRY CHRISTMAS EVERYONE
Shakin' Stevens **2**

1986

11 Jan   **WEST END GIRLS**
Pet Shop Boys **2**
25 Jan   **THE SUN ALWAYS SHINES ON TV**
A-Ha **2**
8 Feb   **WHEN THE GOING GETS
TOUGH, THE TOUGH GET GOING**
Billy Ocean **4**
8 Mar   **CHAIN REACTION** Diana Ross **3**
29 Mar   **LIVING DOLL** Cliff Richard and The
Young Ones, featuring Hank Marvin **3**
19 Apr   **A DIFFERENT CORNER**
George Michael **3**
10 May   **ROCK ME AMADEUS** Falco **1**
17 May   **THE CHICKEN SONG**
Spitting Image **3**

■ 1987: Who's That Girl

MADONNA
Who's
That
Girl

7 Jun   **SPIRIT IN THE SKY**
Doctor and The Medics **3**
28 Jun   **THE EDGE OF HEAVEN** Wham! **2**
12 Jul   **PAPA DON'T PREACH** Madonna **3**
2 Aug   **THE LADY IN RED** Chris de Burgh **3**
23 Aug   **I WANT TO WAKE UP WITH YOU**
Boris Gardiner **3**
13 Sep   **DON'T LEAVE ME THIS WAY**
Communards with
Sarah Jane Morris **4**
11 Oct   **TRUE BLUE** Madonna **1**
18 Oct   **EVERY LOSER WINS** Nick Berry **3**
8 Nov   **TAKE MY BREATH AWAY** Berlin **4**
6 Dec   **THE FINAL COUNTDOWN** Europe **2**
20 Dec   **CARAVAN OF LOVE** Housemartins **1**
27 Dec   **REET PETITE** Jackie Wilson **4**

1987

24 Jan   **JACK YOUR BODY**
Steve 'Silk' Hurley **2**
7 Feb   **I KNEW YOU WERE WAITING
(FOR ME)** George Michael
and Aretha Franklin **2**
21 Feb   **STAND BY ME** Ben E King **3**
14 Mar   **EVERYTHING I OWN** Boy George **2**
28 Mar   **RESPECTABLE** Mel and Kim **1**
4 Apr   **LET IT BE** Ferry Aid **3**
25 Apr   **LA ISLA BONITA** Madonna **2**
9 May   **NOTHING'S GONNA STOP US NOW**
Starship **4**
6 Jun   **I WANNA DANCE WITH SOMEBODY
(WHO LOVES ME)** Whitney Houston **2**
20 Jun   **STAR TREKKIN'** Firm **2**
4 Jul   **IT'S A SIN** Pet Shop Boys **3**
25 Jul   **WHO'S THAT GIRL** Madonna **1**
1 Aug   **LA BAMBA** Los Lobos **2**
15 Aug   **I JUST CAN'T STOP LOVING YOU**
Michael Jackson **2**
29 Aug   **NEVER GONNA GIVE YOU UP**
Rick Astley **5**
3 Oct   **PUMP UP THE VOLUME /
ANITINA (THE FIRST TIME
I SEE SHE DANCE)** M/A/R/R/S **2**
17 Oct   **YOU WIN AGAIN** Bee Gees **4**
14 Nov   **CHINA IN YOUR HAND** T'Pau **5**
19 Dec   **ALWAYS ON MY MIND**
Pet Shop Boys **4**

1988

16 Jan   **HEAVEN IS A PLACE ON EARTH**
Belinda Carlisle **2**
30 Jan   **I THINK WE'RE ALONE NOW**
Tiffany **3**

20 Feb   **I SHOULD BE SO LUCKY**
Kylie Minogue **5**
26 Mar   **DON'T TURN AROUND** Aswad **2**
9 Apr   **HEART** Pet Shop Boys **3**
30 Apr   **THEME FROM S EXPRESS**
S Express **2**
14 May   **PERFECT** Fairground Attraction **1**
21 May   **WITH A LITTLE HELP FROM MY
FRIENDS / SHE'S LEAVING HOME**
Wet Wet Wet / Billy Bragg with
Cara Tivey **4**
18 Jun   **DOCTORIN' THE TARDIS** Timelords **1**
25 Jun   **I OWE YOU NOTHING** Bros **2**
9 Jul   **NOTHING'S GONNA CHANGE MY
LOVE FOR YOU** Glenn Medeiros **4**
6 Aug   **THE ONLY WAY IS UP**
Yazz and The Plastic Population **5**
10 Sep   **A GROOVY KIND OF LOVE**
Phil Collins **2**
24 Sep   **HE AIN'T HEAVY HE'S
MY BROTHER** Hollies **2**
8 Oct   **DESIRE** U2 **1**
15 Oct   **ONE MOMENT IN TIME**
Whitney Houston **2**
29 Oct   **ORINOCO FLOW (SAIL AWAY)**
Enya **3**
19 Nov   **THE FIRST TIME** Robin Beck **3**
10 Dec   **MISTLETOE AND WINE**
Cliff Richard **4**

1989

7 Jan   **ESPECIALLY FOR YOU**
Kylie Minogue and Jason Donovan **3**
28 Jan   **SOMETHING'S GOTTEN HOLD OF
MY HEART** Marc Almond with
special guest Gene Pitney **4**
25 Feb   **BELFAST CHILD**
Simple Minds **2**
11 Mar   **TOO MANY BROKEN HEARTS**
Jason Donovan **2**
25 Mar   **LIKE A PRAYER** Madonna **3**
15 Apr   **ETERNAL FLAME** Bangles **4**
13 May   **HAND ON YOUR HEART**
Kylie Minogue **1**
20 May   **FERRY 'CROSS THE MERSEY**
Christians, Holly Johnson, Paul
McCartney, Gerry Marsden and
Stock Aitken Waterman **3**
10 Jun   **SEALED WITH A KISS**
Jason Donovan **2**
24 Jun   **BACK TO LIFE (HOWEVER DO
YOU WANT ME)** Soul II Soul
featuring Caron Wheeler **4**
22 Jul   **YOU'LL NEVER STOP
ME LOVING YOU** Sonia **2**

5 Aug **SWING THE MOOD**
Jive Bunny and The Mastermixers **5**

9 Sep **RIDE ON TIME** Black Box **6**

21 Oct **THAT'S WHAT I LIKE**
Jive Bunny and The Mastermixers **3**

11 Nov **ALL AROUND THE WORLD**
Lisa Stansfield **2**

25 Nov **YOU GOT IT (THE RIGHT STUFF)**
New Kids on The Block **3**

16 Dec **LET'S PARTY**
Jive Bunny and The Mastermixers **1**

23 Dec **DO THEY KNOW IT'S CHRISTMAS?**
Band Aid II **3**

1990

13 Jan **HANGIN' TOUGH**
New Kids on the Block **2**

27 Jan **TEARS ON MY PILLOW**
Kylie Minogue **1**

3 Feb **NOTHING COMPARES 2 U**
Sinead O'Connor **4**

3 Mar **DUB BE GOOD TO ME**
Beats International
featuring Lindy Layton **4**

31 Mar **THE POWER** Snap! **2**

14 Apr **VOGUE** Madonna **4**

12 May **KILLER** Adamski **4**

9 Jun **WORLD IN MOTION**
Englandneworder **2**

23 Jun **SACRIFICE / HEALING HANDS**
Elton John **5**

28 Jul **TURTLE POWER** Partners In Kryme **4**

25 Aug **ITSY BITSY TEENY WEENY YELLOW
POLKA DOT BIKINI** Bombalurina **3**

15 Sep **THE JOKER** Steve Miller Band **2**

29 Sep **SHOW ME HEAVEN** Maria McKee **4**

27 Oct **A LITTLE TIME** Beautiful South **1**

■ 1990: Killer

3 Nov **UNCHAINED MELODY**
Righteous Brothers **4**

1 Dec **ICE ICE BABY** Vanilla Ice **4**

29 Dec **SAVIOUR'S DAY** Cliff Richard **1**

1991

5 Jan **BRING YOUR DAUGHTER...
TO THE SLAUGHTER** Iron Maiden **2**

19 Jan **SADNESS PART ONE** Enigma **1**

26 Jan **INNUENDO** Queen **1**

2 Feb **3AM ETERNAL** KLF featuring
Children of the Revolution **2**

16 Feb **DO THE BARTMAN** Simpsons **3**

9 Mar **SHOULD I STAY OR SHOULD I GO**
Clash **2**

23 Mar **THE STONK**
Hale and Pace and The Stonkers **1**

30 Mar **THE ONE AND ONLY**
Chesney Hawkes **5**

4 May **THE SHOOP SHOOP SONG
(IT'S IN HIS KISS)** Cher **5**

8 Jun **I WANNA SEX YOU UP**
Color Me Badd **3**

29 Jun **ANY DREAM WILL DO**
Jason Donovan **2**

13 Jul **(EVERYTHING I DO) I DO IT FOR YOU**
Bryan Adams **16**

2 Nov **THE FLY** U2 **1**

9 Nov **DIZZY**
Vic Reeves and The Wonder Stuff **2**

23 Nov **BLACK OR WHITE**
Michael Jackson **2**

7 Dec **DON'T LET THE SUN
GO DOWN ON ME**
George Michael and Elton John **2**

21 Dec **BOHEMIAN RHAPSODY / THESE
ARE THE DAYS OF OUR LIVES**
Queen **5**

1992

25 Jan **GOODNIGHT GIRL** Wet Wet Wet **4**

22 Feb **STAY** Shakespear's Sister **8**

18 Apr **DEEPLY DIPPY** Right Said Fred **3**

9 May **PLEASE DON'T GO /
GAME BOY** KWS **5**

13 Jun **ABBA-ESQUE (EP)** – Erasure **5**

18 Jul **AIN'T NO DOUBT** Jimmy Nail **3**

8 Aug **RHYTHM IS A DANCER** Snap! **6**

19 Sep **EBENEEZER GOODE** Shamen **4**

17 Oct **SLEEPING SATELLITE**
Tasmin Archer **2**

· 31 Oct **THE END OF THE ROAD**
Boyz II Men **3**

■ 1991: Should I Stay or Should I Go

21 Nov **WOULD I LIE TO YOU**
Charles and Eddie **2**

5 Dec **I WILL ALWAYS LOVE YOU**
Whitney Houston **10**

1993

13 Feb **NO LIMIT** 2 Unlimited **5**

20 Mar **OH CAROLINA** Shaggy **2**

3 Apr **YOUNG AT HEART** Bluebells **4**

1 May **FIVE LIVE (EP)** George Michael and
Queen with Lisa Stansfield **3**

22 May **ALL THAT SHE WANTS**
Ace of Base **3**

12 Jun **(I CAN'T HELP) FALLING
IN LOVE WITH YOU** UB40 **2**

26 Jun **DREAMS** Gabrielle **3**

17 Jul **PRAY** Take That **4**

14 Aug **LIVING ON MY OWN** Freddie Mercury **2**

28 Aug **MR VAIN** Culture Beat **4**

25 Sep **BOOM! SHAKE THE ROOM**
Jazzy Jeff and The Fresh Prince **2**

9 Oct **RELIGHT MY FIRE**
Take That featuring Lulu **2**

23 Oct **I'D DO ANYTHING FOR LOVE (BUT
I WON'T DO THAT)** Meat Loaf **7**

11 Dec **MR BLOBBY** Mr Blobby **1**

18 Dec **BABE** Take That **1**

25 Dec **MR BLOBBY** Mr Blobby **2**

1994

8 Jan **TWIST AND SHOUT**
Chaka Demus and Pliers with
Jack Radics and Taxi Gang **2**

22 Jan **THINGS CAN ONLY GET BETTER**
D:Ream **4**

■ 1994: Saturday Night

19 Feb **WITHOUT YOU** Mariah Carey **4**
19 Mar **DOOP** Doop **3**
9 Apr **EVERYTHING CHANGES** Take That **2**
23 Apr **THE MOST BEAUTIFUL**
GIRL IN THE WORLD
Symbol (Prince) **2**
7 May **THE REAL THING** Tony Di Bart **1**
14 May **INSIDE** Stiltskin **1**
21 May **COME ON YOU REDS**
Manchester United Football Squad **2**
4 Jun **LOVE IS ALL AROUND**
Wet Wet Wet **15**
17 Sep **SATURDAY NIGHT** Whigfield **4**
15 Oct **SURE** Take That **2**
29 Oct **BABY COME BACK** Pato Banton **4**
26 Nov **LET ME BE YOUR FANTASY** Baby D **2**
10 Dec **STAY ANOTHER DAY** East 17 **5**

1995

14 Jan **COTTON EYE JOE** Rednex **3**
4 Feb **THINK TWICE** Celine Dion **7**
25 Mar **LOVE CAN BUILD A BRIDGE**
Cher, Chrissie Hynde and Neneh
Cherry with Eric Clapton **1**
1 Apr **DON'T STOP (WIGGLE WIGGLE)**
Outhere Brothers **1**
8 Apr **BACK FOR GOOD** Take That **4**
6 May **SOME MIGHT SAY** Oasis **1**
13 May **DREAMER** Livin' Joy **1**
20 May **UNCHAINED MELODY / (THERE'LL**
BE BLUEBIRDS OVER) THE WHITE
CLIFFS OF DOVER
Robson Green and Jerome Flynn **7**
8 Jul **BOOM BOOM BOOM**
Outhere Brothers **4**
5 Aug **NEVER FORGET** Take That **3**
26 Aug **COUNTRY HOUSE** Blur **2**

9 Sep **YOU ARE NOT ALONE**
Michael Jackson **2**
23 Sep **BOOMBASTIC** Shaggy **1**
30 Sep **FAIRGROUND** Simply Red **4**
28 Oct **GANGSTA'S PARADISE**
Coolio featuring LV **2**
11 Nov **I BELIEVE / UP ON THE ROOF**
Robson Green and Jerome Flynn **4**
9 Dec **EARTH SONG** Michael Jackson **6**

1996

20 Jan **JESUS TO A CHILD**
George Michael **1**
27 Jan **SPACEMAN** Babylon Zoo **5**
2 Mar **DON'T LOOK BACK IN ANGER**
Oasis **1**
9 Mar **HOW DEEP IS YOUR LOVE**
Take That **3**
30 Mar **FIRESTARTER** Prodigy **3**
20 Apr **RETURN OF THE MACK**
Mark Morrison **2**
4 May **FASTLOVE** George Michael **3**
25 May **OOH AAH ... JUST A LITTLE BIT**
Gina G **1**
1 Jun **THREE LIONS (THE OFFICIAL**
SONG OF THE ENGLAND
FOOTBALL TEAM) Baddiel and
Skinner and Lightning Seeds **1**
8 Jun **KILLING ME SOFTLY** Fugees **4**
6 Jul **THREE LIONS (THE OFFICIAL**
SONG OF THE ENGLAND
FOOTBALL TEAM) Baddiel and
Skinner and Lightning Seeds **1**
13 Jul **KILLING ME SOFTLY** Fugees **1**
20 Jul **FOREVER LOVE** Gary Barlow **1**
27 Jul **WANNABE** Spice Girls **7**
14 Sep **FLAVA** Peter Andre **1**
21 Sep **READY OR NOT** Fugees **2**
5 Oct **BREAKFAST AT TIFFANY'S**
Deep Blue Something **1**
12 Oct **SETTING SUN** Chemical Brothers **1**
19 Oct **WORDS** Boyzone **1**
26 Oct **SAY YOU'LL BE THERE**
Spice Girls **2**
9 Nov **WHAT BECOMES OF THE BROKEN**
HEARTED / SATURDAY NIGHT
AT THE MOVIES / YOU'LL
NEVER WALK ALONE
Robson Green and Jerome Flynn **2**
23 Nov **BREATHE** Prodigy **2**
7 Dec **I FEEL YOU** Peter Andre **1**
14 Dec **A DIFFERENT BEAT** Boyzone **1**
21 Dec **KNOCKIN' ON HEAVEN'S DOOR /**
THROW THESE GUNS AWAY
Dunblane **1**

28 Dec **2 BECOME 1** Spice Girls **3**

1997

18 Jan **PROFESSIONAL WIDOW**
(IT'S GOT TO BE BIG) Tori Amos **1**
25 Jan **YOUR WOMAN** White Town **1**
1 Feb **BEETLEBUM** Blur **1**
8 Feb **AIN'T NOBODY** LL Cool J **1**
15 Feb **DISCOTHEQUE** U2 **1**
22 Feb **DON'T SPEAK** No Doubt **3**
15 Mar **MAMA / WHO DO YOU**
THINK YOU ARE Spice Girls **3**
5 Apr **BLOCK ROCKIN' BEATS**
Chemical Brothers **1**
12 Apr **I BELIEVE I CAN FLY** R Kelly **3**
3 May **BLOOD ON THE DANCE FLOOR**
Michael Jackson **1**
10 May **LOVE WON'T WAIT** Gary Barlow **1**
17 May **YOU'RE NOT ALONE** Olive **2**
31 May **I WANNA BE THE ONLY ONE**
Eternal featuring BeBe Winans **1**
7 Jun **MMMBOP** Hanson **3**
28 Jun **I'LL BE MISSING YOU** Puff Daddy
and Faith Evans (featuring 112) **3**
19 Jul **D'YOU KNOW WHAT I MEAN?** Oasis **1**
26 Jul **I'LL BE MISSING YOU** Puff Daddy
and Faith Evans (featuring 112) **3**
16 Aug **MEN IN BLACK** Will Smith **4**
13 Sep **THE DRUGS DON'T WORK** Verve **1**
20 Sep **CANDLE IN THE WIND 1997 /**
SOMETHING ABOUT THE WAY YOU
LOOK TONIGHT Elton John **5**
25 Oct **SPICE UP YOUR LIFE** Spice Girls **1**
1 Nov **BARBIE GIRL** Aqua **4**
29 Nov **PERFECT DAY** Various **2**
13 Dec **TELETUBBIES SAY EH-OH!**
Teletubbies **2**
27 Dec **TOO MUCH** Spice Girls **2**

1998

10 Jan **PERFECT DAY** Various **1**
17 Jan **NEVER EVER** All Saints **1**
24 Jan **ALL AROUND THE WORLD** Oasis **1**
31 Jan **YOU MAKE ME WANNA** Usher **1**
7 Feb **DOCTOR JONES** Aqua **2**
21 Feb **MY HEART WILL GO ON**
Celine Dion **1**
28 Feb **BRIMFUL OF ASHA** Cornershop **1**
7 Mar **FROZEN** Madonna **1**
14 Mar **MY HEART WILL GO ON**
Celine Dion **1**
21 Mar **IT'S LIKE THAT**
Run-DMC vs Jason Nevins **6**

■ 1999: Flat Beat

■ 2000: Don't Call Me Baby

2 May   **ALL THAT I NEED** Boyzone **1**
9 May   **UNDER THE BRIDGE /**
        LADY MARMALADE
        All Saints **1**
16 May **TURN BACK TIME** Aqua **1**
23 May **UNDER THE BRIDGE /**
        LADY MARMALADE All Saints **1**
30 May **FEEL IT**
        Tamperer featuring Maya **1**
6 Jun   **C'EST LA VIE** B*Witched **2**
20 Jun **3 LIONS '98** Baddiel and Skinner
        and Lightning Seeds **3**
11 Jul **BECAUSE WE WANT TO** Billie **1**
18 Jul **FREAK ME** Another Level **1**
25 Jul **DEEPER UNDERGROUND**
        Jamiroquai **1**
1 Aug   **VIVA FOREVER** Spice Girls **2**
15 Aug **NO MATTER WHAT** Boyzone **3**
5 Sep   **IF YOU TOLERATE THIS YOUR**
        CHILDREN WILL BE NEXT
        Manic Street Preachers **1**
12 Sep **BOOTIE CALL** All Saints **1**
19 Sep **MILLENNIUM** Robbie Williams **1**
26 Sep **I WANT YOU BACK**
        Melanie B featuring Missy Elliott **1**
3 Oct   **ROLLERCOASTER** B*Witched **2**
17 Oct **GIRLFRIEND** Billie **1**
24 Oct **GYM AND TONIC** Spacedust **1**
31 Oct **BELIEVE** Cher **7**
19 Dec **TO YOU I BELONG** B*Witched **1**
26 Dec **GOODBYE** Spice Girls **1**

1999

2 Jan   **CHOCOLATE SALTY BALLS (PS I**
        LOVE YOU) Chef **1**
9 Jan   **HEARTBEAT / TRAGEDY** Steps **1**
16 Jan **PRAISE YOU** Fatboy Slim **1**
23 Jan **A LITTLE BIT MORE** 911 **1**

30 Jan **PRETTY FLY (FOR A WHITE GUY)**
        Offspring **1**
6 Feb   **YOU DON'T KNOW ME** Armand Van
        Helden featuring Duane Harden **1**
13 Feb **MARIA** Blondie **1**
20 Feb **FLY AWAY** Lenny Kravitz **1**
27 Feb **BABY ONE MORE TIME**
        Britney Spears **2**
13 Mar **WHEN THE GOING GETS TOUGH**
        Boyzone **2**
27 Mar **BLAME IT ON THE WEATHERMAN**
        B*Witched **1**
3 Apr   **FLAT BEAT** Mr Oizo **2**
17 Apr **PERFECT MOMENT**
        Martine McCutcheon **2**
1 May   **SWEAR IT AGAIN** Westlife **2**
15 May **I WANT IT THAT WAY**
        Backstreet Boys **1**
22 May **YOU NEEDED ME** Boyzone **1**
29 May **SWEET LIKE CHOCOLATE**
        Shanks & Bigfoot **2**
12 Jun **EVERYBODY'S FREE (TO WEAR**
        SUNSCREEN) Baz Luhrmann **1**
19 Jun **BRING IT ALL BACK** S Club 7 **1**
26 Jun **BOOM, BOOM, BOOM, BOOM!!**
        Vengaboys **1**
3 Jul   **(9PM) TILL I COME** ATB **2**
17 Jul **LIVIN' LA VIDA LOCA** Ricky Martin **3**
7 Aug   **WHEN YOU SAY NOTHING AT ALL**
        Ronan Keating **2**
21 Aug **IF I LET YOU GO** Westlife **1**
28 Aug **MI CHICO LATINO** Geri Halliwell **1**
4 Sep   **MAMBO NO.5 (A LITTLE BIT OF...)**
        Lou Bega **2**
18 Sep **WE'RE GOING TO IBIZA!** Vengaboys **1**
25 Sep **BLUE (DA BA DEE)** Eiffel 65 **3**
16 Oct **GENIE IN A BOTTLE**
        Christina Aguilera **2**
30 Oct **FLYING WITHOUT WINGS** Westlife **1**
6 Nov   **KEEP ON MOVIN'** Five **1**
13 Nov **LIFT ME UP** Geri Halliwell **1**
20 Nov **SHE'S THE ONE / IT'S ONLY US**
        Robbie Williams **1**
27 Nov **KING OF THE CASTLE**
        Wamdue Project **1**
4 Dec   **THE MILLENNIUM PRAYER**
        Cliff Richard **3**
25 Dec **I HAVE A DREAM /**
        SEASONS IN THE SUN Westlife **4**

2000

22 Jan **THE MASSES AGAINST THE**
        CLASSES Manic Street Preachers **1**
29 Jan **BORN TO MAKE YOU HAPPY**
        Britney Spears **1**

5 Feb   **RISE** Gabrielle **2**
19 Feb **GO LET IT OUT** Oasis **1**
26 Feb **PURE SHORES** All Saints **2**
11 Mar **AMERICAN PIE** Madonna **1**
18 Mar **DON'T GIVE UP**
        Chicane featuring Bryan Adams **1**
25 Mar **BAG IT UP** Geri Halliwell **1**
1 Apr   **NEVER BE THE SAME AGAIN**
        Melanie C / Lisa 'Left Eye' Lopes **1**
8 Apr   **FOOL AGAIN** Westlife **1**
15 Apr **FILL ME IN** Craig David **1**
22 Apr **TOCA'S MIRACLE** Fragma **2**
6 May   **BOUND 4 DA RELOAD**
        (CASUALTY)
        Oxide & Neutrino **1**
13 May **OOPS! ... I DID IT AGAIN**
        Britney Spears **1**
20 May **DON'T CALL ME BABY**
        Madison Avenue **1**
27 May **DAY & NIGHT** Billie Piper **1**
3 Jun   **IT FEELS SO GOOD** Sonique **3**
24 Jun **YOU SEE THE TROUBLE WITH ME**
        Black Legend **1**

■ 2000: Can't Fight the Moonlight

■ 2001: Rollin'

1 Jul	**SPINNING AROUND** Kylie Minogue **1**	
8 Jul	**THE REAL SLIM SHADY** Eminem **1**	
15 Jul	**BREATHLESS** Corrs **1**	
22 Jul	**LIFE IS A ROLLERCOASTER** Ronan Keating **1**	
29 Jul	**WE WILL ROCK YOU** Five and Queen **1**	
5 Aug	**7 DAYS** Craig David **1**	
12 Aug	**ROCK DJ** Robbie Williams **1**	
19 Aug	**I TURN TO YOU** Melanie C **1**	
26 Aug	**GROOVEJET (IF THIS AIN'T LOVE)** Spiller **1**	
2 Sep	**MUSIC** Madonna **1**	
9 Sep	**TAKE ON ME** A1 **1**	
16 Sep	**LADY (HEAR ME TONIGHT)** Modjo **2**	
30 Sep	**AGAINST ALL ODDS** Mariah Carey and Westlife **2**	
14 Oct	**BLACK COFFEE** All Saints **1**	
21 Oct	**BEAUTIFUL DAY** U2 **1**	

■ 2002: Hero

28 Oct	**STOMP** Steps **1**
4 Nov	**HOLLER / LET LOVE LEAD THE WAY** Spice Girls **1**
11 Nov	**MY LOVE** Westlife **1**
18 Nov	**SAME OLD BRAND NEW YOU** A1 **1**
25 Nov	**CAN'T FIGHT THE MOONLIGHT** LeAnn Rimes **1**
2 Dec	**INDEPENDENT WOMEN PART 1** Destiny's Child **1**
9 Dec	**NEVER HAD A DREAM COME TRUE** S Club 7 **1**
16 Dec	**STAN** Eminem **1**
23 Dec	**CAN WE FIX IT** Bob the Builder **3**

2001

13 Jan	**TOUCH ME** Rui Da Silva featuring Cassandra **1**
20 Jan	**LOVE DON'T COST A THING** Jennifer Lopez **1**
27 Jan	**ROLLIN'** Limp Bizkit **2**
10 Feb	**WHOLE AGAIN** Atomic Kitten **4**
10 Mar	**IT WASN'T ME** Shaggy featuring Ricardo 'Rikrok' Ducent **1**
17 Mar	**UPTOWN GIRL** Westlife **1**
24 Mar	**PURE AND SIMPLE** Hear'Say **3**
14 Apr	**WHAT TOOK YOU SO LONG** Emma Bunton **2**
28 Apr	**SURVIVOR** Destiny's Child **1**
5 May	**DON'T STOP MOVIN'** S Club 7 **1**
12 May	**IT'S RAINING MEN** Geri Halliwell **2**
26 May	**DON'T STOP MOVIN'** S Club 7 **1**
2 Jun	**DO YOU REALLY LIKE IT** DJ Pied Piper and The Masters of Ceremonies **1**
9 Jun	**ANGEL** Shaggy Featuring Rayvon **3**
30 Jun	**LADY MARMALADE** Christina Aguilera, Lil' Kim, Mya and Pink **1**
7 Jul	**WAY TO YOUR LOVE** Hear'Say **1**
14 Jul	**ANOTHER CHANCE** Roger Sanchez **1**
21 Jul	**ETERNITY / ROAD TO MANDALAY** Robbie Williams **2**
4 Aug	**ETERNAL FLAME** Atomic Kitten **2**
18 Aug	**21 SECONDS** So Solid Crew **1**
25 Aug	**LET'S DANCE** Five **2**
8 Sep	**TOO CLOSE** Blue **1**
15 Sep	**MAMBO NO.5** Bob the Builder **1**
22 Sep	**HEY BABY (UHH, AHH)** DJ Otzi **1**
29 Sep	**CAN'T GET YOU OUT OF MY HEAD** Kylie Minogue **4**
27 Oct	**BECAUSE I GOT HIGH** Afroman **3**
17 Nov	**QUEEN OF MY HEART** Westlife **1**
24 Nov	**IF YOU COME BACK** Blue **1**
1 Dec	**HAVE YOU EVER** S Club 7 **1**

8 Dec	**GOTTA GET THRU THIS** Daniel Bedingfield **2**
22 Dec	**SOMETHING STUPID** Robbie Williams and Nicole Kidman **3**

2002

12 Jan	**GOTTA GET THRU THIS** Daniel Bedingfield **1**
19 Jan	**MORE THAN A WOMAN** Aaliyah **1**
26 Jan	**MY SWEET LORD** George Harrison **1**
2 Feb	**HERO** Enrique Iglesias **4**
2 Mar	**WORLD OF OUR OWN** Westlife **1**
9 Mar	**EVERGREEN / ANYTHING IS POSSIBLE** Will Young **3**
30 Mar	**UNCHAINED MELODY** Gareth Gates **4**
27 Apr	**THE HINDU TIMES** Oasis **1**
4 May	**FREAK LIKE ME** Sugababes **1**
11 May	**KISS KISS** Holly Valance **1**
18 May	**IF TOMORROW NEVER COMES** Ronan Keating **1**
25 May	**JUST A LITTLE** Liberty X **1**
1 Jun	**WITHOUT ME** Eminem **1**
8 Jun	**LIGHT MY FIRE** Will Young **2**
22 Jun	**A LITTLE LESS CONVERSATION** Elvis vs JXL **4**
20 Jul	**ANYONE OF US (STUPID MISTAKE)** Gareth Gates **3**
10 Aug	**COLOURBLIND** Darius **2**
24 Aug	**ROUND ROUND** Sugababes **1**
31 Aug	**CROSSROADS** Blazin' Squad **1**
7 Sep	**THE TIDE IS HIGH (GET THE FEELING)** Atomic Kitten **3**
28 Sep	**JUST LIKE A PILL** Pink **1**
5 Oct	**THE LONG AND WINDING ROAD / SUSPICIOUS MINDS** Will Young / Gareth Gates **2**
19 Oct	**THE KETCHUP SONG (ASEREJE)** Las Ketchup **1**
26 Oct	**DILEMMA** Nelly featuring Kelly Rowland **2**
9 Nov	**HEAVEN** DJ Sammy and Yanou featuring Do **1**
16 Nov	**UNBREAKABLE** Westlife **1**
23 Nov	**DIRRTY** Christina Aguilera featuring Redman **2**
7 Dec	**IF YOU'RE NOT THE ONE** Daniel Bedingfield **1**
14 Dec	**LOSE YOURSELF** Eminem **1**
21 Dec	**SORRY SEEMS TO BE THE HARDEST WORD** Blue featuring Elton John **1**
28 Dec	**SOUND OF THE UNDERGROUND** Girls Aloud **4** (3 weeks in 2003)

A-Z BY ARTIST

■ Here starts the listing of every band, solo singer, duo, trio, orchestra, pop star, rock star, DJ, puppet, alien or pensioner that has achieved the distinction of at least one week at No.75 in the UK singles chart

HOW TO USE THIS SECTION

This fictitious entry illustrates how to navigate your way through the information contained in the A-Z by Artist section of the book

Regular readers will notice a few changes to this section. In keeping with traditional alphabetical ordering, artist names consisting of initials (eg ABC, KLF) are dealt with at the beginning of each letter's section, except when the names have become acronyms (ie pronounceable as one word, as in Abba). The only exceptions to this rule are for acts appearing as DJs and MCs where there actual names are listed in alphabetical order. Also, for the first time, re-entries are listed in brackets beside the original entry, denoted as (re) for one re-entry, (2re) for two re-entries, (3re) for three re-entries, and so on. For instance, in the fictional entry below, the hit 'Manflesh' re-entered the chart a further three times, as denoted by (3re). All the weeks on chart for the re-entries are added together with those of the main entry. Elsewhere, when a re-entry is notable for a particular reason, we explain why.

Act name

Indicates position of an act within the list of Top 500 acts of all time, calculated by weeks on chart

KARAOKE KNIFE ATTACK 466 Top 500 *Finland, male / female rock group, originally from London, formed in 1978 out of the ashes of influential prog / ambient trio That Way Lies Madness which imploded in 1979 after they were paid £2,480 to sever their contract by indie label Tourniquet (a record sum at the time). Boasted vocalist Neil Neilson, James 'Smack Hell' Thackwell (g), Jackie D'Arcy (b) and classically trained percussionist Glen Day (d). Their triple album 'Trilogy' was No.1 for 49 weeks in Lithuania. Best-selling single: 'Master of My Domain' 604,391 (118 WEEKS).*

For the first time, selected acts now have their best-selling single listed at the end of their biographies

Total weeks on chart

● UK Top 10 hit

★ UK No.1 hit

pos/wks

Date	Title	pos	wks
19 Mar 80	**DENIAL OF FATE** *HIT Records 008*	18	15
24 Dec 80 ●	**THE JERK STORE** *HIT Records 009*	5	17
2 Feb 81 ★	**MASTER OF MY DOMAIN** *HIT Records 010* ◆	1	26
30 Sep 81 ●	**GANGS OF BALHAM** *HIT Records 011* ▲	8	8
1 Dec 81	**CALZONE FOR CORLEONE** *HIT Records 009*	52	1
12 Jun 82	**POPSTARS – THE REPRISALS** *HIT Records 012* 1	4	20
22 Oct 83 ●	**MANFLESH (3re)** *HIT Records 013*	6	16
3 Dec 83 ★	**PASS THE BUCKFAST** *HIT Records 014* ■	1	23
13 Mar 90	**GIT** *HIT Records 015*	26	3
11 Sep 91	**OL' DIRTY BASTARD TRIBUTE (EP)** *HIT Records 016* 2	74	1
30 Nov 02	**GANGS OF BALHAM (re-mix)** *HIT Records 017*	11	5+

◆ UK million seller

▲ US No.1

■ UK entry at No.1

New listing for re-entries: (3re) here denotes that 'Manflesh' re-entered the Top 75 three times

1 2 etc refers to a footnote indicating a change to the name of the act for a particular single or a collaboration with another artist

1 Karaoke Knife Attack featuring the Chipolataheadz
2 We Fear Change featuring Karaoke Knife Attack

Tracks on Ol' Dirty Bastard Tribute (EP): Brooklyn Zoo / Shimmy Shimmy Ya / Baby I Got Your Money / Free ODB (DJ Deecee Remix)

See also BERSERKER, SERPICO'S BEARD

Cross-reference linking act to associated act or acts

+ Still on chart in Jan 2003

Label / catalogue numbers generally taken from the seven-inch vinyl single before Jan 1993 and CD single after this time

EP track titles

MINI-BIOGRAPHY ABBREVIATIONS

b. – born, d. – died, b – bass guitar, d – drums, fl – flute, g – guitar, k – keyboard, prc – percussion, prog – programming, s – saxophone, syn – synthesizer, t – trumpet, v – vocals

In this edition, for the first time, the act biographies include the real names (if act has a different surname) of all solo artists and duos scoring a Top 75 hit, and the date of death of deceased solo artists

A

A *UK, male vocal / instrumental group (16 WEEKS)* pos/wks

Date	Title	pos	wks
7 Feb 98	FOGHORN *Tycoon TYCD 5*...................................63	63	1
11 Apr 98	NUMBER ONE *Tycoon TYCD 6*...........................47	47	1
27 Jun 98	SING-A-LONG *Tycoon TYCD 7*..........................57	57	1
24 Oct 98	SUMMER ON THE UNDERGROUND *Tycoon TYCD 8* 72	72	1
5 Jun 99	OLD FOLKS *Tycoon TYCD 9*..............................54	54	1
21 Aug 99	I LOVE LAKE TAHOE *Tycoon TYCD 10*...............59	59	1
2 Mar 02 ●	NOTHING *London LONCD 463*..............................9	9	6
1 Jun 02	STARBUCKS *London LONCD 467*.......................20	20	3
30 Nov 02	SOMETHING'S GOIN' ON *London LONCD 471*.......51	51	1

ABC (341) *Top 500* *Glossy but witty pop group formed 1980 in Sheffield, South Yorkshire, UK. Led by stylish vocalist Martin Fry b. 9 Mar 1959. First UK group of the 1980s to prise four Top 20 hits off debut album (1982's 'The Lexicon of Love') and were equally successful Stateside (93 WEEKS)* pos/wks

Date	Title	pos	wks
31 Oct 81	TEARS ARE NOT ENOUGH *Neutron NT 101*.........19	19	8
20 Feb 82 ●	POISON ARROW *Neutron NT 102*..........................6	6	11
15 May 82 ●	THE LOOK OF LOVE (re) *Neutron NT 103*............4	4	12
4 Sep 82 ●	ALL OF MY HEART *Neutron NT 104*......................5	5	8
5 Nov 83	THAT WAS THEN BUT THIS IS NOW *Neutron NT 105*.......18	18	4
21 Jan 84	S.O.S. *Neutron NT 106*.....................................39	39	5
10 Nov 84	HOW TO BE A MILLIONAIRE *Neutron NT 107*......49	49	4
6 Apr 85	BE NEAR ME *Neutron NT 108*............................26	26	4
15 Jun 85	VANITY KILLS *Neutron NT 109*...........................70	70	1
16 Jan 86	OCEAN BLUE *Neutron NT 110*...........................51	51	3
6 Jun 87	WHEN SMOKEY SINGS *Neutron NT 111*.............11	11	10
5 Sep 87	THE NIGHT YOU MURDERED LOVE *Neutron NT 112*.......31	31	8
28 Nov 87	KING WITHOUT A CROWN *Neutron NT 113*.........44	44	3
27 May 89	ONE BETTER WORLD *Neutron NT 114*................32	32	4
23 Sep 89	THE REAL THING *Neutron NT 115*......................68	68	1
14 Apr 90	THE LOOK OF LOVE (re-mix) *Neutron NT 116*.....68	68	1
27 Jul 91	LOVE CONQUERS ALL *Parlophone R 6292*.........47	47	2
11 Jan 92	SAY IT *Parlophone R 6298*................................42	42	3
22 Mar 97	STRANGER THINGS *Blatant / Deconstruction 453632*.......57	57	1

The act was a UK, male vocal / instrumental group for first six hits, and a UK / US, male / female vocal / instrumental group for the next four; male duo 87-92 and Martin Fry alone for 'Stranger Things'

AC/DC (220) *Top 500* *Internationally acclaimed Australia-based quintet: Angus Young (g). Malcolm Young (g), Bon Scott (v) (d. 1980), Cliff Williams (b), Phillip Rudd (d). Brian Johnson (ex-Geordie) replaced Scott in 1980. No act has had more hits (28) without a Top 10 than AC/DC (126 WEEKS)* pos/wks

Date	Title	pos	wks
10 Jun 78	ROCK 'N' ROLL DAMNATION *Atlantic K 11142*.......24	24	9
1 Sep 79	HIGHWAY TO HELL *Atlantic K 11321*...................56	56	4
2 Feb 80	TOUCH TOO MUCH *Atlantic K 11435*.................29	29	9
28 Jun 80	DIRTY DEEDS DONE DIRT CHEAP *Atlantic HM 2*.......47	47	3
28 Jun 80	HIGH VOLTAGE (LIVE VERSION) *Atlantic HM 1*......48	48	3
28 Jun 80	IT'S A LONG WAY TO THE TOP (IF YOU WANNA ROCK 'N' ROLL) *Atlantic HM 3*.......55	55	3
28 Jun 80	WHOLE LOTTA ROSIE *Atlantic HM 4*..................36	36	8
13 Sep 80	YOU SHOOK ME ALL NIGHT LONG *Atlantic K 11600*........38	38	6
29 Nov 80	ROCK 'N' ROLL AIN'T NOISE POLLUTION *Atlantic K 11630*......15	15	8
6 Feb 82	LET'S GET IT UP *Atlantic K 11706*......................13	13	6
3 Jul 82	FOR THOSE ABOUT TO ROCK (WE SALUTE YOU) *Atlantic K 11721*.......15	15	6
29 Oct 83	GUNS FOR HIRE *Atlantic A 9774*.......................37	37	4
4 Aug 84	NERVOUS SHAKEDOWN *Atlantic A 9651*...........35	35	5
6 Jul 85	DANGER *Atlantic A 9532*..................................48	48	4
18 Jan 86	SHAKE YOUR FOUNDATIONS *Atlantic A 9474*.......24	24	5
24 May 86	WHO MADE WHO *Atlantic A 9425*.....................16	16	5
30 Aug 86	YOU SHOOK ME ALL NIGHT LONG (re-issue) *Atlantic A 9377*.......46	46	4
16 Jan 88	HEATSEEKER *Atlantic A 9136*...........................12	12	6
2 Apr 88	THAT'S THE WAY I WANNA ROCK 'N' ROLL *Atlantic A 9098* 22	22	5
22 Sep 90	THUNDERSTRUCK *Atco B 8907*.........................13	13	5
24 Nov 90	MONEYTALKS *Atco B 8886*................................36	36	3
27 Apr 91	ARE YOU READY *Atco B 8830*...........................34	34	3
17 Oct 92	HIGHWAY TO HELL (LIVE) *Atco B 8479*..............14	14	4
6 Mar 93	DIRTY DEEDS DONE DIRT CHEAP (LIVE) *Atco B 6073CD* 68	68	1
10 Jul 93	BIG GUN *Atco B 8396CD*..................................23	23	3
30 Sep 95	HARD AS A ROCK *Atlantic A 4368CD*.................33	33	2
11 May 96	HAIL CAESAR *East West 7559660512*...............56	56	1
15 Apr 00	STIFF UPPER LIP *EMI CDSTIFF 100*...................65	65	1

A CAMP *Sweden / US, female / male vocal / instrumental group leader Nina Persson (1 WEEK)* pos/wks

Date	Title	pos	wks
1 Sep 01	I CAN BUY YOU *Stockholm 0152162*...................46	46	1

A CERTAIN RATIO
UK, male vocal / instrumental group (3 WEEKS) pos/wks

Date	Title	pos	wks
16 Jun 90	WON'T STOP LOVING YOU *A & M ACR 540*.........55	55	3

A.D.A.M. featuring AMY
France, male / female vocal / instrumental duo (11 WEEKS) pos/wks

Date	Title	pos	wks
1 Jul 95	ZOMBIE *Eternal YZ 951CD*................................16	16	11

AFX *UK, male instrumentalist / producer – Richard James (1 WEEK)* pos/wks

Date	Title	pos	wks
11 Aug 01	2 REMIXES BY AFX *MEN1 MEN1CD*△..................69	69	1

See also POLYGON WINDOW; APHEX TWIN

A HOUSE *Ireland, male vocal / instrumental group (8 WEEKS)* pos/wks

Date	Title	pos	wks
13 Jun 92	ENDLESS ART *Setanta AHOU 1*..........................46	46	3
8 Aug 92	TAKE IT EASY ON ME *Setanta AHOU 2*...............55	55	2
25 Jun 94	WHY ME *Setanta CDAHOU 4*.............................52	52	1
1 Oct 94	HERE COME THE GOOD TIMES *Setanta CDAHOUS 5*.......37	37	2

AKA *UK, male vocal group (2 WEEKS)* pos/wks

Date	Title	pos	wks
12 Oct 96	WARNING *RCA 74321360662*.............................43	43	2

a1 (350) *Top 500* *Top UK boy band who have written and played on their recordings: Mark Read, Paul Marazzi, Ben Adams and Norwegian Christian Ingebrigtsen. Quartet, who scored two No.1s in a 10-week period, were winners of 2001 Brits Newcomer award (91 WEEKS)* pos/wks

Date	Title	pos	wks
3 Jul 99 ●	BE THE FIRST TO BELIEVE *Columbia 6674222* 6	6	9
11 Sep 99 ●	SUMMERTIME OF OUR LIVES (re) *Columbia 6678322*.......5	5	8
20 Nov 99 ●	EVERYTIME / READY OR NOT *Columbia 6681872* 3	3	11
4 Mar 00 ●	LIKE A ROSE *Columbia 6689032*.........................6	6	12
9 Sep 00 ★	TAKE ON ME (re) *Columbia 6695902*■................1	1	11
18 Nov 00 ★	SAME OLD BRAND NEW YOU *Columbia 6705202*■.......1	1	10
3 Mar 01 ●	NO MORE (re) *Columbia 6708742*.......................6	6	13
2 Feb 02 ●	CAUGHT IN THE MIDDLE *Columbia 6722322*........2	2	12
25 May 02	MAKE IT GOOD (re) *Columbia 6726182*...............11	11	5

A PERFECT CIRCLE
US, male vocal / instrumental group (2 WEEKS) pos/wks

Date	Title	pos	wks
18 Nov 00	THE HOLLOW *Virgin VUSCD 181*.........................72	72	1
13 Jan 01	3 LIBRAS *Virgin VUSCD 184*..............................49	49	1

A+ *US, male rapper – Andre Levins (9 WEEKS)* pos/wks

Date	Title	pos	wks
13 Feb 99 ●	ENJOY YOURSELF *Universal UND 56230*...............5	5	9

A.R.E. WEAPONS *US, male vocal / insrumental group (1 WEEK)* pos/wks

Date	Title	pos	wks
4 Aug 01	STREET GANG *Rough Trade RTRADESCD 022*.......72	72	1

ASAP *UK, male vocal / instrumental group (4 WEEKS)* pos/wks

Date	Title	pos	wks
14 Oct 89	SILVER AND GOLD *EMI EM 107*..........................60	60	2
3 Feb 90	DOWN THE WIRE *EMI EM 131*...........................67	67	2

ATB *Germany, male producer – Andre Tanneberger (52 WEEKS)* pos/wks

Date	Title	pos	wks
13 Mar 99	(9PM) TILL I COME *Ministry of Sound DATA 1*.......68	68	1
22 May 99	(9PM) TILL I COME (German import) (re) *Club Tools CLU 66066*.......47	47	5

19 Jun 99	**(9PM) TILL I COME (Australian import)** *Dancenet DNET 131*	63	1
3 Jul 99 ★	**(9PM) TILL I COME** *Sound of Ministry MOSCDS 132* ■	1	15
9 Oct 99	**DON'T STOP (import)** *Club Tools CLU 66406*	61	2
23 Oct 99 ●	**DON'T STOP (re)** *Sound of Ministry MOSCDS 134*	3	13
25 Mar 00 ●	**KILLER (re)** *Sound of Ministry MOSCDS 138*	4	9
27 Jan 01	**THE FIELDS OF LOVE** *Club Tools / Edel 0124095 CLU* [1]	16	4
30 Jun 01	**LET U GO** *Kontour 0117335 KTR*	34	2

[1] ATB featuring York

ATC *Italy / New Zealand / UK / Australia, male / female vocal group (4 WEEKS)*

		pos/wks	
17 Aug 02	**AROUND THE WORLD (LA LA LA LA)** *EMI / Liberty CDATC 001*	15	4

A.T.F.C. presents ONEPHATDEEVA
UK, male producer – Aydin Hasirci (10 WEEKS)

		pos/wks	
30 Oct 99	**IN AND OUT OF MY LIFE** *Defected DEFECT 8CDS*	11	5
16 Sep 00	**BAD HABIT** *Defected DFECT 19CDS* [1]	17	3
9 Feb 02	**SLEEP TALK** *Defected DFECT 43CDS* [2]	33	2

[1] A.T.F.C. presents Onephatdeeva featuring Lisa Millett [2] A.T.F.C. featuring Lisa Millett

A.T.G.O.C.
Italy, male instrumentalist / producer – Andrea Mazzali (2 WEEKS)

		pos/wks	
21 Nov 98	**REPEATED LOVE** *Wonderboy WBOYD 012*	38	2

A*TEENS *Sweden, male / female vocal group (19 WEEKS)*

		pos/wks	
4 Sep 99	**MAMMA MIA** *Stockholm 5613432*	12	5
•11 Dec 99	**SUPER TROUPER** *Stockholm 5615002*	21	5
26 May 01 ●	**UPSIDE DOWN** *Stockholm 1588492*	10	7
27 Oct 01	**HALFWAY AROUND THE WORLD** *Stockholm 0153612*	30	2

A vs B *UK, male production duo (1 WEEK)*

		pos/wks	
9 May 98	**RIPPED IN 2 MINUTES** *Positiva CDTIV 89*	49	1

AALIYAH
US, female vocalist – Aaliyah Haughton, d. 25 Aug 2001 (69 WEEKS)

		pos/wks	
2 Jul 94	**BACK AND FORTH** *Jive JIVECD 357*	16	5
15 Oct 94	**(AT YOUR BEST) YOU ARE LOVE** *Jive JIVECD 359*	27	2
11 Mar 95	**AGE AIN'T NOTHING BUT A NUMBER** *Jive JIVECD 369*	32	2
13 May 95	**DOWN WITH THE CLIQUE** *Jive JIVECD 377*	33	2
9 Sep 95	**THE THING I LIKE** *Jive JIVECD 382*	33	2
3 Feb 96	**I NEED YOU TONIGHT** *Big Beat A 8130CD* [1]	66	1
24 Aug 96	**IF YOUR GIRL ONLY KNEW** *Atlantic A 5669CD*	21	2
23 Nov 96	**GOT TO GIVE IT UP** *Atlantic A 5632CD*	37	2
24 May 97	**IF YOUR GIRL ONLY KNEW / ONE IN A MILLION** (re-issue) *Atlantic A 5610CD*	15	3
30 Aug 97	**4 PAGE LETTER** *Atlantic AT 0010CD1*	24	2
22 Nov 97	**THE ONE I GAVE MY HEART TO / HOT LIKE FIRE** *Atlantic AT 0017CD*	30	2
18 Apr 98	**JOURNEY TO THE PAST** *Atlantic AT 0026CD*	22	3
12 Sep 98	**ARE YOU THAT SOMEBODY?** *Atlantic AT 0047CD*	11	4
22 Jul 00 ●	**TRY AGAIN (re)** *Virgin VUSCD 167* ▲	5	12
21 Jul 01	**WE NEED A RESOLUTION (re)** *Blackground VUSCD 206* [2]	20	6
19 Jan 02	**MORE THAN A WOMAN** *Blackground / Virgin VUSCD 230* ■	1	12
18 May 02	**ROCK THE BOAT** *Blackground / Virgin VUSCD 243*	12	7

[1] Junior M.A.F.I.A. featuring Aaliyah [2] Aaliyah featuring Timbaland

ABBA `47` `Top 500` *The most successful Swedish recording act in the UK: Björn Ulvaeus (g/v), Benny Andersson (k/v), Agnetha Fältskog (v), and Norwegian Anni-Frid (Frida) Lyngstad (v). 'Waterloo' was the first Scandinavian No.1 in the UK and the biggest ever Eurovision Song Contest-winning hit in the US (252 WEEKS)*

		pos/wks	
20 Apr 74 ★	**WATERLOO** *Epic EPC 2240*	1	9
13 Jul 74	**RING RING** *Epic EPC 2452*	32	2
12 Jul 75	**I DO, I DO, I DO, I DO, I DO** *Epic EPC 3229*	38	6
20 Sep 75 ●	**S.O.S.** *Epic EPC 3576*	6	10
13 Dec 75 ★	**MAMMA MIA** *Epic EPC 3790*	1	14
27 Mar 76 ★	**FERNANDO** *Epic EPC 4036*	1	15
21 Aug 76 ★	**DANCING QUEEN** *Epic EPC 4499* ▲	1	15
20 Nov 76 ●	**MONEY, MONEY, MONEY** *Epic EPC 4713*	3	12
26 Feb 77 ●	**KNOWING ME, KNOWING YOU** *Epic EPC 4955*	1	13
22 Oct 77 ★	**THE NAME OF THE GAME** *Epic EPC 5750*	1	12
4 Feb 78 ★	**TAKE A CHANCE ON ME** *Epic EPC 5950*	1	10
16 Sep 78 ●	**SUMMER NIGHT CITY** *Epic EPC 6595*	5	9
3 Feb 79 ●	**CHIQUITITA** *Epic EPC 7030*	2	9
5 May 79 ●	**DOES YOUR MOTHER KNOW** *Epic EPC 7316*	4	9
14 Jul 79 ●	**ANGELEYES / VOULEZ-VOUS** *Epic EPC 7499*	3	11
20 Oct 79 ●	**GIMME, GIMME, GIMME (A MAN AFTER MIDNIGHT)** *Epic EPC 7914*	3	12
15 Dec 79 ●	**I HAVE A DREAM** *Epic EPC 8088*	2	10
2 Aug 80 ★	**THE WINNER TAKES IT ALL** *Epic EPC 8835*	1	10
15 Nov 80 ★	**SUPER TROUPER** *Epic EPC 9089*	1	12
18 Jul 81 ●	**LAY ALL YOUR LOVE ON ME** *Epic EPC A13 1456*	7	7
12 Dec 81 ●	**ONE OF US** *Epic EPC A 1740*	3	10
20 Feb 82	**HEAD OVER HEELS** *Epic EPC A 2037*	25	7
23 Oct 82	**THE DAY BEFORE YOU CAME** *Epic EPC A 2847*	32	6
11 Dec 82	**UNDER ATTACK** *Epic EPC A 2971*	26	8
12 Nov 83	**THANK YOU FOR THE MUSIC** *CBS A 3894*	33	6
5 Sep 92	**DANCING QUEEN (re-issue)** *Polydor PO 231*	16	5

'Lay All Your Love on Me' was available only on 12-inch vinyl in the UK

ABBACADABRA
UK, male / female vocal / instrumental group (1 WEEK)

		pos/wks	
5 Sep 92	**DANCING QUEEN** *PWL International PWL 246*	57	1

Russ ABBOT
UK, male comedian / vocalist – Russell Roberts (22 WEEKS)

		pos/wks	
6 Feb 82	**A DAY IN THE LIFE OF VINCE PRINCE (re)** *EMI 5249*	61	2
29 Dec 84 ●	**ATMOSPHERE** *Spirit FIRE 4*	7	13
13 Jul 85	**ALL NIGHT HOLIDAY** *Spirit FIRE 6*	20	7

Gregory ABBOTT *US, male vocalist (13 WEEKS)*

		pos/wks	
22 Nov 86 ●	**SHAKE YOU DOWN** *CBS A 7326* ▲	6	13

Paula ABDUL *US, female vocalist (67 WEEKS)*

		pos/wks	
4 Mar 89 ●	**STRAIGHT UP** *Siren SRN 111* ▲	3	13
3 Jun 89	**FOREVER YOUR GIRL** *Siren SRN 112* ▲	24	6
19 Aug 89	**KNOCKED OUT** *Siren SRN 92*	45	3
2 Dec 89	**(IT'S JUST) THE WAY THAT YOU LOVE ME** *Siren SRN 101*	74	1
7 Apr 90 ●	**OPPOSITES ATTRACT** *Siren SRN 124* [1] ▲	2	13
21 Jul 90	**KNOCKED OUT (re-mix)** *Virgin America VUS 23*	21	5
29 Sep 90	**COLD HEARTED** *Virgin America VUS 27* ▲	46	3
22 Jun 91 ●	**RUSH RUSH** *Virgin America VUS 38* ▲	6	11
31 Aug 91	**THE PROMISE OF A NEW DAY** *Virgin America VUS 44* ▲	52	2
18 Jan 92	**VIBEOLOGY** *Virgin America VUS 53*	19	6
8 Aug 92	**WILL YOU MARRY ME** *Virgin America VUS 58*	73	1
17 Jun 95	**MY LOVE IS FOR REAL** *Virgin America VUSCD 91* [2]	28	3

[1] Paula Abdul with the Wild Pair [2] Paula Abdul featuring Ofra Haza

ABI *UK, male vocalist (2 WEEKS)*

		pos/wks	
13 Jun 98	**COUNTING THE DAYS** *Kuku CDKUKU 1*	44	2

ABIGAIL *UK, female vocalist – Gayle Zsigmond (4 WEEKS)*

		pos/wks	
16 Jul 94	**SMELLS LIKE TEEN SPIRIT** *Klone CDKLONE 25*	29	4

ABNEA – See Johan GIELEN presents ABNEA

Colonel ABRAMS *US, male vocalist (35 WEEKS)*

		pos/wks	
17 Aug 85 ●	**TRAPPED** *MCA MCA 997*	3	23
7 Dec 85	**THE TRUTH** *MCA MCA 1022*	53	3
8 Feb 86	**I'M NOT GONNA LET YOU** *MCA MCA 1031*	24	7
15 Aug 87	**HOW SOON WE FORGET** *MCA MCA 1179*	75	2

ABS *UK, male vocalist / rapper – Richard Breen (8 WEEKS)*

		pos/wks	
31 Aug 02 ●	**WHAT YOU GOT** *S 74321957192*	4	8

See also FIVE

ABSOLUTE *US, male production / instrumental duo –*
Mark Picchiotti and Craig Snider (3 WEEKS)   pos/wks

| 18 Jan 97 | I BELIEVE *AM:PM 5820752* 1 | 38 | 2 |
| 14 Mar 98 | CATCH ME *AM:PM 5825032* | 69 | 1 |

1 Absolute featuring Suzanne Palmer

ABSOLUTELY FABULOUS – *See PET SHOP BOYS*

ACE *UK, male vocal / instrumental group (10 WEEKS)*   pos/wks

| 9 Nov 74 | HOW LONG *Anchor ANC 1002* | 20 | 10 |

Richard ACE *Jamaica, male vocalist (2 WEEKS)*   pos/wks

| 2 Dec 78 | STAYIN' ALIVE *Blue Inc. INC 2* | 66 | 2 |

ACE OF BASE 311 Top 500 *Swedish pop-reggae outfit comprising*
three Berggren family members, Linn (v), Jenny (v), Jonas "Joker" (k) and Ulf
"Buddha" Ekberg (k) all from Gothenburg. Only Swedish act to top the US
album chart with 'The Sign' (titled 'Happy Nation' outside US) in 1994. Best-
selling single: 'All That She Wants' 603,900 (100 WEEKS)   pos/wks

8 May 93	★ ALL THAT SHE WANTS *London 8612702*	1	16
28 Aug 93	WHEEL OF FORTUNE *London 8615452*	20	6
13 Nov 93	HAPPY NATION *London 8619272*	42	3
26 Feb 94	● THE SIGN *London ACECD 1* ▲	2	16
11 Jun 94	● DON'T TURN AROUND *London ACECD 2*	5	11
15 Oct 94	HAPPY NATION (re-issue) *London 8610972*	40	3
14 Jan 95	LIVING IN DANGER *London ACECD 3*	18	4
11 Nov 95	LUCKY LOVE *London ACECD 4*	20	5
27 Jan 96	BEAUTIFUL LIFE *London ACECD 5*	15	6
25 Jul 98	● LIFE IS A FLOWER *London ACECD 7*	5	11
10 Oct 98	● CRUEL SUMMER *London ACECD 8*	8	5
19 Dec 98	ALWAYS HAVE, ALWAYS WILL *London ACECD 9*	12	10
17 Apr 99	EVERYTIME IT RAINS *London ACECD 10*	22	4

ACEN *UK, male producer – Syed Ahsen Razvi (4 WEEKS)*   pos/wks

| 8 Aug 92 | TRIP II THE MOON *Production House PNT 042* | 38 | 3 |
| 10 Oct 92 | TRIP II THE MOON (re-mix) *Production House PNT 042RX* | 71 | 1 |

ACES – *See Desmond DEKKER and the ACES*

Tracy ACKERMAN – *See Q*

ACT *UK / Germany, male / female*
vocal / instrumental group (2 WEEKS)   pos/wks

| 23 May 87 | SNOBBERY AND DECAY *ZTT ZTAS 28* | 60 | 2 |

ACT ONE *US, male / female vocal / instrumental group (6 WEEKS)* pos/wks

| 18 May 74 | TOM THE PEEPER *Mercury 6008 005* | 40 | 6 |

ACZESS *UK, male producer (1 WEEK)*   pos/wks

| 27 Oct 01 | DO WHAT WE WOULD *INCredible 6719782* | 65 | 1 |

ADAM and the ANTS 205 Top 500
Warpaint-wearing, colourfully costumed 'Antmusic' innovators: included
Stuart (Adam Ant) Goddard (v) and Marco Pirroni (g). The London-based act
was 1981's top chart act with nine hits. Also in that year, they amassed 91
chart weeks – a total not bettered until 1996. Best-selling single: 'Stand and
Deliver' 985,000 (130 WEEKS)   pos/wks

2 Aug 80	● KINGS OF THE WILD FRONTIER (re) *CBS 8877*	2	18
11 Oct 80	● DOG EAT DOG *CBS 9039*	4	16
6 Dec 80	● ANTMUSIC *CBS 9352*	2	18
27 Dec 80	● YOUNG PARISIANS *Decca F13803*	9	13
24 Jan 81	CARTROUBLE *Do It DUN 10*	33	9
24 Jan 81	ZEROX *Do It DUN 8*	45	9
9 May 81	★ STAND AND DELIVER *CBS A 1065* ■	1	15
12 Sep 81	★ PRINCE CHARMING *CBS A 1408*	1	12
12 Dec 81	● ANT RAP *CBS A 1738*	3	10
27 Feb 82	DEUTSCHER GIRLS *Ego 5*	13	6

| 13 Mar 82 | THE ANTMUSIC EP (THE B-SIDES) *Do It DUN 20* | 46 | 4 |

'Kings of the Wild Frontier' reached only No.48 on its first visit to the chart, peaking
at No.2 as a re-entry in Feb 1981. Tracks on The Antmusic EP (The B-sides): Friends /
Kick / Physical

See also Adam ANT

Arthur ADAMS *US, male vocalist (5 WEEKS)*   pos/wks

| 24 Oct 81 | YOU GOT THE FLOOR *RCA 146* | 38 | 5 |

Bryan ADAMS 54 Top 500
Globally successful rock singer / songwriter / guitarist, b. 5 Nov 1959,
Kingston, Ontario. He has had more UK hits than any other Canadian artist
and was the biggest-selling singles artist in the UK in 1991 when he hogged
the No.1 spot for a record 16 consecutive weeks. Biggest-selling single:
'(Everything I Do) I Do it for You' 1,527,824 (243 WEEKS)   pos/wks

12 Jan 85	RUN TO YOU *A&M AM 224*	11	12
16 Mar 85	SOMEBODY *A&M AM 236*	35	7
25 May 85	HEAVEN *A&M AM 256* ▲	38	5
10 Aug 85	SUMMER OF '69 *A&M AM 267*	42	7
2 Nov 85	IT'S ONLY LOVE *A&M AM 285* 1	29	6
21 Dec 85	CHRISTMAS TIME *A&M AM 297*	55	2
22 Feb 86	THIS TIME *A&M AM 295*	41	7
12 Jul 86	STRAIGHT FROM THE HEART *A&M AM 322*	51	3
28 Mar 87	HEAT OF THE NIGHT *A&M ADAM 2*	50	2
20 Jun 87	HEARTS ON FIRE *A&M ADAM 3* ▲	57	3
17 Oct 87	VICTIM OF LOVE *A&M AM 407*	68	2
29 Jun 91	★ (EVERYTHING I DO) I DO IT FOR YOU (re) *A&M AM 789* ◆ ▲	1	25
14 Sep 91	CAN'T STOP THIS THING WE STARTED *A&M AM 612*	12	6
23 Nov 91	THERE WILL NEVER BE ANOTHER TONIGHT *A&M AM 838*	32	3
22 Feb 92	● THOUGHT I'D DIED AND GONE TO HEAVEN *A&M AM 848*	8	7
18 Jul 92	ALL I WANT IS YOU *A&M AM 879*	22	5
26 Sep 92	DO I HAVE TO SAY THE WORDS *A&M AM 0068*	30	3
30 Oct 93	● PLEASE FORGIVE ME *A&M 5804232*	2	16
15 Jan 94	● ALL FOR LOVE *A&M 5804772* 2 ▲	2	13
22 Apr 95	HAVE YOU EVER REALLY LOVED A WOMAN *A&M 5810282* ▲	4	9
11 Nov 95	ROCK STEADY *Capitol CDCL 763* 3	50	2
1 Jun 96	● THE ONLY THING THAT LOOKS GOOD ON ME IS YOU *A&M 5813692*	6	7
24 Aug 96	LET'S MAKE A NIGHT TO REMEMBER *A&M 5815672*	10	8
23 Nov 96	STAR *A&M 5820252*	13	4
8 Feb 97	● I FINALLY FOUND SOMEONE *A&M 5820832* 4	10	7
19 Apr 97	18 TIL I DIE *A&M 5821852*	22	3
20 Dec 97	BACK TO YOU *A&M 5824752*	18	7
21 Mar 98	I'M READY *A&M 5825352*	20	4
10 Oct 98	ON A DAY LIKE TODAY *Mercury MERCD 516*	13	5
12 Dec 98	● WHEN YOU'RE GONE *A&M 5828212* 5	3	19
15 May 99	● CLOUD NUMBER 9 *A&M / Mercury 5828492*	6	9
18 Dec 99	THE BEST OF ME (re) *Mercury / A&M 4971952*	47	3
18 Mar 00	★ DON'T GIVE UP *Xtravaganza XTRAV 9CDS* 6 ■	1	14
20 Jul 02	● HERE I AM *A&M 4977442*	5	8

1 Bryan Adams and Tina Turner 2 Bryan Adams, Rod Stewart and Sting
3 Bonnie Raitt and Bryan Adams 4 Barbra Streisand and Bryan Adams
5 Bryan Adams featuring Melanie C 6 Chicane featuring Bryan Adams

Cliff ADAMS ORCHESTRA
UK, orchestra, leader d. 27 Oct 2001 (2 WEEKS)   pos/wks

| 28 Apr 60 | THE LONELY MAN THEME *Pye International 7N 25056* | 39 | 2 |

Gayle ADAMS *US, female vocalist (1 WEEK)*   pos/wks

| 26 Jul 80 | STRETCHIN' OUT *Epic EPC 8791* | 64 | 1 |

Marie ADAMS – *See Johnny OTIS SHOW*

Oleta ADAMS *US, female vocalist (36 WEEKS)*   pos/wks

24 Mar 90	RHYTHM OF LIFE (re) *Fontana OLETA 1*	52	5
12 Jan 91	● GET HERE *Fontana OLETA 3*	4	12
13 Apr 91	YOU'VE GOT TO GIVE ME ROOM / RHYTHM OF LIFE (re-issue) *Fontana OLETA 4*	49	3
29 Jun 91	CIRCLE OF ONE *Fontana OLETA 5*	73	1
28 Sep 91	DON'T LET THE SUN GO DOWN ON ME *Fontana TRIBO 1*	33	5
25 Apr 92	WOMAN IN CHAINS (re-issue) *Fontana IDEA 16* 1	57	1

Date	Title	pos	wks
10 Jul 93	I JUST HAD TO HEAR YOUR VOICE *Fontana OLECD 6*	42	3
7 Oct 95	NEVER KNEW LOVE *Fontana OLECD 9*	22	3
16 Dec 95	RHYTHM OF LIFE (re-mix) *Fontana OLECD 10*	38	2
10 Feb 96	WE WILL MEET AGAIN *Mercury OLECD 11*	51	1

1 Tears for Fears featuring Oleta Adams

The original release of 'Woman in Chains' credited Tears for Fears only

Ryan ADAMS *US, male vocalist (4 WEEKS)* pos/wks

Date	Title	pos	wks
8 Dec 01	NEW YORK NEW YORK *Lost Highway 1722232*	53	1
20 Apr 02	ANSWERING BELL *Lost Highway 1722392*	39	2
28 Sep 02	NUCLEAR *Lost Highway 1722592*	37	1

ADAMSKI
UK, male instrumentalist / producer – Adam Tinley (39 WEEKS) pos/wks

Date	Title	pos	wks
20 Jan 90	N-R-G *MCA MCA 1386*	12	6
7 Apr 90 ★	KILLER *MCA MCA 1400*	1	18
8 Sep 90 ●	THE SPACE JUNGLE *MCA MCA 1435*	7	8
17 Nov 90	FLASHBACK JACK *MCA MCA 1459*	46	2
9 Nov 91	NEVER GOIN' DOWN / BORN TO BE ALIVE *MCA MCS 1578* 1	51	2
4 Apr 92	GET YOUR BODY *MCA MCS 1613* 2	68	1
4 Jul 92	BACK TO FRONT *MCA MCS 1644*	63	1
11 Jul 98	ONE OF THE PEOPLE *ZTT ZTT 101CD* 3	56	1

1 Adamski featuring Jimi Polo / Adamski featuring Soho 2 Adamski featuring Nina Hagen 3 Adamski's Thing

Featured vocalist on 'Killer' was Seal

ADDAMS and GEE *UK, male instrumental duo (1 WEEK)* pos/wks

Date	Title	pos	wks
20 Apr 91	CHUNG KUO (REVISITED) *Debut DEBT 3108*	72	1

ADDIS BLACK WIDOW *US, male rap duo (2 WEEKS)* pos/wks

Date	Title	pos	wks
3 Feb 96	INNOCENT *Mercury Black Vinyl MBVCD 1*	42	2

ADDRISI BROTHERS *US, male vocal duo (3 WEEKS)* pos/wks

Date	Title	pos	wks
6 Oct 79	GHOST DANCER *Scotti Brothers K 11361*	57	3

ADEMA *US, male vocal / instrumental group (2 WEEKS)* pos/wks

Date	Title	pos	wks
16 Mar 02	GIVING IN *Arista 74321924022*	62	1
10 Aug 02	THE WAY YOU LIKE IT *Arista 74321954712*	61	1

ADEVA *US, female vocalist – Patricia Daniels (66 WEEKS)* pos/wks

Date	Title	pos	wks
14 Jan 89	RESPECT *Cooltempo COOL 179*	17	9
25 Mar 89	MUSICAL FREEDOM (MOVING ON UP) *Cooltempo COOL 182* 1	22	8
12 Aug 89	WARNING *Cooltempo COOL 185*	17	8
21 Oct 89	I THANK YOU *Cooltempo COOL 192*	17	7
16 Dec 89	BEAUTIFUL LOVE *Cooltempo COOL 195*	57	5
28 Apr 90	TREAT ME RIGHT *Cooltempo COOL 200*	62	2
6 Apr 91	RING MY BELL *Cooltempo COOL 224* 2	20	5
19 Oct 91	IT SHOULD'VE BEEN ME *Cooltempo COOL 236*	48	3
29 Feb 92	DON'T LET IT SHOW ON YOUR FACE *Cooltempo COOL 248*	34	4
6 Jun 92	UNTIL YOU COME BACK TO ME *Cooltempo COOL 254*	45	3
17 Oct 92	I'M THE ONE FOR YOU *Cooltempo COOL 264*	51	2
11 Dec 93	RESPECT (re-mix) *Network NWKCD 79*	65	1
27 May 95	TOO MANY FISH *Virgin America VUSCD 89* 3	34	2
18 Nov 95	WHADDA U WANT (FROM ME) *Virgin America VUSCD 98* 3	36	2
6 Apr 96	DO WATCHA DO *Avex UK AVEXCD 24* 4	54	1
4 May 96	I THANK YOU (re-mix) *Cooltempo CDCOOLS 318*	37	2
12 Apr 97	DO WATCHA DO (re-mix) *Distinctive DISNCD 28* 4	60	1
26 Jul 97	WHERE IS THE LOVE? / THE WAY THAT YOU FEEL *Distinctive DISNCD 31*	54	1

1 Paul Simpson featuring Adeva 2 Monie Love vs Adeva 3 Frankie Knuckles featuring Adeva 4 Hyper Go Go and Adeva

ADICTS *UK, male vocal / instrumental group (1 WEEK)* pos/wks

Date	Title	pos	wks
14 May 83	BAD BOY *Razor RZS 104*	75	1

ADIEMUS *UK, male instrumental duo (2 WEEKS)* pos/wks

Date	Title	pos	wks
14 Oct 95	ADIEMUS *Venture VEND 4*	48	2

Larry ADLER – See Kate BUSH

ADONIS featuring 2 PUERTO RICANS, A BLACK MAN AND A DOMINICAN *US, male vocal / instrumental group (4 WEEKS)* pos/wks

Date	Title	pos	wks
13 Jun 87	DO IT PROPERLY ('NO WAY BACK') / NO WAY BACK *London LON 136*	47	4

ADRENALIN M.O.D.
UK, male instrumental / production group (5 WEEKS) pos/wks

Date	Title	pos	wks
8 Oct 88	O-O-O *MCA RAGAT 2*	49	5

ADULT NET
UK / US, male / female vocal / instrumental group (2 WEEKS) pos/wks

Date	Title	pos	wks
10 Jun 89	WHERE WERE YOU *Fontana BRX 2*	66	2

ADVENTURES *UK, male vocal / instrumental group (24 WEEKS)* pos/wks

Date	Title	pos	wks
15 Sep 84	ANOTHER SILENT DAY *Chrysalis CHS 2000*	71	2
1 Dec 84	SEND MY HEART *Chrysalis CHS 2001*	62	4
13 Jul 85	FEEL THE RAINDROPS *Chrysalis AD 1*	58	3
9 Apr 88	BROKEN LAND *Elektra EKR 69*	20	10
2 Jul 88	DROWNING IN THE SEA OF LOVE *Elektra EKR 76*	44	4
13 Jun 92	RAINING ALL OVER THE WORLD *Polydor PO 211*	68	1

ADVENTURES OF STEVIE V
UK, male / female vocal / production group (22 WEEKS) pos/wks

Date	Title	pos	wks
21 Apr 90 ●	DIRTY CASH *Mercury MER 311*	2	13
29 Sep 90	BODY LANGUAGE *Mercury MER 331*	29	5
2 Mar 91	JEALOUSY *Mercury MER 337*	58	3
27 Sep 97	DIRTY CASH (re-mix) *Avex Trax AVEXCDX 57*	69	1

ADVERTS
UK, male / female vocal / instrumental group (11 WEEKS) pos/wks

Date	Title	pos	wks
27 Aug 77	GARY GILMORE'S EYES *Anchor ANC 1043*	18	7
4 Feb 78	NO TIME TO BE 21 *Bright BR 1*	34	4

AEROSMITH 349 Top 500
Godfathers of contemporary heavy rock scene, formed 1970 New Hampshire, US. Multi-platinum album act's UK success came only after front men Steven Tyler (v) and Joe Perry (g) teamed with rappers Run-DMC on 'Walk This Way' (1986). Group's first US No.1 single (1998) came 25 years after chart debut. Best-selling single: 'I Don't Want To Miss A Thing' 572,900 (92 WEEKS) pos/wks

Date	Title	pos	wks
17 Oct 87	DUDE (LOOKS LIKE A LADY) *Geffen GEF 29*	45	5
16 Apr 88	ANGEL *Geffen GEF 34*	69	2
9 Sep 89	LOVE IN AN ELEVATOR *Geffen GEF 63*	13	8
24 Feb 90	DUDE (LOOKS LIKE A LADY) (re-issue) *Geffen GEF 72*	20	5
14 Apr 90	RAG DOLL *Geffen GEF 76*	42	4
1 Sep 90	THE OTHER SIDE *Geffen GEF 79*	46	2
10 Apr 93	LIVIN' ON THE EDGE *Geffen GFSTD 35*	19	4
3 Jul 93	EAT THE RICH *Geffen GFSTD 46*	34	3
30 Oct 93	CRYIN' *Geffen GFSTD 56*	17	6
18 Dec 93	AMAZING *Geffen GFSTD 63*	57	3
2 Jul 94	SHUT UP AND DANCE *Geffen GFSTD 75*	24	4
20 Aug 94	SWEET EMOTION *Columbia 6604492*	74	1
5 Nov 94	CRAZY / BLIND MAN *Geffen GFSTD 80*	23	4
8 Mar 97	FALLING IN LOVE (IS HARD ON THE KNEES) *Columbia 6640752*	22	4
21 Jun 97	HOLE IN MY SOUL *Columbia 66645012*	29	2
27 Dec 97	PINK *Columbia 6648722*	38	2
12 Sep 98 ●	I DON'T WANT TO MISS A THING *Columbia 6664082* ▲	4	20
26 Jun 99	PINK (re-issue) *Columbia 6675342*	13	6
17 Mar 01	JADED *Columbia 6709312*	13	7

AFRICAN BUSINESS
Italy, male vocal / instrumental group (1 WEEK) pos/wks

Date	Title	pos	wks
17 Nov 90	IN ZAIRE *Urban URB 64*	73	1

Re-entries are listed as (re), (2re), (3re), etc which signifies that the hit re-entered the chart once, twice or three times, etc

AFRO CELT SOUND SYSTEM UK / Ireland /
France / Guinea, male vocal / instrumental group (1 WEEK) pos/wks

| 29 Apr 00 | RELEASE *Realworld RWSCD 10* | 71 | 1 |

AFRO MEDUSA UK, male production duo – Patrick Cole and
Nick Benneti and Spain, female vocalist – Isabel Fructuoso (2 WEEKS) pos/wks

| 28 Oct 00 | PASILDA *Rulin RULIN 6CDS* | 31 | 2 |

AFROMAN US, male vocalist – Joseph Foreman (30 WEEKS) pos/wks

6 Oct 01	BECAUSE I GOT HIGH (import) *Universal 0152822*	45	3
27 Oct 01 ★	BECAUSE I GOT HIGH (re) *Universal MCSTD 40266* ■ ▲	1	19
2 Feb 02 ●	CRAZY RAP *Universal MCSTD 40273*	10	8

AFTER 7 US, male vocal group (3 WEEKS) pos/wks

| 3 Nov 90 | CAN'T STOP *Virgin America VUS 31* | 54 | 3 |

AFTER THE FIRE
UK, male vocal / instrumental group (12 WEEKS) pos/wks

9 Jun 79	ONE RULE FOR YOU *CBS 7025*	40	6
8 Sep 79	LASER LOVE *CBS 7769*	62	2
9 Apr 83	DER KOMMISSAR *CBS A 2399*	47	4

AFTERNOON BOYS – See Steve WRIGHT

AFTERSHOCK US, male vocal / instrumental
duo – Frost Rivera and Guy Routte (8 WEEKS) pos/wks

| 21 Aug 93 | SLAVE TO THE VIBE *Virgin America VUSCD 75* | 11 | 8 |

AGE OF CHANCE
UK, male / female vocal / instrumental group (13 WEEKS) pos/wks

17 Jan 87	KISS *Fon AGE 5*	50	6
30 May 87	WHO'S AFRAID OF THE BIG BAD NOISE! *Fon VS 962*	65	2
20 Jan 90	HIGHER THAN HEAVEN *Virgin VS 1228*	53	5

AGE OF LOVE Italy, male instrumental / production trio (6 WEEKS) pos/wks

| 5 Jul 97 | THE AGE OF LOVE – THE REMIXES *React CDREACT 100* | 17 | 4 |
| 19 Sep 98 | AGE OF LOVE *React CDREACT 135* | 38 | 2 |

AGENT 00 UK, male production duo (1 WEEK) pos/wks

| 7 Mar 98 | THE MAGNIFICENT *Inferno CDFERN 002* | 65 | 1 |

AGENT PROVOCATEUR
UK, male / female vocal / production group (1 WEEK) pos/wks

| 22 Mar 97 | AGENT DAN *Epic AGENT 3CD* | 49 | 1 |

AGENT SUMO UK, male production duo (4 WEEKS) pos/wks

| 9 Jun 01 | 24 HOURS *Virgin VSCDT 1806* | 44 | 2 |
| 20 Apr 02 | WHY *Virgin VSCDT 1819* | 40 | 2 |

AGNELLI & NELSON
UK, male DJ duo – Chris Agnelli and Robbie Nelson (15 WEEKS) pos/wks

15 Aug 98	EL NINO *Xtravaganza 0091575 EXT*	21	4
11 Sep 99	EVERYDAY *Xtravaganza XTRAV 2CDS*	17	4
17 Jun 00	EMBRACE *Xtravaganza XTRAV 11CDS*	35	2
9 Sep 00	HUDSON STREET *Xtravaganza XTRAV 13CDS*	29	2
7 Apr 01	VEGAS *Xtravaganza XTRAV 23CDS*	48	1
15 Jun 02	EVERYDAY (re-mix) *Xtravaganza XTRAV 31CDS*	33	2

Christina AGUILERA (394) Top 500
Internationally successful photogenic pop vocalist, b. 18 Dec 1980, New York. Four US chart-toppers and the winner of 1999 Best New Artist Grammy and World Music Awards in 2000 and 2001. Best-selling single: 'Genie In A Bottle' 608,100 (85 WEEKS) pos/wks

| 11 Sep 99 | GENIE IN A BOTTLE (import) *RCA 701062* | 50 | 5 |
| 16 Oct 99 ★ | GENIE IN A BOTTLE *RCA 74321705482* ■ ▲ | 1 | 19 |

26 Feb 00 ●	WHAT A GIRL WANTS *RCA 74321737522* ▲	3	13
22 Jul 00	I TURN TO YOU *RCA 74321765472*	19	6
11 Nov 00 ●	COME ON OVER BABY (ALL I WANT IS YOU) (re) *RCA 74321799912* ▲	8	8
10 Mar 01 ●	NOBODY WANTS TO BE LONELY *Columbia 6709462* [1]	4	12
30 Jun 01 ★	LADY MARMALADE *Interscope / Polydor 4975612* [2] ■ ▲	1	16
23 Nov 02 ★	DIRRTY *RCA 74321962722* [3] ■	1	6+

[1] Ricky Martin and Christina Aguilera [2] Christina Aguilera, Lil' Kim, Mya and Pink
[3] Christina Aguilera featuring Redman

A-HA (199) Top 500 Norway's biggest-selling act: Morten Harket (v). Pal
Waaktaar (g). Magna Furuholmen (k). This globally popular teen-targeted trio was noted for its innovative videos and stage shows (133 WEEKS) pos/wks

28 Sep 85 ●	TAKE ON ME *Warner Bros. W 9006* ▲	2	19
28 Dec 85 ★	THE SUN ALWAYS SHINES ON TV *Warner Bros. W 8846*	1	12
5 Apr 86 ●	TRAIN OF THOUGHT *Warner Bros. W 8736*	8	8
14 Jun 86 ●	HUNTING HIGH AND LOW *Warner Bros. W 6663*	5	10
4 Oct 86 ●	I'VE BEEN LOSING YOU *Warner Bros. W 8594*	8	7
6 Dec 86 ●	CRY WOLF *Warner Bros. W 8500*	5	9
28 Feb 87	MANHATTAN SKYLINE *Warner Bros. W 8405*	13	6
4 Jul 87 ●	THE LIVING DAYLIGHTS *Warner Bros. W 8305*	5	9
26 Mar 88 ●	STAY ON THESE ROADS *Warner Bros. W 7936*	5	6
18 Jun 88	THE BLOOD THAT MOVES THE BODY *Warner Bros. W 7840*	25	4
27 Aug 88	TOUCHY! *Warner Bros. W 7749*	11	7
3 Dec 88	YOU ARE THE ONE *Warner Bros. W 7636*	13	10
13 Oct 90	CRYING IN THE RAIN *Warner Bros. W 9547*	13	7
15 Dec 90	I CALL YOUR NAME *Warner Bros. W 9462*	44	5
26 Oct 91	MOVE TO MEMPHIS *Warner Bros. W 0070*	47	2
5 Jun 93	DARK IS THE NIGHT *Warner Bros. W 0175CD*	19	4
18 Sep 93	ANGEL *Warner Bros. W 0195CD*	41	3
26 Mar 94	SHAPES THAT GO TOGETHER *Warner Bros. W 0236CD*	27	3
3 Jun 00	SUMMER MOVED ON *WEA WEA 275CD*	33	2

AHMAD US, male rapper (2 WEEKS) pos/wks

| 9 Jul 94 | BACK IN THE DAY *Giant 74321212042* | 64 | 2 |

AIDA Holland, male production duo (1 WEEK) pos/wks

| 19 Feb 00 | FAR AND AWAY *48K / Perfecto SPECT 03CDS* | 58 | 1 |

AIR France, male instrumental / production duo –
Benoît Dunkel and Nicolas Godin (14 WEEKS) pos/wks

21 Feb 98	SEXY BOY *Virgin VSCDT 1672*	13	4
16 May 98	KELLY WATCH THE STARS *Virgin VSCDT 1690*	18	3
21 Nov 98	ALL I NEED *Virgin VSCDT 1702*	29	3
26 Feb 00	PLAYGROUND LOVE *Virgin VSCDT 1764* [1]	25	2
2 Jun 01	RADIO #1 *Virgin VSCDT 1803*	31	2

[1] Sung by Gordon Tracks

AIR SUPPLY UK / Australia, male vocal / instrumental
group – Russell Hitchcock and Graham Russell (17 WEEKS) pos/wks

27 Sep 80	ALL OUT OF LOVE *Arista ARIST 362*	11	11
2 Oct 82	EVEN THE NIGHTS ARE BETTER *Arista ARIST 474*	44	4
20 Nov 93	GOODBYE *Giant 74321153462*	66	2

AIRHEAD UK, male vocal / instrumental group (10 WEEKS) pos/wks

5 Oct 91	FUNNY HOW *Korova KOW 47*	57	3
21 Dec 91	COUNTING SHEEP *Korova KOW 48*	35	5
7 Mar 92	RIGHT NOW *Korova KOW 49*	50	2

AIRHEADZ UK, male DJ / production duo –
Leigh Guest and Andrew Peach (2 WEEKS) pos/wks

| 28 Apr 01 | STANLEY (HERE I AM) *AM:PM CDAMPM 145* | 36 | 2 |

See also DOUBLE TROUBLE

AIRSCAPE Belgium / Holland, male
instrumental / production group – leader Johan Gielen (5 WEEKS) pos/wks

| 9 Aug 97 | PACIFIC MELODY *Xtravaganza 0091165* | 27 | 2 |

29 Aug 98	AMAZON CHANT *Xtravaganza 0091605 EXT*.........	**46** 1
4 Dec 99	L'ESPERANZA *Xtravaganza EXTRAV 7CD*	**33** 2

See also BLUE BAMBOO; CUBIC 22; TRANSFORMER 2; SVENSON and GIELEN

Laurel AITKEN and the UNITONE
Jamaica / Cuba, male vocal / instrumental group (3 WEEKS) pos/wks

17 May 80	RUDI GOT MARRIED *I-Spy SEE 6*	**60** 3

AKABU featuring Linda CLIFFORD
UK, male producer – Dave Lee and US, female vocalist (1 WEEK) pos/wks

15 Sep 01	RIDE THE STORM *NRK Sound Division NRKCD 053*	**69** 1

See also Joey NEGRO; PHASE II; Z FACTOR; Li KWAN; RAVEN MAIZE; JAKATTA; HED BOYS; IL PADRINOS

Jewel AKENS *US, male vocalist (8 WEEKS)* pos/wks

25 Mar 65	THE BIRDS AND THE BEES *London HLN 9954*	**29** 8

AKIN *UK, female vocal duo (1 WEEK)* pos/wks

14 Jun 97	STAY RIGHT HERE *WEA WEA 117CD*................	**60** 1

ALABAMA 3 *UK, male vocal / instrumental group (3 WEEKS)* pos/wks

22 Nov 97	SPEED AT THE SOUND OF LONELINESS *Elemental ELM 42CDS 1721*.........	**72** 1
11 Apr 98	AIN'T GOIN' TO GOA *Elemental ELM 45CDS1*	**40** 2

ALANA – *See MK*

ALARM *UK, male vocal / instrumental group (64 WEEKS)* pos/wks

24 Sep 83	68 GUNS *IRS PFP 1023*	**17** 7
21 Jan 84	WHERE WERE YOU HIDING WHEN THE STORM BROKE *IRS IRS 101*	**22** 6
31 Mar 84	THE DECEIVER *IRS IRS 103*	**51** 4
3 Nov 84	THE CHANT HAS JUST BEGUN *IRS IRS 104*.........	**48** 4
2 Mar 85	ABSOLUTE REALITY *IRS ALARM 1*	**35** 6
28 Sep 85	STRENGTH *IRS IRM 104*	**40** 4
18 Jan 86	SPIRIT OF '76 *IRS IRM 109*	**22** 5
26 Apr 86	KNIFE EDGE *IRS IRM 112*	**43** 3
17 Oct 87	RAIN IN THE SUMMERTIME *IRS IRM 144*	**18** 5
12 Dec 87	RESCUE ME *IRS IRM 150*	**48** 2
20 Feb 88	PRESENCE OF LOVE *IRS IRM 155*	**44** 3
16 Sep 89	SOLD ME DOWN THE RIVER *IRS EIRS 123*	**43** 3
4 Nov 89	A NEW SOUTH WALES *IRS EIRS 129*.........	**31** 5
3 Feb 90	LOVE DON'T COME EASY *IRS EIRS 134*	**48** 3
27 Oct 90	UNSAFE BUILDING 1990 *IRS ALARM 2*	**54** 2
13 Apr 91	RAW *IRS ALARM 3*	**51** 2

'A New South Wales' features Morriston Orpheus Male Voice Choir. 'Sold Me Down the River' was joined by 'Yn Gymreag' for the first week on chart

Morris ALBERT
Brazil, male vocalist – Morris Kaisermann (10 WEEKS) pos/wks

27 Sep 75	● FEELINGS *Decca F 13591*	**4** 10

ALBERTA *Sierra Leone, female vocalist (3 WEEKS)* pos/wks

26 Dec 98	YOYO BOY *RCA 74321640602*	**48** 3

ALBERTO Y LOS TRIOS PARANOIAS
UK, male vocal / instrumental group (5 WEEKS) pos/wks

23 Sep 78	HEADS DOWN NO NONSENSE MINDLESS BOOGIE *Logo GO 323*	**47** 5

Al ALBERTS – *See FOUR ACES*

ALBION *Holland, male producer – Ferry Corsten (1 WEEK)* pos/wks

3 Jun 00	AIR 2000 *Platipus PLATCD 73*	**59** 1

See also SYSTEM F; VERACOCHA; MOONMAN; GOURYELLA; STARPARTY; Ferry CORSTEN

ALCATRAZ *US, male instrumental / production duo*
– Jean-Philippe Aviance and Victor Imbres (4 WEEKS) pos/wks

17 Feb 96	GIV ME LUV *AM:PM 5814332*	**12** 4

ALCAZAR *Sweden, male / female vocal trio (13 WEEKS)* pos/wks

8 Dec 01	CRYING AT THE DISCOTEQUE *Arista 74321893432*	**13** 11
16 Mar 02	SEXUAL GUARANTEE *Arista 74321920252*	**30** 2

ALDA *Iceland, female vocalist – Alda Olafsdottir (14 WEEKS)* pos/wks

29 Aug 98	● REAL GOOD TIME *Wildstar CDWILD 7*	**7** 7
26 Dec 98	GIRLS NIGHT OUT *Wildstar CDWILD 10*	**20** 7

Cali ALEMAN – *See Tito PUENTE Jr and the LATIN RHYTHM featuring Tito PUENTE, INDIA and Cali ALEMAN*

ALENA *Jamaica, female vocalist (5 WEEKS)* pos/wks

13 Nov 99	TURN IT AROUND *Wonderboy WBOYD 16*	**14** 5

ALESSI *US, male vocal duo – Billy and Bobby Alessi (11 WEEKS)* pos/wks

11 Jun 77	● OH, LORI *A&M AMS 7289*	**8** 11

Hannah ALETHIA – *See SODA CLUB featuring Hannah ALETHIA*

ALEX PARTY *Italy / UK, male / female vocal / instrumental*
group – leader Paolo Visnadi (28 WEEKS) pos/wks

18 Dec 93	SATURDAY NIGHT PARTY (re) *Cleveland City Imports CCICD 17000*	**29** 10
18 Feb 95	● DON'T GIVE ME YOUR LIFE *Systematic SYSCD 7*	**2** 13
18 Nov 95	WRAP ME UP *Systematic SYSCD 22*	**17** 3
19 Oct 96	READ MY LIPS (re-mix) *Systematic SYSCD 30*	**28** 2

'Read My Lips' in 1996 is a remix of the first hit with added vocals

See also LIVIN' JOY

ALEXIA *Italy, female vocalist – Alessia Aquilani (15 WEEKS)* pos/wks

21 Mar 98	● UH LA LA LA *Dance Pool ALEX 1CD*	**10** 9
13 Jun 98	GIMME LOVE *Dance Pool ALEX 2CDZ*	**17** 4
10 Oct 98	THE MUSIC I LIKE *Dance Pool ALEX 3CD*	**31** 2

ALFI and HARRY *US, male vocalist / instumentalist –*
David Seville (d. 16 Jan 1972) under two false names (5 WEEKS) pos/wks

23 Mar 56	THE TROUBLE WITH HARRY *London HLU 8242*	**15** 5

See also David SEVILLE; CHIPMUNKS

ALFIE *UK, male vocal / instrumental group (2 WEEKS)* pos/wks

8 Sep 01	YOU MAKE NO BONES *Twisted Nerve TN 033CD*	**61** 1
16 Mar 02	A WORD IN YOUR EAR *Twisted Nerve TN 037CD*	**66** 1

John ALFORD *UK, male actor / vocalist (12 WEEKS)* pos/wks

17 Feb 96	SMOKE GETS IN YOUR EYES *Love This LUVTHISCD 7*	**13** 5
25 May 96	● BLUE MOON / ONLY YOU *Love This LUVTHISCD 9*	**9** 4
23 Nov 96	IF / KEEP ON RUNNING *Love This LUVTHISCD 15*	**24** 3

ALI *UK, male vocalist (2 WEEKS)* pos/wks

23 May 98	LOVE LETTERS *Wild Card 5698092*	**63** 1
24 Oct 98	FEELIN' YOU *Wild Card 5676992*	**63** 1

Tatyana ALI *US, female vocalist (18 WEEKS)* pos/wks

14 Nov 98	● DAYDREAMIN' *Epic 6665462*	**6** 5
13 Feb 99	● BOY YOU KNOCK ME OUT (re) *MJJ / Epic 6669372* [1]	**3** 9
19 Jun 99	EVERYTIME *Epic / MJJ 674742*	**20** 4

[1] Tatyana Ali featuring Will Smith

ALI and FRAZIER
UK, female vocal duo – Kirsty Ali and Natasha Frazier (4 WEEKS)   pos/wks

7 Aug 93	UPTOWN TOP RANKING *Arista 74321158842*	33 4

ALIBI *UK, male vocal duo (2 WEEKS)*   pos/wks

15 Feb 97	I'M NOT TO BLAME *Urgent 74321434762*	51 1
7 Feb 98	HOW MUCH I FEEL *Urgent 74321548472*	58 1

ALICE BAND
UK / Ireland / US, female vocal / instrumental group (2 WEEKS)   pos/wks

23 Jun 01	ONE DAY AT A TIME *Instant Karma KARMA 5CD*	52 1
27 Apr 02	NOW THAT YOU LOVE ME *Instant Karma KARMA 17CD*	44 1

ALICE DEEJAY
Holland, male / female production / vocal group (50 WEEKS)   pos/wks

31 Jul 99 ●	BETTER OFF ALONE *Positiva CDTIV 113* [1]	2 16
4 Dec 99 ●	BACK IN MY LIFE *Positiva CDTIV 121*	4 15
15 Jul 00 ●	WILL I EVER *Positiva CDTIV 134*	7 10
21 Oct 00	THE LONELY ONE *Positiva CDTIV 145*	16 5
10 Feb 01	CELEBRATE OUR LOVE *Positiva CDTIV 149*	17 4

[1] DJ Jurgen presents Alice Deejay

ALICE IN CHAINS
US, male vocal / instrumental group (14 WEEKS)   pos/wks

23 Jan 93	WOULD *Columbia 6588882*	19 3
20 Mar 93	THEM BONES *Columbia 6590902*	26 3
5 Jun 93	ANGRY CHAIR *Columbia 6593652*	33 2
23 Oct 93	DOWN IN A HOLE *Columbia 6597512*	36 2
11 Nov 95	GRIND *Columbia 6626232*	23 2
10 Feb 96	HEAVEN BESIDE YOU *Columbia 6628935*	35 2

ALIEN ANT FARM
US, male vocal / instrumental group (25 WEEKS)   pos/wks

30 Jun 01	MOVIES *Dreamworks / Polydor 4508992*	53 1
8 Sep 01	SMOOTH CRIMINAL (import) *Dreamworks / Polydor 4508852*	74 2
29 Sep 01 ●	SMOOTH CRIMINAL (re)	
	Dreamworks / Polydor DRMDM 50887	3 13
16 Feb 02 ●	MOVIES (re-issue) *Dreamworks / Polydor 4508492*	5 8
25 May 02	ATTITUDE *Dreamworks / Newnoize 4508292*	66 1

ALIEN VOICES featuring The THREE DEGREES *UK, male*
producer – Andros Georgiou featuring US, female vocal trio (2 WKS)   pos/wks

26 Dec 98	LAST CHRISTMAS *Wildstar CDWILD 15*	54 2

See also Andy G's STARSKY & HUTCH ALL STARS; BOOGIE BOX HIGH

ALISHA *US, female vocalist (2 WEEKS)*   pos/wks

25 Jan 86	BABY TALK *Total Control TOCO 6*	67 2

ALISHA'S ATTIC
UK, female vocal duo – Shellie and Karen Poole (47 WEEKS)   pos/wks

3 Aug 96	I AM I FEEL *Mercury AATCD 1*	14 10
2 Nov 96	ALISHA RULES THE WORLD *Mercury AATCD 2*	12 6
15 Mar 97	INDESTRUCTIBLE *Mercury AATCD 3*	12 6
12 Jul 97	AIR WE BREATHE *Mercury AATCD 4*	12 6
19 Sep 98	THE INCIDENTALS *Mercury AATCD 5*	13 7
9 Jan 99	WISH I WERE YOU *Mercury AATCD 6*	29 5
17 Apr 99	BARBARELLA *Mercury AATCD 7*	34 2
24 Mar 01	PUSH IT ALL ASIDE *Mercury AATCD 8*	24 4
28 Jul 01	PRETENDER GOT MY HEART *Mercury AATCD 9*	43 1

ALIVE featuring D.D. KLEIN
Italy, male production trio and Antigua, female vocalist (1 WEEK)   pos/wks

27 Jul 02	ALIVE *Serious / Universal CDAMPM 153*	49 1

ALIZÉE *France, female vocalist / Alizée Jacotet (9 WEEKS)*   pos/wks

23 Feb 02 ●	MOI … LOLITA *Polydor 5705952*	9 9

ALKALINE TRIO *US, male vocal / instrumental trio (2 WEEKS)*   pos/wks

2 Feb 02	PRIVATE EYE *B Unique / Vagrant BUN 013CDS*	51 1
30 Mar 02	STUPID KID *B Unique / Vagrant BUN 016CDS*	53 1

ALL ABOUT EVE
UK, female / male vocal / instrumental group (47 WEEKS)   pos/wks

31 Oct 87	IN THE CLOUDS *Mercury EVEN 5*	47 5
23 Jan 88	WILD HEARTED WOMAN *Mercury EVEN 6*	33 4
9 Apr 88	EVERY ANGEL *Mercury EVEN 7*	30 5
30 Jul 88 ●	MARTHA'S HARBOUR *Mercury EVEN 8*	10 8
12 Nov 88	WHAT KIND OF FOOL *Mercury EVEN 9*	29 4
30 Sep 89	ROAD TO YOUR SOUL *Mercury EVEN 10*	37 4
16 Dec 89	DECEMBER *Mercury EVEN 11*	34 5
28 Apr 90	SCARLET *Mercury EVEN 12*	34 2
15 Jun 91	FAREWELL MR SORROW *Mercury EVEN 14*	36 2
10 Aug 91	STRANGE WAY *Vertigo EVEN 15*	50 3
19 Oct 91	THE DREAMER *Vertigo EVEN 16*	41 2
10 Oct 92	PHASED (EP) *MCA MCS 1688*	38 2
28 Nov 92	SOME FINER DAY *MCA MCS 1706*	57 1

Tracks on Phased (EP): Phased / Mine / Infra Red / Ascent-Descent

ALL BLUE *UK, male vocal duo (1 WEEK)*   pos/wks

21 Aug 99	PRISONER *WEA WEA 213CD1*	73 1

ALL-4-ONE *US, male vocal group (23 WEEKS)*   pos/wks

2 Apr 94	SO MUCH IN LOVE *Atlantic A 7261CD*	60 1
18 Jun 94 ●	I SWEAR *Atlantic A 7255CD* ▲	2 18
19 Nov 94	SO MUCH IN LOVE (re-mix) *Atlantic A 7216CD*	49 2
15 Jul 95	I CAN LOVE YOU LIKE THAT *Atlantic A 8193CD*	33 2

ALL SAINTS 271 Top 500
*From All Saints Road, London, a cooler, R&B-motivated vocal girl group
in the wake of The Spice Girls. Melanie Blatt, London, Shaznay Lewis,
London and sisters Nicole and Natalie Appleton, Canada. Crowned Best
Breakthrough Artists in the 1998 MTV Europe Music Awards, Group split in
2001. Biggest-selling single: 'Never Ever' 1,254,604 (109 WEEKS)*   pos/wks

6 Sep 97 ●	I KNOW WHERE IT'S AT *London LONCD 398*	4 8
22 Nov 97 ★	NEVER EVER *London LONCD 407* ◆	1 24
9 May 98 ★	UNDER THE BRIDGE / LADY MARMALADE	
	London LONCD 408 ■	1 14
12 Sep 98 ★	BOOTIE CALL *London LONCD 415* ■	1 11
5 Dec 98 ★	WAR OF NERVES *London LONCD 421*	7 11
26 Feb 00 ★	PURE SHORES *London LONCD 444* ■	1 16
14 Oct 00 ★	BLACK COFFEE (2re) *London LONCD 454* ■	1 18
27 Jan 01 ●	ALL HOOKED UP (re) *London LONCD 456*	7 7

See also APPLETON

ALL SEEING I
UK, male vocal / instrumental group (17 WEEKS)   pos/wks

28 Mar 98	BEAT GOES ON *ffrr FCD 334*	11 7
23 Jan 99 ●	WALK LIKE A PANTHER '98 *ffrr FCD 351* [1]	10 7
18 Sep 99	1ST MAN IN SPACE *ffrr FCD 370* [2]	28 3

[1] The All Seeing I featuring Tony Christie [2] The All Seeing I featuring Phil Oakey

ALL SYSTEMS GO
UK, male vocal / instrumental group (2 WEEKS)   pos/wks

18 Jun 88	POP MUZIK *Unique NIQ 03*	63 2

Richard ALLAN *UK, male vocalist (1 WEEK)*   pos/wks

24 Mar 60	AS TIME GOES BY *Parlophone R 4634*	43 1

Steve ALLAN *UK, male vocalist (2 WEEKS)*   pos/wks

27 Jan 79	TOGETHER WE ARE BEAUTIFUL (re) *Creole CR 164*	67 2

Donna ALLEN *US, female vocalist (27 WEEKS)*   pos/wks

18 Apr 87 ●	SERIOUS *Portrait 650744 7*	8 12

		pos/wks
3 Jun 89 ●	JOY AND PAIN *BCM BCM 257*	10 10
21 Jan 95	REAL *Epic 6610992*	34 2
11 Oct 97	SATURDAY *AM:PM 5823752* [1]	29 3

[1] East 57th Street featuring Donna Allen

Keith ALLEN – See BLACK GRAPE; Joe STRUMMER; FAT LES

Dot ALLISON *UK, female vocalist (1 WEEK)*

		pos/wks
17 Aug 02	STRUNG OUT *Mantra MNT 74CD*	67 1

See also ONE DOVE

ALLISONS *UK, male vocal / instrumental duo – John Allison (Brian Alford) and Bob Allison (Colin Day) (27 WEEKS)*

		pos/wks
23 Feb 61 ●	ARE YOU SURE *Fontana H 294*	2 16
18 May 61	WORDS *Fontana H 304*	34 5
15 Feb 62	LESSONS IN LOVE *Fontana H 362*	30 6

ALL STAR CHOIR – See Donna SUMMER

ALLNIGHT BAND *UK, male instrumental group (3 WEEKS)*

		pos/wks
3 Feb 79	THE JOKER (THE WIGAN JOKER) *Casino Classics CC 6*	50 3

ALL-STARS – See Louis ARMSTRONG

ALL-STARS – See Jr WALKER and The ALL-STARS

ALLSTARS *UK, male / female vocal group (22 WEEKS)*

		pos/wks
23 Jun 01	BEST FRIENDS (re) *Islands CID 775*	20 7
22 Sep 01	THINGS THAT GO BUMP IN THE NIGHT / IS THERE SOMETHING I SHOULD KNOW *Island CID 783*	12 4
26 Jan 02 ●	THE LAND OF MAKE BELIEVE (re) *Island CID 791*	9 8
11 May 02	BACK WHEN / GOING ALL THE WAY *Island CID 796*	19 3

ALLURE *US, female vocal group (8 WEEKS)*

		pos/wks
14 Jun 97	HEAD OVER HEELS *Epic 6645942* [1]	18 3
10 Jan 98	ALL CRIED OUT *Epic 6652715* [2]	12 5

[1] Allure featuring NAS [2] Allure featuring 112

ALMIGHTY *UK, male vocal / instrumental group (22 WEEKS)*

		pos/wks
30 Jun 90	WILD AND WONDERFUL *Polydor PO 75*	50 2
2 Mar 91	FREE 'N' EASY *Polydor PO 127*	35 2
11 May 91	DEVIL'S TOY *Polydor PO 144*	36 2
29 Jun 91	LITTLE LOST SOMETIMES *Polydor PO 151*	42 2
3 Apr 93	ADDICTION *Polydor PZCD 261*	38 2
29 May 93	OUT OF SEASON *Polydor PZCD 266*	41 2
30 Oct 93	OVER THE EDGE *Polydor PZCD 298*	38 2
24 Sep 94	WRENCH *Chrysalis CDCHS 5014*	26 2
14 Jan 95	JONESTOWN MIND *Chrysalis CDCHS 5017*	26 3
16 Mar 96	ALL SUSSED OUT *Chrysalis CDCHS 5030*	28 2
25 May 96	DO YOU UNDERSTAND *Raw Power RAWX 1022*	38 1

Marc ALMOND ⟨257 Top 500⟩ *Distinctive vocalist who first found fame fronting chart regulars Soft Cell. b. 9 Jul 1957, Southport, UK. His only No.1 also gave co-vocalist Gene Pitney his first British chart-topper and sold more than one million copies in Europe alone (112 WEEKS)*

		pos/wks
2 Jul 83	BLACK HEART *Some Bizarre BZS 19* [1]	49 3
2 Jun 84	THE BOY WHO CAME BACK *Some Bizarre BZS 23*	52 5
1 Sep 84	YOU HAVE *Some Bizarre BZS 24*	57 3
20 Apr 85 ●	I FEEL LOVE (MEDLEY) *Forbidden Fruit BITE 4* [2]	3 12
24 Aug 85	STORIES OF JOHNNY *Some Bizarre BONK 1*	23 5
26 Oct 85	LOVE LETTER *Some Bizarre BONK 2*	68 3
4 Jan 86	THE HOUSE IS HAUNTED (BY THE ECHO OF YOUR LAST GOODBYE) *Some Bizarre GLOW 1*	55 3
7 Jun 86	A WOMAN'S STORY *Some Bizarre GLOW 2* [3]	41 5
18 Oct 86	RUBY RED *Some Bizarre GLOW 3*	47 3
14 Feb 87	MELANCHOLY ROSE *Some Bizarre GLOW 4*	71 1
3 Sep 88	TEARS RUN RINGS *Parlophone R 6186*	26 7
5 Nov 88	BITTER SWEET *Some Bizarre R 6194*	40 2

		pos/wks
14 Jan 89 ★	SOMETHING'S GOTTEN HOLD OF MY HEART *Parlophone R 6201* [4]	1 12
8 Apr 89	ONLY THE MOMENT *Parlophone R 6210*	45 2
3 Mar 90	A LOVER SPURNED *Some Bizarre R 6229*	29 4
19 May 90	THE DESPERATE HOURS *Some Bizarre R 6252*	45 2
23 Mar 91	SAY HELLO WAVE GOODBYE '91 (re-recording) *Mercury SOFT 1* [5]	38 3
18 May 91 ●	TAINTED LOVE (re-issue) *Mercury SOFT 2* [5]	5 8
28 Sep 91	JACKY *Some Bizarre YZ 610*	17 6
11 Jan 92	MY HAND OVER MY HEART *Some Bizarre YZ 633*	33 5
25 Apr 92 ●	THE DAYS OF PEARLY SPENCER *Some Bizarre YZ 638*	4 7
27 Mar 93	WHAT MAKES A MAN A MAN (LIVE) *Some Bizarre YZ 720CD*	60 2
13 May 95	ADORED AND EXPLORED *Some Bizarre MERCD 431*	25 3
29 Jul 95	THE IDOL *Some Bizarre MERCD 437*	44 2
30 Dec 95	CHILD STAR *Some Bizarre MERCD 450*	41 1
28 Dec 96	YESTERDAY HAS GONE (re) *EMI Premier CDPRESX 13* [6]	58 2

[1] Marc and the Mambas [2] Bronski Beat and Marc Almond [3] Marc Almond and the Willing Sinners [4] Marc Almond featuring special guest star Gene Pitney [5] Soft Cell / Marc Almond [6] PJ Proby and Marc Almond featuring the My Life Story Orchestra

I Feel Love medley comprises: I Feel Love / Love to Love You Baby / Johnny Remember Me. Original hit versions of 'Tainted Love' (1981) and 'Say Hello Wave Goodbye' (1982) credited to Soft Cell alone

ALOOF *UK, male vocal / instrumental group (6 WEEKS)*

		pos/wks
19 Sep 92	ON A MISSION *Cowboy RODEO 5*	64 1
18 May 96	WISH YOU WERE HERE … *East West EW 038CD*	61 1
30 Nov 96	ONE NIGHT STAND *East West EW 067CD*	30 2
1 Mar 97	WISH YOU WERE HERE … (re-mix) *East West EW 083CD1*	43 1
29 Aug 98	WHAT I MISS THE MOST *East West EW 179CD1*	70 1

Herb ALPERT ⟨284 Top 500⟩ *Leader of the US's biggest-selling instrumental act, The Tijuana Brass, b. 31 Mar 1935, Los Angeles. The multi-talented trumpet-toting star's band had four albums simultaneously in the US Top 10 in the mid-1960s. He sold his A&M label for $300m in 1989 and his publishing company for $350m in 2000 (106 WEEKS)*

		pos/wks
3 Jan 63	THE LONELY BULL (EL SOLO TORRO) *Stateside SS 138* [1]	22 9
9 Dec 65 ●	SPANISH FLEA *Pye International 7 N 25335* [2]	3 20
24 Mar 66	TIJUANA TAXI *Pye International 7 N 25352* [2]	37 4
27 Apr 67	CASINO ROYALE *A&M AMS 700* [2]	27 14
3 Jul 68 ●	THIS GUY'S IN LOVE WITH YOU (3re) *A&M AMS 727* ▲	3 19
18 Jun 69	WITHOUT HER *A&M AMS 755* [2]	36 5
12 Dec 70	JERUSALEM (re) *A&M AMS 810* [2]	42 3
13 Oct 79	RISE *A&M AMS 7465* ▲	13 13
19 Jan 80	ROTATION *A&M AMS 7500*	46 3
21 Mar 87	KEEP YOUR EYE ON ME *Breakout USA 602*	19 9
6 Jun 87	DIAMONDS *Breakout USA 605*	27 7

[1] Tijuana Brass [2] Herb Alpert and the Tijuana Brass

Alpert provides vocals on 'This Guy's in Love with You' and 'Without Her'. Janet Jackson and Lisa Keith provide uncredited vocals on 'Diamonds'

ALPHA-BETA – See Izhar COHEN and the ALPHA-BETA

ALPHAVILLE
Germany, male vocal / instrumental group (13 WEEKS)

		pos/wks
18 Aug 84 ●	BIG IN JAPAN *WEA Int. X9505*	8 13

ALPINESTARS featuring Brian MOLKO
UK, male production duo and US, male vocalist (1 WEEK)

		pos/wks
22 Jun 02	CARBON KID *Riverman RMR 11CDS*	63 1

ALSOU *Russia, female vocalist – Alsou Tenisheva (3 WEEKS)*

		pos/wks
12 May 01	BEFORE YOU LOVE ME *Mercury 1589142*	27 3

Gerald ALSTON *US, male vocalist (1 WEEK)*

		pos/wks
15 Apr 89	ACTIVATED *RCA ZB 42681*	73 1

Re-entries are listed as (re), (2re), (3re), etc which signifies that the hit re-entered the chart once, twice or three times, etc

ALTERED IMAGES
UK, male / female vocal / instrumental group (60 WEEKS)   pos/wks

28 Mar 81	DEAD POP STARS *Epic EPC A 1023*	67	2
26 Sep 81 ●	HAPPY BIRTHDAY *Epic EPC A 1522*	2	17
12 Dec 81 ●	I COULD BE HAPPY *Epic EPC A 1834*	7	12
27 Mar 82	SEE THOSE EYES *Epic EPC A 2198*	11	7
22 May 82	PINKY BLUE *Epic EPC A 2426*	35	6
19 Mar 83 ●	DON'T TALK TO ME ABOUT LOVE *Epic EPC A 3083*	7	7
28 May 83	BRING ME CLOSER *Epic EPC A 3398*	29	6
16 Jul 83	LOVE TO STAY *Epic EPC A 3582*	46	3

ALTERN 8
UK, male instrumental / production
duo – Mark Archer and Chris Peat (34 WEEKS)   pos/wks

13 Jul 91	INFILTRATE 202 *Network NWK 24*	28	7
16 Nov 91 ●	ACTIV 8 (COME WITH ME) *Network NWK 34*	3	9
8 Feb 92	FREQUENCY *Network NWKT 37*	41	1
11 Apr 92 ●	EVAPOR 8 *Network NWK 38* [1]	6	6
4 Jul 92	HYPNOTIC ST-8 *Network NWK 49*	16	4
10 Oct 92	SHAME *Network NWKTEN 56* [2]	74	1
12 Dec 92	BRUTAL-8-E *Network NWK 59*	43	5
3 Jul 93	EVERYBODY *Network NWKCD 73*	58	1

[1] Guest vocal 'Evapor 8' – PP Arnold [2] Altern 8 vs Evelyn King

ALTHIA and DONNA
Jamaica, female vocal duo
– Althea Forrest and Donna Reid (11 WEEKS)   pos/wks

24 Dec 77 ★	UPTOWN TOP RANKING *Lightning LIG 506*	1	11

ALVIN and the CHIPMUNKS – See CHIPMUNKS

ALY-US
US, male vocal / instrumental group (3 WEEKS)   pos/wks

21 Nov 92	FOLLOW ME *Cooltempo COOL 266*	43	2
25 May 02	FOLLOW ME (re-mix) *Strictly Rhythm SRUKCD 05*	54	1

Shola AMA
UK, female vocalist – Mathurin Campbell (50 WEEKS)   pos/wks

19 Apr 97 ●	YOU MIGHT NEED SOMEBODY *WEA WEA 097CD1*	4	14
30 Aug 97 ●	YOU'RE THE ONE I LOVE *WEA WEA 121CD1*	3	8
29 Nov 97	WHO'S LOVING MY BABY *WEA WEA 145CD1*	13	7
21 Feb 98	MUCH LOVE *WEA WEA 154CD1*	17	3
11 Apr 98	SOMEDAY I'LL FIND YOU / I'VE BEEN TO A MARVELLOUS PARTY *EMI CDTCB 001* [1]	28	3
17 Apr 99 ●	TABOO *WEA WEA 203CD* [2]	10	8
6 Nov 99	STILL BELIEVE *WEA WEA 239CD1*	26	3
29 Apr 00	IMAGINE *WEA WEA 252 CD*	24	4

[1] Shola Ama and Craig Armstrong / Divine Comedy [2] Glamma Kid featuring Shola Ama

Eddie AMADOR
US, male DJ / producer (5 WEEKS)   pos/wks

24 Oct 98	HOUSE MUSIC *Pukka CDPUKKA 18*	37	2
22 Jan 00	RISE *Defected DEFECT 9CDS*	19	3

AMAR
UK, female vocalist / instrumentalist – Amar Nagi (1 WEEK)   pos/wks

9 Sep 00	SOMETIMES IT SNOWS IN APRIL *Blanco Y Negro NEG 129CD*	48	1

AMAZULU
UK, female / male vocal / instrumental group (57 WEEKS)   pos/wks

6 Jul 85	EXCITABLE *Island IS 201*	12	13
23 Nov 85	DON'T YOU JUST KNOW IT *Island IS 233*	15	11
15 Mar 86	THE THINGS THE LONELY DO *Island IS 267*	43	6
31 May 86 ●	TOO GOOD TO BE FORGOTTEN *Island IS 284*	5	13
13 Sep 86	MONTEGO BAY *Island IS 293*	16	9
10 Oct 87	MONY MONY *EMI EM 32*	38	5

AMBASSADOR
Holland, male DJ / production group (1 WEEK)   pos/wks

12 Feb 00	ONE OF THESE DAYS *Platipus PLATCD 69*	67	1

AMBASSADORS OF FUNK featuring MC MARIO
UK, male DJ and rapper – Simon Harris and Einstein (8 WEEKS)   pos/wks

31 Oct 92 ●	SUPERMARIOLAND *Living Beat SMASH 23*	8	8

See also Simon HARRIS

TOP 10 WELSH ACTS

■ Welsh-born chart champions (calculated by weeks on the UK singles chart) together with each act's highest placed hit

Welsh chart champion Tom Jones tucks into a full Welsh breakfast

1. TOM JONES (392)
   Green, Green Grass of Home

2. SHIRLEY BASSEY (326)
   As I Love You

3. SHAKIN' STEVENS (277)
   This Ole House

4. MANIC STREET PREACHERS (150)
   If You Tolerate This Your Children Will Be Next

5. STEREOPHONICS (108)
   The Bartender and the Thief

6. MALCOLM VAUGHAN (106)
   St Therese of the Roses

7. DAVE EDMUNDS (93)
   I Hear You Knocking

8. BONNIE TYLER (81)
   Total Eclipse of the Heart

9. SCRITTI POLITTI (78)
   The Word Girl

10. MARY HOPKIN (74)
    Those Were the Days

AMBER *Holland, female vocalist – Marie Cremers (2 WEEKS)* pos/wks

24 Jun 00	SEXUAL *Substance SUBS 2CDS*	34	2

AMEN *US, male vocal / instrumental group (2 WEEKS)* pos/wks

17 Feb 01	TOO HARD TO BE FREE *Virgin VUSCD 191*	72	1
21 Jul 01	THE WAITING 18 *Virgin VUSCD 207*	61	1

AMEN CORNER *UK, male vocal / instrumental group*
– lead vocal Andy Fairweather-Low (67 WEEKS) pos/wks

26 Jul 67	GIN HOUSE BLUES *Deram DM 136*	12	10
11 Oct 67	THE WORLD OF BROKEN HEARTS *Deram DM 151*	24	6
17 Jan 68 ●	BEND ME, SHAPE ME *Deram DM 172*	3	12
31 Jan 68 ●	HIGH IN THE SKY *Deram DM 197*	6	13
29 Jan 69 ★	(IF PARADISE IS) HALF AS NICE *Immediate IM 073* ★	1	11
25 Jun 69 ●	HELLO SUZIE *Immediate IM 081*	4	10
14 Feb 76	(IF PARADISE IS) HALF AS NICE (re-issue)		
	Immediate IMS 103	34	5

See also FAIR WEATHER; Andy FAIRWEATHER-LOW

AMEN UK *UK, male / female vocal / production group (6 WEEKS)* pos/wks

8 Feb 97	PASSION *Feverpitch CDFVR 1015*	15	4
28 Jun 97	PEOPLE OF LOVE *Feverpitch CDFVR 18*	36	2

AMERICA *US, male vocal / instrumental group (20 WEEKS)* pos/wks

18 Dec 71 ●	A HORSE WITH NO NAME (re) *Warner Bros. K 16128* ▲	3	13
25 Nov 72	VENTURA HIGHWAY *Warner Bros. K 16219*	43	4
6 Nov 82	YOU CAN DO MAGIC *Capitol CL 264*	59	3

AMERICAN BREED
US, male vocal / instrumental group (6 WEEKS) pos/wks

7 Feb 68	BEND ME SHAPE ME *Stateside SS 2078*	24	6

AMERICAN HEAD CHARGE
US, male vocal / instrumental group (1 WEEK) pos/wks

8 Jun 02	JUST SO YOU KNOW *Mercury 5829622*	52	1

AMERICAN HI-FI *US, male vocal / instrumental group (3 WEEKS)* pos/wks

8 Sep 01	FLAVOR OF THE WEAK *Mercury 5886722*	31	3

AMERICAN MUSIC CLUB
US, male vocal / instrumental group (4 WEEKS) pos/wks

24 Apr 93	JOHNNY MATHIS' FEET *Virgin VSCDG 1445*	58	2
10 Sep 94	WISH THE WORLD AWAY *Virgin VSCDX 1512*	46	2

AMERIE featuring LUDACRIS
US, female vocalist – Amerie Rogers – and male rapper (2 WEEKS) pos/wks

9 Nov 02	WHY DON'T WE FALL IN LOVE *Columbia 6732212*	40	2

AMES BROTHERS *US, male vocal group (6 WEEKS)* pos/wks

4 Feb 55 ●	THE NAUGHTY LADY OF SHADY LANE *HMV B 10800*	6	6

'With Hugo Winterhalter and his Orchestra'

AMIL – *See JAY-Z*

AMILLIONSONS
UK, male production trio and US, female vocalist (2 WEEKS) pos/wks

24 Aug 02	MISTI BLU *London LONCD 468*	39	2

Includes vocal by Taka Boom

AMIRA *US, female vocalist – Amira McNiel (7 WEEKS)* pos/wks

13 Dec 97	MY DESIRE *VC VCRD 27*	51	1
8 Aug 98	MY DESIRE (re-mix) *VC Recordings VCRD 36*	46	2
10 Feb 01	MY DESIRE (2nd re-mix) *VC Recordings VCRD 71*	20	4

AMNESIA – *See Frank'o MOIRAGHI featuring AMNESIA*

Cherie AMORE *France, female vocalist (2 WEEKS)* pos/wks

15 Apr 00	I DON'T WANT NOBODY (TELLIN' ME WHAT TO DO)		
	Eternal / WEA WEA 262CD	33	2

Vanessa AMOROSI *Australia, female vocalist (10 WEEKS)* pos/wks

23 Sep 00 ●	ABSOLUTELY EVERYBODY *Mercury 1582972*	7	10

AMOS
UK, male vocalist / rapper / producer – Amos Pizzey (12 WEEKS) pos/wks

3 Sep 94	ONLY SAW TODAY – INSTANT KARMA *Positiva CDTIV 16*	48	2
25 Mar 95	LET LOVE SHINE *Positiva CDTIV 24*	31	2
7 Oct 95	CHURCH OF FREEDOM *Positiva CDTIV 38*	54	1
12 Oct 96	STAMP! *Positiva CDTIV 65* [1]	11	5
31 May 97	ARGENTINA *Positiva CDTIV 74* [1]	30	2

[1] Jeremy Healy and Amos

Tori AMOS *US, female vocalist / instrumentalist – piano (66 WEEKS)* pos/wks

23 Nov 91	SILENT ALL THESE YEARS *East West YZ 618*	51	3
1 Feb 92	CHINA *East West YZ 7531*	51	2
21 Mar 92	WINTER *East West A 7504*	25	4
20 Jun 92	CRUCIFY *East West A 7479*	15	6
22 Aug 92	SILENT ALL THESE YEARS (re-issue) *East West A 7433*	26	4
22 Jan 94 ●	CORNFLAKE GIRL *East West A 7281CD*	4	6
19 Mar 94 ●	PRETTY GOOD YEAR *East West A 7263CD*	7	4
28 May 94	PAST THE MISSION *East West YZ 7257CD*	31	3
15 Oct 94	GOD *East West A 7251CD*	44	2
13 Jan 96	CAUGHT A LITE SNEEZE *East West A 5524CD1*	20	3
23 Mar 96	TALULA *East West A 8512CD1*	22	2
3 Aug 96	HEY JUPITER / PROFESSIONAL WIDOW		
	East West A 5494CD	20	9
9 Nov 96	BLUE SKIES *Perfecto PERF 130CD1* [1]	26	2
11 Jan 97 ★	PROFESSIONAL WIDOW (IT'S GOT TO BE BIG) (re-mix)		
	East West A 5450CD	1	10
2 May 98	SPARK *Atlantic AT 0031CD*	16	3
13 Nov 99	GLORY OF THE 80'S *Atlantic AT 0077CD1*	46	1
26 Oct 02	A SORTA FAIRYTALE *Epic 6730432*	41	2

[1] BT featuring Tori Amos

AMOURE
UK, male production duo – Rod Edwards and Nick Magnus (2 WEEKS) pos/wks

27 May 00	IS THAT YOUR FINAL ANSWER? (WHO WANTS TO BE A		
	MILLIONAIRE – THE SINGLE) *Celador MILLION 2*	33	2

AMPS *US, male / female vocal / instrumental group (1 WEEK)* pos/wks

21 Oct 95	TIPP CITY *4AD BAD 5015CD*	61	1

AMY – *See A.D.A.M. featuring AMY*

AN EMOTIONAL FISH
Ireland, male vocal / instrumental group (5 WEEKS) pos/wks

23 Jun 90	CELEBRATE *East West YZ 489*	46	5

ANASTACIA
US, female vocalist – Anastacia Newkirk (59 WEEKS) pos/wks

30 Sep 00 ●	I'M OUTTA LOVE *Epic 6695782*	6	17
3 Feb 01	NOT THAT KIND (re) *Epic 6707632*	11	8
2 Jun 01	COWBOYS & KISSES *Epic 6712622*	28	5
25 Aug 01	MADE FOR LOVIN' YOU *Epic 6717172*	27	3
1 Dec 01	PAID MY DUES *Epic 6721252*	14	9
6 Apr 02	ONE DAY IN YOUR LIFE *Epic 6724562*	11	9
21 Sep 02	WHY'D YOU LIE TO ME (re) *Epic 6731112*	25	5
7 Dec 02	YOU'LL NEVER BE ALONE *Epic 6733802*	31	5

AND WHY NOT?
UK, male vocal / instrumental group (18 WEEKS) pos/wks

14 Oct 89	RESTLESS DAYS (SHE CRIES OUT LOUD) *Island IS 426*	38	7
13 Jan 90	THE FACE *Island IS 444*	13	8
21 Apr 90	SOMETHING YOU GOT *Island IS 452*	39	3

... AND YOU WILL KNOW US BY THE TRAIL OF DEAD
US, male vocal / instrumental group (2 WEEKS)   pos/wks

11 Nov 00	MISTAKES AND REGRETS *Domino RUG 114CD*	69	1
11 May 02	ANOTHER MORNING STONER *Interscope / Polydor 4977162*	54	1

Angry ANDERSON *Australia, male vocalist (13 WEEKS)*   pos/wks

19 Nov 88 ●	SUDDENLY *Food For Thought YUM 113*	3	13

Carl ANDERSON *US, male vocalist (4 WEEKS)*   pos/wks

8 Jun 85	BUTTERCUP *Streetwave KHAN 45*	49	4

Carleen ANDERSON *US, female vocalist (17 WEEKS)*   pos/wks

12 Feb 94	NERVOUS BREAKDOWN *Circa YRCDG 112*	27	4
28 May 94	MAMA SAID *Circa YRCD 114*	26	4
13 Aug 94	TRUE SPIRIT *Circa YRCD 118*	24	3
14 Jan 95	LET IT LAST *Circa YRCD 119*	16	3
7 Feb 98	MAYBE I'M AMAZED *Circa YRCD 128*	24	2
25 Apr 98	WOMAN IN ME *Circa YRCD 129*	74	1

See also BRAND NEW HEAVIES; Paul WELLER

Gillian ANDERSON – *See HAL featuring Gillian ANDERSON*

John ANDERSON BIG BAND *UK, big band (5 WEEKS)*   pos/wks

21 Dec 85	GLENN MILLER MEDLEY (re) *Modern GLEN 1*	61	5

Glenn Miller Medley comprises the following tracks: In the Mood / American Patrol / Little Brown Jug / Pennsylvania 65000

Leroy ANDERSON and his POP CONCERT ORCHESTRA
US, orchestra, leader d. 18 May 1975 (4 WEEKS)   pos/wks

28 Jun 57	FORGOTTEN DREAMS (2re) *Brunswick 05485*	24	4

Lynn ANDERSON *US, female vocalist (20 WEEKS)*   pos/wks

20 Feb 71 ●	ROSE GARDEN *CBS 5360*	3	20

Moira ANDERSON *UK, female vocalist (2 WEEKS)*   pos/wks

27 Dec 69	THE HOLY CITY *Decca F 12989*	43	2

Laurie ANDERSON
US, female vocalist / multi-instrumentalist (6 WEEKS)   pos/wks

17 Oct 81 ●	O SUPERMAN *Warner Bros. K 17870*	2	6

Sunshine ANDERSON *US, female vocalist (8 WEEKS)*   pos/wks

2 Jun 01 ●	HEARD IT ALL BEFORE *Atlantic AT 0100CD*	9	7
22 Sep 01	LUNCH OR DINNER *Atlantic AT 0109CD*	57	1

ANDERSON BRUFORD WAKEMAN HOWE
UK, male vocal / instrumental group (2 WEEKS)   pos/wks

24 Jun 89	BROTHER OF MINE *Arista 112379*	63	2

See also YES

Peter ANDRE   408   Top 500
Australian-raised teen-dream vocalist with six-pack stomach, b. 27 Feb 1973, Middlesex, UK. Chart-topping debut album 'Natural' included platinum single 'Mysterious Girl' and two UK No.1s. However, his ventures into more mature R&B-flava'd tracks proved less accessible to his previously large fan base. Best-selling single: 'Mysterious Girl' 750,000 (83 WEEKS)   pos/wks

10 Jun 95	TURN IT UP *Mushroom D 1000*	64	1
16 Sep 95	MYSTERIOUS GIRL *Mushroom D 11921*	53	2
16 Mar 96	ONLY ONE (re) *Mushroom D 1307*	16	4
1 Jun 96 ●	MYSTERIOUS GIRL (re-issue) *Mushroom D 2000* [1]	2	18
14 Sep 96 ★	FLAVA *Mushroom D 2003* ■	1	9
7 Dec 96 ★	I FEEL YOU (2re) *Mushroom D 1521* ■	1	11
8 Mar 97 ●	NATURAL (2re) *Mushroom DX 1577*	6	11
9 Aug 97 ●	ALL ABOUT US (re) *Mushroom MUSH 5CD*	3	9
8 Nov 97 ●	LONELY (re) *Mushroom MUSH 16CD*	6	9

24 Jan 98	ALL NIGHT ALL RIGHT *Mushroom MUSH 21CD* [2]	16	4
25 Jul 98 ●	KISS THE GIRL *Mushroom MUSH 34CDSX*	9	5

[1] Peter Andre featuring Bubbler Ranx [2] Peter Andre featuring Warren G

Chris ANDREWS *UK, male vocalist (36 WEEKS)*   pos/wks

7 Oct 65 ●	YESTERDAY MAN *Decca F 12236*	3	15
2 Dec 65	TO WHOM IT CONCERNS *Decca F 22285*	13	10
14 Apr 66	SOMETHING ON MY MIND (re) *Decca F 22365*	41	3
2 Jun 66	WHAT'CHA GONNA DO NOW? *Decca F 22404*	40	4
25 Aug 66	STOP THAT GIRL *Decca F 22472*	36	4

Eamonn ANDREWS
Ireland, male vocalist, d. 5 Nov 1987 (3 WEEKS)   pos/wks

20 Jan 56	THE SHIFTING WHISPERING SANDS (PARTS 1 & 2) *Parlophone R 4106*	18	3

Hit is credited: 'with Ron Goodwin and his Orchestra and Chorus'

ANEKA *UK, female vocalist – Mary Sandeman (16 WEEKS)*   pos/wks

8 Aug 81 ★	JAPANESE BOY *Hansa HANSA 5*	1	12
7 Nov 81	LITTLE LADY *Hansa HANSA 8*	50	4

Dave ANGEL *UK, male DJ / producer (1 WEEK)*   pos/wks

2 Aug 97	TOKYO STEALTH FIGHTER *Fourth & Broadway BRCD 355*	58	1

Simone ANGEL *Holland, female vocalist (1 WEEK)*   pos/wks

13 Nov 93	LET THIS FEELING *A&M 5803652*	60	1

ANGELETTES *UK, female vocal group (5 WEEKS)*   pos/wks

13 May 72	DON'T LET HIM TOUCH YOU *Decca F 13284*	35	5

ANGELHEART *UK, female producer (2 WEEKS)*   pos/wks

6 Apr 96	COME BACK TO ME *Hi-Life 5776312* [1]	68	1
22 Mar 97	I'M STILL WAITING *Hi-Life 5735452* [2]	74	1

[1] Angelheart featuring Rochelle Harris [2] Angelheart featuring Aletia Bourne

ANGELIC *UK, male / female production / vocal duo*
– Amanda O'Riordan and Darren Tate (16 WEEKS)   pos/wks

17 Jun 00	IT'S MY TURN *Serious MCSTD 40235*	11	10
24 Feb 01	CAN'T KEEP ME SILENT *Serious SERR 023CD*	12	4
10 Nov 01	STAY WITH ME *Serious SERR 35CD*	36	2

See also CITIZEN CANED; Jurgen VRIES

ANGELIC UPSTARTS
UK, male vocal / instrumental group (30 WEEKS)   pos/wks

21 Apr 79	I'M AN UPSTART *Warner Bros. K 17354*	31	8
11 Aug 79	TEENAGE WARNING *Warner Bros. K 17426*	29	6
3 Nov 79	NEVER 'AD NOTHIN' *Warner Bros. K 17476*	52	4
9 Feb 80	OUT OF CONTROL *Warner Bros. K 17558*	58	3
22 Mar 80	WE GOTTA GET OUT OF THIS PLACE *Warner Bros. K 17576*	65	2
2 Aug 80	LAST NIGHT ANOTHER SOLDIER *Zonophone Z 7*	51	4
7 Feb 81	KIDS ON THE STREET *Zonophone Z 16*	57	3

ANGELLE *UK, female vocalist (1 WEEK)*   pos/wks

17 Aug 02	JOY AND PAIN *Innovation CDINNOV 1*	43	1

Bobby ANGELO and the TUXEDOS
UK, male vocal / instrumental group (6 WEEKS)   pos/wks

10 Aug 61	BABY SITTIN' *HMV POP 892*	30	6

ANGELS *US, female vocal group (1 WEEK)*   pos/wks

3 Oct 63	MY BOYFRIEND'S BACK *Mercury AMT 1211* ▲	50	1

ANGELS OF LIGHT – *See PSYCHIC TV*

ANGELS REVERSE Germany, male production duo (1 WEEK)　pos/wks

31 Aug 02	DON'T CARE Inferno CDFERN 46	71	1

ANGELWITCH UK, male vocal / instrumental group (1 WEEK)　pos/wks

7 Jun 80	SWEET DANGER EMI 5064	75	1

ANIMAL
US, male puppet vocalist / instrumentalist – drums (3 WEEKS)　pos/wks

23 Jul 94	WIPE OUT BMG Kidz 74321219532	38	3

ANIMAL NIGHTLIFE
UK, male / female vocal / instrumental group (22 WEEKS)　pos/wks

13 Aug 83	NATIVE BOY (UPTOWN) Innervision A3584	60	3
18 Aug 84	MR SOLITAIRE Island IS 193	25	12
6 Jul 85	LOVE IS JUST THE GREAT PRETENDER Island IS 200	28	6
5 Oct 85	PREACHER, PREACHER Island IS 245	67	1

ANIMALHOUSE UK, male vocal / instrumental group (1 WEEK)　pos/wks

15 Jul 00	READY TO RECEIVE Boilerhouse / Arista 74321771072	61	1

ANIMALS (157 　Top 500)
Ground-breaking Newcastle band: Eric Burdon (v), Alan Price (k), Brian 'Chas' Chandler (b) (d. 1996), Hilton Valentine (g), John Steel (d). They were the first hit act produced by Mickie Most and, after The Tornados and The Beatles, the third UK group to top the US singles chart (147 WEEKS) pos/wks

16 Apr 64	BABY LET ME TAKE YOU HOME Columbia DB 7247	21	8
25 Jun 64	★ THE HOUSE OF THE RISING SUN Columbia DB 7301 ▲	1	12
17 Sep 64	● I'M CRYING Columbia DB 7354	8	10
4 Feb 65	● DON'T LET ME BE MISUNDERSTOOD Columbia DB 7445	3	9
8 Apr 65	● BRING IT ON HOME TO ME Columbia DB 7539	7	11
15 Jul 65	● WE'VE GOTTA GET OUT OF THIS PLACE Columbia DB 7639	2	13
28 Oct 65	● IT'S MY LIFE Columbia DB 7741	7	11
17 Feb 66	INSIDE – LOOKING OUT Decca F 12332	12	8
2 Jun 66	● DON'T BRING ME DOWN Decca F 12407	6	8
27 Oct 66	HELP ME GIRL Decca F 12502 [1]	14	10
15 Jun 67	WHEN I WAS YOUNG MGM 1340 [2]	45	3
6 Sep 67	GOOD TIMES MGM 1344 [2]	20	11
18 Oct 67	● SAN FRANCISCAN NIGHTS MGM 1359 [2]	7	10
14 Feb 68	SKY PILOT MGM 1373 [2]	40	3
15 Jan 69	RING OF FIRE MGM 1461 [2]	35	5
7 Oct 72	THE HOUSE OF THE RISING SUN (re-issue) (re) RAK RR 1	11	16

[1] Eric Burdon and session musicians billed as The Animals [2] Eric Burdon and The Animals

'The House of the Rising Sun' (re-issue) peaked only at No.25 in 1972 and peaked at No.11 as a re-entry in Sep 1982

ANIMOTION
US / UK, male / female vocal / instrumental group (12 WEEKS)　pos/wks

11 May 85	● OBSESSION Mercury PH 34	5	12

Paul ANKA (193 　Top 500) Celebrated Canadian singer / songwriter,
b. 30 Jul 1941, Ottawa. He topped the UK and US charts aged 16 and was the youngest transatlantic chart regular of the 1950s. He also penned big hits for Buddy Holly, Tom Jones, Donny Osmond and 'My Way' for Frank Sinatra. Biggest-selling single: 'Diana' 1,240,000 (134 WEEKS)　pos/wks

9 Aug 57	★ DIANA Columbia DB 3980 ◆ ▲	1	25
8 Nov 57	● I LOVE YOU, BABY Columbia DB 4022	3	15
8 Nov 57	TELL ME THAT YOU LOVE ME Columbia DB 4022	25	2
31 Jan 58	● YOU ARE MY DESTINY Columbia DB 4063	6	13
30 May 58	CRAZY LOVE Columbia DB 4110	26	1
26 Sep 58	MIDNIGHT Columbia DB 4172	26	1
30 Jan 59	● (ALL OF A SUDDEN) MY HEART SINGS Columbia DB 4241	10	13
10 Jul 59	● LONELY BOY Columbia DB 4324 ▲	3	17
30 Oct 59	● PUT YOUR HEAD ON MY SHOULDER Columbia DB 4355	7	12
26 Feb 60	IT'S TIME TO CRY (re) Columbia DB 4390	28	2
31 Mar 60	PUPPY LOVE (re) Columbia DB 4434	33	7

15 Sep 60	HELLO YOUNG LOVERS Columbia DB 4504	44	1
15 Mar 62	LOVE ME WARM AND TENDER RCA 1276	19	11
26 Jul 62	A STEEL GUITAR AND A GLASS OF WINE RCA 1292	41	4
28 Sep 74	● (YOU'RE) HAVING MY BABY United Artists UP 35713 [1] ▲	6	10

[1] Paul Anka featuring Odia Coates

Ana ANN UK, female vocalist – Ana Petrovic (2 WEEKS)　pos/wks

23 Feb 02	RIDE LL RIDELLR 100	24	2

ANOTHER LEVEL (421 　Top 500)
Soulful, teen-targeted UK pop vocal group; Dane Bowers, Wayne Williams, Mark Baron, Bobak Kianoush. Credible quartet, who have had hits with top US rap stars TQ, Jay-Z and Ghostface Killah, were nominated for a Brit award in 1999 but split in 2000 (81 WEEKS)　pos/wks

28 Feb 98	● BE ALONE NO MORE Northwestside 74321551982	6	9
18 Jul 98	★ FREAK ME Northwestside 74321582362 ■	1	12
7 Nov 98	● GUESS I WAS A FOOL Northwestside 74321621202	5	13
23 Jan 99	● I WANT YOU FOR MYSELF Northwestside 74321164632 [1]	2	8
10 Apr 99	● BE ALONE NO MORE Northwestside 74321658472 [2]	11	9
12 Jun 99	● FROM THE HEART (re) Northwestside 74321673012	6	11
4 Sep 99	● SUMMERTIME Northwestside 74321694672 [3]	7	7
13 Nov 99	● BOMB DIGGY Northwestside 74321712212	6	12

[1] Another Level / Ghostface Killah [2] Another Level featuring Jay-Z [3] Another Level featuring TQ

ANOUCHKA – See Terry HALL

Adam ANT Innovative and flamboyant pop idol, b. Stuart Goddard, 3 Nov
1954, London. He left Adam and The Ants at their peak and immediately topped UK chart and scored his first ever US hit. Later made his mark as an actor (69 WEEKS)　pos/wks

22 May 82	★ GOODY TWO SHOES CBS A 2367	1	11
18 Sep 82	● FRIEND OR FOE CBS A 2736	9	8
27 Nov 82	DESPERATE BUT NOT SERIOUS CBS A 2892	33	7
29 Oct 83	● PUSS 'N BOOTS CBS A 3614	5	11
10 Dec 83	STRIP CBS A 3589	41	6
22 Sep 84	APOLLO 9 CBS A 4719	13	8
13 Jul 85	VIVE LE ROCK CBS A 6367	50	4
17 Feb 90	ROOM AT THE TOP MCA MCA 1387	13	7
28 Apr 90	CANT SET RULES ABOUT LOVE MCA MCA 1404	47	2
11 Feb 95	WONDERFUL EMI CDEMS 366	32	3
3 Jun 95	GOTTA BE A SIN EMI CDEMS 379	48	2

See also ADAM and the ANTS

ANT & DEC (348 　Top 500) Newcastle-born child actors and Geordie
jokers Anthony McPartlin and Declan Donnelly (aka PJ & Duncan) initially recorded under their character aliases from the children's TV series Byker Grove. They scored impressive 12 Top 20 entries within three years. These one-time pop idols are now popular TV presenters (92 WEEKS)　pos/wks

18 Dec 93	TONIGHT I'M FREE Telstar CDSTAS 2706	62	3
23 Apr 94	WHY ME Telstar CDSTAS 2719	27	4
23 Jul 94	● LET'S GET READY TO RHUMBLE XSrhythm CDANT 1	9	11
8 Oct 94	IF I GIVE YOU MY NUMBER XSrhythm CDANT 2	15	7
3 Dec 94	ETERNAL LOVE XSrhythm CDANT 3	12	9
25 Feb 95	OUR RADIO ROCKS XSrhythm CDANT 4	15	5
29 Jul 95	STUCK ON U XSrhythm CDANT 5	12	5
14 Oct 95	U KRAZY KATZ XSrhythm CDANT 6	14	4
2 Dec 95	PERFECT Telstar CDANT 7	16	7
20 Mar 96	STEPPING STONE Telstar CDANT 8	11	5
24 Aug 96	● BETTER WATCH OUT Telstar CDANT 9	10	4
23 Nov 96	WHEN I FALL IN LOVE Telstar CDANT 10	12	5
15 Mar 97	● SHOUT Telstar CDDEC 11	10	5
10 May 97	FALLING Telstar CDDEC 12	14	4
8 Jun 02	● WE'RE ON THE BALL Columbia 6727312	3	11

All hits up to and including 20 Mar 96 credited to PJ & Duncan

ANTARCTICA Australia, male producer – Steve Gibbs (2 WEEKS)　pos/wks

29 Jan 00	RETURN TO REALITY React CDREACT 173	53	1
8 Jul 00	ADRIFT (CAST YOUR MIND) React CDREACT 172	72	1

Mark ANTHONI – See FIRE ISLAND

Billie ANTHONY
UK, female vocalist – Philomena Brown d. 1991 (16 WEEKS) pos/wks

15 Oct 54 ●	THIS OLE HOUSE *Columbia DB 3519*	4 16

This release was 'With Eric Jupp and his Orchestra'

Marc ANTHONY
US, male vocalist – Marco Antonio Muniz (3 WEEKS) pos/wks

13 Nov 99	I NEED TO KNOW *Columbia 6683612*	28 3

See also Louie VEGA

Miki ANTHONY *UK, male vocalist (7 WEEKS)* pos/wks

3 Feb 73	IF IT WASN'T FOR THE REASON THAT I LOVE YOU *Bell 1275*	27 7

Ray ANTHONY and His ORCHESTRA *US, orchestra (2 WEEKS)* pos/wks

4 Dec 53 ●	DRAGNET (re) *Capitol CL 13983*	7 2

Richard ANTHONY
France, male vocalist – Richard Anthony Bush (15 WEEKS) pos/wks

12 Dec 63	WALKING ALONE *Columbia DB 7133*	37 5
2 Apr 64	IF I LOVED YOU (re) *Columbia DB 7235*	18 10

ANTHRAX *US, male vocal / instrumental group (37 WEEKS)* pos/wks

28 Feb 87	I AM THE LAW *Island IS LAW 1*	32 5
27 Jun 87	INDIANS *Island IS 325*	44 4
5 Dec 87	I'M THE MAN *Island IS 338*	20 6
10 Sep 88	MAKE ME LAUGH *Island IS 379*	26 3
18 Mar 89	ANTI-SOCIAL *Island IS 409*	44 3
1 Sep 90	IN MY WORLD *Island IS 470*	29 2
5 Jan 91	GOT THE TIME *Island IS 476*	16 4
6 Jul 91	BRING THE NOISE *Island IS 490* [1]	14 5
8 May 93	ONLY *Elektra EKR 166CD*	36 3
11 Sep 93	BLACK LODGE *Elektra EKR 171CD*	53 2

[1] Anthrax featuring Chuck D

ANTICAPPELLA
Italy / UK, male / female vocal / instrumental group (12 WEEKS) pos/wks

16 Nov 91	THE SQUARE ROOT OF 231 *PWL Continental PWL 205*	24 4
18 Apr 92	EVERY DAY *PWL Continental PWL 220*	45 2
25 Jun 94	MOVE YOUR BODY *Media MCSTD 1980* [1]	21 3
1 Apr 95	EXPRESS YOUR FREEDOM *Media MCSTD 2048*	31 2
25 May 96	THE SQUARE ROOT OF 231 / MOVE YOUR BODY (re-mix) *Media MCSTD 40037*	54 1

[1] Anticappella featuring MC Fixx It

ANTI-NOWHERE LEAGUE
UK, male vocal / instrumental group (10 WEEKS) pos/wks

23 Jan 82	STREETS OF LONDON *WXYZ ABCD 1*	48 5
20 Mar 82	I HATE . . . PEOPLE *WXYZ ABCD 2*	46 3
3 Jul 82	WOMAN *WXYZ ABCD 4*	72 2

ANTI-PASTI – See EXPLOITED

ANTONIA – See BOMB THE BASS

ANTS – See ADAM and the ANTS

ANUNA – See Bill WHELAN featuring ANUNA and the RTE CONCERT ORCHESTRA

APACHE INDIAN *UK, male vocalist – Steven Kapur (33 WEEKS)* pos/wks

28 Nov 92	FE' REAL *Ten TEN 416* [1]	33 3
2 Jan 93	ARRANGED MARRIAGE *Island CID 544*	16 6
27 Mar 93	CHOK THERE *Island CID 555*	30 4
14 Aug 93 ●	NUFF VIBES (EP) *Island CID 560*	5 10
22 Oct 93	MOVIN' ON *Island CID 580*	48 2
7 May 94	WRECKX SHOP *MCA MCSTD 1969* [2]	26 2
11 Feb 95	MAKE WAY FOR THE INDIAN *Island CID 586* [3]	29 2
22 Apr 95	RAGGAMUFFIN GIRL *Island CID 606* [4]	31 2
29 Mar 97	LOVIN' (LET ME LOVE YOU) *Coalition COLA 002CD*	53 1
18 Oct 97	REAL PEOPLE *Coalition COLA 019CD*	66 1

[1] Maxi Priest featuring Apache Indian [2] Wreckx-N-Effect featuring Apache Indian [3] Apache Indian and Tim Dog [4] Apache Indian with Frankie Paul

The listed flip side of 'Fe' Real' was 'Just Wanna Know' by Maxi Priest. Tracks on Nuff Vibes (EP): Boom Shack a Lak / Fun / Caste System / Warning

APHEX TWIN
UK, male instrumentalist / producer – Richard James (12 WEEKS) pos/wks

9 May 92	DIGERIDOO *R&S RSUK 12*	55 2
27 Nov 93	ON *Warp WAP 39CD*	32 3
8 Apr 95	VENTOLIN *Warp WAP 60CD*	49 1
26 Oct 96	GIRL / BOY (EP) *Warp WAP 78CD*	64 1
18 Oct 97	COME TO DADDY *Warp WAP 94CD*	36 2
3 Apr 99	WINDOWLICKER *Warp WAP 105CD*	16 3

Tracks on Girl / Boy (EP): Girl / Boy Song / Milkman / Inkey $ / Beatles Under My Carpet. The EP was incorrectly listed in the chart and, because of its length, should have been considered an album

See also POLYGON WINDOW; AFX

APHRODITE featuring WILDFLOWER
UK, male producer and female vocalist (1 WEEK) pos/wks

16 Nov 02	SEE THRU IT *V2 VVR 5020983*	68 1

APHRODITE'S CHILD
Greece, male vocal / instrumental group (7 WEEKS) pos/wks

6 Nov 68	RAIN AND TEARS *Mercury MF 1039*	29 7

APOLLO FOUR FORTY
UK, male instrumental / production group (52 WEEKS) pos/wks

22 Jan 94	ASTRAL AMERICA *Stealth Sonic SSXCD 2* [1]	36 2
5 Nov 94	LIQUID COOL *Stealth Sonic SSXCD 3* [1]	35 2
25 Mar 95	(DON'T FEAR) THE REAPER *Stealth Sonic SSXCD 4* [1]	35 2
27 Jul 96	KRUPA (re) *Stealth Sonic SSXCD 5*	23 8
15 Feb 97 ●	AIN'T TALKIN' 'BOUT DUB *Stealth Sonic SSXCDX 6*	7 7
5 Jul 97	RAW POWER *Stealth Sonic SSXCD 7*	32 3
11 Jul 98	RENDEZ-VOUS '98 *Epic 6661102* [2]	12 6
8 Aug 98 ●	LOST IN SPACE *Stealth Sonic SSX 9CD*	4 9
28 Aug 99 ●	STOP THE ROCK *Epic SSX 10CD*	10 6
27 Nov 99	HEART GO BOOM *Epic SSX 11CD*	57 1
9 Dec 00	CHARLIE'S ANGELS 2000 *Epic SSX 13CD*	29 6

[1] Apollo 440 [2] Jean-Michel Jarre and Apollo 440

APOLLO presents HOUSE OF VIRGINISM *Sweden, male instrumentalist and male vocal / instrumental group (1 WEEK)* pos/wks

17 Feb 96	EXCLUSIVE *Logic 74321324102*	67 1

See also HOUSE OF VIRGINISM

Fiona APPLE *US, female vocalist – Fiona Apple Maggart (2 WEEKS)* pos/wks

26 Feb 00	FAST AS YOU CAN *Columbia 6689962*	33 2

Kim APPLEBY *UK, female vocalist (31 WEEKS)* pos/wks

3 Nov 90 ●	DON'T WORRY *Parlophone R 6272*	2 10
9 Feb 91	G.L.A.D. *Parlophone R 6281*	10 6
29 Jun 91	MAMA *Parlophone R 6291*	19 8
19 Oct 91	IF YOU CARED *Parlophone R 6297*	44 3
31 Jul 93	LIGHT OF THE WORLD *Parlophone CDR 6352*	41 2
13 Nov 93	BREAKAWAY *Parlophone CDR 6362*	56 1
12 Nov 94	FREE SPIRIT *Parlophone CDR 6397*	51 1

See also MEL and KIM

APPLEJACKS
UK, male / female vocal / instrumental group (29 WEEKS) pos/wks

5 Mar 64 ●	TELL ME WHEN *Decca F 11833*	7 13

| 11 Jun 64 | LIKE DREAMERS DO *Decca F 11916* | .20 | 11 |
| 15 Oct 64 | THREE LITTLE WORDS (I LOVE YOU) *Decca F 11981* | .23 | 5 |

APPLES *UK, male vocal / instrumental group (1 WEEK)* pos/wks
| 23 Mar 91 | EYE WONDER *Epic 6566717* | .75 | 1 |

APPLETON *Canada, female vocal duo (10 WEEKS)* pos/wks
| 14 Sep 02 ● | FANTASY *Polydor 5709842* | .2 | 10 |

See also ALL SAINTS

Charlie APPLEWHITE *US, male vocalist, d. 27 Apr 2001 (1 WEEK)* pos/wks
| 23 Sep 55 | BLUE STAR *Brunswick 05416* | .20 | 1 |

This release was 'With Victor Young and Chorus'

Helen APRIL – *See John DUMMER and Helen APRIL*

APRIL WINE *Canada, male vocal / instrumental group (9 WEEKS)* pos/wks
| 15 Mar 80 | I LIKE TO ROCK *Capitol CL 16121* | .41 | 5 |
| 11 Apr 81 | JUST BETWEEN YOU AND ME *Capitol CL 16184* | .52 | 4 |

AQUA (395 Top 500) *Scandinavian Europop: Claus Noreen, Denmark, Soren Rasted, Denmark, fronted by the flame-haired Lene Nystrom, Norway, and the bald-headed Rene Dif, Denmark. Their debut album Aquarium sold more than 14 million worldwide. Ceased to be in 2001 having racked up total album / single sales of more than 28 million. Best-selling single: 'Barbie Girl' 1,722,400 (85 WEEKS)* pos/wks
25 Oct 97 ★	BARBIE GIRL (re) *Universal UMD 80413* ◆	.1	26
7 Feb 98 ★	DOCTOR JONES *Universal UMD 80457* ■	.1	14
16 May 98 ★	TURN BACK TIME *Universal UMD 80490* ■	.1	10
1 Aug 98 ●	MY OH MY (re) *Universal UMD 85058*	.6	11
26 Dec 98	GOOD MORNING SUNSHINE *Universal UMD 85086*	.18	7
26 Feb 00 ●	CARTOON HEROES (re) *Universal MCSTD 40226*	.7	11
10 Jun 00	AROUND THE WORLD *Universal MCSTD 40234*	.26	6

AQUA MARINA – *See FAB*

AQUALUNG
UK, male vocalist / instrumentalist / producer – Matt Hales (7 WEEKS) pos/wks
| 28 Sep 02 ● | STRANGE AND BEAUTIFUL (I'LL PUT A SPELL ON YOU) *B Unique BUN 032CDS* | .7 | 6 |
| 14 Dec 02 | GOOD TIMES GONNA COME *B Unique BUN 043CDS* | .71 | 1 |

AQUANUTS
US / Argentina, male production / instrumental duo (1 WEEK) pos/wks
| 4 May 02 | DEEP SEA *Data DATA 34T* | .74 | 1 |

AQUARIAN DREAM
US, male / female vocal / instrumental group (1 WEEK) pos/wks
| 24 Feb 79 | YOU'RE A STAR *Elektra LV 7* | .67 | 1 |

ARAB STRAP *UK, male vocal / instrumental duo (4 WEEKS)* pos/wks
13 Sep 97	THE GIRLS OF SUMMER (EP) *Chemikal Underground CHEM 017CD*	.74	1
4 Apr 98	HERE WE GO / TRIPPY *Chemikal Underground CHEM 20CD*	.48	1
10 Oct 98	(AFTERNOON) SOAPS *Chemikal Underground CHEM 27CD*	.74	1
10 Feb 01	LOVE DETECTIVE *Chemikal Underground CHEM 049CD*	.66	1

Tracks on The Girls of Summer (EP): Hey! Fever / Girls of Summer / The Beautiful Barmaids of Dundee / One Day After School

ARCADIA *UK, male vocal / instrumental group (13 WEEKS)* pos/wks
26 Oct 85 ●	ELECTION DAY *Odeon NSR 1*	.7	7
25 Jan 86	THE PROMISE *Odeon NSR 2*	.37	4
26 Jul 86	THE FLAME *Odeon NSR 3*	.58	2

Arcadia was Duran Duran sideline band featuring Simon Le Bon, Nick Rhodes and Roger Taylor

Tasmin ARCHER *UK, female vocalist (37 WEEKS)* pos/wks
12 Sep 92 ★	SLEEPING SATELLITE (re) *EMI EM 233*	.1	17
20 Feb 93	IN YOUR CARE *EMI CDEMS 260*	.16	6
29 May 93	LORDS OF THE NEW CHURCH *EMI CDEM 266*	.26	4
21 Aug 93	ARIENNE *EMI CDEM 275*	.30	4
8 Jan 94	SHIPBUILDING *EMI CDEM 302*	.40	4
23 Mar 96	ONE MORE GOOD NIGHT WITH THE BOYS *EMI CDEM 401*	.45	2

ARCHIES *US, male / female cartoon vocal group – lead vocal Ron Dante (26 WEEKS)* pos/wks
| 11 Oct 69 ★ | SUGAR, SUGAR *RCA 1872* ▲ | .1 | 26 |

See also CUFFLINKS

ARCHITECHS
UK, male production duo and female vocalist (19 WEEKS) pos/wks
| 7 Oct 00 ● | BODY GROOVE *Go. Beat / Polydor GOBCD33* 1 | .3 | 14 |
| 7 Apr 01 | SHOW ME THE MONEY (re) *Go. Beat GOBCD 38* | .20 | 5 |

1 Architechs featuring Nana

Jann ARDEN
Canada, female vocalist – Jann Arden Richards (2 WEEKS) pos/wks
| 13 Jul 96 | INSENSITIVE *A&M 5812652* | .40 | 2 |

Tina ARENA *Australia, female vocalist (32 WEEKS)* pos/wks
15 Apr 95	CHAINS *Columbia 6611255*	.6	11
12 Aug 95	HEAVEN HELP MY HEART *Columbia 6620975*	.25	5
2 Dec 95	SHOW ME HEAVEN *Columbia 6626975*	.29	3
3 Aug 96	SORRENTO MOON (I REMEMBER) *Columbia 6635435*	.22	4
27 Jun 98	WHISTLE DOWN THE WIND *Really Useful 5672192*	.24	5
24 Oct 98	IF I WAS A RIVER *Columbia 6665605*	.43	2
13 Mar 99	BURN *Columbia 6667442*	.47	1
20 May 00	LIVE FOR THE ONE I LOVE *Columbia 6691332*	.63	1

ARGENT *UK, male vocal / instrumental group (27 WEEKS)* pos/wks
4 Mar 72 ●	HOLD YOUR HEAD UP *Epic EPC 7786*	.5	12
10 Jun 72	TRAGEDY *Epic EPC 8115*	.34	7
24 Mar 73	GOD GAVE ROCK AND ROLL TO YOU *Epic EPC 1243*	.18	8

See also SAN JOSE featuring Rodriguez ARGENTINA; SILSOE

india.arie
US, female vocalist – India.Arie Simpson (5 WEEKS) pos/wks
| 30 Jun 01 | VIDEO *Motown TMGCD 1505* | .32 | 3 |
| 20 Oct 01 | BROWN SKIN *Motown TMGCD 1507* | .29 | 2 |

ARIEL *UK, male production group (2 WEEKS)* pos/wks
| 27 Mar 93 | LET IT SLIDE *Deconstruction 74321134512* | .57 | 2 |

ARIEL
Argentina, male DJ / producer – Ariel Belloso (4 WEEKS) pos/wks
| 21 Jun 97 | DEEP (I'M FALLING DEEPER) *Wonderboy WBOYD 005* | .47 | 1 |
| 17 Jun 00 | A9 *Essential Recordings ESCD 15* | .28 | 3 |

ARIZONA featuring ZEITIA
UK, male production / instrumental duo and female vocalist (1 WEEK) pos/wks
| 12 Mar 94 | I SPECIALIZE IN LOVE *Union City UCRCD 27* | .74 | 1 |

Ship's Company and Royal Marine Band of HMS ARK ROYAL
UK, male choir and marine band (6 WEEKS) pos/wks
| 23 Dec 78 | THE LAST FAREWELL *BBC RESL 61* | .46 | 6 |

ARKARNA
UK, male vocal / instrumental / production group (3 WEEKS) pos/wks
| 25 Jan 97 | HOUSE ON FIRE *WEA WEA 088CD1* | .33 | 2 |
| 2 Aug 97 | SO LITTLE TIME *WEA WEA 108CD1* | .46 | 1 |

Re-entries are listed as (re), (2re), (3re), etc which signifies that the hit re-entered the chart once, twice or three times, etc

Joan ARMATRADING St Kitts, female vocalist (53 WEEKS)

		pos/wks
16 Oct 76 ●	LOVE AND AFFECTION A&M AMS 7249	10 9
23 Feb 80	ROSIE A&M AMS 7506	49 5
14 Jun 80	ME MYSELF I A&M AMS 7527	21 11
6 Sep 80	ALL THE WAY FROM AMERICA A&M AMS 7552	54 3
12 Sep 81	I'M LUCKY A&M AMS 8163	46 5
16 Jan 82	NO LOVE A&M AMS 8179	50 5
19 Feb 83	DROP THE PILOT A&M AMS 8306	11 10
16 Mar 85	TEMPTATION A&M AM 238	65 2
26 May 90	MORE THAN ONE KIND OF LOVE A&M AM 561	75 1
23 May 92	WRAPPED AROUND HER A&M AM 877	56 2

ARMIN Holland, male DJ / producer – Armin Van Buuren (4 WEEKS)

		pos/wks
14 Feb 98	BLUE FEAR Xtravaganza 0091485 EXT	45 1
12 Feb 00	COMMUNICATION AM:PM CDAMPM 129	18 3

ARMOURY SHOW
UK, male vocal / instrumental group (6 WEEKS)

		pos/wks
25 Aug 84	CASTLES IN SPAIN Parlophone R 6079	69 2
26 Jan 85	WE CAN BE BRAVE AGAIN Parlophone R 6087	66 1
17 Jan 87	LOVE IN ANGER Parlophone R 6149	63 3

Craig ARMSTRONG – See Shola AMA

Louis ARMSTRONG 338 Top 500 Best known jazz artist of the
20th century, b. 4 Aug 1901, New Orleans, US (not 4 Jul 1900 according
to previous claims by the man himself), d. Jul 6 1971. This ground-breaking,
trumpet-toting gravel-voiced vocalist, known as 'Satchmo'. He is the oldest
performer to top either the UK or US charts. (93 WEEKS)

		pos/wks
19 Dec 52 ●	TAKES TWO TO TANGO Brunswick 04995	6 10
13 Apr 56 ●	A THEME FROM THE THREEPENNY OPERA (MACK THE KNIFE) Philips PB 574 [1]	8 11
15 Jun 56	TAKE IT SATCH (EP) Philips BBE 12035 [1]	29 1
13 Jul 56	THE FAITHFUL HUSSAR Philips PB 604 [1]	27 2
6 Nov 59	MACK THE KNIFE (A THEME FROM THE THREEPENNY OPERA) Philips PB 967 [1]	24 1
4 Jun 64 ●	HELLO, DOLLY! London HLR 9878 [2] ▲	4 14
7 Feb 68 ★	WHAT A WONDERFUL WORLD / CABARET HMV POP 1615 [3]	1 29
26 Jun 68	THE SUNSHINE OF LOVE Stateside SS 2116	41 7
16 Apr 88	WHAT A WONDERFUL WORLD (re-issue) A&M AM 435 [3]	53 5
19 Nov 94 ●	WE HAVE ALL THE TIME IN THE WORLD (re) EMI CDEM 357	3 13

[1] Louis Armstrong and his All-Stars [2] Louis Armstrong and the All Stars [3] Louis Armstrong Orchestra and Chorus

Take It Satch (EP) tracks: Tiger Rag / Mack the Knife / The Faithful Hussar / Back
O'Town Blues. 'Mack the Knife' is a re-issue of 'Theme from The Threepenny Opera'
under a different title. 'Cabaret' was not listed with 'What a Wonderful World'
until 14 Feb 1968

ARMY OF LOVERS
Sweden / France, male / female vocal / group (12 WEEKS)

		pos/wks
17 Aug 91	CRUCIFIED Ton Son Ton WOK 2007	47 5
28 Dec 91	OBSESSION Ton Son Ton WOK 2009	67 1
15 Feb 92	CRUCIFIED (re-issue) Ton Son Ton WOK 2017	31 5
18 Apr 92	RIDE THE BULLET Ton Son Ton WOK 2018	67 1

ARNEE and the TERMINATERS
UK, male vocal / instrumental group (7 WEEKS)

		pos/wks
24 Aug 91 ●	I'LL BE BACK Epic 6574177	5 7

ARNIE'S LOVE
US, male / female vocal / instrumental group (3 WEEKS)

		pos/wks
26 Nov 83	I'M OUT OF YOUR LIFE Streetwave WAVE 9	67 3

David ARNOLD – See Nina PERSSON and David ARNOLD; BJÖRK; David
McALMONT; PROPELLERHEADS

Eddy ARNOLD US, male vocalist (21 WEEKS)

		pos/wks
17 Feb 66 ●	MAKE THE WORLD GO AWAY RCA 1496	8 17

| 26 May 66 | I WANT TO GO WITH YOU (re) RCA 1519 | 46 3 |
| 28 Jul 66 | IF YOU WERE MINE MARY RCA 1529 | 49 1 |

PP ARNOLD US, female vocalist (37 WEEKS)

		pos/wks
4 May 67	THE FIRST CUT IS THE DEEPEST Immediate IM 047	18 10
2 Aug 67	THE TIME HAS COME Immediate IM 055	47 2
24 Jan 68	(IF YOU THINK YOU'RE) GROOVY Immediate IM 061	41 4
10 Jul 68	ANGEL OF THE MORNING Immediate IM 067	29 11
24 Sep 88	BURN IT UP Rhythm King LEFT 27 [1]	14 10

[1] Beatmasters with PP Arnold

ARPEGGIO US, male / female vocal group (3 WEEKS)

		pos/wks
31 Mar 79	LOVE AND DESIRE (PART 1) Polydor POSP 40	63 3

ARRESTED DEVELOPMENT
US, male / female vocal / instrumental / rap group (39 WEEKS)

		pos/wks
16 May 92	TENNESSEE (re) Cooltempo COOL 253	46 7
24 Oct 92 ●	PEOPLE EVERYDAY Cooltempo COOL 265	2 14
9 Jan 93 ●	MR WENDAL / REVOLUTION Cooltempo CDCOOL 268	4 9
3 Apr 93	TENNESSEE (re-issue) Cooltempo CDCOOL 270	18 6
28 May 94	EASE MY MIND Cooltempo CDCOOL 293	33 3

Steve ARRINGTON US, male vocalist (19 WEEKS)

		pos/wks
27 Apr 85 ●	FEEL SO REAL Atlantic A 9576	5 10
6 Jul 85	DANCIN' IN THE KEY OF LIFE (re) Atlantic A 9534	21 9

ARRIVAL
UK, male / female vocal / instrumental group (20 WEEKS)

		pos/wks
10 Jan 70 ●	FRIENDS Decca F 12986	8 9
6 Jun 70	I WILL SURVIVE Decca F 13026	16 11

ARROLA – See RUFF DRIVERZ

ARROW Montserrat, male vocalist – Alphonsus Cassell (15 WEEKS)

		pos/wks
28 Jul 84	HOT HOT HOT Cooltempo ARROW 1	59 5
13 Jul 85	LONG TIME London LON 70	30 7
3 Sep 94	HOT HOT HOT (re-mix) The Hit Label HLC 7	38 3

ARROWS US / UK, male vocal / instrumental group (16 WEEKS)

		pos/wks
25 May 74 ●	A TOUCH TOO MUCH RAK 171	8 9
1 Feb 75	MY LAST NIGHT WITH YOU RAK 189	25 7

ARSENAL FC UK, male football team vocal group (16 WEEKS)

		pos/wks
8 May 71	GOOD OLD ARSENAL Pye 7N 45067 [1]	16 7
15 May 93	SHOUTING FOR THE GUNNERS London LONCD 342 [2]	34 3
23 May 98 ●	HOT STUFF Grapevine AFCCD 1	9 5
3 Jun 00	ARSENAL NUMBER ONE / OUR GOAL Grapevine CDGPS280	46 1

[1] Arsenal FC First Team Squad [2] Arsenal FA Cup Squad featuring Tippa Irie and
Peter Hunnigale

ART COMPANY
Holland, male vocal / instrumental group (11 WEEKS)

		pos/wks
26 May 84	SUSANNA Epic A 4174	12 11

ART OF NOISE
UK, male / female instrumental / production group (65 WEEKS)

		pos/wks
24 Nov 84 ●	CLOSE (TO THE EDIT) ZTT ZTPS 01	8 19
13 Apr 85	MOMENTS IN LOVE / BEAT BOX ZTT ZTPS 02	51 4
9 Nov 85	LEGS China WOK 5	69 1
22 Mar 86 ●	PETER GUNN (re-recording) China WOK 6 [1]	8 9
21 Jun 86	PARANOIMIA China WOK 9 [2]	12 9
18 Jul 87	DRAGNET China WOK 14	60 4
29 Oct 88 ●	KISS China CHINA 11 [3]	5 7
12 Aug 89	YEBO China CHINA 18 [4]	63 3
16 Jun 90	ART OF LOVE China CHINA 23	67 1
11 Jan 92	INSTRUMENTS OF DARKNESS (ALL OF US ARE ONE PEOPLE) China WOK 2012	45 5

29 Feb 92	SHADES OF PARANOIMIA *China WOK 2014* 53	2
26 Jun 99	METAFORCE *ZTT ZTT 129CD* 53	1

[1] Art of Noise featuring Duane Eddy [2] Art of Noise featuring Max Headroom
[3] Art of Noise featuring Tom Jones [4] Art of Noise featuring Mahlathini and the Mahotella Queens

ART OF TRANCE
UK, male instrumentalist / producer (6 WEEKS)   pos/wks

31 Oct 98	MADAGASCAR *Platipus PLAT 43CD* 69	1
7 Aug 99	MADAGASCAR (re-mix) *Platipus PLAT 58CD* 48	2
15 Jun 02	MADAGASCAR (2nd re-mix) *Platipus PLATCD 102* 41	2
10 Aug 02	LOVE WASHES OVER *Platipus PLATCD 98* 60	1

ARTEMESIA
Holland, male producer – Patrick Prinz (4 WEEKS)   pos/wks

15 Apr 95	BITS + PIECES (re) *Hooj Choons HOOJ 31CD* 46	3
12 Aug 00	BITS AND PIECES (re-mix) *Tidy Trax TIDT 141CD* 51	1

See also ETHICS; MOVIN' MELODIES; SUBLIMINAL CUTS

ARTFUL DODGER *UK, male production /*
instrumental duo – Mark Hill and Peter Devereux (71 WEEKS)   pos/wks

11 Dec 99 ●	RE-REWIND THE CROWD SAY BO SELECTA		
	Public Demand / Relentless RELENT 1CDS [1] 2	17
4 Mar 00 ●	MOVIN TOO FAST (re) *Locked On XL LOX 117CD* [2] 2	12
15 Jul 00 ●	WOMAN TROUBLE *Public Demand / ffrr FCD 380* [3] 6	10
25 Nov 00 ●	PLEASE DON'T TURN ME ON		
	Public Demand / ffrr FCD 388 [4] 4	10
17 Mar 01	THINK ABOUT ME *ffrr FCD 394* [5] 11	8
15 Sep 01 ●	TWENTYFOURSEVEN *ffrr / Public Demand FCD 400* [6] 6	9
15 Dec 01	IT AIN'T ENOUGH *ffrr / Public Demand FCD 401* [7] 20	5

[1] Artful Dodger featuring Craig David [2] Artful Dodger and Romina Johnson [3] Artful Dodger and Robbie Craig featuring Craig David [4] Artful Dodger featuring Lifford [5] Artful Dodger featuring Michelle Escoffery [6] Artful Dodger featuring Melanie Blatt [7] Dreem Teem vs Artful Dodger featuring MZ May and MC Alistair

Davey ARTHUR – *See FUREYS*

Neil ARTHUR *UK, male vocalist (2 WEEKS)*   pos/wks

5 Feb 94	I LOVE I HATE *Chrysalis CDCHSS 5005* 50	2

ARTIST – *See PRINCE*

ARTISTS AGAINST AIDS WORLDWIDE
US / Ireland, all-star male / female vocal ensemble (12 WEEKS)   pos/wks

17 Nov 01 ●	WHAT'S GOING ON *Columbia 6721172* 6	12

ARTISTS UNITED AGAINST APARTHEID *International*
male / female vocal / instrumental charity assembly (8 WEEKS)   pos/wks

23 Nov 85	SUN CITY *Manhattan MT 7* 21	8

ASCENSION *UK, male production duo*
– Ricky Simmons and Steve Jones (4 WEEKS)   pos/wks

5 Jul 97	SOMEONE *Perfecto PERF 141CD* 55	1
15 Jul 00	SOMEONE (re-mix) *Code Blue BLU 011CD1* 43	2
23 Mar 02	FOR A LIFETIME *Xtravaganza XTRAV 20CDS* [1] 45	1

[1] Ascension featuring Erin Lordan

See also LUSTRAL; ESSENCE; SPACE BROTHERS; CHAKRA

ASH
UK, male / female vocal / instrumental group (58 WEEKS)   pos/wks

1 Apr 95	KUNG FU *Infectious INFECT 21CD* 57	1
12 Aug 95	GIRL FROM MARS *Infectious INFECT 24CD* 11	5
21 Oct 95	ANGEL INTERCEPTOR *Infectious INFECT 27CD* 14	4
27 Apr 96 ●	GOLDFINGER *Infectious INFECT 39CD* 5	5
6 Jul 96	OH YEAH (re) *Infectious INFECT 41CD* 6	8
25 Oct 97 ●	A LIFE LESS ORDINARY *Infectious INFECT 50CD* 10	5
3 Oct 98	JESUS SAYS *Infectious INFECT 59CD* 15	4

5 Dec 98	WILD SURF *Infectious INFECT 61CDS* 31	2
10 Feb 01 ●	SHINING LIGHT *Infectious INFECT 98CD* 8	4
14 Apr 01	BURN BABY BURN *Infectious INFECT 99CDS* 13	6
21 Jul 01	SOMETIMES *Infectious INFECT 101CDS* 21	6
13 Oct 01	CANDY *Infectious INFECT 106CDS* 20	3
12 Jan 02	THERE'S A STAR *Infectious INFECT 112CDS* 13	3
7 Sep 02	ENVY *Infectious INFECT 119CDS* 21	2

Act was a male trio before 1997 hit

ASH – *See QUENTIN and ASH*

ASHA *Italy, female vocalist (2 WEEKS)*   pos/wks

8 Jul 95	JJ TRIBUTE *Ffrreedom TABCD 228* 38	2

ASHANTI *US, female vocalist (49 WEEKS)*   pos/wks

2 Feb 02 ●	ALWAYS ON TIME *Def Jam 5889462* [1] ▲ 6	13
25 May 02 ●	WHAT'S LUV? *Atlantic AT 0128CD* [2] 4	8
8 Jun 02	FOOLISH (import) (re) *Mercury 5829362* 68	3
20 Jul 02 ●	FOOLISH *Murder Inc. / Mercury 0639942* ▲ 4	10
12 Oct 02 ●	DOWN 4 U (re) *Murder Inc 0639002* [3] 4	9
23 Nov 02	HAPPY *Murder Inc / Mercury 0638242* 13	6+

[1] Ja Rule featuring Ashanti [2] Fat Joe featuring Ashanti [3] Irv Gotti presents Ja Rule, Ashanti, Charli Baltimore and Vita

ASHAYE *UK, male vocalist (3 WEEKS)*   pos/wks

15 Oct 83	MICHAEL JACKSON MEDLEY *Record Shack SOHO 10* 45	3

Tracks on medley: Don't Stop Til You Get Enough / Wanna Be Startin' Something / Shake Your Body Down to the Ground / Blame It on the Boogie

Richard ASHCROFT *UK, male vocalist (24 WEEKS)*   pos/wks

15 Apr 00 ●	A SONG FOR THE LOVERS (re)		
	Hut / Virgin HUTCD 128 3	11
24 Jun 00	MONEY TO BURN *Hut / Virgin HUTCD 136* 17	4
23 Sep 00	C'MON PEOPLE (WE'RE MAKING IT NOW)		
	Hut / Virgin HUTCD 138 21	3
19 Oct 02	CHECK THE MEANING (re) *Hut / Virgin HUTCD 161* 11	6

See also VERVE

John ASHER *UK, male vocalist (6 WEEKS)*   pos/wks

15 Nov 75	LET'S TWIST AGAIN *Creole CR 112* 14	6

ASHFORD and SIMPSON *US, male / female*
vocal duo – Nickolas Ashford and Valerie Simpson (22 WEEKS)   pos/wks

18 Nov 78	IT SEEMS TO HANG ON *Warner Bros. K 17237* 48	4
5 Jan 85 ●	SOLID *Capitol CL 345* 3	15
20 Apr 85	BABIES *Capitol CL 355* 56	3

ASHTON, GARDNER AND DYKE
UK, male vocal / instrumental group (14 WEEKS)   pos/wks

16 Jan 71 ●	THE RESURRECTION SHUFFLE *Capitol CL 15665* 3	14

ASIA *UK, male vocal / instrumental group (13 WEEKS)*   pos/wks

3 Jul 82	HEAT OF THE MOMENT *Geffen GEF A2494* 46	5
18 Sep 82	ONLY TIME WILL TELL *Geffen GEF A2228* 54	3
13 Aug 83	DON'T CRY *Geffen A 3580* 33	5

ASIA BLUE *UK, female vocal group (2 WEEKS)*   pos/wks

27 Jun 92	ESCAPING *Atomic WNR 882* 50	2

ASIAN DUB FOUNDATION
UK, male vocal / instrumental group (7 WEEKS)   pos/wks

21 Feb 98	FREE SATPAL RAM *ffrr FCD 326* 56	1
2 May 98	BUZZIN' *ffrr FCD 335* 31	1
4 Jul 98	BLACK WHITE *ffrr FCD 337* 52	1
18 Mar 00	REAL GREAT BRITAIN *ffrr FCD 376* 41	2
3 Jun 00	NEW WAY, NEW LIFE *ffrr FCD 378* 49	1

ASSEMBLY UK, male vocal / instrumental group (10 WEEKS) pos/wks

		pos	wks
12 Nov 83 ●	NEVER NEVER *Mute TINY 1*	4	10

See also ERASURE

ASSOCIATES UK, male vocal / instrumental group (47 WEEKS) pos/wks

		pos	wks
20 Feb 82 ●	PARTY FEARS TWO *Associates ASC 1*	9	10
8 May 82	CLUB COUNTRY *Associates ASC 2*	13	10
7 Aug 82	LOVE HANGOVER / 18 CARAT LOVE AFFAIR *Associates ASC 3*	21	8
16 Jun 84	THOSE FIRST IMPRESSIONS *WEA YZ 6*	43	6
1 Sep 84	WAITING FOR THE LOVEBOAT *WEA YZ 16*	53	4
19 Jan 85	BREAKFAST *WEA YZ 28*	49	6
17 Sep 88	HEART OF GLASS *WEA YZ 310*	56	3

'18 Carat Love Affair' listed until 28 Aug only. Act was duo on 1982 hits

ASSOCIATION US, male vocal / instrumental group (8 WEEKS) pos/wks

		pos	wks
22 May 68	TIME FOR LIVIN' *Warner Bros. WB 7195*	23	8

Rick ASTLEY (351) Top 500

Soulful-voiced pop vocalist , b. 6 Feb 1966, Warrington, UK. Brit award-winning. US chart-topping debut hit was 1987's best-selling UK single. No British solo male can match his seven consecutive (mostly Stock Aitken Waterman produced) Top 10 hits in the 1980s (91 WEEKS) pos/wks

		pos	wks
8 Aug 87 ★	NEVER GONNA GIVE YOU UP *RCA PB 41447* ▲	1	18
31 Oct 87 ●	WHENEVER YOU NEED SOMEBODY *RCA PB 41567*	3	12
12 Dec 87 ●	WHEN I FALL IN LOVE / MY ARMS KEEP MISSING YOU *RCA PB 41683*	2	10
27 Feb 88 ●	TOGETHER FOREVER *RCA PB 41817* ▲	2	9
24 Sep 88 ●	SHE WANTS TO DANCE WITH ME *RCA PB 42189*	6	10
26 Nov 88 ●	TAKE ME TO YOUR HEART *RCA PB 42573*	8	10
11 Feb 89 ●	HOLD ME IN YOUR ARMS *RCA PB 42615*	10	8
26 Jan 91 ●	CRY FOR HELP *RCA PB 44247*	7	7
30 Mar 91	MOVE RIGHT OUT *RCA PB 44407*	58	2
29 Jun 91	NEVER KNEW LOVE *RCA PB 44737*	70	1
4 Sep 93	THE ONES YOU LOVE *RCA 74321160142*	48	2
13 Nov 93	HOPELESSLY *RCA 74321175642*	33	2

Before 9 Jan 1988, 'When I Fall in Love' was listed by itself. After that date 'My Arms Keep Missing You' was the side listed

ASTRO TRAX UK, male / female vocal / production trio (1 WEEK) pos/wks

		pos	wks
24 Oct 98	THE ENERGY (FEEL THE VIBE) *Satellite 74321622052*	74	1

ASWAD (424) Top 500

Seminal reggae outfit formed 1975 London, UK. Featured former child actor Brinsley Forde (v), b. 1952, Guyana. They signed to Island in 1976, topped the chart with an old Tina Turner B-side and followed it into the Top 20 with a Bucks Fizz B-side (81 WEEKS) pos/wks

		pos	wks
3 Mar 84	CHASING FOR THE BREEZE *Island IS 160*	51	3
6 Oct 84	54-46 (WAS MY NUMBER) *Island IS 170*	70	3
27 Feb 88 ★	DON'T TURN AROUND *Mango IS 341*	1	12
21 May 88	GIVE A LITTLE LOVE *Mango IS 358*	11	8
24 Sep 88	SET THEM FREE *Mango IS 383*	70	2
1 Apr 89	BEAUTY'S ONLY SKIN DEEP *Mango MNG 105*	31	6
22 Jul 89	ON AND ON *Mango MNG 708*	25	8
18 Aug 90	NEXT TO YOU *Mango MNG 753*	24	6
17 Nov 90	SMILE *Mango MNG 767* [1]	53	2
30 Mar 91	TOO WICKED (EP) *Mango MNG 771*	61	2
31 Jul 93	HOW LONG *Polydor PZCD 252* [2]	31	5
9 Oct 93	DANCEHALL MOOD *Bubblin' CDBUBB 1*	48	2
18 Jun 94 ●	SHINE *Bubblin' CDBUBB 3*	5	14
17 Sep 94	WARRIORS *Bubblin' CDBUBB 4*	33	3
18 Feb 95	YOU'RE NO GOOD *Bubblin' CDBUBB 5*	35	3
5 Aug 95	IF I WAS *Bubblin' CDBUBB 6*	58	1
31 Aug 02	SHY GUY *Universal TV 0192632* [3]	62	1

[1] Aswad featuring Sweetie Irie [2] Yazz and Aswad [3] Aswad featuring Easther Bennett

Tracks on Too Wicked (EP): Best of My Love / Warrior Re-Charge / Fire / I Shot the Sheriff

AT THE DRIVE-IN US, male vocal / instrumental group (3 WEEKS) pos/wks

		pos	wks
19 Aug 00	ONE ARMED SCISSOR *Grand Royal GR 091CD*	64	1
16 Dec 00	ROLODEX PROPAGANDA *Grand Royal / Virgin VUSCD 189*	54	1
24 Mar 01	INVALID LITTER DEPT *Grand Royal / Virgin VUSCD 193*	50	1

Gali ATARI – See MILK AND HONEY featuring Gali ATARI

ATHLETE UK, male vocal / instrumental group (3 WEEKS) pos/wks

		pos	wks
29 Jun 02	YOU GOT THE STYLE *Parlophone CDATH 001*	37	2
16 Nov 02	BEAUTIFUL *Parlophone CDATH 002*	41	1

Chet ATKINS
US, male instrumentalist – guitar, d. 30 Jun 2001 (2 WEEKS) pos/wks

		pos	wks
17 Mar 60	TEENSVILLE (re) *RCA 1174*	46	2

ATLANTA RHYTHM SECTION
US, male vocal / instrumental group (4 WEEKS) pos/wks

		pos	wks
27 Oct 79	SPOOKY *Polydor POSP 74*	48	4

ATLANTIC OCEAN Holland, male instrumental duo
– Rene Van Der Weyde and Lex Van Coeverden (14 WEEKS) pos/wks

		pos	wks
19 Feb 94	WATERFALL *Eastern Bloc BLOCCD 001*	22	6
2 Jul 94	BODY IN MOTION *Eastern Bloc BLOCCD 009*	15	4
26 Nov 94	MUSIC IS A PASSION *Eastern Bloc BLOCCDX 017*	59	1
30 Nov 96	WATERFALL (re-mix) *Eastern Bloc BLOC 104CD*	21	3

ATLANTIC STARR
US, male / female vocal / instrumental group (48 WEEKS) pos/wks

		pos	wks
9 Sep 78	GIMME YOUR LUVIN' *A&M AMS 7380*	66	3
29 Jun 85	SILVER SHADOW *A&M AM 260*	41	6
7 Sep 85	ONE LOVE *A&M AM 273*	58	4
15 Mar 86 ●	SECRET LOVERS *A&M AM 307*	10	12
24 May 86	IF YOUR HEART ISN'T IN IT *A&M AM 319*	48	4
13 Jun 87 ●	ALWAYS *Warner Bros. W 8455* ▲	3	14
12 Sep 87	ONE LOVER AT A TIME *Warner Bros. W 8327*	57	3
27 Aug 94	EVERYBODY'S GOT SUMMER *Arista 74321228072*	36	2

ATLANTIS vs AVATAR UK, male production
group featuring female vocalist – Miriam Stockley (2 WEEKS) pos/wks

		pos	wks
28 Oct 00	FIJI *Inferno CDFERN 34*	52	2

Natacha ATLAS – See Jean-Michel JARRE

ATMOSFEAR UK, male instrumental group (7 WEEKS) pos/wks

		pos	wks
17 Nov 79	DANCING IN OUTER SPACE *MCA 543*	46	7

ATOMIC KITTEN (320) Top 500 The Liverpool ladies are the only
female trio to amass three No.1 singles. Line-up is Natasha Hamilton, Elizabeth McClarnon and Jenny Frost (who replaced Kerry Katona in 2001). 'Eternal Flame' and 'The Tide Is High' are the only songs to top the chart twice by two different female-fronted acts (97 WEEKS) pos/wks

		pos	wks
11 Dec 99 ●	RIGHT NOW *Innocent SINCD 15*	10	9
8 Apr 00 ●	SEE YA (re) *Innocent SINCD 17*	6	7
15 Jul 00 ●	I WANT YOUR LOVE *Innocent SINCD 18*	10	5
21 Oct 00	FOLLOW ME *Innocent SINCD 22*	20	5
10 Feb 01 ★	WHOLE AGAIN (re) *Innocent SINDX24* ◆ ■	1	23
4 Aug 01 ★	ETERNAL FLAME (re) *Innocent SINCD 27*■	1	15
1 Jun 02 ●	IT'S OK! *Innocent SINCD 36*	3	13
7 Sep 02 ★	THE TIDE IS HIGH (GET THE FEELING) *Innocent SINCD 38*■	1	16
7 Dec 02 ●	THE LAST GOODBYE / BE WITH YOU *Innocent SINDX 42*	2	4+

ATOMIC ROOSTER
UK, male vocal / instrumental group (25 WEEKS) pos/wks

		pos	wks
6 Feb 71	TOMORROW NIGHT *B & C CB 131*	11	12
10 Jul 71 ●	DEVIL'S ANSWER *B & C CB 157*	4	13

ROCK AROUND THE CLOCK

■ The first "teenage anthem" was penned by music business entrepreneur James E Myers (aka Jimmy DeKnight) and veteran Max C Freedman, who had been writing since the 1920s. Haley too was no teenager, being older than previous heartthrobs Eddie Fisher, Johnnie Ray and Guy Mitchell. His version of the song took less than an hour to record and, according to the Comets, has sold (on single and album) close to 200 million copies.

Bill Haley, whose mother came from England, started recording country and western music in the mid-1940s. He had been successfully playing country boogie since the early 1950s, and had first tasted US Top 20 success with the rocking 'Crazy Man Crazy' on Essex Records in 1953.

'Rock Around the Clock', not the first song of that title, was penned in 1953 and first recorded by Sonny Dae and His Knights. Haley's group studied Dae's recording before giving the song their "cowboy jive" arrangement. They played it in their stage act for more than a year before recording it; Essex boss Dave Miller had fallen out with Myers and refused to record any of his songs. However, on 12 April 1954, just four days after they signed with Decca Records, the group finally cut it as the proposed B-side of 'Thirteen Women'. The session was booked for 11am to 5pm at New York's Pythian Temple studios, but the ferry taking the band across the Delaware River got stuck on a sand bar and the group was two hours late. They worked on 'Thirteen Women' until 4.40pm and had just enough time left to do two takes of 'Rock Around the Clock'. On the first the band overpowered Haley's vocal and so only Bill's mike was open on the second.

■ THE SESSION WAS BOOKED FOR 11AM TO 5PM AT NEW YORK'S PYTHIAN TEMPLE STUDIOS, BUT THE FERRY TAKING THE BAND ACROSS THE DELAWARE RIVER GOT STUCK ON A SAND BAR AND THE GROUP WAS TWO HOURS LATE ■

There was no time for either track to be mixed, or for the group to hear them back.

Interestingly, the group decided that guitarist Danny Cedrone should repeat note for note the guitar break he had used on an earlier release, 'Rock the Joint', which resulted in them being sued for lifting it. (It was settled out of court.) It also did not go unnoticed that the song had similarities to Hank Williams's 'Move It on Over' and the old blues number 'My Daddy Rocks Me with a Steady Roll'. Incidentally, Cedrone died in the summer of 1954, unaware of the monster he had helped to create, and three of the other Comets fell out with Haley and split in autumn 1955.

Producer Milt Gabler made up a composite tape using the best parts of both takes and it was released on 6 May 1954. DJs soon flipped it over and 'Rock Around the Clock' reached the bottom

★ ARTIST:	Bill Haley and His Comets
★ LABEL:	Brunswick UK / Decca USA
★ WRITERS:	Max Freedman / Jimmy DeKnight
★ PRODUCER:	Milt Gabler

rungs of both the US and UK charts that year. As part of the promotion Myers sent a copy to MGM which felt it would be ideal as opening music to the juvenile delinquent movie 'The Blackboard Jungle', and the rest is rock 'n' roll history. It was re-issued and rocketed to the top around the globe. It was the first record to sell a million in the UK and is the only single to reach the Top 20 on five separate occasions (not to mention a No.1 visit courtesy of Jive Bunny).

The record, which sold 1,392,000 copies in the UK, might not have been the first rock 'n' roll record but there is no argument that it was the one that spread the music around the globe.

■ Dave McAleer

Disc jockey Pete Murray interviews the man responsible for the first UK million-seller, Bill Haley

Winifred ATWELL `239` `Top 500`

The 'Queen of the Ivories' (and Elton John's early idol) b. 27 Apr 1914, Trinidad, d. 28 Feb 1983. Britain's all-time top female instrumentalist earned a couple of gold discs for her popular party medleys and hosted a very successful TV series in 1957 (117 WEEKS)   pos/wks

12 Dec 52	● BRITANNIA RAG (re) *Decca F 10015*	.5	6
15 May 53	● CORONATION RAG (re) *Decca F 10110*	.5	6
25 Sep 53	● FLIRTATION WALTZ (2re) *Decca F 10161*	.10	3
4 Dec 53	● LET's HAVE A PARTY (re) *Philips PB 213*	.2	15
23 Jul 54	● RACHMANINOFF'S 18TH VARIATION ON A THEME BY PAGANINI (THE STORY OF THREE LOVES) (re) *Philips PB 234*	.9	9
26 Nov 54	★ LET's HAVE ANOTHER PARTY *Philips PB 268*	.1	8
4 Nov 55	● LET's HAVE A DING DONG *Decca F 10634*	.3	10
16 Mar 56	★ THE POOR PEOPLE OF PARIS *Decca F 10681*	.1	16
18 May 56	PORT-AU-PRINCE *Decca F 10727* `1`	.18	6
20 Jul 56	LEFT BANK (C'EST A HAMBOURG) *Decca F 10762*	.14	7
26 Oct 56	● MAKE IT A PARTY *Decca F 10796*	.7	12
22 Feb 57	LET's ROCK 'N' ROLL (re) *Decca F 10852*	.24	4
6 Dec 57	● LET's HAVE A BALL *Decca F 10956*	.4	6
7 Aug 59	THE SUMMER OF THE SEVENTEENTH DOLL *Decca F 11143*	.24	2
27 Nov 59	● PIANO PARTY *Decca F 11183*	.10	7

`1` Winifred Atwell and Frank Chacksfield

Various hits listed above were medleys as follows: Let's Have a Party: If You Knew Suzie / The More We Are Together / That's My Weakness Now / Knees Up Mother Brown / Daisy Bell / Boomps a Daisy / She Was One of the Early Birds / Three O'Clock in the Morning. Let's Have Another Party: Somebody Stole My Gal / I Wonder Where My Baby Is Tonight / When the Red Red Robin / Bye Bye Blackbird / Sheik of Araby / Another Little Drink / Lilly of Laguna / Honeysuckle and the Bee / Broken Doll / Nellie Dean. Let's Have a Ding Dong: Ain't She Sweet / Oh Johnny Oh Johnny Oh / Oh You Beautiful Doll / Yes We Have No Bananas / Happy Days Are Here Again / I'm Forever Blowing Bubbles / I'll Be Your Sweetheart / If These Lips Could Only Speak / Who's Taking You Home Tonight. Make it a Party: Who Were You With Last Night / Hello Hello Who's Your Lady Friend / Yes Sir That's My Baby / Don't Dilly Dally on the Way / Beer Barrel Polka / After the Ball / Peggy O'Neil / Meet Me Tonight in Dreamland / I Belong to Glasgow / Down at the Old Bull and Bush. Let's Rock 'n' Roll: Singin' The Blues / Green Door / See You Later Alligator / Shake Rattle and Roll / Rock Around the Clock / Razzle Dazzle. Let's Have a Ball: Music Music Music / This Ole House / Heartbreaker / Woody Woodpecker / Last Train to San Fernando / Bring a Little Water Sylvie / Puttin' on the Style / Don't You Rock Me Daddy-O. Piano Party: Baby Face / Comin' Thru' the Rye / Annie Laurie / Little Brown Jug / Let Him Go Let Him Tarry / Put Your Arms Around Me Honey / I'll Be With You in Apple Blossom Time / Shine on Harvest Moon / Blue Skies / I'll Never Say 'Never Again' Again / I'll See You in My Dreams.

'Let's Have a Party' re-entered for a second visit peaking at No.14 in Nov 1954

AUDIOWEB *UK, male vocal / instrumental group (12 WEEKS)*   pos/wks

14 Oct 95	SLEEPER *Mother MUMCD 69*	.74	1
9 Mar 96	YEAH *Mother MUMCD 72*	.73	1
15 Jun 96	INTO MY WORLD *Mother MUMCD 76*	.42	1
19 Oct 96	SLEEPER (re-mix) *Mother MUMCD 78*	.50	2
15 Feb 97	BANKROBBER *Mother MUMCD 85*	.19	2
24 May 97	FAKER *Mother MUMCD 91*	.70	1
25 Apr 98	POLICEMAN SKANK … (THE STORY OF MY LIFE) *Mother MUMCD 100*	.21	2
4 Jul 98	PERSONAL FEELING *Mother MUMCD 104*	.65	1
20 Feb 99	TEST THE THEORY *Mother MUMCD 110*	.56	1

Brian AUGER – See Julie DRISCOLL, Brian AUGER and the TRINITY

AURA – See POPPERS presents AURA

AURORA *UK, male production duo – aka Dive (19 WEEKS)*   pos/wks

5 Jun 99	HEAR YOU CALLING *Additive 12AD 040*	.71	1
5 Feb 00	HEAR YOU CALLING (re-issue) *Positiva CDTIV 124*	.17	4
23 Sep 00	● ORDINARY WORLD *Positiva CDTIV 139* `1`	.5	7
13 Apr 02	DREAMING *EMI CDEM 611*	.24	4
6 Jul 02	THE DAY IT RAINED FOR EVER *EMI CDEMS 613*	.29	3

`1` Aurora featuring Naimee Coleman

See also DIVE

AURRA *US, male / female vocal / instrumental group (18 WEEKS)*   pos/wks

4 May 85	LIKE I LIKE IT *10 TEN 45*	.51	5
19 Apr 86	YOU AND ME TONIGHT *10 TEN 71*	.12	8
21 Jun 86	LIKE I LIKE IT (re-issue) *10 TEN 126*	.43	5

Adam AUSTIN *UK, male vocalist (1 WEEK)*   pos/wks

13 Feb 99	CENTERFOLD *Media PSRCA 0107*	.41	1

David AUSTIN *UK, male vocalist (3 WEEKS)*   pos/wks

21 Jul 84	TURN TO GOLD *Parlophone R 6068*	.68	3

Patti AUSTIN *US, female vocalist (11 WEEKS)*   pos/wks

12 Feb 83	BABY COME TO ME *Qwest K 15005* `1` ▲	.11	10
5 Sep 92	I'LL KEEP YOUR DREAMS ALIVE *Ammi AMMI 101* `2`	.68	1

`1` Patti Austin and James Ingram `2` George Benson and Patti Austin

AUTECHRE *UK, male instrumental duo (1 WEEK)*   pos/wks

7 May 94	BASSCADET *Warp WAP 44CD*	.56	1

AUTEURS *UK, male / female vocal / instrumental group (9 WEEKS)*   pos/wks

27 Nov 93	LENNY VALENTINO *Hut HUTCD 36*	.41	2
23 Apr 94	CHINESE BAKERY *Hut HUTDX 41*	.42	2
6 Jan 96	BACK WITH THE KILLER AGAIN *Hut HUTCD 65*	.45	3
24 Feb 96	LIGHT AIRCRAFT ON FIRE *Hut HUTCD 66*	.58	1
3 Jul 99	THE RUBETTES *Hut HUTCD 113*	.66	1

AUTUMN *UK, male vocal / instrumental group (6 WEEKS)*   pos/wks

16 Oct 71	MY LITTLE GIRL *Pye 7N 45090*	.37	6

Peter AUTY and the SINFONIA OF LONDON conducted by Howard BLAKE *UK, male vocalist with UK, orchestra (9 WEEKS)*   pos/wks

14 Dec 85	WALKING IN THE AIR *Stiff LAD 1*	.42	5
19 Dec 87	WALKING IN THE AIR (re-issue) *CBS GA 3950*	.37	4

See also DIGITAL DREAM BABY

AVALANCHES *Australia, male production group (12 WEEKS)*   pos/wks

7 Apr 01	SINCE I LEFT YOU *XL Recordings XLS 128CD*	.16	7
21 Jul 01	FRONTIER PSYCHIATRIST *XL Recordings XLS 134CD*	.18	5

Frankie AVALON
US, male vocalist – Francis Avallone (15 WEEKS)   pos/wks

10 Oct 58	GINGERBREAD *HMV POP 517*	.30	1
24 Apr 59	VENUS *HMV POP 603* ▲	.16	6
22 Jan 60	WHY *HMV POP 688* ▲	.20	4
28 Apr 60	DON'T THROW AWAY ALL THOSE TEARDROPS *HMV POP 727*	.37	4

AVALON BOYS – See LAUREL & HARDY with the AVALON BOYS featuring Chill WILLS

AVERAGE WHITE BAND
UK, male vocal / instrumental group (47 WEEKS)   pos/wks

22 Feb 75	● PICK UP THE PIECES *Atlantic K 10489* ▲	.6	9
26 Apr 75	CUT THE CAKE *Atlantic K 10605*	.31	4
9 Oct 76	QUEEN OF MY SOUL *Atlantic K 10825*	.23	7
28 Apr 79	WALK ON BY *RCA XC 1087*	.46	5
25 Aug 79	WHEN WILL YOU BE MINE *RCA XB 1096*	.49	5
26 Apr 80	LET'S GO ROUND AGAIN PT.1 *RCA AWB 1*	.12	11
26 Jul 80	FOR YOU FOR LOVE *RCA AWB 2*	.46	4
26 Mar 94	LET'S GO ROUND AGAIN (re-mix) *The Hit Label HLC 5*	.56	2

Kevin AVIANCE *US, male vocalist (1 WEEK)*   pos/wks

13 Jun 98	DIN DA DA *Distinctive DISNCD 42*	.65	1

AVONS *UK, male / female vocal trio (22 WEEKS)*   pos/wks

13 Nov 59	● SEVEN LITTLE GIRLS SITTING IN THE BACK SEAT *Columbia DB 4363*	.3	13

7 Jul 60	WE'RE ONLY YOUNG ONCE (re) *Columbia DB 4461*	45	2
27 Oct 60	FOUR LITTLE HEELS (re) *Columbia DB 4522*	45	3
26 Jan 61	RUBBER BALL *Columbia DB 4569*	30	4

AWESOME *UK, male vocal group (2 WEEKS)*
pos/wks

8 Nov 97	RUMOURS *Universal MCSTD 40145*	58	1
21 Mar 98	CRAZY *Universal MCSTD 40195*	63	1

AWESOME 3
UK, male / female vocal / instrumental group (8 WEEKS)
pos/wks

8 Sep 90	HARD UP *A&M AM 591*	55	3
3 Oct 92	DON'T GO *Citybeat CBE 1271*	75	1
4 Jun 94	DON'T GO (re-mix) *XL Recordings CBX 771CD*	45	2
26 Oct 96	DON'T GO (2nd re-mix) *XL Recordings XLS 78CD* [1]	27	2

[1] Awesome 3 featuring Julie McDermott

Hoyt AXTON *US, male vocalist, d. 26 Oct 1999 (4 WEEKS)*
pos/wks

7 Jun 80	DELLA AND THE DEALER *Young Blood YB 82*	48	4

AXUS *UK, male / female vocal / production duo (1 WEEK)*
pos/wks

26 Sep 98	ABACUS (WHEN I FALL IN LOVE) *INCcredible INCRL 8CD*	62	1

Roy AYERS
US, male vocalist / instrumentalist – vibraphone (13 WEEKS)
pos/wks

21 Oct 78	GET ON UP, GET ON DOWN *Polydor AYERS 7*	41	4
13 Jan 79	HEAT OF THE BEAT *Polydor POSP 16* [1]	43	5
2 Feb 80	DON'T STOP THE FEELING *Polydor STEP 6*	56	3
16 May 98	EXPANSIONS *Soma Recordings SOMA 65CDS* [2]	68	1

[1] Roy Ayers and Wayne Henderson [2] Scott Grooves featuring Roy Ayers

AYLA *Germany, male producer – Ingo Kunzi (3 WEEKS)*
pos/wks

4 Sep 99	AYLA *Positiva CDTIV 117*	22	3

AZ *US, male rapper – Anthony Cruz (1 WEEK)*
pos/wks

30 Mar 96	SUGARHILL *Cooltempo CDCOOL 315*	67	1

AZ YET *US, male vocal group (10 WEEKS)*
pos/wks

1 Mar 97	LAST NIGHT *LaFace 74321423202*	21	3
21 Jun 97 ●	HARD TO SAY I'M SORRY *LaFace 74321481482* [1]	7	7

[1] Az Yet featuring Peter Cetera

Charles AZNAVOUR
France, male vocalist – Shanaur Aznavourian (29 WEEKS)
pos/wks

22 Sep 73	THE OLD FASHIONED WAY (LES PLAISIRS DEMODES) (2re) *Barclay BAR 20*	38	15
22 Jun 74 ★	SHE *Barclay BAR 26*	1	14

'The Old Fashioned Way' re-entered the chart in Oct 1973 (at its peak position) and Jul 1974

AZTEC CAMERA (494) `Top 500`
Sensitive, tuneful pop band formed 1980, and centred around teenage singer / songwriter Roddy Frame, b. 29 Jan 1964, East Kilbride, Scotland. Album 'Love' was among nominations for Best British Album at 1989 Brit awards (74 WEEKS)
pos/wks

19 Feb 83	OBLIVIOUS *Rough Trade RT 122*	47	6
4 Jun 83	WALK OUT TO WINTER *Rough Trade RT 132*	64	4
5 Nov 83	OBLIVIOUS (re-issue) *WEA AZTEC 1*	18	11
1 Sep 84	ALL I NEED IS EVERYTHING / JUMP *WEA AC 1*	34	6
13 Feb 88	HOW MEN ARE *WEA YZ 168*	25	9
23 Apr 88 ●	SOMEWHERE IN MY HEART *WEA YZ 181*	3	14
6 Aug 88	WORKING IN A GOLDMINE *WEA YZ 199*	31	5
8 Oct 88	DEEP AND WIDE AND TALL *WEA YZ 154*	55	3
7 Jul 90	THE CRYING SCENE *WEA YZ 492*	70	3
6 Oct 90	GOOD MORNING BRITAIN *WEA YZ 521* [1]	19	8
18 Jul 92	SPANISH HORSES *WEA YZ 688*	52	3

1 May 93	DREAM SWEET DREAMS *WEA YZ 740CD1*	67	2

[1] Aztec Camera and Mick Jones
'Jump' listed only from 22 Sep 1984 to end of chart run

AZTEC MYSTIC – *See DJ ROLANDO AKA AZTEC MYSTIC*

AZURE *Italy / US, male / female vocal / DJ duo (1 WEEK)*
pos/wks

25 Apr 98	MAMA USED TO SAY *Inferno CDFERN 005*	56	1

AZYMUTH *Brazil, male instrumental group (8 WEEKS)*
pos/wks

12 Jan 80	JAZZ CARNIVAL *Milestone MRC 101*	19	8

Bob AZZAM and His ORCHESTRA and CHORUS
Egypt, bandleader and his orchestra (14 WEEKS)
pos/wks

26 May 60	MUSTAPHA *Decca F 21235*	23	1

B

Derek B *UK, male rapper – Derek Boland (15 WEEKS)*
pos/wks

27 Feb 88	GOODGROOVE *Music of Life 7NOTE 12*	16	6
7 May 88	BAD YOUNG BROTHER *Tuff Audio DRKB 1*	16	6
2 Jul 88	WE'VE GOT THE JUICE *Tuff Audio DRKB 2*	56	3

Eric B and RAKIM
US, male DJ / rap duo – Eric Barrier and William Griffin Jr (26 WEEKS)
pos/wks

7 Nov 87	PAID IN FULL *Fourth & Broadway BRW 78*	15	6
20 Feb 88	MOVE THE CROWD *Fourth & Broadway BRW 88*	53	2
12 Mar 88	I KNOW YOU GOT SOUL *Cooltempo COOL 146*	13	6
2 Jul 88	FOLLOW THE LEADER *MCA MCA 1256*	21	5
19 Nov 88	THE MICROPHONE FIEND *MCA MCA 1300*	74	1
12 Aug 89	FRIENDS *MCA MCA 1352* [1]	21	6

[1] Jody Watley with Eric B and Rakim

Howie B
UK, male instrumentalist / producer – Howard Bernstein (4 WEEKS)
pos/wks

19 Jul 97	ANGELS GO BALD: TOO *Polydor 5711672*	36	2
18 Oct 97	SWITCH *Polydor 5717112*	62	1
11 Apr 98	TAKE YOUR PARTNER BY THE HAND *Polydor 5693272* [1]	74	1

[1] Howie B featuring Robbie Robertson

Jazzie B – *See Maxi PRIEST; SOUL II SOUL*

John B *UK, male producer – John B Williams (1 WEEK)*
pos/wks

22 Jun 02	UP ALL NIGHT / TAKE CONTROL *Metalheadz METH 041CD*	58	1

Jon B *US, male vocalist – Jonathan Buck (5 WEEKS)*
pos/wks

17 Oct 98	THEY DON'T KNOW *Epic 6663975*	32	2
26 May 01	DON'T TALK *Epic 6712792*	29	3

Lisa B *US, female vocalist – Lisa Barbuscia (9 WEEKS)*
pos/wks

12 Jun 93	GLAM *ffrr FCD 210*	49	2
25 Sep 93	FASCINATED *ffrr FCD 218*	35	3
8 Jan 94	YOU AND ME *ffrr FCD 226*	39	4

Lorna B *UK, female vocalist (6 WEEKS)*
pos/wks

28 Jan 95	DO YOU WANNA PARTY *Steppin' Out SPONCD 2* [1]	36	3
1 Apr 95	SWEET DREAMS *Steppin' Out SPONCD 3* [1]	37	2
15 Mar 97	FEELS SO GOOD *Avex UK AVEXCD 53*	69	1

[1] DJ Scott featuring Lorna B

Mark B & BLADE *UK, male rap / production duo – Mark Barnes and Vanik Torosian (4 WEEKS)* pos/wks

10 Feb 01	THE UNKNOWN *Wordplay WORDCDS 011*	49	1
26 May 01	YA DON'T SEE THE SIGNS *Wordplay WORDCDSE 019*	23	3

Melanie B *UK, female vocalist – Melanie Brown (36 WEEKS)* pos/wks

26 Sep 98	★ I WANT YOU BACK *Virgin VSCDT 1716* [1] ■	1	9
10 Jul 99	WORD UP (re) *Virgin VSCDT 1735* [2]	14	8
7 Oct 00	● TELL ME *Virgin VSCDT 1777*	4	7
3 Mar 01	● FEELS SO GOOD *Virgin VSCDT 1787*	5	8
16 Jun 01	LULLABY *Virgin VSCDT 1798*	13	4

[1] Melanie B featuring Missy 'Misdemeanor' Elliott [2] Melanie G

See also SPICE GIRLS

Sandy B *US, female vocalist (8 WEEKS)* pos/wks

20 Feb 93	FEEL LIKE SINGIN' *Nervous SANCD 1*	60	1
18 May 96	MAKE THE WORLD GO ROUND *Champion CHAMPCD 322*	73	1
24 May 97	MAKE THE WORLD GO ROUND (re-mix) *Champion CHAMPCD 327*	35	2
8 Nov 97	AIN'T NO NEED TO HIDE *Champion CHAMPCD 331*	60	1
28 Feb 98	MAKE THE WORLD GO ROUND (2nd re-mix) *Champion CHAMPCD 333*	20	3

Stevie B *US, male vocalist – Steven Hill (9 WEEKS)* pos/wks

23 Feb 91	● BECAUSE I LOVE YOU (THE POSTMAN SONG) *Polydor PO 126* ▲	6	9

Tairrie B *US, female rapper (2 WEEKS)* pos/wks

1 Dec 90	MURDER SHE WROTE *MCA MCA 1455*	71	2

B B and Q BAND
US, male vocal / instrumental group (15 WEEKS) pos/wks

18 Jul 81	ON THE BEAT *Capitol CL 202*	41	5
6 Jul 85	GENIE *Cooltempo COOL 110* [1]	40	4
20 Sep 86	(I'M A) DREAMER *Cooltempo COOL 132*	35	5
17 Oct 87	RICOCHET *Cooltempo COOL 154*	71	1

[1] Brooklyn Bronx and Queens

**BBC CONCERT ORCHESTRA,
BBC SYMPHONY CHORUS cond. Stephen JACKSON**
UK, orchestra, chorus and conductor (3 WEEKS) pos/wks

22 Jun 96	ODE TO JOY (FROM BEETHOVEN'S SYMPHONY NO.9) *Virgin VSCDT 1591*	36	3

BBE *France / Italy, male instrumental group (20 WEEKS)* pos/wks

28 Sep 96	● SEVEN DAYS AND ONE WEEK *Positiva CDTIV 67*	3	9
29 Mar 97	● FLASH *Positiva CDTIV 73*	5	5
14 Feb 98	DESIRE *Positiva CDTIV 87*	19	3
30 May 98	DEEPER LOVE (SYMPHONIC PARADISE) *Positiva CDTIV 93*	19	3

BBG *UK, male vocal / instrumental group (10 WEEKS)* pos/wks

28 Apr 90	SNAPPINESS *Urban URB 54* [1]	28	5
11 Aug 90	SOME KIND OF HEAVEN *Urban URB 59*	65	2
23 Mar 96	LET THE MUSIC PLAY *MCA MCSTD 40029* [2]	46	1
18 May 96	SNAPPINESS (re-mix) *Hi-Life 5762972*	50	1
5 Jul 97	JUST BE TONIGHT *Hi-Life 5738972* [2]	45	1

[1] BBG featuring Dina Taylor [2] BBG featuring Erin

BBM *UK, male vocal / instrumental group (2 WEEKS)* pos/wks

6 Aug 94	WHERE IN THE WORLD *Virgin VSCD 1495*	57	2

BBMAK *UK, male vocal group (18 WEEKS)* pos/wks

28 Aug 99	BACK HERE *Telstar CDSTAS 3053*	37	2
24 Feb 01	● BACK HERE (re-issue) *Telstar CDSTAS 3166*	5	10
26 May 01	● STILL ON YOUR SIDE *Telstar CDSTAS 3185*	8	4
16 Nov 02	OUT OF MY HEART *Telstar CDSTAS 3281*	36	2

BEF featuring Lalah HATHAWAY
US, male production duo – Martyn Ware and Ian Craig Marsh – and US, female vocalist (5 WEEKS) pos/wks

27 Jul 91	FAMILY AFFAIR *Ten TEN 369*	37	5

B-15 PROJECT featuring Crissy D and Lady G
UK / Jamaica, male production duo and female vocalists (10 WEEKS) pos/wks

17 Jun 00	● GIRLS LIKE US (re) *Ministry of Sound RELENT 3CDS*	7	10

B-52's *US, male / female vocal / instrumental group (61 WEEKS)* pos/wks

11 Aug 79	ROCK LOBSTER *Island WIP 6506*	37	5
9 Aug 80	GIVE ME BACK MY MAN *Island WIP 6579*	61	3
7 May 83	(SONG FOR A) FUTURE GENERATION *Island IS 107*	63	2
10 May 86	ROCK LOBSTER / PLANET CLAIRE (re-issue) *Island BFT 1*	12	7
3 Mar 90	● LOVE SHACK *Reprise W 9917*	2	13
19 May 90	ROAM *Reprise W 9827*	17	7
18 Aug 90	CHANNEL Z *Reprise W 9737*	61	2
20 Jun 92	GOOD STUFF *Reprise W 0109*	21	6
12 Sep 92	TELL IT LIKE IT T-I-IS *Reprise W 0130*	61	3
9 Jul 94	(MEET) THE FLINTSTONES *MCA MCSTD 1986* [1]	3	12
30 Jan 99	LOVE SHACK 99 *Reprise W 0461CD*	66	1

[1] BC-52's   'Planet Claire' listed only from 17 May 1986

BG THE PRINCE OF RAP *Germany, male rapper (2 WEEKS)* pos/wks

18 Jan 92	TAKE CONTROL OF THE PARTY *Columbia 6576330*	71	2

BK *UK, male producer – Ben Keen (7 WEEKS)* pos/wks

25 Nov 00	HOOVERS AND HORNS *Nukleuz NUKC 0185* [1]	57	2
8 Dec 01	FLASH *Nukleuz NUKP 0361* [2]	67	1
26 Jan 02	ERECTION (TAKE IT TO THE TOP) *Nukleuz NUKC 0352* [3]	48	1
9 Feb 02	FLASH (re-issue) *Nukleuz NUKC 0361* [2]	61	1
7 Dec 02	REVOLUTION *Nukleuz NUKF 0437*	42	2

[1] Fergie and BK [2] BK and Nick Sentience [3] Cortina featuring BK and Madam Friction

BM DUBS present MR RUMBLE featuring BRASSTOOTH and KEE *UK, male production group (2 WEEKS)* pos/wks

17 Mar 01	WHOOMP THERE IT IS *Incentive CENT 16CDS*	32	2

B.M.R. featuring FELICIA *Germany, male producer – Michi Lange featuring female vocalist (2 WEEKS)* pos/wks

1 May 99	CHECK IT OUT (EVERYBODY) *AM:PM CDAMPM 120*	29	2

B.M.U. *US / UK, male vocal group (2 WEEKS)* pos/wks

18 Feb 95	U WILL KNOW *Mercury MERCD 420*	23	2

B REAL / BUSTA RHYMES / COOLIO / LL COOL J / METHOD MAN *US, male rappers (6 WEEKS)* pos/wks

5 Apr 97	● HIT 'EM HIGH (MONSTARS' ANTHEM) *Atlantic A 5449CD*	8	6

BT *US, male producer – Brian Transeau (26 WEEKS)* pos/wks

18 Mar 95	EMBRACING THE SUNSHINE *East West YZ 895CD*	34	2
16 Sep 95	LOVING YOU MORE *Perfecto PERF 110CD* [1]	28	2
10 Feb 96	LOVING YOU MORE (re-mix) *Perfecto PERF 117CD* [1]	14	3
9 Nov 96	BLUE SKIES *Perfecto PERF 130CD* [2]	26	2
19 Jul 97	FLAMING JUNE *Perfecto PERF 145CD1*	19	4
29 Nov 97	LOVE, PEACE & GREASE *Perfecto PERF 153CD1*	41	1
10 Jan 98	FLAMING JUNE (re-mix) *Perfecto PERF 157CD1*	28	4
18 Apr 98	REMEMBER *Perfecto PERF 160CD1*	27	2
21 Nov 98	GODSPEED *Renaissance RENCD 002*	54	1
9 Oct 99	MERCURY AND SOLACE *Headspace HEDSCD 001*	38	2
24 Jun 00	DREAMING *Headspace HEDSCD 002* [3]	38	2
23 Jun 01	NEVER GONNA COME BACK DOWN *Ministry of Sound MOSBT CDS1*	51	1

[1] BT featuring Vincent Covello [2] BT featuring Tori Amos [3] BT featuring Kirsty Hawkshaw

BT EXPRESS US, male instrumental / vocal group (11 WEEKS) pos/wks

29 Mar 75	EXPRESS Pye International 7N 25674	34 6
26 Jul 80	DOES IT FEEL GOOD / GIVE UP THE FUNK (LET'S DANCE) Calibre CAB 503	52 4
23 Apr 94	EXPRESS (re-mix) PWL International PWCD 285	67 1

B BUMBLE and the STINGERS
US, male instrumental group (26 WEEKS) pos/wks

19 Apr 62 ★	NUT ROCKER Top Rank JAR 611	1 15
3 Jun 72	NUT ROCKER (re-issue) Stateside SS 2203	19 11

BC-52's – See B-52's

B-CREW US, female vocal group (1 WEEK) pos/wks

20 Sep 97	PARTAY FEELING Positiva CDTIV 78	45 1

B-MOVIE UK, male vocal / instrumental group (7 WEEKS) pos/wks

18 Apr 81	REMEMBRANCE DAY Deram DM 437	61 3
27 Mar 82	NOWHERE GIRL Some Bizzare B258	67 4

B-TRIBE
Spain, male / female vocal / instrumental group (4 WEEKS) pos/wks

25 Sep 93	!FIESTA FATAL! East West YZ 770CD	64 4

BVSMP US, male rap / vocal group (12 WEEKS) pos/wks

23 Jul 88 ●	I NEED YOU Debut DEBT 3044	3 12

B*WITCHED 〈316 Top 500〉
Ireland's most successful female group, Edele and Keavy Lynch, Sinead O'Carroll and Lindsay Armaou. Youngest girl group to top the chart. They sold more than one million copies of their debut album in the US and were the first act to enter at No.1 with their first four singles. Group split in Sep 2002. Best-selling single: 'C'est La Vie' 850,500 (98 WEEKS) pos/wks

6 Jun 98 ★	C'EST LA VIE Glow Worm / Epic 6660532 ■	1 19
3 Oct 98 ★	ROLLERCOASTER Glow Worm / Epic 6664752 ■	1 15
19 Dec 98 ★	TO YOU I BELONG (re) Glow Worm / Epic 6667712 ■	1 14
27 Mar 99 ★	BLAME IT ON THE WEATHERMAN Glow Worm / Epic 6670335 ■	1 9
10 Apr 99 ●	THANK ABBA FOR THE MUSIC Epic ABCD 1 [1]	4 13
16 Oct 99 ●	JESSE HOLD ON (re) Glow Worm / Epic 6679612	4 12
18 Dec 99	I SHALL BE THERE Glow Worm / Epic 683332 [2]	13 9
8 Apr 00	JUMP DOWN (re) Glow Worm / Epic 6691282	16 7

[1] Steps, Tina Cousins, Cleopatra, B*Witched, Billie [2] B*Witched featuring Ladysmith Black Mambazo

B2K US, male vocal group (2 WEEKS) pos/wks

24 Aug 02	UH HUH Epic 6729512	35 2

BABE INSTINCT UK, female vocal group (2 WEEKS) pos/wks

16 Jan 99	DISCO BABES FROM OUTER SPACE Positiva CDTIV 103	21 2

BABE TEAM UK, female vocal group (2 WEEKS) pos/wks

8 Jun 02	OVER THERE Edel 0140655ERE	45 2

Alice BABS Sweden, female vocalist (1 WEEK) pos/wks

15 Aug 63	AFTER YOU'VE GONE Fontana TF 409	43 1

BABY BUMPS UK, male / female vocal / instrumental
duo – Sean Casey and Lisa Millett (6 WEEKS) pos/wks

8 Aug 98	BURNING Delirious DELICD 10	17 4
26 Feb 00	I GOT THIS FEELING Sound of Ministry MOSCDS 137	22 2

BABY D UK, male / female vocal / instrumental group (45 WEEKS) pos/wks

18 Dec 93	DESTINY Production House PNC 057	69 1
23 Jul 94	CASANOVA Production House PNC 065	67 1

19 Nov 94 ★	LET ME BE YOUR FANTASY Systematic SYSCD 4	1 14
3 Jun 95 ●	(EVERYBODY'S GOT TO LEARN SOMETIME) I NEED YOUR LOVING Systematic SYSCD 11	3 12
13 Jan 96 ●	SO PURE Systematic SYSCD 21	3 7
6 Apr 96	TAKE ME TO HEAVEN Systematic SYSCD 26	15 5
2 Sep 00	LET ME BE YOUR FANTASY (re-mix) Systematic SYSCD 35	16 5

BABY DC featuring IMAJIN
US, male rapper – Derrick Coleman Jr and vocal group (1 WEEK) pos/wks

24 Apr 99	BOUNCE, ROCK, SKATE, ROLL Jive 0522142	45 1

BABY FORD UK, male instrumentalist – keyboards (16 WEEKS) pos/wks

10 Sep 88	OOCHY KOOCHY (F.U. BABY YEAH YEAH) Rhythm King 7BFORD 1	58 6
24 Dec 88	CHIKKI CHIKKI AHH AHH (re) Rhythm King 7BFORD 2	54 4
17 Jun 89	CHILDREN OF THE REVOLUTION Rhythm King 7BFORD 4	53 4
17 Feb 90	BEACH BUMP Rhythm King 7BFORD 6	68 2

BABY JUNE UK, male vocalist – Tim Hegarty (1 WEEK) pos/wks

15 Aug 92	HEY! WHAT'S YOUR NAME Arista 115271	75 1

BABY O US, male / female vocal / instrumental group (5 WEEKS) pos/wks

26 Jul 80	IN THE FOREST Calibre CAB 505	46 5

BABY ROOTS UK, male vocalist (1 WEEK) pos/wks

1 Aug 92	ROCK ME BABY ZYX ZYX 68027	71 1

BABYBIRD UK, male vocalist / instrumentalist (35 WEEKS) pos/wks

10 Aug 96	GOODNIGHT Echo ECSCD 24	28 2
12 Oct 96 ●	YOU'RE GORGEOUS Echo ECSD 26	3 16
1 Feb 97	CANDY GIRL Echo ECSCD 31	14 3
17 May 97	CORNERSHOP Echo ECSCD 33	37 2
9 May 98	BAD OLD MAN Echo ECSCD 60	31 2
22 Aug 98	IF YOU'LL BE MINE Echo ECSCX 65	28 4
27 Feb 99	BACK TOGETHER Echo ECSCD 73	22 3
25 Mar 00	THE F-WORD Echo ECSCD 92	35 2
3 Jun 00	OUT OF SIGHT Echo ECSCD 97	58 1

BABYFACE US, male vocalist – Kenneth Edmonds (23 WEEKS) pos/wks

9 Jul 94	ROCK BOTTOM Epic 6601832	50 4
1 Oct 94	WHEN CAN I SEE YOU Epic 6606592	35 3
9 Nov 96	THIS IS FOR THE LOVER IN YOU Epic 6639352	12 5
8 Mar 97	EVERYTIME I CLOSE MY EYES Epic 6642492	13 4
19 Jul 97 ●	HOW COME, HOW LONG Epic 6646202 [1]	10 5
25 Oct 97	SUNSHINE Northwestside 74321528702 [2]	25 2

[1] Babyface featuring Stevie Wonder [2] Jay-Z featuring Babyface and Foxy Brown

BABYLON ZOO
UK, male vocalist / multi-instrumentalist – Jas Mann (20 WEEKS) pos/wks

27 Jan 96 ★	SPACEMAN EMI CDEM 416 ◆ ■	1 14
27 Apr 96	ANIMAL ARMY EMI CDEM 425	17 3
5 Oct 96	THE BOY WITH THE X-RAY EYES EMI CDEMS 440	32 2
6 Feb 99	ALL THE MONEY'S GONE EMI CDEM 519	46 1

BABYS US / UK, male vocal / instrumental group (3 WEEKS) pos/wks

21 Jan 78	ISN'T IT TIME Chrysalis CHS 2173	45 3

BACCARA Spain, female vocal duo
– Maria Mendiola and Mayte Mateos (25 WEEKS) pos/wks

17 Sep 77 ★	YES SIR, I CAN BOOGIE RCA PB 5526	1 16
14 Jan 78 ●	SORRY I'M A LADY RCA PB 5555	8 9

Burt BACHARACH US, male instrumentalist – piano (12 WEEKS) pos/wks

20 May 65 ●	TRAINS AND BOATS AND PLANES London HL 9968 [1]	4 11
1 May 99	TOLEDO Mercury 8709652 [2]	72 1

[1] Burt Bacharach His Orchestra and Chorus [2] Elvis Costello / Burt Bacharach

UK No.1 ★ UK Top 10 ● Still on chart + UK million seller ◆ UK entry at No.1 ■ US No.1 ▲   67

No.1 ON OTHER CHARTS

■ From time to time fans of our book recall seeing Barry Ryan's 'Eloise', The Allisons' 'Are You Sure' and most regularly 'Please Please Me' by The Beatles at No.1 in some chart or other, but not the one regarded by British Hit Singles as "official". So, for the first time, we publish here a list of all those hits that were chart-toppers in the "other" charts which are not used to create this book.

When the British Market Research Bureau started compiling the Record Retailer Top 50 on 12 February 1969, the argument over which chart would be regarded as "official" by the music industy was settled. Before then, there were several alternatives. The Record Mirror (RM) had its own chart between 1955 and 1962 (when it started using Record Retailer's (RR) chart. The NME chart (which we use from 1952 to 1960) continued throughout the 1960s. Melody Maker (MM) had its own charts from April 1956 onwards, and Disc (D) had its charts from 1958 to August 1967, when it used the same one as MM

The Swinging Blue Jeans, whose 'Hippy Hippy Shake' made No.1 in the Disc magazine chart of 25 Jan 1964, but not in our book

Year	Title	Year	Title
1955	Naughty Lady of Shady Lane Dean Martin (RM)	1963	Do You Want to Know a Secret Billy J Kramer and the Dakotas (NME, MM, D)
1955	Unchained Melody Al Hibbler (RM)	1964	Hippy Hippy Shake Swinging Blue Jeans (D)
1955	Cool Water Frankie Laine (RM)	1964	Bits and Pieces Dave Clark Five (D)
1956	Zambezi Lou Busch (RM)	1965	For Your Love Yardbirds (NME)
1957	Party Elvis Presley (MM)	1965	A World of Our Own Seekers (D)
1958	Ma (He's Making Eyes at Me) Johnny Otis Show (RM, MM)	1965	The Price of Love Everly Brothers (NME)
1958	Bird Dog Everly Brothers (RM, MM, D)	1965	1-2-3 Len Barry (NME)
1960	Stuck on You Elvis Presley (MM, D)	1966	19th Nervous Breakdown Rolling Stones (NME, MM, D)
1960	Mama / Robot Man Connie Francis (D)	1966	I Can't Let Go Hollies (NME)
1960	Mess of Blues / Girl of My Best Friend Elvis Presley (MM)	1966	Sha La La La Lee Small Faces (MM, D)
1961	Are You Sure Allisons (RM, NME, D)	1966	Wild Thing Troggs (D)
1961	A Girl Like You Cliff Richard (D)	1966	I'm a Boy Who (MM)
1961	Wild in the Country Elvis Presley (NME)	1966	Morningtown Ride Seekers (D)
1961	Take Good Care of My Baby Bobby Vee (RM, NME)	1967	Strawberry Fields Forever / Penny Lane Beatles (MM)
1962	Stranger on the Shore Mr Acker Bilk (RM, NME, MM, D)	1967	This Is My Song Harry Secombe (D)
1962	Let's Twist Again Chubby Checker (NME)	1967	Alternate Title Monkees (MM)
1962	March of the Siamese Children Kenny Ball and His Jazzmen (NME, D)	1968	Magical Mystery Tour (double EP) Beatles (MM)
1962	A Picture of You Joe Brown (NME, MM, D)	1968	Delilah Tom Jones (MM)
1962	Speedy Gonzales Pat Boone (D)	1968	Help Yourself Tom Jones (NME)
1963	Please Please Me Beatles (NME, MM, D)	1968	This Guy's in Love with You Herb Alpert (MM)
		1968	Eloise Barry Ryan (NME, MM)

BACHELORS `103` `Top 500`
Irish vocal / instrumental trio, who were one of the few popular non-rock groups of the 1960s: brothers Declan and Con Cluskey and John Stokes. This Dublin act had hits on both sides of the Atlantic with revivals of popular pre-rock ballads (187 WEEKS) pos/wks

24 Jan 63	● CHARMAINE *Decca F 11559*	6	19
4 Jul 63	FARAWAY PLACES *Decca F 11666*	36	3
29 Aug 63	WHISPERING *Decca F 11712*	18	10
23 Jan 64	★ DIANE *Decca F 11799*	1	19
19 Mar 64	● I BELIEVE *Decca F 11857*	2	17
4 Jun 64	● RAMONA *Decca F 11910*	4	13
13 Aug 64	● I WOULDN'T TRADE YOU FOR THE WORLD *Decca F 11949*	4	16
3 Dec 64	● NO ARMS CAN EVER HOLD YOU *Decca F 12034*	7	12
1 Apr 65	TRUE LOVE FOR EVER MORE *Decca F 12108*	34	6
20 May 65	● MARIE *Decca F 12156*	9	12
28 Oct 65	IN THE CHAPEL IN THE MOONLIGHT *Decca F 12256*	27	10
6 Jan 66	HELLO, DOLLY! *Decca F 12309*	38	4
17 Mar 66	● THE SOUND OF SILENCE *Decca F 12351*	3	13
7 Jul 66	CAN I TRUST YOU *Decca F 12417*	26	7
1 Dec 66	WALK WITH FAITH IN YOUR HEART *Decca F 22523*	21	9
6 Apr 67	OH HOW I MISS YOU *Decca F 22592*	30	8
5 Jul 67	MARTA *Decca F 22634*	20	9

Randy BACHMAN – See BUS STOP; BACHMAN-TURNER OVERDRIVE

Tal BACHMAN *Canada, male vocalist / guitarist (2 WEEKS)* pos/wks

30 Oct 99	SHE'S SO HIGH *Columbia 6679932*	30	2

BACHMAN-TURNER OVERDRIVE
Canada, male vocal / instrumental group (18 WEEKS) pos/wks

16 Nov 74	● YOU AIN'T SEEN NOTHING YET *Mercury 6167 025* ▲	2	12
1 Feb 75	ROLL ON DOWN THE HIGHWAY *Mercury 6167 071*	22	6

See also Randy BACHMAN

BACK TO THE PLANET
UK, male / female vocal / instrumental group (2 WEEKS) pos/wks

10 Apr 93	TEENAGE TURTLES *Parallel LLLCD 3*	52	1
4 Sep 93	DAYDREAM *Parallel LLLCD 8*	52	1

BACKBEAT BAND
US, male vocal / instrumental group (5 WEEKS) pos/wks

26 Mar 94	MONEY (re) *Virgin VSCDX 1489*	48	4
14 May 94	PLEASE MR POSTMAN *Virgin VSCDX 1502*	69	1

BACKBEAT DISCIPLES – See Arthur BAKER

BACKROOM BOYS – See Frank IFIELD

BACKSTREET BOYS `134` `Top 500`
American boy band vocal quintet (Brian Littrell, Nick Carter, A J McLean, Howie Dorough, Kevin Richardson) created teen hysteria in Europe before becoming 1999's top-selling act in their homeland. Their 13 consecutive UK Top 10 entries are a record for a US group (161 WEEKS) pos/wks

28 Oct 95	WE'VE GOT IT GOIN' ON *Jive JIVECD 386*	54	1
16 Dec 95	I'LL NEVER BREAK YOUR HEART *Jive JIVECD 389*	42	3
1 Jun 96	GET DOWN (YOU'RE THE ONE FOR ME) *Jive JIVECD 394*	14	8
24 Aug 96	● WE'VE GOT IT GOIN' ON (re-issue) *Jive JIVECD 400*	3	7
16 Nov 96	I'LL NEVER BREAK YOUR HEART (re-issue) *Jive JIVERCD 406*	8	8
18 Jan 97	● QUIT PLAYING GAMES (WITH MY HEART) *Jive JIVECD 409*	2	10
29 Mar 97	● ANYWHERE FOR YOU (2re) *Jive JIVECD 416*	4	8
2 Aug 97	● EVERYBODY (BACKSTREET'S BACK) *Jive JIVECD 426*	3	11
11 Oct 97	● AS LONG AS YOU LOVE ME *Jive JIVECD 434*	3	19
14 Feb 98	● ALL I HAVE TO GIVE *Jive JIVECD 445*	2	12
15 May 99	★ I WANT IT THAT WAY *Jive 0523392* ■	1	14
30 Oct 99	● LARGER THAN LIFE *Jive 0550562*	5	14
26 Feb 00	SHOW ME THE MEANING OF BEING LONELY (import) *Jive IMPORT 9250082*	66	1
4 Mar 00	● SHOW ME THE MEANING OF BEING LONELY (re) *Jive 9250082..3*		11
24 Jun 00	● THE ONE (re) *Jive 9250662*	8	8
18 Nov 00	● SHAPE OF MY HEART *Jive 9251442*	4	9
24 Feb 01	● THE CALL *Jive 9251702*	8	5
7 Jul 01	MORE THAN THAT *Jive 9252342*	12	5
12 Jan 02	● DROWNING *Jive 9252882*	4	7

BACKYARD DOG *UK, male vocal / production group (6 WEEKS)* pos/wks

7 Jul 01	BADDEST RUFFEST (re) *East West EW 233CD*	15	6

BAD ANGEL – See BOOTH and the BAD ANGEL

BAD BOYS INC *UK, male vocal group (31 WEEKS)* pos/wks

14 Aug 93	DON'T TALK ABOUT LOVE *A&M 5803412*	19	5
2 Oct 93	WHENEVER YOU NEED SOMEONE *A&M 5804032*	26	3
11 Dec 93	WALKING ON AIR *A&M 5804692*	24	6
21 May 94	● MORE TO THIS WORLD *A&M 5806072*	8	7
23 Jul 94	TAKE ME AWAY (I'LL FOLLOW YOU) *A&M 5806912*	15	6
17 Sep 94	LOVE HERE I COME *A&M 5807752*	26	4

BAD COMPANY *UK, male vocal / instrumental group (23 WEEKS)* pos/wks

1 Jun 74	CAN'T GET ENOUGH *Island WIP 6191*	15	8
22 Mar 75	GOOD LOVIN' GONE BAD *Island WIP 6223*	31	6
30 Aug 75	FEEL LIKE MAKIN' LOVE *Island WIP 6242*	20	9

BAD COMPANY *UK, male production group (2 WEEKS)* pos/wks

9 Mar 02	SPACEHOPPER / TONIGHT *Ram RAMM 37*	56	1
4 May 02	RUSH HOUR / BLIND *BC Recordings BCRUK 002CD*	59	1

BAD ENGLISH
UK / US, male vocal / instrumental group (3 WEEKS) pos/wks

25 Nov 89	WHEN I SEE YOU SMILE *Epic 655347 1* ▲	61	3

BAD HABIT BOYS *Germany, male production duo (1 WEEK)* pos/wks

1 Jul 00	WEEKEND *Inferno CDFERN 28*	41	1

BAD MANNERS `263` `Top 500` *Good-time ska band fronted by shaven-headed Buster Bloodvessel (b. Douglas Trendle, 6 Sep 1958, London). Spent more weeks on UK chart in 1980 (45) than anyone bar Madness. Even after the hits, they remained a popular live attraction (111 WEEKS)* pos/wks

1 Mar 80	NE-NE NA-NA NA-NA NU-NU *Magnet MAG 164*	28	14
14 Jun 80	LIP UP FATTY *Magnet MAG 175*	15	14
27 Sep 80	● SPECIAL BREW *Magnet MAG 180*	3	13
6 Dec 80	LORRAINE *Magnet MAG 181*	21	12
28 Mar 81	JUST A FEELING *Magnet MAG 187*	13	9
27 Jun 81	● CAN CAN *Magnet MAG 190*	3	13
26 Sep 81	● WALKING IN THE SUNSHINE *Magnet MAG 197*	10	9
21 Nov 81	BUONA SERA *Magnet MAG 211*	34	9
1 May 82	GOT NO BRAINS *Magnet MAG 216*	44	5
31 Jul 82	● MY GIRL LOLLIPOP (MY BOY LOLLIPOP) *Magnet MAG 232*	9	7
30 Oct 82	SAMSON AND DELILAH *Magnet MAG 236*	58	3
14 May 83	THAT'LL DO NICELY *Magnet MAG 243*	49	3

BAD MEETS EVIL featuring EMINEM and ROYCE DA 5'9
US, male producer and male rappers (1 WEEK) pos/wks

1 Sep 01	SCARY MOVIES *Mole UK MOLEUK 045*	63	1

See also EMINEM

BAD NEWS *UK, male vocal group (5 WEEKS)* pos/wks

12 Sep 87	BOHEMIAN RHAPSODY *EMI EM 24*	44	5

BAD RELIGION *US, male vocal / instrumental group (2 WEEKS)* pos/wks

11 Feb 95	21ST CENTURY (DIGITAL BOY) *Columbia 6611435*	41	2

BAD SEEDS – See Nick CAVE and the BAD SEEDS

BAD YARD CLUB – See David MORALES

Angelo BADALAMENTI – *See ORBITAL; BOOTH and the BAD ANGEL*

Wally BADAROU
France, male instrumentalist – keyboards (6 WEEKS)   pos/wks

19 Oct 85	CHIEF INSPECTOR *Fourth & Broadway BRW 37*	46	6

BADDIEL and SKINNER and THE LIGHTNING SEEDS
UK, male vocal group – David Baddiel, Frank Skinner
(aka Christopher Collins) and The Lightning Seeds (34 WEEKS)   pos/wks

1 Jun 96	★ THREE LIONS (THE OFFICIAL SONG OF THE ENGLAND FOOTBALL TEAM) *Epic 6632732* ■	1	15
20 Jun 98	★ THREE LIONS '98 *Epic 6660982* ■	1	13
15 Jun 02	THREE LIONS '98 (re-issue) (re) *Epic 6728152*	16	6

BADFINGER *UK, male vocal / instrumental group (34 WEEKS)*   pos/wks

10 Jan 70	● COME AND GET IT *Apple 20*	4	11
9 Jan 71	● NO MATTER WHAT *Apple 31*	5	12
29 Jan 72	● DAY AFTER DAY *Apple 40*	10	11

BADLY DRAWN BOY *UK, male vocalist /*
producer / instrumentalist – Damon Gough (21 WEEKS)   pos/wks

4 Sep 99	ONCE AROUND THE BLOCK *Twisted Nerve / XL Recordings TNXL 003CD*	46	2
17 Jun 00	ANOTHER PEARL *Twisted Nerve / XL Recordings TNXL 004CD*	41	1
16 Sep 00	DISILLUSION *Twisted Nerve / XL Recordings TNXL 005CD*	26	2
25 Nov 00	ONCE AROUND THE BLOCK (re-issue) *Twisted Nerve / XL Recordings TNXL 009CD*	27	2
19 May 01	PISSING IN THE WIND *Twisted Nerve / XL Recordings TNXL 010CD*	22	2
6 Apr 02	SILENT SIGH *Twisted Nerve / XL Recordings TNXL 012CD*	16	7
22 Jun 02	SOMETHING TO TALK ABOUT *Twisted Nerve / XL Recordings TNXL 014CD*	28	2
26 Oct 02	● YOU WERE RIGHT *Twisted Nerve / XL Recordings TNXL 015CD*	9	3

BADMAN *UK, male producer – Julian Brettle (3 WEEKS)*   pos/wks

2 Feb 91	MAGIC STYLE *Citybeat CBE 759*	61	3

Erykah BADU *US, female vocalist – Erica Wright (17 WEEKS)*   pos/wks

19 Apr 97	ON & ON *Universal UND 561117*	12	4
14 Jun 97	NEXT LIFETIME *Universal UND 56132*	30	3
29 Nov 97	APPLE TREE *Universal UND 56150*	47	1
11 Jul 98	ONE *Elektra E 3833CD1* [1]	23	3
6 Mar 99	YOU GOT ME *MCA MCSTD 48110* [2]	31	2
15 Sep 01	SWEET BABY *Epic 6718822* [3]	23	4

[1] Busta Rhymes featuring Erykah Badu [2] Roots featuring Erykah Badu [3] Macy Gray featuring Erykah Badu

Joan BAEZ *US, female vocalist (47 WEEKS)*   pos/wks

6 May 65	WE SHALL OVERCOME *Fontana TF 564*	26	10
8 Jul 65	● THERE BUT FOR FORTUNE *Fontana TF 587*	8	12
2 Sep 65	IT'S ALL OVER NOW, BABY BLUE *Fontana TF 604*	22	8
23 Dec 65	FAREWELL ANGELINA (re) *Fontana TF 639*	35	4
28 Jul 66	PACK UP YOUR SORROWS *Fontana TF 727*	50	1
9 Oct 71	● THE NIGHT THEY DROVE OLD DIXIE DOWN *Vanguard VS 35138*	6	12

BAHA MEN *Bahamas, male vocal group (35 WEEKS)*   pos/wks

14 Oct 00	● WHO LET THE DOGS OUT *Edel 0115425 ERE*	2	23
3 Feb 01	YOU ALL DAT *Edel 0124855 ERE*	14	5
13 Jul 02	MOVE IT LIKE THIS *S-Curve / EMI CDEM 615*	16	7

'You All Dat' features vocal by Imani Coppola

Carol BAILEY *UK, female vocalist (2 WEEKS)*   pos/wks

25 Feb 95	FEEL IT *Multiply CDMULTY 3*	41	2

Philip BAILEY *US, male vocalist (20 WEEKS)*   pos/wks

9 Mar 85	★ EASY LOVER *CBS A 4915* [1]	1	12
18 May 85	WALKING ON THE CHINESE WALL *CBS A 6202*	34	8

[1] Philip Bailey (duet with Phil Collins)

See also EARTH WIND AND FIRE

Merril BAINBRIDGE *Australia, female vocalist (1 WEEK)*   pos/wks

7 Dec 96	MOUTH *Gotham 74321431012*	51	1

Adrian BAKER *UK, male vocalist (8 WEEKS)*   pos/wks

19 Jul 75	● SHERRY *Magnet MAG 34*	10	8

See also GIDEA PARK

Anita BAKER *US, female vocalist (22 WEEKS)*   pos/wks

15 Nov 86	SWEET LOVE *Elektra EKR 44*	13	10
31 Jan 87	CAUGHT UP IN THE RAPTURE *Elektra EKR 49*	51	5
8 Oct 88	GIVING YOU THE BEST THAT I GOT *Elektra EKR 79*	55	3
30 Jun 90	TALK TO ME *Elektra EKR 111*	68	2
17 Sep 94	BODY & SOUL *Elektra EKR 190CD*	48	2

Arthur BAKER
US, male producer / multi-instrumentalist (8 WEEKS)   pos/wks

20 May 89	IT'S YOUR TIME *Breakout USA 654* [1]	64	2
21 Oct 89	THE MESSAGE IS LOVE *Breakout USA 668* [2]	38	5
30 Nov 02	CONFUSION *Whacked WACKT 002CD* [3]	64	1

[1] Arthur Baker featuring Shirley Lewis [2] Arthur Baker and the Backbeat Disciples featuring Al Green [3] Arthur Baker vs New Order

See also Wally JUMP Jr and the CRIMINAL ELEMENT

Hylda BAKER and Arthur MULLARD
UK, female / male actors / vocal duo (6 WEEKS)   pos/wks

9 Sep 78	YOU'RE THE ONE THAT I WANT *Pye 7N 46121*	22	6

George BAKER SELECTION
Holland, male / female vocal / instrumental group (10 WEEKS)   pos/wks

6 Sep 75	● PALOMA BLANCA *Warner Bros. K 16541*	10	10

BAKSHELF DOG *UK, Male bulldog vocalist – Churchill (2 WEEKS)*   pos/wks

21 Dec 02	NO LIMITS *WVC CDCHURCH 1*	51	2+

BALAAM AND THE ANGEL
UK, male vocal / instrumental group (2 WEEKS)   pos/wks

29 Mar 86	SHE KNOWS *Virgin VS 842*	70	2

Long John BALDRY *UK, male vocalist (36 WEEKS)*   pos/wks

8 Nov 67	★ LET THE HEARTACHES BEGIN *Pye 7N 17385*	1	13
28 Aug 68	WHEN THE SUN COMES SHINING THRU *Pye 7N 17593*	29	7
23 Oct 68	MEXICO *Pye 7N 17563*	15	8
29 Jan 69	IT'S TOO LATE NOW *Pye 7N 17664*	21	8

BALEARIC BILL *Belgium / Holland, male production*
duo – Johan Gielen and Sven Maes (2 WEEKS)   pos/wks

2 Oct 99	DESTINATION SUNSHINE *Xtravaganza XTRAV 3CDS*	36	2

See also SVENSON and GIELEN, BLUE BAMBOO, AIRSCAPE, CUBIC 22, TRANSFORMER 2

Edward BALL *UK, male vocalist (2 WEEKS)*   pos/wks

20 Jul 96	THE MILL HILL SELF HATE CLUB *Creation CRESCD 233*	57	1
22 Feb 97	LOVE IS BLUE *Creation CRESCD 244*	59	1

Kenny BALL and His JAZZMEN   189   Top 500   *Top UK trad jazz band leader, b. 22 May 1930, Essex. His Dixieland band was at the forefront of the early 1960s jazz revival. Their biggest hit, 'Midnight in Moscow', reached runner-up spot on both sides of the Atlantic (136 WEEKS)*   pos/wks

23 Feb 61	SAMANTHA *Pye Jazz Today 7NJ 2040* [1]	13	15
11 May 61	I STILL LOVE YOU ALL *Pye Jazz 7NJ 2042*	24	6
31 Aug 61	SOMEDAY (YOU'LL BE SORRY) *Pye Jazz 7NJ 2047*	28	6

Re-entries are listed as (re), (2re), (3re), etc which signifies that the hit re-entered the chart once, twice or three times, etc

9 Nov 61 ●	MIDNIGHT IN MOSCOW *Pye Jazz 7NJ 2049*	2	21
15 Feb 62 ●	MARCH OF THE SIAMESE CHILDREN *Pye Jazz 7NJ 2051*	4	13
17 May 62 ●	THE GREEN LEAVES OF SUMMER *Pye Jazz 7NJ 2054*	7	14
23 Aug 62	SO DO I *Pye Jazz 7NJ 2056*	14	8
18 Oct 62	THE PAY-OFF (AMOI DE PAYER) *Pye Jazz 7NJ 2061* [2]	23	6
17 Jan 63 ●	SUKIYAKI *Pye Jazz 7NJ 2062*	10	13
25 Apr 63	CASABLANCA *Pye Jazz 7NJ 2064*	21	11
13 Jun 63	RONDO *Pye Jazz 7NJ 2065*	24	8
22 Aug 63	ACAPULCO 1922 *Pye Jazz 7NJ 2067*	27	6
11 Jun 64	HELLO, DOLLY! *Pye Jazz 7NJ 2071*	30	7
19 Jul 67	WHEN I'M SIXTY FOUR *Pye 7N 17348*	43	2

[1] Lonnie Donegan presents Kenny Ball and His Jazz Band [2] Clarinet – Dave Jones

Michael BALL *UK, male actor / vocalist (39 WEEKS)* pos/wks

28 Jan 89 ●	LOVE CHANGES EVERYTHING *Really Useful RUR 3*	2	14
28 Oct 89	THE FIRST MAN YOU REMEMBER *Really Useful RUR 6* [1]	68	2
10 Aug 91	IT'S STILL YOU *Polydor PO 160*	58	2
25 Apr 92	ONE STEP OUT OF TIME *Polydor PO 206*	20	7
12 Dec 92	IF I CAN DREAM (EP) (re) *Polydor PO 248*	51	2
11 Sep 93	SUNSET BOULEVARD *Polydor PZCD 293*	72	1
30 Jul 94	FROM HERE TO ETERNITY *Columbia 6606905*	36	3
17 Sep 94	THE LOVERS WE WERE *Columbia 6607972*	63	2
9 Dec 95	THE ROSE *Columbia 6614535*	42	4
17 Feb 96	(SOMETHING INSIDE) SO STRONG *Columbia 6629005*	40	2

[1] Michael Ball and Diana Morrison

Tracks on If I Can Dream (EP): If I Can Dream / You Don't Have to Say You Love Me / Always on My Mind / Tell Me There's a Heaven

Steve BALSAMO *UK, male vocalist (2 WEEKS)* pos/wks

16 Mar 02	SUGAR FOR THE SOUL *Columbia 6718552*	32	2

BALTIMORA *Ireland, male vocalist – Jimmy McShane (12 WEEKS)* pos/wks

10 Aug 85 ●	TARZAN BOY *Columbia DB 9102*	3	12

Charli BALTIMORE *US, female rapper (13 WEEKS)* pos/wks

1 Aug 98	MONEY *Epic 6662272*	12	4
12 Oct 02 ●	DOWN 4 U (re) *Murder Inc 0639002* [1]	4	9

[1] Irv Gotti presents Ja Rule, Ashanti, Charli Baltimore and Vita

BAM BAM *US, male vocalist / instrumentalist (2 WEEKS)* pos/wks

19 Mar 88	GIVE IT TO ME *Serious 7OUS 10*	65	2

Afrika BAMBAATAA
US, male DJ / producer / rapper – Kevin Donovan (33 WEEKS) pos/wks

28 Aug 82	PLANET ROCK *21 POSP 497* [1]	53	3
10 Mar 84	RENEGADES OF FUNK *Tommy Boy AFR 1* [1]	30	4
1 Sep 84	UNITY (PART 1 – THE THIRD COMING) *Tommy Boy AFR 2* [2]	49	5
27 Feb 88	RECKLESS *EMI EM 41* [3]	17	8
12 Oct 91	JUST GET UP AND DANCE *EMI USA MT 100*	45	3
17 Oct 98	GOT TO GET UP *Multiply CDMULTY 42*	22	4
18 Sep 99	AFRIKA SHOX *Hard Hands HAND 057CD1* [4]	7	5
25 Aug 01	PLANET ROCK *Tommy Boy TBCD 2266* [5]	47	1

[1] Afrika Bambaataa and the Soul Sonic Force [2] Afrika Bambaataa and James Brown [3] Afrika Bambaataa and Family featuring UB40 [4] Leftfield / Bambaataa [5] Paul Oakenfold presents Afrika Bambaataa and Soulsonic Force

BAMBOO *UK, male producer – Andrew Livingstone (12 WEEKS)* pos/wks

17 Jan 98 ●	BAMBOOGIE *VC Recordings VCRD 29*	2	10
4 Jul 98	THE STRUTT *VC Recordings VCRD 35*	36	2

BANANARAMA (90) `Top 500` *Britain's most charted female group: Sarah Dallin, Keren Woodward, Siobhan Fahey. The London-based trio was also a best-selling act in the US, where 'Venus' topped the chart. Fahey, who married Eurythmic Dave Stewart, left in 1988 to form Shakespear's Sister and was replaced by Jacqui O'Sullivan (202 WEEKS)* pos/wks

13 Feb 82 ●	IT AIN'T WHAT YOU DO IT'S THE WAY THAT YOU DO IT *Chrysalis CHS 2570* [1]	4	10

10 Apr 82 ●	REALLY SAYING SOMETHING *Deram NANA 1* [2]	5	10
3 Jul 82 ●	SHY BOY *London NANA 2*	4	11
4 Dec 82	CHEERS THEN *London NANA 3*	45	7
26 Feb 83 ●	NA NA HEY HEY KISS HIM GOODBYE *London NANA 4*	5	10
9 Jul 83 ●	CRUEL SUMMER *London NANA 5*	8	10
3 Mar 84 ●	ROBERT DE NIRO'S WAITING *London NANA 6*	3	11
26 May 84	ROUGH JUSTICE *London NANA 7*	23	7
24 Nov 84	HOTLINE TO HEAVEN *London NANA 8*	58	2
24 Aug 85	DO NOT DISTURB *London NANA 9*	31	6
31 May 86 ●	VENUS *London NANA 10* ▲	8	13
16 Aug 86	MORE THAN PHYSICAL *London NANA 11*	41	5
14 Feb 87	TRICK OF THE NIGHT *London NANA 12*	32	5
11 Jul 87	I HEARD A RUMOUR *London NANA 13*	14	9
10 Oct 87 ●	LOVE IN THE FIRST DEGREE *London NANA 14*	3	12
9 Jan 88	I CAN'T HELP IT *London NANA 15*	20	6
9 Apr 88 ●	I WANT YOU BACK *London NANA 16*	5	10
24 Sep 88	LOVE, TRUTH AND HONESTY *London NANA 17*	23	8
19 Nov 88	NATHAN JONES *London NANA 18*	15	9
25 Feb 89 ●	HELP *London LON 222* [3]	3	9
10 Jun 89	CRUEL SUMMER (re-mix) *London NANA 19*	19	6
28 Jul 90	ONLY YOUR LOVE *London NANA 21*	27	4
5 Jan 91	PREACHER MAN *London NANA 23*	20	6
20 Apr 91	LONG TRAIN RUNNING *London NANA 24*	30	5
29 Aug 92	MOVIN' ON *London NANA 25*	24	5
28 Nov 92	LAST THING ON MY MIND *London NANA 26*	71	2
20 Mar 93	MORE MORE MORE *London NACPD 27*	24	4

[1] Fun Boy Three and Bananarama [2] Bananarama with Fun Boy Three [3] Bananarama / La Na Nee Nee Noo Noo

The listed flip side of 'Love in the First Degree' was 'Mr Sleaze' by Stock Aitken Waterman. Act was a duo for last three hits

BAND *Canada / US, male vocal / instrumental group (18 WEEKS)* pos/wks

18 Sep 68	THE WEIGHT *Capitol CL 15559*	21	9
4 Apr 70	RAG MAMA RAG *Capitol CL 15629*	16	9

BAND AID *International, male / female vocal / instrumental charity assembly (26 WEEKS)* pos/wks

15 Dec 84 ★	DO THEY KNOW IT'S CHRISTMAS? (re) *Mercury FEED 1* ◆ ■	1	20
23 Dec 89 ★	DO THEY KNOW IT'S CHRISTMAS? *PWL/Polydor FEED 2* [1] ■	1	6

[1] Band Aid II

BAND AID: Adam Clayton, Bono (U2); Bob Geldof, Johnny Fingers, Simon Crowe, Peter Briquette (Boomtown Rats); David Bowie; Paul McCartney; Holly Johnson (Frankie Goes To Hollywood); Midge Ure, Chris Cross (Ultravox); Simon Le Bon, Nick Rhodes, Andy Taylor, John Taylor, Roger Taylor (Duran Duran); Paul Young; Tony Hadley, Martin Kemp, John Keeble, Gary Kemp, Steve Norman (Spandau Ballet); Martyn Ware, Glenn Gregory (Heaven 17); Francis Rossi, Rick Parfitt (Status Quo); Sting; Boy George, Jon Moss (Culture Club); Marilyn; Keren Woodward, Sarah Dallin, Siobhan Fahey (Bananarama); Jody Watley (Shalamar); Paul Weller; Robert "Kool" Bell, James Taylor, Dennis Thomas (Kool and the Gang); George Michael and Phil Collins. Band Aid's 1984 'Do They Know It's Christmas?' re-entered the chart and peaked at at No.3 in Dec 1985.

BAND AID II: Bananarama, Big Fun, Bros, Cathy Dennis, D Mob, Jason Donovan, Kevin Godley, Glen Goldsmith, Kylie Minogue, The Pasadenas, Chris Rea, Cliff Richard, Jimmy Somerville, Sonia, Lisa Stansfield, Technotronic, Wet Wet Wet

BAND AKA *US, male vocal / instrumental group (12 WEEKS)* pos/wks

15 May 82	GRACE *Epic EPC A 2376*	41	5
5 Mar 83	JOY *Epic EPC A 3145*	24	7

BAND OF GOLD
Holland, male / female vocal / instrumental group (11 WEEKS) pos/wks

14 Jul 84	LOVE SONGS ARE BACK AGAIN (MEDLEY) *RCA 428*	24	11

BAND OF THIEVES – See Luke GOSS and the BAND OF THIEVES

BANDA SONORA *UK, male producer – Gerald Elms (3 WEEKS)* pos/wks

6 Oct 01	GUITARRA G *Defected DFECT 36CDS*	50	2
19 Oct 02	PRESSURE COOKER *Defected DFTD 060CDS* [1]	46	1

[1] G Club presents Banda Sonora

BANDERAS UK, female vocal / instrumental duo
– Sally Herbert and Caroline Buckley (16 WEEKS)   pos/wks

23 Feb 91	THIS IS YOUR LIFE *London LON 290*	16 10
15 Jun 91	SHE SELLS *London LON 298*	41 6

BANDWAGON – See Johnny JOHNSON

Honey BANE UK, female vocalist – Donna Boylan (8 WEEKS)   pos/wks

24 Jan 81	TURN ME ON TURN ME OFF *Zonophone Z 15*	37 5
18 Apr 81	BABY LOVE *Zonophone Z 19*	58 3

BANG UK, male vocal duo (2 WEEKS)   pos/wks

6 May 89	YOU'RE THE ONE *RCA PB 42715*	74 2

BANGLES   331   Top 500

Originally named The Supersonic Bangs, then Bangs, melodic pop-rock
quartet formed 1981, Los Angeles, California, US. Comprised Susanna Hoffs
(v), sisters Vicki (g) and Debbi Peterson (d) and Michael Steele (b). Split 1989,
having become the most successful all-female band in chart history, then
reformed for a tour in 2000. 'Eternal Flame' returned to top in 2001 by Atomic
Kitten (94 WEEKS)   pos/wks

15 Feb 86 ●	MANIC MONDAY *CBS A 6796*	2 12
26 Apr 86	IF SHE KNEW WHAT SHE WANTS *CBS A 7062*	31 7
5 Jul 86	GOING DOWN TO LIVERPOOL *CBS A 7255*	56 3
13 Sep 86 ●	WALK LIKE AN EGYPTIAN *CBS 650071 7* ▲	3 19
10 Jan 87	WALKING DOWN YOUR STREET *CBS BANGS 1*	16 6
18 Apr 87	FOLLOWING *CBS BANGS 2*	55 3
6 Feb 88	HAZY SHADE OF WINTER *Def Jam BANGS 3*	11 10
5 Nov 88	IN YOUR ROOM *CBS BANGS 4*	35 6
18 Feb 89 ★	ETERNAL FLAME *CBS BANGS 5* ▲	1 18
10 Jun 89	BE WITH YOU *CBS BANGS 6*	23 8
14 Oct 89	I'LL SET YOU FREE *CBS BANGS 7*	74 1
9 Jun 90	WALK LIKE AN EGYPTIAN (re-issue) *CBS BANGS 8*	73 1

Tony BANKS – See FISH

BANNED UK, male vocal / instrumental group (6 WEEKS)   pos/wks

17 Dec 77	LITTLE GIRL *Harvest HAR 5145*	36 6

BANSHEES – See SIOUXSIE and the BANSHEES

Buju BANTON Jamaica, male vocalist (1 WEEK)   pos/wks

7 Aug 93	MAKE MY DAY *Mercury BUJCD 2*	72 1

Pato BANTON UK, male vocalist – Patrick Murray (37 WEEKS)   pos/wks

1 Oct 94 ★	BABY COME BACK *Virgin VSCDT 1522*	1 18
11 Feb 95	THIS COWBOY SONG *A&M 5809652* [1]	15 6
8 Apr 95	BUBBLING HOT *Virgin VSCDT 1530* [2]	15 7
20 Jan 96	SPIRITS IN THE MATERIAL WORLD *MCA MCSTD 2113* [3]	36 2
27 Jul 96	GROOVIN' *IRS CDEIRS 195* [4]	14 4

[1] Sting featuring Pato Banton [2] Pato Banton with Ranking Roger [3] Pato
Banton with Sting [4] Pato Banton and the Reggae Revolution

The sleeve of 'Baby Come Back' credits Ali and Robin Campbell

BAR CODES featuring Alison BROWN
UK, male / female vocal group (1 WEEK)   pos/wks

17 Dec 94	SUPERMARKET SWEEP *Blanca Casa BC 101CD*	72 1

Chris BARBER'S JAZZ BAND
UK, male jazz band, led by Chris Barber – trombone (30 WEEKS)   pos/wks

13 Feb 59 ●	PETITE FLEUR (re) *Pye Nixa NJ 2026* [1]	3 24
9 Oct 59	LONESOME (SI TU VOIS MA MERE) *Columbia DB 4333* [2]	27 2
4 Jan 62	REVIVAL (re) *Columbia SCD 2166*	43 4

[1] Clarinet solo – Monty Sunshine [2] Chris Barber featuring Monty Sunshine

BARBRA and NEIL – See Barbra STREISAND; Neil DIAMOND

BARCLAY JAMES HARVEST
UK, male vocal / instrumental group (9 WEEKS)   pos/wks

2 Apr 77	LIVE (EP) (re) *Polydor 2229 198*	49 2
26 Jan 80	LOVE ON THE LINE *Polydor POSP 97*	63 2
22 Nov 80	LIFE IS FOR LIVING *Polydor POSP 195*	61 3
21 May 83	JUST A DAY AWAY *Polydor POSP 585*	68 2

Tracks on Live (EP): Rock 'n' Roll Star / Medicine Man (Parts 1 & 2)

BARDO UK, male / female vocal duo –
Sally Ann Triplett and Stephen Fischer (8 WEEKS)   pos/wks

10 Apr 82 ●	ONE STEP FURTHER *Epic EPC A2265*	2 8

BARDOT Australia, female vocal group (1 WEEK)   pos/wks

14 Apr 01	POISON *East West EW 229CD*	45 1

BAREFOOT MAN Germany, male vocalist – George Nowak (7 WKS)   pos/wks

5 Dec 98	BIG PANTY WOMAN *Plaza PZACD 082*	21 7

BARENAKED LADIES
Canada, male vocal / instrumental group (12 WEEKS)   pos/wks

20 Feb 99 ●	ONE WEEK *Reprise W 468CD* ▲	5 8
15 May 99	IT'S ALL BEEN DONE *Reprise W 476CD*	28 2
24 Jul 99	CALL AND ANSWER *Reprise W498CD1*	52 1
11 Dec 99	BRIAN WILSON *Reprise W 511CD1*	73 1

BAR-KAYS US, male vocal / instrumental group (15 WEEKS)   pos/wks

23 Aug 67	SOUL FINGER *Stax 601 014*	33 7
22 Jan 77	SHAKE YOUR RUMP TO THE FUNK *Mercury 6167 417*	41 4
12 Jan 85	SEXOMATIC *Club JAB 10*	51 4

BARKIN BROTHERS featuring Johnnie FIORI
UK, male production group and US female vocalist (2 WEEKS)   pos/wks

15 Apr 00	GONNA CATCH YOU *Brothers Organisation BRUVCD 15*	51 2

Gary BARLOW UK, male vocalist (47 WEEKS)   pos/wks

20 Jul 96 ★	FOREVER LOVE *RCA 74321397922* ■	1 16
10 May 97 ★	LOVE WON'T WAIT (2re) *RCA 74321470842* ■	1 9
26 Jul 97	SO HELP ME GIRL (re) *RCA 74321501202*	11 11
15 Nov 97 ●	OPEN ROAD *RCA 74321518292*	7 5
17 Jul 99	STRONGER *RCA 74321682002*	16 4
9 Oct 99	FOR ALL THAT YOU WANT *RCA 74321701012*	24 2

See also TAKE THAT

Gary BARNACLE – See BIG FUN; SONIA

BARNBRACK UK, male vocal / instrumental group (7 WEEKS)   pos/wks

16 Mar 85	BELFAST *Homespun HS 092*	45 7

Jimmy BARNES and INXS Australia, male vocalist
and Australia, vocal / instrumental group (8 WEEKS)   pos/wks

26 Jan 91	GOOD TIMES *Atlantic A 7751*	18 8

Richard BARNES UK, male vocalist (10 WEEKS)   pos/wks

23 May 70	TAKE TO THE MOUNTAINS *Philips BF 1840*	35 6
24 Oct 70	GO NORTH (re) *Philips 6006 039*	38 4

BARRACUDAS
UK / US, male vocal / instrumental group (6 WEEKS)   pos/wks

16 Aug 80	SUMMER FUN *Zonophone Z 5*	37 6

Wild Willy BARRETT – See John OTWAY and Wild Willy BARRETT

Amanda BARRIE and Johnny BRIGGS
UK, female / male vocal duo (3 WEEKS)   pos/wks

16 Dec 95	SOMETHING STUPID *EMI Premier CDEMS 411*	35 3

JJ BARRIE *Canada, male vocalist – Barrie Authors (11 WEEKS)*   pos/wks

24 Apr 76 ★ **NO CHARGE** *Power Exchange PX 209*....................1 11

Featured vocalist is Vicki Brown

Ken BARRIE *UK, male vocalist (15 WEEKS)*   pos/wks

10 Jul 82 **POSTMAN PAT (2re)** *Post Music PP 001*..........................44 15

Re-entries at Christmas 1982 and 1983

BARRON KNIGHTS (333 Top 500) *Britain's princes of pop parody, formed Leighton Buzzard, UK, fronted by Duke D'Mond (b. Richard Palmer). Group's humorous hit medleys proved popular in the 1960s and 1970s and helped to stop pop music taking itself too seriously (94 WEEKS)*   pos/wks

9 Jul 64	● **CALL UP THE GROUPS** *Columbia DB 7317* 1	3	13
22 Oct 64	**COME TO THE DANCE** *Columbia DB 7375* 1	42	2
25 Mar 65	● **POP GO THE WORKERS** *Columbia DB 7525* 1	5	13
16 Dec 65	● **MERRY GENTLE POPS** *Columbia DB 7780* 1	9	7
1 Dec 66	**UNDER NEW MANAGEMENT** *Columbia DB 8071* 1	15	9
23 Oct 68	**AN OLYMPIC RECORD** *Columbia DB 8485*	35	4
29 Oct 77	● **LIVE IN TROUBLE** *Epic EPC 5752*	7	10
2 Dec 78	● **A TASTE OF AGGRO** *Epic EPC 6829*	3	10
8 Dec 79	**FOOD FOR THOUGHT** *Epic EPC 8011*	46	6
4 Oct 80	**THE SIT SONG** *Epic EPC 8994*	44	4
6 Dec 80	**NEVER MIND THE PRESENTS** *Epic EPC 9070*	17	8
5 Dec 81	**BLACKBOARD JUMBLE** *CBS A 1795*	52	5
19 Mar 83	**BUFFALO BILL'S LAST SCRATCH** *Epic EPC A 3208*	49	3

1 The Barron Knights with Duke D'Mond

Joe BARRY *US, male vocalist (1 WEEK)*   pos/wks

24 Aug 61 **I'M A FOOL TO CARE** *Mercury AMT 1149* 49 1

John BARRY ORCHESTRA (445 Top 500) *Early UK rock 'n' roll bandleader, who arranged Adam Faith's hits and found global fame writing film scores (including many for James Bond). b. Jonathan Barry Prendergast, 3 Nov 1933, York, UK. This Oscar and Grammy winner was made an OBE in 1999 (79 WEEKS)*   pos/wks

4 Mar 60	● **HIT AND MISS (re)** *Columbia DB 4414* 1	10	14
28 Apr 60	**BEAT FOR BEATNIKS** *Columbia DB 4446*	40	2
14 Jul 60	**NEVER LET GO** *Columbia DB 4480*	49	1
18 Aug 60	**BLUEBERRY HILL** *Columbia DB 4480*	34	3
8 Sep 60	**WALK DON'T RUN (re)** *Columbia DB 4505* 2	11	14
8 Dec 60	**BLACK STOCKINGS** *Columbia DB 4554* 2	27	9
2 Mar 61	**THE MAGNIFICENT SEVEN (3re)** *Columbia DB 4598* 2	45	5
26 Apr 62	**CUTTY SARK** *Columbia DB 4806* 2	35	2
1 Nov 62	**THE JAMES BOND THEME** *Columbia DB 4898*	13	11
21 Nov 63	**FROM RUSSIA WITH LOVE (re)** *Ember S 181*	39	3
11 Dec 71	**THEME FROM 'THE PERSUADERS'** *CBS 7469* 3	13	15

1 John Barry Seven plus Four 2 John Barry Seven 3 John Barry

Len BARRY *US, male vocalist – Leonard Borisoff (24 WEEKS)*   pos/wks

4 Nov 65	● **1-2-3** *Brunswick 05942*	3	14
13 Jan 66	● **LIKE A BABY** *Brunswick 05949*	10	10

Michael BARRYMORE
UK, male vocalist / comedian – Michael Parker (4 WEEKS)   pos/wks

16 Dec 95 **TOO MUCH FOR ONE HEART** *EMI CDEM 412* 25 4

Lionel BART *UK, male vocalist, d. 3 Apr 1999 (3 WEEKS)*   pos/wks

25 Nov 89 **HAPPY ENDINGS (GIVE YOURSELF A PINCH) (re)** *EMI EM 121* 68 3

BART & HOMER – *See SIMPSONS*

BARTHEZZ *Holland, male producer – Bart Claessen (8 WEEKS)*   pos/wks

22 Sep 01	**ON THE MOVE** *Positiva CDTIV 158*	18	4
20 Apr 02	**INFECTED** *Positiva CDTIVS 168*	25	4

BAS NOIR *US, female vocal duo (1 WEEK)*   pos/wks

11 Feb 89 **MY LOVE IS MAGIC** *10 TEN 257* 73 1

Rob BASE and DJ E-Z ROCK
US, male rap / DJ duo – Robert Ginyard and Rodney Bryce (19 WEEKS) pos/wks

16 Apr 88	**IT TAKES TWO (re)** *Citybeat CBE 724*	24	9
14 Jan 89	**GET ON THE DANCE FLOOR** *Supreme SUPE 139*	14	7
22 Apr 89	**JOY AND PAIN** *Supreme SUPE 143*	47	3

BASEMENT BOYS present Ultra NATÉ
US, male production group and female vocalist (1 WEEK)   pos/wks

23 Feb 91 **IS IT LOVE?** *Eternal YZ 509* 71 1

BASEMENT JAXX *UK, male DJ / production duo – Simon Ratcliffe and Felix Buxton (55 WEEKS)*   pos/wks

31 May 97	**FLY LIFE** *Multiply CDMULTY 21*	19	3
1 May 99	● **RED ALERT** *XL Recordings XLS 100CD*	5	10
14 Aug 99	● **RENDEZ-VU** *XL Recordings XLS 110CD*	4	8
6 Nov 99	**JUMP 'N SHOUT** *XL Recordings XLS 116CD*	12	5
15 Apr 00	**BINGO BANGO** *XL Recordings XLS 120CD*	13	4
16 Jun 01	● **ROMEO** *XL Recordings XLS 132CD*	6	10
6 Oct 01	**JUS 1 KISS (re)** *XL Recordings XLS 136CD*	23	4
8 Dec 01	● **WHERE'S YOUR HEAD AT?** *XL Recordings XLS 140CD*	9	8
29 Jun 02	**GET ME OFF** *XL Recordings XLS 146CD*	22	3

BASIA *Poland, female vocalist (9 WEEKS)*   pos/wks

23 Jan 88	**PROMISES** *Epic BASH 4*	48	4
28 May 88	**TIME AND TIDE** *Epic BASH 5*	61	3
14 Jan 95	**DRUNK ON LOVE** *Epic 6611582*	41	2

Count BASIE – *See Frank SINATRA*

Toni BASIL
US, female vocalist – Antonia Basilotta (16 WEEKS)   pos/wks

6 Feb 82	● **MICKEY** *Radialchoice TIC 4* ▲	2	12
1 May 82	**NOBODY** *Radialchoice TIC 2*	52	4

Olav BASOSKI
Holland, male producer (1 WEEK)   pos/wks

26 Aug 00 **OPIUM SCUMBAGZ** *Defected DFECT 20CDS*.............56 1

Alfie BASS – *See Michael MEDWIN, Bernard BRESSLAW, Alfie BASS and Leslie FYSON*

Fontella BASS *US, female vocalist (15 WEEKS)*   pos/wks

2 Dec 65	**RESCUE ME** *Chess CRS 8023*	11	10
20 Jan 66	**RECOVERY** *Chess CRS 8027*	32	5

Norman BASS
Germany, male producer (4 WEEKS)   pos/wks

21 Apr 01 **HOW U LIKE BASS** *Substance SUBS 10CDS* 17 4

BASS BOYZ
UK, male producer – James Sammon (1 WEEK)   pos/wks

28 Sep 96 **GUNZ AND PIANOZ** *Polydor 5753432* 74 1

See also PIANOMAN

BASS BUMPERS
Germany / UK, male / female vocal / instrumental group (4 WEEKS) pos/wks

25 Sep 93	**RUNNIN'** *Vertigo VERCD 78*	68	1
5 Feb 94	**THE MUSIC'S GOT ME** *Vertigo VERCD 84*	25	3

BASS JUMPERS
Holland, male producer and female vocalist (1 WEEK)   pos/wks

13 Feb 99 **MAKE UP YOUR MIND** *Pepper 0530112* 44 1

Shirley BASSEY 23 Top 500

Internationally acclaimed vocalist and cabaret entertainer, b. 8 Jan 1937, Cardiff, Wales. With 31 hit singles (spanning a record 42-year period for a female) and 35 hit albums, she is Britain's most successful female chart artist. Honoured with a damehood in 2000 (326 WEEKS)   pos/wks

15 Feb 57	● THE BANANA BOAT SONG *Philips PB 668*	8	10
23 Aug 57	FIRE DOWN BELOW *Philips PB 723*	30	1
6 Sep 57	YOU YOU ROMEO *Philips PB 723*	29	2
19 Dec 58	★ AS I LOVE YOU (re) *Philips PB 845*	1	19
26 Dec 58	● KISS ME, HONEY HONEY, KISS ME *Philips PB 860*	3	17
31 Mar 60	WITH THESE HANDS (2re) *Columbia DB 4421*	38	6
4 Aug 60	● AS LONG AS HE NEEDS ME *Columbia DB 4490*	2	30
11 May 61	● YOU'LL NEVER KNOW *Columbia DB 4643*	6	17
27 Jul 61	★ REACH FOR THE STARS / CLIMB EV'RY MOUNTAIN (re) *Columbia DB 4685*	1	18
23 Nov 61	● I'LL GET BY (AS LONG AS I HAVE YOU) *Columbia DB 4737*	10	8
15 Feb 62	TONIGHT *Columbia DB 4777*	21	8
26 Apr 62	AVE MARIA *Columbia DB 4816*	31	4
31 May 62	FAR AWAY *Columbia DB 4836*	24	13
30 Aug 62	● WHAT NOW MY LOVE? *Columbia DB 4882*	5	17
28 Feb 63	WHAT KIND OF FOOL AM I? *Columbia DB 4974*	47	2
26 Sep 63	● I (WHO HAVE NOTHING) *Columbia DB 7113*	6	20
23 Jan 64	MY SPECIAL DREAM *Columbia DB 7185*	32	7
9 Apr 64	GONE *Columbia DB 7248*	36	5
15 Oct 64	GOLDFINGER *Columbia DB 7360*	21	9
20 May 65	NO REGRETS *Columbia DB 7535*	39	4
11 Oct 67	BIG SPENDER *United Artists UP 1192*	21	15
20 Jun 70	● SOMETHING (re) *United Artists UP 35125*	4	22
2 Jan 71	THE FOOL ON THE HILL *United Artists UP 35156*	48	1
27 Mar 71	(WHERE DO I BEGIN) LOVE STORY *United Artists UP 35194*	34	9
7 Aug 71	● FOR ALL WE KNOW (re) *United Artists UP 35267*	6	24
15 Jan 72	DIAMONDS ARE FOREVER *United Artists UP 35293*	38	6
3 Mar 73	● NEVER, NEVER, NEVER (GRANDE, GRANDE, GRANDE) (re) *United Artists UP 35490*	8	19
22 Aug 87	THE RHYTHM DIVINE *Mercury MER 253* [1]	54	2
16 Nov 96	'DISCO' LA PASSIONE *East West EW 072CD* [2]	41	1
20 Dec 97	HISTORY REPEATING *Wall of Sound WALLD 036* [3]	19	7
23 Oct 99	WORLD IN UNION *Universal TV 4669402* [4]	35	3

[1] Yello featuring Shirley Bassey [2] Chris Rea and Shirley Bassey [3] Propellerheads featuring Miss Shirley Bassey [4] Shirley Bassey / Bryn Terfel

BASSHEADS
UK, male / female vocal / instrumental group (19 WEEKS)   pos/wks

16 Nov 91	● IS THERE ANYBODY OUT THERE? *Deconstruction R 6303*	5	8
30 May 92	BACK TO THE OLD SCHOOL *Deconstruction R 6310*	12	4
28 Nov 92	WHO CAN MAKE ME FEEL GOOD *Deconstruction R 6326*	38	2
28 Aug 93	START A BRAND NEW LIFE (SAVE ME) *Deconstruction CDR 6353*	49	2
15 Jul 95	IS THERE ANYBODY OUT THERE? (re-mix) *Deconstruction 74321293882*	24	3

BASS-O-MATIC
UK, male multi-instrumentalist / producer – William Orbit (19 WEEKS) pos/wks

12 May 90	IN THE REALM OF THE SENSES *Virgin VS 1265*	66	3
1 Sep 90	● FASCINATING RHYTHM *Virgin VS 1274*	9	11
22 Dec 90	EASE ON BY *Virgin VS 1295*	61	4
3 Aug 91	FUNKY LOVE VIBRATIONS *Virgin VS 1355*	71	1

See also William ORBIT

BASSTOY *US, male / female production / vocal duo (6 WEEKS)*   pos/wks

27 May 00	RUNNIN *Neo NEOCD 029*	62	1
19 Jan 02	RUNNIN' (re-mix) *Black & White NEOCD 073* [1]	13	5

[1] Mark Picchiotti presents Basstoy featuring Dana

BATES *Germany, male vocal / instrumental group (1 WEEK)*   pos/wks

3 Feb 96	BILLIE JEAN *Virgin International DINSD 151*	67	1

Mike BATT with the NEW EDITION
UK, male vocalist with male / female vocal group (8 WEEKS)   pos/wks

16 Aug 75	● SUMMERTIME CITY *Epic EPC 3460*	4	8

See also WOMBLES

BAUHAUS *UK, male vocal / instrumental group (35 WEEKS)*   pos/wks

18 Apr 81	KICK IN THE EYE *Beggars Banquet BEG 54*	59	3
4 Jul 81	THE PASSION OF LOVERS *Beggars Banquet BEG 59*	56	2
6 Mar 82	KICK IN THE EYE (EP) *Beggars Banquet BEG 74*	45	4
19 Jun 82	SPIRIT *Beggars Banquet BEG 79*	42	5
9 Oct 82	ZIGGY STARDUST *Beggars Banquet BEG 83*	15	7
22 Jan 83	LAGARTIJA NICK *Beggars Banquet BEG 88*	44	4
9 Apr 83	SHE'S IN PARTIES *Beggars Banquet BEG 91*	26	6
29 Oct 83	THE SINGLES 1981-83 *Beggars Banquet BEG 100E*	52	4

Tracks on Kick in the Eye (EP): Kick in the Eye (Searching for Satori) / Harry / Earwax. The Singles 1981-83 was an EP: The Passion of Lovers / Kick in the Eye / Spirit / Ziggy Stardust / Lagartija Nick / She's in Parties

Les BAXTER his Chorus and Orchestra
US, orchestra and chorus, leader d. 15 Jan 1996 (9 WEEKS)   pos/wks

13 May 55	● UNCHAINED MELODY *Capitol CL 14257*	10	9

Tasha BAXTER – *See Roger GOODE featuring Tasha BAXTER*

BAY CITY ROLLERS 243 Top 500
Tartan teen sensations from Edinburgh: Leslie McKeown (v), Eric Faulkner (g), Stuart Wood (g), Alan Longmuir (b), Derek Longmuir (d). They were the first of many acts heralded as 'Biggest Group Since The Beatles' and one of the most screamed-at teeny-bopper acts of the 70s (116 WEEKS)   pos/wks

18 Sep 71	● KEEP ON DANCING *Bell 1164*	9	13
9 Feb 74	● REMEMBER (SHA-LA-LA) *Bell 1338*	6	12
27 Apr 74	● SHANG-A-LANG *Bell 1355*	2	10
27 Jul 74	● SUMMERLOVE SENSATION *Bell 1369*	3	10
12 Oct 74	● ALL OF ME LOVES ALL OF YOU *Bell 1382*	4	10
8 Mar 75	★ BYE BYE BABY *Bell 1409*	1	16
12 Jul 75	★ GIVE A LITTLE LOVE *Bell 1425*	1	9
22 Nov 75	● MONEY HONEY *Bell 1461*	3	9
10 Apr 76	● LOVE ME LIKE I LOVE YOU *Bell 1477*	4	9
11 Sep 76	● I ONLY WANNA BE WITH YOU *Bell 1493*	4	9
7 May 77	IT'S A GAME *Arista 108*	16	6
30 Jul 77	YOU MADE ME BELIEVE IN MAGIC *Arista 127*	34	3

Duke BAYSEE *UK, male vocalist – Kevin Rowe (6 WEEKS)*   pos/wks

3 Sep 94	SUGAR SUGAR *Bell 74321228702*	30	4
21 Jan 95	DO YOU LOVE ME *Double Dekker CDDEK 1*	46	2

BAZ *UK, female vocalist – Baz Gooden (3 WEEKS)*   pos/wks

15 Dec 01	BELIEVERS *One Little Indian 313 TP7CD1*	36	2
30 Mar 02	SMILE TO SHINE *One Little Indian 316 TP7CD*	58	1

BE BOP DELUXE
UK, male vocal / instrumental group (13 WEEKS)   pos/wks

21 Feb 76	SHIPS IN THE NIGHT *Harvest HAR 5104*	23	8
13 Nov 76	HOT VALVES (EP) *Harvest HAR 5117*	36	5

Tracks on Hot Valves (EP): Maid in Heaven / Blazing Apostles / Jet Silver and the Dolls of Venus / Bring Back the Spark

See also Bill NELSON

BEACH BOYS 38 Top 500 *California family band famous for their harmonies. The most successful and consistently popular US group of the rock era: Brian Wilson (b/k/v), Mike Love (v), Carl Wilson (g/v) (d. 1998), Al Jardine (g/v), Dennis Wilson (d/v) (d. 1983) (281 WEEKS)*   pos/wks

1 Aug 63	SURFIN' U.S.A. *Capitol CL 15305*	34	7
9 Jul 64	● I GET AROUND *Capitol CL 15350* ▲	7	13
29 Oct 64	WHEN I GROW UP (TO BE A MAN) (re) *Capitol CL 15361*	27	7
21 Jan 65	DANCE, DANCE, DANCE *Capitol CL 15370*	24	6
3 Jun 65	HELP ME, RHONDA *Capitol CL 15392* ▲	27	10

Date	Title	Pos	Wks
2 Sep 65	CALIFORNIA GIRLS *Capitol CL 15409*	26	8
17 Feb 66 ●	BARBARA ANN *Capitol CL 15432*	3	10
21 Apr 66 ●	SLOOP JOHN B *Capitol CL 15441*	2	15
28 Jul 66 ●	GOD ONLY KNOWS *Capitol CL 15459*	2	14
3 Nov 66 ★	GOOD VIBRATIONS *Capitol CL 15475* ▲	1	13
4 May 67 ●	THEN I KISSED HER *Capitol CL 15502*	4	11
23 Aug 67 ●	HEROES AND VILLAINS *Capitol CL 15510*	8	7
22 Nov 67	WILD HONEY *Capitol CL 15521*	29	6
17 Jan 68	DARLIN' *Capitol CL 15527*	11	14
8 May 68 ●	FRIENDS *Capitol CL 15545*	25	7
24 Jul 68 ★	DO IT AGAIN *Capitol CL 15554*	1	14
25 Dec 68	BLUEBIRDS OVER THE MOUNTAIN *Capitol CL 15572*	33	5
26 Feb 69 ●	I CAN HEAR MUSIC *Capitol CL 15584*	10	13
11 Jun 69 ●	BREAK AWAY *Capitol CL 15598*	6	11
16 May 70 ●	COTTONFIELDS *Capitol CL 15640*	5	17
3 Mar 73	CALIFORNIA SAGA – CALIFORNIA *Reprise K 14232*	37	5
3 Jul 76	GOOD VIBRATIONS (re-issue) *Capitol CL 15875*	18	7
10 Jul 76	ROCK AND ROLL MUSIC *Reprise K 14440*	36	4
31 Mar 79	HERE COMES THE NIGHT *Caribou CRB 7204*	37	8
16 Jun 79 ●	LADY LYNDA *Caribou CRB 7427*	6	11
29 Sep 79	SUMAHAMA *Caribou CRB 7846*	45	4
29 Aug 81	BEACH BOYS MEDLEY *Capitol CL 213*	47	4
22 Aug 87 ●	WIPEOUT *Urban URB 5* [1]	2	12
19 Nov 88	KOKOMO *Elektra EKR 85* ▲	25	9
2 Jun 90	WOULDN'T IT BE NICE *Capitol CL 579*	58	1
29 Jun 91	DO IT AGAIN (re-issue) *Capitol EMCT 1*	61	4
2 Mar 96	FUN FUN FUN *PolyGram TV 5762972* [2]	24	4

[1] Fat Boys and the Beach Boys [2] Status Quo with the Beach Boys

Walter BEASLEY US, male vocalist (3 WEEKS)

		pos/wks
23 Jan 88	I'M SO HAPPY *Urban URB 14*	70 3

BEASTIE BOYS US, male rap group (59 WEEKS)

		pos/wks
28 Feb 87	(YOU GOTTA) FIGHT FOR YOUR RIGHT (TO PARTY) *Def Jam 650418 7*	11 11
30 May 87	NO SLEEP TILL BROOKLYN *Def Jam BEAST 1*	14 7
18 Jul 87 ●	SHE'S ON IT *Def Jam BEAST 2*	10 8
3 Oct 87	GIRLS / SHE'S CRAFTY *Def Jam BEAST 3*	34 4
11 Apr 92	PASS THE MIC *Capitol 12CL 653*	47 2
4 Jul 92	FROZEN METAL HEAD (EP) *Capitol 12CL 665*	55 1
9 Jul 94	GET IT TOGETHER / SABOTAGE *Capitol CDCL 716*	19 4
26 Nov 94	SURE SHOT *Capitol CDCL 726*	27 4
4 Jul 98 ●	INTERGALACTIC *Grand Royal CDCL 803*	5 7
7 Nov 98	BODY MOVIN' (re) *Grand Royal CDCL 809*	15 5
29 May 99	REMOTE CONTROL / 3 MCS & 1 DJ *Grand Royal CDCL 812*	21 3
18 Dec 99	ALIVE *Grand Royal CDCL 818*	28 4

Tracks on Frozen Metal Head (EP): Jimmy James / Jimmy James (Original) / Drinkin' Wine / The Blue Nun

BEAT 347 *Top 500* Birmingham, UK-based band that married ska and new wave influences, formed 1978: Dave Wakeling (v/g), Ranking Roger (v), Andy Cox (g) and David Steele (b). After 1983 break-up, former two launched General Public and latter pair formed Fine Young Cannibals (92 WEEKS)

		pos/wks
8 Dec 79 ●	TEARS OF A CLOWN / RANKING FULL STOP *2 Tone CHSTT 6*	6 11
23 Feb 80 ●	HANDS OFF – SHE'S MINE *Go Feet FEET 1*	9 9
3 May 80 ●	MIRROR IN THE BATHROOM *Go Feet FEET 2*	4 9
16 Aug 80	BEST FRIEND / STAND DOWN MARGARET (DUB) *Go Feet FEET 3*	22 9
13 Dec 80 ●	TOO NICE TO TALK TO *Go Feet FEET 4*	7 11
18 Apr 81	DROWNING / ALL OUT TO GET YOU *Go Feet FEET 6*	22 8
20 Jun 81	DOORS OF YOUR HEART *Go Feet FEET 9*	33 6
5 Dec 81	HIT IT *Go Feet FEET 11*	70 2
17 Apr 82	SAVE IT FOR LATER *Go Feet FEET 333*	47 4
18 Sep 82	JEANETTE *Go Feet FEET 15*	45 3
4 Dec 82	I CONFESS *Go Feet FEET 16*	54 3
30 Apr 83 ●	CAN'T GET USED TO LOSING YOU *Go Feet FEET 17*	3 11
2 Jul 83	ACKEE 1-2-3 *Go Feet FEET 18*	54 4
27 Jan 96	MIRROR IN THE BATHROOM (re-mix) *Go Feet 74321232062*	44 2

THE BEAT BOYS – See Gene VINCENT

BEAT RENEGADES
UK, male production duo – Ian Bland and Paul Fitzpatrick (1 WEEK) pos/wks

19 May 01	AUTOMATIK *Slinky Music SLINKY 014CD*	73	1

See also RED; DREAM FREQUENCY

BEAT SYSTEM UK, male vocal / instrumental group (3 WEEKS) pos/wks

3 Mar 90	WALK ON THE WILD SIDE *Fourth & Broadway BRW 163*	63	2
18 Sep 93	TO A BRIGHTER DAY (O' HAPPY DAY) *ffrr FCD 217*	70	1

BEATCHUGGERS featuring Eric CLAPTON Denmark, male producer – Michael Linde and UK, male vocalist / instrumentalist (2 WEEKS) pos/wks

18 Nov 00	FOREVER MAN (HOW MANY TIMES) *ffrr FCD 386*	26	2

BEATINGS UK, male vocal / instrumental group (1 WEEK) pos/wks

26 Oct 02	BAD FEELING *Fantastic Plastic FPS 034*	68	1

BEATLES 9 *Top 500*
World's most successful group. John Lennon (v/g) b. 9 Oct 1940, Liverpool, d. 8 Dec 1980, New York, Paul McCartney (v/b) b. 18 Jun 1942, Liverpool, George Harrison (v/g) b. 24 Feb 1943, Liverpool, d. 29 Nov 2001, Ringo Starr (Richard Starkey) (v/d) b. 7 Jul 1940, Liverpool. This legendary group changed the face of popular music. Achievements include most No.1 singles and albums in the UK and US. Within three months of their US chart debut in 1964, they held all the Top 5 single chart places, had a record 14 simultaneous entries in Billboard Top 100 and had the two top-selling albums. During those 12 weeks they earned six gold singles and sold four million albums. Their album 'Sgt. Pepper's Lonely Hearts Club Band' is the biggest seller ever in the UK, and the group is the No.1 all-time US best-selling album act. They split in 1970, since when Lennon, McCartney and Harrison have all had No.1 singles. (Starr reached No.2) In 1996, double album 'Anthology' sold 10 million worldwide in only four weeks. 2000's '1' collection is the world's fastest selling album ever with 23.5 million copies sold in the first month and was the top-selling album of 2000 in the UK. The Beatles, who were made MBEs in 1965, have sold an estimated one billion records. Best-selling single in UK: 'She Loves You' 1,890,000 (456 WEEKS) pos/wks

Date	Title	Pos	Wks
11 Oct 62 ●	LOVE ME DO (2re) *Parlophone R 4949* ▲	4	26
17 Jan 63 ●	PLEASE PLEASE ME (re) *Parlophone R 4983*	2	22
18 Apr 63 ★	FROM ME TO YOU (re) *Parlophone R 5015*	1	25
6 Jun 63	MY BONNIE *Polydor NH 66833* [1]	48	1
29 Aug 63 ★	SHE LOVES YOU (2re) *Parlophone R 5055* ◆ ▲	1	36
5 Dec 63 ★	I WANT TO HOLD YOUR HAND (2re) *Parlophone R 5084* ◆ ▲	1	24
26 Mar 64 ★	CAN'T BUY ME LOVE (2re) *Parlophone R 5114* ◆ ▲	1	17
11 Jun 64	AIN'T SHE SWEET *Polydor 52 317*	29	6
16 Jul 64 ★	A HARD DAY'S NIGHT *Parlophone R 5160* ▲	1	15
3 Dec 64 ★	I FEEL FINE (re) *Parlophone R 5200* ◆ ▲	1	14
15 Apr 65 ★	TICKET TO RIDE (re) *Parlophone R 5265* ▲	1	14
29 Jul 65 ★	HELP! (re) *Parlophone R 5305* ▲	1	17
9 Dec 65 ★	DAY TRIPPER / WE CAN WORK IT OUT *Parlophone R 5389* ◆ ▲	1	12
16 Jun 66 ★	PAPERBACK WRITER (re) *Parlophone R 5452* ▲	1	16
11 Aug 66 ★	YELLOW SUBMARINE / ELEANOR RIGBY (re) *Parlophone R 5493*	1	14
23 Feb 67 ●	STRAWBERRY FIELDS FOREVER (re-entry) *Parlophone R 5570* ▲	2	16
12 Jul 67 ★	ALL YOU NEED IS LOVE (re) *Parlophone R 5620* ▲	1	16
29 Nov 67 ★	HELLO, GOODBYE (re) *Parlophone R 5655* ▲	1	13
13 Dec 67 ●	MAGICAL MYSTERY TOUR (DOUBLE EP) *Parlophone SMMT/MMT 1*	2	12
20 Mar 68 ●	LADY MADONNA (re) *Parlophone R 5675*	1	9
4 Sep 68 ★	HEY JUDE (2re) *Apple R 5722* ▲	1	25
23 Apr 69 ★	GET BACK (2re) *Apple R 5777* [2] ■ ▲	1	23
4 Jun 69 ★	THE BALLAD OF JOHN AND YOKO *Apple R 5786*	1	14
8 Nov 69 ●	SOMETHING / COME TOGETHER *Apple R 5814* ▲	4	12
14 Mar 70 ●	LET IT BE (re) *Apple R 5833* ▲	2	10
13 Mar 76 ●	YESTERDAY *Apple R 6013* ▲	8	7
10 Jul 76	BACK IN THE U.S.S.R. *Parlophone R 6016*	19	6
7 Oct 78	SGT. PEPPER'S LONELY HEARTS CLUB BAND – WITH A LITTLE HELP FROM MY FRIENDS *Parlophone R 6022*	63	3
5 Jun 82 ●	BEATLES MOVIE MEDLEY *Parlophone R 6055*	10	9

1 Apr 95	●	BABY IT'S YOU (re) *Apple CDR 6406*	7	7
16 Dec 95	●	FREE AS A BIRD *Apple CDR 6422*	2	8
16 Mar 96	●	REAL LOVE *Apple CDR 6425*	4	7

[1] Tony Sheridan and The Beatles [2] Beatles with Billy Preston

Many Beatles hits re-entered the charts including a large number on the original Parlophone label between 1982 and 1992. The only hit to re-enter inside the Top 20 was 'Hey Jude' on its first re-entry at No.12 in 1976. Tracks on Magical Mystery Tour (EP): Magical Mystery Tour / Your Mother Should Know / I Am the Walrus / Fool on the Hill / Flying / Blue Jay Way

See also Paul McCARTNEY; Ringo STARR; John LENNON; George HARRISON

BEATMASTERS *UK, male / female production group (47 WEEKS)* pos/wks

9 Jan 88	●	ROK DA HOUSE *Rhythm King LEFT 11* [1]	5	11
24 Sep 88		BURN IT UP *Rhythm King LEFT 27* [2]	14	10
22 Apr 89	●	WHO'S IN THE HOUSE *Rhythm King LEFT 31* [3]	8	9
12 Aug 89	●	HEY DJ - I CAN'T DANCE (TO THAT MUSIC YOU'RE PLAYING) / SKA TRAIN *Rhythm King LEFT 34* [4]	7	11
2 Dec 89		WARM LOVE *Rhythm King LEFT 37* [5]	51	2
21 Sep 91		BOULEVARD OF BROKEN DREAMS *Rhythm King 6573617*	62	1
16 May 92		DUNNO WHAT IT IS (ABOUT YOU) *Rhythm King 6580017* [6]	43	3

[1] Beatmasters featuring the Cookie Crew [2] Beatmasters with PP Arnold [3] The Beatmasters with Merlin [4] Beatmasters featuring Betty Boo [5] Beatmasters featuring Claudia Fontaine [6] Beatmasters featuring Elaine Vassell

BEATNUTS *US, male rap duo (1 WEEK)* pos/wks

| 14 Jul 01 | | NO ESCAPIN' THIS *Epic 6713412* | 47 | 1 |

BEATRICE – See Mike KOGLIN

BEATS INTERNATIONAL *UK, male / female vocal / instrumental group, leader – Norman Cook (30 WEEKS)* pos/wks

10 Feb 90	★	DUB BE GOOD TO ME *Go.Beat GOD 39* [1]	1	13
12 May 90	●	WON'T TALK ABOUT IT *Go.Beat GOD 43*	9	7
15 Sep 90		BURUNDI BLUES *Go.Beat GOD 45*	51	3
2 Mar 91		ECHO CHAMBER *Go.Beat GOD 51*	60	2
21 Sep 91		THE SUN DOESN'T SHINE *Go.Beat GOD 59*	66	2
23 Nov 91		IN THE GHETTO *Go.Beat GOD 64*	44	3

[1] Beats International featuring Lindy Layton

See also FREAKPOWER; PIZZAMAN; Norman COOK; FATBOY SLIM; MIGHTY DUB KATZ; HOUSEMARTINS

BEAUTIFUL PEOPLE *UK, male instrumental / production group (1 WEEK)* pos/wks

| 28 May 94 | | IF 60S WERE 90S *Essential ESSX 2037* | 74 | 1 |

BEAUTIFUL SOUTH 147 Top 500

Ex-Housemartins Paul Heaton (v/g) and Dave Hemingway (v) formed the band that featured Briana Corrigan (v) (replaced by Jacqui Abbot 1994-2000). Heaton and Dave Rotheray (g) write the witty and ironic songs (151 WEEKS) pos/wks

3 Jun 89	●	SONG FOR WHOEVER *Go! Discs GOD 32*	2	11
23 Sep 89	●	YOU KEEP IT ALL IN *Go! Discs GOD 35*	8	8
2 Dec 89		I'LL SAIL THIS SHIP ALONE *Go! Discs GOD 38*	31	8
6 Oct 90	★	A LITTLE TIME *Go! Discs GOD 47*	1	14
8 Dec 90		MY BOOK *Go! Discs GOD 48*	43	6
16 Mar 91		LET LOVE SPEAK UP ITSELF *Go! Discs GOD 53*	51	2
11 Jan 92		OLD RED EYES IS BACK *Go! Discs GOD 66*	22	6
14 Mar 92		WE ARE EACH OTHER *Go! Discs GOD 71*	30	3
13 Jun 92		BELL BOTTOMED TEAR *Go! Discs GOD 78*	16	5
26 Sep 92		36D *Go! Discs GOD 88*	46	2
12 Mar 94		GOOD AS GOLD *Go! Discs GODCD 110*	23	5
4 Jun 94		EVERYBODY'S TALKIN' *Go! Discs GODCD 113*	12	8
3 Sep 94		PRETTIEST EYES *Go! Discs GODCD 119*	37	3
12 Nov 94		ONE LAST LOVE SONG *Go! Discs GODCD 122*	14	5
18 Nov 95		PRETENDERS TO THE THRONE *Go! Discs GODCD 134*	18	4
12 Oct 96	●	ROTTERDAM *Go! Discs GODCD 155*	5	9
14 Dec 96	●	DON'T MARRY HER *Go! Discs GODCD 158*	8	10
29 Mar 97		BLACKBIRD ON THE WIRE *Go! Discs 5821252*	23	5
5 Jul 97		LIARS' BAR *Go! Discs 5822492*	43	1

3 Oct 98	●	PERFECT 10 *Go! Discs 5664832*	2	14
19 Dec 98		DUMB (re) *Go! Discs 5667532*	16	8
20 Mar 99		HOW LONG'S A TEAR TAKE TO DRY? *Go! Discs 8708212*	12	6
10 Jul 99		THE TABLE *Go! Discs 5621652*	47	2
7 Oct 00		CLOSER THAN MOST *Go! Discs / Mercury 5629672*	22	4
23 Dec 00		THE RIVER / JUST CHECKIN' *Go! Discs / Mercury 5727552*	59	1
17 Nov 01		THE ROOT OF ALL EVIL *Go! Discs / Mercury 5888702*	50	1

BEAVIS and BUTT-HEAD – See CHER

Gilbert BECAUD *France, male vocalist, d. 18 Dec 2001 (12 WEEKS)* pos/wks

| 29 Mar 75 | ● | A LITTLE LOVE AND UNDERSTANDING *Decca F 13537* | 10 | 12 |

BECK *US, male vocalist – David Campbell (27 WEEKS)* pos/wks

5 Mar 94		LOSER *Geffen GFSTD 67*	15	6
29 Jun 96		WHERE IT'S AT *Geffen GFSTD 22156*	35	2
16 Nov 96		DEVIL'S HAIRCUT *Geffen GFSTD 22183*	22	2
8 Mar 97		THE NEW POLLUTION *Geffen GFSTD 22205*	14	5
24 May 97		SISSYNECK *Geffen GFSTD 22253*	30	2
8 Nov 97		DEADWEIGHT *Geffen GFSTD 22293*	23	3
19 Dec 98		TROPICALIA *Geffen GFSTD 22365*	39	2
20 Nov 99		SEXX LAWS *Geffen 4971812*	27	3
8 Apr 00		MIXED BIZNESS *Geffen 4973002*	34	2

Jeff BECK *UK, male vocalist / instrumentalist – guitar (57 WEEKS)* pos/wks

23 Mar 67		HI-HO SILVER LINING *Columbia DB 8151*	14	14
2 Aug 67		TALLYMAN *Columbia DB 8227*	30	3
28 Feb 68		LOVE IS BLUE (L'AMOUR EST BLEU) *Columbia DB 8359*	23	7
9 Jul 69		GOO GOO BARABAJAGAL (LOVE IS HOT) *Pye 7N 17778* [1]	12	9
4 Nov 72		HI-HO SILVER LINING (re-issue) (re) *RAK RR 3*	17	15
5 May 73		I'VE BEEN DRINKING *RAK RR 4* [2]	27	6
7 Mar 92		PEOPLE GET READY *Epic 6577567* [2]	49	3

[1] Donovan with the Jeff Beck Group [2] Jeff Beck and Rod Stewart

Robin BECK *US, female vocalist (13 WEEKS)* pos/wks

| 22 Oct 88 | ★ | THE FIRST TIME *Mercury MER 270* | 1 | 13 |

Peter BECKETT – See Barry GRAY ORCHESTRA

Victoria BECKHAM *UK, female vocalist (38 WEEKS)* pos/wks

26 Aug 00	●	OUT OF YOUR MIND (re) *Nulife 74321782942* [1]	2	20
29 Sep 01	●	NOT SUCH AN INNOCENT GIRL (2re) *Virgin VSCDT 1816*	6	11
23 Feb 02	●	A MIND OF ITS OWN *Virgin VSCDT 1824*	6	7

[1] True Steppers and Dane Bowers featuring Victoria Beckham

See also SPICE GIRLS

BEDAZZLED *UK, male vocal / instrumental group (1 WEEK)* pos/wks

| 4 Jul 92 | | SUMMER SONG *Columbia 6581627* | 73 | 1 |

Daniel BEDINGFIELD

New Zealand, male vocalist / producer (30 WEEKS) pos/wks

8 Dec 01	★	GOTTA GET THRU THIS *Relentless RELENT 27CD* ■	1	18
24 Aug 02	●	JAMES DEAN (I WANNA KNOW) *Polydor 5709342*	4	8
7 Dec 02	★	IF YOU'RE NOT THE ONE *Polydor 0658632* ■	1	4+

BEDLAM *UK, male DJ / production duo – Alan Thomson and Richard 'Diddy' Dearlove (1 WEEK)* pos/wks

| 6 Feb 99 | | DA-FORCE *Playola 0091695 PLA* | 68 | 1 |

See also DIDDY

BEDLAM AGO GO *UK, male vocal / instrumental group (1 WEEK)* pos/wks

| 4 Apr 98 | | SEASON NO.5 *Sony S2 BDLM 2CD* | 57 | 1 |

BEDROCK *UK, male / female vocal / instrumental duo – John Digweed and Nick Muir (9 WEEKS)* pos/wks

| 1 Jun 96 | | FOR WHAT YOU DREAM OF *Stress CDSTR 23* [1] | 25 | 3 |

Re-entries are listed as (re), (2re), (3re), etc which signifies that the hit re-entered the chart once, twice or three times, etc

Date	Title	Pos	Wks
12 Jul 97	SET IN STONE / FORBIDDEN ZONE *Stress CDSTR 80*	71	1
6 Nov 99	HEAVEN SCENT *Bedrock BEDRCDS 001*	35	3
8 Jul 00	VOICES *Bedrock BEDRCDS 005*	44	2

[1] Bedrock featuring KYO

BEDROCKS UK, male vocal / instrumental group (7 WEEKS)

Date	Title	Pos	Wks
18 Dec 68	OB-LA-DI, OB-LA-DA *Columbia DB 8516*	20	7

Celi BEE and the BUZZY BUNCH
US, male / female vocal / instrumental group (1 WEEK)

Date	Title	Pos	Wks
17 Jun 78	HOLD YOUR HORSES, BABE *TK TKR 6032*	72	1

BEE GEES 18 Top 500
All-time top family recording act, who are members of the exclusive 100 million-plus sales club, are Isle of Man, UK, born and Australian raised Barry, Robin and Maurice Gibb (d. 12 Jan 2003). As composers, they have penned hits for many top acts and had 10 UK No.1s. In 1978 they wrote four consecutive US chart-toppers (three of which they also produced). Their 'Saturday Night Fever' album is the world's biggest selling soundtrack and they were first group to have UK Top 20s in five decades. Distinctive trio has won countless trophies including the World Music Legend Award (1997) and Brits Outstanding Contribution to British Music (1997). (354 WEEKS)

Date	Title	Pos	Wks
27 Apr 67	NEW YORK MINING DISASTER 1941 *Polydor 56 161*	12	10
12 Jul 67	TO LOVE SOMEBODY (re) *Polydor 56 178*	41	5
20 Sep 67 ★	(THE NIGHT THE LIGHTS WENT OUT IN) MASSACHUSETTS *Polydor 56 192*	1	17
22 Nov 67 ●	WORLD *Polydor 56 220*	9	16
31 Jan 68 ●	WORDS *Polydor 56 229*	8	10
27 Mar 68	JUMBO / THE SINGER SANG HIS SONG *Polydor 56 242*	25	7
7 Aug 68 ●	I'VE GOTTA GET A MESSAGE TO YOU *Polydor 56 273*	1	15
19 Feb 69 ●	FIRST OF MAY *Polydor 56 304*	6	11
4 Jun 69	TOMORROW, TOMORROW *Polydor 56 331*	23	8
16 Aug 69 ●	DON'T FORGET TO REMEMBER *Polydor 56 343*	2	15
28 Mar 70	I.O.I.O. *Polydor 56 377*	49	1
5 Dec 70	LONELY DAYS *Polydor 2001 104*	33	9
29 Jan 72	MY WORLD *Polydor 2058 185*	16	9
22 Jul 72 ●	RUN TO ME *Polydor 2058 255*	9	10
28 Jun 75 ●	JIVE TALKIN' *RSO 2090 160* ▲	5	11
31 Jul 76 ●	YOU SHOULD BE DANCING *RSO 2090 195* ▲	5	10
13 Nov 76	LOVE SO RIGHT *RSO 2090 207*	41	4
29 Oct 77 ●	HOW DEEP IS YOUR LOVE *RSO 2090 259* ▲	3	15
4 Feb 78 ●	STAYIN' ALIVE (re) *RSO 2090 267* ▲	4	18
15 Apr 78 ★	NIGHT FEVER *RSO 002* ▲	1	13
25 Nov 78 ●	TOO MUCH HEAVEN *RSO 25* ▲	3	13
17 Feb 79 ★	TRAGEDY *RSO 27* ▲	1	10
14 Apr 79	LOVE YOU INSIDE OUT *RSO 31* ▲	13	9
5 Jan 80	SPIRITS (HAVING FLOWN) *RSO 52*	16	7
17 Sep 83	SOMEONE BELONGING TO SOMEONE *RSO 96*	49	4
26 Sep 87 ★	YOU WIN AGAIN *Warner Bros. W 8351*	1	15
12 Dec 87	E.S.P. *Warner Bros. W 8139*	51	5
15 Apr 89	ORDINARY LIVES *Warner Bros. W 7523*	54	3
24 Jun 89	ONE *Warner Bros. W 2916*	71	1
2 Mar 91 ●	SECRET LOVE *Warner Bros. W 0014*	5	11
21 Aug 93	PAYING THE PRICE OF LOVE *Polydor PZCD 284*	23	5
27 Nov 93 ●	FOR WHOM THE BELL TOLLS *Polydor PZCD 299*	4	14
16 Apr 94	HOW TO FALL IN LOVE PART 1 *Polydor PZDD 311*	30	4
1 Mar 97 ●	ALONE *Polydor 5735272*	5	9
21 Jun 97	I COULD NOT LOVE YOU MORE *Polydor 5712232*	14	3
8 Nov 97	STILL WATERS (RUN DEEP) *Polydor 5718892*	18	3
18 Jul 98 ●	IMMORTALITY *Epic 6661682* [1]	5	12
7 Apr 01	THIS IS WHERE I CAME IN *Polydor 5879772*	18	5

[1] Celine Dion with special guests The Bee Gees

See also Robin GIBB; Barry GIBB

BEENIE MAN
Jamaica, male vocalist / toaster / rapper – Moses David (30 WEEKS)

Date	Title	Pos	Wks
20 Sep 97	DANCEHALL QUEEN *Island Jamaica IJCD 2018* [1]	70	1
7 Mar 98 ●	WHO AM I *Greensleeves GRECD 588*	10	5
8 Aug 98	FOUNDATION *Shocking Vibes SVJCDS1*	69	1
4 Mar 00 ●	MONEY *Parlophone Rhythm Series CDRHYTHM 27* [2]	5	9

Date	Title	Pos	Wks
24 Mar 01	GIRLS DEM SUGAR *Virgin VUSCD 173* [3]	13	5
28 Sep 02 ●	FEEL IT BOY (re) *Virgin VUSCD 258* [4]	9	7
14 Dec 02	DIRTY HARRY'S REVENGE *Kaos KAOS 004* [5]	50	2

[1] Chevelle Franklyn / Beenie Man [2] Jamelia featuring Beenie Man [3] Beenie Man featuring Mya [4] Beenie Man featuring Janet [5] Adam F featuring Beenie Man

Lou BEGA Germany, male vocalist – David Lubega (21 WEEKS)

Date	Title	Pos	Wks
7 Aug 99	MAMBO NO.5 (A LITTLE BIT OF ...) (import) *Ariola 74321658012*	31	4
4 Sep 99 ★	MAMBO NO.5 (A LITTLE BIT OF ...) *RCA 74321696722* ■	1	15
18 Dec 99	I GOT A GIRL *RCA 74321720642*	55	2

BEGGAR and CO UK, male vocal / instrumental group (15 WEEKS)

Date	Title	Pos	Wks
7 Feb 81	(SOMEBODY) HELP ME OUT *Ensign ENY 201*	15	10
12 Sep 81	MULE (CHANT NO.2) *RCA 130*	37	5

BEGINERZ
UK, male production duo – Ibi Tijani and Euen MacNeil (3 WEEKS)

Date	Title	Pos	Wks
13 Jul 02	RECKLESS GIRL *Cheeky / Arista 74321942232*	28	3

BEGINNING OF THE END
US, male vocal / instrumental group (6 WEEKS)

Date	Title	Pos	Wks
23 Feb 74	FUNKY NASSAU *Atlantic K 10021*	31	6

BEIJING SPRING UK, female vocal duo (5 WEEKS)

Date	Title	Pos	Wks
23 Jan 93	I WANNA BE IN LOVE AGAIN *MCA MCSTD 1709*	43	3
8 May 93	SUMMERLANDS *MCA MCSTD 1761*	53	2

BEL AMOUR France, male / female production / vocal trio (3 WEEKS)

Date	Title	Pos	Wks
12 May 01	BEL AMOUR *Credence CDCRED 010*	23	3

BEL CANTO UK, male vocal / instrumental group (1 WEEK)

Date	Title	Pos	Wks
14 Oct 95	WE'VE GOT TO WORK IT OUT *Good Groove CDGG 2*	65	1

Harry BELAFONTE 379 Top 500
Singer / actor, civil rights campaigner and driving force behind USA for Africa b. 1 Mar 1927, New York, US. Started transatlantic calypso craze in 1957 when his LP 'Calypso' topped the US chart for 31 weeks. Became Unicef goodwill ambassador in 1987 (87 WEEKS)

Date	Title	Pos	Wks
1 Mar 57 ●	BANANA BOAT SONG (DAY-O) *HMV POP 308* [1]	2	18
14 Jun 57 ●	ISLAND IN THE SUN *RCA 1007*	3	25
6 Sep 57	SCARLET RIBBONS *HMV POP 360* [2]	18	6
1 Nov 57 ★	MARY'S BOY CHILD (2re) *RCA 1022* ◆	1	19
22 Aug 58	LITTLE BERNADETTE *RCA 1072* [3]	16	7
12 Dec 58	THE SON OF MARY *RCA 1084*	18	4
21 Sep 61	THERE'S A HOLE IN MY BUCKET (re) *RCA 1247* [4]	32	8

[1] Harry Belafonte with Tony Scott's Orchestra and Chorus and Millard Thomas, Guitar [2] Harry Belafonte and Millard Thomas [3] Belafonte [4] Harry Belafonte and Odetta

'Mary's Boy Child' re-entered twice peaking at No.10 in 1958 and at No.30 in 1959

Archie BELL and the DRELLS
US, male vocal / instrumental group (33 WEEKS)

Date	Title	Pos	Wks
7 Oct 72	HERE I GO AGAIN *Atlantic K 10210*	11	10
27 Jan 73	(THERE'S GONNA BE A) SHOWDOWN *Atlantic K 10263*	36	5
8 May 76	THE SOUL CITY WALK *Philadelphia International PIR 4250*	13	10
11 Jun 77	EVERYBODY HAVE A GOOD TIME *Philadelphia International PIR 5179*	43	4
28 Jun 86	DON'T LET LOVE GET YOU DOWN *Portrait A 7254*	49	4

Freddie BELL and the BELLBOYS
US, male vocal / instrumental group (10 WEEKS)

Date	Title	Pos	Wks
28 Sep 56 ●	GIDDY-UP-A DING DONG *Mercury MT 122*	4	10

Maggie BELL UK, female vocalist (12 WEEKS)

Date	Title	Pos	Wks
15 Apr 78	HAZELL (re) *Swansong SSK 19412*	37	4

GOOD VIBRATIONS

■ The Beach Boys' 1966 hit 'Good Vibrations' has long been recognised as one of pop's finest moments. Brian Wilson, one of three Wilson brothers within the group, wrote the major part of The Beach Boys' best work – a lengthy series of classic summer anthems including 'Fun, Fun, Fun', 'I Get Around', 'Help Me, Rhonda' and 'California Girls'. Brian had long since ceased touring with the band due to a fear of flying, and preferred to spend his time writing and recording. The major part of 'Good Vibrations' was written and performed by Brian and studio session musicians, without the participation of the other Beach Boys until the final vocals were added. Wilson was fresh from his work on the group's Pet Sounds album, most of which he'd also recorded himself and presented to the group

when they returned from a tour. Pet Sounds was a radical change of direction from the Beach Boys' usual material based around cars, girls and surfing, and some members of the group, Mike Love in particular, didn't much like the material. Capitol Records, the Beach Boys' record company, didn't like it much either, and spent little time and money on promotion, preferring to release yet another best-of collection instead.

After the relatively low sales of Pet Sounds (which in retrospect was down to Capitol's lack of interest in America –

The Brian-less Beach Boys with 'Good Vibrations' co-writer Mike Love far right

the album was considerably better received and promoted in England), Capitol Records must have been over the moon when it finally received 'Good Vibrations'. Although it was again very different from previous Beach Boys material, anyone with a pair of ears could hear that it was a guaranteed No.1. What made 'Good Vibrations' particularly different was that rather than being one straightforward song, it was a collection of different segments that Brian Wilson had recorded over a period of several months in four different studios, using more than 90 hours of tape at a cost of around $50,000.

The recording also featured a rather unusual electronic effect called a theremin, which exuded an eerie sound and gave the recording a somewhat heavenly aspect. Invented by Franco-Russian Leon Theremin in 1920, the instrument was much featured in horror movies, and during the 1960s Dr Robert Moog had been custom-building theremins before he began working full-time on his own highly successful Moog synthesizer. The person who played the theremin, hired for the recording session from the UCLA music programme, had never even heard of The Beach Boys. Other musicians on

- ★ **ARTIST:** Beach Boys

- ★ **LABEL:** Capitol

- ★ **WRITERS:** Brian Wilson and Mike Love

- ★ **PRODUCER:** Brian Wilson

■ TO THINK THAT INVISIBLE FEELINGS, INVISIBLE VIBRATIONS EXISTED, SCARED ME TO DEATH. BUT SHE [WILSON'S MOTHER] TALKED ABOUT HOW DOGS COULD PICK UP VIBRATIONS FROM PEOPLE; THEY WOULD BARK AT SOME PEOPLE AND NOT BARK AT OTHERS. AND SO IT CAME ABOUT THAT WE TALKED ABOUT GOOD VIBRATIONS ■ BRIAN WILSON, TALKING TO ROLLING STONE MAGAZINE

the track, which was recorded at Western, RCA, Goldstar and Columbia studios, included Glen Campbell, Duane Eddy's mentor, Al Casey, and noted jazz guitarist Barney Kessell.

When Brian Wilson finally edited his 90 hours of recording down to a few minutes, Beach Boys vocalist Mike Love came up with a suitable lyric, after which Brian Wilson edited, remixed and edited some more until he had four different versions, one of which he dispatched to Capitol Records for release. The very next day he changed his mind, recalling the tape, and remixed it one more time until he was finally satisfied. The resulting three minutes and 35 seconds were simply stunning, as all who first heard 'Good Vibrations' in the autumn of 1966 will agree. Remarkably, and despite the acclaim that 'Good Vibrations' has received over the years, Brian Wilson, while modestly maintaining that "it's a good record", still doesn't think that it's anywhere near as good as his own personal favourite, the Ronettes' Phil Spector-produced 'Be My Baby'. Perhaps we should be the judge of that.

■ Tony Burton

| 17 Oct 81 | HOLD ME *Swansong BAM 1* [1] | 11 | 8 |

[1] B A Robertson and Maggie Bell

William BELL *US, male vocalist – William Yarborough (22 WEEKS)* pos/wks
29 May 68	A TRIBUTE TO A KING *Stax 601 038*	31	7
20 Nov 68 ●	PRIVATE NUMBER *Stax 101* [1]	8	14
26 Apr 86	HEADLINE NEWS *Absolute LUTE 1*	70	1

[1] Judy Clay and William Bell

BELL and JAMES *US, male vocal duo (3 WEEKS)* pos/wks
| 31 Mar 79 | LIVIN' IT UP (FRIDAY NIGHT) (re) *A&M AMS 7424* | 59 | 3 |

BELL & SPURLING
UK, male vocal duo – Martin Bellamy and John Spurling (10 WEEKS) pos/wks
| 13 Oct 01 ● | SVEN SVEN SVEN *Eternal WEA 336CD* | 7 | 6 |
| 8 Jun 02 | GOLDENBALLS (MR BECKHAM TO YOU) *Eternal WEA 350CD* | 25 | 4 |

BELL BIV DEVOE *US, male vocal group (29 WEEKS)* pos/wks
30 Jun 90	POISON *MCA MCA 1414*	19	11
22 Sep 90	DO ME *MCA MCA 1440*	56	3
15 Aug 92 ●	THE BEST THINGS IN LIFE ARE FREE *Perspective PERSS 7400* [1]	2	13
9 Oct 93	SOMETHING IN YOUR EYES *MCA MCSTD 1934*	60	2

[1] Luther Vandross and Janet Jackson with special guests BBD and Ralph Tresvant

BELL BOOK & CANDLE
Germany, male / female vocal / instrumental group (1 WEEK) pos/wks
| 17 Oct 98 | RESCUE ME *Logic 74321616882* | 63 | 1 |

BELLAMY BROTHERS
US, male vocal duo – Howard and David Bellamy (29 WEEKS) pos/wks
17 Apr 76 ●	LET YOUR LOVE FLOW *Warner Bros. / Curb K 16690* ▲	7	12
21 Aug 76	SATIN SHEETS *Warner Bros. / Curb K 16775*	43	3
11 Aug 79 ●	IF I SAID YOU HAVE A BEAUTIFUL BODY WOULD YOU HOLD IT AGAINST ME *Warner Bros. / Curb K 17405*	3	14

BELLATRIX *Iceland, male / female vocal / instrumental group (1 WK)* pos/wks
| 16 Sep 00 | JEDI WANNABE *Fierce Panda NING 101CD* | 65 | 1 |

BELLBOYS – *See Freddie BELL and the BELLBOYS*

Regina BELLE *US, female vocalist (13 WEEKS)* pos/wks
| 21 Oct 89 | GOOD LOVIN' *CBS 655230* | 73 | 1 |
| 11 Dec 93 | A WHOLE NEW WORLD (ALADDIN'S THEME) *Columbia 6599002* [1] ▲ | 12 | 12 |

BELLE & SEBASTIAN
UK, male / female vocal / instrumental group (12 WEEKS) pos/wks
24 May 97	DOG ON WHEELS *Jeepster JPRCDS 001*	59	1
9 Aug 97	LAZY LINE PAINTER JANE *Jeepster JPRCDS 002*	41	2
25 Oct 97	3... 6... 9 SECONDS OF LIGHT (EP) *Jeepster JPRCDS 003*	32	2
3 Jun 00	LEGAL MAN *Jeepster JPRCD 018*	15	3
30 Jun 01	JONATHAN DAVID *Jeepster JPRCDS 022*	31	2
8 Dec 01	I'M WAKING UP TO US *Jeepster JPRCDS 023*	39	2

Tracks on 3... 6... 9 Seconds of Light (EP): A Century of Fakers / Le Pastie de la Bourgeoisie / Beautiful / Put the Book Back on the Shelf

BELLE and the DEVOTIONS *UK, female vocal group (8 WEEKS)* pos/wks
| 21 Apr 84 | LOVE GAMES *CBS A 4332* | 11 | 8 |

[1] Regina Belle and Peabo Bryson

BELLE STARS *UK, female vocal / instrumental group (42 WEEKS)* pos/wks
5 Jun 82	IKO IKO *Stiff BUY 150*	35	6
17 Jul 82	THE CLAPPING SONG *Stiff BUY 155*	11	9
16 Oct 82	MOCKINGBIRD *Stiff BUY 159*	51	3

15 Jan 83 ●	SIGN OF THE TIMES *Stiff BUY 167*	3	11
16 Apr 83	SWEET MEMORY *Stiff BUY 174*	22	9
13 Aug 83	INDIAN SUMMER *Stiff BUY 185*	52	3
14 Jul 84	80s ROMANCE *Stiff BUY 200*	71	1

BELLEFIRE *Ireland, female vocal group (8 WEEKS)* pos/wks
| 14 Jul 01 | PERFECT BLISS *Virgin VSCDT 1807* | 18 | 4 |
| 18 May 02 | ALL I WANT IS YOU *Virgin VSCDT 1820* | 18 | 4 |

BELLINI *Germany, male vocal / production group (7 WEEKS)* pos/wks
| 27 Sep 97 ● | SAMBA DE JANEIRO *Virgin DINSD 165* | 8 | 7 |

BELLRAYS
US, male / female vocal / instrumental group (1 WEEK) pos/wks
| 20 Jul 02 | THEY GLUED YOUR HEAD ON UPSIDE DOWN *Poptones MC 5073SCD* | 75 | 1 |

Louis BELLSON – *See Duke ELLINGTON*

BELLY *US, male / female vocal / instrumental group (9 WEEKS)* pos/wks
23 Jan 93	FEED THE TREE *4AD BAD 3001CD*	32	3
10 Apr 93	GEPETTO *4AD BAD 2018CD*	49	2
4 Feb 95	NOW THEY'LL SLEEP *4AD BAD 5003CD*	28	2
22 Jul 95	SEAL MY FATE *4AD BAD 5007CD*	35	2

BELMONTS – *See DION*

BELOUIS SOME – *See Belouis SOME*

BELOVED
UK, male / female vocal / instrumental duo (47 WEEKS) pos/wks
21 Oct 89	THE SUN RISING *WEA YZ 414*	26	7
27 Jan 90	HELLO *WEA YZ 426*	19	7
24 Mar 90	YOUR LOVE TAKES ME HIGHER *East West YZ 463*	39	3
9 Jun 90	TIME AFTER TIME *East West YZ 482*	46	4
10 Nov 90	IT'S ALRIGHT NOW *East West YZ 541*	48	3
23 Jan 93 ●	SWEET HARMONY *East West YZ 709CD*	8	10
10 Apr 93	YOU'VE GOT ME THINKING *East West YZ 738CD*	23	4
14 Aug 93	OUTERSPACE GIRL *East West YZ 726CD*	38	2
30 Mar 96	SATELLITE *East West EW 034CD*	19	3
10 Aug 96	EASE THE PRESSURE *East West EW 058CD*	43	2
30 Aug 97	THE SUN RISING (re-issue) *East West EW 122CD1*	31	2

Act was male only before 1993

BELTRAM *US, male producer – Joey Beltram (4 WEEKS)* pos/wks
| 28 Sep 91 | ENERGY FLASH (EP) *R&S RSUK 3* | 52 | 2 |
| 7 Dec 91 | THE OMEN *R&S RSUK 7* [1] | 53 | 2 |

[1] Program 2 Beltram

Tracks on Energy Flash (EP): Energy Flash / Psycho Bass / My Sound / Sub-Base Experience

Pat BENATAR
US, female vocalist – Patricia Andrzejewski (53 WEEKS) pos/wks
21 Jan 84	LOVE IS A BATTLEFIELD *Chrysalis CHS 2747*	49	5
12 Jan 85	WE BELONG *Chrysalis CHS 2821*	22	9
23 Mar 85	LOVE IS A BATTLEFIELD (re-issue) *Chrysalis PAT 1*	17	10
15 Jun 85	SHADOWS OF THE NIGHT *Chrysalis PAT 2*	50	4
19 Oct 85	INVINCIBLE (THEME FROM 'THE LEGEND OF BILLIE JEAN') *Chrysalis PAT 3*	53	3
15 Feb 86	SEX AS A WEAPON *Chrysalis PAT 4*	67	3
2 Jul 88	ALL FIRED UP *Chrysalis PAT 5*	19	10
1 Oct 88	DON'T WALK AWAY *Chrysalis PAT 6*	42	5
14 Jan 89	ONE LOVE *Chrysalis PAT 7*	59	3
30 Oct 93	SOMEBODY'S BABY *Chrysalis CDCHS 5001*	48	1

David BENDETH
Canada, male vocalist and multi-instrumentalist (5 WEEKS) pos/wks
| 8 Sep 79 | FEEL THE REAL *Sidewalk SID 113* | 44 | 5 |

Re-entries are listed as (re), (2re), (3re), etc which signifies that the hit re-entered the chart once, twice or three times, etc

BENELUX and Nancy DEE
Belgium / Holland / Luxembourg, female vocal group (4 WEEKS)   pos/wks

25 Aug 79	SWITCH *Scope SC 4*	52	4

Eric BENET
US, male vocalist – Eric Bennet Jordan (5 WEEKS)   pos/wks

22 Mar 97	SPIRITUAL THANG *Warner Bros. W 0390CD*	62	1
1 May 99	GEORGY PORGY *Warner Bros. W478CD2* [1]	28	3
5 Feb 00	WHY YOU FOLLOW ME *Warner Bros. W491CD*	48	1

[1] Eric Benet featuring Faith Evans

Nigel BENN – *See PACK featuring Nigel BENN*

Simone BENN – *See VOLATILE AGENTS featuring Simone BENN*

BENNET
UK, male vocal / instrumental group (3 WEEKS)   pos/wks

22 Feb 97	MUM'S GONE TO ICELAND *Roadrunner RR 22853*	34	2
3 May 97	SOMEONE ALWAYS GETS THERE FIRST *Roadrunner RR 22983.*	69	1

Boyd BENNETT and his ROCKETS
US, male vocalist, d. 2 Jun 2002 and male vocal / instrumental group (2 WEEKS)   pos/wks

23 Dec 55	SEVENTEEN *Parlophone R 4063*	16	2

Chris BENNETT – *See MUNICH MACHINE*

Cliff BENNETT and the REBEL ROUSERS
UK, male vocal / instrumental group (23 WEEKS)   pos/wks

1 Oct 64 ●	ONE WAY LOVE *Parlophone R 5173*	9	9
4 Feb 65	I'LL TAKE YOU HOME *Parlophone R 5229*	42	3
11 Aug 66 ●	GOT TO GET YOU INTO MY LIFE *Parlophone R 5489*	6	11

Easther BENNETT – *See ASWAD; ETERNAL*

Peter E BENNETT with the CO-OPERATION CHOIR
UK, male vocalist and choir (1 WEEK)   pos/wks

7 Nov 70	THE SEAGULL'S NAME WAS NELSON *RCA 1991*	45	1

Tony BENNETT
US, male vocalist – Anthony Benedetto (61 WKS)   pos/wks

15 Apr 55 ★	STRANGER IN PARADISE *Philips PB 420*	1	16
16 Sep 55	CLOSE YOUR EYES *Philips PB 445*	18	1
13 Apr 56	COME NEXT SPRING *Philips PB 537*	29	1
5 Jan 61	TILL *Philips PB 1079*	35	2
18 Jul 63	THE GOOD LIFE *CBS AAG 153*	27	13
6 May 65	IF I RULED THE WORLD *CBS 201735*	40	5
27 May 65	(I LEFT MY HEART) IN SAN FRANCISCO (2re) *CBS 201730*	25	14
23 Dec 65	THE VERY THOUGHT OF YOU *CBS 202021*	21	9

Gary BENSON
UK, male vocalist – Harry Hyams (8 WEEKS)   pos/wks

9 Aug 75	DON'T THROW IT ALL AWAY *State STAT 10*	20	8

George BENSON   (175)   Top 500
Grammy-winning guitarist / vocalist, b. 22 Mar 1943, Pennsylvania, US. This one-time child prodigy topped the US chart in 1976 with the triple-platinum album 'Breezin''. He was also a major live attraction in Britain during the 1980s (143 WEEKS)   pos/wks

25 Oct 75	SUPERSHIP *CTI CTSP 002* [1]	30	6
4 Jun 77	NATURE BOY *Warner Bros. K 16921*	26	6
24 Sep 77	THE GREATEST LOVE OF ALL *Arista 133*	27	7
31 Mar 79	LOVE BALLAD *Warner Bros. K 17333*	29	9
26 Jul 80 ●	GIVE ME THE NIGHT *Warner Bros. K 17673*	7	10
4 Oct 80 ●	LOVE X LOVE *Warner Bros. K 17699*	10	8
7 Feb 81	WHAT'S ON YOUR MIND *Warner Bros. K 17748*	45	5
19 Sep 81	LOVE ALL THE HURT AWAY *Arista ARIST 428* [2]	49	3
14 Nov 81	TURN YOUR LOVE AROUND *Warner Bros. K 17877*	29	11
23 Jan 82	NEVER GIVE UP ON A GOOD THING *Warner Bros. K 17902*	14	10
21 May 83	LADY LOVE ME (ONE MORE TIME) *Warner Bros. W 9614*	11	10
16 Jul 83	FEEL LIKE MAKIN' LOVE *Warner Bros. W 9551*	28	7
24 Sep 83 ●	IN YOUR EYES *Warner Bros. W 9487*	7	10
17 Dec 83	INSIDE LOVE (SO PERSONAL) *WEA Int. W 9427*	57	5
19 Jan 85	20 / 20 *Warner Bros. W 9120*	29	9

20 Apr 85	BEYOND THE SEA (LA MER) *Warner Bros. W 9014*	60	3
16 Aug 86	KISSES IN THE MOONLIGHT *Warner Bros. W 8640*	60	4
29 Nov 86	SHIVER *Warner Bros. W 8523*	19	9
14 Feb 87	TEASER *Warner Bros. W 8437*	45	4
27 Aug 88	LET'S DO IT AGAIN *Warner Bros. W 7780*	56	3
5 Sep 92	I'LL KEEP YOUR DREAMS ALIVE *Ammi AMMI 101* [3]	68	1
11 Jul 98	SEVEN DAYS *MCA MCSTD 48083* [4]	22	3

[1] George "Bad" Benson [2] Aretha Franklin and George Benson [3] George Benson and Patti Austin [4] Mary J Blige featuring George Benson

BENTLEY RHYTHM ACE
UK, male instrumental duo – Mike Stokes and Richard March (7 WEEKS)   pos/wks

6 Sep 97	BENTLEY'S GONNA SORT YOU OUT! *Parlophone CDRS 6476*	17	4
27 May 00	THEME FROM GUTBUSTER *Parlophone CDRS 6537*	29	2
2 Sep 00	HOW'D I DO DAT *Parlophone CDRS 6543*	57	1

Brook BENTON
US, male vocalist – Benjamin Peay, d. 9 Apr 1988 (18 WEEKS)   pos/wks

10 Jul 59	ENDLESSLY *Mercury AMT 1043*	28	2
6 Oct 60	KIDDIO (re) *Mercury AMT 1109*	41	6
16 Feb 61	FOOLS RUSH IN *Mercury AMT 1121*	50	1
13 Jul 61	THE BOLL WEEVIL SONG *Mercury AMT 1148*	30	9

BENZ
UK, male rap / vocal group (9 WEEKS)   pos/wks

16 Dec 95	BOOM ROCK SOUL *Hacktown 74321329652*	62	2
16 Mar 96	URBAN CITY GIRL *Hacktown 74321348732*	31	3
25 May 96	MISS PARKER *Hacktown 74321377292*	35	2
29 Mar 97	IF I REMEMBER *Hendricks CDBENZ 1*	59	1
9 Aug 97	ON A SUN-DAY *Hendricks CDBENZ 2*	73	1

Ingrid BERGMAN – *See Dooley WILSON*

BERLIN
US, male / female vocal / instrumental group – lead vocal Terri Nunn (39 WEEKS)   pos/wks

25 Oct 86 ★	TAKE MY BREATH AWAY (LOVE THEME FROM 'TOP GUN') (re) *CBS A 7320* ▲	1	18
17 Jan 87	YOU DON'T KNOW *Mercury MER 237*	39	6
14 Mar 87	LIKE FLAMES *Mercury MER 240*	47	3
13 Oct 90 ●	TAKE MY BREATH AWAY (re-issue) *CBS 656361 7*	3	12

The original 'Take My Breath Away' re-entered at No.52 in 1988

Elmer BERNSTEIN
US, orchestra (11 WEEKS)   pos/wks

18 Dec 59 ●	STACCATO'S THEME (re) *Capitol CL 15101*	4	11

Leonard BERNSTEIN, ORCHESTRA and CHORUS
US, orchestra and chorus, leader d. 14 Oct 1990 (4 WEEKS)   pos/wks

2 Jul 94	AMERICA – WORLD CUP THEME 1994 *Deutsche Grammophon USACD 1*	44	4

BERRI
UK, female vocalist – Beverley Sleight (22 WEEKS)   pos/wks

26 Nov 94	THE SUNSHINE AFTER THE RAIN *Ffrreedom TABCD 223* [1]	26	6
2 Sep 95 ●	THE SUNSHINE AFTER THE RAIN (re-mix) *Ffrreedom TABCD 232*	4	11
2 Dec 95	SHINE LIKE A STAR *Ffrreedom TABCD 239*	20	5

[1] New Atlantic / U4EA featuring Berri

LaKiesha BERRI
US, female vocalist (1 WEEK)   pos/wks

5 Jul 97	LIKE THIS AND LIKE THAT *Adept ADPTCD 7*	54	1

Chuck BERRY   (352)   Top 500
First guitar-playing rock star, b. 18 Oct 1926, Missouri, US. Often called rock 'n' roll's premier poet and most influential instrumentalist. 'Duck walking' legend was among the first acts inducted into the Rock and Roll Hall of Fame (91 WEEKS)   pos/wks

21 Jun 57	SCHOOL DAY (re) *Columbia DB 3951*	24	4
25 Apr 58	SWEET LITTLE SIXTEEN *London HLM 8585*	16	5
11 Jul 63	GO GO GO *Pye International 7N 25209*	38	6

		pos/wks	
10 Oct 63 ●	**LET IT ROCK / MEMPHIS TENNESSEE**		
	Pye International 7N 25218 6	13	
19 Dec 63	**RUN RUDOLPH RUN** *Pye International 7N 25228* 36	6	
13 Feb 64	**NADINE (IS IT YOU) (re)** *Pye International 7N 25236* 27	6	
7 May 64 ●	**NO PARTICULAR PLACE TO GO** *Pye International 7N 25242* 3	12	
20 Aug 64	**YOU NEVER CAN TELL** *Pye International 7N 25257* 23	4	
14 Jan 65	**THE PROMISED LAND** *Pye International 7N 25285* 26	6	
28 Oct 72 ★	**MY DING-A-LING** *Chess 6145 019* ▲ 1	17	
3 Feb 73	**REELIN' AND ROCKIN'** *Chess 6145 020* 18	7	

Dave BERRY (469) Top 500

Unique, charismatic performer b. Dave Grundy, 6 Feb 1941, Sheffield, UK. Major European star, whose 'This Strange Effect' is among Holland's biggest sellers. Stage act influenced Alvin Stardust, and several punk bands acknowledge him as an inspiration (77 WEEKS)

		pos/wks	
19 Sep 63	**MEMPHIS TENNESSEE** *Decca F 11734* 1 19	13	
9 Jan 64	**MY BABY LEFT ME (re)** *Decca F 11803* 1 37	9	
30 Apr 64	**BABY IT'S YOU** *Decca F 11876* 24	6	
6 Aug 64 ●	**THE CRYING GAME** *Decca F 11937* 5	12	
26 Nov 64	**ONE HEART BETWEEN TWO (re)** *Decca F 12020* 41	3	
25 Mar 65 ●	**LITTLE THINGS** *Decca F 12103* 5	12	
22 Jul 65	**THIS STRANGE EFFECT** *Decca F 12188* 37	6	
30 Jun 66 ●	**MAMA** *Decca F 12435* 5	16	

1 Dave Berry and the Cruisers

Mike BERRY *UK, male vocalist (51 WEEKS)*

		pos/wks	
12 Oct 61	**TRIBUTE TO BUDDY HOLLY** *HMV POP 912* 1 24	6	
3 Jan 63 ●	**DON'T YOU THINK IT'S TIME** *HMV POP 1105* 2 6	12	
11 Apr 63	**MY LITTLE BABY** *HMV POP 1142* 2 34	7	
2 Aug 80 ●	**THE SUNSHINE OF YOUR SMILE** *Polydor 2059 261*.....9	12	
29 Nov 80	**IF I COULD ONLY MAKE YOU CARE** *Polydor POSP 202*.....37	9	
5 Sep 81	**MEMORIES** *Polydor POSP 287* 55	5	

1 Mike Berry and the Outlaws 2 Mike Berry & the Outlaws

Nick BERRY *UK, male actor / vocalist (24 WEEKS)*

		pos/wks	
4 Oct 86 ★	**EVERY LOSER WINS (re)** *BBC RESL 204*...........1	13	
13 Jun 92 ●	**HEARTBEAT** *Columbia 6581517* 2	8	
31 Oct 92	**LONG LIVE LOVE** *Columbia 6587597*...........47	3	

Adele BERTEI – *See JELLYBEAN*

BEST COMPANY *UK, male vocal duo (1 WEEK)*

		pos/wks	
27 Mar 93	**DON'T YOU FORGET ABOUT ME** *ZYX ZYX 69468*...........65	1	

BEST SHOT *UK, male rap group (2 WEEKS)*

		pos/wks	
5 Feb 94	**UNITED COLOURS** *East West YZ 795CD* 64	2	

BETA BAND *UK, male vocal / instrumental group (4 WEEKS)*

		pos/wks	
14 Jul 01	**BROKE / WON** *Regal Recordings REG 60CD* 30	2	
27 Oct 01	**HUMAN BEING** *Regal Recordings REG 65CD*...........57	1	
16 Feb 02	**SQUARES** *Regal Recordings REG 69CD* 42	1	

Martin BETTINGHAUS – *See Timo MAAS*

BEVERLEY SISTERS *UK, female vocal trio (34 WEEKS)*

		pos/wks	
27 Nov 53 ●	**I SAW MOMMY KISSING SANTA CLAUS (re)**		
	Philips PB 188 6	5	
13 Apr 56	**WILLIE CAN** *Decca F 10705* 23	4	
1 Feb 57	**I DREAMED** *Decca F 10832* 24	2	
13 Feb 59 ●	**LITTLE DRUMMER BOY** *Decca F 11107* 6	13	
20 Nov 59	**LITTLE DONKEY** *Decca F 11172* 14	7	
23 Jun 60	**GREEN FIELDS (re)** *Columbia DB 4444* 29	3	

Frankie BEVERLY – *See MAZE featuring Frankie BEVERLY*

BEYONCÉ *US, female vocalist – Beyoncé Knowles (11 WEEKS)*

		pos/wks	
27 Jul 02 ●	**WORK IT OUT (re)** *Columbia 6729822* 7	11	

See also DESTINY'S CHILD

BEYOND *UK, male vocal / instrumental group (1 WEEK)*

		pos/wks	
21 Sep 91	**RAGING (EP)** *Harvest HARS 530* 68	1	

Tracks on Raging (EP): Great Indifference / Nail / Eve of My Release

BIBLE *UK, male vocal / instrumental group (8 WEEKS)*

		pos/wks	
20 May 89	**GRACELAND** *Chrysalis BIB 4* 51	4	
26 Aug 89	**HONEY BE GOOD** *Ensign BIB 5* 54	4	

BIBLE OF DREAMS – *See Johnny PANIC and the BIBLE OF DREAMS*

BIDDU ORCHESTRA
UK, orchestra – leader Biddu Appaiah (13 WEEKS)

		pos/wks	
2 Aug 75	**SUMMER OF '42** *Epic EPC 3318* 14	8	
17 Apr 76	**RAIN FOREST** *Epic EPC 4084* 39	4	
11 Feb 78	**JOURNEY TO THE MOON** *Epic EPC 5910* 41	1	

BIFFY CLYRO *UK, male vocal / instrumental trio (1 WEEK)*

		pos/wks	
16 Feb 02	**57** *Beggars Banquet BBQ 358CD* 61	1	

BIG APPLE BAND – *See Walter MURPHY and the BIG APPLE BAND*

BIG AUDIO DYNAMITE
UK / US, male vocal / instrumental group (27 WEEKS)

		pos/wks	
22 Mar 86	**E=MC2** *CBS A 6963* 11	9	
7 Jun 86	**MEDICINE SHOW** *CBS A 7181* 29	5	
18 Oct 86	**C'MON EVERY BEATBOX** *CBS 650147* 51	3	
21 Feb 87	**V THIRTEEN** *CBS BAAD 2* 49	5	
28 May 88	**JUST PLAY MUSIC** *CBS BAAD 4* 51	3	
12 Nov 94	**LOOKING FOR A SONG** *Columbia 6610182* 1 68	2	

1 Big Audio

BIG BAD HORNS – *See LITTLE ANGELS*

BIG BAM BOO
UK / Canada, male vocal / instrumental duo (2 WEEKS)

		pos/wks	
28 Jan 89	**SHOOTING FROM MY HEART** *MCA MCA 1281* 61	2	

BIG BANG THEORY *UK, male producer – Seamus Haji (1 WEEK)*

		pos/wks	
2 Mar 02	**GOD'S CHILD** *Defected DFECT 45CDS*...........51	1	

BIG BASS vs Michelle NARINE
Canada, male production group and female vocalist (1 WEEK)

		pos/wks	
2 Sep 00	**WHAT YOU DO** *Stonebridge / Edel 0110965ERE* 67	1	

BIG BEN *UK, clock (2 WEEKS)*

		pos/wks	
1 Jan 00	**MILLENNIUM CHIMES** *London BIGONE 2000* 53	2	

BIG BEN BANJO BAND *UK, male instrumental group (6 WEEKS)*

		pos/wks	
10 Dec 54 ●	**LET'S GET TOGETHER NO.1** *Columbia DB 3549*...........6	4	
9 Dec 55	**LET'S GET TOGETHER AGAIN NO.1 (re)** *Columbia DB 3676*......18	2	

These hits were both medleys as follows: Let's Get Together No.1: I'm Just Wild About Harry / April Showers / Rock-a-Bye Your Baby / Swanee / Darktown Strutters Ball / For Me and My Gal / Oh You Beautiful Doll / Yes Sir That's My Baby / Let's Get Together

BIG BOPPER
US, male vocalist – JP Richardson, d. 3 Feb 1959 (8 WEEKS)

		pos/wks	
26 Dec 58	**CHANTILLY LACE (re)** *Mercury AMT 1002* 12	8	

BIG BOSS STYLUS presents RED VENOM
UK, male production duo and male rapper – Mike Neilson (1 WEEK)

		pos/wks	
31 Jul 99	**LET'S GET IT ON** *All Around the World CDGLOBE 195* 72	1	

BIG BROVAZ
UK, male / female vocal / rap / production group (10 WEEKS)

		pos/wks	
26 Oct 02 ●	**NU FLOW** *Epic 6730282*...........3	10+	

BIG C – See Alex WHITCOMBE & BIG C

BIG COUNTRY (305) Top 500
Distinctively Scottish-sounding rock quartet from Dunfermline, Scotland: Stuart Adamson b. 11 Apr 1958, d. 16 Dec 2001 (v/g, ex-Skids), Bruce Watson (g), Tony Butler (b), Mark Brzezicki (d). These frequent early-1980s chart visitors achieved five Top 10 albums including the 1984 No.1 'Steeltown' and were well known for Watson's bagpipe-like guitar sound (103 WEEKS)

		pos/wks
26 Feb 83 ●	FIELDS OF FIRE (400 MILES) *Mercury COUNT 2*	10 12
28 May 83	IN A BIG COUNTRY *Mercury COUNT 3*	17 7
3 Sep 83 ●	CHANCE *Mercury COUNT 4*	9 9
21 Jan 84 ●	WONDERLAND *Mercury COUNT 5*	8 8
29 Sep 84	EAST OF EDEN *Mercury MER 175*	17 6
1 Dec 84	WHERE THE ROSE IS SOWN *Mercury MER 185*	29 7
19 Jan 85	JUST A SHADOW *Mercury BCO 8*	26 4
12 Apr 86 ●	LOOK AWAY *Mercury BIGC1*	7 8
21 Jun 86	THE TEACHER *Mercury BIGC 2*	28 4
20 Sep 86	ONE GREAT THING *Mercury BIGC 3*	19 6
29 Nov 86	HOLD THE HEART *Mercury BIGC 4*	55 2
20 Aug 88	KING OF EMOTION (re) *Mercury BIGC 5*	16 6
5 Nov 88	BROKEN HEART (THIRTEEN VALLEYS) *Mercury BIGC 6*	47 4
4 Feb 89	PEACE IN OUR TIME *Mercury BIGC 7*	39 3
12 May 90	SAVE ME *Mercury BIGC 8*	41 3
21 Jul 90	HEART OF THE WORLD *Mercury BIGC 9*	50 2
31 Aug 91	REPUBLICAN PARTY REPTILE (EP) *Vertigo BIC 1*	37 2
19 Oct 91	BEAUTIFUL PEOPLE *Vertigo BIC 2*	72 1
13 Mar 93	ALONE *Compulsion CDPULSS 4*	24 3
1 May 93	SHIPS (WHERE WERE YOU) *Compulsion CDPULSS 6*	29 3
10 Jun 95	I'M NOT ASHAMED *Transatlantic TRAX 1009*	69 1
9 Sep 95	YOU DREAMER *Transatlantic TRAD 1012*	68 1
21 Aug 99	FRAGILE THING *Track TRACK 0004A* [1]	69 1

[1] Big Country featuring Eddi Reader

Tracks on Republican Party Reptile (EP): Republican Party Reptile / Comes a Time / You Me and the Truth

BIG DADDY *US, male vocal group (8 WEEKS)*

		pos/wks
9 Mar 85	DANCING IN THE DARK *Making Waves SURF 1033*	21 8

BIG DADDY KANE *US, male rapper (6 WEEKS)*

		pos/wks
13 May 89	RAP SUMMARY / WRATH OF KANE *Cold Chillin' W 2973*	52 2
26 Aug 89	SMOOTH OPERATOR *Cold Chillin' W 2804*	65 1
13 Jan 90	AIN'T NO STOPPIN' US NOW *Cold Chillin' W 2635*	44 3

BIG DISH *UK, male vocal / instrumental group (5 WEEKS)*

		pos/wks
12 Jan 91	MISS AMERICA *East West YZ 529*	37 5

BIG FAMILY – See JT and the BIG FAMILY

BIG FUN *UK, male vocal group (33 WEEKS)*

		pos/wks
12 Aug 89 ●	BLAME IT ON THE BOOGIE *Jive JIVE 217*	4 11
25 Nov 89 ●	CAN'T SHAKE THE FEELING *Jive JIVE 234*	8 9
17 Mar 90	HANDFUL OF PROMISES *Jive JIVE 243*	21 6
23 Jun 90	YOU'VE GOT A FRIEND *Jive CHILD 90* [1]	14 6
4 Aug 90	HEY THERE LONELY GIRL *Jive JIVE 251*	62 1

[1] Big Fun and Sonia featuring Gary Barnacle

BIG MOUNTAIN
US, male / female vocal / instrumental group (15 WEEKS)

		pos/wks
4 Jun 94 ●	BABY I LOVE YOUR WAY *RCA 74321198062*	2 14
24 Sep 94	SWEET SENSUAL LOVE *Giant 74321234642*	51 1

BIG PUN – See Jennifer LOPEZ

BIG ROLL BAND – See Zoot MONEY and the BIG ROLL BAND

BIG RON
UK, male producer – Aaron Gilbert (aka Jules Verne) (1 WEEK)

		pos/wks
11 Mar 00	LET THE FREAK *48k SPECT 06CDS*	57 1

BIG ROOM GIRL featuring Darryl PANDY
UK, male production / instrumental duo – Robert Chetcutti and Steve McGuinness – and US, male vocalist (2 WEEKS)

		pos/wks
20 Feb 99	RAISE YOUR HANDS *VC Recordings VCRD 44*	40 2

See also RHYTHM MASTERS

BIG SOUND – See Simon DUPREE and the BIG SOUND

BIG SOUND AUTHORITY
UK, male / female vocal / instrumental group (12 WEEKS)

		pos/wks
19 Jan 85	THIS HOUSE (IS WHERE YOUR LOVE STANDS) *Source BSA 1*	21 9
8 Jun 85	A BAD TOWN *Source BSA 2*	54 3

BIG SUPREME *UK, male vocal group (5 WEEKS)*

		pos/wks
20 Sep 86	DON'T WALK *Polydor POSP 809*	58 3
14 Mar 87	PLEASE YOURSELF *Polydor POSP 840*	64 2

BIG THREE *UK, vocal / instrumental group (17 WEEKS)*

		pos/wks
11 Apr 63	SOME OTHER GUY *Decca F 11614*	37 7
11 Jul 63	BY THE WAY *Decca F 11689*	22 10

BIG TIME CHARLIE *UK, male DJ / production duo – Aaron Gilbert and Les Sharma (4 WEEKS)*

		pos/wks
23 Oct 99	ON THE RUN *Inferno CDFERN 18*	22 2
18 Mar 00	MR DEVIL *Inferno CDFERN 24* [1]	39 2

[1] Big Time Charlie featuring Soozy Q

See also BIG RON

BIGFELLA featuring Noel McCALLA
US, male rapper and UK, male vocalist (1 WEEK)

		pos/wks
17 Aug 02	BEAUTIFUL *Nulife 74321942282*	52 1

Barry BIGGS *Jamaica, male vocalist (46 WEEKS)*

		pos/wks
28 Aug 76	WORK ALL DAY *Dynamic DYN 101*	38 5
4 Dec 76 ●	SIDESHOW *Dynamic DYN 118*	3 16
23 Apr 77	YOU'RE MY LIFE *Dynamic DYN 127*	36 4
9 Jul 77	THREE RING CIRCUS *Dynamic DYN 128*	22 8
15 Dec 79	WHAT'S YOUR SIGN GIRL *Dynamic DYN 150*	55 7
20 Jun 81	WIDE AWAKE IN A DREAM *Dynamic DYN 10*	44 6

Ronald BIGGS – See SEX PISTOLS

Ivor BIGGUN *UK, male vocalist – Doc Cox (15 WEEKS)*

		pos/wks
2 Sep 78	THE WINKER'S SONG (MISPRINT) *Beggars Banquet BOP 1* [1]	22 12
12 Sep 81	BRAS ON 45 (FAMILY VERSION) *Dead Badger BOP 6* [2]	50 3

[1] Ivor Biggun and the Red-Nosed Burglars [2] Ivor Biggun and the D Cups

BILBO *UK, male vocal / instrumental group (7 WEEKS)*

		pos/wks
26 Aug 78	SHE'S GONNA WIN *Lightning LIG 548*	42 7

Mr Acker BILK and his PARAMOUNT JAZZ BAND (117) Top 500
First UK act to top US chart in 1960s, b. 28 Jan 1929, Somerset, UK. Band leader / clarinettist / vocalist was at the forefront of the UK trad-jazz revival. 'Stranger on the Shore' spent more than one year on chart, selling 1,130,000, and was voted No.1 instrumental of 1962 in the US. Made an MBE in the 2001 honours list (172 WEEKS)

		pos/wks
22 Jan 60 ●	SUMMER SET *Columbia DB 4382*	5 20
9 Jun 60	GOODNIGHT SWEET PRINCE *Melodisc MEL 1547*	50 1
18 Aug 60	WHITE CLIFFS OF DOVER *Columbia DB 4492*	30 9
8 Dec 60 ●	BUONA SERA *Columbia DB 4544*	7 18
13 Jul 61 ●	THAT'S MY HOME *Columbia DB 4673*	7 17
2 Nov 61	STARS AND STRIPES FOREVER / CREOLE JAZZ *Columbia SCD 2155*	22 10
30 Nov 61 ●	STRANGER ON THE SHORE *Columbia DB 4750* [1] ◆ ▲	2 55

15 Mar 62	FRANKIE AND JOHNNY *Columbia DB 4795*	42	2
26 Jul 62	GOTTA SEE BABY TONIGHT *Columbia SCD 2176*	24	9
27 Sep 62	LONELY *Columbia DB 4897* [1]	14	11
24 Jan 63	A TASTE OF HONEY *Columbia DB 4949* [1]	16	9
21 Aug 76	● ARIA *Pye 7N 45607* [2]	5	11

[1] Mr Acker Bilk with the Leon Young String Chorale [2] Acker Bilk, his Clarinet and Strings

BILL *UK, male vocalist (1 WEEK)*

		pos/wks	
23 Oct 93	CAR BOOT SALE *Mercury MINCD 1*	73	1

BILL & BEN *UK, male flowerpot-dwelling vocalists – voiced by John Thomson (4 WEEKS)*

		pos/wks	
13 Jul 02	FLOBBADANCE *BBC Music WMSS 60552*	23	4

BILLIE – See Billie PIPER; H2O

BIMBO JET
France, male / female vocal / instrumental group (10 WEEKS)

		pos/wks	
26 Jul 75	EL BIMBO *EMI 2317*	12	10

BINARY FINARY *UK, male production duo – Matt Laws and Ricky Grant (9 WEEKS)*

		pos/wks	
10 Oct 98	1998 *Positiva CDTIV 98*	24	3
28 Aug 99	1999 *Positiva CDTIV 118*	11	6

Umberto BINDI *Italy, male vocalist (1 WEEK)*

		pos/wks	
10 Nov 60	IL NOSTRO CONCERTO *Oriole CB 1577*	47	1

BINI & MARTINI *Italy, male production duo (2 WEEKS)*

		pos/wks	
4 Mar 00	HAPPINESS (MY VISION IS CLEAR) *Azuli AZNYCDX 113*	53	1
10 Mar 01	BURNING UP *Azuli AZNY 137*	65	1

See also ECLIPSE; GOODFELLAS featuring Lisa MILLETT; HOUSE OF GLASS

BIOHAZARD *US, male vocal / instrumental group (4 WEEKS)*

		pos/wks	
9 Jul 94	TALES FROM THE HARD SIDE *Warner Bros. W 0254CD*	47	2
20 Aug 94	HOW IT IS *Warner Bros. W 0259CD*	62	2

La BIONDA *Italy, male / female vocal group (4 WEEKS)*

		pos/wks	
7 Oct 78	ONE FOR YOU ONE FOR ME *Philips 6198 227*	54	4

BIOSPHERE
Norway, male instrumentalist – Ger Jenssen, keyboards (2 WEEKS)

		pos/wks	
29 Apr 95	NOVELTY WAVES *Apollo APOLLO 20CDX*	51	2

BIRDLAND *UK, male vocal / instrumental group (7 WEEKS)*

		pos/wks	
1 Apr 89	HOLLOW HEART *Lazy LAZY 13*	70	1
8 Jul 89	PARADISE *Lazy LAZY 14*	70	1
3 Feb 90	SLEEP WITH ME *Lazy LAZY 17*	32	3
22 Sep 90	ROCK 'N' ROLL NIGGER *Lazy LAZY 20*	47	1
2 Feb 91	EVERYBODY NEEDS SOMEBODY *Lazy LAZY 24*	44	1

BIRDS *UK, male vocal / instrumental group (1 WEEK)*

		pos/wks	
27 May 65	LEAVING HERE *Decca F 12140*	45	1

Jane BIRKIN and Serge GAINSBOURG
UK / France, female / male vocal duo (34 WEEKS)

		pos/wks	
30 Jul 69	● JE T'AIME . . . MOI NON PLUS *Fontana TF 1042*	2	11
4 Oct 69	★ JE T'AIME . . . MOI NON PLUS (re-issue) *Major Minor MM 645*	1	14
7 Dec 74	JE T'AIME . . . MOI NON PLUS (2nd re-issue) *Antic K 11511*	31	9

BIS *UK, male / female vocal / instrumental group (9 WEEKS)*

		pos/wks	
30 Mar 96	THE SECRET VAMPIRE SOUNDTRACK (EP) *Chemikal Underground CHEM 003CD*	25	2
22 Jun 96	BIS VS THE DIY CORPS (EP) *Teen-C SKETCH 001CD*	45	1

9 Nov 96	ATOM POWERED ACTION (EP) *Wiiija WIJ 55CD*	54	1
15 Mar 97	SWEET SHOP AVENGERZ *Wiiija WIJ 67CD*	46	1
10 May 97	EVERYBODY THINKS THAT THEY'RE GOING TO GET THEIRS *Wiiija WIJ 69CD*	64	1
14 Nov 98	EURODISCO *Wiiija WIJ 86CD*	37	2
27 Feb 99	ACTION AND DRAMA *Wiiija WIJ 95CD*	50	1

Tracks on The Secret Vampire Soundtrack (EP): Kandy Pop / Secret Vampires / Teen-C Power / Diska. Tracks on Bis vs the DIY Corps (EP): This Is Fake DIY / Burn the Suit / Dance to the Disco Beat. Tracks on Atom Powered Action (EP): Starbright Boy / Wee Love / Team Theme / Cliquesuck

BISCUIT BOY *UK, male vocal / instrumental trio (1 WEEK)*

		pos/wks	
15 Sep 01	MITCH *Mercury 5887582*	75	1

Elvin BISHOP *US, male instrumentalist – guitar (4 WEEKS)*

		pos/wks	
15 May 76	FOOLED AROUND AND FELL IN LOVE *Capricorn 2089 024*	34	4

Hit has uncredited vocal by Mickey Thomas of Starship

BITI – See DEGREES OF MOTION featuring BITI

BIZARRE INC
UK, male / female vocal / instrumental group (49 WEEKS)

		pos/wks	
16 Mar 91	PLAYING WITH KNIVES *Vinyl Solution STORM 25R*	43	5
14 Sep 91	SUCH A FEELING *Vinyl Solution STORM 32S*	13	9
23 Nov 91	● PLAYING WITH KNIVES (re-issue) *Vinyl Solution STORM 38S*	4	8
3 Oct 92	● I'M GONNA GET YOU (re) *Vinyl Solution STORM 46S* [1]	3	13
27 Feb 93	TOOK MY LOVE *Vinyl Solution STORM 60CD* [1]	19	5
23 Mar 96	KEEP THE MUSIC STRONG *Some Bizarre MERCD 451*	33	2
6 Jul 96	SURPRISE *Some Bizarre MERCD 462*	21	3
14 Sep 96	GET UP SUNSHINE STREET *Some Bizarre MERCD 471*	45	2
13 Mar 99	PLAYING WITH KNIVES (re-mix) *Vinyl Solution VC01CD1*	30	2

[1] Bizarre Inc featuring Angie Brown

BIZZ NIZZ
US / Belgium, male / female vocal / instrumental group (11 WEEKS)

		pos/wks	
31 Mar 90	● DON'T MISS THE PARTYLINE *Cooltempo COOL 203*	7	11

BIZZI *UK, male vocalist (1 WEEK)*

		pos/wks	
6 Dec 97	BIZZI'S PARTY *Parlophone Rhythm CDRHYTHM 7*	62	1

BJÖRK 466 Top 500

Captivating, eccentric, uncompromising, female singer / songwriter, b. Björk Gudmundsdottir, 21 Nov 1965, Reykjavik, Iceland. Formerly a member of The Sugarcubes, she was a double Brits winner in 1994 (Best International Female and Best International Newcomer) (77 WEEKS)

		pos/wks	
27 Apr 91	OOOPS *ZTT ZANG 19* [1]	42	3
19 Jun 93	HUMAN BEHAVIOUR *One Little Indian 112 TP7CD*	36	2
4 Sep 93	VENUS AS A BOY *One Little Indian 122 TP7CD*	29	4
23 Oct 93	PLAY DEAD *Island CID 573* [2]	12	6
4 Dec 93	BIG TIME SENSUALITY *One Little Indian 132 TP7CD*	17	8
19 Mar 94	VIOLENTLY HAPPY *One Little Indian 142 TP7CD*	13	4
6 May 95	● ARMY OF ME *One Little Indian 162 TP7CD*	10	5
26 Aug 95	ISOBEL *One Little Indian 172 TP7CD*	23	3
25 Nov 95	● IT'S OH SO QUIET *One Little Indian 182 TP7CD*	4	15
24 Feb 96	● HYPERBALLAD *One Little Indian 192 TP7CD*	8	4
9 Nov 96	POSSIBLY MAYBE *One Little Indian 193 TP7CD*	13	3
1 Mar 97	I MISS YOU *One Little Indian 194 TP7CDL*	36	2
20 Dec 97	BACHELORETTE *One Little Indian 212 TP7CD*	21	5
17 Oct 98	HUNTER *One Little Indian 222 TP7CD*	44	1
12 Dec 98	ALARM CALL *One Little Indian 232 TP7CDL*	33	2
19 Jun 99	ALL IS FULL OF LOVE *One Little Indian 242 TP7CD*	24	2
18 Aug 01	HIDDEN PLACE *One Little Indian 332 TP7CD*	21	2
17 Nov 01	PAGAN POETRY *One Little Indian 352 TP7CD*	38	2
23 Mar 02	COCOON *One Little Indian 322 TP7CD*	35	2
7 Dec 02	IT'S IN OUR HANDS *One Little Indian 366 TP7CD*	37	2

[1] 808 State featuring Björk [2] Björk and David Arnold

BJÖRN AGAIN
Australia, male / female vocal / instrumental group (8 WEEKS) pos/wks

24 Oct 92	ERASURE-ISH (A LITTLE RESPECT / STOP!) *M & G MAGS 32* ..25		3
12 Dec 92	SANTA CLAUS IS COMING TO TOWN *M & G MAGS 35* 55		4
27 Nov 93	FLASHDANCE ... WHAT A FEELING *M & G MAGCD 50* 65		1

BLACK
UK, male vocalist – Colin Vearncombe (35 WEEKS) pos/wks

27 Sep 86	WONDERFUL LIFE *Ugly Man JACK 71* 72		1
27 Jun 87 ●	SWEETEST SMILE *A&M AM 394* 8		10
22 Aug 87 ●	WONDERFUL LIFE *A&M AM 402* 8		9
16 Jan 88	PARADISE *A&M AM 422* 38		3
24 Sep 88	THE BIG ONE *A&M AM 468* 54		4
21 Jan 89	NOW YOU'RE GONE *A&M AM 491* 66		2
4 May 91	FEEL LIKE CHANGE *A&M AM 780* 56		2
15 Jun 91	HERE IT COMES AGAIN *A&M AM 753* 70		1
5 Mar 94	WONDERFUL LIFE (re-issue) *PolyGram TV 5805552* 42		3

'Wonderful Life' on A&M is a re-recording. It was re-issued on PolyGram TV in 1994.

Cilla BLACK 95 Top 500
Undoubtedly one of Britain's favourite female vocalists / entertainers of the past 50 years, b. Priscilla White, 27 May 1943, Liverpool. After handing in her Top 20 season ticket, she has become an award-winning and extremely popular TV presenter (194 WEEKS) pos/wks

17 Oct 63	LOVE OF THE LOVED *Parlophone R 5065* 35		6
6 Feb 64 ★	ANYONE WHO HAD A HEART *Parlophone R 5101* 1		17
7 May 64 ★	YOU'RE MY WORLD *Parlophone R 5133* 1		17
6 Aug 64 ●	IT'S FOR YOU *Parlophone R 5162* 7		10
14 Jan 65 ●	YOU'VE LOST THAT LOVIN' FEELIN' *Parlophone R 5225* 2		9
22 Apr 65	I'VE BEEN WRONG BEFORE *Parlophone R 5269* 17		8
13 Jan 66 ●	LOVE'S JUST A BROKEN HEART *Parlophone R 5395* 5		11
31 Mar 66	ALFIE *Parlophone R 5427* 9		12
9 Jun 66 ●	DON'T ANSWER ME *Parlophone R 5463* 6		10
20 Oct 66	A FOOL AM I (DIMMELO PARLAME) *Parlophone R 5515* 13		9
8 Jun 67	WHAT GOOD AM I? *Parlophone R 5608* 24		7
29 Nov 67	I ONLY LIVE TO LOVE YOU *Parlophone R 5652* 26		11
13 Mar 68 ●	STEP INSIDE LOVE *Parlophone R 5674* 8		9
12 Jun 68	WHERE IS TOMORROW *Parlophone R 5706* 39		3
12 Feb 69 ●	SURROUND YOURSELF WITH SORROW *Parlophone R 5759* 3		12
9 Jul 69 ●	CONVERSATIONS *Parlophone R 5785* 7		12
13 Dec 69	IF I THOUGHT YOU'D EVER CHANGE YOUR MIND *Parlophone R 5820* 20		9
20 Nov 71 ●	SOMETHING TELLS ME (SOMETHING IS GONNA HAPPEN TONIGHT) *Parlophone R 5924* 3		14
2 Feb 74	BABY WE CAN'T GO WRONG *EMI 2107* 36		6
18 Sep 93	THROUGH THE YEARS *Columbia 6596982* 54		1
30 Oct 93	HEART AND SOUL *Columbia 6598562* [1] 75		1

[1] Cilla Black with Dusty Springfield

Frank BLACK
US, male vocalist – Charles Thompson (4 WEEKS) pos/wks

21 May 94	HEADACHE *4AD BAD 4007CD* 53		1
20 Jan 96	MEN IN BLACK *Dragnet 6627862* 37		2
27 Jul 96	I DON'T WANT TO HURT YOU (EVERY SINGLE TIME) *Dragnet 6634635* 63		1

Jeanne BLACK
US, female vocalist (4 WEEKS) pos/wks

23 Jun 60	HE'LL HAVE TO STAY *Capitol CL 15131* 41		4

BLACK & WHITE ARMY
UK, 250 Newcastle United football fan vocalists (2 WEEKS) pos/wks

23 May 98	BLACK & WHITE ARMY *Toon TOON 1CD* 26		2

BLACK BOX 490 Top 500
Although little known in their homeland, house instrumental / production trio (Mirko Limoni, Valerio Semplici, Daniele Davoli) had UK's best-selling single of 1989, using a Loleatta Holloway vocal sample mimed by French model Katrin Quinol. First Italian act to achieve three Top 10 entries. Best-selling single: 'Ride on Time' 973,850 (74 WEEKS) pos/wks

12 Aug 89 ★	RIDE ON TIME *Deconstruction PB 43055* 1		22
17 Feb 90 ●	I DON'T KNOW ANYBODY ELSE *Deconstruction PB 43479* 4		8

2 Jun 90	EVERYBODY EVERYBODY *Deconstruction PB 43715* 16		5
3 Nov 90 ●	FANTASY *Deconstruction PB 43895* 5		11
15 Dec 90	THE TOTAL MIX *Deconstruction PB 44235* 12		8
6 Apr 91	STRIKE IT UP *Deconstruction PB 44459* 16		8
14 Dec 91	OPEN YOUR EYES *Deconstruction PB 45053* 48		4
14 Aug 93	ROCKIN' TO THE MUSIC *Deconstruction 74321158122* 39		2
24 Jun 95	NOT ANYONE *Mercury MERCD 434* 31		2
20 Apr 96	I GOT THE VIBRATION / A POSITIVE VIBRATION *Manifesto MERCD 459* [1] 21		3
22 Feb 97	NATIVE NEW YORKER *Manifesto FESCD 18* [1] 46		1

[1] Blackbox

BLACK BOX RECORDER
UK, male / female vocal / instrumental group (4 WEEKS) pos/wks

22 Apr 00	THE FACTS OF LIFE *Nude NUD 48CD1* 20		3
15 Jul 00	THE ART OF DRIVING *Nude NUD 51CD1* 53		1

BLACK CONNECTION
Italy, male / female vocal / production group (3 WEEKS) pos/wks

14 Mar 98	GIVE ME RHYTHM *Xtravaganza / Edel 0091465 EXT* 32		2
24 Oct 98	I'M GONNA GET YA BABY *Xtravaganza 0091615 EXT* 62		1

BLACK CROWES
US, male vocal / instrumental group (28 WEEKS) pos/wks

1 Sep 90	HARD TO HANDLE *Def American DEFA 6* 45		5
12 Jan 91	TWICE AS HARD *Def American DEFA 7* 47		3
22 Jun 91	JEALOUS AGAIN / SHE TALKS TO ANGELS *Def American DEFA 8* 70		1
24 Aug 91	HARD TO HANDLE (re-issue) *Def American DEFA 10* 39		4
26 Oct 91	SEEING THINGS *Def American DEFA 13* 72		1
2 May 92	REMEDY *Def American DEFA 16* 24		3
26 Sep 92	STING ME *Def American DEFA 21* 42		2
28 Nov 92	HOTEL ILLNESS *Def American DEFA 23* 47		2
11 Feb 95	HIGH HEAD BLUES / A CONSPIRACY *American 74321258492*..25		2
22 Jul 95	WISER TIME *American 74321298272* 34		2
27 Jul 96	ONE MIRROR TOO MANY *American 74321398572* 51		1
7 Nov 98	KICKING MY HEART AROUND *American Recordings 6666665* 55		1

BLACK DIAMOND *US, male vocalist (1 WEEK)* pos/wks

17 Sep 94	LET ME BE *Systematic SYSCD 1* 56		1

BLACK DOG featuring Ofra HAZA
UK, male instrumentalist / producer – Ken Downie and Israel, female vocalist (1 WEEK) pos/wks

3 Apr 99	BABYLON *Warner Esp. WESP 006 CD1* 65		1

BLACK DUCK *UK, male rapper (5 WEEKS)* pos/wks

17 Dec 94	WHIGGLE IN LINE *Flying South CDDUCK 1* 33		5

BLACK EYED PEAS *US, male rap trio (4 WEEKS)* pos/wks

10 Oct 98	JOINTS & JAMS *Interscope IND 95604* 53		1
12 May 01	REQUEST LINE *Interscope 4970532* [1] 31		3

[1] Black Eyed Peas featuring Macy Gray

BLACK GORILLA
UK, male / female vocal / instrumental group (6 WEEKS) pos/wks

27 Aug 77	GIMME DAT BANANA *Response SR 502* 29		6

BLACK GRAPE *UK, male vocal / instrumental group (25 WEEKS)* pos/wks

10 Jun 95 ●	REVEREND BLACK GRAPE *Radioactive RAXTD 16* 9		5
5 Aug 95 ●	IN THE NAME OF THE FATHER *Radioactive RAXTD 19* 8		4
2 Dec 95	KELLY'S HEROES *Radioactive RAXTD 22* 17		5
25 May 96 ●	FAT NECK *Radioactive RAXTD 24* 10		3
29 Jun 96 ●	ENGLAND'S IRIE *Radioactive RAXTD 25* [1] 6		4
1 Nov 97	GET HIGHER *Radioactive RAXTD 32* 24		3
7 Mar 98	MARBLES *Radioactive RAXTD 33* 46		1

[1] Black Grape featuring Joe Strummer and Keith Allen

BLACK LACE `368` `Top 500`

Group formed for 1979 Eurovision Song Contest re-emerged in 1983 as a duo, Colin Routh and Alan Barton (d. 23 Mar 1995). Much maligned 'Superman' and 'Agadoo' have remained popular party favourites (89 WEEKS) pos/wks

31 Mar 79	MARY ANN *EMI 2919*	42	4
24 Sep 83 ●	SUPERMAN (GIOCA JOUER) *Flair FLA 105*	9	18
30 Jun 84 ●	AGADOO *Flair FLA 107*	2	30
24 Nov 84 ●	DO THE CONGA *Flair FLA 108*	10	9
1 Jun 85	EL VINO COLLAPSO *Flair LACE 1*	42	5
7 Sep 85	I SPEAKA DA LINGO *Flair LACE 2*	49	4
7 Dec 85	HOKEY COKEY *Flair LACE 3*	31	6
20 Sep 86	WIG WAM BAM *Flair LACE 5*	63	3
26 Aug 89	I AM THE MUSIC MAN *Flair LACE 10*	52	3
22 Aug 98	AGADOO (re-recording) *NOW CDWAG 260*	64	1

BLACK LEGEND *Italy, male production duo (22 WEEKS)* pos/wks

20 May 00	YOU SEE THE TROUBLE WITH ME (import) *Rise RISECD 072*	52	5
24 Jun 00 ★	YOU SEE THE TROUBLE WITH ME *Eternal WEA 282CD* ■	1	15
4 Aug 01	SOMEBODY *WEA WEA 328CD* `1`	37	2

`1` Shortie vs Black Legend

No.1 version features a 'karaoke' re-recording of the original Barry White vocal by UK vocalist Spoonface

BLACK MACHINE *France / Nigeria, male vocal / instrumental duo – Herry Iyere Innocent and Alasson Wat (5 WEEKS)* pos/wks

9 Apr 94	HOW GEE *London LONCD 348*	17	5

BLACK MAGIC *US, male producer – Marvin Burns (2 WEEKS)* pos/wks

1 Jun 96	FREEDOM (MAKE IT FUNKY) *Positiva CDTIV 51*	41	2

See also LIL' LOUIS

BLACK REBEL MOTORCYCLE CLUB
US, male vocal / instrumental group (6 WEEKS) pos/wks

2 Feb 02	LOVE BURNS *Virgin VUSCD 234*	37	2
1 Jun 02	SPREAD YOUR LOVE *Virgin VUSCD 245*	27	2
28 Sep 02	WHATEVER HAPPENED TO MY ROCK 'N' ROLL (PUNK SONG) *Virgin VUSCD 257*	46	2

BLACK RIOT *US, male producer (3 WEEKS)* pos/wks

3 Dec 88	WARLOCK / A DAY IN THE LIFE *Champion CHAMP 75*	68	3

'A Day in the Life' listed only from 17 Dec 1988

BLACK ROB *US, male rapper – Robert Ross (8 WEEKS)* pos/wks

12 Aug 00	WHOA *Puff Daddy / Arista 74321782732*	44	2
6 Oct 01	BAD BOY FOR LIFE *Bad Boy / Arista 74321889982* `1`	13	6

`1` P Diddy, Black Rob and Mark Curry

BLACK SABBATH
UK / US, vocal / instrumental group (70 WEEKS) pos/wks

29 Aug 70 ●	PARANOID *Vertigo 6059 010*	4	18
3 Jun 78	NEVER SAY DIE *Vertigo SAB 001*	21	8
14 Oct 78	HARD ROAD *Vertigo SAB 002*	33	4
5 Jul 80	NEON KNIGHTS *Vertigo SAB 3*	22	9
16 Aug 80	PARANOID (re-issue) *Nems BSS 101*	14	12
6 Dec 80	DIE YOUNG *Vertigo SAB 4*	41	7
7 Nov 81	MOB RULES *Vertigo SAB 5*	46	4
13 Feb 82	TURN UP THE NIGHT *Vertigo SAB 6*	37	5
15 Apr 89	HEADLESS CROSS *IRS EIRS 107*	62	1
13 Jun 92	TV CRIMES *IRS EIRSP 178*	33	2

Group UK only for first three hits and re-issue of 'Paranoid'

BLACK SHEEP *US, male rap duo (1 WEEK)* pos/wks

19 Nov 94	WITHOUT A DOUBT *Mercury MERCD 417*	60	1

BLACK SLATE
UK / Jamaica, male vocal / instrumental group (15 WEEKS) pos/wks

20 Sep 80 ●	AMIGO *Ensign ENY 42*	9	9
6 Dec 80	BOOM BOOM *Ensign ENY 47*	51	6

BLACK UHURU
Jamaica, male vocal / instrumental group (9 WEEKS) pos/wks

8 Sep 84	WHAT IS LIFE? *Island IS 150*	56	6
31 May 86	THE GREAT TRAIN ROBBERY *Real Authentic Sound RAS 7018*	62	3

Band of the BLACK WATCH *UK, military band (22 WEEKS)* pos/wks

30 Aug 75 ●	SCOTCH ON THE ROCKS *Spark SRL 1128*	8	14
13 Dec 75	DANCE OF THE CUCKOOS (THE 'LAUREL AND HARDY' THEME) *Spark SRL 1135*	37	8

Tony BLACKBURN *UK, male vocalist (7 WEEKS)* pos/wks

24 Jan 68	SO MUCH LOVE *MGM 1375*	31	4
26 Mar 69	IT'S ONLY LOVE *MGM 1467*	42	3

BLACKBYRDS *US, male vocal / instrumental group (6 WEEKS)* pos/wks

31 May 75	WALKING IN RHYTHM *Fantasy FTC 114*	23	6

BLACKFOOT *US, male vocal / instrumental group (5 WEEKS)* pos/wks

6 Mar 82	DRY COUNTY *Atco K 11686*	43	4
18 Jun 83	SEND ME AN ANGEL *Atco B 9880*	66	1

J BLACKFOOT *US, male vocalist (4 WEEKS)* pos/wks

17 Mar 84	TAXI *Allegiance ALES 2*	48	4

BLACKFOOT SUE
UK, male vocal / instrumental group (15 WEEKS) pos/wks

12 Aug 72 ●	STANDING IN THE ROAD *Jam 13*	4	10
16 Dec 72	SING DON'T SPEAK *Jam 29*	36	5

BLACKGIRL *US, female vocal group (3 WEEKS)* pos/wks

16 Jul 94	90s GIRL *RCA 74321217882*	23	3

BLACKHEARTS – See Joan JETT and the BLACKHEARTS

Honor BLACKMAN – See Patrick MacNEE and Honor BLACKMAN

BLACKNUSS
Sweden, male / female vocal / instrumental group (1 WEEK) pos/wks

28 Jun 97	DINAH *Arista 74321479762*	56	1

BLACKOUT *UK, male production / instrumental duo – Marc Dillon and Pat Dickins (1 WEEK)* pos/wks

27 Mar 99	GOTTA HAVE HOPE *Multiply CDMULTY 47*	46	1

BLACKOUT *UK, male / female vocal / rap group (8 WEEKS)* pos/wks

31 Mar 01	MR DJ *Independiente ISOM 48MS*	19	7
6 Oct 01	GET UP *Independiente ISOM 52MS*	67	1

Bill BLACK'S COMBO
US, male instrumental group, leader d. 21 Oct 1965 (8 WEEKS) pos/wks

8 Sep 60	WHITE SILVER SANDS *London HLU 9090*	50	1
3 Nov 60	DON'T BE CRUEL *London HLU 9212*	32	7

BLACKSTREET *US, male vocal group (70 WEEKS)* pos/wks

19 Jun 93	BABY BE MINE *MCA MCSTD 1772* `1`	37	3
13 Aug 94	BOOTI CALL *Interscope A 8250CD*	56	1
11 Feb 95	U BLOW MY MIND *Interscope A 8222CD*	39	2
27 May 95	JOY *Interscope A 8195CD*	56	2
19 Oct 96 ●	NO DIGGITY *Interscope IND 95003* `2` ▲	9	7

8 Mar 97	● GET ME HOME Def Jam DEFCD 32 [3]	11	5
26 Apr 97	● DON'T LEAVE ME Interscope IND 95534	6	10
27 Sep 97	● FIX Interscope IND 97521	7	5
13 Dec 97	(MONEY CAN'T) BUY ME LOVE Interscope IND 95563	18	6
4 Apr 98	● I GET LONELY Virgin VSCDT 1683 [4]	5	7
27 Jun 98	THE CITY IS MINE Northwestside 74321588012 [5]	38	2
12 Dec 98	● TAKE ME THERE Interscope IND 95620 [6]	7	9
17 Apr 99	GIRLFRIEND / BOYFRIEND Interscope IND 95640 [7]	11	7
10 Jul 99	GET READY Puff Daddy / Arista 74321682602 [8]	32	4

[1] BLACKstreet featuring Teddy Riley [2] BLACKstreet featuring Dr Dre [3] Foxy Brown featuring BLACKstreet [4] Janet featuring BLACKstreet [5] Jay-Z featuring BLACKstreet [6] BLACKstreet and Mya featuring Mase and Blinky Blink [7] BLACKstreet with Janet [8] Mase featuring BLACKstreet

BLACKWELLS US, male vocal group (2 WEEKS) · pos/wks

| 18 May 61 | LOVE OR MONEY London HLW 9334 | 46 | 2 |

Richard BLACKWOOD UK, male comedian / rapper (16 WEEKS) pos/wks

17 Jun 00	● MAMA – WHO DA MAN? East West MICKY 01CD1	3	7
16 Sep 00	● 1.2.3.4. GET WITH THE WICKED East West MICKY 05CD1	10	6
25 Nov 00	SOMEONE THERE FOR ME Hopefield / East West MICKY 06CD	23	3

BLADE – See Mark B & BLADE

BLAGGERS I.T.A. UK, male vocal / instrumental group (7 WEEKS) pos/wks

12 Jun 93	STRESSS Parlophone CDITA 1	56	2
9 Oct 93	OXYGEN Parlophone CDITA 2	51	2
8 Jan 94	ABANDON SHIP Parlophone CDITA 3	48	3

BLAHZAY BLAHZAY US, male rap duo (1 WEEK) · pos/wks

| 2 Mar 96 | DANGER Mercury Black Vinyl MBVCD 2 | 56 | 1 |

Vivian BLAINE US, female actor / vocalist – Vivienne Stapleton, d. 13 Dec 1995 (1 WEEK) pos/wks

| 10 Jul 53 | BUSHEL AND A PECK Brunswick 05100 | 12 | 1 |

BLAIR – See Terry HALL

BLAIR UK, male vocalist – Blair Mackichan (5 WEEKS) · pos/wks

| 2 Sep 95 | HAVE FUN GO MAD Mercury MERCD 443 | 37 | 3 |
| 6 Jan 96 | LIFE Mercury MERCD 447 | 44 | 2 |

BLAK TWANG UK, male rapper and female rapper / vocalist (2 WEEKS) pos/wks

| 29 Jun 02 | TRIXSTAR Bad Magic MAGICD 24 [1] | 54 | 1 |
| 26 Oct 02 | SO ROTTEN Bad Magic MAGICD 25 [2] | 48 | 1 |

[1] Blak Twang featuring Est'Elle [2] Blak Twang featuring Jahmali

Peter BLAKE UK, male vocalist (4 WEEKS) · pos/wks

| 8 Oct 77 | LIPSMACKIN' ROCK 'N' ROLLIN' Pepper UP 36295 | 40 | 4 |

BLAME UK, male instrumental / production duo (2 WEEKS) · pos/wks

| 11 Apr 92 | MUSIC TAKES YOU Moving Shadow SHADOW 11 | 48 | 2 |

BLAMELESS UK, male vocal / instrumental group (5 WEEKS) · pos/wks

4 Nov 95	TOWN CLOWNS China WOKCD 2046	56	1
23 Mar 96	BREATHE (A LITTLE DEEPER) China WOKCD 2070	27	3
1 Jun 96	SIGNS... China WOKCD 2077	49	1

BLANCMANGE UK, vocal / instrumental duo (71 WEEKS) · pos/wks

17 Apr 82	GOD'S KITCHEN / I'VE SEEN THE WORD London BLANC 1	65	2
31 Jul 82	FEEL ME London BLANC 2	46	5
30 Oct 82	● LIVING ON THE CEILING London BLANC 3	7	14
19 Feb 83	WAVES London BLANC 4	19	9
7 May 83	● BLIND VISION London BLANC 5	10	8
26 Nov 83	THAT'S LOVE, THAT IT IS London BLANC 6	33	8
14 Apr 84	● DON'T TELL ME London BLANC 7	8	10
21 Jul 84	THE DAY BEFORE YOU CAME London BLANC 8	22	8
7 Sep 85	WHAT'S YOUR PROBLEM London BLANC 9	40	5
10 May 86	I CAN SEE IT London BLANC 11	71	2

Billy BLAND US, male vocalist (10 WEEKS) · pos/wks

| 19 May 60 | LET THE LITTLE GIRL DANCE London HL 9096 | 15 | 10 |

No.1 COLLECTOR

■ British Hit Singles reader Ian Evans owns every UK chart-topper in its original format and he's not alone. Ray Spiller of Romford and Larry Foster of Southend have also collected every one of the 900-plus No.1 hit singles since the chart began in 1952

Six decades of chart-toppers line the walls of Ian Evans's Lincolnshire home

Name: Ian Evans from Donnigton, Lincolnshire

Collection comprises: Every single UK chart-topper, most in their original sleeves

First music memories: Radio Luxembourg on Sunday nights. Listening to Jack Jackson playing late 40s 78s like '12th Street Rag'

No.1s collection started: Late 80s starting buying every new No.1 and began collecting old vinyl chart-toppers

Collected from: Car boot sales, VIP fairs and friends' lofts and attics

Most difficult No.1 to locate: 'How Much Is that Doggie in the Window' by Lita Roza which recently completed the collection. Nearly missed 'Bring Your Daughter to the Slaughter' by Iron Maiden, which fooled me by charting for one week after Christmas one year when I assumed Cliff Richard was still top

Average price of the older 78s and 45s: £5 or £6

Most expensive No.1: 'Rock Around the Clock' by Bill Haley and His Comets, priced at £20

Favourite No.1s: 'I Want to Know What Love Is' by Foreigner and 'Sweets for My Sweet' by The Searchers for the memories they bring back and '(Everything I Do) I Do It For You' by Bryan Adams and 'Love Is All Around' by Wet Wet Wet which saved me a lot of money for obvious reasons

BLANK & JONES
Germany, production duo – Piet Blank and Jaspa Jones (9 WEEKS) pos/wks

26 Jun 99	CREAM *Devia DVNT 31CDS*	.24	3
27 May 00	AFTER LOVE *Nebula NEBCDS 3*	.57	1
30 Sep 00	THE NIGHTFLY *Nebula NEBCD 010*	.55	1
3 Mar 01	BEYOND TIME *Gang Go / Edel 01245115 GAG*	.53	2
29 Jun 02	DJS FANS & FREAKS *Incentive CENT 42CDS*	.45	2

BLAQUE IVORY *US, female vocal group (3 WEEKS)* pos/wks

3 Jul 99	808 *Columbia 6674962*	.31	3

BLAST featuring VDC
Italy, male / female vocal / instrumental group (5 WEEKS) pos/wks

18 Jun 94	CRAYZY MAN *UMM MCSTD 1982*	.22	3
12 Nov 94	PRINCES OF THE NIGHT *UMM MCSTD 2011*	.40	2

Melanie BLATT – *See ALL SAINTS; OUTSIDAZ featuring Rah DIGGA and Melanie BLATT; ARTFUL DODGER*

BLAZE featuring Palmer BROWN
US, male production duo and male vocalist (3 WEEKS) pos/wks

10 Mar 01	MY BEAT *Black & Blue / Kickin' NEOCD 053*	.53	2
21 Sep 02	DO YOU REMEMBER HOUSE *Slip'n'Slide SLIPCD 151*	.55	1

BLAZIN' SQUAD *UK, male vocal / rap group (19 WEEKS)* pos/wks

31 Aug 02	★ CROSSROADS *East West SQUAD 01CD■*	.1	13
23 Nov 02	● LOVE ON THE LINE *East West SQUAD 02CD1*	.6	6+

BLEACHIN' *UK, male vocal / instrumental group (4 WEEKS)* pos/wks

22 Jul 00	PEAKIN' (re) *Boiler House / Arista 74321774812*	.32	4

BLESSID UNION OF SOULS
US, male vocal / instrumental group (6 WEEKS) pos/wks

27 May 95	I BELIEVE *EMI CDEM 374*	.29	5
23 Mar 96	LET ME BE THE ONE *EMI CDEM 387*	.74	1

BLESSING *UK, male vocal / instrumental group (13 WEEKS)* pos/wks

11 May 91	HIGHWAY 5 *MCA MCS 1509*	.42	6
18 Jan 92	HIGHWAY 5 (re-mix) *MCA MCS 1603*	.30	6
19 Feb 94	SOUL LOVE *MCA MCSTD 1940*	.73	1

Mary J BLIGE (218 *Top 500*)
Original queen of hip hop and soul, b. 11 Jan 1971, Atlanta, Georgia, US. Transatlantic chart regular since platinum-selling debut album 'What's the 411?' (1992). Recorded with numerous top acts including Elton John, Puff Daddy, Eric Clapton, Lauryn Hill, Bono, R Kelly, Wyclef Jean, Aretha Franklin and Ja Rule (127 WEEKS) pos/wks

28 Nov 92	REAL LOVE *Uptown MCS 1721*	.68	2
27 Feb 93	REMINISCE *Uptown MCSTD 1731*	.31	4
12 Jun 93	YOU REMIND ME *Uptown MCSTD 1770*	.48	3
28 Aug 93	REAL LOVE (re-mix) *Uptown MCSTD 1922*	.26	4
4 Dec 93	YOU DON'T HAVE TO WORRY *Uptown MCSTD 1948*	.36	2
14 May 94	MY LOVE *Uptown MCSTD 1972*	.29	3
10 Dec 94	BE HAPPY *Uptown MCSTD 2033*	.30	4
15 Apr 95	I'M GOIN' DOWN *Uptown MCSTD 2053*	.12	4
29 Jul 95	● I'LL BE THERE FOR YOU - YOU'RE ALL I NEED TO GET BY *Def Jam DEFDX 11* [1]	.10	5
30 Sep 95	MARY JANE (ALL NIGHT LONG) *Uptown MCSTD 2088*	.17	4
16 Dec 95	(YOU MAKE ME FEEL LIKE A) NATURAL WOMAN *Uptown MCSTD 2108*	.23	3
30 Mar 96	NOT GON' CRY *Arista 74321358252*	.39	2
1 Mar 97	CAN'T KNOCK THE HUSTLE *Northwestside 74321447192* [2]	.30	2
17 May 97	LOVE IS ALL WE NEED *Uptown MCSTD 48053*	.15	4
16 Aug 97	● EVERYTHING *MCA MCSTD 48059*	.6	9
29 Nov 97	MISSING YOU (2re) *MCA MCSTD 48071*	.19	5
11 Jul 98	SEVEN DAYS *MCA MCSTD 48083* [3]	.22	4
13 Mar 99	● AS *Epic 6670122* [4]	.4	10
21 Aug 99	ALL THAT I CAN SAY *MCA MCSTD 40215*	.29	3
11 Dec 99	DEEP INSIDE *MCA MCSTD 40224*	.42	2
29 Apr 00	GIVE ME YOU *MCA MCSTD 40230*	.19	4
16 Dec 00	● 911 *Columbia 6706122* [5]	.9	10
6 Oct 01	● FAMILY AFFAIR *MCA MCSTD 40267* ▲	.8	16
9 Feb 02	DANCE FOR ME *MCA MCSTD 40274* [6]	.13	7
11 May 02	● NO MORE DRAMA *MCA MCSTD 40281*	.9	7
24 Aug 02	RAINY DAYZ *MCA MCSTD 40288* [7]	.17	5

[1] Method Man featuring Mary J Blige [2] Jay-Z featuring Mary J Blige [3] Mary J Blige featuring George Benson [4] George Michael and Mary J Blige [5] Wyclef Jean featuring Mary J Blige [6] Mary J Blige featuring Common [7] Mary J Blige featuring Ja Rule

BLIND MELON *US, male vocal / instrumental group (13 WEEKS)* pos/wks

12 Jun 93	TONES OF HOME *Capitol CDCL 687*	.62	2
11 Dec 93	NO RAIN *Capitol CDCL 699*	.17	6
9 Jul 94	CHANGE *Capitol CDCL 717*	.35	3
5 Aug 95	GALAXIE *Capitol CDCLS 755*	.37	2

BLINK *Ireland, male vocal / instrumental group (1 WEEK)* pos/wks

16 Jul 94	HAPPY DAY *Lime CDR 6385*	.57	1

BLINK 182 *US, male vocal / instrumental group (29 WEEKS)* pos/wks

2 Oct 99	WHAT'S MY AGE AGAIN? *MCA MCSTD 40219*	.38	2
25 Mar 00	● ALL THE SMALL THINGS *MCA MCSTD 40223*	.2	10
8 Jul 00	WHAT'S MY AGE AGAIN? (re-issue) *MCA MCSZD 40219*	.17	6
14 Jul 01	THE ROCK SHOW *MCA MCSTD 40259*	.14	7
6 Oct 01	FIRST DATE (re) *MCA MCSTD 40264*	.31	4

BLINKY BLINK – *See BLACKSTREET*

BLOCKHEADS – *See Ian DURY and the BLOCKHEADS*

BLOCKSTER *UK / Italy, male production group (11 WEEKS)* pos/wks

16 Jan 99	● YOU SHOULD BE ... *Sound of Ministry MOSCDS 128*	.3	9
24 Jul 99	GROOVELINE *Sound of Ministry MOSCDS 131*	.18	2

BLOKES – *See Billy BRAGG*

Kristine BLOND *Denmark, female vocalist (7 WEEKS)* pos/wks

11 Apr 98	LOVE SHY *Reverb BNOISE 1CD*	.22	3
11 Nov 00	LOVE SHY (re-mix) *Relentless RELENT 4CDS*	.28	2
4 May 02	YOU MAKE ME GO OOOH *WEA WEA 343CD*	.35	2

BLONDIE (121 *Top 500*) *Influential New York-based quintet, fronted by ex-Bunny Girl Deborah Harry (v) (b. 1 Jul 1945, Miami) and fiancé Chris Stein (g). Few Acts can match their 20-year span of No.1 hits. Best-selling single: 'Atomic' 1,180,000 (169 WEEKS)* pos/wks

18 Feb 78	● DENIS (DENEE) *Chrysalis CHS 2204*	.2	14
6 May 78	● (I'M ALWAYS TOUCHED BY YOUR) PRESENCE DEAR *Chrysalis CHS 2217*	.10	9
26 Aug 78	PICTURE THIS *Chrysalis CHS 2242*	.12	11
11 Nov 78	● HANGING ON THE TELEPHONE *Chrysalis CHS 2266*	.5	12
27 Jan 79	★ HEART OF GLASS *Chrysalis CHS 2275* ◆ ▲	.1	12
19 May 79	● SUNDAY GIRL *Chrysalis CHS 2320*	.1	13
29 Sep 79	● DREAMING *Chrysalis CHS 2350*	.2	8
24 Nov 79	UNION CITY BLUE *Chrysalis CHS 2400*	.13	10
23 Feb 80	★ ATOMIC *Chrysalis CHS 2410*	.1	9
12 Apr 80	★ CALL ME *Chrysalis CHS 2414*	.1	9
8 Nov 80	★ THE TIDE IS HIGH *Chrysalis CHS 2465* ▲	.1	12
24 Jan 81	● RAPTURE *Chrysalis CHS 2485* ▲	.5	8
8 May 82	ISLAND OF LOST SOULS *Chrysalis CHS 2608*	.11	9
24 Jul 82	WAR CHILD *Chrysalis CHS 2624*	.39	4
3 Dec 88	DENIS (re-mix) *Chrysalis CHS 3328*	.50	3
11 Feb 89	CALL ME (re-mix) *Chrysalis CHS 3342*	.61	2
10 Sep 94	ATOMIC (re-mix) *Chrysalis CDCHS 5013*	.19	4
8 Jul 95	HEART OF GLASS (re-mix) *Chrysalis CSCHS 5023*	.15	3
28 Oct 95	UNION CITY BLUE (re-mix) *Chrysalis CDCHS 5027*	.31	2
13 Feb 99	★ MARIA *Beyond 74321645632* ■	.1	12
12 Jun 99	NOTHING IS REAL BUT THE GIRL *Beyond 74321669472*	.26	3

See also Deborah HARRY

Re-entries are listed as (re), (2re), (3re), etc which signifies that the hit re-entered the chart once, twice or three times, etc

BLOOD SWEAT AND TEARS
US / Canada, male vocal / instrumental group (6 WEEKS)   pos/wks

| 30 Apr 69 | YOU'VE MADE ME SO VERY HAPPY *CBS 4116* | .35 | 6 |

BLOODHOUND GANG
US, male vocal / instrumental group (21 WEEKS)   pos/wks

23 Aug 97	WHY'S EVERYBODY ALWAYS PICKIN' ON ME? *Geffen GFSTD 22252*	.56	1
15 Apr 00 ●	THE BAD TOUCH *Geffen 4972672*	.4	14
2 Sep 00	THE BALLAD OF CHASEY LAIN *Geffen 4973812*	.15	6

Male / female act for 1997 debut hit

BLOODSTONE *US, male vocal / instrumental group (4 WEEKS)*   pos/wks

| 18 Aug 73 | NATURAL HIGH *Decca F 13382* | .40 | 4 |

Bobby BLOOM *US, male vocalist, d. 28 Feb 1974 (24 WEEKS)*   pos/wks

| 29 Aug 70 ● | MONTEGO BAY (2re) *Polydor 2058 051* | .3 | 19 |
| 9 Jan 71 | HEAVY MAKES YOU HAPPY *Polydor 2001 122* | .31 | 5 |

BLOOMSBURY SET
UK, male vocal / instrumental group (3 WEEKS)   pos/wks

| 25 Jun 83 | HANGING AROUND WITH THE BIG BOYS *Stiletto STL 13* | .56 | 3 |

Tanya BLOUNT *US, female vocalist (1 WEEK)*   pos/wks

| 11 Jun 94 | I'M GONNA MAKE YOU MINE *Polydor PZCD 315* | .69 | 1 |

Kurtis BLOW *US, male rapper – Kurtis Walker (23 WEEKS)*   pos/wks

15 Dec 79	CHRISTMAS RAPPIN' *Mercury BLOW 7*	.30	6
11 Oct 80	THE BREAKS *Mercury BLOW 8*	.47	4
16 Mar 85	PARTY TIME (THE GO-GO EDIT) *Club JAB 12*	.67	1
15 Jun 85	SAVE YOUR LOVE (FOR NUMBER 1) *Club JAB 14* [1]	.66	2
18 Jan 86	IF I RULED THE WORLD *Club JAB 26*	.24	8
8 Nov 86	I'M CHILLIN' *Club JAB 42*	.64	2

[1] René and Angela featuring Kurtis Blow

BLOW MONKEYS
UK, male vocal / instrumental group (46 WEEKS)   pos/wks

1 Mar 86	DIGGING YOUR SCENE *RCA PB 40599*	.12	10
17 May 86	WICKED WAYS *RCA MONK 2*	.60	2
31 Jan 87 ●	IT DOESN'T HAVE TO BE THIS WAY *RCA MONK 4*	.5	8
28 Apr 87	OUT WITH HER *RCA MONK 5*	.30	6
30 May 87	(CELEBRATE) THE DAY AFTER YOU *RCA MONK 6* [1]	.52	2
15 Aug 87	SOME KIND OF WONDERFUL *RCA MONK 7*	.67	1
6 Aug 88	THIS IS YOUR LIFE *RCA PB 42149*	.70	2
8 Apr 89	THIS IS YOUR LIFE (re-mix) *RCA PB 42695*	.32	5
15 Jul 89	CHOICE? *RCA PB 42885* [2]	.22	6
14 Oct 89	SLAVES NO MORE *RCA PB 43201* [2]	.73	2
26 May 90	SPRINGTIME FOR THE WORLD *RCA PB 43623*	.69	2

[1] Blow Monkeys with Curtis Mayfield [2] Blow Monkeys featuring Sylvia Tella

BLU PETER *UK, male DJ / producer (1 WEEK)*   pos/wks

| 21 Mar 98 | TELL ME WHAT YOU WANT / JAMES HAS KITTENS *React CDREACT 285* | .70 | 1 |

BLUE *UK, male vocal / instrumental group (8 WEEKS)*   pos/wks

| 30 Apr 77 | GONNA CAPTURE YOUR HEART *Rocket ROKN 522* | .18 | 8 |

BLUE *UK, male vocal group (62 WEEKS)*   pos/wks

2 Jun 01 ●	ALL RISE *Innocent SINCD 28*	.4	13
8 Sep 01 ★	TOO CLOSE *Innocent SINCD 30* ■	.1	13
24 Nov 01 ★	IF YOU COME BACK *Innocent SINCD 32* ■	.1	13
30 Mar 02 ●	FLY BY II *Innocent SINCD 33*	.6	12
2 Nov 02 ●	ONE LOVE *Innocent SINCD 41*	.3	9+
21 Dec 02 ★	SORRY SEEMS TO BE THE HARDEST WORD *Innocent SINDX 43* [1] ■	.1	2+

[1] Blue featuring Elton John

Babbity BLUE *UK, female vocalist (2 WEEKS)*   pos/wks

| 11 Feb 65 | DON'T MAKE ME (FALL IN LOVE WITH YOU) *Decca F 12053* | .48 | 2 |

Barry BLUE *UK, male vocalist – Barry Green (48 WEEKS)*   pos/wks

28 Jul 73 ●	DANCIN' (ON A SATURDAY NIGHT) *Bell 1295*	.2	15
3 Nov 73 ●	DO YOU WANNA DANCE? *Bell 1336*	.7	12
2 Mar 74	SCHOOL LOVE *Bell 1345*	.11	9
3 Aug 74	MISS HIT AND RUN *Bell 1364*	.26	7
26 Oct 74	HOT SHOT *Bell 1379*	.23	5

See also CRY SISCO!

BLUE ADONIS featuring LIL' MISS MAX *Belgium, male production duo, female vocalist – Dirk de Boeck and Wim Perdaen (3 WEEKS)*   pos/wks

| 17 Oct 98 | DISCO COP *Serious SERR 002CD* | .27 | 3 |

BLUE AEROPLANES
UK, male / female vocal / instrumental group (3 WEEKS)   pos/wks

| 17 Feb 90 | JACKET HANGS *Ensign ENY 628* | .72 | 1 |
| 26 May 90 | … AND STONES *Ensign ENY 632* | .63 | 2 |

BLUE AMAZON
UK, male production duo / female vocalist (2 WEEKS)   pos/wks

| 17 May 97 | AND THEN THE RAIN FALLS *Sony S2 BAS 301 CD* | .53 | 1 |
| 1 Jul 00 | BREATHE *Subversive SUB 61D* | .73 | 1 |

BLUE BAMBOO *Belgium, male producer – Johan Gielen (4 WEEKS)*   pos/wks

| 3 Dec 94 | ABC AND D … *Escapade CDJAPE 6* | .23 | 4 |

See also AIRSCAPE; CUBIC 22; TRANSFORMER 2

BLUE BOY *UK, male producer – Alexis Blackmore (16 WEEKS)*   pos/wks

| 1 Feb 97 ● | REMEMBER ME *Pharm CDPHARM 1* | .8 | 13 |
| 23 Aug 97 | SANDMAN *Sidewalk CDSWALK 001* | .25 | 3 |

THE BLUE CAPS – See Gene VINCENT

BLUE FEATHER
Holland, male vocal / instrumental group (4 WEEKS)   pos/wks

| 3 Jul 82 | LET'S FUNK TONIGHT *Mercury MER 109* | .50 | 4 |

BLUE FLAMES – See Georgie FAME

BLUE GRASS BOYS – See Johnny DUNCAN and the BLUE GRASS BOYS

BLUE HAZE *UK, male vocal / instrumental group (6 WEEKS)*   pos/wks

| 18 Mar 72 | SMOKE GETS IN YOUR EYES *A&M AMS 891* | .32 | 6 |

BLUE JEANS – See Bob B SOXX and the BLUE JEANS

BLUE MELONS
UK, male / female vocal / instrumental group (1 WEEK)   pos/wks

| 8 Jun 96 | DO WAH DIDDY DIDDY *Fundamental FUNDCD 1* | .70 | 1 |

BLUE MERCEDES *UK, male vocal / instrumental duo – Duncan Millar and David Titlow (18 WEEKS)*   pos/wks

10 Oct 87	I WANT TO BE YOUR PROPERTY *MCA BONA 1*	.23	11
13 Feb 88	SEE WANT MUST HAVE *MCA BONA 2*	.57	2
23 Jul 88	LOVE IS THE GUN *MCA BONA 3*	.46	5

BLUE MINK 413 Top 500
UK-based session musician supergroup with writers Roger Cook and Roger Greenaway providing the classic pop songs for group members Roger Cook (v), Madeline Bell b. 23 Jul 1942, Newark, New Jersey, US (v), Roger Coulam (k), Herbie Flowers (b), Barry Morgan (d). Greenaway made an OBE in 2001 (83 WEEKS)   pos/wks

| 15 Nov 69 ● | MELTING POT *Philips BF 1818* | .3 | 15 |

28 Mar 70 ●	GOOD MORNING FREEDOM *Philips BF 1838*	10	10
19 Sep 70	OUR WORLD *Philips 6006 042*	17	9
29 May 71 ●	BANNER MAN *Regal Zonophone RZ 3034*	3	14
11 Nov 72	STAY WITH ME (re) *Regal Zonophone RZ 3064*	11	15
3 Mar 73	BY THE DEVIL (I WAS TEMPTED) *EMI 2007*	26	9
23 Jun 73 ●	RANDY *EMI 2028*	9	11

See also PIPKINS; DAVID and JONATHAN

BLUE NILE *UK, male vocal / instrumental group (4 WEEKS)* pos/wks

30 Sep 89	THE DOWNTOWN LIGHTS *Linn LKS 3*	67	1
29 Sep 90	HEADLIGHTS ON THE PARADE *Linn LKS 4*	72	1
19 Jan 91	SATURDAY NIGHT *Linn LKS 5*	50	2

BLUE ÖYSTER CULT
US, male vocal / instrumental group (14 WEEKS) pos/wks

20 May 78	(DON'T FEAR) THE REAPER *CBS 6333*	16	14

BLUE PEARL
UK / US, male / female vocal / instrumental group (29 WEEKS) pos/wks

7 Jul 90 ●	NAKED IN THE RAIN *Big Life BLR 23*	4	13
3 Nov 90	LITTLE BROTHER *Big Life BLR 32*	31	5
11 Jan 92	(CAN YOU) FEEL THE PASSION *Big Life BLR 67*	14	6
25 Jul 92	MOTHER DAWN *Big Life BLR 73*	50	2
27 Nov 93	FIRE OF LOVE *Logic 74321170292* [1]	71	1
4 Jul 98	NAKED IN THE RAIN '98 (re-recording) *Malarky MLKD 7*	22	2

[1] Jungle High with Blue Pearl

BLUE RONDO A LA TURK
UK, male vocal / instrumental group (9 WEEKS) pos/wks

14 Nov 81	ME AND MR SANCHEZ *Virgin VS 463*	40	4
13 Mar 82	KLACTOVEESEDSTEIN *Diable Noir VS 476*	50	5

BLUE ZOO *UK, male vocal / instrumental group (17 WEEKS)* pos/wks

12 Jun 82	I'M YOUR MAN *Magnet MAG 224*	55	3
16 Oct 82	CRY BOY CRY *Magnet MAG 234*	13	10
28 May 83	I JUST CAN'T (FORGIVE AND FORGET) *Magnet MAG 241*	60	4

BLUEBELLS *UK, male vocal / instrumental group (49 WEEKS)* pos/wks

12 Mar 83	CATH / WILL SHE ALWAYS BE WAITING *London LON 20*	62	2
9 Jul 83	SUGAR BRIDGE (IT WILL STAND) *London LON 27*	72	1
24 Mar 84	I'M FALLING *London LON 45*	11	12
23 Jun 84 ●	YOUNG AT HEART *London LON 49*	8	12
1 Sep 84	CATH (re-issue) *London LON 54*	38	7
9 Feb 85	ALL I AM (IS LOVING YOU) *London LON 58*	58	3
27 Mar 93 ★	YOUNG AT HEART (re-issue) *London LONCD 338*	1	12

BLUENOTES – *See Harold MELVIN and the BLUENOTES*

BLUES BAND *UK, male vocal / instrumental group (2 WEEKS)* pos/wks

12 Jul 80	BLUES BAND (EP) *Arista BOOT 2*	68	2

Tracks on Blues Band (EP): Maggie's Farm / Ain't it Tuff / Diddy Wah Diddy / Back Door Man

BLUES BROTHERS *US, male actors / vocal duo – John Belushi and Dan Ackroyd (8 WEEKS)* pos/wks

7 Apr 90	EVERYBODY NEEDS SOMEBODY TO LOVE *East West A7591*	12	8

For the first two weeks, the flip side of 'Everybody Needs Somebody to Love' – 'Think' by Aretha Franklin – was listed

BLUETONES *UK, male vocal / instrumental group (43 WEEKS)* pos/wks

17 Jun 95	ARE YOU BLUE OR ARE YOU BLIND *Superior Quality BLUE 001CD*	31	2
14 Oct 95	BLUETONIC *Superior Quality BLUE 002CD*	19	3
3 Feb 96 ●	SLIGHT RETURN *Superior Quality BLUE 003CD*	2	8
11 May 96 ●	CUT SOME RUG / CASTLE ROCK (re) *Superior Quality BLUE 005CD*	7	6
28 Sep 96 ●	MARBLEHEAD JOHNSON *Superior Quality BLUE 006CD*	7	6

21 Feb 98 ●	SOLOMON BITES THE WORM *Superior Quality BLUED 007*	10	3
9 May 98	IF ... *Superior Quality BLUED 009*	13	5
8 Aug 98	SLEAZY BED TRACK *Superior Quality BLUED 010*	35	2
4 Mar 00	KEEP THE HOME FIRES BURNING *Superior Quality BLUED 012*	13	3
20 May 00	AUTOPHILIA *Superior Quality BLUED 013*	18	3
6 Apr 02	AFTER HOURS *Superior Quality BLUED 016*	26	2

Colin BLUNSTONE *UK, male vocalist (29 WEEKS)* pos/wks

12 Feb 72	SAY YOU DON'T MIND *Epic EPC 7765*	15	9
11 Nov 72	I DON'T BELIEVE IN MIRACLES *Epic EPC 8434*	31	6
17 Feb 73	HOW COULD WE DARE TO BE WRONG *Epic EPC 1197*	45	2
14 Mar 81	WHAT BECOMES OF THE BROKEN HEARTED *Stiff BROKEN 1* [1]	13	10
29 May 82	TRACKS OF MY TEARS *PRT 7P 236*	60	2

[1] Dave Stewart. Guest vocals: Colin Blunstone

See also ARGENT; Neil MacARTHUR; ZOMBIES

BLUR `201` `Top 500` *Prime movers of Britpop: Damon Albarn (v/k), Graham Coxon (g), Alex James (b), Dave Rowntree (d). They won a record four Brit awards in 1995, and their first No.1 caused a media storm when it outpaced 'Roll with It' by Britpop rivals Oasis. Best-selling single: 'Country House' 640,000 (132 WEEKS)* pos/wks

27 Oct 90	SHE'S SO HIGH / I KNOW *Food FOOD 26*	48	3
27 Apr 91 ●	THERE'S NO OTHER WAY *Food FOOD 29*	8	8
10 Aug 91	BANG *Food FOOD 31*	24	4
11 Apr 92	POPSCENE *Food FOOD 37*	32	2
1 May 93	FOR TOMORROW *Food CDFOODS 40*	28	4
10 Jul 93	CHEMICAL WORLD *Food CDFOODS 45*	28	4
16 Oct 93	SUNDAY SUNDAY *Food CDFOOD 46*	26	3
19 Mar 94 ●	GIRLS AND BOYS *Food CDFOODS 47*	5	7
11 Jun 94	TO THE END *Food CDFOODS 50*	16	5
3 Sep 94 ●	PARKLIFE *Food CDFOOD 53*	10	7
19 Nov 94	END OF A CENTURY *Food CDFOOD 56*	19	3
26 Aug 95 ★	COUNTRY HOUSE *Food CDFOODS 63* ■	1	11
9 Sep 95	COUNTRY HOUSE *Food FOODS 63*	57	1
25 Nov 95 ●	THE UNIVERSAL *Food CDFOODS 69*	5	9
24 Feb 96 ●	STEREOTYPES *Food CDFOOD 73*	7	5
11 May 96 ●	CHARMLESS MAN *Food CDFOOD 77*	5	6
1 Feb 97 ★	BEETLEBUM (re) *Food CDFOODS 89* ■	1	7
19 Apr 97 ●	SONG 2 *Food CDFOODS 93*	2	5
28 Jun 97 ●	ON YOUR OWN *Food CDFOOD 98*	5	5
27 Sep 97	MOR *Food CDFOOD 107*	15	3
6 Mar 99 ●	TENDER *Food CDFOODS 117*	2	10
10 Jul 99	COFFEE + TV *Food CDFOODS 122*	11	7
27 Nov 99	NO DISTANCE LEFT TO RUN (re) *Food CDFOOD 123*	14	4
28 Oct 00 ●	MUSIC IS MY RADAR (re) *Food / Parlophone CDFOODS 135*	10	9

Chart rules allow for a maximum of three formats; the 7-inch of 'Country House', already available on two CDs and cassette, was therefore listed separately

BOB and EARL
US, male vocal duo – Bobby Relf and Earl Nelson (13 WEEKS) pos/wks

12 Mar 69 ●	HARLEM SHUFFLE *Island WIP 6053*	7	13

BOB and MARCIA *Jamaica, male / female vocal duo – Bob Andy and Marcia Griffiths (25 WEEKS)* pos/wks

14 Mar 70 ●	YOUNG, GIFTED AND BLACK *Harry J HJ 6605*	5	12
5 Jun 71	PIED PIPER *Trojan TR 7818*	11	13

BOB THE BUILDER *UK, male silicone puppet building contractor – Neil Morrissey (41 WEEKS)* pos/wks

16 Dec 00 ★	CAN WE FIX IT (2re) *BBC Music WMSS 60372* ◆	1	22
15 Sep 01 ★	MAMBO NO.5 *BBC Music WMSS 60442* ■	1	19

BOBBYSOCKS *Norway / Sweden, female vocal duo (4 WEEKS)* pos/wks

25 May 85	LET IT SWING *RCA PB 40127*	44	4

Su Su BOBIEN – *See MASS SYNDICATE featuring Su Su BOBIEN*

Andrea BOCELLI *Italy, male vocalist (24 WEEKS)*   pos/wks
24 May 97 ●	TIME TO SAY GOODBYE (CON TE PARTIRO) *Coalition COLA 003CD* [1]	2 14
25 Sep 99	CANTO DELLA TERRA (re) *Polydor / Sugar 5613192*	24 9
18 Dec 99	AVE MARIA *Philips 4644852*	65 1

[1] Sarah Brightman and Andrea Bocelli

'Canto Della Terra' was originally No.25 before re-entering and peaking one place higher in Jul 2000

Karen BODDINGTON and Mark WILLIAMS
Australia, female / male vocal duo (1 WEEK)   pos/wks
2 Sep 89	HOME AND AWAY *First Night SCORE 19*	73 1

BODY COUNT *US, male rap / instrumental group (4 WEEKS)*   pos/wks
8 Oct 94	BORN DEAD *Rhyme Syndicate SYNDG 4*	28 2
17 Dec 94	NECESSARY EVIL *Virgin VSCDX 1529*	45 2

See also ICE-T

BODYSNATCHERS
UK, female vocal / instrumental group (12 WEEKS)   pos/wks
15 Mar 80	LET'S DO ROCK STEADY *2 Tone CHSTT 9*	22 9
19 Jul 80	EASY LIFE *2 Tone CHSTT 12*	50 3

Humphrey BOGART – *See Dooley WILSON*

Hamilton BOHANNON
US, male vocalist / instrumentalist – drums (38 WEEKS)   pos/wks
15 Feb 75	SOUTH AFRICAN MAN *Brunswick BR 16*	22 8
24 May 75 ●	DISCO STOMP *Brunswick BR 19*	6 12
5 Jul 75	FOOT STOMPIN' MUSIC *Brunswick BR 21*	23 6
6 Sep 75	HAPPY FEELING *Brunswick BR 24*	49 3
26 Aug 78	LET'S START THE DANCE *Mercury 6167 700*	56 4
13 Feb 82	LET'S START TO DANCE AGAIN *London HL 10582*	49 5

BOILING POINT *US, male vocal / instrumental group (6 WEEKS)*   pos/wks
27 May 78	LET'S GET FUNKTIFIED *Bang BANG 1312*	41 6

Marc BOLAN – *See T. REX*

CJ BOLLAND *Belgium, male producer (10 WEEKS)*   pos/wks
5 Oct 96	SUGAR IS SWEETER *Internal LIECD 35*	11 5
17 May 97	THE PROPHET *ffrr FCD 300*	19 3
3 Jul 99	IT AIN'T GONNA BE ME *Essential Recordings ESCD 5*	35 2

See also RAVESIGNAL III

Michael BOLTON   255   Top 500
Soulful rock balladeer / songwriter who initially recorded under his real name, Michael Bolotin (b. 26 Feb 1953, Connecticut, US), and fronted recording groups The Nomads and Blackjack (113 WEEKS)   pos/wks
17 Feb 90 ●	HOW AM I SUPPOSED TO LIVE WITHOUT YOU *CBS 655397 7* ▲	3 10
28 Apr 90 ●	HOW CAN WE BE LOVERS *CBS 655918 7*	10 10
21 Jul 90	WHEN I'M BACK ON MY FEET AGAIN *CBS 656077 7*	44 5
20 Apr 91	LOVE IS A WONDERFUL THING *Columbia 6567717*	23 8
27 Jul 91	TIME LOVE AND TENDERNESS *Columbia 6569897*	28 7
9 Nov 91 ●	WHEN A MAN LOVES A WOMAN *Columbia 6574887* ▲	8 9
8 Feb 92	STEEL BARS *Columbia 6577257*	17 6
9 May 92	MISSING YOU NOW *Columbia 6579917* [1]	28 4
31 Oct 92	TO LOVE SOMEBODY *Columbia 6584557*	16 6
26 Dec 92	DRIFT AWAY *Columbia 6588657*	18 5
13 Mar 93	REACH OUT I'LL BE THERE *Columbia 6588972*	37 4
13 Nov 93	SAID I LOVED YOU BUT I LIED *Columbia 6598762*	15 8
26 Feb 94	SOUL OF MY SOUL *Columbia 6601772*	32 3
14 May 94	LEAN ON ME *Columbia 6604132*	14 7
9 Sep 95 ●	CAN I TOUCH YOU ... THERE *Columbia 6624385*	6 9
2 Dec 95	A LOVE SO BEAUTIFUL *Columbia 6627092*	27 5
16 Mar 96	SOUL PROVIDER *Columbia 6629812*	35 3
8 Nov 97	THE BEST OF LOVE / GO THE DISTANCE *Columbia 6652802*	14 4

[1] Michael Bolton featuring Kenny G

BOMB THE BASS *UK, male producer – Tim Simenon (50 WEEKS)* pos/wks
20 Feb 88 ●	BEAT DIS *Mister-ron DOOD 1*	2 9
27 Aug 88 ●	MEGABLAST / DON'T MAKE ME WAIT *Mister-ron DOOD 2* [1]	6 9
26 Nov 88 ●	SAY A LITTLE PRAYER *Rhythm King DOOD 3* [2]	10 10
27 Jul 91 ●	WINTER IN JULY *Rhythm King 6572757*	7 9
9 Nov 91	THE AIR YOU BREATHE *Rhythm King 6575387*	52 3
2 May 92	KEEP GIVING ME LOVE *Rhythm King 6579887*	62 2
1 Oct 94	BUG POWDER DUST *Stoned Heights BRCD 300* [3]	24 3
17 Dec 94	DARKHEART *Stoned Heights BRCD 305* [4]	35 3
1 Apr 95	1 TO 1 RELIGION *Stoned Heights BRCD 313* [5]	53 1
16 Sep 95	SANDCASTLES *Fourth & Broadway BRCD 324* [6]	54 1

[1] Bomb the Bass featuring Merlin and Antonia / Bomb the Bass featuring Lorraine and Lose [2] Bomb the Bass featuring Maureen [3] Bomb the Bass featuring Justin Warfield [4] Bomb the Bass featuring Spikey Tee [5] Bomb the Bass featuring Carlton [6] Bomb the Bass featuring Bernard Fowler

See also ANTONIA

BOMBALURINA *UK, male / female vocal group (20 WEEKS)*   pos/wks
28 Jul 90 ★	ITSY BITSY TEENY WEENY YELLOW POLKA DOT BIKINI *Carpet CRPT 1*	1 13
24 Nov 90	SEVEN LITTLE GIRLS SITTING IN THE BACKSEAT *Carpet CRPT 2* [1]	18 7

[1] Bombalurina featuring Timmy Mallett

BOMBERS
Canada, male / female vocal / instrumental group (10 WEEKS)   pos/wks
5 May 79	(EVERYBODY) GET DANCIN' *Flamingo FM 1*	37 7
18 Aug 79	LET'S DANCE *Flamingo FM 4*	58 3

BOMFUNK MC'S *Finland, male DJ / rap duo*
– Raymond Ebanks and DJ Gismo (21 WEEKS)   pos/wks
5 Aug 00 ●	FREESTYLER *Dancepool DPS 2CD*	2 12
2 Dec 00	UP ROCKING BEATS *INCredible 6706132*	11 9

BON *Germany, male vocal duo*
– Guy Gross and Claus Capek (5 WEEKS)   pos/wks
3 Feb 01	BOYS *Epic 6707092*	15 5

BON JOVI   69   Top 500
Globally popular New Jersey band: Jon Bon Jovi (v), Richie Sambora (g), David Bryan (k), Alec John Such (b), Tico Torres (d). The UK's biggest-selling album act of 1994. Estimated 75 million albums sold worldwide. Legendary fact: at one of their gigs a pig's head was thrown on stage. Best-selling single: 'Always' 560,500 (223 WEEKS)   pos/wks
31 Aug 85	HARDEST PART IS THE NIGHT *Vertigo VER 22*	68 1
9 Aug 86	YOU GIVE LOVE A BAD NAME *Vertigo VER 26* ▲	14 10
25 Oct 86 ●	LIVIN' ON A PRAYER *Vertigo VER 28* ▲	4 15
11 Apr 87	WANTED DEAD OR ALIVE *Vertigo JOV 1*	13 7
15 Aug 87	NEVER SAY GOODBYE *Vertigo JOV 2*	21 5
24 Sep 88	BAD MEDICINE *Vertigo JOV 3* ▲	17 7
10 Dec 88	BORN TO BE MY BABY *Vertigo JOV 4*	22 7
29 Apr 89	I'LL BE THERE FOR YOU *Vertigo JOV 5* ▲	18 7
26 Aug 89	LAY YOUR HANDS ON ME *Vertigo JOV 6*	18 6
9 Dec 89	LIVING IN SIN *Vertigo JOV 7*	35 6
24 Oct 92 ●	KEEP THE FAITH *Jambco JOV 8*	5 6
23 Jan 93	BED OF ROSES *Jambco JOVCD 9*	13 6
15 May 93 ●	IN THESE ARMS *Jambco JOVCD 10*	9 7
7 Aug 93	I'LL SLEEP WHEN I'M DEAD *Jambco JOVCD 11*	17 5
2 Oct 93	I BELIEVE *Jambco JOVCD 12*	11 6
26 Mar 94 ●	DRY COUNTY *Jambco JOVCD 13*	9 6
24 Sep 94 ●	ALWAYS *Jambco JOVCD 14*	2 18
17 Dec 94 ●	PLEASE COME HOME FOR CHRISTMAS (re) *Jambco JOVCD 16*	7 10
25 Feb 95 ●	SOMEDAY I'LL BE SATURDAY NIGHT *Jambco JOVDD 15*	7 7
10 Jun 95 ●	THIS AIN'T A LOVE SONG *Mercury JOVCD 17*	6 9

30 Sep 95	● SOMETHING FOR THE PAIN *Mercury JOVCD 18*	8	7
25 Nov 95	● LIE TO ME *Mercury JOVCD 19*	10	8
9 Mar 96	● THESE DAYS *Mercury JOVCD 20*	7	6
6 Jul 96	● HEY GOD *Mercury JOVCD 21*	13	5
10 Apr 99	REAL LIFE *Reprise W 479CD*	21	5
3 Jun 00	● IT'S MY LIFE *Mercury 5627682*	3	13
9 Sep 00	● SAY IT ISN'T SO (re) *Mercury 5688972*	10	7
9 Dec 00	THANK YOU FOR LOVING ME *Mercury 5727302*	12	6
19 May 01	ONE WILD NIGHT *Mercury 5729502*	10	7
28 Sep 02	● EVERYDAY (re) *Mercury 0639362*	6	6
21 Dec 02	MISUNDERSTOOD *Mercury 0638152*	21	2

Jon BON JOVI
US, male vocalist / instrumentalist – John Bongiovi Jr (27 WEEKS) pos/wks

4 Aug 90	BLAZE OF GLORY *Vertigo JBJ 1* ▲	13	8
10 Nov 90	MIRACLE *Vertigo JBVJ 2*	29	5
14 Jun 97	● MIDNIGHT IN CHELSEA *Mercury MERCD 488*	4	7
30 Aug 97	● QUEEN OF NEW ORLEANS *Mercury MERCD 493*	10	4
15 Nov 97	JANIE, DON'T TAKE YOUR LOVE TO TOWN *Mercury 5749872*	13	3

Ronnie BOND *UK, male vocalist (5 WEEKS)* pos/wks

| 31 May 80 | IT'S WRITTEN ON YOUR BODY *Mercury MER 13* | 52 | 5 |

Gary 'U.S.' BONDS
US, male vocalist – Gary Anderson (39 WEEKS) pos/wks

19 Jan 61	NEW ORLEANS *Top Rank JAR 527* [1]	16	11
20 Jul 61	● QUARTER TO THREE *Top Rank JAR 575* [2] ▲	7	13
30 May 81	THIS LITTLE GIRL *EMI America EA 122*	43	6
22 Aug 81	JOLE BLON *EMI America EA 127*	51	3
31 Oct 81	IT'S ONLY LOVE *EMI America EA 128*	43	3
17 Jul 82	SOUL DEEP *EMI America EA 140*	59	3

[1] U.S. Bonds [2] US Bonds

BONE *UK, male vocal / instrumental duo (1 WEEK)* pos/wks

| 2 Apr 94 | WINGS OF LOVE *Deconstruction 74321176282* | 55 | 1 |

BONE THUGS-N-HARMONY *US, male rap group (22 WEEKS)* pos/wks

4 Nov 95	1ST OF THA MONTH *Epic 6625172*	32	2
10 Aug 96	● THA CROSSROADS *Epic 6635502* ▲	8	11
9 Nov 96	1ST OF THA MONTH (re-issue) *Epic 6638505*	15	4
15 Feb 97	DAYS OF OUR LIVEZ *East West A 3982CD*	37	2
26 Jul 97	LOOK INTO MY EYES *Epic 6647862*	16	3

Elbow BONES and the RACKETEERS
US, male group leader and female backing group (9 WEEKS) pos/wks

| 14 Jan 84 | A NIGHT IN NEW YORK *EMI America EA 165* | 33 | 9 |

BONEY M [118] Top 500
Internationally successful West Indian vocal group: Bobby Farrell, Marcia Barrett, Liz Mitchell, Maisie Williams. This German-based quartet was assembled by producer Frank Farian (later behind controversial duo Milli Vanilli). Best-selling single: 'Rivers of Babylon' / 'Brown Girl in the Ring' 1,995,000 (171 WEEKS) pos/wks

18 Dec 76	● DADDY COOL *Atlantic K 10827*	6	13
12 Mar 77	● SUNNY *Atlantic K 10892*	3	10
25 Jun 77	● MA BAKER *Atlantic K 10965*	2	13
29 Oct 77	● BELFAST *Atlantic K 11020*	8	13
29 Apr 78	★ RIVERS OF BABYLON / BROWN GIRL IN THE RING *Atlantic / Hansa K 11120* ◆	1	40
7 Oct 78	● RASPUTIN *Atlantic / Hansa K 11192*	2	10
2 Dec 78	★ MARY'S BOY CHILD – OH MY LORD *Atlantic / Hansa K 11221* ◆	1	8
3 Mar 79	● PAINTER MAN *Atlantic / Hansa K 11255*	10	6
28 Apr 79	● HOORAY HOORAY, IT'S A HOLI-HOLIDAY *Atlantic / Hansa K 11279*	3	9
11 Aug 79	GOTTA GO HOME / EL LUTE *Atlantic / Hansa K 11351*	12	11
15 Dec 79	I'M BORN AGAIN *Atlantic / Hansa K 11410*	35	7
26 Apr 80	MY FRIEND JACK *Atlantic / Hansa K 11463*	57	5
14 Feb 81	CHILDREN OF PARADISE *Atlantic / Hansa K 11637*	66	2
21 Nov 81	WE KILL THE WORLD (DON'T KILL THE WORLD) *Atlantic / Hansa K 11689*	39	5
24 Dec 88	MEGAMIX / MARY'S BOY CHILD (re-mix) *Ariola 111947*	52	3
5 Dec 92	● BONEY M MEGAMIX *Arista 74321125127*	7	9
17 Apr 93	BROWN GIRL IN THE RING (re-mix) *Arista 74321137052*	38	3
8 May 99	MA BAKER – SOMEBODY SCREAMED *Logic 74321653872* [1]	22	2
29 Dec 01	DADDY COOL 2001 (re-mix) *BMG 74321913512*	47	2

[1] Boney M vs Horny United

'Brown Girl in the Ring' listed with 'Rivers of Babylon' only from 5 Aug 1978, peaking at No.2. 'El Lute' listed with 'Gotta Go Home' only from 29 Sep 1979. The 1988 and 1992 megamixes are different

BONIFACE *Seychelles, male vocalist – Bruce Boniface (3 WEEKS)* pos/wks

| 31 Aug 02 | CHEEKY *Columbia 6729902* | 25 | 3 |

Guest vocal by Lady Luck

Graham BONNET *UK, male vocalist (15 WEEKS)* pos/wks

| 21 Mar 81 | ● NIGHT GAMES *Vertigo VER 1* | 6 | 11 |
| 13 Jun 81 | LIAR *Vertigo VER 2* | 51 | 4 |

Graham BONNEY *UK, male vocalist – Graham Bradley (8 WEEKS)* pos/wks

| 24 Mar 66 | SUPERGIRL *Columbia DB 7843* | 19 | 8 |

BONO *Ireland, male vocalist – Paul Hewson (25 WEEKS)* pos/wks

25 Jan 86	IN A LIFETIME *RCA PB 40535* [1]	20	5
10 Jun 89	IN A LIFETIME (re-issue) *RCA PB 42873* [1]	17	7
4 Dec 93	● I'VE GOT YOU UNDER MY SKIN *Island CID 578* [2]	4	9
9 Apr 94	IN THE NAME OF THE FATHER *Island CID 593* [3]	46	2
23 Oct 99	NEW DAY *Columbia 6682122* [4]	23	2

[1] Clannad featuring Bono [2] Frank Sinatra with Bono [3] Bono and Gavin Friday [4] Wyclef Jean featuring Bono

I've Got You Under My Skin was the listed B-side of 'Stay (Faraway So Close)' by U2

See also U2

BONZO DOG DOO-DAH BAND
UK, male vocal / instrumental group (14 WEEKS) pos/wks

| 6 Nov 68 | ● I'M THE URBAN SPACEMAN *Liberty LBF 15144* | 5 | 14 |

Betty BOO *UK, female rapper – Alison Clarkson (55 WEEKS)* pos/wks

12 Aug 89	● HEY DJ – I CAN'T DANCE (TO THAT MUSIC YOU'RE PLAYING) / SKA TRAIN *Rhythm King LEFT 34* [1]	7	11
19 May 90	● DOIN' THE DO *Rhythm King LEFT 39*	7	12
11 Aug 90	● WHERE ARE YOU BABY? *Rhythm King LEFT 43*	3	10
1 Dec 90	24 HOURS *Rhythm King LEFT 45*	25	8
8 Aug 92	LET ME TAKE YOU THERE *WEA YZ 677*	12	8
3 Oct 92	I'M ON MY WAY *WEA YZ 693*	44	3
10 Apr 93	HANGOVER *WEA YZ 719CD*	50	3

[1] Beatmasters featuring Betty Boo

BOO RADLEYS *UK, male vocal / instrumental group (27 WEEKS)* pos/wks

20 Jun 92	DOES THIS HURT / BOO! FOREVER *Creation CRE 128*	67	1
23 Oct 93	WISH I WAS SKINNY *Creation CRESCD 169*	75	1
12 Feb 94	BARNEY (... & ME) *Creation CRESCD 178*	48	2
11 Jun 94	LAZARUS *Creation CRESCD 187*	50	2
11 Mar 95	● WAKE UP BOO! *Creation CRESCD 191*	9	8
13 May 95	FIND THE ANSWER WITHIN *Creation CRESCD 202*	37	3
29 Jul 95	IT'S LULU *Creation CRESCD 211*	25	2
7 Oct 95	FROM THE BENCH AT BELVIDERE *Creation CRESCD 214*	24	2
17 Aug 96	WHAT'S IN THE BOX (SEE WATCHA GOT) *Creation CRESCD 220*	25	2
19 Oct 96	C'MON KIDS *Creation CRESCD 236*	18	2
1 Feb 97	RIDE THE TIGER *Creation CRESCD 248X*	38	1
17 Oct 98	FREE HUEY *Creation CRESCD 299X*	54	1

Re-entries are listed as (re), (2re), (3re), etc which signifies that the hit re-entered the chart once, twice or three times, etc

BOO-YAA T.R.I.B.E. US, male rap group (6 WEEKS)

			pos/wks
30 Jun 90	PSYKO FUNK Fourth & Broadway BRW 179	43	3
6 Nov 93	ANOTHER BODY MURDERED Epic 6597942 [1]	26	3

[1] Faith No More and Boo-Yaa T.R.I.B.E.

BOOGIE BOX HIGH UK, male vocal / instrumental
group – leader Andros Georgiou (11 WEEKS)

			pos/wks
4 Jul 87	● JIVE TALKIN' Hardback 7BOSS 4	7	11

See also ALIEN VOICES featuring The THREE DEGREES; Andy G's STARSKY & HUTCH
ALL STARS

BOOGIE DOWN PRODUCTIONS
US, male rap / production duo (2 WEEKS)

			pos/wks
4 Jun 88	MY PHILOSOPHY / STOP THE VIOLENCE Jive JIVEX 170	69	2

BOOKER T and the MG's
US, male instrumental group (43 WEEKS)

			pos/wks
11 Dec 68	SOUL LIMBO Stax 102	30	9
7 May 69	● TIME IS TIGHT Stax 119	4	18
30 Aug 69	SOUL CLAP '69 Stax 127	35	4
15 Dec 79	● GREEN ONIONS Atlantic K 10109	7	12

BOOM! UK, male / female vocal group (5 WEEKS)

			pos/wks
27 Jan 01	FALLING London LONCD 458	11	5

Taka BOOM – See EYE TO EYE featuring Taka BOOM; Joey NEGRO

BOOM BOOM ROOM
UK, male vocal / instrumental group (1 WEEK)

			pos/wks
8 Mar 86	HERE COMES THE MAN Fun After All FUN 101	74	1

BOOMTOWN RATS 224 Top 500 New wave group named after a
band in a Woody Guthrie novel. Fronted by charismatic Bob Geldof (b. 5 Oct
1954, Dublin), who was later knighted for organising Live Aid. The Mutt Lange
produced 'Rat Trap' was the first new wave No.1 (123 WEEKS)

			pos/wks
27 Aug 77	LOOKING AFTER NO.1 Ensign ENY 4	11	9
19 Nov 77	MARY OF THE 4TH FORM Ensign ENY 9	15	9
15 Apr 78	SHE'S SO MODERN Ensign ENY 13	12	11
17 Jun 78	● LIKE CLOCKWORK Ensign ENY 14	6	13
14 Oct 78	★ RAT TRAP Ensign ENY 16	1	15
21 Jul 79	★ I DON'T LIKE MONDAYS Ensign ENY 30	1	12
17 Nov 79	DIAMOND SMILES Ensign ENY 33	13	10
26 Jan 80	● SOMEONE'S LOOKING AT YOU Ensign ENY 34	4	9
22 Nov 80	● BANANA REPUBLIC Mercury BONGO 1	3	11
31 Jan 81	THE ELEPHANT'S GRAVEYARD (GUILTY) Mercury BONGO 2	26	6
12 Dec 81	NEVER IN A MILLION YEARS Mercury MER 87	62	4
20 Mar 82	HOUSE ON FIRE Mercury MER 91	24	8
18 Feb 84	TONIGHT Mercury MER 154	73	1
19 May 84	DRAG ME DOWN Mercury MER 163	50	3
2 Jul 94	I DON'T LIKE MONDAYS (re-issue) Vertigo VERCD 87	38	2

See also Bob GELDOF

Clint BOON EXPERIENCE
UK, male / female vocal / instrumental group (3 WEEKS)

			pos/wks
6 Nov 99	WHITE NO SUGAR Artful CDARTFUL 32	61	1
5 Feb 00	BIGGEST HORIZON Artful CDARTFUL 33	70	1
5 Aug 00	DO WHAT YOU DO (EARWORM SONG) Artful CDARTFUL 34	63	1

Daniel BOONE UK, male vocalist – Peter Lee Stirling (25 WEEKS)

			pos/wks
14 Aug 71	DADDY DON'T YOU WALK SO FAST Penny Farthing PEN 764	17	15
1 Apr 72	BEAUTIFUL SUNDAY (re) Penny Farthing PEN 781	21	10

Debby BOONE US, female vocalist (2 WEEKS)

			pos/wks
24 Dec 77	YOU LIGHT UP MY LIFE Warner Bros. / Curb K 17043 ▲	48	2

Pat BOONE 31 Top 500

Major rival to Elvis in late 1950s, b. 1 Jun 1934, Florida. This clean-cut vocalist
was voted the World's Outstanding Male Singer in the UK in 1957. He was
seldom absent from the UK or US charts during the early rock 'n' roll years
(309 WEEKS)

			pos/wks
18 Nov 55	● AIN'T THAT A SHAME (re) London HLD 8172	7	11
27 Apr 56	★ I'LL BE HOME (re) London HLD 8253	1	24
27 Jul 56	LONG TALL SALLY (re) London HLD 8291	18	7
17 Aug 56	I ALMOST LOST MY MIND London HLD 8303	14	7
7 Dec 56	● FRIENDLY PERSUASION (THEE I LOVE) London HLD 8346	3	21
1 Feb 57	● DON'T FORBID ME London HLD 8370	2	16
26 Apr 57	WHY BABY WHY London HLD 8404	17	7
5 Jul 57	● LOVE LETTERS IN THE SAND London HLD 8445 ▲	2	21
27 Sep 57	● REMEMBER YOU'RE MINE / THERE'S A GOLDMINE IN THE SKY London HLD 8479	5	18
6 Dec 57	● APRIL LOVE London HLD 8512 ▲	7	23
13 Dec 57	WHITE CHRISTMAS London HLD 8520	29	1
4 Apr 58	● A WONDERFUL TIME UP THERE London HLD 8574 (A)	2	17
11 Apr 58	● IT'S TOO SOON TO KNOW London HLD 8574 (B)	7	12
27 Jun 58	● SUGAR MOON London HLD 8640	6	12
29 Aug 58	IF DREAMS CAME TRUE London HLD 8675	16	11
5 Dec 58	GEE, BUT IT'S LONELY London HLD 8739	30	1
16 Jan 59	I'LL REMEMBER TONIGHT (2re) London HLD 8775	18	9
10 Apr 59	WITH THE WIND AND THE RAIN IN YOUR HAIR London HLD 8824	21	3
22 May 59	FOR A PENNY (re) London HLD 8855	19	9
31 Jul 59	'TWIXT TWELVE AND TWENTY (re) London HLD 8910	18	7
23 Jun 60	WALKING THE FLOOR OVER YOU (2re) London HLD 9138	39	6
6 Jul 61	MOODY RIVER London HLD 9350 ▲	18	10
7 Dec 61	● JOHNNY WILL London HLD 9461	4	13
15 Feb 62	I'LL SEE YOU IN MY DREAMS London HLD 9504	27	9
24 May 62	QUANDO, QUANDO, QUANDO London HLD 9543	41	4
12 Jul 62	● SPEEDY GONZALES London HLD 9573	2	19
15 Nov 62	THE MAIN ATTRACTION London HLD 9620	12	11

'There's a Goldmine in the Sky' was listed only for the week of 27 Sep 1957. It
peaked at No.23. 'A Wonderful Time Up There' and 'It's Too Soon to Know' were
both on the same single release

BOOOM – See Boris DLUGOSCH

BOOT ROOM BOYZ – See LIVERPOOL FC

Duke BOOTEE – See GRANDMASTER FLASH, Melle MEL and the FURIOUS FIVE

BOOTH and the BAD ANGEL UK / US, male vocal /
instrumental duo – Tim Booth and Angelo Badalamenti (4 WEEKS)

			pos/wks
22 Jun 96	I BELIEVE Fontana BBCD 1	25	3
11 Jul 98	FALL IN LOVE WITH ME Mercury MERCD 503	57	1

See also JAMES

Ken BOOTHE Jamaica, male vocalist (22 WEEKS)

			pos/wks
21 Sep 74	★ EVERYTHING I OWN Trojan TR 7920	1	12
14 Dec 74	CRYING OVER YOU Trojan TR 7944	11	10

BOOTHILL FOOT-TAPPERS
UK, male / female vocal / instrumental group (3 WEEKS)

			pos/wks
14 Jul 84	GET YOUR FEET OUT OF MY SHOES Go! Discs TAP 1	64	3

BOOTSY'S RUBBER BAND
US, male vocal / instrumental group (3 WEEKS)

			pos/wks
8 Jul 78	BOOTZILLA Warner Bros. K 17196	43	3

BOOTZILLA ORCHESTRA – See Malcolm McLAREN

BOSS US, male producer – David Morales (1 WEEK)

			pos/wks
27 Aug 94	CONGO Cooltempo CDCOOL 296	54	1

See also David MORALES; PULSE featuring Antoinette ROBERSON

BOSTON
US, male vocal / instrumental group (13 WEEKS) — pos/wks

Date	Title	pos	wks
29 Jan 77	**MORE THAN A FEELING** Epic EPC 4658	22	8
7 Oct 78	**DON'T LOOK BACK** Epic EPC 6653	43	5

Eve BOSWELL with Glen SOMERS and his ORCHESTRA
Hungary, female vocalist – Eva Keleti, d. 13 Aug 1998 (13 WEEKS) — pos/wks

Date	Title	pos	wks
30 Dec 55 ●	**PICKIN' A-CHICKEN (2re)** Parlophone R 4082	9	13

Judy BOUCHER St Vincent, female vocalist (23 WEEKS) — pos/wks

Date	Title	pos	wks
4 Apr 87 ●	**CAN'T BE WITH YOU TONIGHT** Orbitone OR 721	2	14
4 Jul 87	**YOU CAUGHT MY EYE** Orbitone OR 722	18	9

Peter BOUNCER – See SHUT UP AND DANCE

BOUNCING CZECKS
UK, male vocal / instrumental group (1 WEEK) — pos/wks

Date	Title	pos	wks
29 Dec 84	**I'M A LITTLE CHRISTMAS CRACKER** RCA 463	72	1

BOUNTY KILLER Jamaica, male rapper – Rodney Price (1 WEEK) — pos/wks

Date	Title	pos	wks
27 Feb 99	**IT'S A PARTY** Edel 0066135 BLA	65	1

BOURGEOIS TAGG US, male vocal / instrumental
duo – Brent Bourgeois and Larry Tagg (6 WEEKS) — pos/wks

Date	Title	pos	wks
6 Feb 88	**I DON'T MIND AT ALL** Island IS 353	35	6

BOURGIE BOURGIE
UK, male vocal / instrumental group (4 WEEKS) — pos/wks

Date	Title	pos	wks
3 Mar 84	**BREAKING POINT** MCA BOU 1	48	4

Toby BOURKE with George MICHAEL
UK, male vocalists (4 WEEKS) — pos/wks

Date	Title	pos	wks
7 Jun 97 ●	**WALTZ AWAY DREAMING** Aegean AECD 01	10	4

Aletia BOURNE – See ANGELHEART

BOW WOW WOW
UK / Burma, female / male vocal / instrumental group (54 WEEKS) — pos/wks

Date	Title	pos	wks
26 Jul 80	**C'30, C'60, C'90, GO** EMI 5088	34	7
6 Dec 80	**YOUR CASSETTE PET** EMI WOW 1	58	6
28 Mar 81	**W.O.R.K. (N.O. NAH NO NO MY DADDY DON'T)** EMI 5153	62	3
15 Aug 81	**PRINCE OF DARKNESS** RCA 100	58	4
7 Nov 81	**CHIHUAHUA** RCA 144	51	4
30 Jan 82 ●	**GO WILD IN THE COUNTRY** RCA 175	7	13
1 May 82	**SEE JUNGLE (JUNGLE BOY) / TV SAVAGE** RCA 220	45	3
5 Jun 82 ●	**I WANT CANDY** RCA 238	9	8
31 Jul 82	**LOUIS QUATORZE** RCA 263	66	2
12 Mar 83	**DO YOU WANNA HOLD ME?** RCA 314	47	4

Your Cassette Pet listed as Louis Quatorze on 6 Dec 1980 only. Tracks on Your Cassette Pet (available only as a cassette) are: Louis Quatorze / Gold He Said / Umo-Sex-Al Apache / I Want My Baby on Mars / Sexy Eiffel Towers / Giant Sized Baby Thing / Fools Rush In / Radio G String. RCA 263 is disc version of track on EMI WOW 1 Cassette

BOWA featuring MALA
US, male / female vocal / instrumental duo (1 WEEK) — pos/wks

Date	Title	pos	wks
7 Dec 91	**DIFFERENT STORY** Dead Dead Good GOOD 8	64	1

Dane BOWERS – See TRUE STEPPERS

David BOWIE ⑩ Top 500

Chameleon-like singer / songwriter / entertainer b. David Jones 8 Jan 1947, Brixton, London. Noted for his changes of character and fashion, he became Ziggy Stardust, Aladdin Sane and The Thin White Duke. His striking appearance was enhanced by an unfortunate school playground incident that changed the colour of one of his blue eyes to green after being stabbed by a compass. Voted most influential artist in an NME poll in 2000. Among his many accolades and awards, for both recording and songwriting, is the 1996

Brit Award for Outstanding Contribution to British Music. (He is the only act to reject induction into the Rock and Roll Hall of Fame.) No UK act can better the 10 albums he charted with simultaneously in the Top 100 in 1983, and no British male can match his eight No.1 albums. This often sampled performer has starred in movies, acted on Broadway, painted and recorded music with many of the world's leading acts. In 1999 he released the first virtual album and became the first major act to make a full album available for download, releasing the first enhanced CD single (1995) and being the first singer / songwriter to go to the stock market selling interest in his back catalogue, raising $55m in the process (451 WEEKS) — pos/wks

Date	Title	pos	wks
6 Sep 69 ●	**SPACE ODDITY (re)** Philips BF 1801	5	14
24 Jun 72 ●	**STARMAN** RCA 2199	10	11
16 Sep 72	**JOHN, I'M ONLY DANCING** RCA 2263	12	10
9 Dec 72 ●	**THE JEAN GENIE** RCA 2302	2	13
14 Apr 73 ●	**DRIVE-IN SATURDAY SEATTLE – PHOENIX)** RCA 2352	3	10
30 Jun 73 ●	**LIFE ON MARS?** RCA 2316	3	13
15 Sep 73 ●	**THE LAUGHING GNOME** Deram DM 123	6	12
20 Oct 73 ●	**SORROW** RCA 2424	3	15
23 Feb 74 ●	**REBEL REBEL** RCA LPBO 5009	5	7
20 Apr 74	**ROCK 'N' ROLL SUICIDE** RCA LPBO 5021	22	7
22 Jun 74	**DIAMOND DOGS** RCA APBO 0293	21	6
28 Sep 74 ●	**KNOCK ON WOOD** RCA 2466	10	6
1 Mar 75	**YOUNG AMERICANS** RCA 2523	18	7
2 Aug 75	**FAME** RCA 2579 ▲	17	8
11 Oct 75 ★	**SPACE ODDITY (re-issue)** RCA 2593	1	10
29 Nov 75 ●	**GOLDEN YEARS** RCA 2640	8	10
22 May 76	**TVC 15** RCA 2682	33	4
19 Feb 77 ●	**SOUND AND VISION** RCA PB 0905	3	11
15 Oct 77	**HEROES** RCA PB 1121	24	8
21 Jan 78	**BEAUTY AND THE BEAST** RCA PB 1190	39	3
2 Dec 78	**BREAKING GLASS (EP)** RCA BOW 1	54	7
5 May 79 ●	**BOYS KEEP SWINGING** RCA BOW 2	7	10
21 Jul 79	**D.J.** RCA BOW 3	29	5
15 Dec 79	**JOHN I'M ONLY DANCING (AGAIN) (1975) / JOHN I'M ONLY DANCING (1972)** RCA BOW 4	12	8
1 Mar 80	**ALABAMA SONG** RCA BOW 5	23	5
16 Aug 80 ★	**ASHES TO ASHES** RCA BOW 6	1	10
1 Nov 80 ●	**FASHION** RCA BOW 7	5	12
10 Jan 81	**SCARY MONSTERS (AND SUPER CREEPS)** RCA BOW 8	20	6
28 Mar 81	**UP THE HILL BACKWARDS** RCA BOW 9	32	6
14 Nov 81 ★	**UNDER PRESSURE** EMI 5250 [1]	1	11
28 Nov 81	**WILD IS THE WIND** RCA BOW 10	24	10
6 Mar 82	**BAAL (EP)** RCA BOW 11	29	5
10 Apr 82	**CAT PEOPLE (PUTTING OUT FIRE)** MCA 770	26	6
27 Nov 82 ●	**PEACE ON EARTH – LITTLE DRUMMER BOY** RCA BOW 12 [2]	3	8
26 Mar 83 ★	**LET'S DANCE** EMI America EA 152 ▲	1	14
11 Jun 83 ●	**CHINA GIRL** EMI America EA 157	2	8
24 Sep 83 ●	**MODERN LOVE** EMI America EA 158	2	8
5 Nov 83	**WHITE LIGHT, WHITE HEAT** RCA 372	46	3
22 Sep 84 ●	**BLUE JEAN** EMI America EA 181	6	8
8 Dec 84	**TONIGHT** EMI America EA 187	53	4
9 Feb 85	**THIS IS NOT AMERICA (THE THEME FROM 'THE FALCON AND THE SNOWMAN')** EMI America EA 190 [3]	14	7
8 Jun 85	**LOVING THE ALIEN (re)** EMI America EA 195	19	7
7 Sep 85 ★	**DANCING IN THE STREET** EMI America EA 204 [4] ■	1	12
15 Mar 86 ●	**ABSOLUTE BEGINNERS** Virgin VS 838	2	9
21 Jun 86	**UNDERGROUND** EMI America EA 216	21	6
8 Nov 86	**WHEN THE WIND BLOWS** Virgin VS 906	44	4
4 Apr 87	**DAY-IN DAY-OUT** EMI America EA 230	17	6
27 Jun 87	**TIME WILL CRAWL** EMI America EA 237	33	4
29 Aug 87	**NEVER LET ME DOWN** EMI America EA 239	34	6
7 Apr 90	**FAME (re-mix)** EMI-USA FAME 90	28	4
22 Aug 92	**REAL COOL WORLD** Warner Bros. W 0127	53	1
27 Mar 93 ●	**JUMP THEY SAY** Arista 74321139422	9	6
12 Jun 93	**BLACK TIE WHITE NOISE** Arista 74321148682 [5]	36	2
23 Oct 93	**MIRACLE GOODNIGHT** Arista 74321162262	40	2
4 Dec 93	**BUDDHA OF SUBURBIA** Arista 74321177052 [6]	35	3
23 Sep 95	**THE HEART'S FILTHY LESSON** RCA 74321307032	35	2
2 Dec 95	**STRANGERS WHEN WE MEET / THE MAN WHO SOLD THE WORLD (LIVE)** RCA 74321329402	39	2
2 Mar 96	**HALLO SPACEBOY** RCA 74321353842	12	4
8 Feb 97	**LITTLE WONDER** RCA 74321452072	14	3
26 Apr 97	**DEAD MAN WALKING** RCA 74321475852	32	2

Re-entries are listed as (re), (2re), (3re), etc which signifies that the hit re-entered the chart once, twice or three times, etc

30 Aug 97	SEVEN YEARS IN TIBET *RCA 74321512542*.........................61	1
21 Feb 98	I CAN'T READ *Velvet ZYX 87578*....................................73	1
2 Oct 99	THURSDAY'S CHILD *Virgin VSCDT 1753*.........................16	3
18 Dec 99	UNDER PRESSURE (re-mix) *Parlophone CDQUEEN 28* [1] 14	7
5 Feb 00	SURVIVE *Virgin VSCDT 1767*.....................................28	2
29 Jul 00	SEVEN *Virgin VSCDT 1776*..32	2
11 May 02	LOVING THE ALIEN (re-mix) *Positiva CDTIV 172* [7]........41	1
28 Sep 02	EVERYONE SAYS 'HI' *Columbia 6731342*.........................20	3

[1] Queen and David Bowie [2] David Bowie and Bing Crosby [3] David Bowie and the Pat Metheny Group [4] David Bowie and Mick Jagger [5] David Bowie featuring Al B Sure! [6] David Bowie featuring Lenny Kravitz [7] Scumfrog vs Bowie

Tracks on Breaking Glass (EP): Breaking Glass / Art Decade / Ziggy Stardust. All three versions of 'John I'm Only Dancing' are different. Tracks on Baal (EP): Baal's Hymn / Remembering Marie A. / Ballad of the Adventurers / The Drowned Girl / Dirty Song

See also TIN MACHINE

BOWLING FOR SOUP *US, male vocal / instrumental group (9 WEEKS)* pos/wks
| 17 Aug 02 | ● GIRL ALL THE BAD GUYS WANT *Music for Nations CDKUT 194* ..8 | 8 |
| 16 Nov 02 | EMILY *Music for Nations CDKUT 198* ....67 | 1 |

George BOWYER *UK, male vocalist (2 WEEKS)* pos/wks
| 22 Aug 98 | GUARDIANS OF THE LAND *Boys BYSCD 01*.........................33 | 2 |

BOX CAR RACER *US, male vocal / instrumental group (1 WEEK)* pos/wks
| 6 Jul 02 | I FEEL SO *MCA MCSTD 40290* ....41 | 1 |

BOX TOPS *US, male vocal / instrumental group (33 WEEKS)* pos/wks
13 Sep 67	● THE LETTER *Stateside SS 2044* ▲ 5	12
20 Mar 68	CRY LIKE A BABY *Bell 1001* 15	12
23 Aug 69	SOUL DEEP *Bell 1068* 22	9

BOY GEORGE *UK, male vocalist – George O'Dowd (46 WEEKS)* pos/wks
7 Mar 87	★ EVERYTHING I OWN *Virgin BOY 100* 1	9
6 Jun 87	KEEP ME IN MIND *Virgin BOY 101* 29	4
18 Jul 87	SOLD *Virgin BOY 102* 24	5
21 Nov 87	TO BE REBORN *Virgin BOY 103* 13	7
5 Mar 88	LIVE MY LIFE *Virgin BOY 105* 62	2
18 Jun 88	NO CLAUSE 28 *Virgin BOY 106* 57	3
8 Oct 88	DON'T CRY *Virgin BOY 107* 60	2
4 Mar 89	DON'T TAKE MY MIND ON A TRIP *Virgin BOY 108* 68	2
19 Sep 92	THE CRYING GAME *Spaghetti CIAO 6* 22	4
12 Jun 93	MORE THAN LIKELY *Gee Street GESCD 49* [1] 40	3
1 Apr 95	FUNTIME *Virgin VSCDG 1538* 45	2
1 Jul 95	IL ADORE *Virgin VSCDX 1543* 50	2
21 Oct 95	SAME THING IN REVERSE *Virgin VSCDT 1561* 56	1

[1] PM Dawn featuring Boy George

See also CULTURE CLUB

BOY MEETS GIRL *US, male / female vocal duo – Shannon Rubicam and George Merrill (13 WEEKS)* pos/wks
| 3 Dec 88 | ● WAITING FOR A STAR TO FALL *RCA PB 49519* ....9 | 13 |

BOY WUNDA – See PROGRESS presents the BOY WUNDA

Jimmy BOYD *US, male vocalist (22 WEEKS)* pos/wks
| 8 May 53 | ● TELL ME A STORY (re) *Philips PB 126* [1] ....5 | 16 |
| 27 Nov 53 | ● I SAW MOMMY KISSING SANTA CLAUS *Columbia DB 3365* ▲ ..3 | 6 |

[1] Jimmy Boyd – Frankie Laine

Jacqueline BOYER *France, female vocalist (2 WEEKS)* pos/wks
| 28 Apr 60 | TOM PILLIBI *Columbia DB 4452*....................................33 | 2 |

BOYS *US, male vocal group (5 WEEKS)* pos/wks
| 12 Nov 88 | DIAL MY HEART *Motown ZB 42245* ....61 | 2 |
| 29 Sep 90 | CRAZY *Motown ZB 44037* ....57 | 3 |

BOYSTOWN GANG *US, male / female vocal group (20 WEEKS)* pos/wks
22 Aug 81	AIN'T NO MOUNTAIN HIGH ENOUGH – REMEMBER ME (MEDLEY) *WEA DICK 1* 46	6
31 Jul 82	● CAN'T TAKE MY EYES OFF YOU *ERC 101* 4	11
9 Oct 82	SIGNED SEALED DELIVERED (I'M YOURS) *ERC 102* 50	3

BOYZ – See HEAVY D and the BOYZ

BOYZ II MEN (425) Top 500 *R&B vocal harmony quartet formed 1988 in Philadelphia (brothers Nathan and Wanya Morris, Shawn Stockman, Michael McCary) were Motown's biggest sellers in the 1990s. The Beatles are the only group to have spent longer at the top of the US chart (81 WEEKS)* pos/wks
5 Sep 92	★ END OF THE ROAD *Motown TMG 1411* ▲ 1	21
19 Dec 92	MOTOWNPHILLY *Motown TMG 1402* 23	6
27 Feb 93	IN THE STILL OF THE NITE (I'LL REMEMBER) *Motown TMGCD 1415* 27	4
3 Sep 94	● I'LL MAKE LOVE TO YOU (re) *Motown TMGCD 1431* ▲ 5	15
26 Nov 94	ON BENDED KNEE *Motown TMGCD 1433* ▲ 20	3
22 Apr 95	THANK YOU *Motown TMGCD 1438* 26	3
8 Jul 95	WATER RUNS DRY *Motown TMGCD 1443* 24	3
9 Dec 95	● ONE SWEET DAY *Columbia 6626035* [1] ▲ 6	11
20 Jan 96	HEY LOVER *Def Jam DEFCD 14* [2] 17	4
20 Sep 97	● 4 SEASONS OF LONELINESS *Motown 8606992* ▲ 10	6
6 Dec 97	A SONG FOR MAMA *Motown 8607372* 34	2
25 Jul 98	CAN'T LET HER GO *Motown 8607952* 23	3

[1] Mariah Carey and Boyz II Men [2] LL Cool J featuring Boyz II Men

BOYZONE (76) Top 500 *Irish boy band vocal quintet who became international teen idols: Ronan Keating, Stephen Gately, Mikey Graham, Keith Duffy, Shane Lynch. They achieved the best ever start to a UK singles career with 16 consecutive Top 5 singles. Best-selling single: 'No Matter What' 1,074,192 (213 WEEKS)* pos/wks
10 Dec 94	● LOVE ME FOR A REASON *Polydor 8512802* 2	13
29 Apr 95	● KEY TO MY LIFE *Polydor PZCD 342* 3	8
12 Aug 95	● SO GOOD *Polydor 5797732* 3	6
25 Nov 95	● FATHER AND SON *Polydor 5775762* 2	16
9 Mar 96	● COMING HOME NOW *Polydor 5775702* 4	9
19 Oct 96	★ WORDS *Polydor 5755372* ■ 1	14
14 Dec 96	★ A DIFFERENT BEAT (2re) *Polydor 5732052* ■ 1	15
22 Mar 97	● ISN'T IT A WONDER (re) *Polydor 5735472* 2	14
2 Aug 97	● PICTURE OF YOU *Polydor 5713112* 2	18
6 Dec 97	● BABY CAN I HOLD YOU / SHOOTING STAR *Polydor 5691672*......2	14
2 May 98	★ ALL THAT I NEED (re) *Polydor 5698732* 1	14
15 Aug 98	■ NO MATTER WHAT *Polydor 5675672* ◆ ■ 1	15
5 Dec 98	● I LOVE THE WAY YOU LOVE ME *Polydor 5631992* 2	13
13 Mar 99	★ WHEN THE GOING GETS TOUGH (re) *Polydor 5699132* ■ 1	16
22 May 99	★ YOU NEEDED ME (re) *Polydor 5639332* ■ 1	15
4 Dec 99	● EVERY DAY I LOVE YOU *Polydor 5615802* 3	13

See also Ronan KEATING; Stephen GATELY; Mikey GRAHAM

BRAD *US, male vocal / instrumental group (1 WEEK)* pos/wks
| 26 Jun 93 | 20TH CENTURY *Epic 6592482* ....64 | 1 |

Scott BRADLEY *UK, male vocalist (1 WEEK)* pos/wks
| 15 Oct 94 | ZOOM *Hidden Agenda HIDDCD 1* ....61 | 1 |

Paul BRADY *UK, male vocalist (1 WEEK)* pos/wks
| 13 Jan 96 | THE WORLD IS WHAT YOU MAKE IT *Mercury PBCD 5* ....67 | 1 |

Billy BRAGG *UK, male vocalist (53 WEEKS)* pos/wks
16 Mar 85	BETWEEN THE WARS (EP) *Go! Discs AGOEP 1* 15	6
28 Dec 85	DAYS LIKE THESE *Go! Discs GOD 8* 43	5
28 Jun 86	LEVI STUBBS' TEARS *Go! Discs GOD 12* 29	6
15 Nov 86	GREETINGS TO THE NEW BRUNETTE *Go! Discs GOD 15* [1] 58	2
14 May 88	★ SHE'S LEAVING HOME *Childline CHILD 1* [2] 1	11
10 Sep 88	WAITING FOR THE GREAT LEAP FORWARDS *Go! Discs GOD 23* 52	3
8 Jul 89	WON'T TALK ABOUT IT *Go.Beat GOD 33* [3] 29	6
6 Jul 91	SEXUALITY *Go! Discs GOD 56* 27	5

Date	Title	pos	wks
7 Sep 91	YOU WOKE UP MY NEIGHBOURHOOD *Go! Discs GOD 60*	54	2
29 Feb 92	ACCIDENT WAITING TO HAPPEN (EP) *Go! Discs GOD 67*	33	3
31 Aug 96	UPFIELD *Cooking Vinyl FRYCD 051*	46	1
17 May 97	THE BOY DONE GOOD *Cooking Vinyl FRYCD 064*	55	1
1 Jun 02	TAKE DOWN THE UNION JACK *Cooking Vinyl FRYCD 131* [4]	22	2

[1] Billy Bragg with Johnny Marr and Kirsty MacColl [2] Billy Bragg with Cara Tivey
[3] Norman Cook featuring Billy Bragg [4] Billy Bragg and the Blokes

Tracks on Between the Wars (EP): Between the Wars / Which Side Are You On / World Turned Upside Down / It Says Here. Tracks on Accident Waiting to Happen (EP): Accident Waiting to Happen / Revolution / Sulk / The Warmest Room. 'She's Leaving Home' was listed with the flip side 'With a Little Help from My Friends' by Wet Wet Wet. 'Won't Talk About It' was listed with the flip side 'Blame It on the Bassline' by Norman Cook featuring MC Wildski

BRAIDS
US, female vocal duo – Zoe Ellis and Caitlin Cornwell (3 WEEKS) pos/wks

2 Nov 96	BOHEMIAN RHAPSODY *Atlantic A 5640CD*	21	3

BRAIN BASHERS
UK, male / female DJ / production duo (1 WEEK) pos/wks

1 Jul 00	DO IT NOW *Tidy Trax TIDY 137 CD*	64	1

BRAINBUG
Italy, male producer – Alberto Bertapelle (7 WEEKS) pos/wks

3 May 97	NIGHTMARE *Positiva CDTIV 76*	11	5
22 Nov 97	BENEDICTUS / NIGHTMARE *Positiva CDTIV 86*	24	2

BRAINCHILD
Germany, male producer – Matthias Hoffmann (2 WEEKS) pos/wks

30 Oct 99	SYMMETRY C *Multiply CDMULTY 55*	31	2

Wilfrid BRAMBELL and Harry H CORBETT
UK, male vocal TV comedy duo (12 WEEKS) pos/wks

28 Nov 63	STEPTOE AND SON AT BUCKINGHAM PALACE (PARTS 1 & 2) *Pye 7N 15588*	25	12

Bekka BRAMLETT – See Joe COCKER

BRAN VAN 3000
Canada, male / female vocal / instrumental group (15 WEEKS) pos/wks

6 Jun 98	DRINKING IN L.A. *Capitol CDCL 802*	34	2
21 Aug 99 ●	DRINKING IN L.A. (re-issue) *Capitol CDCL 811*	3	11
16 Jun 01	ASTOUNDED *Virgin VUSCD 194* [1]	40	2

[1] Bran Van 3000 featuring Curtis Mayfield

BRANCACCIO & AISHER
UK, male production duo – Luke Brancaccio and Bruce Aisher (2 WEEKS) pos/wks

16 Mar 02	IT'S GONNA BE... (A LOVELY DAY) *Credence CDCRED 017*	40	2

Michelle BRANCH
US, female vocalist (14 WEEKS) pos/wks

13 Apr 02	EVERYWHERE *Maverick W 577 CDX*	18	6
3 Aug 02	ALL YOU WANTED *Maverick W 585 CDX*	33	2
23 Nov 02	THE GAME OF LOVE *Arista 74321959442* [1]	16	6+

[1] Santana featuring Michelle Branch

BRAND NEW HEAVIES
UK / US, male / female vocal / instrumental group (68 WEEKS) pos/wks

5 Oct 91	NEVER STOP *ffrr F 165*	43	3
15 Feb 92	DREAM COME TRUE *ffrr F 180*	24	4
18 Apr 92	ULTIMATE TRUNK FUNK (EP) *ffrr F 185*	19	6
1 Aug 92	DON'T LET IT GO TO YOUR HEAD *ffrr BNH 1*	24	4
19 Dec 92	STAY THIS WAY *ffrr BNH 2*	40	5
26 Mar 94	DREAM ON DREAMER *ffrr BNHCD 3*	15	4
11 Jun 94	BACK TO LOVE *ffrr BNHCD 4*	23	4
13 Aug 94	MIDNIGHT AT THE OASIS *ffrr BNHCD 5*	13	4
5 Nov 94	SPEND SOME TIME *ffrr BNHCD 6*	26	4
11 Mar 95	CLOSE TO YOU *ffrr BNHCD 7*	38	3
12 Apr 97	SOMETIMES *ffrr BNHCD 8*	11	5

28 Jun 97	YOU ARE THE UNIVERSE *ffrr GNHCD 9*	21	4
18 Oct 97 ●	YOU'VE GOT A FRIEND *London BNHCD 10*	9	8
10 Jan 98	SHELTER *London BNHCD 11*	31	4
11 Sep 99	SATURDAY NITE *ffrr BNHCD12*	35	2
29 Jan 00	APPARENTLY NOTHING *ffrr BNHCD 13*	32	2

The first 10 hits are credited 'featuring N'Dea Davenport' on either the sleeve or the label. She was replaced by Siedah Garrett from 1997-98 and Carleen Anderson from 1999. Tracks on Ultimate Trunk Funk (EP): Never Stop / Stay This Way / Mr Tanaka. BNH 2 is a re-mixed version of the track on the Ultimate Trunk Funk EP

Johnny BRANDON with The PHANTOMS
UK, male vocalist and instrumental group (12 WEEKS) pos/wks

11 Mar 55 ●	TOMORROW (re) *Polygon P 1131* [1]	8	8
1 Jul 55	DON'T WORRY *Polygon P 1163*	18	4

[1] Johnny Brandon with the Phantoms and the Norman Warren Music

BRANDY (410 *Top 500*)
California-raised female R&B vocalist / actress, b. Brandy Norwood, 1 Feb 1979, Mississippi, US. The star of TV teen drama Moesha had a gold US single before her 16th birthday. Duet with Monica was the top US hit of 1998 (13 weeks at No.1 with more than two million copies sold) (83 WEEKS) pos/wks

10 Dec 94	I WANNA BE DOWN *Atlantic A7217CD*	44	3
3 Jun 95	I WANNA BE DOWN (re-mix) *Atlantic A 7186CD*	36	3
3 Feb 96	SITTIN' UP IN MY ROOM *Arista 74321344012*	30	4
6 Jun 98 ●	THE BOY IS MINE *Atlantic AT 0036CD* [1] ▲	2	20
10 Oct 98 ●	TOP OF THE WORLD (re) *Atlantic AT 0046CD* [2]	2	9
12 Dec 98	HAVE YOU EVER? *Atlantic AT 0058CD* ▲	13	8
19 Jun 99	ALMOST DOESN'T COUNT *Atlantic AT0068CD1*	15	5
16 Jun 01 ●	ANOTHER DAY IN PARADISE *WEA WEA 327CD1* [3]	5	10
23 Feb 02	WHAT ABOUT US? (re) *Atlantic AT 0125CD*	4	11
15 Jun 02	FULL MOON (import) *Atlantic 7567853092*	72	1
29 Jun 02	FULL MOON *Atlantic AT 0130CD*	15	9

[1] Brandy and Monica [2] Brandy featuring Mase [3] Brandy and Ray J

Laura BRANIGAN *US, female vocalist (33 WEEKS)* pos/wks

18 Dec 82 ●	GLORIA *Atlantic K 11759*	6	13
7 Jul 84 ●	SELF CONTROL *Atlantic A 9676*	5	17
6 Oct 84	THE LUCKY ONE *Atlantic A 9636*	56	3

BRASS CONSTRUCTION
US, male vocal / instrumental group (35 WEEKS) pos/wks

3 Apr 76	MOVIN' *United Artists UP 36090*	23	6
5 Feb 77	HA CHA CHA (FUNKTION) *United Artists UP 36205*	37	5
26 Jan 80	MUSIC MAKES YOU FEEL LIKE DANCING *United Artists UP 615*	39	6
28 May 83	WALKIN' THE LINE *Capitol CL 292*	47	3
16 Jul 83	WE CAN WORK IT OUT *Capitol CL 299*	70	2
7 Jul 84	PARTYLINE *Capitol CL 335*	56	4
27 Oct 84	INTERNATIONAL *Capitol CL 341*	70	2
9 Nov 85	GIVE AND TAKE *Capitol CL 377*	62	3
28 May 88	MOVIN' 1988 (re-mix) *Syncopate SY 11*	24	4

BRASSTOOTH – See BM DUBS present MR RUMBLE featuring BRASSTOOTH and KEE

BRAT *UK, male vocalist – Roger Kitter (8 WEEKS)* pos/wks

10 Jul 82	CHALK DUST – THE UMPIRE STRIKES BACK *Hansa SMASH 1*	19	8

BRAVADO
UK, male / female vocal / instrumental group (3 WEEKS) pos/wks

18 Jun 94	HARMONICA MAN *Peach PEACHCD 5*	37	3

BRAVEHEARTS – See QB FINEST featuring NAS & BRAVEHEARTS

BRAVO ALL STARS
UK / US, male / female vocal / instrumental group (2 WEEKS) pos/wks

29 Aug 98	LET THE MUSIC HEAL YOUR SOUL *Edel 0039335 ERE*	36	2

Artists featured: Backstreet Boys, Aaron Carter, Scooter, 'N Sync, Caught in the Act, The Boyz, Blumchen, Gil, Squeezer, Mr President, Touche, R'N'G and the Moffatts

Alan BRAXE and Fred FALKE
France, male production duo (3 WEEKS)   pos/wks

25 Nov 00	INTRO *Vulture / Credence CDCRED 006*	35	3

Dhar BRAXTON *US, female vocalist (8 WEEKS)*   pos/wks

31 May 86	JUMP BACK (SET ME FREE) *Fourth & Broadway BRW 47*	32	8

Toni BRAXTON   `411`   `Top 500`
Sultry, sexy soul / R&B vocalist, b. 7 Oct 1968, Maryland, US, who won Best New Artist Grammy in 1993 and was one of America's top selling pop and R&B artists of the 1990s. Her biggest hits have been ballads from the pens of top writers Babyface, Diane Warren, R Kelly and Rodney Jerkins. Best-selling single: 'Un-break My Heart' 770,000 (83 WEEKS)   pos/wks

18 Sep 93		ANOTHER SAD LOVE SONG *LaFace 74321163502*	51	2
15 Jan 94	●	BREATHE AGAIN *LaFace 74321185442*	2	12
2 Apr 94		ANOTHER SAD LOVE SONG (re-issue)		
		LaFace 74321196682	15	8
9 Jul 94		YOU MEAN THE WORLD TO ME *LaFace 74321214702*	30	5
3 Dec 94		LOVE SHOULDA BROUGHT YOU HOME *LaFace 74321249412*	33	3
13 Jul 96	●	YOU'RE MAKIN' ME HIGH *LaFace 74321395402* ▲	7	11
2 Nov 96	●	UN-BREAK MY HEART *LaFace 74321410632* ▲	2	19
24 May 97	●	I DON'T WANT TO *LaFace 74321468612*	9	8
8 Nov 97		HOW COULD AN ANGEL BREAK MY HEART		
		LaFace 74321531982 `1`	22	4
29 Apr 00	●	HE WASN'T MAN ENOUGH *LaFace 74321757852*	5	11

`1` Toni Braxton with Kenny G

BRAXTONS *US, female vocal group (7 WEEKS)*   pos/wks

1 Feb 97	SO MANY WAYS *Atlantic A 5469CD*	32	2
29 Mar 97	THE BOSS *Atlantic A 5441CD*	31	3
19 Jul 97	SLOW FLOW *Atlantic AT 0001CD*	26	2

BREAD *US, male vocal / instrumental group (46 WEEKS)*   pos/wks

1 Aug 70	●	MAKE IT WITH YOU *Elektra 2101 010* ▲	5	14
15 Jan 72		BABY I'M-A WANT YOU *Elektra K 12033*	14	10
29 Apr 72		EVERYTHING I OWN *Elektra K 12041*	32	6
30 Sep 72		THE GUITAR MAN *Elektra K 12066*	16	9
25 Dec 76		LOST WITHOUT YOUR LOVE *Elektra K 12241*	27	7

BREAK MACHINE *US, male vocal group (32 WEEKS)*   pos/wks

4 Feb 84	●	STREET DANCE *Record Shack SOHO 13*	3	14
12 May 84	●	BREAK DANCE PARTY (re) *Record Shack SOHO 20*	9	10
11 Aug 84		ARE YOU READY? *Record Shack SOHO 24*	27	8

BREAKBEAT ERA
UK, male / female drum and bass trio (5 WEEKS)   pos/wks

18 Jul 98	BREAKBEAT ERA *XL Recordings XLS 95CD*	38	2
21 Aug 99	ULTRA – OBSCENE *XL Recordings XLS 107CD*	48	2
11 Mar 00	BULLITPROOF *XL Recordings XLS 115CD*	65	1

BREAKFAST CLUB
US, male vocal / instrumental group (3 WEEKS)   pos/wks

27 Jun 87	RIGHT ON TRACK *MCA MCA 1146*	54	3

BREATHE *UK, male vocal / instrumental group (27 WEEKS)*   pos/wks

30 Jul 88	●	HANDS TO HEAVEN *Siren SRN 68*	4	12
22 Oct 88		JONAH *Siren SRN 95*	60	3
3 Dec 88		HOW CAN I FALL? *Siren SRN 102*	48	7
11 Mar 89		DON'T TELL ME LIES *Siren SRN 109*	45	5

Freddy BRECK *Germany, male vocalist (4 WEEKS)*   pos/wks

13 Apr 74	SO IN LOVE WITH YOU *Decca F 13481*	44	4

BRECKER BROTHERS *US, male vocal
/ instrumental duo – Randy and Michael Brecker (5 WEEKS)*   pos/wks

4 Nov 78	EAST RIVER *Arista ARIST 211*	34	5

BREEDERS
US / UK, female / male vocal / instrumental group (7 WEEKS)   pos/wks

18 Apr 93	SAFARI (EP) *4AD BAD 2003*	69	1
21 Aug 93	CANNONBALL (EP) *4AD BAD 3011CD*	40	3
6 Nov 93	DIVINE HAMMER *4AD BAD 3017CD*	59	1
23 Jul 94	HEAD TO TOE (EP) *4AD BADD 4012*	68	1
14 Sep 02	SON OF THREE *4AD BAD 2213CD*	72	1

Tracks on Safari (EP): Do You Love Me Now / Don't Call Home / Safari / So Sad About Us. Tracks on Cannonball (EP): Cannonball / Cro-Aloha / Lord of the Thighs / 900. Tracks on Head to Toe (EP): Head to Toe / Shocker in Gloom Town / Freed Pig

See also THROWING MUSES; PIXIES

BREEKOUT KREW *US, male vocal duo (3 WEEKS)*   pos/wks

24 Nov 84	MATT'S MOOD *London LON 59*	51	3

Ann BREEN *Ireland, female vocalist (2 WEEKS)*   pos/wks

19 Mar 83	PAL OF MY CRADLE DAYS (re) *Homespun HS 052*	69	2

Jo BREEZER *UK, female vocalist (2 WEEKS)*   pos/wks

13 Oct 01	VENUS AND MARS *Columbia 6717612*	27	2

BRENDON *UK, male vocalist – Brendon Dunning (9 WEEKS)*   pos/wks

19 Mar 77	GIMME SOME *Magnet MAG 80*	14	9

Maire BRENNAN *Ireland, female vocalist (12 WEEKS)*   pos/wks

16 May 92		AGAINST THE WIND *RCA PB 45399*	64	2
5 Jun 99	●	SALTWATER *Xtravaganza XTRAV 1CDS* `1`	6	10

`1` Chicane featuring Maire Brennan of Clannad

See also CLANNAD

Rose BRENNAN *Ireland, female vocalist (9 WEEKS)*   pos/wks

7 Dec 61	TALL DARK STRANGER *Philips PB 1193*	31	9

Walter BRENNAN *US, male vocalist, d. 21 Sep 1974 (3 WEEKS)*   pos/wks

28 Jun 62	OLD RIVERS *Liberty LIB 55436*	38	3

Tony BRENT
UK, male vocalist – Reginald Bretagne, d. 19 Jun 1993 (52 WEEKS)   pos/wks

19 Dec 52	●	WALKIN' TO MISSOURI (re) *Columbia DB 3147*	7	7
2 Jan 53	●	MAKE IT SOON (re) *Columbia DB 3187*	9	7
23 Jan 53		GOT YOU ON MY MIND *Columbia DB 3226*	12	1
30 Nov 56		CINDY, OH CINDY (re) *Columbia DB 3844*	16	7
28 Jun 57		DARK MOON *Columbia DB 3950*	17	14
28 Feb 58		THE CLOUDS WILL SOON ROLL BY (re) *Columbia DB 4066*	20	5
5 Sep 58		GIRL OF MY DREAMS *Columbia DB 4177*	16	7
24 Jul 59		WHY SHOULD I BE LONELY? *Columbia DB 4304*	24	4

Bernard BRESSLAW
UK, male comedian / actor / vocalist, d. 11 Jun 1993 (11 WEEKS)   pos/wks

5 Sep 58	●	MAD PASSIONATE LOVE *HMV POP 522*	6	11

See also Michael MEDWIN, Bernard BRESSLAW, Alfie BASS and Leslie FYSON

Teresa BREWER *US, female vocalist – Theresa Breuer (53 WKS)* pos/wks

11 Feb 55	●	LET ME GO LOVER *Vogue/Coral Q 72043* `1`	9	10
13 Apr 56	●	A TEAR FELL *Vogue/Coral Q 72146*	2	15
13 Jul 56	●	A SWEET OLD FASHIONED GIRL *Vogue/Coral Q 72172* ..	3	15
10 May 57		NORA MALONE *Vogue/Coral Q 72224*	26	2
23 Jun 60		HOW DO YOU KNOW IT'S LOVE *Coral Q 72396*	21	11

`1` Teresa Brewer with The Lancers

BRIAN and MICHAEL
UK, male vocal duo – Kevin Parrott and Michael Coleman (19 WEEKS) pos/wks

25 Feb 78	★	MATCHSTALK MEN AND MATCHSTALK CATS AND DOGS		
		(LOWRY'S SONG) *Pye 7N 46035*	1	19

JUSTIFIED AND ANCIENT

■ In 1968, Tammy Wynette urged her American sisters to 'Stand By Your Man'. Twenty-three years later and on her fifth marriage, The KLF (aka The JAMS) gave her a ring. If you believe the lyrics, they called her up in Tennessee and said: "Tammy stand by The JAMS." Tammy (after thoroughly checking them out) responded quickly and positively, and one of pop's strangest relationships was born. The KLF (aka The Timelords, aka Bill Drummond and Jimmy Cauty) were sonic terrorists who kept scoring massive chart hits. Tammy Wynette was the First Lady of Country who hadn't charted in the UK for years. Together they took the stadium house track 'Justified and Ancient' to No.2. It stayed in the top 40 for 10 weeks and gave Tammy Wynette her biggest ever US pop hit.

The song describes the roving adventures of the Justified Ancients making their way in an ice-cream van to Mu Mu land, a place where the mythical Mu Mu mate and the children "still cry make mine a 99". Safe to say it was the block-rock beats, and not the Illuminatus-inspired lyrics, which made 'Justified' such an anthem.

"Jimmy and I were about to dump the track," wrote Bill Drummond in his book 45. "We were working in a south London studio, trying to breathe life into a song that had originally been the opening track on our first album. But things turned round after Cauty had the idea of enlisting Tammy. Twenty minutes after he suggested it, Bill, a lifelong fan of country music, was chatting to the heroine of heartache backstage at a Tennessee concert hall. It was going to be the best record we ever made."

■ **MU MU LAND LOOKS A LOT MORE INTERESTING THAN TENNESSEE, BUT I WOULDN'T WANT TO LIVE THERE** ■

Within a week, Drummond had touched down in Nashville, and was taking Wynette through the chords on the grand piano in the lounge of her mansion at First Lady Acres. Her voice was recorded over the backing track; the tapes were taken back to England and The KLF were on the cusp of claiming a Christmas chart-topper with a very different type of country house. It was only Freddie Mercury's untimely death and 'Bohemian Rhapsody''s timely re-release that stopped 'Justified and Ancient' from claiming the top spot.

The First Lady of Country, meanwhile, was standing by the van with a stately but bemused forbearance. "No doubt it will all make sense when they're finished," she told the NME during the filming of the video. "Mu Mu Land looks a lot more interesting than Tennessee, but I wouldn't want to live there."

★ ARTIST:	KLF guest vocals: Tammy Wynette
★ LABEL:	Rough Trade
★ WRITERS:	Jimmy Cauty and Bill Drummond
★ PRODUCER:	Mark Stent

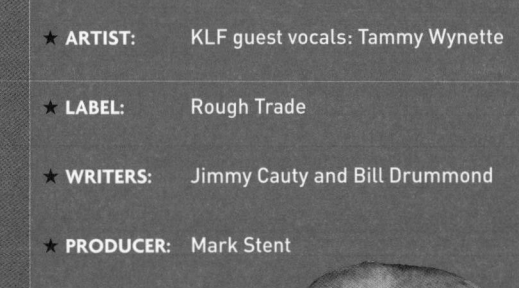

The KLF's Jimmy Cauty (left) and Bill Drummond, whose partnership with Tammy Wynette almost breached the US Top 10

Tammy Wynette was cast in the KLF's video as the Queen of the lost continent of Mu

The video featured a crowned and regally attired Tammy Wynette, hooded guitarists, tribal warriors, Cauty's cop car from the Timelords era and, of course, an ice-cream van. "I'd never heard of a 99 before," said the Queen of Country. "Bill explained it to me and now it makes perfectly good sense." So it was a culinary exchange as well as a musical partnership. After Tammy died in 1998 Drummond wrote, "[She] may have been the greatest female country and western singer of all time, but she is also the only woman who offered to cook me grits for breakfast. There will be one less Christmas card on my mantelpiece this year. Tonight I will go to bed and cry."

■ Daniel Stott / Dave McAleer

BRICK US, male vocal / instrumental group (4 WEEKS)

		pos/wks
5 Feb 77	DAZZ *Bang 004*..	36 4

Edie BRICKELL and the NEW BOHEMIANS
US, female / male vocal / instrumental group (10 WEEKS)

		pos/wks
4 Feb 89	WHAT I AM *Geffen GEF 49*	31 7
27 May 89	CIRCLE *Geffen GEF 51*	74 1
1 Oct 94	GOOD TIMES *Geffen GFSTD 78* [1]	40 2

[1] Edie Brickell

Alicia BRIDGES US, female vocalist (11 WEEKS)

		pos/wks
11 Nov 78	I LOVE THE NIGHTLIFE (DISCO 'ROUND) *Polydor 2066 936*...............................	32 10
8 Oct 94	I LOVE THE NIGHTLIFE (DISCO 'ROUND) (re-mix) *Mother MUMCD 57*	61 1

Johnny BRIGGS – See Amanda BARRIE and Johnny BRIGGS

BRIGHOUSE AND RASTRICK BRASS BAND
UK, male brass band (13 WEEKS)

		pos/wks
12 Nov 77	● THE FLORAL DANCE *Transatlantic BIG 548*..................	2 13

Bette BRIGHT UK, female vocalist (5 WEEKS)

		pos/wks
8 Mar 80	HELLO, I AM YOUR HEART *Korova KOW 3*..................	50 5

Sarah BRIGHTMAN (318) Top 500
Multi-faceted Hot Gossip dancer turned pop and classical star, b. 14 Aug 1960, Hertfordshire, UK. Singer / actress, and ex-wife of Andrew Lloyd Webber. 'Time to Say Goodbye' was the biggest selling single in Germany (2.5 million). At times in 1999 she held three of top four places on US Classical Crossover chart (98 WEEKS)

		pos/wks
11 Nov 78	● I LOST MY HEART TO A STARSHIP TROOPER *Ariola / Hansa AHA 527* [1]	6 14
7 Apr 79	THE ADVENTURES OF THE LOVE CRUSADER *Ariola / Hansa AHA 538* [2]	53 5
30 Jul 83	HIM *Polydor POSP 625* [3]	55 4
23 Mar 85	● PIE JESU *HMV WEBBER 1* [4]	3 8
11 Jan 86	● THE PHANTOM OF THE OPERA *Polydor POSP 800* [5]	7 10
4 Oct 86	● ALL I ASK OF YOU *Polydor POSP 802* [6] ...	3 16
10 Jan 87	● WISHING YOU WERE SOMEHOW HERE AGAIN *Polydor POSP 803*	7 11
11 Jul 92	AMIGOS PARA SIEMPRE (FRIENDS FOR LIFE) *Really Useful RUR 10* [7]	11 11
24 May 97	● TIME TO SAY GOODBYE (CON TE PARTIRO) *Coalition COLA 003CD* [8]	2 14
23 Aug 97	WHO WANTS TO LIVE FOREVER *Coalition COLA 014CD*............	45 1
6 Dec 97	JUST SHOW ME HOW TO LOVE YOU *Coalition COLA 035CD* [9]	54 2
14 Feb 98	STARSHIP TROOPERS *Coalition COLA 040CD*	58 1
13 Feb 99	EDEN *Coalition COLA 065CD*	68 1

[1] Sarah Brightman and Hot Gossip [2] Sarah Brightman and the Starship Troopers [3] Sarah Brightman and the London Philharmonic [4] Sarah Brightman and Paul Miles-Kingston [5] Sarah Brightman and Steve Harley [6] Cliff Richard and Sarah Brightman [7] José Carreras and Sarah Brightman [8] Sarah Brightman and Andrea Bocelli [9] Sarah Brightman and the LSO featuring José Cura

The listed flip side of 'Wishing You Were Somehow Here Again' was 'The Music of the Night' by Michael Crawford. COLA 040CD is a dance re-mix of AHA 527

BRIGHTON AND HOVE ALBION FC
UK, male football team vocalists (2 WEEKS)

		pos/wks
28 May 83	THE BOYS IN THE OLD BRIGHTON BLUE *Energy NRG 2*	65 2

BRILLIANT
UK, male / female vocal / instrumental group (13 WEEKS)

		pos/wks
19 Oct 85	IT'S A MAN'S MAN'S MAN'S WORLD *Food FOOD 5*	58 5
22 Mar 86	LOVE IS WAR *Food FOOD 6*	64 4
2 Aug 86	SOMEBODY *Food FOOD 7*............................	67 4

Danielle BRISEBOIS US, female vocalist (1 WEEK)

		pos/wks
9 Sep 95	GIMME LITTLE SIGN *Epic 6610782*	75 1

Johnny BRISTOL US, male vocalist (16 WEEKS)

		pos/wks
24 Aug 74	● HANG ON IN THERE BABY *MGM 2006 443*	3 11
19 Jul 80	MY GUY – MY GIRL (MEDLEY) *Atlantic / Hansa K 11550* [1]	39 5

[1] Amii Stewart and Johnny Bristol

BRIT PACK UK / Ireland, male vocal group (2 WEEKS)

		pos/wks
12 Feb 00	SET ME FREE *When! WENX 2000*	41 2

BRITS – See VARIOUS ARTISTS (MONTAGES)

BROCK LANDARS UK, male vocal / production duo (2 WEEKS)

		pos/wks
11 Jul 98	S.M.D.U. *Parlophone CDBLUE 001*	49 2

BROKEN ENGLISH
UK, male vocal / instrumental group (13 WEEKS)

		pos/wks
30 May 87	COMIN' ON STRONG *EMI EM 5*...............	18 10
3 Oct 87	LOVE ON THE SIDE *EMI EM 55*..............	69 3

BRONSKI BEAT (451) Top 500
Electronic dance trio formed 1984 London, UK; Steve Bronski (k), Larry Steinbachek (k) and the plaintive falsetto of Jimmy Somerville (v), who left in 1985 for The Communards (replaced by John Foster). First openly gay hit pop group, split in 1989 (78 WEEKS)

		pos/wks
2 Jun 84	● SMALLTOWN BOY *Forbidden Fruit BITE 1*	3 13
22 Sep 84	● WHY? *Forbidden Fruit BITE 2*..................	6 10
1 Dec 84	IT AIN'T NECESSARILY SO *Forbidden Fruit BITE 3*..............	16 11
20 Apr 85	● I FEEL LOVE (MEDLEY) *Forbidden Fruit BITE 4* [1] ...	3 12
30 Nov 85	● HIT THAT PERFECT BEAT *Forbidden Fruit BITE 6*..........	3 14
29 Mar 86	COME ON, COME ON *Forbidden Fruit BITE 7*	20 7
1 Jul 89	CHA CHA HEELS *Arista 112331* [2]	32 7
2 Feb 91	SMALLTOWN BOY (re-mix) *London LON 287* [3]	32 4

[1] Bronski Beat and Marc Almond [2] Eartha Kitt and Bronski Beat [3] Jimmy Somerville with Bronski Beat

Tracks on medley: I Feel Love / Love to Love You Baby / Johnny Remember Me

Jet BRONX and the FORBIDDEN UK, male vocal / instrumental group – featuring TV presenter Loyd Grossman (1 WEEK)

		pos/wks
17 Dec 77	AIN'T DOIN' NOTHIN' *Lightning LIG 50*.................	49 1

BROOK BROTHERS
UK, male vocal duo – Geoff and Ricky Brook (35 WEEKS)

		pos/wks
30 Mar 61	● WARPAINT *Pye 7N 15333*...........................	5 14
24 Aug 61	AIN'T GONNA WASH FOR A WEEK *Pye 7N 15369*.......	13 10
25 Jan 62	HE'S OLD ENOUGH TO KNOW BETTER *Pye 7N 15409*	37 1
16 Aug 62	WELCOME HOME BABY *Pye 7N 15453*	33 6
21 Feb 63	TROUBLE IS MY MIDDLE NAME *Pye 7N 15498*.........	38 4

Bruno BROOKES – See Liz KERSHAW and Bruno BROOKES

BROOKLYN BOUNCE Germany, male production duo and male / female vocal group (1 WEEK)

		pos/wks
30 May 98	THE MUSIC'S GOT ME *Club Tools 0064795 CLU*..........	67 1

BROOKLYN, BRONX and QUEENS – See B B and Q BAND

Elkie BROOKS (356) Top 500
Husky-voiced female vocalist, professional at age 15, b. Elaine Bookbinder, 25 Feb 1945, Salford, UK. Blues, jazz then rock phases (in Vinegar Joe with Robert Palmer) followed by a solo career which featured an impressive 20-year run of 15 hit albums from 1977 (91 WEEKS)

		pos/wks
2 Apr 77	● PEARL'S A SINGER *A&M AMS 7275*	8 9
20 Aug 77	● SUNSHINE AFTER THE RAIN *A&M AMS 7306*	10 9

Date	Title	Pos	Wks
25 Feb 78	LILAC WINE *A&M AMS 7333*	16	7
3 Jun 78	ONLY LOVE CAN BREAK YOUR HEART *A&M AMS 7353*	43	5
11 Nov 78	DON'T CRY OUT LOUD *A&M AMS 7395*	12	11
5 May 79	THE RUNAWAY *A&M AMS 7428*	50	5
16 Jan 82	FOOL IF YOU THINK IT'S OVER *A&M AMS 8187*	17	10
1 May 82	OUR LOVE *A&M AMS 8214*	43	5
17 Jul 82	NIGHTS IN WHITE SATIN *A&M AMS 8235*	33	5
22 Jan 83	GASOLINE ALLEY *A&M AMS 8305*	52	5
22 Nov 86 ●	NO MORE THE FOOL *Legend LM 4*	5	16
4 Apr 87	BREAK THE CHAIN *Legend LM 8*	55	3
11 Jul 87	WE'VE GOT TONIGHT *Legend LM 9*	69	1

Garth BROOKS US, male vocalist (15 WEEKS)

Date	Title	Pos	Wks
1 Feb 92	SHAMELESS *Capitol CL 646*	71	1
22 Jan 94	THE RED STROKES / AIN'T GOING DOWN *Liberty CDCLS 704*	13	5
16 Apr 94	STANDING OUTSIDE THE FIRE *Liberty CDCL 712*	28	4
18 Feb 95	THE DANCE / FRIENDS IN LOW PLACES *Capitol CDCL 735*	36	3
17 Feb 96	SHE'S EVERY WOMAN *Capitol CDCL 767*	55	1
13 Nov 99	LOST IN YOU *Capitol CDCL 814*	70	1

Mel BROOKS
US, male actor / rapper – Melvin Kaminsky (10 WEEKS)

Date	Title	Pos	Wks
18 Feb 84	TO BE OR NOT TO BE (THE HITLER RAP) *Island IS 158*	12	10

Meredith BROOKS *US, female vocal / instrumentalist (13 WEEKS)*

Date	Title	Pos	Wks
2 Aug 97 ●	BITCH *Capital CDCL 790*	6	10
6 Dec 97	I NEED *Capital CDCLS 794*	28	2
7 Mar 98	WHAT WOULD HAPPEN *Capital CDCL 798*	49	1

Norman BROOKS *Canada, male vocalist – Norman Arie (1 WEEK)*

Date	Title	Pos	Wks
12 Nov 54	A SKY-BLUE SHIRT AND A RAINBOW TIE *London L 1228*	17	1

BROS `405` `Top 500`
Top teen appeal act; photogenic twins Matt Goss (v) and Luke Goss (d), b. 29 Sep 1968, London, UK, and Craig Logan (b) – who left in 1989. Sold out tours, broke sales records, created hysteria and won Brits Best Newcomer of 1988 award (84 WEEKS)

Date	Title	Pos	Wks
5 Dec 87	WHEN WILL I BE FAMOUS? (re) *CBS ATOM 2*	2	15
19 Mar 88	DROP THE BOY *CBS ATOM 3*	2	10
18 Jun 88 ★	I OWE YOU NOTHING *CBS ATOM 4*	1	11
17 Sep 88	I QUIT *CBS ATOM 5*	4	8
3 Dec 88 ●	CAT AMONG THE PIGEONS / SILENT NIGHT *CBS ATOM 6*	2	8
29 Jul 89 ●	TOO MUCH *CBS ATOM 7*	2	7
7 Oct 89 ●	CHOCOLATE BOX *CBS ATOM 8*	9	6
16 Dec 89 ●	SISTER *CBS ATOM 9*	10	6
10 Mar 90	MADLY IN LOVE *CBS ATOM 10*	14	4
13 Jul 91	ARE YOU MINE? *Columbia 6569707*	12	5
21 Sep 91	TRY *Columbia 6574047*	27	4

Act was duo for last six hits

BROTHER BEYOND
UK, male vocal / instrumental group (58 WEEKS)

Date	Title	Pos	Wks
4 Apr 87	HOW MANY TIMES *EMI EMI 5591*	62	3
8 Aug 87	CHAIN-GANG SMILE *Parlophone R 6160*	57	3
23 Jan 88	CAN YOU KEEP A SECRET? *Parlophone R 6174*	56	4
30 Jul 88 ●	THE HARDER I TRY *Parlophone R 6184*	2	14
5 Nov 88 ●	HE AIN'T NO COMPETITION *Parlophone R 6193*	6	10
21 Jan 89	BE MY TWIN *Parlophone R 6195*	14	4
1 Apr 89	CAN YOU KEEP A SECRET (re-mix) *Parlophone R 6197*	22	5
28 Oct 89	DRIVE ON *Parlophone R 6233*	39	4
9 Dec 89	WHEN WILL I SEE YOU AGAIN *Parlophone R 6239*	43	5
10 Apr 90	TRUST *Parlophone R 6245*	53	2
19 Jan 91	THE GIRL I USED TO KNOW *Parlophone R 6265*	48	2

BROTHER BROWN featuring FRANK'EE
Denmark, male DJ / production duo and female vocalist (5 WEEKS)

Date	Title	Pos	Wks
2 Oct 99	UNDER THE WATER *ffrr FCD 367*	18	4
24 Nov 01	STAR CATCHING GIRL *Rulin / MOS RULIN 21CDS*	51	1

BROTHER LOVE – See PRATT and McCLAIN with BROTHERLOVE

BROTHERHOOD *UK, male rap group (1 WEEK)*

Date	Title	Pos	Wks
27 Jan 96	ONE SHOT / NOTHING IN PARTICULAR *Bite It BHOODD 3*	55	1

BROTHERHOOD OF MAN `321` `Top 500`
Triple chart-topping UK vocal group formed by producer / composer Tony Hiller, which originally featured Tony Burrows (Edison Lighthouse, White Plains, etc). Their two-boy two-girl line-up in 1976 broke voting record for Eurovision Song Contest. Biggest selling hit: 'Save Your Kisses for Me' 1,006,200 (97 WEEKS)

Date	Title	Pos	Wks
14 Feb 70 ●	UNITED WE STAND *Deram DM 284*	10	9
4 Jul 70	WHERE ARE YOU GOING TO MY LOVE *Deram DM 298*	22	10
13 Mar 76 ★	SAVE YOUR KISSES FOR ME *Pye 7N 45569* ◆	1	16
19 Jun 76	MY SWEET ROSALIE *Pye 7N 45602*	30	7
26 Feb 77	OH BOY (THE MOOD I'M IN) *Pye 7N 45656*	8	12
9 Jul 77 ★	ANGELO *Pye 7N 45699*	1	12
14 Jan 78 ★	FIGARO *Pye 7N 46037*	1	11
27 May 78	BEAUTIFUL LOVER *Pye 7N 46071*	15	12
30 Sep 78	MIDDLE OF THE NIGHT *Pye 7N 46117*	41	6
3 Jul 82	LIGHTNING FLASH *EMI 5309*	67	2

BROTHERS *UK, male vocal group (9 WEEKS)*

Date	Title	Pos	Wks
29 Jan 77 ●	SING ME *Bus Stop Bus 1054*	8	9

BROTHERS FOUR *US, male vocal group (2 WEEKS)*

Date	Title	Pos	Wks
23 Jun 60	GREENFIELDS (re) *Philips PB 1009*	40	2

BROTHERS GRIMM – See JAZZ and the BROTHERS GRIMM

BROTHERS IN RHYTHM *UK, male instrumental / production duo – Dave Seaman and Steve Anderson (12 WEEKS)*

Date	Title	Pos	Wks
16 Mar 91	SUCH A GOOD FEELING *Fourth & Broadway BRW 228*	64	2
14 Sep 91	SUCH A GOOD FEELING (re-issue) *Fourth & Broadway BRW 228 210*	14	8
30 Apr 94	FOREVER AND A DAY *Stress CDSTR 36* 1	51	2

1 Brothers in Rhythm present Charvoni

BROTHERS JOHNSON *US, male vocal / instrumental duo – George and Louis Johnson (34 WEEKS)*

Date	Title	Pos	Wks
9 Jul 77	STRAWBERRY LETTER 23 *A&M AMS 7297*	35	5
2 Sep 78	AIN'T WE FUNKIN' NOW *A&M AMS 7379*	43	6
4 Nov 78	RIDE-O-ROCKET *A&M AMS 7400*	50	4
23 Feb 80 ●	STOMP *A&M AMS 7509*	6	12
31 May 80	LIGHT UP THE NIGHT *A&M AMS 7526*	47	4
25 Jul 81	THE REAL THING *A&M AMS 8149*	50	3

BROTHERS LIKE OUTLAW featuring Alison EVELYN
UK, male / female vocal group (1 WEEK)

Date	Title	Pos	Wks
23 Jan 93	GOOD VIBRATIONS *Gee Street GESCD 44*	74	1

Edgar BROUGHTON BAND
UK, male vocal / instrumental group (10 WEEKS)

Date	Title	Pos	Wks
18 Apr 70	OUT DEMONS OUT *Harvest HAR 5015*	39	5
23 Jan 71	APACHE DROPOUT (3re) *Harvest HAR 5032*	33	5

Alison BROWN – See BAR CODES featuring Alison BROWN

Angie BROWN – See BIZARRE INC; MOTIV 8

Andrea BROWN – See GOLDTRIX presents Andrea Brown

Bobby BROWN `222` `Top 500` *Energetic swingbeat superstar, b. 5 Feb 1969, Massachusetts, who married Whitney Houston in 1992. He joined a re-formed New Edition in 1996, the vocal group in which he topped the chart with 'Candy Girl' as a 14-year-old (125 WEEKS)*

Date	Title	Pos	Wks
6 Aug 88	DON'T BE CRUEL *MCA MCA 1268*	42	7

17 Dec 88 ●	MY PREROGATIVE *MCA MCA 1299* ▲	....	6 17
25 Mar 89	DON'T BE CRUEL (re-issue) *MCA MCA 1310*	13	8
20 May 89 ●	EVERY LITTLE STEP *MCA MCA 1338*	6	9
15 Jul 89 ●	ON OUR OWN (FROM GHOSTBUSTERS II) *MCA MCA 1350*	4	9
23 Sep 89	ROCK WIT'CHA *MCA MCA 1367*	33	6
25 Nov 89	RONI *MCA MCA 1384*	21	7
9 Jun 90	THE FREE STYLE MEGA-MIX *MCA MCA 1421*	14	7
30 Jun 90	SHE AIN'T WORTH IT *London LON 265* [1] ▲	12	9
22 Aug 92	HUMPIN' AROUND *MCA MCS 1680*	19	6
17 Oct 92	GOOD ENOUGH *MCA MCS 1704*	41	4
19 Jun 93	THAT'S THE WAY LOVE IS *MCA MCSTD 1783*	56	2
22 Jan 94	SOMETHING IN COMMON *MCA MCSTD 1957* [2]	16	5
25 Jun 94 ●	TWO CAN PLAY THAT GAME (re) *MCA MCSTD 1973*	3	15
8 Jul 95 ●	HUMPIN' AROUND (re-mix) *MCA MCSTD 2073*	8	6
14 Oct 95	MY PREROGATIVE (re-mix) *MCA MCSTD 2094*	17	3
3 Feb 96	EVERY LITTLE STEP (re-mix) *MCA MCSTD 48004*	25	2
22 Nov 97	FEELIN' INSIDE *MCA MCSTD 48067*	40	1
21 Dec 02	THUG LOVIN' *Def Jam 0637872* [3]	15	2

[1] Glenn Medeiros featuring Bobby Brown [2] Bobby Brown and Whitney Houston
[3] Ja Rule featuring Bobby Brown

'Two Can Play That Game' reached its peak position of No.3 only on its re-entry in Apr 1995

Carl BROWN – *See DOUBLE TROUBLE*

Crazy World of Arthur BROWN
UK, male vocal / instrumental group (14 WEEKS) pos/wks

26 Jun 68 ★	FIRE *Track 604 022*	....	1 14

Dennis BROWN *Jamaica, male vocalist (18 WEEKS)* pos/wks

3 Mar 79	MONEY IN MY POCKET *Lightning LV 5*	14	9
3 Jul 82	LOVE HAS FOUND ITS WAY *A&M AMS 8226*	47	6
11 Sep 82	HALFWAY UP HALFWAY DOWN *A&M AMS 8250*	56	3

Diana BROWN and Barrie K SHARPE
UK, female / male vocal duo (11 WEEKS) pos/wks

2 Jun 90	THE MASTERPLAN *ffrr F 133*	39	6
1 Sep 90	SUN WORSHIPPERS (POSITIVE THINKING) *ffrr F 144*	61	2
23 Mar 91	LOVE OR NOTHING *ffrr F 152*	71	1
27 Jun 92	EATING ME ALIVE *ffrr F 190*	53	2

Errol BROWN *UK, male vocalist (13 WEEKS)* pos/wks

4 Jul 87	PERSONAL TOUCH *WEA YZ 130*	25	8
28 Nov 87	BODY ROCKIN' *WEA YZ 162*	51	2
14 Feb 98	IT STARTED WITH A KISS *EMI CDHOT 101* [1]	18	3

[1] Hot Chocolate featuring Errol Brown

See also HOT CHOCOLATE

Foxy BROWN *US, female rapper – Inga Marchand (25 WEEKS)* pos/wks

21 Sep 96	TOUCH ME TEASE ME *Def Jam DEFCD 18* [1]	26	3
8 Mar 97	GET ME HOME *Def Jam DEFCD 32* [2]	11	5
10 May 97	AIN'T NO PLAYA *Northwestside 74321474842* [3]	31	2
21 Jun 97 ●	I'LL BE *Def Jam 5710432* [4]	9	5
11 Oct 97	BIG BAD MAMMA *Def Jam 5749792* [5]	12	3
25 Oct 97	SUNSHINE *Northwestside 74321528702* [6]	25	2
13 Mar 99	HOT SPOT *Def Jam 8708352*	31	2
8 Sep 01	OH YEAH *Der Jam 5887312*	27	3

[1] Case featuring Foxy Brown [2] Foxy Brown featuring BLACKstreet [3] Jay-Z featuring Foxy Brown [4] Foxy Brown featuring Jay-Z [5] Foxy Brown featuring Dru Hill [6] Jay-Z featuring Babyface and Foxy Brown

Gloria D BROWN *US, female vocalist (3 WEEKS)* pos/wks

8 Jun 85	THE MORE THEY KNOCK, THE MORE I LOVE YOU *10 TEN 52*	57	3

Horace BROWN *US, male vocalist (7 WEEKS)* pos/wks

25 Feb 95	TASTE YOUR LOVE *Uptown MCSTD 2026*	58	1

18 May 96	ONE FOR THE MONEY *Motown 8605232*	12	4
12 Oct 96	THINGS WE DO FOR LOVE *Motown 8605712*	27	2

Ian BROWN *UK, male vocal / instrumentalist (32 WEEKS)* pos/wks

24 Jan 98 ●	MY STAR *Polydor 5719872*	5	4
4 Apr 98	CORPSES *Polydor 5696552*	14	4
20 Jun 98	CAN'T SEE ME *Polydor 5440452*	21	3
20 Feb 99 ●	BE THERE *Mo Wax MW 108CD1* [1]	8	6
6 Nov 99	LOVE LIKE A FOUNTAIN *Polydor 5615162*	23	3
19 Feb 00 ●	DOLPHINS WERE MONKEYS *Polydor 5616372*	5	4
17 Jun 00	GOLDEN GAZE *Polydor 5618442*	29	2
29 Sep 01	F.E.A.R. *Polydor 5872842*	13	4
23 Feb 02	WHISPERS *Polydor 5705382*	33	2

[1] Unkle featuring Ian Brown

See also STONE ROSES

James BROWN (297) Top 500
"Soul Brother No.1", b. 3 May 1928, South Carolina, US. The most charted R&B performer of all time has influenced numerous musical styles since the mid-1950s. Only Elvis Presley has enjoyed more US pop chart entries (104 WEEKS) pos/wks

23 Sep 65	PAPA'S GOT A BRAND NEW BAG *London HL 9990* [1]	25	7
24 Feb 66	I GOT YOU *Pye International 7N 25350* [1]	29	6
16 Jun 66	IT'S A MAN'S MAN'S MAN'S WORLD *Pye International 7N 25371* [1]	13	9
10 Oct 70	GET UP I FEEL LIKE BEING A SEX MACHINE *Polydor 2001 071*	32	7
27 Nov 71	HEY AMERICA *Mojo 2093 006*	47	3
18 Sep 76	GET UP OFFA THAT THING *Polydor 2066 687*	22	6
29 Jan 77	BODY HEAT *Polydor 2066 763*	36	4
10 Jan 81	RAPP PAYBACK (WHERE IZ MOSES?) *RCA 28*	39	5
2 Jul 83	BRING IT ON… BRING IT ON *Sonet SON 2258*	45	4
1 Sep 84	UNITY (PART 1 – THE THIRD COMING) *Tommy Boy AFR 2* [2]	49	5
27 Apr 85	FROGGY MIX *Boiling Point FROG 1*	50	3
1 Jun 85	GET UP I FEEL LIKE BEING A SEX MACHINE (re) *Boiling Point POSP 751*	46	9
25 Jan 86 ●	LIVING IN AMERICA *Scotti Brothers A 6701*	5	10
18 Oct 86	GRAVITY *Scotti Brothers 650059 7*	65	2
30 Jan 88	SHE'S THE ONE *Urban URB 13*	45	3
23 Apr 88	THE PAYBACK MIX *Urban URB 17*	12	6
4 Jun 88	I'M REAL *Scotti Brothers JSB 1* [3]	31	4
23 Jul 88	I GOT YOU (I FEEL GOOD) (re-issue) *A&M AM 444*	52	3
16 Nov 91	GET UP (I FEEL LIKE BEING A) SEX MACHINE (2nd re-issue) *Polydor PO 185*	69	2
24 Oct 92	I GOT YOU (I FEEL GOOD) (re-mix) *FBI FBI 9* [4]	72	1
17 Apr 93	CAN'T GET ANY HARDER *Polydor PZCD 262*	59	2
17 Apr 99	FUNK ON AH ROLL *Inferno / Eagle EAGXA 073*	40	2
22 Apr 00	FUNK ON AH ROLL (re-mix) *Eagle EAGXS 127*	63	1

[1] James Brown and the Famous Flames [2] Afrika Bambaataa and James Brown
[3] James Brown featuring Full Force [4] James Brown vs Dakeyne

'Froggy Mix' is a medley of 12 James Brown songs. The listed flip side of 'I Got You (I Feel Good)' was 'Nowhere to Run' by Martha Reeves and the Vandellas

Jennifer BROWN *Sweden, female vocalist (1 WEEK)* pos/wks

1 May 99	TUESDAY AFTERNOON *RCA 74321604092*	57	1

Joanne BROWN – *See Tony OSBORNE SOUND*

Jocelyn BROWN (443) Top 500
Super session singer from North Carolina who relocated to New York, b. 25 Nov 1950. She has sung backing vocals for such acts as John Lennon, Bruce Springsteen, Luther Vandross, Diana Ross and Bob Dylan and has had UK hits with 11 separate recording acts (79 WEEKS) pos/wks

21 Apr 84	SOMEBODY ELSE'S GUY *Fourth & Broadway BRW 5*	13	9
22 Sep 84	I WISH YOU WOULD *Fourth & Broadway BRW 14*	51	3
15 Mar 86	LOVE'S GONNA GET YOU *Warner Bros. W 8889*	70	1
29 Jun 91 ●	ALWAYS THERE *Talkin Loud TLK 10* [1]	6	9
14 Sep 91	SHE GOT SOUL *A&M AM 819* [2]	57	3
7 Dec 91 ●	DON'T TALK JUST KISS *Tug SNOG 2* [3]	3	11
20 Mar 93	TAKE ME UP *A&M AMCD 210* [4]	61	1

Re-entries are listed as (re), (2re), (3re), etc which signifies that the hit re-entered the chart once, twice or three times, etc

11 Jun 94	NO MORE TEARS (ENOUGH IS ENOUGH)		13	7
	Bell 74321209032 [5]			
8 Oct 94	GIMME ALL YOUR LOVIN' Bell 74321231322 [6]		22	3
13 Jul 96 ●	KEEP ON JUMPIN' Manifesto FESCD 11 [7]		8	6
10 May 97	IT'S ALRIGHT, I FEEL IT! Talkin Loud TLCD 22 [8]		26	2
12 Jul 97	SOMETHING GOIN' ON Manifesto FESCD 25 [7]		5	10
25 Oct 97	I AM THE BLACK GOLD OF THE SUN		31	2
	Talkin Loud TLCD 26 [8]			
22 Nov 97	HAPPINESS Sony S3 KAMCD 2 [9]		45	1
2 May 98	FUN INCredible INCRL 2CD		33	2
29 Aug 98	AIN'T NO MOUNTAIN HIGH ENOUGH		35	2
	INCredible INCRL 7CD			
27 Mar 99	I BELIEVE Playola 0091705 PLA		62	1
3 Jul 99	IT'S ALL GOOD INCredible INCRL 14CD		54	1
11 Mar 00	BELIEVE Defected DFECT 14CD3 [10]		45	2
27 Jan 01	BELIEVE (re-mix) Defected DFECT 26CDS [10]		42	2
7 Sep 02	THAT'S HOW GOOD YOUR LOVE IS		54	1
	Defected DFTD 057CDS [11]			

[1] Incognito featuring Jocelyn Brown [2] Jamestown featuring Jocelyn Brown [3] Right Said Fred. Guest vocals: Jocelyn Brown [4] Sonic Surfers featuring Jocelyn Brown [5] Kym Mazelle and Jocelyn Brown [6] Jocelyn Brown and Kym Mazelle [7] Todd Terry featuring Martha Wash and Jocelyn Brown [8] Nuyorican Soul featuring Jocelyn Brown [9] Kamasutra featuring Jocelyn Brown [10] Ministers De La Funk featuring Jocelyn Brown [11] Il Padrinos featuring Jocelyn Brown

See also Todd TERRY PROJECT

Joe BROWN and the BRUVVERS `346` `Top 500` *Chirpy Cockney singer / guitarist, b. 13 May 1941, Lincolnshire, UK. Brown was one of the original artists managed by early rock impresario Larry Parnes. Voted Top UK Vocal Personality in 1962 NME Poll (92 WEEKS)* pos/wks

17 Mar 60	THE DARKTOWN STRUTTERS' BALL Decca F 11207		34	6
26 Jan 61	SHINE Pye 7N 15322 [1]		33	6
11 Jan 62	WHAT A CRAZY WORLD WE'RE LIVING IN		37	2
	Piccadilly 7N 35024			
17 May 62 ●	A PICTURE OF YOU Piccadilly 7N 35047		2	19
13 Sep 62	YOUR TENDER LOOK Piccadilly 7N 35058		31	6
15 Nov 62 ●	IT ONLY TOOK A MINUTE (re) Piccadilly 7N 35082		6	14
7 Feb 63 ●	THAT'S WHAT LOVE WILL DO Piccadilly 7N 35106		3	14
27 Jun 63	NATURE'S TIME FOR LOVE Piccadilly 7N 35129		26	6
26 Sep 63	SALLY ANN Piccadilly 7N 35138		28	9
29 Jun 67	WITH A LITTLE HELP FROM MY FRIENDS Pye 7N 17339 [1]		32	4
14 Apr 73	HEY MAMA Ammo AMO 101 [1]		33	6

[1] Joe Brown

Karen BROWN – *See DJ's RULE*

Kathy BROWN *US, female vocalist (9 WEEKS)* pos/wks

25 Nov 95	TURN ME OUT Stress CDSTR 40		44	2
20 Sep 97	TURN ME OUT (TURN TO SUGAR) (re-mix) ffrr FCD [1]		35	3
10 Apr 99	JOY Azuli AZNYCDX 094		63	1
5 May 01	LOVE IS NOT A GAME Defected DFECT 31CDS [2]		34	2
2 Jun 01	OVER YOU Defected DFECT 28CDS [3]		42	1

[1] Praxis featuring Kathy Brown [2] J. Majik featuring Kathy Brown [3] Warren Clarke featuring Kathy Brown

Miquel BROWN *US, female vocalist (7 WEEKS)* pos/wks

18 Feb 84	HE'S A SAINT, HE'S A SINNER Record Shack SOHO 15		68	4
24 Aug 85	CLOSE TO PERFECTION Record Shack SOHO 48		63	3

Palmer BROWN – *See BLAZE featuring Palmer BROWN*

Peter BROWN *US, male vocalist (9 WEEKS)* pos/wks

11 Feb 78	DO YA WANNA GET FUNKY WITH ME TK TKR 6009 [1]		43	4
17 Jun 78	DANCE WITH ME TK TKR 6027		57	5

[1] special background vocals: Betty Wright

Polly BROWN *UK, female vocalist (5 WEEKS)* pos/wks

14 Sep 74	UP IN A PUFF OF SMOKE GTO GT 2		43	5

Roy 'Chubby' BROWN *UK, male comedian – Royston Vasey (22 WEEKS)* pos/wks

13 May 95 ●	LIVING NEXT DOOR TO ALICE (WHO THE F**K IS ALICE) (re) N.O.W. CDWAG 245 [1]		3	19
21 Dec 96	ROCKIN' GOOD CHRISTMAS PolyStar 5732612		51	3

[1] Smokie featuring Roy 'Chubby' Brown

Sam BROWN *UK, female vocalist (35 WEEKS)* pos/wks

11 Jun 88 ●	STOP (re) A&M AM 440		4	15
13 May 89	CAN I GET A WITNESS A&M AM 509		15	7
3 Mar 90	WITH A LITTLE LOVE A&M AM 539		44	4
5 May 90	KISSING GATE A&M AM 549		23	8
26 Aug 95	JUST GOOD FRIENDS Dick Bros. DDICK 014CD1 [1]		63	1

[1] Fish featuring Sam Brown

'Stop' reached its peak position of No.4 only on its re-entry in Feb 1989

Sharon BROWN *US, female vocalist (11 WEEKS)* pos/wks

17 Apr 82	I SPECIALIZE IN LOVE Virgin VS 494		38	9
26 Feb 94	I SPECIALIZE IN LOVE (re-mix) Deep Distraxion OILYCD 025		62	2

Sleepy BROWN – *See OUTKAST*

BROWN SAUCE *UK, male / female vocal group (12 WEEKS)* pos/wks

12 Dec 81	I WANNA BE A WINNER BBC RESL 101		15	12

BROWN SUGAR – *See SEX CLUB featuring BROWN SUGAR*

Duncan BROWNE *UK, male vocalist (8 WEEKS)* pos/wks

19 Aug 72	JOURNEY RAK 135		23	6
22 Dec 84	THEME FROM 'THE TRAVELLING MAN' Towerbell TOW 64		68	2

Jackson BROWNE *US, male vocalist (14 WEEKS)* pos/wks

1 Jul 78	STAY Asylum K 13128		12	11
18 Oct 86	IN THE SHAPE OF A HEART Elektra EKR 42		66	2
25 Jun 94	EVERYWHERE I GO Elektra EKR 184CD1		67	1

Ronnie BROWNE – *See SCOTTISH RUGBY TEAM with Ronnie BROWNE*

Tom BROWNE *US, male instrumentalist – trumpet (24 WEEKS)* pos/wks

19 Jul 80 ●	FUNKIN' FOR JAMAICA (N.Y.) Arista ARIST 357		10	11
25 Oct 80	THIGHS HIGH (GRIP YOUR HIPS AND MOVE)		45	5
	Arista ARIST 367			
30 Jan 82	FUNGI MAMA (BEBOPAFUNKADISCOLYPSO)		58	4
	Arista ARIST 450			
11 Jan 92	FUNKIN' FOR JAMAICA (re-mix) Arista 114998		45	4

BROWNS *US, male / female vocal group – Jim Ed, Maxine and Bonnie Brown (13 WEEKS)* pos/wks

18 Sep 59 ●	THE THREE BELLS RCA 1140 ▲		6	13

BROWNSTONE *US, female vocal group (24 WEEKS)* pos/wks

1 Apr 95 ●	IF YOU LOVE ME MJJ 6614135		8	12
15 Jul 95	GRAPEVYNE MJJ 6620942		16	4
23 Sep 95	I CAN'T TELL YOU WHY MJJ 6623775		27	2
17 May 97	5 MILES TO EMPTY Epic 6640962		12	4
27 Sep 97	KISS AND TELL Epic 6649852		21	2

BROWNSVILLE STATION *US, male vocal / instrumental group (6 WEEKS)* pos/wks

2 Mar 74	SMOKIN' IN THE BOYS' ROOM Philips 6073 834		27	6

Dave BRUBECK QUARTET *US, male instrumental group (30 WEEKS)* pos/wks

26 Oct 61 ●	TAKE FIVE Fontana H 339		6	15
8 Feb 62	IT'S A RAGGY WALTZ Fontana H 352		36	3
17 May 62	UNSQUARE DANCE CBS AAG 102		14	12

Tommy BRUCE and the BRUISERS
UK, male vocal / instrumental group (21 WEEKS)   pos/wks

26 May 60	● AIN'T MISBEHAVIN' *Columbia DB 4453*	3	16
8 Sep 60	BROKEN DOLL *Columbia DB 4498*	36	4
22 Feb 62	BABETTE *Columbia DB 4776* [1]	50	1

[1] Tommy Bruce

Claudia BRÜCKEN *Germany, female vocalist (2 WEEKS)*
   pos/wks

| 11 Aug 90 | ABSOLUT(E) *Island IS 471* | 71 | 1 |
| 16 Feb 91 | KISS LIKE ETHER *Island IS 479* | 63 | 1 |

BRUISERS *UK, male instrumental group (7 WEEKS)*
   pos/wks

| 8 Aug 63 | BLUE GIRL (re) *Parlophone R 5042* | 31 | 7 |

Frank BRUNO *UK, male boxer / vocalist (4 WEEKS)*
   pos/wks

| 23 Dec 95 | EYE OF THE TIGER *RCA 74321336282* | 28 | 4 |

BRUNO and LIZ – See Liz KERSHAW and Bruno BROOKES

Tyrone BRUNSON *US, male instrumentalist – bass (5 WEEKS)*
   pos/wks

| 25 Dec 82 | THE SMURF *Epic EPC A 3024* | 52 | 5 |

BRUVVERS – See Joe BROWN and the BRUVVERS

Dora BRYAN
UK, female actor / vocalist – Dora Broadbent (6 WEEKS)   pos/wks

| 5 Dec 63 | ALL I WANT FOR CHRISTMAS IS A BEATLE *Fontana TF 427* | 20 | 6 |

Kéllé BRYAN *UK, female vocalist (4 WEEKS)*
   pos/wks

| 2 Oct 99 | HIGHER THAN HEAVEN *1st Avenue / Mercury MERCD 522* | 14 | 4 |

See also ETERNAL

Anita BRYANT *US, female vocalist (6 WEEKS)*
   pos/wks

| 26 May 60 | PAPER ROSES (2re) *London HLL 9144* | 24 | 4 |
| 6 Oct 60 | MY LITTLE CORNER OF THE WORLD *London HLL 9171* | 48 | 2 |

Peabo BRYSON *US, male vocalist (35 WEEKS)*
   pos/wks

20 Aug 83	● TONIGHT I CELEBRATE MY LOVE *Capitol CL 302* [1]	2	13
16 May 92	BEAUTY AND THE BEAST *Epic 6576607* [2]	9	7
17 Jul 93	BY THE TIME THIS NIGHT IS OVER *Arista 74321157142* [3]	56	3
11 Dec 93	A WHOLE NEW WORLD (ALADDIN'S THEME) *Columbia 6599002* [4] ▲	12	12

[1] Peabo Bryson and Roberta Flack [2] Celine Dion and Peabo Bryson [3] Kenny G with Peabo Bryson [4] Regina Belle and Peabo Bryson

BUBBLEROCK – See Jonathan KING

Catherine BUCHANAN – See JELLYBEAN

Roy BUCHANAN
US, male instrumentalist – guitar, d. 14 Aug 1988 (3 WEEKS)   pos/wks

| 31 Mar 73 | SWEET DREAMS *Polydor 2066 307* | 40 | 3 |

BUCKETHEADS *US, male producer – Kenny Gonzalez (16 WEEKS)* pos/wks

| 4 Mar 95 | ● THE BOMB! (THESE SOUNDS FALL INTO MY MIND) *Positiva CDTIV 33* | 5 | 13 |
| 20 Jan 96 | GOT MYSELF TOGETHER *Positiva CDTIV 48* | 12 | 3 |

Lindsey BUCKINGHAM *US, male vocalist (7 WEEKS)*
   pos/wks

| 16 Jan 82 | TROUBLE *Mercury MER 85* | 31 | 7 |

See also FLEETWOOD MAC

Jeff BUCKLEY *US, male vocalist, d. 29 May 1997 (3 WEEKS)*
   pos/wks

| 27 May 95 | LAST GOODBYE *Columbia 6620422* | 54 | 2 |
| 6 Jun 98 | EVERYBODY HERE WANTS YOU *Columbia 6657912* | 43 | 1 |

BUCKS FIZZ ⟨149⟩ [Top 500]
Chart-topping mixed quartet: Cheryl Baker, Mike Nolan, Jay Aston (replaced by Shelley Preston in 1985) and Bobby G (Gubby). Formed for the 1981 Eurovision Song Contest, they were the last UK winners for 16 years (150 WEEKS)   pos/wks

28 Mar 81	★ MAKING YOUR MIND UP *RCA 56*	1	12
6 Jun 81	PIECE OF THE ACTION *RCA 88*	12	9
15 Aug 81	ONE OF THOSE NIGHTS *RCA 114*	20	10
28 Nov 81	★ THE LAND OF MAKE BELIEVE *RCA 163*	1	16
27 Mar 82	★ MY CAMERA NEVER LIES *RCA 202*	1	8
19 Jun 82	● NOW THOSE DAYS ARE GONE *RCA 241*	8	9
27 Nov 82	● IF YOU CAN'T STAND THE HEAT *RCA 300*	10	11
12 Mar 83	RUN FOR YOUR LIFE *RCA FIZ 1*	14	7
18 Jun 83	● WHEN WE WERE YOUNG *RCA 342*	10	8
1 Oct 83	LONDON TOWN *RCA 363*	34	6
17 Dec 83	RULES OF THE GAME *RCA 380*	57	6
25 Aug 84	TALKING IN YOUR SLEEP *RCA FIZ 2*	15	9
27 Oct 84	GOLDEN DAYS *RCA FIZ 3*	42	4
29 Dec 84	I HEAR TALK *RCA FIZ 4*	34	8
22 Jun 85	YOU AND YOUR HEART SO BLUE *RCA PB 40233*	43	4
14 Sep 85	MAGICAL *RCA PB 40367*	57	3
7 Jun 86	● NEW BEGINNING (MAMBA SEYRA) *Polydor POSP 794*	8	10
30 Aug 86	LOVE THE ONE YOU'RE WITH *Polydor POSP 813*	47	3
15 Nov 86	KEEP EACH OTHER WARM *Polydor POSP 835*	45	4
5 Nov 88	HEART OF STONE *RCA PB 42035*	50	3

BUCKSHOT LEFONQUE
US, male vocal / instrumental group (1 WEEK)   pos/wks

| 6 Dec 97 | ANOTHER DAY *Columbia 6653762* | 65 | 1 |

Roy BUDD *UK, male instrumentalist – piano (1 WEEK)*
   pos/wks

| 10 Jul 99 | GET CARTER *Cinephile CINX 1003* | 68 | 1 |

BUDGIE *UK, male vocal / instrumental group (2 WEEKS)*
   pos/wks

| 3 Oct 81 | KEEPING A RENDEZVOUS *RCA BUDGIE 3* | 71 | 2 |

BUFFALO G *Ireland, female vocal / rap duo*
– Olive Tucker and Naomi Lynch (4 WEEKS)   pos/wks

| 10 Jun 00 | WE'RE REALLY SAYING SOMETHING (re) *Epic 6694182* | 17 | 4 |

BUFFALO TOM *US, male vocal / instrumental group (5 WEEKS)* pos/wks

| 23 Oct 99 | ● GOING UNDERGROUND : CARNATION *Ignition IGNSCD 16* | 6 | 5 |

B-side by: Liam Gallagher and Steve Cradock

BUG KANN and the PLASTIC JAM
UK, male / female vocal / instrumental group (2 WEEKS)   pos/wks

| 31 Aug 91 | MADE IN TWO MINUTES *Optimum Dance BKPJ 1S* [1] | 70 | 1 |
| 26 Feb 94 | MADE IN 2 MINUTES (re-mix) *PWL International PWCD 286* | 64 | 1 |

[1] Bug Kann and Plastic Jam featuring Patti Low and Doogie

BUGGLES *UK, male vocal / instrumental*
duo – Trevor Horn and Geoff Downes (28 WEEKS)   pos/wks

22 Sep 79	★ VIDEO KILLED THE RADIO STAR *Island WIP 6524*	1	11
26 Jan 80	THE PLASTIC AGE *Island WIP 6540*	16	8
5 Apr 80	CLEAN CLEAN *Island WIP 6584*	38	5
8 Nov 80	ELSTREE *Island WIP 6624*	55	4

James BULLER *UK, male vocalist (1 WEEK)*
   pos/wks

| 6 Mar 99 | CAN'T SMILE WITHOUT YOU *BBC Music WMSS 60092* | 51 | 1 |

Silvah BULLET – See Jonny L

BULLETPROOF UK, male producer – Paul Chambers (1 WEEK)   pos/wks
| 10 Mar 01 | SAY YEAH / DANCE TO THE RHYTHM | | |
| | *Tidy Trax TIDY 148CD* | 62 | 1 |

BUMP UK, male instrumental / production
duo – Marc Auerbach and Steve Travell (5 WEEKS)   pos/wks
| 4 Jul 92 | I'M RUSHING *Good Boy EDGE7 1* | 40 | 4 |
| 11 Nov 95 | I'M RUSHING (re-mix) *Deconstruction 74321320692* | 45 | 1 |

BUMP & FLEX UK, male / female vocal / production duo (1 WEEK)   pos/wks
| 23 May 98 | LONG TIME COMING *Heat Recordings HEATCD 014* | 73 | 1 |

BUNKER KRU – See HARLEQUIN 4s / BUNKER KRU

BUNNYMEN – See ECHO and the BUNNYMEN

Emma BUNTON UK, female vocalist (38 WEEKS)   pos/wks
13 Nov 99	● WHAT I AM *VC Recordings VCRD 53* 1	2	12
14 Apr 01	★ WHAT TOOK YOU SO LONG *Virgin VSCDT 1796* ■	1	12
8 Sep 01	● TAKE MY BREATH AWAY *Virgin VSCDT 1814*	5	9
22 Dec 01	WE'RE NOT GONNA SLEEP TONIGHT *Virgin VSCDT 1821*	20	5

1 Tin Tin Out featuring Emma Bunton

See also SPICE GIRLS

Eric BURDON – See ANIMALS

Geoffrey BURGON UK, orchestra (4 WEEKS)   pos/wks
| 26 Dec 81 | BRIDESHEAD THEME *Chrysalis CHS 2562* | 48 | 4 |

Keni BURKE US, male vocalist (4 WEEKS)   pos/wks
| 27 Jun 81 | LET SOMEBODY LOVE YOU *RCA 93* | 59 | 3 |
| 18 Apr 92 | RISIN' TO THE TOP *RCA PB 49103* | 70 | 1 |

BURN UK, male vocal / instrumental group (1 WEEK)   pos/wks
| 8 Jun 02 | THE SMILING FACE *Hut / Virgin HUTCD 155* | 72 | 1 |

Hank C BURNETTE
Sweden, male multi-instrumentalist – Sven-Ake Hogberg (8 WEEKS)   pos/wks
| 30 Oct 76 | SPINNING ROCK BOOGIE *Sonet SON 2094* | 21 | 8 |

Johnny BURNETTE US, male vocalist, d. 1 Aug 1964 (48 WEEKS)   pos/wks
29 Sep 60	● DREAMIN' *London HLG 9172*	5	16
12 Jan 61	● YOU'RE SIXTEEN *London HLG 9254*	3	12
13 Apr 61	LITTLE BOY SAD *London HLG 9315*	12	12
10 Aug 61	GIRLS *London HLG 9388*	37	5
17 May 62	CLOWN SHOES *Liberty LIB 55416*	35	3

Rocky BURNETTE US, male vocalist (7 WEEKS)   pos/wks
| 17 Nov 79 | TIRED OF TOEIN' THE LINE *EMI 2992* | 58 | 7 |

Jerry BURNS UK, female vocalist (1 WEEK)   pos/wks
| 25 Apr 92 | PALE RED *Columbia 6579467* | 64 | 1 |

Ray BURNS UK, male vocalist (19 WEEKS)   pos/wks
| 11 Feb 55 | ● MOBILE *Columbia DB 3563* 1 | 4 | 13 |
| 26 Aug 55 | THAT'S HOW A LOVE SONG WAS BORN *Columbia DB 3640* 2 | 14 | 6 |

1 Ray Burns with Eric Jupp and His Orchestra 2 Ray Burns with the Coronets

BURRELLS – See RESONANCE featuring The BURRELLS

Malandra BURROWS UK, female vocalist (10 WEEKS)   pos/wks
1 Dec 90	JUST THIS SIDE OF LOVE		
	Yorkshire Television DALE 1	11	8
18 Oct 97	CARNIVAL IN HEAVEN *Warner.esp WESP 001CD*	49	1
29 Aug 98	DON'T LEAVE ME *Warner.esp WESP 004CD*	54	1

Jenny BURTON US, female vocalist (2 WEEKS)   pos/wks
| 30 Mar 85 | BAD HABITS *Atlantic A 9583* | 68 | 2 |

BURUNDI STEIPHENSON BLACK Burundi, drummers and chanters
with orchestral additions by Mike Steiphenson of France (14 WEEKS)   pos/wks
| 13 Nov 71 | BURUNDI BLACK *Barclay BAR 3* | 31 | 14 |

BUS 75 – See WHALE

BUS STOP UK, male production group (19 WEEKS)   pos/wks
23 May 98	● KUNG FU FIGHTING		
	All Around the World CDGLOBE 173 1	8	11
24 Oct 98	YOU AIN'T SEEN NOTHIN' YET		
	All Around the World CDGLOBE 187 2	22	4
10 Apr 99	JUMP *All Around the World CDGLOBE 186*	23	3
7 Sep 00	GET IT ON *All Around the World CDGLOBE225* 3	59	1

1 Bus Stop featuring Carl Douglas 2 Bus Stop featuring Randy Bachman 3 Bus Stop featuring T. Rex

See also FLIP & FILL

Lou BUSCH and his Orchestra US, orchestra
and chorus – aka Joe 'Fingers' Carr, d. 19 Sep 1979 (17 WEEKS)   pos/wks
| 27 Jan 56 | ● ZAMBESI *Capitol CL 14504* | 2 | 17 |

BUSH UK, male vocal / instrumental group (13 WEEKS)   pos/wks
8 Jun 96	MACHINEHEAD *Interscope IND 95505*	48	2
1 Mar 97	● SWALLOWED *Interscope IND 95528*	7	5
7 Jun 97	GREEDY FLY *Interscope IND 95536*	22	2
1 Nov 97	BONE DRIVEN *Interscope IND 95553*	49	1
4 Dec 99	THE CHEMICALS BETWEEN US		
	Trauma / Polydor 4972222	46	1
18 Mar 00	WARM MACHINE *Trauma / Polydor 4972752*	45	1
3 Jun 00	LETTING THE CABLES SLEEP *Trauma / Polydor 4973352*	51	1

Kate BUSH ⟨123 Top 500⟩ Unmistakable singer / songwriter with
operatic vocal ability, b. 30 Jul 1958, Kent. Discovered by Dave Gilmour of
Pink Floyd. First British female to top the singles chart with a self-composed
song and the first to have a UK No.1 album (168 WEEKS)   pos/wks
11 Feb 78	★ WUTHERING HEIGHTS (re) *EMI 2719*	1	13
10 Jun 78	● THE MAN WITH THE CHILD IN HIS EYES *EMI 2806*	6	11
11 Nov 78	HAMMER HORROR *EMI 2887*	44	6
17 Mar 79	WOW *EMI 2911*	14	10
15 Sep 79	● ON STAGE (EP) *EMI MIEP 2991*	10	9
26 Apr 80	BREATHING *EMI 5058*	16	7
5 Jul 80	● BABOOSHKA *EMI 5085*	5	10
4 Oct 80	ARMY DREAMERS *EMI 5106*	16	9
6 Dec 80	DECEMBER WILL BE MAGIC AGAIN *EMI 5121*	29	7
11 Jul 81	SAT IN YOUR LAP *EMI 5201*	11	7
7 Aug 82	THE DREAMING *EMI 5296*	48	3
17 Aug 85	● RUNNING UP THAT HILL *EMI KB 1*	3	11
26 Oct 85	CLOUDBUSTING *EMI KB 2*	20	6
1 Mar 86	HOUNDS OF LOVE *EMI KB 3*	18	5
10 May 86	THE BIG SKY *EMI KB 4*	37	3
1 Nov 86	● DON'T GIVE UP *Virgin PGS 2* 1	9	11
8 Nov 86	EXPERIMENT IV *EMI KB 5*	23	4
30 Sep 89	THE SENSUAL WORLD *EMI EM 102*	12	5
2 Dec 89	THIS WOMAN'S WORK *EMI EM 119*	25	5
10 Mar 90	LOVE AND ANGER *EMI EM 134*	38	3
7 Dec 91	ROCKET MAN (I THINK IT'S GOING TO BE A LONG LONG		
	TIME) *Mercury TRIBO 2*	12	8
18 Sep 93	RUBBERBAND GIRL *EMI CDEM 280*	12	5
27 Nov 93	MOMENTS OF PLEASURE *EMI CDEM 297*	26	3
16 Apr 94	THE RED SHOES *EMI CDEMS 316*	21	3
30 Jul 94	THE MAN I LOVE *Mercury MERCD 408* 2	27	2
19 Nov 94	AND SO IS LOVE *EMI CDEMS 355*	26	2

1 Peter Gabriel and Kate Bush 2 Kate Bush and Larry Adler

*Tracks on On Stage (EP): Them Heavy People / Don't Push Your Foot on the
Heartbrake / James and the Cold Gun / L'Amour Looks Something Like You*

BUSTED UK, male vocal / instrumental group (12 WEEKS) pos/wks
28 Sep 02 ● WHAT I GO TO SCHOOL FOR *Universal MCSTD 40294* 3 12

BUSTER UK, male vocal / instrumental group (1 WEEK) pos/wks
19 Jun 76 SUNDAY *RCA 2678*...49 1

Bernard BUTLER UK, male vocal / instrumentalist (9 WEEKS) pos/wks
17 Jan 98 STAY *Creation CRESCD 281* 12 4
28 Mar 98 NOT ALONE *Creation CRESCD 289* 27 3
27 Jun 98 A CHANGE OF HEART *Creation CRESCD 297* 45 1
23 Oct 99 YOU MUST GO ON *Creation CRESCD 324* 44 1

See also SUEDE

Jonathan BUTLER
South Africa, male vocalist / instrumentalist – guitar (18 WEEKS) pos/wks
25 Jan 86 IF YOU'RE READY (COME GO WITH ME) *Jive JIVE 109* [1] 30 7
8 Aug 87 LIES *Jive JIVE 141* 18 11

[1] Ruby Turner featuring Jonathan Butler

BUTTERSCOTCH UK, male vocal group (11 WEEKS) pos/wks
2 May 70 DON'T YOU KNOW *RCA 1937* 17 11

BUTTHOLE SURFERS
US, male vocal / instrumental group (1 WEEK) pos/wks
5 Oct 96 PEPPER *Capitol CDCL 778* 59 1

BUZZCOCKS UK, male vocal / instrumental group (53 WEEKS) pos/wks
18 Feb 78 WHAT DO I GET? *United Artists UP 36348* 37 3
13 May 78 I DON'T MIND *United Artists UP 36386*..............55 2
15 Jul 78 LOVE YOU MORE *United Artists UP 36433* 34 6
23 Sep 78 EVER FALLEN IN LOVE (WITH SOMEONE YOU
SHOULDN'T'VE) *United Artists UP 36455*........12 11
25 Nov 78 PROMISES *United Artists UP 36471* 20 10
10 Mar 79 EVERYBODY'S HAPPY NOWADAYS *United Artists UP 36499*....29 6
21 Jul 79 HARMONY IN MY HEAD *United Artists UP 36541* 32 6
25 Aug 79 SPIRAL SCRATCH (EP) *New Hormones ORG 1* 31 6
6 Sep 80 ARE EVERYTHING / WHY SHE'S A GIRL FROM THE
CHAINSTORE *United Artists BP 365* 61 3

*Tracks on Spiral Scratch (EP): Breakdown / Time's Up / Boredom / Friends of Mine.
Sleeve of EP (not the label) credits Buzzcocks with Howard Devoto. 'Why She's a Girl
from the Chainstore' listed from 13 Sep 1980*

BUZZY BUNCH – See Celi BEE and the BUZZY BUNCH

BY ALL MEANS US, male vocal group (2 WEEKS) pos/wks
18 Jun 88 I SURRENDER TO YOUR LOVE *Fourth & Broadway BRW 102* ..65 2

Max BYGRAVES 204 Top 500 *One of Britain's best-loved
entertainers, b. 16 Oct, 1922, London. The comedian / singer / songwriter
was the only British male in the first UK singles chart. He had five Top 20
'sing-a-long' hit albums in just 15 months of the 1970s (131 WEEKS)* pos/wks
14 Nov 52 ● COWPUNCHER'S CANTATA (3re) *HMV B 10250*...........6 8
14 May 54 ● (THE GANG THAT SANG) HEART OF MY HEART *HMV B 10654* ..7 8
10 Sep 54 ● GILLY GILLY OSSENFEFFER KATZENELLEN BOGEN BY THE
SEA (re) *HMV B 10734*...............................7 8
21 Jan 55 MISTER SANDMAN *HMV B 10801* 16 1
18 Nov 55 ● MEET ME ON THE CORNER *HMV POP 116* 2 11
17 Feb 56 THE BALLAD OF DAVY CROCKETT *HMV POP 153* 20 1
25 May 56 OUT OF TOWN *HMV POP 164* 18 7
5 Apr 57 HEART *Decca F 10862* [1] 14 8
2 May 58 ● YOU NEED HANDS / TULIPS FROM AMSTERDAM
Decca F 11004 [2] 3 25
22 Aug 58 LITTLE TRAIN / GOTTA HAVE RAIN *Decca F 11046*....28 2
2 Jan 59 (I LOVE TO PLAY) MY UKULELE *Decca F 11077*.....19 4
18 Dec 59 ● JINGLE BELL ROCK *Decca F 11176*..................7 4
10 Mar 60 ● FINGS AIN'T WOT THEY USED T'BE *Decca F 11214* 5 15
28 Jul 60 CONSIDER YOURSELF *Decca F 11251*................50 1

1 Jun 61 THE BELLS OF AVIGNON *Decca F 11350* 36 5
19 Feb 69 YOU'RE MY EVERYTHING (re) *Pye 7N 17705*.......34 4
6 Oct 73 DECK OF CARDS *Pye 7N 45276* 13 15
9 Dec 89 WHITE CHRISTMAS *Parkfield PMS 5012* 71 4

[1] Max Bygraves with Malcolm Lockyer and his Orchestra [2] Max Bygraves with
the Clark Bros and both sides with Eric Rodgers and his Orchestra

*Cowpuncher's Cantata is a medley with the following songs: Cry of the Wild Goose /
Riders in the Sky / Mule Train / Jezebel. 'Tulips from Amsterdam' was listed with
'You Need Hands' from 9 May 1958*

BYKER GROOOVE! UK, female vocal group (3 WEEKS) pos/wks
24 Dec 94 LOVE YOUR SEXY … !! *Groove GROVD 01*................48 3

Charlie BYRD – See Stan GETZ

Debra BYRD – See Barry MANILOW

Donald BYRD US, male instrumentalist – trumpet (6 WEEKS) pos/wks
26 Sep 81 LOVING YOU / LOVE HAS COME AROUND *Elektra K 12559*......41 6

Gary BYRD and the GB EXPERIENCE US, male rapper
and male / female vocal / instrumental group (9 WEEKS) pos/wks
23 Jul 83 ● THE CROWN *Motown TMGT 1312*.......................6 9

Features uncredited vocals by Stevie Wonder

BYRDS US, male vocal / instrumental group (52 WEEKS) pos/wks
17 Jun 65 ★ MR TAMBOURINE MAN *CBS 201765* ▲ 1 14
12 Aug 65 ● ALL I REALLY WANT TO DO *CBS 201796* 4 10
11 Nov 65 TURN! TURN! TURN! (TO EVERYTHING THERE IS A
SEASON *CBS 202008* ▲ 26 8
5 May 66 EIGHT MILES HIGH *CBS 202067* 24 9
5 Jun 68 YOU AIN'T GOING NOWHERE *CBS 3411* 45 3
13 Feb 71 CHESTNUT MARE *CBS 5322* 19 8

David BYRNE – See X-PRESS 2; TALKING HEADS

Edward BYRNES and Connie STEVENS US, male / female actors /
vocal duo – Edward Brietenberger and Concetta Ingolia (8 WEEKS) pos/wks
5 May 60 KOOKIE KOOKIE (LEND ME YOUR COMB)
Warner Bros. WB 5 ....27 8

BYSTANDERS UK, male vocal / instrumental group (1 WEEK) pos/wks
9 Feb 67 98.6 *Piccadilly 7N 35363* 45 1

C

Melanie C 487 Top 500 *Former Sporty Spice (b. Melanie Chisholm,
12 Jan 1974, Liverpool, UK) has appeared on 11 No.1 hits – a total never
bettered by any female artist. Only woman to top the UK chart solo and as
part of a duo, quartet and quintet (74 WEEKS)* pos/wks
12 Dec 98 ● WHEN YOU'RE GONE *A&M 5828212* [1] 3 19
9 Oct 99 ● GOIN' DOWN (re) *Virgin VSCDT 1744* 4 6
4 Dec 99 ● NORTHERN STAR *Virgin VSCDT 1748*...............4 11
1 Apr 00 ★ NEVER BE THE SAME AGAIN (re)
Virgin VSCDT 1762 [2] ■ 1 16
19 Aug 00 ★ I TURN TO YOU *Virgin VSCDT 1772* ■ 1 12
9 Dec 00 IF THAT WERE ME (re) *Virgin VSCDT 1786* 18 6

[1] Bryan Adams featuring Melanie C [2] Melanie C / Lisa 'Left Eye' Lopes

See also SPICE GIRLS

Roy C
US, male vocalist – Roy C Hammond (24 WEEKS) pos/wks
21 Apr 66	● SHOTGUN WEDDING *Island WI 273*	6	11
25 Nov 72	● SHOTGUN WEDDING (re-issue) *UK 19*	8	13

C & C MUSIC FACTORY
US, male instrumental / production duo – Robert Clivilles and David Cole featuring male / female vocalists / rappers (53 WEEKS) pos/wks
15 Dec 90	● GONNA MAKE YOU SWEAT (EVERYBODY DANCE NOW) *CBS 6564540* [1] ▲	3	12
30 Mar 91	HERE WE GO *Columbia 6567557* [1]	20	7
6 Jul 91	● THINGS THAT MAKE YOU GO HMMM... *Columbia 6566907*	4	11
23 Nov 91	JUST A TOUCH OF LOVE (EVERYDAY) *Columbia 6575247* [2]	31	3
18 Jan 92	PRIDE (IN THE NAME OF LOVE) *Columbia 6577017* [3]	15	5
14 Mar 92	A DEEPER LOVE *Columbia 6578497* [3]	15	5
3 Oct 92	KEEP IT COMIN' (DANCE TILL YOU CAN'T DANCE NO MORE) *Columbia 6584307* [4]	34	3
27 Aug 94	DO YOU WANNA GET FUNKY *Columbia 6607622*	27	3
18 Feb 95	I FOUND LOVE / TAKE A TOKE *Columbia 6612112* [5]	26	2
11 Nov 95	I'LL ALWAYS BE AROUND *MCA MCSTD 40001*	42	2

[1] C & C Music Factory (featuring Freedom Williams) [2] C & C Music Factory featuring Zelma Davis [3] Clivilles and Cole [4] C & C Music Factory featuring Q Unique and Deborah Cooper [5] C & C Music Factory / C & C Music Factory featuring Martha Wash

C.C.S.
UK, male vocal / instrumental group (55 WEEKS) pos/wks
31 Oct 70	WHOLE LOTTA LOVE *RAK 104*	13	13
27 Feb 71	● WALKIN' *RAK 109*	7	16
4 Sep 71	● TAP TURNS ON THE WATER *RAK 119*	5	13
4 Mar 72	BROTHER *RAK 126*	25	8
4 Aug 73	THE BAND PLAYED THE BOOGIE *RAK 154*	36	5

CJ & CO
US, male vocal / instrumental group (2 WEEKS) pos/wks
30 Jul 77	DEVIL'S GUN *Atlantic K 10956*	43	2

CLS
US, male vocal / production duo (1 WEEK) pos/wks
30 May 98	CAN YOU FEEL IT *Satellite 74321580162*	46	1

ANDY C – See SHIMON & Andy C

C.O.D
US, male vocal / instrumental group (2 WEEKS) pos/wks
14 May 83	IN THE BOTTLE *Streetwave WAVE 2*	54	2

CRW
Italy, male producer – Mauro Picotto (8 WEEKS) pos/wks
26 Feb 00	I FEEL LOVE *VC Recordings VCRD 63*	15	4
25 Nov 00	LOVIN' *VC Recordings VCRD 77*	49	2
27 Apr 02	LIKE A CAT *BXR BXRC 0397* [1]	57	1
26 Oct 02	PRECIOUS LIFE *BXR BXRC 0395* [2]	57	1

[1] CRW featuring Veronika [2] CRW presents Veronika

See also Mauro PICOTTO

CZR featuring DELANO
US, male production group and US, male vocalist (1 WEEK) pos/wks
30 Sep 00	I WANT YOU *Credence CDCRED 002*	57	1

ÇA VA ÇA VA
UK, male vocal / instrumental group (8 WEEKS) pos/wks
18 Sep 82	WHERE'S ROMEO *Regard RG 103*	49	5
19 Feb 83	BROTHER BRIGHT *Regard RG 105*	65	3

Montserrat CABALLÉ – See Freddie MERCURY

CABANA
Brazil, male / female vocal / instrumental duo (1 WEEK) pos/wks
15 Jul 95	BAILANDO CON LOBOS *Hi-Life 5792512*	65	1

CABARET VOLTAIRE
UK, male vocal / instrumental group (8 WEEKS) pos/wks
18 Jul 87	DON'T ARGUE *Parlophone R 6157*	69	2

4 Nov 89	HYPNOTISED *Parlophone R 6227*	66	2
12 May 90	KEEP ON *Parlophone R 6250*	55	2
18 Aug 90	EASY LIFE *Parlophone R 6261*	61	2

CABLE
UK, male vocal / instrumental group (2 WEEKS) pos/wks
14 Jun 97	FREEZE THE ATLANTIC *Infectious INFECT 38CD*	44	2

Albert CABRERA – See David MORALES

CACIQUE
UK, male / female vocal / instrumental group (1 WEEK) pos/wks
1 Jun 85	DEVOTED TO YOU *Diamond Duel DISC 1*	69	1

CACTUS WORLD NEWS
Ireland, male vocal / instrumental group (7 WEEKS) pos/wks
8 Feb 86	YEARS LATER *MCA MCA 1024*	59	3
26 Apr 86	WORLDS APART *MCA MCA 1040*	58	3
20 Sep 86	THE BRIDGE *MCA MCA 1080*	74	1

CADDILLAC TAH – See Jennifer LOPEZ

CADETS with Eileen REID
Ireland, male / female vocal / instrumental group (1 WEEK) pos/wks
3 Jun 65	JEALOUS HEART *Pye 7N 15852*	42	1

Susan CADOGAN
UK, female vocalist (19 WEEKS) pos/wks
5 Apr 75	● HURT SO GOOD *Magnet MAG 23*	4	12
19 Jul 75	LOVE ME BABY *Magnet MAG 36*	22	7

Athena CAGE – See Keith SWEAT

Al CAIOLA
US, orchestra – Al Caiola – guitar (6 WEEKS) pos/wks
15 Jun 61	THE MAGNIFICENT SEVEN *HMV POP 889/LONDON HLT 9294*	34	6

CAKE
US, male vocal / instrumental group (7 WEEKS) pos/wks
22 Mar 97	THE DISTANCE *Capricorn 5742212*	22	3
31 May 97	I WILL SURVIVE *Capricorn 5744712*	29	2
1 May 99	NEVER THERE *Capricorn 8708112*	66	1
3 Nov 01	SHORT SKIRT LONG JACKET *Columbia 6720402*	63	1

CALIBRE CUTS – See VARIOUS ARTISTS (MONTAGES)

CALIFORNIA SUNSHINE
Israel / Italy, male / female DJ / production group (1 WEEK) pos/wks
16 Aug 97	SUMMER '89 *Perfecto PERF 143CD*	56	1

CALL
US, male vocal / instrumental group (6 WEEKS) pos/wks
30 Sep 89	LET THE DAY BEGIN *MCA MCA 1362*	42	6

Terry CALLIER
US, male vocalist (4 WEEKS) pos/wks
13 Dec 97	BEST BIT (EP) *Heavenly HVN 72CD* [1]	36	3
23 May 98	LOVE THEME FROM SPARTACUS *Talkin' Loud TLCD 32*	57	1

[1] Beth Orton featuring Terry Callier

Tracks on Best Bit (EP): Best Bit / Skimming Stone / Dolphins / Lean On Me

CALLING
US, male vocal / instrumental group (15 WEEKS) pos/wks
29 Jun 02	WHEREVER YOU WILL GO (import) *RCA 74321912242*	64	1
6 Jul 02	● WHEREVER YOU WILL GO *RCA 74321947652*	3	11
2 Nov 02	ADRIENNE *RCA 74321968352*	18	3

Eddie CALVERT   432 Top 500
'The Man with the Golden Trumpet', b. 13 Mar 1922, Lancashire, UK, d. 7 Aug 1978, South Africa. First British instrumentalist to achieve two No.1s and first to earn US gold disc. 'Oh Mein Papa' spent nine weeks at the top – a record for an instrumental (80 WEEKS) pos/wks
18 Dec 53	★ OH, MEIN PAPA *Columbia DB 3337*	1	21

8 Apr 55	★ CHERRY PINK AND APPLE BLOSSOM WHITE		
	Columbia DB 3581	1	21
13 May 55	STRANGER IN PARADISE Columbia DB 3594	14	4
29 Jul 55	● JOHN AND JULIE Columbia DB 3624	6	11
9 Mar 56	ZAMBESI (re) Columbia DB 3747	13	7
7 Feb 58	● MANDY (LA PANSE) Columbia DB 3956	9	14
20 Jun 58	LITTLE SERENADE Columbia DB 4105	28	2

Donnie CALVIN – See ROCKER'S REVENGE featuring Donnie CALVIN

CAMEO
US, male vocal / instrumental group (71 WEEKS) pos/wks

31 Mar 84	SHE'S STRANGE Club JAB 2	37	8
13 Jul 85	ATTACK ME WITH YOUR LOVE Club JAB 16	65	2
14 Sep 85	SINGLE LIFE Club JAB 21	15	10
7 Dec 85	SHE'S STRANGE (re-issue) Club JAB 25	22	8
22 Mar 86	A GOODBYE Club JAB 28	65	2
30 Aug 86	● WORD UP Club JAB 38	3	13
29 Nov 86	CANDY Club JAB 43	27	9
25 Apr 87	BACK AND FORTH Club JAB 49	11	9
17 Oct 87	SHE'S MINE Club JAB 57	35	4
29 Oct 88	YOU MAKE ME WORK Club JAB 70	74	1
28 Jul 01	LOVERBOY (re) Virgin VUSCD 211 [1]	12	5

[1] Mariah featuring Cameo

Andy CAMERON UK, male vocalist (8 WEEKS) pos/wks

4 Mar 78	● ALLY'S TARTAN ARMY Klub 03	6	8

CAMILLA – See MOJOLATORS featuring CAMILLA

Tony CAMILLO'S BAZUKA
US, male instrumental / vocal group (5 WEEKS) pos/wks

31 May 75	DYNOMITE (PART 1) A&M AMS 7168	28	5

CAMISRA
UK, male DJ / producer – 'Tall Paul' Newman (12 WEEKS) pos/wks

21 Feb 98	● LET ME SHOW YOU VC Recordings VCRD 31	5	8
11 Jul 98	FEEL THE BEAT VC Recordings VCRD 39	32	2

22 May 99	CLAP YOUR HANDS VC Recordings VCRD 49	34	2

See also PARTIZAN; ESCRIMA; TALL PAUL; GRIFTERS

CAMOUFLAGE featuring MYSTI
UK, male / female vocal / instrumental group (3 WEEKS) pos/wks

24 Sep 77	BEE STING State STAT 58	48	3

CAMP LO US, male rap duo (1 WEEK) pos/wks

16 Aug 97	LUCHINI AKA (THIS IS IT) ffrr FCD 305	74	1

CAMPAG VELOCET
UK, male female vocal / instrumental group (1 WEEK) pos/wks

19 Feb 00	VITO SATAN Pias Recordings PIASX 010CD	75	1

Ali CAMPBELL UK, male vocalist (18 WEEKS) pos/wks

20 May 95	● THAT LOOK IN YOUR EYE Kuff KUFFDG 1	5	10
26 Aug 95	LET YOUR YEAH BE YEAH Kuff KUFFD 2	25	4
9 Dec 95	SOMETHIN' STUPID Kuff KUFFDG 5 [1]	30	4

[1] Ali and Kibibi Campbell

See also Pato BANTON; UB40

Danny CAMPBELL and SASHA
UK, male vocalist and male DJ / producer (1 WEEK) pos/wks

31 Jul 93	TOGETHER ffrr FCD 212	57	1

See also SASHA

Don CAMPBELL – See GENERAL SAINT

Ellie CAMPBELL UK, female vocalist (5 WEEKS) pos/wks

3 Apr 99	SWEET LIES Jive / Eastern Bloc 0519222	42	1
14 Aug 99	SO MANY WAYS Jive / Eastern Bloc 0519362	26	3
9 Jun 01	DON'T WANT YOU BACK Jive 9201302	50	1

Ethna CAMPBELL UK, female vocalist (11 WEEKS) pos/wks

27 Dec 75	THE OLD RUGGED CROSS Philips 6006 475	33	11

Glen CAMPBELL (302 Top 500)
Top session guitarist and singer who became one of the biggest selling country and easy listening artists of the 1960s, b. 22 Apr 1936, Arkansas, US. Other credits include part-time member of The Beach Boys and vocalist with The Crickets (103 WEEKS) pos/wks

29 Jan 69	● WICHITA LINEMAN Ember EMBS 261	7	13
7 May 69	GALVESTON Ember EMBS 263	14	10
6 Dec 69	● ALL I HAVE TO DO IS DREAM Capitol CL 15619 [1]	3	14
7 Feb 70	TRY A LITTLE KINDNESS Capitol CL 15622	45	2
9 May 70	● HONEY COME BACK Capitol CL 15638	4	19
26 Sep 70	EVERYTHING A MAN COULD EVER NEED Capitol CL 15653	32	5
21 Nov 70	● IT'S ONLY MAKE BELIEVE Capitol CL 15663	4	14
27 Mar 71	DREAM BABY (HOW LONG MUST I DREAM) Capitol CL 15674	39	3
4 Oct 75	● RHINESTONE COWBOY Capitol CL 15824 ▲	4	12
26 Mar 77	SOUTHERN NIGHTS Capitol CL 15907 ▲	28	6
30 Nov 02	RHINESTONE COWBOY (GIDDY UP GIDDY UP) Serious SER 059CD [2]	12	5+

[1] Bobbie Gentry and Glen Campbell [2] Rikki and Daz featuring Glen Campbell

Ian CAMPBELL FOLK GROUP
UK, male vocal / instrumental group (5 WEEKS) pos/wks

11 Mar 65	THE TIMES THEY ARE A-CHANGIN' (2re) Transatlantic SP 5	42	5

Jo Ann CAMPBELL US, female vocalist (3 WEEKS) pos/wks

8 Jun 61	MOTORCYCLE MICHAEL HMV POP 873	41	3

Junior CAMPBELL UK, male vocalist (18 WEEKS) pos/wks

14 Oct 72	● HALLELUJAH FREEDOM Deram DM 364	10	9
2 Jun 73	SWEET ILLUSION Deram DM 387	15	9

MOST CHART ENTRIES IN THE TOP 10

■ A list of the acts with the most singles making their chart debut inside the Top 10. Any ties split by number of entries at No.1 and then No.2

Act	Singles entering in the Top 10	
1.	MADONNA	37
2.	U2	20
3.	GEORGE MICHAEL	19
4.	KYLIE MINOGUE	18
5.	BEATLES	18
6.	MICHAEL JACKSON	17
7.	OASIS	16
8.	BOYZONE	16
9.	ROBBIE WILLIAMS	16
10.	PET SHOP BOYS	16

Madonna: whose 37 Top 10 entries included three straight in at No.1

Kibibi CAMPBELL – *See Ali CAMPBELL*

Naomi CAMPBELL *UK, female vocalist (3 WEEKS)*

		pos/wks
24 Sep 94	LOVE AND TEARS *Epic 6608352*	40 3

Pat CAMPBELL *Ireland, male vocalist (5 WEEKS)*

		pos/wks
15 Nov 69	THE DEAL *Major Minor MM 648*....................	31 5

Stan CAMPBELL *UK, male vocalist (3 WEEKS)*

		pos/wks
6 Jun 87	YEARS GO BY *WEA YZ 127*	65 3

Tevin CAMPBELL *US, male vocalist (2 WEEKS)*

		pos/wks
18 Apr 92	TELL ME WHAT YOU WANT ME TO DO *Qwest W 0102*	63 2

CAM'RON

US, male rapper – Cameron Giles (11 WEEKS)

		pos/wks
19 Sep 98	HORSE AND CARRIAGE *Epic 6662612* [1]	12 4
17 Aug 02	OH BOY *Roc-A-Fella 0639642* [2]	13 7

[1] Cam'ron featuring Mase [2] Cam'ron featuring Juelz Santana

CAN *Germany, male vocal / instrumental group (10 WEEKS)*

		pos/wks
28 Aug 76	I WANT MORE *Virgin VS 153*	26 10

CANDIDO *US, male multi-instrumentalist (3 WEEKS)*

		pos/wks
18 Jul 81	JINGO *Excalibur EXC 102*	55 3

CANDLEWICK GREEN

UK, male vocal / instrumental group (8 WEEKS)

		pos/wks
23 Feb 74	WHO DO YOU THINK YOU ARE? *Decca F 13480*	21 8

CANDY FLIP *UK, male vocal / instrumental*

duo – Rick Peel and Danny 'Dizzy' Deo (14 WEEKS)

		pos/wks
17 Mar 90	● STRAWBERRY FIELDS FOREVER *Debut DEBT 3092*	3 10
14 Jul 90	THIS CAN BE REAL *Debut DEBT 3099*	60 4

CANDY GIRLS *UK, male / female instrumental / production*

duo – Rachel Auburn and Paul Masterson (10 WEEKS)

		pos/wks
30 Sep 95	FEE FI FO FUM *VC VCRD 1* [1]	23 4
24 Feb 96	WHAM BAM *VC VCRD 6* [1]	20 4
7 Dec 96	I WANT CANDY *Feverpitch CDFVR 1013* [2]	30 2

[1] Candy Girls featuring Sweet Pussy Pauline [2] Candy Girls featuring Valerie Malcolm

See also YOMANDA; SLEAZESISTERS; CLERGY; DOROTHY; HI-GATE; Paul MASTERSON presents SUSHI

CANDYLAND *UK, male vocal / instrumental group (1 WEEK)*

		pos/wks
9 Mar 91	FOUNTAIN O' YOUTH *Non Fiction YES 4*..........	72 1

CANDYSKINS *UK, male vocal / instrumental group (4 WEEKS)*

		pos/wks
19 Oct 96	MRS HOOVER *Ultimate TOPP 051CD*	65 1
8 Feb 97	MONDAY MORNING *Ultimate TOPP 055CD*	34 2
03 May 97	HANG MYSELF ON YOU *Ultimate TOPP 059CD*	65 1

CANIBUS *US, male rapper – Germaine Williams (3 WEEKS)*

		pos/wks
27 Jun 98	SECOND ROUND KO *Universal UND 56198*	35 2
10 Oct 98	HOW COME *Interscope IND 95598* [1]	52 1

[1] Youssou N'Dour and Canibus

CANNED HEAT

US, male vocal / instrumental group (41 WEEKS)

		pos/wks
24 Jul 68	● ON THE ROAD AGAIN *Liberty LBS 15090*	8 15
1 Jan 69	GOING UP THE COUNTRY *Liberty LBF 15169*	19 10
17 Jan 70	● LET'S WORK TOGETHER *Liberty LBF 15302*	2 15
11 Jul 70	SUGAR BEE *Liberty LBF 15350*	49 1

Freddy CANNON

US, male vocalist – Freddy Picariello (54 WEEKS)

		pos/wks
14 Aug 59	TALLAHASSEE LASSIE *Top Rank JAR 135*	17 8
1 Jan 60	● WAY DOWN YONDER IN NEW ORLEANS *Top Rank JAR 247*.....3 18
4 Mar 60	CALIFORNIA HERE I COME (re) *Top Rank JAR 309*	25 3
17 Mar 60	INDIANA *Top Rank JAR309*	42 1
19 May 60	THE URGE *Top Rank JAR 369*	18 10
20 Apr 61	MUSKRAT RAMBLE *Top Rank JAR 548*	32 5
28 Jun 62	PALISADES PARK *Stateside SS 101*	20 9

Blu CANTRELL *US, female vocalist (9 WEEKS)*

		pos/wks
24 Nov 01	HIT 'EM UP STYLE (OOPS!) *Arista 74321891632*..........	12 9

Jim CAPALDI *UK, male vocalist (17 WEEKS)*

		pos/wks
27 Jul 74	IT'S ALL UP TO YOU *Island WIP 6198*	27 6
25 Oct 75	● LOVE HURTS *Island WIP 6246*	4 11

CAPERCAILLIE

UK / Ireland, male / female vocal / instrumental group (3 WEEKS)

		pos/wks
23 May 92	A PRINCE AMONG ISLANDS (EP) *Survival ZB 45393*	39 2
17 Jun 95	DARK ALAN (AILEIN DUINN) *Survival SURCD 55*	65 1

Tracks on A Prince Among Islands (EP): Coisich a Ruin (Walk My Beloved) / Fagail Bhearnaraid (Leaving Bernaray) / The Lorn Theme / Gun Teann Mi Ris Na Ruinn Tha Seo (Remembrance)

CAPPADONNA – *See WU-TANG CLAN*

CAPPELLA

Italy, male /female / production / vocal group (68 WEEKS)

		pos/wks
9 Apr 88	PUSH THE BEAT / BAUHAUS *Fast Globe FGL 1*	60 2
6 May 89	HELYOM HALIB *Music Man MMPS 7004*	11 9
23 Sep 89	HOUSE ENERGY REVENGE *Music Man MMPS 7009*	73 1
27 Apr 91	EVERYBODY *fffr F158*	66 1
18 Jan 92	TAKE ME AWAY *PWL Continental PWL 210* [1]	25 5
3 Apr 93	● U GOT 2 KNOW *Internal Dance IDC 1*	6 11
14 Aug 93	U GOT 2 KNOW (re-mix) *Internal Dance IDCR 2*	43 3
23 Oct 93	● U GOT 2 LET THE MUSIC *Internal Dance IDC 3*	2 12
19 Feb 94	MOVE ON BABY *Internal Dance IDC 4*	7 7
18 Jun 94	U & ME *Internal Dance IDCC 6*	10 7
15 Oct 94	MOVE IT UP / BIG BEAT *Internal Dance IDC 7*	16 6
16 Sep 95	TELL ME THE WAY *Systematic SYSCD 17*	17 3
6 Sep 97	BE MY BABY *Nukleuz PSNC 0072*	53 1

[1] Cappella featuring Loleatta Holloway

See also 49ers

CAPRICCIO *UK, production duo (2 WEEKS)*

		pos/wks
27 Mar 99	EVERYBODY GET UP *Defected DEFECT 2CDS*	44 2

CAPRICE *US, female vocalist – Caprice Bourret (5 WEEKS)*

		pos/wks
4 Sep 99	OH YEAH *Virgin VSCDT 1745*	24 3
10 Mar 01	ONCE AROUND THE SUN *Virgin VSCDT 1750*	24 2

CAPRICORN *Belgium, male DJ (1 WEEK)*

		pos/wks
29 Nov 97	20 HZ (NEW FREQUENCIES) *R&S RS 97126CD*	73 1

Tony CAPSTICK and the CARLTON MAIN / FRICKLEY COLLIERY BAND *UK, male vocalist and male instrumental band (8 WEEKS)*

		pos/wks
21 Mar 81	● THE SHEFFIELD GRINDER / CAPSTICK COMES HOME *Dingles SID 27*	3 8

CAPTAIN BEAKY – *See Keith MICHELL*

CAPTAIN HOLLYWOOD PROJECT *US / Germany,*

male / female vocal / instrumental group (31 WEEKS)

		pos/wks
22 Sep 90	I CAN'T STAND IT *BCM BCMR 395* [1]	7 10
24 Nov 90	ARE YOU DREAMING *BCM BCM 07504* [1]	17 10
27 Mar 93	ONLY WITH YOU *Pulse 8 CDLOSE 40*	67 1

UK No.1 ★ UK Top 10 ● Still on chart + UK million seller ◆ UK entry at No.1 ■ US No.1 ▲

6 Nov 93	MORE AND MORE *Pulse 8 CDLOSE 50*	23	5
5 Feb 94	IMPOSSIBLE *Pulse 8 CDLOSE 54*	29	3
11 Jun 94	ONLY WITH YOU (re-issue) *Pulse 8 CDLOSE 62*	61	1
1 Apr 95	FLYING HIGH *Pulse 8 CDLOSE 82*	58	1

1 Twenty 4 Seven featuring Captain Hollywood

CAPTAIN SENSIBLE *UK, male vocalist – Ray Burns (31 WEEKS)* pos/wks

26 Jun 82 ★	HAPPY TALK *A&M CAP 1*	1	8
14 Aug 82	WOT! *A&M CAP 2*	26	7
24 Mar 84 ●	GLAD IT'S ALL OVER / DAMNED ON 45 *A&M CAP 6*	6	10
28 Jul 84	THERE ARE MORE SNAKES THAN LADDERS *A&M CAP 7*	57	5
10 Dec 94	THE HOKEY COKEY *Have a Nice Day CDHOKEY 1*	71	1

CAPTAIN and TENNILLE *US, male instrumentalist – keyboards*
– and female vocalist – Daryl Dragon and Toni Tennille (24 WEEKS) pos/wks

2 Aug 75	LOVE WILL KEEP US TOGETHER *A&M AMS 7165* ▲	32	5
24 Jan 76	THE WAY I WANT TO TOUCH YOU *A&M AMS 7203*	28	6
4 Nov 78	YOU NEVER DONE IT LIKE THAT *A&M AMS 7384*	63	3
16 Feb 80 ●	DO THAT TO ME ONE MORE TIME *Casablanca CAN 175* ▲	7	10

Irene CARA *US, female actor / vocalist (33 WEEKS)* pos/wks

3 Jul 82 ★	FAME *RSO 90*	1	16
4 Sep 82	OUT HERE ON MY OWN *RSO 66*	58	3
4 Jun 83 ●	FLASHDANCE . . . WHAT A FEELING *Casablanca CAN 1016* ▲	2	14

CARAMBA *Sweden, male vocalist / multi-instrumentalist*
dog impersonator – Michael Tretow (6 WEEKS) pos/wks

12 Nov 83	FEDORA (I'LL BE YOUR DAWG) *Billco BILL 101*	56	6

CARAVELLES *UK, female vocal duo*
– Lois Wilkinson and Andrea Simpson (13 WEEKS) pos/wks

8 Aug 63 ●	YOU DON'T HAVE TO BE A BABY TO CRY *Decca F 11697*	6	13

CARDIGANS
Sweden, female / male vocal / instrumental group (66 WEEKS) pos/wks

17 Jun 95	CARNIVAL (re) *Trampolene PZCD 345*	35	3
30 Sep 95	SICK AND TIRED *Stockholm 5773112*	34	3
17 Feb 96	RISE AND SHINE *Trampolene 5778252*	29	2
21 Sep 96	LOVEFOOL *Stockholm 5752952*	21	4
7 Dec 96	BEEN IT *Stockholm 5759672*	56	1
3 May 97 ●	LOVEFOOL (re-issue) *Stockholm 5710502*	2	13
6 Sep 97	YOUR NEW CUCKOO *Stockholm 5716632*	35	2
17 Oct 98	MY FAVOURITE GAME *Stockholm 5679912*	14	18
6 Mar 99 ●	ERASE / REWIND *Stockholm 5635332*	7	9
24 Jul 99	HANGING AROUND *Stockholm 5612682*	17	4
25 Sep 99 ●	BURNING DOWN THE HOUSE *Gut CDGUT 26* 1	7	7

1 Tom Jones and The Cardigans

See also A CAMP

CARE *UK, male vocal / instrumental duo (4 WEEKS)* pos/wks

12 Nov 83	FLAMING SWORD *Arista KBIRD 2*	48	4

Mariah CAREY 45 Top 500 *Record-shattering vocalist / songwriter,*
*b. 27 Mar 1970, New York. Since her 1990 chart debut she has sold more than
120 million albums worldwide and has topped the US singles chart 15 times
– only Elvis Presley has spent longer at the top. She had a brief, and much
publicised, $20m-per-album deal with Virgin in 2001. Best-selling single:
'Without You' 559,200 (260 WEEKS)* pos/wks

4 Aug 90 ●	VISION OF LOVE *CBS 6559320* ▲	9	12
10 Nov 90	LOVE TAKES TIME *CBS 6563647* ▲	37	8
26 Jan 91	SOMEDAY *Columbia 6565837* ▲	38	5
1 Jun 91	THERE'S GOT TO BE A WAY *Columbia 6569317*	54	3
5 Oct 91	EMOTIONS *Columbia 6574037* ▲	17	9
11 Jan 92	CAN'T LET GO *Columbia 6576627*	20	7
18 Apr 92	MAKE IT HAPPEN *Columbia 6579417*	17	5
27 Jun 92 ●	I'LL BE THERE *Columbia 6581377* ▲	2	9
21 Aug 93 ●	DREAMLOVER *Columbia 6594445* ▲	9	10

6 Nov 93 ●	HERO *Columbia 6598122* ▲	7	15
19 Feb 94 ★	WITHOUT YOU *Columbia 6599192* ■	1	14
18 Jun 94 ●	ANYTIME YOU NEED A FRIEND *Columbia 6603542*	8	10
17 Sep 94 ●	ENDLESS LOVE (2re) *Epic 6608062* 1	3	16
10 Dec 94 ●	ALL I WANT FOR CHRISTMAS IS YOU (re) *Columbia 6610702*	2	8
23 Sep 95 ●	FANTASY *Columbia 6624952* ▲	4	11
9 Dec 95 ●	ONE SWEET DAY *Columbia 6626035* 2 ▲	6	11
17 Feb 96 ●	OPEN ARMS *Columbia 6629772*	4	6
22 Jun 96 ●	ALWAYS BE MY BABY *Columbia 6633345* ▲	3	10
6 Sep 97 ●	HONEY *Columbia 6650192* ▲	3	8
13 Dec 97	BUTTERFLY *Columbia 6653365*	22	6
13 Jun 98 ●	MY ALL *Columbia 6660592* ▲	4	8
19 Dec 98 ●	WHEN YOU BELIEVE (re) *Columbia 6667522* 3	4	13
10 Apr 99	I STILL BELIEVE *Columbia 6670732*	16	7
6 Nov 99 ●	HEARTBREAKER *Columbia 6683012* 4 ▲	5	13
11 Mar 00 ●	THANK GOD I FOUND YOU (re) *Columbia 6690582* 5 ▲	10	10
30 Sep 00 ★	AGAINST ALL ODDS (re) *Columbia 6698872* 6 ■	1	12
28 Jul 01 ●	LOVERBOY (re) *Virgin VUSCD 211* 7	12	5
29 Dec 01	NEVER TOO FAR / DON'T STOP (FUNKIN' 4 JAMAICA) *Virgin VUSCD 228* 8	32	4
30 Nov 02 ●	THROUGH THE RAIN *Mercury 0638072*	8	5+

1 Luther Vandross and Mariah Carey 2 Mariah Carey and Boyz II Men 3 Mariah Carey and Whitney Houston 4 Mariah Carey featuring Jay-Z 5 Mariah Carey featuring Joe and 98 Degrees 6 Mariah Carey and Westlife 7 Mariah featuring Cameo 8 Mariah Carey / Mariah Carey featuring Mystikal

Although he is uncredited, 'I'll Be There' is a duet with Trey Lorenz

CARL – *See CLUBHOUSE*

Belinda CARLISLE 165 Top 500
*Lead vocalist of the first really successful all-girl rock group, The Go-Go's;
b. 17 Aug 1958, Hollywood. She married the son of British-born film star
James Mason in 1992 and her career fared even better in the UK than in
her homeland. Joined a re-formed Go-Go's in 2001 (145 WEEKS)* pos/wks

12 Dec 87 ★	HEAVEN IS A PLACE ON EARTH *Virgin VS 1036* ▲	1	14
27 Feb 88 ●	I GET WEAK *Virgin VS 1046*	10	9
7 May 88 ●	CIRCLE IN THE SAND *Virgin VS 1074*	4	11
6 Aug 88	MAD ABOUT YOU *IRS IRM 118*	67	3
10 Sep 88	WORLD WITHOUT YOU *Virgin VS 1114*	34	6
10 Dec 88	LOVE NEVER DIES… *Virgin VS 1150*	54	5
7 Oct 89 ●	LEAVE A LIGHT ON *Virgin VS 1210*	4	10
9 Dec 89	LA LUNA *Virgin VS 1230*	38	6
24 Feb 90	RUNAWAY HORSES *Virgin VS 1244*	40	5
26 May 90	VISION OF YOU (re) *Virgin VS 1264*	41	6
13 Oct 90 ●	(WE WANT) THE SAME THING *Virgin VS 1319*	6	10
22 Dec 90	SUMMER RAIN *Virgin VS 1323*	23	10
28 Sep 91	LIVE YOUR LIFE BE FREE *Virgin VS 1370*	12	7
16 Nov 91	DO YOU FEEL LIKE I FEEL *Virgin VS 1383*	29	4
11 Jan 92	HALF THE WORLD *Virgin VS 1388*	35	4
29 Aug 92	LITTLE BLACK BOOK *Virgin VS 1428*	28	5
25 Sep 93	BIG SCARY ANIMAL *Virgin VSCDT 1472*	12	6
27 Nov 93	LAY DOWN YOUR ARMS *Virgin VSCDG 1476*	27	6
13 Jul 96 ●	IN TOO DEEP *Chrysalis CDCHS 5033*	6	7
21 Sep 96 ●	ALWAYS BREAKING MY HEART *Chrysalis CDCHS 5037*	8	6
30 Nov 96	LOVE IN THE KEY OF C *Chrysalis CDCHS 5044*	20	3
1 Mar 97	CALIFORNIA *Chrysalis CDCHSS 5047*	31	2
27 Nov 99	ALL GOD'S CHILDREN *Virgin VSCDT 1756*	66	1

Bob CARLISLE *US, male vocalist (2 WEEKS)* pos/wks

30 Aug 97	BUTTERFLY KISSES *Jive JIVECD 249*	56	2

Don CARLOS – *See SINGING DOGS*

Sara CARLSON – *See MANIC MCs featuring Sara CARLSON*

CARLTON *UK, male vocalist (3 WEEKS)* pos/wks

16 Feb 91	LOVE AND PAIN *Smith & Mighty SNM 4*	56	2
1 Apr 95	1 TO 1 RELIGION *Stoned Heights BRCD 313* 1	53	1

1 Bomb the Bass featuring Carlton

Carl CARLTON *US, male vocalist (8 WEEKS)* pos/wks

18 Jul 81	SHE'S A BAD MAMA JAMA (SHE'S BUILT, SHE'S STACKED) *20th Century TC 2488*	34	8

Larry CARLTON – *See Mike POST*

Vanessa CARLTON *US, female vocalist (14 WEEKS)* pos/wks

3 Aug 02 ●	A THOUSAND MILES *A&M 4977542*	6	13
30 Nov 02	ORDINARY DAY *A&M 4978132*	53	1

CARLTON MAIN / FRICKLEY COLLIERY BAND – *See Tony CAPSTICK and the CARLTON MAIN / FRICKLEY COLLIERY BAND*

CARMEL *UK, female / male vocal / instrumental group (19 WEEKS)* pos/wks

6 Aug 83	BAD DAY *London LON 29*	15	9
11 Feb 84	MORE, MORE, MORE *London LON 44*	23	7
14 Jun 86	SALLY *London LON 90*	60	3

Eric CARMEN *US, male vocalist (7 WEEKS)* pos/wks

10 Apr 76	ALL BY MYSELF *Arista 42*	12	7

Tracey CARMEN – *See RUTHLESS RAP ASSASSINS*

Jean CARN – *See Bobby M featuring Jean CARN*

Kim CARNEGIE *UK, female vocalist (1 WEEK)* pos/wks

19 Jan 91	JAZZ RAP *Best ZB 44085*	73	1

Kim CARNES *US, female vocalist (15 WEEKS)* pos/wks

9 May 81 ●	BETTE DAVIS EYES *EMI America EA 121* ▲	10	9
8 Aug 81	DRAW OF THE CARDS *EMI America EA 125*	49	4
9 Oct 82	VOYEUR *EMI America EA 143*	68	2

CARNIVAL featuring RIP vs RED RAT
UK, male production duo and Jamaica, male vocalist (1 WEEK) pos/wks

12 Sep 98	ALL OF THE GIRLS (ALL AI-DI GIRL DEM) *Pepper 0530072*	51	1

See also RIP PRODUCTIONS

Renato CAROSONE and his SEXTET *Italy, male vocalist (d. 27 Apr 2001) and instrumental backing group (1 WEEK)* pos/wks

4 Jul 58	TORERO – CHA CHA CHA *Parlophone R 4433*	25	1

Mary-Chapin CARPENTER *US, female vocalist (6 WEEKS)* pos/wks

20 Nov 93	HE THINKS HE'LL KEEP HER *Columbia 6598632*	71	1
7 Jan 95	ONE COOL REMOVE *Columbia 6611342* [1]	40	3
3 Jun 95	SHUT UP AND KISS ME *Columbia 6613675*	35	2

[1] Shawn Colvin with Mary-Chapin Carpenter

CARPENTERS 116 `Top 500`

All-time biggest-selling brother / sister duo: Karen Carpenter (v/d)
(d. 4 Feb 1983), Richard Carpenter (k/v). This Connecticut couple was
among the world's most popular pop / MOR acts of the 1970s before
Karen's anorexia-associated death (173 WEEKS) pos/wks

5 Sep 70 ●	(THEY LONG TO BE) CLOSE TO YOU *A&M AMS 800* ▲	6	18
9 Jan 71	WE'VE ONLY JUST BEGUN *A&M AMS 813*	28	7
18 Sep 71	SUPERSTAR / FOR ALL WE KNOW *A&M AMS 864*	18	13
1 Jan 72	MERRY CHRISTMAS DARLING *A&M AME 601*	45	1
23 Sep 72 ●	I WON'T LAST A DAY WITHOUT YOU / GOODBYE TO LOVE *A&M AMS 7023*	9	16
7 Jul 73 ●	YESTERDAY ONCE MORE *A&M AMS 7073*	2	17
20 Oct 73 ●	TOP OF THE WORLD *A&M AMS 7086* ▲	5	18
2 Mar 74	JAMBALAYA (ON THE BAYOU) / MR GUDER *A&M AMS 7098*	12	11
8 Jun 74	I WON'T LAST A DAY WITHOUT YOU (re-issue) *A&M AMS 7111*	32	5
18 Jan 75 ●	PLEASE MR POSTMAN *A&M AMS 7141* ▲	2	12
19 Apr 75 ●	ONLY YESTERDAY *A&M AMS 7159*	7	10
30 Aug 75	SOLITAIRE *A&M AMS 7187*	32	5

20 Dec 75	SANTA CLAUS IS COMIN' TO TOWN *A&M AMS 7144*	37	4
27 Mar 76	THERE'S A KIND OF HUSH (ALL OVER THE WORLD) *A&M AMS 7219*	22	6
3 Jul 76	I NEED TO BE IN LOVE *A&M AMS 7238*	36	5
8 Oct 77 ●	CALLING OCCUPANTS OF INTERPLANETARY CRAFT (THE RECOGNISED ANTHEM OF WORLD CONTACT DAY) *A&M AMS 7318*	9	9
11 Feb 78	SWEET, SWEET SMILE *A&M AMS 7327*	40	4
22 Oct 83	MAKE BELIEVE IT'S YOUR FIRST TIME *A&M AM 147*	60	3
8 Dec 90	MERRY CHRISTMAS DARLING / (THEY LONG TO BE) CLOSE TO YOU (re-issue) *A&M AM 716*	25	5
13 Feb 93	RAINY DAYS AND MONDAYS *A&M AMCD 0180*	63	2
24 Dec 94	TRYIN' TO GET THE FEELING AGAIN *A&M 5807612*	44	2

'I Won't Last a Day Without You' AMS 7023 listed by itself 23 Sep 1972 at No.49.
'Goodbye to Love', the other side, listed by itself from 30 Sep 1972, until the end of
the record's chart run. 'Mr Guder' listed with 'Jambalaya' from 16 Mar 1974, until
the end of the chart run

Dick CARR – *See Slim DUSTY*

Joe 'Fingers' CARR *US, male instrumentalist – piano
– Lou Busch under a false name, d. 19 Sep 1979 (5 WEEKS)* pos/wks

29 Jun 56	PORTUGUESE WASHERWOMAN *Capitol CL 14587*	20	5

See also Lou BUSCH and his Orchestra

Linda CARR *US, female vocalist (12 WEEKS)* pos/wks

12 Jul 75	HIGHWIRE *Chelsea 2005 025* [1]	15	8
5 Jun 76	SOLD MY ROCK 'N' ROLL (GAVE IT FOR FUNKY SOUL) *Spark SRL 1139* [2]	36	4

[1] Linda Carr and the Love Squad [2] Linda and the Funky Boys

Pearl CARR and Teddy JOHNSON
UK, female / male vocal duo (19 WEEKS) pos/wks

20 Mar 59	SING LITTLE BIRDIE *Columbia DB 4275*	12	8
6 Apr 61	HOW WONDERFUL TO KNOW *Columbia DB 4603* [1]	23	11

[1] Teddy Johnson and Pearl Carr

Suzi CARR *US, female vocalist (1 WEEK)* pos/wks

8 Oct 94	ALL OVER ME *Cowboy RODEO 947CD*	45	1

Valerie CARR *US, female vocalist (2 WEEKS)* pos/wks

4 Jul 58	WHEN THE BOYS TALK ABOUT THE GIRLS (re) *Columbia DB 4131*	29	2

Vikki CARR *US, female vocalist –
Florencia Bisenta de Casillas Martinez Cardona (26 WEEKS)* pos/wks

1 Jun 67 ●	IT MUST BE HIM (SEUL SUR SON ETOILE) *Liberty LIB 55917*	2	20
30 Aug 67	THERE I GO *Liberty LBF 15022*	50	1
12 Mar 69	WITH PEN IN HAND (2re) *Liberty LBF 15166*	39	5

Raffaella CARRA *Italy, female vocalist (12 WEEKS)* pos/wks

15 Apr 78 ●	DO IT, DO IT AGAIN *Epic EPC 6094*	9	12

Paul CARRACK *UK, male vocalist (18 WEEKS)* pos/wks

16 May 87	WHEN YOU WALK IN THE ROOM *Chrysalis CHS 3109*	48	5
18 Mar 89	DON'T SHED A TEAR *Chrysalis CHS 3164*	60	3
6 Jan 96	EYES OF BLUE *IRS CDEIRS 192*	40	4
6 Apr 96	HOW LONG *IRS CDEIRS 193*	32	5
24 Aug 96	EYES OF BLUE (re-mix) *IRS CDEIRS 194*	45	1

CARRAPICHO – *See CHILLI featuring CARRAPICHO*

José CARRERAS *Spain, male vocalist (19 WEEKS)* pos/wks

11 Jul 92	AMIGOS PARA SIEMPRE (FRIENDS FOR LIFE) *Really Useful RUR 10* [1]	11	11
30 Jul 94	LIBIAMO / LA DONNA E MOBILE *Teldec YZ 843CD* [2]	21	4

| 25 Jul 98 | YOU'LL NEVER WALK ALONE *Decca 4607982* 3 | 35 | 4 |

1 José Carreras and Sarah Brightman 2 José Carreras featuring Placido Domingo and Luciano Pavarotti with Mehta 3 José Carreras, Placido Domingo and Luciano Pavarotti with Mehta

Tia CARRERE
US, female vocalist – Tia Carrere Samaha (6 WEEKS) pos/wks

| 30 May 92 | BALLROOM BLITZ *Reprise W 0105* | 26 | 6 |

Jim CARREY *Canada, male actor / vocalist (3 WEEKS)* pos/wks

| 21 Jan 95 | CUBAN PETE *Columbia 6606625* | 31 | 3 |

CARRIE *US / UK, male vocal / instrumental group (2 WEEKS)* pos/wks

| 14 Mar 98 | MOLLY *Island CID 687* | 56 | 1 |
| 9 May 98 | CALIFORNIA SCREAMIN' *Island CID 694* | 55 | 1 |

Dina CARROLL (⌐₋₋ Top 500)
Brit award-winning Best Female Vocalist of 1994 b. 21 Aug 1968, Newmarket, UK. Soul / dance vocalist's 'So Close' was the biggest-selling debut album by a British female artist in the 1990s, and she was the only UK woman to have two simultaneous Top 10 singles that decade (in 1993) (99 WEEKS) pos/wks

2 Feb 91	●	IT'S TOO LATE *Mercury ITM 3* 1	8	14
15 Jun 91		NAKED LOVE (JUST SAY YOU WANT ME) *Mercury ITM 4* 2	39	3
11 Jul 92		AIN'T NO MAN *A&M AM 0001*	16	8
10 Oct 92		SPECIAL KIND OF LOVE *A&M AM 0088*	16	5
5 Dec 92		SO CLOSE *A&M AM 0101*	20	8
27 Feb 93		THIS TIME *A&M AMCD 0184*	23	6
15 May 93		EXPRESS *A&M 580262-7*	12	6
16 Oct 93	●	DON'T BE A STRANGER *A&M 5803892*	3	13
11 Dec 93	●	THE PERFECT YEAR *A&M 5804812*	5	11
28 Sep 96	●	ESCAPING *Mercury / First Avenue DCCD 1*	3	8
21 Dec 96		ONLY HUMAN *Mercury / First Avenue DCCD 2*	33	4
24 Oct 98		ONE, TWO, THREE *Mercury / First Avenue MERCD 514*	16	4
24 Jul 99		WITHOUT LOVE *Manifesto / First Avenue FESCD 57*	13	7
16 Jun 01		SOMEONE LIKE YOU *Mercury / First Avenue 5689062*	38	2

1 Quartz introducing Dina Carroll 2 Quartz and Dina Carroll

Ron CARROLL – See SUPERFUNK; KLUSTER featuring Ron CARROLL

Ronnie CARROLL
Ireland, male vocalist – Ronald Cleghorn (50 WEEKS) pos/wks

27 Jul 56	WALK HAND IN HAND *Philips PB 605*	13	8
29 Mar 57	THE WISDOM OF A FOOL *Philips PB 667*	20	2
31 Mar 60	FOOTSTEPS *Philips PB 1004*	36	3
22 Feb 62	RING-A-DING GIRL *Philips PB 1222*	46	3
2 Aug 62	● ROSES ARE RED *Philips 326532 BF*	3	16
15 Nov 62	IF ONLY TOMORROW *Philips 326550 BF*	33	4
7 Mar 63	SAY WONDERFUL THINGS *Philips 326574 BF*	6	14

Jasper CARROTT *UK, male comedian – Bob Davies (15 WEEKS)* pos/wks

| 16 Aug 75 | ● FUNKY MOPED / MAGIC ROUNDABOUT *DJM DJS 388* | 5 | 15 |

CARS *US, male vocal / instrumental group (51 WEEKS)* pos/wks

11 Nov 78	● MY BEST FRIEND'S GIRL *Elektra K 12301*	3	10
17 Feb 79	JUST WHAT I NEEDED *Elektra K 12312*	17	10
28 Jul 79	LET'S GO *Elektra K 12371*	51	4
5 Jun 82	SINCE YOU'RE GONE *Elektra K 13177*	37	4
29 Sep 84	● DRIVE (re) *Elektra E 9706*	4	23

'Drive' originally a No.5 hit re-entered and peaked one place higher in Aug 1985

Aaron CARTER *US, male vocalist (33 WEEKS)* pos/wks

29 Nov 97	● CRUSH ON YOU *Ultra Pop 0099605 ULT*	9	8
7 Feb 98	● CRAZY LITTLE PARTY GIRL *Ultra Pop 0099645 ULT*	7	6
28 Mar 98	I'M GONNA MISS YOU FOREVER *Ultra Pop 0099725 ULT*	24	5
4 Jul 98	SURFIN' USA *Ultra Pop 0099805 ULT*	18	5
16 Sep 00	I WANT CANDY *Jive 9250892*	31	3
28 Oct 00	AARON'S PARTY (COME GET IT) *Jive 9251272*	51	2

| 13 Apr 02 | LEAVE IT UP TO ME *Jive 9253262* | 22 | 4 |

Clarence CARTER *US, male vocalist (13 WEEKS)* pos/wks

| 10 Oct 70 | ● PATCHES *Atlantic 2091 030* | 2 | 13 |

Nick CARTER *US, male vocalist (3 WEEKS)* pos/wks

| 19 Oct 02 | HELP ME *Jive 9254332* | 17 | 3 |

See also BACKSTREET BOYS

CARTER – THE UNSTOPPABLE SEX MACHINE
UK, male vocal / instrumental duo – James 'Jim Bob' Morrison and Leslie 'Fruitbat' Carter (46 WEEKS) pos/wks

26 Jan 91	BLOODSPORT FOR ALL *Rough Trade R 20112687*	48	2
22 Jun 91	SHERIFF FATMAN *Big Cat USM 1*	23	7
26 Oct 91	AFTER THE WATERSHED *Big Cat USM 2*	11	5
11 Jan 92	RUBBISH *Big Cat USM 3*	14	5
25 Apr 92	● THE ONLY LIVING BOY IN NEW CROSS *Big Cat USM 4*	7	5
4 Jul 92	DO RE ME SO FAR SO GOOD *Chrysalis USM 5*	22	3
28 Nov 92	THE IMPOSSIBLE DREAM *Chrysalis USM 6*	21	3
4 Sep 93	LEAN ON ME I WON'T FALL OVER *Chrysalis CDUSM 7*	16	3
16 Oct 93	LENNY AND TERENCE *Chrysalis CDUSM 8*	40	2
12 Mar 94	GLAM ROCK COPS *Chrysalis CDUSMS 10*	24	3
19 Nov 94	LET'S GET TATTOOS *Chrysalis CDUSMS 30*	30	3
4 Feb 95	THE YOUNG OFFENDER'S MUM *Chrysalis CDUSMS 12*	34	3
30 Sep 95	BORN ON THE 5TH OF NOVEMBER *Chrysalis CDUSM 13*	35	2

CARTER TWINS *Ireland, male vocal duo (1 WEEK)* pos/wks

| 8 Mar 97 | THE TWELFTH OF NEVER / TOO RIGHT TO BE *RCA 74321453082* | 61 | 1 |

Junior CARTIER *UK, male producer – Jon Carter (1 WEEK)* pos/wks

| 6 Nov 99 | WOMEN BEAT THEIR MEN *Nucamp CAMPD 3X* | 70 | 1 |

CARTOONS
Denmark, male / female vocal / instrumental group (30 WEEKS) pos/wks

3 Apr 99	● WITCH DOCTOR *Flex / EMI CDTOONS 001*	2	13
19 Jun 99	● DOODAH! (re) *Flex / EMI CDTOON 002*	7	12
4 Sep 99	AISY WAISY *Flex/ EMI CDTOONS 003*	16	5

Sam CARTWRIGHT – See VOLCANO

CARVELLS
UK, male vocalist / instrumentalist – Alan Carvell (4 WEEKS) pos/wks

| 26 Nov 77 | THE L.A. RUN *Creole CR 143* | 31 | 4 |

CASCADES *US, male vocal group (16 WEEKS)* pos/wks

| 28 Feb 63 | ● RHYTHM OF THE RAIN *Warner Bros. WB 88* | 5 | 16 |

CASE *US, male rapper – Case Woodard (15 WEEKS)* pos/wks

21 Sep 96	TOUCH ME TEASE ME *Def Jam DEFCD 18* 1	26	3
10 Nov 01	LIVIN' IT UP *Def Jam 5888142* 2	27	4
3 Aug 02	● LIVIN' IT UP (LIVE) *Def Jam 0639782* 2	5	8

1 Case featuring Foxy Brown 2 Ja Rule featuring Case

Ed CASE *UK, male producer – Edward Makromallies (5 WEEKS)* pos/wks

21 Oct 00	SOMETHING IN YOUR EYES *Red Rose CDRROSE 003*	38	2
15 Sep 01	WHO? *Columbia 6718302* 1	29	2
20 Jul 02	GOOD TIMES *Columbia 6727672* 2	49	1

1 Ed Case and Sweetie Irie 2 Ed Case featuring Skin

Brian and Brandon CASEY – See NIVEA

Natalie CASEY *UK, female vocalist*
– youngest ever chart entrant at three years of age (1 WEEK) pos/wks

| 7 Jan 84 | CHICK CHICK CHICKEN *Polydor CHICK 1* | 72 | 1 |

Johnny CASH US, male vocalist (59 WEEKS)

			pos/wks	
3 Jun 65	IT AIN'T ME BABE *CBS 201760*		28	8
6 Sep 69 ●	A BOY NAMED SUE *CBS 4460*		4	19
23 May 70	WHAT IS TRUTH *CBS 4934*		21	11
15 Apr 72 ●	A THING CALLED LOVE (re) *CBS 7797* 1		4	14
3 Jul 76	ONE PIECE AT A TIME *CBS 4287* 2		32	7

1 Johnny Cash with the Evangel Temple Choir 2 Johnny Cash with the Tennessee Three

Pat CASH – See John McENROE and Pat CASH with the FULL METAL RACKETS

CA$HFLOW US, male vocal / instrumental group (8 WEEKS)

			pos/wks	
24 May 86	MINE ALL MINE / PARTY FREAK *Club JAB 30*		15	8

CASHMERE US, male vocal / instrumental group (11 WEEKS)

			pos/wks	
19 Jan 85	CAN I *Fourth & Broadway BRW 19*		29	8
23 Mar 85	WE NEED LOVE *Fourth & Broadway BRW 22*		52	3

CASINO UK, male vocal / production group (2 WEEKS)

			pos/wks	
17 May 97	SOUND OF EDEN *Worx WORXCD 005*		52	1
10 Jul 99	ONLY YOU *Pow! CDPOW 006*		72	1

CASINOS US, male vocal group (7 WEEKS)

			pos/wks	
23 Feb 67	THEN YOU CAN TELL ME GOODBYE *President PT 123*		28	7

CASSANDRA – See Rui DA SILVA featuring CASSANDRA

David CASSIDY 272 Top 500
Top teen idol of 1970s, b. 12 Apr 1950, New York. This photogenic singer / actor first found fame via the TV series The Partridge Family. His UK chart career took off as his US sales slowed down. Returned to Top 5 album chart in 2001 (109 WEEKS)

			pos/wks	
8 Apr 72 ●	COULD IT BE FOREVER / CHERISH *Bell 1224*		2	17
16 Sep 72 ★	HOW CAN I BE SURE *Bell 1258*		1	11
25 Nov 72	ROCK ME BABY *Bell 1268*		11	9
24 Mar 73 ●	I'M A CLOWN / SOME KIND OF A SUMMER *Bell MABEL 4*		3	12
13 Oct 73 ★	DAYDREAMER / THE PUPPY SONG *Bell 1334*		1	15
11 May 74 ●	IF I DIDN'T CARE *Bell 1350*		9	8
27 Jul 74	PLEASE PLEASE ME *Bell 1371*		16	6
5 Jul 75	I WRITE THE SONGS / GET IT UP FOR LOVE *RCA 2571*		11	8
25 Oct 75	DARLIN' *RCA 2622*		16	8
23 Feb 85 ●	THE LAST KISS *Arista ARIST 589*		6	9
11 May 85	ROMANCE (LET YOUR HEART GO) *Arista ARIST 620*		54	6

See also PARTRIDGE FAMILY

Eva CASSIDY US, female vocalist d. 2 Nov 1996 (9 WEEKS)

			pos/wks	
21 Apr 01	OVER THE RAINBOW (3re) *Blix Street / Hot HIT 16*		42	9

CASSIUS France, DJ production duo
– Philippe Zdar and Hubert Blanc-Francart (13 WEEKS)

			pos/wks	
23 Jan 99 ●	CASSIUS 1999 *Virgin DINSD 177*		7	7
15 May 99	FEELING FOR YOU *Virgin DINSD 181*		16	4
20 Nov 99	LA MOUCHE *Virgin DINSD 188*		53	1
5 Oct 02	THE SOUND OF VIOLENCE *Virgin DISND 241*		49	1

CAST UK, male vocal / instrumental group (55 WEEKS)

			pos/wks	
15 Jul 95	FINETIME *Polydor 5795072*		17	4
30 Sep 95	ALRIGHT *Polydor 5799272*		13	4
20 Jan 96 ●	SANDSTORM *Polydor 5778732*		8	5
30 Mar 96 ●	WALKAWAY *Polydor 5762852*		9	7
26 Oct 96 ●	FLYING *Polydor 5754772*		4	5
5 Apr 97 ●	FREE ME (re) *Polydor 5736512*		7	7
28 Jun 97 ●	GUIDING STAR *Polydor 5711732*		9	6
13 Sep 97 ●	LIVE THE DREAM *Polydor 5716852*		7	5
15 Nov 97	I'M SO LONELY *Polydor 5690592*		14	3
8 May 99 ●	BEAT MAMA *Polydor 5635932*		9	5
7 Aug 99	MAGIC HOUR *Polydor 5612272*		28	3
28 Jul 01	DESERT DROUGHT *Polydor 5871752*		45	1

CAST FROM CASUALTY
UK, male / female actors / vocal group (6 WEEKS)

			pos/wks	
14 Mar 98 ●	EVERLASTING LOVE *Warner.esp WESP 003CD*		5	6

CAST OF THE NEW ROCKY HORROR SHOW
UK, male / female vocal group (1 WEEK)

			pos/wks	
12 Dec 98	THE TIMEWARP *Damn It Janet DAMJAN 1CD*		57	1

Roy CASTLE UK, male vocalist d. 2 Sep 1994 (3 WEEKS)

			pos/wks	
22 Dec 60	LITTLE WHITE BERRY *Philips PB 1087*		40	3

CASUALS UK, male vocal / instrumental group (26 WEEKS)

			pos/wks	
14 Aug 68 ●	JESAMINE *Decca F 22784*		2	18
4 Dec 68	TOY *Decca F 22852*		30	8

CAT UK, male vocalist – Danny John-Jules (4 WEEKS)

			pos/wks	
23 Oct 93	TONGUE TIED *EMI CDEM 286*		17	4

CATATONIA
UK, male / female vocal / instrumental group (50 WEEKS)

			pos/wks	
3 Feb 96	SWEET CATATONIA *Blanco Y Negro NEG 85CD*		61	1
4 May 96	LOST CAT *Blanco Y Negro NEG 88CD1*		41	1
7 Sep 96	YOU'VE GOT A LOT TO ANSWER FOR *Blanco Y Negro NEG 93CD1*		35	2
30 Nov 96	BLEED *Blanco Y Negro NEG 97CD1*		46	1
18 Oct 97	I AM THE MOB *Blanco Y Negro NEG 107CD*		40	2
31 Jan 98 ●	MULDER AND SCULLY *Blanco Y Negro NEG 109CD*		3	10
2 May 98 ●	ROAD RAGE *Blanco Y Negro NEG 112CD*		5	8
1 Aug 98	STRANGE GLUE *Blanco Y Negro NEG 113CD*		11	6
7 Nov 98	GAME ON *WEA NEG 114CD*		33	2
10 Apr 99 ●	DEAD FROM THE WAIST DOWN *Blanco Y Negro NEG 115CD*		7	8
24 Jul 99	LONDINIUM *Blanco Y Negro NEG 117CD*		20	3
13 Nov 99	KARAOKE QUEEN *Blanco Y Negro NEG 119CD*		36	2
4 Aug 01	STONE BY STONE (re) *Blanco Y Negro NEG 134CD*		19	4

See also SPACE

CATCH UK, male vocal / instrumental group (1 WEEK)

			pos/wks	
17 Nov 90	FREE (C'MON) *ffrr F 147*		70	1

CATCH UK, male vocal instrumental group (6 WEEKS)

			pos/wks	
11 Oct 97	BINGO *Virgin VSCDT 1656*		23	4
21 Feb 98	DIVE IN *Virgin VSCDT 1665*		44	2

CATHERINE WHEEL
UK, male vocal / instrumental group (12 WEEKS)

			pos/wks	
23 Nov 91	BLACK METALLIC (EP) *Fontana CW 1*		68	1
8 Feb 92	BALLOON *Fontana CW 2*		59	1
18 Apr 92	I WANT TO TOUCH YOU *Fontana CW 3*		35	2
9 Jan 93	30TH CENTURY MAN *Fontana CWCD 4*		47	2
10 Jul 93	CRANK *Fontana CWCD 5*		66	1
16 Oct 93	SHOW ME MARY *Fontana CWCDA 6*		62	1
5 Aug 95	WAYDOWN *Fontana CWCD 7*		67	1
13 Dec 97	DELICIOUS *Chrysalis CDCHS 5071*		53	1
28 Feb 98	MA SOLITUDA *Chrysalis CDCHS 5077*		53	1
2 May 98	BROKEN NOSE *Chrysalis CDCHS 5086*		48	1

Tracks on Black Metallic (EP): Black Metallic / Crawling Over Me / Let Me Down Again / Saccharine

Lorraine CATO UK, female vocalist (3 WEEKS)

			pos/wks	
6 Feb 93	HOW CAN YOU TELL ME IT'S OVER *Columbia 6587662*		46	2
3 Aug 96	I WAS MADE TO LOVE YOU *MCA MCSTD 40055*		41	1

CATS UK, male instrumental group (2 WEEKS)

			pos/wks	
9 Apr 69	SWAN LAKE (re) *BAF 1*		48	2

CATS U.K. UK, male instrumental group (8 WEEKS)
pos/wks
		pos	wks
6 Oct 79	LUTON AIRPORT WEA K 18075	22	8

Nick CAVE and the BAD SEEDS
Australia / Germany, male vocal / instrumental group (12 WEEKS)
pos/wks
		pos	wks
11 Apr 92	STRAIGHT TO YOU / JACK THE RIPPER Mute MUTE 140	68	1
12 Dec 92	WHAT A WONDERFUL WORLD Mute MUTE 151 [1]	72	1
9 Apr 94	DO YOU LOVE ME Mute MUTE 160	68	1
14 Oct 95	WHERE THE WILD ROSES GROW Mute CDMUTE 185 [2]	11	4
9 Mar 96	HENRY LEE Mute CDMUTE 189 [3]	36	1
22 Feb 97	INTO MY ARMS Mute CDMUTE 192	53	1
31 May 97	(ARE YOU) THE ONE THAT I'VE BEEN… Mute CDMUTE 206	67	1
31 Mar 01	AS I SAT SADLY BY HER SIDE Mute CDMUTE 249	42	1
2 Jun 01	FIFTEEN FEET OF PURE WHITE SNOW Mute CDMUTE 262	52	1

[1] Nick Cave and Shane MacGowan [2] Nick Cave and Kylie Minogue [3] Nick Cave and the Bad Seeds and PJ Harvey

CAVEMAN UK, male rap group (2 WEEKS)
pos/wks
		pos	wks
9 Mar 91	I'M READY Profile PROF 330	65	2

CECIL UK, male vocal / instrumental group (2 WEEKS)
pos/wks
		pos	wks
25 Oct 97	HOSTAGE IN A FROCK Parlophone CDRS 6471	68	1
28 Mar 98	THE MOST TIRING DAY Parlophone CDR 6490	69	1

CELEDA US, female vocalist (5 WEEKS)
pos/wks
		pos	wks
5 Sep 98	MUSIC IS THE ANSWER (DANCIN' AND PRANCIN) Twisted UK TWCD 10038 [1]	36	3
12 Jun 99	BE YOURSELF Twisted UK TWCD 10049	61	1
23 Oct 99	MUSIC IS THE ANSWER (DANCIN' AND PRANCIN) Twisted UK TWCD 10052 [2]	50	1

[1] Danny Tenaglia and Celeda [2] Celeda with Danny Tenaglia

CELETIA UK, female vocalist – Celetia Martin (3 WEEKS)
pos/wks
		pos	wks
11 Apr 98	REWIND Big Life BLRD 142	29	2
8 Aug 98	RUNAWAY SKIES Big Life BLRD 144	66	1

CELTIC CHORUS – See LISBON LIONS featuring Martin O'NEILL & CELTIC CHORUS

CENOGINERZ Holland, male producer – Michel Pollen (1 WEEK)
pos/wks
		pos	wks
2 Feb 02	GIT DOWN Tripoli Trax TTRAX 081CD	75	1

CENTORY US, male rapper (1 WEEK)
pos/wks
		pos	wks
17 Dec 94	POINT OF NO RETURN EMI CDEM 354	67	1

CENTRAL LINE UK, male vocal / instrumental group (30 WEEKS)
pos/wks
		pos	wks
31 Jan 81	(YOU KNOW) YOU CAN DO IT Mercury LINE 7	67	3
15 Aug 81	WALKING INTO SUNSHINE Mercury MER 78	42	10
30 Jan 82	DON'T TELL ME Mercury MER 90	55	3
20 Nov 82	YOU'VE SAID ENOUGH Mercury MER 117	58	3
22 Jan 83	NATURE BOY Mercury MER 131	21	8
11 Jun 83	SURPRISE SURPRISE Mercury MER 133	48	3

CERRONE France, male producer / multi-instrumentalist – Jean-Marc Cerrone (21 WEEKS)
pos/wks
		pos	wks
5 Mar 77	LOVE IN C MINOR Atlantic K 10895	31	4
29 Jul 78	● SUPERNATURE Atlantic K 11089	8	12
13 Jan 79	JE SUIS MUSIC CBS 6918	39	4
10 Aug 96	SUPERNATURE (re-mix) Encore CDCOR 013	66	1

Peter CETERA US, male vocalist (20 WEEKS)
pos/wks
		pos	wks
2 Aug 86	● GLORY OF LOVE Full Moon W 8662 ▲	3	13
21 Jun 97	● HARD TO SAY I'M SORRY La Face 74321481482 [1]	7	7

[1] Az Yet featuring Peter Cetera

See also CHICAGO

Frank CHACKSFIELD and his ORCHESTRA
UK, orchestra, leader d. 9 Jun 1995 (41 WEEKS)
pos/wks
		pos	wks
3 Apr 53	● LITTLE RED MONKEY Parlophone R 3658 [1]	10	3
22 May 53	● TERRY'S THEME FROM 'LIMELIGHT' Decca F 10106	2	24
12 Feb 54	● EBB TIDE Decca F 10122	9	2
24 Feb 56	IN OLD LISBON Decca F 10689	15	4
18 May 56	PORT-AU-PRINCE Decca F 10727 [2]	18	6
31 Aug 56	DONKEY CART Decca F 10743	26	2

[1] Frank Chacksfield's Tunesmiths, featuring Jack Jordan – clavioline [2] Winifred Atwell and Frank Chacksfield

CHAIRMEN OF THE BOARD (463) Top 500
Superior 70s soul group fronted by distinctive singer / songwriter Norman (General) Johnson, b. 23 May 1944, Virginia, US. Detroit-based quartet, who recorded on Holland, Dozier and Holland's Invictus label, are regarded as legends by US "beach" (vintage soul) music fans (77 WEEKS)
pos/wks
		pos	wks
22 Aug 70	● GIVE ME JUST A LITTLE MORE TIME Invictus INV 501	3	13
14 Nov 70	● YOU'VE GOT ME DANGLING ON A STRING Invictus INV 504	5	13
20 Feb 71	EVERYTHING'S TUESDAY Invictus INV 507	12	9
15 May 71	PAY TO THE PIPER Invictus INV 511	34	7
4 Sep 71	CHAIRMAN OF THE BOARD Invictus INV 516	48	2
15 Jul 72	WORKING ON A BUILDING OF LOVE Invictus INV 519	20	8
7 Oct 72	ELMO JAMES Invictus INV 524	21	7
16 Dec 72	I'M ON MY WAY TO A BETTER PLACE (re) Invictus INV 527	30	6
23 Jun 73	FINDERS KEEPERS Invictus INV 530	21	9
13 Sep 86	LOVER BOY EMI EMI 5585 [1]	56	3

[1] Chairmen of the Board featuring General Johnson

CHAKACHAS
Belgium, male / female vocal / instrumental group (8 WEEKS)
pos/wks
		pos	wks
11 Jan 62	TWIST TWIST RCA 1264	48	1
27 May 72	JUNGLE FEVER Polydor 2121 064	29	7

George CHAKIRIS US, male vocalist (1 WEEK)
pos/wks
		pos	wks
2 Jun 60	HEART OF A TEENAGE GIRL Triumph RGM 1010	49	1

CHAKKA BOOM BANG
Holland, male instrumental / production group (1 WEEK)
pos/wks
		pos	wks
20 Jan 96	TOSSING AND TURNING Hooj Choons HOOJCD 39	57	1

CHAKRA UK, male production duo – Ricky Simmons and Steve Jones – and female vocalist (5 WEEKS)
pos/wks
		pos	wks
18 Jan 97	I AM WEA WEA 091CD	24	2
23 Aug 97	HOME WEA WEA 116CD2	46	1
23 Oct 99	LOVE SHINES THROUGH WEA WEA 227CD	67	1
26 Aug 00	HOME (re-mix) WEA WEA 266CD	47	1

See also ESSENCE; SPACE BROTHERS; LUSTRAL; ASCENSION

Sue CHALONER UK, female vocalist (1 WEEK)
pos/wks
		pos	wks
22 May 93	MOVE ON UP Pulse 8 CDLOSE 41	64	1

Richard CHAMBERLAIN US, male actor / vocalist (36 WEEKS)
pos/wks
		pos	wks
7 Jun 62	THEME FROM 'DR KILDARE' (THREE STARS WILL SHINE TONIGHT) MGM 1160	12	10
1 Nov 62	LOVE ME TENDER MGM 1173	15	11
21 Feb 63	HI-LILI, HI-LO MGM 1189	20	9
18 Jul 63	TRUE LOVE MGM 1205	30	6

Bryan CHAMBERS – See CLEPTOMANIACS featuring Bryan CHAMBERS

CHAMELEON UK, male vocal / instrumental group (2 WEEKS)
pos/wks
		pos	wks
18 May 96	THE WAY IT IS Stress CDSTR 65	34	2

CHAMELEONS – See LORI and the CHAMELEONS

CHAMONIX – See Kurtis MANTRONIK

Re-entries are listed as (re), (2re), (3re), etc which signifies that the hit re-entered the chart once, twice or three times, etc

CHAMPAIGN
US, male / female vocal / instrumental group (13 WEEKS) pos/wks
9 May 81 ●	HOW 'BOUT US CBS A 1046	5	13

CHAMPIONSHIP LEGEND – See RAZE

CHAMPS
US, male instrumental group (10 WEEKS) pos/wks
4 Apr 58 ●	TEQUILA London HLU 8580 ▲	5	9
17 Mar 60	TOO MUCH TEQUILA London HLH 9052	49	1

CHAMPS BOYS
France, male instrumental group (6 WEEKS) pos/wks
19 Jun 76	TUBULAR BELLS Philips 6006 519	41	6

CHANCE – See SUNKIDS featuring CHANCE

Gene CHANDLER
US, male vocalist – Eugene Dixon (29 WEEKS) pos/wks
5 Jun 68	NOTHING CAN STOP ME Soul City SC 102	41	4
3 Feb 79	GET DOWN 20th Century BTC 1040	11	11
1 Sep 79	WHEN YOU'RE NUMBER 1 20th Century TC 2411	43	5
28 Jun 80	DOES SHE HAVE A FRIEND? 20th Century TC 2451	28	9

CHANELLE
US, female vocalist – Charlene Munford (9 WEEKS) pos/wks
11 Mar 89	ONE MAN Cooltempo COOL 183	16	8
10 Dec 94	ONE MAN (re-mix) Deep Distraxion OILYCD 031	50	1

CHANGE
US, male / female vocal / instrumental group (43 WEEKS) pos/wks
28 Jun 80	A LOVER'S HOLIDAY / THE GLOW OF LOVE WEA K 79141	14	8
6 Sep 80	SEARCHING WEA K 79156	11	10
2 Jun 84	CHANGE OF HEART WEA YZ 1	17	10
11 Aug 84	YOU ARE MY MELODY WEA YZ 14	48	4
16 Mar 85	LET'S GO TOGETHER Cooltempo COOL 107	37	7
25 May 85	OH WHAT A FEELING Cooltempo COOL 109	56	2
13 Jul 85	MUTUAL ATTRACTION Cooltempo COOL 111	60	2

See also Luther VANDROSS

CHANGING FACES
US, female vocal duo
– Cassandra Lucas and Charisse Rose (12 WEEKS) pos/wks
24 Sep 94	STROKE YOU UP Big Beat A 8251CD	43	3
26 Jul 97 ●	G.H.E.T.T.O.U.T. Atlantic AT 0003CD	10	5
1 Nov 97	I GOT SOMEBODY ELSE Atlantic AT 0014CD	42	1
4 Apr 98	TIME AFTER TIME Atlantic AT 0027CD [1]	35	2
1 Aug 98	SAME TEMPO A&M 5826952	53	1

[1] Changing Faces featuring Jay Z

Bruce CHANNEL
US, male vocalist (28 WEEKS) pos/wks
22 Mar 62 ●	HEY! BABY Mercury AMT 1171 ▲	2	12
26 Jun 68	KEEP ON Bell 1010	12	16

CHANNEL X
Belgium, male / female vocal / instrumental group (1 WEEK) pos/wks
14 Dec 91	GROOVE TO MOVE PWL Continental PWL 209	67	1

CHANSON
US, male / female vocal group (7 WEEKS) pos/wks
13 Jan 79	DON'T HOLD BACK Ariola ARO 140	33	7

CHANTAL – See MOONMAN

CHANTAYS
US, male instrumental group (14 WEEKS) pos/wks
18 Apr 63	PIPELINE London HLD 9696	16	14

CHANTER SISTERS
UK, female vocal group (5 WEEKS) pos/wks
17 Jul 76	SIDESHOW Polydor 2058 735	43	5

CHAOS
UK, male vocal group (2 WEEKS) pos/wks
3 Oct 92	FAREWELL MY SUMMER LOVE Arista 74321116397	55	2

Harry CHAPIN
US, male vocalist d. 16 Jul 1981 (5 WEEKS) pos/wks
11 May 74	W.O.L.D. Elektra K 12133	34	5

Simone CHAPMAN – See ILLEGAL MOTION featuring Simone CHAPMAN

Tracy CHAPMAN
US, female vocalist (15 WEEKS) pos/wks
11 Jun 88 ●	FAST CAR Elektra EKR 73	5	12
30 Sep 89	CROSSROADS Elektra EKR 95	61	3

CHAPTERHOUSE
UK, male vocal / instrumental group (3 WEEKS) pos/wks
30 Mar 91	PEARL Dedicated STONE 003	67	1
12 Oct 91	MESMERISE Dedicated HOUSE 001	60	2

CHAQUITO and his ORCHESTRA
UK, male arranger / conductor – Johnny Gregory (1 WEEK) pos/wks
27 Oct 60	NEVER ON SUNDAY Fontana H 265	50	1

CHARLATANS 462 Top 500
North country boys from Northwich who came to prominence as part of the "Madchester" scene, Tim Burgess (v) b. 30 May 1968, Manchester, UK, and Rob Collins (k) b. 23 Feb 1963, d. 23 Jul 1996. Act has seven Top 10 albums including three No.1s (77 WEEKS) pos/wks
2 Jun 90 ●	THE ONLY ONE I KNOW Situation Two SIT 70T	9	9
22 Sep 90	THEN Situation Two SIT 74T	12	5
9 Mar 91	OVER RISING Situation Two SIT 76	15	5
17 Aug 91	INDIAN ROPE Dead Dead Good GOOD 1T	57	1
9 Nov 91	ME. IN TIME Situation Two SIT 84	28	3
7 Mar 92	WEIRDO Situation Two SIT 88	19	4
18 Jul 92	TREMELO SONG (EP) Situation Two SIT 97T	44	2
5 Feb 94	CAN'T GET OUT OF BED Beggars Banquet BBQ 27CD	24	3
19 Mar 94	I NEVER WANT AN EASY LIFE IF ME AND HE WERE EVER TO GET THERE Beggars Banquet BBQ 31CD	38	1
2 Jul 94	JESUS HAIRDO Beggars Banquet BBQ 32CD1	48	2
7 Jan 95	CRASHIN' IN Beggars Banquet BBQ 44CD	31	2
27 May 95	JUST LOOKIN' / BULLET COMES Beggars Banquet BBQ 55CD	32	3
26 Aug 95	JUST WHEN YOU'RE THINKIN' THINGS OVER Beggars Banquet BBQ 60CD	12	3
7 Sep 96 ●	ONE TO ANOTHER Beggars Banquet BBQ 301CD	3	6
5 Apr 97 ●	NORTH COUNTRY BOY (re) Beggars Banquet BBQ 309CD	4	6
21 Jun 97 ●	HOW HIGH Beggars Banquet BBQ 312CD	6	5
1 Nov 97	TELLIN' STORIES Beggars Banquet BBQ 318CD	16	3
16 Oct 99	FOREVER Universal MCSTD 40220	12	3
18 Dec 99	MY BEAUTIFUL FRIEND Universal MCSTD 40225	31	3
27 May 00	IMPOSSIBLE Universal MCSTD 40231	15	3
8 Sep 01	LOVE IS THE KEY Universal MCSTD 40262	16	3
1 Dec 01	A MAN NEEDS TO BE TOLD Universal MCSTD 40271	31	2

Tracks on Tremelo Song (EP): Tremelo Song / Happen to Die / Normality Swing

CHARLENE
US, female vocalist – Charlene Duncan (12 WEEKS) pos/wks
15 May 82 ★	I'VE NEVER BEEN TO ME Motown TMG 1260	1	12

Alex CHARLES – See DJ INNOCENCE featuring Alex CHARLES

Don CHARLES
UK, male vocalist (5 WEEKS) pos/wks
22 Feb 62	WALK WITH ME MY ANGEL Decca F 11424	39	5

Ray CHARLES 208 Top 500
Rock era's first "genius", b. Ray Charles Robinson, 23 Sep 1930, Georgia. This blind singer / songwriter / pianist and band leader had a US R&B chart career spanning seven decades. In 1994 he received a prestigious National Medal of Arts from US President Clinton (130 WEEKS) pos/wks
1 Dec 60	GEORGIA ON MY MIND (re) HMV POP 792 ▲	24	8
19 Oct 61 ●	HIT THE ROAD JACK HMV POP 935 ▲	6	12
14 Jun 62 ★	I CAN'T STOP LOVING YOU HMV POP 1034 ▲	1	17
13 Sep 62 ●	YOU DON'T KNOW ME HMV POP 1064	9	13
13 Dec 62	YOUR CHEATING HEART HMV POP 1099	13	8
28 Mar 63	DON'T SET ME FREE HMV POP 1133	37	3
16 May 63 ●	TAKE THESE CHAINS FROM MY HEART HMV POP 1161	5	20

12 Sep 63	NO ONE *HMV POP 1202*	35 7
31 Oct 63	BUSTED *HMV POP 1221*	21 10
24 Sep 64	NO ONE TO CRY TO *HMV POP 1333*	38 3
21 Jan 65	MAKIN' WHOOPEE *HMV POP 1383*	42 4
10 Feb 66	CRYIN' TIME *HMV POP 1502* 1	50 1
21 Apr 66	TOGETHER AGAIN *HMV POP 1519*	48 1
5 Jul 67	HERE WE GO AGAIN (re) *HMV POP 1595*	38 3
20 Dec 67	YESTERDAY *Stateside SS 2071*	44 4
31 Jul 68	ELEANOR RIGBY *Stateside SS 2120*	36 9
13 Jan 90	I'LL BE GOOD TO YOU *Qwest W 2697* 2	21 7

1 With the Jack Halloran Singers and the Ray Charles Orchestra with the Raeletts
2 Quincy Jones featuring Ray Charles and Chaka Khan

See also INXS

Suzette CHARLES US, female vocalist (2 WEEKS)

		pos/wks
21 Aug 93	FREE TO LOVE AGAIN *RCA 74321158372*	58 2

Tina CHARLES UK, female vocalist – Tina Hoskins (63 WEEKS)

		pos/wks
7 Feb 76	★ I LOVE TO LOVE (BUT MY BABY LOVES TO DANCE) *CBS 3937*	1 12
1 May 76	LOVE ME LIKE A LOVER *CBS 4237*	31 7
21 Aug 76	● DANCE LITTLE LADY DANCE *CBS 4480*	6 13
4 Dec 76	● DR LOVE *CBS 4779*	4 10
14 May 77	RENDEZVOUS *CBS 5174*	27 6
29 Oct 77	LOVE BUG – SWEETS FOR MY SWEET (MEDLEY) *CBS 5680*	26 4
11 Mar 78	I'LL GO WHERE YOUR MUSIC TAKES ME *CBS 6062*	27 8
30 Aug 86	I LOVE TO LOVE (re-mix) *DMC DECK 1*	67 3

See also 5000 VOLTS

CHARLES and EDDIE US, male vocal duo
– Charles Pettigrew and Eddie Chacon (30 WEEKS)

		pos/wks
31 Oct 92	★ WOULD I LIE TO YOU *Capitol CL 673*	1 17
20 Feb 93	N.Y.C. (CAN YOU BELIEVE THIS CITY) *Capitol CDCL 681*	33 5
22 May 93	HOUSE IS NOT A HOME *Capitol CDCLS 688*	29 4
13 May 95	24-7-365 *Capitol CDCLS 747*	38 4

Dick CHARLESWORTH and his CITY GENTS
UK, male jazz band group – Dick Charlesworth – clarinet (1 WEEK)

		pos/wks
4 May 61	BILLY BOY *Top Rank JAR 558*	43 1

CHARLOTTE UK, female vocalist (4 WEEKS)

		pos/wks
12 Mar 94	QUEEN OF HEARTS *Big Life BLRD 106*	54 1
2 May 98	BE MINE *Parlophone Rhythm CDRHYTHM 10*	59 1
29 May 99	SKIN *Parlophone Rhythm Series CDRHYTHM 20*	56 1
4 Sep 99	SOMEDAY *Parlophone Rhythm Series CDRHYTHM 23*	74 1

CHARME US, male / female vocal group (2 WEEKS)

		pos/wks
17 Nov 84	GEORGY PORGY *RCA 464*	68 2

CHARO and the SALSOUL ORCHESTRA
US, female vocalist and orchestra (4 WEEKS)

		pos/wks
29 Apr 78	DANCE A LITTLE BIT CLOSER *Salsoul SSOL 101*	44 4

CHARVONI *– See BROTHERS IN RHYTHM*

CHAS and DAVE UK, male vocal / instrumental
duo – Chas Hodges and Dave Peacock (66 WEEKS)

		pos/wks
11 Nov 78	STRUMMIN' / I'M IN TROUBLE *EMI 2874* 1	52 3
26 May 79	GERTCHA *EMI 2947*	20 8
1 Sep 79	THE SIDEBOARD SONG (GOT MY BEER IN THE SIDEBOARD HERE) *EMI 2986*	55 3
29 Nov 80	● RABBIT *Rockney 9*	8 11
12 Dec 81	STARS OVER 45 *Rockney KOR 12*	21 8
13 Mar 82	● AIN'T NO PLEASING YOU *Rockney KOR 14*	2 11
17 Jul 82	MARGATE *Rockney KOR 15*	46 4
19 Mar 83	LONDON GIRLS *Rockney KOR 17*	63 3
3 Dec 83	MY MELANCHOLY BABY *Rockney KOR 21*	51 6

3 May 86	● SNOOKER LOOPY *Rockney POT 147* 2	6 9

1 Chas and Dave with Rockney   2 Matchroom Mob with Chas and Dave

See also TOTTENHAM HOTSPUR FA CUP FINAL SQUAD

Tara CHASE *– See Sonny JONES featuring Tara CHASE*

CHEAP TRICK
US, male vocal / instrumental group (14 WEEKS)

		pos/wks
5 May 79	I WANT YOU TO WANT ME *Epic EPC 7258*	29 9
2 Feb 80	WAY OF THE WORLD *Epic EPC 8114*	73 2
31 Jul 82	IF YOU WANT MY LOVE *Epic EPC A 2406*	57 3

Oliver CHEATHAM US, male vocalist (5 WEEKS)

		pos/wks
2 Jul 83	GET DOWN SATURDAY NIGHT *MCA 828*	38 5

CHECK 1-2 *– See Craig McLACHLAN*

Chubby CHECKER (258) Top 500
The "King of the Twist", b. Ernest Evans, 3 Oct 1941, South Carolina, US. This rotund vocalist helped to make the Twist the most popular dance of the rock era. 'The Twist' was the only single to top the US chart on two separate occasions (112 WEEKS)

		pos/wks
22 Sep 60	THE TWIST (2re) *Columbia DB 4503* ▲	14 12
30 Mar 61	PONY TIME *Columbia DB 4591* ▲	27 6
17 Aug 61	● LET'S TWIST AGAIN (3re) *Columbia DB 4691*	2 34
5 Apr 62	SLOW TWISTIN' *Columbia DB 4808*	23 8
19 Apr 62	TEACH ME TO TWIST *Columbia DB 4802* 1	45 1
9 Aug 62	DANCIN' PARTY *Columbia DB 4876*	19 13
1 Nov 62	LIMBO ROCK *Cameo Parkway P 849*	32 10
20 Dec 62	JINGLE BELL ROCK *Cameo Parkway C 205* 1	40 3
31 Oct 63	WHAT DO YA SAY *Cameo Parkway P 806*	37 4
29 Nov 75	● LET'S TWIST AGAIN / THE TWIST (re-issue) *London HLU 10512*	5 10
18 Jun 88	● THE TWIST (YO, TWIST) *Urban URB 20* 2	2 11

1 Chubby Checker and Bobby Rydell   2 Fat Boys and Chubby Checker

'The Twist' made its peak position of No.14 on its 2nd re-entry Jan 1962. 'Lets Twist Again' made its peak position of No.2 on its first re-entry Dec 1961

CHECKMATES *– See Emile FORD and the CHECKMATES*

CHECKMATES LTD
US, male vocal / instrumental group (8 WEEKS)

		pos/wks
15 Nov 69	PROUD MARY *A&M AMS 769*	30 8

Judy CHEEKS US, female vocalist (15 WEEKS)

		pos/wks
13 Nov 93	SO IN LOVE (THE REAL DEAL) *Positiva CDTIV 6*	27 3
7 May 94	REACH *Positiva CDTIV 12*	17 4
4 Mar 95	THIS TIME / RESPECT *Positiva CDTIV 28*	23 2
17 Jun 95	YOU'RE THE STORY OF MY LIFE / AS LONG AS YOU'RE GOOD TO ME *Positiva CDTIV 34*	30 3
13 Jan 96	REACH (re-mix) *Positiva CDTIV 42*	22 3

CHEEKY GIRLS
Romania, female vocal duo – Monica and Gabriella Irimia (3 WEEKS) pos/wks

14 Dec 02	● CHEEKY SONG (TOUCH MY BUM) *Multiply CDMULTY 97*	2 3+

CHEETAHS UK, male vocal / instrumental group (6 WEEKS)

		pos/wks
1 Oct 64	MECCA *Philips BF 1362*	36 3
21 Jan 65	SOLDIER BOY *Philips BF 1383*	39 3

CHEF US, male cartoon vocalist / chef – Isaac Hayes (13 WEEKS)

		pos/wks
26 Dec 98	★ CHOCOLATE SALTY BALLS (PS I LOVE YOU) *Columbia 6667985*	1 13

CHELSEA FC UK, male football team vocalists (22 WEEKS)

		pos/wks
26 Feb 72	● BLUE IS THE COLOUR *Penny Farthing PEN 782*	5 12
14 May 94	NO ONE CAN STOP US NOW *RCA 74321210452*	23 3
17 May 97	BLUE DAY *WEA WEA 112CD* 1	22 5

| 27 May 00 | BLUE TOMORROW *Telstar TV CFCCD 2000* | 22 | 2 |

1 Suggs & Co featuring Chelsea Team

CHEMICAL BROTHERS *UK, male instrumental / production duo – Tom Rowlands and Ed Simons (64 WEEKS)*

pos/wks

17 Jun 95	LEAVE HOME *Junior Boy's Own CHEMSD 1*	17	4
9 Sep 95	LIFE IS SWEET *Junior Boy's Own CHEMSD 2*	25	3
27 Jan 96	LOOPS OF FURY (EP) *Junior Boy's Own CHEMSD 3*	13	1
12 Oct 96	★ SETTING SUN *Junior Boy's Own CHEMSD 4* ■	1	7
5 Apr 97	★ BLOCK ROCKIN' BEATS (re) *Virgin CHEMSD 5* ■	1	7
20 Sep 97	ELEKTROBANK *Virgin CHEMSD 6*	17	4
12 Jun 99	● HEY BOY HEY GIRL *Virgin CHEMSD 8*	3	10
14 Aug 99	● LET FOREVER BE *Virgin CHEMSD 9*	9	7
23 Oct 99	OUT OF CONTROL *Virgin CHEMSD 10*	21	4
22 Sep 01	● IT BEGAN IN AFRIKA (re) *Virgin CHEMSD 12*	8	6
26 Jan 02	● STAR GUITAR (re) *Virgin CHEMSD 14*	8	8
4 May 02	COME WITH US / THE TEST *Virgin CHEMSD 15*	14	3

Tracks on Loops of Fury (EP): Loops of Fury / (The Best Part of) Breaking Up / Get Upon It Like This / Chemical Beats. Uncredited vocal on 'Setting Sun' and 'Let Forever Be' by Noel Gallagher and on 'Out of Control' by Bernard Sumner

CHEQUERS *UK, male vocal / instrumental group (10 WEEKS)*

pos/wks

| 18 Oct 75 | ROCK ON BROTHER *Creole CR 111* | 21 | 5 |
| 28 Feb 76 | HEY MISS PAYNE *Creole CR 116* | 32 | 5 |

CHER (65) Top 500 *Perennially popular vocalist, b. Cherilyn LaPierre, 20 May 1946, California. She was half of the most successful husband / wife duo ever, Sonny and Cher, and had an equally stunning run of solo smashes. At the age of 52 she is the oldest female solo singer to top the chart. Best-selling single: 'Believe', 1,672,108 (229 WEEKS)*

pos/wks

19 Aug 65	● ALL I REALLY WANT TO DO *Liberty LIB 66114*	9	10
31 Mar 66	● BANG BANG (MY BABY SHOT ME DOWN) *Liberty LIB 66160*	3	12
4 Aug 66	I FEEL SOMETHING IN THE AIR *Liberty LIB 12034*	43	2
22 Sep 66	SUNNY *Liberty LIB 12083*	32	5
6 Nov 71	● GYPSYS, TRAMPS AND THIEVES *MCA MU 1142* ▲	4	13
16 Feb 74	DARK LADY (re) *MCA 101* ▲	36	4
19 Dec 87	● I FOUND SOMEONE *Geffen GEF 31*	5	10
2 Apr 88	WE ALL SLEEP ALONE *Geffen GEF 35*	47	4
2 Sep 89	● IF I COULD TURN BACK TIME *Geffen GEF 59*	6	14
13 Jan 90	JUST LIKE JESSE JAMES *Geffen GEF 69*	11	11
7 Apr 90	HEART OF STONE *Geffen GEF 75*	43	5
11 Aug 90	YOU WOULDN'T KNOW LOVE *Geffen GEF 77*	55	3
13 Apr 91	★ THE SHOOP SHOOP SONG (IT'S IN HIS KISS) *Epic 6566737*	1	15
13 Jul 91	● LOVE AND UNDERSTANDING *Geffen GFS 5*	10	8
12 Oct 91	SAVE UP ALL YOUR TEARS *Geffen GFS 11*	37	5
7 Dec 91	LOVE HURTS *Geffen GFS 16*	43	5
18 Apr 92	COULD'VE BEEN YOU *Geffen GFS 19*	31	4
14 Nov 92	OH NO NOT MY BABY *Geffen GFS 29*	33	4
16 Jan 93	MANY RIVERS TO CROSS *Geffen GFSTD 31*	37	3
6 Mar 93	WHENEVER YOU'RE NEAR *Geffen GFSTD 32*	72	1
15 Jan 94	I GOT YOU BABE *Geffen GFSTD 64* 1	35	3
18 Mar 95	★ LOVE CAN BUILD A BRIDGE *London COCD 1* 2	1	8
28 Oct 95	WALKING IN MEMPHIS *WEA WEA 021CD1*	11	7
20 Jan 96	● ONE BY ONE *WEA WEA 032CD*	7	9
27 Apr 96	NOT ENOUGH LOVE IN THE WORLD *WEA WEA 052CD*	31	2
17 Aug 96	THE SUN AIN'T GONNA SHINE ANYMORE *WEA WEA 071CD*	26	3
31 Oct 98	★ BELIEVE *WEA WEA 175CD* ◆ ■ ▲	1	28
6 Mar 99	● STRONG ENOUGH *WEA WEA 201CD1*	5	10
19 Jun 99	ALL OR NOTHING *WEA WEA 212CD1*	12	7
6 Nov 99	DOVE L'AMORE *WEA WEA 230CD1*	21	3
17 Nov 01	● THE MUSIC'S NO GOOD WITHOUT YOU *WEA WEA 337CD*	8	10

1 Cher with Beavis and Butt-Head 2 Cher, Chrissie Hynde and Neneh Cherry with Eric Clapton

See also SONNY and CHER; MEAT LOAF

CHERI *Canada, female vocal duo – Rosalind Hunt and Lyn Cullerier (9 WEEKS)*

pos/wks

| 19 Jun 82 | MURPHY'S LAW *Polydor POSP 459* | 13 | 9 |

CHEROKEES *UK, male vocal / instrumental group (5 WEEKS)*

pos/wks

| 3 Sep 64 | SEVEN DAFFODILS *Columbia DB 7341* | 33 | 5 |

CHERRELLE *US, female vocalist – Cheryl Norton (26 WEEKS)*

pos/wks

28 Dec 85	● SATURDAY LOVE *Tabu A 6829* 1	6	11
1 Mar 86	WILL YOU SATISFY? *Tabu A 6927*	57	3
6 Feb 88	NEVER KNEW LOVE LIKE THIS *Tabu 6513827* 2	26	7
6 May 89	AFFAIR *Tabu 654673 7*	67	2
24 Mar 90	SATURDAY LOVE (re-mix) *Tabu 6558007* 1	55	2
2 Aug 97	BABY COME TO ME *One World OWECD 1* 2	56	1

1 Cherrelle with Alexander O'Neal 2 Alexander O'Neal featuring Cherrelle

Don CHERRY *US, male vocalist d. 19 Oct 1995 (11 WEEKS)*

pos/wks

| 10 Feb 56 | ● BAND OF GOLD *Philips PB 549* | 6 | 11 |

Eagle-Eye CHERRY *Sweden, male vocalist (28 WEEKS)*

pos/wks

4 Jul 98	● SAVE TONIGHT *Polydor 5695952*	6	13
14 Nov 98	● FALLING IN LOVE AGAIN *Polydor 5630252*	8	8
20 Mar 99	PERMANENT TEARS *Polydor 5636752*	43	1
29 Apr 00	ARE YOU STILL HAVING FUN *Polydor 5618032*	21	4
11 Nov 00	LONG WAY AROUND *Polydor 5677812* 1	48	2

1 Eagle-Eye Cherry featuring Neneh Cherry

Neneh CHERRY (317) Top 500 *Sassy, strident rapper-singer, b. 10 Mar 1964, Stockholm, Sweden, raised in New York and relocated to UK early 1980s. Stepdaughter of jazz trumpeter Don Cherry and sister of Eagle-Eye Cherry. Winner 1990 Best New Female in Rolling Stone and the Brits (98 WKS)*

pos/wks

10 Dec 88	● BUFFALO STANCE *Circa YR 21*	3	13
20 May 89	● MANCHILD *Circa YR 30*	5	10
12 Aug 89	KISSES ON THE WIND *Circa YR 33*	20	6
23 Dec 89	INNA CITY MAMMA *Circa YR 42*	31	7
29 Sep 90	I'VE GOT YOU UNDER MY SKIN *Circa YR 53*	25	5
3 Oct 92	MONEY LOVE *Circa YR 83*	23	4
16 Jan 93	BUDDY X *Circa YRCD 98*	35	3
25 Jun 94	● 7 SECONDS (re) *Columbia 6605082* 1	3	25
18 Mar 95	★ LOVE CAN BUILD A BRIDGE *London COCD 1* 2	1	8
3 Aug 96	● WOMAN *Hut HUTCD 70*	9	7
14 Dec 96	KOOTCHI *Hut HUTDG 75*	38	2
22 Feb 97	FEEL IT *Hut HUTCD 79*	68	1
6 Nov 99	BUDDY X 99 *4 Liberty LIBTCD 33* 3	15	5
11 Nov 00	LONG WAY AROUND *Polydor 5677812* 4	48	2

1 Youssou N'Dour (featuring Neneh Cherry) 2 Cher, Chrissie Hynde and Neneh Cherry with Eric Clapton 3 Dreem Teem vs Neneh Cherry 4 Eagle-Eye Cherry featuring Neneh Cherry

CHI-LITES (369) Top 500 *Supreme soft-soul vocal quartet from Chicago, fronted by Eugene Record, b.23 Dec 1940, Illinois, US, who originally formed group with Marshall Thompson as the Hi-Lites. Record also produced and wrote the vast majority of their many transatlantic hits (89 WEEKS)*

pos/wks

28 Aug 71	(FOR GOD'S SAKE) GIVE MORE POWER TO THE PEOPLE *MCA MU 1138*	32	6
15 Jan 72	● HAVE YOU SEEN HER *MCA MU 1146*	3	12
27 May 72	OH GIRL *MCA MU 1156* ▲	14	9
23 Mar 74	● HOMELY GIRL *Brunswick BR 9*	5	13
20 Jul 74	I FOUND SUNSHINE *Brunswick BR 12*	35	5
2 Nov 74	● TOO GOOD TO BE FORGOTTEN *Brunswick BR 13*	10	11
21 Jun 75	● HAVE YOU SEEN HER / OH GIRL (re-issue) *Brunswick BR 20*	5	9
13 Sep 75	● IT'S TIME FOR LOVE *Brunswick BR 25*	5	10
31 Jul 76	● YOU DON'T HAVE TO GO *Brunswick BR 34*	3	11
13 Aug 83	CHANGING FOR YOU *R & B RBS 215*	61	3

CHIC (361) Top 500 *Acclaimed, ground-breaking funk-disco collective, formed 1976, New York City by Nile Rodgers (g), b. 19 Sep 1952 and Bernard Edwards (b), b. 31 Oct 1952; d. 18 Apr 1996, who became one of the top songwriter / production teams of the 80s. 'Good Times' was sampled on first rap hit, 'Rapper's Delight', by Sugarhill Gang (90 WEEKS)*

pos/wks

| 26 Nov 77 | ● DANCE, DANCE, DANCE (YOWSAH, YOWSAH, YOWSAH) *Atlantic K 11038* | 6 | 12 |

1 Apr 78 ●	EVERYBODY DANCE *Atlantic K 11097*	9	11
18 Nov 78 ●	LE FREAK *Atlantic K 11209* ▲	7	16
24 Feb 79 ●	I WANT YOUR LOVE *Atlantic LV 16*	4	11
30 Jun 79 ●	GOOD TIMES *Atlantic K 11310* ▲	5	11
13 Oct 79	MY FORBIDDEN LOVER *Atlantic K 11385*	15	8
8 Dec 79	MY FEET KEEP DANCING *Atlantic K 11415*	21	9
12 Mar 83	HANGIN' *Atlantic A 9898*	64	1
19 Sep 87	JACK LE FREAK *Atlantic A 9198*	19	6
14 Jul 90	MEGACHIC – CHIC MEDLEY *East West A 7949*	58	2
15 Feb 92	CHIC MYSTIQUE *Warner Bros. W 0083*	48	3

CHICAGO 423 Top 500

Pioneering jazz-rock group included Peter Cetera (v / b) b. 13 Sep 1944. Group relocated from city of the same name to California, US, in 1967. Released longest numerical sequence of album titles (majority going platinum in the US) – the most recent being Chicago 26 (1999) (81 WEEKS) pos/wks

10 Jan 70 ●	I'M A MAN *CBS 4715* [1]	8	11
18 Jul 70 ●	25 OR 6 TO 4 *CBS 5076*	7	13
9 Oct 76 ★	IF YOU LEAVE ME NOW *CBS 4603* ▲	1	16
5 Nov 77	BABY, WHAT A BIG SURPRISE *CBS 5672*	41	3
21 Aug 82 ●	HARD TO SAY I'M SORRY *Full Moon K 79301* ▲	4	15
27 Oct 84 ●	HARD HABIT TO BREAK *Full Moon W 9214*	8	13
26 Jan 85	YOU'RE THE INSPIRATION *Warner Bros. W 9126*	14	10

[1] Chicago Transit Authority

CHICANE

UK, male producer / instrumentalist – Nick Bracegirdle (48 WEEKS) pos/wks

21 Dec 96	OFFSHORE *Xtravaganza 0091005*	14	7
14 Jun 97	SUNSTROKE *Xtravaganza 0091125*	21	3
13 Sep 97	OFFSHORE '97 (re-mix) *Xtravaganza 0091255 EXT* [1]	17	4
20 Dec 97	LOST YOU SOMEWHERE *Xtravaganza 0091415*	35	3
10 Oct 98	STRONG IN LOVE *Xtravaganza 0091675EXT* [2]	32	2
5 Jun 99 ●	SALTWATER *Xtravaganza XTRAV 1CDS* [3]	6	10
18 Mar 00 ★	DON'T GIVE UP *Xtravaganza XTRAV 9CDS* [4] ■	1	14
22 Jul 00	NO ORDINARY MORNING / HALCYON		
	Xtravaganza XTRAV 12CDS	28	3
28 Oct 00	AUTUMN TACTICS *Xtravaganza XTRAV 17CDS*	44	2

[1] Chicane with Power Circle [2] Chicane featuring Mason [3] Chicane featuring Maire Brennan of Clannad [4] Chicane featuring Bryan Adams

Chicane are Disco Citizens under another name

CHICKEN SHACK

UK, male / female vocal / instrumental group (19 WEEKS) pos/wks

7 May 69	I'D RATHER GO BLIND *Blue Horizon 57-3153*	14	13
6 Sep 69	TEARS IN THE WIND *Blue Horizon 57-3160*	29	6

CHICKEN SHED *UK, youth theatre company (6 WEEKS)* pos/wks

27 Dec 97	I AM IN LOVE WITH THE WORLD *Columbia 6654172*	15	6

CHICORY TIP

UK, male vocal / instrumental group (34 WEEKS) pos/wks

29 Jan 72 ★	SON OF MY FATHER *CBS 7737*	1	13
20 May 72	WHAT'S YOUR NAME *CBS 8021*	13	8
31 Mar 73	GOOD GRIEF CHRISTINA *CBS 1258*	17	13

CHIEFTAINS

Ireland, male vocal / instrumental group (4 WEEKS) pos/wks

18 Mar 95	HAVE I TOLD YOU LATELY THAT I LOVE YOU		
	RCA 74321271702 [1]	71	1
12 Jun 99	I KNOW MY LOVE *RCA Victor 74321670622* [2]	37	3

[1] Chieftains with Van Morrison [2] Chieftains featuring The Corrs

CHIFFONS *US, female vocal group (40 WEEKS)* pos/wks

11 Apr 63	HE'S SO FINE *Stateside SS 172* ▲	16	12
18 Jul 63	ONE FINE DAY *Stateside SS 202*	29	6
26 May 66	SWEET TALKIN' GUY *Stateside SS 512*	31	8
18 Mar 72 ●	SWEET TALKIN' GUY (re-issue) *London HL 10271*	4	14

CHILD *UK, male vocal / instrumental group (22 WEEKS)* pos/wks

29 Apr 78	WHEN YOU WALK IN THE ROOM *Ariola Hansa AHA 511*	38	5
22 Jul 78 ●	IT'S ONLY MAKE BELIEVE *Ariola Hansa AHA 522*	10	12
28 Apr 79	ONLY YOU (AND YOU ALONE) *Ariola Hansa AHA 536* ...	33	5

Jane CHILD *Canada, female vocalist (8 WEEKS)* pos/wks

12 May 90	DON'T WANNA FALL IN LOVE *Warner Bros. W 9817*	22	8

CHILDLINERS

UK / Australia, male / female vocal group (6 WEEKS) pos/wks

16 Dec 95 ●	THE GIFT OF CHRISTMAS *London LONCD 376*	9	6

CHILDREN FOR RWANDA *UK, male / female choir (2 WEEKS)* pos/wks

10 Sep 94	LOVE CAN BUILD A BRIDGE *East West YZ 849CD*	57	2

CHILDREN OF THE NIGHT

UK, male vocalist / producer (2 WEEKS) pos/wks

26 Nov 88	IT'S A TRIP (TUNE IN, TURN ON, DROP OUT)		
	Jive JIVE 189	52	2

CHILDREN OF THE REVOLUTION – *See KLF*

Toni CHILDS *US, female vocalist (4 WEEKS)* pos/wks

25 Mar 89	DON'T WALK AWAY *A&M AM 462*	53	4

CHILI HI FLY *Australia, male DJ / production

duo – Simon Lewicki and Noel Burgess (2 WEEKS) pos/wks

18 Mar 00	IS IT LOVE *Ministry of Sound MOSCDS 141*	37	2

CHILL FAC-TORR *US, male vocal / instrumental group (8 WEEKS)* pos/wks

2 Apr 83	TWIST (ROUND 'N' ROUND) *Phillyworld PWS 109*	37	8

CHILLI featuring CARRAPICHO *US / Ghana / Brazil,

male / female vocal / instrumental group (1 WEEK) pos/wks

20 Sep 97	TIC, TIC TAC *Arista 74321511332*	59	1

CHIMES *UK, male / female vocal / instrumental group (28 WEEKS)* pos/wks

19 Aug 89	1-2-3 *CBS 655166 7*	60	3
2 Dec 89	HEAVEN (re) *CBS 655432 7*	66	5
19 May 90 ●	I STILL HAVEN'T FOUND WHAT I'M LOOKING FOR		
	CBS CHIM 1	6	9
28 Jul 90	TRUE LOVE *CBS CHIM 2*	48	3
29 Sep 90	HEAVEN (re-issue) *CBS CHIM 3*	24	6
1 Dec 90	LOVE COMES TO MIND *CBS CHIM 4*	49	5

CHIMIRA *South Africa, female vocalist (1 WEEK)* pos/wks

6 Dec 97	SHOW ME HEAVEN *Neoteric NRDCD 11*	70	1

CHINA BLACK *UK, male vocal / instrumental

duo – Errol Reid and Simon Fung (35 WEEKS) pos/wks

16 Jul 94 ●	SEARCHING (re) *Wild Card CARDD 7*	4	20
29 Oct 94	STARS *Wild Card CARDD 9*	19	7
11 Feb 95	ALMOST SEE YOU (SOMEWHERE) *Wild Card CARDW 15* ...	31	2
3 Jun 95	SWING LOW SWEET CHARIOT *PolyGram TV SWLOW 2* [1]	15	6

[1] Ladysmith Black Mambazo featuring China Black

CHINA CRISIS *UK, male vocal / instrumental group (66 WEEKS)* pos/wks

7 Aug 82	AFRICAN AND WHITE *Inevitable INEV 011*	45	5
22 Jan 83	CHRISTIAN *Virgin VS 562*	12	9
21 May 83	TRAGEDY AND MYSTERY *Virgin VS 587*	46	6
15 Oct 83	WORKING WITH FIRE AND STEEL *Virgin VS 620*	48	5
14 Jan 84 ●	WISHFUL THINKING *Virgin VS 647*	9	8
10 Mar 84	HANNA HANNA *Virgin VS 665*	44	3
30 Mar 85	BLACK MAN RAY *Virgin VS 752*	14	9
1 Jun 85	KING IN A CATHOLIC STYLE (WAKE UP) *Virgin VS 765* ...	19	9
7 Sep 85	YOU DID CUT ME *Virgin VS 799*	54	3

Re-entries are listed as (re), (2re), (3re), etc which signifies that the hit re-entered the chart once, twice or three times, etc

8 Nov 86	ARIZONA SKY *Virgin VS 898*....................	47	4
24 Jan 87	BEST KEPT SECRET *Virgin VS 926*	36	5

CHINA DRUM *UK, male vocal / instrumental group (4 WEEKS)*

		pos/wks	
2 Mar 96	CAN'T STOP THESE THINGS *Mantra MNT 8CD*	65	1
20 Apr 96	LAST CHANCE *Mantra MNT 10CD*	60	1
9 Aug 97	FICTION OF LIFE *Mantra MNT 21CD*	65	1
27 Sep 97	SOMEWHERE ELSE *Mantra MNT 022CD1*	74	1

Jonny CHINGAS *US, male instrumentalist (6 WEEKS)*

		pos/wks	
19 Feb 83	PHONE HOME *CBS A 3121*	43	6

CHIPMUNKS *US, chipmunk vocal trio (12 WEEKS)*

		pos/wks	
24 Jul 59	RAGTIME COWBOY JOE *London HLU 8916* [1]	11	8
19 Dec 92	ACHY BREAKY HEART *Epic 6588837* [2]	53	3
14 Dec 96	MACARENA *Sony Wonder 6639981* [3]	65	1

[1] David Seville and the Chipmunks [2] Alvin and the Chipmunks featuring Billy Ray Cyrus [3] Los Del Chipmunks

The Chipmunk characters were created by David Seville, who died in 1972. His son resurrected the act in 1980

See also David SEVILLE

CHIPPENDALES *UK / US, male vocal group (4 WEEKS)*

		pos/wks	
31 Oct 92	GIVE ME YOUR BODY *XSrhythm XSR 3*	28	4

George CHISHOLM – See JOHNSTON BROTHERS

CHOCOLATE PUMA *Holland, male production duo – DJ Dobri and DJ Zki (Rene ter Horst and Gaston Steenkist) (9 WEEKS)*

		pos/wks	
24 Mar 01 ●	I WANNA BE U (re) *Cream / Parlophone CREAM 13CD*	6	9

See also JARK PRONGO; TOMBA VIRA; RHYTHMKILLAZ; RIVA featuring Dannii MINOGUE; GOODMEN

CHOO CHOO PROJECT *US, male / female production / instrumental vocal duo – Harry Romero and Octahvia Lambert (3 WEEKS)*

		pos/wks	
15 Jan 00	HAZIN' & PHAZIN' *Defected DEFECT 10CDS*	21	3

See also Harry 'Choo-Choo' ROMERO; Jose NUNEZ featuring OCTAHVIA

CHOPS-EMC + EXTENSIVE
UK, male instrumental group and rapper (1 WEEK)

		pos/wks	
8 Aug 92	ME' ISRAELITES *Faze 2 FAZE 6*	60	1

CHORDETTES *US, female vocal group (25 WEEKS)*

17 Dec 54	MR SANDMAN *Columbia DB 3553* ▲	11	8
31 Aug 56 ●	BORN TO BE WITH YOU *London HLA 8302*	8	9
18 Apr 58 ●	LOLLIPOP *London HLD 8584*	6	8

CHORDS *UK, male vocal / instrumental group (17 WEEKS)*

		pos/wks	
6 Oct 79	NOW IT'S GONE *Polydor 2059 141*	63	2
2 Feb 80	MAYBE TOMORROW *Polydor POSP 101*	40	5
26 Apr 80	SOMETHING'S MISSING *Polydor POSP 146*	55	3
12 Jul 80	THE BRITISH WAY OF LIFE *Polydor 2059 258*	54	3
18 Oct 80	IN MY STREET *Polydor POSP 185*	50	4

CHRIS and JAMES *UK, male instrumental/production duo (3 WKS)*

		pos/wks	
17 Sep 94	CALM DOWN (BASS KEEPS PUMPIN') *Stress 12STR 38*	74	1
4 Nov 95	FOX FORCE FIVE *Stress CDSTR 61*	71	1
7 Nov 98	CLUB FOR LIFE '98 *Stress CDSTR 85*	66	1

Neil CHRISTIAN *UK, male vocalist - Christopher Tidmarsh (10 WKS)*

		pos/wks	
7 Apr 66	THAT'S NICE *Strike JH 301*	14	10

Roger CHRISTIAN *UK, male vocalist (3 WEEKS)*

		pos/wks	
30 Sep 89	TAKE IT FROM ME *Island IS 427*	63	3

CHRISTIANS (406) Top 500

Soul / gospel-influenced UK pop group: vocalist brothers Russell, Roger (who went solo in 1986) and Garry Christian plus Henry Priestman (k/v). In 1974, the brothers appeared on TV talent show Opportunity Knocks. Their self-titled debut album went double platinum (84 WEEKS)

		pos/wks	
31 Jan 87	FORGOTTEN TOWN *Island IS 291*	22	11
13 Jun 87	HOOVERVILLE (AND THEY PROMISED US THE WORLD) *Island IS 326*	21	10
26 Sep 87	WHEN THE FINGERS POINT *Island IS 335*	34	7
5 Dec 87	IDEAL WORLD *Island IS 347*	14	13
23 Apr 88	BORN AGAIN *Island IS 365*	25	7
15 Oct 88 ●	HARVEST FOR THE WORLD *Island IS 395*	8	7
20 May 89 ★	FERRY 'CROSS THE MERSEY *PWL PWL 41* [1] ■	1	7
23 Dec 89	WORDS *Island IS 450*	18	8
7 Apr 90	I FOUND OUT *Island IS 453*	56	2
15 Sep 90	GREENBANK DRIVE *Island IS 466*	63	2
5 Sep 92	WHAT'S IN A WORD *Island IS 536*	33	5
14 Nov 92	FATHER *Island IS 543*	55	2
6 Mar 93	THE BOTTLE *Island CID 549*	39	3

[1] Christians, Holly Johnson, Paul McCartney, Gerry Marsden and Stock Aitken Waterman

CHRISTIE *UK, male vocal / instrumental group (37 WEEKS)*

		pos/wks	
2 May 70 ★	YELLOW RIVER *CBS 4911*	1	22
10 Oct 70 ●	SAN BERNADINO (re) *CBS 5169*	7	14
25 Mar 72	IRON HORSE *CBS 7747*	47	1

David CHRISTIE *France, male vocalist (12 WEEKS)*

		pos/wks	
14 Aug 82 ●	SADDLE UP *KR KR 9*	9	12

John CHRISTIE *Australia, male vocalist (6 WEEKS)*

		pos/wks	
25 Dec 76	HERE'S TO LOVE (AULD LANG SYNE) *EMI 2554*	24	6

Lou CHRISTIE
US, male vocalist – Lugee Sacco (35 WEEKS)

		pos/wks	
24 Feb 66	LIGHTNIN' STRIKES *MGM 1297* ▲	11	8
28 Apr 66	RHAPSODY IN THE RAIN *MGM 1308*	37	2
13 Sep 69 ●	I'M GONNA MAKE YOU MINE *Buddah 201 057*	2	17
27 Dec 69	SHE SOLD ME MAGIC *Buddah 201 073*	25	8

Tony CHRISTIE
UK, male vocalist – Tony Fitzgerald (54 WEEKS)

		pos/wks	
9 Jan 71	LAS VEGAS *MCA MK 5058*	21	9
8 May 71 ●	I DID WHAT I DID FOR MARIA *MCA MK 5064*	2	17
20 Nov 71	(IS THIS THE WAY TO) AMARILLO *MCA MKS 5073*	18	13
10 Feb 73	AVENUES AND ALLEYWAYS *MCA MKS 5101*	37	4
17 Jan 76	DRIVE SAFELY DARLIN' *MCA 219*	35	4
23 Jan 99 ●	WALK LIKE A PANTHER '98 *ffrr FCD 351* [1]	10	7

[1] The All Seeing I featuring Tony Christie

Shawn CHRISTOPHER *US, female vocalist (10 WEEKS)*

		pos/wks	
4 May 91	ANOTHER SLEEPLESS NIGHT *Arista 114186*	50	4
21 Mar 92	DON'T LOSE THE MAGIC *Arista 115097*	30	5
2 Jul 94	MAKE MY LOVE *BTB BTBCD 502*	57	1

CHUCKS *UK, male / female vocal group (7 WEEKS)*

		pos/wks	
24 Jan 63	LOO-BE-LOO *Decca F 11569*	22	7

CHUMBAWAMBA
UK, male / female vocal / instrumental group (31 WEEKS)

		pos/wks	
18 Sep 93	ENOUGH IS ENOUGH *One Little Indian 79 TP7CD* [1]	56	2
4 Dec 93	TIMEBOMB *One Little Indian 89 TP7CD*	59	1
23 Aug 97 ●	TUBTHUMPING *EMI CDEM 486*	2	20
31 Jan 98 ●	AMNESIA *EMI CDEM 498*	10	5
13 Jun 98	TOP OF THE WORLD (OLE, OLE, OLE) *EMI CDEM 511*	21	3

[1] Chumbawamba and Credit to the Nation

Chubby CHUNKS
UK, male instrumentalist / producer (2 WEEKS)   pos/wks

4 Jun 94	TESTAMENT 4 *Cleveland City CLECD 13017* [1]	52	1
29 May 99	I'M TELLIN YOU (re-mix)		
	Cleveland City CLECD 13052 [2]	61	1

[1] Chubby Chunks Volume II [2] Chubby Chunks featuring Kim Ruffin

CHUPITO *Spain, male vocalist (2 WEEKS)*   pos/wks

| 23 Sep 95 | AMERICAN PIE *Eternal WEA 018CD* | 54 | 2 |

Charlotte CHURCH *UK, female vocalist (4 WEEKS)*   pos/wks

| 25 Dec 99 | JUST WAVE HELLO *Sony Classical 6685312* | 31 | 4 |

CHYNA – See INCOGNITO

CICA – See PQM featuring CICA

CICERO *UK, male vocalist – Dave Cicero (12 WEEKS)*   pos/wks

18 Jan 92	LOVE IS EVERYWHERE *Spaghetti CIAO 3*	19	8
18 Apr 92	THAT LOVING FEELING *Spaghetti CIAO 4*	46	3
1 Aug 92	HEAVEN MUST HAVE SENT YOU BACK *Spaghetti CIAO 5*	70	1

CINDERELLA *US, male vocal / instrumental group (7 WEEKS)*   pos/wks

6 Aug 88	GYPSY ROAD *Vertigo VER 40*	54	2
4 Mar 89	DON'T KNOW WHAT YOU GOT (TILL IT'S GONE)		
	Vertigo VER 43	54	2
17 Nov 90	SHELTER ME *Vertigo VER 51*	55	2
27 Apr 91	HEARTBREAK STATION *Vertigo VER 53*	63	1

CINDY and the SAFFRONS *UK, female vocal group (3 WEEKS)*   pos/wks

| 15 Jan 83 | PAST, PRESENT AND FUTURE *Stiletto STL 9* | 56 | 3 |

CINERAMA *UK, male / female vocal / instrumental duo (1 WEEK)*   pos/wks

| 18 Jul 98 | KERRY KERRY *Cooking Vinyl FRYCD 072* | 71 | 1 |

Gigliola CINQUETTI *Italy, female vocalist (27 WEEKS)*   pos/wks

| 23 Apr 64 | NON HO L'ETA PER AMARTI *Decca F 21882* | 17 | 17 |
| 4 May 74 ● | GO (BEFORE YOU BREAK MY HEART) *CBS 2294* | 8 | 10 |

CIRCA featuring DESTRY
UK, male production group and US, male vocalist (1 WEEK)   pos/wks

| 27 Nov 99 | SUN SHINING DOWN *Inferno CDFERN 22* | 70 | 1 |

CIRCUIT
UK, male / female vocal / instrumental group (3 WEEKS)   pos/wks

| 20 Jul 91 | SHELTER ME *Cooltempo COOL 237* | 44 | 2 |
| 1 Apr 95 | SHELTER ME (re-issue) *Pukka CDPUKA 2* | 50 | 1 |

CIRCULATION *UK, male production duo (1 WEEK)*   pos/wks

| 1 Sep 01 | TURQUOISE *Hooj Choons HOOJ 109* | 64 | 1 |

CIRRUS *UK, male vocal group (1 WEEK)*   pos/wks

| 30 Sep 78 | ROLLIN' ON *Jet 123* | 62 | 1 |

CITIZEN CANED *UK, male producer – Darren Tate (2 WEEKS)*   pos/wks

| 7 Apr 01 | THE JOURNEY *Serious SERR 029CD* | 41 | 2 |

See also Jurgen VRIES; ANGELIC; ORION

CITY BOY *UK, male vocal / instrumental group (20 WEEKS)*   pos/wks

8 Jul 78 ●	5.7.0.5. *Vertigo 6059 207*	8	12
28 Oct 78	WHAT A NIGHT *Vertigo 6059 211*	39	5
15 Sep 79	THE DAY THE EARTH CAUGHT FIRE *Vertigo 6059 238*	67	3

CITY GENTS – See Dick CHARLESWORTH and his CITY GENTS

CITY HIGH *US, male / female vocal / rap trio (27 WEEKS)*   pos/wks

6 Oct 01 ●	WHAT WOULD YOU DO?		
	Interscope / Polydor IND 97617	3	17
16 Mar 02 ●	CARAMEL *Interscope / Polydor 4976742* [1]	9	10

[1] City High featuring Eve

CITY SPUD – See NELLY

Gary CLAIL ON-U SOUND SYSTEM
UK, male vocal / instrumental group (19 WEEKS)   pos/wks

14 Jul 90	BEEF *RCA PB 43843* [1]	64	2
30 Mar 91 ●	HUMAN NATURE *Perfecto PB 44401*	10	9
8 Jun 91	ESCAPE *Perfecto PB 44563*	44	3
14 Nov 92	WHO PAYS THE PIPER *Perfecto 74321117017*	31	3
22 May 93	THESE THINGS ARE WORTH FIGHTING FOR		
	Perfecto 74321147222	45	2

[1] Gary Clail On-U Sound System featuring Bim Sherman

See also PRIMAL SCREAM

CLAIRE and FRIENDS
UK, female vocalist and young male / female friends (11 WEEKS)   pos/wks

| 7 Jun 86 | IT'S 'ORRIBLE BEING IN LOVE (WHEN YOU'RE 8 1/2) | | |
| | *BBC RESL 189* | 13 | 11 |

CLANNAD
Ireland, male / female vocal / instrumental group (29 WEEKS)   pos/wks

6 Nov 82 ●	THEME FROM 'HARRY'S GAME' *RCA 292*	5	10
2 Jul 83	NEW GRANGE *RCA 340*	65	1
12 May 84	ROBIN (THE HOODED MAN) *RCA HOOD 1*	42	5
25 Jan 86	IN A LIFETIME *RCA PB 40535* [1]	20	5
10 Jun 89	IN A LIFETIME (re-issue) *RCA PB 42873* [1]	17	7
10 Aug 91	BOTH SIDES NOW *MCA MCS 1546* [2]	74	1

[1] Clannad featuring Bono [2] Clannad and Paul Young

Jimmy CLANTON *US, male vocalist (1 WEEK)*   pos/wks

| 21 Jul 60 | ANOTHER SLEEPLESS NIGHT *Top Rank JAR 382* | 50 | 1 |

Eric CLAPTON `151` `Top 500`
Rock guitar player, b. Eric Clapp, 30 Mar 1945, Surrey, nicknamed 'Slowhand'. Prior to long and lucrative solo career he recorded with hitmakers The Yardbirds, Cream, Blind Faith and Derek and the Dominoes. Multi-Grammy-winning singer-guitarist and mega-grossing live performer who made the Albert Hall his second home (150 WEEKS)   pos/wks

20 Dec 69	COMIN' HOME *Atlantic 584 308* [1]	16	9
12 Aug 72 ●	LAYLA *Polydor 2058 130* [2]	7	11
27 Jul 74 ●	I SHOT THE SHERIFF *RSO 2090 132* ▲	9	9
10 May 75	SWING LOW SWEET CHARIOT *RSO 2090 158*	19	9
16 Aug 75	KNOCKIN' ON HEAVEN'S DOOR *RSO 2090 166*	38	4
24 Dec 77	LAY DOWN SALLY *RSO 2090 264*	39	6
21 Oct 78	PROMISES *RSO 21*	37	7
6 Mar 82 ●	LAYLA (re-issue) *RSO 87* [2]	4	10
5 Jun 82	I SHOT THE SHERIFF (re-issue) *RSO 88*	64	2
23 Apr 83	THE SHAPE YOU'RE IN *Duck W 9701*	75	1
16 Mar 85	FOREVER MAN *Warner Bros. W 9069*	51	4
4 Jan 86	EDGE OF DARKNESS *BBC RESL 178* [3]	65	3
17 Jan 87	BEHIND THE MASK *Duck W 8461*	15	11
20 Jun 87	TEARING US APART *Duck W 8299* [4]	56	3
27 Jan 90	BAD LOVE *Duck W 2644*	25	7
14 Apr 90	NO ALIBIS *Duck W 9981*	53	3
16 Nov 91	WONDERFUL TONIGHT (LIVE) *Duck W 0069*	30	7
8 Feb 92 ●	TEARS IN HEAVEN (re) *Reprise W 0081*	5	12
1 Aug 92	RUNAWAY TRAIN *Rocket EJS 29* [5]	31	4
29 Aug 92	IT'S PROBABLY ME *A&M AM 883* [6]	30	5
3 Oct 92	LAYLA (ACOUSTIC) (re-recording) *Duck W 0134*	45	3
15 Oct 94	MOTHERLESS CHILD *Duck W 0271CD*	63	1
18 Mar 95 ★	LOVE CAN BUILD A BRIDGE *London COCD 1* [7]	1	8
20 Jul 96	CHANGE THE WORLD *Reprise W 0358CD*	18	5
4 Apr 98	MY FATHER'S EYES *Duck W 0443CD*	33	2

4 Jul 98	CIRCUS Duck W 0447CD	.39	2	
18 Nov 00	FOREVER MAN (HOW MANY TIMES) ffrr FCD 386 [8]	26	2	

[1] Delaney and Bonnie and Friends featuring Eric Clapton [2] Derek and the Dominoes [3] Eric Clapton featuring Michael Kamen [4] Eric Clapton and Tina Turner [5] Elton John and Eric Clapton [6] Sting with Eric Clapton [7] Cher, Chrissie Hynde and Neneh Cherry with Eric Clapton [8] Beatchuggers featuring Eric Clapton

CLARISSA – See DJ VISAGE featuring CLARISSA

Dee CLARK US, male vocalist d. 7 Dec 1990 (9 WEEKS) pos/wks

2 Oct 59	JUST KEEP IT UP (AND SEE WHAT HAPPENS)		
	London HL 8915	26	1
11 Oct 75	RIDE A WILD HORSE Chelsea 2005 037	16	8

Gary CLARK UK, male vocalist (8 WEEKS) pos/wks

30 Jan 93	WE SAIL ON THE STORMY WATERS Circa YRCDX 93	34	4
3 Apr 93	FREEFLOATING Circa YRCDX 94	50	3
19 Jun 93	MAKE A FAMILY Circa YRCDX 105	70	1

Loni CLARK US, female vocalist (6 WEEKS) pos/wks

5 Jun 93	RUSHING A&M 5802862	37	2
22 Jan 94	U A&M 5804752	28	3
17 Dec 94	LOVE'S GOT ME ON A TRIP SO HIGH A&M 5808872	59	1

Petula CLARK (51 Top 500)
Britain's most consistently successful female vocalist, b. 15 Nov 1932, Surrey. Before her 34-year chart span, she starred in movies and was voted Britain's Top TV Personality. First UK female to win a Grammy and to be named Top Female Vocalist of the Year in the US in 1966 (247 WEEKS)   pos/wks

11 Jun 54 ●	THE LITTLE SHOEMAKER (re) Polygon P 1117	7	10
18 Feb 55	MAJORCA (re) Polygon P 1146	12	5
25 Nov 55 ●	SUDDENLY THERE'S A VALLEY Pye Nixa N 15013	7	10
26 Jul 57 ●	WITH ALL MY HEART Pye Nixa N 15096	4	18
15 Nov 57 ●	ALONE Pye Nixa N 15112	8	12
28 Feb 58	BABY LOVER Pye Nixa N 15126	12	7
26 Jan 61 ★	SAILOR Pye 7N 15324	1	15
13 Apr 61	SOMETHING MISSING Pye 7N 15337	44	1
13 Jul 61 ●	ROMEO Pye 7N 15361	3	15
16 Nov 61 ●	MY FRIEND THE SEA Pye 7N 15389	7	13
8 Feb 62	I'M COUNTING ON YOU Pye 7N 15407	41	2
28 Jun 62	YA YA TWIST (re) Pye 7N 15448	14	13
2 May 63	CASANOVA / CHARIOT Pye 7N 15522	39	7
12 Nov 64 ●	DOWNTOWN Pye 7N 15722 ▲	2	15
11 Mar 65	I KNOW A PLACE Pye 7N 15772	17	8
12 Aug 65	YOU BETTER COME HOME Pye 7N 15864	44	3
14 Oct 65	ROUND EVERY CORNER Pye 7N 15945	43	3
4 Nov 65	YOU'RE THE ONE Pye 7N 15991	23	9
10 Feb 66 ●	MY LOVE Pye 7N 17038 ▲	4	9
21 Apr 66	A SIGN OF THE TIMES Pye 7N 17071	49	1
30 Jun 66 ●	I COULDN'T LIVE WITHOUT YOUR LOVE Pye 7N 17133	6	11
2 Feb 67 ★	THIS IS MY SONG Pye 7N 17258	1	14
25 May 67	DON'T SLEEP IN THE SUBWAY Pye 7N 17325	12	11
13 Dec 67	THE OTHER MAN'S GRASS (IS ALWAYS GREENER)		
	Pye 7N 17416	20	9
6 Mar 68	KISS ME GOODBYE Pye 7N 17466	50	1
30 Jan 71	THE SONG OF MY LIFE Pye 7N 45026	32	12
15 Jan 72	I DON'T KNOW HOW TO LOVE HIM (re) Pye 7N 45112	47	2
19 Nov 88 ●	DOWNTOWN '88 (re-mix) PRT PYS 19	10	11

Roland CLARK – See Armand VAN HELDEN; Azzido DA BASS

Dave CLARKE UK, male producer (8 WEEKS) pos/wks

30 Sep 95 ●	RED THREE: THUNDER / STORM Deconstruction 74321306992	45	2
3 Feb 96	SOUTHSIDE Bush 74321335382	34	2
15 Jun 96	NO ONE'S DRIVING Bush 74321380162	37	2
8 Dec 01	THE COMPASS Skint SKINT 73CD	46	1
28 Dec 02	THE WOLF Skint SKINT 78	66	1+

John Cooper CLARKE UK, male vocalist (3 WEEKS) pos/wks

10 Mar 79	¡GIMMIX! PLAY LOUD Epic EPC 7009	39	3

Rick CLARKE UK, male vocalist (2 WEEKS) pos/wks

30 Apr 88	I'LL SEE YOU ALONG THE WAY WA WA 1	63	2

Sharon D CLARKE – See FPI PROJECT; SERIOUS ROPE

Warren CLARKE featuring Kathy BROWN
UK, male producer and US, female vocalist (1 WEEK)   pos/wks

2 Jun 01	OVER YOU Defected DFECT 28CDS	42	1

Dave CLARK FIVE (115 Top 500)
Beat Boom superstars from Tottenham, London: Dave Clark (d), Mike Smith (v/k), Lenny Davidson (g), Denis Payton (s), Rick Huxley (g). In the first years of the "British Invasion", this foot-stomping quintet was second only to The Beatles in the US (174 WEEKS)   pos/wks

3 Oct 63	DO YOU LOVE ME Columbia DB 7112	30	6
21 Nov 63 ★	GLAD ALL OVER Columbia DB 7154	1	19
20 Feb 64 ●	BITS AND PIECES Columbia DB 7210	2	11
28 May 64 ●	CAN'T YOU SEE THAT SHE'S MINE Columbia DB 7291	10	11
13 Aug 64	THINKING OF YOU BABY Columbia DB 7335	26	4
22 Oct 64	ANYWAY YOU WANT IT Columbia DB 7377	25	5
14 Jan 65	EVERYBODY KNOWS Columbia DB 7453	37	4
11 Mar 65	REELIN' AND ROCKIN' Columbia DB 7503	24	8
27 May 65	COME HOME Columbia DB 7580	16	8
15 Jul 65 ●	CATCH US IF YOU CAN Columbia DB 7625	5	11
11 Nov 65	OVER AND OVER Columbia DB 7744 ▲	45	4
19 May 66	LOOK BEFORE YOU LEAP Columbia DB 7909	50	1
16 Mar 67	YOU GOT WHAT IT TAKES Columbia DB 8152	28	8
1 Nov 67 ●	EVERYBODY KNOWS Columbia DB 8286	2	14
28 Feb 68	NO ONE CAN BREAK A HEART LIKE YOU		
	Columbia DB 8342	28	7
18 Sep 68 ●	THE RED BALLOON Columbia DB 8465	7	11
27 Nov 68	LIVE IN THE SKY Columbia DB 8505	39	6
25 Oct 69	PUT A LITTLE LOVE IN YOUR HEART Columbia DB 8624	31	4
6 Dec 69 ●	GOOD OLD ROCK 'N' ROLL Columbia DB 8638	7	12
7 Mar 70 ●	EVERYBODY GET TOGETHER Columbia DB 8660	8	8
4 Jul 70	HERE COMES SUMMER Columbia DB 8689	44	3
7 Nov 70	MORE GOOD OLD ROCK 'N' ROLL Columbia DB 8724	34	6
1 May 93	GLAD ALL OVER (re-issue) EMI CDEMCT 8	37	3

'Everybody Knows' on DB 7453 and 'Everybody Knows' on DB 8286 are two different songs. The two Rock 'n' Roll titles are medleys as follows: Good Old Rock 'n' Roll / Sweet Little Sixteen / Long Tall Sally / Whole Lotta Shakin' Goin' On / Blue Suede Shoes / Lucille / Reelin' and Rockin' / Memphis Tennessee. More Good Old Rock 'n' Roll Music / Blueberry Hill / Good Golly Miss Molly / My Blue Heaven / Keep a Knockin' / Loving You / One Night / Lawdy Miss Clawdy

Julian CLARY – See JOAN COLLINS FAN CLUB

CLASH (191 Top 500)
Leading lights of the UK punk rock explosion: Joe Strummer (b. John Mellor, d. 23 Dec 2002) (v/g), Mick Jones (g/v), Paul Simonon (b), Topper Headon (d). Their third LP, 'London Calling' (first released 1979), was voted Best Album of the 1980s by Rolling Stone magazine (135 WEEKS)   pos/wks

2 Apr 77	WHITE RIOT CBS 5058	38	3
8 Oct 77	COMPLETE CONTROL CBS 5664	28	2
4 Mar 78	CLASH CITY ROCKERS CBS 5834	35	4
24 Jun 78	(WHITE MAN) IN HAMMERSMITH PALAIS CBS 6383	32	7
2 Dec 78	TOMMY GUN CBS 6788	19	10
3 Mar 79	ENGLISH CIVIL WAR (JOHNNY COMES MARCHING HOME)		
	CBS 7082	25	6
19 May 79	THE COST OF LIVING (EP) CBS 7324	22	8
15 Dec 79	LONDON CALLING CBS 8087	11	10
9 Aug 80	BANKROBBER CBS 8323	12	10
6 Dec 80	THE CALL UP CBS 9339	40	6
24 Jan 81	HITSVILLE UK CBS 9480	56	4
25 Apr 81	THE MAGNIFICENT SEVEN CBS 1133	34	5
28 Nov 81	THIS IS RADIO CLASH CBS A 1797	47	6
1 May 82	KNOW YOUR RIGHTS CBS A 2309	43	3
26 Jun 82	ROCK THE CASBAH CBS A 2429	30	10
25 Sep 82	SHOULD I STAY OR SHOULD I GO / STRAIGHT TO HELL		
	CBS A 2646	17	9
12 Oct 85	THIS IS ENGLAND CBS A 6122	24	5

		pos/wks
12 Mar 88	I FOUGHT THE LAW *CBS CLASH 1*	29 5
7 May 88	LONDON CALLING (re-issue) *CBS CLASH 2*	46 3
21 Jul 90	RETURN TO BRIXTON *CBS 656072 7*	57 2
2 Mar 91	★ SHOULD I STAY OR SHOULD I GO (re-issue) *Columbia 6566677*	1 9
13 Apr 91	ROCK THE CASBAH (re-issue) *Columbia 6568147*	15 6
8 Jun 91	LONDON CALLING (re-issue) *Columbia 6569467*	64 2

Tracks on The Cost of Living (EP): I Fought the Law / Groovy Times / Gates of the West / Capital Radio. CBS CLASH 1 is a re-issue of a track from The Cost of Living (EP)

CLASS ACTION featuring Chris WILTSHIRE
US, female vocal group (3 WEEKS) pos/wks

7 May 83	WEEKEND *Jive JIVE 35*	49 3

CLASSICS IV *US, male vocal / instrumental group (1 WEEK)* pos/wks

28 Feb 68	SPOOKY *Liberty LBS 15051*	46 1

CLASSIX NOUVEAUX
UK, male vocal / instrumental group (34 WEEKS) pos/wks

28 Feb 81	GUILTY *Liberty BP 388*	43 7
16 May 81	TOKYO *Liberty BP 397*	67 3
8 Aug 81	INSIDE OUTSIDE *Liberty BP 403*	45 5
7 Nov 81	NEVER AGAIN (THE DAYS TIME ERASED) *Liberty BP 406*	44 4
13 Mar 82	IS IT A DREAM *Liberty BP 409*	11 9
29 May 82	BECAUSE YOU'RE YOUNG *Liberty BP 411*	43 4
30 Oct 82	THE END ... OR THE BEGINNING *Liberty BP 414*	60 2

See also Sal SOLO

CLAWFINGER
Norway / Sweden, male vocal / instrumental group (1 WEEK) pos/wks

19 Mar 94	WARFAIR *East West YZ 804CD1*	54 1

Judy CLAY – See William BELL

Adam CLAYTON and Larry MULLEN
Ireland, male instrumental duo (12 WEEKS) pos/wks

15 Jun 96	● THEME FROM 'MISSION: IMPOSSIBLE' *Mother MUMCD 75*	7 12

See also U2

Merry CLAYTON *US, female vocalist (1 WEEK)* pos/wks

21 May 88	YES *RCA PB 49563*	70 1

CLAYTOWN TROUPE
UK, male vocal / instrumental group (3 WEEKS) pos/wks

16 Jun 90	WAYS OF LOVE *Island IS 464*	57 2
14 Mar 92	WANTED IT ALL *EMI USA MT 102*	74 1

Johnny CLEGG and SAVUKA
UK / South Africa, male vocal / instrumental group (1 WEEK) pos/wks

16 May 87	SCATTERLINGS OF AFRICA *EMI EMI 5605*	75 1

See also JULUKA

CLEOPATRA *UK, female vocal group*
– Cleopatra, Zainam and Yonah Higgins (44 WEEKS) pos/wks

14 Feb 98	● CLEOPATRA'S THEME *WEA WEA 133CD*	3 10
16 May 98	● LIFE AIN'T EASY *WEA WEA 159CD1*	4 7
22 Aug 98	● I WANT YOU BACK *WEA WEA 172CD1*	4 7
6 Mar 99	A TOUCH OF LOVE *WEA WEA 199CD1*	24 4
10 Apr 99	● THANK ABBA FOR THE MUSIC *Epic ABCD 1* [1]	4 13
29 Jul 00	COME AND GET ME *WEA WEA 216CD1*	29 3

[1] Steps, Tina Cousins, Cleopatra, B*Witched, Billie

CLEPTOMANIACS featuring Bryan CHAMBERS
UK, male production group and vocalist (3 WEEKS) pos/wks

3 Feb 01	ALL I DO *Defected DFECT 27 CDS*	23 3

CLERGY
UK, male production duo – Paul Masterson and Judge Jules (1 WEEK) pos/wks

20 Jul 02	THE OBOE SONG *ffrr DFCD 005*	50 1

See also HI-GATE; SLEAZESISTERS; YOMANDA; CANDY GIRLS; DOROTHY; Paul MASTERSON presents SUSHI

CLICK *US, male rap group (1 WEEK)* pos/wks

29 Jun 96	SCANDALOUS *Jive JIVECD 393*	54 1

Jimmy CLIFF
Jamaica, male vocalist – James Chambers (33 WEEKS) pos/wks

25 Oct 69	● WONDERFUL WORLD, BEAUTIFUL PEOPLE *Trojan TR 690*	6 13
14 Feb 70	VIETNAM (re) *Trojan TR 7722*	46 3
8 Aug 70	● WILD WORLD *Island WIP 6087*	8 12
19 Mar 94	I CAN SEE CLEARLY NOW *Columbia 6601982*	23 5

Buzz CLIFFORD *US, male vocalist (13 WEEKS)* pos/wks

2 Mar 61	BABY SITTIN' BOOGIE *Fontana H 297*	17 13

Linda CLIFFORD *US, female vocalist (13 WEEKS)* pos/wks

10 Jun 78	IF MY FRIENDS COULD SEE ME NOW *Curtom K 17163*	50 5
5 May 79	BRIDGE OVER TROUBLED WATER *RSO 30*	28 7
15 Sep 01	RIDE THE STORM *NRK Sound Division NRKCD 053* [1]	69 1

[1] Akabu featuring Linda Clifford

CLIMAX BLUES BAND
UK, male vocal / instrumental group (9 WEEKS) pos/wks

9 Oct 76	● COULDN'T GET IT RIGHT *BTM SBT 105*	10 9

Simon CLIMIE *UK, male vocalist (2 WEEKS)* pos/wks

19 Sep 92	SOUL INSPIRATION *Epic 6582837*	60 2

CLIMIE FISHER *UK, male vocal / instrumental*
duo – Simon Climie and Rob Fisher (44 WEEKS) pos/wks

5 Sep 87	LOVE CHANGES (EVERYTHING) *EMI EM 15*	67 2
12 Dec 87	● RISE TO THE OCCASION *EMI EM 33*	10 11
12 Mar 88	● LOVE CHANGES (EVERYTHING) (re-mix) *EMI EM 47*	2 12
21 May 88	THIS IS ME *EMI EM 58*	22 5
20 Aug 88	I WON'T BLEED FOR YOU *EMI EM 66*	35 4
24 Dec 88	LOVE LIKE A RIVER *EMI EM 81*	22 7
23 Sep 89	FACTS OF LOVE *EMI EM 103*	50 3

Patsy CLINE
US, female vocalist – Virginia Hensley d. 5 Mar 1963 (17 WEEKS) pos/wks

26 Apr 62	SHE'S GOT YOU *Brunswick 05866*	43 1
29 Nov 62	HEARTACHES *Brunswick 05878*	31 5
8 Dec 90	CRAZY *MCA MCA 1465*	14 11

CLINIC *UK, male vocal / instrumental group (3 WEEKS)* pos/wks

22 Apr 00	THE RETURN OF EVIL BILL *Domino RUG 093CD*	70 1
4 Nov 00	THE SECOND LINE *Domino RUG 116CD*	56 1
2 Mar 02	WALKING WITH THEE *Domino RUG 134CD*	65 1

George CLINTON *US, male vocalist (10 WEEKS)* pos/wks

4 Dec 82	LOOPZILLA *Capitol CL 271*	57 5
26 Apr 86	DO FRIES GO WITH THAT SHAKE *Capitol CL 402*	57 2
27 Aug 94	BOP GUN (ONE NATION) *Fourth & Broadway BRCD 308* [1]	22 3

[1] Ice Cube featuring George Clinton

CLIVILLES & COLE – See C & C MUSIC FACTORY

CLOCK *UK, male production / vocal / instrumental duo (70 WEEKS)* pos/wks

30 Oct 93	HOLDING ON *Media MRLCD 007*	66 1
21 May 94	THE RHYTHM *Media MCSTD 1971*	28 2
10 Sep 94	KEEP THE FIRES BURNING *Media MCSTD 1998*	36 3
4 Mar 95	● AXEL F / KEEP PUSHIN' *Media MCSTD 2041*	7 9

EUROVISION TOP 20

■ Here are the best performing Eurovision winners ranked by the songs' UK singles chart stats

1. 1976 (UK) **Brotherhood of Man** SAVE YOUR KISSES FOR ME
   (6 weeks at No.1, 16 weeks on chart)

2. 1967 (UK) **Sandie Shaw** PUPPET ON A STRING
   (3 weeks at No.1, 18 weeks on chart)

3. 1981 (UK) **Bucks Fizz** MAKING YOUR MIND UP
   (3 weeks at No.1, 12 weeks on chart)

4. 1970 (IRELAND) **Dana** ALL KINDS OF EVERYTHING
   (2 weeks at No.1, 16 weeks on chart)

=5. 1974 (SWEDEN) **Abba** WATERLOO
   (2 weeks at No.1, 9 weeks on chart)

=5. 1982 (GERMANY) **Nicole** A LITTLE PEACE
   (2 weeks at No.1, 9 weeks on chart)

7. 1980 (IRELAND) **Johnny Logan** WHAT'S ANOTHER YEAR
   (2 weeks at No.1, 8 weeks on chart)

8. 1972 (LUXEMBOURG) **Vicky Leandros** COME WHAT MAY
   (No.2, 16 weeks on chart)

9. 1969 (UK) **Lulu** BOOM BANG-A-BANG (No.2, 13 weeks on chart)

10. 1987 (IRELAND) **Johnny Logan** HOLD ME NOW
    (No.2, 11 weeks on chart)

11. 1997 (UK) **Katrina and the Waves** LOVE SHINE A LIGHT
    (No.3, 12 weeks on chart)

12. 1979 (ISRAEL) **Milk and Honey featuring Gali Atari** HALLELUJAH
    (No.5, 8 weeks on chart)

13. 1971 (MONACO) **Séverine** UN BANC, UN ARBRE, UNE RUE
    (No.9, 11 weeks on chart)

14. 1998 (ISRAEL) **Dana International** DIVA (No.11, 4 weeks on chart)

15. 1973 (LUXEMBOURG) **Anne Marie David**
    TU TE RECONNAITRAS (No.13, 9 weeks on chart)

16. 1975 (NETHERLANDS) **Teach-In** DING-A-DONG
    (No.13, 7 weeks on chart)

17. 1964 (ITALY) **Gigliola Cinquetti** NON HO L'ETA
    (No.17, 17 weeks on chart)

18. 1978 (ISRAEL) **Izhar Cohen and Alpha-Beta** A BA NI BI
    (No.20, 7 weeks on chart)

19. 1999 (SWEDEN) **Charlotte Nilsson** TAKE ME TO YOUR HEAVEN
    (No.20, 4 weeks on chart)

20. 1993 (IRELAND) **Niamh Kavanagh** IN YOUR EYES
    (No.24, 5 weeks on chart)

Sandie Shaw does her "look, no strings" impression for the 1967 Eurovision audience

EUROVISION FOOTNOTES

Celine Dion, one of the most successful singers on the UK chart, failed to chart with her 1988 Eurovision winner

In the first 11 years of the contest, only two winners made the Top 75 in the UK

Six of the seven Irish winning entries have made the UK Top 75

The UK has won Eurovision five times and all five winners have reached the Top 3 in the UK singles chart

1 Jul 95 ●	WHOOMPH! (THERE IT IS) *Media MCSTD 2059*	4 9
26 Aug 95 ●	EVERYBODY *Media MCSTD 2077*	6 5
18 Nov 95	IN THE HOUSE *Media MCSTD 40005*	23 3
24 Feb 96	HOLDING ON 4 U (re-mix) *Media MCSTD 40019*	27 2
7 Sep 96	OH WHAT A NIGHT *Power Station MCSTD 40057*	13 10
22 Mar 97 ●	IT'S OVER *Media MCSTD 40100*	10 5
18 Oct 97	U SEXY THING *Media MCSTD 40138*	11 9
17 Jan 98	THAT'S THE WAY (I LIKE IT) *Media MCSTD 40148*	11 4
11 Jul 98	ROCK YOUR BODY *Media MCSTD 40160*	30 3
28 Nov 98	BLAME IT ON THE BOOGIE *Media MCSTD 40191*	16 4
31 Jul 99	SUNSHINE DAY *Media MCSTD 40208*	58 1

Rosemary CLOONEY (419) Top 500

Top 50s female vocalist and 90s Grammy-nominated granny. b. 23 May 1928, Kentucky, US. d. 29 Jun 2002. Award-winning balladeer and jazz song stylist was at the forefront of first mambo craze in mid-1950s. Sampled on original Shaft 1999 recording '(Mucho Mambo) Sway' which has appeared on a number of compilation albums (81 WEEKS)

		pos/wks
14 Nov 52 ●	HALF AS MUCH *Columbia DB 3129*	3 9
5 Feb 54 ●	MAN (UH-HUH) *Philips PB 220*	7 5
8 Oct 54 ★	THIS OLE HOUSE *Philips PB 336* ▲	1 18
17 Dec 54 ★	MAMBO ITALIANO *Philips PB 382* [1]	1 16
20 May 55 ●	WHERE WILL THE DIMPLE BE? *Philips PB 428* [1]	6 13
30 Sep 55 ●	HEY THERE *Philips PB 494* ▲	4 11
29 Mar 57	MANGOS (re) *Philips PB 671*	17 9

[1] Rosemary Clooney and the Mellomen

From 19 Feb 1954, other side of 'Man (Uh-Huh)', 'Woman (Uh-Huh)', by Jose Ferrer was also credited

CLOUD *UK, male instrumental group (1 WEEK)*

		pos/wks
31 Jan 81	ALL NIGHT LONG / TAKE IT TO THE TOP *UK Champagne FUNK 1*	72 1

CLOUDBURST – See DISCO TEX presents CLOUDBURST

CLOUT *South Africa, female vocal / instrumental group (15 WEEKS)* pos/wks

17 Jun 78 ●	SUBSTITUTE *Carrere EMI 2788*	2 15

CLUB NOUVEAU
US, male / female vocal / instrumental group (12 WEEKS)

		pos/wks
21 Mar 87 ●	LEAN ON ME *King Jay W 8430* ▲	3 12

CLUB 69 *Austria / US, male producer / instrumentalist – Peter Rauhofer (6 WEEKS)*

		pos/wks
5 Dec 92	LET ME BE YOUR UNDERWEAR *ffrr F 204*	33 5
14 Nov 98	ALRIGHT *Twisted UK TWCD 10039* [1]	70 1

[1] Club 69 featuring Suzanne Palmer

CLUBHOUSE
Italy, male vocal / instrumental group (40 WEEKS)

		pos/wks
23 Jul 83	DO IT AGAIN – BILLIE JEAN (MEDLEY) *Island IS 132*	11 6
3 Dec 83	SUPERSTITION – GOOD TIMES (MEDLEY) *Island IS 147*	59 3
1 Jul 89	I'M A MAN – YEKE YEKE (MEDLEY) *Music Man MMPS 7003*	69 3
20 Apr 91	DEEP IN MY HEART (re) *ffrr F 157*	55 4
4 Sep 93	LIGHT MY FIRE (2re) *PWL Continental PWCD 272* [1]	45 12
30 Apr 94 ●	LIGHT MY FIRE (re-mix) *PWL Continental PWCD 288* [1]	7 8
23 Jul 94	LIVING IN THE SUNSHINE *PWL Continental PWCD 309* [1]	21 3
11 Mar 95	NOWHERE LAND *PWL International PWCD 318* [1]	56 1

[1] Clubhouse featuring Carl

CLUBZONE
UK / Germany, male vocal / instrumental group (1 WEEK)

		pos/wks
19 Nov 94	HANDS UP *Logic 74321236982*	50 1

CLUELESS *US, male / female vocal / production group (1 WEEK)* pos/wks

5 Apr 97	DON'T SPEAK *ZYX ZYX 660738*	61 1

Jeremy CLYDE – See Chad STUART and Jeremy CLYDE

CLYDE VALLEY STOMPERS
UK, male instrumental group (8 WEEKS)

		pos/wks
9 Aug 62	PETER AND THE WOLF *Parlophone R 4928*	25 8

CO-CO *UK, male / female vocal / instrumental group (7 WEEKS)* pos/wks

22 Apr 78	BAD OLD DAYS *Ariola Hansa AHA 513*	13 7

COAST 2 COAST featuring DISCOVERY
Ireland, male production duo and female vocalist (1 WEEK)

		pos/wks
16 Jun 01	HOME *Religion RLG 0126955*	44 1

COAST TO COAST
UK, male vocal / instrumental group (22 WEEKS)

		pos/wks
31 Jan 81 ●	(DO) THE HUCKLEBUCK *Polydor POSP 214*	5 15
23 May 81	LET'S JUMP THE BROOMSTICK *Polydor POSP 249*	28 7

COASTERS *US, male vocal group (32 WEEKS)*

		pos/wks
27 Sep 57	SEARCHIN' *London HLE 8450*	30 1
15 Aug 58	YAKETY YAK *London HLE 8665*	12 8
27 Mar 59 ●	CHARLIE BROWN *London HLE 8819*	6 12
30 Oct 59	POISON IVY *London HLE 8938*	15 7
9 Apr 94	SORRY BUT I'M GONNA HAVE TO PASS *Rhino A 4519CD*	41 4

Odia COATES – See Paul ANKA

Luis COBOS featuring Placido DOMINGO *Spain, male orchestra conductor and Spain, male vocalist (2 WEEKS)* pos/wks

16 Jun 90	NESSUN DORMA FROM 'TURANDOT' *Epic 656005 7*	59 2

Eddie COCHRAN (359) Top 500

Legendary rock 'n' roll singer / songwriter and guitarist b. 3 Oct 1938, Oklahoma, US. d. 17 Apr 1960, Wiltshire, UK. Distinctive and influential 'teen rebel' rocker, whose songs have been recorded by such stars as Cliff Richard, Beach Boys, Sex Pistols and The Who (90 WEEKS)

		pos/wks
7 Nov 58	SUMMERTIME BLUES *London HLU 8702*	18 6
13 Mar 59 ●	C'MON EVERYBODY *London HLU 8792*	6 13
16 Oct 59	SOMETHIN' ELSE *London HLU 8944*	22 3
22 Jan 60	HALLELUJAH, I LOVE HER SO (re) *London HLW 9022*	22 4
12 May 60 ★	THREE STEPS TO HEAVEN *London HLG 9115*	1 15
6 Oct 60	SWEETIE PIE *London HLG 9196*	38 3
3 Nov 60	LONELY *London HLG 9196*	41 1
15 Jun 61	WEEKEND *London HLG 9362*	15 16
30 Nov 61	JEANNIE, JEANNIE, JEANNIE *London HLG 9460*	31 4
25 Apr 63	MY WAY *Liberty LIB 10088*	23 10
24 Apr 68	SUMMERTIME BLUES (re-issue) *Liberty LBF 15071*	34 8
13 Feb 88	C'MON EVERYBODY (re-issue) *Liberty EDDIE 501*	14 7

Tom COCHRANE *Canada, male vocalist (2 WEEKS)*

		pos/wks
27 Jun 92	LIFE IS A HIGHWAY *Capitol CL 660*	62 2

COCK ROBIN
US, male / female vocal / instrumental group (12 WEEKS)

		pos/wks
31 May 86	THE PROMISE YOU MADE *CBS A 6764*	28 12

Joe COCKER (364) Top 500 *Throaty, emotive pop / rock singer b. 20 May 1944, Sheffield, UK, whose first single was released in 1964. Remembered for a memorable performance at Woodstock, Cocker is still scoring Top 20 albums across Europe in the 21st century (89 WEEKS)*

		pos/wks
22 May 68	MARJORINE *Regal-Zonophone RZ 3006*	48 1
2 Oct 68 ★	WITH A LITTLE HELP FROM MY FRIENDS *Regal-Zonophone RZ 3013*	1 13
27 Sep 69 ●	DELTA LADY *Regal-Zonophone RZ 3024*	10 11
4 Jul 70	THE LETTER *Regal-Zonophone RZ 3027*	39 6
26 Sep 81	I'M SO GLAD I'M STANDING HERE TODAY *MCA 741* [1]	61 3

Re-entries are listed as (re), (2re), (3re), etc which signifies that the hit re-entered the chart once, twice or three times, etc

15 Jan 83 ●	UP WHERE WE BELONG Island WIP 6830 [2] ▲	7	13
14 Nov 87	UNCHAIN MY HEART Capitol CL 465	46	4
13 Jan 90	WHEN THE NIGHT COMES Capitol CL 535	65	2
7 Mar 92	(ALL I KNOW) FEELS LIKE FOREVER Capitol CL 645	25	5
9 May 92	NOW THAT THE MAGIC HAS GONE Capitol CL 657	28	6
4 Jul 92	UNCHAIN MY HEART (re-issue) Capitol CL 664	17	6
21 Nov 92	WHEN THE NIGHT COMES (re-issue) Capitol CL 674	61	3
13 Aug 94	THE SIMPLE THINGS Capitol CDCLS 722	17	5
22 Oct 94	TAKE ME HOME Capitol CDCLS 729 [3]	41	3
17 Dec 94	LET THE HEALING BEGIN Capitol CDCLS 727	32	5
23 Sep 95	HAVE A LITTLE FAITH Capitol CDCLS 744	67	2
12 Oct 96	DON'T LET ME BE MISUNDERSTOOD Parlophone CDCLS 779	53	1

[1] Crusaders, featured vocalist Joe Cocker [2] Joe Cocker and Jennifer Warnes
[3] Joe Cocker featuring Bekka Bramlett

COCKEREL CHORUS UK, male Tottenham
Hotspur Football Club Supporters vocal group (12 WEEKS)   pos/wks

| 24 Feb 73 | NICE ONE CYRIL Youngblood YB 1017 | ....14 | 12 |

COCKNEY REBEL – See Steve HARLEY and COCKNEY REBEL

COCKNEY REJECTS
UK, male vocal / instrumental group (22 WEEKS)   pos/wks

1 Dec 79	I'M NOT A FOOL EMI 5008	65	2
16 Feb 80	BADMAN EMI 5035	65	3
26 Apr 80	THE GREATEST COCKNEY RIP-OFF Zonophone Z 2	21	7
17 May 80	I'M FOREVER BLOWING BUBBLES Zonophone Z 4	35	5
12 Jul 80	WE CAN DO ANYTHING Zonophone Z 6	65	2
25 Oct 80	WE ARE THE FIRM Zonophone Z 10	54	3

COCO UK, female vocalist (2 WEEKS)   pos/wks

| 8 Nov 97 | I NEED A MIRACLE Positiva CDTIV 81 | ....39 | 2 |

See also FRAGMA

COCONUTS US, female vocal group (3 WEEKS)   pos/wks

| 11 Jun 83 | DID YOU HAVE TO LOVE ME LIKE YOU DID EMI America EA 156 | ....60 | 3 |

See also Kid CREOLE and the COCONUTS

COCTEAU TWINS
UK, male / female vocal / instrumental group (25 WEEKS)   pos/wks

28 Apr 84	PEARLY-DEWDROPS' DROPS 4AD 405	29	5
30 Mar 85	AIKEA-GUINEA 4AD AD 501	41	3
23 Nov 85	TINY DYNAMINE (EP) 4AD BAD 510	52	2
7 Dec 85	ECHOES IN A SHALLOW BAY (EP) 4AD BAD 511	65	1
25 Oct 86	LOVE'S EASY TEARS 4AD AD 610	53	1
8 Sep 90	ICEBLINK LUCK 4AD AD 0011	38	3
2 Oct 93	EVANGELINE Fontana CTCD 1	34	2
18 Dec 93	WINTER WONDERLAND / FROSTY THE SNOWMAN Fontana COCCD 1	58	1
26 Feb 94	BLUEBEARD Fontana CTCD 2	33	2
7 Oct 95	TWINLIGHTS (EP) Fontana CTCD 3	59	1
4 Nov 95	OTHERNESS (EP) Fontana CTCD 4	59	1
30 Mar 96	TISHBITE Fontana CTCD 5	34	2
20 Jul 96	VIOLAINE Fontana CTCD 6	56	1

Tracks on Tiny Dynamine (EP): Pink Orange Red / Ribbed and Veined / Plain Tiger / Sultitan Itan. Tracks on Echoes in a Shallow Bay (EP): Great Spangled Fritillary / Melonella / Pale Clouded White / Eggs and Their Shells. Tracks on Twinlights (EP): Golden-Vein / Half-Gifts / Pink Orange Red / Rilkean Heart. Tracks on Otherness (EP): Cherry Coloured Funk / Feet Like Fins / Seekers Who Are Lovers / Violaine

CODE RED UK, male vocal group (7 WEEKS)   pos/wks

6 Jul 96	I GAVE YOU EVERYTHING Polydor 5763992	50	1
16 Nov 96	THIS IS OUR SONG Polydor 5756332	59	1
14 Jun 97	CAN WE TALK… Polydor 5710992	29	2
9 Aug 97	IS THERE SOMEONE OUT THERE? Polydor 5714652	34	2
4 Jul 98	WHAT WOULD YOU DO IF…? Polydor 569932	55	1

COFFEE US, female vocal group (13 WEEKS)   pos/wks

| 27 Sep 80 | CASANOVA De-Lite MER 38 | ....13 | 10 |
| 6 Dec 80 | SLIP AND DIP / I WANNA BE WITH YOU De-Lite DE 1 | ....57 | 3 |

Alma COGAN 268 Top 500
Very popular 1950s radio, TV and recording star. b. 19 May 1932, d. 26 Oct 1966. The singer, who was renowned for her glamour and was known as the "gal with the giggle in her voice", was the youngest English female to top the chart in the 1950s (110 WEEKS)   pos/wks

19 Mar 54 ●	BELL BOTTOM BLUES HMV B 10653	4	9
27 Aug 54	LITTLE THINGS MEAN A LOT (2re) HMV B 10717	11	5
3 Dec 54 ●	I CAN'T TELL A WALTZ FROM A TANGO HMV B 10786	6	11
27 May 55 ★	DREAMBOAT HMV B 10872	1	16
23 Sep 55	THE BANJO'S BACK IN TOWN HMV B 10917 (A)	17	1
14 Oct 55	GO ON BY HMV B 10917 (B)	16	4
16 Dec 55	TWENTY TINY FINGERS HMV POP 129(A)	17	1
23 Dec 55 ●	NEVER DO A TANGO WITH AN ESKIMO HMV POP 129(B)	6	5
30 Mar 56	WILLIE CAN HMV POP 187 [1]	13	8
13 Jul 56	THE BIRDS AND THE BEES HMV POP 223	25	4
10 Aug 56	WHY DO FOOLS FALL IN LOVE HMV POP 223	22	3
2 Nov 56	IN THE MIDDLE OF THE HOUSE (re) HMV POP 261	20	4
18 Jan 57	YOU, ME AND US HMV POP 284	18	6
29 Mar 57	WHATEVER LOLA WANTS (LOLA GETS) HMV POP 317	26	2
31 Jan 58	THE STORY OF MY LIFE HMV POP 433	25	2
14 Feb 58	SUGARTIME (re) HMV POP 450	16	11
23 Jan 59	LAST NIGHT ON THE BACK PORCH HMV POP 573	27	2
18 Dec 59	WE GOT LOVE HMV POP 670	26	4
12 May 60	DREAM TALK HMV POP 728	48	1
11 Aug 60	TRAIN OF LOVE HMV POP 760	27	5
20 Apr 61	COWBOY JIMMY JOE Columbia DB 4607	37	6

[1] Alma Cogan with Desmond Lane – penny whistle

Shaye COGAN US, female vocalist (1 WEEK)   pos/wks

| 24 Mar 60 | MEAN TO ME MGM 1063 | ....40 | 1 |

Izhar COHEN and the ALPHA-BETA
Israel, male / female vocal group (7 WEEKS)   pos/wks

| 13 May 78 | A-BA-NI-BI Polydor 2001 781 | ....20 | 7 |

Marc COHN US, male vocalist (15 WEEKS)   pos/wks

25 May 91	WALKING IN MEMPHIS Atlantic A 7747	66	4
10 Aug 91	SILVER THUNDERBIRD Atlantic A 7657	54	3
12 Oct 91	WALKING IN MEMPHIS (re-issue) Atlantic A 7585	22	5
29 May 93	WALK THROUGH THE WORLD Atlantic A 7340CD	37	3

COLA BOY UK, male / female vocal / instrumental
duo – Andrew Midgely and Janey Lee Grace (7 WEEKS)   pos/wks

| 6 Jul 91 ● | 7 WAYS TO LOVE Arista 114526 | ....8 | 7 |

COLD JAM featuring GRACE
US, male / female vocal / instrumental group (2 WEEKS)   pos/wks

| 28 Jul 90 | LAST NIGHT A DJ SAVED MY LIFE Big Wave BWR 39 | ....64 | 2 |

COLDCUT UK, male production duo
– Matt Black and Jonathan Moore (39 WEEKS)   pos/wks

20 Feb 88 ●	DOCTORIN' THE HOUSE Ahead of Our Time CCUT 27 [1]	6	9
10 Sep 88	STOP THIS CRAZY THING Ahead of Our Time CCUT 4 [2]	21	7
25 Mar 89	PEOPLE HOLD ON Ahead of Our Time CCUT 5 [3]	11	9
3 Jun 89	MY TELEPHONE Ahead of Our Time CCUT 6	52	2
16 Dec 89	COLDCUT'S CHRISTMAS BREAK Ahead of Our Time CCUT 7	67	3
26 May 90	FIND A WAY Ahead of Our Time CCUT 8 [4]	52	2
4 Sep 93	DREAMER Arista 74321156642	54	2
22 Jan 94	AUTUMN LEAVES Arista 74321171052	50	2
16 Aug 97	MORE BEATS & PIECES Ninja Tune ZENCDS 58	37	2
16 Jun 01	REVOLUTION Ninja Tune ZENCDS 88	67	1

[1] Coldcut featuring Yazz and the Plastic Population [2] Coldcut featuring Junior Reid and the Ahead of Our Time Orchestra [3] Coldcut featuring Lisa Stansfield [4] Coldcut featuring Queen Latifah

COLDPLAY UK, male vocal / instrumental group (39 WEEKS)　pos/wks

18 Mar 00	SHIVER *Parlophone CDR 6536*	35	3
8 Jul 00 ●	YELLOW *Parlophone CDR 6538*	4	11
4 Nov 00 ●	TROUBLE *Parlophone CDR 6549*	10	9
17 Aug 02 ●	IN MY PLACE *Parlophone CDRS 6579*	2	10
23 Nov 02 ●	THE SCIENTIST *Parlophone CDR 6588*	10	6+

Andy COLE UK, male vocalist / footballer (1 WEEK)　pos/wks

18 Sep 99	OUTSTANDING *WEA WEA 224CD*	68	1

Cozy COLE
US, male instrumentalist – drums, d. 9 Jan 1981 (1 WEEK)　pos/wks

5 Dec 58	TOPSY (PARTS 1 AND 2) *London HL 8750*	29	1

George COLE – See Dennis WATERMAN

Lloyd COLE UK, male vocalist (62 WEEKS)　pos/wks

26 May 84	PERFECT SKIN (re) *Polydor COLE 1* [1]	26	9
25 Aug 84	FOREST FIRE *Polydor COLE 2* [1]	41	6
17 Nov 84	RATTLESNAKES *Polydor COLE 3* [1]	65	2
14 Sep 85	BRAND NEW FRIEND *Polydor COLE 4* [1]	19	8
9 Nov 85	LOST WEEKEND *Polydor COLE 5* [1]	17	7
18 Jan 86	CUT ME DOWN *Polydor COLE 6* [1]	38	4
3 Oct 87	MY BAG *Polydor COLE 7* [1]	46	4
9 Jan 88	JENNIFER SHE SAID *Polydor COLE 8* [1]	31	5
23 Apr 88	FROM THE HIP (EP) *Polydor COLE 9* [1]	59	2
3 Feb 90	NO BLUE SKIES *Polydor COLE 11*	42	4
7 Apr 90	DON'T LOOK BACK *Polydor COLE 12*	59	3
31 Aug 91	SHE'S A GIRL AND I'M A MAN *Polydor COLE 14*	55	2
25 Sep 93	SO YOU'D LIKE TO SAVE THE WORLD *Fontana VIBE D1*	72	2
16 Sep 95	LIKE LOVERS DO *Fontana LCDD 1*	24	3
2 Dec 95	SENTIMENTAL FOOL *Fontana LCDD 2*	73	1

[1] Lloyd Cole and the Commotions

Tracks on From the Hip (EP): From the Hip / Please / Lonely Mile / Love Your Wife

MJ COLE UK, male producer – Matt Coleman (16 WEEKS)　pos/wks

23 May 98	SINCERE *AM:PM 5826912*	38	2
6 May 00 ●	CRAZY LOVE *Talkin Loud TLCD 59*	10	7
12 Aug 00	SINCERE (re-mix) *Talkin Loud TLCD 60*	13	5
2 Dec 00	HOLD ON TO ME *Talkin Loud TLCD 62* [1]	35	2

[1] MJ Cole featuring Elizabeth Troy

Nat 'King' COLE ⟨ 49 ⟩ Top 500
One of the 20th century's most distinctive song stylists, b. 17 Mar 1917, Alabama, d. 15 Feb 1965. His 41-year chart span is proof that the highly regarded vocalist's recordings are timeless (249 WEEKS)　pos/wks

14 Nov 52 ●	SOMEWHERE ALONG THE WAY *Capitol CL 13774*	3	7
19 Dec 52 ●	BECAUSE YOU'RE MINE (2re) *Capitol CL 13811*	6	4
2 Jan 53 ●	FAITH CAN MOVE MOUNTAINS (2re) *Capitol CL 13811*	10	4
24 Apr 53 ●	PRETEND *Capitol CL 13878*	2	18
14 Aug 53 ●	CAN'T I (2re) *Capitol CL 13937*	6	8
18 Sep 53 ●	MOTHER NATURE AND FATHER TIME *Capitol CL 13912*	7	7
16 Apr 54 ●	TENDERLY *Capitol CL 14061*	10	1
10 Sep 54 ●	SMILE *Capitol CL 14149*	2	14
8 Oct 54	MAKE HER MINE *Capitol CL 14149*	11	2
25 Feb 55 ●	A BLOSSOM FELL *Capitol CL 14235*	3	10
26 Aug 55	MY ONE SIN (re) *Capitol CL 14327*	17	2
27 Jan 56 ●	DREAMS CAN TELL A LIE *Capitol CL 14513*	10	9
11 May 56 ● ★	TOO YOUNG TO GO STEADY *Capitol CL 14573*	8	14
14 Sep 56	LOVE ME AS THOUGH THERE WERE NO TOMORROW (re) *Capitol CL 14621*	11	15
19 Apr 57 ●	WHEN I FALL IN LOVE *Capitol CL 14709*	2	20
5 Jul 57	WHEN ROCK AND ROLL CAME TO TRINIDAD *Capitol CL 14733*	28	1
18 Oct 57	MY PERSONAL POSSESSION *Capitol CL 14765* [1]	21	2
25 Oct 57	STARDUST *Capitol CL 14787*	24	2
29 May 59	YOU MADE ME LOVE YOU *Capitol CL 15017*	22	3
4 Sep 59	MIDNIGHT FLYER (re) *Capitol CL 15056*	23	4
12 Feb 60	TIME AND THE RIVER (2re) *Capitol CL 15111*	23	5

26 May 60 ●	THAT'S YOU *Capitol CL 15129*	10	8
10 Nov 60 ●	JUST AS MUCH AS EVER *Capitol CL 15163*	18	10
2 Feb 61	THE WORLD IN MY ARMS *Capitol CL 15178*	36	10
16 Nov 61	LET TRUE LOVE BEGIN *Capitol CL 15224*	29	10
22 Mar 62	BRAZILIAN LOVE SONG (ANDORHINA PRETA) *Capitol CL 15241*	34	4
31 May 62	THE RIGHT THING TO SAY *Capitol CL 15250*	42	4
19 Jul 62	LET THERE BE LOVE *Capitol CL 15257* [2]	11	14
27 Sep 62 ●	RAMBLIN' ROSE *Capitol CL 15270*	5	14
20 Dec 62	DEAR LONELY HEARTS *Capitol CL 15280*	37	3
12 Dec 87 ●	WHEN I FALL IN LOVE (re-issue) *Capitol CL 15975*	4	7
22 Jun 91	UNFORGETTABLE *Elektra EKR 128* [3]	19	8
14 Dec 91	THE CHRISTMAS SONG *Capitol CL 641*	69	2
19 Mar 94	LET'S FACE THE MUSIC AND DANCE *EMI CDEM 312*	30	3

[1] Nat 'King' Cole and the Four Knights [2] Nat 'King' Cole with George Shearing
[3] Natalie Cole and Nat 'King' Cole

Natalie COLE ⟨ 384 ⟩ Top 500
Daughter of legendary Nat 'King' Cole who has a 20-year Grammy-winning span of her own. b. 6 Feb 1950, Los Angeles, US. 'Unforgettable' in 1991 was an electronically recorded duet with her late father. Nat and Natalie are the only dad and daughter who both have No.1 US albums (87 WEEKS)　pos/wks

11 Oct 75	THIS WILL BE *Capitol CL 15834*	32	5
8 Aug 87	JUMP START *Manhattan MT 22*	44	4
26 Mar 88 ●	PINK CADILLAC *Manhattan MT 35*	5	12
25 Jun 88	EVERLASTING *Manhattan MT 46*	28	6
20 Aug 88	JUMP START (re-issue) *Manhattan MT 50*	36	5
26 Nov 88	I LIVE FOR YOUR LOVE *Manhattan MT 57*	23	14
15 Apr 89 ●	MISS YOU LIKE CRAZY *EMI-USA MT 63*	2	15
22 Jul 89	REST OF THE NIGHT *EMI-USA MT 69*	56	2
16 Dec 89	STARTING OVER AGAIN *EMI-USA MT 77*	56	4
21 Apr 90	WILD WOMEN DO *EMI-USA MT 81*	16	7
22 Jun 91	UNFORGETTABLE *Elektra EKR 128* [1]	19	8
16 May 92	THE VERY THOUGHT OF YOU *Elektra EKR 147*	71	1

[1] Natalie Cole and Nat 'King' Cole

Paula COLE US, female vocalist (9 WEEKS)　pos/wks

28 Jun 97	WHERE HAVE ALL THE COWBOYS GONE? *Warner Bros. W 0406CD*	15	8
1 Aug 98	I DON'T WANT TO WAIT *Warner Bros. W 0422CD*	43	1

Naimee COLEMAN – See AURORA

COLETTE – See SISTER BLISS

John Ford COLEY – See ENGLAND DAN and John Ford COLEY

COLLAGE
US / Canada / Philippines, male vocal / instrumental group (5 WEEKS)　pos/wks

21 Sep 85	ROMEO WHERE'S JULIET? *MCA MCA 1006*	46	5

COLLAPSED LUNG
UK, male vocal / instrumental group (8 WEEKS)　pos/wks

22 Jun 96	LONDON TONIGHT / EAT MY GOAL *Deceptive BLUFF 029CD*	31	3
30 May 98	EAT MY GOAL (re-issue) *Deceptive BLUFF 060CD*	18	5

Dave and Ansil COLLINS *Jamaica, male vocal / instrumental duo – Dave Barker and Ansil Collins (27 WEEKS)*　pos/wks

27 Mar 71 ★	DOUBLE BARREL *Technique TE 901*	1	15
26 Jun 71 ●	MONKEY SPANNER *Technique TE 914* [1]	7	12

[1] Dave and Ansel Collins

Edwyn COLLINS
UK, male vocalist / instrumentalist (25 WEEKS)　pos/wks

11 Aug 84	PALE BLUE EYES *Swamplands SWP 1*	72	2
12 Nov 94	EXPRESSLY (EP) *Setanta ZOP 001CD1*	42	3
17 Jun 95 ●	A GIRL LIKE YOU (re-issue) *Setanta ZOP 003CD*	4	14
2 Mar 96	KEEP ON BURNING *Setanta ZOP 004CD1*	45	2

2 Aug 97	THE MAGIC PIPER (OF LOVE) *Setanta SETCDA 041*	32	3
18 Oct 97	ADIDAS WORLD *Setanta SETCDB 045*	71	1

The only track on all formats of Expressly (EP) was 'A Girl Like You'

See also ORANGE JUICE

Felicia COLLINS – *See LUKK featuring Felicia COLLINS*

Jeff COLLINS *UK, male vocalist (8 WEEKS)*　pos/wks

18 Nov 72	ONLY YOU *Polydor 2058 287*	40	8

Judy COLLINS (391 Top 500) Distinctive folk / pop singer born 1 May 1939, Washington, US, and raised in Colorado. 'Both Sides Now' was the first Joni Mitchell composition to chart and 'Amazing Grace' spent longer on the chart than any other single by a female artist (86 WEEKS)　pos/wks

17 Jan 70	BOTH SIDES NOW *Elektra EKSN 45043*	14	11
5 Dec 70 ●	AMAZING GRACE (7re) *Elektra 2101 020*	5	67
17 May 75 ●	SEND IN THE CLOWNS *Elektra K 12177*	6	8

'Amazing Grace' re-entered in Jul, Sep, Nov, Dec 1971 and Apr, Sep, Dec 1972

Michelle COLLINS *UK, female vocalist (3 WEEKS)*　pos/wks

27 Feb 99	SUNBURN *BBC Music WMSS 60082*	28	3

Phil COLLINS (64 Top 500) Continually popular singer / songwriter (b. 31 Jan 1951, London) who simultaneously fronted Genesis (until 1996) and managed a successful solo career. Only members of The Beatles have appeared on more UK No.1 albums (230 WEEKS)　pos/wks

17 Jan 81	IN THE AIR TONIGHT *Virgin VS102*	2	10
7 Mar 81	I MISSED AGAIN *Virgin VS 402*	14	8
30 May 81	IF LEAVING ME IS EASY *Virgin VS 423*	17	8
23 Oct 82	THRU' THESE WALLS *Virgin VS 524*	56	2
4 Dec 82 ★	YOU CAN'T HURRY LOVE *Virgin VS 531*	1	16
19 Mar 83	DON'T LET HIM STEAL YOUR HEART AWAY *Virgin VS 572*	45	5
7 Apr 84 ●	AGAINST ALL ODDS (TAKE A LOOK AT ME NOW) *Virgin VS 674* ▲	2	14
26 Jan 85	SUSSUDIO *Virgin VS 736* ▲	12	9
9 Mar 85 ★	EASY LOVER *CBS A 4915* [1]	1	12
13 Apr 85 ●	ONE MORE NIGHT *Virgin VS 755* ▲	4	9
27 Jul 85	TAKE ME HOME *Virgin VS 777*	19	9
23 Nov 85 ●	SEPARATE LIVES *Virgin VS 818* [2] ▲	4	13
18 Jun 88 ●	IN THE AIR TONIGHT (re-mix) *Virgin VS 102*	4	9
3 Sep 88 ★	A GROOVY KIND OF LOVE *Virgin VS 1117* ▲	1	13
26 Nov 88 ●	TWO HEARTS *Virgin VS 1141* ▲	6	11
4 Nov 89 ●	ANOTHER DAY IN PARADISE *Virgin VS 1234* ▲	2	11
27 Jan 90 ●	I WISH IT WOULD RAIN DOWN *Virgin VS 1240*	7	9
28 Apr 90	SOMETHING HAPPENED ON THE WAY TO HEAVEN *Virgin VS 1251*	15	7
28 Jul 90	THAT'S JUST THE WAY IT IS *Virgin VS 1277*	26	5
6 Oct 90	HANG IN LONG ENOUGH *Virgin VS 1300*	34	3
8 Dec 90	DO YOU REMEMBER (LIVE) *Virgin VS 1305*	57	5
15 May 93	HERO *Atlantic A 7360* [3]	56	1
30 Oct 93 ●	BOTH SIDES OF THE STORY (re) *Virgin VSCDT 1500*	7	6
15 Jan 94	EVERYDAY *Virgin VSCDT 1505*	15	6
7 May 94	WE WAIT AND WE WONDER *Virgin VSCDT 1510*	45	2
5 Oct 96 ●	DANCE INTO THE LIGHT *Face Value EW 066CD*	9	6
14 Dec 96	IT'S IN YOUR EYES *Face Value EW 076CD1*	30	4
12 Jul 97	WEAR MY HAT *Face Value EW 113CD*	43	2
7 Nov 98	TRUE COLORS *Virgin VSCDT 1715*	26	4
6 Nov 99	YOU'LL BE IN MY HEART *Edel / Walt Disney 0100735 DNY*	17	6
22 Sep 01	IN THE AIR TONITE *WEA WEA 331CD* [4]	26	2
16 Nov 02	CAN'T STOP LOVING YOU *Face Value EW 254CD*	28	2

[1] Philip Bailey (duet with Phil Collins) [2] Phil Collins and Marilyn Martin [3] David Crosby featuring Phil Collins [4] Lil' Kim featuring Phil Collins

See also GENESIS

Rodger COLLINS *US, male vocalist (6 WEEKS)*　pos/wks

3 Apr 76	YOU SEXY SUGAR PLUM (BUT I LIKE IT) *Fantasy FTC 132*	22	6

Willie COLLINS *US, male vocalist (4 WEEKS)*　pos/wks

28 Jun 86	WHERE YOU GONNA BE TONIGHT? *Capitol CL 410*	46	4

Willie COLON *US, male vocalist (7 WEEKS)*　pos/wks

28 Jun 86	SET FIRE TO ME *A&M AM 330*	41	7

COLOR ME BADD *US, male vocal group (31 WEEKS)*　pos/wks

18 May 91 ★	I WANNA SEX YOU UP *Giant W 0036*	1	14
3 Aug 91 ●	ALL 4 LOVE *Giant W 0053* ▲	5	10
12 Oct 91	I ADORE MI AMOR *Giant W 0067* ▲	44	2
9 Nov 91	I ADORE MI AMOR (re-issue) *Giant W 0076*	59	2
22 Feb 92	HEARTBREAKER *Giant W 0078*	58	1
20 Nov 93	TIME AND CHANCE *Giant 74321168992*	62	1
16 Apr 94	CHOOSE *Giant 74321199432*	65	1

COLORADO *UK, female vocal group (3 WEEKS)*　pos/wks

21 Oct 78	CALIFORNIA DREAMING *Pinnacle PIN 67*	45	3

COLOUR FIELD *UK, male vocal / instrumental group (18 WEEKS)*　pos/wks

21 Jan 84	THE COLOUR FIELD *Chrysalis COLF 1*	43	4
28 Jul 84	TAKE *Chrysalis COLF 2*	70	1
26 Jan 85	THINKING OF YOU *Chrysalis COLF 3*	12	10
13 Apr 85	CASTLES IN THE AIR *Chrysalis COLF 4*	51	3

COLOUR GIRL
UK, female vocalist – Rebecca Skingley (5 WEEKS)　pos/wks

11 Mar 00	CAN'T GET USED TO LOSING YOU *4 Liberty LIBT CD037*	31	3
9 Sep 00	JOYRIDER (YOU'RE PLAYING WITH FIRE) *4 Liberty LIBT CD039*	51	1
3 Feb 01	MAS QUE NADA *4 Liberty LIBTCD 040* [1]	57	1

[1] Colour Girl featuring PSG

COLOURS featuring EMMANUEL & ESKA
UK, male instrumentalist / producer and female vocalist (1 WEEK)　pos/wks

27 Feb 99	WHAT U DO *Inferno CDFERN 12*	51	1

See also Nitin SAWHNEY featuring ESKA; EN-CORE featuring Stephen EMMANUEL & ESKA

COLOURSOUND *UK, male production duo (2 WEEKS)*　pos/wks

28 Sep 02	FLY WITH ME *City Rockers ROCKERS 20CD*	49	2

COLUMBO featuring OOE *UK, male production duo (1 WEEK)*　pos/wks

15 May 99	ROCKABILLY BOB *V2 / Milkgems VVR 5006903*	59	1

Shawn COLVIN *US, female vocalist (12 WEEKS)*　pos/wks

27 Nov 93	I DON'T KNOW WHY *Columbia 6598272*	62	1
12 Feb 94	ROUND OF BLUES *Columbia 6594282*	73	1
3 Sep 94	EVERY LITTLE THING HE DOES IS MAGIC *Columbia 6607742*	65	2
7 Jan 95	ONE COOL REMOVE *Columbia 6611342* [1]	40	3
12 Aug 95	I DON'T KNOW WHY (re-issue) *Columbia 6622725*	52	1
15 Mar 97	GET OUT OF THIS HOUSE *Columbia 6638522*	70	1
30 May 98	SUNNY CAME HOME *Columbia 6648022*	29	3

[1] Shawn Colvin with Mary-Chapin Carpenter

COMETS – *See Bill HALEY and his COMETS*

COMING OUT CREW *US, male / female vocal duo (1 WEEK)*　pos/wks

18 Mar 95	FREE, GAY AND HAPPY *Out on Vinyl CDOOV 002*	50	1

COMMANDER TOM
Germany, male producer – Tom Weyer (1 WEEK)　pos/wks

23 Dec 00	EYE BEE M *Tripoli Trax TTRAX 069CD*	75	1

COMMENTATORS
UK, male impressionist – Rory Bremner (7 WEEKS)　pos/wks

22 Jun 85	N-N-NINETEEN NOT OUT *Oval 100*	13	7

COMMITMENTS
Ireland, male / female vocal / instrumental group (1 WEEK)　pos/wks

30 Nov 91	MUSTANG SALLY *MCA MCS 1598*	63	1

COMMODORES 228 Top 500
Top-notch US R&B combo: Lionel Richie (v/k), William King (t), Thomas McClary (g), Milan Williams (var), Ronald LaPread (b), Walter Orange (d). They were among the 1970s' biggest-selling groups, but lost ground when songwriter Richie went solo in 1982 (121 WEEKS)　pos/wks

24 Aug 74	MACHINE GUN *Tamla Motown TMG 902*	20	11
23 Nov 74	THE ZOO (THE HUMAN ZOO) *Tamla Motown TMG 924*	44	2
2 Jul 77 ●	EASY *Motown TMG 1073*	9	10
8 Oct 77	SWEET LOVE / BRICK HOUSE *Motown TMG 1086*	32	6
11 Mar 78	TOO HOT TA TROT / ZOOM *Motown TMG 1096*	38	4
24 Jun 78	FLYING HIGH *Motown TMG 1111*	37	7
5 Aug 78 ★	THREE TIMES A LADY *Motown TMG 1113* ▲	1	14
25 Nov 78	JUST TO BE CLOSE TO YOU *Motown TMG 1127*	62	4
25 Aug 79 ●	SAIL ON *Motown TMG 1155*	8	10
3 Nov 79 ●	STILL *Motown TMG 1166* ▲	4	11
19 Jan 80	WONDERLAND *Motown TMG 1172*	40	4
1 Aug 81	LADY (YOU BRING ME UP) *Motown TMG 1238*	56	5
21 Nov 81	OH NO *Motown TMG 1245*	44	3
26 Jan 85 ●	NIGHTSHIFT *Motown TMG 1371*	3	14
11 May 85	ANIMAL INSTINCT *Motown ZB 40097*	74	1
25 Oct 86	GOIN' TO THE BANK *Polydor POSPA 826*	43	4
13 Aug 88	EASY (re-issue) *Motown ZB 41793*	15	11

Group was US / UK for 1985 and 1986 hits

COMMON *US, male rapper – Rasheed Lynn (10 WEEKS)*　pos/wks

8 Nov 97	REMINDING ME (OF SEF) *Relativity 6560762* 1	59	1
14 Oct 00	THE LIGHT / THE 6TH SENSE *MCA MCSTD 40237*	56	1
28 Apr 01	GETO HEAVEN *MCA MCSTD 40246* 2	48	1
9 Feb 02	DANCE FOR ME *MCA MCSTD 40274* 3	13	7

1 Common featuring Chantay Savage 2 Common featuring Macy Gray 3 Mary J Blige featuring Common

COMMOTIONS – See Lloyd COLE

COMMUNARDS 470 Top 500
Controversial, melodic pop duo consisted of Bronski Beat's Jimmy Somerville (v) b. 22 Jun 1961, Glasgow, Scotland, and Richard Coles (k), b. 23 Jun 1962, Northampton, UK. Their No.1 cover marked the song's third Top 20 reading within a decade (76 WEEKS)　pos/wks

12 Oct 85	YOU ARE MY WORLD *London LON 77*	30	8
24 May 86	DISENCHANTED *London LON 89*	29	5
23 Aug 86 ★	DON'T LEAVE ME THIS WAY *London LON 103* 1	1	14
29 Nov 86 ●	SO COLD THE NIGHT *London LON 110*	8	10
21 Feb 87	YOU ARE MY WORLD (87) (re-mix) *London LON 123*	21	6
12 Sep 87	TOMORROW *London LON 143*	23	7
7 Nov 87 ●	NEVER CAN SAY GOODBYE *London LON 158*	4	11
20 Feb 88	FOR A FRIEND *London LON 166*	28	7
11 Jun 88	THERE'S MORE TO LOVE *London LON 173*	20	8

1 Communards with Sarah Jane Morris

Perry COMO 24 Top 500
One of the 20th century's most enduring entertainers, b. 18 May 1912, Pennsylvania, d. 12 May 2001. This easy-on-the-ear relaxed balladeer launched his career in 1933, collected 150 US chart entries, hosted an Emmy-winning TV series, and continued to score hits past the age of 60 (323 WEEKS)　pos/wks

16 Jan 53 ★	DON'T LET THE STARS GET IN YOUR EYES *HMV B 10400* 1 ▲1	15
4 Jun 54 ●	WANTED (re) *HMV B 10691* ▲	4	15
25 Jun 54 ●	IDLE GOSSIP *HMV B 10667*	3	15
10 Dec 54	PAPA LOVES MAMBO *HMV B 10776*	16	1
30 Dec 55	TINA MARIE *HMV POP 103*	24	1
27 Apr 56	JUKE BOX BABY *HMV POP 191*	22	6
25 May 56 ●	HOT DIGGITY (DOG ZIGGITY BOOM) *HMV POP 212*	4	13
21 Sep 56 ●	MORE (re) *HMV POP 240*	10	12
28 Sep 56	GLENDORA *HMV POP 240*	18	6
7 Feb 58 ★	MAGIC MOMENTS *RCA 1036*	1	17
7 Mar 58 ●	CATCH A FALLING STAR *RCA 1036*	9	10
9 May 58 ●	KEWPIE DOLL *RCA 1055*	9	7
30 May 58	I MAY NEVER PASS THIS WAY AGAIN *RCA 1062*	15	8
5 Sep 58	MOON TALK *RCA 1071*	17	11
7 Nov 58 ●	LOVE MAKES THE WORLD GO ROUND *RCA 1086*	6	14
21 Nov 58	MANDOLINS IN THE MOONLIGHT *RCA 1086*	13	12
27 Feb 59	TOMBOY *RCA 1111*	10	12
10 Jul 59	I KNOW *RCA 1126*	13	16
26 Feb 60 ●	DELAWARE *RCA 1170*	3	14
10 May 62	CATERINA (re) *RCA 1283*	37	6
30 Jan 71 ●	IT'S IMPOSSIBLE *RCA 2043*	4	23
15 May 71	I THINK OF YOU *RCA 2075*	14	11
21 Apr 73 ●	AND I LOVE YOU SO (re) *RCA 2346*	3	35
25 Aug 73 ●	FOR THE GOOD TIMES *RCA 2402*	7	27
8 Dec 73	WALK RIGHT BACK *RCA 2432*	33	10
25 May 74	I WANT TO GIVE *RCA LPBO 7518*	31	6

1 Perry Como with the Ramblers

LES COMPAGNONS DE LA CHANSON
France, male vocal group (3 WEEKS)　pos/wks

9 Oct 59	THE THREE BELLS (THE JIMMY BROWN SONG) (re) *Columbia DB 4358*	21	3

COMSAT ANGELS
UK, male vocal / instrumental group (2 WEEKS)　pos/wks

21 Jan 84	INDEPENDENCE DAY (re) *Jive JIVE 54*	71	2

CON FUNK SHUN
US, male vocal / instrumental group (2 WEEKS)　pos/wks

19 Jul 86	BURNIN' LOVE *Club JAB 32*	68	2

CONCEPT
US, male vocalist / instrumentalist – Eric Reed (6 WEEKS)　pos/wks

14 Dec 85	MR DJ *Fourth & Broadway BRW 40*	27	6

CONDUCTOR & THE COWBOY
UK, male production duo – Lee Hallett and Adam Pracy (2 WEEKS)　pos/wks

20 May 00	FEELING THIS WAY *Serious SERR 016CD*	35	2

CONFEDERATES – See Elvis COSTELLO

CONGREGATION
UK, male / female choir (14 WEEKS)　pos/wks

27 Nov 71 ●	SOFTLY WHISPERING I LOVE YOU *Columbia DB 8830*	4	14

CONGRESS
UK, male / female vocal / instrumental group (4 WEEKS)　pos/wks

26 Oct 91	40 MILES *Inner Rhythm 7HEART 01*	26	4

Arthur CONLEY *US, male vocalist (15 WEEKS)*　pos/wks

27 Apr 67 ●	SWEET SOUL MUSIC *Atlantic 584 083*	7	14
10 Apr 68	FUNKY STREET *Atlantic 583 175*	46	1

CONNELLS *US, male vocal / instrumental group (11 WEEKS)*　pos/wks

12 Aug 95	74–75 (re) *TVT LONCD 369*	14	11

Harry CONNICK Jr *US, male vocalist (11 WEEKS)*　pos/wks

25 May 91	RECIPE FOR LOVE / IT HAD TO BE YOU *Columbia 6568907*	32	6
3 Aug 91	WE ARE IN LOVE *Columbia 6572847*	62	2
23 Nov 91	BLUE LIGHT RED LIGHT (SOMEONE'S THERE) *Columbia 6575367*	54	3

Billy CONNOLLY
UK, male comedian / vocalist / instrumentalist (31 WEEKS)　pos/wks

1 Nov 75 ★	D.I.V.O.R.C.E. *Polydor 2058 652*	1	10

17 Jul 76	NO CHANCE (NO CHARGE) *Polydor 2058 748*	24	5
25 Aug 79	IN THE BROWNIES *Polydor 2059 160*	38	7
9 Mar 85	SUPER GRAN *Stiff BUY 218*	32	9

Sarah CONNOR featuring TQ
Germany, female vocalist and US, male rapper (5 WEEKS) pos/wks

13 Oct 01	LET'S GET BACK TO BED ...BOY *Epic 67 18662*	16	5

CONQUERING LION *UK, male vocal group (1 WEEK)* pos/wks

8 Oct 94	CODE RED *Mango CIDM 821*	53	1

Leena CONQUEST and HIP HOP FINGER
US, female vocalist and male rapper (1 WEEK) pos/wks

18 Jun 94	BOUNDARIES *Natural Response 74321208522*	67	1

Jess CONRAD *UK, male vocalist (13 WEEKS)* pos/wks

30 Jun 60	CHERRY PIE *Decca F 1123*	39	1
26 Jan 61	MYSTERY GIRL (re) *Decca F 11315*	18	10
11 Oct 62	PRETTY JENNY *Decca F 11511*	50	2

CONSORTIUM *UK, male vocal group (9 WEEKS)* pos/wks

12 Feb 69	ALL THE LOVE IN THE WORLD *Pye 7N 17635*	22	9

Ann CONSUELO – See SUBTERRANIA featuring Ann CONSUELO

CONTOURS *US, male vocal group (6 WEEKS)* pos/wks

24 Jan 70	JUST A LITTLE MISUNDERSTANDING *Tamla Motown TMG 723*	31	6

CONTRABAND
Germany / US, male / female vocal / instrumental group (2 WEEKS) pos/wks

20 Jul 91	ALL THE WAY FROM MEMPHIS *Impact American EM 195*	65	2

CONTROL
UK, male / female vocal / instrumental group (5 WEEKS) pos/wks

2 Nov 91	DANCE WITH ME (I'M YOUR ECSTASY) *All Around the World GLOBE 105*	17	5

CONVERT *Belgium, male instrumental / production duo*
– Peter Ramson and Danny Van Wauwe (7 WEEKS) pos/wks

11 Jan 92	NIGHTBIRD *A&M AM 845*	39	4
29 May 93	ROCKIN' TO THE RHYTHM *A&M 5802532*	42	2
31 Jan 98	NIGHTBIRD (re-issue) *Wonderboy WBOYD 008*	45	1

See also TRANSFORMER 2

Russ CONWAY ⟨111⟩ Top 500
Popular pianist and composer, b. Trevor Stanford, 2 Sep 1925, Bristol,
d. 16 Nov 2000. Against the trends of the day this MOR piano player was
the UK's top-selling artist in 1959 (179 WEEKS) pos/wks

29 Nov 57	PARTY POPS *Columbia DB 4031*	24	5
29 Aug 58	GOT A MATCH *Columbia DB 4166*	30	1
28 Nov 58 ●	MORE PARTY POPS *Columbia DB 4204*	10	7
23 Jan 59	THE WORLD OUTSIDE (re) *Columbia DB 4234*	24	4
20 Feb 59 ★	SIDE SADDLE *Columbia DB 4256*	1	30
15 May 59 ★	ROULETTE *Columbia DB 4298*	1	19
21 Aug 59 ●	CHINA TEA *Columbia DB 4337*	5	13
13 Nov 59 ●	SNOW COACH *Columbia DB 4368*	7	9
20 Nov 59 ●	MORE AND MORE PARTY POPS *Columbia DB 4373*	5	8
4 Mar 60	ROYAL EVENT *Columbia DB 4418*	15	8
21 Apr 60	FINGS AIN'T WOT THEY USED T'BE *Columbia DB 4422*	47	1
19 May 60	LUCKY FIVE *Columbia DB 4457*	14	9
29 Sep 60	PASSING BREEZE *Columbia DB 4508*	16	10
24 Nov 60	EVEN MORE PARTY POPS *Columbia DB 4535*	27	8
19 Jan 61	PEPE *Columbia DB 4564*	19	9
25 May 61	PABLO *Columbia DB 4649*	45	2
24 Aug 61	SAY IT WITH FLOWERS *Columbia DB 4665* [1]	23	10
30 Nov 61 ●	TOY BALLOONS *Columbia DB 4738*	7	11

22 Feb 62	LESSON ONE *Columbia DB 4784*	21	7
29 Nov 62	ALWAYS YOU AND ME (re) *Columbia DB 4934*	33	7

[1] Dorothy Squires and Russ Conway

'Always You and Me' featured Russ Conway talking as well as playing piano. Several of the discs were medleys as follows: Party Pops: When You're Smiling / I'm Looking over a Four-Leafed Clover / When You Wore a Tulip / Row Row Row / For Me and My Girl / Shine on Harvest Moon / By the Light of the Silvery Moon / Side By Side. More Party Pops: Music Music Music / If You Were the Only Girl in the World / Nobody's Sweetheart / Yes Sir That's My Baby / Some of these Days / Honeysuckle and the Bee / Hello Hello Who's Your Lady Friend / Shanty in Old Shanty Town. More and More Party Pops: Sheik of Araby / Who Were You With Last Night / Any Old Iron / Tiptoe Through the Tulips / If You Were the Only Girl in the World / When I Leave the World Behind. Even More Party Pops: Ain't She Sweet / I Can't Give You Anything But Love / Yes We Have No Bananas / I May Be Wrong / Happy Days And Lonely Nights / Glad Rag Doll

CONWAY BROTHERS *US, male vocal group (10 WEEKS)* pos/wks

22 Jun 85	TURN IT UP *10 TEN 57*	11	10

Martin COOK – See Richard DENTON and Martin COOK

Norman COOK
UK, male producer / multi-instrumentalist (10 WEEKS) pos/wks

8 Jul 89	WON'T TALK ABOUT IT / BLAME IT ON THE BASSLINE *Go.Beat GOD 33* [1]	29	6
21 Oct 89	FOR SPACIOUS LIES *Go.Beat GOD 37* [2]	48	4

[1] Norman Cook featuring Billy Bragg / Norman Cook featuring MC Wildski
[2] Norman Cook featuring Lester

See also FATBOY SLIM; FREAKPOWER; MIGHTY DUB KATZ; PIZZAMAN; BEATS INTERNATIONAL; HOUSEMARTINS

Peter COOK
UK, male comedian / vocalist d. 9 Jan 1995 (15 WEEKS) pos/wks

17 Jun 65	GOODBYE-EE *Decca F 12158* [1]	18	10
15 Jul 65	THE BALLAD OF SPOTTY MULDOON *Decca F 12182*	34	5

[1] Peter Cook and Dudley Moore

Brandon COOKE featuring Roxanne SHANTE
UK, male producer and US, female rapper (3 WEEKS) pos/wks

29 Oct 88	SHARP AS A KNIFE *Club JAB 73* [1]	45	3

[1] Brandon Cooke featuring Roxanne Shante

See also Roxanne SHANTE

Sam COOKE ⟨417⟩ Top 500
Gospel great turned soul superstar. b. 22 Jan 1931, Mississippi, US,
d. 11 Dec 1964. Former leader of the Soul Stirrers and transatlantic hitmaker.
Acclaimed singer / songwriter who influenced many R&B and pop vocalists
including Otis Redding and Rod Stewart (82 WEEKS) pos/wks

17 Jan 58	YOU SEND ME *London HLU 8506* ▲	29	1
14 Aug 59	ONLY SIXTEEN *HMV POP 642*	23	4
7 Jul 60	WONDERFUL WORLD *HMV POP 754*	27	8
29 Sep 60 ●	CHAIN GANG *RCA 1202*	9	11
27 Jul 61 ●	CUPID *RCA 1242*	7	14
8 Mar 62 ●	TWISTIN' THE NIGHT AWAY *RCA 1277*	6	14
16 May 63	ANOTHER SATURDAY NIGHT *RCA 1341*	23	12
5 Sep 63	FRANKIE AND JOHNNY *RCA 1361*	30	6
22 Mar 86 ●	WONDERFUL WORLD (re-issue) *RCA PB 49871*	2	11
10 May 86	ANOTHER SATURDAY NIGHT (re-issue) *RCA PB 49849*	75	1

COOKIE CREW *UK, female rap duo (31 WEEKS)* pos/wks

9 Jan 88 ●	ROK DA HOUSE *Rhythm King LEFT 11* [1]	5	11
7 Jan 89	BORN THIS WAY (LET'S DANCE) *ffrr FFR 19*	23	5
1 Apr 89	GOT TO KEEP ON *ffrr FFR 25*	17	9
15 Jul 89	COME AND GET SOME *ffrr F 110*	42	3
27 Jul 91	SECRETS (OF SUCCESS) *ffrr F159* [2]	53	3

[1] Beatmasters featuring the Cookie Crew [2] Cookie Crew featuring Danny D

EVERY BREATH YOU TAKE

■ Aside from writing the song that tops the list of songs Paul McCartney wishes he'd written (the magnificent 'Fields of Gold'), Gordon Sumner, alias Sting, has built an impressive song catalogue since his emergence with The Police in 1978. However, the song that probably accrues the most annual royalties for Mr Sumner is his 1983 Grammy award-winning classic 'Every Breath You Take' – not least due to the 1997 adaptation by Puff Daddy and Faith Evans as 'I'll

Be Missing You', a tribute to the murdered rap star Notorious B.I.G.

The Police, comprising Sumner, Andy Summers and Stewart Copeland, signed to A&M Records in London in 1978 and the group hit their stride in 1979, enjoying five No.1 singles and four chart-topping albums in Britain between 1979 and 1983. Featured on their fifth and final album, Synchronicity, 'Every Breath You Take' was undoubtedly the group's chart 'pièce de résistance'. Sting wrote the song on a piano once

Sting, flanked by Andy Summers (left) and Stewart Copeland (right), created the song borrowed by Puff Daddy and influenced by his wife, James Bond and Noël Coward along the way

STING WROTE THE SONG WHILE HOLIDAYING AT JAMES BOND AUTHOR IAN FLEMING'S FORMER HOME GOLDENEYE IN JAMAICA

owned by Noël Coward while holidaying at James Bond author Ian Fleming's former home Goldeneye in Jamaica. According to Sting, his most popular song came to him in the middle of the night and virtually wrote itself. He rose, went to the piano, wrote the song within 10 minutes, and returned to bed. He also wrote two other Synchronicity hits, 'King of Pain' and 'Wrapped Around Your Finger', in the same house.

While 'Every Breath You Take' might have been an easy song to write, it was far from easy to record. During sessions at George Martin's Air Studios on the Caribbean island of Montserrat, the song received a decidedly lukewarm reception. Relations between Sting and Stewart Copeland in particular were heated, to say the least. Copeland initially hated the song, but following some discussion and rearrangement, the song began to take on a life of its own and soon all the band members agreed that they'd recorded a major hit.

Based in part on the break-up of Sting's first marriage to the actress Frances Tomelty, 'Every Breath You Take' is a prime example of the old music business adage that simple songs are

often the best. As Sting himself has freely admitted, the lyrics are virtually taken "straight out of a rhyming dictionary", while the melody is about as basic as it gets.

In the middle of the song where one would normally expect an outbreak of distorted guitar there is a repetitive one-note piano solo, and with the exception of the bridge, the song meanders along in the same key. While 'Every Breath You Take' at first listen would appear to be a love song, Sting has always emphasised its ominous side, pointing out in a Rolling Stone interview: "I consider it a fairly nasty song. It's about surveillance and ownership and jealousy." Summing up his most popular work Sting says, "It's very simple, laughably simple, and at the same time it does have some kind of emotional relevance. It's kind of mysterious that way."

■ Tony Burton

* **ARTIST:** Police
* **LABEL:** A&M
* **WRITER:** Sting
* **PRODUCERS:** Hugh Padgham and The Police

COOKIES
US, female vocal group (1 WEEK) pos/wks

10 Jan 63	**CHAINS** *London HLU 9634*	**50**	1

COOL DOWN ZONE
UK, male / female vocal / instrumental group (4 WEEKS) pos/wks

30 Jun 90	**HEAVEN KNOWS** *10 TEN 309*	**52**	4

COOL JACK
Italy, male instrumental / production duo (1 WEEK) pos/wks

9 Nov 96	**JUS' COME** *AM:PM 5819892*	**44**	1

COOL NOTES
UK, male / female vocal / instrumental group (28 WEEKS) pos/wks

18 Aug 84	**YOU'RE NEVER TOO YOUNG** *Abstract Dance AD 1*	**42**	5
17 Nov 84	**I FORGOT** *Abstract Dance AD 2*	**63**	2
23 Mar 85	**SPEND THE NIGHT** *Abstract Dance AD 3*	**11**	9
13 Jul 85	**IN YOUR CAR** *Abstract Dance AD 4*	**13**	9
19 Oct 85	**HAVE A GOOD FOREVER** *Abstract Dance AD 5*	**73**	1
17 May 86	**INTO THE MOTION** *Abstract Dance AD 8*	**66**	2

COOL, the FAB, and the GROOVY present Quincy JONES
UK, male production duo, US, male band
and US, male producer / instrumentalist (1 WEEK) pos/wks

1 Aug 98	**SOUL BOSSA NOVA** *Manifesto FESCD 48* [1]	**47**	1

[1] Cool, the Fab and the Groovy present Quincy Jones

Rita COOLIDGE
US, female vocalist (24 WEEKS) pos/wks

25 Jun 77 ●	**WE'RE ALL ALONE** *A&M AMS 7295*	**6**	13
15 Oct 77	**(YOUR LOVE HAS LIFTED ME) HIGHER AND HIGHER (re)** *A&M AMS 7315*	**48**	2
4 Feb 78	**WORDS** *A&M AMS 7330*	**25**	8
25 Jun 83	**ALL TIME HIGH** *A&M AM 007*	**75**	1

COOLIO
US, male rapper – Artis Ivey Jr (62 WEEKS) pos/wks

23 Jul 94	**FANTASTIC VOYAGE** *Tommy Boy TB 0617CD*	**41**	2
15 Oct 94	**I REMEMBER** *Tommy Boy TBXCD 635*	**73**	1
28 Oct 95 ★	**GANGSTA'S PARADISE** *Tommy Boy MCSTD 2104* [1] ◆ ■ ▲ 1		20
20 Jan 96 ●	**TOO HOT** *Tommy Boy TBCD 718*	**9**	6
6 Apr 96	**1234 (SUMPIN' NEW)** *Tommy Boy TBCD 7721*	**13**	7
17 Aug 96	**IT'S ALL THE WAY LIVE (NOW)** *Tommy Boy TBCD 7731*	**34**	2
5 Apr 97 ●	**HIT EM HIGH (THE MONSTARS' ANTHEM)** *Atlantic A 5449CD* [2]	**8**	6
7 Jun 97	**THE WINNER** *Atlantic A 5433CD*	**53**	1
19 Jul 97 ●	**C U WHEN U GET THERE** *Tommy Boy TBCD 785* [3]	**3**	12
11 Oct 97	**OOH LA LA** *Tommy Boy TBCD 799*	**14**	5

[1] Coolio featuring LV [2] B Real / Busta Rhymes / Coolio / LL Cool J / Method Man
[3] Coolio featuring 40 Thevz

COOLY'S HOT BOX – *See Roger SANCHEZ*

Alice COOPER ⬭ 293 Top 500
The alter ego of shock-rock vocalist Vincent Furnier, b. 4 Feb 1948, Detroit, US. Transatlantic chart-topper whose group was voted World's Top Band in 1972 in UK. Renowned for on-stage shock-horror theatrics (104 WEEKS) pos/wks

15 Jul 72 ★	**SCHOOL'S OUT** *Warner Bros. K 16188*	**1**	12
7 Oct 72 ●	**ELECTED** *Warner Bros. K 16214*	**4**	10
10 Feb 73 ●	**HELLO HURRAY** *Warner Bros. K 16248*	**6**	12
21 Apr 73 ●	**NO MORE MR NICE GUY** *Warner Bros. K 16262*	**10**	10
19 Jan 74	**TEENAGE LAMENT '74** *Warner Bros. K 16345*	**12**	7
21 May 77	**(NO MORE) LOVE AT YOUR CONVENIENCE** *Warner Bros. K 16935*	**44**	2
23 Dec 78	**HOW YOU GONNA SEE ME NOW** *Warner Bros. K 17270*	**61**	6
6 Mar 82	**SEVEN AND SEVEN IS (live version)** *Warner Bros. K 17924*	**62**	1
8 May 82	**FOR BRITAIN ONLY / UNDER MY WHEELS** *Warner Bros. K 17940*	**66**	2
18 Oct 86	**HE'S BACK (THE MAN BEHIND THE MASK)** *MCA MCA 1090*	**61**	2
9 Apr 88	**FREEDOM** *MCA MCA 1241*	**50**	3
29 Jul 89 ●	**POISON** *Epic 655061 7*	**2**	11
7 Oct 89	**BED OF NAILS** *Epic ALICE 3*	**38**	5

2 Dec 89	**HOUSE OF FIRE** *Epic ALICE 4*	**65**	2
22 Jun 91	**HEY STOOPID** *Epic 6569837*	**21**	6
5 Oct 91	**LOVE'S A LOADED GUN** *Epic 6574387*	**38**	3
6 Jun 92	**FEED MY FRANKENSTEIN** *Epic 6580927*	**27**	3
28 May 94	**LOST IN AMERICA** *Epic 6603472*	**22**	3
23 Jul 94	**IT'S ME** *Epic 6605632*	**34**	2

For the first five hits, 'Alice Cooper' was the name of the entire group, not just of the lead vocalist

Deborah COOPER – *See C & C MUSIC FACTORY*

CO-OPERATION CHOIR – *See Peter E BENNETT with the CO-OPERATION CHOIR*

Tommy COOPER
UK, male comedian / vocalist, d. 15 Apr 1984 (3 WEEKS) pos/wks

29 Jun 61	**DON'T JUMP OFF THE ROOF DAD (re)** *Palette PG 9019*	**40**	3

COOPER TEMPLE CLAUSE
UK, male vocal / instrumental group (6 WEEKS) pos/wks

29 Sep 01	**LET'S KILL MUSIC** *Morning MORNING 9*	**41**	1
9 Feb 02	**FILM MAKER / BEEN TRAINING DOGS** *Morning MORNING 15*	**20**	3
18 May 02	**WHO NEEDS ENEMIES?** *Morning MORNING 23*	**22**	2

CO-ORDINATE – *See PESHAY*

Julian COPE
UK, male vocalist (59 WEEKS) pos/wks

19 Nov 83	**SUNSHINE PLAYROOM** *Mercury COPE 1*	**64**	1
31 Mar 84	**THE GREATNESS AND PERFECTION OF LOVE** *Mercury MER 155*	**52**	5
27 Sep 86	**WORLD SHUT YOUR MOUTH** *Island IS 290*	**19**	8
17 Jan 87	**TRAMPOLENE** *Island IS 305*	**31**	6
11 Apr 87	**EVE'S VOLCANO (COVERED IN SIN)** *Island IS 318*	**41**	5
24 Sep 88	**CHARLOTTE ANNE** *Island IS 380*	**35**	6
21 Jan 89	**5 O'CLOCK WORLD** *Island IS 399*	**42**	4
24 Jun 89	**CHINA DOLL** *Island IS 406*	**53**	2
9 Feb 91	**BEAUTIFUL LOVE** *Island IS 483*	**32**	6
20 Apr 91	**EAST EASY RIDER** *Island IS 492*	**51**	3
3 Aug 91	**HEAD** *Island IS 497*	**57**	2
8 Aug 92	**WORLD SHUT YOUR MOUTH (re-issue)** *Island IS 534*	**44**	3
17 Oct 92	**FEAR LOVES THIS PLACE** *Island IS 545*	**42**	2
12 Aug 95	**TRY TRY TRY** *Echo ECSCD 11*	**24**	3
27 Jul 96	**I COME FROM ANOTHER PLANET BABY** *Echo ECSCD 22*	**34**	2
5 Oct 96	**PLANETARY SIT-IN (EVERY GIRL HAS YOUR NAME)** *Echo ECSCD 25*	**34**	1

See also TEARDROP EXPLODES

Imani COPPOLA
US, female vocalist / instrumentalist (3 WEEKS) pos/wks

28 Feb 98	**LEGEND OF A COWGIRL** *Columbia 6656015*	**32**	3

See also BAHA MEN

The CORAL
UK, male vocal / instrumental group (7 WEEKS) pos/wks

27 Jul 02	**GOODBYE** *Deltasonic DLTCD 2005*	**21**	2
19 Oct 02	**DREAMING OF YOU** *Deltasonic DLTCD 2008*	**13**	5

Harry H CORBETT – *See Wilfrid BRAMBELL and Harry H CORBETT*

Frank CORDELL and his ORCHESTRA
UK, orchestra, leader d. 6 Jul 1980 (4 WEEKS) pos/wks

24 Aug 56	**SADIE'S SHAWL** *HMV POP 229*	**29**	2
16 Feb 61	**THE BLACK BEAR** *HMV POP 824*	**44**	2

Louise CORDET
UK, female vocalist – Louise Boisot (13 WEEKS) pos/wks

5 Jul 62	**I'M JUST A BABY** *Decca F 11476*	**13**	13

Chris CORNELL
US, male vocalist (1 WEEK) pos/wks

23 Oct 99	**CAN'T CHANGE ME** *A&M 4971732*	**62**	1

See also SOUNDGARDEN

Re-entries are listed as (re), (2re), (3re), etc which signifies that the hit re-entered the chart once, twice or three times, etc

Don CORNELL
US, male vocalist – Luigi Varlaro (23 WEEKS)   pos/wks

| 3 Sep 54 | ★ HOLD MY HAND *Vogue Q 2013* | 1 | 21 |
| 22 Apr 55 | STRANGER IN PARADISE *Vogue Q 72073* | 19 | 2 |

Lynn CORNELL
UK, female vocalist (9 WEEKS)   pos/wks

| 20 Oct 60 | NEVER ON SUNDAY *Decca F 11277* | 30 | 9 |

CORNERSHOP
UK, male vocal / instrumental duo (18 WEEKS)   pos/wks

30 Aug 97	BRIMFUL OF ASHA *Wiiija WIJ 75CD*	60	1
28 Feb 98	★ BRIMFUL OF ASHA (re-mix) *Wiiija WIJ 81CD* ■	1	12
16 May 98	SLEEP ON THE LEFT SIDE *Wiiija WIJ 80CD*	23	3
16 Mar 02	LESSONS LEARNED FROM ROCKY I TO ROCKY III *Wiiija WIJ 129CD*	37	2

Charlotte CORNWELL – See Julie COVINGTON, Rula LENSKA, Charlotte CORNWELL and Sue JONES-DAVIES

Hugh CORNWELL
UK, male vocalist / instrumentalist – guitar (3 WEEKS)   pos/wks

| 24 Jan 87 | FACTS + FIGURES *Virgin VS 922* | 61 | 2 |
| 7 May 88 | ANOTHER KIND OF LOVE *Virgin VS 945* | 71 | 1 |

See also STRANGLERS

CO-RO featuring TARLISA
Germany, male / female vocal / production group (1 WEEK)   pos/wks

| 12 Dec 92 | BECAUSE THE NIGHT *ZYX ZYX 68227* | 61 | 1 |

CORONA
Brazil, male producer and female vocalist – Francesco Bontempi and Olga de Souza (44 WEEKS)   pos/wks

10 Sep 94	● THE RHYTHM OF THE NIGHT (re) *WEA YZ 837CD1*	2	18
8 Apr 95	● BABY BABY *Eternal YZ 919CD*	5	8
22 Jul 95	● TRY ME OUT *Eternal YZ 955CD*	6	10
23 Dec 95	I DON'T WANNA BE A STAR *Eternal WEA 029CD*	22	6
22 Feb 97	MEGAMIX *Eternal WEA 092CD*	36	2

CORONATION STREET CAST featuring Bill WADDINGTON
UK, male / female actors / vocal group (3 WEEKS)   pos/wks

| 16 Dec 95 | ALWAYS LOOK ON THE BRIGHT SIDE OF LIFE *EMI Premier CDEMS 411* | 35 | 3 |

The listed flip side of 'Always Look on the Bright Side of Life' was 'Something Stupid' by Amanda Barrie and Johnny Briggs

CORONETS
UK, male / female vocal group (7 WEEKS)   pos/wks

| 26 Aug 55 | THAT'S HOW A LOVE SONG WAS BORN *Columbia DB 3640* [1] | 14 | 6 |
| 25 Nov 55 | TWENTY TINY FINGERS *Columbia DB 3671* | 20 | 1 |

[1] Ray Burns with the Coronets

Briana CORRIGAN
UK, female vocalist (2 WEEKS)   pos/wks

| 11 May 96 | LOVE ME NOW *East West EW 041CD1* | 48 | 2 |

See also BEAUTIFUL SOUTH

CORRS (344) Top 500
Internationally successful Irish sisters and brother group: Andrea, Caroline, Sharon and Jim Corr. Quartet, which has sold more than five million albums in the UK, was voted Best International Group at 1999 Brits. 'Talk on Corners' was the top UK album in 1998 (92 WEEKS)   pos/wks

17 Feb 96	RUNAWAY (re) *Atlantic A 5727CD*	49	3
1 Feb 97	LOVE TO LOVE YOU / RUNAWAY (re-issue) *Atlantic A 5621CD*	62	1
25 Oct 97	ONLY WHEN I SLEEP *Atlantic AT 0015CD*	58	1
20 Dec 97	I NEVER LOVED YOU ANYWAY *Atlantic AT 0018CD*	43	2
28 Mar 98	WHAT CAN I DO *Atlantic AT 0029CD*	53	1
16 May 98	● DREAMS *Atlantic AT 0032CD*	6	10
29 Aug 98	● WHAT CAN I DO (re-mix) *Atlantic AT 0044CD*	3	11
28 Nov 98	● SO YOUNG *Atlantic AT 0057CD1*	6	13
27 Feb 99	● RUNAWAY (re-mix) *Atlantic AT 0062CD*	2	11

12 Jun 99	I KNOW MY LOVE *RCA Victor 74321670622* [1]	37	3
11 Dec 99	RADIO *Atlantic AT 0079CD*	18	9
15 Jul 00	★ BREATHLESS *Atlantic AT 0084CD* ■	1	13
11 Nov 00	IRRESISTIBLE *Atlantic AT 0089CD*	20	7
28 Apr 01	GIVE ME A REASON *Atlantic AT 0097CD*	27	2
10 Nov 01	WOULD YOU BE HAPPIER? *Atlantic AT 0115CD*	14	5

[1] Chieftains featuring The Corrs

CORRUPTED CRU featuring MC NEAT
UK, male rap / production duo – Scott Garcia and Michael Wood and male rapper (1 WEEK)   pos/wks

| 2 Mar 02 | G.A.R.A.G.E. *Red Rose CDRROSE 011* | 59 | 1 |

See also Scott GARCIA featuring MC STYLES

Ferry CORSTEN
Holland, male producer (3 WEEKS)   pos/wks

| 8 Jun 02 | PUNK *Positiva CDTIV 173* | 29 | 3 |

See also GOURYELLA; SYSTEM F; VERACOCHA; MOONMAN; ALBION; STARPARTY

CORTINA
UK, male producer – Ben Keen (3 WEEKS)   pos/wks

| 24 Mar 01 | MUSIC IS MOVING *Nukleuz NUKC 0159* | 42 | 2 |
| 26 Jan 02 | ERECTION (TAKE IT TO THE TOP) *Nukleuz NUKC 0352* [1] | 48 | 1 |

[1] Cortina featuring BK and Madam Friction

See also BK

Vladimir COSMA
Hungary, orchestra (1 WEEK)   pos/wks

| 14 Jul 79 | DAVID'S SONG (MAIN THEME FROM 'KIDNAPPED') *Decca FR 13841* | 64 | 1 |

COSMIC BABY
Germany, male producer (1 WEEK)   pos/wks

| 26 Feb 94 | LOOPS OF INFINITY *Logic 74321191432* | 70 | 1 |

COSMIC GATE
Germany, male production trio (10 WEEKS)   pos/wks

| 4 Aug 01 | ● FIRE WIRE *Data DATA 24 CDS* | 9 | 7 |
| 11 May 02 | EXPLORATION OF SPACE *Data DATA 30 CDS* | 29 | 3 |

COSMIC ROUGH RIDERS
UK, male vocal / instrumental group (2 WEEKS)   pos/wks

| 4 Aug 01 | REVOLUTION (IN THE SUMMERTIME) *Poptones MC 5047SCD* | 35 | 1 |
| 29 Sep 01 | THE PAIN INSIDE *Poptones MC 5052SCD* | 36 | 1 |

COSMOS
UK, male producer / instrumentalist – Tom Middleton (3 WEEKS)   pos/wks

| 18 Sep 99 | SUMMER IN SPACE *Island Blue PFACD 3* | 49 | 1 |
| 5 Oct 02 | TAKE ME WITH YOU *Polydor 659952* | 32 | 2 |

See also GLOBAL COMMUNICATION

Don COSTA
US, orchestra, leader d. 19 Jan 1983 (10 WEEKS)   pos/wks

| 13 Oct 60 | NEVER ON SUNDAY (re) *London HLT 9195* | 27 | 10 |

Nikka COSTA
US, female vocalist (1 WEEK)   pos/wks

| 11 Aug 01 | LIKE A FEATHER *Virgin VUSCD 199* | 53 | 1 |

Elvis COSTELLO (109) Top 500
Acclaimed singer / songwriter, b. Declan McManus, 25 Aug 1955, Liverpool, UK. He emerged during the punk explosion of 1976, but was soon accepted as a mainstream artist. Has clocked up 13 US Top 40 albums (180 WEEKS)   pos/wks

5 Nov 77	WATCHING THE DETECTIVES *Stiff BUY 20*	15	11
11 Mar 78	(I DON'T WANT TO GO TO) CHELSEA *Radar ADA 3* [1]	16	10
13 May 78	PUMP IT UP *Radar ADA 10* [1]	24	10
28 Oct 78	RADIO RADIO *Radar ADA 24* [1]	29	7
10 Feb 79	● OLIVER'S ARMY *Radar ADA 31* [1]	2	12
12 May 79	ACCIDENTS WILL HAPPEN *Radar ADA 35* [1]	28	8
16 Feb 80	I CAN'T STAND UP FOR FALLING DOWN *F. Beat XX 1* [1]	4	8
12 Apr 80	HIGH FIDELITY *F. Beat XX 3*	30	5
7 Jun 80	NEW AMSTERDAM *F. Beat XX 5*	36	6

Date	Title / Label	pos	wks
20 Dec 80	CLUBLAND *F. Beat XX 12* [1]	60	4
3 Oct 81	● A GOOD YEAR FOR THE ROSES *F. Beat XX 17*	6	11
12 Dec 81	SWEET DREAMS *F. Beat XX 19*	42	8
10 Apr 82	I'M YOUR TOY *F. Beat XX 21* [2]	51	3
19 Jun 82	YOU LITTLE FOOL *F. Beat XX 26*	52	3
31 Jul 82	MAN OUT OF TIME *F. Beat XX 28*	58	2
25 Sep 82	FROM HEAD TO TOE *F. Beat XX 30*	43	4
11 Dec 82	PARTY PARTY *A&M AMS 8267* [3]	48	6
11 Jun 83	PILLS AND SOAP *Imp IMP 001* [4]	16	4
9 Jul 83	EVERYDAY I WRITE THE BOOK *F. Beat XX 32*	28	8
17 Sep 83	LET THEM ALL TALK *F. Beat XX 33*	59	2
28 Apr 84	PEACE IN OUR TIME *Imposter TRUCE 1* [4]	48	3
16 Jun 84	I WANNA BE LOVED / TURNING THE TOWN RED *F. Beat XX 35*	25	6
25 Aug 84	THE ONLY FLAME IN TOWN *F. Beat XX 37*	71	2
4 May 85	GREEN SHIRT (re) *F. Beat ZB 40085*	68	2
1 Feb 86	DON'T LET ME BE MISUNDERSTOOD *F. Beat ZB 40555* [5]	33	4
30 Aug 86	TOKYO STORM WARNING *Imp IMP 007*	73	1
4 Mar 89	VERONICA *Warner Bros. W 7558*	31	6
20 May 89	BABY PLAYS AROUND (EP) *Warner Bros. W 2949*	65	1
4 May 91	THE OTHER SIDE OF SUMMER *Warner Bros. W 0025*	43	4
5 Mar 94	SULKY GIRL *Warner Bros. W 0234CD* [1]	22	3
30 Apr 94	13 STEPS LEAD DOWN *Warner Bros. W 0245CD* [1]	59	1
26 Nov 94	LONDON'S BRILLIANT PARADE *Warner Bros. W 0270CD1* [1]	48	2
11 May 96	IT'S TIME *Warner Bros. W 0348CD* [1]	58	1
1 May 99	TOLEDO *Mercury 8709652* [6]	72	1
31 Jul 99	SHE (re) *Mercury MERCD 521*	19	10
20 Apr 02	TEAR OFF YOUR OWN HEAD (IT'S A DOLL REVOLUTION) *Mercury 5828872*	58	1

[1] Elvis Costello and the Attractions [2] Elvis Costello and the Attractions with the Royal Philharmonic Orchestra [3] Elvis Costello and the Attractions with the Royal Horn Guards [4] Imposter [5] The Costello Show featuring the Confederates [6] Elvis Costello / Burt Bacharach

Tracks on Baby Plays Around (EP): Baby Plays Around / Poisoned Rose / Almost Blue / My Funny Valentine

COTTAGERS – See Tony REES and the COTTAGERS

Billy COTTON and His BAND
UK, male bandleader / vocalist (d. 25 Mar 1969), with band and chorus (25 WEEKS) pos/wks

Date	Title / Label	pos	wks
1 May 53	● IN A GOLDEN COACH (THERE'S A HEART OF GOLD) *Decca F 10058* [1]	3	10
18 Dec 53	I SAW MOMMY KISSING SANTA CLAUS *Decca F 10206* [2]	11	3
30 Apr 54	● FRIENDS AND NEIGHBOURS (re) *Decca F 10299* [3]	3	12

[1] Billy Cotton and His Band, vocals by Doreen Stephens [2] Billy Cotton and His Band, vocals by the Mill Girls and the Bandits [3] Billy Cotton and His Band, vocals by the Bandits

Mike COTTON'S JAZZMEN
UK, male instrumental band – Mike Cotton – trumpet (4 WEEKS) pos/wks

Date	Title / Label	pos	wks
20 Jun 63	SWING THAT HAMMER *Columbia DB 7029*	36	4

John COUGAR – See John Cougar MELLENCAMP

COUGARS
UK, male instrumental group (8 WEEKS) pos/wks

Date	Title / Label	pos	wks
28 Feb 63	SATURDAY NITE AT THE DUCK-POND *Parlophone R 4989*	33	8

COUNCIL COLLECTIVE
UK / US, male / female vocal / instrumental group (6 WEEKS) pos/wks

Date	Title / Label	pos	wks
22 Dec 84	SOUL DEEP (PART 1) *Polydor MINE 1*	24	6

COUNT INDIGO
UK, male vocalist (1 WEEK) pos/wks

Date	Title / Label	pos	wks
9 Mar 96	MY UNKNOWN LOVE *Cowboy RODEO 952CD*	59	1

COUNTING CROWS
US, male vocal / instrumental group (13 WEEKS) pos/wks

Date	Title / Label	pos	wks
30 Apr 94	MR JONES *Geffen GFSTD 69*	28	2
9 Jul 94	ROUND HERE *Geffen GFSTD 74*	70	1
15 Oct 94	RAIN KING *Geffen GFSTD 82*	49	3

Date	Title / Label	pos	wks
19 Oct 96	ANGELS OF THE SILENCES *Geffen GFSTD 22182*	41	1
14 Dec 96	A LONG DECEMBER (re) *Geffen GFSTD 22190*	62	2
31 May 97	DAYLIGHT FADING *Geffen GFSTD 22247*	54	1
30 Oct 99	HANGINAROUND *Geffen 4971842*	46	1
29 Jun 02	AMERICAN GIRLS *Geffen 4977402*	33	2

COUNTRYMEN
UK, male vocal group (2 WEEKS) pos/wks

Date	Title / Label	pos	wks
3 May 62	I KNOW WHERE I'M GOING *Piccadilly 7N 35029*	45	2

COURSE
Holland, male / female vocal / DJ / production group (15 WEEKS) pos/wks

Date	Title / Label	pos	wks
19 Apr 97	● READY OR NOT *The Brothers Organisation CDBRUV 2*	5	7
5 Jul 97	● AIN'T NOBODY *The Brothers Organisation CDBRUV 3*	8	6
20 Dec 97	BEST LOVE *The Brothers Organisation CDBRUV 6*	51	2

Michael COURTNEY – See LINCOLN CITY FC featuring Michael COURTNEY

Tina COUSINS
UK, female vocalist (42 WEEKS) pos/wks

Date	Title / Label	pos	wks
15 Aug 98	● MYSTERIOUS TIMES *Multiply CDMULTY 40* [1]	2	12
21 Nov 98	PRAY *Jive 0519162*	20	3
27 Mar 99	KILLIN' TIME *Jive / Eastern Bloc 0519232*	15	4
10 Apr 99	● THANK ABBA FOR THE MUSIC *ABCD 1 Epic* [2]	4	13
10 Jul 99	FOREVER *Jive 0519332*	45	1
9 Oct 99	ANGEL *Ebul / Jive 0519432*	46	1
22 Apr 00	● JUST AROUND THE HILL *Multiply CDMULTY 62* [1]	8	7

[1] Sash! featuring Tina Cousins [2] Starring Steps, Tina Cousins, Cleopatra, B*Witched, Billie

Don COVAY
US, male vocalist (6 WEEKS) pos/wks

Date	Title / Label	pos	wks
7 Sep 74	IT'S BETTER TO HAVE (AND DON'T NEED) *Mercury 6052 634*	29	6

Vincent COVELLO – See BT

COVENTRY CITY CUP FINAL SQUAD
UK, male football team vocalists (2 WEEKS) pos/wks

Date	Title / Label	pos	wks
23 May 87	GO FOR IT! *Sky Blue SKB 1*	61	2

COVER GIRLS
US, female vocal group (4 WEEKS) pos/wks

Date	Title / Label	pos	wks
1 Aug 92	WISHING ON A STAR *Epic 6581437*	38	4

David COVERDALE and WHITESNAKE
UK, male vocalist and UK, male vocal / instrumental group (1 WEEK) pos/wks

Date	Title / Label	pos	wks
7 Jun 97	TOO MANY TEARS *EMI CDEM 471*	46	1

See also COVERDALE PAGE; WHITESNAKE; DEEP PURPLE

COVERDALE PAGE
UK, male vocal / instrumental duo – David Coverdale and Jimmy Page (3 WEEKS) pos/wks

Date	Title / Label	pos	wks
3 Jul 93	TAKE ME FOR A LITTLE WHILE *EMI CDEM 270*	29	2
23 Oct 93	TAKE A LOOK AT YOURSELF *EMI CDEM 279*	43	1

Julie COVINGTON
UK, female actor / vocalist (29 WEEKS) pos/wks

Date	Title / Label	pos	wks
25 Dec 76	★ DON'T CRY FOR ME ARGENTINA (re) *MCA 260*	1	18
3 Dec 77	ONLY WOMEN BLEED *Virgin VS 196*	12	11

See also Julie COVINGTON, Rula LENSKA, Charlotte CORNWELL and Sue JONES-DAVIES

Julie COVINGTON, Rula LENSKA, Charlotte CORNWELL and Sue JONES-DAVIES
UK, female actors / vocal group (6 WEEKS) pos/wks

Date	Title / Label	pos	wks
21 May 77	● OK? *Polydor 2001 714*	10	6

See also Julie COVINGTON

Warren COVINGTON – See Tommy DORSEY ORCHESTRA starring Warren COVINGTON

Patrick COWLEY – See SYLVESTER

Re-entries are listed as (re), (2re), (3re), etc which signifies that the hit re-entered the chart once, twice or three times, etc

Carl COX UK, male producer (19 WEEKS)

		pos/wks	
28 Sep 91	I WANT YOU (FOREVER) Perfecto PB 44885 [1]	23	7
8 Aug 92	DOES IT FEEL GOOD TO YOU Perfecto PB 74321102877 [1]	35	3
6 Nov 93	THE PLANET OF LOVE Perfecto 74321161772	44	2
9 Mar 96	TWO PAINTINGS AND A DRUM (EP) Edel 0090715COX	24	2
8 Jun 96	SENSUAL SOPHIS-TI-CAT / THE PLAYER Ultimatum 0090875COX	25	2
12 Dec 98	THE LATIN THEME Edel 0091685 COX	52	1
22 May 99	PHUTURE 2000 Worldwide Ultimatum / Edel 0091715 COX	40	2

[1] DJ Carl Cox

Tracks on Two Paintings and a Drum (EP): Phoebus Apollo / Yum Yum / Siberian Snow Storm

Deborah COX Canada, female vocalist (8 WEEKS)

		pos/wks	
11 Nov 95	SENTIMENTAL Arista 74321324962	34	3
24 Feb 96	WHO DO U LOVE Arista 74321337942	31	3
31 Jul 99	IT'S OVER NOW Arista 74321686942	49	1
9 Oct 99	NOBODY'S SUPPOSED TO BE HERE Arista 74321702102	55	1

Michael COX UK, male vocalist (15 WEEKS)

		pos/wks	
9 Jun 60 ●	ANGELA JONES Triumph RGM 1011	7	13
20 Oct 60	ALONG CAME CAROLINE HMV POP 789	41	2

Peter COX UK, male vocalist (6 WEEKS)

		pos/wks	
2 Aug 97	AIN'T GONNA CRY AGAIN Chrysalis CDCHS 5056	37	2
15 Nov 97	IF YOU WALK AWAY Chrysalis CDCHSS 5069	24	2
20 Jun 98	WHAT A FOOL BELIEVES Chrysalis CDCHS 5089	39	2

See also GO WEST

CRACKER US, male vocal / instrumental group (9 WEEKS)

		pos/wks	
28 May 94	LOW (re) Virgin America VUSDG 80	43	6
23 Jul 94	GET OFF THIS Virgin America VUSCD 83	41	3

Sarah CRACKNELL UK, female vocalist (1 WEEK)

		pos/wks	
14 Sep 96	ANYMORE Gut CDGUT 3	39	1

See also SAINT ETIENNE

CRACKOUT UK, male vocal / instrumental group (1 WEEK)

		pos/wks	
22 Jun 02	I AM THE ONE Hut / Virgin HUTCD 156	72	1

STEVE CRADOCK – See OCEAN COLOUR SCENE; BUFFALO TOM

CRAIG UK, male vocalist – Craig Phillips (6 WEEKS)

		pos/wks	
23 Dec 00	AT THIS TIME OF YEAR (re) WEA WEA 321CD	14	6

Robbie CRAIG – See ARTFUL DODGER

Floyd CRAMER
US, male instrumentalist – piano d. 31 Dec 1997 (24 WEEKS)

		pos/wks	
13 Apr 61 ★	ON THE REBOUND RCA 1231	1	14
20 Jul 61	SAN ANTONIO ROSE RCA 1241	36	8
23 Aug 62	HOT PEPPER RCA 1301	46	2

CRAMPS US, male / female vocal / instrumental group (4 WEEKS)

		pos/wks	
9 Nov 85	CAN YOUR PUSSY DO THE DOG? Big Beat NS 110	68	1
10 Feb 90	BIKINI GIRLS WITH MACHINE GUNS Enigma ENV 17	35	3

CRANBERRIES
Ireland, female / male vocal / instrumental group (50 WEEKS)

		pos/wks	
27 Feb 93	LINGER Island CID 556	74	1
12 Feb 94	LINGER (re-issue) Island CID 559	14	11
7 May 94	DREAMS Island CIDX 594	27	5
1 Oct 94	ZOMBIE Island CID 600	14	6
3 Dec 94	ODE TO MY FAMILY Island CIDX 601	26	6
11 Mar 95	I CAN'T BE WITH YOU Island CID 605	23	5
12 Aug 95	RIDICULOUS THOUGHTS Island CID 616	20	3

20 Apr 96	SALVATION Island CID 633	13	5
13 Jul 96	FREE TO DECIDE Island CID 637	33	3
17 Apr 99	PROMISES Island US / Mercury 5725912	13	4
17 Jul 99	ANIMAL INSTINCT Island US / Mercury 5621972	54	1

Les CRANE US, male vocalist (14 WEEKS)

		pos/wks	
19 Feb 72 ●	DESIDERATA Warner Bros. K 16119	7	14

Whitfield CRANE – See ICE-T; MOTORHEAD

CRANES UK, male / female vocal / instrumental group (2 WEEKS)

		pos/wks	
25 Sep 93	JEWEL Dedicated CRANE 007CD	29	1
3 Sep 94	SHINING ROAD Dedicated CRANE 008CD1	57	1

CRASH TEST DUMMIES
Canada, male / female vocal / instrumental group (20 WEEKS)

		pos/wks	
23 Apr 94 ●	MMM MMM MMM MMM RCA 74321201512	2	11
16 Jul 94	AFTERNOONS & COFFEESPOONS RCA 74321219622	23	5
15 Apr 95	THE BALLAD OF PETER PUMPKINHEAD RCA 74321276772 [1]	30	4

[1] Crash Test Dummies featuring Ellen Reid

Beverley CRAVEN UK, female vocalist (33 WEEKS)

		pos/wks	
20 Apr 91 ●	PROMISE ME Epic 6559437	3	13
20 Jul 91	HOLDING ON Epic 6565507	32	7
5 Oct 91	WOMAN TO WOMAN Epic 6574647	40	5
7 Dec 91	MEMORIES Epic 6576617	68	2
25 Sep 93	LOVE SCENES Epic 6595952	34	4
20 Nov 93	MOLLIE'S SONG Epic 6598132	61	2

Billy CRAWFORD US, male vocalist (2 WEEKS)

		pos/wks	
10 Oct 98	URGENTLY IN LOVE V2 VVR 5003063	48	2

Jimmy CRAWFORD UK, male vocalist - Ronald Lindsey (11 WKS)

		pos/wks	
8 Jun 61	LOVE OR MONEY Columbia DB 4633	49	1
16 Nov 61	I LOVE HOW YOU LOVE ME Columbia DB 4717	18	10

Michael CRAWFORD
UK, male actor / vocalist – Michael Dumble-Smith (14 WEEKS)

		pos/wks	
10 Jan 87 ●	THE MUSIC OF THE NIGHT Polydor POSP 803 [1]	7	11
15 Jan 94	THE MUSIC OF THE NIGHT Columbia 6597382 [2]	54	3

[1] Michael Crawford with the Royal Philharmonic Orchestra, conducted by David Caddick [2] Barbra Streisand (duet with Michael Crawford)

The flip side of POSP 803 – 'Wishing You Were Somehow Here Again' by Sarah Brightman – was also listed

Randy CRAWFORD (481 Top 500) Soulful jazz-slanted song stylist, b. 18 Feb 1952, Georgia, US. Has surprisingly proved more successful in Europe than her homeland, where she has yet to crack the pop Top 100. Winner of Brits Best Female Artist award in 1982 (75 WEEKS)

		pos/wks	
21 Jun 80	LAST NIGHT AT DANCELAND Warner Bros. K 17631	61	2
30 Aug 80	ONE DAY I'LL FLY AWAY Warner Bros. K 17680	2	11
30 May 81	YOU MIGHT NEED SOMEBODY Warner Bros. K 17803	11	13
8 Aug 81	RAINY NIGHT IN GEORGIA Warner Bros. K 17840	18	9
31 Oct 81	SECRET COMBINATION Warner Bros. K 17872	48	3
30 Jan 82	IMAGINE (re) Warner Bros. K 17906	60	2
5 Jun 82	ONE HELLO Warner Bros. K 17948	48	4
19 Feb 83	HE REMINDS ME Warner Bros. K 17970	65	2
8 Oct 83	NIGHT LINE Warner Bros. W 9530	51	4
29 Nov 86 ●	ALMAZ Warner Bros. W 8583	4	17
18 Jan 92	DIAMANTE London LON 313 [1]	44	7
15 Nov 97	GIVE ME THE NIGHT WEA WEA 142CD	60	1

[1] Zucchero with Randy Crawford

See also CRUSADERS

Robert CRAY BAND US, male vocal / instrumental group (5 WKS)

		pos/wks	
20 Jun 87	RIGHT NEXT DOOR (BECAUSE OF ME) Mercury CRAY 3	50	4

| 20 Apr 96 | | BABY LEE *Silvertone ORECD 81* [1] | .....65 | 1 |

[1] John Lee Hooker with Robert Cray

CRAZY ELEPHANT *US, male vocal group (13 WEEKS)*
			pos/wks
21 May 69		GIMME GIMME GOOD LOVIN' *Major Minor MM 609*	.....12 13

CRAZY TOWN
US, male vocal / rap / instrumental group (19 WEEKS) — pos/wks
7 Apr 01	●	BUTTERFLY *Columbia 6710012* ▲	3	13
11 Aug 01		REVOLVING DOOR *Columbia 6714942*	23	5
30 Nov 02		DROWNING *Columbia 6733262*	50	1

CRAZYHEAD *UK, male vocal / instrumental group (4 WEEKS)* — pos/wks
16 Jul 88		TIME HAS TAKEN ITS TOLL ON YOU *Food FOOD 12*	65	2
25 Feb 89		HAVE LOVE, WILL TRAVEL (EP) *Food SGE 2025*	68	2

Tracks on Have Love, Will Travel (EP): Have Love Will Travel / Out on a Limb (Live) / Baby Turpentine (Live) / Snake Eyes (Live)

CREAM *UK, male vocal / instrumental group (59 WEEKS)* — pos/wks
20 Oct 66		WRAPPING PAPER *Reaction 591 007*	34	6
15 Dec 66		I FEEL FREE *Reaction 591 011*	11	12
8 Jun 67		STRANGE BREW *Reaction 591 015*	17	9
5 Jun 68		ANYONE FOR TENNIS (THE SAVAGE SEVEN THEME) *Polydor 56 258*	40	3
9 Oct 68		SUNSHINE OF YOUR LOVE *Polydor 56 286*	25	7
15 Jan 69		WHITE ROOM *Polydor 56 300*	28	8
9 Apr 69		BADGE *Polydor 56 315*	18	10
28 Oct 72		BADGE (re-issue) *Polydor 2058 285*	42	4

See also Eric CLAPTON

CREATION *UK, male vocal / instrumental group (3 WEEKS)* — pos/wks
7 Jul 66		MAKING TIME *Planet PLF 116*	49	1
3 Nov 66		PAINTER MAN *Planet PLF 119*	36	2

CREATURES
UK, male / female vocal / instrumental group (27 WEEKS) — pos/wks
3 Oct 81		MAD EYED SCREAMER *Polydor POSPD 354*	24	7
23 Apr 83		MISS THE GIRL *Wonderland SHE 1*	21	7
16 Jul 83		RIGHT NOW *Wonderland SHE 2*	14	10
14 Oct 89		STANDING THERE *Wonderland SHE 17*	53	2
27 Mar 99		SAY *Sioux SIOUX 6CD*	72	1

See also SIOUXSIE and the BANSHEES

CREDIT TO THE NATION *UK, male rap group (11 WEEKS)* — pos/wks
22 May 93		CALL IT WHAT YOU WANT *One Little Indian 94 TP7CD*	57	3
18 Sep 93		ENOUGH IS ENOUGH *One Little Indian 79 TP7CD* [1]	56	2
12 Mar 94		TEENAGE SENSATION *One Little Indian 124 TP7CD*	24	3
14 May 94		SOWING THE SEEDS OF HATRED *One Little Indian 134 TP7CD*	72	1
22 Jul 95		LIAR LIAR *One Little Indian 144 TP7CD*	60	1
12 Sep 98		TACKY LOVE SONG *Chrysalis CDCHS 5097*	60	1

[1] Chumbawamba and Credit to the Nation

CREED *US, male vocal / instrumental group (13 WEEKS)* — pos/wks
15 Jan 00		HIGHER *Epic 6683152*	47	1
20 Jan 01		WITH ARMS WIDE OPEN *Epic 6706952* ▲	13	5
29 Sep 01		HIGHER (re-issue) *Epic 6710642*	64	1
16 Mar 02		MY SACRIFICE *Epic 6723162*	18	5
3 Aug 02		ONE LAST BREATH / BULLETS *Epic 6728262*	47	1

CREEDENCE CLEARWATER REVIVAL `332` `Top 500`
Internationally successful combo which cleverly created original songs with 50s rock 'n' roll feel, fronted by John Fogerty b. 28 May 1945, California, US. Voted World's Top Group in UK Polls 1970/71 (beating The Beatles and The Rolling Stones) (94 WEEKS) — pos/wks
28 May 69	●	PROUD MARY *Liberty LBF 15223*	8	13

16 Aug 69	★	BAD MOON RISING *Liberty LBF 15230*	1	15
15 Nov 69		GREEN RIVER *Liberty LBF 15250*	19	11
14 Feb 70		DOWN ON THE CORNER *Liberty LBF 15283*	31	6
4 Apr 70	●	TRAVELLIN' BAND (re) *Liberty LBF 15310*	8	13
20 Jun 70		UP AROUND THE BEND *Liberty LBF 15354*	3	12
5 Sep 70		LONG AS I CAN SEE THE LIGHT *Liberty LBF 15384*	20	9
20 Mar 71		HAVE YOU EVER SEEN THE RAIN *Liberty LBF 15440*	36	6
24 Jul 71		SWEET HITCH-HIKER *United Artists UP 35261*	36	8
2 May 92		BAD MOON RISING (re-issue) *Epic 6580047*	71	1

Kid CREOLE and the COCONUTS
US, male vocalist and female vocal group (58 WEEKS) — pos/wks
13 Jun 81		ME NO POP I *Ze WIP 6711* [1]	32	7
15 May 82	●	I'M A WONDERFUL THING, BABY *Ze WIP 6756*	4	11
24 Jul 82	●	STOOL PIGEON *Ze WIP 6793*	7	9
9 Oct 82	●	ANNIE I'M NOT YOUR DADDY *Ze WIP 6801*	2	8
11 Dec 82		DEAR ADDY *Ze WIP 6840*	29	7
10 Sep 83		THERE'S SOMETHING WRONG IN PARADISE *Island IS 130*	35	5
19 Nov 83		THE LIFEBOAT PARTY *Island IS 142*	49	4
14 Apr 90		THE SEX OF IT *CBS 655698 7*	29	5
10 Apr 93		I'M A WONDERFUL THING BABY (re-mix) *Island CID 551*	60	2

[1] Kid Creole and the Coconuts present Coati Mundi

See also COCONUTS

CRESCENDO *UK / US, male / female vocal / instrumental duo – Serena and Steve Hitchcock (5 WEEKS)* — pos/wks
23 Dec 95		ARE YOU OUT THERE *ffrr FCD 270*	20	5

CRESCENT *UK, male vocal / instrumental group (3 WEEKS)* — pos/wks
18 May 02		ON THE RUN *Hut / Virgin HUTCD 153*	49	1
27 Jul 02		TEST OF TIME *Hut / Virgin HUTCD 157*	60	1
28 Sep 02		SPINNIN' WHEELS *Hut / Virgin HUTCD 160*	61	1

CRESTERS – See Mike SAGAR and the CRESTERS

CREW CUTS *Canada, male vocal group (29 WEEKS)* — pos/wks
1 Oct 54		SH-BOOM *Mercury MB 3140* ▲	12	9
15 Apr 55	●	EARTH ANGEL *Mercury MB 3202*	4	20

Bernard CRIBBINS *UK, male actor / vocalist (29 WEEKS)* — pos/wks
15 Feb 62	●	HOLE IN THE GROUND *Parlophone R 4869*	9	13
5 Jul 62	●	RIGHT, SAID FRED *Parlophone R 4923*	10	10
13 Dec 62		GOSSIP CALYPSO *Parlophone R 4961*	25	6

CRICKETS `322` `Top 500`
Band that originally featured Buddy Holly formed in Lubbock, Texas, US, best known members being Jerry Allison (d), Joe B Mauldin (b) and Sonny Curtis (g/v). Without Holly they recorded original versions of Top 10 hits 'I Fought the Law', 'Someone Someone', 'When You Ask About Love' and 'More Than I Can Say' (97 WEEKS) — pos/wks
27 Sep 57	★	THAT'LL BE THE DAY (re) *Vogue Coral Q 72279* ▲	1	15
27 Dec 57	●	OH BOY *Coral Q 72298*	3	15
14 Mar 58	●	MAYBE BABY *Coral Q 72307*	4	10
25 Jul 58		THINK IT OVER *Coral Q 72329*	11	7
24 Apr 59		LOVE'S MADE A FOOL OF YOU (re) *Coral Q 72365*	26	2
15 Jan 60		WHEN YOU ASK ABOUT LOVE *Coral Q 72382*	27	1
12 May 60		MORE THAN I CAN SAY *Coral Q 72395*	42	1
26 May 60		BABY MY HEART *Coral Q 72395*	33	4
21 Jun 62	●	DON'T EVER CHANGE *Liberty LIB 55441*	5	15
24 Jan 63		MY LITTLE GIRL *Liberty LIB 10067*	17	9
6 Jun 63		DON'T TRY TO CHANGE ME *Liberty LIB 10092*	37	4
14 May 64		YOU'VE GOT LOVE *Coral Q 72472* [1]	40	6
2 Jul 64		(THEY CALL HER) LA BAMBA *Liberty LIB 55696*	21	10

[1] Buddy Holly and the Crickets

Although not credited on the records, Buddy Holly was featured on the first four hits

CRIMINAL ELEMENT ORCHESTRA – See Wally JUMP Jr and the CRIMINAL ELEMENT

CRISPY AND COMPANY
US, male vocal / instrumental group (11 WEEKS)   pos/wks

16 Aug 75	**BRAZIL** *Creole CR 109*	26	5
27 Dec 75	**GET IT TOGETHER** *Creole CR 114* 1	21	6

1 Crispy & Co

CRITTERS *US, male vocal / instrumental group (5 WEEKS)*   pos/wks

30 Jun 66	**YOUNGER GIRL** *London HL 10047*	38	5

Tony CROMBIE and His ROCKETS *UK, male vocal / instrumental*
group – Tony Crombie – drums, d. 18 Oct 1999 (2 WEEKS)   pos/wks

19 Oct 56	**TEACH YOU TO ROCK / SHORT'NIN' BREAD** *Columbia DB 3822*	25	2

Bing CROSBY (325 Top 500)
The King of the Crooners. Bing released 2,500 tracks, 299 of which reached the US Top 20 (1931-1961) with estimated sales of more than 300,000,000. b. 3 May 1903, Washington, US, d.14 Oct 1977, Spain. 'White Christmas' (the most charted single in the US) is the No.2 all-time best-seller (97 WEEKS) pos/wks

14 Nov 52 ●	**THE ISLE OF INNISFREE** *Brunswick 04900*	3	12
5 Dec 52 ●	**ZING A LITTLE ZONG** *Brunswick 04981* 1	10	2
19 Dec 52 ●	**SILENT NIGHT, HOLY NIGHT** *Brunswick 03929*	8	2
19 Mar 54 ●	**CHANGING PARTNERS** (2re) *Brunswick 05244*	9	3
7 Jan 55	**COUNT YOUR BLESSINGS INSTEAD OF SHEEP** (re) *Brunswick 05339*	11	3
29 Apr 55	**STRANGER IN PARADISE** *Brunswick 05410*	17	2
27 Apr 56	**IN A LITTLE SPANISH TOWN** *Brunswick 05543*	22	3
23 Nov 56 ●	**TRUE LOVE** *Capitol CL 14645* 2	4	27
24 May 57 ●	**AROUND THE WORLD** *Brunswick 05674*	5	15
9 Aug 75	**THAT'S WHAT LIFE IS ALL ABOUT** *United Artists UP 35852*	41	4
3 Dec 77 ●	**WHITE CHRISTMAS** *MCA 111* ▲	5	7
27 Nov 82 ●	**PEACE ON EARTH – LITTLE DRUMMER BOY** *RCA BOW 12* 3	3	8
17 Dec 83	**TRUE LOVE** (re-issue) *Capitol CL 315* 2	70	3
21 Dec 85 ●	**WHITE CHRISTMAS** (re-issue) *MCA BING 1*	69	2
19 Dec 98	**WHITE CHRISTMAS** (2nd re-issue) *MCA MCSRD 48105*	29	4

1 Bing Crosby and Jane Wyman 2 Bing Crosby and Grace Kelly 3 David Bowie and Bing Crosby

David CROSBY featuring Phil COLLINS
US / UK, male vocalist / instrumentalists (3 WEEKS)   pos/wks

15 May 93	**HERO** *Atlantic A 7360* 1	56	3

1 David Crosby featuring Phil Collins

See also CROSBY, STILLS, NASH and YOUNG; Phil COLLINS

CROSBY, STILLS, NASH and YOUNG
US / UK / Canada, male vocal / instrumental group (12 WEEKS)   pos/wks

16 Aug 69	**MARRAKESH EXPRESS** *Atlantic 584 283* 1	17	9
21 Jan 89	**AMERICAN DREAM** *Atlantic A 9003*	55	3

1 Crosby, Stills and Nash

See also Stephen STILLS; Neil YOUNG; David CROSBY featuring Phil COLLINS

CROSS *UK / US, male vocal / instrumental group (1 WEEK)*   pos/wks

17 Oct 87	**COWBOYS AND INDIANS** *Virgin VS 1007*	74	1

Christopher CROSS
US, male vocalist – Christopher Geppert (27 WEEKS)   pos/wks

19 Apr 80	**RIDE LIKE THE WIND** *Warner Bros. K 17582*	69	1
14 Feb 81	**SAILING** *Warner Bros. K 17695* ▲	48	6
17 Oct 81 ●	**ARTHUR'S THEME (BEST THAT YOU CAN DO)** (re) *Warner Bros. K 17847* ▲	7	15
5 Feb 83	**ALL RIGHT** *Warner Bros. W 9843*	51	5

It was not until 'Arthur's Theme' re-entered in Jan 1982 that it reached the peak position of No.7

CROW *Germany, male production duo*
– David Rzenno and David Nothroff (1 WEEK)   pos/wks

19 May 01	**WHAT YA LOOKIN' AT** *Tidy Trax TIDY 153CD*	60	1

Sheryl CROW (390 Top 500)
Multi-Grammy-winning pop singer / songwriter / instrumentalist – guitar, born 11 Feb 1962, Missouri, US. The one-time backing singer for Michael Jackson and George Harrison became the first US female soloist to score six UK hits off debut LP (1993's Tuesday Night Music Club) (86 WEEKS) pos/wks

18 Jun 94	**LEAVING LAS VEGAS** *A&M 5806472*	66	1
5 Nov 94 ●	**ALL I WANNA DO** *A&M 5808452*	4	13
11 Feb 95	**STRONG ENOUGH** *A&M 5809212*	33	4
27 May 95	**CAN'T CRY ANYMORE** *A&M 5810552*	33	3
29 Jul 95	**RUN BABY RUN** *A&M 5811492*	24	4
11 Nov 95	**WHAT I CAN DO FOR YOU** *A&M 5812292*	43	1
21 Sep 96 ●	**IF IT MAKES YOU HAPPY** *A&M 5819032*	9	6
30 Nov 96 ●	**EVERYDAY IS A WINDING ROAD** *A&M 5820232*	12	6
29 Mar 97	**HARD TO MAKE A STAND** *A&M 5821492*	22	3
12 Jul 97 ●	**A CHANGE WOULD DO YOU GOOD** *A&M 5822092*	8	5
18 Oct 97	**HOME** *A&M 0440312*	25	2
13 Dec 97	**TOMORROW NEVER DIES** *A&M 5824572*	12	9
12 Sep 98 ●	**MY FAVORITE MISTAKE** *Polydor 5827632*	9	6
5 Dec 98	**THERE GOES THE NEIGHBORHOOD** *A&M 5828092*	19	7
6 Mar 99	**ANYTHING BUT DOWN** *A&M / Polydor 5828272*	19	4
11 Sep 99	**SWEET CHILD O' MINE** *Columbia 6678882*	30	3
13 Apr 02	**SOAK UP THE SUN** *A&M 4977042*	16	8
13 Jul 02	**STEVE MCQUEEN** *A&M 4977422*	44	1

CROWD *International, male / female vocal*
/ instrumental charity assembly (11 WEEKS)   pos/wks

1 Jun 85 ★	**YOU'LL NEVER WALK ALONE** *Spartan BRAD 1*	1	11

CROWDED HOUSE
New Zealand / Australia, male vocal / instrumental group (64 WEEKS) pos/wks

6 Jun 87	**DON'T DREAM IT'S OVER** *Capitol CL 438*	27	8
22 Jun 91	**CHOCOLATE CAKE** *Capitol CL 618*	69	2
2 Nov 91	**FALL AT YOUR FEET** *Capitol CL 626*	17	7
29 Feb 92 ●	**WEATHER WITH YOU** *Capitol CL 643*	7	9
20 Jun 92	**FOUR SEASONS IN ONE DAY** *Capitol CL 655*	26	5
26 Sep 92	**IT'S ONLY NATURAL** *Capitol CL 661*	24	4
2 Oct 93	**DISTANT SUN** *Capitol CDCLS 697*	19	6
20 Nov 93	**NAILS IN MY FEET** *Capitol CDCLS 701*	22	4
19 Feb 94	**LOCKED OUT** *Capitol CDCLS 707*	12	4
11 Jun 94	**FINGERS OF LOVE** *Capitol CDCLS 715*	25	3
24 Sep 94	**PINEAPPLE HEAD** *Capitol CDCLS 723*	27	3
22 Jun 96	**INSTINCT** *Capitol CDCLS 774*	12	4
17 Aug 96	**NOT THE GIRL YOU THINK YOU ARE** *Capitol CDCLS 776*	20	3
9 Nov 96	**DON'T DREAM IT'S OVER** (re-issue) *Capitol CDCL 780*	25	2

See also FINN; Neil FINN; Tim FINN

CROWN HEIGHTS AFFAIR
US, male vocal / instrumental group (34 WEEKS)   pos/wks

19 Aug 78	**GALAXY OF LOVE** *Mercury 6168 801*	24	10
11 Nov 78	**I'M GONNA LOVE YOU FOREVER** *Mercury 6168 803*	47	4
14 Apr 79	**DANCE LADY DANCE** *Mercury 6168 804*	44	4
3 May 80 ●	**YOU GAVE ME LOVE** *De-Lite MER 9*	10	12
9 Aug 80	**YOU'VE BEEN GONE** *De-Lite MER 28*	44	4

Julee CRUISE *US, female vocalist (14 WEEKS)*   pos/wks

10 Nov 90 ●	**FALLING** *Warner Bros. W 9544*	7	11
2 Mar 91	**ROCKIN' BACK INSIDE MY HEART** *Warner Bros. W 0004*	66	2
11 Sep 99	**IF I SURVIVE** *Distinctive DISNCD 55* 1	52	1

1 Hybrid featuring Julee Cruise

CRUISERS – See Dave BERRY

CRUSADERS *US, male vocal / instrumental group (16 WEEKS)* pos/wks

18 Aug 79 ●	**STREET LIFE** *MCA 513*	5	11

| 26 Sep 81 | I'M SO GLAD I'M STANDING HERE TODAY *MCA 741* [1] | 61 | 3 |
| 7 Apr 84 | NIGHT LADIES *MCA MCA 853* | 55 | 2 |

[1] Crusaders, featured vocalist Joe Cocker

Vocalist on 'Street Life' was Randy Crawford, though uncredited

CRUSH UK, female vocal duo (3 WEEKS)
pos/wks
| 24 Feb 96 | JELLYHEAD *Telstar CDSTAS 2809* | 50 | 2 |
| 3 Aug 96 | LUV'D UP *Telstar CDSTAS 2833* | 45 | 1 |

Bobby CRUSH UK, male instrumentalist – piano (4 WEEKS)
pos/wks
| 4 Nov 72 | BORSALINO *Philips 6006 248* | 37 | 4 |

CRY BEFORE DAWN
Ireland, male vocal / instrumental group (2 WEEKS)
| 17 Jun 89 | WITNESS FOR THE WORLD *Epic GONE 3* | 67 | 2 |

CRY OF LOVE
US, male / female vocal / instrumental group (1 WEEK)
pos/wks
| 15 Jan 94 | BAD THING *Columbia 6600462* | 60 | 1 |

CRY SISCO! UK, male producer – Barry Blue (9 WEEKS)
pos/wks
| 2 Sep 89 | AFRO DIZZI ACT (re) *Escape AWOL 1* | 42 | 9 |

See also Barry BLUE

CRYIN' SHAMES UK, male vocal / instrumental group (7 WEEKS)
pos/wks
| 31 Mar 66 | PLEASE STAY *Decca F 12340* | 26 | 7 |

CRYPT-KICKERS – See Bobby 'Boris' PICKETT and the CRYPT-KICKERS

CRYSTAL METHOD US, male instrumental duo (4 WEEKS)
pos/wks
11 Oct 97	(CAN'T YOU) TRIP LIKE I DO *Epic 6650862* [1]	39	2
7 Mar 98	KEEP HOPE ALIVE *Sony S2 CM 3CD*	71	1
8 Aug 98	COMIN' BACK *Sony S2 CM 4CD*	73	1

[1] Filter and The Crystal Method

CRYSTAL PALACE WITH THE FAB FOUR
UK, male football team vocalists and UK male group (2 WEEKS)
pos/wks
| 12 May 90 | GLAD ALL OVER / WHERE EAGLES FLY *Parkfield PMS 5019* | 50 | 2 |

CRYSTALS US, female vocal group (54 WEEKS)
pos/wks
22 Nov 62	HE'S A REBEL *London HLU 9611* ▲	19	13
20 Jun 63	● DA DOO RON RON *London HLU 9732*	5	16
19 Sep 63	● THEN HE KISSED ME *London HLU 9773*	2	14
5 Mar 64	I WONDER *London HLU 9852*	36	3
19 Oct 74	DA DOO RON RON (re-issue) *Warner Spector K 19010*	15	8

CSILLA Hungary, female vocalist (1 WEEK)
pos/wks
| 13 Jul 96 | MAN IN THE MOON *Worx WORXCD 001* | 69 | 1 |

CUBAN BOYS UK, male / female production group (9 WEEKS)
pos/wks
| 25 Dec 99 | ● COGNOSCENTI VS INTELLIGENTSIA (re) *EMI CDCUBAN 001* | 4 | 9 |

CUBIC 22 Belgium, male instrumental / production duo
– Peter Ramson and Danny van Wauwe (7 WEEKS)
pos/wks
| 22 Jun 91 | NIGHT IN MOTION *XL Recordings XLS 20* | 15 | 7 |

See also AIRSCAPE; BLUE BAMBOO; TRANSFORMER 2

CUD UK, male vocal / instrumental group (16 WEEKS)
pos/wks
19 Oct 91	OH NO WON'T DO (EP) *A&M AMB 829*	49	2
28 Mar 92	THROUGH THE ROOF *A&M AM 857*	44	2
30 May 92	RICH AND STRANGE *A&M AM 871*	24	3
15 Aug 92	PURPLE LOVE BALLOON *A&M AM 0024*	27	3

10 Oct 92	ONCE AGAIN *A&M AM 0081*	45	1
12 Feb 94	NEUROTICA *A&M 5805172*	37	2
2 Apr 94	STICKS AND STONES *A&M 5805472*	68	1
3 Sep 94	ONE GIANT LOVE *A&M 5807292*	52	2

Tracks on Oh No Won't Do (EP): Oh No Won't Do / Profession / Ariel / Price of Love

CUFFLINKS US, male vocal group, leader – Ron Dante (30 WEEKS)
pos/wks
| 29 Nov 69 | ● TRACY *MCA MU 1101* | 4 | 16 |
| 14 Mar 70 | ● WHEN JULIE COMES AROUND *MCA MU 1112* | 10 | 14 |

See also ARCHIES

The CULT (435 Top 500)
UK gothic rock stars who became US heavy rock heroes, previously recorded as Southern Death Cult and Death Cult. West Yorkshire band's constant members Ian Astbury (v) and Billy Duffy (g). Group, who relocated to US in 1988, topped the UK album chart with hits collection in 1993 (80 WEEKS)
pos/wks
22 Dec 84	RESURRECTION JOE *Beggars Banquet BEG 122*	74	2
25 May 85	SHE SELLS SANCTUARY (re) *Beggars Banquet BEG 135*	15	19
5 Oct 85	RAIN *Beggars Banquet BEG 147*	17	8
30 Nov 85	REVOLUTION *Beggars Banquet BEG 152*	30	7
28 Feb 87	LOVE REMOVAL MACHINE *Beggars Banquet BEG 182*	18	7
2 May 87	LIL' DEVIL *Beggars Banquet BEG 188*	11	7
22 Aug 87	WILD FLOWER (DOUBLE SINGLE) *Beggars Banquet BEG 195D*	24	7
29 Aug 87	WILD FLOWER *Beggars Banquet BEG 195*	30	4
1 Apr 89	FIRE WOMAN *Beggars Banquet BEG 228*	15	4
8 Jul 89	EDIE (CIAO BABY) *Beggars Banquet BEG 230*	32	5
18 Nov 89	SUN KING / EDIE (CIAO BABY) (re-issue) *Beggars Banquet BEG 235*	39	2
10 Mar 90	SWEET SOUL SISTER *Beggars Banquet BEG 241*	42	4
14 Sep 91	WILD HEARTED SON *Beggars Banquet BEG 255*	40	2
29 Feb 92	HEART OF SOUL *Beggars Banquet BEG 260*	51	1
30 Jan 93	SHE SELLS SANCTUARY (re-mix) *Beggars Banquet BEG 253CD*	15	4
8 Oct 94	COMING DOWN *Beggars Banquet BBQ 40CD*	50	1
7 Jan 95	STAR *Beggars Banquet BBQ 45CD*	65	1

Tracks on double single: Wild Flower / Love Trooper / Outlaw (live) / Horse Nation (live)

CULT JAM – See LISA LISA

Smiley CULTURE UK, male vocalist – David Emanuel (13 WEEKS)
pos/wks
15 Dec 84	POLICE OFFICER *Fashion FAD 7012*	12	10
6 Apr 85	COCKNEY TRANSLATION *Fashion FAD 7028*	71	1
13 Sep 86	SCHOOLTIME CHRONICLE *Polydor POSP 815*	59	2

CULTURE BEAT UK / US / Germany, male
/ female vocal / instrumental group (46 WEEKS)
pos/wks
3 Feb 90	CHERRY LIPS (DER ERDBEERMUND) *Epic 6556337*	55	3
7 Aug 93	★ MR VAIN *Epic 6594682*	1	15
6 Nov 93	● GOT TO GET IT *Epic 6597212*	4	11
15 Jan 94	● ANYTHING *Epic 6600252*	5	8
2 Apr 94	WORLD IN YOUR HANDS *Epic 6602292*	20	4
27 Jan 96	INSIDE OUT *Epic 6626562*	32	2
15 Jun 96	CRYING IN THE RAIN *Epic 6633582*	29	2
28 Sep 96	TAKE ME AWAY *Epic 6637552*	52	1

CULTURE CLUB (233 Top 500)
Internationally successful London-based quartet, whose flamboyant lead singer, Boy George (b. George O'Dowd, 14 Jun 1961, Kent), attracted considerable media attention. In 1984, they won both Brit (Best Group) and Grammy Awards (Best New Artist). Original members reunited for late 1990s tours. Best-selling single: 'Karma Chameleon' 1,405,000 (119 WEEKS)
pos/wks
18 Sep 82	★ DO YOU REALLY WANT TO HURT ME *Virgin VS 518*	1	18
27 Nov 82	● TIME (CLOCK OF THE HEART) *Virgin VS 558*	3	12
9 Apr 83	● CHURCH OF THE POISON MIND *Virgin VS 571*	2	9
17 Sep 83	★ KARMA CHAMELEON *Virgin VS 612* ◆ ▲	1	20
10 Dec 83	● VICTIMS *Virgin VS 641*	3	10
24 Mar 84	● IT'S A MIRACLE *Virgin VS 662*	4	9

6 Oct 84 ●	THE WAR SONG *Virgin VS 694*	2	8
1 Dec 84	THE MEDAL SONG (re) *Virgin VS 730*	...32	5
15 Mar 86 ●	MOVE AWAY *Virgin VS 845*	...7	7
31 May 86	GOD THANK YOU WOMAN *Virgin VS 861*	...31	5
31 Oct 98 ●	I JUST WANNA BE LOVED *Virgin VSCDT 1710*	...4	10
7 Aug 99	YOUR KISSES ARE CHARITY *Virgin VSCDT 1736*	...25	4
27 Nov 99	COLD SHOULDER / STARMAN *Virgin VSCDT 1758*	...43	2

See also BOY GEORGE

Larry CUNNINGHAM and the MIGHTY AVONS
Ireland, male vocal / instrumental group (11 WEEKS) pos/wks

10 Dec 64	TRIBUTE TO JIM REEVES (re) *King KG 1016*	40	11

CUPID'S INSPIRATION
UK, male vocal / instrumental group (19 WEEKS) pos/wks

19 Jun 68 ●	YESTERDAY HAS GONE *Nems 56 3500*	4	11
2 Oct 68	MY WORLD *Nems 56 3702*	...33	8

José CURA – See Sarah BRIGHTMAN

Mike CURB Congregation – See Little Jimmy OSMOND

CURE (166 [Top 500]) Goth rock giants: Robert Smith (v/g), Lol Tolhurst (k), Simon Gallup (b), Porl Thompson (g), Boris Williams (d), who went from UK cult heroes to stadium-packing supergroup. Voted Best Group at 1991 Brit Awards (145 WEEKS)
pos/wks

12 Apr 80	A FOREST *Fiction FICS 10*	...31	8
4 Apr 81	PRIMARY *Fiction FICS 12*	...43	6
17 Oct 81	CHARLOTTE SOMETIMES *Fiction FICS 14*	...44	4
24 Jul 82	HANGING GARDEN *Fiction FICS 15*	...34	4
27 Nov 82	LET'S GO TO BED (re) *Fiction FICS 17*	...44	5
9 Jul 83	THE WALK *Fiction FICS 18*	...12	8
29 Oct 83 ●	THE LOVE CATS *Fiction FICS 19*	...7	11
7 Apr 84	THE CATERPILLAR *Fiction FICS 20*	...14	7
27 Jul 85	IN BETWEEN DAYS *Fiction FICS 22*	...15	10
21 Sep 85	CLOSE TO ME *Fiction FICS 23*	...24	8
3 May 86	BOYS DON'T CRY *Fiction FICS 24*	...22	6
18 Apr 87	WHY CAN'T I BE YOU? *Fiction FICS 25*	...21	5
4 Jul 87	CATCH *Fiction FICS 26*	...27	6
17 Oct 87	JUST LIKE HEAVEN *Fiction FICS 27*	...29	5
20 Feb 88	HOT HOT HOT!!! *Fiction FICSX 28*	...45	3
22 Apr 89 ●	LULLABY *Fiction FICS 29*	...5	6
2 Sep 89	LOVESONG *Fiction FICS 30*	...18	7
31 Mar 90	PICTURES OF YOU *Fiction FICS 34*	...24	6
29 Sep 90	NEVER ENOUGH *Fiction FICS 35*	...13	5
3 Nov 90	CLOSE TO ME (re-mix) *Fiction FICS 36*	...13	5
28 Mar 92 ●	HIGH *Fiction FICS 39*	...8	3
11 Apr 92	HIGH (re-mix) *Fiction FICSX 41*	...44	1
23 May 92 ●	FRIDAY I'M IN LOVE *Fiction FICS 42*	...6	7
17 Oct 92	A LETTER TO ELISE *Fiction FICS 46*	...28	2
4 May 96	THE 13TH *Fiction 5764692*	...15	2
29 Jun 96	MINT CAR *Fiction FISCD 52*	...31	2
14 Dec 96	GONE *Fiction FICD 53*	...60	1
29 Nov 97	WRONG NUMBER *Fiction FICD 54*	...62	1
10 Nov 01	CUT HERE *Fiction 5873892*	...54	1

See also GLOVE

CURIOSITY *UK, male vocal / instrumental group (58 WEEKS)*
pos/wks

13 Dec 86 ●	DOWN TO EARTH *Mercury CAT 2* [1]	...3	18
4 Apr 87	ORDINARY DAY *Mercury CAT 3* [1]	...11	7
20 Jun 87 ●	MISFIT *Mercury CAT 4* [1]	...7	9
19 Sep 87	FREE *Mercury CAT 5* [1]	...56	2
16 Sep 89	NAME AND NUMBER *Mercury CAT 6*	...14	9
25 Apr 92 ●	HANG ON IN THERE BABY *RCA PB 45377*	...3	10
29 Aug 92	I NEED YOUR LOVIN' *RCA 74321111377*	...47	2
30 Oct 93	GIMME THE SUNSHINE *RCA 74321168602*	...73	1

[1] Curiosity Killed the Cat

CURLS – See Paul EVANS

Mark CURRY – See PUFF DADDY

Chantal CURTIS *France, female vocalist (3 WEEKS)* pos/wks

14 Jul 79	GET ANOTHER LOVE *Pye 7P 5003*	...51	3

TC CURTIS *Jamaica, male vocalist / instrumentalist (4 WEEKS)* pos/wks

23 Feb 85	YOU SHOULD HAVE KNOWN BETTER *Hot Melt VS 754*	...50	4

CURVE *UK, male / female vocal / instrumental duo – Toni Halliday and Dean Garcia (14 WEEKS)* pos/wks

16 Mar 91	THE BLINDFOLD (EP) *AnXious ANX 27*	...68	1
25 May 91	COAST IS CLEAR *AnXious ANX 30*	...34	3
9 Nov 91	CLIPPED *AnXious ANX 35*	...36	2
7 Mar 92	FAIT ACCOMPLI *AnXious ANXT 36*	...22	3
18 Jul 92	HORROR HEAD (EP) *AnXious ANXT 38*	...31	2
4 Sep 93	BLACKERTHREETRACKER (EP) *AnXious ANXCD 42*	...39	2
16 May 98	COMING UP ROSES *Universal UND 80489*	...51	1

Tracks on The Blindfold (EP): Ten Little Girls / I Speak Your Every Word / Blindfold / No Escape from Heaven. Tracks on Horror Head (EP): Horror Head / Falling Free / Mission from God / Today Is Not the Day. Only track available on all formats of Blackerthreetracker (EP): Missing Link

CURVED AIR
UK, male / female vocal / instrumental group (12 WEEKS) pos/wks

7 Aug 71 ●	BACK STREET LUV *Warner Bros. K 16092*	...4	12

CUT 'N' MOVE
Denmark, male / female vocal / instrumental group (4 WEEKS) pos/wks

2 Oct 93	GIVE IT UP *EMI CDEM 273*	...61	2
9 Sep 95	I'M ALIVE *EMI CDEM 375*	...49	2

Frankie CUTLASS *US, male rapper (1 WEEK)* pos/wks

5 Apr 97	THE CYPHER: PART 3 *Epic 6641445*	...59	1

Adge CUTLER – See WURZELS

Jon CUTLER featuring E-MAN
US, male producer and male vocalist – Eric Clark (2 WEEKS) pos/wks

19 Jan 02	IT'S YOURS *Direction 6720532*	...38	2

CUTTING CREW
UK / Canada, male vocal / instrumental group (37 WEEKS) pos/wks

16 Aug 86 ●	(I JUST) DIED IN YOUR ARMS *Siren SIREN 21* ▲	...4	12
25 Oct 86	I'VE BEEN IN LOVE BEFORE (re) *Siren SIREN 29*	...31	10
7 Mar 87	ONE FOR THE MOCKINGBIRD *Siren SIREN 40*	...52	5
21 Nov 87	I'VE BEEN IN LOVE BEFORE (re-mix) *Siren SRN 29*	...24	8
22 Jul 89	(BETWEEN A) ROCK AND A HARD PLACE *Siren SRN 108*	...66	2

CYBERSONIK *US, male instrumentalist / producers (1 WEEK)* pos/wks

10 Nov 90	TECHNARCHY *Champion CHAMP 264*	...73	1

CYCLEFLY *Ireland, male vocal / instrumental group (1 WEEK)* pos/wks

6 Apr 02	NO STRESS *Radioactive RAXTD 41*	...68	1

CYGNUS X *Germany, male producer – A C Bousten (5 WEEKS)* pos/wks

11 Mar 00	THE ORANGE THEME *Hooj Choons HOOJ 88CD*	...43	2
18 Aug 01	SUPERSTRING *Xtravaganza XTRAV 28CDS*	...33	3

Johnny CYMBAL
Canada, male vocalist d. 16 Mar 1993 (10 WEEKS) pos/wks

14 Mar 63	MR BASS MAN *London HLR 9682*	...24	10

CYPRESS HILL *US, male rap group (44 WEEKS)* pos/wks

31 Jul 93	INSANE IN THE BRAIN *Ruff House 6595332*	...32	4
2 Oct 93	WHEN THE SH.. GOES DOWN *Ruff House 6596702*	...19	4
11 Dec 93	I AIN'T GOIN' OUT LIKE THAT *Ruff House 6596902*	...15	7

26 Feb 94	INSANE IN THE BRAIN (re-issue)		
	Ruff House 6601762	21	4
7 May 94	LICK A SHOT Ruff House 6603192	20	3
7 Oct 95	THROW YOUR SET IN THE AIR Ruff House 6623542	15	3
17 Feb 96	ILLUSIONS Columbia 6629052	23	2
10 Oct 98	TEQUILA SUNRISE Columbia 6664935	23	2
10 Apr 99	DR GREENTHUMB Columbia 6671202	34	2
26 Jun 99	INSANE IN THE BRAIN INCredible INCRL 17CD [1]	19	3
29 Apr 00	(RAP) SUPERSTAR / (ROCK) SUPERSTAR		
	Columbia 6692642	13	5
16 Sep 00	HIGHLIFE / CAN'T GET THE BEST OF ME		
	Columbia 6697892	35	2
8 Dec 01	LOWRIDER / TROUBLE (re) Columbia 6721662	33	3

[1] Jason Nevins vs Cypress Hill

Billy Ray CYRUS US, male vocalist (18 WEEKS)

		pos/wks	
25 Jul 92	● ACHY BREAKY HEART Mercury MER 373	3	10
10 Oct 92	COULD'VE BEEN ME Mercury MER 378	24	4
28 Nov 92	THESE BOOTS ARE MADE FOR WALKIN' Mercury MER 384	63	1
19 Dec 92	ACHY BREAKY HEART Epic 6588837 [1]	53	3

[1] Alvin and the Chipmunks featuring Billy Ray Cyrus

D

Asher D UK, male rapper (2 WEEKS)

		pos/wks	
4 Aug 01	BABY, CAN I GET YOUR NUMBER East West EW 235CD [1]	75	1
8 Jun 02	BACK IN THE DAY / WHY ME Independiente ISOM 57MS	43	1

[1] OBI Project featuring Harry, Asher D and DJ What?

See also SO SOLID CREW

DB BOULEVARD
Italy, male production trio and female vocalist (12 WEEKS)

		pos/wks	
23 Feb 02	● POINT OF VIEW Illustrious CDILL 002	3	12

Chuck D US, male rapper – Carlton Ridenhour (9 WEEKS)

		pos/wks	
6 Jul 91	BRING THE NOISE Island IS 490 [1]	14	5
26 Oct 96	NO Mercury MERCD 476	55	1
23 Jun 01	ROCK DA FUNKY BEATS Xtrahard / Xtravaganza X2H3 CDS [2]	19	3

[1] Anthrax featuring Chuck D [2] Public Domain featuring Chuck D

See also PUBLIC ENEMY

Crissy D – See B-15 PROJECT featuring Crissy D and Lady G

Danny D – See COOKIE CREW

Dimples D US, female rapper – Crystal Smith (10 WEEKS)

		pos/wks	
17 Nov 90	SUCKER DJ FBI FBI 11	17	10

Longsy D UK, male instrumentalist / producer (7 WEEKS)

		pos/wks	
4 Mar 89	THIS IS SKA Big One VBIG 13	56	7

Maxwell D UK, male rapper – Maxwell Donaldson (2 WEEKS)

		pos/wks	
15 Sep 01	SERIOUS 4 Liberty LIBTCD 046	38	2

Nikki D US, female rapper – Nichelle Strong (6 WEEKS)

		pos/wks	
6 May 89	MY LOVE IS SO RAW Def Jam 6548987 [1]	34	5
30 Mar 91	DADDY'S LITTLE GIRL Def Jam 6567347	75	1

[1] Alyson Williams featuring Nikki D

Vicky D US, female vocalist (6 WEEKS)

		pos/wks	
13 Mar 82	THIS BEAT IS MINE Virgin VS 486	42	6

DBM
Germany, male / female vocal / instrumental group (3 WEEKS)

		pos/wks	
12 Nov 77	DISCO BEATLEMANIA Atlantic K 11027	45	3

D, B, M and T UK, male vocal / instrumental group (8 WEEKS)

		pos/wks	
1 Aug 70	MR PRESIDENT Fontana 6007 022	33	8

See also Dave DEE, DOZY, BEAKY, MICK and TICH

D BO GENERAL – See URBAN SHAKEDOWN

D4 New Zealand, male vocal / instrumental group (2 WEEKS)

		pos/wks	
28 Sep 02	GET LOOSE Infectious INFEC 117CDS	64	1
7 Dec 02	COME ON! Infectious INFEC 121CDS	50	1

D.H.S. US, male producer – Ben Stokes (1 WEEK)

		pos/wks	
9 Feb 02	HOUSE OF GOD Club Tools 0135825 CLU	72	1

D MOB UK, male producer – Danny D (48 WEEKS)

		pos/wks	
15 Oct 88	● WE CALL IT ACIEED fffr FFR 13 [1]	3	12
3 Jun 89	● IT IS TIME TO GET FUNKY fffr F 107 [2]	9	10
21 Oct 89	C'MON AND GET MY LOVE fffr F 117 [3]	15	10
6 Jan 90	● PUT YOUR HANDS TOGETHER fffr F 124 [4]	7	8
7 Apr 90	THAT'S THE WAY OF THE WORLD fffr F 132 [3]	48	3
12 Feb 94	WHY fffr FCD 227 [3]	23	3
3 Sep 94	ONE DAY fffr FCDP 239	41	2

[1] D Mob featuring Gary Haisman [2] D Mob featuring LRS [3] D Mob with Cathy Dennis [4] D Mob featuring Nuff Juice

DMX US, male rapper – Earl Simmons (6 WEEKS)

		pos/wks	
15 May 99	SLIPPIN' Def Jam 8707552	30	2
15 Dec 01	WHO WE BE Def Jam 5888512	34	4

DNA
UK, male production duo – Neal Slateford and Nick Bett (29 WEEKS)

		pos/wks	
28 Jul 90	● TOM'S DINER (re-mix) A&M AM 592 [1]	2	10
18 Aug 90	LA SERENISSIMA Raw Bass RBASS 006	34	8
3 Aug 91	REBEL WOMAN DNA 7DNA 001 [2]	42	4
1 Feb 92	CAN YOU HANDLE IT (re-recording) EMI EM 219 [3]	17	5
9 May 92	BLUE LOVE (CALL MY NAME) EMI EM 226 [4]	66	2

[1] DNA featuring Suzanne Vega [2] DNA featuring Jazzi P [3] DNA featuring Sharon Redd [4] DNA featuring Joe Nye

D*NOTE UK, male producer – Matt Winn (3 WEEKS)

		pos/wks	
12 Jul 97	WAITING HOPEFULLY A&M 5822792	46	1
15 Nov 97	LOST AND FOUND VC VCRD 25	59	1
27 Apr 02	SHED MY SKIN Channel 4 Music C4M 00182	73	1

D.O.P. UK, male instrumental / production duo (2 WEEKS)

		pos/wks	
3 Feb 96	STOP STARTING TO START STOPPING (EP)		
	Hi-Life 5779472	58	1
13 Jul 96	GROOVY BEAT Hi-Life 5750652	54	1

Tracks on Stop Starting to Stop Stopping (EP): Gusta / Dance to the House / Can You Feel It / How Do Y'All Feel

D.O.S.E. – See Mark E SMITH

D:REAM 491 Top 500 Uplifting pop / dance act featuring Ulster-born Peter Cunnah (v) and Scotsman Al Mackenzie (k) who left 1993. 'Things Can Only Get Better' (first three-time Top 30 entrant in the 1990s) used as theme for Labour Party's 1997 general election campaign (74 WEEKS)

		pos/wks	
4 Jul 92	U R THE BEST THING FXU FXU 3	72	1
30 Jan 93	THINGS CAN ONLY GET BETTER Magnet MAG 1010CD	24	5

Re-entries are listed as (re), (2re), (3re), etc which signifies that the hit re-entered the chart once, twice or three times, etc

				pos/wks
24 Apr 93	U R THE BEST THING (re-issue) *Magnet MAG 1011CD*	19	8
31 Jul 93	UNFORGIVEN *Magnet MAG 1016CD*	29	3
2 Oct 93	STAR / I LIKE IT *Magnet MAG 1019CD*	26	4
8 Jan 94 ★	THINGS CAN ONLY GET BETTER (re-issue) *Magnet MAG 1020CD*	1	16
26 Mar 94 ●	U R THE BEST THING (re-mix) *Magnet MAG 1021CD*	4	10
18 Jun 94	TAKE ME AWAY *Magnet MAG 1025CD*	18	5
10 Sep 94	BLAME IT ON ME *Magnet MAG 1027CD*	25	5
8 Jul 95 ●	SHOOT ME WITH YOUR LOVE *Magnet MAG 1034CD*	7	7
9 Sep 95	PARTY UP THE WORLD *Magnet MAG 1037CD*	20	6
11 Nov 95	THE POWER (OF ALL THE LOVE IN THE WORLD) *Magnet MAG 1039CD*	40	1
3 May 97	THINGS CAN ONLY GET BETTER (2nd re-issue) *Magnet MAG 1050CD*	19	3

D-SHAKE
Holland, male producer – Adrianus De Mooy (8 WEEKS) pos/wks

2 Jun 90	YAAAH / TECHNO TRANCE *Cooltempo COOL 213*	20	6
2 Feb 91	MY HEART THE BEAT *Cooltempo COOL 228*	42	2

DSK
UK, male / female vocal / instrumental / production group (4 WEEKS) pos/wks

31 Aug 91	WHAT WOULD WE DO / READ MY LIPS *Boy's Own BOI 6*	46	3
22 Nov 97	WHAT WOULD WE DO (re-mix) *Fresh FRSHD 63*	55	1

DSM *US, male rap group (4 WEEKS)* pos/wks

7 Dec 85	WARRIOR GROOVE *10 DAZZ 45-7*	68	4

DSP – See Matt DAREY

DTI *US, male vocal / instrumental group (1 WEEK)* pos/wks

16 Apr 88	KEEP THIS FREQUENCY CLEAR *Premiere UK ERE 501*	73	1

D-TEK *UK, male instrumental / production group (1 WEEK)* pos/wks

6 Nov 93	DROP THE ROCK (EP) *Positiva 12TIV 5*	70	1

Tracks on Drop the Rock (EP): Drop the Rock / Chunkafunk / Drop the Rock (re-mix) / Don't Breathe

D TRAIN *US, male vocal / instrumental duo*
– James Williams and Hubert Eaves III (36 WEEKS) pos/wks

6 Feb 82	YOU'RE THE ONE FOR ME *Epic EPC A 2016*	30	8
8 May 82	WALK ON BY *Epic EPC A 2298*	44	6
7 May 83	MUSIC PART 1 *Prelude A 3332*	23	7
16 Jul 83	KEEP GIVING ME LOVE *Prelude A 3497*	65	2
27 Jul 85	YOU'RE THE ONE FOR ME (re-mix) *Prelude ZB 40302*	15	11
12 Oct 85	MUSIC (re-mix) *Prelude ZB 40431*	62	2

D12 *US, male rap group (24 WEEKS)* pos/wks

17 Mar 01 ●	SHIT ON YOU *Interscope 4974962*	10	7
21 Jul 01 ●	PURPLE PILLS *Shady / Interscope 4975692*	2	12
17 Nov 01	FIGHT MUSIC *Shady / Interscope 4976522*	11	5

Azzido DA BASS
Germany, male DJ / producer – Ingo Martens (13 WEEKS) pos/wks

4 Mar 00	DOOMS NIGHT (re) *Club Tools 0067285 CLU*	46	3
21 Oct 00 ●	DOOMS NIGHT (re-mix) (re) *Club Tools 0120285 CLU*	8	9
23 Mar 02	SPEED (CAN YOU FEEL IT) *Club Tools 0135815 CLU* [1]	68	1

[1] Azzido Da Bass featuring Roland Clark

DA BRAT *US, female rapper (1 WEEK)* pos/wks

22 Oct 94	FUNKDAFIED *Columbia 6609212*	65	1

DA CLICK *UK, male rap group / female vocalist (8 WEEKS)* pos/wks

16 Jan 99	GOOD RHYMES *ffrr FCD 353*	14	6
29 May 99	WE ARE DA CLICK *ffrr FCD 363*	38	2

DA FOOL *US, male DJ / producer – Mike Stewart (2 WEEKS)* pos/wks

16 Jan 99	NO GOOD *ffrr FCD 352*	38	2

Ricardo DA FORCE *UK, male rapper – Ricardo Lyte (14 WEEKS)* pos/wks

18 Mar 95	PUMP UP THE VOLUME *Stress CDSTR 49* [1]	51	2
16 Sep 95 ●	STAYIN' ALIVE *All Around the World CDGLOBE 131* [2]	2	11
31 Aug 96	WHY *ffrr FCD 280*	58	1

[1] Greed featuring Ricardo Da Force [2] N-Trance featuring Ricardo Da Force

DA HOOL *Germany, male instrumentalist / producer*
– Frank Tomiczek (13 WEEKS) pos/wks

14 Feb 98	MEET HER AT THE LOVE PARADE *Manifesto FESCD 39*	15	4
22 Aug 98	BORA BORA *Manifesto FESCD 47*	35	3
28 Jul 01	MEET HER AT THE LOVE PARADE 2001 *Manifesto FESCD 85*	11	6

DA LENCH MOB *US, male rap group (2 WEEKS)* pos/wks

20 Mar 93	FREEDOM GOT AN A.K. *East West America A 8431CD*	51	2

DA MOB featuring JOCELYN BROWN
US, male / female vocal / instrumental group (3 WEEKS) pos/wks

2 May 98	FUN *INCredible INCRL 2CD*	33	2
3 Jul 99	IT'S ALL GOOD *INCredible INCRL 14CD*	54	1

DA MUTTZ
UK, male production duo – Elliot Ireland and Alex Rizzo (10 WEEKS) pos/wks

9 Dec 00	WASSUUP *Eternal WEA 319CD*	11	10

See also SHAFT

TOP 10 NORTHERN IRISH ACTS

■ Northern Irish-born chart champions (calculated by weeks on the UK singles chart) together with each act's highest placed hit

1. **RUBY MURRAY (114)**
Softly, Softly

2. **GARY MOORE (103)**
Out in the Fields

3. **D:REAM (74)**
Things Can Only Get Better

4. **UNDERTONES (67)**
My Perfect Cousin

5. **FEARGAL SHARKEY (58)**
A Good Heart

6. **ASH (56)**
Goldfinger

7. **STIFF LITTLE FINGERS (39)**
At the Edge

8. **THERAPY? (33)**
Shortsharpshock (EP)

9. **THEM (23)**
Here Comes the Night

10. **VAN MORRISON (21)**
Whenever God Shines His Light

TV star and chart-topping Northern Irish songstress, Belfast-born Ruby Murray, who died in 1996

Rui DA SILVA featuring CASSANDRA *Portugal, male producer and UK, female vocalist – Cassandra Fox (14 WEEKS)* pos/wks
13 Jan 01 ★ TOUCH ME *Kismet / Arista 74321823992* ■ 1 14

DA SLAMMIN' PHROGZ *France, male production duo (1 WEEK)* pos/wks
29 Apr 00 SOMETHING ABOUT THE MUSIC *WEA WEA 251CD*.................53 1

DA TECHNO BOHEMIAN *Holland, male production trio (1 WEEK)* pos/wks
25 Jan 97 BANGIN' BASS *Hi-Life 5731772*..63 1

Paul DA VINCI *UK, male vocalist – Paul Prewer (8 WEEKS)* pos/wks
20 Jul 74 YOUR BABY AIN'T YOUR BABY ANYMORE
Penny Farthing PEN 843 ....20 8

See also RUBETTES

Terry DACTYL and the DINOSAURS
UK, male vocal / instrumental group (16 WEEKS) pos/wks
15 Jul 72 ● SEASIDE SHUFFLE *UK 5* 2 12
13 Jan 73 ON A SATURDAY NIGHT *UK 21* 45 4

Terry Dactyl is Jona Lewie

DADA *US, male vocal / instrumental group (1 WEEK)* pos/wks
4 Dec 93 DOG *IRS CDEIRSS 185*..71 1

DADDY FREDDY – See Simon HARRIS

DADDY'S FAVOURITE *UK, male DJ / producer (3 WEEKS)* pos/wks
21 Nov 98 I FEEL GOOD THINGS FOR YOU *Go.Beat GONCD 12* 44 2
9 Oct 99 I FEEL GOOD THINGS FOR YOU (re-issue)
Go.Beat GOBCD 22 ....50 1

DAFFY DUCK featuring the GROOVE GANG
Germany, male instrumental / production group (3 WEEKS) pos/wks
6 Jul 91 PARTY ZONE *East West YZ 592* 58 3

DAFT PUNK *France, male instrumental / production duo –*
Thomas Bangalter and Guy Manuel de Homem-Christo (35 WEEKS) pos/wks
22 Feb 97 ● DA FUNK / MUSIQUE *Soma / Virgin VSCDT 1625* 7 5
26 Apr 97 ● AROUND THE WORLD *Virgin VSCDT 1633* 5 5
4 Oct 97 BURNIN' *Virgin VSCDT 1649* 30 2
28 Feb 98 REVOLUTION 909 *Virgin VSCDT 1682* 47 1
25 Nov 00 ● ONE MORE TIME *Virgin VSCDT 1791* 2 12
23 Jun 01 DIGITAL LOVE *Virgin VSCDT 1810* 14 7
17 Nov 01 HARDER BETTER FASTER STRONGER *Virgin VSCDT 1822* 25 3

Etienne DAHO – See SAINT ETIENNE

DAINTEES – See Martin STEPHENSON and the DAINTEES

DAISY CHAINSAW
UK, male / female vocal / instrumental group (6 WEEKS) pos/wks
18 Jan 92 LOVE YOUR MONEY *Deva DEVA 001* 26 5
28 Mar 92 PINK FLOWER / ROOM ELEVEN *Deva 82 TP7* 65 1

DAJAE – See Junior SANCHEZ featuring DAJAE

DAKEYNE – See James BROWN; TINMAN

DAKOTAS *UK, male instrumental group (13 WEEKS)* pos/wks
11 Jul 63 THE CRUEL SEA *Parlophone R 5044* 18 13

See also Billy J KRAMER and the DAKOTAS

Jim DALE *UK, male vocalist – James Smith (22 WEEKS)* pos/wks
11 Oct 57 ● BE MY GIRL *Parlophone R 4343*....................................2 16
10 Jan 58 JUST BORN (TO BE MY BABY) *ParlophoneR 4376*...............27 1

17 Jan 58 CRAZY DREAM *Parlophone R 4376* 24 2
7 Mar 58 SUGARTIME *Parlophone R 4402* 25 3

DALE and GRACE *US, male / female vocal duo (2 WEEKS)* pos/wks
9 Jan 64 I'M LEAVING IT UP TO YOU *London HL 9807* ▲ 42 2

DALE SISTERS
UK, female vocal trio – Julie, Hazel and Betty Dunderdale (7 WEEKS) pos/wks
17 Mar 60 HEARTBEAT *HMV POP 710* 1 ....33 1
23 Nov 61 MY SUNDAY BABY *Ember S 140* 36 6

1 England Sisters

DALI'S CAR *UK, male vocal / instrumental duo (2 WEEKS)* pos/wks
3 Nov 84 THE JUDGEMENT IS THE MIRROR *Paradox DOX 1* 66 2

Roger DALTREY *UK, male vocalist (46 WEEKS)* pos/wks
14 Apr 73 ● GIVING IT ALL AWAY *Track 2094 110* 5 11
4 Aug 73 I'M FREE *Ode ODS 66302* 1 ....13 10
14 May 77 WRITTEN ON THE WIND *Polydor 2121 319*......................46 2
2 Aug 80 FREE ME *Polydor 2001 980* 39 6
11 Oct 80 WITHOUT YOUR LOVE *Polydor POSP 181* 55 4
3 Mar 84 WALKING IN MY SLEEP *WEA U 9686* 56 3
5 Oct 85 AFTER THE FIRE *10 TEN 69* 50 5
8 Mar 86 UNDER A RAGING MOON *10 TEN 81* 43 5

1 With London Symphony Orchestra and English Chamber Choir – conducted by David Measham

See also WHO

DAMAGE *UK, male vocal group (59 WEEKS)* pos/wks
20 Jul 96 ANYTHING *Big Life BLRD 129* 68 1
12 Oct 96 LOVE II LOVE *Big Life BLRD 131* 12 6
14 Dec 96 ● FOREVER *Big Life BLRD 132* 6 9
22 Mar 97 ● LOVE GUARANTEED (re) *Big Life BLRDA 133* 7 5
17 May 97 ● WONDERFUL TONIGHT *Big Life BLRDA 134* 3 8
9 Aug 97 LOVE LADY *Big Life BLRDB 137* 33 2
1 Jul 00 ● GHETTO ROMANCE *Cooltempo CDCOOL 347* 7 7
28 Oct 00 RUMOURS *Cooltempo CDCOOLS 352* 22 4
31 Mar 01 STILL BE LOVIN' YOU (re) *Cooltempo CDCOOLS 355* 11 7
14 Jul 01 SO WHAT IF I (re) *Cooltempo CDCOOLS 357* 12 6
15 Dec 01 AFTER THE LOVE HAS GONE *Cooltempo CDCOOL 360*..........42 2

Carolina DAMAS – See SUENO LATINO

Bobby D'AMBROSIO featuring Michelle WEEKS
US, male DJ / producer and female vocalist (3 WEEKS) pos/wks
2 Aug 97 MOMENT OF MY LIFE *Ministry of Sound MOSCDS 1*.................23 3

DAMIAN *UK, male vocalist – Damian Davis (26 WEEKS)* pos/wks
26 Dec 87 THE TIME WARP 2 *Jive JIVE 160* 51 6
27 Aug 88 THE TIME WARP 2 (re-issue) *Jive JIVE 182* 64 3
19 Aug 89 ● THE TIME WARP (re-mix) *Jive JIVE 209* 7 13
16 Dec 89 WIG WAM BAM *Jive JIVE 236*.......................................49 4

'The Time Warp' is a re-mix of 'The Time Warp 2'

DAMNED (464 *Top 500*) *Anarchic stalwarts of the UK punk rock scene: Dave Vanian (v), Brian James (g), Captain Sensible (b) and Rat Scabies (d). London-based band released the first UK punk single 'New Rose' (1976) and album 'Damned, Damned, Damned' (1977) (77 WEEKS)* pos/wks
5 May 79 LOVE SONG *Chiswick CHIS 112*......................................20 8
20 Oct 79 SMASH IT UP *Chiswick CHIS 116*....................................35 5
1 Dec 79 I JUST CAN'T BE HAPPY TODAY *Chiswick CHIS 120* 46 5
4 Oct 80 HISTORY OF THE WORLD (PART 1) *Chiswick CHIS 135* 51 4
28 Nov 81 FRIDAY 13TH (EP) *Stale One TRY 1* 50 4
10 Jul 82 LOVELY MONEY *Bronze BRO 149* 42 4
9 Jun 84 THANKS FOR THE NIGHT *Damned DAMNED 1* 43 4
30 Mar 85 GRIMLY FIENDISH *MCA GRIM 1*......................................21 7
22 Jun 85 THE SHADOW OF LOVE (EDITION PREMIERE) *MCA GRIM 2* 25 8

Re-entries are listed as (re), (2re), (3re), etc which signifies that the hit re-entered the chart once, twice or three times, etc

Date	Title	pos	wks
21 Sep 85	IS IT A DREAM *MCA GRIM 3*	34	4
8 Feb 86 ●	ELOISE (re) *MCA GRIM 4*	3	10
22 Nov 86	ANYTHING *MCA GRIM 5*	32	4
7 Feb 87	GIGOLO *MCA GRIM 6*	29	3
25 Apr 87	ALONE AGAIN OR *MCA GRIM 7*	27	6
28 Nov 87	IN DULCE DECORUM *MCA GRIM 8*	72	1

Tracks on Friday 13th (EP): Disco Man / Limit Club / Billy Bad Breaks / Citadel

Kenny DAMON *US, male vocalist (1 WEEK)*

Date	Title	pos	wks
19 May 66	WHILE I LIVE *Mercury MF 907*	48	1

Vic DAMONE *US, male vocalist – Vito Farinola (22 WEEKS)*

Date	Title	pos	wks
6 Dec 57	AN AFFAIR TO REMEMBER (OUR LOVE AFFAIR) (re) *Philips PB 745*	29	2
9 May 58 ★	ON THE STREET WHERE YOU LIVE *Philips PB 819*	1	17
1 Aug 58	THE ONLY MAN ON THE ISLAND *Philips PB 837*	24	3

Richie DAN
UK, male DJ / producer – Richard Gittens (3 WEEKS)

Date	Title	pos	wks
12 Aug 00	CALL IT FATE *Pure Silk CDPSR 1*	34	3

DANA – *See Mark PICCHIOTTI presents BASSTOY featuring DANA*

DANA `479` `Top 500`

Petite teenager won Eurovision Song Contest for Ireland with her first hit in 1970. Born Rosemary Brown (later Scallon), 30 Aug 1951, London, UK. Winning debut hit sold more than two million and was also successful in Australia and South Africa. Ran for Irish presidency in 1997 (75 WEEKS)

Date	Title	pos	wks
4 Apr 70 ★	ALL KINDS OF EVERYTHING (re) *Rex R 11054*	1	16
13 Feb 71	WHO PUT THE LIGHTS OUT *Rex R 11062*	14	11
25 Jan 75 ●	PLEASE TELL HIM THAT I SAID HELLO *GTO GT 6*	8	14
13 Dec 75 ●	IT'S GONNA BE A COLD COLD CHRISTMAS *GTO GT 45*	4	6
6 Mar 76	NEVER GONNA FALL IN LOVE AGAIN *GTO GT 55*	31	4
16 Oct 76	FAIRYTALE *GTO GT 66*	13	16
31 Mar 79	SOMETHING'S COOKIN' IN THE KITCHEN *GTO GT 243*	44	5
15 May 82	I FEEL LOVE COMIN' ON *Creole CR 32*	66	3

DANA INTERNATIONAL
Israel, transgender vocalist – Yaron Cohen (4 WEEKS)

Date	Title	pos	wks
27 Jun 98	DIVA *Dance Pool DANA 1CD*	11	4

DANCE CONSPIRACY
UK, male instrumental / production duo (1 WEEK)

Date	Title	pos	wks
3 Oct 92	DUB WAR *XL Recordings XLT 34*	72	1

DANCE FLOOR VIRUS
Italy, male vocal / instrumental group (2 WEEKS)

Date	Title	pos	wks
21 Oct 95	MESSAGE IN A BOTTLE *Epic 6623742*	49	2

DANCE 2 TRANCE *Germany, male instrumental / production duo – Rolf Ellmer and Dag Lerner (8 WEEKS)*

Date	Title	pos	wks
24 Apr 93	P.OWER OF A.MERICAN N.ATIVES *Logic 74321139582*	25	4
24 Jul 93	TAKE A FREE FALL *Logic 74321153602*	36	3
4 Feb 95	WARRIOR *Logic 74321257722*	56	1

See also JAM & SPOON featuring PLAVKA

Evan DANDO – *See LEMONHEADS; Kirsty MacCOLL*

DANDY WARHOLS
US, male / female vocal / instrumental group (24 WEEKS)

Date	Title	pos	wks
28 Feb 98	EVERY DAY SHOULD BE A HOLIDAY *Capitol CDCL 797*	29	2
2 May 98	NOT IF YOU WERE THE LAST JUNKIE ON EARTH *Capitol CDCL 800*	13	4
8 Aug 98	BOYS BETTER *Capitol CDCLS 805*	36	2
10 Jun 00	GET OFF *Capitol CDCLS 821*	38	2
9 Sep 00	BOHEMIAN LIKE YOU *Capitol CDCLS823*	42	1
7 Jul 01	GODLESS *Capitol CDCL 829*	66	1

Date	Title	pos	wks
10 Nov 01 ●	BOHEMIAN LIKE YOU (re-issue) *Parlophone / Capitol CDCLX 823*	5	10
16 Mar 02	GET OFF (re-issue) *Parlophone / Capitol CDCL 835*	34	2

DANDYS *UK, male vocal / instrumental group (2 WEEKS)*

Date	Title	pos	wks
14 Mar 98	YOU MAKE ME WANT TO SCREAM *Artificial ATFCD 3*	71	1
30 May 98	ENGLISH COUNTRY GARDEN *Artificial ATFCD 4*	57	1

DANE *UK, male vocalist – Dane Bowers (38 WEEKS)*

Date	Title	pos	wks
29 Apr 00 ●	BUGGIN *Nulife 74321753342* [1]	6	8
26 Aug 00 ●	OUT OF YOUR MIND (re) *Nulife 74321782942* [2]	2	20
3 Mar 01 ●	SHUT UP AND FORGET ABOUT IT *Arista 74321835342*	9	5
7 Jul 01 ●	ANOTHER LOVER *Arista 74321863412*	9	5

[1] True Steppers featuring Dane Bowers [2] True Steppers and Dane Bowers featuring Victoria Beckham

D'ANGELO *US, male vocalist – Michael D'Angelo (11 WEEKS)*

Date	Title	pos	wks
28 Oct 95	BROWN SUGAR *Cooltempo CDCOOL 307*	24	3
2 Mar 96	CRUISIN' *Cooltempo CDCOOL 316*	31	2
2 Mar 96	COLD WORLD *Geffen GFSTD 22114* [1]	40	2
15 Jun 96	LADY *Cooltempo CDCOOLS 323*	21	2
22 May 99	BREAK UPS 2 MAKE UPS *Def Jam 8709272* [2]	33	2

[1] Genius / GZA featuring D'Angelo [2] Method Man featuring D'Angelo

DANGER DANGER
US, male vocal / instrumental group (5 WEEKS)

Date	Title	pos	wks
8 Feb 92	MONKEY BUSINESS *Epic 6577517*	42	2
28 Mar 92	I STILL THINK ABOUT YOU *Epic 6578387*	46	2
13 Jun 92	COMIN' HOME *Epic 6581337*	75	1

DAN-I *UK, male vocalist – Selmore Lewinson (9 WEEKS)*

Date	Title	pos	wks
10 Nov 79	MONKEY CHOP *Island WIP 6520*	30	9

Charlie DANIELS BAND
US, male vocal / instrumental group (10 WEEKS)

Date	Title	pos	wks
22 Sep 79	THE DEVIL WENT DOWN TO GEORGIA *Epic EPC 7737*	14	10

Johnny DANKWORTH and His ORCHESTRA *UK, male orchestral group leader / instrumentalist – alto sax (33 WEEKS)*

Date	Title	pos	wks
22 Jun 56 ●	EXPERIMENTS WITH MICE *Parlophone R 4185*	7	12
23 Feb 61 ●	AFRICAN WALTZ *Columbia DB 4590*	9	21

DANNII – *See Dannii MINOGUE*

DANNY and the JUNIORS *US, male vocal group (19 WEEKS)*

Date	Title	pos	wks
17 Jan 58 ●	AT THE HOP *HMV POP 436* ▲	3	14
10 Jul 76	AT THE HOP (re-issue) *ABC 4123*	39	5

DANNY WILSON
UK, male vocal / instrumental group (28 WEEKS)

Date	Title	pos	wks
22 Aug 87 ●	MARY'S PRAYER (re) *Virgin VS 934*	3	18
17 Jun 89	THE SECOND SUMMER OF LOVE *Virgin VS 1186*	23	9
16 Sep 89	NEVER GONNA BE THE SAME *Virgin VS 1203*	69	1

It was not until 'Mary's Prayer' re-entered in Apr 1988 that it reached its peak position of No.3

DANSE SOCIETY
UK, male vocal / instrumental group (5 WEEKS)

Date	Title	pos	wks
27 Aug 83	WAKE UP *Society SOC 5*	61	3
5 Nov 83	HEAVEN IS WAITING *Society SOC 6*	60	2

Steven DANTE *UK, male vocalist – Steven Dennis (16 WEEKS)*

Date	Title	pos	wks
26 Sep 87	THE REAL THING *Chrysalis CHS 3167* [1]	13	10
9 Jul 88	I'M TOO SCARED *Cooltempo DANTE 1*	34	6

[1] Jellybean featuring Steven Dante

Tonja DANTZLER US, female vocalist (1 WEEK)

		pos/wks
17 Dec 94	**IN AND OUT OF MY LIFE** *ffrr FCD 246*	66 1

DANY – See DOUBLE DEE featuring DANY

DANZIG US, male vocal / instrumental group (1 WEEK)

		pos/wks
14 May 94	**MOTHER** *American MOMDD 1*	62 1

DAPHNE US, female vocalist (1 WEEK)

		pos/wks
9 Dec 95	**CHANGE** *Stress CDSTR 54*	71 1

DAPHNE & CELESTE US, female vocal duo
– Daphne DeConcetto and Celeste Cruz (28 WEEKS)

		pos/wks
5 Feb 00 ●	**OOH STICK YOU!** *Universal MCSTD 40209*	8 12
17 Jun 00	**UGLY** *Universal MCSTD 40232*	18 12
2 Sep 00	**SCHOOL'S OUT** *Universal MCSTD 40238*	12 4

Terence Trent D'ARBY (460) Top 500 Unpredictable
US pop / soul singer / songwriter, b. 15 Mar 1962, New York, US, whose success came after relocating to UK. Multi-million-selling, Grammy-winning debut album, 'Introducing the Hardline...', was a worldwide hit. Winner of 1988 Brit award for Best International Newcomer (77 WEEKS)

		pos/wks
14 Mar 87 ●	**IF YOU LET ME STAY** *CBS TRENT 1*	7 13
20 Jun 87 ●	**WISHING WELL** *CBS TRENT 2* ▲	4 11
10 Oct 87	**DANCE LITTLE SISTER (PART ONE)** *CBS TRENT 3*	20 7
9 Jan 88 ●	**SIGN YOUR NAME** *CBS TRENT 4*	2 10
20 Jan 90	**TO KNOW SOMEONE DEEPLY IS TO KNOW SOMEONE SOFTLY** *CBS TRENT 6*	55 3
17 Apr 93	**DO YOU LOVE ME LIKE YOU SAY** *Columbia 6590732*	14 6
19 Jun 93	**DELICATE** *Columbia 6593312* [1]	14 6
28 Aug 93	**SHE KISSED ME** *Columbia 6595922*	16 7
20 Nov 93	**LET HER DOWN EASY** *Columbia 6598642*	18 7
8 Apr 95	**HOLDING ON TO YOU** *Columbia 6614235*	20 6
5 Aug 95	**VIBRATOR** *Columbia 6622585*	57 1

[1] Terence Trent D'Arby featuring Des'ree

Richard DARBYSHIRE UK, male vocalist (7 WEEKS)

		pos/wks
20 Aug 88	**COMING BACK FOR MORE** *Chrysalis JEL 4* [1]	41 3
24 Jul 93	**THIS I SWEAR** *Dome CDDOME 1003*	50 3
12 Feb 94	**WHEN ONLY LOVE WILL DO** *Dome CDDOME 1008*	54 1

[1] Jellybean featuring Richard Darbyshire

DARE UK, male vocal / instrumental group (7 WEEKS)

		pos/wks
29 Apr 89	**THE RAINDANCE** *A&M AM 483*	62 2
29 Jul 89	**ABANDON** *A&M AM 519*	71 2
10 Aug 91	**WE DON'T NEED A REASON** *A&M AM 755*	52 2
5 Oct 91	**REAL LOVE** *A&M AM 824*	67 1

Matt DAREY UK, male producer / instrumentalist (17 WEEKS)

		pos/wks
9 Oct 99	**LIBERATION (TEMPTATION – FLY LIKE AN EAGLE)** *Incentive CENT 1CDS* [1]	19 3
22 Apr 00	**FROM RUSSIA WITH LOVE** *Liquid Asset ASSET CD003* [2]	40 2
15 Jul 00	**BEAUTIFUL** *Incentive CENT 7CDS* [3]	21 4
20 Apr 02 ●	**BEAUTIFUL (re-mix)** *Incentive CENT 38CDS* [4]	10 6
14 Dec 02	**U SHINE ON** *Incentive CENT 50CDS* [5]	34 2

[1] Matt Darey presents Mash Up [2] Matt Darey presents DSP [3] Matt Darey's Mash Up presents Marcella Woods [4] Matt Darey featuring Marcella Woods [5] Matt Darey and Marcella Woods

See also SUNBURST; MELT featuring Little Ms MARCIE; MDM

Bobby DARIN (133) Top 500
Singer / songwriter / actor and multi-instrumentalist who had pop, rock, R&B, country and MOR hits, b. Walden Robert Cassotto, 14 May 1936, New York, d. 20 Dec 1973. This Grammy winner was posthumously inducted into the Rock and Roll Hall of Fame in 1990 (162 WEEKS)

		pos/wks
1 Aug 58	**SPLISH SPLASH (re)** *London HLE 8666*	18 7
9 Jan 59	**QUEEN OF THE HOP** *London HLE 8737*	24 2
29 May 59 ★	**DREAM LOVER** *London HLE 8867*	1 19
25 Sep 59 ★	**MACK THE KNIFE (2re)** *London HLK 8939* ▲	1 18
29 Jan 60 ●	**LA MER (BEYOND THE SEA) (re)** *London HLK 9034*	8 13
31 Mar 60 ●	**CLEMENTINE** *London HLK 9086*	8 12
30 Jun 60	**BILL BAILEY (re)** *London HLK 9142*	34 2
16 Mar 61 ●	**LAZY RIVER** *London HLK 9303*	2 13
6 Jul 61	**NATURE BOY** *London HLK 9375*	24 7
12 Oct 61 ●	**YOU MUST HAVE BEEN A BEAUTIFUL BABY** *London HLK 9429*	10 11
26 Oct 61	**THEME FROM 'COME SEPTEMBER'** *London HLK 9407* [1]	50 1
21 Dec 61 ●	**MULTIPLICATION** *London HLK 9474*	5 13
19 Jul 62 ●	**THINGS** *London HLK 9575*	2 17
4 Oct 62	**IF A MAN ANSWERS** *Capitol CL 15272*	24 6
29 Nov 62	**BABY FACE** *London HLK 9624*	40 4
25 Jul 63	**EIGHTEEN YELLOW ROSES** *Capitol CL 15306*	37 4
13 Oct 66 ●	**IF I WERE A CARPENTER** *Atlantic 584 051*	9 12
14 Apr 79	**DREAM LOVER / MACK THE KNIFE (re-issue)** *Lightning LIG 9017*	64 1

[1] Bobby Darin Orchestra

DARIO G UK, male DJ / production trio (42 WEEKS)

		pos/wks
27 Sep 97 ●	**SUNCHYME** *Eternal WEA 130CD*	2 18
20 Jun 98 ●	**CARNAVAL DE PARIS** *Eternal WEA 162CD*	5 9
12 Sep 98	**SUNMACHINE** *Eternal WEA 173CD*	17 4
25 Mar 00	**VOICES** *Eternal WEA 256CD*	37 2
3 Feb 01 ●	**DREAM TO ME** *Manifesto FESCD 79*	9 6
8 Jun 02	**CARNAVAL 2002 (re-mix)** *Eternal WEA 349CD*	34 3

DARIUS UK, male vocalist – Darius Danesh (20 WEEKS)

		pos/wks
10 Aug 02 ★	**COLOURBLIND** *Mercury 639652* ■	1 16
7 Dec 02 ●	**RUSHES** *Mercury 0638042*	5 4+

DARK MONKS UK, male production duo (1 WEEK)

		pos/wks
14 Sep 02	**INSANE** *Incentive CENT 45CDS*	62 1

DARK STAR
UK, male vocal / instrumental group (6 WEEKS)

		pos/wks
26 Jun 99	**ABOUT 3AM** *Harvest CDEM 545*	50 1
15 Jan 00	**GRACEADELICA** *Harvest CDEMS 556*	25 3
13 May 00	**I AM THE SUN** *Harvest CDEMS 566*	31 2

DARKMAN
UK, male rapper – Brian Mitchell (7 WEEKS)

		pos/wks
14 May 94	**YABBA DABBA DOO** *Wild Card CARDD 6*	49 2
20 Aug 94	**WHO'S THE DARKMAN** *Wild Card CARDD 8*	46 2
3 Dec 94	**YABBA DABBA DOO (re-issue)** *Wild Card CARDD 11*	37 2
21 Oct 95	**BRAND NEW DAY** *Wild Card 5771892*	74 1

DARLING BUDS
UK, male / female vocal / instrumental group (20 WEEKS)

		pos/wks
8 Oct 88	**BURST** *Epic BLOND 1*	50 5
7 Jan 89	**HIT THE GROUND** *CBS BLOND 2*	27 5
25 Mar 89	**LET'S GO ROUND THERE** *CBS BLOND 3*	49 4
22 Jul 89	**YOU'VE GOT TO CHOOSE** *CBS BLOND 4*	45 3
2 Jun 90	**TINY MACHINE** *CBS BLOND 5*	60 2
12 Sep 92	**SURE THING** *Epic 6582157*	71 1

Guy DARRELL UK, male vocalist (13 WEEKS)

		pos/wks
18 Aug 73	**I'VE BEEN HURT** *Santa Ponsa PNS 4*	12 13

James DARREN
US, male vocalist – James Ercolani (25 WEEKS)

		pos/wks
11 Aug 60	**BECAUSE THEY'RE YOUNG** *Pye International 7N 25059*	29 7
14 Dec 61	**GOODBYE CRUEL WORLD** *Pye International 7N 25116*	28 9
29 Mar 62	**HER ROYAL MAJESTY** *Pye International 7N 25125*	36 3
21 Jun 62	**CONSCIENCE** *Pye International 7N 25138*	30 6

DARTS (241) [Top 500] *Britain's best-known doo-wop vocal group; line-up included Den Hegarty, Griff Fender, Rita Ray and Bob Fish. The popular London-based eight-piece band had three successive No.2 hits with revivals of early US rock 'n' roll and R&B songs (117 WEEKS)* pos/wks

		pos	wks
5 Nov 77 ●	DADDY COOL / THE GIRL CAN'T HELP IT *Magnet MAG 100*	6	13
28 Jan 78 ●	COME BACK MY LOVE *Magnet MAG 110*	2	12
6 May 78 ●	THE BOY FROM NEW YORK CITY *Magnet MAG 116*	2	13
5 Aug 78 ●	IT'S RAINING *Magnet MAG 126*	2	11
11 Nov 78	DON'T LET IT FADE AWAY *Magnet MAG 134*	18	11
10 Feb 79 ●	GET IT *Magnet MAG 140*	10	9
21 Jul 79 ●	DUKE OF EARL *Magnet MAG 147*	6	11
20 Oct 79	CAN'T GET ENOUGH OF YOUR LOVE *Magnet MAG 156*	43	6
1 Dec 79	REET PETITE *Magnet MAG 160*	51	7
31 May 80	LET'S HANG ON *Magnet MAG 174*	11	14
6 Sep 80	PEACHES *Magnet MAG 179*	66	3
29 Nov 80	WHITE CHRISTMAS / SH-BOOM (LIFE COULD BE A DREAM) *Magnet MAG 184*	48	7

DARUDE *Finland, male producer – Ville Virtanen (29 WEEKS)* pos/wks

		pos	wks
24 Jun 00 ●	SANDSTORM *Neo NEOCD 033*	3	15
25 Nov 00 ●	FEEL THE BEAT *Neo NEOCD 045*	5	10
15 Sep 01	OUT OF CONTROL (BACK FOR MORE) *Neo NEOCD 067*	13	4

DAS EFX *US, male production / rap duo (5 WEEKS)* pos/wks

		pos	wks
7 Aug 93	CHECK YO SELF *Fourth & Broadway BRCD 283* [1]	36	4
25 Apr 98	RAP SCHOLAR *East West E 3853CD* [2]	42	1

[1] Ice Cube featuring Das EFX [2] Das EFX featuring Redman

The DATSUNS
New Zealand, male vocal / instrumental group (2 WEEKS)

		pos	wks
5 Oct 02	IN LOVE *V2 VVR 5020953*	25	2

N'Dea DAVENPORT *US, female vocalist (7 WEEKS)* pos/wks

		pos	wks
11 Sep 93	TRUST ME *Cooltempo CDCOOL 278* [1]	34	2
20 Jun 98	BRING IT ON *Gee Street VVR5002033*	52	1
15 Dec 01	YOU CAN'T CHANGE ME *Defected DFECT 41CDS* [2]	25	4

[1] Guru featuring N'Dea Davenport [2] Roger Sanchez featuring Armand Van Helden and N'Dea Davenport

See also BRAND NEW HEAVIES; GURU

Anne-Marie DAVID *France, female vocalist (9 WEEKS)* pos/wks

		pos	wks
28 Apr 73	WONDERFUL DREAM *Epic EPC 1446*	13	9

Craig DAVID (377) [Top 500] *Critically lauded singer / songwriter, b. 5 May 1981, Southampton, UK. At 18 years, 11 months and 10 days he was the youngest British male to write and sing a No.1. Won numerous awards for his songs, records and videos. Debut album 'Born To Do It' went gold in 24 countries with UK sales exceeding 1.5 million (87 WEEKS)* pos/wks

		pos	wks
11 Dec 99 ●	RE-REWIND THE CROWD SAY BO SELECTA *Public Demand / Relentless RELENT 1CDS* [1]	2	17
15 Apr 00 ★	FILL ME IN *Wildstar CDWILD 28* ■	1	14
15 Jul 00 ●	WOMAN TROUBLE *Public Demand / ffrr FCD 380* [2]	6	10
5 Aug 00 ★	7 DAYS (re) *Wildstar CDWILD 30* ■	1	15
2 Dec 00 ●	WALKING AWAY *Wildstar CDWILD 35*	3	13
31 Mar 01 ●	RENDEZVOUS *Wildstar CDWILD 36*	8	10
9 Nov 02 ●	WHAT'S YOUR FLAVA? *Wildstar CDWILD 43*	8	8+

[1] Artful Dodger featuring Craig David [2] Artful Dodger and Robbie Craig featuring Craig David

FR DAVID *France, male vocalist – Robert Fitoussi (13 WEEKS)* pos/wks

		pos	wks
2 Apr 83 ●	WORDS *Carrere CAR 248*	2	12
18 Jun 83	MUSIC *Carrere CAR 282*	71	1

DAVID and JONATHAN
UK, male vocal duo – Roger Greenaway and Roger Cook (22 WEEKS) pos/wks

		pos	wks
13 Jan 66	MICHELLE *Columbia DB 7800*	11	6

		pos	wks
7 Jul 66 ●	LOVERS OF THE WORLD UNITE *Columbia DB 7950*	7	16

See also BLUE MINK; PIPKINS

Jim DAVIDSON *UK, male vocalist (4 WEEKS)* pos/wks

		pos	wks
27 Dec 80	WHITE CHRISTMAS / TOO RISKY *Scratch SCR 001*	52	4

Paul DAVIDSON *Jamaica, male vocalist (10 WEEKS)* pos/wks

		pos	wks
27 Dec 75 ●	MIDNIGHT RIDER *Tropical ALO 56*	10	10

Dave DAVIES *UK, male vocalist (17 WEEKS)* pos/wks

		pos	wks
19 Jul 67 ●	DEATH OF A CLOWN *Pye 7N 17356*	3	10
6 Dec 67	SUZANNAH'S STILL ALIVE *Pye 7N 17429*	20	7

See also KINKS

Windsor DAVIES and Don ESTELLE
UK, male actors / vocal duo (16 WEEKS) pos/wks

		pos	wks
17 May 75 ★	WHISPERING GRASS *EMI 2290* [1]	1	12
25 Oct 75	PAPER DOLL *EMI 2361* [2]	41	4

[1] Windsor Davies as BSM Williams and Don Estelle as Gunner Sugden (Lofty)
[2] Don Estelle and Windsor Davies

Billie DAVIS *UK, female vocalist – Carol Hedges (33 WEEKS)* pos/wks

		pos	wks
30 Aug 62	WILL I WHAT *Parlophone R 4932* [1]	18	10
7 Feb 63 ●	TELL HIM *Decca F 11572*	10	12
30 May 63	HE'S THE ONE *Decca F 11658*	40	3
9 Oct 68	I WANT YOU TO BE MY BABY *Decca F 12823*	33	8

[1] Mike Sarne with Billie Davis

Billy DAVIS Jr – See Marilyn McCOO and Billy DAVIS Jr

Darlene DAVIS *US, female vocalist (5 WEEKS)* pos/wks

		pos	wks
7 Feb 87	I FOUND LOVE *Serious 70US 1*	55	5

John DAVIS and the MONSTER ORCHESTRA
US, male vocal / instrumental group (2 WEEKS) pos/wks

		pos	wks
10 Feb 79	AIN'T THAT ENOUGH FOR YOU *Miracle M 2*	70	2

Mac DAVIS *US, male vocalist (22 WEEKS)* pos/wks

		pos	wks
4 Nov 72	BABY DON'T GET HOOKED ON ME *CBS 8250* ▲	29	6
15 Nov 80	IT'S HARD TO BE HUMBLE *Casablanca CAN 210*	27	16

Richie DAVIS – See SHUT UP AND DANCE

Roy DAVIS Jr featuring Peven EVERETT
US, male producer, male vocalist (4 WEEKS) pos/wks

		pos	wks
1 Nov 97	GABRIEL *XL XLS 88CD*	22	4

Ruth DAVIS – See Bo KIRKLAND and Ruth DAVIS

Sammy DAVIS Jr *US, male vocalist, d. 16 May 1990 (37 WEEKS)* pos/wks

		pos	wks
29 Jul 55	SOMETHING'S GOTTA GIVE (re) *Brunswick LAT 8296*	11	7
9 Sep 55 ●	LOVE ME OR LEAVE ME (re) *Brunswick 05428*	8	8
30 Sep 55	THAT OLD BLACK MAGIC *Brunswick 05450*	16	1
7 Oct 55	HEY THERE *Brunswick 05469*	19	1
20 Apr 56	IN A PERSIAN MARKET *Brunswick 05518*	28	1
28 Dec 56	ALL OF YOU *Brunswick 05629*	28	1
16 Jun 60	HAPPY TO MAKE YOUR ACQUAINTANCE *Brunswick 05830* [1]	46	1
22 Mar 62	WHAT KIND OF FOOL AM I? / GONNA BUILD A MOUNTAIN *Reprise R 20048*	26	8
13 Dec 62	ME AND MY SHADOW (re) *Reprise R 20128* [2]	20	9

[1] Sammy Davis Jr and Carmen McRae [2] Frank Sinatra and Sammy Davis Jr

Skeeter DAVIS *US, female vocalist – Mary Penick (13 WEEKS)* pos/wks

		pos	wks
14 Mar 63	END OF THE WORLD *RCA 1328*	18	13

Zelma DAVIS – See C & C MUSIC FACTORY

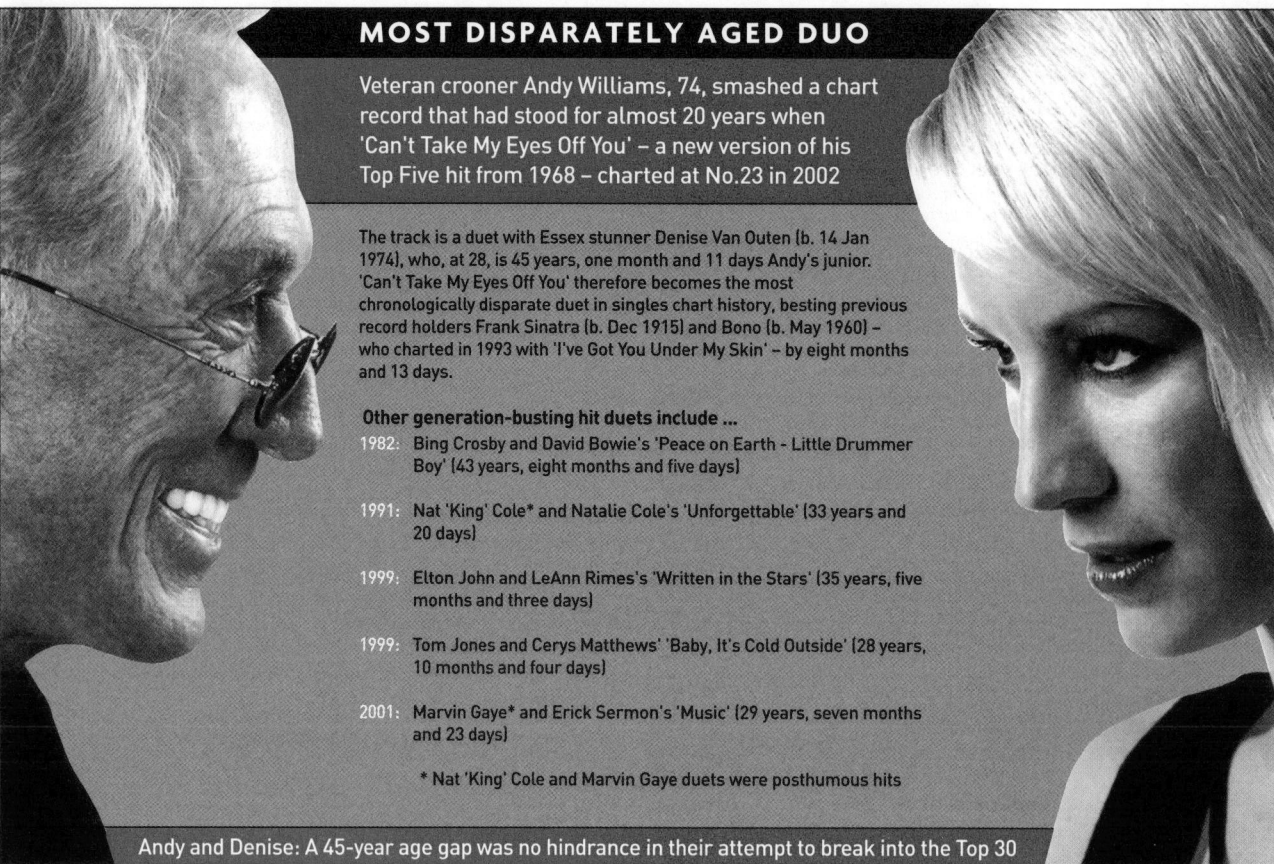

MOST DISPARATELY AGED DUO

Veteran crooner Andy Williams, 74, smashed a chart record that had stood for almost 20 years when 'Can't Take My Eyes Off You' – a new version of his Top Five hit from 1968 – charted at No.23 in 2002

The track is a duet with Essex stunner Denise Van Outen (b. 14 Jan 1974), who, at 28, is 45 years, one month and 11 days Andy's junior. 'Can't Take My Eyes Off You' therefore becomes the most chronologically disparate duet in singles chart history, besting previous record holders Frank Sinatra (b. Dec 1915) and Bono (b. May 1960) – who charted in 1993 with 'I've Got You Under My Skin' – by eight months and 13 days.

Other generation-busting hit duets include ...

1982: Bing Crosby and David Bowie's 'Peace on Earth - Little Drummer Boy' (43 years, eight months and five days)

1991: Nat 'King' Cole* and Natalie Cole's 'Unforgettable' (33 years and 20 days)

1999: Elton John and LeAnn Rimes's 'Written in the Stars' (35 years, five months and three days)

1999: Tom Jones and Cerys Matthews' 'Baby, It's Cold Outside' (28 years, 10 months and four days)

2001: Marvin Gaye* and Erick Sermon's 'Music' (29 years, seven months and 23 days)

* Nat 'King' Cole and Marvin Gaye duets were posthumous hits

Andy and Denise: A 45-year age gap was no hindrance in their attempt to break into the Top 30

8 Jun 96	SUMMER HOLIDAY MEDLEY *RCA 74321384472*	**17** 4
9 May 98	HOW CAN I BE SURE ? *Eastcoast DDCD 001*	**71** 1

Doris DAY (159 Top 500) *The Fifties' favourite singer / actress, b. Doris Kappelhoff, 3 Apr 1924, Cincinnati. The No.1 female movie star of that era, she also had numerous British hits (not to mention 25 US bestsellers) before the UK chart first started (146 WEEKS)* pos/wks

14 Nov 52	● SUGARBUSH (re) *Columbia DB 3123* [1]	**8** 8
21 Nov 52	● MY LOVE AND DEVOTION *Columbia DB 3157*	**10** 2
3 Apr 53	MA SAYS, PA SAYS *Columbia DB3242* [2]	**12** 1
17 Apr 53	FULL TIME JOB *Columbia DB 3242* [2]	**11** 1
24 Jul 53	● LET'S WALK THAT-A-WAY *Philips PB 157* [2]	**4** 14
2 Apr 54	★ SECRET LOVE *Philips PB 230* ▲	**1** 29
27 Aug 54	● THE BLACK HILLS OF DAKOTA *Philips PB 287*	**7** 8
1 Oct 54	● IF I GIVE MY HEART TO YOU *Philips PB 325* [3]	**4** 11
8 Apr 55	● READY, WILLING AND ABLE *Philips PB 402*	**7** 9
9 Sep 55	LOVE ME OR LEAVE ME *Philips PB 479*	**20** 1
21 Oct 55	I'LL NEVER STOP LOVING YOU (re) *Philips PB 497*	**17** 3
29 Jun 56	★ WHATEVER WILL BE, WILL BE (QUE SERA, SERA) *Philips PB 586*	**1** 22
13 Jun 58	A VERY PRECIOUS LOVE *Philips PB 799*	**16** 11
15 Aug 58	EVERYBODY LOVES A LOVER (re) *Philips PB 843*	**25** 4
12 Mar 64	● MOVE OVER DARLING *CBS AAG 183*	**8** 16
18 Apr 87	● MOVE OVER DARLING (re-issue) *CBS LEGS 1*	**45** 6

[1] Doris Day and Frankie Laine [2] Doris Day and Johnnie Ray [3] Doris Day with The Mellomen

Inaya DAY *US, female vocalist – Inaya Davis (3 WEEKS)* pos/wks

22 May 99	JUST CAN'T GET ENOUGH *AM:PM CDAMPM 121* [1]	**39** 2
7 Oct 00	FEEL IT *Positiva CDTIV 141*	**51** 1

[1] Harry 'Choo Choo' Romero presents Inaya Day

See also Boris DLUGOSCH

Patti DAY *US, female vocalist (1 WEEK)* pos/wks

9 Dec 89	RIGHT BEFORE MY EYES *Debut DEBT 3080*	**69** 1

DAY ONE *UK, male vocal / instrumental duo (1 WEEK)* pos/wks

13 Nov 99	I'M DOIN' FINE *Melankolic / Virgin SADD6*	**68** 1

DAYEENE *Sweden, female vocal duo (1 WEEK)* pos/wks

17 Jul 99	AND IT HURTS *Pukka CDPUKKA 20*	**63** 1

Taylor DAYNE
US, female vocalist – Leslie Wundermann (54 WEEKS) pos/wks

23 Jan 88	● TELL IT TO MY HEART *Arista 109616*	**3** 13
19 Mar 88	● PROVE YOUR LOVE *Arista 109830*	**8** 10
11 Jun 88	I'LL ALWAYS LOVE YOU *Arista 111536*	**41** 7
18 Nov 89	WITH EVERY BEAT OF MY HEART *Arista 112760*	**53** 2
14 Apr 90	I'LL BE YOUR SHELTER *Arista 112996*	**43** 5
4 Aug 90	LOVE WILL LEAD YOU BACK *Arista 113277* ▲	**69** 1
3 Jul 93	CAN'T GET ENOUGH OF YOUR LOVE *Arista 74321147852*	**14** 8
16 Apr 94	I'LL WAIT *Arista 74321203472*	**29** 3
4 Feb 95	ORIGINAL SIN (THEME FROM 'THE SHADOW') *Arista 74321223462*	**63** 1
18 Nov 95	SAY A PRAYER *Arista 74321324292*	**58** 1
13 Jan 96	TELL IT TO MY HEART (re-mix) *Arista 74321335962*	**23** 3

DAYTON *US, male vocal group (1 WEEK)* pos/wks

10 Dec 83	THE SOUND OF MUSIC *Capitol CL 318*	**75** 1

DAZZ BAND *US, male vocal / instrumental group (12 WEEKS)* pos/wks

3 Nov 84	LET IT ALL BLOW *Motown TMG 1361*	**12** 12

Darryl D'BONNEAU – See Barbara TUCKER; FONTANA featuring Darryl D'BONNEAU

D'BORA *US, female vocalist – Deborah Walker (4 WEEKS)* pos/wks

14 Sep 91	DREAM ABOUT YOU *Polydor PO 161*	**75** 1

1 Jul 95	GOING ROUND *Vibe MCSTD 2055*	**40** 2
30 Mar 96	GOOD LOVE REAL LOVE *Music Plant MCSTD 40023*	**58** 1

Nino DE ANGELO *Germany, male vocalist (5 WEEKS)* pos/wks

21 Jul 84	GUARDIAN ANGEL *Carrere CAR 335*	**57** 5

DE BOS *Holland, male DJ / producer (1 WEEK)* pos/wks

25 Oct 97	ON THE RUN *Jive JIVECD 433*	**51** 1

Chris DE BURGH *Ireland, male vocalist (71 WEEKS)* pos/wks

23 Oct 82	DON'T PAY THE FERRYMAN *A&M AMS 8256*	**48** 5
12 May 84	HIGH ON EMOTION *A&M AM 190*	**44** 5
12 Jul 86	★ THE LADY IN RED (re) *A&M AM 331*	**1** 15
20 Sep 86	FATAL HESITATION *A&M AM 346*	**44** 4
13 Dec 86	A SPACEMAN CAME TRAVELLING / THE BALLROOM OF ROMANCE *A&M AM 365*	**40** 5
12 Dec 87	THE SIMPLE TRUTH (A CHILD IS BORN) (re) *A&M AM 427*	**55** 3
29 Oct 88	● MISSING YOU *A&M AM 474*	**3** 12
7 Jan 89	TENDER HANDS *A&M AM 486*	**43** 6
14 Oct 89	THIS WAITING HEART *A&M AM 528*	**59** 3
25 May 91	THE SIMPLE TRUTH (A CHILD IS BORN) (re-issue) *A&M RELF 1*	**36** 2
11 Apr 92	SEPARATE TABLES *A&M AM 863*	**30** 4
21 May 94	BLONDE HAIR BLUE JEANS *A&M 5805932*	**51** 1
9 Dec 95	THE SNOWS OF NEW YORK *A&M 5813132*	**60** 1
27 Sep 97	SO BEAUTIFUL *A&M 5823932*	**29** 4
18 Sep 99	WHEN I THINK OF YOU *A&M / Mercury 4971302*	**59** 1

DE CASTRO SISTERS *Cuba, female vocal group (1 WEEK)* pos/wks

11 Feb 55	TEACH ME TONIGHT *London HL 8104*	**20**

DE-CODE featuring Beverli SKEETE
UK, male / female vocal / instrumental group (1 WEEK) pos/wks

18 May 96	WONDERWALL / SOME MIGHT SAY *Neoteric NRCD 2*	**69** 1

Etienne DE CRECY
France, male DJ / producer (3 WEEKS) pos/wks

28 Mar 98	PRIX CHOC REMIXES *Different DIF 007CD*	**60** 1
20 Jan 01	AM I WRONG *XL Recordings XLS 127 CD*	**44** 2

DE FUNK featuring F45
Italy / UK, male production / vocal group (1 WEEK) pos/wks

25 Sep 99	PLEASURE LOVE *INCredible INCS 3CD*	**49** 1

Lennie DE ICE *UK, male producer (1 WEEK)* pos/wks

17 Apr 99	WE ARE I. E. *Distinctive DISNCD 50*	**61** 1

DE LA SOUL *US, male rap group (63 WEEKS)* pos/wks

8 Apr 89	ME MYSELF AND I *Big Life BLR 7*	**22** 8
8 Jul 89	SAY NO GO *Big Life BLR 10*	**18** 7
21 Oct 89	EYE KNOW *Big Life BLR 13*	**14** 7
23 Dec 89	● THE MAGIC NUMBER / BUDDY *Big Life BLR 14*	**7** 8
24 Mar 90	MAMA GAVE BIRTH TO THE SOUL CHILDREN *Gee Street GEE 26* [1]	**14** 7
27 Apr 91	● RING RING RING (HA HA HEY) *Big Life BLR 42*	**10** 7
3 Aug 91	A ROLLER SKATING JAM NAMED 'SATURDAYS' *Big Life BLR 55*	**22** 5
23 Nov 91	KEEPIN' THE FAITH *Big Life BLR 64*	**50** 2
18 Sep 93	BREAKADAWN *Big Life BLRD 103*	**39** 3
2 Apr 94	FALLIN' *Epic 6602622* [2]	**59** 1
29 Jun 96	STAKES IS HIGH *Tommy Boy TBCD 7730*	**55** 1
8 Mar 97	4 MORE *Tommy Boy TBCD 7779A* [3]	**52** 1
22 Jul 00	OOOH *Tommy Boy TBCD 2102* [4]	**29** 2
11 Nov 00	ALL GOOD *Tommy Boy TBCD 2154B* [5]	**33** 3
2 Mar 02	BABY PHAT *Tommy Boy TBCD 2359A*	**55** 1

[1] Queen Latifah + De La Soul [2] Teenage Fanclub and De La Soul [3] De La Soul featuring Zhané [4] De La Soul featuring Redman [5] De La Soul featuring Chaka Khan. *'Buddy' listed only until 6 Jan 1990, peaking at No.8*

Donna DE LORY US, female vocalist (1 WEEK)
pos/wks
24 Jul 93	JUST A DREAM MCA MCSTD 1750	71 1

Vincent DE MOOR Holland, male producer (4 WEEKS)
pos/wks
16 Aug 97	FLOWTATION XL Recordings XLS 89CD	54 1
7 Apr 01	FLY AWAY VC Recordings VCRD 87	30 3

See also VERACOCHA

DE NADA UK, male / female production / vocal group (7 WEEKS)
pos/wks
25 Aug 01	LOVE YOU ANYWAY Wildstar CDWILD 37	15 4
9 Feb 02	BRING IT ON TO MY LOVE Wildstar CDWILD 39	24 3

DE NUIT Italy, male production duo
– Fabio Seveso and Francesco de Leo (2 WEEKS)
pos/wks
23 Nov 02	ALL THAT MATTERED (LOVE YOU DOWN) Credence CDCRED 029	38 2

Lynsey DE PAUL
UK, female vocalist / songwriter – Lynsey Rubin (54 WEEKS)
19 Aug 72 ●	SUGAR ME MAM 81	5 11
2 Dec 72	GETTING A DRAG MAM 88	18 8
27 Oct 73	WON'T SOMEBODY DANCE WITH ME MAM 109	14 7
8 Jun 74	OOH I DO Warner Bros. K 16401	25 6
2 Nov 74 ●	NO HONESTLY Jet 747	7 11
22 Mar 75	MY MAN AND ME Jet 750	40 4
26 Mar 77	ROCK BOTTOM Polydor 2058 859 [1]	19 7

[1] Lynsey De Paul and Mike Moran

Tullio DE PISCOPO Italy, male vocalist (4 WEEKS)
pos/wks
28 Feb 87	STOP BAJON ... PRIMAVERA Greyhound GREY 9	58 4

Rebecca DE RUVO Sweden, female vocalist (1 WEEK)
pos/wks
1 Oct 94	I CAUGHT YOU OUT Arista 74321230782	72 1

Teri DE SARIO US, female vocalist (5 WEEKS)
pos/wks
2 Sep 78	AIN'T NOTHING GONNA KEEP ME FROM YOU Casablanca CAN 128	52 5

Stephanie DE SYKES
UK, female vocalist – Stephanie Ryton (17 WEEKS)
pos/wks
20 Jul 74 ●	BORN WITH A SMILE ON MY FACE Bradley's BRAD 7409 [1]	2 10
19 Apr 75	WE'LL FIND OUR DAY Bradley's BRAD 7509	17 7

[1] Stephanie De Sykes with Rain

Tony DE VIT UK, male DJ / producer, d. 2 Jul 1998 (12 WEEKS)
pos/wks
4 Mar 95	BURNING UP Icon ICONCD 001	25 3
12 Aug 95	HOOKED Labello Dance LAD 18CD [1]	28 2
9 Sep 95	TO THE LIMIT X:Plode BANG 1CD	44 2
30 May 96	I'LL BE THERE Labello Dance LAD 25CD1 [1]	37 2
28 Oct 00	DAWN Tidy Trax TIDY 140CD	56 2
21 Dec 02	I DON'T CARE Tidy Trax TIDY 181T	65 1

[1] 99th Floor Elevators featuring Tony De Vit

DEACON BLUE 259 Top 500
Scottish sextet with fervent following, led by singer / songwriter Ricky Ross (v) and featuring his wife Lorraine McIntosh (v). Named after the Steely Dan song, they achieved five Top 5 albums, including the million-selling 'When the World Knows Your Name' (112 WEEKS)
pos/wks
23 Jan 88	DIGNITY CBS DEAC 4	31 8
9 Apr 88	WHEN WILL YOU MAKE MY TELEPHONE RING CBS DEAC 5	34 7
16 Jul 88	CHOCOLATE GIRL CBS DEAC 6	43 7
15 Oct 88 ●	REAL GONE KID CBS DEAC 7	8 13
4 Mar 89	WAGES DAY CBS DEAC 8	18 6
20 May 89	FERGUS SINGS THE BLUES CBS DEAC 9	14 6
16 Sep 89	LOVE AND REGRET CBS DEAC 10	28 5

6 Jan 90	QUEEN OF THE NEW YEAR CBS DEAC 11	21	5
25 Aug 90 ●	FOUR BACHARACH AND DAVID SONGS (EP) CBS DEAC 12	2	9
25 May 91	YOUR SWAYING ARMS Columbia 6568937	23	4
27 Jul 91 ●	TWIST AND SHOUT Columbia 6573027	10	9
12 Oct 91	CLOSING TIME Columbia 6575027	42	3
14 Dec 91	COVER FROM THE SKY Columbia 6576737	31	4
28 Nov 92	YOUR TOWN Columbia 6587867	14	8
13 Feb 93	WILL WE BE LOVERS Columbia 6589732	31	4
24 Apr 93	ONLY TENDER LOVE Columbia 6591842	22	4
17 Jul 93	HANG YOUR HEAD Columbia 6594602	21	3
2 Apr 94	I WAS RIGHT AND YOU WERE WRONG Columbia 6602222	32	3
28 May 94	DIGNITY (re-issue) Columbia 6604485	20	3
28 Apr 01	EVERYTIME YOU SLEEP Papillon BTFLY 0011	64	1

Tracks on Four Bacharach and David Songs (EP): I'll Never Fall in Love Again / The Look of Love / Message to Michael / Are You There (With Another Girl). 'Dignity' in 1994 was the original recording of the song first issued in 1987 when it failed to chart

DEAD DRED UK, male instrumental / production duo (2 WEEKS)
pos/wks
5 Nov 94	DRED BASS Moving Shadow SHADOW 50CD	60 2

DEAD END KIDS UK, male vocal / instrumental group (10 WKS)
pos/wks
26 Mar 77 ●	HAVE I THE RIGHT CBS 4972	6 10

DEAD KENNEDYS US, male vocal / instrumental group (9 WKS)
pos/wks
1 Nov 80	KILL THE POOR Cherry Red CHERRY 16	49 3
30 May 81	TOO DRUNK TO FUCK Cherry Red CHERRY 24	36 6

DEAD OR ALIVE UK, male vocal / instrumental group (70 WEEKS)
pos/wks
24 Mar 84	THAT'S THE WAY (I LIKE IT) Epic A 4271	22	9
1 Dec 84 ★	YOU SPIN ME ROUND (LIKE A RECORD) Epic A 4861	1	23
20 Apr 85	LOVER COME BACK TO ME Epic A 6086	11	8
29 Jun 85	IN TOO DEEP Epic A 6360	14	8
21 Sep 85	MY HEART GOES BANG (GET ME TO THE DOCTOR) Epic A 6571	23	6
20 Sep 86	BRAND NEW LOVER Epic A 650075 7	31	4
10 Jan 87	SOMETHING IN MY HOUSE Epic BURNS 1	12	7
4 Apr 87	HOOKED ON LOVE Epic BURNS 2	69	2
3 Sep 88	TURN ROUND AND COUNT 2 TEN Epic BURNS 4	70	1
22 Jul 89	COME HOME WITH ME BABY Epic BURNS 5	62	2

DEAD PREZ US, male rap duo (2 WEEKS)
pos/wks
11 Mar 00	HIP HOP Epic 6689862	41 2

DEADLY SINS
UK / Italy, male vocal / instrumental duo (2 WEEKS)
pos/wks
30 Apr 94	WE ARE GOING ON DOWN Ffrreedom TABCD 220	45 2

Hazell DEAN UK, female vocalist (71 WEEKS)
pos/wks
18 Feb 84	EVERGREEN / JEALOUS LOVE Proto ENA 114	63 3
21 Apr 84 ●	SEARCHIN' (I GOTTA FIND A MAN) Proto ENA 109	6 15
28 Jul 84 ●	WHATEVER I DO (WHEREVER I GO) Proto ENA 119	4 11
3 Nov 84	BACK IN MY ARMS (ONCE AGAIN) Proto ENA 122	41 4
2 Mar 85	NO FOOL (FOR LOVE) Proto ENA 123	41 5
12 Oct 85	THEY SAY IT'S GONNA RAIN Parlophone R 6107	58 4
2 Apr 88 ●	WHO'S LEAVING WHO EMI EM 45	4 11
25 Jun 88	MAYBE (WE SHOULD CALL IT A DAY) EMI EM 62	15 6
24 Sep 88	TURN IT INTO LOVE EMI EM 71	21 7
26 Aug 89	LOVE PAINS Lisson DOLE 12	48 4
23 Mar 91	BETTER OFF WITHOUT YOU Lisson DOLE 19	72 1

Jimmy DEAN US, male vocalist – Seth Ward (17 WEEKS)
pos/wks
26 Oct 61 ●	BIG BAD JOHN Philips PB 1187 ▲	2 13
8 Nov 62	LITTLE BLACK BOOK CBS AAG 122	33 4

Letitia DEAN and Paul MEDFORD
UK, female / male vocal duo (7 WEEKS)
pos/wks
25 Oct 86	SOMETHING OUTA NOTHING BBC RESL 203	12 7

Re-entries are listed as (re), (2re), (3re), etc which signifies that the hit re-entered the chart once, twice or three times, etc

Sheryl DEANE – See THRILLSEEKERS

DEANNA – See David MORALES

DEAR JON *UK, female / male vocal / instrumental group (1 WEEK)* pos/wks
22 Apr 95	ONE GIFT OF LOVE *MDMC DEVCS 2*	68	1

DEATH IN VEGAS *UK, male instrumental / production*
duo – Richard Fearless and Tim Holmes (10 WEEKS) pos/wks
2 Aug 97	DIRT *Concrete HARD 27CD*	61	1
1 Nov 97	ROCCO *Concrete HARD 29CD*	51	1
12 Feb 00 ●	AISHA *Concrete HARD 43CD*	9	4
6 May 00	DIRGE *Concrete HARD 44CD*	24	2
21 Sep 02	HANDS AROUND MY THROAT *Concrete HARD 48CD*	36	1
28 Dec 02	SCORPIO RISING *Concrete HARD 54CD1* 1	14	1+

1 Death In Vegas with Liam Gallagher

Uncredited vocal on 'Aisha' by Iggy Pop

DeBARGE *US, male / female vocal group (17 WEEKS)* pos/wks
6 Apr 85 ●	RHYTHM OF THE NIGHT *Gordy TMG 1376*	4	14
21 Sep 85	YOU WEAR IT WELL *Gordy ZB 40345* 1	54	3

1 El DeBarge with DeBarge

See also El DeBARGE; Chico DeBARGE

Chico DeBARGE *US, male vocalist (1 WEEK)* pos/wks
14 Mar 98	IGGIN' ME *Universal UND 56170*	50	1

See also DeBARGE

El DeBARGE *US, male vocalist (3 WEEKS)* pos/wks
28 Jun 86	WHO'S JOHNNY ('SHORT CIRCUIT' THEME) *Gordy ELD 1*	60	2
31 Mar 90	SECRET GARDEN *Qwest W 9992* 1	67	1

1 Quincy Jones featuring Al B Sure!, James Ingram, El DeBarge and Barry White

See also DeBARGE

Diana DECKER *US, female vocalist (10 WEEKS)* pos/wks
23 Oct 53 ●	POPPA PICCOLINO (re) *Columbia DB 3325*	2	10

DECLAN featuring YOUNG VOICES CHOIR
UK, male vocalist – Declan Galbraith (2 WEEKS) pos/wks
21 Dec 02	TELL ME WHY *EMI / Liberty CDDECS 004*	29	2+

Dave DEE *UK, male vocalist (4 WEEKS)* pos/wks
14 Mar 70	MY WOMAN'S MAN *Fontana TF 1074*	42	4

See also Dave DEE, DOZY, BEAKY, MICK and TICH

Dave DEE, DOZY, BEAKY, MICK and TICH 177 Top 500
*Quirkily named UK quintet was very popular in late 1960s: Dave Dee
(David Harman) (v), Dozy (Trevor Davies) (b), Beaky (John Dymond) (g),
Mick (Michael Wilson) (d), Tich (Ian Amey) (g). Catchy productions and
ultra-commercial songs (penned by managers Howard and Blaikley)
ensured string of hits (141 WEEKS)* pos/wks
23 Dec 65	YOU MAKE IT MOVE *Fontana TF 630*	26	8
3 Mar 66 ●	HOLD TIGHT! *Fontana TF 671*	4	17
9 Jun 66 ●	HIDEAWAY *Fontana TF 711*	10	11
15 Sep 66 ●	BEND IT! *Fontana TF 746*	2	12
8 Dec 66 ●	SAVE ME *Fontana TF 775*	3	10
9 Mar 67	TOUCH ME, TOUCH ME *Fontana TF 798*	13	9
18 May 67 ●	OKAY! *Fontana TF 830*	4	11
11 Oct 67 ●	ZABADAK! *Fontana TF 873*	3	14
14 Feb 68 ★	THE LEGEND OF XANADU *Fontana TF 903*	1	12
3 Jul 68 ●	LAST NIGHT IN SOHO *Fontana TF 953*	8	11
2 Oct 68	THE WRECK OF THE 'ANTOINETTE' *Fontana TF 971*	14	9
5 Mar 69	DON JUAN *Fontana TF 1000*	23	9
14 May 69	SNAKE IN THE GRASS *Fontana TF 1020*	23	8

Jazzy DEE *US, male rapper / instrumentalist (5 WEEKS)* pos/wks
5 Mar 83	GET ON UP *Laurie LRS 101*	53	5

Joey DEE and the STARLITERS
US, male vocal / instrumental group (8 WEEKS) pos/wks
8 Feb 62	PEPPERMINT TWIST *Columbia DB 4758* ▲	33	8

Kiki DEE 438 Top 500
*First white UK artist to secure a recording deal with Tamla Motown,
b. Pauline Matthews, 6 Mar 1947, Bradford, UK. The vocalist received an
Olivier Award nomination in 1989 for her acting skills demonstrated in Willy
Russell's West End stage hit 'Blood Brothers' (79 WEEKS)* pos/wks
10 Nov 73	AMOUREUSE *Rocket PIG 4*	13	13
7 Sep 74	I'VE GOT THE MUSIC IN ME *Rocket PIG 12* 1	19	8
12 Apr 75	(YOU DONT KNOW) HOW GLAD I AM *Rocket PIG 16* 1	33	4
3 Jul 76 ★	DON'T GO BREAKING MY HEART *Rocket ROKN 512* 2 ▲	1	14
11 Sep 76	LOVING AND FREE / AMOUREUSE (re-issue) *Rocket ROKN 515*	13	8
19 Feb 77	FIRST THING IN THE MORNING *Rocket ROKN 520*	32	5
11 Jun 77	CHICAGO *Rocket ROKN 526*	28	4
21 Feb 81	STAR *Ariola ARO 251*	13	10
23 May 81	PERFECT TIMING *Ariola ARO 257*	66	3
20 Nov 93 ●	TRUE LOVE *Rocket EJSCX 32* 2	2	10

1 Kiki Dee Band 2 Elton John and Kiki Dee

*On 18 Sep, 25 Sep and 2 Oct 1976, 'Loving and Free' was listed by itself. 'Chicago'
was one side of a double-sided chart entry, the other being 'Bite Your Lip (Get Up
and Dance)' by Elton John*

Nancy DEE – See BENELUX and Nancy DEE

DEE DEE *Belgium, male production trio*
and female vocalist – Diana Trippaers (7 WEEKS) pos/wks
20 Jul 02	FOREVER *Incentive CENT 43CDS*	12	7

Trio includes Christophe Chantzis and Eric Vanspauwen (Ian Van Dahl)

DEEE-LITE *US / Russia / Japan, male*
/ female vocal / instrumental group (30 WEEKS) pos/wks
18 Aug 90 ●	GROOVE IS IN THE HEART / WHAT IS LOVE *Elektra EKR 114*	2	13
24 Nov 90	POWER OF LOVE / DEEE-LITE THEME *Elektra EKR 117*	25	7
23 Feb 91	HOW DO YOU SAY ... LOVE / GROOVE IS IN THE HEART (re-mix) *Elektra EKR 118*	52	2
27 Apr 91	GOOD BEAT *Elektra EKR 122*	53	3
13 Jun 92	RUNAWAY *Elektra EKR 148*	45	3
30 Jul 94	PICNIC IN THE SUMMERTIME *Elektra EKR 186CD1*	43	2

'What Is Love' listed only from 25 Aug 1990

DEEJAY PUNK-ROC *US, male DJ / producer (5 WEEKS)* pos/wks
21 Mar 98	DEAD HUSBAND *Independiente ISOM 9MS*	71	1
9 May 98	MY BEATBOX *Independiente ISOM 12MS*	43	1
8 Aug 98	FAR OUT *Independiente ISOM 17MS*	43	2
20 Feb 99	ROC-IN-IT *Independiente ISOM 21MS* 1	59	1

1 Deejay Punk-Roc vs Onyx

DEEJAY SVEN – See MC MIKER 'G' and Deejay SVEN

Carol DEENE *UK, female vocalist (25 WEEKS)* pos/wks
26 Oct 61	SAD MOVIES (MAKE ME CRY) *HMV POP 922*	44	3
25 Jan 62	NORMAN *HMV POP 973*	24	8
5 Jul 62	JOHNNY GET ANGRY *HMV POP 1027*	32	4
23 Aug 62	SOME PEOPLE *HMV POP 1058*	25	10

Scotti DEEP
US, male producer / instrumentalist (1 WEEK) pos/wks
15 Mar 97	BROOKLYN BEATS *Xtravaganza 0090095*	67	1

MACK THE KNIFE

■ In 1959, with rock 'n' roll at its peak, the idea of a hitmaking rocker recording a finger-snapping, Sinatra-styled version of a 30-year-old German operatic aria couldn't have sounded like a very commercial proposition. Add to this the fact that it involved a gory story about a Victorian murderer in London, and that it had been a big hit three years earlier, then the chances of it selling well must have seemed small.

Kurt Weill and Berthold Brecht wrote 'Mack the Knife' as 'Mordtat' (translated as "murder deed") in 1928 as an 11th-hour addition to their modern opera 'Die Dreigroschenoper', based on English writer John Gay's 'The Beggar's Opera'. American Marc Blitzstein was most impressed with the show, and in 1950 suggested to Weill that he write an English lyric. Weill, who relocated to the US in 1935 to escape the Nazis, was keen on Blitzstein's involvement, but died before hearing the unique lyric Blitzstein penned for the song then known as 'The Ballad of Mac the Knife'. Blitzstein first staged 'The Threepenny Opera' in 1952. His prodigy Leonard 'West Side Story' Bernstein was the conductor, and it featured one of the original 1928 stars, Weill's widow Lotte Lenya. It opened off-Broadway in March 1954 and ran for 2,706 performances. In 1956, the year Brecht died, Louis Armstrong's vocal version of 'Mack the Knife' was a UK Top 10 hit, and joined three instrumental recordings (recorded as 'Moritat' or 'Theme from The Three Penny Opera') in the US Top 20.

In 1958, Lotte Lenya asked Atlantic Records head Ahmet Ertegun if any of his acts could record Weill's composition. Quite coincidentally, her wish came true when Bobby Darin, who loved the

■ THE SONG INVOLVED A GORY STORY ABOUT A VICTORIAN MURDERER IN LONDON. THIS, COUPLED WITH THE FACT THAT IT HAD BEEN A BIG HIT THREE YEARS EARLIER, MADE THE CHANCES OF IT SELLING WELL VERY SMALL ■

show and had added 'Mack the Knife' to his stage repertoire, included it in his adult-aimed That's All album. It was Armstrong's version that inspired Darin, who even added Satchmo's ad-lib reference to Lotte Lenya (as well as to her stage character Jenny Diver) in the list of Mackie's conquests. It was certainly not in the original lyric.

Despite being banned by some US stations, which thought it might promote juvenile delinquency (especially after two New York teenagers were stabbed to death), 'Mack' topped the US chart during the week in which Darin became the youngest ever Las Vegas headliner. It

Singer, actor, multi-instrumentalist and double UK chart-topper Bobby Darin

stayed there for nine weeks and its sales of more than two million helped to convince other rock stars, including Elvis, also to record with the older generation in mind. The single headed the UK chart and picked up the Record of the Year Grammy while Darin scooped the award for Best New Artist. 'Mack', which became Darin's signature tune and the first of his many big band swing revival hits, is among America's Top 20 records of the rock era.

It should be noted that from an early age Darin knew his bad health would result in his early death, and as he told Life magazine, "I'd like to be a legend by the time I'm 25." At age 23, he already had a string of hits but it was 'Mack' that lifted him to near-legendary status by the time of his death in 1973 at the age of 37.

Look out, old Mackie is back! In 2002, exactly 50 years after the vocal version was first performed, the song returned and topped the UK album chart when recorded by both Robbie Williams and Gareth Gates.

■ Dave McAleer

★ ARTIST:	Bobby Darin
★ LABEL:	London American/Atco USA
★ WRITERS:	Kurt Weill/Berthold Brecht/Marc Blitzstein
★ PRODUCER:	Ahmet Ertegun

DEEP BLUE
UK, male producer – Sean O'Keefe (2 WEEKS) pos/wks
16 Apr 94	HELICOPTER TUNE *Moving Shadow SHADOW 41CD*	68	2

DEEP BLUE SOMETHING
US, male vocal / instrumental group (17 WEEKS) pos/wks
6 Jul 96 ★	BREAKFAST AT TIFFANY'S (re) *Interscope IND 80032*	1	14
7 Dec 96	JOSEY *Interscope IND 95518*	27	3

DEEP C
UK, male / female vocal / instrumental group (3 WEEKS) pos/wks
19 Jan 91	AFRICAN REIGN *M & G MAGS 4*	75	1
8 Jun 91	CHILL TO THE PANIC *M & G MAGS 10*	73	2

DEEP COVER
UK, male production duo
– Scott Anderson and Leon McCormack (1 WEEK) pos/wks
11 May 02	SOUNDS OF EDEN (EVERYTIME I SEE THE GIRL) *Attitude! 0158392*	63	1

DEEP CREED '94
US, male producer – Armand Van Helden (1 WEEK) pos/wks
7 May 94	CAN U FEEL IT *Eastern Bloc BLOCCD 005*	59	1

DEEP DISH
Iran, male instrumental / production
duo – Ali Shirazinia and Sharam Tayebi (4 WEEKS) pos/wks
26 Oct 96	STAY GOLD *Deconstruction 74321418222*	41	1
1 Nov 97	STRANDED *Deconstruction 74321512232*	60	1
3 Oct 98	THE FUTURE OF THE FUTURE (STAY GOLD) *Deconstruction 74321616252* [1]	31	2

[1] Deep Dish with Everything but the Girl

DEEP FEELING
UK, male vocal / instrumental group (5 WEEKS) pos/wks
25 Apr 70	DO YOU LOVE ME (re) *Page One POF 165*	34	5

DEEP FOREST
France, male instrumental duo
– Eric Mouquet and Michael Sanchez (14 WEEKS) pos/wks
5 Feb 94 ●	SWEET LULLABY *Columbia 6599242*	10	6
21 May 94	DEEP FOREST *Columbia 6604115*	20	4
23 Jul 94	SAVANNA DANCE *Columbia 6606355*	28	2
24 Jun 95	MARTA'S SONG *Columbia 6621402*	26	2

DEEP PURPLE (397) Top 500
Long-running legendary heavy rock group. London band's ever-changing line-up ensured many spin-off groups, among them Rainbow (founded by ex-guitarist Ritchie Blackmore), Whitesnake (featuring ex-vocalist David Coverdale) and Gillan (started by ex-vocalist Ian Gillan) (85 WEEKS) pos/wks
15 Aug 70 ●	BLACK NIGHT *Harvest HAR 5020*	2	21
27 Feb 71 ●	STRANGE KIND OF WOMAN *Harvest HAR 5033*	8	12
13 Nov 71	FIREBALL *Harvest HAR 5045*	15	13
1 Apr 72	NEVER BEFORE *Purple PUR 102*	35	6
16 Apr 77	SMOKE ON THE WATER *Purple PUR 132*	21	7
15 Oct 77	NEW LIVE AND RARE (EP) *Purple PUR 135*	31	4
7 Oct 78	NEW LIVE AND RARE II (EP) *Purple PUR 137*	45	3
2 Aug 80	BLACK NIGHT (re-issue) *Harvest HAR 5210*	43	6
1 Nov 80	NEW LIVE AND RARE III (EP) *Harvest SHEP 101*	48	3
26 Jan 85	PERFECT STRANGERS *Polydor POSP 719*	48	3
15 Jun 85	KNOCKING AT YOUR BACK DOOR / PERFECT STRANGERS *Polydor POSP 749*	68	1
18 Jun 88	HUSH *Polydor PO 4*	62	2
20 Oct 90	KING OF DREAMS *RCA PB 49247*	70	1
2 Mar 91	LOVE CONQUERS ALL *RCA PB 49225*	57	2
24 Jun 95	BLACK NIGHT (re-mix) *EMI CDEM 382*	66	1

Tracks on New Live and Rare (EP): Black Night (Live) / Painted Horse / When a Blind Man Cries. New Live and Rare II (EP): Burn (Edited Version) / Coronarias Redig / Mistreated (Interpolating Rock Me Baby). New Live and Rare Volume 3 (EP): Smoke on the Water / Bird Has Flown / Grabsplatter

DEEP RIVER BOYS
US, male vocal group (1 WEEK) pos/wks
7 Dec 56	THAT'S RIGHT *HMV POP 263*	29	1

Rick DEES and his CAST OF IDIOTS
US, male DJ / vocalist with male / female vocal / instrumental group (9 WEEKS) pos/wks
18 Sep 76 ●	DISCO DUCK (PART ONE) *RSO 2090 204* ▲	6	9

DEETAH
Chile, female vocalist (10 WEEKS) pos/wks
26 Sep 98	RELAX *ffrr FCDP 345*	11	8
1 May 99	EL PARAISO RICO *ffrr FCD 356*	39	2

DEF LEPPARD (250) Top 500
Mainstream UK rock stalwarts who wooed US before their homeland: Joe Elliott (v), Phil Collen (g from 1983), Steve Clark (g) (d. 1991), Rick Savage (b), Rick Allen (d). In US achieved feat of two consecutive albums selling more than eight million (114 WEEKS) pos/wks
17 Nov 79	WASTED *Vertigo 6059 247*	61	3
23 Feb 80	HELLO AMERICA *Vertigo LEPP 1*	45	4
5 Feb 83	PHOTOGRAPH *Vertigo VER 5*	66	3
27 Aug 83	ROCK OF AGES *Vertigo VER 6*	41	4
1 Aug 87 ●	ANIMAL *Bludgeon Riffola LEP 1*	6	9
19 Sep 87	POUR SOME SUGAR ON ME *Bludgeon Riffola LEP 2*	18	6
28 Nov 87	HYSTERIA (re) *Bludgeon Riffola LEP 3*	26	6
9 Apr 88	ARMAGEDDON IT *Bludgeon Riffola LEP 4*	20	5
16 Jul 88	LOVE BITES *Bludgeon Riffola LEP 5* ▲	11	8
11 Feb 89	ROCKET *Bludgeon Riffola LEP 6*	15	7
28 Mar 92 ●	LET'S GET ROCKED *Bludgeon Riffola DEF 7*	2	7
27 Jun 92	MAKE LOVE LIKE A MAN *Bludgeon Riffola LEP 7*	12	5
12 Sep 92	HAVE YOU EVER NEEDED SOMEONE SO BAD *Bludgeon Riffola LEP 8*	16	5
30 Jan 93	HEAVEN IS *Bludgeon Riffola LEPCD 9*	13	5
1 May 93	TONIGHT *Bludgeon Riffola LEPCD 10*	34	3
18 Sep 93	TWO STEPS BEHIND *Bludgeon Riffola LEPCD 12*	32	4
15 Jan 94	ACTION *Bludgeon Riffola LEPCD 13*	14	5
14 Oct 95 ●	WHEN LOVE AND HATE COLLIDE *Bludgeon Riffola LEPCD 14*	2	10
4 May 96	SLANG *Bludgeon Riffola LEPCD 15*	17	5
13 Jul 96	WORK IT OUT *Bludgeon Riffola LEPCD 16*	22	3
28 Sep 96	ALL I WANT IS EVERYTHING *Bludgeon Riffola LEPCD 17*	38	2
30 Nov 96	BREATHE A SIGH *Bludgeon Riffola LEPCD 18*	43	1
24 Jul 99	PROMISES *Bludgeon Riffola 5621362*	41	1
9 Oct 99	GOODBYE *Bludgeon Riffola 5622892*	54	1
17 Aug 02	NOW *Bludgeon Riffola / Mercury 0639692*	23	2

See also Mick RONSON with Joe ELLIOTT

DEFINITION OF SOUND
UK, male rap duo – Donald Weekes and Kevin Clark (25 WEEKS) pos/wks
9 Mar 91	WEAR YOUR LOVE LIKE HEAVEN *Circa YR 61*	17	9
1 Jun 91	NOW IS TOMORROW *Circa YR 66*	46	4
8 Feb 92	MOIRA JANE'S CAFE *Circa YR 80*	34	4
19 Sep 92	WHAT ARE YOU UNDER *Circa YR 95*	68	1
14 Nov 92	CAN I GET OVER *Circa YR 97*	61	2
20 May 95	BOOM BOOM *Fontana DOSCD 1*	59	1
2 Dec 95	PASS THE VIBES *Fontana DOSCD 2*	23	3
24 Feb 96	CHILD *Fontana DOSCD 3*	48	1

DEFTONES
US, male vocal / instrumental group (4 WEEKS) pos/wks
21 Mar 98	MY OWN SUMMER (SHOVE IT) *Maverick W 0432CD*	29	2
11 Jul 98	BE QUIET AND DRIVE (FAR AWAY) *Maverick W 0445CD*	50	1
26 Aug 00	CHANGE (IN THE HOUSE OF FLIES) *Maverick W531CD*	53	1

DEGREES OF MOTION featuring BITI
US, female vocal group (21 WEEKS) pos/wks
25 Apr 92	DO YOU WANT IT RIGHT NOW *ffrr F 184*	31	5
18 Jul 92	SHINE ON *ffrr F 192* [1]	43	3
7 Nov 92	SOUL FREEDOM – FREE YOUR SOUL *ffrr FX 201*	64	1
19 Mar 94 ●	SHINE ON (re-mix) *ffrr FCD 229*	8	8
25 Jun 94	DO YOU WANT IT RIGHT NOW (re-mix) *ffrr FCD 236*	26	4

[1] Degrees of Motion featuring Biti with Kit West

DEJA
US, male / female vocal duo (1 WEEK) pos/wks
29 Aug 87	SERIOUS *10 TEN 132*	75	1

DEJA VU UK, male vocal / instrumental duo (1 WEEK)

		pos/wks
5 Feb 94	WHY WHY WHY *Cowboy CDRODEO 941* 57	1

Desmond DEKKER and the ACES
Jamaica, vocal / instrumental group (71 WEEKS)

		pos/wks
12 Jul 67	007 (SHANTY TOWN) *Pyramid PYR 6004* 14	11
19 Mar 69	★ ISRAELITES (re) *Pyramid PYR 6058* 1	15
25 Jun 69	● IT MIEK *Pyramid PYR 6068* 7	11
10 Jan 70	PICKNEY GAL *Pyramid PYR 6078* 42	3
22 Aug 70	● YOU CAN GET IT IF YOU REALLY WANT *Trojan TR 7777* [1] 2	15
10 May 75	● ISRAELITES (re-recording) *Cactus CT 57* [1] 10	9
30 Aug 75	SING A LITTLE SONG *Cactus CT 73* [1] 16	7

[1] Desmond Dekker

DEL AMITRI
UK, male vocal / instrumental group (71 WEEKS)

		pos/wks
19 Aug 89	KISS THIS THING GOODBYE *A&M AM 515* 59	2
13 Jan 90	NOTHING EVER HAPPENS *A&M AM 536* 11	9
24 Mar 90	KISS THIS THING GOODBYE (re-issue) *A&M AM 551* 43	4
16 Jun 90	MOVE AWAY JIMMY BLUE *A&M AM 555* 36	6
3 Nov 90	SPIT IN THE RAIN *A&M AM 589* 21	6
9 May 92	ALWAYS THE LAST TO KNOW *A&M AM 870* 13	7
11 Jul 92	BE MY DOWNFALL *A&M AM 884* 30	4
12 Sep 92	JUST LIKE A MAN *A&M AM 0057* 25	4
23 Jan 93	WHEN YOU WERE YOUNG *A&M AMCD 0132* 20	3
18 Feb 95	HERE AND NOW *A&M 5809692* 21	4
29 Apr 95	DRIVING WITH THE BRAKES ON *A&M 5810072* 18	4
8 Jul 95	ROLL TO ME *A&M 5811312* 22	4
28 Oct 95	TELL HER THIS *A&M 5812172* 32	2
21 Jun 97	NOT WHERE IT'S AT *A&M 5822532* 21	3
6 Dec 97	SOME OTHER SUCKER'S PARADE *A&M 5824352* 46	1
13 Jun 98	DON'T COME HOME TOO SOON *A&M 5827052* 15	4
5 Sep 98	CRY TO BE FOUND *A&M MERCD 513* 40	2
13 Apr 02	JUST BEFORE YOU LEAVE *Mercury 4976972* 37	2

DE'LACY
US, male / female vocal / instrumental group (16 WEEKS)

		pos/wks
2 Sep 95	● HIDEAWAY *Slip 'N' Slide 74321310472* 9	10
31 Aug 96	THAT LOOK *Slip 'N' Slide 74321398322* 19	4
14 Feb 98	HIDEAWAY 1998 (re-mix) *Slip 'N'Slide 74321561052* 21	2

DELAGE UK, female vocal group (2 WEEKS)

		pos/wks
15 Dec 90	ROCK THE BOAT *PWL / Polydor PO 113* 63	2

DELAKOTA UK, male vocal / instrumental duo (3 WEEKS)

		pos/wks
18 Jul 98	THE ROCK *Go.Beat GOBCD 10* 60	1
19 Sep 98	C'MON CINCINNATI *Go.Beat GOBCD 11* [1] 55	1
13 Feb 99	555 *Go.Beat GOBCD 14* 42	1

[1] Delakota featuring Rose Smith

DELANEY and BONNIE and FRIENDS *US, male / female vocal duo –*
Delaney and Bonnie Bramlett, and instrumental group (9 WEEKS)

		pos/wks
20 Dec 69	COMIN' HOME *Atlantic 584 308* [1] 16	9

[1] Delaney and Bonnie and Friends featuring Eric Clapton

See also Eric CLAPTON

DELANO – *See CZR featuring DELANO*

DELEGATION UK, male vocal / instrumental group (7 WEEKS)

		pos/wks
23 Apr 77	WHERE IS THE LOVE (WE USED TO KNOW)	
	State STAT 40 22	6
20 Aug 77	YOU'VE BEEN DOING ME WRONG *State STAT 55* 49	1

DELERIUM *Canada, male production duo*
– Rhys Fulber and Bill Leeb (23 WEEKS)

		pos/wks
12 Jun 99	SILENCE *Nettwerk 398152* 73	1
5 Feb 00	HEAVEN'S EARTH *Nettwerk 331032* 44	1

		pos/wks
14 Oct 00	● SILENCE (re-mix) *Nettwerk 331072* [1] 3	16
7 Jul 01	INNOCENTE (FALLING IN LOVE) *Nettwerk 331172* [2] 32	3
24 Nov 01	UNDERWATER *Nettwerk 331422* [3] 33	2

[1] Delerium featuring Sarah McLachlan [2] Delerium featuring Leigh Nash [3] Delerium featuring Rani

Sarah McLachlan's vocals also featured, uncredited, on original hit version of 'Silence'

DELFONICS US, male vocal group (23 WEEKS)

		pos/wks
10 Apr 71	DIDN'T I (BLOW YOUR MIND THIS TIME) (re) *Bell 1099* 22	9
10 Jul 71	LA-LA MEANS I LOVE YOU *Bell 1165* 19	10
16 Oct 71	READY OR NOT HERE I COME (CAN'T HIDE	
	FROM LOVE) *Bell 1175* 41	4

DELGADOS
UK, male / female vocal / instrumental group (2 WEEKS)

		pos/wks
23 May 98	PULL THE WIRES FROM THE WALL	
	Chemikal CHEM 023CD 69	1
3 Jun 00	AMERICAN TRILOGY	
	Chemikal Underground CHEM 039CD 61	1

DELIRIOUS? *UK, male vocal / instrumental group (17 WEEKS)*

		pos/wks
1 Mar 97	WHITE RIBBON DAY *Furious? CDFURY 1* 41	2
17 May 97	DEEPER *Furious? CDFURY 2* 20	3
26 Jul 97	PROMISE *Furious? CDFURY 3* 20	2
15 Nov 97	DEEPER (EP) *Furious? CXFURY 4* 36	2
27 Mar 99	SEE THE STAR *Furious? CDFURY 5* 16	2
4 Mar 00	IT'S OK *Furious? CDFURY 6* 18	2
16 Jun 01	WAITING FOR THE SUMMER *Furious? CDFURY 7* 26	2
22 Dec 01	I COULD SING OF YOUR LOVE FOREVER	
	Furious? CDFURY 9 40	2

Tracks on Deeper (EP): Deeper / Summer of Love / Touch / Sanctify

'DELIVERANCE' SOUNDTRACK *US, male instrumental duo –*
Eric Weissberg on banjo and Steve Mandell on guitar (7 WEEKS)

		pos/wks
31 Mar 73	DUELLING BANJOS *Warner Bros. K 16223* 17	7

DELLS US, male vocal group (9 WEEKS)

		pos/wks
16 Jul 69	I CAN SING A RAINBOW – LOVE IS BLUE (MEDLEY)	
	Chess CRS 8099 15	9

DELORES – *See MONOBOY featuring DELORES*

DELRONS – *See REPARATA and the DELRONS*

DELSENA – *See Oris JAY presents DELSENA*

DELTA – *See David MORALES; Crystal WATERS*

DELUXE US, female vocalist (1 WEEK)

		pos/wks
18 Mar 89	JUST A LITTLE MORE *Unyque UNQ 5* 74	1

Tim DELUXE featuring Sam OBERNIK
UK, male DJ / producer – Tim Liken and female vocalist (7 WEEKS) pos/wks

20 Jul 02	IT JUST WON'T DO *Underwater H20 016CD* 14	7

DEM 2 UK, male production duo (2 WEEKS)

		pos/wks
24 Oct 98	DESTINY *Locked On LOX 101CD* 58	2

DEMETREUS – *See Christian FALK featuring DEMETREUS*

DEMOLITION MAN – *See PRIZNA featuring DEMOLITION MAN*

DEMON vs HEARTBREAKER
France, male production group (1 WEEK) pos/wks

19 May 01	YOU ARE MY HIGH *Source SOURCDSE 1032* 70	1

D'EMPRESS – *See 187 LOCKDOWN*

Chaka DEMUS and PLIERS
Jamaica, male vocal duo (55 WEEKS) pos/wks

12 Jun 93	● TEASE ME *Mango CIDM 806*	3 15
18 Sep 93	● SHE DON'T LET NOBODY *Mango CIDM 810*	4 10
18 Dec 93	★ TWIST AND SHOUT (re) *Mango CIDM 814* [1]	1 14
12 Mar 94	MURDER SHE WROTE *Mango CIDM 812*	27 4
18 Jun 94	I WANNA BE YOUR MAN *Mango CIDM 817*	19 6
27 Aug 94	GAL WINE *Mango CIDM 820*	20 4
31 Aug 96	EVERY KINDA PEOPLE *Island Jamaica IJCD 2005*	47 1
30 Aug 97	EVERY LITTLE THING SHE DOES IS MAGIC *Virgin VSCDT 1654*	51 1

[1] Chaka Demus and Pliers featuring Jack Radics and Taxi Gang

Terry DENE *UK, male vocalist – Terry Williams (20 WEEKS)* pos/wks

7 Jun 57	A WHITE SPORT COAT (re) *Decca F 10895*	18 7
19 Jul 57	START MOVIN' *Decca F 10914*	15 8
16 May 58	STAIRWAY OF LOVE *Decca F 11016*	16 5

DENISE and JOHNNY *UK, male / female vocal duo – Denise Van Outen and Johnny Vaughan (12 WEEKS)* pos/wks

26 Dec 98	● ESPECIALLY FOR YOU (re) *RCA 74321644722*	3 12

See also THOSE 2 GIRLS

Cathy DENNIS *UK, female vocalist (68 WEEKS)* pos/wks

21 Oct 89	C'MON AND GET MY LOVE *ffrr F 117* [1]	15 10
7 Apr 90	THAT'S THE WAY OF THE WORLD *ffrr F 132* [1]	48 3
4 May 91	● TOUCH ME (ALL NIGHT LONG) *Polydor CATH 3*	5 10
20 Jul 91	JUST ANOTHER DREAM *Polydor CATH 2*	13 7
5 Oct 91	TOO MANY WALLS *Polydor CATH 4*	17 7
7 Dec 91	EVERYBODY MOVE *Polydor CATH 5*	25 8
29 Aug 92	YOU LIED TO ME *Polydor CATH 6*	34 4
21 Nov 92	IRRESISTIBLE *Polydor CATH 7*	24 6
6 Feb 93	FALLING *Polydor CATHD 8*	32 2
12 Feb 94	WHY *ffrr FCD 227* [1]	23 3
10 Aug 96	WEST END PAD *Polydor 5752812*	25 2
1 Mar 97	WATERLOO SUNSET *Polydor 5759612*	11 5
21 Jun 97	WHEN DREAMS TURN TO DUST *Polydor 5711852*	43 1

[1] D Mob with Cathy Dennis

Jackie DENNIS *UK, male vocalist (10 WEEKS)* pos/wks

14 Mar 58	● LA DEE DAH *Decca F 10992*	4 9
27 Jun 58	THE PURPLE PEOPLE EATER *Decca F 11033*	29 1

Stefan DENNIS *Australia, male vocalist (8 WEEKS)* pos/wks

6 May 89	DON'T IT MAKE YOU FEEL GOOD *Sublime LIME 105*	16 7
7 Oct 89	THIS LOVE AFFAIR *Sublime LIME 113*	67 1

DENNISONS *UK, male vocal / instrumental group (13 WEEKS)* pos/wks

15 Aug 63	BE MY GIRL *Decca F 11691*	46 6
7 May 64	WALKING THE DOG *Decca F 11880*	36 7

Richard DENTON and Martin COOK *UK, male orchestra leaders – instrumental duo, guitar and keyboards (7 WEEKS)* pos/wks

15 Apr 78	THEME FROM 'HONG KONG BEAT' *BBC RESL 52*	25 7

John DENVER
US, male vocalist – Henry Deutschendorf, d. 12 Oct 1997 (22 WEEKS) pos/wks

17 Aug 74	★ ANNIE'S SONG *RCA APBO 0295* ▲	1 13
12 Dec 81	PERHAPS LOVE *CBS A 1905* [1]	46 9

[1] Placido Domingo with John Denver

Karl DENVER ⟨219 Top 500⟩ *Versatile Scottish singer with multi-octave vocal range, b. Angus McKenzie, 16 Dec 1934, Glasgow (d. 21 Dec 1998). This unique artist, whose yodel-laced style added colour and contrast to the charts, reached the Top 20 with his first five singles (127 WEEKS)* pos/wks

22 Jun 61	● MARCHETA *Decca F 11360*	8 20
19 Oct 61	● MEXICALI ROSE *Decca F 11395*	8 11

25 Jan 62	● WIMOWEH *Decca F 11420*	4 17
22 Feb 62	● NEVER GOODBYE *Decca F 11431*	9 18
7 Jun 62	A LITTLE LOVE A LITTLE KISS *Decca F 11470*	19 10
20 Sep 62	BLUE WEEK-END *Decca F 11505*	33 5
21 Mar 63	CAN YOU FORGIVE ME *Decca F 11608*	32 8
13 Jun 63	INDIAN LOVE CALL *Decca F 11674*	32 8
22 Aug 63	STILL *Decca F 11720*	13 15
5 Mar 64	MY WORLD OF BLUE *Decca F 11828*	29 6
4 Jun 64	LOVE ME WITH ALL YOUR HEART *Decca F 11905*	37 6
9 Jun 90	LAZYITIS - ONE ARMED BOXER *Factory FAC 2227* [1]	46 3

[1] Happy Mondays and Karl Denver

DENZIE – *See MONSTA BOY featuring DENZIE*

DEODATO
US, male multi-instrumentalist – Eumir Deodato (9 WEEKS) pos/wks

5 May 73	● ALSO SPRACH ZARATHUSTRA (2001) *Creed Taylor CTI 4000*	7 9

DEPARTMENT S *UK, male vocal / instrumental group (13 WEEKS)* pos/wks

4 Apr 81	IS VIC THERE? *RCA1003*	22 10
11 Jul 81	GOING LEFT RIGHT *Stiff BUY 118*	55 3

DEPECHE MODE ⟨55 Top 500⟩
Consistently successful synth-led Essex band: Dave Gahan (v), Martin Gore (syn), Andy Fletcher (b, syn), Vince Clarke (syn, replaced 1982 by Alan Wilder). One of the world's best-selling groups, who reached the UK Top 10 with their first 13 albums (240 WEEKS) pos/wks

4 Apr 81	DREAMING OF ME *Mute MUTE 013*	57 4
13 Jun 81	NEW LIFE *Mute MUTE 014*	11 15
19 Sep 81	● JUST CAN'T GET ENOUGH *Mute MUTE 016*	8 10
13 Feb 82	● SEE YOU *Mute MUTE 018*	6 10
8 May 82	THE MEANING OF LOVE *Mute MUTE 022*	12 8
28 Aug 82	LEAVE IN SILENCE *Mute BONG 1*	18 10
12 Feb 83	GET THE BALANCE RIGHT *Mute 7BONG 2*	13 8
23 Jul 83	● EVERYTHING COUNTS *Mute 7BONG 3*	6 11
1 Oct 83	LOVE IN ITSELF *Mute 7BONG 4*	21 7
24 Mar 84	● PEOPLE ARE PEOPLE *Mute 7BONG 5*	4 10
1 Sep 84	● MASTER AND SERVANT *Mute 7BONG 6*	9 9
10 Nov 84	SOMEBODY / BLASPHEMOUS RUMOURS *Mute 7BONG 7*	16 6
11 May 85	SHAKE THE DISEASE *Mute BONG 8*	18 9
28 Sep 85	IT'S CALLED A HEART *Mute BONG 9*	18 4
22 Feb 86	STRIPPED *Mute BONG 10*	15 5
26 Apr 86	A QUESTION OF LUST *Mute BONG 11*	28 5
23 Aug 86	A QUESTION OF TIME *Mute BONG 12*	17 6
9 May 87	STRANGELOVE *Mute BONG 13*	16 5
5 Sep 87	NEVER LET ME DOWN AGAIN *Mute BONG 14*	22 4
9 Jan 88	BEHIND THE WHEEL *Mute BONG 15*	21 5
28 May 88	LITTLE 15 (import) *Mute LITTLE 15*	60 2
25 Feb 89	EVERYTHING COUNTS *Mute BONG 16*	22 7
9 Sep 89	PERSONAL JESUS *Mute BONG 17*	13 6
17 Feb 90	● ENJOY THE SILENCE *Mute BONG 18*	6 9
19 May 90	POLICY OF TRUTH *Mute BONG 19*	16 6
29 Sep 90	WORLD IN MY EYES *Mute BONG 20*	17 6
27 Feb 93	● I FEEL YOU *Mute CDBONG 21*	8 7
8 May 93	WALKING IN MY SHOES *Mute CDBONG 22*	14 4
25 Sep 93	● CONDEMNATION *Mute CDBONG 23*	9 4
22 Jan 94	● IN YOUR ROOM *Mute CDBONG 24*	8 4
15 Feb 97	● BARREL OF A GUN *Mute CDBONG 25*	4 4
12 Apr 97	● IT'S NO GOOD *Mute CDBONG 26*	5 5
28 Jun 97	HOME *Mute CDBONG 27*	23 4
1 Nov 97	USELESS *Mute CDBONG 28*	28 2
19 Sep 98	ONLY WHEN I LOSE MYSELF *Mute CDBONG 29*	17 3
5 May 01	● DREAM ON (re) *Mute CDBONG 30*	6 5
11 Aug 01	I FEEL LOVED *Mute CDBONG 31*	12 6
17 Nov 01	FREELOVE *Mute CDBONG 32*	19 3

'BONG 16' is a live version of 'BONG 3'

DEPTH CHARGE *UK, male producer – Jonathan Kane (1 WEEK)* pos/wks

29 Jul 95	LEGEND OF THE GOLDEN SNAKE *DC DC 01CD*	75 1

DER DRITTE RAUM
Germany, male producer – Andreas Kruger (1 WEEK)   pos/wks

4 Sep 99	HALLE BOPP *Additive 12AD 042*	75	1

DEREK and the DOMINOES – *See Eric CLAPTON*

Yves DERUYTER *Belgium, male DJ / producer (3 WEEKS)*
14 Apr 01	BACK TO EARTH *UK Bonzai UKBONZAI CD01*	63	1
19 Jan 02	BACK TO EARTH (re-mix) *UK Bonzai UKBONZAI 109CD*	56	2

DESERT *UK, male production duo (1 WEEK)*   pos/wks
20 Oct 01	LETTIN' YA MIND GO *Future Groove CDFGR 017*	74	1

DESIDERIO
UK / Holland, male production duo / female vocalist (1 WEEK)   pos/wks
3 Jun 00	STARLIGHT *Code Blue BLU 010CD*	57	1

Kevin DESIMONE – *See Barry MANILOW*

DESIRELESS *France, female vocalist (19 WEEKS)*   pos/wks
31 Oct 87	VOYAGE VOYAGE *CBS DESI 1*	53	6
14 May 88	● VOYAGE VOYAGE (re-mix) *CBS DESI 2*	5	13

DESIYA featuring Melissa YIANNAKOU
UK, male / female vocal / instrumental duo (1 WEEK)   pos/wks
1 Feb 92	COMIN' ON STRONG *Black Market 12MKT 2*	74	1

DESKEE *UK, male instrumentalist (3 WEEKS)*
3 Feb 90	LET THERE BE HOUSE *Big One VBIG 19*	52	2
8 Sep 90	DANCE, DANCE *Big One VBIG 22*	74	1

DES'REE *UK, female vocalist (72 WEEKS)*   pos/wks
31 Aug 91	FEEL SO HIGH *Dusted Sound 6573667*	51	5
11 Jan 92	FEEL SO HIGH (re-issue) *Dusted Sound 6576897*	13	9
21 Mar 92	MIND ADVENTURES *Dusted Sound 6578637*	43	3
27 Jun 92	WHY SHOULD I LOVE YOU *Dusted Sound 6580917*	44	3
19 Jun 93	DELICATE *Columbia 6593312* [1]	14	6
9 Apr 94	YOU GOTTA BE *Dusted Sound 6601342*	20	7
18 Jun 94	I AIN'T MOVIN' *Dusted Sound 6604672*	44	3
3 Sep 94	LITTLE CHILD *Dusted Sound 6604515*	69	1
11 Mar 95	YOU GOTTA BE (re-mix) *Dusted Sound 6613215*	14	8
20 Jun 98	● LIFE *Sony S2 6659302*	8	15
7 Nov 98	WHAT'S YOUR SIGN? *Sony S2 6665162*	19	4
3 Apr 99	● YOU GOTTA BE (2nd re-mix) *Dusted Sound / Sony S2 6668935* .	10	8
16 Oct 99	AIN'T NO SUNSHINE *Universal Music TV 1564332* [2]	42	2

[1] Terence Trent D'Arby featuring Des'ree [2] Ladysmith Black Mambazo featuring Des'ree

DESTINY'S CHILD (265 Top 500)
Texas-based female R&B quartet turned trio, fronted by Beyoncé Knowles, who also co-writes and co-produces these independent women responsible for four US No.1s. The only US girl group to top the UK chart twice (110 WEEKS) pos/wks
28 Mar 98	● NO, NO, NO *Columbia 6656592* [1]	5	8
11 Jul 98	WITH ME *Columbia 6661472*	19	3
7 Nov 98	SHE'S GONE *Columbia 6664915* [2]	24	3
23 Jan 99	GET ON THE BUS *East West E 3780CD* [3]	15	5
24 Jul 99	● BILLS, BILLS, BILLS *Columbia 6676902* ▲	6	9
30 Oct 99	● BUG A BOO *Columbia 6681882*	9	7
8 Apr 00	● SAY MY NAME *Columbia 6691882* ▲	3	11
29 Jul 00	● JUMPIN' JUMPIN' *Columbia 6696292*	5	11
2 Dec 00	★ INDEPENDENT WOMEN PART 1 *Columbia 6705932* ■ ▲	1	15
28 Apr 01	★ SURVIVOR *Columbia 6711732* ■	1	13
4 Aug 01	● BOOTYLICIOUS *Columbia 6717382* ▲	2	11
24 Nov 01	● EMOTION *Columbia 6721112*	3	14

[1] Destiny's Child featuring Wyclef Jean [2] Matthew Marsden featuring Destiny's Child [3] Destiny's Child featuring Timbaland

See also BEYONCÉ; Kelly ROWLAND

DESTRY – *See CIRCA featuring DESTRY; ZOO EXPERIENCE featuring DESTRY*

Marcella DETROIT
US, female vocalist – Marcella Levy (16 WEEKS)   pos/wks
12 Mar 94	I BELIEVE *London LONCD 347*	11	8
14 May 94	AIN'T NOTHING LIKE THE REAL THING		
	London LONCD 350 [1]	24	4
16 Jul 94	I'M NO ANGEL *London LOCDP 351*	33	4

[1] Marcella Detroit and Elton John

DETROIT EMERALDS *US, male vocal group (44 WEEKS)*   pos/wks
10 Feb 73	● FEEL THE NEED IN ME *Janus 6146 020*	4	15
5 May 73	YOU WANT IT, YOU GOT IT *Westbound 6146 103*	12	9
11 Aug 73	I THINK OF YOU *Westbound 6146 104*	27	9
18 Jun 77	FEEL THE NEED (re-recording) *Atlantic K 10945*	12	11

DETROIT GRAND PU BAHS
US, male production / vocal group (3 WEEKS)   pos/wks
8 Jul 00	SANDWICHES *Jive Electro 9230252*	29	3

DETROIT SPINNERS (340 Top 500)
Detroit-based R&B quintet known as The Spinners in US. Lead singers included G C Cameron, Phillippe Wynne (died on stage 1984) and John Edwards. Unusually, the group fared better after leaving Motown, and has a 33-year US Top 40 span (93 WEEKS)   pos/wks
14 Nov 70	IT'S A SHAME *Tamla Motown TMG 755* [1]	20	11
21 Apr 73	COULD IT BE I'M FALLING IN LOVE *Atlantic K 10283*	11	11
29 Sep 73	● GHETTO CHILD *Atlantic K 10359*	7	10
19 Oct 74	THEN CAME YOU *Atlantic K 10495* [2] ▲	29	6
11 Sep 76	THE RUBBERBAND MAN *Atlantic K 10807*	16	11
29 Jan 77	WAKE UP SUSAN *Atlantic K 10799*	29	6
7 May 77	COULD IT BE I'M FALLING IN LOVE (EP) *Atlantic K 10935*	32	3
23 Feb 80	★ WORKING MY WAY BACK TO YOU – FORGIVE ME GIRL –		
	(MEDLEY) *Atlantic K 11432*	1	14
10 May 80	BODY LANGUAGE *Atlantic K 11392*	40	7
28 Jun 80	● CUPID – I'VE LOVED YOU FOR A LONG TIME (MEDLEY)		
	Atlantic K 11498	4	10
24 Jun 95	I'LL BE AROUND *Cooltempo CDCOOL 306* [3]	30	4

[1] Motown Spinners [2] Dionne Warwicke and the Detroit Spinners [3] Rappin' 4-Tay featuring the Spinners

Tracks on Could It Be I'm Falling in Love (EP): Could It Be I'm Falling in Love / You're Throwing a Good Love Away / Games People Play / Lazy Susan

DETROIT WHEELS – *See Mitch RYDER and the DETROIT WHEELS*

DEUCE *UK, male / female vocal group (23 WEEKS)*   pos/wks
21 Jan 95	CALL IT LOVE *London LONCD 355*	11	10
22 Apr 95	● I NEED YOU *London LONCD 365*	10	5
19 Aug 95	ON THE BIBLE *London LONCD 368*	13	6
29 Jun 96	NO SURRENDER *Love This LUVTHISCD 10*	29	2

SHORTEST-NAMED HITS

■ Surprisingly, there are just four single-letter or number chart hits and all of them are from the past 10 years

X	XZIBIT featuring SNOOP DOGG – peak position 14
7	PRINCE AND THE NEW POWER GENERATION – peak position 27
U	LONI CLARK – peak position 28
I	PETEY PABLO – peak position 51

---

dEUS *Belgium, male vocal / instrumental group (7 WEEKS)*

		pos/wks	
11 Feb 96	HOTEL LOUNGE (BE THE DEATH OF ME) *Island CID 603*	55	1
13 Jul 96	THEME FROM TURNPIKE (EP) *Island CID 630*	68	1
19 Oct 96	LITTLE ARITHMETICS *Island CID 643*	44	2
15 Mar 97	ROSES *Island CID 645*	56	1
24 Apr 99	INSTANT STREET *Island CID 742*	49	1
3 Jul 99	SISTER DEW *Island CID 750*	62	1

Tracks on Theme from Turnpike (EP): Theme from Turnpike / Worried About Satan / Overflow / My Little Contessa

David DEVANT & HIS SPIRIT WIFE
UK, male vocal / instrumental group (2 WEEKS)

		pos/wks	
5 Apr 97	GINGER *Rhythm King KIND 4CD*	54	1
21 Jun 97	THIS IS FOR REAL *Rhythm King KIND 5CD*	61	1

William DEVAUGHN *US, male vocalist (10 WEEKS)*

		pos/wks	
6 Jul 74	BE THANKFUL FOR WHAT YOU'VE GOT *Chelsea 2005 002*	31	5
20 Sep 80	BE THANKFUL FOR WHAT YOU'VE GOT (re-recording) *EMI 5101*	44	5

Sidney DEVINE *UK, male vocalist (1 WEEK)*

		pos/wks	
1 Apr 78	SCOTLAND FOREVER (EP) *Philips SCOT 1*	48	1

Tracks on Scotland Forever (EP): Scots Wha' Hae, Flower of Scotland, Scottish Trilogy

DEVO *US, male vocal / instrumental group (23 WEEKS)*

		pos/wks	
22 Apr 78	(I CAN'T ME GET NO) SATISFACTION *Stiff BOY 1*	41	8
13 May 78	JOCKO HOMO *Stiff DEV 1*	62	3
12 Aug 78	BE STIFF *Stiff BOY 2*	71	1
2 Sep 78	COME BACK JONEE *Virgin VS 223*	60	4
22 Nov 80	WHIP IT *Virgin VS 383*	51	7

DEVOTIONS – See BELLE and the DEVOTIONS

Howard DEVOTO – See BUZZCOCKS; MAGAZINE

DEXY'S MIDNIGHT RUNNERS ⟨337 Top 500⟩
Maverick Birmingham, UK-based post-punk group which split up in 1987. Led throughout radical personnel and stylistic changes by Kevin Rowland (v/g), b 17 Aug 1953. Transatlantic No.1, 'Come On Eileen', was the top selling UK single of 1982, selling 1,201,000 (93 WEEKS)

		pos/wks	
19 Jan 80	DANCE STANCE *Oddball Productions R 6028*	40	6
22 Mar 80 ★	GENO *Late Night Feelings R 6033*	1	14
12 Jul 80 ●	THERE THERE MY DEAR *Late Night Feelings R 6038*	7	9
21 Mar 81	PLAN B *Parlophone R 6046*	58	2
11 Jul 81	SHOW ME *Mercury DEXYS 6*	16	9
20 Mar 82	THE CELTIC SOUL BROTHERS *Mercury DEXYS 8* [1]	45	4
3 Jul 82 ★	COME ON EILEEN *Mercury DEXYS 9* [1] ◆ ▲	1	17
2 Oct 82 ●	JACKIE WILSON SAID (I'M IN HEAVEN WHEN YOU SMILE) *Mercury DEXYS 10* [2]	5	7
4 Dec 82	LET'S GET THIS STRAIGHT (FROM THE START) / OLD *Mercury DEXYS 11* [2]	17	9
2 Apr 83	THE CELTIC SOUL BROTHERS *Mercury DEXYS 12* [2]	20	6
22 Nov 86	BECAUSE OF YOU *Mercury BRUSH 1*	13	10

[1] Dexy's Midnight Runners with the Emerald Express [2] Kevin Rowland and Dexy's Midnight Runners

DEXYS 12 is a different version from DEXYS 8

DHANY – See KMC featuring DHANY

DI – See SHY FX & T-POWER

Tony DI BART *UK, male vocalist (19 WEEKS)*

		pos/wks	
9 Apr 94 ★	THE REAL THING *Cleveland City Blues CCBCD 15001*	1	12
20 Aug 94	DO IT *Cleveland City Blues CCBCD 15003*	21	4
20 May 95	WHY DID YA *Cleveland City Blues CCBCD 15004*	46	1
2 Mar 96	TURN YOUR LOVE AROUND *Cleveland City Blues CCBCD 15006*	66	1
17 Oct 98	THE REAL THING (re-mix) *Cleveland City CLECD 13050*	51	1

Gregg DIAMOND BIONIC BOOGIE
US, male / female vocal group, leader d. 14 Mar 1999 (3 WEEKS)

		pos/wks	
20 Jan 79	CREAM (ALWAYS RISES TO THE TOP) *Polydor POSP 18*	61	3

Jim DIAMOND *UK, male vocalist (30 WEEKS)*

		pos/wks	
3 Nov 84 ★	I SHOULD HAVE KNOWN BETTER *A&M AM 220*	1	13
2 Feb 85	I SLEEP ALONE AT NIGHT *A&M AM 229*	72	1
18 May 85	REMEMBER I LOVE YOU *A&M AM 247*	42	5
22 Feb 86 ●	HI HO SILVER *A&M AM 296*	5	11

See also PhD

Neil DIAMOND ⟨229 Top 500⟩
World-renowned singer / guitarist / songwriter, b. 24 Jan 1941, Brooklyn, US. First found international fame as writer of 'I'm a Believer' (Monkees), before going on to become one of the world's most popular live artists and biggest-selling album acts (20 platinum and 17 gold albums) (121 WEEKS)

		pos/wks	
7 Nov 70 ●	CRACKLIN' ROSIE *Uni UN 529* ▲	3	17
20 Feb 71 ●	SWEET CAROLINE *Uni UN 531*	8	11
8 May 71 ●	I AM … I SAID *Uni UN 532*	4	12
13 May 72	SONG SUNG BLUE *Uni UN 538* ▲	14	13
14 Aug 76	IF YOU KNOW WHAT I MEAN *CBS 4398*	35	4
23 Oct 76	BEAUTIFUL NOISE *CBS 4601*	13	9
24 Dec 77	DESIREE *CBS 5869*	39	6
25 Nov 78 ●	YOU DON'T BRING ME FLOWERS *CBS 6803* [1] ▲	5	12
3 Mar 79	FOREVER IN BLUE JEANS *CBS 7047*	16	12
15 Nov 80	LOVE ON THE ROCKS *Capitol CL 16173*	17	12
14 Feb 81	HELLO AGAIN *Capitol CL 16176*	51	4
20 Nov 82	HEARTLIGHT *CBS A 2814*	47	7
21 Nov 92	MORNING HAS BROKEN *Columbia 6588267*	36	2

[1] Barbra and Neil

Barbra was Barbra Streisand

DIAMOND HEAD
UK, male vocal / instrumental group (2 WEEKS)

		pos/wks	
11 Sep 82	IN THE HEAT OF THE NIGHT *MCA DHM 102*	67	2

DIAMONDS *Canada / US, male vocal group (17 WEEKS)*

		pos/wks	
31 May 57 ●	LITTLE DARLIN' *Mercury MT 148*	3	17

DIANA – See Diana ROSS

DICK and DEEDEE *US, male / female vocal duo*
– Dick St John and Deedee Sperling (3 WEEKS)

		pos/wks	
26 Oct 61	THE MOUNTAIN'S HIGH *London HLG 9408*	37	3

Charles DICKENS *UK, male vocalist – David Anthony (8 WEEKS)* pos/wks

1 Jul 65	THAT'S THE WAY LOVE GOES *Pye 7N 15887*	37	8

Gwen DICKEY *US, female vocalist (13 WEEKS)*

		pos/wks	
27 Jan 90	CAR WASH *Swanyard SYR 7*	72	1
2 Jul 94	AIN'T NOBODY (LOVES ME BETTER) *X-clusive XCLU 010CD* [1]	21	4
14 Feb 98	WISHING ON A STAR *Northwestside 74321554632* [2]	13	4
31 Oct 98	CAR WASH (re-recording) *MCA MCSTD 48096* [3]	18	3

[1] KWS and Gwen Dickey [2] Jay-Z featuring Gwen Dickey [3] Rose Royce featuring Gwen Dickey

See also ROSE ROYCE

Neville DICKIE *UK, male instrumentalist – piano (10 WEEKS)*

		pos/wks	
25 Oct 69	ROBIN'S RETURN (re) *Major Minor MM 644*	33	10

DICKIES *US, male vocal / instrumental group (28 WEEKS)*

		pos/wks	
16 Dec 78	SILENT NIGHT *A&M AMS 7403*	47	4
21 Apr 79 ●	BANANA SPLITS (THE TRA LA LA SONG) *A&M AMS 7431*	7	8
21 Jul 79	PARANOID *A&M AMS 7368*	45	6

15 Sep 79	NIGHTS IN WHITE SATIN *A&M AMS 7469*	39	5
16 Feb 80	FAN MAIL *A&M AMS 7504*	57	3
19 Jul 80	GIGANTOR *A&M AMS 7544*	72	2

Bruce DICKINSON *UK, male vocalist (23 WEEKS)*   pos/wks

28 Apr 90	TATTOOED MILLIONAIRE *EMI EM 138*	18	5
23 Jun 90	ALL THE YOUNG DUDES *EMI EM 142*	23	5
25 Aug 90	DIVE! DIVE! DIVE! *EMI EM 151*	45	2
4 Apr 92 ●	(I WANT TO BE) ELECTED *London LON 319* [1]	9	5
28 May 94	TEARS OF THE DRAGON *EMI CDEM 322*	28	2
8 Oct 94	SHOOT ALL THE CLOWNS *EMI CDEMS 341*	37	2
13 Apr 96	BACK FROM THE EDGE *Raw Power RAWX 1012*	68	1
3 May 97	ACCIDENT OF BIRTH *Raw Power RAWX 1042*	54	1

[1] Mr Bean and Smear Campaign featuring Bruce Dickinson

See also IRON MAIDEN

Barbara DICKSON *UK, female vocalist (49 WEEKS)*   pos/wks

17 Jan 76 ●	ANSWER ME *RSO 2090 174*	9	7
26 Feb 77	ANOTHER SUITCASE IN ANOTHER HALL *MCA 266*	18	7
19 Jan 80	CARAVAN SONG *Epic EPC 8103*	41	7
15 Mar 80	JANUARY FEBRUARY *Epic EPIC 8115*	11	10
14 Jun 80	IN THE NIGHT *Epic EPC 8593*	48	2
5 Jan 85 ★	I KNOW HIM SO WELL *RCA CHESS 3* [1]	1	16

[1] Elaine Paige and Barbara Dickson

DICTATORS *US, male vocal / instrumental group (2 WEEKS)*   pos/wks

17 Sep 77	SEARCH AND DESTROY (re) *Asylum K 13091*	49	2

Bo DIDDLEY
US, male vocalist / instrumentalist, guitar – Ellas McDaniel (10 WEEKS) pos/wks

10 Oct 63	PRETTY THING *Pye International 7N 25217*	34	6
18 Mar 65	HEY GOOD LOOKIN' *Chess 8000*	39	4

DIDDY *UK, male producer – Richard 'Diddy' Dearlove (3 WEEKS)*   pos/wks

19 Feb 94	GIVE ME LOVE *Positiva CDTIV 8*	52	1
12 Jul 97	GIVE ME LOVE (re-mix) *Feverpitch CDFVR 19*	23	2

See also BEDLAM

P DIDDY – *See PUFF DADDY*

DIDO *UK, female vocalist – Florian Cloud*
de Bounevialle Armstrong (33 WEEKS)   pos/wks

24 Apr 01 ●	HERE WITH ME *Cheeky / Arista 74321832732*	4	12
2 Jun 01 ●	THANK YOU *Cheeky / Arista 74321853042*	3	10
22 Sep 01	HUNTER *Cheeky / Arista 74321885452*	17	8
20 Apr 02 ●	ONE STEP TOO FAR *Cheeky / Arista 74321926412* [1]	6	3

[1] Faithless featuring Dido

DIESEL PARK WEST
UK, male vocal / instrumental group (15 WEEKS)   pos/wks

4 Feb 89	ALL THE MYTHS ON SUNDAY *Food FOOD 17*	66	2
1 Apr 89	LIKE PRINCES DO *Food FOOD 19*	58	3
5 Aug 89	WHEN THE HOODOO COMES *Food FOOD 20*	62	2
18 Jan 92	FALL TO LOVE *Food FOOD 35*	48	3
21 Mar 92	BOY ON TOP OF THE NEWS *Food FOOD 36*	58	2
5 Sep 92	GOD ONLY KNOWS *Food FOOD 39*	57	3

DIFFERENT GEAR vs POLICE *UK / Italy, male production*
group and UK / US, male vocal / instrumental trio (3 WEEKS)   pos/wks

5 Aug 00	WHEN THE WORLD IS RUNNING DOWN *Pagan PAGAN039CDS*	28	3

DIFFORD and TILBROOK
UK, male vocal / instrumental duo (2 WEEKS)   pos/wks

30 Jun 84	LOVE'S CRASHING WAVES *A&M AM 193*	57	2

See also SQUEEZE

DIGABLE PLANETS
US, male / female vocal / instrumental group (2 WEEKS)   pos/wks

13 Feb 93	REBIRTH OF SLICK (COOL LIKE DAT) *Pendulum EKR 159CD*	67	2

Rah DIGGA – *See OUTSIDAZ featuring Rah DIGGA and Melanie BLATT*

DIGITAL DREAM BABY
UK, male producer – Steven Teear (4 WEEKS)   pos/wks

14 Dec 91	WALKING IN THE AIR *Columbia 6576067*	49	4

Hit is a dance re-mix of 'Walking in the Air' by vocalist Peter Auty

See also Peter AUTY and the SINFONIA OF LONDON conducted by Howard BLAKE

DIGITAL EXCITATION
Belgium, male producer – Frank de Wulf (2 WEEKS)   pos/wks

29 Feb 92	PURE PLEASURE *R&S RSUK 10*	37	2

DIGITAL ORGASM
Belgium, male / female vocal / instrumental group (14 WEEKS)   pos/wks

7 Dec 91	RUNNING OUT OF TIME *Dead Dead Good GOOD 009*	16	9
18 Apr 92	STARTOUCHERS *DDG International GOOD 13*	31	3
25 Jul 92	MOOG ERUPTION *DDG International GOOD 17*	62	2

DIGITAL UNDERGROUND *US, male rap group (4 WEEKS)*   pos/wks

16 Mar 91	SAME SONG *Big Life BLR 40*	52	4

DILATED PEOPLES
US, male vocal / DJ / production group (3 WEEKS)   pos/wks

23 Feb 02	WORST COMES TO WORST *Capitol CDCL 834*	29	3

DILEMMA *Italy, male instrumental / production group (1 WEEK)*   pos/wks

6 Apr 96	IN SPIRIT *ffrr FCD 274*	42	1

Ricky DILLARD – *See Farley 'Jackmaster' FUNK*

DILLINJA *UK, male producer – Karl Francis (2 WEEKS)*   pos/wks

9 Nov 02	TWIST 'EM OUT *Renegade Hardware RH 40*	50	1
21 Dec 02	LIVE OR DIE / SOUTH MANZ *Valve VLV 007*	53	1

DIMESTARS
UK, male / female vocal / instrumental group (1 WEEK)   pos/wks

16 Jun 01	MY SUPERSTAR *Polydor 5870912*	72	1

D'INFLUENCE
UK, male / female vocal / instrumental group (10 WEEKS)   pos/wks

20 Jun 92	GOOD LOVER *East West A 8573* [1]	46	2
27 Mar 93	GOOD LOVER (re-mix) *East West America A 8439CD* [1]	61	1
24 Jun 95	MIDNITE *East West A 4418CD* [2]	58	1
16 Aug 97	HYPNOTIZE *Echo ECSCD 41*	33	2
11 Oct 97	MAGIC *Echo ECSCD 45*	45	1
5 Sep 98	ROCK WITH YOU *Echo ECSCD 56*	30	3

[1] D-Influence [2] D*Influence

Paolo DINI – *See FPI PROJECT*

Mark DINNING *US, male vocalist, d. 22 Mar 1986 (4 WEEKS)*   pos/wks

10 Mar 60	TEEN ANGEL (re) *MGM 1053* ▲	37	4

DINOSAUR JR *US, male vocal / instrumental group (13 WEEKS)*   pos/wks

2 Feb 91	THE WAGON *Blanco Y Negro NEG 48*	49	2
14 Nov 92	GET ME *Blanco Y Negro NEG 60*	44	1
30 Jan 93	START CHOPPIN' *Blanco Y Negro NEG 61CD*	20	3
12 Jun 93	OUT THERE *Blanco Y Negro NEG 63CD*	44	2
27 Aug 94	FEEL THE PAIN *Blanco Y Negro NEG 74CD*	25	3
11 Feb 95	I DON'T THINK SO *Blanco Y Negro NEG 77CD*	67	1
5 Apr 97	TAKE A RUN AT THE SUN *Blanco Y Negro NEG 103CD*	53	1

DINOSAURS – See Terry DACTYL and the DINOSAURS

DIO UK / US, male vocal / instrumental group (22 WEEKS)

pos/wks

20 Aug 83	HOLY DIVER *Vertigo DIO 1*	72	2
29 Oct 83	RAINBOW IN THE DARK *Vertigo DIO 2*	46	3
11 Aug 84	WE ROCK *Vertigo DIO 3*	42	3
29 Sep 84	MYSTERY *Vertigo DIO 4*	34	4
10 Aug 85	ROCK 'N' ROLL CHILDREN *Vertigo DIO 5*	26	6
2 Nov 85	HUNGRY FOR HEAVEN *Vertigo DIO 6*	72	1
17 May 86	HUNGRY FOR HEAVEN (re-issue) *Vertigo DIO 7*	56	2
1 Aug 87	I COULD HAVE BEEN A DREAMER *Vertigo DIO 8*	69	1

DION US, male vocalist – Dion DiMucci (35 WEEKS)

pos/wks

26 Jun 59	A TEENAGER IN LOVE *London HLU 8874* [1]	28	2
19 Jan 61	LONELY TEENAGER *Top Rank JAR 521*	47	1
2 Nov 61	RUNAROUND SUE *Top Rank JAR 586* ▲	11	9
15 Feb 62 ●	THE WANDERER *HMV POP 971*	10	12
22 May 76	THE WANDERER (re-issue) *Philips 6146 700*	16	9
19 Aug 89	KING OF THE NEW YORK STREETS *Arista 112556*	74	2

[1] Dion and the Belmonts

Celine DION ⟨ 50 ⟩ Top 500

French-Canadian vocalist who won the 1988 Eurovision Song Contest (for Switzerland), b. 30 Mar 1968, Quebec. She has sold a reported 130 million albums worldwide and is the only female with two UK million-selling singles as a solo artist. Best-selling single: 'My Heart Will Go On' 1,312,551 (248 WEEKS)

pos/wks

16 May 92 ●	BEAUTY AND THE BEAST *Epic 6576607* [1]	9	7
4 Jul 92	IF YOU ASKED ME TO (re) *Epic 6581927*	57	5
14 Nov 92	LOVE CAN MOVE MOUNTAINS *Epic 6587787*	46	2
3 Apr 93	WHERE DOES MY HEART BEAT NOW *Epic 6563265*	72	1
29 Jan 94 ●	THE POWER OF LOVE *Epic 6597992* ▲	4	10
23 Apr 94	MISLED *Epic 6602922*	40	3
22 Oct 94 ★	THINK TWICE *Epic 6606422* ◆	1	31
20 May 95 ●	ONLY ONE ROAD *Epic 6613535*	8	8
9 Sep 95 ●	TU M'AIMES ENCORE (TO LOVE ME AGAIN) *Epic 6624255*	7	9
2 Dec 95	MISLED (re-issue) *Epic 6626495*	15	6
2 Mar 96 ●	FALLING INTO YOU *Epic 6629795*	10	10
1 Jun 96 ●	BECAUSE YOU LOVED ME (THEME FROM 'UP CLOSE AND PERSONAL') *Epic 6632382* ▲	5	16
5 Oct 96 ●	IT'S ALL COMING BACK TO ME NOW *Epic 6637112*	3	14
21 Dec 96 ●	ALL BY MYSELF (re) *Epic 6640622*	6	13
28 Jun 97	CALL THE MAN *Epic 6646922*	11	6
15 Nov 97 ●	TELL HIM *Epic 6653052* [2]	3	15
20 Dec 97	THE REASON *Epic 6653812*	11	8
21 Feb 98 ★	MY HEART WILL GO ON *Epic 6655472* ◆ ■ ▲	1	20
18 Jul 98 ●	IMMORTALITY *Epic 6661682* [3]	5	12
28 Nov 98 ●	I'M YOUR ANGEL *Epic 6666282* [4] ▲	3	13
10 Jul 99	TREAT HER LIKE A LADY *Epic 6675522*	29	3
11 Dec 99	THAT'S THE WAY IT IS *Epic 6684622*	12	11
8 Apr 00	THE FIRST TIME EVER I SAW YOUR FACE (re) *Epic 6691942*	19	7
23 Feb 02 ●	A NEW DAY HAS COME *Epic 6725032*	7	10
31 Aug 02	I'M ALIVE *Epic 6730652*	17	6
7 Dec 02	GOODBYE'S (THE SADDEST WORD) *Epic 6733732*	38	2

[1] Celine Dion and Peabo Bryson [2] Barbra Streisand and Celine Dion [3] Celine Dion with Bee Gees [4] Celine Dion and R Kelly

Kathryn DION – See 2 FUNKY 2 starring Kathryn DION

DIONNE Canada, female vocalist (2 WEEKS)

pos/wks

23 Sep 89	COME GET MY LOVIN' *Citybeat CBC 745*	69	2

Wasis DIOP featuring Lena FIAGBE
Senegal, male producer and UK, female singer (2 WEEKS)

pos/wks

10 Feb 96	AFRICAN DREAM *Mercury MERCD 453*	44	2

DIPPY – See Keith HARRIS and ORVILLE

DIRE STRAITS ⟨ 236 ⟩ Top 500

Multi-Brit and Grammy-award-winning group led by vocalist / lead guitarist / songwriter Mark Knopfler, b. 12 Aug 1949, Glasgow. This London-based band, whose world tours attracted millions, is among the top five album-selling acts in the UK. Knopfler was made an MBE in 2000 and, shortly afterwards, had a dinosaur named after him (119 WEEKS)

pos/wks

10 Mar 79 ●	SULTANS OF SWING *Vertigo 6059 206*	8	11
28 Jul 79	LADY WRITER *Vertigo 6059 230*	51	6
17 Jan 81 ●	ROMEO AND JULIET *Vertigo MOVIE 1*	8	11
4 Apr 81	SKATEAWAY *Vertigo MOVIE 2*	37	5
10 Oct 81	TUNNEL OF LOVE *Vertigo MUSIC 3*	54	3
4 Sep 82 ●	PRIVATE INVESTIGATIONS *Vertigo DSTR 1*	2	8
22 Jan 83	TWISTING BY THE POOL *Vertigo DSTR 2*	14	7
18 Feb 84	LOVE OVER GOLD (LIVE) / SOLID ROCK (LIVE) *Vertigo DSTR 6*	50	3
20 Apr 85	SO FAR AWAY *Vertigo DSTR 9*	20	6
6 Jul 85 ●	MONEY FOR NOTHING *Vertigo DSTR 10* ▲	4	16
26 Oct 85	BROTHERS IN ARMS *Vertigo DSTR 11*	16	13
11 Jan 86 ●	WALK OF LIFE *Vertigo DSTR 12*	2	11
3 May 86	YOUR LATEST TRICK *Vertigo DSTR 13*	26	6
5 Nov 88	SULTANS OF SWING (re-issue) *Vertigo DSTR 15*	62	1
31 Aug 91	CALLING ELVIS *Vertigo DSTR 16*	21	4
2 Nov 91	HEAVY FUEL *Vertigo DSTR 17*	55	2
29 Feb 92	ON EVERY STREET *Vertigo DSTR 18*	42	2
27 Jun 92	THE BUG *Vertigo DSTR 19*	67	1
22 May 93	ENCORES (EP) *Vertigo DSCD 20*	31	3

Tracks on Encores (EP): Your Latest Trick / The Bug / Solid Rock / Local Hero (Wild Theme)

See also Mark KNOPFLER

DIRECKT UK, male instrumental / production duo
– Mike 'E-Bloc' Kirwin and Danny 'Hibrid' Bennett (2 WEEKS)

pos/wks

13 Aug 94	TWO FATT GUITARS (REVISITED) *UFG UFG 7CD*	36	2

See also E-LUSTRIOUS

DIRECT DRIVE
UK, male / female vocal / instrumental group (3 WEEKS)

pos/wks

26 Jan 85	ANYTHING? *Polydor POSP 728*	67	2
4 May 85	A.B.C. (FALLING IN LOVE'S NOT EASY) *Boiling Point POSP 742*	75	1

DIRT DEVILS UK / Finland, male production
duo – Jon Grant and Paavo Siljamaki (6 WEEKS)

pos/wks

2 Feb 02	THE DRILL *NuLife / Arista 74321915262*	15	6

DIRTY ROTTEN SCOUNDRELS – See Lisa STANSFIELD

DIRTY VEGAS UK, male production trio (11 WEEKS)

pos/wks

19 May 01	DAYS GO BY *Credence CDCRED 011*	27	4
3 Aug 02	GHOSTS *Credence CDCRED 028*	31	3
12 Oct 02	DAYS GO BY (re-issue) *Credence CDCRED 030*	16	4

DISCHARGE UK, male vocal / instrumental group (3 WEEKS)

pos/wks

24 Oct 81	NEVER AGAIN *Clay CLAY 6*	64	3

DISCO ANTHEM
Holland, male producer – Lex van Coeverden (2 WEEKS)

pos/wks

18 Jun 94	SCREAM *Sweat MCSTD 1977*	47	2

DISCO CITIZENS
UK, male producer – Nick Bracegirdle (5 WEEKS)

pos/wks

22 Jul 95	RIGHT HERE RIGHT NOW *Deconstruction 74321293872*	40	1
12 Apr 97	FOOTPRINT *Xtravaganza 0091115*	34	2
4 Jul 98	NAGASAKI BADGER *Xtravaganza 0091595 EXT*	56	1

See also CHICANE

DISCO EVANGELISTS
UK, male instrumental / production group (2 WEEKS) pos/wks
8 May 93	DE NIRO Positiva CDTIV 2	59	2

DISCO TEX & the SEX-O-LETTES
US, male vocalist / female vocal group (22 WEEKS) pos/wks
23 Nov 74	● GET DANCIN' Chelsea 2005 013	8	12
26 Apr 75	● I WANNA DANCE WIT CHOO (DOO DAT DANCE) – PART 1 Chelsea 2005 024 [1]	6	10

[1] Disco Tex and the Sex-O-Lettes featuring Sir Monti Rock III

DISCO TEX presents CLOUDBURST
UK, male / female production / vocal group (2 WEEKS) pos/wks
24 Mar 01	I CAN CAST A SPELL Absolution CDABSOL 1	35	2

See also FULL INTENTION; HUSTLERS CONVENTION featuring Dave LAUDAT and Ondrea DUVERNEY; SEX-O-SONIQUE

DISCOVERY – See COAST 2 COAST featuring DISCOVERY

DISPOSABLE HEROES OF HIPHOPRISY
US, male rap / instrumental duo (7 WEEKS) pos/wks
4 Apr 92	TELEVISION THE DRUG OF THE NATION (re) Fourth & Broadway BRW 241	44	6
30 May 92	LANGUAGE OF VIOLENCE Fourth & Broadway 12BRW 248	68	1

First hit peaked when re-entered in Dec 1992

DISTANT SOUNDZ UK, male production / vocal trio (4 WEEKS) pos/wks
9 Mar 02	TIME AFTER TIME W10 / Incentive CENT 36CDS	20	4

Sacha DISTEL France, male vocalist (27 WEEKS) pos/wks
10 Jan 70	● RAINDROPS KEEP FALLING ON MY HEAD (4re) Warner Bros. WB 7345	10	27

DISTURBED US, male vocal / instrumental group (4 WEEKS) pos/wks
7 Apr 01	VOICES Giant 74321848962	52	1
28 Sep 02	PRAYER Reprise W 591CD1	31	2
14 Dec 02	REMEMBER Reprise W 596CD1	56	1

DIVA Norway, female vocal duo (2 WEEKS) pos/wks
7 Oct 95	THE SUN ALWAYS SHINES ON TV East West YZ 947CD	53	1
20 Jul 96	EVERYBODY (MOVE YOUR BODY) East West EW 035CD	44	1

DIVA SURPRISE featuring Georgia JONES
US / Spain, male production duo – Walter Taieb and Giuseppe Nuzzo and US, female vocalist (2 WEEKS) pos/wks
14 Nov 98	ON THE TOP OF THE WORLD Positiva CDTIV 100	29	2

See also ORIGINAL

DIVE UK, male production duo – Sacha Collisson and Simon Greenaway (1 WEEK) pos/wks
21 Feb 98	BOOGIE WEA WEA 147CD1	35	1

Hit featured vocalist Nasreen Shah

See also AURORA

DIVERSIONS UK, male / female vocal / instrumental group (3 WKS) pos/wks
20 Sep 75	FATTIE BUM BUM Gull GULS 18	34	3

DIVINE
US, male vocalist – Harris Milstead, d. 7 Mar 1988 (24 WEEKS) pos/wks
15 Oct 83	LOVE REACTION Design Communication DES 4	65	2
14 Jul 84	YOU THINK YOU'RE A MAN Proto ENA 118	16	10
20 Oct 84	I'M SO BEAUTIFUL Proto ENA 121	52	2
27 Apr 85	WALK LIKE A MAN Proto ENA 125	23	7
20 Jul 85	TWISTIN' THE NIGHT AWAY Proto ENA 127	47	3

DIVINE US, female vocal group (1 WEEK) pos/wks
16 Oct 99	LATELY Mushroom / Red Ant RA 002CDS ▲	52	1

DIVINE COMEDY
UK, male vocalist / instrumentalist – Neil Hannon (38 WEEKS) pos/wks
29 Jun 96	SOMETHING FOR THE WEEKEND Setanta SETCD 26	14	5
24 Aug 96	BECOMING MORE LIKE ALFIE Setanta SETCD 27	27	2
16 Nov 96	THE FROG PRINCESS Setanta SETCD 32	15	2
22 Mar 97	EVERYBODY KNOWS (EXCEPT YOU) Setanta SETCDA 038	14	4
11 Apr 98	SOMEDAY I'LL FIND YOU / I'VE BEEN TO A MARVELLOUS PARTY EMI CDTCB 001 [1]	28	3
26 Sep 98	GENERATION SEX Setanta SETCDA 050	19	3
28 Nov 98	THE CERTAINTY OF CHANCE Setanta SETCDA 067	49	1
6 Feb 99	● NATIONAL EXPRESS Setanta SETCDA 069	8	7
21 Aug 99	THE POP SINGER'S FEAR OF THE POLLEN COUNT Setanta SETCDA 070	17	4
13 Nov 99	GIN SOAKED BOY Setanta SETCDA 071	38	2
10 Mar 01	LOVE WHAT YOU DO Parlophone CDRS 6554	26	2
26 May 01	BAD AMBASSADOR Parlophone CRDS 6558	34	2
10 Nov 01	PERFECT LOVESONG Parlophone CDR 6561	42	1

[1] Shola Ama and Craig Armstrong / Divine Comedy

DIVINYLS
Australia, male / female vocal / instrumental duo (12 WEEKS) pos/wks
18 May 91	● I TOUCH MYSELF Virgin America VUS 36	10	12

DIXIE CHICKS US, female vocal group (6 WEEKS) pos/wks
3 Jul 99	THERE'S YOUR TROUBLE Epic 6675162	26	5
6 Nov 99	READY TO RUN Epic 6682472	53	1

DIXIE CUPS US, female vocal group (16 WEEKS) pos/wks
18 Jun 64	CHAPEL OF LOVE Pye International 7N 25245 ▲	22	8
13 May 65	IKO IKO Red Bird RB 10024	23	8

DIZZY HEIGHTS UK, male rapper (4 WEEKS) pos/wks
18 Dec 82	CHRISTMAS RAPPING Polydor WRAP 1	49	4

DJ ALIGATOR PROJECT
Denmark, male producer – Aliasghar Movasat (11 WEEKS) pos/wks
7 Sep 00	THE WHISTLE SONG EMI CDBLOW 001	57	1
19 Jan 02	● THE WHISTLE SONG (BLOW MY WHISTLE BITCH) (re-mix) All Around the World CDGLOBE 247	5	10

DJ ARABESQUE – See Mario PIU

DJ BADMARSH and SHRI featuring UK APACHE India / Yemen,
male instrumental / production duo and UK, male rapper (1 WEEK) pos/wks
28 Jul 01	SIGNS Outcaste OUT 38CD1	63	1

DJ BOBO
Switzerland, male producer – Rene Baumann (4 WEEKS) pos/wks
24 Sep 94	EVERYBODY PWL Continental PWCD 312	47	2
17 Jun 95	LOVE IS ALL AROUND Avex UK AXEXCD 7	49	2

DJ CHUS presents GROOVE FOUNDATION
Spain, male DJ / production duo (1 WEEK) pos/wks
2 Nov 02	THAT FEELING Defected DFTD 055R	65	1

DJ DADO Italy, male producer – Roberto Gallo (9 WEEKS) pos/wks
6 Apr 96	● X-FILES ZYX ZYX 8065R8	8	6
14 Mar 98	COMING BACK ffrr TABCD 247	63	1
11 Jul 98	GIVE ME LOVE VC Recordings VCRD 37 [1]	59	1
8 May 99	READY OR NOT Chemistry CDKEM 006 [2]	51	1

[1] DJ Dado vs Michelle Weeks [2] DJ Dado and Simone Jay

DJ DAN presents NEEDLE DAMAGE
US, male DJ / production group (1 WEEK) pos/wks
5 May 01   THAT ZIPPER TRACK *Duty Free DF 026CD*..........**53** 1

DJ DEE KLINE *UK, male DJ / producer – Nick Annand (6 WEEKS)* pos/wks
3 Jun 00   I DON'T SMOKE *East West EW 213CD*.....................**11** 6

DJ DISCIPLE *US, male DJ / producer (1 WEEK)* pos/wks
12 Nov 94   ON THE DANCEFLOOR *Mother MUMCD 55* **67** 1

DJ DUKE *Denmark, male producer – Ken Larson (7 WEEKS)* pos/wks
8 Jan 94   BLOW YOUR WHISTLE *ffrr FCD 228* **15** 5
16 Jul 94   TURN IT UP (SAY YEAH) *ffrr FCD 235* **31** 2

DJ E-Z ROCK – See Rob BASE and DJ E-Z ROCK

DJ EMPIRE presents Giorgio MORODER
Germany, male producer – Alexander Wilkie (1 WEEK)
12 Feb 00   THE CHASE (re-recording) *LOGIC 731482* **46** 1

DJ ERIC *UK, male production trio (3 WEEKS)* pos/wks
13 Feb 99   WE ARE LOVE *Distinctive DISNCD 49* **37** 2
10 Jun 00   DESIRE *Distinctive DISNCD 56*..........................**67** 1

DJ 'FAST' EDDIE *US, male producer (15 WEEKS)* pos/wks
11 Apr 87   CAN U DANCE (re) *Champion CHAMP 41* [1] **67** 4
21 Jan 89   HIP HOUSE / I CAN DANCE *DJ International DJIN 5*.......**47** 4
11 Mar 89   YO YO GET FUNKY *DJ International DJIN 7* **54** 3
28 Oct 89   GIT ON UP *DJ International 655366 7* [2] **49** 4

[1] Kenny 'Jammin' Jason and 'Fast' Eddie Smith [2] DJ 'Fast' Eddie featuring Sundance

DJ FLAVOURS *UK, male producer – Neil Rumney (4 WEEKS)* pos/wks
11 Oct 97   YOUR CARESS (ALL I NEED)
        All Around the World CDGLOBE 160..........................**19** 4

DJ GARRY *Belgium, male producer – Marino Stephano (2 WEEKS)* pos/wks
19 Jan 02   DREAM UNIVERSE *Xtravaganza XTRAV 32CDS*....................**36** 2

DJ GERT
Belgium, male DJ / producer – Gert Rossenbacker (1 WEEK) pos/wks
26 May 01   GIVE ME SOME MORE *Mostika 23200253* **50** 1

DJ GREGORY *France, male producer (1 WEEK)* pos/wks
9 Nov 02   TROPICAL SOUNDCLASH *Defected DFTD 061CD* **59** 1

DJ HYPE *UK, male producer (2 WEEKS)* pos/wks
20 Mar 93   SHOT IN THE DARK *Suburban Base SUBBASE 20CD*........**63** 1
2 Jun 01   CASINO ROYALE / DEAD A'S *True Playaz TPRCD 004* [1] **58** 1

[1] DJ Zinc / DJ Hype

DJ INNOCENCE featuring Alex CHARLES
UK, male producer and male vocalist (1 WEEK) pos/wks
6 Apr 02   SO BEAUTIFUL *Echo ECSCD 119* **51** 1

DJ JAZZY JEFF & the FRESH PRINCE – See JAZZY JEFF & the FRESH PRINCE

DJ JEAN *Holland, DJ / producer – Jan Engelaar (11 WEEKS)* pos/wks
11 Sep 99 ● THE LAUNCH *AM:PM CDAMPM 123* **2** 11

DJ JURGEN presents Alice DEEJAY
Holland, male DJ / production group and female vocalist (16 WEEKS) pos/wks
31 Jul 99 ● BETTER OFF ALONE *Positiva CDTIV 113*..........................**2** 16

See also ALICE DEEJAY

DJ KOOL
US, male rapper / DJ / producer – John Bowman (7 WEEKS) pos/wks
22 Feb 97 ● LET ME CLEAR MY THROAT *American 74321452092* **8** 7

DJ KRUSH *Japan, male producer (2 WEEKS)* pos/wks
16 Mar 96   MEISO *Mo Wax MW 042CD*...............................**52** 1
12 Oct 96   ONLY THE STRONG SURVIVE *Mo Wax MW 060CD* **71** 1

DJ LUCK & MC NEAT
UK, male DJ / producers – Joel Samuels and Michael Rose (44 WEEKS) pos/wks
25 Dec 99 ● A LITTLE BIT OF LUCK *Red Rose CORROSLE 1*....................**9** 15
27 May 00 ● MASTERBLASTER 2000 *Red Rose RROSE 002CD* [1] **5** 8
7 Oct 00 ● AIN'T NO STOPPIN' US *Red Rose CDRRROSE 004* [2] **8** 6
17 Mar 01   PIANO LOCO *Island CID 773* **12** 8
8 Sep 01   I'M ALL ABOUT YOU (re) *Island CID 781* [3] **18** 5
25 May 02   IRIE *Island CID 795* [4] **31** 2

[1] DJ Luck and MC Neat featuring JJ [2] DJ Luck & MC Neat featuring JJ [3] DJ Luck and MC Neat featuring Ari Gold [4] Luck & Neat

DJ MANTA *Holland, male / female DJ / production trio (1 WEEK)* pos/wks
9 Oct 99   HOLDING ON *AM:PM CDAMPM 125* **47** 1

DJ MARKY & XRS *Brazil, male DJ / production
duo - Marco Da Silva and Michael Nicassio (7 WEEKS)* pos/wks
20 Jul 02   LK 'CAROLINA CAROL BELA' *V Recordings V 035* [1] **17** 6
16 Nov 02   LK (re-mix) *V Recordings V 038* **45** 1

[1] DJ Marky & XRS and Stamina MC

DJ MIKO
Italy, male producer – Quartobaro Manier (10 WEEKS) pos/wks
13 Aug 94 ● WHAT'S UP *Systematic SYSCD 2*.........................**6** 10

DJ MILANO featuring SAMANTHA FOX
Italy, male DJ / producer and UK, female vocalist (2 WEEKS) pos/wks
28 Mar 98   SANTA MARIA *All Around the World CDGLOBE 163*................**31** 2

See also Samantha FOX

DJ MISJAH and DJ TIM *Holland, male instrumental / production
duo – Misjah Van Der Heiden and Tim Hoogestegger (4 WEEKS)* pos/wks
23 Mar 96   ACCESS *Ffrreedom TABCD 240*..............................**16** 3
27 May 00   ACCESS (re-mix) *Tripoli Trax TTRAXCD 063* **45** 1

DJ OTZI *Austria, male DJ / producer – Gerry Friedle (48 WEEKS)* pos/wks
18 Aug 01   HEY BABY *EMI 8892462*..................................**41** 5
22 Sep 01 ★ HEY BABY (UHH, AHH) (re) *EMI CDOTZI 001* ■.....**1** 24
1 Dec 01 ● DO WAH DIDDY *EMI CDOTZI 002* **9** 9
29 Dec 01   X-MAS TIME *EMI CDOTZI 003*.............................**51** 2
8 Jun 02   HEY BABY (THE UNOFFICIAL WORLD CUP REMIX) (re-mix)
        (2re) *EMI Austria / Liberty CDOTZI 004*......................**10** 7
28 Dec 02   LIVE IS LIFE *EMI / Liberty CDLIVE 001* [1] ....**50** 1+

[1] Hermes House Band and DJ Otzi

DJ PIED PIPER and The MASTERS OF CEREMONIES
UK, male rap / production group (14 WEEKS) pos/wks
2 Jun 01 ★ DO YOU REALLY LIKE IT *Relentless MOS RELMOS 1CDS* [1] ■ **1** 14

[1] Dj Pied Piper and The Masters of Ceremonies

DJ POWER
Italy, male producer – Steve Gambaroli (2 WEEKS) pos/wks
7 Mar 92   EVERYBODY PUMP *Cooltempo COOL 252*....................**46** 2

DJ PROFESSOR *Italy, male producer (6 WEEKS)* pos/wks
10 Aug 91   WE GOTTA DO IT *Fourth & Broadway BRW 225* [1] **57** 2
28 Mar 92   ROCK ME STEADY *PWL Continental PWL 219* **49** 2

		pos/wks
8 Oct 94	ROCKIN' ME *Citra CITRA 1CD* [2]	**56** 1
1 Mar 97	WALKIN' ON UP *Nukleuz MCSTD 40098* [3]	**64** 1

[1] DJ Professor featuring Francesco Zappala [2] Professor [3] DJ PROF-X-OR

DJ QUICKSILVER *Turkey / Belgium, male DJ / producer duo – Ohran Terzi and Tomasso De Donatis (29 WEEKS)*
		pos/wks
5 Apr 97	● BELLISSIMA *Positiva CDTIV 72*	**4** 17
6 Sep 97	● FREE *Positiva CDTIVS 77*	**7** 7
21 Feb 98	PLANET LOVE *Positiva CDTIV 88*	**12** 5

DJ QUIK – See TONY TONI TONÉ

DJ RAP
UK, female vocalist / DJ / producer – Charissa Saverio (5 WEEKS)
		pos/wks
4 Jul 98	BAD GIRL *Higher Ground HIGHS 8CD*	**32** 2
17 Oct 98	GOOD TO BE ALIVE *Higher Ground HIGHS 14CD*	**36** 2
3 Apr 99	EVERYDAY GIRL *Higher Ground HIGHS 19CD*	**47** 1

DJ ROLANDO AKA AZTEC MYSTIC
US, male DJ / producer – Rolando Rocha (2 WEEKS)
		pos/wks
21 Oct 00	JAGUAR *430 West 430 WUKTCD1*	**43** 2

DJ SAKIN & FRIENDS
Germany, DJ / producer – Sakin Botzkurt (18 WEEKS)
		pos/wks
20 Feb 99	● PROTECT YOUR MIND (FOR THE LOVE OF A PRINCESS) (re) *Positiva CDTIV 107*	**4** 11
5 Jun 99	NOMANSLAND (DAVID'S SONG) *Positiva CDTIV 112*	**14** 7

DJ SAMMY AND YANOU featuring DO *Spain / Germany, male DJ production duo and Holland, female vocalist (8 WEEKS)*
		pos/wks
9 Nov 02	★ HEAVEN *Data / MOS DATA 45CDS* ■	**1** 8+

DJ SANDY vs HOUSETRAP *Germany, female DJ / producer – Sande De Sutter, and vocalist (2 WEEKS)*
		pos/wks
1 Jul 00	OVERDRIVE *Positiva CDTIV 133*	**32** 2

DJ SCOT PROJECT *Germany, male DJ / producer (2 WEEKS)*
		pos/wks
27 Jul 96	U (I GOT THE FEELING) *Positiva CDTIV 55* [1]	**66** 1
14 Feb 98	Y (HOW DEEP IS YOUR LOVE) *Perfecto PERF 158CD1*	**57** 1

[1] Scot Project

DJ Doc SCOTT *UK, male producer (2 WEEKS)*
		pos/wks
1 Feb 92	NHS (EP) *Absolute 2 ABS 001DJ*	**64** 2

Tracks on NHS (EP): Surgery / Night Nurse

DJ SCOTT featuring Lorna B
UK, male DJ – Scott Robertson, and female vocalist (5 WEEKS)
		pos/wks
28 Jan 95	DO YOU WANNA PARTY *Steppin' Out SPONCD 2*	**36** 3
1 Apr 95	SWEET DREAMS *Steppin' Out SPONCD 3*	**37** 2

DJ SEDUCTION
UK, male producer – John Kallum (8 WEEKS)
		pos/wks
22 Feb 92	HARDCORE HEAVEN / YOU AND ME *Ffrreedom TAB 103*	**26** 5
11 Jul 92	COME ON *Ffrreedom TAB 111*	**37** 3

DJ SHADOW *US, male producer – Josh Davis (11 WEEKS)*
		pos/wks
25 Mar 95	WHAT DOES YOUR SOUL LOOK LIKE *Mo Wax MW 027CD*	**59** 1
14 Sep 96	MIDNIGHT IN A PERFECT WORLD *Mo Wax MW 057CD*	**54** 1
9 Nov 96	STEM *Mo Wax MW 058CD*	**74** 1
11 Oct 97	HIGH NOON *Mo Wax MW 063CD*	**22** 2
20 Dec 97	CAMEL BOBSLED RACE *Mo Wax MW 084CD*	**62** 1
24 Jan 98	WHAT DOES YOUR SOUL LOOK LIKE (PART 1) *Mo Wax MW 087*	**54** 1
1 Jun 02	YOU CAN'T GO HOME AGAIN *Mo Wax CID 797*	**30** 2
2 Nov 02	SIX DAYS *Island CID 807*	**28** 2

DJ SHOG *Germany, male DJ / producer – Sven Greiner (2 WEEKS)*
		pos/wks
20 Jul 02	THIS IS MY SOUND *Nu Life 74321942272*	**40** 2

DJ SHORTY – See Lenny FONTANA and DJ SHORTY

DJ SS *UK, male DJ / producer (1 WEEK)*
		pos/wks
20 Apr 02	THE LIGHTER *Formation FORM 12093*	**63** 1

DJ SUPREME *UK, male producer – Nick Destri (11 WEEKS)*
		pos/wks
5 Oct 96	THA WILD STYLE *Distinctive DISNCD 19*	**39** 2
3 May 97	THA WILD STYLE (re-issue) *Distinctive DISNCD 29*	**24** 2
6 Dec 97	ENTER THE SCENE *Distinctive DISNCD 40* [1]	**49** 1
21 Feb 98	THA HORNS OF JERICHO *All Around the World CDGLOBE 164*	**29** 2
16 Jan 99	● UP TO THE WILDSTYLE *All Around the World CDGLOBE 170* [2]	**10** 4

[1] DJ Supreme vs the Rhythm Masters [2] Porn Kings vs DJ Supreme

DJ TAUCHER
German, male DJ / producer – Ralf Armand Beck (1 WEEK)
		pos/wks
8 May 99	CHILD OF THE UNIVERSE *Additive 12AD 037*	**74** 1

DJ TIESTO *Holland, male producer – Tijs Verwest (10 WEEKS)*
		pos/wks
12 May 01	FLIGHT 643 *Nebula NEBCD 016*	**56** 1
29 Sep 01	URBAN TRAIN *Nebula VCRD 95* [1]	**22** 3
13 Apr 02	LETHAL INDUSTRY *Nebula VCRD 103*	**25** 3
29 Jun 02	643 (LOVE'S ON FIRE) (re-recording) *Nebula VCRD 106* [3]	**36** 2
30 Nov 02	OBSESSION *Nebula NEBCD 029* [2]	**56** 1

[1] DJ Tiesto featuring Kirsty Hawshaw [2] Tiesto and Junkie XL [3] DJ Tiesto featuring Suzanne Palmer

See also GOURYELLA

DJ TIM – See DJ MISJAH and DJ TIM

DJ VISAGE featuring CLARISSA
Denmark / Germany, male DJ / producer / female vocalist (1 WEEK) pos/wks
		pos/wks
10 Jun 00	THE RETURN (TIME TO SAY GOODBYE) *One Step Music OSMCDS 13*	**58** 1

DJ WHAT? – See OBI PROJECT featuring HARRY, ASHER D and DJ WHAT?

DJ ZINC *UK, male DJ / producer – Benjamin Pettit (6 WEEKS)*
		pos/wks
18 Nov 00	138 TREK *Phaze One PHAZE CDX03*	**27** 3
2 Jun 01	CASINO ROYALE / DEAD A'S *True Playaz TPRCD 004* [1]	**58** 1
13 Apr 02	REACHOUT *True Playaz TPR 12039*	**73** 1
21 Sep 02	FAIR FIGHT / AS WE DO *Bingo Beats BING 008*	**72** 1

[1] DJ Zinc / DJ Hype

DJAIMIN *Switzerland, male producer (2 WEEKS)*
		pos/wks
19 Sep 92	GIVE YOU *Cooltempo COOL 262*	**45** 2

DJD presents HYDRAULIC DOGS
UK, male production duo (1 WEEK)
		pos/wks
8 Jun 02	SHAKE IT BABY *Direction 6721812*	**56** 1

DJH featuring STEFY
Italy, male instrumental / production group (14 WEEKS)
		pos/wks
16 Feb 91	THINK ABOUT ... *RCA PB 44385*	**22** 6
13 Jul 91	I LIKE IT *RCA PB 44741*	**16** 7
19 Oct 91	MOVE YOUR LOVE *RCA PB 44965*	**73** 1

DJPC *Belgium, male producer (5 WEEKS)*
		pos/wks
26 Oct 91	INSSOMNIAK *Hype 7PUM 005*	**62** 4
29 Feb 92	INSSOMNIAK (re-issue) *Hype PUMR 005*	**64** 1

GOD SAVE THE QUEEN

■ It was EMI Records (representing the likes of Cliff Richard and Des O'Connor) that, as it turned out, drew the short straw in signing The Sex Pistols, the most infamous new group of the mid-70s punk explosion. Virgin Records owner Richard Branson had already been on the phone to EMI head Leslie Hill offering to take The Sex Pistols off his hands, but had been tersely turned down. This was before the infamous Bill Grundy interview that forced EMI to change its tune as a result of the Today broadcast on London's Thames Television (owned, ironically, by EMI). Since the group's reputation preceded them, it was unwise to have them on the show in the first place (they were actually last-minute replacements for Queen), but Grundy proceeded to goad them into a profanity-filled "live" interview which shocked tea-time viewers, and made the front page of the national tabloids the next day. A 47-year-old lorry driver from Essex was so enraged that he smashed his television with his foot.

Inevitably, Grundy's TV contract was not renewed and EMI chief Leslie Hill didn't waste much time phoning Richard Branson to offer Virgin the Pistols. EMI had released only one record with the group, 'Anarchy in the UK', but it then decided to wash its hands of them due to so-called "adverse publicity". However, just when Branson thought he had a deal, McLaren announced that the group had signed with rival A&M Records. Their second single, 'God Save the Queen' (originally entitled 'No Future'), had been in the can since December 1976 and was now controversially scheduled for release to coincide with Queen Elizabeth's Silver Jubilee celebrations.

■ SEEMINGLY UNSUBSTANTIATED RUMOURS SPREAD THAT THE POWERS THAT BE HAD RIGGED THE CHART SO THAT 'GOD SAVE THE QUEEN' WOULD NOT BE NO.1 IN JUBILEE WEEK ■

Appropriately, the signing ceremony with A&M took place outside Buckingham Palace on 10 March 1977. Six days later the A&M contract was also terminated, making this one of the shortest recording contracts in pop music history. Following a riotous party at A&M's HQ to celebrate the signing, the company's employees were so disgusted at the group's behaviour that the band was dropped before any product was released. There had also been pressure from other A&M artists and the company's head office in Los Angeles. The Pistols and McLaren received another golden handshake for doing nothing. A&M had already pressed 25,000 copies of the single, which had to be destroyed, although some are still in circulation and among the most collectable rarities. An A&M single of 'God Save the Queen' was sold for £2,820 at Sotheby's in 2001.

Reluctant to sign with another major company, but desperate to get 'God Save the Queen' out in

★ ARTIST:	Sex Pistols
★ LABEL:	Virgin
★ WRITERS:	Jones/Cook/Matlock/Rotten
★ PRODUCER:	Chris Thomas

time for the jubilee, McLaren finally signed with Branson and 'God Save the Queen' was duly released. Virgin had considerable problems getting the notorious record manufactured – packing ladies at CBS agreed to handle the record only after reportedly being threatened with the sack – and while it received minimum radio play, the wave of publicity surrounding the group made sure that it sold 150,000 copies in five days. It looked set to top the chart but the single stalled at No.2 on the officially recognised BBC/British Market Research Bureau chart. Seemingly unsubstantiated rumours spread that the powers that be had rigged the chart so that 'God Save the Queen' would not be No.1 in jubilee week. Considering these circumstances, the actual chart-topper, Rod Stewart's 'I Don't Want to Talk About It'/'First Cut Is the Deepest', was a suitable alternative.

'God Save the Queen' was issued once more by Virgin in May 2002 in time for Queen Elizabeth's Golden Jubilee celebrations providing no controversy whatsoever, peaking at No.15.

■ Tony Burton

In front of Buckingham Palace and the eyes of the law, the Pistols sign for A&M

DJ's RULE *Canada, male instrumental / production duo (2 WEEKS)* pos/wks

2 Mar 96	GET INTO THE MUSIC *Distinctive DISNCD 9*	72	1
5 Apr 97	GET INTO THE MUSIC (re-mix) *Distinctive DISNCDD27* [1]	65	1

[1] DJ's Rule featuring Karen Brown

DJUM DJUM – *See LEFTFIELD*

Boris DLUGOSCH *Germany, male producer (8 WEEKS)* pos/wks

7 Dec 96	KEEP PUSHIN' *Manifesto FESCD 17* [1]	41	2
13 Sep 97	HOLD YOUR HEAD UP HIGH *Positiva CDTIV 79* [1]	23	4
16 Jun 01	NEVER ENOUGH *Positiva CDTIV 156* [2]	16	4

[1] Boris Dlugosch presents Booom! Vocals by Inaya Davis (aka Inaya Day) [2] Boris Dlugosch featuring Roisin Murphy

D'LUX *UK, male / female vocal / instrumental group (1 WEEK)* pos/wks

22 Jun 96	LOVE RESURRECTION *Logic 74321371012*	58	1

DMAC *UK, male vocalist – Derek McDonald (2 WEEKS)* pos/wks

27 Jul 02	THE WORLD SHE KNOWS *Chrysalis CDCHS 5140*	33	2

D'MENACE
UK, male production duo – Sandy Rivera and John Alvarez (3 WEEKS) pos/wks

8 Aug 98	DEEP MENACE (SPANK) *Inferno CDFERN 8*	20	3

DO – *See DJ SAMMY & YANOU featuring DO*

Carl DOBKINS Jr *US, male vocalist (1 WEEK)* pos/wks

31 Mar 60	LUCKY DEVIL *Brunswick 05817*	44	1

Anita DOBSON *UK, female actor / vocalist (13 WEEKS)* pos/wks

9 Aug 86	● ANYONE CAN FALL IN LOVE *BBC RESL 191* [1]	4	9
18 Jul 87	TALKING OF LOVE *Parlophone R 6159*	43	4

[1] Anita Dobson featuring the Simon May Orchestra

DR ALBAN *Nigeria, male vocalist – Alban Nwapa (28 WEEKS)* pos/wks

5 Sep 92	● IT'S MY LIFE *Logic 115330*	2	12
14 Nov 92	ONE LOVE *Logic 74321108727*	45	2
10 Apr 93	SING HALLELUJAH! *Logic 74321136202*	16	8
26 Mar 94	LOOK WHO'S TALKING *Logic 74321195342*	55	3
13 Aug 94	AWAY FROM HOME *Logic 74321222682*	42	2
29 Apr 95	SWEET DREAMS *Logic 74321251552* [1]	59	1

[1] Swing featuring Dr Alban

DOCTOR and the MEDICS *UK, male / female vocal / instrumental group – lead vocal Clive Jackson (25 WEEKS)* pos/wks

10 May 86	★ SPIRIT IN THE SKY *IRS IRM 113*	1	15
9 Aug 86	BURN *IRS IRM 119*	29	6
22 Nov 86	WATERLOO *IRS IRM 125* [1]	45	4

[1] Doctor and the Medics featuring Roy Wood

DR DRE (472) Top 500

Controversial rapper / producer and architect of West Coast gangsta rap, b. Andre Young, 18 Feb 1965, Los Angeles. Former member of rap group NWA and founder of the Death Row record label, whose protégés include Snoop Dogg and Eminem (76 WEEKS) pos/wks

22 Jan 94	NUTHIN' BUT A 'G' THANG / LET ME RIDE *Death Row A 8328CD*	31	3
3 Sep 94	DRE DAY *Death Row A 8292CD*	59	2
15 Apr 95	NATURAL BORN KILLAZ *Death Row A 8197CD* [1]	45	2
10 Jun 95	KEEP THEIR HEADS RINGIN' *Priority PTYCD 103*	25	4
13 Apr 96	● CALIFORNIA LOVE *Death Row DRWCD 3* [2]	6	8
19 Oct 96	● NO DIGGITY *Interscope IND 95003* [3] ▲	9	7
11 Jul 98	ZOOM *Interscope IND 95594* [4]	15	3
14 Aug 99	● GUILTY CONSCIENCE *Interscope IND 4971282* [5]	5	8
25 Mar 00	● STILL D.R.E. *Interscope 4972742* [6]	6	10
10 Jun 00	● FORGOT ABOUT DRE *Interscope 4973412* [7]	7	9

3 Feb 01	● THE NEXT EPISODE *Interscope 4974762* [6]	3	10
19 Jan 02	● BAD INTENTIONS *Interscope 4973932* [8]	4	10

[1] Dr Dre and Ice Cube [2] 2Pac featuring Dr Dre [3] BLACKstreet featuring Dr Dre [4] Dr Dre and LL Cool J [5] Eminem featuring Dr Dre [6] Dr Dre featuring Snoop Dogg [7] Dr Dre featuring Eminem [8] Dr. Dre featuring Knoc-Turn'al

DR FEELGOOD *UK, male vocal / instrumental group (29 WEEKS)* pos/wks

11 Jun 77	SNEAKIN' SUSPICION *United Artists UP 36255*	47	3
24 Sep 77	SHE'S A WIND UP *United Artists UP 36304*	34	5
30 Sep 78	DOWN AT THE DOCTORS *United Artists UP 36444*	48	5
20 Jan 79	● MILK AND ALCOHOL *United Artists UP 36468*	9	9
5 May 79	AS LONG AS THE PRICE IS RIGHT *United Artists YUP 36506*	40	6
8 Dec 79	PUT HIM OUT OF YOUR MIND *United Artists BP 306*	73	1

DR HOOK (292) Top 500

Distinctive group fronted by vocalists Dennis Locorriere and Ray Sawyer; had eight years of regular UK / US hits. Early recordings often featured humorous anarchic Shel Silverstein songs, but this good-time New Jersey act had greater success with later gentler material (104 WEEKS) pos/wks

24 Jun 72	● SYLVIA'S MOTHER *CBS 7929* [1]	2	13
26 Jun 76	● A LITTLE BIT MORE *Capitol CL 15871*	2	14
30 Oct 76	● IF NOT YOU *Capitol CL 15885*	5	10
25 Mar 78	MORE LIKE THE MOVIES *Capitol CL 15967*	14	10
22 Sep 79	★ WHEN YOU'RE IN LOVE WITH A BEAUTIFUL WOMAN *Capitol CL 16039*	1	17
5 Jan 80	● BETTER LOVE NEXT TIME *Capitol CL 16112*	8	8
29 Mar 80	● SEXY EYES *Capitol CL 16127*	4	9
23 Aug 80	YEARS FROM NOW *Capitol CL 16154*	47	6
8 Nov 80	SHARING THE NIGHT TOGETHER *Capitol CL 16171*	43	4
22 Nov 80	GIRLS CAN GET IT *Mercury MER 51*	40	5
1 Feb 92	WHEN YOU'RE IN LOVE WITH A BEAUTIFUL WOMAN (re-issue) *Capitol EMCT 4*	44	4
6 Jun 92	A LITTLE BIT MORE (re-issue) *EMI EMCT 6*	47	4

[1] Dr Hook and the Medicine Show

DR MOUTHQUAKE – *See E-ZEE POSSEE*

DR OCTAGON *US, male producer – Keith Thornton (1 WEEK)* pos/wks

7 Sep 96	BLUE FLOWERS *Mo Wax MW 055CD*	66	1

DOCTOR SPIN *UK, male instrumental / production duo (8 WEEKS)* pos/wks

3 Oct 92	● TETRIS *Carpet CRPT 4*	6	8

Ken DODD (62) Top 500

Seasoned stand-up comedian-cum-balladeer, b. 8 Nov 1929, Liverpool. The tickling-stick-wielding troubadour was one of the most successful Merseyside acts in the mid-1960s, at times enjoying two Top 10 singles simultaneously. Biggest-selling single: 'Tears' 1,521,000 (233 WEEKS) pos/wks

7 Jul 60	● LOVE IS LIKE A VIOLIN *Decca F 11248*	8	18
15 Jun 61	ONCE IN EVERY LIFETIME (2re) *Decca F 11355*	28	18
1 Feb 62	PIANISSIMO *Decca F 11422*	21	15
29 Aug 63	STILL *Columbia DB 7094*	35	10
6 Feb 64	EIGHT BY TEN *Columbia DB 7191*	22	11
23 Jul 64	HAPPINESS *Columbia DB 7325*	31	13
26 Nov 64	SO DEEP IS THE NIGHT *Columbia DB 7398*	31	7
2 Sep 65	★ TEARS *Columbia DB 7659* ◆	1	24
18 Nov 65	● THE RIVER (LE COLLINE SONO IN FIORO) *Columbia DB 7750*	3	14
12 May 66	● PROMISES *Columbia DB 7914*	6	14
4 Aug 66	MORE THAN LOVE *Columbia DB 7976*	14	11
27 Oct 66	IT'S LOVE *Columbia DB 8031*	36	7
19 Jan 67	LET ME CRY ON YOUR SHOULDER *Columbia DB 8101*	11	10
30 Jul 69	TEARS WON'T WASH AWAY THESE HEARTACHES *Columbia DB 8600*	22	11
5 Dec 70	BROKEN HEARTED (re) *Columbia DB 8725*	15	10
10 Jul 71	WHEN LOVE COMES ROUND AGAIN (L'ARCA DI NOE) *Columbia DB 8796*	19	16
18 Nov 72	JUST OUT OF REACH (OF MY TWO EMPTY ARMS) *Columbia DB 8947*	29	11

Re-entries are listed as (re), (2re), (3re), etc which signifies that the hit re-entered the chart once, twice or three times, etc

| 29 Nov 75 | THINK OF ME (WHEREVER YOU ARE) *EMI 2342* | .21 | 8 |
| 26 Dec 81 | HOLD MY HAND *Images IMGS 0002* | .44 | 5 |

Rory DODD – See Jim STEINMAN

DODGY *UK, male vocal / instrumental group (41 WEEKS)*
pos/wks

8 May 93	LOVEBIRDS *A&M AMCD 0177*	.65	2
3 Jul 93	I NEED ANOTHER (EP) *A&M 5803172*	.67	2
6 Aug 94	THE MELOD-EP *Bostin 5806772*	.53	1
1 Oct 94	STAYING OUT FOR THE SUMMER *Bostin 5807972*	.38	2
7 Jan 95	SO LET ME GO FAR *Bostin 5809032*	.30	3
11 Mar 95	MAKING THE MOST OF *Bostin 5809892* [1]	.22	3
10 Jun 95	STAYING OUT FOR THE SUMMER (re-mix) *Bostin 5810952*	.19	5
8 Jun 96	IN A ROOM *A&M 5816252*	.12	6
10 Aug 96 ●	GOOD ENOUGH *A&M 5818152*	.4	8
16 Nov 96	IF YOU'RE THINKING OF ME *A&M 5819992*	.11	4
15 Mar 97	FOUND YOU *A&M 5821332*	.19	3
26 Sep 98	EVERY SINGLE DAY *A&M MERCD 512*	.32	2

[1] Dodgy with the Kick Horns

Tracks on I Need Another (EP): I Need Another / If I Fall / Hendre DDU. Tracks on The Melod-EP: Melodies Haunt You / The Snake / Don't Go / Summer Fayre

Tim DOG *US, male rapper (3 WEEKS)*
pos/wks

| 29 Oct 94 | BITCH WITH A PERM *Dis-stress DISCD 1* | .49 | 1 |
| 11 Feb 95 | MAKE WAY FOR THE INDIAN *Island CID 586* [1] | .29 | 2 |

[1] Apache Indian and Tim Dog

DOG EAT DOG *US, male vocal / instrumental group (7 WEEKS)*
pos/wks

| 19 Aug 95 ● | NO FRONTS (re) *Roadrunner RR 23312* | .9 | 6 |
| 13 Jul 96 | ISMS *Roadrunner RR 23083* | .43 | 1 |

It was not until the Apr 1996 re-entry that 'No Fronts' reached its peak position of No.9

Nate DOGG *US, male rapper – Nathan Hale (28 WEEKS)*
pos/wks

23 Jul 94 ●	REGULATE *Death Row A 8290CD* [1]	.5	14
3 Feb 01	OH NO *Rawkus RWK 302* [2]	.24	4
25 Aug 01	WHERE I WANNA BE (re) *London LONCD 461* [3]	.14	7
29 Sep 01	AREA CODES *Def Jam 5887722* [4]	.25	3

[1] Warren G and Nate Dogg [2] Mos Def and Nate Dogg featuring Pharoahe Monch [3] Shade Sheist featuring Nate Dogg and Kurupt [4] Ludacris featuring Nate Dogg

DOGS D'AMOUR *UK, male vocal / instrumental group (15 WEEKS)*
pos/wks

4 Feb 89	HOW COME IT NEVER RAINS *China CHINA 13*	.44	3
5 Aug 89	SATELLITE KID *China CHINA 17*	.26	3
14 Oct 89	TRAIL OF TEARS *China CHINA 20*	.47	3
23 Jun 90	VICTIMS OF SUCCESS *China CHINA 24*	.36	3
15 Sep 90	EMPTY WORLD *China CHINA 27*	.61	2
19 Jun 93	ALL OR NOTHING *China WOKCD 2033*	.53	1

Ken DOH *UK, male producer – Michael Devlin (7 WEEKS)*
pos/wks

| 30 Mar 96 ● | NAGASAKI (EP) *ffrr FCD 272* | .7 | 7 |

Tracks on Nagasaki (EP): Nagasaki (2 mixes) / I Need A Lover Tonight (2 mixes) / Kaki Traki

Joe DOLAN *Ireland, male vocalist (40 WEEKS)*
pos/wks

25 Jun 69 ●	MAKE ME AN ISLAND (re) *Pye 7N 17738*	.3	19
1 Nov 69	TERESA *Pye 7N 17833*	.20	7
28 Feb 70	YOU'RE SUCH A GOOD LOOKING WOMAN *Pye 7N 17891*	.17	13
17 Sep 77	I NEED YOU *Pye 7N 45702*	.43	1

Thomas DOLBY *UK, male vocalist / multi-instrumentalist – Thomas Robertson (51 WEEKS)*
pos/wks

3 Oct 81	EUROPA AND THE PIRATE TWINS *Parlophone R 6051*	.48	3
14 Aug 82	WINDPOWER *Venice In Peril VIPS 103*	.31	8
6 Nov 82	SHE BLINDED ME WITH SCIENCE *Venice In Peril VIPS 104*	.49	4
16 Jul 83	SHE BLINDED ME WITH SCIENCE (re-issue) *Venice In Peril VIPS 105*	.56	4

21 Jan 84	HYPERACTIVE *Parlophone Odeon R 6065*	.17	9
31 Mar 84	I SCARE MYSELF *Parlophone Odeon R 6067*	.46	5
16 Apr 88	AIRHEAD *Manhattan MT 38*	.53	3
9 May 92	CLOSE BUT NO CIGAR *Virgin VS 1410*	.22	5
11 Jul 92	I LOVE YOU GOODBYE *Virgin VS 1417*	.36	4
26 Sep 92	SILK PYJAMAS *Virgin VS 1430*	.62	2
22 Jan 94	HYPERACTIVE! (re-mix) *Parlophone CDEMCTS 10*	.23	4

Joe DOLCE MUSIC THEATRE *US, male vocalist (10 WEEKS)*
pos/wks

| 7 Feb 81 ★ | SHADDAP YOU FACE *Epic EPC 9518* | .1 | 10 |

DOLL *UK, male / female vocal / instrumental group (8 WEEKS)*
pos/wks

| 13 Jan 79 | DESIRE ME *Beggars Banquet BEG 11* | .28 | 8 |

DOLLAR (211) Top 500
Photogenic teen-targeted UK vocal duo, who were originally one third of Guys and Dolls: David Van Day and Thereze Bazar. Their Top 10 hits came from writers as diverse as John Lennon, Paul McCartney, Trevor Horn, Erasure and themselves (128 WEEKS) pos/wks

11 Nov 78	SHOOTING STAR *EMI 2871*	.14	12
19 May 79	WHO WERE YOU WITH IN THE MOONLIGHT *Carrere CAR 110*	.14	12
18 Aug 79 ●	LOVE'S GOTTA HOLD ON ME *Carrere CAR 122*	.4	13
24 Nov 79 ●	I WANNA HOLD YOUR HAND *Carrere CAR 131*	.9	14
25 Oct 80	TAKIN' A CHANCE ON YOU *WEA K 18353*	.62	3
15 Aug 81	HAND HELD IN BLACK AND WHITE *WEA BUCK 1*	.19	12
14 Nov 81 ●	MIRROR MIRROR (MON AMOUR) *WEA BUCK 2*	.4	17
20 Mar 82	RING RING *Carrere CAR 225*	.61	2
27 Mar 82 ●	GIVE ME BACK MY HEART *WEA BUCK 3*	.4	9
19 Jun 82	VIDEOTHEQUE *WEA BUCK 4*	.17	10
18 Sep 82	GIVE ME SOME KINDA MAGIC *WEA BUCK 5*	.34	6
16 Aug 86	WE WALKED IN LOVE *Arista DIME 1*	.61	4
26 Dec 87 ●	O L'AMOUR *London LON 146*	.7	11
16 Jul 88	IT'S NATURE'S WAY (NO PROBLEM) *London LON 179*	.58	3

Placido DOMINGO *Spain, male vocalist (28 WEEKS)*
pos/wks

12 Dec 81	PERHAPS LOVE *CBS A 1905* [1]	.46	9
27 May 89	TILL I LOVED YOU *CBS 654843 7* [2]	.24	9
16 Jun 90	NESSUN DORMA FROM 'TURANDOT' *Epic 656005 7* [3]	.59	2
30 Jul 94	LIBIAMO / LA DONNA E MOBILE *Teldec YZ 843CD* [4]	.21	4
25 Jul 98	YOU'LL NEVER WALK ALONE *Decca 4607982* [5]	.35	4

[1] Placido Domingo with John Denver [2] Placido Domingo and Jennifer Rush [3] Luis Cobos featuring Placido Domingo [4] José Carreras featuring Placido Domingo and Luciano Pavarotti with Mehta [5] José Carreras, Placido Domingo and Luciano Pavarotti with Mehta

DOMINO *US, male rapper / vocalist – Shawn Ivy (6 WEEKS)*
pos/wks

| 22 Jan 94 | GETTO JAM *Chaos 6600402* | .33 | 4 |
| 14 May 94 | SWEET POTATOE PIE *Chaos 6603292* | .42 | 2 |

Fats DOMINO (264) Top 500
Pioneering rock 'n' roll singer / songwriter and pianist, b. 26 Feb 1928, New Orleans. Sold millions of rockin' records in pre-Haley / Presley years and is still among the biggest-selling artists and most successful composers of the rock era (111 WEEKS) pos/wks

27 Jul 56	I'M IN LOVE AGAIN (re) *London HLU 8280*	.12	14
30 Nov 56 ●	BLUEBERRY HILL (re) *London HLU 8330*	.6	15
25 Jan 57	AIN'T THAT A SHAME *London HLU 8173*	.23	2
1 Feb 57	HONEY CHILE *London HLU 8356*	.29	1
29 Mar 57	BLUE MONDAY (re) *London HLP 8377*	.23	2
19 Apr 57	I'M WALKIN' *London HLP 8407*	.19	7
19 Jul 57	VALLEY OF TEARS *London HLP 8449*	.25	1
28 Mar 58	THE BIG BEAT *London HLP 8575*	.20	4
4 Jul 58	SICK AND TIRED *London HLP 8628*	.26	1
22 May 59	MARGIE *London HLP 8865*	.18	5
16 Oct 59	I WANT TO WALK YOU HOME *London HLP 8942*	.14	5
18 Dec 59	BE MY GUEST (re) *London HLP 9005*	.11	13
17 Mar 60	COUNTRY BOY *London HLP 9073*	.19	11
21 Jul 60	WALKING TO NEW ORLEANS *London HLP 9163*	.19	10
10 Nov 60	THREE NIGHTS A WEEK *London HLP 9198*	.45	4
5 Jan 61	MY GIRL JOSEPHINE *London HLP 9244*	.32	4

UK No.1 ★   UK Top 10 ●   Still on chart +   UK million seller ◆   UK entry at No.1 ■   US No.1 ▲

27 Jul 61	IT KEEPS RAININ' *London HLP 9374*	49	1
30 Nov 61	WHAT A PARTY *London HLP 9456*	43	1
29 Mar 62	JAMBALAYA *London HLP 9520*	41	1
31 Oct 63	RED SAILS IN THE SUNSET *HMV POP 1219*	34	6
24 Apr 76	BLUEBERRY HILL (re-issue) *United Artists UP 35797*	41	5

DON PABLO'S ANIMALS
Italy, male production group (10 WEEKS)   pos/wks

19 May 90 ●	VENUS *Rumour RUMA 18*	4	10

DON-E
UK, male vocalist – Donald McLean (8 WEEKS)   pos/wks

9 May 92	LOVE MAKES THE WORLD GO ROUND *Fourth & Broadway BRW 242*	18	6
25 Jul 92	PEACE IN THE WORLD *Fourth & Broadway BRW 256*	41	1
28 Feb 98	DELICIOUS *Mushroom MUSH 20CD* [1]	52	1

[1] Deni Hines featuring Don-E

Lonnie DONEGAN (27) Top 500
The 'King of Skiffle', b. 29 Apr 1931, d. 3 Nov 2002, Glasgow, Scotland. Britain's most successful and influential recording artist before The Beatles. Chalked up 28 successive Top 30 hits, and was the first UK male to score two US Top 10s. Album with Van Morrison and Chris Barber reached Top 20 in 2000 (321 WEEKS)   pos/wks

6 Jan 56 ●	ROCK ISLAND LINE (2re) *Decca F 10647* [1]	8	22
20 Apr 56 ●	STEWBALL *Pye Nixa N 15036* [1]	2	18
6 Jul 56	SKIFFLE SESSION (EP) *Pye Nixa NJE 1017* [1]	20	2
7 Sep 56	BRING A LITTLE WATER, SYLVIE / DEAD OR ALIVE (re) *Pye Nixa N 15071*	7	13
21 Dec 56	LONNIE DONEGAN SHOWCASE (LP) *Pye Nixa NPT 19012* [2]	26	3
18 Jan 57 ●	DON'T YOU ROCK ME DADDY-O *Pye Nixa N 15080* [2]	4	17
5 Apr 57 ★	CUMBERLAND GAP *Pye Nixa N 15087* [2]	1	12
7 Jun 57 ★	GAMBLIN' MAN / PUTTIN' ON THE STYLE *Pye Nixa N 15093* [2]	1	19
11 Oct 57 ●	MY DIXIE DARLING *Pye Nixa N 15108* [2]	10	15
20 Dec 57	JACK O' DIAMONDS *Pye Nixa 7N 15116* [2]	14	7
11 Apr 58 ●	THE GRAND COOLIE DAM *Pye Nixa 7N 15129* [2]	6	15
11 Jul 58	SALLY DON'T YOU GRIEVE / BETTY, BETTY, BETTY *Pye Nixa 7N 15148* [2]	11	7
26 Sep 58	LONESOME TRAVELLER *Pye Nixa 7N 15158* [2]	28	1
14 Nov 58	LONNIE'S SKIFFLE PARTY *Pye Nixa 7N 15165* [2]	23	5
21 Nov 58 ●	TOM DOOLEY *Pye Nixa 7N 15172* [2]	3	14
6 Feb 59 ●	DOES YOUR CHEWING GUM LOSE ITS FLAVOUR (ON THE BEDPOST OVERNIGHT) *Pye Nixa 7N 15181* [2]	3	12
8 May 59	FORT WORTH JAIL *Pye Nixa 7N 15198* [2]	14	5
26 Jun 59 ●	BATTLE OF NEW ORLEANS *Pye Nixa 7N 15206* [2]	2	16
11 Sep 59	SAL'S GOT A SUGAR LIP *Pye Nixa 7N 15223* [2]	13	4
4 Dec 59	SAN MIGUEL *Pye 7N 15237* [2]	19	4
24 Mar 60 ★	MY OLD MAN'S A DUSTMAN *Pye 7N 15256* [3]	1	13
26 May 60 ●	I WANNA GO HOME (THE WRECK OF THE 'JOHN B') *Pye 7N 15267* [4]	5	17
25 Aug 60 ●	LORELEI *Pye 7N 15275*	10	8
24 Nov 60 ●	LIVELY *Pye 7N 15312* [3]	13	9
8 Dec 60	VIRGIN MARY *Pye 7N 15315*	27	5
11 May 61 ●	HAVE A DRINK ON ME *Pye 7N 15354* [3]	8	15
31 Aug 61 ●	MICHAEL, ROW THE BOAT / LUMBERED *Pye 7N 15371* [3]	6	11
18 Jan 62 ●	THE COMANCHEROS *Pye 7N 15410*	14	10
5 Apr 62 ●	THE PARTY'S OVER *Pye 7N 15424*	9	12
16 Aug 62 ●	PICK A BALE OF COTTON *Pye 7N 15455* [3]	11	10

[1] Lonnie Donegan Skiffle Group [2] Lonnie Donegan and His Skiffle Group [3] Lonnie Donegan and His Group [4] Lonnie Donegan and Wally Stott's Orchestra

'Stewball' had one week on the chart by itself on 20 Apr 1956. 'Lost John', the other side, replaced it on 27 Apr 1956, but 'Stewball' was given co-billing with 'Lost John' for the weeks of 11, 18 and 25 May 1956, peaking only at No.7. 'Dead or Alive' was not listed with 'Bring a Little Water Sylvie' for the week 7 Sep 1956. 'Putting on the Style' was not listed with 'Gamblin' Man' for the weeks of 7 and 14 Jun 1956. Tracks on Skiffle Session (EP): Railroad Bill / Stockalee / Ballad of Jesse James / Ol' Riley. Tracks on Lonnie Donegan Showcase (LP): Wabash Cannonball / How Long / How Long Blues / Nobody's Child / I Shall Not Be Moved / I'm Alabammy Bound / I'm a Rambling Man / Wreck of the Old '97 / Frankie and Johnny

Tanya DONELLY
US, female vocalist / instrumentalist (2 WEEKS)   pos/wks

30 Aug 97	PRETTY DEEP *4AD BAD 7007CD*	55	1
6 Dec 97	THE BRIGHT LIGHT *4AD BAD 7012CD*	64	1

Ral DONNER
US, male vocalist, d. 6 Apr 1984 (10 WEEKS)   pos/wks

21 Sep 61	YOU DON'T KNOW WHAT YOU'VE GOT (UNTIL YOU LOSE IT) *Parlophone R 4820*	25	10

DONOVAN (312) Top 500
Acclaimed Celtic singer / songwriter, b. Donovan Leitch, 10 May 1946, Glasgow. Initially dubbed British version of Bob Dylan, he enjoyed massive fame on both sides of the Atlantic in the 'flower power' years of the late 1960s (100 WEEKS)   pos/wks

25 Mar 65 ●	CATCH THE WIND *Pye 7N 15801*	4	13
3 Jun 65 ●	COLOURS *Pye 7N 15866*	4	12
11 Nov 65	TURQUOISE *Pye 7N 15984*	30	6
8 Dec 66 ●	SUNSHINE SUPERMAN *Pye 7N 17241* ▲	2	11
9 Feb 67 ●	MELLOW YELLOW *Pye 7N 17267*	8	8
25 Oct 67 ●	THERE IS A MOUNTAIN *Pye 7N 17403*	8	11
21 Feb 68 ●	JENNIFER JUNIPER *Pye 7N 17457*	5	11
29 May 68 ●	HURDY GURDY MAN *Pye 7N 17537*	4	10
4 Dec 68	ATLANTIS *Pye 7N 17660*	23	8
9 Jul 69	GOO GOO BARABAJAGAL (LOVE IS HOT) *Pye 7N 17778* [1]	12	9
1 Dec 90	JENNIFER JUNIPER *Fontana SYP 1*	68	1

[1] Donovan with the Jeff Beck Group

Jason DONOVAN (184) Top 500
The top teen idol of the late 1980s, b. 1 Jun 1968, Melbourne. The Australian actor turned singer had an impressive array of UK hits after leaving TV soap 'Neighbours'. His debut LP, 'Ten Good Reasons', was the UK's top-selling album of 1989 (137 WEEKS)   pos/wks

10 Sep 88 ●	NOTHING CAN DIVIDE US *PWL PWL 17*	5	12
10 Dec 88 ●	ESPECIALLY FOR YOU *PWL PWL 24* [1]	1	14
4 Mar 89 ★	TOO MANY BROKEN HEARTS *PWL PWL 32*	1	13
10 Jun 89 ★	SEALED WITH A KISS *PWL PWL 39* ■	1	10
9 Sep 89 ●	EVERY DAY (I LOVE YOU MORE) *PWL PWL 43*	2	9
9 Dec 89 ●	WHEN YOU COME BACK TO ME *PWL PWL 46*	2	11
7 Apr 90 ●	HANG ON TO YOUR LOVE *PWL PWL 51*	8	7
30 Jun 90	ANOTHER NIGHT *PWL PWL 58*	18	5
1 Sep 90 ●	RHYTHM OF THE RAIN *PWL PWL 60*	9	6
27 Oct 90	I'M DOING FINE *PWL PWL 69*	22	6
18 May 91	RSVP *PWL PWL 80*	17	5
22 Jun 91 ★	ANY DREAM WILL DO *Really Useful RUR 7*	1	12
24 Aug 91 ●	HAPPY TOGETHER *PWL PWL 203*	10	6
7 Dec 91	JOSEPH MEGA REMIX *Really Useful RUR 9* [2]	13	8
18 Jul 92	MISSION OF LOVE *Polydor PO 222*	26	4
28 Nov 92	AS TIME GOES BY *Polydor PO 245*	26	6
7 Aug 93	ALL AROUND THE WORLD *Polydor PZCD 278*	41	3

[1] Kylie Minogue and Jason Donovan [2] Jason Donovan and Original London Cast featuring Linzi Hately, David Easter and Johnny Amobi

DOOBIE BROTHERS
US, male vocal / instrumental group (45 WEEKS)   pos/wks

9 Mar 74	LISTEN TO THE MUSIC *Warner Bros. K 16208*	29	7
7 Jun 75	TAKE ME IN YOUR ARMS (ROCK ME A LITTLE WHILE) *Warner Bros. K 16559*	29	5
17 Feb 79	WHAT A FOOL BELIEVES (re) *Warner Bros. K 17314* ▲	31	11
14 Jul 79	MINUTE BY MINUTE *Warner Bros. K 17411*	47	4
24 Jan 87	WHAT A FOOL BELIEVES (re-issue) *Warner Bros. W 8451* [1]	57	3
29 Jul 89	THE DOCTOR *Capitol CL 536*	73	2
27 Nov 93 ●	LONG TRAIN RUNNIN' *Warner Bros. W 0217CD*	7	10
14 May 94	LISTEN TO THE MUSIC (re-mix) *Warner Bros. W 0228CD*	37	3

[1] Doobie Brothers featuring Michael McDonald

DOOGIE – See BUG KANN and the PLASTIC JAM

DOOLALLY
UK, male production duo – Stephen Mende and Daniel Langsmen (16 WEEKS)   pos/wks

14 Nov 98	STRAIGHT FROM THE HEART (re) *Locked On LOX 104CD*	20	10

   Re-entries are listed as (re), (2re), (3re), etc which signifies that the hit re-entered the chart once, twice or three times, etc

7 Aug 99 ● **STRAIGHT FROM THE HEART (re-issue)**
Chocolate Boy / Locked On LOX 112CD 9 6

See also SHANKS & BIGFOOT

DOOLEYS 413 Top 500
*Largest UK family act to chart (seven members at times); Jim, John, Frank,
Kathy, Helen, Anne Dooley plus Anne's husband Bob, and Alan Bogan. First
mixed UK family group to notch up five Top 20 entries (83 WEEKS)* pos/wks

13 Aug 77	THINK I'M GONNA FALL IN LOVE WITH YOU *GTO GT 95*	13	10
12 Nov 77 ●	LOVE OF MY LIFE *GTO GT 110*	9	11
13 May 78	DON'T TAKE IT LYIN' DOWN *GTO GT 220*	60	3
2 Sep 78	A ROSE HAS TO DIE *GTO GT 229*	11	11
10 Feb 79	HONEY I'M LOST *GTO GT 242*	24	9
16 Jun 79 ●	WANTED *GTO GT 249*	3	14
22 Sep 79	THE CHOSEN FEW *GTO GT 258*	7	11
8 Mar 80	LOVE PATROL *GTO GT 260*	29	7
6 Sep 80	BODY LANGUAGE *GTO GT 276*	46	4
10 Oct 81	AND I WISH *GTO GT 300*	52	3

Val DOONICAN 172 Top 500 *Popular balladeer and TV host, b.*
*3 Feb 1928, Waterford, Ireland. This relaxed crooner, who was known for his
rocking chair and multicoloured jumpers, had five successive Top 10 albums
in the Swinging Sixties (143 WEEKS)* pos/wks

15 Oct 64 ●	WALK TALL *Decca F 11982*	3	21
21 Jan 65 ●	THE SPECIAL YEARS (re) *Decca F 12049*	7	13
8 Apr 65	I'M GONNA GET THERE SOMEHOW *Decca F 12118*	25	5
17 Mar 66 ●	ELUSIVE BUTTERFLY *Decca F 12358*	5	12
3 Nov 66 ●	WHAT WOULD I BE *Decca F 12505*	2	17
23 Feb 67	MEMORIES ARE MADE OF THIS *Decca F 12566*	11	12
25 May 67	TWO STREETS *Decca F 12608*	39	4
18 Oct 67 ●	IF THE WHOLE WORLD STOPPED LOVIN' *Pye 7N 17396*	3	19
21 Feb 68	YOU'RE THE ONLY ONE *Pye 7N 17465*	37	4
12 Jun 68	NOW *Pye 7N 17534*	43	2
23 Oct 68	IF I KNEW THEN WHAT I KNOW NOW *Pye 7N 17616*	14	13
23 Apr 69	RING OF BRIGHT WATER *Pye 7N 17713*	48	1
4 Dec 71	MORNING *Philips 6006 177*	12	13
10 Mar 73	HEAVEN IS MY WOMAN'S LOVE (re) *Philips 6028 031*	34	7

DOOP *Holland, male instrumental duo*
– Ferry Ridderhof and Peter Garnefski (12 WEEKS) pos/wks

12 Mar 94 ★	DOOP *Citybeat CBE 774CD*	1	12

DOORS *US, male vocal / instrumental group (42 WEEKS)* pos/wks

16 Aug 67	LIGHT MY FIRE *Elektra EKSN 45014* ▲	49	1
28 Aug 68	HELLO, I LOVE YOU *Elektra EKSN 45037* ▲	15	12
16 Oct 71	RIDERS ON THE STORM (re) *Elektra K 12021*	22	11
20 Mar 76	RIDERS ON THE STORM (re-issue) *Elektra K 12203*	33	5
3 Feb 79	HELLO I LOVE YOU (re-issue) *Elektra K 12215*	71	2
27 Apr 91	BREAK ON THROUGH *Elektra EKR 121*	64	2
1 Jun 91 ●	LIGHT MY FIRE (re-issue) *Elektra EKR 125*	7	8
10 Aug 91	RIDERS ON THE STORM (2nd re-issue) *Elektra EKR 131*	68	1

DOPE SMUGGLAZ *UK, male DJ / production trio (5 WEEKS)* pos/wks

5 Dec 98	THE WORD *Mushroom PERFCDS 1*	62	1
7 Aug 99	DOUBLE DOUBLE DUTCH *Perfecto PERF2CDS*	15	4

Charlie DORE *UK, female vocalist (2 WEEKS)* pos/wks

17 Nov 79	PILOT OF THE AIRWAVES *Island WIP 6526*	66	2

DOROTHY *UK, male producer /*
instrumentalist – Paul Masterson (5 WEEKS) pos/wks

9 Dec 95	WHAT'S THAT TUNE (DOO DOO DOO DOO DOO-DOO-DOO-DOO-DOO-DOO) *RCA 74321330912*	31	5

*See also SLEAZESISTERS; CANDY GIRLS; YOMANDA; HI-GATE; CLERGY; Paul
MASTERSON presents SUSHI*

Lee DORSEY *US, male vocalist, d. 1 Dec 1986 (36 WEEKS)* pos/wks

3 Feb 66	GET OUT OF MY LIFE, WOMAN *Stateside SS 485*	22	7

5 May 66	CONFUSION *Stateside SS 506*	38	6
11 Aug 66 ●	WORKING IN THE COALMINE *Stateside SS 528*	8	11
27 Oct 66 ●	HOLY COW *Stateside SS 552*	6	12

Marc DORSEY *US, male vocalist (1 WEEK)* pos/wks

19 Jun 99	IF YOU REALLY WANNA KNOW *Jive 0522592*	58	1

Tommy DORSEY ORCHESTRA starring Warren COVINGTON
*US, orchestra with Warren Covington, male instrumentalist – trombone,
leader Tommy Dorsey d. 26 Nov 1956 (19 WEEKS)* pos/wks

17 Oct 58 ●	TEA FOR TWO CHA CHA *Brunswick 05757*	3	19

DOUBLE *Switzerland, male vocal / instrumental
duo – Kurt Maloo and Felix Haug (10 WEEKS)* pos/wks

25 Jan 86 ●	THE CAPTAIN OF HER HEART *Polydor POSP 779*	8	9
5 Dec 87	DEVIL'S BALL *Polydor POSP 888*	71	1

DOUBLE DEE featuring DANY *Italy, male vocal / instrumental
duo – Davide Domenella and Danny Losito (4 WEEKS)* pos/wks

1 Dec 90	FOUND LOVE *Epic 6563766*	63	2
25 Nov 95	FOUND LOVE (re-mix) *Sony S3 DANUCD 1*	33	2

DOUBLE 99 *UK, male instrumental /
production duo – Tim Liken and Omar Adimora (9 WEEKS)* pos/wks

31 May 97	RIPGROOVE *Satellite 74321485132*	31	3
1 Nov 97	RIPGROOVE (re-mix) *Satellite 74321529322*	14	6

See also RIP PRODUCTIONS

007 – *See RED RAW featuring 007*

DOUBLE SIX *UK, male vocal / instrumental group (2 WEEKS)* pos/wks

19 Sep 98	REAL GOOD *Multiply CDMULTY 39*	66	1
12 Jun 99	BREAKDOWN *Multiply CDMULTY 50*	59	1

DOUBLE TROUBLE *UK, male instrumental /
production duo – Leigh Guest and Michael Menson (35 WEEKS)* pos/wks

27 May 89	JUST KEEP ROCKIN' *Desire WANT 9* [1]	11	12
7 Oct 89 ●	STREET TUFF *Desire WANT 18* [2]	3	14
12 May 90	TALK BACK *Desire WANT 27* [3]	71	1
30 Jun 90	LOVE DON'T LIVE HERE ANYMORE *Desire WANT 32* [4]	21	6
15 Jun 91	RUB-A-DUB *Desire WANT 41*	66	2

[1] Double Trouble and the Rebel MC [2] Rebel MC and Double Trouble [3] With
vocals by Janette Sewell [4] Double Trouble featuring Janette Sewell and Carl
Brown

See also AIRHEADZ

DOUBLE YOU?
Italy, male vocalist – Willie Morales (3 WEEKS) pos/wks

2 May 92	PLEASE DON'T GO *ZYX ZYX 67487*	41	3

Rob DOUGAN
Australia, male vocalist / instrumentalist / producer (4 WEEKS) pos/wks

4 Apr 98	FURIOUS ANGELS *Cheeky CHEKCD 025*	62	1
6 Jul 02	CLUBBED TO DEATH *Cheeky / Arista 74321941702*	24	3

See also OUR TRIBE / ONE TRIBE; SPHINX

Carl DOUGLAS *Jamaica, male vocalist (39 WEEKS)* pos/wks

17 Aug 74 ★	KUNG FU FIGHTING *Pye 7N 45377* ▲	1	13
30 Nov 74	DANCE THE KUNG FU *Pye 7N 45418*	35	5
3 Dec 77	RUN BACK *Pye 7N 46018*	25	10
23 May 98 ●	KUNG FU FIGHTING *All Around the World CDGLOBE 173* [1]	8	11

[1] Bus Stop featuring Carl Douglas

*Second listing for Kung Fu Fighting was not a re-mix of the original but Douglas'
1974 hit vocal sampled and used in a new recording by Bus Stop*

Carol DOUGLAS *US, female vocalist (4 WEEKS)* pos/wks

22 Jul 78	NIGHT FEVER *Gull GULS 61*	66 4

Craig DOUGLAS `252` `Top 500`

Clean-cut early Sixties teen idol, b. Terence Perkins, 12 Aug 1941, Isle of Wight. Voted Best New Singer of 1959; had eight cover versions among his nine Top 20 entries. He topped the bill on The Beatles' first major stage show (113 WEEKS) pos/wks

12 Jun 59	A TEENAGER IN LOVE *Top Rank JAR 133*	13 11
7 Aug 59	★ ONLY SIXTEEN *Top Rank JAR 159*	1 15
22 Jan 60	● PRETTY BLUE EYES *Top Rank JAR 268*	4 15
28 Apr 60	● THE HEART OF A TEENAGE GIRL *Top Rank JAR 340*	10 9
11 Aug 60	OH! WHAT A DAY *Top Rank JAR 406*	43 1
20 Apr 61	● A HUNDRED POUNDS OF CLAY *Top Rank JAR 556*	9 9
29 Jun 61	● TIME *Top Rank JAR 569*	9 14
22 Mar 62	● WHEN MY LITTLE GIRL IS SMILING *Top Rank JAR 610*	9 13
28 Jun 62	● OUR FAVOURITE MELODIES *Columbia DB 4854*	9 10
18 Oct 62	OH, LONESOME ME *Decca F 11523*	15 12
28 Feb 63	TOWN CRIER *Decca F 11575*	36 4

DOVE *Ireland, male / female vocal group (2 WEEKS)* pos/wks

11 Sep 99	DON'T DREAM *ZTT 135CD*	37 2

DOVES *UK, male vocal / instrumental group (15 WEEKS)* pos/wks

14 Aug 99	HERE IT COMES *Casino CHIP 003CD*	73 1
1 Apr 00	THE CEDAR ROOM *Heavenly HVN 95CD*	33 2
10 Jun 00	CATCH THE SUN *Heavenly HVN 96CD*	32 2
11 Nov 00	THE MAN WHO TOLD EVERYTHING *Heavenly HVN 98CD*	32 2
27 Apr 02	● THERE GOES THE FEAR *Heavenly HVN 111CD*	3 3
3 Aug 02	POUNDING *Heavenly HVN 116CD*	21 3
26 Oct 02	CAUGHT BY THE RIVER *Heavenly HVN 126CDS*	29 2

DOWLANDS *UK, male vocal group (7 WEEKS)* pos/wks

9 Jan 64	ALL MY LOVING *Oriole CB 1897*	33 7

Robert DOWNEY Jr *US, male actor / vocalist (1 WEEK)* pos/wks

30 Jan 93	SMILE *Epic 6589052*	68 1

Don DOWNING *US, male vocalist (10 WEEKS)* pos/wks

10 Nov 73	LONELY DAYS, LONELY NIGHTS *People PEO 102*	32 10

Will DOWNING *US, male vocalist (35 WEEKS)* pos/wks

2 Apr 88	A LOVE SUPREME *Fourth & Broadway BRW 90*	14 10
25 Jun 88	IN MY DREAMS *Fourth & Broadway BRW 104*	34 6
1 Oct 88	FREE *Fourth & Broadway BRW 112*	58 5
21 Jan 89	WHERE IS THE LOVE *Fourth & Broadway BRW 122* [1]	19 7
28 Oct 89	TEST OF TIME *Fourth & Broadway BRW 146*	67 2
24 Feb 90	COME TOGETHER AS ONE *Fourth & Broadway BRW 159*	48 4
18 Sep 93	THERE'S NO LIVING WITHOUT YOU *Fourth & Broadway BRCD 278*	67 1

[1] Mica Paris and Will Downing

Jason DOWNS featuring MILK
US, male vocalist and US, male rapper (6 WEEKS) pos/wks

12 May 01	WHITE BOY WITH A FEATHER *Pepper 9230412*	19 5
14 Jul 01	CATS IN THE CRADLE *Pepper 9230442*	65 1

Lamont DOZIER – See HOLLAND-DOZIER featuring Lamont DOZIER

Charlie DRAKE
UK, male comedian / vocalist – Charles Sprigall (37 WEEKS) pos/wks

8 Aug 58	● SPLISH SPLASH *Parlophone R 4461*	7 11
24 Oct 58	VOLARE *Parlophone R 4478*	28 2
27 Oct 61	MR CUSTER *Parlophone R 4701*	12 12
5 Oct 61	MY BOOMERANG WON'T COME BACK *Parlophone R 4824*	14 11
1 Jan 72	PUCKWUDGIE *Columbia DB 8829*	47 1

DRAMATIS *UK, male vocal / instrumental group (8 WEEKS)* pos/wks

5 Dec 81	LOVE NEEDS NO DISGUISE *Beggars Banquet BEG 68* [1]	33 7
13 Nov 82	I CAN SEE HER NOW *Rocket XPRES 83*	57 1

[1] Gary Numan and Dramatis

Rusty DRAPER *US, male vocalist (4 WEEKS)* pos/wks

11 Aug 60	MULE SKINNER BLUES *Mercury AMT 1101*	39 4

DREAD ZEPPELIN
US, male vocal / instrumental group (3 WEEKS) pos/wks

1 Dec 90	YOUR TIME IS GONNA COME *IRS DREAD 1*	59 1
13 Jul 91	STAIRWAY TO HEAVEN *IRS DREAD 2*	62 2

DREADZONE *UK, male instrumental group (15 WEEKS)* pos/wks

6 May 95	ZION YOUTH *Virgin VSCDG 1537*	49 2
29 Jul 95	CAPTAIN DREAD *Virgin VSCDG 1541*	49 2
23 Sep 95	MAXIMUM (EP) *Virgin VSCDT 1555*	56 2
6 Jan 96	LITTLE BRITAIN *Virgin VSCDG 1565*	20 6
30 Mar 96	LIFE LOVE AND UNITY *Virgin VSCDT 1583*	56 1
10 May 97	EARTH ANGEL *Virgin VSCDT 1593*	51 1
26 Jul 97	MOVING ON *Virgin VSCDT 1635*	58 1

Tracks on Maximum (EP): Maximum / Fight the Power 95 / One Way

DREAM *US, female vocal group (7 WEEKS)* pos/wks

17 Mar 01	HE LOVES U NOT *Puff Daddy / Arista 74321823542*	17 7

DREAM ACADEMY
UK, male / female vocal / instrumental group (10 WEEKS) pos/wks

30 Mar 85	LIFE IN A NORTHERN TOWN *Blanco Y Negro NEG 10*	15 8
14 Sep 85	THE LOVE PARADE *Blanco Y Negro NEG 16*	68 2

DREAM FREQUENCY *UK, male producer – Ian Bland (12 WEEKS)* pos/wks

12 Jan 91	LOVE PEACE AND HARMONY *Citybeat CBE 756*	71 2
25 Jan 92	FEEL SO REAL *Citybeat CBE 763* [1]	23 5
25 Apr 92	TAKE ME *Citybeat CBE 768*	39 3
21 May 94	GOOD TIMES / THE DREAM *Citybeat CBE 773CD*	67 1
10 Sep 94	YOU MAKE ME FEEL MIGHTY REAL *Citybeat CBE 775CD*	65 1

[1] Dream Frequency featuring Debbie Sharp

See also BEAT RENEGADES; RED

DREAM WARRIORS *Canada, male rap group (19 WEEKS)* pos/wks

14 Jul 90	WASH YOUR FACE IN MY SINK *Fourth & Broadway BRW 183*	16 8
24 Nov 90	MY DEFINITION OF A BOOMBASTIC JAZZ STYLE *Fourth & Broadway BRW 197*	13 8
2 Mar 91	LUDI *Fourth & Broadway BRW 206*	39 3

DREAMCATCHER
UK, male / female production / vocal trio (4 WEEKS) pos/wks

12 Jan 02	I DON'T WANNA LOSE MY WAY *Positiva CDTIVS 157*	14 4

DREAMERS – See FREDDIE and the DREAMERS

DREAMHOUSE *UK, male vocal / instrumental group (2 WEEKS)* pos/wks

3 Jun 95	STAY *Chase CDPALACE 1*	62 2

DREAMWEAVERS *US, male / female vocal group (18 WEEKS)* pos/wks

10 Feb 56	★ IT'S ALMOST TOMORROW *Brunswick 05515*	1 18

DREEM TEEM *UK, male DJ / production trio (14 WEEKS)* pos/wks

13 Dec 97	THE THEME *4 Liberty 74321542032*	34 4
6 Nov 99	BUDDY X 99 *4 Liberty LIBTCD 33* [1]	15 5
15 Dec 01	IT AIN'T ENOUGH *ffrr / Public Demand FCD 401* [2]	20 5

[1] Dreem Teem vs Neneh Cherry [2] Dreem Teem vs Artful Dodger featuring MZ May and MC Alistair

DRELLS – See Archie BELL and the DRELLS

Eddie DRENNON and B.B.S. UNLIMITED
US, male vocal / instrumental group (6 WEEKS)   pos/wks
28 Feb 76	LET'S DO THE LATIN HUSTLE		
	Pye International 7N 25702	20	6

Alan DREW *UK, male vocalist (2 WEEKS)*   pos/wks
26 Sep 63	ALWAYS THE LONELY ONE *Columbia DB 7090*........	48	2

DRIFTERS 114 Top 500
Ever changing, ever popular US group, founded in 1953 by Clyde McPhatter (d. 1972) and still active today, with erstwhile members including Ben E King, Johnny Moore (d. 1998) and Rudy Lewis (d. 1964). Inducted into Rock and Roll Hall of Fame in 1988 (176 WEEKS)   pos/wks
8 Jan 60	DANCE WITH ME (re) *London HLE 8988*	17	5
3 Nov 60 ●	SAVE THE LAST DANCE FOR ME *London HLK 9201* ▲	2	18
16 Mar 61	I COUNT THE TEARS *London HLK 9287*	28	6
5 Apr 62	WHEN MY LITTLE GIRL IS SMILING *London HLK 9522*	31	3
10 Oct 63	I'LL TAKE YOU HOME *London HLK 9785*	37	5
24 Sep 64	UNDER THE BOARDWALK *Atlantic AT 4001*	45	4
8 Apr 65	AT THE CLUB *Atlantic AT 4019*	35	7
29 Apr 65	COME ON OVER TO MY PLACE *Atlantic AT 4023*	40	5
2 Feb 67	BABY WHAT I MEAN *Atlantic 584 065*	49	1
25 Mar 72 ●	AT THE CLUB *Atlantic K 10148*	3	20
26 Aug 72 ●	COME ON OVER TO MY PLACE (re-issue) *Atlantic K 10216*	9	11
4 Aug 73 ●	LIKE SISTER AND BROTHER *Bell 1313*	7	12
15 Jun 74 ●	KISSIN' IN THE BACK ROW OF THE MOVIES *Bell 1358*.............	2	13
12 Oct 74 ●	DOWN ON THE BEACH TONIGHT *Bell 1381*	7	9
8 Feb 75	LOVE GAMES *Bell 1396*	33	6
6 Sep 75 ●	THERE GOES MY FIRST LOVE *Bell 1433*	3	12
29 Nov 75 ●	CAN I TAKE YOU HOME LITTLE GIRL *Bell 1462*	10	10
13 Mar 76	HELLO HAPPINESS *Bell 1469*	12	8
11 Sep 76	EVERY NITE'S A SATURDAY NIGHT WITH YOU *Bell 1491*.............	29	7
18 Dec 76 ●	YOU'RE MORE THAN A NUMBER IN MY LITTLE RED BOOK		
	Arista 78	5	12
14 Apr 79	SAVE THE LAST DANCE FOR ME / WHEN MY LITTLE GIRL		
	IS SMILING (re-issue) *Lightning LIG 9014*	69	2

'Saturday Night at the Movies' received chart credit with 'At the Club' only after the re-issue's return to the chart on 8 Apr 1972

DRIFTERS – See SHADOWS

Julie DRISCOLL, Brian AUGER and the TRINITY
UK, female vocalist / male instrumental group (16 WEEKS)   pos/wks
17 Apr 68 ●	THIS WHEEL'S ON FIRE *Marmalade 598 006*.............	5	16

DRIVER 67 *UK, male vocalist – Paul Phillips (12 WEEKS)*   pos/wks
23 Dec 78 ●	CAR 67 *Logo GO 336*	7	12

DRIZABONE
UK / US, male / female vocal / instrumental group (18 WEEKS)   pos/wks
22 Jun 91	REAL LOVE *Fourth & Broadway BRW 223* [1]	16	8
26 Oct 91	CATCH THE FIRE *Fourth & Broadway BRW 232* [1]	54	2
23 Apr 94	PRESSURE *Fourth & Broadway BRCD 264*.............	33	2
15 Oct 94	BRIGHTEST STAR *Fourth & Broadway BRCD 293*	45	2
4 Mar 95	REAL LOVE (re-recording)		
	Fourth & Broadway BRCD 311.............	24	4

[1] Driza Bone

Frank D'RONE *US, male vocalist (6 WEEKS)*   pos/wks
22 Dec 60	STRAWBERRY BLONDE (THE BAND ROCKED ON)		
	Mercury AMT 1123	24	6

DROWNING POOL
US, male vocal / instrumental group (3 WEEKS)   pos/wks
27 Apr 02	BODIES *Epic 6723172*	34	2
10 Aug 02	TEAR AWAY *Epic 6729832*	65	1

DRU HILL *US, male vocal group (42 WEEKS)*   pos/wks
15 Feb 97	TELL ME *Fourth & Broadway BRCD 342*.............	30	3
10 May 97	IN MY BED *Fourth & Broadway BRCD 353*	16	3
11 Oct 97	BIG BAD MAMMA *Def Jam 5749792* [1]	12	3
6 Dec 97	5 STEPS *Island Black Music CID 675*.............	22	3
24 Oct 98 ●	HOW DEEP IS YOUR LOVE (re)		
	Island Black Music CID 725 [2]	9	8
6 Feb 99	THESE ARE THE TIMES *Island Black Music CID 733*	4	6
10 Jul 99	WILD WILD WEST *Columbia 6675962* [3] ▲	2	16

[1] Foxy Brown featuring Dru Hill [2] Dru Hill featuring Redman [3] Will Smith featuring Dru Hill – additional vocals Kool Moe Dee

See also SISQO

DRUGSTORE
UK / US / Brazil, male / female vocal / instrumental group (5 WEEKS)   pos/wks
10 Jun 95	FADER *Honey HONCD 7*	72	1
2 May 98	EL PRESIDENT *Roadrunner RR 22369* [1]	20	3
4 Jul 98	SOBER *Roadrunner RR22303*.............	68	1

[1] Additional vocals by Thom Yorke

DRUM CLUB *UK, male instrumental / production duo (1 WEEK)*   pos/wks
6 Nov 93	SOUND SYSTEM *Butterfly BFLD 10*	62	1

DRUM THEATRE *UK, male vocal / instrumental group (8 WEEKS)* pos/wks
15 Feb 86	LIVING IN THE PAST *Epic A 6798*	67	2
17 Jan 87	ELDORADO *Epic EMU 1*.............	44	6

DRUPI *Italy, male vocalist – Giampiero Anelli (12 WEEKS)*   pos/wks
1 Dec 73	VADO VIA *A&M AMS 7083*.............	17	12

DTOX *UK, male / female vocal / instrumental group (1 WEEK)*   pos/wks
21 Nov 92	SHATTERED GLASS *Vitality VITal 1*.............	75	1

John DU CANN *UK, male vocalist (6 WEEKS)*   pos/wks
22 Sep 79	DON'T BE A DUMMY *Vertigo 6059 241*	33	6

John DU PREZ – See MODERN ROMANCE

DUB CONSPIRACY – See TRU FAITH & DUB CONSPIRACY

DUB PISTOLS
UK, male vocal / instrumental / production group (1 WEEK)   pos/wks
10 Oct 98	CYCLONE *CONCRETE HARD 36CD*.............	63	1

DUB WAR *UK, male vocal / instrumental group (5 WEEKS)*   pos/wks
3 Jun 95	STRIKE IT *Earache MOSH 138CD*.............	70	1
27 Jan 96	ENEMY MAKER *Earache MOSH 147CD*.............	41	2
24 Aug 96	CRY DIGNITY *Earache MOSH 163CDD*.............	59	1
29 Mar 97	MILLION DOLLAR LOVE *Earache MOSH 170CD1*	73	1

DUBLINERS *Ireland, male vocal / instrumental group (45 WEEKS)* pos/wks
30 Mar 67 ●	SEVEN DRUNKEN NIGHTS *Major Minor MM 506*	7	17
30 Aug 67	BLACK VELVET BAND *Major Minor MM 530*	15	15
20 Dec 67	MAIDS, WHEN YOU'RE YOUNG NEVER WED AN OLD MAN		
	Major Minor MM 551	43	3
28 Mar 87 ●	THE IRISH ROVER *Stiff BUY 258* [1]	8	8
16 Jun 90	JACK'S HEROES / WHISKEY IN THE JAR		
	Pogue Mahone YZ 500 [1]	63	2

[1] Pogues and the Dubliners

DUBSTAR
UK, female / male vocal / instrumental group (26 WEEKS)   pos/wks
8 Jul 95	STARS *Food CDFOOD 61*.............	40	3
30 Sep 95	ANYWHERE *Food CDFOOD 67*	37	3
6 Jan 96	NOT SO MANIC NOW *Food CDFOOD 71*	18	5
30 Mar 96	STARS (re-issue) *Food CDFOODS 75*	15	6

POST-WAR POP HITS

■ The first chart that reflected British sheet music sales appeared in the late 1930s. Not surprisingly, between 1939 and 1945 as the bombs fell around them, people had a few more important things to do than calculate the top tunes. Therefore, the charts were sporadic during the Second World War and did not become a regular weekly event until the autumn of 1945. It should be remembered that sheet music sold in similar quantities to records nowadays. A top hit could sell 10,000 a day and million sellers were not that unusual – the last probably being 'How Much is That Doggie in the Window' in 1953.

Below are listed all the No.1 songs from August 1945 until the launch of the Record Best Sellers chart in November 1952, together with act/s that helped to popularise them in the UK. It should be noted that in those days it was the norm for a hit song to be recorded by at least half a dozen acts, and since no accurate record sales totals were kept, informed guesses have been made in a few cases as to the most popular version/s. Readers (or their parents/grandparents) in their 50s will at last be able to see what was No.1 on the day they were born

31 Aug 1945	**Let Him Go Let Him Tarry** Joe Loss / Nat Gonella
14 Sep 1945	**The Gypsy** Dorothy Squires / Ink Spots
19 Oct 1945	**I'm In Love with Two Sweethearts** Issy Bonn
11 Jan 1946	**It's Been a Long Long Time** Bing Crosby / Squadronaires
18 Jan 1946	**Cruising Down the River** Lou Preager / Primo Scala
25 Jan 1946	**It's Been a Long Long Time** Bing Crosby / Squadronaires
1 Feb 1946	**Kentucky** Squadronaires
22 Feb 1946	**Cruising Down the River** Lou Preager / Primo Scala
1 Mar 1946	**Kentucky** Squadronaires
8 Mar 1946	**Chickery Chick** Evelyn Knight and the Jesters
29 Mar 1946	**Cruising Down the River** Lou Preager / Primo Scala
5 Apr 1946	**Chickery Chick** Evelyn Knight and the Jesters
16 May 1946	**Along the Navajo Trail** Bing Crosby and Andrews Sisters / Steve Conway
23 May 1946	**In the Land of Beginning Again** Archie Lewis / Turner Layton
30 May 1946	**Mary Lou** Skyrockets / Denny Dennis
4 Jul 1946	**Bless You** Ink Spots
22 Aug 1946	**Bless You** Ink Spots / **Primrose Hill** Turner Layton / Skyrockets **tied**
29 Aug 1946	**Bless You** Ink Spots
31 Oct 1946	**Let It Be Soon** Skyrockets
7 Nov 1946	**Bless You** Ink Spots / **All Through the Day** Dick Haymes and Helen Forrest **tied**
14 Nov 1946	**Bless You** Ink Spots
5 Dec 1946	**Five Minutes More** Frank Sinatra
12 Dec 1946	**Five Minutes More** Frank Sinatra / **Sweetheart You'll Never Grow Old** Issy Bonn **tied**
19 Dec 1946	**Five Minutes More** Frank Sinatra
6 Feb 1947	**The Old Lamplighter** Geraldo / Joe Loss
13 Feb 1947	**Five Minutes More** Frank Sinatra / **To Each His Own** Ink Spots **tied**
20 Feb 1947	**Anniversary Song** Anne Shelton / Al Jolson
27 Feb 1947	**The Old Lamplighter** Geraldo / Joe Loss
10 Apr 1947	**Anniversary Song** Anne Shelton / Al Jolson
22 May 1947	**Among My Souvenirs** Bing Crosby / Squadronaires
26 Jun 1947	**Among My Souvenirs** Bing Crosby / Squadronaires / **A Gal in Calico** Bing Crosby **tied**
3 Jul 1947	**Tell Me Marianne** Mantovani / Monte Rey
10 Jul 1947	**Among My Souvenirs** Bing Crosby / Squadronaires
31 Jul 1947	**Among My Souvenirs** Bing Crosby / Squadronaires / **A Gal in Calico** Bing Crosby **tied**
7 Aug 1947	**Now Is the Hour** Gracie Fields
21 Aug 1947	**Come Back to Sorrento** Gracie Fields / Josef Locke
4 Sep 1947	**Now Is the Hour** Gracie Fields
11 Dec 1947	**An Apple Blossom Wedding** Lou Preager / Jimmy Leach
5 Feb 1948	**A Tree in the Meadow** Hutch / Dorothy Squires
19 Feb 1948	**A Tree in the Meadow** Hutch / Dorothy Squires / **Near You** Andrews Sisters / Francis Craig **tied**
26 Feb 1948	**A Tree in the Meadow** Hutch / Dorothy Squires
22 Apr 1948	**A Tree in the Meadow** Hutch / Dorothy Squires / **Near You** Andrews Sisters / Francis Craig **tied**

29 Apr 1948	**Galway Bay** Bing Crosby / Anne Shelton
30 Sep 1948	**So Tired** Russ Morgan / Reggie Goff
18 Nov 1948	**Buttons and Bows** Dinah Shore / Evelyn Knight
3 Feb 1949	**On a Slow Boat to China** Kay Kyser / Geraldo
24 Mar 1949	**Far Away Places** Bing Crosby / Radio Revellers
7 Apr 1949	**Twelfth Street Rag** Pee Wee Hunt
19 May 1949	**Lavender Blue** Donald Peers / Burl Ives
25 Jun 1949	**The Wedding of Lilli Marlene** Anne Shelton / Steve Conway
13 Aug 1949	**Riders in the Sky** Vaughn Monroe / Bing Crosby
15 Oct 1949	**I Don't See Me in Your Eyes Any More** Perry Como / The Stardusters
29 Oct 1949	**Forever and Ever** Russ Morgan / Dinah Shore
5 Nov 1949	**You're Breaking My Heart** Ink Spots / Reggie Goff
31 Dec 1949	**The Harry Lime Theme** Anton Karas
7 Jan 1950	**You're Breaking My Heart** Andrews Sisters / Francis Craig
21 Jan 1950	**The Hop Scotch Polka** Guy Lombardo / Tanner Sisters
28 Jan 1950	**The Harry Lime Theme** Anton Karas
4 Feb 1950	**Dear Hearts and Gentle People** Bing Crosby / Donald Peers
11 Feb 1950	**The Harry Lime Theme** Anton Karas
25 Feb 1950	**Dear Hearts and Gentle People** Bing Crosby / Donald Peers
11 Mar 1950	**Music! Music! Music!** Teresa Brewer
22 Apr 1950	**I'd've Baked a Cake** Eve Young / Donald Peers
29 Apr 1950	**My Foolish Heart** Billy Eckstine / Steve Conway
8 Jul 1950	**Bewitched** Doris Day / Bill Snyder
15 Jul 1950	**My Foolish Heart** Billy Eckstine / Steve Conway
22 Jul 1950	**Bewitched** Doris Day / Bill Snyder
9 Sep 1950	**Silver Dollar** Eve Young
28 Oct 1950	**Goodnight Irene** Weavers and Gordon Jenkins / Jo Stafford
25 Nov 1950	**Rudolph the Red-Nosed Reindeer** Gene Autry / Bing Crosby
6 Jan 1951	**I Taut I Taw a Puddy Tat** Mel Blanc
27 Jan 1951	**Beloved, Be Faithful** Teddy Johnson / Donald Peers
3 Feb 1951	**The Petite Waltz** Billy Cotton / Ken Griffin
17 Feb 1951	**The Tennessee Waltz** Les Paul and Mary Ford / Teddy Johnson

Top 1940s orchestra leader and BBC wireless favourite Geraldo, who recorded popular versions of both 'Slow Boat to China' and 'The Old Lamplighter'

21 Apr 1951	**Mockin' Bird Hill** Les Paul and Mary Ford / Ronnie Ronalde
30 Jun 1951	**With These Hands** Lee Lawrence / David Hughes
21 Jul 1951	**My Resistance Is Low** Hoagy Carmichael / Dorothy Squires
18 Aug 1951	**Too Young** Jimmy Young / Nat 'King' Cole
10 Nov 1951	**Longing for You** Teddy Johnson / Teresa Brewer
12 Jan 1952	**The Loveliest Night of the Year** Mario Lanza
19 Jan 1952	**Longing for You** Teddy Johnson / Teresa Brewer
2 Feb 1952	**The Loveliest Night of the Year** Mario Lanza
23 Feb 1952	**There's Always Room at Our House** Guy Mitchell
22 Mar 1952	**Unforgettable** Nat 'King' Cole
24 May 1952	**A-round the Corner** Jo Stafford / Stargazers
14 Jun 1952	**Auf Wiederseh'n Sweetheart** Vera Lynn
23 Aug 1952	**The Homing Waltz** Vera Lynn
25 Oct 1952	**Here in My Heart** Al Martino

3 Aug 96	ELEVATOR SONG *Food CDFOOD 80*	25	2
19 Jul 97	NO MORE TALK *Food CDFOOD 96*	20	3
20 Sep 97	CATHEDRAL PARK *Food CDFOOD 104*	41	1
7 Feb 98	I WILL BE YOUR GIRLFRIEND *Food CDFOODS 108*	28	2
27 May 00	I (FRIDAY NIGHT) *Food CDFOODS 128*	37	1

Ricardo 'Rikrok' DUCENT – *See SHAGGY*

Mary DUFF – *See Daniel O'DONNELL*

DUFFO *Australia, male vocalist (2 WEEKS)* pos/wks
24 Mar 79	GIVE ME BACK ME BRAIN *Beggars Banquet BEG 15*	60	2

Stephen 'Tin Tin' DUFFY *UK, male vocalist (24 WEEKS)* pos/wks
9 Jul 83	HOLD IT *Curve X 9763* [1]	55	4
2 Mar 85 ●	KISS ME *10 TIN 2*	4	11
18 May 85	ICING ON THE CAKE *10 TIN 3*	14	9

[1] Tin Tin

DUKE *UK, male vocalist (6 WEEKS)* pos/wks
25 May 96	SO IN LOVE WITH YOU *Encore CDCOR 009*	66	1
26 Oct 96	SO IN LOVE WITH YOU (re-issue) *Pukka CDPUKKA 11*	22	4
11 Nov 00	SO IN LOVE WITH YOU (re-mix) *48k / Perfecto SPECT 08CDS*	65	1

George DUKE *US, male vocalist / instrumentalist (6 WEEKS)* pos/wks
12 Jul 80	BRAZILIAN LOVE AFFAIR *Epic EPC 8751*	36	6

DUKES *UK, male vocal duo (13 WEEKS)* pos/wks
17 Oct 81	MYSTERY GIRL *WEA K 18867*	47	7
1 May 82	THANK YOU FOR THE PARTY *WEA K 19136*	53	6

Candy DULFER
Holland, female instrumentalist – saxophone (14 WEEKS) pos/wks
24 Feb 90 ●	LILY WAS HERE *RCA ZB 43045* [1]	6	12
4 Aug 90	SAXUALITY *RCA PB 43769*	60	2

[1] David A Stewart featuring Candy Dulfer

DUM DUMS
UK, male vocal / instrumental group (15 WEEKS) pos/wks
11 Mar 00	EVERYTHING *Good Behavior CDGOOD 1*	21	5
8 Jul 00	CAN'T GET YOU OUT OF MY THOUGHTS *Good Behaviour GD GOOD 2*	18	5
23 Sep 00	YOU DO SOMETHING TO ME *Good Behaviour CD GOLD 3*	27	3
17 Feb 01	ARMY OF TWO *Good Behaviour CDGOOD 5*	27	2

Thuli DUMAKUDE
South Africa, female vocalist (1 WEEK) pos/wks
2 Jan 88	THE FUNERAL (SEPTEMBER 25, 1977) *MCA MCA 1228*	75	1

The listed flip side of 'The Funeral' was 'Cry Freedom' by George Fenton and Jonas Gwangwa

John DUMMER and Helen APRIL
UK, male / female vocal duo (3 WEEKS) pos/wks
28 Aug 82	BLUE SKIES *Speed SPEED 8*	54	3

DUMONDE
Germany, male / female production / vocal group (3 WEEKS) pos/wks
27 Jan 01	TOMORROW *Variation VART 6*	60	1
19 May 01	NEVER LOOK BACK *Manifesto FESCD 83*	36	2

DUNBLANE
UK, male / female vocal / instrumental group (15 WEEKS) pos/wks
21 Dec 96 ★	KNOCKIN' ON HEAVEN'S DOOR / THROW THESE GUNS AWAY *BMG 74321442182* ■	1	15

Johnny DUNCAN and the BLUE GRASS BOYS *US, male vocalist (d. 15 Jul 2000) and UK, instrumental group (20 WEEKS)* pos/wks
26 Jul 57	LAST TRAIN TO SAN FERNANDO *Columbia DB 3959*	2	17
25 Oct 57	BLUE, BLUE HEARTACHES *Columbia DB 3996*	27	1
29 Nov 57	FOOTPRINTS IN THE SNOW (re) *Columbia DB 4029*	27	2

David DUNDAS *UK, male vocalist (14 WEEKS)* pos/wks
24 Jul 76 ●	JEANS ON *Air CHS 2094*	3	9
9 Apr 77	ANOTHER FUNNY HONEYMOON *Air CHS 2136*	29	5

Errol DUNKLEY *Jamaica, male vocalist (14 WEEKS)* pos/wks
22 Sep 79	OK FRED *Scope SC 6*	11	11
2 Feb 80	SIT DOWN AND CRY *Scope SC 11*	52	3

Clive DUNN *UK, male actor / vocalist (28 WEEKS)* pos/wks
28 Nov 70 ★	GRANDAD (re) *Columbia DB 8726*	1	28

Simon DUPREE and the BIG SOUND
UK, male vocal / instrumental group (16 WEEKS) pos/wks
22 Nov 67 ●	KITES *Parlophone R 5646*	9	13
3 Apr 68	FOR WHOM THE BELL TOLLS *Parlophone R 5670*	43	3

DURAN DURAN (70) [Top 500] *New Romantics turned teen idols: Simon Le Bon (v), Nick Rhodes (k), John Taylor (b), Andy Taylor (g), Roger Taylor (d). The Birmingham band's successive Top 10 hits included 'A View to a Kill', the best-selling James Bond theme ever in the UK and the US. The three Taylors were unrelated (222 WEEKS)* pos/wks
21 Feb 81	PLANET EARTH *EMI 5137*	12	11
9 May 81	CARELESS MEMORIES *EMI 5168*	37	7
25 Jul 81 ●	GIRLS ON FILM *EMI 5206*	5	11
28 Nov 81	MY OWN WAY *EMI 5254*	14	11
15 May 82 ●	HUNGRY LIKE THE WOLF *EMI 5295*	5	12
21 Aug 82 ●	SAVE A PRAYER *EMI 5327*	2	9
13 Nov 82 ●	RIO *EMI 5346*	9	11
26 Mar 83 ★	IS THERE SOMETHING I SHOULD KNOW? *EMI 5371* ■	1	9
29 Oct 83 ●	UNION OF THE SNAKE (re) *EMI 5429*	3	11
4 Feb 84 ●	NEW MOON ON MONDAY *EMI DURAN 1*	9	7
28 Apr 84 ★	THE REFLEX *EMI DURAN 2* ▲	1	14
3 Nov 84 ●	THE WILD BOYS *Parlophone DURAN 3*	2	14
18 May 85 ●	A VIEW TO A KILL *Parlophone DURAN 007* ▲	2	16
1 Nov 86	NOTORIOUS (re) *EMI DDN 45*	7	7
21 Feb 87	SKIN TRADE *EMI TRADE 1*	22	6
25 Apr 87	MEET EL PRESIDENTE *EMI TOUR 1*	24	5
1 Oct 88	I DON'T WANT YOUR LOVE *EMI YOUR 1*	14	5
7 Jan 89 ●	ALL SHE WANTS IS *EMI DD 11*	9	5
22 Apr 89	DO YOU BELIEVE IN SHAME? *EMI DD 12*	30	4
16 Dec 89	BURNING THE GROUND *EMI DD 13*	31	5
4 Aug 90	VIOLENCE OF SUMMER (LOVE'S TAKING OVER) *Parlophone DD 14*	20	4
17 Nov 90	SERIOUS *Parlophone DD 15*	48	3
30 Jan 93 ●	ORDINARY WORLD *Parlophone CDDDS 16*	6	9
10 Apr 93	COME UNDONE *Parlophone CDDDS 17*	13	8
4 Sep 93	TOO MUCH INFORMATION *Parlophone CDDDS 18*	35	3
25 Mar 95	PERFECT DAY *Parlophone CDDDS 20*	28	4
17 Jun 95	WHITE LINES (DON'T DO IT) *Parlophone CDDD 19* [1]	17	5
24 May 97	OUT OF MY MIND *Virgin VSCDT 1639*	21	2
30 Jan 99	ELECTRIC BARBARELLA *EMI CDELEC 2000*	23	3
10 Jun 00	SOMEONE ELSE NOT ME *Hollywood / Edel 0108845 HWR*	53	1

[1] Duran Duran featuring Melle Mel and Grandmaster Flash and the Furious Five

Group was UK / US from 'Burning the Ground'. See also POWER STATION; ARCADIA

Jimmy DURANTE *US, male vocalist, d. 29 Jan 1980 (1 WEEK)* pos/wks
14 Dec 96	MAKE SOMEONE HAPPY *Warner Bros. W 0385CD*	69	1

Judith DURHAM *Australia, female vocalist (5 WEEKS)* pos/wks
15 Jun 67	THE OLIVE TREE *Columbia DB 8207*	33	5

See also SEEKERS

Re-entries are listed as (re), (2re), (3re), etc which signifies that the hit re-entered the chart once, twice or three times, etc

Ian DURY and the BLOCKHEADS
UK, male vocal / instrumental group, leader d. 27 Mar 2000 (56 WEEKS) pos/wks

		pos	wks
29 Apr 78 ●	WHAT A WASTE! *Stiff BUY 27*	9	12
9 Dec 78 ★	HIT ME WITH YOUR RHYTHM STICK *Stiff BUY 38* [1]	1	15
4 Aug 79 ●	REASONS TO BE CHEERFUL (PT. 3) *Stiff BUY 50*	3	8
30 Aug 80	I WANT TO BE STRAIGHT *Stiff BUY 90*	22	7
15 Nov 80	SUPERMAN'S BIG SISTER *Stiff BUY 100*	51	3
25 May 85	HIT ME WITH YOUR RHYTHM STICK (re-mix) *Stiff BUY 214*	55	4
26 Oct 85	PROFOUNDLY IN LOVE WITH PANDORA *EMI EMI 5534* [2]	45	5
27 Jul 91	HIT ME WITH YOUR RHYTHM STICK '91 *Flying FLYR 1*	73	1
11 Mar 00	DRIP FED FRED *Virgin VSCDT 1768* [3]	55	1

[1] Ian and the Blockheads [2] Ian Dury [3] Madness featuring Ian Dury

DUST BROTHERS
US, male production duo (1 WEEK) pos/wks

		pos	wks
11 Dec 99	THIS IS YOUR LIFE *Restless 74321713962*	60	1

DUST JUNKYS
UK, male vocal / instrumental group (5 WEEKS) pos/wks

		pos	wks
15 Nov 97	(NONSTOPOPERATION) *Polydor 5719732*	47	2
28 Feb 98	WHAT TIME IS IT? *Polydor 5694912*	39	2
16 May 98	NOTHIN' PERSONAL *Polydor 5699092*	62	1

DUSTED
*UK, male production / instrumental duo
– Roland Armstrong and Mark Bates (2 WEEKS)* pos/wks

		pos	wks
20 Jan 01	ALWAYS REMEMBER TO RESPECT AND HONOUR YOUR MOTHER *Go! Beat / Polydor GOBCD 36*	31	2

Vocal by 12-year-old choir boy Alan Young

See also SPHINX; OUR TRIBE / ONE TRIBE; FAITHLESS; ROLLO

Slim DUSTY
Australia, male vocalist – David Kirkpatrick (15 WEEKS) pos/wks

		pos	wks
30 Jan 59 ●	A PUB WITH NO BEER *Columbia DB 4212* [1]	3	15

[1] Slim Dusty with Dick Carr and his Bushlanders

DUTCH FORCE
Holland, male producer – Benno De Goeij (2 WEEKS) pos/wks

		pos	wks
6 May 00	DEADLINE *Inferno CDFERN 27*	35	2

Ondrea DUVERN – *See HUSTLERS CONVENTION featuring Dave LAUDAT and Ondrea DUVERNEY*

DWEEB
UK, male / female vocal / instrumental trio (2 WEEKS) pos/wks

		pos	wks
22 Feb 97	SCOOBY DOO *Blanco Y Negro NEG 100CD*	63	1
7 Jun 97	OH YEAH, BABY *Blanco Y Negro NEG 102CD1*	70	1

Sarah DWYER – *See LANGE*

Bob DYLAN
(187 | Top 500) *The most influential folk / rock vocalist / guitarist ever, b. Robert Zimmerman, 24 May 1941, Minnesota, US. The legendary performer, who led the 1960s folk music movement, redefined the term and, indeed, image of the singer / songwriter. He was still adding to his impressive tally of Top 5 UK and US albums in 2001 (137 WEEKS)* pos/wks

		pos	wks
25 Mar 65 ●	TIMES THEY ARE A-CHANGIN' *CBS 201751*	9	11
29 Apr 65 ●	SUBTERRANEAN HOMESICK BLUES *CBS 201753*	9	9
17 Jun 65	MAGGIE'S FARM *CBS 201781*	22	8
19 Aug 65 ●	LIKE A ROLLING STONE *CBS 201811*	4	12
28 Oct 65 ●	POSITIVELY 4TH STREET *CBS 201824*	8	12
27 Jan 66	CAN YOU PLEASE CRAWL OUT YOUR WINDOW *CBS 201900*	17	5
14 Apr 66	ONE OF US MUST KNOW (SOONER OR LATER) *CBS 202053*	33	5
12 May 66 ●	RAINY DAY WOMEN NOS. 12 & 35 *CBS 202307*	7	8
21 Jul 66	I WANT YOU *CBS 202258*	16	9
14 May 69	I THREW IT ALL AWAY *CBS 4219*	30	6
13 Sep 69 ●	LAY LADY LAY *CBS 4434*	5	12
10 Jul 71	WATCHING THE RIVER FLOW *CBS 7329*	24	9
6 Oct 73	KNOCKIN' ON HEAVEN'S DOOR *CBS 1762*	14	9
7 Feb 76	HURRICANE *CBS 3878*	43	4
29 Jul 78	BABY STOP CRYING *CBS 6499*	13	11
28 Oct 78	IS YOUR LOVE IN VAIN? *CBS 6718*	56	3

		pos	wks
20 May 95	DIGNITY *Columbia 6620762*	33	2
11 Jul 98	LOVE SICK *Columbia 6659972*	64	1
14 Oct 00	THINGS HAVE CHANGED *Columbia 6693792*	58	1

DYNAMIX II featuring TOO TOUGH TEE
US, male vocal / instrumental group and rapper (4 WEEKS) pos/wks

		pos	wks
8 Aug 87	JUST GIVE THE DJ A BREAK *Cooltempo COOL 151*	50	4

DYNASTY
US, male / female vocal / instrumental group (20 WEEKS) pos/wks

		pos	wks
13 Oct 79	I DON'T WANT TO BE A FREAK (BUT I CAN'T HELP MYSELF) *Solar FB 1694*	20	13
9 Aug 80	I'VE JUST BEGUN TO LOVE YOU *Solar SO 10*	51	4
21 May 83	DOES THAT RING A BELL *Solar E 9911*	53	3

Ronnie DYSON
US, male vocalist d. 10 Nov 1990 (6 WEEKS) pos/wks

		pos	wks
4 Dec 71	WHEN YOU GET RIGHT DOWN TO IT *CBS 7449*	34	6

E

Katherine E
US, female vocalist (7 WEEKS) pos/wks

		pos	wks
6 Apr 91	I'M ALRIGHT *Dead Dead Good GOOD 2*	41	5
18 Jan 92	THEN I FEEL GOOD *PWL Continental PWL 13*	56	2

Lizz E – *See FRESH 4 featuring Lizz E*

Sheila E
*US, female vocalist / instrumentalist
– percussion – Sheila Escovedo (9 WEEKS)* pos/wks

		pos	wks
23 Feb 85	THE BELLE OF ST MARK *Warner Bros. W 9180*	18	9

E-LUSTRIOUS
UK, male instrumental / production duo – Mike Kirwin and Danny Bennett (2 WEEKS) pos/wks

		pos	wks
15 Feb 92	DANCE NO MORE *MOS MOS 001T* [1]	58	1
2 Jul 94	IN YOUR DANCE *UFG UFG 6CD*	69	1

[1] E-Lustrious featuring Deborah French

See also DIRECKT

EMF
UK, male vocal / instrumental group (50 WEEKS) pos/wks

		pos	wks
3 Nov 90 ●	UNBELIEVABLE *Parlophone R 6273* ▲	3	13
2 Feb 91	I BELIEVE *Parlophone R 6279*	6	7
27 Apr 91	CHILDREN *Parlophone R 6288*	19	5
31 Aug 91	LIES *Parlophone R 6295*	28	3
2 May 92	UNEXPLAINED (EP) *Parlophone SGE 2026*	18	4
19 Sep 92	THEY'RE HERE *Parlophone R 6321*	29	3
21 Nov 92	IT'S YOU *Parlophone R 6327*	23	3
25 Feb 95	PERFECT DAY *Parlophone CDRS 6401*	27	3
8 Jul 95 ●	I'M A BELIEVER *Parlophone CDR 6412* [1]	3	8
28 Oct 95	AFRO KING *Parlophone CDRS 6416*	51	1

[1] EMF and Reeves and Mortimer

Tracks on Unexplained (EP): Getting Through / Far From Me / The Same / Search and Destroy

E-MALE
UK, male vocal / instrumental group (1 WEEK) pos/wks

		pos	wks
31 Jan 98	WE ARE E-MALE *East West EW 137CD*	44	1

E-MAN – *See Jon CUTLER*

E-MOTION
UK, male vocal / instrumental
duo – Alan Angus and Justin Oliver (7 WEEKS) pos/wks

3 Feb 96	THE NAUGHTY NORTH AND THE SEXY SOUTH		
	Soundproof MCSTD 40017	**20**	3
17 Aug 96	I STAND ALONE *Soundproof MCSTD 40061*	**60**	1
26 Oct 96	THE NAUGHTY NORTH AND THE SEXY SOUTH (re-mix)		
	Soundproof MCSTD 40076	**17**	3

EPMD
US, male rap / DJ duo (1 WEEK) pos/wks

15 Aug 98	STRICTLY BUSINESS *Parlophone CDR 6502* [1]	**43**	1

[1] Kurtis Mantronik vs EPMD

See also Kurtis MANTRONIK

E-ROTIC
Germany / US, male / female vocal / instrumental group (2 WEEKS) pos/wks

3 Jun 95	MAX DON'T HAVE SEX WITH YOUR EX *Stip CDSTIP 2*	**45**	2

E-SMOOVE featuring Latanza WATERS
US, male producer – Eric Miller and and US, female vocalist (1 WEEK) pos/wks

15 Aug 98	DEJA VU *AM:PM 5827671*	**63**	1

See also THICK D; PRAISE CATS

E-TRAX *Germany, male production duo (1 WEEK)* pos/wks

9 Jun 01	LET'S ROCK *Tidy Trax TIDY 155CD*	**60**	1

E-TYPE *Sweden, male vocalist (2 WEEKS)* pos/wks

23 Sep 95	THIS IS THE WAY *Ffrreedom TABCD 237*	**53**	1
24 Jun 00	CAMPIONE 2000 *Polydor 1580822*	**58**	1

E.U. *– See SALT-N-PEPA*

EYC *US, male vocal group (36 WEEKS)* pos/wks

11 Dec 93	FEELIN' ALRIGHT *MCA MCSTD 1952*	**16**	8
5 Mar 94	THE WAY YOU WORK IT *MCA MCSTD 1963*	**14**	7
14 May 94	NUMBER ONE *MCA MCSTD 1976*	**27**	5
30 Jul 94	BLACK BOOK *MCA MCSTD 1987*	**13**	6
10 Dec 94	ONE MORE CHANCE *MCA MCSTD 2025*	**26**	6
23 Sep 95	OOH-AH-AA (I FEEL IT) *Gasoline Alley MCSTD 2096*	**33**	2
2 Dec 95	IN THE BEGINNING *Gasoline Alley MCSTD 2107*	**41**	2

E-ZEE POSSEE
UK, male / female vocal / instrumental group (16 WEEKS) pos/wks

26 Aug 89	EVERYTHING STARTS WITH AN 'E' (re)		
	More Protein PROT 1	**15**	9
20 Jan 90	LOVE ON LOVE *More Protein PROT 3* [1]	**59**	3
30 Jun 90	THE SUN MACHINE *More Protein PROT 4*	**62**	3
21 Sep 91	BREATHING IS E-ZEE *More Protein PROT 12* [2]	**72**	1

[1] With Dr Mouthquake [2] E-Zee Possee featuring Tara Newley

'Everything Starts with an 'E' did not reach its peak position until it re-entered in Mar 1990

E-Z ROLLERS
UK, male / female vocal / instrumental group (3 WEEKS) pos/wks

24 Apr 99	WALK THIS LAND *Moving Shadow 130CD1*	**18**	3

EAGLES *US, male vocal / instrumental group (51 WEEKS)* pos/wks

9 Aug 75	ONE OF THESE NIGHTS *Asylum AYM 543* ▲	**23**	7
1 Nov 75	LYIN' EYES *Asylum AYM 548*	**23**	7
6 Mar 76	TAKE IT TO THE LIMIT *Asylum K 13029*	**12**	7
15 Jan 77	NEW KID IN TOWN *Asylum K 13069* ▲	**20**	7
16 Apr 77	● HOTEL CALIFORNIA *Asylum K 13079* ▲	**8**	10
16 Dec 78	PLEASE COME HOME FOR CHRISTMAS *Asylum K 13145*	**30**	5
13 Oct 79	HEARTACHE TONIGHT *Asylum K 12394* ▲	**40**	5
1 Dec 79	THE LONG RUN *Elektra K 12404*	**66**	2
13 Jul 96	LOVE WILL KEEP US ALIVE *Geffen GFSTD 21980*	**52**	1

Robert EARL *UK, male vocalist – Brian Budge (27 WEEKS)* pos/wks

25 Apr 58	I MAY NEVER PASS THIS WAY AGAIN *Philips PB 805*	**14**	13
24 Oct 58	MORE THAN EVER (COME PRIMA) (re) *Philips PB 867*	**26**	4
13 Feb 59	THE WONDERFUL SECRET OF LOVE *Philips PB 891*	**17**	10

Charles EARLAND
US, male instrumentalist – keyboards, d. 11 Dec 1999 (5 WEEKS) pos/wks

19 Aug 78	LET THE MUSIC PLAY *Mercury 6167 703*	**46**	5

Steve EARLE
US, male vocalist / instrumentalist – guitar (7 WEEKS) pos/wks

15 Oct 88	COPPERHEAD ROAD *MCA MCA 1280*	**45**	6
31 Dec 88	JOHNNY COME LATELY *MCA MCA 1301*	**75**	1

EARLY MUSIC CONSORT directed by David MUNROW
UK, male / female instrumental group (1 WEEK) pos/wks

3 Apr 71	HENRY VIII SUITE (EP) *BBC RESL 1*	**49**	1

Tracks on Henry VIII Suite (EP): Fanfare, Passomezo du Roy, Gaillarde d'Escosse / Pavane, Mille Ducats / Larocque Gaillarde / Allemande / Wedding March, La Mourisque / If Love Now Reigned / Ronde, Pourquoi

EARTH WIND AND FIRE (210) [Top 500]
Colourful, mystical, Los Angeles-based group noted for flamboyant stage performances. Formed by Maurice White (d/v) and included Philip Bailey (v), Ronnie Laws (s/fl) and Verdine White (b). Few R&B acts outsold them in the late 1970s, when they achieved eight successive US Top 10 albums (128 WEEKS) pos/wks

12 Feb 77	SATURDAY NITE *CBS 4835*	**17**	9
11 Feb 78	FANTASY *CBS 6056*	**14**	10
13 May 78	JUPITER *CBS 6267*	**41**	5
29 Jul 78	MAGIC MIND (re) *CBS 6490*	**54**	5
7 Oct 78	GOT TO GET YOU INTO MY LIFE *CBS 6553*	**33**	7
9 Dec 78	● SEPTEMBER *CBS 6922*	**3**	13
12 May 79	● BOOGIE WONDERLAND *CBS 7292* [1]	**4**	13
28 Jul 79	AFTER THE LOVE HAS GONE *CBS 7721*	**4**	10
6 Oct 79	STAR *CBS 7902*	**16**	8
15 Dec 79	CAN'T LET GO *CBS 8077*	**46**	7
8 Mar 80	IN THE STONE *CBS 8252*	**53**	3
11 Oct 80	LET ME TALK *CBS 8982*	**29**	5
20 Dec 80	BACK ON THE ROAD *CBS 9377*	**63**	4
7 Nov 81	● LET'S GROOVE *CBS A 1679*	**3**	13
6 Feb 82	I'VE HAD ENOUGH *CBS A 1959*	**29**	6
5 Feb 83	FALL IN LOVE WITH ME *CBS A 2927*	**47**	4
7 Nov 87	SYSTEM OF SURVIVAL *CBS EWF 1*	**54**	3
31 Jul 99	SEPTEMBER (re-mix) *INCredible INCR 24CD*	**25**	3

[1] Earth Wind and Fire with The Emotions

EARTHLING *UK, male vocal / instrumental duo (2 WEEKS)* pos/wks

14 Oct 95	ECHO ON MY MIND PART II *Cooltempo CDCOOL 312*	**61**	1
1 Jun 96	BLOOD MUSIC (EP) *Cooltempo CDCOOL 319*	**69**	1

Tracks on Blood Music (EP): First Transmission / Because the Night / Soup or No Soup / Infinite M

EAST 57th STREET featuring Donna ALLEN
UK, male production trio and US, female vocalist (3 WEEKS) pos/wks

11 Oct 97	SATURDAY *AM:PM 5823752*	**29**	3

EAST OF EDEN *UK, male instrumental group (12 WEEKS)* pos/wks

17 Apr 71	● JIG-A-JIG *Deram DM 297*	**7**	12

EAST 17 (120) [Top 500]
London-based singing, rapping and dancing lads with international teen appeal: Tony Mortimer (v/k), Brian Harvey (v), John Hendy (v), Terry Coldwell (v). Bad press and personal problems resulted in main songwriter Mortimer quitting, and a name change to E-17 for their short-lived 1998 comeback. Best-selling single: 'Stay Another Day' 910,000 (170 WEEKS) pos/wks

29 Aug 92	● HOUSE OF LOVE *London LON 325*	**10**	9
14 Nov 92	GOLD (re) *London LON 331*	**28**	8

30 Jan 93 ●	DEEP *London LOCDP 334*.....................	5	10
10 Apr 93	SLOW IT DOWN *London LONCD 339*........	13	7
26 Jun 93	WEST END GIRLS *London LONCD 344*.....	11	7
4 Dec 93 ●	IT'S ALRIGHT *London LONCD 345*............	3	14
14 May 94 ●	AROUND THE WORLD *London LONCD 349*..	3	13
1 Oct 94 ●	STEAM *London LONCD 353*....................	7	8
3 Dec 94 ★	STAY ANOTHER DAY (re) *London LONCD 354*..	1	16
25 Mar 95	LET IT RAIN *London LONCD 363*.............	10	7
17 Jun 95	HOLD MY BODY TIGHT *London LONCD 367*..	12	7
4 Nov 95 ●	THUNDER *London LONCD 373*................	4	14
10 Feb 96 ●	DO U STILL *London LONCD 379*..............	7	7
10 Aug 96 ●	SOMEONE TO LOVE *London LONCD 385*...	16	8
2 Nov 96 ●	IF YOU EVER *London LONCD 388* 1	2	15
18 Jan 97 ●	HEY CHILD *London LONCD 390*..............	3	5
14 Nov 98 ●	EACH TIME *Telstar CDSTAS 3017* 2	2	10
13 Mar 99	BETCHA CAN'T WAIT *Telstar CDSTAS 3031* 2 ..	12	5

1 East 17 featuring Gabrielle 2 E-17

EAST SIDE BEAT *Italy, male vocal / instrumental*
duo – Carl Fanini and Francesco Petrocchi (18 WEEKS) pos/wks

30 Nov 91 ●	RIDE LIKE THE WIND *ffrr F 176*.............	3	11
19 Dec 92	ALIVE AND KICKING *ffrr F 206*.............	26	6
29 May 93	YOU'RE MY EVERYTHING *ffrr FCD 207*....	65	1

Sheena EASTON 296 Top 500
Scotland's most successful act Stateside, b. Sheena Orr, 27 Apr 1959, Glasgow. This vocalist was first seen in TV documentary 'The Big Time'. Reached the big time on both sides of the Atlantic and won the Grammy for Best New Artist of 1981 (104 WEEKS) pos/wks

5 Apr 80 ●	MODERN GIRL (re) *EMI 5042*	8	15
19 Jul 80 ●	9 TO 5 *EMI 5066* ▲	3	15
25 Oct 80	ONE MAN WOMAN *EMI 5114*	14	6
14 Feb 81	TAKE MY TIME *EMI 5135*	44	5
2 May 81	WHEN HE SHINES *EMI 5166*	12	8
27 Jun 81 ●	FOR YOUR EYES ONLY *EMI 5195*	8	13
12 Sep 81	JUST ANOTHER BROKEN HEART *EMI 5232*..	33	8
5 Dec 81	YOU COULD HAVE BEEN WITH ME *EMI 5252*..	54	3
31 Jul 82	MACHINERY *EMI 5326*........................	38	5
12 Feb 83	WE'VE GOT TONIGHT *Liberty UP 658* 1 ..	28	7
21 Jan 89	THE LOVER IN ME *MCA MCA 1289*	15	8
18 Mar 89	DAYS LIKE THIS *MCA MCA 1325*	43	3
15 Jul 89	101 *MCA MCA 1348*	54	2
18 Nov 89	THE ARMS OF ORION *Warner Bros. W 2757* 2 ..	27	5
9 Dec 00	GIVING UP GIVING IN *Universal MCSTD 40244* ..	54	1

1 Kenny Rogers and Sheena Easton 2 Prince with Sheena Easton

See also PRINCE

EASTSIDE CONNECTION
US, disco aggregation (3 WEEKS) pos/wks

8 Apr 78	YOU'RE SO RIGHT FOR ME *Creole CR 149* ...	44	3

Clint EASTWOOD
US, male actor / vocalist (2 WEEKS) pos/wks

7 Feb 70	I TALK TO THE TREES *Paramount PARA 3004*	18	2

This is the flip of 'Wand'rin Star' by Lee Marvin and was listed with Marvin's A-side for two weeks only

Clint EASTWOOD and GENERAL SAINT
UK, male vocal duo (8 WEEKS) pos/wks

29 Sep 84	LAST PLANE (ONE WAY TICKET) *MCA MCA 910* ..	51	3
2 Apr 94	OH CAROL! *Copasetic COPCD 0009*	54	5

EASY RIDERS – See Frankie LAINE

EASYBEATS *Australia /*
Holland / UK, male vocal / instrumental group (24 WEEKS) pos/wks

27 Oct 66 ●	FRIDAY ON MY MIND *United Artists UP 1157*...	6	15
10 Apr 68	HELLO, HOW ARE YOU *United Artists UP 2209* ..	20	9

EASYWORLD *UK, male vocal / instrumental trio (2 WEEKS)* pos/wks

1 Jun 02	BLEACH *Jive 9253552*.........................	67	1
21 Sep 02	YOU & ME *Jive 9254092*......................	57	1

EAT *UK / US, male / female vocal / instrumental group (1 WEEK)* pos/wks

12 Jun 93	BLEED ME WHITE *Fiction FICCD 48*.........	73	1

EAT STATIC *UK, male production duo (3 WEEKS)* pos/wks

22 Feb 97	HYBRID *Planet Dog BARK 024CD*...........	41	1
27 Sep 97	INTERCEPTOR *Planet Dog BARK 030CD*....	44	1
27 Jun 98	CONTACT... *Planet Dog BARK 033CD*......	67	1

Cleveland EATON
US, male instrumentalist – keyboards (6 WEEKS) pos/wks

23 Sep 78	BAMA BOOGIE WOOGIE *Gull GULS 63*	35	6

EAV *Austria, male vocal / instrumental group (4 WEEKS)* pos/wks

27 Sep 86	BA-BA-BANKROBBERY (ENGLISH VERSION) *Columbia DB 9139*.............................	63	4

EAZY-E *US, male rapper – Eric Wright, d. 26 Mar 1995 (3 WEEKS)* pos/wks

6 Jan 96	JUST TAH LET YOU KNOW *Epic 6628162*	30	3

ECHO and the BUNNYMEN 392 Top 500
Cult alternative rock group originally from Liverpool, UK, who named themselves after their drum machine. Ian McCulloch (v), b. 5 May 1959, frontman of this moody and atmospheric group, went solo 1988. Original line-up regrouped in 1997 (86 WEEKS) pos/wks

17 May 80	RESCUE *Korova KOW 1*.......................	62	1
18 Apr 81	SHINE SO HARD (EP) *Korova ECHO 1*......	37	4
18 Jul 81	A PROMISE *Korova KOW 15*.................	49	4
29 May 82	THE BACK OF LOVE *Korova KOW 24*.......	19	7
22 Jan 83 ●	THE CUTTER *Korova KOW 26*...............	8	8
16 Jul 83	NEVER STOP *Korova KOW 28*...............	15	7
28 Jan 84 ●	THE KILLING MOON *Korova KOW 32*.......	9	6
21 Apr 84	SILVER *Korova KOW 34*......................	30	5
14 Jul 84	SEVEN SEAS *Korova KOW 35*	16	7
19 Oct 85	BRING ON THE DANCING HORSES *Korova KOW 43*..	21	7
13 Jun 87	THE GAME *WEA YZ 134*......................	28	4
1 Aug 87	LIPS LIKE SUGAR *WEA YZ 144*	36	4
20 Feb 88	PEOPLE ARE STRANGE *WEA YZ 175*	29	5
2 Mar 91	PEOPLE ARE STRANGE (re-issue) *East West YZ 567*...	34	4
28 Jun 97 ●	NOTHING LASTS FOREVER *London LOCDP 396* ..	8	6
13 Sep 97	I WANT TO BE THERE WHEN YOU COME *London LONCD 399*............................	30	2
8 Nov 97	DON'T LET IT GET YOU DOWN *London LOCDP 406*..	50	1
27 Mar 99	RUST *London LONCD 424*....................	22	3
5 May 01	IT'S ALRIGHT *Cooking Vinyl FRYCD 104*	41	1

Tracks on 'Shine So Hard' (EP): Crocodiles, All That Jazz, Zimbo, Over the Wall

ECHOBASS *UK, male producer – Simon Woodgate (1 WEEK)* pos/wks

14 Jul 01	YOU ARE THE WEAKEST LINK *House of Bush CDANNE 001*................	53	1

ECHOBEATZ *UK, male DJ / production*
duo – Dave De Braie and Paul Moody (5 WEEKS) pos/wks

25 Jul 98 ●	MAS QUE NADA *Eternal WEA 176CD*	10	5

ECHOBELLY
UK / Sweden, male / female vocal / instrumental group (16 WEEKS) pos/wks

2 Apr 94	INSOMNIAC *Fauve FAUV 1CD*...............	47	1
2 Jul 94	I CAN'T IMAGINE THE WORLD WITHOUT ME *Fauve FAUV 2CD*.............................	39	2
5 Nov 94	CLOSE... BUT *Fauve FAUV 4CD*.............	59	1
2 Sep 95	GREAT THINGS *Fauve FAUV 5CD*	13	3
4 Nov 95	KING OF THE KERB *Fauve FAUV 7CD*......	25	3
2 Mar 96	DARK THERAPY *Fauve FAUV 8CD*..........	20	3

23 Aug 97	THE WORLD IS FLAT *Epic 6648152*		31	2
8 Nov 97	HERE COMES THE BIG RUSH *Epic 6652452*		56	1

See also LITHIUM and Sonya MADAN

Billy ECKSTINE *US, male vocalist, d. 8 Mar 1993 (48 WEEKS)*
pos/wks

12 Nov 54 ●	NO ONE BUT YOU *MGM 763*		3	17
27 Sep 57	PASSING STRANGERS *Mercury MT 164* [1]		22	2
13 Feb 59 ●	GIGI *Mercury AMT 1018*		8	14
12 Mar 69	PASSING STRANGERS (re-issue) *Mercury MF 1082* [1]		20	15

[1] Billy Eckstine and Sarah Vaughan

ECLIPSE
Italy, male producer / instrumentalist – Gianni Bini (4 WEEKS)
pos/wks

14 Aug 99	MAKES ME LOVE YOU *Azuli AZNYCDX 100*		25	4

See also BINI & MARTINI; GOODFELLAS featuring Lisa MILLETT; HOUSE OF GLASS

Silvio ECOMO *Holland, male producer (1 WEEK)*
pos/wks

15 Jul 00	STANDING *Hooj Choons HOOJ 098CD*		70	1

EDDIE and the HOT RODS
UK, male vocal / instrumental group (26 WEEKS)
pos/wks

11 Sep 76	LIVE AT THE MARQUEE (EP) *Island IEP 2*		43	5
13 Nov 76	TEENAGE DEPRESSION *Island WIP 6354*		35	4
23 Apr 77	I MIGHT BE LYING *Island WIP 6388*		44	3
13 Aug 77 ●	DO ANYTHING YOU WANNA DO *Island WIP 6401* [1]		9	10
21 Jan 78	QUIT THIS TOWN *Island WIP 6411*		36	4

[1] Rods

Tracks on Live at the Marquee (EP): 96 Tears / Get out of Denver / Medley: Gloria / Satisfaction

EDDY *UK, female vocalist (2 WEEKS)*
pos/wks

9 Jul 94	SOMEDAY *Positiva CDTIV 14*		49	2

Duane EDDY （89 Top 500）
Twangy guitar legend, b. 26 Apr 1938, New York. Early rock's No.1 solo instrumentalist assembled a long string of UK and US hit singles and was one of the first rock acts to score on the album charts (202 WEEKS)
pos/wks

5 Sep 58	REBEL-ROUSER *London HL 8669* [1]		19	10
2 Jan 59	CANNONBALL *London HL 8764* [2]		22	4
19 Jun 59 ●	PETER GUNN (re) *London HLW 8879*		6	11
24 Jul 59	YEP! *London HLW B8879*		17	5
4 Sep 59	FORTY MILES OF BAD ROAD *London HLW 8929*		11	9
18 Dec 59	SOME KIND-A EARTHQUAKE *London HLW 9007*		12	5
19 Feb 60	BONNIE CAME BACK *London HLW 9050*		12	11
28 Apr 60 ●	SHAZAM! *London HLW 9104*		4	13
21 Jul 60 ●	BECAUSE THEY'RE YOUNG *London HLW 9162*		2	18
10 Nov 60	KOMMOTION *London HLW 9225*		13	10
12 Jan 61 ●	PEPE *London HLW 9257*		2	14
20 Apr 61 ●	THEME FROM DIXIE *London HLW 9324*		7	10
22 Jun 61	RING OF FIRE *London HLW 9370*		17	10
14 Sep 61	DRIVIN' HOME *London HLW 9406*		30	4
5 Oct 61	CARAVAN *Parlophone R 4826*		42	3
24 May 62	DEEP IN THE HEART OF TEXAS *RCA 1288*		19	8
23 Aug 62 ●	BALLAD OF PALADIN *RCA 1300* [3]		10	10
8 Nov 62 ●	(DANCE WITH THE) GUITAR MAN *RCA 1316*		4	16
14 Feb 63	BOSS GUITAR *RCA 1329* [4]		27	8
30 May 63	LONELY BOY LONELY GUITAR *RCA 1344*		35	4
29 Aug 63	YOUR BABY'S GONE SURFIN' *RCA 1357*		49	1
8 Mar 75 ●	PLAY ME LIKE YOU PLAY YOUR GUITAR *GTO GT 11* [4]		9	9
22 Mar 86 ●	PETER GUNN (re-recording) *China WOK 6* [5]		8	9

[1] Duane Eddy and His Twangy Guitar [2] Duane Eddy His Twangy Guitar & The Rebels [3] Duane Eddy – Orchestra conducted by Bob Thompson [4] Duane Eddy and the Rebelettes [5] Art of Noise featuring Duane Eddy

EDDY and the SOUL BAND
US, male / female vocal / instrumental group (7 WEEKS)
pos/wks

23 Feb 85	THE THEME FROM 'SHAFT' *Club JAB 11*		13	7

Randy EDELMAN
US, male vocalist / instrumentalist – piano (18 WEEKS)
pos/wks

6 Mar 76	CONCRETE AND CLAY *20th Century BTC 2261*		11	7
18 Sep 76	UPTOWN UPTEMPO WOMAN *20th Century BTC 2225*		25	7
15 Jan 77	YOU *20th Century BTC 2253*		49	2
17 Jul 82	NOBODY MADE ME *Rocket XPRES 81*		60	2

EDELWEISS
Austria, male / female vocal / instrumental group (10 WEEKS)
pos/wks

29 Apr 89 ●	BRING ME EDELWEISS *WEA YZ 353*		5	10

EDEN *UK / Australia, male / female vocal / instrumental group (2 WEEKS)*
pos/wks

6 Mar 93	DO U FEEL 4 ME *Logic 74321135422*		51	2

Lyn EDEN – See SMOKIN BEATS featuring Lyn EDEN

EDISON LIGHTHOUSE *UK, male vocal / instrumental group – lead vocal Tony Burrows (13 WEEKS)*
pos/wks

24 Jan 70 ★	LOVE GROWS (WHERE MY ROSEMARY GOES) *Bell 1091*		1	12
30 Jan 71	IT'S UP TO YOU PETULA *Bell 1136*		49	1

Dave EDMUNDS （339 Top 500） *Former member of one-hit wonders Love Sculpture, b. 15 Apr 1944, Cardiff, Wales. Singer / guitarist and retro-sounding performer / producer's debut solo hit sold three million worldwide. He has produced many top acts including Dion, Everly Brothers, Del Shannon, Status Quo, Shakin' Stevens and Stray Cats (93 WEEKS)*
pos/wks

21 Nov 70 ★	I HEAR YOU KNOCKING *MAM 1* [1]		1	14
20 Jan 73 ●	BABY I LOVE YOU *Rockfield ROC 1*		8	13
9 Jun 73 ●	BORN TO BE WITH YOU *Rockfield ROC 2*		5	12
2 Jul 77	I KNEW THE BRIDE *Swansong SSK 19411*		26	8
30 Jun 79 ●	GIRLS TALK *Swansong SSK 19418*		4	11
22 Sep 79	QUEEN OF HEARTS *Swansong SSK 19419*		11	9
24 Nov 79	CRAWLING FROM THE WRECKAGE *Swansong SSK 19420*		59	4
9 Feb 80	SINGING THE BLUES *Swansong SSK 19422*		28	8
28 Mar 81	ALMOST SATURDAY NIGHT *Swansong SSK 19424*		58	3
20 Jun 81	THE RACE IS ON *Swansong SSK 19425* [2]		34	6
26 Mar 83	SLIPPING AWAY *Arista ARIST 522*		60	4
7 Apr 90	KING OF LOVE *Capitol CL 568*		68	1

[1] Dave Edmunds' Rockpile [2] Dave Edmunds and the Stray Cats

Alton EDWARDS *Zimbabwe, male vocalist (9 WEEKS)*
pos/wks

9 Jan 82	I JUST WANNA (SPEND SOME TIME WITH YOU) *Streetwave STRA 1897*		20	9

Dennis EDWARDS featuring Siedah GARRETT
US, male / female vocal duo (10 WEEKS)
pos/wks

24 Mar 84	DON'T LOOK ANY FURTHER (re) *Gordy TMG 1334*		45	10

The re-entry peaked at No.55 in June 1987

Rupie EDWARDS *Jamaica, male vocalist (16 WEEKS)*
pos/wks

23 Nov 74 ●	IRE FEELINGS (SKANGA) *Cactus CT 38*		9	10
8 Feb 75	LEGO SKANGA *Cactus CT 51*		32	6

Tommy EDWARDS *US, male vocalist, d. 23 Oct 1969 (18 WEEKS)*
pos/wks

3 Oct 58 ★	IT'S ALL IN THE GAME *MGM 989* ▲		1	17
7 Aug 59	MY MELANCHOLY BABY *MGM 1020*		29	1

EELS *US, male vocal / instrumental group (23 WEEKS)*
pos/wks

15 Feb 97 ●	NOVOCAINE FOR THE SOUL *Dreamworks DRMCD 22174*		10	5
17 May 97 ●	SUSAN'S HOUSE *Dreamworks DRMCD 22238*		9	5
13 Sep 97	YOUR LUCKY DAY IN HELL *Dreamworks DRMCD 22277*		35	2
26 Sep 98	LAST STOP: THIS TOWN *Dreamworks DRMCD 22346*		23	3
12 Dec 98	CANCER FOR THE CURE *Dreamworks DRMCD 22373*		60	1
26 Feb 00	MR E'S BEAUTIFUL BLUES *Dreamworks DRMCD 4509762*		11	4
24 Jun 00	FLYSWATTER *Dreamworks DRMCD 4509462*		55	1
22 Sep 01	SOULJACKER PART 1 *Dreamworks DRMCD 4508922*		30	2

Re-entries are listed as (re), (2re), (3re), etc which signifies that the hit re-entered the chart once, twice or three times, etc

EFUA
UK, female vocalist (5 WEEKS)

			pos/wks
3 Jul 93	SOMEWHERE *Virgin VSCDT 1463*	42	5

EGG
UK, male vocal / instrumental group (1 WEEK)

			pos/wks
30 Jan 99	GETTING AWAY WITH IT *Indochina ID 079CD*	58	1

EGGS ON LEGS
UK, male vocalist (1 WEEK)

			pos/wks
23 Sep 95	COCK A DOODLE DO IT *Avex UK AVEXCD 18*	42	1

EGYPTIAN EMPIRE
UK, male producer – Tim Taylor (2 WEEKS)

			pos/wks
24 Oct 92	THE HORN TRACK *Ffrreedom TAB 115*	61	2

EIFFEL 65
Italy, male vocal trio (36 WEEKS)

			pos/wks
21 Aug 99	BLUE (DA BA DEE) (import) *Logic 74321688212*	39	5
25 Sep 99	★ BLUE (DA BA DEE) *Eternal WEA 226CD1* ◆ ■	1	21
19 Feb 00	● MOVE YOUR BODY *Eternal WEA 255CD1*	3	10

808 STATE
UK, DJ / production / instrumental group (70 WEEKS)

			pos/wks
18 Nov 89	● PACIFIC *ZTT ZANG 1*	10	9
31 Mar 90	THE EXTENDED PLEASURE OF DANCE (EP) *ZTT ZANG 2T*	56	1
2 Jun 90	● THE ONLY RHYME THAT BITES *ZTT ZANG 3* [1]	10	10
15 Sep 90	TUNES SPLITS THE ATOM *ZTT ZANG 6* [1]	18	7
10 Nov 90	● CUBIK / OLYMPIC *ZTT ZANG 5*	10	10
16 Feb 91	● IN YER FACE *ZTT ZANG 14*	9	6
27 Apr 91	OOOPS *ZTT ZANG 19* [2]	42	3
17 Aug 91	LIFT / OPEN YOUR MIND *ZTT ZANG 20*	38	4
29 Aug 92	TIME BOMB / NIMBUS *ZTT ZANG 33*	59	1
12 Dec 92	ONE IN TEN (re-mix) *ZTT ZANG 39* [3]	17	8
30 Jan 93	PLAN 9 *ZTT ZANG 38CD*	50	2
26 Jun 93	10 X 10 *ZTT ZANG 42CD*	67	1
13 Aug 94	BOMBADIN *ZTT ZANG 54CD*	67	1
29 Jun 96	BOND *ZTT ZANG 80CD*	57	1
8 Feb 97	LOPEZ *ZTT ZANG 87CD*	20	2
16 May 98	PACIFIC / CUBIK (re-mixes) *ZTT ZTT 98CD1*	21	3
6 Mar 99	THE ONLY RHYME THAT BITES 99 *ZTT ZTT 125CD* [1]	53	1

[1] MC Tunes versus 808 State [2] 808 State featuring Björk [3] 808 State vs UB40

Tracks on The Extended Pleasure of Dance (EP): Cobra Bora / Ancodia / Cubik.
'Cubik' is a re-issue of one of the tracks from The Extended Pleasure of Dance (EP).
'Lopez' features the uncredited vocals of James Dean Bradfield, lead singer of The Manic Street Preachers

18 WHEELER
UK, male vocal / instrumental group (1 WEEK)

			pos/wks
15 Mar 97	STAY *Creation CRESCD 249*	59	1

EIGHTH WONDER
UK, male / female vocal / instrumental group (25 WEEKS)

			pos/wks
2 Nov 85	STAY WITH ME *CBS A 6594*	65	2
20 Feb 88	● I'M NOT SCARED *CBS SCARE 1*	7	13
25 Jun 88	CROSS MY HEART *CBS 651552 7*	13	8
1 Oct 88	BABY BABY *CBS BABE 1*	65	2

EIGHTIES MATCHBOX B-LINE DISASTER
UK, male vocal / instrumental group (1 WEEK)

			pos/wks
28 Sep 02	CELEBRATE YOUR MOTHER *No Death / Island MCSTD 40296*	66	1

88.3 – See Lisa MAY

EINSTEIN
UK, male rapper (6 WEEKS)

			pos/wks
18 Nov 89	ANOTHER MONSTERJAM *ffrr F 116* [1]	65	1
15 Dec 90	TURN IT UP *Swanyard SYD 9* [2]	42	4
24 Aug 96	THE POWER 96 *Arista 74321398672* [3]	42	1

[1] Simon Harris featuring Einstein [2] Technotronic featuring Melissa and Einstein
[3] Snap featuring Einstein

See also AMBASSADORS OF FUNK featuring MC MARIO

EL COCO
US, male vocal / instrumental group (4 WEEKS)

			pos/wks
14 Jan 78	COCOMOTION *Pye International 7N 25761*	31	4

EL MARIACHI
US, male producer – Roger Sanchez (2 WEEKS)

			pos/wks
9 Nov 96	CUBA *ffrr FCD 286*	38	2

See also FUNK JUNKEEZ; Roger SANCHEZ

ELASTICA
UK, female / male vocal / instrumental group (12 WEEKS)

			pos/wks
12 Feb 94	LINE UP *Deceptive BLUFF 004CD*	20	3
22 Oct 94	CONNECTION *Deceptive BLUFF 010CD*	17	4
25 Feb 95	WAKING UP *Deceptive BLUFF 011CD*	13	4
24 Jun 00	MAD DOG *Deceptive BLUFF 077CD*	44	1

ELATE
UK, male / female vocal / instrumental trio (2 WEEKS)

			pos/wks
26 Jul 97	SOMEBODY LIKE YOU *VC VCRD 22*	38	2

Donnie ELBERT
US, male vocalist d. 26 Jan 1989 (29 WEEKS)

			pos/wks
8 Jan 72	● WHERE DID OUR LOVE GO? *London HL 10352*	8	10
26 Feb 72	I CAN'T HELP MYSELF *Avco 6105 009*	11	10
29 Apr 72	A LITTLE PIECE OF LEATHER *London HL 10370*	27	9

ELBOW
UK, male vocal / instrumental group (6 WEEKS)

			pos/wks
5 May 01	RED *V2 VVR 5016153*	36	1
21 Jul 01	POWDER BLUE *V2 VVR 5016163*	41	1
20 Oct 01	NEWBORN *V2 VVR 5016173*	42	1
16 Feb 02	ASLEEP IN THE BACK / COMING SECOND *V2 VVR 5018703*	19	3

ELECTRA
UK, male vocal / instrumental group (7 WEEKS)

			pos/wks
6 Aug 88	JIBARO *ffrr FFR 9*	54	3
30 Dec 89	IT'S YOUR DESTINY / AUTUMN LOVE *London F 121*	51	4

ELECTRAFIXION
UK, male vocal / instrumental group (6 WEEKS)

			pos/wks
19 Nov 94	ZEPHYR *WEA YZ 865CD*	47	2
9 Sep 95	LOWDOWN *WEA YZ 977CD*	54	2
4 Nov 95	NEVER *Spacejunk WEA 022CD*	58	1
16 Mar 96	SISTER PAIN *Spacejunk WEA 037CD1*	27	1

ELECTRASY
UK, male vocal / instrumental group (7 WEEKS)

			pos/wks
13 Jun 98	LOST IN SPACE *MCA MCSTD 40171*	60	1
5 Sep 98	MORNING AFTERGLOW *MCA MCSTD 40184*	19	4
28 Nov 98	BEST FRIEND'S GIRL *MCA MCSXD 40195*	41	2

ELECTRIBE 101
UK / Germany, male / female vocal / instrumental group (15 WEEKS)

			pos/wks
28 Oct 89	TELL ME WHEN THE FEVER ENDED *Mercury MER 310*	32	5
24 Feb 90	TALKING WITH MYSELF *Mercury MER 316*	23	5
22 Sep 90	YOU'RE WALKING *Mercury MER 328*	50	3
10 Oct 98	TALKING WITH MYSELF (re-mix) *Manifesto FESDD 49*	39	2

ELECTRIC LIGHT ORCHESTRA 46 Top 500

Ground-breaking and innovative UK group, fronted by multi-talented Jeff Lynne (v/g) from Birmingham and originally included Roy Wood (The Move). Their unique sound, which featured an orchestral string section, helped them to achieve numerous transatlantic hits (255 WEEKS)

			pos/wks
29 Jul 72	● 10538 OVERTURE *Harvest HAR 5053*	9	8
27 Jan 73	● ROLL OVER BEETHOVEN *Harvest HAR 5063*	6	10
6 Oct 73	SHOWDOWN *Harvest HAR 5077*	12	10
9 Mar 74	MA-MA-MA-BELLE *Warner Bros. K 16349*	22	8
10 Jan 76	● EVIL WOMAN *Jet 764*	10	8
3 Jul 76	STRANGE MAGIC *Jet 779*	38	2
13 Nov 76	● LIVIN' THING *Jet UP 36184*	4	12
19 Feb 77	● ROCKARIA! *Jet UP 36209*	9	9
21 May 77	● TELEPHONE LINE *Jet UP 36254*	8	10
29 Oct 77	TURN TO STONE *Jet UP 36313*	18	12

			pos/wks
28 Jan 78 ●	MR. BLUE SKY *Jet UP 36342*	......	6 11
10 Jun 78 ●	WILD WEST HERO *Jet JET 109*	......	6 14
7 Oct 78 ●	SWEET TALKIN' WOMAN *Jet 121*	......	6 9
9 Dec 78	THE ELO EP *Jet ELO 1*	......	34 8
19 May 79 ●	SHINE A LITTLE LOVE *Jet 144*	......	6 10
21 Jul 79 ●	THE DIARY OF HORACE WIMP *Jet 150*	......	8 9
1 Sep 79	DON'T BRING ME DOWN *Jet 153*	......	3 9
17 Nov 79 ●	CONFUSION / LAST TRAIN TO LONDON *Jet 166*	......	8 10
24 May 80	I'M ALIVE *Jet 179*	......	20 9
21 Jun 80 ★	XANADU *Jet 185* [1]	......	1 11
2 Aug 80	ALL OVER THE WORLD *Jet 195*	......	11 8
22 Nov 80	DON'T WALK AWAY *Jet 7004*	......	21 10
1 Aug 81 ●	HOLD ON TIGHT *Jet 7011* [2]	......	4 12
24 Oct 81	TWILIGHT *Jet 7015*	......	30 7
9 Jan 82	TICKET TO THE MOON / HERE IS THE NEWS *Jet 7018* [3]	......	24 8
18 Jun 83	ROCK 'N' ROLL IS KING *Jet A 3500*	......	13 9
3 Sep 83	SECRET MESSAGES *Jet A 3720*	......	48 3
1 Mar 86	CALLING AMERICA *Epic A 6844*	......	28 7
11 May 91	HONEST MEN *Telstar ELO 100* [4]	......	60 1

[1] Olivia Newton-John and Electric Light Orchestra [2] ELO [3] ELO ('Here Is the News' only) [4] Electric Light Orchestra Part 2

'Here Is the News' listed from 16 Jan 1982. Tracks on the ELO EP: Can't Get It Out of My Head / Strange Magic / Ma-Ma-Ma-Belle / Evil Woman

ELECTRIC PRUNES *US, male vocal / instrumental group (5 WKS)* pos/wks

			pos/wks
9 Feb 67	I HAD TOO MUCH TO DREAM (LAST NIGHT) *Reprise RS 20532*	......	49 1
11 May 67	GET ME TO THE WORLD ON TIME *Reprise RS 20564*	......	42 4

ELECTRIC SOFT PARADE *UK, male vocal / instrumental group – led by Alex and Tom White (5 WEEKS)* pos/wks

			pos/wks
4 Aug 01	EMPTY AT THE END / SUMATRAN *DB DB 006CD7* [1]	......	65 1
10 Nov 01	THERE'S A SILENCE *DB DB 007CD7*	......	52 1
16 Mar 02	SILENT TO THE DARK II *DB DB 008CD7*	......	23 2
1 Jun 02	EMPTY AT THE END / THIS GIVEN LINE *DB DB 009CD7*	......	39 1

[1] Soft Parade

The 2002 version of 'Empty at the End' is a re-recording

ELECTRIQUE BOUTIQUE
UK / France, male production group (2 WEEKS) pos/wks

			pos/wks
26 Aug 00	REVELATION *Data DATA 14CDS*	......	37 2

ELECTRONIC *UK, male vocal / instrumental group (36 WEEKS)* pos/wks

			pos/wks
16 Dec 89	GETTING AWAY WITH IT *Factory FAC 2577*	......	12 9
27 Apr 91 ●	GET THE MESSAGE *Factory FAC 2877*	......	8 7
21 Sep 91	FEEL EVERY BEAT *Factory FAC 3287*	......	39 4
4 Jul 92 ●	DISAPPOINTED *Parlophone R 6311*	......	6 5
6 Jul 96	FORBIDDEN CITY *Parlophone CDR 6436*	......	14 4
28 Sep 96	FOR YOU *Parlophone CDR 6445*	......	16 2
15 Feb 97	SECOND NATURE *Parlophone CDR 6455*	......	35 2
24 Apr 99	VIVID *Parlopbone CDR 6514*	......	17 3

ELECTRONICAS *Holland, male instrumental group (8 WEEKS)* pos/wks

			pos/wks
19 Sep 81	ORIGINAL BIRD DANCE *Polydor POSP 360*	......	22 8

ELECTROSET
UK, male instrumental / production group (4 WEEKS) pos/wks

			pos/wks
21 Nov 92	HOW DOES IT FEEL *ffrr F 203*	......	27 3
15 Jul 95	SENSATION *Ffrreedom TABCD 231*	......	69 1

ELEGANTS *US, male vocal group (2 WEEKS)* pos/wks

			pos/wks
26 Sep 58	LITTLE STAR *HMV POP 520* ▲	......	25 2

ELEMENT FOUR *UK, male production duo – Paul Oakenfold and Andy Gray (11 WEEKS)* pos/wks

			pos/wks
9 Sep 00 ●	BIG BROTHER UK TV THEME (re) *Channel 4 Music C4M 00072*	......	4 11

ELEVATION *UK, male instrumental / production duo (1 WEEK)* pos/wks

			pos/wks
23 May 92	CAN U FEEL IT *Nova Mute 12NOMU 3*	......	62 1

ELEVATOR SUITE
UK, male production / instrumental trio (1 WEEK) pos/wks

			pos/wks
12 Aug 00	BACK AROUND *Infectious INFECT 85CDS*	......	71 1

ELEVATORMAN
UK, male instrumental / production group (4 WEEKS) pos/wks

			pos/wks
14 Jan 95	FUNK AND DRIVE *Wired WIRED 211*	......	37 3
1 Jul 95	FIRED UP *Wired WIRED 216*	......	44 1

ELGINS *US, male / female vocal group (20 WEEKS)* pos/wks

			pos/wks
1 May 71 ●	HEAVEN MUST HAVE SENT YOU *Tamla Motown TMG 771*	......	3 13
9 Oct 71	PUT YOURSELF IN MY PLACE *Tamla Motown TMG 787*	......	28 7

ELIAS and his ZIG-ZAG JIVE FLUTES
South Africa, male instrumental group (14 WEEKS) pos/wks

			pos/wks
25 Apr 58 ●	TOM HARK *Columbia DB 4109*	......	2 14

Yvonne ELLIMAN *US, female vocalist (44 WEEKS)* pos/wks

			pos/wks
29 Jan 72	I DON'T KNOW HOW TO LOVE HIM *MCA MMKS 5077*	......	47 1
6 Nov 76 ●	LOVE ME *RSO 2090 205*	......	6 13
7 May 77	HELLO STRANGER *RSO 2090 236*	......	26 5
13 Aug 77	I CAN'T GET YOU OUT OF MY MIND *RSO 2090 251*	......	17 13
6 May 78 ●	IF I CAN'T HAVE YOU *RSO 2090 266* ▲	......	4 12

'I Don't Know How to Love Him' was one of four tracks on a maxi-single, two of which were credited during the disc's one week on the chart. The other track credited was 'Superstar' by Murray Head

Duke ELLINGTON *US, male band leader / instrumentalist – piano, d. 24 May 1974 (4 WEEKS)* pos/wks

			pos/wks
5 Mar 54 ●	SKIN DEEP *Philips PB 243* [1]	......	7 4

[1] Duke Ellington and his Orchestra with Louis Bellson (drums)

Lance ELLINGTON *UK, male vocalist (1 WEEK)* pos/wks

			pos/wks
21 Aug 93	LONELY (HAVE WE LOST OUR LOVE) *RCA 74321158332*	......	57 1

Ray ELLINGTON
UK, male vocal / instrumental group, leader d. 27 Feb 1985 (4 WEEKS) pos/wks

			pos/wks
15 Nov 62	THE MADISON (re) *Ember S 102*	......	36 4

Bern ELLIOTT and the FENMEN
UK, male vocal / instrumental group (22 WEEKS) pos/wks

			pos/wks
21 Nov 63	MONEY *Decca F 11770*	......	14 13
19 Mar 64	NEW ORLEANS *Decca F 11852*	......	24 9

Joe ELLIOTT – See Mick RONSON with Joe ELLIOTT

Missy 'Misdemeanor' ELLIOTT ⟨416⟩ Top 500
Leading female rapper / songwriter / producer / arranger and record label (Gold Mind) boss, b. Melissa Elliott, Virginia, 1 Jul 1972. Award-winning hip hop / R&B legend, who first surfaced in group Sista in 1992, has recorded with countless artists and charted with 14 of them (82 WEEKS) pos/wks

			pos/wks
30 Aug 97	THE RAIN (SUPA DUPA FLY) *East West E 3919 CD*	......	16 3
29 Nov 97	SOCK IT 2 ME *East West E 3890CD*	......	33 2
25 Apr 98	BEEP ME 911 *East West E 3859CD*	......	14 3
22 Aug 98	MAKE IT HOT *East West E 3821 CD* [1]	......	22 4
22 Aug 98	HIT 'EM WIT DA HEE *East West E3824 CD1* [2]	......	25 3
26 Sep 98 ★	I WANT YOU BACK *Virgin VSCDT 1716* [3] ■	......	1 9
21 Nov 98	5 MINUTES *Elektra E 3803CD* [4]	......	72 1
13 Mar 99	HERE WE COME *Virgin DINSD 179* [5]	......	43 1
25 Sep 99	ALL N MY GRILL *Elektra E 3742 CD* [6]	......	20 4
22 Jan 00	HOT BOYZ *Elektra E 7002CD* [7]	......	18 3
28 Apr 01 ●	GET UR FREAK ON *East West / Elektra E 7206CD*	......	4 11
18 Aug 01 ●	ONE MINUTE MAN *Elektra E 7245CD* [8]	......	10 8

13 Oct 01	**SUPERFREAKON** *East West / Elektra 7559672550*	..........**72**	1
22 Dec 01	**SON OF A GUN (I BETCHA THINK THIS SONG**		
	IS ABOUT YOU) (re) *Virgin VUSCD 232* 9	..........**13**	9
6 Apr 02	● **4 MY PEOPLE** *Goldmind / Elektra E 7286CD*	..........**5**	13
16 Nov 02	● **WORK IT** *Goldmind / Elektra E7344CD* 10	..........**6**	7+

1 Nicole featuring Missy 'Misdemeanor' Elliott and Mocha 2 Missy 'Misdemeanor' Elliott featuring Lil' Kim 3 Melanie B featuring Missy 'Misdemeanor' Elliott 4 Lil' Mo featuring Missy 'Misdemeanor' Elliott 5 Timbaland / Missy Elliott and Magoo 6 Missy 'Misdemeanor' Elliott featuring MC Solaar 7 Missy 'Misdemeanor' Elliott featuring Nas, Eve and Q Tip 8 Missy 'Misdemeanor' Elliott featuring Ludacris 9 Janet with Carly Simon featuring Missy Elliott 10 Missy Elliott

Greg ELLIS – *See Reva RICE and Greg ELLIS*

Joey B ELLIS *US, male rapper (10 WEEKS)* pos/wks

16 Feb 91	**GO FOR IT (HEART AND FIRE)** *Capitol CL 601* 1	..........**20**	8
18 May 91	**THOUGHT U WERE THE ONE FOR ME** *Capitol CL 614*	..........**58**	2

1 Rocky V featuring Joey B Ellis and Tynetta Hare

Shirley ELLIS *US, female vocalist (17 WEEKS)* pos/wks

6 May 65	● **THE CLAPPING SONG** *London HLR 9961*	..........**6**	13
8 Jul 78	**THE CLAPPING SONG (EP)** *MCA MCEP 1*	..........**59**	4

Tracks on The Clapping Song (EP): The Clapping Song / Ever See a Diver Kiss His Wife While the Bubbles Bounce Above the Water / The Name Game / The Nitty Gritty. 'The Clapping Song' itself qualifies as a re-issue

ELLIS, BEGGS and HOWARD
UK, male vocal / instrumental group (8 WEEKS) pos/wks

2 Jul 88	**BIG BUBBLES, NO TROUBLES (re)** *RCA PB 42089*	..........**41**	8

Peak position reached on its re-entry in Mar 89

Sophie ELLIS BEXTOR *UK, female vocalist (48 WEEKS)* pos/wks

25 Aug 01	● **TAKE ME HOME (A GIRL LIKE ME)** *Polydor 5872312*	..........**2**	12
15 Dec 01	● **MURDER ON THE DANCEFLOOR** *Polydor 5704942*	..........**2**	16
22 Jun 02	● **GET OVER YOU / MOVE THIS MOUNTAIN** *Polydor 5708332*	.......**3**	13
16 Nov 02	**MUSIC GETS THE BEST OF ME** *Polydor 0659222*	..........**14**	7+

See also THEAUDIENCE; SPILLER

ELWOOD *US, male rapper / vocalist – Elwood Strickland (1 WEEK)* pos/wks

26 Aug 00	**SUNDOWN** *Palm Pictures PPCD 70342*	..........**72**	1

EMBRACE *UK, male vocal / instrumental group (38 WEEKS)* pos/wks

17 May 97	**FIREWORKS (EP)** *Hut HUTCD 84*	..........**34**	2
19 Jul 97	**ONE BIG FAMILY (EP)** *Hut HUTCD 86*	..........**21**	3
8 Nov 97	● **ALL YOU GOOD GOOD PEOPLE (EP)** *Hut HUTCD 90*	..........**8**	4
6 Jun 98	● **COME BACK TO WHAT YOU KNOW** *Hut HUTCD 93*	..........**6**	8
29 Aug 98	● **MY WEAKNESS IS NONE OF YOUR BUSINESS**		
	Hut HUTCD 103	..........**9**	4
13 Nov 99	**HOOLIGAN** *Hut HUTCD 123*	..........**18**	3
25 Mar 00	● **YOU'RE NOT ALONE** *Hut / Virgin HUTCD 126*	..........**14**	3
10 Jun 00	**SAVE ME (re)** *Hut / Virgin HUTCD 133*	..........**29**	3
19 Aug 00	**I WOULDN'T WANNA HAPPEN TO YOU**		
	Hut / Virgin HUTCD 137	..........**23**	2
1 Sep 01	**WONDER (re)** *Hut / Virgin HUTCD 142*	..........**14**	4
17 Nov 01	**MAKE IT LAST** *Hut / Virgin HUTCD 144*	..........**35**	2

Tracks on Fireworks (EP): The Last Gas / Now You're Nobody / Blind / Fireworks. Tracks on One Big Family (EP): One Big Family / Dry Kids / You've Only Got to Stop to Get Better / Butter Wouldn't Melt. Tracks on All You Good Good People (EP): All You Good Good People / You Don't Amount To Anything – This Time / The Way I Do / Free Ride

EMERSON – *See SASHA*

Keith EMERSON
UK, male instrumentalist – keyboards (5 WEEKS) pos/wks

10 Apr 76	**HONKY TONK TRAIN BLUES** *Manticore K 13513*	..........**21**	5

See also EMERSON, LAKE and PALMER

EMERSON, LAKE and PALMER
UK, male instrumental group (13 WEEKS) pos/wks

4 Jun 77	● **FANFARE FOR THE COMMON MAN** *Atlantic K 10946*	.....**2**	13

See also Keith EMERSON; Greg LAKE; ASIA

Dick EMERY *UK, male actor / vocalist, d. 2 Jan 1983 (8 WEEKS)* pos/wks

26 Feb 69	**IF YOU LOVE HER** *Pye 7N 17644*	..........**32**	4
13 Jan 73	**YOU ARE AWFUL** *Pye 7N 45202*	..........**43**	4

EMILIA *Sweden, female vocalist – Emilia Rydberg (14 WEEKS)* pos/wks

12 Dec 98	● **BIG BIG WORLD** *Universal UMD 87190*	..........**5**	13
1 May 99	**GOOD SIGN** *Universal UMD 87206*	..........**54**	1

EMINEM 306 Top 500

Controversy-courting, chainsaw-wielding, multi-award-winning rap superstar, whose real name is Marshall Mathers (aka Slim Shady) b. 17 Oct 1974, Detroit. He has had more UK No.1 singles and albums than any rap act (102 WEEKS) pos/wks

10 Apr 99	● **MY NAME IS (re)** *Interscope IND 95638*	..........**2**	12
14 Aug 99	● **GUILTY CONSCIENCE** *Interscope IND 4971282* 1	..........**5**	8
10 Jun 00	● **FORGOT ABOUT DRE** *Interscope 4973412* 2	..........**7**	9
8 Jul 00	★ **THE REAL SLIM SHADY** *Interscope 4973792* ■	..........**1**	15
14 Oct 00	● **THE WAY I AM** *Interscope 4974252*	..........**8**	9
16 Dec 00	★ **STAN (re)** *Interscope IND 97470* ■	..........**1**	17
1 Sep 01	**SCARY MOVIES** *Mole UK MOLEUK 045* 3	..........**63**	1
1 Jun 02	★ **WITHOUT ME** *Interscope 4977282* ■	..........**1**	16
28 Sep 02	● **CLEANIN' OUT MY CLOSET** *Interscope 4973942*	..........**4**	12
14 Dec 02	★ **LOSE YOURSELF** *Interscope 4978282* ■ ▲	..........**1**	3+

1 Eminem featuring Dr Dre 2 Dr Dre featuring Eminem 3 Bad meets Evil featuring Eminem & Royce Da 5'9"

'Stan' features uncredited vocal by Dido

EMMA *UK, female vocalist – Emma Booth (6 WEEKS)* pos/wks

28 Apr 90	**GIVE A LITTLE LOVE BACK TO THE WORLD**		
	Big Wave BWR 33	..........**33**	6

EMMANUEL & ESKA – *See COLOURS featuring EMMANUEL & ESKA; EN-CORE featuring Stephen EMMANUEL & ESKA*

EMMIE *UK, female vocalist – Emma Norton-Smith (9 WEEKS)* pos/wks

23 Jan 99	● **MORE THAN THIS** *Indirect / Manifesto FESCD 52*	..........**5**	8
16 Feb 02	**I WON'T LET YOU DOWN**		
	Decode / Telstar CDSTAS 3210 1	..........**53**	1

1 W.I.P. featuring Emmie

EMOTIONS *US, female vocal group (28 WEEKS)* pos/wks

10 Sep 77	● **BEST OF MY LOVE** *CBS 5555* ▲	..........**4**	10
24 Dec 77	**I DON'T WANNA LOSE YOUR LOVE** *CBS 5819*	..........**40**	5
12 May 79	● **BOOGIE WONDERLAND** *CBS 7292* 1	..........**4**	13

1 Earth Wind and Fire with The Emotions

Alec EMPIRE *Germany, male producer (1 WEEK)* pos/wks

13 Apr 02	**ADDICTED TO YOU** *Digital Hardcore DHRMCD 38*	..........**64**	1

EMPIRION *UK, male instrumental / production group (2 WEEKS)* pos/wks

6 Jul 96	**NARCOTIC INFLUENCE** *XL XLS 72CD*	..........**64**	1
21 Jun 97	**BETA** *XL XLS 77CD*	..........**75**	1

EN VOGUE 414 Top 500

Very influential post-feminist R&B vocal quartet formed Oakland, California, US; Terry Ellis, Maxine Jones, Dawn Robinson (left 1995) and ex-beauty pageant winner Cindy Herron. Award-winning team blended hip hop and R&B and helped to launch the New Jill Swing movement (83 WEEKS) pos/wks

5 May 90	● **HOLD ON** *East West America 7908*	..........**5**	11
21 Jul 90	**LIES** *East West America 7893*	..........**44**	4

		pos/wks
4 Apr 92	● MY LOVIN' (re) *East West America A 8578*..............4 12	
15 Aug 92	GIVING HIM SOMETHING HE CAN FEEL	
	East West America A 8524..............44 3	
7 Nov 92	FREE YOUR MIND / GIVING HIM SOMETHING HE CAN	
	FEEL (re-issue) *East West America A 8468*.......16 8	
16 Jan 93	GIVE IT UP TURN IT LOOSE	
	East West America A 8445CD..............22 4	
10 Apr 93	LOVE DON'T LOVE YOU *East West America A 8424CD*...64 1	
9 Oct 93	RUNAWAY LOVE *East West America A 8359CD*......36 3	
19 Mar 94	● WHATTA MAN *ffrr FCD 222* [1]..............7 10	
11 Jan 97	● DON'T LET GO (LOVE) *East West A 3976CD*........5 16	
14 Jun 97	WHATEVER *East West E 3642CD*..............14 5	
6 Sep 97	TOO GONE, TOO LONG *East West E 3908CD*........20 3	
28 Nov 98	HOLD ON (re-mix) *East West E 3796 CD*..............53 1	
1 Jul 00	RIDDLE *Elektra E 7053CD*..............33 2	

[1] Salt-N-Pepa with En Vogue

EN-CORE featuring Stephen EMMANUEL & ESKA
UK, male producer – Stephen Boreland
and female vocalist – Eska Mtungwazi (2 WEEKS)   pos/wks

9 Sep 00	COOCHY COO *VC Recordings VCRD 72*..............32 2

ENCORE
France, female vocalist – Sabine Ohmes (4 WEEKS)   pos/wks

14 Feb 98	LE DISC JOCKEY *Sum CDSUM 2*..............12 4

ENERGISE *UK, male vocal / instrumental group (1 WEEK)*   pos/wks

16 Feb 91	REPORT TO THE DANCEFLOOR *Network NWKT 16*.......69 1

ENERGY 52
Germany, male DJ / producer – Paul Schmitz-Moormann (11 WEEKS) pos/wks

8 Mar 97	CAFE DEL MAR *Hooj Choons HOOJCD 51*..............51 1
25 Jul 98	CAFE DEL MAR '98 (re-mix) *Hooj Choons HOOJ 64CD*...12 6
12 Oct 02	CAFE DEL MAR (re-mix) *Lost Language LOST 019CD*...24 4

ENERGY ORCHARD
Ireland, male vocal / instrumental group (6 WEEKS)   pos/wks

27 Jan 90	BELFAST *MCA MCA 1392*..............52 4
7 Apr 90	SAILORTOWN *MCA MCA 1402*..............73 2

Harry ENFIELD *UK, male comedian / vocalist (7 WEEKS)*   pos/wks

7 May 88	● LOADSAMONEY (DOIN' UP THE HOUSE) *Mercury DOSH 1* 4 7

ENGLAND BOYS *UK, male vocal group (3 WEEKS)*   pos/wks

8 Jun 02	GO ENGLAND *Phonogram 5829592*..............26 3

ENGLAND DAN and John Ford COLEY
US, male vocal duo – Dan Seals and John Ford Coley (12 WEEKS) pos/wks

25 Sep 76	I'D REALLY LOVE TO SEE YOU TONIGHT	
	Atlantic K 10810..............26 7	
23 Jun 79	LOVE IS THE ANSWER *Big Tree K 11296*..............45 5	

ENGLAND RUGBY WORLD CUP SQUAD – See UNION featuring the ENGLAND WORLD CUP SQUAD

ENGLAND SISTERS – See DALE SISTERS

ENGLAND SUPPORTERS' BAND
UK, male instrumental group (4 WEEKS)   pos/wks

27 Jun 98	THE GREAT ESCAPE *V2 VVR 5002163*..............46 2	
24 Jun 00	THE GREAT ESCAPE 2000 (re-recording)	
	V2 VVR 5014293..............26 2	

ENGLAND UNITED
UK, male / female vocal / instrumental group (11 WEEKS)   pos/wks

13 Jun 98	● (HOW DOES IT FEEL TO BE) ON TOP OF THE WORLD	
	(re) *London LONCD 414*..............9 11	

ENGLAND WORLD CUP SQUAD
UK, male football team vocalists (48 WEEKS)   pos/wks

18 Apr 70	★ BACK HOME (re) *Pye 7N 17920*..............1 17	
10 Apr 82	● THIS TIME (WE'LL GET IT RIGHT) / ENGLAND, WE'LL	
	FLY THE FLAG *England ER 1*..............2 13	
19 Apr 86	WE'VE GOT THE WHOLE WORLD AT OUR FEET / WHEN WE	
	ARE FAR FROM HOME *Columbia DB 9128*..............66 2	
21 May 88	ALL THE WAY *MCA GOAL 1* [1]..............64 2	
2 Jun 90	★ WORLD IN MOTION ... *Factory / MCA FAC 2937* [2]...1 12	
15 Jun 02	WORLD IN MOTION (re-issue)	
	London / MCA NUDOCD 12 [2]..............43 2	

[1] England Football Team and the 'sound' of Stock, Aitken and Waterman
[2] Englandneworder

ENGLAND'S BARMY ARMY
UK, 5,000 male / female vocal cricket supporters (1 WEEK)   pos/wks

12 Jun 99	COME ON ENGLAND! *Wildstar CDWILD 20*..............45 1

Kim ENGLISH *US, female vocalist (7 WEEKS)*   pos/wks

23 Jul 94	NITE LIFE *Hi-Life PZCD 323*..............35 2
4 Mar 95	TIME FOR LOVE *Hi-Life HICD 8*..............48 1
9 Sep 95	I KNOW A PLACE *Hi-Life 5798072*..............52 1
30 Nov 96	NITE LIFE (re-mix) *Hi-Life 5755332*..............35 2
26 Apr 97	SUPERNATURAL *Hi-Life 5736972*..............50 1

Scott ENGLISH *US, male vocalist (10 WEEKS)*   pos/wks

9 Oct 71	BRANDY *Horse HOSS 7*..............12 10

ENIAC – See Tom NOVY

ENIGMA
UK, male / female vocal / instrumental group (15 WEEKS)   pos/wks

23 May 81	AIN'T NO STOPPING *Creole CR 9*..............11 8
8 Aug 81	I LOVE MUSIC *Creole CR 14*..............25 7

ENIGMA *Germany / Romania, male*
/ female vocal / instrumental duo (45 WEEKS)   pos/wks

15 Dec 90	★ SADNESS PART 1 *Virgin International DINS 101*..............1 12	
30 Mar 91	MEA CULPA PART II *Virgin International DINS 104*.......55 3	
10 Aug 91	PRINCIPLES OF LUST *Virgin International DINS 110*.......59 2	
11 Jan 92	THE RIVERS OF BELIEF	
	Virgin International DINS 112..............68 2	
29 Jan 94	● RETURN TO INNOCENCE	
	Virgin International DINSD 123..............3 14	
14 May 94	THE EYES OF TRUTH *Virgin International DINSD 126*......21 4	
20 Aug 94	AGE OF LONELINESS *Virgin International DINSD 135*......21 5	
25 Jan 97	BEYOND THE INVISIBLE	
	Virgin International DINSD 155..............26 2	
19 Apr 97	TNT FOR THE BRAIN *Virgin International DINSD 161*......60 1	

ENYA *Ireland, female vocalist / instrumentalist*
– Eithne Ni Bhraonain (65 WEEKS)   pos/wks

15 Oct 88	★ ORINOCO FLOW *WEA YZ 312*..............1 13
24 Dec 88	EVENING FALLS . . . *WEA YZ 356*..............20 4
10 Jun 89	STORMS IN AFRICA (PART II) *WEA YZ 368*..............41 4
19 Oct 91	CARIBBEAN BLUE *WEA YZ 604*..............13 7
7 Dec 91	HOW CAN I KEEP FROM SINGING? *WEA YZ 365*......32 5
1 Aug 92	● BOOK OF DAYS *WEA YZ 640*..............10 6
14 Nov 92	THE CELTS *WEA YZ 705*..............29 4
18 Nov 95	● ANYWHERE IS *WEA WEA 023CD*..............7 12
7 Dec 96	ON MY WAY HOME *WEA WEA 047CD*..............26 2
13 Dec 97	ONLY IF... *WEA WEA 143CD*..............43 2
25 Nov 00	ONLY TIME *WEA WEA 316CD*..............32 3
31 Mar 01	WILD CHILD *WEA WEA 324CD*..............72 1
2 Feb 02	MAY IT BE *WEA W 578CD*..............50 2

EON *UK, male producer – Ian Bela (1 WEEK)*   pos/wks

17 Aug 91	FEAR: THE MINDKILLER *Vinyl Solution STORM 33*..............63 1

   Re-entries are listed as (re), (2re), (3re), etc which signifies that the hit re-entered the chart once, twice or three times, etc

EQUALS
UK, male vocal / instrumental group (69 WEEKS)   pos/wks

21 Feb 68	I GET SO EXCITED *President PT 180*	44 4
1 May 68 ★	BABY COME BACK (re) *President PT 135*	1 18
21 Aug 68	LAUREL AND HARDY *President PT 200*	35 5
27 Nov 68	SOFTLY SOFTLY *President PT 222*	48 3
2 Apr 69	MICHAEL AND THE SLIPPER TREE *President PT 240*	24 7
30 Jul 69 ●	VIVA BOBBY JOE *President PT 260*	6 14
27 Dec 69	RUB A DUB DUB *President PT 275*	34 7
19 Dec 70 ●	BLACK SKIN BLUE EYED BOYS *President PT 325*	9 11

ERASURE   86   Top 500
Award-winning UK duo formed by Vince Clarke (k) and Andy Bell (v). After hits with Depeche Mode, Yazoo and The Assembly, this act was Clarke's greatest success, scoring 15 Top 10 singles and having five albums enter at No.1 (203 WEEKS)   pos/wks

5 Oct 85	WHO NEEDS LOVE LIKE THAT *Mute MUTE 40*	55 2
25 Oct 86 ●	SOMETIMES *Mute MUTE 51*	2 17
28 Feb 87	IT DOESN'T HAVE TO BE *Mute MUTE 56*	12 9
30 May 87 ●	VICTIM OF LOVE *Mute MUTE 61*	7 9
3 Oct 87 ●	THE CIRCUS *Mute MUTE 66*	6 10
5 Mar 88 ●	SHIP OF FOOLS *Mute MUTE 74*	6 8
11 Jun 88	CHAINS OF LOVE *Mute MUTE 83*	11 7
1 Oct 88 ●	A LITTLE RESPECT *Mute MUTE 85*	4 10
10 Dec 88 ●	CRACKERS INTERNATIONAL (EP) *Mute MUTE 93*	2 13
30 Sep 89 ●	DRAMA! *Mute MUTE 89*	4 9
9 Dec 89	YOU SURROUND ME *Mute MUTE 99*	15 9
10 Mar 90 ●	BLUE SAVANNAH *Mute MUTE 109*	3 10
2 Jun 90	STAR *Mute MUTE 111*	11 7
29 Jun 91 ●	CHORUS *Mute MUTE 125*	3 9
21 Sep 91 ●	LOVE TO HATE YOU *Mute MUTE 131*	4 9
7 Dec 91	AM I RIGHT? (EP) *Mute MUTE 134*	15 6
11 Jan 92	AM I RIGHT (EP) (re-mix) *Mute L12MUTE 134*	22 3
28 Mar 92 ●	BREATH OF LIFE *Mute MUTE 142*	8 6
13 Jun 92 ★	ABBA-ESQUE (EP) *Mute MUTE 144* ■	1 12
7 Nov 92 ●	WHO NEEDS LOVE (LIKE THAT) (re-mix) *Mute MUTE 150*	10 4
23 Apr 94 ●	ALWAYS *Mute CDMUTE 152*	4 9
30 Jul 94 ●	RUN TO THE SUN *Mute CDMUTE 153*	6 5
3 Dec 94	I LOVE SATURDAY *Mute CDMUTE 166*	20 6
23 Sep 95	STAY WITH ME *Mute CDMUTE 174*	15 4
9 Dec 95	FINGERS AND THUMBS (COLD SUMMER'S DAY) *Mute CDMUTE 178*	20 3
18 Jan 97	IN MY ARMS *Mute CDMUTE 190*	13 4
8 Mar 97	DON'T SAY YOUR LOVE IS KILLING ME *Mute CDMUTE 195*	23 2
21 Oct 00	FREEDOM *Mute CDMUTE 244*	27 2

Tracks on Crackers International (EP): Stop / The Hardest Part / Knocking on Your Door / She Won't Be Home. Tracks on Am I Right (EP): Am I Right / Carry On Clangers / Let It Flow / Waiting for Sex. Tracks on Am I Right (Re-mix EP): Am I Right / Chorus / Love to Hate You / Perfect Stranger. Tracks on Abba-esque (EP): Lay All Your Love on Me / SOS / Take a Chance on Me / Voulez-Vous. 'Take a Chance On Me' credits MC Kinky

See also KINKY

ERIC and the GOOD GOOD FEELING
UK, male / female vocal / instrumental group (1 WEEK)   pos/wks

3 Jun 89	GOOD GOOD FEELING *Equinox EQN 1*	73 1

ERIK
UK, female vocalist (5 WEEKS)   pos/wks

10 Apr 93	LOOKS LIKE I'M IN LOVE AGAIN *PWL Sanctuary PWCD 252* [1]	46 2
29 Jan 94	GOT TO BE REAL *PWL International PWCD 278*	42 2
1 Oct 94	WE GOT THE LOVE *PWL International PWCD 305*	55 1

[1] Key West featuring Erik

ERIN – See BBG; SHUT UP AND DANCE; Erin LORDAN

ERIRE – See SCIENCE DEPARTMENT featuring ERIRE

EROTIC DRUM BAND
Canada, male / female vocal / instrumental group (3 WEEKS)   pos/wks

9 Jun 79	LOVE DISCO STYLE *Scope SC 1*	47 3

ERUPTION
Jamaica, male / female vocal / instrumental group (21 WEEKS)   pos/wks

18 Feb 78 ●	I CAN'T STAND THE RAIN *Atlantic K 11068* [1]	5 11
21 Apr 79 ●	ONE WAY TICKET *Atlantic / Hansa K 11266*	9 10

[1] Eruption featuring Precious Wilson

Michelle ESCOFFERY – See ARTFUL DODGER

Shaun ESCOFFERY
UK, male vocalist (2 WEEKS)   pos/wks

10 Mar 01	SPACE RIDER *Oyster Music OYSCD 4*	52 1
20 Jul 02	DAYS LIKE THIS *Oyster Music OYSCDS 8*	53 1

ESCORTS
UK, male vocal / instrumental group (2 WEEKS)   pos/wks

2 Jul 64	THE ONE TO CRY *Fontana TF 474*	49 2

ESCRIMA
UK, male producer – Paul Newman (4 WEEKS)   pos/wks

11 Feb 95	TRAIN OF THOUGHT *Ffrreedom TABCD 225*	36 2
7 Oct 95	DEEPER *Hooj Choons TABCD 236*	27 2

See also TALL PAUL; PARTIZAN; CAMISRA; GRIFTERS

ESKA – See EN-CORE featuring Stephen EMMANUEL & ESKA; COLOURS featuring EMMANUEL & ESKA; Nitin SAWHNEY featuring ESKA

ESKIMOS & EGYPT
UK, male vocal / instrumental group (4 WEEKS)   pos/wks

13 Feb 93	FALL FROM GRACE *One Little Indian EEF 96CD*	51 2
29 May 93	UK-USA *One Little Indian 99 TP7CD*	52 2

ESPIRITU
UK / France, male / female vocal / instrumental duo – Vanessa Quinones and Chris Chaplin (10 WEEKS)   pos/wks

6 Mar 93	CONQUISTADOR *Heavenly HVN 28CD*	47 2
7 Aug 93	LOS AMERICANOS *Heavenly HVN 33CD*	45 2
20 Aug 94	BONITA MANANA *Columbia 6606925*	50 1
25 Mar 95	ALWAYS SOMETHING THERE TO REMIND ME *WEA YZ 911CD* [1]	14 5

[1] Tin Tin Out featuring Espiritu

ESSENCE
UK, male production group – Ricky Simmonds and Stephen Jones, and female vocalist (2 WEEKS)   pos/wks

21 Mar 98	THE PROMISE *Innocent SINCD 1*	27 2

See also CHAKRA; SPACE BROTHERS; LUSTRAL; ASCENSION

ESSEX
US, male / female vocal group (5 WEEKS)   pos/wks

8 Aug 63	EASIER SAID THAN DONE *Columbia DB 7077* ▲	41 5

David ESSEX   92   Top 500
Actor / teeny-bop star turned popular entertainer. b. David Cook, 23 Jul 1947, London. This singer / songwriter was voted No.1 British Male Vocalist (1974) and was a teen idol for more than a decade. Starred in the stage show 'Godspell' and graduated successfully to films (199 WEEKS)   pos/wks

18 Aug 73 ●	ROCK ON *CBS 1693*	3 11
10 Nov 73 ●	LAMPLIGHT *CBS 1902*	7 15
11 May 74	AMERICA *CBS 2176*	32 5
12 Oct 74 ★	GONNA MAKE YOU A STAR *CBS 2492*	1 17
14 Dec 74 ●	STARDUST *CBS 2828*	7 10
5 Jul 75 ●	ROLLING STONE *CBS 3425*	5 7
13 Sep 75 ★	HOLD ME CLOSE *CBS 3572*	1 10
6 Dec 75	IF I COULD *CBS 3776*	13 8
20 Mar 76	CITY LIGHTS *CBS 4050*	24 4
16 Oct 76	COMING HOME *CBS 4486*	24 6
17 Sep 77	COOL OUT TONIGHT *CBS 5495*	23 6
11 Mar 78	STAY WITH ME BABY *CBS 6063*	45 5
19 Aug 78 ●	OH WHAT A CIRCUS *Mercury 6007 185*	3 11
21 Oct 78	BRAVE NEW WORLD *CBS 6705*	55 3
3 Mar 79	IMPERIAL WIZARD *Mercury 6007 202*	32 8
5 Apr 80 ●	SILVER DREAM MACHINE (PART 1) *Mercury BIKE 1*	4 11

			pos/wks	
14 Jun 80		HOT LOVE *Mercury HOT 11*	57	4
26 Jun 82		ME AND MY GIRL (NIGHT-CLUBBING) *Mercury MER 107*	13	10
11 Dec 82	●	A WINTER'S TALE *Mercury MER 127*	2	10
4 Jun 83		THE SMILE *Mercury ESSEX 1*	52	4
27 Aug 83	●	TAHITI (FROM 'MUTINY ON THE BOUNTY') *Mercury BOUNT 1*	8	11
26 Nov 83		YOU'RE IN MY HEART (re) *Mercury ESSEX 2*	59	6
23 Feb 85		FALLING ANGELS RIDING *Mercury ESSEX 5*	29	7
18 Apr 87		MYFANWY *Arista RIS 11*	41	7
26 Nov 94		TRUE LOVE WAYS *PolyGram TV TLWCD 2* [1]	38	3

[1] David Essex and Catherine Zeta Jones

Gloria ESTEFAN [108] Top 500

Latin music's leading lady, b. Gloria Fajardo, 1 Dec 1957, Cuba. Successes in the dance and MOR fields have pushed her world sales to more than 35 million, with two of the vocalist's albums passing the one-million sales mark in the UK (182 WEEKS)

			pos/wks	
16 Jul 88	●	ANYTHING FOR YOU *Epic 651673 7* [1] ▲	10	16
22 Oct 88		1-2-3 (re) *Epic 652958 7* [1]	9	10
17 Dec 88		RHYTHM IS GONNA GET YOU *Epic 654514 7* [1]	16	9
11 Feb 89	●	CAN'T STAY AWAY FROM YOU *Epic 651444 7* [1]	7	12
15 Jul 89	●	DON'T WANNA LOSE YOU *Epic 655054 0* ▲	6	10
16 Sep 89		OYE MI CANTO (HEAR MY VOICE) *Epic 655287 7*	16	8
25 Nov 89		GET ON YOUR FEET *Epic 655450 7*	23	7
3 Mar 90		HERE WE ARE *Epic 6554737*	23	6
26 May 90		CUTS BOTH WAYS *Epic 655982 7*	49	5
26 Jan 91		COMING OUT OF THE DARK *Epic 6565747* ▲	25	5
6 Apr 91		SEAL OUR FATE *Epic 6567737*	24	7
8 Jun 91		REMEMBER ME WITH LOVE *Epic 6569687*	22	6
21 Sep 91		LIVE FOR LOVING YOU *Epic 6573827*	33	5
24 Oct 92		ALWAYS TOMORROW *Epic 6583977*	24	4
12 Dec 92	●	MIAMI HIT MIX / CHRISTMAS THROUGH YOUR EYES *Epic 6588377*	8	9
13 Feb 93		I SEE YOUR SMILE *Epic 6589612*	48	2
3 Apr 93		GO AWAY *Epic 6590952*	13	6
3 Jul 93		MI TIERRA *Epic 6593512*	36	3
14 Aug 93		IF WE WERE LOVERS / CON LOS ANOS QUE ME QUEDAN *Epic 6595702*	40	3
18 Dec 93		MONTUNO *Epic 6599972*	55	2
15 Oct 94		TURN THE BEAT AROUND *Epic 6606822*	21	6
3 Dec 94		HOLD ME THRILL ME KISS ME (re) *Epic 6610802*	11	11
18 Feb 95		EVERLASTING LOVE *Epic 6611595*	19	5
25 May 96		REACH (2re) *Epic 6632642*	15	8
24 Aug 96		YOU'LL BE MINE (PARTY TIME) *Epic 6636505*	18	3
14 Dec 96		I'M NOT GIVING YOU UP *Epic 6640222*	28	3
6 Jun 98		HEAVEN'S WHAT I FEEL *Epic 6660042*	17	4
10 Oct 98		OYE *Epic 6664645*	33	2
16 Jan 99		DON'T LET THIS MOMENT END *Epic 6667472*	28	2
8 Jan 00		MUSIC OF MY HEART *Epic 6685272* [2]	34	3

[1] Gloria Estefan and Miami Sound Machine [2] 'N Sync / Gloria Estefan

'Christmas Through Your Eyes' was listed only from 19 Dec 1992

See also MIAMI SOUND MACHINE

EST'ELLE – See BLACK TWANG

Don ESTELLE – See Windsor DAVIES and Don ESTELLE

ESTHERO – See Ian POOLEY

Deon ESTUS

US, male vocalist / instrumentalist – bass (7 WEEKS)

			pos/wks	
25 Jan 86		MY GUY – MY GIRL (MEDLEY) *Sedition EDIT 3310* [1]	63	3
29 Apr 89		HEAVEN HELP ME *Mika MIKA 2*	41	4

[1] Amii Stewart and Deon Estus

ETA

Denmark, male instrumental group (5 WEEKS)

		pos/wks	
28 Jun 97	CASUAL SUB (BURNING SPEAR) *East West EW 110CD*	28	3
31 Jan 98	CASUAL SUB (BURNING SPEAR) (re-mix) *East West Dance EW 145CD*	28	2

ETERNAL [194] Top 500

London-based vocal group with across-the-board appeal: sisters Easther and Vernett Bennett, Kéllé Bryan, Louise Nurding. First all-female act to shift more than one million copies of an album in the UK. Louise left for a successful solo career in 1995 followed by Kéllé four years later . Best-selling single: 'I Wanna Be The Only One' 600,000 (134 WEEKS)

			pos/wks	
2 Oct 93	●	STAY *EMI CDEM 283*	4	9
15 Jan 94	●	SAVE OUR LOVE *EMI CDEM 296*	8	7
30 Apr 94	●	JUST A STEP FROM HEAVEN *EMI CDEM 311*	8	10
20 Aug 94		SO GOOD *EMI CDEMS 339*	13	7
5 Nov 94	●	OH BABY I . . . *EMI CDEM 353*	4	13
24 Dec 94		CRAZY *EMI CDEMX 364*	15	7
21 Oct 95	●	POWER OF A WOMAN *EMI CDEM 396*	5	8
9 Dec 95	●	I AM BLESSED *EMI CDEMS 408*	7	12
9 Mar 96	●	GOOD THING *EMI CDEM 419*	8	6
17 Aug 96	●	SOMEDAY *EMI CDEMS 439*	4	9
7 Dec 96	●	SECRETS *EMI CDEM 459*	9	7
8 Mar 97	●	DON'T YOU LOVE ME *EMI CDEMS 465*	3	7
31 May 97	★	I WANNA BE THE ONLY ONE *EMI CDEM 472* [1] ■	1	15
11 Oct 97	●	ANGEL OF MINE *EMI CDEM 493*	4	13
30 Oct 99		WHAT 'CHA GONNA DO *EMI CDEM 552*	16	4

[1] Eternal featuring BeBe Winans

ETHER *UK, male vocal / instrumental group (1 WEEK)*

		pos/wks	
28 Mar 98	WATCHING YOU *Parlophone CDR 6491*	74	1

ETHICS *Holland, male producer – Patrick Prinz (5 WEEKS)*

		pos/wks	
25 Nov 95	TO THE BEAT OF THE DRUM (LA LUNA) *VC VCRD 5*	13	5

See also ARTEMESIA; MOVIN' MELODIES; SUBLIMINAL CUTS

ETHIOPIANS *Jamaica, male vocal / instrumental group (6 WEEKS)*

		pos/wks	
13 Sep 67	TRAIN TO SKAVILLE *Rio RIO 130*	40	6

Tony ETORIA *UK, male vocalist (8 WEEKS)*

		pos/wks	
4 Jun 77	I CAN PROVE IT *GTO GT 89*	21	8

EUROGROOVE *UK, male / female vocal group (7 WEEKS)*

		pos/wks	
20 May 95	MOVE YOUR BODY *Avex UK AVEXCD 4*	29	2
5 Aug 95	DIVE TO PARADISE *Avex UK AVEXCD 10*	31	2
21 Oct 95	IT'S ON YOU (SCAN ME) *Avex UK AVEXCD 17*	25	2
3 Feb 96	MOVE YOUR BODY (re-mix) *Avex UK AVEXCD 22*	44	1

EUROPE *Sweden, male vocal / instrumental group – lead vocalist Joey Tempest (50 WEEKS)*

			pos/wks	
1 Nov 86	★	THE FINAL COUNTDOWN *Epic A 7127*	1	15
31 Jan 87		ROCK THE NIGHT *Epic EUR 1*	12	9
18 Apr 87		CARRIE *Epic EUR 2*	22	8
20 Aug 88		SUPERSTITIOUS *Epic EUR 3*	34	5
1 Feb 92		I'LL CRY FOR YOU *Epic 6576977*	28	5
21 Mar 92		HALFWAY TO HEAVEN *Epic 6578517*	42	4
25 Dec 99		THE FINAL COUNTDOWN 2000 (re-recording) *Epic 6685042*	36	4

EURYTHMICS [83] Top 500

Innovative and internationally popular duo formed by Brit award-winning Scottish vocalist Annie Lennox and multi-instrumentalist / songwriter / producer Dave Stewart, formerly known as The Tourists. The most charted male / female duo in the UK, whose greatest hits album sold more than two million copies in the UK and in Europe (208 WEEKS)

			pos/wks	
4 Jul 81		NEVER GONNA CRY AGAIN *RCA 68*	63	3
20 Nov 82	●	LOVE IS A STRANGER (re) *RCA DA 1*	6	13
12 Feb 83	●	SWEET DREAMS (ARE MADE OF THIS) *RCA DA 2* ▲	2	14
9 Jul 83	●	WHO'S THAT GIRL? *RCA DA 3*	3	10
5 Nov 83	●	RIGHT BY YOUR SIDE *RCA DA 4*	10	11
21 Jan 84	●	HERE COMES THE RAIN AGAIN *RCA DA 5*	8	8
3 Nov 84	●	SEXCRIME (NINETEEN EIGHTY FOUR) *Virgin VS 728*	4	13
19 Jan 85		JULIA *Virgin VS 734*	44	4

Re-entries are listed as (re), (2re), (3re), etc which signifies that the hit re-entered the chart once, twice or three times, etc

20 Apr 85	WOULD I LIE TO YOU? *RCA PB 40101*	17	8
6 Jul 85	★ THERE MUST BE AN ANGEL (PLAYING WITH MY HEART)		
	RCA PB 40247	1	13
2 Nov 85	● SISTERS ARE DOIN' IT FOR THEMSELVES *RCA PB 40339* [1]	9	11
11 Jan 86	IT'S ALRIGHT (BABY'S COMING BACK) *RCA PB 40375*	12	8
14 Jun 86	WHEN TOMORROW COMES *RCA DA 7*	30	6
6 Sep 86	● THORN IN MY SIDE *RCA DA 8*	5	11
29 Nov 86	THE MIRACLE OF LOVE *RCA DA 9*	23	9
28 Feb 87	MISSIONARY MAN *RCA DA 10*	31	4
24 Oct 87	BEETHOVEN (I LOVE TO LISTEN TO) *RCA DA 11*	25	5
26 Dec 87	SHAME *RCA DA 14*	41	6
9 Apr 88	I NEED A MAN *RCA DA 15*	26	5
11 Jun 88	YOU HAVE PLACED A CHILL IN MY HEART *RCA DA 16*	16	8
26 Aug 89	REVIVAL *RCA DA 17*	26	6
4 Nov 89	DON'T ASK ME WHY *RCA DA 19*	25	6
3 Feb 90	THE KING AND QUEEN OF AMERICA *RCA DA 20*	29	5
12 May 90	ANGEL *RCA DA 21*	23	6
9 Mar 91	LOVE IS A STRANGER (re-issue) *RCA PB 44265*	46	3
16 Nov 91	SWEET DREAMS (ARE MADE OF THIS) '91 *RCA PB 45031*	48	2
16 Oct 99	I SAVED THE WORLD TODAY *RCA 74321695632*	11	6
5 Feb 00	17 AGAIN *RCA 74321726262*	27	4

[1] Eurythmics and Aretha Franklin

'Love Is a Stranger' reached its peak position when it re-entered in Apr 1983

See also Dave STEWART; Annie LENNOX; VEGAS

EUSEBE *UK, male / female vocal group (3 WEEKS)*   pos/wks

| 26 Aug 95 | SUMMERTIME HEALING *Mama's Yard CDMAMA 4* | 32 | 3 |

EVANGEL TEMPLE CHOIR – See Johnny CASH

Faith EVANS *US, female vocalist (40 WEEKS)*   pos/wks

14 Oct 95	YOU USED TO LOVE ME *Puff Daddy 74321299812*	42	2
23 Nov 96	STRESSED OUT *Jive JIVECD 404* [1]	33	4
28 Jun 97	★ I'LL BE MISSING YOU *Puff Daddy 74321499102* [2] ◆ ■ ▲	1	21
14 Nov 98	LOVE LIKE THIS *Puff Daddy 74321625592*	24	4
1 May 99	ALL NIGHT LONG *Puff Daddy / Arista 74321665692* [3]	23	3
1 May 99	GEORGY PORGY *Warner Bros. W478CD2* [4]	28	3
30 Dec 00	HEARTBREAK HOTEL *Arista 74321820572* [5]	25	5

[1] A Tribe Called Quest featuring Faith Evans and Raphael Saadiq [2] Puff Daddy and Faith Evans featuring 112 [3] Faith Evans featuring Puff Daddy [4] Eric Benet featuring Faith Evans [5] Whitney Houston featuring Faith Evans and Kelly Price

Maureen EVANS *UK, female vocalist (37 WEEKS)*   pos/wks

22 Jan 60	THE BIG HURT *Oriole CB 1533*	26	2
17 Mar 60	LOVE KISSES AND HEARTACHES *Oriole CB 1540*	44	1
2 Jun 60	PAPER ROSES *Oriole CB 1550*	40	5
29 Nov 62	● LIKE I DO *Oriole CB 1760*	3	18
27 Feb 64	I LOVE HOW YOU LOVE ME (re) *Oriole CB 1906*	34	11

Paul EVANS *US, male vocalist (14 WEEKS)*   pos/wks

27 Nov 59	SEVEN LITTLE GIRLS SITTING IN THE BACK SEAT		
	London HLL 8968 [1]	25	1
31 Mar 60	MIDNITE SPECIAL *London HLL 9045*	41	1
16 Dec 78	● HELLO, THIS IS JOANNIE (THE TELEPHONE ANSWERING		
	MACHINE SONG) *Spring 2066 932*	6	12

[1] Paul Evans and The Curls

EVASIONS

UK, male / female vocal / rap / instrumental group (8 WEEKS)   pos/wks

| 13 Jun 81 | WIKKA WRAP *Groove GP 107* | 20 | 8 |

E.V.E. *UK / US, female vocal group (5 WEEKS)*   pos/wks

| 1 Oct 94 | GROOVE OF LOVE *Gasoline Alley MCSTD 2007* | 30 | 3 |
| 28 Jan 95 | GOOD LIFE *Gasoline Alley MCSTD 2038* | 39 | 2 |

EVE *US, female rapper – Eve Jeffers (40 WEEKS)*   pos/wks

| 19 May 01 | ● WHO'S THAT GIRL *Interscope 4975572* | 6 | 8 |
| 25 Aug 01 | ● LET ME BLOW YA MIND *Interscope / Polydor 4975932* [1] | 4 | 12 |

9 Mar 02	BROTHA PART II *J 74321922142* [2]	37	2
16 Mar 02	● CARAMEL *Interscope / Polydor 4976742* [3]	9	10
5 Oct 02	● GANGSTA LOVIN' *Ruff Ryders / Interscope 4978042* [4]	6	8

[1] Eve featuring Gwen Stefani [2] Angie Stone featuring Alicia Keys and Eve [3] City High featuring Eve [4] Eve featuring Alicia Keys

See also Missy 'Misdemeanor' ELLIOTT

Jessica EVE – See WHO DA FUNK featuring Jessica EVE

Alison EVELYN – See BROTHERS LIKE OUTLAW featuring Alison EVELYN

EVERCLEAR *US, male vocal / instrumental group (7 WEEKS)*   pos/wks

1 Jun 96	HEARTSPARK DOLLARSIGN *Capitol CDCLS 773*	48	2
31 Aug 96	SANTA MONICA (WATCH THE WORLD DIE)		
	Capitol CDCL 775	40	2
9 May 98	EVERYTHING TO EVERYONE *Capitol CDCL 799*	41	1
14 Oct 00	WONDERFUL *Capital CDCLS 824*	36	2

Betty EVERETT *US, female vocalist, d. 18 Aug 2001 (14 WEEKS)*   pos/wks

14 Jan 65	GETTING MIGHTY CROWDED *Fontana TF 520*	29	7
30 Oct 68	IT'S IN HIS KISS (THE SHOOP SHOOP SONG)		
	President PT 215	34	7

Kenny EVERETT *UK, male DJ / vocalist, d. 4 Apr 1995 (12 WEEKS)*   pos/wks

| 12 Nov 77 | CAPTAIN KREMMEN (RETRIBUTION) *DJM DJS 10810* [1] | 32 | 4 |
| 26 Mar 83 | ● SNOT RAP *RCA KEN 1* | 9 | 8 |

[1] Kenny Everett and Mike Vickers

Peven EVERETT – See Roy DAVIS Jr featuring Peven EVERETT

EVERLAST *US, male vocalist – Erik Schrody (5 WEEKS)*   pos/wks

27 Feb 99	WHAT IT'S LIKE *Tommy Boy TBCD 7470*	34	2
3 Jul 99	ENDS *Tommy Boy TBCD 346*	47	1
20 Jan 01	BLACK JESUS *Tommy Boy TBCD 2180*	37	2

See also HOUSE OF PAIN

EVERLY BROTHERS (19) Top 500

Rock 'n' roll's foremost vocal duo: Don b. 1 Feb 1937 and Phil Everly b. 19 Jan 1939. The Kentucky-based brothers' distinctive harmony sound has influenced scores of later groups including The Beatles. The duo, voted World's Top Group by NME readers in 1958, was supported by The Rolling Stones on 1963 UK tour. They achieved long string of transatlantic hits, many of which were self-composed. They were the first duo / group inducted in Rock and Roll Hall of Fame, and were awarded a Lifetime Grammy in 1997. In 2001 they were elected into the Country Music Hall of Fame and their home state erected statues in their honour (345 WEEKS)   pos/wks

12 Jul 57	● BYE BYE LOVE *London HLA 8440*	6	16
8 Nov 57	● WAKE UP LITTLE SUSIE *London HLA 8498* ▲	2	13
23 May 58	★ ALL I HAVE TO DO IS DREAM / CLAUDETTE		
	London HLA 8618 ▲	1	21
12 Sep 58	● BIRD DOG *London HLA 8685* ▲	2	16
23 Jan 59	● PROBLEMS *London HLA 8781*	6	12
22 May 59	TAKE A MESSAGE TO MARY (2re) *London HLA 8863*	20	10
29 May 59	POOR JENNY *London B-HLA 8863*	14	11
11 Sep 59	● ('TIL) I KISSED YOU *London HLA 8934*	2	15
12 Feb 60	LET IT BE ME (re) *London HLA 9039*	13	10
14 Apr 60	★ CATHY'S CLOWN *Warner Bros. WB 1* ▲	1	18
14 Jul 60	● WHEN WILL I BE LOVED *London HLA 9157*	4	16
22 Sep 60	● LUCILLE / SO SAD (TO WATCH GOOD LOVE GO BAD)		
	Warner Bros. WB 19	4	15
15 Dec 60	LIKE STRANGERS *London HLA 9250*	11	10
9 Feb 61	★ WALK RIGHT BACK / EBONY EYES *Warner Bros. WB 33*	1	16
15 Jun 61	★ TEMPTATION *Warner Bros. WB 42*	1	15
5 Oct 61	MUSKRAT / DON'T BLAME ME *Warner Bros. WB 50*	20	6
18 Jan 62	● CRYING IN THE RAIN *Warner Bros. WB 56*	6	15
17 May 62	HOW CAN I MEET HER *Warner Bros. WB 67*	12	10
25 Oct 62	NO ONE CAN MAKE MY SUNSHINE SMILE		
	Warner Bros. WB 79	11	11
21 Mar 63	SO IT WILL ALWAYS BE *Warner Bros. WB 94*	23	11

13 Jun 63	IT'S BEEN NICE (GOODNIGHT) *Warner Bros. WB 99*	26	5
17 Oct 63	THE GIRL SANG THE BLUES *Warner Bros. WB 109*	25	9
16 Jul 64	THE FERRIS WHEEL *Warner Bros. WB 135*	22	10
3 Dec 64	GONE, GONE, GONE *Warner Bros. WB 146*	36	7
6 May 65	THAT'LL BE THE DAY *Warner Bros. WB 158*	30	4
20 May 65 ●	THE PRICE OF LOVE *Warner Bros. WB 161*	2	14
26 Aug 65	I'LL NEVER GET OVER YOU *Warner Bros. WB 5639*	35	5
21 Oct 65	LOVE IS STRANGE *Warner Bros. WB 5649*	11	9
8 May 68	IT'S MY TIME *Warner Bros. WB 7192*	39	6
22 Sep 84	ON THE WINGS OF A NIGHTINGALE *Mercury MER 170*	41	9

'All I Have to Do Is Dream' was listed without Claudette for its first week on the chart but, from 30 May 1958, both sides charted for 20 more weeks

See also Phil EVERLY

Phil EVERLY *US, male vocalist (24 WEEKS)*
			pos/wks
6 Nov 82	LOUISE *Capitol CL 266*	47	6
19 Feb 83 ●	SHE MEANS NOTHING TO ME *Capitol CL 276* [1]	9	9
10 Dec 94	ALL I HAVE TO DO IS DREAM (re) *EMI CDEMS 359* [2]	14	9

[1] Phil Everly and Cliff Richard [2] Cliff Richard and Phil Everly

'All I Have to Do Is Dream' was listed with its flip side 'Miss You Nights' by Cliff Richard

See also EVERLY BROTHERS

EVERTON FOOTBALL CLUB
UK, male football team vocalists (8 WEEKS)
			pos/wks
11 May 85	HERE WE GO *Columbia DB 9106* [1]	14	5
20 May 95	ALL TOGETHER NOW *MDMC DEVCS 3*	24	3

[1] Everton 1985

EVERYTHING BUT THE GIRL `327` `Top 500`
Introspective pop duo formed 1982, Hull, UK; Tracey Thorn (v) b. 26 Sep 1962. Ben Watt (k) b. 6 Dec 1962. Gained greatest popularity after mid-90s conversion to low-key dance music. Remix of 'Missing' was the first single to spend an uninterrupted year on the US chart. Best-selling single: 'Missing' 870,000 (96 WEEKS) pos/wks
12 May 84	EACH AND EVERY ONE *Blanco Y Negro NEG 1*	28	7
21 Jul 84	MINE *Blanco Y Negro NEG 3*	58	2
6 Oct 84	NATIVE LAND *Blanco Y Negro NEG 6*	73	2
2 Aug 86	COME ON HOME *Blanco Y Negro NEG 21*	44	7
11 Oct 86	DON'T LEAVE ME BEHIND *Blanco Y Negro NEG 23*	72	2
13 Feb 88	THESE EARLY DAYS *Blanco Y Negro NEG 30*	75	1
9 Jul 88 ●	I DON'T WANT TO TALK ABOUT IT *Blanco Y Negro NEG 34*	3	9
27 Jan 90	DRIVING *Blanco Y Negro NEG 40*	54	2
22 Feb 92	COVERS (EP) *Blanco Y Negro NEG 54*	13	6
24 Apr 93	THE ONLY LIVING BOY IN NEW YORK (EP) *Blanco Y Negro NEG 62CD*	42	5
19 Jun 93	I DIDN'T KNOW I WAS LOOKING FOR LOVE (EP) *Blanco Y Negro NEG 64CD*	72	1
4 Jun 94	ROLLERCOASTER (EP) *Blanco Y Negro NEG 69CD*	65	1
20 Aug 94	MISSING *Blanco Y Negro NEG 71CD1*	69	1
28 Oct 95 ●	MISSING (re-mix) *Blanco Y Negro NEG 84CD*	3	22
20 Apr 96 ●	WALKING WOUNDED *Virgin VSCDT 1577*	6	6
29 Jun 96 ●	WRONG *Virgin VSCDT 1589*	8	7
5 Oct 96	SINGLE *Virgin VSCDT 1600*	20	2
7 Dec 96	DRIVING (re-mix) *Blanco Y Negro NEG 99CD1*	36	2
1 Mar 97	BEFORE TODAY *Virgin VSCDT 1624*	25	2
3 Oct 98	THE FUTURE OF THE FUTURE (STAY GOLD) *Deconstruction 74321616252* [1]	31	2
25 Sep 99	FIVE FATHOMS *Virgin VSCDT 1742*	27	3
4 Mar 00	TEMPERAMENTAL *Virgin VSCDT 1761*	72	1
27 Jan 01	TRACEY IN MY ROOM *VC Recordings VCRD 78* [2]	34	2

[1] Deep Dish with Everything but the Girl [2] EBTG vs Soul Vision

Tracks on Covers (EP): Love Is Strange / Tougher Than the Rest / Time After Time / Alison. Tracks on The Only Living Boy in New York (EP): The Only Living Boy in New York / Birds / Gabriel / Horses in the Room. Tracks on I Didn't Know I Was Looking For Love (EP): I Didn't Know I Was Looking for Love / My Head Is My Only House Unless It Rains / Political Science / A Piece of My Mind. Tracks on Rollercoaster (EP): Rollercoaster / Straight Back to You / Lights of Te Touan / I Didn't Know I Was Looking for Love (demo)

E'VOKE
UK, female vocal duo – Marlaine Gordon and Kerry Potter (9 WEEKS) pos/wks
25 Nov 95	RUNAWAY *Ffrreedom TABCD 238*	30	3
24 Aug 96	ARMS OF LOREN *Manifesto FESCD 10*	25	3
2 Feb 02	ARMS OF LOREN (re-mix) *Inferno CDFERN 001*	31	3

EVOLUTION
UK, male / female vocal / instrumental group (12 WEEKS) pos/wks
20 Mar 93	LOVE THING *Deconstruction 74321134272*	32	2
3 Jul 93	EVERYBODY DANCE *Deconstruction 74321152012*	19	5
8 Jan 94	EVOLUTIONDANCE PART ONE (EP) *Deconstruction 74321171912*	52	3
4 Nov 95	LOOK UP TO THE LIGHT *Deconstruction 74321318042*	55	1
19 Oct 96	YOUR LOVE IS CALLING *Deconstruction 74321422872*	60	1

Tracks on Evolutiondance Part One (EP): Escape 2 Alcatraz (remix) / Everybody / Don't Stop the Rain

EX PISTOLS *UK, male vocal / instrumental group (2 WEEKS)* pos/wks
2 Feb 85	LAND OF HOPE AND GLORY *Virginia PISTOL 76*	69	2

EXCITERS *US, male / female vocal group (7 WEEKS)* pos/wks
21 Feb 63	TELL HIM *United Artists UP 1011*	46	1
4 Oct 75	REACHING FOR THE BEST *20th Century BTC 1005*	31	6

EXETER BRAMDEAN BOYS' CHOIR *UK, male choir (3 WEEKS)* pos/wks
18 Dec 93	REMEMBERING CHRISTMAS *Golden Sounds DSCC 1*	46	3

EXILE *US, male vocal / instrumental group (18 WEEKS)* pos/wks
19 Aug 78 ●	KISS YOU ALL OVER *RAK 279* ▲	6	12
12 May 79	HOW COULD THIS GO WRONG *RAK 293*	67	2
12 Sep 81	HEART AND SOUL *RAK 333*	54	4

EXOTERIX *UK, male producer – Duncan Millar (2 WEEKS)* pos/wks
24 Apr 93	VOID *Positiva CDTIV 1*	58	1
5 Feb 94	SATISFY MY LOVE *Union UCRCD 26*	62	1

EXOTICA featuring Itsy FOSTER
UK / Italy, male / female vocal / instrumental group (1 WEEK) pos/wks
16 Sep 95	THE SUMMER IS MAGIC *Polydor 5798392*	68	1

EXPLOITED *UK, male vocal / instrumental group (13 WEEKS)* pos/wks
18 Apr 81	DOGS OF WAR *Secret SHH 110*	63	4
17 Oct 81	DEAD CITIES *Secret SHH 120*	31	5
5 Dec 81	DON'T LET 'EM GRIND YOU DOWN *Superville EXP 1003* [1]	70	1
8 May 82	ATTACK *Secret SHH 130*	50	3

[1] Exploited and Anti-Pasti

EXPOSÉ *US, female vocal group (1 WEEK)* pos/wks
28 Aug 93	I'LL NEVER GET OVER YOU (GETTING OVER ME) *Arista 74321158962*	75	1

EXPRESS OF SOUND
Italy, male instrumental / production group (1 WEEK) pos/wks
2 Nov 96	REAL VIBRATION (WANT LOVE) *Positiva CDTIV 66*	45	1

EXPRESSOS
UK, male / female vocal / instrumental group (5 WEEKS) pos/wks
21 Jun 80	HEY GIRL *WEA K 18246*	60	3
14 Mar 81	TANGO IN MONO *WEA K 18431*	70	2

EXTENSIVE – See CHOPS-EMC + EXTENSIVE

EXTREME *US, male vocal / instrumental group (46 WEEKS)* pos/wks
8 Jun 91	GET THE FUNK OUT *A&M AM 737*	19	7
27 Jul 91 ●	MORE THAN WORDS *A&M AM 792* ▲	2	11

Re-entries are listed as (re), (2re), (3re), etc which signifies that the hit re-entered the chart once, twice or three times

12 Oct 91	DECADENCE DANCE *A&M AM 773*	36	3
23 Nov 91	HOLE HEAZE *A&M AM 698*	12	6
5 Sep 92	REST IN PEACE *A&M AM 0055*	13	5
14 Nov 92	STOP THE WORLD *A&M AM 0096*	22	2
6 Feb 93	TRAGIC COMIC *A&M AMCD 0156*	15	4
11 Mar 95	HIP TODAY *A&M 5809932*	44	1

EYE TO EYE featuring Taka BOOM *UK, male producer – Stuart Crichton, and US, female vocalist (2 WEEKS)* pos/wks

9 Jun 01	JUST CAN'T GET ENOUGH (NO NO NO NO) *Xtravaganza XTRAV 25CD*	36	2

See also UMBOZA; MUKKAA

EYES CREAM *Italy, male producer – Agostino Carollo (1 WEEK)* pos/wks

16 Oct 99	FLY AWAY (BYE BYE) *Accolade CDAC 001*	53	1

F

Adam F *UK, male producer – Adam Fenton (22 WEEKS)* pos/wks

27 Sep 97	CIRCLES *Positiva CDFJ 002*	20	3
7 Mar 98	MUSIC IN MY MIND *Positiva CDFJ 003*	27	3
15 Sep 01	SMASH SUMTHIN' *Def Jam 5886932* [1]	11	7
1 Dec 01	STAND CLEAR *Chrysalis CDEM 597* [2]	43	1
6 Apr 02	WHERE'S MY...? *EMI CDEMS 598* [3]	37	1
27 Apr 02	METROSOUND *Kaos KAOS 001P* [4]	54	1
8 Jun 02	STAND CLEAR (re-mix) *Kaos KAOSCD 002* [2]	50	1
31 Aug 02	SMASH SUMTHIN' (re-mix) *Kaos KAOSCD 003* [1]	47	2
14 Dec 02	DIRTY HARRY'S REVENGE *Kaos KAOS 004* [5]	50	1

[1] Redman featuring Adam F [2] Adam F featuring M.O.P. [3] Adam F featuring Lil' Mo [4] Adam F and J Majik [5] Adam F featuring Beenie Man

FBI – *See REDHEAD KINGPIN and the FBI*

FC KAHUNA *UK, male production duo (2 WEEKS)* pos/wks

6 Apr 02	GLITTERBALL *City Rockers ROCKERS 11CD*	64	1
20 Jul 02	MACHINE SAYS YES *City Rockers ROCKERS 18CD*	58	1

F45 – *See DE FUNK featuring F45*

FKW *UK, male vocal / instrumental group (8 WEEKS)* pos/wks

2 Oct 93	NEVER GONNA (GIVE YOU UP) *PWL International PWCD 273*	48	2
11 Dec 93	SEIZE THE DAY *PWL International PWCD 279*	45	2
5 Mar 94	JINGO *PWL International PWCD 283*	30	3
4 Jun 94	THIS IS THE WAY *PWL International PWCD 307*	63	1

FLB – *See FAT LARRY'S BAND*

F.L.O. – *See Rahni HARRIS and F.L.O.*

FM *UK, male vocal / instrumental group (11 WEEKS)* pos/wks

31 Jan 87	FROZEN HEART *Portrait DIDGE 1*	64	2
20 Jun 87	LET LOVE BE THE LEADER *Portrait MERV 1*	71	2
5 Aug 89	BAD LUCK *Epic 655031 7*	54	4
7 Oct 89	SOMEDAY (YOU'LL COME RUNNING) *CBS DINK 1*	64	2
10 Feb 90	EVERYTIME I THINK OF YOU *Epic DINK 2*	73	1

FPI PROJECT
Italy, male instrumental / production group (17 WEEKS) pos/wks

9 Dec 89	● GOING BACK TO MY ROOTS / RICH IN PARADISE *Rumour RUMAT 9*	9	12

9 Mar 91	EVERYBODY (ALL OVER THE WORLD) *Rumour RUMA 29*	65	3
7 Aug 93	COME ON (AND DO IT) *Synthetic SYNTH 006CD*	59	1
13 Mar 99	EVERYBODY (ALL OVER) (re-mix) *99 North CDNTH 14*	67	1

'Going Back to My Roots' was a vocal track available in two formats and featured either Paolo Dini or Sharon Dee Clarke

FAB *UK, male producers (11 WEEKS)* pos/wks

7 Jul 90	● THUNDERBIRDS ARE GO *Brothers Organisation FAB 1* [1]	5	8
20 Oct 90	THE PRISONER *Brothers Organisation FAB 6* [2]	56	2
1 Dec 90	THE STINGRAY MEGAMIX *Brothers Organisation FAB 2* [3]	66	1

[1] FAB featuring MC Parker [2] FAB featuring MC Number 6 [3] FAB featuring Aqua Marina

FAB! *Ireland, female vocal group (1 WEEK)* pos/wks

1 Aug 98	TURN AROUND *Break Records BRCX 107*	59	1

Shelley FABARES *US, female vocalist (4 WEEKS)* pos/wks

26 Apr 62	JOHNNY ANGEL *Pye International 7N 25132* ▲	41	4

FABIAN *US, male vocalist (1 WEEK)* pos/wks

10 Mar 60	HOUND DOG MAN *HMV POP 695*	46	1

Lara FABIAN *Belgium, female vocalist (1 WEEK)* pos/wks

28 Oct 00	I WILL LOVE AGAIN *Columbia 6694062*	63	1

FABULOUS BAKER BOYS
UK, male DJ / production trio (2 WEEKS) pos/wks

15 Nov 97	OH BOY *Multiply CDMULTY 28*	34	2

FACE – *See David MORALES*

FACES
UK, male vocal / instrumental group (46 WEEKS) pos/wks

18 Dec 71	● STAY WITH ME *Warner Bros. K 16136*	6	14
17 Feb 73	● CINDY INCIDENTALLY *Warner Bros. K 16247*	2	9
8 Dec 73	● POOL HALL RICHARD / I WISH IT WOULD RAIN *Warner Bros. K 16341*	8	11
7 Dec 74	YOU CAN MAKE ME DANCE SING OR ANYTHING (EVEN TAKE THE DOG FOR A WALK, MEND A FUSE, FOLD AWAY THE IRONING BOARD, OR ANY OTHER DOMESTIC SHORT COMINGS) *Warner Bros. K 16494* [1]	12	9
4 Jun 77	THE FACES (EP) *Riva 8*	41	3

[1] Faces / Rod Stewart

Tracks on The Faces (EP): Memphis / You Can Make Me Dance Sing or Anything / Stay with Me / Cindy Incidentally

See also Rod STEWART

FACTORY OF UNLIMITED RHYTHM
Jamaica, male / female vocal / instrumental group (1 WEEK) pos/wks

1 Jun 96	THE SWEETEST SURRENDER *Kuff KUFFD 6*	59	1

Donald FAGEN *US, male vocalist (2 WEEKS)* pos/wks

3 Jul 93	TOMORROW'S GIRLS *Reprise W 0180CDX*	46	2

See also STEELY DAN

Joe FAGIN *UK, male vocalist (20 WEEKS)* pos/wks

7 Jan 84	● THAT'S LIVIN' ALRIGHT *Towerbell TOW 46*	3	11
5 Apr 86	BACK WITH THE BOYS AGAIN / GET IT RIGHT *Towerbell TOW 84*	53	9

Jad FAIR – *See TEENAGE FANCLUB*

Yvonne FAIR
US, female vocalist, d. 6 Mar 1994 (11 WEEKS) pos/wks

24 Jan 76	● IT SHOULD HAVE BEEN ME *Tamla Motown TMG 1013*	5	11

BITTER SWEET SYMPHONY

■ Considering the aftermath of The Verve's recording of this song, a more apt title would be hard to find. Although 'Bitter Sweet Symphony' helped to shift seven million copies of their LP Urban Hymns, the use of a short musical sample resulted in a whirlwind of legal activity. This ultimately cost its writer, Richard Ashcroft, 100 per cent of his royalties, and led to his departure from and dissolution of the band in 1999. Ashcroft was no stranger to legal problems. Formed in 1991 in Wigan as simply Verve, the group had a lengthy legal battle with Verve Records which resulted in their name being elongated to The Verve. Ashcroft also got into deep trouble for pinching half of poet William Blake's 'London' for the song 'History' which appeared on their second album, A Northern Soul, in 1995. However, 'Bitter Sweet Symphony' was to incur the wrath of a number of music business giants.

While the infamous sample seems central to the song, few realise that 'Bitter Sweet Symphony' was written and considered finished before the producer Youth heard the track and suggested adding the string break. The contentious musical sequence was sourced from a 1965 album by the Andrew Oldham Orchestra. This might sound innocuous enough until one discovers that Andrew Oldham was at that time manager of The Rolling Stones, and the piece in question was an orchestrated version of their 1965 No.1 'The Last Time'. The Verve's record company, Virgin Records, had actually paid Decca, which released the original, for permission to use the offending sample, but one of the music industry's best known wheelers and dealers got wind of the affair. His name was Allen Klein, another former Stones manager, who owned the rights to their

■ **THIS WAS CASH THAT ASHCROFT WOULD SOON NEED BECAUSE THE NEXT MAN TO ARRIVE ON THE SCENE WAS A WRIT-BEARING ANDREW LOOG OLDHAM** ■

songs from the 1960s, and if The Verve were going to use part of 'The Last Time', then it was going to cost them ... everything. A plea to Mick Jagger and Keith Richards fell on deaf ears; there was no way they were going to get involved in a legal spectacle with Klein. Thus Mr Klein demanded – and received - the majority of the publishing royalties. Graciously, he did allow Richard Ashcroft to lay claim to the lyrics, although this didn't involve any royalties, just a relatively small one-off payment.

This was cash that Ashcroft would soon need because the next man to arrive on the scene was a writ-bearing Andrew Loog Oldham, who had unearthed a contract stating that Decca had lost the rights. He threatened to have Urban Hymns withdrawn from the market unless he received his percentage for the sample from his recording. Since the song-publishing royalties had all disappeared in Mr Klein's direction, he demanded a slice of the record royalties. The upshot of Klein and Oldham's legal intervention was that the sleeve credits on Urban Hymns now declare that

'Bitter Sweet Symphony' was "written by" Mick Jagger and Keith Richards, "performed by" The Andrew Oldham Orchestra and "produced by" Andrew Loog Oldham. The legal wranglings continue to this day, and the issue is rumoured to have cost The Verve £1m. For a few thousand pounds, the sample could have been re-recorded by an orchestra, avoiding many of the problems which ensued.

There is an ironic twist in this story. While the whole sordid business was based around the rights to the Mick Jagger and Keith Richards composition 'The Last Time', were these rights really theirs to claim in the first place? It seems that the two Stones had reportedly "borrowed" the idea themselves from a song by the Staple Singers called, 'This May Be the Last Time'. However, the Staples never sued the Stones and, anyway, who knows where they got the idea from?

■ Tony Burton

★ **ARTIST:**   The Verve

★ **LABEL:**   Hut UK/VC/Hut USA

★ **WRITERS:**   Mick Jagger and Keith Richards
                    Lyric by Richard Ashcroft

★ **PRODUCER:**   Andrew Loog Oldham courtesy of
                    The Decca Record Company Ltd.
                    (Actual producers of The Verve's
                    studio recording were Martin
                    Glover and The Verve.)

Richard Ashcroft looks understandably pensive

FAIR WEATHER UK, male vocal / instrumental group (12 WEEKS)pos/wks

18 Jul 70 ●	NATURAL SINNER RCA 1977	6	12

Fair Weather is led by Andy Fairweather-Low

See also Andy FAIRWEATHER-LOW; AMEN CORNER

FAIRGROUND ATTRACTION UK, female / male
vocal / instrumental group – lead vocal Eddi Reader (27 WEEKS) pos/wks

16 Apr 88 ★	PERFECT RCA PB 41845	1	13
30 Jul 88 ●	FIND MY LOVE RCA PB 42079	7	10
19 Nov 88	A SMILE IN A WHISPER RCA PB 42249	75	1
28 Jan 89	CLARE RCA PB 42607	49	3

See also Eddi READER

FAIRPORT CONVENTION
UK, male / female vocal / instrumental group (9 WEEKS) pos/wks

23 Jul 69	SI TU DOIS PARTIR (re) Island WIP 6064	21	9

Andy FAIRWEATHER-LOW UK, male vocalist (18 WEEKS) pos/wks

21 Sep 74 ●	REGGAE TUNE A&M AMS 7129	10	8
6 Dec 75 ●	WIDE EYED AND LEGLESS A&M AMS 7202	6	10

See also AMEN CORNER; FAIR WEATHER

Adam FAITH 48 Top 500

Teen-idol vocalist turned top actor then financial wizard, b. Terence Nelhams, 23 Jun 1940, London, d. 8 Mar 2003. One of the most charted acts of the 1960s; became the first UK artist to lodge initial seven hits in the Top 5. Also one of the first UK acts to record original songs regularly (252 WKS) pos/wks

20 Nov 59 ★	WHAT DO YOU WANT? Parlophone R 4591	1	19
22 Jan 60 ★	POOR ME Parlophone R 4623	1	18
14 Apr 60 ●	SOMEONE ELSE'S BABY Parlophone R 4643	2	13
30 Jun 60 ●	JOHNNY COMES MARCHING HOME / MADE YOU Parlophone R 4665 1	5	13
15 Sep 60 ●	HOW ABOUT THAT! Parlophone R 4689 1	4	14
17 Nov 60 ●	LONELY PUP (IN A CHRISTMAS SHOP) Parlophone R 4708	4	11
9 Feb 61 ●	WHO AM I! / THIS IS IT! Parlophone R 4735	5	14
27 Apr 61	EASY GOING ME Parlophone R 4766	12	10
20 Jul 61	DON'T YOU KNOW IT Parlophone R 4807	12	10
26 Oct 61 ●	THE TIME HAS COME Parlophone R 4837	4	14
18 Jan 62	LONESOME Parlophone R 4864 1	12	9
3 May 62 ●	AS YOU LIKE IT Parlophone R 4896 1	5	15
30 Aug 62 ●	DON'T THAT BEAT ALL Parlophone R 4930 2	8	11
13 Dec 62	BABY TAKE A BOW Parlophone R 4964	22	6
31 Jan 63	WHAT NOW Parlophone R 4990 2	31	5
11 Jul 63	WALKIN' TALL Parlophone R 5039	23	6
19 Sep 63 ●	THE FIRST TIME Parlophone R 5061 3	5	13
12 Dec 63	WE ARE IN LOVE Parlophone R 5091 3	11	12
12 Mar 64	IF HE TELLS YOU Parlophone R 5109 3	25	9
28 May 64	I LOVE BEING IN LOVE WITH YOU Parlophone R 5138 3	33	6
26 Nov 64	A MESSAGE TO MARTHA (KENTUCKY BLUEBIRD) Parlophone R 5201	12	11
11 Feb 65	STOP FEELING SORRY FOR YOURSELF Parlophone R 5235	23	6
17 Jun 65	SOMEONE'S TAKEN MARIA AWAY Parlophone R 5289	34	5
20 Oct 66	CHERYL'S GOIN' HOME Parlophone R 5516	46	2

1 With John Barry and His Orchestra 2 Adam Faith with Johnny Keating and His Orchestra 3 Adam Faith and The Roulettes

Horace FAITH Jamaica, male vocalist – Horace Smith (10 WEEKS) pos/wks

12 Sep 70	BLACK PEARL Trojan TR 7790	13	10

Percy FAITH Canada, orchestra, leader d. 9 Feb 1976 (31 WEEKS) pos/wks

4 Mar 60 ●	THE THEME FROM 'A SUMMER PLACE' Philips PB 989 ▲	2	31

FAITH BROTHERS
UK, male vocal / instrumental group (6 WEEKS) pos/wks

13 Apr 85	THE COUNTRY OF THE BLIND Siren SIREN 2	63	3

6 Jul 85	A STRANGER ON HOME GROUND Siren SIREN 4	69	3

FAITH, HOPE AND CHARITY
US, male / female vocal group (4 WEEKS) pos/wks

31 Jan 76	JUST ONE LOOK RCA 2632	38	4

FAITH, HOPE AND CHARITY
UK, female vocal group (3 WEEKS) pos/wks

23 Jun 90	BATTLE OF THE SEXES WEA YZ 480	53	3

FAITH NO MORE
US, male vocal / instrumental group (65 WEEKS) pos/wks

6 Feb 88	WE CARE A LOT Slash LASH 17	53	3
10 Feb 90	EPIC Slash LASH 21	37	4
14 Apr 90	FROM OUT OF NOWHERE Slash LASH 24	23	6
14 Jul 90	FALLING TO PIECES Slash LASH 25	41	3
8 Sep 90	EPIC (re-issue) Slash LASH 26	25	5
6 Jun 92 ●	MIDLIFE CRISIS Slash LASH 37	10	5
8 Aug 92	A SMALL VICTORY Slash LASH 39	29	5
12 Sep 92	A SMALL VICTORY (re-mix) Slash LASHX 40	55	1
21 Nov 92	EVERYTHING'S RUINED Slash LASH 43	28	3
16 Jan 93 ●	I'M EASY / BE AGGRESSIVE (re) Slash LACDP 44	3	8
6 Nov 93	ANOTHER BODY MURDERED Epic 6597942 1	26	3
11 Mar 95	DIGGING THE GRAVE Slash LASCD 51	16	4
27 May 95	RICOCHET Slash LASCD 53	27	2
29 Jul 95	EVIDENCE Slash LASCD 54	32	3
31 May 97	ASHES TO ASHES Slash LASCD 61	15	3
16 Aug 97	LAST CUP OF SORROW Slash LASCD 62	51	2
13 Dec 97	THIS TOWN AIN'T BIG ENOUGH FOR BOTH OF US Roadrunner RR 22513 2	40	2
17 Jan 98	ASHES TO ASHES (re-issue) Slash LACDP 63	29	3
7 Nov 98	I STARTED A JOKE Slash LASCD 65	49	1

1 Faith No More and Boo-Yaa T.R.I.B.E. 2 Sparks vs Faith No More

Marianne FAITHFULL UK, female vocalist (59 WEEKS) pos/wks

13 Aug 64 ●	AS TEARS GO BY Decca F 11923	9	13
18 Feb 65 ●	COME AND STAY WITH ME Decca F 12075	4	13
6 May 65 ●	THIS LITTLE BIRD Decca F 12162	6	11
22 Jul 65 ●	SUMMER NIGHTS Decca F 12193	10	10
4 Nov 65	YESTERDAY Decca F 12268	36	4
9 Mar 67	IS THIS WHAT I GET FOR LOVING YOU? Decca F 22524	43	2
24 Nov 79	THE BALLAD OF LUCY JORDAN Island WIP 6491	48	6

FAITHLESS
UK, male / female vocal / instrumental group (72 WEEKS) pos/wks

5 Aug 95	SALVA MEA (SAVE ME) Cheeky CHEKCD 008	30	2
9 Dec 95	INSOMNIA Cheeky CHEKCD 010	27	2
23 Mar 96	DON'T LEAVE Cheeky CHEKCD 012	34	2
26 Oct 96 ●	INSOMNIA (re-issue) Cheeky CHEKCD 017	3	13
21 Dec 96 ●	SALVA MEA (re-mix) Cheeky CHEKCD 018	9	7
26 Apr 97 ●	REVERENCE Cheeky CHEKCD 019	10	3
15 Nov 97	DON'T LEAVE (re-mix) Cheeky CHEKXCD 024	21	2
5 Sep 98 ●	GOD IS A DJ Cheeky CHEKCD 028	6	8
5 Dec 98	TAKE THE LONG WAY HOME Cheeky CHEKCD 031	15	6
1 May 99	BRING MY FAMILY BACK Cheeky CHEKCD 035	14	5
16 Jun 01 ●	WE COME 1 Cheeky 74321850842	3	10
29 Sep 01	MUHAMMAD ALI (re) Cheeky 74321886442	29	4
29 Dec 01	TARANTULA (re) Cheeky 74321903592	29	5
20 Apr 02 ●	ONE STEP TOO FAR Cheeky / Arista 74321926412 1	6	3

1 Faithless featuring Dido

See also ROLLO; DUSTED; OUR TRIBE / ONE TRIBE; SPHINX

FALCO
Austria, male vocalist – Johann Holzel, d. 6 Feb 1998 (26 WEEKS) pos/wks

22 Mar 86 ★	ROCK ME AMADEUS A&M AM 278 ▲	1	15
31 May 86 ●	VIENNA CALLING A&M AM 318	10	8
2 Aug 86	JEANNY A&M AM 333	68	1
27 Sep 86	THE SOUND OF MUSIK WEA U 8591	61	2

Re-entries are listed as (re), (2re), (3re), etc which signifies that the hit re-entered the chart once, twice or three times, etc

Christian FALK featuring DEMETREUS
Sweden, male producer and Sweden, male vocalist (3 WEEKS)   pos/wks

26 Aug 00	**MAKE IT RIGHT** *London LONCD 452*	**22** 3

Fred FALKE – *See Alan BRAXE and Fred FALKE*

FALL *UK, male / female vocal / instrumental group – leader Mark E Smith (26 WEEKS)*   pos/wks

13 Sep 86	**MR PHARMACIST** *Beggars Banquet BEG 168*	**75** 1
20 Dec 86	**HEY! LUCIANI** *Beggars Banquet BEG 176*	**59** 1
9 May 87	**THERE'S A GHOST IN MY HOUSE** *Beggars Banquet BEG 187*	**30** 4
31 Oct 87	**HIT THE NORTH** *Beggars Banquet BEG 200*	**57** 5
30 Jan 88	**VICTORIA** *Beggars Banquet BEG 206*	**35** 3
26 Nov 88	**BIG NEW PRINZ / JERUSALEM (DOUBLE SINGLE)** *Beggars Banquet FALL 2/3*	**59** 2
27 Jan 90	**TELEPHONE THING** *Cog Sinister SIN 4*	**58** 1
8 Sep 90	**WHITE LIGHTNING** *Cog Sinister SIN 6*	**56** 2
14 Mar 92	**FREE RANGE** *Cog Sinister SINS 8*	**40** 1
17 Apr 93	**WHY ARE PEOPLE GRUDGEFUL** *Permanent CDSPERM 9*	**43** 1
25 Dec 93	**BEHIND THE COUNTER** *Permanent CDSPERM 13*	**75** 1
30 Apr 94	**15 WAYS** *Permanent CDSPERM 14*	**65** 1
17 Feb 96	**THE CHISELERS** *Jet JETSCD 500*	**60** 1
21 Feb 98	**MASQUERADE** *Artful CDARTFUL 1*	**69** 1
14 Dec 02	**FALL VS 2003** *Action TAKE 020CD*	**64** 1

Tracks on 'Big New Prinz / Jerusalem' double single: Big New Prinz / Wrong Place Right Time Number Two / Jerusalem / Acid Priest 2088

See also Mark E SMITH

FALLACY & FUSION *UK, male production / rap duo (2 WEEKS)*   pos/wks

22 Jun 02	**THE GROUNDBREAKER** *Wordplay WORDCD 036*	**47** 2

Harold FALTERMEYER
Germany, male instrumentalist – keyboards (23 WEEKS)   pos/wks

23 Mar 85 ●	**AXEL F (re)** *MCA MCA 949*	**2** 22
24 Aug 85	**FLETCH THEME** *MCA MCA 991*	**74** 1

'Axel F' reached its peak position only in Jun 1985

Agnetha FALTSKOG *Sweden, female vocalist (12 WEEKS)*   pos/wks

28 May 83	**THE HEAT IS ON** *Epic A 3436*	**35** 6
13 Aug 83	**WRAP YOUR ARMS AROUND ME** *Epic A 3622*	**44** 5
22 Oct 83	**CAN'T SHAKE LOOSE** *Epic A 3812*	**63** 1

See also ABBA

Georgie FAME   245   Top 500
Critically acclaimed R&B / jazz vocalist / keyboard player, b. Clive Powell, 26 Jun 1943, Lancashire, UK. The one-time rock 'n' roll tour musician, who had a string of Sixties hits, is still a popular performer, often working with contemporaries such as Van Morrison and Bill Wyman (115 WEEKS) pos/wks

17 Dec 64 ★	**YEH, YEH** *Columbia DB 7428* [1]	**1** 12
4 Mar 65	**IN THE MEANTIME** *Columbia DB 7494* [1]	**22** 8
29 Jul 65	**LIKE WE USED TO BE** *Columbia DB 7633* [1]	**33** 7
28 Oct 65	**SOMETHING** *Columbia DB 7727* [1]	**23** 7
23 Jun 66 ★	**GET AWAY** *Columbia DB 7946* [1]	**1** 11
22 Sep 66	**SUNNY** *Columbia DB 8015*	**13** 8
22 Dec 66	**SITTING IN THE PARK** *Columbia DB 8096* [1]	**12** 10
23 Mar 67	**BECAUSE I LOVE YOU** *CBS 202587*	**15** 8
13 Sep 67	**TRY MY WORLD** *CBS 2945*	**37** 5
13 Dec 67 ★	**THE BALLAD OF BONNIE AND CLYDE** *CBS 3124*	**1** 13
9 Jul 69	**PEACEFUL** *CBS 4295*	**16** 9
13 Dec 69	**SEVENTH SON** *CBS 4459*	**25** 7
10 Apr 71	**ROSETTA** *CBS 7108* [2]	**11** 10

[1] Georgie Fame and The Blue Flames   [2] Fame and Price Together

FAMILY *UK, male vocal / instrumental group (44 WEEKS)*   pos/wks

1 Nov 69	**NO MULE'S FOOL** *Reprise RS 27001*	**29** 7
22 Aug 70	**STRANGE BAND** *Reprise RS 27009*	**11** 12

17 Jul 71 ●	**IN MY OWN TIME** *Reprise K 14090*	**4** 13
23 Sep 72	**BURLESQUE** *Reprise K 14196*	**13** 12

FAMILY CAT *UK, male vocal / instrumental group (4 WEEKS)*   pos/wks

28 Aug 93	**AIRPLANE GARDENS / ATMOSPHERIC ROAD** *Dedicated FCUK 003CD*	**69** 1
21 May 94	**WONDERFUL EXCUSE** *Dedicated 74321208432*	**48** 1
30 Jul 94	**GOLDENBOOK** *Dedicated 74321220072*	**42** 2

FAMILY COOKIN' – *See LIMMIE and the FAMILY COOKIN'*

FAMILY DOGG *UK, male / female vocal group (14 WEEKS)*   pos/wks

28 May 69 ●	**A WAY OF LIFE** *Bell 1055*	**6** 14

FAMILY FOUNDATION
UK, male / female vocal / instrumental group (4 WEEKS)   pos/wks

13 Jun 92	**XPRESS YOURSELF** *380 PEW 1*	**42** 4

FAMILY STAND
US, male / female vocal / instrumental group (13 WEEKS)   pos/wks

31 Mar 90 ●	**GHETTO HEAVEN** *East West A 7997*	**10** 11
17 Jan 98	**GHETTO HEAVEN (re-mix)** *Perfecto PERF 156CD1*	**30** 2

FAMILY STONE – *See SLY and the FAMILY STONE*

FAMOUS FLAMES – *See James BROWN*

FANTASTIC FOUR *US, male vocal group (4 WEEKS)*   pos/wks

24 Feb 79	**B.Y.O.F. (BRING YOUR OWN FUNK)** *Atlantic LV 14*	**62** 4

FANTASTICS *US, male vocal group (12 WEEKS)*   pos/wks

27 Mar 71 ●	**SOMETHING OLD, SOMETHING NEW** *Bell 1141*	**9** 12

FANTASY UFO *UK, male instrumental group (6 WEEKS)*   pos/wks

29 Sep 90	**FANTASY** *XL XLT 15*	**56** 3
10 Aug 91	**MIND BODY SOUL** *Strictly Underground YZ 591* [1]	**50** 3

[1] Fantasy UFO featuring Jay Groove

FAR CORPORATION *UK / US / Germany / Switzerland, male vocal / instrumental group (11 WEEKS)*   pos/wks

26 Oct 85 ●	**STAIRWAY TO HEAVEN** *Arista ARIST 639*	**8** 11

Don FARDON *UK, male vocalist – Donald Maughn (22 WEEKS)*   pos/wks

18 Apr 70	**BELFAST BOY** *Young Blood YB 1010*	**32** 5
10 Oct 70 ●	**INDIAN RESERVATION** *Young Blood YB 1015*	**3** 17

FARGETTA *Italy / UK, male producer – Mario Fargetta (3 WEEKS)*   pos/wks

23 Jan 93	**MUSIC** *Synthetic CDR 6334* [1]	**34** 2
10 Aug 96	**THE MUSIC IS MOVING** *Arista 74321381572*	**74** 1

[1] Fargetta and Anne-Marie Smith

See also TAMPERER featuring MAYA

Chris FARLOWE *UK, male vocalist – John Deighton (36 WEEKS)*   pos/wks

27 Jan 66	**THINK (re)** *Immediate IM 023*	**37** 3
23 Jun 66 ★	**OUT OF TIME** *Immediate IM 035*	**1** 13
27 Oct 66	**RIDE ON BABY** *Immediate IM 038*	**31** 7
16 Feb 67	**MY WAY OF GIVING IN** *Immediate IM 041*	**48** 1
29 Jun 67	**MOANIN'** *Immediate IM 056*	**46** 2
13 Dec 67	**HANDBAGS AND GLADRAGS** *Immediate IM 065*	**33** 6
27 Sep 75	**OUT OF TIME (re-issue)** *Immediate IMS 101*	**44** 4

FARM *UK, male vocal / instrumental group (54 WEEKS)*   pos/wks

5 May 90	**STEPPING STONE / FAMILY OF MAN** *Produce MILK 101*	**58** 4
1 Sep 90 ●	**GROOVY TRAIN** *Produce MILK 102*	**6** 10
8 Dec 90 ●	**ALL TOGETHER NOW** *Produce MILK 103*	**4** 12

13 Apr 91	**SINFUL! (SCARY JIGGIN' WITH DR LOVE)**				
	Siren SRN 138 1			28	5
4 May 91	**DON'T LET ME DOWN** *Produce MILK 104*			36	3
24 Aug 91	**MIND** *Produce MILK 105*			31	4
14 Dec 91	**LOVE SEE NO COLOUR** *Produce MILK 106*			58	4
4 Jul 92	**RISING SUN** *End Product 6581737*			48	3
17 Oct 92	**DON'T YOU WANT ME** *End Product 6584687*			18	5
2 Jan 93	**LOVE SEE NO COLOUR (re-mix)**				
	End Product 6588682			35	4

1 Pete Wylie with The Farm

FARMERS BOYS
UK, male vocal / instrumental group (17 WEEKS) — pos/wks

9 Apr 83	**MUCK IT OUT** *EMI 5380*	48	6
30 Jul 83	**FOR YOU** *EMI 5401*	66	3
4 Aug 84	**IN THE COUNTRY** *EMI FAB 2*	44	5
3 Nov 84	**PHEW WOW** *EMI FAB 3*	59	3

John FARNHAM *Australia, male vocalist (17 WEEKS)* — pos/wks

25 Apr 87 ●	**YOU'RE THE VOICE** *Wheatley PB 41093*	6	17

Joanne FARRELL *US, female vocalist (2 WEEKS)* — pos/wks

24 Jun 95	**ALL I WANNA DO** *Big Beat A 8194CD*	40	2

Joe FARRELL
US, male instrumentalist – saxophone, d. 10 Jan 1986 (4 WEEKS) — pos/wks

16 Dec 78	**NIGHT DANCING** *Warner Bros. LV 2*	57	4

Dionne FARRIS *US, female vocalist (6 WEEKS)* — pos/wks

18 Mar 95	**I KNOW (re)** *Columbia 6613542*	41	5
7 Jun 97	**HOPELESS** *Columbia 6645165*	42	1

Gene FARROW with the GF BAND
UK, male vocal / instrumental group (8 WEEKS) — pos/wks

1 Apr 78	**MOVE YOUR BODY (re)** *Magnet MAG 109*	33	6
5 Aug 78	**DON'T STOP NOW (re)** *Magnet MAG 125*	71	2

FASCINATIONS *US, female vocal group (6 WEEKS)* — pos/wks

3 Jul 71	**GIRLS ARE OUT TO GET YOU** *Mojo 2092 004*	32	6

FASHION
UK, male vocal / instrumental group (12 WEEKS) — pos/wks

3 Apr 82	**STREETPLAYER (MECHANIK)** *Arista ARIST 456*	46	5
21 Aug 82	**LOVE SHADOW** *Arista ARIST 483*	51	5
18 Feb 84	**EYE TALK** *Epic A 4106*	69	2

Susan FASSBENDER *UK, female vocalist (8 WEEKS)* — pos/wks

17 Jan 81	**TWILIGHT CAFE** *CBS 9468*	21	8

FASTBALL *US, male vocal / instrumental trio (5 WEEKS)* — pos/wks

3 Oct 98	**THE WAY** *Polydor 5699472*	21	5

FASTWAY *UK, male vocal / instrumental group (1 WEEK)* — pos/wks

2 Apr 83	**EASY LIVIN'** *CBS A 3196*	74	1

FAT BOYS *US, male rap group (29 WEEKS)* — pos/wks

4 May 85	**JAIL HOUSE RAP** *Sutra U 9123*	63	2
22 Aug 87 ●	**WIPEOUT** *Urban URB 5* 1	2	12
18 Jun 88 ●	**THE TWIST (YO, TWIST)** *Urban URB 20* 2	2	11
5 Nov 88	**LOUIE LOUIE** *Urban URB 26*	46	4

1 Fat Boys and The Beach Boys 2 Fat Boys and Chubby Checker

FAT JOE *US, male rapper (17 WEEKS)* — pos/wks

1 Apr 00	**FEELIN' SO GOOD** *Columbia 6691972* 1	15	6
30 Mar 02	**WE THUGGIN'** *Atlantic AT 0124CD*	48	1

25 May 02 ●	**WHAT'S LUV?** *Atlantic AT 0128CD* 2		4	8
14 Dec 02	**CRUSH TONIGHT** *Atlantic AT 0142CD* 3		42	2

1 Jennifer Lopez featuring Big Pun and Fat Joe 2 Fat Joe featuring Ashanti
3 Fat Joe featuring Ginuwine

FAT LADY SINGS
Ireland, male vocal / instrumental group (2 WEEKS) — pos/wks

17 Jul 93	**DRUNKARD LOGIC** *East West YZ 756CD*	56	2

FAT LARRY'S BAND
US, male vocal / instrumental group (26 WEEKS) — pos/wks

2 Jul 77	**CENTER CITY** *Atlantic K 10951*	31	5
10 Mar 79	**BOOGIE TOWN** *Fantasy FTC 168* 1	46	4
18 Aug 79	**LOOKING FOR LOVE TONIGHT** *Fantasy FTC 179* 2	46	4
18 Sep 82	**ZOOM** *Virgin VS 546*	2	11

1 FLB 2 Fat Larry's Band (FLB)

FAT LES *UK, male / female vocal group (22 WEEKS)* — pos/wks

20 Jun 98 ●	**VINDALOO** *Telstar CDSTAS 2982*	2	12
19 Dec 98	**NAUGHTY CHRISTMAS (GOBLIN IN THE OFFICE)**		
	Turtleneck NECKCD 001	21	5
17 Jun 00 ●	**JERUSALEM (re)** *Parlophone CDR 6540* 1	10	5

1 Fat Les 2000

FATBACK BAND
US, male vocal / instrumental group (67 WEEKS) — pos/wks

6 Sep 75	**YUM, YUM (GIMME SOME)** *Polydor 2066 590*	40	6
6 Dec 75	**(ARE YOU READY) DO THE BUS STOP** *Polydor 2066 637*	18	10
21 Feb 76 ●	**(DO THE) SPANISH HUSTLE** *Polydor 2066 656*	10	7
29 May 76	**PARTY TIME** *Polydor 2066 682*	41	4
14 Aug 76	**NIGHT FEVER** *Spring 2066 706*	38	4
12 Mar 77	**DOUBLE DUTCH** *Spring 2066 777*	31	4
9 Aug 80	**BACKSTROKIN'** *Spring POSP 149* 1	41	9
23 Jun 84 ●	**I FOUND LOVIN' (re)** *Master Mix CHE 8401*	7	16
4 May 85	**GIRLS ON MY MIND** *Atlantic/Cotillion FBACK 1* 1	69	2
6 Sep 86	**I FOUND LOVIN' (re-issue)** *Important TAN 10*	55	5

1 Fatback

FATBOY SLIM (497) Top 500

Multi-aliased, superstar DJ / producer Norman Cook (b. Quentin Cook, 31 Jul 1963, Bromley, Kent, UK) finally achieved a solo No.1 in this guise, having already topped the chart with Housemartins and Beats International. Married TV / radio presenter Zoë Ball in 1999 (73 WEEKS) — pos/wks

3 May 97	**GOING OUT OF MY HEAD** *Skint SKINT 19CD*	57	1
1 Nov 97	**EVERYBODY NEEDS A 303** *Skint SKINT 31CD*	34	2
20 Jun 98 ●	**THE ROCKAFELLER SKANK** *Skint SKINT 35CD*	6	10
17 Oct 98 ●	**GANGSTER TRIPPIN'** *Skint SKINT 39CD*	3	8
16 Jan 99 ★	**PRAISE YOU** *Skint SKINT 42CD* ■	1	12
1 May 99 ●	**RIGHT HERE RIGHT NOW** *Skint SKINT 46CD*	2	10
1 May 99	**BADDER BADDER SCHWING** *Eye Q EYEUK 040CD* 1	34	2
28 Oct 00 ●	**SUNSET (BIRD OF PREY) (re)** *Skint SKINT 58CD*	9	13
20 Jan 01	**DEMONS** *Skint SKINT 60CD* 2	16	5
5 May 01 ●	**STAR 69** *Skint SKINT 64CD*	10	7
15 Sep 01	**YA MAMA / SONG FOR SHELTER** *Skint SKINT 71CD*	30	2
26 Jan 02	**RETOX** *Skint SKINT FAT 18*	73	1

1 Freddy Fresh featuring Fatboy Slim 2 Fatboy Slim featuring Macy Gray

*See also Norman COOK; BEATS INTERNATIONAL; MIGHTY DUB KATZ;
HOUSEMARTINS; FREAKPOWER; PIZZAMAN; URBAN ALL STARS*

FATHER ABRAHAM – See SMURFS

FATHER ABRAPHART and the SMURPS – See Jonathan KING

FATIMA MANSIONS
Ireland, male vocal / instrumental group (11 WEEKS) — pos/wks

23 May 92	**EVIL MAN** *Radioactive SKX 56*	59	1
1 Aug 92	**1000 %** *Radioactive SKX 59*	61	3

| 19 Sep 92 ● | (EVERYTHING I DO) I DO IT FOR YOU *Columbia 6583827* | 7 | 6 |
| 6 Aug 94 | THE LOYALISER *Kitchenware SKCD 67* | 58 | 1 |

'(Everything I Do) I Do It For You' was listed with 'Theme From M.A.S.H. (Suicide Is Painless)' by Manic Street Preachers

FEAR FACTORY *US, male vocal / instrumental group (1 WEEK)* pos/wks
| 9 Oct 99 | CARS *Roadrunner RR 21893* | 57 | 1 |

Phil FEARON *UK, male vocalist (63 WEEKS)* pos/wks
23 Apr 83 ●	DANCING TIGHT *Ensign ENY 501* [1]	4	11
30 Jul 83	WAIT UNTIL TONIGHT (MY LOVE) *Ensign ENY 503* [1]	20	8
22 Oct 83	FANTASY REAL *Ensign ENY 507* [2]	41	6
10 Mar 84 ●	WHAT DO I DO *Ensign ENY 510* [2]	5	10
14 Jul 84 ●	EVERYBODY'S LAUGHING *Ensign ENY 514* [2]	10	10
15 Jun 85	YOU DON'T NEED A REASON *Ensign ENY 517* [2]	42	4
27 Jul 85	THIS KIND OF LOVE *Ensign ENY 521* [3]	70	3
2 Aug 86 ●	I CAN PROVE IT *Ensign PF 1*	8	9
15 Nov 86	AIN'T NOTHING BUT A HOUSEPARTY *Ensign PF 2*	60	2

[1] Galaxy featuring Phil Fearon [2] Phil Fearon and Galaxy [3] Phil Fearon and Galaxy featuring Dee Galdes

FEEDER *UK, male vocal / instrumental group (42 WEEKS)* pos/wks
8 Mar 97	TANGERINE *Echo ECSCD 32*	60	1
10 May 97	CEMENT *Echo ECSCX 36*	53	1
23 Aug 97	CRASH *Echo ECSCD 42*	48	1
18 Oct 97	HIGH *Echo ECSCD 44*	24	2
28 Feb 98	SUFFOCATE *Echo ECSCX 52*	37	1
3 Apr 99	DAY IN DAY OUT *Echo ECSCD 75*	31	2
12 Jun 99	INSOMNIA *Echo ECSCD 77*	22	3
21 Aug 99	YESTERDAY WENT TOO SOON *Echo ECSCD 79*	20	3
20 Nov 99	PAPERFACES *Echo ECSCD 85*	41	2
20 Jan 01 ●	BUCK ROGERS *Echo ECSCD 106*	5	6
14 Apr 01	SEVEN DAYS IN THE SUN (re) *Echo ECSCD 107*	14	6
14 Jul 01	TURN *Echo ECSCD 116*	27	2
22 Dec 01	JUST A DAY (EP) *Echo ECSCD 121*	12	7
12 Oct 02	COME BACK AROUND (re) *Echo ECSCD 130*	14	5

Tracks on 'Just a Day' (EP): 'Just a Day', 'Can't Stop Losing You', 'Piece By Piece' (last two tracks are video only)

Wilton FELDER *US, male instrumentalist – tenor sax (7 WEEKS)* pos/wks
| 1 Nov 80 | INHERIT THE WIND *MCA 646* | 39 | 5 |
| 16 Feb 85 | (NO MATTER HOW HIGH I GET) I'LL STILL BE LOOKIN' UP TO YOU *MCA MCA 919* [1] | 63 | 2 |

[1] Featuring Bobby Womack and introducing Alltrina Grayson

FELICIA – See B.M.R. featuring FELICIA

José FELICIANO
US, male vocalist / instrumentalist – guitar (23 WEEKS) pos/wks
| 18 Sep 68 ● | LIGHT MY FIRE *RCA 1715* | 6 | 16 |
| 18 Oct 69 | AND THE SUN WILL SHINE *RCA 1871* | 25 | 7 |

FELIX *UK, male producer – Francis Wright (29 WEEKS)* pos/wks
8 Aug 92 ●	DON'T YOU WANT ME *Deconstruction 74321110507*	6	11
24 Oct 92	IT WILL MAKE ME CRAZY *Deconstruction 74321118137*	11	6
22 May 93	STARS *Deconstruction 74321147102*	29	3
12 Aug 95 ●	DON'T YOU WANT ME (re-mix) *Deconstruction 74321293972*	10	5
19 Oct 96	DON'T YOU WANT ME (2nd Re-Mix) *Deconstruction 74321418142*	17	4

Julie FELIX *US, female vocalist (19 WEEKS)* pos/wks
| 18 Apr 70 | IF I COULD (EL CONDOR PASA) *RAK 101* | 19 | 11 |
| 17 Oct 70 | HEAVEN IS HERE *RAK 105* | 22 | 8 |

FELIX DA HOUSECAT
US, male producer – Felix Stallings Jr (5 WEEKS) pos/wks
| 6 Sep 97 | DIRTY MOTHA *Manifesto FESCD 29* | 66 | 1 |

14 Jul 01	SILVER SCREEN SHOWER SCENE *City Rockers ROCKERS 1CD*	55	1
2 Mar 02	WHAT DOES IT FEEL LIKE? *City Rockers ROCKERS 8CD*	66	1
5 Oct 02	SILVER SCREEN SHOWER SCENE (re-mix) *City Rockers ROCKERS 19CD*	39	2

FELLY – See TECHNOTRONIC

FELON *UK, female vocalist – Simone Locker (2 WEEKS)* pos/wks
| 23 Mar 02 | GET OUT *Serious SERR 032CD* | 31 | 2 |

FE-M@IL *UK, female vocal group (2 WEEKS)* pos/wks
| 5 Aug 00 | FLEE FLY FLO *Jive 9250592* | 46 | 2 |

FEMME FATALE
US, male / female vocal / instrumental group (2 WEEKS) pos/wks
| 11 Feb 89 | FALLING IN AND OUT OF LOVE *MCA MCA 1309* | 69 | 2 |

FENDERMEN *US, male vocal / instrumental duo*
– Phil Humphrey and Jim Sundquist – guitars (9 WEEKS) pos/wks
| 18 Aug 60 | MULE SKINNER BLUES (2re) *Top Rank JAR 395* | 32 | 9 |

FENIX TX *US, male vocal / instrumental group (1 WEEK)* pos/wks
| 11 May 02 | THREESOME *MCA MCSTD 40279* | 66 | 1 |

FENMEN – See Bern ELLIOTT and the FENMEN

George FENTON and Jonas GWANGWA
UK / South Africa, male instrumental / production duo (1 WEEK) pos/wks
| 2 Jan 88 | CRY FREEDOM *MCA MCA 1228* | 75 | 1 |

The listed flip side of 'Cry Freedom' was 'The Funeral' by Thuli Dumakude

Peter FENTON *UK, male vocalist (3 WEEKS)* pos/wks
| 10 Nov 66 | MARBLE BREAKS IRON BENDS *Fontana TF 748* | 46 | 3 |

Shane FENTON and The FENTONES
UK, male instrumental group (32 WEEKS) pos/wks
26 Oct 61	I'M A MOODY GUY *Parlophone R 4827*	22	8
1 Feb 62	WALK AWAY *Parlophone R 4866*	38	5
5 Apr 62	IT'S ALL OVER NOW *Parlophone R 4883*	29	7
19 Apr 62	THE MEXICAN *Parlophone R 4899* [1]	41	3
12 Jul 62	CINDY'S BIRTHDAY *Parlophone R 4921*	19	8
27 Sep 62	THE BREEZE AND I *Parlophone R 4937* [1]	48	1

[1] The Fentones

See Shane FENTON and The FENTONES; Alvin STARDUST

FERGIE
Ireland, male DJ / producer – Robert Ferguson (5 WEEKS) pos/wks
9 Sep 00	DECEPTION *Duty Free DF 020CD*	47	1
25 Nov 00	HOOVERS & HORNS *Nukleuz NUKC 0185* [1]	57	2
10 Aug 02	THE BASS EP *Duty Free / Decode DFTELCX 004*	47	2

[1] Fergie & BK

Tracks on The Bass EP: Mixes of 'Bass Generator' / 'Bass Has Got Me On'

Sheila FERGUSON *US, female vocalist (1 WEEK)* pos/wks
| 5 Feb 94 | WHEN WILL I SEE YOU AGAIN *XSrhythm CDSTAS 2711* | 60 | 1 |

See also THREE DEGREES

FERKO STRING BAND *US, male instrumental group (2 WEEKS)* pos/wks
| 12 Aug 55 | ALABAMA JUBILEE *London HL 8140* | 20 | 2 |

Luisa FERNANDEZ *Spain, female vocalist (8 WEEKS)* pos/wks
| 11 Nov 78 | LAY LOVE ON YOU *Warner Bros. K 17061* | 31 | 8 |

Pamela FERNANDEZ
US, female vocalist (3 WEEKS)   pos/wks

| 17 Sep 94 | KICKIN' IN THE BEAT *Ore AG 5CD* .... | 43 | 2 |
| 3 Jun 95 | LET'S START OVER / KICKIN' IN THE BEAT (re-mix) *Ore AG 9CD* .... | 59 | 1 |

FERRANTE and TEICHER
US, male instrumental duo – Arthur Ferrante and Louis Teicher – pianos (18 WEEKS)   pos/wks

| 18 Aug 60 | THEME FROM 'THE APARTMENT' *London HLT 9164* .... | 44 | 1 |
| 9 Mar 61 | ● EXODUS (THEME FROM 'EXODUS') *London HLT 9298 and HMV POP 881* .... | 6 | 17 |

Exodus (Theme from 'Exodus') available first on London, then on HMV when the US label, United Artists, changed its UK outlet

Jose FERRER
US, male actor / vocalist – Jose Vincente Ferrer y Centron, d. 26 Jan 1992 (3 WEEKS)   pos/wks

| 19 Feb 54 | ● WOMAN (UH-HUH) *Philips PB220* .... | 7 | 3 |

'Woman (Uh-Huh)' coupled with 'Man (Uh-Huh)' by Rosemary Clooney

Tony FERRINO
UK, male vocalist – comedian Steve Coogan (2 WEEKS)   pos/wks

| 23 Nov 96 | HELP YOURSELF / BIGAMY AT CHRISTMAS *RCA 74321430302* .... | 42 | 2 |

Bryan FERRY (200) (Top 500)
Stylish UK vocalist / songwriter, b. 26 Sep 1945, Tyne and Wear. Sophisticated singer who split his time between solo career and fronting the visually stimulating Roxy Music. Still having Top 20 albums in 2002 (133 WEEKS)   pos/wks

29 Sep 73	● A HARD RAIN'S A-GONNA FALL *Island WIP 6170*	10	9
25 May 74	THE 'IN' CROWD *Island WIP 6196*	13	6
31 Aug 74	SMOKE GETS IN YOUR EYES *Island WIP 6205*	17	8
5 Jul 75	YOU GO TO MY HEAD *Island WIP 6234*	33	3
12 Jun 76	● LET'S STICK TOGETHER (LET'S WORK TOGETHER) *Island WIP 6307*	4	10
7 Aug 76	● EXTENDED PLAY (EP) *Island IEP 1*	7	9
5 Feb 77	● THIS IS TOMORROW *Polydor 2001 704*	9	9
14 May 77	TOKYO JOE *Polydor 2001 711*	15	7
13 May 78	WHAT GOES ON *Polydor POSP 3*	67	2
5 Aug 78	SIGN OF THE TIMES *Polydor 2001 798*	37	8
11 May 85	● SLAVE TO LOVE *EG FERRY 1*	10	9
31 Aug 85	DON'T STOP THE DANCE *EG FERRY 2*	21	7
7 Dec 85	WINDSWEPT *EG FERRY 3*	46	3
29 Mar 86	IS YOUR LOVE STRONG ENOUGH? *EG FERRY 4*	22	7
10 Oct 87	THE RIGHT STUFF *Virgin VS 940*	37	6
13 Feb 88	KISS AND TELL *Virgin VS 1034*	41	5
29 Oct 88	LET'S STICK TOGETHER (re-mix) *EG EGO 44*	12	7
11 Feb 89	THE PRICE OF LOVE (re-mix) *EG EGO 46*	49	3
22 Apr 89	HE'LL HAVE TO GO *EG EGO 48*	63	1
6 Mar 93	I PUT A SPELL ON YOU *Virgin VSCDG 1400*	18	5
29 May 93	WILL YOU LOVE ME TOMORROW *Virgin VSCDG 1455* ...	23	5
4 Sep 93	GIRL OF MY BEST FRIEND *Virgin VSCDG 1488*	57	2
29 Oct 94	YOUR PAINTED SMILE *Virgin VSCDG 1508*	52	1
11 Feb 95	MAMOUNA *Virgin VSCDG 1528*	57	1

Tracks on Extended Play (EP): Price of Love / Shame Shame Shame / Heart on My Sleeve / It's Only Love

See also ROXY MUSIC

FERRY AID
International, male / female charity ensemble (7 WEEKS)   pos/wks

| 4 Apr 87 | ★ LET IT BE *The Sun AID 1* ■ .... | 1 | 7 |

FEVER featuring Tippa IRIE
UK, male production / instrumental group with male vocalist (1 WEEK)   pos/wks

| 8 Jul 95 | STAYING ALIVE 95 *Telstar CDSTAS 2776* .... | 48 | 1 |

Lena FIAGBE
UK, female vocalist (13 WEEKS)   pos/wks

24 Jul 93	YOU COME FROM EARTH *Mother MUMCD 42* [1]	69	1
23 Oct 93	GOTTA GET IT RIGHT *Mother MUMCD 44*	20	5
16 Apr 94	WHAT'S IT LIKE TO BE BEAUTIFUL *Mother MUMCD 49* ...	52	3
25 Jun 94	VISIONS *Mother MUMCD 53*	48	2
10 Feb 96	AFRICAN DREAM *Mercury MERCD 453* [2]	44	2

[1] Lena [2] Wasis Diop featuring Lena Fiagbe

Karel FIALKA
UK, male vocalist / multi-instrumentalist (12 WEEKS)   pos/wks

| 17 May 80 | THE EYES HAVE IT *Blueprint BLU 2005* .... | 52 | 4 |
| 5 Sep 87 | ● HEY MATTHEW *IRS IRM 140* .... | 9 | 8 |

FIAT LUX
UK, male vocal / instrumental group (4 WEEKS)   pos/wks

| 28 Jan 84 | SECRETS *Polydor FIAT 2* .... | 65 | 3 |
| 17 Mar 84 | BLUE EMOTION *Polydor FIAT 3* .... | 59 | 1 |

FICTION FACTORY
UK, male vocal / instrumental group (11 WEEKS)   pos/wks

| 14 Jan 84 | ● (FEELS LIKE) HEAVEN *CBS A 3996* .... | 6 | 9 |
| 17 Mar 84 | GHOST OF LOVE *CBS A 3819* .... | 64 | 2 |

FIDDLER'S DRAM
UK, male / female vocal / instrumental group (9 WEEKS)   pos/wks

| 15 Dec 79 | ● DAYTRIP TO BANGOR (DIDN'T WE HAVE A LOVELY TIME) *Dingle's SID 211* .... | 3 | 9 |

FIDELFATTI featuring RONNETTE
Italy, male producer and female vocalist (1 WEEK)   pos/wks

| 27 Jan 90 | JUST WANNA TOUCH ME *Urban URB 46* .... | 65 | 1 |

Billy FIELD
Australia, male vocalist (3 WEEKS)   pos/wks

| 12 Jun 82 | YOU WEREN'T IN LOVE WITH ME *CBS A 2344* .... | 67 | 3 |

Ernie FIELDS and his ORCHESTRA
US, orchestra, leader d. 11 May 1997 (8 WEEKS)   pos/wks

| 25 Dec 59 | IN THE MOOD *London HL 8985* .... | 13 | 8 |

Gracie FIELDS
UK, female vocalist – Grace Stansfield, d. 27 Sep 1979 (15 WEEKS)   pos/wks

| 31 May 57 | ● AROUND THE WORLD (re) *Columbia DB 3953* .... | 8 | 9 |
| 6 Nov 59 | LITTLE DONKEY (re) *Columbia DB 4360* .... | 20 | 6 |

Richard 'Dimples' FIELDS
US, male vocalist, d. 15 Jan 2000 (4 WEEKS)   pos/wks

| 20 Feb 82 | I'VE GOT TO LEARN TO SAY NO *Epic EPC A 1918* ..... | 56 | 4 |

FIELDS OF THE NEPHILIM
UK, male vocal / instrumental group (10 WEEKS)   pos/wks

24 Oct 87	BLUE WATER *Situation Two SIT 48*	75	1
4 Jun 88	MOONCHILD *Situation Two SIT 52*	28	3
27 May 89	PSYCHONAUT *Situation Two SIT 57*	35	3
4 Aug 90	FOR HER LIGHT *Beggars Banquet BEG 244T*	54	1
24 Nov 90	SUMERLAND (DREAMED) *Beggars Banquet BEG 250* ...	37	1
28 Sep 02	FROM THE FIRE *Jungle JUNG 65CD*	62	1

FIERCE
UK, female vocal group (23 WEEKS)   pos/wks

9 Jan 99	RIGHT HERE RIGHT NOW *Wildstar CDWILD 13*	25	5
15 May 99	DAYZ LIKE THAT *Wildstar CDWILD 19*	11	5
14 Aug 99	SO LONG *Wildstar CDWILD 27*	15	5
12 Feb 00	● SWEET LOVE 2K *Wildstar CDWILD 34*	3	8

5TH DIMENSION
US, male / female vocal group (21 WEEKS)   pos/wks

| 16 Apr 69 | AQUARIUS / LET THE SUNSHINE IN (MEDLEY) *Liberty LBF 15193* ▲ .... | 11 | 12 |
| 17 Jan 70 | WEDDING BELL BLUES *Liberty LBF 15288* ▲ .... | 16 | 9 |

Re-entries are listed as (re), (2re), (3re), etc which signifies that the hit re-entered the chart once, twice or three times, etc

5050 *UK, male production duo*
– Jason Powell and Andy Lysandrou (2 WEEKS) pos/wks

13 Oct 01	WHO'S COMING ROUND *Obsessive FIFTYCD 01*	54	1
23 Mar 02	BAD BOYS HOLLER BOO *Logic 74321910202*	73	1

50 GRIND featuring POKEMON ALLSTARS *UK, male*
vocal / instrumental group and Pokémon popsters (1 WEEK) pos/wks

22 Dec 01	GOTTA CATCH 'EM ALL *Recognition CDREC 21*	57	1

52ND STREET
UK, male / female vocal / instrumental group (13 WEEKS) pos/wks

2 Nov 85	TELL ME (HOW IT FEELS) *10 TEN 74*	54	5
11 Jan 86	YOU'RE MY LAST CHANCE *10 TEN 89*	49	4
8 Mar 86	I CAN'T LET YOU GO *10 TEN 114*	57	4

53RD & 3RD *– See Jonathan KING*

FILTER *US, male vocal / instrumental duo*
– Richard Patrick and Brian Liesgang (5 WEEKS) pos/wks

11 Oct 97	(CAN'T YOU) TRIP LIKE I DO *Epic 6650862* [1]	39	2
18 Mar 00	TAKE A PICTURE *Reprise W 515CD*	25	3

[1] Filter and The Crystal Method

FINAL CUT *– See TRUE FAITH and Bridgette GRACE with FINAL CUT*

FINE YOUNG CANNIBALS (430 Top 500)
Politically aware pop / soul trio from Birmingham, UK; Roland Gift (v), ex-
Beat members Andy Cox (g) and David Steele (b). Unmistakable vocalist Gift
also acted in films, most notably 1989's Scandal. FYC, who were among
1989's biggest selling acts worldwide, won (and returned) two Brit awards in
1990 (81 WEEKS) pos/wks

8 Jun 85	● JOHNNY COME HOME *London LON 68*	8	13
9 Nov 85	BLUE *London LON 79*	41	6
11 Jan 86	● SUSPICIOUS MINDS *London LON 82*	8	9
12 Apr 86	FUNNY HOW LOVE IS *London LON 88*	58	4
21 Mar 87	● EVER FALLEN IN LOVE *London LON 121*	9	10
7 Jan 89	● SHE DRIVES ME CRAZY *London LON 199* ▲	5	11
15 Apr 89	● GOOD THING *London LON 218* ▲	7	8
19 Aug 89	DON'T LOOK BACK *London LON 220*	34	4
18 Nov 89	I'M NOT THE MAN I USED TO BE *London LON 244*	20	8
24 Feb 90	I'M NOT SATISFIED *London LON 252*	46	3
16 Nov 96	THE FLAME *ffrr LONCD 389*	17	3
11 Jan 97	SHE DRIVES ME CRAZY (re-mix) *ffrr LONCD 391*	36	2

See also TWO MEN, A DRUM MACHINE AND A TRUMPET

FINITRIBE *UK, male instrumental / production group (2 WEEKS)* pos/wks

11 Jul 92	FOREVERGREEN *One Little Indian 74 TP12F*	51	1
19 Nov 94	BRAND NEW *ffrr FCD 247*	69	1

FINK BROTHERS *UK, male vocal / instrumental duo (4 WEEKS)* pos/wks

9 Feb 85	MUTANTS IN MEGA CITY ONE *Zarjazz JAZZ 2*	50	4

FINN *New Zealand, male vocal /*
instrumental duo – Neil and Tim Finn (5 WEEKS) pos/wks

14 Oct 95	SUFFER NEVER *Parlophone CDRS 6417*	29	3
9 Dec 95	ANGEL'S HEAP *Parlophone CDRS 6421*	41	2

See also CROWDED HOUSE; Neil FINN; Tim FINN

Micky FINN *– See URBAN SHAKEDOWN*

Neil FINN *New Zealand, male vocalist / instrumentalist (6 WEEKS)* pos/wks

13 Jun 98	SHE WILL HAVE HER WAY *Parlophone CDR 6495*	26	2
17 Oct 98	SINNER *Parlophone CDR 6505*	39	1
7 Apr 01	WHEREVER YOU ARE *Parlophone CDRS 6557*	32	2
22 Sep 01	HOLE IN THE ICE *Parlophone CDRS 6563*	43	1

See also CROWDED HOUSE; FINN

Tim FINN *New Zealand, male vocalist (6 WEEKS)* pos/wks

26 Jun 93	PERSUASION *Capitol 6592482*	43	3
18 Sep 93	HIT THE GROUND RUNNING *Capitol CDCLS 694*	50	3

See also CROWDED HOUSE; FINN

Johnnie FIORI *– See BARKIN BROTHERS featuring Johnnie FIORI*

Elisa FIORILLO *US, female vocalist (14 WEEKS)* pos/wks

28 Nov 87	● WHO FOUND WHO *Chrysalis CHS JEL 1* [1]	10	10
13 Feb 88	HOW CAN I FORGET YOU *Chrysalis ELISA 1*	50	4

[1] Jellybean featuring Elisa Fiorillo

FIRE INC *– See Jim STEINMAN*

FIRE ISLAND *UK, male instrumental / production group (7 WKS)* pos/wks

8 Aug 92	IN YOUR BONES / FIRE ISLAND *Boy's Own BOIX 11*	66	1
12 Mar 94	THERE BUT FOR THE GRACE OF GOD		
	Junior Boy's Own JBO 18CD [1]	32	3
4 Mar 95	IF YOU SHOULD NEED A FRIEND		
	Junior Boy's Own JBO 26CDS [2]	51	1
11 Apr 98	SHOUT TO THE TOP *JBO JNR 5001573* [3]	23	2

[1] Fire Island featuring Love Nelson [2] Fire Island featuring Mark Anthoni [3] Fire
Island featuring Loleatta Holloway

See also HELLER & FARLEY PROJECT; Pete HELLER; STYLUS TROUBLE

FIREBALLS *US, male vocal / instrumental group (17 WEEKS)* pos/wks

27 Jul 61	QUITE A PARTY *Pye International 7N 25092*	29	9
14 Nov 63	SUGAR SHACK (re) *London HLD 9789* [1] ▲	45	8

[1] Jimmy Gilmer and The Fireballs

FIREHOUSE *US, male vocal / instrumental group (2 WEEKS)* pos/wks

13 Jul 91	DON'T TREAT ME BAD *Epic 6567807*	71	1
19 Dec 92	WHEN I LOOK INTO YOUR EYES *Epic 6588347*	65	1

FIRM *UK, male vocal / instrumental group (21 WEEKS)* pos/wks

17 Jul 82	ARTHUR DALEY ('E'S ALRIGHT) *Bark HID 1*	14	9
6 Jun 87	★ STAR TREKKIN' *Bark TREK 1*	1	12

FIRM featuring Dawn ROBINSON
US, male rap group, and US, female vocalist (3 WEEKS) pos/wks

29 Nov 97	FIRM BIZ *Columbia 6651612*	18	3

FIRST CHOICE *US, female vocal group (21 WEEKS)* pos/wks

19 May 73	ARMED AND EXTREMELY DANGEROUS *Bell 1297*	16	10
4 Aug 73	● SMARTY PANTS *Bell 1324*	9	11

FIRST CLASS *UK, male vocal group (10 WEEKS)* pos/wks

15 Jun 74	BEACH BABY *UK 66*	13	10

FIRST EDITION *– See Kenny ROGERS*

FIRST LIGHT *UK, male vocal / instrumental duo (5 WEEKS)* pos/wks

21 May 83	EXPLAIN THE REASONS *London LON 26*	65	3
28 Jan 84	WISH YOU WERE HERE *London LON 43*	71	2

FIRSTBORN *Ireland, male producer – Oisin Lunny (1 WEEK)* pos/wks

19 Jun 99	THE MOOD CLUB *Independiente ISOM 28MS*	69	1

FISCHERSPOONER *US, male vocal / instrumental*
duo – Warren Fischer and Casey Spooner (3 WEEKS) pos/wks

20 Jul 02	EMERGE *Ministry of Sound FSMOS 1CDS*	25	3

FISCHER-Z *UK, male vocal / instrumental group (7 WEEKS)* pos/wks

26 May 79	THE WORKER *United Artists UP 36509*	53	5
3 May 80	SO LONG *United Artists BP 342*	72	2

FISH UK, male vocalist – Derek Dick (20 WEEKS) pos/wks

18 Oct 86	**SHORT CUT TO SOMEWHERE** Charisma CB 426 [1] **75**	1
28 Oct 89	**STATE OF MIND** EMI EM 109 ....**32**	3
6 Jan 90	**BIG WEDGE** EMI EM 125 ....**25**	4
17 Mar 90	**A GENTLEMAN'S EXCUSE ME** EMI EM 135 ......**30**	3
28 Sep 91	**INTERNAL EXILE** Polydor FISHY 1 ....**37**	2
11 Jan 92	**CREDO** Polydor FISHY 2 ....**38**	2
4 Jul 92	**SOMETHING IN THE AIR** Polydor FISHY 3 ....**51**	2
16 Apr 94	**LADY LET IT LIE** Dick Bros. DDICK 3CD1 .....**46**	1
1 Oct 94	**FORTUNES OF WAR** Dick Bros. DDICK 008CD1 ....**67**	1
26 Aug 95	**JUST GOOD FRIENDS** Dick Bros. DDICK 014CD1 [2] **63**	1

[1] Fish and Tony Banks [2] Fish featuring Sam Brown

See also MARILLION

FISHBONE US, male vocal / instrumental group (3 WEEKS) pos/wks

1 Aug 92	**EVERYDAY SUNSHINE / FIGHT THE YOUTH**	
	Columbia 6581937 ....**60**	2
28 Aug 93	**SWIM** Columbia 6596252 ....**54**	1

Cevin FISHER US, male DJ / producer (9 WEEKS) pos/wks

3 Oct 98	**THE FREAKS COME OUT**	
	Ministry of Sound MOSCDS 127 [1] **34**	2
20 Feb 99	**(YOU GOT ME) BURNING UP**	
	Wonderboy WBOYD 013 [2] **14**	4
7 Aug 99	**MUSIC SAVED MY LIFE**	
	Sm:)e Communications SM 90982 ....**67**	1
20 Jan 01	**IT'S A GOOD LIFE** Wonderboy WBOYD 022 [3] **54**	1
24 Feb 01	**LOVE YOU SOME MORE** Subversive SUB 68D [4] **60**	1

[1] Cevin Fisher's Big Break [2] Cevin Fisher / Loleatta Holloway [3] Cevin Fisher
featuring Ramona Kelly [4] Cevin Fisher featuring Shelia Smith

Eddie FISHER ⟨ 288 ⟩ Top 500
*Leading 1950s heart-throb, b. 10 Aug 1929, Philadelphia. The US's most
successful male singer between 1950 and 1954; accumulated many more UK
hits in the pre-chart years. Married Elizabeth Taylor, Debbie Reynolds and
Connie Stevens and is father of the actress Carrie Fisher (105 WEEKS)* pos/wks

2 Jan 53	★ **OUTSIDE OF HEAVEN (re)** HMV B 10362 ......**1**	17
23 Jan 53	● **EVERYTHING I HAVE IS YOURS (re)** HMV B 10398 ....**8**	5
1 May 53	● **DOWNHEARTED** HMV B 10450 ....**3**	15
22 May 53	★ **I'M WALKING BEHIND YOU** HMV B 10489 [1] ▲ **1**	18
6 Nov 53	● **WISH YOU WERE HERE** HMV B 10564 ....**8**	9
22 May 54	● **OH MY PAPA (O MEIN PAPA) (3re)** HMV B 10614 ▲ **9**	4
29 Oct 54	**I NEED YOU NOW (2re)** HMV B 10755 ▲ **13**	10
18 Mar 55	● **(I'M ALWAYS HEARING) WEDDING BELLS** HMV B 10839 ....**5**	11
23 Nov 56	● **CINDY, OH CINDY** HMV POP 273 ....**5**	16

[1] Eddie Fisher with Sally Sweetland (soprano)

Mark FISHER featuring Dotty GREEN UK, male
instrumentalist – keyboards and female vocalist (2 WEEKS) pos/wks

29 Jun 85	**LOVE SITUATION** Total Control TOCO 3 ....**59**	2

Toni FISHER US, female vocalist, d. 12 Feb 1999 (1 WEEK) pos/wks

12 Feb 60	**THE BIG HURT** Top Rank JAR 261 ....**30**	1

FITS OF GLOOM UK / Italy, male vocal duo (4 WEEKS) pos/wks

4 Jun 94	**HEAVEN** Media MCSTD 1981 ....**47**	2
5 Nov 94	**THE POWER OF LOVE** Media MCSTD 2016 [1] **49**	2

[1] Fits of Gloom featuring Lizzy Mack

Ella FITZGERALD
US, female vocalist, d. 15 June 1996 (29 WEEKS) pos/wks

23 May 58	**THE SWINGIN' SHEPHERD BLUES** HMV POP 486 ....**15**	5
16 Oct 59	**BUT NOT FOR ME (re)** HMV POP 657 ....**25**	3
21 Apr 60	**MACK THE KNIFE** HMV POP 736 ....**19**	9
6 Oct 60	**HOW HIGH THE MOON** HMV POP 782 ....**46**	1
22 Nov 62	**DESAFINADO (re)** Verve VS 502 ....**38**	6
30 Apr 64	**CAN'T BUY ME LOVE** Verve VS 519 ....**34**	5

Scott FITZGERALD
UK, male vocalist – William McPhail (12 WEEKS) pos/wks

14 Jan 78	● **IF I HAD WORDS** Pepper UP 36333 [1] **3**	10
7 May 88	● **GO** PRT PYS 10 ....**52**	2

[1] Scott Fitzgerald and Yvonne Keeley with the St Thomas More School Choir

FIVE ⟨ 197 ⟩ Top 500
*Superior all-boy vocal group: 'Abs' Breen, 'J' Brown, Sean Conlon, Rich
Neville, Scott Robinson. Eponymous debut album sold more than four million
worldwide. The only UK act to reach the Top 10 with every one of their first 11
releases split in 2001 (133 WEEKS)* pos/wks

13 Dec 97	● **SLAM DUNK (DA FUNK)** RCA 74321537352 ....**10**	9
14 Mar 98	● **WHEN THE LIGHTS GO OUT** RCA 74321562312 ....**4**	9
20 Jun 98	● **GOT THE FEELIN'** RCA 74321584892 ....**3**	13
12 Sep 98	● **EVERYBODY GET UP** RCA 74321613752 ....**2**	12
28 Nov 98	● **UNTIL THE TIME IS THROUGH** RCA 74321632602 ....**2**	12
31 Jul 99	● **IF YA GETTIN' DOWN** RCA 74321689692 ....**2**	12
6 Nov 99	★ **KEEP ON MOVIN'** RCA 74321709862 ■ **1**	17
18 Mar 00	● **DON'T WANNA LET YOU GO** RCA 74321745292 ....**9**	12
29 Jul 00	★ **WE WILL ROCK YOU (re)** RCA 74321774022 [1] ■ **1**	13
25 Aug 01	★ **LET'S DANCE** RCA 74321875962 ■ **1**	12
3 Nov 01	● **CLOSER TO ME (re)** RCA 74321900742 ....**4**	12

[1] Five and Queen

See also ABS

FIVE FOR FIGHTING
US, male vocalist / instrumentalist – John Ondrasik (1 WEEK) pos/wks

1 Jun 02	**SUPERMAN (IT'S NOT EASY)** Columbia 6727202 ....**48**	1

FIVE SMITH BROTHERS UK, male vocal group (1 WEEK) pos/wks

22 Jul 55	**I'M IN FAVOUR OF FRIENDSHIP** Decca F 10527 ....**20**	1

FIVE STAR ⟨ 179 ⟩ Top 500
*Britain's best known black family act: Deniece, Doris, Stedman, Lorraine and
Delroy Pearson. The Essex-based group became the youngest act to top the
LP chart with the UK million-seller 'Silk and Steel'. In 1987 they were voted
Top British Group in Smash Hits and at the Brit Awards. They relocated to the
US and had some R&B chart success (140 WEEKS)* pos/wks

4 May 85	**ALL FALL DOWN** Tent PB 40039 ....**15**	12
20 Jul 85	**LET ME BE THE ONE** Tent PB 40193 ....**18**	9
14 Sep 85	**LOVE TAKE OVER** Tent PB 40353 ....**25**	9
16 Nov 85	**RSVP** Tent PB 40445 ....**45**	5
11 Jan 86	● **SYSTEM ADDICT** Tent PB 40515 ....**3**	11
12 Apr 86	● **CAN'T WAIT ANOTHER MINUTE** Tent PB 40697 ....**7**	10
26 Jul 86	● **FIND THE TIME** Tent PB 40799 ....**7**	10
13 Sep 86	● **RAIN OR SHINE** Tent PB 40901 ....**2**	11
22 Nov 86	**IF I SAY YES** Tent PB 40981 ....**15**	9
7 Feb 87	● **STAY OUT OF MY LIFE** Tent PB 41131 ....**9**	8
18 Apr 87	● **THE SLIGHTEST TOUCH** Tent PB 41265 ....**4**	9
22 Aug 87	**WHENEVER YOU'RE READY** Tent PB 41477 ....**11**	6
10 Oct 87	**STRONG AS STEEL** Tent PB 41565 ....**16**	7
5 Dec 87	**SOMEWHERE SOMEBODY** Tent PB 41661 ....**23**	6
4 Jun 88	**ANOTHER WEEKEND** Tent PB 42081 ....**18**	4
6 Aug 88	**ROCK MY WORLD** Tent PB 42145 ....**28**	4
17 Sep 88	**THERE'S A BRAND NEW WORLD** Tent PB 42235 ....**61**	2
19 Nov 88	**LET ME BE YOURS** Tent PB 42343 ....**51**	3
8 Apr 89	**WITH EVERY HEARTBEAT** Tent PB 42693 ....**49**	2
10 Mar 90	**TREAT ME LIKE A LADY** Tent FIVE 1 ....**54**	2
7 Jul 90	**HOT LOVE** Tent FIVE 2 ....**68**	1

FIVE THIRTY
UK, male vocal / instrumental group (4 WEEKS) pos/wks

4 Aug 90	**ABSTAIN** East West YZ 530 ....**75**	1
25 May 91	**13TH DISCIPLE** East West YZ 577 ....**67**	1
3 Aug 91	**SUPERNOVA** East West YZ 594 ....**75**	1
2 Nov 91	**YOU (EP)** East West YZ 624 ....**72**	1

Tracks on You (EP): You / Cuddly Drug / Slow Train into the Ocean

5000 VOLTS
UK, male / female vocal / instrumental group (18 WEEKS) pos/wks

| 6 Sep 75 | ● I'M ON FIRE *Philips 6006 464* | 4 | 9 |
| 24 Jul 76 | ● DOCTOR KISS-KISS *Philips 6006 533* | 8 | 9 |

Vocals (uncredited) on 'I'm on Fire' by Tina Charles

FIXATE
UK, male vocal group (1 WEEK) pos/wks

| 14 Jul 01 | 24/7 *Epark EPKFIX CD1* | 42 | 1 |

FIXX
UK, male vocal / instrumental group (8 WEEKS) pos/wks

| 24 Apr 82 | STAND OR FALL *MCA FIXX 2* | 54 | 4 |
| 17 Jul 82 | RED SKIES *MCA FIXX 3* | 57 | 4 |

Roberta FLACK 441 Top 500
Ground-breaking, song stylist / pianist, b. 10 Feb 1939, North Carolina, US. Recorded original hit 'Killing Me Softly with His Song' (written about Don McLean) and was the first black female soloist to top the US album chart, with 'First Take' in 1972 (79 WEEKS) pos/wks

27 May 72	THE FIRST TIME EVER I SAW YOUR FACE *Atlantic K 10161* ▲	14	14
5 Aug 72	WHERE IS THE LOVE *Atlantic K 10202* [1]	29	7
17 Feb 73	● KILLING ME SOFTLY WITH HIS SONG *Atlantic K 10282* ▲	6	14
24 Apr 74	FEEL LIKE MAKIN' LOVE *Atlantic K 10467* ▲	34	7
6 May 78	THE CLOSER I GET TO YOU *Atlantic K 11099* [2]	42	4
17 May 80	● BACK TOGETHER AGAIN *Atlantic K 11481* [1]	3	11
30 Aug 80	DON'T MAKE ME WAIT TOO LONG *Atlantic K 11555*	44	7
20 Aug 83	● TONIGHT I CELEBRATE MY LOVE *Capitol CL 302* [3]	2	13
29 Jul 89	UH-UH OOH OOH LOOK OUT (HERE IT COMES) *Atlantic A 8941*	72	2

[1] Roberta Flack and Donny Hathaway [2] Roberta Flack with Donny Hathaway
[3] Peabo Bryson and Roberta Flack

FLAJ – *See GETO BOYS featuring FLAJ*

FLAMING LIPS
US, male vocal / instrumental group (6 WEEKS) pos/wks

9 Mar 96	THIS HERE GIRAFFE *Warner Bros. W 0335CD*	72	1
26 Jun 99	RACE FOR THE PRIZE *Warner Bros. W 494CD1*	39	2
20 Nov 99	WAITIN' FOR A SUPERMAN *Warner Bros. W 505CD1*	73	1
31 Aug 02	DO YOU REALIZE?? *Warner Bros. WEA W 586CD*	32	2

FLAMINGOS *US, male vocal group (5 WEEKS)* pos/wks

| 4 Jun 69 | THE BOOGALOO PARTY *Philips BF 1786* | 26 | 5 |

Michael FLANDERS
UK, male vocalist, d. 14 Apr 1975 (3 WEEKS) pos/wks

| 27 Feb 59 | THE LITTLE DRUMMER BOY (re) *Parlophone R 4528* | 20 | 3 |

With the Michael Sammes Singers

FLASH and the PAN
Australia, male vocal / instrumental group (15 WEEKS) pos/wks

| 23 Sep 78 | AND THE BAND PLAYED ON (DOWN AMONG THE DEAD MEN)
Ensign ENY 15 | 54 | 4 |
| 21 May 83 | ● WAITING FOR A TRAIN *Easybeat EASY 1* | 7 | 11 |

Lester FLATT and Earl SCRUGGS
US, male instrumental duo – banjos (6 WEEKS) pos/wks

| 15 Nov 67 | FOGGY MOUNTAIN BREAKDOWN
CBS 3038 and Mercury MF 1007 | 39 | 6 |

The versions on the two labels were not the same cuts; CBS had a 1965 recording, Mercury a 1949 recording. The chart did not differentiate and listed both together

Fogwell FLAX and the ANKLEBITERS from FREEHOLD JUNIOR SCHOOL *UK, male vocalist and school choir (2 WEEKS)* pos/wks

| 26 Dec 81 | ONE NINE FOR SANTA *EMI 5255* | 68 | 2 |

FLEE-REKKERS *UK, male instrumental group (13 WEEKS)* pos/wks

| 19 May 60 | GREEN JEANS *Triumph RGM 1008* | 23 | 13 |

FLEETWOOD MAC 68 Top 500
Record-breaking Anglo-American act. Members included: Mick Fleetwood (d), John McVie (b), Peter Green (g), Christine McVie (k/v), Lindsey Buckingham (g/v), Stevie Nicks (v). Grammy-winning album 'Rumours' sold more than 18 million copies in the US alone and has spent longer on the UK album chart than any other LP (223 WEEKS) pos/wks

10 Apr 68	BLACK MAGIC WOMAN *Blue Horizon 57 3138*	37	7
17 Jul 68	NEED YOUR LOVE SO BAD *Blue Horizon 57 3139*	31	13
4 Dec 68	★ ALBATROSS *Blue Horizon 57 3145*	1	20
16 Apr 69	● MAN OF THE WORLD *Immediate IM 080*	2	14
23 Jul 69	NEED YOUR LOVE SO BAD (re-issue) (re) *Blue Horizon 57 3157*	32	9
4 Oct 69	● OH WELL *Reprise RS 27000*	2	16
23 May 70	● THE GREEN MANALISHI (WITH THE TWO-PRONG CROWN) *Reprise RS 27007*	10	12
12 May 73	● ALBATROSS (re-issue) *CBS 8306*	2	15
13 Nov 76	SAY YOU LOVE ME *Reprise K 14447*	40	4
19 Feb 77	GO YOUR OWN WAY *Warner Bros. K 16872*	38	4
30 Apr 77	DON'T STOP *Warner Bros. K 16930*	32	5
9 Jul 77	DREAMS *Warner Bros. K 16969* ▲	24	9
22 Oct 77	YOU MAKE LOVING FUN *Warner Bros. K 17013*	45	2
11 Mar 78	RHIANNON *Reprise K 14430*	46	3
6 Oct 79	● TUSK *Warner Bros. K 17468*	6	10
22 Dec 79	SARA *Warner Bros. K 17533*	37	8
25 Sep 82	GYPSY *Warner Bros. K 17997*	46	3
18 Dec 82	● OH DIANE *Warner Bros. FLEET 1*	9	15
4 Apr 87	● BIG LOVE *Warner Bros. W 8398*	9	12
11 Jul 87	SEVEN WONDERS *Warner Bros. W 8317*	56	4
26 Sep 87	● LITTLE LIES *Warner Bros. W 8291*	5	12
26 Dec 87	FAMILY MAN *Warner Bros. W 8114*	54	5
2 Apr 88	● EVERYWHERE *Warner Bros. W 8143*	4	10
18 Jun 88	ISN'T IT MIDNIGHT *Warner Bros. W 7860*	60	2
17 Dec 88	AS LONG AS YOU FOLLOW *Warner Bros. W 7644*	66	3
5 May 90	SAVE ME *Warner Bros. W 9866*	53	3
25 Aug 90	IN THE BACK OF MY MIND *Warner Bros. W 9739*	58	3

Group was UK and male only up to and including the re-issue of 'Albatross'

FLEETWOODS
US, male / female vocal group (8 WEEKS) pos/wks

| 24 Apr 59 | ● COME SOFTLY TO ME *London HLU 8841* ▲ | 6 | 8 |

John 'OO' FLEMING *UK, male DJ / producer (3 WEEKS)* pos/wks

25 Dec 99	LOST IN EMOTION *React CDREACT 170*	74	1
12 Aug 00	FREE *React CDREACT 186*	61	1
2 Feb 02	BELFAST TRANCE *Nebula BELFCD 001* [1]	74	1

[1] John 'OO' Fleming vs Simple Minds

FLESH & BONES
Belgium, male / female production / vocal trio (1 WEEK) pos/wks

| 10 Aug 02 | I LOVE YOU *Multiply CDMULTY 86* | 70 | 1 |

La FLEUR
Holland, male / female vocal / instrumental group (4 WEEKS) pos/wks

| 30 Jul 83 | BOOGIE NIGHTS *Proto ENA 111* | 51 | 4 |

FLICKMAN *Italy, male production duo*
– Andreas Mazzali and Giuliano Orlandi (6 WEEKS) pos/wks

| 4 Mar 00 | THE SOUND OF BAMBOO *Inferno CDFERN 25* | 11 | 5 |
| 28 Apr 01 | HEY! PARADISE *Inferno CDFERN 37* | 69 | 1 |

KC FLIGHTT *US, male rapper (5 WEEKS)* pos/wks

| 1 Apr 89 | PLANET E *RCA PT 49404* | 48 | 4 |
| 12 May 01 | VOICES *Hooj Choons HOOJ 106CD* [1] | 59 | 1 |

[1] KC Flightt vs Funky Junction

Dread FLIMSTONE and the MODERN TONE AGE FAMILY
US, male vocal / instrumental group (1 WEEK)   pos/wks

| 30 Nov 91 | FROM THE GHETTO *Urban URB 87* | 66 | 1 |

Berni FLINT *UK, male vocalist (11 WEEKS)*   pos/wks

| 19 Mar 77 ● | I DON'T WANT TO PUT A HOLD ON YOU *EMI 2599* | 3 | 10 |
| 23 Jul 77 | SOUTHERN COMFORT *EMI 2621* | 48 | 1 |

FLINTLOCK *UK, male vocal / instrumental group (5 WEEKS)*   pos/wks

| 29 May 76 | DAWN *Pinnacle P 8419* | 30 | 5 |

FLIP & FILL
UK, male production duo – Graham Turner and Mark Hall (23 WEEKS) pos/wks

24 Mar 01	TRUE LOVE NEVER DIES *All Around the World CDGLOBE 240* [1]	34	3
2 Feb 02 ●	TRUE LOVE NEVER DIES (re-mix) *All Around the World CDGLOBE 248* [1]	7	10
27 Jul 02 ●	SHOOTING STAR *All Around the World CDGLOBE 258*	3	10

[1] Flip and Fill featuring Kelly Llorenna

'Shooting Star' features uncredited vocal Karen Parry

See also BUS STOP

FLIPMODE SQUAD
US, male / female production / rap group (1 WEEK)   pos/wks

| 31 Oct 98 | CHA CHA CHA *Elektra E 3810CD* | 54 | 1 |

FLOATERS *US, male vocal group (11 WEEKS)*   pos/wks

| 23 Jul 77 ★ | FLOAT ON *ABC 4187* | 1 | 11 |

A FLOCK OF SEAGULLS
UK, male vocal / instrumental group (46 WEEKS)   pos/wks

27 Mar 82	I RAN *Jive JIVE 14*	43	6
12 Jun 82	SPACE AGE LOVE SONG *Jive JIVE 17*	34	6
6 Nov 82 ●	WISHING (IF I HAD A PHOTOGRAPH OF YOU) *Jive JIVE 25*	10	12
23 Apr 83	NIGHTMARES *Jive JIVE 33*	53	3
25 Jun 83	TRANSFER AFFECTION *Jive JIVE 41*	38	5
14 Jul 84	THE MORE YOU LIVE, THE MORE YOU LOVE *Jive JIVE 62*	26	11
19 Oct 85	WHO'S THAT GIRL (SHE'S GOT IT) *Jive JIVE 106*	66	3

FLOORPLAY *UK, male instrumental / production duo (1 WEEK)*   pos/wks

| 27 Jan 96 | AUTOMATIC *Perfecto PERF 115CD* | 50 | 1 |

FLOWERED UP *UK, male vocal / instrumental group (17 WEEKS)* pos/wks

28 Jul 90	IT'S ON *Heavenly HVN 3*	54	4
24 Nov 90	PHOBIA *Heavenly HVN 7*	75	1
11 May 91	TAKE IT *London FUP 1*	34	4
17 Aug 91	IT'S ON / EGG RUSH (re-recording) *London FUP 2*	38	3
2 May 92	WEEKENDER *Heavenly HVN 16*	20	5

FLOWERPOT MEN *UK, male vocal group (12 WEEKS)*   pos/wks

| 23 Aug 67 ● | LET'S GO TO SAN FRANCISCO *Deram DM 142* | 4 | 12 |

Mike FLOWERS POPS
UK, male / female vocal / instrumental group (14 WEEKS) pos/wks

30 Dec 95 ●	WONDERWALL (re) *London LONCD 378*	2	9
8 Jun 96	LIGHT MY FIRE / PLEASE RELEASE ME *London LONCD 384*	39	2
28 Dec 96	DON'T CRY FOR ME ARGENTINA *Love This LUVTHIS 16*	30	3

Eddie FLOYD *US, male vocalist (29 WEEKS)*   pos/wks

2 Feb 67	KNOCK ON WOOD (re) *Atlantic 584 041*	19	18
16 Mar 67	RAISE YOUR HAND *Stax 601 001*	42	3
9 Aug 67	THINGS GET BETTER *Stax 601 016*	31	8

FLUFFY *UK, female vocal / instrumental group (2 WEEKS)*   pos/wks

| 17 Feb 96 | HUSBAND *Parkway PARK 006CD* | 58 | 1 |
| 5 Oct 96 | NOTHING *Virgin VSCDT 1614* | 52 | 1 |

FLUKE *UK, male instrumental / production group (20 WEEKS)*   pos/wks

20 Mar 93	SLID *Circa YRCD 103*	59	1
19 Jun 93	ELECTRIC GUITAR *Circa YRCD 104*	58	2
11 Sep 93	GROOVY FEELING *Circa YRCD 106*	45	3
23 Apr 94	BUBBLE *Circa YRCD 110*	37	2
29 Jul 95	BULLET *Circa YRCD 121*	23	3
16 Dec 95	TOSH *Circa YRCD 122*	32	3
16 Nov 96	ATOM BOMB *Circa YRCD 125*	20	3
31 May 97	ABSURD *Virgin YRCD 126*	25	2
27 Sep 97	SQUIRT *Circa YRCD 127*	46	1

See also LUCKY MONKEYS

FLUSH – *See SLADE*

FLYING LIZARDS
UK, male / female vocal / instrumental group (16 WEEKS)   pos/wks

| 4 Aug 79 ● | MONEY *Virgin VS 276* | 5 | 10 |
| 9 Feb 80 | TV *Virgin VS 325* | 43 | 6 |

FLYING PICKETS *UK, male vocal group (20 WEEKS)*   pos/wks

26 Nov 83 ★	ONLY YOU *10 TEN 14*	1	11
21 Apr 84 ●	WHEN YOU'RE YOUNG AND IN LOVE *10 TEN 20*	7	8
8 Dec 84	WHO'S THAT GIRL *10 GIRL 1*	71	1

Jerome FLYNN – *See ROBSON and JEROME*

FLYTRONIX – *See PESHAY*

FOCUS *Holland, male instrumental group (21 WEEKS)*   pos/wks

| 20 Jan 73 | HOCUS POCUS *Polydor 2001 211* | 20 | 10 |
| 27 Jan 73 ● | SYLVIA *Polydor 2001 422* | 4 | 11 |

FOG *US, male DJ / producer – Ralph Falcon (4 WEEKS)*   pos/wks

| 19 Feb 94 | BEEN A LONG TIME *Columbia 6601212* | 44 | 2 |
| 6 Jun 98 | BEEN A LONG TIME (re-mix) *Pukka CDPUKKA 16* | 27 | 2 |

See also FUNKY GREEN DOGS

Dan FOGELBERG *US, male vocalist (4 WEEKS)*   pos/wks

| 15 Mar 80 | LONGER *Epic EPC 8230* | 59 | 4 |

Ben FOLDS *US, male singer / instrumentalist – piano (1 WEEK)*   pos/wks

| 29 Sep 01 | ROCKIN' THE SUBURBS *Epic 6718492* | 53 | 1 |

Ben FOLDS FIVE *US, male vocal / instrumental group (12 WEEKS)* pos/wks

14 Sep 96	UNDERGROUND *Caroline CDCAR 008*	37	2
1 Mar 97	BATTLE OF WHO COULD CARE LESS *Epic 6642302*	26	3
7 Jun 97	KATE *Epic 6645365*	39	2
18 Apr 98	BRICK *Epic 6656612*	26	3
24 Apr 99	ARMY *Epic 6672182*	28	2

FOLK IMPLOSION *US, male vocal / instrumental duo (1 WEEK)*   pos/wks

| 15 Jun 96 | NATURAL ONE *London LONCD 382* | 45 | 1 |

Claudia FONTAINE – *See BEATMASTERS*

FONTANA featuring Darryl D'BONNEAU
US, male producer and male vocalist (1 WEEK)   pos/wks

| 24 Mar 01 | POW POW POW *Strictly Rhythm SRUKCD 01* | 62 | 1 |

Lenny FONTANA and DJ SHORTY *US, male production duo – Lenny Fontana and Dominik Huebler (2 WEEKS)*   pos/wks

| 4 Mar 00 | CHOCOLATE SENSATION *ffrr FCD 375* | 39 | 2 |

Re-entries are listed as (re), (2re), (3re), etc which signifies that the hit re-entered the chart once, twice or three times, etc

Wayne FONTANA (471) Top 500

UK, male vocalist b. Glyn Ellis 28 October 1945, Manchester, backed by the Mindbenders. Appropriately all his hits were recorded on the Fontana label, as a result creating a classic pop quiz question (76 WEEKS) pos/wks

11 Jul 63	HELLO JOSEPHINE *Fontana TF 404* [1]	46 2
28 May 64	STOP LOOK AND LISTEN *Fontana TF 451* [1]	37 4
8 Oct 64 ●	UM, UM, UM, UM, UM, UM *Fontana TF 497* [1]	5 15
4 Feb 65 ●	GAME OF LOVE *Fontana TF 535* [1] ▲	2 11
17 Jun 65	JUST A LITTLE BIT TOO LATE *Fontana TF 579* [1]	20 7
30 Sep 65	SHE NEEDS LOVE *Fontana TF 611* [1]	32 6
9 Dec 65	IT WAS EASIER TO HURT HER *Fontana TF 642*	36 6
21 Apr 66	COME ON HOME *Fontana TF 684*	16 12
25 Aug 66	GOODBYE BLUEBIRD *Fontana TF 737*	49 1
8 Dec 66	PAMELA, PAMELA *Fontana TF 770*	11 12

[1] Wayne Fontana and The Mindbenders

See also MINDBENDERS

FOO FIGHTERS *US, male vocal / instrumental group (41 WEEKS)* pos/wks

1 Jul 95 ●	THIS IS A CALL *Roswell CDCL 753*	5 4
16 Sep 95	I'LL STICK AROUND *Roswell CDCL 757*	18 3
2 Dec 95	FOR ALL THE COWS *Roswell CDCL 762*	28 2
6 Apr 96	BIG ME *Roswell CDCL 768*	19 3
10 May 97	MONKEY WRENCH *Roswell CDCLS 788*	12 4
30 Aug 97	EVERLONG *Roswell CDCL 792*	18 3
31 Jan 98	MY HERO *Roswell CDCL 796*	21 2
29 Aug 98	WALKING AFTER YOU; BEACON LIGHT *Elektra E 4100CD* [1]	20 4
30 Oct 99	LEARN TO FLY *RCA 74321706622*	21 3
30 Sep 00	BREAKOUT *RCA 74321790102*	29 3
16 Dec 00	NEXT YEAR *RCA 74321809262*	42 2
19 Oct 02 ●	ALL MY LIFE *RCA 74321973152*	5 9

[1] Foo Fighters: Ween

FOOL BOONA *UK, male DJ / producer – Colin Tevendale (1 WEEK)* pos/wks

10 Apr 99	POPPED!! *Virgin / VC Recordings / Uber Disko VCRD 46*	52 1

FOOL'S GARDEN
Germany, male vocal / instrumental group (4 WEEKS) pos/wks

25 May 96	LEMON TREE *Encore CDCOR 014*	61 1
3 Aug 96	LEMON TREE (re-issue) *Encore CDCOR 018*	26 3

FOR REAL *US, female vocal group (2 WEEKS)* pos/wks

1 Jul 95	YOU DON'T KNOW NOTHIN' *A&M 5811232*	54 1
12 Jul 97	LIKE I DO *Rowdy 74321486582*	45 1

Bill FORBES *UK, male vocalist (1 WEEK)* pos/wks

15 Jan 60	TOO YOUNG *Columbia DB 4386*	29 1

David FORBES *UK, male producer (1 WEEK)* pos/wks

25 Aug 01	QUESTIONS (MUST BE ASKED) *Serious SERR 031CD*	57 1

FORBIDDEN – *See Jet BRONX and the FORBIDDEN*

FORCE & STYLES featuring Kelly LLORENNA
UK, male DJ duo and female vocalist (1 WEEK) pos/wks

25 Jul 98	HEART OF GOLD *Diverse VERSE 2CD*	55 1

FORCE MD'S *US, male vocal group (9 WEEKS)* pos/wks

12 Apr 86	TENDER LOVE *Tommy Boy IS 269*	23 9

Clinton FORD
UK, male vocalist – Ian Stopford Harrison (25 WEEKS) pos/wks

23 Oct 59	OLD SHEP *Oriole CB 1500*	27 1
17 Aug 61	TOO MANY BEAUTIFUL GIRLS *Oriole CB 1623*	48 1
8 Mar 62	FANLIGHT FANNY *Oriole CB 1706*	22 10
5 Jan 67	RUN TO THE DOOR *Piccadilly 7N 35361*	25 13

Emile FORD and the CHECKMATES (363) Top 500

First group to top the chart in the 1960s, fronted by vocalist b. Emile Sweatman 16 Oct 1937, Bahamas. UK-based multiracial act had five consecutive Top 20 entries – three with updates of oldies. NME readers voted them Best New Act 1960 (89 WEEKS) pos/wks

30 Oct 59 ★	WHAT DO YOU WANT TO MAKE THOSE EYES AT ME FOR? *Pye 7N 15225*	1 26
5 Feb 60 ●	ON A SLOW BOAT TO CHINA *Pye 7N 15245*	3 15
26 May 60	YOU'LL NEVER KNOW WHAT YOU'RE MISSING ('TIL YOU TRY) *Pye 7N 15268*	12 9
1 Sep 60	THEM THERE EYES *Pye 7N 15282* [1]	18 16
8 Dec 60 ●	COUNTING TEARDROPS *Pye 7N 15314*	4 12
2 Mar 61	WHAT AM I GONNA DO *Pye 7N 15331*	33 6
18 May 61	HALF OF MY HEART (re) *Piccadilly 7N 35003* [2]	42 4
8 Mar 62	I WONDER WHO'S KISSING HER NOW *Piccadilly 7N 35033* [2]	43 1

[1] Emile Ford: The Babs Knight Group and Johnny Keating Music [2] Emile Ford

Lita FORD *UK, female vocalist (7 WEEKS)* pos/wks

17 Dec 88	KISS ME DEADLY *RCA PB 49575*	75 1
20 May 89	CLOSE MY EYES FOREVER *Dreamland PB 49409* [1]	47 3
11 Jan 92	SHOT OF POISON *RCA PB 49145*	63 3

[1] Lita Ford duet with Ozzy Osbourne

Martyn FORD ORCHESTRA *UK, orchestra (3 WEEKS)* pos/wks

14 May 77	LET YOUR BODY GO DOWNTOWN *Mountain TOP 26*	38 3

Mary FORD – *See Les PAUL and Mary FORD*

Penny FORD *US, female vocalist (7 WEEKS)* pos/wks

4 May 85	DANGEROUS *Total Experience FB 49975* [1]	43 5
29 May 93	DAYDREAMING *Columbia 6590592*	43 2

[1] Pennye Ford

See also SNAP!

Tennessee Ernie FORD
US, male vocalist, d. 17 Oct 1991 (42 WEEKS) pos/wks

21 Jan 55 ★	GIVE ME YOUR WORD *Capitol CL 14005*	1 24
6 Jan 56 ★	SIXTEEN TONS *Capitol CL 14500* ▲	1 11
13 Jan 56 ●	THE BALLAD OF DAVY CROCKETT *Capitol CL 14506*	3 7

Julia FORDHAM *UK, female vocalist (32 WEEKS)* pos/wks

2 Jul 88	HAPPY EVER AFTER *Circa YR 15*	27 9
25 Feb 89	WHERE DOES THE TIME GO? *Circa YR 23*	41 5
31 Aug 91	I THOUGHT IT WAS YOU *Circa YR 69*	64 2
18 Jan 92	LOVE MOVES (IN MYSTERIOUS WAYS) *Circa YR 73*	19 9
30 May 92	I THOUGHT IT WAS YOU (re-mix) *Circa YR 90*	45 3
30 Apr 94	DIFFERENT TIME DIFFERENT PLACE *Circa YRCD 111*	41 3
23 Jul 94	I CAN'T HELP MYSELF *Circa YRCD 116*	62 1

FOREIGNER (447) Top 500

Melodic Anglo-American rock group which amassed six US Top 10 albums. Featured Londoner Mick Jones (g) and New York native Lou Gramm (v). 'Waiting for a Girl Like You' stayed at No.2 in the US for a record-breaking 10 weeks (78 WEEKS) pos/wks

6 May 78	FEELS LIKE THE FIRST TIME *Atlantic K 11086*	39 6
15 Jul 78	COLD AS ICE *Atlantic K 10986*	24 10
28 Oct 78	HOT BLOODED *Atlantic K 11167*	42 3
24 Feb 79	BLUE MORNING, BLUE DAY *Atlantic K 11236*	45 4
29 Aug 81	URGENT *Atlantic K 11665*	54 4
10 Oct 81	JUKE BOX HERO *Atlantic K 11678*	48 4
12 Dec 81 ●	WAITING FOR A GIRL LIKE YOU *Atlantic K 11696*	8 13
8 May 82	URGENT (re-issue) *Atlantic K 11728*	45 5
8 Dec 84 ★	I WANT TO KNOW WHAT LOVE IS *Atlantic A 9596* ▲	1 16
6 Apr 85	THAT WAS YESTERDAY *Atlantic A 9571*	28 6
22 Jun 85	COLD AS ICE (re-mix) *Atlantic A 9539*	64 2
19 Dec 87	SAY YOU WILL *Atlantic A 91691*	71 4
22 Oct 94	WHITE LIE *Arista 74321232862*	58 1

FORMATIONS US, male vocal group (11 WEEKS) — pos/wks

		pos/wks
31 Jul 71	AT THE TOP OF THE STAIRS (re) Mojo 2027 001	**28** 11

George FORMBY UK, male vocalist / instrumentalist
– ukulele – George Hoy Booth, d. 6 Mar 1961 (3 WEEKS) — pos/wks

		pos/wks
21 Jul 60	HAPPY GO LUCKY ME / BANJO BOY Pye 7N 15269	**40** 3

See also 2 IN A TENT

FORREST US, male vocalist – Forrest M Thomas Jr (20 WEEKS) — pos/wks

		pos/wks
26 Feb 83 ●	ROCK THE BOAT CBS A 3163	**4** 10
14 May 83	FEEL THE NEED IN ME CBS A 3411	**17** 8
17 Sep 83	ONE LOVER (DON'T STOP THE SHOW) CBS A 3734	**67** 2

Sharon FORRESTER Jamaica, female vocalist (1 WEEK) — pos/wks

		pos/wks
11 Feb 95	LOVE INSIDE ffrr FCD 253	**50** 1

Lance FORTUNE UK, male vocalist – Chris Morris (18 WEEKS) — pos/wks

		pos/wks
19 Feb 60 ●	BE MINE Pye 7N 15240	**4** 13
5 May 60	THIS LOVE I HAVE FOR YOU Pye 7N 15260	**26** 5

FORTUNES UK, male vocal / instrumental group (65 WEEKS) — pos/wks

		pos/wks
8 Jul 65 ●	YOU'VE GOT YOUR TROUBLES Decca F 12173	**2** 14
7 Oct 65 ●	HERE IT COMES AGAIN Decca F 12243	**4** 14
3 Feb 66	THIS GOLDEN RING Decca F 12321	**15** 9
11 Sep 71 ●	FREEDOM COME, FREEDOM GO Capitol CL 15693	**6** 17
29 Jan 72 ●	STORM IN A TEACUP Capitol CL 15707	**7** 11

45 KING (DJ MARK THE 45 KING)
US, male producer – Mark James (6 WEEKS) — pos/wks

		pos/wks
28 Oct 89	THE KING IS HERE / THE 900 NUMBER (re) Dance Trax DRX 9	**60** 6

49ers
Italy, male producer – Gianfranco Bortolotti (27 WEEKS) — pos/wks

		pos/wks
16 Dec 89 ●	TOUCH ME Fourth & Broadway BRW 157	**3** 13
17 Mar 90	DON'T YOU LOVE ME Fourth & Broadway BRW 167	**12** 6
9 Jun 90	GIRL TO GIRL Fourth & Broadway BRW 174	**31** 3
6 Jun 92	GOT TO BE FREE Fourth & Broadway BRW 255	**46** 2
29 Aug 92	THE MESSAGE Fourth & Broadway BRW 257	**68** 1
18 Mar 95	ROCKIN' MY BODY Media MCSTD 2021 [1]	**31** 2

[1] 49ers featuring Ann-Marie Smith

See also CAPPELLA

Itsy FOSTER – See EXOTICA featuring Itsy FOSTER

FOSTER and ALLEN
Ireland, male vocal duo – Mike Foster and Tony Allen (47 WEEKS) — pos/wks

		pos/wks
27 Feb 82	A BUNCH OF THYME Ritz RITZ 5	**18** 11
30 Oct 82	OLD FLAMES Ritz RITZ 028	**51** 8
19 Feb 83	MAGGIE Ritz RITZ 025	**27** 9
29 Oct 83	I WILL LOVE YOU ALL MY LIFE Ritz RITZ 056	**49** 6
30 Jun 84	JUST FOR OLD TIME'S SAKE Ritz RITZ 066	**47** 6
29 Mar 86	AFTER ALL THESE YEARS Ritz RITZ 106	**43** 7

FOUNDATIONS West Indies / UK / Sri Lanka,
male vocal / instrumental group (57 WEEKS) — pos/wks

		pos/wks
27 Sep 67 ★	BABY NOW THAT I'VE FOUND YOU Pye 7N 17366	**1** 16
24 Jan 68	BACK ON MY FEET AGAIN Pye 7N 17417	**18** 10
1 May 68	ANY OLD TIME (YOU'RE LONELY AND SAD) (re) Pye 7N 17503	**48** 2
20 Nov 68 ●	BUILD ME UP BUTTERCUP Pye 7N 17636	**2** 15
12 Mar 69 ●	IN THE BAD BAD OLD DAYS (BEFORE YOU LOVED ME) Pye 7N 17702	**8** 10
13 Sep 69	BORN TO LIVE, BORN TO DIE Pye 7N 17809	**46** 3
12 Dec 98	BUILD ME UP BUTTERCUP (re-issue) Castle NEEX 1001	**71** 1

FOUNTAINS OF WAYNE
US, male vocal / instrumental group (7 WEEKS) — pos/wks

		pos/wks
22 Mar 97	RADIATION VIBE Atlantic 7567956262	**32** 2
10 May 97	SINK TO THE BOTTOM Atlantic A 5612CD	**42** 1
26 Jul 97	SURVIVAL CAR Atlantic AT 0004CD	**53** 1
27 Dec 97	I WANT AN ALIEN FOR CHRISTMAS Atlantic AT 0020CD	**36** 2
20 Mar 99	DENISE Atlantic AT 0053CD	**57** 1

FOUR ACES US, male vocal group (40 WEEKS) — pos/wks

		pos/wks
30 Jul 54 ●	THREE COINS IN THE FOUNTAIN (re) Brunswick 05308 [1]	**5** 6
7 Jan 55 ●	MISTER SANDMAN Brunswick 05355 [1]	**9** 5
20 May 55	STRANGER IN PARADISE Brunswick 05418	**6** 6
18 Nov 55 ●	LOVE IS A MANY SPLENDORED THING Brunswick 05480 [1] ▲**2** 13
19 Oct 56	A WOMAN IN LOVE Brunswick 05589 [1]	**19** 3
4 Jan 57	FRIENDLY PERSUASION (THEE I LOVE) Brunswick 05623 [1]	**29** 1
23 Jan 59	THE WORLD OUTSIDE Brunswick 05773	**18** 6

[1] Four Aces featuring Al Alberts

FOUR BUCKETEERS UK, male / female vocal group (6 WEEKS) — pos/wks

		pos/wks
3 May 80	THE BUCKET OF WATER SONG CBS 8393	**26** 6

FOUR ESQUIRES US, male vocal group (2 WEEKS) — pos/wks

		pos/wks
31 Jan 58	LOVE ME FOREVER London HLO 8533	**23** 2

4 HERO UK, male instrumental group (6 WEEKS) — pos/wks

		pos/wks
24 Nov 90	MR KIRK'S NIGHTMARE Reinforced RIVET 1203	**73** 2
9 May 92	COOKIN' UP YAH BRAIN Reinforced RIVET 1216	**59** 2
15 Aug 98	STAR CHASERS Talkin' Loud TLCD 36	**41** 1
3 Nov 01	LES FLEUR Talkin' Loud TLCD 66	**53** 1

'Mr Kirk's Nightmare' was titled 'Combat Dancing (EP)' in its first week on chart

400 BLOWS UK, male vocal / instrumental duo (4 WEEKS) — pos/wks

		pos/wks
29 Jun 85	MOVIN' Illuminated ILL 61	**54** 4

FOUR JAYS – See Billy FURY

FOUR KESTRELS – See Billy FURY

FOUR KNIGHTS US, male vocal group (11 WEEKS) — pos/wks

		pos/wks
4 Jun 54 ●	(OH BABY MINE) I GET SO LONELY (re) Capitol CL 14076	**5** 11

FOUR LADS Canada, male vocal group (23 WEEKS) — pos/wks

		pos/wks
19 Dec 52 ●	FAITH CAN MOVE MOUNTAINS (re) Columbia DB 3154 [1]	**7** 3
22 Oct 54 ●	RAIN, RAIN, RAIN Philips PB 311 [2]	**8** 16
28 Apr 60	STANDING ON THE CORNER Philips PB 1000	**34** 4

[1] Johnnie Ray and The Four Lads [2] Frankie Laine and The Four Lads

4 NON BLONDES
US, female / male vocal / instrumental group (19 WEEKS) — pos/wks

		pos/wks
19 Jun 93 ●	WHAT'S UP Interscope A 8412CD	**2** 17
16 Oct 93	SPACEMAN Interscope A 8349CD	**53** 2

4 OF US
Ireland, male vocal / instrumental group (6 WEEKS) — pos/wks

		pos/wks
27 Feb 93	SHE HITS ME Columbia 6589192	**35** 4
1 May 93	I MISS YOU Columbia 6591722	**62** 2

FOUR PENNIES UK, male vocal / instrumental
group – lead vocal Lionel Morton (56 WEEKS) — pos/wks

		pos/wks
16 Jan 64	DO YOU WANT ME TO (re) Philips BF 1296	**47** 2
2 Apr 64 ★	JULIET Philips BF 1322	**1** 15
16 Jul 64	I FOUND OUT THE HARD WAY Philips BF 1349	**14** 11
29 Oct 64	BLACK GIRL Philips BF 1366	**20** 12
7 Oct 65	UNTIL IT'S TIME FOR YOU TO GO Philips BF 1435	**19** 11
17 Feb 66	TROUBLE IS MY MIDDLE NAME Philips BF 1469	**32** 5

Re-entries are listed as (re), (2re), (3re), etc which signifies that the hit re-entered the chart once, twice or three times, etc

TOP 30 TRIBUTES

SINGLE TITLE - RECORDED BY - PEAK POSITION - WEEKS ON CHART

#	Title	Peak	Weeks
1.	GENO [Geno Washington] Dexy's Midnight Runners	1	(14)
2.	ABBA-ESQUE (EP) Erasure	1	(12)
3.	FOUR BACHARACH AND DAVID SONGS (EP) Deacon Blue	2	(9)
4.	THANK ABBA FOR THE MUSIC Steps, Tina Cousins, Cleopatra, B*Witched, Billie	4	(13)
5.	BO DIDDLEY Buddy Holly	4	(12)
6.	I REMEMBER ELVIS PRESLEY (THE KING IS DEAD) Danny Mirror	4	(9)
7.	THE BALLAD OF TOM JONES Space with Cerys of Catatonia	4	(8)
8.	JACKIE WILSON SAID (I'M IN HEAVEN WHEN YOU SMILE) Dexy's Midnight Runners	5	(7)
9.	I FEEL LIKE BUDDY HOLLY Alvin Stardust	7	(11)
10.	LULU SELLING TEA* Proclaimers	9	(8)
11.	WOOD BEEZ (PRAY LIKE ARETHA FRANKLIN) Scritti Politti	10	(12)
12.	BEACH BOY GOLD Gidea Park	11	(13)
13.	WHEN SMOKEY SINGS [Smokey Robinson] ABC	11	(10)
14.	BUDDY HOLLY Weezer	12	(7)
15.	THERE'S A GUY WORKS DOWN THE CHIP SHOP SWEARS HE'S ELVIS Kirsty MacColl	14	(9)
=16.	NOW I KNOW WHAT MADE OTIS BLUE [Otis Redding] Paul Young	14	(7)
=16.	STARS ON STEVIE [Stevie Wonder] Starsound	14	(7)
18.	ALL I WANT FOR CHRISTMAS IS A BEATLE Dora Bryan	20	(6)
19.	CALLING ELVIS Dire Straits	21	(4)
20.	TRIBUTE TO BUDDY HOLLY Mike Berry and the Outlaws	24	(6)
21.	IF MADONNA CALLS Junior Vasquez	24	(2)
22.	ERASURE-ISH (A LITTLE RESPECT / STOP!) Bjorn Again	25	(3)
23.	LIKE MARVIN GAYE SAID (WHAT'S GOING ON) Speech	35	(2)
24.	BEATLES AND THE STONES House of Love	36	(4)
25.	TRIBUTE TO JIM REEVES Larry Cunningham and the Mighty Avons	40	(11)
26.	DISCO BEATLEMANIA DBM	45	(3)
27.	THE MONKEES Rampage	51	(1)
28.	THE FRANK SONATA [Frank Sinatra] Longpigs	57	(1)
29.	JOHNNY MATHIS' FEET American Music Club	58	(2)
30.	SMELLS LIKE NIRVANA Weird Al Yankovic	58	(1)

* Included on the 'King of the Road' EP

Geno Washington started his singing career when he was a US serviceman stationed in East Anglia and was immortalised by Dexy's Midnight Runners at No.1 in this tribute chart

FOUR PREPS US, male vocal group (23 WEEKS)

		pos/wks
13 Jun 58 ●	BIG MAN (re) *Capitol CL 14873*..................................2 14	
26 May 60	GOT A GIRL (re) *Capitol CL 15128*.............................28 7	
2 Nov 61	MORE MONEY FOR YOU AND ME (MEDLEY) *Capitol CL 15217*...39 2	

Tracks on medley: *Mr Blue / Alley Oop / Smoke Gets in Your Eyes / In This Whole Wide World / A Worried Man / Tom Dooley / A Teenager in Love – all songs feature new lyrics*

FOUR SEASONS 148 Top 500

No.1 US group of the early 1960s: Frankie Valli (v), Bob Gaudio (k/v), Nick Massi (b/v) (died 2000), Tommy DeVito (g/v). Falsetto-voiced Valli's quartet, the first group to score three US No.1s in succession, has a chart span there of almost 40 years (151 WEEKS) pos/wks

4 Oct 62 ●	SHERRY *Stateside SS 122* ▲ 8 16
17 Jan 63	BIG GIRLS DON'T CRY *Stateside SS 145* ▲ 13 10
28 Mar 63	WALK LIKE A MAN *Stateside SS 169* ▲...............12 12
27 Jun 63	AIN'T THAT A SHAME *Stateside SS 194* 38 3
27 Aug 64 ●	RAG DOLL *Philips BF 1347* 1 ▲ 2 13
18 Nov 65 ●	LET'S HANG ON *Philips BF 1439* 1 ....4 16
31 Mar 66	WORKIN' MY WAY BACK TO YOU *Philips BF 1474* 2 ....50 3
2 Jun 66	OPUS 17 (DON'T YOU WORRY 'BOUT ME) *Philips BF 1493* 2 ....20 9
29 Sep 66	I'VE GOT YOU UNDER MY SKIN *Philips BF 1511* 2 ...12 11
12 Jan 67	TELL IT TO THE RAIN *Philips BF 1538* 2 ....37 5
19 Apr 75 ●	THE NIGHT *Mowest MW 3024* 3 ....7 9
20 Sep 75 ★	WHO LOVES YOU *Warner Bros. / Curb K 16602* 6 9
31 Jan 76 ★	DECEMBER, 1963, (OH, WHAT A NIGHT) *Warner Bros. / Curb K 16688* ▲ 1 10
24 Apr 76 ●	SILVER STAR *Warner Bros. / Curb K 16742* 3 9
27 Nov 76	WE CAN WORK IT OUT *Warner Bros. / Curb K 16845* 34 4
18 Jun 77	RHAPSODY *Warner Bros. / Curb K 16932* 37 3
20 Aug 77	DOWN THE HALL *Warner Bros. / Curb K 16982* 34 5
29 Oct 88	DECEMBER, 1963, (OH, WHAT A NIGHT) (re-mix) *BR 45277* 3 ....49 4

1 Four Seasons with the sound of Frankie Valli 2 Four Seasons with Frankie Valli 3 Frankie Valli and The Four Seasons

4 STRINGS
Holland, male / female production / vocal duo (12 WEEKS) pos/wks

23 Dec 00	DAY TIME *AM:PM 139*.....................................48 3
11 May 02	(TAKE ME AWAY) INTO THE NIGHT (re) *Nebula / Virgin CDRD 107* 15 7
14 Sep 02	DIVING *Nebula VCRD 108* 38 2

See also MADELYNE

4 THE CAUSE US, male / female vocal group (9 WEEKS) pos/wks

10 Oct 98	STAND BY ME *RCA 74321622442* 12 9

FOUR TOPS 29 Top 500

Unmistakable R&B vocal group from Detroit: Levi Stubbs, Renaldo Benson, Lawrence Payton (d. 1997), Abdul Fakir. The legendary Motown act performed together for a record 44 years (until Payton's death) and were inducted into the Rock and Roll Hall of Fame in 1990 (318 WEEKS) pos/wks

1 Jul 65	I CAN'T HELP MYSELF *Tamla Motown TMG 515* ▲ 23 9
2 Sep 65	IT'S THE SAME OLD SONG *Tamla Motown TMG 528*.....34 8
21 Jul 66	LOVING YOU IS SWEETER THAN EVER *Tamla Motown TMG 568*.................................21 12
13 Oct 66 ★	REACH OUT I'LL BE THERE *Tamla Motown TMG 579* ▲.....1 16
12 Jan 67 ●	STANDING IN THE SHADOWS OF LOVE *Tamla Motown TMG 589* 6 8
30 Mar 67 ●	BERNADETTE *Tamla Motown TMG 601* 8 10
15 Jun 67	SEVEN ROOMS OF GLOOM *Tamla Motown TMG 612* 12 9
11 Oct 67	YOU KEEP RUNNING AWAY *Tamla Motown TMG 623* ...26 7
13 Dec 67 ●	WALK AWAY RENEE *Tamla Motown TMG 634* 3 11
13 Mar 68 ●	IF I WERE A CARPENTER *Tamla Motown TMG 647* 7 11
21 Aug 68	YESTERDAY'S DREAMS *Tamla Motown TMG 665* 23 15
13 Nov 68	I'M IN A DIFFERENT WORLD *Tamla Motown TMG 675*....27 13
28 May 69	WHAT IS A MAN *Tamla Motown TMG 698* 16 11

27 Sep 69	DO WHAT YOU GOTTA DO *Tamla Motown TMG 710* 11 11
21 Mar 70 ●	I CAN'T HELP MYSELF (re-issue) *Tamla Motown TMG 732* 10 11
30 May 70 ●	IT'S ALL IN THE GAME (re) *Tamla Motown TMG 736* 5 16
3 Oct 70 ●	STILL WATER (LOVE) (re) *Tamla Motown TMG 752*....10 12
1 May 71	JUST SEVEN NUMBERS (CAN STRAIGHTEN OUT MY LIFE) *Tamla Motown TMG 770* 36 5
26 Jun 71	RIVER DEEP MOUNTAIN HIGH *Tamla Motown TMG 777* 1 ....11 10
25 Sep 71 ●	SIMPLE GAME *Tamla Motown TMG 785* 3 11
20 Nov 71	YOU GOTTA HAVE LOVE IN YOUR HEART *Tamla Motown TMG 793* 1 ....25 10
11 Mar 72	BERNADETTE (re-issue) *Tamla Motown TMG 803* ...23 7
5 Aug 72	WALK WITH ME TALK WITH ME DARLING *Tamla Motown TMG 823* 32 6
18 Nov 72	KEEPER OF THE CASTLE *Probe PRO 575*................18 9
10 Nov 73	SWEET UNDERSTANDING LOVE *Probe PRO 604* 29 10
17 Oct 81 ●	WHEN SHE WAS MY GIRL *Casablanca CAN 1005* 3 10
19 Dec 81	DON'T WALK AWAY *Casablanca CAN 1006* 16 11
6 Mar 82	TONIGHT I'M GONNA LOVE YOU ALL OVER *Casablanca CAN 1008*.............................43 4
26 Jun 82	BACK TO SCHOOL AGAIN *RSO 89* 62 2
23 Jul 88	REACH OUT I'LL BE THERE (re-mix) *Motown ZB 41943*....11 9
17 Sep 88	INDESTRUCTIBLE *Arista 111717* 2 ....55 4
3 Dec 88 ●	LOCO IN ACAPULCO *Arista 111850* 7 13
25 Feb 89	INDESTRUCTIBLE *Arista 112074* 2 ....30 7

1 Supremes and The Four Tops 2 Four Tops featuring Smokey Robinson

The original US recording of 'Indestructible' was not issued until after the chart run of the UK-only mix

4 VINI featuring Elisabeth TROY
UK, male vocal / production group and UK, female vocalist (1 WEEK) pos/wks

18 May 02	FOREVER YOUNG *Botchit & Scarper BOS 2CD033*.......75 1

4CLUBBERS Germany, male production group (1 WEEK) pos/wks

14 Sep 02	CHILDREN *Code Blue BLUO 26CD*.......................45 1

See also FUTURE BREEZE

4MANDU UK, male vocal group (6 WEEKS) pos/wks

29 Jul 95	THIS IS IT *Final Vinyl 74321291222* 45 3
17 Feb 96	DO IT FOR LOVE *Arista 74321343902* 45 2
15 Jun 96	BABY DON'T GO *Arista 74321375914*..................47 1

FOURMOST UK, male vocal / instrumental group (64 WEEKS) pos/wks

12 Sep 63 ●	HELLO LITTLE GIRL *Parlophone R 5056* 9 17
26 Dec 63	I'M IN LOVE *Parlophone R 5078*........................17 12
23 Apr 64 ●	A LITTLE LOVING *Parlophone R 5128*...................6 13
13 Aug 64	HOW CAN I TELL HER *Parlophone R 5157* 33 4
26 Nov 64	BABY I NEED YOUR LOVIN' *Parlophone R 5194*......24 12
9 Dec 65	GIRLS, GIRLS, GIRLS *Parlophone R 5379*...............33 6

14-18 UK, male vocalist – Peter Waterman (4 WEEKS) pos/wks

1 Nov 75	GOODBYE-EE *Magnet MAG 48* 33 4

See also STOCK AITKEN WATERMAN

40 THEVZ – See COOLIO

Bernard FOWLER – See BOMB THE BASS

FOX UK / US, male / female vocal / instrumental group (29 WEEKS) pos/wks

15 Feb 75 ●	ONLY YOU CAN *GTO GT 8* 3 11
10 May 75	IMAGINE ME IMAGINE YOU *GTO GT 21* 15 8
10 Apr 76 ●	S-S-S-SINGLE BED *GTO GT 57* 4 10

Noosha FOX UK, female vocalist (6 WEEKS) pos/wks

12 Nov 77	GEORGINA BAILEY *GTO GT 106* 31 6

Samantha FOX UK, female artist (73 WEEKS) pos/wks

22 Mar 86 ●	TOUCH ME (I WANT YOUR BODY) *Jive FOXY 1* 3 10

28 Jun 86 ●	DO YA DO YA (WANNA PLEASE ME) *Jive FOXY 2*	10	7
6 Sep 86	HOLD ON TIGHT *Jive FOXY 3*	26	5
13 Dec 86	I'M ALL YOU NEED *Jive FOXY 4*	41	6
30 May 87 ●	NOTHING'S GONNA STOP ME NOW *Jive FOXY 5*	8	9
25 Jul 87	I SURRENDER (TO THE SPIRIT OF THE NIGHT) *Jive FOXY 6*	25	7
17 Oct 87	I PROMISE YOU (GET READY) *Jive FOXY 7*	58	3
19 Dec 87	TRUE DEVOTION *Jive FOXY 8*	62	3
21 May 88	NAUGHTY GIRLS (NEED LOVE TOO) *Jive FOXY 9*	31	5
19 Nov 88	LOVE HOUSE *Jive FOXY 10*	32	6
28 Jan 89	I ONLY WANNA BE WITH YOU *Jive FOXY 11*	16	8
17 Jun 89	I WANNA HAVE SOME FUN *Jive FOXY 12*	63	2
28 Mar 98	SANTA MARIA *All Around the World CDGLOBE 163*	31	2

See also SOX

Bruce FOXTON *UK, male vocalist (9 WEEKS)*

				pos/wks
30 Jul 83	FREAK *Arista BFOX 1*		23	5
29 Oct 83	THIS IS THE WAY *Arista BFOX 2*		56	3
21 Apr 84	IT MAKES ME WONDER *Arista BFOX 3*		74	1

See also JAM

Inez FOXX *US, female vocalist (8 WEEKS)*

				pos/wks
23 Jul 64	HURT BY LOVE *Sue WI 323*		40	3
19 Feb 69	MOCKINGBIRD (re) *United Artists UP 2269* 1		33	5

1 Inez and Charlie Foxx

John FOXX *UK, male vocalist – Dennis Leigh (31 WEEKS)*

				pos/wks
26 Jan 80	UNDERPASS *Virgin VS 318*		31	8
29 Mar 80	NO-ONE DRIVING (DOUBLE SINGLE) *Virgin VS 338*		32	4
19 Jul 80	BURNING CAR *Virgin VS 360*		35	7
8 Nov 80	MILES AWAY *Virgin VS 382*		51	3
29 Aug 81	EUROPE (AFTER THE RAIN) *Virgin VS 393*		40	5
2 Jul 83	ENDLESSLY *Virgin VS 543*		66	3
17 Sep 83	YOUR DRESS *Virgin VS 615*		61	1

Tracks on double single: No One Driving / Glimmer / This City / Mr No

FRAGGLES *UK / US, puppets from TV series (8 WEEKS)*

				pos/wks
18 Feb 84	'FRAGGLE ROCK' THEME *RCA 389*		33	8

FRAGMA *Germany / Spain, male / female production / vocal group (45 WEEKS)*

				pos/wks
25 Sep 99	TOCA ME *Positiva CDTIV 120*		11	6
22 Apr 00 ★	TOCA'S MIRACLE (re-mix) (re) *Positiva CDTIV 128* 1 ■		1	17
13 Jan 01 ●	EVERYTIME YOU NEED ME *Positiva CDTIV 147* 2		3	11
19 May 01 ●	YOU ARE ALIVE *Positiva CDTIVS 153*		4	9
8 Dec 01	SAY THAT YOU'RE HERE *Illustrious CDILLS 001*		25	2

1 Vocals by Co Co 2 Fragma featuring Maria Rubia

Roddy FRAME *UK, male vocalist / instrumentalist (2 WEEKS)*

				pos/wks
19 Sep 98	REASON FOR LIVING *Independiente ISOM 18MS*		45	2

See also AZTEC CAMERA

Peter FRAMPTON *UK, male vocalist (24 WEEKS)*

				pos/wks
1 May 76 ●	SHOW ME THE WAY *A&M AMS 7218*		10	12
11 Sep 76	BABY I LOVE YOUR WAY *A&M AMS 7246*		43	5
6 Nov 76	DO YOU FEEL LIKE WE DO *A&M AMS 7260*		39	4
23 Jul 77	I'M IN YOU *A&M AMS 7298*		41	1

Connie FRANCIS 53 Top 500

The original Italian-American queen of pop, b. Concetta Franconero, 12 Dec 1938, New Jersey. The most successful international female vocalist of the 1950s and 1960s, the first female teenager to register a UK No.1 single and the first female solo artist to top the UK album chart (244 WEEKS) pos/wks

4 Apr 58 ★	WHO'S SORRY NOW *MGM 975*	1	25
27 Jun 58	I'M SORRY I MADE YOU CRY *MGM 982*	11	10
22 Aug 58 ★	CAROLINA MOON / STUPID CUPID *MGM 985*	1	19

31 Oct 58	I'LL GET BY *MGM 993*	19	6
21 Nov 58	FALLIN' *MGM 993*	20	5
26 Dec 58	YOU ALWAYS HURT THE ONE YOU LOVE *MGM 998*	13	7
13 Feb 59 ●	MY HAPPINESS (re) *MGM 1001*	4	15
3 Jul 59 ●	LIPSTICK ON YOUR COLLAR *MGM 1018*	3	16
11 Sep 59	PLENTY GOOD LOVIN' *MGM 1036*	18	6
4 Dec 59	AMONG MY SOUVENIRS *MGM 1046*	11	10
17 Mar 60	VALENTINO *MGM 1060*	27	8
19 May 60 ●	MAMA / ROBOT MAN *MGM 1076*	2	19
18 Aug 60 ●	EVERYBODY'S SOMEBODY'S FOOL *MGM 1086* ▲	5	13
3 Nov 60 ●	MY HEART HAS A MIND OF ITS OWN *MGM 1100* ▲	3	15
12 Jan 61	MANY TEARS AGO *MGM 1111*	12	9
16 Mar 61 ●	WHERE THE BOYS ARE / BABY ROO *MGM 1121*	5	14
15 Jun 61	BREAKIN' IN A BRAND NEW BROKEN HEART *MGM 1136*	12	11
14 Sep 61 ●	TOGETHER *MGM 1138*	6	11
14 Dec 61	BABY'S FIRST CHRISTMAS *MGM 1145*	30	4
26 Apr 62	DON'T BREAK THE HEART THAT LOVES YOU *MGM 1157* ▲	39	3
2 Aug 62 ●	VACATION *MGM 1165*	10	9
20 Dec 62	I'M GONNA BE WARM THIS WINTER *MGM 1185*	48	1
10 Jun 65	MY CHILD *MGM 1271*	26	6
20 Jan 66	JEALOUS HEART *MGM 1293*	44	2

Baby Roo listed with 'Where the Boys Are' for first eight weeks only

Jill FRANCIS *UK, female vocalist (1 WEEK)*

				pos/wks
3 Jul 93	MAKE LOVE TO ME *Glady Wax GW 003CD*		70	1

Claude FRANÇOIS
France, male vocalist, d. 11 Mar 1978 (4 WEEKS) pos/wks

10 Jan 76	TEARS ON THE TELEPHONE *Bradley's BRAD 7528*	35	4

Girl vocal: Kathy Barnet

Joe FRANK – See HAMILTON, Joe FRANK and REYNOLDS

FRANK AND WALTERS
Ireland, male vocal / instrumental group (13 WEEKS) pos/wks

21 Mar 92	HAPPY BUSMAN *Setanta HOO 2*	49	2
12 Sep 92	THIS IS NOT A SONG *Setanta HOO 3*	46	3
9 Jan 93	AFTER ALL *Setanta HOOCD 4*	11	5
17 Apr 93	FASHION CRISIS HITS NEW YORK *Setanta HOOCD 5*	42	3

FRANKE *UK, male vocalist – Franke Pharoah (3 WEEKS)*

				pos/wks
7 Nov 92	UNDERSTAND THIS GROOVE *China WOK 2028*		60	2
21 May 94	LOVE COME HOME *Triangle BLUESCD 001* 1		73	1

1 Our Tribe with Franke Pharoah and Kristine W

FRANK'EE – See BROTHER BROWN featuring FRANK'EE

FRANKIE GOES TO HOLLYWOOD 155 Top 500

Fiercely marketed, controversial and regularly re-mixed Merseyside-based quintet fronted by Holly Johnson (b. 19 Feb 1960, Sudan). First act since Gerry and the Pacemakers to hit No.1 with initial three releases. During July 1984, 'Two Tribes' and 'Relax' held top two places in the chart. Best-selling single: 'Relax' 1,910,000 (147 WEEKS) pos/wks

26 Nov 83 ★	RELAX (re) *ZTT ZTAS 1* ◆	1	52
16 Jun 84 ★	TWO TRIBES (re) *ZTT ZTAS 3* ◆ ■	1	21
1 Dec 84 ★	THE POWER OF LOVE (re) *ZTT ZTAS 5*	1	12
30 May 85 ●	WELCOME TO THE PLEASURE DOME *ZTT ZTAS 7*	2	11
6 Sep 86 ●	RAGE HARD *ZTT ZTAS 22*	4	7
22 Nov 86	WARRIORS (OF THE WASTELAND) *ZTT ZTAS 25*	19	8
7 Mar 87	WATCHING THE WILDLIFE *ZTT ZTAS 26*	28	6
2 Oct 93 ●	RELAX (re-issue) *ZTT FGTH 1CD*	5	7
20 Nov 93	WELCOME TO THE PLEASURE DOME (re-mix) *ZTT FGTH 2CD*	18	3
18 Dec 93 ●	THE POWER OF LOVE (re-issue) *ZTT FGTH 3CD*	10	7
26 Feb 94	TWO TRIBES (re-mix) *ZTT FGTH 4CD*	16	3
1 Jul 00 ●	THE POWER OF LOVE (re-mix) *ZTT ZTT 150CD*	6	6
9 Sep 00	TWO TRIBES (re-mix) *ZTT ZTT 154CD*	17	3
18 Nov 00	WELCOME TO THE PLEASURE DOME (re-mix) *ZTT ZTT 166CD*	45	1

Aretha FRANKLIN (107) Top 500

The 'Queen of Soul Music', b. 25 Mar 1942, Tennessee, US. With six decades of recording behind her, this legendary gospel-influenced vocalist has won countless awards and amassed more R&B hits than any other female in her homeland (182 WEEKS) pos/wks

			pos	wks
8 Jun 67	●	RESPECT *Atlantic 584 115* ▲	10	14
23 Aug 67		BABY I LOVE YOU *Atlantic 584 127*	39	4
20 Dec 67		SATISFACTION *Atlantic 584 157*	37	7
13 Mar 68		SINCE YOU'VE BEEN GONE (SWEET SWEET BABY) *Atlantic 584 172*	47	1
22 May 68		THINK *Atlantic 584 186*	26	9
7 Aug 68	●	I SAY A LITTLE PRAYER *Atlantic 584 206*	4	14
22 Aug 70		DON'T PLAY THAT SONG *Atlantic 2091 027*	13	11
2 Oct 71		SPANISH HARLEM *Atlantic 2091 138*	14	9
8 Sep 73		ANGEL *Atlantic K 10346*	37	5
16 Feb 74		UNTIL YOU COME BACK TO ME (THAT'S WHAT I'M GONNA DO) *Atlantic K 10399*	26	8
6 Dec 80		WHAT A FOOL BELIEVES *Arista ARIST 377*	46	7
19 Sep 81		LOVE ALL THE HURT AWAY *Arista ARIST 428* 1	49	3
4 Sep 82		JUMP TO IT *Arista ARIST 479*	42	5
23 Jul 83		GET IT RIGHT *Arista ARIST 537*	74	2
13 Jul 85		FREEWAY OF LOVE (re) *Arista ARIST 624*	51	6
2 Nov 85	●	SISTERS ARE DOIN' IT FOR THEMSELVES *RCA PB 40339* 2	9	11
23 Nov 85		WHO'S ZOOMIN' WHO *Arista ARIST 633*	11	14
22 Feb 86		ANOTHER NIGHT *Arista ARIST 657*	54	6
25 Oct 86		JUMPIN' JACK FLASH *Arista ARIST 678*	58	3
31 Jan 87	★	I KNEW YOU WERE WAITING (FOR ME) *Epic DUET 1* 3 ▲	1	9
14 Mar 87		JIMMY LEE *Arista RIS 6*	46	4
6 May 89		THROUGH THE STORM *Arista 112185* 4	41	3
9 Sep 89		IT ISN'T, IT WASN'T, IT AIN'T NEVER GONNA BE *Arista 112545* 5	29	5
7 Apr 90		THINK *East West A 7951*	31	2
27 Jul 91		EVERYDAY PEOPLE *Arista 114420*	69	1
12 Feb 94	●	A DEEPER LOVE *Arista 74321187022*	5	7
25 Jun 94		WILLING TO FORGIVE *Arista 74321213342*	17	7
9 May 98		A ROSE IS STILL A ROSE *Arista 74321569742*	22	4
26 Sep 98		HERE WE GO AGAIN *Arista 74321612742*	68	1

1 Aretha Franklin and George Benson 2 Eurythmics and Aretha Franklin 3 Aretha Franklin and George Michael 4 Aretha Franklin and Elton John 5 Aretha Franklin and Whitney Houston

'Think' on East West is a re-recording. It was the flip side of 'Everybody Needs Somebody to Love' by Blues Brothers and was listed for the first two weeks of that record's run

Erma FRANKLIN
US, female vocalist, d. 7 Sep 2002 (10 WEEKS) pos/wks

			pos	wks
10 Oct 92	●	(TAKE A LITTLE) PIECE OF MY HEART *Epic 6583847*	9	10

Rodney FRANKLIN
US, male instrumentalist – piano (9 WEEKS) pos/wks

			pos	wks
19 Apr 80	●	THE GROOVE *CBS 8529*	7	9

Chevelle FRANKLYN / BEENIE MAN
Jamaica, female / male vocalists (1 WEEK) pos/wks

			pos	wks
20 Sep 97		DANCEHALL QUEEN *Island Jamaica IJCD 2018* 1	70	1

FRANTIC FIVE – See Don LANG

FRANTIQUE *US, female vocal group (12 WEEKS)* pos/wks

			pos	wks
11 Aug 79	●	STRUT YOUR FUNKY STUFF *Philadelphia Int. PIR 7728*	10	12

Elizabeth FRASER – See COCTEAU TWINS; MASSIVE ATTACK; Ian McCULLOCH; FUTURE SOUND OF LONDON

Wendy FRASER – See Patrick SWAYZE featuring Wendy FRASER

FRASH *UK, male vocal / instrumental group (1 WEEK)* pos/wks

			pos	wks
18 Feb 95		HERE I GO AGAIN *PWL International FLIPCD 1*	69	1

FRAZIER CHORUS
UK, male / female vocal / instrumental group (14 WEEKS) pos/wks

			pos	wks
4 Feb 89		DREAM KITCHEN *Virgin VS 1145*	57	3
15 Apr 89		TYPICAL! *Virgin VS 1174*	53	2
15 Jul 89		SLOPPY HEART *Virgin VS 1192*	73	1
9 Jun 90		CLOUD 8 *Virgin VS 1252*	52	3
25 Aug 90		NOTHING *Virgin VS 1284*	51	3
16 Feb 91		WALKING ON AIR *Virgin VS 1330*	60	2

FREAKPOWER
UK / Canada, male vocal / instrumental group (20 WEEKS) pos/wks

			pos	wks
16 Oct 93		TURN ON TUNE IN COP OUT *Fourth & Broadway BRCD 284* 1	29	5
26 Feb 94		RUSH *Fourth & Broadway BRCD 291*	62	2
18 Mar 95	●	TURN ON TUNE IN COP OUT (re-issue) *Fourth & Broadway BRCD 317*	3	9
8 Jun 96		NEW DIRECTION *Fourth & Broadway BRCD 331*	60	1
9 May 98		NO WAY *Deconstruction 74321578572*	29	3

1 Freak Power

See also Norman COOK; BEATS INTERNATIONAL; PIZZAMAN; FATBOY SLIM; MIGHTY DUB KATZ; HOUSEMARTINS

FREAKY REALISTIC
UK / Japan, male / female vocal / instrumental group (3 WEEKS) pos/wks

			pos	wks
3 Apr 93		KOOCHIE RYDER *Realism FRECD 2*	52	2
3 Jul 93		LEONARD NIMOY *Realism FRECD 3*	71	1

FREAKYMAN
Holland, male producer – Andre Van Den Bosch (1 WEEK) pos/wks

			pos	wks
27 Sep 97		DISCOBUG '97 *Xtravaganza 0091285 EXT*	68	1

Stan FREBERG
US, male vocalist / comedian (5 WEEKS) pos/wks

			pos	wks
19 Nov 54		SH-BOOM *Capitol CL 14187* 1	15	2
27 Jul 56		ROCK ISLAND LINE / HEARTBREAK HOTEL (re) *Capitol CL 14608* 2	24	2
12 May 60		THE OLD PAYOLA ROLL BLUES *Capitol CL 15122* 3	40	1

1 Stan Freberg with the Toads 2 Stan Freberg and his Sniffle Group 3 Stan Freberg with Jesse White

FRED & ROXY
UK, female vocal duo – Phaedra and Roxanna Aslami (2 WEEKS) pos/wks

			pos	wks
5 Feb 00		SOMETHING FOR THE WEEKEND *Echo ECSCD 81*	36	2

John FRED and the PLAYBOY BAND
US, male vocal / instrumental group (12 WEEKS) pos/wks

			pos	wks
3 Jan 68	●	JUDY IN DISGUISE (WITH GLASSES) *Pye International 7N 25442* ▲	3	12

FREDDIE and the DREAMERS (396) Top 500

Fun beat group fronted and founded by the leaping, laughing Freddie Garrity, b. 14 Nov 1940, Manchester, UK. Immortalised in the 1965 film 'Every Day's a Holiday', which was re-titled 'Seaside Swingers' in the US where they topped the charts with 'I'm Telling You Now' (85 WEEKS) pos/wks

			pos	wks
9 May 63	●	IF YOU GOTTA MAKE A FOOL OF SOMEBODY *Columbia DB 7032*	3	14
8 Aug 63	●	I'M TELLING YOU NOW *Columbia DB 7086* ▲	2	11
7 Nov 63	●	YOU WERE MADE FOR ME *Columbia DB 7147*	3	15
20 Feb 64		OVER YOU *Columbia DB 7214*	13	11
14 May 64		I LOVE YOU BABY *Columbia DB 7286*	16	8
16 Jul 64		JUST FOR YOU *Columbia DB 7322*	41	3
5 Nov 64	●	I UNDERSTAND *Columbia DB 7381*	5	15
22 Apr 65		A LITTLE YOU *Columbia DB 7526*	26	5
4 Nov 65		THOU SHALT NOT STEAL *Columbia DB 7720*	44	3

FREDERICK – See NINA and FREDERICK

Dee FREDRIX UK, female vocalist (5 WEEKS)

			pos/wks
27 Feb 93	**AND SO I WILL WAIT FOR YOU** East West YZ 725CD	**56**	4
3 Jul 93	**DIRTY MONEY** East West YZ 750CD	**74**	1

FREE `482` `Top 500` Blues-orientated London rock quartet; Paul Rodgers (v), Paul Kossoff (g), Andy Fraser (b) and Simon Kirke (d); split 1973 when Rodgers and Kirke formed Bad Company (75 WEEKS)

			pos/wks
6 Jun 70	● **ALL RIGHT NOW (re)** Island WIP 6082	**2**	25
1 May 71	● **MY BROTHER JAKE** Island WIP 6100	**4**	11
27 May 72	**LITTLE BIT OF LOVE** Island WIP 6129	**13**	10
13 Jan 73	● **WISHING WELL** Island WIP 6146	**7**	10
18 Feb 78	**FREE (EP) (re)** Island IEP 6	**11**	10
9 Feb 91	● **ALL RIGHT NOW (re-mix)** Island IS 486	**8**	9

'All Right Now' re-entry peaked at No.15 in Jul 1973 and the 'Free' (EP) re-entered in Oct 1982 peaking at No.57. Tracks on the 'Free' (EP): All Right Now (long version) / My Brother Jake (re-issue) / Wishing Well (re-issue)

FREE – See QUEEN; Wyclef JEAN; Pras MICHEL; QUEEN LATIFAH

FREE SPIRIT UK, male / female vocal duo (1 WEEK)

			pos/wks
13 May 95	**NO MORE RAINY DAYS** Columbia 6612822	**68**	1

FREEEZ UK, male vocal / instrumental group (48 WEEKS)

			pos/wks
7 Jun 80	**KEEP IN TOUCH** Calibre CAB 103	**49**	3
7 Feb 81	● **SOUTHERN FREEEZ** Beggars Banquet BEG 51 `1`	**8**	11
18 Apr 81	**FLYING HIGH** Beggars Banquet BEG 55	**35**	5
18 Jun 83	● **I.O.U.** Beggars Banquet BEG 96	**2**	15
1 Oct 83	**POP GOES MY LOVE** Beggars Banquet BEG 98	**26**	6
17 Jan 87	**I.O.U. (re-mix)** Citybeat CBE 709 `2`	**23**	6
30 May 87	**SOUTHERN FREEEZ (re-mix)** Total Control TOCO 14 `1`	**63**	2

`1` Freeez featuring Ingrid Mansfield Allman `2` Freeez featuring John Rocca

FREEFALL featuring Jan JOHNSTON
UK / Australia, male DJ / production duo – Alan Bremner and Anthony Pappalardo, and female vocalist (5 WEEKS)

			pos/wks
28 Nov 98	**SKYDIVE** Stress CDSTR 89	**75**	1
22 Jul 00	**SKYDIVE (re-mix)** Renaissance Recordings RENCDS 002	**43**	2
8 Sep 01	**SKYDIVE (I FEEL WONDERFUL) (2nd re-mix)** Incentive CENT 22CDS `1`	**35**	2

`1` Freefall featuring Jan Johnston

FREEFALL featuring PSYCHOTROPIC
UK / US, male instrumental / production group (1 WEEK)

			pos/wks
27 Jul 91	**FEEL SURREAL** ffrr FX 160	**63**	1

FREEHOLD JUNIOR SCHOOL – See Fogwell FLAX and the ANKLEBITERS from FREEHOLD JUNIOR SCHOOL

Claire FREELAND UK, female vocalist (1 WEEK)

			pos/wks
10 Jul 01	**FREE** Statuesque CDSTATU 1	**44**	1

FREESTYLERS UK, male instrumental / vocal group (5 WEEKS)

			pos/wks
7 Feb 98	**B-BOY STANCE** Freskanova FND 7 `1`	**23**	3
14 Nov 98	**WARNING** Freskanova FND 14 `2`	**68**	1
24 Jul 99	**HERE WE GO** Freskanova FND 19	**45**	1

`1` Freestylers featuring Tenor Fly `2` Freestylers featuring Navigator

FREIHEIT Germany, male vocal / instrumental group (9 WEEKS)

			pos/wks
17 Dec 88	**KEEPING THE DREAM ALIVE** CBS 652989 7	**14**	9

Deborah FRENCH – See E-LUSTRIOUS

Nicki FRENCH UK, female vocalist (18 WEEKS)

			pos/wks
15 Oct 94	● **TOTAL ECLIPSE OF THE HEART (re)** Bags of Fun BAGSCD 1	**5**	13
22 Apr 95	**FOR ALL WE KNOW** Bags of Fun BAGSCD 4	**42**	2
15 Jul 95	**DID YOU EVER REALLY LOVE ME** Love This LUVTHISCD 2	**55**	1
27 May 00	**DON'T PLAY THAT SONG AGAIN** RCA 74321764572	**34**	2

'Total Eclipse of the Heart' peaked at No.5 on re-entry in Jan 1995

FRENCH AFFAIR
France, male production duo / female vocalist (3 WEEKS)

			pos/wks
16 Sep 00	**MY HEART GOES BOOM** Arista 74321780562	**44**	3

Doug E FRESH and the GET FRESH CREW
US, male rap / DJ group (11 WEEKS)

			pos/wks
9 Nov 85	● **THE SHOW** Cooltempo COOL 116	**7**	11

Freddy FRESH US, male producer – Frederick Schmid (3 WEEKS)

			pos/wks
1 May 99	**BADDER BADDER SCHWING** Eye Q EYEUK 040CD `1`	**34**	2
31 Jul 99	**WHAT IT IS** Eye Q EYEUK 043CD	**63**	1

`1` Freddy Fresh featuring Fatboy Slim

FRESH 4 featuring Lizz E
UK, male DJ / production group and female vocalist (9 WEEKS)

			pos/wks
7 Oct 89	● **WISHING ON A STAR** 10 TEN 287	**10**	9

FRESH PRINCE – See JAZZY JEFF & the FRESH PRINCE

FRESHIES UK, male vocal / instrumental group (3 WEEKS)

			pos/wks
14 Feb 81	**I'M IN LOVE WITH THE GIRL ON A CERTAIN MANCHESTER MEGASTORE CHECKOUT DESK** MCA 670	**54**	3

Matt FRETTON UK, male vocalist (5 WEEKS)

			pos/wks
11 Jun 83	**IT'S SO HIGH** Chrysalis MATT 1	**50**	5

FREUR UK, male vocal / instrumental group (4 WEEKS)

			pos/wks
23 Apr 83	**DOOT DOOT** CBS A 3141	**59**	4

Glenn FREY US, male vocalist (20 WEEKS)

			pos/wks
2 Mar 85	**THE HEAT IS ON** MCA MCA 941	**12**	12
22 Jun 85	**SMUGGLER'S BLUES** BBC RESL 170	**22**	8

See also EAGLES

FRIDA Norway, female vocalist (12 WEEKS)

			pos/wks
21 Aug 82	**I KNOW THERE'S SOMETHING GOING ON** Epic EPC A2603	**43**	7
17 Dec 83	**TIME** Epic A 3983 `1`	**45**	5

`1` Frida and B A Robertson

See also ABBA

Gavin FRIDAY – See BONO

Ralph FRIDGE
Germany, male producer – Ralf Fritsch (4 WEEKS)

			pos/wks
24 Apr 99	**PARADISE** Additive 12AD 036	**68**	1
8 Apr 00	**ANGEL** Incentive CENT 6CDS	**20**	3

Dean FRIEDMAN US, male vocalist (22 WEEKS)

			pos/wks
3 Jun 78	**WOMAN OF MINE** Lifesong LS 401	**52**	5
23 Sep 78	● **LUCKY STARS** Lifesong LS 402	**3**	10
18 Nov 78	**LYDIA** Lifesong LS 403	**31**	7

'Lucky Stars' features uncredited vocals by Denise Marsa

FRIENDS AGAIN
UK, male vocal / instrumental group (3 WEEKS)

			pos/wks
4 Aug 84	**THE FRIENDS AGAIN EP** Mercury FA 1	**59**	3

Tracks on The Friends Again EP: Lullaby on Board / Wand You Wave / Thank You for Being an Angel

FRIENDS OF MATTHEW
UK, male / female vocal / instrumental group (1 WEEK) pos/wks

| 10 Jul 99 | **OUT THERE** *Serious SERR 007CD* .... | 61 | 1 |

FRIGID VINEGAR
UK, male rap / production duo (1 WEEK) pos/wks

| 21 Aug 99 | **DOGMONAUT 2000 (IS THERE ANYONE OUT THERE?)** *Gut CDGUT 27* .... | 53 | 1 |

FRIJID PINK *US, male vocal / instrumental group (16 WEEKS)* pos/wks

| 28 Mar 70 ● | **THE HOUSE OF THE RISING SUN** *Deram DMR 288* .... | 4 | 16 |

Robert FRIPP – *See David SYLVIAN*

Jane FROMAN *US, female vocalist, d. 22 Apr 1980 (4 WEEKS)* pos/wks

| 17 Jun 55 | **I WONDER** *Capitol CL 14254* .... | 14 | 4 |

FRONT 242
Belgium / US, male vocal / instrumental group (1 WEEK) pos/wks

| 1 May 93 | **RELIGION** *RRE RRE 106CD* .... | 46 | 1 |

FROU FROU
UK, male / female production / vocal duo (1 WEEK) pos/wks

| 6 Jul 02 | **BREATHE IN** *Island CID 799* .... | 44 | 1 |

Christian FRY *UK, male vocalist (3 WEEKS)* pos/wks

| 14 Nov 98 | **YOU GOT ME** *Mushroom MUSH 33CDS* .... | 45 | 2 |
| 3 Apr 99 | **WON'T YOU SAY** *Mushroom MUSH 46CDS* .... | 48 | 1 |

FUGAZI *US, male vocal / instrumental group (1 WEEK)* pos/wks

| 20 Oct 01 | **FURNITURE** *Dischord DIS 129CD* .... | 61 | 1 |

FUGEES
US / Haiti, male / female vocal / rap / production group (65 WEEKS) pos/wks

6 Apr 96	**FU-GEE-LA** *Columbia 6630662*	21	5
8 Jun 96 ★	**KILLING ME SOFTLY** *Columbia 6633435* ◆ ■	1	20
14 Sep 96 ★	**READY OR NOT** *Columbia 6637215*	1	12
30 Nov 96 ●	**NO WOMAN, NO CRY** *Columbia 6639925*	2	9
15 Mar 97 ●	**RUMBLE IN THE JUNGLE** *Mercury 5740692*	3	8
28 Jun 97	**WE TRYING TO STAY ALIVE** *Columbia 6646815* [1]	13	5
6 Sep 97	**THE SWEETEST THING** *Columbia 6649785* [2]	18	4
27 Sep 97	**GUANTANAMERA** *Columbia 6650852* [1]	25	2

[1] Wyclef Jean and The Refugee Allstars [2] Refugee Camp Allstars featuring Lauryn Hill

See also Lauryn HILL; Wyclef JEAN; Pras MICHEL

FULL CIRCLE *US, male vocal group (5 WEEKS)* pos/wks

| 7 Mar 87 | **WORKIN' UP A SWEAT** *EMI America EA 229* .... | 41 | 5 |

FULL FORCE
US, male vocal / instrumental group (37 WEEKS) pos/wks

4 May 85	**I WONDER IF I TAKE YOU HOME (re)** *CBS A 6057* [1]	12	17
21 Dec 85 ●	**ALICE I WANT YOU JUST FOR ME** *CBS A 6640*	9	11
21 May 88	**NAUGHTY GIRLS (NEED LOVE TOO)** *Jive FOXY 9*	31	5
4 Jun 88	**I'M REAL** *Scotti Brothers JSB 1* [2]	31	4

[1] Lisa Lisa and Cult Jam with Full Force [2] James Brown featuring Full Force

FULL INTENTION
UK, male instrumental / production group (8 WEEKS) pos/wks

6 Apr 96	**AMERICA (I LOVE AMERICA)** *Stress CDSTR 56*	32	2
10 Aug 96	**UPTOWN DOWNTOWN** *Stress CDSTR 67*	61	1
26 Jul 97	**SHAKE YOUR BODY (DOWN TO THE GROUND)** *Sugar Daddy CDSTR 82*	34	2
22 Nov 97	**AMERICA (I LOVE AMERICA) (re-mix)** *Sugar Daddy CDSTRX 56*	56	1
6 Jun 98	**YOU ARE SOMEBODY** *Sugar Daddy CDSD 001*	75	1

| 1 Sep 01 | **I'LL BE WAITING** *Rulin RULIN 17CDS* [1] .... | 44 | 1 |

[1] Full Intention presents Shena

See also SEX-O-SONIQUE; HUSTLERS CONVENTION featuring Dave LAUDAT and Ondrea DUVERNEY; DISCO TEX presents CLOUDBURST; SHENA

FULL METAL RACKETS – *See John McENROE and Pat CASH with the FULL METAL RACKETS*

FULL MONTY ALLSTARS featuring TJ DAVIS
UK, male vocal / instrumental group with female vocalist (1 WEEK) pos/wks

| 27 Jul 96 | **BRILLIANT FEELING** *Arista 74321380902* .... | 72 | 1 |

Bobby FULLER FOUR
US, male vocal / instrumental group, leader d. 18 Jul 1966 (4 WEEKS) pos/wks

| 14 Apr 66 | **I FOUGHT THE LAW** *London HL 10030* .... | 33 | 4 |

FUN BOY THREE
UK, male vocal / instrumental trio – leader Terry Hall (70 WEEKS) pos/wks

7 Nov 81	**THE LUNATICS (HAVE TAKEN OVER THE ASYLUM)** *Chrysalis CHS 2563*	20	12
13 Feb 82 ●	**IT AIN'T WHAT YOU DO IT'S THE WAY THAT YOU DO IT** *Chrysalis CHS 2570* [1]	4	10
10 Apr 82 ●	**REALLY SAYING SOMETHING** *Deram NANA 1* [2]	5	10
8 May 82	**THE TELEPHONE ALWAYS RINGS** *Chrysalis CHS 2609* ...	17	9
31 Jul 82	**SUMMERTIME** *Chrysalis CHS 2629*	18	8
15 Jan 83	**THE MORE I SEE (THE LESS I BELIEVE)** *Chrysalis CHS 2664*	68	1
5 Feb 83 ●	**TUNNEL OF LOVE** *Chrysalis CHS 2678*	10	10
30 Apr 83	**OUR LIPS ARE SEALED** *Chrysalis FUNB 1*	7	10

[1] Fun Boy Three and Bananarama [2] Bananarama with Fun Boy Three

See also SPECIALS; COLOUR FIELD

FUN LOVIN' CRIMINALS
US, male vocal / rap / instrumental trio (31 WEEKS) pos/wks

8 Jun 96	**THE GRAVE AND THE CONSTANT** *Chrysalis CDCHS 5031*	72	1
17 Aug 96	**SCOOBY SNACKS** *Chrysalis CDCHS 5034*	22	3
16 Nov 96	**THE FUN LOVIN' CRIMINAL** *Chrysalis CDCHS 5040*	26	3
29 Mar 97	**KING OF NEW YORK** *Chrysalis CDCHS 5049*	28	3
5 Jul 97	**I'M NOT IN LOVE / SCOOBY SNACKS** *Chrysalis CDCHS 5060*	12	5
15 Aug 98	**LOVE UNLIMITED** *Chrysalis CDCHS 5096*	18	4
17 Oct 98	**BIG NIGHT OUT** *Chrysalis CDCHSS 5101*	29	2
8 May 99	**KOREAN BODEGA** *Chrysalis CDCHS 5108*	15	3
17 Feb 01 ●	**LOCO** *Chrysalis CDCHSS 5121*	5	6
1 Sep 01	**BUMP / RUN DADDY RUN** *Chrysalis CDCHSS 5128*	50	1

Farley 'Jackmaster' FUNK
US, male producer – Farley Williams (16 WEEKS) pos/wks

23 Aug 86 ●	**LOVE CAN'T TURN AROUND** *DJ International LON 105*	10	12
11 Feb 89	**AS ALWAYS** *Champion CHAMP 90* [1]	49	2
14 Dec 96	**LOVE CAN'T TURN AROUND** *4 Liberty LIBTCD 27* [2]	40	2

[1] Farley 'Jackmaster' Funk presents Ricky Dillard [2] Farley 'Jackmaster' Funk with Darryl Pandy

'Love Can't Turn Around' in 1996 is a re-recording

FUNK D'VOID *Sweden, male producer – Lars Sandberg (1 WEEK)* pos/wks

| 20 Oct 01 | **DIABLA** *Soma SOMA 112* .... | 70 | 1 |

FUNK JUNKEEZ
US, male DJ / producer – Roger Sanchez (1 WEEK) pos/wks

| 21 Feb 98 | **GOT FUNK** *Evocative EVOKE 1CDS* .... | 57 | 1 |

See also EL MARIACHI; Roger SANCHEZ

FUNK MASTERS
UK, male / female vocal / instrumental group (12 WEEKS) pos/wks

| 18 Jun 83 ● | **IT'S OVER** *Master Funk Records 7MP 004* [1] .... | 8 | 12 |

[1] Features Gonzales on horns

Re-entries are listed as (re), (2re), (3re), etc which signifies that the hit re-entered the chart once, twice or three times, etc

FUNKADELIC US, male vocal / instrumental group (13 WEEKS) pos/wks

			pos	wks
9 Dec 78 ●	ONE NATION UNDER A GROOVE (PART 1)			
	Warner Bros. K 17246		9	12
21 Aug 99	MOTHERSHIP RECONNECTION Virgin DINSD 185 [1]		55	1

[1] Scott Grooves featuring Parliament / Funkadelic

FUNKAPOLITAN UK, male vocal / instrumental group (7 WEEKS) pos/wks

			pos	wks
22 Aug 81	AS TIME GOES BY London LON 001		41	7

FUNKDOOBIEST US, male rap group (6 WEEKS) pos/wks

			pos	wks
11 Dec 93	WOPBABALUBOP Immortal 6597112		37	4
5 Mar 94	BOW WOW WOW Immortal 6594052		34	2

FUNKSTAR DE LUXE
Denmark, male producer / instrumentalist – Matt Ottesen (18 WEEKS) pos/wks

			pos	wks
25 Sep 99 ●	SUN IS SHINING Club Tools / Edel oo66895 CLU [1]		3	10
22 Jan 00	RAINBOW COUNTRY Club Tools 0067225CLU [1]		11	6
13 May 00	WALKIN IN THE NAME Club Tools 0067375 CLU [2]		42	1
25 Nov 00	PULL UP TO THE BUMPER Club Tools 0120375 CLU [3]		60	1

[1] Bob Marley vs Funkstar De Luxe [2] Funkstar De Luxe vs Terry Maxx [3] Grace Jones vs Funkstar De Luxe

FUNKY BOYS – See Linda CARR

FUNKY BUNCH – See MARKY MARK and the FUNKY BUNCH

FUNKY CHOAD featuring Nick SKITZ Australia / Italy.
male production duo and Australia, male vocalist (1 WEEK) pos/wks

			pos	wks
29 Aug 98	THE ULTIMATE ffrr FCD 341		51	1

FUNKY GREEN DOGS US, male / female vocal / production
group – Oscar Gaetan, Ralph Falcon and Tamara. (6 WEEKS) pos/wks

			pos	wks
12 Apr 97	FIRED UP! Twisted UK TWCD 10016		17	3
28 Jun 97	THE WAY Twisted UK TWCD 10026		43	1
20 Jun 98	UNTIL THE DAY Twisted UK TWCD 10034		75	1
27 Feb 99	BODY Twisted UK TWCD 110041		46	1

See also FOG

FUNKY JUNCTION – See KC FLIGHTT

FUNKY POETS US, male vocal group (1 WEEK) pos/wks

			pos	wks
7 May 94	BORN IN THE GHETTO Epic 6603522		72	1

FUNKY WORM
UK, male / female vocal / instrumental group (14 WEEKS) pos/wks

			pos	wks
30 Jul 88	HUSTLE! (TO THE MUSIC . . .) Fon FON 15		13	8
26 Nov 88	THE SPELL! Fon FON 16		61	3
20 May 89	U + ME = LOVE Fon FON 19		46	3

FUREYS Ireland, male vocal group (14 WEEKS) pos/wks

			pos	wks
10 Oct 81	WHEN YOU WERE SWEET SIXTEEN Ritz RITZ 003 [1]		14	11
3 Apr 82	I WILL LOVE YOU (EV'RY TIME WHEN WE ARE GONE)			
	Ritz RITZ 012		54	3

[1] Fureys with Davey Arthur

FURIOUS FIVE – See GRANDMASTER FLASH, Melle MEL and the FURIOUS FIVE

FURNITURE
UK, male / female vocal / instrumental group (10 WEEKS) pos/wks

			pos	wks
14 Jun 86	BRILLIANT MIND Stiff BUY 251		21	10

Nelly FURTADO Canada, female vocalist (31 WEEKS) pos/wks

			pos	wks
10 Mar 01 ●	I'M LIKE A BIRD Dreamworks 4509192		5	16
1 Sep 01 ●	TURN OFF THE LIGHT Dreamworks DRMDM 50891		4	10
19 Jan 02	...ON THE RADIO (REMEMBER THE DAYS) (re)			
	Dreamworks DRMDM 50856		18	5

Billy FURY 39 Top 500
Early British rock 'n' roll star, b. Ronald Wycherley, 17 Apr 1940, Liverpool, d. 28 Jan 1983. Equalled The Beatles' record of 24 hits in the 1960s, and spent 281 weeks on chart but without ever without reaching No.1 (281 WEEKS) pos/wks

			pos	wks
27 Feb 59	MAYBE TOMORROW (re) Decca F 11102		18	9
26 Jun 59	MARGO Decca F 11128		28	1
10 Mar 60 ●	COLETTE Decca F 11200		9	10
26 May 60	THAT'S LOVE Decca F 11237 [1]		19	11
22 Sep 60	WONDROUS PLACE Decca F 11267		25	9
19 Jan 61	A THOUSAND STARS Decca F 11311		14	10
27 Apr 61	DON'T WORRY Decca F 11334 [2]		40	2
11 May 61 ●	HALFWAY TO PARADISE Decca F 11349		3	23
7 Sep 61 ●	JEALOUSY Decca F 11384		2	12
14 Dec 61 ●	I'D NEVER FIND ANOTHER YOU Decca F 11409		5	15
15 Mar 62	LETTER FULL OF TEARS Decca F 11437		32	6
3 May 62 ●	LAST NIGHT WAS MADE FOR LOVE Decca F 11458		4	16
19 Jul 62 ●	ONCE UPON A DREAM Decca F 11485		7	13
25 Oct 62	BECAUSE OF LOVE Decca F 11508		18	14
14 Feb 63 ●	LIKE I'VE NEVER BEEN GONE Decca F11582		3	15
16 May 63 ●	WHEN WILL YOU SAY I LOVE YOU Decca F 11655		3	12
25 Jul 63 ●	IN SUMMER Decca F 11701		5	11
3 Oct 63	SOMEBODY ELSE'S GIRL Decca F 11744		18	7
2 Jan 64	DO YOU REALLY LOVE ME TOO? (FOOLS ERRAND)			
	Decca F 11792		13	10
30 Apr 64	I WILL Decca F 11888		14	12
23 Jul 64 ●	IT'S ONLY MAKE BELIEVE Decca F 11939		10	10
14 Jan 65	I'M LOST WITHOUT YOU Decca F 12048		16	10
22 Jul 65 ●	IN THOUGHTS OF YOU Decca F 12178		9	11
16 Sep 65	RUN TO MY LOVIN' ARMS Decca F 12230		25	7
10 Feb 66	I'LL NEVER QUITE GET OVER YOU Decca F 12325		35	5
4 Aug 66	GIVE ME YOUR WORD Decca F 12459		27	7
4 Sep 82	LOVE OR MONEY Polydor POSP 457		57	5
13 Nov 82	DEVIL OR ANGEL Polydor POSP 528		58	4
4 Jun 83	FORGET HIM Polydor POSP 558		59	4

[1] Billy Fury with The Four Jays [2] Billy Fury with The Four Kestrels

FUSED Sweden, male instrumental
/ production duo / female vocalist (1 WEEK) pos/wks

			pos	wks
20 Mar 99	THIS PARTY SUCKS! Columbia 6669302		64	1

FUTURE BREEZE Germany, male production
duo – Markus Boehme and Martin Hensing (9 WEEKS) pos/wks

			pos	wks
6 Sep 97	WHY DON'T YOU DANCE WITH ME AM:PM 5823312		50	1
20 Jan 01	SMILE Nebula NEBCD 014		67	1
13 Apr 02	TEMPLE OF DREAMS Ministry of Sound / DATA DATA 31 CDS		21	6
28 Dec 02	OCEAN OF ETERNITY Ministry of Sound / DATA DATA 44 CDS		46	1+

See also 4CLUBBERS

FUTURE FORCE UK / US, male / female vocal / instrumental duo (1 WK) pos/wks

			pos	wks
17 Aug 96	WHAT YOU WANT AM:PM 5816592		47	1

FUTURE SOUND OF LONDON UK, male instrumental /
production duo – Brian Dougans and Gary Cobain (25 WEEKS) pos/wks

			pos	wks
23 May 92	PAPUA NEW GUINEA Jumpin' & Pumpin' TOT 17		22	6
6 Nov 93	CASCADE Virgin VSCDT 1478		27	3
30 Jul 94	EXPANDER Jumpin' & Pumpin' CDSTOT 37		72	1
13 Aug 94	LIFEFORMS Virgin VSCDT 1484 [1]		14	3
27 May 95	FAR-OUT SON OF LUNG AND THE RAMBLINGS OF A			
	MADMAN Virgin VSCDT 1540		22	3
26 Oct 96	MY KINGDOM Virgin VSCDT 1605		13	3
12 Apr 97	WE HAVE EXPLOSIVE Virgin VSCDX 1616		12	3
29 Sep 01	PAPUA NEW GUINEA 2001 (re-mix)			
	Jumpin' & Pumpin' CDSTOT 44		28	3

[1] F.S.O.L. vocals by Elizabeth Fraser

See also HUMANOID

FUZZBOX – See WE'VE GOT A FUZZBOX AND WE'RE GONNA USE IT

Leslie FYSON – See Michael MEDWIN, Bernard BRESSLAW, Alfie BASS and Leslie FYSON

G

Ali G and SHAGGY *UK, male comedian / rapper – Sacha Baron Cohen – and Jamaica, male vocalist – Orville Burrell (14 WEEKS)*   pos/wks
23 Mar 02	●	ME JULIE *Island CID 793*	2 14

Andy G's STARSKY & HUTCH ALL STARS
UK, male producer (1 WEEK)   pos/wks
3 Oct 98	STARSKY & HUTCH – THE THEME *Virgin VSCDT 1708*	51 1

Bobby G *UK, male vocalist (12 WEEKS)*   pos/wks
1 Dec 84	BIG DEAL (2re) *BBC RESL 151*	46 12

See also BUCKS FIZZ

Dennis G – *See WIDEBOYS featuring Dennis G*

Gina G *Australia, female vocalist – Gina Gardiner (51 WEEKS)*   pos/wks
6 Apr 96	★ OOH AAH...JUST A LITTLE BIT (2re)	
	Eternal WEA 041CD	1 25
9 Nov 96	● I BELONG TO YOU *Eternal WEA 081CD*	6 11
22 Mar 97	● FRESH! *Eternal WEA 095CD*	6 7
7 Jun 97	TI AMO *Eternal WEA 107CD1*	11 5
6 Sep 97	GIMME SOME LOVE *Eternal WEA 101CD1*	25 2
15 Nov 97	EVERY TIME I FALL *Eternal WEA 134CD*	52 1

Hurricane G – *See PUFF DADDY*

Kenny G
US, male instrumentalist, saxophone – Kenny Gorelick (26 WEEKS) pos/wks
21 Apr 84	HI! HOW YA DOIN'? *Arista ARIST 561*	70 3
30 Aug 86	WHAT DOES IT TAKE (TO WIN YOUR LOVE)	
	Arista ARIST 672	64 2
4 Jul 87	SONGBIRD *Arista RIS 18*................................	22 7
9 May 92	MISSING YOU NOW *Columbia 6579917* [1]	28 4
24 Apr 93	FOREVER IN LOVE *Arista 74321145552*	47 3
17 Jul 93	BY THE TIME THIS NIGHT IS OVER *Arista 74321157142* [2]	56 3
8 Nov 97	HOW COULD AN ANGEL BREAK MY HEART	
	LaFace 74321531982 [3]	22 4

[1] Michael Bolton featuring Kenny G [2] Kenny G with Peabo Bryson [3] Toni Braxton with Kenny G

Warren G *US, male rapper – Warren Griffin (60 WEEKS)*   pos/wks
23 Jul 94	●	REGULATE *Death Row A 8290CD* [1]	5 14
12 Nov 94		THIS DJ (re) *RAL RALCD 1*	12 7
25 Mar 95		DO YOU SEE *RAL RALCD 3*	29 2
23 Nov 96	●	WHAT'S LOVE GOT TO DO WITH IT *Interscope IND 97008* [2]	2 12
22 Feb 97	●	I SHOT THE SHERIFF *Mercury DEFCD 31*	2 8
31 May 97		SMOKIN' ME OUT *Def Jam 5744432* [3]	14 5
10 Jan 98		PRINCE IGOR *Def Jam 5749652* [4]	15 7
24 Jan 98		ALL NIGHT ALL RIGHT *Mushroom MUSH 21CD* [5]	16 4
16 Mar 02		LOOKIN' AT YOU *Universal MCSTD 40275* [6]	60 1

[1] Warren G and Nate Dogg [2] Warren G featuring Adina Howard [3] Warren G featuring Ron Isley [4] Warren G featuring Sissel [5] Peter Andre featuring Warren G [6] Warren G featuring Toi

GBH *UK, male vocal / instrumental group (5 WEEKS)*   pos/wks
6 Feb 82	NO SURVIVORS *Clay CLAY 8*	63 2
20 Nov 82	GIVE ME FIRE *Clay CLAY 16*	69 3

G-CLEFS *US, male vocal group (12 WEEKS)*   pos/wks
30 Nov 61	I UNDERSTAND *London HLU 9433*	17 12

G CLUB presents BANDA SONORA
UK, male producer – Gerald Elms (1 WEEK)   pos/wks
19 Oct 02	PRESSURE COOKER *Defected DFTD 060CDS*	46 1

G NATION featuring ROSIE *UK, male production duo – Jake Moses and Mark Smith – and UK, female vocalist (1 WEEK)*   pos/wks
9 Aug 97	FEEL THE NEED *Cooltempo CDCOOL 327*	58 1

G.O.S.H. *UK, male / female charity ensemble (11 WEEKS)*   pos/wks
28 Nov 87	THE WISHING WELL *MBS GOSH 1*	22 11

G.Q. *US, male vocal / instrumental group (6 WEEKS)*   pos/wks
10 Mar 79	DISCO NIGHTS – (ROCK FREAK) *Arista ARIST 245*	42 6

GSP *UK, male instrumental / production duo – Ian Gallivan and Justin Stride (3 WEEKS)*   pos/wks
3 Oct 92	THE BANANA SONG *Yoyo YOYO 1*	37 3

GTO *UK, male / female instrumental / production duo – Lee Newman and Michael Wells (7 WEEKS)*   pos/wks
4 Aug 90	PURE *Cooltempo COOL 218*	57 3
7 Sep 91	LISTEN TO THE RHYTHM FLOW / BULLFROG	
	React REACT 7001	72 2
2 May 92	ELEVATION *React REACT 4*	59 2

See also TECHNOHEAD; TRICKY DISCO

Eric GABLE *US, male vocalist (1 WEEK)*   pos/wks
19 Mar 94	PROCESS OF ELIMINATION *Epic 6602282*	63 1

Peter GABRIEL (260 Top 500)
Award-winning singer / songwriter, b. 13 Feb 1950, Surrey, UK. Fronted Genesis until 1975, when replaced by Phil Collins. He broke through internationally with 'Sledgehammer', which also made him a video innovator. He is the driving force behind the Womad festival and is a tireless Amnesty International supporter (112 WEEKS)   pos/wks
9 Apr 77		SOLSBURY HILL *Charisma CB 301*	13 9
9 Feb 80	●	GAMES WITHOUT FRONTIERS *Charisma CB 354*	4 11
10 May 80		NO SELF CONTROL *Charisma CB 360*	33 6
23 Aug 80		BIKO *Charisma CB 370*	38 3
25 Sep 82		SHOCK THE MONKEY *Charisma SHOCK 1* ...	58 5
9 Jul 83		I DON'T REMEMBER *Charisma GAB 1*	62 3
2 Jun 84		WALK THROUGH THE FIRE *Virgin VS 689* ...	69 3
26 Apr 86	●	SLEDGEHAMMER *Virgin PGS 1* ▲	4 16
1 Nov 86	●	DON'T GIVE UP *Virgin PGS 2* [1]	9 11
28 Mar 87		BIG TIME *Charisma PGS 3*	13 7
11 Jul 87		RED RAIN *Charisma PGS 4*	46 3
21 Nov 87		BIKO (LIVE) *Charisma PGS 6*	49 6
3 Jun 89		SHAKIN' THE TREE *Virgin VS 1167* [2]	61 3
22 Dec 90		SOLSBURY HILL / SHAKING THE TREE (re-issue)	
		Virgin VS 1322 [3]	57 4
19 Sep 92		DIGGING IN THE DIRT *Realworld PGS 7*	24 4
16 Jan 93	●	STEAM *Realworld PGSDG 8*	10 7
3 Apr 93		BLOOD OF EDEN *Realworld PGSDG 9*	43 4
25 Sep 93		KISS THAT FROG *Realworld PGSDG 10*	46 3
25 Jun 94		LOVETOWN *Epic 6604802*	49 2
3 Sep 94		SW LIVE (EP) *Realworld PGSCD 11*	39 2

[1] Peter Gabriel and Kate Bush [2] Youssou N'Dour and Peter Gabriel [3] Peter Gabriel / Youssou N'Dour and Peter Gabriel

Tracks available on all formats of SW Live (EP): Red Rain / San Jacinto

GABRIELLE (167 Top 500) *Eyepatch-wearing soul / pop vocalist, born Louisa Gabrielle Bobb, 16 May 1970, London, UK. Broke record for highest chart debut when 'Dreams' entered at No.2. Voted Best British Newcomer at 1994 Brit Awards and Best British Female Vocalist in 1997. Best-selling single: 'Dreams' 513,200 (144 WEEKS)*   pos/wks
19 Jun 93	★ DREAMS *Go.Beat GODCD 99*	1 15

			pos/wks
2 Oct 93 ●	GOING NOWHERE Go.Beat GODCD 106	9	7
11 Dec 93	I WISH Go.Beat GODCD 108	26	5
26 Feb 94	BECAUSE OF YOU Go.Beat GODCD 109	24	5
24 Feb 96 ●	GIVE ME A LITTLE MORE TIME Go.Beat GODCD 139	5	18
22 Jun 96	FORGET ABOUT THE WORLD Go.Beat GODCD 146	23	5
5 Oct 96	IF YOU REALLY CARED Go.Beat GODCD 153	15	5
2 Nov 96 ●	IF YOU EVER London LONCD 388 [1]	2	15
1 Feb 97 ●	WALK ON BY Go.Beat GODCD 159	7	8
9 Oct 99 ●	SUNSHINE Go.Beat GOBCD 23	9	8
5 Feb 00 ★	RISE Go.Beat GOBCD 25 ■	1	15
17 Jun 00 ●	WHEN A WOMAN Go.Beat / Polydor GOBCD 27	6	8
4 Nov 00	SHOULD I STAY Go.Beat / Polydor GOBCD 32	13	7
21 Apr 01 ●	OUT OF REACH Go.Beat / Polydor GOLCD 39	4	16
3 Nov 01 ●	DON'T NEED THE SUN TO SHINE (TO MAKE ME SMILE) Go.Beat / Polydor GOBCD 47	9	7

[1] East 17 featuring Gabrielle

Yvonne GAGE US, female vocalist (4 WEEKS)
			pos/wks
16 Jun 84	DOIN' IT IN A HAUNTED HOUSE Epic A 4519	45	4

Danni'elle GAHA Australia, female vocalist (7 WEEKS)
			pos/wks
1 Aug 92	STUCK IN THE MIDDLE Epic 6581247	68	2
27 Feb 93	DO IT FOR LOVE Epic 6584612	52	2
12 Jun 93	SECRET LOVE Epic 6592212	41	3

Billy and Sarah GAINES US, male / female vocal duo (1 WEEK)
			pos/wks
14 Jun 97	I FOUND SOMEONE Expansion CDEXP 27	48	1

Rosie GAINES US, female vocalist (15 WEEKS)
			pos/wks
11 Nov 95	I WANT U Motown 8604852	70	1
31 May 97 ●	CLOSER THAN CLOSE Big Bang CDBBANG 1	4	12
29 Nov 97	I SURRENDER Big Bang CDBBANG 2	39	2

Serge GAINSBOURG – See Jane BIRKIN and Serge GAINSBOURG

GALA Italy, female vocalist – Gala Rizzatto (24 WEEKS)
			pos/wks
19 Jul 97 ●	FREED FROM DESIRE Big Life BLRD 135	2	14
6 Dec 97	LET A BOY CRY Big Life BLRD 140	11	8
22 Aug 98	COME INTO MY LIFE Big Life BLRD 147	38	2

GALAXY – See Phil FEARON

Dee GALDES – See Phil FEARON

Eve GALLAGHER UK, female vocalist (8 WEEKS)
			pos/wks
1 Dec 90	LOVE COME DOWN (re) More Protein PROT 6	61	4
15 Apr 95	YOU CAN HAVE IT ALL Cleveland City CLECD 13023	43	2
28 Oct 95	LOVE COME DOWN (re-recording) Cleveland City CLECD 13028	57	1
6 Jul 96	HEARTBREAK React CDREACT 78 [1]	44	1

[1] Mrs Wood featuring Eve Gallagher

Liam GALLAGHER – See OASIS; BUFFALO TOM; DEATH IN VEGAS

GALLAGHER and LYLE UK, male vocal / instrumental duo – Benny Gallagher and Graham Lyle (27 WEEKS)
			pos/wks
28 Feb 76 ●	I WANNA STAY WITH YOU A&M AMS 7211	6	9
22 May 76 ●	HEART ON MY SLEEVE A&M AMS 7227	6	10
11 Sep 76	BREAKAWAY A&M AMS 7245	35	4
29 Jan 77	EVERY LITTLE TEARDROP A&M AMS 7274	32	4

Patsy GALLANT Canada, female vocalist (9 WEEKS)
			pos/wks
10 Sep 77 ●	FROM NEW YORK TO L.A. EMI 2620	6	9

GALLEON France, male production duo (2 WEEKS)
			pos/wks
20 Apr 02	SO I BEGIN Epic 6724102	36	2

Luke GALLIANA UK, male vocalist (1 WEEK)
			pos/wks
12 May 01	TO DIE FOR Jive 9201272	42	1

GALLIANO UK, male / female vocal / instrumental group (14 WEEKS)
			pos/wks
30 May 92	SKUNK FUNK Talkin Loud TLK 23	41	2
1 Aug 92	PRINCE OF PEACE Talkin Loud TLK 24	47	3
10 Oct 92	JUS' REACH (RECYCLED) Talkin Loud TLK 29	66	2
28 May 94	LONG TIME GONE Talkin Loud TLKCD 48	15	3
30 Jul 94	TWYFORD DOWN Talkin Loud TLKCD 49	37	2
27 Jul 96	EASE YOUR MIND Talkin Loud TLCD 10	45	2

James GALWAY UK, male instrumentalist – flute (13 WEEKS)
			pos/wks
27 May 78 ●	ANNIE'S SONG RCA Red Seal RB 5085 [1]	3	13

[1] James Galway, flute, National Philharmonic Orchestra; Charles Gerhart, conductor

GAMBAFREAKS Italy, male production duo (2 WEEKS)
			pos/wks
12 Sep 98	INSTANT REPLAY Evocative EVOKE 7CDS [1]	57	1
13 May 00	DOWN DOWN DOWN Azuli AZNYCDX 116	57	1

[1] Gambafreaks featuring Paco Rivaz

GANG OF FOUR UK, male vocal / instrumental group (5 WEEKS)
			pos/wks
16 Jun 79	AT HOME HE'S A TOURIST EMI 2956	58	3
22 May 82	I LOVE A MAN IN UNIFORM EMI 5299	65	2

GANG STARR US, male rap duo – Guru and DJ Premier (8 WEEKS)
			pos/wks
13 Oct 90	JAZZ THING CBS 356377 7	66	2
23 Feb 91	TAKE A REST Cooltempo COOL 230	63	1
25 May 91	LOVESICK Cooltempo COOL 234	50	3
13 Jun 92	2 DEEP Cooltempo COOL 256	67	2

GANT UK, production duo – Julian Jonah and Danny Harrison (1 WEEK)
			pos/wks
27 Dec 97	SOUND BWOY BURIAL / ALL NIGHT LONG Positiva CDTIV 85	67	1

GAP BAND 418 Top 500
Soul / funk / disco outfit from Tulsa, Oklahoma, US, featuring brothers Charlie, Ronnie and Robert Wilson. Named after Greenwood, Archer and Pine – three streets in their hometown. First British hit launched a 'rowing-boat' craze on UK dancefloors (82 WEEKS)
			pos/wks
12 Jul 80 ●	OOPS UP SIDE YOUR HEAD Mercury MER 22	6	14
27 Sep 80	PARTY LIGHTS Mercury MER 37	30	8
27 Dec 80	BURN RUBBER ON ME (WHY YOU WANNA HURT ME) Mercury MER 52	22	11
11 Apr 81	HUMPIN' Mercury MER 63	36	6
27 Jun 81	YEARNING FOR YOUR LOVE Mercury MER 73	47	4
5 Jun 82	EARLY IN THE MORNING Mercury MER 97	55	3
19 Feb 83	OUTSTANDING Total Experience TE 001	68	2
31 Mar 84	SOMEDAY Total Experience TE 5	17	8
23 Jun 84	JAMMIN' IN AMERICA Total Experience TE 6	64	2
13 Dec 86 ●	BIG FUN Total Experience FB 49779	4	12
14 Mar 87	HOW MUSIC CAME ABOUT (BOP B DA B DA DA) Total Experience FB 49755	61	2
11 Jul 87	OOPS UPSIDE YOUR HEAD (re-mix) Club JAB 54	20	8
18 Feb 89	I'M GONNA GIT YOU SUCKA Arista 112016	63	2

GARBAGE US / UK, male / female vocal / instrumental group (66 WEEKS)
			pos/wks
19 Aug 95	SUBHUMAN Mushroom D 1138	50	1
30 Sep 95	ONLY HAPPY WHEN IT RAINS Mushroom D 1199	29	3
2 Dec 95	QUEER Mushroom D 1237	13	4
23 Mar 96 ●	STUPID GIRL Mushroom D 1271	4	7
23 Nov 96 ●	MILK (re) Mushroom D 1494 [1]	10	8
9 May 98 ●	PUSH IT Mushroom MUSH 28CDS	9	5
18 Jul 98 ●	I THINK I'M PARANOID Mushroom MUSH 35CDS	9	5

17 Oct 98	SPECIAL *Mushroom MUSH 39CDS*	15	4
6 Feb 99 ●	WHEN I GROW UP *Mushroom MUSH 43CDS*	9	7
5 Jun 99	YOU LOOK SO FINE *Mushroom MUSH 49CDS*	19	4
27 Nov 99	THE WORLD IS NOT ENOUGH *Radioactive RAXTD 40*	11	9
6 Oct 01	ANDROGYNY *Mushroom MUSH 94CDS*	24	2
2 Feb 02	CHERRY LIPS (GO BABY GO!) *Mushroom MUSH 98CDS*	22	4
20 Apr 02	BREAKING UP THE GIRL *Mushroom MUSH 101CDS*	27	2
5 Oct 02	SHUT YOUR MOUTH *Mushroom MUSH 106CDS*	20	1

1 Garbage featuring Tricky

Adam GARCIA *Australia, male vocalist (5 WEEKS)* pos/wks

16 May 98	NIGHT FEVER *Polydor 5697972*	15	5

Scott GARCIA featuring MC STYLES *UK, male producer and UK, male rapper – Scott Garcia and Daryl Turner (3 WEEKS)* pos/wks

1 Nov 97	A LONDON THING *Connected CDCONNECT 1*	29	3

See also CORRUPTED CRU featuring MC NEAT

Boris GARDINER
Jamaica, male vocalist / instrumentalist (38 WEEKS) pos/wks

17 Jan 70	ELIZABETHAN REGGAE (re) *Duke DU 39*	14	14
26 Jul 86 ★	I WANT TO WAKE UP WITH YOU *Revue REV 733*	1	15
4 Oct 86	YOU'RE EVERYTHING TO ME *Revue REV 735*	11	8
27 Dec 86	THE MEANING OF CHRISTMAS *Revue REV 740*	69	1

The first copies of 'Elizabethan Reggae', an instrumental, were printed with the label incorrectly crediting Byron Lee as the performer. The charts for the first entry, and the first four weeks of the re-entry, all reprinted this error. All charts and discs printed after 28 Feb 1970 gave Boris Gardiner the credit he deserved

Paul GARDINER *UK, male instrumentalist – bass (4 WEEKS)* pos/wks

25 Jul 81	STORMTROOPER IN DRAG *Beggars Banquet BEG 61*	49	4

Uncredited vocalist is Gary Numan

Art GARFUNKEL *US, male vocalist (37 WEEKS)* pos/wks

13 Sep 75 ★	I ONLY HAVE EYES FOR YOU *CBS 3575*	1	11
3 Mar 79 ★	BRIGHT EYES *CBS 6947* ♦	1	19
7 Jul 79	SINCE I DON'T HAVE YOU *CBS 7371*	38	7

See also SIMON and GARFUNKEL

Judy GARLAND
US, female vocalist – Frances Gumm, d. 22 Jan 1969 (2 WEEKS) pos/wks

10 Jun 55	THE MAN THAT GOT AWAY *Philips PB 366*	18	2

Jessica GARLICK *UK, female vocalist (6 WEEKS)* pos/wks

25 May 02	COME BACK *Columbia 6725662*	13	6

Laurent GARNIER *France, male DJ / producer (4 WEEKS)* pos/wks

15 Feb 97	CRISPY BACON *F Communications F 055CD*	60	1
22 Apr 00	MAN WITH THE RED FACE *F Communications F 119CD*	65	1
11 Nov 00	GREED / THE MAN WITH THE RED FACE (re-issue) *F Communications F 127CDUK*	36	2

Lee GARRETT *US, male vocalist (7 WEEKS)* pos/wks

29 May 76	YOU'RE MY EVERYTHING *Chrysalis CHS 2087*	15	7

Leif GARRETT *US, male vocalist (14 WEEKS)* pos/wks

20 Jan 79 ●	I WAS MADE FOR DANCIN' *Scotti Brothers K 11202*	4	10
21 Apr 79	FEEL THE NEED *Scotti Brothers K 11274*	38	4

Lesley GARRETT and Amanda THOMPSON
UK, female vocal / instrumental duo (10 WEEKS) pos/wks

6 Nov 93	AVE MARIA *Internal Affairs KGBD 012*	16	10

Siedah GARRETT – See BRAND NEW HEAVIES; Michael JACKSON; Dennis EDWARDS featuring Siedah GARRETT

David GARRICK *UK, male vocalist – Philip Core (16 WEEKS)* pos/wks

9 Jun 66	LADY JANE *Piccadilly 7N 35317*	28	7
22 Sep 66	DEAR MRS APPLEBEE *Piccadilly 7N 35335*	22	9

GARY'S GANG *US, male vocal / instrumental group (18 WEEKS)* pos/wks

24 Feb 79 ●	KEEP ON DANCIN' *CBS 7109*	8	10
2 Jun 79	LET'S LOVEDANCE TONIGHT *CBS 7328*	49	4
6 Nov 82	KNOCK ME OUT *Arista ARIST 499*	45	4

Barbara GASKIN – See Dave STEWART

GAT DECOR
UK, male instrumental / production group (10 WEEKS) pos/wks

16 May 92	PASSION *Effective EFFS 1*	29	4
9 Mar 96 ●	PASSION (re-mix) *Way Of Life WAYDA 1*	6	6

See also PHUNKY PHANTOM; REST ASSURED

Stephen GATELY *Ireland, male vocalist (19 WEEKS)* pos/wks

10 Jun 00 ●	NEW BEGINNING / BRIGHT EYES *A&M / Polydor 5618192*	3	11
14 Oct 00	I BELIEVE *Polydor 5877472*	11	4
12 May 01	STAY *A&M / Mercury 5870672*	13	4

See also BOYZONE

David GATES *US, male vocalist (2 WEEKS)* pos/wks

22 Jul 78	TOOK THE LAST TRAIN *Elektra K 12307*	50	2

See also BREAD

Gareth GATES *UK, male vocalist (57 WEEKS)* pos/wks

30 Mar 02 ★	UNCHAINED MELODY (re) *S 74321930882* ♦ ■	1	27
20 Jul 02 ★	ANYONE OF US (STUPID MISTAKE) *S 74321950602* ■	1	15
5 Oct 02 ★	THE LONG AND WINDING ROAD / SUSPICIOUS MINDS *S 74321965972* 1 ■	1	13+
21 Dec 02 ●	WHAT MY HEART WANTS TO SAY *S 743211985592*	5	2+

1 Will Young and Gareth Gates / Gareth Gates

GAY DAD
UK, male / female vocal / instrumental group (10 WEEKS) pos/wks

30 Jan 99 ●	TO EARTH WITH LOVE *London LONCD 413*	10	4
5 Jun 99	JOY! *London LONCD 428*	22	3
14 Aug 99	OH JIM *London LONCD 437*	47	1
31 Mar 01	NOW ALWAYS AND FOREVER *B Unique BUN 004CD*	41	1
22 Sep 01	TRANSMISSION *B Unique BUN 009CD*	58	1

GAY GORDON and the MINCE PIES
UK, male / female vocal / instrumental group (5 WEEKS) pos/wks

6 Dec 86	THE ESSENTIAL WALLY PARTY MEDLEY *Lifestyle XY 2*	60	5

Marvin GAYE 88 Top 500
One of soul's most innovative and successful singer / songwriters, b. 2 Apr 1939, Washington DC, d. 1 Apr 1984. He went from doo-wop group member and session drummer to superstar. Posthumously awarded a Lifetime Achievement Grammy Award in 1996 (202 WEEKS) pos/wks

30 Jul 64	ONCE UPON A TIME *Stateside SS 316* 1	50	1
10 Dec 64	HOW SWEET IT IS *Stateside SS 360*	49	1
29 Sep 66	LITTLE DARLIN' (I NEED YOU) *Tamla Motown TMG 574*	50	1
26 Jan 67	IT TAKES TWO *Tamla Motown TMG 590* 2	16	11
17 Jan 68	IF I COULD BUILD MY WHOLE WORLD AROUND YOU *Tamla Motown TMG 635* 3	41	7
12 Jun 68	AIN'T NOTHIN' LIKE THE REAL THING *Tamla Motown TMG 655* 3	34	7
2 Oct 68	YOU'RE ALL I NEED TO GET BY *Tamla Motown TMG 668* 3	19	19
22 Jan 69	YOU AIN'T LIVIN' TILL YOU'RE LOVIN' *Tamla Motown TMG 681* 3	21	8
12 Feb 69 ★	I HEARD IT THROUGH THE GRAPEVINE *Tamla Motown TMG 686* ▲	1	15
4 Jun 69	GOOD LOVIN' AIN'T EASY TO COME BY (re) *Tamla Motown TMG 697* 3	26	8

			pos/wks
23 Jul 69 ●	TOO BUSY THINKING 'BOUT MY BABY		
	Tamla Motown TMG 705	5	16
15 Nov 69 ●	ONION SONG Tamla Motown TMG 715 [3]	9	12
9 May 70 ●	ABRAHAM, MARTIN AND JOHN Tamla Motown TMG 734	9	14
11 Dec 71	SAVE THE CHILDREN Tamla Motown TMG 796	41	6
22 Sep 73	LET'S GET IT ON Tamla Motown TMG 868 ▲	31	7
23 Mar 74 ●	YOU ARE EVERYTHING Tamla Motown TMG 890 [4]	5	12
20 Jul 74	STOP LOOK LISTEN (TO YOUR HEART)		
	Tamla Motown TMG 906 [4]	25	8
7 May 77 ●	GOT TO GIVE IT UP (PT.1) Motown TMG 1069 ▲	7	10
24 Feb 79	POPS, WE LOVE YOU Motown TMG 1136 [5]	66	5
30 Oct 82 ●	(SEXUAL) HEALING CBS A 2855	4	14
8 Jan 83	MY LOVE IS WAITING CBS A 3048	34	5
18 May 85	SANCTIFIED LADY CBS A 4894	51	4
26 Apr 86 ●	I HEARD IT THROUGH THE GRAPEVINE (re-issue)		
	Tamla Motown ZB 40701	8	8
14 May 94	LUCKY LUCKY ME Motown TMGCD 1426	67	1
6 Oct 01	MUSIC Polydor 4976222 [6]	36	2

[1] Marvin Gaye and Mary Wells [2] Marvin Gaye and Kim Weston [3] Marvin Gaye
and Tammi Terrell [4] Diana Ross and Marvin Gaye [5] Diana Ross, Marvin Gaye,
Smokey Robinson and Stevie Wonder [6] Erick Sermon featuring Marvin Gaye

GAYE BYKERS ON ACID
UK, male vocal / instrumental group (2 WEEKS) pos/wks

31 Oct 87	GIT DOWN (SHAKE YOUR THANG) Purple Fluid VS 1008	54	2

Crystal GAYLE
US, female vocalist – Brenda Gail Webb (28 WEEKS) pos/wks

12 Nov 77 ●	DON'T IT MAKE MY BROWN EYES BLUE		
	United Artists UP 36307	5	14
26 Aug 78	TALKING IN YOUR SLEEP United Artists UP 36422	11	14

Michelle GAYLE UK, female actor / vocalist (52 WEEKS) pos/wks

7 Aug 93	LOOKING UP RCA 74321154532	11	6
24 Sep 94 ●	SWEETNESS RCA 74321230192	4	16
17 Dec 94	I'LL FIND YOU RCA 74321247762	26	7
27 May 95	FREEDOM RCA 74321284692	16	6
26 Aug 95	HAPPY JUST TO BE WITH YOU RCA 74321302692	11	7
8 Feb 97 ●	DO YOU KNOW RCA 74321419282	6	6
26 Apr 97	SENSATIONAL RCA 74321419302	14	4

Roy GAYLE – See MIRAGE

GAYLE & GILLIAN Australia, female vocal duo (2 WEEKS) pos/wks

3 Jul 93	MAD IF YA DON'T Mushroom CDMUSH 1	75	1
19 Mar 94	WANNA BE YOUR LOVER Mushroom D 11598	62	1

Gloria GAYNOR (498 Top 500) Legendary disco diva, b. 7 Sep 1949,
New Jersey, US. Her transatlantic chart-topping feminist anthem and
karaoke favourite proved it would survive by returning to the Top 5, in
remixed form, 14 years after reaching No.1 (73 WEEKS) pos/wks

7 Dec 74 ●	NEVER CAN SAY GOODBYE MGM 2006 463	2	13
8 Mar 75	REACH OUT, I'LL BE THERE MGM 2006 499	14	8
9 Aug 75	ALL I NEED IS YOUR SWEET LOVIN' MGM 2006 531	44	3
17 Jan 76	HOW HIGH THE MOON MGM 2006 558	33	4
3 Feb 79 ★	I WILL SURVIVE Polydor 2095 017 ▲	1	15
6 Oct 79	LET ME KNOW (I HAVE A RIGHT) Polydor STEP 5	32	7
24 Dec 83	I AM WHAT I AM (FROM 'LA CAGE AUX FOLLES')		
	Chrysalis CHS 2765	13	12
26 Jun 93	I WILL SURVIVE (re-mix) Polydor PZCD 270	5	10
3 Jun 00	LAST NIGHT Logic 74321738082	67	1

GAZ US, male vocal / instrumental group (4 WEEKS) pos/wks

24 Feb 79	SING SING Salsoul SSOL 116	60	4

GAZZA UK, male footballer / vocalist – Paul Gascoigne (14 WEEKS) pos/wks

10 Nov 90 ●	FOG ON THE TYNE (REVISITED) Best ZB 44083 [1]	2	9
22 Dec 90	GEORDIE BOYS (GAZZA RAP) Best ZB 44229	31	5

[1] Gazza and Lindisfarne

Nigel GEE UK, male producer (1 WEEK) pos/wks

27 Jan 01	HOOTIN' Neo NEOCD 040	57	1

J GEILS BAND US, male vocal / instrumental group (20 WEEKS) pos/wks

9 Jun 79	ONE LAST KISS EMI America AM 507	74	1
13 Feb 82 ●	CENTERFOLD EMI America EA 135 ▲	3	9
10 Apr 82	FREEZE-FRAME EMI America EA 134	27	7
26 Jun 82	ANGEL IN BLUE EMI America EA 138	55	3

Bob GELDOF Ireland, male vocalist (15 WEEKS) pos/wks

1 Nov 86	THIS IS THE WORLD CALLING Mercury BOB 101	25	5
21 Feb 87	LOVE LIKE A ROCKET Mercury BOB 102	61	3
23 Jun 90	THE GREAT SONG OF INDIFFERENCE Mercury BOB 104	15	6
7 May 94	CRAZY Vertigo VERCX 85	65	1

See also BOOMTOWN RATS

GEM – See OUR TRIBE / ONE TRIBE

GEMINI
UK, male vocal duo – Michael and David Smallwood (7 WEEKS) pos/wks

30 Sep 95	EVEN THOUGH YOU BROKE MY HEART EMI CDEMS 391	40	3
10 Feb 96	STEAL YOUR LOVE AWAY EMI CDEMS 407	37	2
29 Jun 96	COULD IT BE FOREVER EMI CDEMS 426	38	2

GEMS FOR JEM UK, male instrumental / production
duo – Steve McCutcheon and Darren Pearce (2 WEEKS) pos/wks

6 May 95	LIFTING ME HIGHER Box 21 CDSBOKS 3	28	2

GENE UK, male vocal / instrumental group (22 WEEKS) pos/wks

13 Aug 94	BE MY LIGHT BE MY GUIDE Costermonger COST 002CD	54	1
12 Nov 94	SLEEP WELL TONIGHT Costermonger COST 003CD	36	2
4 Mar 95	HAUNTED BY YOU Costermonger COST 004CD	32	2
22 Jul 95	OLYMPIAN Costermonger COST 005CD	18	2
13 Jan 96	FOR THE DEAD Costermonger COST 006CD	14	3
2 Nov 96	FIGHTING FIT Costermonger COST 009CD	22	2
1 Feb 97	WE COULD BE KINGS Polydor COSCD 10	17	2
10 May 97	WHERE ARE THEY NOW? Polydor COSCD 11	22	2
9 Aug 97	SPEAK TO ME SOMEONE Polydor COSCD 12	30	2
27 Feb 99	AS GOOD AS IT GETS Polydor COSCD 14	23	2
24 Apr 99	FILL HER UP Polydor COSCD 15	36	2

GENE AND JIM ARE INTO SHAKES
UK, male vocal / instrumental duo (2 WEEKS) pos/wks

19 Mar 88	SHAKE! (HOW ABOUT A SAMPLING, GENE?)		
	Rough Trade RT 216	68	2

GENE LOVES JEZEBEL
UK, male vocal / instrumental group (7 WEEKS) pos/wks

29 Mar 86	SWEETEST THING Beggars Banquet BEG 156	75	1
14 Jun 86	HEARTACHE Beggars Banquet BEG 161	71	2
5 Sep 87	THE MOTION OF LOVE Beggars Banquet BEG 192	56	3
5 Dec 87	GORGEOUS Beggars Banquet BEG 202	68	1

GENERAL DEGREE – See Richie STEPHENS

GENERAL LEVY UK, male vocalist – Paul Levy (13 WEEKS) pos/wks

4 Sep 93	MONKEY MAN ffrr FCD 214	75	1
18 Jun 94	INCREDIBLE Renk RENK 42 CD [1]	39	3
10 Sep 94 ●	INCREDIBLE (re-mix) Renk CD RENK 44 [1]	8	9

[1] M-Beat featuring General Levy

GENERAL PUBLIC
UK, male vocal / instrumental group (4 WEEKS) pos/wks

10 Mar 84	GENERAL PUBLIC Virgin VS 659	60	3
2 Jul 94	I'LL TAKE YOU THERE Epic 6605532	73	1

See also BEAT

THE TWIST

■ Dance crazes have come and gone in the rock era, but without doubt the Twist was the most successful. It started internationally with Chubby Checker's 'The Twist', the only single to top the US chart twice.

Top R&B performer Hank Ballard wrote 'The Twist' in 1958, although it had a similar tune to The Drifters' 1955 hit 'What'cha Gonna Do'. He penned it in about 20 minutes and said it was inspired by the stage movements of his group The Midnighters. Ballard and his band released it in January 1959 and Billboard suggested it could "probably add a new dance step to teenagers' repertoires". Even though it was only a B-side, it reached the R&B Top 20 and earned a UK release. It might not have been a pop hit in 1959, but two US groups which tagged themselves The Twisters charted that year.

Slowly, the Twist's popularity spread, and by 1960 the dance and Ballard's record came to the attention of Dick Clark, the influential US pop TV show host. Clark decided he would rather promote a cover version, and remembered local lad Ernest Evans who had recorded a "musical" Christmas card especially for Clark, which contained impersonations of various singers. (When released commercially, 'The Class' reached the US Top 40.) In fact, it was Clark's wife Bobbie who renamed the ex-chicken plucker Chubby Checker. It took just three takes and 34 minutes for Checker and vocal group The Dreamlovers to record the song that has kept him fully employed for more than 40 years. According to Ballard, "Checker did an absolute clone", and he swore that when he first heard it he thought he was listening to his own recording.

■ **CHUBBY CHECKER IS KING OF THE WAY WE DANCE WORLDWIDE SINCE 1959. WHATEVER DANCES CAME AFTER THE TWIST, IT ALL STARTED HERE** ■

Either way, after Checker demonstrated the dance on Clark's American Bandstand his version overtook Ballard's on the chart and hit the top in September 1960.

The Twist was not the first dance you did without a partner, nor even the first of that name (several 1940s R&B records also mentioned "little sis doing the twist"), but none of them had anything like the same impact. Anyone could twist instantly; you didn't need lessons. As Checker said: "It's like putting out a cigarette with both feet, or coming out of a shower and wiping your bottom with a towel to music."

The story does not end there. The following year American adults discovered the dance and then the rest of the world climbed on the bandwagon. 'The Twist' returned to top the US chart in January 1962, and before long everyone from Sinatra to Presley was recording Twist tunes, and Checker had four albums simultaneously in the US Top 10. Britain too caught twist fever, although 'The Twist' itself reached only No.14 then. However, Checker and rotund rappers The Fat Boys took it to No.2 in 1988.

Ernest Evans had the stage name
Chubby Checker bestowed on him by
disc jockey Dick Clark's wife, who
was inspired by Fats (Chubby)
Domino (Checker)

★ **ARTIST:** Chubby Checker

★ **LABEL:** Cameo Parkway
USA/Columbia
(EMI) UK

★ **WRITER:** Hank Ballard

★ **PRODUCER:** Kal Mann

Ballard, who earned a small
fortune in royalties, was not
bitter, saying, "There wouldn't be
a 'Twist' if it hadn't have been for
Checker and Clark." According
to Checker, Clark said: "The
three most important
things that ever
happened in the
music industry
are Elvis
Presley, The
Beatles and Chubby Checker."
Checker added: "Chubby Checker is
king of the way we dance worldwide
since 1959. Whatever dances came
after the Twist, it all started here."
Twist in the tale: in 1991 Checker
sued McDonald's for using a sound-
alike version of 'The Twist' in a
commercial without his permission. They
agreed it was a sound-alike, but one trying
to sound like Ballard, not Checker, and he
had granted permission.

■ Dave McAleer

GENERAL SAINT UK, male vocalist (9 WEEKS)

		pos/wks	
29 Sep 84	LAST PLANE (ONE WAY TICKET) MCA MCA 910 [1]	...51	3
2 Apr 94	OH CAROL! Copasetic COPCD 0009 [1]	...54	5
6 Aug 94	SAVE THE LAST DANCE FOR ME Copasetic COPCD 12 [2]	...75	1

[1] Clint Eastwood and General Saint [2] General Saint featuring Don Campbell

GENERATION X UK, male vocal / instrumental group (31 WEEKS) pos/wks

		pos/wks	
17 Sep 77	YOUR GENERATION Chrysalis CHS 2165	...36	4
11 Mar 78	READY STEADY GO Chrysalis CHS 2207	...47	3
20 Jan 79	KING ROCKER Chrysalis CHS 2261	...11	9
7 Apr 79	VALLEY OF THE DOLLS Chrysalis CHS 2310	...23	7
30 Jun 79	FRIDAY'S ANGELS Chrysalis CHS 2330	...62	2
18 Oct 80	DANCING WITH MYSELF Chrysalis CHS 2444 [1]	...62	2
24 Jan 81	DANCING WITH MYSELF (EP) Chrysalis CHS 2488 [1]	...60	4

[1] Gen X

Tracks on Dancing With Myself (EP): Dancing With Myself / Untouchables / Rock On / King Rocker

See also Billy IDOL

GENERATOR Holland, male producer – Robert Smit (1 WEEK)

		pos/wks	
23 Oct 99	WHERE ARE YOU NOW? Tidy Trax TIDY 130CD	...60	1

GENESIS (105 Top 500)

Perennially popular UK group. Stalwart members are Tony Banks (k) and Mike Rutherford (g); others included Peter Gabriel (v), Phil Collins (v/d), Steve Hackett (g). These progressive 1970s rockers became a major act in the 1980s and had 10 consecutive Top 3 albums (187 WEEKS) pos/wks

		pos/wks	
6 Apr 74	I KNOW WHAT I LIKE (IN YOUR WARDROBE) Charisma CB 224	...21	7
26 Feb 77	YOUR OWN SPECIAL WAY Charisma CB 300	...43	3
28 May 77	SPOT THE PIGEON (EP) Charisma GEN 001	...14	7
11 Mar 78 ●	FOLLOW YOU FOLLOW ME Charisma CB 309	...7	13
8 Jul 78	MANY TOO MANY Charisma CB 315	...43	5
15 Mar 80 ●	TURN IT ON AGAIN Charisma CB 356	...8	10
17 May 80	DUCHESS Charisma CB 363	...46	5
13 Sep 80	MISUNDERSTANDING Charisma CB 369	...42	5
22 Aug 81 ●	ABACAB Charisma CB 388	...9	8
31 Oct 81	KEEP IT DARK Charisma CB 391	...33	4
13 Mar 82	MAN ON THE CORNER Charisma CB 393	...41	5
22 May 82 ●	3 X 3 (EP) Charisma GEN 1	...10	8
3 Sep 83 ●	MAMA Virgin / Charisma MAMA 1	...4	10
12 Nov 83	THAT'S ALL Charisma / Virgin TATA 1	...16	11
11 Feb 84	ILLEGAL ALIEN (re) Charisma / Virgin AL1	...46	4
31 May 86	INVISIBLE TOUCH Virgin GENS 1 ▲	...15	8
30 Aug 86	IN TOO DEEP Virgin GENS 2	...19	9
22 Nov 86	LAND OF CONFUSION Virgin GENS 3	...14	12
14 Mar 87	TONIGHT TONIGHT TONIGHT Virgin GENS 4	...18	6
20 Jun 87	THROWING IT ALL AWAY Virgin GENS 5	...22	8
2 Nov 91 ●	NO SON OF MINE (re) Virgin GENS 6	...6	7
11 Jan 92 ●	I CAN'T DANCE Virgin GENS 7	...7	9
18 Apr 92	HOLD ON MY HEART Virgin GENS 8	...16	5
25 Jul 92	JESUS HE KNOWS ME Virgin GENS 9	...20	7
21 Nov 92 ●	INVISIBLE TOUCH (LIVE) Virgin GENS 10	...7	4
20 Feb 93	TELL ME WHY Virgin GENDG 11	...40	3
27 Sep 97	CONGO Virgin GENSD 12	...29	2
13 Dec 97	SHIPWRECKED Virgin GENDX14	...54	1
7 Mar 98	NOT ABOUT US Virgin GENSD 15	...66	1

Tracks on Spot the Pigeon (EP): Match of the Day / Pigeons / Inside and Out. Tracks on 3 x 3 (EP): Paperlate / You Might Recall / Me and Virgil

See also MIKE and the MECHANICS; Phil COLLINS; Steve HACKETT; FISH; Peter GABRIEL

Lee A GENESIS – See Bob SINCLAR

GENEVA UK, male vocal / instrumental group (9 WEEKS)

		pos/wks	
26 Oct 96	NO ONE SPEAKS Nude NUD 22CD	...32	2
8 Feb 97	INTO THE BLUE Nude NUD 25CD	...26	2
31 May 97	TRANQUILIZER Nude NUD 28 CD1	...24	2

		pos/wks	
16 Aug 97	BEST REGRETS Nude NUD 31CD1	...38	1
27 Nov 99	DOLLARS IN THE HEAVENS Nude NUD 46CD1	...59	1
11 Mar 00	IF YOU HAVE TO GO Nude NUD 49CD1	...69	1

GENEVIEVE UK, female vocalist – Susan Hunt (1 WEEK)

		pos/wks	
5 May 66	ONCE CBS 202061	...43	1

GENIUS CRU UK, male production group (7 WEEKS)

		pos/wks	
3 Feb 01	BOOM SELECTION Incentive CENT 17CDS	...12	5
27 Oct 01	COURSE BRUV Incentive CENT 28CDS	...39	2

GENIUS / GZA featuring D'ANGELO US, male rapper and US male vocalist – Gary Grice and Michael D'Angelo (2 WEEKS) pos/wks

		pos/wks	
2 Mar 96	COLD WORLD Geffen GFSTD 22114	...40	2

Bobbie GENTRY
US, female vocalist – Roberta Streeter (48 WEEKS) pos/wks

		pos/wks	
13 Sep 67	ODE TO BILLY JOE Capitol CL 15511 ▲	...13	11
30 Aug 69 ★	I'LL NEVER FALL IN LOVE AGAIN Capitol CL 15606	...1	19
6 Dec 69 ●	ALL I HAVE TO DO IS DREAM Capitol CL 15619 [1]	...3	14
21 Feb 70	RAINDROPS KEEP FALLING ON MY HEAD Capitol CL 15626	...40	4

[1] Bobbie Gentry and Glen Campbell

GEORDIE UK, male vocal / instrumental group (35 WEEKS)

		pos/wks	
2 Dec 72	DON'T DO THAT Regal Zonophone RZ 3067	...32	7
17 Mar 73 ●	ALL BECAUSE OF YOU EMI 2008	...6	13
16 Jun 73	CAN YOU DO IT EMI 2031	...13	9
25 Aug 73	ELECTRIC LADY EMI 2048	...32	6

Robin GEORGE UK, male vocalist (2 WEEKS)

		pos/wks	
27 Apr 85	HEARTLINE Bronze BRO 191	...68	2

Sophia GEORGE Jamaica, female vocalist (11 WEEKS)

		pos/wks	
7 Dec 85 ●	GIRLIE GIRLIE Winner WIN 01	...7	11

GEORGIA SATELLITES
US, male vocal / instrumental group (8 WEEKS) pos/wks

		pos/wks	
7 Feb 87	KEEP YOUR HANDS TO YOURSELF Elektra EKR 50	...69	1
16 May 87	BATTLESHIP CHAINS Elektra EKR 58	...44	4
21 Jan 89	HIPPY HIPPY SHAKE Elektra EKR 86	...63	3

GEORGIE PORGIE US, male producer (3 WEEKS)

		pos/wks	
12 Aug 95	EVERYBODY MUST PARTY Vibe MCSTD 2068	...61	1
4 May 96	TAKE ME HIGHER Music Plant MCSTD 40031	...61	1
26 Aug 00	LIFE GOES ON Neo NEOCD 039	...54	1

GEORGIO US, male vocalist (3 WEEKS)

		pos/wks	
20 Feb 88	LOVER'S LANE Motown ZB 41611	...54	3

Danyel GERARD France, male vocalist (12 WEEKS)

		pos/wks	
18 Sep 71	BUTTERFLY CBS 7454	...11	12

GERIDEAU US, male vocalist (2 WEEKS)

		pos/wks	
27 Aug 94	BRING IT ALL BACK 2 LUV Fruittree FTREE 10CD [1]	...65	1
4 Jul 98	MASQUERADE Inferno CDFERN7	...63	1

[1] Project featuring Gerideau

GERRY and the PACEMAKERS (246 Top 500)
Record-breaking Merseybeat band: Gerry Marsden (v/g), Les Chadwick (b), Les McGuire (p), Freddie Marsden (d). Second Liverpool group to chart (after The Beatles), but first to reach No.1 and first act ever to top UK chart with their initial three singles (114 WEEKS) pos/wks

		pos/wks	
14 Mar 63 ★	HOW DO YOU DO IT? Columbia DB 4987	...1	18
30 May 63 ★	I LIKE IT Columbia DB 7041	...1	15

Re-entries are listed as (re), (2re), (3re), etc which signifies that the hit re-entered the chart once, twice or three times, etc

10 Oct 63	★ YOU'LL NEVER WALK ALONE *Columbia DB 7126*........	1	19
16 Jan 64	● I'M THE ONE *Columbia DB 7189*	2	15
16 Apr 64	● DON'T LET THE SUN CATCH YOU CRYING		
	Columbia DB 7268........	6	11
3 Sep 64	IT'S GONNA BE ALL RIGHT *Columbia DB 7353*........	24	7
17 Dec 64	● FERRY 'CROSS THE MERSEY *Columbia DB 7437*........	8	13
25 Mar 65	I'LL BE THERE *Columbia DB 7504*........	15	9
18 Nov 65	WALK HAND IN HAND *Columbia DB 7738*........	29	7

GET FRESH CREW – *See Doug E FRESH and the GET FRESH CREW*

GET READY *UK, male vocal group (1 WEEK)*
pos/wks
3 Jun 95	WILD WILD WEST *Mega GACXCD 2698*........	65	1

GETO BOYS featuring FLAJ *US, male rap group (1 WEEK)*
pos/wks
11 May 96	THE WORLD IS A GHETTO *Virgin America VUSCD 104*........	49	1

Stan GETZ *US, male instrumentalist – tenor*
sax – Stanley Gayetzsky, b. 6 Jun 1991 (29 WEEKS)
pos/wks
8 Nov 62	DESAFINADO *HMV POP 1061* [1]........	11	13
23 Jul 64	THE GIRL FROM IPANEMA (GAROTA DE IPANEMA)		
	Verve VS 520 [2]........	29	10
25 Aug 84	THE GIRL FROM IPANEMA (re-issue) *Verve IPA 1* [3]........	55	6

[1] Stan Getz and Charlie Byrd [2] Stan Getz and Joao Gilberto [3] Astrud Gilberto

The re-issue of 'The Girl from Ipanema' was credited only to Astrud Gilberto, the vocalist, even though it was exactly the same recording as the original hit

Amanda GHOST *UK, female vocalist (1 WEEK)*
pos/wks
8 Apr 00	IDOL *Warner Brothers W 518CD*........	63	1

GHOST DANCE *UK, male vocal / instrumental group (2 WEEKS)*
pos/wks
17 Jun 89	DOWN TO THE WIRE *Chrysalis CHS 3376*........	66	2

GHOSTFACE KILLAH
US, male rapper – Dennis Coles (13 WEEKS)
pos/wks
12 Jul 97	ALL THAT I GOT IS YOU *Epic 6646842*........	11	4
23 Jan 99	● I WANT YOU FOR MYSELF *Northwestside 74321643632* [1]........	2	8
4 Nov 00	MISS FAT BOOTY – PART II *Rawkus RWK 282CD* [2]........	64	1

[1] Another Level / Ghostface Killah [2] Mos Def featuring Ghostface Killah

Andy GIBB *UK, male vocalist, d. 10 Mar 1988 (30 WEEKS)*
pos/wks
25 Jun 77	I JUST WANNA BE YOUR EVERYTHING *RSO 2090 237* ▲........	26	7
13 May 78	SHADOW DANCING *RSO 001* ▲........	42	6
12 Aug 78	● AN EVERLASTING LOVE *RSO 015*........	10	10
27 Jan 79	(OUR LOVE) DON'T THROW IT ALL AWAY *RSO 26*........	32	7

Barry GIBB – *See BEE GEES; Barbra STREISAND*

Robin GIBB *UK, male vocalist (21 WEEKS)*
pos/wks
9 Jul 69	● SAVED BY THE BELL (re) *Polydor 56-337*........	2	17
7 Feb 70	AUGUST OCTOBER *Polydor 56-371*........	45	3
11 Feb 84	ANOTHER LONELY NIGHT IN NEW YORK		
	Polydor POSP 668........	71	1

See also BEE GEES

Steve GIBBONS BAND
UK, male vocal / instrumental group (14 WEEKS)
pos/wks
6 Aug 77	TULANE *Polydor 2058 889*........	12	10
13 May 78	EDDY VORTEX *Polydor 2059 017*........	56	4

Georgia GIBBS *US, female vocalist – Freda Gibbons (2 WEEKS)*
pos/wks
22 Apr 55	TWEEDLE DEE *Mercury MB 3196*........	20	1
13 Jul 56	KISS ME ANOTHER *Mercury MT 110*........	24	1

Debbie GIBSON *US female vocalist / producer (70 WEEKS)*
pos/wks
26 Sep 87	ONLY IN MY DREAMS (re) *Atlantic A 9322*........	11	12

23 Jan 88	● SHAKE YOUR LOVE *Atlantic A 9187*........	7	8
7 May 88	OUT OF THE BLUE *Atlantic A 9091*........	19	7
9 Jul 88	● FOOLISH BEAT *Atlantic A 9059* ▲........	9	9
15 Oct 88	STAYING TOGETHER *Atlantic A 9020*........	53	2
28 Jan 89	LOST IN YOUR EYES *Atlantic A 8970* ▲........	34	7
29 Apr 89	ELECTRIC YOUTH *Atlantic A 8919*........	14	8
19 Aug 89	WE COULD BE TOGETHER *Atlantic A 8896*........	22	8
9 Mar 91	ANYTHING IS POSSIBLE *Atlantic A 7735*........	51	2
3 Apr 93	SHOCK YOUR MAMA *Atlantic A 7386CD*........	74	1
24 Jul 93	YOU'RE THE ONE THAT I WANT *Epic 6595222* [1]........	13	6

[1] Craig McLachlan and Debbie Gibson

'Only In My Dreams' made its peak position on re-entry in Mar 1988

Don GIBSON *US, male vocalist (16 WEEKS)*
pos/wks
31 Aug 61	SEA OF HEARTBREAK *RCA 1243*........	14	13
1 Feb 62	LONESOME NUMBER ONE *RCA 1272*........	47	3

Wayne GIBSON *UK, male vocalist (13 WEEKS)*
pos/wks
3 Sep 64	KELLY *Pye 7N 15680*........	48	2
23 Nov 74	UNDER MY THUMB *Pye Disco Demand DDS 2001*........	17	11

GIBSON BROTHERS
Martinique, male vocal / instrumental group (54 WEEKS)
pos/wks
10 Mar 79	CUBA *Island WIP 6483*........	41	9
21 Jul 79	● OOH! WHAT A LIFE *Island WIP 6503*........	10	12
17 Nov 79	● QUE SERA MI VIDA (IF YOU SHOULD GO)		
	Island WIP 6525........	5	11
23 Feb 80	CUBA / BETTER DO IT SALSA (re-issue)		
	Island WIP 6561........	12	9
12 Jul 80	MARIANA *Island WIP 6617*........	11	10
9 Jul 83	MY HEART'S BEATING WILD (TIC TAC TIC TAC)		
	Stiff BUY 184........	56	3

GIDEA PARK
UK, male vocal / instrumentalist – Adrian Baker (19 WEEKS)
pos/wks
4 Jul 81	BEACH BOY GOLD *Sonet SON 2162*........	11	13
12 Sep 81	SEASONS OF GOLD *Polo POLO 14*........	28	6

Johan GIELEN presents ABNEA
Belgium, male producer (1 WEEK)
pos/wks
18 Aug 01	VELVET MOODS *Data DATA 17T*........	74	1

See also SVENSON and GIELEN; BLUE BAMBOO; AIRSCAPE; BALEARIC BILL

GIFTED *UK, male instrumentalist (1 WEEK)*
pos/wks
23 Aug 97	DO I *Perfecto PERF 140CD*........	60	1

GIGOLO AUNTS *US, male vocal / instrumental group (4 WEEKS)*
pos/wks
23 Apr 94	MRS WASHINGTON *Fire BLAZE 68CD*........	74	1
13 May 95	WHERE I FIND MY HEAVEN *Fire BLAZE 87CD*........	29	3

Astrud GILBERTO – *See Stan GETZ*

Joao GILBERTO – *See Stan GETZ*

Donna GILES *US, female vocalist (4 WEEKS)*
pos/wks
13 Aug 94	AND I'M TELLING YOU I'M NOT GOING *Ore AG 4CD*........	43	2
10 Feb 96	AND I'M TELLING YOU I'M NOT GOING (re-issue)		
	Ore AGR 4CD........	27	2

Johnny GILL *US, male vocalist (12 WEEKS)*
pos/wks
23 Feb 91	WRAP MY BODY TIGHT *Motown ZB 44271*........	57	2
28 Nov 92	SLOW AND SEXY *Epic 6587727* [1]........	17	7
17 Jul 93	THE FLOOR *Motown TMGCD 1416*........	53	1
29 Jan 94	A CUTE SWEET LOVE ADDICTION *Motown TMGCD 1420*........	46	2

[1] Shabba Ranks featuring Johnny Gill

Vince GILL – *See Amy GRANT; Barbra STREISAND*

GILLAN
UK, male vocal / instrumental group (46 WEEKS)   pos/wks

14 Jun 80	SLEEPING ON THE JOB *Virgin VS 355*	55	3
4 Oct 80	TROUBLE *Virgin VS 377*	14	6
14 Feb 81	MUTUALLY ASSURED DESTRUCTION *Virgin VSK 103*	32	5
21 Mar 81	NEW ORLEANS *Virgin VS 406*	17	10
20 Jun 81	NO LAUGHING IN HEAVEN *Virgin VS 425*	31	6
10 Oct 81	NIGHTMARE *Virgin VS 441*	36	6
23 Jan 82	RESTLESS *Virgin VS 465*	25	7
4 Sep 82	LIVING FOR THE CITY *Virgin VS 519*	50	3

GILLETTE – *See 20 FINGERS*

Stuart GILLIES
UK, male vocalist (10 WEEKS)   pos/wks

| 31 Mar 73 | AMANDA *Philips 6006 293* | 13 | 10 |

Jimmy GILMER – *See FIREBALLS*

James GILREATH
US, male vocalist (10 WEEKS)   pos/wks

| 2 May 63 | LITTLE BAND OF GOLD *Pye International 7N 25190* | 29 | 10 |

Jim GILSTRAP
US, male vocalist (11 WEEKS)   pos/wks

| 15 Mar 75 ● | SWING YOUR DADDY *Chelsea 2005 021* | 4 | 11 |

Gordon GILTRAP
UK, male instrumentalist – guitar (10 WEEKS)   pos/wks

| 14 Jan 78 | HEARTSONG *Electric WOT 19* | 21 | 7 |
| 28 Apr 79 | FEAR OF THE DARK *Electric WOT 29* 1 | 58 | 3 |

1 Gordon Giltrap Band

GIN BLOSSOMS
US, male vocal / instrumental group (12 WEEKS)   pos/wks

5 Feb 94	HEY JEALOUSY *Fontana GINCD 3*	24	5
16 Apr 94	FOUND OUT ABOUT YOU *Fontana GINCD 4*	40	3
10 Feb 96	TIL I HEAR IT FROM YOU *A&M 5812272*	39	2
27 Apr 96	FOLLOW YOU DOWN *A&M 5815512*	30	2

GINGERBREADS – *See GOLDIE and the GINGERBREADS*

GINUWINE
US, male rapper – Elgin Lumpkin (24 WEEKS)   pos/wks

25 Jan 97	PONY *Epic 6641282*	16	6
24 May 97	TELL ME DO U WANNA *Epic 6645272*	16	3
6 Sep 97 ●	WHEN DOVES CRY *Epic 6649245*	10	5
14 Mar 98	HOLLER *Epic 6653372*	13	4
13 Mar 99 ●	WHAT'S SO DIFFERENT? *Epic 6670522*	10	4
14 Dec 02	CRUSH TONIGHT *Atlantic AT 0142CD* 1	42	2

1 Fat Joe featuring Ginuwine

GIPSY KINGS
France, male vocal / instrumental group (2 WEEKS)   pos/wks

| 3 Sep 94 | HITS MEDLEY *Columbia 6606022* | 53 | 2 |

Martine GIRAULT
UK, female vocalist (7 WEEKS)   pos/wks

29 Aug 92	REVIVAL *ffrr FX 195*	53	2
30 Jan 93	REVIVAL (re-issue) *ffrr FCD 205*	37	3
28 Oct 95	BEEN THINKING ABOUT YOU *RCA 74321316142*	63	1
1 Feb 97	REVIVAL (re-mix) *RCA 74321432162*	61	1

GIRESSE
UK, male DJ / production duo (1 WEEK)   pos/wks

| 14 Apr 01 | MON AMI *Inferno CDFERN 36* | 61 | 1 |

GIRL
UK, male vocal / instrumental group (3 WEEKS)   pos/wks

| 12 Apr 80 | HOLLYWOOD TEASE *Jet 176* | 50 | 3 |

GIRL NEXT DOOR – *See M&S presents GIRL NEXT DOOR*

GIRL THING
UK / Holland, female vocal group (13 WEEKS)   pos/wks

| 1 Jul 00 ● | LAST ONE STANDING (re) *RCA 74321762412* | 8 | 10 |
| 18 Nov 00 | GIRLS ON TOP *RCA 74321801162* | 25 | 3 |

GIRLFRIEND
Australia, female vocal group (6 WEEKS)   pos/wks

| 30 Jan 93 | TAKE IT FROM ME *Arista 74321114252* | 47 | 4 |
| 15 May 93 | GIRL'S LIFE *Arista 74321138452* | 68 | 2 |

GIRLS ALOUD
UK, female vocal group (1 WEEK)   pos/wks

| 28 Dec 02 ★ | SOUND OF THE UNDERGROUND *Polydor 0658272* ■ | 1 | 1+ |

GIRLS @ PLAY
UK, female vocal group (7 WEEKS)   pos/wks

| 24 Feb 01 | AIRHEAD *GSM GSMCDR 1* | 18 | 5 |
| 13 Oct 01 | RESPECTABLE *Redbus RBMCD101* | 29 | 2 |

GIRLSCHOOL
UK, female vocal / instrumental group (25 WEEKS)   pos/wks

2 Aug 80	RACE WITH THE DEVIL *Bronze BRO 100*	49	6
21 Feb 81 ●	ST VALENTINE'S DAY MASSACRE (EP) *Bronze BRO 116* 1	5	8
11 Apr 81	HIT AND RUN *Bronze BRO 118*	32	6
11 Jul 81	C'MON LET'S GO *Bronze BRO 126*	42	3
3 Apr 82	WILDLIFE (EP) *Bronze BRO 144*	58	2

1 Motörhead and Girlschool (also known as Headgirl)

Tracks on St Valentine's Day Massacre (EP): Please Don't Touch / Emergency / Bomber. Tracks on Wildlife (EP): Don't Call It Love / Wildlife / Don't Stop

Junior GISCOMBE – *See JUNIOR*

GITTA
Denmark / Italy, male / female / instrumental group (1 WEEK) pos/wks

| 19 Aug 00 | NO MORE TURNING BACK *Pepper 9230302* | 54 | 1 |

GLADIATORS – *See NERO and the GLADIATORS*

GLADIATORS
UK, male / female vocal group (1 WEEK)   pos/wks

| 30 Nov 96 | THE BOYS ARE BACK IN TOWN *RCA 74321417002* | 70 | 1 |

GLAM
Italy, male instrumental / production group (2 WEEKS)   pos/wks

| 1 May 93 | HELL'S PARTY *Six6 SIXCD 001* | 42 | 2 |

GLAM METAL DETECTIVES
UK, male / female vocal group (2 WEEKS)   pos/wks

| 11 Mar 95 | EVERYBODY UP! *ZTT ZANG 62CD* | 29 | 2 |

GLAMMA KID
UK, male vocalist / rapper – Yael Constable (25 WEEKS)   pos/wks

21 Nov 98	FASHION '98 *WEA WEA 179CD*	49	1
17 Apr 99 ●	TABOO *WEA WEA 203CD* 1	10	8
27 Nov 99 ●	WHY *WEA WEA 229 CD1*	10	10
2 Sep 00	BILLS 2 PAY (re) *WEA WEA 268CD*	17	6

1 Glamma Kid featuring Shola Ama

GLASS TIGER
Canada, male vocal / instrumental group (18 WEEKS)   pos/wks

18 Oct 86	DON'T FORGET ME (WHEN I'M GONE) *Manhattan MT 13*	29	9
31 Jan 87	SOMEDAY *Manhattan MT 17*	66	2
26 Oct 91	MY TOWN *EMI EM 212*	33	7

'My Town' features the uncredited vocals of Rod Stewart

Mayson GLEN ORCHESTRA – *See Paul HENRY and the Mayson GLEN ORCHESTRA*

GLENN and CHRIS
UK, male footballers / vocal duo – Glenn Hoddle and Chris Waddle (8 WEEKS)   pos/wks

| 18 Apr 87 | DIAMOND LIGHTS *Record Shack KICK 1* | 12 | 8 |

Gary GLITTER (119) Top 500 *Glitter rock giant, b. Paul Gadd, 8 May 1940, Oxfordshire, UK. Started recording in 1960 (as Paul Raven), and was the first act to put his first 11 hits into the Top 10. This singer / songwriter remained a popular live performer until he was jailed in 1999. Biggest-selling single: 'I Love You Love Me Love' 1,140,000 (170 WEEKS)* pos/wks

10 Jun 72	● ROCK AND ROLL (PARTS 1 & 2) *Bell 1216*	2 15
23 Sep 72	● I DIDN'T KNOW I LOVED YOU (TILL I SAW YOU ROCK 'N' ROLL) *Bell 1259*	4 11
20 Jan 73	● DO YOU WANNA TOUCH ME? (OH YEAH) *Bell 1280*	2 11
7 Apr 73	● HELLO! HELLO! I'M BACK AGAIN *Bell 1299*	2 14
21 Jul 73	★ I'M THE LEADER OF THE GANG (I AM) *Bell 1321*	1 12
17 Nov 73	★ I LOVE YOU LOVE ME LOVE *Bell 1337* ◆ ■	1 14
30 Mar 74	● REMEMBER ME THIS WAY *Bell 1349*	3 8
15 Jun 74	★ ALWAYS YOURS *Bell 1359*	1 9
23 Nov 74	● OH YES! YOU'RE BEAUTIFUL *Bell 1391*	2 10
3 May 75	● LOVE LIKE YOU AND ME *Bell 1423*	10 6
21 Jun 75	● DOING ALRIGHT WITH THE BOYS *Bell 1429*	6 7
8 Nov 75	PAPA OOM MOW MOW *Bell 1451*	38 5
13 Mar 76	YOU BELONG TO ME *Bell 1473*	40 5
22 Jan 77	IT TAKES ALL NIGHT LONG *Arista 85*	25 6
16 Jul 77	A LITTLE BOOGIE WOOGIE IN THE BACK OF MY MIND *Arista 112*	31 5
20 Sep 80	GARY GLITTER (EP) *GTO GT 282*	57 3
10 Oct 81	AND THEN SHE KISSED ME *Bell BELL 1497*	39 5
5 Dec 81	ALL THAT GLITTERS *Bell BELL 1498*	48 5
23 Jun 84	DANCE ME UP *Arista ARIST 570*	25 5
1 Dec 84	● ANOTHER ROCK AND ROLL CHRISTMAS *Arista ARIST 592*	7 7
10 Oct 92	AND THE LEADER ROCKS ON *EMI EM 252*	58 2
21 Nov 92	THROUGH THE YEARS *EMI EM 256*	49 3
16 Dec 95	HELLO HELLO I'M BACK AGAIN (AGAIN!) *Carlton Sounds 3036000192*	50 2

'Rock and Roll Part 1' not listed with 'Part 2' for weeks of 10 and 17 Jun 1972. Tracks on Gary Glitter (EP): I'm the Leader of the Gang (I Am) / Rock and Roll (Part 2) / Hello Hello I'm Back Again / Do You Wanna Touch Me? (Oh Yeah). All were re-issues. 'Hello Hello I'm Back Again (Again!)' in 1995 is a re-recording

GLITTER BAND
UK, male vocal / instrumental group (60 WEEKS) pos/wks

23 Mar 74	● ANGEL FACE *Bell 1348*	4 10
3 Aug 74	● JUST FOR YOU *Bell 1368*	10 8
19 Oct 74	● LET'S GET TOGETHER AGAIN *Bell 1383*	8 8
18 Jan 75	● GOODBYE MY LOVE *Bell 1395*	2 9
12 Apr 75	● THE TEARS I CRIED *Bell 1416*	8 8
9 Aug 75	LOVE IN THE SUN *Bell 1437*	15 8
28 Feb 76	● PEOPLE LIKE YOU AND PEOPLE LIKE ME *Bell 1471*	5 9

See also Gary GLITTER

GLOBAL COMMUNICATION
UK, male instrumental / production duo (1 WEEK) pos/wks

11 Jan 97	THE WAY / THE DEEP *Dedicated GLOBA 002CD*	51 1

See also COSMOS

GLOVE *UK, male vocal / instrumental group (3 WEEKS)* pos/wks

20 Aug 83	LIKE AN ANIMAL *Wonderland SHE 3*	52 3

See also SIOUXSIE and the BANSHEES; CURE

GLOWORM *UK / US, male vocal / instrumental group (17 WEEKS)* pos/wks

6 Feb 93	I LIFT MY CUP *Pulse 8 CDLOSE 37*	20 4
14 May 94	● CARRY ME HOME *Go.Beat GODCD 112*	9 11
6 Aug 94	I LIFT MY CUP (re-issue) *Pulse 8 CDLOSE 67*	46 2

GO GO LORENZO and the DAVIS PINCKNEY PROJECT
US, male vocal / instrumental group (8 WEEKS) pos/wks

6 Dec 86	YOU CAN DANCE IF YOU WANT TO *Boiling Point POSP 836*	46 8

GO-GO's *US, female vocal / instrumental group (10 WEEKS)* pos/wks

15 May 82	OUR LIPS ARE SEALED *IRS GDN 102*	47 6

26 Jan 91	COOL JERK *IRS AM 712*	60 1
18 Feb 95	THE WHOLE WORLD LOST ITS HEAD *IRS CDEIRS 190*	29 3

See also Jane WIEDLIN; Belinda CARLISLE

GO WEST (403) Top 500
Songwriting duo specialising in radio-friendly white soul sounds; Peter Cox (v) and Richard Drummie (g/k/v). Best Newcomers at the 1986 Brit awards had US Top 10 hit with 'King of Wishful Thinking', from the soundtrack of Pretty Woman (85 WEEKS) pos/wks

23 Feb 85	● WE CLOSE OUR EYES *Chrysalis CHS 2850*	5 14
11 May 85	CALL ME *Chrysalis GOW 1*	12 10
3 Aug 85	GOODBYE GIRL *Chrysalis GOW 2*	25 7
23 Nov 85	DON'T LOOK DOWN – THE SEQUEL *Chrysalis GOW 3*	13 10
29 Nov 86	TRUE COLOURS *Chrysalis GOW 4*	48 7
9 May 87	I WANT TO HEAR IT FROM YOU *Chrysalis GOW 5*	43 3
12 Sep 87	THE KING IS DEAD *Chrysalis GOW 6*	67 2
28 Jul 90	THE KING OF WISHFUL THINKING *Chrysalis GOW 8*	18 10
17 Oct 92	FAITHFUL *Chrysalis GOW 9*	13 6
16 Jan 93	WHAT YOU WON'T DO FOR LOVE *Chrysalis CDGOWS 10*	15 5
27 Mar 93	STILL IN LOVE *Chrysalis CDGOWS 11*	43 3
2 Oct 93	TRACKS OF MY TEARS *Chrysalis CDGOWS 12*	16 5
4 Dec 93	WE CLOSE OUR EYES (re-mix) *Chrysalis CDGOWS 13*	40 3

GOATS *US, male rap group (2 WEEKS)* pos/wks

29 May 93	AAAH D YAAA / TYPICAL AMERICAN *Ruff House 6593032*	53 2

'Typical American' listed only from 5 Jun 1993, peaking at No.65

GOD MACHINE *US, male vocal / instrumental group (2 WEEKS)* pos/wks

30 Jan 93	HOME *Fiction FICCD 47*	65 2

GODIEGO
Japan / US, male vocal / instrumental group (11 WEEKS) pos/wks

15 Oct 77	THE WATER MARGIN *BBC RESL 50*	37 4
16 Feb 80	GANDHARA *BBC RESL 66*	56 7

'The Water Margin' is the English version of the song, which shared chart credit with the Japanese language version by Pete Mac Jr

GODLEY and CREME *UK, male vocal / instrumental duo – Kevin Godley and Lol Creme (36 WEEKS)* pos/wks

12 Sep 81	● UNDER YOUR THUMB *Polydor POSP 322*	3 11
21 Nov 81	● WEDDING BELLS *Polydor POSP 369*	7 11
30 Mar 85	CRY (re) *Polydor POSP 732*	19 14

See also 10 CC

GOD'S PROPERTY *US, male / female gospel choir (1 WEEK)* pos/wks

22 Nov 97	STOMP *B-rite Music IND 95559*	60 1

Andrew GOLD
US, male vocalist / instrumentalist – piano (36 WEEKS) pos/wks

2 Apr 77	LONELY BOY *Asylum K 13076*	11 9
25 Mar 78	● NEVER LET HER SLIP AWAY *Asylum K 13112*	5 13
24 Jun 78	HOW CAN THIS BE LOVE *Asylum K 13126*	19 10
14 Oct 78	THANK YOU FOR BEING A FRIEND *Asylum K 13135*	42 4

See also WAX

Ari GOLD – *See DJ LUCK & MC NEAT*

Brian and Tony GOLD – *See RED DRAGON with Brian and Tony GOLD; SHAGGY*

GOLD BLADE *UK, male vocal / instrumental group (1 WEEK)* pos/wks

22 Mar 97	STRICTLY HARDCORE *Ultimate TOPP 056CD*	64 1

GOLDBUG
UK, male / female vocal / instrumental group (5 WEEKS) pos/wks

27 Jan 96	● WHOLE LOTTA LOVE *Acid Jazz JAZID 125CD*	3 5

GOLDEN BOY with MISS KITTEN
Germany, male producer and France, female vocalist (1 WEEK) pos/wks

7 Sep 02	RIPPIN KITTEN *Illustrious CDILL 007*	67 1

GOLDEN EARRING
Holland, male vocal / instrumental group (16 WEEKS) pos/wks

8 Dec 73 ●	RADAR LOVE *Track 2094 116* ●	7 13
8 Oct 77	RADAR LOVE *Polydor 2121 335*	44 3

The 8 Oct 1977 version of Radar Love credits Golden Earring 'Live'

GOLDEN GIRLS
UK, male producer / instrumentalist – Mike Hazell (3 WEEKS) pos/wks

3 Oct 98	KINETIC *Distinctive DISNCD 46*	38 2
4 Dec 99	KINETIC (re-mix) *Distinctive DISNCD 59*	56 1

GOLDENSCAN *UK, male DJ / production duo (1 WEEK)* pos/wks

11 Nov 00	SUNRISE *VC Recordings VCRD 79*	52 1

GOLDFINGER
US, male vocal / instrumental group (1 WEEK) pos/wks

22 Jun 02	OPEN YOUR EYES *Jive 9270052*	75 1

GOLDFRAPP
UK, male / female vocal / instrumental group (2 WEEKS) pos/wks

23 Jun 01	UTOPIA *Mute CDMUTE 264*	62 1
17 Nov 01	PILOTS *Mute CDMUTE 267*	68 1

GOLDIE *UK, male vocal / instrumental group (11 WEEKS)* pos/wks

27 May 78 ●	MAKING UP AGAIN *Bronze BRO 50*	7 11

GOLDIE *UK, male producer – Clifford Price (16 WEEKS)* pos/wks

3 Dec 94	INNER CITY LIFE *ffrr FCD 251* [1]	49 2
9 Sep 95	ANGEL *ffrr FCD 266*	41 3
11 Nov 95	INNER CITY LIFE (re-mix) *ffrr FCD 267*	39 2
1 Nov 97	DIGITAL *ffrr FCD 316* [2]	13 3
24 Jan 98	TEMPERTEMPER *ffrr FCD 325* [2]	13 4
18 Apr 98	BELIEVE *ffrr FCD 332*	36 2

[1] Goldie presents Metalheadz [2] Goldie featuring KRS One

GOLDIE and the GINGERBREADS
US, female vocal / instrumental group (5 WEEKS) pos/wks

25 Feb 65	CAN'T YOU HEAR MY HEART BEAT? *Decca F 12070*	25 5

GOLDRUSH
UK, male vocal / instrumental group (2 WEEKS) pos/wks

22 Jun 02	SAME PICTURE *Virgin VSCDT 1833*	64 1
7 Sep 02	WIDE OPEN SKY *Virgin VSCDT 1834*	70 1

Bobby GOLDSBORO *US, male vocalist (47 WEEKS)* pos/wks

17 Apr 68 ●	HONEY *United Artists UP2215* ▲	2 15
4 Aug 73 ●	SUMMER (THE FIRST TIME) *United Artists UP35558*	9 10
3 Aug 74	HELLO, SUMMERTIME *United Artists UP35705*	14 10
29 Mar 75 ●	HONEY (re-issue) *United Artists UP35633*	2 12

Glen GOLDSMITH *UK, male vocalist (24 WEEKS)* pos/wks

7 Nov 87	I WON'T CRY *Reproduction PB 41493*	34 7
12 Mar 88	DREAMING *Reproduction PB 41711*	12 11
11 Jun 88	WHAT YOU SEE IS WHAT YOU GET *Reproduction PB 42075*	33 5
3 Sep 88	SAVE A LITTLE BIT *Reproduction PB 42147*	73 1

GOLDTRIX presents Andrea BROWN *UK, male*
production / instrumental duo and US, female vocalist (9 WEEKS) pos/wks

19 Jan 02 ●	IT'S LOVE (TRIPPIN') (re) *AM:PM / Serious / Evolve CDAMPM 152*	6 9

GOMEZ
UK, male vocal / instrumental group (16 WEEKS) pos/wks

11 Apr 98	78 STONE WOBBLE *Hut HUTCD 95*	44 1
13 Jun 98	GET MYSELF ARRESTED *Hut HUTCD 97*	45 1
12 Sep 98	WHIPPIN' PICCADILLY *Hut HUTCD 105*	35 3
10 Jul 99	BRING IT ON *Hut HUTCD 112*	21 3
11 Sep 99	RHYTHM & BLUES ALIBI *Hut HUTCD 114*	18 3
27 Nov 99	WE HAVEN'T TURNED AROUND *Hut HUTCD 117*	38 2
16 Mar 02	SHOT SHOT *Hut / Virgin HUTCD 149*	28 2
15 Jun 02	SOUND OF SOUNDS / PING ONE DOWN *Hut / Virgin HUTCD 154*	48 1

Leroy GOMEZ – See SANTA ESMERALDA and Leroy GOMEZ

GOMPIE
Holland, male vocal / instrumental group (12 WEEKS) pos/wks

20 May 95	ALICE (WHO THE X IS ALICE) (LIVING NEXT DOOR TO ALICE) (re) *Habana HABSCD 5*	17 12

GONZALES – See FUNK MASTERS

GONZALEZ
UK / US, male vocal / instrumental group (11 WEEKS) pos/wks

31 Mar 79	HAVEN'T STOPPED DANCING YET *Sidewalk SID 102*	15 11

GOO GOO DOLLS
US, male vocal / instrumental trio (4 WEEKS) pos/wks

1 Aug 98	IRIS *Reprise W 0449CD*	50 1
27 Mar 99	SLIDE *Edel / Hollywood / Third Rail 0102035 HWR*	43 1
17 Jul 99	IRIS (re-issue) *Hollywood 0102485 HWR*	26 2

GOOD GIRLS *US, female vocal group (1 WEEK)* pos/wks

24 Jul 93	JUST CALL ME *Motown TMGCD 1417*	75 1

GOODBYE MR MACKENZIE
UK, male / female vocal / instrumental group (13 WEEKS) pos/wks

20 Aug 88	GOODBYE MR MACKENZIE *Capitol CL 501*	62 2
11 Mar 89	THE RATTLER *Capitol CL 522*	37 6
29 Jul 89	GOODWILL CITY / I'M SICK OF YOU *Capitol CL 538*	49 2
21 Apr 90	LOVE CHILD *Parlophone R 6247*	52 2
23 Jun 90	BLACKER THAN BLACK *Parlophone R 6257*	61 2

Roger GOODE featuring Tasha BAXTER
South Africa, male DJ / producer and female vocalist (2 WEEKS) pos/wks

13 Apr 02	IN THE BEGINNING *ffrr DFCD 004*	33 2

GOODFELLAS featuring Lisa MILLETT *Italy, male production duo*
– Paolo Martini and Gianni Bini – and UK, female vocalist (2 WEEKS) pos/wks

21 Jul 01	SOUL HEAVEN *Direction 6713852*	27 2

See also ECLIPSE; BINI & MARTINI; HOUSE OF GLASS

GOODFELLAZ *US, male vocal trio (2 WEEKS)* pos/wks

10 May 97	SUGAR HONEY ICE TEA *Wild Card 5736132*	25 2

GOODIES
UK, male comedy / vocal group (38 WEEKS) pos/wks

7 Dec 74 ●	THE INBETWEENIES / FATHER CHRISTMAS DO NOT TOUCH ME *Bradley's BRAD 7421*	7 9
15 Mar 75 ●	FUNKY GIBBON / SICK-MAN BLUES *Bradley's BRAD 7504*	4 10
21 Jun 75	BLACK PUDDING BERTHA (THE QUEEN OF NORTHERN SOUL) *Bradley's BRAD 7517*	19 7
27 Sep 75	NAPPY LOVE / WILD THING *Bradley's BRAD 7524*	21 4
13 Dec 75	MAKE A DAFT NOISE FOR CHRISTMAS *Bradley's BRAD 7533*	20 6

Cuba GOODING *US, male vocalist (2 WEEKS)* pos/wks

19 Nov 83	HAPPINESS IS JUST AROUND THE BEND *London LON 41*	72 2

GOODMEN Holland, male instrumental / production
duo – Rene Terhorst and Gaston Steenkist (19 WEEKS)   pos/wks

| 7 Aug 93 | ● | GIVE IT UP (re) Fresh Fruit TABCD 118 | 5 | 19 |

See also RIVA featuring Dannii MINOGUE; JARK PRONGO; TOMBA VIRA; RHYTHMKILLAZ; CHOCOLATE PUMA

Ron GOODWIN and His ORCHESTRA
UK, orchestra (24 WEEKS)   pos/wks

| 15 May 53 | ● | TERRY'S THEME FROM 'LIMELIGHT' Parlophone R 3686 | 3 | 23 |
| 28 Oct 55 | | BLUE STAR (THE MEDIC THEME) Parlophone R 4074 | 20 | 1 |

See also Eamonn ANDREWS

GOODY GOODY US, female vocal duo (5 WEEKS)   pos/wks

| 2 Dec 78 | | NUMBER ONE DEE JAY Atlantic LV 3 | 55 | 5 |

GOOMBAY DANCE BAND Germany / Montserrat,
male / female vocal / instrumental group (16 WEEKS)   pos/wks

| 27 Feb 82 | ★ | SEVEN TEARS Epic EPC A 1242 | 1 | 12 |
| 15 May 82 | | SUN OF JAMAICA Epic EPC A 2345 | 50 | 4 |

GOONS UK, male comedy / vocal group (30 WEEKS)   pos/wks

29 Jun 56	●	I'M WALKING BACKWARDS FOR CHRISTMAS / BLUEBOTTLE BLUES Decca F 10756	4	10
14 Sep 56	●	BLOODNOK'S ROCK 'N' ROLL CALL / THE YING TONG SONG Decca E 10780	3	10
21 Jul 73	●	YING TONG SONG (re-issue) Decca F 13414	9	10

'Bluebottle Blues' listed only from 13 Jul 1956. It peaked at No.5

Lonnie GORDON US, female vocalist (23 WEEKS)   pos/wks

24 Jun 89		(I'VE GOT YOUR) PLEASURE CONTROL ffrr F 106 [1]	60	3
27 Jan 90	●	HAPPENIN' ALL OVER AGAIN Supreme SUPE 159	4	10
11 Aug 90		BEYOND YOUR WILDEST DREAMS Supreme SUPE 167	48	2
17 Nov 90		IF I HAVE TO STAND ALONE Supreme SUPE 181	68	1
4 May 91		GONNA CATCH YOU Supreme SUPE 185	32	5
7 Oct 95		LOVE EVICTION X:Plode BANG 2CD [2]	32	2

[1] Simon Harris featuring Lonnie Gordon [2] Quartz Lock featuring Lonnie Gordon

Lesley GORE US, female vocalist (20 WEEKS)   pos/wks

| 20 Jun 63 | ● | IT'S MY PARTY Mercury AMT 1205 ▲ | 9 | 12 |
| 24 Sep 64 | | MAYBE I KNOW Mercury MF 829 | 20 | 8 |

GORILLAZ UK / US, animated male vocal
/ instrumental / production group (39 WEEKS)   pos/wks

17 Mar 01	●	CLINT EASTWOOD Parlophone CDR 6552	4	17
7 Jul 01	●	19/2000 Parlophone CDR 6559	6	10
3 Nov 01		ROCK THE HOUSE Parlophone CDRS 6565	18	8
9 Mar 02		TOMORROW COMES TODAY (re) Parlophone CDR 6573	33	3
3 Aug 02		LIL' DUB CHEFIN' Parlophone CDR 6584 [1]	73	1

[1] Space Monkeyz vs Gorillaz

GORKY'S ZYGOTIC MYNCI
UK, male / female vocal / instrumental group (8 WEEKS)   pos/wks

9 Nov 96		PATIO SONG Fontana GZMCD 1	41	1
29 Mar 97		DIAMOND DEW Fontana GZMCD 2	42	1
21 Jun 97		YOUNG GIRLS & HAPPY ENDINGS / DARK NIGHT Fontana GZMCD 3	49	1
6 Jun 98		SWEET JOHNNY Fontana GZMCD 4	60	1
29 Aug 98		LET'S GET TOGETHER (IN OUR MINDS) Fontana GZMCD 5	43	1
2 Oct 99		SPANISH DANCE TROUPE Mantra / Beggars Banquet MNT 47CD	47	1
4 Mar 00		POODLE ROCKIN' Mantra / Beggars Banquet MNT 52CD	52	1
15 Sep 01		STOOD ON GOLD Mantra / Beggars Banquet MNT 64CD	65	1

Eydie GORME US, female vocalist (33 WEEKS)   pos/wks

| 24 Jan 58 | | LOVE ME FOREVER HMV POP 432 | 21 | 5 |
| 21 Jun 62 | ● | YES MY DARLING DAUGHTER CBS AAG 105 | 10 | 9 |

| 31 Jan 63 | | BLAME IT ON THE BOSSA NOVA CBS AAG 131 | 32 | 6 |
| 22 Aug 63 | ● | I WANT TO STAY HERE CBS AAG 163 [1] | 3 | 13 |

[1] Steve and Eydie

Luke GOSS and the BAND OF THIEVES
UK, male vocal / instrumental group (3 WEEKS)   pos/wks

| 12 Jun 93 | | SWEETER THAN THE MIDNIGHT RAIN Sabre CDSAB 1 | 52 | 2 |
| 21 Aug 93 | | GIVE ME ONE MORE CHANCE Sabre CDSAB 2 | 68 | 1 |

See also BROS

Matt GOSS UK, male vocalist (5 WEEKS)   pos/wks

| 26 Aug 95 | | THE KEY Atlas 5811532 | 40 | 2 |
| 27 Apr 96 | | IF YOU WERE HERE TONIGHT Atlas 5762932 | 23 | 3 |

See also BROS

Irv GOTTI presents JA RULE, ASHANTI, Charli BALTIMORE & VITA
US, male producer and male / female vocalists / rappers (9 WEEKS) pos/wks

| 12 Oct 02 | ● | DOWN 4 U (re) Murder Inc 0639002 | 4 | 9 |

Nigel GOULDING – See Abigail MEAD and Nigel GOULDING

Graham GOULDMAN UK, male vocalist (4 WEEKS)   pos/wks

| 23 Jun 79 | | SUNBURN Mercury SUNNY 1 | 52 | 4 |

See also 10 CC; WAX

GOURYELLA Holland, male production duo
– Tijs Verwest and Ferry Corsten (11 WEEKS)   pos/wks

10 Jul 99		GOURYELLA Code Blue BLU 001CD	15	7
4 Dec 99		WALHALLA Code Blue BLU 006CD	27	2
23 Dec 00		TENSHI Code Blue BLUE 017CD	45	2

See also MOONMAN; SYSTEM F; VERACOCHA; ALBION; STARPARTY; Ferry CORSTEN

GRACE UK, female vocalist – Dominique Atkins (24 WEEKS)   pos/wks

8 Apr 95	●	NOT OVER YET Perfecto PERF 104CD	6	8
23 Sep 95		I WANT TO LIVE Perfecto PERF 109CD	30	2
24 Feb 96		SKIN ON SKIN Perfecto PERF 116CD	21	3
1 Jun 96		DOWN TO EARTH Perfecto PERF 120CD	20	2
28 Sep 96		IF I COULD FLY Perfecto PERF 127CD	29	2
3 May 97		HAND IN HAND Perfecto PERF 129CD	38	1
26 Jul 97		DOWN TO EARTH (re-mix) Perfecto PERF 142CD1	29	2
14 Aug 99		NOT OVER YET 99 Code Blue BLU 004CD1 [1]	16	4

[1] Planet Perfecto featuring Grace

Bridgette GRACE – See TRUE FAITH and Bridgette GRACE with FINAL CUT

GRACE BROTHERS UK, male instrumental duo (1 WEEK)   pos/wks

| 20 Apr 96 | | ARE YOU BEING SERVED EMI Premier PRESCD 1 | 51 | 1 |

Charlie GRACIE US, male vocalist – Charlie Graci (41 WEEKS)   pos/wks

19 Apr 57		BUTTERFLY Parlophone R 4290	12	8
14 Jun 57	●	FABULOUS Parlophone R 4313	8	16
23 Aug 57	●	WANDERIN' EYES London HLU 8467	6	16
10 Jan 58		COOL BABY London HLU 8521	26	1

'I Love You So Much It Hurts' and 'Wanderin' Eyes' were listed together for two weeks, then listed separately for a further two and 12 weeks respectively

Eve GRAHAM – See NEW SEEKERS

Jaki GRAHAM   485   Top 500
Britain's foremost black female vocalist of the 1980s, b. 15 Sep 1956, Birmingham, UK, who was first introduced to the public via a duet with ex-Linx vocalist David Grant. The one-time UB40 backing vocalist helped to open doors for other UK female soul singers (75 WEEKS)   pos/wks

| 23 Mar 85 | ● | COULD IT BE I'M FALLING IN LOVE Chrysalis GRAN 6 [1] | 5 | 11 |
| 29 Jun 85 | ● | ROUND AND ROUND EMI JAKI 4 | 9 | 11 |

31 Aug 85	HEAVEN KNOWS *EMI JAKI 5*	59	3
16 Nov 85	MATED *EMI JAKI 6* [1]	20	10
3 May 86 ●	SET ME FREE *EMI JAKI 7*	7	12
9 Aug 86	BREAKING AWAY *EMI JAKI 8*	16	8
15 Nov 86	STEP RIGHT UP *EMI JAKI 9*	15	12
9 Jul 88	NO MORE TEARS *EMI JAKI 12*	60	2
24 Jun 89	FROM NOW ON *EMI JAKI 15*	73	2
16 Jul 94	AIN'T NOBODY *Pulse 8 CDLOSE 64*	44	2
4 Feb 95	YOU CAN COUNT ON ME *Avex UK AVEXCD 1*	62	1
8 Jul 95	ABSOLUTE E-SENSUAL *Avex UK AVEXCD 5*	69	1

[1] David Grant and Jaki Graham

Larry GRAHAM
US, male vocalist / instrumentalist – bass (4 WEEKS) pos/wks

3 Jul 82	SOONER OR LATER *Warner Bros. K 17925*	54	4

Mikey GRAHAM *Ireland, male vocalist (6 WEEKS)* pos/wks

10 Jun 00	YOU'RE MY ANGEL *Public PR 001CDS*	13	5
14 Apr 01	YOU COULD BE MY EVERYTHING *Public PR 003CDS*	62	1

See also BOYZONE

Ron GRAINER ORCHESTRA
UK, orchestra, leader d. 21 Feb 1981 (7 WEEKS) pos/wks

9 Dec 78	A TOUCH OF VELVET – A STING OF BRASS *Casino Classics CC 5*	60	7

GRAM'MA FUNK – See GROOVE ARMADA; ILLICIT featuring GRAM'MA FUNK

GRAND FUNK RAILROAD
US, male vocal / instrumental group (1 WEEK) pos/wks

6 Feb 71	INSIDE LOOKING OUT *Capitol CL 15668*	40	1

GRAND PLAZ *UK, male instrumental / production group (4 WEEKS)* pos/wks

8 Sep 90	WOW WOW – NA NA *Urban URB 60*	41	4

GRAND PRIX *UK, male vocal / instrumental group (1 WEEK)* pos/wks

27 Feb 82	KEEP ON BELIEVING *RCA 162*	75	1

GRAND PUBA *US, male rapper – Maxwell Dixon (6 WEEKS)* pos/wks

13 Jan 96	WHY YOU TREAT ME SO BAD *Virgin VSCDT 1566* [1]	11	5
30 Mar 96	WILL YOU BE MY BABY *GHQ 74321339092* [2]	53	1

[1] Shaggy featuring Grand Puba [2] Infiniti featuring Grand Puba

GRAND THEFT AUDIO
UK, male vocal / instrumental group (1 WEEK) pos/wks

24 Mar 01	WE LUV U *Sci-Fi SCIFI 1CD*	70	1

GRANDAD ROBERTS AND HIS SON ELVIS
UK, male vocal duo (1 WEEK) pos/wks

20 Jun 98	MEAT PIE SAUSAGE ROLL *WEA WEA 160CD*	67	1

GRANDADDY *US, male vocal / instrumental group (3 WEEKS)* pos/wks

2 Sep 00	HEWLETT'S DAUGHTER *V2 VVR 5014333*	71	1
10 Feb 01	THE CRYSTAL LAKE *V2 VVR 5015153*	38	2

GRANDMASTER FLASH,
Melle MEL and the FURIOUS FIVE `388` `Top 500`
Pioneering rap act who led the genre into more serious subjects. New York act fronted by Grandmaster Flash (Joseph Saddler) and Melle Mel (Melvin Glover). 'White Lines' took a record 25 weeks to make the Top 10 (87 WEEKS) pos/wks

28 Aug 82 ●	THE MESSAGE *Sugarhill SHL 117* [1]	8	9
22 Jan 83	MESSAGE II (SURVIVAL) *Sugarhill SH 119* [2]	74	2
19 Nov 83 ●	WHITE LINES (DON'T DON'T DO IT) (3re) *Sugarhill SH 130* [3]	7	43
30 Jun 84	BEAT STREET BREAKDOWN *Atlantic A 9659* [4]	42	7
22 Sep 84	WE DON'T WORK FOR FREE *Sugarhill SH 136* [4]	45	4
15 Dec 84 ●	STEP OFF (PART 1) *Sugarhill SH 139* [4]	8	12

16 Feb 85	SIGN OF THE TIMES *Elektra E 9677* [5]	72	1
16 Mar 85	PUMP ME UP *Sugarhill SH 141* [4]	45	6
8 Jan 94	WHITE LINES (DON'T DO IT) (re-mix) *WGAF WGAFCD 103* [3] 59		3

[1] Grandmaster Flash and the Furious Five [2] Melle Mel and Duke Bootee
[3] Grandmaster and Melle Mel [4] Grandmaster Melle Mel and the Furious Five
[5] Grandmaster Flash

'White Lines (Don't, Don't Do It) re-entered in 1984 (twice), 1985 and 1994

See also DURAN DURAN

GRANDMIXER D.ST.
US, male DJ / producer – Derek Howells (3 WEEKS) pos/wks

24 Dec 83	CRAZY CUTS (re) *Island IS 146*	71	3

GRANGE HILL CAST
UK, male / female TV show cast / vocal charity assembly (6 WEEKS) pos/wks

19 Apr 86 ●	JUST SAY NO *BBC RESL 183*	5	6

Gerri GRANGER *US, female vocalist (3 WEEKS)* pos/wks

30 Sep 78	I GO TO PIECES (EVERYTIME) *Casino Classics CC3*	50	3

Amy GRANT *US, female vocalist (39 WEEKS)* pos/wks

11 May 91 ●	BABY BABY *A&M AM 727* ▲	2	13
3 Aug 91	EVERY HEARTBEAT *A&M AM 783*	25	7
2 Nov 91	THAT'S WHAT LOVE IS FOR *A&M AM 666*	60	3
15 Feb 92	GOOD FOR ME *A&M AM 810*	60	1
13 Aug 94	LUCKY ONE *A&M 5807322*	60	1
22 Oct 94	SAY YOU'LL BE MINE *A&M 5808292*	41	2
24 Jun 95	BIG YELLOW TAXI *A&M 5809972*	20	10
14 Oct 95	HOUSE OF LOVE *A&M 5812332* [1]	46	2

[1] Amy Grant with Vince Gill

Andrea GRANT *UK, female vocalist (1 WEEK)* pos/wks

14 Nov 98	REPUTATIONS (JUST BE GOOD TO ME) *WEA WEA 192CD*	75	1

Boysie GRANT – See Ezz RECO and the LAUNCHERS with Boysie GRANT

David GRANT *UK, male vocalist (59 WEEKS)* pos/wks

30 Apr 83	STOP AND GO *Chrysalis GRAN 1*	19	9
16 Jul 83 ●	WATCHING YOU WATCHING ME *Chrysalis GRAN 2*	10	13
8 Oct 83	LOVE WILL FIND A WAY *Chrysalis GRAN 3*	24	6
26 Nov 83	ROCK THE MIDNIGHT *Chrysalis GRAN 4*	46	4
23 Mar 85	COULD IT BE I'M FALLING IN LOVE *Chrysalis GRAN 6* [1]	5	11
16 Nov 85	MATED *EMI JAKI 6* [1]	20	10
1 Aug 87	CHANGE *Polydor POSP 871*	55	4
12 May 90	KEEP IT TOGETHER *Fourth & Broadway BRW 169*	56	4

[1] David Grant and Jaki Graham

Eddy GRANT `278` `Top 500` *Former lead guitarist and songwriter for UK group The Equals, b. 5 Mar 1948, Plaisance, Guyana. Left group 1972, went into production and formed own label, Ice. Remix of transatlantic No.2 'Electric Avenue' returned him to the heights in 2001 (107 WEEKS)* pos/wks

2 Jun 79	LIVING ON THE FRONT LINE *Ensign ENY 26*	11	11
15 Nov 80 ●	DO YOU FEEL MY LOVE? *Ensign ENY 45*	8	11
4 Apr 81	CAN'T GET ENOUGH OF YOU *Ensign ENY 207*	13	10
25 Jul 81	I LOVE YOU, YES I LOVE YOU *Ensign ENY 216*	37	6
16 Oct 82 ★	I DON'T WANNA DANCE *Ice ICE 56*	1	15
15 Jan 83 ●	ELECTRIC AVENUE *Ice ICE 57*	2	9
19 Mar 83	LIVING ON THE FRONT LINE / DO YOU FEEL MY LOVE (re-issue) *Mercury MER 135*	47	4
23 Apr 83	WAR PARTY *Ice ICE 58*	42	4
29 Oct 83	TILL I CAN'T TAKE LOVE NO MORE *Ice ICE 60*	42	7
19 May 84	ROMANCING THE STONE *Ice ICE 61*	52	3
23 Jan 88 ●	GIMME HOPE JO'ANNA *Ice ICE 78701*	7	11
27 May 89	WALKING ON SUNSHINE *Blue Wave R 6217*	63	2
9 Jun 01 ●	ELECTRIC AVENUE (re-mix) (re) *Ice / East West EW 232CD*	5	14
24 Nov 01	WALKING ON SUNSHINE (re-mix) *Ice / East West EW 242CD*	57	1

Gogi GRANT
US, female vocalist – Audrey Arinsberg (11 WEEKS) pos/wks

29 Jun 56 ●	THE WAYWARD WIND *London HLB 8282* ▲	9	11

Julie GRANT
UK, female vocalist – Vivienne Foreman (17 WEEKS) pos/wks

3 Jan 63	UP ON THE ROOF *Pye 7N 15483*	33	3
28 Mar 63	COUNT ON ME *Pye 7N 15508*	24	9
24 Sep 64	COME TO ME *Pye 7N 15684*	31	5

Rudy GRANT
Guyana, male vocalist (3 WEEKS) pos/wks

14 Feb 81	LATELY *Ensign ENY 202*	58	3

GRAPEFRUIT
UK, male vocal / instrumental group (19 WEEKS) pos/wks

14 Feb 68	DEAR DELILAH *RCA 1656*	21	9
14 Aug 68	C'MON MARIANNE *RCA 1716*	31	10

GRASS-SHOW
Sweden, male vocal / instrumental group (2 WEEKS) pos/wks

22 Mar 97	1962 *Food CDFOOD 90*	53	1
23 Aug 97	OUT OF THE VOID *Food CDFOOD 103*	75	1

GRAVEDIGGAZ
US, male rap group (6 WEEKS) pos/wks

11 Mar 95	SIX FEET DEEP (EP) *Gee Street GESCD 62*	64	1
5 Aug 95	THE HELL (EP) *Fourth & Broadway BRCD 326* [1]	12	3
24 Jan 98	THE NIGHT THE EARTH CRIED *Gee Street GEE 5001013*	44	1
25 Apr 98	UNEXPLAINED *Gee Street GEE 5001623*	48	1

[1] Tricky vs the Gravediggaz

Tracks on Six Feet Deep (EP): Bang Your Head / Mommy / Suicide. Tracks on The Hell (EP): Hell Is Round the Corner / Hell Is Round the Corner (remix) / Psychosis / Tonite Is a Special Nite

David GRAY
UK, male vocalist (36 WEEKS) pos/wks

4 Dec 99	PLEASE FORGIVE ME *IHT IHTCDS 003*	72	1
1 Jul 00 ●	BABYLON *IHT / East West EW 215CD1*	5	12
28 Oct 00	PLEASE FORGIVE ME (re-issue) *IHT / East West EW 219CD*	18	6
17 Mar 01	THIS YEAR'S LOVE *IHT / East West EW 228CD1*	20	5
28 Jul 01	SAIL AWAY *IHT / East West EW 234CD*	26	6
29 Dec 01	SAY HELLO WAVE GOODBYE *IHT / East West EW 244CD*	26	4
21 Dec 02	THE OTHER SIDE *IHT / East West EW 259CD*	35	2+

See also ORBITAL

Dobie GRAY
US, male vocalist – Lawrence Brown (11 WEEKS) pos/wks

25 Feb 65	THE 'IN' CROWD *London HL 9953*	25	7
27 Sep 75	OUT ON THE FLOOR *Black Magic BM 107*	42	4

Dorian GRAY
UK, male vocalist (7 WEEKS) pos/wks

27 Mar 68	I'VE GOT YOU ON MY MIND *Parlophone R 5667*	36	7

Les GRAY
UK, male vocalist (5 WEEKS) pos/wks

26 Feb 77	A GROOVY KIND OF LOVE *Warner Bros. K 16883*	32	5

See also MUD

Macy GRAY
US, female vocalist – Natalie McIntyre (49 WEEKS) pos/wks

3 Jul 99	DO SOMETHING *Epic 6675932*	51	1
9 Oct 99 ●	I TRY *Epic 6681832*	6	22
25 Mar 00	STILL (re) *Epic 6689822*	18	9
5 Aug 00	WHY DIDN'T YOU CALL ME (re) *Epic 6696682*	38	3
20 Jan 01	DEMONS *Skint SKINT 60CD*	16	5
28 Apr 01	GETO HEAVEN *MCA MCSTD 40246* [2]	48	1
12 May 01	REQUEST + LINE *Interscope 4970532* [3]	31	3
15 Sep 01	SWEET BABY *Epic 6718822* [4]	23	4
8 Dec 01	SEXUAL REVOLUTION *Epic 6721462*	45	1

[1] Fatboy Slim featuring Macy Gray [2] Common featuring Macy Gray [3] Black Eyed Peas featuring Macy Gray [4] Macy Gray featuring Erykah Badu

Barry GRAY ORCHESTRA
UK, orchestra (8 WEEKS) pos/wks

11 Jul 81	THUNDERBIRDS *PRT 7P 216*	61	2
14 Jun 86	JOE 90 (THEME) / CAPTAIN SCARLET THEME *PRT 7PX 354* [1]	53	6

[1] Barry Gray Orchestra with Peter Beckett – keyboards

Alltrinna GRAYSON – *See Wilton FELDER*

GREAT WHITE
US, male vocal / instrumental group (5 WEEKS) pos/wks

24 Feb 90	HOUSE OF BROKEN LOVE *Capitol CL 562*	44	2
16 Feb 91	CONGO SQUARE *Capitol CL 605*	62	1
7 Sep 91	CALL IT ROCK 'N'ROLL *Capitol CL 625*	67	2

Martin GRECH
UK, male vocalist (1 WEEK) pos/wks

12 Oct 02	OPEN HEART ZOO *DTOX / Island CID 811*	68	1

Buddy GRECO
US, male vocalist – Armando Greco (8 WEEKS) pos/wks

7 Jul 60	THE LADY IS A TRAMP *Fontana H 255*	26	8

GREED featuring Ricardo DA FORCE
UK, male instrumental duo and UK, male rapper (2 WEEKS) pos/wks

18 Mar 95	PUMP UP THE VOLUME *Stress CDSTR 49*	51	2

GREEDIES
Ireland / UK / US, male vocal / instrumental group (5 WEEKS) pos/wks

15 Dec 79	A MERRY JINGLE *Vertigo GREED 1*	28	5

Al GREEN
US, male vocalist (68 WEEKS) pos/wks

9 Oct 71 ●	TIRED OF BEING ALONE *London HLU 10337*	4	13
8 Jan 72 ●	LET'S STAY TOGETHER *London HLU 10348* ▲	7	12
20 May 72	LOOK WHAT YOU DONE FOR ME *London HLU 10369*	44	4
19 Aug 72	I'M STILL IN LOVE WITH YOU *London HLU 10382*	35	5
16 Nov 74	SHA-LA-LA (MAKE ME HAPPY) *London HLU 10470*	20	11
15 Mar 75	L.O.V.E. (LOVE) *London HLU 10482*	24	8
3 Dec 88	PUT A LITTLE LOVE IN YOUR HEART *A&M AM 484* [1]	28	8
21 Oct 89	THE MESSAGE IS LOVE *Breakout USA 668* [2]	38	5
2 Oct 93	LOVE IS A BEAUTIFUL THING *Arista 74321162692*	56	2

[1] Annie Lennox and Al Green [2] Arthur Baker and the Backbeat Disciples featuring Al Green

Dotty GREEN – *See Mark FISHER featuring Dotty GREEN*

Jesse GREEN
Jamaica, male vocalist (26 WEEKS) pos/wks

7 Aug 76	NICE AND SLOW *EMI 2492*	17	12
18 Dec 76	FLIP *EMI 2564*	26	8
11 Jun 77	COME WITH ME *EMI 2615*	29	6

Robson GREEN and Jerome FLYNN – *See ROBSON and JEROME*

GREEN DAY
US, male vocal / instrumental group (43 WEEKS) pos/wks

20 Aug 94	BASKET CASE *Reprise W 0257CD*	55	2
29 Oct 94	WELCOME TO PARADISE *Reprise W 0269CDX*	20	3
28 Jan 95 ●	BASKET CASE (re-issue) *Reprise W 0279CD*	7	6
18 Mar 95	LONGVIEW *Reprise W 0278CD*	30	3
20 May 95	WHEN I COME AROUND *Reprise W 0294CD*	27	3
7 Oct 95	GEEK STINK BREATH *Reprise W 0320CD*	16	3
6 Jan 96	STUCK WITH ME *Reprise W 0327CD*	24	3
6 Jul 96	BRAIN STEW / JADED *Reprise W 0339CD*	28	2
11 Oct 97	HITCHIN' A RIDE *Reprise W 0424CD*	25	2
31 Jan 98	TIME OF YOUR LIFE (GOOD RIDDANCE) *Reprise W 0430CD1*	11	5
9 May 98	REDUNDANT *Reprise W 0438CD1*	27	2
30 Sep 00	MINORITY *Reprise W 532CD*	18	3
23 Dec 00	WARNING *Reprise W 548CD1*	27	4
10 Nov 01	WAITING *Reprise W 570CD*	34	2

GREEN JELLY US, male vocal / instrumental group (15 WEEKS)

			pos/wks	
5 Jun 93	● THREE LITTLE PIGS Zoo 74321151422		5	8
14 Aug 93	ANARCHY IN THE UK Zoo 74321159052		27	3
25 Dec 93	I'M THE LEADER OF THE GANG			
	Arista 74321174892 [1]		25	4

[1] Hulk Hogan with Green Jelly

GREEN VELVET
US, male DJ / producer – Curtis Jones (2 WEEKS)

			pos/wks	
25 May 02	LA LA LAND Credence CDCRED 025		29	2

Norman GREENBAUM US, male vocalist (20 WEEKS)

			pos/wks	
21 Mar 70	★ SPIRIT IN THE SKY Reprise RS 20885		1	20

Lorne GREENE
Canada, male actor / vocalist, d. 11 Sep 1987 (8 WEEKS)

			pos/wks	
17 Dec 64	RINGO RCA 1428 ▲		22	8

Lee GREENWOOD US, male vocalist (6 WEEKS)

			pos/wks	
19 May 84	THE WIND BENEATH MY WINGS MCA 877		49	6

Iain GREGORY UK, male vocalist (2 WEEKS)

			pos/wks	
4 Jan 62	CAN'T YOU HEAR THE BEAT OF A BROKEN HEART			
	Pye 7N 15397		39	2

Johnny GREGORY – See CHAQUITO and his ORCHESTRA; Russ HAMILTON

Band of the GRENADIER GUARDS – See ST JOHN'S COLLEGE SCHOOL CHOIR and the Band of the GRENADIER GUARDS

GREYHOUND
Jamaica, male vocal / instrumental group (33 WEEKS)

			pos/wks	
26 Jun 71	● BLACK AND WHITE Trojan TR 7820		6	13
8 Jan 72	MOON RIVER Trojan TR 7848		12	11
25 Mar 72	I AM WHAT I AM Trojan TR 7853		20	9

GRID UK, male instrumental / production
duo – Richard Norris and Dave Ball (47 WEEKS)

			pos/wks	
7 Jul 90	FLOATATION East West YZ 475		60	2
29 Sep 90	A BEAT CALLED LOVE East West YZ 498		64	4
25 Jul 92	FIGURE OF 8 Virgin VSTG 1421		50	3
3 Oct 92	HEARTBEAT Virgin VST 1427		72	2
13 Mar 93	CRYSTAL CLEAR Virgin VSCDT 1442		27	4
30 Oct 93	TEXAS COWBOYS Deconstruction 74321167762		21	3
4 Jun 94	● SWAMP THING Deconstruction 74321205842		3	17
17 Sep 94	ROLLERCOASTER Deconstruction 74321230772		19	4
3 Dec 94	TEXAS COWBOYS (re-issue)			
	Deconstruction 74321244032		17	6
23 Sep 95	DIABLO Deconstruction 74321308402		32	2

Zaine GRIFF New Zealand, male vocalist (6 WEEKS)

			pos/wks	
16 Feb 80	TONIGHT Automatic K 17547		54	3
31 May 80	ASHES AND DIAMONDS Automatic K 17610		68	3

Billy GRIFFIN US, male vocalist (12 WEEKS)

			pos/wks	
8 Jan 83	HOLD ME TIGHTER IN THE RAIN CBS A 2935		17	9
14 Jan 84	SERIOUS CBS A 4053		64	3

See also MIRACLES

Clive GRIFFIN UK, male vocalist (5 WEEKS)

			pos/wks	
24 Jun 89	HEAD ABOVE WATER Mercury STEP 4		60	2
11 May 91	I'LL BE WAITING Mercury STEP 6		56	3

Roni GRIFFITH US, female vocalist (4 WEEKS)

			pos/wks	
30 Jun 84	(THE BEST PART OF) BREAKING UP			
	Making Waves SURF 101		63	4

GRIFTERS UK, male production duo
– Paul Newman and Brandon Block (1 WEEK)

			pos/wks	
20 Feb 99	FLASH Duty Free DF 004CD		63	1

See also TALL PAUL; ESCRIMA; CAMISRA; PARTIZAN

GRIMETHORPE COLLIERY BAND – See Peter SKELLERN

Jay GROOVE – See FANTASY UFO

GROOVE ARMADA UK, male production /
instrumental duo – Andy Cato and Tom Findlay (24 WEEKS)

			pos/wks	
8 May 99	IF EVERYBODY LOOKED THE SAME Pepper 0530292		25	2
7 Aug 99	AT THE RIVER Pepper 0530062		19	5
27 Nov 99	I SEE YOU BABY (re) Pepper 9230002 [1]		17	6
25 Aug 01	SUPERSTYLIN' (re) Pepper 9230472		12	7
17 Nov 01	MY FRIEND Pepper 9230532		36	2
2 Nov 02	PURPLE HAZE Pepper 9230642		36	2

[1] Groove Armada featuring Gram'ma Funk

See also WEEKEND PLAYERS

GROOVE CONNEKTION 2
UK, male producer / instrumentalist (1 WEEK)

			pos/wks	
11 Apr 98	CLUB LONELY XL Recordings XLT 94CD		54	1

GROOVE CORPORATION
UK / Italy, male / female vocal / instrumental group (1 WEEK)

			pos/wks	
16 Apr 94	RAIN Six6 SIXCD 109		71	1

GROOVE FOUNDATION – See DJ CHUS presents GROOVE FOUNDATION

GROOVE GANG – See DAFFY DUCK featuring the GROOVE GANG

GROOVE GENERATION featuring Leo SAYER
UK, male production group (3 WEEKS)

			pos/wks	
8 Aug 98	YOU MAKE ME FEEL LIKE DANCING			
	Brothers Org. CDBRUV 8		32	3

GROOVE THEORY US, male / female production
vocal duo – Bryce Wilson and Amel Larrieaux (3 WEEKS)

			pos/wks	
18 Nov 95	TELL ME Epic 6623882		31	3

See also MANTRONIX

GROOVERIDER
UK, male DJ / producer – Ray Bingham (3 WEEKS)

			pos/wks	
26 Sep 98	RAINBOWS OF COLOUR Higher Ground HIGHS 13CD		40	2
19 Jun 99	WHERE'S JACK THE RIPPER			
	Higher Ground HIGHS 20CD		61	1

Scott GROOVES US, male DJ / producer (3 WEEKS)

			pos/wks	
16 May 98	EXPANSIONS Soma Recordings SOMA 65CDS [1]		68	1
28 Nov 98	MOTHERSHIP RECONNECTION			
	Soma Recordings SOMA 71CDS		55	1
21 Aug 99	MOTHERSHIP RECONNECTION Virgin DINSD 185 [2]		55	1

[1] Scott Grooves featuring Roy Ayers [2] Scott Grooves featuring Parliament / Funkadelic

Henry GROSS US, male vocalist (4 WEEKS)

			pos/wks	
28 Aug 76	SHANNON Life Song ELS 45002		32	4

GROUND LEVEL
Australia, male instrumental / production group (2 WEEKS)

			pos/wks	
30 Jan 93	DREAMS OF HEAVEN Faze 2 CDFAZE 14		54	2

GROUP THERAPY US, male rap group (1 WEEK)

			pos/wks	
30 Nov 96	EAST COAST / WEST COAST KILLAS Interscope IND 95516		51	1

Re-entries are listed as (re), (2re), (3re), etc which signifies that the hit re-entered the chart once, twice or three times, etc

Boring Bob GROVER – See PIRANHAS

GUESS WHO Canada, male vocal / instrumental group (14 WEEKS) pos/wks

16 Feb 67	HIS GIRL King KG 1044	45	1
9 May 70	AMERICAN WOMAN (re) RCA 1943 ▲	19	13

David GUETTA featuring Chris WILLIS
France, male producer and US, male vocalist (1 WEEK)   pos/wks

31 Aug 02	LOVE, DON'T LET ME GO Virgin DINSD 243	46	1

GUN UK, male vocal / instrumental trio (11 WEEKS) pos/wks

20 Nov 68 ●	RACE WITH THE DEVIL CBS 3734	8	11

GUN UK, male vocal / instrumental group (46 WEEKS) pos/wks

1 Jul 89	BETTER DAYS A&M AM 505	33	9
16 Sep 89	MONEY (EVERYBODY LOVES HER) A&M AM 520	73	2
11 Nov 89	INSIDE OUT A&M AM 531	57	2
10 Feb 90	TAKING ON THE WORLD A&M AM 541	50	3
14 Jul 90	SHAME ON YOU A&M AM 573	33	4
14 Mar 92	STEAL YOUR FIRE A&M AM 851	24	4
2 May 92	HIGHER GROUND A&M AM 869	48	2
4 Jul 92	WELCOME TO THE REAL WORLD A&M AM 885	43	2
9 Jul 94 ●	WORD UP A&M 5806672	8	7
24 Sep 94	DON'T SAY IT'S OVER A&M 5807572	19	3
25 Feb 95	THE ONLY ONE A&M 5809552	29	3
15 Apr 95	SOMETHING WORTHWHILE A&M 5810452	39	2
26 Apr 97	CRAZY YOU A&M 5821932 [1]	21	2
12 Jul 97	MY SWEET JANE A&M 5822792 [1]	51	1

[1] G.U.N.

GUNS N' ROSES (279 Top 500) Often controversial Los Angeles-based
band. Best known line-up included W Axl Rose (b. William Bailey) (v), Slash
(b. Saul Hudson) (g), Izzy Stradlin (b. Jeffrey Isbell) (g). The only act to hold
the top two album spots in both the UK and the US on the week of releasing
both records: Use Your Illusion 1 and 2 in 1991 (107 WEEKS)   pos/wks

3 Oct 87	WELCOME TO THE JUNGLE Geffen GEF 30	67	2
20 Aug 88	SWEET CHILD O' MINE Geffen GEF 43 ▲	24	8
29 Oct 88	WELCOME TO THE JUNGLE / NIGHTRAIN (re-issue)		
	Geffen GEF 47	24	5
18 Mar 89 ●	PARADISE CITY Geffen GEF 50	6	9
3 Jun 89 ●	SWEET CHILD O' MINE (re-issue) Geffen GEF 55	6	9
1 Jul 89 ●	PATIENCE Geffen GEF 56	10	7
2 Sep 89	NIGHTRAIN (re-issue) Geffen GEF 60	17	5
13 Jul 91 ●	YOU COULD BE MINE Geffen GFS 6	3	10
21 Sep 91 ●	DON'T CRY Geffen GFS 9	8	4
21 Dec 91 ●	LIVE AND LET DIE Geffen GFS 17	5	7
7 Mar 92 ●	NOVEMBER RAIN Geffen GFS 18	4	5
23 May 92 ●	KNOCKIN' ON HEAVEN'S DOOR Geffen GFS 21	2	9
21 Nov 92 ●	YESTERDAYS / NOVEMBER RAIN (re-issue) Geffen GFS 27	8	9
29 May 93	THE CIVIL WAR (EP) Geffen GFSTD 43	11	3
20 Nov 93 ●	AIN'T IT FUN Geffen GFSTD 62	9	3
4 Jun 94 ●	SINCE I DON'T HAVE YOU Geffen GFSTD 70	10	6
14 Jan 95 ●	SYMPATHY FOR THE DEVIL Geffen GFSTD 86	9	6

The re-issue of 'November Rain' was listed only from 28 Nov 1992. Tracks on The
Civil War (EP): Civil War / Garden of Eden / Dead Horse / Interview

Peter GUNZ – See LORD TARIQ

GURU US, male rapper / producer – Keith Allam (12 WEEKS) pos/wks

11 Sep 93	TRUST ME Cooltempo CDCOOL 278 [1]	34	2
13 Nov 93	NO TIME TO PLAY Cooltempo CDCOOL 282 [2]	25	3
19 Aug 95	WATCH WHAT YOU SAY Cooltempo CDCOOL 308 [3]	28	3
18 Nov 95	FEEL THE MUSIC Cooltempo CDCOOLS 313	34	2
13 Jul 96	LIVIN' IN THIS WORLD / LIFESAVER		
	Cooltempo CDCOOL 320	61	1
16 Dec 00	KEEP YOUR WORRIES Virgin VUSCD 177 [4]	57	1

[1] Guru featuring N'Dea Davenport [2] Guru featuring Dee C Lee [3] Guru
featuring Chaka Khan [4] Guru's Jazzmatazz featuring Angie Stone

See also GANG STARR

GURU JOSH UK, male producer – Paul Walden (14 WEEKS) pos/wks

24 Feb 90 ●	INFINITY Deconstruction PB 43475	5	10
16 Jun 90	WHOSE LAW (IS IT ANYWAY)?		
	Deconstruction PB 43647	26	4

Adrian GURVITZ UK, male vocalist (16 WEEKS) pos/wks

30 Jan 82 ●	CLASSIC RAK 339	8	13
12 Jun 82	YOUR DREAM RAK 343	61	3

GUS GUS
Iceland, male / female vocal / instrumental group (3 WEEKS)   pos/wks

21 Feb 98	POLYESTERDAY 4AD BAD 8002CD	55	1
13 Mar 99	LADYSHAVE 4AD BAD 9001CD	64	1
24 Apr 99	STARLOVERS 4AD BADD 9004CD	62	1

TOP 20 FLYING RECORDS

■ In 2003 it's the 100th
anniversary of man's first
powered flight on 24 August.
We've checked the black box and
OK'd the propellerheads, jets
and wings for take-off, so it's up,
up and away with the 20 best-
performing aviation chart hits

R Kelly believes he can fly

1. I BELIEVE I CAN FLY – R Kelly – 1
2. FLYING WITHOUT WINGS – Westlife – 1
3. FLY AWAY – Lenny Kravitz – 1
4. LEAVING ON A JET PLANE – Peter Paul and Mary – 2
5. ONE DAY I'LL FLY AWAY – Randy Crawford – 2
6. WIND BENEATH MY WINGS – Steven Houghton – 3
7. AIRPORT – Motors – 4
8. FLYING – Cast – 4
9. I'M MANDY FLY ME – 10cc – 6
10. INTERNATIONAL JET SET – Specials – 6
11. HIGH IN THE SKY – Amen Corner – 6
12. JET – Paul McCartney and Wings – 7
13. I'LL FLY FOR YOU – Spandau Ballet – 9
14. THIS FLIGHT TONIGHT – Nazareth – 11
15. AEROPLANE – Red Hot Chili Peppers – 11
16. DROP THE PILOT – Joan Armatrading – 11
17. WISH I COULD FLY – Roxette – 11
18. 747 (STRANGERS IN THE NIGHT) – Saxon – 13
19. LUTON AIRPORT – Cats UK – 22
20. PREPARE TO LAND – Supernaturals – 48

GUSTO US, male producer – Edward Green (8 WEEKS) pos/wks

| 2 Mar 96 ● | DISCO'S REVENGE Manifesto FESCD 6 | 9 | 5 |
| 7 Sep 96 | LET'S ALL CHANT Manifesto FESCD 13 | 21 | 3 |

Gwen GUTHRIE US, female vocalist, d. 9 Feb 1999 (25 WEEKS) pos/wks

19 Jul 86 ●	AIN'T NOTHIN' GOIN' ON BUT THE RENT Boiling Point POSP 807	5	12
11 Oct 86	(THEY LONG TO BE) CLOSE TO YOU Boiling Point POSP 822	25	7
14 Feb 87	GOOD TO GO LOVER / OUTSIDE IN THE RAIN Boiling Point POSP 841	37	4
4 Sep 93	AIN'T NOTHIN' GOIN' ON BUT THE RENT (re-mix) Polydor PZCD 276	42	2

GUY US, male vocal group (4 WEEKS) pos/wks

| 4 May 91 | HER MCA MCS 1575 | 58 | 4 |

A GUY CALLED GERALD
UK, male producer – Gerald Simpson (23 WEEKS) pos/wks

| 8 Apr 89 | VOODOO RAY (re) Rham! RS 804 | 12 | 18 |
| 16 Dec 89 | FX / EYES OF SORROW Subscape AGCG 1 | 52 | 5 |

GUYS 'N' DOLLS UK, male / female vocal group (33 WEEKS) pos/wks

1 Mar 75 ●	THERE'S A WHOLE LOT OF LOVING Magnet MAG 20 [1]	2	11
17 May 75	HERE I GO AGAIN Magnet MAG 30	33	5
21 Feb 76 ●	YOU DON'T HAVE TO SAY YOU LOVE ME Magnet MAG 50	5	8
6 Nov 76	STONEY GROUND Magnet MAG 76	38	4
13 May 78	ONLY LOVING DOES IT Magnet MAG 115	42	5

[1] Guys & Dolls

Jonas GWANGWA – See George FENTON and Jonas GWANGWA

GYPSYMEN US, male producer – Todd Terry (2 WEEKS) pos/wks

| 11 Aug 01 | BABARABATIRI Sound Design SDES 09CDS | 32 | 2 |

See also Todd TERRY PROJECT

GYRES UK, male vocal / instrumental group (2 WEEKS) pos/wks

| 13 Apr 96 | POP COP Sugar SUGA 9CD | 71 | 1 |
| 6 Jul 96 | ARE YOU READY Sugar SUGA 11CD | 71 | 1 |

H

H & CLAIRE UK, male / female vocal duo
– Ian Watkins and Claire Richards (23 WEEKS) pos/wks

18 May 02 ●	DJ WEA WEA 347CD	3	11
24 Aug 02 ●	HALF A HEART (re) WEA WEA 359CDX	8	6
16 Nov 02 ●	ALL OUT OF LOVE (re) WEA WEA 360CD	10	6+

See also STEPS

HHC UK, male DJ / production duo (1 WEEK) pos/wks

| 19 Apr 97 | WE'RE NOT ALONE Perfecto PERF 138CD | 44 | 1 |

H 20 UK, male vocal / instrumental group (16 WEEKS) pos/wks

| 21 May 83 | DREAM TO SLEEP RCA 330 | 17 | 10 |
| 13 Aug 83 | JUST OUTSIDE OF HEAVEN RCA 349 | 38 | 6 |

H20 US / Switzerland, male / female vocal / instrumental group (4 WKS) pos/wks

| 14 Sep 96 | NOBODY'S BUSINESS AM:PM 5818832 [1] | 19 | 3 |
| 30 Aug 97 | SATISFIED (TAKE ME HIGHER) AM:PM 5823252 | 66 | 1 |

[1] H20 featuring Billie

HWA featuring SONIC THE HEDGEHOG
UK, male producer – Jeremy Healy (6 WEEKS) pos/wks

| 5 Dec 92 | SUPERSONIC Internal Affairs KGB 008 | 33 | 6 |

See also Jeremy HEALY and AMOS

HABIT UK, male vocal / instrumental group (2 WEEKS) pos/wks

| 30 Apr 88 | LUCY Virgin VS 1063 | 56 | 2 |

Steve HACKETT
UK, male vocalist / instrumentalist – guitar (2 WEEKS) pos/wks

| 2 Apr 83 | CELL 151 Charisma CELL 1 | 66 | 2 |

See also GENESIS

HADDAWAY
Trinidad and Tobago, male vocalist – Nester Haddaway (52 WEEKS) pos/wks

5 Jun 93 ●	WHAT IS LOVE Logic 74321148502	2	15
25 Sep 93 ●	LIFE Logic 74321164212	6	9
18 Dec 93 ●	I MISS YOU Logic 74321181522	9	14
2 Apr 94 ●	ROCK MY HEART Logic 74321194122	9	9
24 Jun 95	FLY AWAY Logic 74321286942	20	3
23 Sep 95	CATCH A FIRE Logic 74321306652	39	2

Tony HADLEY UK, male vocalist (9 WEEKS) pos/wks

7 Mar 92	LOST IN YOUR LOVE EMI EM 222	42	4
29 Aug 92	FOR YOUR BLUE EYES ONLY EMI EM 234	67	2
16 Jan 93	THE GAME OF LOVE EMI CDEM 254	72	1
10 May 97	DANCE WITH ME VC VCRD 17 [1]	35	2

[1] Tin Tin Out featuring Tony Hadley

See also SPANDAU BALLET

Sammy HAGAR
US, male vocalist / instrumentalist – guitar (15 WEEKS) pos/wks

15 Dec 79	THIS PLANET'S ON FIRE (BURN IN HELL) / SPACE STATION NO.5 Capitol CL 16114	52	5
16 Feb 80	I'VE DONE EVERYTHING FOR YOU Capitol CL 16120	36	5
24 May 80	HEARTBEAT / LOVE OR MONEY Capitol RED 1	67	2
16 Jan 82	PIECE OF MY HEART (re) Geffen GEFA 1884	67	3

See also VAN HALEN; MONTROSE

Paul HAIG UK, male vocalist (3 WEEKS) pos/wks

| 28 May 83 | HEAVEN SENT Island IS 111 | 74 | 3 |

HAIRCUT 100 UK, male vocal / instrumental group (47 WEEKS) pos/wks

24 Oct 81 ●	FAVOURITE SHIRTS (BOY MEETS GIRL) Arista CLIP 1	4	14
30 Jan 82 ●	LOVE PLUS ONE Arista CLIP 2	3	12
10 Apr 82 ●	FANTASTIC DAY Arista CLIP 3	9	9
21 Aug 82 ●	NOBODY'S FOOL Arista CLIP 4	9	7
6 Aug 83	PRIME TIME Polydor HC 1	46	5

Curtis HAIRSTON US, male vocalist (16 WEEKS) pos/wks

15 Oct 83	I WANT YOU (ALL TONIGHT) RCA 368	44	5
27 Apr 85	I WANT YOUR LOVIN' (JUST A LITTLE BIT) London LON 66	13	7
6 Dec 86	CHILLIN' OUT Atlantic A 9335	57	4

Gary HAISMAN – See D MOB

HAL featuring Gillian ANDERSON
UK, male production trio and US, female vocalist (3 WEEKS) pos/wks

| 24 May 97 | EXTREMIS Virgin VSCDT 1636 | 23 | 3 |

HALE and PACE and the STONKERS UK, male comedy
duo – Gareth Hale and Norman Pace, and backing group (7 WEEKS) pos/wks

| 9 Mar 91 ★ | THE STONK London LON 296 | 1 | 7 |

Bill HALEY and His COMETS 〔93〕 Top 500

Original 'King of Rock 'n' Roll', b. 6 Jul 1925, Detroit, d. 9 Feb 1981. The kiss-curl hairstyled frontman introduced rock to the world via a string of 1950s smashes, including 'Rock Around the Clock', the only record to return to the Top 20 on five occasions, selling 1,392,000 (199 WEEKS)
pos/wks

17 Dec 54 ●	SHAKE, RATTLE AND ROLL *Brunswick 05338*	4 14
7 Jan 55 ★	ROCK AROUND THE CLOCK (5re)	
	Brunswick 05317 ◆ ▲	1 36
15 Apr 55	MAMBO ROCK *Brunswick 05405*	14 2
30 Dec 55 ●	ROCK-A-BEATIN' BOOGIE *Brunswick 05509*	4 9
9 Mar 56 ●	SEE YOU LATER, ALLIGATOR (re) *Brunswick 05530*	7 21
25 May 56 ●	THE SAINTS ROCK 'N ROLL *Brunswick 05565*	5 24
17 Aug 56 ●	ROCKIN' THROUGH THE RYE (re) *Brunswick 05582*	3 23
14 Sep 56	RAZZLE DAZZLE *Brunswick 05453*	13 8
9 Nov 56 ●	RIP IT UP *Brunswick 05615*	4 18
9 Nov 56	ROCK 'N' ROLL STAGE SHOW (LP)	
	Brunswick LAT 8139	30 1
23 Nov 56	RUDY'S ROCK (re) *Brunswick 05616*	26 5
1 Feb 57	ROCK THE JOINT *London HLF 8371*	20 4
8 Feb 57 ●	DON'T KNOCK THE ROCK *Brunswick 05640*	7 8
3 Apr 68	ROCK AROUND THE CLOCK (re-issue) *MCA MU 1013*	20 11
16 Mar 74	ROCK AROUND THE CLOCK (2nd re-issue) *MCA 128*	12 10
25 Apr 81	HALEY'S GOLDEN MEDLEY *MCA 694*	50 5

'Rock Around the Clock' re-entries were in Oct 1955 when it peaked at No.1, twice in 1956 and twice in 1957. Tracks on Rock 'n' Roll Stage Show (LP): Calling All Comets / Rockin' Through the Rye / A Rockin' Little Tune / Hide and Seek / Hey There Now / Goofin' Around / Hook Line and Sinker / Rudy's Rock / Choo Choo Ch'Boogie / Blue Comets Rock / Hot Dog Buddy Buddy / Tonight's the Night. Occasionally, some of the 'Rock Around the Clock' labels billed the song as '(We're Gonna) Rock Around the Clock'

Aaron HALL *US, male vocalist (3 WEEKS)*
pos/wks

13 Jun 92	DON'T BE AFRAID *MCA MCS 1632*	56 2
23 Oct 93	GET A LITTLE FREAKY WITH ME *MCA MCSTD 1936*	66 1

Audrey HALL *Jamaica, female vocalist (20 WEEKS)*
pos/wks

25 Jan 86	ONE DANCE WON'T DO *Germain DG7-1985*	20 11
5 Jul 86	SMILE *Germain DG 15*	14 9

Daryl HALL *US, male vocalist (26 WEEKS)*
pos/wks

2 Aug 86	DREAMTIME *RCA HALL 1*	28 8
25 Sep 93	I'M IN A PHILLY MOOD (re) *Epic 6595555*	52 4
8 Jan 94	STOP LOVING ME STOP LOVING YOU *Epic 6599982*	30 6
14 May 94	HELP ME FIND A WAY TO YOUR HEART *Epic 6604102*	70 1
2 Jul 94	GLORYLAND *Mercury MERCD 404* 〔1〕	36 4
10 Jun 95	WHEREVER WOULD I BE *Columbia 6620592* 〔2〕	44 3

〔1〕 Daryl Hall and the Sounds of Blackness 〔2〕 Dusty Springfield and Daryl Hall

See also Daryl HALL and John OATES

Daryl HALL and John OATES 〔407〕 Top 500

White, soul-influenced US duo: Daryl Hall (v), b. 11 Oct 1948, Philadelphia and John Oates (g) b. 7 Apr 1949, New York. Met at university in 1967, eventually becoming the most successful duo in US singles chart history, with 16 Top 10s and six No.1s (84 WEEKS)
pos/wks

16 Oct 76	SHE'S GONE *Atlantic K 10828*	42 4
14 Jun 80	RUNNING FROM PARADISE *RCA RUN 1*	41 6
20 Sep 80	YOU'VE LOST THAT LOVIN' FEELIN' *RCA 1*	55 3
15 Nov 80	KISS ON MY LIST *RCA 15* ▲	33 8
23 Jan 82 ●	I CAN'T GO FOR THAT (NO CAN DO) *RCA 172* ▲	8 10
10 Apr 82	PRIVATE EYES *RCA 134* ▲	32 7
30 Oct 82 ●	MANEATER *RCA 290* ▲	6 11
22 Jan 83	ONE ON ONE *RCA 305*	63 3
30 Apr 83	FAMILY MAN *RCA 323*	15 7
12 Nov 83	SAY IT ISN'T SO *RCA 375*	69 3
10 Mar 84	ADULT EDUCATION *RCA 396*	63 2
20 Oct 84	OUT OF TOUCH *RCA 449* ▲	48 5
9 Feb 85	METHOD OF MODERN LOVE *RCA 472*	21 8
22 Jun 85	OUT OF TOUCH (re-mix) *RCA PB 49967*	62 3
21 Sep 85	A NIGHT AT THE APOLLO LIVE! *RCA PB 49935* 〔1〕	58 2

29 Sep 90	SO CLOSE *Arista 113600* 〔2〕	69 1
26 Jan 91	EVERYWHERE I LOOK *Arista 113980*	74 1

〔1〕 Daryl Hall and John Oates featuring David Ruffin and Eddie Kendrick 〔2〕 Hall and Oates

'A Night at the Apollo Live!' is a medley of 'The Way You Do the Things You Do' and 'My Girl'

Lynden David HALL
UK, male vocalist / instrumentalist (12 WEEKS)
pos/wks

25 Oct 97	SEXY CINDERELLA *Cooltempo CDCOOL 328*	45 2
14 Mar 98	DO I QUALIFY? *Cooltempo CDCOOLS 331*	26 2
4 Jul 98	CRESCENT MOON *Cooltempo CDCOOL 333*	45 1
31 Oct 98	SEXY CINDERELLA (re-issue) *Cooltempo CDCOOLS 340*	17 3
11 Mar 00	FORGIVE ME *Cooltempo CDCOOLS 346*	30 2
27 May 00	SLEEPING WITH VICTOR *Cooltempo CDCOOL 348*	49 1
23 Sep 00	LET'S DO IT AGAIN *Cooltempo CDCOOL 351*	69 1

Pam HALL *Jamaica, female vocalist (4 WEEKS)*
pos/wks

16 Aug 86	DEAR BOOPSIE *Bluemountain BM 027*	54 4

Terry HALL *UK, male vocalist (6 WEEKS)*
pos/wks

11 Nov 89	MISSING *Chrysalis CHS 3381*	75 1
27 Aug 94	FOREVER J *AnXious ANX 1024CDX*	67 1
12 Nov 94	SENSE *AnXious ANX 1027CD*	54 2
28 Oct 95	RAINBOWS (EP) *AnXious ANX 1033CD1*	62 1
14 Jun 97	BALLAD OF A LANDLORD *Southsea Bubble CDBUBBLE 1*	50 1

The sleeve, not the label, of 'Missing' credits Terry, Blair and Anouchka. Tracks on Rainbows (EP) CD1: Chasing a Rainbow / Mistakes / See No Evil (live) / Ghost Town (live) and CD2: Chasing a Rainbow / Our Lips Are Sealed (live) / Thinking of You (live) / Ghost Town (live)

See also FUN BOY THREE; SPECIALS; VEGAS

Toni HALLIDAY – *See LEFTFIELD; Paul VAN DYK*

Geri HALLIWELL 〔335〕 Top 500

Headline-grabbing former Ginger Spice (b. 6 Aug 1972, Watford, UK) sang on seven Spice Girls chart-toppers before achieving more solo No.1s than any other UK female. She is the only person to score as many as four consecutive No.1s both as a solo artist and as part of group (93 WEEKS)
pos/wks

22 May 99 ●	LOOK AT ME (re) *EMI CDEM 542*	2 14
28 Aug 99 ★	MI CHICO LATINO *EMI CDEM 548* ■	1 13
13 Nov 99 ★	LIFT ME UP *EMI CDEM 554* ■	1 13
25 Mar 00 ★	BAG IT UP (re) *EMI CDEMS 560* ■	1 13
12 May 01 ★	IT'S RAINING MEN *EMI CDEMS 584* ■	1 15
11 Aug 01 ●	SCREAM IF YOU WANNA GO FASTER (re) *EMI CDEMS 595*	8 11
8 Dec 01 ●	CALLING *EMI CDEMS 606*	7 10

See also SPICE GIRLS

HALO *UK, male vocal / instrumental group (3 WEEKS)*
pos/wks

16 Feb 02	COLD LIGHT OF DAY *S2 6723072*	49 1
1 Jun 02	SANCTIMONIOUS *S2 6725962*	44 1
7 Sep 02	NEVER ENDING *S2 6730125*	56 1

HALO JAMES
UK, male vocal / instrumental group (24 WEEKS)
pos/wks

7 Oct 89	WANTED *Epic HALO 1*	45 5
23 Dec 89 ●	COULD HAVE TOLD YOU SO *Epic HALO 2*	6 12
17 Mar 90	BABY *Epic HALO 3*	43 4
19 May 90	MAGIC HOUR *Epic HALO 4*	59 3

George HAMILTON IV *US, male vocalist (13 WEEKS)*
pos/wks

7 Mar 58	WHY DON'T THEY UNDERSTAND *HMV POP 429*	22 9
18 Jul 58	I KNOW WHERE I'M GOIN' (re) *HMV POP 505*	23 4

Lynne HAMILTON *UK, female vocalist (11 WEEKS)*
pos/wks

29 Apr 89 ●	ON THE INSIDE (THEME FROM 'PRISONER: CELL BLOCK H') *A1 A1 311*	3 11

Russ HAMILTON UK, male vocalist – Ronald Hulme (26 WEEKS) pos/wks

			pos	wks
24 May 57	●	WE WILL MAKE LOVE *Oriole CB 1359*	2	20
27 Sep 57		WEDDING RING *Oriole CB 1388* [1]	20	6

[1] Russ Hamilton with Johnny Gregory and His Orchestra with The Tonettes

HAMILTON, Joe FRANK and REYNOLDS
US, male vocal group (6 WEEKS) pos/wks

			pos	wks
13 Sep 75		FALLIN' IN LOVE *Pye International 7N 25690* ▲	33	6

Marvin HAMLISCH US, male instrumentalist – piano (13 WEEKS) pos/wks

			pos	wks
30 Mar 74		THE ENTERTAINER *MCA 121*	25	13

HAMMER US, male rapper – Stanley Burrell (68 WEEKS) pos/wks

			pos	wks
9 Jun 90	●	U CAN'T TOUCH THIS *Capitol CL 578* [1]	3	16
6 Oct 90	●	HAVE YOU SEEN HER *Capitol CL 590* [1]	8	7
8 Dec 90	●	PRAY *Capitol CL 599* [1]	8	10
23 Feb 91		HERE COMES THE HAMMER *Capitol CL 610* [1]	15	5
1 Jun 91		YO!! SWEETNESS *Capitol CL 616* [1]	16	5
20 Jul 91		(HAMMER HAMMER) THEY PUT ME IN THE MIX *Capitol CL 607* [1]	20	4
26 Oct 91		2 LEGIT 2 QUIT *Capitol CL 636*	60	2
21 Dec 91	●	ADDAMS GROOVE *Capitol CL 642*	4	9
21 Mar 92		DO NOT PASS ME BY *Capitol CL 650*	14	6
12 Mar 94		IT'S ALL GOOD *RCA 74321188612*	52	2
13 Aug 94		DON'T STOP *RCA 74321220012*	72	1
3 Jun 95		STRAIGHT TO MY FEET *Priority PTYCD 102* [2]	57	1

[1] MC Hammer [2] Hammer featuring Deion Saunders

Jan HAMMER
Czech Republic, male instrumentalist – keyboards (26 WEEKS) pos/wks

			pos	wks
12 Oct 85	●	MIAMI VICE THEME *MCA MCA 1000* ▲	5	8
19 Sep 87	●	CROCKETT'S THEME *MCA MCA 1193*	2	12
1 Jun 91		CROCKETT'S THEME (re-issue) / CHANCER *MCA MCS 1541*	47	6

Albert HAMMOND Gibraltar, male vocalist (11 WEEKS) pos/wks

			pos	wks
30 Jun 73		FREE ELECTRIC BAND *Mums 1494*	19	11

Beres HAMMOND – See Maxi PRIEST

HAMPENBERG Denmark, male / female
vocal / instrumental / production group (2 WEEKS) pos/wks

			pos	wks
21 Sep 02		DUCKTOY *Serious SERR 49CD*	30	2

Herbie HANCOCK
US, male vocalist / instrumentalist – keyboards (41 WEEKS) pos/wks

			pos	wks
26 Aug 78		I THOUGHT IT WAS YOU *CBS 6530*	15	9
3 Feb 79		YOU BET YOUR LOVE *CBS 7010*	18	10
30 Jul 83	●	ROCKIT *CBS A 3577*	8	12
8 Oct 83		AUTODRIVE *CBS A 3802*	33	4
21 Jan 84		FUTURE SHOCK *CBS A 4075*	54	3
4 Aug 84		HARDROCK *CBS A 4616*	65	3

HANDBAGGERS
UK, male / female vocal / instrumental group (1 WEEK) pos/wks

			pos	wks
15 Jun 96		U FOUND OUT *Tidy Trax TIDY 104CD*	55	1

HANDLEY FAMILY UK, male / female vocal group (7 WEEKS) pos/wks

			pos	wks
7 Apr 73		WAM BAM *GL 100*	30	7

HANI US, male DJ / producer (1 WEEK) pos/wks

			pos	wks
11 Mar 00		BABY WANTS TO RIDE *Neo NEO CD025*	70	1

Jayn HANNA UK, female vocalist (2 WEEKS) pos/wks

			pos	wks
13 Apr 96		LOVELIGHT (RIDE ON A LOVE TRAIN) *VC VCRD 10*	42	1
1 Feb 97		LOST WITHOUT YOU *VC VCRD 16*	44	1

HANNAH – See MAN WITH NO NAME

HANNAH
UK, female vocalist – Hannah Waddingham (2 WEEKS) pos/wks

			pos	wks
21 Oct 00		OUR KIND OF LOVE *Telstar CDSTAS 3149*	41	2

HANNAH and her SISTERS – See Hannah JONES

HANOI ROCKS
Finland / UK, male vocal / instrumental group (2 WEEKS) pos/wks

			pos	wks
7 Jul 84		UP AROUND THE BEND *CBS A 4513*	61	2

HANSON US, male vocal / instrumental group (47 WEEKS) pos/wks

			pos	wks
7 Jun 97	★	MMMBOP *Mercury 5745012* ■ ▲	1	13
13 Sep 97	●	WHERE'S THE LOVE *Mercury 5749032*	4	9
22 Nov 97	●	I WILL COME TO YOU *Mercury 5680672*	5	9
28 Mar 98		WEIRD *Mercury 5685412*	19	5
4 Jul 98		THINKING OF YOU (re) *Mercury 5688132*	23	7
29 Apr 00		IF ONLY *Mercury 5627502*	15	4

HAPPENINGS US, male vocal group (14 WEEKS) pos/wks

			pos	wks
18 May 67		I GOT RHYTHM *Stateside SS 2013*	28	9
16 Aug 67		MY MAMMY *Pye International 7N 25501 and BT Puppy BTS 45530*	34	5

Pye gave the US BT Puppy label its own identification halfway through the success of 'My Mammy'

HAPPY CLAPPERS
UK, male / female vocal / instrumental group (19 WEEKS) pos/wks

			pos	wks
3 Jun 95		I BELIEVE *Shindig SHIN 4CD*	21	3
26 Aug 95		HOLD ON *Shindig SHIN 7CD*	27	2
18 Nov 95	●	I BELIEVE (re-issue) *Shindig SHIN 9CD*	7	8
15 Jun 96		CAN'T HELP IT *Coliseum TOGA 004CD*	18	3
21 Dec 96		NEVER AGAIN *Coliseum TOGA 012CD*	49	1
22 Nov 97		I BELIEVE (re-mix) *Coalition COLA 027CD*	28	2

HAPPY MONDAYS
UK, male vocal / instrumental group (53 WEEKS) pos/wks

			pos	wks
30 Sep 89		WFL *Factory FAC 2327*	68	2
25 Nov 89		MADCHESTER RAVE ON (EP) *Factory FAC 2427*	19	14
7 Apr 90	●	STEP ON *Factory FAC 2727*	5	11
9 Jun 90		LAZYITIS – ONE ARMED BOXER *Factory FAC 2227* [1]	46	3
20 Oct 90	●	KINKY AFRO *Factory FAC 3027*	5	7
9 Mar 91		LOOSE FIT *Factory FAC 3127*	17	7
30 Nov 91		JUDGE FUDGE *Factory FAC 3327*	24	3
19 Sep 92		STINKIN THINKIN *Factory FAC 3627*	31	3
21 Nov 92		SUNSHINE AND LOVE *Factory FAC 3727*	62	1
22 May 99		THE BOYS ARE BACK IN TOWN *London LONCD 432*	24	2

[1] Happy Mondays and Karl Denver

Tracks on Madchester Rave On (EP): Hallelujah / Holy Ghost / Clap Your Hands / Rave On

See also BLACK GRAPE

Ed HARCOURT UK, male vocalist (1 WEEK) pos/wks

			pos	wks
2 Feb 02		APPLE OF MY EYE *Heavenly HVN 107CDS*	61	1

Paul HARDCASTLE UK, male producer (66 WEEKS) pos/wks

			pos	wks
7 Apr 84		YOU'RE THE ONE FOR ME – DAYBREAK – AM *Total Control TOCO 1*	41	4
28 Jul 84		GUILTY *Total Control TOCO 2*	55	3
22 Sep 84		RAIN FOREST *Bluebird BR 8* ▲	41	5
17 Nov 84		EAT YOUR HEART OUT *Cooltempo COOL 102*	59	4
4 May 85	★	19 *Chrysalis CHS 2860*	1	16
15 Jun 85		RAIN FOREST (re-issue) *Bluebird / 10 BR 15*	53	4
9 Nov 85		JUST FOR MONEY *Chrysalis CASH 1*	19	5
1 Feb 86	●	DON'T WASTE MY TIME *Chrysalis PAUL 1* [1]	8	11
21 Jun 86		FOOLIN' YOURSELF *Chrysalis PAUL 2*	51	3
11 Oct 86		THE WIZARD *Chrysalis PAUL 3*	15	6

		pos/wks
9 Apr 88	**WALK IN THE NIGHT** *Chrysalis PAUL 4*	54 3
4 Jun 88	**40 YEARS** *Chrysalis PAUL 5*	53 2

1 Paul Hardcastle featuring Carol Kenyon

'Just for Money' features the voices of Laurence Olivier, Bob Hoskins, Ed O'Ross and Alan Talbot, who are credited on the sleeve only

See also SILENT UNDERDOG

HARDCORE RHYTHM TEAM
UK, male vocal / production group (1 WEEK)   pos/wks

14 Mar 92	**HARDCORE – THE FINAL CONFLICT** *Furious FRUT 001*	69 1

Duane HARDEN – *See Armand VAN HELDEN; POWERHOUSE*

HARDFLOOR
Germany, male instrumental / production group (6 WEEKS)   pos/wks

26 Dec 92	**HARDTRANCE ACPERIENCE** *Harthouse UK HARTUK 1*	56 4
10 Apr 93	**TRANCESCRIPT** *Harthouse UK HARTUK 5CD*	72 1
25 Oct 97	**ACPERIENCE (re-mix)** *Eye-q EYEUK 018CD1*	60 1

Tim HARDIN *US, male vocalist, d. 29 Dec 1980 (1 WEEK)*   pos/wks

5 Jan 67	**HANG ON TO A DREAM** *Verve VS 1504*	50 1

Carolyn HARDING – *See PROSPECT PARK / Carolyn HARDING*

Mike HARDING
UK, male vocalist / comedian (8 WEEKS)   pos/wks

2 Aug 75	**ROCHDALE COWBOY** *Rubber ADUB 3*	22 8

Françoise HARDY *France, female vocalist (27 WEEKS)*   pos/wks

25 Jun 64	**TOUS LES GARÇONS ET LES FILLES** *Pye 7N 15653*	36 7
31 Dec 64	**ET MÊME** *Pye 7N 15740*	31 5
25 Mar 65	**ALL OVER THE WORLD** *Pye 7N 15802*	16 15

Tynetta HARE – *See Joey B ELLIS*

NIKI HARIS – *See SNAP!*

Morten HARKET *Norway, male vocalist (1 WEEK)*   pos/wks

19 Aug 95	**A KIND OF CHRISTMAS CARD** *Warner Bros. W 0304CD*	53 1

See also A-HA

HARLEM COMMUNITY CHOIR – *See John LENNON*

HARLEQUIN 4s / BUNKER KRU *US, male / female vocal*
/ instrumental group with UK, male production duo (4 WEEKS)   pos/wks

19 Mar 88	**SET IT OFF** *Champion CHAMP 64*	55 4

Steve HARLEY and COCKNEY REBEL
UK, male vocal / instrumental group – leader Steve Nice (69 WEEKS) pos/wks

11 May 74	● **JUDY TEEN** *EMI 2128* 1	5 11
10 Aug 74	● **MR SOFT** *EMI 2191* 1	8 9
8 Feb 75	★ **MAKE ME SMILE (COME UP AND SEE ME)** *EMI 2263*	1 9
7 Jun 75	**MR RAFFLES (MAN, IT WAS MEAN)** *EMI 2299*	13 6
31 Jul 76	● **HERE COMES THE SUN** *EMI 2505* 2	10 7
6 Nov 76	**(I BELIEVE) LOVE'S A PRIMA DONNA** *EMI 2539* 2	41 4
20 Oct 79	**FREEDOM'S PRISONER** *EMI 2994* 2	58 3
13 Aug 83	**BALLERINA (PRIMA DONNA)** *Stiletto STL 14* 2	51 5
11 Jan 86	● **THE PHANTOM OF THE OPERA** *Polydor POSP 800* 3	7 10
25 Apr 92	**MAKE ME SMILE (COME UP AND SEE ME) (re-issue)** *EMI EMCT 5* 2	46 2
30 Dec 95	**MAKE ME SMILE (COME UP AND SEE ME) (2nd re-issue)** *EMI CDHARLEY 1*	33 3

1 Cockney Rebel 2 Steve Harley 3 Sarah Brightman and Steve Harley

HARLEY QUINNE *UK, male vocal group (8 WEEKS)*   pos/wks

14 Oct 72	**NEW ORLEANS** *Bell 1255*	19 8

HARMONIX *UK, male producer – Hamish Brown (2 WEEKS)*   pos/wks

30 Mar 96	**LANDSLIDE** *Deconstruction 74321330762*	28 2

HARMONY GRASS
UK, male vocal / instrumental group (7 WEEKS)   pos/wks

29 Jan 69	**MOVE IN A LITTLE CLOSER BABY** *RCA 1772*	24 7

Ben HARPER *US, male vocalist / instrumentalist (1 WEEK)*   pos/wks

4 Apr 98	**FADED** *Virgin VUSCD 134*	54 1

Charlie HARPER *UK, male vocalist (1 WEEK)*   pos/wks

19 Jul 80	**BARMY LONDON ARMY** *Gem GEMS 35*	68 1

HARPERS BIZARRE *US, male vocal group (13 WEEKS)*   pos/wks

30 Mar 67	**59TH STREET BRIDGE SONG (FEELIN' GROOVY)** *Warner Bros. WB 5890*	34 7
4 Oct 67	**ANYTHING GOES** *Warner Bros. WB 7063*	33 6

HARPO *Sweden, male vocalist – Jan Svensson (6 WEEKS)*   pos/wks

17 Apr 76	**MOVIE STAR** *DJM DJS 400*	24 6

T HARRINGTON – *See Rahni HARRIS and F.L.O.*

Anita HARRIS *UK, female vocalist (50 WEEKS)*   pos/wks

29 Jun 67	● **JUST LOVING YOU** *CBS 2724*	6 30
11 Oct 67	**THE PLAYGROUND** *CBS 2991*	46 3
24 Jan 68	**ANNIVERSARY WALTZ** *CBS 3211*	21 9
14 Aug 68	**DREAM A LITTLE DREAM OF ME** *CBS 3637*	33 8

Emmylou HARRIS *US, female vocalist (6 WEEKS)*   pos/wks

6 Mar 76	**HERE, THERE & EVERYWHERE** *Reprise K 14415*	30 6

Jet HARRIS *UK, male instrumentalist – bass (18 WEEKS)*   pos/wks

24 May 62	**BESAME MUCHO** *Decca F 11466*	22 7
16 Aug 62	**MAIN TITLE THEME (FROM 'THE MAN WITH THE GOLDEN ARM')** *Decca F 11488*	12 11

See also Jet HARRIS and Tony MEEHAN; SHADOWS

Jet HARRIS and Tony MEEHAN
UK, male instrumental duo – bass and drums (39 WEEKS)   pos/wks

10 Jan 63	★ **DIAMONDS** *Decca F 11563*	1 13
25 Apr 63	● **SCARLETT O'HARA** *Decca F 11644*	2 13
5 Sep 63	● **APPLEJACK** *Decca F 11710*	4 13

See also Jet HARRIS; Tony MEEHAN; SHADOWS

Keith HARRIS and ORVILLE
UK, male ventriloquist vocalist with duck (20 WEEKS)   pos/wks

18 Dec 82	● **ORVILLE'S SONG** *BBC RESL 124*	4 11
24 Dec 83	**COME TO MY PARTY** *BBC RESL 138* 1	44 4
14 Dec 85	**WHITE CHRISTMAS** *Columbia DB 9121*	40 5

1 Keith Harris and Orville with Dippy

Major HARRIS *US, male vocalist (9 WEEKS)*   pos/wks

9 Aug 75	**LOVE WON'T LET ME WAIT** *Atlantic K 10585*	37 7
5 Nov 83	**ALL MY LIFE** *London LON 37*	61 2

Max HARRIS *UK, orchestra (10 WEEKS)*   pos/wks

1 Dec 60	**GURNEY SLADE** *Fontana H 282*	11 10

Rahni HARRIS and F.L.O.
US, male instrumental group (7 WEEKS)   pos/wks

16 Dec 78	**SIX MILLION STEPS (WEST RUNS SOUTH)** *Mercury 6007 198*	43 7

Hit has credit 'vocals by T Harrington and O Rasbury'

Richard HARRIS
Ireland, male actor / vocalist, d. 25 Oct 2002 (18 WEEKS)   pos/wks

| 26 Jun 68 | ● MACARTHUR PARK *RCA 1699* | 4 12 |
| 8 Jul 72 | MACARTHUR PARK (re-issue) *Probe GFF 101* | 38 6 |

Rochelle HARRIS – See ANGELHEART

Rolf HARRIS (455 Top 500)
Lovable Australian musician, artist and presenter, b. 30 Mar 1930, can lay claim to having some of the unlikeliest hits in the history of the UK charts. His only No.1 was a song written in 1903 by Theodore F Morse and Edward Madden and was the final chart-topper of the 60s (77 WEEKS)   pos/wks

21 Jul 60	● TIE ME KANGAROO DOWN SPORT *Columbia DB 4483* [1]	9 13
25 Oct 62	● SUN ARISE *Columbia DB 4888*	3 16
28 Feb 63	JOHNNY DAY *Columbia DB 4979*	44 2
16 Apr 69	BLUER THAN BLUE *Columbia DB 8553*	30 8
22 Nov 69	★ TWO LITTLE BOYS (re) *Columbia DB 8630*	1 25
13 Feb 93	● STAIRWAY TO HEAVEN *Vertigo VERCD 73*	7 6
1 Jun 96	BOHEMIAN RHAPSODY *Living Beat LBECD 41*	50 1
25 Oct 97	SUN ARISE (re-recording) *EMI CDROO 001*	26 3
14 Oct 00	FINE DAY *Tommy Boy TBCD 2155*	24 3

[1] Rolf Harris with his wobble board and The Rhythm Spinners

Ronnie HARRIS *UK, male vocalist (3 WEEKS)*   pos/wks

| 24 Sep 54 | THE STORY OF TINA *Columbia DB 3499* | 12 3 |

Sam HARRIS *US, male vocalist (2 WEEKS)*   pos/wks

| 9 Feb 85 | HEARTS ON FIRE / OVER THE RAINBOW *Motown TMG 1370* | 67 2 |

Simon HARRIS *UK, male / DJ producer (17 WEEKS)*   pos/wks

19 Mar 88	BASS (HOW LOW CAN YOU GO) *ffrr FFR 4*	12 6
29 Oct 88	HERE COMES THAT SOUND *ffrr FFR 12*	38 4
24 Jun 89	(I'VE GOT YOUR) PLEASURE CONTROL *ffrr F 106* [1]	60 3
18 Nov 89	ANOTHER MONSTERJAM *ffrr F 116* [2]	65 1
10 Mar 90	RAGGA HOUSE (ALL NIGHT LONG) *Living Beat 7SMASH 9* [3]	56 3

[1] Simon Harris featuring Lonnie Gordon [2] Simon Harris featuring Einstein [3] Simon Harris featuring Daddy Freddy

See also AMBASSADORS OF FUNK featuring MC MARIO

George HARRISON (342 Top 500)
Former Beatles guitarist, much inspired by Eastern musicians, born 25 Feb 1943, Liverpool, UK, died 29 Nov 2001. First ex-Beatle to score a solo UK No.1 single, only soloist to top chart twice with same single and only act to make UK and US Top 5 with back-to-back triple albums (92 WEEKS)   pos/wks

23 Jan 71	★ MY SWEET LORD *Apple R 5884* ▲	1 17
14 Aug 71	● BANGLA-DESH *Apple R 5912*	10 9
2 Jun 73	● GIVE ME LOVE (GIVE ME PEACE ON EARTH) *Apple R 5988* ▲	8 10
21 Dec 74	DING DONG *Apple R 6002*	38 5
11 Oct 75	YOU *Apple R 6007*	38 5
10 Mar 79	BLOW AWAY *Dark Horse K 17327*	51 5
23 May 81	ALL THOSE YEARS AGO *Dark Horse K 17807*	13 7
24 Oct 87	● GOT MY MIND SET ON YOU *Dark Horse W 8178* ▲	2 14
6 Feb 88	WHEN WE WAS FAB *Dark Horse W 8131*	25 7
25 Jun 88	THIS IS LOVE *Dark Horse W 7913*	55 3
26 Jan 02	★ MY SWEET LORD (re-issue) *Parlophone CDR 6571* ■	1 10

Noel HARRISON *UK, male vocalist (14 WEEKS)*   pos/wks

| 26 Feb 69 | ● THE WINDMILLS OF YOUR MIND *Reprise RS 20758* | 8 14 |

HARRY – See OBI PROJECT featuring HARRY, ASHER D and DJ WHAT?

HARRY *UK, female vocalist – Victoria Harrison (1 WEEK)*   pos/wks

| 2 Nov 02 | SO REAL *Dirty Word DWRCD 003* | 53 1 |

Deborah HARRY *US, female vocalist (52 WEEKS)*   pos/wks

1 Aug 81	BACKFIRED *Chrysalis CHS 2526* [1]	32 6
15 Nov 86	● FRENCH KISSIN' IN THE USA *Chrysalis CHS 3066* [1]	8 10
28 Feb 87	FREE TO FALL *Chrysalis CHS 3093* [1]	46 4
9 May 87	IN LOVE WITH LOVE *Chrysalis CHS 3128* [1]	45 5
7 Oct 89	I WANT THAT MAN *Chrysalis CHS 3369*	13 10
2 Dec 89	BRITE SIDE *Chrysalis CHS 3452*	59 4
31 Mar 90	SWEET AND LOW *Chrysalis CHS 3491*	57 3
5 Jan 91	WELL DID YOU EVAH! *Chrysalis CHS 3646* [2]	42 4
3 Jul 93	I CAN SEE CLEARLY NOW *Chrysalis CDCHSS 4900*	23 4
18 Sep 93	STRIKE ME PINK *Chrysalis CDCHSS 5000*	46 2

[1] Debbie Harry [2] Deborah Harry and Iggy Pop

See also BLONDIE

HARRY J ALL STARS
Jamaica, male instrumental group (25 WEEKS)   pos/wks

| 25 Oct 69 | ● LIQUIDATOR *Trojan TR 675* | 9 20 |
| 29 Mar 80 | LIQUIDATOR (re-issue) *Trojan TRO 9063* | 42 5 |

Re-issue of 'Liquidator' coupled with re-issue of 'Long Shot Kick De Bucket' by The Pioneers

Richard HARTLEY / Michael REED ORCHESTRA
UK, male instrumentalist – synthesizer, orchestra (10 WEEKS)   pos/wks

| 25 Feb 84 | ● THE MUSIC OF TORVILL AND DEAN (EP) *Safari SKATE 1* | 9 10 |

Tracks on The Music of Torvill and Dean (EP): Bolero / Capriccio Espagnole Opus 34 (Nos. 4 and 5) by Richard Hartley; Barnum on Ice / Discoskate by the Michael Reed Orchestra

Dan HARTMAN *US, male vocalist (34 WEEKS)*   pos/wks

21 Oct 78	● INSTANT REPLAY *Blue Sky SKY 6706*	8 15
13 Jan 79	THIS IS IT *Blue Sky SKY 6999*	17 8
18 May 85	SECOND NATURE *MCA MCA 957*	66 2
24 Aug 85	I CAN DREAM ABOUT YOU *MCA MCA 988*	12 8
1 Apr 95	KEEP THE FIRE BURNIN' *Columbia 6611552* [1]	49 1

[1] Dan Hartman starring Loleatta Holloway

HARVEY *UK, male rapper – Michael Harvey (2 WEEKS)*   pos/wks

| 7 Sep 02 | GET UP AND MOVE *Go! Beat GOBCD 52* | 24 2 |

Alex HARVEY BAND – See SENSATIONAL ALEX HARVEY BAND

Brian HARVEY *UK, male vocalist (5 WEEKS)*   pos/wks

| 28 Apr 01 | STRAIGHT UP NO BENDS *Edel 0126605 ERE* | 26 2 |
| 27 Oct 01 | LOVING YOU (OLE OLE OLE) *Blacklist 0132325 ERE* [1] | 20 3 |

[1] Brian Harvey and the Refugee Crew

See also TRUE STEPPERS; EAST 17

Lee HARVEY – See N*E*R*D

PJ HARVEY *UK, female vocalist – Polly Jean Harvey (22 WEEKS)* pos/wks

29 Feb 92	SHEELA-NA-GIG *Too Pure PURE 008*	69 1
1 May 93	50 FT QUEENIE *Island CID 538*	27 2
17 Jul 93	MAN-SIZE *Island CID 569*	42 2
18 Feb 95	DOWN BY THE WATER *Island CID 607*	38 2
22 Jul 95	C'MON BILLY *Island CID 614*	29 2
28 Oct 95	SEND HIS LOVE TO ME *Island CID 610*	34 2
9 Mar 96	HENRY LEE *Mute CDMUTE 189* [1]	36 1
23 Nov 96	THAT WAS MY VEIL *Island CID 648*	75 1
26 Sep 98	A PERFECT DAY ELISE *Island CID 718*	25 2
23 Jan 99	THE WIND *Island CID 730*	29 2
25 Nov 00	GOOD FORTUNE *Island CID 769*	41 2
10 Mar 01	A PLACE CALLED HOME *Island CID 771*	43 2
20 Oct 01	THIS IS LOVE *Island CID 785*	41 1

[1] Nick Cave and the Bad Seeds and PJ Harvey

For the first three hits PJ Harvey was the name of the entire group, not just the lead singer

Steve HARVEY UK, male vocalist (6 WEEKS)

		pos/wks
28 May 83	SOMETHING SPECIAL London LON 25	46 4
29 Oct 83	TONIGHT London LON 36	63 2

HARVEY DANGER US, male vocal / instrumental group (1 WEEK)

		pos/wks
1 Aug 98	FLAGPOLE SITTA Slash LASCD 64	57 1

Gordon HASKELL UK, male vocalist (6 WEEKS)

		pos/wks
29 Dec 01	● HOW WONDERFUL YOU ARE Flying Sparks TDBCDS 04	2 6

David HASSELHOFF US, male vocalist (2 WEEKS)

		pos/wks
13 Nov 93	IF I COULD ONLY SAY GOODBYE Arista 74321172262	35 2

Tony HATCH UK, orchestra (1 WEEK)

		pos/wks
4 Oct 62	OUT OF THIS WORLD Pye 7N 15460	50 1

Juliana HATFIELD US, female vocalist / instrumentalist (2 WEEKS)

		pos/wks
11 Sep 93	MY SISTER Mammoth YZ 767CD [1]	71 1
18 Mar 95	UNIVERSAL HEART-BEAT East West YZ 916CD	65 1

[1] Juliana Hatfield Three

Donny HATHAWAY – See Roberta FLACK

Lalah HATHAWAY US, female vocalist (10 WEEKS)

		pos/wks
1 Sep 90	HEAVEN KNOWS Virgin America VUS 28	66 2
2 Feb 91	BABY DON'T CRY Virgin America VUS 35	54 3
27 Jul 91	FAMILY AFFAIR Ten TEN 369	37 5

HATIRAS featuring SLARTA JOHN Canada, male producer – George Hatiris and UK, male rapper – Mark James (5 WEEKS)

		pos/wks
27 Jan 01	SPACED INVADER Defected DFECT 25CDS	14 5

HAVANA UK, male instrumental / production group (1 WEEK)

		pos/wks
6 Mar 93	ETHNIC PRAYER Limbo LIMBO 007CD	71 1

HAVEN UK, male vocal / instrumental group (6 WEEKS)

		pos/wks
22 Sep 01	LET IT LIVE Radiate RDT 3	72 1
2 Feb 02	SAY SOMETHING Radiate RDT 4	24 3
4 May 02	TIL THE END Radiate RDT 6	28 2

Nic HAVERSON UK, male vocalist (3 WEEKS)

		pos/wks
30 Jan 93	HEAD OVER HEELS Telstar CDHOH 1	48 3

Chesney HAWKES UK, male vocalist (26 WEEKS)

		pos/wks
23 Feb 91	★ THE ONE AND ONLY Chrysalis CHS 3627	1 16
22 Jun 91	I'M A MAN NOT A BOY Chrysalis CHS 3708	27 5
28 Sep 91	SECRETS OF THE HEART Chrysalis CHS 3681	57 3
29 May 93	WHAT'S WRONG WITH THIS PICTURE Chrysalis CDCHS 3969	63 1
12 Jan 02	STAY AWAY BABY JANE Arc DSART 13	74 1

Screamin' Jay HAWKINS US, male vocalist, d. 12 Feb 2000 (3 WEEKS)

		pos/wks
3 Apr 93	HEART ATTACK AND VINE Columbia 6591092	42 3

Sophie B HAWKINS US, female vocalist (37 WEEKS)

		pos/wks
4 Jul 92	DAMN I WISH I WAS YOUR LOVER Columbia 6581077	14 9
12 Sep 92	CALIFORNIA HERE I COME Columbia 6583177	53 3
6 Feb 93	I WANT YOU Columbia 6587772	49 2
13 Aug 94	RIGHT BESIDE YOU Columbia 6606915	13 12
26 Nov 94	DON'T DON'T TELL ME NO Columbia 6610152	36 5
11 Mar 95	AS I LAY ME DOWN Columbia 6612125	24 6

Edwin HAWKINS SINGERS US, male / female vocal group (13 WEEKS)

		pos/wks
21 May 69	● OH HAPPY DAY (re) Buddah 201 048	2 13

Kirsty HAWKSHAW UK, female vocalist (7 WEEKS)

		pos/wks
24 Jun 00	DREAMING Headspace HEDSCD 002 [1]	38 2
29 Sep 01	URBAN TRAIN Nebula VCRD 95 [2]	22 3
21 Sep 02	STEALTH Distinctive Breaks DISNCD 90 [3]	67 1
23 Nov 02	FINE DAY Mainline CDMAIN 002	62 1

[1] BT featuring Kirsty Hawkshaw [2] DJ Tiesto featuring Kirsty Hawshaw [3] Way Out West featuring Kirsty Hawkshaw

See also OPUS III

HAWKWIND UK, male vocal / instrumental group with female dancer (28 WEEKS)

		pos/wks
1 Jul 72	● SILVER MACHINE (2re) United Artists UP 35381	3 22
11 Aug 73	URBAN GUERRILLA United Artists UP 35566	39 3
19 Jul 80	SHOT DOWN IN THE NIGHT Bronze BRO 98	59 3

'Silver Machine' re-entries were in 1978 and 1983

Bill HAYES US, male vocalist (9 WEEKS)

		pos/wks
6 Jan 56	● THE BALLAD OF DAVY CROCKETT London HLA 8220 ▲	2 9

With Archie Bleyer's Orchestra

Darren HAYES Australia, male vocalist (26 WEEKS)

		pos/wks
30 Mar 02	● INSATIABLE Columbia 6723995	8 14
20 Jul 02	STRANGE RELATIONSHIP Columbia 6728685	15 8
16 Nov 02	I MISS YOU Columbia 6733312	20 4

See also SAVAGE GARDEN

Gemma HAYES Ireland, female vocalist (2 WEEKS)

		pos/wks
25 May 02	HANGING AROUND Source SOURCD 046	62 1
10 Aug 02	LET A GOOD THING GO Source SOURCD 051	54 1

Isaac HAYES US, male vocalist / multi-instrumentalist (35 WEEKS)

		pos/wks
4 Dec 71	● THEME FROM 'SHAFT' Stax 2025 069 ▲	4 12
3 Apr 76	● DISCO CONNECTION ABC 4100 [1]	10 9
26 Dec 98	★ CHOCOLATE SALTY BALLS (PS I LOVE YOU) Columbia 6667985 [2]	1 13
30 Sep 00	THEME FROM SHAFT (re-recording) LaFace / Arista 74321792582	53 1

[1] Isaac Hayes Movement [2] Chef

HAYSI FANTAYZEE UK, male / female production / vocal duo – Jeremy Healy and Kate Garner (25 WEEKS)

		pos/wks
24 Jul 82	JOHN WAYNE IS BIG LEGGY Regard RG 100	11 10
13 Nov 82	HOLY JOE Regard RG 104	51 3
22 Jan 83	SHINY SHINY Regard RG 106	16 10
25 Jun 83	SISTER FRICTION Regard RG 108	62 2

Justin HAYWARD UK, male vocalist (20 WEEKS)

		pos/wks
25 Oct 75	● BLUE GUITAR Threshold TH 21 [1]	8 7
8 Jul 78	● FOREVER AUTUMN CBS 6368 [2]	5 13

[1] Justin Hayward and John Lodge [2] From Jeff Wayne's 'War of the Worlds' featuring Justin Hayward

See also MOODY BLUES

Leon HAYWOOD US, male vocalist (11 WEEKS)

		pos/wks
15 Mar 80	DON'T PUSH IT DON'T FORCE IT 20th Century Fox TC 2443	12 11

HAYWOODE UK, female vocalist – Sharon Haywoode (31 WEEKS)

		pos/wks
17 Sep 83	A TIME LIKE THIS CBS A 3651	48 7

29 Sep 84	I CAN'T LET YOU GO *CBS A 4664*	**63** 4
13 Apr 85	ROSES *CBS A 6069*	**65** 3
5 Oct 85	GETTING CLOSER *CBS A 6582*	**67** 2
21 Jun 86	ROSES (re-issue) *CBS A 7224*	**11** 11
13 Sep 86	I CAN'T LET YOU GO (re-issue) *CBS 650076 7*	**50** 4

Ofra HAZA *Israel, female vocalist, d. 23 Feb 2000 (12 WEEKS)* pos/wks

30 Apr 88	IM NIN'ALU *WEA YZ 190*	**15** 8
17 Jun 95	MY LOVE IS FOR REAL *Virgin America VUSCD 91* 1	**28** 3
3 Apr 99	BABYLON *Warner Esp. WESP 006CD1* 2	**65** 1

1 Paula Abdul featuring Ofra Haza 2 Black Dog featuring Ofra Haza

HAZIZA *Sweden, male production duo (1 WEEK)* pos/wks

28 Apr 01	ONE MORE *Tidy Trax TIDY 152T*	**75** 1

Lee HAZLEWOOD – See Nancy SINATRA

Murray HEAD *UK, male vocalist (15 WEEKS)* pos/wks

29 Jan 72	SUPERSTAR *MCA MMKS 5077*	**47** 1
10 Nov 84	ONE NIGHT IN BANGKOK (re) *RCA CHESS 1*	**12** 14

'Superstar' was one of four tracks on a maxi single, two of which were credited during the disc's one week on the chart. The other track credited was 'I Don't Know How to Love Him' by Yvonne Elliman

Roy HEAD *US, male vocalist (5 WEEKS)* pos/wks

4 Nov 65	TREAT HER RIGHT *Vocalion V-P 9248*	**30** 5

HEADBANGERS *UK, male vocal / instrumental group (3 WEEKS)* pos/wks

10 Oct 81	STATUS ROCK *Magnet MAG 206*	**60** 3

HEADBOYS *UK, male vocal / instrumental group (8 WEEKS)* pos/wks

22 Sep 79	THE SHAPE OF THINGS TO COME *RSO 40*	**45** 8

HEADGIRL – See MOTÖRHEAD; GIRLSCHOOL

Max HEADROOM – See ART OF NOISE

HEADS *UK, male instrumental group (4 WEEKS)* pos/wks

21 Jun 86	AZTEC LIGHTNING (THEME FROM BBC WORLD CUP GRANDSTAND) *BBC RESL 184*	**45** 4

HEADS with Shaun RYDER
US / UK, male / female vocal / instrumental group (1 WEEK) pos/wks

9 Nov 96	DON'T TAKE MY KINDNESS FOR WEAKNESS *Radioactive MCSTD 48024*	**60** 1

Heads are Talking Heads minus lead singer David Byrne

See also TALKING HEADS

HEADSWIM
UK, male vocal / instrumental group (5 WEEKS) pos/wks

25 Feb 95	CRAWL *Epic 6612252*	**64** 1
14 Feb 98	TOURNIQUET *Epic 6650442*	**30** 3
16 May 98	BETTER MADE *Epic 6658402*	**42** 1

Jeremy HEALY and AMOS *UK, male production / vocal duo – Jeremy Healy and Amos Pizzey (7 WEEKS)* pos/wks

12 Oct 96	STAMP! *Positiva CDTIV 65*	**11** 5
31 May 97	ARGENTINA *Positiva CDTIV 74*	**30** 2

See also HWA featuring SONIC THE HEDGEHOG

Imogen HEAP – See URBAN SPECIES

HEAR 'N' AID *International, male / female vocal / instrumental charity assembly (6 WEEKS)* pos/wks

19 Apr 86	STARS *Vertigo HEAR 1*	**26** 6

HEAR'SAY *UK, male / female vocal group (60 WEEKS)* pos/wks

24 Mar 01	★ PURE AND SIMPLE *Polydor 5870069* ◆ ■	**1** 25
7 Jul 01	★ THE WAY TO YOUR LOVE (re) *Polydor 5871482* ■	**1** 17
8 Dec 01	● EVERYBODY *Polydor 5705122*	**4** 11
24 Aug 02	● LOVIN' IS EASY (re) *Polydor 5708542*	**6** 7

HEART `474` `Top 500`
Giants of Stateside AOR, who first tasted success in Canada and are regarded as key players on the Seattle music scene. Fronted by Californian-born Wilson sisters Ann (v/g/f) b. 19 Jun 1951 and Nancy (g/v) b. 16 Mar 1954. UK chart career began a full decade after US debut (76 WEEKS) pos/wks

29 Mar 86	THESE DREAMS *Capitol CL 394* ▲	**62** 4
13 Jun 87	● ALONE *Capitol CL 448* ▲	**3** 16
19 Sep 87	WHO WILL YOU RUN TO *Capitol CL 457*	**30** 7
12 Dec 87	THERE'S THE GIRL *Capitol CL 473*	**34** 7
5 Mar 88	● NEVER / THESE DREAMS (re-issue) *Capitol CL 482*	**8** 9
14 May 88	WHAT ABOUT LOVE *Capitol CL 487*	**14** 6
22 Oct 88	NOTHIN' AT ALL *Capitol CL 507*	**38** 3
24 Mar 90	● ALL I WANNA DO IS MAKE LOVE TO YOU *Capitol CL 569*	**8** 13
28 Jul 90	I DIDN'T WANT TO NEED YOU *Capitol CL 580*	**47** 3
17 Nov 90	STRANDED *Capitol CL 595*	**60** 2
14 Sep 91	YOU'RE THE VOICE *Capitol CLS 624*	**56** 2
20 Nov 93	WILL YOU BE THERE (IN THE MORNING) *Capitol CDCLS 700*	**19** 4

HEARTBEAT
UK, male / female vocal / instrumental group (5 WEEKS) pos/wks

24 Oct 87	TEARS FROM HEAVEN *Priority P 17*	**32** 4
23 Apr 88	THE WINNER *Priority P 19*	**70** 1

HEARTBEAT COUNTRY
UK, male vocalist – Bill Maynard (1 WEEK) pos/wks

31 Dec 94	HEARTBEAT *MMM MMM 01CD*	**75** 1

HEARTBREAKER – See DEMON vs HEARTBREAKER

HEARTBREAKERS – See Tom PETTY and the HEARTBREAKERS; Stevie NICKS

HEARTISTS *Italy, male DJ / production trio (5 WEEKS)* pos/wks

9 Aug 97	BELO HORIZONTI *VC VCRD 23*	**42** 3
31 Jan 98	BELO HORIZONTI (re-mix) *VC VCRD 28*	**40** 2

HEARTLESS CREW *UK, male DJ / production trio (3 WEEKS)* pos/wks

25 May 02	THE HEARTLESS THEME AKA 'THE SUPERGLUE RIDDIM' *East West HEART 02CD*	**21** 3

Ted HEATH and his MUSIC
UK, orchestra, leader d. 18 Nov 1969 (56 WEEKS) pos/wks

16 Jan 53	VANESSA *Decca F 9983*	**11** 1
3 Jul 53	● HOT TODDY *Decca F 10093*	**6** 11
23 Oct 53	● DRAGNET (4re) *Decca F 10176*	**9** 5
12 Feb 54	● SKIN DEEP *Decca F 10246*	**9** 3
6 Jul 56	THE FAITHFUL HUSSAR *Decca F 10746*	**18** 9
14 Mar 58	● SWINGIN' SHEPHERD BLUES *Decca F 11000*	**3** 14
11 Apr 58	TEQUILA *Decca F 11003*	**21** 6
4 Jul 58	TOM HARK *Decca F 11025*	**24** 2
5 Oct 61	SUCU SUCU (re) *Decca F 11392*	**36** 5

HEATWAVE `433` `Top 500`
Internationally successful UK-based soul / disco band formed Germany 1973 by brothers Johnnie and Keith Wilder (Ohio, US). Group's keyboard player and main songwriter, UK-born Rod Temperton, later penned many hits including several for Michael Jackson (80 WEEKS) pos/wks

22 Jan 77	● BOOGIE NIGHTS *GTO GT 77*	**2** 14
7 May 77	TOO HOT TO HANDLE / SLIP YOUR DISC TO THIS *GTO GT 91*	**15** 11
14 Jan 78	THE GROOVE LINE *GTO GT 115*	**12** 8
3 Jun 78	MIND BLOWING DECISIONS *GTO GT 226*	**12** 11
4 Nov 78	● ALWAYS AND FOREVER / MIND BLOWING DECISIONS (re-mix) *GTO GT 236*	**9** 14
26 May 79	RAZZLE DAZZLE *GTO GT 248*	**43** 5

17 Jan 81	GANGSTERS OF THE GROOVE *GTO GT 285*	**19** 8
21 Mar 81	JITTERBUGGIN' *GTO GT 290*	**34** 7
1 Sep 90	MIND BLOWING DECISIONS (re-recording)	
	Brothers Organisation HW 1	**65** 2

HEAVEN 17 `382` `Top 500`

Politically astute electronic pop trio from Sheffield, UK; Martyn Ware (k), Ian Craig Marsh (k) (both previously in Human League) and Glenn Gregory (v). Act, named after a fictional band in cult film A Clockwork Orange, reunited and played first ever gigs in 1997 (87 WEEKS) — pos/wks

21 Mar 81	(WE DON'T NEED THIS) FASCIST GROOVE THANG	
	Virgin VS 400	**45** 5
5 Sep 81	PLAY TO WIN *Virgin VS 433*	**46** 7
14 Nov 81	PENTHOUSE AND PAVEMENT *Virgin VS 455*	**57** 3
30 Oct 82	LET ME GO *Virgin VS 532*	**41** 6
16 Apr 83	● TEMPTATION *Virgin VS 570*	**2** 13
25 Jun 83	● COME LIVE WITH ME *Virgin VS 607*	**5** 11
10 Sep 83	CRUSHED BY THE WHEELS OF INDUSTRY *Virgin VS 628*	**17** 7
1 Sep 84	SUNSET NOW *Virgin VS 708*	**24** 6
27 Oct 84	THIS IS MINE *Virgin VS 722*	**23** 7
19 Jan 85	… (AND THAT'S NO LIE) *Virgin VS 740*	**52** 5
17 Jan 87	TROUBLE *Virgin VS 920*	**51** 3
21 Nov 92	● TEMPTATION (re-mix) *Virgin VS 1446*	**4** 11
27 Feb 93	(WE DON'T NEED THIS) FASCIST GROOVE THANG	
	(re-mix) *Virgin VSCDT 1451*	**40** 2
10 Apr 93	PENTHOUSE AND PAVEMENT (re-mix) *Virgin VSCDT 1457*	**54** 1

Carol Kenyon is the uncredited vocalist on 'Temptation'. 'Fascist Groove Thang' in 1993 is a re-recording

HEAVENS CRY *Holland, male production duo (2 WEEKS)* — pos/wks

6 Oct 01	TILL TEARS DO US PART (re) *Tidy Trax 158 CD*	**68** 2

HEAVY D and the BOYZ
Jamaica / US, male rap / vocal duo (28 WEEKS) — pos/wks

6 Dec 86	MR BIG STUFF *MCA MCA 1106*	**61** 8
15 Jul 89	WE GOT OUR OWN THANG *MCA MCA 23942*	**69** 2
6 Jul 91	● NOW THAT WE FOUND LOVE *MCA MCS 1550*	**2** 12
28 Sep 91	IS IT GOOD TO YOU *MCA MCS 1564*	**46** 3
8 Oct 94	THIS IS YOUR NIGHT *MCA MCSTD 2010*	**30** 3

HEAVY PETTIN' *UK, male vocal / instrumental group (2 WEEKS)* — pos/wks

17 Mar 84	LOVE TIMES LOVE *Polydor HEP 3*	**69** 2

HEAVY STEREO
UK, male vocal / instrumental group (4 WEEKS) — pos/wks

22 Jul 95	SLEEP FREAK *Creation CRESCD 203*	**46** 1
28 Oct 95	SMILER *Creation CRESCD 213*	**46** 1
10 Feb 96	CHINESE BURN *Creation CRESCD 218*	**45** 1
24 Aug 96	MOUSE IN A HOLE *Creation CRESCD 230*	**53** 1

HEAVY WEATHER *US, male vocalist – Peter Lee (1 WEEK)* — pos/wks

29 Jun 96	LOVE CAN'T TURN AROUND *Pukka CDPUKKA 6*	**56** 1

Bobby HEBB *US, male vocalist (15 WEEKS)* — pos/wks

8 Sep 66	SUNNY *Philips BF 1503*	**12** 9
19 Aug 72	LOVE LOVE LOVE *Philips 6051 023*	**32** 6

HED BOYS *UK, male instrumental / production
duo – Dave Lee and Andrew Livingstone (6 WEEKS)* — pos/wks

6 Aug 94	GIRLS + BOYS *Deconstruction 74321223322*	**21** 4
4 Nov 95	GIRLS + BOYS (re-mix) *Deconstruction 74321322032*	**36** 2

See also PHASE II; Z FACTOR; Joey NEGRO; JAKATTA; Li KWAN; RAVEN MAIZE; AKABU featuring Linda CLIFFORD; IL PADRINOS

HEDGEHOPPERS ANONYMOUS
UK, male vocal / instrumental group (12 WEEKS) — pos/wks

30 Sep 65	● IT'S GOOD NEWS WEEK *Decca F 12241*	**5** 12

HEFNER *UK, male vocal / instrumental group (3 WEEKS)* — pos/wks

26 Aug 00	GOOD FRUIT *Too Pure PURE 108CDS*	**50** 1
14 Oct 00	THE GREEDY UGLY PEOPLE *Too Pure PURE 111CDS*	**64** 1
8 Sep 01	ALAN BEAN *Too Pure PURE 118CDS*	**58** 1

Neal HEFTI *US, male orchestra (4 WEEKS)* — pos/wks

9 Apr 88	BATMAN THEME *RCA PB 49571*	**55** 4

Den HEGARTY *UK, male vocalist (2 WEEKS)* — pos/wks

31 Mar 79	VOODOO VOODOO *Magnet MAG 143*	**73** 2

See also DARTS

Anita HEGERLAND – See Mike OLDFIELD

HEINZ *UK, male vocalist – Heinz Burt, d. 7 Apr 2000 (35 WEEKS)* — pos/wks

8 Aug 63	● JUST LIKE EDDIE *Decca F 11693*	**5** 15
28 Nov 63	COUNTRY BOY *Decca F 11768*	**26** 9
27 Feb 64	YOU WERE THERE *Decca F 11831*	**26** 8
15 Oct 64	QUESTIONS I CAN'T ANSWER *Columbia DB 7374*	**39** 2
18 Mar 65	DIGGIN' MY POTATOES *Columbia DB 7482* [1]	**49** 1

[1] Heinz and the Wild Boys

HELICOPTER *UK, male instrumental /
production duo – Dylan Barnes and Rob Davy (4 WEEKS)* — pos/wks

27 Aug 94	ON YA WAY *Helicopter TIG 007CD*	**32** 2
22 Jun 96	ON YA WAY (re-mix) *Systematic SYSCD 27*	**37** 2

See also MUTINY UK

HELIOCENTRIC WORLD
UK, male / female vocal / instrumental group (2 WEEKS) — pos/wks

14 Jan 95	WHERE'S YOUR LOVE BEEN *Talkin Loud TLKCD 51*	**71** 2

HELIOTROPIC featuring Verna V *UK, male production
duo – Nick Hale and Gez Dewar – with female vocalist (2 WEEKS)* — pos/wks

16 Oct 99	ALIVE *Multiply CDMULTY 52*	**33** 2

HELL IS FOR HEROES
UK, male vocal / instrumental group (4 WEEKS) — pos/wks

9 Feb 02	YOU DROVE ME TO IT *Wishakismo CDWISH 003*	**63** 1
17 Aug 02	I CAN CLIMB MOUNTAINS *Chrysalis CDCHS 5143*	**41** 2
2 Nov 02	NIGHT VISION *Chrysalis CDCHSS 5147*	**38** 1

See also SYMPOSIUM

Pete HELLER *UK, male DJ / producer (7 WEEKS)* — pos/wks

15 May 99	BIG LOVE *Essential Recordings ESCD 4*	**12** 7

HELLER & FARLEY PROJECT *UK, male instrumental /
production duo – Pete Heller and Terry Farley (7 WEEKS)* — pos/wks

24 Feb 96	ULTRA FLAVA *AM:PM 5814372*	**22** 3
28 Dec 96	ULTRA FLAVA (re-mix) *AM:PM 5820552*	**32** 4

See also FIRE ISLAND; Pete HELLER; STYLUS TROUBLE

HELLO *UK, male vocal / instrumental group (21 WEEKS)* — pos/wks

9 Nov 74	● TELL HIM *Bell 1377*	**6** 12
18 Oct 75	● NEW YORK GROOVE *Bell 1438*	**9** 9

HELLOWEEN
US, male vocal / instrumental group (7 WEEKS) — pos/wks

27 Aug 88	DR STEIN *Noise International 7HELLO 1*	**57** 3
12 Nov 88	I WANT OUT *Noise International 7HELLO 2*	**69** 2
2 Mar 91	KIDS OF THE CENTURY *EMI EM 178*	**56** 2

Bobby HELMS *US, male vocalist, d. 19 Jun 1997 (7 WEEKS)* — pos/wks

29 Nov 57	MY SPECIAL ANGEL *Brunswick 05721* [1]	**22** 3

SLAVE TO THE RHYTHM

■ Jamaican-born Grace Mendoza spent her teenage years in New York where she began her career as a fashion model in the early 1970s. Jet-setting around the world, she appeared on the covers of Vogue and Elle. Paris became a particularly popular habitat and party animal Jones, who shared a flat with fellow model Jerry Hall, was soon spotted about town and signed by a small French label for a series of disco records that attracted some attention on the New York scene. This led to her signing by Chris Blackwell on his Island Records label in 1977.

With her shaved head, minimal apparel, robot stance and extrovert personality, Grace Jones could best be described as a "difficult" artist but Chris Blackwell was one of the few record company bosses who had a respect and understanding of his artists' flamboyant behaviour.

Though signed to Island, at the end of her contract she was lent to Trevor Horn's ZTT for 'Slave to the Rhythm', a one-off single which turned into an entire album courtesy of Horn's studio trickery. 'Slave' is probably Grace Jones's finest musical moment, although its success undoubtedly owed more to Horn's studio production than it did to Ms Jones's noteworthy performance.

The song had been around Mr Horn's studio for some time. Written by members of his studio team, it had originally been scheduled as a possible follow-up to 'Relax' by Frankie Goes To Hollywood, but was at the time deemed to be unsuitable. Horn and co-producer/guitarist Stephen Lipson took some four months

■ IT SHOULD BE NOTED THAT ONE OF THE HIRED HANDS ON THE RECORDING WAS NONE OTHER THAN PINK FLOYD GUITARIST DAVID GILMOUR ■

perfecting this one song to their satisfaction. Apparently the cost of studio time and musicians wasn't a high priority, and it should be noted that one of the hired hands on the recording was none other than Pink Floyd guitarist David Gilmour.

According to ZTT creative guru Paul Morley: "Horn was at the cutting edge of inventing a whole new way of making modern records, involving the use of the studio as a musical instrument." Indeed, so great was Horn's input on the song that the man himself recalls: "When we recorded 'Slave' I was almost like the artist, while he [Lipson] was the producer." Such was the volume of work involved on the song that ZTT ended up with an entire album's worth of alternative mixes which made No.12 on the UK

album chart in 1985. Aside from a later greatest
hits compilation, this became Grace Jones's
most successful album.

Grace Jones's career since 1985 has certainly
had its ups and downs. She appeared in a
number of films including 'Conan the Destroyer'
with Arnold Schwarzenegger and the 1985
James Bond adventure 'A View to a Kill' starring
Roger Moore as 007. Her personal life was not
free of problems, with reported cocaine and
bankruptcy stories, and she made herself
particularly unpopular by being kicked off an
American Airlines flight in Jamaica for creating
something of a disturbance after her boyfriend
had complained to the pilot about a flight delay.
In the UK Jones will be best remembered for an
incident on live television, rather than her music.
A guest on chat-show host Russell Harty's
programme, the late Mr Harty got fed up with her
monosyllabic responses to his questions and
moved on to his next guest. An enraged Grace
Jones proceeded to clobber the poor man with
her handbag.

■ Tony Burton

For reasons best known to
herself, Grace Jones
disguises herself on stage
with a Grace Jones mask

★ ARTIST:	Grace Jones
★ LABEL:	ZTT/Island
★ WRITERS:	Bruce Woolley, Simon Darlow, Stephen Lipson and Trevor Horn
★ PRODUCERS:	Trevor Horn assisted by Stephen Lipson

| 21 Feb 58 | NO OTHER BABY *Brunswick 05730* .... | **30** | 1 |
| 1 Aug 58 | JACQUELINE *Brunswick 05748* [1] .... | **20** | 3 |

[1] Bobby Helms with the Anita Kerr Singers

Jimmy HELMS *US, male vocalist (10 WEEKS)* pos/wks

| 24 Feb 73 | ● GONNA MAKE YOU AN OFFER YOU CAN'T REFUSE *Cube BUG 27*..**8** 10 |

HELTAH SKELTAH and ORIGINOO GUNN CLAPPAZ as the FABULOUS FIVE *US, male rap / vocal / production group (1 WEEK)* pos/wks

| 1 Jun 96 | BLAH *Priority PTYCD 117* .... | **60** | 1 |

Eddie HENDERSON
US, male instrumentalist – trumpet (6 WEEKS) pos/wks

| 28 Oct 78 | PRANCE ON *Capitol CL 16015* .... | **44** | 6 |

Joe 'Mr Piano' HENDERSON
UK, male instrumentalist – piano, d. 4 May 1980 (23 WEEKS) pos/wks

3 Jun 55	SING IT WITH JOE *Polygon P 1167*	**14**	4
2 Sep 55	SING IT AGAIN WITH JOE *Polygon P 1184*	**18**	3
25 Jul 58	TRUDIE (re) *Pye Nixa N 15147*	**14**	14
23 Oct 59	TREBLE CHANCE *Pye 7N 15224*	**28**	1
24 Mar 60	OOH! LA! LA! *Pye 7N 15257*	**44**	1

First two hits are medleys as follows: Sing It with Joe: Margie / I'm Nobody's Sweetheart / Somebody Stole My Gal / Moonlight Bay / By the Light of the Silvery Moon / Cuddle Up a Little Closer. Sing It Again with Joe: Put Your Arms Around Me Honey / Ain't She Sweet / When You're Smiling / Shine on Harvest Moon / My Blue Heaven / Show Me the Way to Go Home

Wayne HENDERSON – *See Roy AYERS*

Billy HENDRIX
Germany, male producer – Sharam Khososi (2 WEEKS) pos/wks

| 12 Sep 98 | THE BODY SHINE (EP) *Hooj Choons HOOJ 65CD* .... | **55** | 2 |

Tracks on The Body Shine (EP): The Body Shine / Funky Shine / Colour Systems Inc's Amber Dub / Timewriter re-mix

See also THREE 'N ONE

Jimi HENDRIX EXPERIENCE (374) [Top 500]
Guitar ace and hugely influential 20th-century icon, b. Johnny Allen Hendrix, 27 Nov 1942, Seattle, US, renamed James Marshall Hendrix, d. 18 Sep 1970, London. After being 'discovered' and then managed by Animals' bassist Chas Chandler, the left-handed guitarist and vocalist formed The Jimi Hendrix Experience, featuring Mitch Mitchell (d) and Noel Redding (b). His timeless appeal consistently generates annual global sales of about three million albums (88 WEEKS) pos/wks

29 Dec 66	● HEY JOE *Polydor 56 139*	**6**	11
23 Mar 67	● PURPLE HAZE *Track 604 001*	**3**	14
11 May 67	● THE WIND CRIES MARY *Track 604 004*	**6**	11
30 Aug 67	BURNING OF THE MIDNIGHT LAMP *Track 604 007*	**18**	9
23 Oct 68	● ALL ALONG THE WATCHTOWER *Track 604 025*	**5**	11
16 Apr 69	CROSSTOWN TRAFFIC *Track 604 029*	**37**	3
7 Nov 70	★ VOODOO CHILE *Track 2095 001*	**1**	13
30 Oct 71	GYPSY EYES / REMEMBER *Track 2094 010*	**35**	5
12 Feb 72	JOHNNY B GOODE *Polydor 2001 277* [1]	**35**	5
21 Apr 90	CROSSTOWN TRAFFIC (re-issue) *Polydor PO 71* [1]	**61**	3
20 Oct 90	ALL ALONG THE WATCHTOWER (EP) *Polydor PO 100* [1]	**52**	3

[1] Jimi Hendrix

Tracks on All Along the Watchtower (EP): All Along the Watchtower / Voodoo Chile / Hey Joe (re-issues)

Nona HENDRYX *US, female vocalist (2 WEEKS)* pos/wks

| 16 May 87 | WHY SHOULD I CRY *EMI America EA 234* .... | **60** | 2 |

Don HENLEY *US, male vocalist (30 WEEKS)* pos/wks

| 12 Feb 83 | DIRTY LAUNDRY *Asylum E 9894* .... | **59** | 3 |
| 9 Feb 85 | THE BOYS OF SUMMER *Geffen A 4945* .... | **12** | 10 |

29 Jul 89	THE END OF THE INNOCENCE *Geffen GEF 57*	**48**	5
3 Oct 92	SOMETIMES LOVE JUST AIN'T ENOUGH *MCA MCS 1692* [1]	**22**	6
18 Jul 98	BOYS OF SUMMER (re-issue) *Geffen GFSTD 22350*	**12**	6

[1] Patty Smyth with Don Henley

See also EAGLES

Cassius HENRY *UK, male vocalist (2 WEEKS)* pos/wks

| 30 Mar 02 | BROKE *Blacklist 0130265 ERE* .... | **31** | 2 |

Clarence 'Frogman' HENRY *US, male vocalist (35 WEEKS)* pos/wks

4 May 61	● BUT I DO *Pye International 7N 25078*	**3**	19
13 Jul 61	● YOU ALWAYS HURT THE ONE YOU LOVE *Pye International 7N 25089*	**6**	12
21 Sep 61	LONELY STREET / WHY CAN'T YOU *Pye International 7N 25108*	**42**	2
17 Jul 93	(I DON'T KNOW WHY) BUT I DO (re-issue) *MCA MCSTD 1797*	**65**	2

Kevin HENRY – *See LA MIX*

Paul HENRY and the Mayson GLEN ORCHESTRA
UK, male vocalist / orchestra (2 WEEKS) pos/wks

| 14 Jan 78 | BENNY'S THEME *Pye 7N 46027* .... | **39** | 2 |

Pauline HENRY *UK, female vocalist (21 WEEKS)* pos/wks

18 Sep 93	TOO MANY PEOPLE *Sony S2 6595942*	**38**	2
6 Nov 93	FEEL LIKE MAKING LOVE *Sony S2 6597972*	**12**	7
29 Jan 94	CAN'T TAKE YOUR LOVE *Sony S2 6599902*	**30**	3
21 May 94	WATCH THE MIRACLE START *Sony S2 6602772*	**54**	1
30 Sep 95	SUGAR FREE *Sony S2 6624362*	**57**	2
23 Dec 95	LOVE HANGOVER *Sony S2 6626132*	**37**	3
24 Feb 96	NEVER KNEW LOVE LIKE THIS *Sony S2 6629382* [1] ...	**40**	2
1 Jun 96	HAPPY *Sony S2 6630692*	**46**	1

[1] Pauline Henry featuring Wayne Marshall

Pierre HENRY *France, male instrumentalist (1 WEEK)* pos/wks

| 4 Oct 97 | PSYCHE ROCK *Hi-Life 4620312* .... | **58** | 1 |

HEPBURN *UK, female vocal / instrumental group (15 WEEKS)* pos/wks

29 May 99	● I QUIT *Columbia 6674012*	**8**	7
28 Aug 99	BUGS *Columbia 6677382*	**14**	5
19 Feb 00	DEEP DEEP DOWN *Columbia 6683382*	**16**	3

HERD *UK, male vocal / instrumental group (35 WEEKS)* pos/wks

13 Sep 67	● FROM THE UNDERWORLD *Fontana TF 856*	**6**	13
20 Dec 67	PARADISE LOST *Fontana TF 887*	**15**	9
10 Apr 68	● I DON'T WANT OUR LOVING TO DIE *Fontana TF 925*	**5**	13

HERMAN'S HERMITS (79) [Top 500]
Manchester quintet fronted by teenage vocalist Peter Noone, b. 5 Nov 1947, whose US popularity in the mid-1960s rivalled The Beatles. This band sold more than 40 million records and at times had three singles simultaneously in the US Top 20 (211 WEEKS) pos/wks

20 Aug 64	★ I'M INTO SOMETHING GOOD *Columbia DB 7338*	**1**	15
19 Nov 64	SHOW ME GIRL *Columbia DB 7408*	**19**	9
18 Feb 65	● SILHOUETTES *Columbia DB 7475*	**3**	12
29 Apr 65	● WONDERFUL WORLD *Columbia DB 7546*	**7**	9
2 Sep 65	JUST A LITTLE BIT BETTER *Columbia DB 7670*	**15**	9
23 Dec 65	● A MUST TO AVOID *Columbia DB 7791*	**6**	11
24 Mar 66	YOU WON'T BE LEAVING *Columbia DB 7861*	**20**	7
23 Jun 66	THIS DOOR SWINGS BOTH WAYS *Columbia DB 7947* ...	**18**	7
6 Oct 66	● NO MILK TODAY *Columbia DB 8012*	**7**	11
1 Dec 66	EAST WEST *Columbia DB 8076*	**37**	7
9 Feb 67	● THERE'S A KIND OF HUSH *Columbia DB 8123*	**7**	11
17 Jan 68	I CAN TAKE OR LEAVE YOUR LOVING *Columbia DB 8327*	**11**	7
1 May 68	SLEEPY JOE *Columbia DB 8404*	**12**	10
17 Jul 68	● SUNSHINE GIRL *Columbia DB 8446*	**8**	14
18 Dec 68	● SOMETHING'S HAPPENING *Columbia DB 8504*	**6**	15

Re-entries are listed as (re), (2re), (3re), etc which signifies that the hit re-entered the chart once, twice or three times, etc

23 Apr 69 ●	MY SENTIMENTAL FRIEND *Columbia DB 8563*	2	12
8 Nov 69	HERE COMES THE STAR *Columbia DB 8626*	33	9
7 Feb 70 ●	YEARS MAY COME, YEARS MAY GO (re)		
	Columbia DB 8656	7	12
23 May 70	BET YER LIFE I DO *RAK 102*	22	10
14 Nov 70	LADY BARBARA *RAK 106* 1	13	12

1 Peter Noone and Herman's Hermits

See also Peter NOONE

HERMES HOUSE BAND
Holland, male / female vocal / instrumental group (14 WEEKS)   pos/wks

15 Dec 01 ●	COUNTRY ROADS *EMI / Liberty CDHHB 001*	7	12
13 Apr 02	QUE SERA SERA *EMI / Liberty CDHHB 002*	53	1
28 Dec 02	LIVE IS LIFE *EMI / Liberty CDLIVE 001* 1	50	1+

1 Hermes House Band and DJ Otzi

HERNANDEZ *UK, male vocalist (3 WEEKS)*   pos/wks

15 Apr 89	ALL MY LOVE *Epic HER 1*	58	3

Patrick HERNANDEZ
Guadeloupe, male vocalist (14 WEEKS)   pos/wks

16 Jun 79 ●	BORN TO BE ALIVE *Gem GEM 4*	10	14

HERREYS *Sweden, male vocal group (3 WEEKS)*   pos/wks

26 May 84	DIGGI LOO-DIGGI LEY *Panther PAN 5*	46	3

Kristin HERSH *US, female vocalist (3 WEEKS)*   pos/wks

22 Jan 94	YOUR GHOST *4AD BAD 4001CD*	45	2
16 Apr 94	STRINGS *4AD BAD 4006CD*	60	1

Nick HEYWARD *UK, male vocalist (65 WEEKS)*   pos/wks

19 Mar 83	WHISTLE DOWN THE WIND *Arista HEY 1*	13	8
4 Jun 83	TAKE THAT SITUATION *Arista HEY 2*	11	10
24 Sep 83	BLUE HAT FOR A BLUE DAY *Arista HEY 3*	14	8
3 Dec 83	ON A SUNDAY *Arista HEY 4*	52	5
2 Jun 84	LOVE ALL DAY *Arista HEY 5*	31	6
3 Nov 84	WARNING SIGN (re) *Arista HEY 6*	25	9
8 Jun 85	LAURA *Arista HEY 8*	45	4
10 May 86	OVER THE WEEKEND *Arista HEY 9*	43	5
10 Sep 88	YOU'RE MY WORLD *Warner Bros. W 7758*	67	2
21 Aug 93	KITE *Epic 6594882*	44	2
16 Oct 93	HE DOESN'T LOVE YOU LIKE I DO *Epic 6597282*	58	2
30 Sep 95	THE WORLD *Epic 6623845*	47	2
13 Jan 96	ROLLERBLADE *Epic 6627912*	37	2

See also HAIRCUT 100

HI-FIVE *US, male vocal group (8 WEEKS)*   pos/wks

1 Jun 91	I LIKE THE WAY (THE KISSING GAME) *Jive JIVE 271* ▲	43	6
24 Oct 92	SHE'S PLAYING HARD TO GET *Jive JIVE 316*	55	2

HI-GATE *UK, male production duo – Julius (Judge Jules) O'Riordan and Paul Masterson (14 WEEKS)*   pos/wks

29 Jan 00 ●	PITCHIN' (IN EVERY DIRECTION) *Incentice CENT 3CD*	6	6
26 Aug 00	I CAN HEAR VOICES / CANED AND UNABLE		
	Incentive CENT 9 CDS	12	5
7 Apr 01	GONNA WORK IT OUT *Incentive CENT 20CDS*	25	3

See also YOMANDA; CANDY GIRLS; CLERGY; DOROTHY; SLEAZESISTERS; Paul MASTERSON presents SUSHI

HI GLOSS *US, disco aggregation (13 WEEKS)*   pos/wks

8 Aug 81	YOU'LL NEVER KNOW *Epic EPC A 1387*	12	13

HI-LUX *UK, male instrumental / production duo (3 WEEKS)*   pos/wks

18 Feb 95	FEEL IT *Cheeky CHEKCD 006*	41	2
2 Sep 95	NEVER FELT THIS WAY / FEEL IT (re-issue)		
	Champion CHAMPCD 319	58	1

HI POWER *Germany, male rap group (1 WEEK)*   pos/wks

1 Sep 90	CULT OF SNAP / SIMBA GROOVE *Rumour RUMAT 24*	73	1

HI-TEK featuring JONELL
US, male producer – Tony Cottrell (1 WEEK)   pos/wks

20 Oct 01	ROUND & ROUND *Rawkus RWK 3432*	73	1

HI-TEK 3 featuring YA KID K
Belgium, male / female vocal / instrumental group (10 WEEKS)   pos/wks

3 Feb 90	SPIN THAT WHEEL *Brothers Organisation BORG 1*	69	3
29 Sep 90	SPIN THAT WHEEL (TURTLES GET REAL) (re-issue)		
	Brothers Organisation BORG 16	15	7

See also TECHNOTRONIC

HI TENSION *UK, male vocal / instrumental group (23 WEEKS)*   pos/wks

6 May 78	HI TENSION *Island WIP 6422*	13	12
12 Aug 78 ●	BRITISH HUSTLE / PEACE ON EARTH *Island WIP 6446*	8	11

'Peace on Earth' credited with 'British Hustle' from 2 Sep 1978 to end of record's chart run

Al HIBBLER *US, male vocalist, d. 24 Apr 2001 (17 WEEKS)*   pos/wks

13 May 55 ●	UNCHAINED MELODY *Brunswick 05420*	2	17

Hinda HICKS *UK, female vocalist (15 WEEKS)*   pos/wks

7 Mar 98	IF YOU WANT ME *Island CID 689*	25	3
16 May 98	YOU THINK YOU OWN ME *Island CID 700*	19	4
15 Aug 98	I WANNA BE YOUR LADY *Island CID 709*	14	5
24 Oct 98	TRULY *Island CID 721*	31	2
14 Oct 00	MY REMEDY *Island CID 765*	61	1

Bertie HIGGINS *US, male vocalist (4 WEEKS)*   pos/wks

5 Jun 82	KEY LARGO *Epic EPC A 2168*	60	4

HIGH *UK, male vocal group (11 WEEKS)*   pos/wks

25 Aug 90	UP AND DOWN *London LON 272*	53	4
27 Oct 90	TAKE YOUR TIME *London LON 280*	56	2
12 Jan 91	BOX SET GO *London LONG 286*	28	3
6 Apr 91	MORE . . . *London LON 297*	67	2

HIGH CONTRAST
UK, male producer – Lincoln Barrett (1 WEEK)   pos/wks

1 Jun 02	GLOBAL LOVE *Hospital NHS 44CD*	68	1

HIGH FIDELITY *UK, male vocal / instrumental group (1 WEEK)*   pos/wks

25 Jul 98	LUV DUP *Plastique FAKE 03CDS*	70	1

HIGH NUMBERS
UK, male vocal / instrumental group (4 WEEKS)   pos/wks

5 Apr 80	I'M THE FACE *Back Door DOOR 4*	49	4

The High Numbers were an early version of The Who

HIGH SOCIETY *UK, male vocal / instrumental group (4 WEEKS)*   pos/wks

15 Nov 80	I NEVER GO OUT IN THE RAIN *Eagle ERS 002*	53	4

HIGHLY LIKELY *UK, male vocal / instrumental group (4 WEEKS)*   pos/wks

21 Apr 73	WHATEVER HAPPENED TO YOU ('LIKELY LADS' THEME)		
	BBC RESL 10	35	4

HIGHWAYMEN *US, male vocal group (18 WEEKS)*   pos/wks

7 Sep 61 ★	MICHAEL *HMV POP 910* ▲	1	14
7 Dec 61	THE GYPSY ROVER (re) *HMV POP 948*	41	4

HIJACK *UK, male rap group (3 WEEKS)*   pos/wks

6 Jan 90	THE BADMAN IS ROBBIN' *Rhyme Syndicate 655517 7*	56	3

UK No.1 ★   UK Top 10 ●   Still on chart +   UK million seller ◆   UK entry at No.1 ■   US No.1 ▲   **233**

Benny HILL
UK, male comedian / vocalist, d. 20 Apr 1992 (43 WEEKS) pos/wks

16 Feb 61	**GATHER IN THE MUSHROOMS** *Pye 7N 15327* 12	8
1 Jun 61	**TRANSISTOR RADIO** *Pye 7N 15359* 24	6
16 May 63	**HARVEST OF LOVE** *Pye 7N 15520* 20	8
13 Nov 71 ★	**ERNIE (THE FASTEST MILKMAN IN THE WEST)**	
	Columbia DB 8833 1	17
30 May 92	**ERNIE (THE FASTEST MILKMAN IN THE WEST)**	
	(re-issue) *EMI ERN 1* 29	4

Chris HILL
UK, male vocalist / DJ / producer (14 WEEKS) pos/wks

6 Dec 75 ●	**RENTA SANTA** *Philips 6006 491* 10	7
4 Dec 76 ●	**BIONIC SANTA** *Philips 6006 551* 10	7

Dan HILL
Canada, male vocalist (13 WEEKS) pos/wks

18 Feb 78	**SOMETIMES WHEN WE TOUCH (re)**	
	20th Century BTC 2355 13	13

Faith HILL
US, female vocalist (34 WEEKS) pos/wks

14 Nov 98	**THIS KISS** *Warner Brothers W463CD* 13	11
17 Apr 99	**LET ME LET GO** *Warner Bros. W473CD* 72	1
20 May 00	**BREATHE** *WEA WEA 520CD* 33	2
21 Apr 01	**THE WAY YOU LOVE ME** *Warner Brothers W51CD* 15	5
30 Jun 01 ●	**THERE YOU'LL BE** *Warner Brothers W 563CD* 3	11
13 Oct 01	**BREATHE (re-mix)** *Warner Brothers W 572CD* 36	2
26 Oct 02	**CRY** *Warner Brothers W 593CD* 25	2

Lauryn HILL
US, female vocalist (35 WEEKS) pos/wks

6 Sep 97	**THE SWEETEST THING** *Columbia 6649785* [1] 18	4
27 Dec 97	**ALL MY TIME** *World Entertainment OWECD 2* 57	1
3 Oct 98 ●	**DOO WOP (THAT THING)** *Ruffhouse 6665152* ▲ 3	7
27 Feb 99 ●	**EX-FACTOR (re)** *Columbia / Ruffhouse 6669452* 4	10
10 Jul 99	**EVERYTHING IS EVERYTHING**	
	Columbia / Ruffhouse 6675742 19	6
11 Dec 99	**TURN YOUR LIGHTS DOWN LOW**	
	Columbia 6684362 [2] 15	7

[1] Refugee Camp Allstars featuring Lauryn Hill [2] Bob Marley featuring Lauryn Hill

See also FUGEES

Lonnie HILL
US, male vocalist (4 WEEKS) pos/wks

22 Mar 86	**GALVESTON BAY** *10 TEN 111* 51	4

Roni HILL
US, female vocalist (4 WEEKS) pos/wks

7 May 77	**YOU KEEP ME HANGIN' ON – STOP IN THE**	
	NAME OF LOVE (MEDLEY) *Creole CR 138* 36	4

Vince HILL (354) Top 500
*Easy listening balladeer, b. 16 Apr 1937, Coventry, UK. Member of critically
acclaimed Raindrops (with Jackie Lee and composer Johnny Worth) and
regularly heard on 'live' radio before starting 60s chart run (91 WKS)* pos/wks

7 Jun 62	**THE RIVER'S RUN DRY (re)** *Piccadilly 7N 35043* 41	2
6 Jan 66	**TAKE ME TO YOUR HEART AGAIN** *Columbia DB 7781* 13	11
17 Mar 66	**HEARTACHES** *Columbia DB 7852* 28	5
2 Jun 66	**MERCI CHERI** *Columbia DB 7924* 36	6
9 Feb 67 ●	**EDELWEISS** *Columbia DB 8127* 2	17
11 May 67	**ROSES OF PICARDY** *Columbia DB 8185* 13	11
27 Sep 67	**LOVE LETTERS IN THE SAND** *Columbia DB 8268* 23	9
26 Jun 68	**THE IMPORTANCE OF YOUR LOVE**	
	Columbia DB 8414 32	12
12 Feb 69	**DOESN'T ANYBODY KNOW MY NAME?**	
	Columbia DB 8515 50	1
25 Oct 69	**LITTLE BLUE BIRD** *Columbia DB 8616* 42	1
25 Sep 71	**LOOK AROUND (AND YOU'LL FIND ME THERE)**	
	Columbia DB 8804 12	16

HILLMAN MINX
UK / France, male / female vocal / instrumental group (1 WEEK) pos/wks

5 Sep 98	**I'VE HAD ENOUGH** *Mercury MERCD 509* 72	1

HILLTOPPERS
US, male vocal group (30 WEEKS) pos/wks

27 Jan 56 ●	**ONLY YOU (AND YOU ALONE) (re)** *London HLD 8221* 3	23
14 Sep 56	**TRYIN'** *London HLD 8298* 30	1
5 Apr 57	**MARIANNE (re)** *London HLD 8381* 20	6

Ronnie HILTON (188) Top 500
*Favourite 1950s balladeer, b. Adrian Hill,
26 Jan 1926, Hull, UK, d. 21 Feb 2001. Despite the rise of rock 'n' roll, he
amassed a formidable selection of best-sellers, albeit mainly with cover
versions (the customary UK practice in the 1950s) (136 WEEKS)* pos/wks

26 Nov 54 ●	**I STILL BELIEVE** *HMV B 10785* 3	14
10 Dec 54	**VENI VIDI VICI** *HMV B 10785* 12	8
11 Mar 55 ●	**A BLOSSOM FELL** *HMV B 10808* 10	5
26 Aug 55	**STARS SHINE IN YOUR EYES** *HMV B 10901* 13	7
11 Nov 55	**THE YELLOW ROSE OF TEXAS** *HMV B 10924* 15	2
10 Feb 56	**YOUNG AND FOOLISH (2re)** *HMV POP 154* 17	3
20 Apr 56 ★	**NO OTHER LOVE** *HMV POP 198* 1	14
29 Jun 56 ●	**WHO ARE WE** *HMV POP 221* 6	12
21 Sep 56	**A WOMAN IN LOVE** *HMV POP 248* 30	1
9 Nov 56	**TWO DIFFERENT WORLDS** *HMV POP 274* 13	13
24 May 57 ●	**AROUND THE WORLD** *HMV POP 338* 4	18
2 Aug 57	**WONDERFUL! WONDERFUL!** *HMV POP 364* 27	2
21 Feb 58	**MAGIC MOMENTS** *HMV POP 446* 22	2
18 Apr 58	**I MAY NEVER PASS THIS WAY AGAIN (2re)**	
	HMV POP 468 [1] 27	3
9 Jan 59	**THE WORLD OUTSIDE** *HMV POP 559* [1] 18	6
21 Aug 59	**THE WONDER OF YOU** *HMV POP 638* 22	3
21 May 64	**DON'T LET THE RAIN COME DOWN** *HMV POP 1291* 21	10
11 Feb 65	**A WINDMILL IN OLD AMSTERDAM** *HMV POP 1378* 23	13

[1] Ronnie Hilton with the Michael Sammes Singers

HINDSIGHT
UK, male vocal / instrumental group (3 WEEKS) pos/wks

5 Sep 87	**LOWDOWN** *Circa YR 5* 62	3

Deni HINES
Australia, female vocalist (6 WEEKS) pos/wks

14 Jun 97	**IT'S ALRIGHT** *Mushroom D 1593* 35	2
20 Sep 97	**I LIKE THE WAY** *Mushroom MUSH 7CDX* 37	2
28 Feb 98	**DELICIOUS** *Mushroom MUSH 20CD* [1] 52	1
23 May 98	**JOY** *Mushroom MUSH 30CDS* 47	1

[1] Deni Hines featuring Don-E

Gregory HINES – *See Luther VANDROSS*

HIPSWAY
UK, male vocal / instrumental group (21 WEEKS) pos/wks

13 Jul 85	**THE BROKEN YEARS** *Mercury MER 193* 72	3
14 Sep 85	**ASK THE LORD** *Mercury MER 195* 72	1
22 Feb 86	**THE HONEYTHIEF** *Mercury MER 212* 17	9
10 May 86	**ASK THE LORD (re-recording)** *Mercury LORD 1* 50	5
20 Sep 86	**LONG WHITE CAR** *Mercury MER 230* 55	2
1 Apr 89	**YOUR LOVE** *Mercury MER 279* 66	1

HISTORY featuring Q-TEE
UK, male production duo and female rapper (5 WEEKS) pos/wks

21 Apr 90	**AFRIKA** *SBK SBK 7008* 42	5

Carol HITCHCOCK
Australia, female vocalist (5 WEEKS) pos/wks

30 May 87	**GET READY** *A&M AM 391* 56	5

HITHOUSE
Holland, male producer – Peter Slaghuis (13 WEEKS) pos/wks

5 Nov 88	**JACK TO THE SOUND OF THE UNDERGROUND**	
	Supreme SUPE 137 14	12
19 Aug 89	**MOVE YOUR FEET TO THE RHYTHM OF THE BEAT**	
	Supreme SUPE 149 69	1

HITMAN HOWIE TEE – *See REAL ROXANNE*

The HIVES
Sweden, male vocal / instrumental group (5 WEEKS) pos/wks

23 Feb 02	**HATE TO SAY I TOLD YOU SO** *Burning Heart BHR 1059* 23	3
18 May 02	**MAIN OFFENDER** *Poptones MC 5076SCD* 24	2

Helen HOBSON – See Cliff RICHARD

Edmund HOCKRIDGE *Canada, male vocalist (18 WEEKS)*
pos/wks

17 Feb 56 ●	YOUNG AND FOOLISH (2re) *Nixa N 15039*	**10**	9
11 May 56	NO OTHER LOVE (2re) *Nixa N 15048*	**24**	4
31 Aug 56	BY THE FOUNTAINS OF ROME *Pye Nixa N 15063*	**17**	5

Eddie HODGES *US, male vocalist (10 WEEKS)*
pos/wks

28 Sep 61	I'M GONNA KNOCK ON YOUR DOOR *London HLA 9369*	**37**	6
9 Aug 62	(GIRLS GIRLS GIRLS) MADE TO LOVE *London HLA 9576*	**37**	4

Roger HODGSON – See SUPERTRAMP

Mani HOFFMAN – See SUPERMEN LOVERS featuring Mani HOFFMAN

Susanna HOFFS *US, female vocalist (8 WEEKS)*
pos/wks

2 Mar 91	MY SIDE OF THE BED *Columbia 6565547*	**44**	4
11 May 91	UNCONDITIONAL LOVE *Columbia 6567827*	**65**	2
19 Oct 96	ALL I WANT *London LONCD 387*	**32**	2

See also BANGLES

Hulk HOGAN with GREEN JELLY *US, male wrestler / vocalist –*
Terry Bollea, and US, male vocal / instrumental group (4 WEEKS)
pos/wks

25 Dec 93	I'M THE LEADER OF THE GANG *Arista 74321174892*	**25**	4

HOGGBOY *UK, male vocal / instrumental group (1 WEEK)*
pos/wks

27 Apr 02	SHOULDN'T LET THE SIDE DOWN *04L SOB4 CDA*	**74**	1

Demi HOLBORN *UK, female vocalist (2 WEEKS)*
pos/wks

27 Jul 02	I'D LIKE TO TEACH THE WORLD TO SING *Universal Classics & Jazz 0190982*	**27**	2

HOLE *US, female / male vocal / instrumental group (15 WEEKS)*
pos/wks

17 Apr 93	BEAUTIFUL SON *City Slang EFA 0491603*	**54**	1
9 Apr 94	MISS WORLD *City Slang EFA 049362*	**64**	1
15 Apr 95	DOLL PARTS *Geffen GFSTD 91*	**16**	3
29 Jul 95	VIOLET *Geffen GFSTD 94*	**17**	2
12 Sep 98	CELEBRITY SKIN *Geffen GFSTD 22345*	**19**	4
30 Jan 99	MALIBU *Geffen GFSTD 22369*	**22**	2
10 Jul 99	AWFUL *Geffen INTDE 97098*	**42**	2

HOLE IN ONE *Holland, male DJ / producer – Marcel Hol (2 WEEKS)*
pos/wks

15 Feb 97	LIFE'S TOO SHORT *Manifesto FESCD 21*	**36**	2

Jools HOLLAND and JAMIROQUAI
UK, male instrumentalist – piano and male vocalist (3 WEEKS)
pos/wks

24 Feb 01	I'M IN THE MOOD FOR LOVE *Warner Esp WSMS 001CD*	**29**	3

See also SQUEEZE; JAMIROQUAI

HOLLAND-DOZIER featuring Lamont DOZIER
US, male vocal duo (5 WEEKS)
pos/wks

28 Oct 72	WHY CAN'T WE BE LOVERS *Invictus INV 525*	**29**	5

Jennifer HOLLIDAY *US, female vocalist (6 WEEKS)*
pos/wks

4 Sep 82	AND I'M TELLING YOU I'M NOT GOING *Geffen GEF A 2644*	**32**	6

Michael HOLLIDAY
UK, male vocalist – Norman Milne, d. 29 Oct 1963 (66 WEEKS)
pos/wks

30 Mar 56	NOTHIN' TO DO (re) *Columbia DB 3746*	**20**	3
15 Jun 56	THE GAL WITH THE YALLER SHOES *Columbia DB 3783*	**13**	11
5 Oct 56	TEN THOUSAND MILES *Columbia DB 3813*	**24**	3
17 Jan 58 ★	THE STORY OF MY LIFE *Columbia DB 4058*	**1**	15
14 Mar 58	IN LOVE *Columbia DB 4087*	**26**	3
16 May 58 ●	STAIRWAY OF LOVE *Columbia DB 4121*	**3**	13
11 Jul 58	I'LL ALWAYS BE IN LOVE WITH YOU *Columbia DB 4155*	**27**	1
1 Jan 60 ★	STARRY EYED *Columbia DB 4378* [1]	**1**	13

14 Apr 60	SKYLARK *Columbia DB 4437*	**39**	3
1 Sep 60	LITTLE BOY LOST *Columbia DB 4475*	**50**	1

[1] Michael Holliday with the Michael Sammes Singers

When 'Hot Diggity (Dog Ziggity Boom) / Gal With the Yaller Shoes' re-entered the chart on 3 Aug 1956, 'Hot Diggity (Dog Ziggity Boom)' was listed by itself on 3 Aug and 10 Aug. Both sides were listed on 17 Aug – 'Gal With the Yaller Shoes' peaking at No.25

HOLLIES [28] [Top 500] *Distinctive, influential and well-respected Manchester group: Allan Clarke (v), Graham Nash (g), Tony Hicks (g), Eric Haydock (b), Bobby Elliott (d). They were among the most regular chart visitors of the 1960s, and their No.1s span 23 years (318 WEEKS)*
pos/wks

30 May 63	(AIN'T THAT) JUST LIKE ME *Parlophone R 5030*	**25**	10
29 Aug 63	SEARCHIN' *Parlophone R 5052*	**12**	14
21 Nov 63 ●	STAY *Parlophone R 5077*	**8**	16
27 Feb 64 ●	JUST ONE LOOK *Parlophone R 5104*	**2**	13
21 May 64 ●	HERE I GO AGAIN *Parlophone R 5137*	**4**	12
17 Sep 64 ●	WE'RE THROUGH *Parlophone R 5178*	**7**	11
28 Jan 65	YES I WILL *Parlophone R 5232*	**9**	13
27 May 65 ★	I'M ALIVE *Parlophone R 5287*	**1**	14
2 Sep 65 ●	LOOK THROUGH ANY WINDOW *Parlophone R 5322*	**4**	11
9 Dec 65	IF I NEEDED SOMEONE *Parlophone R 5392*	**20**	9
24 Feb 66 ●	I CAN'T LET GO *Parlophone R 5409*	**2**	10
23 Jun 66 ●	BUS STOP *Parlophone R 5469*	**5**	9
13 Oct 66 ●	STOP STOP STOP *Parlophone R 5508*	**2**	12
16 Feb 67 ●	ON A CAROUSEL *Parlophone R 5562*	**4**	11
1 Jun 67 ●	CARRIE-ANNE *Parlophone R 5602*	**3**	11
27 Sep 67	KING MIDAS IN REVERSE *Parlophone R 5637*	**18**	8
27 Mar 68 ●	JENNIFER ECCLES *Parlophone R 5680*	**7**	11
2 Oct 68	LISTEN TO ME *Parlophone R 5733*	**11**	11
5 Mar 69 ●	SORRY SUZANNE *Parlophone R 5765*	**3**	12
4 Oct 69 ●	HE AIN'T HEAVY, HE'S MY BROTHER *Parlophone R 5806*	**3**	15
18 Apr 70 ●	I CAN'T TELL THE BOTTOM FROM THE TOP *Parlophone R 5837*	**7**	10
3 Oct 70	GASOLINE ALLEY BRED *Parlophone R 5862*	**14**	7
22 May 71	HEY WILLY *Parlophone R 5905*	**22**	7
26 Feb 72	THE BABY *Polydor 2058 199*	**26**	6
2 Sep 72	LONG COOL WOMAN IN A BLACK DRESS *Parlophone R 5939*	**32**	8
13 Oct 73	THE DAY THAT CURLY BILLY SHOT DOWN CRAZY SAM MCGHEE *Polydor 2058 403*	**24**	6
9 Feb 74 ●	THE AIR THAT I BREATHE *Polydor 2058 435*	**2**	13
14 Jun 80	SOLDIER'S SONG *Polydor 2059 246*	**58**	3
29 Aug 81	HOLLIEDAZE (MEDLEY) *EMI 5229*	**28**	7
3 Sep 88 ★	HE AIN'T HEAVY, HE'S MY BROTHER (re-issue) *EMI EM 74*	**1**	11
3 Dec 88	THE AIR THAT I BREATHE (re-issue) *EMI EM 80*	**60**	5
20 Mar 93	THE WOMAN I LOVE *EMI CDEM 264*	**42**	2

The 1972 hit 'The Baby' featured Swedish lead vocalist Mikael Rickfors

Loleatta HOLLOWAY *US, female vocalist (21 WEEKS)*
pos/wks

31 Aug 91	GOOD VIBRATIONS *Interscope A 8764* [1] ▲	**14**	7
18 Jan 92	TAKE ME AWAY *PWL Continental PWL 210* [2]	**25**	1
26 Mar 94	STAND UP *Six6 SIXCD 111*	**68**	1
1 Apr 95	KEEP THE FIRE BURNIN' *Columbia 6611552* [3]	**49**	1
11 Apr 98	SHOUT TO THE TOP *JBO JNR 5001573* [4]	**23**	2
20 Feb 99	(YOU GOT ME) BURNING UP *Wonderboy WBOYD 013* [5]	**14**	4
25 Nov 00	DREAMIN' *Defected DFECT 22CDS*	**59**	1

[1] Marky Mark and the Funky Bunch featuring Loleatta Holloway [2] Cappella featuring Loleatta Holloway [3] Dan Hartman starring Loleatta Holloway [4] Fire Island featuring Loleatta Holloway [5] Cevin Fisher / Loleatta Holloway

HOLLOWAY & CO *UK, male producer – Nicky Holloway (1 WEEK)*
pos/wks

21 Aug 99	I'LL DO ANYTHING – TO MAKE YOU MINE *INCredible INCS 2CD*	**58**	1

Buddy HOLLY [100] [Top 500]
Highly respected and exceptionally influential singer / songwriter, b. Charles Hardin Holley, 7 Sep 1936, Texas, US, d. 3 Feb 1959 (aka 'the day the music died'). Despite a relatively brief career, his records and songs are still frequently heard around the globe (190 WEEKS)
pos/wks

6 Dec 57 ●	PEGGY SUE *Coral Q 72293*	**6**	17
14 Mar 58	LISTEN TO ME *Coral Q 72288*	**16**	2

UK No.1 ★ UK Top 10   Still on chart ✛ UK million seller ◆ UK entry at No.1 ■ US No.1 ▲

20 Jun 58 ●	RAVE ON *Coral Q 72325*	5	14
29 Aug 58	EARLY IN THE MORNING *Coral Q 72333*	17	4
16 Jan 59	HEARTBEAT *Coral Q 72346*	30	1
27 Feb 59 ★	IT DOESN'T MATTER ANYMORE *Coral Q 72360*	1	21
31 Jul 59	MIDNIGHT SHIFT *Brunswick 05800*	26	3
11 Sep 59	PEGGY SUE GOT MARRIED *Coral Q 72376*	13	10
28 Apr 60	HEARTBEAT (re-issue) *Coral Q 72392*	30	3
26 May 60	TRUE LOVE WAYS *Coral Q 72397*	25	7
20 Oct 60	LEARNING THE GAME *Coral Q 72411*	36	3
26 Jan 61	WHAT TO DO *Coral Q 72419*	34	6
6 Jul 61	BABY I DON'T CARE / VALLEY OF TEARS *Coral Q 72432*	12	14
15 Mar 62	LISTEN TO ME (re-issue) *Coral Q 72449*	48	1
13 Sep 62	REMINISCING *Coral Q 72455*	17	11
14 Mar 63 ●	BROWN-EYED HANDSOME MAN *Coral Q 72459*	3	17
6 Jun 63 ●	BO DIDDLEY *Coral Q 72463*	4	12
5 Sep 63 ●	WISHING *Coral Q 72466*	10	11
19 Dec 63	WHAT TO DO (re-recording) *Coral Q 72469*	27	8
14 May 64	YOU'VE GOT LOVE *Coral Q 72472* [1]	40	6
10 Sep 64	LOVE'S MADE A FOOL OF YOU *Coral Q 72475*	39	6
3 Apr 68	PEGGY SUE / RAVE ON (re-issue) *MCA MU 1012*	32	9
10 Dec 88	TRUE LOVE WAYS (re-issue) *MCA MCA 1302*	65	4

[1] Buddy Holly and The Crickets

Buddy Holly's version of 'Love's Made a Fool of You' is not the same version as the Crickets' hit of 1959, on which Holly did not appear. 'Valley of Tears' was not listed together with 'Baby I Don't Care' until 13 Jul 1961

HOLLY and the IVYS
UK, male / female vocal / instrumental group (4 WEEKS) pos/wks

19 Dec 81	CHRISTMAS ON 45 *Decca SANTA 1*	40	4

HOLLYWOOD ARGYLES *US, male vocal group (10 WEEKS)* pos/wks

21 Jul 60	ALLEY-OOP *London HLU 9146* ▲	24	10

HOLLYWOOD BEYOND *UK, male group (14 WEEKS)* pos/wks

12 Jul 86 ●	WHAT'S THE COLOUR OF MONEY? *WEA YZ 76*	7	10
20 Sep 86	NO MORE TEARS *WEA YZ 81*	47	4

Eddie HOLMAN *US, male vocalist (13 WEEKS)* pos/wks

19 Oct 74 ●	(HEY THERE) LONELY GIRL *ABC 4012*	4	13

Dave HOLMES *UK, male producer (1 WEEK)* pos/wks

26 May 01	DEVOTION *Tidy Trax TIDY 154CD*	66	1

David HOLMES *UK, male producer (8 WEEKS)* pos/wks

6 Apr 96	GONE *Go! Discs GODCD 140*	75	1
23 Aug 97	GRITTY SHAKER *Go.Beat GOBCD 2*	53	1
10 Jan 98	DON'T DIE JUST YET *Go.Beat GOLCD 6*	33	3
4 Apr 98	MY MATE PAUL *Go.Beat GOBCD 8*	39	2
19 Aug 00	69 POLICE *Go.Beat / Polydor GOBCD 30*	53	1

Rupert HOLMES *US, male vocalist (14 WEEKS)* pos/wks

12 Jan 80	ESCAPE (THE PINA COLADA SONG) *Infinity INF 120* ▲	23	7
22 Mar 80	HIM *MCA 565*	31	7

Adele HOLNESS – *See Ben SHAW featuring Adele HOLNESS*

John HOLT *Jamaica, male vocalist (14 WEEKS)* pos/wks

14 Dec 74 ●	HELP ME MAKE IT THROUGH THE NIGHT *Trojan TR 7909*	6	14

Nichola HOLT *UK, female vocalist (1 WEEK)* pos/wks

21 Oct 00	THE GAME *RCA 74321798992*	72	1

A HOMEBOY, a HIPPIE and a FUNKI DREDD
UK, male vocal / instrumental group (9 WEEKS) pos/wks

13 Oct 90	TOTAL CONFUSION *Tam Tam 7TTT 031*	56	3
29 Dec 90	FREEDOM *Tam Tam 7TTT 039*	68	4
8 Jan 94	HERE WE GO AGAIN *Polydor PZCD 302*	57	2

HONDY *Italy, male / female production / vocal group (2 WEEKS)* pos/wks

12 Apr 97	HONDY (NO ACCESS) *Manifesto FESCD 20*	26	2

HONEYBUS *UK, male vocal / instrumental group (12 WEEKS)* pos/wks

20 Mar 68 ●	I CAN'T LET MAGGIE GO *Deram DM 182*	8	12

HONEYCOMBS *UK, male / female vocal / instrumental group – lead vocal Dennis D'Ell (Dalziel) (39 WEEKS)* pos/wks

23 Jul 64 ★	HAVE I THE RIGHT *Pye 7N 15664*	1	15
22 Oct 64	IS IT BECAUSE *Pye 7N 15705*	38	6
29 Apr 65	SOMETHING BETTER BEGINNING *Pye 7N 15827*	39	4
5 Aug 65	THAT'S THE WAY *Pye 7N 15890*	12	14

HONEYCRACK *UK, male vocal / instrumental group (9 WEEKS)* pos/wks

4 Nov 95	SITTING AT HOME *Epic 6625382*	42	2
24 Feb 96	GO AWAY *Epic 6628642*	41	2
11 May 96	KING OF MISERY *Epic 6631472*	32	2
20 Jul 96	SITTING AT HOME (re-issue) *Epic 6635032*	32	2
16 Nov 96	ANYWAY *EG EGO 52A*	67	1

HONEYDRIPPERS
UK / US, male vocal / instrumental group (3 WEEKS) pos/wks

2 Feb 85	SEA OF LOVE *Es Paranza YZ 33*	56	3

See also Robert PLANT

HONEYZ *UK / France, female vocal trio (57 WEEKS)* pos/wks

5 Sep 98 ●	FINALLY FOUND *1st Avenue / Mercury HNZCD 1*	4	12
19 Dec 98 ●	END OF THE LINE (re) *1st Avenue / Mercury HNZCD 2*	5	14
24 Apr 99 ●	LOVE OF A LIFETIME *1st Avenue / Mercury HNZCD 3*	9	9
23 Oct 99 ●	NEVER LET YOU DOWN *1st Avenue / Mercury HNZCD 4*	7	6
11 Mar 00 ●	WON'T TAKE IT LYING DOWN (re) *1st Avenue / Mercury HNZCD 5*	7	8
28 Oct 00	NOT EVEN GONNA TRIP (2re) *1st Avenue / Mercury HNZCD 7*	24	5
18 Aug 01	I DON'T KNOW *1st Avenue / Mercury HNZCD 8*	28	3

HONKY *UK, male vocal / instrumental group (5 WEEKS)* pos/wks

28 May 77	JOIN THE PARTY *Creole CR 137*	28	5

HONKY *UK, male vocal / instrumental group (5 WEEKS)* pos/wks

30 Oct 93	THE HONKY DOODLE DAY EP *ZTT ZANG 45CD*	61	1
19 Feb 94	THE WHISTLER *ZTT ZANG 48CD*	41	2
20 Apr 96	HIP HOP DON'T YA DROP *Higher Ground HIGHS 1CD*	70	1
10 Aug 96	WHAT'S GOIN DOWN *Higher Ground HIGHS 2CD*	49	1

Tracks on The Honky Doodle Day EP: KKK (Boom Boom Tra La La La) / Honky Doodle Dub / Chains

HOOBASTANK
US, male vocal / instrumental group (2 WEEKS) pos/wks

13 Apr 02	CRAWLING IN THE DARK *Mercury 5828622*	47	2

Frank HOOKER and POSITIVE PEOPLE
US, male / female vocal / instrumental group (4 WEEKS) pos/wks

5 Jul 80	THIS FEELIN' *DJM DJS 10947*	48	4

John Lee HOOKER
US, male vocalist, d. 21 Jun 2001 (23 WEEKS) pos/wks

11 Jun 64	DIMPLES *Stateside SS 297*	23	10
24 Oct 92	BOOM BOOM *Pointblank POB 3*	16	5
16 Jan 93	BOOGIE AT RUSSIAN HILL *Pointblank POBDX 4*	53	2
15 May 93	GLORIA *Exile VANCD 11* [1]	31	3
11 Feb 95	CHILL OUT (THINGS GONNA CHANGE) *Pointblank POBD 10*	45	2
20 Apr 96	BABY LEE *Silvertone ORECD 81* [2]	65	1

[1] Van Morrison and John Lee Hooker [2] John Lee Hooker with Robert Cray

Re-entries are listed as (re), (2re), (3re), etc which signifies that the hit re-entered the chart once, twice or three times, etc

HOOTERS US, male vocal / instrumental group (9 WEEKS)

		pos/wks
21 Nov 87	SATELLITE CBS 651168 7	22 9

HOOTIE & THE BLOWFISH
US, male vocal / instrumental group (6 WEEKS)

		pos/wks
25 Feb 95	HOLD MY HAND Atlantic A 7230CD	50 3
27 May 95	LET HER CRY Atlantic A 7188CD	75 1
4 May 96	OLD MAN AND ME (WHEN I GET TO HEAVEN) Atlantic A 5513CD	57 1
7 Nov 98	I WILL WAIT Atlantic AT 0048CD	57 1

HOPE A.D. UK, male producer – David Hope (1 WEEK)

		pos/wks
4 Jun 94	TREE FROG Sun-Up SUN 003CD	73 1

See also MIND OF KANE

Mary HOPKIN (488 Top 500) Propelled to stardom from TV talent show 'Opportunity Knocks' witnessed by Twiggy who recommended the Welsh singer (b. 3 May 1950) to Paul McCartney. The Beatle produced 'Those Were the Days', originally a Russian folk song, which ironically knocked 'Hey Jude' from the No.1 spot (74 WEEKS)

		pos/wks
4 Sep 68 ★	THOSE WERE THE DAYS Apple 2........................	1 21
2 Apr 69 ●	GOODBYE Apple 10	2 14
31 Jan 70 ●	TEMMA HARBOUR Apple 22	6 11
28 Mar 70 ●	KNOCK KNOCK WHO'S THERE Apple 26	2 14
31 Oct 70	THINK ABOUT YOUR CHILDREN (re) Apple 30......	19 9
31 Jul 71	LET MY NAME BE SORROW Apple 34	46 1
20 Mar 76	IF YOU LOVE ME (I WON'T CARE) Good Earth GD 2....	32 4

Anthony HOPKINS UK, male actor / vocalist (1 WEEK)

		pos/wks
27 Dec 86	DISTANT STAR Juice AA 5	75 1

Nick HORNBY – See PRETENDERS

Bruce HORNSBY and the RANGE
US, male vocal / instrumental group (15 WEEKS)

		pos/wks
2 Aug 86	THE WAY IT IS RCA PB 49805 ▲	15 10
25 Apr 87	MANDOLIN RAIN RCA PB 49769	70 1
28 May 88	THE VALLEY ROAD RCA PB 49561	44 4

HORNY UNITED – See BONEY M

HORSE UK, female / male vocal / instrumental group (10 WEEKS)

		pos/wks
24 Nov 90	CAREFUL Capitol CL 587	52 3
21 Aug 93	SHAKE THIS MOUNTAIN Oxygen GASPD 7	52 1
23 Oct 93	GOD'S HOME MOVIE Oxygen GASXD 10	56 1
15 Jan 94	CELEBRATE Oxygen GASPD 11	49 2
5 Apr 97	CAREFUL (re-mix) Stress CDSTRX 79	44 2

Johnny HORTON US, male vocalist, d. 5 Nov 1960 (15 WEEKS)

		pos/wks
26 Jun 59	THE BATTLE OF NEW ORLEANS Philips PB 932 ▲	16 4
19 Jan 61	NORTH TO ALASKA Philips PB 1062	23 11

HOT BLOOD France, male instrumental group (5 WEEKS)

		pos/wks
9 Oct 76	SOUL DRACULA Creole CR 132	32 5

HOT BUTTER US, production duo – Bill and Steve Jerome featuring Stan Free (19 WEEKS)

		pos/wks
22 Jul 72 ●	POPCORN (re) Pye International 7N 25583................	5 19

HOT CHOCOLATE (36 Top 500) London-based band who were chart regulars throughout the 1970s and 1980s. Group founders were West Indian-born Errol Brown (v) and Tony Wilson (b/v). The act had at least one hit every year between 1970 and 1984 and 'You Sexy Thing' made the Top 10 in three decades: 70s, 80s and 90s (283 WEEKS)

		pos/wks
15 Aug 70 ●	LOVE IS LIFE RAK 103	6 12
6 Mar 71	YOU COULD HAVE BEEN A LADY RAK 110.............	22 9
28 Aug 71 ●	I BELIEVE (IN LOVE) RAK 118	8 11
28 Oct 72	YOU'LL ALWAYS BE A FRIEND RAK 139	23 8
14 Apr 73 ●	BROTHER LOUIE RAK 149	7 10
18 Aug 73	RUMOURS RAK 157	44 3
16 Mar 74 ●	EMMA RAK 168	3 10
30 Nov 74	CHERI BABE RAK 188	31 9
24 May 75	DISCO QUEEN RAK 202	11 7
9 Aug 75 ●	A CHILD'S PRAYER RAK 212	7 10
8 Nov 75 ●	YOU SEXY THING RAK 221	2 12
20 Mar 76	DON'T STOP IT NOW RAK 230	11 8
26 Jun 76	MAN TO MAN RAK 238	14 8
21 Aug 76	HEAVEN IS IN THE BACK SEAT OF MY CADILLAC RAK 240	25 8
18 Jun 77 ★	SO YOU WIN AGAIN RAK 259	1 11
26 Nov 77 ●	PUT YOUR LOVE IN ME RAK 266	10 9
4 Mar 78	EVERY 1'S A WINNER RAK 270	12 11
2 Dec 78	I'LL PUT YOU TOGETHER AGAIN (FROM DEAR ANYONE) RAK 286	13 11
19 May 79	MINDLESS BOOGIE RAK 292	46 5
28 Jul 79	GOING THROUGH THE MOTIONS RAK 296	53 4
3 May 80 ●	NO DOUBT ABOUT IT RAK 310	2 11
19 Jul 80	ARE YOU GETTING ENOUGH OF WHAT MAKES YOU HAPPY RAK 318	17 7
13 Dec 80	LOVE ME TO SLEEP RAK 324	50 5
30 May 81	YOU'LL NEVER BE SO WRONG RAK 331	52 4
17 Apr 82 ●	GIRL CRAZY RAK 341	7 11
10 Jul 82 ●	IT STARTED WITH A KISS RAK 344	5 12
25 Sep 82	CHANCES RAK 350	32 5
7 May 83	WHAT KINDA BOY YOU LOOKING FOR (GIRL) RAK 357	10 9
17 Sep 83	TEARS ON THE TELEPHONE RAK 363	37 5
4 Feb 84	I GAVE YOU MY HEART (DIDN'T I) RAK 369	13 10
17 Jan 87 ●	YOU SEXY THING (re-mix) EMI 5592	10 10
4 Apr 87	EVERY 1'S A WINNER (re-mix) EMI 5607	69 2
6 Mar 93	IT STARTED WITH A KISS (re-issue) EMI CDEMCTS 7	31 5
22 Nov 97	YOU SEXY THING (re-issue) EMI CDHOT 100	6 8
14 Feb 98	IT STARTED WITH A KISS (2nd re-issue) EMI CDHOT 101 [1]	18 3

[1] Hot Chocolate featuring Errol Brown

HOT GOSSIP – See Sarah BRIGHTMAN

HOT HOUSE
UK, male / female vocal / instrumental group (3 WEEKS)

		pos/wks
14 Feb 87	DON'T COME TO STAY Deconstruction CHEZ 1	74 1
24 Sep 88	DON'T COME TO STAY (re-issue) Deconstruction PB 42233......	70 2

HOT 'N' JUICY – See MOUSSE T

HOT RODS – See EDDIE and the HOT RODS

HOT STREAK US, male vocal / instrumental group (8 WEEKS)

		pos/wks
10 Sep 83	BODY WORK Polydor POSP 642..................	19 8

HOTHOUSE FLOWERS
Ireland, male vocal / instrumental group (36 WEEKS)

		pos/wks
14 May 88	DON'T GO London LON 174	11 8
23 Jul 88	I'M SORRY London LON 187	53 3
12 May 90	GIVE IT UP London LON 258	30 5
28 Jul 90	I CAN SEE CLEARLY NOW London LON 269	23 7
20 Oct 90	MOVIES London LON 276	68 2
13 Feb 93	EMOTIONAL TIME London LONCD 335	38 4
8 May 93	ONE TONGUE London LOCDP 340	45 3
19 Jun 93	ISN'T IT AMAZING London LOCDP 343	46 2
27 Nov 93	THIS IS IT (YOUR SOUL) London LONCD 346	67 1
16 May 98	YOU CAN LOVE ME NOW London LONCD 410	65 1

HOTLEGS UK, male vocal / instrumental group (14 WEEKS)

		pos/wks
4 Jul 70 ●	NEANDERTHAL MAN Fontana 6007 019................	2 14

HOTSHOTS UK, male vocal group (15 WEEKS)

		pos/wks
2 Jun 73 ●	SNOOPY VS THE RED BARON Mooncrest MOON 5	4 15

Steven HOUGHTON UK, male actor / vocalist (22 WEEKS)

			pos/wks
29 Nov 97 ●	WIND BENEATH MY WINGS *RCA 74321529272*	3	15
7 Mar 98	TRULY (re) *RCA 74321558552*	23	7

HOUSE – See A HOUSE

HOUSE ENGINEERS UK, male vocal / instrumental duo (2 WKS) pos/wks

5 Dec 87	GHOST HOUSE *Syncopate SY 8*	69	2

HOUSE OF GLASS
Italy, male production duo – Gianni Bini and Paolo Martini (1 WEEK) pos/wks

14 Apr 01	DISCO DOWN *Azuli AZNY 138*	72	1

See also ECLIPSE; BINI & MARTINI; GOODFELLAS featuring Lisa MILLETT

HOUSE OF LOVE UK, male vocal / instrumental group (21 WKS) pos/wks

22 Apr 89	NEVER *Fontana HOL 1*	41	2
18 Nov 89	I DON'T KNOW WHY I LOVE YOU *Fontana HOL 2*	41	3
3 Feb 90	SHINE ON *Fontana HOL 3*	20	4
7 Apr 90	BEATLES AND THE STONES *Fontana HOL 4*	36	4
26 Oct 91	THE GIRL WITH THE LONELIEST EYES *Fontana HOL 5*	58	1
2 May 92	FEEL *Fontana HOL 6*	45	3
27 Jun 92	YOU DON'T UNDERSTAND *Fontana HOL 7*	46	3
5 Dec 92	CRUSH ME *Fontana HOL 810*	67	1

HOUSE OF PAIN US, male rap group (24 WEEKS) pos/wks

10 Oct 92	JUMP AROUND *Ruffness XLS 32*	32	4
22 May 93 ●	JUMP AROUND / TOP O' THE MORNING TO YA (re-issue) *Ruffness XL 43CD*	8	7
23 Oct 93	SHAMROCKS AND SHENANIGANS / WHO'S THE MAN *Ruffness XLS 46CD*	23	4
16 Jul 94	ON POINT *Ruffness XLS 52CD*	19	3
12 Nov 94	IT AIN'T A CRIME *Ruffness XLS 55CD1*	37	2
1 Jul 95	OVER THERE (I DON'T CARE) *Ruffness XLS 61CD1*	20	3
5 Oct 96	FED UP *Tommy Boy TBCD 7744*	68	1

HOUSE OF VIRGINISM
Sweden, male vocal / instrumental group (6 WEEKS) pos/wks

20 Nov 93	I'LL BE THERE FOR YOU (DOYA DODODO DOYA) *ffrr FCD 221*	29	3
30 Jul 94	REACHIN *ffrr FCD 238*	35	2
17 Feb 96	EXCLUSIVE *Logic 74321324102*	67	1

HOUSE OF ZEKKARIYAS – See WOMACK and WOMACK

HOUSE TRAFFIC
Italy / UK, male / female vocal / production group (3 WEEKS) pos/wks

4 Oct 97	EVERY DAY OF MY LIFE *Logic 74321249442*	24	3

HOUSEMARTINS UK, male vocal / instrumental group
fronted by Norman Cook (b) and Paul Heaton (v) (59 WEEKS) pos/wks

8 Mar 86	SHEEP (re) *Go! Discs GOD 9*	54	4
7 Jun 86 ●	HAPPY HOUR *Go! Discs GOD 11*	3	13
4 Oct 86	THINK FOR A MINUTE *Go! Discs GOD 13*	18	8
6 Dec 86 ★	CARAVAN OF LOVE *Go! Discs GOD 16*	1	11
23 May 87	FIVE GET OVER EXCITED *Go! Discs GOD 18*	11	6
5 Sep 87	ME AND THE FARMER *Go! Discs GOD 19*	15	5
21 Nov 87	BUILD *Go! Discs GOD 21*	15	8
23 Apr 88	THERE IS ALWAYS SOMETHING THERE TO REMIND ME *Go! Discs GOD 22*	35	4

HOUSEMASTER BOYZ and the RUDE BOY OF HOUSE
US, male vocal / instrumental group (14 WEEKS) pos/wks

9 May 87 ●	HOUSE NATION (re) *Magnetic Dance MAGD 1*	8	14

HOUSETRAP – See DJ SANDY vs HOUSETRAP

Thelma HOUSTON US, female vocalist (22 WEEKS) pos/wks

5 Feb 77	DON'T LEAVE ME THIS WAY *Motown TMG 1060* ▲	13	8

27 Jun 81	IF YOU FEEL IT *RCA 77*	48	4
1 Dec 84	YOU USED TO HOLD ME SO TIGHT *MCA MCA 932*	49	8
21 Jan 95	DON'T LEAVE ME THIS WAY (re-recording) *Dynamo DYND 001*	35	2

Whitney HOUSTON ⟨30⟩ ⟨Top 500⟩ Multi-award-winning,
record-shattering vocalist b. 9 Aug 1963, New Jersey, US. She recorded the second biggest selling UK single by a female, and scored a record seven successive No.1s in the US. In 2001, with sales exceeding 140 million behind her. she signed a record-breaking $100m recording deal. Best-selling single: 'I Will Always Love You' 1,355,055 (315 WEEKS) pos/wks

16 Nov 85 ★	SAVING ALL MY LOVE FOR YOU *Arista ARIST 640* ▲	1	16
25 Jan 86 ●	HOW WILL I KNOW *Arista ARIST 656* ▲	5	12
25 Jan 86	HOLD ME *Asylum EKR 32* [1]	44	5
12 Apr 86 ●	GREATEST LOVE OF ALL *Arista ARIST 658* ▲	8	11
23 May 87 ★	I WANNA DANCE WITH SOMEBODY (WHO LOVES ME) *Arista RIS 1* ▲	1	16
22 Aug 87	DIDN'T WE ALMOST HAVE IT ALL *Arista RIS 31* ▲	14	8
14 Nov 87 ●	SO EMOTIONAL *Arista RIS 43* ▲	5	11
12 Mar 88	WHERE DO BROKEN HEARTS GO *Arista 109793* ▲	14	8
28 May 88 ●	LOVE WILL SAVE THE DAY *Arista 111516*	10	7
24 Sep 88 ★	ONE MOMENT IN TIME *Arista 111613*	1	12
9 Sep 89	IT ISN'T, IT WASN'T, IT AIN'T NEVER GONNA BE *Arista 112545* [2]	29	5
20 Oct 90 ●	I'M YOUR BABY TONIGHT (re) *Arista 113594* ▲	5	10
22 Dec 90	ALL THE MAN THAT I NEED *Arista 114000* ▲	13	10
6 Jul 91	MY NAME IS NOT SUSAN *Arista 114510*	29	5
28 Sep 91	I BELONG TO YOU *Arista 114727*	54	2
14 Nov 92 ★	I WILL ALWAYS LOVE YOU (re) *Arista 74321120657* ◆ ▲	1	29
20 Feb 93 ●	I'M EVERY WOMAN *Arista 74321131502*	4	11
24 Apr 93 ●	I HAVE NOTHING *Arista 74321146142*	3	10
31 Jul 93	RUN TO YOU *Arista 74321153332*	15	6
6 Nov 93	QUEEN OF THE NIGHT *Arista 74321169302*	14	5
22 Jan 94	SOMETHING IN COMMON *MCA MCSTD 1957* [3]	16	5
18 Nov 95	EXHALE (SHOOP SHOOP) *Arista 74321332472* ▲	11	9
24 Feb 96	COUNT ON ME *Arista 74321345842* [4]	12	6
21 Dec 96	STEP BY STEP *Arista 74321449332*	13	13
29 Mar 97	I BELIEVE IN YOU AND ME *Arista 74321468602*	16	5
19 Dec 98 ●	WHEN YOU BELIEVE (re) *Columbia 6667522* [5]	4	13
6 Mar 99 ●	IT'S NOT RIGHT (BUT IT'S OK) *Arista 74321652402*	3	15
3 Jul 99 ●	MY LOVE IS YOUR LOVE *Arista 74321672862*	2	12
11 Dec 99	I LEARNED FROM THE BEST *Arista 74321723992*	19	11
17 Jun 00 ●	IF I TOLD YOU THAT (re) *Arista 74321766262* [6]	9	11
14 Oct 00 ●	COULD I HAVE THIS KISS FOREVER *Arista 74321795992* [7]	7	8
30 Dec 00	HEARTBREAK HOTEL *Arista 74321820572* [8]	25	5
9 Nov 02	WHATCHULOOKINAT *Arista 74321973062*	13	3

[1] Teddy Pendergrass with Whitney Houston [2] Aretha Franklin and Whitney Houston [3] Bobby Brown and Whitney Houston [4] Whitney Houston and CeCe Winans [5] Mariah Carey and Whitney Houston [6] Whitney Houston / George Michael [7] Whitney Houston and Enrique Iglesias [8] Whitney Houston featuring Faith Evans and Kelly Price

'I Will Always Love You' re-entered peaking at No.25 in Dec 1993

Adina HOWARD US, female vocalist (16 WEEKS) pos/wks

4 Mar 95	FREAK LIKE ME (re) *East West A 4473CD*	33	4
23 Nov 96 ●	WHAT'S LOVE GOT TO DO WITH IT *Interscope IND 97008* [1]	2	12

[1] Warren G featuring Adina Howard

Billy HOWARD UK, male comedian / vocalist (12 WEEKS) pos/wks

13 Dec 75 ●	KING OF THE COPS *Penny Farthing PEN 892*	6	12

Miki HOWARD US, female vocalist (2 WEEKS) pos/wks

26 May 90	UNTIL YOU COME BACK (THAT'S WHAT I'M GONNA DO) *East West 7935*	67	2

Nick HOWARD Australia, male vocalist (1 WEEK) pos/wks

21 Jan 95	EVERYBODY NEEDS SOMEBODY *Bell 74321220942*	64	1

Robert HOWARD – See Kym MAZELLE

HOWLIN' WOLF
US, male vocalist – Chester Burnette, d. 10 Jan 1976 (5 WEEKS) pos/wks

4 Jun 64	SMOKESTACK LIGHTNIN' *Pye International 7N 25244*	42	5

Al HUDSON *US, male vocalist (20 WEEKS)* pos/wks

9 Sep 78	DANCE, GET DOWN (FEEL THE GROOVE) / HOW DO YOU DO *ABC 4229*	57	4
15 Sep 79	YOU CAN DO IT *MCA 511* [1]	15	10
8 Dec 79	MUSIC *MCA 542* [2]	56	6

[1] Al Hudson and the Partners [2] One Way featuring Al Hudson

Lavine HUDSON *UK, female vocalist (3 WEEKS)* pos/wks

21 May 88	INTERVENTION *Virgin VS 1067*	57	3

HUDSON-FORD *UK, male vocal / instrumental*
duo – Richard Hudson and John Ford (20 WEEKS) pos/wks

18 Aug 73	● PICK UP THE PIECES *A&M AMS 7078*	8	9
16 Feb 74	BURN BABY BURN *A&M AMS 7096*	15	9
29 Jun 74	FLOATING IN THE WIND *A&M AMS 7116*	35	2

See also MONKS

HUE AND CRY
UK, male vocal / instrumental duo – Pat and Greg Kane (59 WEEKS) pos/wks

13 Jun 87	● LABOUR OF LOVE *Circa YR 4*	6	16
19 Sep 87	STRENGTH TO STRENGTH *Circa YR 6*	46	5
30 Jan 88	I REFUSE *Circa YR 8*	47	3
22 Oct 88	ORDINARY ANGEL *Circa YR 18*	42	6
28 Jan 89	LOOKING FOR LINDA *Circa YR 24*	15	9
6 May 89	VIOLENTLY (EP) *Circa YR 29*	21	6
30 Sep 89	SWEET INVISIBILITY *Circa YR 37*	55	3
25 May 91	MY SALT HEART *Circa YR 64*	47	3
3 Aug 91	LONG TERM LOVERS OF PAIN (EP) *Circa YR 71*	48	1
11 Jul 92	PROFOUNDLY YOURS *Fidelity FIDEL 1*	74	1
13 Mar 93	LABOUR OF LOVE (re-mix) *Circa HUESCD 1*	25	4

Tracks on Violently (EP): Violently / The Man with the Child In His Eyes / Calamity John. Tracks on Long Term Lovers of Pain (EP): Long Term Lovers of Pain / Heart of Saturday Night / Remembrance and Gold / Stars Crash Down

HUES CORPORATION *US, male / female vocal group (16 WEEKS)* pos/wks

27 Jul 74	● ROCK THE BOAT *RCA APBO 0232* ▲	6	10
19 Oct 74	ROCKIN' SOUL *RCA PB 10066*	24	6

HUFF & HERB *UK, male DJ / production duo*
– Ben Langmaid and Jeff Patterson (8 WEEKS) pos/wks

2 Nov 96	HELP ME MAKE IT *Skyway SKYWCD 4* [1]	31	2
21 Jun 97	HELP ME MAKE IT (re-mix) *Skyway SKYWCD 8* [1]	37	2
6 Dec 97	FEELING GOOD *Planet 3 GXY 2018CD*	31	3
7 Nov 98	FEELING GOOD '98 (re-mix) *Planet 3 GXY 2020CD*	69	1

[1] Huff & Puff (Ben Langmaid and Roland Armstrong).

See also FAITHLESS; ROLLO; DUSTED ; OUR TRIBE / ONE TRIBE; SPHINX

David HUGHES
UK, male vocalist – Geoffrey Paddison, d. 19 Oct 1972 (1 WEEK) pos/wks

21 Sep 56	BY THE FOUNTAINS OF ROME *Philips PB 606*	27	1

HUGO and LUIGI *US, orchestra*
and chorus – leaders Hugo Peretti and Luigi Creatore (2 WEEKS) pos/wks

24 Jul 59	LA PLUME DE MA TANTE *RCA 1127*	29	2

HUMAN LEAGUE [139] [Top 500] *Early-1980s UK pop sensation.*
Fronted by Phil Oakey (b. 2 Oct 1955, Sheffield) (v/syn) and joined in 1980 by vocalists Joanne Catherall and Susanne Sulley. The group, which also topped the US chart, won Best Newcomers at the 1982 Brit Awards. Best-selling single: 'Don't You Want Me' 1,430,000 (156 WEEKS) pos/wks

3 May 80	HOLIDAY 80 (DOUBLE SINGLE) (re) *Virgin SV 105*	46	10
21 Jun 80	EMPIRE STATE HUMAN *Virgin VS 351*	62	2
28 Feb 81	BOYS AND GIRLS *Virgin VS 395*	48	4
2 May 81	THE SOUND OF THE CROWD *Virgin VS 416*	12	10
8 Aug 81	● LOVE ACTION (I BELIEVE IN LOVE) *Virgin VS 435*	3	13
10 Oct 81	● OPEN YOUR HEART *Virgin VS 453*	6	9
5 Dec 81	★ DON'T YOU WANT ME *Virgin VS 466* ◆ ▲	1	13
9 Jan 82	● BEING BOILED *EMI FAST 4*	6	9
20 Nov 82	● MIRROR MAN *Virgin VS 522*	2	10
23 Apr 83	● (KEEP FEELING) FASCINATION *Virgin VS 569*	2	9
5 May 84	THE LEBANON (re) *Virgin VS 672*	11	7
30 Jun 84	LIFE ON YOUR OWN *Virgin VS 688*	16	6
17 Nov 84	LOUISE *Virgin VS 723*	13	10
23 Aug 86	● HUMAN *Virgin VS 880* ▲	8	8
22 Nov 86	I NEED YOUR LOVING *Virgin VS 900*	72	1
15 Oct 88	LOVE IS ALL THAT MATTERS *Virgin VS 1025*	41	5
18 Aug 90	HEART LIKE A WHEEL *Virgin VS 1262*	29	5
7 Jan 95	● TELL ME WHEN *East West YZ 882CD1*	6	9
18 Mar 95	ONE MAN IN MY HEART *East West YZ 904CD1*	13	8
17 Jun 95	FILLING UP WITH HEAVEN *East West YZ 944CD1*	36	2
28 Oct 95	DON'T YOU WANT ME (re-mix) *Virgin VSCDT 1557*	16	3
20 Jan 96	STAY WITH ME TONIGHT *East West EW 020CD*	40	1
11 Aug 01	ALL I EVER WANTED *Papillon BTFLYS 0012*	47	1

'Holiday 80 (Double Single)' reached its peak position on re-entry in Feb 1982. Tracks on double single: Being Boiled / Marianne / Rock and Roll – Nightclubbing / Dancevision

HUMAN MOVEMENT featuring Sophie MOLETA
UK, male production duo and Australia, female vocalist (1 WEEK) pos/wks

3 Feb 01	LOVE HAS COME AGAIN *Renaissance Recordings RENCDS 005*	53	1

HUMAN NATURE *Australia, male vocal group (7 WEEKS)* pos/wks

10 May 97	WISHES *Epic 6644485*	44	1
30 Aug 97	WHISPER YOUR NAME *Epic 6649465*	53	1
10 Mar 01	HE DON'T LOVE YOU *Epic 6708922*	18	4
30 Jun 01	WHEN WE WERE YOUNG *Epic 6713792*	43	1

HUMAN RESOURCE
Holland, male instrumental / production group (14 WEEKS) pos/wks

14 Sep 91	DOMINATOR *R&S RSUK 4*	36	7
21 Dec 91	THE COMPLETE DOMINATOR (re-mix) *R&S RSUK 4X*	18	7

HUMANOID *UK, male producer – Brian Dougans (14 WEEKS)* pos/wks

26 Nov 88	STAKKER HUMANOID *Westside WSR 12*	17	8
22 Apr 89	SLAM *Westside WSR 14*	54	2
8 Aug 92	STAKKER HUMANOID (re-issue) *Jumpin' + Pumpin' TOT 27*	40	3
3 Mar 01	STAKKER HUMANOID (re-mix) *Jumpin' + Pumpin' CDSTOT 43*	65	1

See also FUTURE SOUND OF LONDON

HUMATE *Germany, male production trio (4 WEEKS)* pos/wks

30 Jan 99	LOVE STIMULATION *Deviant DVNT 22CDS*	18	4

HUMBLE PIE *UK, male vocal / instrumental group (10 WEEKS)* pos/wks

23 Aug 69	● NATURAL BORN BUGIE *Immediate IM 082*	4	10

Engelbert HUMPERDINCK [56] [Top 500]
Internationally popular cabaret entertainer and easy-on-the-ear vocalist, b. Arnold Dorsey, 2 May 1936, Madras, India. After a slow career start, an unlikely name change helped him to become one of the biggest-earning performers of the 1960s. This Vegas veteran was the UK's biggest-selling artist of 1967 and has reportedly amassed a personal fortune of £100m. Best-selling single: 'Release Me' 1,365,000 (239 WEEKS) pos/wks

26 Jan 67	★ RELEASE ME *Decca F 12541* ◆	1	56
25 May 67	● THERE GOES MY EVERYTHING *Decca F 12610*	2	29
23 Aug 67	★ THE LAST WALTZ *Decca F 12655* ◆	1	27
10 Jan 68	● AM I THAT EASY TO FORGET *Decca F 12722*	3	13
24 Apr 68	● A MAN WITHOUT LOVE *Decca F 12770*	2	15
25 Sep 68	● LES BICYCLETTES DE BELSIZE *Decca F 12834*	5	15

		pos/wks
5 Feb 69 ●	THE WAY IT USED TO BE *Decca F 12879*	3 14
9 Aug 69	I'M A BETTER MAN (FOR HAVING LOVED YOU) *Decca F 12957*	15 13
15 Nov 69 ●	WINTER WORLD OF LOVE *Decca F 12980*	7 13
30 May 70	MY MARIE *Decca F 13032*	31 7
12 Sep 70	SWEETHEART (re) *Decca F 13068*	22 7
11 Sep 71	ANOTHER TIME, ANOTHER PLACE *Decca F 13212*	13 12
4 Mar 72	TOO BEAUTIFUL TO LAST *Decca F 13281*	14 10
20 Oct 73	LOVE IS ALL (re) *Decca F 13443*	44 4
30 Jan 99	QUANDO QUANDO QUANDO *The Hit Label HLC 15*	40 3
6 May 00	HOW TO WIN YOUR LOVE *Universal TV 8822682*	59 1

HUNDRED REASONS
UK, male vocal / instrumental group (10 WEEKS)

		pos/wks
18 Aug 01	EP TWO *Columbia 6713922*	47 1
15 Dec 01	EP THREE *Columbia 6720782*	37 2
16 Mar 02	IF I COULD *Columbia 6724402*	19 3
18 May 02	SILVER *Columbia 6726642*	15 3
28 Sep 02	FALTER *Columbia 6731452*	38 1

Tracks on EP Two: Remmus / Soapbox / Shine. Tracks on EP Three: I'll Find You / Sunny / Slow Motion

Peter HUNNIGALE – See ARSENAL FC

Geraldine HUNT *Canada, female vocalist (5 WEEKS)*

		pos/wks
25 Oct 80	CAN'T FAKE THE FEELING *Champagne FIZZ 501*	44 5

Lisa HUNT – See LOVESTATION

Marsha HUNT *US, female vocalist (3 WEEKS)*

		pos/wks
21 May 69	WALK ON GILDED SPLINTERS *Track 604 030*	46 2
2 May 70	KEEP THE CUSTOMER SATISFIED *Track 604 037*	41 1

Tommy HUNT *US, male vocalist (17 WEEKS)*

		pos/wks
11 Oct 75	CRACKIN' UP *Spark SRL 1132*	39 5
21 Aug 76	LOVING ON THE LOSING SIDE *Spark SRL 1146*	28 9
4 Dec 76	ONE FINE MORNING *Spark SRL 1148*	44 3

Alfonzo HUNTER *US, male rap / instrumentalist (2 WEEKS)*

		pos/wks
22 Feb 97	JUST THE WAY *Cooltempo CDCOOL 326*	38 2

HUNTER featuring Ruby TURNER
UK, male gladiator / vocalist and UK, female vocalist (1 WEEK)

		pos/wks
9 Dec 95	SHAKABOOM! *Telstar HUNTCD 1*	64 1

Ian HUNTER *UK, male vocalist (10 WEEKS)*

		pos/wks
3 May 75	ONCE BITTEN TWICE SHY *CBS 3194*	14 10

See also MOTT THE HOOPLE

Tab HUNTER
US, male actor / vocalist – Andrew Arthur Kelm (30 WEEKS)

		pos/wks
8 Feb 57 ★	YOUNG LOVE *London HLD 8380* ▲	1 18
12 Apr 57 ●	NINETY-NINE WAYS (re) *London HLD 8410*	5 12

Terry HUNTER *US, male DJ / producer (1 WEEK)*

		pos/wks
26 Jul 97	HARVEST FOR THE WORLD *Delirious DELICD 4*	48 1

HURLEY & TODD *UK / South Africa, male
production duo – Ross Hurley and Drew Todd (2 WEEKS)*

		pos/wks
29 Apr 00	SUNSTORM *Multiply CDMULTY 58*	38 2

Steve 'Silk' HURLEY *US, male producer (9 WEEKS)*

		pos/wks
10 Jan 87 ★	JACK YOUR BODY *DJ International LON 117*	1 9

See also VOICES OF LIFE

HURRICANE – See PUFF DADDY

HURRICANE #1
UK, male vocal / instrumental group (17 WEEKS)

		pos/wks
10 May 97	STEP INTO MY WORLD *Creation CRESCD 253*	29 2
5 Jul 97	JUST ANOTHER ILLUSION *Creation CRESCD 264*	35 2
6 Sep 97	CHAIN REACTION *Creation CRESCD 271*	30 2
1 Nov 97	STEP INTO MY WORLD (re-mix) *Creation CRESCD 276*	19 3
21 Feb 98	ONLY THE STRONGEST WILL SURVIVE *Creation CRERSCD 285.*	19 6
24 Oct 98	RISING SIGN *Creation CRESCD 303*	47 1
3 Apr 99	THE GREATEST HIGH *Creation CRESCD 309*	43 1

HURRICANE SMITH
UK, male vocalist – Norman Smith (35 WEEKS)

		pos/wks
12 Jun 71 ●	DON'T LET IT DIE *Columbia DB 8785*	2 12
29 Apr 72 ●	OH BABE, WHAT WOULD YOU SAY? *Columbia DB 8878*	4 16
2 Sep 72	WHO WAS IT *Columbia DB 8916*	23 7

HURRICANES – See JOHNNY and the HURRICANES

Phil HURTT *US, male vocalist (5 WEEKS)*

		pos/wks
11 Nov 78	GIVING IT BACK *Fantasy FTC 161*	36 5

HUSTLERS CONVENTION featuring Dave LAUDAT
and Ondrea DUVERNEY *UK, male production duo
with male vocalist and US, female vocalist (1 WEEK)*

		pos/wks
20 May 95	DANCE TO THE MUSIC *Stress CDSTR 53*	71 1

See also SEX-O-SONIQUE; FULL INTENTION; DISCO TEX presents CLOUDBURST

Willie HUTCH *US, male vocalist (8 WEEKS)*

		pos/wks
4 Dec 82	IN AND OUT *Motown TMG 1285*	51 7
6 Jul 85	KEEP ON JAMMIN' *Motown ZB 40173*	73 1

June HUTTON *US, female vocalist, d. 2 May 1973 (7 WEEKS)*

		pos/wks
7 Aug 53 ●	SAY YOU'RE MINE AGAIN (re) *Capitol CL 13918*	6 7

With 'Alex Stordahl with the Boys Next Door'

HYBRID *UK, male production trio (4 WEEKS)*

		pos/wks
10 Jul 99	FINISHED SYMPHONY *Distinctive DISNCD 52*	58 1
11 Sep 99	IF I SURVIVE *Distinctive DISNCD 55* [1]	52 1
3 Jun 00	KID 2000 *Virgin / EMI VTS CD2* [2]	32 2

[1] Hybrid featuring Julee Cruise [2] Hybrid featuring Chrissie Hynde

HYDRAULIC DOGS – See DJD presents HYDRAULIC DOGS

Brian HYLAND *US, male vocalist (72 WEEKS)*

		pos/wks
7 Jul 60 ●	ITSY BITSY TEENIE WEENIE YELLOW POLKADOT BIKINI *London HLR 9161* ▲	8 13
20 Oct 60	FOUR LITTLE HEELS *London HLR 9203*	29 6
10 May 62 ●	GINNY COME LATELY *HMV POP 1013*	5 15
2 Aug 62 ●	SEALED WITH A KISS *HMV POP 1051*	3 15
8 Nov 62	WARMED OVER KISSES *HMV POP 1079*	28 6
27 Mar 71	GYPSY WOMAN (re) *Uni UN 530*	42 6
28 Jun 75	SEALED WITH A KISS (re-issue) *ABC 4059*	7 11

Sheila HYLTON *Jamaica, female vocalist (12 WEEKS)*

		pos/wks
15 Sep 79	BREAKFAST IN BED *United Artists BP 304*	57 5
17 Jan 81	THE BED'S TOO BIG WITHOUT YOU *Island WIP 6671*	35 7

Phyllis HYMAN *US, female vocalist, d. 30 Jun 1995 (9 WEEKS)*

		pos/wks
16 Feb 80	YOU KNOW HOW TO LOVE ME *Arista ARIST 323*	47 6
12 Sep 81	YOU SURE LOOK GOOD TO ME *Arista ARIST 424*	56 3

Dick HYMAN TRIO
US, male instrumental trio – Dick Hyman, keyboards (10 WEEKS)

		pos/wks
16 Mar 56 ●	THEME FROM 'THE THREEPENNY OPERA' *MGM 890*	9 10

Re-entries are listed as (re), (2re), (3re), etc which signifies that the hit re-entered the chart

Chrissie HYNDE US, female vocalist / instrumentalist (38 WEEKS)

		pos/wks
3 Aug 85	★ I GOT YOU BABE *DEP International DEP20* [1]	1 13
18 Jun 88	● BREAKFAST IN BED *DEP International DEP29* [1]	6 11
12 Oct 91	SPIRITUAL HIGH (STATE OF INDEPENDENCE) *Arista 114528* [2]	66 2
23 Jan 93	SPIRITUAL HIGH (STATE OF INDEPENDENCE) (re-mix) *Arista 74321 127712* [2]	47 2
18 Mar 95	★ LOVE CAN BUILD A BRIDGE *London CO CD1* [3]	1 8
3 Jun 00	KID 2000 *Virgin / EMI VTS CD2* [4]	32 2

[1] UB40 featuring Chrissie Hynde [2] Moodswings featuring Chrissie Hynde
[3] Cher, Chrissie Hynde and Neneh Cherry with Eric Clapton [4] Hybrid featuring Chrissie Hynde

See also PRETENDERS

HYPER GO GO UK, male instrumental / production duo – Jamie Diplock and Alex Bell (15 WEEKS)

		pos/wks
22 Aug 92	HIGH *Deconstruction 74321110497*	30 5
31 Jul 93	NEVER LET GO *Positiva CDTIV 3*	45 3
5 Feb 94	RAISE *Positiva CDTIV 9*	36 2
26 Nov 94	IT'S ALRIGHT *Positiva CDTIV 20*	49 1
6 Apr 96	DO WATCHA DO *Avex UK AVEXCD 24* [1]	54 1
12 Oct 96	HIGH (re-mix) *Distinctive DISNCD 24*	32 2
12 Apr 97	DO WATCHA DO (re-mix) *Distinctive DISNCD 28* [1]	60 1

[1] Hyper Go Go and Adeva

HYPERLOGIC UK, male instrumental / production trio (3 WEEKS)

		pos/wks
29 Jul 95	ONLY ME *Systematic SYSCD 15*	35 2
9 May 98	ONLY ME (re-mix) *Tidy Trax TIDY 113CD1*	48 1

HYPERSTATE UK, male / female vocal / instrumental duo (1 WK)

		pos/wks
6 Feb 93	TIME AFTER TIME *M & G MAGCD 34*	71 1

HYPNOTIST UK, male producer – Caspar Pound (5 WEEKS)

		pos/wks
28 Sep 91	THE HOUSE IS MINE *Rising High RSN 4*	65 2
21 Dec 91	THE HARDCORE EP *Rising High RSN 13*	68 3

Tracks on The Hardcore EP: Hardcore U Know the Score / The Ride / Night of the Livin' E Heads / God of the Universe

HYSTERIC EGO UK, male producer – Rob White (8 WEEKS)

		pos/wks
31 Aug 96	WANT LOVE *WEA WEA 070CD*	28 4
21 Jun 97	MINISTRY OF LOVE *WEA WEA 094CD*	39 2
28 Feb 98	WANT LOVE – THE REMIXES *WEA WEA 150CD*	46 1
13 Feb 99	TIME TO GET BACK *WEA WEA 198CD*	50 1

HYSTERICS UK, male vocal / instrumental group (5 WEEKS)

		pos/wks
12 Dec 81	JINGLE BELLS LAUGHING ALL THE WAY *Record Delivery KA 5*	44 5

HYSTERIX UK, male / female vocal / instrumental group (4 WEEKS)

		pos/wks
7 May 94	MUST BE THE MUSIC *Deconstruction 74321207362*	40 3
18 Feb 95	EVERYTHING *Deconstruction 74321236882*	65 1

I-LEVEL UK, male vocal / instrumental group (9 WEEKS)

		pos/wks
16 Apr 83	MINEFIELD *Virgin VS 563*	52 6
18 Jun 83	TEACHER *Virgin VS 595*	56 3

I MONSTER UK, male production / vocal duo – Dean Honer and Jarrod Gosling (6 WEEKS)

		pos/wks
16 Jun 01	DAYDREAM IN BLUE *Instant Karma KARMA 7 CD*	20 6

Janis IAN US, female vocalist (10 WEEKS)

		pos/wks
17 Nov 79	FLY TOO HIGH *CBS 7936*	44 7
28 Jun 80	THE OTHER SIDE OF THE SUN *CBS 8611*	44 3

IAN VAN DAHL Belgium, male / female production / vocal group – leader AnneMie Coenen (42 WEEKS)

		pos/wks
21 Jul 01	● CASTLES IN THE SKY *Nulife 74321867142*	3 16
22 Dec 01	● WILL I *Nulife 74321903402*	5 13
1 Jun 02	● REASON *Nulife 74321938722*	8 8
12 Oct 02	TRY *Nulife 74321967942*	15 5

ICE CUBE US, male rapper – O'Shea Jackson (23 WEEKS)

		pos/wks
27 Mar 93	IT WAS A GOOD DAY *Fourth & Broadway BRCD 270*	27 4
7 Aug 93	CHECK YO SELF *Fourth & Broadway BRCD 283* [1]	36 4
11 Sep 93	WICKED *Fourth & Broadway BRCD 282*	62 1
18 Dec 93	REALLY DOE *Fourth & Broadway BRCD 302*	66 1
26 Mar 94	YOU KNOW HOW WE DO IT (re) *Fourth & Broadway BRCD 303*	41 5
27 Aug 94	BOP GUN (ONE NATION) *Fourth & Broadway BRCD 308* [2]	22 3
11 Mar 95	HAND OF THE DEAD BODY *Virgin America VUSCD 88* [3]	41 2
15 Apr 95	NATURAL BORN KILLAZ *Death Row A 8197CD* [4]	45 2
22 Mar 97	THE WORLD IS MINE *Jive JIVECD 419*	60 1

[1] Ice Cube featuring Das EFX [2] Ice Cube featuring George Clinton [3] Scarface featuring Ice Cube [4] Dr Dre and Ice Cube

ICE MC UK, male rapper – Ian Campbell (5 WEEKS)

		pos/wks
6 Aug 94	THINK ABOUT THE WAY (BOM DIGI DIGI BOM...) *WEA YZ 829CD*	42 2
8 Apr 95	IT'S A RAINY DAY *Eternal YZ 902CD*	73 1
14 Sep 96	BOM DIGI BOM (THINK ABOUT THE WAY) (re-issue) *Eternal WEA 073CD*	38 2

ICE-T US, male rapper – Tracy Morrow (29 WEEKS)

		pos/wks
18 Mar 89	HIGH ROLLERS *Sire W 7574*	63 2
17 Feb 90	YOU PLAYED YOURSELF *Sire W 9994*	64 2
29 Sep 90	SUPERFLY 1990 *Capitol CL 586* [1]	48 3
8 May 93	I AIN'T NEW TA THIS *Rhyme Syndicate SYNDD 1*	62 2
18 Dec 93	THAT'S HOW I'M LIVIN' *Rhyme Syndicate SYNDD 2*	21 6
9 Apr 94	GOTTA LOTTA LOVE *Rhyme Syndicate SYNDD 3*	24 4
10 Dec 94	BORN TO RAISE HELL *Fox 74321230152* [2]	47 2
1 Jun 96	I MUST STAND *Rhyme Syndicate SYNDD 5*	23 3
7 Dec 96	THE LANE *Rhyme Syndicate SYNDD 6*	18 5

[1] Curtis Mayfield and Ice-T [2] Motörhead / Ice-T / Whitfield Crane

ICEBERG SLIMM UK, male rapper – Duane Dyer (2 WEEKS)

		pos/wks
7 Oct 00	NURSERY RHYMES *Polydor 5877632*	37 2

ICEHOUSE Australia, male vocal / instrumental group (28 WEEKS)

		pos/wks
5 Feb 83	HEY LITTLE GIRL *Chrysalis CHS 2670*	17 10
23 Apr 83	STREET CAFE *Chrysalis COOL 1*	62 4
3 May 86	NO PROMISES *Chrysalis CHS 2978*	72 1
29 Aug 87	CRAZY (re) *Chrysalis CHS 3156*	38 9
14 May 88	ELECTRIC BLUE *Chrysalis CHS 3239*	53 4

'Crazy' peaked when it returned to the chart in Feb 1988

ICICLE WORKS UK, male vocal / instrumental group – lead vocal Ian McNabb (28 WEEKS)

		pos/wks
24 Dec 83	LOVE IS A WONDERFUL COLOUR *Beggars Banquet BEG 99*	15 8
10 Mar 84	BIRDS FLY (WHISPER TO A SCREAM) / IN THE CAULDRON OF LOVE *Beggars Banquet BEG 108*	53 4
26 Jul 86	UNDERSTANDING JANE *Beggars Banquet BEG 160*	52 3
4 Oct 86	WHO DO YOU WANT FOR YOUR LOVE? *Beggars Banquet BEG 172*	54 4
14 Feb 87	EVANGELINE *Beggars Banquet BEG 181*	53 4

Still on chart ↓ UK million seller ◆ UK entry at No.1 ■ US No.1 ▲

A WHITER SHADE OF PALE

■ Classical melodies have often been adapted, or simply stolen, in the creation of popular songs, but seldom as successfully as in the case of 'A Whiter Shade of Pale', Procol Harum's international hit from 1967. Most classical music is long out of copyright, and can be freely used without the necessity of expensive royalty payments to the long-dead composer. Thus Beethoven, Tchaikovsky, Chopin, Rachmaninov and several others will have had cause to turn in their graves over adaptations by Eric Carmen/Celine Dion ('All By Myself'), Barry Manilow/Donna Summer/Take That ('Could it Be Magic'), B Bumble and the Stingers ('Nut Rocker') and the Beach Boys ('Lady Lynda') to name but a few. The music to 'A Whiter Shade of Pale' was an adaptation of Bach's 'Air on a G String'; the lyrics were something else entirely.

Procol Harum as a group didn't exist at all when the recording was made, being more a studio session unit brought together via an advertisement in Melody Maker to record the songs that vocalist Gary Brooker had written with lyricist Keith Reid. 'A Whiter Shade of Pale' was duly recorded under the production supervision of Denny Cordell, a former manager of the Moody Blues. (The group name Procol Harum was the misspelt Latin name of a friend's pedigree cat.)

To say that Keith Reid's lyrics were surreal would be an understatement, since particularly in the case of 'A Whiter Shade of Pale' with its vestal virgins, light fandangos and millers telling tales, they remain incomprehensible. (It's rumoured that another verse was edited out to reduce the length of the song. This, of course, might have

■ THE GROUP'S FRIEND GUY STEVENS HAD SPOTTED HIS WIFE LOOKING SOMEWHAT THE WORSE FOR WEAR AND COMMENTED, "MY GOD, YOU'VE JUST TURNED A WHITER SHADE OF PALE" ■

been the verse that explained it all.) At the time, the lyrics were described as "psychedelic" and the title of the song was actually a phrase that Keith Reid overheard at a late-night party. The group's friend, noted DJ turned producer Guy Stevens, had spotted his wife looking somewhat the worse for wear and commented, "My God, you've just turned a whiter shade of pale."

There was no doubt that the recording, with its haunting organ, strange lyric and a drum arrangement borrowed from Percy Sledge's 1966 hit 'When a Man Loves a Woman', was very different from anything else on the market. So different in fact that Decca Records, a conservative label at the best of times, had no idea what to do with it, and was extremely unsure if it had any hit potential at all.

Fortunately, producer Denny Cordell had a few

promotional ideas of his own, and he sent a test pressing of the record to pirate radio station Radio London situated three miles off Britain's east coast. Decca was forced to rush-release it due to public demand, and in just three weeks it reached No.1, also topping the charts in Germany, Belgium, Italy and twice in Holland.

Over the years, Gary Brooker has remained the key figure in a constantly changing Procol Harum line-up. The group followed 'A Whiter Shade of Pale' with two strong follow-ups: 'Homburg' and 'A Salty Dog'. Virtually dismissed in their home country as a one-hit-wonder, the group was more successful in America where a live album recorded with the Edmonton Symphony Orchestra in 1972 reached No.5, and 'A Whiter Shade of Pale' returned to the UK Top 20 at this time. Since then the group has split and reformed on several occasions. Brooker has made a number of solo albums and toured with Eric Clapton, and more recently as a member of Bill Wyman's Rhythm Kings. Procol Harum continue to tour on a regular basis, mostly in continental Europe.

■ Tony Burton

★ **ARTIST:**   Procol Harum

★ **LABEL:**   Deram UK/London USA

★ **WRITERS:**   Gary Brooker and Keith Reid

★ **PRODUCER:**   Denny Cordell

They skipped the light fandango: Procol Harum

243

30 Apr 88	**LITTLE GIRL LOST** *Beggars Banquet BEG 215*	**59** 4
17 Mar 90	**MOTORCYCLE RIDER** *Epic WORKS 100*	**73** 1

ICON *UK, male / female vocal / instrumental duo (1 WEEK)*   pos/wks
15 Jun 96	**TAINTED LOVE** *Eternal WEA 057CD*	**51** 1

IDEAL *UK, male producer – Jon Da Silva (2 WEEKS)*   pos/wks
6 Aug 94	**HOT** *Cleveland City CLECD 13019*	**49** 2

IDEAL U.S. featuring LIL' MO
US, male vocal group and female vocalist (3 WEEKS)   pos/wks
23 Sep 00	**WHATEVER** *Virgin VUSCD172*	**31** 3

IDES OF MARCH *US, male vocal / instrumental group (9 WEEKS)* pos/wks
6 Jun 70	**VEHICLE** *Warner Bros. WB 7378*	**31** 9

Eric IDLE featuring Richard WILSON
UK, male actors / vocalists (3 WEEKS)   pos/wks
17 Dec 94	**ONE FOOT IN THE GRAVE** *Victa CDVICTA 1*	**50** 3

IDLEWILD *UK, male vocal / instrumental group (28 WEEKS)*   pos/wks
9 May 98	**A FILM FOR THE FUTURE** *Food CDFOOD 111*	**53** 1
25 Jul 98	**EVERYONE SAYS YOU'RE SO FRAGILE** *Food CDFOOD 113*	**47** 1
24 Oct 98	**I'M A MESSAGE** *Food CDFOOD 114*	**41** 1
13 Feb 99	**WHEN I ARGUE I SEE SHAPES** *Food CDFOOD 116*	**19** 2
2 Oct 99	**LITTLE DISCOURAGE** *Food CDFOOD 124*	**24** 2
8 Apr 00	**ACTUALLY IT'S DARKNESS** *Food CDFOOD127*	**23** 3
24 Jun 00	**THESE WOODEN IDEAS** *Food CDFOOD 132*	**32** 3
28 Oct 00	**ROSEABILITY** *Food CDFOODS 134*	**38** 2
4 May 02	● **YOU HELD THE WORLD IN YOUR ARMS** *Parlophone CDRS 6575*	**9** 4
13 Jul 02	**AMERICAN ENGLISH** *Parlophone CDRS 6582*	**15** 7
2 Nov 02	**LIVE IN A HIDING PLACE** *Parlophone CDRS 6587*	**26** 2

Billy IDOL (287) Top 500
Snarling rock 'n' roll rebel of the 1980s. Former vocalist of punk hitmakers Generation X, b. William Broad, 30 Nov 1955, Middlesex, UK. He had his greatest success in the US, where four singles reached the Top 10 and 'Mony Mony' reached No.1 (106 WEEKS)   pos/wks
11 Sep 82	**HOT IN THE CITY** *Chrysalis CHS 2625*	**58** 4
24 Mar 84	**REBEL YELL** *Chrysalis IDOL 2*	**62** 2
30 Jun 84	**EYES WITHOUT A FACE** *Chrysalis IDOL 3*	**18** 11
29 Sep 84	**FLESH FOR FANTASY** *Chrysalis IDOL 4*	**54** 3
13 Jul 85	● **WHITE WEDDING** *Chrysalis IDOL 5*	**6** 15
14 Sep 85	● **REBEL YELL (re-issue)** *Chrysalis IDOL 6*	**6** 12
4 Oct 86	**TO BE A LOVER** *Chrysalis IDOL 8*	**22** 8
7 Mar 87	**DON'T NEED A GUN** *Chrysalis IDOL 9*	**26** 5
13 Jun 87	**SWEET SIXTEEN** *Chrysalis IDOL 10*	**17** 9
3 Oct 87	● **MONY MONY** *Chrysalis IDOL 11* ▲	**7** 10
16 Jan 88	**HOT IN THE CITY (re-mix)** *Chrysalis IDOL 12*	**13** 9
13 Aug 88	**CATCH MY FALL** *Chrysalis IDOL 13*	**63** 3
28 Apr 90	**CRADLE OF LOVE** *Chrysalis IDOL 14*	**34** 4
11 Aug 90	**L.A. WOMAN** *Chrysalis IDOL 15*	**70** 2
22 Dec 90	**PRODIGAL BLUES** *Chrysalis IDOL 16*	**47** 4
26 Jun 93	**SHOCK TO THE SYSTEM** *Chrysalis CDCHS 3994*	**30** 3
10 Sep 94	**SPEED** *Fox 74321223472*	**47** 2

Frank IFIELD (130) Top 500   Early 60s superstar, b. 30 Nov 1937,
Coventry, UK, and raised in Australia. This pop vocalist / yodeller had four No.1s in 12 months with revivals of US standards. Unlike many of his early 1960s UK contemporaries, his records also did well internationally. Best-selling single: 'I Remember You' 1,096,000 (163 WEEKS)   pos/wks
19 Feb 60	**LUCKY DEVIL (re)** *Columbia DB 4399*	**22** 8
29 Sep 60	**GOTTA GET A DATE** *Columbia DB 4496*	**49** 1
5 Jul 62	★ **I REMEMBER YOU** *Columbia DB 4856* ◆	**1** 28
25 Oct 62	★ **LOVESICK BLUES** *Columbia DB 4913*	**1** 17
24 Jan 63	★ **THE WAYWARD WIND** *Columbia DB 4960*	**1** 13
11 Apr 63	● **NOBODY'S DARLIN' BUT MINE** *Columbia DB 7007*	**4** 16

27 Jun 63	★ **CONFESSIN' (THAT I LOVE YOU)** *Columbia DB 7062*.........	**1** 16
17 Oct 63	**MULE TRAIN** *Columbia DB 7131*	**22** 6
9 Jan 64	● **DON'T BLAME ME** *Columbia DB 7184*	**8** 13
23 Apr 64	**ANGRY AT THE BIG OAK TREE** *Columbia DB 7263* ...	**25** 8
23 Jul 64	**I SHOULD CARE** *Columbia DB 7319*	**33** 3
1 Oct 64	**SUMMER IS OVER** *Columbia DB 7355*	**25** 6
19 Aug 65	**PARADISE** *Columbia DB 7655*	**26** 9
23 Jun 66	**NO ONE WILL EVER KNOW** *Columbia DB 7940*	**25** 4
8 Dec 66	**CALL HER YOUR SWEETHEART** *Columbia DB 8078* ...	**24** 11
7 Dec 91	**SHE TAUGHT ME HOW TO YODEL** *EMI 7YODEL 1* [1]	**40** 4

[1] Frank Ifield featuring the Backroom Boys

Enrique IGLESIAS *Spain, male vocalist (65 WEEKS)*   pos/wks
11 Sep 99	● **BAILAMOS** *Interscope IND 97131* ▲	**4** 9
18 Dec 99	**RHYTHM DIVINE** *Interscope 4972242*	**45** 2
14 Oct 00	● **COULD I HAVE THIS KISS FOREVER** *Arista 74321795992* [1]	**7** 8
2 Feb 02	★ **HERO** *Interscope IND 97671* [2] ■	**1** 19
27 Apr 02	**ESCAPE (import)** *Interscope 4976922* [2]	**71** 2
25 May 02	**ESCAPE** *Interscope 4977062* [2]	**3** 14
7 Sep 02	**LOVE TO SEE YOU CRY** *Interscope IND 97760* [2] ...	**12** 7
7 Dec 02	**MAYBE** *Interscope 4978222* [2]	**12** 4+

[1] Whitney Houston and Enrique Iglesias [2] Enrique

Julio IGLESIAS (478) Top 500
Spain's most successful vocalist of all time with reported world sales of more than 225 million albums; b. 23 Sep 1943, Madrid. Suave singer was still adding to his hits and awards in late 1990s, and his son Enrique is currently one of the world's top-selling artists (75 WEEKS)   pos/wks
24 Oct 81	★ **BEGIN THE BEGUINE (VOLVER A EMPEZAR)** *CBS A 1612*	**1** 14
6 Mar 82	● **QUIEREME MUCHO (YOURS)** *CBS A 1939*	**3** 9
9 Oct 82	**AMOR** *CBS A 2801*	**32** 7
9 Apr 83	**HEY!** *CBS JULIO 1*	**31** 7
7 Apr 84	**TO ALL THE GIRLS I'VE LOVED BEFORE** *CBS A 4252* [1]	**17** 10
7 Jul 84	**ALL OF YOU** *CBS A 4522* [2]	**43** 8
6 Aug 88	● **MY LOVE** *CBS JULIO 2* [3]	**5** 11
4 Jun 94	**CRAZY (re)** *Columbia 6603695*	**43** 5
26 Nov 94	**FRAGILE (re)** *Columbia 6610192*	**53** 4

[1] Julio Iglesias and Willie Nelson [2] Julio Iglesias and Diana Ross [3] Julio Iglesias featuring Stevie Wonder

IGNORANTS *UK, male vocal duo (3 WEEKS)*   pos/wks
25 Dec 93	**PHAT GIRLS** *Spaghetti CIOCD 8*	**59** 3

IIO *US, male / female production duo – Marcus Moser and Nadia Li (12 WEEKS)*   pos/wks
10 Nov 01	● **RAPTURE** *Made / Data / MoS DATA 27CDS*	**2** 12

IKARA COLT
UK, male / female vocal / instrumental group (1 WEEK)   pos/wks
2 Mar 02	**RUDD** *Fantastic Plastic FPS 029*	**72** 1

IL PADRINOS featuring Jocelyn BROWN
UK, male production duo – Dave Lee and Danny Rampling (1 WEEK) pos/wks
7 Sep 02	**THAT'S HOW GOOD YOUR LOVE IS** *Defected DFTD 057CDS*	**54** 1

See also Joey NEGRO; JAKATTA; HED BOYS; AKABU featuring Linda CLIFFORD; Li KWAN; RAVEN MAIZE; Z FACTOR; PHASE II

ILLEGAL MOTION featuring Simone CHAPMAN
UK, male / female vocal / instrumental duo (1 WEEK)   pos/wks
9 Oct 93	**SATURDAY LOVE** *Arista 74321163032*	**67** 1

ILLICIT featuring GRAM'MA FUNK
UK, male production duo with US, female vocalist (1 WEEK)   pos/wks
2 Sep 00	**CHEEKY ARMADA** *Yola YOLACDX 01*	**72** 1

ILS *UK, male producer (1 WEEK)* pos/wks

23 Feb 02	NEXT LEVEL *Marine Parade MAPA 012*	75	1

IMAANI
UK, female vocalist – Imaani Saleem (aka Melanie Crosdale) (7 WEEKS) pos/wks

9 May 98	WHERE ARE YOU *EMI CDEM 510*	15	7

IMAGINATION `289` `Top 500`

Distinctive London-based trio, which created a unique blend of soul and dance music: Leee John (v), Ashley Ingram (v/k), Errol Kennedy (d). One of the most original British acts of the early 1980s, they were fronted by a charismatic and flamboyant lead singer (105 WEEKS) pos/wks

16 May 81 ●	BODY TALK *R & B RBS 201*	4	18
5 Sep 81	IN AND OUT OF LOVE *R & B RBS 202*	16	9
14 Nov 81	FLASHBACK *R & B RBS 206*	16	13
6 Mar 82 ●	JUST AN ILLUSION *R & B RBS 208*	2	11
26 Jun 82 ●	MUSIC AND LIGHTS *R & B RBS 210*	5	9
25 Sep 82	IN THE HEAT OF THE NIGHT *R & B RBS 211*	22	8
11 Dec 82	CHANGES *R & B RBS 213*	31	8
4 Jun 83	LOOKING AT MIDNIGHT *R & B RBS 214*	29	7
5 Nov 83	NEW DIMENSIONS *R & B RBS 216*	56	3
26 May 84	STATE OF LOVE *R & B RBS 218*	67	2
24 Nov 84	THANK YOU MY LOVE *R & B RBS 219*	22	15
16 Jan 88	INSTINCTUAL *RCA PB 41697*	62	2

IMAJIN *US, male vocal group (7 WEEKS)* pos/wks

27 Jun 98	SHORTY (YOU KEEP PLAYIN' WITH MY MIND) *Jive 0521212* [1]	22	3
20 Feb 99	NO DOUBT *Jive 0521772*	42	2
24 Apr 99	BOUNCE, ROCK, SKATE, ROLL *Jive 0522142* [2]	45	1
12 Feb 00	FLAVA *Jive 9250012*	64	1

[1] Imajin featuring Keith Murray [2] Baby DC featuring Imajin

Natalie IMBRUGLIA *Australia, female actor / vocalist (53 WEEKS)* pos/wks

8 Nov 97 ●	TORN *RCA 74321527982*	2	17
14 Mar 98 ●	BIG MISTAKE *RCA 74321566782*	2	10
6 Jun 98	WISHING I WAS THERE *RCA 74321585062*	19	5
17 Oct 98 ●	SMOKE *RCA 74321621942*	5	7
10 Nov 01	THAT DAY (re) *RCA 74321896792*	11	5
23 Mar 02 ●	WRONG IMPRESSION *RCA 74321928352*	10	7
3 Aug 02	BEAUTY ON THE FIRE *RCA 74321947022*	26	2

IMMACULATE FOOLS
UK, male vocal / instrumental group (4 WEEKS) pos/wks

26 Jan 85	IMMACULATE FOOLS *A&M AM 227*	51	4

IMMATURE featuring SMOOTH
US, male vocal group and US, female vocalist (2 WEEKS) pos/wks

16 Mar 96	WE GOT IT *MCA MCSTD 48009*	26	2

IMPALAS *US, male vocal group (1 WEEK)* pos/wks

21 Aug 59	SORRY (I RAN ALL THE WAY HOME) *MGM 1015*	28	1

IMPEDANCE *UK, male producer – Daniel Haydon (4 WEEKS)* pos/wks

11 Nov 89	TAINTED LOVE *Jumpin' & Pumpin' TOT 4*	54	4

IMPERIAL DRAG *UK, male vocal / instrumental group (1 WEEK)* pos/wks

12 Oct 96	BOY OR A GIRL *Columbia 6632992*	54	1

IMPERIAL TEEN
US, male / female vocal / instrumental group (1 WEEK) pos/wks

7 Sep 96	YOU'RE ONE *Slash LASCD 57*	69	1

See also FAITH NO MORE

IMPERIALS *US, male vocal group (9 WEEKS)* pos/wks

24 Dec 77	WHO'S GONNA LOVE ME *Power Exchange PX 266*	17	9

IMPERIALS QUARTET – *See Elvis PRESLEY*

IMPOSTER – *See Elvis COSTELLO*

IMPRESSIONS *US, male vocal group (10 WEEKS)* pos/wks

22 Nov 75	FIRST IMPRESSIONS *Curtom K 16638*	16	10

IN CROWD *UK, male vocal / instrumental group (1 WEEK)* pos/wks

20 May 65	THAT'S HOW STRONG MY LOVE IS *Parlophone R 5276*	48	1

IN TUA NUA
Ireland, male / female vocal / instrumental group (2 WEEKS) pos/wks

14 May 88	ALL I WANTED *Virgin VS 1072*	69	2

INAURA *UK, male vocal / instrumental group (1 WEEK)* pos/wks

18 May 96	COMA AROMA *EMI CDEM 421*	57	1

INCANTATION
UK, male instrumental group (12 WEEKS) pos/wks

4 Dec 82	CACHARPAYA (ANDES PUMPSA DAESI) *Beggars Banquet BEG 84*	12	12

INCOGNITO
UK, male / female vocal / instrumental group (38 WEEKS) pos/wks

15 Nov 80	PARISIENNE GIRL *Ensign ENY 44*	73	2
29 Jun 91 ●	ALWAYS THERE *Talkin Loud TLK 10* [1]	6	9
14 Sep 91	CRAZY FOR YOU *Talkin Loud TLK 14* [2]	59	2
6 Jun 92	DON'T YOU WORRY 'BOUT A THING *Talkin Loud TLK 21*	19	6
15 Aug 92	CHANGE *Talkin Loud TLK 26*	52	2
21 Aug 93	STILL A FRIEND OF MINE *Talkin Loud TLKCD 42*	47	2
20 Nov 93	GIVIN' IT UP *Talkin Loud TLKCD 44*	43	2
12 Mar 94	PIECES OF A DREAM *Talkin Loud TLKCD 46*	35	2
27 May 95	EVERYDAY *Talkin Loud TLKCD 55*	23	3
5 Aug 95	I HEAR YOUR NAME *Talkin Loud TLKCD 56*	42	2
11 May 96	JUMP TO MY LOVE / ALWAYS THERE (re-recording) *Talkin Loud TLCD 7*	29	3
26 Oct 96	OUT OF THE STORM *Talkin Loud TLCD 14*	57	1
10 Apr 99	NIGHTS OVER EGYPT *Talkin Loud TLCD 40*	56	1

[1] Incognito featuring Jocelyn Brown [2] Incognito featuring Chyna

INCUBUS *US, male vocal / instrumental group (8 WEEKS)* pos/wks

20 May 00	PARDON ME *Epic 6693462*	61	1
23 Jun 01	DRIVE *Epic 6713782*	40	2
2 Feb 02	WISH YOU WERE HERE *Epic 6722552*	27	3
14 Sep 02	ARE YOU IN? *Epic 6728482*	34	2

INDEEP *US, male / female vocal / rap group (11 WEEKS)* pos/wks

22 Jan 83	LAST NIGHT A DJ SAVED MY LIFE *Sound of New York SNY 1*	13	9
14 May 83	WHEN BOYS TALK *Sound of New York SNY 3*	67	2

INDIA *US, female vocalist – Linda Caballero (15 WEEKS)* pos/wks

26 Feb 94	LOVE AND HAPPINESS (YEMAYA Y OCHUN) *Cooltempo CDCOOL 287* [1]	50	2
5 Aug 95	I CAN'T GET NO SLEEP *A&M 5811412* [2]	44	2
16 Mar 96	OYE COMO VA *Media MCSTD 40013* [3]	36	2
8 Feb 97	RUNAWAY *Talkin Loud TLCD20* [4]	24	4
19 Jul 97	OYE COMO VA (re-issue) *Nukleuz MCSTD 40120* [3]	56	1
31 Jul 99	TO BE IN LOVE *Defected DEFECT 5CDS* [5]	23	3
6 Jul 02	BACKFIRED *SuSu CDSUSU 4* [6]	62	1

[1] River Ocean featuring India [2] Masters at Work presents India [3] Tito Puente Jr and the Latin Rhythm featuring Tito Puente, India and Cali Aleman [4] Nuyorican Soul featuring India [5] MAW presents India [6] Masters at Work featuring India

INDIAN VIBES *UK, male vocal / instrumental group (2 WEEKS)* pos/wks

24 Sep 94	MATHAR *Virgin International DINSD 136*	68	1
2 May 98	MATHAR (re-mix) *VC Recordings VCRD 32*	52	1

INDO US, female vocal duo (3 WEEKS)
pos/wks

18 Apr 98	R U SLEEPING Satellite 74321568212	31	3

INDUSTRY STANDARD UK, male DJ / production duo – Clayton Mitchell and Dave Dellar (3 WEEKS)
pos/wks

10 Jan 98	VOLUME 1 (WHAT YOU WANT WHAT YOU NEED) Satellite 74321543742	34	3

INFINITI – See GRAND PUBA

INGRAM US, male vocal / instrumental group (2 WEEKS)
pos/wks

11 Jun 83	SMOOTHIN' GROOVIN' Streetwave WAVE 3	56	2

James INGRAM US, male vocalist (42 WEEKS)
pos/wks

12 Feb 83	BABY COME TO ME Qwest K 15005 [1] ▲	11	10
18 Feb 84	YAH MO B THERE (re) Qwest W 9293947 [2]	44	8
12 Jan 85	YAH MO B THERE (remix) Qwest W 9202887 [2]	12	8
11 Jul 87 ●	SOMEWHERE OUT THERE MCA MCA 1132 [3]	8	13
31 Mar 90	SECRET GARDEN Qwest W 9992 [4]	67	1
16 Apr 94	THE DAY I FALL IN LOVE Columbia 6600282 [5]	64	2

[1] Patti Austin and James Ingram [2] James Ingram with Michael McDonald [3] Linda Ronstadt and James Ingram [4] Quincy Jones featuring Al B Sure!, James Ingram, El DeBarge and Barry White [5] Dolly Parton and James Ingram

'Yah Mob B There' original chart peak was No.44, then No. 69 on first re-entry in Apr 1984 and No.12 on the second re-entry in Jan 1985

INK SPOTS US, male vocal group (4 WEEKS)
pos/wks

29 Apr 55 ●	MELODY OF LOVE Parlophone R 3977	10	4

John INMAN UK, male actor / vocalist (6 WEEKS)
pos/wks

25 Oct 75	ARE YOU BEING SERVED SIR? DJM DJS 602	39	6

INMATES UK, male vocal / instrumental group (9 WEEKS)
pos/wks

8 Dec 79	THE WALK Radar ADA 47	36	9

INME UK, male vocal / instrumental group (2 WEEKS)
pos/wks

27 Jul 02	UNDERDOSE Music For Nations CDKUT 195	66	1
28 Sep 02	FIREFLY Music For Nations CDKUT 197	43	1

INNER CIRCLE
Jamaica, male vocal / instrumental group (35 WEEKS)
pos/wks

24 Feb 79	EVERYTHING IS GREAT Island WIP 6472	37	8
12 May 79	STOP BREAKING MY HEART Island WIP 6488	50	3
31 Oct 92 ●	SWEAT (A LA LA LA LA LONG) (re) Magnet 9031776802	3	19
31 Jul 93	BAD BOYS Magnet MAG 1017CD	52	3
10 Sep 94	GAMES PEOPLE PLAY Magnet MAG 1026CD	67	2

'Sweat (A La La La La Long)' made peak position on re-entry in May 1993

INNER CITY ⟨428 Top 500⟩ House act from Detroit, US, formed by New York-born producer and club DJ Kevin Saunderson, b. 9 May 1964, which featured distinctive vocalist Paris Grey. Quickly became first house act to reach the UK Top 10 with initial three hits (81 WEEKS)
pos/wks

3 Sep 88 ●	BIG FUN 10 TEN 240 [1]	8	14
10 Dec 88 ●	GOOD LIFE 10 TEN 249	4	12
22 Apr 89 ●	AIN'T NOBODY BETTER 10 TEN 252	10	7
29 Jul 89	DO YOU LOVE WHAT YOU FEEL 10 TEN 273	16	7
18 Nov 89	WATCHA GONNA DO WITH MY LOVIN' 10 TEN 290	12	9
13 Oct 90	THAT MAN (HE'S ALL MINE) 10 TEN 334	42	4
23 Feb 91	TILL WE MEET AGAIN Ten TEN 337	47	2
7 Dec 91	LET IT REIGN Ten TEN 392	51	2
4 Apr 92	HALLELUJAH '92 Ten TEN 398	22	4
13 Jun 92	PENNIES FROM HEAVEN Ten TEN 405	24	4
12 Sep 92	PRAISE Ten TENX 408	59	2
27 Feb 93	TILL WE MEET AGAIN (re-mix) Ten TENCD 414	55	1
14 Aug 93	BACK TOGETHER AGAIN Six6 SIXCD 104	49	1
5 Feb 94	DO YA Six6 SIXCD 107	44	2

9 Jul 94	SHARE MY LIFE Six6 SIXCD 114	62	1
10 Feb 96	YOUR LOVE Six6 SIXCD 127	28	2
5 Oct 96	DO ME RIGHT Six6 SIXXCD 2	47	1
6 Feb 99 ●	GOOD LIFE (BUENA VIDA) (re-recording) Pias Recordings PIASX 002CD	10	6

[1] Inner City featuring Kevin Saunderson

INNER SANCTUM
Canada, male producer – Steve Bolton (1 WEEK)
pos/wks

23 May 98	HOW SOON IS NOW Malarky MLKD 6	75	1

INNERZONE ORCHESTRA
US, male producer – Carl Craig (1 WEEK)
pos/wks

28 Sep 96	BUG IN THE BASSBIN Mo Wax MW 049CD	68	1

INNOCENCE
UK, male / female vocal / instrumental group (33 WEEKS)
pos/wks

3 Mar 90	NATURAL THING Cooltempo COOL 201	16	7
21 Jul 90	SILENT VOICE Cooltempo COOL 212	37	5
13 Oct 90	LET'S PUSH IT Cooltempo COOL 220	25	6
8 Dec 90	A MATTER OF FACT Cooltempo COOL 223	37	7
30 Mar 91	REMEMBER THE DAY Cooltempo COOL 226	56	2
20 Jun 92	I'LL BE THERE Cooltempo COOL 255	26	3
3 Oct 92	ONE LOVE IN MY LIFETIME Cooltempo COOL 263	40	2
21 Nov 92	BUILD Cooltempo COOL 267	72	1

INSANE CLOWN POSSE US, male rap duo (2 WEEKS)
pos/wks

17 Jan 98	HALLS OF ILLUSION Island CID 685	56	1
6 Jun 98	HOKUS POKUS Island CIDX 705	53	1

INSPIRAL CARPETS
UK, male vocal / instrumental group (50 WEEKS)
pos/wks

18 Nov 89	MOVE Cow DUNG 6	49	2
17 Mar 90	THIS IS HOW IT FEELS Cow DUNG 7	14	8
30 Jun 90	SHE COMES IN THE FALL Cow DUNG 10	27	6
17 Nov 90	ISLAND HEAD (EP) Cow DUNG 11	21	4
30 Mar 91	CARAVAN Cow DUNG 13	30	5
22 Jun 91	PLEASE BE CRUEL Cow DUNG 15	50	2
29 Feb 92	DRAGGING ME DOWN Cow DUNG 16	12	5
30 May 92	TWO WORLDS COLLIDE Cow DUNG 17	32	2
19 Sep 92	GENERATIONS Cow DUNG 18T	28	3
14 Nov 92	BITCHES BREW Cow DUNG 20T	36	2
5 Jun 93	HOW IT SHOULD BE Cow DUNG 22CD	49	1
22 Jan 94	SATURN 5 Cow DUNG 23CD	20	4
5 Mar 94	I WANT YOU Cow DUNG 24CD [1]	18	3
7 May 94	UNIFORM Cow DUNG 26CD	51	1
16 Sep 95	JOE Cow DUNG 27CD	37	2

[1] Inspiral Carpets featuring Mark E Smith

Tracks on Island Head (EP): Biggest Mountain / Gold Top / Weakness / I'll Keep It In Mind

INSPIRATIONAL CHOIR US, male / female choir (11 WEEKS)
pos/wks

22 Dec 84	ABIDE WITH ME Epic A 4997	44	5
14 Dec 85	ABIDE WITH ME (re-issue) Portrait A 4997	36	6

Label credits the Royal Choral Society

INSTANT FUNK US, male vocal / instrumental group (5 WEEKS)
pos/wks

20 Jan 79	GOT MY MIND MADE UP Salsoul SSOL 114	46	5

INTASTELLA
UK, male / female vocal / instrumental group (6 WEEKS)
pos/wks

25 May 91	DREAM SOME PARADISE MCA MCS 1520	69	1
24 Aug 91	PEOPLE MCA MCS 1559	74	2
16 Nov 91	CENTURY MCA MCS 1585	70	2
23 Sep 95	THE NIGHT Planet 3 GXY 2005CD	60	1

INTELLIGENT HOODLUM US, male rapper (3 WEEKS)
pos/wks

6 Oct 90	BACK TO REALITY A&M AM 598	55	3

Re-entries are listed as (re), (2re), (3re), etc which signifies that the hit re-entered the chart once, twice or three times, etc

INTENSO PROJECT
UK, male production / vocal group (2 WEEKS)   pos/wks

17 Aug 02	LUV DA SUNSHINE *Inferno CDFERN 47*.....................	22	2

INTERACTIVE
Germany, male instrumental / production group (4 WEEKS)   pos/wks

13 Apr 96	FOREVER YOUNG *Ffrreedom TABCD 235*....................	28	4

INTERPOL *US, male vocal / instrumental group (1 WEEK)*   pos/wks

23 Nov 02	OBSTACLE 1 *Matador OLE 5702*...................	72	1

INTRUDERS *US, male vocal group (21 WEEKS)*   pos/wks

13 Apr 74	I'LL ALWAYS LOVE MY MAMA *Philadelphia International PIR 2159*..........	32	7
6 Jul 74	WIN, PLACE OR SHOW (SHE'S A WINNER) *Philadelphia International PIR 2212*..........	14	9
22 Dec 84	WHO DO YOU LOVE? *Streetwave KHAN 34*	65	5

INVADERS OF THE HEART – See Jah WOBBLE'S INVADERS of the HEART

INVISIBLE GIRLS – See Pauline MURRAY and the INVISIBLE GIRLS

INVISIBLE MAN *UK, male producer – Graham Mew (1 WEEK)*   pos/wks

17 Apr 99	GIVE A LITTLE LOVE *Serious SERR 006CD*	48	1

INXS `202` `Top 500`
Stadium-packing rock sextet led by Australian Michael Hutchence (b. 22 Jan 1960, Sydney; d. 22 Nov 1997). Both Hutchence and group won Brit awards in 1991, and the video for their US chart-topper 'Need You Tonight' won five MTV awards in 1988 (132 WEEKS)   pos/wks

19 Apr 86	WHAT YOU NEED *Mercury INXS 5*................	51	6
28 Jun 86	LISTEN LIKE THIEVES *Mercury INXS 6*	46	7
30 Aug 86	KISS THE DIRT (FALLING DOWN THE MOUNTAIN) *Mercury INXS 7*................	54	3
24 Oct 87	NEED YOU TONIGHT *Mercury INXS 8* ▲	58	3
9 Jan 88	NEW SENSATION *Mercury INXS 9*................	25	6
12 Mar 88	DEVIL INSIDE *Mercury INXS 10*................	47	5
25 Jun 88	NEVER TEAR US APART *Mecury INXS 11*.........	24	7
12 Nov 88 ●	NEED YOU TONIGHT (re-issue) *Mercury INXS 12*.........	2	11
8 Apr 89	MYSTIFY *Mercury INXS 13*................	14	7
15 Sep 90	SUICIDE BLONDE *Mercury INXS 14*.........	11	6
8 Dec 90	DISAPPEAR *Mercury INXS 15*................	21	8
26 Jan 91	GOOD TIMES *Atlantic A 7751* `1`	18	8
30 Mar 91	BY MY SIDE *Mercury INXS 16*................	42	4
13 Jul 91	BITTER TEARS *Mercury INXS 17*................	30	3
2 Nov 91	SHINING STAR (EP) *Mercury INXS 18*.........	27	3
18 Jul 92	HEAVEN SENT *Mercury INXS 19*................	31	3
5 Sep 92	BABY DON'T CRY *Mercury INXS 20*.........	20	5
14 Nov 92	TASTE IT *Mercury INXS 23*................	21	4
13 Feb 93	BEAUTIFUL GIRL *Mercury INXCD 24*.........	23	5
23 Oct 93	THE GIFT *Mercury INXCD 25*................	11	4
11 Dec 93	PLEASE (YOU GOT THAT . . .) *Mercury INXCD 26*	50	1
22 Oct 94	THE STRANGEST PARTY (THESE ARE THE TIMES) *Mercury INXCD 27*................	15	5
22 Mar 97	ELEGANTLY WASTED *Mercury INXCD 28*.........	20	4
7 Jun 97	EVERYTHING *Mercury INXDD 29*................	71	1
18 Aug 01	PRECIOUS HEART (re) *Duty Free / Decode DFTELCD 001* `2`	14	5
3 Nov 01	I'M SO CRAZY (re) *Credence CDCRED 016* `3`	19	6

`1` Jimmy Barnes and INXS `2` Tall Paul vs Inxs `3` Par-T-One vs Inxs

Tracks on Shining Star (EP): Shining Star / Send a Message (Live) / Faith in Each Other (Live) / Bitter Tears (Live). Although uncredited, 'Please (You Got That...)' is a duet with Ray Charles

Sweetie IRIE – See ASWAD; SCRITTI POLITTI; Ed CASE

Tippa IRIE *UK, male vocalist – Anthony Henry (14 WEEKS)*   pos/wks

22 Mar 86	HELLO DARLING *Greensleeves / UK Bubblers TIPPA 4*	22	7
19 Jul 86	HEARTBEAT *Greensleeves / UK Bubblers TIPPA 5*	59	3

15 May 93	SHOUTING FOR THE GUNNERS *London LONCD 342* `1`	34	3
8 Jul 95	STAYING ALIVE 95 *Telstar CDSTAS 2776* `2`	48	1

`1` Arsenal FA Cup Squad featuring Tippa Irie and Peter Hunnigale `2` Fever featuring Tippa Irie

IRON MAIDEN `138` `Top 500`
Legendary London-based group named after a medieval torture device. Lead vocalists have included Paul Di'Anno and Blaze Bayley, but it was with frontman Bruce Dickinson that they enjoyed a period as one of the world's top metal bands (158 WEEKS)   pos/wks

23 Feb 80	RUNNING FREE *EMI 5032*................	34	5
7 Jun 80	SANCTUARY *EMI 5065*................	29	5
8 Nov 80	WOMEN IN UNIFORM *EMI 5105*................	35	4
14 Mar 81	TWILIGHT ZONE / WRATH CHILD *EMI 5145*.........	31	5
27 Jun 81	PURGATORY *EMI 5184*................	52	3
26 Sep 81	MAIDEN JAPAN (EP) *EMI 5219*................	43	4
20 Feb 82 ●	RUN TO THE HILLS *EMI 5263*................	7	10
15 May 82	THE NUMBER OF THE BEAST *EMI 5287*.........	18	8
23 Apr 83	FLIGHT OF ICARUS *EMI 5378*................	11	6
2 Jul 83	THE TROOPER *EMI 5397*................	12	7
18 Aug 84	2 MINUTES TO MIDNIGHT *EMI 5849*.........	11	6
3 Nov 84	ACES HIGH *EMI 5502*................	20	5
5 Oct 85	RUNNING FREE (LIVE) *EMI 5532*.........	19	5
14 Dec 85	RUN TO THE HILLS (LIVE) *EMI 5542*.........	26	6
6 Sep 86	WASTED YEARS *EMI 5583*................	18	4
22 Nov 86	STRANGER IN A STRANGE LAND (re) *EMI 5589*.........	22	6
26 Mar 88 ●	CAN I PLAY WITH MADNESS *EMI EM 49*	3	6
13 Aug 88 ●	THE EVIL THAT MEN DO *EMI EM 64*	5	6
19 Nov 88 ●	THE CLAIRVOYANT *EMI EM 79*................	6	6
18 Nov 89 ●	INFINITE DREAMS (re) *EMI EM 117*.........	6	6
22 Sep 90 ●	HOLY SMOKE *EMI EM 153*................	3	4
5 Jan 91 ★	BRING YOUR DAUGHTER . . . TO THE SLAUGHTER *EMI EMPD 171* ■	1	5
25 Apr 92 ●	BE QUICK OR BE DEAD *EMI EM 229*	2	4
11 Jul 92	FROM HERE TO ETERNITY *EMI EMS 240*	21	4
13 Mar 93 ●	FEAR OF THE DARK (LIVE) *EMI CDEMS 263*	8	3
16 Oct 93 ●	HALLOWED BE THY NAME (LIVE) *EMI CDEM 288*	9	3
7 Oct 95 ●	MAN ON THE EDGE *EMI CDEMS 398*.........	10	3
21 Sep 96	VIRUS *EMI CDEM 443*................	16	3
21 Mar 98	THE ANGEL AND THE GAMBLER *EMI CDEM 507*	18	3
20 May 00 ●	THE WICKER MAN *EMI CDEMS 568*.........	9	4
4 Nov 00	OUT OF THE SILENT PLANET *EMI CDEM 576*	20	3
23 Mar 02 ●	RUN TO THE HILLS (re-recording) *EMI CDEM 612*	9	4

'Run To The Hills' (re-recording) is a live version

IRONHORSE
Canada, male vocal / instrumental group (3 WEEKS)   pos/wks

5 May 79	SWEET LUI-LOUISE *Scotti Brothers K 11271*................	60	3

Big Dee IRWIN
US, male vocalist – Difosco Erwin, d. 27 Aug 1995 (17 WEEKS)   pos/wks

21 Nov 63 ●	SWINGING ON A STAR *Colpix PX 11010*	7	17

Single was a vocal duet by Big Dee Irwin and Little Eva (uncredited)

Chris ISAAK
US, male vocalist (22 WEEKS)   pos/wks

24 Nov 90 ●	WICKED GAME *London LON 279*	10	10
2 Feb 91	BLUE HOTEL *Reprise W 0005*	17	7
3 Apr 93	CAN'T DO A THING (TO STOP ME) *Reprise W 0161CD*	36	3
10 Jul 93	SAN FRANCISCO DAYS *Reprise W 0182CD*	62	1
2 Oct 99	BABY DID A BAD BAD THING *Reprise W 503CD*	44	1

ISHA-D *UK, male / female vocal / instrumental duo – Phil Coxon and Beverley Reppion (4 WEEKS)*   pos/wks

22 Jul 95	STAY (TONIGHT) *Cleveland City Blues CCBCD 15005*	28	3
5 Jul 97	STAY (re-issue) *Satellite 74321498212*	58	1

Ronald ISLEY – See ISLEY BROTHERS; Rod STEWART; R KELLY; Warren G

ISLEY BROTHERS 277 Top 500

Cincinnati brothers who have had five decades of US hits: Ronald, O'Kelly (d. 1986) and Rudolph Isley. These influential singers / songwriters / producers and label-owners penned pop anthem 'Shout', and have US hits covering six decades. On 14 Jul 2001, the Isley Brothers became the first act in history to have six decades of US Hot 100 hits (108 WEEKS)   pos/wks

25 Jul 63	TWIST AND SHOUT *Stateside SS 112*	42	1
28 Apr 66 ●	THIS OLD HEART OF MINE (IS WEAK FOR YOU) (re) *Tamla Motown TMG 555*	3	17
1 Sep 66	I GUESS I'LL ALWAYS LOVE YOU *Tamla Motown TMG 572*	45	2
15 Jan 69	I GUESS I'LL ALWAYS LOVE YOU (re-issue) *Tamla Motown TMG 683*	11	9
16 Apr 69 ●	BEHIND A PAINTED SMILE *Tamla Motown TMG 693*	5	12
25 Jun 69	IT'S YOUR THING *Major Minor MM 621*	30	5
30 Aug 69	PUT YOURSELF IN MY PLACE *Tamla Motown TMG 708*	13	11
22 Sep 73	THAT LADY *Epic EPC 1704*	14	9
19 Jan 74	HIGHWAYS OF MY LIFE *Epic EPC 1980*	25	8
25 May 74	SUMMER BREEZE *Epic EPC 2244*	16	8
10 Jul 76 ●	HARVEST FOR THE WORLD *Epic EPC 4369*	10	8
13 May 78	TAKE ME TO THE NEXT PHASE *Epic EPC 6292*	50	4
3 Nov 79	IT'S A DISCO NIGHT (ROCK DON'T STOP) *Epic EPC 7911*	14	11
16 Jul 83	BETWEEN THE SHEETS *Epic A 3513*	52	3

'This Old Heart of Mine (Is Weak for You)' originally peaked at No.47 before making No.3 in Nov 1968

ISLEY JASPER ISLEY

US, male vocal / instrumental group (5 WEEKS)   pos/wks

| 23 Nov 85 | CARAVAN OF LOVE *Epic A 6612* | 52 | 5 |

ISOTONIK *UK, male producer – Chris Paul (9 WEEKS)*   pos/wks

| 11 Jan 92 | DIFFERENT STROKES *Ffrreedom TAB 101* | 12 | 5 |
| 2 May 92 | EVERYWHERE I GO / LET'S GET DOWN *Ffrreedom TAB 108* | 25 | 4 |

'Let's Get Down' listed only from 9 May 1992

See also Chris PAUL

IT BITES *UK, male vocal / instrumental group (21 WEEKS)*   pos/wks

12 Jul 86 ●	CALLING ALL THE HEROES *Virgin VS 872*	6	12
18 Oct 86	WHOLE NEW WORLD *Virgin VS 896*	54	3
23 May 87	THE OLD MAN AND THE ANGEL *Virgin VS 941*	72	1
13 May 89	STILL TOO YOUNG TO REMEMBER *Virgin VS 1184*	66	3
24 Feb 90	STILL TOO YOUNG TO REMEMBER (re-issue) *Virgin VS 1238*	60	2

IT'S IMMATERIAL

UK, male vocal / instrumental group (10 WEEKS)   pos/wks

| 12 Apr 86 | DRIVING AWAY FROM HOME (JIM'S TUNE) *Siren SIREN 15* | 18 | 7 |
| 2 Aug 86 | ED'S FUNKY DINER (FRIDAY NIGHT, SATURDAY MORNING) *Siren SIREN 24* | 65 | 3 |

ITTY BITTY BOOZY WOOZY *Holland, male instrumental / production duo – Addy Van Der Zwan and Koen Groeneveld (2 WEEKS)*   pos/wks

| 25 Nov 95 | TEMPO FIESTA (PARTY TIME) *Systematic SYSCD 23* | 34 | 2 |

See also KLUBBHEADS

Burl IVES *US, male vocalist, d. 14 Apr 1995 (25 WEEKS)*   pos/wks

| 25 Jan 62 ● | A LITTLE BITTY TEAR *Brunswick 05863* | 9 | 15 |
| 17 May 62 | FUNNY WAY OF LAUGHIN' *Brunswick 05868* | 29 | 10 |

IVY LEAGUE *UK, male vocal group (31 WEEKS)*   pos/wks

4 Feb 65 ●	FUNNY HOW LOVE CAN BE *Piccadilly 7N 35222*	8	9
6 May 65	THAT'S WHY I'M CRYING *Piccadilly 7N 35228*	22	8
24 Jun 65 ●	TOSSING AND TURNING *Piccadilly 7N 35251*	3	13
14 Jul 66	WILLOW TREE *Piccadilly 7N 35326*	50	1

IZIT *UK, male / female vocal / instrumental group (3 WEEKS)*   pos/wks

| 2 Dec 89 | STORIES *ffrr F 122* | 52 | 3 |

J

Ray J *US, male vocalist – Willie Ray Norwood Jr. (12 WEEKS)*   pos/wks

17 Oct 98	THAT'S WHY I LIE *Atlantic AT 0049CD*	71	1
16 Jun 01 ●	ANOTHER DAY IN PARADISE *WEA WEA 327CD1* [1]	5	10
11 Aug 01	WAIT A MINUTE *Atlantic AT 0106CD* [2]	54	1

[1] Brandy and Ray J [2] Ray J featuring Lil' Kim

J.A.L.N. BAND

UK / Jamaica, male vocal / instrumental group (17 WEEKS)   pos/wks

11 Sep 76	DISCO MUSIC / I LIKE IT *Magnet MAG 73*	21	9
27 Aug 77	I GOT TO SING *Magnet MAG 97*	40	4
1 Jul 78	GET UP (AND LET YOURSELF GO) *Magnet MAG 118*	53	4

JB's ALL STARS

UK, male / female vocal / instrumental group (4 WEEKS)   pos/wks

| 11 Feb 84 | BACKFIELD IN MOTION *RCA Victor RCA 384* | 48 | 4 |

JC *UK, male producer (1 WEEK)*   pos/wks

| 7 Feb 98 | SO HOT *East West EW 146CD* | 74 | 1 |

JC001 *UK, male rapper (4 WEEKS)*   pos/wks

| 24 Apr 93 | NEVER AGAIN *AnXious ANX 1012CD* | 67 | 2 |
| 26 Jun 93 | CUPID *AnXious ANX 1014CD* | 56 | 2 |

JD – *See SNOOP DOGGY DOGG*

JDS *Italy / UK, male DJ / production duo – Julian Napolitano and Darren Pearce (3 WEEKS)*   pos/wks

27 Sep 97	NINE WAYS *ffrr FCD 310*	61	1
23 May 98	LONDON TOWN *Jive 0530042*	49	1
3 Mar 01	NINE WAYS (re-mix) *ffrr FCD 391*	47	1

JFK *UK, male producer (3 WEEKS)*   pos/wks

15 Sep 01	GOOD GOD *Y2K Y2K 025CD*	71	1
26 Jan 02	WHIPLASH *Y2K Y2K 027CD*	47	1
4 May 02	THE SOUND OF BLUE *Y2K Y2K 030CD*	55	1

JJ *UK, male / female vocal / instumental duo (3 WEEKS)*   pos/wks

| 9 Feb 91 | IF THIS IS LOVE *Columbia 6566097* | 55 | 3 |

JJ – *See also J LUCK & MC NEAT*

JJ72

Ireland, male / female vocal / instrumental group (12 WEEKS)   pos/wks

3 Jun 00	LONG WAY SOUTH *Lakota LAK 0015CD*	68	1
26 Aug 00	OXYGEN *Lakota LAK 0016CD*	23	3
4 Nov 00	OCTOBER SWIMMER *Lakota LAK 0018CD*	29	3
10 Feb 01	SNOW *Lakota LAK 0019CD*	21	3
12 Oct 02	FORMULAE *Lakota / Columbia 6731592*	28	2

JKD BAND *UK, male vocal / instrumental group (4 WEEKS)*   pos/wks

| 1 Jul 78 | DRAGON POWER *Satril SAT 132* | 58 | 4 |

JM SILK *US, male vocal / instrumental duo (6 WEEKS)*   pos/wks

| 25 Oct 86 | I CAN'T TURN AROUND *RCA PB 49793* | 62 | 3 |
| 7 Mar 87 | LET THE MUSIC TAKE CONTROL *RCA PB 49767* | 47 | 3 |

JMD – *See TYREE*

J MAGIK – *See Ian POOLEY*

J PAC UK, male vocal / instrumental duo (2 WEEKS)
pos/wks
22 Jul 95	ROCK 'N' ROLL (DOLE) East West YZ 953CD	51	2

JT and the BIG FAMILY
Italy, male / female vocal / instrumental group (8 WEEKS)
pos/wks
3 Mar 90 ●	MOMENTS IN SOUL Champion CHAMP 237	7	8

JT PLAYAZ UK, male production trio (4 WEEKS)
pos/wks
5 Apr 97	JUST PLAYIN' Pukka CDJTP 1	30	3
2 May 98	LET'S GET DOWN MCA MCSTD 40161	64	1

JTQ UK, male instrumental group (6 WEEKS)
pos/wks
3 Apr 93	LOVE THE LIFE Big Life BLRD 93 [1]	34	3
3 Jul 93	SEE A BRIGHTER DAY Big Life BLRDA 97 [1]	49	2
25 Feb 95	LOVE WILL KEEP US TOGETHER Acid Jazz JAZID 112CD [2]	63	1

[1] JTQ with Noel McKoy [2] JTQ featuring Alison Limerick

JX UK, male producer – Jake Williams (33 WEEKS)
pos/wks
2 Apr 94	SON OF A GUN Internal Dance IDC 5	13	6
1 Apr 95	YOU BELONG TO ME Ffrreedom TABCD 227	17	5
19 Aug 95 ●	SON OF A GUN (re-mix) Ffrreedom TABCD 233	6	6
18 May 96 ●	THERE'S NOTHING I WON'T DO Ffrreedom TABCD 241	4	13
8 Mar 97	CLOSE TO YOUR HEART Ffrreedom TABCD 245	18	3

JXL – See JUNKIE XL

JA RULE ⟨484⟩ [Top 500]
Mobo winner Jeffrey Atkins (hence JA), b. New York, 29 Feb 1976. One of this millennium's most regular transatlantic chart entrants, and one of just five acts to replace themselves at the top of the US chart (75 WEEKS)
pos/wks
13 Mar 99	CAN I GET A... Def Jam 5668472 [1]	24	3
3 Mar 01	BETWEEN YOU AND ME Def Jam 5727402 [2]	26	3
10 Nov 01	LIVIN' IT UP Def Jam 5888142 [3]	27	4
10 Nov 01 ●	I'M REAL Epic 6720322 [4]	4	15
2 Feb 02 ●	ALWAYS ON TIME Def Jam 5889462 [5] ▲	6	13
23 Mar 02 ●	AIN'T IT FUNNY Epic 6724922 [6] ▲	4	13
3 Aug 02 ●	LIVIN' IT UP (re-issue) Def Jam 0639782 [3]	5	8
24 Aug 02	RAINY DAYZ MCA MCSTD 40288 [7]	17	5
12 Oct 02 ●	DOWN 4 U (re) Murder Inc 0639002 [8]	4	9
21 Dec 02	THUG LOVIN' Def Jam 0637872 [9]	15	2+

[1] Jay-Z featuring Amil & Ja Rule [2] Ja Rule featuring Christina Milian [3] Ja Rule featuring Case [4] Jennifer Lopez featuring Ja Rule [5] Ja Rule featuring Ashanti [6] Jennifer Lopez featuring Ja Rule & Cadillac Tah [7] Mary J Blige featuring Ja Rule [8] Irv Gotti presents Ja Rule, Ashanti, Charli Baltimore and Vita [9] Ja Rule featuring Bobby Brown

JACK 'N' CHILL UK, male instrumental group (21 WEEKS)
pos/wks
6 Jun 87 ●	THE JACK THAT HOUSE BUILT (re) Oval / 10 / Virgin TEN 174.	6	16
9 Jul 88	BEATIN' THE HEAT 10 TEN 234	42	5

'The Jack That House Built' reached its peak position only on re-entry in Jan 1988

Terry JACKS Canada, male vocalist (21 WEEKS)
pos/wks
23 Mar 74 ★	SEASONS IN THE SUN Bell 1344 ▲	1	12
29 Jun 74	IF YOU GO AWAY Bell 1362	8	9

See also POPPY FAMILY

Chad JACKSON
UK, male DJ / producer – Mark Chadwick (10 WEEKS)
pos/wks
2 Jun 90 ●	HEAR THE DRUMMER (GET WICKED) Big Wave BWR 36	3	10

Dee D JACKSON
UK, female vocalist – Deirdre Cozier (14 WEEKS)
pos/wks
22 Apr 78 ●	AUTOMATIC LOVER Mercury 6007 171	4	9
2 Sep 78	METEOR MAN Mercury 6007 182	48	5

Freddie JACKSON US, male vocalist (31 WEEKS)
pos/wks
23 Nov 85	YOU ARE MY LADY Capitol CL 379	49	4
22 Feb 86	ROCK ME TONIGHT (FOR OLD TIME'S SAKE) Capitol CL 358	18	9
11 Oct 86	TASTY LOVE Capitol CL 428	73	1
7 Feb 87	HAVE YOU EVER LOVED SOMEBODY Capitol CL 437	33	6
9 Jul 88	NICE 'N' SLOW Capitol CL 502	56	2
15 Oct 88	CRAZY (FOR ME) Capitol CL 510	41	3
5 Sep 92	ME AND MRS JONES Capitol CL 668	32	5
15 Jan 94	MAKE LOVE EASY RCA 74321179162	70	1

Gisele JACKSON US, female vocalist (1 WEEK)
pos/wks
30 Aug 97	LOVE COMMANDMENTS Manifesto FESCD 28	54	1

Janet JACKSON ⟨35⟩ [Top 500]
Multi-award-winning, record-breaking vocalist / performer, b. 16 May 1966, Indiana, US. Although not an overnight sensation, the youngest of the talented Jackson family became one of the world's biggest-selling recording artists and has amassed a staggering collection of gold albums and singles. Best-selling single: 'Together Again' 741,000 (288 WEEKS)
pos/wks
22 Mar 86 ●	WHAT HAVE YOU DONE FOR ME LATELY A&M AM 308	3	14
31 May 86	NASTY A&M AM 316	19	9
9 Aug 86 ●	WHEN I THINK OF YOU A&M AM 337 ▲	10	10
1 Nov 86	CONTROL A&M AM 359	42	9
21 Mar 87 ●	LET'S WAIT AWHILE Breakout USA 601	3	10
13 Jun 87	PLEASURE PRINCIPLE Breakout USA 604	24	5
14 Nov 87	FUNNY HOW TIME FLIES (WHEN YOU'RE HAVING FUN) A&M Breakout USA 613	59	2
2 Sep 89 ●	MISS YOU MUCH Breakout USA 663 ▲	22	7
4 Nov 89	RHYTHM NATION Breakout USA 673	23	5
27 Jan 90	COME BACK TO ME Breakout USA 681	20	7
31 Mar 90	ESCAPADE Breakout USA 684 ▲	17	7
7 Jul 90	ALRIGHT A&M USA 693	20	5
8 Sep 90	BLACK CAT A&M AM 587 ▲	15	6
27 Oct 90	LOVE WILL NEVER DO (WITHOUT YOU) A&M AM 700 ▲	34	4
15 Aug 92 ●	THE BEST THINGS IN LIFE ARE FREE Perspective PERSS 7400 ●	2	13
8 May 93 ●	THAT'S THE WAY LOVE GOES Virgin VSCDG 1460 ▲	2	10
31 Jul 93	IF Virgin VSCDT 1474	14	7
20 Nov 93 ●	AGAIN Virgin VSCDG 1481 ▲	6	11
12 Mar 94	BECAUSE OF LOVE Virgin VSCDG 1488	19	4
18 Jun 94	ANY TIME ANY PLACE Virgin VSCDT 1501	13	5
26 Nov 94	YOU WANT THIS Virgin VSCDT 1519	14	3
18 Mar 95 ●	WHOOPS NOW / WHAT'LL I DO Virgin VSCDT 1533	9	8
10 Jun 95 ●	SCREAM (re) Epic 6620222 [2]	3	13
24 Jun 95	SCREAM (re-mix) Epic 6621277 [2]	43	2
23 Sep 95 ●	RUNAWAY Virgin VSCDT 1972	6	7
16 Dec 95 ●	THE BEST THINGS IN LIFE ARE FREE (re-mix) A&M 5813092 [3]	7	7
6 Apr 96	TWENTY FOREPLAY A&M 5815112	22	4
4 Oct 97 ●	GOT 'TIL IT'S GONE Virgin VSCDG 1666 [4]	6	9
13 Dec 97 ●	TOGETHER AGAIN Virgin VSCDG 1670 [5] ▲	4	19
4 Apr 98 ●	I GET LONELY Virgin VSCDT 1683 [6]	5	7
27 Jun 98	GO DEEP Virgin VSCDT 1680 [5]	13	5
19 Dec 98	EVERY TIME Virgin VSCDT 1720 [5]	46	1
17 Apr 99	GIRLFRIEND / BOYFRIEND Interscope IND 95640 [7]	11	7
1 May 99 ●	WHAT'S IT GONNA BE?! Elektra E3762CD1 [8]	6	7
19 Aug 00 ●	DOESN'T REALLY MATTER Def Soul 5629152 ▲	5	11
21 Apr 01 ●	ALL FOR YOU Virgin VSCDT 1801 ▲	3	11
11 Aug 01	SOMEONE TO CALL MY LOVER Virgin VSCDT 1813	11	5
22 Dec 01	SON OF A GUN (I BETCHA THINK THIS SONG IS ABOUT YOU) (re) Virgin VUSCD 232 [9]	13	9
28 Sep 02 ●	FEEL IT BOY (re) Virgin VUSCD 258 [10]	9	7

[1] Luther Vandross and Janet Jackson with special guests BBD and Ralph Tresvant [2] Michael Jackson and Janet Jackson [3] Luther Vandross and Janet Jackson [4] Janet featuring Q-Tip and Joni Mitchell [5] Janet [6] Janet featuring BLACKstreet [7] BLACKstreet with Janet [8] Busta Rhymes featuring Janet [9] Janet with Carly Simon featuring Missy Elliott [10] Beenie Man featuring Janet

See also Herb ALPERT

Jermaine JACKSON US, male vocalist (43 WEEKS)

		pos/wks
10 May 80 ●	LET'S GET SERIOUS Motown TMG 1183	8 11
26 Jul 80	BURNIN' HOT Motown TMG 1194	32 6
30 May 81	YOU LIKE ME DON'T YOU Motown TMG 1222	41 5
12 May 84	SWEETEST SWEETEST Arista JJK 1	52 4
27 Oct 84	WHEN THE RAIN BEGINS TO FALL Arista ARIST 584 [1]	68 2
16 Feb 85 ●	DO WHAT YOU DO Arista ARIST 609	6 13
21 Oct 89	DON'T TAKE IT PERSONAL Arista 112634	69 2

[1] Jermaine Jackson and Pia Zadora

'Let's Get Serious' features uncredited vocals of Stevie Wonder

See also JACKSONS

Joe JACKSON UK, male vocalist (49 WEEKS)

		pos/wks
4 Aug 79	IS SHE REALLY GOING OUT WITH HIM? A&M AMS 7459	13 9
12 Jan 80 ●	IT'S DIFFERENT FOR GIRLS A&M AMS 7493	5 9
4 Jul 81	JUMPIN' JIVE A&M AMS 8145 [1]	43 5
8 Jan 83 ●	STEPPIN' OUT A&M AMS 8262	6 8
12 Mar 83	BREAKING US IN TWO A&M AM 101	59 4
28 Apr 84	HAPPY ENDING A&M AM 186	58 3
7 Jul 84	BE MY NUMBER TWO A&M AM 200	70 2
7 Jun 86	LEFT OF CENTER A&M AM 320 [2]	32 9

[1] Joe Jackson's Jumpin' Jive [2] Suzanne Vega featuring Joe Jackson

Michael JACKSON [7] Top 500

The self-proclaimed "King of Pop" b. 29 Aug 1958, Indiana, US, is arguably the best-known living musical entertainer. The youngest vocalist (age 11, fronting the Jackson Five) to top the US singles chart, he was also the first artist to enter that chart at No.1 (with 'You Are Not Alone'). In 1991 he became the first US act to enter the UK chart at No.1 since Elvis Presley in 1960 (whose daughter, Lisa Marie, he married in 1994). This outstanding, innovative singer / songwriter and performer has broken countless other records for his singles, albums, videos and tours. 'Thriller' is the world's biggest-selling record with global sales of more than 47 million, including 26 million in the US alone. It topped the US album chart for an unprecedented 37 weeks and had a record 12 Grammy nominations. Also on the album front, 'History' sold more copies in its first week than any previous double album. 'Dangerous' sold a staggering 10 million worldwide in its first month and 'Invincible' returned him to the top in 2001. Both 'Thriller' and 'Bad' have sold more than three million copies in the UK. Jackson, whose private life and physical appearance have attracted much media attention, was the first entertainer to earn more than $100m in a year, and the first to receive an award for selling at least 100 million albums outside of the US. Best-selling single: 'Earth Song' 1,038,821 (508 WEEKS)

		pos/wks
12 Feb 72 ●	GOT TO BE THERE Tamla Motown TMG 797	5 11
20 May 72 ●	ROCKIN' ROBIN Tamla Motown TMG 816	3 14
19 Aug 72 ●	AIN'T NO SUNSHINE Tamla Motown TMG 826	8 11
25 Nov 72 ●	BEN Tamla Motown TMG 834 ▲	7 14
18 Nov 78	EASE ON DOWN THE ROAD MCA 396 [1]	45 4
15 Sep 79 ●	DON'T STOP 'TIL YOU GET ENOUGH Epic EPC 7763 ▲	3 12
24 Nov 79 ●	OFF THE WALL Epic EPC 8045	7 10
9 Feb 80 ●	ROCK WITH YOU Epic EPC 8206 ▲	7 9
3 May 80 ●	SHE'S OUT OF MY LIFE Epic EPC 8384	3 9
26 Jul 80	GIRLFRIEND Epic EPC 8782	41 5
23 May 81 ★	ONE DAY IN YOUR LIFE Motown TMG 976	1 14
1 Aug 81	WE'RE ALMOST THERE Motown TMG 977	46 4
6 Nov 82 ●	THE GIRL IS MINE (re) Epic EPC A 2729 [2]	8 10
29 Jan 83 ★	BILLIE JEAN Epic EPC A 3084 ▲	1 15
9 Apr 83 ●	BEAT IT Epic EPC A 3258 ▲	3 12
11 Jun 83 ●	WANNA BE STARTIN' SOMETHIN' Epic A 3427	8 9
23 Jul 83	HAPPY (LOVE THEME FROM 'LADY SINGS THE BLUES') Tamla Motown TMG 986	52 3
15 Oct 83 ●	SAY SAY SAY Parlophone R 6062 [3] ▲	2 15
19 Nov 83 ●	THRILLER Epic A 3643	10 18
31 Mar 84	P.Y.T. (PRETTY YOUNG THING) Epic A 4136	11 8
2 Jun 84 ●	FAREWELL MY SUMMER LOVE Motown TMG 1342	7 12
11 Aug 84	GIRL YOU'RE SO TOGETHER Motown TMG 1355	33 8
8 Aug 87 ★	I JUST CAN'T STOP LOVING YOU Epic 650202 7 ▲	1 9

		pos/wks
26 Sep 87 ●	BAD Epic 651155 7 ▲	3 11
5 Dec 87 ●	THE WAY YOU MAKE ME FEEL Epic 651275 7 ▲	3 10
20 Feb 88	MAN IN THE MIRROR Epic 651388 7 ▲	21 5
16 Apr 88	I WANT YOU BACK Motown ZB 41919 [4]	8 9
28 May 88	GET IT Motown ZB 41883 [5]	37 4
16 Jul 88 ●	DIRTY DIANA Epic 651546 7 ▲	4 8
10 Sep 88	ANOTHER PART OF ME Epic 652844 7	15 6
26 Nov 88 ●	SMOOTH CRIMINAL Epic 653026 7	8 10
25 Feb 89 ●	LEAVE ME ALONE Epic 654672 7	2 9
15 Jul 89	LIBERIAN GIRL Epic 654947 0	13 6
23 Nov 91 ★	BLACK OR WHITE Epic 6575987 ■ ▲	1 10
18 Jan 92	BLACK OR WHITE (re-mix) Epic 6577316	14 4
15 Feb 92 ●	REMEMBER THE TIME / COME TOGETHER Epic 6577747	3 8
2 May 92 ●	IN THE CLOSET Epic 6580187	8 6
25 Jul 92 ●	WHO IS IT Epic 6581797	10 7
12 Sep 92	JAM Epic 6583607	13 5
5 Dec 92 ●	HEAL THE WORLD Epic 6584887	2 15
27 Feb 93 ●	GIVE IN TO ME Epic 6590692	2 9
10 Jul 93 ●	WILL YOU BE THERE Epic 6592222	9 8
18 Dec 93	GONE TOO SOON Epic 6599762	33 5
10 Jun 95 ●	SCREAM (re) Epic 6620222 [6]	3 13
24 Jun 95	SCREAM (re-mix) Epic 6621277 [6]	43 2
2 Sep 95 ★	YOU ARE NOT ALONE Epic 6623102 ▲	1 15
9 Dec 95 ★	EARTH SONG Epic 6626955 ◆ ■	1 17
20 Apr 96 ●	THEY DON'T CARE ABOUT US (2re) Epic 6629502	4 14
24 Aug 96 ●	WHY Epic 6629502 [7]	2 9
16 Nov 96	STRANGER IN MOSCOW (re) Epic 6637872	4 11
3 May 97 ★	BLOOD ON THE DANCEFLOOR Epic 6644625 ■	1 9
19 Jul 97 ●	HISTORY / GHOSTS Epic 6647962	5 8
20 Oct 01 ●	YOU ROCK MY WORLD Epic 6720292	2 15
22 Dec 01	CRY Epic 6721822	25 4

[1] Diana Ross and Michael Jackson [2] Michael Jackson and Paul McCartney [3] Paul McCartney and Michael Jackson [4] Michael Jackson with the Jackson Five [5] Stevie Wonder and Michael Jackson [6] Michael Jackson and Janet Jackson [7] 3T featuring Michael Jackson

The sleeve of 'I Just Can't Stop Loving You' credits Siedah Garrett but the label does not. 'Come Together' was listed only from 7 Mar 1992. It peaked at No.10. Chart rules allow for a maximum of three formats; the additional three formats of 'Scream' – which each included re-mixed versions – were therefore listed separately (see 24 Jun 1995)

Mick JACKSON UK, male vocalist (16 WEEKS)

		pos/wks
30 Sep 78	BLAME IT ON THE BOOGIE Atlantic K 11102	15 8
3 Feb 79	WEEKEND Atlantic K 11224	38 8

Millie JACKSON US, female vocalist (8 WEEKS)

		pos/wks
18 Nov 72	MY MAN, A SWEET MAN Mojo 2093 022	50 1
10 Mar 84	I FEEL LIKE WALKIN' IN THE RAIN Sire W 9348	55 2
15 Jun 85	ACT OF WAR Rocket EJS 8 [1]	32 5

[1] Elton John and Millie Jackson

Stonewall JACKSON US, male vocalist (2 WEEKS)

		pos/wks
17 Jul 59	WATERLOO Philips PB 941	24 2

Tony JACKSON – See Q

Tony JACKSON and the VIBRATIONS
UK, male vocal / instrumental group (3 WEEKS)

		pos/wks
8 Oct 64	BYE BYE BABY Pye 7N 15685	38 3

See also SEARCHERS

Wanda JACKSON US, female vocalist (11 WEEKS)

		pos/wks
1 Sep 60	LET'S HAVE A PARTY Capitol CL 15147	32 8
26 Jan 61	MEAN MEAN MAN (re) Capitol CL 15176	40 3

JACKSON SISTERS US, female vocal group (2 WEEKS)

		pos/wks
20 Jun 87	I BELIEVE IN MIRACLES Urban URB 4	72 2

Re-entries are listed as (re), (2re), (3re), etc which signifies that the hit re-entered the chart once, twice or three times, etc

JACKSONS `60` `Top 500`

One of the world's biggest-selling and most popular groups: brothers Jackie, Tito, Jermaine, Marlon and solo superstar Michael Jackson, with Randy joining in 1977. The Indiana quintet topped the US chart with their first four hits, and have reportedly sold more than 100 million records (235 WEEKS)

		pos/wks
31 Jan 70 ●	I WANT YOU BACK *Tamla Motown TMG 724* [1] ▲	2 13
16 May 70 ●	ABC *Tamla Motown TMG 738* [1] ▲	8 11
1 Aug 70 ●	THE LOVE YOU SAVE *Tamla Motown TMG 746* [1] ▲	7 9
21 Nov 70 ●	I'LL BE THERE *Tamla Motown TMG 758* [1] ▲	4 16
10 Apr 71	MAMA'S PEARL *Tamla Motown TMG 769* [1]	25 7
17 Jul 71	NEVER CAN SAY GOODBYE *Tamla Motown TMG 778* [1]	33 7
11 Nov 72 ●	LOOKIN' THROUGH THE WINDOWS *Tamla Motown TMG 833* [1]	9 11
23 Dec 72	SANTA CLAUS IS COMING TO TOWN *Tamla Motown TMG 837* [1]	43 3
17 Feb 73 ●	DOCTOR MY EYES *Tamla Motown TMG 842* [1]	9 10
9 Jun 73	HALLELUJAH DAY *Tamla Motown TMG 856* [1]	20 9
8 Sep 73	SKYWRITER *Tamla Motown TMG 865* [1]	25 8
9 Apr 77	ENJOY YOURSELF *Epic EPC 5063*	42 4
4 Jun 77 ★	SHOW YOU THE WAY TO GO *Epic EPC 5266*	1 10
13 Aug 77	DREAMER *Epic EPC 5458*	22 9
5 Nov 77	GOIN' PLACES *Epic EPC 5732*	26 7
11 Feb 78	EVEN THOUGH YOU'VE GONE *Epic EPC 5919*	31 4
23 Sep 78 ●	BLAME IT ON THE BOOGIE *Epic EPC 6683*	8 12
3 Feb 79	DESTINY *Epic EPC 6983*	39 6
24 Mar 79 ●	SHAKE YOUR BODY (DOWN TO THE GROUND) *Epic EPC 7181*	4 12
25 Oct 80	LOVELY ONE *Epic EPC 9302*	29 6
13 Dec 80	HEARTBREAK HOTEL *Epic EPC 9391*	44 6
28 Feb 81 ●	CAN YOU FEEL IT *Epic EPC 9554*	6 15
4 Jul 81 ●	WALK RIGHT NOW *Epic EPC A 1294*	7 11
7 Jul 84	STATE OF SHOCK *Epic A 4431* [2]	14 8
8 Sep 84	TORTURE *Epic A 4675*	26 6
16 Apr 88 ●	I WANT YOU BACK (re-mix) *Motown ZB 41913* [3]	8 9
13 May 89	NOTHIN' (THAT COMPARES 2 U) *Epic 654808 7*	33 6

[1] Jackson Five [2] Jacksons, lead vocals Mick Jagger and Michael Jackson
[3] Michael Jackson with the Jackson Five

JACKY – See Jackie LEE

JACQUELINE – See MACK VIBE featuring JACQUELINE

JADA – See SKIP RAIDERS featuring JADA

JADE *US, female vocal group (28 WEEKS)*

		pos/wks
20 Mar 93 ●	DON'T WALK AWAY *Giant W 0160CD*	7 8
3 Jul 93	I WANNA LOVE YOU *Giant 74321151662*	13 7
18 Sep 93	ONE WOMAN *Giant 74321165122*	22 5
5 Feb 94	ALL THRU THE NITE *Giant 74321187552* [1]	32 3
11 Feb 95	EVERY DAY OF THE WEEK *Giant 74321260242*	19 5

[1] P.O.V. featuring Jade

JADE 4 U – See Praga KHAN

JAGGED EDGE
UK, male vocal / instrumental group (2 WEEKS)

		pos/wks
15 Sep 90	YOU DON'T LOVE ME *Polydor PO 97*	66 2

JAGGED EDGE featuring NELLY
US, male vocal group and male rapper (3 WEEKS)

		pos/wks
27 Oct 01	WHERE THE PARTY AT? *Columbia 6719012*	25 3

See also NELLY

Mick JAGGER *UK, male vocalist (43 WEEKS)*

		pos/wks
14 Nov 70	MEMO FROM TURNER *Decca F 13067*	32 5
7 Jul 84	STATE OF SHOCK *Epic A 4431* [1]	14 8
16 Feb 85	JUST ANOTHER NIGHT *CBS A 4722*	32 6
7 Sep 85 ★	DANCING IN THE STREET *EMI America EA 204* [2] ■	1 12
12 Sep 87	LET'S WORK *CBS 651028 7*	31 7

		pos/wks
6 Feb 93	SWEET THING *Atlantic A 7410CD*	24 4
23 Mar 02	VISIONS OF PARADISE *Virgin VUSCD 240*	43 1

[1] Jacksons, lead vocals Mick Jagger and Michael Jackson [2] David Bowie and Mick Jagger

See also ROLLING STONES

JAGS *UK, male vocal / instrumental group (11 WEEKS)*

		pos/wks
8 Sep 79	BACK OF MY HAND *Island WIP 6501*	17 10
2 Feb 80	WOMAN'S WORLD *Island WIP 6531*	75 1

JAHEIM *US, male rapper – Jaheim Hoagland (8 WEEKS)*

		pos/wks
24 Mar 01	COULD IT BE *Warner Brothers W 551CD*	33 3
11 Aug 01	JUST IN CASE *Warner Brothers W 564CD*	34 2
29 Jun 02	JUST IN CASE (re-mix) *Warner Brothers WEA W 581CD*	38 3

JAHMALI – See BLAK TWANG

JAKATTA *UK, male producer – Dave Lee (28 WEEKS)*

		pos/wks
24 Feb 01 ●	AMERICAN DREAM (re) *Rulin RULIN 15CDS*	3 14
11 Aug 01	AMERICAN DREAM (re-mix) *Rulin RULIN 20CDS*	63 1
16 Feb 02	SO LONELY *Rulin RULIN 25CDS*	8 5
12 Oct 02 ●	MY VISION *Rulin RULIN 26CDS* [1]	6 8

[1] Jakatta featuring Seal

See also Z FACTOR; PHASE II; Li KWAN; HED BOYS; SEAL; Joey NEGRO; RAVEN MAIZE; AKABU featuring Linda CLIFFORD; IL PADRINOS

JAM `85` `Top 500`
Influential and extremely popular punk-based mod trio from Surrey: Paul Weller (v/g), Bruce Foxton (b), Rick Buckler (d). They hold the record for the most simultaneous Top 75 singles with 13 (all reactivated by their 1982 dissolution). Mass waves of re-entries dominated the charts on 26 Apr 1980 and 22 Jan 1983 (206 WEEKS)

		pos/wks
7 May 77	IN THE CITY (2re) *Polydor 2058 866*	40 14
23 Jul 77	ALL AROUND THE WORLD (2re) *Polydor 2058 903*	13 15
5 Nov 77	THE MODERN WORLD (2re) *Polydor 2058 945*	36 11
11 Mar 78	NEWS OF THE WORLD (2re) *Polydor 2058 995*	27 12
26 Aug 78	DAVID WATTS / 'A' BOMB IN WARDOUR STREET (2re) *Polydor 2059 054*	25 15
21 Oct 78	DOWN IN THE TUBE STATION AT MIDNIGHT (re) *Polydor POSP 8*	15 13
17 Mar 79	STRANGE TOWN (2re) *Polydor POSP 34*	15 18
25 Aug 79	WHEN YOU'RE YOUNG (re) *Polydor POSP 69*	17 11
3 Nov 79 ●	THE ETON RIFLES (re) *Polydor POSP 83*	3 15
22 Mar 80 ★	GOING UNDERGROUND / DREAMS OF CHILDREN (re) *Polydor POSP 113* ■	1 15
23 Aug 80 ★	START (re) *Polydor 2059 266*	1 10
7 Feb 81	THAT'S ENTERTAINMENT (import) *Metronome 0030 364*	21 7
6 Jun 81 ●	FUNERAL PYRE *Polydor POSP 257*	4 6
24 Oct 81 ●	ABSOLUTE BEGINNERS *Polydor POSP 350*	4 6
13 Feb 82 ★	TOWN CALLED MALICE / PRECIOUS (re) *Polydor POSP 400* ■	1 9
3 Jul 82 ●	JUST WHO IS THE FIVE O'CLOCK HERO *Polydor 2059 504*	8 5
18 Sep 82 ●	THE BITTEREST PILL (I EVER HAD TO SWALLOW) *Polydor POSP 505*	2 7
4 Dec 82 ★	BEAT SURRENDER *Polydor POSP 540* ■	1 9
29 Jan 83	THAT'S ENTERTAINMENT *Polydor POSP 482*	60 3
29 Jun 91	THAT'S ENTERTAINMENT (re-issue) *Polydor PO 155*	57 2
11 Oct 97	THE BITTEREST PILL (I EVER HAD TO SWALLOW) (re-issue) *Polydor 5715992*	30 2
11 May 02	IN THE CITY (re-issue) *Polydor 5876117*	36 1

See also Paul WELLER; Bruce FOXTON

JAM & SPOON *Germany, male production duo – Rolf Ellmer and Markus Löeffel (26 WEEKS)*

		pos/wks
2 May 92	TALES FROM A DANCEOGRAPHIC OCEAN (EP) *R&S RSUK 14*	49 1
6 Jun 92	THE COMPLETE STELLA (re-mix) *R&S RSUK 14X*	66 2
26 Feb 94	RIGHT IN THE NIGHT (FALL IN LOVE WITH MUSIC) *Epic 6600822* [1]	31 4
24 Sep 94	FIND ME (ODYSSEY TO ANYOONA) *Epic 6608082* [1]	37 3

10 Jun 95 ●	RIGHT IN THE NIGHT (FALL IN LOVE WITH MUSIC)		
	(re-issue) *Epic 6620182* [1]	10	8
16 Sep 95	FIND ME (ODYSSEY TO ANYOONA) (re-issue) *Epic 6623242* [1]	22	3
25 Nov 95	ANGEL (LADADI O-HEYO) *Epic 6626382* [1]	26	2
30 Aug 97	KALEIDOSCOPE SKIES *Epic 6647614* [1]	48	1
2 Mar 02	BE ANGELED *Nulife / Arista 74321878992* [2]	31	2

[1] Jam & Spoon featuring Plavka [2] Jam & Spoon featuring Rea

Tracks on Tales From a Danceographic Ocean (EP): Stella / Keep on Movin' / My First Fantastic FF. 'The Complete Stella' is a re-mix of a track from the EP

See also TOKYO GHETTO PUSSY; STORM; DANCE 2 TRANCE

JAM MACHINE
Italy / US, male vocal / instrumental group (1 WEEK) pos/wks

23 Dec 89	EVERYDAY *Deconstruction PB 43299*	68	1

JAM ON THE MUTHA *UK, male vocal / instrumental group (2 WKS)* pos/wks

11 Aug 90	HOTEL CALIFORNIA *M & G MAGS 3*	62	2

JAM TRONIK
Germany, male / female vocal / instrumental group (7 WEEKS) pos/wks

24 Mar 90	ANOTHER DAY IN PARADISE *Debut DEBT 3093*	19	7

JAMAICA UNITED *Jamaica, male vocal ensemble (1 WEEK)* pos/wks

4 Jul 98	RISE UP *Columbia 6660522*	54	1

JAMELIA *UK, female vocalist – Jamelia Davis (18 WEEKS)* pos/wks

31 Jul 99	I DO *Parlophone Rhythm Series CDRHYTHM 21*	36	2
4 Mar 00 ●	MONEY *Parlophone Rhythm Series CDRHYTHM 27* [1]	5	9
24 Jun 00	CALL ME *Parlophone Rhythm Series CDRHYTHM 28*	11	5
21 Oct 00	BOY NEXT DOOR		
	Parlophone Rhythm Series CDRHYTHM 29	42	2

[1] Jamelia featuring Beenie Man

JAMES 367 Top 500
Anthemic indie pop band formed 1982 in Manchester, UK, by mainstays Tim Booth (v) and Larry Gott (g). After several hitless years, critically acclaimed releases and record company changes, they became one of the most consistently successful acts of the 1990s (89 WEEKS) pos/wks

12 May 90	HOW WAS IT FOR YOU? *Fontana JIM 5*	32	3
7 Jul 90	COME HOME *Fontana JIM 6*	32	4
8 Dec 90	LOSE CONTROL *Fontana JIM 7*	38	5
30 Mar 91 ●	SIT DOWN *Fontana JIM 8*	2	10
30 Nov 91	SOUND *Fontana JIM 9*	9	7
1 Feb 92	BORN OF FRUSTRATION *Fontana JIM 10*	13	6
4 Apr 92	RING THE BELLS *Fontana JIM 11*	37	2
18 Jul 92	SEVEN (EP) *Fontana JIM 12*	46	2
11 Sep 93	SOMETIMES *Fontana JIMCD 13*	18	4
13 Nov 93	LAID *Fontana JIMCD 14*	25	4
2 Apr 94	JAM J / SAY SOMETHING *Fontana JIMCD 15*	24	4
22 Feb 97 ●	SHE'S A STAR *Fontana JIMCD 16*	9	5
3 May 97	TOMORROW *Fontana JIMCD 17*	12	3
5 Jul 97	WALTZING ALONG *Fontana JIMCD 18*	23	4
21 Mar 98	DESTINY CALLING *Fontana JIMCD 19*	17	4
6 Jun 98	RUNAGROUND *Fontana JIMCD 20*	29	2
21 Nov 98 ●	SIT DOWN (re-mix) *Fontana JIMCD 21*	7	7
31 Jul 99	I KNOW WHAT I'M HERE FOR *Mercury JIMCD22*	22	5
16 Oct 99	JUST LIKE FRED ASTAIRE *Mercury JIMCD 23*	17	3
25 Dec 99	WE'RE GOING TO MISS YOU *Mercury JIMCD 24*	48	2
7 Jul 01	GETTING AWAY WITH IT (ALL MESSED UP)		
	Mercury JIMCD 25	22	3

Tracks on Seven (EP): Seven / Goalie's Ball / William Burroughs / Still Alive. 'Say Something' listed with 'Jam J' only for first two weeks of record's run

JAMES – See CHRIS and JAMES

David JAMES *UK, male DJ / producer (1 WEEK)* pos/wks

11 Aug 01	ALWAYS A PERMANENT STATE *Hooj Choons HOOJ 108CD*	60	1

Dick JAMES
UK, male vocalist – Isaac Vapnic, d. 1 Feb 1986 (13 WEEKS) pos/wks

20 Jan 56	ROBIN HOOD (re) / THE BALLAD OF DAVY CROCKETT		
	Parlophone R 4117	14	9
11 Jan 57	GARDEN OF EDEN *Parlophone R 4255*	18	4

'Robin Hood' is with Stephen James and his Chums. 'The Ballad of Davy Crockett' was listed only from 18 May 1956

Etta JAMES *US, female vocalist – Jamesetta Hawkins (7 WEEKS)* pos/wks

10 Feb 96 ●	I JUST WANT TO MAKE LOVE TO YOU *MCA MCSTD 48003*	5	7

Freddie JAMES *Canada, male vocalist (3 WEEKS)* pos/wks

24 Nov 79	GET UP AND BOOGIE *Warner Bros. K 17478*	54	3

Joni JAMES *US, female vocalist – Joan Babbo (2 WEEKS)* pos/wks

6 Mar 53	WHY DON'T YOU BELIEVE ME? *MGM 582* ▲	11	1
30 Jan 59	THERE MUST BE A WAY *MGM 1002*	24	1

Rick JAMES *US, male vocalist (30 WEEKS)* pos/wks

8 Jul 78	YOU AND I *Motown TMG 1110*	46	7
7 Jul 79	I'M A SUCKER FOR YOUR LOVE *Motown TMG 1146* [1]	43	8
6 Sep 80	BIG TIME *Motown TMG 1198*	41	6
4 Jul 81	GIVE IT TO ME BABY *Motown TMG 1229*	47	3
12 Jun 82	STANDING ON THE TOP (PART 1) *Motown TMG 1263* [2]	53	3
3 Jul 82	DANCE WIT' ME *Motown TMG 1266*	53	3

[1] Teena Marie, co-lead vocals Rick James [2] Temptations featuring Rick James

Sonny JAMES *US, male vocalist – James Loden (8 WEEKS)* pos/wks

30 Nov 56	THE CAT CAME BACK *Capitol CL 14635*	30	1
8 Feb 57	YOUNG LOVE *Capitol CL 14683*	11	7

Wendy JAMES *UK, female vocalist (4 WEEKS)* pos/wks

20 Feb 93	THE NAMELESS ONE *MCA MCSTD 1732*	34	3
17 Apr 93	LONDON'S BRILLIANT *MCA MCSTD 1763*	62	1

Jimmy JAMES and the VAGABONDS
UK, male vocal / instrumental group (25 WEEKS) pos/wks

11 Sep 68	RED RED WINE *Pye 7N 17579*	36	8
24 Apr 76	I'LL GO WHERE YOUR MUSIC TAKES ME *Pye 7N 45585*	23	8
17 Jul 76 ●	NOW IS THE TIME *Pye 7N 45606*	5	9

Tommy JAMES and the SHONDELLS
US, male vocal / instrumental group (25 WEEKS) pos/wks

21 Jul 66	HANKY PANKY *Roulette RK 7000* ▲	38	7
5 Jun 68 ★	MONY MONY *Major Minor MM 567*	1	18

JAMES BOYS
UK, male vocal duo – Bradley and Stewart Palmer (6 WEEKS) pos/wks

19 May 73	OVER AND OVER *Penny Farthing PEN 806*	39	6

JAMESON & VIPER *UK, male DJ / production / vocal duo (1 WEEK)* pos/wks

14 Sep 02	SELECTA (URBAN HEROES) *Soundproof / Island SPR 1CD*	51	1

JAMESTOWN featuring JOCELYN BROWN *US, male instrumentalist / producer – Kent Brainerd and US, female vocalist (1 WEEK)* pos/wks

27 Mar 99	I BELIEVE *Playola 0091705 PLA*	62	1

JAMIROQUAI 178 Top 500
One of world's biggest-selling acts of the late 1990s features headdress-wearing vocalist Jay Kay, b. 30 Dec 1969, Manchester, UK. Group, whose videos have also earned numerous accolades, sold seven million copies of 1996 album 'Travelling Without Moving' and 1999 album 'Synkronized' topped many European charts (141 WEEKS) pos/wks

31 Oct 92	WHEN YOU GONNA LEARN (re) *Acid Jazz JAZID 46*	52	3
13 Mar 93 ●	TOO YOUNG TO DIE *Sony S2 6590112*	10	7

5 Jun 93	BLOW YOUR MIND *Sony S2 6592972*.......................	12	6
14 Aug 93	EMERGENCY ON PLANET EARTH *Sony S2 6595782*	32	3
25 Sep 93	WHEN YOU GONNA LEARN (re-issue) *Sony S2 6596952*	28	3
8 Oct 94	SPACE COWBOY *Sony S2 6608512*....................	17	5
19 Nov 94	HALF THE MAN *Sony S2 6610032*...................	15	8
1 Jul 95 ●	STILLNESS IN TIME *Sony S2 6620255*................	9	5
1 Jun 96	DO U KNOW WHERE YOU'RE COMING FROM		
	Renk CDRENK 63 [1]	12	5
31 Aug 96 ●	VIRTUAL INSANITY *Sony S2 6636132*................	3	11
7 Dec 96 ●	COSMIC GIRL *Sony S2 6638292*...................	6	10
10 May 97 ●	ALRIGHT *Sony S2 6643252*.......................	6	5
13 Dec 97	HIGH TIMES *Sony S2 6653702*....................	20	6
25 Jul 98 ★	DEEPER UNDERGROUND *Sony S2 6662182*■	1	11
5 Jun 99 ●	CANNED HEAT *Sony S2 6673022*..................	4	10
25 Sep 99	SUPERSONIC *Sony S2 6678392*...................	22	4
11 Dec 99	KING FOR A DAY *Sony S2 6679732*................	20	7
24 Feb 01	I'M IN THE MOOD FOR LOVE *Warner Esp WSMS 001CD* [2] ...29		3
25 Aug 01 ●	LITTLE L *Sony S2 6717182*......................	5	11
1 Dec 01	YOU GIVE ME SOMETHING *Sony S2 6720072*.........	16	9
9 Mar 02	LOVE FOOLOSOPHY (re) *Sony S2 6723252*..........	14	6
20 Jul 02	CORNER OF THE EARTH *Sony S2 6727882*..........	31	3

[1] M-Beat featuring Jamiroquai [2] Jools Holland and Jamiroquai

JAMMERS *US, male vocal / instrumental group (2 WEEKS)*
pos/wks
29 Jan 83	BE MINE TONIGHT *Salsoul Sal 101*	65	2

JAMX & DeLEON *Germany, male production duo*
– Jürgen Mutschall and Dominik DeLeon (2 WEEKS)
pos/wks
7 Sep 02	CAN U DIG IT? *Serious SERR 052CD*	40	2

JAN and DEAN
US, male vocal duo – Jan Berry and Dean Torrence (18 WEEKS)
pos/wks
24 Aug 61	HEART AND SOUL *London HLH 9395*..............	24	8
15 Aug 63	SURF CITY *Liberty LIB 55580* ▲	26	10

JAN and KJELD
Denmark, male vocal duo – Jan and Kjeld Wennick (4 WEEKS)
pos/wks
21 Jul 60	BANJO BOY *Ember S 101*	36	4

JANE'S ADDICTION *US, male vocal / instrumental group (4 WKS)*
pos/wks
23 Mar 91	BEEN CAUGHT STEALING *Warner Bros. W 0011*	34	3
1 Jun 91	CLASSIC GIRL *Warner Bros. W 0031*	60	1

Horst JANKOWSKI, His Orchestra and Chorus
Germany, male instrumentalist – piano (18 WEEKS)
pos/wks
29 Jul 65 ●	A WALK IN THE BLACK FOREST *Mercury MF 861*	3	18

Samantha JANUS *UK, female vocalist (3 WEEKS)*
pos/wks
11 May 91	A MESSAGE TO YOUR HEART *Hollywood HWD 104*	30	3

Philip JAP *UK, male vocalist (8 WEEKS)*
pos/wks
31 Jul 82	SAVE US *A&M AMS 8217*	53	4
25 Sep 82	TOTAL ERASURE *A&M JAP 1*	41	4

JAPAN `431` `Top 500`
*Rock quintet which subsequently became New Romantic figureheads
fronted by David Sylvian (v), b. David Batt, 23 Feb 1958, London, UK, who
later recorded critically acclaimed solo work. Group folded in 1982, but full
line-up briefly reconvened as Rain Tree Crow in 1991 (81 WEEKS)*
pos/wks
18 Oct 80	GENTLEMEN TAKE POLAROIDS *Virgin VS 379*........	60	2
9 May 81	THE ART OF PARTIES *Virgin VS 409*...............	48	5
19 Sep 81	QUIET LIFE *Hansa HANSA 6*	19	9
7 Nov 81	VISIONS OF CHINA *Virgin VS 436*	32	12
23 Jan 82	EUROPEAN SON *Hansa HANSA 10*.................	31	4
20 Mar 82 ●	GHOSTS *Virgin VS 472*..........................	5	8
22 May 82	CANTONESE BOY *Virgin VS 502*..................	24	6
3 Jul 82 ●	I SECOND THAT EMOTION *Hansa HANSA 12*.........	9	11
9 Oct 82	LIFE IN TOKYO *Hansa HANSA 17*	28	6

20 Nov 82	NIGHT PORTER *Virgin VS 554*	29	9
12 Mar 83	ALL TOMORROW'S PARTIES *Hansa HANSA 18*	38	4
21 May 83	CANTON (LIVE) *Virgin VS 581*	42	3

See also RAIN TREE CROW

JARK PRONGO *Holland, male production duo*
– René ter Horst and Gaston Steenkist (1 WEEK)
pos/wks
3 Apr 99	MOVIN' THRU YOUR SYSTEM *Hooj Choons HOOJ 72CD*...58		1

See also GOODMEN; TOMBA VIRA; RHYTHMKILLAZ; RIVA featuring Dannii
MINOGUE; CHOCOLATE PUMA

Jean-Michel JARRE
France, male instrumentalist / producer (40 WEEKS)
pos/wks
27 Aug 77 ●	OXYGENE PART IV *Polydor 2001 721*..............	4	9
20 Jan 79	EQUINOXE PART 5 *Polydor POSP 20*...............	45	5
23 Aug 86	FOURTH RENDEZ-VOUS *Polydor POSP 788*..........	65	4
5 Nov 88	REVOLUTIONS *Polydor PO 25*	52	2
7 Jan 89	LONDON KID *Polydor PO 32* [1]	52	3
7 Oct 89	OXYGENE PART IV (re-mix) *Polydor PO 55*	65	2
26 Jun 93	CHRONOLOGIE PART 4 *Polydor POCS 274*..........	55	2
30 Oct 93	CHRONOLOGIE PART 4 (re-mix) *Polydor POCS 274* ...	56	1
22 Mar 97	OXYGENE 8 *Epic 6643232*......................	17	3
5 Jul 97	OXYGENE 10 *Epic 6647152*.....................	21	2
11 Jul 98	RENDEZ-VOUS '98 *Epic 6661102* [2]	12	6
26 Feb 00	C'EST LA VIE *Epic 6689302* [3]	40	1

[1] Jean-Michel Jarre featuring Hank Marvin [2] Jean-Michel Jarre and Apollo 440
[3] Jean-Michel Jarre featuring Natacha Atlas

Al JARREAU *US, male vocalist (30 WEEKS)*
pos/wks
26 Sep 81	WE'RE IN THIS LOVE TOGETHER *Warner Bros. K 17849*	55	4
14 May 83	MORNIN' *WEA U9929*	28	6
16 Jul 83	TROUBLE IN PARADISE *WEA Int. U9871*	36	5
24 Sep 83	BOOGIE DOWN *WEA U9814*	63	3
16 Nov 85	DAY BY DAY *Polydor POSP 770* [1]	53	3
5 Apr 86	THE MUSIC OF GOODBYE (LOVE THEME FROM 'OUT OF		
	AFRICA') *MCA MCA 1038* [2]	75	1
7 Mar 87 ●	'MOONLIGHTING' THEME *WEA U8407*	8	8

[1] Shakatak featuring Al Jarreau [2] Melissa Manchester and Al Jarreau

Kenny 'Jammin' JASON and DJ 'Fast' Eddie SMITH
US, male DJ / production duo (4 WEEKS)
pos/wks
11 Apr 87	CAN U DANCE (re) *Champion CHAMP 41*	67	4

JAVELLS featuring Nosmo KING
UK, male vocalist – Stephen Gold (8 WEEKS)
pos/wks
9 Nov 74	GOODBYE NOTHING TO SAY *Pye Disco Demand DDS 2003*.....26		8

See also TRUTH

Peter JAY and the JAYWALKERS
UK, male instrumental group – Peter Jay – drums (11 WEEKS)
pos/wks
8 Nov 62	CAN CAN '62 *Decca F 11531*.....................	31	11

Oris JAY presents DELSENA *Holland, male producer*
– Peran van Dijk – and UK, female vocalist (2 WEEKS)
pos/wks
23 Mar 02	TRIPPIN' *Gusto CDGUS 3*	42	2

Simone JAY – See DJ DADO

JAYDEE *Holland, male DJ / producer – Robin Albers (3 WEEKS)*
pos/wks
20 Sep 97	PLASTIC DREAMS *R&S RS 97117CD*................	18	3

Ollie JAYE – See JON THE DENTIST vs Ollie JAYE

JAYHAWKS
US, male / female vocal / instrumental group (1 WEEK)
pos/wks
15 Jul 95	BAD TIME *American 74321291632*................	70	1

US CHART-TOPPERS BUT UK FAILURES

■ All of these US No.1s since November 1952 failed to chart or were unreleased in the UK, which must have been particularly frustrating for the British-born acts among these hitmakers

22/11/52	IT'S IN THE BOOK (PARTS 1 & 2) Johnny Standley
16/05/53	THE SONG FROM MOULIN ROUGE (WHERE IS YOUR HEART) Percy Faith and His Orchestra
10/10/53	ST GEORGE AND THE DRAGONET Stan Freberg
21/11/53	RAGS TO RICHES Tony Bennett
05/02/55	HEARTS OF STONE Fontane Sisters
29/10/55	AUTUMN LEAVES Roger Williams
25/02/56	LISBON ANTIGUA Nelson Riddle
24/03/56	THE POOR PEOPLE OF PARIS Les Baxter
06/04/57	ROUND AND ROUND Perry Como
22/12/58	THE CHIPMUNK SONG Chipmunks
11/05/59	THE HAPPY ORGAN Dave 'Baby' Cortez
18/05/59	KANSAS CITY Wilbert Harrison
16/11/59	MR BLUE Fleetwoods
10/10/60	MR CUSTER Larry Verne
09/01/61	WONDERLAND BY NIGHT Bert Kaempfert
13/02/61	CALCUTTA Lawrence Welk
10/07/61	TOSSIN' AND TURNIN' Bobby Lewis
28/08/61	WOODEN HEART Joe Dowell
11/12/61	PLEASE MR POSTMAN Marvelettes
07/07/62	THE STRIPPER David Rose and His Orchestra
12/01/63	GO AWAY LITTLE GIRL Steve Lawrence
27/04/63	I WILL FOLLOW HIM Little Peggy March
10/08/63	FINGERTIPS (PT. 2) Little Stevie Wonder
12/12/64	MR LONELY Bobby Vinton
20/02/65	THIS DIAMOND RING Gary Lewis and the Playboys
13/03/65	EIGHT DAYS A WEEK Beatles*
01/05/65	MRS BROWN YOU'VE GOT A LOVELY DAUGHTER Herman's Hermits*
07/08/65	I'M HENRY VIII I AM Herman's Hermits*
01/01/66	THE SOUND OF SILENCE Simon and Garfunkel
30/04/66	GOOD LOVIN' Young Rascals
24/09/66	CHERISH Association
12/11/66	POOR SIDE OF TOWN Johnny Rivers
18/02/67	KIND OF A DRAG Buckinghams
01/07/67	WINDY Association
21/10/67	TO SIR WITH LOVE Lulu*
25/11/67	INCENSE AND PEPPERMINTS Strawberry Alarm Clock
18/05/68	TIGHTEN UP Archie Bell and the Drells
20/07/68	GRAZING IN THE GRASS Hugh Masekela
17/08/68	PEOPLE GOT TO BE FREE Rascals
01/02/69	CRIMSON AND CLOVER Tommy James and the Shondells
28/06/69	LOVE THEME FROM ROMEO AND JULIET Henry Mancini and His Orchestra
14/02/70	THANK YOU (FALETTINME BE MICE ELF AGIN) / EVERYBODY IS A STAR Sly and the Family Stone
13/06/70	THE LONG AND WINDING ROAD / FOR YOU BLUE Beatles*
13/02/71	ONE BAD APPLE Osmonds
20/03/71	ME AND BOBBY MCGEE Janis Joplin
12/06/71	WANT ADS Honey Cone
24/07/71	INDIAN RESERVATION (THE LAMENT OF THE CHEROKEE RESERVATION INDIAN) Raiders
07/08/71	HOW CAN YOU MEND A BROKEN HEART Bee Gees*
04/09/71	UNCLE ALBERT / ADMIRAL HALSEY Paul and Linda McCartney*
11/09/71	GO AWAY LITTLE GIRL Donny Osmond
10/06/72	THE CANDY MAN Sammy Davis Jr
26/08/72	BRANDY (YOU'RE A FINE GIRL) Looking Glass
16/09/72	BLACK AND WHITE Three Dog Night
09/12/72	I AM WOMAN Helen Reddy
07/04/73	THE NIGHT THE LIGHTS WENT OUT IN GEORGIA Vicki Lawrence
07/07/73	WILL IT GO ROUND IN CIRCLES Billy Preston
21/07/73	BAD, BAD LEROY BROWN Jim Croce
04/08/73	THE MORNING AFTER Maureen McGovern
25/08/73	BROTHER LOUIE Stories
15/09/73	DELTA DAWN Helen Reddy
29/09/73	WE'RE AN AMERICAN BAND Grand Funk
06/10/73	HALF-BREED Cher
29/12/73	TIME IN A BOTTLE Jim Croce
19/01/74	SHOW AND TELL Al Wilson

30/03/74	**SUNSHINE ON MY SHOULDERS** John Denver
06/04/74	**HOOKED ON A FEELING** Blue Swede
04/05/74	**THE LOCO-MOTION** Grand Funk
15/06/74	**BILLY, DON'T BE A HERO**
	Bo Donaldson and the Heywoods
19/10/74	**NOTHING FROM NOTHING** Billy Preston
21/12/74	**CAT'S IN THE CRADLE** Harry Chapin
08/02/75	**FIRE** Ohio Players
15/02/75	**YOU'RE NO GOOD** Linda Ronstadt
01/03/75	**BEST OF MY LOVE** Eagles
08/03/75	**HAVE YOU NEVER BEEN MELLOW**
	Olivia Newton-John*
15/03/75	**BLACK WATER** Doobie Brothers
26/04/75	**(HEY WON'T YOU PLAY) ANOTHER SOMEBODY**
	DONE SOMEBODY WRONG SONG BJ Thomas
03/05/75	**HE DON'T LOVE YOU (LIKE I LOVE YOU)**
	Tony Orlando and Dawn

Escape Club, from London and Leeds, were US chart-toppers without one entry in the UK singles chart of any description

24/05/75	**SHINING STAR** Earth Wind and Fire
31/05/75	**BEFORE THE NEXT TEARDROP FALLS**
	Freddy Fender
07/06/75	**THANK GOD I'M A COUNTRY BOY** John Denver
14/06/75	**SISTER GOLDEN HAIR** America
27/09/75	**I'M SORRY / CALYPSO** John Denver
11/10/75	**BAD BLOOD** Neil Sedaka
27/12/75	**LET'S DO IT AGAIN** Staple Singers
03/01/76	**SATURDAY NIGHT** Bay City Rollers*
17/01/76	**I WRITE THE SONGS** Barry Manilow
31/01/76	**LOVE ROLLERCOASTER** Ohio Players
28/02/76	**THEME FROM S.W.A.T.** Rhythm Heritage
08/05/76	**WELCOME BACK** John Sebastian
15/05/76	**BOOGIE FEVER** Sylvers
26/03/77	**RICH GIRL** Daryl Hall and John Oates
02/07/77	**GONNA FLY NOW (THEME FROM 'ROCKY')**
	Bill Conti
16/07/77	**DA DOO RON RON** Shaun Cassidy
23/07/77	**LOOKS LIKE WE MADE IT** Barry Manilow
04/03/78	**(LOVE IS) THICKER THAN WATER** Andy Gibb*
28/10/78	**HOT CHILD IN THE CITY** Nick Gilder
25/07/81	**THE ONE THAT YOU LOVE** Air Supply**
08/11/86	**AMANDA** Boston

06/12/86	**THE NEXT TIME I FALL**
	Peter Cetera and Amy Grant
24/01/87	**AT THIS MOMENT** Billy Vera and Beaters
14/03/87	**JACOB'S LADDER** Huey Lewis and the News
20/06/87	**HEAD TO TOE** Lisa Lisa and Cult Jam
01/08/87	**SHAKEDOWN**
	Bob Seger and the Silver Bullet Band
20/02/88	**SEASONS CHANGE** Exposé
09/07/88	**THE FLAME** Cheap Trick
12/11/88	**WILD WILD WEST** Escape Club*
10/12/88	**LOOK AWAY** Chicago
04/02/89	**WHEN I'M WITH YOU** Sheriff
03/06/89	**ROCK ON** Michael Damian
01/09/90	**IF WISHES CAME TRUE** Sweet Sensation
20/10/90	**I DON'T HAVE THE HEART** James Ingram
23/03/91	**ONE MORE TRY** Timmy-T
25/05/91	**I DON'T WANNA CRY** Mariah Carey
14/11/92	**HOW DO YOU TALK TO AN ANGEL** Heights
24/06/00	**BE WITH YOU** Enrique Iglesias
22/07/00	**BENT** Matchbox Twenty

* = British-born acts ** = British / Australian act

JAY-Z `383` Top 500

Foremost East Coast rapper, b. Shawn Carter, 4 Dec 1969, New York, whose original rap name was "Jazzy". The owner of Roc-A-Fella Records has had UK hits with a dozen acts, six simultaneous US R&B chart entries (2001), and saw saw his last five studio recorded albums top the US charts (87 WEEKS) pos/wks

Date	Title	pos	wks
1 Mar 97	CAN'T KNOCK THE HUSTLE *Northwestside 74321447192* [1]	30	2
10 May 97	AIN'T NO PLAYA *Northwestside 74321474842* [2]	31	2
21 Jun 97 ●	I'LL BE *Def Jam 75710432* [3]	9	5
23 Aug 97	WHO YOU WIT *Qwest W 0411CD*	65	1
25 Oct 97	SUNSHINE *Northwestside 74321528702* [4]	25	2
14 Feb 98	WISHING ON A STAR *Northwestside 74321554632* [5]	13	4
27 Jun 98	THE CITY IS MINE *Northwestside 74321588012* [6]	38	2
12 Dec 98 ●	HARD KNOCK LIFE (GHETTO ANTHEM) *Northwestside 74321635332*	2	11
13 Mar 99	CAN I GET A... *Def Jam 5668472* [7]	24	3
10 Apr 99	BE ALONE NO MORE *Northwestside 74321658472* [8]	11	9
19 Jun 99	LOBSTER & SCRIMP *Virgin DINSD 186* [9]	48	1
6 Nov 99 ●	HEARTBREAKER *Columbia 6683012* [10] ▲	5	13
4 Dec 99	WHAT YOU THINK OF THAT *Def Jam 8708292*	58	1
26 Feb 00	ANYTHING *Def Jam 5626502*	18	4
24 Jun 00	BIG PIMPIN' *Def Jam 5627742*	29	3
16 Dec 00	I JUST WANNA LOVE U (GIVE IT 2 ME) *Def Jam 5727462*	17	8
23 Jun 01	FIESTA *Jive 9252142* [11]	23	3
27 Oct 01	IZZO (H.O.V.A.) *Roc-A-Fella / Def Jam 5888152*	21	4
19 Jan 02	GIRLS, GIRLS, GIRLS (re) *Roc-A-Fella / Def Jam 5889062*	11	7
25 May 02	HONEY *Jive 9253662* [12]	35	2

[1] Jay-Z featuring Mary J Blige [2] Jay-Z featuring Foxy Brown [3] Foxy Brown featuring Jay-Z [4] Jay-Z featuring Babyface and Foxy Brown [5] Jay-Z featuring Gwen Dickey [6] Jay-Z featuring BLACKstreet [7] Jay-Z featuring Amil & Ja Rule [8] Another Level featuring Jay-Z [9] Timbaland featuring Jay-Z [10] Mariah Carey featuring Jay-Z [11] R Kelly featuring Jay-Z [12] R. Kelly & Jay-Z

JAZZ and the BROTHERS GRIMM
UK, male vocal / instrumental group (2 WEEKS) pos/wks

Date	Title	pos	wks
9 Jul 88	(LET'S ALL GO BACK) DISCO NIGHTS *Ensign ENY 616*	57	2

JAZZY JEFF & the FRESH PRINCE
US, male rap / DJ duo – Jeff Townes and Will Smith (49 WEEKS) pos/wks

Date	Title	pos	wks
4 Oct 86	GIRLS AIN'T NOTHING BUT TROUBLE *Champion Champ 18* [1]	21	8
3 Aug 91 ●	SUMMERTIME (re) *Jive JIVECD 279* [1]	8	12
9 Nov 91	RING MY BELL *Jive JIVECD 288* [1]	53	2
11 Sep 93 ★	BOOM! SHAKE THE ROOM *Jive JIVECD 335*	1	13
20 Nov 93	I'M LOOKING FOR THE ONE (TO BE WITH ME) *Jive JIVECD 345*	24	4
19 Feb 94	CAN'T WAIT TO BE WITH YOU *Jive JIVECD 348*	29	4
4 Jun 94	TWINKLE TWINKLE (I'M NOT A STAR) *Jive JIVECD 354*	62	2
2 Dec 95	BOOM! SHAKE THE ROOM (re-mix) *Jive JIVECD 387*	40	2
11 Jul 98	LOVELY DAZE *Jive 0518902* [1]	37	2

[1] DJ Jazzy Jeff and the Fresh Prince

'Summertime' re-entered and peaked at No.29 in Aug 1994

See also Will SMITH

JAZZY M *UK, male DJ / producer – Michael Connelly (2 WEEKS)* pos/wks

Date	Title	pos	wks
21 Oct 00	JAZZIN' THE WAY YOU KNOW *Perfecto PERF 08CDS*	47	2

Norma JEAN – See Romina JOHNSON

Wyclef JEAN `483` Top 500
Production pioneer and ex-Fugee, b. 17 Oct 1972, Haiti, and was the first hip hop act to headline at Carnegie Hall. New Jersey-based prolific rapper / vocalist / instrumentalist / composer with a social conscience has fused hip-hop with acts as diverse as Santana, Tom Jones, Whitney Houston and wrestler The Rock (75 WEEKS) pos/wks

Date	Title	pos	wks
28 Jun 97	WE TRYING TO STAY ALIVE *Columbia 6646815* [1]	13	5
27 Sep 97	GUANTANAMERA *Columbia 6650852* [1]	25	2
28 Mar 98 ●	NO, NO, NO *Columbia 6656592* [2]	5	8
16 May 98 ●	GONE TILL NOVEMBER *Columbia 6658712*	3	9

Date	Title	pos	wks
14 Nov 98 ●	ANOTHER ONE BITES THE DUST *Dreamworks DRMCD 22364* [3]	5	6
23 Oct 99	NEW DAY *Columbia 6682122* [4]	23	2
16 Sep 00 ●	IT DOESN'T MATTER *Columbia 6697782* [5]	3	8
16 Dec 00 ●	911 *Columbia 6706122* [6]	9	10
21 Jul 01 ●	PERFECT GENTLEMEN *Columbia 6710522*	4	14
8 Dec 01	WISH YOU WERE HERE (re) *Columbia 6721562*	28	5
6 Jul 02	TWO WRONGS (DON'T MAKE A RIGHT) *Columbia 6728902* [7]	14	6

[1] Wyclef Jean and The Refugee Allstars [2] Destiny's Child featuring Wyclef Jean [3] Queen with Wyclef Jean featuring Pras and Free [4] Wyclef Jean featuring Bono [5] Wyclef Jean featuring The Rock and Melky Sedeck [6] Wyclef Jean featuring Mary J Blige [7] Wyclef Jean featuring Claudette Ortiz

See also FUGEES

JEFFERSON *UK, male vocalist – Geoff Turton (8 WEEKS)* pos/wks

Date	Title	pos	wks
9 Apr 69	COLOUR OF MY LOVE *Pye 7N 17706*	22	8

JEFFERSON STARSHIP – See STARSHIP

Garland JEFFREYS *US, male vocalist (1 WEEK)* pos/wks

Date	Title	pos	wks
8 Feb 92	HAIL HAIL ROCK 'N' ROLL *RCA PB 49171*	72	1

JELLYBEAN *US, male producer – John Benitez (47 WEEKS)* pos/wks

Date	Title	pos	wks
1 Feb 86	SIDEWALK TALK *EMI America EA 210* [1]	47	4
26 Sep 87	THE REAL THING *Chrysalis CHS 3167* [2]	13	10
28 Nov 87 ●	WHO FOUND WHO *Chrysalis CHS JEL 1* [3]	10	10
12 Dec 87	JINGO *Chrysalis JEL 2*	12	10
12 Mar 88	JUST A MIRAGE *Chrysalis JEL 3* [4]	13	10
20 Aug 88	COMING BACK FOR MORE *Chrysalis JEL 4* [5]	41	3

[1] Jellybean featuring Catherine Buchanan [2] Jellybean featuring Steven Dante [3] Jellybean featuring Elisa Fiorillo [4] Jellybean featuring Adele Bertei [5] Jellybean featuring Richard Darbyshire

JELLYFISH *US, male vocal / instrumental group (20 WEEKS)* pos/wks

Date	Title	pos	wks
26 Jan 91	THE KING IS HALF UNDRESSED *Charisma CUSS 1*	39	6
27 Apr 91	BABY'S COMING BACK *Charisma CUSS 2*	51	4
3 Aug 91	THE SCARY-GO-ROUND EP *Charisma CUSS 3*	49	3
26 Oct 91	I WANNA STAY HOME *Charisma CUSS 4*	59	2
1 May 93	THE GHOST AT NUMBER ONE *Charisma CUSDG 10*	43	3
17 Jul 93	NEW MISTAKE *Charisma CUSDG 11*	55	2

Tracks on The Scary-Go-Round EP: Now She Knows She's Wrong / Bedspring Kiss / She Still Loves Him (Live) / Baby's Coming Back (Live)

JERU THE DAMAJA *US, male rapper (1 WEEK)* pos/wks

Date	Title	pos	wks
7 Dec 96	YA PLAYIN YASELF *ffrr FCD 289*	67	1

JESSICA *Sweden, female vocalist (1 WEEK)* pos/wks

Date	Title	pos	wks
20 Mar 99	HOW WILL I KNOW (WHO YOU ARE) *Jive 0522412*	47	1

JESUS AND MARY CHAIN
UK, male vocal / instrumental group (59 WEEKS) pos/wks

Date	Title	pos	wks
2 Mar 85	NEVER UNDERSTAND *Blanco Y Negro NEG 8*	47	4
8 Jun 85	YOU TRIP ME UP *Blanco Y Negro NEG 13*	55	3
12 Oct 85	JUST LIKE HONEY *Blanco Y Negro NEG 17*	45	3
26 Jul 86	SOME CANDY TALKING *Blanco Y Negro NEG 19*	13	5
2 May 87 ●	APRIL SKIES *Blanco Y Negro NEG 24*	8	6
15 Aug 87	HAPPY WHEN IT RAINS *Blanco Y Negro NEG 25*	25	5
7 Nov 87	DARKLANDS *Blanco Y Negro NEG 29*	33	4
9 Apr 88	SIDEWALKING *Blanco Y Negro NEG 32*	30	3
23 Sep 89	BLUES FROM A GUN *Blanco Y Negro NEG 41*	32	2
18 Nov 89	HEAD ON *Blanco Y Negro NEG 42*	57	2
8 Sep 90	ROLLERCOASTER (EP) *Blanco Y Negro NEG 45*	46	2
15 Feb 92 ●	REVERENCE *Blanco Y Negro NEG 55*	10	4
14 Mar 92	FAR GONE AND OUT *Blanco Y Negro NEG 56*	23	3
4 Apr 92	ALMOST GOLD *Blanco Y Negro NEG 57*	41	2
10 Jul 93	SOUND OF SPEED (EP) *Blanco Y Negro NEG 66CD*	30	3
30 Jul 94	SOMETIMES ALWAYS *Blanco Y Negro NEG 70CD*	22	3
22 Oct 94	COME ON *Blanco Y Negro NEG 73CD1*	52	2

Re-entries are listed as (re), (2re), (3re), etc which signifies that the hit re-entered the chart once, twice or three times, etc

17 Jun 95	I HATE ROCK 'N' ROLL *Blanco Y Negro NEG 81CD*		61	1
18 Apr 98	CRACKING UP *Creation CRESCD 292*		35	2
30 May 98	ILOVEROCKNROLL *Creation CRESCD 296*		38	1

Tracks on Rollercoaster (EP): Rollercoaster / Silverblade / Lowlife / Tower of Song.
Tracks on Sound of Speed (EP): Snakedriver / Something I Can't Have / Write Record
Release Blues / Little Red Rooster

JESUS JONES *UK, male vocal / instrumental group (52 WEEKS)* pos/wks

25 Feb 89	INFO-FREAKO *Food FOOD 18*		42	3
8 Jul 89	NEVER ENOUGH *Food FOOD 21*		42	3
23 Sep 89	BRING IT ON DOWN *Food FOOD 22*		46	3
7 Apr 90	REAL REAL REAL *Food FOOD 24*		19	8
6 Oct 90	RIGHT HERE RIGHT NOW *Food FOOD 25*		31	4
12 Jan 91 ●	INTERNATIONAL BRIGHT YOUNG THING *Food FOOD 27*		7	7
2 Mar 91	WHO? WHERE? WHY? *Food FOOD 28*		21	7
20 Jul 91	RIGHT HERE RIGHT NOW (re-issue) *Food FOOD 30*		31	4
9 Jan 93 ●	THE DEVIL YOU KNOW *Food CDPERV 1*		10	5
10 Apr 93	THE RIGHT DECISION *Food CDPERV 2*		36	3
10 Jul 93	ZEROES & ONES *Food CDFOODS 44*		30	3
14 Jun 97	THE NEXT BIG THING *Food CDFOOD 95*		49	1
16 Aug 97	CHEMICAL #1 *Food CDFOOD 102*		71	1

JESUS LIZARD *US, male vocal / instrumental group (2 WEEKS)* pos/wks

6 Mar 93	PUSS *Touch And Go TG 83CD*		12	2

The listed flip side of 'Puss' was 'Oh, the Guilt' by Nirvana

JESUS LOVES YOU *UK, male vocalist – Boy George (18 WEEKS)* pos/wks

11 Nov 89	AFTER THE LOVE *More Protein PROT 2*		68	1
23 Feb 91	BOW DOWN MISTER *More Protein PROT 8*		27	8
8 Jun 91	GENERATIONS OF LOVE *More Protein PROT 10*		35	8
12 Dec 92	SWEET TOXIC LOVE *Virgin VS 1449*		65	1

See also BOY GEORGE; CULTURE CLUB

JETHRO TULL *UK, male vocal / instrumental group (68 WEEKS)* pos/wks

1 Jan 69	LOVE STORY *Island WIP 6048*		29	8
14 May 69 ●	LIVING IN THE PAST *Island WIP 6056*		3	14
1 Nov 69 ●	SWEET DREAM *Chrysalis WIP 6070*		7	11
24 Jan 70 ●	TEACHER / THE WITCH'S PROMISE *Chrysalis WIP 6077*		4	9
18 Sep 71	LIFE IS A LONG SONG / UP THE POOL *Chrysalis WIP 6106*		11	8
11 Dec 76	RING OUT SOLSTICE BELLS (EP) *Chrysalis CXP 2*		28	6
15 Sep 84	LAP OF LUXURY *Chrysalis TULL 1*		70	2
16 Jan 88	SAID SHE WAS A DANCER *Chrysalis TULL 4*		55	4
21 Mar 92	ROCKS ON THE ROAD *Chrysalis TULL 7*		47	3
22 May 93	LIVING IN THE (SLIGHTLY MORE RECENT) PAST *Chrysalis CDCHSS 3970*		32	3

Tracks on Ring Out Solstice Bells (EP): Ring Out Solstice Bells / March the Mad
Scientist / The Christmas Song / Pan Dance. 'Living in the (Slightly More Recent) Past'
is a live version of the original

JETS *UK, male vocal / instrumental group (38 WEEKS)* pos/wks

22 Aug 81	SUGAR DOLL *EMI 5211*		55	3
31 Oct 81	YES TONIGHT JOSEPHINE *EMI 5247*		25	11
6 Feb 82	LOVE MAKES THE WORLD GO ROUND *EMI 5262*		21	9
24 Apr 82	THE HONEYDRIPPER *EMI 5289*		58	3
9 Oct 82	SOMEBODY TO LOVE *EMI 5342*		56	3
6 Aug 83	BLUE SKIES *EMI 5405*		53	3
17 Dec 83	ROCKIN' AROUND THE CHRISTMAS TREE *PRT 7P 297*		62	4
13 Oct 84	PARTY DOLL *PRT JETS 2*		72	2

JETS *US, male / female vocal / instrumental group (19 WEEKS)* pos/wks

31 Jan 87 ●	CRUSH ON YOU *MCA MCA 1048*		5	13
25 Apr 87	CURIOSITY *MCA MCA 1119*		41	4
28 May 88	ROCKET 2 U *MCA MCA 1226*		69	2

Joan JETT and the BLACKHEARTS *US, female vocalist with male vocal / instrumental group (21 WEEKS)* pos/wks

24 Apr 82 ●	I LOVE ROCK 'N' ROLL *Epic EPC A 2152* ▲		4	10

---

10 Jul 82	CRIMSON AND CLOVER *Epic EPC A 2485*		60	3
20 Aug 88	I HATE MYSELF FOR LOVING YOU *London LON 195*		46	6
31 Mar 90	DIRTY DEEDS *Chrysalis CHS 3518* [1]		69	1
19 Feb 94	I LOVE ROCK & ROLL (re-issue) *Reprise W 0232CD*		75	1

[1] Joan Jett

JEWEL *US, female vocalist – Jewel Kilcher (8 WEEKS)* pos/wks

14 Jun 97	WHO WILL SAVE YOUR SOUL *Atlantic A 8514CD*		52	1
9 Aug 97	YOU WERE MEANT FOR ME (re) *Atlantic A 5463CD*		32	3
21 Nov 98	HANDS *Atlantic AT 0055CD*		41	2
26 Jun 99	DOWN SO LONG *Atlantic AT 0069CD*		38	2

JEZ & CHOOPIE *UK / Israel, male DJ / production duo – Jeremy Ansell and David Geyra (2 WEEKS)* pos/wks

21 Mar 98	YIM *Multiply CDMULTY 31*		36	2

JHELISA *US, female vocalist (1 WEEK)* pos/wks

1 Jul 95	FRIENDLY PRESSURE *Dorado DOR 040CD*		75	1

JIGSAW
UK, male vocal / instrumental group (16 WEEKS) pos/wks

1 Nov 75 ●	SKY HIGH *Splash CP1 1*		9	11
6 Aug 77	IF I HAVE TO GO AWAY *Splash CP 11*		36	5

JILTED JOHN
UK, male vocalist – Graham Fellows (12 WEEKS) pos/wks

12 Aug 78 ●	JILTED JOHN *EMI International INT 567*		4	12

JIMMY EAT WORLD
US, male vocal / instrumental group (6 WEEKS) pos/wks

17 Nov 01	SALT SWEAT SUGAR *Dreamworks 4508782*		60	1
9 Feb 02	THE MIDDLE *Dreamworks 4508482*		26	3
15 Jun 02	SWEETNESS *Dreamworks 4508342*		38	2

JIMMY THE HOOVER
UK, male / female vocal / instrumental group (8 WEEKS) pos/wks

25 Jun 83	TANTALISE (WO WO EE YEH YEH) *Innervision A 3406*		18	8

JINGLE BELLES *US / UK, female vocal group (4 WEEKS)* pos/wks

17 Dec 83	CHRISTMAS SPECTRE *Passion PASH 14*		37	4

JINNY *Italy, female vocalist – Janine Brown (16 WEEKS)* pos/wks

29 Jun 91	KEEP WARM *Virgin VS 1356*		68	3
22 May 93	FEEL THE RHYTHM *Logic 401633001022*		74	1
15 Jul 95	KEEP WARM (re-mix) *Multiply CDMULTY 5*		11	8
16 Dec 95	WANNA BE WITH YOU *Multiply CDMULTY 8*		30	4

JIVE BUNNY and the MASTERMIXERS *UK, male DJ / production duo – Andy Pickles and Les Hemstock (68 WEEKS)* pos/wks

15 Jul 89 ★	SWING THE MOOD *Music Factory Dance MFD 001*		1	19
14 Oct 89 ★	THAT'S WHAT I LIKE *Music Factory Dance MFD 002*		1	12
16 Dec 89 ★	LET'S PARTY *Music Factory Dance MFD 003* ■		1	6
17 Mar 90 ●	THAT SOUNDS GOOD TO ME *Music Factory Dance MFD 004*		4	6
25 Aug 90 ●	CAN CAN YOU PARTY *Music Factory Dance MFD 007*		8	6
17 Nov 90	LET'S SWING AGAIN *Music Factory Dance MFD 009*		19	5
22 Dec 90	THE CRAZY PARTY MIXES *Music Factory Dance MFD 010*		13	5
23 Mar 91	OVER TO YOU JOHN (HERE WE GO AGAIN) *Music Factory Dance MFD 012*		28	5
20 Jul 91	HOT SUMMER SALSA *Music Factory Dance MFD 013*		43	2
23 Nov 91	ROCK 'N' ROLL DANCE PARTY *Music Factory Dance MFD 015*		48	2

See also Liz KERSHAW and Bruno BROOKES

JO JO GUNNE
US, male vocal / instrumental group (12 WEEKS) pos/wks

25 Mar 72 ●	RUN RUN RUN *Asylum AYM 501*		6	12

UK No.1 ★   UK Top 10 ●   Still on chart +   UK million seller ◆   UK entry at No.1 ■   US No.1 ▲

JOAN COLLINS FAN CLUB
UK, male comedian / vocalist – Julian Clary (3 WEEKS) pos/wks

18 Jun 88	LEADER OF THE PACK *10 TEN 227*	60	3

John Paul JOANS *UK, male vocalist (7 WEEKS)*
pos/wks

19 Dec 70	THE MAN FROM NAZARETH (re) *RAK 107*	25	7

JOBOXERS *UK, male vocal / instrumental group (33 WEEKS)*
pos/wks

19 Feb 83 ●	BOXERBEAT *RCA BOX 1*	3	15
21 May 83 ●	JUST GOT LUCKY *RCA BOXX 2*	7	9
13 Aug 83	JOHNNY FRIENDLY *RCA BOXX 3*	31	8
12 Nov 83	JEALOUS LOVE *RCA BOXX 4*	72	1

JOCASTA *UK, male vocal / instrumental group (2 WEEKS)*
pos/wks

15 Feb 97	GO *Epic 6641415*	50	1
3 May 97	CHANGE ME *Epic 6643902*	60	1

JOCKMASTER B.A. – See MAD JOCKS featuring JOCKMASTER B.A.

JOCKO
US, male DJ / rapper – Jocko Henderson, d. 15 Jul 2000 (3 WEEKS) pos/wks

23 Feb 80	RHYTHM TALK *Philadelphia International PIR 8222*	56	3

JODE featuring YO-HANS *UK, male / female vocal duo (2 WKS)* pos/wks

19 Dec 98	WALK...(THE DOG) LIKE AN EGYPTIAN *Logic 74321640332*	48	2

JODECI *US, male vocal group (19 WEEKS)*
pos/wks

16 Jan 93	CHERISH *Uptown MCSTD 1726*	56	2
11 Dec 93	CRY FOR YOU *Uptown MCSTD 1951*	56	1
16 Jul 94	FEENIN' *Uptown MCSTD 1984*	18	3
28 Jan 95	CRY FOR YOU (re-issue) *Uptown MCSTD 2039*	20	3
24 Jun 95	FREEK 'N YOU *Uptown MCSTD 2072*	17	5
9 Dec 95	LOVE U 4 LIFE *Uptown MCSTD 2105*	23	3
25 May 96	GET ON UP *MCA MCSTD 48010*	20	2

JODIE *Australia, female vocalist (1 WEEK)*
pos/wks

25 Feb 95	ANYTHING YOU WANT *Mercury MERCD 423*	47	1

JOE *US, male vocalist – Joseph Thomas (45 WEEKS)*
pos/wks

22 Jan 94	I'M IN LUV *Mercury JOECD 1*	22	4
25 Jun 94	THE ONE FOR ME *Mercury JOECD 2*	34	2
22 Oct 94	ALL OR NOTHING *Mercury JOECD 3*	56	1
27 Apr 96	ALL THE THINGS (YOUR MAN WON'T DO) *Island CID 634*	34	3
14 Jun 97	DON'T WANNA BE A PLAYER *Jive JIVECD 410*	16	3
27 Sep 97	THE LOVE SCENE *Jive JIVECD 430*	22	2
10 Jan 98	GOOD GIRLS *Jive JIVECD 442*	29	2
22 Aug 98	NO ONE ELSE COMES CLOSE *Jive 0521682*	41	2
31 Oct 98	ALL THAT I AM *Jive 0518532*	52	1
11 Mar 00 ●	THANK GOD I FOUND YOU (re) *Columbia 6690582* [1] ▲	10	10
15 Jul 00	TREAT HER LIKE A LADY *Jive 9250772*	60	1
17 Feb 01 ●	STUTTER *Jive 9251632* [2] ▲	7	8
5 May 01	I WANNA KNOW *Jive 9252102*	37	2
16 Feb 02	LET'S STAY HOME TONIGHT *Jive 9253222*	29	2
14 Sep 02	WHAT IF A WOMAN *Jive 9253962*	53	1

[1] Mariah Carey featuring Joe and 98 Degrees [2] Joe featuring Mystikal

JOE PUBLIC *US, male rap group (5 WEEKS)*
pos/wks

11 Jul 92	LIVE AND LEARN *Columbia 6575267*	43	4
28 Nov 92	I'VE BEEN WATCHIN' *Columbia 6587657*	75	1

Billy JOEL (161 Top 500)
Platinum-plated singer / songwriter / pianist, b. 9 May 1949, Long Island, US. This relatively youthful Grammy Living Legend Award recipient was the first artist to have five albums pass the seven-million mark Stateside. Best-selling single: 'Uptown Girl' 974,000 (146 WEEKS) pos/wks

11 Feb 78	JUST THE WAY YOU ARE *CBS 5872*	19	9
24 Jun 78	MOVIN' OUT (ANTHONY'S SONG) *CBS 6412*	35	6

2 Dec 78	MY LIFE *CBS 6821*	12	15
28 Apr 79	UNTIL THE NIGHT *CBS 7242*	50	3
12 Apr 80	ALL FOR LEYNA *CBS 8325*	40	4
9 Aug 80	IT'S STILL ROCK AND ROLL TO ME *CBS 8753* ▲	14	11
15 Oct 83 ★	UPTOWN GIRL *CBS A 3775*	1	17
10 Dec 83 ●	TELL HER ABOUT IT *CBS A 3655* ▲	4	10
18 Feb 84 ●	AN INNOCENT MAN *CBS A 4142*	8	10
28 Apr 84	THE LONGEST TIME *CBS A 4280*	25	8
23 Jun 84	LEAVE A TENDER MOMENT ALONE / GOODNIGHT SAIGON *CBS A 4521*	29	7
22 Feb 86	SHE'S ALWAYS A WOMAN / JUST THE WAY YOU ARE (re-issue) *CBS A 6862*	53	1
20 Sep 86	A MATTER OF TRUST *CBS 650057 7*	52	4
30 Sep 89 ●	WE DIDN'T START THE FIRE *CBS JOEL 1* ▲	7	10
16 Dec 89	LENINGRAD *CBS JOEL 2*	53	4
10 Mar 90	I GO TO EXTREMES *CBS JOEL 2*	70	2
29 Aug 92	ALL SHOOK UP *Columbia 6583437*	27	4
31 Jul 93 ●	THE RIVER OF DREAMS *Columbia 6595432*	3	14
23 Oct 93	ALL ABOUT SOUL *Columbia 6597362*	32	4
26 Feb 94	NO MAN'S LAND *Columbia 6599202*	50	3

'Goodnight Saigon' listed only from 30 Jun 1984

JOHANN *Germany, male producer – Johann Bley (1 WEEK)*
pos/wks

16 Mar 96	NEW KICKS *Perfecto PERF 118CD*	54	1

Angela JOHN – See José PADILLA featuring Angela JOHN

Elton JOHN (4 Top 500)
Flamboyant singer / songwriter / pianist, b. Reginald Dwight, 25 Mar 1947, Pinner, Middlesex, UK. Almost as famous for his outrageous wardrobe as his music, Elton was the biggest-selling pop act of the 1970s, and has sold more albums in the UK and US than any British male singer, with total worldwide sales exceeding 150 million. He is the only British act to enter the US singles chart at No.1 and also recorded the first two albums to enter the US chart at No.1. He holds the record for headlining appearances at New York's Madison Square Garden. Elton, twice chairman of Watford Football Club, is the only act to chart every year from 1971 to 1999 in the UK and US. His Greatest Hits album has sold more than 15 million in the US and he has topped the US adult contemporary chart a record 16 times. 'Candle in the Wind 1997' (which he performed at the funeral of Diana, Princess of Wales) topped the chart in almost every country. In the UK it sold nearly five million in six weeks and in the US had record advance orders of 8.7 million (and total sales in excess of 11 million). It also spent a staggering three years in the Canadian Top 20, which included 45 weeks at No.1. It is the world's biggest-selling single, with sales of 33 million (4,864,611 in the UK). His lyric-writing partners have included, most influentially, Bernie Taupin and, more recently, Sir Tim Rice. He became Sir Elton John in 1998 (593 WEEKS) pos/wks

23 Jan 71 ●	YOUR SONG *DJM DJS 233*	7	12
22 Apr 72 ●	ROCKET MAN (I THINK IT'S GOING TO BE A LONG LONG TIME) *DJM DJX 501*	2	13
9 Sep 72	HONKY CAT *DJM DJS 269*	31	6
4 Nov 72 ●	CROCODILE ROCK *DJM DJS 271* ▲	5	14
20 Jan 73 ●	DANIEL *DJM DJS 275*	4	10
7 Jul 73 ●	SATURDAY NIGHT'S ALRIGHT FOR FIGHTING *DJM DJX 502*	7	9
29 Sep 73 ●	GOODBYE YELLOW BRICK ROAD *DJM DJS 285*	6	16
8 Dec 73	STEP INTO CHRISTMAS *DJM DJS 290*	24	7
2 Mar 74	CANDLE IN THE WIND *DJM DJS 297*	11	9
1 Jun 74	DON'T LET THE SUN GO DOWN ON ME *DJM DJS 302*	16	8
14 Sep 74	THE BITCH IS BACK *DJM DJS 322*	15	7
23 Nov 74 ●	LUCY IN THE SKY WITH DIAMONDS *DJM DJS 340* ▲	10	10
8 Mar 75	PHILADELPHIA FREEDOM *DJM DJS 354* [1] ▲	12	9
28 Jun 75	SOMEONE SAVED MY LIFE TONIGHT *DJM DJS 385*	22	5
4 Oct 75	ISLAND GIRL *DJM DJS 610* ▲	14	8
20 Mar 76 ●	PINBALL WIZARD *DJM DJS 652*	7	7
3 Jul 76 ★	DON'T GO BREAKING MY HEART *Rocket ROKN 512* [2] ▲	1	14
25 Sep 76	BENNIE AND THE JETS *DJM DJS 10705* ▲	37	5
13 Nov 76	SORRY SEEMS TO BE THE HARDEST WORD *Rocket ROKN 517*	11	10
26 Feb 77	CRAZY WATER *Rocket ROKN 521*	27	6
11 Jun 77	BITE YOUR LIP (GET UP AND DANCE) *Rocket ROKN 526*	28	4
15 Apr 78	EGO *Rocket ROKN 538*	34	6

Re-entries are listed as (re), (2re), (3re), etc which signifies that the hit re-entered the chart once, twice or three times

21 Oct 78	PART TIME LOVE *Rocket XPRES 1*	15	13
16 Dec 78 ●	SONG FOR GUY *Rocket XPRES 5*	4	10
12 May 79	ARE YOU READY FOR LOVE *Rocket XPRES 13*	42	6
24 May 80	LITTLE JEANNIE *Rocket XPRES 32*	33	7
23 Aug 80	SARTORIAL ELOQUENCE *Rocket XPRES 41*	44	5
21 Mar 81	I SAW HER STANDING THERE *DJM DJS 10965* [3]	40	4
23 May 81	NOBODY WINS *Rocket XPRES 54*	42	5
27 Mar 82 ●	BLUE EYES *Rocket XPRES 71*	8	10
12 Jun 82	EMPTY GARDEN *Rocket XPRES 77*	51	4
30 Apr 83 ●	I GUESS THAT'S WHY THEY CALL IT THE BLUES		
	Rocket XPRES 91	5	15
30 Jul 83 ●	I'M STILL STANDING *Rocket EJS 1*	4	11
15 Oct 83	KISS THE BRIDE *Rocket EJS 2*	20	7
10 Dec 83	COLD AS CHRISTMAS (IN THE MIDDLE OF THE YEAR)		
	Rocket EJS 3	33	6
26 May 84 ●	SAD SONGS (SAY SO MUCH) *Rocket PH 7*	7	12
11 Aug 84 ●	PASSENGERS *Rocket EJS 5*	5	11
20 Oct 84	WHO WEARS THESE SHOES *Rocket EJS 6*	50	3
2 Mar 85	BREAKING HEARTS (AIN'T WHAT IT USED TO BE)		
	Rocket EJS 7	59	3
15 Jun 85	ACT OF WAR *Rocket EJS 8* [4]	32	5
12 Oct 85 ●	NIKITA *Rocket EJS 9*	3	13
9 Nov 85	THAT'S WHAT FRIENDS ARE FOR *Arista ARIST 638* [5] ▲	16	9
7 Dec 85	WRAP HER UP *Rocket EJS 10*	12	10
1 Mar 86	CRY TO HEAVEN *Rocket EJS 11*	47	4
4 Oct 86	HEARTACHE ALL OVER THE WORLD *Rocket EJS 12*	45	4
29 Nov 86	SLOW RIVERS *Rocket EJS 13* [6]	44	8
20 Jun 87	FLAMES OF PARADISE *CBS 6508657* [7]	59	3
16 Jan 88 ●	CANDLE IN THE WIND *Rocket EJS 15*	5	11
4 Jun 88	I DON'T WANNA GO ON WITH YOU LIKE THAT		
	Rocket EJS 16	30	8
3 Sep 88	TOWN OF PLENTY *Rocket EJS 17*	74	1
6 May 89	THROUGH THE STORM *Arista 112185* [8]	41	3
26 Aug 89	HEALING HANDS *Rocket EJS 19*	45	5
4 Nov 89	SACRIFICE *Rocket EJS 20*	55	3
9 Jun 90 ★	SACRIFICE / HEALING HANDS (re-issue) *Rocket EJS 22*	1	15
18 Aug 90	CLUB AT THE END OF THE STREET / WHISPERS		
	Rocket EJS 23	47	3
20 Oct 90	YOU GOTTA LOVE SOMEONE *Rocket EJS 24*	33	4
15 Dec 90	EASIER TO WALK AWAY (re) *Rocket EJS 25*	63	2
7 Dec 91 ●	DON'T LET THE SUN GO DOWN ON ME *Epic 6576467* [9] ■ ▲	1	10
6 Jun 92 ●	THE ONE *Rocket EJS 28*	10	8
1 Aug 92	RUNAWAY TRAIN *Rocket EJS 29* [10]	31	4
7 Nov 92	THE LAST SONG *Rocket EJS 30*	21	4
22 May 93	SIMPLE LIFE *Rocket EJS 31*	44	4
20 Nov 93	TRUE LOVE *Rocket EJSCX 32* [2]	2	10
26 Feb 94	DON'T GO BREAKING MY HEART (re-recording)		
	Rocket EJRCD 33 [11]	7	7
14 May 94	AIN'T NOTHING LIKE THE REAL THING		
	London LONCD 350 [12]	24	4
9 Jul 94	CAN YOU FEEL THE LOVE TONIGHT *Mercury EJCD 34*	14	9
8 Oct 94	CIRCLE OF LIFE *Rocket EJSCD 35*	11	12
4 Mar 95	BELIEVE *Rocket EJSCD 36*	15	7
20 May 95	MADE IN ENGLAND *Rocket EJSCD 37*	18	5
3 Feb 96	PLEASE *Rocket EJSCD 40*	33	3
14 Dec 96 ●	LIVE LIKE HORSES *Rocket LLHDD 1* [13]	9	6
20 Sep 97 ★	CANDLE IN THE WIND 1997 / SOMETHING ABOUT		
	THE WAY YOU LOOK TONIGHT *Rocket PTCD 1* ◆ ■ ▲	1	24
14 Feb 98	RECOVER YOUR SOUL *Rocket EJSCD 42*	16	3
13 Jun 98	IF THE RIVER CAN BEND *Rocket EJSDD 43*	32	2
6 Mar 99 ●	WRITTEN IN THE STARS (re) *Mercury EJSCD 45* [14]	10	8
6 Oct 01 ●	I WANT LOVE *Rocket / Mercury 5887062*	9	10
26 Jan 02	THIS TRAIN DON'T STOP THERE ANYMORE		
	Rocket / Mercury 588962	24	4
13 Apr 02	ORIGINAL SIN *Rocket / Mercury 5889992*	39	2
27 Jul 02 ●	YOUR SONG (re-recording) *Mercury 639972* [15]	4	9
21 Dec 02 ★	SORRY SEEMS TO BE THE HARDEST WORD (re-recording)		
	Innocent SINDX 43 ■ [16]	1	2+

[1] Elton John Band [2] Elton John and Kiki Dee [3] Elton John Band featuring John Lennon and the Muscle Shoals Horns [4] Elton John and Millie Jackson [5] Dionne Warwick and Friends featuring Elton John, Stevie Wonder and Gladys Knight [6] Elton John and Cliff Richard [7] Jennifer Rush and Elton John [8] Aretha Franklin and Elton John [9] George Michael and Elton John [10] Elton John and Eric Clapton [11] Elton John with RuPaul [12] Marcella Detroit and Elton John [13] Elton John and

Luciano Pavarotti [14] Elton John and LeAnn Rimes [15] Elton John and Alessandro Safina [16] Blue featuring Elton John

'Bite Your Lip (Get Up and Dance)' was one side of a double-sided chart entry, the other being 'Chicago' by Kiki Dee. 'Wrap Her Up' features George Michael as uncredited co-vocalist. 'Candle in the Wind' 1988 was a live recording

Robert JOHN *US, male vocalist - Robert John Pedrick (13 WEEKS)* pos/wks

17 Jul 68	IF YOU DON'T WANT MY LOVE *CBS 3436*	42	5
20 Oct 79	SAD EYES *EMI American EA 101* ▲	31	8

JOHNNA *US, female vocalist (3 WEEKS)* pos/wks

10 Feb 96	DO WHAT YOU FEEL *PWL International PWL 323CD*	43	2
11 May 96	IN MY DREAMS *PWL International PWL 325CD*	66	1

JOHNNY and CHARLEY *Spain, male vocal duo (1 WEEK)* pos/wks

14 Oct 65	LA YENKA *Pye International 7N 25326*	49	1

JOHNNY and the HURRICANES (375) Top 500

Internationally successful instrumental quintet formed 1957, Ohio, US. Featured saxophonist Johnny Paris (born Pocisk) and organist Paul Tesluk. Specialised in rocking retreads of old standards. The Beatles supported them in Hamburg in Dec 1962 (88 WEEKS) pos/wks

9 Oct 59 ●	RED RIVER ROCK *London HL 8948*	3	16
25 Dec 59	REVEILLE ROCK *London HL 9017*	14	5
17 Mar 60 ●	BEATNIK FLY *London HLI 9072*	8	19
16 Jun 60 ●	DOWN YONDER *London HLX 9134*	8	11
29 Sep 60 ●	ROCKING GOOSE *London HLX 9190*	3	20
2 Mar 61	JA-DA *London HLX 9289*	14	9
6 Jul 61	OLD SMOKIE / HIGH VOLTAGE *London HLX 9378*	24	8

JOHNNY CORPORATE *US, male production duo (2 WEEKS)* pos/wks

28 Oct 00	SUNDAY SHOUTIN' *Defected DFECT 21CDS*	45	2

JOHNNY HATES JAZZ
UK, male vocal / instrumental group (45 WEEKS) pos/wks

11 Apr 87 ●	SHATTERED DREAMS *Virgin VS 948*	5	14
29 Aug 87	I DON'T WANT TO BE A HERO *Virgin VS 1000*	11	10
21 Nov 87	TURN BACK THE CLOCK *Virgin VS 1017*	12	11
27 Feb 88	HEART OF GOLD *Virgin VS 1045*	19	7
9 Jul 88	DON'T SAY IT'S LOVE *Virgin VS 1081*	48	3

JOHNSON *UK, male / female vocal / instrumental duo (1 WEEK)* pos/wks

27 Mar 99	SAY YOU LOVE ME		
	Higher Ground HIGHS 18CD	56	1

Andreas JOHNSON *Sweden, male vocalist (12 WEEKS)* pos/wks

5 Feb 00 ●	GLORIOUS *WEA WEA 254CD*	4	11
27 May 00	THE GAMES WE PLAY *WEA WEA 264*	41	1

Bryan JOHNSON *UK, male vocalist, d. 18 Oct 1995 (11 WEEKS)* pos/wks

10 Mar 60	LOOKING HIGH, HIGH, HIGH *Decca F 11213*	20	11

Carey JOHNSON *Australia, male vocalist (8 WEEKS)* pos/wks

25 Apr 87	REAL FASHION REGGAE STYLE *Oval TEN 170*	19	8

Denise JOHNSON *UK, female vocalist (4 WEEKS)* pos/wks

24 Aug 91	DON'T FIGHT IT FEEL IT *Creation CRE 110* [1]	41	2
14 May 94	RAYS OF THE RISING SUN *Magnet MAG 1022CD*	45	2

[1] Primal Scream featuring Denise Johnson

Don JOHNSON *US, male vocalist (12 WEEKS)* pos/wks

18 Oct 86	HEARTBEAT *Epic 650064 7*	46	5
5 Nov 88	TILL I LOVED YOU (LOVE THEME FROM 'GOYA')		
	CBS BARB 2 [1]	16	7

[1] Barbra Streisand and Don Johnson

General JOHNSON – See CHAIRMEN OF THE BOARD

Holly JOHNSON *UK, male vocalist (38 WEEKS)*

		pos/wks
14 Jan 89	● LOVE TRAIN *MCA MCA 1306*	4 11
1 Apr 89	● AMERICANOS *MCA MCA 1323*	4 11
20 May 89	★ FERRY 'CROSS THE MERSEY *PWL PWL 41* [1] ■	1 7
24 Jun 89	ATOMIC CITY *MCA MCA 1342*	18 4
30 Sep 89	HEAVEN'S HERE *MCA MCA 1365*	62 2
1 Dec 90	WHERE HAS LOVE GONE? *MCA MCA 1460*	73 1
25 Dec 99	THE POWER OF LOVE *Pleasure Dome PLDCD 1005*	56 2

[1] Christians, Holly Johnson, Paul McCartney, Gerry Marsden and Stock Aitken Waterman

See also FRANKIE GOES TO HOLLYWOOD

Howard JOHNSON *US, male vocalist (6 WEEKS)*

		pos/wks
4 Sep 82	KEEPIN' LOVE NEW / SO FINE *A&M USA 1221*	45 6

'Keepin' Love New' listed 4 Sep 1982 only

Johnny JOHNSON and the BANDWAGON
US, male vocal group (50 WEEKS)

		pos/wks
16 Oct 68	● BREAKIN' DOWN THE WALLS OF HEARTACHE *Direction 58-3670* [1]	4 15
5 Feb 69	YOU *Direction 58-3923*	34 4
28 May 69	LET'S HANG ON *Direction 58-4180*	36 6
25 Jul 70	● SWEET INSPIRATION (re) *Bell 1111*	10 13
28 Nov 70	● (BLAME IT) ON THE PONY EXPRESS *Bell 1128*	7 12

[1] Bandwagon

Kevin JOHNSON *Australia, male vocalist (6 WEEKS)*

		pos/wks
11 Jan 75	ROCK 'N ROLL (I GAVE YOU THE BEST YEARS OF MY LIFE) *UK UKR 84*	23 6

Laurie JOHNSON *UK, orchestra (14 WEEKS)*

		pos/wks
28 Sep 61	● SUCU SUCU *Pye 7N 15383*	9 12
17 May 97	THEME FROM 'THE PROFESSIONALS' *Virgin VSCDT 1643* [1]	36 2

[1] Laurie Johnson's London Big Band

LJ JOHNSON *US, male vocalist (6 WEEKS)*

		pos/wks
7 Feb 76	YOUR MAGIC PUT A SPELL ON ME *Philips 6006 492*	27 6

Lou JOHNSON *US, male vocalist (2 WEEKS)*

		pos/wks
26 Nov 64	A MESSAGE TO MARTHA (KENTUCKY BLUEBIRD) *London HL 9929*	36 2

Marv JOHNSON *US, male vocalist, d. 16 May 1993 (40 WEEKS)*

		pos/wks
12 Feb 60	● YOU GOT WHAT IT TAKES *London HLT 9013*	7 17
5 May 60	I LOVE THE WAY YOU LOVE *London HLT 9109*	35 3
11 Aug 60	AIN'T GONNA BE THAT WAY *London HLT 9165*	50 1
22 Jan 69	● I'LL PICK A ROSE FOR MY ROSE *Tamla Motown TMG 680*	10 11
25 Oct 69	I MISS YOU BABY *Tamla Motown TMG 713*	25 8

Orlando JOHNSON – See SECCHI featuring Orlando JOHNSON

Paul JOHNSON *UK, male vocalist (7 WEEKS)*

		pos/wks
21 Feb 87	WHEN LOVE COMES CALLING *CBS PJOHN 1*	52 5
25 Feb 89	NO MORE TOMORROWS *CBS PJOHN 7*	67 2

Paul JOHNSON *US, male producer / instrumentalist (8 WEEKS)*

		pos/wks
25 Sep 99	● GET GET DOWN *Defected DEFECT 7CDS*	5 8

Puff JOHNSON *US, female vocalist (6 WEEKS)*

		pos/wks
18 Jan 97	OVER AND OVER *Columbia 6640345*	20 4
12 Apr 97	FOREVER MORE *Work 644075*	29 2

Romina JOHNSON *UK, female vocalist (13 WEEKS)*

		pos/wks
4 Mar 00	● MOVIN TOO FAST (re) *Locked On XL LOX 117CD* [1]	2 12
17 Jun 00	MY FORBIDDEN LOVER *51 Lexington CDLEX 1* [2]	59 1

[1] Artful Dodger and Romina Johnson [2] Romina Johnson featuring Luci Martin and Norma Jean

Syleena JOHNSON *US, female vocalist (2 WEEKS)*

		pos/wks
26 Oct 02	TONIGHT I'M GONNA LET GO *Jive 9254252*	38 2

Sleeve credits Syleena Johnson featuring Busta Rhymes, Rampage, Sham & Spliff Star (of Flipmode Squad)

Teddy JOHNSON – See Pearl CARR and Teddy JOHNSON

Bruce JOHNSTON
US, male instrumentalist – keyboards (4 WEEKS)

		pos/wks
27 Aug 77	PIPELINE *CBS 5514*	33 4

Jan JOHNSTON *UK, female vocalist (12 WEEKS)*

		pos/wks
8 Feb 97	TAKE ME BY THE HAND *AM:PM 5821012* [1]	28 2
28 Nov 98	SKYDIVE *Stress CDSTR 89* [2]	75 1
12 Feb 00	LOVE WILL COME *Xtravaganza XTRAV6CDS* [3]	31 2
22 Jul 00	SKYDIVE (re-mix) *Renaissance Recordings RENCDS 002* [2]	43 2
21 Apr 01	FLESH *Perfecto PERF 05CDS*	36 2
28 Jul 01	SILENT WORDS *Perfecto PERF 16CDS*	57 1
8 Sep 01	SKYDIVE (I FEEL WONDERFUL) (2nd re-mix) *Incentive CENT 22CDS* [2]	35 2

[1] Submerge featuring Jan Johnston [2] Freefall featuring Jan Johnston [3] Tomski featuring Jan Johnston

Sabrina JOHNSTON *US, female vocalist (19 WEEKS)*

		pos/wks
7 Sep 91	● PEACE *East West YZ 616*	8 10
7 Dec 91	FRIENDSHIP *East West YZ 637*	58 4
11 Jul 92	I WANNA SING *East West YZ 661*	46 2
3 Oct 92	PEACE (re-mix) *Epic 6584377*	35 2
13 Aug 94	SATISFY MY LOVE *Champion CHAMPCD 311*	62 1

The listed flipside of 'Peace' (re-mix) in 1992, was 'Gypsy Woman' (re-mix) by Crystal Waters

JOHNSTON BROTHERS *UK, male vocal group*
– leader Johnny Johnston (Johnny Reine) (33 WEEKS)

		pos/wks
3 Apr 53	● OH, HAPPY DAY *Decca F 10071*	4 8
5 Nov 54	WAIT FOR ME, DARLING *Decca F 10362* [1]	18 1
21 Jan 55	HAPPY DAYS AND LONELY NIGHTS *Decca F 10389*	14 2
7 Oct 55	★ HERNANDO'S HIDEAWAY *Decca F 10608*	1 13
30 Dec 55	● JOIN IN AND SING AGAIN *Decca F 10636* [2]	9 1
13 Apr 56	NO OTHER LOVE *Decca F 10721*	22 1
30 Nov 56	IN THE MIDDLE OF THE HOUSE *Decca F 10781*	27 1
7 Dec 56	JOIN IN AND SING NO.3 (re) *Decca F 10814*	24 2
8 Feb 57	GIVE HER MY LOVE *Decca F 10828*	27 1
19 Apr 57	HEART *Decca F 10860*	23 3

[1] Joan Regan with the Johnston Brothers [2] Johnson Brothers and The George Chisholm Sour-Note Six

The following two hits were medleys: Join In and Sing Again: Sheik of Araby / Yes Sir That's My Baby / California Here I Come / Some of These Days / Charleston / Margie. Join In and Sing (No.3): Coal Black Morning / When You're Smiling / Alexander's Ragtime Band / Sweet Sue Just You / When You Wore a Tulip / If You Were the Only Girl in the World

JOJO – See 2PAC; K-CI & JOJO

James JOLIS – See Barry MANILOW

JOLLY BROTHERS
Jamaica, male vocal / instrumental group (7 WEEKS)

		pos/wks
28 Jul 79	CONSCIOUS MAN *United Artists UP 36415*	46 7

Re-entries are listed as (re), (2re), (3re), etc which signifies that the hit re-entered the chart once, twice or three times

JOLLY ROGER
UK, male instrumentalist / producer – Eddie Richards (12 WEEKS) pos/wks

10 Sep 88	ACID MAN *10 TEN 236*	23	12

JOMALSKI – *See WILDCHILD*

JOMANDA
US, female vocal group (10 WEEKS) pos/wks

22 Apr 89	MAKE MY BODY ROCK *RCA PB 42749*	44	3
29 Jun 91	GOT A LOVE FOR YOU *Giant W 0040*	43	4
11 Sep 93	I LIKE IT *Big Beat A 8377CD*	67	1
13 Nov 93	NEVER *Big Beat A 8347CD*	40	2

JON and VANGELIS
UK, male vocalist and Greece, male multi-instrumentalist –
Jon Anderson and Evangelos Papathanassiou (28 WEEKS) pos/wks

5 Jan 80	● I HEAR YOU NOW *Polydor POSP 96*	8	11
12 Dec 81	● I'LL FIND MY WAY HOME *Polydor JV 1*	6	13
30 Jul 83	HE IS SAILING *Polydor JV 4*	61	2
18 Aug 84	STATE OF INDEPENDENCE *Polydor JV 5*	67	2

See also VANGELIS

JON OF THE PLEASED WIMMIN
UK, male DJ / producer – Jonathan Cooper (5 WEEKS) pos/wks

18 Feb 95	PASSION *Perfecto YZ 884CD*	27	3
6 Apr 96	GIVE ME STRENGTH *Perfecto PERF 119CD*	30	2

JON THE DENTIST vs Ollie JAYE
UK, male DJs / producers (2 WEEKS) pos/wks

24 Jul 99	IMAGINATION *Tidy Trax TIDY 126CD*	72	1
10 Jun 00	FEEL SO GOOD *Tidy Trax TIDY 135CD*	72	1

JONAH
Holland, male production group (4 WEEKS) pos/wks

22 Jul 00	SSSST (LISTEN) *VC Recordings VCRD 69*	25	4

JONELL – *See HI-TEK featuring JONELL*

Aled JONES *UK, male vocalist (24 WEEKS)* pos/wks

20 Jul 85	MEMORY: THEME FROM THE MUSICAL 'CATS' *BBC RESL 175*	42	4
30 Nov 85	● WALKING IN THE AIR *HMV ALED 1*	5	11
14 Dec 85	PICTURES IN THE DARK *Virgin VS 836* [1]	50	6
20 Dec 86	A WINTER STORY *HMV ALED 2*	51	3

[1] Mike Oldfield featuring Aled Jones, Anita Hegerland and Barry Palmer

Barbara JONES
Jamaica, female vocalist – Barbara Nation (7 WEEKS) pos/wks

31 Jan 81	JUST WHEN I NEEDED YOU MOST *Sonet SON 2221*	31	7

Catherine Zeta JONES
UK, female actor / vocalist (9 WEEKS) pos/wks

19 Sep 92	FOR ALL TIME *Columbia 6583547*	36	5
26 Nov 94	TRUE LOVE WAYS *PolyGram TV TLWCD 2* [1]	38	3
1 Apr 95	IN THE ARMS OF LOVE *Wow! WOWCD 7101*	72	1

[1] David Essex and Catherine Zeta Jones

Donell JONES *US, male vocalist (20 WEEKS)* pos/wks

15 Feb 97	KNOCKS ME OFF MY FEET *LaFace 74321458502*	58	1
22 Jan 00	● U KNOW WHAT'S UP *LaFace 74321722752*	2	11
20 May 00	SHORTY (GOT HER EYES ON ME) *Laface 74321748902*	19	3
2 Dec 00	TRUE STEP TONIGHT *Nulife 74321811312* [1]	25	3
24 Aug 02	YOU KNOW THAT I LOVE YOU *Arista 74321956962*	41	2

[1] True Steppers featuring Brian Harvey and Donell Jones

Georgia JONES – *See PLUX featuring Georgia JONES; DIVA SURPRISE featuring Georgia JONES*

Grace JONES
Jamaica, female vocalist – Grace Mendoza (46 WEEKS) pos/wks

26 Jul 80	PRIVATE LIFE *Island WIP 6629*	17	8
20 Jun 81	PULL UP TO THE BUMPER *Island WIP 6696*	53	4
30 Oct 82	THE APPLE STRETCHING / NIPPLE TO THE BOTTLE *Island WIP 6779*	50	4
9 Apr 83	MY JAMAICAN GUY *Island IS 103*	56	3
12 Oct 85	SLAVE TO THE RHYTHM *ZTT IS 206*	12	8
18 Jan 86	PULL UP TO THE BUMPER / LA VIE EN ROSE (re-issue) *Island IS 240*	12	9
1 Mar 86	LOVE IS THE DRUG *Island IS 266*	35	4
15 Nov 86	I'M NOT PERFECT (BUT I'M PERFECT FOR YOU) *Manhattan MT 15*	56	3
7 May 94	SLAVE TO THE RHYTHM (re-mix) *Zance ZANG 50CD1*	28	2
25 Nov 00	PULL UP TO THE BUMPER *Club Tools 0120375 CLU* [1]	60	1

[1] Grace Jones vs Funkstar De Luxe

'La Vie En Rose' was listed only from 1 Feb 1986

Hannah JONES *US, female vocalist (9 WEEKS)* pos/wks

14 Sep 91	BRIDGE OVER TROUBLED WATER *Dance Pool 6565467* [1]	21	8
30 Jan 93	KEEP IT ON *TMRC CDTMRC 7*	67	1

[1] PJB featuring Hannah and her Sisters

Howard JONES 300 Top 500 *Accomplished singer / songwriter, b. 23 Feb 1955, Southampton, UK, who was a regular chart visitor in the mid-1980s with his brand of synth-based pop. Jones, who was equally popular in the US, appeared at Live Aid (103 WEEKS)* pos/wks

17 Sep 83	● NEW SONG (re) *WEA HOW 1*	3	15
26 Nov 83	● WHAT IS LOVE *WEA HOW 2*	2	15
18 Feb 84	HIDE AND SEEK *WEA HOW 3*	12	9
26 May 84	● PEARL IN THE SHELL *WEA HOW 4*	7	10
11 Aug 84	● LIKE TO GET TO KNOW YOU WELL *WEA HOW 5*	4	12
9 Feb 85	● THINGS CAN ONLY GET BETTER *WEA HOW 6*	6	8
20 Apr 85	● LOOK MAMA *WEA HOW 7*	10	6
29 Jun 85	LIFE IN ONE DAY *WEA HOW 8*	14	7
15 Mar 86	NO ONE IS TO BLAME *WEA HOW 9*	16	7
4 Oct 86	ALL I WANT *WEA HOW 10*	35	4
29 Nov 86	YOU KNOW I LOVE YOU...DON'T YOU? *WEA HOW 11*	43	3
21 Mar 87	LITTLE BIT OF SNOW *WEA HOW 12*	70	1
4 Mar 89	EVERLASTING LOVE *WEA HOW 13*	62	3
11 Apr 92	LIFT ME UP *East West HOW 15*	52	3

Janie JONES *UK, female vocalist (3 WEEKS)* pos/wks

27 Jan 66	WITCHES BREW *HMV POP 1495*	46	3

Jimmy JONES *US, male vocalist (47 WEEKS)* pos/wks

17 Mar 60	● HANDY MAN (re) *MGM 1051*	3	24
16 Jun 60	★ GOOD TIMIN' *MGM 1078*	1	15
8 Sep 60	I JUST GO FOR YOU *MGM 1091*	35	4
17 Nov 60	READY FOR LOVE *MGM 1103*	46	1
30 Mar 61	I TOLD YOU SO *MGM 1123*	33	3

Juggy JONES
US, male multi-instrumentalist – Henry Murray (4 WEEKS) pos/wks

7 Feb 76	INSIDE AMERICA *Contempo CS 2080*	39	4

Kelly JONES – *See MANCHILD*

Lavinia JONES *South Africa, female vocalist (2 WEEKS)* pos/wks

18 Feb 95	SING IT TO YOU (DEE-DOOB-DEE-DOO) *Virgin International DINDG 142*	45	2

Mick JONES – *See AZTEC CAMERA; CLASH*

Norah JONES *US, female vocalist / instrumentalist (2 WEEKS)* pos/wks

25 May 02	DON'T KNOW WHY *Parlophone CDCL 836*	59	1
17 Aug 02	FEELIN' THE SAME WAY *Parlophone CDCL 838*	72	1

Oran 'Juice' JONES US, male vocalist (14 WEEKS)
pos/wks
| 15 Nov 86 | ● | THE RAIN Def Jam A 7303 | 4 | 14 |

Paul JONES UK, male vocalist – Paul Pond (34 WEEKS)
pos/wks
6 Oct 66	●	HIGH TIME HMV POP 1554	4	15
19 Jan 67	●	I'VE BEEN A BAD, BAD BOY HMV POP 1576	5	9
23 Aug 67		THINKIN' AIN'T FOR ME (re) HMV POP 1602	32	8
5 Feb 69		AQUARIUS Columbia DB 8514	45	2

See also MANFRED MANN; BLUES BAND

Quincy JONES
US, male producer / instrumentalist – keyboards (42 WEEKS)
pos/wks
29 Jul 78		STUFF LIKE THAT A&M AMS 7367	34	9
11 Apr 81		AI NO CORRIDA (I-NO-KO-REE-DA) A&M AMS 8109 [1]	14	10
20 Jun 81		RAZZAMATAZZ A&M AMS 8140	11	9
5 Sep 81		BETCHA' WOULDN'T HURT ME A&M AMS 8157	52	3
13 Jan 90		I'LL BE GOOD TO YOU Qwest W 2697 [2]	21	7
31 Mar 90		SECRET GARDEN Qwest W 9992 [3]	67	1
14 Sep 96		STOMP Qwest W 0372CD [4]	28	2
1 Aug 98		SOUL BOSSA NOVA Manifesto FESCD 48 [5]	47	1

[1] Quincy Jones featuring Dune [2] Quincy Jones featuring Ray Charles and Chaka Khan [3] Quincy Jones featuring Al B Sure!, James Ingram, El DeBarge and Barry White [4] Quincy Jones featuring Melle Mel, Coolio, Yo-Yo, Shaquille O'Neal, The Luniz [5] Cool, the Fab and the Groovy present Quincy Jones

Uncredited vocals on 'Stuff Like That' were by Ashford and Simpson and Chaka Khan, and on 'Razzamatazz' and 'Betcha' Wouldn't Hurt Me' by Patti Austin.

Rickie Lee JONES US, female vocalist (9 WEEKS)
pos/wks
| 23 Jun 79 | | CHUCK E'S IN LOVE Warner Bros. K 17390 | 18 | 9 |

Shirley JONES – See PARTRIDGE FAMILY

Sonny JONES featuring Tara CHASE
Germany, male vocalist and Canada, female rapper (2 WEEKS)
pos/wks
| 7 Oct 00 | | FOLLOW YOU FOLLOW ME Logic 74321772892 | 42 | 2 |

Tammy JONES UK, female vocalist (10 WEEKS)
pos/wks
| 26 Apr 75 | ● | LET ME TRY AGAIN Epic EPC 3211 | 5 | 10 |

Tom JONES 16 Top 500
Unmistakable entertainer who has been an international headliner for five decades, b Thomas Woodward, 7 Jun, 1940, South Wales (re-named after the popular 1963 film). Despite failure of his first two Joe Meek-produced singles, the Welsh wonder became one of world's most popular singers, with hits in the pop, country, R&B and easy listening fields. The Vegas veteran, who hosted his very successful late-1960s TV series, has had hits on 10 labels. This 60-something sex symbol, who was the top British solo singer of the 1960s on both sides of Atlantic, had his biggest-selling album in 1999 with 'Reload'. Best-selling single: 'Green, Green Grass of Home' 1,205,000 (392 WEEKS)
pos/wks
11 Feb 65	★	IT'S NOT UNUSUAL Decca F 12062	1	14
6 May 65		ONCE UPON A TIME Decca F 12121	32	4
8 Jul 65		WITH THESE HANDS Decca F 12191	13	11
12 Aug 65		WHAT'S NEW PUSSYCAT? Decca F 12203	11	10
13 Jan 66		THUNDERBALL Decca F 12292	35	4
19 May 66		ONCE THERE WAS A TIME / NOT RESPONSIBLE Decca F 12390	18	9
18 Aug 66		THIS AND THAT Decca F 12461	44	3
10 Nov 66	★	GREEN, GREEN GRASS OF HOME Decca F 22511 ◆	1	22
16 Feb 67	●	DETROIT CITY Decca F 22555	8	10
13 Apr 67	●	FUNNY FAMILIAR FORGOTTEN FEELINGS Decca F 12599	7	10
26 Jul 67	●	I'LL NEVER FALL IN LOVE AGAIN Decca F 12639	2	25
22 Nov 67	●	I'M COMING HOME Decca F 12693	2	16
28 Feb 68	●	DELILAH Decca F 12747	2	17
17 Jul 68	●	HELP YOURSELF Decca F 12812	5	26
27 Nov 68		A MINUTE OF YOUR TIME Decca F 12854	14	15
14 May 69	●	LOVE ME TONIGHT Decca F 12924	9	12
13 Dec 69	●	WITHOUT LOVE (re) Decca F 12990	10	12

18 Apr 70	●	DAUGHTER OF DARKNESS Decca F 13013	5	15
15 Aug 70		I (WHO HAVE NOTHING) (re) Decca F 13061	16	11
16 Jan 71		SHE'S A LADY (re) Decca F 13113	13	10
5 Jun 71		PUPPET MAN (re) Decca F 13183	49	2
23 Oct 71		TILL Decca F 13236	2	15
1 Apr 72	●	THE YOUNG NEW MEXICAN PUPPETEER Decca F 13298	6	12
14 Apr 73		LETTER TO LUCILLE Decca F 13393	31	8
7 Sep 74		SOMETHING 'BOUT YOU BABY I LIKE Decca F 13550	36	5
16 Apr 77		SAY YOU'LL STAY UNTIL TOMORROW EMI 2583	40	3
18 Apr 87	●	A BOY FROM NOWHERE Epic OLE 1	2	12
30 May 87		IT'S NOT UNUSUAL (re-issue) Decca F 103	17	8
2 Jan 88		I WAS BORN TO BE ME Epic OLE 4	61	1
29 Oct 88	●	KISS China CHINA 11 [1]	5	7
29 Apr 89		MOVE CLOSER Jive 203	49	3
26 Jan 91		COULDN'T SAY GOODBYE Dover ROJ 10	51	2
16 Mar 91		CARRYING A TORCH Dover ROJ 12	57	2
4 Jul 92		DELILAH (re-issue) The Hit Label TOM 10	68	2
6 Feb 93		ALL YOU NEED IS LOVE Childline CHILDCD 93	19	4
5 Nov 94		IF I ONLY KNEW ZTT ZANG 59CD	11	9
25 Sep 99	●	BURNING DOWN THE HOUSE Gut CDGUT 26 [2]	7	7
18 Dec 99		BABY, IT'S COLD OUTSIDE Gut CDGUT 29 [3]	17	7
18 Mar 00	●	MAMA TOLD ME NOT TO COME Gut CDGUT 031 [4]	4	7
20 May 00	●	SEX BOMB Gut CDGUT 33 [5]	3	10
18 Nov 00		YOU NEED LOVE LIKE I DO GUT CDGUT 36 [6]	24	3
9 Nov 02		TOM JONES INTERNATIONAL V2 VVR5021083	31	2

[1] Art of Noise featuring Tom Jones [2] Tom Jones and The Cardigans [3] Tom Jones and Cerys Matthews [4] Tom Jones and Stereophonics [5] Tom Jones and Mousse T [6] Tom Jones and Heather Small

Sue JONES-DAVIES – See Julie COVINGTON, Rula LENSKA, Charlotte CORNWELL and Sue JONES-DAVIES

JONESTOWN US, male vocal duo (1 WEEK)
pos/wks
| 13 Jun 98 | | SWEET THANG Universal UMD 70376 | 49 | 1 |

Alison JORDAN UK, female vocalist (4 WEEKS)
pos/wks
| 9 May 92 | | BOY FROM NEW YORK CITY Arista 74321100427 | 23 | 4 |

Dick JORDAN UK, male vocalist (4 WEEKS)
pos/wks
| 17 Mar 60 | | HALLELUJAH, I LOVE HER SO Oriole CB 1534 | 47 | 1 |
| 9 Jun 60 | | LITTLE CHRISTINE Oriole CB 1548 | 39 | 3 |

Jack JORDAN – See Frank CHACKSFIELD and his ORCHESTRA

Montell JORDAN US, male vocalist (21 WEEKS)
pos/wks
13 May 95		THIS IS HOW WE DO IT Def Jam DEFCD 07 ▲	11	8
2 Sep 95		SOMETHIN' 4 DA HONEYZ Def Jam DEFCD 10	15	4
19 Oct 96		I LIKE Def Jam DEFCD 19 [1]	24	3
23 May 98		LET'S RIDE Def Jam 5686912 [2]	25	2
8 Apr 00		GET IT ON TONITE Def Soul 5627222	15	4

[1] Montell Jordan featuring Slick Rick [2] Montell Jordan featuring Master P and Silkk the Shocker

Ronny JORDAN
UK, male instrumentalist – guitar – Ronnie Simpson (7 WEEKS)
pos/wks
1 Feb 92		SO WHAT! Antilles ANN 14	32	4
25 Sep 93		UNDER YOUR SPELL Island CID 565	72	1
15 Jan 94		TINSEL TOWN Island CID 566	64	1
28 May 94		COME WITH ME Island CID 584	63	1

JORDANAIRES – See Elvis PRESLEY

JORIO US, male producer – Fred Jorio (1 WEEK)
pos/wks
| 24 Feb 01 | | REMEMBER ME Wonderboy WBOYD 021 | 54 | 1 |

David JOSEPH UK, male vocalist (21 WEEKS)
pos/wks
26 Feb 83		YOU CAN'T HIDE (YOUR LOVE FROM ME) Island IS 101	13	9
28 May 83		LET'S LIVE IT UP (NITE PEOPLE) Island IS 116	26	5
18 Feb 84		JOYS OF LIFE Island IS 153	61	2

Re-entries are listed as (re), (2re), (3re), etc which signifies that the hit re-entered the chart once, twice or three times, etc

JUNGLE HIGH with BLUE PEARL
UK / Germany, male production / instrumental duo and
UK / US, male / female vocal / instrumental group (1 WEEK)   pos/wks
27 Nov 93   FIRE OF LOVE *Logic 74321170292* **71** 1

JUNIOR *UK, male vocalist – Norman Giscombe (57 WEEKS)*   pos/wks
24 Apr 82 ● MAMA USED TO SAY *Mercury MER 98* **7** 13
10 Jul 82   TOO LATE *Mercury MER 112* **20** 9
25 Sep 82   LET ME KNOW / I CAN'T HELP IT *Mercury MER 116*........**53** 3
23 Apr 83   COMMUNICATION BREAKDOWN *Mercury MER 134* **57** 3
8 Sep 84   SOMEBODY *London LON 50* **64** 2
9 Feb 85   DO YOU REALLY (WANT MY LOVE) *London LON 60* **47** 4
30 Nov 85   OH LOUISE *London LON 75* **74** 3
4 Apr 87   ● ANOTHER STEP (CLOSER TO YOU) *MCA KIM 5* 1 ......**6** 11
25 Aug 90   STEP OFF *MCA MCA 1432* 2 ....**63** 3
15 Aug 92   THEN CAME YOU *MCA MCS 1676* 2 ....**32** 5
31 Oct 92   ALL OVER THE WORLD *MCA MCS 1691* 2 ....**74** 1

1 Kim Wilde and Junior 2 Junior Giscombe

JUNIOR JACK *Italy, male producer – Vito Lucente (7 WEEKS)*   pos/wks
16 Dec 00   MY FEELING *Defected DFECT 24CDS* **31** 4
2 Mar 02   THRILL ME *VC Recordings VCRD 102* **29** 3

JUNIOR M.A.F.I.A. *US, male / female rap ensemble (2 WEEKS)*   pos/wks
3 Feb 96   I NEED YOU TONIGHT *Big Beat A 8130CD* 1 ....**66** 1
19 Oct 96   GETTIN' MONEY *Big Beat A 5674CD* **63** 1

1 Junior M.A.F.I.A. featuring Aaliyah

JUNIORS – See DANNY and the JUNIORS

JUNKIE XL *Holland, male producer – Tom Holkenborg (14 WEEKS)* pos/wks
22 Jul 00   ZEROTONINE *Manifesto FESCD71* **63** 1
22 Jun 02 ★ A LITTLE LESS CONVERSATION *RCA 742194572* 1 ■ **1** 12
30 Nov 02   OBSESSION *Nebula NEBCD 029* 2 ....**56** 1

1 Elvis vs JXL 2 Tiesto and Junkie XL

JUNO REACTOR *UK / Germany, male production duo (1 WEEK)* pos/wks
8 Feb 97   JUNGLE HIGH *Perfecto PERF 133CD* **45** 1

JURASSIC 5 *US, male rap group (4 WEEKS)*   pos/wks
25 Jul 98   JAYOU *Pan PAN 018CD*..**56** 1
24 Oct 98   CONCRETE SCHOOLYARD *Pan PAN 020CD* **35** 3

Christopher JUST *Austria, male producer (2 WEEKS)*   pos/wks
13 Dec 97   I'M A DISCO DANCER *Slut Trax SLUT 001CD*................**72** 1
6 Feb 99   I'M A DISCO DANCER (re-mix) *XL Recordings XLS 105CD* **69** 1

JUST 4 JOKES featuring MC RB
UK, male production duo and male rapper (1 WEEK)   pos/wks
28 Sep 02   JUMP UP *Serious SERR 050CD* **67** 1

JUST LUIS
Spain, male vocalist – Luis Sierra Pizarro (3 WEEKS)   pos/wks
14 Oct 95   AMERICAN PIE (re) *Pro-Activ CDPTV 1*........................**31** 3

Jimmy JUSTICE *UK, male vocalist – James Little (35 WEEKS)* pos/wks
29 Mar 62 ● WHEN MY LITTLE GIRL IS SMILING *Pye 7N 15421* **9** 13
14 Jun 62 ● AIN'T THAT FUNNY *Pye 7N 15443* **8** 11
23 Aug 62   SPANISH HARLEM *Pye 7N 15457* **20** 11

JUSTIFIED ANCIENTS OF MU MU
UK, male production duo (6 WEEKS)   pos/wks
9 Nov 91   ● IT'S GRIM UP NORTH (re)
              KLF Communications JAMS 028..................................**10** 6

See also KLF; 2K; TIMELORDS

JUSTIN *UK, male vocalist – Justin Osuji (13 WEEKS)*   pos/wks
22 Aug 98   THIS BOY *Virgin STCDT 1* **34** 2
16 Jan 99   OVER YOU *Virgin STCDT 2* **11** 4
17 Jul 99   IT'S ALL ABOUT YOU *Innocent STCDT 3*......................**34** 3
22 Jan 00   LET IT BE ME *Innocent STCDTX 4* **15** 4

Bill JUSTIS
US, male instrumentalist – alto sax, d. 15 Jul 1982 (8 WEEKS)   pos/wks
10 Jan 58   RAUNCHY (re) *London HLS 8517*................................**11** 8

Patrick JUVET *Switzerland, male vocalist (19 WEEKS)*   pos/wks
2 Sep 78   GOT A FEELING *Casablanca CAN 127*........................**34** 7
4 Nov 78   I LOVE AMERICA *Casablanca CAN 132* **12** 12

Frank K featuring Wiston OFFICE
Italy / US, male vocal / instrumental duo (1 WEEK)   pos/wks
26 Jan 91   EVERYBODY LET'S SOMEBODY LOVE *Urban URB 66*.............**61** 1

Leila K
Sweden, female rapper – Leila El Khalifi (22 WEEKS)   pos/wks
25 Nov 89 ● GOT TO GET *Arista 112696* 1 ....**8** 14
17 Mar 90   ROK THE NATION *Arista 112971* 1 ....**41** 3
23 Jan 93   OPEN SESAME *Polydor PQCD 1* **23** 4
3 Jul 93   ÇA PLANE POUR MOI *Polydor PQCD 3* **69** 1

1 Rob 'n' Raz featuring Leila K

KC & SUNSHINE BAND (294 Top 500)
Red-hot disco act from Florida, US, fronted by KC (b. Harry Wayne Casey,
31 Jan 1951, Florida) and including co-writer / producer Richard Finch (b.).
The internationally successful group's wall-to-wall late 1970s hits
included five US No.1s (104 WEEKS)   pos/wks
17 Aug 74 ● QUEEN OF CLUBS *Jayboy BOY 88*............................**7** 12
23 Nov 74   SOUND YOUR FUNKY HORN *Jayboy BOY 83* **17** 9
29 Mar 75   GET DOWN TONIGHT *Jayboy BOY 93* ▲ **21** 9
2 Aug 75   ● THAT'S THE WAY (I LIKE IT) *Jayboy BOY 99* ▲ **4** 10
22 Nov 75   I'M SO CRAZY ('BOUT YOU) *Jayboy BOY 101*............**34** 3
17 Jul 76   (SHAKE, SHAKE, SHAKE) SHAKE YOUR BOOTY
              Jayboy BOY 110 ▲ **22** 8
11 Dec 76   KEEP IT COMIN' LOVE *Jayboy BOY 112*....................**31** 8
30 Apr 77   I'M YOUR BOOGIE MAN *TK XB 2167* ▲ **41** 4
6 May 78   BOOGIE SHOES *TK TKR 6025* **34** 5
22 Jul 78   IT'S THE SAME OLD SONG *TK TKR 6037* **47** 5
8 Dec 79   ● PLEASE DON'T GO *TK TKR 7558* ▲ **3** 12
16 Jul 83   ★ GIVE IT UP *Epic EPC A 3017*......................................**1** 14
24 Sep 83   (YOU SAID) YOU'D GIMME SOME MORE *Epic A 2760*............**41** 3
11 May 91   THAT'S THE WAY I LIKE IT (re-mix)
              Music Factory Dance M7FAC 2 ....**59** 2

K-CI & JOJO
US, male vocal duo – Cedric and Joel Hailey (29 WEEKS)   pos/wks
27 Jul 96   HOW DO YOU WANT IT *Death Row DRWCD 4* 1 ▲ **17** 4
23 Aug 97   YOU BRING ME UP *MCA MCSTD 48057*....................**21** 2
18 Apr 98 ● ALL MY LIFE *MCA MCSTD 48076* ▲ **8** 11
19 Sep 98   DON'T RUSH (TAKE LOVE SLOWLY)
              MCA MCSTD 48090 ....**16** 3
2 Oct 99   TELL ME IT'S REAL *MCA MCSTD 40211*......................**40** 2
23 Sep 00   TELL ME IT'S REAL (re-mix) *AM:PM CDAMPM 135* **16** 5
12 May 01   CRAZY *MCA MCSTD 40253* **35** 2

1 2Pac featuring K-Ci and JoJo

K CREATIVE UK, male vocal / instrumental group (2 WEEKS)
pos/wks

| 7 Mar 92 | THREE TIMES A MAYBE *Talkin Loud TLK 17* | 58 | 2 |

The listed flipside of 'Three Times a Maybe' was 'Feed the Feeling' by Perception

Ernie K-DOE
US, male vocalist – Ernest Kador, d. 5 Jul 2001 (7 WEEKS)
pos/wks

| 11 May 61 | MOTHER-IN-LAW *London HLU 9330* ▲ | 29 | 7 |

K-GEE UK, male producer – Karl Gordon (3 WEEKS)
pos/wks

| 4 Nov 00 | I DON'T REALLY CARE *Instant Karma KARMA 3CD* | 22 | 3 |

K.I.D. *Antilles, male / female vocal / instrumental group (4 WEEKS)*
pos/wks

| 28 Feb 81 | DON'T STOP *EMI 5143* | 49 | 4 |

K-KLASS
UK, male / female vocal / instrumental group (31 WEEKS)
pos/wks

4 May 91	RHYTHM IS A MYSTERY *Deconstruction CREED 11* [1]	61	2
9 Nov 91 ●	RHYTHM IS A MYSTERY (re-issue) *Deconstruction R 6302* [2]	3	10
25 Apr 92	SO RIGHT *Deconstruction R 6309*	20	5
7 Nov 92	DON'T STOP *Deconstruction R 6325*	32	3
27 Nov 93	LET ME SHOW YOU *Deconstruction CDR 6367*	13	7
28 May 94	WHAT YOU'RE MISSING *Deconstruction CDRS 6380*	24	3
1 Aug 98	BURNIN' *Parlophone CDK 2001*	45	1

[1] K-Klass featuring Bobbie Depasois [2] K-Klass with vocals by Bobby Depasois

KLF *UK, male vocal / instrumental duo*
– Bill Drummond and Jimmy Cauty (51 WEEKS)
pos/wks

11 Aug 90 ●	WHAT TIME IS LOVE? (LIVE AT TRANCENTRAL) *KLF Communications KLF 004* [1]	5	12
19 Jan 91 ★	3 AM ETERNAL *KLF Communications KLF 005* [1]	1	11
4 May 91 ●	LAST TRAIN TO TRANCENTRAL *KLF Communications KLF 008*	2	9
7 Dec 91 ●	JUSTIFIED AND ANCIENT *KLF Communications KLF 099* [2]	2	12
7 Mar 92 ●	AMERICA: WHAT TIME IS LOVE? (re-mix) *KLF Communications KLFUSA 004*	4	7

[1] KLF featuring the Children of the Revolution [2] KLF guest vocals: Tammy Wynette

See also JUSTIFIED ANCIENTS OF MU MU; TIMELORDS; 2K

KMC featuring DHANY
Italy, male production duo and female vocalist (2 WEEKS)
pos/wks

| 25 May 02 | I FEEL SO FINE *Incentive CENT 39CDS* | 33 | 2 |

KP & ENVYI *US, female vocal / rap duo*
– Kia Philips and Susan Hedgepath (4 WEEKS)
pos/wks

| 13 Jun 98 | SWING MY WAY *East West E 3849 CD* | 14 | 4 |

KRS ONE *US, male rapper – Lawrence Parker (8 WEEKS)*
pos/wks

18 May 96	RAPPAZ R N DAINJA *Jive JIVECD 396*	47	1
8 Feb 97	WORD PERFECT *Jive JIVECD 418*	70	1
26 Apr 97	STEP INTO A WORLD (RAPTURE'S DELIGHT) *Jive JIVECD 411*	24	2
20 Sep 97	HEARTBEAT / A FRIEND *Jive JIVECD 431*	66	1
1 Nov 97	DIGITAL *ffrr FCD 316* [1]	13	3

[1] Goldie featuring KRS One

K7 *US, male vocal / rap group (22 WEEKS)*
pos/wks

11 Dec 93 ●	COME BABY COME *Big Life BLRD 105*	3	16
2 Apr 94	HI DE HO *Big Life BLRD 108* [1]	17	5
25 Jun 94	ZUNGA ZENG *Big Life BLRD 111* [1]	63	1

[1] K7 and the Swing Kids

K3M *Italy, male / female vocal / instrumental duo (1 WEEK)*
pos/wks

| 21 Mar 92 | LISTEN TO THE RHYTHM *PWL Continental PWL 214* | 71 | 1 |

K2 FAMILY UK, male production / rap / vocal group (3 WEEKS)
pos/wks

| 27 Oct 01 | BOUNCING FLOW *Relentless RELENT 22CD* | 27 | 3 |

K-WARREN featuring LEE-0 *UK, male producer – Kevin Warren*
Williams and UK, male vocalist – Leo Ihenacho (2 WEEKS)
pos/wks

| 5 May 01 | COMING HOME *Go! Beat GOBCD 41* | 32 | 2 |

KWS *UK, male vocal / instrumental group (36 WEEKS)*
pos/wks

25 Apr 92 ★	PLEASE DON'T GO / GAME BOY *Network NWK 46*	1	16
22 Aug 92 ●	ROCK YOUR BABY *Network NWK 54*	8	7
12 Dec 92	HOLD BACK THE NIGHT *Network NWK 65* [1]	30	5
5 Jun 93	CAN'T GET ENOUGH OF YOUR LOVE *Network NWKCD 72*	71	1
9 Apr 94	IT SEEMS TO HANG ON *X-clusive XCLU 006CD*	58	1
2 Jul 94	AIN'T NOBODY (LOVES ME BETTER) *X-clusive XCLU 010CD* [2]	21	4
19 Nov 94	THE MORE I GET THE MORE I WANT *X-clusive XCLU 011CD* [3]	35	2

[1] KWS features guest vocal from The Trammps [2] KWS and Gwen Dickey [3] KWS featuring Teddy Pendergrass

'Game Boy' was listed only from 9 May 1992

KYO – *See BEDROCK*

KACI *US, female vocalist – Kaci Battaglia (22 WEEKS)*
pos/wks

10 Mar 01	PARADISE *Curb / London CUBC 61*	11	9
28 Jul 01	TU AMOR *Curb / London CUBC 71*	24	3
2 Feb 02 ●	I THINK I LOVE YOU *Curb / London CUBC 076*	10	10

Joshua KADISON *US, male vocalist (19 WEEKS)*
pos/wks

26 Feb 94	JESSIE (re) *SBK CDSBK 43*	48	5
12 Nov 94	BEAUTIFUL IN MY EYES *SBK CDSBK 50*	65	1
29 Apr 95	JESSIE (re-issue) *SBK CDSBK 53*	15	10
12 Aug 95	BEAUTIFUL IN MY EYES (re-issue) *SBK CDSBK 55*	37	3

KADOC
UK / Spain, male vocal / instrumental group (11 WEEKS)
pos/wks

6 Apr 96	THE NIGHTTRAIN *Positiva CDTIV 26*	14	8
17 Aug 96	YOU GOT TO BE THERE *Positiva CDTIV 58*	45	1
23 Aug 97	ROCK THE BELLS *Manifesto FESCD 30*	34	2

Bert KAEMPFERT & His Orchestra
Germany, orchestra, leader d. 21 Jun 1980 (10 WEEKS)
pos/wks

| 23 Dec 65 | BYE BYE BLUES *Polydor BM 56 504* | 24 | 10 |

KAJAGOOGOO
UK, male vocal / instrumental group – lead vocal Limahl (50 WEEKS) pos/wks

22 Jan 83 ★	TOO SHY *EMI 5359*	1	13
2 Apr 83 ●	OOH TO BE AH *EMI 5383*	7	8
4 Jun 83	HANG ON NOW *EMI 5394*	13	7
17 Sep 83 ●	BIG APPLE *EMI 5423*	8	8
3 Mar 84	THE LION'S MOUTH *EMI 5449*	25	7
5 May 84	TURN YOUR BACK ON ME *EMI 5646*	47	4
21 Sep 85	SHOULDN'T DO THAT *Parlophone R 6106* [1]	63	3

[1] Kaja

KALEEF *UK, male rap / vocal group (12 WEEKS)*
pos/wks

30 Mar 96	WALK LIKE A CHAMPION *Payday KACD 5* [1]	23	3
7 Dec 96	GOLDEN BROWN *Unity UNITY 010CD*	22	4
14 Jun 97	TRIALS OF LIFE *Unity UNITY 012CD*	75	1
11 Oct 97	I LIKE THE WAY (THE KISSING GAME) *Unity UNITY 015CD1*	58	1
24 Jan 98	SANDS OF TIME *Unity UNITY 016CD*	26	3

[1] Kaliphz featuring Prince Naseem

Preeya KALIDAS *UK, female vocalist (1 WEEK)*
pos/wks

| 13 Jul 02 | SHAKALAKA BABY *Sony Classical 6726322* | 38 | 1 |

UK No.1 ★   UK Top 10 ●   Still on chart +   UK million seller ◆   UK entry at No.1 ■   US No.1 ▲

BLUE MONDAY

■ Now regarded as a sort of synth-pop 'Stairway to Heaven', New Order's 'Blue Monday' has a story every bit as mysterious as anything in rock's satanic lore.

Retreating from the bleak beauty of previous incarnation Joy Division (brought to a tragic end by singer Ian Curtis's suicide), New Order were now toying with sequencers and disco. In contrast to their decidedly ramshackle early efforts, 'Blue Monday' oozed sophistication, from its startling floppy-disc cut-out sleeve (blank, except for basic information in a "colour alphabet" devised by Factory designer Peter Saville)

to the sleek mechanical beats within. Typically, those beats were accidental, originating when drummer Stephen Morris was testing a new drum machine.

'Blue Monday' had its roots in the ultra-primitive 'Prime 586', a slab of electronic twiddling that was distilled in the excellent '586' on New Order's second album Power, Corruption and Lies (1983). New Order didn't release singles from albums and this track was reworked, retaining the earlier song's eerie Kraftwerkesque Mellotron choir and sense of menace. More mysterious was the origin of the song's lyrics. Despite singer Bernard Sumner's assertion that "it's about nowt, really", debate raged on the song's subject matter. Theories ranged from an anti-Falklands War message to "not wanting to get up and go to work" (bassist Peter Hook). Another rumour, given credence by the band's manager, the late Rob Gretton, was that the song was about the true story of a spate of student suicides in 1950s Sweden, apparently sparked by listening to a Fats Domino song. The title? 'Blue Monday'.

A critical success on its release in March 1983, 'Blue Monday' boldly eschewed the radio/chart-friendly seven-inch format, opting for a lengthy 12-inch vinyl workout. Factory plugger Tony Michaledes bent the ear of radio DJs, sending the single to No.12, and later selling 600,000 copies on 12-inch (a record) and 1,001,400 copies in total.

Bernard Sumner surrounded by the gloomy figures of Peter Hook, Gillian Gilbert and Stephen Morris

However, sales of the record surely couldn't have been boosted by New Order's appearance on Top of the Pops. Previously barred from the show due to their insistence on playing live, they found the BBC relenting now they'd broken the Top 20. They celebrated their success with a less than confident performance that looked like four schoolchildren performing in morning assembly. Depressingly, any fiscal rewards from the record were reduced by Saville's expensive sleeve, which meant that the label lost around 5p on every copy sold. Meanwhile, the running costs of the new Manchester enormo-club The Hacienda were draining the coffers of both the label and New Order, co-owners of the venue. Thankfully, 'Blue Monday' got a second lease of life and with a cheaper sleeve.

Having disappeared from view in Britain, the record had become a 1983 summer disco staple around Europe. Inebriated Brits had transformed this oddball electronics experiment into a monster holiday anthem. It re-entered the UK chart to peak at No.9 in October and reappeared again in January

★ **ARTIST:** New Order

★ **LABEL:** Factory/London Records

★ **WRITERS:** Bernard Sumner, Peter Hook, Stephen Morris, Gillian Gilbert

★ **PRODUCER:** New Order

RUMOUR WAS THAT THE SONG WAS ABOUT THE TRUE STORY OF A SPATE OF STUDENT SUICIDES IN 1950s SWEDEN, APPARENTLY SPARKED BY LISTENING TO A **FATS DOMINO** SONG

1984. New Order shrugged and got on with something else. But while the band moved on, it seemed the rest of the world couldn't. In 1988, producer Quincy Jones, head of the band's US label Qwest, supervised a remix aimed at the American R&B chart, resulting in the seven-inch 'Blue Monday 88' and a UK No.3 placing in May.

The band was persuaded to record a version of 'Blue Monday' for a Sunkist commercial (see 1993's New Order Story documentary), although, with typical perversity, they changed their mind at the last minute only to permit an American Express ad featuring the tune years later. Now regarded as a classic dance track, 'Blue Monday' returned to the chart yet again in 1995, courtesy of German hard-house types Hardfloor. In 2002, Kylie Minogue worked the song into live performances of 'Can't Get You Out of My Head', which blossomed into the bonus track 'Can't Get Blue Monday Out of My Head' on her single 'Love at First Sight' – a compliment repaid by a freshly reformed New Order at their gigs.

■ Mark Bennett

KALIN TWINS
US, male vocal duo – Herb and Hal Kalin (18 WEEKS) pos/wks
18 Jul 58 ★ WHEN *Brunswick 05751* 1 18

KALLAGHAN – See N'n'G featuring KALLAGHAN

Kitty KALLEN *US, female vocalist (23 WEEKS)* pos/wks
2 Jul 54 ★ LITTLE THINGS MEAN A LOT *Brunswick 05287* ▲ 1 23

Gunter KALLMAN CHOIR
Germany, male / female vocal group (3 WEEKS) pos/wks
24 Dec 64 ELISABETH SERENADE *Polydor NH 24678* 39 3

KAMASUTRA featuring Jocelyn BROWN
Italy, male DJ / production duo and US, female vocalist (1 WEEK) pos/wks
22 Nov 97 HAPPINESS *Sony S2 KAMCD 2* 45 1

Nick KAMEN *UK, male vocalist (33 WEEKS)* pos/wks
8 Nov 86 ● EACH TIME YOU BREAK MY HEART *WEA YZ 90*.....................5 12
28 Feb 87 LOVING YOU IS SWEETER THAN EVER *WEA YZ 106*.............16 9
16 May 87 NOBODY ELSE *WEA YZ 122* 47 3
28 May 88 TELL ME *WEA YZ 184* 40 5
28 Apr 90 I PROMISED MYSELF *WEA YZ 454* 50 4

Ini KAMOZE *Jamaica, male vocalist (15 WEEKS)* pos/wks
7 Jan 95 ● HERE COMES THE HOTSTEPPER *Columbia 6610472* ▲ 4 15

KANDI *US, female vocalist – Kandi Burruss (10 WEEKS)* pos/wks
11 Nov 00 ● DON'T THINK I'M NOT *Columbia 6705102* 9 10

KANDIDATE *UK, male vocal / instrumental group (28 WEEKS)* pos/wks
19 Aug 78 DON'T WANNA SAY GOODNIGHT *RAK 280* 47 6
17 Mar 79 I DON'T WANNA LOSE YOU *RAK 289* 11 12
4 Aug 79 GIRLS GIRLS GIRLS *RAK 295*...34 7
22 Mar 80 LET ME ROCK YOU *RAK 306*...58 3

Eden KANE (500) [Top 500] *Last teen idol before The Beatles, b. Richard Sarstedt, 29 Mar 1942, Delhi, India. Stylish pop beat singer who, like Adam Faith, had many of his hits penned for him by Johnny Worth. Brothers Peter and Robin Sarstedt also had Top 3 entries (73 WEEKS)* pos/wks
1 Jun 61 ★ WELL I ASK YOU *Decca F 11353* 1 21
14 Sep 61 ● GET LOST *Decca F 11381* 10 11
18 Jan 62 ● FORGET ME NOT *Decca F 11418* 3 14
10 May 62 ● I DON'T KNOW WHY *Decca F 11460* 7 13
30 Jan 64 ● BOYS CRY *Fontana TF 438* 8 14

KANE GANG *UK, male vocal / instrumental group (37 WEEKS)* pos/wks
19 May 84 SMALLTOWN CREED *Kitchenware SK 11* 60 2
7 Jul 84 CLOSEST THING TO HEAVEN *Kitchenware SK 15*.................12 11
10 Nov 84 RESPECT YOURSELF (re) *Kitchenware SK 16* 21 11
9 Mar 85 GUN LAW *Kitchenware SK 20* 53 4
27 Jun 87 MOTORTOWN *Kitchenware SK 30* 45 5
16 Apr 88 DON'T LOOK ANY FURTHER *Kitchenware SK 33* 52 4

KANSAS *US, male vocal / instrumental group (7 WEEKS)* pos/wks
1 Jul 78 CARRY ON WAYWARD SON *Kirshner KIR 4932*........................51 7

Mory KANTE *Guinea, male vocalist (14 WEEKS)* pos/wks
23 Jul 88 YEKE YEKE *London LON 171* 29 9
11 Mar 95 YEKE YEKE (re-issue) *Ffrreedom TABCD 226* 25 3
30 Nov 96 YEKE YEKE (re-mix) *ffrr FCD 288* 28 2

KAOMA
France, male / female vocal / instrumental group (20 WEEKS) pos/wks
21 Oct 89 ● LAMBADA *CBS 655011 7*...4 18
27 Jan 90 DANCANDO LAMBADA *CBS 655235 7*.................................62 2

KAOTIC CHEMISTRY *UK, male instrumental / production group (1 WK)* pos/wks
31 Oct 92 LSD (EP) *Moving Shadow SHADOW 20*................................68 1
Tracks on LSD (EP): Space Cakes / LSD / Illegal Substances / Drumtrip II

KARAJA *Germany, female vocalist (1 WEEK)* pos/wks
19 Oct 02 SHE MOVES (LA LA LA)
Ministry of Sound / Substance SUBS 14CDS 42 1

KARIN – See UNIQUE 3

KARIYA *US, female vocalist (9 WEEKS)* pos/wks
8 Jul 89 LET ME LOVE YOU FOR TONIGHT (re) *Sleeping Bag SBUK 4* 44 9

Mick KARN
UK, male instrumentalist – bass – Anthony Michaelides (6 WEEKS) pos/wks
9 Jul 83 AFTER A FASHION *Musicfest FEST 1* [1] 39 4
17 Jan 87 BUOY *Virgin VS 910* [2] 63 2
[1] Midge Ure and Mick Karn [2] Mick Karn featuring David Sylvian
See also JAPAN

KARTOON KREW *US, rap / instrumental group (6 WEEKS)* pos/wks
7 Dec 85 INSPECTOR GADGET *Champion CHAMP 6*............................58 6

KASENETZ-KATZ SINGING ORCHESTRAL CIRCUS
US, male vocal / instrumental group (15 WEEKS) pos/wks
20 Nov 68 QUICK JOEY SMALL (RUN JOEY RUN) *Buddah 201 022*...........19 15

KATCHA *UK, male DJ / producer (1 WEEK)* pos/wks
21 Aug 99 TOUCHED BY GOD *Hooj Choons HOOJ 77CD* 57 1

KATRINA and the WAVES
US / UK, female / male vocal / instrumental group (34 WEEKS) pos/wks
4 May 85 ● WALKING ON SUNSHINE *Capitol CL 354* 8 12
5 Jul 86 SUN STREET *Capitol CL 407* 22 9
8 Jun 96 WALKING ON SUNSHINE (re-issue) *EMI Premier PRESCD 2* ..53 1
10 May 97 ● LOVE SHINE A LIGHT *Eternal WEA 106CD1* 3 12

KAVANA *UK, male vocalist – Anthony Kavanagh (26 WEEKS)* pos/wks
11 May 96 CRAZY CHANCE *Nemesis NMSD 1* 35 3
24 Aug 96 WHERE ARE YOU *Nemesis NMSD 2* 26 2
11 Jan 97 ● I CAN MAKE YOU FEEL GOOD *Nemesis NMSDX 3* 8 5
19 Apr 97 ● MFEO *Nemesis NMSD 4* 8 4
13 Sep 97 CRAZY CHANCE 97 (re-recording) *Nemesis NMSD 5* 16 3
29 Aug 98 SPECIAL KIND OF SOMETHING *Virgin VSCDT 1704* 13 4
12 Dec 98 FUNKY LOVE (re) *Virgin VSCDT 1711* 32 3
20 Mar 99 WILL YOU WAIT FOR ME *Virgin VSCDT 1726* 29 3

Niamh KAVANAGH *Ireland, female vocalist (5 WEEKS)* pos/wks
12 Jun 93 IN YOUR EYES *Arista 74321154152* 24 5

KAWALA
UK, male vocal / instrumental / production group (1 WEEK) pos/wks
26 Feb 00 HUMANISTIC *Pepper 9230022* 68 1

Janet KAY *UK, female vocalist – Janet Bogle (24 WEEKS)* pos/wks
9 Jun 79 ● SILLY GAMES *Scope SC 2* 2 14
11 Aug 90 SILLY GAMES *Arista 113452* [1] 22 7
11 Aug 90 SILLY GAMES (re-mix) *Music Factory Dance MFD 006*............62 3
[1] Lindy Layton featuring Janet Kay

Danny KAYE
US, male actor / vocalist – David Kaminsky, d. 3 Mar 1987 (10 WEEKS) pos/wks
27 Feb 53 ● WONDERFUL COPENHAGEN *Brunswick 05023* 5 10
With Gordon Jenkins and his Orchestra and Chorus

KAYE SISTERS *UK, female vocal group (45 WEEKS)*

		pos/wks
25 May 56	IVORY TOWER *HMV POP 209* [1]	20 5
1 Nov 57 ●	GOT-TA HAVE SOMETHING IN THE BANK, FRANK *Philips PB 751* [2]	8 11
3 Jan 58	SHAKE ME I RATTLE / ALONE *Philips PB 752*	27 1
1 May 59 ●	COME SOFTLY TO ME *Philips PB 913* [2]	9 9
7 Jul 60 ●	PAPER ROSES *Philips PB 1024*	7 19

[1] Three Kayes [2] Frankie Vaughan and the Kaye Sisters

KAYESTONE *UK, male DJ / production duo (1 WEEK)*

		pos/wks
29 Jul 00	ATMOSPHERE *Distinctive DISNCD 62*	55 1

KÉ *US, male vocalist (1 WEEK)*

		pos/wks
13 Apr 96	STRANGE WORLD *Venture 74321349412*	73 1

Johnny KEATING *UK, orchestra (14 WEEKS)*

		pos/wks
1 Mar 62 ●	THEME FROM 'Z CARS' (JOHNNY TODD) *Piccadilly 7N 35032*	8 14

Ronan KEATING (393) Top 500

Record-setting Irish vocalist, b. 3 Mar 1977, Dublin, who is still adding to his unprecedented chart start of 23 Top 10 entries (22 of them making the Top 5) including those as a member of Boyzone. In addition his six albums (including two solo) entered at No.1. He formerly co-managed Westlife. Best-selling single: 'When You Say Nothing At All' 528,600 (85 WKS) pos/wks

		pos/wks
7 Aug 99 ★	WHEN YOU SAY NOTHING AT ALL (2re) *Polydor 5612902* ■	1 17
22 Jul 00 ★	LIFE IS A ROLLERCOASTER *Polydor 5619362* ■	1 14
2 Dec 00 ●	THE WAY YOU MAKE ME FEEL (re) *Polydor 5878852*	6 12
28 Apr 01 ●	LOVIN' EACH DAY *Polydor 5876872*	2 14
18 May 02 ★	IF TOMORROW NEVER COMES *Polydor 5707182* ■	1 15
21 Sep 02 ●	I LOVE IT WHEN WE DO (re) *Polydor 5709032*	5 9
7 Dec 02 ●	WE'VE GOT TONIGHT *Polydor 0658612* [1]	4 4+

[1] Ronan Keating featuring Lulu

See also BOYZONE

KEE – See BM DUBS present MR RUMBLE featuring BRASSTOOTH and KEE

Kevin KEEGAN *UK, male footballer / vocalist (6 WEEKS)*

		pos/wks
9 Jun 79	HEAD OVER HEELS IN LOVE *EMI 2965*	31 6

Yvonne KEELEY – See Scott FITZGERALD

Nelson KEENE
UK, male vocalist – Malcolm Holland (5 WEEKS)

		pos/wks
25 Aug 60	IMAGE OF A GIRL (re) *HMV POP 771*	37 5

KEITH *US, male vocalist – James Keefer (8 WEEKS)*

		pos/wks
26 Jan 67	98.6 *Mercury MF 955*	24 7
16 Mar 67	TELL ME TO MY FACE *Mercury MF 968*	50 1

KEITH 'N' SHANE
Ireland, male vocal duo – Keith Duffy and Shane Lynch (3 WEEKS)

		pos/wks
23 Dec 00	GIRL YOU KNOW IT'S TRUE *Polydor 5879462*	36 3

See also BOYZONE

KELIS *US, female vocalist – Kelis Rogers (30 WEEKS)*

		pos/wks
26 Feb 00	CAUGHT OUT THERE (import) *Virgin 8965102CD*	52 1
4 Mar 00 ●	CAUGHT OUT THERE (re) *Virgin VUSCD 158*	4 12
17 Jun 00	GOOD STUFF *Virgin VUSCD 164*	19 5
8 Jul 00	GOT YOUR MONEY *Elektra E 7077CD* [1]	11 8
21 Oct 00	GET ALONG WITH YOU *Virgin VUSCD 174*	51 1
3 Nov 01	YOUNG FRESH N' NEW *Virgin VUSCD 212*	32 2
5 Oct 02	HELP ME *Perfecto PERF 42CDS* [2]	65 1

[1] Ol' Dirty Bastard featuring Kelis [2] Timo Maas featuring Kelis

Jerry KELLER *US, male vocalist (14 WEEKS)*

		pos/wks
28 Aug 59 ★	HERE COMES SUMMER *London HLR 8890*	1 14

Frank KELLY
Ireland, male actor / vocalist – Francis O'Kelly (5 WEEKS)

		pos/wks
24 Dec 83	CHRISTMAS COUNTDOWN (re) *Ritz RITZ 062*	26 5

Re-entry peaked at No.54 in Dec 1984

Frankie KELLY *US, male vocalist / instrumentalist (2 WEEKS)*

		pos/wks
2 Nov 85	AIN'T THAT THE TRUTH *10 TEN 87*	65 2

Grace KELLY – See Bing CROSBY

Keith KELLY *UK, male vocalist – Michael Pailthorpe (5 WEEKS)*

		pos/wks
5 May 60	TEASE ME (MUST YOU ALWAYS) (re) *Parlophone R 4640*	27 4
18 Aug 60	LISTEN LITTLE GIRL *Parlophone R 4676*	47 1

R KELLY (124) Top 500

Phenomenally successful R&B vocalist, b. Robert Kelly 8 Jan 1971, Chicago, US, whose writing and production skills are constantly in demand by other top artists. Amazingly, 1998 album 'R' yielded seven Top 20 hits but never reached the Top 20 itself. Best-selling single: 'I Believe I Can Fly' 673,000 (167 WEEKS) pos/wks

		pos/wks
9 May 92	SHE'S GOT THAT VIBE *Jive JIVET 292* [1]	57 2
20 Nov 93	SEX ME *Jive JIVECD 346* [1]	75 1
14 May 94	YOUR BODY'S CALLIN' *Jive JIVECD 353*	19 4
3 Sep 94	SUMMER BUNNIES *Jive JIVECD 358*	23 3
22 Oct 94 ●	SHE'S GOT THAT VIBE (re-issue) *Jive JIVECD 364*	3 13
21 Jan 95	BUMP 'N' GRIND *Jive JIVECD 368* ▲	8 9
6 May 95	THE 4 PLAY EP *Jive JIVECD 376*	23 3
11 Nov 95	YOU REMIND ME OF SOMETHING *Jive JIVECD 388*	24 3
2 Mar 96	DOWN LOW (NOBODY HAS TO KNOW) *Jive JIVECD 392* [2]	23 3
22 Jun 96	THANK GOD IT'S FRIDAY *Jive JIVECD 395*	14 4
29 Mar 97 ★	I BELIEVE I CAN FLY *Jive JIVECD 415*	1 17
19 Jul 97 ●	GOTHAM CITY *Jive JIVECD 428*	9 8
18 Jul 98 ●	BE CAREFUL (re) *Jive 0521452* [3]	7 7
26 Sep 98	HALF ON A BABY *Jive 0521802*	16 4
14 Nov 98	HOME ALONE *Jive 0522392* [4]	17 5
28 Nov 98 ●	I'M YOUR ANGEL *Epic 6666282* [5] ▲	3 13
31 Jul 99	DID YOU EVER THINK *Jive 0523612*	20 5
16 Oct 99	IF I COULD TURN BACK THE HANDS OF TIME *Jive 0523182*	2 21
19 Feb 00	SATISFY YOU (IMPORT) (re) *Bad Boy / Arista 792832* [6]	73 2
11 Mar 00 ●	SATISFY YOU *Bad Boy / Arista 74321745592* [6]	8 8
22 Apr 00	ONLY THE LOOT CAN MAKE ME HAPPY / WHEN A WOMAN'S FED UP / I CAN'T SLEEP BABY (IF I) *Jive 9250282*	24 3
21 Oct 00	I WISH *Jive 9251262*	12 6
31 Mar 01	THE STORM IS OVER NOW *Jive 9251782*	18 6
23 Jun 01	FIESTA *Jive 9252142* [7]	23 3
2 Mar 02 ●	THE WORLD'S GREATEST *Jive 9253242*	4 12
25 May 02	HONEY *Jive 9253662* [8]	35 2

[1] R Kelly and Public Announcement [2] R Kelly featuring Ronald Isley [3] Sparkle featuring R Kelly [4] R Kelly featuring Keith Murray [5] Celine Dion and R Kelly [6] Puff Daddy featuring R Kelly [7] R Kelly featuring Jay-Z [8] R Kelly & Jay-Z

The 4 Play EP was available on two CDs, each featuring 'Your Body's Callin'' and three further tracks

See also PUBLIC ANNOUNCEMENT

Ramona KELLY – See Cevin FISHER

Roberta KELLY *US, female vocalist (3 WEEKS)*

		pos/wks
21 Jan 78	ZODIACS (re) *Oasis/Hansa 3*	44 3

KELLY FAMILY
Ireland, male / female vocal / instrumental group (1 WEEK)

		pos/wks
21 Oct 95	AN ANGEL *EMI CDEM 390*	69 1

Tricia Lee KELSHALL – See WAY OUT WEST

Johnny KEMP Barbados, male vocalist (1 WEEK)

		pos/wks
27 Aug 88	JUST GOT PAID CBS 651470 7	68 1

Tara KEMP US, female vocalist (2 WEEKS)

		pos/wks
20 Apr 91	HOLD YOU TIGHT Giant W 0020	69 2

Graham KENDRICK UK, male vocalist (4 WEEKS)

		pos/wks
9 Sep 89	LET THE FLAME BURN BRIGHTER Power P 30	55 4

Eddie KENDRICKS US, male vocalist, d. 5 Oct 1992 (20 WEEKS)

		pos/wks
3 Nov 73	KEEP ON TRUCKIN' Tamla Motown TMG 873 ▲	18 14
16 Mar 74	BOOGIE DOWN Tamla Motown TMG 888	39 4
21 Sep 85	A NIGHT AT THE APOLLO LIVE! RCA PB 49935 [1]	58 2

[1] Daryl Hall and John Oates featuring David Ruffin and Eddie Kendrick

A Night at the Apollo Live! is a medley of 'The Way You Do the Things You Do' and 'My Girl'. Kendricks dropped the 's' from his name for last hit

See also TEMPTATIONS

KENICKIE UK, female / male vocal / instrumental group (13 WKS)

		pos/wks
14 Sep 96	PUNKA Emidisc CDDISC 001	43 2
16 Nov 96	MILLIONAIRE SWEEPER Emidisc CDDISC 002	60 1
11 Jan 97	IN YOUR CAR Emidisc CDDISC 005	24 3
3 May 97	NIGHTLIFE Emidisc CDDISC 006	27 2
5 Jul 97	PUNKA (re-issue) Emidisc CDDISC 007	38 2
6 Jun 98	I WOULD FIX YOU EMI CDEM 513	36 2
22 Aug 98	STAY IN THE SUN EMI CDEMS 520	43 1

Jane KENNAWAY and STRANGE BEHAVIOUR
UK, female vocalist with male instrumental group (3 WEEKS)

		pos/wks
24 Jan 81	I.O.U. Deram DM 436	65 3

Brian KENNEDY Ireland, male vocalist (8 WEEKS)

		pos/wks
22 Jun 96	A BETTER MAN RCA 74321382642	28 3
21 Sep 96	LIFE, LOVE AND HAPPINESS RCA 74321409921	27 3
5 Apr 97	PUT THE MESSAGE IN THE BOX RCA 74321462272	37 2

Kevin KENNEDY UK, male actor / vocalist (1 WEEK)

		pos/wks
24 Jun 00	BULLDOG NATION D2m 74321759742	70 1

KENNY Ireland, male vocalist – Tony Kenny (16 WEEKS)

		pos/wks
3 Mar 73	HEART OF STONE RAK 144	11 13
30 Jun 73	GIVE IT TO ME NOW RAK 153	38 3

KENNY UK, male vocal / instrumental group (39 WEEKS)

		pos/wks
7 Dec 74	● THE BUMP RAK 186	3 15
8 Mar 75	● FANCY PANTS RAK 196	4 9
7 Jun 75	BABY I LOVE YOU, OK! RAK 207	12 7
16 Aug 75	● JULIE ANNE RAK 214	10 8

Gerard KENNY US, male vocalist (21 WEEKS)

		pos/wks
9 Dec 78	NEW YORK, NEW YORK RCA PB 5117	43 8
21 Jun 80	FANTASY (re) RCA PB 5256	34 6
18 Feb 84	THE OTHER WOMAN, THE OTHER MAN Impression IMS 3	69 4
4 May 85	NO MAN'S LAND WEA YZ 38	56 3

KENT Sweden, male vocal / instrumental group (1 WEEK)

		pos/wks
13 Mar 99	747 RCA 74321645912	61 1

Klark KENT US, male vocalist / multi-instrumentalist – Stewart Copeland (4 WEEKS)

		pos/wks
26 Aug 78	DON'T CARE A&M AMS 7376	48 4

See also POLICE

Carol KENYON – See Paul HARDCASTLE; HEAVEN 17; RAPINATION

KERBDOG Ireland, male vocal / instrumental group (5 WEEKS)

		pos/wks
12 Mar 94	DRY RISER Vertigo VERCC 83	60 1
6 Aug 94	DUMMY CRUSHER Vertigo VERCD 86	37 2
12 Oct 96	SALLY Fontana KERCD 2	69 1
29 Mar 97	MEXICAN WAVE Fontana KERCD 3	49 1

Dick KERR – See Slim DUSTY

Anita KERR SINGERS – See Bobby HELMS

KERRI and MICK Australia, female / male vocal duo (3 WEEKS)

		pos/wks
28 Apr 84	'SONS AND DAUGHTERS' THEME A1 A1 286	68 3

KERRI-ANN Ireland, female vocalist (1 WEEK)

		pos/wks
8 Aug 98	DO YOU LOVE ME BOY? Raglan Road 5671012	58 1

Liz KERSHAW and Bruno BROOKES
UK, male / female DJ / vocal duo (3 WEEKS)

		pos/wks
2 Dec 89	IT TAKES TWO BABY Spartan CIN 101 [1]	53 2
1 Dec 90	LET'S DANCE Jive BRUNO 1 [2]	54 1

[1] Liz Kershaw, Bruno Brookes, Jive Bunny and Londonbeat [2] Bruno and Liz and the Radio 1 DJ Posse

Nik KERSHAW (366) Top 500
One time jazz-funk guitarist whose melodic pop repertoire made him a mid-1980s teen idol, b. 1 Mar 1958, Bristol, UK. His 50 weeks on the singles chart in 1984 beat all other soloists. He appeared at Live Aid, and penned hits for Let Loose, The Hollies and a No.1 for Chesney Hawkes (89 WEEKS) pos/wks

		pos/wks
19 Nov 83	I WON'T LET THE SUN GO DOWN ON ME MCA MCA 816	47 5
28 Jan 84	● WOULDN'T IT BE GOOD MCA NIK 2	4 14
14 Apr 84	DANCING GIRLS MCA NIK 3	13 9
16 Jun 84	● I WON'T LET THE SUN GO DOWN ON ME (re-issue) MCA NIK 4	2 13
15 Sep 84	HUMAN RACING MCA NIK 5	19 7
17 Nov 84	● THE RIDDLE MCA NIK 6	3 11
16 Mar 85	● WIDE BOY MCA NIK 7	9 8
3 Aug 85	● DON QUIXOTE MCA NIK 8	10 7
30 Nov 85	WHEN A HEART BEATS MCA NIK 9	27 7
11 Oct 86	NOBODY KNOWS MCA NIK 10	44 3
13 Dec 86	RADIO MUSICOLA MCA NIK 11	43 2
4 Feb 89	ONE STEP AHEAD MCA NIK 12	55 1
27 Feb 99	SOMEBODY LOVES YOU Eagle EAGXA 023	70 1
7 Aug 99	SOMETIMES Wall of Sound WALLD 054 [1]	56 1

[1] Les Rythmes Digitales featuring Nik Kershaw

KEVIN and PERRY – See PRECOCIOUS BRATS featuring KEVIN and PERRY

KEVIN THE GERBIL UK, male gerbil vocalist (6 WEEKS)

		pos/wks
4 Aug 84	SUMMER HOLIDAY Magnet RAT 3	50 6

KEY WEST – See ERIK

KEYNOTES – See Dave KING

Alicia KEYS US, female vocalist (35 WEEKS)

		pos/wks
10 Nov 01	● FALLIN' J 74321903692 ▲	3 10
9 Mar 02	BROTHA PART II J 74321922142 [1]	37 2
30 Mar 02	A WOMAN'S WORTH J 74321928692	18 8
20 Jul 02	HOW COME YOU DON'T CALL ME J 74321943122	26 3
5 Oct 02	● GANGSTA LOVIN' Ruff Ryders / Interscope 4978042 [2]	6 8
7 Dec 02	GIRLFRIEND J 74321974972	24 4+

[1] Angie Stone featuring Alicia Keys and Eve [2] Eve featuring Alicia Keys

Chaka KHAN (324) Top 500 *Powerful and influential soul diva b. Yvette Stevens, 23 Mar 1953, Illinois, US. Fronted funk troupe Rufus for six years, went solo 1978. Prince-penned 'I Feel For You' was the first UK No.1 to feature rap elements (courtesy of Grandmaster Melle Mel) (97 WKS)* pos/wks

		pos/wks
2 Dec 78	I'M EVERY WOMAN Warner Bros. K 17269	11 13

31 Mar 84 ●	AIN'T NOBODY *Warner Bros. RCK 1* [1]	.........8 12
20 Oct 84 ★	I FEEL FOR YOU *Warner Bros. W 9209*	....1 16
19 Jan 85	THIS IS MY NIGHT *Warner Bros. W 9097*	....14 6
20 Apr 85	EYE TO EYE *Warner Bros. W 9009*	....16 7
12 Jul 86	LOVE OF A LIFETIME *Warner Bros. W 8671*	....52 4
21 Jan 89	IT'S MY PARTY *Warner Bros. W 7678*	....71 2
6 May 89 ●	I'M EVERY WOMAN (re-mix) *Warner Bros. W 2963*....8 8
8 Jul 89 ●	AIN'T NOBODY (re-mix) *Warner Bros. W 2880* [1]	....6 9
7 Oct 89	I FEEL FOR YOU (re-mix) *Warner Bros. W 2764*	....45 2
13 Jan 90	I'LL BE GOOD TO YOU *Qwest W 2697* [2]	....21 7
28 Mar 92	LOVE YOU ALL MY LIFETIME *Warner Bros. W 0087*....49 3
17 Jul 93	DON'T LOOK AT ME THAT WAY *Warner Bros. W 0192CD*....73 1
19 Aug 95	WATCH WHAT YOU SAY *Cooltempo CDCOOL 308* [3]....28 3
1 Mar 97	NEVER MISS THE WATER *Reprise W 1393CD* [4]	....59 1
11 Nov 00	ALL GOOD *Tommy Boy TBCD 2154B* [5]	....33 3

[1] Rufus and Chaka Khan [2] Quincy Jones featuring Ray Charles and Chaka Khan
[3] Guru featuring Chaka Khan [4] Chaka Khan featuring Me'Shell Ndegeocello
[5] De La Soul featuring Chaka Khan

See also Quincy JONES

Praga KHAN
Belgium, male producer – Maurice Engelen (9 WEEKS) pos/wks

4 Apr 92	FREE YOUR BODY / INJECTED WITH A POISON	
	Profile PROFT 347 [1]	....16 6
11 Jul 92	RAVE ALERT *Profile PROF 369*	....39 2
24 Nov 01	INJECTED WITH A POISON (re-mix) *Nukleuz NUKC 0238*....52 1

[1] Praga Khan featuring Jade 4 U

Mary KIANI *UK, female vocalist (15 WEEKS)* pos/wks

12 Aug 95	WHEN I CALL YOUR NAME *Mercury MERCD 440*	....18 4
23 Dec 95	I GIVE IT ALL TO YOU / I IMAGINE	
	Mercury MERCD 449	....35 4
27 Apr 96	LET THE MUSIC PLAY *Mercury MERCD 456*	....19 3
18 Jan 97	100% *Mercury MERCD 469*	....23 3
21 Jun 97	WITH OR WITHOUT YOU *Mercury MERCD 487*	....46 1

KICK HORNS – *See DODGY*

KICK SQUAD
UK / Germany, male vocal / instrumental group (2 WEEKS) pos/wks

| 10 Nov 90 | SOUND CLASH (CHAMPION SOUND) *Kickin KICK 2*....59 2 |

KICKING BACK with TAXMAN *UK, male / female*
vocal / instrumental duo with male rapper (8 WEEKS) pos/wks

| 17 Mar 90 | DEVOTION *10 TEN 297* | ....47 4 |
| 7 Jul 90 | EVERYTHING *10 TEN 307* | ....54 4 |

KICKS LIKE A MULE *UK, male instrumental / production*
duo – Nick Halkes and Richard Russell (6 WEEKS) pos/wks

| 1 Feb 92 ● | THE BOUNCER *Tribal Bass TRIBE 3S* | ....7 6 |

KID 'N' PLAY *US, male rap duo (7 WEEKS)* pos/wks

18 Jul 87	LAST NIGHT *Cooltempo COOL 148*	....71 1
26 Mar 88	DO THIS MY WAY *Cooltempo COOL 164*	....48 3
17 Sep 88	GITTIN' FUNKY *Cooltempo COOL 168*	....55 3

KID ROCK *US, male vocalist / rapper – Robert Ritchie (8 WEEKS)* pos/wks

23 Oct 99	COWBOY *Atlantic AT 0076CD*	....36 2
9 Sep 00	AMERICAN BAD ASS *Atlantic AT 0085CD*	....25 4
12 May 01	BAWITDABA *Atlantic AT 0098CD*	....41 2

KID UNKNOWN *UK, male producer – Paul Fitzpatrick (1 WEEK)* pos/wks

| 2 May 92 | NIGHTMARE *Warp WAP 20CD* | ....64 1 |

Carol KIDD featuring Terry WAITE
UK, female / male vocal duo (3 WEEKS) pos/wks

| 17 Oct 92 | WHEN I DREAM *The Hit Label HLS 1* | ....58 3 |

Johnny KIDD and the PIRATES *UK, male vocal*
/ instrumental group, leader d. 7 Oct 1966 (62 WEEKS) pos/wks

12 Jun 59	PLEASE DON'T TOUCH (re) *HMV POP 615* [1]....25 5
12 Feb 60	YOU GOT WHAT IT TAKES *HMV POP 698*	....25 3
16 Jun 60 ★	SHAKIN' ALL OVER *HMV POP 753*	....1 19
6 Oct 60	RESTLESS *HMV POP 790*	....22 7
13 Apr 61	LINDA LU *HMV POP 853*	....47 1
10 Jan 63	A SHOT OF RHYTHM AND BLUES *HMV POP 1088*....48 1
25 Jul 63 ●	I'LL NEVER GET OVER YOU *HMV POP 1173*....4 15
28 Nov 63	HUNGRY FOR LOVE *HMV POP 1228*	....20 10
30 Apr 64	ALWAYS AND EVER *HMV POP 1269*	....46 1

[1] Johnny Kidd

Nicole KIDMAN *Australia, female actor / vocalist (17 WEEKS)* pos/wks

| 6 Oct 01 | COME WHAT MAY *Interscope / Polydor 4976302* [1]....27 5 |
| 22 Dec 01 ★ | SOMETHIN' STUPID *Chrysalis CDCHS 5132* [2] ■....1 12 |

[1] Nicole Kidman and Ewan McGregor [2] Robbie Williams and Nicole Kidman

KIDS FROM 'FAME'
US, male / female actors / vocal group (36 WEEKS) pos/wks

14 Aug 82 ●	HI-FIDELITY *RCA 254* [1]	....5 10
2 Oct 82 ●	STARMAKER *RCA 280*	....3 10
11 Dec 82	MANNEQUIN *RCA 299* [2]	....50 6
9 Apr 83	FRIDAY NIGHT (LIVE VERSION) *RCA 320*	....13 10

[1] Kids from Fame featuring Valerie Landsberg [2] Kids from Fame featuring Gene Anthony Ray

Greg KIHN BAND *US, male vocal / instrumental group (2 WEEKS)* pos/wks

| 23 Apr 83 | JEOPARDY *Beserkley E 9847* | ....63 2 |

KILLAH PRIEST *US, male rapper (1 WEEK)* pos/wks

| 7 Feb 98 | ONE STEP *Geffen GFSTD 22318* | ....45 1 |

KILLER MIKE – *See OUTKAST*

KILLING JOKE *UK, male vocal / instrumental group (48 WEEKS)* pos/wks

23 May 81	FOLLOW THE LEADERS *Malicious Damage EGMDS 101*....55 5
20 Mar 82	EMPIRE SONG *Malicious Damage EGO 4*	....43 4
30 Oct 82	BIRDS OF A FEATHER *EG EGO 10*	....64 2
25 Jun 83	LET'S ALL (GO TO THE FIRE DANCES) *EG EGO 11*....51 3
15 Oct 83	ME OR YOU? *EG EGO 14*	....57 1
7 Apr 84	EIGHTIES *EG EGO 16*	....60 5
21 Jul 84	A NEW DAY *EG EGO 17*	....56 2
2 Feb 85	LOVE LIKE BLOOD *EG EGO 20*	....16 9
30 Mar 85	KINGS AND QUEENS *EG EGO 21*	....58 3
16 Aug 86	ADORATIONS *EG EGO 27*	....42 6
18 Oct 86	SANITY *EG EGO 30*	....70 1
7 May 94	MILLENNIUM *Butterfly BFLD 12*	....34 2
16 Jul 94	THE PANDEMONIUM SINGLE *Butterfly BFLD 17*....28 3
4 Feb 95	JANA *Butterfly BFLDA 21*	....54 1
23 Mar 96	DEMOCRACY *Butterfly BFLDA 33*	....39 1

Andy KIM
Canada, male vocalist – Andrew Joachim (12 WEEKS) pos/wks

| 24 Aug 74 ● | ROCK ME GENTLY *Capitol CL 15787* ▲ | ....2 12 |

KINANE *Ireland, female vocalist (4 WEEKS)* pos/wks

18 May 96	ALL THE LOVER I NEED *Coliseum TOGA 003CD* [1]....59 1
21 Sep 96	THE WOMAN IN ME *Coliseum TOGA 007CD* [1]....73 1
16 May 98	HEAVEN *Coalition COLA 047CD*	....49 1
22 Aug 98	SO FINE *Coalition COLA 055CD1*	....63 1

[1] Bianca Kinane

KING *UK / Ireland, male vocal / instrumental group (44 WEEKS)* pos/wks

12 Jan 85 ●	LOVE AND PRIDE *CBS A 4988*	....2 14
23 Mar 85	WON'T YOU HOLD MY HAND NOW *CBS A 6094*....24 8
17 Aug 85 ●	ALONE WITHOUT YOU *CBS A 6308*	....8 9

UK No.1 ★   UK Top 10 ●   Still on chart +   UK million seller ◆   UK entry at No.1 ■   US No.1 ▲

| 19 Oct 85 | THE TASTE OF YOUR TEARS *CBS A 6618* | 11 | 9 |
| 11 Jan 86 | TORTURE *CBS A 6761* | 23 | 4 |

See also Paul KING

Albert KING – *See Gary MOORE*

B.B. KING
US, male vocalist / instrumentalist – guitar – Riley King (10 WEEKS) pos/wks
| 15 Apr 89 | ● WHEN LOVE COMES TO TOWN *Island IS 411* [1] | 6 | 7 |
| 18 Jul 92 | SINCE I MET YOU BABY *Virgin VS 1423* [2] | 59 | 3 |

[1] U2 with B.B. King [2] Gary Moore and B.B. King

Ben E KING
US, male vocalist – Benjamin Nelson (35 WEEKS) pos/wks
2 Feb 61	FIRST TASTE OF LOVE *London HLK 9258*	27	11
22 Jun 61	STAND BY ME (re) *London HLK 9358*	27	7
5 Oct 61	AMOR, AMOR *London HLK 9416*	38	4
14 Feb 87	★ STAND BY ME (re-issue) *Atlantic A 9361*	1	11
4 Jul 87	SAVE THE LAST DANCE FOR ME *Manhattan MT 25*	69	2

See also DRIFTERS

Carole KING *US, female vocalist – Carole Klein (29 WEEKS)* pos/wks
20 Sep 62	● IT MIGHT AS WELL RAIN UNTIL SEPTEMBER		
	London HLU 9591	3	13
7 Aug 71	● IT'S TOO LATE *A&M AMS 849* ▲	6	12
28 Oct 72	IT MIGHT AS WELL RAIN UNTIL SEPTEMBER (re-issue)		
	London HL 10391	43	4

Dave KING *UK, male vocalist, d. 17 Apr 2002 (29 WEEKS)* pos/wks
17 Feb 56	● MEMORIES ARE MADE OF THIS *Decca F 10684* [1]	5	15
13 Apr 56	YOU CAN'T BE TRUE TO TWO *Decca F 10720* [1]	11	9
21 Dec 56	CHRISTMAS AND YOU *Decca F 10791*	23	2
24 Jan 58	THE STORY OF MY LIFE *Decca F 10973*	20	3

[1] Dave King featuring The Keynotes

Denis KING – *See STUTZ BEARCATS and the Denis KING ORCHESTRA; KING BROTHERS*

Diana KING *Jamaica, female vocalist (22 WEEKS)* pos/wks
8 Jul 95	● SHY GUY *Columbia 6621682*	2	13
28 Oct 95	AIN'T NOBODY *Columbia 6625495*	13	5
1 Nov 97	I SAY A LITTLE PRAYER *Columbia 6651472*	17	4

Evelyn 'Champagne' KING (476 Top 500)
Bubbly soul / disco vocalist b. 29 Jun 1960, New York , US. Ground-breaking debut hit 'Shame' was the biggest selling transatlantic 12-inch single at the time. It earned her a US gold record and a silver disc in the UK despite failing to reach the Top 30 (76 WEEKS) pos/wks
13 May 78	SHAME *RCA PC 1122*	39	23
3 Feb 79	I DON'T KNOW IF IT'S RIGHT *RCA PB 1386*	67	2
27 Jun 81	I'M IN LOVE *RCA 95* [1]	27	11
26 Sep 81	IF YOU WANT MY LOVIN' *RCA 131* [1]	43	6
28 Aug 82	● LOVE COME DOWN *RCA 249* [1]	7	13
20 Nov 82	BACK TO LOVE *RCA 287* [1]	40	4
19 Feb 83	GET LOOSE *RCA 315* [1]	45	5
9 Nov 85	YOUR PERSONAL TOUCH *RCA PB 49915*	37	5
29 Mar 86	HIGH HORSE *RCA PB 49891*	55	3
23 Jul 88	HOLD ON TO WHAT YOU'VE GOT *Manhattan MT 49*	47	3
10 Oct 92	SHAME (re-mix) *Network NWKTEN 56* [2]	74	1

[1] Evelyn King [2] Altern 8 vs Evelyn King

Jonathan KING (212 Top 500) *King of the pseudonyms, b. 6 Dec 1944, London, UK. A multi-faceted pop maestro who masterminded numerous hits and helped to guide the early careers of Genesis, Bay City Rollers and 10cc. Was Jailed in 2001 (128 WEEKS)* pos/wks
| 29 Jul 65 | ● EVERYONE'S GONE TO THE MOON *Decca F 12187* | 4 | 11 |
| 10 Jan 70 | LET IT ALL HANG OUT *Decca F 12988* | 26 | 7 |

16 Jan 71	IT'S THE SAME OLD SONG *B & C CB 139* [1]	19	9
3 Apr 71	SUGAR SUGAR *RCA 2064* [2]	12	14
29 May 71	LAZY BONES *Decca F 13177*	23	8
20 Nov 71	HOOKED ON A FEELING *Decca F 13241*	23	10
5 Feb 72	FLIRT! *Decca F 13276*	22	9
14 Oct 72	● LOOP DI LOVE *UK 7* [3]	4	13
26 Jan 74	(I CAN'T GET NO) SATISFACTION *UK 53* [4]	29	5
6 Sep 75	● UNA PALOMA BLANCA (WHITE DOVE) *UK 105*	5	11
20 Sep 75	CHICK-A-BOOM (DON'T YA JES LOVE IT) *UK 2012 002* [5]	36	4
7 Feb 76	IN THE MOOD *UK 121* [6]	46	3
26 Jun 76	● IT ONLY TAKES A MINUTE *UK 135* [7]	9	9
7 Oct 78	ONE FOR YOU, ONE FOR ME *GTO GT 237*	29	6
16 Dec 78	LICK A SMURP FOR CHRISTMAS (ALL FALL DOWN)		
	Petrol GAS 1 / Magnet MAG 139 [8]	58	4
16 Jun 79	YOU'RE THE GREATEST LOVER *UK International INT 586*	67	2
3 Nov 79	GLORIA *Ariola ARO 198*	65	3

[1] Weathermen [2] Sakkarin [3] Shag [4] Bubblerock [5] 53rd and 3rd featuring the Sound of Shag [6] Sound 9418 [7] One Hundred Ton and a Feather [8] Father Abraphart and the Smurps

Nosmo KING – *See JAVELLS featuring Nosmo KING*

Paul KING *UK, male vocalist (3 WEEKS)* pos/wks
| 2 May 87 | I KNOW *CBS PKING 1* | 59 | 3 |

See also KING

Solomon KING *US, male vocalist (28 WEEKS)* pos/wks
| 3 Jan 68 | ● SHE WEARS MY RING *Columbia DB 8325* | 3 | 18 |
| 1 May 68 | WHEN WE WERE YOUNG *Columbia DB 8402* | 21 | 10 |

Tony KING – *See VISIONMASTERS; Kylie MINOGUE*

KING ADORA *UK, male vocal / instrumental group (5 WEEKS)* pos/wks
4 Nov 00	SMOULDER *Superior Quality / A&M RQSD 010CD*	62	1
3 Mar 01	SUFFOCATE *Superior Quality / A&M RQS 11DD*	39	2
26 May 01	BIONIC *Superior Quality / A&M RQS 012CD*	30	2

KING BEE *UK, male rapper (6 WEEKS)* pos/wks
| 26 Jan 91 | MUST BEE THE MUSIC *Columbia 6565827* [1] | 44 | 4 |
| 23 Mar 91 | BACK BY DOPE DEMAND *First Bass 7RUFF 6X* | 61 | 2 |

[1] King Bee featuring Michele

KING BROTHERS (495 Top 500) *Britain's top male group before The Beatles; brothers Denis (v/p), Michael (v/g) and Tony (v/b) King from Essex, UK. Poll-winning MOR trio made first of many TV appearances in 1953 (when Denis was 14). Denis became one of the UK's top TV theme writers (74 WKS)* pos/wks
31 May 57	● A WHITE SPORT COAT (AND A PINK CARNATION)		
	Parlophone R 4310	6	14
9 Aug 57	IN THE MIDDLE OF AN ISLAND *Parlophone R 4338*	19	13
6 Dec 57	WAKE UP LITTLE SUSIE *Parlophone R 4367*	22	3
31 Jan 58	PUT A LIGHT IN THE WINDOW (2re) *Parlophone R 4389*	25	4
14 Apr 60	● STANDING ON THE CORNER *Parlophone R 4639*	4	11
28 Jul 60	MAIS OUI *Parlophone R 4672*	16	10
12 Jan 61	DOLL HOUSE *Parlophone R 4715*	21	8
2 Mar 61	76 TROMBONES *Parlophone R 4737*	19	11

KING KURT *UK, male vocal / instrumental group (16 WEEKS)* pos/wks
15 Oct 83	DESTINATION ZULULAND *Stiff BUY 189*	36	6
28 Apr 84	MACK THE KNIFE *Stiff BUY 199*	55	4
4 Aug 84	BANANA BANANA *Stiff BUY 206*	54	4
15 Nov 86	AMERICA *Polydor KURT 1*	73	1
2 May 87	THE LAND OF RING DANG DO *Polydor KURT 2*	67	1

KING SUN-D'MOET *US, male rap / DJ duo (3 WEEKS)* pos/wks
| 11 Jul 87 | HEY LOVE *Flame MELT 5* | 66 | 3 |

KING TRIGGER *UK, male / female vocal / instrumental group (4 WKS)* pos/wks
| 14 Aug 82 | THE RIVER *Chrysalis CHS 2623* | 57 | 4 |

Re-entries are listed as (re), (2re), (3re), etc which signifies that the hit re-entered the chart once, twice or three times

KINGDOM COME US, male vocal / instrumental group (2 WEEKS) pos/wks

16 Apr 88	GET IT ON Polydor KCS 1	75	1
6 May 89	DO YOU LIKE IT Polydor KCS 3	73	1

KINGMAKER UK, male vocal / instrumental group (22 WEEKS) pos/wks

18 Jan 92	IDIOTS AT THE WHEEL (EP) Scorch SCORCH 3	30	3
23 May 92	EAT YOURSELF WHOLE Scorch SCORCHG 5	15	3
31 Oct 92	ARMCHAIR ANARCHIST Scorch SCORCHG 6	47	2
8 May 93	10 YEARS ASLEEP Scorch CDSCORCHS 8	15	4
19 Jun 93	QUEEN JANE Scorch CDSCORS 9	29	4
30 Oct 93	SATURDAY'S NOT WHAT IT USED TO BE Scorch CDSCORCH 10	63	1
15 Apr 95	YOU AND I WILL NEVER SEE THINGS EYE TO EYE Scorch CDSCORCHS 11	33	3
3 Jun 95	IN THE BEST POSSIBLE TASTE (PART 2) Scorch CDSCORCHS 12	41	2

Tracks on Idiots at the Wheel (EP): Really Scrape the Sky / Revelation / Every Teenage Suicide / Strip Away

KINGS OF CONVENIENCE
Norway, male vocal / instrumental duo (2 WEEKS) pos/wks

21 Apr 01	TOXIC GIRL Source SOURCDSE 1025	44	1
14 Jul 01	FAILURE Source SOURCD 036	63	1

KINGS OF SWING ORCHESTRA Australia, orchestra (5 WEEKS) pos/wks

1 May 82	SWITCHED ON SWING Philips Swing 1	48	5

KINGS OF TOMORROW US, male production / instrumental duo – Sandy Rivera and Jason Sealee (6 WEEKS) pos/wks

14 Apr 01	FINALLY Distance DI 2029 [1]	54	1
29 Sep 01	FINALLY (re-mix) Defected DFECT 37CDS [1]	24	3
13 Apr 02	YOUNG HEARTS Defected DFECT 46CDS	45	2

[1] Kings of Tomorrow featuring Julie McKnight

KINGSMEN US, male vocal / instrumental group (7 WEEKS) pos/wks

30 Jan 64	LOUIE LOUIE Pye International 7N 25231	26	7

KINGSTON TRIO US, male vocal / instrumental group (15 WEEKS) pos/wks

21 Nov 58	● TOM DOOLEY Capitol CL 14951 ▲	5	14
4 Dec 59	SAN MIGUEL Capitol CL 15073	29	1

KINKS 74 Top 500

Well-respected and innovative London band, who had few equals in the 1960s: Ray Davies (v/g), Dave Davies (g), Pete Quaife (b), Mick Avory (d). Ray Davies, regarded as one of rock's premier songwriters, remains active almost 40 years after the group's first hit (215 WEEKS) pos/wks

13 Aug 64	★ YOU REALLY GOT ME Pye 7N 15673	1	12
29 Oct 64	● ALL DAY AND ALL OF THE NIGHT Pye 7N 15714	2	14
21 Jan 65	● TIRED OF WAITING FOR YOU Pye 7N 15759	1	10
25 Mar 65	EVERYBODY'S GONNA BE HAPPY Pye 7N 15813	17	8
27 May 65	● SET ME FREE Pye 7N 15854	9	11
5 Aug 65	● SEE MY FRIEND Pye 7N 15919	10	9
2 Dec 65	● TILL THE END OF THE DAY Pye 7N 15981	8	12
3 Mar 66	● DEDICATED FOLLOWER OF FASHION Pye 7N 17064	4	11
9 Jun 66	★ SUNNY AFTERNOON Pye 7N 17125	1	13
24 Nov 66	● DEAD END STREET Pye 7N 17222	5	11
11 May 67	● WATERLOO SUNSET Pye 7N 17321	2	11
18 Oct 67	● AUTUMN ALMANAC Pye 7N 17400	3	11
17 Apr 68	WONDERBOY Pye 7N 17468	36	5
17 Jul 68	DAYS Pye 7N 17573	12	10
16 Apr 69	PLASTIC MAN Pye 7N 17724	31	4
10 Jan 70	VICTORIA Pye 7N 17865	33	4
4 Jul 70	● LOLA Pye 7N 17961	2	14
12 Dec 70	● APEMAN Pye 7N 45016	5	14
27 May 72	SUPERSONIC ROCKET SHIP RCA 2211	16	8
27 Jun 81	BETTER THINGS Arista ARIST 415	46	5
6 Aug 83	COME DANCING Arista ARIST 502	12	9
15 Oct 83	DON'T FORGET TO DANCE Arista ARIST 524	58	3
15 Oct 83	YOU REALLY GOT ME (re-issue) PRT KD1	47	4
18 Jan 97	THE DAYS EP When! WENX 1016	35	2

Tracks on The Days EP: Days / You Really Got Me / Dead End Street / Lola

KINKY UK, female rapper (1 WEEK) pos/wks

24 Aug 96	EVERYBODY Feverpitch CDFVR 1009	71	1

See also ERASURE

KINKY MACHINE UK, male vocal / instrumental group (4 WEEKS) pos/wks

6 Mar 93	SUPERNATURAL GIVER Lemon LEMON 006CD	70	1
29 May 93	SHOCKAHOLIC Oxygen GASPD 5	70	1
14 Aug 93	GOING OUT WITH GOD Oxygen GASPD 9	74	1
2 Jul 94	10 SECOND BIONIC MAN Oxygen GASPD 14	66	1

Fern KINNEY US, female vocalist – Fern Kinney-Lewis (11 WEEKS) pos/wks

16 Feb 80	★ TOGETHER WE ARE BEAUTIFUL WEA K 79111	1	11

KINSHASA BAND – See Johnny WAKELIN

KIOKI Japan, male vocalist (1 WEEK) pos/wks

17 Aug 02	DO & DON'T FOR LOVE V2 VVR 5020803	66	1

Kathy KIRBY UK, female vocalist (54 WEEKS) pos/wks

15 Aug 63	DANCE ON Decca F 11682	11	13
7 Nov 63	● SECRET LOVE Decca F 11759	4	18
20 Feb 64	LET ME GO LOVER! Decca F 11832	10	11
7 May 64	YOU'RE THE ONE Decca F 11892	17	9
4 Mar 65	I BELONG Decca F 12087	36	3

Bo KIRKLAND and Ruth DAVIS
US, male / female vocal duo (9 WEEKS) pos/wks

4 Jun 77	YOU'RE GONNA GET NEXT TO ME EMI International INT 532	12	9

KISS US / Israel, male vocal / instrumental group (57 WEEKS) pos/wks

30 Jun 79	I WAS MADE FOR LOVIN' YOU Casablanca CAN 152	50	7
20 Feb 82	A WORLD WITHOUT HEROES Casablanca KISS 002	55	3
30 Apr 83	CREATURES OF THE NIGHT Casablanca KISS 4	34	4
29 Oct 83	LICK IT UP Vertigo KISS 5	31	5
8 Sep 84	HEAVEN'S ON FIRE Vertigo VER 12	43	3
9 Nov 85	TEARS ARE FALLING Vertigo KISS 6	57	2
3 Oct 87	● CRAZY CRAZY NIGHTS Vertigo KISS 7	4	9
5 Dec 87	REASON TO LIVE Vertigo KISS 8	33	7
10 Sep 88	TURN ON THE NIGHT Vertigo KISS 9	41	3
18 Nov 89	HIDE YOUR HEART Vertigo KISS 10	59	2
31 Mar 90	FOREVER Vertigo KISS 11	65	2
11 Jan 92	● GOD GAVE ROCK AND ROLL TO YOU II Interscope A 8696	4	8
9 May 92	UNHOLY Mercury KISS 12	26	2

KISS AMC UK, female rap duo (5 WEEKS) pos/wks

1 Jul 89	A BIT OF …(re) Syncopate SY 29	58	4
3 Feb 90	MY DOCS Syncopate XAMC 1	66	1

Before its re-entry in Aug 89 'A Bit of U2' was unable to be given its full title due to copyright problems

KISSING THE PINK
UK, male / female vocal / instrumental group (14 WEEKS) pos/wks

5 Mar 83	LAST FILM Magnet KTP 3	19	14

Mac and Katie KISSOON
Trinidad / UK, male / female vocal duo (33 WEEKS) pos/wks

19 Jun 71	CHIRPY CHIRPY CHEEP CHEEP Young Blood YB 1026	41	1
18 Jan 75	● SUGAR CANDY KISSES Polydor 2058 531	3	10
3 May 75	● DON'T DO IT BABY State STAT 4	9	8
30 Aug 75	LIKE A BUTTERFLY State STAT 9	18	9
15 May 76	THE TWO OF US State STAT 21	46	5

Kevin KITCHEN UK, male vocalist (3 WEEKS)

		pos/wks
20 Apr 85	PUT MY ARMS AROUND YOU *China WOK 1*	64 3

Joy KITIKONTI Italy, male producer – Massimo Chiticonti (2 WEEKS)

		pos/wks
17 Nov 01	JOYENERGIZER *BXR BXRC 0347*	57 2

Eartha KITT US, female vocalist (34 WEEKS)

		pos/wks
1 Apr 55 ●	UNDER THE BRIDGES OF PARIS (re) *HMV B 10647*	7 10
3 Dec 83	WHERE IS MY MAN *Record Shack SOHO 11*	36 11
7 Jul 84	I LOVE MEN *Record Shack SOHO 21*	50 3
12 Apr 86	THIS IS MY LIFE *Record Shack SOHO 61*	73 1
1 Jul 89	CHA CHA HEELS *Arista 112331* [1]	32 7
5 Mar 94	IF I LOVE YA THEN I NEED YA IF I NEED YA THEN I WANT YOU AROUND *RCA 74321190342*	43 2

[1] Eartha Kitt and Bronski Beat

KITTIE Canada, female vocal / instrumental group (2 WEEKS)

		pos/wks
25 Mar 00	BRACKISH *Epic 6691292*	46 1
22 Jul 00	CHARLOTTE *Epic 6696222*	60 1

KLAXONS Belgium, male vocal / instrumental group (6 WEEKS)

		pos/wks
10 Dec 83	THE CLAP CLAP SOUND *PRT 7P 290*	45 6

KLEA UK, male / female production / vocal / rap trio (1 WEEK)

		pos/wks
7 Sep 02	TIC TOC *Incentive CENT 41CDS*	61 1

KLEEER US, male / female vocal / instrumental group (10 WEEKS)

		pos/wks
17 Mar 79	KEEEP YOUR BODY WORKIN' *Atlantic LV 21*	51 6
14 Mar 81	GET TOUGH *Atlantic 11560*	49 4

D.D. KLEIN – See ALIVE featuring D.D. KLEIN

KLESHAY UK, female vocal trio (5 WEEKS)

		pos/wks
19 Sep 98	REASONS *Epic KLE 1CD*	33 2
20 Feb 99	RUSH *Epic KLE 2CD*	19 3

KLUBBHEADS
Holland, male instrumental / production group (10 WEEKS)

		pos/wks
11 May 96 ●	KLUBBHOPPING *AM:PM 5815572*	10 6
16 Aug 97	DISCOHOPPING *AM:PM 5823032*	35 2
15 Aug 98	KICKIN' HARD *Wonderboy WBOYD 011*	36 2

See also ITTY BITTY BOOZY WOOZY

KLUSTER featuring Ron CARROLL
France, male DJ / production duo (1 WEEK)

		pos/wks
28 Apr 01	MY LOVE *Scorpio Music 1928112*	73 1

KNACK US, male vocal / instrumental group (12 WEEKS)

		pos/wks
30 Jun 79 ●	MY SHARONA *Capitol CL 16087* ▲	6 10
13 Oct 79	GOOD GIRLS DON'T *Capitol CL 16097*	66 2

KNACK – See MOUNT RUSHMORE presents THE KNACK

Beverley KNIGHT
UK, female vocalist – Beverley Smith (39 WEEKS)

		pos/wks
8 Apr 95	FLAVOUR OF THE OLD SCHOOL *Dome CDDOME 101*	50 2
2 Sep 95	DOWN FOR THE ONE *Dome CDDOME 102*	55 1
21 Oct 95	FLAVOUR OF THE OLD SCHOOL (re-mix) *Dome CDDOME 105*	33 2
23 Mar 96	MOVING ON UP (ON THE RIGHT SIDE) *Dome CDDOME 107*	42 1
30 May 98	MADE IT BACK *Parlophone Rhythm CDRHYTHM 11* [1]	21 3
22 Aug 98	REWIND (FIND A WAY) *Parlophone Rhythm CDRHYTHS 13*	40 2
10 Apr 99	MADE IT BACK 99 (re-mix) *Parlophone Rhythm CDRHYTM 18*	19 5
17 Jul 99	GREATEST DAY *Parlophone Rhythm CDRHYTHS 22*	14 5
4 Dec 99	SISTA SISTA *Parlophone Rhythm CDRHYTHM 26*	31 2

		pos/wks
17 Nov 01	GET UP *Parlophone CDRS 6564*	17 4
9 Mar 02 ●	SHOULDA WOULDA COULDA *Parlophone CDRS 6570*	10 8
6 Jul 02	GOLD *Parlophone CDRS 6580*	27 4

[1] Beverley Knight featuring Redman

Frederick KNIGHT US, male vocalist (10 WEEKS)

		pos/wks
10 Jun 72	I'VE BEEN LONELY SO LONG *Stax 2025 098*	22 10

Gladys KNIGHT and the PIPS 104 Top 500

One of soul music's foremost female singers for almost 40 years; b. 28 May 1944, Georgia, US. The celebrated vocalist (who first appeared on US TV aged eight) and her family quartet The Pips (they split in 1989) were inducted into the Rock and Roll Hall of Fame in 1996 (187 WEEKS)

		pos/wks
8 Jun 67	TAKE ME IN YOUR ARMS AND LOVE ME *Tamla Motown TMG 604*	13 15
27 Dec 67	I HEARD IT THROUGH THE GRAPEVINE *Tamla Motown TMG 629*	47 1
17 Jun 72	JUST WALK IN MY SHOES *Tamla Motown TMG 813*	35 8
25 Nov 72	HELP ME MAKE IT THROUGH THE NIGHT *Tamla Motown TMG 830*	11 17
3 Mar 73	THE LOOK OF LOVE *Tamla Motown TMG 844*	21 9
26 May 73	NEITHER ONE OF US (WANTS TO BE THE FIRST TO SAY GOODBYE) *Tamla Motown TMG 855*	31 7
5 Apr 75 ●	THE WAY WE WERE – TRY TO REMEMBER *Buddah BDS 428*	4 15
2 Aug 75 ●	BEST THING THAT EVER HAPPENED TO ME *Buddah BDS 432*	7 10
15 Nov 75	PART TIME LOVE *Buddah BDS 438*	30 5
8 May 76 ●	MIDNIGHT TRAIN TO GEORGIA *Buddah BDS 444* ▲	10 9
21 Aug 76	MAKE YOURS A HAPPY HOME *Buddah BDS 447*	35 4
6 Nov 76	SO SAD THE SONG *Buddah BDS 448*	20 9
15 Jan 77	NOBODY BUT YOU *Buddah BDS 451*	34 2
28 May 77 ●	BABY DON'T CHANGE YOUR MIND *Buddah BDS 458*	4 12
24 Sep 77	HOME IS WHERE THE HEART IS *Buddah BDS 460*	35 4
8 Apr 78	THE ONE AND ONLY (re) *Buddah BDS 470*	32 5
24 Jun 78	COME BACK AND FINISH WHAT YOU STARTED *Buddah BDS 473*	15 13
30 Sep 78	IT'S A BETTER THAN GOOD TIME *Buddah BDS 478*	59 4
30 Aug 80	TASTE OF BITTER LOVE *CBS 8890*	35 6
8 Nov 80	BOURGIE, BOURGIE *CBS 9081*	32 6
26 Dec 81	WHEN A CHILD IS BORN *CBS S 1758* [1]	74 2
9 Nov 85	THAT'S WHAT FRIENDS ARE FOR *Arista ARIST 638* [2] ▲	16 9
16 Jan 88	LOVE OVERBOARD *MCA MCA 1223*	42 4
10 Jun 89 ●	LICENCE TO KILL *MCA MCA 1339* [3]	6 11

[1] Johnny Mathis and Gladys Knight [2] Dionne Warwick and Friends featuring Elton John, Stevie Wonder and Gladys Knight [3] Gladys Knight

Jordan KNIGHT US, male vocalist (9 WEEKS)

		pos/wks
16 Oct 99 ●	GIVE IT TO YOU (re) *Interscope 4971672*	5 9

See also NEW KIDS ON THE BLOCK

Robert KNIGHT US, male vocalist (26 WEEKS)

		pos/wks
17 Jan 68	EVERLASTING LOVE *Monument MON 1008*	40 2
24 Nov 73 ●	LOVE ON A MOUNTAIN TOP *Monument MNT 1875*	10 16
9 Mar 74	EVERLASTING LOVE (re-issue) *Monument MNT 2106*	19 8

KNOC-TURN'AL – See DR DRE

Mark KNOPFLER
UK, male vocalist / instrumentalist – guitar (7 WEEKS)

		pos/wks
12 Mar 83	GOING HOME (THEME OF 'LOCAL HERO') *Vertigo DSTR 4*	56 3
16 Mar 96	DARLING PRETTY *Vertigo VERCD 88*	33 2
25 May 96	CANNIBALS *Vertigo VERCD 89*	42 2

See also DIRE STRAITS

KNOWLEDGE Italy, male production duo (1 WEEK)

		pos/wks
8 Nov 97	AS (UNTIL THE DAY) *ffrr FCD 312*	70 1

Buddy KNOX US, male vocalist, d. 14 Feb 1999 (5 WEEKS)

		pos/wks
10 May 57	PARTY DOLL Columbia DB 3914 ▲	29 3
16 Aug 62	SHE'S GONE Liberty LIB 55473	45 2

Frankie KNUCKLES US, male producer (19 WEEKS)

		pos/wks
17 Jun 89	TEARS ffrr F 108 [1]	50 3
21 Oct 89	YOUR LOVE Trax TRAXT 3	59 4
27 Jul 91	THE WHISTLE SONG Virgin America VUS 47	17 5
23 Nov 91	IT'S HARD SOMETIMES Virgin America VUS 52	67 1
6 Jun 92	RAIN FALLS Virgin America VUST 60 [2]	48 2
27 May 95	TOO MANY FISH Virgin America VUSCD 89 [3]	34 2
18 Nov 95	WHADDA U WANT (FROM ME) Virgin America VUSCD 98 [3]	36 2

[1] Frankie Knuckles presents Satoshi Tomiie [2] Frankie Knuckles featuring Lisa Michaelis [3] Frankie Knuckles featuring Adeva

Moe KOFFMAN QUARTETTE Canada, male instrumental group, Moe Koffman – flute, d. 28 Mar 2001 (2 WEEKS)

		pos/wks
28 Mar 58	SWINGIN' SHEPHERD BLUES London HLJ 8549	23 2

Mike KOGLIN Germany, male producer (4 WEEKS)

		pos/wks
28 Nov 98	THE SILENCE Multiply CDMULTY 44	20 2
29 May 99	ON MY WAY Multiply CDMULTY 51 [1]	28 2

[1] Mike Koglin featuring Beatrice

KOKOMO US, male instrumentalist – piano (7 WEEKS)

		pos/wks
13 Apr 61	ASIA MINOR London HLU 9305	35 7

KOKOMO UK, male / female vocal / instrumental group (3 WEEKS)

		pos/wks
29 May 82	A LITTLE BIT FURTHER AWAY CBS A 2064	45 3

KON KAN Canada, male vocal / instrumental duo – Barry Harris and Kevin Wynne (13 WEEKS)

		pos/wks
4 Mar 89 ●	I BEG YOUR PARDON Atlantic A 8969	5 13

John KONGOS
South Africa, male vocalist / multi-instrumentalist (25 WEEKS)

		pos/wks
22 May 71 ●	HE'S GONNA STEP ON YOU AGAIN Fly BUG 8	4 14
20 Nov 71 ●	TOKOLOSHE MAN Fly BUG 14	4 11

KONKRETE UK, female production duo (1 WEEK)

		pos/wks
22 Sep 01	LAW UNTO MYSELF Perfecto PERF 23CDS	60 1

KOOL and the GANG (84 Top 500)
One of the most consistently successful R&B acts, hailing from New Jersey and including Robert 'Kool' Bell (b) and James 'JT' Taylor (v). The band spent 10 years as top US R&B stars before starting their impressive run of international hits (207 WEEKS)

		pos/wks
27 Oct 79 ●	LADIES NIGHT Mercury KOOL 7	9 12
19 Jan 80	TOO HOT Mercury KOOL 8	23 8
12 Jul 80	HANGIN' OUT De-Lite KOOL 9	52 4
1 Nov 80 ●	CELEBRATION De-Lite KOOL 10 ▲	7 13
21 Feb 81	JONES VS JONES / SUMMER MADNESS De-Lite KOOL 11	17 11
30 May 81	TAKE IT TO THE TOP De-Lite DE 2	15 9
31 Oct 81	STEPPIN' OUT De-Lite DE 4	12 13
19 Dec 81 ●	GET DOWN ON IT De-Lite DE 5	3 12
6 Mar 82	TAKE MY HEART (YOU CAN HAVE IT IF YOU WANT IT) De-Lite DE 6	29 7
7 Aug 82	BIG FUN De-Lite DE 7	14 8
16 Oct 82 ●	OOH LA LA LA (LET'S GO DANCIN') De-Lite DE 9	6 9
4 Dec 82	HI DE HI, HI DE HO De-Lite DE 14	29 8
10 Dec 83	STRAIGHT AHEAD De-Lite DE 15	15 10
11 Feb 84 ●	JOANNA / TONIGHT De-Lite DE 16	2 11
14 Apr 84	(WHEN YOU SAY YOU LOVE SOMEBODY) IN THE HEART De-Lite DE 17	7 8
24 Nov 84	FRESH De-Lite DE 18	11 12
9 Feb 85	MISLED De-Lite DE 19	28 5
11 May 85 ●	CHERISH De-Lite DE 20	4 22

		pos/wks
2 Nov 85	EMERGENCY De-Lite DE 21	50 3
22 Nov 86	VICTORY (re) Club JAB 44	30 12
21 Mar 87	STONE LOVE Club JAB 47	45 4
31 Dec 88	CELEBRATION (re-mix) Club JAB 78	56 5
6 Jul 91	GET DOWN ON IT (re-mix) Mercury MER 346	69 1

'Jones vs Jones' and 'Summer Madness' were labelled as A and B sides with 'Funky Stuff' and 'Hollywood Swinging' as the C and D sides of a two-disc release

KOOL ROCK STEADY – See TYREE

KOON + STEPHENSON – See WESTBAM

KORGIS UK, male vocal / instrumental duo (27 WEEKS)

		pos/wks
23 Jun 79	IF I HAD YOU Rialto TREB 103	13 12
24 May 80 ●	EVERYBODY'S GOT TO LEARN SOMETIME Rialto TREB 115	5 12
30 Aug 80	IF IT'S ALRIGHT WITH YOU BABY Rialto TREB 118	56 3

KORN US, male vocal / instrumental group (21 WEEKS)

		pos/wks
19 Oct 96	NO PLACE TO HIDE Epic 6638452	26 2
15 Feb 97	A.D.I.D.A.S. Epic 6642042	22 2
7 Jun 97	GOOD GOD Epic 6646585	25 2
22 Aug 98	GOT THE LIFE Epic 6663912	23 2
8 May 99	FREAK ON A LEASH Epic 6672522	24 2
12 Feb 00	FALLING AWAY FROM ME Epic 6688692	24 2
3 Jun 00	MAKE ME BAD Epic 6694332	25 2
1 Jun 02	HERE TO STAY Epic 6727425	12 5
21 Sep 02	THOUGHTLESS Epic 6731572	37 2

KOSHEEN UK, male / female production / vocal trio (23 WEEKS)

		pos/wks
17 Jun 00	EMPTY SKIES / HIDE U Moksha Recordings MOKSHA 05CD	73 1
14 Apr 01	(SLIP & SLIDE) SUICIDE Moksha Recordings MOKSHA 07CD	50 2
1 Sep 01 ●	HIDE U (re-mix) (re) Arista 74321879412	6 7
22 Dec 01	CATCH Moksha / Arista 74321913722	15 8
4 May 02	HUNGRY Moksha / Arista 74321934382	13 4
31 Aug 02	HARDER Moksha / Arista 74321954452	53 1

KOWDEAN – See OXIDE & NEUTRINO

KRAFTWERK Germany, vocal / instrumental group (72 WEEKS)

		pos/wks
10 May 75	AUTOBAHN Vertigo 6147 012	11 9
28 Oct 78	NEON LIGHTS Capitol CL 15998	53 3
9 May 81	POCKET CALCULATOR EMI 5175	39 6
11 Jul 81 ★	COMPUTER LOVE / THE MODEL (re) EMI 5207	1 21
20 Feb 82	SHOWROOM DUMMIES EMI 5272	25 5
6 Aug 83	TOUR DE FRANCE (re) EMI 5413	22 19
1 Jun 91	THE ROBOTS EMI EM 192	20 4
2 Nov 91	RADIOACTIVITY (re-mix) EMI EM 201	43 2
23 Oct 99	TOUR DE FRANCE (re-issue) EMI 8874210	61 1
18 Mar 00	EXPO 2000 EMI CDEM 562	27 2

'Computer Love / The Model' did not make No.1 until re-entry in Dec 1981

'Tour de France' also peaked at No.24 after re-entering in Aug 1984

Billy J KRAMER and the DAKOTAS
UK, male vocal / instrumental group (71 WEEKS)

		pos/wks
2 May 63 ●	DO YOU WANT TO KNOW A SECRET? Parlophone R 5023	2 15
1 Aug 63 ★	BAD TO ME Parlophone R 5049	1 14
7 Nov 63 ●	I'LL KEEP YOU SATISFIED Parlophone R 5073	4 13
27 Feb 64 ★	LITTLE CHILDREN Parlophone R 5105	1 13
23 Jul 64 ●	FROM A WINDOW Parlophone R 5156	10 8
20 May 65	TRAINS AND BOATS AND PLANES Parlophone R 5285	12 8

KRANKIES UK, male / female vocal duo (6 WEEKS)

		pos/wks
7 Feb 81	FAN'DABI'DOZI (re) Monarch MON 21	46 6

Lenny KRAVITZ US, male vocalist (69 WEEKS)

		pos/wks
2 Jun 90	MR CABDRIVER Virgin America VUS 20	58 2
4 Aug 90	LET LOVE RULE Virgin America VUS 26	39 4
30 Mar 91	ALWAYS ON THE RUN Virgin America VUS 34	41 3

TOP 100 BEST-SELLING SINGLES

■ No discussion. This is the chart which, surely, no one can argue with: the top 100 singles since 1952 according to the number of copies sold. Debate will rage, though, as to why surprise offerings from Teletubbies and Ken Dodd are included but nothing from Abba nor The Rolling Stones

1. 4,864,611 CANDLE IN THE WIND 1997 / SOMETHING ABOUT THE WAY YOU LOOK TONIGHT Elton John
2. 3,550,000 DO THEY KNOW IT'S CHRISTMAS? Band Aid
3. 2,130,000 BOHEMIAN RHAPSODY Queen
4. 2,050,000 MULL OF KINTYRE / GIRLS' SCHOOL Wings
5. 1,985,000 RIVERS OF BABYLON / BROWN GIRL IN THE RING Boney M
6. 1,975,000 YOU'RE THE ONE THAT I WANT John Travolta and Olivia Newton-John
7. 1,910,000 RELAX Frankie Goes To Hollywood
8. 1,890,000 SHE LOVES YOU Beatles
9. 1,843,700 UNCHAINED MELODY / (THERE'LL BE BLUEBIRDS OVER) THE WHITE CLIFFS OF DOVER Robson Green and Jerome Flynn
10. 1,790,000 MARY'S BOY CHILD – OH MY LORD Boney M
11. 1,783,827 LOVE IS ALL AROUND Wet Wet Wet
12. 1,779,900 ANYTHING IS POSSIBLE / EVERGREEN Will Young
13. 1,775,000 I JUST CALLED TO SAY I LOVE YOU Stevie Wonder
14. 1,750,000 I WANT TO HOLD YOUR HAND Beatles
15. 1,722,400 BARBIE GIRL Aqua
16. 1,672,108 BELIEVE Cher
17. 1,548,500 PERFECT DAY Various artists
18. 1,527,800 (EVERYTHING I DO) I DO IT FOR YOU Bryan Adams
19. 1,521,000 TEARS Ken Dodd
20. 1,520,000 CAN'T BUY ME LOVE Beatles
21. 1,515,000 SUMMER NIGHTS John Travolta and Olivia Newton-John
22. 1,510,000 TWO TRIBES Frankie Goes To Hollywood
23. 1,486,600 IMAGINE John Lennon
24. 1,450,154 ...BABY ONE MORE TIME Britney Spears
25. 1,430,000 DON'T YOU WANT ME Human League
26. 1,420,000 LAST CHRISTMAS / EVERYTHING SHE WANTS Wham!

27. 1,410,000 I FEEL FINE Beatles
28. 1,409,688 I'LL BE MISSING YOU Puff Daddy and Faith Evans featuring 112
29. 1,405,000 KARMA CHAMELEON Culture Club
30. 1,400,000 THE CARNIVAL IS OVER Seekers
31. 1,392,000 ROCK AROUND THE CLOCK Bill Haley and His Comets
32. 1,385,000 WE CAN WORK IT OUT / DAY TRIPPER Beatles
33. 1,380,000 Y.M.C.A. Village People
34. 1,365,995 CARELESS WHISPER George Michael
35. 1,365,000 RELEASE ME Engelbert Humperdinck
36. 1,355,055 I WILL ALWAYS LOVE YOU Whitney Houston
37. 1,321,500 THE POWER OF LOVE Jennifer Rush
38. 1,318,700 UNCHAINED MELODY Gareth Gates
39. 1,312,551 MY HEART WILL GO ON Celine Dion
40. 1,269,841 WANNABE Spice Girls
41. 1,268,200 KILLING ME SOFTLY Fugees
42. 1,254,604 NEVER EVER All Saints
43. 1,246,300 GANGSTA'S PARADISE Coolio featuring LV
44. 1,240,000 DIANA Paul Anka
45. 1,235,000 THINK TWICE Celine Dion
46. 1,210,000 IT'S NOW OR NEVER Elvis Presley
47. 1,205,000 GREEN, GREEN GRASS OF HOME Tom Jones
48. 1,201,000 COME ON EILEEN Dexy's Midnight Runners
49. 1,180,700 IT WASN'T ME Shaggy featuring Ricardo 'Rikrok' Ducent
50. 1,180,000 HEART OF GLASS Blondie
51. 1,175,000 MARY'S BOY CHILD Harry Belafonte
52. 1,160,000 THE LAST WALTZ Engelbert Humperdinck
53. 1,155,000 BRIGHT EYES Art Garfunkel
54. 1,150,285 HEARTBEAT / TRAGEDY Steps
55. 1,145,000 DON'T GIVE UP ON US David Soul
56. 1,140,000 I LOVE YOU LOVE ME LOVE Gary Glitter
57. 1,135,000 TAINTED LOVE Soft Cell
58. 1,130,000 STRANGER ON THE SHORE Mr Acker Bilk
59. 1,119,900 IT'S LIKE THAT Run-DMC vs Jason Nevins
60. 1,107,200 TELETUBBIES SAY EH-OH! Teletubbies
61. 1,098,900 SPACEMAN Babylon Zoo
62. 1,096,000 I REMEMBER YOU Frank Ifield
63. 1,094,000 I BELIEVE / UP ON THE ROOF Robson and Jerome

64. 1,092,300 SATURDAY NIGHT Whigfield
65. 1,078,400 PURE AND SIMPLE Hear'Say
66. 1,074,192 NO MATTER WHAT Boyzone
67. 1,072,100 2 BECOME 1 Spice Girls
68. 1,052,000 THE YOUNG ONES Cliff Richard and The Shadows
69. 1,038,821 EARTH SONG Michael Jackson
70. 1,037,235 CAN'T GET YOU OUT OF MY HEAD Kylie Minogue
71. 1,023,500 BLUE (DA BA DEE) Eiffel 65
72. 1,008,800 CAN WE FIX IT? Bob the Builder
73. 1,006,500 MERRY XMAS EVERYBODY Slade
74. 1,006,200 SAVE YOUR KISSES FOR ME Brotherhood of Man
75. 1,005,500 EYE LEVEL Simon Park Orchestra
76. 1,001,400 BLUE MONDAY New Order
77. 998,000 LONG HAIRED LOVER FROM LIVERPOOL Little Jimmy Osmond
78. 995,000 ANOTHER BRICK IN THE WALL (PART 2) Pink Floyd
79. 993,000 DON'T CRY FOR ME ARGENTINA Julie Covington
80. 990,000 EYE OF THE TIGER Survivor
81. 990,000 I'D LIKE TO TEACH THE WORLD TO SING New Seekers
82. 988,000 TIE A YELLOW RIBBON ROUND THE OLE OAK TREE Dawn featuring Tony Orlando
83. 985,000 STAND AND DELIVER Adam and The Ants
84. 985,000 UNDER THE MOON OF LOVE Showaddywaddy
85. 982,300 TORN Natalie Imbruglia
86. 982,000 ESPECIALLY FOR YOU Kylie Minogue and Jason Donovan
87. 979,100 HIT ME WITH YOUR RHYTHM STICK Ian and The Blockheads
88. 979,000 SUGAR SUGAR Archies
89. 978,000 THE LION SLEEPS TONIGHT Tight Fit
90. 976,000 THE NEXT TIME / BACHELOR BOY Cliff Richard and The Shadows
91. 975,000 FAME Irene Cara
92. 974,000 GHOSTBUSTERS Ray Parker Jr
93. 974,000 UPTOWN GIRL Billy Joel
94. 973,850 RIDE ON TIME Black Box
95. 967,000 TELSTAR Tornados
96. 966,940 WONDERWALL Oasis
97. 962,000 AMAZING GRACE Royal Scots Dragoon Guards
98. 959,582 BACK FOR GOOD Take That
99. 955,000 SAILING Rod Stewart
100. 947,000 MISSISSIPPI Pussycat

Further information on the stories behind the UK's best selling Singles can be found in the Chrysalis publication 'Top 100 Singles: The Definitive Chart of the UK's best-selling songs – ever'

276

15 Jun 91		IT AIN'T OVER TIL IT'S OVER *Virgin America VUS 43*	11	8
14 Sep 91		STAND BY MY WOMAN *Virgin America VUS 45*	55	3
20 Feb 93	●	ARE YOU GONNA GO MY WAY *Virgin America VUSDG 65*	4	11
22 May 93		BELIEVE *Virgin America VUSCD 72*	30	5
28 Aug 93		HEAVEN HELP *Virgin America VUSDG 73*	20	7
4 Dec 93		IS THERE ANY LOVE IN YOUR HEART *Virgin America VUSDG 76*	52	2
4 Dec 93		BUDDHA OF SUBURBIA *Arista 74321177052* [1]	35	3
9 Sep 95		ROCK AND ROLL IS DEAD *Virgin America VUSCD 93*	22	3
23 Dec 95		CIRCUS *Virgin America VUSCD 96*	54	2
2 Mar 96		CAN'T GET YOU OFF MY MIND *Virgin America VUSCD 100*	54	2
16 May 98		IF YOU CAN'T SAY NO *Virgin VUSCD 130*	48	2
10 Oct 98		I BELONG TO YOU *Virgin VUSCD 138*	75	1
20 Feb 99	★	FLY AWAY *Virgin VUSCD 141* ■	1	10
6 Apr 02		STILLNESS OF HEART *Virgin VUSCD 236*	44	1

[1] David Bowie featuring Lenny Kravitz

KRAZE *US, male / female vocal / instrumental group (6 WEEKS)* pos/wks

22 Oct 88		THE PARTY *MCA MCA 1288*	29	5
17 Jun 89		LET'S PLAY HOUSE *MCA MCA 1337*	71	1

KREUZ *UK, male vocal group (1 WEEK)* pos/wks

8 Jul 95		PARTY ALL NIGHT *Diesel DES 004C*	75	1

Chantal KREVIAZUK *Canada, female vocalist (1 WEEK)* pos/wks

6 Mar 99		LEAVING ON A JET PLANE *Epic 6666272*	59	1

KREW-KATS *UK, male instrumental group (10 WEEKS)* pos/wks

9 Mar 61		TRAMBONE (re) *HMV POP 840*	33	10

KRIS KROSS
US, male rap duo – Chris Kelly and Chris Smith (22 WEEKS) pos/wks

30 May 92	●	JUMP *Ruff House 6578547* ▲	2	8
25 Jul 92		WARM IT UP *Ruff House 6582187*	16	6
17 Oct 92		I MISSED THE BUS *Ruff House 6583927*	57	1
19 Dec 92		IT'S A SHAME *Ruff House 6588587*	31	5
11 Sep 93		ALRIGHT *Ruff House 6595652*	47	2

Marty KRISTIAN – See NEW SEEKERS

Chad KROEGER featuring Josey SCOTT
US, male vocal / instrumental duo (14 WEEKS) pos/wks

22 Jun 02	●	HERO *Roadrunner RR 20463*	4	14

KROKUS
Switzerland / Malta, male vocal / instrumental group (2 WEEKS) pos/wks

16 May 81		INDUSTRIAL STRENGTH (EP) *Ariola ARO 258*	62	2

Tracks on Industrial Strength (EP): Bedside Radio / Easy Rocker / Celebration / Bye Bye Baby

KRUSH *UK, male / female vocal / instrumental group (16 WEEKS)* pos/wks

5 Dec 87	●	HOUSE ARREST *Club JAB 63*	3	15
14 Nov 92		WALKING ON SUNSHINE *Network NWK 55*	71	1

KRUSH PERSPECTIVE *US, female vocal group (2 WEEKS)* pos/wks

16 Jan 93		LET'S GET TOGETHER (SO GROOVY NOW) *Perspective PERD 7416*	61	2

KRUST *UK, male producer / instrumentalist – Keith Thompson (2 WEEKS)* pos/wks

23 Oct 99		CODED LANGUAGE *Talkin Loud TLCD 51* [1]	66	1
26 Jan 02		SNAPPED IT *Full Cycle FCY 034*	58	1

[1] Krust featuring Saul Williams

KULA SHAKER *UK, male vocal / instrumental group (48 WEEKS)* pos/wks

4 May 96		GRATEFUL WHEN YOU'RE DEAD – JERRY WAS THERE *Columbia KULACD 2*	35	3
6 Jul 96	●	TATTVA *Columbia KULACD 3*	4	8
7 Sep 96	●	HEY DUDE *Columbia KULACD 4*	2	7
23 Nov 96	●	GOVINDA *Columbia KULACD 5*	7	8
8 Mar 97	●	HUSH (re) *Columbia KULACD 6*	2	9
2 May 98	●	SOUND OF DRUMS *Columbia KULA 21CD*	3	6
6 Mar 99		MYSTICAL MACHINE GUN *Columbia KULA 22CD*	14	3
15 May 99		SHOWER YOUR LOVE *Columbia KULA 23CD*	14	4

KULAY *Philippines, male / female vocal group (1 WEEK)* pos/wks

12 Sep 98		DELICIOUS *INCredible INCRL 4CD*	73	1

KUMARA *Holland, male production duo (1 WEEK)* pos/wks

7 Sep 00		SNAP YOUR FINGAZ *Y2K Y2K 018CD*	70	1

Charlie KUNZ
US, male instrumentalist – piano, d. 16 Mar 1958 (4 WEEKS) pos/wks

17 Dec 54		PIANO MEDLEY NO.114 (re) *Decca F 10419*	16	4

Medley titles: There Must be a Reason / Hold My Hand / If I Give My Heart to You / Little Things Mean a Lot / Make Her Mine / My Son My Son

KURSAAL FLYERS
UK, male vocal / instrumental group (10 WEEKS) pos/wks

20 Nov 76		LITTLE DOES SHE KNOW *CBS 4689*	14	10

KURUPT *US, male rapper (10 WEEKS)* pos/wks

25 Aug 01		WHERE I WANNA BE (re) *London LONCD461* [1]	14	7
13 Oct 01		IT'S OVER *Pias Recordings PIASB 024CD*	21	3

[1] Shade Sheist featuring Nate Dogg and Kurupt

KUT KLOSE *US, female vocal group (1 WEEK)* pos/wks

29 Apr 95		I LIKE *Elektra EKR 200CD*	72	1

Li KWAN *UK, male producer – Dave Lee (2 WEEKS)* pos/wks

17 Dec 94		I NEED A MAN *Deconstruction 74321252192*	51	2

See also Joey NEGRO; PHASE II; Z FACTOR; AKABU featuring Linda CLIFFORD; HED BOYS; IL PADRINOS; RAVEN MAIZE; JAKATTA

KY-MANI – See PM DAWN

Jonny L *UK, male vocalist / instrumentalist / producer (2 WEEKS)* pos/wks

28 Aug 93		OOH I LIKE IT *XL Recordings XLS 44CD*	73	1
31 Oct 98		20 DEGREES *XL Recordings XLS 103CD* [1]	66	1

[1] Jonny L featuring Silvah Bullet

LA GANZ *US, male vocal / instrumental group (1 WEEK)* pos/wks

9 Nov 96		LIKE A PLAYA *Jive JIVECD 405*	75	1

L.A. GUNS
US, male / female vocal / instrumental group (4 WEEKS) pos/wks

30 Nov 91		SOME LIE 4 LOVE *Mercury MER 358*	61	1
21 Dec 91		THE BALLAD OF JAYNE *Mercury MER 361*	53	3

LA MIX *UK, male / female vocal / instrumental duo (25 WEEKS)* pos/wks

10 Oct 87		DON'T STOP (JAMMIN') *Breakout USA 615*	47	4
21 May 88	●	CHECK THIS OUT *Breakout USA 629*	6	7

8 Jul 89	**GET LOOSE** *Breakout USA 659* [1]	....	.25	6
16 Sep 89	**LOVE TOGETHER** *Breakout USA 662* [2]	......	.66	2
15 Sep 90	**COMING BACK FOR MORE** *A&M AM 579*	....	.50	3
19 Jan 91	**MYSTERIES OF LOVE** *A&M AM 707*	....	.46	2
23 Mar 91	**WE SHOULDN'T HOLD HANDS IN THE DARK** *A&M AM 755*	..	.69	1

[1] LA Mix featuring Jazzi P [2] LA Mix featuring Kevin Henry

LCD *UK, male production group (9 WEEKS)*
pos/wks

27 Jun 98	**ZORBA'S DANCE** *Virgin VSCDT 1693*	....	.20	5
9 Oct 99	**ZORBA'S DANCE (re-issue)** *Virgin VSCDT 1757*	....	.22	4

LFO *UK, male instrumental group (15 WEEKS)*
pos/wks

14 Jul 90	**LFO** *Warp WAP 5*	....	.12	10
6 Jul 91	**WE ARE BACK / NURTURE** *Warp 7WAP 14*	...	.47	3
1 Feb 92	**WHAT IS HOUSE (EP)** *Warp WAP 17*	....	.62	2

Tracks on What Is House (EP): Tan Ta Ra / Mashed Potato / What Is House / Syndrome

LL COOL J (409) Top 500

With a moniker abbreviated from Ladies Love Cool James, this whizz kid was born James Todd Smith, 18 Jun 1968, New York, US. The first solo rap act to score a UK Top 10 hit with 'I Need Love', which was also the first successful rap 'ballad', he has amassed a record eight US No.1 rap hits (83 WEEKS) pos/wks

4 Jul 87	**I'M BAD** *Def Jam 650856 7*	....	.71	1
12 Sep 87 ●	**I NEED LOVE** *Def Jam 651101 7*	....	.8	10
21 Nov 87	**GO CUT CREATOR GO** *Def Jam LLCJ 1*	....	.66	2
13 Feb 88	**GOING BACK TO CALI / JACK THE RIPPER** *Def Jam LLCJ 2*	..	.37	4
10 Jun 89	**I'M THAT TYPE OF GUY** *Def Jam LLCJ 3*	.....	.43	5
1 Dec 90	**AROUND THE WAY GIRL / MAMA SAID KNOCK YOU OUT** *Def Jam 6564470*	....	.41	4
9 Mar 91	**AROUND THE WAY GIRL (re-mix)** *Columbia 6564470*	...	.36	4
10 Apr 93	**HOW I'M COMIN'** *Def Jam 6591692*	....	.37	2
20 Jan 96	**HEY LOVER** *Def Jam DEFCD 14* [1]	....	.17	4
1 Jun 96	**DOIN' IT** *Def Jam DEFCD 15* [2]	....	.15	3
5 Oct 96 ●	**LOUNGIN'** *Def Jam DEFCD 30*	....	.7	8
8 Feb 97 ★	**AIN'T NOBODY** *Geffen GFSTD 22195* ■	....	.1	9
5 Apr 97	**HIT EM HIGH (THE MONSTARS' ANTHEM)** *Atlantic A 5449CD* [3]	....	.8	6
1 Nov 97 ●	**PHENOMENON** *Def Jam 5681172*	....	.9	5
28 Mar 98 ●	**FATHER** *Def Jam 5685292*	....	.10	5
11 Jul 98	**ZOOM** *Interscope IND 95594* [4]	....	.15	3
5 Dec 98	**INCREDIBLE** *Jive 0522102* [5]	....	.52	1
26 Oct 02 ●	**LUV U BETTER** *Def Jam 0638722*	....	.7	7

[1] LL Cool J featuring Boyz II Men [2] LL Cool J, guest vocals by LeShaun [3] B Real / Busta Rhymes / Coolio / LL Cool J / Method Man [4] Dr Dre and LL Cool J [5] Keith Murray featuring LL Cool J

'Jack the Ripper' listed only from 20 Feb 1988

LNR *US, male vocal / instrumental duo (2 WEEKS)*
pos/wks

3 Jun 89	**WORK IT TO THE BONE** *Kool Kat KOOL 501*	....	.64	2

LRS – *See D MOB*

LSG *Germany, male DJ / producer – Oliver Lieb (1 WEEK)*
pos/wks

10 May 97	**NETHERWORLD** *Hooj Choons HOOJCD 52*	....	.63	1

L7 *US, female vocal / instrumental group (18 WEEKS)*
pos/wks

4 Apr 92	**PRETEND WE'RE DEAD** *Slash LASH 34*	....	.21	7
30 May 92	**EVERGLADE** *Slash LASH 36*	....	.27	3
12 Sep 92	**MONSTER** *Slash LASH 38*	....	.33	3
28 Nov 92	**PRETEND WE'RE DEAD (re-issue)** *Slash LASH 42*	.....	.50	3
9 Jul 94	**ANDRES** *Slash LASCD 48*	....	.34	2

L.T.D. *US, male vocal / instrumental group (3 WEEKS)*
pos/wks

9 Sep 78	**HOLDING ON (WHEN LOVE IS GONE)** *A&M AMS 7378*	....	.70	3

LV *US, male vocalist – Larry Sanders (25 WEEKS)*
pos/wks

28 Oct 95 ★	**GANGSTA'S PARADISE** *Tommy Boy MCSTD 2104* [1] ◆ ■ ▲	1	20

23 Dec 95	**THROW YOUR HANDS UP / GANGSTA'S PARADISE** *Tommy Boy TBCD 699*	.....	.24	4
4 May 96	**I AM LV** *Tommy Boy TBCD 7724*	....	.64	1

[1] Coolio featuring LV

The version of 'Gangsta's Paradise' coupled with 'Throw Your Hands Up' is a re-recorded version without Coolio's vocals

LWS *Italy, male instrumental group (1 WEEK)*
pos/wks

29 Oct 94	**GOSP** *Transworld TRANNY 4CD*	....	.65	1

LA BELLE EPOQUE *France, female vocal duo (14 WEEKS)*
pos/wks

27 Aug 77 ●	**BLACK IS BLACK (re)** *Harvest HAR 5133*	....	.2	14

LA BOUCHE *US, male / female rap / vocal duo – Lane McCray and Melanie Thornton (12 WEEKS)*
pos/wks

24 Sep 94	**SWEET DREAMS** *Bell 74321223912*	....	.63	1
15 Jul 95	**BE MY LOVER** *Arista 74321265402*	....	.27	4
30 Sep 95	**FALLING IN LOVE** *Arista 74321305102*	.....	.43	2
2 Mar 96	**BE MY LOVER (re-mix)** *Arista 74321339822*	.....	.25	4
7 Sep 96	**SWEET DREAMS (re-issue)** *Arista 74321398542*	.....	.44	1

LA NA NEE NEE NOO NOO – *See BANANARAMA*

Danny LA RUE *UK, male vocalist – Daniel Carroll (9 WEEKS)*
pos/wks

18 Dec 68	**ON MOTHER KELLY'S DOORSTEP** *Page One POF 108*	....	.33	9

LA TREC – *See SASH!*

LaBELLE
US, female vocal group – lead vocal Patti LaBelle (9 WEEKS)
pos/wks

22 Mar 75	**LADY MARMALADE (VOULEZ-VOUS COUCHER AVEC MOI CE SOIR?)** *Epic EPC 2852* ▲	...17	9

See also Patti LaBELLE

Patti LaBELLE
US, female vocalist – Patricia Holt (21 WEEKS)
pos/wks

3 May 86 ●	**ON MY OWN** *MCA MCA 1045* [1] ▲	.....	.2	13
2 Aug 86	**OH, PEOPLE** *MCA MCA 1075*	....	.26	6
3 Sep 94	**THE RIGHT KINDA LOVER** *MCA MCSTD 1995*	....	.50	2

[1] Patti LaBelle and Michael McDonald

See also LaBELLE

Tiff LACEY – *See REDD SQUARE featuring Tiff LACEY*

LADIES CHOICE
UK, male vocal / instrumental group (4 WEEKS)
pos/wks

25 Jan 86	**FUNKY SENSATION** *Sure Delight SD 01*	....	.41	4

LADIES FIRST *UK, female vocal trio (8 WEEKS)*
pos/wks

24 Nov 01	**MESSIN'** *Polydor 5873422*	....	.30	2
13 Apr 02	**I CAN'T WAIT** *Polydor 5706912*	....	.19	6

LADY G – *See B-15 PROJECT featuring Crissy D and Lady G*

LADY J – *See RAZE*

LADY OF RAGE *US, female rapper (1 WEEK)*
pos/wks

8 Oct 94	**AFRO PUFFS** *Interscope A 8288CD*	....	.72	1

LADY SAW *Jamaica, female vocalist – Marion Hall (3 WEEKS)*
pos/wks

16 Dec 00	**BUMP N GRIND (I AM FEELING HOT TONIGHT)** *Telstar CDSTAS 3129* [1]	.....	.59	1
20 Oct 01	**SINCE I MET YOU LADY / SPARKLE OF MY EYES** *DEP International DEPD 55* [2]	.....	.40	2

[1] M Dubs featuring Lady Saw [2] UB40 featuring Lady Saw

Re-entries are listed as (re), (2re), (3re), etc which signifies that the hit re-entered the chart once, twice or three times, etc

LADYSMITH BLACK MAMBAZO
South Africa, male vocal group (26 WEEKS) pos/wks

3 Jun 95	SWING LOW SWEET CHARIOT *PolyGram TV SWLOW 2* [1]	15 6
3 Jun 95	WORLD IN UNION '95 *PolyGram TV RUGBY 2* [2]	47 5
15 Nov 97	INKANYEZI NEZAZI (THE STAR AND THE WISEMAN) *A&M 5823892*	33 3
11 Jul 98	THE STAR AND THE WISEMAN (re-issue) *AM:PM 5825692*	63 1
16 Oct 99	AIN'T NO SUNSHINE *Universal Music TV 1564332* [3]	42 2
18 Dec 99	I SHALL BE THERE *Glow Worm / Epic 6683332* [4]	13 9

[1] Ladysmith Black Mambazo featuring China Black [2] Ladysmith Black Mambazo featuring PJ Powers [3] Ladysmith Black Mambazo featuring Des'ree [4] B*Witched featuring Ladysmith Black Mambazo

LADYTRON
UK / Bulgaria, male / female vocal production group (1 WEEK) pos/wks

7 Dec 02	SEVENTEEN *Telstar / Invicta Hi-Fi CDSTAS 3284*	68 1

LAGUNA *Italy, male DJ / production duo*
– Cristiano Spiller and Tommy Vee (2 WEEKS) pos/wks

1 Nov 97	SPILLER FROM RIO (DO IT EASY) *Positiva CDTIV 83*	40 2

See also SPILLER

LAID BACK *Denmark, male vocal / instrumental duo (4 WEEKS)* pos/wks

5 May 90	BAKERMAN *Arista 112356*	44 4

LAIN – See WOOKIE

Cleo LAINE
UK, female vocalist – Clementina Campbell (14 WEEKS) pos/wks

29 Dec 60	LET'S SLIP AWAY *Fontana H 269*	42 1
14 Sep 61	● YOU'LL ANSWER TO ME *Fontana H 326*	5 13

Frankie LAINE ⟨ 37 | Top 500 ⟩
Powerful-voiced No.1 hitmaker of the pre-rock years, b. Frank Lovecchio, 30 Mar 1913, Chicago, US. He spent an unequalled 27 weeks at the top of the UK chart in 1953, including a record 18 by 'I Believe'. At one time he had three singles in the Top 5 (282 WEEKS) pos/wks

14 Nov 52	● HIGH NOON (DO NOT FORSAKE ME) *Columbia DB 3113*	7 7
14 Nov 52	● SUGARBUSH (re) *Columbia DB 3123* [1]	8 8
20 Mar 53	THE GIRL IN THE WOOD *Columbia DB 2907*	11 1
3 Apr 53	★ I BELIEVE *Philips PB 117*	1 36
8 May 53	● TELL ME A STORY (re) *Philips PB 126* [2]	5 16
4 Sep 53	● WHERE THE WINDS BLOW *Philips PB 167*	2 12
16 Oct 53	★ HEY JOE! *Philips PB 172*	1 8
30 Oct 53	★ ANSWER ME *Philips PB 196*	1 17
8 Jan 54	● BLOWING WILD *Philips PB 207*	2 12
26 Mar 54	● GRANADA (re) *Philips PB 242*	9 2
16 Apr 54	● THE KID'S LAST FIGHT *Philips PB 258*	3 10
13 Aug 54	● MY FRIEND *Philips PB 316*	3 15
8 Oct 54	● THERE MUST BE A REASON *Philips PB 306*	9 9
22 Oct 54	● RAIN, RAIN, RAIN *Philips PB 311* [3]	8 16
11 Mar 55	IN THE BEGINNING *Philips PB 404*	20 1
24 Jun 55	● COOL WATER *Philips PB 465* [4]	2 22
15 Jul 55	● STRANGE LADY IN TOWN *Philips PB 478*	6 13
11 Nov 55	HUMMING BIRD *Philips PB 498*	16 1
25 Nov 55	● HAWK-EYE *Philips PB 519*	7 8
20 Jan 56	● SIXTEEN TONS *Philips PB 539* [4]	10 3
4 May 56	HELL HATH NO FURY *Philips PB 585*	28 1
7 Sep 56	★ A WOMAN IN LOVE *Philips PB 617*	1 21
28 Dec 56	● MOONLIGHT GAMBLER (re) *Philips PB 638*	13 13
26 Apr 57	LOVE IS A GOLDEN RING *Philips PB 676* [5]	19 5
4 Oct 57	GOOD EVENING FRIENDS / UP ABOVE MY HEAD, I HEAR MUSIC IN THE AIR *Philips PB 708* [6]	25 4
13 Nov 59	● RAWHIDE (re) *Philips PB 965*	6 20
11 May 61	GUNSLINGER *Philips PB 1135*	50 1

[1] Doris Day and Frankie Laine [2] Jimmy Boyd – Frankie Laine [3] Frankie Laine and the Four Lads [4] Frankie Laine with The Mellomen [5] Frankie Laine and The Easy Riders [6] Frankie Laine and Johnnie Ray

Greg LAKE *UK, male vocalist (12 WEEKS)* pos/wks

6 Dec 75	● I BELIEVE IN FATHER CHRISTMAS (2re) *Manticore K 13511*	2 12

Re-entries occurred in Dec '82 and Dec '83

See also EMERSON, LAKE and PALMER

LAMB *UK, male / female vocal / production duo*
– Andy Barlow and Louise Rhodes (4 WEEKS) pos/wks

29 Mar 97	GORECKI *Fontana LAMCD 4*	30 2
3 Apr 99	B LINE *Fontana LAMCD 5*	52 1
22 May 99	ALL IN YOUR HANDS *Fontana LAMCD 6*	71 1

Annabel LAMB *UK, female vocalist (7 WEEKS)* pos/wks

27 Aug 83	RIDERS ON THE STORM *A&M AM 131*	27 7

LAMBCHOP
US, male / female vocal / instrumental group (1 WEEK) pos/wks

20 May 00	UP WITH PEOPLE *City Slang 201592*	66 1

LAMBRETTAS *UK, male vocal / instrumental group (24 WEEKS)* pos/wks

1 Mar 80	● POISON IVY *Rocket XPRESS 25*	7 12
24 May 80	D-A-A-ANCE *Rocket XPRESS 33*	12 8
23 Aug 80	ANOTHER DAY (ANOTHER GIRL) *Rocket XPRESS 36*	49 4

LAMPIES *US, male / female / canine cartoon vocal group (3 WEEKS)* pos/wks

22 Dec 01	LIGHT UP THE WORLD FOR CHRISTMAS *Bluecrest LAMPCD 001*	48 3

LANCASTRIANS *UK, male vocal / instrumental group (2 WEEKS)* pos/wks

24 Dec 64	WE'LL SING IN THE SUNSHINE *Pye 7N 15732*	44 2

Major LANCE *US, male vocalist d. 3 Sep 1994 (2 WEEKS)* pos/wks

13 Feb 64	UM, UM, UM, UM, UM, UM *Columbia DB 7205*	40 2

LANCERS – See Teresa BREWER

Valerie LANDSBERG – See KIDS FROM 'FAME'

LANDSCAPE *UK, male vocal / instrumental group (20 WEEKS)* pos/wks

28 Feb 81	● EINSTEIN A GO-GO *RCA 22*	5 13
23 May 81	NORMAN BATES *RCA 60*	40 7

Desmond LANE – See Alma COGAN; Cyril STAPLETON and his Orchestra

Ronnie LANE and SLIM CHANCE *UK, male vocalist*
(d. 4 Jun 1997) and male instrumental group (12 WEEKS) pos/wks

12 Jan 74	HOW COME? *GM GMS 011* [1]	11 8
15 Jun 74	THE POACHER *GM GMS 024*	36 4

[1] Ronnie Lane accompanied by the band Slim Chance

See also SMALL FACES

Emma LANFORD – See MOUSSE T

Don LANG
UK, male vocalist – Gordon Langhorn d. 3 Aug 1992 (18 WEEKS) pos/wks

4 Nov 55	CLOUDBURST (2re) *HMV POP 115*	16 4
5 Jul 57	SCHOOL DAY (RING! RING! GOES THE BELL) *HMV POP 350* [1]	26 2
23 May 58	● WITCH DOCTOR *HMV POP 488* [1]	5 11
10 Mar 60	SINK THE BISMARCK *HMV POP 714*	43 1

[1] Don Lang and his Frantic Five

kd lang
Canada, female vocalist – Katherine Dawn Lang (25 WEEKS) pos/wks

16 May 92	CONSTANT CRAVING *Sire W 0100*	52 4

22 Aug 92	CRYING *Virgin America VUS 63* [1]		.13	6
27 Feb 93	CONSTANT CRAVING (re-issue) *Sire W 0157CD*		.15	8
1 May 93	THE MIND OF LOVE (WHERE IS YOUR HEAD, KATHRYN?)			
	Sire W 0170CD1		.72	1
26 Jun 93	MISS CHATELAINE *Sire W 0181CDX*		.68	2
11 Dec 93	JUST KEEP ME MOVING *Sire W 0227CD*		.59	1
30 Sep 95	IF I WERE YOU *Sire W 0319CD*		.53	1
18 May 96	YOU'RE OK *Warner Bros. W 0332CD*		.44	2

[1] Roy Orbison (duet with kd lang)

Thomas LANG *UK, male vocalist (3 WEEKS)* pos/wks
30 Jan 88	THE HAPPY MAN *Epic VOW 4*		.67	3

LANGE *UK, male producer – Stuart Langelaan and female vocalist (7 WEEKS)* pos/wks
19 Jun 99	I BELIEVE *Additive 12 AD039* [1]		.68	1
19 Jan 02 ●	DRIFTING AWAY *VC Recordings VCRD 101* [2]		.9	6

[1] Lange featuring Sarah Dwyer [2] Lange featuring Skye

LANTERNS *UK, male / female vocal / instrumental trio (1 WEEK)* pos/wks
6 Feb 99	HIGHRISE TOWN *Columbia 6665712*		.50	1

Mario LANZA *US, male vocalist – Alfredo Cocozza d. 7 Oct 1959 (32 WEEKS)* pos/wks
14 Nov 52 ●	BECAUSE YOU'RE MINE *HMV DA 2017*		.3	24
4 Feb 55	DRINKING SONG *HMV DA 2065*		.13	1
18 Feb 55	I'LL WALK WITH GOD (re) *HMV DA 2062*		.18	2
22 Apr 55	SERENADE (re) *HMV DA 2065*		.15	3
14 Sep 56	SERENADE (re) *HMV DA 2085*		.25	2

DA 2065 and DA 2085 are two different songs

LAPTOP *US, male vocalist / instrumentalist – Jesse Hartman (1 WEEK)* pos/wks
12 Jun 99	NOTHING TO DECLARE *Island CID 744*		.74	1

Julius LAROSA *US, male vocalist (9 WEEKS)* pos/wks
4 Jul 58	TORERO *RCA 1063*		.15	9

LA's *UK, male vocal / instrumental group (20 WEEKS)* pos/wks
14 Jan 89	THERE SHE GOES *Go! Discs GOLASEP 2*		.59	4
15 Sep 90	TIMELESS MELODY *Go! Discs GOLAS 4*		.57	2
3 Nov 90	THERE SHE GOES (re-issue) *Go! Discs GOLAS 5*		.13	9
16 Feb 91	FEELIN' *Go! Discs GOLAS 6*		.43	3
10 May 97	FEVER PITCH THE EP *Blanco Y Negro NEG 104CD* [1]		.65	1
2 Oct 99	THERE SHE GOES (2nd re-issue) *Polydor 5614032*		.65	1

[1] Pretenders, La's, Orlando, Neil MacColl, Nick Hornby

Tracks on Fever Pitch the EP: Goin' Back – Pretenders / There She Goes – La's / How Can We Hang on to a Dream – Orlando / Football – Neill MacColl, Boo Hewerdine and Nick Hornby

LAS KETCHUP *Spain, female vocal trio (15 WEEKS)* pos/wks
2 Sep 02	THE KETCHUP SONG (ASEREJE) (import)			
	Columbia 6729602CD		.49	4
19 Oct 02 ★	THE KETCHUP SONG (ASEREJE) *Columbia 6731932* ■		.1	11+

Denise LASALLE *US, female vocalist – Denise Craig (13 WEEKS)* pos/wks
15 Jun 85 ●	MY TOOT TOOT *Epic A 6334*		.6	13

LASGO *Belgium, male / female production / vocal / instrumental trio (28 WEEKS)* pos/wks
9 Mar 02 ●	SOMETHING *Positiva CDTIV 169*		.4	15
24 Aug 02 ●	ALONE *Positiva CDTIVS 176*		.7	8
30 Nov 02	PRAY *Positiva CDTIVS 182*		.17	5+

Lisa LASHES *UK, female DJ / producer (1 WEEK)* pos/wks
8 Jul 00	UNBELIEVABLE *Tidy Trax TIDY 138CD*		.63	1

James LAST BAND *Germany, male orchestra (4 WEEKS)* pos/wks
3 May 80	THE SEDUCTION (LOVE THEME) *Polydor PD 2071*		.48	4

LAST RHYTHM *Italy, male instrumental / production group (1 WEEK)* pos/wks
14 Sep 96	LAST RHYTHM *Stress CDSTR 76*		.62	1

LATANZA WATERS – See E-SMOOVE featuring Latanza WATERS

LATE SHOW *UK, male vocal / instrumental group (6 WEEKS)* pos/wks
3 Mar 79	BRISTOL STOMP *Decca F 13822*		.40	6

LATIN QUARTER *UK, male / female vocal / instrumental group (10 WEEKS)* pos/wks
18 Jan 86	RADIO AFRICA *Rockin' Horse RH 102*		.19	9
18 Apr 87	NOMZAMO (ONE PEOPLE ONE CAUSE)			
	Rockin' Horse RH 113		.73	1

LATIN RHYTHM – See Tito PUENTE Jr and the LATIN RHYTHM featuring Tito PUENTE, INDIA and Cali ALEMAN

LATIN THING *Canada / Spain, male / female vocal / instrumental group (1 WEEK)* pos/wks
13 Jul 96	LATIN THING *Faze 2 CDFAZE 33*		.41	1

Gino LATINO *Italy, male producer – Lorenzo Cherubini (7 WEEKS)* pos/wks
20 Jan 90	WELCOME *ffrr F 126*		.17	7

LATINO RAVE – See VARIOUS ARTISTS (MONTAGES)

LATOUR *US, male vocalist / producer – William LaTour (7 WEEKS)* pos/wks
8 Jun 91	PEOPLE ARE STILL HAVING SEX *Polydor PO 147*		.15	7

Stacy LATTISAW *US, female vocalist (14 WEEKS)* pos/wks
14 Jun 80 ●	JUMP TO THE BEAT *Atlantic / Cotillion K 11496*		.3	11
30 Aug 80	DYNAMITE *Atlantic K 11554*		.51	3

Dave LAUDAT – See HUSTLERS CONVENTION featuring Dave LAUDAT and Ondrea DUVERNEY

LAUNCHERS – See Ezz RECO and the LAUNCHERS with Boysie GRANT

Cyndi LAUPER (299 Top 500)
Flamboyant and versatile singer / songwriter. b. 20 Jun 1953, New York, US. Her debut album, 'She's So Unusual' (1983), spawned four Top 5 US singles, and she won a Grammy for Best New Artist of 1984 (easily outpacing her major female rival, Madonna) (103 WEEKS) pos/wks
14 Jan 84 ●	GIRLS JUST WANT TO HAVE FUN *Portrait A 3943*		.2	12
24 Mar 84 ●	TIME AFTER TIME (re) *Portrait A 4290* ▲		.3	17
1 Sep 84	SHE BOP *Portrait A 4620*		.46	5
17 Nov 84	ALL THROUGH THE NIGHT *Portrait A 4849*		.64	2
20 Sep 86	TRUE COLOURS *Portrait 650026 7* ▲		.12	11
27 Dec 86	CHANGE OF HEART (re) *Portrait CYNDI 1*		.67	2
28 Mar 87	WHAT'S GOING ON *Portrait CYN 1*		.57	3
20 May 89 ●	I DROVE ALL NIGHT *Epic CYN 4*		.7	12
5 Aug 89	MY FIRST NIGHT WITHOUT YOU *Epic CYN 5*		.53	4
30 Dec 89	HEADING WEST *Epic CYN 6*		.68	1
6 Jun 92	THE WORLD IS STONE *Epic 6579707*		.15	7
13 Nov 93	THAT'S WHAT I THINK *Epic 6598782*		.31	4
8 Jan 94	WHO LET IN THE RAIN *Epic 6590392*		.32	4
17 Sep 94 ●	HEY NOW (GIRLS JUST WANT TO HAVE FUN)			
	Epic 6608072		.4	13
11 Feb 95	I'M GONNA BE STRONG *Epic 6611962*		.37	2
26 Aug 95	COME ON HOME *Epic 6614255*		.39	2
1 Feb 97	YOU DON'T KNOW *Epic 6641845*		.27	2

'Hey Now (Girls Just Want to Have Fun)' is a re-recording of her first hit

Re-entries are listed as (re), (2re), (3re), etc which signifies that the hit re-entered the chart

LAUREL and HARDY
UK, male vocal / instrumental duo (2 WEEKS)   pos/wks

| 2 Apr 83 | CLUNK CLINK *CBS A 3213* | 65 | 2 |

LAUREL and HARDY with the AVALON BOYS
featuring Chill WILLS
UK / US, male vocal duo – Stan Laurel and Oliver Hardy, with US, male vocal group (10 WEEKS)   pos/wks

| 22 Nov 75 ● | THE TRAIL OF THE LONESOME PINE *United Artists UP 36026* | 2 | 10 |

LAURNEA
US, female vocalist – Laurnea Wilkinson (2 WEEKS)   pos/wks

| 12 Jul 97 | DAYS OF YOUTH *Epic 6646932* | 36 | 2 |

Lauren LAVERNE – See KENICKIE; MINT ROYALE

Avril LAVIGNE
Canada, female vocalist (12 WEEKS)   pos/wks

7 Sep 02	COMPLICATED (import) (re) *RCA 74321955782*	64	2
5 Oct 02 ●	COMPLICATED *Arista 74321985962*	3	9
28 Dec 02 ●	SK8ER BOI *Arista 74321979782*	9	1+

Joanna LAW
UK, female vocalist (8 WEEKS)   pos/wks

| 7 Jul 90 | FIRST TIME EVER *Citybeat CBE 752* | 67 | 3 |
| 14 Sep 96 | THE GIFT *Deconstruction 74321401912* [1] | 15 | 5 |

[1] Way Out West featuring Miss Joanna Law

Law's contribution to 'The Gift' is a sample from 'First Time Ever'

Steve LAWLER
UK, male DJ / producer (1 WEEK)   pos/wks

| 11 Nov 00 | RISE 'IN *Bedrock BEDRCDS 008* | 50 | 1 |

Belle LAWRENCE
UK, female vocalist (1 WEEK)   pos/wks

| 30 Mar 02 | EVERGREEN *Euphoric CDUPH 024* | 73 | 1 |

Billy LAWRENCE – See RAMPAGE featuring Billy LAWRENCE

Joey LAWRENCE
US, male vocalist (15 WEEKS)   pos/wks

26 Jun 93	NOTHIN' MY LOVE CAN'T FIX *EMI CDEM 271*	13	7
28 Aug 93	I CAN'T HELP MYSELF *EMI CDEM 277*	27	4
30 Oct 93	STAY FOREVER *EMI CDEM 289*	41	3
19 Sep 98	NEVER GONNA CHANGE MY MIND *Curb CUBC 34*	49	1

Lee LAWRENCE
UK, male vocalist – Leon Siroto d. Feb 1961 (10 WEEKS)   pos/wks

| 20 Nov 53 ● | CRYING IN THE CHAPEL (re) *Decca F 10177* | 7 | 6 |
| 2 Dec 55 | SUDDENLY THERE'S A VALLEY (re) *Columbia DB 3681* | 14 | 4 |

With Ray Martin and his Orchestra

Sophie LAWRENCE
UK, female vocalist (7 WEEKS)   pos/wks

| 3 Aug 91 | LOVE'S UNKIND *IQ ZB 44821* | 21 | 7 |

Steve LAWRENCE
US, male vocalist – Sidney Leibowitz (27 WEEKS)   pos/wks

21 Apr 60 ●	FOOTSTEPS *HMV POP 726*	4	13
18 Aug 60	GIRLS, GIRLS, GIRLS *London HLT 9166*	49	1
22 Aug 63 ●	I WANT TO STAY HERE *CBS AAG 163* [1]	3	13

[1] Steve and Eydie

LAYO & BUSHWACKA!
UK, male DJ / production duo – Layo Paskin and Matthew Benjamin (2 WEEKS)   pos/wks

| 22 Jun 02 | LOVE STORY *XL Recordings XLS 144CD* | 30 | 2 |

Lindy LAYTON
UK, female vocalist (28 WEEKS)   pos/wks

10 Feb 90 ★	DUB BE GOOD TO ME *Go. Beat GOD 39* [1]	1	13
11 Aug 90	SILLY GAMES *Arista 113452* [2]	22	7
26 Jan 91	ECHO MY HEART *Arista 113845*	42	2
31 Aug 91	WITHOUT YOU (ONE AND ONE) *Arista 114636*	71	2

| 24 Apr 93 | WE GOT THE LOVE *PWL International PWCD 250* | 38 | 3 |
| 30 Oct 93 | SHOW ME *PWL International PWCD 275* | 47 | 1 |

[1] Beats International featuring Lindy Layton [2] Lindy Layton featuring Janet Kay

Peter LAZONBY
UK, male DJ / producer (1 WEEK)   pos/wks

| 10 Jun 00 | SACRED CYCLES *Hooj Choons HOOJ 93CD* | 49 | 1 |

Doug LAZY
US, male rapper – Gene Finley (9 WEEKS)   pos/wks

15 Jul 89	LET IT ROLL *Atlantic A 8866* [1]	27	5
4 Nov 89	LET THE RHYTHM PUMP *Atlantic A 8784*	45	3
26 May 90	LET THE RHYTHM PUMP (re-mix) *East West A 7919*	63	1

[1] Raze presents Doug Lazy

Keith LE BLANC – See Malcolm X

LE CLICK
Sweden / US, male / female vocal duo – Kayo Shekoni and Robert Haynes (2 WEEKS)   pos/wks

| 30 Aug 97 ● | CALL ME *Logic 74321509672* | 38 | 2 |

Kele LE ROC
UK, female vocalist – Kelly Biggs (15 WEEKS)   pos/wks

31 Oct 98 ●	LITTLE BIT OF LOVIN' *1st Avenue / Wild Card / Polydor 5672812*	8	7
27 Mar 99 ●	MY LOVE *1st Avenue / Wild Card / Polydor 5636112*	8	7
30 Sep 00	THINKING OF YOU *Telstar CDSTAS 3136* [1]	70	1

[1] Curtis Lynch Jr featuring Kele Le Roc and Red Rat

Vicky LEANDROS
Greece, female vocalist (29 WEEKS)   pos/wks

8 Apr 72 ●	COME WHAT MAY *Philips 6000 049*	2	16
23 Dec 72	THE LOVE IN YOUR EYES (2re) *Philips 6000 081*	40	8
7 Jul 73	WHEN BOUZOUKIS PLAYED (re) *Philips 6000 111*	44	5

Denis LEARY
US, male vocalist / comedian (2 WEEKS)   pos/wks

| 13 Jan 96 | ASSHOLE *A&M 5813352* | 58 | 2 |

LEAVES
Iceland, male vocal / instrumental group (1 WEEK)   pos/wks

| 18 May 02 | RACE *B Unique BUN 020CDS* | 66 | 1 |

LED ZEPPELIN
UK, male vocal / instrumental group (2 WEEKS)   pos/wks

| 13 Sep 97 | WHOLE LOTTA LOVE *Atlantic ATT00 13CD* | 21 | 2 |

See also Robert PLANT

Angel LEE
UK, female vocalist – Angelique Beckford (1 WEEK)   pos/wks

| 3 Jun 00 | WHAT'S YOUR NAME? *WEA WEA 258CD* | 39 | 1 |

Ann LEE
UK, female vocalist – Annerley Gordon (21 WEEKS)   pos/wks

11 Sep 99	2 TIMES (import) *ZYX ZYX 90188*	57	2
16 Oct 99 ●	2 TIMES *Systematic SYSCD 31*	2	16
4 Mar 00	VOICES *Systematic SYSCD 32*	27	3

Brenda LEE   80   Top 500
Biggest-selling teenage female vocalist of the early rock years; b. Brenda Tarpley, 11 Dec 1944, Georgia, US. 'Little Miss Dynamite', who first recorded aged 11, had back-to-back UK / US hits in the early 1960s. She was inducted into the Country Music Hall of Fame in 1997 (210 WEEKS)   pos/wks

17 Mar 60 ●	SWEET NUTHIN'S (re) *Brunswick 05819*	4	19
30 Jun 60	I'M SORRY *Brunswick 05833* ▲	12	16
20 Oct 60	I WANT TO BE WANTED *Brunswick 05839* ▲	31	6
19 Jan 61	LET'S JUMP THE BROOMSTICK *Brunswick 05823*	12	15
6 Apr 61	EMOTIONS *Brunswick 05847*	45	1
20 Jul 61	DUM DUM *Brunswick 05854*	22	8
16 Nov 61	FOOL NUMBER ONE *Brunswick 05860*	38	3
8 Feb 62	BREAK IT TO ME GENTLY *Brunswick 05864*	46	2
5 Apr 62	SPEAK TO ME PRETTY *Brunswick 05867*	3	12
21 Jun 62	HERE COMES THAT FEELING *Brunswick 05871*	5	12
13 Sep 62	IT STARTED ALL OVER AGAIN *Brunswick 05876*	15	11

				pos/wks
29 Nov 62 ●	ROCKIN' AROUND THE CHRISTMAS TREE			
	Brunswick 05880			6 7
17 Jan 63 ●	ALL ALONE AM I *Brunswick 05882*			7 17
28 Mar 63 ●	LOSING YOU *Brunswick 05886*			10 16
18 Jul 63	I WONDER *Brunswick 05891*			14 9
31 Oct 63	SWEET IMPOSSIBLE YOU *Brunswick 05896*			28 6
9 Jan 64 ●	AS USUAL *Brunswick 05899*			5 15
9 Apr 64	THINK *Brunswick 05903*			26 8
10 Sep 64	IS IT TRUE *Brunswick 05915*			17 8
10 Dec 64	CHRISTMAS WILL BE JUST ANOTHER LONELY DAY			
	Brunswick 05921			25 5
4 Feb 65	THANKS A LOT *Brunswick 05927*			41 2
29 Jul 65	TOO MANY RIVERS *Brunswick 05936*			22 12

Byron LEE – *See Boris GARDINER*

Curtis LEE *US, male vocalist (2 WEEKS)*
			pos/wks
31 Aug 61	PRETTY LITTLE ANGEL EYES (re) *London HLX 9397*		47 2

Dave LEE – *See Joey NEGRO; JAKATTA; HED BOYS; AKABU featuring Linda CLIFFORD; Li KWAN; RAVEN MAIZE; IL PADRINOS; Z FACTOR*

Dee C LEE *UK, female vocalist – Diane Sealey (20 WEEKS)*
			pos/wks
9 Nov 85 ●	SEE THE DAY *CBS A 6570*		3 12
8 Mar 86	COME HELL OR WATERS HIGH *CBS A 6869*		46 5
13 Nov 93	NO TIME TO PLAY *Cooltempo CDCOOL 282* [1]		25 3

[1] Guru featuring Dee C Lee

See also STYLE COUNCIL

Garry LEE and SHOWDOWN
Canada, male vocal / instrumental group (3 WEEKS)
			pos/wks
31 Jul 93	THE RODEO SONG *Party Dish VCD 101*		44 3

Jackie LEE *UK, female vocalist – Jackie Hopkins (31 WEEKS)*
			pos/wks
10 Apr 68 ●	WHITE HORSES *Philips BF 1647* [1]		10 14
2 Jan 71	RUPERT *Pye 7N 45003*		14 17

[1] Jacky

Leapy LEE *UK, male vocalist – Lee Graham (28 WEEKS)*
			pos/wks
21 Aug 68 ●	LITTLE ARROWS *MCA MU 1028*		2 21
20 Dec 69	GOOD MORNING (re) *MCA MK 5021*		29 7

Peggy LEE *US, female vocalist – Norma Jean Egstrom d. 22 Jan 2002 (29 WEEKS)*
			pos/wks
24 May 57 ●	MR WONDERFUL *Brunswick 05671*		5 13
15 Aug 58 ●	FEVER *Capitol CL 14902*		5 11
23 Mar 61	TILL THERE WAS YOU (re) *Capitol CL 15184*		30 4
22 Aug 92	FEVER (re-issue) *Capitol PEG 1*		75 1

Toney LEE *US, male vocalist (4 WEEKS)*
			pos/wks
29 Jan 83	REACH UP *TMT TMT 2*		64 4

Tracey LEE *US, male vocalist (1 WEEK)*
			pos/wks
19 Jul 97	THE THEME *Universal UND 56133*		51 1

LEEDS UNITED FC
UK, male football team vocalists (13 WEEKS)
			pos/wks
29 Apr 72 ●	LEEDS UNITED *Chapter One SCH 168*		10 10
25 Apr 92	LEEDS, LEEDS, LEEDS (re) *Q Music LUFC 2*		54 3

Carol LEEMING – *See STAXX featuring Carol LEEMING*

LEE-O – *See K-WARREN featuring LEE-O*

Raymond LEFEVRE *France, orchestra (2 WEEKS)*
			pos/wks
15 May 68	SOUL COAXING *Major Minor MM 559*		46 2

LEFTFIELD *UK, male instrumental / production duo – Neil Barnes and Paul Daley (23 WEEKS)*
			pos/wks
12 Dec 92	SONG OF LIFE *Hard Hands HAND 002T*		59 1
13 Nov 93	OPEN UP *Hard Hands HAND 009CD* [1]		13 5
25 Mar 95	ORIGINAL *Hard Hands HAND 18CD* [2]		18 3
5 Aug 95	THE AFRO-LEFT EP		
	Hard Hands HAND 23CD [3]		22 3
20 Jan 96	RELEASE THE PRESSURE		
	Hard Hands HAND 29CD		13 3
18 Sep 99 ●	AFRIKA SHOX *Hard Hands HAND 057CD1* [4]		7 5
11 Dec 99	DUSTED (re) *Hard Hands HAND 058CD1* [5]		28 3

[1] Leftfield Lydon [2] Leftfield Halliday [3] Leftfield featuring Djum Djum [4] Leftfield / Bambaataa [5] Leftfield / Roots Manuva

Tracks on The Afro-Left EP: Afro-Left / Afro Ride / Afro Central / Afro Sol

LEGEND B *Germany, male production duo (1 WEEK)*
			pos/wks
22 Feb 97	LOST IN LOVE *Perfecto PERF 132CD*		45 1

LEILANI *UK, female vocalist – Leilani Sen (7 WEEKS)*
			pos/wks
6 Feb 99	MADNESS THING *ZTT ZTT 124CD*		19 4
12 Jun 99	DO YOU WANT ME? *ZTT ZTT 134CD*		40 2
3 Jun 00	FLYING ELVIS *ZTT ZTT 145CD*		73 1

Paul LEKAKIS *US, male vocalist (4 WEEKS)*
			pos/wks
30 May 87	BOOM BOOM (LET'S GO BACK TO MY ROOM)		
	Champion CHAMP 43		60 4

LEMON JELLY *UK, male production duo – Fred Deakin and Nick Franglan (2 WEEKS)*
			pos/wks
19 Oct 02	SPACE WALK		
	Impotent Fury / XL Recordings IFXLS 150CD		36 2

LEMON PIPERS
US, male vocal / instrumental group (16 WEEKS)
			pos/wks
7 Feb 68 ●	GREEN TAMBOURINE		
	Pye International 7N 25444 ▲		7 11
1 May 68	RICE IS NICE *Pye International 7N 25454*		41 5

LEMON TREES
UK, male vocal / instrumental group (9 WEEKS)
			pos/wks
26 Sep 92	LOVE IS IN YOUR EYES *Oxygen GASP 1*		75 1
7 Nov 92	THE WAY I FEEL *Oxygen GASP 2*		62 2
13 Feb 93	LET IT LOOSE *Oxygen GASPD 3*		55 2
17 Apr 93	CHILD OF LOVE *Oxygen GASPD 4*		55 3
3 Jul 93	I CAN'T FACE THE WORLD *Oxygen GASPD 6*		52 1

LEMONESCENT *UK, female vocal group (2 WEEKS)*
			pos/wks
29 Jun 02	BEAUTIFUL *Supertone SUPTCD 1*		70 1
9 Nov 02	SWING MY HIPS (SEX DANCE) *Supertone SUPTCD 2*		48 1

LEMONHEADS *US / Australia, male vocal / instrumental group – lead vocal Evan Dando (26 WEEKS)*
			pos/wks
17 Oct 92	IT'S A SHAME ABOUT RAY *Atlantic A 7423*		70 1
5 Dec 92	MRS ROBINSON / BEIN' AROUND *Atlantic A 7401*		19 9
6 Feb 93	CONFETTI / MY DRUG BUDDY *Atlantic A 7430CD*		44 2
10 Apr 93	IT'S A SHAME ABOUT RAY (re-issue) *Atlantic A 5764CD*		31 3
16 Oct 93	INTO YOUR ARMS *Atlantic A 7302CD*		14 4
27 Nov 93	IT'S ABOUT TIME *Atlantic A 7296CD*		57 2
14 May 94	BIG GAY HEART *Atlantic A 7259CD*		55 2
28 Sep 96	IF I COULD TALK I'D TELL YOU *Atlantic A 5561CD*		39 2
14 Dec 96	IT'S ALL TRUE *Atlantic A 5635CD*		61 1

LEN *Canada, male / female DJ / vocal group (15 WEEKS)*
			pos/wks
18 Dec 99 ●	STEAL MY SUNSHINE *Columbia 6685062*		8 13
10 Jun 00	CRYPTIK SOULS CREW *Columbia 6693832*		28 2

LENA – *See Lena FIAGBE*

Re-entries are listed as (re), (2re), (3re), etc which signifies that the hit re-entered the chart once, twice or three times, etc

John LENNON 94 `Top 500`

One of the century's greatest musical talents, b. 9 Oct 1940, Liverpool, d. 8 Dec 1980. World-famous singer / songwriter who, together with Paul McCartney, fronted The Beatles and penned their hits. Three of his singles topped the UK chart in the two months after his murder in New York. He was recently included in the BBC's Top 10 Great Britons of all time. Best-selling single: 'Imagine' 1,486,581 (197 WEEKS)

		pos/wks
9 Jul 69 ●	GIVE PEACE A CHANCE (re) *Apple 13* [1]	2 18
1 Nov 69	COLD TURKEY *Apple APPLES 1001* [1]	14 8
21 Feb 70 ●	INSTANT KARMA *Apple APPLES 1003* [2]	5 9
20 Mar 71 ●	POWER TO THE PEOPLE *Apple R 5892* [3]	7 9
9 Dec 72 ●	HAPPY XMAS (WAR IS OVER) (4re) *Apple R 5970* [4]	2 26
24 Nov 73	MIND GAMES *Apple R 5994*	26 9
19 Oct 74	WHATEVER GETS YOU THRU' THE NIGHT *Apple R 5998* [5] ▲	36 4
8 Feb 75	#9 DREAM *Apple R 6003*	23 8
3 May 75	STAND BY ME *Apple R 6005*	30 7
1 Nov 75 ★	IMAGINE (re) *Apple R 6009* ◆	1 24
8 Nov 80 ★	(JUST LIKE) STARTING OVER *Geffen K 79186* ▲	1 15
24 Jan 81 ★	WOMAN *Geffen K 79195*	1 11
21 Mar 81	I SAW HER STANDING THERE *DJM DJS 10965* [6]	40 4
4 Apr 81	WATCHING THE WHEELS *Geffen K 79207*	30 6
20 Nov 82	LOVE *Parlophone R 6059*	41 7
21 Jan 84 ●	NOBODY TOLD ME *Ono Music / Polydor POSP 700*	6 6
17 Mar 84	BORROWED TIME *Polydor POSP 701*	32 6
30 Nov 85	JEALOUS GUY *Parlophone R 6117*	65 2
10 Dec 88	IMAGINE / JEALOUS GUY / HAPPY XMAS (WAR IS OVER) (re-issue) *Parlophone R 6199*	45 5
25 Dec 99 ●	IMAGINE (re-issue) (re) *Parlophone CDR 6534*	3 13

[1] Plastic Ono Band [2] Lennon, Ono and the Plastic Ono Band [3] John Lennon / Plastic Ono Band [4] John and Yoko and the Plastic Ono Band with the Harlem Community Choir [5] John Lennon with the Plastic Ono Nuclear Band [6] Elton John Band featuring John Lennon and the Muscle Shoals Horns

'Give Peace a Chance' re-entered at No.33 in Jan 1981. 'Happy Xmas (War Is Over)' peaked at No.4 in Dec '1972, No.48 in Jan 1975, and No.2 in Dec 1980, and the re-entry made No.28 in Dec 1981 and peaked at No.56 in Dec 1982. 'Imagine' peaked at No.6 in 1975, and topped the chart on re-entry in Dec 1980

See also BEATLES

Julian LENNON *UK, male vocalist (47 WEEKS)*

		pos/wks
6 Oct 84 ●	TOO LATE FOR GOODBYES *Charisma JL 1*	6 11
15 Dec 84	VALOTTE *Charisma JL 2*	55 6
9 Mar 85	SAY YOU'RE WRONG *Charisma JL 3*	75 1
7 Dec 85	BECAUSE *EMI 5538*	40 7
11 Mar 89	NOW YOU'RE IN HEAVEN *Virgin VS 1154*	59 3
24 Aug 91 ●	SALTWATER *Virgin VS 1361*	6 13
30 Nov 91	HELP YOURSELF *Virgin VS 1379*	53 2
25 Apr 92	GET A LIFE *Virgin VS 1398*	56 3
23 May 98	DAY AFTER DAY *Music from Another JULIAN 4CD*	66 1

Annie LENNOX *UK, female songwriter / vocalist (68 WEEKS)*

		pos/wks
3 Dec 88	PUT A LITTLE LOVE IN YOUR HEART *A&M AM 484* [1]	28 8
28 Mar 92 ●	WHY *RCA PB 45317*	5 8
6 Jun 92	PRECIOUS *RCA 74321100257*	23 5
22 Aug 92 ●	WALKING ON BROKEN GLASS *RCA 74321107227*	8 8
31 Oct 92	COLD *RCA 74321116902*	26 4
13 Feb 93 ●	LITTLE BIRD / LOVE SONG FOR A VAMPIRE *RCA 74321133832*	3 12
18 Feb 95 ●	NO MORE 'I LOVE YOU'S *RCA 74321257162*	2 12
10 Jun 95	A WHITER SHADE OF PALE *RCA 74321284822*	16 6
30 Sep 95	WAITING IN VAIN *RCA 74321316132*	31 3
9 Dec 95	SOMETHING SO RIGHT *RCA 74321332392* [2]	44 2

[1] Annie Lennox and Al Green [2] Annie Lennox featuring Paul Simon

See also EURYTHMICS

Dino LENNY *UK, male producer (1 WEEK)*

		pos/wks
4 May 02	I FEEL STEREO *Incentive CENT 40CDS*	60 1

Rula LENSKA – See Julie COVINGTON, Rula LENSKA, Charlotte CORNWELL and Sue JONES-DAVIES

Phillip LEO *UK, male vocalist (3 WEEKS)*

		pos/wks
23 Jul 94	SECOND CHANCE *EMI CDEM 327*	57 2
25 Mar 95	THINKING ABOUT YOUR LOVE *EMI CDEM 358*	64 1

LES RYTHMES DIGITALES

UK, male DJ / producer – Jacques Lu Cont (Stuart Price) (3 WEEKS)

		pos/wks
25 Apr 98	MUSIC MAKES YOU LOSE CONTROL *Wall of Sound WALLD 037*	69 1
7 Aug 99	SOMETIMES *Wall of Sound WALLD 054* [1]	56 1
30 Oct 99	JACQUES YOUR BODY (MAKE ME SWEAT) *Wall of Sound WALLD 060*	60 1

[1] Les Rythmes Digitales featuring Nik Kershaw

LeSHAUN – See LL COOL J

LESS THAN JAKE *US, male vocal / instrumental group (2 WEEKS)*

		pos/wks
5 Aug 00	ALL MY BEST FRIENDS ARE METALHEADS *Golf CDSHOLE 027*	51 1
8 Sep 01	GAINESVILLE ROCK CITY *Golf CDSHOLE 48*	57 1

LESTER – See Norman COOK

Ketty LESTER *US, female vocalist – Revoyda Frierson (16 WEEKS)*

		pos/wks
19 Apr 62 ●	LOVE LETTERS *London HLN 9527*	4 12
19 Jul 62	BUT NOT FOR ME *London HLN 9574*	45 4

LET LOOSE *UK, male vocal / instrumental group (62 WEEKS)*

		pos/wks
24 Apr 93	CRAZY FOR YOU *Vertigo VERCD 74*	44 3
9 Apr 94	SEVENTEEN *Mercury MERCD 400*	44 2
25 Jun 94 ●	CRAZY FOR YOU (re-issue) (re) *Mercury MERCD 402*	2 24
22 Oct 94	SEVENTEEN (re-mix) (re) *Mercury MERCD 406*	11 9
28 Jan 95	ONE NIGHT STAND *Mercury MERCD 419*	12 6
29 Apr 95 ●	BEST IN ME *Mercury MERCD 428*	8 5
4 Nov 95	EVERYBODY SAY EVERYBODY DO (re) *Mercury MERCD 446*	29 4
22 Jun 96 ●	MAKE IT WITH YOU *Mercury MERCD 464*	7 6
7 Sep 96	TAKE IT EASY *Mercury MERCD 472*	25 2
16 Nov 96	DARLING BE HOME SOON *Mercury MERCD 475*	65 1

Gerald LETHAN – See WALL OF SOUND featuring Gerald LETHAN

LETTERMEN *US, male vocal group (3 WEEKS)*

		pos/wks
23 Nov 61	THE WAY YOU LOOK TONIGHT *Capitol CL 15222*	36 3

LEVEL 42 113 `Top 500`

Critically acclaimed Isle of Wight / Hong Kong / London band: Mark King (v/b), Boon Gould (g), Mike Lindup (k/v), Phil Gould (d). Boasting a world-class bass player in King, they went from Brit-funk cult heroes to international stardom (177 WEEKS)

		pos/wks
30 Aug 80	LOVE MEETING LOVE *Polydor POSP 170*	61 4
18 Apr 81	LOVE GAMES *Polydor POSP 234*	38 6
8 Aug 81	TURN IT ON *Polydor POSP 286*	57 6
14 Nov 81	STARCHILD *Polydor POSP 343*	47 4
8 May 82	ARE YOU HEARING (WHAT I HEAR?) *Polydor POSP 396*	49 5
2 Oct 82	WEAVE YOUR SPELL *Polydor POSP 500*	43 4
15 Jan 83	THE CHINESE WAY *Polydor POSP 538*	24 8
16 Apr 83	OUT OF SIGHT, OUT OF MIND *Polydor POSP 570*	41 4
30 Jul 83 ●	THE SUN GOES DOWN (LIVING IT UP) *Polydor POSP 622*	10 12
22 Oct 83	MICRO KID *Polydor POSP 643*	37 5
1 Sep 84	HOT WATER *Polydor POSP 697*	18 9
3 Nov 84	THE CHANT HAS BEGUN *Polydor POSP 710*	41 5
21 Sep 85 ●	SOMETHING ABOUT YOU *Polydor POSP 759*	6 17
7 Dec 85	LEAVING ME NOW *Polydor POSP 776*	15 11
26 Apr 86 ●	LESSONS IN LOVE *Polydor POSP 790*	3 13
14 Feb 87 ●	RUNNING IN THE FAMILY *Polydor POSP 842*	6 10
25 Apr 87 ●	TO BE WITH YOU AGAIN *Polydor POSP 855*	10 7
12 Sep 87 ●	IT'S OVER *Polydor POSP 900*	10 8
12 Dec 87	CHILDREN SAY *Polydor POSP 911*	22 6
3 Sep 88	HEAVEN IN MY HANDS *Polydor PO 14*	12 5
29 Oct 88	TAKE A LOOK *Polydor PO 24*	32 4
21 Jan 89	TRACIE *Polydor PO 34*	25 5

28 Oct 89	TAKE CARE OF YOURSELF *Polydor PO 58*	39	3
17 Aug 91	GUARANTEED *RCA PB 44745*	17	4
19 Oct 91	OVERTIME *RCA PB 44997*	62	2
18 Apr 92	MY FATHER'S SHOES *RCA PB 45271*	55	1
26 Feb 94	FOREVER NOW *RCA 74321190272*	19	4
30 Apr 94	ALL OVER YOU *RCA 74321205662*	26	4
6 Aug 94	LOVE IN A PEACEFUL WORLD *RCA 74321220332*	31	3

LEVELLERS *UK, male vocal / instrumental group (57 WEEKS)* pos/wks

21 Sep 91	ONE WAY *China WOK 2008*	51	2
7 Dec 91	FAR FROM HOME *China WOK 2010*	71	1
23 May 92	15 YEARS (EP) *China WOKX 2020*	11	5
10 Jul 93	BELARUSE *China WOKCD 2034*	12	5
30 Oct 93	THIS GARDEN *China WOKCD 2039*	12	4
14 May 94	JULIE (EP) *China WOKCD 2042*	17	3
12 Aug 95	HOPE ST *China WOKCD 2059*	12	5
14 Oct 95	FANTASY *China WOKCD 2067*	16	3
23 Dec 95	JUST THE ONE *China WOKCD 2076* [1]	12	8
20 Jul 96	EXODUS – LIVE *China WOKCD 2082*	24	2
9 Aug 97	WHAT A BEAUTIFUL DAY *China WOKCD 2088*	13	5
18 Oct 97	CELEBRATE *China WOKCD 2089*	28	2
20 Dec 97	DOG TRAIN *China WOKCD 2090*	24	5
14 Mar 98	TOO REAL *China WOKCD 2091*	46	1
24 Oct 98	BOZOS *China WOKCD 2096*	44	2
6 Feb 99	ONE WAY (re-recording) *China WOKCD 2102*	33	2
9 Sep 00	HAPPY BIRTHDAY REVOLUTION *China EW218CD*	57	1
21 Sep 02	COME ON *Eagle / Hag EHAGXS 001*	44	1

[1] Levellers, special guest Joe Strummer

Tracks on 15 Years (EP): 15 Years / Dance Before the Storm / The River Flow (Live) / Plastic Jeezus. Tracks on Julie (EP): Julie / English Civil War / Lowlands of Holland / 100 Years of Solitude

LEVERT *US, male vocal group (10 WEEKS)* pos/wks

| 22 Aug 87 | ● CASANOVA *Atlantic A 9217* | 9 | 10 |

LEVERT SWEAT GILL *US, male vocal group (7 WEEKS)* pos/wks

14 Mar 98	MY BODY *East West E 3857CD*	21	3
6 Jun 98	CURIOUS *East West E 3842CD*	23	2
12 Sep 98	DOOR #1 *East West E 3817CD*	45	2

Hank LEVINE *US, orchestra (4 WEEKS)* pos/wks

| 21 Dec 61 | IMAGE *HMV POP 947* | 45 | 4 |

LEVITICUS *UK, male producer (1 WEEK)* pos/wks

| 25 Mar 95 | BURIAL *ffrr FCD 255* | 66 | 1 |

Barrington LEVY *Jamaica, male vocalist (13 WEEKS)* pos/wks

2 Feb 85	HERE I COME *London LON 62*	41	4
15 Jun 91	TRIBAL BASE *Desire WANT 44* [1]	20	6
24 Sep 94	WORK *MCA MCSTD 2003*	65	1
13 Oct 01	HERE I COME (SING DJ) *Nulife / Arista 74321895622* [2]	37	2

[1] Rebel MC featuring Tenor Fly and Barrington Levy [2] Talisman P featuring Barrington Levy

Here I Come (Sing DJ) is a re-recording of Here I Come

Jona LEWIE *UK, male vocalist – John Lewis (20 WEEKS)* pos/wks

| 10 May 80 | YOU'LL ALWAYS FIND ME IN THE KITCHEN AT PARTIES *Stiff BUY 73* | 16 | 9 |
| 29 Nov 80 | ● STOP THE CAVALRY *Stiff BUY 104* | 3 | 11 |

On some copies first title was simply 'Kitchen at Parties'

See also Terry DACTYL and the DINOSAURS

CJ LEWIS *UK, male vocalist (32 WEEKS)* pos/wks

23 Apr 94	● SWEETS FOR MY SWEET *Black Market BMITD 017*	3	13
23 Jul 94	● EVERYTHING IS ALRIGHT (UPTIGHT) *Black Market BMITD 019*	10	7
8 Oct 94	BEST OF MY LOVE *Black Market BMITD 021*	13	6
17 Dec 94	DOLLARS *Black Market BMITD 023*	34	4
9 Sep 95	R TO THE A *Black Market BMITD 030*	34	2

Danny J LEWIS *UK, male producer (2 WEEKS)* pos/wks

| 20 Jun 98 | SPEND THE NIGHT *Locked On LOX 98CD* | 29 | 2 |

Darlene LEWIS *US, female vocalist (4 WEEKS)* pos/wks

| 16 Apr 94 | LET THE MUSIC (LIFT YOU UP) *KMS / Eastern Bloc KMSCD 10* | 16 | 4 |

All formats of 'Let the Music Lift You Up' featured versions by Loveland featuring Rachel McFarlane and also by Darlene Lewis

Dee LEWIS *UK, female vocalist (5 WEEKS)* pos/wks

| 18 Jun 88 | BEST OF MY LOVE *Mercury DEE 3* | 47 | 5 |

Donna LEWIS *UK, female vocalist (16 WEEKS)* pos/wks

| 7 Sep 96 | ● I LOVE YOU ALWAYS FOREVER *Atlantic A 5495CD* | 5 | 14 |
| 8 Feb 97 | WITHOUT LOVE *Atlantic A 5468CD* | 39 | 2 |

Gary LEWIS and the PLAYBOYS *US, male vocal / instrumental group, leader – Gary Levitch (7 WEEKS)* pos/wks

| 8 Feb 75 | MY HEART'S SYMPHONY *United Artists UP 35780* | 36 | 7 |

Huey LEWIS and the NEWS
US, male vocal / instrumental group (66 WEEKS) pos/wks

27 Oct 84	IF THIS IS IT *Chrysalis CHS 2803*	39	6
31 Aug 85	THE POWER OF LOVE *Chrysalis HUEY 1* ▲	11	10
23 Nov 85	HEART AND SOUL (EP) *Chrysalis HUEY 2*	61	4
8 Feb 86	● THE POWER OF LOVE / DO YOU BELIEVE IN LOVE (re-issue) *Chrysalis HUEY 3*	9	12
10 May 86	THE HEART OF ROCK AND ROLL *Chrysalis HUEY 4*	49	3
23 Aug 86	STUCK WITH YOU *Chrysalis HUEY 5* ▲	12	12
6 Dec 86	HIP TO BE SQUARE *Chrysalis HUEY 6*	41	8
21 Mar 87	SIMPLE AS THAT *Chrysalis HUEY 7*	47	5
16 Jul 88	PERFECT WORLD *Chrysalis HUEY 10*	48	6

Tracks on Heart and Soul (EP): Heart and Soul / Hope You Love Me Like You Say You Do / Heart of Rock and Roll / Buzz Buzz Buzz. 'Do You Believe in Love' listed only from 15 Feb 1986

Jerry LEWIS
US, male actor / vocalist – Joseph Levitch (8 WEEKS) pos/wks

| 8 Feb 57 | ROCK-A-BYE YOUR BABY WITH A DIXIE MELODY (re) *Brunswick 05636* | 12 | 8 |

Jerry Lee LEWIS *US, male vocalist (68 WEEKS)* pos/wks

27 Sep 57	● WHOLE LOTTA SHAKIN' GOIN' ON (re) *London HLS 8457*	8	11
20 Dec 57	★ GREAT BALLS OF FIRE *London HLS 8529*	1	12
11 Apr 58	● BREATHLESS *London HLS 8592*	8	7
23 Jan 59	HIGH SCHOOL CONFIDENTIAL *London HLS 8780*	12	6
1 May 59	LOVIN' UP A STORM *London HLS 8840*	28	1
9 Jun 60	BABY, BABY, BYE BYE *London HLS 9131*	47	1
4 May 61	● WHAT'D I SAY (re) *London HLS 9335*	10	14
6 Sep 62	SWEET LITTLE SIXTEEN *London HLS 9584*	38	5
14 Mar 63	GOOD GOLLY MISS MOLLY *London HLS 9688*	31	6
6 May 72	CHANTILLY LACE *Mercury 6052 141*	33	5

Linda LEWIS *UK, female vocalist (31 WEEKS)* pos/wks

2 Jun 73	ROCK-A-DOODLE-DOO *Raft RA 18502*	15	11
12 Jul 75	● IT'S IN HIS KISS *Arista 17*	6	6
17 Apr 76	BABY I'M YOURS *Arista 43*	33	6
2 Jun 79	I'D BE SURPRISINGLY GOOD FOR YOU *Ariola ARO 166*	40	5
19 Aug 00	REACH OUT *Skint SKINT 54CD* [1]	61	1

[1] Midfield General featuring Linda Lewis

Ramsey LEWIS
US, male instrumentalist – piano (8 WEEKS) pos/wks

| 15 Apr 72 | WADE IN THE WATER *Chess 6145 004* | 31 | 8 |

Shirley LEWIS – See Arthur BAKER

John LEYTON UK male vocalist / actor (70 WEEKS)
pos/wks

3 Aug 61 ★	JOHNNY REMEMBER ME *Top Rank JAR 577*	1	15
5 Oct 61 ●	WILD WIND *Top Rank JAR 585*	2	10
28 Dec 61	SON THIS IS SHE *HMV POP 956*	15	10
15 Mar 62	LONE RIDER *HMV POP 992*	40	5
3 May 62	LONELY CITY *HMV POP 1014*	14	11
23 Aug 62	DOWN THE RIVER NILE *HMV POP 1054*	42	3
21 Feb 63	CUPBOARD LOVE *HMV POP 1122*	22	12
18 Jul 63	I'LL CUT YOUR TAIL OFF (re) *HMV POP 1175*	36	3
20 Feb 64	MAKE LOVE TO ME *HMV POP 1264* [1]	49	1

[1] John Leyton and the LeRoys

LEYTON BUZZARDS UK, male vocal / instrumental group (5 WEEKS)
pos/wks

3 Mar 79	SATURDAY NIGHT (BENEATH THE PLASTIC PALM TREES) *Chrysalis CHS 2288*	53	5

LIBERACE US, male instrumentalist – piano
(Wladziu Valentino Liberace) d. 4 Feb 1987 (2 WEEKS)
pos/wks

17 Jun 55	UNCHAINED MELODY *Philips PB 430*	20	1
19 Oct 56	I DON'T CARE (AS LONG AS YOU CARE FOR ME) *Columbia DB 3834*	28	1

'I Don't Care' featured Liberace as vocalist too

LIBERATION UK, male instrumental / production
duo – William Linch and David Cooper (3 WEEKS)
pos/wks

24 Oct 92	LIBERATION *ZYX ZYX 68657*	28	3

The LIBERTINES UK, male vocal / instrumental group (4 WEEKS)
pos/wks

15 Jun 02	WHAT A WASTER *Rough Trade RTRADESCD 054*	37	2
12 Oct 02	UP THE BRACKET *Rough Trade RTRADESCD 064*	29	2

LIBERTY X UK, male / female vocal group (45 WEEKS)
pos/wks

6 Oct 01 ●	THINKING IT OVER *V2 VVR 5017773* [1]	5	8
15 Dec 01 ●	DOIN' IT *V2 VVR 5017793* [1]	14	6
25 May 02 ★	JUST A LITTLE *V2 VVR 5018963* ■	1	16
21 Sep 02 ●	GOT TO HAVE YOUR LOVE *V2 VVR 5020503*	2	12
14 Dec 02 ●	HOLDING ON FOR YOU *V2 VVR 5020763*	5	3+

[1] Liberty

LIBIDO Norway, male vocal / instrumental group (1 WEEK)
pos/wks

31 Jan 98	OVERTHROWN *Fire BLAZE 119CD*	53	1

LIBRA presents TAYLOR
US, male / female production / vocal trio (3 WEEKS)
pos/wks

26 Oct 96	ANOMALY – CALLING YOUR NAME *Platipus PLATCD 24*	71	1
18 Mar 00	ANOMALY – CALLING YOUR NAME (re-mix) *Platipus PLATCD 56*	43	2

LICK THE TINS
UK, male / female vocal / instrumental group (8 WEEKS)
pos/wks

29 Mar 86	CAN'T HELP FALLING IN LOVE *Sedition EDIT 3308*	42	8

Oliver LIEB presents SMOKED
Germany, male producer (1 WEEK)
pos/wks

30 Sep 00	METROPOLIS *Duty Free DF 019CD*	72	1

See also LSG

Ben LIEBRAND
Holland, male DJ / producer (2 WEEKS)
pos/wks

9 Jun 90	PULS(T)AR *Epic LIEB 1*	68	2

LIEUTENANT PIGEON
UK, male / female instrumental group (29 WEEKS)
pos/wks

16 Sep 72 ★	MOULDY OLD DOUGH *Decca F 13278*	1	19
16 Dec 72	DESPERATE DAN *Decca F 13365*	17	10

LIFEHOUSE US, male vocal / instrumental group (4 WEEKS)
pos/wks

8 Sep 01	HANGING BY A MOMENT *Dreamworks / Polydor 4975612*	25	4

LIFFORD – See ARTFUL DODGER

LIGHT OF THE WORLD
UK, male vocal / instrumental group (25 WEEKS)
pos/wks

14 Apr 79	SWINGIN' *Ensign ENY 22*	45	5
14 Jul 79	MIDNIGHT GROOVIN' *Ensign ENY 29*	72	1
18 Oct 80	LONDON TOWN *Ensign ENY 43*	41	5
17 Jan 81	I SHOT THE SHERIFF *Ensign ENY 46*	40	5
28 Mar 81	I'M SO HAPPY / TIME *Ensign MER 64*	35	6
21 Nov 81	RIDE THE LOVE TRAIN *EMI 5242*	49	3

LIGHTER SHADE OF BROWN US, male vocal duo (3 WEEKS)
pos/wks

9 Jul 94	HEY DJ *Mercury MERCD 401*	33	3

Gordon LIGHTFOOT Canada, male vocalist (26 WEEKS)
pos/wks

19 Jun 71	IF YOU COULD READ MY MIND *Reprise RS 20974*	30	9
3 Aug 74	SUNDOWN *Reprise K 14327* ▲	33	7
15 Jan 77	THE WRECK OF THE EDMUND FITZGERALD *Reprise K 14451*	40	4
16 Sep 78	DAYLIGHT KATY *Warner Bros. K 17214*	41	6

Terry LIGHTFOOT'S NEW ORLEANS JAZZMEN
UK, vocalist / instrumentalist – clarinet – and male band (17 WEEKS)
pos/wks

7 Sep 61	TRUE LOVE *Columbia DB 4696*	33	4
23 Nov 61	KING KONG *Columbia SCD 2165*	29	12
3 May 62	TAVERN IN THE TOWN *Columbia DB 4822*	49	1

LIGHTFORCE Germany, male production duo (1 WEEK)
pos/wks

28 Oct 00	JOIN ME *Slinky Music SLINKY 004CD*	53	1

LIGHTHOUSE FAMILY (371 Top 500)
Smooth, easy-on-the-ear pop / soul duo formed in Newcastle-upon-Tyne,
UK; Nigerian-born Tunde Baiyewu (v) and Londoner Paul Tucker (k). After
slow start, debut album 'Ocean Drive' (1995) sold more than 1.6 million in
UK and made a name for them in the rest of Europe (89 WEEKS)
pos/wks

27 May 95	LIFTED *Wild Card CARDW 17*	61	2
14 Oct 95	OCEAN DRIVE *Wild Card 5797072*	34	3
10 Feb 96 ●	LIFTED (re-issue) *Wild Card 5779432*	4	10
1 Jun 96	OCEAN DRIVE (re-issue) *Wild Card 5766192*	11	8
21 Sep 96	GOODBYE HEARTBREAK *Wild Card 5753492*	14	6
21 Dec 96	LOVING EVERY MINUTE *Wild Card 5731012*	20	7
11 Oct 97 ●	RAINCLOUD *Wild Card 5717932*	6	7
10 Jan 98 ●	HIGH *Polydor 5691492*	4	14
27 Jun 98 ●	LOST IN SPACE *Wild Card 5670592*	6	8
10 Oct 98	QUESTION OF FAITH *Wild Card 5673932*	21	5
9 Jan 99	POSTCARD FROM HEAVEN *Wild Card 5633952*	24	6
24 Nov 01 ●	(I WISH I KNEW HOW IT WOULD FEEL TO BE) FREE – ONE *Wild Card / Polydor 5873812*	6	9
9 Mar 02	RUN *Wild Card / Polydor 5705702*	30	3
6 Jul 02	HAPPY *Wild Card / Polydor 5707902*	51	1

LIGHTNING SEEDS (291 Top 500)
Conceived as a 'perfect pop' studio project by producer and group veteran
Ian Broudie (v/g) 4 Aug 1958, Liverpool, UK. England's most popular
footballing anthem, 'Three Lions', became the first song to top the charts
twice with different lyrics (104 WEEKS)
pos/wks

22 Jul 89	PURE *Ghetto GTG 4*	16	8
14 Mar 92	THE LIFE OF RILEY *Virgin VS 1402*	28	8
30 May 92	SENSE *Virgin VS 1414*	31	5
20 Aug 94	LUCKY YOU *Epic 6606282*	43	2
14 Jan 95	CHANGE *Epic 6609865*	13	6

HEARTBREAK HOTEL

■ One of the most important days in popular music history was Tuesday 10 January 1956, the day Elvis Aaron Presley first recorded for RCA at their Nashville studios. Chet Atkins was in attendance at that legendary session, together with Elvis's regular group, Scotty Moore on guitar, Bill Black on bass and drummer DJ Fontana, with the addition of Floyd Cramer on piano. Steve Sholes, who was to oversee the session, had no idea how it would turn out, and RCA's engineers had admitted that they were mystified as to how Sam Phillips had created Elvis's trademark sound previously at Sun's studios.

The picture raises the question, did Elvis ever sing in the shower?

He needn't have worried. The session was a classic, starting with Elvis hymn-singing as a studio warm-up before a performance that resulted in ripped trousers and bleeding fingers from his high-energy guitar playing. Even Chet Atkins, who'd seen it all before, called his wife up and told her to get down to the studio right away. "I told her she'd never see anything like this again. It was just so damned exciting!" Among the songs recorded on the session was 'Heartbreak Hotel'. Elvis had first been presented with the song by one of its writers, Mae Axton, at a DJ convention the previous November, and liking the song immediately had promised to record it as his next single. Rockabilly singer Glen Glenn, who demoed the song for Elvis the way he imagined he would do it, said of the composition, "It was the silliest song I ever heard."

Axton wrote the song watched by her 17-year-old son Hoyt, after co-writer Tommy Durden showed her a newspaper article about a suicide. The victim had left a one-line suicide note: "I walk a lonely street." Axton suggested they place a "Heartbreak Hotel" at the end of this lonely street, and the two wrote the rest of the song in half an hour. In order to persuade Presley to

■ MAE AXTON WROTE THE SONG AFTER CO-WRITER TOMMY DURDEN SHOWED HER A NEWSPAPER ARTICLE ABOUT A SUICIDE ■

record the song, Axton had offered to give him a co-writing credit, and thus a cut of the royalties. This was a common practice in the 1950s whereby major artists were offered writing credits in return for recording a song, and it may well often have been a demand by record companies or managers as a condition of recording. Elvis Presley is credited as co-writer of several of his hits and made these songs famous, but he had nothing whatsoever to do with their writing.

When Steve Sholes presented the results of his first session with Elvis to the powers that be at RCA in New York, they were not impressed, telling him he had nothing worth releasing and had better get back in the studio again as soon as possible. The next session included a version of 'Blue Suede Shoes' (which Sholes had previously promised Sam Phillips that Elvis would not record). However, in the absence of anything better, RCA reluctantly released 'Heartbreak Hotel', which Phillips described as a "morbid mess". The record took five weeks to make the US chart, and a further six weeks to hit US No.1, where it remained for eight weeks. "The King" had arrived.

■ Tony Burton / Dave McAleer

★ ARTIST:	Elvis Presley
★ LABEL:	RCA USA/HMV UK
★ WRITERS:	Mae Axton, Tommy Durden and Elvis Presley
★ PRODUCER:	Steve Sholes

15 Apr 95	MARVELLOUS *Epic 6614265*....................	24	5
22 Jul 95	PERFECT *Epic 6621792*	18	5
21 Oct 95	LUCKY YOU (re-issue) *Epic 6625182*	15	6
9 Mar 96	READY OR NOT *Epic 6629672*	20	4
1 Jun 96	★ THREE LIONS (THE OFFICIAL SONG OF THE ENGLAND FOOTBALL TEAM) *Epic 6632732* [1] ■	1	15
2 Nov 96	WHAT IF... (re) *Epic 6638635*................	14	4
18 Jan 97	SUGAR COATED ICEBERG *Epic 6640432*.......	12	4
26 Apr 97	● YOU SHOWED ME *Epic 6643282*.............	8	5
13 Dec 97	WHAT YOU SAY *Epic 6653572*...............	41	5
20 Jun 98	★ THREE LIONS '98 *Epic 6660982* [1] ■	1	13
27 Nov 99	LIFE'S TOO SHORT (re) *Epic 6681502*.........	27	4
18 Mar 00	SWEETEST SOUL SENSATIONS *Epic 6689422*...	67	1
15 Jun 02	THREE LIONS '98 (re-issue) (re) *Epic 6728152* [2]	16	6

[1] Baddiel and Skinner and The Lightning Seeds [2] Baddiel, Skinner and The Lightning Seeds

LIL BOW WOW *US, male rapper – Rashad Moss (9 WEEKS)* pos/wks

14 Apr 01	● BOW WOW (THAT'S MY NAME) *So So Def / Columbia 6709832*...............	6	9

LIL' DEVIOUS *UK, male production duo (1 WEEK)* pos/wks

15 Sep 01	COME HOME *Rulin RULIN 16CDS*	55	1

LIL' KIM *US, female vocalist – Kimberly Jones (40 WEEKS)* pos/wks

26 Apr 97	NO TIME *Atlantic A 5594CD* [1]	45	1
5 Jul 97	CRUSH ON YOU (re) *Atlantic AT 0002CD*........	23	5
16 Aug 97	NOT TONIGHT *Atlantic AT 0007CD*	11	5
22 Aug 97	HIT 'EM WIT DA HEE *East West E3824 CD1* [2] ...	25	3
5 Feb 00	NOTORIOUS B.I.G. *Puff Daddy / Arista 747321737312* [3]	16	5
2 Sep 00	NO MATTER WHAT THEY SAY *Atlantic 7567846972*...	35	2
30 Jun 01	★ LADY MARMALADE *Interscope / Polydor 4975612* [4] ■ ▲	1	16
11 Aug 01	WAIT A MINUTE *Atlantic AT 0106CD* [5]	54	1
22 Sep 01	IN THE AIR TONITE *WEA WEA 331CD* [6]	26	2

[1] Lil' Kim featuring Puff Daddy [2] Missy 'Misdemeanor' Elliott featuring Lil' Kim [3] Notorious B.I.G. featuring Puff Daddy and Lil' Kim [4] Christina Aguilera, Lil' Kim, Mya and Pink [5] Ray J featuring Lil' Kim [6] Lil' Kim featuring Phil Collins

LIL' LOUIS
US, male producer – Marvin Burns (21 WEEKS)

29 Jul 89	● FRENCH KISS *ffrr FX 115*.................	2	11
13 Jan 90	I CALLED U *ffrr F 123*	16	6
26 Sep 92	SAVED MY LIFE *ffrr FX 197* [1]	74	1
12 Aug 00	HOW'S YOUR EVENING SO FAR *ffrr FCD 384* [2]	23	3

[1] Lil' Louis and the World [2] Josh Wink and Lil' Louis

See also BLACK MAGIC

LIL' MISS MAX – See BLUE ADONIS featuring LIL' MISS MAX

LIL' MO *US, female vocalist – Cynthia Long (6 WEEKS)* pos/wks

21 Nov 98	5 MINUTES *Elektra E 3803CD* [1]	72	1
23 Sep 00	WHATEVER *Virgin VUSCD 172* [2]	31	3
6 Apr 02	WHERE'S MY...? *EMI CDEMS 598* [3]	37	2

[1] Lil' Mo featuring Missy 'Misdemeanor' Elliott [2] Ideal U.S. featuring Lil' Mo [3] Adam F featuring Lil' Mo

LIL' MO' YIN YANG *US, male instrumental / production duo – Erick 'More' Morillo and 'Lil' Louis Vega (2 WEEKS)* pos/wks

9 Mar 96	REACH *Multiply CDMULTY 9*.................	28	2

See also Erick 'More' MORILLO presents RAW; REEL 2 REAL; PIANOHEADZ

LIL' ROMEO *US, male rapper (1 WEEK)* pos/wks

22 Sep 01	MY BABY *Priority PTYCD 136*...............	67	1

LILY – See MAXIMA featuring LILY

LILYS *US, male vocal / instrumental group (4 WEEKS)* pos/wks

21 Feb 98	A NANNY IN MANHATTAN *Che CHE 77CD*.......	16	4

LIMA – See Tom NOVY

LIMAHL *UK, male vocalist – Chris Hamill (25 WEEKS)* pos/wks

5 Nov 83	ONLY FOR LOVE (re) *EMI LML 1*	16	8
2 Jun 84	TOO MUCH TROUBLE *EMI LML 2*.............	64	3
13 Oct 84	● NEVER ENDING STORY *EMI LML 3*	4	14

See also KAJAGOOGOO

Alison LIMERICK *UK, female vocalist (39 WEEKS)* pos/wks

30 Mar 91	WHERE LOVE LIVES *Arista 144208*	27	8
12 Oct 91	COME BACK (FOR REAL LOVE) *Arista 114530*....	53	2
21 Dec 91	MAGIC'S BACK (THEME FROM 'THE GHOSTS OF OXFORD STREET') *RCA PB 45223* [1]	42	4
29 Feb 92	MAKE IT ON MY OWN *Arista 114996*.........	16	6
18 Jul 92	GETTIN' IT RIGHT *Arista 74321102867*.......	57	2
28 Nov 92	HEAR MY CALL *Arista 115337*..............	73	1
8 Jan 94	TIME OF OUR LIVES *Arista 74321180332*......	36	4
19 Mar 94	LOVE COME DOWN *Arista 74321191952*......	36	2
25 Feb 95	LOVE WILL KEEP US TOGETHER *Acid Jazz JAZID 112CD* [2] ..	63	1
6 Jul 96	● WHERE LOVE LIVES (re-mix) *Arista 74321381592* ...	9	6
14 Sep 96	MAKE IT ON MY OWN (re-mix) *Arista 74321407812* ..	30	2
23 Aug 97	PUT YOUR FAITH IN ME *MBA XES 9001*	42	1

[1] Malcolm McLaren featuring Alison Limerick [2] JTQ featuring Alison Limerick

LIMIT *Holland, male vocal / instrumental duo – Bernard Oates and Rob van Schaik (8 WEEKS)* pos/wks

5 Jan 85	SAY YEAH *Portrait A 4808*.................	17	8

LIMMIE and the FAMILY COOKIN'
US, male / female vocal group (28 WEEKS)

21 Jul 73	● YOU CAN DO MAGIC *Avco 6105 019*........	3	13
20 Oct 73	DREAMBOAT *Avco 6105 025*...............	31	5
6 Apr 74	● A WALKIN' MIRACLE *Avco 6105 027*........	6	10

LIMP BIZKIT *US, male vocal / instrumental group (49 WEEKS)* pos/wks

15 Jul 00	● TAKE A LOOK AROUND (THEME FROM 'MI:2') *Interscope 4973682*...................	3	13
11 Nov 00	MY GENERATION (re) *Interscope IND 97448* ...	15	8
27 Jan 01	★ ROLLIN' *Interscope IND 97474* ■	1	13
23 Jun 01	MY WAY *Interscope 4975732*	6	10
10 Nov 01	BOILER *Interscope 4976362*...............	18	5

LINA *US, female vocalist (1 WEEK)* pos/wks

3 Mar 01	PLAYA NO MO' *Atlantic AT 0094CD*..........	46	1

LINCOLN CITY F.C. featuring Michael COURTNEY
UK, male football team and male vocalist (1 WEEK) pos/wks

4 May 02	CHIRPY CHIRPY CHEEP CHEEP / JAGGED END *Nap Music SLCPD 0001*	64	1

Bob LIND *US, male vocalist (10 WEEKS)* pos/wks

10 Mar 66	● ELUSIVE BUTTERFLY *Fontana TF 670*	5	9
26 May 66	REMEMBER THE RAIN *Fontana TF 702*........	46	1

LINDA and the FUNKY BOYS – See Linda CARR

LINDISFARNE *UK, male vocal / instrumental group (55 WEEKS)* pos/wks

26 Feb 72	● MEET ME ON THE CORNER *Charisma CB 173* ...	5	11
13 May 72	● LADY ELEANOR *Charisma CB 153*	3	11
23 Sep 72	ALL FALL DOWN *Charisma CB 191*	34	5
3 Jun 78	● RUN FOR HOME *Mercury 6007 177*.........	10	15
7 Oct 78	JUKE BOX GYPSY *Mercury 6007 187*.........	56	4
10 Nov 90	● FOG ON THE TYNE (REVISITED) *Best ZB 44083* [1] ..	2	9

[1] Gazza and Lindisfarne

LINDSAY UK, female vocalist (4 WEEKS) — pos/wks

		pos	wks
12 May 01	NO DREAM IMPOSSIBLE *Universal TV 1589562*	32	4

LINER UK, male vocal / instrumental group (6 WEEKS) — pos/wks

		pos	wks
10 Mar 79	KEEP REACHING OUT FOR LOVE *Atlantic K 11235*	49	3
26 May 79	YOU AND ME *Atlantic K 11285*	44	3

Andy LING UK, male producer (1 WEEK) — pos/wks

		pos	wks
13 May 00	FIXATION *Hooj Choons HOOJ 094CD*	55	1

Laurie LINGO and the DIPSTICKS UK, male DJ / vocal duo – Dave Lee Travis and Paul Burnett (7 WEEKS) — pos/wks

		pos	wks
17 Apr 76 ●	CONVOY GB *State STAT 23*	4	7

LINK US, male rapper (1 WEEK) — pos/wks

		pos	wks
7 Nov 98	WHATCHA GONE DO? *Relativity 6666055*	48	1

LINKIN PARK US, male vocal / instrumental group (33 WEEKS) — pos/wks

		pos	wks
27 Jan 01	ONE STEP CLOSER *Warner Brothers W 550CD*	24	4
21 Apr 01	CRAWLING *Warner Brothers W 556CD*	16	8
30 Jun 01	PAPERCUT *Warner Brothers W 562CD*	14	6
20 Oct 01 ●	IN THE END *Warner Brothers W 569CD*	8	9
3 Aug 02 ●	H! VLTG3 / PTS.OF.ATHRTY *Warner Brothers W 588CD*	9	6

LINOLEUM UK, male / female vocal / instrumental group (1 WEEK) pos/wks

		pos	wks
12 Jul 97	MARQUIS *Lino Vinyl LINO 004CD1*	73	1

LINX UK, male vocal / instrumental duo – David Grant and Peter Martin (45 WEEKS) — pos/wks

		pos	wks
20 Sep 80	YOU'RE LYING *Chrysalis CHS 2461*	15	10
7 Mar 81 ●	INTUITION *Chrysalis CHS 2500*	7	11
13 Jun 81	THROW AWAY THE KEY *Chrysalis CHS 2519*	21	9
5 Sep 81	SO THIS IS ROMANCE *Chrysalis CHS 2546*	15	9
21 Nov 81	CAN'T HELP MYSELF *Chrysalis CHS 2565*	55	3
10 Jul 82	PLAYTHING *Chrysalis CHS 2621*	48	3

LIONROCK UK, male producer – Justin Robertson (14 WEEKS) — pos/wks

		pos	wks
5 Dec 92	LIONROCK *Deconstruction 74321124381*	63	1
8 May 93	PACKET OF PEACE *Deconstruction 74321144372*	32	3
23 Oct 93	CARNIVAL *Deconstruction 74321164862*	34	2
27 Aug 94	TRIPWIRE *Deconstruction 74321204702*	44	1
6 Apr 96	STRAIGHT AT YER HEAD *Deconstruction 74321342972*	33	2
27 Jul 96	FIRE UP THE SHOESAW *Deconstruction 74321382652*	43	1
14 Mar 98	RUDE BOY ROCK *Concrete HARD 31CD*	20	3
30 May 98	SCATTER & SWING *Concrete HARD 35CD*	54	1

LIPPS INC US, male / female vocal / instrumental group (13 WEEKS) — pos/wks

		pos	wks
17 May 80 ●	FUNKYTOWN *Casablanca CAN 194* ▲	2	13

LIQUID UK, male producer – Eamon Downes (20 WEEKS) — pos/wks

		pos	wks
21 Mar 92	SWEET HARMONY *XL Recordings XLS 28*	15	6
5 Sep 92	THE FUTURE MUSIC (EP) *XL Recordings XLT 33*	59	2
20 Mar 93	TIME TO GET UP *XL Recordings XLS 40CD*	46	2
8 Jul 95	SWEET HARMONY (re-mix) / ONE LOVE FAMILY *XL Recordings XLS 65CD*	14	6
21 Oct 95	CLOSER *XL Recordings XLS 66CD*	47	2
25 Jul 98	STRONG *Higher Ground HIGHS 7CD*	59	1
21 Oct 00	ORLANDO DAWN *Xtravaganza XTRAV 16CDS*	53	1

Tracks on The Future Music (EP): Liquid Is Liquid / Music / House (Is a Feeling) / The Year 3000. On the first two hits act also included Shane Heneghan

LIQUID CHILD Germany, male production duo – Tobias Menguser and Jürgen Herbarth (2 WEEKS) — pos/wks

		pos	wks
23 Oct 99	DIVING FACES *Essential Recordings ESCD 9*	25	2

LIQUID GOLD UK, male / female vocal / instrumental group (46 WEEKS) — pos/wks

		pos	wks
2 Dec 78	ANYWAY YOU DO IT *Creole CR 159*	41	7
23 Feb 80 ●	DANCE YOURSELF DIZZY *Polo POLO 1*	2	14
31 May 80 ●	SUBSTITUTE *Polo POLO 4*	8	9
1 Nov 80	THE NIGHT THE WINE AND THE ROSES *Polo 6*	32	7
28 Mar 81	DON'T PANIC *Polo POLO 8*	42	5
21 Aug 82	WHERE DID WE GO WRONG *Polo POLO 23*	56	4

LIQUID OXYGEN US, male producer (2 WEEKS) — pos/wks

		pos	wks
28 Apr 90	THE PLANET DANCE (MOVE YA BODY) *Champion CHAMP 242*	56	2

LIQUID PEOPLE vs SIMPLE MINDS UK, male production duo and UK, male vocal / instrumental group (1 WEEK) — pos/wks

		pos	wks
20 Jul 02	MONSTER *Defected DFECT 49*	67	1

LIQUID STATE featuring Marcella WOODS UK, male production duo and female vocalist (1 WEEK) — pos/wks

		pos	wks
30 Mar 02	FALLING *Perfecto PERF 29CDS*	60	1

LISA LISA US, female vocalist – Lisa Velez (32 WEEKS) — pos/wks

		pos	wks
4 May 85	I WONDER IF I TAKE YOU HOME (re) *CBS A 6057* [1]	12	17
31 Oct 87	LOST IN EMOTION *CBS 651036 7* [2] ▲	58	4
13 Jul 91	LET THE BEAT HIT 'EM *Columbia 6572867* [2]	17	6
24 Aug 91	LET THE BEAT HIT 'EM PART 2 *Columbia 6573747* [2]	49	2
26 Mar 94	SKIP TO MY LU *Chrysalis CDCHS 5006*	34	3

[1] Lisa Lisa and Cult Jam with Full Force [2] Lisa Lisa and Cult Jam

LISA MARIE – See Malcolm McLAREN

LISA MARIE EXPERIENCE UK, male instrumental / production duo – Dean Marriot and Neil Hynde (15 WEEKS) — pos/wks

		pos	wks
27 Apr 96 ●	KEEP ON JUMPIN' (re) *ffrr FCD 271*	7	13
10 Aug 96	DO THAT TO ME *Positiva CDTIV 57*	33	2

LISBON LIONS featuring Martin O'NEILL & CELTIC CHORUS UK, male football supporters vocal group (4 WEEKS) — pos/wks

		pos	wks
11 May 02	THE BEST DAY OF OUR LIVES *Concept CDCON 32*	17	4

LIT US, male vocal / instrumental group (7 WEEKS) — pos/wks

		pos	wks
26 Jun 99	MY OWN WORST ENEMY *RCA 74321669992*	16	4
25 Sep 99	ZIP – LOCK *RCA 74321701852*	60	1
19 Aug 00	OVER MY HEAD *Capitol 8889532*	37	2

LITHIUM and Sonya MADAN US, male producer – Victor Imbres and UK, female vocalist (2 WEEKS) pos/wks

		pos	wks
1 Mar 97	RIDE A ROCKET *ffrr FCD 293*	40	2

See also ECHOBELLY

De Etta LITTLE and Nelson PIGFORD US, female / male vocal duo (5 WEEKS) — pos/wks

		pos	wks
13 Aug 77	YOU TAKE MY HEART AWAY *United Artists UP 36257*	35	5

LITTLE ANGELS UK, male vocal / instrumental group (41 WEEKS) pos/wks

		pos	wks
4 Mar 89	BIG BAD EP *Polydor LTLEP 2*	74	1
24 Feb 90	KICKING UP DUST *Polydor LTL 5*	46	4
12 May 90	RADICAL YOUR LOVER *Polydor LTL 6* [1]	34	4
4 Aug 90	SHE'S A LITTLE ANGEL *Polydor LTL 7*	21	3
2 Feb 91	BONEYARD *Polydor LTL 8*	33	4
30 Mar 91	PRODUCT OF THE WORKING CLASS *Polydor LTL 9*	40	2
1 Jun 91	YOUNG GODS *Polydor LTL 10*	34	2
20 Jul 91	I AIN'T GONNA CRY *Polydor LTL 11*	26	3
7 Nov 92	TOO MUCH TOO YOUNG *Polydor LTL 12*	22	3
9 Jan 93	WOMANKIND *Polydor LTLCD 13*	12	5
24 Apr 93	SOAPBOX *Polydor LTLCD 14*	33	4

25 Sep 93	**SAIL AWAY** *Polydor LTLCD 15*	....**45**	3
9 Apr 94	**TEN MILES HIGH** *Polydor LTLCD 16*	....**18**	3

[1] Little Angels featuring the Big Bad Horns

Tracks on Big Bad EP: She's a Little Angel / Don't Waste My Time / Better Than the Rest / Sex in Cars

LITTLE ANTHONY and the IMPERIALS
US, male vocal group (4 WEEKS) pos/wks

31 Jul 76	**BETTER USE YOUR HEAD** *United Artists UP 36141*	....**42**	4

LITTLE BENNY and the MASTERS *US, male rapper / instrumentalist – trumpet – and male instrumental group (7 WEEKS)* pos/wks

2 Feb 85	**WHO COMES TO BOOGIE** *Bluebird 10 BR 13*	....**33**	7

LITTLE CAESAR *UK, male vocalist (3 WEEKS)* pos/wks

9 Jun 90	**THE WHOLE OF THE MOON** *A1 EAU 1*	....**68**	3

LITTLE EVA *US, female vocalist – Eva Boyd (45 WEEKS)* pos/wks

6 Sep 62	● **THE LOCO-MOTION (re)** *London HL 9581* ▲	....**2**	28
3 Jan 63	**KEEP YOUR HANDS OFF MY BABY** *London HLU 9633*	....**30**	5
7 Mar 63	**LET'S TURKEY TROT** *London HLU 9687*	....**13**	12

'Loco-motion' re-entry peaked at No.11 in Jul 1972

See also Big Dee IRWIN

LITTLE LOUIE – See Louie VEGA

LITTLE MS MARCIE – See MELT featuring Little Ms MARCIE

LITTLE RICHARD (244) Top 500 *Frantic, no-holds-barred rock 'n' roll singer / songwriter and piano-pounder, b. Richard Penniman, 5 Dec 1932, Georgia, US. This legendary performer's wild vocals and unrestrained stage show influenced many later stars. Both The Beatles and The Rolling Stones supported him on tour (116 WEEKS)* pos/wks

14 Dec 56	**RIP IT UP** *London HLO 8336*	....**30**	1
8 Feb 57	● **LONG TALL SALLY** *London HLO 8366*	....**3**	16
22 Feb 57	**TUTTI FRUTTI** *London HLO 8366*	....**29**	1
8 Mar 57	**SHE'S GOT IT (re)** *London HLO 8382*	....**15**	9
15 Mar 57	● **THE GIRL CAN'T HELP IT** *London HLO 8382*	....**9**	11
28 Jun 57	● **LUCILLE** *London HLO 8446*	....**10**	9
13 Sep 57	**JENNY JENNY** *London HLO 8470*	....**11**	5
29 Nov 57	**KEEP A KNOCKIN'** *London HLO 8509*	....**21**	7
28 Feb 58	● **GOOD GOLLY MISS MOLLY** *London HLU 8560*	....**8**	9
11 Jul 58	**OOH! MY SOUL (re)** *London HLO 8647*	....**22**	4
2 Jan 59	● **BABY FACE** *London HLU 8770*	....**2**	15
3 Apr 59	**BY THE LIGHT OF THE SILVERY MOON** *London HLU 8831*	....**17**	5
5 Jun 59	**KANSAS CITY** *London HLU 8868*	....**26**	5
11 Oct 62	**HE GOT WHAT HE WANTED (BUT HE LOST WHAT HE HAD)** *Mercury AMT 1189*	....**38**	4
4 Jun 64	**BAMA LAMA BAMA LOO** *London HL 9896*	....**20**	7
2 Jul 77	**GOOD GOLLY MISS MOLLY / RIP IT UP** *Creole CR 140*	....**37**	4
14 Jun 86	**GREAT GOSH A'MIGHTY! (IT'S A MATTER OF TIME)** *MCA MCA 1049*	....**62**	2
25 Oct 86	**OPERATOR** *WEA YZ 89*	....**67**	2

The 1977 versions of 'Good Golly Miss Molly' and 'Rip It Up' on Creole are re-recordings

LITTLE STEVEN *US, male vocalist/instrumentalist – guitar (3 WKS)* pos/wks

23 May 87	**BITTER FRUIT** *Manhattan MT 21*	....**66**	3

LITTLE T – See REBEL MC

LITTLE TONY and his BROTHERS
Italy, male vocal group, leader – Anthony Ciacci (3 WEEKS) pos/wks

15 Jan 60	**TOO GOOD** *Decca F 11190*	....**19**	3

LITTLE TREES *Denmark, female vocal group (7 WEEKS)* pos/wks

1 Sep 01	**HELP! I'M A FISH** *RCA 74321874652*	....**11**	7

LIVE *US, male vocal / instrumental group (13 WEEKS)* pos/wks

18 Feb 95	**I ALONE** *Radioactive RAXTD 13*	....**48**	4
1 Jul 95	**SELLING THE DRAMA** *Radioactive RAXTD 17*	....**30**	2
7 Oct 95	**ALL OVER YOU** *Radioactive RAXTD 20*	....**48**	1
13 Jan 96	**LIGHTNING CRASHES** *Radioactive RAXTD 23*	....**33**	2
15 Mar 97	**LAKINI'S JUICE** *Radioactive RAD 49023*	....**29**	2
12 Jul 97	**FREAKS** *Radioactive RAXTD 29*	....**60**	1
5 Feb 00	**THE DOLPHIN'S CRY** *Radioactive RAXTD 39*	....**62**	1

LIVE ELEMENT *US, male production duo – Greg Bahary and Chris Malinchak (2 WEEKS)* pos/wks

26 Jan 02	**BE FREE** *Strictly Rhythm SRUKCD 11*	....**26**	2

LIVE REPORT
UK, male vocal / instrumental group (1 WEEK) pos/wks

20 May 89	**WHY DO I ALWAYS GET IT WRONG** *Brouhaha CUE 7*	....**73**	1

LIVERPOOL EXPRESS
UK, male vocal / instrumental group (26 WEEKS) pos/wks

26 Jun 76	**YOU ARE MY LOVE** *Warner Bros. K 16743*	....**11**	9
16 Oct 76	**HOLD TIGHT** *Warner Bros. K 16799*	....**46**	2
18 Dec 76	**EVERY MAN MUST HAVE A DREAM** *Warner Bros. K 16854*	....**17**	11
4 Jun 77	**DREAMIN'** *Warner Bros. K 16933*	....**40**	4

LIVERPOOL FC
UK, male football team vocalists (21 WEEKS) pos/wks

28 May 77	**WE CAN DO IT (EP)** *State STAT 50*	....**15**	4
23 Apr 83	**LIVERPOOL (WE'RE NEVER GONNA...) / LIVERPOOL (ANTHEM)** *Mean MEAN 102*	....**54**	4
17 May 86	**SITTING ON TOP OF THE WORLD** *Columbia DB 9116*	....**50**	2
14 May 88	● **ANFIELD RAP (RED MACHINE IN FULL EFFECT)** *Virgin LFC 1*	....**3**	6
18 May 96	● **PASS AND MOVE (IT'S THE LIVERPOOL GROOVE)** *Telstar LFCCD 96* [1]	....**4**	5

[1] Liverpool FC and the Boot Room Boyz

Tracks on We Can Do It (EP): We Can Do It / Liverpool Lou / We Shall Not Be Moved / You'll Never Walk Alone

LIVIN' JOY *US / Italy, male / female vocal / instrumental group – leader Paolo Visnadi (44 WEEKS)* pos/wks

3 Sep 94	**DREAMER** *Undiscovered MCSTD 1993*	....**18**	6
13 May 95	★ **DREAMER (re-mix)** *Undiscovered MCSTD 2056* ■	....**1**	11
15 Jun 96	● **DON'T STOP MOVIN'** *Undiscovered MCSTD 40041*	....**5**	14
2 Nov 96	● **FOLLOW THE RULES** *Undiscovered MCSTD 40081*	....**9**	5
5 Apr 97	**WHERE CAN I FIND LOVE** *Undiscovered MCSTD 40108*	....**12**	4
23 Aug 97	**DEEP IN YOU** *Universal MCSTD 40136*	....**17**	4

See also ALEX PARTY

LIVING COLOUR
US, male vocal / instrumental group (22 WEEKS) pos/wks

27 Oct 90	**TYPE** *Epic LCL 7*	....**75**	1
2 Feb 91	**LOVE REARS ITS UGLY HEAD** *Epic 6565937*	....**12**	11
1 Jun 91	**SOLACE OF YOU** *Epic 6569087*	....**33**	5
26 Oct 91	**CULT OF PERSONALITY** *Epic 6575357*	....**67**	2
20 Feb 93	**LEAVE IT ALONE** *Epic 6589762*	....**34**	2
17 Apr 93	**AUSLANDER** *Epic 6591732*	....**53**	1

LIVING IN A BOX
UK, male vocal / instrumental group (62 WEEKS) pos/wks

4 Apr 87	● **LIVING IN A BOX** *Chrysalis LIB 1*	....**5**	13
13 Jun 87	**SCALES OF JUSTICE** *Chrysalis LIB 2*	....**30**	6
26 Sep 87	**SO THE STORY GOES** *Chrysalis LIB 3* [1]	....**34**	8
30 Jan 88	**LOVE IS THE ART** *Chrysalis LIB 4*	....**44**	4
18 Feb 89	● **BLOW THE HOUSE DOWN** *Chrysalis LIB 5*	....**10**	9
10 Jun 89	**GATECRASHING** *Chrysalis LIB 6*	....**36**	6
23 Sep 89	● **ROOM IN YOUR HEART** *Chrysalis LIB 7*	....**5**	13
30 Dec 89	**DIFFERENT AIR (re)** *Chrysalis LIB 8*	....**57**	3

[1] Living in a Box featuring Bobby Womack

Dandy LIVINGSTONE
Jamaica, male vocalist – Robert Livingstone Thompson (19 WEEKS) pos/wks

2 Sep 72	SUZANNE BEWARE OF THE DEVIL *Horse HOSS 16*	14 11
13 Jan 73	BIG CITY / THINK ABOUT THAT *Horse HOSS 25*	26 8

LLAMA FARMERS
UK, male / female vocal / instrumental group (2 WEEKS) pos/wks

6 Feb 99	BIG WHEELS *Beggars Banquet BBQ 333CD*	67 1
15 May 99	GET THE KEYS AND GO *Beggars Banquet BBQ 335CD*	74 1

Kelly LLORENNA *UK, female vocalist (32 WEEKS)* pos/wks

7 May 94	SET YOU FREE *All Around the World CDGLOBE 124* [1]	39 4
24 Feb 96	BRIGHTER DAY *Pukka CDPUKKA 5*	43 2
25 Jul 98	HEART OF GOLD *Diverse VERSE 2CD* [2]	55 1
24 Mar 01	TRUE LOVE NEVER DIES	
	All Around the World CDGLOBE 240 [3]	34 3
2 Feb 02 ●	TRUE LOVE NEVER DIES (re-mix)	
	All Around the World CDGLOBE 248 [3]	7 10
6 Jul 02 ●	TELL IT TO MY HEART	
	All Around the World CDGLOBE 256	9 8
30 Nov 02	HEART OF GOLD *All Around the World CDGLOBE 271*	19 4

[1] N-Trance featuring Kelly Llorenna [2] Force and Styles featuring Kelly Llorenna
[3] Flip and Fill featuring Kelly Llorenna

See also N-TRANCE

Don LLOYDIE – *See SOUNDMAN and Don LLOYDIE with Elisabeth TROY*

LO FIDELITY ALLSTARS
UK, male vocal / instrumental group (5 WEEKS) pos/wks

11 Oct 97	DISCO MACHINE GUN *Skint SKINT 30CD*	50 1
2 May 98	VISION INCISION *Skint SKINT 33CD*	30 2
28 Nov 98	BATTLEFLAG *Skint SKINT 38CD* [1]	36 2

[1] Lo Fidelity Allstars featuring Pigeonhed

LOBO *US, male vocalist – Kent LaVoie (25 WEEKS)* pos/wks

19 Jun 71 ●	ME AND YOU AND A DOG NAMED BOO	
	Philips 6073 801	4 14
8 Jun 74 ●	I'D LOVE YOU TO WANT ME *UK 68*	5 11

LOBO *Holland, male vocalist – Imrich Lobo (11 WEEKS)* pos/wks

25 Jul 81 ●	THE CARIBBEAN DISCO SHOW *Polydor POSP 302*	8 11

LOCK 'N' LOAD
Holland, male DJ / production duo – Francis Rooijen and Nilz Pijpers (13 WEEKS) pos/wks

15 Apr 00 ●	BLOW YA MIND (re) *Pepper 9230162*	6 11
3 Mar 01	HOUSE SOME MORE *Pepper 9230422*	45 2

Hank LOCKLIN *US, male vocalist (41 WEEKS)* pos/wks

11 Aug 60 ●	PLEASE HELP ME, I'M FALLING *RCA 1188*	9 19
15 Feb 62	FROM HERE TO THERE TO YOU *RCA 1273*	44 3
15 Nov 62	WE'RE GONNA GO FISHIN' *RCA 1305*	18 11
5 May 66	I FEEL A CRY COMING ON *RCA 1510*	29 8

LOCKSMITH
US, male vocal / instrumental group (6 WEEKS) pos/wks

23 Aug 80	UNLOCK THE FUNK *Arista ARIST 364*	42 6

LOCOMOTIVE
UK, male vocal / instrumental group (8 WEEKS) pos/wks

16 Oct 68	RUDI'S IN LOVE *Parlophone R 5718*	25 8

John LODGE – *See Justin HAYWARD; MOODY BLUES*

LODGER
UK, male / female vocal / instrumental group (2 WEEKS) pos/wks

2 May 98	I'M LEAVING *Island CID 693*	40 2

Lisa LOEB and NINE STORIES
US, female / male vocal / instrumental group (17 WEEKS) pos/wks

3 Sep 94 ●	STAY (I MISSED YOU) *RCA 74321212522* ▲	6 15
16 Sep 95	DO YOU SLEEP? *Geffen GFSTD 96*	45 2

Nils LOFGREN
US, male vocalist / instrumentalist – guitar (3 WEEKS) pos/wks

8 Jun 85	SECRETS IN THE STREET *Towerbell TOW 68*	53 3

Johnny LOGAN
Ireland, male vocalist – Sean Sherrard (24 WEEKS) pos/wks

3 May 80 ★	WHAT'S ANOTHER YEAR *Epic EPC 8572*	1 8
23 May 87 ●	HOLD ME NOW *Epic LOG 1*	2 11
22 Aug 87	I'M NOT IN LOVE *Epic LOG 2*	51 5

Kenny LOGGINS
US, male vocalist / instrumentalist (21 WEEKS) pos/wks

28 Apr 84 ●	FOOTLOOSE *CBS A 4101* ▲	6 10
1 Nov 86	DANGER ZONE *CBS A 7188*	45 11

LOGO featuring Dawn JOSEPH
UK, male production duo and female vocalist (1 WEEK) pos/wks

8 Dec 01	DON'T PANIC *Manifesto FESCD 89*	42 1

LOLA *US, female vocalist (1 WEEK)* pos/wks

28 Mar 87	WAX THE VAN *Syncopate SY 1*	65 1

LOLLY
UK, female vocalist – Anna Klumby (44 WEEKS) pos/wks

10 Jul 99 ●	VIVA LA RADIO *Polydor 5639492*	6 9
18 Sep 99 ●	MICKEY *Polydor 5613682*	4 10
4 Dec 99 ●	BIG BOYS DON'T CRY / ROCKIN' ROBIN *Polydor 5615552*	10 9
6 May 00	PER SEMPRE AMORE (FOREVER IN LOVE) (re)	
	Polydor 5617882	11 10
9 Sep 00	GIRLS JUST WANNA HAVE FUN *Polydor 5619762*	14 6

Alain LOMBARD – *See Mady MESPLE and Danielle MILLET with the PARIS OPERA-COMIQUE ORCHESTRA conducted by Alain LOMBARD*

LONDON BOYS *UK, male vocal duo*
– Edam Phillips and Dennis George (46 WEEKS) pos/wks

10 Dec 88 ●	REQUIEM (re) *WEA YZ 345*	4 21
1 Jul 89 ●	LONDON NIGHTS *WEA YZ 393*	2 9
16 Sep 89	HARLEM DESIRE *WEA YZ 415*	17 7
2 Dec 89	MY LOVE *WEA YZ 433*	46 6
16 Jun 90	CHAPEL OF LOVE *East West YZ 458*	75 1
19 Jan 91	FREEDOM *East West YZ 554*	54 2

'Requiem' peaked at No.4 after re-entry in Apr '89

LONDON COMMUNITY GOSPEL CHOIR – *See Sal SOLO*

Julie LONDON
US, female vocalist – Julie Peck d. 18 Oct 2000 (3 WEEKS) pos/wks

5 Apr 57	CRY ME A RIVER *London HLU 8240*	22 3

Laurie LONDON *UK, male vocalist (12 WEEKS)* pos/wks

8 Nov 57	HE'S GOT THE WHOLE WORLD IN HIS HANDS	
	Parlophone R 4359	12 12

With Geoff Love his Orchestra and Chorus

LONDON PHILHARMONIC ORCHESTRA – *See Cliff RICHARD*

LONDON STRING CHORALE
UK, orchestra / choir (13 WEEKS) pos/wks

15 Dec 73	GALLOPING HOME (re) *Polydor 2058 280*	31 13

LONDON SYMPHONY ORCHESTRA UK, orchestra (7 WEEKS) pos/wks

		pos	wks
6 Jan 79	**THEME FROM 'SUPERMAN' (MAIN TITLE)** *Warner Bros. K 17292*	32	5
6 Dec 97	**JUST SHOW ME HOW TO LOVE YOU** *Coaltion COLA 035CD* [1]	54	2

[1] Sarah Brightman and the LSO featuring José Cura

Orchestra conducted by John Williams

LONDONBEAT UK / US, male vocal group (47 WEEKS) pos/wks

		pos	wks
26 Nov 88	**9 AM (THE COMFORT ZONE)** *AnXious ANX 008*	19	10
18 Feb 89	**FAILING IN LOVE AGAIN** *AnXious ANX 007*	60	2
2 Dec 89	**IT TAKES TWO BABY** *Spartan CIN 101* [1]	53	2
1 Sep 90 ●	**I'VE BEEN THINKING ABOUT YOU** *AnXious ANX 14* ▲	2	13
24 Nov 90	**A BETTER LOVE** *AnXious ANX 21*	52	5
2 Mar 91	**NO WOMAN NO CRY** *AnXious ANX 25*	64	2
20 Jul 91	**A BETTER LOVE** (re-issue) *AnXious ANX 32*	23	6
27 Jun 92	**YOU BRING ON THE SUN** *AnXious ANX 37*	32	4
24 Oct 92	**THAT'S HOW I FEEL ABOUT YOU** *AnXious ANX 40*	69	1
8 Apr 95	**I'M JUST YOUR PUPPET ON A … (STRING)** *AnXious 74321270982*	55	1
20 May 95	**COME BACK** *AnXious 74321226682*	69	1

[1] Liz Kershaw, Bruno Brookes, Jive Bunny and Londonbeat

LONE JUSTICE
US, female / male vocal / instrumental group (4 WEEKS) pos/wks

		pos	wks
7 Mar 87	**I FOUND LOVE** *Geffen GEF 18*	45	4

LONESTAR US, male vocal / instrumental group (24 WEEKS) pos/wks

		pos	wks
15 Apr 00	**AMAZED** *BMG / Grapevine 74321742582* ▲	21	22
7 Sep 00	**SMILE** *BMG / Grapevine 74321786132*	55	2

Shorty LONG
US, male vocalist – Frederick Long d. 29 Jun 1969 (7 WEEKS) pos/wks

		pos	wks
17 Jul 68	**HERE COMES THE JUDGE** *Tamla Motown TMG 663*	30	7

LONG AND THE SHORT
UK, male vocal / instrumental group (8 WEEKS) pos/wks

		pos	wks
10 Sep 64	**THE LETTER** *Decca F 11964*	35	5
24 Dec 64	**CHOC ICE** *Decca F 12043*	40	3

LONG RYDERS
US, male vocal / instrumental group (4 WEEKS) pos/wks

		pos	wks
5 Oct 85	**LOOKING FOR LEWIS AND CLARKE** *Island IS 237*	59	4

LONGPIGS UK, male vocal / instrumental group (17 WEEKS) pos/wks

		pos	wks
22 Jul 95	**SHE SAID** *Mother MUMCD 66*	67	1
28 Oct 95	**JESUS CHRIST** *Mother MUMCD 68*	61	1
17 Feb 96	**FAR** *Mother MUMCD 71*	37	2
13 Apr 96	**ON AND ON** *Mother MUMCD 74*	16	3
22 Jun 96	**SHE SAID** (re-issue) *Mother MUMCD 77*	16	4
5 Oct 96	**LOST MYSELF** *Mother MUMCD 82*	22	3
9 Oct 99	**BLUE SKIES** *Mother MUMCD 113*	21	2
18 Dec 99	**THE FRANK SONATA** *Mother MUMCD 114*	57	1

Joe LONGTHORNE UK, male vocalist (6 WEEKS) pos/wks

		pos	wks
30 Apr 94	**YOUNG GIRL** *EMI CDEM 310*	61	2
10 Dec 94	**PASSING STRANGERS** *EMI CDEM 362* [1]	34	4

[1] Joe Longthorne and Liz Dawn

LONGVIEW UK, male vocal / instrumental group (1 WEEK) pos/wks

		pos	wks
26 Oct 02	**WHEN YOU SLEEP** *4:45 Recordings LVIEW 02CD*	74	1

LONYO UK, male vocalist / producer – Lonyo Engele (9 WEEKS) pos/wks

		pos	wks
8 Jul 00 ●	**SUMMER OF LOVE** *Riverhorse RIVH CD3* [1]	8	7
7 Apr 01	**GARAGE GIRLS** *Riverhorse RIVHCD 12* [2]	39	2

[1] Lonyo – Comme Ci Comme Ça [2] Lonyo featuring MC Onyx Stone

LOOK UK, male vocal / instrumental group (15 WEEKS) pos/wks

		pos	wks
20 Dec 80 ●	**I AM THE BEAT** *MCA 647*	6	12
29 Aug 81	**FEEDING TIME** *MCA 736*	50	3

LOON – *See PUFF DADDY*

LOOP DA LOOP UK, male producer – Nick Dresti (4 WEEKS) pos/wks

		pos	wks
7 Jun 97	**GO WITH THE FLOW** *Manifesto FESCD 24*	47	1
20 Feb 99	**HAZEL** *Manifesto FESCD 53*	20	3

LOOSE ENDS (475) **Top 500** Soul / disco trio formed in London; Carl
McIntosh (v/g), Jane Eugene (v) and Steve Nichol (k) – the last two leaving
in 1990. The first UK group to top the US R&B chart achieved this feat with
US-produced 'Hangin' on a String' and 'Slow Down' (76 WEEKS) pos/wks

		pos	wks
25 Feb 84	**TELL ME WHAT YOU WANT** *Virgin VS 658*	74	1
28 Apr 84	**EMERGENCY (DIAL 999)** *Virgin VS 677*	41	6
21 Jul 84	**CHOOSE ME (RESCUE ME)** *Virgin VS 697*	59	3
23 Feb 85	**HANGIN' ON A STRING (CONTEMPLATING)** *Virgin VS 748*	13	13
11 May 85	**MAGIC TOUCH** *Virgin VS 761*	16	7
27 Jul 85	**GOLDEN YEARS** *Virgin VS 795*	59	4
14 Jun 86	**STAY A LITTLE WHILE, CHILD** *Virgin VS 819*	52	5
20 Sep 86	**SLOW DOWN** *Virgin VS 884*	27	7
29 Nov 86	**NIGHTS OF PLEASURE** *Virgin VS 919*	42	7
4 Jun 88	**MR BACHELOR** *Virgin VS 1080*	50	4
25 Aug 90	**DON'T BE A FOOL** *10 TEN 312*	13	9
17 Nov 90	**LOVE'S GOT ME** *10 TEN 330*	40	4
20 Jun 92	**HANGIN' ON A STRING** (re-mix) *Ten TEN 406*	25	5
5 Sep 92	**MAGIC TOUCH** (re-mix) *Ten TEN 409*	75	1

Lisa 'Left Eye' LOPES
US, female vocalist, d. 25 Apr 2002 (20 WEEKS) pos/wks

		pos	wks
1 Apr 00 ★	**NEVER BE THE SAME AGAIN** (re) *Virgin VSCDT 1762* [1] ■	1	16
27 Oct 01	**THE BLOCK PARTY** *La Face / Arista 74321895912*	16	4

[1] Melanie C / Lisa 'Left Eye' Lopes

See also TLC

Jennifer LOPEZ (281) **Top 500**
*Globally successful, photogenic singer / actress. J.Lo, b. 24 Jul 1970, Bronx,
New York, starred in such movies as 'The Wedding Planner', 'The Cell' and
'Selena' (life story of an earlier Latin superstar) (106 WEEKS)* pos/wks

		pos	wks
3 Jul 99 ●	**IF YOU HAD MY LOVE** *Columbia 6675772* ▲	4	13
13 Nov 99 ●	**WAITING FOR TONIGHT** *Columbia 6683072*	5	12
1 Apr 00	**FEELIN' SO GOOD** *Columbia 6691972* [1]	15	6
20 Jan 01 ★	**LOVE DON'T COST A THING** (re) *Epic 6707282* ■	1	11
12 May 01	**PLAY** (re) *Epic 6712272*	3	12
18 Aug 01	**AIN'T IT FUNNY** *Epic 6717592*	3	9
10 Nov 01	**I'M REAL** *Epic 6720322* [2]	4	15
23 Mar 02 ●	**AIN'T IT FUNNY** (re-mix) *Epic 6724922* [3] ▲	4	13
13 Jul 02	**I'M GONNA BE ALRIGHT** *Epic 6728442* [4]	3	10
30 Nov 02	**JENNY FROM THE BLOCK** *Epic 6733572*	3	5+

[1] Jennifer Lopez featuring Big Pun and Fat Joe [2] Jennifer Lopez featuring Ja Rule
[3] Jennifer Lopez featuring Ja Rule & Caddillac Tah [4] Jennifer Lopez featuring Nas

Trini LOPEZ US, male vocalist (37 WEEKS) pos/wks

		pos	wks
12 Sep 63 ●	**IF I HAD A HAMMER** *Reprise R 20198*	4	17
12 Dec 63	**KANSAS CITY** *Reprise R 20236*	35	5
12 May 66	**I'M COMING HOME CINDY** *Reprise R 20455*	28	5
6 Apr 67	**GONNA GET ALONG WITHOUT YA NOW** *Reprise R 20547*	41	5
19 Dec 81	**TRINI TRAX** *RCA 154*	59	5

LO-PRO – *See X-PRESS 2*

LORD ROCKINGHAM'S XI UK, male / female
instrumental group – leader Harry Robinson (21 WEEKS) pos/wks

		pos	wks
24 Oct 58 ★	**HOOTS MON** *Decca F 11059* [1]	1	17
6 Feb 59	**WEE TOM** *Decca F 11104* [1]	16	3
25 Sep 93	**HOOTS MON** (re-issue) *Decca 8820982*	60	1

[1] Jack Good presents Lord Rockingham's XI

LORD TANAMO *Trinidad and Tobago, male vocalist (2 WEEKS)* pos/wks
1 Dec 90   **I'M IN THE MOOD FOR LOVE** *Mooncrest MOON 1009* **58** 2

LORD TARIQ and Peter GUNZ *US, male vocal / rap duo – Sean Hamilton and Peter Panky (3 WEEKS)* pos/wks
2 May 98   **DEJA VU (UPTOWN BABY)** *Columbia 6658722*......................**21** 3

Erin **LORDAN** – *See SHUT UP AND DANCE; BBG; ASCENCION*

Jerry LORDAN *UK, male vocalist d. 24 Jul 1995 (16 WEEKS)* pos/wks
8 Jan 60   **I'LL STAY SINGLE** (re) *Parlophone R 4588* **26** 3
26 Feb 60   **WHO COULD BE BLUER** (re) *Parlophone R 4627* **16** 11
2 Jun 60   **SING LIKE AN ANGEL** *Parlophone R 4653* **36** 2

Traci LORDS *US, female vocalist (1 WEEK)* pos/wks
7 Oct 95   **FALLEN ANGEL** *Radioactive RAXTD 18* **72** 1

Sophia LOREN – *See Peter SELLERS*

Trey LORENZ *US, male vocalist – Lloyd Lorenz Smith (5 WEEKS)* pos/wks
21 Nov 92   **SOMEONE TO HOLD** *Epic 6587857*..................**65** 2
30 Jan 93   **PHOTOGRAPH OF MARY** *Epic 6589542* **38** 3

See also Mariah CAREY

LORI and the CHAMELEONS *UK, female / male vocal / instrumental group (1 WEEK)* pos/wks
8 Dec 79   **TOUCH** *Sire SIR 4025*.................................**70** 1

LORRAINE – *See BOMB THE BASS*

LOS BRAVOS *Spain / Germany, male vocal / instrumental group (24 WEEKS)* pos/wks
30 Jun 66 ●   **BLACK IS BLACK** *Decca F 22419* **2** 13
8 Sep 66   **I DON'T CARE** *Decca F 22484* **16** 11

LOS DEL CHIPMUNKS – *See CHIPMUNKS*

LOS DEL MAR featuring Wil VELOZ *Cuba / Canada, male vocal / instrumental group (7 WEEKS)* pos/wks
8 Jun 96   **MACARENA** (re) *Pulse 8 CDLOSE 101*...............**43** 7

LOS DEL RIO *Spain, male vocal / instrumental duo – Antonio Monge and Rafael Perdigones (19 WEEKS)* pos/wks
1 Jun 96 ●   **MACARENA** (re) *RCA 74321345372* ▲ **2** 19

LOS INDIOS TABAJARAS *Brazil, male instrumental guitar duo – Natalicio and Antenor Lima (17 WEEKS)* pos/wks
31 Oct 63 ●   **MARIA ELENA** *RCA 1365* **5** 17

LOS LOBOS *US, male vocal / instrumental group – lead vocal David Hildago (24 WEEKS)* pos/wks
6 Apr 85   **DON'T WORRY BABY / WILL THE WOLF SURVIVE**
       London LASH 4 ....**57** 4
18 Jul 87 ★   **LA BAMBA** *Slash LASH 13* ▲ **1** 11
26 Sep 87   **COME ON LET'S GO** *Slash LASH 14* **18** 9

LOS POP TOPS *Spain, male vocal group (6 WEEKS)* pos/wks
9 Oct 71   **MAMY BLUE** *A&M AMS 859* **35** 6

LOS UMBRELLOS *Denmark, male / female vocal trio (2 WEEKS)* pos/wks
3 Oct 98   **NO TENGO DINERO** *Virgin VUSCD 139* **33** 2

Joe LOSS and His Orchestra *UK, orchestra, leader d. 6 Jun 1990 (53 WEEKS)* pos/wks
29 Jun 61   **WHEELS CHA CHA** *HMV POP 880* **21** 21

---

19 Oct 61   **SUCU SUCU** *HMV POP 937*..........................**48** 1
29 Mar 62   **THE MAIGRET THEME** *HMV POP 995* **20** 10
1 Nov 62   **MUST BE MADISON** *HMV POP 1075* **20** 13
5 Nov 64   **MARCH OF THE MODS** (re) *HMV POP 1351* **31** 8

LOST *UK, male / instrumental / production duo (1 WEEK)* pos/wks
22 Jun 91   **TECHNO FUNK** *Perfecto PT 44560*.................**75** 1

LOST BOYZ *US, male rap group (2 WEEKS)* pos/wks
2 Nov 96   **MUSIC MAKES ME HIGH** *Universal MCSTD 48015*..**42** 1
12 Jul 97   **LOVE, PEACE & NAPPINESS** *Universal UND 56131* ..**57** 1

LOST IT.COM *UK, male vocal / production duo (1 WEEK)* pos/wks
7 Apr 01   **ANIMAL** *Perfecto PERF 13CDS* **70** 1

LOST TRIBE
UK, male production duo – Matt Darey and Red Jerry (3 WEEKS) pos/wks
11 Sep 99   **GAMEMASTER** *Hooj Choons HOOJ 81CD* **24** 3

See also Matt DAREY; SUNBURST; MELT; MDM

LOST WITNESS
UK, male production duo and female vocalist (13 WEEKS) pos/wks
29 May 99   **HAPPINESS HAPPENING**
       Ministry of Sound MOSCDS 129...................**18** 4
18 Sep 99   **RED SUN RISING** *Ministry of Sound MOSCDS 133* ..**22** 3
16 Dec 00   **7 COLOURS** *Data DATA 15CDS*..................**28** 3
18 May 02   **DID I DREAM (SONG TO THE SIREN)**
       Ministry of Sound / Data DATA 28CDS **28** 3

LOSTPROPHETS
UK, male vocal / instrumental group (5 WEEKS) pos/wks
8 Dec 01   **SHINOBI VS DRAGON NINJA**
       Visible Noise TORMENT 16 ....**41** 2
23 Mar 02   **THE FAKE SOUND OF PROGRESS**
       Visible Noise TORMENT 19 ....**21** 3

LOTUS EATERS *UK, male vocal / instrumental duo – Peter Coyle and Jerry Kelley (16 WEEKS)* pos/wks
2 Jul 83   **FIRST PICTURE OF YOU** *Sylvan SYL 1*..........**15** 12
8 Oct 83   **YOU DON'T NEED SOMEONE NEW** *Sylvan SYL 2*..**53** 4

Bonnie LOU *US, female vocalist – Bonnie Lou Kath (10 WEEKS)* pos/wks
5 Feb 54 ●   **TENNESSEE WIG WALK** *Parlophone R 3730* **4** 10

Lippy LOU *UK, female rapper (2 WEEKS)* pos/wks
22 Apr 95   **LIBERATION** *More Protein PROCD 105*............**57** 2

Louchie LOU and Michie ONE
UK, female rap duo – Louise Gold and Michelle Charles (36 WEEKS) pos/wks
29 May 93 ●   **SHOUT** *ffrr FCD 211* **7** 8
14 Aug 93   **SOMEBODY ELSE'S GUY** *ffrr FCD 216* **54** 2
26 Aug 95   **GET DOWN ON IT** *China WOKCD 2054*..........**58** 1
13 Apr 96 ●   **CECILIA** (2re) *WEA WEA 042CD1* [1] **4** 19
15 Jun 96   **GOOD SWEET LOVIN'** *Indochina ID 050CD* **34** 2
21 Sep 96   **NO MORE ALCOHOL** *WEA WEA 065CD1* [1] **24** 4

[1] Suggs featuring Louchie Lou and Michie One

LOUD *UK, male vocal / instrumental group (2 WEEKS)* pos/wks
28 Mar 92   **EASY** *China WOK 2016* **67** 2

John D LOUDERMILK *US, male vocalist (10 WEEKS)* pos/wks
4 Jan 62   **THE LANGUAGE OF LOVE** *RCA 1269*..............**13** 10

Louie LOUIE *US, male vocalist (5 WEEKS)* pos/wks
19 Dec 92   **THE THOUGHT OF IT** *Hardback YZ 724* **34** 5

LOUISE 451 Top 500 First British female to have a string of Top 20s as both a group member (exited Eternal in July 1995) and solo singer, b. Louise Nurding, 4 Nov 1974, south London. Photogenic vocalist, who has sung on 17 Top 20 entries, is married to footballer Jamie Redknapp (78 WEEKS) pos/wks

7 Oct 95	●	LIGHT OF MY LIFE EMI CDEMS 397	8	8
16 Mar 96	●	IN WALKED LOVE EMI CDEMS 413	17	6
8 Jun 96	●	NAKED EMI CDEM 431	5	8
31 Aug 96	●	UNDIVIDED LOVE EMI CDEM 441	5	6
30 Nov 96	●	ONE KISS FROM HEAVEN EMI CDEM 454	9	7
4 Oct 97	●	ARMS AROUND THE WORLD EMI CDEM 490	4	7
29 Nov 97	●	LET'S GO ROUND AGAIN EMI CDEM 500	10	9
4 Apr 98		ALL THAT MATTERS (re) 1st Avenue CDEM 506	11	6
29 Jul 00	●	2 FACED 1st Avenue / EMI CDEMS 570	3	8
11 Nov 00		BEAUTIFUL INSIDE 1st Avenue / EMI CDEMS 575	13	4
8 Sep 01	●	STUCK IN THE MIDDLE WITH YOU 1st Avenue / EMI CDEM 600	4	9

See also ETERNAL

Darlene LOVE US, female vocalist – Darlene Wright (5 WEEKS) pos/wks

| 19 Dec 92 | ALL ALONE ON CHRISTMAS (re) Arista 74321124767 | 31 | 5 |

Re-entry made No.72 in Jan 1994

Geoff LOVE – See MANUEL and THE MUSIC OF THE MOUNTAINS; Laurie LONDON

Helen LOVE
UK, male / female vocal / instrumental group (2 WEEKS) pos/wks

| 20 Sep 97 | DOES YOUR HEART GO BOOM Che CHE 72CD | 71 | 1 |
| 19 Sep 98 | LONG LIVE THE UK MUSIC SCENE Che CHE 82CD | 65 | 1 |

Monie LOVE UK, female rapper – Simone Johnson (51 WEEKS) pos/wks

4 Feb 89	I CAN DO THIS Cooltempo COOL 177	37	4
24 Jun 89	GRANDPA'S PARTY Cooltempo COOL 184	16	9
14 Jul 90	MONIE IN THE MIDDLE Cooltempo COOL 210	46	3
22 Sep 90	IT'S A SHAME (MY SISTER) Cooltempo COOL 219 [1]	12	8
1 Dec 90	DOWN TO EARTH Cooltempo COOL 222	31	6
6 Apr 91	RING MY BELL Cooltempo COOL 224 [2]	20	5
25 Jul 92	FULL TERM LOVE Cooltempo COOL 258	34	4
13 Mar 93	BORN 2 B.R.E.E.D. Cooltempo CDCOOL 269	18	5
12 Jun 93	IN A WORD OR 2 / THE POWER Cooltempo CDCOOL 273	33	3
21 Aug 93	NEVER GIVE UP Cooltempo CDCOOL 276	41	2
22 Apr 00	SLICE OF DA PIE Relentless RELENT 2CDS	29	2

[1] Monie Love featuring True Image [2] Monie Love vs Adeva

LOVE AFFAIR UK, male vocal / instrumental group – lead vocal Steve Ellis (56 WEEKS) pos/wks

3 Jan 68	★	EVERLASTING LOVE CBS 3125	1	12
17 Apr 68	●	RAINBOW VALLEY CBS 3366	5	13
11 Sep 68	●	A DAY WITHOUT LOVE CBS 3674	6	12
19 Feb 69	●	ONE ROAD CBS 3994	16	9
16 Jul 69	●	BRINGING ON BACK THE GOOD TIMES CBS 4300	9	10

Vikki LOVE – See JUNGLE BROTHERS; NUANCE featuring Vikki LOVE

LOVE AND MONEY
UK, male vocal / instrumental group (23 WKS) pos/wks

24 May 86	CANDYBAR EXPRESS Mercury MONEY 1	56	4
25 Apr 87	LOVE AND MONEY Mercury MONEY 4	68	4
17 Sep 88	HALLELUIAH MAN Fontana MONEY 5	63	4
14 Jan 89	STRANGE KIND OF LOVE Fontana MONEY 6	45	5
25 Mar 89	JOCELYN SQUARE Fontana MONEY 7	51	4
16 Nov 91	WINTER Fontana MONEY 9	52	2

LOVE BITE Italy, male / female production / vocal group (1 WEEK) pos/wks

| 7 Oct 00 | TAKE YOUR TIME AM:PM CDAMPM134 | 56 | 1 |

LOVE CITY GROOVE
UK, male / female vocal / rap / instrumental group (11 WEEKS) pos/wks

| 8 Apr 95 | ● | LOVE CITY GROOVE Planet 3 GXY 2003CD | 7 | 11 |

LOVE CONNECTION
Italy / Germany, male / female vocal / production group (1 WEEK) pos/wks

| 2 Dec 00 | THE BOMB Multiply CDMULTY 63 | 53 | 1 |

LOVE DECADE
UK, male / female vocal / instrumental group (14 WEEKS) pos/wks

6 Jul 91	DREAM ON (IS THIS A DREAM) All Around the World GLOBE 100	52	2
23 Nov 91	SO REAL All Around the World GLOBE 106	14	7
11 Apr 92	I FEEL YOU All Around the World GLOBE 107	34	3
6 Feb 93	WHEN THE MORNING COMES All Around the World CDGLOBE 114	69	1
17 Feb 96	IS THIS A DREAM All Around the World CDGLOBE 132	39	1

'Is This a Dream' in 1996 is a re-recording

LOVE DECREE UK, male vocal / instrumental group (4 WEEKS) pos/wks

| 16 Sep 89 | SOMETHING SO REAL (CHINHEADS THEME) Ariola 112642 | 61 | 4 |

LOVE / HATE US, male vocal / instrumental group (4 WEEKS) pos/wks

| 30 Nov 91 | EVIL TWIN Columbia 6575967 | 59 | 1 |
| 4 Apr 92 | WASTED IN AMERICA Columbia 6578897 | 38 | 3 |

LOVE INC. Jamaica / Canada, male / female production / vocal duo – Chris Sheppard and Simone Denny (1 WEEK) pos/wks

| 28 Dec 02 | ● | YOU'RE A SUPERSTAR Nulife / Arista 74321973842 | 7 | 1+ |

LOVE INCORPORATED featuring MC NOISE
UK, male vocal / production duo (3 WEEKS) pos/wks

| 9 Feb 91 | LOVE IS THE MESSAGE Love EVOL 1 | 59 | 3 |

LOVE NELSON – See FIRE ISLAND

LOVE REACTION – See ZODIAC MINDWARP and the LOVE REACTION

LOVE SCULPTURE UK, instrumental group (14 WEEKS) pos/wks

| 27 Nov 68 | ● | SABRE DANCE Parlophone R 5744 | 5 | 14 |

See also Dave EDMUNDS

LOVE SQUAD – See Linda CARR

A LOVE SUPREME
UK, male vocal / instrumental group (2 WEEKS) pos/wks

| 17 Apr 99 | NIALL QUINN'S DISCO PANTS A Love Supreme / Cherry Red CDVINNIE 3 | 59 | 2 |

[LOVE] TATTOO
Australia, male producer – Stephen Allkins (1 WEEK) pos/wks

| 6 Oct 01 | DROP SOME DRUMS Positiva CDTIV 162 | 58 | 1 |

LOVE TO INFINITY
UK, male / female vocal / instrumental group (4 WEEKS) pos/wks

24 Jun 95	KEEP LOVE TOGETHER Mushroom D 00467	38	2
18 Nov 95	SOMEDAY Mushroom D 1143	75	1
3 Aug 96	PRAY FOR LOVE Mushroom D 1213	69	1

LOVE TRIBE US, male / female vocal / instrumental duo – Tanya Walters and Dewey Bullock (3 WEEKS) pos/wks

| 29 Jun 96 | STAND UP AM:PM 5816272 | 23 | 3 |

LOVE UNLIMITED US, female vocal group (19 WEEKS) pos/wks

| 17 Jun 72 | WALKIN' IN THE RAIN WITH THE ONE I LOVE Uni UN 539 | 14 | 10 |
| 25 Jan 75 | IT MAY BE WINTER OUTSIDE (BUT IN MY HEART IT'S SPRING) 20th Century BTC 2149 | 11 | 9 |

Re-entries are listed as (re), (2re), (3re), etc which signifies that the hit re-entered the chart once, twice or three times, etc

LOVE UNLIMITED ORCHESTRA *US, orchestra (10 WEEKS)* pos/wks

2 Feb 74 ● LOVE'S THEME *Pye International 7N 25635* ▲ 10 10

LOVEBUG STARSKI
US, male rapper – Kevin Smith (9 WEEKS) pos/wks

31 May 86 AMITYVILLE (THE HOUSE ON THE HILL) *Epic A 7182*.........12 9

LOVEDEEJAY AKEMI – *See YOSH presents LOVEDEEJAY AKEMI*

LOVEHAPPY
US / UK, male / female vocal / instrumental group (3 WEEKS) pos/wks

18 Feb 95 MESSAGE OF LOVE *MCA MCSTD 2040* 37 2
20 Jul 96 MESSAGE OF LOVE (re-mix) *MCA MCSTD 40052* ...70 1

Bill LOVELADY *UK, male vocalist (10 WEEKS)* pos/wks

18 Aug 79 REGGAE FOR IT NOW *Charisma CB 337* 12 10

LOVELAND featuring the voice of Rachel McFARLANE
UK, male / female vocal / instrumental group (15 WEEKS) pos/wks

16 Apr 94 LET THE MUSIC (LIFT YOU UP)
            KMS / Eastern Bloc KMSCD 10 ....16 4
 5 Nov 94 (KEEP ON) SHINING / HOPE (NEVER GIVE UP)
            Eastern Bloc BLOCCD 016 ....37 2
14 Jan 95 I NEED SOMEBODY *Eastern Bloc BLOCCD 019* 21 3
10 Jun 95 DON'T MAKE ME WAIT *Eastern Bloc BLOC 20CD* ..22 3
 2 Sep 95 THE WONDER OF LOVE *Eastern Bloc BLOC 22CD*....53 1
11 Nov 95 I NEED SOMEBODY (re-mix) *Eastern Bloc BLOC 23CD*.........38 2

All formats of 'Let the Music (Lift You Up)' featured versions by Loveland featuring Rachel McFarlane and also by Darlene Lewis

LOVER SPEAKS *UK, male vocal / instrumental duo (5 WEEKS)* pos/wks

16 Aug 86 NO MORE 'I LOVE YOU'S' *A&M AM 326* 58 5

Michael LOVESMITH *US, male vocalist (1 WEEK)* pos/wks

 5 Oct 85 ● AIN'T NOTHIN' LIKE IT *Motown ZB 40369* 75 1

LOVESTATION
UK, male / female vocal / instrumental group (21 WEEKS) pos/wks

13 Mar 93 SHINE ON ME *RCA 743211337912* [1] 71 1
13 Nov 93 BEST OF MY LOVE *Fresh FRSHD 1* 73 1
18 Mar 95 LOVE COME RESCUE ME *Fresh FRSHD 22*.............42 2
 1 Aug 98 TEARDROPS *Fresh FRSHD 65*.......................14 6
 5 Dec 98 SENSUALITY *Fresh FRSHD 71*......................16 7
 5 Feb 00 TEARDROPS (re-mix) *Fresh FRSHD 79* 24 4

[1] Lovestation featuring Lisa Hunt

Lene LOVICH *US, female vocalist – Lili Premilovich (38 WEEKS)* pos/wks

17 Feb 79 ● LUCKY NUMBER *Stiff BUY 42*......................3 11
12 May 79 SAY WHEN *Stiff BUY 46*...........................19 10
20 Oct 79 BIRD SONG *Stiff BUY 53*..........................39 7
29 Mar 80 WHAT WILL I DO WITHOUT YOU *Stiff BUY 69*.......58 3
14 Mar 81 NEW TOY *Stiff BUY 97*............................53 5
27 Nov 82 IT'S YOU ONLY YOU (MEIN SCHMERZ) *Stiff BUY 164*.......68 2

LOVIN' SPOONFUL
US / Canada, male vocal / instrumental group (33 WEEKS) pos/wks

14 Apr 66 ● DAYDREAM *Pye International 7N 25361* 2 13
14 Jul 66 ● SUMMER IN THE CITY *Kama Sutra KAS 200* ▲ 8 11
 5 Jan 67 NASHVILLE CATS *Kama Sutra KAS 204* 26 7
 9 Mar 67 DARLING BE HOME SOON *Kama Sutra KAS 207* 44 2

LOVINDEER *Jamaica, male vocalist (3 WEEKS)* pos/wks

27 Sep 86 MAN SHORTAGE *TSOJ TS 1* 69 3

Gary LOW *Italy, male vocalist (3 WEEKS)* pos/wks

 8 Oct 83 I WANT YOU *Savoir Faire FAIS 004* 52 3

Patti LOW – *See BUG KANN and the PLASTIC JAM*

Jim LOWE *US, male vocalist (9 WEEKS)* pos/wks

26 Oct 56 ● THE GREEN DOOR *London HLD 8317* [1] 8 9

[1] Jim Lowe and the High Fives

Nick LOWE *UK, male vocalist (27 WEEKS)* pos/wks

11 Mar 78 ● I LOVE THE SOUND OF BREAKING GLASS *Radar ADA 1*...........7 8
 9 Jun 79 CRACKING UP *Radar ADA 34*........................34 5
25 Aug 79 CRUEL TO BE KIND *Radar ADA 43*..................12 11
26 May 84 HALF A BOY AND HALF A MAN *F. Beat XX 34*........53 3

LOWGOLD *UK, male vocal / instrumental group (4 WEEKS)* pos/wks

30 Sep 00 BEAUTY DIES YOUNG *Nude NUD 52CD* 67 1
10 Feb 01 MERCURY *Nude NUD 53CD*...........................48 1
12 May 01 COUNTERFEIT *Nude NUD 55CD*.......................52 1
 8 Sep 01 BEAUTY DIES YOUNG (re-mix) *Nude NUD 59CD*.......40 1

LOWRELL *US, male vocalist – Lowrell Simon (9 WEEKS)* pos/wks

24 Nov 79 MELLOW MELLOW RIGHT ON *AVI AVIS 108* 37 9

LUCAS *Denmark, male vocalist – Lucas Secon (4 WEEKS)* pos/wks

 6 Aug 94 LUCAS WITH THE LID OFF *WEA YZ 832CD* 37 4

Carrie LUCAS *US, female vocalist (6 WEEKS)* pos/wks

16 Jun 79 DANCE WITH YOU *Solar FB 1482*...................40 6

Tammy LUCAS – *See Teddy RILEY*

LUCIANA *UK, female vocalist (5 WEEKS)* pos/wks

23 Apr 94 GET IT UP FOR LOVE *Chrysalis CDCHS 5008* 55 2
 6 Aug 94 IF YOU WANT *Chrysalis CDCHS 5009* 47 2
 5 Nov 94 WHAT GOES AROUND / ONE MORE RIVER
            Chrysalis CDCHS 5015 ....67 1

LUCID
UK, male / female vocal / instrumental group (15 WEEKS) pos/wks

 8 Aug 98 ● I CAN'T HELP MYSELF *ffrr FCD 339* 7 8
27 Feb 99 CRAZY *ffrr / Delirious / Indirect FCD 355* 14 5
16 Oct 99 STAY WITH ME TILL DAWN *ffrr FCD 368* 25 2

LUCKY MONKEYS *UK, male instrumental group (1 WEEK)* pos/wks

 9 Nov 96 BJANGO *Hi-Life 5757132* 50 1

See also FLUKE

LUCY PEARL
US, male / female vocal / rap / instrumental / production trio (7 WEEKS) pos/wks

29 Jul 00 DANCE TONIGHT *Virgin VSCDT 1775* 36 2
25 Nov 00 DON'T MESS WITH MY MAN *Virgin VSCDT 1778* 20 4
28 Jul 01 WITHOUT YOU *Virgin VSCDT 1805*..................51 1

LUDACRIS *US, male rapper – Christopher Bridges (26 WEEKS)* pos/wks

 9 Jun 01 WHAT'S YOUR FANTASY *Def Jam 5729842* 19 5
18 Aug 01 ● ONE MINUTE MAN *Elektra E 7245CD* [1] 10 8
29 Sep 01 AREA CODES *Def Jam 5887722* [2] 25 3
22 Jun 02 ROLLOUT (MY BUSINESS) *Def Jam 5829632*..........20 7
 5 Oct 02 SATURDAY (OOOH OOOH) *Def Jam 0639142* 31 1
 9 Nov 02 WHY DON'T WE FALL IN LOVE *Columbia 6732212* [3] 40 2

[1] Missy 'Misdemeanor' Elliott featuring Ludacris [2] Ludacris featuring Nate Dogg
[3] Amerie featuring Ludacris

Baz LUHRMANN *Australia, male producer (16 WEEKS)* pos/wks

12 Jun 99 ★ EVERYBODY'S FREE (TO WEAR SUNSCREEN)
            EMI CDBAZ 001 ■ 1 16

Uncredited vocals by actor Lee Perry

Robin LUKE US, male vocalist (6 WEEKS)

		pos/wks
17 Oct 58	SUSIE DARLIN' (2re) London HLD 8676	23 6

LUKK featuring Felicia COLLINS
US, male / female vocal / instrumental group (1 WEEK)

		pos/wks
28 Sep 85	ON THE ONE Important TAN 6	72 1

LULU 112 Top 500
One of Scotland's best-known female vocalists, b. Marie Lawrie, 3 Nov 1948, Strathclyde. She scored her first hit aged 15, had a US chart-topper ('To Sir with Love') aged 18, won the Eurovision Song Contest aged 20, and finally reached No.1 aged 44 (179 WEEKS)

		pos/wks
14 May 64 ●	SHOUT Decca F 11884 1	7 13
12 Nov 64	HERE COMES THE NIGHT Decca F 12017	50 1
17 Jun 65 ●	LEAVE A LITTLE LOVE Decca F 12169	8 11
2 Sep 65	TRY TO UNDERSTAND Decca F 12214	25 8
13 Apr 67 ●	THE BOAT THAT I ROW Columbia DB 8169	6 11
29 Jun 67	LET'S PRETEND Columbia DB 8221	11 11
8 Nov 67	LOVE LOVES TO LOVE LOVE Columbia DB 8295	32 6
28 Feb 68 ●	ME, THE PEACEFUL HEART Columbia DB 8358	9 9
5 Jun 68	BOY Columbia DB 8425	15 7
6 Nov 68 ●	I'M A TIGER Columbia DB 8500	9 13
12 Mar 69 ●	BOOM BANG-A-BANG Columbia DB 8550	2 13
22 Nov 69	OH ME OH MY (I'M A FOOL FOR YOU BABY) Atco 226008	47 2
26 Jan 74 ●	THE MAN WHO SOLD THE WORLD Polydor 2001 490	3 9
19 Apr 75	TAKE YOUR MAMA FOR A RIDE Chelsea 2005 022	37 4
12 Dec 81	I COULD NEVER MISS YOU (MORE THAN I DO) (re) Alfa ALFA 1700	62 5
19 Jul 86 ●	SHOUT Jive LULU1 / Decca SHOUT 1	8 11
30 Jan 93	INDEPENDENCE Dome CDDOME 1001	11 5
3 Apr 93	I'M BACK FOR MORE Dome CDDOME 1002 2	27 5
4 Sep 93	LET ME WAKE UP IN YOUR ARMS Dome CDDOME 1005	51 2
9 Oct 93 ★	RELIGHT MY FIRE RCA 74321167722 3 ■	1 14
27 Nov 93	HOW 'BOUT US Dome CDDOME 1007	46 3
27 Aug 94	GOODBYE BABY AND AMEN Dome CDDOME 1011	40 2
26 Nov 94	EVERY WOMAN KNOWS Dome CDDOME 1013	44 2
29 May 99	HURT ME SO BAD Rocket / Mercury 5726132	42 2
8 Jan 00	BETTER GET READY Mercury 5625852	59 1
18 Mar 00	WHERE THE POOR BOYS DANCE Mercury 1568452	24 5
7 Dec 02 ●	WE'VE GOT TONIGHT Polydor 0658612 4	4 4+

1 Lulu and The Luvvers 2 Lulu and Bobby Womack 3 Take That featuring Lulu
4 Ronan Keating featuring Lulu

The newly recorded 'Shout' entered the chart on 19 Jul 1986, and the next week the original Decca version by Lulu and The Luvvers also charted. For all subsequent weeks Gallup amalgamated both versions under one entry and we have added an extra week on chart for the 'double week' to take account of this

Bob LUMAN US, male vocalist d. 27 Dec 1978 (21 WEEKS)

		pos/wks
8 Sep 60 ●	LET'S THINK ABOUT LIVING Warner Bros. WB 18	6 18
15 Dec 60	WHY, WHY, BYE, BYE Warner Bros. WB 28	46 1
4 May 61	THE GREAT SNOWMAN Warner Bros. WB 37	49 2

LUMINAIRE – See Jonathan PETERS presents LUMINAIRE

LUNIZ US, male rap duo – Jerrold 'Yukmouth' Ellis Jr and Garrick 'Knumbskull' Husbands (18 WEEKS)

		pos/wks
17 Feb 96 ●	I GOT 5 ON IT Virgin America VUSCD 101	3 13
11 May 96	PLAYA HATA Virgin America VUSCD 103	20 3
31 Oct 98	I GOT 5 ON IT (re-mix) Virgin VCRD 41	28 2

LUPINE HOWL UK, male vocal / instrumental group (1 WEEK)

		pos/wks
22 Jan 00	VAPORIZER Vinyl Hiss VHISSCD 001	68 1

LURKERS UK, male vocal / instrumental group (11 WEEKS)

		pos/wks
3 Jun 78	AIN'T GOT A CLUE Beggars Banquet BEG 6	45 4
5 Aug 78	I DON'T NEED TO TELL HER Beggars Banquet BEG 9	49 4
3 Feb 79	JUST THIRTEEN Beggars Banquet BEG 14	66 2
9 Jun 79	OUT IN THE DARK / CYANIDE Beggars Banquet BEG 19	72 1
17 Nov 79	NEW GUITAR IN TOWN Beggars Banquet BEG 28	72 1

LUSCIOUS JACKSON
US, female vocal / instrumental group (5 WEEKS)

		pos/wks
18 Mar 95	DEEP SHAG / CITYSONG Capitol CDCL 739	69 1
21 Oct 95	HERE Capitol CDCL 758	59 1
12 Apr 97	NAKED EYE Capitol CDCL 786	25 2
3 Jul 99	LADYFINGERS Grand Royal / Parlophone CDCL 813	43 1

LUSH UK, female / male vocal / instrumental group (19 WEEKS)

		pos/wks
10 Mar 90	MAD LOVE (EP) 4AD BAD 003	55 1
27 Oct 90	SWEETNESS AND LIGHT 4AD BAD 0013	47 2
19 Oct 91	NOTHING NATURAL 4AD AD 1016	43 2
11 Jan 92	FOR LOVE (EP) 4AD BAD 2001	35 2
11 Jun 94	HYPOCRITE 4AD BAD 4008CD	52 2
11 Jun 94	DESIRE LINES 4AD BAD 4010CD	60 1
20 Jan 96	SINGLE GIRL 4AD BAD 6001CD	21 3
9 Mar 96	LADYKILLERS 4AD BAD 6002CD	22 3
27 Jul 96	500 (SHAKE BABY SHAKE) 4AD BAD 6009CD	21 3

Tracks on Mad Love (EP): De-Luxe / Leaves Me Cold / Downer / Thoughtforms. Tracks on For Love (EP): For Love / Starlust / Outdoor Miner / Astronaut

LUSTRAL UK, male DJ / production duo
– Ricky Simmons and Steve Jones (3 WEEKS)

		pos/wks
18 Oct 97	EVERYTIME Hooj Choons HOOJCD 55	60 1
4 Dec 99	EVERYTIME (re-mix) Hooj Choons HOOJ 83CD	30 2

See also SPACE BROTHERS; CHAKRA; ASCENSION

LUVVERS – See LULU

LUZON US, male producer – Stacy Burket (1 WEEK)

		pos/wks
14 Jul 01	THE BAGUIO TRACK Renaissance RENCDS 006	67 1

Annabella LWIN Burma, female vocalist (1 WEEK)

		pos/wks
28 Jan 95	DO WHAT YOU DO Sony S2 6611235	61 1

John LYDON UK, male vocalist (6 WEEKS)

		pos/wks
13 Nov 93	OPEN UP Hard Hands HAND 009CD 1	13 5
2 Aug 97	SUN Virgin VUSCD 122	42 1

1 Leftfield Lydon

See also PUBLIC IMAGE LTD; SEX PISTOLS

Frankie LYMON and the TEENAGERS
US, male vocal group, leader d. 28 Feb 1968 (38 WEEKS)

		pos/wks
29 Jun 56 ★	WHY DO FOOLS FALL IN LOVE Columbia DB 3772 1	1 16
29 Mar 57	I'M NOT A JUVENILE DELINQUENT Columbia 33 DB 3878	12 7
12 Apr 57 ●	BABY, BABY Columbia DB 3878	4 12
20 Sep 57	GOODY GOODY Columbia DB 3983	24 3

1 Teenagers featuring Frankie Lymon

Des LYNAM featuring WIMBLEDON CHORAL SOCIETY
UK, male vocalist / TV presenter with choir (3 WEEKS)

		pos/wks
12 Dec 98	IF – READ TO FAURE'S 'PAVANE' BBC Worldwide WMSS 60062	45 3

Curtis LYNCH Jr featuring Kele LE ROC and RED RAT UK, male producer and female vocalist and Jamaica, male vocalist (1 WEEK)

		pos/wks
30 Sep 00	THINKING OF YOU Telstar CDSTAS3136	70 1

Kenny LYNCH UK, male vocalist (59 WEEKS)

		pos/wks
30 Jun 60	MOUNTAIN OF LOVE HMV POP 751	33 3
13 Sep 62	PUFF (re) HMV POP 1057	33 6
6 Dec 62 ●	UP ON THE ROOF HMV POP 1090	10 12
20 Jun 63 ●	YOU CAN NEVER STOP ME LOVING YOU HMV POP 1165	10 14
16 Apr 64	STAND BY ME HMV POP 1280	39 7
27 Aug 64	WHAT AM I TO YOU (re) HMV POP 1321	37 6
17 Jun 65	I'LL STAY BY YOU HMV POP 1430	29 7

Re-entries are listed as (re), (2re), (3re), etc which signifies that the hit re-entered the chart once, twice or three times, etc

| 20 Aug 83 | HALF THE DAY'S GONE AND WE HAVEN'T EARNED A PENNY *Satril SAT 510* | 50 | 4 |

Liam LYNCH *US, male vocalist (4 WEEKS)* pos/wks

| 7 Dec 02 ● | UNITED STATES OF WHATEVER *Global Warming WARMCD 17* | 10 | 4+ |

Cheryl LYNN *US, female vocalist (2 WEEKS)* pos/wks

| 8 Sep 84 | ENCORE *Streetwave KHAN 23* | 68 | 2 |

Patti LYNN *UK, female vocalist (5 WEEKS)* pos/wks

| 10 May 62 | JOHNNY ANGEL *Fontana H 391* | 37 | 5 |

Tami LYNN *US, female vocalist (20 WEEKS)* pos/wks

| 22 May 71 ● | I'M GONNA RUN AWAY FROM YOU *Mojo 2092 001* | 4 | 14 |
| 3 May 75 | I'M GONNA RUN AWAY FROM YOU (re-issue) *Contempo Raries CS 9026* | 36 | 6 |

Vera LYNN
UK, female vocalist – Vera Welsh (46 WEEKS) pos/wks

14 Nov 52 ●	AUF WIEDERSEH'N SWEETHEART *Decca F 9927* ▲	10	1
14 Nov 52 ●	FORGET-ME-NOT (re) *Decca F 9985*	5	6
14 Nov 52 ●	THE HOMING WALTZ *Decca F 9959*	9	3
5 Jun 53	THE WINDSOR WALTZ *Decca F 10092*	11	1
15 Oct 54 ★	MY SON, MY SON *Decca F 10372* [1]	1	14
8 Jun 56	WHO ARE WE *Decca F 10715*	30	1
26 Oct 56	A HOUSE WITH LOVE IN IT *Decca F 10799*	17	13
15 Mar 57	THE FAITHFUL HUSSAR (DON'T CRY MY LOVE) *Decca F 10846*	29	2
21 Jun 57	TRAVELLIN' HOME *Decca F 10903*	20	5

[1] Vera Lynn with Frank Weir, his saxophone, his Orchestra and Chorus

Jeff LYNNE *UK, male vocalist (4 WEEKS)* pos/wks

| 30 Jun 90 | EVERY LITTLE THING *Reprise W 9799* | 59 | 4 |

See also ELECTRIC LIGHT ORCHESTRA

Shelby LYNNE *US, female vocalist (1 WEEK)* pos/wks

| 29 Apr 00 | LEAVIN' *Mercury 5627372* | 73 | 1 |

Philip LYNOTT *Ireland, male vocalist d. 4 Jan 1986 (36 WEEKS)* pos/wks

5 Apr 80	DEAR MISS LONELY HEARTS *Vertigo SOLO 1*	32	6
21 Jun 80	KING'S CALL *Vertigo SOLO 2*	35	6
21 Mar 81	YELLOW PEARL (re) *Vertigo SOLO 3*	14	12
18 May 85 ●	OUT IN THE FIELDS *10 TEN 49* [1]	5	10
24 Jan 87	KING'S CALL (re-mix) *Vertigo LYN 1*	68	2

[1] Gary Moore and Phil Lynott

'Yellow Pearl' made its peak position on re-entry in Dec 1981

See also THIN LIZZY

LYNYRD SKYNYRD
US, male vocal / instrumental group (21 WEEKS) pos/wks

| 11 Sep 76 | SWEET HOME ALABAMA / DOUBLE TROUBLE (2re) *MCA 251* | 21 | 21 |

Sweet Home Alabama / Double Trouble was the chart listing for what was also alternatively listed as the Freebird EP for the two re-entries which peaked at No.43 in Dec 1979 and No.21 in 1982. 1976 chart peak was No.31

Barbara LYON
US, female vocalist d. 10 Jul 1985 (12 WEEKS) pos/wks

| 24 Jun 55 | STOWAWAY *Columbia DB 3619* | 12 | 8 |
| 21 Dec 56 | LETTER TO A SOLDIER *Columbia DB 3865* | 27 | 4 |

LYTE FUNKIE ONES
US, male vocal / rap group (20 WEEKS) pos/wks

| 22 May 99 | CAN'T HAVE YOU *Logic 74321649152* | 54 | 1 |

18 Sep 99	SUMMER GIRLS *Logic 74321701152*	16	7
5 Feb 00 ●	GIRL ON TV *Logic 74321717582*	6	9
27 Apr 02	EVERY OTHER TIME *Logic 74321925502*	24	3

Humphrey LYTTELTON BAND
UK, male jazz band – Humphrey Lyttelton – trumpet (6 WEEKS) pos/wks

| 13 Jul 56 | BAD PENNY BLUES *Parlophone R 4184* | 19 | 6 |

M

M
UK, male vocalist / multi-instrumentalist – Robin Scott (39 WEEKS) pos/wks

7 Apr 79 ●	POP MUZIK *MCA 413* ▲	2	14
8 Dec 79	MOONLIGHT AND MUZAK *MCA 541*	33	9
15 Mar 80	THAT'S THE WAY THE MONEY GOES *MCA 570*	45	5
22 Nov 80	OFFICIAL SECRETS *MCA 650*	64	2
10 Jun 89	POP MUZIK (re-mix) *Freestyle FRS 1*	15	9

Bobby M featuring Jean CARN
US, male / female vocal / instrumental duo (3 WEEKS) pos/wks

| 29 Jan 83 | LET'S STAY TOGETHER *Gordy TMG 1288* | 53 | 3 |

M and O BAND *UK, male vocal / instrumental duo – Muff Murfin and Colin Owen (6 WEEKS)* pos/wks

| 28 Feb 76 | LET'S DO THE LATIN HUSTLE *Creole CR 120* | 16 | 6 |

M&S presents GIRL NEXT DOOR
UK, male production duo and female vocalist (13 WEEKS) pos/wks

| 7 Apr 01 ● | SALSOUL NUGGET (IF U WANNA) *ffrr FCD 393* | 6 | 13 |

MBD – See SO SOLID CREW

M-BEAT
UK, male producer – Marlon Hart (24 WEEKS) pos/wks

18 Jun 94	INCREDIBLE *Renk RENK 42CD* [1]	39	3
10 Sep 94 ●	INCREDIBLE (re-mix) *Renk CDRENK 44* [1]	8	9
17 Dec 94	SWEET LOVE *Renk CDRENK 49* [2]	18	7
1 Jun 96	DO U KNOW WHERE YOU'RE COMING FROM *Renk CDRENK 63* [3]	12	5

[1] M-Beat featuring General Levy [2] M-Beat featuring Nazlyn [3] M-Beat featuring Jamiroquai

M-D-EMM
UK, male producer – Mark Ryder (3 WEEKS) pos/wks

| 22 Feb 92 | GET DOWN *Strictly Underground 7STUR 13* | 55 | 2 |
| 30 May 92 | MOVE YOUR FEET *Strictly Underground STUR 15* | 67 | 1 |

See also Mark RYDER

MDM
UK, male producer – Matt Darey (1 WEEK) pos/wks

| 27 Oct 01 | MASH IT UP *Nulife / Arista 74321870472* | 66 | 1 |

See also Matt DAREY; SUNBURST; MELT featuring Little Ms MARCIE

M DUBS featuring LADY SAW
UK / Jamaica, male producer / female vocalist (1 WEEK) pos/wks

| 16 Dec 00 | BUMP N GRIND (I AM FEELING HOT TONIGHT) *Telstar CDSTAS 3129* | 59 | 1 |

MFSB US, orchestra (18 WEEKS)
		pos/wks	
27 Apr 74	**TSOP (THE SOUND OF PHILADELPHIA)**		
	Philadelphia International PIR 2289 [1] ▲	**22**	9
26 Jul 75	**SEXY** *Philadelphia International PIR 3381*	**37**	5
31 Jan 81	**MYSTERIES OF THE WORLD** *Sound of Philadelphia PIR 9501*	**41**	4

[1] MFSB featuring the Three Degrees

M FACTOR UK, male DJ / production duo
– Danny Harrison and Julian Jonah (4 WEEKS)
		pos/wks	
6 Jul 02	**MOTHER** *Serious SERR 042CD*	**18**	4

MG's – See BOOKER T and the MG's

MK US, male producer – Mark Kinchen (3 WEEKS)
		pos/wks	
4 Feb 95	**ALWAYS** *Activ CDTV 3* [1]	**69**	1
27 May 95	**BURNING '95** *Activ CDTVR 6*	**44**	2

[1] MK featuring Alana

Alana appears on both hits, although she is credited only on the first

M + M Canada, male / female vocal duo (4 WEEKS)
		pos/wks	
28 Jul 84	**BLACK STATIONS WHITE STATIONS** *RCA 426*	**46**	4

M + M are Martha and a Muffin

See also MARTHA and the MUFFINS

MN8 UK / Trinidad, male vocal group (38 WEEKS)
		pos/wks	
4 Feb 95	● **I'VE GOT A LITTLE SOMETHING FOR YOU** *Columbia 6608802*	**2**	13
29 Apr 95	● **IF YOU ONLY LET ME IN** *Columbia 6613252*	**6**	7
15 Jul 95	● **HAPPY** *Columbia 6622192*	**8**	7
4 Nov 95	**BABY IT'S YOU (re)** *Columbia 6624522*	**22**	3
24 Feb 96	**PATHWAY TO THE MOON** *Columbia 6629212*	**25**	2
31 Aug 96	**TUFF ACT TO FOLLOW** *Columbia 6635345*	**15**	3
26 Oct 96	**DREAMING** *Columbia 6638302*	**21**	3

MNO Belgium, male instrumental / production group (2 WEEKS)
		pos/wks	
28 Sep 91	**GOD OF ABRAHAM** *A&M AM 820*	**66**	2

M.O.P.
US, male rap duo – Jamal Grinnage and Eric Murry (19 WEEKS)
		pos/wks	
12 May 01	● **COLD AS ICE** *Epic 6711762*	**4**	10
18 Aug 01	● **ANTE UP (re)** *Epic 6717882* [1]	**7**	8
1 Dec 01	**STAND CLEAR** *Chrysalis CDEM 597* [2]	**43**	1
8 Jun 02	**STAND CLEAR (re-issue)** *Kaos KAOSCD 002* [2]	**50**	1

[1] M.O.P. featuring Busta Rhymes [2] Adam F featuring M.O.P.

M PEOPLE 186 Top 500
Clubland favourites turned pop soul sophisticates: Heather Small (v), backed by Paul Heard and Mike Pickering (both k / prog). In 1994 this Manchester act was voted Best British Dance Act at the Brits and won the 1993 Mercury Music Prize for their LP 'Elegant Slumming' (137 WEEKS)
		pos/wks	
26 Oct 91	**HOW CAN I LOVE YOU MORE?** *Deconstruction PB 44855*	**29**	9
7 Mar 92	**COLOUR MY LIFE** *Deconstruction PB 45241*	**35**	4
18 Apr 92	**SOMEDAY** *Deconstruction PB 45369* [1]	**38**	3
10 Oct 92	**EXCITED** *Deconstruction 74321116337*	**29**	5
6 Feb 93	● **HOW CAN I LOVE YOU MORE? (re-mix)**		
	Deconstruction 74321130232	**8**	8
26 Jun 93	● **ONE NIGHT IN HEAVEN** *Deconstruction 74321151852*	**6**	11
25 Sep 93	● **MOVING ON UP** *Deconstruction 74321166162*	**2**	11
4 Dec 93	● **DON'T LOOK ANY FURTHER** *Deconstruction 74321177112*	**9**	10
12 Mar 94	● **RENAISSANCE** *Deconstruction 74321194132*	**5**	7
17 Sep 94	**ELEGANTLY AMERICAN: ONE NIGHT IN HEAVEN / MOVING ON UP (EP) (re-mix)** *Deconstruction 74321231882*	**31**	2
19 Nov 94	● **SIGHT FOR SORE EYES** *Deconstruction 74321245472*	**6**	9
4 Feb 95	● **OPEN YOUR HEART** *Deconstruction 74321261532*	**9**	7
24 Jun 95	● **SEARCH FOR THE HERO** *Deconstruction 74321287962*	**9**	7
14 Oct 95	**LOVE RENDEZVOUS** *Deconstruction 74321319282*	**32**	4
25 Nov 95	**ITCHYCOO PARK** *Deconstruction 74321330732*	**11**	8
4 Oct 97	● **JUST FOR YOU** *BMG 74321523002*	**8**	7
6 Dec 97	**FANTASY ISLAND (re)** *BMG 74321542932*	**33**	9
28 Mar 98	● **ANGEL STREET** *M People 74321564182*	**8**	6
7 Nov 98	**TESTIFY** *M People 74321621742*	**12**	6
13 Feb 99	**DREAMING** *M People 74321645352*	**13**	4

[1] M People with Heather Small

M3 UK, male / female production / vocal trio (2 WEEKS)
		pos/wks	
30 Oct 99	**BAILAMOS** *Inferno CDFERN 21*	**40**	2

M2M Norway, female vocal / instrumental
duo – Marit Larsen and Marion Raven (6 WEEKS)
		pos/wks	
1 Apr 00	**DON'T SAY YOU LOVE ME** *Atlantic AT 0081CD*	**16**	6

MXM Italy, male / female vocal / instrumental group (1 WEEK)
		pos/wks	
2 Jun 90	**NOTHING COMPARES 2 U** *London LON 267*	**68**	1

Timo MAAS Germany, male DJ / producer (10 WEEKS)
		pos/wks	
1 Apr 00	**DER SCHIEBER** *48k / Perfecto SPECT 07CDS*	**50**	1
30 Sep 00	**UBIK** *Perfecto PERF 10CDS* [1]	**33**	2
23 Feb 02	**TO GET DOWN** *Perfecto PERF 30CDS*	**14**	4
11 May 02	**SHIFTER** *Perfecto PERF 31CDS* [2]	**38**	2
5 Oct 02	**HELP ME** *Perfecto PERF 42CDS* [3]	**65**	1

[1] Timo Mass featuring Martin Bettinghaus [2] Timo Maas featuring MC Chickaboo
[3] Timo Maas featuring Kelis

Pete MAC Jr US, male vocalist (4 WEEKS)
		pos/wks	
15 Oct 77	**THE WATER MARGIN** *BBC RESL 50*	**37**	4

This is the Japanese version of the song which shared chart credit with the English-language version by Godiego

See also GODIEGO

Scott MAC – See SIGNUM

MAC BAND featuring the McCAMPBELL BROTHERS
US, male vocal group (17 WEEKS)
		pos/wks	
18 Jun 88	● **ROSES ARE RED** *MCA MCA 1264*	**8**	13
10 Sep 88	**STALEMATE** *MCA MCA 1271*	**40**	4

'Stalemate' credits the McCampbell Brothers on the sleeve only, not on the label

Keith MAC PROJECT
UK, male / female vocal / instrumental group (1 WEEK)
		pos/wks	
25 Jun 94	**DE DAH DAH (SPICE OF LIFE)** *Public Demand PPDCD 3*	**66**	1

David McALMONT UK, male vocalist (5 WEEKS)
		pos/wks	
27 Apr 96	**HYMN** *Blanco Y Negro NEG 87CD* [1]	**65**	1
9 Aug 97	**LOOK AT YOURSELF** *Hut HUTCD 87*	**40**	2
22 Nov 97	**DIAMONDS ARE FOREVER** *East West EW 141CD* [2]	**39**	2

[1] Ultramarine featuring David McAlmont [2] David McAlmont / David Arnold

See also McALMONT & BUTLER

McALMONT & BUTLER
UK, male vocal / instrumental duo (17 WEEKS)
		pos/wks	
27 May 95	● **YES** *Hut HUTCD 53*	**8**	8
4 Nov 95	**YOU DO** *Hut HUTCD 57*	**17**	4
10 Aug 02	**FALLING** *Chrysalis CDCHS 5141*	**23**	3
9 Nov 02	**BRING IT BACK** *Chrysalis CDCHSS 5145*	**36**	2

See also David McALMONT; Bernard BUTLER

Neil MacARTHUR UK, male vocalist – Colin Blunstone (5 WEEKS)
		pos/wks	
5 Feb 69	**SHE'S NOT THERE** *Deram DM 225*	**34**	5

David MacBETH UK, male vocalist (4 WEEKS)
		pos/wks	
30 Oct 59	**MR BLUE** *Pye 7N 15231*	**18**	4

Nicko McBRAIN
UK, male vocalist / instrumentalist – drums (1 WEEK)   pos/wks

13 Jul 91	RHYTHM OF THE BEAST *EMI NICK 01*..................	72 1

Frankie McBRIDE *Ireland, male vocalist (15 WEEKS)*   pos/wks

9 Aug 67	FIVE LITTLE FINGERS *Emerald MD 1081*....................	19 15

Dan McCAFFERTY *UK, male vocalist (3 WEEKS)*   pos/wks

13 Sep 75	OUT OF TIME *Mountain TOP 1*	41 3

CW McCALL *US, male vocalist – William Fries (10 WEEKS)*   pos/wks

14 Feb 76 ●	CONVOY *MGM 2006 560* ▲	2 10

Noel McCALLA – See BIGFELLA featuring Noel McCALLA

David McCALLUM *UK, male actor / vocalist (4 WEEKS)*   pos/wks

14 Apr 66	COMMUNICATION *Capitol CL 15439*	32 4

McCAMPBELL BROTHERS – See MAC BAND featuring the McCAMPBELL BROTHERS

Linda McCARTNEY
US, female vocalist – Linda Eastman, d. 17 Apr 1998 (7 WEEKS)   pos/wks

28 Aug 71	BACK SEAT OF MY CAR *Apple R 5914* [1]	39 5
21 Nov 98	WIDE PRAIRIE *Parlophone CDR 6510*	74 1
6 Feb 99	THE LIGHT COMES FROM WITHIN *Parlophone CDR 6513*	56 1

[1] Paul and Linda McCartney

See also Paul McCARTNEY

Paul McCARTNEY   ⬭15⬭   `Top 500`
Pop's most successful singer / songwriter and the richest man in British music, b. 18 Jun, 1942, Liverpool. His composition 'Yesterday' is the world's most recorded song and has had more than seven million plays on US radio alone. This entertainer, known for his charitable work, has broken attendance records around the world: his 50-date 2002 US tour grossed a record $100m and a 1999 internet show attracted at least 50 million hits. Winner of a record number of Ivor Novello Awards, he was awarded the only Rhodium record (from Guinness) to honour outstanding sales and received Lifetime Achievement Grammy (1990) and knighthood (1997). He has reportedly amassed a personal fortune of £500m. Sir Paul is the only artist to have No.1s as a solo artist, part of a duo, trio, quartet, quintet and charity group. Best-selling single: 'Mull of Kintyre / Girls' School' 2,050,000 (410 WEEKS)   pos/wks

27 Feb 71 ●	ANOTHER DAY *Apple R 5889*	2 12
28 Aug 71	BACK SEAT OF MY CAR *Apple R 5914* [1]	39 5
26 Feb 72	GIVE IRELAND BACK TO THE IRISH *Apple R 5936* [2]	16 8
27 May 72 ●	MARY HAD A LITTLE LAMB *Apple R 5949* [2]	9 11
9 Dec 72 ●	HI, HI, HI / C MOON *Apple R 5973* [2]	5 13
7 Apr 73 ●	MY LOVE *Apple R 5985* [3] ▲	9 11
9 Jun 73 ●	LIVE AND LET DIE (re) *Apple R 5987* [2]	9 14
3 Nov 73	HELEN WHEELS *Apple R 5993* [3]	12 12
2 Mar 74	JET *Apple R 5996* [3]	7 9
6 Jul 74 ●	BAND ON THE RUN *Apple R 5997* [3] ▲	3 11
9 Nov 74	JUNIOR'S FARM *Apple R 5999* [3]	16 10
31 May 75 ●	LISTEN TO WHAT THE MAN SAID *Capitol R 6006* [2] ▲	6 8
18 Oct 75	LETTING GO *Capitol R 6008* [2]	41 3
15 May 76 ●	SILLY LOVE SONGS *Parlophone R 6014* [2] ▲	2 11
7 Aug 76 ●	LET 'EM IN *Parlophone R 6015* [2]	2 10
19 Feb 77	MAYBE I'M AMAZED *Parlophone R 6017* [2]	28 5
19 Nov 77 ★	MULL OF KINTYRE / GIRLS' SCHOOL *Capitol R 6018* [2] ◆	1 17
1 Apr 78 ●	WITH A LITTLE LUCK *Parlophone R 6019* [2] ▲	5 9
1 Jul 78	I'VE HAD ENOUGH *Parlophone R 6020* [2]	42 7
9 Sep 78	LONDON TOWN *Parlophone R 6021* [2]	60 4
7 Apr 79 ●	GOODNIGHT TONIGHT *Parlophone R 6023* [2]	5 10
16 Jun 79	OLD SIAM SIR *Parlophone R 6026* [2]	35 6
1 Sep 79	GETTING CLOSER / BABY'S REQUEST *Parlophone R 6027* [2] 60 3
1 Dec 79 ●	WONDERFUL CHRISTMASTIME *Parlophone R 6029*	6 8
19 Apr 80 ●	COMING UP *Parlophone R 6035* ▲	2 9
21 Jun 80 ●	WATERFALLS *Parlophone R 6037*	9 8
10 Apr 82 ★	EBONY AND IVORY *Parlophone 6054* [4] ▲	1 10

3 Jul 82	TAKE IT AWAY *Parlophone R 6056*	15 10
9 Oct 82	TUG OF WAR *Parlophone R 6057*	53 3
6 Nov 82 ●	THE GIRL IS MINE (re) *Epic EPC A 2729* [5]	8 10
15 Oct 83 ●	SAY SAY SAY *Parlophone R 6062* [6] ▲	2 15
17 Dec 83 ★	PIPES OF PEACE *Parlophone R 6064*	1 12
6 Oct 84 ●	NO MORE LONELY NIGHTS (BALLAD) *Parlophone R 6080*	2 15
24 Nov 84 ●	WE ALL STAND TOGETHER (re) *Parlophone R 6086* [7]	3 18
30 Nov 85	SPIES LIKE US *Parlophone R 6118*	13 10
26 Jul 86	PRESS *Parlophone R 6133*	25 8
13 Dec 86	ONLY LOVE REMAINS *Parlophone R 6148*	34 5
28 Nov 87 ●	ONCE UPON A LONG AGO *Parlophone R 6170*	10 7
20 May 89	MY BRAVE FACE *Parlophone R 6213*	18 5
20 May 89 ★	FERRY 'CROSS THE MERSEY *PWL PWL 41* [8] ■	1 7
29 Jul 89	THIS ONE *Parlophone R 6223*	18 6
25 Nov 89	FIGURE OF EIGHT *Parlophone R 6235*	42 3
17 Feb 90	PUT IT THERE *Parlophone R 6246*	32 2
20 Oct 90	BIRTHDAY *Parlophone R 6271*	29 3
8 Dec 90	ALL MY TRIALS *Parlophone CDR 6278*	35 5
9 Jan 93	HOPE OF DELIVERANCE *Parlophone CDR 6330*	18 6
6 Mar 93	C'MON PEOPLE *Parlophone CDRS 6338*	41 3
10 May 97	YOUNG BOY *Parlophone CDRS 6462*	19 3
19 Jul 97	THE WORLD TONIGHT *Parlophone CDR 6472*	23 2
27 Dec 97	BEAUTIFUL NIGHT *Parlophone CDR 6489*	25 4
6 Nov 99	NO OTHER BABY / BROWN EYED HANDSOME MAN *Parlophone CDR 6527*	42 2
10 Nov 01	FROM A LOVER TO A FRIEND *Parlophone CDR 6567*	45 2

[1] Paul and Linda McCartney [2] Wings [3] Paul McCartney and Wings [4] Paul McCartney with Stevie Wonder [5] Michael Jackson and Paul McCartney [6] Paul McCartney and Michael Jackson [7] Paul McCartney and the Frog Chorus [8] Christians, Holly Johnson, Paul McCartney, Gerry Marsden and Stock Aitken Waterman

R 6027 credits no label at all, although the number is a Parlophone one

See also BEATLES

TOP 10 SCOTTISH ACTS

■ Scottish-born chart champions (calculated by weeks on the UK singles chart) together with each act's highest placed hit

1. **LONNIE DONEGAN (321)**
   Gamblin' Man / Putting on the Style

2. **WET WET WET (209)**
   Love Is All Around

3. **SIMPLE MINDS (190)**
   Belfast Child

4. **LULU (178)**
   Relight My Fire

5. **MARMALADE (130)**
   Ob-La-Di, Ob-La-Da

6. **TEXAS (127)**
   Say What You Want

7. **KARL DENVER (127)**
   Wimoweh

8. **BAY CITY ROLLERS (116)**
   Bye Bye Baby

9. **DEACON BLUE (112)**
   Four Bacharach and David Songs (EP)

10. **SHEENA EASTON (104)**
    9 to 5

The 'King of Skiffle' and top of the Scots: Glasgow-born Lonnie Donegan, who died in 2002

Kirsty MacCOLL UK, female vocalist d. 18 Dec 2000 (65 WEEKS) pos/wks

13 Jun 81	THERE'S A GUY WORKS DOWN THE CHIPSHOP SWEARS HE'S ELVIS *Polydor POSP 250*	14	9
19 Jan 85 ●	A NEW ENGLAND *Stiff BUY 216*	7	10
15 Nov 86	GREETINGS TO THE NEW BRUNETTE *Go! Discs GOD 15* [1]	58	2
5 Dec 87 ●	FAIRYTALE OF NEW YORK *Pogue Mahone NY 7* [2]	2	9
8 Apr 89	FREE WORLD *Virgin KMA 1*	43	6
1 Jul 89	DAYS *Virgin KMA 2*	12	9
25 May 91	WALKING DOWN MADISON *Virgin VS 1348*	23	7
17 Aug 91	MY AFFAIR *Virgin VS 1354*	56	4
14 Dec 91	FAIRYTALE OF NEW YORK (re-issue) *PM YZ 628* [2]	36	5
4 Mar 95	CAROLINE *Virgin VSCDX 1517*	58	2
24 Jun 95	PERFECT DAY *Virgin VSCDT 1552* [3]	75	1
29 Jul 95	DAYS (re-issue) *Virgin VSCDT 1558*	42	3

[1] Billy Bragg with Johnny Marr and Kirsty MacColl [2] Pogues featuring Kirsty MacColl [3] Kirsty MacColl and Evan Dando

Neil MacCOLL – See LA's; PRETENDERS

Marilyn McCOO and Billy DAVIS Jr
US, female / male vocal duo (9 WEEKS) pos/wks

19 Mar 77 ●	YOU DON'T HAVE TO BE A STAR (TO BE IN MY SHOW) *ABC 4147* ▲	7	9

Van McCOY US, orchestra, leader d. 6 Jul 1979 (36 WEEKS) pos/wks

31 May 75 ●	THE HUSTLE *Avco 6105 038* [1] ▲	3	12
1 Nov 75	CHANGE WITH THE TIMES *Avco 6105 042*	36	4
12 Feb 77	SOUL CHA CHA *H & L 6105 065*	34	6
9 Apr 77 ●	THE SHUFFLE *H & L 6105 076*	4	14

[1] Van McCoy with the Soul City Symphony

McCOYS US, male vocal / instrumental group (18 WEEKS) pos/wks

2 Sep 65 ●	HANG ON SLOOPY *Immediate IM 001* ▲	5	14
16 Dec 65	FEVER *Immediate IM 021*	44	4

George McCRAE US, male vocalist (62 WEEKS) pos/wks

29 Jun 74 ★	ROCK YOUR BABY *Jayboy BOY 85* ▲	1	14
5 Oct 74 ●	I CAN'T LEAVE YOU ALONE *Jayboy BOY 90*	9	9
14 Dec 74	YOU CAN HAVE IT ALL *Jayboy BOY 92*	23	9
22 Mar 75	SING A HAPPY SONG *Jayboy BOY 95*	38	4
19 Jul 75 ●	IT'S BEEN SO LONG *Jayboy BOY 100*	4	11
18 Oct 75	I AIN'T LYIN' *Jayboy BOY 105*	12	7
24 Jan 76	HONEY I *Jayboy BOY 107*	33	4
25 Feb 84	ONE STEP CLOSER (TO LOVE) *President PT 522*	57	4

Gwen McCRAE US, female vocalist (5 WEEKS) pos/wks

30 Apr 88	ALL THIS LOVE THAT I'M GIVING *Flame MELT 7*	63	2
13 Feb 93	ALL THIS LOVE I'M GIVING *KTDA CDKTDA 2* [1]	36	3

[1] Music and Mystery featuring Gwen McCrae

McCRARYS US, male / female vocal group (4 WEEKS) pos/wks

31 Jul 82	LOVE ON A SUMMER NIGHT *Capitol CL 251*	52	4

Mindy McCREADY US, female vocalist (3 WEEKS) pos/wks

1 Aug 98	OH ROMEO *BNA 74321597242*	41	3

Ian McCULLOCH UK, male vocalist (14 WEEKS) pos/wks

15 Dec 84	SEPTEMBER SONG *Korova KOW 40*	51	5
2 Sep 89	PROUD TO FALL *WEA YZ 417*	51	4
12 May 90	CANDLELAND (THE SECOND COMING) *East West YZ 452* [1]	75	1
22 Feb 92	LOVER LOVER LOVER *East West YZ 643*	47	4

[1] Ian McCulloch featuring Elizabeth Fraser

See also ECHO and the BUNNYMEN

Martine McCUTCHEON UK, female actor / vocalist (65 WEEKS) pos/wks

18 Nov 95	ARE YOU MAN ENOUGH *Avex UK AVEX CD 14* [1]	62	1

17 Apr 99 ★	PERFECT MOMENT (re) *Innocent SINCD 7* ■	1	20
11 Sep 99 ●	I'VE GOT YOU *Innocent SINCD 12*	6	10
4 Dec 99 ●	TALKING IN YOUR SLEEP / LOVE ME *Innocent SINCD 14*	6	16
4 Nov 00 ●	I'M OVER YOU *Innocent SINCD 20*	2	10
3 Feb 01 ●	ON THE RADIO *Innocent SINCD 21*	7	8

[1] Uno Clio featuring Martine McCutcheon

Gene McDANIELS US, male vocalist (2 WEEKS) pos/wks

16 Nov 61	TOWER OF STRENGTH (re) *London HLG 9448*	49	2

Julie McDERMOTT – See THIRD DIMENSION featuring Julie McDERMOTT; AWESOME 3

Charles McDEVITT SKIFFLE GROUP featuring Nancy WHISKEY
UK, male / female vocal / instrumental group (20 WEEKS) pos/wks

12 Apr 57 ●	FREIGHT TRAIN (re) *Oriole CB 1352*	5	18
14 Jun 57	GREENBACK DOLLAR (re) *Oriole CB 1371*	28	2

Jane McDONALD UK, female vocalist (7 WEEKS) pos/wks

26 Dec 98 ●	CRUISE INTO CHRISTMAS MEDLEY *Focus Music Int CDFM 2*	10	7

Michael McDONALD
US, male vocalist / instrumentalist (49 WEEKS) pos/wks

18 Feb 84	YAH MO B THERE (re) *Qwest 9293947* [1]	44	8
12 Jan 85	YAH MO B THERE (remix) *Qwest 9202887* [1]	12	8
3 May 86 ●	ON MY OWN *MCA MCA 1045* [2] ▲	2	13
26 Jul 86	I KEEP FORGETTIN' *Warner Bros K 17992*	43	6
6 Sep 86	SWEET FREEDOM *MCA MCA 1073*	12	10
24 Jan 87	WHAT A FOOL BELIEVES (re-issue) *Warner Bros. W 8451* [3]	57	3
5 Oct 02	SWEET FREEDOM (re-mix) *Serious SERR 55CD* [4]	54	1

[1] James Ingram with Michael McDonald [2] Patti LaBelle and Michael McDonald [3] Doobie Brothers featuring Michael McDonald [4] Safri Duo featuring Michael McDonald

See also DOOBIE BROTHERS

Carrie McDOWELL US, female vocalist (3 WEEKS) pos/wks

26 Sep 87	UH UH NO NO CASUAL SEX *Motown ZV 41501*	68	3

John McENROE and Pat CASH with the FULL METAL RACKETS
US / Australia, male vocal / instrumental duo with UK, backing group (1 WEEK) pos/wks

13 Jul 91	ROCK 'N' ROLL *Music for Nations KUT 141*	66	1

Reba McENTIRE US, female vocalist (1 WEEK) pos/wks

19 Jun 99	DOES HE LOVE YOU *MCA Nashville MCSTD 55569*	62	1

MACEO & THE MACKS
US male vocal / instrumental group (5 WEEKS) pos/wks

16 May 87	CROSS THE TRACK (WE BETTER GO BACK) *Urban URBX1*	54	5

McFADDEN and WHITEHEAD US, male vocal
duo – Gene McFadden and John Whitehead (10 WEEKS) pos/wks

19 May 79 ●	AIN'T NO STOPPIN' US NOW *Philadelphia International PIR 7365*	5	10

Rachel McFARLANE UK, female vocalist (2 WEEKS) pos/wks

1 Aug 98	LOVER *Multiply CDMULTY 37*	38	2

See also LOVELAND featuring the voice of Rachel McFARLANE

Bobby McFERRIN US, male vocalist (15 WEEKS) pos/wks

24 Sep 88 ●	DON'T WORRY BE HAPPY *Manhattan MT 56* ▲	2	11
17 Dec 88	THINKIN' ABOUT YOUR BODY *Manhattan BLUE 6*	46	4

McGANNS UK, male actors / vocal trio (4 WEEKS)

			pos/wks
14 Nov 98	JUST MY IMAGINATION Coalition COLA 062CD	59	1
6 Feb 99	A HEARTBEAT AWAY Coalition COLA 069CD	42	3

Mike McGEAR UK, male vocalist – Michael McCartney (4 WEEKS)

			pos/wks
5 Oct 74	LEAVE IT Warner Bros. K 16446	36	4

See also SCAFFOLD

Maureen McGOVERN US, female vocalist (8 WEEKS)

			pos/wks
5 Jun 76	THE CONTINENTAL 20th Century BTC 2222	16	8

Shane MacGOWAN UK, male vocalist (9 WEEKS)

			pos/wks
12 Dec 92	WHAT A WONDERFUL WORLD Mute MUTE 151 [1]	72	1
3 Sep 94	THE CHURCH OF THE HOLY SPOOK ZTT ZANG 57CD [2]	74	1
15 Oct 94	THAT WOMAN'S GOT ME DRINKING ZTT ZANG 56CD [2]	34	3
29 Apr 95	HAUNTED ZTT ZANG 65CD [3]	30	2
20 Apr 96	MY WAY ZTT ZANG 79CD	29	2

[1] Nick Cave and Shane MacGowan [2] Shane MacGowan and the Popes [3] Shane MacGowan and Sinead O'Connor

See also POGUES

Ewan McGREGOR – See PF PROJECT featuring Ewan McGREGOR; Nicole KIDMAN

Freddie McGREGOR Jamaica, male vocalist (16 WEEKS)

			pos/wks
27 Jun 87	● JUST DON'T WANT TO BE LONELY Germain DG 24	9	11
19 Sep 87	THAT GIRL (GROOVY SITUATION) Polydor POSP 884	47	5

Mary MacGREGOR US, female vocalist (10 WEEKS)

			pos/wks
19 Feb 77	● TORN BETWEEN TWO LOVERS Ariola America AA 111 ▲	4	10

McGUINNESS FLINT
UK, male vocal / instrumental group (26 WEEKS)

			pos/wks
21 Nov 70	● WHEN I'M DEAD AND GONE Capitol CL 15662	2	14
1 May 71	● MALT AND BARLEY BLUES Capitol CL 15682	5	12

Barry McGUIRE US, male vocalist (13 WEEKS)

			pos/wks
9 Sep 65	● EVE OF DESTRUCTION RCA 1469 ▲	3	13

McGUIRE SISTERS US, female vocal group (24 WEEKS)

			pos/wks
1 Apr 55	NO MORE Vogue Coral Q 72050	20	1
15 Jul 55	SINCERELY Vogue Coral Q 72050 ▲	14	4
1 Jun 56	DELILAH JONES Vogue Coral Q 72161	24	2
14 Feb 58	SUGARTIME Coral Q 72305	14	6
1 May 59	MAY YOU ALWAYS (re) Coral Q 72356	15	11

MACHEL Trinidad, male vocalist (2 WEEKS)

			pos/wks
14 Sep 96	COME DIG IT London LONCD 386	56	2

MACHINE HEAD UK, male vocal / instrumental group (4 WEEKS)

			pos/wks
27 May 95	OLD Roadrunner RR 23403	43	2
6 Dec 97	TAKE MY SCARS Roadrunner RR 22573	73	1
18 Dec 99	FROM THIS DAY Roadrunner RR 21383	74	1

Craig MACK US, male rapper (5 WEEKS)

			pos/wks
12 Nov 94	FLAVA IN YA EAR Bad Boy 74321242582	57	2
1 Apr 95	GET DOWN Puff Daddy 74321263402	54	1
7 Jun 97	SPIRIT Perspective 5822312 [1]	35	2

[1] Sound of Blackness featuring Craig Mack

Lizzy MACK UK, female vocalist (3 WEEKS)

			pos/wks
5 Nov 94	THE POWER OF LOVE Media MCSTD 2016 [1]	49	2
4 Nov 95	DON'T GO Power Station MCSTD 40004	52	1

[1] Fits of Gloom featuring Lizzy Mack

Lonnie MACK US, male instrumentalist – guitar (3 WEEKS)

			pos/wks
14 Apr 79	MEMPHIS Lightning LIG 9011	47	3

'Memphis' was coupled with 'Let's Dance' by Chris Montez as a double A-side

MACK VIBE featuring JACQUELINE
US, male / female vocal / instrumental duo (1 WEEK)

			pos/wks
4 Feb 95	I CAN'T LET YOU GO MCA MCSTD 20020	53	1

Maria McKEE US, female vocalist (23 WEEKS)

			pos/wks
15 Sep 90	★ SHOW ME HEAVEN Epic 656303 7	1	14
26 Jan 91	BREATHE Geffen GFS 1	59	1
1 Aug 92	SWEETEST CHILD Geffen GFS 23	45	4
22 May 93	I'M GONNA SOOTHE YOU Geffen GFSTD 39	35	3
18 Sep 93	I CAN'T MAKE IT ALONE Geffen GFSTD 53	74	1

Kenneth McKELLAR UK, male vocalist (4 WEEKS)

			pos/wks
10 Mar 66	A MAN WITHOUT LOVE Decca F 12341	30	4

Terence McKENNA – See SHAMEN

Gisele MacKENZIE
Canada, female vocalist – Gisele LeFleche (6 WEEKS)

			pos/wks
17 Jul 53	● SEVEN LONELY DAYS (re) Capitol CL 13920	6	6

Scott McKENZIE
US, male vocalist – Philip Blondheim (18 WEEKS)

			pos/wks
12 Jul 67	★ SAN FRANCISCO (BE SURE TO WEAR SOME FLOWERS IN YOUR HAIR) CBS 2816	1	17
1 Nov 67	LIKE AN OLD TIME MOVIE CBS 3009 [1]	50	1

[1] The Voice of Scott McKenzie

Ken MACKINTOSH his SAXOPHONE and his ORCHESTRA
UK, orchestra (9 WEEKS)

			pos/wks
15 Jan 54	● THE CREEP (re) HMV BD 1295	10	2
7 Feb 58	RAUNCHY HMV POP 426	19	6
10 Mar 60	NO HIDING PLACE HMV POP 713	45	1

Brian McKNIGHT US, male vocalist (4 WEEKS)

			pos/wks
6 Jun 98	ANYTIME Motown 8607752	48	2
3 Oct 98	YOU SHOULD BE MINE Motown 8608412	36	2

Julie McKNIGHT US, female vocalist (6 WEEKS)

			pos/wks
14 Apr 01	FINALLY Distance DI 2029 [1]	54	1
29 Sep 01	FINALLY (re-mix) Defected DFECT 37CDS [1]	24	3
15 Jun 02	HOME Defected DFECT 51 CDS	61	1
23 Nov 02	DIAMOND LIFE Distance DI 2409 [2]	52	1

[1] Kings of Tomorrow featuring Julie McKnight [2] Louie Vega and Jay 'Sinister' Sealee starring Julie McKnight

Vivienne McKONE UK, female vocalist (5 WEEKS)

			pos/wks
25 Jul 92	SING (OOH-EE-OOH) ffrr F 183	47	4
31 Oct 92	BEWARE ffrr F 202	69	1

McKOY UK, male / female vocal group (2 WEEKS)

			pos/wks
6 Mar 93	FIGHT Rightrack CDTUM 1	54	2

Noel McKOY – See JTQ; McKOY

Craig McLACHLAN
Australia, male actor / vocalist (40 WEEKS)

			pos/wks
16 Jun 90	● MONA Epic 655784 7 [1]	2	11
4 Aug 90	AMANDA Epic 656170 7 [1]	19	6
10 Nov 90	I ALMOST FELT LIKE CRYING Epic 656310 7 [1]	50	3
23 May 92	ONE REASON WHY Epic 6580677	29	6
14 Nov 92	ON MY OWN Epic 6584677	59	2

24 Jul 93	YOU'RE THE ONE THAT I WANT *Epic 6595222* 2	13	6
25 Dec 93	GREASE *Epic 6600242*	44	4
8 Jul 95	EVERYDAY *MDMC DEVCS 6* 3	65	2

1 Craig McLachlan and Check 1-2 2 Craig McLachlan and Debbie Gibson 3 Craig McLachlan and the Culprits

Sarah McLACHLAN
Canada, female vocalist / instrumentalist (24 WEEKS)   pos/wks

3 Oct 98	ADIA *Arista 74321613902*	18	5
14 Oct 00 ●	SILENCE (re-mix) *Nettwerk 331072* 1	3	16
2 Feb 02	ANGEL (re-mix) *Nettwerk 331482*	36	3

1 Delerium featuring Sarah McLachlan

Tommy McLAIN
US, male vocalist (1 WEEK)   pos/wks

8 Sep 66	SWEET DREAMS *London HL 10065*	49	1

Malcolm McLAREN
UK, male vocalist (65 WEEKS)   pos/wks

4 Dec 82 ●	BUFFALO GALS *Charisma MALC 1* 1	9	12
26 Feb 83	SOWETO *Charisma MALC 2* 2	32	5
2 Jul 83 ●	DOUBLE DUTCH *Charisma MALC 3*	3	13
17 Dec 83	DUCK FOR THE OYSTER *Charisma MALC 4*	54	5
1 Sep 84	MADAM BUTTERFLY (UN BEL DI VEDREMO) *Charisma MALC 5*	13	9
27 May 89	WALTZ DARLING *Epic WALTZ 2* 3	31	8
19 Aug 89	SOMETHING'S JUMPIN' IN YOUR SHIRT *Epic WALTZ 3* 4	29	7
25 Nov 89	HOUSE OF THE BLUE DANUBE *Epic WALTZ 4* 3	73	1
21 Dec 91	MAGIC'S BACK (THEME FROM 'THE GHOSTS OF OXFORD STREET') *RCA PB 45223* 5	42	4
3 Oct 98	BUFFALO GALS STAMPEDE *Virgin VSCDT 1717* 6	65	1

1 Malcolm McLaren and the World's Famous Supreme Team 2 Malcolm McLaren and the McLarenettes 3 Malcolm McLaren and the Bootzilla Orchestra 4 Malcolm McLaren and the Bootzilla Orchestra featuring Lisa Marie 5 Malcolm McLaren featuring Alison Limerick 6 Malcolm McLaren and the World's Famous Supreme Team plus Rakim and Roger Sanchez

Bitty McLEAN
UK, male vocalist (50 WEEKS)   pos/wks

31 Jul 93 ●	IT KEEP RAININ' (TEARS FROM MY EYES) *Brilliant CDBRIL 1*	2	15
30 Oct 93	PASS IT ON *Brilliant CDBRIL 2*	35	3
15 Jan 94 ●	HERE I STAND *Brilliant CDBRIL 3*	10	6
9 Apr 94 ●	DEDICATED TO THE ONE I LOVE *Brilliant CDBRIL 4*	6	10
6 Aug 94	WHAT GOES AROUND *Brilliant CDBRIL 5*	36	3
8 Apr 95	OVER THE RIVER *Brilliant CDBRIL 9*	27	4
17 Jun 95	WE'VE ONLY JUST BEGUN *Brilliant CDBRIL 10*	23	5
30 Sep 95	NOTHING CAN CHANGE THIS LOVE *Brilliant CDBRIL 11*	55	2
27 Jan 96	NATURAL HIGH *Brilliant CDBRIL 12*	63	1
5 Oct 96	SHE'S ALRIGHT *Kuff KUFFD 9*	53	1

Don McLEAN
US, male vocalist / instrumentalist (68 WEEKS)   pos/wks

22 Jan 72 ●	AMERICAN PIE *United Artists UP 35325* ▲	2	16
13 May 72 ★	VINCENT *United Artists UP 35359*	1	15
14 Apr 73	EVERYDAY *United Artists UP 35519*	38	5
10 May 80 ★	CRYING *EMI 5051*	1	14
17 Apr 82	CASTLES IN THE AIR *EMI 5258*	47	8
5 Oct 91	AMERICAN PIE (re-issue) *Liberty EMCT 3*	12	10

Jackie McLEAN
US, male instrumentalist – alto sax (4 WEEKS)   pos/wks

7 Jul 79	DOCTOR JACKYLL AND MISTER FUNK *RCA PB 1575*	53	4

Phil McLEAN
US, male vocalist (4 WEEKS)   pos/wks

18 Jan 62	SMALL SAD SAM *Top Rank JAR 597*	34	4

Ian McNABB
UK, male vocalist (6 WEEKS)   pos/wks

23 Jan 93	IF LOVE WAS LIKE GUITARS *This Way Up WAY 233*	67	1
2 Jul 94	YOU MUST BE PREPARED TO DREAM *This Way Up WAY 3199* 1	54	1
17 Sep 94	GO INTO THE LIGHT *This Way Up WAY 3699*	66	2

27 Apr 96	DON'T PUT YOUR SPELL ON ME *This Way Up WAY 5033*	72	1
6 Jul 96	MERSEYBEAST *This Way Up WAY 5266*	74	1

1 Ian McNabb featuring Ralph Molina and Billy Talbot

See also ICICLE WORKS

Lutricia McNEAL
US, female vocalist (43 WEEKS)   pos/wks

29 Nov 97 ●	AIN'T THAT JUST THE WAY *Wildstar CXSTAS 2907*	6	18
23 May 98 ●	STRANDED *Wildstar CXSTAS 2973*	3	12
26 Sep 98 ●	SOMEONE LOVES YOU HONEY *Wildstar CDWILD 9*	9	7
19 Dec 98	THE GREATEST LOVE YOU'LL NEVER KNOW *Wildstar CDWILD 11*	17	6

Patrick MacNEE and Honor BLACKMAN
UK, male / female actors / vocal duo (7 WEEKS)   pos/wks

1 Dec 90 ●	KINKY BOOTS *Deram KINKY 1*	5	7

Rita MacNEIL
Canada, female vocalist (10 WEEKS)   pos/wks

6 Oct 90	WORKING MAN *Polydor PO 98*	11	10

Clyde McPHATTER
US, male vocalist d. 13 Jun 1972 (1 WEEK)   pos/wks

24 Aug 56	TREASURE OF LOVE *London HLE 8293*	27	1

Carmen McRAE – See Sammy DAVIS Jr

Ralph McTELL
UK, male vocalist – Ralph May (18 WEEKS)   pos/wks

7 Dec 74 ●	STREETS OF LONDON *Reprise K 14380*	2	12
20 Dec 75	DREAMS OF YOU *Warner Bros. K 16648*	36	6

MAD COBRA featuring Richie STEPHENS
Jamaica / UK, male vocal duo (2 WEEKS)   pos/wks

15 May 93	LEGACY *Columbia 6592852*	64	2

MAD DONNA
UK, female vocalist (4 WEEKS)   pos/wks

4 May 02	THE WHEELS ON THE BUS *Star Harbour / All Around the World DISCO 0202R*	17	4

MAD JOCKS featuring JOCKMASTER B.A.
UK, male vocal / instrumental group (9 WEEKS)   pos/wks

19 Dec 87	JOCK MIX 1 *Debut DEBT 3037*	46	5
18 Dec 93	PARTY FOUR (EP) *SMP CDSSKM 24*	57	4

Tracks on Party Four (EP): No Lager / Here We Go Again / Jock Party Mix / Jock Jak Mix

MAD MOSES
US, male DJ / producer – 'Mad' Mitch Moses (1 WEEK)   pos/wks

16 Aug 97	PANTHER PARTY *Hi-Life 5744932*	50	1

MAD STUNTMAN – See REEL 2 REAL

MADAM FRICTION – See CORTINA

Sonya MADAN – See LITHIUM and Sonya MADAN

MADASUN
UK, female vocal group (13 WEEKS)   pos/wks

11 Mar 00	DON'T YOU WORRY *V2 VVR 5011523*	14	6
27 May 00	WALKING ON WATER *V2 VVR 5012418*	14	4
2 Sep 00	FEEL GOOD *V2 VVR 5012983*	29	3

Danny MADDEN
US, male vocalist (2 WEEKS)   pos/wks

14 Jul 90	THE FACTS OF LIFE *Eternal YZ 473*	72	2

MADDER ROSE
US, male / female vocal / instrumental group (2 WEEKS)   pos/wks

26 Mar 94	PANIC ON *Atlantic A 8301CD*	65	1
16 Jul 94	CAR SONG *Seed A 7256CD*	68	1

Re-entries are listed as (re), (2re), (3re), etc which signifies that the hit re-entered the chart once, twice or three times, etc

MADDOG – See STRETCH 'N' VERN present MADDOG

MADE IN LONDON
UK / Norway, female vocal group (6 WEEKS) pos/wks

13 May 00	DIRTY WATER *RCA 74321746192*	**15**	5
9 Sep 00	SHUT YOUR MOUTH *RCA 74321772602*	**74**	1

MADELYNE
Holland, male producer – Carlo Resoort (1 WEEK) pos/wks

7 Sep 02	BEAUTIFUL CHILD (A DEEPER LOVE) *Xtravaganza XTRAV 36CDS*	**63**	1

See also 4 STRINGS

MADEMOISELLE
France, male production / instrumental duo (1 WEEK) pos/wks

8 Sep 01	DO YOU LOVE ME *RCA 74321878952*	**56**	1

MAD'HOUSE
France / Holland, male / female production / vocal group (14 WEEKS) pos/wks

17 Aug 02	● LIKE A PRAYER *Serious SERR 046CD*	**3**	11
9 Nov 02	HOLIDAY *Serious SERR 058CD*	**24**	3

MADISON AVENUE
Australia, male producer – Andy Van Dorsselaer – and female vocalist – Cheyne Coates (25 WEEKS) pos/wks

13 Nov 99	DON'T CALL ME BABY (2re) *VC Recordings VCRD 56*	**30**	6
20 May 00	★ DON'T CALL ME BABY (re-issue) *VC Recordings VCRD 64* ■	**1**	12
21 Oct 00	● WHO THE HELL ARE YOU *VC Recordings VCRD 70*	**10**	5
27 Jan 01	EVERYTHING YOU NEED *VC Recordings VCRD 82*	**33**	2

MADNESS ⟨42⟩ Top 500
London-based band whose ska-rooted 'nutty' sound earned them a huge haul of hits. This good-time septet fronted by Graham 'Suggs' McPherson (b. 13 Jan 1961) spent more weeks on the chart in the 1980s than any other group (268 WEEKS) pos/wks

1 Sep 79	THE PRINCE *2 Tone TT 3*	**16**	11
10 Nov 79	● ONE STEP BEYOND... *Stiff BUY 56*	**7**	14
5 Jan 80	● MY GIRL *Stiff BUY 62*	**3**	10
5 Apr 80	● WORK REST AND PLAY (EP) *Stiff BUY 71*	**6**	8
13 Sep 80	● BAGGY TROUSERS *Stiff BUY 84*	**3**	20
22 Nov 80	● EMBARRASSMENT *Stiff BUY 102*	**4**	12
24 Jan 81	● THE RETURN OF THE LOS PALMAS SEVEN *Stiff BUY 108*	**7**	11
25 Apr 81	● GREY DAY *Stiff BUY 112*	**4**	10
26 Sep 81	● SHUT UP *Stiff BUY 126*	**7**	9
5 Dec 81	● IT MUST BE LOVE *Stiff BUY 134*	**4**	12
20 Feb 82	CARDIAC ARREST *Stiff BUY 140*	**14**	10
22 May 82	★ HOUSE OF FUN *Stiff BUY 146*	**1**	9
24 Jul 82	● DRIVING IN MY CAR *Stiff BUY 153*	**4**	8
27 Nov 82	● OUR HOUSE *Stiff BUY 163*	**5**	13
19 Feb 83	● TOMORROW'S (JUST ANOTHER DAY) / MADNESS (IS ALL IN THE MIND) *Stiff BUY 169*	**8**	9
20 Aug 83	● WINGS OF A DOVE *Stiff BUY 181*	**2**	10
5 Nov 83	● THE SUN AND THE RAIN *Stiff BUY 192*	**5**	10
11 Feb 84	MICHAEL CAINE *Stiff BUY 196*	**11**	8
2 Jun 84	ONE BETTER DAY *Stiff BUY 201*	**17**	7
31 Aug 85	YESTERDAY'S MEN *Zarjazz JAZZ 5*	**18**	7
26 Oct 85	UNCLE SAM *Zarjazz JAZZ 7*	**21**	11
1 Feb 86	SWEETEST GIRL *Zarjazz JAZZ 8*	**35**	6
8 Nov 86	(WAITING FOR) THE GHOST TRAIN (re) *Zarjazz JAZZ 9*	**18**	8
19 Mar 88	I PRONOUNCE YOU *Virgin VS 1054* [1]	**44**	4
15 Feb 92	● IT MUST BE LOVE (re-issue) *Virgin VS 1405*	**6**	9
25 Apr 92	HOUSE OF FUN (re-issue) *Virgin VS 1413*	**40**	3
8 Aug 92	MY GIRL (re-issue) *Virgin VS 1425*	**27**	4
28 Nov 92	THE HARDER THEY COME *Go! Discs GOD 93*	**44**	3
27 Feb 93	NIGHT BOAT TO CAIRO *Virgin VSCDT 1447*	**56**	2
31 Jul 99	● LOVESTRUCK *Virgin VSCDT 1737*	**10**	7
6 Nov 99	JOHNNY THE HORSE *Virgin VSCDT 1740*	**44**	2
11 Mar 00	DRIP FED FRED *Virgin VSCDT 1768* [2]	**55**	1

[1] The Madness [2] Madness featuring Ian Dury

Tracks on Work Rest and Play (EP): Night Boat to Cairo / Deceives the Eye / The Young and the Old / Don't Quote Me on That. 'Night Boat to Cairo' in 1993 is a re-issue of a track from the Work Rest and Play EP

See also SUGGS

MADONNA ⟨5⟩ Top 500
The most successful female chart act of all time in the UK and US, with world sales in excess of 140 million records, b. Madonna Ciccone, 16 Aug 1958, Michigan. Continually ground-breaking and trend-setting, this often controversial artist has amassed an unequalled 35 consecutive UK Top 10 singles (includes two re-entries, a remix and a re-issue) and an unbeatable tally of Top 5 entries. She has also had more UK No.1 singles and albums than any other female soloist, and at one time held the top two slots on the singles chart (1985). Her accumulated UK Top 10 entries are more than The Beatles and Rolling Stones combined, and her album 'The Immaculate Collection' has sold more than 3.3 million copies in the UK alone. In the US, the multi-award-winning singer holds the female record for 27 consecutive Top 20 entries and 16 successive Top 5s plus a dozen No.1s – 10 of which she wrote. Madonna has produced more No.1s than any female, played to packed stadiums around the globe and starred in several successful films. Her 2000 album 'Music' topped the chart in 26 countries and shipped five million albums. She was again voted Best International Female Singer at the 2001 Brits and grossed £40m for the 28 US dates of her Drowned World Tour – the highest figure for a female performer in that year. She is also the most performed artist on the TV show 'Stars In Their Eyes', with eight impressions in the first 14 series' (576 WEEKS) pos/wks

14 Jan 84	● HOLIDAY (re) *Sire W 9405*	**2**	21
17 Mar 84	LUCKY STAR *Sire W 9522*	**14**	9
2 Jun 84	● BORDERLINE (re) *Sire W 9260*	**2**	13
17 Nov 84	● LIKE A VIRGIN *Sire W 9210* ▲	**3**	18
2 Mar 85	● MATERIAL GIRL *Sire W 9083*	**3**	10
8 Jun 85	● CRAZY FOR YOU *Geffen A 6323* ▲	**2**	15
27 Jul 85	★ INTO THE GROOVE *Sire W 8934*	**1**	14
21 Sep 85	● ANGEL *Sire W 8881*	**5**	9
12 Oct 85	● GAMBLER (re) *Geffen A 6585*	**4**	12
7 Dec 85	● DRESS YOU UP *Sire W 8848*	**5**	11
26 Apr 86	● LIVE TO TELL *Sire W 8717* ▲	**2**	12
28 Jun 86	★ PAPA DON'T PREACH *Sire W 8636* ▲	**1**	14
4 Oct 86	★ TRUE BLUE *Sire W 8550*	**1**	15
13 Dec 86	● OPEN YOUR HEART *Sire W 8480* ▲	**4**	9
4 Apr 87	● LA ISLA BONITA *Sire W 8378*	**1**	11
18 Jul 87	★ WHO'S THAT GIRL *Sire W 8341* ▲	**1**	10
19 Sep 87	● CAUSING A COMMOTION *Sire W 8224*	**4**	9
12 Dec 87	● THE LOOK OF LOVE *Sire W 8115*	**9**	7
18 Mar 89	★ LIKE A PRAYER *Sire W 7539* ▲	**1**	12
3 Jun 89	● EXPRESS YOURSELF *Sire W 2948*	**5**	10
16 Sep 89	● CHERISH *Sire W 2883*	**3**	8
16 Dec 89	● DEAR JESSIE *Sire W 2668*	**5**	9
7 Apr 90	★ VOGUE *Sire W 9851* ▲	**1**	14
21 Jul 90	● HANKY PANKY *Sire W 9789*	**2**	9
8 Dec 90	● JUSTIFY MY LOVE *Sire W 9000* ▲	**2**	10
2 Mar 91	● CRAZY FOR YOU (re-mix) *Sire W 0008*	**2**	8
13 Apr 91	● RESCUE ME *Sire W 0024*	**3**	8
8 Jun 91	● HOLIDAY (re-issue) *Sire W 0037*	**5**	7
25 Jul 92	● THIS USED TO BE MY PLAYGROUND *Sire W 0122* ▲	**3**	9
17 Oct 92	● EROTICA (re) *Maverick W 0138*	**3**	9
12 Dec 92	● DEEPER AND DEEPER *Maverick W 0146*	**6**	9
6 Mar 93	● BAD GIRL *Maverick W 0145CD*	**10**	7
3 Apr 93	● FEVER *Maverick W 0168CD*	**6**	6
31 Jul 93	● RAIN *Maverick W 0190CD*	**7**	8
2 Apr 94	● I'LL REMEMBER *Maverick W 0240CD*	**7**	8
8 Oct 94	● SECRET *Maverick W 0268CD*	**5**	9
17 Dec 94	TAKE A BOW *Maverick W 0278CD* ▲	**16**	9
25 Feb 95	● BEDTIME STORY (re) *Maverick W 0285CD*	**4**	9
26 Aug 95	● HUMAN NATURE *Maverick W 0300CD*	**8**	5
4 Nov 95	● YOU'LL SEE *Maverick W 0324CD*	**5**	13
6 Jan 96	OH FATHER *Maverick W 0326CD*	**16**	6
23 Mar 96	ONE MORE CHANCE *Maverick W 0337CD*	**11**	4
2 Nov 96	● YOU MUST LOVE ME (2re) *Warner Bros. W 0378CD*	**10**	6
28 Dec 96	● DON'T CRY FOR ME ARGENTINA *Warner Bros. W 0384CD*	**3**	12
29 Mar 97	● ANOTHER SUITCASE IN ANOTHER HALL *Warner Bros. W 0388CD*	**7**	5
7 Mar 98	★ FROZEN *Maverick W 0433CD* ■	**1**	13
9 May 98	● RAY OF LIGHT (re) *Maverick W 0444CD*	**2**	10
5 Sep 98	● DROWNED WORLD (SUBSTITUTE FOR LOVE) *Maverick W 0453CD1*	**10**	5

5 Dec 98 ●	THE POWER OF GOODBYE / LITTLE STAR		
	Maverick W 459CD	6	9
13 Mar 99 ●	NOTHING REALLY MATTERS (re) Maverick W 471CD	7	9
19 Jun 99 ●	BEAUTIFUL STRANGER Maverick W 495CD	2	16
11 Mar 00 ★	AMERICAN PIE (re) Maverick W 519CD ■	1	14
2 Sep 00 ★	MUSIC Maverick W 537CD1 ▲	1	23
9 Dec 00 ●	DON'T TELL ME Maverick W 547CD1	4	10
28 Apr 01 ●	WHAT IT FEELS LIKE FOR A GIRL (re)		
	Maverick W 533CD	7	11
9 Nov 02 ●	DIE ANOTHER DAY Warner W 595CD	3	8+

Re-entries: 'Holiday' originally peaked at No.6 in 1984 making No.2 only on re-entry in Aug 1985. 'Borderline' peaked at No.56 on its first chart visit before making No.2 on re-entry in Jan 1986

MAGAZINE UK, male vocal / instrumental
group – lead vocal Howard Devoto (7 WEEKS)   pos/wks

11 Feb 78	SHOT BY BOTH SIDES Virgin VS 200	41	4
26 Jul 80	SWEET HEART CONTRACT Virgin VS 368	54	3

MAGIC AFFAIR
US / Germany, male / female vocal / instrumental group (8 WEEKS) pos/wks

4 Jun 94	OMEN III EMI CDEM 317	17	4
27 Aug 94	GIVE ME ALL YOUR LOVE EMI CDEM 340	30	2
5 Nov 94	IN THE MIDDLE OF THE NIGHT EMI CDEM 349	38	2

MAGIC LADY US, female vocal duo (3 WEEKS)   pos/wks

14 May 88	BETCHA CAN'T LOSE (WITH MY LOVE) Motown ZB 42003	58	3

MAGIC LANTERNS
UK, male vocal / instrumental group (3 WEEKS)   pos/wks

7 Jul 66	EXCUSE ME BABY (2re) CBS 202094	44	3

Magik J – See Ian POOLEY

MAGNUM UK, male vocal / instrumental group (26 WEEKS)   pos/wks

22 Mar 80	MAGNUM (DOUBLE SINGLE) Jet 175	47	6
12 Jul 86	LONELY NIGHT Polydor POSP 798	70	2
19 Mar 88	DAYS OF NO TRUST Polydor POSP 910	32	4
7 May 88	START TALKING LOVE Polydor POSP 920	22	4
2 Jul 88	IT MUST HAVE BEEN LOVE Polydor POSP 930	33	4
23 Jun 90	ROCKIN' CHAIR Polydor PO 88	27	4
25 Aug 90	HEARTBROKE AND BUSTED Polydor PO 94	49	2

Tracks on double single: Invasion / Kingdom of Madness / All of My Life /
Great Adventure

MAGOO UK, male vocal / instrumental group (1 WEEK)   pos/wks

4 Apr 98	BLACK SABBATH / SWEET LEAF		
	Fierce Panda NING 47CD [1]	60	1

[1] Magoo : Mogwai

MAGOO – See TIMBALAND; Missy 'Misdemeanor' ELLIOTT

Sean MAGUIRE UK, male vocalist (34 WEEKS)   pos/wks

20 Aug 94	SOMEONE TO LOVE Parlophone CDR 6390	14	7
5 Nov 94	TAKE THIS TIME (re) Parlophone CDR 6395	27	5
25 Mar 95	SUDDENLY Parlophone CDR 6403	18	5
24 Jun 95	NOW I'VE FOUND YOU Parlophone CDLEEPYS 1	22	3
18 Nov 95	YOU TO ME ARE EVERYTHING Parlophone CDR 6420	16	3
25 May 96	GOOD DAY Parlophone CDR 6432	12	4
3 Aug 96	DON'T PULL YOUR LOVE Parlophone CDR 6440	14	4
29 Mar 97	TODAY'S THE DAY Parlophone CDR 6459	27	3

Siobhan MAHER – See OCEANIC

MAHLATHINI and the MAHOTELLA QUEENS – See ART OF NOISE

MAI TAI Guyana, female vocal group (30 WEEKS)   pos/wks

25 May 85 ●	HISTORY Virgin VS 773	8	13

3 Aug 85 ●	BODY AND SOUL Virgin VS 801	9	13
15 Feb 86	FEMALE INTUITION Virgin VS 844	54	4

MAIN INGREDIENT US, male vocal group (7 WEEKS)   pos/wks

29 Jun 74	JUST DON'T WANT TO BE LONELY RCA APBO 0205	27	7

MAISONETTES UK, male / female vocal group (12 WEEKS)   pos/wks

11 Dec 82 ●	HEARTACHE AVENUE Ready Steady Go! RSG 1	7	12

J MAJIK UK, male producer – Jamie Spratling (3 WEEKS)   pos/wks

5 May 01	LOVE IS NOT A GAME Defected DFECT 31CDS [1]	34	2
27 Apr 02	METROSOUND Kaos KAOS 001P [2]	54	1

[1] J Majik featuring Kathy Brown [2] Adam F and J Majik

MAKADOPOULOS and his GREEK SERENADERS
Greece, male vocal / instrumental group (14 WEEKS)   pos/wks

20 Oct 60	NEVER ON SUNDAY Palette PG 9005	36	14

MAKAVELI – See 2PAC

Jack E MAKOSSA Kenya, male producer (5 WEEKS)   pos/wks

12 Sep 87	THE OPERA HOUSE Champion CHAMP 50	48	5

MALA – See BOWA featuring MALA

MALAIKA US, female vocalist (1 WEEK)   pos/wks

31 Jul 93	GOTTA KNOW (YOUR NAME) A&M 5802732	68	1

Carl MALCOLM Jamaica, male vocalist (8 WEEKS)   pos/wks

13 Sep 75 ●	FATTIE BUM BUM UK 108	8	8

Valerie MALCOLM – See CANDY GIRLS

Stephen MALKMUS US, male vocalist (1 WEEK)   pos/wks

28 Apr 01	DISCRETION GROVE Domino RUG 123CD	60	1

Timmy MALLETT – See BOMBALURINA

Raul MALO US, male vocalist (1 WEEK)   pos/wks

18 May 02	I SAID I LOVE YOU Gravity 74321923082	57	1

See also MAVERICKS

MAMA CASS
US, female vocalist – Ellen Cohen, d. 29 Jul 1974 (27 WEEKS)   pos/wks

14 Aug 68	DREAM A LITTLE DREAM OF ME RCA 1726	11	12
16 Aug 69 ●	IT'S GETTING BETTER Stateside SS 8021	8	15

See also MAMAS and the PAPAS

MAMAS and the PAPAS
US, vocal / instrumental group (71 WEEKS)   pos/wks

28 Apr 66	CALIFORNIA DREAMIN' RCA 1503	23	9
12 May 66 ●	MONDAY MONDAY RCA 1516 ▲	3	13
28 Jul 66	I SAW HER AGAIN RCA 1533	11	11
9 Feb 67	WORDS OF LOVE RCA 1564	47	3
6 Apr 67 ●	DEDICATED TO THE ONE I LOVE RCA 1576	2	17
26 Jul 67 ●	CREEQUE ALLEY RCA 1613	9	11
2 Aug 97 ●	CALIFORNIA DREAMIN' (re-issue) MCA MCSTD 48058	9	7

See also MAMA CASS

MAMBAS – See Marc ALMOND

Cheb MAMI – See STING

A MAN CALLED ADAM
UK, male / female vocal / instrumental group (4 WEEKS)   pos/wks

29 Sep 90	BAREFOOT IN THE HEAD (re) Big Life BLR 28	60	4

MAN TO MAN
US, male vocal / instrumental duo (19 WEEKS)   pos/wks

13 Sep 86 ●	MALE STRIPPER (2re) *Bolts BOLTS 4* [1]	4 16
4 Jul 87	I NEED A MAN / ENERGY'S EUROBEAT *Bolts BOLTS 5*	43 3

[1] Man 2 Man meet Man Parrish

'Male Stripper' reached its peak on second re-entry in Feb 1987

MAN WITH NO NAME
UK, male producer – Martin Freeland (6 WEEKS)   pos/wks

30 Sep 95	FLOOR-ESSENCE *Perfecto PERF 108CD*	68 1
20 Jan 96	PAINT A PICTURE *Perfecto PERF 114CD* [1]	42 2
12 Oct 96	TELEPORT / SUGAR RUSH *Perfecto PERF 126CD*	55 1
2 May 98	VAVOOM! *Perfecto PERF 159CD1*	43 1
18 Jul 98	THE FIRST DAY (HORIZON) *Perfecto PERF 164CD*	72 1

[1] Man with No Name featuring Hannah

Melissa MANCHESTER – See Al JARREAU

MANCHESTER UNITED FOOTBALL CLUB
UK, male football team vocalists (56 WEEKS)   pos/wks

8 May 76	MANCHESTER UNITED *Decca F 13633*	50 1
21 May 83	GLORY GLORY MAN UNITED *EMI 5390*	13 5
18 May 85 ●	WE ALL FOLLOW MAN UNITED *Columbia DB 9107*	10 5
19 Jun 93	UNITED (WE LOVE YOU) *Living Beat LBECD 026* [1]	37 2
30 Apr 94 ★	COME ON YOU REDS *PolyGram TV MANU 2*	1 15
13 May 95 ●	WE'RE GONNA DO IT AGAIN *PolyGram TV MANU 952* [2]	6 6
4 May 96 ●	MOVE MOVE MOVE (THE RED TRIBE) (re) *Music Collection MANUCD 1* [3]	6 15
29 May 99	LIFT IT HIGH (ALL ABOUT BELIEF) (re) *Music Collection MANUCD 4* [4]	11 7

[1] Manchester United and the Champions [2] Manchester United Football Squad featuring Stryker [3] 1996 Manchester United FA Cup Squad [4] 1999 Manchester United Squad

MANCHILD
UK, male production duo – Max Odell and Brett Parker (2 WEEKS)   pos/wks

16 Sep 00	THE CLICHES ARE TRUE *One Little Indian 176 TP7CD* [1]	60 1
25 Aug 01	NOTHING WITHOUT ME *One Little Indian 183 TP7CD*	40 1

[1] Manchild featuring Kelly Jones

See also STEREOPHONICS

Henry MANCINI
US, orchestra / chorus, leader d. 14 Jun 1994 (23 WEEKS)   pos/wks

7 Dec 61	MOON RIVER (re) *RCA 1256*	44 3
24 Sep 64 ●	HOW SOON *RCA 1414*	10 12
25 Mar 72	THEME FROM 'CADE'S COUNTY' *RCA 2182*	42 1
11 Feb 84	MAIN THEME FROM 'THE THORN BIRDS' *Warner Bros. 9677*	23 7

Steve MANDELL – See 'DELIVERANCE' SOUNDTRACK

MANFRED MANN (72) Top 500
One of the most regular chart entrants of the 1960s: Manfred Mann (k), Mike Vickers (g), Tom McGuinness (b), Mike Hugg (d), Paul Jones (v) – Jones was replaced by Mike D'Abo in 1966. They were the first group from the south of England to top the US charts during 1964's so-called 'British Invasion' (217 WEEKS)   pos/wks

23 Jan 64 ●	5-4-3-2-1 *HMV POP 1252*	5 13
16 Apr 64	HUBBLE BUBBLE (TOIL AND TROUBLE) *HMV POP 1282*	11 8
16 Jul 64 ★	DO WAH DIDDY DIDDY *HMV POP 1320* ▲	1 14
15 Oct 64 ●	SHA LA LA *HMV POP 1346*	3 12
14 Jan 65 ●	COME TOMORROW *HMV POP 1381*	4 9
15 Apr 65	OH NO, NOT MY BABY *HMV POP 1413*	11 10
16 Sep 65 ●	IF YOU GOTTA GO, GO NOW *HMV POP 1466*	2 12
21 Apr 66 ★	PRETTY FLAMINGO *HMV POP 1523*	1 12
7 Jul 66	YOU GAVE ME SOMEBODY TO LOVE *HMV POP 1541*	36 4
4 Aug 66 ●	JUST LIKE A WOMAN *Fontana TF 730*	10 10
27 Oct 66 ●	SEMI-DETACHED SUBURBAN MR JAMES *Fontana TF 757*	2 12
30 Mar 67 ●	HA! HA! SAID THE CLOWN *Fontana TF 812*	4 11

25 May 67	SWEET PEA *Fontana TF 828*	36 4
24 Jan 68 ★	MIGHTY QUINN *Fontana TF 897*	1 11
12 Jun 68 ●	MY NAME IS JACK *Fontana TF 943*	8 11
18 Dec 68 ●	FOX ON THE RUN *Fontana TF 985*	5 12
30 Apr 69 ●	RAGAMUFFIN MAN *Fontana TF 1013*	8 11
8 Sep 73 ●	JOYBRINGER *Vertigo 6059 083* [1]	9 10
28 Aug 76 ●	BLINDED BY THE LIGHT *Bronze BRO 29* [1] ▲	6 10
20 May 78 ●	DAVY'S ON THE ROAD AGAIN *Bronze BRO 52* [1]	6 12
17 Mar 79	YOU ANGEL YOU *Bronze BRO 68* [1]	54 5
7 Jul 79	DON'T KILL IT CAROL *Bronze BRO 77* [1]	45 4

[1] Manfred Mann's Earth Band

MANHATTAN TRANSFER
US, vocal quartet (72 WEEKS)   pos/wks

7 Feb 76	TUXEDO JUNCTION *Atlantic K 10670*	24 6
5 Feb 77 ★	CHANSON D'AMOUR *Atlantic K 10886*	1 13
28 May 77	DON'T LET GO *Atlantic K 10930*	32 6
18 Feb 78	WALK IN LOVE (re) *Atlantic K 11075*	12 12
20 May 78	ON A LITTLE STREET IN SINGAPORE *Atlantic K 11136*	20 9
16 Sep 78	WHERE DID OUR LOVE GO / JE VOULAIS (TE DIRE QUE JE T'ATTENDS) *Atlantic K 11182*	40 4
23 Dec 78	WHO, WHAT, WHEN, WHERE, WHY *Atlantic K 11233*	49 6
17 May 80	TWILIGHT ZONE – TWILIGHT TONE (MEDLEY) *Atlantic K 11476*	25 8
21 Jan 84	SPICE OF LIFE *Atlantic A 9728*	19 8

MANHATTANS
US, male vocal group (31 WEEKS)   pos/wks

19 Jun 76 ●	KISS AND SAY GOODBYE *CBS 4317* ▲	4 11
2 Oct 76 ●	HURT *CBS 4562*	4 11
23 Apr 77	IT'S YOU *CBS 5093*	43 3
26 Jul 80	SHINING STAR *CBS 8624*	45 4
6 Aug 83	CRAZY *CBS A 3578*	63 2

M.A.N.I.C.
UK, male vocal / production duo (1 WEEK)   pos/wks

18 Apr 92	I'M COMIN' HARDCORE *Union City UCRT 2*	60 1

MANIC MCs featuring Sara CARLSON
UK, male production duo and female vocalist (5 WEEKS)   pos/wks

12 Aug 89	MENTAL *RCA PB 43037*	30 5

MANIC STREET PREACHERS (150) Top 500
Best-selling Welsh act of the 1990s: James Dean Bradfield (v/g), Nicky Wire (b), Sean Moore (d) and Richey Edwards (v/g – missing since 1995 and officially declared dead in 2002). Won trophies for the Best British Group and Best Album at the 1997 and 1999 Brit Awards (150 WEEKS)   pos/wks

25 May 91	YOU LOVE US *Heavenly HVN 10*	62 2
10 Aug 91	STAY BEAUTIFUL *Columbia 6573377*	40 3
9 Nov 91	LOVE'S SWEET EXILE / REPEAT *Columbia 6575827*	26 3
1 Feb 92	YOU LOVE US (re-issue) *Columbia 6577247*	16 4
28 Mar 92	SLASH 'N' BURN *Columbia 6578737*	20 4
13 Jun 92	MOTORCYCLE EMPTINESS *Columbia 6580837*	17 6
19 Sep 92 ●	THEME FROM M.A.S.H. (SUICIDE IS PAINLESS) *Columbia 6583827*	7 6
21 Nov 92	LITTLE BABY NOTHING *Columbia 6587967*	29 3
12 Jun 93	FROM DESPAIR TO WHERE *Columbia 6593372*	25 4
31 Jul 93	LA TRISTESSE DURERA (SCREAM TO A SIGH) *Columbia 6594772*	22 5
2 Oct 93	ROSES IN THE HOSPITAL *Columbia 6597272*	15 3
12 Feb 94	LIFE BECOMING A LANDSLIDE *Columbia 6600702*	36 2
11 Jun 94	FASTER / PCP *Epic 6604472*	16 3
13 Aug 94	REVOL *Epic 6606862*	22 3
15 Oct 94	SHE IS SUFFERING *Epic 6608952*	25 3
27 Apr 96 ●	A DESIGN FOR LIFE (re) *Epic 6630705*	2 11
3 Aug 96 ●	EVERYTHING MUST GO *Epic 6634685*	5 6
12 Oct 96 ●	KEVIN CARTER *Epic 6637752*	9 4
14 Dec 96 ●	AUSTRALIA *Epic 6640442*	7 7
13 Sep 97	MOTORCYCLE EMPTINESS (re-issue) *Epic MANIC 5CD*	41 2
13 Sep 97	YOU LOVE US (2nd re-issue) *Epic MANIC 3CD*	49 1
13 Sep 97	LITTLE BABY NOTHING (re-issue) *Epic MANIC 6CD*	50 1
13 Sep 97	STAY BEAUTIFUL (re-issue) *Epic MANIC 1CD*	52 1
13 Sep 97	SLASH 'N' BURN (re-issue) *Epic MANIC 4CD*	54 1

13 Sep 97	LOVE'S SWEET EXILE (re-issue) *Epic MANIC 2CD*	55	1
5 Sep 98	★ IF YOU TOLERATE THIS YOUR CHILDREN WILL BE NEXT (re) *Epic 6663452* ■	1	11
12 Dec 98	THE EVERLASTING *Epic 6666862*	11	8
20 Mar 99	● YOU STOLE THE SUN FROM MY HEART *Epic 6669532*	5	8
17 Jul 99	TSUNAMI *Epic 6674112*	11	5
22 Jan 00	★ THE MASSES AGAINST THE CLASSES (re) *Epic 6685302* ■	1	7
10 Mar 01	● FOUND THAT SOUL (re) *Epic 6708332*	9	4
10 Mar 01	● SO WHY SO SAD *Epic 6708322*	8	7
16 Jun 01	OCEAN SPRAY *Epic 6712532*	15	4
22 Sep 01	LET ROBESON SING *Epic 6717732*	19	2
26 Oct 02	● THERE BY THE GRACE OF GOD (re) *Epic 6731662*	6	5

The listed flipside of 'Theme From M.A.S.H. (Suicide Is Painless)' was '(Everything I Do) I Do It for You' by Fatima Mansions

Barry MANILOW 190 Top 500

Middle-of-the-road superstar. b. Barry Pincus, 17 Jun 1946, Brooklyn, US. This crowd-pulling singer / songwriter / pianist with a vast and loyal following on both sides of the Atlantic has sold in excess of 50 million albums (136 WEEKS)

		pos/wks	
22 Feb 75	MANDY *Arista 1* ▲	11	9
6 May 78	CAN'T SMILE WITHOUT YOU *Arista 176*	43	7
29 Jul 78	SOMEWHERE IN THE NIGHT / COPACABANA (AT THE COPA) *Arista 196*	42	10
23 Dec 78	COULD IT BE MAGIC *Arista ARIST 229*	25	10
8 Nov 80	LONELY TOGETHER *Arista ARIST 373*	21	13
7 Feb 81	I MADE IT THROUGH THE RAIN *Arista ARIST 384*	37	6
11 Apr 81	BERMUDA TRIANGLE *Arista ARIST 406*	15	9
26 Sep 81	LET'S HANG ON *Arista ARIST 429*	12	11
12 Dec 81	THE OLD SONGS *Arista ARIST 443*	48	8
20 Feb 82	IF I SHOULD LOVE AGAIN *Arista ARIST 453*	66	2
17 Apr 82	STAY *Arista ARIST 464* [1]	23	8
16 Oct 82	● I WANNA DO IT WITH YOU *Arista ARIST 495*	8	8
4 Dec 82	I'M GONNA SIT RIGHT DOWN AND WRITE MYSELF A LETTER *Arista ARIST 503*	36	7
25 Jun 83	SOME KIND OF FRIEND *Arista ARIST 516*	48	2
27 Aug 83	YOU'RE LOOKING HOT TONIGHT *Arista ARIST 542*	47	6
10 Dec 83	READ 'EM AND WEEP *Arista ARIST 551*	17	7
8 Apr 89	PLEASE DON'T BE SCARED *Arista 112186*	35	5
10 Apr 93	COPACABANA (AT THE COPA) (re-mix) *Arista 74321136912*	22	4
20 Nov 93	COULD IT BE MAGIC (re-recording) *Arista 74321174882*	36	3
6 Aug 94	LET ME BE YOUR WINGS *EMI CDEM 336* [2]	73	1

[1] Barry Manilow featuring Kevin Desimone and James Jolis [2] Barry Manilow and Debra Byrd

ARIST 464 was available as both a live and studio recording

MANIX
UK, male / female vocal / instrumental group (6 WEEKS)

		pos/wks	
23 Nov 91	MANIC MINDS *Reinforced RIVET 1209*	63	2
7 Mar 92	OBLIVION (HEAD IN THE CLOUDS) (EP) *Reinforced RIVET 1212*	43	3
8 Aug 92	RAINBOW PEOPLE *Reinforced RIVET 1221*	57	1

Tracks on Oblivion (Head in the Clouds) (EP): Oblivion (Head in the Clouds) / Never Been to Belgium (Gotta Rush) / I Can't Stand It / You Held My Hand

MANKEY *UK, male producer – Andy Manston (1 WEEK)*

		pos/wks	
16 Nov 96	BELIEVE IN ME *Frisky DISKY 3*	74	1

MANKIND *UK, male instrumental group (12 WEEKS)*

		pos/wks	
25 Nov 78	DR WHO *Pinnacle PIN 71*	25	12

Aimee MANN *US, female vocalist (9 WEEKS)*

		pos/wks	
31 Oct 87	TIME STAND STILL *Vertigo RUSH 13* [1]	42	3
28 Aug 93	I SHOULD'VE KNOWN *Imago 72787250437*	55	2
20 Nov 93	STUPID THING *Imago 72787250527*	47	2
5 Mar 94	I SHOULD'VE KNOWN (re-issue) *Imago 72787250602*	45	2

[1] Rush with Aimee Mann

Johnny MANN SINGERS
US, male / female vocal group (13 WEEKS)

		pos/wks	
12 Jul 67	● UP-UP AND AWAY *Liberty LIB 55972*	6	13

MANSUN
UK, male vocal / instrumental group (44 WEEKS)

		pos/wks	
6 Apr 96	ONE (EP) *Parlophone CDR 6430*	37	2
15 Jun 96	TWO (EP) *Parlophone CDR 6437*	32	2
21 Sep 96	THREE (EP) *Parlophone CDR 6447*	19	3
17 Dec 96	WIDE OPEN SPACE *Parlophone CDR 6453*	15	4
15 Feb 97	● SHE MAKES MY NOSE BLEED *Parlophone CDR 6453*	9	5
10 May 97	TAXLOSS *Parlophone CDRS 6465*	15	3
18 Oct 97	● CLOSED FOR BUSINESS *Parlophone CDRS6482*	10	3
11 Jul 98	● LEGACY (EP) *Parlophone CDRS 6497*	7	4
5 Sep 98	BEING A GIRL (PART ONE) (EP) *Parlophone CDR 6503*	13	3
7 Nov 98	NEGATIVE *Parlophone CDR 6508*	27	2
13 Feb 99	SIX *Parlophone CDR 6511*	16	3
12 Aug 00	● I CAN ONLY DISAPPOINT U *Parlophone CDR 6544*	8	6
18 Nov 00	ELECTRIC MAN *Parlophone CDR 6550*	23	2
10 Feb 01	FOOL *Parlophone CDRS 6553*	28	2

Tracks on One (EP): Egg Shaped Fred / Ski Jump Nose / Lemonade Secret Drinker / Thief. Tracks on Two (EP): Take It Easy Chicken / Drastic Sturgeon / The Greatest Pain / Moronica. Tracks on Three (EP): Stripper Vicar / An Open Letter to the Lyrical Trainspotter / No One Knows Us / Things Keep Falling Off Buildings. Tracks on Legacy (EP): CD#1 Legacy (Extended version) / Can't Afford to Die / Spasm of Identity / Check Under the Bed. CD#2 Legacy / Wide Open Space (The Perfecto Remix) / GSOH / Face in the Crowd. Tracks on Being a Girl (Part One) (EP): Being a Girl / I Care / Been Here Before / Hideout / Railings

MANTOVANI and his ORCHESTRA *UK, orchestra,*
leader – Annunzio Paolo Mantovani d. 29 Mar 1980 (52 WEEKS)

		pos/wks	
19 Dec 52	● WHITE CHRISTMAS *Decca F 10017*	6	3
29 May 53	★ THE SONG FROM THE MOULIN ROUGE (2re) *Decca F 10094*	1	23
23 Oct 53	● SWEDISH RHAPSODY (re) *Decca F 10168*	2	18
11 Feb 55	LONELY BALLERINA (re) *Decca F 10395*	16	4
31 May 57	AROUND THE WORLD *Decca F 10888*	20	4

See also David WHITFIELD

Kurtis MANTRONIK
US, male vocalist / instrumentalist / producer (2 WEEKS)

		pos/wks	
15 Aug 98	STRICTLY BUSINESS *Parlophone CDR 6502* [1]	43	1
9 Nov 02	77 STRINGS *Southern Fried ECB 35* [2]	71	1

[1] Kurtis Mantronik vs EPMD [2] Kurtis Mantronik presents Chamonix

MANTRONIX
US / Jamaica, male vocal / instrumental duo – Curtis Kahleel, MC Tee (Toure Embden) replaced Bryce Wilson (1989) (48 WEEKS)

		pos/wks	
22 Feb 86	LADIES *10 TEN 116*	55	4
17 May 86	BASSLINE *10 TEN 118*	34	6
7 Feb 87	WHO IS IT? *10 TEN 137*	40	6
4 Jul 87	SCREAM (PRIMAL SCREAM) *10 TEN 169*	46	4
30 Jan 88	SING A SONG (BREAK IT DOWN) *10 TEN 206*	61	4
12 Mar 88	SIMPLE SIMON (YOU GOTTA REGARD) *10 TEN 217*	72	2
6 Jan 90	● GOT TO HAVE YOUR LOVE *Capitol CL 559* [1]	4	11
12 May 90	● TAKE YOUR TIME *Capitol CL 573* [1]	10	7
2 Mar 91	DON'T GO MESSIN' WITH MY HEART *Capitol CL 608*	22	5
22 Jun 91	STEP TO ME (DO ME) *Capitol CL 613*	59	1

[1] Mantronix featuring Wondress

MANUEL and The MUSIC OF THE MOUNTAINS
UK, orchestra, leader – Geoff Love d. 8 Jul 1991 (31 WEEKS)

		pos/wks	
28 Aug 59	THE HONEYMOON SONG (2re) *Columbia DB 4323*	22	9
13 Oct 60	NEVER ON SUNDAY *Columbia DB 4515*	29	10
13 Oct 66	SOMEWHERE MY LOVE *Columbia DB 7969*	42	2
31 Jan 76	● RODRIGO'S GUITAR CONCERTO DE ARANJUEZ (THEME FROM 2ND MOVEMENT) *EMI 2383*	3	10

Re-entries are listed as (re), (2re), (3re), etc which signifies that the hit re-entered the chart

Roots MANUVA
UK, male rapper – Rodney Hylton Smith (6 WEEKS)   pos/wks

11 Dec 99	DUSTED (re) *Hard Hands HAND 058CD1* [1]	28	3
4 Aug 01	WITNESS (1 HOPE) *Big Dada BDCDS 022*	45	2
20 Oct 01	DREAMY DAYS *Big Dada BDCDS 033*	53	1

[1] Leftfield / Roots Manuva

MARATHON
Germany / UK, male vocal / instrumental group (3 WEEKS)   pos/wks

25 Jan 92	MOVIN' *Ten TEN 395*	36	3

MARAUDERS *UK, male vocal / instrumental group (4 WEEKS)*   pos/wks

8 Aug 63	THAT'S WHAT I WANT (re) *Decca F 11695*	43	4

MARBLES *UK, male vocal duo – Graham*
Bonnet and Trevor Gordon (18 WEEKS)   pos/wks

25 Sep 68 ●	ONLY ONE WOMAN *Polydor 56 272*	5	12
26 Mar 69	THE WALLS FELL DOWN *Polydor 56 310*	28	6

MARC and the MAMBAS – See Marc ALMOND

MARC et CLAUDE *Germany, male DJ / production*
duo – Marc Romboy and Klaus Derichs (13 WEEKS)   pos/wks

21 Nov 98	LA *Positiva CDTIV 104*	28	3
22 Jul 00	I NEED YOUR LOVIN' (LIKE THE SUNSHINE) *Positiva CDTIV 136*	12	7
6 Apr 02	TREMBLE *Positiva CDTIVS 170*	29	3

MARCELS *US, male vocal group*
– lead vocal Cornelius Harp (17 WEEKS)   pos/wks

13 Apr 61 ★	BLUE MOON *Pye International 7N 25073* ▲	1	13
8 Jun 61	SUMMERTIME *Pye International 7N 25083*	46	4

Little Peggy MARCH
US, female vocalist – Margaret Battavio (7 WEEKS)   pos/wks

12 Sep 63	HELLO HEARTACHE, GOODBYE LOVE *RCA 1362*	29	7

MARCO POLO *Italy, male instrumental / production duo (1 WEEK)* pos/wks

8 Apr 95	A PRAYER TO THE MUSIC *Hi-Life HICD 7*	65	1

MARCY PLAYGROUND
US, male vocal / instrumental trio (3 WEEKS)   pos/wks

18 Apr 98	SEX AND CANDY *EMI CDEM 508*	29	3

MARDI GRAS *UK, male vocal / instrumental group (9 WEEKS)*   pos/wks

5 Aug 72	TOO BUSY THINKING ABOUT MY BABY *Bell 1226*	19	9

MARIA – See Maria NAYLER

Kelly MARIE *UK, female vocalist – Jacqueline McKinnon (36 WKS)* pos/wks

2 Aug 80 ★	FEELS LIKE I'M IN LOVE *Calibre PLUS 1*	1	16
18 Oct 80	LOVING JUST FOR FUN *Calibre PLUS 4*	21	7
7 Feb 81	HOT LOVE *Calibre PLUS 5*	22	10
30 May 81	LOVE TRIAL *Calibre PLUS 7*	51	3

Rose MARIE *Ireland, female vocalist (5 WEEKS)*   pos/wks

19 Nov 83	WHEN I LEAVE THE WORLD BEHIND (2re) *A1 284*	63	5

Teena MARIE *US, female vocalist – Mary Brockert (28 WEEKS)*   pos/wks

7 Jul 79	I'M A SUCKER FOR YOUR LOVE *Motown TMG 1146* [1]	43	8
31 May 80 ●	BEHIND THE GROOVE *Motown TMG 1185*	6	10
11 Oct 80	I NEED YOUR LOVIN' *Motown TMG 1203*	28	6
26 Mar 88	OOO LA LA LA *Epic 651423 7*	74	2
10 Nov 90	SINCE DAY ONE *Epic 656429 7*	69	2

[1] Teena Marie, co-lead vocals Rick James

MARILLION (301) Top 500 *Progressive rock group formed in*
Buckinghamshire and originally named after Tolkien's novel Silmarillion.
They reached their peak of popularity in the 80s, when fronted by Scottish
vocalist / songwriter Fish (b. Derek Dick, 25 Apr 1958). When Fish left in
1989 the band continued to make regular visits to the charts with Steve
Hogarth in the role of vocalist / songwriter (103 WEEKS)   pos/wks

20 Nov 82	MARKET SQUARE HEROES (re) *EMI 5351*	53	8
12 Feb 83	HE KNOWS YOU KNOW *EMI 5362*	35	4
18 Jun 83	GARDEN PARTY *EMI 5393*	16	5
11 Feb 84	PUNCH AND JUDY *EMI MARIL 1*	29	4
12 May 84	ASSASSING *EMI MARIL 2.*	22	5
18 May 85 ●	KAYLEIGH *EMI MARIL 3.*	2	14
7 Sep 85 ●	LAVENDER *EMI MARIL 4.*	5	9
30 Nov 85	HEART OF LOTHIAN *EMI MARIL 5.*	29	6
23 May 87 ●	INCOMMUNICADO *EMI MARIL 6.*	6	5
25 Jul 87	SUGAR MICE *EMI MARIL 7.*	22	5
7 Nov 87	WARM WET CIRCLES *EMI MARIL 8.*	22	4
26 Nov 88	FREAKS (LIVE) *EMI MARIL 9*	24	3
9 Sep 89	HOOKS IN YOU *Capitol MARIL 10.*	30	3
9 Dec 89	UNINVITED GUEST *EMI MARIL 11.*	53	2
14 Apr 90	EASTER *EMI MARIL 12.*	34	2
8 Jun 91	COVER MY EYES (PAIN AND HEAVEN) *EMI MARIL 13*	34	4
3 Aug 91	NO ONE CAN *EMI MARIL 14.*	33	4
5 Oct 91	DRY LAND *EMI MARIL 15.*	34	2
23 May 92	SYMPATHY *EMI MARIL 16.*	17	3
1 Aug 92	NO ONE CAN (re-issue) *EMI MARIL 17.*	26	4
26 Mar 94	THE HOLLOW MAN *EMI CDEMS 307.*	30	2
7 May 94	ALONE AGAIN IN THE LAP OF LUXURY *EMI CDEMS 318*	53	3
10 Jun 95	BEAUTIFUL *EMI CDMARILS 18*	29	2

See also FISH

MARILYN *UK, male vocalist – Peter Robinson (26 WEEKS)*   pos/wks

5 Nov 83 ●	CALLING YOUR NAME *Mercury MAZ 1*	4	12
11 Feb 84	CRY AND BE FREE *Mercury MAZ 2*	31	6
21 Apr 84	YOU DON'T LOVE ME *Mercury MAZ 3*	40	7
13 Apr 85	BABY U LEFT ME (IN THE COLD) *Mercury MAZ 4*	70	1

MARILYN MANSON
US, male vocal / instrumental group (29 WEEKS)   pos/wks

7 Jun 97	THE BEAUTIFUL PEOPLE *Nothing 95541*	18	3
20 Sep 97	TOURNIQUET *Nothing 95552*	28	2
21 Nov 98	THE DOPE SHOW *Nothing 95610*	12	3
26 Jun 99	ROCK IS DEAD *Maverick W 486CD*	23	2
18 Nov 00	DISPOSABLE TEENS *Nothing 4974372*	12	3
3 Mar 01	THE FIGHT SONG *Nothing / Interscope 4974902*	24	3
15 Sep 01	THE NOBODIES *Nothing IND97604*	34	2
30 Mar 02 ●	TAINTED LOVE *Maverick / Warner Bros. W 579CD*	5	11

Marino MARINI and his QUARTET
Italy, male vocalist and instrumental group (23 WEEKS)   pos/wks

3 Oct 58	VOLARE (NEL BLU DIPINTO DI BLU) *Durium DC 16632*	13	7
10 Oct 58 ●	COME PRIMA *Durium DC 16632.*	2	14
20 Mar 59	CIAO CIAO BAMBINA (PIOVE) (re) *Durium DC 16636*	24	2

MARION *UK, male vocal / instrumental group (9 WEEKS)*   pos/wks

25 Feb 95	SLEEP *London LONCD 360*	53	1
13 May 95	TOYS FOR BOYS *London LONCD 366*	57	1
21 Oct 95	LET'S ALL GO TOGETHER *London LONCD 371*	37	2
3 Feb 96	TIME *London LONCD 377*	29	2
30 Mar 96	SLEEP (re-mix) *London LONCD 381*	17	2
7 Mar 98	MIYAKO HIDEAWAY *London LONCD 403*	45	1

MARK 'OH *Germany, male producer – Marko Albrecht (3 WEEKS)* pos/wks

6 May 95	TEARS DON'T LIE *Systematic SYSCD 9*	24	3

Pigmeat MARKHAM
US, male vocalist / comedian d. 13 Dec 1981 (8 WEEKS)   pos/wks

17 Jul 68	HERE COMES THE JUDGE *Chess CRS 8077*	19	8

Biz MARKIE US, male rapper (2 WEEKS)
		pos/wks
26 May 90	JUST A FRIEND *Cold Chillin'* W 9823	55 2

Yannis MARKOPOULOS Greece, orchestra (8 WEEKS)
		pos/wks
17 Dec 77	WHO PAYS THE FERRYMAN? *BBC RESL 51*	11 8

Guy MARKS
US, male vocalist – Mario Scarpo d. 28 Nov 1987 (8 WEEKS)
		pos/wks
13 May 78	LOVING YOU HAS MADE ME BANANAS *ABC 4211*	25 8

MARKSMEN – See Houston WELLS and the MARKSMEN

MARKY MARK and the FUNKY BUNCH
US, male / female vocal / rap / instrumental group (14 WEEKS)
		pos/wks
31 Aug 91	GOOD VIBRATIONS *Interscope A 8764* [1] ▲	14 7
2 Nov 91	WILDSIDE *Interscope A 8674*	42 3
12 Dec 92	YOU GOTTA BELIEVE *Interscope A 8480*	54 4

[1] Marky Mark and the Funky Bunch featuring Loleatta Holloway

Bob MARLEY and the WAILERS `125` `Top 500`
Legendary, globally successful Jamaican group, fronted by Bob Marley, nicknamed 'Tuff Gong'. b. 6 Apr 1945, Jamaica, d. 11 May 1981, Miami, (v/g). Varying line-up included Peter Tosh b. 19 Oct 1944, Jamaica, d. 11 Sep 1987, Jamaica (v/g), Bunny Wailer (v/prc). Their compilation 'Legend' is the biggest-selling reggae album in the UK and the US with combined sales of more than 12 million (167 WEEKS)
		pos/wks
27 Sep 75	● NO WOMAN NO CRY (re) *Island WIP 6244*	8 18
25 Jun 77	EXODUS *Island WIP 6390*	14 9
10 Sep 77	WAITING IN VAIN *Island WIP 6402*	27 6
10 Dec 77	● JAMMING / PUNKY REGGAE PARTY *Island WIP 6410*	9 12
25 Feb 78	● IS THIS LOVE *Island WIP 6420*	9 9
10 Jun 78	SATISFY MY SOUL *Island WIP 6440*	21 10
20 Oct 79	SO MUCH TROUBLE IN THE WORLD *Island WIP 6510*	56 4
21 Jun 80	● COULD YOU BE LOVED *Island WIP 6610*	5 12
13 Sep 80	THREE LITTLE BIRDS *Island WIP 6641*	17 9
7 May 83	● BUFFALO SOLDIER *Island/Tuff Gong IS 108*	4 12
21 Apr 84	● ONE LOVE – PEOPLE GET READY *Island IS 169*	5 11
23 Jun 84	WAITING IN VAIN (re-issue) *Island IS 180*	31 7
8 Dec 84	COULD YOU BE LOVED (re-issue) *Island IS 210*	71 2
18 May 91	ONE LOVE – PEOPLE GET READY (re-issue) *Tuff Gong TGX 1*	42 3
19 Sep 92	● IRON LION ZION *Tuff Gong TGX 2*	5 9
28 Nov 92	WHY SHOULD I / EXODUS (re) *Tuff Gong TGX 3*	42 4
20 May 95	KEEP ON MOVING *Tuff Gong TGXCD 4*	17 4
8 Jun 96	WHAT GOES AROUND COMES AROUND *Anansi ANACS 002*	42 1
25 Sep 99	● SUN IS SHINING *Club Tools / Edel 0066895 CLU* [1]	3 10
11 Dec 99	TURN YOUR LIGHTS DOWN LOW *Columbia 6684362* [2]	15 7
22 Jan 00	RAINBOW COUNTRY *Club Tools 0067225CLU* [1]	11 6
24 Jun 00	JAMMIN' *Tuff Gong TGXCD 9* [3]	42 2

[1] Bob Marley vs Funkstar De Luxe [2] Bob Marley featuring Lauryn Hill [3] Bob Marley featuring MC Lyte

'No Woman No Cry' on first chart visit made No.22 before making its peak position on re-entry in Jun 1981. 'Exodus' on Tuff Gong TGX 3 listed with 'Why Should I' only from 5 Dec 1992, and is a different version from the Island hit. It peaked at No.53

Ziggy MARLEY and the MELODY MAKERS
Jamaica, male / female vocal / instrumental group (11 WEEKS)
		pos/wks
11 Jun 88	TOMORROW PEOPLE *Virgin VS 1049*	22 10
23 Sep 89	LOOK WHO'S DANCING *Virgin America VUS 5*	65 1

Lene MARLIN
Norway, female vocalist – Lene Marlin Pederson (19 WEEKS)
		pos/wks
11 Mar 00	● SITTING DOWN HERE *Virgin DINSD 183*	5 11
16 Sep 00	UNFORGIVABLE SINNER *Virgin DINSD 202*	13 6
13 Jan 01	WHERE I'M HEADED *Virgin DINSD 196*	31 2

MARLO UK, male vocal / instrumental group (1 WEEK)
		pos/wks
24 Jul 99	HOW DO I KNOW? *Polydor 5611362*	56 1

MARMALADE `207` `Top 500`
The first Scottish group to top the chart: included Dean Ford (v), Junior Campbell (g/p/v). Alan Whitehead (d). This pop quintet, which first recorded as Dean Ford and The Gaylords, had a large late-1960s teen following (130 WEEKS)
		pos/wks
22 May 68	● LOVIN' THINGS *CBS 3412*	6 13
23 Oct 68	WAIT FOR ME MARIANNE *CBS 3708*	30 5
4 Dec 68	★ OB-LA-DI, OB-LA-DA *CBS 3892*	1 20
11 Jun 69	● BABY MAKE IT SOON *CBS 4287*	9 13
20 Dec 69	● REFLECTIONS OF MY LIFE *Decca F 12982*	3 12
18 Jul 70	● RAINBOW *Decca F 13035*	3 14
27 Mar 71	MY LITTLE ONE *Decca F 13135*	15 11
4 Sep 71	● COUSIN NORMAN *Decca F 13214*	6 11
27 Nov 71	BACK ON THE ROAD (re) *Decca F 13251*	35 8
1 Apr 72	● RADANCER *Decca F 13297*	6 12
21 Feb 76	● FALLING APART AT THE SEAMS *Target TGT 105*	9 11

MARMION
Spain / Holland, male instrumental / production duo (2 WEEKS)
		pos/wks
18 May 96	SCHONEBERG *Hooj Choons HOOJCD 43*	53 1
14 Feb 98	SCHONEBERG (re-mix) *ffrr FCD 324*	56 1

Johnny MARR – See Billy BRAGG; Kirsty MacCOLL; ELECTRONIC; SMITHS

MARRADONA UK, male DJ / production group (5 WEEKS)
		pos/wks
26 Feb 94	OUT OF MY HEAD *Peach PWCD 282*	38 3
26 Jul 97	OUT OF MY HEAD 97 (re-mix) *Soopa SPCD 1*	39 2

M/A/R/R/S
UK, male instrumental / production group (14 WEEKS)
		pos/wks
5 Sep 87	★ PUMP UP THE VOLUME / ANITINA (THE FIRST TIME I SEE SHE DANCE) *4AD AD 70*	1 14

Gerry MARSDEN – See CHRISTIANS; Holly JOHNSON; Paul McCARTNEY; STOCK AITKEN WATERMAN; GERRY and the PACEMAKERS

Matthew MARSDEN UK, male actor / vocalist (10 WEEKS)
		pos/wks
11 Jul 98	THE HEART'S LONE DESIRE *Columbia 6661152*	13 7
7 Nov 98	SHE'S GONE *Columbia 6664915* [1]	24 3

[1] Matthew Marsden featuring Destiny's Child

Stevie MARSH UK, female vocalist (4 WEEKS)
		pos/wks
4 Dec 59	IF YOU WERE THE ONLY BOY IN THE WORLD (re) *Decca F 11181*	24 4

MARSHA – See SHAGGY

MARSHALL HAIN
UK, male / female vocal / instrumental duo – Julian Marshall and Kit Hain (19 WEEKS)
		pos/wks
3 Jun 78	● DANCING IN THE CITY *Harvest HAR 5157*	3 15
14 Oct 78	COMING HOME *Harvest HAR 5168*	39 4

Joy MARSHALL UK, female vocalist (2 WEEKS)
		pos/wks
23 Jun 66	THE MORE I SEE YOU *Decca F 12422*	34 2

Keith MARSHALL UK, male vocalist (10 WEEKS)
		pos/wks
4 Apr 81	ONLY CRYING *Arrival PIK 2*	12 10

Louise Clare MARSHALL – See SILICONE SOUL featuring Louise Clare MARSHALL

Wayne MARSHALL UK, male vocalist (7 WEEKS)
		pos/wks
1 Oct 94	OOH AAH (G-SPOT) *Soultown SOULCDS 322*	29 3
3 Jun 95	SPIRIT *Soultown SOULCDS 00352*	58 1

Re-entries are listed as (re). (2re). (3re). etc which signifies that the hit re-entered the chart

| 24 Feb 96 | NEVER KNEW LOVE LIKE THIS *Sony S2 6629382* [1] | 40 | 2 |
| 7 Dec 96 | G SPOT (re-mix) *MBA INTER 9006* | 50 | 1 |

[1] Pauline Henry featuring Wayne Marshall

MARTAY featuring ZZ TOP *UK, female rapper – Melone McKenzy and US, male vocal / instrumental trio (2 WEEKS)*

		pos/wks
16 Oct 99	GIMME ALL YOUR LOVIN' 2000 *Riverhorse RIVHCD 2* 28	2

Lena MARTELL *UK, female vocalist – Helen Thomson (18 WEEKS)*

		pos/wks
29 Sep 79	★ ONE DAY AT A TIME *Pye 7N 46021* 1	18

MARTHA and the MUFFINS *Canada, female / male vocal / instrumental group (10 WEEKS)*

		pos/wks
1 Mar 80	● ECHO BEACH *Dindisc DIN 9* 10	10

See also M + M

MARTHA and the VANDELLAS – *See Martha REEVES and the VANDELLAS*

MARTIKA *US, female vocalist – Marta Marrera (57 WEEKS)*

		pos/wks
29 Jul 89	● TOY SOLDIERS *CBS 655049 7* ▲ 5	11
14 Oct 89	● I FEEL THE EARTH MOVE *CBS 655294 7* 7	14
13 Jan 90	MORE THAN YOU KNOW *CBS 655526 7* 15	7
17 Mar 90	WATER *CBS 655731 7* 59	3
17 Aug 91	● LOVE . . . THY WILL BE DONE *Columbia 6573137* 9	9
30 Nov 91	MARTIKA'S KITCHEN *Columbia 6575687* 17	10
22 Feb 92	COLOURED KISSES *Columbia 6577097* 41	3

Billie Ray MARTIN *Germany, female vocalist – Birgit Dieckmann (20 WEEKS)*

		pos/wks
19 Nov 94	YOUR LOVING ARMS *Magnet MAG 1028CD* 38	3
20 May 95	● YOUR LOVING ARMS (re-mix) *Magnet MAG 1031CD* 6	10
2 Sep 95	RUNNING AROUND TOWN *Magnet MAG 1035CD* 29	2
6 Jan 96	IMITATION OF LIFE *Magnet MAG 1040CD* 29	3
6 Apr 96	SPACE OASIS *Magnet MAG 1042CD* 66	1
21 Aug 99	HONEY *React CDREACT 129* 54	1

Dean MARTIN (131) Top 500 *Acclaimed vocalist / entertainer / film actor and cabaret performer, b. Dino Crocetti, 7 Jun 1917, Ohio, d. 25 Dec 1995. He first found fame partnering Jerry Lewis (1946-56), and had a long and successful solo career. He was a member of Frank Sinatra's 'Rat Pack' and had an impressive 46-year chart span (163 WEEKS)*

		pos/wks
18 Sep 53	● KISS (re) *Capitol CL 13893* 5	8
22 Jan 54	● THAT'S AMORE *Capitol CL 14008* 2	11
1 Oct 54	● SWAY *Capitol CL 14138* 6	7
22 Oct 54	HOW DO YOU SPEAK TO AN ANGEL (re) *Capitol CL 14150* 15	6
28 Jan 55	● THE NAUGHTY LADY OF SHADY LANE *Capitol CL 14226.* 5	10
4 Feb 55	MAMBO ITALIANO *Capitol CL 14227* 14	2
25 Feb 55	● LET ME GO, LOVER *Capitol CL 14226* 3	9
1 Apr 55	● UNDER THE BRIDGES OF PARIS *Capitol CL 14255* 6	8
10 Feb 56	★ MEMORIES ARE MADE OF THIS *Capitol CL 14523* ▲ 1	16
2 Mar 56	YOUNG AND FOOLISH *Capitol CL 14519* 20	1
27 Apr 56	INAMORATA *Capitol CL 14507* 21	3
22 Mar 57	THE MAN WHO PLAYS THE MANDOLINO *Capitol CL 14690* 21	2
13 Jun 58	● RETURN TO ME *Capitol CL 14844* 2	22
29 Aug 58	● VOLARE (NEL BLU DIPINTO DI BLU) *Capitol CL 14910* 2	14
27 Aug 64	EVERYBODY LOVES SOMEBODY *Reprise R 20281* ▲ 11	13
12 Nov 64	THE DOOR IS STILL OPEN TO MY HEART *Reprise R 20307* 42	4
5 Feb 69	● GENTLE ON MY MIND (re) *Reprise RS 23343* 2	24
22 Jun 96	THAT'S AMORE (re-issue) *EMI Premier PRESCD 3* 43	2
21 Aug 99	SWAY (re-issue) *Capitol CDSWAY 001* 66	1

Juan MARTIN *Spain, male instrumentalist – guitar (7 WEEKS)*

		pos/wks
28 Jan 84	● LOVE THEME FROM 'THE THORN BIRDS' *WEA X 9518* 10	7

Linda MARTIN *Ireland, female vocalist (2 WEEKS)*

		pos/wks
30 May 92	WHY ME *Columbia 6581317* 59	2

Luci MARTIN – *See Romina JOHNSON*

Marilyn MARTIN – *See Phil COLLINS*

Ray MARTIN and his Chorus and Orchestra *UK, orchestra, leader d. 7 Feb 1988 (11 WEEKS)*

		pos/wks
14 Nov 52	● BLUE TANGO (re) *Columbia DB 3051* 8	4
4 Dec 53	● SWEDISH RHAPSODY (re) *Columbia DB 3346* 4	4
15 Jun 56	THE CAROUSEL WALTZ (re) *Columbia DB 3771* 24	3

See also Lee LAWRENCE

Ricky MARTIN (477) Top 500 *Bon-bon shaking, ex-boy band singer and soap star b. Enrique Martin Morales, 24 Dec 1971, Puerto Rico. The performer who put the Latin into platinum sold 15 million of his eponymous album, recorded the world's biggest-selling football single ('The Cup of Life') and has the world's biggest-selling Spanish language album ('Vuelve'). Best-selling single: 'Livin' La Vida Loca' 775,700 (75 WEEKS)*

		pos/wks
20 Sep 97	● (UN, DOS, TRES) MARIA *Columbia 6649595* 6	6
11 Jul 98	THE CUP OF LIFE *Columbia 6661502* 29	3
17 Jul 99	★ LIVIN' LA VIDA LOCA *Columbia 6676402* ■ ▲ 1	17
20 Nov 99	SHAKE YOUR BON-BON *Columbia 6683412* 12	9
29 Apr 00	● PRIVATE EMOTION *Columbia 6692692* [1] 9	9
4 Nov 00	● SHE BANGS *Columbia 6705422* 3	15
10 Mar 01	● NOBODY WANTS TO BE LONELY *Columbia 6709462* [2] 4	12
28 Jul 01	LOADED *Columbia 6714642* 19	4

[1] Ricky Martin featuring Meja [2] Ricky Martin and Christina Aguilera

Tony MARTIN *US, male vocalist – Alvin Morris Jr. (28 WEEKS)*

		pos/wks
22 Apr 55	● STRANGER IN PARADISE *HMV B 10849* 6	13
13 Jul 56	● WALK HAND IN HAND *HMV POP 222* 2	15

Both with Hugo Winterhalter's Orchestra and Chorus

Vince MARTIN – *See TARRIERS*

Wink MARTINDALE *US, male vocalist (41 WEEKS)*

		pos/wks
4 Dec 59	● DECK OF CARDS (3re) *London HLD 8962* 5	29
20 Oct 73	DECK OF CARDS (re-issue) *Dot DOT 109* 22	12

'Deck of Cards' on the London label made No.18 in 1959 re-entering at No.28 in Jan 1960, again at No.45 in Mar 1960 before making No.5 with the third re-entry in Apr 1963

Alice MARTINEAU *US, female vocalist (1 WEEK)*

		pos/wks
23 Nov 02	IF I FALL *Epic 6732332* 45	1

Al MARTINO (380) Top 500 *Big-voiced balladeer b. Alfred Cini, 7 Oct 1927, Philadelphia, US. First release topped the US chart and was the first UK No.1. After a few lean years, he returned to become one of the 1960s, top-selling easy listening acts in the US (87 WEEKS)*

		pos/wks
14 Nov 52	★ HERE IN MY HEART *Capitol CL 13779* ▲ 1	18
21 Nov 52	● TAKE MY HEART *Capitol CL 13769* 9	1
30 Jan 53	● NOW *Capitol CL 13835* 3	12
10 Jul 53	● RACHEL (re) *Capitol CL 13879* 10	5
4 Jun 54	● WANTED (2re) *Capitol CL 14128* 4	16
1 Oct 54	● THE STORY OF TINA *Capitol CL 14163* 10	8
23 Sep 55	THE MAN FROM LARAMIE *Capitol CL 14343* 19	3
31 Mar 60	SUMMERTIME *Top Rank JAR 312* 49	1
29 Aug 63	I LOVE YOU BECAUSE *Capitol CL 15300* 48	1
22 Aug 70	● SPANISH EYES (re) *Capitol CL 15430* 5	22

'Spanish Eyes' peaked only at No.49 in 1970 before re-entering in Jul 1973 to make No.5

John MARTYN – *See SISTER BLISS*

MARVELETTES *US, female vocal group (10 WEEKS)*

		pos/wks
15 Jun 67	WHEN YOU'RE YOUNG AND IN LOVE *Tamla Motown TMG 609* 13	10

PASS THE DUTCHIE

■ "A dutchie is a big steel stockpot. Made in Holland – hence dutchie," explains Dennis Seaton, former lead vocalist with Musical Youth. A kutchie, on the other hand, is a water pipe used for smoking marijuana. But bongs and Blue Peter don't mix, so it was obvious early on that Birmingham's biggest boy band had to find a new title for their version of the infectious Mighty Diamonds track 'Pass the Kutchie'.

"We used to hear 'Kutchie' on the radio round about that time and we loved it," says Seaton, who joined the band in 1981, replacing ex-Techniques vocalist Freddie Waite. "So we wanted to record our own version. Our manager, Tony Owens, wanted the title and some of the lyrics changed. He was standing by the controls repeating that word kutchie, messing around with it, and then pretty quickly came up with 'dutchie'.

"Another change we made was replacing the chorus lyric. That changed from 'how does it feel when you've got no herb' to 'how does it feel when you've got no food'." The cleaned-up, instantly memorable pop version powered its way up the charts, hitting the top spot in September 1982. At this point Musical Youth was a family affair, comprising Michael Grant on keyboards and his brother Kelvin on the guitar. Patrick Waite was the group's bassist and his brother Freddie was the drummer. The Waite brothers and vocalist Dennis Seaton were all friends from Duddeston Manor School in Birmingham. Michael and Kelvin Grant, meanwhile, had been recruited from a Midlands musical workshop by Freddie Waite senior, the band's musical mentor who had pieced the band together in 1978.

■ GETTING TO MEET PETER DUNCAN WAS SOON TRUMPED BY MEETING PETER TOSH ■

When 'Pass the Dutchie' went to No.1 in the UK (rising from No.27 to No.1 in the process), the band was aged between 11 and 15. Dennis was just 13, still young enough, he remembers, to get excited about a Blue Peter badge. "When we got asked to sing on the show, we were all like 'wow'. Yes! We're going to get a badge."

The group eventually made three appearances on Blue Peter during the early 1980s and they were rewarded on their last show with a special badge for "outstanding endeavour". Appearances on Razzmatazz, Saturday Swapshop and Jim'll Fix It soon followed. "People asked us a lot about what the song meant, though no one was really that bothered," says Dennis. Getting to meet Blue Peter presenter Peter Duncan was soon trumped by meeting Peter Tosh at Jamaica's famous Reggae Sunsplash festival. "We got to know loads of people playing there, all of our heroes basically, Gregory Isaacs, Bunny Lee, Joe Gibbs, Yellowman, Eek-a-Mouse," says Dennis.

The band enjoyed huge success, playing in Jamaica and then in the States, where they were nominated for a Grammy. But it didn't last long. 'Pass the Dutchie' was to be the band's first and last No.1. A string of less successful hits followed, including a surprise collaboration with Donna Summer on 'Unconditional Love' and a cover version of the Desmond Dekker classic '007'. The band released their second and last album, 'Different Style', in 1985. They split the same year. Dennis Seaton now runs a car hire firm, but still performs and writes music. In 1990 he released a solo album, Imagine, which featured the track 'Whatcha Talkin' 'Bout?', a song which had been written and produced for Dennis by Stevie Wonder. Seaton still tours with his band XMY. Patrick Waite died in 1993, and his brother Freddie junior is no longer involved in the music business. Michael Grant now runs his own label, and his

★ **ARTIST:** Musical Youth

★ **LABEL:** MCA

★ **WRITERS:** Jackie Mitto, Fitzroy Simpson and Lloyd Ferguson

★ **PRODUCER:** Peter Collins

brother Kelvin is a DJ. The band recently won a long-running dispute over royalty payments, and is planning to reform to celebrate its 21st anniversary with a greatest hits release.

■ Daniel Stott

The Grammy-nominated, Blue Peter badge-scooping Musical Youth

Hank MARVIN
UK, male vocalist / instrumentalist – guitar – Brian Rankin (36 WEEKS)

		pos/wks	
13 Sep 69 ●	THROW DOWN A LINE Columbia DB 8615 [1]	7	9
21 Feb 70	THE JOY OF LIVING Columbia DB 8657 [1]	25	8
6 Mar 82	DON'T TALK Polydor POSP 420	49	4
22 Mar 86 ★	LIVING DOLL WEA YZ 65 [2]	1	11
7 Jan 89	LONDON KID Polydor PO 32 [3]	52	3
17 Oct 92	WE ARE THE CHAMPIONS PolyGram TV PO 229 [4]	66	1

[1] Cliff and Hank [2] Cliff Richard and the Young Ones featuring Hank B Marvin [3] Jean-Michel Jarre featuring Hank Marvin [4] Hank Marvin featuring Brian May

See also SHADOWS

Lee MARVIN
US, male actor / vocalist – d. 28 Aug 1987 (23 WEEKS)

		pos/wks	
7 Feb 70 ★	WAND'RIN' STAR (2re) Paramount PARA 3004	1	23

'I Talk to the Trees' by Clint Eastwood, the flip side of 'Wand'rin' Star', was listed with 'Wand'rin' Star' for 7 Feb and 14 Feb 1970 only

MARVIN and TAMARA
UK, male / female vocal duo – Marvin Simmonds and Tamara Nicole (9 WEEKS)

		pos/wks	
7 Aug 99	GROOVE MACHINE Epic 6675582	11	5
25 Dec 99	NORTH, SOUTH, EAST, WEST Epic 6684902	38	4

MARVIN THE PARANOID ANDROID
UK, male robot (4 WEEKS) pos/wks

		pos/wks	
16 May 81	MARVIN Polydor POSP 261	53	4

Richard MARX (480 Top 500)
Child jingle singer turned session singer turned singer / songwriter. b. 16 Sep 1962, Chicago, US. He scored 12 consecutive Top 20 entries in the US (first six hits in the Top 3) and sold more than 15 million albums. Married Cynthia Rhodes, lead singer of Animotion. Produced and wrote for 'N Sync in 2000 (75 WEEKS)

		pos/wks	
27 Feb 88	SHOULD'VE KNOWN BETTER Manhattan MT 32	50	5
14 May 88	ENDLESS SUMMER NIGHTS Manhattan MT 39	50	3
17 Jun 89	SATISFIED EMI-USA MT 64 ▲	52	4
2 Sep 89 ●	RIGHT HERE WAITING EMI-USA MT 72 ▲	2	10
11 Nov 89	ANGELIA EMI-USA MT 74	45	4
24 Mar 90	TOO LATE TO SAY GOODBYE EMI-USA MT 80	38	3
7 Jul 90	CHILDREN OF THE NIGHT EMI-USA MT 84	54	4
1 Sep 90	ENDLESS SUMMER NIGHTS / HOLD ON TO THE NIGHTS (re-issue) EMI-USA MT 89 ▲	60	2
19 Oct 91	KEEP COMING BACK Capitol CL 634	55	2
9 May 92 ●	HAZARD Capitol CL 654	3	15
29 Aug 92	TAKE THIS HEART Capitol CL 667	13	6
28 Nov 92	CHAINS AROUND MY HEART Capitol CL 676	29	6
29 Jan 94	NOW AND FOREVER Capitol CDCLS 703	13	6
30 Apr 94	SILENT SCREAM Capitol CDCLS 714	32	4
13 Aug 94	THE WAY SHE LOVES ME Capitol CDCL 721	38	3

MARXMAN
UK / Ireland, rap / instrumental group (5 WEEKS)

		pos/wks	
6 Mar 93	ALL ABOUT EVE Talkin Loud TLKCD 35	28	4
1 May 93	SHIP AHOY Talkin Loud TLKCD 39	64	1

Sinead O'Connor provides uncredited vocals on 'Ship Ahoy'

MARY JANE GIRLS
US, female vocal group (15 WEEKS)

		pos/wks	
21 May 83	CANDY MAN Motown TMG 1301	60	4
25 Jun 83	ALL NIGHT LONG Gordy TMG 1309	13	9
8 Oct 83	BOYS Gordy TMG 1315	74	1
18 Feb 95	ALL NIGHT LONG (re-mix) Motown TMGCD 1436	51	1

MARY MARY
US, female vocal duo – Erica and Tina Atkins (14 WEEKS)

		pos/wks	
10 Jun 00 ●	SHACKLES (PRAISE YOU) Columbia 6694202	5	12
18 Nov 00	I SINGS Columbia 6699742	32	2

Carolyne MAS
US, female vocalist (2 WEEKS)

		pos/wks	
2 Feb 80	QUOTE GOODBYE QUOTE Mercury 6167 873	71	2

MASE
US, male rapper – Mason Betha (53 WEEKS)

		pos/wks	
29 Mar 97	CAN'T NOBODY HOLD ME DOWN Arista 74321464552 [1] ▲	19	4
9 Aug 97 ●	MO MONEY MO PROBLEMS Puff Daddy 74321492492 [2] ▲	6	10
27 Dec 97	FEEL SO GOOD Puff Daddy 74321526442	10	8
18 Apr 98	WHAT YOU WANT Puff Daddy 74321578772 [3]	15	5
19 Sep 98	HORSE AND CARRIAGE Epic 6662612 [4]	12	4
10 Oct 98 ●	TOP OF THE WORLD (re) Atlantic AT 0046CD [5]	2	9
12 Dec 98 ●	TAKE ME THERE Interscope IND 95620 [6]	7	9
10 Jul 99	GET READY Puff Daddy / Arista 74321682602 [7]	32	4

[1] Puff Daddy featuring Mase [2] Notorious B.I.G. featuring Puff Daddy and Mase [3] Mase featuring Total [4] Cam'ron featuring Mase [5] Brandy featuring Mase [6] BLACKstreet and Mya featuring Mase and Blinky Blink [7] Mase featuring BLACKstreet

MASH
US, male vocal / instrumental group (12 WEEKS)

		pos/wks	
10 May 80 ★	THEME FROM M*A*S*H (SUICIDE IS PAINLESS) CBS 8536	1	12

MASH!
UK / US, male / female vocal group (3 WEEKS)

		pos/wks	
21 May 94	U DON'T HAVE TO SAY U LOVE ME React CDREACT 37	37	2
4 Feb 95	LET'S SPEND THE NIGHT TOGETHER Playa CDXPLAYA 2	66	1

MASH UP – See Matt DAREY

MASON – See CHICANE

Barbara MASON
US, female vocalist (5 WEEKS)

		pos/wks	
21 Jan 84	ANOTHER MAN Streetwave KHAN 3	45	5

Glen MASON
UK, male vocalist – Tommy Lennon (7 WEEKS)

		pos/wks	
28 Sep 56	GLENDORA Parlophone R 4203	28	2
16 Nov 56	THE GREEN DOOR Parlophone R 4244	24	5

Mary MASON
UK, female vocalist (6 WEEKS)

		pos/wks	
8 Oct 77	ANGEL OF THE MORNING – ANY WAY THAT YOU WANT ME (MEDLEY) Epic EPC 5552	27	6

MASQUERADE
UK, male / female vocal group (10 WEEKS)

		pos/wks	
11 Jan 86	ONE NATION Streetwave KHAN 59	54	6
5 Jul 86	(SOLUTION TO) THE PROBLEM (re) Streetwave KHAN 67	64	4

MASS ORDER
US, male vocal / instrumental duo – Eugene Hanes and Marc Valentine (5 WEEKS)

		pos/wks	
14 Mar 92	LIFT EVERY VOICE (TAKE ME AWAY) Columbia 6577487	35	3
23 May 92	LET'S GET HAPPY Columbia 6580737	45	2

MASS PRODUCTION
US, male vocal / instrumental group (7 WEEKS)

		pos/wks	
12 Mar 77	WELCOME TO OUR WORLD (OF MERRY MUSIC) Atlantic K 10898	44	3
17 May 80	SHANTE Atlantic K 11475	59	4

MASS SYNDICATE featuring Su Su BOBIEN
US, male producer and US, female vocalist (1 WEEK)

		pos/wks	
24 Oct 98	YOU DON'T KNOW fffr FCD 347	71	1

Zeitia MASSIAH
UK, female vocalist (2 WEEKS)

		pos/wks	
12 Mar 94	I SPECIALIZE IN LOVE Union City UCRCD 27	74	1
24 Sep 94	THIS IS THE PLACE Virgin VSCDT 1511	62	1

MASSIEL
Spain, female vocalist (4 WEEKS)

		pos/wks	
24 Apr 68	LA LA LA Philips BF 1667	35	4

Re-entries are listed as (re), (2re), (3re), etc which signifies that the hit re-entered the chart once, twice or th...

MASSIVE ATTACK
UK, male / female vocal / instrumental group (42 WEEKS)   pos/wks

23 Feb 91	**UNFINISHED SYMPATHY** *Wild Bunch WBRS 2* [1]	13	9
8 Jun 91	**SAFE FROM HARM** *Wild Bunch WBRS 3*	25	6
22 Feb 92	**MASSIVE ATTACK (EP)** *Wild Bunch WBRS 4*	27	4
29 Oct 94	**SLY** *Wild Bunch WBRDX 5*	24	4
21 Jan 95	**PROTECTION** *Wild Bunch WBRX 6* [2]	14	4
1 Apr 95	**KARMACOMA** *Wild Bunch WBRX 7*	28	4
19 Jul 97	**RISINGSON** *Circa WBRX 8*	11	3
9 May 98 ●	**TEARDROP** *Virgin WBRX 9*	10	6
25 Jul 98	**ANGEL** *Virgin WBRX 10*	30	2

[1] Massive [2] Massive Attack featuring Tracey Thorn

Vocals on first three releases by Shara Nelson. Tracks on Massive Attack (EP): Hymn of the Big Wheel / Home of the Whale / Be Thankful / Any Love. Teardrop features an uncredited vocal by Elizabeth Fraser from Cocteau Twins

See also Shara NELSON

MASSIVO featuring TRACY
UK, male / female vocal / instrumental group (11 WEEKS)   pos/wks

26 May 90	**LOVING YOU** *Debut DEBT 3097*	25	11

MASTER P – *See Montell JORDAN*

MASTER SINGERS *UK, male vocal group (8 WEEKS)*   pos/wks

14 Apr 66	**HIGHWAY CODE** *Parlophone R 5428*	25	6
17 Nov 66	**WEATHER FORECAST (re)** *Parlophone R 5523*	45	2

MASTERMIXERS – *See JIVE BUNNY and the MASTERMIXERS*

MASTERS AT WORK *US, male production / instrumental duo – 'Lil' Louis Vega and Kenny 'Dope' Gonzales (6 WEEKS)*   pos/wks

5 Aug 95	**I CAN'T GET NO SLEEP** *A&M 5811412* [1]	44	2
31 Jul 99	**TO BE IN LOVE** *Defected DEFECT 5CDS* [2]	23	3
6 Jul 02	**BACKFIRED** *SuSu CDSUSU 4* [3]	62	1

[1] Masters at Work presents India [2] MAW presents India [3] Masters at Work featuring India

See also NUYORICAN SOUL

Sammy MASTERS
US, male vocalist – Samuel Lawmaster (5 WEEKS)   pos/wks

9 Jun 60	**ROCKIN' RED WING** *Warner Bros. WB 10*	36	5

MASTERS of CEREMONIES – *See DJ PIED PIPER and The MASTERS OF CEREMONIES*

Paul MASTERSON presents SUSHI
UK, male producer (2 WEEKS)   pos/wks

2 Nov 02	**THE EARTHSHAKER** *Nulife 74321970372*	35	2

See also YOMANDA; HI-GATE; SLEAZESISTERS; DOROTHY; CLERGY; CANDY GIRLS

MATCH *UK, male vocal / instrumental group (3 WEEKS)*   pos/wks

16 Jun 79	**BOOGIE MAN** *Flamingo FM 2*	48	3

MATCHBOX *UK, male vocal / instrumental group (66 WEEKS)*   pos/wks

3 Nov 79	**ROCKABILLY REBEL** *Magnet MAG 155*	18	12
19 Jan 80	**BUZZ BUZZ A DIDDLE IT** *Magnet MAG 157*	22	8
10 May 80	**MIDNITE DYNAMOS** *Magnet MAG 169*	14	12
27 Sep 80 ●	**WHEN YOU ASK ABOUT LOVE** *Magnet MAG 191*	4	12
29 Nov 80	**OVER THE RAINBOW – YOU BELONG TO ME (MEDLEY)** *Magnet MAG 192*	15	11
4 Apr 81	**BABES IN THE WOOD** *Magnet MAG 193*	46	6
1 Aug 81	**LOVE'S MADE A FOOL OF YOU** *Magnet MAG 194*	63	3
29 May 82	**ONE MORE SATURDAY NIGHT** *Magnet MAG 223*	63	2

MATCHBOX 20
US, male vocal / instrumental group (4 WEEKS)   pos/wks

11 Apr 98	**PUSH** *Atlantic AT 0021CD*	38	2
4 Jul 98	**3 AM** *Atlantic AT 0034CD*	64	1
17 Feb 01	**IF YOU'RE GONE** *Atlantic AT 0090CD*	50	1

MATCHROOM MOB – *See CHAS and DAVE*

Mireille MATHIEU *France, female vocalist (7 WEEKS)*   pos/wks

13 Dec 67	**LA DERNIERE VALSE** *Columbia DB 8323*	26	7

Johnny MATHIS ⟨182 Top 500⟩ *Legendary MOR vocal superstar, b. 30 Sep 1935, San Francisco, US. Frank Sinatra and Elvis Presley are the only males with more hit albums in the US, where his greatest hits album charted for almost 10 years – a record for a solo performer (138 WEEKS)*   pos/wks

23 May 58	**TEACHER, TEACHER** *Fontana H 130*	27	5
26 Sep 58 ●	**A CERTAIN SMILE** *Fontana H 142*	4	16
19 Dec 58	**WINTER WONDERLAND** *Fontana H 165*	17	3
7 Aug 59 ●	**SOMEONE** *Fontana H 199*	6	15
27 Nov 59	**THE BEST OF EVERYTHING** *Fontana H 218*	30	1
29 Jan 60	**MISTY (re)** *Fontana H 219*	12	12
24 Mar 60	**YOU ARE BEAUTIFUL (re)** *Fontana H 234*	38	9
28 Jul 60	**STARBRIGHT** *Fontana H 254*	47	2
6 Oct 60 ●	**MY LOVE FOR YOU** *Fontana H 267*	9	18
4 Apr 63	**WHAT WILL MARY SAY** *CBS AAG 135*	49	1
25 Jan 75 ●	**I'M STONE IN LOVE WITH YOU** *CBS 2653*	10	12
13 Nov 76 ★	**WHEN A CHILD IS BORN (SOLEADO)** *CBS 4599*	1	12
25 Mar 78 ●	**TOO MUCH, TOO LITTLE, TOO LATE** *CBS 6164* [1] ▲	3	14
29 Jul 78	**YOU'RE ALL I NEED TO GET BY** *CBS 6483* [1]	45	6
11 Aug 79	**GONE, GONE, GONE** *CBS 7730*	15	10
26 Dec 81	**WHEN A CHILD IS BORN** *CBS S 1758* [2]	74	2

[1] Johnny Mathis and Deniece Williams [2] Johnny Mathis and Gladys Knight

Ivan MATIAS *US, male vocalist (1 WEEK)*   pos/wks

6 Apr 96	**SO GOOD (TO COME HOME TO) / I'VE HAD ENOUGH** *Arista 74321345072*	69	1

MATT BIANCO
UK, male / female vocal / instrumental duo (65 WEEKS)   pos/wks

11 Feb 84	**GET OUT OF YOUR LAZY BED** *WEA BIANCO 1*	15	8
14 Apr 84	**SNEAKING OUT THE BACK DOOR / MATT'S MOOD** *WEA YZ 3*	44	7
10 Nov 84	**HALF A MINUTE** *WEA YZ 26*	23	10
2 Mar 85	**MORE THAN I CAN BEAR** *WEA YZ 34*	50	7
5 Oct 85	**YEH YEH** *WEA YZ 46*	13	10
1 Mar 86	**JUST CAN'T STAND IT** *WEA YZ 62*	66	2
14 Jun 86	**DANCING IN THE STREET** *WEA YZ 72*	64	3
4 Jun 88	**DON'T BLAME IT ON THAT GIRL / WAP-BAM-BOOGIE** *WEA YZ 188*	11	13
27 Aug 88	**GOOD TIMES** *WEA YZ 302*	55	3
4 Feb 89	**NERVOUS / WAP-BAM-BOOGIE (re-mix)** *WEA YZ 328*	59	2

'Matt's Mood' credited only from 5 May 1984. Act was a UK / Poland, male / female vocal / instrumental group on first five hits

Al MATTHEWS *US, male vocalist (8 WEEKS)*   pos/wks

23 Aug 75	**FOOL** *CBS 3429*	16	8

Cerys MATTHEWS – *See CATATONIA; Tom JONES; SPACE*

John MATTHEWS – *See UNDERCOVER*

Dave MATTHEWS BAND
US, male vocal / instrumental group (2 WEEKS)   pos/wks

1 Dec 01	**THE SPACE BETWEEN** *RCA 74321883192*	35	2

MATTHEWS' SOUTHERN COMFORT *UK, male vocal / instrumental group – lead vocalist Ian Matthews (18 WEEKS)*   pos/wks

26 Sep 70 ★	**WOODSTOCK** *Uni UNS 526*	1	18

MATUMBI *UK, male vocal / instrumental group (7 WEEKS)*   pos/wks

29 Sep 79	**POINT OF VIEW (SQUEEZE A LITTLE LOVIN)** *Matumbi RIC 101*	35	7

Susan MAUGHAN UK, female vocalist (25 WEEKS)

		pos/wks
11 Oct 62 ●	BOBBY'S GIRL *Philips 326544 BF*	...3 19
14 Feb 63	HAND A HANDKERCHIEF TO HELEN *Philips 326562 BF*	...41 3
9 May 63	SHE'S NEW TO YOU *Philips 326586 BF*	...45 3

MAUREEN UK, female vocalist – Maureen Walsh (22 WEEKS)

		pos/wks
26 Nov 88 ●	SAY A LITTLE PRAYER *Rhythm King DOOD 3* [1]	...10 10
16 Jun 90	THINKING OF YOU *Urban URB 55*	...11 9
12 Jan 91	WHERE HAS ALL THE LOVE GONE *Urban URB 65*	...51 3

[1] Bomb the Bass featuring Maureen

Some copies of 'Thinking of You' are credited to the fuller name of Maureen Walsh

Paul MAURIAT and his Orchestra
France, orchestra (14 WEEKS)

		pos/wks
21 Feb 68	LOVE IS BLUE (L'AMOUR EST BLEU) *Philips BF 1637* ▲	...12 14

MAVERICKS
US, male vocal / instrumental group (23 WEEKS)

		pos/wks
2 May 98 ●	DANCE THE NIGHT AWAY *MCA Nashville MCSTD 48081*	...4 18
26 Sep 98	I'VE GOT THIS FEELING *MCA Nashville MCSTD 48095*	...27 4
5 Jun 99	SOMEONE SHOULD TELL HER	
	MCA Nashville MCSTD 55567	...45 1

See also Raul MALO

MAW – *See MASTERS AT WORK*

MAX LINEN UK, male production duo (1 WEEK)

		pos/wks
17 Nov 01	THE SOULSHAKER *Global Cuts GC 73CD*	...55 1

MAX Q Australia, male vocal / instrumental duo (3 WEEKS)

		pos/wks
17 Feb 90	SOMETIMES *Mercury MXQ 2*	...53 3

MAX WEBSTER
Canada, male vocal / instrumental group (3 WEEKS)

		pos/wks
19 May 79	PARADISE SKIES *Capitol CL 16079*	...43 3

MAXEE US, female vocalist (1 WEEK)

		pos/wks
17 Mar 01	WHEN I LOOK INTO YOUR EYES *Mercury 5628702*	...55 1

MAXIM UK, male producer / vocalist – Keith Palmer (3 WEEKS)

		pos/wks
10 Jun 00	CARMEN QUEASY *XL Recordings XLS 119CD*	...33 2
23 Sep 00	SCHEMING *XL Recordings XLS 121CD*	...53 1

Sleeve of 'Carmen Queasy' credits 'vocal by Skin' (from Skunk Anansie)

See also PRODIGY

MAXIMA featuring LILY
UK / Spain, male / female vocal / instrumental duo (2 WEEKS)

		pos/wks
14 Aug 93	IBIZA *Yo! Yo! CDLILY 1*	...55 2

MAXTREME Holland, male production group (1 WEEK)

		pos/wks
9 Mar 02	MY HOUSE IS YOUR HOUSE *Y2K Y2K 028CD*	...66 1

MAXWELL US, male vocalist – Maxwell Menard (10 WEEKS)

		pos/wks
11 May 96	...TIL THE COPS COME KNOCKIN' *Columbia 6631792*	...63 1
24 Aug 96	ASCENSION NO ONE'S GONNA LOVE YOU SO DON'T EVER	
	WONDER *Columbia 6636265*	...39 3
1 Mar 97	SUMTHIN' SUMTHIN' THE MANTRA *Columbia 6638642*	...27 3
24 May 97	ASCENSION DON'T EVER WONDER (re-issue)	
	Columbia 6645952	...28 3

MAXX UK / Sweden / Germany, male
/ female vocal / instrumental group (24 WEEKS)

		pos/wks
21 May 94 ●	GET-A-WAY *Pulse 8 CDLOSE 59*	...4 12
6 Aug 94 ●	NO MORE (I CAN'T STAND IT) *Pulse 8 CDLOSE 66*	...8 8

29 Oct 94	YOU CAN GET IT *Pulse 8 CDLOSE 75*	...21 3
22 Jul 95	I CAN MAKE YOU FEEL LIKE *Pulse 8 CDLOSE 88*	...56 1

Terry MAXX – *See FUNKSTAR DE LUXE*

Billy MAY and his Orchestra US, orchestra (10 WEEKS)

		pos/wks
27 Apr 56 ●	MAIN TITLE THEME FROM 'MAN WITH THE GOLDEN ARM'	
	Capitol CL 14551	...9 10

Brian MAY UK, male vocalist / instrumentalist – guitar (33 WEEKS)

		pos/wks
5 Nov 83	STAR FLEET *EMI 5436* [1]	...65 3
7 Dec 91 ●	DRIVEN BY YOU *Parlophone R 6304*	...6 9
5 Sep 92 ●	TOO MUCH LOVE WILL KILL YOU *Parlophone R 6320*	...5 9
17 Oct 92	WE ARE THE CHAMPIONS *PolyGram TV PO 229* [2]	...66 1
21 Nov 92	BACK TO THE LIGHT *Parlophone R 6329*	...19 4
19 Jun 93	RESURRECTION *Parlophone CDRS 6351* [3]	...23 3
18 Dec 93	LAST HORIZON *Parlophone CDR 6371*	...51 2
6 Jun 98	THE BUSINESS *Parlophone CDR 6498*	...51 1
12 Sep 98	WHY DON'T WE TRY AGAIN *Parlophone CDR 6504*	...44 1

[1] Brian May and Friends [2] Hank Marvin featuring Brian May [3] Brian May with Cozy Powell

See also QUEEN

Lisa MAY UK, female vocalist (2 WEEKS)

		pos/wks
15 Jul 95	WISHING ON A STAR *Urban Gorilla UG 3CD* [1]	...61 1
14 Sep 96	THE CURSE OF VOODOO RAY *Fontana VOOCD 1*	...64 1

[1] 88.3 featuring Lisa MAY

Mary MAY UK, female vocalist (1 WEEK)

		pos/wks
27 Feb 64	ANYONE WHO HAD A HEART *Fontana TF 440*	...49 1

Shernette MAY UK, female vocalist (1 WEEK)

		pos/wks
6 Jun 98	ALL THE MAN THAT I NEED *Virgin VSCDT 1691*	...50 1

Simon MAY UK, male vocalist (21 WEEKS)

		pos/wks
9 Oct 76 ●	THE SUMMER OF MY LIFE *Pye 7N 45627*	...7 8
21 May 77	WE'LL GATHER LILACS – ALL MY LOVING (MEDLEY)	
	(re) *Pye 7N 45688*	...49 2
26 Oct 85	HOWARD'S WAY *BBC RESL 174* [1]	...21 11

[1] Simon May Orchestra

See also Anita DOBSON; Marti WEBB

MAYA – *See TAMPERER featuring MAYA*

Curtis MAYFIELD US, male vocalist d. 26 Dec 1999 (20 WEEKS)

		pos/wks
31 Jul 71	MOVE ON UP *Buddah 2011 080*	...12 10
2 Dec 78	NO GOODBYES *Atlantic LV 1*	...65 3
30 May 87	(CELEBRATE) THE DAY AFTER YOU *RCA MONK 6* [1]	...52 2
29 Sep 90	SUPERFLY 1990 *Capitol CL 586* [2]	...48 3
16 Jun 01	ASTOUNDED *Virgin VUSCD 194* [3]	...40 2

[1] Blow Monkeys with Curtis Mayfield [2] Curtis Mayfield and Ice-T [3] Bran Van 3000 featuring Curtis Mayfield

MAYTALS Jamaica, male vocal / instrumental group (4 WEEKS)

		pos/wks
25 Apr 70	MONKEY MAN (re) *Trojan TR 7711*	...47 4

MAYTE US, female vocalist (1 WEEK)

		pos/wks
18 Nov 95	IF EYE LOVE U 2 NIGHT *NPG 0061635*	...67 1

MAZE featuring Frankie BEVERLY
US, male vocal / instrumental group (14 WEEKS)

		pos/wks
20 Jul 85	TOO MANY GAMES *Capitol CL 363*	...36 7
23 Aug 86	I WANNA BE WITH YOU *Capitol CL 421*	...55 3
27 May 89	JOY AND PAIN *Capitol CL 531* [1]	...57 4

[1] Maze

Re-entries are listed as (re), (2re), (3re), etc which signifies that the hit re-entered the chart once, twice or three times, etc

Kym MAZELLE
US, female vocalist – Kimberley Grigsby (66 WEEKS)   pos/wks

12 Nov 88	USELESS (I DON'T NEED YOU NOW) *Syncopate SY 18*	53	3
14 Jan 89	● WAIT *RCA PB 42595* [1]	7	10
25 Mar 89	GOT TO GET YOU BACK *Syncopate SY 25*	29	4
7 Oct 89	LOVE STRAIN *Syncopate SY 30*	52	3
20 Jan 90	WAS THAT ALL IT WAS *Syncopate SY 32*	33	6
26 May 90	USELESS (I DON'T NEED YOU NOW) (re-mix) *Syncopate SY 36*	48	2
24 Nov 90	MISSING YOU *Ten TEN 345* [2]	22	7
25 May 91	NO ONE CAN LOVE YOU MORE THAN ME *Parlophone R 6287*	62	2
26 Dec 92	LOVE ME THE RIGHT WAY *Arista 74321128097* [3]	22	10
11 Jun 94	NO MORE TEARS (ENOUGH IS ENOUGH) *Bell 74321209032* [4]	13	7
8 Oct 94	GIMME ALL YOUR LOVIN' *Bell 74321231322* [5]	22	3
23 Dec 95	SEARCHING FOR THE GOLDEN EYE *Eternal WEA 027CD* [6]	40	3
28 Sep 96	LOVE ME THE RIGHT WAY (re-mix) *Logic 74321404442* [3]	55	1
16 Aug 97	YOUNG HEARTS RUN FREE *EMI CDEM 488*	20	4
19 Feb 00	TRULY *Island Blue PFACD 4* [7]	55	1

[1] Robert Howard and Kym Mazelle [2] Soul II Soul featuring Kym Mazelle [3] Rapination and Kym Mazelle [4] Kym Mazelle and Jocelyn Brown [5] Jocelyn Brown and Kym Mazelle [6] Motiv 8 and Kym Mazelle [7] Peshay featuring Kym Mazelle

MAZZY STAR
US, male / female vocal / instrumental group (3 WEEKS)   pos/wks

27 Aug 94	FADE INTO YOU *Capitol CDCL 720*	48	1
2 Nov 96	FLOWERS IN DECEMBER *Capitol CDCL 781*	40	2

MC ALISTAIR – *See DREEM TEEM*

MC CHICKABOO – *See Timo MAAS*

MC DUKE *UK, male rapper (1 WEEK)*   pos/wks

11 Mar 89	I'M RIFFIN (ENGLISH RASTA) *Music of Life 7NOTE 25*	75	1

MC ERIC – *See TECHNOTRONIC*

MC FIXX IT – *See ANTICAPPELLA*

MC HAMMER – *See HAMMER*

MC IMAGE – *See Jhay PALMER featuring MC IMAGE*

MC KIE – *See TEEBONE featuring MC KIE and MC SPARKS*

MC LETHAL *UK, male producer (1 WEEK)*   pos/wks

14 Nov 92	THE RAVE DIGGER *Network NWKT 60*	66	1

MC LYTE *US, female rapper – Lana Moorer (16 WEEKS)*   pos/wks

15 Jan 94	RUFFNECK *Atlantic A 8336CD*	67	1
29 Jun 96	KEEP ON KEEPIN' ON *East West A 4287CD* [1]	39	2
18 Jan 97	COLD ROCK A PARTY *East West A 3975CD*	15	4
19 Apr 97	KEEP ON KEEPIN' ON (re-issue) *East West A 3950CD1* [1]	27	2
5 Sep 98	I CAN'T MAKE A MISTAKE *Elektra E 3813CD*	46	1
19 Dec 98	IT'S ALL YOURS *East West E 3789CD* [2]	36	4
24 Jun 00	JAMMIN' *Tuff Gong TGXCD 9* [3]	42	2

[1] MC Lyte featuring Xscape [2] MC Lyte featuring Gina Thompson [3] Bob Marley featuring MC Lyte

MC MALIBU – *See ROUND SOUND presents ONYX STONE & MC MALIBU*

MC MARIO – *See AMBASSADORS OF FUNK featuring MC MARIO*

MC MIKEE FREEDOM – *See NOMAD*

MC MIKER 'G' and Deejay SVEN *Holland, male vocal / instrumental rap duo – Lucien Witteveen and Sven Van Veen (7 WEEKS)*   pos/wks

6 Sep 86	● HOLIDAY RAP *Debut DEBT 3008*	6	7

MC NEAT – *See CORRUPTED CRU featuring MC NEAT; DJ LUCK & MC NEAT*

MC NOISE – *See LOVE INCORPORATED featuring MC NOISE*

MC NUMBER 6 – *See FAB*

MC ONYX STONE – *See LONYO; ROUND SOUND presents ONYX STONE and MC MALIBU*

MC PARKER – *See FAB*

MC RB – *See SUNSHIP featuring MCRB; JUST 4 JOKES featuring MC RB*

MC SAR – *See REAL McCOY*

MC SKAT KAT and the STRAY MOB
US, male cartoon feline rap / vocal group (2 WEEKS)   pos/wks

9 Nov 91	SKAT STRUT *Virgin America VUS 51*	64	2

MC SOLAAR – *See URBAN SPECIES; Missy 'Misdemeanor' ELLIOTT*

MC SPARKS – *See TEEBONE featuring MC KIE and MC SPARKS*

MC SPY-D + FRIENDS
UK, male / female vocal / instrumental group (2 WEEKS)   pos/wks

11 Mar 95	THE AMAZING SPIDER-MAN *Parlophone CDR 6404*	37	2

MC STYLES – *See Scott GARCIA featuring MC STYLES*

MC TUNES *UK, male rapper – Nicholas Lockett (19 WEEKS)*   pos/wks

2 Jun 90	● THE ONLY RHYME THAT BITES *ZTT ZANG 3* [1]	10	10
15 Sep 90	TUNES SPLITS THE ATOM *ZTT ZANG 6* [1]	18	7
1 Dec 90	PRIMARY RHYMING *ZTT ZANG 10*	67	1
6 Mar 99	THE ONLY RHYME THAT BITES 99 *ZTT ZTT 125CD* [1]	53	1

[1] MC Tunes versus 808 State

MC VIPER – *See REFLEX featuring MC VIPER*

MC WILDSKI *UK, male rapper (10 WEEKS)*   pos/wks

8 Jul 89	BLAME IT ON THE BASSLINE *Go.Beat GOD 33* [1]	29	6
3 Mar 90	WARRIOR *Arista 112956*	49	4

[1] Norman Cook featuring MC Wildski

'Blame It on the Bassline' was listed with 'Won't Talk About It' by Norman Cook featuring Billy Bragg

ME AND YOU featuring WE THE PEOPLE BAND
Jamaica / UK, male / female vocal / instrumental group (9 WEEKS)   pos/wks

28 Jul 79	YOU NEVER KNOW WHAT YOU'VE GOT *Laser LAS 8*	31	9

ME ME ME *UK, male vocal / instrumental group (4 WEEKS)*   pos/wks

17 Aug 96	HANGING AROUND *Indolent DUFF 005CD*	19	4

Abigail MEAD and Nigel GOULDING *UK / US, female / male producers – Vivian Kubrick and Nigel Goulding (10 WEEKS)*   pos/wks

26 Sep 87	● FULL METAL JACKET (I WANNA BE YOUR DRILL INSTRUCTOR) *Warner Bros. W 8187*	2	10

MEAT BEAT MANIFESTO *UK, male production duo (1 WEEK)*   pos/wks

20 Feb 93	MINDSTREAM *Play It Again Sam BIAS 232CD*	55	1

MEAT LOAF (160) [Top 500] *Larger-than-life vocalist / actor: b. Marvin Lee Aday, 27 Sep 1948, Dallas, US. His collaborations with producer / songwriter Jim Steinman resulted in some of rock's finest recordings. His album 'Bat Out of Hell' sold more than 25 million copies and spent almost 10 years in total in the UK chart. Best-selling single: 'I'd Do Anything For Love (But I Won't Do That)' 761,200 (146 WEEKS)*   pos/wks

20 May 78	YOU TOOK THE WORDS RIGHT OUT OF MY MOUTH *Epic EPC 5980*	33	8
19 Aug 78	TWO OUT OF THREE AIN'T BAD *Epic EPC 6281*	32	8
10 Feb 79	BAT OUT OF HELL *Epic EPC 7018*	15	7
26 Sep 81	I'M GONNA LOVE HER FOR BOTH OF US *Epic EPCA 1580*	62	3
28 Nov 81 ●	DEAD RINGER FOR LOVE *Epic EPCA 1697*	5	17
28 May 83	IF YOU REALLY WANT TO *Epic A 3357*	59	2
24 Sep 83	MIDNIGHT AT THE LOST AND FOUND *Epic A 3748*	17	8
14 Jan 84	RAZOR'S EDGE *Epic A 4080*	41	3
6 Oct 84	MODERN GIRL *Arista ARIST 585*	17	9
22 Dec 84	NOWHERE FAST *Arista ARIST 600*	67	4
23 Mar 85	PIECE OF THE ACTION *Arista ARIST 603*	47	5
30 Aug 86	ROCK 'N' ROLL MERCENARIES *Arista ARIST 666* [1]	31	6
22 Jun 91	DEAD RINGER FOR LOVE (re-issue) *Epic 6569827*	53	2
27 Jun 92	TWO OUT OF THREE AIN'T BAD (re-issue) *Epic 6574917*	69	1
9 Oct 93 ★	I'D DO ANYTHING FOR LOVE (BUT I WON'T DO THAT) *Virgin VSCDT 1443* ▲	1	19
18 Dec 93 ●	BAT OUT OF HELL (re-issue) *Epic 6600062*	8	9
19 Feb 94	ROCK AND ROLL DREAMS COME THROUGH *Virgin VSCDT 1479*	11	7
7 May 94	OBJECTS IN THE REAR VIEW MIRROR MAY APPEAR CLOSER THAN THEY ARE *Virgin VSCDT 1492*	26	4
28 Oct 95 ●	I'D LIE FOR YOU (AND THAT'S THE TRUTH) *Virgin VSCDT 1563*	2	11
27 Jan 96 ●	NOT A DRY EYE IN THE HOUSE *Virgin VSCDT 1567*	7	6
27 Apr 96	RUNNIN' FOR THE RED LIGHT (I GOTTA LIFE) *Virgin VSCDX 1582*	21	3
17 Apr 99	IS NOTHING SACRED *Virgin VSCDT 1734* [2]	15	4

[1] Meat Loaf featuring John Parr [2] Meat Loaf featuring Patti Russo

'Dead Ringer for Love' features Cher as uncredited co-vocalist. 'I'd Do Anything for Love (But I Won't Do That) features uncredited vocals by Lorraine Crosby (aka Mrs Loud)

MECHANICS – See MIKE and the MECHANICS

MECO *US, orchestra – leader Meco Monardo (9 WEEKS)*   pos/wks

1 Oct 77 ●	STAR WARS THEME – CANTINA BAND *RCA XB 1028* ▲	7	9

Glenn MEDEIROS *US, male vocalist (26 WEEKS)*   pos/wks

18 Jun 88 ★	NOTHING'S GONNA CHANGE MY LOVE FOR YOU *London LON 184*	1	13
3 Sep 88	LONG AND LASTING LOVE (ONCE IN A LIFETIME) *London LON 202*	42	4
30 Jun 90	SHE AIN'T WORTH IT *London LON 265* [1] ▲	12	9

[1] Glenn Medeiros featuring Bobby Brown

Paul MEDFORD – See Letitia DEAN and Paul MEDFORD

MEDICINE HEAD *UK, male vocal / instrumental duo – John Fiddler and Peter Hope Evans (37 WEEKS)*   pos/wks

26 Jun 71	(AND THE) PICTURES IN THE SKY *Dandelion DAN 7003*	22	8
5 May 73 ●	ONE AND ONE IS ONE *Polydor 2001 432*	3	13
4 Aug 73	RISING SUN *Polydor 2058 389*	11	9
9 Feb 74	SLIP AND SLIDE *Polydor 2058 436*	22	7

MEDICINE SHOW – See DR HOOK

Bill MEDLEY *US, male vocalist (29 WEEKS)*   pos/wks

31 Oct 87 ●	(I'VE HAD) THE TIME OF MY LIFE (re) *RCA PB 49625* [1] ▲	6	23
27 Aug 88	HE AIN'T HEAVY, HE'S MY BROTHER *Scotti Brothers PO 10*	25	6

[1] Bill Medley and Jennifer Warnes

'(I've Had) The Time of My Life' re-entered in Dec 1990 peaking at No.8

See also RIGHTEOUS BROTHERS

MEDWAY *US, male producer – Jesse Skeens (2 WEEKS)*   pos/wks

29 Apr 00	FAT BASTARD (EP) *Hooj Choons HOOJ 92CD*	69	1
10 Mar 01	RELEASE *Hooj Choons HOOJ 105*	67	1

Tracks on Fat Bastard (EP): Release / Flanker / Faith

Michael MEDWIN, Bernard BRESSLAW, Alfie BASS and Leslie FYSON *UK, male actors / vocalists (9 WEEKS)*   pos/wks

30 May 58 ●	THE SIGNATURE TUNE OF 'THE ARMY GAME' *HMV POP 490*	5	9

See also Bernard BRESSLAW

MEECHIE *US, female vocalist (1 WEEK)*   pos/wks

2 Sep 95	YOU BRING ME JOY *Vibe MCSTD 2069*	74	1

Tony MEEHAN
UK, male instrumental group – Tony Meehan – drums (4 WEEKS)   pos/wks

16 Jan 64	SONG OF MEXICO *Decca F 11801*	39	4

See also Jet HARRIS and Tony MEEHAN; SHADOWS

MEEKER *UK, female vocal / production duo (1 WEEK)*   pos/wks

26 Feb 00	SAVE ME *Underwater H20 009 CD*	60	1

MEGA CITY FOUR
UK, male vocal / instrumental group (7 WEEKS)   pos/wks

19 Oct 91	WORDS THAT SAY *Big Life MEGA 2*	66	1
8 Feb 92	STOP (EP) *Big Life MEGA 3*	36	2
16 May 92	SHIVERING SAND *Big Life MEGA 4*	35	2
1 May 93	IRON SKY *Big Life MEGAD 5*	48	1
17 Jul 93	WALLFLOWER *Big Life MEGAD 6*	69	1

Tracks on Stop (EP): Stop / Desert Song / Back to Zero / Overlap

MEGABASS – See VARIOUS ARTISTS (MONTAGES)

MEGADETH *US, male vocal / instrumental group (32 WEEKS)*   pos/wks

19 Dec 87	WAKE UP DEAD *Capitol CL 476*	65	2
27 Feb 88	ANARCHY IN THE UK *Capitol CL 480*	45	3
21 May 88	MARY JANE *Capitol CL 489*	46	2
13 Jan 90	NO MORE MR NICE GUY *SBK SBK 4*	13	6
29 Sep 90	HOLY WARS . . . THE PUNISHMENT DUE *Capitol CLP 588*	24	3
16 Mar 91	HANGAR 18 *Capitol CLS 604*	26	4
27 Jun 92	SYMPHONY OF DESTRUCTION *Capitol CLS 662*	15	3
24 Oct 92	SKIN O' MY TEETH *Capitol CLP 669*	13	3
29 May 93	SWEATING BULLETS *Capitol CDCL 682*	26	3
7 Jan 95	TRAIN OF CONSEQUENCES *Capitol CDCL 730*	22	3

MEGAMAN – See OXIDE & NEUTRINO

MEHTA – See José CARRERAS

Dieter MEIER – See YELLO; X-PRESS 2

MEJA *Sweden, female vocalist – Meja Beckman (14 WEEKS)*   pos/wks

24 Oct 98	ALL 'BOUT THE MONEY *Columbia 6665662*	12	5
29 Apr 00 ●	PRIVATE EMOTION *Columbia 6692692* [1]	9	9

[1] Ricky Martin featuring Meja

MEKKA *UK, male producer – Jake Williams (1 WEEK)*   pos/wks

24 Mar 01	DIAMOND BACK *Perfecto PERF 12CDS*	67	1

MEKON featuring Roxanne SHANTE
UK, male producer – John Gosling and US, female rapper (1 WEEK)   pos/wks

23 Sep 00	WHAT'S GOING ON *Wall of Sound WALD 064*	43	1

Melle MEL – See GRANDMASTER FLASH, Melle MEL and the FURIOUS FIVE

MEL and KIM
UK, female vocal duo – Mel and Kim Appleby (51 WEEKS)   pos/wks

20 Sep 86	●	SHOWING OUT (GET FRESH AT THE WEEKEND)		
		Supreme SUPE 107	**3**	19
7 Mar 87	★	RESPECTABLE *Supreme SUPE 111*	**1**	15
11 Jul 87	●	F.L.M. *Supreme SUPE 113*	**7**	10
27 Feb 88	●	THAT'S THE WAY IT IS *Supreme SUPE 117*	**10**	7

See also Kim APPLEBY

MEL and KIM – *See Mel SMITH; Kim WILDE*

George MELACHRINO ORCHESTRA
UK, orchestra, leader d. 18 Jun 1965 (9 WEEKS)   pos/wks

12 Oct 56	AUTUMN CONCERTO *HMV B 10958*	**18**	9

MELANIE
US, female vocalist – Melanie Safka (35 WEEKS)   pos/wks

26 Sep 70	●	RUBY TUESDAY (re) *Buddah 2011 038*	**9**	15
16 Jan 71		WHAT HAVE THEY DONE TO MY SONG MA *Buddah 2011038*	**39**	1
1 Jan 72	●	BRAND NEW KEY *Buddah 2011 105* ▲	**4**	12
16 Feb 74		WILL YOU LOVE ME TOMORROW *Neighbourhood NBH 9*	**37**	5
24 Sep 83		EVERY BREATH OF THE WAY *Neighbourhood HOOD NB1*	**70**	2

MELKY SEDECK
US, male / female vocal / instrumental duo – Melky and Sedeck Jean (9 WEEKS)   pos/wks

8 May 99		RAW *MCA MCSTD 48107*	**50**	1
16 Sep 00	●	IT DOESN'T MATTER *Columbia 6697782* [1]	**3**	8

[1] Wyclef Jean featuring The Rock and Melky Sedeck

John Cougar MELLENCAMP
US, male vocalist (18 WEEKS)   pos/wks

23 Oct 82		JACK AND DIANE *Riva RIVA 37* [1] ▲	**25**	8
1 Feb 86		SMALL TOWN *Riva JCM 5*	**53**	4
10 May 86		R.O.C.K. IN THE USA *Riva JCM 6*	**67**	3
3 Sep 94		WILD NIGHT *Mercury MERCD 409* [2]	**34**	3

[1] John Cougar [2] John Mellencamp featuring Me'Shell Ndegeocello

MELLOMEN – *See Rosemary CLOONEY; Frankie LAINE; Doris DAY*

Will MELLOR
UK, male actor / vocalist (9 WEEKS)   pos/wks

28 Feb 98	●	WHEN I NEED YOU *Unity UNITY 017RCD*	**5**	6
27 Jun 98		NO MATTER WHAT I DO *Jive 0540012*	**23**	3

MELLOW TRAX
Germany, male producer – Christian Schwarnweber (2 WEEKS)   pos/wks

14 Oct 00	OUTTA SPACE *Substance SUBS 3CDS*	**41**	2

MELODIANS
Jamaica, male vocal / instrumental group (1 WEEK)   pos/wks

10 Jan 70	SWEET SENSATION *Trojan TR 695*	**41**	1

MELODY MAKERS – *See Ziggy MARLEY and the MELODY MAKERS*

MELT featuring Little Ms MARCIE
UK, male producer – Matt Darey – and female vocalist (1 WEEK)   pos/wks

8 Apr 00	HARD HOUSE MUSIC *WEA WEA 257CD*	**59**	1

See also Matt DAREY; SUNBURST; MDM; Marcella WOODS

MELTDOWN
UK / US, male instrumental / production duo (1 WEEK)   pos/wks

27 Apr 96	MY LIFE IS IN YOUR HANDS *Sony S3 DANU 7CD*	**44**	1

Harold MELVIN and The BLUENOTES
US, male vocal group, leader d. 24 Mar 1997 (52 WEEKS)   pos/wks

13 Jan 73	●	IF YOU DON'T KNOW ME BY NOW *CBS 8496*	**9**	9
12 Jan 74		THE LOVE I LOST (PART 1)		
		Philadelphia International PIR 1879	**21**	8
13 Apr 74		SATISFACTION GUARANTEED (OR TAKE YOUR LOVE BACK)		
		Philadelphia International PIR 2187	**32**	6
31 May 75		GET OUT (AND LET ME CRY) *Route RT 06* [1]	**35**	5
28 Feb 76		WAKE UP EVERYBODY (PART 1)		
		Philadelphia International PIR 3866	**23**	7
22 Jan 77	●	DON'T LEAVE ME THIS WAY		
		Philadelphia International PIR 4909 [2]	**5**	10
2 Apr 77		REACHING FOR THE WORLD *ABC 4161* [1]	**48**	1
28 Apr 84		DON'T GIVE ME UP *London LON 47* [1]	**59**	4
4 Aug 84		TODAY'S YOUR LUCKY DAY *London LON 52* [3]	**66**	2

[1] Harold Melvin and The Blue Notes [2] Harold Melvin and The Bluenotes featuring Theodore Pendergrass [3] Harold Melvin and The Blue Notes featuring Nikko

MEMBERS
UK, male vocal / instrumental group (14 WEEKS)   pos/wks

3 Feb 79	THE SOUND OF THE SUBURBS *Virgin VS 242*	**12**	9
7 Apr 79	OFFSHORE BANKING BUSINESS *Virgin VS 248*	**31**	5

MEMBERS OF MAYDAY
Germany, male production duo – Klaus Jankuhn and Maximilian Lenz (4 WEEKS)   pos/wks

23 Jun 01	10 IN 01 *Deviant DVNT 42CDS*	**31**	3
13 Apr 02	SONIC EMPIRE *Low Spirit DVNT 49CDS*	**59**	1

MEMPHIS BLEEK featuring JAY-Z
US, male rappers (1 WEEK)   pos/wks

4 Dec 99	WHAT YOU THINK OF THAT *Def Jam 8708292*	**58**	1

MEN AT WORK
Australia / UK, male vocal / instrumental group – lead vocal Colin James Hay (39 WEEKS)   pos/wks

30 Oct 82		WHO CAN IT BE NOW? *Epic EPC A 2392* ▲	**45**	5
8 Jan 83	★	DOWN UNDER *Epic EPC A 1980* ▲	**1**	12
9 Apr 83		OVERKILL *Epic EPC A 3220*	**21**	10
2 Jul 83		IT'S A MISTAKE *Epic EPC A 3475*	**33**	6
10 Sep 83		DR HECKYLL AND MR JIVE *Epic EPC A 3668*	**31**	6

MEN OF VIZION
US, male vocal group (2 WEEKS)   pos/wks

27 Mar 99	DO YOU FEEL ME? (...FREAK YOU)		
	MJJ / Epic 6670912	**36**	2

MEN THEY COULDN'T HANG
UK, male vocal / instrumental group (4 WEEKS)   pos/wks

2 Apr 88	THE COLOURS *Magnet SELL 6*	**61**	4

MEN WITHOUT HATS
Canada, male vocal / instrumental group (11 WEEKS)   pos/wks

8 Oct 83 ●	THE SAFETY DANCE *Statik TAK 1*	6 11

Sergio MENDES *Brazil, male conductor (5 WEEKS)*
   pos/wks

9 Jul 83	NEVER GONNA LET YOU GO *A&M AM 118*	45 5

Uncredited vocals by Joe Pizzulo and Leza Miller

Andrea MENDEZ *UK, female vocalist (1 WEEK)*
   pos/wks

3 Aug 96	BRING ME LOVE *AM:PM 5817872*	44 1

MENSWEAR *UK, male vocal / instrumental group (18 WEEKS)*
   pos/wks

15 Apr 95	I'LL MANAGE SOMEHOW *Laurel LAUCD 4*	49 1
1 Jul 95	DAYDREAMER *Laurel LAUCD 5*	14 4
30 Sep 95	STARDUST *Laurel LAUCD 6*	16 3
16 Dec 95	SLEEPING IN *Laurel LAUCD 7*	24 3
23 Mar 96 ●	BEING BRAVE *Laurel LAUCD 8*	10 4
7 Sep 96	WE LOVE YOU *Laurel LAUCD 11*	22 3

MENTAL AS ANYTHING
Australia, male vocal / instrumental group (13 WEEKS)   pos/wks

7 Feb 87 ●	LIVE IT UP *Epic ANY 1*	3 13

Freddie MERCURY   (437   Top 500)   *Gregarious, versatile lead singer of Queen, b. Faroukh Bulsara, 5 Sep 1946, Zanzibar, Africa, d. 24 Nov 1991. UK-based performer was one of rock music's all-time great showmen, whose music has raised millions of pounds for Aids charities (79 WEEKS)*   pos/wks

22 Sep 84 ●	LOVE KILLS *CBS A 4735*	10 8
20 Apr 85	I WAS BORN TO LOVE YOU *CBS A 6019*	11 10
13 Jul 85	MADE IN HEAVEN *CBS A 6413*	57 4
21 Sep 85	LIVING ON MY OWN *CBS A 6555*	50 3
24 May 86	TIME *EMI EMI 5559*	32 5
7 Mar 87 ●	THE GREAT PRETENDER *Parlophone R 6151*	4 9
7 Nov 87 ●	BARCELONA *Polydor POSP 887* 1	8 9
8 Aug 92 ●	BARCELONA (re-issue) *Polydor PO 221* 1	2 8
12 Dec 92 ●	IN MY DEFENCE *Parlophone R 6331*	8 7
6 Feb 93	THE GREAT PRETENDER (re-issue) *Parlophone CDR 6336*	29 3
31 Jul 93 ★	LIVING ON MY OWN (re-mix) *Parlophone CDR 6355*	1 13

1 Freddie Mercury and Montserrat Caballé

See also QUEEN

MERCURY REV *US, male vocal / instrumental group (12 WEEKS)* pos/wks

14 Nov 98	GODDESS ON A HIWAY *V2 VVR 5003323*	51 1
6 Feb 99	DELTA SUN BOTTLENECK STOMP *V2 VVR 5005413*	26 2
22 May 99	OPUS 40 *V2 VVR 5006963*	31 2
28 Aug 99	GODDESS ON A HIWAY (re-issue) *V2 VVR 5008493*	26 2
6 Oct 01	NITE AND FOG *V2 VVR 5017723*	47 1
26 Jan 02	THE DARK IS RISING *V2 VVR 5018713*	16 3
27 Jul 02	LITTLE RHYMES *V2 VVR 5019783*	51 1

MERCY MERCY *UK, male vocal / instrumental group (2 WEEKS)* pos/wks

21 Sep 85	WHAT ARE WE GONNA DO ABOUT IT? *Ensign ENY 522*	59 2

MERLIN – *See BOMB THE BASS; BEATMASTERS*

MERO *UK, male vocal duo – Tommy Clark and Derek McDonald (2 WEEKS)*
   pos/wks

25 Mar 00	IT MUST BE LOVE *RCA 74321664772*	33 2

Tony MERRICK *UK, male vocalist (1 WEEK)*
   pos/wks

2 Jun 66	LADY JANE *Columbia DB 7913*	49 1

MERSEYBEATS *UK, male vocal / instrumental group (64 WEEKS)* pos/wks

12 Sep 63	IT'S LOVE THAT REALLY COUNTS *Fontana TF 412*	24 12
16 Jan 64 ●	I THINK OF YOU *Fontana TF 431*	5 17

16 Apr 64	DON'T TURN AROUND *Fontana TF 459*	13 11
9 Jul 64	WISHIN' AND HOPIN' *Fontana TF 482*	13 10
5 Nov 64	LAST NIGHT *Fontana TF 504*	40 3
14 Oct 65	I LOVE YOU, YES I DO *Fontana TF 607*	22 8
20 Jan 66	I STAND ACCUSED *Fontana TF 645*	38 3

MERSEYS *UK, male vocal duo (13 WEEKS)* pos/wks

28 Apr 66 ●	SORROW *Fontana TF 694*	4 13

MERTON PARKAS
UK, male vocal / instrumental group (6 WEEKS)   pos/wks

4 Aug 79	YOU NEED WHEELS *Beggars Banquet BEG 22*	40 6

MERZ *UK, male vocalist / instrumentalist – Conrad Lambert (2 WEEKS)*
   pos/wks

17 Jul 99	MANY WEATHERS APART *Epic 6674972*	48 1
16 Oct 99	LOVELY DAUGHTER *Epic 6679132*	60 1

Mady MESPLE and Danielle MILLET with the PARIS OPERA-COMIQUE ORCHESTRA conducted by Alain LOMBARD
France, female vocal duo and orchestra (4 WEEKS)   pos/wks

6 Apr 85	FLOWER DUET (FROM 'LAKME') *EMI 5481*	47 4

MESSIAH *UK, male instrumental / production group (13 WEEKS)* pos/wks

20 Jun 92	TEMPLE OF DREAMS *Kickin KICK 12S*	20 5
26 Sep 92	I FEEL LOVE *Kickin KICK 22S* 1	19 5
27 Nov 93	THUNDERDOME *WEA YZ 790CD1*	29 3

1 Messiah featuring Precious Wilson

METAL GURUS *UK, male vocal / instrumental group (2 WEEKS)* pos/wks

8 Dec 90	MERRY XMAS EVERYBODY *Mercury GURU 1*	55 2

METALHEADZ – *See GOLDIE*

METALLICA
US / Denmark, male vocal / instrumental group (59 WEEKS)   pos/wks

22 Aug 87	THE $5.98 EP – GARAGE DAYS RE-REVISITED *Vertigo METAL 112*	27 4
3 Sep 88	HARVESTER OF SORROW *Vertigo METAL 212*	20 3
22 Apr 89	ONE *Vertigo METAL 5*	13 7
10 Aug 91 ●	ENTER SANDMAN *Vertigo METAL 7*	5 4
9 Nov 91	THE UNFORGIVEN *Vertigo METAL 8*	15 4
2 May 92 ●	NOTHING ELSE MATTERS *Vertigo METAL 10*	6 6
31 Oct 92	WHEREVER I MAY ROAM *Vertigo METAL 9*	25 4
20 Feb 93	SAD BUT TRUE *Vertigo METAL 11*	20 3
1 Jun 96 ●	UNTIL IT SLEEPS *Vertigo METCD 12*	5 4
28 Sep 96	HERO OF THE DAY *Vertigo METCD 13*	17 4
7 Dec 96	MAMA SAID *Vertigo METCD 14*	19 2
22 Nov 97	THE MEMORY REMAINS *Vertigo METCD 15*	13 3
7 Mar 98	THE UNFORGIVEN II *Vertigo METDD 17*	15 4
4 Jul 98	FUEL *Vertigo METCD 16*	31 2
27 Feb 99	WHISKEY IN THE JAR *Vertigo METCD 19*	29 2
12 Aug 00	I DISAPPEAR *Hollywood 0113875 HWR*	35 3

Tracks on The $5.98 EP: Garage Days Re-Revisited : Helpless / Crash Course in Brain Surgery / The Small Hours / Last Caress / Green Hell

METEOR SEVEN
Germany, male producer – Jans Ebert (1 WEEK)   pos/wks

18 May 02	UNIVERSAL MUSIC *Bulletproof PROOF 16CD*	71 1

METEORS *UK, male vocal / instrumental group (2 WEEKS)* pos/wks

26 Feb 83	JOHNNY REMEMBER ME *ID EYE 1*	66 2

Pat METHENY GROUP – *See David BOWIE*

METHOD MAN *US, male rapper – Clifford Smith (14 WEEKS)* pos/wks

29 Apr 95	RELEASE YO' SELF *Def Jam DEFCD 6*	46 1

29 Jul 95 ●	I'LL BE THERE FOR YOU – YOU'RE ALL I NEED TO GET BY		
	Def Jam DEFCD 11 [1]	10	5
5 Apr 97 ●	HIT EM HIGH (THE MONSTARS' ANTHEM)		
	Atlantic A 5449CD [2]	8	6
22 May 99	BREAK UPS 2 MAKE UPS *Def Jam 8709272* [3]	33	2

[1] Method Man featuring Mary J Blige [2] B Real / Busta Rhymes / Coolio / LL Cool J / Method Man [3] Method Man featuring D'Angelo

MEZZOFORTE *Iceland, male instrumental group (10 WEEKS)*
pos/wks

5 Mar 83	GARDEN PARTY *Steinar STE 705*	17	9
11 Jun 83	ROCKALL *Steinar STE 710*	75	1

MIAMI SOUND MACHINE
Cuba, male / female vocal / instrumental group (72 WEEKS)
pos/wks

11 Aug 84 ●	DR BEAT *Epic A 4614*	6	14
17 May 86	BAD BOY *Epic A 6537*	16	11
16 Jul 88 ●	ANYTHING FOR YOU *Epic 651673 7* [1] ▲	10	16
22 Oct 88 ●	1-2-3 (re) *Epic 652958 7* [1]	9	10
17 Dec 88 ●	RHYTHM IS GONNA GET YOU *Epic 654514 7* [1]	16	9
11 Feb 89 ●	CAN'T STAY AWAY FROM YOU *Epic 651 444 7* [1]	7	12

[1] Gloria Estefan and Miami Sound Machine

See also Gloria ESTEFAN

George MICHAEL (44) Top 500
Previously half of internationally celebrated duo Wham!, b. Georgios Panayiotou, 25 Jun 1963, London, UK. This multi-talented, award-winning singer / songwriter / producer / arranger and instrumentalist has successfully made the difficult transition from teeny-bopper hero to world-renowned solo star. Best-selling single: 'Careless Whisper' 1,365,995 (264 WEEKS)
pos/wks

4 Aug 84 ★	CARELESS WHISPER *Epic A 4603* ◆ ▲	1	17
5 Apr 86 ★	A DIFFERENT CORNER *Epic A 7033*	1	10
31 Jan 87 ★	I KNEW YOU WERE WAITING (FOR ME) *Epic DUET 2* [1] ▲	1	9
13 Jun 87 ●	I WANT YOUR SEX *Epic LUST 1*	3	10
24 Oct 87 ●	FAITH *Epic EMU 3* ▲	2	12
9 Jan 88	FATHER FIGURE *Epic EMU 4* ▲	11	6
23 Apr 88 ●	ONE MORE TRY *Epic EMU 5* ▲	8	7
16 Jul 88	MONKEY *Epic EMU 6* ▲	13	6
3 Dec 88	KISSING A FOOL *Epic EMU 7*	18	6
25 Aug 90 ●	PRAYING FOR TIME *Epic GEO 1* ▲	6	7
27 Oct 90	WAITING FOR THAT DAY *Epic GEO 2*	23	5
15 Dec 90	FREEDOM! *Epic GEO 3*	28	6
16 Feb 91	HEAL THE PAIN *Epic 6566477*	31	4
30 Mar 91	COWBOYS AND ANGELS *Epic 6567747*	45	3
7 Dec 91 ★	DON'T LET THE SUN GO DOWN ON ME *Epic 6576467* [2] ■ ▲	1	10
13 Jun 92	TOO FUNKY *Epic 6580587*	4	9
1 May 93 ★	FIVE LIVE (EP) (re) *Parlophone CDRS 6340* [3] ■	1	12
20 Jan 96 ★	JESUS TO A CHILD (2re) *Virgin VSCDG 1571* ■	1	13
4 May 96 ★	FASTLOVE *Virgin VSCDG 1579* ■	1	14
31 Aug 96 ★	SPINNING THE WHEEL *Virgin VSCDG 1595*	2	12
1 Feb 97 ●	OLDER / I CAN'T MAKE YOU LOVE ME (re)		
	Virgin VSCDG 1626	3	9
10 May 97 ●	STAR PEOPLE '97 (re) *Virgin VSCDG 1641*	2	13
7 Jun 97 ●	WALTZ AWAY DREAMING *Aegean AECD 01* [4]	10	4
20 Sep 97 ●	YOU HAVE BEEN LOVED / THE STRANGEST THING '97		
	Virgin VSCD 1663	2	8
31 Oct 98 ●	OUTSIDE (re) *Epic 6665625*	2	16
13 Mar 99 ●	AS *Epic 6670122* [5]	4	10
17 Jun 00 ●	IF I TOLD YOU THAT (re) *Arista 74321766282* [6]	9	11
30 Mar 02 ●	FREEEK! *Polydor 5706812*	7	10
10 Aug 02	SHOOT THE DOG (re) *Polydor 5709242*	12	5

[1] Aretha Franklin and George Michael [2] George Michael and Elton John [3] George Michael and Queen with Lisa Stansfield [4] Toby Bourke with George Michael [5] George Michael and Mary J Blige [6] Whitney Houston / George Michael

Tracks on Five Live (EP): Somebody to Love / These Are the Days of Our Lives / Calling You / Papa Was a Rolling Stone – Killer (medley). The first track on the EP features Queen, the second Queen and Lisa Stansfield

See also Lisa MOORISH; Elton JOHN

MICHAEL SCHENKER GROUP – *See Michael SCHENKER GROUP*

MICHAELA *UK, female vocalist (6 WEEKS)*
pos/wks

2 Sep 89	H-A-P-P-Y RADIO *London H 1*	62	4
28 Apr 90	TAKE GOOD CARE OF MY HEART *London WAC 90*	66	2

Lisa MICHAELIS – *See Frankie KNUCKLES*

Pras MICHEL
US, male rapper / producer – Prakazrel Michael (36 WEEKS)
pos/wks

27 Jun 98 ●	GHETTO SUPASTAR (THAT IS WHAT YOU ARE)		
	Interscope IND 95593 [1]	2	17
7 Nov 98 ●	BLUE ANGELS *Ruffhouse 6666215* [2]	6	10
14 Nov 98 ●	ANOTHER ONE BITES THE DUST		
	Dreamworks DRMCD 22364 [3]	5	6
1 Sep 01	MISS CALIFORNIA *Elektra E 7192CD* [4]	25	3

[1] Pras Michel featuring Ol' Dirty Bastard introducing Mya [2] Pras [3] Queen with Wyclef Jean featuring Pras and Free [4] Dante Thomas featuring Pras

MICHELE – *See KING BEE*

Keith MICHELL *Australia, male actor / vocalist (25 WEEKS)*
pos/wks

27 Mar 71	I'LL GIVE YOU THE EARTH (TOUS LES BATEAUX, TOUS		
	LES OISEAUX) (re) *Spark SRL 1046*	30	11
26 Jan 80 ●	CAPTAIN BEAKY / WILFRED THE WEASEL		
	Polydor POSP 106	5	10
29 Mar 80	THE TRIAL OF HISSING SID *Polydor HISS 1* [1]	53	4

[1] Keith Michell, Captain Beaky and his Band

MICHELLE *Trinidad, female vocalist (1 WEEK)*
pos/wks

8 Jun 96	STANDING HERE ALL ALONE *Positiva CDTIV 54*	69	1

Yvette MICHELLE *US, female vocalist – Michele Bryant (3 WEEKS)* pos/wks

5 Apr 97	I'M NOT FEELING YOU *Loud 74321465222*	36	3

Lloyd MICHELS – *See MISTURA featuring Lloyd MICHELS*

MICK and PAT – *See PAT and MICK*

MICROBE *UK, male vocalist – Ian Doody (7 WEEKS)*
pos/wks

14 May 69	GROOVY BABY *CBS 4158*	29	7

MICRODISNEY
Ireland, male vocal / instrumental group (3 WEEKS)
pos/wks

21 Feb 87	TOWN TO TOWN *Virgin VS 927*	55	3

MIDDLE OF THE ROAD (470) Top 500
Scottish vocal / instrumental pop quartet which relocated to Italy and was extremely successful across Europe. Fronted by sole female Sally Carr (Sarah Young) b. 28 Mar 1945, Glasgow. First hit reportedly sold close to 10 million copies worldwide (76 WEEKS)
pos/wks

5 Jun 71 ★	CHIRPY CHIRPY CHEEP CHEEP *RCA 2047*	1	34
4 Sep 71 ●	TWEEDLE DEE, TWEEDLE DUM *RCA 2110*	2	17
11 Dec 71 ●	SOLEY SOLEY *RCA 2151*	5	12
25 Mar 72	SACRAMENTO (A WONDERFUL TOWN) (re) *RCA 2184*	23	7
29 Jul 72	SAMSON AND DELILAH *RCA 2237*	26	6

MIDDLESBROUGH FC featuring Bob MORTIMER and Chris REA
UK, male football team / vocal group (1 WEEK)
pos/wks

24 May 97	LET'S DANCE *Magnet EW 112CD*	44	1

MIDFIELD GENERAL featuring LINDA LEWIS
UK, male producer – Damian Harris and female vocalist (1 WEEK) pos/wks

19 Aug 00	REACH OUT *Skint / SKINT 54CD*	61	1

MIDGET *UK, male vocal / instrumental group (2 WEEKS)*
pos/wks

31 Jan 98	ALL FALL DOWN *Radarscope TINYCDS 6X*	57	1
18 Apr 98	INVISIBLE BALLOON *Radarscope TINYCDS 7*	66	1

MIDI XPRESS UK, male vocal / instrumental duo (1 WEEK)
pos/wks
| 11 May 96 | CHASE *Labello Dance LAD 26CD* | 73 | 1 |

Bette MIDLER US, female vocalist (27 WEEKS)
pos/wks
17 Jun 89	● WIND BENEATH MY WINGS *Atlantic A 8972* ▲	5	12
13 Oct 90	● FROM A DISTANCE (re) *Atlantic A 7820*	6	14
5 Dec 98	MY ONE TRUE FRIEND *Warner Brothers W 460CD*	58	1

'From a Distance' peaked at No.5 on re-entry in Jun 1991

MIDNIGHT COWBOY SOUNDTRACK US, orchestra (4 WEEKS) pos/wks
| 8 Nov 80 | MIDNIGHT COWBOY *United Artists UP 634* | 47 | 4 |

MIDNIGHT OIL
Australia, male vocal / instrumental group (32 WEEKS)
pos/wks
23 Apr 88	BEDS ARE BURNING *Sprint OIL 1*	48	5
2 Jul 88	THE DEAD HEART *Sprint OIL 2*	62	4
25 Mar 89	● BEDS ARE BURNING (re-issue) *Sprint OIL 3*	6	13
1 Jul 89	THE DEAD HEART (re-issue) *Sprint OIL 4*	62	4
10 Feb 90	BLUE SKY MINE *CBS OIL 5*	66	2
17 Apr 93	TRUGANINI *Columbia 6590492*	29	4
3 Jul 93	MY COUNTRY *Columbia 6593702*	66	1
6 Nov 93	IN THE VALLEY *Columbia 6598492*	60	1

MIDNIGHT STAR
US, male / female vocal / instrumental group (26 WEEKS)
pos/wks
23 Feb 85	OPERATOR *Solar MCA 942*	66	2
28 Jun 86	HEADLINES *Solar MCA 1065*	16	8
4 Oct 86	● MIDAS TOUCH *Solar MCA 1096*	8	10
7 Feb 87	ENGINE NO.9 *Solar MCA 1117*	64	3
2 May 87	WET MY WHISTLE *Solar MCA 1127*	60	3

MIDNITE BAND – See Tony RALLO and the MIDNITE BAND

MIGHTY AVENGERS
UK, male vocal / instrumental group (2 WEEKS)
pos/wks
| 26 Nov 64 | SO MUCH IN LOVE *Decca F 11962* | 46 | 2 |

MIGHTY AVONS – See Larry CUNNINGHAM and the MIGHTY AVONS

MIGHTY DUB KATZ UK, male producer – Norman Cook (6 WKS) pos/wks
7 Dec 96	JUST ANOTHER GROOVE *ffrr FCD 287*	43	1
2 Aug 97	MAGIC CARPET RIDE *ffrr FCD 306*	24	4
7 Dec 02	LET THE DRUMS SPEAK *Southern Fried ECB 31X*	73	1

See also Norman COOK; BEATS INTERNATIONAL; HOUSEMARTINS; FATBOY SLIM; PIZZAMAN; FREAKPOWER

MIGHTY LEMON DROPS
UK, male vocal / instrumental group (6 WEEKS)
pos/wks
13 Sep 86	THE OTHER SIDE OF YOU *Blue Guitar AZUR 1*	67	1
18 Apr 87	OUT OF HAND *Blue Guitar AZUR 4*	66	3
23 Jan 88	INSIDE OUT *Blue Guitar AZUR 6*	74	2

MIGHTY MIGHTY BOSSTONES
US, male vocal / instrumental group (6 WEEKS)
pos/wks
| 25 Apr 98 | THE IMPRESSION THAT I GET *Mercury 5748432* | 12 | 5 |
| 27 Jun 98 | THE RASCAL KING *Mercury 5661092* | 63 | 1 |

MIGHTY MORPH'N POWER RANGERS
US, male / female vocal group (13 WEEKS)
pos/wks
| 17 Dec 94 | ● POWER RANGERS (3re) *RCA 74321253022* | 3 | 13 |

MIGHTY WAH – See WAH!

MIGIL FIVE UK, male vocal / instrumental group (20 WEEKS)
pos/wks
| 19 Mar 64 | ● MOCKINGBIRD HILL *Pye 7N 15597* | 10 | 13 |
| 4 Jun 64 | NEAR YOU *Pye 7N 15645* | 31 | 7 |

MIG29 Italy, male instrumental / production group (2 WEEKS)
pos/wks
| 22 Feb 92 | MIG29 *Champion CHAMP 292* | 62 | 2 |

MIKAELA – See SUPERCAR

MIKE UK, male producer – Mark Jolley (2 WEEKS)
pos/wks
| 19 Nov 94 | TWANGLING THREE FINGERS IN A BOX *Pukka CDMIKE 100* | 40 | 2 |

MIKE and the MECHANICS
UK, male vocal / instrumental group (67 WEEKS)
pos/wks
15 Feb 86	SILENT RUNNING (ON DANGEROUS GROUND) *WEA U 8908*	21	9
31 May 86	ALL I NEED IS A MIRACLE *WEA U 8765*	53	4
14 Jan 89	● THE LIVING YEARS *WEA U 7717* ▲	2	11
16 Mar 91	WORD OF MOUTH *Virgin VS 1345*	13	10
15 Jun 91	A TIME AND PLACE *Virgin VS 1351*	58	3
8 Feb 92	EVERYBODY GETS A SECOND CHANCE *Virgin VS 1396*	56	4
25 Feb 95	OVER MY SHOULDER *Virgin VSCDT 1526*	12	9
17 Jun 95	A BEGGAR ON A BEACH OF GOLD *Virgin VSCDT 1535*	33	5
2 Sep 95	ANOTHER CUP OF COFFEE *Virgin VSCDT 1554*	51	4
17 Feb 96	ALL I NEED IS A MIRACLE (re-mix) *Virgin VSCDT 1576*	27	4
1 Jun 96	SILENT RUNNING (re-issue) *Virgin VSCDT 1585*	61	1
5 Jun 99	NOW THAT YOU'VE GONE *Virgin VSCDT 1732*	35	2
28 Aug 99	WHENEVER I STOP *Virgin VSCDT 1743*	73	1

See also GENESIS

MIKI and GRIFF
UK, female / male vocal duo – Miki and Griff Griffiths (25 WEEKS)
pos/wks
2 Oct 59	HOLD BACK TOMORROW *Pye 7N 15213*	26	2
13 Oct 60	ROCKIN' ALONE *Pye 7N 15296*	44	3
1 Feb 62	A LITTLE BITTY TEAR *Pye 7N 15412*	16	13
22 Aug 63	I WANT TO STAY HERE *Pye 7N 15555*	23	7

John MILES
UK, male vocalist / multi-instrumentalist (30 WEEKS)
pos/wks
18 Oct 75	HIGHFLY *Decca F 13595*	17	6
20 Mar 76	● MUSIC *Decca F 13627*	3	9
16 Oct 76	REMEMBER YESTERDAY *Decca F 13667*	32	5
18 Jun 77	● SLOW DOWN *Decca F 13709*	10	10

Robert MILES Italy, male instrumentalist – keyboards – Roberto
Concina. Best-selling single: 'Children' 770,000 (49 WEEKS)
pos/wks
24 Feb 96	● CHILDREN *Deconstruction 74321348322*	2	18
8 Jun 96	● FABLE (2re) *Deconstruction 74321382622*	7	9
16 Nov 96	● ONE & ONE *Deconstruction 74321427692* [1]	3	17
29 Nov 97	FREEDOM *Deconstruction 74321536952* [2]	15	4
28 Jul 01	PATHS *Salt SALT 002CD* [3]	74	1

[1] Robert Miles featuring Maria Nayler [2] Robert Miles featuring Kathy Sledge
[3] Robert Miles featuring Nina Miranda

June MILES-KINGSTON – See Jimmy SOMERVILLE

Paul MILES-KINGSTON – See Sarah BRIGHTMAN

Christina MILIAN US, female vocalist (27 WEEKS)
pos/wks
26 Jan 02	● AM TO PM *Def Soul 5889332*	3	11
29 Jun 02	● WHEN YOU LOOK AT ME *Def Soul 5829802*	3	10
9 Nov 02	● IT'S ALL GRAVY *Relentless RELENT 32CD* [1]	9	6

[1] Romeo featuring Christina Milian

See also JA RULE

MILK – See Jason DOWNS featuring MILK

MILK AND HONEY featuring Gali ATARI
Israel, male / female vocal / instrumental group (8 WEEKS)
pos/wks
| 14 Apr 79 | ● HALLELUJAH *Polydor 2001 870* | 5 | 8 |

Re-entries are listed as (re), (2re), (3re), etc which signifies that the hit re-entered the chart

MILK & SUGAR vs John Paul YOUNG
Germany, male production duo – Michael Kronenberger and Steffan Harning and Australia, male vocalist (3 WEEKS) pos/wks

12 Jan 02		LOVE IS IN THE AIR *Positiva CDTIV 166*	25	3

MILK INC.
Belgium, male / female production / vocal duo – Regi Penxten and An Vervoort (14 WEEKS) pos/wks

25 May 02	●	IN MY EYES *All Around the World CDGLOBE 252*	9	8
21 Sep 02	●	WALK ON WATER *Positiva CDTIV 179*	10	6

MILK INCORPORATED
Belgium, male / female vocal / production group (3 WEEKS) pos/wks

28 Feb 98		GOOD ENOUGH (LA VACHE) *Malarky MLKD 5*	23	3

MILKY
Italy, male production duo and Egypt, female vocalist (7 WEEKS) pos/wks

31 Aug 02	●	JUST THE WAY YOU ARE *Multiply CDMULTY 87*	8	6
7 Dec 02		IN MY MIND *Multiply CDMULTY 92*	48	1

MILL GIRLS – See Billy COTTON and his BAND

MILLA *US, female vocalist (1 WEEK)* pos/wks

18 Jun 94		GENTLEMAN WHO FELL *SBK CDSBK 49*	65	1

Frankie MILLER *UK, male vocalist (32 WEEKS)* pos/wks

4 Jun 77		BE GOOD TO YOURSELF *Chrysalis CHS 2147*	27	6
14 Oct 78	●	DARLIN' *Chrysalis CHS 2255*	6	15
20 Jan 79		WHEN I'M AWAY FROM YOU *Chrysalis CHS 2276*	42	5
21 Mar 92		CALEDONIA *MCS MCS 2001*	45	6

Gary MILLER
UK, male vocalist – Neville Williams d. 15 Jun 1968 (35 WEEKS) pos/wks

21 Oct 55		THE YELLOW ROSE OF TEXAS *Nixa N 15004*	13	5
13 Jan 56	●	ROBIN HOOD *Nixa N 15020*	10	6
11 Jan 57		GARDEN OF EDEN (re) *Pye Nixa N 15070*	14	7
19 Jul 57		WONDERFUL, WONDERFUL *Pye Nixa N 15094*	29	1
17 Jan 58		THE STORY OF MY LIFE *Pye Nixa N 15120*	14	6
21 Dec 61		THERE GOES THAT SONG AGAIN (re-entry) *Pye 7N 15404*	29	10

'The Night Is Young' listed with 'There Goes That Song Again' only for weeks 21 and 28 Dec 1961 and 4 Jan 1962. It peaked at No.32

Glenn MILLER and his ORCHESTRA
US, orchestra, Glenn Miller – trombone, d. 15 Dec 1944 (9 WEEKS) pos/wks

12 Mar 54		MOONLIGHT SERENADE *HMV BD 5942*	12	1
24 Jan 76		MOONLIGHT SERENADE (re-Issue) / LITTLE BROWN JUG / IN THE MOOD *RCA 2644* ▲	13	8

US No.1 symbol refers only to 'In the Mood' which hit the top spot in 1939

Jody MILLER *US, female vocalist (1 WEEK)* pos/wks

21 Oct 65		HOME OF THE BRAVE *Capitol CL 15415*	49	1

Leza MILLER – See Sergio MENDES

Mitch MILLER his Orchestra and Chorus
US, orchestra and chorus (13 WEEKS) pos/wks

7 Oct 55	●	THE YELLOW ROSE OF TEXAS *Philips PB 505* ▲	2	13

Ned MILLER *US, male vocalist (22 WEEKS)* pos/wks

14 Feb 63	●	FROM A JACK TO A KING *London HL 9658*	2	21
18 Feb 65		DO WHAT YOU DO DO WELL *London HL 9937*	48	1

Roger MILLER *US, male vocalist d. 25 Oct 1992 (42 WEEKS)* pos/wks

18 Mar 65	★	KING OF THE ROAD *Philips BF 1397*	1	15
3 Jun 65		ENGINE ENGINE NO.9 *Philips BF 1416*	33	5
21 Oct 65		KANSAS CITY STAR *Philips BF 1437*	48	1

16 Dec 65		ENGLAND SWINGS (re) *Philips BF 1456*	13	8
27 Mar 68		LITTLE GREEN APPLES (2re) *Mercury MF 1021*	19	13

Steve MILLER BAND
US, male vocal / instrumental group (36 WEEKS) pos/wks

23 Oct 76		ROCK 'N ME *Mercury 6078 804* ▲	11	9
19 Jun 82	●	ABRACADABRA *Mercury STEVE 3* ▲	2	11
4 Sep 82		KEEPS ME WONDERING WHY *Mercury STEVE 4*	52	3
11 Aug 90	★	THE JOKER *Capitol CL 583* ▲	1	13

Suzi MILLER and the JOHNSTON BROTHERS
UK, female vocalist – Renee Lester and male vocal group (2 WEEKS) pos/wks

21 Jan 55		HAPPY DAYS AND LONELY NIGHTS *Decca F 10389*	14	2

Lisa MILLETT – See SHEER BRONZE featuring Lisa MILLETT; GOODFELLAS featuring Lisa MILLETT; A.T.F.C. presents ONEPHATDEEVA; BABY BUMPS

MILLI VANILLI *France / Germany, male duo – Rob Pilatus (d. 2 Apr 1998) and Fabrice Morvan (50 WEEKS)* pos/wks

1 Oct 88	●	GIRL YOU KNOW IT'S TRUE *Cooltempo COOL 170*	3	13
17 Dec 88		BABY DON'T FORGET MY NUMBER *Cooltempo COOL 178* ▲	16	11
22 Jul 89		BLAME IT ON THE RAIN (re) *Cooltempo COOL 180* ▲	52	10
30 Sep 89	●	GIRL I'M GONNA MISS YOU *Cooltempo COOL 191* ▲	2	15
10 Mar 90		ALL OR NOTHING *Cooltempo COOL 199*	74	1

MILLICAN and NESBITT
UK, male vocal duo – Alan Millican and Tim Nesbitt (14 WEEKS) pos/wks

1 Dec 73		VAYA CON DIOS (MAY GOD BE WITH YOU) *Pye 7N 45310*	20	11
18 May 74		FOR OLD TIME'S SAKE *Pye 7N 45357*	38	3

MILLIE *Jamaica, female vocalist – Millie Small (33 WEEKS)* pos/wks

12 Mar 64	●	MY BOY LOLLIPOP *Fontana TF 449*	2	18
25 Jun 64		SWEET WILLIAM *Fontana TF 479*	30	9
11 Nov 65		BLOODSHOT EYES *Fontana TF 617*	48	1
25 Jul 87		MY BOY LOLLIPOP (re-issue) *Island WIP 6574*	46	5

MILLIONAIRE HIPPIES
UK, male producer – Danny Rampling (4 WEEKS) pos/wks

18 Dec 93		I AM THE MUSIC HEAR ME! *Deconstruction 74321175432*	52	3
10 Sep 94		C'MON *Deconstruction 74321229372*	59	1

Garry MILLS *UK, male vocalist (31 WEEKS)* pos/wks

7 Jul 60	●	LOOK FOR A STAR *Top Rank JAR 336*	7	14
20 Oct 60		TOP TEEN BABY *Top Rank JAR 500*	24	12
22 Jun 61		I'LL STEP DOWN *Decca F 11358*	39	5

Hayley MILLS *UK, female actor / vocalist (11 WEEKS)* pos/wks

19 Oct 61		LET'S GET TOGETHER *Decca F 21396*	17	11

Stephanie MILLS *US, female vocalist (33 WEEKS)* pos/wks

18 Oct 80	●	NEVER KNEW LOVE LIKE THIS BEFORE *20th Century TC 2460*	4	14
23 May 81		TWO HEARTS *20th Century TC 2492* [1]	49	5
15 Sep 84		THE MEDICINE SONG *Club JAB 8*	29	9
5 Sep 87		(YOU'RE PUTTIN') A RUSH ON ME *MCA MCA 1187*	62	2
1 May 93		NEVER DO YOU WRONG *MCA MCSTD 1767*	57	2
10 Jul 93		ALL DAY ALL NIGHT *MCA MCSTD 1778*	68	1

[1] Stephanie Mills featuring Teddy Pendergrass

Warren MILLS *Zambia, male vocalist (1 WEEK)* pos/wks

28 Sep 85		SUNSHINE *Jive JIVE 99*	74	1

MILLS BROTHERS *US, male vocal group (1 WEEK)* pos/wks

9 Jan 53	●	THE GLOW WORM *Brunswick 05007*	10	1

With Hal McIntyre and his Orchestra

MILLTOWN BROTHERS
UK, male vocal / instrumental group (16 WEEKS)   pos/wks

2 Feb 91	WHICH WAY SHOULD I JUMP? *A&M AM 711*	38 5
13 Apr 91	HERE I STAND *A&M AM 758*	41 4
6 Jul 91	APPLE GREEN *A&M AM 787*	43 4
22 May 93	TURN OFF *A&M 5802692*	55 1
17 Jul 93	IT'S ALL OVER NOW BABY BLUE *A&M 5803332*	48 2

CB MILTON *Holland, male vocalist (5 WEEKS)*   pos/wks

21 May 94	IT'S A LOVING THING *Logic 74321208062*	49 2
25 Mar 95	IT'S A LOVING THING (re-mix) *Logic 74321267212*	34 2
19 Aug 95	HOLD ON *Logic 74321292112*	62 1

Garnet MIMMS and TRUCKIN' CO
US, male vocalist and male instrumental group (1 WEEK)   pos/wks

25 Jun 77	WHAT IT IS *Arista 109*	44 1

MIND OF KANE *UK, male producer – David Hope (1 WEEK)*   pos/wks

27 Jul 91	STABBED IN THE BACK *Deja Vu DJV 007*	64 1

See also HOPE A.D.

MINDBENDERS   440   Top 500
UK, male vocal / instrumental group (79 WEEKS)   pos/wks

11 Jul 63	HELLO JOSEPHINE *Fontana TF 404* [1]	46 2
28 May 64	STOP LOOK AND LISTEN *Fontana TF 451* [1]	37 4
8 Oct 64 ●	UM, UM, UM, UM, UM, UM *Fontana TF 497* [1]	5 15
4 Feb 65 ●	GAME OF LOVE *Fontana TF 535* [1] ▲	2 11
17 Jun 65	JUST A LITTLE BIT TOO LATE *Fontana TF 579* [1]	20 7
30 Sep 65	SHE NEEDS LOVE *Fontana TF 611* [1]	32 6
13 Jan 66 ●	A GROOVY KIND OF LOVE *Fontana TF 644*	2 14
5 May 66	CAN'T LIVE WITH YOU CAN'T LIVE WITHOUT YOU *Fontana TF 697*	28 7
25 Aug 66	ASHES TO ASHES *Fontana TF 731*	14 9
20 Sep 67	THE LETTER *Fontana TF 869*	42 4

[1] Wayne Fontana and The Mindbenders

See also Wayne FONTANA

MINDS OF MEN
UK, male / female vocal / instrumental group (1 WEEK)   pos/wks

22 Jun 96	BRAND NEW DAY *Perfecto PERF 121CD*	41 1

Sal MINEO *US, male actor / vocalist d. 12 Feb 1976 (11 WEEKS)*   pos/wks

12 Jul 57	START MOVIN' (IN MY DIRECTION) *Philips PB 707*	16 11

Marcello MINERBI *Italy, orchestra (16 WEEKS)*   pos/wks

22 Jul 65 ●	ZORBA'S DANCE *Durium DRS 54001*	6 16

MINI POPS *UK, male / female vocal group (2 WEEKS)*   pos/wks

26 Dec 87	SONGS FOR CHRISTMAS '87 (EP) *Bright BULB 9*	39 2

Tracks on Songs for Christmas '87 (EP): Thanks for Giving Us Christmas / The Man in Red / Christmas Time Around the World / Shine On

MINIMAL FUNK 2 *Italy, male production duo (2 WEEKS)*   pos/wks

18 Jul 98	THE GROOVY THANG *Cleveland City CLECD 13046*	65 1
18 May 02	DEFINITION OF HOUSE *Junior BRG 033* [1]	63 1

[1] Minimal Funk

MINIMALISTIX *Belgium, male production group (5 WEEKS)*   pos/wks

16 Mar 02	CLOSE COVER *Data DATA 32CDS*	12 5

MINISTERS DE LA FUNK *US, male production trio (4 WEEKS)*   pos/wks

11 Mar 00	BELIEVE *Defected DFECT 14CDS*	45 2
27 Jan 01	BELIEVE (re-mix) *Defected DFECT 26CDS* [1]	42 2

[1] Ministers De La Funk featuring Jocelyn Brown

MINISTRY *US, male vocal / instrumental group (3 WEEKS)*   pos/wks

8 Aug 92	NWO *Sire W 0125TE*	49 1
6 Jan 96	THE FALL *Warner Bros. W 0328CD*	53 2

See also REVOLTING COCKS

MINK DeVILLE *US, male vocal / instrumental group (9 WEEKS)*   pos/wks

6 Aug 77	SPANISH STROLL *Capitol CLX 103*	20 9

MINKY *UK, male producer – Gary Dedman (1 WEEK)*   pos/wks

30 Oct 99	THE WEEKEND HAS LANDED *Offbeat OFFCD 1001*	70 1

Liza MINNELLI *US, female vocalist (15 WEEKS)*   pos/wks

12 Aug 89 ●	LOSING MY MIND *Epic ZEE 1*	6 7
7 Oct 89	DON'T DROP BOMBS *Epic ZEE 2*	46 3
25 Nov 89	SO SORRY I SAID *Epic ZEE 3*	62 2
3 Mar 90	LOVE PAINS *Epic ZEE 4*	41 3

Dannii MINOGUE   370   Top 500
Australia, singer / actor, b. 20 Oct 1971, who like older sister Kylie had a chart comeback in 2001. The Minogues have had more singles success than any other sisters (89 WEEKS) pos/wks

30 Mar 91 ●	LOVE AND KISSES *MCA MCS 1529*	8 8
18 May 91	SUCCESS *MCA MCS 1538*	11 7
27 Jul 91 ●	JUMP TO THE BEAT *MCA MCS 1556*	8 6
19 Oct 91	BABY LOVE *MCA MCS 1580*	14 6
14 Dec 91	I DON'T WANNA TAKE THIS PAIN *MCA MCS 1600*	40 5
1 Aug 92	SHOW YOU THE WAY TO GO *MCA MCS 1671*	30 3
12 Dec 92	LOVE'S ON EVERY CORNER *MCA MCSR 1723*	44 4
17 Jul 93 ●	THIS IS IT *MCA MCSTD 1790*	10 8
2 Oct 93	THIS IS THE WAY *MCA MCSTD 1935*	27 3
11 Jun 94	GET INTO YOU *Mushroom D 11751*	36 2
23 Aug 97 ●	ALL I WANNA DO *Eternal WEA 119CD* [1]	4 8
1 Nov 97	EVERYTHING I WANTED *Eternal WEA 137CD* [1]	15 4
28 Mar 98	DISREMEMBRANCE *Eternal WEA 153CD* [1]	21 3
1 Dec 01 ●	WHO DO YOU LOVE NOW (STRINGER) *fffr DFCD 002* [2]	3 15
16 Nov 02 ●	PUT THE NEEDLE ON IT *London LONCD 470*	7 7+

[1] Dannii [2] Riva featuring Dannii Minogue

Kylie MINOGUE   25   Top 500
Biggest-selling female vocalist of the late 1980s, b. 28 May 1968, Melbourne, Australia. She has had the best ever chart start for a female soloist with 13 successive Top 10 entries. Best-selling single: 'Can't Get You Out of My Head' 1,037,235 (322 WEEKS) pos/wks

23 Jan 88 ★	I SHOULD BE SO LUCKY *PWL PWL 8*	1 16
14 May 88 ●	GOT TO BE CERTAIN *PWL PWL 12*	2 12
6 Aug 88 ●	THE LOCO-MOTION *PWL PWL 14*	2 11
22 Oct 88 ●	JE NE SAIS PAS POURQUOI *PWL PWL 21*	2 13
10 Dec 88 ★	ESPECIALLY FOR YOU *PWL PWL 24* [1]	1 14
6 May 89 ★	HAND ON YOUR HEART *PWL PWL 35*	1 11
5 Aug 89 ●	WOULDN'T CHANGE A THING *PWL PWL 42*	2 9
4 Nov 89 ●	NEVER TOO LATE *PWL PWL 45*	4 10
20 Jan 90 ★	TEARS ON MY PILLOW *PWL PWL 47*	1 8
12 May 90 ●	BETTER THE DEVIL YOU KNOW *PWL PWL 56*	2 10
3 Nov 90 ●	STEP BACK IN TIME *PWL PWL 64*	4 8
2 Feb 91 ●	WHAT DO I HAVE TO DO *PWL PWL 72*	6 8
1 Jun 91 ●	SHOCKED *PWL PWL 81*	6 7
7 Sep 91	WORD IS OUT *PWL PWL 204*	16 5
2 Nov 91 ●	IF YOU WERE WITH ME NOW *PWL PWL 208* [2]	4 7
30 Nov 91	KEEP ON PUMPIN' IT *PWL PWL 207* [3]	49 1
25 Jan 92 ●	GIVE ME JUST A LITTLE MORE TIME *PWL PWL 212*	2 8
25 Apr 92	FINER FEELINGS *PWL International PWL 227*	11 6
22 Aug 92	WHAT KIND OF FOOL (HEARD ALL THAT BEFORE) *PWL International PWL 241*	14 5
28 Nov 92	CELEBRATION *PWL International PWL 257*	20 7
10 Sep 94 ●	CONFIDE IN ME *Deconstruction 74321227482*	2 9
26 Nov 94	PUT YOURSELF IN MY PLACE *Deconstruction 74321246572*	11 9
22 Jul 95	WHERE IS THE FEELING *Deconstruction 74321293612*	16 3
14 Oct 95	WHERE THE WILD ROSES GROW *Mute CDMUTE 185* [4]	11 4
20 Sep 97	SOME KIND OF BLISS *Deconstruction 74321517252*	22 5
6 Dec 97	DID IT AGAIN *Deconstruction 74321535702*	14 6
21 Mar 98	BREATHE *Deconstruction 74321570132*	14 4

		pos/wks
31 Oct 98	**GBI** Arthrob ART 021CD [5]	.63 1
1 Jul 00 ★	**SPINNING AROUND** Parlophone CDRS 6542 ■	.1 11
23 Sep 00 ●	**ON A NIGHT LIKE THIS** (re) Parlophone CDRS 6546	.2 8
21 Oct 00 ●	**KIDS** (2re) Chrysalis CDCHS 5119 [6]	.2 19
23 Dec 00 ●	**PLEASE STAY** Parlophone CDRS 6551	.10 7
29 Sep 01 ★	**CAN'T GET YOU OUT OF MY HEAD**	
	Parlophone CDRS 6562 ◆ ■	.1 25
2 Mar 02 ●	**IN YOUR EYES** Parlophone CDRS 6569	.3 17
22 Jun 02 ●	**LOVE AT FIRST SIGHT** Parlophone CDRS 6577	.2 12
23 Nov 02 ●	**COME INTO MY WORLD** Parlophone CDR 6590	.8 6+

[1] Kylie Minogue and Jason Donovan [2] Kylie Minogue and Keith Washington
[3] Visionmasters with Tony King and Kylie Minogue [4] Nick Cave and Kylie Minogue [5] Towa Tei featuring Kylie Minogue [6] Robbie Williams / Kylie Minogue

Morris MINOR and the MAJORS
UK, male vocal / rap group (11 WEEKS)   pos/wks

19 Dec 87 ●	**STUTTER RAP (NO SLEEP 'TIL BEDTIME)** 10 TEN 203	.4 11

Sugar MINOTT *Jamaica, male vocalist (16 WEEKS)*   pos/wks

28 Mar 81 ●	**GOOD THING GOING (WE'VE GOT A GOOD THING GOING)**	
	RCA 58	.4 12
17 Oct 81	**NEVER MY LOVE** RCA 138	.52 4

MINT CONDITION *US, male vocal group (3 WEEKS)*   pos/wks

21 Jun 97	**WHAT KIND OF MAN WOULD I BE** Wild Card 5710492	.38 2
4 Oct 97	**LET ME BE THE ONE** Wild Card 5717132	.63 1

MINT JULEPS *UK, female vocal group (7 WEEKS)*   pos/wks

22 Mar 86	**ONLY LOVE CAN BREAK YOUR HEART** Stiff BUY 241	.62 2
30 May 87	**EVERY KINDA PEOPLE** Stiff BUY 257	.58 5

MINT ROYALE
UK, male production duo – Neil Claxton and Chris Baker (8 WEEKS)   pos/wks

5 Feb 00	**DON'T FALTER** Faith & Hope FHCD 014 [1]	.15 4
6 May 00	**TAKE IT EASY** Faith & Hope FHCD 016	.66 1
7 Sep 02	**SEXIEST MAN IN JAMAICA** Faith & Hope FHCD 025	.20 3

[1] Mint Royale featuring Lauren Laverne

MINTY *Australia, female vocalist – Angela Kelly (1 WEEK)*   pos/wks

23 Jan 99	**I WANNA BE FREE** Virgin VSCDT 1728	.67 1

MINUTEMAN *UK, male vocal / instrumental group (2 WEEKS)*   pos/wks

20 Jul 02	**BIG BOY** Ignition IGNSCD 225	.69 1
21 Sep 02	**5000 MINUTES OF PAIN** Ignition IGNSCD 227	.75 1

MIRACLES (423) `Top 500` *Motown's first US Top 10 act was fronted, between 1955 and 1972, by Smokey Robinson who wrote and produced hits for many Motown acts including this quartet (81 WEEKS)*   pos/wks

24 Feb 66	**GOING TO A GO-GO** Tamla Motown TMG 547	.44 5
22 Dec 66	**(COME 'ROUND HERE) I'M THE ONE YOU NEED**	
	Tamla Motown TMG 584	.45 2
27 Dec 67	**I SECOND THAT EMOTION** Tamla Motown TMG 631 [1]	.27 11
3 Apr 68	**IF YOU CAN WANT** Tamla Motown TMG 648 [2]	.50 1
7 May 69 ●	**TRACKS OF MY TEARS** Tamla Motown TMG 696 [1]	.9 13
1 Aug 70 ★	**THE TEARS OF A CLOWN** Tamla Motown TMG 745 [1] ▲	.1 14
30 Jan 71	**(COME 'ROUND HERE) I'M THE ONE YOU NEED**	
	(re-issue) Tamla Motown TMG 761 [1]	.13 9
5 Jun 71	**I DON'T BLAME YOU AT ALL** Tamla Motown TMG 774 [1]	.11 10
10 Jan 76 ●	**LOVE MACHINE** Tamla Motown TMG 1015 ▲	.3 10
2 Oct 76	**THE TEARS OF A CLOWN** (re-issue)	
	Tamla Motown TMG 1048 [1]	.34 6

[1] Smokey Robinson and The Miracles [2] Smokey Robinson & The Miracles

See also Smokey ROBINSON and the MIRACLES

MIRAGE *UK, male vocal / instrumental group (35 WEEKS)*   pos/wks

14 Jan 84	**GIVE ME THE NIGHT (MEDLEY)** Passion PASH 15 [1]	.49 4
9 May 87 ●	**JACK MIX II / III** Debut DEBT 3022	.4 11
25 Jul 87	**SERIOUS MIX** Debut DEBT 3028	.42 4
7 Nov 87 ●	**JACK MIX IV** Debut DEBT 3035	.8 10
27 Feb 88	**JACK MIX VII** Debut DEBT 3042	.50 3
2 Jul 88	**PUSH THE BEAT** Debut DEBT 3050	.67 2
11 Nov 89	**LATINO HOUSE** Debut DEBT 3085	.70 1

[1] Mirage featuring Roy Gayle

'Jack Mix III' listed with 'Jack Mix II' only from 6 Jun 1987

Nina MIRANDA – See Robert MILES

Danny MIRROR *Holland, male vocalist – Eddy Ouwens (9 WEEKS)* pos/wks

17 Sep 77 ●	**I REMEMBER ELVIS PRESLEY (THE KING IS DEAD)**	
	Sonet SON 2121	.4 9

MIRRORBALL *UK, male production duo – Jamie White and Jamie Ford – and female vocalist (5 WEEKS)*   pos/wks

13 Feb 99	**GIVEN UP** Multiply CDMULTY 46	.12 4
24 Jun 00	**BURNIN'** Multiply CDMULTY 56	.47 1

See also TZANT; PF PROJECT featuring Ewan McGREGOR

MIRWAIS
France, male producer – Mirwais Ahmadzais (3 WEEKS)   pos/wks

20 May 00	**DISCO SCIENCE** Epic 6693102	.68 1
23 Dec 00	**NAIVE SONG** Epic 6706922	.50 2

MISHKA
Bermuda, male vocalist – Alexander Mishka Frith (2 WEEKS) pos/wks

15 May 99	**GIVE YOU ALL THE LOVE** Creation CRESCD 311	.34 2

MISS JANE *UK, female vocalist (1 WEEK)*   pos/wks

30 Oct 99	**IT'S A FINE DAY** G1 Recordings G 1001CD	.62 1

MISS KITTIN – See GOLDEN BOY featuring MISS KITTIN

MISS SHIVA
Germany, female DJ / producer – Khadra Bungardt (2 WEEKS)   pos/wks

10 Nov 01	**DREAMS** VC Recordings VCRD 99	.30 2

MISS X *UK, female vocalist – Joyce Blair (6 WEEKS)*   pos/wks

1 Aug 63	**CHRISTINE** Ember S 175	.37 6

MS DYNAMITE *UK, female rapper / vocalist (29 WEEKS)*   pos/wks

23 Jun 01	**BOOO!** ffrr / Public Demand / Social Circles FCD 399 [1]	.12 6
1 Jun 02 ●	**IT TAKES MORE** Polydor 5707982	.7 10
7 Sep 02 ●	**DY-NA-MI-TEE** Polydor 5709782	.5 10
14 Dec 02	**PUT HIM OUT** Polydor 0658942	.19 3+

[1] Sticky featuring Ms Dynamite

MISSION *UK, male vocal / instrumental group (58 WEEKS)*   pos/wks

14 Jun 86	**SERPENTS KISS** Chapter 22 CHAP 6	.70 3
26 Jul 86	**GARDEN OF DELIGHT / LIKE A HURRICANE**	
	Chapter 22 CHAP 7	.49 4
18 Oct 86	**STAY WITH ME** Mercury MYTH 1	.30 4
17 Jan 87	**WASTELAND** Mercury MYTH 2	.11 6
14 Mar 87	**SEVERINA** Mercury MYTH 3	.25 5
13 Feb 88	**TOWER OF STRENGTH** Mercury MYTH 4	.12 7
23 Apr 88	**BEYOND THE PALE** Mercury MYTH 6	.32 4
13 Jan 90	**BUTTERFLY ON A WHEEL** Mercury MYTH 8	.12 4
10 Mar 90	**DELIVERANCE** Mercury MYTH 9	.27 4
2 Jun 90	**INTO THE BLUE** Mercury MYTH 10	.32 3
17 Nov 90	**HANDS ACROSS THE OCEAN** Mercury MYTH 11	.28 2
25 Apr 92	**NEVER AGAIN** Mercury MYTH 12	.34 3
20 Jun 92	**LIKE A CHILD AGAIN** Mercury MYTH 13	.30 2
17 Oct 92	**SHADES OF GREEN** Vertigo MYTH 14	.49 2
8 Jan 94	**TOWER OF STRENGTH** (re-mix) Vertigo MYTCD 15	.33 3
26 Mar 94	**AFTERGLOW** Vertigo MYTCD 16	.53 1
4 Feb 95	**SWOON** Neverland HOOKCD 002	.73 1

MISS JONES US. female vocalist (1 WEEK)   pos/wks
10 Oct 98   **2 WAY STREET** Motown 8608572 ....49 1

MISTA E UK. male producer – Damon Rochefort (5 WEEKS)   pos/wks
10 Dec 88   **DON'T BELIEVE THE HYPE** Urban URB 28 ....41 5

MIS-TEEQ UK. female vocal group (45 WEEKS)   pos/wks
20 Jan 01 ● **WHY** Inferno / Telstar CDFERN 35...8 7
23 Jun 01 ● **ALL I WANT** Inferno / Telstar CDSTAS 3184 ....2 11
27 Oct 01 ● **ONE NIGHT STAND** Inferno / Telstar CDSTAS 3208 ....5 12
2 Mar 02 ● **B WITH ME** Inferno / Telstar CDSTAS 3243 ....5 8
29 Jun 02 ● **ROLL ON / THIS IS HOW WE DO IT**
        Inferno / Telstar CDSTAS 3255 ....7 7

MR and MRS SMITH
UK. male / female instrumental / production group (1 WEEK)   pos/wks
12 Oct 96   **GOTTA GET LOOSE** Hooj Choons HOOJCD 46..........................70 1

MR BEAN and SMEAR CAMPAIGN featuring Bruce DICKINSON
UK. male comedian – Rowan Atkinson and male vocalist (5 WEEKS) pos/wks
4 Apr 92 ● **(I WANT TO BE) ELECTED** London LON 319 ....9 5

MR BIG UK. male vocal / instrumental group (14 WEEKS)   pos/wks
12 Feb 77 ● **ROMEO** EMI 2567...4 10
21 May 77   **FEEL LIKE CALLING HOME** EMI 2610..................................35 4

MR BIG US. male vocal / instrumental group (17 WEEKS)   pos/wks
7 Mar 92 ● **TO BE WITH YOU** Atlantic A 7514 ▲ 3 11
23 May 92   **JUST TAKE MY HEART** Atlantic A 7490 ....26 4
8 Aug 92   **GREEN TINTED SIXTIES MIND** Atlantic A 7468.............72 1
20 Nov 93   **WILD WORLD** Atlantic A 7310CD..59 1

MR BLOBBY
UK. male pink and yellow spotted blob vocalist (16 WEEKS)   pos/wks
4 Dec 93 ★ **MR BLOBBY** Destiny Music CDDMUS 104............................1 12
16 Dec 95   **CHRISTMAS IN BLOBBYLAND** Destiny DMUSCD 108 ....36 4

MR BLOE UK. male instrumental group (18 WEEKS)   pos/wks
9 May 70 ● **GROOVIN' WITH MR BLOE** DJM DJS 216 ....2 18

MR FINGERS US. male producer – Larry Heard (5 WEEKS)   pos/wks
17 Mar 90   **WHAT ABOUT THIS LOVE** ffrr F 131 ....74 1
7 Mar 92   **CLOSER** MCA MCS 1601 ....50 3
23 May 92   **ON MY WAY** MCA MCS 1630 ....71 1

MR FOOD UK. male vocalist (3 WEEKS)   pos/wks
9 Jun 90   **...AND THAT'S BEFORE ME TEA!** Tangible TGB 005...............62 3

Mr HAHN – See X-ECUTIONERS featuring Mike SHINODA and Mr. HAHN of LINKIN PARK; LINKIN PARK

MR HANKEY US. male Christmas excrement vocalist (6 WEEKS)   pos/wks
25 Dec 99 ● **MR HANKEY THE CHRISTMAS POO** Columbia 6685582 ....4 6

MR JACK Belgium. male producer – Lucente Vito (2 WEEKS)   pos/wks
25 Jan 97   **WIGGLY WORLD** Extravaganza 0090965...32 2

MR LEE US. male producer – Leroy Haggard (6 WEEKS)   pos/wks
6 Aug 88   **PUMP UP LONDON** Breakout USA 639..64 2
11 Nov 89   **GET BUSY (re)** Jive JIVE 231...41 4

MR MISTER US. male vocal / instrumental group (22 WEEKS)   pos/wks
21 Dec 85 ● **BROKEN WINGS** RCA PB 49945 ▲ 4 13
1 Mar 86   **KYRIE** RCA PB 49927 ▲ 11 9

MR OIZO France. male producer – Quentin Dupieux (15 WEEKS)   pos/wks
3 Apr 99 ★ **FLAT BEAT (re)**
        F Communications / Pias Recordings F 104CDUK ■ 1 15

MR PINK presents The PROGRAM
UK. male producer – Leiam Sullivan (4 WEEKS)   pos/wks
19 Jan 02   **LOVE AND AFFECTION** Manifesto FESCD 90 ....22 4

MR PRESIDENT Germany. male / female vocal group (13 WEEKS) pos/wks
14 Jun 97 ● **COCO JAMBOO** WEA WEA 110CD 8 11
20 Sep 97   **I GIVE YOU MY HEART** WEA WEA 126CD...........................52 1
25 Apr 98   **JOJO ACTION** WEA WEA 156CD...73 1

MR ROY UK. male instrumental / production group (6 WEEKS)   pos/wks
7 May 94   **SOMETHING ABOUT YOU** Fresh FRSHD 11 ....74 1
21 Jan 95   **SAVED** Fresh FRSHD 21..24 4
16 Dec 95   **SOMETHING ABOUT U (CAN'T BE BEAT) (re-mix)**
        Fresh FRSHCD 33 ....49 1

MR RUMBLE – See BM DUBS present MR RUMBLE featuring BRASSTOOTH and KEE

MR SCRUFF UK. male producer (1 WEEK)   pos/wks
14 Dec 02   **SWEETSMOKE** Ninja Tune ZENCDS 12124...............................75 1

MR SHABZ – See SO SOLID CREW

MR SMASH & FRIENDS featuring THE ENGLAND SUPPORTERS' BAND UK. male vocal football supporters group (1 WEEK)   pos/wks
8 Jun 02   **WE'RE COMING OVER** RGR RGRCD 2 ....67 1
See also MADNESS

MR V UK. male producer – Rob Villiers (2 WEEKS)   pos/wks
6 Aug 94   **GIVE ME LIFE** Cheeky CHEKCD 005..40 2

MR VEGAS Jamaica. male vocalist – Clifford Smith (7 WEEKS)   pos/wks
22 Aug 98   **HEADS HIGH** Greensleeves GRECD 650 ....71 1
13 Nov 99   **HEADS HIGH (re-issue)** Greensleeves GRECD 785..................16 6

MRS MILLS
UK. female instrumentalist – piano – Gladys Mills d. 1978 (6 WEEKS) pos/wks
14 Dec 61   **MRS MILLS MEDLEY** Parlophone R 4856 ....18 5
31 Dec 64   **MRS MILLS PARTY MEDLEY** Parlophone R 5214................50 1

Mrs Mills' Medley consisted of the following tunes: I Want to Be Happy / Sheik of Araby / Baby Face / Somebody Stole My Gal / Ma (He's Making Eyes At Me) / Swanee / Ain't She Sweet / California Here I Come

MRS WOOD UK. female producer – Jane Wood (6 WEEKS)   pos/wks
16 Sep 95   **JOANNA** React CDREACT 066 ....40 2
6 Jul 96   **HEARTBREAK** React CDREACT 78 ⃞1 ....44 1
4 Oct 97   **JOANNA (re-mix)** React CDREACT 107.......................................34 2
15 Aug 98   **1234** React CDREACT 121..54 1

⃞1 Mrs Wood featuring Eve Gallagher

MISTURA featuring Lloyd MICHELS
US. male instrumental group, Lloyd Michels – trumpet (10 WEEKS)   pos/wks
15 May 76   **THE FLASHER** Route RT 30 ....23 10

Des MITCHELL UK / Belgium. male DJ / production trio (5 WKS)   pos/wks
29 Jan 00 ● **(WELCOME) TO THE DANCE** Code Blue BLUE 0087CD1 ....5 5

Guy MITCHELL ⟨127⟩ ⟨Top 500⟩ Extremely popular pre-rock vocalist, b. Al Cernik, 27 Feb 1927, Detroit, US, d. 1 Jul 1999. He appeared on the first and last charts of the 1950s, and was one of most consistently successful singers and performers of that decade (165 WEEKS)   pos/wks
14 Nov 52 ● **FEET UP!** Columbia DB 3151 ....2 10

Re-entries are listed as (re), (2re), (3re), etc which signifies that the hit re-entered the chart once, twice or three ti...

13 Feb 53	★ SHE WEARS RED FEATHERS (re) *Columbia DB 3238*	1	16
24 Apr 53	● PRETTY LITTLE BLACK-EYED SUSIE *Columbia DB 3255*	2	11
28 Aug 53	★ LOOK AT THAT GIRL *Philips PB 162*	1	14
6 Nov 53	● CHICKA BOOM (re) *Philips PB 178*	4	15
18 Dec 53	● CLOUD LUCKY SEVEN *Philips PB 210A*	2	16
19 Feb 54	● THE CUFF OF MY SHIRT (2re) *Philips PB 225*	9	3
26 Feb 54	SIPPIN' SODA *Philips PB 210B*	11	1
30 Apr 54	● A DIME AND A DOLLAR (re) *Philips PB 248*	8	5
7 Dec 56	★ SINGING THE BLUES *Philips PB 650* ▲	1	22
15 Feb 57	● KNEE DEEP IN THE BLUES *Philips PB 669*	3	12
26 Apr 57	★ ROCK-A-BILLY *Philips PB 685*	1	14
26 Jul 57	IN THE MIDDLE OF A DARK, DARK NIGHT / SWEET STUFF (re) *Philips PB 712*	25	4
11 Oct 57	CALL ROSIE ON THE PHONE *Philips PB 743*	17	6
27 Nov 59	● HEARTACHES BY THE NUMBER (re) *Philips PB 964* ▲	5	16

Joni MITCHELL
Canada, female vocalist – Roberta Anderson (24 WEEKS)   pos/wks

13 Jun 70	BIG YELLOW TAXI *Reprise RS 20906*	11	15
4 Oct 97	● GOT 'TIL IT'S GONE *Virgin VSCDG 1666* [1]	6	9

[1] Janet featuring Q-Tip and Joni Mitchell

VSCDG 1666 uses samples from RS 20906

Willie MITCHELL *US, male instrumentalist – guitar (3 WEEKS)*   pos/wks

24 Apr 68	SOUL SERENADE *London HLU 10186*	43	1
11 Dec 76	THE CHAMPION *London HL 10545*	47	2

MIX FACTORY
UK, male / female vocal / instrumental group (2 WEEKS)   pos/wks

30 Jan 93	TAKE ME AWAY (PARADISE) *All Around the World CDGLOBE 120*	51	2

MIXMASTER *Italy, male producer – Daniele Davoli (10 WEEKS)*   pos/wks

4 Nov 89	● GRAND PIANO *BCM BCM 344*	9	10

MIXTURES *Australia, male vocal / instrumental group (21 WEEKS)* pos/wks

16 Jan 71	● THE PUSHBIKE SONG *Polydor 2058 083*	2	21

Hank MIZELL *US, male vocalist d. Dec 1992 (13 WEEKS)*   pos/wks

20 Mar 76	● JUNGLE ROCK *Charly CS 1005*	3	13

MOBILES
UK, male / female vocal / instrumental group (14 WEEKS)   pos/wks

9 Jan 82	● DROWNING IN BERLIN *Rialto RIA 3*	9	10
27 Mar 82	AMOUR AMOUR *Rialto RIA 5*	45	4

MOBO ALLSTARS
UK / US, male / female vocal / instrumental group (3 WEEKS)   pos/wks

26 Dec 98	AIN'T NO STOPPING US NOW *PolyGram TV 5632302*	47	3

Artists featured include: Another Level, Shola Ama, Kéllé Bryan, Celetia, Cleopatra, Damage, Des'ree, D'Influence, E17, Michelle Gayle, Glamma Kid, Lynden David Hall, Hinda Hicks, Honeyz, Kle'Shay, Kele Le Roc, Beverley Knight, Tony Momrelle, Nine Yards, Mica Paris, Karen Ramirez, Connor Reeves, Roachford, 7th Son, Byron Stingily, Truce, Soundproof, Ultimate Kaos

MOBY *US, male producer – Richard Hall (70 WEEKS)*   pos/wks

27 Jul 91	● GO (re) *Outer Rhythm FOOT 15*	10	10
3 Jul 93	I FEEL IT *Equinox AXISCD 001*	38	3
11 Sep 93	MOVE *Mute CDMUTE 158*	21	5
28 May 94	HYMN *Mute CDMUTE 161*	31	2
29 Oct 94	FEELING SO REAL *Mute CDMUTE 173*	30	2
25 Feb 95	EVERY TIME YOU TOUCH ME *Mute CDMUTE 176*	28	3
1 Jul 95	INTO THE BLUE *Mute CDMUTE 179A*	34	2
7 Sep 96	THAT'S WHEN I REACH FOR MY REVOLVER *Mute CDMUTE 184*	50	1
15 Nov 97	● JAMES BOND THEME (re) *Mute CDMUTE 210*	8	8
5 Sep 98	HONEY *Mute CDMUTE 218*	33	2

8 May 99	RUN ON *Mute CDMUTE 221*	33	2
24 Jul 99	BODYROCK *Mute CDMUTE 225*	38	2
23 Oct 99	WHY DOES MY HEART FEEL SO BAD *Mute CDMUTE 230*	16	4
18 Mar 00	NATURAL BLUES *Mute CDMUTE 251*	11	6
24 Jun 00	PORCELAIN *Mute CDMUTE 252*	5	6
28 Oct 00	WHY DOES MY HEART FEEL SO BAD (re-issue) *Mute CDMUTE 255*	17	5
11 May 02	WE ARE ALL MADE OF STARS *Mute CDMUTE 268*	11	4
31 Aug 02	EXTREME WAYS *Mute CDMUTE 270*	39	1
16 Nov 02	IN THIS WORLD *Mute CDMUTE 276*	35	2

MOCA – *See David MORALES*

MOCHA – *See Missy 'Misdemeanor' ELLIOTT; Nicole RAY*

MOCK TURTLES
UK, male / female vocal / instrumental group (15 WEEKS)   pos/wks

9 Mar 91	CAN YOU DIG IT? *Siren SRN 136*	18	11
29 Jun 91	AND THEN SHE SMILES *Siren SRN 139*	44	4

MODERN LOVERS – *See Jonathan RICHMAN and the MODERN LOVERS*

MODERN ROMANCE (467) Top 500
Latin-tinged London pop group which evolved out of new wave band The Leyton Buzzards. Lead singer Geoff Deane, who was replaced in 1982 by Michael J Mullins, later became a top TV scriptwriter (Birds of a Feather, Chef!, Babes in the Wood) (77 WEEKS)   pos/wks

15 Aug 81	EVERYBODY SALSA *WEA K 18815*	12	10
7 Nov 81	● AY AY AY AY MOOSEY *WEA K 18883*	10	12
30 Jan 82	QUEEN OF THE RAPPING SCENE (NOTHING EVER GOES THE WAY YOU PLAN) *WEA K 18928*	37	8
14 Aug 82	CHERRY PINK AND APPLE BLOSSOM WHITE *WEA K 19245* [1]	15	8
13 Nov 82	● BEST YEARS OF OUR LIVES *WEA ROM 1*	4	13
26 Feb 83	● HIGH LIFE *WEA ROM 2*	8	8
7 May 83	DON'T STOP THAT CRAZY RHYTHM *WEA ROM 3*	14	6
6 Aug 83	● WALKING IN THE RAIN *WEA X 9733*	7	12

[1] Modern Romance featuring John du Prez

MODERN TALKING *Germany, male vocal / instrumental duo – Thomas Anders and Dieter Bohlen (22 WEEKS)*   pos/wks

15 Jun 85	YOU'RE MY HEART, YOU'RE MY SOUL (re) *Magnet MAG 277*	56	7
12 Oct 85	YOU CAN WIN IF YOU WANT *Magnet MAG 282*	70	2
16 Aug 86	● BROTHER LOUIE *RCA PB 40875*	4	10
4 Oct 86	ATLANTIS IS CALLING (S.O.S. FOR LOVE) *RCA PB 40969*	55	3

MODETTES *UK, female vocal / instrumental group (6 WEEKS)*   pos/wks

12 Jul 80	PAINT IT BLACK *Deram DET-R 1*	42	5
18 Jul 81	TONIGHT *Deram DET 3*	68	1

MODJO *France, male production / vocal duo – Yann Destangol and Romain Tranchart (29 WEEKS)*   pos/wks

16 Sep 00	★ LADY (HEAR ME TONIGHT) *Polydor 5877582* ■	1	20
14 Apr 01	CHILLIN' *Polydor 5870092*	12	8
6 Oct 01	WHAT I MEAN *Polydor 5873462*	59	1

Domenico MODUGNO *Italy, male vocalist d. 6 Aug 1994 (13 WKS)* pos/wks

5 Sep 58	● VOLARE (NEL BLU DIPINTO DI BLU) *Oriole ICB 5000* ▲	10	12
27 Mar 59	CIAO CIAO BAMBINA (PIOVE) *Oriole CB 1489*	29	1

MOFFATTS *Canada, male vocal / instrumental group (6 WEEKS)* pos/wks

20 Feb 99	CRAZY *Chrysalis CDEM 533*	16	3
26 Jun 99	UNTIL YOU LOVED ME *Chrysalis CDEM 541*	36	2
23 Oct 99	MISERY *EMI CDEM 551*	47	1

MOGWAI *UK, male instrumental group (3 WEEKS)*

4 Apr 98	SWEET LEAF / BLACK SABBATH *Fierce Panda NING 47CD* [1]	60	1

(I CAN'T GET NO) SATISFACTION

■ Keith Richards had the basic idea for '(I Can't Get No) Satisfaction' at the Gulf Motel in Clearwater, Florida, in May 1965 while the Rolling Stones were on tour in the US. Waking up in the middle of the night, he had the basic riff and the one line "I can't get no satisfaction", which he quickly recorded on to a cassette. According to Keith, "It was very funny 'cause that night I was so tired. I pushed the button and I got the guitar and I ran through the sequence once. On the tape

Keith Richards (left) was less convinced than fellow Stones Charlie Watts (centre) and Mick Jagger (right) about the merits of 'Satisfaction' as a hit single

★ ARTIST:	Rolling Stones
★ LABEL:	Decca UK/London US
★ WRITERS:	Mick Jagger and Keith Richards
★ PRODUCER:	Andrew Loog Oldham

you can hear me drop the pick and the rest of the tape is me snoring!" It was only by chance that Richards came across his recording the next morning, and while not thinking too much of it, he gave it to Mick Jagger who quickly wrote the rest. While on tour the Stones would habitually drop into recording studios along the way, and on 10 May 1965 they visited the famous Chess Studios in Chicago for a nine-hour session. It was here, the previous year, the group had been stunned to be greeted by legendary bluesman Muddy Waters who was up a ladder painting the studio façade – he even helped the group to carry their gear into the studio. Several songs were recorded that day, among them a semi-acoustic version of 'Satisfaction' to which the band didn't really give a second thought.

Two days later, arriving in Hollywood, the band tried an entirely different version of the song at RCA Studios, with drummer Charlie Watts playing a different drum tempo and Keith Richards playing that famous fuzz guitar line.

Richards later admitted he'd adapted the idea from Martha and the Vandellas' Motown hit 'Dancing in the Street'. This time it really worked and most of the band and their entourage were convinced it was the best thing they'd recorded and should be released as a single. Keith Richards, however, wasn't convinced, thinking the song might be a B-side, or an album track, but certainly not a hit. Richards recalls, "If I'd had my way, 'Satisfaction' would never have been released. The song was basic as the hills and I thought the fuzz guitar thing was a bit of a gimmick. So when they said they wanted it as a single, I got up on my hind legs for the first time and said no way!"

Fortunately for posterity, the Stones were a five-way democracy: the other four members voted Richards down and 'Satisfaction' was rush-released in the States and came out in June, barely a month after it was recorded, and became their first chart-topper Stateside. In the UK and the rest of the world the release was delayed for two months until the middle of August. Richards never liked the Stones' recording, particularly the fuzz guitar, which he doesn't play any more. In fact he always thought 'Satisfaction' would have sounded better with a horn section, so he was probably very happy when Otis Redding's punchy brass-driven version came out one year later.

■ I THOUGHT THE FUZZ GUITAR THING WAS A BIT OF A GIMMICK. SO WHEN THEY SAID THEY WANTED IT AS A SINGLE, I GOT UP ON MY HIND LEGS FOR THE FIRST TIME AND SAID NO WAY! ■
KEITH RICHARDS

■ Tony Burton

11 Apr 98	FEAR SATAN *Eye-Q EYEUK 032CD*	57	1
11 Jul 98	NO EDUCATION NO FUTURE (F**K THE CURFEW)		
	Chemikal CHEM 026CD	68	1

[1] Mogwai: Magoo

MOHAWKS
Jamaica, male vocal / instrumental group (2 WEEKS)   pos/wks

| 24 Jan 87 | THE CHAMP *Pama PM 1* .... | 58 | 2 |

Frank'o MOIRAGHI featuring AMNESIA
Italy, male / female vocal / instrumental duo (4 WEEKS)   pos/wks

| 1 Jun 96 | FEEL MY BODY *Multiply CDMULTY 10* .... | 39 | 2 |
| 26 Oct 96 | FEEL MY BODY (re-mix) *Multiply CDMULTY 15* ... | 40 | 2 |

MOIST
Canada, male vocal / instrumental group (10 WEEKS)   pos/wks

12 Nov 94	PUSH *Chrysalis CDCHS 5016*	35	3
25 Feb 95	SILVER *Chrysalis CDCHS 5019*	50	2
29 Apr 95	FREAKY BE BEAUTIFUL *Chrysalis CDCHS 5022*	47	2
19 Aug 95	PUSH (re-issue) *Chrysalis CDCHS 5024*	20	3

MOJO
UK, male instrumental group (3 WEEKS)   pos/wks

| 22 Aug 81 | DANCE ON *Creole CR 17* .... | 70 | 3 |

MOJOLATORS featuring CAMILLA
US, male production duo and female vocalist (1 WEEK)   pos/wks

| 6 Oct 01 | DRIFTING *Multiply CDMULTY 81* .... | 52 | 1 |

MOJOS
UK, male vocal / instrumental group (26 WEEKS)   pos/wks

26 Mar 64 ●	EVERYTHING'S ALRIGHT *Decca F 11853*	9	11
11 Jun 64	WHY NOT TONIGHT *Decca F 11918*	25	10
10 Sep 64	SEVEN DAFFODILS *Decca F 11959*	30	5

MOKENSTEF
US, female vocal group (1 WEEK)   pos/wks

| 23 Sep 95 | HE'S MINE *Def Jam DEFCD 13* .... | 70 | 1 |

MOLELLA featuring the OUTHERE BROTHERS
Italy, male producer and US, male rap / vocal duo (10 WEEKS)   pos/wks

| 16 Dec 95 ● | IF YOU WANNA PARTY *Eternal WEA 030CD* ..... | 9 | 10 |

Sophie MOLETA – See HUMAN MOVEMENT featuring Sophie MOLETA

Ralph MOLINA – See Ian McNABB

Brian MOLKO – See ALPINESTARS featuring Brian MOLKO

Sam MOLLISON – See SASHA

MOLLY HALF HEAD
UK, male vocal / instrumental group (1 WEEK)   pos/wks

| 3 Jun 95 | SHINE *Columbia 6620732* .... | 73 | 1 |

MOLOKO
Ireland / UK, male / female vocal /
instrumental duo – Roisin Murphy and Mark Brydon (31 WEEKS)   pos/wks

24 Feb 96	DOMINOID *Echo ECSCD 016*	65	1
25 May 96	FUN FOR ME *Echo ECSCD 20*	36	2
20 Jun 98	THE FLIPSIDE *Echo ECSCD 54*	53	1
27 Mar 99	SING IT BACK *Echo ECSCD 71*	45	2
4 Sep 99 ●	SING IT BACK (re-mix) *Echo ECSCD 82*	4	9
1 Apr 00 ●	THE TIME IS NOW *Echo ECSCD 88*	2	10
5 Aug 00	PURE PLEASURE SEEKER *Echo ECSCD 99*	21	5
25 Nov 00	INDIGO *Echo ECSCD 104*	51	1

See also PSYCHEDELIC WALTONS featuring Roisin MURPHY

MOMBASSA
UK, male production duo (1 WEEK)   pos/wks

| 8 Mar 97 | CRY FREEDOM *Soundproof SPCD 021* .... | 63 | 1 |

MOMENTS
US, male vocal group (32 WEEKS)   pos/wks

8 Mar 75 ●	GIRLS *All Platinum 6146 302* [1]	3	10
19 Jul 75 ●	DOLLY MY LOVE *All Platinum 6146 306*	10	9
25 Oct 75	LOOK AT ME (I'M IN LOVE) *All Platinum 6146 309* ...	42	4
22 Jan 77 ●	JACK IN THE BOX *All Platinum 6146 318*	7	9

[1] Moments and Whatnauts

Tony MOMRELLE
UK, male vocalist (1 WEEK)   pos/wks

| 15 Aug 98 | LET ME SHOW YOU *Art & Soul ART 1CDS* .... | 67 | 1 |

MONACO
UK, male vocal / instrumental
duo – Peter Hook and David Potts (11 WEEKS)   pos/wks

15 Mar 97	WHAT DO YOU WANT FROM ME? *Polydor 5731912* ...	11	6
31 May 97	SWEET LIPS *Polydor 5710552*	18	4
20 Sep 97	SHINE (SOMEONE WHO NEEDS ME) *Polydor 5714182* ...	55	1

See also NEW ORDER

Pharoahe MONCH
US, male rapper – Troy Jamerson (11 WEEKS)   pos/wks

19 Feb 00	SIMON SAYS *Rawkus RWK 205CD*	24	2
19 Aug 00	LIGHT *Rawkus RWK 259CD*	72	1
3 Feb 01	OH NO *Rawkus RWK 302* [1]	24	4
1 Dec 01	GOT YOU *Priority PTYCD 145*	27	3
14 Sep 02	THE LIFE *MCA MCSTD 402292* [2]	60	1

[1] Mos Def and Nate Dogg featuring Pharoahe Monch [2] Styles and Pharoahe Monch

Jay MONDI and the LIVING BASS
US, male / female vocal / instrumental group (3 WEEKS)   pos/wks

| 24 Mar 90 | ALL NIGHT LONG *10 TEN 304* .... | 63 | 3 |

MONDO KANE
UK, male vocal / instrumental group (3 WEEKS)   pos/wks

| 16 Aug 86 | NEW YORK AFTERNOON *Lisson DOLE 2* .... | 70 | 3 |

MONE
US, female vocalist (2 WEEKS)   pos/wks

| 12 Aug 95 | WE CAN MAKE IT *A&M 5811592* .... | 64 | 1 |
| 16 Mar 96 | MOVIN' *A&M:PM 5814392* .... | 48 | 1 |

Zoot MONEY and the BIG ROLL BAND
UK, male vocal
/ instrumental group, leader – George Bruno Money (8 WEEKS)   pos/wks

| 18 Aug 66 | BIG TIME OPERATOR *Columbia DB 7975* .... | 25 | 8 |

MONEY MARK
US, male vocal / instrumentalist
/ producer – Mark Ramos-Nishita (3 WEEKS)   pos/wks

| 28 Feb 98 | HAND IN YOUR HEAD *Mo Wax MW 066CD* .... | 40 | 2 |
| 6 Jun 98 | MAYBE I'M DEAD *Mo Wax MW 089CD1* .... | 45 | 1 |

MONICA
US, female vocalist – Monica Arnold (37 WEEKS)   pos/wks

29 Jul 95	DON'T TAKE IT PERSONAL (JUST ONE OF DEM DAYS)		
	Arista 74321301452	32	3
17 Feb 96	LIKE THIS AND LIKE THAT *Rowdy 74321344222* ...	33	2
8 Jun 96	BEFORE YOU WALK OUT OF MY LIFE *Rowdy 74321374042* ...	22	3
24 May 97	FOR YOU I WILL *Atlantic A 5437CD*	27	3
6 Jun 98 ●	THE BOY IS MINE *Atlantic AT 0036 CD* [1] ▲ ...	2	20
17 Oct 98 ●	THE FIRST NIGHT *Rowdy 74321619342* ▲	6	6
4 Sep 99	ANGEL OF MINE *Arista 74321692892* ▲	55	1

[1] Brandy and Monica

MONIFAH
US, female vocalist – Monifah Carter (2 WEEKS)   pos/wks

| 30 Jan 99 | TOUCH IT *Universal UND 56218* .... | 29 | 2 |

TS MONK
US, male / female vocal / instrumental group (6 WEEKS)   pos/wks

| 7 Mar 81 | BON BON VIE *Mirage K 11653* .... | 63 | 2 |
| 25 Apr 81 | CANDIDATE FOR LOVE *Mirage K 11648* .... | 58 | 4 |

MONKEES (308) Top 500
The world's top act of 1967: Davy Jones (v/g), Mike Nesmith (v/g), Peter Tork (v/k), Mickey Dolenz (v/d). This Anglo-American quartet was hand-picked for a Beatles-style TV series, which helped to rocket them, albeit briefly, to the very top (101 WEEKS)　pos/wks

Date		Title	pos	wks
5 Jan 67	★	I'M A BELIEVER *RCA 1560* ▲	1	17
26 Jan 67		LAST TRAIN TO CLARKSVILLE *RCA 1547* ▲	23	7
6 Apr 67	●	A LITTLE BIT ME, A LITTLE BIT YOU *RCA 1580*	3	12
22 Jun 67	●	ALTERNATE TITLE *RCA 1604*	2	13
16 Aug 67		PLEASANT VALLEY SUNDAY *RC 1620*	11	8
15 Nov 67	●	DAYDREAM BELIEVER *RCA 1645* ▲	5	17
27 Mar 68		VALLERI *RCA 1673*	12	8
26 Jun 68		DW WASHBURN *RCA 1706*	17	6
26 Mar 69		TEAR DROP CITY *RCA 1802*	46	1
25 Jun 69		SOMEDAY MAN *RCA 1824*	47	1
15 Mar 80		THE MONKEES EP *Arista ARIST 326*	33	9
18 Oct 86		THAT WAS THEN, THIS IS NOW *Arista ARIST 673*	68	1
1 Apr 89		THE MONKEES EP *Arista 112157*	62	2

Tracks on Arista 326 EP: I'm a Believer / Daydream Believer / Last Train to Clarksville / A Little Bit Me a Little Bit You. Tracks on Arista 112157 EP: Daydream Believer / Monkees Theme / Last Train to Clarksville

MONKEY MAFIA
UK, male vocal / instrumental / DJ / production group (3 WEEKS)　pos/wks

Date	Title	pos	wks
10 Aug 96	WORK MI BODY *Heavenly HVN 53CD* [1]	75	1
7 Jun 97	15 STEPS (EP) *Heavenly HVN 67CD*	67	1
2 May 98	LONG AS I CAN SEE THE LIGHT *Heavenly HVN 84CD*	51	1

[1] Monkey Mafia featuring Patra

Tracks on 15 Steps (EP): Lion in the Hall / Krash the Decks: Slaughter the Vinyl / Metro Love / Beats in the Hall

MONKS *UK, male vocal / instrumental duo – Richard Hudson and John Ford (9 WEEKS)*　pos/wks

Date	Title	pos	wks
21 Apr 79	NICE LEGS SHAME ABOUT HER FACE *Carrere CAR 104*	19	9

The Monks were Hudson-Ford under a different name

MONO
UK, male / female vocal / instrumental duo (1 WEEK)　pos/wks

Date	Title	pos	wks
2 May 98	LIFE IN MONO *Echo ECSCD 64*	60	1

MONOBOY featuring DELORES *Ireland, male producer – Ian Masterson and female vocalist (1 WEEK)*　pos/wks

Date	Title	pos	wks
7 Jul 01	THE MUSIC IN YOU *Perfecto PERF 18CDS*	50	1

Matt MONRO (217) Top 500
Superior British balladeer, b. Terence Parsons, 1 Dec 1930, London, d. 7 Feb 1985. This Sinatra-styled vocalist, who was renamed by hitmaker Winifred Atwell, had few MOR equals in the 1960s. In 1961, Billboard magazine named him Top International Act and Most Promising Male Singer (127 WEEKS)　pos/wks

Date		Title	pos	wks
15 Dec 60	●	PORTRAIT OF MY LOVE *Parlophone R 4714*	3	16
9 Mar 61	●	MY KIND OF GIRL *Parlophone R 4755*	5	12
18 May 61		WHY NOT NOW / CAN THIS BE LOVE *Parlophone R 4775*	24	9
28 Sep 61		GONNA BUILD A MOUNTAIN *Parlophone R 4819*	44	3
8 Feb 62	●	SOFTLY AS I LEAVE YOU *Parlophone R 4868*	10	18
14 Jun 62		WHEN LOVE COMES ALONG *Parlophone R 4911*	46	3
8 Nov 62		MY LOVE AND DEVOTION *Parlophone R 4954*	29	5
14 Nov 63		FROM RUSSIA WITH LOVE *Parlophone R 5068*	20	13
17 Sep 64	●	WALK AWAY *Parlophone R 5171*	4	20
24 Dec 64		FOR MAMA *Parlophone R 5215*	23	4
25 Mar 65		WITHOUT YOU *Parlophone R 5251*	37	4
21 Oct 65	●	YESTERDAY *Parlophone R 5348*	8	12
24 Nov 73		AND YOU SMILED *EMI 2091*	28	8

Gerry MONROE *UK, male vocalist (57 WEEKS)*　pos/wks

Date		Title	pos	wks
23 May 70	●	SALLY *Chapter One CH 122*	4	20
19 Sep 70		CRY *Chapter One CH 128*	38	5
14 Nov 70	●	MY PRAYER *Chapter One CH 132*	9	12
17 Apr 71		IT'S A SIN TO TELL A LIE *Chapter One CH 144*	13	12
21 Aug 71		LITTLE DROPS OF SILVER *Chapter One CH 152*	37	6
12 Feb 72		GIRL OF MY DREAMS *Chapter One CH 159*	43	2

Hollis P MONROE *Canada, male producer (1 WEEK)*　pos/wks

Date	Title	pos	wks
24 Apr 99	I'M LONELY *City Beat CBE 778CD*	51	1

MONSOON
UK, male / female vocal / instrumental group (12 WEEKS)　pos/wks

Date	Title	pos	wks
3 Apr 82	EVER SO LONELY *Mobile Suit Corp CORP 2*	12	9
5 Jun 82	SHAKTI (THE MEANING OF WITHIN) *Mobile Suit Corp CORP 4*	41	3

MONSTA BOY featuring DENZIE
UK, male production / vocal instrumental duo (3 WEEKS)　pos/wks

Date	Title	pos	wks
7 Oct 00	SORRY (I DIDN'T KNOW) *Locked On LOX 125CD*	25	3

MONSTER MAGNET
US, male vocal / instrumental group (6 WEEKS)　pos/wks

Date	Title	pos	wks
29 May 93	TWIN EARTH *A&M 5802812*	67	1
18 Mar 95	NEGASONIC TEENAGE WARHEAD *A&M 5809812*	49	1
6 May 95	DOPES TO INFINITY *A&M 5810332*	58	1
23 Jan 99	POWERTRIP *A&M 5828232*	39	2
6 Mar 99	SPACE LORD *A&M 5632752*	45	1

MONTAGE *UK, female vocal trio (1 WEEK)*　pos/wks

Date	Title	pos	wks
15 Feb 97	THERE AIN'T NOTHIN' LIKE THE LOVE *Wildcard 5733172*	64	1

MONTANA SEXTET *US, male instrumental group (1 WEEK)*　pos/wks

Date	Title	pos	wks
15 Jan 83	HEAVY VIBES *Virgin VS 560*	59	1

MONTANO vs THE TRUMPET MAN
UK, male production / instrumental duo (1 WEEK)　pos/wks

Date	Title	pos	wks
18 Sep 99	ITZA TRUMPET THING *Serious SERR 010CD*	46	1

Hugo MONTENEGRO his Orchestra and Chorus
US, orchestra, leader d. 6 Feb 1981 (26 WEEKS)　pos/wks

Date		Title	pos	wks
11 Sep 68	★	THE GOOD, THE BAD AND THE UGLY (re) *RCA 1727*	1	25
8 Jan 69		HANG 'EM HIGH *RCA 1771*	50	1

Chris MONTEZ
US, male vocalist – Ezekiel Montanez (61 WEEKS)　pos/wks

Date		Title	pos	wks
4 Oct 62	●	LET'S DANCE *London HLU 9596*	2	18
17 Jan 63	●	SOME KINDA FUN *London HLU 9650*	10	9
30 Jun 66	●	THE MORE I SEE YOU *Pye International 7N 25369*	3	13
22 Sep 66		THERE WILL NEVER BE ANOTHER YOU *Pye International 7N 25381*	37	4
14 Oct 72	●	LET'S DANCE (re-issue) *London HLU 10205*	9	14
14 Apr 79	●	LET'S DANCE (2nd re-issue) *Lightning LIG 9011*	47	3

The second re-issue of 'Let's Dance' on Lightning was coupled with 'Memphis' by Lonnie Mack as a double A-side

MONTROSE
US, male vocal / instrumental group (2 WEEKS)　pos/wks

Date	Title	pos	wks
28 Jun 80	SPACE STATION NUMBER 5 / GOOD ROCKIN' TONIGHT *Warner Brothers WB HM 9*	71	2

MONTROSE AVENUE
UK, male vocal / instrumental group (4 WEEKS)　pos/wks

Date	Title	pos	wks
28 Mar 98	WHERE DO I STAND? *Columbia 6656072*	38	2
20 Jun 98	SHINE *Columbia 6660012*	58	1
17 Oct 98	START AGAIN *Columbia 6664255*	59	1

MONTY PYTHON *UK, male vocal comedy group (9 WEEKS)*　pos/wks

Date		Title	pos	wks
5 Oct 91	●	ALWAYS LOOK ON THE BRIGHT SIDE OF LIFE *Virgin PYTH 1*	3	9

MONYAKA
US / Jamaica, male vocal / instrumental group (8 WEEKS) pos/wks

10 Sep 83	**GO DEH YAKA (GO TO THE TOP)** *Polydor POSP 641*	14	8

MOOD
UK, male vocal / instrumental group (10 WEEKS) pos/wks

6 Feb 82	**DON'T STOP** *RCA 171*	59	4
22 May 82	**PARIS IS ONE DAY AWAY** *RCA 211*	42	5
30 Oct 82	**PASSION IN DARK ROOMS** *RCA 276*	74	1

MOODSWINGS / CHRISSIE HYNDE
UK, male / instrumental group and US, female vocalist / instrumentalist (4 WEEKS) pos/wks

12 Oct 91	**SPIRITUAL HIGH (STATE OF INDEPENDENCE)** *Arista 114528*	66	2
23 Jan 93	**SPIRITUAL HIGH (STATE OF INDEPENDENCE) (re-mix)** *Arista 74321127712*	47	2

See also PRETENDERS

MOODY BLUES `248` `Top 500`
Long-lived and internationally popular cosmic rock quintet from Birmingham, UK. Line-up has included Denny Laine (v/g), Ray Thomas (fl/v), Mike Pinder, (k/v), Graeme Edge (d), Justin Hayward (v/g) and John Lodge (b/v). This album-orientated act has sold more than 50 million records worldwide (114 WEEKS) pos/wks

10 Dec 64	★ **GO NOW** *Decca F 12022*	1	14
4 Mar 65	**I DON'T WANT TO GO ON WITHOUT YOU** *Decca F 12095*	33	9
10 Jun 65	**FROM THE BOTTOM OF MY HEART** *Decca F 12166*	22	9
18 Nov 65	**EVERYDAY** *Decca F 12266*	44	2
27 Dec 67	● **NIGHTS IN WHITE SATIN (2re)** *Deram DM 161*	9	34
7 Aug 68	**VOICES IN THE SKY** *Deram DM 196*	27	10
4 Dec 68	**RIDE MY SEE-SAW** *Deram DM 213*	42	1
2 May 70	● **QUESTION** *Threshold TH 4*	2	12
6 May 72	**ISN'T LIFE STRANGE** *Threshold TH 9*	13	10
10 Feb 73	**I'M JUST A SINGER (IN A ROCK & ROLL BAND)** *Threshold TH 13*	36	4
20 Aug 83	**BLUE WORLD** *Threshold TH 30*	35	5
25 Jun 88	**I KNOW YOU'RE OUT THERE SOMEWHERE** *Polydor POSP 921*	52	4

'Nights in White Satin' peaked at No.19 on its original chart visit then peaked at No.9 in Dec 1972 and peaked at No.14 on re-entry in Nov 1979

Michael MOOG
US, male producer – Shivaun Gaines (3 WEEKS) pos/wks

11 Dec 99	**THAT SOUND** *ffrr FCD 374*	32	2
25 Aug 01	**YOU BELONG TO ME** *Strictly Rhythm SRUKECD 04*	62	1

MOOGWAI
Switzerland / Holland, production duo (2 WEEKS) pos/wks

6 May 00	**VIOLA** *Platipus PLATCD 71*	55	1
26 May 01	**THE LABYRINTH** *Platipus PLATCD 83*	68	1

MOONMAN
Holland, male DJ / producer – Ferry Corsten (4 WEEKS) pos/wks

9 Aug 97	**DON'T BE AFRAID** *Heat Recordings HEATCD 009*	60	1
27 Nov 99	**DON'T BE AFRAID '99 (re-mix)** *Heat Recordings HEATCD 022*	41	2
7 Oct 00	**GALAXIA** *Heat Recordings HEATCD 025* `1`	50	1

`1` Moonman featuring Chantal

See also VERACOCHA; GOURYELLA; SYSTEM F; Ferry CORSTEN; ALBION; STARPARTY

MOONTREKKERS
UK, male instrumental group (1 WEEK) pos/wks

2 Nov 61	**NIGHT OF THE VAMPIRE** *Parlophone R 4814*	50	1

MOONY
Italy, female vocalist – Monica Bragato (8 WEEKS) pos/wks

15 Jun 02	● **DOVE (I'LL BE LOVING YOU)** *Positiva / Cream CDMNY 1*	9	8

Chanté MOORE
US, female vocalist (11 WEEKS) pos/wks

20 Mar 93	**LOVE'S TAKEN OVER** *MCA MCSTD 1744*	54	3
4 Mar 95	**FREE / SAIL ON** *MCA MCSTD 2042*	69	1
7 Apr 01	**STRAIGHT UP (re)** *MCA MCSTD 40250*	11	7

Dorothy MOORE
US, female vocalist (24 WEEKS) pos/wks

19 Jun 76	● **MISTY BLUE** *Contempo CS 2087*	5	12
16 Oct 76	**FUNNY HOW TIME SLIPS AWAY** *Contempo CS 2092*	38	3
15 Oct 77	**I BELIEVE YOU** *Epic EPC 5573*	20	9

Dudley MOORE – *See Peter COOK*

Gary MOORE `304` `Top 500`
Noted blues guitarist, b. 4 Apr 1952, Belfast. Played in early 1970s Irish band Skid Row (with Phil Lynott) as well as Thin Lizzy and Colosseum II, before successfully launching his solo career (103 WEEKS) pos/wks

21 Apr 79	● **PARISIENNE WALKWAYS** *MCA 419*	8	11
21 Jan 84	**HOLD ON TO LOVE** *10 TEN 13*	65	3
11 Aug 84	**EMPTY ROOMS** *10 TEN 25*	51	5
18 May 85	● **OUT IN THE FIELDS** *10 TEN 49* `1`	5	10
27 Jul 85	**EMPTY ROOMS (re-issue)** *10 TEN 58*	23	8
20 Dec 86	**OVER THE HILLS AND FAR AWAY** *10 TEN 134*	20	8
28 Feb 87	**WILD FRONTIER** *10 TEN 159*	35	5
9 May 87	**FRIDAY ON MY MIND** *10 TEN 164*	26	6
29 Aug 87	**THE LONER** *10 TEN 178*	53	5
5 Dec 87	**TAKE A LITTLE TIME (DOUBLE SINGLE)** *10 TEN 190*	75	1
14 Jan 89	**AFTER THE WAR** *Virgin GMS 1*	37	4
18 Mar 89	**READY FOR LOVE** *Virgin GMS 2*	56	2
24 Mar 90	**OH PRETTY WOMAN** *Virgin VS 1233* `2`	48	3
12 May 90	**STILL GOT THE BLUES (FOR YOU)** *Virgin VS 1267*	31	7
18 Aug 90	**WALKING BY MYSELF** *Virgin VS 1281*	48	5
15 Dec 90	**TOO TIRED** *Virgin VS 1306*	71	1
22 Feb 92	**COLD DAY IN HELL** *Virgin VS 1393*	24	5
9 May 92	**STORY OF THE BLUES** *Virgin VS 1412*	40	4
18 Jul 92	**SINCE I MET YOU BABY** *Virgin VS 1423* `3`	59	3
24 Oct 92	**SEPARATE WAYS** *Virgin VS 1437*	59	1
8 May 93	**PARISIENNE WALKWAYS (re-recording)** *Virgin VSCDX 1456*	32	4
17 Jun 95	**NEED YOUR LOVE SO BAD** *Virgin VSCDG 1546*	48	2

`1` Gary Moore and Phil Lynott `2` Gary Moore featuring Albert King `3` Gary Moore and B.B. King

'Parisienne Walkways' features uncredited vocals by Phil Lynott. Tracks on double single: Take a Little Time / Out in the Fields / All Messed Up / Thunder Rising

Jackie MOORE
US, female vocalist (5 WEEKS) pos/wks

15 Sep 79	**THIS TIME BABY** *CBS 7722*	49	5

Lynsey MOORE – *See RAMSEY and FEN featuring Lynsey MOORE*

Mandy MOORE
US, female vocalist (18 WEEKS) pos/wks

6 May 00	● **CANDY** *Epic 6693452*	6	13
19 Aug 00	**I WANNA BE WITH YOU** *Epic 6695922*	21	5

Mark MOORE – *See S EXPRESS*

Melba MOORE
US, female vocalist – Melba Hill (29 WEEKS) pos/wks

15 May 76	● **THIS IS IT** *Buddah BDS 443*	9	8
26 May 79	**PICK ME UP, I'LL DANCE** *Epic EPC 7234*	48	5
9 Oct 82	**LOVE'S COMIN' AT YA** *EMI America EA 146*	15	8
15 Jan 83	**MIND UP TONIGHT** *Capitol CL 272*	22	6
5 Mar 83	**UNDERLOVE** *Capitol CL 281*	60	2

Ray MOORE
UK, male DJ / vocalist d. Jan 1989 (9 WEEKS) pos/wks

29 Nov 86	**O' MY FATHER HAD A RABBIT** *Play PLAY 213*	24	7
5 Dec 87	**BOG EYED JOG** *Play PLAY 224*	61	2

Sam MOORE and LOU REED
US, male vocalists (10 WEEKS) pos/wks

17 Jan 87	**SOUL MAN** *A&M AM 364*	30	10

See also SAM and DAVE

Tina MOORE
US, female vocalist (18 WEEKS) pos/wks

30 Aug 97	● **NEVER GONNA LET YOU GO** *Delirious 74321511052*	7	15
25 Apr 98	**NOBODY BETTER** *RCA 74321571612*	20	3

Lisa MOORISH UK, female vocalist – Lisa Morrish (11 WEEKS)

		pos/wks
7 Jan 95	JUST THE WAY IT IS Go.Beat GODCD 123	42 3
19 Aug 95	I'M YOUR MAN Go.Beat GODCD 128	24 3
3 Feb 96	MR FRIDAY NIGHT Go.Beat GODCD 137	24 3
18 May 96	LOVE FOR LIFE Go.Beat GODCD 145	37 2

'I'm Your Man' features the uncredited vocals of George Michael

Angel MORAES US, male producer (2 WEEKS)

		pos/wks
16 Nov 96	HEAVEN KNOWS – DEEP DEEP DOWN ffrr FCD 282	72 1
17 May 97	I LIKE IT AM:PM 5871792	70 1

David MORALES US, male DJ / producer (21 WEEKS)

		pos/wks
10 Jul 93	GIMME LUV (EENIE MEENIE MINY MO) Mercury MERCD 390	37 3
20 Nov 93	THE PROGRAM Mercury MERCD 396	66 1
24 Aug 96	IN DE GHETTO Manifesto FESCD 12 [1]	35 2
15 Aug 98 ●	NEEDIN' U Manifesto FESCD 46 [2]	8 8
24 Jun 00	HIGHER Azuli AZNYCDX 120 [3]	41 2
20 Jan 01	NEEDIN' YOU II Manifesto FESCD 78 [4]	11 5

[1] David Morales and the Bad Yard Club featuring Crystal Waters and Delta [2] David Morales presents The Face [3] David Morales and Albert Cabrera present Moca featuring Deanna [4] David Morales presents The Face featuring Juliet Roberts

See also BOSS; PULSE featuring Antoinette ROBERSON

Mike MORAN – See Lynsey DE PAUL

MORCHEEBA
UK, male / female vocal / instrumental group (14 WEEKS)

		pos/wks
13 Jul 96	TAPE LOOP Indochina ID 045CD	42 1
5 Oct 96	TRIGGER HIPPIE Indochina ID 052CD	40 2
15 Feb 97	THE MUSIC THAT WE HEAR (MOOG ISLAND) Indochina ID 054CD	47 1
11 Oct 97	SHOULDER HOLSTER Indochina ID 064CD	53 1
11 Apr 98	BLINDFOLD Indochina ID 070CD	56 1
20 Jun 98	LET ME SEE Indochina ID 076CD	46 1
29 Aug 98	PART OF THE PROCESS China WOKCD 2097	38 2
5 Aug 00	ROME WASN'T BUILT IN A DAY East West EW 214CD	34 3
31 Mar 01	WORLD LOOKING IN East West EW 225CD	48 1
6 Jul 02	OTHERWISE East West EW 247CD	64 1

MORE UK, male vocal / instrumental group (2 WEEKS)

		pos/wks
14 Mar 81	WE ARE THE BAND Atlantic K 11561	59 2

MORE FIRE CREW – See PLATINUM 45 featuring MORE FIRE CREW

MOREL
US, male vocalist / producer – Richard Morel (1 WEEK)

		pos/wks
12 Aug 00	TRUE (THE FAGGOT IS YOU) Hooj Choons HOOJ 097CD	64 1

George MOREL featuring Heather WILDMAN
US, male / female vocal / instrumental duo (2 WEEKS)

		pos/wks
26 Oct 96	LET'S GROOVE Positiva CDTIV 62	42 2

MORGAN UK, male vocal / instrumental duo (1 WEEK)

		pos/wks
27 Nov 99	MISS PARKER Source CDSOUR 002	74 1

Debelah MORGAN US, female vocalist (9 WEEKS)

		pos/wks
24 Feb 01 ●	DANCE WITH ME Atlantic AT 0087CD	10 9

Derrick MORGAN Jamaica, male vocalist (1 WEEK)

		pos/wks
17 Jan 70	MOON HOP Crab 32	49 1

Jamie J MORGAN US, male vocalist (6 WEEKS)

		pos/wks
10 Feb 90	WALK ON THE WILD SIDE Tabu 655596 7	27 6

Jane MORGAN
US, female vocalist – Jane Currier (22 WEEKS)

		pos/wks
5 Dec 58 ★	THE DAY THE RAINS CAME London HLR 8751	1 16
22 May 59	IF ONLY I COULD LIVE MY LIFE AGAIN London HLR 8810	27 1
21 Jul 60	ROMANTICA London HLR 9120	39 5

Meli'sa MORGAN US, female vocalist (7 WEEKS)

		pos/wks
9 Aug 86	FOOL'S PARADISE Capitol CL 415	41 5
25 Jun 88	GOOD LOVE Capitol CL 483	59 2

Ray MORGAN UK, male vocalist (6 WEEKS)

		pos/wks
25 Jul 70	THE LONG AND WINDING ROAD B & C CB 128	32 6

Erick 'More' MORILLO presents RAW
US, male DJ / producer / instrumentalist and female vocalist (1 WEEK) pos/wks

4 Feb 95	HIGHER (FEEL IT) A&M 5809412	74 1

See also PIANOHEADZ; REAL TO REEL; LIL MO' YIN YANG

Alanis MORISSETTE
Canada, female vocalist / instrumentalist (53 WEEKS)

		pos/wks
5 Aug 95	YOU OUGHTA KNOW Maverick W 0307CD	22 7
28 Oct 95	HAND IN MY POCKET Maverick W 0312CD	26 3
24 Feb 96	YOU LEARN Maverick W 0334CD	24 4
20 Apr 96	IRONIC Maverick W 0343CD	11 9
3 Aug 96 ●	HEAD OVER FEET Maverick W 0355CD	7 7
7 Dec 96	ALL I REALLY WANT Maverick W 0382CD	59 1
31 Oct 98 ●	THANK U Maverick W 0458CD	5 10
13 Mar 99	JOINING YOU Maverick W 472CD1	28 2
31 Jul 99	SO PURE Maverick W 492CD1	38 2
2 Mar 02	HANDS CLEAN Maverick W 574CD	12 7
17 Aug 02	PRECIOUS ILLUSIONS Maverick W 582CD	53 1

Giorgio MORODER
Italy, male instrumentalist – synthesizer (36 WEEKS)

		pos/wks
24 Sep 77	FROM HERE TO ETERNITY Oasis 1 [1]	16 10
17 Mar 79	CHASE Casablanca CAN 144	48 6
22 Sep 84 ●	TOGETHER IN ELECTRIC DREAMS Virgin VS 713 [2]	3 13
29 Jun 85	GOOD-BYE BAD TIMES Virgin VS 772 [3]	44 5
11 Jul 98	CARRY ON Almighty CDALMY 120 [4]	65 1
12 Feb 00	THE CHASE (re-recording) Logic 74321732112 [5]	46 1

[1] Giorgio [2] Giorgio Moroder and Phil Oakey [3] Philip Oakey and Giorgio Moroder [4] Donna Summer and Giorgio Moroder [5] DJ Empire presents Giorgio Moroder

Ennio MORRICONE Italy, orchestra (12 WEEKS)

		pos/wks
11 Apr 81 ●	CHI MAI (THEME FROM THE TV SERIES 'THE LIFE AND TIMES OF DAVID LLOYD GEORGE') BBC RESL 92	2 12

Sarah Jane MORRIS – See COMMUNARDS

Diana MORRISON – See Michael BALL

Dorothy Combs MORRISON – See Edwin HAWKINS SINGERS

Mark MORRISON UK, male vocalist – Abdul Rahman.
Best-selling single: 'Return Of The Mack' 837,000 (68 WEEKS)

		pos/wks
22 Apr 95	CRAZY WEA YZ 907CD	19 4
16 Sep 95	LET'S GET DOWN WEA WEA 001CD	39 2
16 Mar 96 ★	RETURN OF THE MACK (re) WEA WEA 040CD	1 24
27 Jul 96 ●	CRAZY (re-mix) (re) WEA WEA 054CD1	6 9
19 Oct 96 ●	TRIPPIN' WEA WEA 079CD1	8 6
21 Dec 96 ●	HORNY WEA WEA 090CD1	5 9
15 Mar 97 ●	MOAN & GROAN WEA WEA 096CD1	7 6
20 Sep 97	WHO'S THE MACK! WEA WEA 128CD1	13 5
4 Sep 99	BEST FRIEND WEA WEA 221CD1 [1]	23 3

[1] Mark Morrison and Conner Reeves

Van MORRISON UK, male vocalist – George Ivan (21 WEEKS)

			pos/wks	
20 Oct 79	BRIGHT SIDE OF THE ROAD *Mercury 6001 121*		63	3
1 Jul 89	HAVE I TOLD YOU LATELY *Polydor VANS 1*		74	1
9 Dec 89	WHENEVER GOD SHINES HIS LIGHT			
	Polydor VANS 2 [1]		20	6
15 May 93	GLORIA *Exile VANCD 11* [2]		31	3
18 Mar 95	HAVE I TOLD YOU LATELY THAT I LOVE YOU			
	RCA 74321271702 [3]		71	1
10 Jun 95	DAYS LIKE THIS *Exile VANCD 12*		65	1
2 Dec 95	NO RELIGION *Exile 5775792*		54	1
1 Mar 97	THE HEALING GAME *Exile 5733912*		46	1
6 Mar 99	PRECIOUS TIME *Pointblank / Virgin POBD 14*		36	2
22 May 99	BACK ON TOP *Exile / Pointblank / Virgin POBD 15*		69	1
18 May 02	HEY MR DJ *Polydor / Exile 5705962*		58	1

[1] Van Morrison with Cliff Richard [2] Van Morrison and John Lee Hooker
[3] Chieftains with Van Morrison

'Have I Told You Lately That I Love You' is a re-recording of his second hit

See also THEM

MORRISSEY (496) Top 500

Witty, often provocative vocalist / lyricist and former frontman of The Smiths, born Stephen Morrissey, 22 May 1959, Manchester, UK. The first of 15 successive Top 40 singles entered at No.6, thereby immediately outdoing his previous band's chart peak (74 WEEKS)

			pos/wks	
27 Feb 88 ●	SUEDEHEAD *HMV POP 1618*		5	6
11 Jun 88 ●	EVERYDAY IS LIKE SUNDAY *HMV POP 1619*		9	6
11 Feb 89 ●	LAST OF THE FAMOUS INTERNATIONAL PLAYBOYS			
	HMV POP 1620.		6	5
29 Apr 89 ●	INTERESTING DRUG *HMV POP 1621*		9	4
25 Nov 89	OUIJA BOARD OUIJA BOARD *HMV POP 1622*		18	4
5 May 90	NOVEMBER SPAWNED A MONSTER *HMV POP 1623*		12	4
20 Oct 90	PICCADILLY PALARE *HMV POP 1624*		18	2
23 Feb 91	OUR FRANK *HMV POP 1625*		26	3
13 Apr 91	SING YOUR LIFE *HMV POP 1626*		33	2
27 Jul 91	PREGNANT FOR THE LAST TIME *HMV POP 1627*		25	4
12 Oct 91	MY LOVE LIFE *HMV POP 1628*		29	2
9 May 92	WE HATE IT WHEN OUR FRIENDS BECOME SUCCESSFUL			
	HMV POP 1629.		17	3
18 Jul 92	YOU'RE THE ONE FOR ME, FATTY *HMV POP 1630*		19	3
19 Dec 92	CERTAIN PEOPLE I KNOW *HMV POP 1631*		35	4
12 Mar 94 ●	THE MORE YOU IGNORE ME THE CLOSER I GET			
	Parlophone CDR 6372		8	3
11 Jun 94	HOLD ON TO YOUR FRIENDS *Parlophone CDR 6383*		47	2
20 Aug 94	INTERLUDE *Parlophone CDR 6365* [1]		25	2
28 Jan 95	BOXERS *Parlophone CDR 6400*		23	3
2 Sep 95	DAGENHAM DAVE *RCA Victor 74321299802*		26	2
9 Dec 95	THE BOY RACER *RCA Victor 74321332952*		36	2
23 Dec 95	SUNNY *Parlophone CDR 6243*		42	2
2 Aug 97	ALMA MATTERS *Island CID 667*		16	3
18 Oct 97	ROY'S KEEN *Island CID 671*		42	1
10 Jan 98	SATAN REJECTED MY SOUL *Island CID 686*		39	2

[1] Morrissey and Siouxsie

See also SMITHS

MORRISTON ORPHEUS MALE VOICE CHOIR – See ALARM

Buddy MORROW US, orchestra – Muni Zudecoff (1 WEEK)

			pos/wks	
20 Mar 53	NIGHT TRAIN *HMV B 10347*		12	1

Bob MORTIMER – See EMF; MIDDLESBROUGH FC featuring Bob MORTIMER and Chris REA

MOS DEF US male rapper – Dante Smith (6 WEEKS)

			pos/wks	
24 Jun 00	UMI SAYS *Rawkus RWK 232CD*		60	1
4 Nov 00	MISS FAT BOOTY – PART II *Rawkus RWK 282CD* [1]		64	1
3 Feb 01	OH NO *Rawkus RWK 302* [2]		24	4

[1] Mos Def featuring Ghostface Killah [2] Mos Def and Nate Dogg featuring Pharoahe Monch

Mickie MOST UK, male vocalist (1 WEEK)

			pos/wks	
25 Jul 63	MR PORTER *Decca F 11664*		45	1

MOTELS

US / UK, male / female vocal / instrumental group (7 WEEKS)

			pos/wks	
11 Oct 80	WHOSE PROBLEM? *Capitol CL 16162*		42	4
10 Jan 81	DAYS ARE O.K. *Capitol CL 16149*		41	3

Wendy MOTEN US, female vocalist (13 WEEKS)

			pos/wks	
5 Feb 94 ●	COME IN OUT OF THE RAIN *EMI-USA CDMT 105*		8	9
14 May 94	SO CLOSE TO LOVE *EMI-USA CDMTS 106*		35	4

MOTHER UK, male instrumental / production

duo – Jools Brettle and Lee Fisher (4 WEEKS)

			pos/wks	
12 Jun 93	ALL FUNKED UP *Bosting BYSNCD 101*		34	2
1 Oct 94	GET BACK *Six6 SIXT 119*		73	1
31 Aug 96	ALL FUNKED UP (re-mix) *Six6 SIXXCD 1*		66	1

MOTHER'S PRIDE UK, male DJ / production duo (2 WEEKS)

			pos/wks	
21 Mar 98	FLORIBUNDA *Heat Recordings HEATCD 013*		42	1
6 Nov 99	LEARNING TO FLY *Devolution DEVR 001CDS*		54	1

MOTIV 8 UK, male producer – Steve Rodway (10 WEEKS)

			pos/wks	
17 Jul 93	ROCKIN' FOR MYSELF *Nuff Respect NUFF 002CD* [1]		67	1
7 May 94	ROCKIN' FOR MYSELF (re-mix) *WEA YZ 814CD*		18	4
21 Oct 95	BREAK THE CHAIN *Eternal WEA 010CD*		31	2
23 Dec 95	SEARCHING FOR THE GOLDEN EYE *Eternal WEA 027CD* [2]		40	1

[1] Motiv 8 featuring Angie Brown [2] Motiv 8 and Kym Mazelle

MOTIVATION Holland, male producer – Francis Louwers (1 WEEK)

			pos/wks	
17 Nov 01	PARA MI *Definitive CDDEF 1*		71	1

MÖTLEY CRÜE US, male vocal / instrumental group (28 WEEKS)

			pos/wks	
24 Aug 85	SMOKIN' IN THE BOYS ROOM *Elektra EKR 16*		71	2
8 Feb 86	HOME SWEET HOME / SMOKIN' IN THE BOYS ROOM			
	(re-issue) *Elektra EKR 33*		51	3
1 Aug 87	GIRLS, GIRLS, GIRLS *Elektra EKR 59*		26	6
16 Jan 88	YOU'RE ALL I NEED / WILD SIDE *Elektra EKR 65*		23	4
4 Nov 89	DR FEELGOOD *Elektra EKR 97*		50	3
12 May 90	WITHOUT YOU *Elektra EKR 109*		39	3
7 Sep 91	PRIMAL SCREAM *Elektra EKR 133*		32	2
11 Jan 92	HOME SWEET HOME (re-mix) *Elektra EKR 136.*		37	2
5 Mar 94	HOOLIGAN'S HOLIDAY *Elektra EKR 180CDX*		36	2
19 Jul 97	AFRAID *Elektra E 3936 CD1*		58	1

'Wild Side' listed with 'You're All I Need' only from 30 Jan 1988. It peaked at No.26

See also Vince NEIL

MOTÖRHEAD (429) Top 500

Unashamedly loud mainstays of UK heavy rock formed in 1975 after Lemmy (v/b) (b. Ian Kilmister 24 Dec 1945, Stoke-on-Trent, UK) left Hawkwind. Much admired in punk circles, they helped to show the way to 1980s heavy metal bands such as Metallica (81 WEEKS)

			pos/wks	
16 Jul 78	LOUIE LOUIE (re) *Bronze BRO 60*		68	2
10 Mar 79	OVERKILL (re) *Bronze BRO 67*		39	7
30 Jun 79	NO CLASS *Bronze BRO 78*		61	4
1 Dec 79	BOMBER *Bronze BRO 85*		34	7
3 May 80 ●	THE GOLDEN YEARS (EP) *Bronze BRO 92*		8	7
1 Nov 80	ACE OF SPADES *Bronze BRO 106*		15	12
22 Nov 80	BEER DRINKERS AND HELL RAISERS *Big Beat SWT 61*		43	4
21 Feb 81 ●	ST VALENTINE'S DAY MASSACRE (EP) *Bronze BRO 116* [1]		5	8
11 Jul 81 ●	MOTÖRHEAD (LIVE) *Bronze BRO 124*		6	7
3 Apr 82	IRON FIST *Bronze BRO 146*		29	5
21 May 83	I GOT MINE *Bronze BRO 165*		46	2
30 Jul 83	SHINE *Bronze BRO 167*		59	2
1 Sep 84	KILLED BY DEATH *Bronze BRO 185*		51	2
5 Jul 86	DEAF FOREVER *GWR GWR 2*		67	1
5 Jan 91	THE ONE TO SING THE BLUES *Epic 6565787*		45	3

14 Nov 92	'92 TOUR (EP) *Epic 6588096*	63	1
11 Sep 93	ACE OF SPADES (re-issue) *WGAF CDWGAF 101*	23	5
10 Dec 94	BORN TO RAISE HELL *Fox 74321230152* [2]	47	2

[1] Motörhead and Girlschool (also known as Headgirl) [2] Motörhead / Ice-T / Whitfield Crane

Tracks on The Golden Years (EP): Dead Men Tell No Tales / Too Late Too Late / Leaving Here / Stone Dead Forever. Tracks on St Valentine's Day Massacre (EP): Please Don't Touch / Emergency / Bomber. Tracks on '92 Tour (EP): Hellraiser / You Better Run / Going to Brazil / Ramones

MOTORS *UK, male vocal / instrumental group (29 WEEKS)* pos/wks

24 Sep 77	DANCING THE NIGHT AWAY *Virgin VS 186*	42	4
10 Jun 78 ●	AIRPORT *Virgin VS 219*	4	13
19 Aug 78	FORGET ABOUT YOU *Virgin VS 222*	13	9
12 Apr 80	LOVE AND LONELINESS *Virgin VS 263*	58	3

MOTOWN SPINNERS – *See DETROIT SPINNERS*

MOTT THE HOOPLE
UK, male vocal / instrumental group (55 WEEKS) pos/wks

12 Aug 72 ●	ALL THE YOUNG DUDES *CBS 8271*	3	11
16 Jun 73	HONALOOCHIE BOOGIE *CBS 1530*	12	9
8 Sep 73 ●	ALL THE WAY FROM MEMPHIS *CBS 1764*	10	8
24 Nov 73 ●	ROLL AWAY THE STONE *CBS 1895*	8	12
30 Mar 74	THE GOLDEN AGE OF ROCK 'N' ROLL *CBS 2177*	16	7
22 Jun 74	FOXY, FOXY *CBS 2439*	33	5
2 Nov 74	SATURDAY GIG *CBS 2754*	41	3

See also Ian HUNTER

MOUNT RUSHMORE presents The KNACK
UK, male production duo / female vocalist (1 WEEK) pos/wks

3 Apr 99	YOU BETTER *Universal MCSTD 40192*	53	1

Nana MOUSKOURI *Greece, female vocalist (11 WEEKS)* pos/wks

11 Jan 86 ●	ONLY LOVE *Philips PH 38*	2	11

MOUSSE T
Germany, male producer – Mustafa Gundogdu (28 WEEKS) pos/wks

6 Jun 98 ●	HORNY *AM:PM 5826712* [1]	2	17
20 May 00 ●	SEX BOMB *Gut CDGUT 33* [2]	3	10
10 Aug 02	FIRE *Serious SERR 44CD* [3]	58	1

[1] Mousse T vs Hot 'N' Juicy [2] Tom Jones and Mousse T [3] Mousse T featuring Emma Lanford

MOUTH and MACNEAL
Holland, male / female vocal duo (10 WEEKS) pos/wks

4 May 74 ●	I SEE A STAR *Decca F 13504*	8	10

MOVE `267` `Top 500` *Innovative and influential Birmingham band, included Carl Wayne (v), Roy Wood (v/g). They were the first group heard on BBC Radio 1 ('Flowers in the Rain'), and had eight consecutive Top 20 entries. Wood later moved on to a successful solo career, helped to form ELO and went on to front Wizzard (110 WEEKS)* pos/wks

5 Jan 67 ●	NIGHT OF FEAR *Deram DM 109*	2	10
6 Apr 67 ●	I CAN HEAR THE GRASS GROW *Deram DM 117*	5	10
6 Sep 67 ●	FLOWERS IN THE RAIN *Regal Zonophone RZ3001*	2	13
7 Feb 68 ●	FIRE BRIGADE *Regal Zonophone RZ3005*	3	11
25 Dec 68 ★	BLACKBERRY WAY *Regal Zonophone RZ3015*	1	12
23 Jul 69	CURLY *Regal Zonophone RZ3021*	12	12
25 Apr 70 ●	BRONTOSAURUS *Regal Zonophone RZ3026*	7	10
3 Jul 71	TONIGHT *Harvest HAR 5038*	11	10
23 Oct 71	CHINATOWN *Harvest HAR 5043*	23	8
13 May 72 ●	CALIFORNIA MAN *Harvest HAR 5050*	7	14

MOVEMENT *US, male vocal / instrumental group (2 WEEKS)* pos/wks

24 Oct 92	JUMP! *Arista 74321116677*	57	2

MOVEMENT 98 featuring Carroll THOMPSON
UK, male / female vocal / instrumental group (8 WEEKS) pos/wks

19 May 90	JOY AND HEARTBREAK *Circa YR 45*	27	5
15 Sep 90	SUNRISE *Circa YR 51*	58	3

MOVIN' MELODIES
Holland, male producer – Patrick Prinz (3 WEEKS) pos/wks

22 Oct 94	LA LUNA *Effective EFFS 017CD* [1]	64	1
29 Jun 96	INDICA *Hooj Choons HOOJCD 44*	62	1
26 Jul 97	ROLLERBLADE *Movin' Melodies 5822352*	71	1

[1] Movin' Melodies Production

See also ARTEMESIA; ETHICS; SUBLIMINAL CUTS

Alison MOYET `280` `Top 500` *After five Top 20 hits with Yazoo, the distinctive, bluesy-voiced vocalist (b. 18 Jun 1961, Essex, UK), nicknamed Alf, enjoyed a string of solo successes. Her biggest hits included revivals of songs made popular by Billie Holiday and Ketty Lester (107 WEEKS)* pos/wks

23 Jun 84 ●	LOVE RESURRECTION *CBS A 4497*	10	11
13 Oct 84 ●	ALL CRIED OUT *CBS A 4757*	8	11
1 Dec 84	INVISIBLE *CBS A 4930*	21	10
16 Mar 85 ●	THAT OLE DEVIL CALLED LOVE *CBS A 6044*	2	10
29 Nov 86 ●	IS THIS LOVE? *CBS MOYET 1*	3	16
7 Mar 87 ●	WEAK IN THE PRESENCE OF BEAUTY *CBS MOYET 2*	6	10
30 May 87	ORDINARY GIRL *CBS MOYET 3*	43	4
28 Nov 87 ●	LOVE LETTERS *CBS MOYET 5*	4	10
6 Apr 91	IT WON'T BE LONG *Columbia 6567577*	50	4
1 Jun 91	WISHING YOU WERE HERE *Columbia 6569397*	72	1
12 Oct 91	THIS HOUSE *Columbia 6575157*	40	5
16 Oct 93	FALLING *Columbia 6595962*	42	3
12 Mar 94	WHISPERING YOUR NAME *Columbia 6601622*	18	7
28 May 94	GETTING INTO SOMETHING *Columbia 6603565*	51	2
22 Oct 94	ODE TO BOY *Columbia 6607952*	59	1
26 Aug 95	SOLID WOOD *Columbia 6623265*	44	2

See also YAZOO

MOZAIC *UK, female vocal group (7 WEEKS)* pos/wks

5 Aug 95	SING IT (THE HALLELUJAH SONG) *Perfecto PERF 106CD*	14	4
10 Aug 96	RAYS OF THE RISING SUN *Perfecto PERF 123CD*	32	2
30 Nov 96	MOVING UP MOVING ON *Perfecto PERF 131CD*	62	1

MTUME *US, male / female vocal / instrumental group (12 WEEKS)* pos/wks

14 May 83	JUICY FRUIT *Epic A 3424*	34	9
22 Sep 84	PRIME TIME *Epic A 4720*	57	3

MUD `180` `Top 500` *Rock 'n' roll-influenced Seventies stars: Les Gray (v), Rob Davis (g/v), Ray Stiles (b/v), Dave Mount (d/v). After joining RAK Records and teaming with writers / producers Nicky Chinn and Mike Chapman, this good-time British band had a noteworthy run of hits, including three No.1s. Davis is now one of the UK's most successful songwriters, writing No.1 hits for Kylie Minogue and Spiller (139 WEEKS)* pos/wks

10 Mar 73	CRAZY *RAK 146*	12	12
23 Jun 73	HYPNOSIS *RAK 152*	16	13
27 Oct 73 ●	DYNA-MITE *RAK 159*	4	12
19 Jan 74 ★	TIGER FEET *RAK 166*	1	11
13 Apr 74 ●	THE CAT CREPT IN *RAK 170*	2	9
27 Jul 74 ●	ROCKET *RAK 178*	6	9
30 Nov 74 ★	LONELY THIS CHRISTMAS (re) *RAK 187*	1	13
15 Feb 75 ●	THE SECRETS THAT YOU KEEP *RAK 194*	3	9
26 Apr 75 ★	OH BOY *RAK 201*	1	9
21 Jun 75 ●	MOONSHINE SALLY *RAK 208*	10	7
2 Aug 75	ONE NIGHT *RAK 213*	32	4
4 Oct 75 ●	L'L'LUCY *Private Stock PVT 41*	10	6
29 Nov 75 ●	SHOW ME YOU'RE A WOMAN *Private Stock PVT 45*	8	8
15 May 76	SHAKE IT DOWN *Private Stock PVT 65*	12	8
27 Nov 76 ●	LEAN ON ME *Private Stock PVT 85*	7	9

'Lonely This Christmas' re-entered peaking at No.61 in Dec 1985

MUDHONEY US, male vocal / instrumental group (2 WEEKS)

		pos/wks
17 Aug 91	**LET IT SLIDE** Subpop SP 15154	**60** 1
24 Oct 92	**SUCK YOU DRY** Reprise W 0137	**65** 1

MUDLARKS UK, male / female vocal group (19 WEEKS)

		pos/wks
2 May 58 ●	**LOLLIPOP** Columbia DB 4099	**2** 9
6 Jun 58 ●	**BOOK OF LOVE** Columbia DB 4133	**8** 9
27 Feb 59	**THE LOVE GAME** Columbia DB 4250	**30** 1

MUFFINS – See MARTHA and the MUFFINS

Idris MUHAMMAD
US, male instrumentalist – drums (3 WEEKS)

		pos/wks
17 Sep 77	**COULD HEAVEN EVER BE LIKE THIS** Kudu 935	**42** 3

Vocal by Frank Floyd

MUKKAA UK, male instrumental / production
duo – Stuart Crichton and Billy Kiltie (1 WEEK)

		pos/wks
27 Feb 93	**BURUCHACCA** Limbo LIMBO 008	**74** 1

See also EYE TO EYE featuring Taka BOOM; UMBOZA

Maria MULDAUR
US, female vocalist – Maria D'Amato (8 WEEKS)

		pos/wks
29 Jun 74	**MIDNIGHT AT THE OASIS** Reprise K 14331	**21** 8

MULL HISTORICAL SOCIETY
UK, male vocal / instrumental group (3 WEEKS)

		pos/wks
21 Jul 01	**ANIMAL CANNABUS** Rough Trade RTRADESCD 021	**53** 1
9 Feb 02	**WATCHING XANADU** Blanco Y Negro NEG 138CD	**36** 2

Arthur MULLARD – See Hylda BAKER and Arthur MULLARD

Larry MULLEN – See Adam CLAYTON and Larry MULLEN

Shawn MULLINS US, male vocalist (11 WEEKS)

		pos/wks
6 Mar 99 ●	**LULLABY** Columbia 6669592	**9** 10
2 Oct 99	**WHAT IS LIFE** Columbia 6678212	**62** 1

MULU UK, male / female vocal / instrumental duo (1 WEEK)

		pos/wks
2 Aug 97	**PUSSYCAT** Dedicated MULU 003CD1	**50** 1

Omera MUMBA Ireland, male vocalist (2 WEEKS)

		pos/wks
20 Jul 02	**LIL' BIG MAN** Polydor 5708852	**42** 2

Samantha MUMBA Ireland, female vocalist (69 WEEKS)

		pos/wks
8 Jul 00 ●	**GOTTA TELL YOU** Wild Card / Polydor 5618832	**2** 12
28 Oct 00 ●	**BODY II BODY** Wild Card / Polydor 5877742	**5** 12
3 Mar 01 ●	**ALWAYS COME BACK TO YOUR LOVE** Wild Card / Polydor 5879252	**3** 15
22 Sep 01 ●	**BABY COME ON OVER** Wild Card / Polydor 5872352	**5** 10
22 Dec 01 ●	**LATELY** Wild Card / Polydor 5705232	**6** 12
26 Oct 02 ●	**I'M RIGHT HERE (re)** Wild Card / Polydor 0659372	**5** 8

Coati MUNDI – See Kid CREOLE and the COCONUTS

MUNDY Ireland, male vocalist (2 WEEKS)

		pos/wks
3 Aug 96	**TO YOU I BESTOW** Epic MUNDY 1CD	**60** 1
5 Oct 96	**LIFE'S A CINCH** Epic MUNDY 2CD	**75** 1

MUNGO JERRY `372` `Top 500` London-based good-time jug band,
fronted by singer / songwriter Ray Dorset, b. 21 Mar 1946, Middlesex, UK. 'In
the Summertime', the first three-track No.1, sold seven million worldwide,
and their first two singles topped the chart. Dorset also penned Kelly Marie's
No.1 'Feels Like I'm in Love' (88 WEEKS)

		pos/wks
6 Jun 70 ★	**IN THE SUMMERTIME** Dawn DNX 2502	**1** 20

		pos/wks
6 Feb 71 ★	**BABY JUMP (re)** Dawn DNX 2505	**1** 13
29 May 71 ●	**LADY ROSE** Dawn DNX 2510	**5** 12
18 Sep 71	**YOU DON'T HAVE TO BE IN THE ARMY TO FIGHT IN THE WAR** Dawn DNX 2513	**13** 8
22 Apr 72	**OPEN UP** Dawn DNX 2514	**21** 8
7 Jul 73 ●	**ALRIGHT, ALRIGHT, ALRIGHT** Dawn DNS 1037	**3** 12
10 Nov 73	**WILD LOVE** Dawn DNS 1051	**32** 5
6 Apr 74	**LONG LEGGED WOMAN DRESSED IN BLACK** Dawn DNS 1067	**13** 9
29 May 99	**SUPPORT THE TOON – IT'S YOUR DUTY (EP)** Saraja TOONCD 001 `1`	**57** 1

`1` Mungo Jerry and Toon Travellers

Tracks on Support the Toon – It's Your Duty (EP): Blaydon Races / Going to
Wembley / Bottle of Beer

MUNICH MACHINE
Germany, male instrumental group (8 WEEKS)

		pos/wks
10 Dec 77	**GET ON THE FUNK TRAIN** Oasis OASIS 2	**41** 4
4 Nov 78	**A WHITER SHADE OF PALE** Oasis OASIS 5 `1`	**42** 4

`1` Munich Machine introducing Chris Bennett

David MUNROW – See EARLY MUSIC CONSORT directed by David MUNROW

MUPPETS US, frog-fronted puppet ensemble (15 WEEKS)

		pos/wks
28 May 77 ●	**HALFWAY DOWN THE STAIRS** Pye 7N 45698	**7** 8
17 Dec 77	**THE MUPPET SHOW MUSIC HALL EP** Pye 7NX 8004	**19** 7

'Halfway Down the Stairs' is sung by Jerry Nelson as Kermit the Frog's nephew,
Robin. Tracks on The Muppet Show Music Hall EP: Don't Dilly Dally on the Way /
Waiting at the Church / The Boy in the Gallery / Wotcher (Knocked 'Em in the Old
Kent Road)

MURDERDOLLS US, male vocal / instrumental group (1 WEEK)

		pos/wks
16 Nov 02	**DEAD IN HOLLYWOOD** Roadrunner RR 20223	**54** 1

Lydia MURDOCK US, female vocalist (9 WEEKS)

		pos/wks
24 Sep 83	**SUPERSTAR** Korova KOW 30	**14** 9

Shirley MURDOCK US, female vocalist (2 WEEKS)

		pos/wks
12 Apr 86	**TRUTH OR DARE** Elektra EKR 36	**60** 2

Eddie MURPHY – See Shabba RANKS

Noel MURPHY Ireland, male vocalist (4 WEEKS)

		pos/wks
27 Jun 87	**MURPHY AND THE BRICKS** Murphy's STACK 1	**57** 4

Roisin MURPHY – See MOLOKO; PSYCHEDELIC WALTONS featuring Roisin
MURPHY

Walter MURPHY and the BIG APPLE BAND
US, orchestra (9 WEEKS)

		pos/wks
10 Jul 76	**A FIFTH OF BEETHOVEN** Private Stock PVT 59 ▲	**28** 9

Anne MURRAY Canada, female vocalist (40 WEEKS)

		pos/wks
24 Oct 70	**SNOWBIRD** Capitol CL 15654	**23** 17
21 Oct 72	**DESTINY** Capitol CL 15734	**41** 4
9 Dec 78	**YOU NEEDED ME** Capitol CL 16011 ▲	**22** 14
21 Apr 79	**I JUST FALL IN LOVE AGAIN** Capitol CL 16069	**58** 2
19 Apr 80	**DAYDREAM BELIEVER** Capitol CL 16123	**61** 3

Keith MURRAY US, male rapper (10 WEEKS)

		pos/wks
2 Nov 96	**THE RHYME** Jive JIVECD 407	**59** 1
27 Jun 98	**SHORTY (YOU KEEP PLAYIN' WITH MY MIND)** Jive 0521212 `1`	**22** 3
14 Nov 98	**HOME ALONE** Jive 0522392 `2`	**17** 5
5 Dec 98	**INCREDIBLE** Jive 0522102 `3`	**52** 1

`1` Imajin featuring Keith Murray `2` R Kelly featuring Keith Murray `3` Keith
Murray featuring LL Cool J

Pauline MURRAY and the INVISIBLE GIRLS UK, female
vocalist with male (really) vocal / instrumental group (2 WEEKS) pos/wks

2 Aug 80	DREAM SEQUENCE (ONE) *Illusive IVE 1*		67	2

Ruby MURRAY (249) Top 500 *Singing sensation of 1955, b. 29 Mar 1935,*
Belfast, d. 17 Dec 1996. The name of this nasal-sounding 'girl next door',
who became the first artist to have five simultaneous Top 20 hits, has become a part
of the English language (rhyming slang for a curry) (114 WEEKS) pos/wks

3 Dec 54	● HEARTBEAT *Columbia DB 3542*		3	16
28 Jan 55	★ SOFTLY, SOFTLY (re) *Columbia DB 3558*		1	23
4 Feb 55	● HAPPY DAYS AND LONELY NIGHTS *Columbia DB 3577*		6	8
4 Mar 55	● LET ME GO LOVER *Columbia DB 3577*		5	7
18 Mar 55	● IF ANYONE FINDS THIS, I LOVE YOU *Columbia DB 3580* [1]		4	11
1 Jul 55	● EVERMORE *Columbia DB 3617*		3	17
14 Oct 55	● I'LL COME WHEN YOU CALL *Columbia DB 3643*		6	7
31 Aug 56	YOU ARE MY FIRST LOVE (re) *Columbia DB 3770*		16	5
12 Dec 58	REAL LOVE *Columbia DB 4192*		18	6
5 Jun 59	GOODBYE JIMMY, GOODBYE (re) *Columbia DB 4305*		10	14

[1] Ruby Murray with Anne Warren

Junior MURVIN *Jamaica, male vocalist – Mervin Smith (9 WEEKS)* pos/wks

3 May 80	POLICE AND THIEVES *Island WIP 6539*		23	9

MUSE *UK, male vocal / instrumental group (30 WEEKS)* pos/wks

26 Jun 99	UNO *Mushroom / Taste Media MUSH 50CDS*		73	1
18 Sep 99	CAVE *Mushroom / Taste Media MUSH 58CDS*		52	1
4 Dec 99	MUSCLE MUSEUM *Mushroom / Taste Media MUSH 66CDS*		43	2
4 Mar 00	SUNBURN *Mushroom / Taste Media MUSH 68CDS*		22	2
17 Jun 00	UNINTENDED *Mushroom / Taste Media MUSH 72CDS*		20	4
21 Oct 00	MUSCLE MUSEUM (re-issue) *Mushroom / Taste Media MUSH 84CDS*		25	3
24 Mar 01	PLUG IN BABY *Mushroom / Taste Media MUSH 89CDS*		11	5
16 Jun 01	NEW BORN *Mushroom / Taste Media MUSH 92CDS*		12	4
1 Sep 01	BLISS *Mushroom / Taste Media MUSH 96CDS*		22	2
1 Dec 01	HYPER MUSIC / FEELING GOOD *Mushroom MUSH 97CDS*		24	3
29 Jun 02	DEAD STAR / IN YOUR WORLD *Mushroom MUSH 104CDS*		13	3

The MUSIC *UK, male vocal / instrumental group (5 WEEKS)* pos/wks

31 Aug 02	TAKE THE LONG ROAD AND WALK IT *Hut / Virgin HUTCD 158*		14	3
30 Nov 02	GETAWAY *Hut / Virgin HUTCD162*		26	2

MUSIC and MYSTERY featuring Gwen McCRAE
UK, male production group and US, female vocalist (3 WEEKS) pos/wks

13 Feb 93	ALL THIS LOVE I'M GIVING *KTDA CDKTDA 2*		36	3

MUSIC RELIEF '94 *UK, male / female vocal group (1 WEEK)* pos/wks

5 Nov 94	WHAT'S GOING ON *Jive RWANDACD 1*		70	1

MUSICAL YOUTH *UK, male vocal / instrumental*
group – lead vocal Dennis Seaton (55 WEEKS) pos/wks

25 Sep 82	★ PASS THE DUTCHIE (re) *MCA YOU 1*		1	13
20 Nov 82	YOUTH OF TODAY *MCA YOU 2*		13	9
12 Feb 83	● NEVER GONNA GIVE YOU UP *MCA YOU 3*		6	10
16 Apr 83	HEARTBREAKER *MCA YOU 4*		44	3
9 Jul 83	TELL ME WHY *MCA YOU 5*		33	6
22 Oct 83	007 *MCA YOU 6*		26	6
14 Jan 84	SIXTEEN *MCA YOU 7*		23	8

See also Donna SUMMER

MUSIQUE *US, female vocal group (12 WEEKS)* pos/wks

18 Nov 78	IN THE BUSH *CBS 6791*		16	12

See also PF PROJECT featuring Ewan McGREGOR

MUSIQUE vs U2 *UK, male production duo – Nick Hanson and Moussa*
Clarke – and Ireland, male vocal / instrumental group (5 WEEKS) pos/wks

2 Jun 01	NEW YEAR'S DUB (re) *Serious SERR 030CD*		15	5

MUSTAFAS – *See STAIFFI and his MUSTAFAS*

MUTINY UK
UK, male production duo – Dylan Barnes and Rob Davy (3 WEEKS) pos/wks

19 May 01	SECRETS *Sunflower VCRD 86* [1]		47	1
25 Aug 01	VIRUS *VC Recordings VCRD 91*		42	2

[1] Vocals by Lorraine Cato

See also HELICOPTER

MY BLOODY VALENTINE
UK, male / female vocal / instrumental group (5 WEEKS) pos/wks

5 May 90	SOON *Creation CRE 073*		41	3
16 Feb 91	TO HERE KNOWS WHEN *Creation CRE 085*		29	2

MY LIFE STORY
UK, male / female vocal / instrumental group (12 WEEKS) pos/wks

17 Aug 96	12 REASONS WHY I LOVE HER *Parlophone CDR 6442*		32	2
9 Nov 96	SPARKLE *Parlophone CDR 6450*		34	2
1 Mar 97	THE KING OF KISSINGDOM *Parlophone CDRS 6457*		35	1
17 May 97	STRUMPET *Parlophone CDR 6464*		27	2
23 Aug 97	DUCHESS *Parlophone CDR 6474*		39	1
19 Jun 99	IT'S A GIRL THING *IT ITR 001*		37	2
30 Oct 99	EMPIRE LINE *IT ITR 003*		58	1
19 Feb 00	WALK / DON'T wALK *IT ITR 007*		48	1

MY VITRIOL *UK, male / female vocal / instrumental group (7 WKS)* pos/wks

22 Jul 00	CEMENTED SHOES *Infectious INFECT 89CDS*		65	1
11 Nov 00	PIECES *Infectious INFECT 94CDS*		56	1
24 Feb 01	ALWAYS YOUR WAY *Infectious INFECT 95CDS*		31	2
19 May 01	GROUNDED *Infectious INFECT 97CD*		29	2
27 Jul 02	MOODSWINGS / THE GENTLE ART OF CHOKING *Infectious INFECT 107CDSX*		39	1

MYA *US, female vocalist – Mya Harrison (64 WEEKS)* pos/wks

27 Jun 98	● GHETTO SUPASTAR (THAT IS WHAT YOU ARE) *Interscope IND 95593* [1]		2	17
12 Dec 98	● TAKE ME THERE *Interscope IND 95620* [2]		7	9
10 Feb 01	● CASE OF THE EX *Interscope 4974772*		3	11
24 Mar 01	GIRLS DEM SUGAR *Virgin VUSCD 173* [3]		13	5
9 Jun 01	FREE *Interscope 4975002*		11	6
30 Jun 01	★ LADY MARMALADE *Interscope / Polydor 4975612* [4] ■ ▲		1	16

[1] Pras Michel featuring Ol' Dirty Bastard introducing Mya [2] BLACKstreet and Mya featuring Mase and Blinky Blink [3] Beenie Man featuring Mya [4] Christina Aguilera, Lil' Kim, Mya and Pink

Tim MYCROFT – *See SOUNDS NICE featuring Tim MYCROFT*

Alicia MYERS *US, female vocalist (3 WEEKS)* pos/wks

1 Sep 84	YOU GET THE BEST FROM ME (SAY, SAY, SAY) *MCA MCA 914*		58	3

Billie MYERS *UK, female vocalist (12 WEEKS)* pos/wks

11 Apr 98	● KISS THE RAIN *Universal UND 56182*		4	9
25 Jul 98	TELL ME *Universal UND 56201*		28	3

Richard MYHILL *UK, male vocalist (9 WEEKS)* pos/wks

1 Apr 78	IT TAKES TWO TO TANGO *Mercury 6007 167*		17	9

Alannah MYLES *Canada, female vocalist (17 WEEKS)* pos/wks

17 Mar 90	● BLACK VELVET *East West A 8742* ▲		2	15
16 Jun 90	LOVE IS *East West A 8918*		61	2

Marie MYRIAM *France, female vocalist (4 WEEKS)* pos/wks

28 May 77	L'OISEAU ET L'ENFANT *Polydor 2056 634*		42	4

MYRON *US male vocalist (1 WEEK)* pos/wks

22 Nov 97	WE CAN GET DOWN *Island Black Music CID 677*		74	1

MYSTERIANS – See ? (QUESTION MARK) and the MYSTERIANS

MYSTERY *Holland, male production duo (2 WEEKS)*

		pos/wks	
6 Oct 01	MYSTERY *Inferno CDFERN 42*	56	1
10 Aug 02	ALL I EVER WANTED (DEVOTION) *Xtravaganza XTRAV 33CDS*	57	1

MYSTI – See CAMOUFLAGE featuring MYSTI

MYSTIC MERLIN
US, male vocal / instrumental group (9 WEEKS)

		pos/wks	
26 Apr 80	JUST CAN'T GIVE YOU UP *Capitol CL 16133*	20	9

MYSTIC 3
UK / Italy, male production group (aka Blockster) (1 WEEK)

		pos/wks	
24 Jun 00	SOMETHING'S GOIN' ON *Rulin RULIN 2CDS*	63	1

MYSTICA *Israel, male production trio (2 WEEKS)*

		pos/wks	
24 Jan 98	EVER REST *Perfecto PERF 152CD*	62	1
9 May 98	AFRICAN HORIZON *Perfecto PERF 161CD*	59	1

MYSTIKAL *US, male rapper – Michael Tyler (17 WEEKS)*

		pos/wks	
9 Dec 00	SHAKE YA ASS *Jive 9251552*	30	5
17 Feb 01 ●	STUTTER *Jive 9251632* [1] ▲	7	8
3 Mar 01	DANGER (BEEN SO LONG) *Jive 9251722* [2]	28	3
23 Feb 02	BOUNCIN' BACK (BUMPIN' ME AGAINST THE WALL) *Jive 9253272*	45	1

[1] Joe featuring Mystikal [2] Mystikal featuring Nivea

See also Mariah CAREY

MYTOWN *Ireland, male vocal group (2 WEEKS)*

		pos/wks	
13 Mar 99	PARTY ALL NIGHT *Universal UND 56231*	22	2

MZ MAY – See DREEM TEEM

N-JOI
UK, male instrumental / production group (28 WEEKS)

		pos/wks	
27 Oct 90	ANTHEM *Deconstruction PB 44041*	45	5
2 Mar 91	ADRENALIN (EP) *Deconstruction PT 44344*	23	5
6 Apr 91 ●	ANTHEM (re-issue) *Deconstruction PB 44445*	8	8
22 Feb 92	LIVE IN MANCHESTER (PARTS 1 + 2) *Deconstruction PT 45252*	12	5
24 Jul 93	THE DRUMSTRUCK EP *Deconstruction 74321154832*	33	3
17 Dec 94	PAPILLON *Deconstruction 74321252132*	70	1
8 Jul 95	BAD THINGS *Deconstruction 74321277292*	57	1

Tracks on Adrenalin (EP): Adrenalin / The Kraken / Rhythm Zone / Phoenix. Tracks on The Drumstruck EP: The Void / Boom Bass / Drumstruck

NKOTB – See NEW KIDS ON THE BLOCK

N'n'G featuring KALLAGHAN
UK, male / female production / vocal group (6 WEEKS)

		pos/wks	
1 Apr 00	RIGHT BEFORE MY EYES *Urban Heat UHTCD 003*	12	6

N.O.R.E. *US, male rapper – Victor Santiago (7 WEEKS)*

		pos/wks	
21 Sep 02	NOTHIN' *Def Jam 639262*	11	7

NRG *UK, male DJ / production duo (2 WEEKS)*

		pos/wks	
29 Mar 97	NEVER LOST HIS HARDCORE *Top Banana TOPCD 04*	71	1
12 Dec 98	NEVER LOST HIS HARDCORE '98 (re-mix) *Top Banana TOPCD 010*	61	1

'N SYNC (441 [Top 500]) *Record-breaking Florida-based boy band: Justin Timberlake, Lance Bass, Chris Kirkpatrick, Josh Chasez and Joey Fatone. Their 2000 album 'No Strings Attached' sold a record 2.4 million in its first week in the US and, in one day, the group sold an unprecedented one million tour tickets grossing $40m (79 WEEKS)*

		pos/wks	
13 Sep 97	TEARIN' UP MY HEART *Arista 74321505152*	40	2
22 Nov 97	I WANT YOU BACK *Arista 74321541122*	62	1
27 Feb 99 ●	I WANT YOU BACK (re-issue) *Transcontinental / Northwestside 74321646972*	5	10
26 Jun 99 ●	TEARIN' UP MY HEART (re-issue) (re) *Northwestside / Arista 74321675832*	9	10
8 Jan 00	MUSIC OF MY HEART *Epic 6685272* [1]	34	3
11 Mar 00 ●	BYE BYE BYE *Jive 9250202*	3	8
22 Jul 00	I'LL NEVER STOP *Jive 9250762*	13	6
16 Sep 00 ●	IT'S GONNA BE ME *Jive 9251082* ▲	9	8
2 Dec 00	THIS I PROMISE YOU *Jive 9251302*	21	7
21 Jul 01 ●	POP *Jive 9252422*	9	8
8 Dec 01	GONE (re) *Jive 9252772*	24	4
27 Apr 02 ●	GIRLFRIEND *Jive 9253312* [2]	2	12+

[1] 'N Sync / Gloria Estefan [2] 'N Sync featuring Nelly

See also Justin TIMBERLAKE

NT GANG *Germany, male vocal / instrumental group (1 WEEK)*

		pos/wks	
2 Apr 88	WAM BAM *Cooltempo COOL 163*	71	1

N-TRANCE (426 [Top 500]) *Producers Dale Longworth and Kevin O'Toole are the nucleus of this multi-faceted Manchester act who emerged from the trance scene (81 WEEKS)*

		pos/wks	
7 May 94	SET YOU FREE *All Around the World CDGLOBE 124* [1]	39	4
22 Oct 94	TURN UP THE POWER *All Around the World CDGLOBE 125*	23	3
14 Jan 95 ●	SET YOU FREE (re-mix) *All Around the World CDGLOBE 126*	2	15
16 Sep 95 ●	STAYIN' ALIVE *All Around the World CDGLOBE 131* [2]	2	11
24 Feb 96	ELECTRONIC PLEASURE *All Around the World CDGLOBE 135*	11	4
5 Apr 97	D.I.S.C.O. *All Around the World CDGLOBE 153*	11	6
23 Aug 97	THE MIND OF THE MACHINE *All Around the World CDGLOBE 159*	15	4
1 Nov 97 ●	DA YA THINK I'M SEXY *All Around the World CDGLOBE 150* [3]	7	10
12 Sep 98	PARADISE CITY *All Around the World CDGLOBE 140*	28	3
19 Dec 98	TEARS IN THE RAIN *All Around the Globe CDGLOBE 185*	53	1
20 May 00	SHAKE YA BODY *All Around the World CDGLOBE 204*	37	1
22 Sep 01 ●	SET YOU FREE (2nd re-mix) *All Around the World CDGLOBE 242*	4	11
14 Sep 02 ●	FOREVER (re) *All Around the World CDGLOBE 257*	6	8

[1] N-Trance featuring Kelly Llorenna [2] N-Trance featuring Ricardo Da Force [3] N-Trance featuring Rod Stewart

Although she is vocalist on all versions of 'Set You Free', Kelly Llorenna is given label credit only on the first entry. Similarly, Ricardo da Force appears on several tracks but receives label credit only for 'Stayin' Alive'

N-TYCE *UK, female vocal group (15 WEEKS)*

		pos/wks	
5 Jul 97	HEY DJ! (PLAY THAT SONG) *Telstar CDSTAS 2885*	20	2
13 Sep 97	WE COME TO PARTY *Telstar CDSTAS 2915*	12	4
28 Feb 98	TELEFUNKIN' *Telstar CDSTAS 2944*	16	5
6 Jun 98	BOOM BOOM *Telstar CDSTAS 2971*	18	4

NWA *US, male rap group (15 WEEKS)*

		pos/wks	
9 Sep 89	EXPRESS YOURSELF (re) *Fourth & Broadway BRW 144*	26	9
1 Sep 90	GANGSTA, GANGSTA *Fourth & Broadway BRW 191*	70	1
10 Nov 90	100 MILES AND RUNNIN' *Fourth & Broadway BRW 200*	38	3
23 Nov 91	ALWAYZ INTO SOMETHIN' *Fourth & Broadway BRW 238*	60	2

'Express Yourself' made No.50 on its first visit and peaked at No.26 on re-entry in May 1990

Re-entries are listed as (re), (2re), (3re), etc which signifies that the hit re-entered the chart once, twice or three times, etc

NYCC *Germany, male rap trio (6 WEEKS)*   pos/wks

30 May 98	FIGHT FOR YOUR RIGHT (TO PARTY)		
	Control 0042645 CON	14	5
19 Sep 98	CAN YOU FEEL IT (ROCK DA HOUSE)		
	Control 0042785 CON	68	1

Jimmy NAIL (499) *Top 500* *Singer / songwriter, b. James Michael Aloysius Bradford, 1954, Newcastle, UK, whose R&B mixed with a Geordie take on country provided a flip-side to his acting career which included key characters in both 'Auf Wiedersehen Pet' and 'Spender'. His longest stay on the charts was courtesy of another TV series, 'Crocodile Shoes', in which he combined acting and singing (73 WEEKS)*   pos/wks

27 Apr 85 ●	LOVE DON'T LIVE HERE ANYMORE *Virgin VS 764*	3	11
11 Jul 92 ★	AIN'T NO DOUBT *East West YZ 686*	1	12
3 Oct 92	LAURA *East West YZ 702*	58	2
26 Nov 94	CROCODILE SHOES (2re) *East West YZ 867CD*	4	20
11 Feb 95	COWBOY DREAMS *East West YZ 878CD*	13	7
6 May 95	CALLING OUT YOUR NAME *East West YZ 935CD*	65	1
28 Oct 95	BIG RIVER *East West EW 008CD*	18	5
23 Dec 95	LOVE *East West EW 018CD*	33	4
3 Feb 96	BIG RIVER (re-mix) *East West EW 024CD*	72	2
16 Nov 96	COUNTRY BOY *East West EW 070CD*	25	8
21 Nov 98	THE FLAME STILL BURNS *London LONCD 420* [1]	47	1

[1] Jimmy Nail with Strange Fruit

NAKATOMI
UK, male / female production group (4 WEEKS)   pos/wks

7 Feb 98	CHILDREN OF THE NIGHT *Peach PCHCD 006*	47	2
26 Oct 02	CHILDREN OF THE NIGHT (re-mix) *Jive 9254212*	31	2

NAKED EYES *UK, male vocal / instrumental duo (3 WEEKS)*   pos/wks

23 Jul 83	ALWAYS SOMETHING THERE TO REMIND ME *RCA 348*	59	3

NALIN I.N.C. *Germany, male production duo (1 WEEK)*   pos/wks

28 Mar 98	PLANET VIOLET *Logic 74321565702*	51	1

See also NALIN & KANE

NALIN & KANE *Germany, male DJ / production duo – Andy Nalin and Harry Cane (6 WEEKS)*   pos/wks

1 Nov 97	BEACHBALL *ffrr FCD 318*	48	1
3 Oct 98	BEACHBALL (re-mix) *LONDON FCD349*	17	5

See also NALIN I.N.C.

NANA – See ARCHITECHS

NAPOLEON XIV
US, male vocalist – Jerry Samuels (10 WEEKS)   pos/wks

4 Aug 66 ●	THEY'RE COMING TO TAKE ME AWAY, HA-HAAA!		
	Warner Bros. WB 5831	4	10

NARADA – See Narada Michael WALDEN

NARCOTIC THRUST
UK, male / female production duo and female vocalist (3 WEEKS)   pos/wks

10 Aug 02	SAFE FROM HARM *ffrr FCD 406*	24	3

Michelle NARINE – See BIG BASS vs Michelle NARINE

NAS *US, male rapper – Nasir Jones (45 WEEKS)*   pos/wks

28 May 94	IT AIN'T HARD TO TELL *Columbia 6604702*	64	1
17 Aug 96	IF I RULED THE WORLD *Columbia 6634022*	12	7
25 Jan 97	STREET DREAMS *Columbia 6641302*	12	4
14 Jun 97	HEAD OVER HEELS *Epic 6645942* [1]	18	3
29 May 99	HATE ME NOW *Columbia 6672562* [2]	14	6
15 Jan 00	NASTRADAMUS *Columbia 6685572*	24	3
22 Jan 00	HOT BOYZ *Elektra E 7002CD* [3]	18	3
21 Apr 01	OOCHIE WALLY *Columbia 67010852* [4]	30	3
2 Feb 02	GOT UR SELF A ... (re) *Columbia 6723022*	30	5
13 Jul 02 ●	I'M GONNA BE ALRIGHT *Epic 6728442* [5]	3	10

[1] Allure featuring NAS [2] Nas featuring Puff Daddy [3] Missy 'Misdemeanor' Elliott featuring Nas, Eve and Q Tip [4] QB Finest featuring Nas & Bravehearts [5] Jennifer Lopez featuring Nas

Johnny NASH (282) *Top 500* *US singer / songwriter / actor and label co-owner, b. 19 Aug 1940, Texas. This versatile vocalist first charted in his homeland in 1957. After recording in Jamaica in the late 1960s, he helped to popularise reggae on both sides of the Atlantic and introduced the public to Bob Marley's songs (106 WEEKS)*   pos/wks

7 Aug 68 ●	HOLD ME TIGHT *Regal Zonophone RZ 3010*	5	16
8 Jan 69 ●	YOU GOT SOUL *Major Minor MM 586*	6	12
2 Apr 69 ●	CUPID (re) *Major Minor MM 603*	6	12
1 Apr 72	STIR IT UP *CBS 7800*	13	12
24 Jun 72 ●	I CAN SEE CLEARLY NOW *CBS 8113* ▲	5	15
7 Oct 72 ●	THERE ARE MORE QUESTIONS THAN ANSWERS *CBS 8351*	9	9
14 Jun 75 ★	TEARS ON MY PILLOW *CBS 3220*	1	11
11 Oct 75	LET'S BE FRIENDS *CBS 3597*	42	3
12 Jun 76	(WHAT A) WONDERFUL WORLD *Epic EPC 4294*	25	7
9 Nov 85	ROCK ME BABY *2000 AD FED 19*	47	4
15 Apr 89	I CAN SEE CLEARLY NOW (re-mix) *Epic JN 1*	54	5

Leigh NASH – See DELERIUM

NASHVILLE TEENS
UK, male vocal / instrumental group (37 WEEKS)   pos/wks

9 Jul 64 ●	TOBACCO ROAD *Decca F 11930*	6	13
22 Oct 64 ●	GOOGLE EYE *Decca F 12000*	10	11
4 Mar 65	FIND MY WAY BACK HOME *Decca F 12089*	34	6
20 May 65	THIS LITTLE BIRD *Decca F 12143*	38	4
3 Feb 66	THE HARD WAY (re) *Decca F 12316*	45	3

NATASHA *UK, female vocalist – Natasha England (16 WEEKS)*   pos/wks

5 Jun 82	IKO IKO *Towerbell TOW 22*	10	11
4 Sep 82	THE BOOM BOOM ROOM *Towerbell TOW 25*	44	5

Ultra NATE *US, female vocalist – Ultra Nate Wyche (39 WEEKS)*   pos/wks

9 Dec 89	IT'S OVER NOW *Eternal YZ 440*	62	3
23 Feb 91	IS IT LOVE? *Eternal YZ 509*	71	1
29 Jan 94	SHOW ME *Warner Bros. W 0219CD*	62	1
14 Jun 97 ●	FREE *AM:PM 5822432*	4	17
24 Jan 98	FREE (re-mix) *AM:PM 5825012*	33	2
18 Apr 98 ●	FOUND A CURE *AM:PM 5826452*	6	7
25 Jul 98	NEW KIND OF MEDICINE *AM:PM 5827492*	14	5
22 Jul 00	DESIRE *AM:PM CDAMPM133*	40	2
9 Jun 01	GET IT UP (THE FEELING) *AM:PM CDAMPM 140*	51	1

NATIONAL PHILHARMONIC ORCHESTRA – See James GALWAY

NATIVE *UK, male production duo (2 WEEKS)*   pos/wks

10 Feb 01	FEEL THE DRUMS *Slinky Music SLINKY 009 CD*	46	2

NATURAL *US, male vocal group (2 WEEKS)*   pos/wks

10 Aug 02	PUT YOUR ARMS AROUND ME *Ariola 74321947892*	32	2

NATURAL BORN CHILLERS
UK, male production duo – Arif Salih and Lee Parker (3 WEEKS)   pos/wks

1 Nov 97	ROCK THE FUNKY BEAT *East West EW 138CD1*	30	3

NATURAL BORN GROOVES *Belgium, male DJ / production duo – Burn Boon and Jaco van Rijsvijck (3 WEEKS)*   pos/wks

2 Nov 96	FORERUNNER *XL XLS 76CD*	64	1
19 Apr 97	GROOVEBIRD *Positiva CDTIV 75*	21	2

NATURAL LIFE
UK, male / female vocal / instrumental group (3 WEEKS)   pos/wks

7 Mar 92	NATURAL LIFE *Tribe NLIFE 3*	47	3

NATURAL SELECTION
US, male vocal / instrumental duo (2 WEEKS)   pos/wks
9 Nov 91   DO ANYTHING East West A 8724 ....69 2

NATURALS UK, male vocal / instrumental group (9 WEEKS)   pos/wks
20 Aug 64   I SHOULD HAVE KNOWN BETTER Parlophone R 5165..........24 9

David NAUGHTON US, male actor / vocalist (6 WEEKS)   pos/wks
25 Aug 79   MAKIN' IT RSO 32 ....44 6

NAUGHTY BY NATURE US, male rap group (18 WEEKS)   pos/wks
9 Nov 91   O.P.P. Big Life BLR 62 ....73 1
20 Jun 92   O.P.P. (re-issue) Big Life BLR 74 ....35 3
30 Jan 93   HIP HOP HOORAY Big Life BLRD 89 ....22 3
19 Jun 93   IT'S ON Big Life BLRD 99 ....48 2
27 Nov 93   HIP HOP HOORAY (re-mix) Big Life BLRDA 104 ....20 4
29 Apr 95   FEEL ME FLOW Big Life BLRD 115 ....23 3
11 Sep 99   JAMBOREE Arista 74321692882 [1] 51 1
19 Oct 02   FEELS GOOD (DON'T WORRY BOUT A THING)
            Island CID 806 [2] 44 1

[1] Naughty By Nature featuring Zhane [2] Naughty By Nature featuring 3LW

NAVIGATOR – See FREESTYLERS

Maria NAYLER UK, female vocalist (26 WEEKS)   pos/wks
9 Mar 96   BE AS ONE Deconstruction 74321342962 [1] 17 4
16 Nov 96 ● ONE & ONE Deconstruction 74321427692 [2] 3 17
7 Mar 98   NAKED AND SACRED Deconstruction 74321534242..........32 3
5 Sep 98   WILL YOU BE WITH ME / LOVE IS THE GOD
            Deconstruction 74321591772 ....65 1
27 May 00   ANGRY SKIES Deconstruction 74321759492 ....42 1

[1] Sasha and Maria [2] Robert Miles featuring Maria Nayler

NAZARETH (486 Top 500) Earthy, versatile rock band formed 1969 in
Dunfermline, Scotland, which throughout its 30-year career has been led by
Dan McCafferty (v). Sole US Top 10 hit 'Love Hurts' also spent a record-
shattering 60 weeks on the Norwegian chart (75 WEEKS)   pos/wks
5 May 73 ● BROKEN DOWN ANGEL Mooncrest MOON 1 ....9 11
21 Jul 73 ● BAD BAD BOY Mooncrest MOON 9 ....10 9
13 Oct 73   THIS FLIGHT TONIGHT Mooncrest MOON 14 ....11 13
23 Mar 74   SHANGHAI'D IN SHANGHAI Mooncrest MOON 22 ....41 4
14 Jun 75   MY WHITE BICYCLE Mooncrest MOON 47....................14 8
15 Nov 75   HOLY ROLLER Mountain TOP 3 ....36 4
24 Sep 77   HOT TRACKS (EP) Mountain NAZ 1 ....15 11
18 Feb 78   GONE DEAD TRAIN Mountain NAZ 002 ....49 2
13 May 78   PLACE IN YOUR HEART (re) Mountain TOP 37 ....70 2
27 Jan 79   MAY THE SUNSHINE Mountain NAZ 003 ....22 8
28 Jul 79   STAR Mountain TOP 45 ....54 3

Tracks on Hot Tracks (EP): Love Hurts / This Flight Tonight / Broken Down Angel /
Hair of the Dog

NAZLYN – See M-BEAT

Me'Shell NDEGEOCELLO
US, female vocalist / instrumentalist – bass (5 WEEKS)   pos/wks
12 Feb 94   IF THAT'S YOUR BOYFRIEND (HE WASN'T LAST NIGHT)
            Maverick W 0223CD1 ....74 1
3 Sep 94   WILD NIGHT Mercury MERCD 409 [1] 34 3
1 Mar 97   NEVER MISS THE WATER Reprise W 0393CD [2] 59 1

[1] John Mellencamp featuring Me'Shell Ndegeocello [2] Chaka Khan featuring
Me'Shell Ndegeocello

Youssou N'DOUR Senegal, male vocalist (35 WEEKS)   pos/wks
3 Jun 89   SHAKIN' THE TREE Virgin VS 1167 [1] 61 3
22 Dec 90   SHAKIN' THE TREE (re-issue)
            Virgin VS 1322 [1] 57 4
25 Jun 94 ● 7 SECONDS (re) Columbia 6605082 [2] 3 25

14 Jan 95   UNDECIDED Columbia 6609712 ....53 2
10 Oct 98   HOW COME Interscope IND 95598 [3] 52 1

[1] Youssou N'Dour and Peter Gabriel [2] Youssou N'Dour (featuring Neneh Cherry)
[3] Youssou N'Dour and Canibus

The re-issue of 'Shaking the Tree' was listed with its flip side, 'Solsbury Hill' by
Peter Gabriel

NEARLY GOD
UK, male / female vocal / instrumental group (2 WEEKS)   pos/wks
20 Apr 96   POEMS Durban Poison DPCD 3 ....28 2

Terry NEASON UK, female vocalist (1 WEEK)   pos/wks
25 Jun 94   LIFEBOAT WEA YZ 830 ....72 1

NEBULA II UK, male instrumental / production group (3 WEEKS) pos/wks
1 Feb 92   SEANCE / ATHEAMA Reinforced RIVET 1211 ....55 2
16 May 92   FLATLINERS J4M 12NEBULA 2 ....54 1

NED'S ATOMIC DUSTBIN
UK, male vocal / instrumental group (24 WEEKS)   pos/wks
14 Jul 90   KILL YOUR TELEVISION Chapter 22 CHAP 48 ....53 2
27 Oct 90   UNTIL YOU FIND OUT Chapter 22 CHAP 52 ....51 2
9 Mar 91   HAPPY Columbia 6566807 ....16 4
21 Sep 91   TRUST Furtive 6574627 ....21 4
10 Oct 92   NOT SLEEPING AROUND Furtive 6583866 ....19 3
5 Dec 92   INTACT Furtive 6588166 ....36 6
25 Mar 95   ALL I ASK OF MYSELF IS THAT I HOLD TOGETHER
            Furtive 6613565 ....33 2
15 Jul 95   STUCK Furtive 6620562 ....64 1

NEEDLE DAMAGE – See DJ DAN presents NEEDLE DAMAGE

Joey NEGRO UK, male producer – Dave Lee (15 WEEKS)   pos/wks
16 Nov 91   DO WHAT YOU FEEL Ten TEN 391 [1] 36 3
21 Dec 91   REACHIN' (re-mix) Republic LIC 160 [1] 70 1
18 Jul 92   ENTER YOUR FANTASY (EP) Ten TEN 397 ....35 3
25 Sep 93   WHAT HAPPENED TO THE MUSIC Virgin VSCD 1466 ......51 2
19 Feb 00 ● MUST BE THE MUSIC Incentive CENT 4CDS [2] 8 5
16 Sep 00   SATURDAY Yola YOLA CDX03 [2] 41 1

[1] Joey Negro presents Phase II [2] Joey Negro featuring Taka Boom

Tracks on Enter Your Fantasy (EP): Love Fantasy / Get Up / Enter Your Mind /
Everybody

See also Z FACTOR; Li KWAN; PHASE II; RAVEN MAIZE; AKABU featuring Linda
CLIFFORD; JAKATTA; HED BOYS; IL PADRINOS

neil UK, male actor / hippie / vocalist – Nigel Planer (10 WEEKS) pos/wks
14 Jul 84 ● HOLE IN MY SHOE WEA YZ 10................................2 10

Vince NEIL US, male vocalist (1 WEEK)   pos/wks
3 Oct 92   YOU'RE INVITED (BUT YOUR FRIEND CAN'T COME)
            Hollywood HWD 123 ....63 1

See also MÖTLEY CRÜE

NEJA Italy, female vocalist (1 WEEK)   pos/wks
26 Sep 98   RESTLESS (I KNOW YOU KNOW) Panorama CDPAN 1..........47 1

NEK Italy, male vocalist (1 WEEK)   pos/wks
29 Aug 98   LAURA Coalition COLA 054CD 59 1

NELLY US, male rapper – Cornell Haynes (69 WEEKS)   pos/wks
11 Nov 00 ● (HOT S**T) COUNTRY GRAMMAR Universal MCSTD 40242........7 9
24 Feb 01   EI Universal MCSTD 40249 ....11 5
19 May 01 ● RIDE WIT ME Universal MCSTD 40252 [1] 3 12
15 Sep 01   BATTER UP Universal MCSTD 40261 [2] 28 3
27 Oct 01   WHERE THE PARTY AT? Columbia MCSTD 6719012 [3] 25 3

Re-entries are listed as (re), (2re), (3re), etc which signifies that the hit re-entered the

27 Apr 02 ● GIRLFRIEND *Jive 9253312* 4	2	12
29 Jun 02 ● HOT IN HERRE *Universal MCSTD 40289* ▲	4	15
26 Oct 02 ★ DILEMMA *Universal MCSTD 40299* 5 ■ ▲	1	10+

1 Nelly featuring City Spud 2 Nelly and St Lunatics 3 Jagged Edge featuring Nelly 4 'N Sync featuring Nelly 5 Nelly featuring Kelly Rowland

NELSON *US, male vocal duo (3 WEEKS)*

pos/wks

27 Oct 90	(CAN'T LIVE WITHOUT YOUR) LOVE AND AFFECTION *DGC GEF 82* ▲	54	3

Bill NELSON *UK, male vocalist / instrumentalist – guitar and synthesizer (12 WEEKS)*

pos/wks

24 Feb 79	FURNITURE MUSIC *Harvest HAR 5176* 1	59	3
5 May 79	REVOLT INTO STYLE *Harvest HAR 5183* 1	69	2
5 Jul 80	DO YOU DREAM IN COLOUR? *Cocteau COQ 1*	52	4
13 Jun 81	YOUTH OF NATION ON FIRE *Mercury WILL 2*	73	3

1 Bill Nelson's Red Noise

See also BE BOP DELUXE

Phyllis NELSON *US, female vocalist (24 WEEKS)*

pos/wks

23 Feb 85 ★ MOVE CLOSER *Carrere CAR 337*	1	21
21 May 94	MOVE CLOSER (re-issue) *EMI CDEMCT 9*	34	3

Ricky NELSON 152 Top 500 *TV star turned teen idol and later singer / songwriter b. 8 May 1940, New Jersey, d. 31 Dec 1985. He was virtually raised on a US radio / TV family show. In the 1950s, he enjoyed sales on a par with Elvis Presley and Pat Boone. Both his father and his two sons also topped the US chart (1935 and 1990) (150 WEEKS)*

pos/wks

21 Feb 58	STOOD UP (re) *London HLP 8542*	27	2
22 Aug 58 ● POOR LITTLE FOOL (re) *London HLP 8670* ▲	4	14
7 Nov 58 ● SOMEDAY *London HLP 8732*	9	13
21 Nov 58	I GOT A FEELING *London HLP 8732*	27	1
17 Apr 59 ● IT'S LATE *London HLP 8817*	3	20
15 May 59	NEVER BE ANYONE ELSE BUT YOU (re) *London HLP 8817*	14	10
4 Sep 59	SWEETER THAN YOU *London HLP 8927*	19	3
11 Sep 59	JUST A LITTLE TOO MUCH *London HLP 8927*	11	8
15 Jan 60	I WANNA BE LOVED *London HLP 9021*	30	1
7 Jul 60	YOUNG EMOTIONS *London HLP 9121*	48	1
1 Jun 61 ● HELLO MARY LOU / TRAVELLIN' MAN *London HLP 9347* ▲	2	18
16 Nov 61	EVERLOVIN' *London HLP 9440* 1	23	5
29 Mar 62	YOUNG WORLD *London HLP 9524*	19	13
30 Aug 62	TEENAGE IDOL *London HLP 9583* 1	39	4
17 Jan 63	IT'S UP TO YOU *London HLP 9648* 1	22	9
17 Oct 63	FOOLS RUSH IN *Brunswick 05895* 1	12	9
30 Jan 64	FOR YOU *Brunswick 05900* 1	14	10
21 Oct 72	GARDEN PARTY *MCA MU 1165* 1	41	4
24 Aug 91	HELLO MARY LOU (GOODBYE HEART) (re-issue) *Liberty EMCT 2*	45	5

1 Rick Nelson

Sandy NELSON *US, male instrumentalist – drums (42 WEEKS)*

pos/wks

6 Nov 59 ● TEEN BEAT (re) *Top Rank JAR 197*	9	12
14 Dec 61 ● LET THERE BE DRUMS *London HLP 9466*	3	16
22 Mar 62	DRUMS ARE MY BEAT *London HLP 9521*	30	6
7 Jun 62	DRUMMIN' UP A STORM *London HLP 9558*	39	8

Shara NELSON *UK, female vocalist (23 WEEKS)*

pos/wks

24 Jul 93	DOWN THAT ROAD *Cooltempo CDCOOL 275*	19	6
18 Sep 93	ONE GOODBYE IN TEN *Cooltempo CDCOOL 279*	21	5
12 Feb 94	UPTIGHT *Cooltempo CDCOOL 286*	19	5
4 Jun 94	NOBODY *Cooltempo CDCOOL 290*	49	1
10 Sep 94	INSIDE OUT / DOWN THAT ROAD (re-mix) *Cooltempo CDCOOLX 295*	34	3
16 Sep 95	ROUGH WITH THE SMOOTH *Cooltempo CDCOOL 311*	30	2
5 Dec 98	SENSE OF DANGER *Pagan PAGAN 024CDS* 1	61	1

1 Presence featuring Shara Nelson

See also MASSIVE ATTACK

IVOR NOVELLO AWARDS

■ The annual Ivor Novello Awards are internationally respected as Britain's major platform for recognising its songwriting talents.

The Ivors are presented by the British Academy of Composers and Songwriters in association with the Performing Rights Society. The winners are chosen by committees of voters made up of composers from across the range of musical genres. The academy began its campaigning life as the British Songwriters Protective Association in 1947 in response to the domination of American pop music in the UK, particularly on the airwaves of the BBC. The PRS has guaranteed the financial support necessary to stage the awards since 1974.

Ivor Novello, the British musician and songwriter whose memory is honoured by these awards, died in 1951, hours after starring in a performance of his own King's Rhapsody. Paul McCartney remains top dog in the numbers stakes with 20 awards, followed by John Lennon with 15 and then Andrew Lloyd Webber with 14.

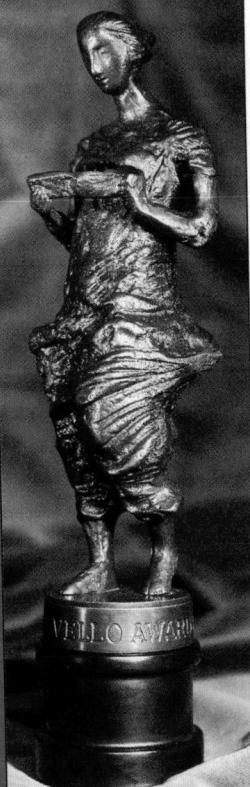

The Ivor Novello award: a bronze, 12-inch, 7lb 2oz statuette depicting Euterpe, the Greek muse of music and lyric poetry

The top award winners are:

20	PAUL McCARTNEY	8	PETE WATERMAN
15	JOHN LENNON	7	LIONEL BART
14	ANDREW LLOYD WEBBER	7	LESLIE BRICUSSE
12	TIM RICE	6	PHIL COLLINS
11	BARRY GIBB	6	GEORGE FENTON
11	ROBIN GIBB	6	MICHAEL KAMEN
11	ELTON JOHN	6	GEORGE MICHAEL
10	MAURICE GIBB	5	MIKE BATT
8	MATT AITKEN	5	DON BLACK
8	TONY MACAULEY	5	ROGER COOK
8	STING	5	ROGER GREENAWAY
8	MIKE STOCK	5	BARRY MASON
8	BERNIE TAUPIN	5	LES REED
		5	PADDY ROBERTS

Shelley NELSON – See TIN TIN OUT

Willie NELSON US, male vocalist (13 WEEKS)

		pos/wks
31 Jul 82	ALWAYS ON MY MIND CBS A 2511	49 3
7 Apr 84	TO ALL THE GIRLS I'VE LOVED BEFORE CBS A 4252 [1]	17 10

[1] Julio Iglesias and Willie Nelson

NENA Germany, female / male vocal / instrumental group – lead vocal Gabriele (Nena) Kerner (14 WEEKS)

		pos/wks
4 Feb 84	★ 99 RED BALLOONS Epic A 4074	1 12
5 May 84	JUST A DREAM Epic H 3249	70 2

NEPTUNES – See PUFF DADDY

N*E*R*D US, male vocal / production trio (6 WEEKS)

		pos/wks
9 Jun 01	LAPDANCE Virgin VUSCD 196 [1]	33 2
10 Aug 02	ROCK STAR Virgin VUSCD 253	15 4

[1] N*E*R*D featuring Lee Harvey and Vita

NERIO'S DUBWORK – See Darryl PANDY

Frances NERO US, female vocalist (9 WEEKS)

		pos/wks
13 Apr 91	FOOTSTEPS FOLLOWING ME Debut DEBT 3109	17 9

NERO and the GLADIATORS
UK, male instrumental group (6 WEEKS)

		pos/wks
23 Mar 61	ENTRY OF THE GLADIATORS (re) Decca F 11329	37 5
27 Jul 61	IN THE HALL OF THE MOUNTAIN KING Decca F 11367	48 1

Ann NESBY US, female vocalist (3 WEEKS)

		pos/wks
21 Dec 96	WITNESS (EP) A&M:PM 5875612	42 2
17 May 97	HOLD ON (EP) A&M:PM 5822332	75 1

Tracks on Witness (EP): Can I Get a Witness I (mix) I In the Spirit I I'm Still Wearing Your Name. Tracks on Hold On (EP): Hold On (Mousse T's Uplifting Garage Edit) I Hold On (Mousse T's Hard Soul Remix) I Hold On (Klub Head Mix) I This Weekend (Laidback Mix)

Michael NESMITH US, male vocalist (6 WEEKS)

		pos/wks
26 Mar 77	RIO Island WIP 6373	28 6

See also MONKEES

NETWORK UK, male vocal / instrumental group (4 WEEKS)

		pos/wks
12 Dec 92	BROKEN WINGS Chrysalis CHS 3923	46 4

NEVADA UK, male / female vocal / instrumental group (1 WEEK)

		pos/wks
8 Jan 83	IN THE BLEAK MID WINTER Polydor POSP 203	71 1

Robbie NEVIL US, male vocalist (24 WEEKS)

		pos/wks
20 Dec 86	● C'EST LA VIE Manhattan MT 14	3 11
2 May 87	DOMINOES Manhattan MT 19	26 6
11 Jul 87	WOT'S IT TO YA Manhattan MT 24	43 7

Aaron NEVILLE – See Linda RONSTADT; NEVILLE BROTHERS

NEVILLE BROTHERS
US, male vocal / instrumental group (7 WEEKS)

		pos/wks
25 Nov 89	WITH GOD ON OUR SIDE A&M AM 545	47 6
7 Jul 90	BIRD ON A WIRE A&M AM 568	72 1

Jason NEVINS US, male DJ / producer (24 WEEKS)

		pos/wks
21 Feb 98	IT'S LIKE THAT (German import) Columbia 6652932 [1]	63 3
14 Mar 98	IT'S LIKE THAT (US import) Columbia 6652932 [1]	65 1
21 Mar 98	★ IT'S LIKE THAT Sm:)e Communications SM 90652 [1] ◆ ■	1 16
18 Apr 98	IT'S TRICKY (import) Epidrome EPD 6656982 [1]	74 1
26 Jun 99	INSANE IN THE BRAIN INCredible INCRL 17CD [2]	19 3

[1] Run-DMC vs Jason Nevins [2] Jason Nevins vs Cypress Hill

NEW ATLANTIC UK, male instrumental / production duo – Richard Lloyd and Cameron Saunders (15 WEEKS)

		pos/wks
29 Feb 92	I KNOW 3 Beat 3BT 1	12 7
3 Oct 92	INTO THE FUTURE 3 Beat 3BT 2 [1]	70 1
13 Feb 93	TAKE OFF SOME TIME 3 Beat 3BTCD 14	64 1
26 Nov 94	THE SUNSHINE AFTER THE RAIN Ffrreedom TABCD 223 [2]	26 6

[1] New Atlantic featuring Linda Wright [2] New Atlantic / U4EA featuring Berri

'The Sunshine After the Rain' was re-issued in 1995, credited simply to the vocalist Berri

NEW BOHEMIANS – See Edie BRICKELL and the NEW BOHEMIANS

NEW EDITION US, male vocal group (36 WEEKS)

		pos/wks
16 Apr 83	★ CANDY GIRL London LON 21	1 13
13 Aug 83	POPCORN LOVE London LON 31	43 5
23 Feb 85	MR TELEPHONE MAN MCA MCA 938	19 9
15 Apr 89	CRUCIAL MCA MCA 23934	70 1
10 Aug 96	HIT ME OFF MCA MCSTD 48014	20 4
7 Jun 97	SOMETHING ABOUT YOU MCA MCSTD 48032	16 4

See also BELL BIV DEVOE; Ralph TRESVANT; Bobby BROWN; Johnny GILL

NEW FOUND GLORY
US, male / female vocal group (5 WEEKS)

		pos/wks
16 Jun 01	HIT OR MISS (WAITED TOO LONG) MCA 1558232	58 1
3 Aug 02	MY FRIENDS OVER YOU MCA MCSTD 40286	30 3
19 Oct 02	HEAD ON COLLISION MCA MCSTD 40298	64 1

A NEW GENERATION
UK, male vocal / instrumental group (5 WEEKS)

		pos/wks
26 Jun 68	SMOKEY BLUES AWAY Spark SRL 1007	38 5

NEW KIDS ON THE BLOCK (357) Top 500

Highest earning boy band of all time: Jordan and Jon Knight, Donnie Wahlberg, Danny Wood, Joey McIntyre. Formed Boston, US, by producer / manager Maurice Starr as pop version of his act New Edition. In 1990, they grossed a reported $861m and became the first group to score eight UK Top 10 entries in a year (90 WEEKS)

		pos/wks
16 Sep 89	HANGIN' TOUGH CBS BLOCK 1	52 4
11 Nov 89	★ YOU GOT IT (THE RIGHT STUFF) CBS BLOCK 2	1 13
6 Jan 90	★ HANGIN' TOUGH (re-issue) CBS BLOCK 3 ▲	1 9
17 Mar 90	● I'LL BE LOVING YOU (FOREVER) CBS BLOCK 4 ▲	5 8
12 May 90	COVER GIRL CBS BLOCK 5	4 8
16 Jun 90	● STEP BY STEP CBS BLOCK 6 ▲	2 7
4 Aug 90	● TONIGHT CBS BLOCK 7	3 10
13 Oct 90	● LET'S TRY AGAIN / DIDN'T I BLOW YOUR MIND CBS BLOCK 8	8 5
8 Dec 90	● THIS ONE'S FOR THE CHILDREN CBS BLOCK 9	9 7
9 Feb 91	GAMES CBS 6566267	14 4
18 May 91	CALL IT WHAT YOU WANT Columbia 6567857	12 5
14 Dec 91	● IF YOU GO AWAY Columbia 6576667	9 5
19 Feb 94	DIRTY DAWG Columbia 6600362 [1]	27 3
26 Mar 94	NEVER LET YOU GO Columbia 6602072 [1]	42 2

[1] NKOTB

NEW MODEL ARMY
UK, male vocal / instrumental group (33 WEEKS)

		pos/wks
27 Apr 85	NO REST EMI NMA 1	28 5
3 Aug 85	BETTER THAN THEM / NO SENSE EMI NMA 2	49 2
30 Nov 85	BRAVE NEW WORLD EMI NMA 3	57 1
8 Nov 86	51ST STATE EMI NMA 4	71 2
28 Feb 87	POISON STREET EMI NMA 5	64 1
26 Sep 87	WHITE COATS (EP) EMI NMA 6	50 3
21 Jan 89	STUPID QUESTIONS EMI NMA 7	31 3
11 Mar 89	VAGABONDS EMI NMA 8	37 3
10 Jun 89	GREEN AND GREY EMI NMA 9	37 3
8 Sep 90	GET ME OUT EMI NMA 10	34 3
3 Nov 90	PURITY EMI NMA 11	61 2
8 Jun 91	SPACE EMI NMA 12	39 2

Re-entries are listed as (re). (2re). (3re). etc which signifies that the hit re-entered the chart

| 20 Feb 93 | HERE COMES THE WAR *Epic 6589352* | 25 | 2 |
| 24 Jul 93 | LIVING IN THE ROSE (THE BALLADS EP) *Epic 6592492* | 51 | 1 |

Better Than Them / No Sense are the lead tracks from The Acoustic EP which included the following tracks: Better Than Them / No Sense / Adrenalin / Trust. Tracks on White Coats (EP): White Coats / The Charge / Chinese Whispers / My Country. Tracks on Living in the Rose (The Ballads EP): Living in the Rose / Drummy B / Marry the Sea / Sleepwalking

NEW MUSIK *UK, male vocal / instrumental group (27 WEEKS)*

pos/wks

6 Oct 79	STRAIGHT LINES *GTO GT 255*	53	5
19 Jan 80	LIVING BY NUMBERS *GTO GT 261*	13	8
26 Apr 80	THIS WORLD OF WATER *GTO GT 268*	31	7
12 Jul 80	SANCTUARY *GTO GT 275*	31	7

NEW ORDER ⟨ 98 ⟩ Top 500

Innovative Mancunian group featuring three former members of critically acclaimed Joy Division: Bernard Sumner (v/g), Peter Hook (b), Stephen Morris (d), and augmented by Gillian Gilbert (k). 'Blue Monday' remains the UK's biggest-selling 12-inch single of all time. The band was the only new entry in the 2002 / 2003 British Hit Singles All-Time Top 100 Acts listing. Best-selling single (all formats): 'Blue Monday' 1,001,400 (191 WEEKS)

pos/wks

14 Mar 81	CEREMONY *Factory FAC 33*	34	5
3 Oct 81	PROCESSION / EVERYTHING'S GONE GREEN *Factory FAC 53*	38	5
22 May 82	TEMPTATION *Factory FAC 63*	29	7
19 Mar 83 ●	BLUE MONDAY (2re) *Factory FAC 73* ◆	9	38
3 Sep 83	CONFUSION *Factory FAC 93*	12	7
28 Apr 84	THIEVES LIKE US *Factory FAC 103*	18	5
25 May 85	THE PERFECT KISS *Factory FAC 123*	46	4
9 Nov 85	SUB-CULTURE *Factory FAC 133*	63	4
29 Mar 86	SHELLSHOCK *Factory FAC 143*	28	5
27 Sep 86	STATE OF THE NATION *Factory FAC 153*	30	3
27 Sep 86	THE PEEL SESSIONS (1ST JUNE 1982) *Strange Fruit SFPS 001*	54	1
15 Nov 86	BIZARRE LOVE TRIANGLE *Factory FAC 163*	56	2
1 Aug 87 ●	TRUE FAITH *Factory FAC 183/7*	4	10
19 Dec 87	TOUCHED BY THE HAND OF GOD *Factory FAC 1937*	20	7
7 May 88 ●	BLUE MONDAY (re-mix) *Factory FAC 737*	3	11
10 Dec 88	FINE TIME *Factory FAC 2237*	11	8
11 Mar 89	ROUND AND ROUND *Factory FAC 2637*	21	7
9 Sep 89	RUN 2 *Factory FAC 273*	49	2
2 Jun 90 ★	WORLD IN MOTION . . . *Factory / MCA FAC 2937* [1]	1	12
17 Apr 93 ●	REGRET *Centredate Co. NUOCD 1*	4	7
3 Jul 93	RUINED IN A DAY *Centredate Co. NUOCD 2*	22	4
4 Sep 93	WORLD (THE PRICE OF LOVE) *Centredate Co. NUOCD 3*	13	5
18 Dec 93	SPOOKY *Centredate Co. NUOCD 4*	22	4
19 Nov 94 ●	TRUE FAITH (re-mix) *Centredate Co. NUOCD 5*	9	8
21 Jan 95	NINETEEN63 *London NUOCD 6*	21	4
5 Aug 95	BLUE MONDAY (2nd) (re-mix) *London NUOCD 7*	17	4
25 Aug 01 ●	CRYSTAL *London NUOCD 8*	8	4
1 Dec 01	60 MILES AN HOUR *London NUOCD 9*	29	2
27 Apr 02	HERE TO STAY *London NUOCD 11*	15	3
15 Jun 02	WORLD IN MOTION (re-issue) *London NUDOCD 12* [1]	43	2
30 Nov 02	CONFUSION (re-mix) *Whacked WACKT 002CD* [2]	64	1

[1] Englandneworder [2] Arthur Baker vs New Order

Group was male only on first hit. 'Blue Monday''s first visit to the chart peaked at No.12 with the first re-entry making No.9 in Oct 1983 and the second peaking at No.52 after re-entering in Jan 1984. 'Blue Monday' in 1988 is a re-mixed version of the original 1983 hit which was made available on seven-inch for the first time, hence the slight difference in catalogue number. Sales for the re-mix and the original were combined from 7 May 1988 onwards when calculating its chart position. Tracks on The Peel Sessions (1st June 1982) EP: Turn the Heater On / We All Stand / Too Late / 5-8-6

See also JOY DIVISION; MONACO; ELECTRONIC; OTHER TWO

NEW ORLEANS JAZZMEN – *See Terry LIGHTFOOT'S NEW ORLEANS JAZZMEN*

NEW POWER GENERATION
US, male / female vocal / instrumental group (64 WEEKS)

pos/wks

31 Aug 91 ●	GETT OFF *Paisley Park W 0056* [1]	4	8
21 Sep 91	CREAM *Paisley Park W 0061* [1] ▲	15	7
7 Dec 91	DIAMONDS AND PEARLS *Paisley Park W 0075* [1]	25	6

28 Mar 92	MONEY DON'T MATTER 2 NIGHT *Paisley Park W 0091* [1]	19	5
27 Jun 92	THUNDER *Paisley Park W 0113* [1]	28	3
18 Jul 92 ●	SEXY MF / STROLLIN' *Paisley Park W 0123* [1]	4	7
10 Oct 92 ●	MY NAME IS PRINCE *Paisley Park W 0132* [1]	7	5
14 Nov 92	MY NAME IS PRINCE (re-mix) *Paisley Park W 0142T* [1]	51	1
5 Dec 92	7 *Paisley Park W 0147* [1]	27	6
13 Mar 93	THE MORNING PAPERS *Paisley Park W 0162CD* [1]	52	3
1 Apr 95	GET WILD *NPG 0061045*	19	4
19 Aug 95	THE GOOD LIFE (re) *NPG 0061515*	15	8
21 Nov 98	COME ON *RCA 74321634722*	65	1

[1] Prince and the New Power Generation

'The Good Life' peaked at No.29 on its first visit before re-entering at the peak position in Jul 1995

See also PRINCE

NEW RADICALS *US, male vocalist – Gregg Alexander (18 WEEKS)*

pos/wks

| 3 Apr 99 ● | YOU GET WHAT YOU GIVE *MCA MCSTD 48111* | 5 | 17 |
| 25 Sep 99 | SOMEDAY WE'LL KNOW *MCA MCSTD 40217* | 48 | 1 |

NEW SEEKERS ⟨ 170 ⟩ Top 500

Anglo-Australian vocal group formed by ex-Seeker Keith Potger with Eve Graham, Lyn Paul, Peter Doyle, Paul Layton and Marty Kristian. Hits included a Coca-Cola advertisement and a Eurovision entry. The group sold more than 25 million records worldwide and equalled the eight Top 20 entries by The Seekers. Biggest-selling single 'I'd Like to Teach the World to Sing' 990,000 (143 WEEKS)

pos/wks

17 Oct 70	WHAT HAVE THEY DONE TO MY SONG MA (re) *Philips 6006 027*	44	2
10 Jul 71 ●	NEVER ENDING SONG OF LOVE *Philips 6006 125*	2	19
18 Dec 71 ★	I'D LIKE TO TEACH THE WORLD TO SING (IN PERFECT HARMONY) *Polydor 2058 184*	1	21
4 Mar 72 ●	BEG, STEAL OR BORROW *Polydor 2058 201*	2	13
10 Jun 72 ●	CIRCLES *Polydor 2058 242*	4	16
2 Dec 72	COME SOFTLY TO ME *Polydor 2058 315* [1]	20	11
24 Feb 73	PINBALL WIZARD – SEE ME, FEEL ME (MEDLEY) *Polydor 2058 338*	16	8
7 Apr 73	NEVERTHELESS (I'M IN LOVE WITH YOU) *Polydor 2068 340* [2]	34	5
16 Jun 73	GOODBYE IS JUST ANOTHER WORD *Polydor 2058 368*	36	5
24 Nov 73 ★	YOU WON'T FIND ANOTHER FOOL LIKE ME *Polydor 2058 421* [3]	1	16
9 Mar 74	I GET A LITTLE SENTIMENTAL OVER YOU *Polydor 2058 439* [3] 5	9
14 Aug 76	IT'S SO NICE (TO HAVE YOU HOME) *CBS 4391*	44	4
29 Jan 77	I WANNA GO BACK *CBS 4786*	25	4
15 Jul 78	ANTHEM (ONE DAY IN EVERY WEEK) *CBS 6413*	21	10

[1] New Seekers featuring Marty Kristian [2] Eve Graham and The New Seekers
[3] New Seekers featuring Lyn Paul

NEW TONE AGE FAMILY – *See Dread FLIMSTONE and the MODERN TONE AGE FAMILY*

NEW VAUDEVILLE BAND
UK, male vocal / instrumental group (43 WEEKS)

pos/wks

8 Sep 66 ●	WINCHESTER CATHEDRAL *Fontana TF 741* ▲	4	19
26 Jan 67 ●	PEEK-A-BOO *Fontana TF 784* [1]	7	11
11 May 67	FINCHLEY CENTRAL *Fontana TF 824*	11	9
2 Aug 67	GREEN STREET GREEN *Fontana TF 853*	37	4

[1] New Vaudeville Band featuring Tristram

NEW VISION *US, male vocal / instrumental duo –*
Samuel Morales and Albert Cabrerra (2 WEEKS)

pos/wks

| 29 Jan 00 | (JUST) YOU AND ME *AM:PM CDAMPM 128* | 23 | 2 |

NEW WORLD
Australia, male vocal / instrumental group (53 WEEKS)

pos/wks

27 Feb 71	ROSE GARDEN *RAK 111*	15	11
3 Jul 71 ●	TOM-TOM TURNAROUND *RAK 117*	6	15
4 Dec 71	KARA, KARA *RAK 123*	17	13
13 May 72 ●	SISTER JANE *RAK 130*	9	13
12 May 73	ROOFTOP SINGING *RAK 148*	50	1

NEW YORK CITY US, male vocal group (11 WEEKS)

		pos/wks
21 Jul 73	I'M DOIN' FINE NOW RCA 2351	20 11

NEW YORK SKYY
US, male / female vocal / instrumental group (2 WEEKS)

		pos/wks
16 Jan 82	LET'S CELEBRATE (re) Epic EPC A 1898	67 2

NEWBEATS US, male vocal group (22 WEEKS)

		pos/wks
10 Sep 64	BREAD AND BUTTER Hickory 1269	15 9
23 Oct 71 ●	RUN, BABY, RUN London HLE 10341	10 13

Booker NEWBERRY III US, male vocalist (11 WEEKS)

		pos/wks
28 May 83 ●	LOVE TOWN Polydor POSP 613	6 8
8 Oct 83	TEDDY BEAR Polydor POSP 637	44 3

Mickey NEWBURY US, male vocalist d. 28 Sep 2002 (5 WEEKS)

		pos/wks
1 Jul 72	AMERICAN TRILOGY Elektra K 12047	42 5

NEWCLEUS US, male rap / instrumental group (6 WEEKS)

		pos/wks
3 Sep 83	JAM ON REVENGE (THE WIKKI WIKKI SONG) Beckett BKS 8	44 6

Anthony NEWLEY 206 Top 500

Acclaimed actor / vocalist and composer. b. 24 Sep 1931, London, UK, d. 14 Apr 1999. He appeared in more than 20 films before his singing career started. He was among the most innovative UK acts of the early rock years before moving into musicals and cabaret (130 WEEKS)

		pos/wks
1 May 59 ●	I'VE WAITED SO LONG Decca F 11127	3 15
8 May 59	IDLE ON PARADE (EP) Decca DFE 6566	13 4
12 Jun 59 ●	PERSONALITY Decca F 11142	6 12
15 Jan 60 ★	WHY Decca F 11194	1 18
24 Mar 60 ★	DO YOU MIND Decca F 11220	1 15
14 Jul 60 ●	IF SHE SHOULD COME TO YOU Decca F 11254	4 15
24 Nov 60 ●	STRAWBERRY FAIR Decca F 11295	3 11
16 Mar 61 ●	AND THE HEAVENS CRIED Decca F 11331	6 12
15 Jun 61	POP GOES THE WEASEL / BEE BOM Decca F 11362	12 9
3 Aug 61	WHAT KIND OF FOOL AM I? Decca F 11376 ...	36 4
25 Jan 62	D-DARLING Decca F 11419	25 6
26 Jul 62	THAT NOISE Decca F 11486	34 5

'Bee Bom' listed together with 'Pop Goes the Weasel' only for weeks of 15 and 22 Jun 1961. It peaked at No.15. Tracks on Idle on Parade (EP): I've Waited So Long / Idle Rock-a-Boogie / Idle on Parade / Saturday Night Rock-a-Boogie

Tara NEWLEY – See E-ZEE POSSEE

Brad NEWMAN UK, male vocalist (1 WEEK)

		pos/wks
22 Feb 62	SOMEBODY TO LOVE Fontana H 357	47 1

Dave NEWMAN UK, male vocalist (6 WEEKS)

		pos/wks
15 Apr 72	THE LION SLEEPS TONIGHT (WIMOWEH) (re) Pye 7N 45134	34 6

Paul NEWMAN – See CAMISRA; ESCRIMA; PARTIZAN; TALL PAUL; GRIFTERS

NEWS – See Huey LEWIS and the NEWS

NEWS UK, male vocal / instrumental group (3 WEEKS)

		pos/wks
29 Aug 81	AUDIO VIDEO George GEORGE 1	52 3

NEWTON UK, male vocalist – William Myers (6 WEEKS)

		pos/wks
15 Jul 95	SKY HIGH Bags Of Fun BAGSCD 6	56 2
15 Feb 97	SOMETIMES WHEN WE TOUCH Dominion CDDMIN 202	32 3
16 Aug 97	DON'T WORRY Dominion CDDMIN 206	61 1

Juice NEWTON US, female vocalist (6 WEEKS)

		pos/wks
2 May 81	ANGEL OF THE MORNING Capitol CL 16189 ...	43 6

Olivia NEWTON-JOHN 61 Top 500

Top female vocalist in the US in the 1970s, b. 26 Sep 1948, Cambridge, UK. This photogenic Australian-raised singer / actress has won numerous pop and country awards and was the first female to score a dozen US Top 5 singles (234 WEEKS)

		pos/wks
20 Mar 71 ●	IF NOT FOR YOU Pye International 7N 25543	7 11
23 Oct 71 ●	BANKS OF THE OHIO Pye International 7N 25568 ...	6 17
11 Mar 72	WHAT IS LIFE Pye International 7N 25575	16 8
13 Jan 73	TAKE ME HOME COUNTRY ROADS Pye International 7N 25599	15 13
16 Mar 74	LONG LIVE LOVE Pye International 7N 25638 ..	11 8
12 Oct 74	I HONESTLY LOVE YOU EMI 2216 ▲	22 6
11 Jun 77 ●	SAM EMI 2616	6 11
20 May 78 ★	YOU'RE THE ONE THAT I WANT RSO 006 1 ◆ ▲	1 26
16 Sep 78 ★	SUMMER NIGHTS RSO 18 2 ◆	1 19
4 Nov 78 ●	HOPELESSLY DEVOTED TO YOU RSO 17	2 11
16 Dec 78 ●	A LITTLE MORE LOVE EMI 2879	4 12
30 Jun 79	DEEPER THAN THE NIGHT EMI 2954	64 3
21 Jun 80 ★	XANADU Jet 185 3	1 11
23 Aug 80	MAGIC Jet 196 ▲	32 7
25 Oct 80	SUDDENLY Jet 7002 4	15 7
10 Oct 81 ●	PHYSICAL EMI 5234 ▲	7 16
16 Jan 82	LANDSLIDE EMI 5257	18 9
17 Apr 82	MAKE A MOVE ON ME EMI 5291	43 3
23 Oct 82	HEART ATTACK EMI 5347	46 4
15 Jan 83	I HONESTLY LOVE YOU (re-issue) EMI 5360 ...	52 4
12 Nov 83	TWIST OF FATE EMI 5438	57 2
22 Dec 90	THE GREASE MEGAMIX Polydor PO 114 1 ...	3 10
23 Mar 91	GREASE – THE DREAM MIX PWL / Polydor PO 136 5 ...	47 2
4 Jul 92	I NEED LOVE Mercury MER 370	75 1
9 Dec 95	HAD TO BE EMI CDEMS 410 6	22 4
25 Jul 98 ●	YOU'RE THE ONE THAT I WANT (re-issue) Polydor 0441332 1 ..	4 9

1 John Travolta and Olivia Newton-John 2 John Travolta, Olivia Newton-John and Cast 3 Olivia Newton-John and Electric Light Orchestra 4 Olivia Newton-John and Cliff Richard 5 Frankie Valli, John Travolta and Olivia Newton-John 6 Cliff Richard and Olivia Newton-John

NEXT US, male vocal trio (8 WEEKS)

		pos/wks
6 Jun 98	TOO CLOSE Arista 74321580672 ▲	24 3
16 Sep 00	WIFEY Arista 74321790912	19 5

NEXT OF KIN UK, male vocal / instrumental group (6 WEEKS)

		pos/wks
20 Feb 99	24 HOURS FROM YOU Universal MCSTD 40201 ...	13 4
19 Jun 99	MORE LOVE Universal MCSTD 40207	33 2

NIAGRA UK, male / female vocal / DJ / production duo (1 WEEK)

		pos/wks
27 Sep 97	CLOUDBURST Freeflow FLOW CD2	65 1

NICE UK, male instrumental group (15 WEEKS)

		pos/wks
10 Jul 68	AMERICA Immediate IM 068	21 15

Paul NICHOLAS
UK, male actor / vocalist – Paul Beuselinck (31 WEEKS)

		pos/wks
17 Apr 76	REGGAE LIKE IT USED TO BE RSO 2090 185 ...	17 8
9 Oct 76 ●	DANCING WITH THE CAPTAIN RSO 2090 206 ..	8 9
4 Dec 76 ●	GRANDMA'S PARTY RSO 2090 216	9 11
9 Jul 77	HEAVEN ON THE 7TH FLOOR RSO 2090 249 ..	40 3

Sue NICHOLLS UK, female actor / vocalist (8 WEEKS)

		pos/wks
3 Jul 68	WHERE WILL YOU BE Pye 7N 17565	17 8

NICKELBACK Canada, male vocal / instrumental group (34 WKS)

		pos/wks
23 Feb 02	HOW YOU REMIND ME (import) Roadrunner 23203323CD ...	65 2
9 Mar 02 ●	HOW YOU REMIND ME Roadrunner 23203320 ▲	4 21
7 Sep 02 ●	TOO BAD (re) Roadrunner 20373	9 9
7 Dec 02	NEVER AGAIN Roadrunner RR 20253	30 2

Stevie NICKS US, female vocalist (30 WEEKS)

		pos/wks
15 Aug 81	STOP DRAGGIN' MY HEART AROUND WEA K 79231 1 ...	50 4
25 Jan 86	I CAN'T WAIT Parlophone R 6110	54 4

Re-entries are listed as (re), (2re), (3re) etc which signifies the

29 Mar 86	TALK TO ME *Parlophone R 6124*	68	2
6 May 89	ROOMS ON FIRE *EMI EM 90*	16	7
12 Aug 89	LONG WAY TO GO *EMI EM 97*	60	2
11 Nov 89	WHOLE LOTTA TROUBLE *EMI EM 114*	62	2
24 Aug 91	SOMETIMES IT'S A BITCH *EMI EM 203*	40	4
9 Nov 91	I CAN'T WAIT (re-issue) *EMI EM 214*	47	2
2 Jul 94	MAYBE LOVE *EMI CDEMS 328*	42	3

1 Stevie Nicks with Tom Petty and the Heartbreakers

See also FLEETWOOD MAC

NICOLE
Germany, female vocalist – Nicole Hohloch (10 WEEKS) pos/wks

8 May 82 ★	A LITTLE PEACE *CBS A 2365*	1	9
21 Aug 82	GIVE ME MORE TIME *CBS A 2467*	75	1

NICOLE *US, female vocalist – Nicole McLeod (9 WEEKS)* pos/wks

28 Dec 85	NEW YORK EYES *Portrait A 6805* 1	41	7
26 Dec 92	ROCK THE HOUSE *React 12REACT 12* 2	63	1
6 Jul 96	RUNNIN' AWAY *Ore AG 18CD*	69	1

1 Nicole with Timmy Thomas 2 Source featuring Nicole

NICOLETTE *UK, female vocalist (1 WEEK)* pos/wks

23 Dec 95	NO GOVERNMENT *Talkin Loud TLCD 1*	67	1

NIGEL & MARVIN
Trinidad, male vocal duo – Nigel and Marvin Lewis (10 WEEKS) pos/wks

18 May 02 ●	FOLLOW DA LEADER *Relentless RELENT 19CD*	5	10

NIGHTCRAWLERS featuring John REID
UK, house collective, leader – John Reid (36 WEEKS) pos/wks

15 Oct 94	PUSH THE FEELING ON *ffrr FCD 245* 1	22	5
4 Mar 95 ●	PUSH THE FEELING ON (re-mix) *ffrr FCD 257*	3	11
27 May 95 ●	SURRENDER YOUR LOVE *Final Vinyl 74321283982*	7	7
9 Sep 95	DON'T LET THE FEELING GO *Final Vinyl 7432129882*	13	4
20 Jan 96	LET'S PUSH IT *Final Vinyl 74321328142*	23	4
20 Apr 96	SHOULD I EVER (FALL IN LOVE) *Arista 74321358072*	34	2
27 Jul 96	KEEP ON PUSHING OUR LOVE *Arista 74321390422* 2	30	2
3 Jul 99	NEVER KNEW LOVE *Riverhorse RIVHCD 1* 1	59	1

1 Nightcrawlers 2 Nightcrawlers featuring John Reid and Alysha Warren

Maxine NIGHTINGALE *UK, female vocalist (16 WEEKS)* pos/wks

1 Nov 75 ●	RIGHT BACK WHERE WE STARTED FROM *United Artists UP 36015*	8	8
12 Mar 77	LOVE HIT ME *United Artists UP 36215*	11	8

NIGHTMARES ON WAX *UK, male DJ / producer / instrumentalist / vocalist – George Evelyn (6 WEEKS)* pos/wks

27 Oct 90	AFTERMATH / I'M FOR REAL *Warp WAP 6*	38	5
26 Jun 99	FINER *Warp WAP 123CD*	63	1

NIGHTWRITERS *US, male vocal / instrumental duo (2 WEEKS)* pos/wks

23 May 92	LET THE MUSIC USE YOU *Ffrreedom TABX 112*	51	2

NIKKE? NICOLE! *US, female rapper (1 WEEK)* pos/wks

1 Jun 91	NIKKE DOES IT BETTER *Love EVOL 5*	73	1

Markus NIKOLAI *Germany, male producer (1 WEEK)* pos/wks

6 Oct 01	BUSHES *SOUTHERN FRIED ECB 24CD*	74	1

NILSSON
US, male vocalist – Harry Nilsson d. 15 Jan 1994 (55 WEEKS) pos/wks

27 Sep 69	EVERYBODY'S TALKIN' (2re) *RCA 1876*	23	15
5 Feb 72 ★	WITHOUT YOU *RCA 2165* ▲	1	20
3 Jun 72	COCONUT *RCA 2214*	42	5
16 Oct 76	WITHOUT YOU (re-issue) *RCA 2733*	22	8

20 Aug 77	ALL I THINK ABOUT IS YOU *RCA PB 9104*	43	3
19 Feb 94	WITHOUT YOU (2nd re-issue) *RCA 74321193092*	47	4

'Everybody's Talkin' made No.50 on its first visit, followed by No.23 on first re-entry in Oct 1969 and No.39 on second re-entry in Mar 1970

Charlotte NILSSON *Sweden, female vocalist (4 WEEKS)* pos/wks

3 Jul 99	TAKE ME TO YOUR HEAVEN *Arista 74321686952*	20	4

NINA and FREDERIK *Denmark, female / male vocal duo*
– Baroness Nina and Baron Frederik Van Pallandt (29 WEEKS) pos/wks

18 Dec 59	MARY'S BOY CHILD *Columbia DB 4375*	26	1
10 Mar 60	LISTEN TO THE OCEAN (re) *Columbia DB 4332*	46	2
17 Nov 60 ●	LITTLE DONKEY *Columbia DB 4536*	3	10
28 Sep 61	LONGTIME BOY *Columbia DB 4703*	43	3
5 Oct 61	SUCU-SUCU *Columbia DB 4632*	23	13

NINE INCH NAILS *US, male vocal / instrumental group – leader – Trent Reznor (15 WEEKS)* pos/wks

14 Sep 91	HEAD LIKE A HOLE *TVT IS 484*	45	4
16 Nov 91	SIN *TVT IS 508*	35	2
9 Apr 94	MARCH OF THE PIGS *TVT CID 592*	45	3
18 Jun 94	CLOSER *TVT CIDX 596*	25	3
13 Sep 97	THE PERFECT DRUG *Interscope IND 95542*	43	1
18 Dec 99	WE'RE IN THIS TOGETHER *Island 4971402*	39	2

999 *UK, male vocal / instrumental group (13 WEEKS)* pos/wks

25 Nov 78	HOMICIDE *United Artists UP 36467*	40	3
27 Oct 79	FOUND OUT TOO LATE *Radar ADA 46*	69	2
16 May 81	OBSESSED *Albion ION 1011*	71	1
18 Jul 81	LIL RED RIDING HOOD *Albion ION 1017*	59	3
14 Nov 81	INDIAN RESERVATION *Albion ION 1023*	51	4

911 ⟨ 330 ⟩ `Top 500`

Leading UK boy band: Lee Brennan, Jimmy Constable, Simon 'Spike' Dawbarn. Vocal trio formed in 1996, when they won GMTV 'Search for the Next Big Thing' contest. Tally of 10 consecutive Top 10s is among the best chart runs in history. The group split in 1999 (94 WEEKS) pos/wks

11 May 96	NIGHT TO REMEMBER *Ginga CDGINGA 1*	38	2
10 Aug 96	LOVE SENSATION *Ginga CDGINGA 2*	21	4
9 Nov 96 ●	DON'T MAKE ME WAIT (re) *Ginga VSCDT 1618*	10	8
22 Feb 97 ●	THE DAY WE FIND LOVE *Virgin VSCDT 1619*	4	8
3 May 97 ●	BODYSHAKIN' *Virgin VSCDT 1634*	3	7
12 Jul 97 ●	THE JOURNEY *Virgin VSCDT 1645*	3	7
1 Nov 97 ●	PARTY PEOPLE...FRIDAY NIGHT (re) *Ginga / Virgin VSCDT 1658*	5	10
4 Apr 98 ●	ALL I WANT IS YOU (re) *Virgin VSCDT 1681*	4	7
4 Jul 98 ●	HOW DO YOU WANT ME TO LOVE YOU? (re) *Ginga VSCDT 1686*	10	9
24 Oct 98 ●	MORE THAN A WOMAN (re) *Virgin VSCDT 1707*	2	13
23 Jan 99 ★	A LITTLE BIT MORE *Virgin VSCDT 1719* ■	1	9
15 May 99 ●	PRIVATE NUMBER *Virgin VSCDT 1730*	3	7
23 Oct 99	WONDERLAND *Virgin VSCDT 1755*	13	1

9.9 *US, female vocal group (3 WEEKS)* pos/wks

6 Jul 85	ALL OF ME FOR ALL OF YOU *RCA PB 49951*	53	3

NINE YARDS *UK, male vocal group (3 WEEKS)* pos/wks

21 Nov 98	LONELINESS IS GONE *Virgin VSCDT 1696*	70	1
10 Apr 99	MATTER OF TIME *Virgin VSCDT 1723*	59	1
28 Aug 99	ALWAYS FIND A WAY *Virgin VSCDT 1746*	50	1

1910 FRUITGUM CO.
US, male vocal / instrumental group (16 WEEKS) pos/wks

20 Mar 68 ●	SIMON SAYS *Pye International 7N 25447*	2	16

1927 *Australia, male vocal / instrumental group (6 WEEKS)* pos/wks

22 Apr 89	THAT'S WHEN I THINK OF YOU *WEA YZ 351*	46	6

98°
US, male vocal group (17 WEEKS)
pos/wks

29 Nov 97	INVISIBLE MAN *Motown 8607092*	66	1
31 Oct 98	TRUE TO YOUR HEART *Motown 8608832* [1]	51	1
13 Mar 99	BECAUSE OF YOU *Motown 8609012*	36	2
11 Mar 00	● THANK GOD I FOUND YOU (re) *Columbia 6690582* [2] ▲	10	10
11 Mar 00	THE HARDEST THING *Universal MCSTD 40228*	29	2
2 Dec 00	GIVE ME JUST ONE MORE NIGHT (UNA NOCHE) *Universal MCSTD 40243*	61	1

[1] 98 Degrees featuring Stevie Wonder [2] Mariah Carey featuring Joe and 98 Degrees

99TH FLOOR ELEVATORS
UK, male DJ / production duo (5 WEEKS)
pos/wks

12 Aug 95	HOOKED *Labello Dance LAD 18CD* [1]	28	2
30 May 96	I'LL BE THERE *Labello Dance LAD 25CD1* [1]	37	2
8 Apr 00	HOOKED (re-mix) *Tripoli Trax TTRAX 061CD*	66	1

[1] 99th Floor Elevators featuring Tony De Vit

NIRVANA
UK / Ireland, male vocal / instrumental duo (6 WEEKS)
pos/wks

| 15 May 68 | RAINBOW CHASER *Island WIP 6029* | 34 | 6 |

NIRVANA
US, male vocal / instrumental group (36 WEEKS)
pos/wks

30 Nov 91	● SMELLS LIKE TEEN SPIRIT *DGC DGCS 5*	7	6
14 Mar 92	● COME AS YOU ARE *DGC DGCS 7*	9	5
25 Jul 92	LITHIUM *DGC DGCS 9*	11	6
12 Dec 92	IN BLOOM *Geffen GFS 34*	28	7
6 Mar 93	OH THE GUILT *Touch And Go TG 83CD*	12	2
11 Sep 93	● HEART-SHAPED BOX *Geffen GFSTD 54*	5	5
18 Dec 93	ALL APOLOGIES / RAPE ME *Geffen GFSTD 66*	32	5

The listed flip side of 'Oh the Guilt' was 'Puss' by Jesus Lizard

NITRO DELUXE
US, male multi-instrumentalist – Lee Junior (16 WEEKS)
pos/wks

| 14 Feb 87 | THIS BRUTAL HOUSE (re) *Cooltempo COOL 142* | 47 | 11 |
| 6 Feb 88 | LET'S GET BRUTAL (re-mix) *Cooltempo COOL* | 24 | 5 |

'Let's Get Brutal' is a re-mixed version of 'This Brutal House'

NITZER EBB
UK, male vocal / instrumental group (3 WEEKS)
pos/wks

11 Jan 92	GODHEAD *Mute 1MUTE 135T*	56	1
11 Apr 92	ASCEND *Mute 110MUTE 145*	52	1
4 Mar 95	KICK IT *Mute LCDMUTE 155*	75	1

NIVEA
US, female vocalist – Nivea Hamilton (3 WEEKS)
pos/wks

| 4 May 02 | RUN AWAY (I WANNA BE WITH U) / DON'T MESS WITH THE RADIO *Jive 9253362* | 48 | 1 |
| 21 Sep 02 | DON'T MESS WITH MY MAN *Jive 9254082* [1] | 41 | 2 |

[1] Nivea featuring Brian and Brandon Casey

See also MYSTIKAL

NO AUTHORITY
US, male vocal group (1 WEEK)
pos/wks

| 14 Mar 98 | DON'T STOP *EPIC 6655592* | 54 | 1 |

NO DICE
UK, male vocal / instrumental group (2 WEEKS)
pos/wks

| 5 May 79 | COME DANCING *EMI 2927* | 65 | 2 |

NO DOUBT
US, male / female vocal / instrumental group – lead vocal Gwen Stefani (60 WEEKS)
pos/wks

26 Oct 96	JUST A GIRL *Interscope IND 80034*	38	2
22 Feb 97	★ DON'T SPEAK *Interscope IND 95515* ■	1	18
5 Jul 97	● JUST A GIRL (re-issue) *Interscope IND 95539*	3	7
4 Oct 97	SPIDERWEBS *Interscope IND 95551*	16	3
20 Dec 97	SUNDAY MORNING *Interscope IND 95566*	50	3
12 Jun 99	NEW *Higher Ground HIGHS 22CD*	30	2
25 Mar 00	EX-GIRLFRIEND *Interscope 4972992*	23	3
7 Oct 00	SIMPLE KIND OF LIFE *Interscope 4974162*	69	1

16 Feb 02	● HEY BABY *Interscope 4976682*	2	9
15 Jun 02	● HELLA GOOD *Interscope 4977362*	12	7
12 Oct 02	UNDERNEATH IT ALL *Interscope 4977792*	18	5

NO MERCY
US, male vocal / instrumental group (26 WEEKS)
pos/wks

18 Jan 97	● WHERE DO YOU GO *Arista 74321401502*	2	15
24 May 97	● PLEASE DON'T GO *Arista 74321481372*	4	7
6 Sep 97	KISS YOU ALL OVER *Arista 7432151452*	16	4

NO ONE DRIVING – *See NOVACANE vs NO ONE DRIVING*

NO SWEAT
Ireland, male vocal / instrumental group (5 WEEKS)
pos/wks

| 13 Oct 90 | HEART AND SOUL *London LON 274* | 64 | 4 |
| 2 Feb 91 | TEAR DOWN THE WALLS *London LON 257* | 61 | 1 |

NO WAY JOSÉ
US, male instrumental group (6 WEEKS)
pos/wks

| 3 Aug 85 | TEQUILA *Fourth & Broadway BRW 28* | 47 | 6 |

NO WAY SIS
UK, male vocal / instrumental group (4 WEEKS)
pos/wks

| 21 Dec 96 | I'D LIKE TO TEACH THE WORLD TO SING *EMI CDEM 461* | 27 | 4 |

NOLANS 360 Top 500
Dublin-born singing sisters with considerable MOR / pop appeal. Personnel on most hits: Anne, Maureen, Bernadette, Linda and Coleen Nolan. First European act to win the Grand Prize at the prestigious Tokyo Music Festival (1981) (90 WEEKS)
pos/wks

6 Oct 79	SPIRIT, BODY AND SOUL *Epic EPC 7796* [1]	34	6
22 Dec 79	● I'M IN THE MOOD FOR DANCING *Epic EPC 8068*	3	15
12 Apr 80	DON'T MAKE WAVES *Epic EPC 8349*	12	11
13 Sep 80	● GOTTA PULL MYSELF TOGETHER *Epic EPC 8878*	9	13
6 Dec 80	WHO'S GONNA ROCK YOU *Epic EPC 9325*	12	11
14 Mar 81	● ATTENTION TO ME *Epic EPC 9571*	9	13
15 Aug 81	CHEMISTRY *Epic EPC A 1485*	15	8
20 Feb 82	DON'T LOVE ME TOO HARD *Epic EPC A 1927*	14	12
1 Apr 95	I'M IN THE MOOD FOR DANCING (re-recording) *Living Beat LBECD 31*	51	1

[1] Nolan Sisters

NOMAD
UK, male / female vocal / instrumental duo – Damon Rochefort and Sharon Dee Clarke (22 WEEKS)
pos/wks

2 Feb 91	● (I WANNA GIVE YOU) DEVOTION *Rumour RUMA 25* [1]	2	10
4 May 91	JUST A GROOVE *Rumour RUMA 33*	16	6
28 Sep 91	SOMETHING SPECIAL *Rumour RUMA 35*	73	1
25 Apr 92	YOUR LOVE IS LIFTING ME *Rumour RUMA 48*	60	2
7 Nov 92	24 HOURS A DAY *Rumour RUMA 60*	61	1
25 Nov 95	(I WANNA GIVE YOU) DEVOTION (re-mix) *Rumour RUMACD 75*	42	2

[1] Nomad featuring MC Mikee Freedom

NONCHALANT
US, female vocalist (1 WEEK)
pos/wks

| 29 Jun 96 | 5 O'CLOCK *MCA MCSTD 48011* | 44 | 1 |

Peter NOONE
UK, male vocalist (9 WEEKS)
pos/wks

| 22 May 71 | OH YOU PRETTY THING *RAK 114* | 12 | 9 |

See also HERMAN'S HERMITS

NOOTROPIC
UK, male instrumental / production duo (1 WEEK)
pos/wks

| 16 Mar 96 | I SEE ONLY YOU *Hi-Life 5779832* | 42 | 1 |

Ken NORDENE – *See Billy VAUGHN and his Orchestra*

Chris NORMAN – *See Suzi QUATRO; SMOKIE*

NORTH AND SOUTH
UK, male vocal / instrumental group (16 WEEKS)
pos/wks

| 17 May 97 | ● I'M A MAN NOT A BOY *RCA 74321461142* | 7 | 5 |
| 9 Aug 97 | TARANTINO'S NEW STAR *RCA 7432150124 2* | 18 | 5 |

Re-entries are listed as (re), (2re), (3re), etc which signifies that the hit re-entered the chart once, twice or thrice...

Date	Title	pos/wks
8 Nov 97	**BREATHING** *RCA 74321528422*	27 2
4 Apr 98	**NO SWEAT '98** *RCA 74321562212*	29 4

NORTHERN LINE
UK / South Africa, male vocal group (12 WEEKS) pos/wks

9 Oct 99	**RUN FOR YOUR LIFE** *Global Talent GTR 002CDS1*	18 4
11 Mar 00	**LOVE ON THE NORTHERN LINE** *Global Talent GTR 003CDS1*	15 5
17 Jun 00	**ALL AROUND THE WORLD** *Global Talent GTR 004CDS1*	27 3

NORTHERN UPROAR
UK, male vocal / instrumental group (11 WEEKS) pos/wks

21 Oct 95	**ROLLERCOASTER / ROUGH BOYS** *Heavenly HVN 047CD*	41 2
3 Feb 96	**FROM A WINDOW / THIS MORNING** *Heavenly HVN 051CD*	17 3
20 Apr 96	**LIVIN' IT UP** *Heavenly HVN 52CD*	24 2
22 Jun 96	**TOWN** *Heavenly HVN 54CD*	48 1
7 Jun 97	**ANY WAY YOU LOOK** *Heavenly HVN 70CD*	36 2
23 Aug 97	**A GIRL I ONCE KNEW** *Heavenly HVN 73CD*	63 1

NORTHSIDE *UK, male vocal / instrumental group (12 WEEKS)* pos/wks

9 Jun 90	**SHALL WE TAKE A TRIP / MOODY PLACES** *Factory FAC 268*	50 5
3 Nov 90	**MY RISING STAR** *Factory FAC 2987*	32 3
1 Jun 91	**TAKE 5** *Factory FAC 3087*	40 4

Freddie NOTES and the RUDIES
Jamaica, male vocal / instrumental group (2 WEEKS) pos/wks

10 Oct 70	**MONTEGO BAY** *Trojan TR 7791*	45 2

NOTORIOUS B.I.G.
US, male rapper – Christopher Wallace d. 9 Mar 1997 (30 WEEKS) pos/wks

29 Oct 94	**JUICY** *Bad Boy 74321240102*	72 1
1 Apr 95	**BIG POPPA** *Puff Daddy 74321263412*	63 1
15 Jul 95	**CAN'T YOU SEE** *Tommy Boy TBCD 700* [1]	43 2
19 Aug 95	**ONE MORE CHANCE / STAY WITH ME** *Puff Daddy 74321300782*	34 2
3 May 97	● **HYPNOTIZE** *Arista 74321466412* ▲	10 4
9 Aug 97	● **MO MONEY MO PROBLEMS** *Puff Daddy 74321492492* [2] ▲	6 10
14 Feb 98	**SKY'S THE LIMIT** *Puff Daddy 74321561992* [3]	35 2
18 Jul 98	**RUNNIN'** *Black Jam BJAM 9005* [4]	15 3
5 Feb 00	**NOTORIOUS B.I.G** *Puff Daddy / Arista 74321737312* [5]	16 5

[1] Total featuring the Notorious B.I.G. [2] Notorious B.I.G. featuring Puff Daddy and Mase [3] Notorious B.I.G. featuring 112 [4] 2Pac and Notorious B.I.G. [5] Notorious B.I.G. featuring Puff Daddy and Lil' Kim

NOTTINGHAM FOREST with PAPER LACE
UK, football team with male vocal / instrumental group (6 WEEKS) pos/wks

4 Mar 78	**WE'VE GOT THE WHOLE WORLD IN OUR HANDS** *Warner Bros. K 17110*	24 6

Heather NOVA *Bermuda, female vocalist (1 WEEK)* pos/wks

25 Feb 95	**WALK THIS WORLD** *Butterfly BFLD 19*	69 1

Nancy NOVA *UK, female vocalist (2 WEEKS)* pos/wks

4 Sep 82	**NO, NO, NO** *EMI 5328*	63 2

NOVACANE vs NO ONE DRIVING
UK, male production group (1 WEEK) pos/wks

15 Jun 02	**LOVE BE MY LOVER (PLAYA SOL)** *Direction 6727792*	69 1

Tom NOVY *Germany, male producer (8 WEEKS)* pos/wks

2 May 98	**SUPERSTAR** *D:disco 74321569352* [1]	32 3
3 Jun 00	**PUMPIN** *Positiva CDTIV 132* [1]	19 3
2 Sep 00	**I ROCK** *Rulin RULIN 3CDS* [2]	55 1
4 Aug 01	**NOW OR NEVER** *Rulin RULIN 14CDS* [3]	64 1

[1] Novy vs Eniac [2] Tom Novy featuring Virginia [3] Tom Novy featuring Lima

NU COLOURS
UK, male / female vocal / instrumental group (11 WEEKS) pos/wks

6 Jun 92	**TEARS** *Wild Card CARD 1*	55 2
10 Oct 92	**POWER** *Wild Card CARD 3*	64 1
5 Jun 93	**WHAT IN THE WORLD** *Wild Card CARDD 4*	57 2
27 Nov 93	**POWER (re-mix)** *Wild Card CARDD 5*	40 2
25 May 96	**DESIRE** *Wild Card 5763652*	31 2
24 Aug 96	**SPECIAL KIND OF LOVER** *Wild Card 5752012*	38 2

NU GENERATION *UK, male producer – Aston Harvey (9 WEEKS)* pos/wks

29 Jan 00	● **IN YOUR ARMS (RESCUE ME)** *Concept CDCON 7*	8 8
21 Oct 00	**NOWHERE TO RUN 2000** *Concept CDCON 16*	66 1

NU MATIC *UK, male instrumental / production duo (1 WEEK)* pos/wks

8 Aug 92	**SPRING IN MY STEP** *XL Recordings XLS 31*	58 1

NU SHOOZ *US, male / female vocal duo*
– John Smith and Valerie Day (17 WEEKS) pos/wks

24 May 86	● **I CAN'T WAIT** *Atlantic A 9446*	2 14
26 Jul 86	**POINT OF NO RETURN** *Atlantic A 9392*	48 3

NU SOUL featuring Kelli RICH *US, male / female vocal /*
instrumental duo – Carnell Newbill and Kelli Richardson (2 WEEKS) pos/wks

13 Jan 96	**HIDE-A-WAY** *ffrr FCD 269*	27 2

NUANCE featuring Vikki LOVE
US, male / female vocal / instrumental group (3 WEEKS) pos/wks

19 Jan 85	**LOVERIDE** *Fourth & Broadway BRW 20*	59 3

NUBIAN PRINZ – See POWERCUT featuring NUBIAN PRINZ

NU-BIRTH *UK, male production duo (2 WEEKS)* pos/wks

6 Sep 97	**ANYTIME** *XL XLS 85CD*	48 1
6 Jun 98	**ANYTIME (re-issue)** *Locked On LOX 97CD*	41 1

NUFF JUICE – See D MOB

NUKLEUZ DJ'S *UK, collection of DJs / producers (2 WEEKS)* pos/wks

24 Aug 02	**DJ NATION** *Nukleuz NUKF 0440*	40 2

Three 12-inch singles released featuring various Nukleuz DJ / producers each including the track 'DJ Nation'

Gary NUMAN (126 Top 500) *The moody, synthesized sound of London-born Gary Webb (b. 8 Mar 1958) first hit the charts in 1979 under the group name Tubeway Army. Five-times chart hit 'Cars' was also the basis of Armand Van Helden's Top 20 hit 'Koochy' in 2000 (166 WEEKS)* pos/wks

19 May 79	★ **ARE 'FRIENDS' ELECTRIC?** *Beggars Banquet BEG 18* [1]	1 16
1 Sep 79	★ **CARS** *Beggars Banquet BEG 23*	1 11
24 Nov 79	● **COMPLEX** *Beggars Banquet BEG 29*	6 9
24 May 80	● **WE ARE GLASS** *Beggars Banquet BEG 35*	5 7
30 Aug 80	● **I DIE: YOU DIE** *Beggars Banquet BEG 46*	6 7
20 Dec 80	**THIS WRECKAGE** *Beggars Banquet BEG 50*	20 7
29 Aug 81	● **SHE'S GOT CLAWS** *Beggars Banquet BEG 62*	6 6
5 Dec 81	**LOVE NEEDS NO DISGUISE** *Beggars Banquet BEG 68* [2]	33 7
6 Mar 82	**MUSIC FOR CHAMELEONS** *Beggars Banquet BEG 72*	19 7
19 Jun 82	● **WE TAKE MYSTERY (TO BED)** *Beggars Banquet BEG 77*	9 4
28 Aug 82	**WHITE BOYS AND HEROES** *Beggars Banquet BEG 81*	20 4
3 Sep 83	**WARRIORS** *Beggars Banquet BEG 95*	20 5
22 Oct 83	**SISTER SURPRISE** *Beggars Banquet BEG 101*	32 5
3 Nov 84	**BERSERKER** *Numa NU 4*	32 5
22 Dec 84	**MY DYING MACHINE** *Numa NU 6*	66 1
9 Feb 85	**CHANGE YOUR MIND** *Polydor POSP 722* [3]	17 8
25 May 85	**THE LIVE EP** *Numa NUM 7*	27 4
10 Aug 85	**YOUR FASCINATION** *Numa NU 9*	46 5
21 Sep 85	**CALL OUT THE DOGS** *Numa NU 11*	49 2
16 Nov 85	**MIRACLES** *Numa NU 13*	49 3
19 Apr 86	**THIS IS LOVE** *Numa NU 16*	28 3
28 Jun 86	**I CAN'T STOP** *Numa NU 17*	27 4

		pos/wks
4 Oct 86	NEW THING FROM LONDON TOWN *Numa NU 19* [3]	52 3
6 Dec 86	I STILL REMEMBER *Numa NU 21*	74 1
28 Mar 87	RADIO HEART *GFM GFM 109* [4]	35 6
13 Jun 87	LONDON TIMES *GFM GFM 112* [4]	48 2
19 Sep 87	CARS (E REG MODEL) / ARE 'FRIENDS' ELECTRIC? (re-mix) *Beggars Banquet BEG 199*	16 7
30 Jan 88	NO MORE LIES *Polydor POSP 894* [3]	34 3
1 Oct 88	NEW ANGER *Illegal ILS 1003*	46 4
3 Dec 88	AMERICA *Illegal ILS 1004*	49 1
3 Jun 89	I'M ON AUTOMATIC *Polydor PO 43* [3]	44 2
16 Mar 91	HEART *IRS Numan 1*	43 1
21 Mar 92	THE SKIN GAME *Numa NU 23*	68 1
1 Aug 92	MACHINE + SOUL *Numa NUM 124*	72 1
4 Sep 93	CARS (2nd re-mix) *Beggars Banquet BEG 264CD*	53 1
16 Mar 96	CARS (re-issue of re-mix) *PolyGram TV PRMCD 1*	17 4
13 Jul 02	RIP *Jagged Halo JHCD 5*	29 2

[1] Tubeway Army [2] Gary Numan and Dramatis [3] Sharpe and Numan [4] Radio Heart featuring Gary Numan

Tracks on The Live EP: Are 'Friends' Electric? / Berserker / Cars / We Are Glass. 'Cars' in 1996 is a re-issue of the 1987 remix

See also Paul GARDINER

NUMBER ONE CUP
US, male vocal / instrumental group (1 WEEK)

		pos/wks
2 Mar 96	DIVEBOMB *Blue Rose BRRC 10032*	61 1

Jose NUNEZ featuring OCTAHVIA
US, male DJ / producer (2 WEEKS)

		pos/wks
5 Sep 98	IN MY LIFE *Ministry of Sound MOSCDS 126*	56 1
5 Jun 99	HOLD ON *Ministry of Sound MOSCDS 130*	44 1

See also CHOO CHOO PROJECT

Bobby NUNN
US, male vocalist / multi-instrumentalist d. 5 Nov 1986 (3 WEEKS)

		pos/wks
4 Feb 84	DON'T KNOCK IT (UNTIL YOU TRY IT) *Motown TMG 1323*	65 3

NUSH
UK, male instrumental / production duo – Danny Matlock and Danny Harrison (7 WEEKS)

		pos/wks
23 Jul 94	U GIRLS *Blunted Vinyl BLNCDX 006*	58 1
22 Apr 95	MOVE THAT BODY *Blunted Vinyl BLNCD 012*	46 2
16 Sep 95	U GIRLS (LOOK SO SEXY) (re-mix) *Blunted Vinyl BLNCD 13*	15 4

NUT
UK, female vocalist (4 WEEKS)

		pos/wks
8 Jun 96	BRAINS *Epic NUTCD 2*	64 1
21 Sep 96	CRAZY *Epic NUTCD 5*	56 1
11 Jan 97	SCREAM *Epic NUTCD 6*	43 2

NUTTIN' NYCE
US, female vocal group (2 WEEKS)

		pos/wks
10 Jun 95	DOWN 4 WHATEVA *Jive JIVECD 365*	62 1
12 Aug 95	FROGGY STYLE *Jive JIVECD 381*	68 1

NUYORICAN SOUL
US, male DJ / production group (8 WEEKS)

		pos/wks
8 Feb 97	RUNAWAY *Talkin Loud TLCD20* [1]	24 4
10 May 97	IT'S ALRIGHT, I FEEL IT! *Talkin Loud TLCD 22* [2]	26 2
25 Oct 97	I AM THE BLACK GOLD OF THE SUN *Talkin Loud TLCD 26* [2]	31 2

[1] Nuyorican Soul featuring India [2] Nuyorican Soul featuring Jocelyn Brown

See also MASTERS AT WORK

Joe NYE *– See DNA*

NYLON MOON
Italy, male instrumental duo (2 WEEKS)

		pos/wks
13 Apr 96	SKY PLUS *Positiva CDTIV 50*	43 2

Michael NYMAN
UK, male instrumentalist – piano (2 WEEKS)

		pos/wks
19 Mar 94	THE HEART ASKS PLEASURE FIRST / THE PROMISE *Virgin VEND 3*	60 2

O

OMC
New Zealand, male vocalist – Paul Fuemana Lawrence (17 WEEKS)

		pos/wks
20 Jul 96	● HOW BIZARRE *Polydor 5776202*	5 16
18 Jan 97	ON THE RUN *Polydor 5732452*	56 1

OMD *– See ORCHESTRAL MANOEUVRES IN THE DARK*

OPM
US, male vocal / instrumental group (18 WEEKS)

		pos/wks
14 Jul 01	● HEAVEN IS A HALFPIPE *Atlantic AT 0107CD*	4 14
12 Jan 02	EL CAPITAN (re) *Atlantic AT 0118CD*	20 4

O.T. QUARTET *– See OUR TRIBE / ONE TRIBE*

O-TOWN
US, male vocal group (26 WEEKS)

		pos/wks
28 Apr 01	● LIQUID DREAMS *J 74321853202*	3 10
4 Aug 01	● ALL OR NOTHING *J 74321875822*	4 10
3 Nov 01	WE FIT TOGETHER (re) *J 74321893692*	20 4
23 Feb 02	LOVE SHOULD BE A CRIME *J 74321920232*	38 2

OTT
Ireland, male vocal group (18 WEEKS)

		pos/wks
15 Feb 97	LET ME IN *Epic 6642052*	12 5
17 May 97	FOREVER GIRL *Epic 6645082*	24 3
23 Aug 97	ALL OUT OF LOVE *Epic 6649152*	11 4
24 Jan 98	THE STORY OF LOVE *Epic OTT 1CD*	11 6

OAKENFOLD
UK, male DJ / producer – Paul Oakenfold (13 WEEKS)

		pos/wks
25 Aug 01	PLANET ROCK *Tommy Boy TBCD2266* [1]	47 1
22 Jun 02	SOUTHERN SUN / READY STEADY GO *Perfecto PERF 17CDS*	16 4
31 Aug 02	● STARRY EYED SURPRISE *Perfecto PERF 27CDS*	6 8

[1] Paul Oakenfold presents Afrika Bambaataa

See also VIRUS

Phil OAKEY *– See HUMAN LEAGUE; Giorgio MORODER*

OASIS [21] [Top 500] *Peerless Manchester-based, Beatles-influenced band: Liam (v) and Noel (g/v) Gallagher, Gem Archer (g), Andy Bell (b), Alan White (d). Tony McCarroll was replaced by Alan White in 1994. In 1999 Paul 'Bonehead' Arthurs was replaced by Gem Archer and Paul McGuigan was replaced by Andy Bell. The often controversial Britpop group smashed the record for most weeks on the chart in one year (134 in 1996). Best-selling single: 'Wonderwall' 966,940 (338 WEEKS)*

		pos/wks
23 Apr 94	SUPERSONIC (5re) *Creation CRESCD 176*	31 14
2 Jul 94	SHAKERMAKER (5re) *Creation CRESCD 182*	11 15
20 Aug 94	● LIVE FOREVER (6re) *Creation CRESCD 185*	10 18
22 Oct 94	● CIGARETTES AND ALCOHOL (9re) *Creation CRESCD 190*	7 35
31 Dec 94	● WHATEVER (8re) *Creation CRESCD 195*	3 50
6 May 95	★ SOME MIGHT SAY (6re) *Creation CRESCD 204* ■	1 27
13 May 95	SOME MIGHT SAY *Creation CRE 204T*	71 1
26 Aug 95	● ROLL WITH IT (3re) *Creation CRESCD 212*	2 18
11 Nov 95	● WONDERWALL (2re) *Creation CRESCD 215*	2 34
25 Nov 95	WIBBLING RIVALRY (INTERVIEWS WITH NOEL AND LIAM GALLAGHER) *Fierce Panda NING 12CD* [1]	52 2
2 Mar 96	★ DON'T LOOK BACK IN ANGER (2re) *Creation CRESCD 221* ■	1 24
19 Jul 97	★ D'YOU KNOW WHAT I MEAN? *Creation CRESCD 256* ■	1 18
4 Oct 97	● STAND BY ME *Creation CRESCD 278*	2 18
24 Jan 98	★ ALL AROUND THE WORLD (re) *Creation CRESCD 282* ■	1 9
19 Feb 00	★ GO LET IT OUT (re) *Big Brother RKIDSCD 001* ■	1 12
29 Apr 00	● WHO FEELS LOVE? (re) *Big Brother RKIDSCD 003*	4 8
15 Jul 00	● SUNDAY MORNING CALL *Big Brother RKIDSCD004*	4 6

Re-entries are listed as (re), (2re), (3re), etc which signifies that the hit re-entered the

27 Apr 02	★ THE HINDU TIMES *Big Brother RKIDSCD 23* ■	1 11
29 Jun 02	● STOP CRYING YOUR HEART OUT *Big Brother RKIDSCD 24*	2 10
5 Oct 02	● LITTLE BY LITTLE / SHE IS LOVE *Big Brother RKIDSCD 26*	2 8

1 Oas*s

Chart rules allow for a maximum of three formats; the 12-inch of 'Some Might Say' – already available on CD, seven-inch and cassette – was therefore listed separately. Oasis had a record number of re-entries between 1995 and 1997 as new releases were accompanied by the regular return of singles from their back catalogue

John OATES – See Daryl HALL and John OATES

Sam OBERNIK – See Tim DELUXE featuring Sam OBERNIK

OBERNKIRCHEN CHILDREN'S CHOIR
Germany, children's choir (26 WEEKS) pos/wks

| 22 Jan 54 | ● THE HAPPY WANDERER (re) *Parlophone R 3799* | 2 26 |

OBI PROJECT featuring HARRY, ASHER D and DJ WHAT?
UK, male vocal / rap / production group (1 WEEK) pos/wks

| 4 Aug 01 | BABY, CAN I GET YOUR NUMBER *East West EW 235CD* | 75 1 |

Dermot O'BRIEN and his CLUBMEN
Ireland, male vocal / instrumental group (2 WEEKS) pos/wks

| 20 Oct 66 | THE MERRY PLOUGHBOY (re) *Envoy ENV 016* | 46 2 |

Billy OCEAN 144 Top 500
Top British-based R&B singer / songwriter of the 1980s, b. Leslie Charles, 21 Jan 1950, Trinidad. He waited seven years after scoring his first four UK Top 20 hits before accumulating an impressive run of transatlantic successes, which included three US No.1s (153 WEEKS) pos/wks

21 Feb 76	● LOVE REALLY HURTS WITHOUT YOU *GTO GT 52*	2 10
10 Jul 76	● L.O.D. (LOVE ON DELIVERY) *GTO GT 62*	19 8
13 Nov 76	STOP ME (IF YOU'VE HEARD IT ALL BEFORE) *GTO GT 72*	12 11
19 Mar 77	● RED LIGHT SPELLS DANGER *GTO GT 85*	2 10
1 Sep 79	AMERICAN HEARTS *GTO GT 244*	54 5
19 Jan 80	ARE YOU READY *GTO GT 259*	42 7
13 Oct 84	● CARIBBEAN QUEEN (NO MORE LOVE ON THE RUN) *Jive JIVE 77* ▲	6 14
19 Jan 85	LOVERBOY *Jive JIVE 80*	15 10
11 May 85	● SUDDENLY *Jive JIVE 90*	4 14
17 Aug 85	MYSTERY LADY *Jive JIVE 98*	49 4
25 Jan 86	★ WHEN THE GOING GETS TOUGH, THE TOUGH GET GOING *Jive JIVE 114*	1 13
12 Apr 86	THERE'LL BE SAD SONGS (TO MAKE YOU CRY) *Jive JIVE 117* ▲	12 13
9 Aug 86	LOVE ZONE *Jive JIVE 124*	49 3
11 Oct 86	BITTERSWEET *Jive JIVE 133*	44 4
10 Jan 87	LOVE IS FOREVER *Jive JIVE 134*	34 7
6 Feb 88	● GET OUTTA MY DREAMS GET INTO MY CAR *Jive BOS 1* ▲	3 11
7 May 88	CALYPSO CRAZY *Jive BOS 2*	35 4
6 Aug 88	THE COLOUR OF LOVE *Jive BOS 3*	65 3
6 Feb 93	PRESSURE *Jive BOSCD 6*	55 2

OCEAN COLOUR SCENE
UK, male vocal / instrumental group (62 WEEKS) pos/wks

23 Mar 91	YESTERDAY TODAY *!Phfft FIT 2*	49 1
17 Feb 96	THE RIVERBOAT SONG *MCA MCSTD 40021*	15 5
6 Apr 96	● YOU'VE GOT IT BAD *MCA MCSTD 40036*	7 4
15 Jun 96	● THE DAY WE CAUGHT THE TRAIN *MCA MCSTD 40046*	4 11
28 Sep 96	● THE CIRCLE *MCA MCSTD 40077*	6 6
28 Jun 97	● HUNDRED MILE HIGH CITY *MCA MCSTD 40133*	4 7
6 Sep 97	● TRAVELLERS TUNE *MCA MCSTD 40144*	5 5
22 Nov 97	● BETTER DAY *MCA MCSTD 40151*	9 5
28 Feb 98	IT'S A BEAUTIFUL THING *MCA MCSTD 40157*	12 4
4 Sep 99	PROFIT IN PEACE *Island CID 757*	13 5
27 Nov 99	SO LOW *Island CID 759*	34 2
8 Jul 00	JULY / I AM THE NEWS *Island CID 763*	31 2
7 Apr 01	UP ON THE DOWN SIDE *Island CID 774*	19 3
14 Jul 01	MECHANICAL WONDER *Island CID 779*	49 1
22 Dec 01	CRAZY LOWDOWN WAYS *Island CID 787*	64 1

OCEANIC
UK, male / female vocal / instrumental group (26 WEEKS) pos/wks

24 Aug 91	● INSANITY *Dead Dead Good GOOD 4*	3 15
30 Nov 91	WICKED LOVE (re) *Dead Dead Good GOOD 5*	25 5
13 Jun 92	CONTROLLING ME *Dead Dead Good GOOD 14*	14 5
14 Nov 92	IGNORANCE *Dead Dead Good GOOD 22* 1	72 1

1 Oceanic featuring Siobhan Maher

OCEANLAB featuring Justine SUISSA
UK, male production trio and female vocalist (1 WEEK) pos/wks

| 27 Apr 02 | CLEAR BLUE WATER *Code Blue BLU 024CD* | 48 1 |

Des O'CONNOR 240 Top 500
Entertainer, comedian and MOR vocalist, b. 12 Jan 1932. This London-based all-rounder toured with Buddy Holly and Lonnie Donegan in the 1950s, had a series of hits in the 1960s and has been a top-rated TV star for the past four decades (117 WEEKS) pos/wks

1 Nov 67	● CARELESS HANDS *Columbia DB 8275* 1	6 17
8 May 68	★ I PRETEND *Columbia DB 8397*	1 36
20 Nov 68	● ONE, TWO THREE O'LEARY *Columbia DB 8492*	4 11
7 May 69	DICK-A-DUM-DUM (KING'S ROAD) *Columbia DB 8566*	14 10
29 Nov 69	LONELINESS *Columbia DB 8632*	18 11
14 Mar 70	I'LL GO ON HOPING *Columbia DB 8661*	30 7
26 Sep 70	THE TIP OF MY FINGERS *Columbia DB 8713*	15 15
8 Nov 86	● THE SKYE BOAT SONG *Tembo TML119* 2	10 10

1 Des O'Connor with the Michael Sammes Singers 2 Roger Whittaker and Des O'Connor

Hazel O'CONNOR *UK, female vocalist (46 WEEKS)* pos/wks

16 Aug 80	● EIGHTH DAY *A&M AMS 7553*	5 11
25 Oct 80	GIVE ME AN INCH *A&M AMS 7569*	41 4
21 Mar 81	● D-DAYS *Albion ION 1009*	10 9
23 May 81	● WILL YOU *A&M AMS 8131*	8 10
1 Aug 81	(COVER PLUS) WE'RE ALL GROWN UP *Albion ION 1018*	41 6
3 Oct 81	HANGING AROUND *Albion ION 1022*	45 3
23 Jan 82	CALLS THE TUNE *A&M AMS 8203*	60 3

Sinead O'CONNOR *Ireland, female vocalist (65 WEEKS)* pos/wks

16 Jan 88	MANDINKA *Ensign ENY 611*	17 9
20 Jan 90	★ NOTHING COMPARES 2 U *Ensign ENY 630* ▲	1 14
21 Jul 90	THE EMPEROR'S NEW CLOTHES *Ensign ENY 633*	31 5
20 Oct 90	THREE BABIES *Ensign ENY 635*	42 4
8 Jun 91	MY SPECIAL CHILD *Ensign ENY 646*	42 3
14 Dec 91	SILENT NIGHT *Ensign ENY 652*	60 4
12 Sep 92	SUCCESS HAS MADE A FAILURE OF OUR HOME *Ensign ENY 656*	18 4
12 Dec 92	DON'T CRY FOR ME ARGENTINA *Ensign ENY 657*	53 4
19 Feb 94	YOU MADE ME THE THIEF OF YOUR HEART *Island CID 588*	42 3
26 Nov 94	THANK YOU FOR HEARING ME *Ensign CDENYS 662*	13 7
29 Apr 95	HAUNTED *ZTT ZANG 65CD* 1	30 2
26 Aug 95	FAMINE *Ensign CDENY 663*	51 1
17 May 97	GOSPEL OAK (EP) *Chrysalis CDCHS 5051*	28 3
6 Dec 97	THIS IS A REBEL SONG *Columbia 6652992*	60 1
24 Aug 02	TROY (THE PHOENIX FROM THE FLAME) *Devolution DEVR 003CDS*	48 1

1 Shane MacGowan and Sinead O'Connor

Tracks on Gospel Oak (EP): This Is to Mother You / I Am Enough for Myself / Petit Poulet / 4 My Love

See also MARXMAN; Jah WOBBLE'S INVADERS of the HEART

OCTAHVIA – See Jose NUNEZ featuring OCTAHVIA; CHOO CHOO PROJECT

OCTAVE ONE featuring Ann SAUNDERSON
US, male production trio and US, female vocalist (2 WEEKS) pos/wks

| 16 Feb 02 | BLACKWATER *Concept / 430 West CDCON 26* | 47 1 |
| 28 Sep 02 | BLACKWATER (re-mix) *Concept / 430 CDCON 34* | 69 1 |

OCTOPUS UK / France, male vocal / instrumental group (5 WEEKS) pos/wks

22 Jun 96	YOUR SMILE Food CDFOOD 78	42	2
14 Sep 96	SAVED Food CDFOODS 84	40	2
23 Nov 96	JEALOUSY Food CDFOODS 87	59	1

Alan O'DAY US, male vocalist (3 WEEKS) pos/wks

| 2 Jul 77 | UNDERCOVER ANGEL Atlantic K 10926 ▲ | 43 | 3 |

ODETTA – See Harry BELAFONTE

Daniel O'DONNELL Ireland, male vocalist (64 WEEKS) pos/wks

12 Sep 92	I JUST WANT TO DANCE WITH YOU Ritz RITZ 250P	20	7
2 Jan 93	THE THREE BELLS Ritz RITZCD 239	71	1
8 May 93	THE LOVE IN YOUR EYES Ritz RITZCD 257	47	3
7 Aug 93	WHAT EVER HAPPENED TO OLD FASHIONED LOVE Ritz RITZCD 262	21	5
16 Apr 94	SINGING THE BLUES Ritz RITZCD 270	23	3
26 Nov 94	THE GIFT Ritz RITZCD 275	46	3
10 Jun 95	SECRET LOVE Ritz RITZCD 285 [1]	28	3
9 Mar 96	TIMELESS Ritz RITZCD 293 [1]	32	3
28 Sep 96	FOOTSTEPS Ritz RITZCD 300	25	5
7 Jun 97	THE LOVE SONGS EP Ritz RITZCD 306	27	4
11 Apr 98 ●	GIVE A LITTLE LOVE Ritz RITZCD 315	7	5
17 Oct 98	THE MAGIC IS THERE Ritz RZCD 320	16	4
20 Mar 99	THE WAY DREAMS ARE Ritz RZCD 325	18	3
24 Jul 99	UNO MAS Ritz RZCD 326	25	3
18 Dec 99	A CHRISTMAS KISS Ritz RZCD 330	20	4
15 Apr 00	LIGHT A CANDLE Ritz RZCD 335	23	4
16 Dec 00	MORNING HAS BROKEN Ritz RZCD 341	32	4

[1] Daniel O'Donnell and Mary Duff

Tracks on The Love Songs EP: Save the Last Dance for Me / I Can't Stop Loving You / You're the Only Good Thing / Limerick You're a Lady

ODYSSEY 415 Top 500 Soul / disco vocal trio formed in New York, US, by non-natives Lillian and Louise Lopez (from Connecticut) and Manila-born Tony Reynolds (replaced 1978 by Bill McEachern). UK success not mirrored in US, where only their debut hit reached the Top 40 (82 WEEKS) pos/wks

24 Dec 77 ●	NATIVE NEW YORKER RCA PC 1129	5	11
21 Jun 80 ★	USE IT UP AND WEAR IT OUT RCA PB 1962	1	12
13 Sep 80 ●	IF YOU'RE LOOKIN' FOR A WAY OUT RCA 5	6	15
17 Jan 81	HANG TOGETHER RCA 23	36	7
30 May 81 ●	GOING BACK TO MY ROOTS RCA 85	4	12
19 Sep 81 ●	IT WILL BE ALRIGHT RCA 128	43	5
12 Jun 82 ●	INSIDE OUT RCA 226	3	11
11 Sep 82	MAGIC TOUCH RCA 275	41	5
17 Aug 85	(JOY) I KNOW IT Mirror BUTCH 12	51	4

Esther and Abi OFARIM Israel, female / male vocal duo – Esther Zaled and Abraham Reichstadt (22 WEEKS) pos/wks

| 14 Feb 68 ★ | CINDERELLA ROCKEFELLA Philips BF 1640 | 1 | 13 |
| 19 Jun 68 | ONE MORE DANCE Philips BF 1678 | 13 | 9 |

Wiston OFFICE – See Frank K featuring Wiston OFFICE

OFF-SHORE Germany, male instrumental / production duo – Jens Lissat and Peter Harder (12 WEEKS) pos/wks

| 22 Dec 90 ● | I CAN'T TAKE THE POWER CBS 6565707 | 7 | 11 |
| 17 Aug 91 | I GOT A LITTLE SONG Dance Pool 6568257 | 64 | 1 |

OFFSPRING US, male vocal / instrumental group – lead vocal Dexter Holland (56 WEEKS) pos/wks

25 Feb 95	SELF ESTEEM Golf CDSHOLE 001	37	3
19 Aug 95	GOTTA GET AWAY Out Of Step WOOS 2CDS	43	2
1 Feb 97	ALL I WANT Epitaph 64912	31	2
26 Apr 97	GONE AWAY Epitaph 64982	42	1
30 Jan 99 ★	PRETTY FLY (FOR A WHITE GUY) Columbia 666802 ■	1	11
8 May 99 ●	WHY DON'T YOU GET A JOB? Columbia 6673542	2	8
11 Sep 99	THE KIDS AREN'T ALRIGHT Columbia 6677632	11	6
4 Dec 99	SHE'S GOT ISSUES Columbia 6683772	41	2

18 Nov 00 ●	ORIGINAL PRANKSTER Columbia 6699972	6	8
31 Mar 01	WANT YOU BAD (re) Columbia 6709292	15	9
7 Jul 01	MILLION MILES AWAY Columbia 6714082	21	4

OH WELL Germany, male producer – Ackim Faulker (7 WEEKS) pos/wks

| 14 Oct 89 | OH WELL Parlophone R 6236 | 28 | 6 |
| 3 Mar 90 | RADAR LOVE Parlophone R 6244 | 65 | 1 |

OHIO EXPRESS US, male vocal / instrumental group (15 WEEKS) pos/wks

| 5 Jun 68 ● | YUMMY YUMMY YUMMY Pye International 7N 25459 | 5 | 15 |

OHIO PLAYERS US, male vocal / instrumental group (4 WEEKS) pos/wks

| 10 Jul 76 | WHO'D SHE COO? Mercury PLAY 001 | 43 | 4 |

O'JAYS US, male vocal group (72 WEEKS) pos/wks

23 Sep 72	BACK STABBERS CBS 8270	14	9
3 Mar 73 ●	LOVE TRAIN CBS 1181 ▲	9	13
31 Jan 76	I LOVE MUSIC Philadelphia International PIR 3879	13	9
12 Feb 77	DARLIN' DARLIN' BABY (SWEET, TENDER, LOVE) Philadelphia International PIR 4834	24	6
8 Apr 78	I LOVE MUSIC (re-issue) Philadelphia International PIR 6093	36	3
17 Jun 78	USED TA BE MY GIRL Philadelphia International PIR 6332	12	12
30 Sep 78	BRANDY Philadelphia International PIR 6658	21	9
29 Sep 79	SING A HAPPY SONG Philadelphia International PIR 7825	39	6
30 Jul 83	PUT OUR HEADS TOGETHER Philadelphia International A 3642	45	5

John O'KANE UK, male vocalist (4 WEEKS) pos/wks

| 9 May 92 | STAY WITH ME Circa YR 88 | 41 | 4 |

OL' DIRTY BASTARD US, male rapper – Russell Jones (25 WEEKS) pos/wks

| 27 Jun 98 ● | GHETTO SUPERSTAR (THAT IS WHAT YOU ARE) Interscope IND 95593 [1] | 2 | 17 |
| 8 Jul 00 | GOT YOUR MONEY Elektra E 7077CD [2] | 11 | 8 |

[1] Pras Michel featuring Ol' Dirty Bastard introducing Mya [2] Ol' Dirty Bastard featuring Kelis

See also WU-TANG CLAN

OLD SKOOL ORCHESTRA UK, male DJ / production duo (1 WEEK) pos/wks

| 23 Jan 99 | B-BOY HUMP East West EW 186CD1 | 55 | 1 |

See also STRETCH 'N' VERN present MADDOG

Mike OLDFIELD 254 Top 500 Composer / producer / multi-instrumentalist, b. 15 May 1953, Reading, UK. His chart-topping 1973 debut album, 'Tubular Bells', spent five years on the chart, and the belated 'Tubular Bells II' also reached UK No.1 (1992) (113 WEEKS) pos/wks

13 Jul 74	MIKE OLDFIELD'S SINGLE (THEME FROM TUBULAR BELLS) Virgin VS 101	31	6
20 Dec 75 ●	IN DULCE JUBILO / ON HORSEBACK Virgin VS 131	4	10
27 Nov 76 ●	PORTSMOUTH Virgin VS 163	3	12
23 Dec 78	TAKE 4 (EP) Virgin VS 238	72	3
21 Apr 79	GUILTY Virgin VS 245	22	8
8 Dec 79	BLUE PETER Virgin VS 317	19	9
20 Mar 82	FIVE MILES OUT Virgin VS 464 [1]	43	6
12 Jun 82	FAMILY MAN Virgin VS 489 [1]	45	6
28 May 83 ●	MOONLIGHT SHADOW Virgin VS 586 [2]	4	17
14 Jan 84	CRIME OF PASSION Virgin VS 648 [1]	61	3
30 Jun 84	TO FRANCE Virgin VS 686 [1]	48	7
14 Dec 85	PICTURES IN THE DARK Virgin VS 836 [3]	50	6
3 Oct 92 ●	SENTINEL WEA YZ 698	10	6
19 Dec 92	TATTOO WEA YZ 708	33	5
17 Apr 93	THE BELL WEA YZ 737CD	50	2
9 Oct 93	MOONLIGHT SHADOW (re-issue) Virgin VSCDT 1477	52	2

Re-entries are listed as (re), (2re), (3re), etc which signifies that the hit re-entered the chart

			pos/wks
7 Dec 94	**HIBERNACULUM** *WEA YZ 871CD*	47	3
2 Sep 95	**LET THERE BE LIGHT** *WEA YZ 880CD*	51	1
22 Nov 97	**WOMEN OF IRELAND** *WEA WEA 093CD*	70	1
24 Apr 99	**FAR ABOVE THE CLOUDS** *WEA WEA 206CD1*	53	1

1 Mike Oldfield featuring Maggie Reilly 2 Mike Oldfield with vocals by Maggie Reilly 3 Mike Oldfield featuring Aled Jones, Anita Hegerland and Barry Palmer

Tracks on Take 4 (EP): Portsmouth / In Dulce Jubilo / Wrekorder Wrondo / Sailors Hornpipe. 'The Bell' credits Vivian Stanshall

Sally OLDFIELD *UK, female vocalist (13 WEEKS)*
			pos/wks
9 Dec 78	**MIRRORS** *Bronze BRO 66*	19	13

Misty OLDLAND *UK, female vocalist (7 WEEKS)*
			pos/wks
16 Oct 93	**GOT ME A FEELING** *Columbia 6597872*	59	2
12 Mar 94	**A FAIR AFFAIR (JE T'AIME)** *Columbia 6601612*	49	4
9 Jul 94	**I WROTE YOU A SONG** *Columbia 6603732*	73	1

OLGA *Italy, female vocalist (1 WEEK)*
			pos/wks
1 Oct 94	**I'M A BITCH** *UMM UMM 144UKCD*	68	1

OLIVE *UK, male / female vocal / instrumental group – vocal Ruth Ann Boyle (24 WEEKS)*
			pos/wks
7 Sep 96	**YOU'RE NOT ALONE** *RCA 74321406272*	42	4
15 Mar 97	**MIRACLE** *RCA 74321461242*	41	2
17 May 97	★ **YOU'RE NOT ALONE** (re-issue) *RCA 74321473232* ■	1	13
16 Aug 97	**OUTLAW** *RCA 74321508372*	14	4
8 Nov 97	**MIRACLE** (re-mix) *RCA 74321530842*	41	1

OLIVER *US, male vocalist – William Swofford (18 WEEKS)*
			pos/wks
9 Aug 69	● **GOOD MORNING STARSHINE** (re) *CBS 4435*	6	18

Frankie OLIVER *UK, male vocalist (1 WEEK)*
			pos/wks
7 Jun 97	**GIVE HER WHAT SHE WANTS** *Island Jamaica IJCD 2011*	58	1

OLLIE and JERRY
US, male vocal duo – Ollie Brown and Jerry Knight (14 WEEKS)
			pos/wks
23 Jun 84	● **BREAKIN' . . . THERE'S NO STOPPING US** *Polydor POSP 690*	5	11
9 Mar 85	**ELECTRIC BOOGALOO** *Polydor POSP 730*	57	3

OLYMPIC ORCHESTRA *UK, orchestra (15 WEEKS)*
			pos/wks
1 Oct 83	**REILLY** *Red Bus RBUS 82*	26	15

OLYMPIC RUNNERS
UK, male vocal / instrumental group (21 WEEKS)
			pos/wks
13 May 78	**WHATEVER IT TAKES** *RCA PC 5078*	61	2
14 Oct 78	**GET IT WHILE YOU CAN** *Polydor RUN 7*	35	6
20 Jan 79	**SIR DANCEALOT** *Polydor POSP 17*	35	6
28 Jul 79	**THE BITCH** *Polydor POSP 63*	37	7

OLYMPICS *US, male vocal group (9 WEEKS)*
			pos/wks
3 Oct 58	**WESTERN MOVIES** *HMV POP 528*	12	8
19 Jan 61	**I WISH I COULD SHIMMY LIKE MY SISTER KATE** *Vogue V 9174*	40	1

OMAR *UK, male vocalist – Omar Hammer (18 WEEKS)*
			pos/wks
22 Jun 91	**THERE'S NOTHING LIKE THIS** *Talkin Loud TLK 9*	14	7
23 May 92	**YOUR LOSS MY GAIN** *Talkin Loud TLK 22*	47	2
26 Sep 92	**MUSIC** *Talkin Loud TLK 28*	53	2
23 Jul 94	**OUTSIDE / SATURDAY** *RCA 74321213982*	43	2
15 Oct 94	**KEEP STEPPIN'** *RCA 74321233682*	57	1
2 Aug 97	**SAY NOTHIN'** *RCA 74321502872*	29	2
18 Oct 97	**GOLDEN BROWN** *RCA 74321525422*	37	2

OMNI TRIO *UK, male producer – Rob Haigh (3 WEEKS)*
			pos/wks
7 Jul 01	**THE ANGELS & SHADOWS PROJECT** *Moving Shadow SHADOW 150CD*	44	3

ONE *UK, male vocal group (2 WEEKS)*
			pos/wks
11 Jan 97	**ONE MORE CHANCE** *Mercury MERDD 478*	31	2

Michie ONE – See Louchie LOU and Michie ONE

ONE DOVE *UK, male / female vocal / instrumental group (9 WEEKS)*
			pos/wks
7 Aug 93	**WHITE LOVE** *Boy's Own BOICD 14*	43	3
16 Oct 93	**BREAKDOWN** *Boy's Own BOICD 15*	24	3
15 Jan 94	**WHY DON'T YOU TAKE ME** *Boy's Own BOICD 16*	30	3

See also Dot ALLISON

187 LOCKDOWN *UK, male production duo – Danny Harrison and Julian Jonah (16 WEEKS)*
			pos/wks
15 Nov 97	**GUNMAN** *East West EW 140CD*	16	4
25 Apr 98	● **KUNG-FU** *East West EW 155CD*	9	5
25 Jul 98	**GUNMAN** (re-mix) *East West EW 176CD*	17	4
3 Oct 98	**THE DON** *East West EW 180CD*	29	2
13 Feb 99	**ALL 'N' ALL** *East West EW 194CD* 1	43	1

1 187 Lockdown (featuring D'Empress)

See also REFLEX featuring MC VIPER

1 GIANT LEAP *UK, male production duo – Jamie Catto and Duncan Bridgeman (6 WEEKS)*
			pos/wks
20 Apr 02	● **MY CULTURE** *Palm Pictures PPCD 70732*	9	6

Vocals by Robbie Williams and Maxi Jazz (Faithless)

See also FAITHLESS; Robbie WILLIAMS

ONE HUNDRED TON AND A FEATHER – See Jonathan KING

ONE MINUTE SILENCE
UK, male vocal / rap / instrumental group (1 WEEK)
			pos/wks
20 Jan 01	**FISH OUT OF WATER** *V2 VVR 5013213*	56	1

112 *US, male vocal / instrumental group (34 WEEKS)*
			pos/wks
28 Jun 97	★ **I'LL BE MISSING YOU** *Puff Daddy 74321499102* 1 ◆ ■ ▲	1	21
10 Jan 98	**ALL CRIED OUT** *Epic 6652715* 2	12	5
14 Feb 98	**SKY'S THE LIMIT** *Puff Daddy 74321561992* 3	35	2
30 Jun 01	**IT'S OVER NOW** *Puff Daddy/Arista 74321849912*	22	3
8 Sep 01	**PEACHES & CREAM** *ARISTA 74321882632*	32	3

1 Puff Daddy and Faith Evans featuring 112 2 Allure featuring 112 3 Notorious B.I.G. featuring 112

ONE THE JUGGLER
UK, male vocal / instrumental group (1 WEEK)
			pos/wks
19 Feb 83	**PASSION KILLER** *Regard RG 107*	71	1

1000 CLOWNS *US, male / female vocal / rap group (4 WEEKS)*
			pos/wks
22 May 99	**(NOT THE) GREATEST RAPPER** *Elektra E 3759CD*	23	4

ONE TRIBE – See OUR TRIBE / ONE TRIBE

ONE TRUE VOICE *UK, male vocal group (1 WEEK)*
			pos/wks
28 Dec 02	● **SACRED TRUST / AFTER YOU'RE GONE (I'LL STILL BE LOVING YOU)** *Ebul / Jive 9201532*	2	1+

ONE 2 MANY
Norway, male / female vocal / instrumental group (11 WEEKS)
			pos/wks
12 Nov 88	**DOWNTOWN** *A&M AM 476*	65	4
3 Jun 89	**DOWNTOWN** (re-issue) *A&M AM 456*	43	7

ONE WAY *US, male vocal / instrumental group (8 WEEKS)*
			pos/wks
8 Dec 79	**MUSIC** *MCA 542* 1	56	6
29 Jun 85	**LET'S TALK ABOUT SHHH** *MCA 972*	64	2

1 One Way featuring Al Hudson

HANDLE WITH CARE

■ Of all the so-called supergroups put together over the years, there can be none more star-studded than The Traveling Wilburys, who appeared out of nowhere in 1988. The quintet consisted of former Beatle George Harrison, ex-Electric Light Orchestra frontman Jeff Lynne, Bob Dylan, Roy Orbison and Tom Petty, and although the five had all crossed musical paths over the years, their coming together as a unit was the result of a string of coincidences.

As Jeff Lynne explained, the idea began as a joke between himself and George Harrison. "While we were doing Cloud Nine [Harrison's 1987 album] we'd sort of finish work most nights, have a few beers, listen back to the stuff, and have these silly little ideas about making our fantasy group, which would be like a group of all your favourite people – which started out as being The Trembling Wilburys!"

Some months later, Lynne was busy working in Los Angeles on Roy Orbison's album Mystery Girl when George Harrison got in touch, and the three went to lunch. Harrison revealed that he needed to record a "bonus" track for a 12-inch single ('When We Was Fab') that he was releasing and during the course of conversation Orbison volunteered to join on vocals. In need of a studio to record in, Harrison called his friend Bob Dylan who had a home studio in his garage. George Harrison recalled: "My guitar was at Tom Petty's house for some reason, and I had to go there and get it." Thus Petty joined Harrison, Lynne and Orbison on their way to Dylan's house, and the five future Wilburys convened for the first time.

At this point, Harrison had only half a song, and

■ **HARRISON HAD ONLY HALF A SONG, AND LOOKING ROUND DYLAN'S GARAGE FOR INSPIRATION SAW A CARTON MARKED "HANDLE WITH CARE"** ■

looking round Dylan's garage for inspiration saw a carton marked "handle with care". With five world-renowned songwriters sitting around in Dylan's garden with their acoustic guitars, and a working title, the song didn't take long to complete. With a little help from his friends, George Harrison had his song, and that would have been the end of the story had it not been for the reaction of Warner Bros, Harrison's record label. Jeff Lynne takes up the story: "George took it to the record company saying, 'Here's that track you were talking about', and they said, 'Aw no, you can't use that. It's too good for that – you know, you want to make an album of that!'"

★ ARTIST:	Traveling Wilburys
★ LABEL:	Wilbury
★ WRITERS:	Traveling Wilburys
★ PRODUCER:	George Harrison

Harrison and Lynne discussed the idea, and the other three quickly agreed. "So we went in and we did nine songs in 10 days, which is really quick," says Lynne. "It was great fun, and it was so easy, you see, because we had five songwriters all sitting around in a circle. There's no way you can't finish a song, because when you're writing on your own you might get stuck but when there's five of you there's always someone who's going to come up with an answer."

During the album's recording the group's name eventually evolved from "Trembling" to "Traveling Wilburys", while the members all adopted pseudonyms; Harrison became "Nelson"

Wilbury, while Dylan was "Lucky", Lynne "Otis", Orbison "Lefty" and Petty "Charlie T Jr". 'Handle with Care', originally recorded as a George Harrison B-side, launched the Wilburys' career and became their first hit, while the Grammy-winning album was a popular worldwide seller and reached No.3 in the US.

■ Tony Burton

Left to right: Dylan, Lynne, Petty, Orbison and Harrison

Alexander O'NEAL `270` `Top 500`

Soulful ex-vocalist with Minneapolis-based Flyte Time (line-up featured star producers Jimmy Jam and Terry Lewis, who worked on most of his hits), b. 15 Nov 1953, Mississippi, US. Co-wrote his biggest hit and clocked up impressive five Top 20 albums between 1985 and 1993 (110 WEEKS) pos/wks

28 Dec 85 ●	SATURDAY LOVE *Tabu A 6829* `1`	6	11
15 Feb 86	IF YOU WERE HERE TONIGHT *Tabu A 6391*	13	10
5 Apr 86	A BROKEN HEART CAN MEND *Tabu A 6244*	53	4
6 Jun 87	FAKE *Tabu 650891 7*	33	6
31 Oct 87 ●	CRITICIZE *Tabu 651211 7*	4	14
6 Feb 88	NEVER KNEW LOVE LIKE THIS *Tabu 651382 7* `2`	26	7
28 May 88	THE LOVERS *Tabu 6515957*	28	4
23 Jul 88	(WHAT CAN I SAY) TO MAKE YOU LOVE ME *Tabu 652852 7*	27	5
24 Sep 88	FAKE '88 (re-mix) *Tabu 652949 7*	16	7
10 Dec 88	CHRISTMAS SONG (CHESTNUTS ROASTING ON AN OPEN FIRE) / THANK YOU FOR A GOOD YEAR *Tabu 653182 7*	30	5
25 Feb 89	HEARSAY '89 *Tabu 654667 7*	56	2
2 Sep 89	SUNSHINE *Tabu 655191 7*	72	1
9 Dec 89	HITMIX (OFFICIAL BOOTLEG MEGA-MIX) *Tabu 655504 7*	19	7
24 Mar 90	SATURDAY LOVE (re-mix) *Tabu 655680 7* `1`	55	2
12 Jan 91	ALL TRUE MAN *Tabu 6565717*	18	6
23 Mar 91	WHAT IS THIS THING CALLED LOVE? *Tabu 6567317*	53	2
11 May 91	SHAME ON ME *Tabu 6568737*	71	1
9 May 92	SENTIMENTAL *Tabu 6580147*	53	2
30 Jan 93	LOVE MAKES NO SENSE *Tabu AMCD 7708*	28	6
3 Jul 93	IN THE MIDDLE *Tabu 5877152*	32	3
25 Sep 93	ALL THAT MATTERS TO ME *Tabu 6577232*	67	1
2 Nov 96	LET'S GET TOGETHER *EMI Premier PRESCD 11*	38	2
2 Aug 97	BABY COME TO ME *One World OWECD 1* `2`	56	1
12 Dec 98	CRITICIZE '98 MIX (re-recording) *One World OWECD 3*	51	1

`1` Cherrelle with Alexander O'Neal `2` Alexander O'Neal featuring Cherrelle

Shaquille O'NEAL *US, male rapper (4 WEEKS)* pos/wks

26 Mar 94	I'M OUTSTANDING *Jive JIVECD 349*	70	1
1 Feb 97	YOU CAN'T STOP THE REIGN *Interscope IND 95522*	40	2
17 Oct 98	THE WAY IT'S GOIN' DOWN (T.W.I.S.M. FOR LIFE) *A&M 5827932*	62	1

Martin O'NEILL – See LISBON LIONS featuring Martin O'NEILL & CELTIC CHORUS

ONEPHATDEEVA – See A.T.F.C. presents ONEPHATDEEVA

ONES *US, male production trio (12 WEEKS)* pos/wks

20 Oct 01 ●	FLAWLESS (re) *Positiva CDTIV 164*	7	12

ONLY ONES *UK, male vocal / instrumental group (2 WEEKS)* pos/wks

1 Feb 92	ANOTHER GIRL – ANOTHER PLANET *Columbia 6577507*	57	2

Yoko ONO *Japan, female vocalist (5 WEEKS)* pos/wks

28 Feb 81	WALKING ON THIN ICE *Geffen K 79202*	35	5

See also John LENNON

ONSLAUGHT *UK, male vocal / instrumental group (3 WEEKS)* pos/wks

6 May 89	LET THERE BE ROCK *London LON 224*	50	3

ONYX *US, male rap group (8 WEEKS)* pos/wks

28 Aug 93	SLAM *Columbia 6596302*	31	4
27 Nov 93	THROW YA GUNZ *Columbia 6598312*	34	3
20 Feb 99	ROC-IN-IT *Independiente ISOM 21MS* `1`	59	1

`1` Deejay Punk-Roc vs Onyx

ONYX STONE – See ROUND SOUND presents ONYX STONE & MC MALIBU

OO LA LA *UK, male vocal / instrumental group (2 WEEKS)* pos/wks

5 Sep 92	OO … AH … CANTONA *North Speed OOAH 1*	64	2

OOBERMAN *UK, male / female vocal / instrumental group (5 WEEKS)* pos/wks

8 May 99	BLOSSOMS FALLING *Independiente ISOM 26MS*	39	2
17 Jul 99	MILLION SUNS *Independiente ISOM 30MS*	43	1
23 Oct 99	TEARS FROM A WILLOW *Independiente ISOM 37MS*	63	1
8 Apr 00	SHORLEY WALL *Independiente ISOM 41MS*	47	1

OOE – See COLUMBO featuring OOE

OPEN ARMS featuring ROWETTA *UK, male / female vocal / instrumental group (1 WEEK)* pos/wks

15 Jun 96	HEY MR DJ *All Around the World CDGLOBE 136*	62	1

OPERA BABES *UK, female vocal duo (1 WEEK)* pos/wks

6 Jul 02	ONE FINE DAY *Sony Classical 6727062*	54	1

OPTICAL – See Ed RUSH & OPTICAL / UNIVERSAL PROJECT

OPTIMYSTIC *UK, male / female vocal group (6 WEEKS)* pos/wks

17 Sep 94	CAUGHT UP IN MY HEART *WEA YZ 841CD*	49	3
10 Dec 94	NOTHING BUT LOVE *WEA 864CD1*	37	2
13 May 95	BEST THING IN THE WORLD *WEA YZ 920CD*	70	1

OPUS *Austria, male vocal / instrumental group (15 WEEKS)* pos/wks

15 Jun 85 ●	LIVE IS LIFE *Polydor POSP 743*	6	15

OPUS III *UK, male / female vocal / instrumental group (10 WEEKS)* pos/wks

22 Feb 92 ●	IT'S A FINE DAY *PWL International PWL 215*	5	8
27 Jun 92	I TALK TO THE WIND *PWL International PWL 235*	52	1
11 Jun 94	WHEN YOU MADE THE MOUNTAIN *PWL International PWCD 302*	71	1

ORANGE *UK, male vocal / instrumental group (1 WEEK)* pos/wks

8 Oct 94	JUDY OVER THE RAINBOW *Chrysalis CDCHS 5012*	73	1

ORANGE JUICE *UK, male vocal / instrumental group (34 WEEKS)* pos/wks

7 Nov 81	L.O.V.E. … LOVE *Polydor POSP 357*	65	2
30 Jan 82	FELICITY *Polydor POSP 386*	63	3
21 Aug 82	TWO HEARTS TOGETHER / HOKOYO *Polydor POSP 470*	60	2
23 Oct 82	I CAN'T HELP MYSELF *Polydor POSP 522*	42	3
19 Feb 83	RIP IT UP *Polydor POSP 547*	8	11
4 Jun 83	FLESH OF MY FLESH *Polydor OJ 4*	41	6
25 Feb 84	BRIDGE *Polydor OJ 5*	67	2
12 May 84	WHAT PRESENCE? *Polydor OJ 6*	47	4
27 Oct 84	LEAN PERIOD *Polydor OJ 7*	74	1

See also Edwyn COLLINS

ORB *UK, male instrumental / production duo – Dr Alex Paterson and Kris Weston (32 WEEKS)* pos/wks

15 Jun 91	PERPETUAL DAWN (re) *Big Life BLRD 46*	18	6
20 Jun 92 ●	BLUE ROOM *Big Life BLRT 75*	8	6
17 Oct 92	ASSASSIN *Big Life BLRT 81*	12	5
13 Nov 93 ●	LITTLE FLUFFY CLOUDS *Big Life BLRD 98*	10	5
27 May 95	OXBOW LAKES *Island CID 609*	38	2
8 Feb 97 ●	TOXYGENE *Island CID 652*	4	4
24 May 97	ASYLUM *Island CID 657*	20	2
24 Feb 01	ONCE MORE *Island CID 767*	38	2

'Perpetual Dawn' made No.61 on its original visit to the chart before re-entering in Feb 1994 and making its peak position

Roy ORBISON `20` `Top 500`

Unmistakable vocalist, b. 23 Apr 1936, Texas, d. 6 Dec 1988. The "Big O" recorded for legendary Sun label in the mid-1950s, and was the most popular US singer in Britain during the Beat Boom era (1963-65), when The Beatles supported him on tour. The performer, whose trademark was his dark glasses, had a hit span of 33 years, and was enjoying a successful comeback, both as a soloist and member of The Traveling Wilburys, when he died. This multi-award-winner is in the Grammy Hall of Fame as well as the Songwriters' and Rock and Roll Halls of Fame (345 WEEKS)　pos/wks

28 Jul 60	★ ONLY THE LONELY (KNOW HOW I FEEL) (re)		
	London HLU 9149	1	24
27 Oct 60	● BLUE ANGEL *London HLU 9207*	11	16
25 May 61	● RUNNING SCARED *London HLU 9342* ▲	9	15
21 Sep 61	CRYIN' *London HLU 9405*	25	9
8 Mar 62	● DREAM BABY *London HLU 9511*	2	14
28 Jun 62	THE CROWD *London HLU 9561*	40	4
8 Nov 62	WORKIN' FOR THE MAN *London HLU 9607*	50	1
28 Feb 63	● IN DREAMS *London HLU 9676*	6	23
30 May 63	● FALLING *London HLU 9727*	9	11
19 Sep 63	● BLUE BAYOU / MEAN WOMAN BLUES *London HLU 9777*	3	19
20 Feb 64	● BORNE ON THE WIND *London HLU 9845*	15	10
30 Apr 64	★ IT'S OVER *London HLU 9882*	1	18
10 Sep 64	★ OH, PRETTY WOMAN *London HLU 9919* ▲	1	18
19 Nov 64	● PRETTY PAPER *London HLU 9930*	6	11
11 Feb 65	GOODNIGHT *London HLU 9951*	14	9
22 Jul 65	(SAY) YOU'RE MY GIRL *London HLU 9978*	23	8
9 Sep 65	RIDE AWAY *London HLU 9986*	34	6
4 Nov 65	CRAWLING BACK *London HLU 10000*	19	9
27 Jan 66	BREAKIN' UP IS BREAKIN' MY HEART		
	London HLU 10015	22	6
7 Apr 66	TWINKLE TOES *London HLU 10034*	29	5
16 Jun 66	LANA *London HLU 10051*	15	9
18 Aug 66	● TOO SOON TO KNOW *London HLU 10067*	3	17
1 Dec 66	THERE WON'T BE MANY COMING HOME *London HLU 10096*	12	9
23 Feb 67	SO GOOD *London HLU 10113*	32	6
24 Jul 68	WALK ON *London HLU 10206*	39	10
25 Sep 68	HEARTACHE *London HLU 10222*	44	4
30 Apr 69	MY FRIEND *London HLU 10261*	35	4
13 Sep 69	PENNY ARCADE (re) *London HLU 10285*	27	14
14 Jan 89	● YOU GOT IT *Virgin VS 1166*	3	10
1 Apr 89	SHE'S A MYSTERY TO ME *Virgin VS 1173*	27	5
4 Jul 92	● I DROVE ALL NIGHT *MCA MCS 1652*	7	10
22 Aug 92	CRYING *Virgin America VUS 63* [1]	13	6
7 Nov 92	HEARTBREAK RADIO *Virgin America VUS 68*	36	3
13 Nov 93	I DROVE ALL NIGHT (re-issue)		
	Virgin America VUSCD 79	47	2

[1] Roy Orbison (duet with kd lang)

William ORBIT

UK, male producer – William Wainwright (18 WEEKS)　pos/wks

26 Jun 93	WATER FROM A VINE LEAF *Guerilla VSCDT 1465*	59	1
18 Dec 99	● BARBER'S ADAGIO FOR STRINGS (re) *WEA WEA 247 CD*	4	15
6 May 00	RAVEL'S PAVANE POUR UNE INFANTE DEFUNTE		
	WEA WEA 269CD	31	2

ORBITAL

UK, male instrumental duo – Paul and Phil Hartnoll (56 WEEKS)　pos/wks

24 Mar 90	CHIME *ffrr F B5*	17	7
22 Sep 90	OMEN *ffrr F 145*	46	3
19 Jan 91	SATAN *ffrr FX 149*	31	4
15 Feb 92	MUTATIONS (EP) *ffrr FCD 181*	24	3
26 Sep 92	RADICCIO (EP) *Internal LIARX 1*	37	2
21 Aug 93	LUSH *Internal LIECD 7*	43	2
24 Sep 94	ARE WE HERE *Internal LIECD 15*	33	2
27 May 95	BELFAST *Volume VOLCD 1*	53	1
27 Apr 96	THE BOX *Internal LIECD 30*	11	4
11 Jan 97	● SATAN (re-recording) *Internal LIECD 37*	3	6
19 Apr 97	● THE SAINT *ffrr FCD 296*	3	7
20 Mar 99	STYLE *ffrr FCD 358*	13	4
17 Jul 99	NOTHING LEFT *ffrr FCD 365*	32	2
11 Mar 00	BEACHED *ffrr FCD 377* [1]	36	3

28 Apr 01	FUNNY BREAK (ONE IS ENOUGH) *ffrr FCD 395*	21	3
8 Jun 02	REST & PLAY (EP) *ffrr FCD 407*	33	3

[1] Orbital and Angelo Badalamenti

Tracks on Mutations (EP): Chime Crime / Oolaa / Farenheit 3D 3 / Speed Freak. Tracks on Radiccio (EP): Halcyon / The Naked and the Dead / Sunday. The listed flip side of 'Belfast' was 'Innocent X' by Therapy?. Tracks on Rest & Play (EP): 'Frenetic' / 'Illuminate' (featuring David Gray) / 'Chime'

ORCHESTRA ON THE HALF SHELL

US, male vocal / instrumental group (6 WEEKS)　pos/wks

15 Dec 90	TURTLE RHAPSODY *SBK SBK 17*	36	6

ORCHESTRAL MANOEUVRES IN THE DARK `91` `Top 500`

One of the most regular chart visitors of the 1980s had a nucleus of Andy McCluskey (v/syn/b) and Paul Humphries (syn), who left in 1989. This Liverpool-based synthesizer band had numerous international hits including 'Maid of Orleans', which was Germany's biggest seller in 1982 (201 WEEKS)　pos/wks

9 Feb 80	RED FRAME WHITE LIGHT *Dindisc DIN 6*	67	2
10 May 80	MESSAGES *Dindisc DIN 15*	13	11
4 Oct 80	● ENOLA GAY *Dindisc DIN 22*	8	15
29 Aug 81	● SOUVENIR *Dindisc DIN 24*	3	12
24 Oct 81	● JOAN OF ARC *Dindisc DIN 36*	5	14
23 Jan 82	● MAID OF ORLEANS (THE WALTZ JOAN OF ARC)		
	Dindisc DIN 40	4	10
19 Feb 83	● GENETIC ENGINEERING *Virgin VS 527*	20	8
9 Apr 83	TELEGRAPH *Virgin VS 580*	42	4
14 Apr 84	● LOCOMOTION *Virgin VS 660*	5	11
16 Jun 84	TALKING LOUD AND CLEAR *Virgin VS 685*	11	10
8 Sep 84	TESLA GIRLS *Virgin VS 705*	21	8
10 Nov 84	NEVER TURN AWAY *Virgin VS 727*	70	2
25 May 85	SO IN LOVE *Virgin VS 766*	27	7
20 Jul 85	SECRET *Virgin VS 796*	34	7
26 Oct 85	LA FEMME ACCIDENT *Virgin VS 811*	42	4
3 May 86	IF YOU LEAVE *Virgin VS 843*	48	4
6 Sep 86	(FOREVER) LIVE AND DIE *Virgin VS 888*	11	10
15 Nov 86	WE LOVE YOU *Virgin VS 911*	54	5
2 May 87	SHAME *Virgin VS 938*	52	3
6 Feb 88	DREAMING (re) *Virgin VS 987*	50	6
30 Mar 91	● SAILING ON THE SEVEN SEAS *Virgin VS 1310*	3	13
6 Jul 91	● PANDORA'S BOX *Virgin VS 1331*	7	10
14 Sep 91	THEN YOU TURN AWAY *Virgin VS 1368*	50	4
7 Dec 91	CALL MY NAME *Virgin VS 1380*	50	2
15 May 93	STAND ABOVE ME *Virgin VSCDG 1444*	21	4
17 Jul 93	DREAM OF ME (BASED ON LOVE'S THEME)		
	Virgin VSCDT 1461	24	5
18 Sep 93	EVERYDAY *Virgin VSCDT 1471*	59	2
17 Aug 96	WALKING ON THE MILKY WAY		
	Virgin VSCDT 1599	17	5
2 Nov 96	UNIVERSAL *Virgin VSCDT 1606*	55	1
26 Sep 98	THE OMD REMIXES (EP) (re-mix)		
	Virgin VSCDT 1694	35	2

Group often known as OMD. Tracks on the OMD Remixes (EP): Enola Gay / Souvenir / Electricity

Raul ORELLANA *Spain, male producer (8 WEEKS)*　pos/wks

30 Sep 89	THE REAL WILD HOUSE *RCA BCM 322*	29	8

O.R.G.A.N.

Spain, male DJ / producer – Vidana Crespo (2 WEEKS)　pos/wks

16 May 98	TO THE WORLD *Multiply CDMULTY 34*	33	2

ORIGIN *UK, male production duo (1 WEEK)*　pos/wks

12 Aug 00	WIDE EYED ANGEL *Lost Language LOST 001CD*	73	1

ORIGIN UNKNOWN

UK, male instrumental / production duo (2 WEEKS)　pos/wks

13 Jul 96	VALLEY OF THE SHADOWS *Ram RAMM 16CD*	60	1
11 May 02	TRULY ONE *Ram RAMM 38CD*	53	1

ORIGINAL *US, male vocal / instrumental duo*
– Everett Bradley and Walter Taieb (14 WEEKS) pos/wks

14 Jan 95	I LUV U BABY *Ore AG 8CD*	31 3
19 Aug 95 ●	I LUV U BABY (re-mix) *Ore AGR 8CD*	2 9
11 Nov 95	B 2 GETHER *Ore AG 12CD*	29 2

See also DIVA SURPRISE featuring Georgia JONES

ORIGINOO GUNN CLAPPAZ – *See HELTAH SKELTAH and ORIGINOO GUNN CLAPPAZ as the FABULOUS FIVE*

ORION *UK, male / female production / vocal / instrumental duo – Darren Tate and Sarah J (2 WEEKS)* pos/wks

7 Oct 00	ETERNITY *Incentive CENT 11CDS*	38 2

ORION TOO
Belgium, male producer and female vocalist (1 WEEK) pos/wks

9 Nov 02	HOPE AND WAIT *Data DATA 40CDS*	46 1

See also Jurgen VRIES; ANGELIC; CITIZEN CANED

ORLANDO – *See PRETENDERS; LA's*

Tony ORLANDO
US, male vocalist – Michael Anthony Orlando Cassavitis (11 WEEKS) pos/wks

5 Oct 61 ●	BLESS YOU *Fontana H 330*	5 11

See also DAWN

ORLONS *US, female / male vocal group (3 WEEKS)* pos/wks

27 Dec 62	DON'T HANG UP (re) *Cameo Parkway C 231*	39 3

ORN *UK, male DJ / producer – Omio Nourizadeh (1 WEEK)* pos/wks

1 Mar 97	SNOW *Deconstruction 74321447612*	61 1

Claudette ORTIZ – *See Wyclef JEAN*

Beth ORTON *UK, female vocalist (12 WEEKS)* pos/wks

1 Feb 97	TOUCH ME WITH YOUR LOVE *Heavenly HVN 64CD*	60 1
5 Apr 97	SOMEONE'S DAUGHTER *Heavenly HVN 65CD*	49 1
14 Jun 97	SHE CRIES YOUR NAME *Heavenly HVN 68CD*	40 2
13 Dec 97	BEST BIT (EP) *Heavenly HVN 72CD* [1]	36 3
13 Mar 99	STOLEN CAR *Heavenly HVN 89CD*	34 2
25 Sep 99	CENTRAL RESERVATION *Heavenly HVN 92CD*	37 2
16 Nov 02	ANYWHERE *Heavenly HVN 125CDS*	55 1

[1] Beth Orton featuring Terry Callier

Tracks on Best Bit (EP): Best Bit / Skimming Stone / Dolphins / Lean on Me

ORVILLE – *See Keith HARRIS and ORVILLE*

Jeffrey OSBORNE *US, male vocalist (38 WEEKS)* pos/wks

17 Sep 83	DON'T YOU GET SO MAD *A&M AM 140*	54 2
14 Apr 84	STAY WITH ME TONIGHT *A&M AM 188*	18 11
23 Jun 84	ON THE WINGS OF LOVE *A&M AM 198*	11 14
20 Oct 84	DON'T STOP *A&M AM 222*	61 2
26 Jul 86	SOWETO (re) *A&M AM 334*	44 6
15 Aug 87	LOVE POWER *Arista RIS 27* [1]	63 3

[1] Dionne Warwick and Jeffrey Osborne

Joan OSBORNE *US, female vocalist (13 WEEKS)* pos/wks

10 Feb 96 ●	ONE OF US *Blue Gorilla JOACD 1*	6 10
8 Jun 96	ST TERESA *Blue Gorilla JOACD 3*	33 3

Tony OSBORNE SOUND *UK, orchestra (3 WEEKS)* pos/wks

23 Feb 61	THE MAN FROM MADRID *HMV POP 827* [1]	50 1
3 Feb 73	THE SHEPHERD'S SONG *Philips 6006 266*	46 2

[1] Tony Osborne Sound featuring Joanne Brown

Kelly OSBOURNE *UK, female vocalist (13 WEEKS)* pos/wks

24 Aug 02	PAPA DON'T PREACH (import) *Epic 6729152*	65 3
21 Sep 02 ●	PAPA DON'T PREACH (re) *Epic 6731602*	3 10

Ozzy OSBOURNE *UK, male vocalist (48 WEEKS)* pos/wks

13 Sep 80	CRAZY TRAIN *Jet 197* [1]	49 4
15 Nov 80	MR CROWLEY *Jet 7003* [1]	46 3
26 Nov 83	BARK AT THE MOON *Epic A 3915*	21 8
2 Jun 84	SO TIRED *Epic A 4452*	20 9
1 Feb 86	SHOT IN THE DARK *Epic A 6859*	20 6
9 Aug 86	THE ULTIMATE SIN / LIGHTNING STRIKES *Epic A 7311*	72 1
20 May 89	CLOSE MY EYES FOREVER *Dreamland PB 49409* [2]	47 3
28 Sep 91	NO MORE TEARS *Epic 6574407*	32 2
30 Nov 91	MAMA I'M COMING HOME *Epic 6576177*	46 2
25 Nov 95	PERRY MASON *Epic 6626395*	23 2
31 Aug 96	I JUST WANT YOU *Epic 6635702*	43 1
8 Jun 02	DREAMER / GETS ME THROUGH *Epic 6724122*	18 6

[1] Ozzy Osbourne Blizzard of Ozz [2] Lita Ford duet with Ozzy Osbourne

See also BLACK SABBATH

OSIBISA
Ghana / Nigeria, male vocal / instrumental group (12 WEEKS) pos/wks

17 Jan 76	SUNSHINE DAY *Bronze BRO 20*	17 6
5 Jun 76	DANCE THE BODY MUSIC *Bronze BRO 26*	31 6

Donny OSMOND (237) `Top 500`

Teenage teen-idol vocalist, b. 9 Dec 1957, Utah, US. The main focal point of the hitmaking family act The Osmonds, he was one of the most popular pin-ups of the 1970s, had three solo No.1s before his 16th birthday and returned to the album Top 20 in 2002 (118 WEEKS) pos/wks

17 Jun 72 ★	PUPPY LOVE (3re) *MGM 2006 104*	1 23
16 Sep 72 ●	TOO YOUNG (re) *MGM 2006 113*	5 15
11 Nov 72 ●	WHY *MGM 2006 119*	3 20
10 Mar 73 ●	THE TWELFTH OF NEVER *MGM 2006 199*	1 14
18 Aug 73 ★	YOUNG LOVE *MGM 2006 300*	1 10
10 Nov 73 ●	WHEN I FALL IN LOVE *MGM 2006 365*	4 13
9 Nov 74	WHERE DID ALL THE GOOD TIMES GO *MGM 2006 468*	18 10
26 Sep 87	I'M IN IT FOR LOVE *Virgin VS 994*	70 1
6 Aug 88	SOLDIER OF LOVE *Virgin VS 1094*	29 8
12 Nov 88	IF IT'S LOVE THAT YOU WANT *Virgin VS 1140*	70 2
9 Feb 91	MY LOVE IS A FIRE *Capitol CL 600*	64 2

See also Donny and Marie OSMOND; OSMONDS

Donny and Marie OSMOND
US, male / female vocal duo (37 WEEKS) pos/wks

3 Aug 74 ●	I'M LEAVING IT (ALL) UP TO YOU *MGM 2006 446*	2 12
14 Dec 74 ●	MORNING SIDE OF THE MOUNTAIN *MGM 2006 474*	5 12
21 Jun 75	MAKE THE WORLD GO AWAY *MGM 2006 523*	18 6
17 Jan 76	DEEP PURPLE *MGM 2006 561*	25 7

See also Donny OSMOND; Marie OSMOND

Little Jimmy OSMOND *US, male vocalist (50 WEEKS)* pos/wks

25 Nov 72 ★	LONG HAIRED LOVER FROM LIVERPOOL (re) *MGM 2006 109* [1]	1 27
31 Mar 73 ●	TWEEDLEE DEE *MGM 2006 175*	4 13
23 Mar 74	I'M GONNA KNOCK ON YOUR DOOR *MGM 2006 389* [2]	11 10

[1] Little Jimmy Osmond with the Mike Curb Congregation [2] Jimmy Osmond

Marie OSMOND *US, female vocalist (15 WEEKS)* pos/wks

17 Nov 73 ●	PAPER ROSES *MGM 2006 315*	2 15

See also Donny and Marie OSMOND

OSMOND BOYS *US, male vocal group (6 WEEKS)* pos/wks

9 Nov 91	BOYS WILL BE BOYS *Curb 6573847*	65 2
11 Jan 92	SHOW ME THE WAY *Curb 6577227*	60 4

OSMONDS 329 Top 500 Top teeny-bop act, brothers Donny, Alan, Wayne, Merrill and Jay Osmond from Utah, US. Polished pop quintet created hysteria wherever they appeared. Osmond family (including Marie and Little Jimmy) had a record 13 UK hits in 1973 (94 WEEKS)

		pos/wks
5 Mar 72	DOWN BY THE LAZY RIVER *MGM 2006 096*	40 5
1 Nov 72 ●	CRAZY HORSES *MGM 2006 142*	2 18
4 Jul 73 ●	GOIN' HOME *MGM 2006 288*	4 10
7 Oct 73 ●	LET ME IN *MGM 2006 321*	2 14
0 Apr 74	I CAN'T STOP *MCA 129*	12 10
4 Aug 74 ★	LOVE ME FOR A REASON *MGM 2006 458*	1 9
1 Mar 75	HAVING A PARTY *MGM 2006 492*	28 8
4 May 75 ●	THE PROUD ONE *MGM 2006 520*	5 8
5 Nov 75	I'M STILL GONNA NEED YOU *MGM 2006 551*	32 4
0 Oct 76	I CAN'T LIVE A DREAM *Polydor 2066 726*	37 5
3 Sep 95	CRAZY HORSES (re-mix) *Polydor 5793212*	50 1
2 Jun 99	CRAZY HORSES (re-issue of re-mix)	
	Polydor 5611372	34 2

See also Donny OSMOND; Donny and Marie OSMOND

Gilbert O'SULLIVAN 164 Top 500

Distinctive Irish singer / songwriter / pianist, b. Raymond O'Sullivan, 1 Dec 1946, Waterford. His unusual image – short trousers, flat cap and pudding-basin haircut – helped to launch the successful international career of the performer voted No.1 UK Male Singer of 1972 (145 WEEKS)

		pos/wks
8 Nov 70 ●	NOTHING RHYMED *MAM 3*	8 11
3 Apr 71	UNDERNEATH THE BLANKET GO (re) *MAM 13*	40 4
4 Jul 71	WE WILL *MAM 30*	16 11
7 Nov 71 ●	NO MATTER HOW I TRY *MAM 53*	5 15
4 Mar 72 ●	ALONE AGAIN (NATURALLY) *MAM 66* ▲	3 12
7 Jun 72 ●	OOH-WAKKA-DOO-WAKKA-DAY *MAM 78*	8 11
1 Oct 72 ★	CLAIR *MAM 84*	1 14
7 Mar 73 ★	GET DOWN *MAM 96*	1 13
5 Sep 73	OOH BABY *MAM 107*	18 7
0 Nov 73 ●	WHY, OH WHY, OH WHY *MAM 111*	6 14
9 Feb 74	HAPPINESS IS ME AND YOU *MAM 114*	19 7
4 Aug 74	A WOMAN'S PLACE *MAM 122*	42 3
4 Dec 74	CHRISTMAS SONG *MAM 124*	12 6
4	I DON'T LOVE YOU BUT I THINK I LIKE YOU *MAM 130*	14 6
7 Sep 80	WHAT'S IN A KISS *CBS 8929*	19 9
4 Feb 90	SO WHAT *Dover ROJ 3*	70 2

OTHER TWO *UK, male / female vocal / instrumental duo – Stephen Morris and Gillian Gilbert (5 WEEKS)*

		pos/wks
9 Nov 91	TASTY FISH *Factory FAC 3297*	41 3
6 Nov 93	SELFISH *London TWOCD 1*	46 2

See also NEW ORDER

Johnny OTIS SHOW *US, band – leader John Veliotes (22 WEEKS)*

		pos/wks
2 Nov 57 ●	MA (HE'S MAKING EYES AT ME)	
	Capitol CL 14794 [1]	2 15
0 Jan 58	BYE BYE BABY *Capitol CL 14817* [2]	20 7

[1] Johnny Otis and His Orchestra with Marie Adams and the Three Tons of Joy [2] Johnny Otis Show, vocals by Marie Adams and Johnny Otis

OTTAWAN *France, male / female vocal duo (45 WEEKS)*

		pos/wks
3 Sep 80 ●	D.I.S.C.O. *Carrere CAR 161*	2 18
3 Dec 80	YOU'RE OK *Carrere CAR 168*	56 6
9 Aug 81 ●	HANDS UP (GIVE ME YOUR HEART)	
	Carrere CAR 183	3 15
5 Dec 81	HELP, GET ME SOME HELP! *Carrere CAR 215*	49 6

John OTWAY and Wild Willy BARRETT *UK, male vocal / instrumental duo (15 WEEKS)*

		pos/wks
3 Dec 77	REALLY FREE *Polydor 2058 951*	27 8
5 Jul 80	DK 50–80 *Polydor 2059 250* [1]	45 4
2 Oct 02 ●	BUNSEN BURNER *U-Vibe OTWAY 02X* [2]	9 3

[1] Otway and Barrett [2] John Otway

OUI 3 *UK / US / Switzerland, male / female rap / instrumental group (21 WEEKS)*

		pos/wks
20 Feb 93	FOR WHAT IT'S WORTH *MCA MCSTD 1736*	28 6
24 Apr 93	ARMS OF SOLITUDE *MCA MCSTD 1759*	54 2
17 Jul 93	BREAK FROM THE OLD ROUTINE *MCA MCSTD 1793*	17 6
23 Oct 93	FOR WHAT IT'S WORTH (re-mix) *MCA MCSTD 1941*	26 3
29 Jan 94	FACT OF LIFE *MCA MCSTD 1939*	38 2
27 May 95	JOY OF LIVING *MCA MCSTD 2057*	55 2

OUR DAUGHTER'S WEDDING *US, male vocal / instrumental group (6 WEEKS)*

		pos/wks
1 Aug 81	LAWNCHAIRS *EMI America EA 124*	49 6

OUR HOUSE *Australia, male instrumental production duo (1 WEEK)*

		pos/wks
31 Aug 96	FLOOR SPACE *Perfecto PERF 125CD*	52 1

OUR KID *UK, male vocal group (11 WEEKS)*

		pos/wks
29 May 76 ●	YOU JUST MIGHT SEE ME CRY *Polydor 2058 729*	2 11

OUR LADY PEACE *Canada, male vocal / instrumental group (1 WEEK)*

		pos/wks
15 Jan 00	ONE MAN ARMY *Epic 6688662*	70 1

OUR TRIBE / ONE TRIBE *UK / US, male / female vocal / instrumental group (13 WEEKS)*

		pos/wks
20 Jun 92	WHAT HAVE YOU DONE (IS THIS ALL)	
	Inner Rhythm HEART 03 [1]	52 2
27 Mar 93	I BELIEVE IN YOU *Ffrreedom TABCD 117* [2]	42 2
30 Apr 94	HOLD THAT SUCKER DOWN *Cheeky CHEKCD 004* [3]	24 3
21 May 94	LOVE COME HOME *Triangle BLUESCD 001* [4]	73 1
13 May 95	HIGH AS A KITE *ffrr FCD 259* [5]	55 1
30 Sep 95	HOLD THAT SUCKER DOWN (re-mix) *Cheeky CHEKCD 009* [3]	26 3
9 Dec 00	HOLD THAT SUCKER DOWN (re-issue)	
	Champion CHAMPCD 786 [3]	45 1

[1] One Tribe featuring Gem [2] Our Tribe [3] OT Quartet [4] Our Tribe with Franke Pharoah and Kristine W [5] One Tribe featuring Roger

See also ROLLO; DUSTED; FAITHLESS; SPHINX

OUT OF MY HAIR *UK, male vocal / instrumental group (1 WEEK)* pos/wks

1 Jul 95	MISTER JONES *RCA 74321267812*	73 1

OUTHERE BROTHERS *US, male rap / vocal duo (50 WEEKS) – Lamar Mahone and Craig Simpkins*

		pos/wks
18 Mar 95 ★	DON'T STOP (WIGGLE WIGGLE) *Eternal YZ 917CD*	1 15
17 Jun 95 ★	BOOM BOOM BOOM *Eternal YZ 938CD*	1 15
23 Sep 95 ●	LA LA LA HEY HEY *Eternal YZ 974CD*	7 7
16 Dec 95 ●	IF YOU WANNA PARTY *Eternal WEA 030CD* [1]	9 10
25 Jan 97	LET ME HEAR YOU SAY 'OLE OLE' *WEA 089CD*	18 3

[1] Molella featuring The Outhere Brothers

OUTKAST *US, male rap / vocal duo (29 WEEKS)* pos/wks

23 Dec 00	B.O.B (BOMBS OVER BAGHDAD)	
	Laface / Arista 74321822942	61 1
3 Feb 01	MS JACKSON (import) *Laface 73008245252*	48 4
3 Mar 01 ●	MS JACKSON *Laface / Arista 74321836822* ▲	2 10
9 Jun 01	SO FRESH, SO CLEAN *Laface / Arista 74321863402*	16 8
6 Apr 02	THE WHOLE WORLD *Laface 74321917592* [1]	19 5
27 Jul 02	LAND OF A MILLION DRUMS *Atlantic AT 0134CD* [2]	46 1

[1] Outkast featuring Killer Mike [2] Outkast featuring Killer Mike and Sleepy Brown

OUTLANDER *Belgium, male producer – Marcos Salon (3 WEEKS)* pos/wks

31 Aug 91	VAMP *R&S RSUK 1*	51 2
7 Feb 98	THE VAMP (REVAMPED) *R&S RS 97113CDX*	62 1

OUTLAWS UK, male instrumental group (4 WEEKS)   pos/wks

| 13 Apr 61 | SWINGIN' LOW *HMV POP 844* .... | 46 | 2 |
| 8 Jun 61 | AMBUSH *HMV POP 877* .... | 43 | 2 |

See also Mike BERRY

OUTRAGE US, male vocalist (2 WEEKS)   pos/wks

| 11 Mar 95 | TALL 'N' HANDSOME *Effective ECFL 001CD* .... | 57 | 1 |
| 23 Nov 96 | TALL 'N' HANDSOME (re-mix) *Positiva CDTIV 64* .... | 51 | 1 |

OUTSIDAZ featuring Rah DIGGA and Melanie BLATT US, male rap group and female rapper and UK, female vocalist (2 WEEKS)   pos/wks

| 2 Mar 02 | I'M LEAVIN' *Rufflife RLCDM 03* .... | 41 | 2 |

OVERLANDERS UK, male vocal / instrumental group – lead vocal Paul Arnold (10 WEEKS)   pos/wks

| 13 Jan 66 | ★ MICHELLE *Pye 7N 17034* .... | 1 | 10 |

OVERWEIGHT POOCH featuring Ce Ce PENISTON US, female rapper and female vocalist (2 WEEKS)   pos/wks

| 18 Jan 92 | I LIKE IT *A&M AM 847* .... | 58 | 2 |

Mark OWEN UK, male vocalist (24 WEEKS)   pos/wks

30 Nov 96	● CHILD (re) *RCA 74321424422*	3	15
15 Feb 97	● CLEMENTINE *RCA 74321454982*	3	6
23 Aug 97	I AM WHAT I AM *RCA 74321501222*	29	3

See also TAKE THAT

Reg OWEN and his Orchestra UK, orchestra, leader d. 1978 (10 WEEKS)   pos/wks

27 Feb 59	MANHATTAN SPIRITUAL		
	Pye International 7N 25009	20	8
27 Oct 60	OBSESSION *Palette PG 9004*	43	2

Sid OWEN UK, male actor / vocalist (6 WEEKS)   pos/wks

16 Dec 95	BETTER BELIEVE IT (CHILDREN IN NEED)		
	Trinity TDM 001CD [1]	60	1
8 Jul 00	GOOD THING GOING *Mushroom MUSH 74CDS*	14	5

[1] Sid Owen and Patsy Palmer

Robert OWENS US, male vocalist (5 WEEKS)   pos/wks

7 Dec 91	I'LL BE YOUR FRIEND *Perfecto PB 45161*	75	2
26 Apr 97	I'LL BE YOUR FRIEND (re-mix)		
	Perfecto PERF 137CD1	25	2
24 Feb 01	MINE TO GIVE *Science QEDCD 10* [1]	44	1

[1] Photek featuring Robert Owens

OXIDE & NEUTRINO UK, male production / rap duo – Alex Rivers and Mark Oseitutu (45 WEEKS)   pos/wks

6 May 00	★ BOUND 4 DA RELOAD (CASUALTY)		
	East West OXIDE 01CD1 ■	1	11
30 Dec 00	● NO GOOD 4 ME *East West OXIDE 02CD* [1]	6	8
26 May 01	● UP MIDDLE FINGER *East West OXIDE 03CD*	7	7
28 Jul 01	DEVIL'S NIGHTMARE *East West OXIDE 07CD1*	16	5
8 Dec 01	RAP DIS / ONLY WANNA KNOW U COS URE FAMOUS		
	East West OXIDE 08CD	12	8
28 Sep 02	● DEM GIRLZ (I DON'T KNOW WHY) (re)		
	East West OXIDE 09CD1 [2]	10	6

[1] Oxide & Neutrino featuring Megaman, Romeo and Lisa Maffia [2] Oxide & Neutrino featuring Kowdean

OZOMATLI US, male vocal / instrumental group (2 WEEKS)   pos/wks

| 20 Mar 99 | CUT CHEMIST SUITE *Almo Sounds CDALM 62* .... | 58 | 1 |
| 22 May 99 | SUPER BOWL SUNDAE *Almo Sounds CDALM 63* .... | 68 | 1 |

P

Jazzi P UK, female rapper – Pauline Bennett (12 WEEKS)   pos/wks

8 Jul 89	GET LOOSE *Breakout USA 659* [1]	25	6
9 Jun 90	FEEL THE RHYTHM *A&M USA 691*	51	2
3 Aug 91	REBEL WOMAN *DNA 7DNA 001* [2]	42	4

[1] LA Mix featuring Jazzi P [2] DNA featuring Jazzi P

PF PROJECT featuring Ewan McGREGOR UK, male production duo – Jamie White and Moussa Clarke – and UK, male actor (11 WEEKS)   pos/wks

| 15 Nov 97 | ● CHOOSE LIFE *Positiva CDTIV 84* .... | 6 | 11 |

See also TZANT; MUSIQUE VS U2

PhD UK, male vocal / instrumental trio – leader Jim Diamond (14 WEEKS) pos/wks

| 3 Apr 82 | ● I WON'T LET YOU DOWN *WEA K 79209* .... | 3 | 14 |

See also Jim DIAMOND

P.I.L. – *See PUBLIC IMAGE LTD*

PJ Canada, male producer – Paul Jacobs (2 WEEKS)   pos/wks

| 20 Sep 97 | HAPPY DAYS *Deconstruction 74321511822* .... | 72 | 1 |
| 4 Sep 99 | HAPPY DAYS (re-mix) *Defected DEFECT 6CDS* .... | 57 | 1 |

PJ & DUNCAN – *See ANT & DEC*

PJB featuring HANNAH and her SISTERS Germany, male production group and US, female vocalists (8 WEEKS)   pos/wks

| 14 Sep 91 | BRIDGE OVER TROUBLED WATER *Dance Pool 6565467* .... | 21 | 8 |

See also Hannah JONES

PKA UK, male producer – Phil Kelsey (2 WEEKS)   pos/wks

| 20 Apr 91 | TEMPERATURE RISING *Stress SS 4* .... | 68 | 1 |
| 7 Mar 92 | POWERGEN (ONLY YOUR LOVE) *Stress PKA 1* .... | 70 | 1 |

PM DAWN US, male vocal / instrumental / rap duo – Attrell and Jarrett Cordes (39 WEEKS)   pos/wks

8 Jun 91	A WATCHER'S POINT OF VIEW (DON'T CHA THINK)		
	Gee Street GEE 32	36	5
17 Aug 91	● SET ADRIFT ON MEMORY BLISS *Gee Street GEE 33* ▲	3	8
19 Oct 91	PAPER DOLL *Gee Street GEE 35*	49	3
22 Feb 92	REALITY USED TO BE A FRIEND OF MINE		
	Gee Street GEE 37	29	4
7 Nov 92	I'D DIE WITHOUT YOU *Gee Street GEE 39*	30	5
13 Mar 93	LOOKING THROUGH PATIENT EYES		
	Gee Street GESCD 47	11	7
12 Jun 93	MORE THAN LIKELY *Gee Street GESCD 49* [1]	40	3
30 Sep 95	DOWNTOWN VENUS *Gee Street GESCD 63*	58	2
6 Apr 96	SOMETIMES I MISS YOU SO MUCH *Gee Street GESCD 65*	58	1
31 Oct 98	GOTTA BE...MOVIN' ON UP *Gee Street GEE 5003933* [2]	68	1

[1] PM Dawn featuring Boy George [2] PM Dawn featuring Ky-Mani

POB featuring DJ Patrick REID UK , male producer – Paul Brogden and male DJ (1 WEEK)   pos/wks

| 11 Dec 99 | BLUEBOTTLE / FLY *Platipus PLAT 63CD* .... | 74 | 1 |

P.O.D. US, male vocal / instrumental group (8 WEEKS)   pos/wks

| 2 Feb 02 | ALIVE *Atlantic AT 0119CD* .... | 19 | 6 |
| 18 May 02 | YOUTH OF THE NATION *Atlantic AT 0127CD* .... | 36 | 2 |

P.O.V. featuring JADE *US, male vocal group and female vocal group (3 WEEKS)* pos/wks
5 Feb 94   **ALL THRU THE NITE** *Giant 74321187552* **32** 3

PPK *Russia, male production / instrumental duo – Sergey Pimenov and Alexander Polyakov (17 WEEKS)* pos/wks
8 Dec 01 ● **RESURECTION** *Perfecto PERF 32CDS* **3** 15
26 Oct 02   **RELOAD** *Perfecto PERF 41CDS* **39** 2

PQM featuring CICA *US, male producer and female vocalist (1 WEEK)* pos/wks
9 Dec 00   **THE FLYING SONG** *Renaissance / Yoshitoshi RENCDS 004* **68** 1

PSG – See COLOUR GIRL

Petey PABLO *US, male rapper (1 WEEK)* pos/wks
9 Feb 02   **I** *Jive 9253092* **51** 1

Thom PACE *US, male vocalist (15 WEEKS)* pos/wks
19 May 79   **MAYBE** *RSO 34* **14** 15

PACEMAKERS – See GERRY and the PACEMAKERS

PACIFICA *UK, male production duo (1 WEEK)* pos/wks
31 Jul 99   **LOST IN THE TRANSLATION** *Wildstar CDWILD 25* **54** 1

PACK featuring Nigel BENN *UK, male vocal / instrumental group and boxer / rapper (2 WEEKS)* pos/wks
8 Dec 90   **STAND AND FIGHT** *IQ ZB 44237* **61** 2

PACKABEATS *UK, male instrumental group (1 WEEK)* pos/wks
23 Feb 61   **GYPSY BEAT** *Parlophone R 4729* **49** 1

José PADILLA featuring Angela JOHN *Spain, male DJ and UK, female vocalist (1 WEEK)* pos/wks
8 Aug 98   **WHO DO YOU LOVE** *Manifesto FESCD 45* **59** 1

PAFFENDORF *Germany, male production duo – Gottfried Engels and Ramon Zenker (7 WEEKS)* pos/wks
15 Jun 02 ● **BE COOL** *Data DATA 29CDS* **7** 7

PAGANINI TRAXX *Italy, male DJ / producer (1 WEEK)* pos/wks
1 Feb 97   **ZOE** *Sony S3 DANUCD 18X* **47** 1

Jimmy PAGE *UK, male instrumentalist – guitar (16 WEEKS)* pos/wks
17 Dec 94   **GALLOWS POLE** *Fontana PPCD 2* 1 ....**35** 3
11 Apr 98   **MOST HIGH** *Mercury 5687512* 2 ....**26** 2
1 Aug 98   **COME WITH ME (import)** *Epic 34K78954* 3 ....**75** 1
8 Aug 98 ● **COME WITH ME** *Epic 6662842* 3 ....**2** 10

1 Jimmy Page and Robert Plant 2 Page and Plant 3 Puff Daddy featuring Jimmy Page

See also LED ZEPPELIN

Patti PAGE *US, female vocalist – Clara Ann Fowler (5 WEEKS)* pos/wks
27 Mar 53 ● **(HOW MUCH IS) THAT DOGGIE IN THE WINDOW** *Oriole CB 1156* ▲ **9** 5

Tommy PAGE *US, male vocalist (3 WEEKS)* pos/wks
26 May 90   **I'LL BE YOUR EVERYTHING** *Sire W 9959* ▲ **53** 3

Wendy PAGE – See TIN TIN OUT

PAGLIARO *Canada, male vocalist – Michel Pagliaro (6 WEEKS)* pos/wks
19 Feb 72   **LOVIN' YOU AIN'T EASY** *Pye 7N 45111* **31** 6

PAID & LIVE featuring Lauryn HILL *US, male production duo and female rapper / vocalist (1 WEEK)* pos/wks
27 Dec 97   **ALL MY TIME** *World Entertainment OWECD 2* **57** 1

Elaine PAIGE *UK, female vocalist – Elaine Bickerstaff (41 WEEKS)* pos/wks
21 Oct 78   **DON'T WALK AWAY TILL I TOUCH YOU** *EMI 2862* **46** 5
6 Jun 81 ● **MEMORY (re)** *Polydor POSP 279* **6** 15
14 Apr 84   **SOMETIMES (THEME FROM 'CHAMPIONS')** *Island IS 174* **72** 1
5 Jan 85 ★ **I KNOW HIM SO WELL** *RCA CHESS 3* 1 ....**1** 16
21 Nov 87   **THE SECOND TIME (THEME FROM 'BILITIS')** *WEA YZ 163*....**69** 1
21 Jan 95   **HYMNE A L'AMOUR (IF YOU LOVE ME)** *WEA YZ 899CD* **68** 1
24 Oct 98   **MEMORY (re-recording)** *WEA WEA 197CD* **36** 2

1 Elaine Paige and Barbara Dickson

Hal PAIGE and the WHALERS *US, male vocal / instrumental group (1 WEEK)* pos/wks
25 Aug 60   **GOING BACK TO MY HOME TOWN** *Melodisc MEL 1553*....**50** 1

Jennifer PAIGE *US, female vocalist (13 WEEKS)* pos/wks
12 Sep 98 ● **CRUSH** *EAR 0039425* **4** 12
20 Mar 99   **SOBER** *EAR / Edel 0044185 ERE* **68** 1

Orchestre de Chambre Jean-François PAILLARD *France, male conductor and orchestra (3 WEEKS)* pos/wks
20 Aug 88   **THEME FROM 'VIETNAM' (CANON IN D)** *Debut DEBT 3053* **61** 3

PALE *Ireland, male vocal / instrumental group (2 WEEKS)* pos/wks
13 Jun 92   **DOGS WITH NO TAILS** *A&M AM 866* **51** 2

PALE FOUNTAINS *UK, male vocal / instrumental group (6 WEEKS)* pos/wks
27 Nov 82   **THANK YOU** *Virgin VS 557* **48** 6

PALE SAINTS *UK, male / female vocal / instrumental group (1 WEEK)* pos/wks
6 Jul 91   **KINKY LOVE** *4AD AD 1009* **72** 1

PALE X *Holland, male producer (1 WEEK)* pos/wks
3 Feb 01   **NITRO** *Nukleuz NUKP 0280* **74** 1

Nerina PALLOT *UK, female vocalist (1 WEEK)* pos/wks
18 Aug 01   **PATIENCE** *Polydor 5872122* **61** 1

Barry PALMER – See Mike OLDFIELD

Jhay PALMER featuring MC IMAGE *UK, male producer / vocalist and UK, male rapper (1 WEEK)* pos/wks
27 Apr 02   **HELLO** *Bagatrix CDBTX 002* **69** 1

Patsy PALMER – See Sid OWEN

Robert PALMER ⟨213 | Top 500⟩
Grammy-winning UK rock-group veteran, b. 19 Jan 1949, Yorkshire. This vocalist's hottest run of transatlantic hits came after he fronted short-lived Anglo-American supergroup Power Station in 1985. He benefited from some striking award-winning videos featuring an all-female backing band (parodied in a 1999 Shania Twain video) (128 WEEKS) pos/wks
20 May 78   **EVERY KINDA PEOPLE** *Island WIP 6425*....................**53** 4
7 Jul 79   **BAD CASE OF LOVIN' YOU (DOCTOR DOCTOR)** *Island WIP 6481* **61** 2
6 Sep 80   **JOHNNY AND MARY** *Island WIP 6638*....................**44** 8
22 Nov 80   **LOOKING FOR CLUES** *Island WIP 6651*....................**33** 9
13 Feb 82   **SOME GUYS HAVE ALL THE LUCK** *Island WIP 6754* **16** 8
2 Apr 83   **YOU ARE IN MY SYSTEM** *Island IS 104* **53** 4
18 Jun 83   **YOU CAN HAVE IT (TAKE MY HEART)** *Island IS 121*....................**66** 2

		pos/wks
10 May 86 ●	ADDICTED TO LOVE *Island IS 270* ▲	**5** 15
19 Jul 86 ●	I DIDN'T MEAN TO TURN YOU ON *Island IS 283*	**9** 9
1 Nov 86	DISCIPLINE OF LOVE *Island IS 242*	**68** 1
26 Mar 88	SWEET LIES *Island IS 352*	**58** 3
11 Jun 88	SIMPLY IRRESISTIBLE *EMI EM 61*	**44** 4
15 Oct 88 ●	SHE MAKES MY DAY *EMI EM 65*	**6** 12
13 May 89	CHANGE HIS WAYS *EMI EM 85*	**28** 7
26 Aug 89	IT COULD HAPPEN TO YOU *EMI EM 99*	**71** 1
3 Nov 90 ●	I'LL BE YOUR BABY TONIGHT *EMI EM 167* 1	**6** 10
5 Jan 91 ●	MERCY MERCY ME – I WANT YOU *EMI EM 173*	**9** 9
15 Jun 91	DREAMS TO REMEMBER *EMI EM 193*	**68** 1
7 Mar 92	EVERY KINDA PEOPLE (re-mix) *Island IS 498*	**43** 3
17 Oct 92	WITCHCRAFT *EMI EM 251*	**50** 3
9 Jul 94	GIRL U WANT *EMI CDEMS 331*	**57** 2
3 Sep 94	KNOW BY NOW *EMI CDEMS 343*	**25** 5
24 Dec 94	YOU BLOW ME AWAY *EMI CDEMS 350*	**38** 4
14 Oct 95	RESPECT YOURSELF *EMI CDEMS 399*	**45** 2

1 Robert Palmer and UB40

Suzanne PALMER – See CLUB 69; ABSOLUTE; DJ TIESTO

Tyrone 'Visionary' PALMER – See SLAM

PAN POSITION
Italy / Venezuela, male instrumental / production group (1 WEEK)   pos/wks

18 Jun 94	ELEPHANT PAW (GET DOWN TO THE FUNK)	
	Positiva CDTIV 13	**55** 1

PANDORA'S BOX
US, male / female vocal / instrumental group (3 WEEKS)   pos/wks

21 Oct 89	IT'S ALL COMING BACK TO ME NOW *Virgin VS 1216*	**51** 3

Darryl PANDY *US, male vocalist (5 WEEKS)*   pos/wks

14 Dec 96	LOVE CAN'T TURN AROUND *4 Liberty LIBTCD 27* 1	**40** 2
20 Feb 99	RAISE YOUR HANDS *VC Recordings VCRD 44* 2	**40** 2
2 Oct 99	SUNSHINE & HAPPINESS *Azuli AZNYCD 103* 3	**68** 1

1 Farley 'Jackmaster' Funk with Darryl Pandy. 2 Big Room Girl featuring Darryl Pandy 3 Darryl Pandy / Nerio's Dubwork

Johnny PANIC and the BIBLE OF DREAMS
UK, male / female vocal / instrumental group (2 WEEKS)   pos/wks

2 Feb 91	JOHNNY PANIC AND THE BIBLE OF DREAMS	
	Fontana PANIC 1	**70** 2

See also TEARS FOR FEARS

PANTERA *US, male vocal / instrumental group (8 WEEKS)*   pos/wks

10 Oct 92	MOUTH FOR WAR *Atco A 5845T*	**73** 1
27 Feb 93	WALK *Atco B 6076CD*	**35** 2
19 Mar 94	I'M BROKEN *Atco B 5932CD1*	**19** 2
22 Oct 94	PLANET CARAVAN *East West A 5836CD1*	**26** 3

PAPA ROACH
US, male vocal / instrumental group (25 WEEKS)   pos/wks

17 Feb 01 ●	LAST RESORT *Dreamworks / Polydor 4509212*	**3** 10
5 May 01	BETWEEN ANGELS & INSECTS	
	Dreamworks / Polydor 4509082	**17** 6
22 Jun 02	SHE LOVES ME NOT *Dreamworks / Polydor 4508182*	**14** 8
2 Nov 02	TIME AND TIME AGAIN *Dreamworks / Polydor 4508052*	**54** 1

PAPER DOLLS *UK, female vocal group (13 WEEKS)*   pos/wks

13 Mar 68	SOMETHING HERE IN MY HEART (KEEPS A-TELLIN' ME NO) *Pye 7N 17456*	**11** 13

PAPER LACE *UK, male vocal / instrumental group – lead vocal Phil Wright (41 WEEKS)*   pos/wks

23 Feb 74 ★	BILLY DON'T BE A HERO *Bus Stop BUS 1014*	**1** 14
4 May 74 ●	THE NIGHT CHICAGO DIED *Bus Stop BUS 1016* ▲	**3** 11
24 Aug 74	THE BLACK EYED BOYS *Bus Stop BUS 1019*	**11** 10

4 Mar 78	WE GOT THE WHOLE WORLD IN OUR HANDS	
	Warner Bros. K 17110 1	**24** 6

1 Nottingham Forest with Paper Lace

PAPERDOLLS *UK, female vocal group (1 WEEK)*   pos/wks

12 Sep 98	GONNA MAKE YOU BLUSH *MCA MCSTD 40175*	**65** 1

PAPPA BEAR featuring VAN DER TOORN
Germany, male rapper and Holland, male vocalist (1 WEEK)   pos/wks

16 May 98	CHERISH *Universal UMD 70316*	**47** 1

PAR-T-ONE vs INXS *Italy, male production trio and Australia, male vocal / instrumental group (6 WEEKS)*   pos/wks

3 Nov 01	I'M SO CRAZY (re) *Credence CDCRED 016*	**19** 6

Vanessa PARADIS *France, female vocalist (30 WEEKS)*   pos/wks

13 Feb 88 ●	JOE LE TAXI *FA Productions POSP 902*	**3** 10
10 Oct 92 ●	BE MY BABY *Remark PO 235*	**6** 15
27 Feb 93	SUNDAY MONDAYS *Remark PZCD 251*	**49** 4
24 Jul 93	JUST AS LONG AS YOU ARE THERE *Remark PZCD 272*	**57** 1

PARADISE *UK, male vocal / instrumental group (4 WEEKS)*   pos/wks

10 Sep 83	ONE MIND, TWO HEARTS *Priority P 1*	**42** 4

PARADISE LOST *UK, male vocal / instrumental group (3 WEEKS)* pos/wks

20 May 95	THE LAST TIME *Music for Nations CDKUT 165*	**60** 1
7 Oct 95	FOREVER FAILURE *Music for Nations CDKUT 169*	**66** 1
28 Jun 97	SAY JUST WORDS *Music for Nations CDKUT 174*	**53** 1

PARADISE ORGANISATION
UK, male instrumental / production group (1 WEEK)   pos/wks

23 Jan 93	PRAYER TOWER *Cowboy RODEO 13*	**70** 1

PARADOX *UK, male instrumental duo (2 WEEKS)*   pos/wks

24 Feb 90	JAILBREAK *Ronin 7R2*	**66** 2

Norrie PARAMOR
UK, orchestra, leader – d. 9 Sep 1979 (8 WEEKS)   pos/wks

17 Mar 60	THEME FROM 'A SUMMER PLACE' *Columbia DB 4419*	**36** 2
22 Mar 62	THEME FROM 'Z CARS' *Columbia DB 4789*	**33** 6

PARAMOUNT JAZZ BAND – See Mr Acker BILK and his PARAMOUNT JAZZ BAND

PARAMOUNTS *UK, male vocal / instrumental group (7 WEEKS)*   pos/wks

16 Jan 64	POISON IVY *Parlophone R 5093*	**35** 7

PARCHMENT
UK, male / female vocal / instrumental group (5 WEEKS)   pos/wks

16 Sep 72	LIGHT UP THE FIRE *Pye 7N 45178*	**31** 5

PARIS *UK, male / female vocal group (4 WEEKS)*   pos/wks

19 Jun 82	NO GETTING OVER YOU *RCA 222*	**49** 4

PARIS *US, male vocalist – Oscar Jackson (2 WEEKS)*   pos/wks

21 Jan 95	GUERRILLA FUNK *Priority PTYCD 100*	**38** 2

Mica PARIS *UK, female vocalist – Michelle Wallen (63 WEEKS)*   pos/wks

7 May 88 ●	MY ONE TEMPTATION *Fourth & Broadway BRW 85*	**7** 11
30 Jul 88	LIKE DREAMERS DO *Fourth & Broadway BRW 108* 1	**26** 5
22 Oct 88	BREATHE LIFE INTO ME *Fourth & Broadway BRW 115*	**26** 10
21 Jan 89	WHERE IS THE LOVE *Fourth & Broadway BRW 122* 2	**19** 7
6 Oct 90	CONTRIBUTION *Fourth & Broadway BRW 188*	**33** 4
1 Dec 90	SOUTH OF THE RIVER *Fourth & Broadway BRW 199*	**50** 2
23 Feb 91	IF I LOVE U 2 NITE *Fourth & Broadway BRW 207*	**43** 3
31 Aug 91	YOUNG SOUL REBELS *Big Life BLR 57*	**61** 3

Re-entries are listed as (re), (2re), (3re), etc which signifies that the hit re-entered the chart once, twice, three times

	3 Apr 93	I NEVER FELT LIKE THIS BEFORE		
		Fourth & Broadway BRCD 263	**15**	5
	5 Jun 93	I WANNA HOLD ON TO YOU *Fourth & Broadway BRCD 275*	**27**	3
	7 Aug 93	TWO IN A MILLION *Fourth & Broadway BRCD 285*	**51**	2
	4 Dec 93	WHISPER A PRAYER *Fourth & Broadway BRCD 287*	**65**	1
	8 Apr 95	ONE *Cooltempo CDCOOL 304*	**29**	4
	16 May 98	STAY *Cooltempo CDCOOL 334*	**40**	2
	14 Nov 98	BLACK ANGEL *Cooltempo CDCOOL 341*	**72**	1

1 Mica Paris featuring Courtney Pine 2 Mica Paris and Will Downing

Ryan PARIS *France, male vocalist – Fabio Roscioli (10 WEEKS)*   pos/wks
	3 Sep 83	● DOLCE VITA *Carrere CAR 289*	**5**	10

PARIS & SHARP *UK, male production duo (1 WEEK)*   pos/wks
	1 Dec 01	APHRODITE *Cream / Parlophone CREAM 16CD*	**61**	1

PARIS ANGELS
UK, male / female vocal / instrumental group (5 WEEKS)
	3 Nov 90	SCOPE *Sheer Joy SHEER 0047*	**75**	1
	20 Jul 91	PERFUME *Virgin VS 1360*	**55**	3
	21 Sep 91	FADE *Virgin VS 1365*	**70**	1

PARIS RED
US / Germany, male / female vocal / instrumental duo (2 WEEKS)   pos/wks
	29 Feb 92	GOOD FRIEND *Columbia 6569417*	**61**	1
	15 May 93	PROMISES *Columbia 6592342*	**59**	1

John PARISH and Polly Jean HARVEY *US, male*
producer / instrumentalist and UK, female vocalist (1 WEEK)   pos/wks
	23 Nov 96	THAT WAS MY VEIL *Island CID 648*	**75**	1

See also PJ HARVEY

Simon PARK *UK, orchestra (24 WEEKS)*   pos/wks
	25 Nov 72	★ EYE LEVEL (THEME FROM THE TV SERIES `VAN DER VALK' (re)		
		Columbia DB 8946 ◆	**1**	24

'Eye Level' made No.41 on its original visit to the chart before re-entering and peaking at No.1 in Sep 1973

Graham PARKER and the RUMOUR
UK, male vocal / instrumental group (16 WEEKS)   pos/wks
	19 Mar 77	THE PINK PARKER EP *Vertigo PARK 001*	**24**	5
	22 Apr 78	HEY LORD, DON'T ASK ME QUESTIONS *Vertigo PARK 002*	**32**	7
	20 Mar 82	TEMPORARY BEAUTY *RCA PARK 100* 1	**50**	4

1 Graham Parker

Tracks on The Pink Parker EP: Hold Back the Night / (Let Me Get) Sweet on You / White Honey / Soul Shoes

Ray PARKER Jr *US, male vocalist (47 WEEKS)*   pos/wks
	25 Aug 84	● GHOSTBUSTERS *Arista ARIST 580* ▲	**2**	31
	18 Jan 86	GIRLS ARE MORE FUN *Arista ARIST 641*	**46**	4
	3 Oct 87	I DON'T THINK THAT MAN SHOULD SLEEP ALONE		
		Geffen GEF 27	**13**	10
	30 Jan 88	OVER YOU *Geffen GEF 33*	**65**	2

See also RAYDIO

Robert PARKER *US, male vocalist (8 WEEKS)*   pos/wks
	4 Aug 66	BAREFOOTIN' *Island WI 286*	**24**	8

Sara PARKER *US, female vocalist (2 WEEKS)*   pos/wks
	12 Apr 97	MY LOVE IS DEEP *Manifesto FESCD 22*	**22**	2

Jimmy PARKINSON *Australia, male vocalist (19 WEEKS)*   pos/wks
	2 Mar 56	● THE GREAT PRETENDER *Columbia DB 3729*	**9**	13
	17 Aug 56	WALK HAND IN HAND (re) *Columbia DB 3775*	**26**	2
	9 Nov 56	IN THE MIDDLE OF THE HOUSE (re) *Columbia DB 3833*	**20**	4

PARKS & WILSON *UK, male production duo*
– Michael Parks and Michael Wilson (1 WEEK)   pos/wks
	9 Sep 00	FEEL THE DRUM (EP) *Hooj Choons HOOJ 099*	**71**	1

Tracks on Feel the Drum (EP): My Orbit / The Dragon / My Orbit (remix) / Drum Parade (No UFOs)

PARLIAMENT – See Scott GROOVES

John PARR *UK, male vocalist (22 WEEKS)*   pos/wks
	14 Sep 85	● ST ELMO'S FIRE (MAN IN MOTION)		
		London LON 73 ▲	**6**	13
	18 Jan 86	NAUGHTY NAUGHTY *London LON 80*	**58**	3
	30 Aug 86	ROCK 'N' ROLL MERCENARIES *Arista ARIST 666* 1	**31**	6

1 Meat Loaf featuring John Parr

Dean PARRISH *US, male vocalist (5 WEEKS)*   pos/wks
	8 Feb 75	I'M ON MY WAY *UK USA 2*	**38**	5

Man PARRISH *US, male DJ / producer (26 WEEKS)*   pos/wks
	26 Mar 83	HIP HOP, BE BOP (DON'T STOP) *Polydor POSP 575*	**41**	6
	23 Mar 85	BOOGIE DOWN (BRONX) *Boiling Point POSP 731*	**56**	4
	13 Sep 86	● MALE STRIPPER (2re) *Bolts BOLTS 4* 1	**4**	16

1 Man 2 Man meet Man Parrish

'Male Stripper' made No.64 on its first chart visit followed by No.63 in Jan 1987 and No.4 on its second re-entry in Feb 1987

Karen PARRY – See PASCAL featuring Karen PARRY

Bill PARSONS *US, male vocalist (2 WEEKS)*   pos/wks
	10 Apr 59	THE ALL AMERICAN BOY *London HL 8798*	**22**	2

Record erroneously credited to Bill Parsons; actual vocalist is Bobby Bare

Alan PARSONS PROJECT
UK, male vocal / instrumental group (4 WEEKS)   pos/wks
	15 Jan 83	OLD AND WISE *Arista ARIST 494*	**74**	1
	10 Mar 84	DON'T ANSWER ME *Arista ARIST 553*	**58**	3

PARTIZAN *UK, male DJ / production duo – 'Tall*
Paul' Newman and Craig Daniel-Yefet (3 WEEKS)   pos/wks
	8 Feb 97	DRIVE ME CRAZY *Multiply CDMULTY 17*	**36**	2
	6 Dec 97	KEEP YOUR LOVE *Multiply CDMULTY 29* 1	**53**	1

1 Partizan featuring Natalie Robb

See also TALL PAUL; ESCRIMA; CAMISRA; GRIFTERS

PARTNERS IN KRYME *US, male rap duo*
– James Alpem and Richard Usher (10 WEEKS)   pos/wks
	21 Jul 90	★ TURTLE POWER *SBK TURTLE 1*	**1**	10

David PARTON *UK, male vocalist (9 WEEKS)*   pos/wks
	15 Jan 77	● ISN'T SHE LOVELY *Pye 7N 45663*	**4**	9

Dolly PARTON *US, female vocalist (34 WEEKS)*   pos/wks
	15 May 76	● JOLENE *RCA 2675*	**7**	10
	21 Feb 81	9 TO 5 *RCA 25* ▲	**47**	5
	12 Nov 83	● ISLANDS IN THE STREAM *RCA 378* 1 ▲	**7**	15
	7 Apr 84	HERE YOU COME AGAIN *RCA 395*	**75**	1
	16 Apr 94	THE DAY I FALL IN LOVE *Columbia 6600282* 2	**64**	2
	19 Oct 02	IF *Sanctuary SANX 139*	**73**	1

1 Kenny Rogers and Dolly Parton 2 Dolly Parton and James Ingram

Stella PARTON
US, female vocalist (4 WEEKS)   pos/wks
	22 Oct 77	THE DANGER OF A STRANGER *Elektra K 12272*	**35**	4

Don PARTRIDGE
UK, male vocalist / instrumentalist – one-man band (32 WEEKS)   pos/wks

7 Feb 68	● ROSIE *Columbia DB 8330*	4	12
29 May 68	● BLUE EYES *Columbia DB 8416*	3	13
19 Feb 69	BREAKFAST ON PLUTO *Columbia DB 8538*	26	7

PARTRIDGE FAMILY
US, male / female actor / vocal group (53 WEEKS)   pos/wks

13 Feb 71	I THINK I LOVE YOU *Bell 1130* [1] ▲	18	9
26 Feb 72	IT'S ONE OF THOSE NIGHTS (YES LOVE) *Bell 1203* [1]	11	11
8 Jul 72	● BREAKING UP IS HARD TO DO *Bell MABEL 1* [1]	3	13
3 Feb 73	● LOOKING THRU THE EYES OF LOVE *Bell 1278* [2]	9	9
19 May 73	● WALKING IN THE RAIN *Bell 1293* [2]	10	11

[1] Partridge Family starring Shirley Jones featuring David Cassidy [2] Partridge Family starring David Cassidy

See also David CASSIDY

PARTY ANIMALS
Holland, male instrumental / production duo (3 WEEKS)   pos/wks

1 Jun 96	HAVE YOU EVER BEEN MELLOW *Mokum DB 17553*	56	1
19 Oct 96	HAVE YOU EVER BEEN MELLOW (EP) *Mokum DB 17413*	43	2

Tracks on Have You Ever Been Mellow (EP): Have You Ever Been Mellow / Hava Naquilla / Aquarius

PARTY FAITHFUL
UK, male / female vocal / instrumental group (1 WEEK)   pos/wks

22 Jul 95	BRASS: LET THERE BE HOUSE *Ore AG 10CD*	54	1

PASADENAS
UK, male vocal group (57 WEEKS)   pos/wks

28 May 88	● TRIBUTE (RIGHT ON) *CBS PASA 1*	5	14
17 Sep 88	RIDING ON A TRAIN *CBS PASA 2*	13	9
26 Nov 88	ENCHANTED LADY *CBS PASA 3*	31	6
12 May 90	LOVE THING *CBS PASA 4*	22	5
14 Jul 90	REELING *CBS PASA 5*	75	1
1 Feb 92	● I'M DOING FINE NOW *Columbia 6577187*	4	10
4 Apr 92	MAKE IT WITH YOU *Columbia 6579257*	20	4
6 Jun 92	I BELIEVE IN MIRACLES *Columbia 6580567*	34	3
29 Aug 92	MOVING IN THE RIGHT DIRECTION *Columbia 6583417*	49	2
21 Nov 92	LET'S STAY TOGETHER *Columbia 6587747*	22	3

PASCAL featuring Karen PARRY
UK, male producer and female vocalist (1 WEEK)   pos/wks

28 Dec 02	I THINK WE'RE ALONE NOW *All Around the World CDGLOBE 267*	23	1+

PASSENGERS
Ireland / UK / Italy, male vocal / instrumental group (9 WEEKS)   pos/wks

2 Dec 95	● MISS SARAJEVO *Island CID 625*	6	9

PASSION
UK, male vocal / rap group (1 WEEK)   pos/wks

25 Jan 97	SHARE YOUR LOVE (NO DIGGITY) *Charm CRTCDS 269*	62	1

PASSIONS
UK, male / female vocal / instrumental group (8 WEEKS)   pos/wks

31 Jan 81	I'M IN LOVE WITH A GERMAN FILM STAR *Polydor POSP 222*	25	8

PAT and MICK
UK, male DJ / vocal duo – Pat Sharp and Mick Brown (27 WEEKS)   pos/wks

9 Apr 88	LET'S ALL CHANT / ON THE NIGHT *PWL PWL 10* [1]	11	9
25 Mar 89	● I HAVEN'T STOPPED DANCING YET *PWL PWL 33*	9	8
14 Apr 90	USE IT UP AND WEAR IT OUT *PWL PWL 55*	22	6
23 Mar 91	GIMME SOME *PWL PWL 75*	53	2
15 May 93	HOT HOT HOT *PWL International PARKCD 1*	47	2

[1] Mick and Pat

'On the Night' listed only from 4 Jun 1988. It peaked at No.70

PATIENCE and PRUDENCE
US, female vocal duo – Patience and Prudence McIntyre (8 WEEKS)   pos/wks

2 Nov 56	TONIGHT YOU BELONG TO ME *London HLU 8321*	28	3
1 Mar 57	GONNA GET ALONG WITHOUT YA NOW (re) *London HLU 8369*	22	5

PATRA *Jamaica, female vocalist (11 WEEKS)*   pos/wks

25 Dec 93	FAMILY AFFAIR *Polydor PZCD 304* [1]	18	8
30 Sep 95	PULL UP TO THE BUMPER *Epic 6623942*	50	2
10 Aug 96	WORK MI BODY *Heavenly HVN 53CD* [2]	75	1

[1] Shabba Ranks featuring Patra and Terri & Monica [2] Monkey Mafia featuring Patra

PATRIC *UK, male vocalist (2 WEEKS)*   pos/wks

9 Jul 94	LOVE ME *Bell 7432125352*	54	2

Dee PATTEN *UK, male DJ / producer (1 WEEK)*   pos/wks

30 Jan 99	WHO'S THE BAD MAN? *Higher Ground HIGHS 15CD*	42	1

Kellee PATTERSON *US, female vocalist (7 WEEKS)*   pos/wks

18 Feb 78	IF IT DON'T FIT DON'T FORCE IT *EMI International INT 544*	44	7

Rahsaan PATTERSON *US, male vocalist (2 WEEKS)*   pos/wks

26 Jul 97	STOP BY *MCA MCSTD 48055*	50	1
21 Mar 98	WHERE YOU ARE *MCA MCSTD 48073*	55	1

Billy PAUL *US, male vocalist – Paul Williams (44 WEEKS)*   pos/wks

13 Jan 73	ME AND MRS JONES *Epic EPC 1055* ▲	12	9
12 Jan 74	THANKS FOR SAVING MY LIFE *Philadelphia International PIR 1928*	33	6
22 May 76	LET'S MAKE A BABY *Philadelphia International PIR 4144*	30	5
30 Apr 77	LET 'EM IN *Philadelphia International PIR 5143*	26	5
16 Jul 77	YOUR SONG *Philadelphia International PIR 5391*	37	5
19 Nov 77	ONLY THE STRONG SURVIVE *Philadelphia International PIR 5699*	33	7
14 Jul 79	BRING THE FAMILY BACK *Philadelphia International PIR 7456*	51	5

Chris PAUL
UK, male producer / instrumentalist – guitar (8 WEEKS)   pos/wks

31 May 86	EXPANSIONS '86 (EXPAND YOUR MIND) *Fourth & Broadway BRW 48* [1]	58	5
21 Nov 87	BACK IN MY ARMS *Syncopate SY 5*	74	2
13 Aug 88	TURN THE MUSIC UP *Syncopate SY 13*	73	1

[1] Chris Paul featuring David Joseph

See also ISOTONIK

Frankie PAUL – *See APACHE INDIAN*

Les PAUL and Mary FORD
US, male instrumentalist – guitar, and female vocalist (4 WEEKS)   pos/wks

20 Nov 53	● VAYA CON DIOS (MAY GOD BE WITH YOU) *Capitol CL 13943* ▲	7	4

Lyn PAUL
UK, female vocalist – Lynda Belcher (6 WEEKS)   pos/wks

28 Jun 75	IT OUGHTA SELL A MILLION *Polydor 2058 602*	37	6

See also NEW SEEKERS

Owen PAUL *UK, male vocalist – Owen McGee (14 WEEKS)*   pos/wks

31 May 86	● MY FAVOURITE WASTE OF TIME *Epic A 7125*	3	14

Sean PAUL
Jamaica, male vocalist – Sean Paul Henriques (7 WEEKS)   pos/wks

21 Sep 02	GIMME THE LIGHT (re) *VP VPCD 6400*	32	7

PAUL and PAULA US, male / female vocal
duo – Ray Hildebrand and Jill Jackson (31 WEEKS)   pos/wks

| 14 Feb 63 ● | HEY PAULA (re) *Philips 304012 BF* ▲ | 8 17 |
| 18 Apr 63 ● | YOUNG LOVERS *Philips 304016 BF* | 9 14 |

Luciano PAVAROTTI Italy, male vocalist (30 WEEKS)   pos/wks

16 Jun 90 ●	NESSUN DORMA *Decca PAV 03*	2 11
24 Oct 92	MISERERE *London LON 329* [1]	15 5
30 Jul 94	LIBIAMO / LA DONNA E MOBILE *Teldec YZ 843CD* [2]	21 4
14 Dec 96 ●	LIVE LIKE HORSES *Rocket LLHDD 1* [3]	9 6
25 Jul 98	YOU'LL NEVER WALK ALONE *Decca 4607982* [4]	35 4

[1] Zucchero with Luciano Pavarotti [2] José Carreras featuring Placido Domingo and Luciano Pavarotti with Mehta [3] Elton John and Luciano Pavarotti [4] José Carreras, Placido Domingo and Luciano Pavarotti with Mehta

PAVEMENT US, male vocal / instrumental group (6 WEEKS)   pos/wks

28 Nov 92	WATERY, DOMESTIC (EP) *Big Cat ABB 38T*	58 1
12 Feb 94	CUT YOUR HAIR *Big Cat ABB 55SCD*	52 1
8 Feb 97	STEREO *Domino RUG 51CD*	48 1
3 May 97	SHADY LANE *Domino RUG 53CD*	40 1
22 May 99	CARROT ROPE *Domino RUG 90CD1*	27 2

Tracks on Watery, Domestic (EP): Texas Never Whispers / Frontwards / Feed 'Em / The Linden Lions / Shoot the Singer (1 Sick Verse)

Rita PAVONE Italy, female vocalist (19 WEEKS)   pos/wks

| 1 Dec 66 | HEART *RCA 1553* | 27 12 |
| 19 Jan 67 | YOU ONLY YOU *RCA 1561* | 21 7 |

PAY AS U GO UK, male rap / production group (4 WEEKS)   pos/wks

| 27 Apr 02 | CHAMPAGNE DANCE *So Urban 6721362* | 13 4 |

Freda PAYNE US, female vocalist (30 WEEKS)   pos/wks

5 Sep 70 ★	BAND OF GOLD *Invictus INV 502*	1 19
21 Nov 70	DEEPER AND DEEPER *Invictus INV 505*	33 9
27 Mar 71	CHERISH WHAT IS DEAR TO YOU (WHILE IT'S NEAR TO YOU) *Invictus INV 509*	46 2

Tammy PAYNE UK, female vocalist (2 WEEKS)   pos/wks

| 20 Jul 91 | TAKE ME NOW *Talkin Loud TLK 12* | 55 2 |

Heather PEACE UK, female vocalist (1 WEEK)   pos/wks

| 13 May 00 | THE ROSE *RCA 74321742892* | 56 1 |

PEACE BY PIECE UK, male vocal group (2 WEEKS)   pos/wks

| 21 Sep 96 | SWEET SISTER *Blanco Y Negro NEG 94CD* | 46 1 |
| 25 Apr 98 | NOBODY'S BUSINESS *Blanco Y Negro NEG 110CD1* | 50 1 |

PEACH UK / Belgium, female / male vocal / production group (1 WEEK)   pos/wks

| 17 Jan 98 | ON MY OWN *Mute CDMUTE 215* | 69 1 |

PEACHES
Canada, female producer / vocalist – Merrill Nisker (2 WEEKS)   pos/wks

| 15 Jun 02 | SET IT OFF *Epic 6726862* | 36 2 |

PEACHES and HERB US, female / male vocal
duo – Linda Green and Herbert Feemster (23 WEEKS)   pos/wks

| 20 Jan 79 | SHAKE YOUR GROOVE THING *Polydor 2066 992* | 26 10 |
| 21 Apr 79 ● | REUNITED *Polydor POSP 43* ▲ | 4 13 |

Mary PEARCE – See UP YER RONSON featuring Mary PEARCE

Natasha PEARL – See TASTE XPERIENCE featuring Natasha PEARL

PEARL JAM US, male vocal / instrumental group (43 WEEKS)   pos/wks

15 Feb 92	ALIVE *Epic 6575727*	16 6
18 Apr 92	EVEN FLOW *Epic 6578577*	27 3
26 Sep 92	JEREMY *Epic 6582587*	15 4
1 Jan 94	DAUGHTER *Epic 6600202*	18 5
28 May 94	DISSIDENT *Epic 6604415*	14 4
26 Nov 94 ●	SPIN THE BLACK CIRCLE *Epic 6610362*	10 3
25 Feb 95	NOT FOR YOU *Epic 6612032*	34 2
16 Dec 95	MERKINBALL *Epic 6627162*	25 2
17 Aug 96	WHO YOU ARE *Epic 6635392*	18 2
31 Jan 98	GIVEN TO FLY *Epic 6653942*	12 3
23 May 98	WISHLIST *Epic 6657902*	30 2
14 Aug 99	LAST KISS *Epic 6674791*	42 1
13 May 00	NOTHING AS IT SEEMS *Epic 6693742*	22 2
22 Jul 00	LIGHT YEARS *Epic 6696282*	52 1
9 Nov 02	I AM MINE *Epic 6733082*	26 2

'Merkinball' is the title of the single featuring 'I Got Id' and 'Long Road'

PEARLS UK, female vocal duo (24 WEEKS)   pos/wks

27 May 72	THIRD FINGER, LEFT HAND *Bell 1217*	31 6
23 Sep 72	YOU CAME, YOU SAW, YOU CONQUERED *Bell 1254*	32 5
24 Mar 73	YOU ARE EVERYTHING *Bell 1284*	41 3
1 Jun 74 ●	GUILTY *Bell 1352*	10 10

Johnny PEARSON ORCHESTRA
UK, orchestra – Johnny Pearson – piano (15 WEEKS)   pos/wks

| 18 Dec 71 ● | SLEEPY SHORES *Penny Farthing PEN 778* | 8 15 |

PEBBLES US, female vocalist – Perri McKissack (17 WEEKS)   pos/wks

19 Mar 88 ●	GIRLFRIEND *MCA MCA 1233*	8 11
28 May 88	MERCEDES BOY *MCA MCA 1248*	42 4
27 Oct 90	GIVING YOU THE BENEFIT *MCA MCA 1448*	73 2

PEDDLERS UK, male vocal / instrumental group (14 WEEKS)   pos/wks

7 Jan 65	LET THE SUNSHINE IN *Philips BF 1375*	50 1
23 Aug 69	BIRTH *CBS 4449*	17 9
31 Jan 70	GIRLIE *CBS 4720*	34 4

PEE BEE SQUAD UK, male vocalist – Paul Burnett (3 WEEKS)   pos/wks

| 5 Oct 85 | RUGGED AND MEAN, BUTCH AND ON SCREEN *Project PRO 3* | 52 3 |

Ann PEEBLES US, female vocalist (3 WEEKS)   pos/wks

| 20 Apr 74 | I CAN'T STAND THE RAIN (re) *London HLU 10428* | 41 3 |

PEECH BOYS US, male vocal / instrumental group (3 WEEKS)   pos/wks

| 30 Oct 82 | DON'T MAKE ME WAIT *TMT TMT 7001* | 49 3 |

Donald PEERS UK, male vocalist d. 9 Aug 1973 (28 WEEKS)   pos/wks

29 Dec 66	GAMES THAT LOVERS PLAY *Columbia DB 8079*	46 1
18 Dec 68 ●	PLEASE DON'T GO (re) *Columbia DB 8502*	3 21
24 Jun 72	GIVE ME ONE MORE CHANCE *Decca F 13302*	36 6

PELE UK, male / female / instrumental group (3 WEEKS)   pos/wks

15 Feb 92	MEGALOMANIA *M & G MAGS 20*	73 1
13 Jun 92	FAIR BLOWS THE WIND FOR FRANCE *M & G MAGS 24*	62 1
31 Jul 93	FAT BLACK HEART *M & G MAGCD 43*	75 1

Marti PELLOW UK, male vocalist (8 WEEKS)   pos/wks

| 16 Jun 01 ● | CLOSE TO YOU *Mercury MERCD 532* | 9 6 |
| 1 Dec 01 | I'VE BEEN AROUND THE WORLD *Mercury 5887772* | 28 2 |

See also WET WET WET

Debbie PENDER US, female vocalist (1 WEEK)   pos/wks

| 30 May 98 | MOVIN' ON *AM:PM 5826492* | 41 1 |

CHART-TOPPING FIRSTS

■ Here, in a list of achievements that can never be bettered, are the earliest No.1 chart stars in a variety of different categories

George McCrae: responsible for the first disco chart-topper

First male solo No.1 1952
AL MARTINO – 'HERE IN MY HEART'

First female solo No.1 1953
JO STAFFORD – 'YOU BELONG TO ME'

First UK-born male No.1 1953
DAVID WHITFIELD – 'ANSWER ME'

First US-born male No.1 1952
AL MARTINO – 'HERE IN MY HEART'

First UK-born female No.1 1953
LITA ROZA – (HOW MUCH IS)
THAT DOGGIE IN THE WINDOW

First US-born female No.1 1953
JO STAFFORD –
'YOU BELONG TO ME'

First male teenager at No.1 1956
Teenagers featuring FRANKIE LYMON –
'WHY DO FOOLS FALL IN LOVE'

First female teenager at No.1 1958
CONNIE FRANCIS –
'WHO'S SORRY NOW'

First UK group No.1 1953
STARGAZERS – 'BROKEN WINGS'

First duo No.1 1958
EVERLY BROTHERS –
'ALL I HAVE TO DO IS DREAM'

First trio No.1 1964
SUPREMES – 'BABY LOVE'

First male group No.1 1955
JOHNSTON BROTHERS –
'HERNANDO'S HIDEAWAY'

First female group No.1 1964
SUPREMES – 'BABY LOVE'

First mixed group No.1 1953
STARGAZERS – 'BROKEN WINGS'

First female duo No.1 1977
BACCARA – 'YES SIR, I CAN BOOGIE'

First a cappella No.1 1983
FLYING PICKETS – 'ONLY YOU'

First instrumental No.1 1953
MANTOVANI AND HIS ORCHESTRA –
'THE SONG FROM THE MOULIN ROUGE'

First non-human No.1 1969
ARCHIES – 'SUGAR SUGAR'

First Motown No.1 1964
SUPREMES – 'BABY LOVE'

First No.1 including samples 1987
M/A/R/R/S – 'PUMP UP THE VOLUME'

First transatlantic No.1 1952
AL MARTINO – 'HERE IN MY HEART'

First Eurovision No.1 1967
SANDIE SHAW – 'PUPPET ON A STRING'

First self-penned No.1 1956
DREAMWEAVERS –
'IT'S ALMOST TOMORROW'

First posthumous No.1 1959
BUDDY HOLLY –
'IT DOESN'T MATTER ANYMORE'

First No.1 to include rap 1983
NEW EDITION – 'CANDY GIRL'

First new wave/punk No.1 1978
BOOMTOWN RATS – 'RAT TRAP'

First house No.1 1987
STEVE 'SILK' HURLEY –
'JACK YOUR BODY'

First disco No.1 1974
GEORGE McCRAE – 'ROCK YOUR BABY'

First country No.1 1955 – TENNESSEE
ERNIE FORD – 'GIVE ME YOUR WORD'

First rock 'n' roll No.1 1955
BILL HALEY AND HIS COMETS –
'ROCK AROUND THE CLOCK'

First film theme No.1 1953
MANTOVANI AND HIS ORCHESTRA –
'THE SONG FROM THE MOULIN ROUGE'

California-born Jo Stafford: the first US female to top the UK singles chart as a solo artist

Teddy PENDERGRASS US, male vocalist (24 WEEKS)

		pos/wks
21 May 77	THE WHOLE TOWN'S LAUGHING AT ME	
	Philadelphia International PIR 5116 ....44 3	
28 Oct 78	ONLY YOU / CLOSE THE DOOR	
	Philadelphia International PIR 6713 ....41 6	
23 May 81	TWO HEARTS *20th Century TC 2492* [1] 49 5	
25 Jan 86	HOLD ME *Asylum EKR 32* [2] 44 5	
28 May 88	JOY *Elektra EKR 75* 58 3	
19 Nov 94	THE MORE I GET THE MORE I WANT	
	X-clusive XCLU 011CD [3] 35 2	

[1] Stephanie Mills featuring Teddy Pendergrass [2] Teddy Pendergrass with Whitney Houston [3] KWS featuring Teddy Pendergrass

Ce Ce PENISTON US, female vocalist (53 WEEKS)

		pos/wks
12 Oct 91	FINALLY *A&M AM 822* 29 7	
11 Jan 92 ●	WE GOT A LOVE THANG *A&M AM 846* 6 8	
18 Jan 92	I LIKE IT *A&M AM 847* [1] 58 2	
21 Mar 92 ●	FINALLY (re-issue) *A&M AM 858* 2 8	
23 May 92 ●	KEEP ON WALKIN' *A&M AM 878* 10 6	
5 Sep 92	CRAZY LOVE *A&M AM 0060* 44 3	
12 Dec 92	INSIDE THAT I CRIED *A&M AM 0121* 42 2	
15 Jan 94	I'M IN THE MOOD *A&M 5804552* 16 4	
2 Apr 94	KEEP GIVIN' ME YOUR LOVE *A&M 5805492* 36 2	
6 Aug 94	HIT BY LOVE *A&M 5806932* 33 2	
13 Sep 97	FINALLY (re-mix) *AM:PM 5823432* 26 5	
7 Feb 98	SOMEBODY ELSE'S GUY *AM:PM 5825112* 13 4	

[1] Overweight Pooch featuring Ce Ce Peniston

Dawn PENN
Jamaica, female vocalist – Dawn Pickering (12 WEEKS)

		pos/wks
11 Jun 94 ●	YOU DON'T LOVE ME (NO, NO, NO) *Big Beat A 8295CD* 3 12	

Barbara PENNINGTON US, female vocalist (8 WEEKS)

		pos/wks
27 Apr 85	FAN THE FLAME *Record Shack SOHO 37* 62 3	
27 Jul 85	ON A CROWDED STREET *Record Shack SOHO 49* 57 5	

Tricia PENROSE UK, female vocalist (2 WEEKS)

		pos/wks
7 Dec 96	WHERE DID OUR LOVE GO *RCA 74321428152* 71 1	
4 Mar 00	DON'T WANNA BE ALONE *Doop DP 2001CD* 44 1	

PENTANGLE
UK, male / female vocal / instrumental group (4 WEEKS)

		pos/wks
28 May 69	ONCE I HAD A SWEETHEART *Big T BIG 124* 46 1	
14 Feb 70	LIGHT FLIGHT (re) *Big T BIG 128* 43 3	

PENTHOUSE 4 UK, male vocal / instrumental duo (3 WEEKS)

		pos/wks
23 Apr 88	BUST THIS HOUSE DOWN *Syncopate SY 10* 56 3	

PEOPLES CHOICE
US, male vocal / instrumental group (9 WEEKS)

		pos/wks
20 Sep 75	DO IT ANY WAY YOU WANNA	
	Philadelphia International PIR 3500 ....36 5	
21 Jan 78	JAM, JAM, JAM (ALL NIGHT LONG)	
	Philadelphia International PIR 5891 [1] 40 4	

[1] People's Choice

PEPE DELUXE Finland, male DJ / production group (3 WEEKS)

		pos/wks
26 May 01	BEFORE YOU LEAVE *Catskills / Incredible 6712392* 20 3	

Danny PEPPERMINT and the JUMPING JACKS US, male
vocal / instrumental group, leader – Danny Lamego (8 WEEKS)

		pos/wks
18 Jan 62	THE PEPPERMINT TWIST *London HLL 9478* 26 8	

PEPPERS France, male instrumental group (12 WEEKS)

		pos/wks
26 Oct 74 ●	PEPPER BOX *Spark SRL 1100* 6 12	

PEPSI and SHIRLIE UK, female vocal duo
– Helen DeMacque and Shirley Holliman (24 WEEKS)

		pos/wks
17 Jan 87 ●	HEARTACHE *Polydor POSP 837* 2 12	
30 May 87 ●	GOODBYE STRANGER *Polydor POSP 865* 9 7	
26 Sep 87	CAN'T GIVE ME LOVE *Polydor POSP 885* 58 3	
12 Dec 87	ALL RIGHT NOW *Polydor POSP 896* 50 2	

PERAN Holland, male producer – Peran van Dijk (2 WEEKS)

		pos/wks
23 Mar 02	GOOD TIME *Incentive CENT 37CDS* 37 2	

PERCEPTION UK, male vocal group (2 WEEKS)

		pos/wks
7 Mar 92	FEED THE FEELING *Talkin Loud TLK 17* 58 2	

The listed flip side of 'Feed the Feeling' was 'Three Times a Maybe' by K-Creative

Lance PERCIVAL UK, male vocalist (3 WEEKS)

		pos/wks
28 Oct 65	SHAME AND SCANDAL IN THE FAMILY	
	Parlophone R 5335 ....37 3	

PERFECT CIRCLE – See A PERFECT CIRCLE

PERFECT DAY
UK, male vocal / instrumental group (4 WEEKS)

		pos/wks
21 Jan 89	LIBERTY TOWN *London LON 214* 58 3	
1 Apr 89	JANE *London LON 188* 68 1	

PERFECT PHASE Holland, male production duo
– Freek Fontein and Willem Faber (7 WEEKS)

		pos/wks
25 Dec 99	HORNY HORNS *Positiva CDTIV 123* 21 7	

PERFECTLY ORDINARY PEOPLE
UK, male vocal / instrumental group (3 WEEKS)

		pos/wks
22 Oct 88	THEME FROM P.O.P. *Urban URB 25* 61 3	

PERFECTO ALLSTARZ UK, male instrumental /
production duo – Paul Oakenfold and Steve Osborne (11 WEEKS)

		pos/wks
4 Feb 95 ●	REACH UP (PAPA'S GOT A BRAND NEW PIG BAG)	
	Perfecto YZ 892CD 6 11	

PERFUME UK, male vocal / instrumental group (1 WEEK)

		pos/wks
10 Feb 96	HAVEN'T SEEN YOU *Aromasound AROMA 005CDS* 71 1	

Emilio PERICOLI Italy, male vocalist (14 WEEKS)

		pos/wks
28 Jun 62	AL DI LA *Warner Bros. WB 69* 30 14	

Carl PERKINS US, male vocalist d. 19 Jan 1988 (8 WEEKS)

		pos/wks
18 May 56 ●	BLUE SUEDE SHOES *London HLU 8271* 10 8	

PERPETUAL MOTION
UK, male instrumental / production group (5 WEEKS)

		pos/wks
2 May 98	KEEP ON DANCIN' (LET'S GO) *Positiva CDTIV 90* 12 5	

Steve PERRY UK, male vocalist (1 WEEK)

		pos/wks
4 Aug 60	STEP BY STEP *HMV POP 745* 41 1	

Nina PERSSON and David ARNOLD Sweden, female
vocalist and UK, male instrumentalist / producer (1 WEEK)

		pos/wks
29 Apr 00	THEME FROM 'RANDALL & HOPKIRK (DECEASED)'	
	Island CID 762 ....49 1	

See also CARDIGANS

Jon PERTWEE
UK, male actor / vocalist d. 20 May 1996 (7 WEEKS)

		pos/wks
1 Mar 80	WORZEL'S SONG *Decca F 13885* 33 7	

PESHAY
UK, male DJ / producer – Paul Pesce (6 WEEKS)   pos/wks

9 May 98	MILES FROM HOME *Mo Wax MW 092*	.75	1
17 Jul 99	SWITCH *Island Blue PFACD 1*	.59	1
19 Feb 00	TRULY *Island Blue PFACD 4* [1]	.55	1
4 May 02	YOU GOT ME BURNING / FUZION		
	Cubik Music CUBIKSAMP CD001CD [2]	.41	2
24 Aug 02	SATISFY MY LOVE *Cubik Music CUBIK 002CD* [3]	.67	1

[1] Peshay featuring Kym Mazelle [2] Peshay featuring Co-ordinate [3] Peshay vs Flytronix

PET SHOP BOYS 59 Top 500
Critically acclaimed and quintessentially English duo: former assistant editor of Smash Hits, Neil Tennant (v), and Chris Lowe (k). No duo has amassed more chart entries than this act, whose first hit was voted Best British Single at the 1987 Brit Awards (236 WEEKS)   pos/wks

23 Nov 85	★ WEST END GIRLS *Parlophone R 6115* ▲	.1	15
8 Mar 86	LOVE COMES QUICKLY *Parlophone R 6116*	.19	9
31 May 86	OPPORTUNITIES (LET'S MAKE LOTS OF MONEY)		
	Parlophone R 6129	.11	8
4 Oct 86	● SUBURBIA *Parlophone R 6140*	.8	9
27 Jun 87	★ IT'S A SIN *Parlophone R 6158*	.1	11
22 Aug 87	● WHAT HAVE I DONE TO DESERVE THIS?		
	Parlophone R 6163 [1]	.2	9
24 Oct 87	● RENT *Parlophone R 6168*	.8	7
12 Dec 87	★ ALWAYS ON MY MIND *Parlophone R 6171*	.1	11
2 Apr 88	★ HEART *Parlophone R 6177*	.1	10
24 Sep 88	● DOMINO DANCING *Parlophone R 6190*	.7	8
26 Nov 88	● LEFT TO MY OWN DEVICES *Parlophone R 6198*	.4	8
8 Jul 89	● IT'S ALRIGHT *Parlophone R 6220*	.5	8
6 Oct 90	● SO HARD *Parlophone R 6269*	.4	6
24 Nov 90	BEING BORING *Parlophone R 6275*	.20	8
23 Mar 91	● WHERE THE STREETS HAVE NO NAME – CAN'T TAKE MY		
	EYES OFF YOU / HOW CAN YOU EXPECT TO BE		
	TAKEN SERIOUSLY *Parlophone R 6285*	.4	8
8 Jun 91	JEALOUSY *Parlophone R 6283*	.12	5
26 Oct 91	DJ CULTURE *Parlophone R 6301*	.13	3
23 Nov 91	DJ CULTURE (re-mix) *Parlophone 12RX 6301*	.40	2
21 Dec 91	WAS IT WORTH IT? *Parlophone R 6306*	.24	4
12 Jun 93	● CAN YOU FORGIVE HER *Parlophone CDR 6348*	.7	7
18 Sep 93	● GO WEST *Parlophone CDR 6356*	.2	9
11 Dec 93	I WOULDN'T NORMALLY DO THIS KIND OF THING		
	Parlophone CDR 6370	.13	7
16 Apr 94	LIBERATION *Parlophone CDR 6377*	.14	5
11 Jun 94	● ABSOLUTELY FABULOUS *Spaghetti CDR 6382* [2]	.6	7
10 Sep 94	YESTERDAY WHEN I WAS MAD *Parlophone CDR 6386*	.13	4
5 Aug 95	PANINARO *Parlophone CDR 6414*	.15	4
4 May 96	● BEFORE *Parlophone CDR 6431*	.7	5
24 Aug 96	SE A VIDE E (THAT'S THE WAY LIFE IS) *Parlophone CDR 6443*	.8	8
23 Nov 96	SINGLE *Parlophone CDR 6452*	.14	3
29 Mar 97	● A RED LETTER DAY *Parlophone CDR 6460*	.9	3
5 Jul 97	● SOMEWHERE *Parlophone CDR 6470*	.9	5
31 Jul 99	I DON'T KNOW WHAT YOU WANT BUT I CAN'T GIVE IT		
	ANYMORE *Parlophone CDR 6523*	.15	3
9 Oct 99	NEW YORK CITY BOY *Parlophone CDR 6525*	.14	4
15 Jan 00	● YOU ONLY TELL ME YOU LOVE ME WHEN YOU'RE DRUNK		
	Parlophone CDR 6533	.8	4
30 Mar 02	HOME AND DRY *Parlophone CDRS 6572*	.14	6
27 Jul 02	I GET ALONG *Parlophone CDRS 6581*	.18	3

[1] Pet Shop Boys and Dusty Springfield [2] Absolutely Fabulous

PETER and GORDON 454 Top 500 UK duo, Peter Asher and Gordon
Waller, who had transatlantic No.1 with debut single (penned, as were two other hits, by Asher's sister's boyfriend, Paul McCartney). Peter became a highly regarded Grammy-winning producer (77 WEEKS)   pos/wks

12 Mar 64	★ A WORLD WITHOUT LOVE *Columbia DB 7225* ▲	.1	14
4 Jun 64	NOBODY I KNOW *Columbia DB 7292*	.10	11
8 Apr 65	● TRUE LOVE WAYS *Columbia DB 7524*	.2	15
24 Jun 65	● TO KNOW YOU IS TO LOVE YOU *Columbia DB 7617*	.5	10
21 Oct 65	BABY I'M YOURS *Columbia DB 7729*	.19	9
24 Feb 66	WOMAN *Columbia DB 7834*	.28	7
22 Sep 66	LADY GODIVA *Columbia DB 8003*	.16	11

PETER, PAUL and MARY
US, male / female vocal / instrumental group (38 WEEKS)   pos/wks

10 Oct 63	BLOWING IN THE WIND *Warner Bros. WB 104*	.13	16
16 Apr 64	TELL IT ON THE MOUNTAIN *Warner Bros. WB 127*	.33	4
15 Oct 64	THE TIMES THEY ARE A-CHANGIN'		
	Warner Bros. WB 142	.44	2
17 Jan 70	● LEAVING ON A JET PLANE *Warner Bros. WB 7340* ▲	.2	16

PETERS and LEE
UK, male / female vocal duo – Lennie Peters and Dianne Lee (57 WEEKS)   pos/wks

26 May 73	★ WELCOME HOME *Philips 6006 307*	.1	24
3 Nov 73	BY YOUR SIDE *Philips 6006 339*	.39	4
20 Apr 74	● DON'T STAY AWAY TOO LONG *Philips 6006 388*	.3	15
17 Aug 74	RAINBOW *Philips 6006 406*	.17	7
6 Mar 76	HEY MR MUSIC MAN *Philips 6006 502*	.16	7

Jonathan PETERS presents LUMINAIRE
US, male DJ / producer (1 WEEK)   pos/wks

| 24 Jul 99 | FLOWER DUET *Pelican PELID 001* | .75 | 1 |

Ray PETERSON US, male vocalist (9 WEEKS)   pos/wks

4 Sep 59	THE WONDER OF YOU *RCA 1131*	.23	1
24 Mar 60	ANSWER ME *RCA 1175*	.47	1
19 Jan 61	CORRINE, CORRINA (re) *London HLX 9246*	.41	7

Tom PETTY and the HEARTBREAKERS
US, male vocal / instrumental group (43 WEEKS)   pos/wks

25 Jun 77	ANYTHING THAT'S ROCK 'N' ROLL *Shelter WIP 6396*	.36	3
13 Aug 77	AMERICAN GIRL *Shelter WIP 6403*	.40	5
15 Aug 81	STOP DRAGGIN' MY HEART AROUND		
	WEA K 79231 [1]	.50	4
13 Apr 85	DON'T COME AROUND HERE NO MORE *MCA MCA 926*	.50	4
13 May 89	I WON'T BACK DOWN *MCA MCA 1334* [2]	.28	10
12 Aug 89	RUNNIN' DOWN A DREAM *MCA MCA 1359* [2]	.55	4
25 Nov 89	FREE FALLIN' *MCA MCA 1381* [2]	.64	2
29 Jun 91	LEARNING TO FLY *MCA MCS 1555*	.46	4
4 Apr 92	TOO GOOD TO BE TRUE *MCA MCS 1616*	.34	3
30 Oct 93	SOMETHING IN THE AIR *MCA MCSTD 1945* [2]	.53	2
12 Mar 94	MARY JANE'S LAST DANCE *MCA MCSTD 1966*	.52	2

[1] Stevie Nicks with Tom Petty and the Heartbreakers [2] Tom Petty

PHANTOMS – See Johnny BRANDON with The PHANTOMS

PHARAO
Germany, male / female vocal / instrumental group (2 WEEKS)   pos/wks

| 4 Mar 95 | THERE IS A STAR *Epic 6611832* | .43 | 2 |

PHARAOHS – See SAM THE SHAM and the PHARAOHS

PHARCYDE US, male rap group (6 WEEKS)   pos/wks

31 Jul 93	PASSIN' ME BY *Atlantic A 8360CD*	.55	3
6 Apr 96	RUNNIN' *Go.Beat GODCD 142*	.36	2
10 Aug 96	SHE SAID *Go.Beat GODCD 144*	.51	1

Franke PHAROAH – See FRANKE

PHARRELL – See Pharrell WILLIAMS

PHASE II UK, male producer – Dave Lee (2 WEEKS)   pos/wks

| 18 Mar 89 | REACHIN' *Republic LICT 006* | .70 | 1 |
| 21 Dec 91 | REACHIN' (re-mix) *Republic LIC 160* [1] | .70 | 1 |

[1] Joey Negro presents Phase II

See also Z FACTOR; HED BOYS; Li KWAN; RAVEN MAIZE; JAKATTA; AKABU featuring Linda CLIFFORD; Joey NEGRO; IL PADRINOS

PHAT 'N' PHUNKY UK, male production duo (1 WEEK)   pos/wks

| 14 Jun 97 | LET'S GROOVE *Chase CDCHASE 8* | .61 | 1 |

PHATS & SMALL UK, male DJ / production
duo – Jason Hayward and Russell Small (36 WEEKS)   pos/wks

10 Apr 99 ●	TURN AROUND Multiply CDMULTY 49	2 16
14 Aug 99 ●	FEEL GOOD Multiply CDMULTY 54	7 8
4 Dec 99	TONITE Multiply CDMULTY 57	11 6
30 Jun 01	THIS TIME AROUND Multiply CDMULTY 75	15 5
24 Nov 01	CHANGE Multiply CDMULTY 80	45 1

PHATT B
Holland, male DJ / producer – Bernsquil Verndoom (1 WEEK)   pos/wks

11 Nov 00	AND DA DRUM MACHINE Nulife / Arista 74321801902	58 1

Barrington PHELOUNG Australia, male conductor (2 WEEKS)   pos/wks

13 Mar 93	'INSPECTOR MORSE' THEME Virgin VSCDT 1458	61 2

PHILADELPHIA INTERNATIONAL ALL-STARS
US, male / female vocal / instrumental group (8 WEEKS)   pos/wks

13 Aug 77	LET'S CLEAN UP THE GHETTO	
	Philadelphia International PIR 5451	34 8

PHILHARMONIA ORCHESTRA, conductor Lorin MAAZEL
UK, orchestra and US, male conductor (7 WEEKS)   pos/wks

30 Jul 69	THUS SPAKE ZARATHUSTRA Columbia DB 8607	33 7

Chynna PHILLIPS US, female vocalist (1 WEEK)   pos/wks

3 Feb 96	NAKED AND SACRED EMI CDEM 409	62 1

Esther PHILLIPS
US, female vocalist – Esther Mae Jones d. 7 Aug 1984 (8 WEEKS)   pos/wks

4 Oct 75 ●	WHAT A DIFFERENCE A DAY MADE Kudu 925	6 8

PHOEBE ONE UK, female rapper – Phoebe Espirit (3 WEEKS)   pos/wks

12 Dec 98	DOIN' OUR THING / ONE MAN'S BITCH	
	Mecca Recordings MECX 1020	59 1
15 May 99	GET ON IT Mecca Recordings MECX 1026	38 2

PHOENIX France, male vocal / instrumental group (1 WEEK)   pos/wks

3 Feb 01	IF I EVER FEEL BETTER Source DINSD 210	65 1

Paul PHOENIX UK, male vocalist (4 WEEKS)   pos/wks

3 Nov 79	NUNC DIMITTIS Different HAVE 20	56 4

Full artist credit on hit as follows: Paul Phoenix (treble) with Instrumental Ensemble – James Watson (trumpet), John Scott (organ), conducted by Barry Rose

PHOTEK UK, male producer – Rupert Parkes (4 WEEKS)   pos/wks

22 Mar 97	NI-TEN-ICHI-RYU (TWO SWORDS TECHNIQUE)	
	Science QEDCD 2	37 2
28 Feb 98	MODUS OPERANDI Virgin QEDCD 6	66 1
24 Feb 01	MINE TO GIVE Science QEDCD 10 [1]	44 1

[1] Photek featuring Robert Owens

PHOTOS UK, male / female vocal / instrumental group (4 WEEKS) pos/wks

17 May 80	IRENE Epic EPC 8517	56 4

PHUNKY PHANTOM
UK, male producer – Lawrence Nelson (3 WEEKS)   pos/wks

16 May 98	GET UP STAND UP Club for Life DISNCD 44	27 3

See also GAT DECOR; REST ASSURED

PHUTURE ASSASSINS
UK, male instrumental / production group (1 WEEK)   pos/wks

6 Jun 92	FUTURE SOUND (EP) Suburban Base SUBBASE 010	64 1

Tracks on Future Sound (EP): Future Sound / African Sanctus / Rydim Come Foward / Freedom Sound

PIA – See Pia ZADORA

Edith PIAF France, female vocalist
– Edith Gassion d. 11 Oct 1963 (15 WEEKS)   pos/wks

12 May 60	MILORD (re) Columbia DC 754	24 15

PIANOHEADZ US, male DJ / production
duo – Erick Morillo and Jose Nunez (2 WEEKS)   pos/wks

11 Jul 98	IT'S OVER (DISTORTION) Incredible Music INCRL 3CD	39 2

See also REAL TO REEL; Erick 'More' MORILLO presents RAW; LIL MO' YIN YANG

PIANOMAN UK, male producer – James Sammon (8 WEEKS)   pos/wks

15 Jun 96 ●	BLURRED Ffrreedom TABCD 243	6 7
26 Apr 97	PARTY PEOPLE (LIVE YOUR LIFE BE FREE) 3 Beat 3 BTCD1	43 1

See also BASS BOYZ

Mark PICCHIOTTI presents BASSTOY featuring DANA
US, male / female production / vocal duo (5 WEEKS)   pos/wks

19 Jan 02	RUNNIN' Black & Blue NEOCD 73	13 5

See also SANDSTORM

Bobby 'Boris' PICKETT and the CRYPT-KICKERS
US, male vocal / instrumental group (13 WEEKS)   pos/wks

1 Sep 73 ●	MONSTER MASH London HLU 10320 ▲	3 13

Wilson PICKETT US, male vocalist (61 WEEKS)   pos/wks

23 Sep 65	IN THE MIDNIGHT HOUR Atlantic AT 4036	12 11
25 Nov 65	DON'T FIGHT IT Atlantic AT 4052	29 8
10 Mar 66	634-5789 Atlantic AT 4072	36 5
1 Sep 66	LAND OF 1000 DANCES Atlantic 584 039	22 9
15 Dec 66	MUSTANG SALLY Atlantic 584 066	28 7
27 Sep 67	FUNKY BROADWAY Atlantic 584 130	43 3
11 Sep 68	I'M A MIDNIGHT MOVER Atlantic 584 203	38 6
8 Jan 69	HEY JUDE Atlantic 584 236	16 9
21 Nov 87	IN THE MIDNIGHT HOUR (re-recording) Motown ZB 41583	62 3

PICKETTYWITCH
UK, male / female vocal / instrumental group (34 WEEKS)   pos/wks

28 Feb 70 ●	THAT SAME OLD FEELING Pye 7N 17887	5 14
4 Jul 70	(IT'S LIKE A) SAD OLD KINDA MOVIE Pye 7N 17951	16 10
7 Nov 70	BABY I WON'T LET YOU DOWN Pye 7N 45002	27 10

Mauro PICOTTO Italy, male producer (23 WEEKS)   pos/wks

12 Jun 99	LIZARD (GONNA GET YOU) VC Recordings VCRD 50	27 3
20 Nov 99	LIZARD (GONNA GET YOU) (re-mix)	
	VC Recordings VCRD 57	33 2
15 Jul 00	IGUANA VC Recordings VCRD 68	33 3
13 Jan 01	KOMODO (SAVE A SOUL) VC Recordings VCRD 85	13 5
11 Aug 01	LIKE THIS LIKE THAT VC Recordings VCRD 92	21 4
25 Aug 01	VERDI BXR BXRP 0318	74 1
16 Mar 02	PULSAR 2002 BXR BXRC 0162	35 2
3 Aug 02	BACK TO CALI BXR BXRC 0433	42 2

See also CRW; RAF

PIGBAG UK, male instrumental group (20 WEEKS)   pos/wks

7 Nov 81	SUNNY DAY Y Records Y 12	53 3
27 Feb 82	GETTING UP Y Records Y 16	61 3
3 Apr 82 ●	PAPA'S GOT A BRAND NEW PIGBAG Y Records Y 10	3 11
10 Jul 82	THE BIG BEAN Y Records Y 24	40 3

PIGEON HED – See LO FIDELITY ALLSTARS

Nelson PIGFORD – See De Etta LITTLE and Nelson PIGFORD

PIGLETS UK, female vocal group (12 WEEKS)   pos/wks

6 Nov 71 ●	JOHNNY REGGAE Bell 1180	3 12

Dick PIKE – *See Ruby WRIGHT*

PILOT *UK, male vocal / instrumental group (29 WEEKS)*

			pos/wks
2 Nov 74	MAGIC *EMI 2217*		11 11
18 Jan 75 ★	JANUARY *EMI 2255*		1 10
19 Apr 75	CALL ME ROUND *EMI 2287*		34 4
27 Sep 75	JUST A SMILE *EMI 2338*		31 4

PILTDOWN MEN *US, male instrumental group (36 WEEKS)*

			pos/wks
8 Sep 60	MCDONALD'S CAVE *Capitol CL 15149*		14 18
12 Jan 61	PILTDOWN RIDES AGAIN *Capitol CL 15175*		14 10
9 Mar 61	GOODNIGHT MRS. FLINTSTONE *Capitol CL 15186*		18 8

Courtney PINE
UK, male instrumentalist – saxophone (6 WEEKS)

			pos/wks
30 Jul 88	LIKE DREAMERS DO *Fourth & Broadway BRW 108* [1]		26 5
7 Jul 90	I'M STILL WAITING *Mango MNG 749* [2]		66 1

[1] Mica Paris featuring Courtney Pine [2] Courtney Pine featuring Carroll Thompson

"PING PING" and Al VERLAINE
Belgium, male vocal duo (4 WEEKS)

			pos/wks
28 Sep 61	SUCU SUCU *Oriole CB 1589*		41 4

PINK 436 Top 500
R&B / pop diva whose hair colour regularly matches her name, b. Alecia Moore, 8 Sep 1979, Pennsylvania, US. Rock-influenced UK million-selling 'M!ssundaztood' was 2002's top-selling album by a female artist in both the US and UK. Seven UK Top 10 hits with her first seven releases is a total unbeaten by any other US female (79 WEEKS)

			pos/wks
10 Jun 00 ●	THERE YOU GO *LaFace / Arista 74321757602*		6 9
30 Sep 00 ●	MOST GIRLS *LaFace / Arista 74321792012*		5 8
27 Jan 01 ●	YOU MAKE ME SICK *LaFace / Arista 74321828702*		9 6
30 Jun 01 ★	LADY MARMALADE *Interscope / Polydor 4975612* [1] ■ ▲		1 16
26 Jan 02 ●	GET THE PARTY STARTED *LaFace / Arista 74321913372*		2 15
25 May 02 ●	DON'T LET ME GET ME *Arista 74321939212*		6 11
28 Sep 02 ★	JUST LIKE A PILL *Arista 74321959652* ■		1 11
14 Dec 02	FAMILY PORTRAIT, (import) *Arista 74321982102*		66 1
21 Dec 02	FAMILY PORTRAIT *Arista 74321982052*		11 2+

[1] Christina Aguilera, Lil' Kim, Mya and Pink

PINK FLOYD *UK, male vocal / instrumental group (55 WEEKS)*

			pos/wks
30 Mar 67	ARNOLD LAYNE *Columbia DB 8156*		20 8
22 Jun 67 ●	SEE EMILY PLAY *Columbia DB 8214*		6 12
1 Dec 79 ★	ANOTHER BRICK IN THE WALL (PART 2) *Harvest HAR 5194* ▲		1 12
7 Aug 82	WHEN THE TIGERS BROKE FREE *Harvest HAR 5222*		39 5
7 May 83	NOT NOW JOHN *Harvest HAR 5224*		30 4
19 Dec 87	ON THE TURNING AWAY *EMI EM 34*		55 4
25 Jun 88	ONE SLIP *EMI EM 52*		50 3
4 Jun 94	TAKE IT BACK *EMI CDEMS 309*		23 4
29 Oct 94	HIGH HOPES / KEEP TALKING *EMI CDEMS 342*		26 3

PINKEES *UK, male vocal / instrumental group (9 WEEKS)*

			pos/wks
18 Sep 82 ●	DANGER GAMES *Creole CR 39*		8 9

PINKERTON'S ASSORTED COLOURS
UK, male vocal / instrumental group (12 WEEKS)

			pos/wks
13 Jan 66 ●	MIRROR MIRROR *Decca F 12307*		9 11
21 Apr 66	DON'T STOP LOVING ME BABY *Decca F 12377*		50 1

PINKY and PERKY *UK, pork puppet duo (3 WEEKS)*

			pos/wks
29 May 93	REET PETITE *Telstar CDPIGGY 1*		47 3

Lisa PIN-UP *UK, female DJ / producer – Lisa Chilcott (3 WEEKS)* pos/wks

25 May 02	TURN UP THE SOUND *Nukleuz NUK 0406*		60 1
21 Dec 02	BLOW YOUR MIND (I AM THE WOMAN) *Nukleuz 0450 FNUK*		60 2+

PIONEERS *Jamaica, male vocal / instrumental group (34 WEEKS)* pos/wks

18 Oct 69	LONG SHOT KICK DE BUCKET (re) *Trojan TR 672*		21 11
31 Jul 71 ●	LET YOUR YEAH BE YEAH *Trojan TR 7825*		5 12
15 Jan 72	GIVE AND TAKE *Trojan TR 7846*		35 6
29 Mar 80	LONG SHOT KICK DE BUCKET (re-issue) *Trojan TRO 9063*		42 5

Re-issue of 'Long Shot Kick De Bucket' coupled with re-issue of Liquidator by Harry J All Stars

Billie PIPER 376 Top 500
Youngest solo act to debut at No.1, b. 22 Sep 1982, Swindon, UK. One-time 'Smash Hits' model topped the chart at 15. Singer who is married to DJ / entrepreneur Chris Evans holds the record for being the only female to score three chart-toppers before her 18th birthday (87 WEEKS)

			pos/wks
11 Jul 98 ★	BECAUSE WE WANT TO *Innocent SINCD 2* [1] ■		1 12
17 Oct 98 ★	GIRLFRIEND (re) *Innocent SINCD 3* [1] ■		1 12
19 Dec 98	SHE WANTS YOU (re) *Innocent SINDXX 6* [1]		3 13
3 Apr 99 ●	HONEY TO THE BEE (re) *Innocent SINCD 8* [1]		3 11
10 Apr 99 ●	THANK ABBA FOR THE MUSIC *Epic ABCD 1* [2]		4 13
27 May 00 ★	DAY & NIGHT (re) *Innocent SINCD 11* [1]		1 12
30 Sep 00 ●	SOMETHING DEEP INSIDE (re) *Innocent SINCD 19*		4 9
23 Dec 00	WALK OF LIFE *Innocent SINCD 23*		25 5

[1] Billie [2] Steps, Tina Cousins, Cleopatra, B*Witched, Billie

PIPKINS *UK, male vocal duo – Roger Greenaway and Tony Burrows (10 WEEKS)*

			pos/wks
28 Mar 70 ●	GIMME DAT DING *Columbia DB 8662*		6 10

See also DAVID and JONATHAN; BLUE MINK

PIPS – *See Gladys KNIGHT and the PIPS*

PIRANHAS *UK, male vocal / instrumental group (21 WEEKS)* pos/wks

2 Aug 80 ●	TOM HARK *Sire SIR 4044*		6 12
16 Oct 82	ZAMBESI *Dakota DAK 6* [1]		17 9

[1] Piranhas featuring Boring Bob Grover

PIRATES – *See Johnny KIDD and the PIRATES*

PITCHSHIFTER *UK, male vocal / instrumental group (4 WEEKS)* pos/wks

28 Feb 98	GENIUS *Geffen GFSTD 22324*		71 1
26 Sep 98	MICROWAVED *Geffen GFSTD 22348*		54 1
21 Oct 00	DEAD BATTERY *MCA MCSTD 40241*		71 1
29 Jun 02	SHUTDOWN *Mayan MYNX 008*		66 1

Gene PITNEY 77 Top 500
Leading US performer in the 1960s, b. 17 Feb 1941, Connecticut. This unmistakable vocalist and songwriter had a longer and more impressive track record in the UK than in his homeland. Nonetheless, it took him 28 years to reach No.1 (212 WEEKS)

			pos/wks
23 Mar 61	(I WANNA) LOVE MY LIFE AWAY *London HL 9270*		26 11
8 Mar 62	TOWN WITHOUT PITY *HMV POP 952*		32 6
5 Dec 63 ●	TWENTY FOUR HOURS FROM TULSA *United Artists UP 1035*		5 19
5 Mar 64 ●	THAT GIRL BELONGS TO YESTERDAY *United Artists UP 1045*		7 12
15 Oct 64	IT HURTS TO BE IN LOVE *United Artists UP 1063*		36 4
12 Nov 64 ●	I'M GONNA BE STRONG *Stateside SS 358*		2 14
18 Feb 65	I MUST BE SEEING THINGS *Stateside SS 390*		6 10
10 Jun 65 ●	LOOKING THRU THE EYES OF LOVE *Stateside SS 420*		3 12
4 Nov 65 ●	PRINCESS IN RAGS *Stateside SS 471*		9 12
17 Feb 66	BACKSTAGE *Stateside SS 490*		4 10
9 Jun 66 ●	NOBODY NEEDS YOUR LOVE *Stateside SS 518*		2 13
10 Nov 66 ●	JUST ONE SMILE *Stateside SS 558*		8 12
23 Feb 67	(IN THE) COLD LIGHT OF DAY *Stateside SS 597*		38 6
15 Nov 67 ●	SOMETHING'S GOTTEN HOLD OF MY HEART *Stateside SS 2060*		5 13
3 Apr 68	SOMEWHERE IN THE COUNTRY *Stateside SS 2103*		19 9
27 Nov 68	YOURS UNTIL TOMORROW *Stateside SS 2131*		34 7
5 Mar 69	MARIA ELENA *Stateside SS 2142*		25 6
14 Mar 70	A STREET CALLED HOPE *Stateside SS 2164*		37 5
3 Oct 70	SHADY LADY *Stateside SS 2177*		29 8
28 Apr 73	24 SYCAMORE *Pye International 7N 25606*		34 7

Re-entries are listed as (re) (2re) (3re) etc which signifies that the

			pos/wks	
2 Nov 74		BLUE ANGEL (re) *Bronze BRO 11*	**39**	4
14 Jan 89 ★		SOMETHING'S GOTTEN HOLD OF MY HEART		
		Parlophone R 6201 [1]	**1**	12

[1] Marc Almond featuring special guest star Gene Pitney

Mario PIU *Italy, male DJ / producer (14 WEEKS)* pos/wks
11 Dec 99 ●	COMMUNICATION (SOMEBODY ANSWER THE PHONE)			
	Incentive CENT 2CDS	**5**	9	
10 Mar 01	THE VISION (re) *BXR BXRC 0253* [1]	**16**	5	

[1] Mario Piu presents DJ Arabesque

PIXIES *US, male / female vocal / instrumental group (13 WEEKS)* pos/wks
1 Apr 89	MONKEY GONE TO HEAVEN *4AD AD 904*	**60**	3
1 Jul 89	HERE COMES YOUR MAN *4AD AD 909*	**54**	1
28 Jul 90	VELOURIA *4AD AD 0009*	**28**	3
10 Nov 90	DIG FOR FIRE *4AD AD 0014*	**62**	1
8 Jun 91	PLANET OF SOUND *4AD AD 1008*	**27**	3
4 Oct 97	DEBASER *4AD BAD 7010CD*	**23**	2

PIZZAMAN *UK, male producer – Norman Cook (18 WEEKS)* pos/wks
27 Aug 94	TRIPPIN' ON SUNSHINE *Cowboy Records CDLOAD 16*	**33**	2
10 Jun 95	SEX ON THE STREETS (re) *Cowboy Records CDLOAD 24*....	**23**	8
18 Nov 95	HAPPINESS *Cowboy Records CDLOAD 29*	**19**	4
1 Jun 96	TRIPPIN' ON SUNSHINE (re-issue)		
	Cowboy Records CDLOAD 32	**18**	3
14 Sep 96	HELLO HONKY TONKS (ROCK YOUR BODY)		
	Cowboy Records CDLOAD 39	**41**	1

See also MIGHTY DUB KATZ; FREAKPOWER; HOUSEMARTINS; Norman COOK; BEATS INTERNATIONAL; Norman COOK

PIZZICATO FIVE
Japan, male / female vocal / instrumental group (1 WEEK) pos/wks
1 Nov 97	MON AMOUR TOKYO *Matador OLE 2902*.................	**72**	1

Joe PIZZULO – *See Sergio MENDES*

PLACEBO
US / Sweden / UK, male vocal / instrumental group (37 WEEKS) pos/wks
28 Sep 96	TEENAGE ANGST *Elevator Music FLOORCD 3*...........	**30**	3
1 Feb 97 ●	NANCY BOY *Elevator Music FLOORCD 4*.................	**4**	6
24 May 97	BRUISE PRISTINE *Elevator Music FLOORCD 5*	**14**	3
15 Aug 98 ●	PURE MORNING *Hut FLOORCD 6*	**4**	6
10 Oct 98 ●	YOU DON'T CARE ABOUT US *Hut FLOORCD 7*........	**5**	5
6 Feb 99	EVERY YOU EVERY ME *Hut / Virgin FLOORCD 9*	**11**	5
29 Jul 00	TASTE IN MEN *Hut / Virgin FLOORCD 11*	**16**	6
7 Oct 00	SLAVE TO THE WAGE *Hut / Virgin FLOORCD 12*	**19**	3

PLANET FUNK *Italy / UK / Finland, male*
/ female vocal / production group (9 WEEKS) pos/wks
10 Feb 01 ●	CHASE THE SUN (re) *Virgin VSCDT 1794*	**5**	9

PLANET PATROL
US, male vocal / instrumental group (3 WEEKS) pos/wks
17 Sep 83	CHEAP THRILLS *Polydor POSP 639*	**64**	3

PLANET PERFECTO *UK, male production group (15 WEEKS)* pos/wks
14 Aug 99	NOT OVER YET 99 *Code Blue BLU 004CD1* [1]	**16**	4
13 Nov 99	BULLET IN THE GUN *Perfecto PERF 3CDS*	**15**	4
16 Sep 00 ●	BULLET IN THE GUN 2000 (re-mix)		
	Perfecto PERF 03CDSX	**7**	6
29 Sep 01	BITES DA DUST *Perfecto PERF 19CDS*	**52**	1

[1] Planet Perfecto featuring Grace

PLANETS *UK, male vocal / instrumental group (8 WEEKS)* pos/wks
18 Aug 79	LINES *Rialto TREB 104*	**36**	6
25 Oct 80	DON'T LOOK DOWN *Rialto TREB 116*	**66**	2

PLANK *UK, male producer – Andrew Holt (1 WEEK)* pos/wks
2 Feb 02	STRINGS OF LIFE *Multiply CDMULTY 82*.................	**60**	1

Robert PLANT *UK, male vocalist (33 WEEKS)* pos/wks
9 Oct 82	BURNING DOWN ONE SIDE *Swansong SSK 19429* ...	**73**	1
16 Jul 83	BIG LOG *WEA B 9848*	**11**	10
30 Jan 88	HEAVEN KNOWS *Es Paranza A 9373*	**33**	5
28 Apr 90	HURTING KIND (I'VE GOT MY EYES ON YOU)		
	Es Paranza A 8985	**45**	3
8 May 93	29 PALMS *Fontana FATEX 1*	**21**	5
3 Jul 93	I BELIEVE *Fontana FATEX 2*	**64**	1
25 Dec 93	IF I WERE A CARPENTER *Fontana FATEX 4*	**63**	2
17 Dec 94	GALLOWS POLE *Fontana PPCD 2* [1]	**35**	3
11 Apr 98	MOST HIGH *Mercury 5687512* [2]	**26**	2

[1] Jimmy Page and Robert Plant [2] Page and Plant

See also LED ZEPPELIN

PLASMATICS
US, female / male vocal / instrumental group (4 WEEKS) pos/wks
26 Jul 80	BUTCHER BABY *Stiff BUY 76*	**55**	4

PLASTIC BERTRAND
Belgium, male vocalist – Roger Jouret (17 WEEKS) pos/wks
13 May 78 ●	ÇA PLANE POUR MOI *Sire 6078 616*	**8**	12
5 Aug 78	SHA LA LA LA LEE *Vertigo 6059 209*	**39**	5

PLASTIC JAM – *See BUG KANN and the PLASTIC JAM*

PLASTIC ONO BAND – *See John LENNON*

PLASTIC PENNY
UK, male vocal / instrumental group (10 WEEKS) pos/wks
3 Jan 68 ●	EVERYTHING I AM *Page One POF 051*.................	**6**	10

PLASTIC POPULATION – *See YAZZ*

PLATINUM 45 featuring MORE FIRE CREW
UK, male producer and male rap / vocal trio (8 WEEKS) pos/wks
16 Mar 02 ●	Oi! *Go Beat GOBCD 48*	**8**	8

PLATINUM HOOK *US, male vocal / instrumental group (1 WEEK)* pos/wks
2 Sep 78	STANDING ON THE VERGE (OF GETTING IT ON)		
	Motown TMG 1115.................	**72**	1

PLATTERS `345` `Top 500` *World's biggest-selling vocal group in late 1950s, fronted by tenor Tony Williams b. 5 Apr 1928, New Jersey, US, d.14 Aug 1992. Male / female doo-wop quintet appeared in more countries than any of their 1950s contemporaries (92 WEEKS)* pos/wks
7 Sep 56 ●	THE GREAT PRETENDER / ONLY YOU (re) *Mercury MT 117*	**5**	13
2 Nov 56 ●	MY PRAYER (2re) *Mercury MT 120* ▲	**4**	13
25 Jan 57	YOU'LL NEVER NEVER KNOW / IT ISN'T RIGHT (2re)		
	Mercury MT 130	**23**	3
29 Mar 57	ONLY YOU (AND YOU ALONE) *Mercury MT 117.*	**18**	3
17 May 57	I'M SORRY (2re) *Mercury MT 145.*	**18**	4
16 May 58 ●	TWILIGHT TIME *Mercury MT 214* ▲	**3**	18
16 Jan 59 ★	SMOKE GETS IN YOUR EYES *Mercury AMT 1016* ▲	**1**	20
28 Aug 59	REMEMBER WHEN *Mercury AMT 1053*	**25**	2
29 Jan 60	HARBOUR LIGHTS *Mercury AMT 1081*	**11**	12

PLAVKA – *See JAM & SPOON featuring PLAVKA*

PLAYBOY BAND – *See John FRED and the PLAYBOY BAND*

PLAYBOYS – *See Gary LEWIS and the PLAYBOYS*

PLAYER *US / UK, male vocal / instrumental group (7 WEEKS)* pos/wks
25 Feb 78	BABY COME BACK *RSO 2090 254* ▲	**32**	7

PLAYERS ASSOCIATION
US, male vocal / instrumental group (17 WEEKS)

			pos/wks
10 Mar 79	●	TURN THE MUSIC UP! *Vanguard VS 5011* 8	9
5 May 79		RIDE THE GROOVE *Vanguard VS 5012* 42	5
9 Feb 80		WE GOT THE GROOVE *Vanguard VS 5016* 61	3

PLAYGROUP *UK, male producer – Trevor Jackson (1 WEEK)*

		pos/wks
24 Nov 01	NUMBER ONE *Source SOURCD 026* 66	1

PLAYTHING *Italy, male production duo*
– Luca Moretti and Riccardo Romanini (6 WEEKS)

		pos/wks
5 May 01	INTO SPACE *Manifesto FESCD 81* 48	1
24 Aug 02	DO YOU SEE THE LIGHT? *Data DATA 33CDS* 1 14	5

1 Snap! vs Plaything

See also TRIPLE X

PLUS ONE featuring SIRRON
UK, male / female vocal / instrumental group (4 WEEKS)

		pos/wks
19 May 90	IT'S HAPPENIN' *MCA MCA 1405* 40	4

PLUTO – See Pluto SHERVINGTON

PLUX featuring Georgia JONES
US, male / female vocal / instrumental group (2 WEEKS)

		pos/wks
4 May 96	OVER AND OVER *ffrr FCD 277* 33	2

POETS *UK, male vocal / instrumental group (5 WEEKS)*

		pos/wks
29 Oct 64	NOW WE'RE THRU *Decca F 11995* 31	5

POGUES *Ireland, male vocal / instrumental group (70 WEEKS)*

			pos/wks
6 Apr 85		A PAIR OF BROWN EYES *Stiff BUY 220* 72	2
22 Jun 85		SALLY MACLENNANE *Stiff BUY 224* 51	4
14 Sep 85		DIRTY OLD TOWN *Stiff BUY 229* 62	3
8 Mar 86		POGUETRY IN MOTION (EP) *Stiff BUY 243* 29	6
30 Aug 86		HAUNTED *MCA MCA 1084* 42	4
28 Mar 87	●	THE IRISH ROVER *Stiff BUY 258* 1 8	8
5 Dec 87	●	FAIRYTALE OF NEW YORK *Pogue Mahone NY 7* 2 2	9
5 Mar 88		IF I SHOULD FALL FROM GRACE WITH GOD *Pogue Mahone PG 1* 58	3
16 Jul 88		FIESTA *Pogue Mahone PG 2* 24	5
17 Dec 88		YEAH, YEAH, YEAH, YEAH *Pogue Mahone YZ 355* 43	4
8 Jul 89		MISTY MORNING, ALBERT BRIDGE *PM YZ 407* 41	3
16 Jun 90		JACK'S HEROES / WHISKEY IN THE JAR *PM YZ 500* 1 63	2
15 Sep 90		SUMMER IN SIAM *PM YZ 519* 64	2
21 Sep 91		A RAINY NIGHT IN SOHO *PM YZ 603* 67	1
14 Dec 91		FAIRYTALE OF NEW YORK (re-issue) *PM YZ 628* 2 36	5
30 May 92		HONKY TONK WOMEN *PM YZ 673* 56	2
21 Aug 93		TUESDAY MORNING *PM YZ 758 CD* 18	5
22 Jan 94		ONCE UPON A TIME *PM YZ 771CD* 66	2

1 Pogues and The Dubliners 2 Pogues featuring Kirsty MacColl

Tracks on Poguetry in Motion (EP): London Girl / The Body of an American / A Rainy Night in Soho / Planxty Noel Hill

POINT BREAK *UK, male vocal group (21 WEEKS)*

			pos/wks
9 Oct 99		DO WE ROCK *Eternal WEA 216CD1* 29	2
22 Jan 00	●	STAND TOUGH *Eternal WEA 248CD1* 7	5
22 Apr 00		FREAKYTIME *Eternal WEA 265CD1* 13	6
5 Aug 00		YOU *Eternal WEA 290CD1* 14	5
2 Dec 00		WHAT ABOUT US *Eternal WEA 314CD1* 24	3

POINTER SISTERS 385 Top 500
Talented sibling vocal quartet formed 1971, Oakland, California, US, whose recordings touched many musical bases. Reduced to trio – June, Anita and Ruth – when Bonnie left in 1978. Soulful sisters surprisingly won a country music Grammy for 'Fairytale' in 1974 (87 WEEKS)

		pos/wks
3 Feb 79	EVERYBODY IS A STAR *Planet K 12324* 61	3
17 Mar 79	FIRE *Planet K 12339* 34	8

			pos/wks
22 Aug 81	●	SLOWHAND *Planet K 12530* 10	11
5 Dec 81		SHOULD I DO IT? *Planet K 12578* 50	5
14 Apr 84	●	AUTOMATIC *Planet RPS 105* 2	15
23 Jun 84	●	JUMP (FOR MY LOVE) *Planet RPS 106* 6	10
11 Aug 84		I NEED YOU *Planet RPS 107* 25	9
27 Oct 84		I'M SO EXCITED *Planet RPS 108* 11	11
12 Jan 85		NEUTRON DANCE *Planet RPS 109* 31	7
20 Jul 85		DARE ME *RCA PB 49957* 17	8

POISON *US, male vocal / instrumental group (43 WEEKS)*

		pos/wks
23 May 87	TALK DIRTY TO ME *Music For Nations KUT 125* 67	1
7 May 88	NOTHIN' BUT A GOOD TIME *Capitol CL 486* 35	3
5 Nov 88	FALLEN ANGEL *Capitol CL 500* 59	1
11 Feb 89	EVERY ROSE HAS ITS THORN *Capitol CL 520* ▲ 13	9
29 Apr 89	YOUR MAMA DON'T DANCE *Capitol CL 523* 13	7
23 Sep 89	NOTHIN' BUT A GOOD TIME (re-issue) *Capitol CL 539* 48	3
30 Jun 90	UNSKINNY BOP *Capitol CL 582* 15	7
27 Oct 90	SOMETHING TO BELIEVE IN *Enigma CL 594* 35	4
23 Nov 91	SO TELL ME WHY *Capitol CL 640* 25	2
13 Feb 93	STAND *Capitol CDCL 679* 25	3
24 Apr 93	UNTIL YOU SUFFER SOME (FIRE AND ICE) *Capitol CDCL 685* 32	3

POKEMON ALLSTARS – See 50 GRIND featuring POKEMON ALLSTARS

POLECATS *UK, male vocal / instrumental group (18 WEEKS)*

		pos/wks
7 Mar 81	JOHN I'M ONLY DANCING / BIG GREEN CAR *Mercury POLE 1* 35	8
16 May 81	ROCKABILLY GUY *Mercury POLE 2* 35	6
22 Aug 81	JEEPSTER / MARIE CELESTE *Mercury POLE 3* 53	4

POLICE 143 Top 500
World-famous Anglo-American rock trio: Sting (b. Gordon Sumner) (v/b), Andy Summers (g/v), Stewart Copeland (d/v). These Brit and Grammy award winners were one of the 1980s' most popular acts. They had five successive albums entering the UK chart at No.1 (153 WEEKS)

			pos/wks
7 Oct 78	●	CAN'T STAND LOSING YOU (re) *A&M AMS 7381* 2	16
28 Apr 79		ROXANNE *A&M AMS 7348* 12	9
22 Sep 79	★	MESSAGE IN A BOTTLE *A&M AMS 7474* 1	11
17 Nov 79		FALL OUT *Illegal IL 001* 47	4
1 Dec 79	★	WALKING ON THE MOON *A&M AMS 7494* 1	10
16 Feb 80	●	SO LONELY *A&M AMS 7402* 6	10
14 Jun 80		SIX PACK *A&M AMPP 6001* 17	4
27 Sep 80	★	DON'T STAND SO CLOSE TO ME *A&M AMS 7564* ■ 1	10
13 Dec 80	●	DE DO DO DO, DE DA DA DA *A&M AMS 7578* 5	8
26 Sep 81		INVISIBLE SUN *A&M AMS 8164* 2	8
24 Oct 81	★	EVERY LITTLE THING SHE DOES IS MAGIC *A&M AMS 8174* 1	13
12 Dec 81		SPIRITS IN THE MATERIAL WORLD *A&M AMS 8194* 12	8
28 May 83	★	EVERY BREATH YOU TAKE *A&M AM 117* ▲ 1	11
23 Jul 83	●	WRAPPED AROUND YOUR FINGER *A&M AM 127* 7	7
5 Nov 83		SYNCHRONICITY II *A&M AM 153* 17	4
14 Jan 84		KING OF PAIN *A&M AM 176* 17	5
11 Oct 86		DON'T STAND SO CLOSE TO ME '86 (re-mix) *A&M AM 354* 24	4
13 May 95		CAN'T STAND LOSING YOU (LIVE) *A&M 5810372* 27	2
20 Dec 97		ROXANNE '97 (re-mix) *A&M 5824552* 1 17	6
5 Aug 00		WHEN THE WORLD IS RUNNING DOWN *Pagan PAGAN 039CDS* 2 28	3

1 Sting and The Police 2 Different Gear vs The Police

'Can't Stand Losing You' made No.42 on its first visit and peaked at No.2 only on re-entry in Jul 1979. Six Pack consists of six separate Police singles as follows: The Bed's Too Big Without You / Roxanne / Message in a Bottle / Walking on the Moon / So Lonely / Can't Stand Losing You. The last five titles were re-issues

See also STING; Klark KENT

Su POLLARD *UK, female actor / vocalist (11 WEEKS)*

			pos/wks
5 Oct 85		COME TO ME (I AM WOMAN) *Rainbow RBR 1* 71	1
1 Feb 86	●	STARTING TOGETHER *Rainbow RBR 4* 2	10

Jimi POLO *US, male vocalist (5 WEEKS)*

		pos/wks
9 Nov 91	NEVER GOIN' DOWN *MCA MCS 1578* 1 51	2

Re-entries are listed as (re), (2re), (3re), etc which signifies that the hit re-entered the chart

			pos/wks
1 Aug 92	**EXPRESS YOURSELF** *Perfecto 74321101827*	**59**	2
9 Aug 97	**EXPRESS YOURSELF (re-issue)** *Perfecto PERF 146CD1*	**62**	1

[1] Adamski featuring Jimi Polo

The listed flip side of 'Never Goin' Down' was 'Born to Be Alive' by Adamski featuring Soho

POLTERGEIST *UK, male producer – Simon Berry (2 WEEKS)*
			pos/wks
6 Jul 96	**VICIOUS CIRCLES** *Manifesto FESCD 8*	**32**	2

See also VICIOUS CIRCLES

Peter POLYCARPOU *UK, male actor / vocalist (4 WEEKS)*
			pos/wks
20 Feb 93	**LOVE HURTS** *Soundtrack Music CDEM 259*	**26**	4

POLYGON WINDOW
UK, male producer – Richard James (1 WEEK)
			pos/wks
3 Apr 93	**QUOTH** *Warp WAP 33CD*	**49**	1

See also APHEX TWIN; AFX

POLYPHONIC SPREE
US, male / female vocal / instrumental ensemble (1 WEEK)
			pos/wks
2 Nov 02	**HANGING AROUND** *679 Recordings 679L 012CD*	**39**	1

PONI-TAILS *US, female vocal group (14 WEEKS)*
			pos/wks
19 Sep 58 ●	**BORN TOO LATE** *HMV POP 516*	**5**	11
10 Apr 59	**EARLY TO BED** *HMV POP 596*	**26**	3

Brian POOLE and The TREMELOES – See TREMELOES

Glyn POOLE *UK, male vocalist (8 WEEKS)*
			pos/wks
20 Oct 73	**MILLY MOLLY MANDY** *York SYK 565*	**35**	8

Ian POOLEY *Germany, male DJ / producer (3 WEEKS)*
			pos/wks
10 Mar 01	**900 DEGREES** *V2 VVR 5015143*	**57**	1
11 Aug 01	**BALMES** *V2 VVR 5016613* [1]	**65**	1
23 Nov 02	**PIHA** *Honchos Music HONMO 019CD* [2]	**53**	1

[1] Ian Pooley featuring Esthero [2] Ian Pooley and J Magik

Iggy POP *US, male vocalist – James Jewel Osterburg (28 WEEKS)* pos/wks
13 Dec 86 ●	**REAL WILD CHILD (WILD ONE)** *A&M AM 368*	**10**	11
10 Feb 90	**LIVIN' ON THE EDGE OF THE NIGHT** *Virgin America VUS 18*	**51**	4
13 Oct 90	**CANDY** *Virgin America VUS 29*	**67**	1
5 Jan 91	**WELL DID YOU EVAH!** *Chrysalis CHS 3646* [1]	**42**	4
4 Sep 93	**THE WILD AMERICA (EP)** *Virgin America VUSCD 74*	**63**	1
21 May 94	**BESIDE YOU** *Virgin America VUSCD 77*	**47**	2
23 Nov 96	**LUST FOR LIFE** *Virgin America VUSCD 116*	**26**	2
7 Mar 98	**THE PASSENGER** *Virgin VSCDT 1689*	**22**	3

[1] Deborah Harry and Iggy Pop

Tracks on The Wild America (EP): Wild America / Credit Card / Come Back Tomorrow / My Angel

POP WILL EAT ITSELF
UK, male vocal / instrumental group (43 WEEKS)
			pos/wks
30 Jan 88	**THERE IS NO LOVE BETWEEN US ANYMORE** *Chapter 22 CHAP 20*	**66**	1
23 Jul 88	**DEF CON ONE** *Chapter 22 PWEI 001*	**63**	4
11 Feb 89	**CAN U DIG IT?** *RCA PB 42621*	**38**	4
22 Apr 89	**WISE UP! SUCKER** *RCA PB 42761*	**41**	3
2 Sep 89	**VERY METAL NOISE POLLUTION (EP)** *RCA PB 42883*	**45**	3
9 Jun 90	**TOUCHED BY THE HAND OF CICCIOLINA** *RCA PB 43735*	**28**	4
13 Oct 90	**DANCE OF THE MAD** *RCA PB 44023*	**32**	2
12 Jan 91	**X Y & ZEE** *RCA PB 44243*	**15**	4
1 Jun 91	**92º F** *RCA PB 44555*	**23**	3
6 Jun 92	**KARMADROME / EAT ME DRINK ME LOVE ME** *RCA PB 45467*	**17**	2
29 Aug 92	**BULLETPROOF!** *RCA 74321110137*	**24**	3
16 Jan 93 ●	**GET THE GIRL! KILL THE BADDIES!** *RCA 74321128802*	**9**	4
16 Oct 93	**RSVP / FAMILIUS HORRIBILUS** *Infectious INFECT 1CD*	**27**	2

12 Mar 94	**ICH BIN EIN AUSLANDER** *Infectious INFECT 4CD*	**28**	2
10 Sep 94	**EVERYTHING'S COOL** *Infectious INFECT 9CD*	**23**	2

Tracks on Very Metal Noise Pollution (EP): Def Con 1989 AD including the Twilight Zone / Preaching to the Perverted / PWEI-zation / 92°F

POPES – See Shane MacGOWAN

POPPERS presents AURA
UK, male production trio and UK, female vocalist (1 WEEK)
			pos/wks
25 Oct 97	**EVERY LITTLE TIME** *VC VCRD 26*	**44**	1

POPPY FAMILY *Canada, male / female vocal / instrumental*
group – Terry Jacks and Susan Peklevits (14 WEEKS) pos/wks
15 Aug 70 ●	**WHICH WAY YOU GOIN' BILLY?** *Decca F 22976*	**7**	14

See also Terry JACKS

PORN KINGS
UK, male instrumental / production group (10 WEEKS) pos/wks
28 Sep 96	**UP TO NO GOOD** *All Around the World CDGLOBE 145*	**28**	2
21 Jun 97	**AMOUR (C'MON)** *All Around the World CDGLOBE 152*	**17**	3
16 Jan 99 ●	**UP TO THE WILDSTYLE** *All Around the World CDGLOBE 170* [1]	**10**	4
10 Feb 01	**SLEDGER** *All Around the World CDGLOBE 229*	**71**	1

[1] Porn Kings vs DJ Supreme

PORNO FOR PYROS *US, male vocal / instrumental group (2 WKS)* pos/wks
5 Jun 93	**PETS** *Warner Bros. W 0177 CD*	**53**	2

PORTISHEAD
UK, male / female vocal / instrumental group (20 WEEKS) pos/wks
13 Aug 94	**SOUR TIMES (re)** *Go.Beat GODCD 116*	**13**	5
14 Jan 95	**GLORY BOX** *Go.Beat GODCD 120*	**13**	7
20 Sep 97 ●	**ALL MINE** *Go.Beat 5715972*	**8**	4
22 Nov 97	**OVER** *Go.Beat 5719932*	**25**	2
14 Mar 98	**ONLY YOU** *Go.Beat 5694752*	**35**	2

'Sour Times' made No.57 on its first visit peaking at No.13 in Apr 1995

Gary PORTNOY *US, male vocalist (3 WEEKS)* pos/wks
25 Feb 84	**THEME FROM 'CHEERS'** *Starblend CHEER 1*	**58**	3

PORTRAIT *US, male vocal group (6 WEEKS)* pos/wks
27 Mar 93	**HERE WE GO AGAIN** *Capitol CDCL 683*	**37**	3
8 Apr 95	**I CAN CALL YOU** *Capitol CDCL 740*	**61**	1
8 Jul 95	**HOW DEEP IS YOUR LOVE** *Capitol CDCL 751*	**41**	2

PORTSMOUTH SINFONIA *UK, orchestra (4 WEEKS)* pos/wks
12 Sep 81	**CLASSICAL MUDDLY** *Island WIP 6736*	**38**	4

Sandy POSEY *US, female vocalist (32 WEEKS)* pos/wks
15 Sep 66	**BORN A WOMAN** *MGM 1321*	**24**	11
5 Jan 67	**SINGLE GIRL** *MGM 1330*	**15**	13
13 Apr 67	**WHAT A WOMAN IN LOVE WON'T DO** *MGM 1335*	**48**	3
6 Sep 75	**SINGLE GIRL (re-issue)** *MGM 2006 533*	**35**	5

POSIES *US, male vocal / instrumental group (1 WEEK)* pos/wks
19 Mar 94	**DEFINITE DOOR** *Geffen GFSTD 68*	**67**	1

POSITIVE FORCE *US, female vocal duo*
– Brenda Reynolds and Vicki Drayton (9 WEEKS) pos/wks
22 Dec 79	**WE GOT THE FUNK** *Sugarhill SHL 102*	**18**	9

POSITIVE GANG
UK, male / female instrumental / vocal group (5 WEEKS) pos/wks
17 Apr 93	**SWEET FREEDOM** *PWL Continental PWCD 261*	**34**	4
31 Jul 93	**SWEET FREEDOM PART 2** *PWL Continental PWCD 264*	**67**	1

POSITIVE K US, male rapper (2 WEEKS)

			pos/wks
15 May 93	I GOT A MAN *Fourth & Broadway BRCD 280*	43	2

Mike POST US, orchestra (18 WEEKS)

			pos/wks
9 Aug 75	AFTERNOON OF THE RHINO (re) *Warner Bros. K 16588* [1]	47	2
16 Jan 82	THEME FROM 'HILL STREET BLUES' *Elektra K 12576* [2]	25	11
29 Sep 84	THE A TEAM *RCA 443*	45	5

[1] Mike Post Coalition [2] Mike Post featuring Larry Carlton

POTTERS
UK, male Stoke City football supporters vocal group (2 WEEKS)

			pos/wks
1 Apr 72	WE'LL BE WITH YOU *Pye JT 100*	34	2

POWDER UK, male / female vocal / instrumental group (1 WEEK)

			pos/wks
24 Jun 95	AFRODISIAC *Parkway PARK 002CD*	72	1

Bryan POWELL UK, male vocalist (3 WEEKS)

			pos/wks
13 Mar 93	IT'S ALRIGHT *Talkin' Loud TLKCD 34*	73	1
15 May 93	I THINK OF YOU *Talkin' Loud TLKCD 38*	61	1
7 Aug 93	NATURAL *Talkin' Loud TLKCD 41*	73	1

Cozy POWELL UK, male instrumentalist – drums – Colin Flooks d. 5 Apr 1998 (38 WEEKS)

			pos/wks
8 Dec 73	● DANCE WITH THE DEVIL *RAK 164*	3	15
25 May 74	THE MAN IN BLACK *RAK 173*	18	8
10 Aug 74	● NA NA NA *RAK 180*	10	10
10 Nov 79	THEME ONE *Ariola ARO 189*	62	2
19 Jun 93	RESURRECTION *Parlophone CDRS 6351* [1]	23	3

[1] Brian May with Cozy Powell

Kobie POWELL – See US3

POWER CIRCLE – See CHICANE

POWER OF DREAMS
Ireland, male vocal / instrumental group (2 WEEKS)

			pos/wks
19 Jan 91	AMERICAN DREAM *Polydor PO 117*	74	1
11 Apr 92	THERE I GO AGAIN *Polydor PO 200*	65	1

POWER STATION
UK / US, male vocal / instrumental group (17 WEEKS)

			pos/wks
16 Mar 85	SOME LIKE IT HOT *Parlophone R 6091*	14	8
11 May 85	GET IT ON *Parlophone R 6096*	22	7
9 Nov 85	COMMUNICATION *Parlophone R 6114*	75	1
12 Oct 96	SHE CAN ROCK IT *Chrysalis CDCHS 5039*	63	1

POWERCUT featuring NUBIAN PRINZ
US, male vocal / instrumental group (4 WEEKS)

			pos/wks
22 Jun 91	GIRLS *Eternal YZ 570*	50	4

POWERHOUSE UK, male production duo (4 WEEKS)

			pos/wks
20 Dec 97	RHYTHM OF THE NIGHT *Satellite 74321522592*	38	4

POWERHOUSE featuring Duane HARDEN
US, male producer – Lenny Fontana male vocalist (5 WEEKS)

			pos/wks
22 May 99	WHAT YOU NEED *Defected DEFECT 3CDS*	13	5

POWERPILL UK, male instrumental / production group (3 WEEKS)

			pos/wks
6 Jun 92	PAC-MAN *Ffrreedom TABX 110*	43	3

P J POWERS – See LADYSMITH BLACK MAMBAZO

Will POWERS US, female vocalist – Lyn Goldsmith (9 WEEKS)

			pos/wks
1 Oct 83	KISSING WITH CONFIDENCE *Island IS 134*	17	9

Hit features uncredited vocals by Carly Simon

Perez PRADO and His Orchestra
Cuba, orchestra, leader d. 14 Sep 1989 (57 WEEKS)

			pos/wks
25 Mar 55	★ CHERRY PINK AND APPLE BLOSSOM WHITE *HMV B 10833* [1] ▲	1	17
25 Jul 58	● PATRICIA *RCA 1067*	8	16
10 Dec 94	● GUAGLIONE (2re) *RCA 74321250192* [2]	2	24

[1] Perez 'Prez' Prado and his Orchestra, the King of the Mambo [2] Perez 'Prez' Prado and His Orchestra

'Guaglione' did not made its peak position until its second re-entry in May 1995 after first making No.41 in 1994 and No.58 on its first re-entry

PRAISE UK, male / female vocal / instrumental group (7 WEEKS)

			pos/wks
2 Feb 91	● ONLY YOU *Epic 6566117*	4	7

Uncredited vocals by Miriam Stockley

PRAISE CATS
US, male producer – Eric 'E-Smoove' Miller (1 WEEK)

			pos/wks
26 Oct 02	SHINED ON ME *Pias PIAS 028CD*	56	1

See also THICK D; E-SMOOVE featuring Latanza WATERS

PRAS – See Pras MICHEL

PRATT and McCLAIN with BROTHERLOVE US, male vocal duo – Truett
Pratt and Jerry McClain with male instrumental group (6 WEEKS)

			pos/wks
1 Oct 77	HAPPY DAYS *Reprise K 14435*	31	6

PRAXIS featuring KATHY BROWN
UK, male producer – David Shaw and US, female vocalist (5 WEEKS)

			pos/wks
25 Nov 95	TURN ME OUT *Stress CDSTR 40*	44	2
20 Sep 97	TURN ME OUT (TURN TO SUGAR) (re-mix) *ffrr FCD 314*	35	3

PRAYING MANTIS
UK, male vocal / instrumental group (2 WEEKS)

			pos/wks
31 Jan 81	CHEATED *Arista ARIST 378*	69	2

PRECIOUS UK, female vocal group (20 WEEKS)

			pos/wks
29 May 99	● SAY IT AGAIN (re) *EMI CDEM 544*	6	11
1 Apr 00	REWIND *EMI CDEM 557*	11	5
15 Jul 00	IT'S GONNA BE MY WAY *EMI CDEM 569*	27	3
25 Nov 00	NEW BEGINNING *EMI CDEM 573*	50	1

PRECOCIOUS BRATS featuring KEVIN and PERRY UK, male
production duo – Julius O'Riordan (Judge Jules) and Matt Smith with male / female vocal / comedy duo – Harry Enfield and Kathy Burke (4 WEEKS)

			pos/wks
6 May 00	BIG GIRL *Virgin / EMI VTSCD 1*	16	4

PREFAB SPROUT
UK, male / female vocal / instrumental group (60 WEEKS)

			pos/wks
28 Jan 84	DON'T SING *Kitchenware SK 9*	62	2
20 Jul 85	FARON YOUNG *Kitchenware SK 22*	74	1
9 Nov 85	WHEN LOVE BREAKS DOWN *Kitchenware SK 21*	25	10
8 Feb 86	JOHNNY JOHNNY *Kitchenware SK 24*	64	2
13 Feb 88	CARS AND GIRLS *Kitchenware SK 35*	44	5
30 Apr 88	● THE KING OF ROCK 'N' ROLL *Kitchenware SK 37*	7	10
23 Jul 88	HEY MANHATTAN! *Kitchenware SK 38*	72	2
18 Aug 90	LOOKING FOR ATLANTIS *Kitchenware SK 47*	51	3
20 Oct 90	WE LET THE STARS GO *Kitchenware SK 48*	50	3
5 Jan 91	JORDAN: THE EP *Kitchenware SK 49*	35	4
13 Jun 92	THE SOUND OF CRYING *Kitchenware SK 58*	23	5
8 Aug 92	IF YOU DON'T LOVE ME *Kitchenware SK 60*	33	4
3 Oct 92	ALL THE WORLD LOVES LOVERS *Kitchenware SK 62*	61	2
9 Jan 93	LIFE OF SURPRISES *Kitchenware SKCD 63*	24	4
10 May 97	A PRISONER OF THE PAST *Columbia SKZD 70*	30	2
2 Aug 97	ELECTRIC GUITARS *Columbia SKZD 71*	53	1

Tracks on Jordan: The EP: Carnival 2000 / The Ice Maiden / One of the Broken / Jordan: The Comeback

Re-entries are listed as (re), (2re), (3re), etc which signifies that the hit re-entered the chart

PRELUDE UK, male / female vocal group (26 WEEKS) pos/wks

26 Jan 74		AFTER THE GOLDRUSH *Dawn DNS 1052*	21	9
26 Apr 80		PLATINUM BLONDE *EMI 5046*	45	7
22 May 82		AFTER THE GOLDRUSH (re-recording) *After Hours AFT 02*	28	7
31 Jul 82		ONLY THE LONELY *After Hours AFT 06*	55	3

PRESENCE UK, male / female vocal / production group (2 WEEKS) pos/wks

5 Dec 98		SENSE OF DANGER *Pagan PAGAN 024CDS* 1	61	1
19 Jun 99		FUTURE LOVE *Pagan PAGAN 028CDS*	66	1

1 Presence featuring Shara Nelson

PRESIDENT BROWN – See SABRE featuring PRESIDENT BROWN

PRESIDENTS OF THE UNITED STATES OF AMERICA
US, male vocal / instrumental trio (21 WEEKS) pos/wks

6 Jan 96		LUMP *Columbia 6624962*	15	7
20 Apr 96	●	PEACHES *Columbia 6631072*	8	7
20 Jul 96		DUNE BUGGY *Columbia 6634892*	15	4
2 Nov 96		MACH 5 *Columbia 6638812*	29	2
1 Aug 98		VIDEO KILLED THE RADIO STAR *Maverick W 0450CD*	52	1

Elvis PRESLEY 1 Top 500

The most important, most influential and most impersonated artist of the 20th century, b. 8 Jan 1935, Mississippi, US, d. 16 Aug 1977. The singer, whose first five US singles failed to reach the pop charts, went from rock 'n' roll rebel to Las Vegas veteran and on the way sold more records than any other performer in history. He holds, or has held, almost every chart-related record including perhaps the most important: more No.1s than any act in chart history. No other solo artist of the rock era can match his number of best-selling singles and albums in the UK or US, nor his collection of platinum and gold records. The "King of Rock 'n' Roll" was the first artist to enter the UK chart at No.1, and the first to amass US advance orders in excess of one million copies for a single. He now has a 46-year span of UK No.1 albums and also holds the record for most simultaneous UK album chart entries (27 in the Top 100) and held the record for the most entries on the UK single chart (nine). The most documented entertainer ever has won hundreds of awards, starred in dozens of successful films, broken numerous box office records in North America (the only continent he ever performed in), made Memphis a major tourist attraction and was the first artist credited with sales of one billion records (20 million of which were reportedly sold the day after his death). In 2002, after a 25-year gap, he returned to top the UK singles chart and his album 'ELV1S' entered at No.1 in 17 countries. Best-selling single (UK): 'It's Now or Never' 1,210,000 (1185 WEEKS) pos/wks

11 May 56	●	HEARTBREAK HOTEL (re) *HMV POP 182* ▲	2	22
25 May 56	●	BLUE SUEDE SHOES (re) *HMV POP 213*	9	10
13 Jul 56		I WANT YOU, I NEED YOU, I LOVE YOU (re) *HMV POP 235* ▲	14	11
21 Sep 56	●	HOUND DOG *HMV POP 249* ▲	2	23
16 Nov 56		BLUE MOON *HMV POP 272*	9	11
23 Nov 56		I DON'T CARE IF THE SUN DON'T SHINE (re) *HMV POP 272*	23	4
7 Dec 56		LOVE ME TENDER *HMV POP 253* ▲	11	9
15 Feb 57		MYSTERY TRAIN *HMV POP 295*	25	5
8 Mar 57		RIP IT UP *HMV POP 305*	27	1
10 May 57	●	TOO MUCH (re) *HMV POP 330* 1 ▲	6	9
14 Jun 57	★	ALL SHOOK UP (re) *HMV POP 359* 1 ▲	1	21
12 Jul 57	●	(LET ME BE YOUR) TEDDY BEAR *RCA1013* 1 ▲	3	19
30 Aug 57		PARALYZED *HMV POP 378*	8	10
4 Oct 57	●	PARTY *RCA 1020* 1	2	15
18 Oct 57		GOT A LOT O' LIVIN' TO DO *RCA 1020.* 1	17	4
1 Nov 57		LOVING YOU *RCA 1013* 1	24	2
1 Nov 57		TRYING TO GET TO YOU *HMV POP 408*	16	4
8 Nov 57		LAWDY MISS CLAWDY *HMV POP 408*	15	5
15 Nov 57	●	SANTA BRING MY BABY BACK (TO ME) *RCA 1025*	7	8
17 Jan 58		I'M LEFT, YOU'RE RIGHT, SHE'S GONE (re) *HMV POP 428*	21	3
24 Jan 58	★	JAILHOUSE ROCK (re) *RCA 1028* ■ ▲	1	20
31 Jan 58		JAILHOUSE ROCK (EP) *RCA RCX 106* 1	18	5
28 Feb 58	●	DON'T *RCA 1043* 1	2	11
2 May 58	●	WEAR MY RING AROUND YOUR NECK *RCA 1058* 1	3	10
25 Jul 58	●	HARD HEADED WOMAN *RCA 1070* 1 ▲	2	11
3 Oct 58	●	KING CREOLE *RCA 1081* 1	2	15
23 Jan 59	★	ONE NIGHT / I GOT STUNG *RCA 1100*	1	12

24 Apr 59	★	A FOOL SUCH AS I / I NEED YOUR LOVE TONIGHT *RCA 1113* 1	1	15
24 Jul 59	●	A BIG HUNK O' LOVE *RCA 1136* 1 ▲	4	9
12 Feb 60		STRICTLY ELVIS (EP) *RCA RCX 175*	26	1
7 Apr 60	●	STUCK ON YOU *RCA 1187* 1 ▲	3	14
28 Jul 60	●	A MESS OF BLUES *RCA 1194* 1	2	18
3 Nov 60	●	IT'S NOW OR NEVER *RCA 1207* 1 ◆ ■ ▲	1	19
19 Jan 61	●	ARE YOU LONESOME TONIGHT? *RCA 1216* 1 ▲	1	15
9 Mar 61	★	WOODEN HEART *RCA 1226*	1	27
25 May 61	★	SURRENDER *RCA 1227* 1 ▲	1	15
7 Sep 61	●	WILD IN THE COUNTRY / I FEEL SO BAD *RCA 1244* 1	4	12
2 Nov 61	★	(MARIE'S THE NAME) HIS LATEST FLAME / LITTLE SISTER *RCA 1258*	1	13
1 Feb 62	★	ROCK-A-HULA BABY / CAN'T HELP FALLING IN LOVE *RCA 1270* 1	1	20
10 May 62	★	GOOD LUCK CHARM *RCA 1280* 1 ▲	1	17
21 Jun 62		FOLLOW THAT DREAM (EP) *RCA RCX 211*	34	2
30 Aug 62		SHE'S NOT YOU *RCA 1303* 1	1	14
29 Nov 62	★	RETURN TO SENDER *RCA 1320* 1	1	14
28 Feb 63		ONE BROKEN HEART FOR SALE *RCA 1337* 2	12	9
4 Jul 63	★	(YOU'RE THE) DEVIL IN DISGUISE *RCA 1355* 1	1	12
24 Oct 63		BOSSA NOVA BABY *RCA 1374* 1	13	8
19 Dec 63		KISS ME QUICK *RCA 1375*	14	10
12 Mar 64		VIVA LAS VEGAS *RCA 1390* 1	17	12
25 Jun 64		KISSIN' COUSINS *RCA 1404* 1	10	11
20 Aug 64		SUCH A NIGHT *RCA 1411* 1	13	10
29 Oct 64		AIN'T THAT LOVING YOU BABY *RCA 1422*	15	8
3 Dec 64		BLUE CHRISTMAS *RCA 1430*	11	7
11 Mar 65		DO THE CLAM *RCA 1443* 3	19	8
27 May 65	★	CRYING IN THE CHAPEL *RCA 1455* 1	1	15
11 Nov 65		TELL ME WHY *RCA 1489* 1	15	10
24 Feb 66		BLUE RIVER *RCA 1504*	22	7
7 Apr 66		FRANKIE AND JOHNNY *RCA 1509*	21	9
7 Jul 66	●	LOVE LETTERS *RCA 1526*	6	10
13 Oct 66		ALL THAT I AM *RCA 1545* 1	18	8
1 Dec 66		IF EVERY DAY WAS LIKE CHRISTMAS *RCA 1557* 4	9	7
9 Feb 67		INDESCRIBABLY BLUE *RCA 1565* 4	21	5
11 May 67		YOU GOTTA STOP / THE LOVE MACHINE *RCA 1593*	38	5
16 Aug 67		LONG LEGGED GIRL (WITH THE SHORT DRESS ON) *RCA RCA 1616* 1	49	2
21 Feb 68		GUITAR MAN *RCA 1663.*	19	9
15 May 68		U.S. MALE *RCA 1688* 1	15	8
17 Jul 68		YOUR TIME HASN'T COME YET BABY *RCA 1714* 1	22	11
16 Oct 68		YOU'LL NEVER WALK ALONE *RCA 1747* 1	44	3
26 Feb 69		IF I CAN DREAM *RCA 1795*	11	10
11 Jun 69	●	IN THE GHETTO (re) *RCA 1831*	2	17
6 Sep 69		CLEAN UP YOUR OWN BACK YARD *RCA 1869*	21	7
29 Nov 69	●	SUSPICIOUS MINDS *RCA 1900* ▲	2	14
28 Feb 70		DON'T CRY DADDY *RCA 1916*	8	11
16 May 70		KENTUCKY RAIN *RCA 1949*	21	12
11 Jul 70	★	THE WONDER OF YOU (re) *RCA 1974*	1	21
14 Nov 70		I'VE LOST YOU *RCA 1999*	9	12
9 Jan 71	●	YOU DON'T HAVE TO SAY YOU LOVE ME (re) *RCA 2046*	9	10
20 Mar 71		THERE GOES MY EVERYTHING *RCA 2060* 5	6	11
15 May 71		RAGS TO RICHES *RCA 2084* 5	9	11
17 Jul 71	●	HEARTBREAK HOTEL / HOUND DOG (re-issue) *RCA Maximillion 2104*	10	12
2 Oct 71		I'M LEAVIN' *RCA 2125* 5	23	9
4 Dec 71	●	I JUST CAN'T HELP BELIEVING *RCA 2158* 6	6	16
11 Dec 71		JAILHOUSE ROCK (re-issue) *RCA Maximillion 2153*	42	5
1 Apr 72	●	UNTIL IT'S TIME FOR YOU TO GO *RCA 2188* 5	5	9
17 Jun 72	●	AN AMERICAN TRILOGY *RCA 2229*	8	11
30 Sep 72	●	BURNING LOVE *RCA 2267* 7	7	9
16 Dec 72	●	ALWAYS ON MY MIND *RCA 2304* 7	9	13
26 May 73		POLK SALAD ANNIE *RCA 2359*	23	7
11 Aug 73		FOOL *RCA 2393* 1	15	10
24 Nov 73		RAISED ON ROCK *RCA 2435.*	36	7
16 Mar 74		I'VE GOT A THING ABOUT YOU BABY *RCA APBO 0196* 7	33	5
13 Jul 74		IF YOU TALK IN YOUR SLEEP *RCA APBO 0280*	40	3
16 Nov 74	●	MY BOY *RCA 2458*	5	13
18 Jan 75		PROMISED LAND *RCA PB 10074*	9	8
24 May 75		T.R.O.U.B.L.E. *RCA 2562*	31	4
29 Nov 75		GREEN GREEN GRASS OF HOME *RCA 2635.*	29	7
1 May 76		HURT *RCA 2674*	37	5

			pos/wks
4 Sep 76 ●	THE GIRL OF MY BEST FRIEND *RCA 2729*		9 12
25 Dec 76 ●	SUSPICION *RCA 2768*		9 12
5 Mar 77 ●	MOODY BLUE *RCA PB 0857* [8]		6 9
13 Aug 77 ★	WAY DOWN *RCA PB 0998* [9]		1 13
3 Sep 77	ALL SHOOK UP (re-issue) *RCA PB 2694* [1]		41 2
3 Sep 77	ARE YOU LONESOME TONIGHT? (re-issue) *RCA PB 2699* [1]		46 1
3 Sep 77	CRYING IN THE CHAPEL (re-issue) *RCA PB 2708* [1]		43 2
3 Sep 77	IT'S NOW OR NEVER (re-issue) *RCA PB 2698* [1]		39 2
3 Sep 77	JAILHOUSE ROCK (2nd re-issue) *RCA PB 2695* [1]		44 2
3 Sep 77	RETURN TO SENDER (re-issue) *RCA PB 2706* [1]		42 3
3 Sep 77	THE WONDER OF YOU (re-issue) *RCA PB 2709*		48 1
3 Sep 77	WOODEN HEART (re-issue) *RCA PB 2700*		49 1
10 Dec 77 ●	MY WAY *RCA 1165* [10]		9 8
24 Jun 78	DON'T BE CRUEL *RCA PB 9265*		24 12
15 Dec 79	IT WON'T SEEM LIKE CHRISTMAS (WITHOUT YOU) *RCA PB 9464*		13 6
30 Aug 80 ●	IT'S ONLY LOVE / BEYOND THE REEF *RCA 4*		3 10
6 Dec 80	SANTA CLAUS IS BACK IN TOWN *RCA 16*		41 6
14 Feb 81	GUITAR MAN *RCA 43*		43 4
18 Apr 81	LOVING ARMS *RCA 48*		47 6
13 Mar 82	ARE YOU LONESOME TONIGHT? (LIVE) *RCA 196* [10]		25 7
26 Jun 82	THE SOUND OF YOUR CRY *RCA 232* [5]		59 2
7 May 83	BABY I DON'T CARE *RCA 332*		61 3
3 Dec 83	I CAN HELP *RCA 369* [11]		30 9
10 Nov 84	THE LAST FAREWELL *RCA 459* [8]		48 6
19 Jan 85	THE ELVIS MEDLEY *RCA 476* [1]		51 3
10 Aug 85	ALWAYS ON MY MIND (re-mix) *RCA PB 49944*		59 4
11 Apr 87	AIN'T THAT LOVIN' YOU BABY / BOSSA NOVA BABY (re-recording) *RCA ARON 1*		47 5
22 Aug 87	LOVE ME TENDER / IF I CAN DREAM (re-issue)*RCA ARON 2*		56 3
16 Jan 88	STUCK ON YOU (re-issue) *RCA PB 49595* [1]		58 2
17 Aug 91	ARE YOU LONESOME TONIGHT (LIVE) (re-issue) *RCA PB 49177*		68 2
29 Aug 92	DON'T BE CRUEL (re-issue) *RCA 7431110777* [1]		42 2
11 Nov 95	THE TWELFTH OF NEVER *RCA 74321320122* [11]		21 3
18 May 96	HEARTBREAK HOTEL / I WAS THE ONE (2nd re-issue) *RCA 74321336862*		45 1
24 May 97	ALWAYS ON MY MIND (re-issue of re-mix) *RCA 74321485412*		13 6
14 Apr 01	SUSPICIOUS MINDS (Live) *RCA 74321855822*		15 4
10 Nov 01	AMERICA THE BEAUTIFUL *RCA 74321904022*		69 1
22 Jun 02 ★	A LITTLE LESS CONVERSATION *RCA 74321943572* ■ [12]		1 12

[1] With The Jordanaires [2] With The Mellomen [3] With The Jordanaires Jubilee Four and Carol Lombard Trio [4] With The Jordanaires and Imperials Quartet [5] Vocal accompaniment: The Imperial Quartet [6] Vocal acc. The Imperials Quartet and The Sweet Inspirations [7] Vocal acc. JD Sumner and The Stamps [8] Vocal acc. JD Sumner and The Stamps Qt. Kathy Westmoreland, Myrna Smith [9] Vocal acc. JD Sumner and The Stamps Qt. K Westmoreland, S Neilson and M Smith [10] Vocal acc. JD Sumner and the Stamps, the Sweet Inspirations and Kathy Westmoreland [11] Vocal accompaniment The Voice [12] Elvis vs JXL

'Jailhouse Rock' re-entry was in Feb 1983 peaking at No.27. Tracks on *Jailhouse Rock* (EP): Jailhouse Rock / Young and Beautiful / I Want to Be Free / Don't Leave Me Now / Baby I Don't Care. Tracks on *Strictly Elvis* (EP): Old Shep / Any Place Is Paradise / Paralyzed / Is It So Strange. Tracks on *Follow That Dream* (EP): Follow That Dream / Angel / What a Wonderful Life / I'm Not the Marrying Kind. On 5 Jul 1962, a note on the Top 50 for that week stated: "Due to difficulties in assessing returns of Follow That Dream EP, it has been decided not to include it in Britain's Top 50. It is of course No.1 in the EP charts." Therefore this EP had only a two-week run on the chart when its sales would certainly have justified a much longer one. 'Beyond the Reef' listed only from 30 Aug to 13 Sep 1980. It peaked at No.7. RCA PB 49177 is a re-issue of RCA 196. 'Can't Help Falling in Love' credited from 1 Mar 1962. Tracks on *The Elvis Medley*: Jailhouse Rock / Teddy Bear / Hound Dog / Don't Be Cruel / Burning Love / Suspicious Minds. 'Guitar Man' on 14 Feb 1981 is an overdubbed release

Sharp-eyed readers will have counted 17 US No.1 hits listed for 'The King'. However, he actually scored 18 chart-toppers – with 'Don't Be Cruel' which gets an individual top placing in the US in addition to a joint listing with 'Hound Dog'

PRESSURE DROP *UK, male vocal / instrumental duo (2 WEEKS)* pos/wks

21 Mar 98	SILENTLY BAD MINDED *Higher Ground HIGHS6 CD*	53 1
17 Mar 01	WARRIOR SOUND *Higher Ground 6697192*	72 1

Billy PRESTON
US, male vocalist / instrumentalist – keyboards (51 WEEKS) pos/wks

23 Apr 69 ★	GET BACK (2re) *Apple R 5777* [1] ■ ▲	1 23
2 Jul 69	THAT'S THE WAY GOD PLANNED IT *Apple 12*	11 10
16 Sep 72	OUTA SPACE *A&M AMS 7007*	44 3
15 Dec 79 ●	WITH YOU I'M BORN AGAIN *Motown TMG 1159* [2]	2 11
8 Mar 80	IT WILL COME IN TIME *Motown TMG 1175* [2]	47 4

[1] Beatles with Billy Preston [2] Billy Preston and Syreeta

Johnny PRESTON
US, male vocalist – Johnny Courville (46 WEEKS) pos/wks

12 Feb 60 ★	RUNNING BEAR (re) *Mercury AMT 1079* ▲	1 16
21 Apr 60 ●	CRADLE OF LOVE *Mercury AMT 1092*	2 16
28 Jul 60	I'M STARTING TO GO STEADY *Mercury AMT 1104*	49 1
11 Aug 60	FEEL SO FINE *Mercury AMT 1104*	18 10
8 Dec 60	CHARMING BILLY (re) *Mercury AMT 1114*	34 3

Mike PRESTON *UK, male vocalist – Jack Davis (33 WEEKS)* pos/wks

30 Oct 59	MR BLUE *Decca F 11167*	12 8
25 Aug 60	I'D DO ANYTHING *Decca F 11255*	23 10
22 Dec 60	TOGETHERNESS *Decca F 11287*	41 5
9 Mar 61	MARRY ME *Decca F 11335*	14 10

PRETENDERS 201 Top 500

Internationally successful. British-based post-punk group with an ever-changing line-up, but with ex-NME journalist Chrissie Hynde (b. 7 Sep 1951, Ohio, US) (v/g) as a common factor. Hynde was briefly married to the lead singer of Simple Minds, Jim Kerr, and had a child with Ray Davies of The Kinks (132 WEEKS) pos/wks

10 Feb 79	STOP YOUR SOBBING *Real ARE 6*	34 9
14 Jul 79	KID *Real ARE 9*	33 7
17 Nov 79 ★	BRASS IN POCKET *Real ARE 11*	1 17
5 Apr 80 ●	TALK OF THE TOWN *Real ARE 12*	8 8
14 Feb 81	MESSAGE OF LOVE *Real ARE 15*	11 7
12 Sep 81	DAY AFTER DAY *Real ARE 17*	45 4
14 Nov 81 ●	I GO TO SLEEP *Real ARE 18*	7 10
2 Oct 82	BACK ON THE CHAIN GANG *Real ARE 19*	17 9
26 Nov 83	2000 MILES *Real ARE 20*	15 9
9 Jun 84	THIN LINE BETWEEN LOVE AND HATE *Real ARE 22*	49 3
11 Oct 86 ●	DON'T GET ME WRONG *Real YZ 85*	10 9
13 Dec 86	HYMN TO HER *Real YZ 93*	8 12
15 Aug 87	IF THERE WAS A MAN *Real YZ 149* [1]	49 6
23 Apr 94	I'LL STAND BY YOU *WEA YZ 815CD*	10 10
2 Jul 94	NIGHT IN MY VEINS *WEA YZ 825CD*	25 5
15 Oct 94	977 *WEA YZ 848CD1*	66 2
14 Oct 95	KID (re-recording) *WEA 014CD*	73 1
10 May 97	FEVER PITCH THE EP *Blanco Y Negro NEG 104CD* [2]	65 1
15 May 99	HUMAN *WEA WEA 207CD*	33 3

[1] Pretenders for 007 [2] Pretenders, La's, Orlando, Neil MacColl, Nick Hornby

Tracks on *Fever Pitch the EP*: Goin' Back – Pretenders; There She Goes – La's; How Can We Hang on to a Dream – Orlando; Football – Neil MacColl; Boo Hewerdine – Nick Hornby. 'Kid' in 1995 is a re-recording

See also Chrissie HYNDE

PRETTY BOY FLOYD
US, male vocal / instrumental group (1 WEEK) pos/wks

10 Mar 90	ROCK AND ROLL (IS GONNA SET THE NIGHT ON FIRE) *MCA MCA 1393*	75 1

PRETTY THINGS
UK, male vocal / instrumental group (41 WEEKS) pos/wks

18 Jun 64	ROSALYN *Fontana TF 469*	41 5
22 Oct 64 ●	DON'T BRING ME DOWN *Fontana TF 503*	10 11
25 Feb 65	HONEY I NEED *Fontana TF 537*	13 10
15 Jul 65	CRY TO ME *Fontana TF 585*	28 7
20 Jan 66	MIDNIGHT TO SIX MAN *Fontana TF 647*	46 1
5 May 66	COME SEE ME *Fontana TF 688*	43 5
21 Jul 66	A HOUSE IN THE COUNTRY (re) *Fontana TF 722*	50 2

Re-entries are listed as (re) (2re) (3re) etc which signifies that the hit

Alan PRICE `387` `Top 500`

One-time leader of The Animals (first called Alan Price Combo), who left in 1965, b. 19 Apr 1942, Durham, UK. Best known for keyboards and vocals but wrote the 1973 Bafta-winning film score for 'O Lucky Man!' and won Most Promising New Actor award in 1975 (87 WEEKS)

		pos/wks	
31 Mar 66 ●	I PUT A SPELL ON YOU *Decca F 12367* [1]	9	10
14 Jul 66	HI LILI, HI LO *Decca F 12442* [1]	11	12
2 Mar 67 ●	SIMON SMITH AND HIS AMAZING DANCING BEAR *Decca F 12570* [1]	4	12
2 Aug 67 ●	THE HOUSE THAT JACK BUILT *Decca F 12641* [1]	4	10
15 Nov 67	SHAME *Decca F 12691* [1]	45	2
31 Jan 68	DON'T STOP THE CARNIVAL *Decca F 12731* [1]	13	8
10 Apr 71	ROSETTA *CBS 7108* [2]	11	10
25 May 74 ●	JARROW SONG *Warner Bros. K 16372*	6	9
29 Apr 78	JUST FOR YOU *Jet UP 36358*	43	7
17 Feb 79	BABY OF MINE / JUST FOR YOU (re-issue) *Jet 135*	32	3
30 Apr 88	CHANGES *Ariola 109911*	54	4

[1] Alan Price Set [2] Fame and Price Together

Kelly PRICE *US, female vocalist (10 WEEKS)*

		pos/wks	
7 Nov 98	FRIEND OF MINE *Island Black Music CID 723*	25	3
8 May 99	SECRET LOVE *Island Black Music CID 739*	26	2
30 Dec 00	HEARTBREAK HOTEL *Arista 74321820572* [1]	25	5

[1] Whitney Houston featuring Faith Evans and Kelly Price

Lloyd PRICE *US, male vocalist (36 WEEKS)*

		pos/wks	
13 Feb 59 ●	STAGGER LEE *HMV POP 580* ▲	7	14
15 May 59	WHERE WERE YOU (ON OUR WEDDING DAY)? *HMV POP 598*	15	6
12 Jun 59 ●	PERSONALITY (re) *HMV POP 626*	9	10
11 Sep 59	I'M GONNA GET MARRIED *HMV POP 650*	23	5
21 Apr 60	LADY LUCK *HMV POP 712*	45	1

PRICKLY HEAT *UK, male producer (1 WEEK)*

		pos/wks	
26 Dec 98	OOOIE, OOOIE, OOOIE *Virgin VSCDT 1727*	57	1

Dickie PRIDE

UK, male vocalist – Richard Knellar d. May 1969 (1 WEEK)

		pos/wks	
30 Oct 59	PRIMROSE LANE *Columbia DB 4340*	28	1

Maxi PRIEST `286` `Top 500`

Popular dancehall reggae star, b. Max Elliott, 10 Jun 1960, London, UK. This internationally acclaimed vocalist is one of only two UK reggae acts to top the US chart ('Close to You', 1990). A duet with Roberta Flack, 'Set the Night to Music', also reached the US Top 10 in 1991 (106 WEEKS)

		pos/wks	
29 Mar 86	STROLLIN' ON *10 TEN 84*	32	9
12 Jul 86	IN THE SPRINGTIME *10 TEN 127*	54	3
8 Nov 86	CRAZY LOVE *10 TEN 135*	67	5
4 Apr 87	LET ME KNOW *10 TEN 156*	49	4
24 Oct 87	SOME GUYS HAVE ALL THE LUCK *10 TEN 198*	12	12
20 Feb 88	HOW CAN WE EASE THE PAIN *10 TEN 207*	41	6
4 Jun 88 ●	WILD WORLD *10 TEN 221*	5	9
27 Aug 88	GOODBYE TO LOVE AGAIN *10 TEN 238*	57	3
9 Jun 90 ●	CLOSE TO YOU *10 TEN 294* ▲	7	10
1 Sep 90	PEACE THROUGHOUT THE WORLD *10 TEN 317* [1]	41	4
1 Dec 90	HUMAN WORK OF ART (re) *10 TEN 328*	71	4
24 Aug 91	HOUSECALL *Epic 6573477* [2]	31	7
5 Oct 91	JUST A LITTLE BIT LONGER (EP) *Ten TEN 343*	62	3
26 Sep 92	GROOVIN' IN THE MIDNIGHT *Ten TEN 412*	50	2
28 Nov 92	JUST WANNA KNOW / FE' REAL *Ten TEN 416* [3]	33	3
20 Mar 93	ONE MORE CHANCE *Ten TENCD 420*	40	3
8 May 93 ●	HOUSECALL (re-mix) *Epic 6592842* [2]	8	8
31 Jul 93	WAITING IN VAIN *GRP MCSTD 1921* [4]	65	2
22 Jun 96	THAT GIRL *Virgin America VUSCD 106* [5]	15	7
21 Sep 96	WATCHING THE WORLD GO BY *Virgin America VUSCD 108*	36	2

[1] Maxi Priest featuring Jazzie B [2] Shabba Ranks featuring Maxi Priest [3] Maxi Priest / Maxi Priest featuring Apache Indian [4] Lee Ritenour and Maxi Priest [5] Maxi Priest featuring Shaggy

Tracks on Just a Little Bit Longer (EP): Just a Little Bit Longer / Best of Me / Searching / Fever

Louis PRIMA *US, male vocalist d. 24 Aug 1978 (1 WEEK)*

		pos/wks	
21 Feb 58	BUONA SERA *Capitol CL 14821*	25	1

PRIMA DONNA *UK, male / female vocal group (4 WEEKS)*

		pos/wks	
26 Apr 80	LOVE ENOUGH FOR TWO *Ariola ARO 221*	48	4

PRIMAL SCREAM
UK, male vocal / instrumental group (52 WEEKS)

		pos/wks	
3 Mar 90	LOADED *Creation CRE 070*	16	9
18 Aug 90	COME TOGETHER *Creation CRE 078*	26	6
22 Jun 91	HIGHER THAN THE SUN *Creation CRE 096*	40	2
24 Aug 91	DON'T FIGHT IT FEEL IT *Creation CRE 110* [1]	41	2
8 Feb 92	DIXIE-NARCO (EP) *Creation CRE 117*	11	6
12 Mar 94	ROCKS / FUNKY JAM *Creation CRESCD 129*	7	5
18 Jun 94	JAILBIRD *Creation CRESCD 145*	29	2
10 Dec 94	(I'M GONNA) CRY MYSELF BLIND *Creation CRESCD 183*	49	2
15 Jun 96	THE BIG MAN AND THE SCREAM TEAM MEET THE BARMY ARMY UPTOWN *Creation CRESCD 194* [2]	17	2
17 May 97 ●	KOWALSKI *Creation CRESCD 245*	8	3
28 Jun 97	STAR *Creation CRESCD 263*	16	2
25 Oct 97	BURNING WHEEL *Creation CRESCD 272*	17	2
20 Nov 99	SWASTIKA EYES *Creation CRESCD 326*	22	2
1 Apr 00	KILL ALL HIPPIES *Creation CRESCD 332*	24	2
23 Sep 00	ACCELERATOR *Creation CRESCD 333*	34	1
3 Aug 02	MISS LUCIFER *Columbia 6728252*	25	2
9 Nov 02	AUTOBAHN 66 *Columbia 6733122*	44	1

[1] Primal Scream featuring Denise Johnson [2] Primal Scream, Irvine Welsh and On-U Sound

Tracks on Dixie-Narco (EP): Movin' On Up / Stone My Soul / Carry Me Home / Screamadelica

See also Gary CLAIL ON-U SOUND SYSTEM

PRIME MOVERS *US, male vocal / instrumental group (1 WEEK)*

		pos/wks	
8 Feb 86	ON THE TRAIL *Island IS 263*	74	1

PRIMITIVE RADIO GODS
US, male vocalist – Chris O'Connor (1 WEEK)

		pos/wks	
30 Mar 96	STANDING OUTSIDE A BROKEN PHONE BOOTH WITH MONEY IN MY HAND *Columbia 6627692*	74	1

PRIMITIVES
UK, male / female vocal / instrumental group (27 WEEKS)

		pos/wks	
27 Feb 88 ●	CRASH *Lazy PB 41761*	5	10
30 Apr 88	OUT OF REACH *Lazy PB 42011*	25	4
3 Sep 88	WAY BEHIND ME *Lazy PB 42209*	36	4
29 Jul 89	SICK OF IT *Lazy PB 42947*	24	4
30 Sep 89	SECRETS *Lazy PB 43173*	49	3
3 Aug 91	YOU ARE THE WAY *RCA PB 44481*	58	2

PRINCE `33` `Top 500`

Prolific singer / songwriter / producer / multi-instrumentalist / actor / label and studio owner, b. Prince Rogers Nelson, 7 Jun 1958, Minneapolis, US. This often controversial entertainer has packed stadiums and collected awards worldwide. He has recorded under a variety of monikers including a symbol and "The Artist Formerly Known As Prince" (305 WEEKS)

		pos/wks	
19 Jan 80	I WANNA BE YOUR LOVER *Warner Bros. K 17537*	41	3
29 Jan 83	1999 *Warner Bros. W 9896*	25	7
30 Apr 83	LITTLE RED CORVETTE *Warner Bros. W 9688*	54	6
26 Nov 83	LITTLE RED CORVETTE (re-issue) *Warner Bros. W 9436*	66	2
30 Jun 84 ●	WHEN DOVES CRY *Warner Bros. W 9286* ▲	4	15
22 Sep 84 ●	PURPLE RAIN *Warner Bros. W 9174* [1]	8	9
8 Dec 84	I WOULD DIE 4 U *Warner Bros. W 9121* [1]	58	6
19 Jan 85	1999 / LITTLE RED CORVETTE (re-issue) *Warner Bros. W 1999*	2	10
23 Feb 85 ●	LET'S GO CRAZY / TAKE ME WITH U *Warner Bros. W 2000* [1] ▲	7	9
25 May 85	PAISLEY PARK *WEA W 9052* [1]	18	10
27 Jul 85	RASPBERRY BERET *WEA W 8929* [1]	25	8

I WILL SURVIVE

■ Had it not been for a personal crusade by Gloria Gaynor, 'I Will Survive' might never have been a hit at all. The song was written as a throwaway B-side. The New Jersey-born singer first found international success with a 1974 up-tempo remake of the Jackson Five ballad 'Never Can Say Goodbye', and this led to her being crowned Queen of Disco by the National Association of Discotheque DJs in 1975. Despite this success, and partly because of a number of personal problems, Gaynor had some difficulty in finding a follow-up and soon lost her disco crown to Donna Summer. However, she was to make a remarkable comeback and temporarily reclaim her throne with a vengeance with 'I Will Survive'.

Assigned to producer Freddie Perren, she began work on a new single in 1978. Perren was an industry veteran who had co-written the first three US Jackson Five chart-toppers and had written and produced a string of hits for Tavares. The song to be recorded at the session was a cover of a Righteous Brothers track, 'Substitute', that had been a recent UK No.2 hit for the South African group Clout. Perren had agreed to produce the sessions, only if he could supply the B-side. This was common music business practice. The profits on singles were divided 50/50 between both sides, which meant that the writer of the backside of a huge hit received the same remuneration as the writers of the hit side. Thus producers were often given (or demanded) the opportunity to cash in on this potential money-spinner with an inferior piece cobbled together in next to no time. The B-side to 'Substitute' proved to be an exception to the rule.

'I Will Survive' was especially written for Gloria

■ HOW COULD THIS BE A B-SIDE? SURELY IT WAS A MAJOR HIT? THE RECORD COMPANY DIDN'T AGREE AND 'SUBSTITUTE' WAS RELEASED AS GLORIA GAYNOR'S NEXT SINGLE ■

Gaynor, and before beginning the lyric, Freddie Perren's partner Dino Fekaris consulted her about subject matter that might appeal to her. However, when Fekaris arrived at the session he'd forgotten to bring the lyrics with him, and had to jot them down quickly on a brown paper bag he found in the studio. As soon as she read them, and without even hearing the melody, Gaynor was immediately hooked. She was also stunned. How could this be a B-side? Surely it was a major hit? The record company didn't agree and 'Substitute' was released as her next single with 'I Will Survive' hidden away on the flip side. Not even the writers, Perren and Fekaris, saw the potential in what has become their most successful song.

Gaynor and her husband decided to take matters into their own hands. She began featuring the song as the finale at concerts to a great response. Club DJs were persuaded to "flip" the

★ **ARTIST:**   Gloria Gaynor

★ **LABEL:**   Polydor

★ **WRITERS:**   Dino Fekaris and Freddie Perren

★ **PRODUCERS:**   Dino Fekaris and Freddie Perren

record, and eventually it became a popular favourite at New York's influential Studio 54 discotheque. After months of persuasion (and when it became apparent that 'Substitute' wasn't going to make it), 'I Will Survive' was re-released as the A-side and promptly shot to the top of the charts on both sides of the Atlantic, winning a Grammy award for Best Disco Record. Despite several attempts including 'I Am What I Am', Gloria Gaynor has never been able to better the success of this career blockbuster which has since become a gay and feminist anthem. A re-mixed recording returned to the UK Top Five in 1993 and, to this day, gets massive exposure as one of the most frequently performed karaoke numbers.

■ Tony Burton

Gloria Gaynor shows a million karaoke pretenders just how 'I Will Survive' should really be done

26 Oct 85	POP LIFE *Paisley Park W 8858* [1]	60	2
8 Mar 86 ●	KISS *Paisley Park W 8751* [1] ▲	6	9
14 Jun 86	MOUNTAINS *Paisley Park W 8711* [1]	45	4
16 Aug 86	GIRLS AND BOYS *Paisley Park W 8586* [1]	11	8
1 Nov 86	ANOTHERLOVERHOLENYOHEAD *Paisley Park W 8521* [1]	...36	3
14 Mar 87	SIGN 'O' THE TIMES *Paisley Park W 8399*	10	9
20 Jun 87	IF I WAS YOUR GIRLFRIEND *Paisley Park W 8334*	20	6
15 Aug 87	U GOT THE LOOK *Paisley Park W 8289*	11	9
28 Nov 87	I COULD NEVER TAKE THE PLACE OF YOUR MAN *Paisley Park W 8288*	29	6
7 May 88 ●	ALPHABET STREET *Paisley Park W 7900*	9	4
23 Jul 88	GLAM SLAM *Paisley Park W 7806*	29	4
5 Nov 88	I WISH U HEAVEN *Paisley Park W 7745*	24	5
24 Jun 89 ●	BATDANCE *Warner Bros. W 2924* ▲	2	12
9 Sep 89	PARTYMAN *Warner Bros. W 2814*	14	6
18 Nov 89	THE ARMS OF ORION *Warner Bros. W 2757* [2]	27	5
4 Aug 90 ●	THIEVES IN THE TEMPLE *Paisley Park W 9751*	7	6
10 Nov 90	NEW POWER GENERATION *Paisley Park W 9525*	26	4
31 Aug 91 ●	GETT OFF *Paisley Park W 0056* [3]	4	8
21 Sep 91	CREAM *Paisley Park W 0061* [3] ▲	15	7
7 Dec 91	DIAMONDS AND PEARLS *Paisley Park W 0075* [3]	25	6
28 Mar 92	MONEY DON'T MATTER 2 NIGHT *Paisley Park W 0091* [3]	...19	5
27 Jun 92	THUNDER *Paisley Park W 0113* [3]	28	3
18 Jul 92 ●	SEXY MF / STROLLIN' *Paisley Park W 0123* [3]	4	7
10 Oct 92 ●	MY NAME IS PRINCE *Paisley Park W 0132* [3]	7	5
14 Nov 92	MY NAME IS PRINCE (re-mix) *Paisley Park W 0142T* [3]	...51	1
5 Dec 92	7 *Paisley Park W 0147* [3]	27	6
13 Mar 93	THE MORNING PAPERS *Paisley Park W 0162CD* [3]	52	3
16 Oct 93	PEACH *Paisley Park W 0210CD*	14	5
11 Dec 93 ●	CONTROVERSY *Paisley Park W 0215CD1*	5	5
9 Apr 94 ★	THE MOST BEAUTIFUL GIRL IN THE WORLD *NPG NPG 60155*...1		12
4 Jun 94	THE BEAUTIFUL EXPERIENCE (re-mix) *NPG NPG 60212*........18		3
10 Sep 94	LETITGO *Warner Bros. W 0260CD*	30	4
18 Mar 95	PURPLE MEDLEY *Warner Bros. W 0289CD*	33	2
23 Sep 95	EYE HATE U *Warner Bros. W 0315CD*	20	3
9 Dec 95 ●	GOLD *Warner Bros. W 0325CD*	10	6
3 Aug 96	DINNER WITH DELORES *Warner Bros. 9362437422*......36		2
14 Dec 96	BETCHA BY GOLLY WOW *NPG CDEM 463* [4]	11	7
8 Mar 97	THE HOLY RIVER *EMI CDEM 467* [4]	19	3
9 Jan 99 ●	1999 (re-issue) (re) *Warner Bros. W 467CD*	10	9
26 Feb 00	THE GREATEST ROMANCE EVER SOLD *NPG / Arista 74321745002* [4]	65	1

[1] Prince and The Revolution [2] Prince with Sheena Easton [3] Prince and The New Power Generation [4] The Artist

Although uncredited, Sheena Easton also sings on 'U Got the Look'. 'The Beautiful Experience' was a seven-track CD featuring 'The Most Beautiful Girl in the World' and six further mixes of the track

PRINCE BUSTER
Jamaica, male vocalist – Buster Campbell (16 WEEKS) pos/wks

23 Feb 67	AL CAPONE *Blue Beat BB 324*	18	13
4 Apr 98	WHINE AND GRINE *Island CID 691*	21	3

PRINCE CHARLES and the CITY BEAT BAND
US, male vocal / instrumental group (2 WEEKS) pos/wks

22 Feb 86	WE CAN MAKE IT HAPPEN *PRT 7P 348*	56	2

PRINCE NASEEM – *See KALEEF*

PRINCESS
UK, female vocalist – Desiree Heslop (44 WEEKS) pos/wks

3 Aug 85 ●	SAY I'M YOUR NUMBER ONE *Supreme SUPE 101*	7	12
9 Nov 85	AFTER THE LOVE HAS GONE *Supreme SUPE 103*	28	13
19 Apr 86	I'LL KEEP ON LOVING YOU *Supreme SUPE 105*	16	8
5 Jul 86	TELL ME TOMORROW *Supreme SUPE 106*	34	5
25 Oct 86	IN THE HEAT OF A PASSIONATE MOMENT *Supreme SUPE 109*	74	1
13 Jun 87	RED HOT *Polydor POSP 868*	58	5

PRINCESS IVORI
US, female rapper (2 WEEKS) pos/wks

17 Mar 90	WANTED *Supreme SUPE 163*	69	2

PRINCESS SUPERSTAR
US, female vocalist – Concetta Kirschner (7 WEEKS) pos/wks

2 Mar 02	BAD BABYSITTER *Rapster RR 007CDM*	11	7

Patrick PRINZ – *See ARTEMESIA; ETHICS; MOVIN' MELODIES; SUBLIMINAL CUTS*

Maddy PRIOR – *See STATUS QUO; STEELEYE SPAN*

PRIVATE LIVES
UK, male vocal / instrumental duo (4 WEEKS) pos/wks

11 Feb 84	LIVING IN A WORLD (TURNED UPSIDE DOWN) *EMI PRIV 2*......53		4

PRIZNA featuring DEMOLITION MAN
UK, male vocal / instrumental group (2 WEEKS) pos/wks

29 Apr 95	FIRE *Labello Blanco NLBCDX 18*	33	2

PJ PROBY (355) Top 500
Controversial pony tail-wearing, trouser-splitting teen idol, b. James Marcus Smith, 6 Nov 1938, Texas, US. Mannered vocalist found success after relocating to UK, and adopting Tom Jones (the successful 60s film, not the singer) attire. Voted Brightest Hope of 1964 by Melody Maker readers (91 WEEKS) pos/wks

28 May 64 ●	HOLD ME *Decca F 11904*	3	15
3 Sep 64 ●	TOGETHER *Decca F 11967*	8	11
10 Dec 64 ●	SOMEWHERE *Liberty LIB 10182*	6	12
25 Feb 65	I APOLOGISE *Liberty LIB 10188*	11	8
8 Jul 65	LET THE WATER RUN DOWN *Liberty LIB 10206*	19	8
30 Sep 65	THAT MEANS A LOT *Liberty LIB 10215*	30	6
25 Nov 65	MARIA *Liberty LIB 10218*	8	9
10 Feb 66	YOU'VE COME BACK *Liberty LIB 10223*	25	7
16 Jun 66	TO MAKE A BIG MAN CRY *Liberty LIB 10236*	34	3
27 Oct 66	I CAN'T MAKE IT ALONE *Liberty LIB 10250*	37	5
6 Mar 68	IT'S YOUR DAY TODAY *Liberty LBF 15046*	32	5
28 Dec 96	YESTERDAY HAS GONE (re) *EMI Premier CDPRESX 13* [1]......58		2

[1] PJ Proby and Marc Almond featuring the My Life Story Orchestra

PROCLAIMERS
UK, male vocal / instrumental duo – Charlie and Craig Reid (50 WEEKS) pos/wks

14 Nov 87 ●	LETTER FROM AMERICA *Chrysalis CHS 3178*	3	10
5 Mar 88	MAKE MY HEART FLY *Chrysalis CLAIM 1*	63	3
27 Aug 88	I'M GONNA BE (500 MILES) *Chrysalis CLAIM 2*	11	11
12 Nov 88	SUNSHINE ON LEITH *Chrysalis CLAIM 3*	41	5
11 Feb 89	I'M ON MY WAY *Chrysalis CLAIM 4*	43	4
24 Nov 90 ●	KING OF THE ROAD (EP) *Chrysalis CLAIM 5*	9	8
19 Feb 94	LET'S GET MARRIED *Chrysalis CDCLAIMS 6*	21	4
16 Apr 94	WHAT MAKES YOU CRY *Chrysalis CDCLAIMS 7*	38	3
22 Oct 94	THESE ARMS OF MINE *Chrysalis CDCLAIM 8*	51	2

Tracks on King of the Road (EP): King of the Road / Long Black Veil / Lulu Selling Tea / Not Ever

PROCOL HARUM
UK, male vocal / instrumental group – lead vocal Gary Brooker (56 WEEKS) pos/wks

25 May 67 ★	A WHITER SHADE OF PALE *Deram DM 126*	1	15
4 Oct 67 ●	HOMBURG *Regal Zonophone RZ 3003*	6	10
24 Apr 68	QUITE RIGHTLY SO *Regal Zonophone RZ 3007*	50	1
18 Jun 69	A SALTY DOG (2re) *Regal Zonophone RZ 3019*	44	3
22 Apr 72	A WHITER SHADE OF PALE (re-issue) *Fly Magnify ECHO 101*..13		13
5 Aug 72	CONQUISTADOR *Chrysalis CHS 2003*	22	7
23 Aug 75	PANDORA'S BOX *Chrysalis CHS 2073*	16	7

Michael PROCTOR – *See URBAN BLUES PROJECT presents Michael PROCTER*

PRODIGY (163) Top 500
Confrontational dance-rock collision masterminded by Liam Howlett (k/prog) and featuring charismatic Keith Flint (v). This act has achieved a run of 12 successive Top 20 singles, while their 1997 album, 'Fat of the Land', debuted at No.1 in more than 20 countries, including the US and the UK. MC / dancer Maxim went solo in 2000. Best-selling single: 'Breathe' 709,000 (145 WEEKS) pos/wks

24 Aug 91 ●	CHARLY (re) *XL XL Recordings 21CD*	3	11
4 Jan 92 ●	EVERYBODY IN THE PLACE (EP) (re) *XL XL Recordings 26CD1*..2		10

26 Sep 92 ●	FIRE / JERICHO (re) *XL XL Recordings 30CD*..............	11	5
21 Nov 92 ●	OUT OF SPACE / RUFF IN THE JUNGLE BIZNESS (re)		
	XL XL Recordings 35CD..............	5	14
17 Apr 93	WIND IT UP (REWOUND) (re) *XL XL Recordings 39CD*	11	8
16 Oct 93 ●	ONE LOVE *XL XL Recordings 47CD*..............	8	6
28 May 94 ●	NO GOOD (START THE DANCE) (re)		
	XL XL Recordings 51CD..............	4	14
24 Sep 94 ●	VOODOO PEOPLE (re) *XL XL Recordings 54CD*.........13	13	6
18 Mar 95 ●	POISON (re) *XL XL Recordings 58CD*..............	15	7
30 Mar 96 ★	FIRESTARTER (2re) *XL XL Recordings 70CD* ■..............	1	30
23 Nov 96 ★	BREATHE (re) *XL XL Recordings 80CD* ■..............	1	18
29 Nov 97 ●	SMACK MY BITCH UP *XL XL Recordings 90CD*..............	8	10
13 Jul 02 ●	BABY'S GOT A TEMPER *XL Recordings XLS 145CD*	5	6

Tracks on Everybody in the Place (EP): Everybody in the Place / Crazy Man / G-Force (Energy Flow) / Rip Up the Sound System

Eight of their singles re-entered in Apr 1996

PRODUCT G&B – *See SANTANA*

PROFESSIONALS
UK, male vocal / instrumental group (4 WEEKS)   pos/wks

11 Oct 80	1-2-3 *Virgin VS 376*	43	4

PROFESSOR – *See DJ PROFESSOR*

PROFESSOR T – *See SHUT UP AND DANCE*

PROGRAM – *See MR PINK presents The PROGRAM*

PROGRAM 2 BELTRAM – *See BELTRAM*

PROGRESS FUNK *Italy, male production trio (1 WEEK)*   pos/wks

11 Oct 97	AROUND MY BRAIN *Deconstruction 74321518182*	73	1

PROGRESS presents the BOY WUNDA
UK, male DJ / producer – Robert Webster (10 WEEKS)   pos/wks

18 Dec 99 ●	EVERYBODY *Manifesto FESCD 65*	7	10

PROJECT featuring GERIDEAU
US, male vocal / instrumental duo (1 WEEK)   pos/wks

27 Aug 94	BRING IT BACK 2 LUV *Fruittree FTREE 10CD*	65	1

PROJECT 1 *UK, male producer – Mark Williams (3 WEEKS)*   pos/wks

16 May 92	ROUGH NECK (EP) *Rising High RSN 22*	49	2
29 Aug 92	DON GARGON COMIN' *Rising High RSN 35*	64	1

Tracks on Roughneck (EP): Come My Selector / Can't Take the Heartbreak / Live Vibe 4 (Summer Vibes)

PRONG *US, male vocal / instrumental group (1 WEEK)*   pos/wks

25 Apr 92	WHOSE FIST IS THIS ANYWAY (EP) *Epic 6580026*	58	1

Tracks on Whose Fist Is This Anyway (EP): Prove You Wrong / Hell If I Could / (Get a) Grip (On Yourself) / Prove You Wrong (re-mix)

PROPAGANDA
Germany, male / female vocal / instrumental group (35 WEEKS)   pos/wks

17 Mar 84	DR MABUSE *ZTT ZTAS 2*..............	27	9
4 May 85	DUEL *ZTT ZTAS 8*..............	21	12
10 Aug 85	P MACHINERY *ZTT ZTAS 12*..............	50	5
28 Apr 90	HEAVEN GIVE ME WORDS *Virgin VS 1245*	36	5
8 Sep 90	ONLY ONE WORD *Virgin VS 1271*	71	4

PROPELLERHEADS *UK, male instrumental /
production duo – Alex Gifford and Will White (15 WEEKS)*   pos/wks

7 Dec 96	TAKE CALIFORNIA *Wall of Sound WALLD 024*	69	1
17 May 97	SPYBREAK! *Wall of Sound WALLD 029X*	40	1
18 Oct 97 ●	ON HER MAJESTY'S SECRET SERVICE		
	East West EW 136CD [1]	7	5

20 Dec 97	HISTORY REPEATING *Wall of Sound WALLD 036* [2]	19	7
27 Jun 98	BANG ON! *Wall of Sound WALLD 039*..............	53	1

[1] Propellerheads / David Arnold [2] Propellerheads featuring Miss Shirley Bassey

PROPHETS OF SOUND
UK, male instrumental / production duo (2 WEEKS)   pos/wks

14 Nov 98	HIGH *Distinctive DISNCD 47*..............	73	1
23 Feb 02	NEW DAWN *Ink NIBNE 10CD*..............	51	1

PROSPECT PARK / Carolyn HARDING
UK, male / female vocal / production duo (1 WEEK)   pos/wks

8 Aug 98	MOVIN' ON *AM:PM 5827312*..............	55	1

Shaila PROSPERE – *See RIMES featuring Shaila PROSPERE*

Brian PROTHEROE *UK, male vocalist (6 WEEKS)*   pos/wks

7 Sep 74	PINBALL *Chrysalis CHS 2043*	22	6

PROUD MARY
UK, male vocal / instrumental group (1 WEEK)   pos/wks

25 Aug 01	VERY BEST FRIEND *Sour Mash JDNCSCD 004*	75	1

Dorothy PROVINE *US, female actor / vocalist (15 WEEKS)*   pos/wks

7 Dec 61	DON'T BRING LULU *Warner Bros. WB 53*	17	12
28 Jun 62	CRAZY WORDS, CRAZY TUNE *Warner Bros. WB 70*	45	3

PSEUDO ECHO
Australia, male vocal / instrumental group (12 WEEKS)   pos/wks

18 Jul 87 ●	FUNKY TOWN *RCA PB 49705*..............	8	12

PSYCHEDELIC FURS
UK, male vocal / instrumental group (31 WEEKS)   pos/wks

2 May 81	DUMB WAITERS *CBS A 1166*	59	2
27 Jun 81	PRETTY IN PINK *CBS A 1327*	43	5
31 Jul 82	LOVE MY WAY *CBS A 2549*	42	6
31 Mar 84	HEAVEN *CBS A 4300*	29	6
16 Jun 84	GHOST IN YOU *CBS A 4470*	68	2
23 Aug 86	PRETTY IN PINK (re-recording) *CBS A 7242*	18	9
9 Jul 88	ALL THAT MONEY WANTS *CBS FURS 4*	75	1

PSYCHEDELIC WALTONS featuring Roisin MURPHY
UK, male production duo – Nellee Hooper and Fabien Waltmann – and Ireland, female vocalist (2 WEEKS)   pos/wks

19 Jan 02	WONDERLAND *Echo ECSCD 120*..............	37	2

See also SOUL II SOUL; MOLOKO

PSYCHIC TV
UK, male / female vocal / instrumental group (4 WEEKS)   pos/wks

26 Apr 86	GODSTAR *Temple TOPY 009* [1]	67	2
20 Sep 86	GOOD VIBRATIONS / ROMAN P *Temple TOPY 23*	65	2

[1] Psychic TV and the Angels of Light

PSYCHOTROPIC – *See FREEFALL featuring PSYCHOTROPIC; SALT-N-PEPA*

PUBLIC ANNOUNCEMENT
US, male vocal / instrumental group (5 WEEKS)   pos/wks

9 May 92	SHE'S GOT THAT VIBE *Jive JIVET 292* [1]	57	2
20 Nov 93	SEX ME *Jive JIVECD 346* [1]	75	1
4 Jul 98	BODY BUMPIN' (YIPPEE-YI-YO) *A&M 5826972*..............	38	2

[1] R Kelly and Public Announcement

See also R KELLY

PUBLIC DEMAND *UK, male vocal group (2 WEEKS)*   pos/wks

15 Feb 97	INVISIBLE *ZTT ZANG 85CD*..............	41	2

PUBLIC DOMAIN *UK, male production / vocal group (18 WEEKS)* pos/wks

Date	Title	pos	wks
2 Dec 00	● OPERATION BLADE (BASS IN THE PLACE) *Xtrahard / Xtravaganza X2H1 CDS*	5	13
23 Jun 01	ROCK DA FUNKY BEATS *Xtrahard / Xtravaganza X2H3 CDS* [1]	19	3
12 Jan 02	TOO MANY MC'S / LET ME CLEAR MY THROAT *Xtrahard / Xtravaganza X2H 8CDS*	34	2

[1] Public Domain featuring Chuck D

PUBLIC ENEMY *US, male rap group (53 WEEKS)* pos/wks

Date	Title	pos	wks
21 Nov 87	REBEL WITHOUT A PAUSE (re) *Def Jam 651245 7*	37	7
9 Jan 88	BRING THE NOISE *Def Jam 651335 7*	32	5
2 Jul 88	DON'T BELIEVE THE HYPE *Def Jam 652833 7*	18	5
15 Oct 88	NIGHT OF THE LIVING BASEHEADS *Def Jam 6530460*	63	2
24 Jun 89	FIGHT THE POWER *Motown ZB 42877*	29	5
20 Jan 90	WELCOME TO THE TERRORDOME *Def Jam 655476 0*	18	4
7 Apr 90	911 IS A JOKE *Def Jam 655830 7*	41	3
23 Jun 90	BROTHERS GONNA WORK IT OUT *Def Jam 656018 1*	46	2
3 Nov 90	CAN'T DO NUTTIN' FOR YA MAN *Def Jam 656385 7*	53	2
12 Oct 91	CAN'T TRUSS IT *Def Jam 6575307*	22	4
25 Jan 92	SHUT 'EM DOWN *Def Jam 6577617*	21	3
11 Apr 92	NIGHTTRAIN *Def Jam 6578647*	55	2
13 Aug 94	GIVE IT UP *Def Jam DEFCD 1*	18	3
29 Jul 95	SO WATCHA GONNA DO NOW *Def Jam DEFCD 5*	50	1
6 Jun 98	HE GOT GAME *Def Jam 5689852* [1]	16	4
25 Sep 99	DO YOU WANNA GO OUR WAY??? *Pias Recordings PIASX 005CDX*	66	1

[1] Public Enemy featuring Stephen Stills

PUBLIC IMAGE LTD
UK, male vocal / instrumental group (61 WEEKS) pos/wks

Date	Title	pos	wks
21 Oct 78	● PUBLIC IMAGE *Virgin VS 228*	9	8
7 Jul 79	DEATH DISCO *Virgin VS 274*	20	7
20 Oct 79	MEMORIES *Virgin VS 299*	60	2
4 Apr 81	FLOWERS OF ROMANCE *Virgin VS 397*	24	7
17 Sep 83	● THIS IS NOT A LOVE SONG *Virgin VS 529*	5	10
19 May 84	BAD LIFE *Virgin VS 675*	71	2
1 Feb 86	RISE *Virgin VS 841*	11	8
3 May 86	HOME *Virgin VS 855*	75	1
22 Aug 87	SEATTLE *Virgin VS 988*	47	4
6 May 89	DISAPPOINTED *Virgin VS 1181*	38	5
20 Oct 90	DON'T ASK ME *Virgin VS 1231*	22	5
22 Feb 92	CRUEL *Virgin VS 1390*	49	2

Group often known as P.I.L.

See also John LYDON

Gary PUCKETT – *See UNION GAP featuring Gary PUCKETT*

PUDDLE OF MUDD
US, male vocal / instrumental group (21 WEEKS) pos/wks

Date	Title	pos	wks
23 Feb 02	CONTROL (re) *Flawless / Geffen 4976822*	15	5
15 Jun 02	● BLURRY *Flawless / Geffen 4977342*	8	9
28 Sep 02	SHE HATES ME *Flawless / Geffen 4977982*	14	7

Tito PUENTE Jr and The LATIN RHYTHM featuring Tito PUENTE, INDIA and Cali ALEMAN
US, male / female vocal / instrumental group (3 WEEKS) pos/wks

Date	Title	pos	wks
16 Mar 96	OYE COMO VA *Media MCSTD 40013*	36	2
19 Jul 97	OYE COMA VA (re-mix) *Nukleuz MCSTD 40120*	56	1

PUFF DADDY 238 Top 500
World Music Award-winning rapper / songwriter / producer and record label owner now known as P Diddy, b. Sean Combs 1970, New York, US. Only producer to score three successive US No.1 singles in the 1990s. 'I'll Be Missing You', a tribute to (his discovery) Notorious B.I.G., is the most successful rap single of all time and sold 1,409,688 copies in the UK (118 WEEKS) pos/wks

Date	Title	pos	wks
29 Mar 97	CAN'T NOBODY HOLD ME DOWN *Arista 74321464552* [1] ▲	19	4
26 Apr 97	NO TIME *Atlantic A 5594CD* [2]	45	1
28 Jun 97	★ I'LL BE MISSING YOU *Puff Daddy 74321499102* [3] ◆ ■ ▲	1	21
9 Aug 97	● MO MONEY MO PROBLEMS *Puff Daddy 74321492492* [4] ▲	6	10
13 Sep 97	SOMEONE *RCA 74321513942* [5]	34	2
1 Nov 97	BEEN AROUND THE WORLD (re) *Puff Daddy 74321539442* [6]	20	6
7 Feb 98	IT'S ALL ABOUT THE BENJAMINS *Puff Daddy 74321561972* [6]	18	3
1 Aug 98	COME WITH ME (import) *Epic 34K78954* [7]	75	1
8 Aug 98	● COME WITH ME *Epic 6662842* [7]	2	10
1 May 99	ALL NIGHT LONG *Puff Daddy / Arista 74321665692* [8]	23	3
29 May 99	HATE ME NOW *Columbia 6672562* [9]	14	6
21 Aug 99	P.E. 2000 *Puff Daddy / Arista 74321694972* [10]	13	4
20 Nov 99	BEST FRIEND *Puff Daddy / Arista 74321712312* [11]	24	4
5 Feb 00	NOTORIOUS B.I.G. *Puff Daddy / Arista 74321737312* [12]	16	5
19 Feb 00	SATISFY YOU (import) (re) *Bad Boy / Arista 7928322* [13]	73	2
11 Mar 00	SATISFY YOU *Puff Daddy / Arista 74321745592* [13]	8	8
6 Oct 01	BAD BOY FOR LIFE *Bad Boy / Arista 74321889982* [14]	13	6
26 Jan 02	DIDDY *Puff Daddy / Arista 74321911652* [15]	19	4
8 Jun 02	PASS THE COURVOISIER – PART II *J 74321937902* [16]	16	7
10 Aug 02	● I NEED A GIRL (PART ONE) *Puff Daddy / Arista 74321947242* [17]	4	11

[1] Puff Daddy featuring Mase [2] Lil' Kim featuring Puff Daddy [3] Puff Daddy and Faith Evans featuring 112 [4] Notorious B.I.G. featuring Puff Daddy and Mase [5] SWV featuring Puff Daddy [6] Puff Daddy and the Family [7] Puff Daddy featuring Jimmy Page [8] Faith Evans featuring Puff Daddy [9] Nas featuring Puff Daddy [10] Puff Daddy featuring Hurricane G [11] Puff Daddy featuring Mario Winans [12] Notorious B.I.G. featuring Puff Daddy and Lil' Kim [13] Puff Daddy featuring R Kelly [14] P Diddy, Black Rob and Mark Curry [15] P Diddy featuring The Neptunes [16] Busta Rhymes featuring P Diddy and Pharrell [17] P Diddy featuring Usher and Loon

PULP 493 Top 500
Jarvis Cocker b. 19 Sep 1963, Sheffield, UK, is frontman of Pulp, or Arabacus Pulp as his band was called in 1978. After countless line-up changes and modest commercial success, 17 years passed before No.1 album 'Different Class' and a string of Top 10 singles troubled the charts. Cocker's unique brand of wit and wisdom was then exposed to the wider world culminating in the legendary bottom-wiggling "protest" at Michael Jackson's 1996 Brit Awards performance (74 WEEKS) pos/wks

Date	Title	pos	wks
27 Nov 93	LIP GLOSS *Island CID 567*	50	2
2 Apr 94	DO YOU REMEMBER THE FIRST TIME (re) *Island CID 574*	33	5
4 Jun 94	THE SISTERS (EP) *Island CID 595*	19	4
3 Jun 95	● COMMON PEOPLE *Island CID 613*	2	13
7 Oct 95	● MIS-SHAPES / SORTED FOR E'S AND WIZZ (re) *Island CID 620*	2	11
9 Dec 95	● DISCO 2000 *Island CID 623*	7	11
6 Apr 96	● SOMETHING CHANGED (2re) *Island CID 632*	10	7
22 Nov 97	● HELP THE AGED (re) *Island CID 679*	8	9
28 Mar 98	THIS IS HARDCORE *Island CID 695*	12	4
20 Jun 98	A LITTLE SOUL *Island CID 708*	22	2
19 Sep 98	PARTY HARD *Island CID 719*	29	2
20 Oct 01	SUNRISE / THE TREES *Island CID 786*	23	2
27 Apr 02	BAD COVER VERSION *Island CID 794*	27	2

Tracks on The Sisters (EP): Babies / Your Sister's Clothes / Seconds / His 'n' Hers

'Do You Remember The First Time' entered for a second time in Sep 1996

PULSE featuring Antoinette ROBERSON *US, male / female vocal / production duo – David Morales and Antoinette Roberson (3 WEEKS)* pos/wks

Date	Title	pos	wks
25 May 96	THE LOVER THAT YOU ARE *ffrr FCD 278*	22	3

See also BOSS; David MORALES

PUNK CHIC *Sweden, male producer – Johan Strandkvist (1 WEEK)* pos/wks

Date	Title	pos	wks
6 Oct 01	DJ SPINNIN' *WEA WEA 333CD*	69	1

PUNX *Germany, male production trio (1 WEEK)* pos/wks

Date	Title	pos	wks
16 Nov 02	THE ROCK *Data / Ministry of Sound DATA 38CDS*	59	1

PURE SUGAR *UK, male / female vocal / instrumental trio (1 WEEK)* pos/wks

Date	Title	pos	wks
24 Oct 98	DELICIOUS *Geffen GFSTD 22355*	70	1

PURESSENCE *UK, male vocal / instrumental group (6 WEEKS)* pos/wks

Date	Title	pos	wks
23 May 98	THIS FEELING *Island CID 688*	33	2

8 Aug 98	IT DOESN'T MATTER ANYMORE *Island CID 703*	47	1
21 Nov 98	ALL I WANT *Island CID 722*	39	2
5 Oct 02	WALKING DEAD *Island CID 803*	40	1

PURETONE
Australia, male producer – Josh Abrahams (15 WEEKS)   pos/wks

12 Jan 02 ●	ADDICTED TO BASS *Gusto CDGUS 6*	2	15

James and Bobby PURIFY
US, male vocal duo – James Purify and Robert Dickey (16 WEEKS)   pos/wks

24 Apr 76	I'M YOUR PUPPET *Mercury 6167 324*	12	10
7 Aug 76	MORNING GLORY *Mercury 6167 380*	27	6

PURPLE HEARTS
UK, male vocal / instrumental group (5 WEEKS)   pos/wks

22 Sep 79	MILLIONS LIKE US *Fiction FICS 003*	57	3
8 Mar 80	JIMMY *Fiction FICS 9*	60	2

PURPLE KINGS *UK, male vocal / instrumental*
duo – Rob Tillen and Glen Williamson (3 WEEKS)   pos/wks

15 Oct 94	THAT'S THE WAY YOU DO IT *Positiva CDTIV 21*	26	3

PUSH *Belgium, male producer – Dirk Dierickx (18 WEEKS)*   pos/wks

15 May 99	UNIVERSAL NATION *Bonzai / Inferno CDFERN 16*	36	2
9 Oct 99	UNIVERSAL NATION '99 (re-mix) *Inferno CDFERN 20*	35	2
23 Sep 00	TILL WE MEET AGAIN *Inferno CDFERN 29*	46	1
12 May 01	STRANGE WORLD *Inferno CDFERN 38*	21	4
20 Oct 01	PLEASE SAVE ME *Inferno / Five AM FAMFERN 1CD* [1]	36	2
3 Nov 01	THE LEGACY *Inferno CDFERN 43*	22	4
4 May 02	TRANZY STATE OF MIND *Inferno CDFERN 45*	31	2
5 Oct 02	STRANGE WORLD / THE LEGACY *Inferno CDFERN 49*	55	1

[1] Sunscreem vs Push

PUSSY 2000 *UK, male production duo (1 WEEK)*   pos/wks

3 Nov 01	IT'S GONNA BE ALRIGHT *Ink NIBNE 9CD*	70	1

PUSSYCAT
Holland, male / female vocal / instrumental group (30 WEEKS)   pos/wks

28 Aug 76 ★	MISSISSIPPI *Sonet SON 2077*	1	22
25 Dec 76	SMILE *Sonet SON 2096*	24	8

PYRAMIDS *Jamaica, male vocal / instrumental group (4 WEEKS)*   pos/wks

22 Nov 67	TRAIN TOUR TO RAINBOW CITY *President PT 161*	35	4

PYTHON LEE JACKSON
Australia, male vocal / instrumental group (12 WEEKS)   pos/wks

30 Sep 72 ●	IN A BROKEN DREAM *Youngblood YB 1002*	3	12

Uncredited lead vocals by Rod Stewart

Q

Q *UK, male instrumental / production duo (6 WEEKS)*   pos/wks

5 Jun 93	GET HERE *Arista 74321145972* [1]	37	4
12 Mar 94	(EVERYTHING I DO) I DO IT FOR YOU *Bell 74321193062* [2]	47	2

[1] Q featuring Tracy Ackerman [2] Q featuring Tony Jackson

QB FINEST featuring NAS & BRAVEHEARTS
US, male rappers (3 WEEKS)   pos/wks

21 Apr 01	OOCHIE WALLY *Columbia 6710852*	30	3

Q-BASS *UK, male production / instrumental group (1 WEEK)*   pos/wks

8 Feb 92	HARDCORE WILL NEVER DIE		
	Suburban Base SUBBASE 007	64	1

Q-CLUB *Italy, male / female vocal / instrumental group (3 WEEKS)* pos/wks

6 Jan 96	TELL IT TO MY HEART *Manifesto FESCD 5*	28	3

QFX *UK, male vocal / instrumental group (16 WEEKS)*   pos/wks

6 May 95	FREEDOM (EP) *Epidemic EPICD 004*	41	3
3 Feb 96	EVERYTIME YOU TOUCH ME *Epidemic EPICD 006*	22	4
3 Aug 96	YOU GOT THE POWER *Epidemic EPICD 007*	33	3
18 Jan 97	FREEDOM 2 (re-mix) *Epidemic EPICD 008*	21	4
20 Mar 99	SAY YOU'LL BE MINE *Quality Recordings QUAL 005CD*	34	2

Tracks on Freedom (EP): Freedom / Metropolis / Sianora Baby / The Machine

Q-TEE *UK, female rapper – Tatiana Mais (7 WEEKS)*   pos/wks

21 Apr 90	AFRIKA *SBK SBK 7008* [1]	42	5
10 Feb 96	GIMME THAT BODY *Heavenly HVN 48CD*	40	2

[1] History featuring Q-Tee

Q-TEX *UK, male / female vocal / instrumental group (7 WEEKS)*   pos/wks

9 Apr 94	THE POWER OF LOVE *Stoatin' STOAT 002CD*	65	1
26 Nov 94	BELIEVE *23rd Precinct THIRD 2CD*	41	2
15 Jun 96	LET THE LOVE *23rd Precinct THIRD 4CD*	30	2
30 Nov 96	DO YOU WANT ME *23rd Precinct THIRD 5CD*	48	1
28 Jun 97	POWER OF LOVE '97 (re-mix)		
	23rd Precinct THIRD 7CD	49	1

Q-TIP *US, male rapper – John Davis (23 WEEKS)*   pos/wks

4 Oct 97 ●	GOT 'TIL IT'S GONE *Virgin VSCDG 1666* [1]	6	9
19 Jun 99	GET INVOLVED *Hollywood 0101185 HWR* [2]	36	2
22 Jan 00	HOT BOYZ *Elektra E7002CD* [3]	18	3
12 Feb 00	BREATHE AND STOP *Arista 74321727062*	12	7
6 May 00	VIVRANT THING *Arista 74321751302*	39	2

[1] Janet featuring Q-Tip and Joni Mitchell [2] Raphael Saadiq and Q-Tip [3] Missy 'Misdemeanor' Elliott featuring Nas, Eve and Q-Tip

See also A TRIBE CALLED QUEST; DEEE-LITE

Q UNIQUE – *See C & C MUSIC FACTORY*

QATTARA *UK, male production duo*
– Andy Cato and Alex Whitcombe (2 WEEKS)   pos/wks

15 Mar 97	COME WITH ME *Positiva CDTIV 71*	31	2

QUAD CITY DJs *US, male rap duo (1 WEEK)*   pos/wks

15 Nov 97	SPACE JAM *Atlantic EW773*	57	1

See also TAG TEAM

QUADROPHONIA
Belgium, male instrumental / production group (15 WEEKS)   pos/wks

13 Apr 91	QUADROPHONIA *ARS 6567687*	14	9
6 Jul 91	THE WAVE OF THE FUTURE *ARS 6569937*	40	3
21 Dec 91	FIND THE TIME (PART ONE) *ARS 6576260*	41	3

QUADS *UK, male vocal / instrumental group (2 WEEKS)*   pos/wks

22 Sep 79	THERE MUST BE THOUSANDS *Big Bear BB 23*	66	2

QUAKE featuring Marcia RAE
UK, male producer and UK, female vocalist (1 WEEK)   pos/wks

29 Aug 98	THE DAY WILL COME *ffrr FCD 344*	53	1

QUANTUM JUMP
UK, male vocal / instrumental group (10 WEEKS)   pos/wks

2 Jun 79 ●	THE LONE RANGER *Electric WOT 33*	5	10

QUARTERFLASH
US, male / female vocal / instrumental group (5 WEEKS)   pos/wks

| 27 Feb 82 | HARDEN MY HEART *Geffen GEF A 1838* | 49 | 5 |

QUARTZ *UK, male instrumental group (19 WEEKS)*   pos/wks

17 Mar 90	WE'RE COMIN' AT YA *Mercury ITMR 2* 1	65	2
2 Feb 91 ●	IT'S TOO LATE *Mercury ITM 3* 2	8	14
15 Jun 91	NAKED LOVE (JUST SAY YOU WANT ME) *Mercury ITM 4* 3	39	3

1 Quartz featuring Stepz 2 Quartz introducing Dina Carroll 3 Quartz and Dina Carroll

Jakie QUARTZ *France, female vocalist (3 WEEKS)*   pos/wks

| 11 Mar 89 | A LA VIE, A L'AMOUR *PWL PWL 30* | 55 | 3 |

QUARTZ LOCK featuring Lonnie GORDON
UK, male production / instrumental duo – Mark Andrews and Donald Lynch – and US, female vocalist (2 WEEKS)   pos/wks

| 7 Oct 95 | LOVE EVICTION *X:Plode BANG 2CD* | 32 | 2 |

Suzi QUATRO   227   Top 500
Leather-clad US rock singer / guitarist, b. Suzi Quatrocchio, 3 Jun 1950, Detroit. Thanks partly to ultra-commercial songs and productions by Nicky Chinn and Mike Chapman, she was a regular hitmaker in Europe. In her homeland, however, only 'Stumblin' In' reached the Top 40 (122 WEEKS)   pos/wks

19 May 73	CAN THE CAN *RAK 150*	1	14
28 Jul 73 ●	48 CRASH *RAK 158*	3	9
27 Oct 73	DAYTONA DEMON *RAK 161* ■	14	13
9 Feb 74 ★	DEVIL GATE DRIVE *RAK 167* ■	1	11
29 Jun 74	TOO BIG *RAK 175*	14	6
9 Nov 74	THE WILD ONE *RAK 185*	7	10
8 Feb 75	YOUR MAMMA WON'T LIKE ME *RAK 191*	31	5
5 Mar 77	TEAR ME APART *RAK 248*	27	6
18 Mar 78 ●	IF YOU CAN'T GIVE ME LOVE *RAK 271*	4	13
22 Jul 78	THE RACE IS ON *RAK 278* 1	43	5
11 Nov 78	STUMBLIN' IN *RAK 285* 1	41	8
20 Oct 79	SHE'S IN LOVE WITH YOU *RAK 299*	11	9
19 Jan 80	MAMA'S BOY *RAK 303*	34	5
5 Apr 80	I'VE NEVER BEEN IN LOVE *RAK 307*	56	3
25 Oct 80	ROCK HARD *Dreamland DLSP 6*	68	2
13 Nov 82	HEART OF STONE *Polydor POSP 477*	60	3

1 Suzi Quatro and Chris Norman

Finley QUAYE *UK, male vocal / instrumentalist (23 WEEKS)*   pos/wks

21 Jun 97	SUNDAY SHINING *Epic 6644552*	16	6
13 Sep 97 ●	EVEN AFTER ALL *Epic 6649712*	10	5
29 Nov 97	IT'S GREAT WHEN WE'RE TOGETHER *Epic 6653382*	29	3
7 Mar 98	YOUR LOVE GETS SWEETER *Epic 6656065*	16	5
15 Aug 98	ULTRA STIMULATION *Epic 6660792*	51	1
23 Sep 00	SPIRITUALIZED *Epic 6698032*	26	3

QUEEN   12   Top 500   *World-renowned British quartet: Freddie Mercury (v) (d. 1991), Brian May (g/v), John Deacon (b/v), Roger Taylor (d/v). 'Bohemian Rhapsody', voted BHS readers' No.1 single, was the first of only two records to top the chart on two occasions (selling more than a million each time) and was No.1 in a record two calendar years. First act to have chart-topping singles in the 70s, 80s, 90s and 21st century, and sold more than 25 million Greatest Hits albums worldwide. They were given the Brits Outstanding Contribution to British Music Award (1992) and were inducted into the Rock and Roll Hall of Fame (2000). Queen musical 'We Will Rock You' penned by Ben Elton and backed by Robert De Niro opened in 2002. Best-selling single: 'Bohemian Rhapsody' 2,130,000 (419 WEEKS)*   pos/wks

9 Mar 74 ●	SEVEN SEAS OF RHYE *EMI 2121*	10	10
26 Oct 74 ●	KILLER QUEEN *EMI 2229*	2	12
25 Jan 75	NOW I'M HERE *EMI 2256*	11	7
8 Nov 75 ★	BOHEMIAN RHAPSODY *EMI 2375* ◆	1	17
3 Jul 76 ●	YOU'RE MY BEST FRIEND *EMI 2494*	7	8
27 Nov 76 ●	SOMEBODY TO LOVE *EMI 2565*	2	9
19 Mar 77	TIE YOUR MOTHER DOWN *EMI 2593*	31	4

4 Jun 77	QUEEN'S FIRST EP *EMI 2623*	17	10
22 Oct 77 ●	WE ARE THE CHAMPIONS *EMI 2708*	2	11
25 Feb 78	SPREAD YOUR WINGS *EMI 2757*	34	4
28 Oct 78	BICYCLE RACE / FAT BOTTOMED GIRLS *EMI 2870*	11	12
10 Feb 79 ●	DON'T STOP ME NOW *EMI 2910*	9	12
14 Jul 79	LOVE OF MY LIFE *EMI 2959*	63	2
20 Oct 79 ●	CRAZY LITTLE THING CALLED LOVE *EMI 5001* ▲	2	14
2 Feb 80	SAVE ME *EMI 5022*	11	6
14 Jun 80	PLAY THE GAME *EMI 5076*	14	8
6 Sep 80 ●	ANOTHER ONE BITES THE DUST *EMI 5102* ▲	7	9
6 Dec 80	FLASH *EMI 5126*	10	13
14 Nov 81 ★	UNDER PRESSURE *EMI 5250* 1	1	11
1 May 82	BODY LANGUAGE *EMI 5293*	25	6
12 Jun 82	LAS PALABRAS DE AMOR *EMI 5316*	17	8
21 Aug 82	BACKCHAT *EMI 5325*	40	4
4 Feb 84 ●	RADIO GAGA *EMI QUEEN 1*	2	9
14 Apr 84 ●	I WANT TO BREAK FREE *EMI QUEEN 2*	3	15
28 Jul 84 ●	IT'S A HARD LIFE *EMI QUEEN 3*	6	9
22 Sep 84	HAMMER TO FALL *EMI QUEEN 4*	13	7
8 Dec 84	THANK GOD IT'S CHRISTMAS *EMI QUEEN 5*	21	6
16 Nov 85 ●	ONE VISION *EMI QUEEN 6*	7	10
29 Mar 86 ●	A KIND OF MAGIC *EMI QUEEN 7*	3	11
21 Jun 86	FRIENDS WILL BE FRIENDS *EMI QUEEN 8*	14	8
27 Sep 86	WHO WANTS TO LIVE FOREVER *EMI QUEEN 9*	24	5
13 May 89 ●	I WANT IT ALL *Parlophone QUEEN 10*	3	7
1 Jul 89 ●	BREAKTHRU' *Parlophone QUEEN 11*	7	7
19 Aug 89	THE INVISIBLE MAN *Parlophone QUEEN 12*	12	6
21 Oct 89	SCANDAL *Parlophone QUEEN 14*	25	4
9 Dec 89	THE MIRACLE *Parlophone QUEEN 15*	21	5
26 Jan 91 ★	INNUENDO *Parlophone QUEEN 16* ■	1	6
25 May 91	I'M GOING SLIGHTLY MAD *Parlophone QUEEN 17*	22	5
25 May 91	HEADLONG *Parlophone QUEEN 18*	14	4
26 Oct 91	THE SHOW MUST GO ON (re) *Parlophone QUEEN 19*	16	10
21 Dec 91 ★	BOHEMIAN RHAPSODY / THESE ARE THE DAYS OF OUR LIVES (re-issue) *Parlophone QUEEN 20* ◆ ■	1	14
1 May 93 ★	FIVE LIVE (EP) (re) *Parlophone CDRS 6340* 2 ■	1	12
4 Nov 95 ●	HEAVEN FOR EVERYONE *Parlophone CDQUEEN 21*	2	12
23 Dec 95 ●	A WINTER'S TALE *Parlophone CDQUEEN 22*	6	6
9 Mar 96	TOO MUCH LOVE WILL KILL YOU *Parlophone CDQUEEN 23*	15	6
29 Jun 96 ●	LET ME LIVE *Parlophone CDQUEEN 24*	9	4
30 Nov 96	YOU DON'T FOOL ME *Parlophone CDQUEEN 25*	17	4
17 Jan 98	NO ONE BUT YOU / TIE YOUR MOTHER DOWN *Parlophone CDQUEEN 27*	13	4
14 Nov 98 ●	ANOTHER ONE BITES THE DUST *Dreamworks DRMCD 22364* 3	5	6
18 Dec 99	UNDER PRESSURE (re-mix) *Parlophone CDQUEEN 28* 1	14	7
29 Jul 00 ★	WE WILL ROCK YOU (re) *RCA 74321774022* 4 ■	1	13

1 Queen and David Bowie 2 George Michael and Queen with Lisa Stansfield 3 Queen with Wyclef Jean featuring Pras and Free 4 Five and Queen

Tracks on Queen's First EP: Good Old Fashioned Lover Boy / Death on Two Legs (Dedicated to...) / Tenement Funster / White Queen (As it Began). Tracks on Five Live (EP): Somebody to Love / These Are the Days of Our Lives / Calling You / Papa Was a Rolling Stone – Killer (medley). Queen appear only on the first two tracks. The first credits George Michael and Queen and the second George Michael with Lisa Stansfield

See also Freddie MERCURY

QUEEN LATIFAH
US, female rapper – Dana Owens (17 WEEKS)   pos/wks

24 Mar 90	MAMA GAVE BIRTH TO THE SOUL CHILDREN *Gee Street GEE 26* 1	14	7
26 May 90	FIND A WAY *Ahead of Our Time CCUT 8* 2	52	2
31 Aug 91	FLY GIRL *Gee Street GEE 34*	67	1
26 Jun 93	WHAT'CHA GONNA DO *Epic 6593072* 3	21	4
26 Mar 94	U.N.I.T.Y. *Motown TMGCD 1422*	74	1
12 Apr 97	MR BIG STUFF *Motown 5736572* 4	31	2

1 Queen Latifah + De La Soul 2 Coldcut featuring Queen Latifah 3 Shabba Ranks featuring Queen Latifah 4 Queen Latifah, Shades and Free

QUEEN PEN *US, female rapper – Lynise Walters (10 WEEKS)*   pos/wks

| 7 Mar 98 | MAN BEHIND THE MUSIC *Interscope IND 95562* | 38 | 2 |

| 9 May 98 | ALL MY LOVE *Interscope IND 95584* [1] | 11 | 5 |
| 5 Sep 98 | IT'S TRUE *Interscope IND 95597* | 24 | 3 |

[1] Queen Pen featuring Eric Williams

QUEENS OF THE STONE AGE
US, male vocal / instrumental group (9 WEEKS) pos/wks

| 26 Aug 00 | THE LOST ART OF KEEPING A SECRET *Interscope 4973912* | 31 | 2 |
| 16 Nov 02 | NO ONE KNOWS *Interscope / Polydor 4978122* | 15 | 7+ |

QUEENSRŸCHE
US, male vocal / instrumental group (21 WEEKS) pos/wks

13 May 89	EYES OF A STRANGER *EMI USA MT 65*	59	1
10 Nov 90	EMPIRE *EMI USA MT 90*	61	1
20 Apr 91	SILENT LUCIDITY *EMI USA MT 94*	34	5
6 Jul 91	BEST I CAN *EMI USA MT 97*	36	3
7 Sep 91	JET CITY WOMAN *EMI USA MT 98*	39	2
8 Aug 92	SILENT LUCIDITY (re-issue) *EMI USA MT 104*	18	4
28 Jan 95	I AM I *EMI CDMT 109*	40	2
25 Mar 95	BRIDGE *EMI CDMT 111*	40	3

QUENCH
Australia, male instrumental / production duo (1 WEEK) pos/wks

| 17 Feb 96 | DREAMS *Infectious INFECT 3CD* | 75 | 1 |

QUENTIN and ASH
UK, female actor / vocal duo – Caroline Quentin and Leslie Ash (3 WEEKS) pos/wks

| 6 Jul 96 | TELL HIM *East West EW 049CD* | 25 | 3 |

? (QUESTION MARK) and the MYSTERIANS
US, male vocal / instrumental group (4 WEEKS) pos/wks

| 17 Nov 66 | 96 TEARS *Cameo Parkway C428* ▲ | 37 | 4 |

QUESTIONS
UK, male vocal / instrumental group (8 WEEKS) pos/wks

23 Apr 83	PRICE YOU PAY *Respond KOB 702*	56	3
17 Sep 83	TEAR SOUP *Respond KOB 705*	66	1
10 Mar 84	TUESDAY SUNSHINE *Respond KOB 707*	46	4

QUICK
UK, male vocal / instrumental group (7 WEEKS) pos/wks

| 15 May 82 | RHYTHM OF THE JUNGLE *Epic EPC A 2013* | 41 | 7 |

Tommy QUICKLY and The REMO FOUR
UK, male vocalist (8 WEEKS) pos/wks

| 22 Oct 64 | WILD SIDE OF LIFE *Pye 7N 15708* | 33 | 8 |

QUIET FIVE
UK, male vocal / instrumental group (3 WEEKS) pos/wks

| 13 May 65 | WHEN THE MORNING SUN DRIES THE DEW *Parlophone R 5273* | 45 | 1 |
| 21 Apr 66 | HOMEWARD BOUND *Parlophone R 5421* | 44 | 2 |

QUIET RIOT
US, male vocal / instrumental group (5 WEEKS) pos/wks

| 3 Dec 83 | METAL HEALTH / CUM ON FEEL THE NOIZE *Epic A 3968* | 45 | 5 |

'Cum on Feel the Noize' credited only from 10 Dec 1983

Eimear QUINN
Ireland, female vocalist (2 WEEKS) pos/wks

| 15 Jun 96 | THE VOICE *Polydor 5768842* | 40 | 2 |

Paul QUINN and EDWYN COLLINS
UK, male vocalists / instrumentalists (2 WEEKS) pos/wks

| 11 Aug 84 | PALE BLUE EYES *Swamplands SWP 1* | 72 | 2 |

QUIREBOYS
UK, male vocal / instrumental group (27 WEEKS) pos/wks

4 Nov 89	7 O'CLOCK *Parlophone R 6230*	36	4
6 Jan 90	HEY YOU *Parlophone R 6241*	14	7
7 Apr 90	I DON'T LOVE YOU ANYMORE *Parlophone R 6248*	24	6

8 Sep 90	THERE SHE GOES AGAIN / MISLED *Parlophone R 6267*	37	4
10 Oct 92	TRAMPS AND THIEVES *Parlophone RS 6323*	41	3
20 Feb 93	BROTHER LOUIE *Parlophone CDR 6335*	31	3

QUIVER – *See* SUTHERLAND BROTHERS

QUIVVER
UK, male instrumental / production duo (3 WEEKS) pos/wks

| 5 Mar 94 | SAXY LADY *A&M 5805152* | 56 | 2 |
| 18 Nov 95 | BELIEVE IN ME *Perfecto PERF 111CD* | 56 | 1 |

QUO VADIS
UK, male production trio (1 WEEK) pos/wks

| 16 Dec 00 | SONIC BOOM (LIFE'S TOO SHORT) *Serious SERR 028CD* | 49 | 1 |

QWILO – *See* FELIX DA HOUSECAT

R

RAF
Italy, male producer – Mauro Picotto (6 WEEKS) pos/wks

14 Mar 92	WE'VE GOT TO LIVE TOGETHER *PWL Continental PWL 218*	34	3
5 Mar 94	TAKE ME HIGHER *Media MRLCD 0012*	71	1
23 Mar 96	TAKE ME HIGHER (re-mix) *Media MCSTD 40026*	59	1
27 Jul 96	ANGEL'S SYMPHONY *Media MCSTD 40051*	73	1

R.E.M. `129` `Top 500`
"America's Best Rock Band", according to Rolling Stone: Michael Stipe (v), Peter Buck (g), Mike Mills (b), Bill Berry (d). This Georgia group went from the US college circuit to packing stadiums worldwide. In 1996, the award-winning, platinum-album-earning quartet signed an $80m record deal (164 WEEKS) pos/wks

28 Nov 87	THE ONE I LOVE *IRS IRM 46*	51	8
30 Apr 88	FINEST WORKSONG *IRS IRM 161*	50	2
4 Feb 89	STAND *Warner Bros. W 7577*	51	3
3 Jun 89	ORANGE CRUSH *Warner Bros. W 2960*	28	5
12 Aug 89	STAND (re-issue) *Warner Bros. W 2833*	48	2
9 Mar 91	LOSING MY RELIGION *Warner Bros. W 0015*	19	9
18 May 91 ●	SHINY HAPPY PEOPLE *Warner Bros. W 0027*	6	11
17 Aug 91	NEAR WILD HEAVEN *Warner Bros. W 0055*	27	4
21 Sep 91	THE ONE I LOVE (re-issue) *IRS IRM 178*	16	6
16 Nov 91	RADIO SONG *Warner Bros. W 0072*	28	3
14 Dec 91	IT'S THE END OF THE WORLD AS WE KNOW IT *IRS IRM 180*	39	4
3 Oct 92	DRIVE *Warner Bros. W 0136*	11	5
28 Nov 92	MAN ON THE MOON *Warner Bros. W 0143*	18	8
20 Feb 93	THE SIDEWINDER SLEEPS TONITE *Warner Bros. W 0152CD1*	17	6
17 Apr 93 ●	EVERYBODY HURTS *Warner Bros W 0169CD1*	7	12
24 Jul 93	NIGHTSWIMMING *Warner Bros. W 0184CD*	27	5
11 Dec 93	FIND THE RIVER *Warner Bros. W 0211CD*	54	1
17 Sep 94 ●	WHAT'S THE FREQUENCY, KENNETH *Warner Bros. W 0265CD*	9	7
12 Nov 94	BANG AND BLAME *Warner Bros. W 0275CD*	15	4
4 Feb 95	CRUSH WITH EYELINER *Warner Bros. W 0281CD*	23	3
15 Apr 95 ●	STRANGE CURRENCIES *Warner Bros. W 0290CD*	9	4
29 Jul 95	TONGUE *Warner Bros. W 0308CD*	13	5
31 Aug 96 ●	E-BOW THE LETTER *Warner Bros. W 0369CD*	4	5
2 Nov 96	BITTERSWEET ME *Warner Bros. W 0377CD*	19	2
14 Dec 96	ELECTROLITE *Warner Bros. W 0383CD*	29	2
24 Oct 98 ●	DAYSLEEPER *Warner Bros. W 0455CD*	6	6
19 Dec 98	LOTUS *Warner Bros. W 466CD*	26	5
20 Mar 99	AT MY MOST BEAUTIFUL *Warner Bros. W 477CD*	10	4
5 Feb 00 ●	THE GREAT BEYOND *Warner Bros. W 516CD*	3	10
12 May 01 ●	IMITATION OF LIFE *Warner Bros. W 559CD*	6	9
4 Aug 01	ALL THE WAY TO RENO *Warner Bros. W 568CD*	24	3
1 Dec 01	I'LL TAKE THE RAIN *Warner Bros. W 573CD*	44	1

REO SPEEDWAGON
US, male vocal / instrumental group (38 WEEKS)   pos/wks

11 Apr 81	● KEEP ON LOVING YOU *Epic EPC 9544* ▲	7	14
27 Jun 81	TAKE IT ON THE RUN *Epic EPC A 1207*	19	14
16 Mar 85	CAN'T FIGHT THIS FEELING *Epic A 4880* ▲	16	10

RHC *Belgium, male / female vocal / instrumental duo (1 WEEK)*   pos/wks

| 11 Jan 92 | FEVER CALLED LOVE *R&S RSUK 9* | 65 | 1 |

RIP PRODUCTIONS *UK, production duo (1 WEEK)*   pos/wks

| 29 Nov 97 | THE CHANT (WE R) / RIP PRODUCTIONS *Satellite 74321534022* | 58 | 1 |

See also DOUBLE 99; CARNIVAL featuring RIP vs RED RAT

RM PROJECT *UK, production group (1 WEEK)*   pos/wks

| 3 Jul 99 | GET IT UP *Inferno CDFERN 15* | 49 | 1 |

RTE CONCERT ORCHESTRA – See Bill WHELAN featuring ANUNA and the RTE CONCERT ORCHESTRA

Eddie RABBITT *US, male vocalist, d. 7 May 1998 (14 WEEKS)*   pos/wks

| 27 Jan 79 | EVERY WHICH WAY BUT LOOSE *Elektra K 12331* | 41 | 9 |
| 28 Feb 81 | I LOVE A RAINY NIGHT *Elektra K 12498* ▲ | 53 | 5 |

Steve RACE *UK, male instrumentalist – piano (9 WEEKS)*   pos/wks

| 28 Feb 63 | PIED PIPER (THE BEEJE) *Parlophone R 4981* | 29 | 9 |

RACEY *UK, male vocal / instrumental group (44 WEEKS)*   pos/wks

25 Nov 78	● LAY YOUR LOVE ON ME *RAK 284*	3	14
31 Mar 79	● SOME GIRLS *RAK 291*	2	11
18 Aug 79	BOY OH BOY *RAK 297*	22	9
20 Dec 80	RUNAROUND SUE *RAK 325*	13	10

RACING CARS
UK, male vocal / instrumental group (7 WEEKS)   pos/wks

| 12 Feb 77 | THEY SHOOT HORSES DON'T THEY? *Chrysalis CHS 2129* | 14 | 7 |

RACKETEERS – See Elbow BONES and the RACKETEERS

Jimmy RADCLIFFE
US, male vocalist, d. 27 Jul 1973 (2 WEEKS)   pos/wks

| 4 Feb 65 | LONG AFTER TONIGHT IS ALL OVER *Stateside SS 374* | 40 | 2 |

RADHA KRISHNA TEMPLE
UK, male / female vocal / instrumental group (17 WEEKS)   pos/wks

| 13 Sep 69 | HARE KRISHNA MANTRA *Apple 15* | 12 | 9 |
| 28 Mar 70 | GOVINDA *Apple 25* | 23 | 8 |

RADICAL ROB *UK, male producer – Rob McLuan (1 WEEK)*   pos/wks

| 11 Jan 92 | MONKEY WAH *R&S RSUK 8* | 67 | 1 |

Jack RADICS – See Chaka DEMUS and PLIERS; SUPERCAT

RADIO HEART featuring Gary NUMAN *UK, male instrumental group and male vocalist / instrumentalist (8 WEEKS)*   pos/wks

| 28 Mar 87 | RADIO HEART *GFM GFM 109* | 35 | 6 |
| 13 Jun 87 | LONDON TIMES *GFM GFM 112* | 48 | 2 |

RADIO 1 DJ POSSE – See Liz KERSHAW and Bruno BROOKES

RADIO REVELLERS – See Anthony STEEL and the RADIO REVELLERS

RADIO STARS
UK, male vocal / instrumental group (3 WEEKS)   pos/wks

| 4 Feb 78 | NERVOUS WRECK *Chiswick NS 23* | 39 | 3 |

RADIOHEAD *UK, male vocal / instrumental group (52 WEEKS)*   pos/wks

13 Feb 93	ANYONE CAN PLAY GUITAR *Parlophone CDR 6333*	32	2
22 May 93	POP IS DEAD *Parlophone CDR 6345*	42	2
18 Sep 93	● CREEP *Parlophone CDR 6359*	7	6
8 Oct 94	MY IRON LUNG *Parlophone CDR 6394*	24	2
11 Mar 95	HIGH AND DRY / PLANET TELEX *Parlophone CDR 6405*	17	4
27 May 95	FAKE PLASTIC TREES *Parlophone CDR 6411*	20	4
2 Sep 95	JUST *Parlophone CDR 6415*	19	3
3 Feb 96	● STREET SPIRIT (FADE OUT) *Parlophone CDR 6419*	5	4
7 Jun 97	● PARANOID ANDROID *Parlophone CDODATA S 01*	3	5
6 Sep 97	● KARMA POLICE *Parlophone CDODATAS 03*	8	4
24 Jan 98	● NO SURPRISES (re) *Parlophone CDODATAS 04*	4	7
2 Jun 01	● PYRAMID SONG *Parlophone CDSFHEIT 45102*	5	5
18 Aug 01	KNIVES OUT *Parlophone CDFHEIT 45103*	13	4

RADISH *US, male vocal / instrumental group (3 WEEKS)*   pos/wks

| 30 Aug 97 | LITTLE PINK STARS *Mercury MERCD 494* | 32 | 2 |
| 15 Nov 97 | SIMPLE SINCERITY *Mercury MERCD 498* | 50 | 1 |

Fonda RAE *US, female vocalist (4 WEEKS)*   pos/wks

| 6 Oct 84 | TUCH ME *Streetwave KHAN 28* | 49 | 4 |

Jesse RAE *UK, male vocalist (2 WEEKS)*   pos/wks

| 11 May 85 | OVER THE SEA *Scotland-Video YZ 36* | 65 | 2 |

Marcia RAE – See QUAKE featuring Marcia RAE

RAE & CHRISTIAN featuring VEBA
UK, male production duo and UK, female vocalist (1 WEEK)   pos/wks

| 6 Mar 99 | ALL I ASK *Grand Central GCCD 120* | 67 | 1 |

Gerry RAFFERTY *UK, male vocalist (47 WEEKS)*   pos/wks

18 Feb 78	● BAKER STREET *United Artists UP 36346*	3	15
26 May 79	● NIGHT OWL *United Artists UP 36512*	5	13
18 Aug 79	GET IT RIGHT NEXT TIME *United Artists BP 301*	30	9
22 Mar 80	BRING IT ALL HOME *United Artists BP 340*	54	4
21 Jun 80	ROYAL MILE *United Artists BP 354*	67	2
10 Mar 90	BAKER STREET (re-mix) *EMI EM 132*	53	4

RAGE *UK, male vocal / instrumental group (15 WEEKS)*   pos/wks

31 Oct 92	● RUN TO YOU *Pulse 8 LOSE 33*	3	11
27 Feb 93	WHY DON'T YOU *Pulse 8 CDLOSE 39*	44	2
15 May 93	HOUSE OF THE RISING SUN *Pulse 8 CDLOSE 43*	41	2

RAGE AGAINST THE MACHINE
US, male vocal / instrumental group (19 WEEKS)   pos/wks

27 Feb 93	KILLING IN THE NAME *Epic 6584922*	25	4
8 May 93	BULLET IN THE HEAD *Epic 6592582*	16	4
4 Sep 93	BOMBTRACK *Epic 6594712*	37	2
13 Apr 96	● BULLS ON PARADE *Epic 6631522*	8	3
7 Sep 96	PEOPLE OF THE SUN *Epic 6636282*	26	2
6 Nov 99	GUERRILLA RADIO *Epic 6683142*	32	2
15 Apr 00	SLEEP NOW IN THE FIRE *Epic 6691362*	43	2

RAGGA TWINS *UK, male vocal group (10 WEEKS)*   pos/wks

10 Nov 90	ILLEGAL GUNSHOT / SPLIFFHEAD *Shut Up and Dance SUAD 7*	51	2
6 Apr 91	WIPE THE NEEDLE / JUGGLING *Shut Up and Dance SUAD 12S*	71	2
6 Jul 91	HOOLIGAN 69 *Shut Up and Dance SUAD 16S*	56	2
7 Mar 92	MIXED TRUTH / BRING UP THE MIC SOME MORE *Shut Up and Dance SUAD 27S*	65	2
11 Jul 92	SHINE EYE *Shut Up and Dance SUAD 32S* [1]	63	2

[1] Ragga Twins featuring Junior Reid

RAGING SPEEDHORN
UK, male vocal / instrumental group (2 WEEKS)   pos/wks

| 16 Jun 01 | THE GUSH *ZTT GIR 004CD* | 47 | 1 |
| 6 Jul 02 | THE HATE SONG *ZTT RSH 001CD* | 69 | 1 |

Re-entries are listed as (re), (2re), (3re), etc which signifies that the hit re-entered the chart once, twice or three times, etc

RAGTIMERS UK, male instrumental group (8 WEEKS)

			pos/wks
6 Mar 74	THE STING (re) *Pye 7N 45323*........................	31	8

RAH BAND UK, male / female vocal / instrumental group, leaders – Richard A and Liz Hewson (50 WEEKS)

			pos/wks
9 Jul 77 ●	THE CRUNCH *Good Earth GD 7*	6	12
1 Nov 80	FALCON *DJM DJS 10954*	35	7
7 Feb 81	SLIDE *DJM DJS 10964*	50	7
1 May 82	PERFUMED GARDEN *KR KR 5*.........................	45	7
9 Jul 83	MESSAGES FROM THE STARS *TMT TMT 5*........	42	5
19 Jan 85	ARE YOU SATISFIED? (FUNKA NOVA) *RCA RCA 470*	70	2
30 Mar 85 ●	CLOUDS ACROSS THE MOON *RCA PB 40025*	6	10

RAHSAAN – See US3

RAILWAY CHILDREN
UK, male vocal / instrumental group (13 WEEKS)

			pos/wks
24 Mar 90	EVERY BEAT OF THE HEART (re) *Virgin VS 1237*............	24	8
2 Jun 90	MUSIC STOP *Virgin VS 1255*...........................	66	2
20 Oct 90	SO RIGHT *Virgin VS 1289*	68	1
20 Apr 91	SOMETHING SO GOOD *Virgin VS 1318*	57	2

'Every Beat of the Heart' debuted on the chart at No.68 before making its peak position after re-entry in Feb 1991

RAIN – See Stephanie DE SYKES

RAIN TREE CROW UK, male vocal / instrumental group (1 WEEK)

			pos/wks
30 Mar 91	BLACKWATER *Virgin VS 1340*	62	1

Group is Japan under an assumed name

See also JAPAN

RAINBOW UK, male vocal / instrumental group (62 WEEKS)

			pos/wks
17 Sep 77	-KILL THE KING *Polydor 2066 845*	44	3
8 Apr 78	LONG LIVE ROCK 'N' ROLL *Polydor 2066 913*	33	3
30 Sep 78	L.A. CONNECTION *Polydor 2066 968*.............	40	4
15 Sep 79 ●	SINCE YOU'VE BEEN GONE *Polydor POSP 70*	6	10
16 Feb 80 ●	ALL NIGHT LONG *Polydor POSP 104*	5	11
31 Jan 81 ●	I SURRENDER *Polydor POSP 221*	3	10
20 Jun 81	CAN'T HAPPEN HERE *Polydor POSP 251*.........	20	8
11 Jul 81	KILL THE KING (re-issue) *Polydor POSP 274*	41	4
3 Apr 82	STONE COLD *Polydor POSP 421*	34	4
27 Aug 83	STREET OF DREAMS *Polydor POSP 631*..........	52	3
5 Nov 83	CAN'T LET YOU GO *Polydor POSP 654*	43	2

RAINBOW UK, male puppet rappers – DJ George and MC Zippy (Roy Skelton) (3 WEEKS)

			pos/wks
14 Dec 02	IT'S A RAINBOW *BBC Music ZIPPCD 1*	15	3+

RAINBOW COTTAGE
UK, male vocal / instrumental group (4 WEEKS)

			pos/wks
6 Mar 76	SEAGULL *Penny Farthing PEN 906*................	33	4

RAINMAKERS US, male vocal / instrumental group (11 WEEKS)

			pos/wks
7 Mar 87	LET MY PEOPLE GO-GO *Mercury MER 238*	18	11

Marvin RAINWATER
US, male vocalist – Marvin Percy (22 WEEKS)

			pos/wks
7 Mar 58 ★	WHOLE LOTTA WOMAN *MGM 974*	1	15
6 Jun 58	I DIG YOU BABY *MGM 980*............................	19	7

RAISSA UK, female vocalist – Raissa Khan-Panni (1 WEEK)

			pos/wks
12 Feb 00	HOW LONG DO I GET *Polydor 5616282*...........	47	1

Bonnie RAITT US, female vocalist / instrumentalist (9 WEEKS)

			pos/wks
14 Dec 91	I CAN'T MAKE YOU LOVE ME *Capitol CL 639*	50	4
9 Apr 94	LOVE SNEAKIN' UP ON YOU *Capitol CDCL 713*	69	1
18 Jun 94	YOU *Capitol CDCLS 718*...............................	31	2
11 Nov 95	ROCK STEADY *Capitol CDCL 763* [1]	50	2

[1] Bonnie Raitt and Bryan Adams

RAJA NEE US, female vocalist (2 WEEKS)

			pos/wks
4 Mar 95	TURN IT UP *Perspective 5874872*	42	2

Dionne RAKEEM UK, female vocalist (2 WEEKS)

			pos/wks
4 Aug 01	SWEETER THAN WINE *Virgin VSCDT 1809*.......	46	2

RAKIM US, male rapper – William Griffin (17 WEEKS)

			pos/wks
27 Dec 97	GUESS WHO'S BACK *Universal UND 56151*	32	3
22 Aug 98	STAY A WHILE *Universal UND 56203*	53	1
3 Oct 98	BUFFALO GIRLS STAMPEDE *Virgin VSCDT 1717* [1]	65	1
31 Aug 02 ●	ADDICTIVE *Aftermath / Interscope 4977782* [2]	3	12

[1] Malcolm McLaren and the World's Famous Supreme Team plus Rakim and Roger Sanchez [2] Truth Hurts featuring Rakim

See also Eric B and RAKIM

Tony RALLO and the MIDNITE BAND
France / US, male vocal / instrumental group (8 WEEKS)

			pos/wks
23 Feb 80	HOLDIN' ON *Calibre CAB 150*........................	34	8

Sheryl Lee RALPH US, female vocalist (2 WEEKS)

			pos/wks
26 Jan 85	IN THE EVENING *Arista ARIST 595*	64	2

RAM JAM US, male vocal / instrumental group (20 WEEKS)

			pos/wks
10 Sep 77 ●	BLACK BETTY *Epic EPC 5492*	7	12
17 Feb 90	BLACK BETTY (re-mix) *Epic 655430 7*.............	13	8

RAM JAM BAND – See Geno WASHINGTON and the RAM JAM BAND

RAM TRILOGY UK, male production trio (3 WEEKS)

			pos/wks
6 Jul 02	CHAPTER FOUR *Ram RAMM 39*.......................	71	1
20 Jul 02	CHAPTER 5 *Ram RAMM 40*	62	1
3 Aug 02	CHAPTER 6 *Ram RAMM 41*	60	1

RAMBLERS – See Perry COMO

RAMBLERS (from the Abbey Hey Junior School)
UK, children's choir (15 WEEKS)

			pos/wks
13 Oct 79	THE SPARROW *Decca F 13860*........................	11	15

Karen RAMIREZ
UK, female vocalist – Karen Ramelize (15 WEEKS)

			pos/wks
28 Mar 98	TROUBLED GIRL *Manifesto FESCD 31*	50	1
27 Jun 98 ●	LOOKING FOR LOVE *Manifesto FESCD 44*	8	11
21 Nov 98	IF WE TRY *Manifesto FESCD 50*	23	3

RAMMSTEIN
Germany, male vocal / instrumental group (4 WEEKS)

			pos/wks
25 May 02	ICH WILL *Motor / Universal MCSTD 40280*........	30	2
23 Nov 02	FEUER FREI *Universal MCSTD 40302*	35	2

RAMONES US, male vocal / instrumental group (32 WEEKS)

			pos/wks
21 May 77	SHEENA IS A PUNK ROCKER *Sire RAM 001*	22	7
6 Aug 77	SWALLOW MY PRIDE *Sire 6078 607*	36	3
30 Sep 78	DON'T COME CLOSE *Sire SRE 1031*	39	5
8 Sep 79	ROCK 'N' ROLL HIGH SCHOOL *Sire SIR 4021*	67	2
26 Jan 80 ●	BABY, I LOVE YOU *Sire SIR 4031*	8	9
19 Apr 80	DO YOU REMEMBER ROCK 'N' ROLL RADIO? *Sire SIR 4037*	54	3
10 May 86	SOMEBODY PUT SOMETHING IN MY DRINK / SOMETHING TO BELIEVE IN *Beggars Banquet BEG 157*	69	1
19 Dec 92	POISON HEART *Chrysalis CHS 3917*	69	2

RAMP *UK, male instrumental / production*
duo – Shem McCauley and Simon Rogers (1 WEEK) pos/wks
| 8 Jun 96 | ROCK THE DISCOTEK *Loaded LOADCD 30* | 49 | 1 |

See also SLACKER

RAMPAGE *UK, male DJ / production group (1 WEEK)* pos/wks
| 25 Nov 95 | THE MONKEES *Almo Sounds CDALMOS 017* | 51 | 1 |

RAMPAGE featuring Billy LAWRENCE
US male rapper – Roger McNair and US, male vocalist (1 WEEK) pos/wks
| 18 Oct 97 | TAKE IT TO THE STREETS *Elektra E 3914CD* | 58 | 1 |

RAMRODS
US, male / female instrumental group (12 WEEKS) pos/wks
| 23 Feb 61 | ● RIDERS IN THE SKY *London HLU 9282* | 8 | 12 |

RAMSEY and FEN featuring Lynsey MOORE
UK, male production duo and female vocalist (1 WEEK) pos/wks
| 10 Jun 00 | LOVE BUG *Nebula VCNEBD 4* | 75 | 1 |

RANCID *US, male vocal / instrumental group (1 WEEK)* pos/wks
| 7 Oct 95 | TIME BOMB *Out Of Step WOOS 8CDS* | 56 | 1 |

RANGE – *See Bruce HORNSBY and the RANGE*

RANGERS FC *UK, male football team vocalists (2 WEEKS)* pos/wks
| 4 Oct 97 | GLASGOW RANGERS (NINE IN A ROW) *Gers GERSCD 1* | 54 | 2 |

RANI – *See DELERIUM*

RANK 1 *Holland, male production duo*
– Piet Bervoets and Benno de Goeij (5 WEEKS) pos/wks
| 15 Apr 00 | ● AIRWAVE *Manifesto FESCD 69* | 10 | 5 |

RANKING ANN – *See SCRITTI POLITTI*

RANKING ROGER – *See Pato BANTON*

Shabba RANKS *Jamaica, male vocalist*
– Rexton Rawlston Fernando Gordon (67 WEEKS) pos/wks
16 Mar 91	SHE'S A WOMAN *Virgin VS 1333* [1]	20	7
18 May 91	TRAILER LOAD A GIRLS *Epic 6568747*	63	2
24 Aug 91	HOUSECALL *Epic 6573477* [2]	31	7
8 Aug 92	MR LOVERMAN *Epic 6582517*	23	7
28 Nov 92	SLOW AND SEXY *Epic 6587727* [3]	17	7
6 Mar 93	I WAS A KING *Motown TMGCD 1414* [4]	64	1
13 Mar 93	● MR LOVERMAN (re-issue) *Epic 6590782*	3	11
8 May 93	● HOUSECALL (re-mix) *Epic 6592842* [2]	8	8
26 Jun 93	WHAT'CHA GONNA DO *Epic 6593072* [5]	21	4
25 Dec 93	FAMILY AFFAIR *Polydor PZCD 304* [6]	18	8
29 Apr 95	LET'S GET IT ON *Epic 6614122*	22	3
5 Aug 95	SHINE EYE GAL *Epic 6622332* [7]	46	2

[1] Scritti Politti featuring Shabba Ranks [2] Shabba Ranks featuring Maxi Priest
[3] Shabba Ranks featuring Johnny Gill [4] Eddie Murphy featuring Shabba Ranks
[5] Shabba Ranks featuring Queen Latifah [6] Shabba Ranks featuring Patra and
Terri & Monica [7] Shabba Ranks (featuring Mykal Rose)

Bubbler RANX – *See Peter ANDRE*

RAPINATION *Italy, male instrumental / production*
duo – Marco Sabiu and Charlie Mallozzi (12 WEEKS) pos/wks
26 Dec 92	LOVE ME THE RIGHT WAY *Logic 74321128097* [1]	22	10
10 Jul 93	HERE'S MY A *Logic 74321153092* [2]	69	1
28 Sep 96	LOVE ME THE RIGHT WAY (re-mix) *Logic 7432140442* [1]	55	1

[1] Rapination featuring Kym Mazelle [2] Rapination featuring Carol Kenyon

RAPPIN' 4-TAY *US, male rapper – Anthony Forte (5 WEEKS)* pos/wks
| 24 Jun 95 | I'LL BE AROUND *Cooltempo CDCOOL 306* [1] | 30 | 4 |
| 30 Sep 95 | PLAYAZ CLUB *Cooltempo CDCOOL 310* | 63 | 1 |

[1] Rappin' 4-Tay featuring The Spinners

The Spinners on 'I'll Be Around' are The Detroit Spinners

RARE *UK, male / female vocal / instrumental group (1 WEEK)* pos/wks
| 17 Feb 96 | SOMETHING WILD *Equator AXISCD 011* | 57 | 1 |

RARE BIRD *UK, male vocal / instrumental group (8 WEEKS)* pos/wks
| 14 Feb 70 | SYMPATHY *Charisma CB 120* | 27 | 8 |

O RASBURY – *See Rahni HARRIS and F.L.O.*

RASHAAN – *See US3*

Roland RAT SUPERSTAR
UK, male rodent vocalist / rapper (20 WEEKS) pos/wks
19 Nov 83	RAT RAPPING *Rodent RAT 1*	14	12
28 Apr 84	LOVE ME TENDER *Rodent RAT 2*	32	7
2 Mar 85	NO.1 RAT FAN *Rodent RAT 4*	72	1

RATPACK *UK, male instrumental / production duo (3 WEEKS)* pos/wks
| 6 Jun 92 | SEARCHIN' FOR MY RIZLA *Big Giant BIGT 02* | 58 | 3 |

RATTLES *Germany, male vocal / instrumental group (15 WEEKS)* pos/wks
| 3 Oct 70 | ● THE WITCH *Decca F 23058* | 8 | 15 |

RATTY *Germany, male production group (1 WEEK)* pos/wks
| 24 Mar 01 | SUNRISE (HERE I AM) *Neo NEOCD 051* | 51 | 1 |

RAVEN MAIZE *UK, male producer – Dave Lee (9 WEEKS)* pos/wks
5 Aug 89	FOREVER TOGETHER *Republic LIC 014*	67	1
18 Aug 01	THE REAL LIFE (re) *Rulin / MoS / Credence RULIN 18CDS*	12	6
17 Aug 02	FASCINATED *Ministry of Sound / Rulin RULIN 27CDS*	37	2

*See also Joey NEGRO; Z FACTOR; PHASE II; Li KWAN; AKABU featuring Linda
CLIFFORD; IL PADRINOS; JAKATTA; HED BOYS*

The RAVEONETTES
Denmark, male / female vocal / instrumental group (1 WEEK) pos/wks
| 21 Dec 02 | ATTACK OF THE GHOSTRIDERS *Columbia 6733892* | 73 | 1 |

RAVESIGNAL III
Belgium, male producer – Christian Bolland (2 WEEKS) pos/wks
| 14 Dec 91 | HORSEPOWER *R&S RSUK 6* | 61 | 2 |

See also CJ BOLLAND

RAW – *See Erick 'More' MORILLO presents RAW*

RAW SILK *US, female vocal group (12 WEEKS)* pos/wks
| 16 Oct 82 | DO IT TO THE MUSIC *KR KR 14* | 18 | 9 |
| 10 Sep 83 | JUST IN TIME *West End WEND 2* | 49 | 3 |

RAW STYLUS *UK, male / female vocal / instrumental duo (1 WEEK)* pos/wks
| 26 Oct 96 | BELIEVE IN ME *Wired WIRED 234* | 66 | 1 |

Lou RAWLS *US, male vocalist (10 WEEKS)* pos/wks
| 31 Jul 76 | ● YOU'LL NEVER FIND ANOTHER LOVE LIKE MINE *Philadelphia International PIR 4372* | 10 | 10 |

Gene Anthony RAY – *See KIDS FROM 'FAME'*

Jimmy RAY *UK, male vocalist – James Edwards (6 WEEKS)* pos/wks
| 25 Oct 97 | ARE YOU JIMMY RAY? *Sony S2 6650125* | 13 | 5 |
| 14 Feb 98 | GOIN' TO VEGAS *Sony S2 6654652* | 49 | 1 |

Johnnie RAY (122) Top 500
A sensation in the 1950s, the heart-wrenching vocal delivery of the 'Cry Guy' (b. 10 Jan 1927, Oregon, US, d. 25 Feb 1990) influenced many acts, including Elvis, and Ray was the prime target for teen hysteria in pre-Presley days (168 WEEKS)

pos/wks

Date	Title	pos	wks
14 Nov 52	WALKIN' MY BABY BACK HOME *Columbia DB 3060*	12	1
19 Dec 52 ●	FAITH CAN MOVE MOUNTAINS (re) *Columbia DB 3154* [1]	7	3
3 Apr 53	MA SAYS, PA SAYS *Columbia DB3242* [2]	12	1
10 Apr 53 ●	SOMEBODY STOLE MY GAL (3re) *Philips PB 123*	6	7
17 Apr 53	FULL TIME JOB *Columbia DB 3242* [2]	11	1
24 Jul 53 ●	LET'S WALK THAT-A-WAY *Philips PB 157* [2]	4	14
9 Apr 54 ★	SUCH A NIGHT *Philips PB 244*	1	18
8 Apr 55 ●	IF YOU BELIEVE (re) *Philips PB 379*	7	11
20 May 55	PATHS OF PARADISE *Philips PB 441*	20	1
7 Oct 55	HERNANDO'S HIDEAWAY *Philips PB 495*	11	5
14 Oct 55 ●	HEY THERE *Philips PB 495*	5	9
28 Oct 55 ●	SONG OF THE DREAMER *Philips PB 516*	10	5
17 Feb 56	WHO'S SORRY NOW *Philips PB 546*	17	2
20 Apr 56	AIN'T MISBEHAVIN' (re) *Philips PB 580*	17	7
12 Oct 56 ★	JUST WALKING IN THE RAIN *Philips PB 624*	1	19
18 Jan 57	YOU DON'T OWE ME A THING *Philips PB 655*	12	15
8 Feb 57 ●	LOOK HOMEWARD ANGEL *Philips PB 655*	7	16
10 May 57 ★	YES TONIGHT JOSEPHINE *Philips PB 686*	1	16
6 Sep 57	BUILD YOUR LOVE (ON A STRONG FOUNDATION) *Philips PB 721*	17	7
4 Oct 57	GOOD EVENING FRIENDS / UP ABOVE MY HEAD, I HEAR MUSIC IN THE AIR *Philips PB 708* [3]	25	4
4 Dec 59	I'LL NEVER FALL IN LOVE AGAIN (2re) *Philips PB 952*	26	6

[1] Johnnie Ray and The Four Lads [2] Doris Day and Johnnie Ray [3] Frankie Laine and Johnnie Ray

The chart history of 'You Don't Owe Me a Thing / Look Homeward Angel' is complicated and is as follows: 'You Don't Owe Me a Thing' entered the chart by itself on 18 Jan 1957. On 8 and 15 Feb 1957, 'Look Homeward Angel' was coupled with 'You Don't Owe Me a Thing', but from 22 Feb 1957 the two sides went their individual ways on the chart and were listed separately: 'You Don't Owe Me a Thing' for a further 10 weeks and 'Look Homeward Angel' for a further 14 weeks

Nicole RAY *US, female vocalist – Nicole Wray (5 WEEKS)*
pos/wks

Date	Title	pos	wks
22 Aug 98	MAKE IT HOT *East West E 3821CD* [1]	22	4
5 Dec 98	I CAN'T SEE *East West E 3801CD*	55	1

[1] Nicole featuring Missy 'Misdemeanor' Elliott and Mocha

RAYDIO *US, male vocal / instrumental group (21 WEEKS)*
pos/wks

Date	Title	pos	wks
8 Apr 78	JACK AND JILL *Arista 161*	11	12
8 Jul 78	IS THIS A LOVE THING *Arista 193*	27	9

See also Ray PARKER Jr

RAYVON
Barbados, male rapper / vocalist – Bruce Brewster (26 WEEKS)
pos/wks

Date	Title	pos	wks
8 Jul 95 ●	IN THE SUMMERTIME *Virgin VSCDT 1542* [1]	5	9
9 Jun 01 ★	ANGEL *MCA MCSTD 40257* [1] ■ ▲	1	16
3 Aug 02	2-WAY *MCA MCSTD 40287*	67	1

[1] Shaggy featuring Rayvon

RAZE *US, male / female vocal / instrumental group (47 WEEKS)*
pos/wks

Date	Title	pos	wks
1 Nov 86	JACK THE GROOVE (re) *Champion CHAMP 23*	20	15
28 Feb 87	LET THE MUSIC MOVE U *Champion CHAMP 27*	57	3
31 Dec 88	BREAK 4 LOVE (re) *Champion CHAMP 67*	28	16
15 Jul 89	LET IT ROLL *Atlantic A 8866* [1]	27	5
27 Jan 90	ALL 4 LOVE (BREAK 4 LOVE 1990) *Champion CHAMP 228* [2]	30	5
10 Feb 90	CAN YOU FEEL IT / CAN YOU FEEL IT *Champion CHAMP 227* [3]	62	1
24 Sep 94	BREAK 4 LOVE (re-mix) *Champion CHAMPCD 314*	44	2

[1] Raze presents Doug Lazy [2] Raze featuring Lady J and Secretary of Entertainment [3] Raze / Championship Legend

'Can You Feel It' by Championship Legend is a montage of six Raze tracks

REA – See JAM & SPOON

Chris REA (232) Top 500
One of the most popular UK singer / songwriters of the late 1980s, b. 4 Mar 1951, Middlesbrough. He was already a major European star by the time he finally cracked the UK Top 10 with his 18th chart entry, 'The Road to Hell (Part 2)' (120 WEEKS)
pos/wks

Date	Title	pos	wks
7 Oct 78	FOOL (IF YOU THINK IT'S OVER) *Magnet MAG 111*	30	7
21 Apr 79	DIAMONDS *Magnet MAG 144*	44	3
27 Mar 82	LOVING YOU *Magnet MAG 215*	65	3
1 Oct 83	I CAN HEAR YOUR HEARTBEAT *Magnet MAG 244*	60	2
17 Mar 84	I DON'T KNOW WHAT IT IS BUT I LOVE IT *Magnet MAG 255*	65	2
30 Mar 85	STAINSBY GIRLS *Magnet MAG 276*	26	10
29 Jun 85	JOSEPHINE *Magnet MAG 280*	67	2
29 Mar 86	IT'S ALL GONE *Magnet MAG 283*	69	1
31 May 86	ON THE BEACH (2re) *Magnet MAG 294*	57	8
6 Jun 87	LET'S DANCE *Magnet MAG 299*	12	10
29 Aug 87	LOVING YOU AGAIN *Magnet MAG 300*	47	4
5 Dec 87	JOYS OF CHRISTMAS *Magnet MAG 314*	67	1
13 Feb 88	QUE SERA *Magnet MAG 318*	73	2
13 Aug 88	ON THE BEACH SUMMER '88 *WEA YZ 195*	12	6
22 Oct 88	I CAN HEAR YOUR HEARTBEAT *WEA YZ 320*	74	2
17 Dec 88	THE CHRISTMAS EP *WEA YZ 325*	53	3
18 Feb 89	WORKING ON IT *WEA YZ 350*	53	3
14 Oct 89 ●	THE ROAD TO HELL (PART 2) *WEA YZ 431*	10	9
10 Feb 90	TELL ME THERE'S A HEAVEN *East West YZ 455*	24	6
5 May 90	TEXAS *East West YZ 468*	69	1
16 Feb 91	AUBERGE *East West YZ 555*	16	6
6 Apr 91	HEAVEN *East West YZ 566*	57	2
29 Jun 91	LOOKING FOR THE SUMMER *East West YZ 584*	49	3
9 Nov 91	WINTER SONG *East West YZ 629*	27	4
24 Oct 92	NOTHING TO FEAR *East West YZ 699*	16	4
28 Nov 92	GOD'S GREAT BANANA SKIN *East West YZ 706*	31	3
30 Jan 93	SOFT TOP HARD SHOULDER *East West YZ 710CD*	53	2
23 Oct 93	JULIA *East West YZ 772CD*	18	5
12 Nov 94	YOU CAN GO YOUR OWN WAY *East West YZ 835CD*	28	3
24 Dec 94	TELL ME THERE'S A HEAVEN (re-issue) *East West YZ 885CD*	70	1
16 Nov 96	'DISCO' LA PASSIONE *East West EW 072CD* [1]	41	1
24 May 97	LET'S DANCE *Magnet EW 112CD* [2]	44	1

[1] Chris Rea and Shirley Bassey [2] Middlesbrough FC featuring Bob Mortimer and Chris Rea

Both 'On the Beach Summer '88' and 'I Can Hear Your Heartbeat' in 1988 are re-recordings. Tracks on Driving Home for Christmas (EP): Driving Home for Christmas / Footsteps in the Snow / Joys of Christmas / Smile

REACT 2 RHYTHM *UK, male production group (1 WEEK)*
pos/wks

Date	Title	pos	wks
28 Jun 97	INTOXICATION *Jackpot WIN 014CD*	73	1

Eileen READ – See CADETS with Eileen REID

Eddi READER *UK, female vocalist (14 WEEKS)*
pos/wks

Date	Title	pos	wks
4 Jun 94	PATIENCE OF ANGELS *Blanco Y Negro NEG 68CD*	33	5
13 Aug 94	JOKE (I'M LAUGHING) *Blanco Y Negro NEG 72CD*	42	3
5 Nov 94	DEAR JOHN *Blanco Y Negro NEG 75CD1*	48	2
22 Jun 96	TOWN WITHOUT PITY *Blanco Y Negro NEG 90CD1*	26	3
21 Aug 99	FRAGILE THING *Track TRACK 0004A* [1]	69	1

[1] Big Country featuring Eddi Reader

See also FAIRGROUND ATTRACTION

READY FOR THE WORLD
US, male vocal / instrumental group (8 WEEKS)
pos/wks

Date	Title	pos	wks
26 Oct 85	OH SHEILA *MCA MCA 1005* ▲	50	5
14 Mar 87	LOVE YOU DOWN *MCA MCA 1110*	60	3

REAL EMOTION
UK, male / female vocal / instrumental group (1 WEEK)
pos/wks

Date	Title	pos	wks
1 Jul 95	BACK FOR GOOD *Living Beat LBECD 34*	67	1

REAL McCOY
Germany / US, male / female vocal / instrumental duo (36 WEEKS) pos/wks

Date	Title	pos	wks
6 Nov 93	ANOTHER NIGHT *Logic 74321173732* [1]	61	1

			pos/wks
5 Nov 94 ●	ANOTHER NIGHT (re-issue) *Logic 74321236992* [1]	..............2 12
28 Jan 95 ●	RUN AWAY *Logic 74321258822* [1]	..............6 10
22 Apr 95	LOVE AND DEVOTION *Logic 74321272702* [1]	..............11 8
26 Aug 95	COME AND GET YOUR LOVE *Logic 74321301272*	..............19 4
11 Nov 95	AUTOMATIC LOVER (CALL FOR LOVE) *Logic 74321325042*	......58 1

[1] (MC Sar &) The Real McCoy

REAL PEOPLE
UK, male vocal / instrumental group (8 WEEKS) pos/wks

16 Feb 91	OPEN UP YOUR MIND (LET ME IN) *CBS 6566127*	..............70 1
20 Apr 91	THE TRUTH *Columbia 6567877*	..............73 1
6 Jul 91	WINDOW PANE (EP) *Columbia 6569327*	..............60 1
11 Jan 92	THE TRUTH (re-issue) *Columbia 6576987*	..............41 3
23 May 92	BELIEVER *Columbia 6580067*	..............38 2

Tracks on Window Pane (EP): Window Pane / See Through You / Everything Must Change

REAL ROXANNE
US, female rapper – Joanne Martinez (10 WEEKS) pos/wks

28 Jun 86	(B ANG ZOOM) LET'S GO-GO *Cooltempo COOL 124* [1]	..........11 9
12 Nov 88	RESPECT *Cooltempo COOL 176*	..............71 1

[1] Real Roxanne with Hitman Howie Tee

REAL THING (247) [Top 500]
Liverpool vocal quartet comprising brothers Chris and Eddie Amoo, Ray Lake and Dave Smith. They were the UK's best-selling black group of the late 1970s, whose biggest hits returned to the Top 10 (when re-mixed) in the 1980s (114 WEEKS) pos/wks

5 Jun 76 ★	YOU TO ME ARE EVERYTHING *Pye International 7N 25709*	.........1 11
4 Sep 76 ●	CAN'T GET BY WITHOUT YOU *Pye 7N 45618*	..............2 10
12 Feb 77	YOU'LL NEVER KNOW WHAT YOU'RE MISSING *Pye 7N 45662*	.16 9
30 Jul 77	LOVE'S SUCH A WONDERFUL THING *Pye 7N 45701*	.......33 5
4 Mar 78	WHENEVER YOU WANT MY LOVE *Pye 7N 46045*	.......18 9
3 Jun 78	LET'S GO DISCO *Pye 7N 46078*	..............39 7
12 Aug 78	RAININ' THROUGH MY SUNSHINE *Pye 7N 46113*	......40 8
17 Feb 79 ●	CAN YOU FEEL THE FORCE? *Pye 7N 46147*	..............5 11
21 Jul 79	BOOGIE DOWN (GET FUNKY NOW) *Pye 7P 109*	......33 6
22 Nov 80	SHE'S A GROOVY FREAK *Calibre CAB 105*	..............52 4
8 Mar 86 ●	YOU TO ME ARE EVERYTHING (THE DECADE RE-MIX 76-86) *PRT 7P 349*	.........5 13
24 May 86 ●	CAN'T GET BY WITHOUT YOU (THE SECOND DECADE REMIX) *PRT 7P 352*	......6 13
2 Aug 86	CAN YOU FEEL THE FORCE ('86 REMIX) *PRT 7P 358*	...24 6
25 Oct 86	STRAIGHT TO THE HEART *Jive JIVE 129*	..............71 2

REAL TO REEL
US, male vocal / instrumental group (2 WEEKS) pos/wks

21 Apr 84	LOVE ME LIKE THIS *Arista ARIST 565*	..............68 2

See also PIANOHEADZ; Erick 'More' MORILLO presents RAW; LIL MO' YIN YANG

REBEL MC
UK, male rapper – Mike West (52 WEEKS) pos/wks

27 May 89	JUST KEEP ROCKIN' *Desire WANT 9* [1]	..............11 12
7 Oct 89 ●	STREET TUFF *Desire WANT 18* [2]	..............3 14
31 Mar 90	BETTER WORLD *Desire WANT 25*	..............20 6
2 Jun 90	REBEL MUSIC *Desire WANT 31*	..............53 2
6 Apr 91	WICKEDEST SOUND *Desire WANT 40* [3]	..............43 6
15 Jun 91	TRIBAL BASE *Desire WANT 44* [4]	..............20 6
31 Aug 91	BLACK MEANING GOOD *Desire WANT 47*	..............73 1
21 Mar 92	RICH AH GETTING RICHER *Big Life BLR 70* [5]	..........48 4
8 Aug 92	HUMANITY *Big Life BLR 78* [6]	..............62 1

[1] Double Trouble and the Rebel MC [2] Rebel MC and Double Trouble [3] Rebel MC featuring Tenor Fly [4] Rebel MC featuring Tenor Fly and Barrington Levy [5] Rebel MC introducing Little T [6] Rebel MC featuring Lincoln Thompson

REBEL ROUSERS – See Cliff BENNETT and the REBEL ROUSERS

REBELETTES – See Duane EDDY

REBELS – See Duane EDDY

Ezz RECO and The LAUNCHERS with Boysie GRANT
Jamaica, male vocal / instrumental group (4 WEEKS) pos/wks

5 Mar 64	KING OF KINGS *Columbia DB 7217*	..............44 4

RECOIL
UK, male vocal / instrumental group (1 WEEK) pos/wks

21 Mar 92	FAITH HEALER *Mute MUTE 110*	..............60 1

RED
UK, male production duo – Ian Bland and Paul Fitzpatrick (1 WEEK) pos/wks

20 Jan 01	HEAVEN & EARTH *Slinky Music SLINKY 008CD*	......41 1

See also BEAT RENEGADES; DREAM FREQUENCY

RED BOX *UK, male vocal / instrumental duo – Julian Close and Simon Toulson (28 WEEKS)* pos/wks

24 Aug 85 ●	LEAN ON ME (AH-LI-AYO) *Sire W 8926*	..............3 14
25 Oct 86 ●	FOR AMERICA *Sire YZ 84*	..............10 12
31 Jan 87	HEART OF THE SUN *Sire YZ 100*	..............71 2

RED CAR AND THE BLUE CAR
UK, male vocal / instrumental group (4 WEEKS) pos/wks

14 Dec 91	HOME FOR CHRISTMAS DAY *Virgin VS 1394*	......44 4

RED DRAGON with Brian and Tony GOLD
Jamaica, male vocal group (15 WEEKS) pos/wks

30 Jul 94 ●	COMPLIMENTS ON YOUR KISS (re) *Mango CIDM 820*	....2 15

RED EYE *UK, male instrumental / production duo (1 WEEK)* pos/wks

3 Dec 94	KUT IT *Champion CHAMPCD 315*	..............62 1

RED 5 *Germany, male producer – Thomas Kukula (10 WEEKS)* pos/wks

10 May 97	I LOVE YOU ... STOP! *Multiply CDMULTY 20*	..........11 5
20 Dec 97	LIFT ME UP *Multiply CDMULTY 30*	..............26 5

RED HED – See VINYLGROOVER and The RED HED

RED HILL CHILDREN *UK, male / female children's choir (2 WKS)* pos/wks

30 Nov 96	WHEN CHILDREN RULE THE WORLD *Really Useful 5797262*	...40 2

RED HOT CHILI PEPPERS (461) [Top 500]
Los Angeles-based funk / punk rock quartet formed by high school pals Anthony Kiedis (v) and Michael "Flea" Balzary (b) (currently featuring John Frusciante (g) and Chad Smith (d)). Their 'By the Way' album sold more than a million copies in both the US and UK in 2002, taking their worldwide album sales tally to more than 30 million (77 WEEKS) pos/wks

10 Feb 90	HIGHER GROUND *EMI-USA MT 75*	..............55 3
23 Jun 90	TASTE THE PAIN *EMI-USA MT 85*	..............29 3
8 Sep 90	HIGHER GROUND (re-issue) *EMI-USA MT 88*	......54 3
14 Mar 92	UNDER THE BRIDGE *Warner Bros. W 0084*	......26 4
15 Aug 92	BREAKING THE GIRL *Warner Bros. W 0126*	......41 3
5 Feb 94 ●	GIVE IT AWAY *Warner Bros. W 0225CD1*	..............9 4
30 Apr 94	UNDER THE BRIDGE (re-issue) *Warner Bros. W 0237CD*	...13 6
2 Sep 95	WARPED *Warner Bros. W 0316CD*	..............31 2
21 Oct 95	MY FRIENDS *Warner Bros. W 0317CD*	..............29 2
17 Feb 96	AEROPLANE *Warner Bros. W 0331CD*	..............11 3
14 Jun 97 ●	LOVE ROLLERCOASTER *Geffen GFSTD 22188*	......7 8
12 Jun 99	SCAR TISSUE *Warner Bros. W 490CD*	..............15 6
4 Sep 99	AROUND THE WORLD *Warner Bros. W 500CD1*	...35 2
12 Feb 00	OTHERSIDE *Warner Bros. W 510CD1*	..............33 2
19 Aug 00	CALIFORNICATION *Warner Bros. W 534CD*	......16 5
13 Jan 01	ROAD TRIPPIN' *Warner Bros. W 546CD1*	..............30 2
13 Jul 02 ●	BY THE WAY *Warner Bros. W 580CD*	..............2 10
2 Nov 02	THE ZEPHYR SONG *Warner Bros. W 592CD*	......11 9+

RED JERRY – See WESTBAM; LOST TRIBE

RED RAT – See CARNIVAL featuring RIP vs RED RAT; Curtis LYNCH Jr featuring Kele LE ROC and RED RAT

Re-entries are listed as (re), (2re), (3re), etc which signifies that the hit re-entered the chart...

RED RAW featuring 007
UK, male vocal / instrumental duo (1 WEEK) pos/wks

28 Oct 95	OOH LA LA LA *Media MCSTD 2065*	59	1

RED SNAPPER
UK, male vocal / instrumental / production group (1 WEEK) pos/wks

21 Nov 98	IMAGE OF YOU *Warp WAP 111CD*	60	1

RED VENOM – See BIG BOSS STYLUS presents RED VENOM

REDBONE *US, male vocal / instrumental group (12 WEEKS)* pos/wks

25 Sep 71 ●	THE WITCH QUEEN OF NEW ORLEANS *Epic EPC 7351*	2	12

REDD KROSS *US, male vocal / instrumental group (4 WEEKS)* pos/wks

5 Feb 94	VISIONARY *This Way Up WAY 2733*	75	1
10 Sep 94	YESTERDAY ONCE MORE *A&M 5807932*	45	2
1 Feb 97	GET OUT OF MYSELF *This Way Up WAY 5466*	63	1

The listed flip side of 'Yesterday Once More' was 'Superstar' by Sonic Youth

Sharon REDD *US, female vocalist, d. 1 May 1992 (32 WEEKS)* pos/wks

28 Feb 81	CAN YOU HANDLE IT *Epic EPC 9572*	31	8
2 Oct 82	NEVER GIVE YOU UP *Prelude PRL A2755*	20	9
15 Jan 83	IN THE NAME OF LOVE *Prelude PRL A2905*	31	5
22 Oct 83	LOVE HOW YOU FEEL *Prelude A3868*	39	5
1 Feb 92	CAN YOU HANDLE IT (re-recording) *EMI EM 219* [1]	17	5

[1] DNA featuring Sharon Redd

REDD SQUARE featuring Tiff LACEY
UK, male production group and female vocalist (1 WEEK) pos/wks

26 Oct 02	IN YOUR HANDS *Inferno CDFERN 50*	64	1

Otis REDDING ⟨223⟩ [Top 500]
Peerless singer / songwriter, b. 9 Sep 1941, Georgia, US, d. 10 Dec 1967. He was one of the first and most influential Sixties soul stars. He replaced Elvis as the World's Top Male Singer in a Melody Maker poll shortly before his death in a plane crash (124 WEEKS) pos/wks

25 Nov 65	MY GIRL *Atlantic AT 4050*	11	16
7 Apr 66	(I CAN'T GET NO) SATISFACTION *Atlantic AT 4080*	33	4
14 Jul 66	MY LOVER'S PRAYER *Atlantic 584 019*	37	6
25 Aug 66	I CAN'T TURN YOU LOOSE *Atlantic 584 030*	29	8
24 Nov 66	FA FA FA FA FA (SAD SONG) *Atlantic 584 049*	23	9
26 Jan 67	TRY A LITTLE TENDERNESS *Atlantic 584 070*	46	4
23 Mar 67	DAY TRIPPER *Stax 601 005*	43	6
4 May 67	LET ME COME ON HOME *Stax 601 007*	48	1
15 Jun 67	SHAKE *Stax 601 011*	28	10
19 Jul 67	TRAMP *Stax 601 012* [1]	18	11
11 Oct 67	KNOCK ON WOOD *Stax 601 021* [1]	35	5
14 Feb 68	MY GIRL (re-issue) *Atlantic 584 092*	36	9
21 Feb 68 ●	(SITTIN' ON) THE DOCK OF THE BAY *Stax 601 031* ▲	3	15
29 May 68	THE HAPPY SONG (DUM-DUM) *Stax 601 040*	24	5
31 Jul 68	HARD TO HANDLE *Atlantic 584 199*	15	12
9 Jul 69	LOVE MAN *Atco 226 001*	43	3

[1] Otis Redding and Carla Thomas

Helen REDDY *Australia, female vocalist (18 WEEKS)* pos/wks

18 Jan 75 ●	ANGIE BABY *Capitol CL 15799* ▲	5	10
28 Nov 81	I CAN'T SAY GOODBYE TO YOU *MCA 744*	43	8

REDHEAD KINGPIN and The FBI
US, male rapper – David Guppy – and rap group (11 WEEKS) pos/wks

22 Jul 89	DO THE RIGHT THING *10 TEN 271*	13	10
2 Dec 89	SUPERBAD SUPERSLICK *10 TEN 286*	68	1

REDMAN *US, male rapper – Reggie Noble (30 WEEKS)* pos/wks

25 Apr 98	RAP SCHOLAR *East West E 3853CD* [1]	42	1
30 May 98	MADE IT BACK *Parlophone Rhythm CDRHYTHM 11* [2]	21	3
24 Oct 98 ●	HOW DEEP IS YOUR LOVE (re) *Island Black Music CID 725* [3]	..9	8
12 Jun 99	DA GOODNESS *Def Jam 8709232*	52	1
22 Jul 00	OOOH *Tommy Boy TBCD 2102* [4]	29	2
15 Sep 01	SMASH SUMTHIN' *Def Jam 5886932* [5]	11	7
31 Aug 02	SMASH SUMTHIN' (re-mix) *Kaos KAOSCD 003* [5]	47	2
23 Nov 02 ★	DIRRTY *RCA 74321962722* [6] ■	1	6+

[1] Das EFX featuring Redman [2] Beverley Knight featuring Redman [3] Dru Hill featuring Redman [4] De La Soul featuring Redman [5] Redman featuring Adam F [6] Christina Aguilera featuring Redman

REDNEX *Sweden, male / female vocal / instrumental group (23 WEEKS)* pos/wks

17 Dec 94 ★	COTTON EYE JOE *Internal Affairs KGBCD 016*	1	16
25 Mar 95	OLD POP IN AN OAK *Internal Affairs KGBD 019*	12	6
21 Oct 95	WILD 'N FREE *Internal Affairs KGBD 024*	55	1

REDS UNITED
UK, male vocal group – 40 Manchester United FC fans (13 WEEKS) pos/wks

6 Dec 97	SING UP FOR THE CHAMPIONS *Music Collection MANUCDP 2*	12	9
9 May 98	UNITED CALYPSO '98 *Music Collection MANUCDP 3*	33	4

REDSKINS *UK, male vocal / instrumental trio (12 WEEKS)* pos/wks

10 Nov 84	KEEP ON KEEPIN' ON *Decca F 1*	43	5
22 Jun 85	BRING IT DOWN (THIS INSANE THING) *Decca F 2*	33	5
22 Feb 86	THE POWER IS YOURS *Decca F 3*	59	2

Alex REECE *UK, male producer (7 WEEKS)* pos/wks

16 Dec 95	FEEL THE SUNSHINE *Blunted Vinyl BLNCD 016*	69	1
11 May 96	FEEL THE SUNSHINE (re-mix) *Fourth & Broadway BRCD 332*	26	3
27 Jul 96	CANDLES *Fourth & Broadway BRCD 333*	33	2
18 Nov 96	ACID LAB *Fourth & Broadway BRCD 344*	64	1

Jimmy REED *US, male vocalist, d. 29 Aug 1976 (2 WEEKS)* pos/wks

10 Sep 64	SHAME, SHAME, SHAME *Stateside SS 330*	45	2

Lou REED *US, male vocalist – Lou Firbank (19 WEEKS)* pos/wks

12 May 73 ●	WALK ON THE WILD SIDE *RCA 2303*	10	9
17 Jan 87	SOUL MAN *A&M AM 364* [1]	30	10

[1] Sam Moore and Lou Reed

Dan REED NETWORK
US, male vocal / instrumental group (16 WEEKS) pos/wks

20 Jan 90	COME BACK BABY *Mercury DRN 2*	51	3
17 Mar 90	RAINBOW CHILD *Mercury DRN 3*	60	3
21 Jul 90	STARDATE 1990 / RAINBOW CHILD (re-issue) *Mercury DRN 4*	39	4
8 Sep 90	LOVER / MONEY *Mercury DRN 5*	45	3
13 Jul 91	MIX IT UP *Mercury MER 345*	49	2
21 Sep 91	BABY NOW I *Mercury MER 352*	65	1

Michael REED ORCHESTRA – See Richard HARTLEY / Michael REED ORCHESTRA

REEF *UK, male vocal / instrumental group (46 WEEKS)* pos/wks

15 Apr 95	GOOD FEELING *Sony S2 6613602*	24	4
3 Jun 95	NAKED *Sony S2 6620622*	11	5
5 Aug 95	WEIRD *Sony S2 6622772*	19	3
2 Nov 96 ●	PLACE YOUR HANDS *Sony S2 6635712*	6	7
25 Jan 97 ●	COME BACK BRIGHTER *Sony S2 6640972*	8	5
5 Apr 97	CONSIDERATION *Sony S2 6643125*	13	4
2 Aug 97	YER OLD *Sony S2 6647032*	21	3
10 Apr 99	I'VE GOT SOMETHING TO SAY *Sony S2 6669542*	15	6
5 Jun 99	SWEETY *Sony S2 6673732*	46	1
11 Sep 99	NEW BIRD *Sony S2 6678512*	73	1
12 Aug 00	SET THE RECORD STRAIGHT *Sony S2 6695952*	19	5
16 Dec 00	SUPERHERO *Sony S2 66999382*	55	1
19 May 01	ALL I WANT *Sony S2 6708222*	51	1

POP PLACE NAMES

■ If you like driving in your car like those nutty boys Madness and want to take in a few locations immortalised in song titles, check out our very own British Hit Singles atlas of hit singles featuring UK place names in the titles. You will, of course, notice that the London area is not represented. Look out for this in a future edition

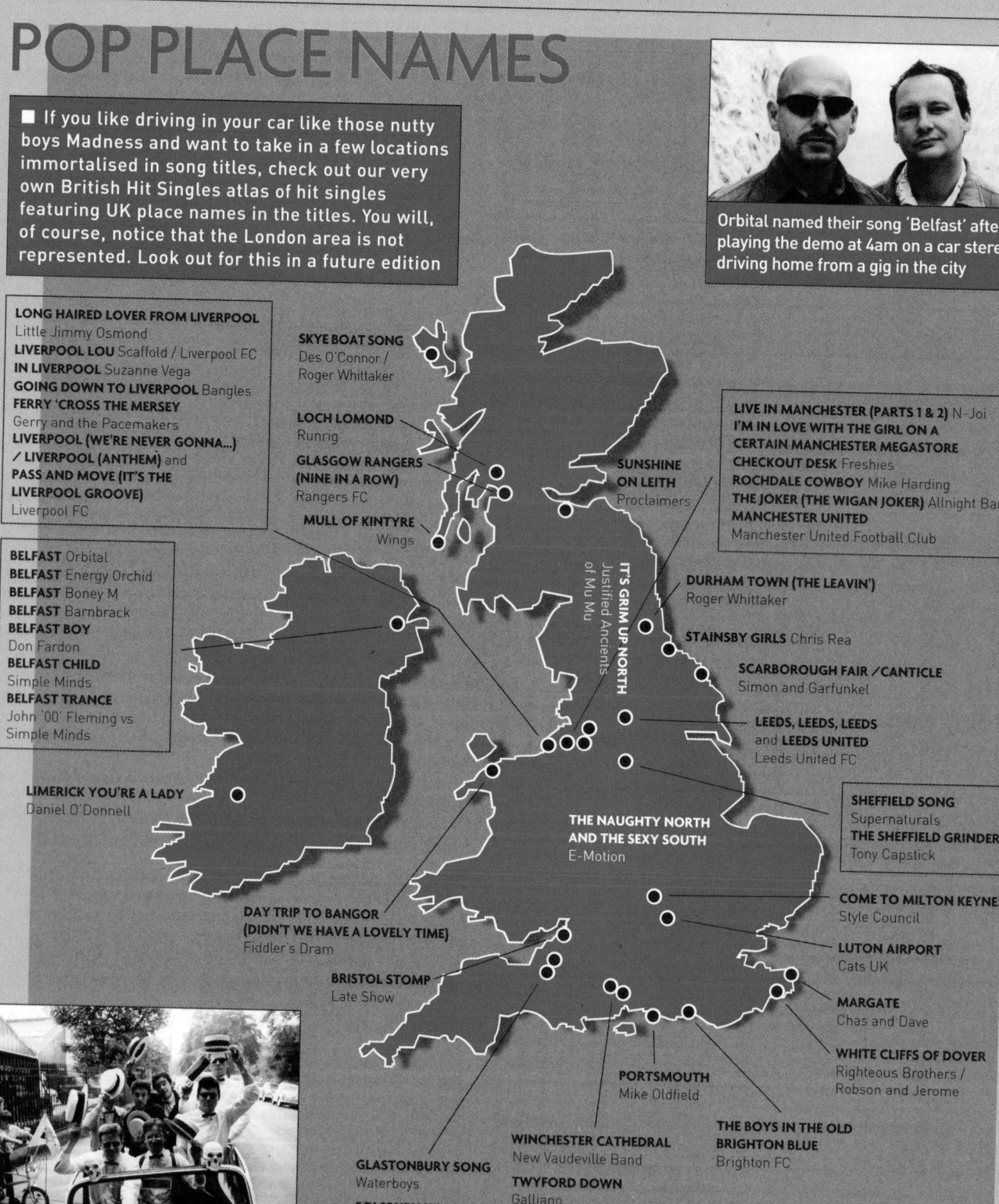

Orbital named their song 'Belfast' after playing the demo at 4am on a car stereo, driving home from a gig in the city

LONG HAIRED LOVER FROM LIVERPOOL
Little Jimmy Osmond
LIVERPOOL LOU Scaffold / Liverpool FC
IN LIVERPOOL Suzanne Vega
GOING DOWN TO LIVERPOOL Bangles
FERRY 'CROSS THE MERSEY
Gerry and the Pacemakers
LIVERPOOL (WE'RE NEVER GONNA...)
/ **LIVERPOOL (ANTHEM)** and
**PASS AND MOVE (IT'S THE
LIVERPOOL GROOVE)**
Liverpool FC

SKYE BOAT SONG
Des O'Connor /
Roger Whittaker

LOCH LOMOND
Runrig

**GLASGOW RANGERS
(NINE IN A ROW)**
Rangers FC

MULL OF KINTYRE
Wings

**SUNSHINE
ON LEITH**
Proclaimers

LIVE IN MANCHESTER (PARTS 1 & 2) N-Joi
**I'M IN LOVE WITH THE GIRL ON A
CERTAIN MANCHESTER MEGASTORE
CHECKOUT DESK** Freshies
ROCHDALE COWBOY Mike Harding
THE JOKER (THE WIGAN JOKER) Allnight Band
MANCHESTER UNITED
Manchester United Football Club

BELFAST Orbital
BELFAST Energy Orchid
BELFAST Boney M
BELFAST Barnbrack
BELFAST BOY
Don Fardon
BELFAST CHILD
Simple Minds
BELFAST TRANCE
John '00' Fleming vs
Simple Minds

IT'S GRIM UP NORTH
Justified Ancients
of Mu Mu

DURHAM TOWN (THE LEAVIN')
Roger Whittaker

STAINSBY GIRLS Chris Rea

SCARBOROUGH FAIR / CANTICLE
Simon and Garfunkel

LEEDS, LEEDS, LEEDS
and **LEEDS UNITED**
Leeds United FC

LIMERICK YOU'RE A LADY
Daniel O'Donnell

**THE NAUGHTY NORTH
AND THE SEXY SOUTH**
E-Motion

SHEFFIELD SONG
Supernaturals
THE SHEFFIELD GRINDER
Tony Capstick

**DAY TRIP TO BANGOR
(DIDN'T WE HAVE A LOVELY TIME)**
Fiddler's Dram

COME TO MILTON KEYNES
Style Council

LUTON AIRPORT
Cats UK

BRISTOL STOMP
Late Show

MARGATE
Chas and Dave

WHITE CLIFFS OF DOVER
Righteous Brothers /
Robson and Jerome

PORTSMOUTH
Mike Oldfield

**THE BOYS IN THE OLD
BRIGHTON BLUE**
Brighton FC

WINCHESTER CATHEDRAL
New Vaudeville Band
TWYFORD DOWN
Galliano

GLASTONBURY SONG
Waterboys

SOLSBURY HILL
Peter Gabriel

Madness: they like driving in their car

REEL Ireland, male vocal group (3 WEEKS) pos/wks

| 24 Nov 01 | LIFT ME UP *Universal TV 0154632* | 39 | 1 |
| 8 Jun 02 | YOU TAKE ME AWAY *Universal TV 0190172* | 31 | 2 |

REEL BIG FISH US, male vocal / instrumental group (1 WEEK) pos/wks

| 6 Apr 02 | SOLD OUT (EP) *Jive 9270002* | 62 | 1 |

Tracks on Sold Out (EP): Sell Out / Take On Me / Hungry Like the Wolf

REEL 2 REAL US, male vocal / production duo – Erick Morillo and Mark 'The Mad Stuntman' Quashie (53 WEEKS) pos/wks

12 Feb 94 ●	I LIKE TO MOVE IT *Positiva CDTIV 10* [1]	5	20
2 Jul 94 ●	GO ON MOVE *Positiva CDTIV 15* [1]	7	9
1 Oct 94	CAN YOU FEEL IT *Positiva CDTIV 22* [1]	13	5
3 Dec 94	RAISE YOUR HANDS *Positiva CDTIV 27* [1]	14	6
1 Apr 95	CONWAY *Positiva CDTIVS 30* [1]	27	4
6 Jul 96 ●	JAZZ IT UP *Positiva CDTIV 59*	7	7
5 Oct 96	ARE YOU READY FOR SOME MORE *Positiva CDTIV 56*	24	2

[1] Reel 2 Real featuring The Mad Stuntman

See also Erick 'More' MORILLO presents RAW; LIL 'MO' YIN YANG

REELISTS UK, male vocal / production duo – Kaywan Qazzaz and Saif Naqui (13 WEEKS) pos/wks

| 19 Jan 02 ● | HATERS *Relentless RELENT 23CD* [1] | 8 | 7 |
| 25 May 02 | FREAK MODE (re) *Go Beat GOBCD 45* | 16 | 6 |

[1] So Solid Crew presents Mr Shabz featuring MBD and The Reelists

See also SO SOLID CREW

Maureen REES
UK, female vocalist / TV learner driver (4 WEEKS) pos/wks

| 20 Dec 97 | DRIVING IN MY CAR *Eagle EAGXS 014* | 49 | 4 |

Tony REES and The COTTAGERS
UK, male vocal group (1 WEEK) pos/wks

| 10 May 75 | VIVA EL FULHAM *Sonet SON 2059* | 46 | 1 |

REESE PROJECT
US, male producer – Kevin Saunderson (7 WEEKS) pos/wks

8 Aug 92	THE COLOUR OF LOVE *Network NWK 51*	52	2
12 Dec 92	I BELIEVE *Network NWKT 63*	74	1
13 Mar 93	SO DEEP *Network NWKCD 68*	54	2
24 Sep 94	THE COLOUR OF LOVE (re-mix) *Network NWKCD 81*	55	1
6 May 95	DIRECT-ME *Network NWKCD 87*	44	1

Conner REEVES UK, male vocalist (18 WEEKS) pos/wks

30 Aug 97	MY FATHER'S SON *Wildstar CDWILD 1*	12	5
22 Nov 97	EARTHBOUND *Wildstar CDWILD 2*	14	4
11 Apr 98	READ MY MIND *Wildstar CXWILD 4*	19	4
3 Oct 98	SEARCHING FOR A SOUL *Wildstar CDWILD 6*	28	2
4 Sep 99	BEST FRIEND *WEA WEA 221CD1* [1]	23	3

[1] Mark Morrison and Conner Reeves

Jim REEVES ⟨ 26 ⟩ **Top 500**

Internationally acclaimed velvet-voiced vocalist b. 20 Aug 1924, Texas, US, d. 31 Jul 1964. 'Gentleman Jim' had an impressive portfolio of posthumous hits, including a record-breaking eight albums simultaneously on the UK chart three months after his death (322 WEEKS) pos/wks

24 Mar 60	HE'LL HAVE TO GO (re) *RCA 1168*	12	31
16 Mar 61	WHISPERING HOPE *RCA 1223*	50	1
23 Nov 61	YOU'RE THE ONLY GOOD THING (THAT HAPPENED TO ME) *RCA 1261*	17	19
28 Jun 62	ADIOS AMIGO *RCA 1293*	23	21
22 Nov 62	I'M GONNA CHANGE EVERYTHING *RCA 1317*	42	2
13 Jun 63 ●	WELCOME TO MY WORLD *RCA 1342*	6	15
17 Oct 63	GUILTY *RCA 1364*	29	7
20 Feb 64 ●	I LOVE YOU BECAUSE *RCA 1385*	5	39
18 Jun 64 ●	I WON'T FORGET YOU (re) *RCA 1400*	3	26

5 Nov 64 ●	THERE'S A HEARTACHE FOLLOWING ME *RCA 1423*	6	13
4 Feb 65 ●	IT HURTS SO MUCH (TO SEE YOU GO) *RCA 1437*	8	10
15 Apr 65	NOT UNTIL THE NEXT TIME *RCA 1446*	13	12
6 May 65	HOW LONG HAS IT BEEN *RCA 1445*	45	5
15 Jul 65	THIS WORLD IS NOT MY HOME *RCA 1412*	22	9
11 Nov 65	IS IT REALLY OVER *RCA 1488*	17	9
18 Aug 66 ★	DISTANT DRUMS *RCA 1537*	1	25
2 Feb 67	I WON'T COME IN WHILE HE'S THERE *RCA 1563*	12	11
26 Jul 67	TRYING TO FORGET *RCA 1611*	33	5
22 Nov 67	I HEARD A HEART BREAK LAST NIGHT *RCA 1643*	38	6
27 Mar 68	PRETTY BROWN EYES *RCA 1672*	33	5
25 Jun 69	WHEN TWO WORLDS COLLIDE *RCA 1830*	17	17
6 Dec 69	BUT YOU LOVE ME DADDY *RCA 1899*	15	16
21 Mar 70	NOBODY'S FOOL *RCA 1915*	32	5
12 Sep 70	ANGELS DON'T LIE (re) *RCA 1997*	32	3
26 Jun 71	I LOVE YOU BECAUSE (re-issue) / HE'LL HAVE TO GO (re-issue) / MOONLIGHT & ROSES *RCA Maximillion 2092*	34	8
19 Feb 72	YOU'RE FREE TO GO *RCA 2174*	48	2

Martha REEVES and the VANDELLAS ⟨ 402 ⟩ **Top 500**

Fronted by Martha Reeves, b. 18 Jul 1941, Alabama, US, previously a secretary and backing vocalist for the Motown label. The female trio made their UK Top 20 debut six years after doing the same in the US and were inducted into the Rock and Roll Hall of Fame in 1995 (85 WEEKS) pos/wks

29 Oct 64	DANCING IN THE STREET *Stateside SS 345* [1]	28	8
1 Apr 65	NOWHERE TO RUN *Tamla Motown TMG 502* [1]	26	8
1 Dec 66	I'M READY FOR LOVE *Tamla Motown TMG 582* [1]	22	8
30 Mar 67	JIMMY MACK (re) *Tamla Motown TMG 599* [1]	21	21
17 Jan 68	HONEY CHILE *Tamla Motown TMG 636*	30	9
15 Jan 69 ●	DANCING IN THE STREET (re-issue) *Tamla Motown TMG 684*	4	12
16 Apr 69	NOWHERE TO RUN (re-issue) *Tamla Motown TMG 694*	42	3
13 Feb 71	FORGET ME NOT *Tamla Motown TMG 762*	11	8
8 Jan 72	BLESS YOU *Tamla Motown TMG 794*	33	5
23 Jul 88	NOWHERE TO RUN (2nd re-issue) *A&M AM 444*	52	3

[1] Martha and The Vandellas

The listed flip side of 'Nowhere to Run' in 1988 was 'I Got You (I Feel Good)' by James Brown

'Jimmy Mack' also peaked at No.21 during the Aug 1970 re-entry

Vic REEVES UK, male comedian / vocalist – Jim Moir (29 WEEKS) pos/wks

27 Apr 91 ●	BORN FREE *Sense SIGH 710* [1]	6	6
26 Oct 91 ★	DIZZY *Sense SIGH 712* [2]	1	12
14 Dec 91	ABIDE WITH ME *Sense SIGH 713*	47	3
8 Jul 95 ●	I'M A BELIEVER *Parlophone CDR 6412* [3]	3	8

[1] Vic Reeves and The Roman Numerals [2] Vic Reeves and The Wonder Stuff [3] EMF and Reeves and Mortimer

RE-FLEX UK, male vocal / instrumental group (9 WEEKS) pos/wks

| 28 Jan 84 | THE POLITICS OF DANCING *EMI FLEX 2* | 28 | 9 |

REFLEX featuring MC VIPER UK, male production duo – Danny Harrison and Julian Jonah, and male rapper (1 WEEK) pos/wks

| 19 May 01 | PUT YOUR HANDS UP *Gusto CDGUS 2* | 72 | 1 |

See also 187 LOCKDOWN

REFUGEE ALLSTARS – See Wyclef JEAN; FUGEES

REFUGEE CAMP ALLSTARS – See Lauryn HILL

Joan REGAN UK, female vocalist (62 WEEKS) pos/wks

11 Dec 53 ●	RICOCHET (re) *Decca F 10193* [1]	8	5
14 May 54 ●	SOMEONE ELSE'S ROSES *Decca F 10257*	5	8
1 Oct 54 ●	IF I GIVE MY HEART TO YOU (re) *Decca F 10373*	3	11
5 Nov 54	WAIT FOR ME, DARLING *Decca F 10362* [2]	18	1
25 Mar 55	PRIZE OF GOLD *Decca F 10432*	6	8
6 May 55	OPEN UP YOUR HEART *Decca F 10474* [3]	19	1
1 May 59 ●	MAY YOU ALWAYS *HMV POP 593*	9	16
5 Feb 60	HAPPY ANNIVERSARY (re) *Pye 7N 15238*	29	2

28 Jul 60	PAPA LOVES MAMA *Pye 7N 15278*	29	8
24 Nov 60	ONE OF THE LUCKY ONES *Pye 7N 15310*	47	1
5 Jan 61	IT MUST BE SANTA *Pye 7N 15303*	42	1

[1] Joan Regan with The Squadronaires [2] Joan Regan with The Johnston Brothers
[3] Joan and Rusty Regan

REGENTS *UK, male / female vocal / instrumental group (14 WKS)* pos/wks

| 22 Dec 79 | 7 TEEN *Rialto TREB 111* | 11 | 12 |
| 7 Jun 80 | SEE YOU LATER *Arista ARIST 350* | 55 | 2 |

REGGAE BOYZ
Jamaica, male vocal / instrumental group (1 WEEK) pos/wks

| 27 Jun 98 | KICK IT *Universal MCSTD 40167* | 59 | 1 |

REGGAE PHILHARMONIC ORCHESTRA
UK, male / female vocal / instrumental group (11 WEEKS) pos/wks

| 19 Nov 88 | MINNIE THE MOOCHER *Mango IS 378* | 35 | 9 |
| 28 Jul 90 | LOVELY THING *Mango MNG 742* [1] | 71 | 2 |

[1] Featuring Jazzy Joyce

REGGAE REVOLUTION – *See Pato BANTON*

REGGIE – *See TECHNOTRONIC*

REGINA *US, female vocalist (3 WEEKS)* pos/wks

| 1 Feb 86 | BABY LOVE *Funkin' Marvellous MARV 01* | 50 | 3 |

REID *UK, male vocal group (12 WEEKS)* pos/wks

8 Oct 88	ONE WAY OUT *Syncopate SY 16*	66	2
11 Feb 89	REAL EMOTION *Syncopate SY 24*	65	2
15 Apr 89	GOOD TIMES *Syncopate SY 27*	55	6
21 Oct 89	LOVIN' ON THE SIDE *Syncopate REID 1*	71	2

Ellen REID – *See CRASH TEST DUMMIES*

John REID – *See NIGHTCRAWLERS featuring John REID*

Junior REID – *See COLDCUT; RAGGA TWINS; SOUP DRAGONS*

Mike REID *UK, male actor / comedian (10 WEEKS)* pos/wks

| 22 Mar 75 | ● THE UGLY DUCKLING *Pye 7N 45434* | 10 | 8 |
| 24 Apr 99 | THE MORE I SEE YOU *Telstar TV CDSTAS 3049* [1] | 46 | 2 |

[1] Barbara Windsor and Mike Reid

Neil REID *UK, male vocalist (26 WEEKS)* pos/wks

| 1 Jan 72 | ● MOTHER OF MINE *Decca F 13264* | 2 | 20 |
| 8 Apr 72 | THAT'S WHAT I WANT TO BE (re) *Decca F 13300* | 45 | 6 |

Patrick REID – *See POB featuring DJ Patrick REID*

Maggie REILLY – *See Mike OLDFIELD*

Keith RELF *UK, male vocalist, d. 14 May 1976 (1 WEEK)* pos/wks

| 26 May 66 | MR ZERO *Columbia DB 7920* | 50 | 1 |

See also YARDBIRDS

REMBRANDTS *US, male vocal / instrumental group (28 WEEKS)* pos/wks

| 2 Sep 95 | ● I'LL BE THERE FOR YOU (THEME FROM 'FRIENDS') (re) *East West A 4390CD* | 3 | 27 |
| 20 Jan 96 | THIS HOUSE IS NOT A HOME *East West A 4336CD* | 58 | 1 |

'I'll Be There For You' re-entry made No.5 in May 1997

REMO FOUR – *See Tommy QUICKLY and The REMO FOUR*

REMY ZERO *US, male vocal / instrumental group (1 WEEK)* pos/wks

| 27 Apr 02 | SAVE ME *Elektra E 7297CD* | 55 | 1 |

RENAISSANCE
UK, male / female vocal / instrumental group (11 WEEKS) pos/wks

| 15 Jul 78 | ● NORTHERN LIGHTS *Warner Bros. K 17177* | 10 | 11 |

RENÉ and ANGELA *US, male / female vocal duo – Réne Moore and Angela Winbush (15 WEEKS)* pos/wks

15 Jun 85	SAVE YOUR LOVE (FOR NUMBER 1) *Club JAB 14* [1]	66	2
7 Sep 85	I'LL BE GOOD *Club JAB 18*	22	10
2 Nov 85	SECRET RENDEZVOUS *Champion CHAMP 5*	54	3

[1] René and Angela featuring Kurtis Blow

RENÉ and YVETTE *UK, male / female vocal duo (4 WEEKS)* pos/wks

| 22 Nov 86 | JE T'AIME ('ALLO 'ALLO) / RENE DMC (DEVASTATING MACHO CHARISMA) *Sedition EDIT 3319* | 57 | 4 |

Nicole RENEE *US, female vocalist (1 WEEK)* pos/wks

| 12 Dec 98 | STRAWBERRY *Atlantic AT 0050CD* | 55 | 1 |

RENÉE and RENATO *UK / Italy, female / male vocal duo – Hilary Lester and Renato Pagliari (22 WEEKS)* pos/wks

| 30 Oct 82 | ★ SAVE YOUR LOVE *Hollywood HWD 003* | 1 | 16 |
| 12 Feb 83 | JUST ONE MORE KISS *Hollywood HWD 006* | 48 | 6 |

RENEGADE SOUNDWAVE *UK, male vocal / instrumental group (7 WEEKS)* pos/wks

| 3 Feb 90 | PROBABLY A ROBBERY *Mute MUTE 102* | 38 | 6 |
| 5 Feb 94 | RENEGADE SOUNDWAVE *Mute CDMUTE 146* | 64 | 1 |

REPARATA and The DELRONS
US, female vocal group (12 WEEKS) pos/wks

| 20 Mar 68 | CAPTAIN OF YOUR SHIP *Bell 1002* | 13 | 10 |
| 18 Oct 75 | SHOES *Dart 2066 562* [1] | 43 | 2 |

[1] Reparata

REPRAZENT – *See Roni SIZE / REPRAZENT*

REPUBLICA
UK, male / female vocal / instrumental group (18 WEEKS) pos/wks

27 Apr 96	READY TO GO *Deconstruction 74321326132*	43	2
1 Mar 97	READY TO GO (re-issue) *Deconstruction 74321421332*	13	6
3 May 97	● DROP DEAD GORGEOUS *Deconstruction 74321408442*	7	7
3 Oct 98	FROM RUSH HOUR WITH LOVE *Deconstruction 74321610472*	20	3

See also SAFFRON

RESONANCE featuring The BURRELLS
US, male producer and male vocal duo (1 WEEK) pos/wks

| 26 May 01 | DJ *Strictly Rhythm SRUKCD 02* | 67 | 1 |

REST ASSURED *UK, male production trio (7 WEEKS)* pos/wks

| 28 Feb 98 | TREAT INFAMY *ffrr FCD 333* | 14 | 7 |

See also GAT DECOR; PHUNKY PHANTOM

REUNION *US, male vocal group (4 WEEKS)* pos/wks

| 21 Sep 74 | LIFE IS A ROCK (BUT THE RADIO ROLLED ME) *RCA PB 10056* | 33 | 4 |

REVILLOS – *See REZILLOS*

REVIVAL 3000 *UK, male DJ / production trio (1 WEEK)* pos/wks

| 1 Nov 97 | THE MIGHTY HIGH *Hi-Life 5718092* | 47 | 1 |

REVOLTING COCKS
US, male vocal / instrumental group (1 WEEK) pos/wks

| 18 Sep 93 | DA YA THINK I'M SEXY *Devotion CDDVN 111* | 61 | 1 |

Re-entries are listed as (re), (2re), (3re), etc which signifies that the hit re-entered the chart once, twice or three times, etc

REVOLUTION – See PRINCE

Debbie REYNOLDS US, female actor / vocalist (17 WEEKS)   pos/wks
30 Aug 57 ● TAMMY Vogue-Coral Q 72274 ▲ **2** 17

Jody REYNOLDS US, male vocalist (1 WEEK)   pos/wks
14 Apr 79   ENDLESS SLEEP Lightning LIG 9015 ....**66** 1

'Endless Sleep' was coupled with 'To Know Him Is to Love Him' by the Teddy Bears
as a double A-side

LJ REYNOLDS US, male vocalist (3 WEEKS)   pos/wks
30 Jun 84   DON'T LET NOBODY HOLD YOU DOWN Club JAB 5 ....**53** 3

REYNOLDS GIRLS
UK, female vocal duo – Linda and Aisling Reynolds (12 WEEKS)   pos/wks
25 Feb 89 ● I'D RATHER JACK PWL PWL 25..**8** 12

REZILLOS
UK, male / female vocal / instrumental group (21 WEEKS)   pos/wks
12 Aug 78   TOP OF THE POPS Sire SIR 4001 ....**17** 9
25 Nov 78   DESTINATION VENUS Sire SIR 4008 ....**43** 4
18 Aug 79   I WANNA BE YOUR MAN / I CAN'T STAND MY BABY (re)
             Sensible SAB 1 ....**71** 2
26 Jan 80   MOTORBIKE BEAT Dindisc DIN 5 [1] **45** 6

[1] Revillos

RHIANNA UK, female vocalist – Rhianna Kelly (6 WEEKS)   pos/wks
1 Jun 02   OH BABY S2 6726232..**18** 5
14 Sep 02   WORD LOVE S2 6730112......................................**41** 1

RHODA with The SPECIAL AKA
UK, female vocalist and male vocal / instrumental group (5 WEEKS) pos/wks
23 Jan 82   THE BOILER 2 Tone CHSTT 18 ....**35** 5

See also SPECIALS

Busta RHYMES US, male rapper – Trevor Smith (72 WEEKS)   pos/wks
11 May 96 ● WOO-HAH!! GOT YOU ALL IN CHECK Elektra EKR 220CD **8** 7
21 Sep 96   IT'S A PARTY Elektra EKR 226CD [1] **23** 2
5 Apr 97 ● HIT EM HIGH (THE MONSTARS' ANTHEM)
             Atlantic A 5449CD [2] **8** 6
3 May 97   DO MY THING Elektra EKR 235CD **39** 1
18 Oct 97   PUT YOUR HANDS WHERE MY EYES COULD SEE
             Elektra E 3900CD **16** 3
20 Dec 97   DANGEROUS Elektra E 3877CD **32** 4
18 Apr 98 ● TURN IT UP / FIRE IT UP Elektra E 3847CD **2** 10
11 Jul 98   ONE Elektra E 3833CD1 [3] **23** 3
30 Jan 99 ● GIMME SOME MORE Elektra E 3782CD **5** 6
1 May 99 ● WHAT'S IT GONNA BE?! Elektra E 3762CD1 [4] **6** 7
22 Jul 00   GET OUT Elektra E 7075CD **57** 1
16 Dec 00   FIRE East West E 7136 ....**60** 1
18 Aug 01 ● ANTE UP (re) Epic 6717882 [5] **7** 8
16 Mar 02   BREAK YA NECK J 74321922332 ....**11** 6
8 Jun 02   PASS THE COURVOISIER – PART II J 74321937902 [6] **16** 7

[1] Busta Rhymes featuring Zhane [2] B Real / Busta Rhymes / Coolio / LL Cool J /
Method Man [3] Busta Rhymes featuring Erykah Badu [4] Busta Rhymes featuring
Janet [5] M.O.P. featuring Busta Rhymes [6] Busta Rhymes featuring P Diddy & Pharrell

See also Syleena JOHNSON

RHYTHIM IS RHYTHIM US, male production group (1 WEEK)   pos/wks
11 Nov 89   STRINGS OF LIFE Kool Kat KOOL 509.........................**74** 1

RHYTHM BANGERS – See Robbie RIVERA

RHYTHM ETERNITY
UK, male / female vocal / instrumental group (1 WEEK)   pos/wks
23 May 92   PINK CHAMPAGNE Dead Dead Good GOOD 15T **72** 1

RHYTHM FACTOR
US, male / female vocal / instrumental group (2 WEEKS)   pos/wks
29 Apr 95   YOU BRING ME JOY Multiply CDMULTY 4.......................**53** 2

RHYTHM MASTERS
UK / Malta, male DJ / production duo (4 WEEKS)   pos/wks
16 Aug 97   COME ON Y'ALL Faze 2 CDFAZE 37............................**49** 1
6 Dec 97   ENTER THE SCENE Distinctive DISNCD 40 [1] **49** 1
18 Aug 01   UNDERGROUND Black & Blue NEOCD 056 ....**50** 1
30 Mar 02   GHETTO Black & Blue NEOCD 074 [2] **71** 1

[1] DJ Supreme vs The Rhythm Masters [2] Rhythm Masters featuring Joe Watson

See also BIG ROOM GIRL featuring Darryl PANDY; RHYTHMATIC JUNKIES

RHYTHM-N-BASS UK, male vocal group (4 WEEKS)   pos/wks
19 Sep 92   ROSES Epic 6582907 ....**56** 2
3 Jul 93   CAN'T STOP THIS FEELING Epic 6592002......................**59** 2

RHYTHM OF LIFE
UK, male DJ / producer – Steve Burgess (2 WEEKS)   pos/wks
13 May 00   YOU PUT ME IN HEAVEN WITH YOUR TOUCH
             Xtravaganza XTRAV 4CDS **24** 2

RHYTHM ON THE LOOSE
UK, male producer – Geoff Hibbert (2 WEEKS)   pos/wks
19 Aug 95   BREAK OF DAWN Six6 SIXCD 126..............................**36** 2

RHYTHM QUEST UK, male producer – Mark Hadfield (2 WEEKS)   pos/wks
20 Jun 92   CLOSER TO ALL YOUR DREAMS Network NWK 40..................**45** 2

RHYTHM SECTION UK, male vocal / instrumental group (1 WEEK) pos/wks
18 Jul 92   MIDSUMMER MADNESS (EP) Rhythm Section RSEC 006..........**66** 1

Tracks on Midsummer Madness (EP): Dreamworld / Burnin' Up / Perfect Love 2am /
Perfect Love 8am

RHYTHM SOURCE
UK, male / female vocal / instrumental group (1 WEEK)   pos/wks
17 Jun 95   LOVE SHINE A&M 5810672....................................**74** 1

RHYTHM SPINNERS – See Rolf HARRIS

RHYTHMATIC
UK, male instrumental / production duo (3 WEEKS)   pos/wks
12 May 90   TAKE ME BACK (re) Network NWK 8 ....**71** 2
3 Nov 90   FREQUENCY Network NWK 13 ....**62** 1

RHYTHMATIC JUNKIES
UK, male vocal / production group (1 WEEK)   pos/wks
15 May 99   THE FEELIN (CLAP YOUR HANDS)
             Sound of Ministry RIDE 2CDS **67** 1

RHYTHMKILLAZ Holland, male production duo
– Rene ter Horst and Gaston Steenkist (2 WEEKS)   pos/wks
31 Mar 01   WACK ASS MF Incentive CENT 18 CDS.........................**32** 2

See also CHOCOLATE PUMA; JARK PRONGO; TOMBA VIRA; GOODMEN; RIVA
featuring Dannii MINOGUE

RIALTO UK, male vocal / instrumental group (8 WEEKS)   pos/wks
8 Nov 97   MONDAY MORNING 5:19 East West EW 116CD **37** 2
17 Jan 98   UNTOUCHABLE East West EW 107CD1 ....**20** 3
28 Mar 98   DREAM ANOTHER DREAM East West EW 156CD1 ....**39** 2
17 Oct 98   SUMMER'S OVER China WOKCDR 2099 ....**60** 1

Rosie RIBBONS UK, female vocalist (4 WEEKS)   pos/wks
2 Nov 02   BLINK T2 / Telstar CDSTAS 3288............................**12** 4

Reva RICE and Greg ELLIS
UK, male / female vocal duo (2 WEEKS)   pos/wks

| 27 Mar 93 | NEXT TIME YOU FALL IN LOVE *Really Useful RURCD 12* | 59 | 2 |

Charlie RICH
US, male vocalist, d. 25 July 1995 (29 WEEKS)   pos/wks

16 Feb 74	● THE MOST BEAUTIFUL GIRL *Epic EPC 1897* ▲	2	14
13 Apr 74	BEHIND CLOSED DOORS *Epic EPC 1539*	16	10
1 Feb 75	WE LOVE EACH OTHER *Epic EPC 2868*	37	5

Kelli RICH – See NU SOUL featuring Kelli RICH

Richie RICH
UK, male DJ / producer (16 WEEKS)   pos/wks

16 Jul 88	TURN IT UP *Club JAB 68*	48	3
22 Oct 88	I'LL HOUSE YOU *Gee Street GEE 003* 1	22	5
10 Dec 88	MY DJ (PUMP IT UP SOME) *Gee Street GEE 7*	74	1
2 Sep 89	SALSA HOUSE *ffrr F 113*	50	3
9 Mar 91	YOU USED TO SALSA *ffrr F 156* 2	52	3
29 Mar 97	STAY WITH ME *Castle CATX 1001* 3	58	1

1 Richie Rich meets The Jungle Brothers 2 Richie Rich featuring Ralphi Rosario
3 Richie Rich and Esera Tuaolo

'You Used to Salsa' is a remix of 'Salsa House'

RICH KIDS
UK, male vocal / instrumental group (5 WEEKS)   pos/wks

| 28 Jan 78 | RICH KIDS *EMI 2738* | 24 | 5 |

Tony RICH PROJECT
US, male vocalist – Antonio Jeffries (22 WEEKS)   pos/wks

4 May 96	● NOBODY KNOWS *LaFace 74321356422*	4	17
31 Aug 96	LIKE A WOMAN *LaFace 74321401612*	27	4
14 Dec 96	LEAVIN' *LaFace 74321438382*	52	1

Cliff RICHARD ☐2 **Top 500**
'The Peter Pan of Pop' - Britain's most successful solo vocalist, b. Harry Webb, 14 Oct 1940, Lucknow, India. Ex-member of Dick Teague Skiffle Group was instantly successful, and almost overnight became the UK's No.1 rock 'n' roll star despite bad press due to "too sexy" live performances. Many successes on film, stage, TV, radio and video. He has had hits in every major market around the globe and was named World's No.1 Artist by Billboard in 1963 (with Elvis second and Shadows third). Between 1959 and 2002, Cliff had a staggering 35 Top 10 albums including seven No.1s, and had more Top 10 albums in the 1980s than any other artist. He was seen on the first 'Top of the Pops' and has appeared on the TV show more often than any other artist. He is one of the few performers to top the chart with two different recordings of the same song (Living Doll). This seemingly ageless entertainer's record number of 64 Top 10 entries now spans 43 years, and at times he held the record for being the youngest (1959) and oldest (1999) British singer to top the singles chart. Cliff, who has sold more than 260 million records (singles, albums, EPs) worldwide, was awarded the Outstanding Contribution to British Music trophy at the 1989 Brits, was made an MBE in 1980, was knighted in 1995, and holds the unique achievement of a UK No.1 single in five different decades. Best-selling single: 'The Young Ones' 1,052,000 (1152 WEEKS)   pos/wks

12 Sep 58	● MOVE IT! *Columbia DB 4178* 1	2	17
21 Nov 58	● HIGH CLASS BABY *Columbia DB 4203* 1	7	10
30 Jan 59	LIVIN' LOVIN' DOLL *Columbia DB 4249* 1	20	6
8 May 59	● MEAN STREAK *Columbia DB 4290 A* 1	10	9
15 May 59	NEVER MIND *Columbia DB 4290 B* 1	21	2
10 Jul 59	★ LIVING DOLL (2re) *Columbia DB 4306* 1	1	23
9 Oct 59	★ TRAVELLIN' LIGHT *Columbia DB 4351 B* 2	1	17
9 Oct 59	DYNAMITE (re) *Columbia DB 4351 A* 2	16	4
15 Jan 60	EXPRESSO BONGO (EP) *Columbia SEG 7971* 2	14	7
22 Jan 60	● A VOICE IN THE WILDERNESS (re) *Columbia DB 4398* 2	2	16
24 Mar 60	● FALL IN LOVE WITH YOU *Columbia DB 4431* 2	2	15
30 Jun 60	★ PLEASE DON'T TEASE *Columbia DB 4479* 2	1	18
22 Sep 60	● NINE TIMES OUT OF TEN *Columbia DB 4506* 2	3	12
1 Dec 60	★ I LOVE YOU *Columbia DB 4547* 2	1	16
2 Mar 61	● THEME FOR A DREAM *Columbia DB 4593* 2	3	14
30 Mar 61	● GEE WHIZ IT'S YOU *Columbia DC 756* 2	4	14
22 Jun 61	● A GIRL LIKE YOU *Columbia DB 4667* 2	3	14

19 Oct 61	● WHEN THE GIRL IN YOUR ARMS IS THE GIRL IN YOUR HEART *Columbia DB 4716*	3	15
11 Jan 62	★ THE YOUNG ONES *Columbia DB 4761* 2 ◆ ■	1	21
10 May 62	● I'M LOOKING OUT THE WINDOW / DO YOU WANT TO DANCE *Columbia DB 4828* 3	2	17
6 Sep 62	● I'LL BE ME *Columbia DB 4886* 2	2	12
6 Dec 62	★ THE NEXT TIME / BACHELOR BOY *Columbia DB 4950* 2	1	18
21 Feb 63	★ SUMMER HOLIDAY *Columbia DB 4977* 2	1	18
9 May 63	● LUCKY LIPS *Columbia DB 7034* 2	4	15
22 Aug 63	● IT'S ALL IN THE GAME *Columbia DB 7089*	2	13
7 Nov 63	● DON'T TALK TO HIM (re) *Columbia DB 7150* 2	2	14
6 Feb 64	● I'M THE LONELY ONE *Columbia DB 7203* 2	8	10
30 Apr 64	● CONSTANTLY *Columbia DB 7272*	4	13
2 Jul 64	● ON THE BEACH *Columbia DB 7305* 2	7	13
8 Oct 64	● THE TWELFTH OF NEVER *Columbia DB 7372*	8	11
10 Dec 64	● I COULD EASILY FALL *Columbia DB 7420* 2	6	11
11 Mar 65	★ THE MINUTE YOU'RE GONE *Columbia DB 7496*	1	14
10 Jun 65	ON MY WORD *Columbia DB 7596*	12	10
19 Aug 65	THE TIME IN BETWEEN *Columbia DB 7660* 2	22	8
4 Nov 65	● WIND ME UP (LET ME GO) *Columbia DB 7745* 2	2	16
24 Mar 66	BLUE TURNS TO GREY *Columbia DB 7866* 2	15	9
21 Jul 66	● VISIONS *Columbia DB 7968*	7	12
13 Oct 66	● TIME DRAGS BY *Columbia DB 8017* 2	10	12
15 Dec 66	● IN THE COUNTRY *Columbia DB 8094* 2	6	10
16 Mar 67	● IT'S ALL OVER *Columbia DB 8150*	9	10
8 Jun 67	I'LL COME RUNNIN' *Columbia DB 8210*	26	8
16 Aug 67	● THE DAY I MET MARIE *Columbia DB 8245*	10	14
15 Nov 67	● ALL MY LOVE *Columbia DB 8293*	6	12
20 Mar 68	★ CONGRATULATIONS *Columbia DB 8376*	1	13
26 Jun 68	I'LL LOVE YOU FOREVER TODAY *Columbia DB 8437*	27	6
25 Sep 68	MARIANNE *Columbia DB 8476*	22	8
27 Nov 68	DON'T FORGET TO CATCH ME *Columbia DB 8503* 2	21	10
26 Feb 69	GOOD TIMES (BETTER TIMES) *Columbia DB 8548*	12	11
28 May 69	● BIG SHIP *Columbia DB 8581*	8	10
13 Sep 69	● THROW DOWN A LINE *Columbia DB 8615* 4	7	9
6 Dec 69	WITH THE EYES OF A CHILD *Columbia DB 8641*	20	11
21 Feb 70	THE JOY OF LIVING *Columbia DB 8657* 4	25	8
6 Jun 70	● GOODBYE SAM, HELLO SAMANTHA *Columbia DB 8685*	6	15
5 Sep 70	I AIN'T GOT TIME ANYMORE *Columbia DB 8708*	21	7
23 Jan 71	SUNNY HONEY GIRL *Columbia DB 8747*	19	6
10 Apr 71	SILVERY RAIN *Columbia DB 8774*	27	6
17 Jul 71	FLYING MACHINE *Columbia DB 8797*	37	7
13 Nov 71	SING A SONG OF FREEDOM *Columbia DB 8836*	13	12
11 Mar 72	JESUS *Columbia DB 8864*	35	3
26 Aug 72	LIVING IN HARMONY *Columbia DB 8917*	12	10
17 Mar 73	● POWER TO ALL OUR FRIENDS *EMI 2012*	4	12
12 May 73	HELP IT ALONG / TOMORROW RISING *EMI 2022*	29	6
1 Dec 73	TAKE ME HIGH *EMI 2088*	27	12
18 May 74	(YOU KEEP ME) HANGIN' ON *EMI 2150*	13	8
7 Feb 76	MISS YOU NIGHTS *EMI 2376*	15	10
8 May 76	● DEVIL WOMAN *EMI 2458*	9	8
21 Aug 76	I CAN'T ASK FOR ANYTHING MORE THAN YOU *EMI 2499*	17	8
4 Dec 76	HEY MR DREAM MAKER *EMI 2559*	31	5
5 Mar 77	MY KINDA LIFE *EMI 2584*	15	8
16 Jul 77	WHEN TWO WORLDS DRIFT APART *EMI 2633*	46	3
31 Mar 79	GREEN LIGHT *EMI 2920*	57	3
21 Jul 79	★ WE DON'T TALK ANYMORE *EMI 2975*	1	14
3 Nov 79	HOT SHOT *EMI 5003*	46	5
2 Feb 80	● CARRIE *EMI 5006*	4	10
16 Aug 80	● DREAMIN' *EMI 5095*	8	10
25 Oct 80	SUDDENLY *Jet 7002* 5	15	7
24 Jan 81	A LITTLE IN LOVE *EMI 5123*	15	8
29 Aug 81	● WIRED FOR SOUND *EMI 5221*	4	9
21 Nov 81	● DADDY'S HOME *EMI 5251*	2	12
17 Jul 82	● THE ONLY WAY OUT *EMI 5318*	10	8
25 Sep 82	WHERE DO WE GO FROM HERE *EMI 5341*	60	3
4 Dec 82	LITTLE TOWN *EMI 5348*	11	7
19 Feb 83	● SHE MEANS NOTHING TO ME *Capitol CL 276* 6	9	9
16 Apr 83	● TRUE LOVE WAYS *EMI 5385* 7	8	8
4 Jun 83	DRIFTING *DJM SHEIL 1* 8	64	2
3 Sep 83	NEVER SAY DIE (GIVE A LITTLE BIT MORE) *EMI 5415*	15	7
26 Nov 83	● PLEASE DON'T FALL IN LOVE *EMI 5437*	7	9
31 Mar 84	OCEAN DEEP (re) / BABY YOU'RE DYNAMITE (re) *EMI 5457*	27	7
3 Nov 84	SHOOTING FROM THE HEART *EMI RICH 1*	51	4

9 Feb 85	HEART USER *EMI RICH 2*	46	3
14 Sep 85	SHE'S SO BEAUTIFUL *EMI 5531*	17	9
7 Dec 85	IT'S IN EVERY ONE OF US *EMI 5537*	45	6
22 Mar 86 ★	LIVING DOLL *WEA YZ 65* [9]	1	11
4 Oct 86 ●	ALL I ASK OF YOU *Polydor POSP 802* [10]	3	16
29 Nov 86	SLOW RIVERS *Rocket EJS 13* [11]	44	8
20 Jun 87 ●	MY PRETTY ONE *EMI EM 4*	6	10
29 Aug 87 ●	SOME PEOPLE *EMI EM 18*	3	10
31 Oct 87	REMEMBER ME *EMI EM 31*	35	4
13 Feb 88	TWO HEARTS *EMI EM 42*	34	3
3 Dec 88 ★	MISTLETOE AND WINE *EMI EM 78*	1	8
10 Jun 89 ●	THE BEST OF ME *EMI EM 92*	2	7
26 Aug 89 ●	I JUST DON'T HAVE THE HEART *EMI EM 101*	3	8
14 Oct 89	LEAN ON YOU *EMI EM 105*	17	6
9 Dec 89	WHENEVER GOD SHINES HIS LIGHT *Polydor VANS 2* [12]	20	6
24 Feb 90	STRONGER THAN THAT *EMI EM 129*	14	5
25 Aug 90 ●	SILHOUETTES *EMI EM 152*	10	7
13 Oct 90	FROM A DISTANCE *EMI EM 155*	11	6
8 Dec 90 ★	SAVIOUR'S DAY *EMI XMAS 90*	1	7
14 Sep 91	MORE TO LIFE *EMI EM 205*	23	5
7 Dec 91	WE SHOULD BE TOGETHER *EMI XMAS 91*	10	4
11 Jan 92	THIS NEW YEAR *EMI EMS 218*	30	2
5 Dec 92 ●	I STILL BELIEVE IN YOU *EMI EM 255*	7	6
27 Mar 93 ●	PEACE IN OUR TIME *EMI EM 265*	8	5
12 Jun 93	HUMAN WORK OF ART *EMI CDEM 267*	24	4
2 Oct 93	NEVER LET GO *EMI CDEM 281*	32	3
18 Dec 93	HEALING LOVE *EMI CDEM 294*	19	5
10 Dec 94	ALL I HAVE TO DO IS DREAM / MISS YOU NIGHTS (re) *EMI CDEM 359* [13]	14	9
2 Oct 95	MISUNDERSTOOD MAN *EMI CDEM 394*	19	3
9 Dec 95	HAD TO BE *EMI CDEM 410* [14]	22	4
30 Mar 96	THE WEDDING *EMI CDEM 422* [15]	40	1
25 Jan 97	BE WITH ME ALWAYS *EMI CDEM 453*	52	1
24 Oct 98 ●	CAN'T KEEP THIS FEELING IN *EMI CDEM 526*	10	4
7 Aug 99	THE MIRACLE *EMI / Blacknight CDEM 546*	23	2
27 Nov 99 ★	THE MILLENNIUM PRAYER *Papillon PROMISECD 01*	1	16
15 Dec 01	SOMEWHERE OVER THE RAINBOW / WHAT A WONDERFUL WORLD *Papillon CLIFF CD 1*	11	6
13 Apr 02	LET ME BE THE ONE *Papillon CLIFF CD2*	29	3

[1] Cliff Richard and The Drifters [2] Cliff Richard and The Shadows [3] Cliff Richard / The Shadows [4] Cliff and Hank [5] Olivia Newton-John and Cliff Richard [6] Phil Everly and Cliff Richard [7] Cliff Richard with the London Philharmonic Orchestra [8] Sheila Walsh and Cliff Richard [9] Cliff Richard and The Young Ones featuring Hank B Marvin [10] Cliff Richard and Sarah Brightman [11] Elton John and Cliff Richard [12] Van Morrison with Cliff Richard [13] Cliff Richard with Phil Everly / Cliff Richard [14] Cliff Richard and Olivia Newton-John [15] Cliff Richard featuring Helen Hobson

Tracks on Expresso Bongo (EP): Love / A Voice in the Wilderness / The Shrine on the Second Floor / Bongo Blues. 'Gee Whiz It's You' was an 'export' single. 'Bongo Blues' features only The Shadows. 'Bachelor Boy' was listed with 'The Next Time' from 10 Jan 1963. 'Ocean Deep' listed from 28 Apr 1984 onwards. It peaked at No.41

Wendy RICHARD – See Mike SARNE

Lionel RICHIE `106` `Top 500`

Singer / composer / producer, b. 20 Jun 1949, Alabama, US. Launched a solo career in 1982 after 12 years fronting The Commodores. Arguably the most successful US songwriter of the 1980s, who composed at least one US chart-topper per year for a record nine successive years (182 WEEKS) pos/wks

12 Sep 81 ●	ENDLESS LOVE *Motown TMG 1240* [1] ▲	7	12
20 Nov 82 ●	TRULY *Motown TMG 1284* ▲	6	11
29 Jan 83	YOU ARE *Motown TMG 1290*	43	7
9 May 83	MY LOVE *Motown TMG 1300*	70	3
1 Oct 83 ●	ALL NIGHT LONG (ALL NIGHT) *Motown TMG 1319* ▲	2	16
3 Dec 83 ●	RUNNING WITH THE NIGHT *Motown TMG 1324*	9	12
10 Mar 84 ★	HELLO *Motown TMG 1330* ▲	1	15
23 Jun 84	STUCK ON YOU *Motown TMG 1341*	12	10
20 Oct 84	PENNY LOVER *Motown TMG 1356*	18	7
16 Nov 85 ●	SAY YOU, SAY ME *Motown ZB 40421* ▲	8	11
26 Jul 86 ●	DANCING ON THE CEILING *Motown LIO1*	7	11
11 Oct 86	LOVE WILL CONQUER ALL *Motown LIO 2*	45	5
20 Dec 86	BALLERINA GIRL / DEEP RIVER WOMAN *Motown LIO3*	17	8
28 Mar 87	SELA *Motown LIO4*	43	6

9 May 92	DO IT TO ME *Motown TMG 1407*	33	6
22 Aug 92 ●	MY DESTINY *Motown TMG 1408*	7	13
28 Nov 92	LOVE OH LOVE (re) *Motown TMG 1413*	52	4
6 Apr 96	DON'T WANNA LOSE YOU *Mercury MERCD 461*	17	5
23 Nov 96	STILL IN LOVE *Mercury MERCD 477*	66	1
27 Jun 98	CLOSEST THING TO HEAVEN *Mercury 5661312*	26	2
21 Oct 00	ANGEL *Mercury 5726702*	18	5
23 Dec 00	DON'T STOP THE MUSIC *Mercury 5688992*	34	5
17 Mar 01	TENDER HEART *Mercury 5728462*	29	3
23 Jun 01	I FORGOT *Mercury 5729922*	34	2

[1] Diana Ross and Lionel Richie

'Deep River Woman' was listed only from 17 Jan 1987. It has the following credit: background vocal 'Alabama'

Jonathan RICHMAN and the MODERN LOVERS

US, male vocal / instrumental group (27 WEEKS) pos/wks

16 Jul 77	ROADRUNNER *Beserkley BZZ 1*	11	9
29 Oct 77 ●	EGYPTIAN REGGAE *Beserkley BZZ 2*	5	14
21 Jan 78	THE MORNING OF OUR LIVES *Beserkley BZZ 7* [1]	29	4

[1] Modern Lovers

Adam RICKITT *UK, male actor / vocalist (19 WEEKS)* pos/wks

26 Jun 99 ●	I BREATHE AGAIN *Polydor 5611862*	5	10
16 Oct 99	EVERYTHING MY HEART DESIRES *Polydor 5614392*	15	6
5 Feb 00	BEST THING *Polydor 5616132*	25	3

RICO – See SPECIALS

RIDE *UK, male vocal / instrumental group (22 WEEKS)* pos/wks

27 Jan 90	RIDE (EP) *Creation CRE 072T*	71	2
14 Apr 90	PLAY (EP) *Creation CRE 075T*	32	3
29 Sep 90	FALL (EP) *Creation CRE 087T*	34	3
16 Mar 91	TODAY FOREVER (EP) *Creation CRE 100T*	14	4
15 Feb 92 ●	LEAVE THEM ALL BEHIND *Creation CRE 123T*	9	3
25 Apr 92	TWISTERELLA *Creation CRE 150T*	36	2
30 Apr 94	BIRDMAN *Creation CRESCD 155*	38	2
25 Jun 94	HOW DOES IT FEEL TO FEEL *Creation CRESCD 184*	58	1
8 Oct 94	I DON'T KNOW WHERE IT COMES FROM *Creation CRESCD 189R*	46	1
24 Feb 96	BLACK NITE CRASH *Creation CRESCD 199*	67	1

Tracks on Ride (EP): Chelsea Girl / Drive Blind / All I Can See / Close My Eyes. Tracks on Play (EP): Like a Daydream / Silver / Furthest Sense / Perfect Time. Tracks on Fall (EP): Dreams Burn Down / Taste / Hear and Now / Nowhere. Tracks on Today Forever (EP): Unfamiliar / Sennen / Beneath / Today

RIDER & Terry VENABLES *UK, male vocal / instrumental group and soccer-styled vocalist (2 WEEKS)* pos/wks

1 Jun 02	ENGLAND CRAZY *East West EW 248CD*	46	2

Andrew RIDGELEY *UK, male vocalist (3 WEEKS)* pos/wks

31 Mar 90	SHAKE *Epic AJR 1*	58	3

See also WHAM!

Stan RIDGWAY *US, male vocalist (12 WEEKS)* pos/wks

5 Jul 86 ●	CAMOUFLAGE *IRS IRM 114*	4	12

RIGHEIRA *Italy, male vocal duo (3 WEEKS)* pos/wks

24 Sep 83	VAMOS A LA PLAYA *A&M AM 137*	53	3

RIGHT SAID FRED *UK, male vocal / instrumental group – lead vocal Richard Fairbrass (66 WEEKS)* pos/wks

27 Jul 91	I'M TOO SEXY *Tug SNOG 1* ▲	2	16
7 Dec 91	DON'T TALK JUST KISS *Tug SNOG 2* [1]	3	11
21 Mar 92 ★	DEEPLY DIPPY *Tug SNOG 3*	1	14
1 Aug 92	THOSE SIMPLE THINGS / DAYDREAM *Tug SNOG 4*	29	5
27 Feb 93 ●	STICK IT OUT *Tug CDCOMIC 1* [2]	4	7
23 Oct 93	BUMPED *Tug CDSNOG 7*	32	4

18 Dec 93	HANDS UP (4 LOVERS) *Tug CDSNOG 8*	60	3
19 Mar 94	WONDERMAN *Tug CDSNOG 9*	55	1
13 Oct 01	YOU'RE MY MATE *Kingsize 74321895632*	18	5

1 Right Said Fred. Guest vocals: Jocelyn Brown 2 Right Said Fred and Friends

RIGHTEOUS BROTHERS (389 Top 500)
Pioneering, influential blue-eyed soul duo, Bill Medley b. 19 Sep 1940, California, US, and Bobby Hatfield b. 10 Aug 1940, Wisconsin, US. 'You've Lost That Lovin' Feelin', has an unsurpassed eight million US radio plays and reached the UK Top 10 three times. (86 WEEKS) pos/wks

14 Jan 65	★ YOU'VE LOST THAT LOVIN' FEELIN' *London HLU 9943* ▲	1	10
12 Aug 65	UNCHAINED MELODY *London HL 9975*	14	12
13 Jan 66	EBB TIDE *London HL 10011*	48	2
14 Apr 66	(YOU'RE MY) SOUL AND INSPIRATION *Verve VS 535* ▲	15	10
10 Nov 66	THE WHITE CLIFFS OF DOVER *London HL 10086*	21	9
22 Dec 66	ISLAND IN THE SUN *Verve VS 547*	24	5
12 Feb 69	● YOU'VE LOST THAT LOVIN' FEELIN' (re-issue) *London HL 10241*	10	11
19 Nov 77	YOU'VE LOST THAT LOVIN' FEELIN' (2nd re-issue) *Phil Spector International 2010 022*	42	4
27 Oct 90	★ UNCHAINED MELODY (re-issue) *Verve / Polydor PO 101*	1	14
15 Dec 90	● YOU'VE LOST THAT LOVIN' FEELIN' / EBB TIDE (3rd re-issue) *Verve / Polydor PO 116*	3	9

RIKKI and DAZ featuring Glen CAMPBELL *UK, male production duo – John Matthews and Darren Sampson and US, male vocalist (5 WKS)* pos/wks

30 Nov 02	RHINESTONE COWBOY (GIDDY UP GIDDY UP) *Serious SER 059CD*	12	5+

Cheryl Pepsii RILEY *US, female vocalist (1 WEEK)* pos/wks

28 Jan 89	THANKS FOR MY CHILD *CBS 653153 7*	75	1

Jeannie C RILEY
US, female vocalist – Jeanne C Stephenson (15 WEEKS) pos/wks

16 Oct 68	HARPER VALLEY P.T.A. *Polydor 56748* ▲	12	15

Teddy RILEY *US, male producer (5 WEEKS)* pos/wks

21 Mar 92	IS IT GOOD TO YOU *MCA MCS 1611* 1	53	2
19 Jun 93	BABY BE MINE *MCA MCSTD 1772* 2	37	3

1 Teddy Riley featuring Tammy Lucas 2 BLACKstreet featuring Teddy Riley

RIMES featuring Shaila PROSPERE
UK, male rapper – Julian Johnson (1 WEEK) pos/wks

22 May 99	IT'S OVER *Universal MCSTD 40199*	51	1

LeAnn RIMES (365 Top 500)
Teenage queen of country music, b. 28 Aug 1982, Mississippi. She first recorded at age 11; three years later she became both the youngest act to enter US album chart at No.1 and Best New Artist Grammy winner. At 15, 'How Do I Live' broke several longevity records on the US chart. Best-selling single: 'How Do I Live' 713,900 (89 WEEKS) pos/wks

7 Mar 98	● HOW DO I LIVE (re) *Curb CUBCX 30*	7	34
12 Sep 98	LOOKING THROUGH YOUR EYES / COMMITMENT *Curb CUBC 32*	38	2
12 Dec 98	BLUE *Curb CUBC 39*	23	6
6 Mar 99	● WRITTEN IN THE STARS (re) *Mercury EJSCD 45* 1	10	8
18 Dec 99	CRAZY *Curb CUBC 52*	36	3
25 Nov 00	★ CAN'T FIGHT THE MOONLIGHT *Curb CUBC 58* ■	1	17
31 Mar 01	I NEED YOU (re) *Curb CUBC 60*	13	7
23 Feb 02	BUT I DO LOVE YOU *London / Curb CUBC 075*	20	4
12 Oct 02	LIFE GOES ON *Curb CUBC 085*	11	8

1 Elton John and LeAnn Rimes

RIMSHOTS
US, male / female instrumental / vocal group (5 WEEKS) pos/wks

19 Jul 75	7-6-5-4-3-2-1 (BLOW YOUR WHISTLE) *All Platinum 6146 304*	26	5

RIO and MARS
France / UK, male / female vocal / instrumental duo (3 WEEKS) pos/wks

28 Jan 95	BOY I GOTTA HAVE YOU *Dome CDDOME 1014*	43	2
13 Apr 96	BOY I GOTTA HAVE YOU (re-issue) *Feverpitch CDFVR 1007*	46	1

Miguel RIOS *Spain, male vocalist (12 WEEKS)* pos/wks

11 Jul 70	SONG OF JOY *A&M AMS 790*	16	12

Waldo de los RIOS
Argentina, orchestra, leader – Osvaldo Ferraro Guiterrez (16 WEEKS) pos/wks

10 Apr 71	● MOZART SYMPHONY NO.40 IN G MINOR K550 1ST MOVEMENT (ALLEGRO MOLTO) *A&M AMS 836*	5	16

Minnie RIPERTON *US, female vocalist, d. 12 Jul 1979 (10 WEEKS)* pos/wks

12 Apr 75	● LOVIN' YOU *Epic EPC 3121* ▲	2	10

RISE *UK, male production duo – Paul Oakenfold and Steve Osborne (1 WEEK)* pos/wks

3 Sep 94	THE SINGLE *East West YZ 839CD*	70	1

RITCHIE FAMILY *US, female vocal group (19 WEEKS)* pos/wks

23 Aug 75	BRAZIL *Polydor 2058 625*	41	4
18 Sep 76	● THE BEST DISCO IN TOWN *Polydor 2058 777*	10	9
17 Feb 79	AMERICAN GENERATION *Mercury 6007 199*	49	6

Lee RITENOUR and Maxi PRIEST
US, male instrumentalist – guitar and UK, male vocalist (2 WEEKS) pos/wks

31 Jul 93	WAITING IN VAIN *GRP MCSTD 1921* 1	65	2

1 Lee Ritenour and Maxi Priest

Tex RITTER *US, male vocalist, 3 Jan 1974 (14 WEEKS)* pos/wks

22 Jun 56	● THE WAYWARD WIND *Capitol CL 14581*	8	14

RIVA featuring Dannii MINOGUE *Holland, male production duo – Rene ter Horst and Gaston Steenkist, and Australia, female vocalist (15 WEEKS)* pos/wks

1 Dec 01	● WHO DO YOU LOVE NOW (STRINGER) *ffrr DFCD 002*	3	15

See also JARK PRONGO; GOODMEN; RHYTHMKILLAZ; TOMBA VIRA; CHOCOLATE PUMA

RIVAL SCHOOLS *US, male vocal / instrumental group (2 WEEKS)* pos/wks

30 Mar 02	USED FOR GLUE *Mercury 5889652*	42	1
20 Jul 02	GOOD THINGS *Mercury 5829662*	74	1

Paco RIVAZ – See GAMBAFREAKS

RIVER CITY PEOPLE
UK, male / female vocal / instrumental group (27 WEEKS) pos/wks

12 Aug 89	(WHAT'S WRONG WITH) DREAMING? *EMI EM 95*	70	3
3 Mar 90	WALKING ON ICE *EMI EM 130*	62	2
30 Jun 90	CARRY THE BLAME / CALIFORNIA DREAMIN' *EMI EM 145*	13	10
22 Sep 90	(WHAT'S WRONG WITH) DREAMING? (re-issue) *EMI EM 156*	40	3
2 Mar 91	WHEN I WAS YOUNG *EMI EM 176*	62	2
28 Sep 91	SPECIAL WAY *EMI EM 207*	44	3
22 Feb 92	STANDING IN THE NEED OF LOVE *EMI EM 216*	36	4

RIVER DETECTIVES
UK, male vocal / instrumental duo (4 WEEKS) pos/wks

29 Jul 89	CHAINS *WEA YZ 383*	51	4

RIVER OCEAN featuring INDIA
US, male producer – Louie Vega – and female vocalist (2 WEEKS) pos/wks

26 Feb 94	LOVE AND HAPPINESS (YEMAYA Y OCHUN) *Cooltempo CDCOOL 287*	50	2

See also INDIA; Louie VEGA

Robbie RIVERA *Puerto Rico, male producer (8 WEEKS)*

			pos/wks
2 Sep 00	**BANG** *Multiply CDMULTY 64* [1]	**13**	7
12 Oct 02	**SEX** *352 Recordings 352CD 001* [2]	**55**	1

[1] Robbie Rivera presents Rhythm Bangers [2] Robbie Rivera featuring Billy Paul W

Danny RIVERS *UK, male vocalist (3 WEEKS)*

			pos/wks
12 Jan 61	**CAN'T YOU HEAR MY HEART** *Decca F 11294*	**36**	3

ROACH MOTEL
UK, male instrumental / production group (2 WEEKS)

			pos/wks
21 Aug 93	**AFRO SLEEZE / TRANSATLANTIC** *Junior Boy's Own JBO 1412*	**73**	1
10 Dec 94	**HAPPY BIZZNESS / WILD LUV** *Junior Boy's Own JBO 24*	**75**	1

ROACHFORD *UK, male / female vocal / instrumental*
group – leader Andrew Roachford (61 WEEKS)

			pos/wks
18 Jun 88	**CUDDLY TOY** *CBS ROA 2*	**61**	4
14 Jan 89 ●	**CUDDLY TOY (re-issue)** *CBS ROA 4*	**4**	9
18 Mar 89	**FAMILY MAN** *CBS ROA 5*	**25**	6
1 Jul 89	**KATHLEEN** *CBS ROA 6*	**43**	5
13 Apr 91	**GET READY!** *Columbia 6567057*	**22**	8
19 Mar 94	**ONLY TO BE WITH YOU** *Columbia 6601562*	**21**	7
18 Jun 94	**LAY YOUR LOVE ON ME** *Columbia 6603722*	**36**	5
20 Aug 94	**THIS GENERATION** *Columbia 6607452*	**38**	4
3 Dec 94	**CRY FOR ME** *Columbia 6610742*	**46**	2
1 Apr 95	**I KNOW YOU DON'T LOVE ME** *Columbia 6612525*	**42**	2
11 Oct 97	**THE WAY I FEEL** *Columbia 6651042*	**20**	4
14 Feb 98	**HOW COULD I? (INSECURITY)** *Columbia 6653462*	**34**	3
11 Jul 98	**NAKED WITHOUT YOU** *Columbia 6659362*	**53**	2

ROB 'N' RAZ featuring Leila K
Sweden, male production duo and female rapper (17 WEEKS)

			pos/wks
25 Nov 89 ●	**GOT TO GET** *Arista 112696*	**8**	14
17 Mar 90	**ROK THE NATION** *Arista 112971*	**41**	3

Kate ROBBINS and BEYOND
UK, female / male vocal / instrumental group (10 WEEKS)

			pos/wks
30 May 81 ●	**MORE THAN IN LOVE** *RCA 69*	**2**	10

Marty ROBBINS
US, male vocalist – Marty Robinson, d. 8 Dec 1982 (33 WEEKS)

			pos/wks
29 Jan 60 ●	**EL PASO (re)** *Fontana H 233* ▲	**19**	9
26 May 60	**BIG IRON** *Fontana H 229*	**48**	1
27 Sep 62 ●	**DEVIL WOMAN** *CBS AAG 114*	**5**	17
17 Jan 63	**RUBY ANN** *CBS AAG 128*	**24**	6

Antoinette ROBERSON – See PULSE featuring Antoinette ROBERSON

Austin ROBERTS *US, male vocalist (7 WEEKS)*

			pos/wks
25 Oct 75	**ROCKY** *Private Stock PVT 33*	**22**	7

Joe ROBERTS *UK, male vocalist (17 WEEKS)*

			pos/wks
28 Aug 93	**BACK IN MY LIFE** *ffrr FCD 215*	**59**	1
29 Jan 94	**LOVER** *ffrr FCD 220*	**22**	5
14 May 94	**BACK IN MY LIFE (re-issue)** *ffrr FCD 230*	**39**	3
6 Aug 94	**ADORE** *ffrr FCD 240*	**45**	3
18 Feb 95	**YOU ARE EVERYTHING** *Columbia 6611755* [1]	**28**	4
24 Feb 96	**HAPPY DAYS** *Grass Green GRASS 10CD* [2]	**63**	1

[1] Melanie Williams and Joe Roberts [2] Sweet Mercy featuring Joe Roberts

Juliet ROBERTS *UK, female vocalist (34 WEEKS)*

			pos/wks
31 Jul 93	**CAUGHT IN THE MIDDLE** *Cooltempo CDCOOL 272*	**24**	6
6 Nov 93	**FREE LOVE** *Cooltempo CDCOOL 281*	**25**	3
19 Mar 94	**AGAIN / I WANT YOU** *Cooltempo CDCOOL 285*	**33**	3
2 Jul 94	**CAUGHT IN THE MIDDLE (re-mix)** *Cooltempo CDCOOL 291*	**14**	5
15 Oct 94	**I WANT YOU (re-issue)** *Cooltempo CDCOOL 297*	**28**	3
31 Jan 98	**SO GOOD / FREE LOVE 98 (re-mix)** *Delirious 74321554002*	**15**	4

			pos/wks
23 Jan 99	**BAD GIRLS / I LIKE** *Delirious DELICD 11*	**17**	5
20 Jan 01	**NEEDIN' YOU II** *Manifesto FESCD 78* [1]	**11**	5

[1] David Morales presents The Face featuring Juliet Roberts

Malcolm ROBERTS
UK, male vocalist d. 7 Feb 2003 (29 WEEKS)

			pos/wks
11 May 67	**TIME ALONE WILL TELL** *RCA 1578*	**45**	2
30 Oct 68 ●	**MAY I HAVE THE NEXT DREAM WITH YOU (re)** *Major Minor MM 581*	**8**	15
22 Nov 69	**LOVE IS ALL** *Major Minor MM 637*	**12**	12

B A ROBERTSON *UK, male vocalist (60 WEEKS)*

			pos/wks
28 Jul 79 ●	**BANG BANG** *Asylum K 13152*	**2**	12
27 Oct 79 ●	**KNOCKED IT OFF** *Asylum K 12396*	**8**	12
1 Mar 80	**KOOL IN THE KAFTAN** *Asylum K 12427*	**17**	12
31 May 80 ●	**TO BE OR NOT TO BE** *Asylum K 12449*	**9**	11
17 Oct 81	**HOLD ME** *Swansong BAM 1* [1]	**11**	8
17 Dec 83	**TIME** *Epic A 3983* [2]	**45**	5

[1] B A Robertson and Maggie Bell [2] Frida and B A Robertson

Don ROBERTSON
US, male instrumentalist – piano and whistle (9 WEEKS)

			pos/wks
11 May 56 ●	**THE HAPPY WHISTLER** *Capitol CL 14575*	**8**	9

Robbie ROBERTSON
Canada, male vocalist / instrumentalist (11 WEEKS)

			pos/wks
23 Jul 88	**SOMEWHERE DOWN THE CRAZY RIVER** *Geffen GEF 40*	**15**	10
11 Apr 98	**TAKE YOUR PARTNER BY THE HAND** *Polydor 5693272* [1]	**74**	1

[1] Howie B featuring Robbie Robertson

Ivo ROBIC *Croatia, male vocalist (1 WEEK)*

			pos/wks
6 Nov 59	**MORGEN** *Polydor 23923*	**23**	1

Dawn ROBINSON – See FIRM

Floyd ROBINSON *US, male vocalist (9 WEEKS)*

			pos/wks
16 Oct 59 ●	**MAKIN' LOVE** *RCA 1146*	**9**	9

Smokey ROBINSON *US, male vocalist (45 WEEKS)*

			pos/wks
23 Feb 74	**JUST MY SOUL RESPONDING** *Tamla Motown TMG 883*	**35**	6
24 Feb 79	**POPS, WE LOVE YOU** *Motown TMG 1136* [1]	**66**	5
9 May 81 ★	**BEING WITH YOU** *Motown TMG 1223*	**1**	13
13 Mar 82	**TELL ME TOMORROW** *Motown TMG 1255*	**51**	4
28 Mar 87	**JUST TO SEE HER** *Motown ZB 41147*	**52**	6
17 Sep 88	**INDESTRUCTIBLE** *Arista 111717* [2]	**55**	4
25 Feb 89	**INDESTRUCTIBLE** *Arista 112074* [2]	**30**	7

[1] Diana Ross, Marvin Gaye, Smokey Robinson and Stevie Wonder [2] Four Tops featuring Smokey Robinson

The original US recording of 'Indestructible' was not issued until after the chart run of the UK-only mix

See also Smokey ROBINSON and the MIRACLES; MIRACLES

Smokey ROBINSON and The MIRACLES
US, male vocal group (64 WEEKS)

			pos/wks
27 Dec 67	**I SECOND THAT EMOTION** *Tamla Motown TMG 631*	**27**	11
3 Apr 68	**IF YOU CAN WANT** *Tamla Motown TMG 648*	**50**	1
7 May 69 ●	**TRACKS OF MY TEARS** *Tamla Motown TMG 696*	**9**	13
1 Aug 70 ★	**THE TEARS OF A CLOWN** *Tamla Motown TMG 745* ▲	**1**	14
30 Jan 71	**(COME 'ROUND HERE) I'M THE ONE YOU NEED (re-issue)** *Tamla Motown TMG 761*	**13**	9
5 Jun 71	**I DON'T BLAME YOU AT ALL** *Tamla Motown TMG 774*	**11**	10
2 Oct 76	**THE TEARS OF A CLOWN (re-issue)** *Tamla Motown TMG 1048*	**34**	6

1976 re-issue of 'The Tears of a Clown' was a double A-side with 'Tracks of My Tears'

See also MIRACLES; Smokey ROBINSON

UK No.1 ★   UK Top 10 ●   Still on chart +   UK million seller ◆   UK entry at No.1 ■   US No.1 ▲

Tom ROBINSON
UK, male vocalist / instrumentalist (41 WEEKS)   pos/wks

22 Oct 77	● 2-4-6-8 MOTORWAY *EMI 2715* [1]	5	9
18 Feb 78	RISING FREE (EP) *EMI 2749* [1]	18	6
13 May 78	UP AGAINST THE WALL *EMI 2787* [1]	33	6
17 Mar 79	BULLY FOR YOU *EMI 2916* [1]	68	2
25 Jun 83	● WAR BABY *Panic NIC 2*	6	9
12 Nov 83	LISTEN TO THE RADIO: ATMOSPHERICS *Panic NIC 3*.........	39	6
15 Sep 84	RIKKI DON'T LOSE THAT NUMBER *Castaway TR 2*..........	58	3

[1] Tom Robinson Band

Tracks on Rising Free (EP): Don't Take No for an Answer / Sing If You're Glad to Be Gay / Martin / Right on Sister

Vicki Sue ROBINSON
US, female vocalist, d. 27 Apr 2000 (1 WEEK)   pos/wks

27 Sep 97	HOUSE OF JOY *Logic 74321511492*	48	1

ROBO BABE – *See SIR KILLALOT vs ROBO BABE*

ROBSON and JEROME *UK, male actors / vocal*
duo – Robson Green and Jerome Flynn (45 WEEKS)   pos/wks

20 May 95	★ UNCHAINED MELODY / (THERE'LL BE BLUEBIRDS OVER) THE WHITE CLIFFS OF DOVER (re) *RCA 74321284362* [1] ◆ ■	1	17
11 Nov 95	★ I BELIEVE / UP ON THE ROOF *RCA 74321326882* ◆ ■	1	14
9 Nov 96	★ WHAT BECOMES OF THE BROKENHEARTED / SATURDAY NIGHT AT THE MOVIES / YOU'LL NEVER WALK AGAIN *RCA 74321424732* ■	1	14

[1] Robson Green and Jerome Flynn

ROBYN *Sweden, female vocalist – Robyn Carlsson (14 WEEKS)*   pos/wks

20 Jul 96	YOU'VE GOT THAT SOMETHIN' *RCA 74321393462*..............	54	1
16 Aug 97	DO YOU KNOW (WHAT IT TAKES) *RCA 74321509932*...........	26	3
7 Mar 98	● SHOW ME LOVE *RCA 74321555032*	8	6
30 May 98	DO YOU REALLY WANT ME *RCA 74321582982*................	20	4

John ROCCA – *See FREEEZ*

ROCHELLE *US, female vocalist (6 WEEKS)*   pos/wks

1 Feb 86	MY MAGIC MAN *Warner Bros. W 8838*	27	6

ROCK – *See Wyclef JEAN*

Chubb ROCK *US, male rapper (1 WEEK)*   pos/wks

19 Jan 91	TREAT 'EM RIGHT *Champion CHAMP 272*	67	1

Sir Monti ROCK III – *See DISCO TEX and the SEX-O-LETTES*

ROCK AID ARMENIA
UK, male vocal / instrumental charity ensemble (5 WEEKS)   pos/wks

16 Dec 89	SMOKE ON THE WATER *Life Aid Armenia ARMEN 001*	39	5

ROCK CANDY
UK, male vocal / instrumental group (6 WEEKS)   pos/wks

11 Sep 71	REMEMBER *MCA MK 5069*	32	6

ROCK GODDESS
UK, female vocal / instrumental group (5 WEEKS)   pos/wks

5 Mar 83	MY ANGEL *A&M AMS 8311*...............................	64	2
24 Mar 84	I DIDN'T KNOW I LOVED YOU (TILL I SAW YOU ROCK 'N' ROLL) *A&M AMS 185*	57	3

ROCKER'S REVENGE featuring Donnie CALVIN
US, male / female vocal / instrumental group (20 WEEKS)   pos/wks

14 Aug 82	● WALKING ON SUNSHINE *London LON 11*	4	13
29 Jan 83	THE HARDER THEY COME *London LON 18*	30	7

ROCKET FROM THE CRYPT
US, male vocal / instrumental group (7 WEEKS)   pos/wks

27 Jan 96	BORN IN 69 *Elemental ELM 32CD*	68	1
13 Apr 96	YOUNG LIVERS *Elemental ELM 33CDS*....................	67	1
14 Sep 96	ON A ROPE *Elemental ELM 38CDS1*	12	4
29 Aug 98	LIPSTICK *Elemental ELM 48CDS1*.......................	64	1

ROCKETS – *See Tony CROMBIE and his ROCKETS*

ROCKFORD FILES
UK, male instrumental / production duo (4 WEEKS)   pos/wks

11 Mar 95	YOU SEXY DANCER *Escapade CDJAPE 7*	34	3
6 Apr 96	YOU SEXY DANCER (re-issue) *Escapade CDJAPE 14*	59	1

ROCKIN' BERRIES
UK, male vocal / instrumental group (41 WEEKS)   pos/wks

1 Oct 64	I DIDN'T MEAN TO HURT YOU *Piccadilly 7N 35197*	43	1
15 Oct 64	● HE'S IN TOWN *Piccadilly 7N 35203*	3	13
21 Jan 65	WHAT IN THE WORLD'S COME OVER YOU *Piccadilly 7N 35217*	23	7
13 May 65	● POOR MAN'S SON *Piccadilly 7N 35236*	5	11
26 Aug 65	YOU'RE MY GIRL *Piccadilly 7N 35254*	40	7
6 Jan 66	THE WATER IS OVER MY HEAD (re) *Piccadilly 7N 35270*	43	2

ROCKNEY – *See CHAS and DAVE*

ROCKSTEADY CREW *US, male / female vocal group (16 WEEKS)* pos/wks

1 Oct 83	● (HEY YOU) THE ROCKSTEADY CREW *Charisma / Virgin RSC 1* ..6	12
5 May 84	UPROCK *Charisma / Virgin RSC 2*......................	64	4

ROCKWELL *US, male vocalist – Kennedy Gordy (11 WEEKS)*   pos/wks

4 Feb 84	● SOMEBODY'S WATCHING ME *Motown TMG 1331*	6	11

'Somebody's Watching Me' features uncredited vocal by Michael Jackson

ROCKY V – *See Joey B ELLIS*

ROCOCO
UK / Italy, male / female vocal / instrumental group (5 WEEKS)   pos/wks

16 Dec 89	ITALO HOUSE MIX *Mercury MER 314*	54	5

RODEO JONES
UK / Grenada, male / female vocal / instrumental group (2 WEEKS) pos/wks

30 Jan 93	NATURAL WORLD *A&M AMCD 0165*........................	75	1
3 Apr 93	SHADES OF SUMMER *A&M AMCD 212*......................	59	1

Clodagh RODGERS *Ireland, female vocalist (59 WEEKS)*   pos/wks

26 Mar 69	● COME BACK AND SHAKE ME *RCA 1792*	3	14
9 Jul 69	● GOODNIGHT MIDNIGHT (re) *RCA 1852*	4	12
8 Nov 69	BILJO *RCA 1891*	22	9
4 Apr 70	EVERYBODY GO HOME THE PARTY'S OVER *RCA 1930*	47	2
20 Mar 71	● JACK IN THE BOX *RCA 2066*	4	10
9 Oct 71	LADY LOVE BUG *RCA 2117*..............................	28	12

Jimmie RODGERS *US, male vocalist (37 WEEKS)*   pos/wks

1 Nov 57	HONEYCOMB *Columbia DB 3986* ▲	30	1
20 Dec 57	● KISSES SWEETER THAN WINE *Columbia DB 4052*.........	7	11
28 Mar 58	OH-OH, I'M FALLING IN LOVE AGAIN *Columbia DB 4078*	18	6
19 Dec 58	WOMAN FROM LIBERIA *Columbia DB 4206*.................	18	6
14 Jun 62	● ENGLISH COUNTRY GARDEN *Columbia DB 4847*	5	13

Paul RODGERS *UK, male vocalist (2 WEEKS)*   pos/wks

12 Feb 94	MUDDY WATER BLUES *Victory ROGCD 1*	45	2

See also FREE; BAD COMPANY

RODRIGUEZ – *See SASH!*

RODS – *See EDDIE and the HOT RODS*

Re-entries are listed as (re), (2re), (3re), etc which signifies that the hit re-entered the chart once, twice or three times, etc

Tommy ROE `489` `Top 500`
One of the 1960s' most successful male solo pop singer / songwriters b. 9 May 1942, Georgia, US. Initially recorded Buddy Holly-influenced 'Sheila' with his group The Satins two years before solo version. Co-wrote twice-chart-topping song 'Dizzy' (74 WEEKS) pos/wks

6 Sep 62 ●	SHEILA *HMV POP 1060* ▲	3	14
6 Dec 62	SUSIE DARLIN' *HMV POP 1092*	37	5
21 Mar 63 ●	THE FOLK SINGER *HMV POP 1138*	4	13
26 Sep 63 ●	EVERYBODY (re) *HMV POP 1207*	9	14
16 Apr 69 ★	DIZZY *Stateside SS 2143* ▲	1	19
23 Jul 69	HEATHER HONEY *Stateside SS 2152*	24	9

ROFO
UK, male instrumental / production duo (3 WEEKS) pos/wks

1 Aug 92	ROFO'S THEME *PWL Continental PWLT 236*	44	3

ROGER
US, male vocalist – Roger Troutman, d. 24 Apr 1999 (8 WEEKS) pos/wks

17 Oct 87	I WANT TO BE YOUR MAN *Reprise W 8229*	61	4
12 Nov 88	BOOM! THERE SHE WAS *Virgin VS 1143*	55	3
13 May 95	HIGH AS A KITE *ffrr FCD 259* [1]	55	1

[1] One Tribe featuring Roger

Julie ROGERS UK, female vocalist – Julie Rolls (38 WEEKS) pos/wks

13 Aug 64 ●	THE WEDDING *Mercury MF 820* [1]	3	23
10 Dec 64	LIKE A CHILD *Mercury MF 838*	20	9
25 Mar 65	HAWAIIAN WEDDING SONG *Mercury MF 849*	31	6

[1] Julie Rogers with Johnny Arthey and his Orchestra and Chorus

Kenny ROGERS `273` `Top 500`
Celebrated crossover country vocalist / actor, who was one of the US's top-selling artists of the past 30 years, b. 21 Aug 1938, Houston. This Grammy-winning ex-New Christy Minstrel has collected more than 20 US gold albums and is a household name in many countries (109 WEEKS) pos/wks

18 Oct 69 ●	RUBY, DON'T TAKE YOUR LOVE TO TOWN *Reprise RS 20829* [1]	2	23
7 Feb 70 ●	SOMETHING'S BURNING *Reprise RS 20888* [1]	8	14
30 Apr 77 ★	LUCILLE *United Artists UP 36242*	1	14
17 Sep 77	DAYTIME FRIENDS *United Artists UP 36289*	39	4
2 Jun 79	SHE BELIEVES IN ME *United Artists UP 36533*	42	7
26 Jan 80 ★	COWARD OF THE COUNTY *United Artists UP 614*	1	12
15 Nov 80	LADY *United Artists UP 635* ▲	12	12
12 Feb 83	WE'VE GOT TONIGHT *Liberty UP 658* [2]	28	7
22 Oct 83	EYES THAT SEE IN THE DARK *RCA 358*	61	1
12 Nov 83 ●	ISLANDS IN THE STREAM *RCA 378* [3] ▲	7	15

[1] Kenny Rogers and the First Edition [2] Kenny Rogers and Sheena Easton
[3] Kenny Rogers and Dolly Parton

ROKOTTO UK, male vocal / instrumental group (10 WEEKS) pos/wks

22 Oct 77	BOOGIE ON UP *State STAT 62*	40	4
10 Jun 78	FUNK THEORY *State STAT 80*	49	6

ROLLERGIRL Germany, female vocalist – Nicci Juice (3 WEEKS) pos/wks

16 Sep 00	DEAR JESSIE *Neo NEOCD 038*	22	3

ROLLING STONES `17` `Top 500`
'World's No. 1 rock group': Mick Jagger (v), Keith Richard (g), Brian Jones (g, d. 1969), Bill Wyman (b) (left 1991), Charlie Watts (d) – Ron Wood (g) joined 1975. No group has accumulated more UK or US Top 10 albums (they have a record 30 US platinum and 9 US gold albums) or grossed more income from touring than this legendary British band which has broken box office records on every continent and is still the world's highest earning live band. Ever controversial group became early members of Rock and Roll Hall of Fame. Jagger and Richard, nicknamed The Glimmer Twins, were inducted into the Songwriters' Hall of Fame and the group received a Grammy Lifetime Achievement award (1986) (367 WEEKS) pos/wks

25 Jul 63	COME ON *Decca F 11675*	21	14
14 Nov 63	I WANNA BE YOUR MAN *Decca F 11764*	12	16
27 Feb 64 ●	NOT FADE AWAY *Decca F 11845*	3	15
2 Jul 64 ★	IT'S ALL OVER NOW *Decca F 11934*	1	15
19 Nov 64 ★	LITTLE RED ROOSTER *Decca F 12014*	1	12
4 Mar 65 ★	THE LAST TIME *Decca F 12104*	1	13
26 Aug 65 ★	(I CAN'T GET NO) SATISFACTION *Decca F 12220* ▲	1	12
28 Oct 65 ★	GET OFF OF MY CLOUD *Decca F 12263* ▲	1	12
10 Feb 66 ●	NINETEENTH NERVOUS BREAKDOWN *Decca F 12331*	2	8
19 May 66 ●	PAINT IT BLACK *Decca F 12395* ▲	1	10
29 Sep 66 ●	HAVE YOU SEEN YOUR MOTHER BABY STANDING IN THE SHADOW *Decca F 12497*	5	8
19 Jan 67 ●	LET'S SPEND THE NIGHT TOGETHER / RUBY TUESDAY *Decca F 12546* ▲	3	10
23 Aug 67 ●	WE LOVE YOU / DANDELION *Decca F 12654*	8	8
29 May 68 ★	JUMPIN' JACK FLASH *Decca F 12782*	1	11
9 Jul 69 ★	HONKY TONK WOMEN *Decca F 12952* ▲	1	17
24 Apr 71 ●	BROWN SUGAR / BITCH / LET IT ROCK *Rolling Stones RS 19100* ▲	2	13
3 Jul 71	STREET FIGHTING MAN *Decca F 13195*	21	8
29 Apr 72 ●	TUMBLING DICE *Rolling Stones RS 19103*	5	8
1 Sep 73 ●	ANGIE *Rolling Stones RS 19105* ▲	5	10
3 Aug 74 ●	IT'S ONLY ROCK AND ROLL *Rolling Stones RS 19114*	10	7
20 Sep 75	OUT OF TIME *Decca F 13597*	45	2
1 May 76 ●	FOOL TO CRY *Rolling Stones RS 19121*	6	10
3 Jun 78 ●	MISS YOU / FARAWAY EYES *Rolling Stones EMI 2802* ▲	3	13
30 Sep 78	RESPECTABLE *Rolling Stones EMI 2861*	23	9
5 Jul 80 ●	EMOTIONAL RESCUE *Rolling Stones RSR 105*	9	8
4 Oct 80	SHE'S SO COLD *Rolling Stones RSR 106*	33	6
29 Aug 81 ●	START ME UP *Rolling Stones RSR 108*	7	9
12 Dec 81	WAITING ON A FRIEND *Rolling Stones RSR 109*	50	6
12 Jun 82	GOING TO A GO GO *Rolling Stones RSR 110*	26	6
2 Oct 82	TIME IS ON MY SIDE *Rolling Stones RSR 111*	62	2
12 Nov 83	UNDERCOVER OF THE NIGHT *Rolling Stones RSR 113*	11	9
11 Feb 84	SHE WAS HOT *Rolling Stones RSR 114*	42	4
21 Jul 84	BROWN SUGAR (re-issue) *Rolling Stones SUGAR 1*	58	2
15 Mar 86	HARLEM SHUFFLE *Rolling Stones A 6864*	13	7
2 Sep 89	MIXED EMOTIONS *Rolling Stones 655193 7*	36	5
2 Dec 89	ROCK AND A HARD PLACE *Rolling Stones 655422 7*	63	1
23 Jun 90	PAINT IT BLACK (re-issue) *London LON 264*	61	3
30 Jun 90	ALMOST HEAR YOU SIGH *Rolling Stones 656065 7*	31	5
30 Mar 91	HIGHWIRE *Rolling Stones 6567567*	29	4
1 Jun 91	RUBY TUESDAY (LIVE) *Rolling Stones 6568927*	59	2
16 Jul 94	LOVE IS STRONG *Virgin VSCDT 1503*	14	5
8 Oct 94	YOU GOT ME ROCKING *Virgin VSCDG 1518*	23	3
10 Dec 94	OUT OF TEARS *Virgin VSCDT 1524*	36	4
15 Jul 95	I GO WILD *Virgin VSCDX 1539*	29	3
11 Nov 95	LIKE A ROLLING STONE *Virgin VSCDT 1562*	12	5
4 Oct 97	ANYBODY SEEN MY BABY? *Virgin VSCDT 1653*	22	3
7 Feb 98	SAINT OF ME *Virgin VSCDT 1667*	26	2
22 Aug 98	OUT OF CONTROL *Virgin VSCDT 1700*	51	1
28 Dec 02	DON'T STOP *Virgin VCSDT 1838*	36	1+

US No.1 symbol referring to 'Let's Spend the Night Together / Ruby Tuesday' applies to Ruby Tuesday which hit the top spot in 1967

'Faraway Eyes' was listed from 15 July 1978, with a peak position of No.10

ROLLINS BAND
US, male vocal / instrumental group (4 WEEKS) pos/wks

12 Sep 92	TEARING *Imago 72787250187*	54	2
10 Sep 94	LIAR / DISCONNECTED *Imago 74321213052*	27	2

ROLLO UK, male producer – Roland Armstrong (8 WEEKS) pos/wks

29 Jan 94	GET OFF YOUR HIGH HORSE (re) *Cheeky CHEKCD 003* [1]	43	4
10 Jun 95	LOVE LOVE LOVE – HERE I COME *Cheeky CHEKCD 007* [2]	32	2
8 Jun 96	LET THIS BE A PRAYER *Cheeky CHEKCD 013* [3]	26	2

[1] Rollo Goes Camping [2] Rollo Goes Mystic [3] Rollo Goes Spiritual with Pauline Taylor

See also DUSTED; SPHINX; OUR TRIBE / ONE TRIBE; FAITHLESS

ROMAN HOLLIDAY
UK, male vocal / instrumental group (19 WEEKS) pos/wks

2 Apr 83	STAND BY *Jive JIVE 31*	61	3

| 2 Jul 83 | DON'T TRY TO STOP IT *Jive JIVE 39* | 14 | 9 |
| 24 Sep 83 | MOTORMANIA *Jive JIVE 49* | 40 | 7 |

ROMAN NUMERALS – *See Vic REEVES*

ROMANTICS – *See RUBY and the ROMANTICS*

ROMEO *UK, male rapper – Marvin Dawkins (23 WEEKS)* pos/wks

30 Dec 00	● NO GOOD 4 ME *East West OXIDE 02CD* [1]	6	8
24 Aug 02	● ROMEO DUNN *Relentless RELENT 29CD*	3	9
9 Nov 02	● IT'S ALL GRAVY *Relentless RELENT 32CD* [2]	9	6

[1] Oxide & Neutrino featuring Megaman, Romeo and Lisa Maffia [2] Romeo featuring Christina Milian

See also SO SOLID CREW

Max ROMEO
Jamaica, male vocalist – Maxie Smith (25 WEEKS) pos/wks

| 28 May 69 | ● WET DREAM (re) *Unity UN 503* | 10 | 25 |

Harry 'Choo-Choo' ROMERO
US, male producer (3 WEEKS) pos/wks

| 22 May 99 | JUST CAN'T GET ENOUGH *AM:PM CDAMPM 121* [1] | 39 | 2 |
| 1 Sep 01 | I WANT OUT (I CAN'T BELIEVE) *Perfecto PERF 22CDS* | 51 | 1 |

[1] Harry 'Choo Choo' Romero presents Inaya Day

See also CHOO CHOO PROJECT

RONALDO'S REVENGE
UK, male production duo – Mike Gray and Jean Pearn (2 WEEKS) pos/wks

| 1 Aug 98 | MAS QUE MANCADA *AM:PM 5827532* | 37 | 2 |

See also FULL INTENTION

RONDO VENEZIANO *Italy, orchestra (3 WEEKS)* pos/wks

| 22 Oct 83 | LA SERENISSIMA (THEME FROM 'VENICE IN PERIL') *Ferroway 7 RON 1* | 58 | 3 |

RONETTES *US, female vocal group (34 WEEKS)* pos/wks

17 Oct 63	● BE MY BABY *London HLU 9793*	4	13
9 Jan 64	BABY, I LOVE YOU *London HLU 9826*	11	14
27 Aug 64	(THE BEST PART OF) BREAKIN' UP *London HLU 9905*	43	3
8 Oct 64	DO I LOVE YOU *London HLU 9922*	35	4

RONNETTE – *See FIDELFATTI featuring RONNETTE*

Mick RONSON with Joe ELLIOTT
UK, male instrumental / vocal duo (1 WEEK) pos/wks

| 7 May 94 | DON'T LOOK DOWN *Epic 6603582* | 55 | 1 |

See also DEF LEPPARD

Linda RONSTADT *US, female vocalist (34 WEEKS)* pos/wks

8 May 76	TRACKS OF MY TEARS *Asylum K 13034*	42	3
28 Jan 78	BLUE BAYOU *Asylum K 13106*	35	4
26 May 79	ALISON *Asylum K 13149*	66	2
11 Jul 87	● SOMEWHERE OUT THERE *MCA MCA 1132* [1]	8	13
11 Nov 89	● DON'T KNOW MUCH *Elektra EKR 101* [2]	2	12

[1] Linda Ronstadt and James Ingram [2] Linda Ronstadt featuring Aaron Neville

ROOFTOP SINGERS
US, male / female vocal group (12 WEEKS) pos/wks

| 31 Jan 63 | ● WALK RIGHT IN *Fontana 271700 TF* ▲ | 10 | 12 |

ROOTJOOSE *UK, male vocal / instrumental group (3 WEEKS)* pos/wks

17 May 97	CAN'T KEEP LIVING THIS WAY *Rage RAGECD 2*	73	1
2 Aug 97	MR FIXIT *Rage RAGECDX 3*	54	1
4 Oct 97	LONG WAY *Rage RAGECD 5*	68	1

ROOTS *US, male rap / production group (3 WEEKS)* pos/wks

| 3 May 97 | WHAT THEY DO *Geffen GFSTD 22240* | 49 | 1 |
| 6 Mar 99 | YOU GOT ME *MCA MCSTD 48110* [1] | 31 | 2 |

[1] Roots featuring Erykah Badu

Ralphi ROSARIO – *See Richie RICH*

Mykal ROSE – *See Shabba RANKS*

ROSE OF ROMANCE ORCHESTRA *UK, orchestra (1 WEEK)* pos/wks

| 9 Jan 82 | TARA'S THEME FROM 'GONE WITH THE WIND' *BBC RESL 108* | 71 | 1 |

ROSE ROYCE (253 Top 500)

The best-selling nine-piece soul / dance combo from Los Angeles, whose biggest hits featured vocalist Gwen Dickey, started as a backing band for Motown acts and topped the UK album chart with their Greatest Hits collection in 1980 (113 WEEKS) pos/wks

25 Dec 76	● CAR WASH *MCA 267* ▲	9	12
22 Jan 77	PUT YOUR MONEY WHERE YOUR MOUTH IS *MCA 259*	44	5
2 Apr 77	I WANNA GET NEXT TO YOU *MCA 278*	14	8
24 Sep 77	DO YOUR DANCE *Whitfield K 17006*	30	6
14 Jan 78	WISHING ON A STAR *Warner Bros. K 17060*	3	14
6 May 78	IT MAKES YOU FEEL LIKE DANCIN' *Warner Bros. K 17148*	16	10
16 Sep 78	● LOVE DON'T LIVE HERE ANYMORE *Whitfield K 17236*	2	10
3 Feb 79	I'M IN LOVE (AND I LOVE THE FEELING) *Whitfield K 17291*	51	4
17 Nov 79	IS IT LOVE YOU'RE AFTER *Whitfield K 17456*	13	13
8 Mar 80	OOH BOY *Whitfield K 17575*	46	7
21 Nov 81	R.R. EXPRESS *Warner Bros. K 17875*	52	3
1 Sep 84	MAGIC TOUCH *Streetwave KHAN 21*	43	8
6 Apr 85	LOVE ME RIGHT NOW *Streetwave KHAN 39*	60	1
11 Jun 88	CAR WASH / IS IT LOVE YOU'RE AFTER (re-issue) *MCA MCA 1253*	20	7
31 Oct 98	CAR WASH (re-recording) *MCA MCSTD 48096* [1]	18	3

[1] Rose Royce featuring Gwen Dickey

ROSE TATTOO
Australia, male vocal / instrumental group (4 WEEKS) pos/wks

| 11 Jul 81 | ROCK 'N' ROLL OUTLAW *Carrere CAR 200* | 60 | 4 |

Jimmy ROSELLI *US, male vocalist (8 WEEKS)* pos/wks

| 5 Mar 83 | WHEN YOUR OLD WEDDING RING WAS NEW *A1 282* | 51 | 5 |
| 20 Jun 87 | WHEN YOUR OLD WEDDING RING WAS NEW (re-issue) *First Night SCORE 9* | 52 | 3 |

ROSIE – *See G NATION featuring ROSIE*

Diana ROSS (6 Top 500)

Perennially popular ex-leader of The Supremes, the most successful girl group of all time, b. Diane Earle, 26 Mar 1944, Detroit, US. Ross continued to clock up worldwide hits after leaving trio in 1970 and sang lead on at least one hit every year for a record 33 years (1964-1996). The classy vocalist has also had more albums on the UK chart than any other American female artist. Diana, who starred in the movies 'Lady Sings the Blues' (1972), 'Mahogany' (76) and 'The Wiz' (78), moved from Motown to RCA in 1981 for a (female) record $20m. In 1994, she was the star of the opening ceremony of football's World Cup, and in 1998 was sampled on US chart-topping singles by Puff Daddy and Monica. In her homeland this supreme song stylist has collected a staggering 22 Top 5 entries during her career, even though she has not had a major hit there since 1984. She has been inducted into the Soul Train and Songwriters' Hall of Fame and was the recipient of a Lifetime Achievement trophy at the World Music Awards in 1996 (560 WEEKS) pos/wks

30 Aug 67	● REFLECTIONS *Tamla Motown TMG 616* [1]	5	14
29 Nov 67	IN AND OUT OF LOVE *Tamla Motown TMG 632* [1]	13	13
10 Apr 68	FOREVER CAME TODAY *Tamla Motown TMG 650* [1]	28	8
3 Jul 68	SOME THINGS YOU NEVER GET USED TO *Tamla Motown TMG 662* [1]	34	6
20 Nov 68	LOVE CHILD *Tamla Motown TMG 677* [1] ▲	15	14

Re-entries are listed as (re), (2re), (3re), etc which signifies that the hit re-entered the chart once, twice or three times, etc

Date	Title	pos	wks
29 Jan 69 ●	I'M GONNA MAKE YOU LOVE ME (re) *Tamla Motown TMG 685* [2]	3	12
23 Apr 69	I'M LIVIN' IN SHAME (re) *Tamla Motown TMG 695* [1]	14	10
16 Jul 69	NO MATTER WHAT SIGN YOU ARE *Tamla Motown TMG 704*	37	7
20 Sep 69	I SECOND THAT EMOTION *Tamla Motown TMG 709* [2]	18	8
13 Dec 69	SOMEDAY WE'LL BE TOGETHER *Tamla Motown TMG 721*	13	13
21 Mar 70	WHY (MUST WE FALL IN LOVE) *Tamla Motown TMG 730* [2]	31	7
18 Jul 70	REACH OUT AND TOUCH *Tamla Motown TMG 743*	33	5
12 Sep 70 ●	AIN'T NO MOUNTAIN HIGH ENOUGH *Tamla Motown TMG 751* ▲	6	12
3 Apr 71	REMEMBER ME *Tamla Motown TMG 768*	7	12
31 Jul 71 ★	I'M STILL WAITING *Tamla Motown TMG 781*	1	14
30 Oct 71 ●	SURRENDER *Tamla Motown TMG 792*	10	11
13 May 72	DOOBEDOOD'NDOOBE DOOBEDOOD'NDOOBE *Tamla Motown TMG 812*	12	9
14 Jul 73 ●	TOUCH ME IN THE MORNING (re) *Tamla Motown TMG 861* ▲	9	13
5 Jan 74 ●	ALL OF MY LIFE *Tamla Motown TMG 880*	9	13
23 Mar 74 ●	YOU ARE EVERYTHING *Tamla Motown TMG 890* [3]	5	12
4 May 74	LAST TIME I SAW HIM *Tamla Motown TMG 893*	35	4
20 Jul 74	STOP LOOK LISTEN (TO YOUR HEART) *Tamla Motown TMG 906* [3]	25	8
24 Aug 74	BABY LOVE (re-issue) *Tamla Motown TMG 915* [1]	12	10
28 Sep 74	LOVE ME *Tamla Motown TMG 917*	38	5
29 Mar 75	SORRY DOESN'T ALWAYS MAKE IT RIGHT *Tamla Motown TMG 941*	23	9
3 Apr 76 ●	THEME FROM 'MAHOGANY' (DO YOU KNOW WHERE YOU'RE GOING TO) *Tamla Motown TMG 1010* ▲	5	8
24 Apr 76 ●	LOVE HANGOVER *Tamla Motown TMG 1024* ▲	10	10
10 Jul 76	I THOUGHT IT TOOK A LITTLE TIME (BUT TODAY I FELL IN LOVE) *Tamla Motown TMG 1032*	32	5
16 Oct 76	I'M STILL WAITING (re-issue) *Tamla Motown TMG 1041*	41	4
19 Nov 77	GETTIN' READY FOR LOVE *Motown TMG 1090*	23	7
22 Jul 78	LOVIN', LIVIN' AND GIVIN' *Motown TMG 1112*	54	6
18 Nov 78	EASE ON DOWN THE ROAD *MCA 396* [4]	45	4
24 Feb 79	POPS, WE LOVE YOU *Motown TMG 1136* [5]	66	5
21 Jul 79	THE BOSS *Motown TMG 1150*	40	7
6 Oct 79	NO ONE GETS THE PRIZE *Motown TMG 1160*	59	3
24 Nov 79	IT'S MY HOUSE *Motown TMG 1169*	32	10
19 Jul 80 ●	UPSIDE DOWN *Motown TMG 1195* ▲	2	12
20 Sep 80	MY OLD PIANO *Motown TMG 1202*	5	9
15 Nov 80	I'M COMING OUT *Motown TMG 1210*	13	10
17 Jan 81	IT'S MY TURN *Motown TMG 1217*	16	8
28 Mar 81	ONE MORE CHANCE *Motown TMG 1227*	49	5
13 Jun 81	CRYIN' MY HEART OUT FOR YOU *Motown TMG 1233*	58	3
12 Sep 81 ●	ENDLESS LOVE *Motown TMG 1240* [6] ▲	7	12
7 Nov 81 ●	WHY DO FOOLS FALL IN LOVE *Capitol CL 226*	4	12
23 Jan 82	TENDERNESS (re) *Motown TMG 1248*	73	2
30 Jan 82	MIRROR MIRROR *Capitol CL 234*	36	5
29 May 82 ●	WORK THAT BODY *Capitol CL 241*	7	11
7 Aug 82	IT'S NEVER TOO LATE *Capitol CL 256*	41	4
23 Oct 82	MUSCLES *Capitol CL 268*	15	9
15 Jan 83	SO CLOSE *Capitol CL 277*	43	4
23 Jul 83	PIECES OF ICE *Capitol CL 298*	46	3
7 Jul 84	ALL OF YOU *CBS A 4522* [7]	43	8
15 Sep 84	TOUCH BY TOUCH *Capitol CL 337*	47	6
28 Sep 85	EATEN ALIVE *Capitol CL 372*	71	1
25 Jan 86 ★	CHAIN REACTION *Capitol CL 386*	1	17
3 May 86	EXPERIENCE *Capitol CL 400*	47	3
13 Jun 87	DIRTY LOOKS *EMI EM 2*	49	3
8 Oct 88	MR LEE *EMI EM 73*	58	2
26 Nov 88	LOVE HANGOVER (re-mix) *Motown ZB 42307*	75	1
18 Feb 89	STOP! IN THE NAME OF LOVE (re-issue) *Motown ZB 41963* [1]	62	1
6 May 89	WORKIN' OVERTIME *EMI EM 91*	32	5
29 Jul 89	PARADISE *EMI EM 94*	61	2
7 Jul 90	I'M STILL WAITING (re-mix) *Motown ZB 43781*	21	6
30 Nov 91 ●	WHEN YOU TELL ME THAT YOU LOVE ME *EMI EM 217*	2	11
15 Feb 92	THE FORCE BEHIND THE POWER *EMI EM 221*	27	3
20 Jun 92 ●	ONE SHINING MOMENT *EMI EM 239*	10	8
28 Nov 92	IF WE HOLD ON TOGETHER *EMI EM 257*	11	10
13 Mar 93	HEART (DON'T CHANGE MY MIND) *EMI CDEM 261*	31	3
9 Oct 93	CHAIN REACTION (re-issue) *EMI CDEM 290*	20	5
11 Dec 93	YOUR LOVE *EMI CDEM 299*	14	8
2 Apr 94	THE BEST YEARS OF MY LIFE *EMI CDEM 305*	28	4
9 Jul 94	WHY DO FOOLS FALL IN LOVE (re-issue) / I'M COMING OUT (re-mix) *EMI CDEM 332*	36	4
2 Sep 95	TAKE ME HIGHER *EMI CDEM 388*	32	4
25 Nov 95	I'M GONE *EMI CDEM 402*	36	3
17 Feb 96	I WILL SURVIVE *EMI CDEM 415* [8]	14	4
21 Dec 96	IN THE ONES YOU LOVE *EMI CDEM 457*	34	4
6 Nov 99 ●	NOT OVER YOU YET (re) *EMI CDEMS 553*	9	7

[1] Diana Ross and The Supremes [2] Diana Ross and The Supremes and The Temptations [3] Diana Ross and Marvin Gaye [4] Diana Ross and Michael Jackson [5] Diana Ross, Marvin Gaye, Smokey Robinson and Stevie Wonder [6] Diana Ross and Lionel Richie [7] Julio Iglesias and Diana Ross [8] Diana

See also SUPREMES

Ricky ROSS *UK, male vocalist (3 WEEKS)*

Date	Title	pos	wks
18 May 96	RADIO ON *Epic 6631352*	35	2
10 Aug 96	GOOD EVENING PHILADELPHIA *Epic 6635335*	58	1

See also DEACON BLUE

Francis ROSSI *UK, male vocalist (6 WEEKS)*

Date	Title	pos	wks
11 May 85	MODERN ROMANCE (I WANT TO FALL IN LOVE AGAIN) *Vertigo FROS 1* [1]	54	4
3 Aug 96	GIVE MYSELF TO LOVE *Virgin VSCDT 1594* [2]	42	2

[1] Francis Rossi and Bernard Frost [2] Francis Rossi of Status Quo

See also STATUS QUO

Nini ROSSO *Italy, male instrumentalist – trumpet (14 WEEKS)*

Date	Title	pos	wks
26 Aug 65 ●	IL SILENZIO *Durium DRS 54000*	8	14

David Lee ROTH *US, male vocalist (15 WEEKS)*

Date	Title	pos	wks
23 Feb 85	CALIFORNIA GIRLS *Warner Bros. W 9102*	68	2
5 Mar 88	JUST LIKE PARADISE *Warner Bros. W 8119*	27	7
3 Sep 88	DAMN GOOD / STAND UP *Warner Bros. W 7753*	72	1
12 Jan 91	A LIL' AIN'T ENOUGH *Warner Bros. W 0002*	32	3
19 Feb 94	SHE'S MY MACHINE *Reprise W 0229CD*	64	1
28 May 94	NIGHT LIFE *Reprise W 0249CD*	72	1

See also VAN HALEN

ROTTERDAM TERMINATION SOURCE *Holland, male instrumental / production duo – Maurice Steenbergen and Danny Scholte (6 WEEKS)* pos/wks

Date	Title	pos	wks
7 Nov 92	POING *SEP EDGE 74*	27	4
25 Dec 93	MERRY X-MESS *React CDREACT 33*	73	2

ROULA – *See 20 FINGERS*

ROULETTES – *See Adam FAITH*

ROUND SOUND presents ONYX STONE & MC MALIBU
UK, male production trio and male rappers (1 WEEK) pos/wks

Date	Title	pos	wks
16 Mar 02	WHADDA WE LIKE? *Cooltempo CDCOOL 358*	69	1

Demis ROUSSOS *Greece, male vocalist (44 WEEKS)*

Date	Title	pos	wks
22 Nov 75 ●	HAPPY TO BE ON AN ISLAND IN THE SUN *Philips 6042 033*	5	10
28 Feb 76	CAN'T SAY HOW MUCH I LOVE YOU *Philips 6042 114*	35	5
26 Jun 76 ★	THE ROUSSOS PHENOMENON (EP) *Philips DEMIS 001*	1	12
2 Oct 76 ●	WHEN FOREVER HAS GONE *Philips 6042 186*	2	10
19 Mar 77	BECAUSE *Philips 6042 245*	39	4
18 Jun 77	KYRILA (EP) *Philips Demis 002*	33	3

Tracks on The Roussos Phenomenon (EP): Forever and Ever / Sing an Ode to Love / So Dreamy / My Friend the Wind. Tracks on Kyrila (EP): Kyrila / I'm Gonna Fall in Love / I Dig You / Sister Emilyne

ROUTERS *US, male instrumental group (7 WEEKS)*

Date	Title	pos	wks
27 Dec 62	LET'S GO *Warner Bros. WB 77*	32	7

Maria ROWE *UK, female vocalist (2 WEEKS)* pos/wks
20 May 95   SEXUAL *ffrr FCD 248* **67** 2

ROWETTA – *See OPEN ARMS featuring ROWETTA*

Kelly ROWLAND *US, female vocalist (11 WEEKS)* pos/wks
26 Oct 02 ★ DILEMMA *Universal MCSTD 40299* [1] ■ ▲ ....**1** 10+
28 Dec 02   STOLE (import) *Columbia 6732122* ....**61** 1+

[1] Nelly featuring Kelly Rowland

See also DESTINY'S CHILD

Kevin ROWLAND – *See DEXY'S MIDNIGHT RUNNERS*

John ROWLES *New Zealand, male vocalist (28 WEEKS)* pos/wks
13 Mar 68 ● IF I ONLY HAD TIME *MCA MU 1000* **3** 18
19 Jun 68   HUSH ... NOT A WORD TO MARY *MCA MU 1023* **12** 10

Lisa ROXANNE
UK, female vocalist – Lisa Roxanne Naraine (2 WEEKS) pos/wks
9 Jun 01   NO FLOW *Palm Pictures PPCD 70542* **18** 2

ROXETTE (174 Top 500) *The most successful Scandinavian act in the US singles chart: Marie Fredriksson (v), Per Gessle (v/g). The duo, who have even appeared on postage stamps in their homeland, can claim total worldwide sales in excess of 40 million (143 WEEKS)* pos/wks
22 Apr 89 ● THE LOOK *EMI EM 87* ▲ **7** 10
15 Jul 89   DRESSED FOR SUCCESS *EMI EM 96* **48** 5
28 Oct 89   LISTEN TO YOUR HEART *EMI EM 108* ▲ **62** 3
2 Jun 90 ● IT MUST HAVE BEEN LOVE *EMI EM 141* ▲ **3** 14
11 Aug 90 ● LISTEN TO YOUR HEART / DANGEROUS (re-issue)
             EMI EM 149 ....**6** 9
27 Oct 90   DRESSED FOR SUCCESS (re-issue) *EMI EM 162* **18** 7
9 Mar 91 ● JOYRIDE *EMI EM 177* ▲ **4** 10
11 May 91   FADING LIKE A FLOWER (EVERY TIME YOU LEAVE)
             EMI EM 190 ....**12** 6
7 Sep 91   THE BIG L *EMI EM 204* **21** 6
23 Nov 91   SPENDING MY TIME *EMI EM 215* **22** 4
28 Mar 92   CHURCH OF YOUR HEART *EMI EM 227* **21** 4
1 Aug 92   HOW DO YOU DO! *EMI EM 241* **13** 7
7 Nov 92   QUEEN OF RAIN *EMI EM 253* **28** 4
24 Jul 93 ● ALMOST UNREAL *EMI CDEM 268* **7** 9
18 Sep 93 ● IT MUST HAVE BEEN LOVE (re-issue) *EMI CDEM 285* ...**10** 8
26 Mar 94   SLEEPING IN MY CAR *EMI CDEM 314* **14** 6
4 Jun 94   CRASH! BOOM! BANG! *EMI CDEM 324* **26** 5
17 Sep 94   FIREWORKS *EMI CDEM 345* **30** 4
3 Dec 94   RUN TO YOU *EMI CDEM 360* **27** 6
8 Apr 95   VULNERABLE *EMI CDEM 369* **44** 2
25 Nov 95   THE LOOK (re-mix) *EMI CDEM 406* **28** 3
30 Mar 96   YOU DON'T UNDERSTAND ME *EMI CDEM 418* **42** 2
20 Jul 96   JUNE AFTERNOON *EMI CDEM 437* **52** 1
20 Mar 99   WISH I COULD FLY *EMI CDEM 537* **11** 7
9 Oct 99   STARS *EMI CDEM 550* **56** 1

ROXY MUSIC (141 Top 500)
Stylish art-rock group regarded as highly influential pioneers. Nucleus of oft-changing group line-up: Bryan Ferry (v), Andy Mackay (sax), Phil Manzanera (g). A major act of its time, this group amassed 11 Top 10 albums (155 WEEKS) pos/wks
19 Aug 72 ● VIRGINIA PLAIN *Island WIP 6144* **4** 12
10 Mar 73 ● PYJAMARAMA *Island WIP 6159* **10** 12
17 Nov 73 ● STREET LIFE *Island WIP 6173* **9** 12
12 Oct 74   ALL I WANT IS YOU *Island WIP 6208* **12** 8
11 Oct 75 ● LOVE IS THE DRUG *Island WIP 6248* **2** 10
27 Dec 75   BOTH ENDS BURNING *Island WIP 6262* **25** 7
22 Oct 77   VIRGINIA PLAIN (re-issue) *Polydor 2001 739* **11** 6
3 Mar 79   TRASH *Polydor POSP 32* **40** 6
28 Apr 79 ● DANCE AWAY *Polydor POSP 44* **2** 14
11 Aug 79 ● ANGEL EYES *Polydor POSP 67* **4** 11
17 May 80 ● OVER YOU *Polydor POSP 93* **5** 9
2 Aug 80 ● OH YEAH (ON THE RADIO) *Polydor 2001 972* **5** 8

8 Nov 80   THE SAME OLD SCENE *Polydor ROXY 1* **12** 7
21 Feb 81 ★ JEALOUS GUY *EG ROXY 2* **1** 11
3 Apr 82 ● MORE THAN THIS *EG ROXY 3* **6** 8
19 Jun 82   AVALON *EG ROXY 4* **13** 6
25 Sep 82   TAKE A CHANCE WITH ME *EG ROXY 5* **26** 6
27 Apr 96   LOVE IS THE DRUG (re-mix) *EG VSCDT 1580* **33** 2

See also Bryan FERRY

Billy Joe ROYAL *US, male vocalist (4 WEEKS)* pos/wks
7 Oct 65   DOWN IN THE BOONDOCKS *CBS 201802* **38** 4

**Central Band of the ROYAL AIR FORCE,
Conductor W/Cdr AE SIMS OBE** *UK, military band (1 WEEK)* pos/wks
21 Oct 55   THE DAM BUSTERS MARCH *HMV B 10877* **18** 1

ROYAL GUARDSMEN
US, male vocal / instrumental group (17 WEEKS) pos/wks
19 Jan 67 ● SNOOPY VS THE RED BARON *Stateside SS 574* **8** 13
6 Apr 67   RETURN OF THE RED BARON *Stateside SS 2010* **37** 4

ROYAL HOUSE *US, male DJ / producer – Todd Terry (18 WEEKS)* pos/wks
10 Sep 88   CAN YOU PARTY *Champion CHAMP 79* **14** 14
7 Jan 89   YEAH! BUDDY *Champion CHAMP 91* **35** 4

**ROYAL PHILHARMONIC ORCHESTRA arranged and conducted
by Louis CLARK** *UK, orchestra and conductor (19 WEEKS)* pos/wks
25 Jul 81 ● HOOKED ON CLASSICS *RCA 109* **2** 11
24 Oct 81   HOOKED ON CAN-CAN *RCA 151* **47** 3
10 Jul 82   BBC WORLD CUP GRANDSTAND *BBC RESL 116* **61** 3
7 Aug 82   IF YOU KNEW SOUSA (AND FRIENDS) *RCA 256* **71** 2

Louis Clark did not conduct the third hit

See also Elvis COSTELLO

**Pipes and Drums and Military Band of the ROYAL
SCOTS DRAGOON GUARDS** *UK, military band (43 WEEKS)* pos/wks
1 Apr 72 ★ AMAZING GRACE (re) *RCA 2191* **1** 27
19 Aug 72   HEYKENS SERENADE (STANDCHEN) / THE DAY IS ENDED
             (THE DAY THOU GAVE US LORD, IS ENDED) *RCA 2251* ...**30** 7
2 Dec 72   LITTLE DRUMMER BOY *RCA 2301* **13** 9

ROYALLE DELITE *US, female vocal group (6 WEEKS)* pos/wks
14 Sep 85   (I'LL BE A) FREAK FOR YOU *Streetwave KHAN 51* **45** 6

ROYCE DA 5'9" – *See BAD MEETS EVIL featuring EMINEM & ROYCE DA 5'9*

RÖYKSOPP *Norway, male production duo (6 WEEKS)* pos/wks
15 Dec 01   POOR LENO *Wall of Sound WALLD 073* **59** 1
17 Aug 02   REMIND ME / SO EASY *Wall of Sound WALLD 074* **21** 3
30 Nov 02   POOR LENO (re-issue) *Wall of Sound WALLD 079CD* ...**38** 2

Lita ROZA *UK, female vocalist (18 WEEKS)* pos/wks
13 Mar 53 ★ (HOW MUCH IS) THAT DOGGIE IN THE WINDOW
             Decca F 10070 ....**1** 11
7 Oct 55   HEY THERE *Decca F 10611* **17** 2
23 Mar 56   JIMMY UNKNOWN *Decca F 10679* **15** 5

ROZALLA *Zimbabwe, female vocalist – Rozalla Miller (48 WEEKS)* pos/wks
27 Apr 91   FAITH (IN THE POWER OF LOVE) *Pulse 8 LOSE 7* **65** 2
7 Sep 91 ● EVERYBODY'S FREE (TO FEEL GOOD) *Pulse 8 LOSE 13* **6** 11
16 Nov 91   FAITH (IN THE POWER OF LOVE) (re-issue) *Pulse 8 LOSE 15* ..**11** 6
22 Feb 92   ARE YOU READY TO FLY *Pulse 8 LOSE 21* **14** 6
9 May 92   LOVE BREAKDOWN *Pulse 8 LOSE 25* **65** 2
15 Aug 92   IN 4 CHOONS LATER *Pulse 8 LOSE 29* **50** 2
30 Oct 93   DON'T PLAY WITH ME *Pulse 8 CDLOSE 52* **50** 1
5 Feb 94   I LOVE MUSIC *Epic 6598932* **18** 5
6 Aug 94   THIS TIME I FOUND LOVE *Epic 6603742* **33** 3
29 Oct 94   YOU NEVER LOVE THE SAME WAY TWICE *Epic 6609052* ...**16** 5

4 Mar 95	**BABY** *Epic 6611955*	26	3
31 Aug 96	**EVERYBODY'S FREE (re-mix)** *Pulse 8 CDLOSE 110*	30	2

RUBBADUBB
UK, male / female vocal / instrumental group (1 WEEK)   pos/wks

18 Jul 98	**TRIBUTE TO OUR ANCESTORS** *Perfecto PERF 165CD*	56	1

RUBETTES
Ex-Barry Blue backing band fronted by Alan Williams, b. 22 Dec 1950, Hertfordshire, UK, whose brand of 1970s good-time rock 'n' roll produced a string of European hits. Distinctive falsetto Paul Da Vinci left the group after singing on their three-million-selling debut hit (68 WEEKS)   pos/wks

4 May 74	★ **SUGAR BABY LOVE** *Polydor 2058 442*	1	10
13 Jul 74	**TONIGHT** *Polydor 2058 499*	12	9
16 Nov 74	● **JUKE BOX JIVE** *Polydor 2058 529*	3	12
8 Mar 75	● **I CAN DO IT** *State STAT 1*	7	9
21 Jun 75	**FOE-DEE-O-DEE** *State STAT 7*	15	6
22 Nov 75	**LITTLE DARLING** *State STAT 13*	30	5
1 May 76	**YOU'RE THE REASON WHY** *State STAT 20*	28	4
25 Sep 76	**UNDER ONE ROOF** *State STAT 27*	40	3
12 Feb 77	● **BABY I KNOW** *State STAT 37*	10	10

Maria RUBIA *UK, female vocalist (2 WEEKS)*   pos/wks

19 May 01	**SAY IT** *Neo NEOCD 055*	40	2

See also FRAGMA

Paulina RUBIO
Mexico, female vocalist (1 WEEK)   pos/wks

28 Sep 02	**DON'T SAY GOODBYE** *Universal MCSTD 40291*	68	1

RUBY and The ROMANTICS
US, female / male vocal group (6 WEEKS)   pos/wks

28 Mar 63	**OUR DAY WILL COME** *London HLR 9679* ▲	38	6

RUDE BOY OF HOUSE – *See HOUSEMASTER BOYZ and the RUDE BOY OF HOUSE*

RUDIES – *See Freddie NOTES and the RUDIES*

RUFF DRIVERZ
UK, male / female vocal / production trio (21 WEEKS)   pos/wks

7 Feb 98	**DON'T STOP** *Inferno CDFERN 003*	30	2
23 May 98	**DEEPER LOVE** *Inferno CDFERN 006*	19	3
24 Oct 98	**SHAME** *Inferno CXFERN 9*	51	2
28 Nov 98	● **DREAMING** *Inferno CXFERN 11* [1]	10	8
24 Apr 99	**LA MUSICA** *Inferno CDFERN 14* [1]	14	4
2 Oct 99	**WAITING FOR THE SUN** *Inferno CDFERN 19*	37	2

[1] Ruff Driverz presents Arrola

RUFF ENDZ
US, male vocal duo – David Chance and Dante Jordan (5 WEEKS)   pos/wks

19 Aug 00	**NO MORE** *Epic 6696202*	11	5

Frances RUFFELLE *UK, female vocalist (6 WEEKS)*   pos/wks

16 Apr 94	**LONELY SYMPHONY** *Virgin VSCDT 1499*	25	6

Bruce RUFFIN
Jamaica, male vocalist – Bernard Downer (23 WEEKS)   pos/wks

1 May 71	**RAIN** *Trojan TR 7814*	19	11
24 Jun 72	● **MAD ABOUT YOU** *Rhino RNO 101*	9	12

David RUFFIN
US, male vocalist, d. 1 Jun 1991 (10 WEEKS)   pos/wks

17 Jan 76	● **WALK AWAY FROM LOVE** *Tamla Motown TMG 1017*	10	8
21 Sep 85	**A NIGHT AT THE APOLLO LIVE!** *RCA PB 49935* [1]	58	2

[1] Daryl Hall and John Oates featuring David Ruffin and Eddie Kendrick

See also TEMPTATIONS

Jimmy RUFFIN ⟨285 Top 500⟩
Major Motown hitmaker, b. 7 May 1939, Mississippi, US. After rejecting a job as the lead vocalist of The Temptations (taken by his brother David), he had a handful of UK / US hits (several charting twice). He relocated to the UK, and was in a one-off hit act, Council Collective, a Paul Weller project. Son Ray produced chart toppers Blue (106 WKS)   pos/wks

27 Oct 66	● **WHAT BECOMES OF THE BROKENHEARTED**		
	Tamla Motown TMG 577	8	15
9 Feb 67	**I'VE PASSED THIS WAY BEFORE** *Tamla Motown TMG 593*	29	7
20 Apr 67	**GONNA GIVE HER ALL THE LOVE I'VE GOT**		
	Tamla Motown TMG 603	26	6
9 Aug 69	**I'VE PASSED THIS WAY BEFORE (re-issue)**		
	Tamla Motown TMG 703	33	6
28 Feb 70	● **FAREWELL IS A LONELY SOUND** *Tamla Motown TMG 726*	8	16
4 Jul 70	**I'LL SAY FOREVER MY LOVE** *Tamla Motown TMG 740*	7	12
17 Oct 70	● **IT'S WONDERFUL (TO BE LOVED BY YOU)**		
	Tamla Motown TMG 753	6	14
27 Jul 74	● **WHAT BECOMES OF THE BROKENHEARTED (re-issue)**		
	Tamla Motown TMG 911	4	12
2 Nov 74	**FAREWELL IS A LONELY SOUND (re-issue)**		
	Tamla Motown TMG 922	30	5
16 Nov 74	**TELL ME WHAT YOU WANT** *Polydor 2058 433*	39	4
3 May 80	● **HOLD ON TO MY LOVE** *RSO 57*	7	8
26 Jan 85	**THERE WILL NEVER BE ANOTHER YOU** *EMI 5541*	68	1

Kim RUFFIN – *See Chubby CHUNKS*

RUFFNECK featuring YAVAHN
US, male production group featuring US female vocalist (6 WEEKS)   pos/wks

11 Nov 95	**EVERYBODY BE SOMEBODY** *Positiva CDTIV 46*	13	4
7 Sep 96	**MOVE YOUR BODY** *Positiva CDTIV 61*	60	1

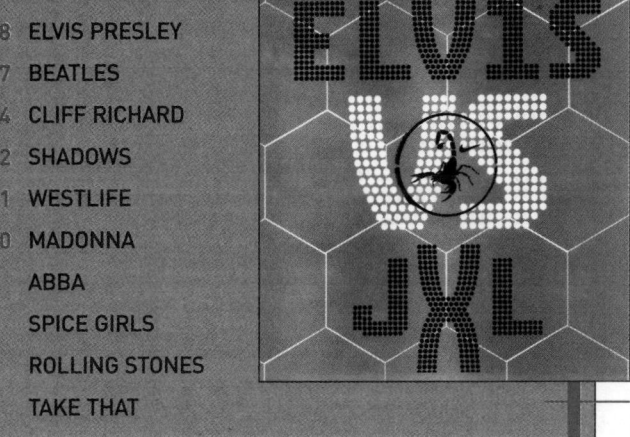

MOST No.1 HITS

■ After years of parity between the Fab Four and Elvis, the King has gone clear at the top of this list of acts with the most No.1 singles. 'A Little Less Conversation' (CD sleeve below) was the single that made the difference. The remix with JXL was a re-working of the original Elvis release that amazingly failed to chart at all in the UK back in the late 1960s and peaked only at 69 in the US.

In 2002 the track was given a new lease of chart life when it became the soundtrack to a major TV advertising campaign by Nike before and during the summer's football World Cup

18	ELVIS PRESLEY
17	BEATLES
14	CLIFF RICHARD
12	SHADOWS
11	WESTLIFE
10	MADONNA
9	ABBA
9	SPICE GIRLS
8	ROLLING STONES
8	TAKE THAT

1 Dec 01	**EVERYBODY BE SOMEBODY (re-mix)**		
	Strictly Rhythm SRUKCD 08 ....**66**	1

Re-entries are listed as (re), (2re), (3re), etc which signifies that the hit re-entered the chart once, twice or three times, etc

		pos/wks
19 Apr 80	STARING AT THE RUDE BOYS *Virgin VS 327*	22 8
30 Aug 80	WEST ONE (SHINE ON ME) *Virgin VS 370*	43 4

Barry RYAN *UK, male vocalist – Barry Sapherson (33 WEEKS)* pos/wks

23 Oct 68 ●	ELOISE *MGM 1442*	2 12
19 Feb 69	LOVE IS LOVE *MGM 1464*	25 4
4 Oct 69	THE HUNT *Polydor 56 348*	34 5
21 Feb 70	MAGICAL SPIEL *Polydor 56 370*	49 1
16 May 70	KITSCH *Polydor 2001 035*	37 6
15 Jan 72	CAN'T LET YOU GO *Polydor 2001 256*	32 5

See also Paul and Barry RYAN

Joshua RYAN *US, male producer (3 WEEKS)* pos/wks

27 Jan 01	PISTOL WHIP *Nulife/Arista 74321825482*	29 3

Marion RYAN
UK, female vocalist – Marion Sapherson, d. 15 Jan 1999 (11 WEEKS) pos/wks

24 Jan 58 ●	LOVE ME FOREVER *Pye Nixa N 15121*	5 11

With the Peter Knight Orchestra and the Beryl Stott Chorus

Paul and Barry RYAN
UK, male vocal duo – Paul and Barry Sapherson (43 WEEKS) pos/wks

11 Nov 65	DON'T BRING ME YOUR HEARTACHES *Decca F 12260*	13 9
3 Feb 66	HAVE PITY ON THE BOY *Decca F 12319*	18 6
12 May 66	I LOVE HER *Decca F 12391*	17 8
14 Jul 66	I LOVE HOW YOU LOVE ME *Decca F 12445*	21 7
29 Sep 66	HAVE YOU EVER LOVED SOMEBODY *Decca F 12494*	49 1
8 Dec 66	MISSY MISSY *Decca F 12520*	43 4
2 Mar 67	KEEP IT OUT OF SIGHT *Decca F 12567*	30 6
29 Jun 67	CLAIRE *Decca F 12633*	47 2

See also Barry RYAN

Rebekah RYAN *UK, female vocalist (5 WEEKS)* pos/wks

18 May 96	YOU LIFT ME UP *MCA MCSTD 40022*	26 3
7 Sep 96	JUST A LITTLE BIT OF LOVE *MCA MCSTD 40063*	51 1
17 May 97	WOMAN IN LOVE *MCA MCSTD 40109*	64 1

Bobby RYDELL *US, male vocalist – Robert Ridarelli (60 WEEKS)* pos/wks

10 Mar 60 ●	WILD ONE (re) *Columbia DB 4429*	7 15
30 Jun 60	SWINGIN' SCHOOL *Columbia DB 4471*	44 1
1 Sep 60	VOLARE (re) *Columbia DB 4495*	22 6
15 Dec 60	SWAY *Columbia DB 4545*	12 13
23 Mar 61	GOOD TIME BABY *Columbia DB 4600*	42 7
19 Apr 62	TEACH ME TO TWIST *Columbia DB 4802* [1]	45 1
20 Dec 62	JINGLE BELL ROCK *Cameo Parkway C 205* [1]	40 3
23 May 63	FORGET HIM *Cameo Parkway C 108*	13 14

[1] Chubby Checker and Bobby Rydell

Mitch RYDER and the DETROIT WHEELS
US, male vocal / instrumental group (5 WEEKS) pos/wks

10 Feb 66	JENNY TAKE A RIDE (re) *Stateside SS 481*	33 5

Mark RYDER *UK, male producer – Mark Rydquist (2 WEEKS)* pos/wks

31 Mar 01	JOY *Relentless Public Demand RELENT 9CDS*	34 2

See also M-D-EMM

Shaun RYDER – *See BLACK GRAPE; HAPPY MONDAYS; HEADS with Shaun RYDER; Russell WATSON*

RYTHM SYNDICATE
US, male vocal / instrumental group (5 WEEKS) pos/wks

27 Jul 91	P.A.S.S.I.O.N. *Impact American EM 197*	58 5

RYZE *UK, male vocal trio (1 WEEK)* pos/wks

2 Nov 02	IN MY LIFE *Inferno Cool CDFERN 48*	46 1

S

Robin S *US, female vocalist – Robin Stone (38 WEEKS)* pos/wks

16 Jan 93 ●	SHOW ME LOVE (re) *Champion CHAMPCD 300*	6 17
31 Jul 93	LUV 4 LUV *Champion CHAMPCD 301*	11 7
4 Dec 93	WHAT I DO BEST *Champion CHAMPCD 307*	43 2
19 Mar 94	I WANT TO THANK YOU *Champion CHAMPCD 310*	48 1
5 Nov 94	BACK IT UP *Champion CHAMPCD 312*	43 2
8 Mar 97 ●	SHOW ME LOVE (re-mix) *Champion CHAMPCD 326*	9 5
12 Jul 97	IT MUST BE LOVE *Atlantic A 5596CD*	37 2
4 Oct 97	YOU GOT THE LOVE *Champion CHAMPCD 330*	62 1
7 Dec 02	SHOW ME LOVE (2nd re-mix) *Champion CHAMPCD 796*	61 1

S CLUB JUNIORS *UK, male / female vocal group (42 WEEKS)* pos/wks

4 May 02 ●	ONE STEP CLOSER *Polydor 5707322*	2 16
3 Aug 02 ●	AUTOMATIC HIGH *Polydor 5708922*	2 13
19 Oct 02 ●	NEW DIRECTION *Polydor 0659692*	2 11+
21 Dec 02 ●	PUPPY LOVE / SLEIGH RIDE *Polydor 0658442*	6 2+

S CLUB 7 168 Top 500

Made-for-TV act (series seen in more than 100 countries) had the best start to its career of any mixed vocal group, with eight Top 3 hits from first eight releases including four No.1s. Award-winning septet is the largest vocal group ever to top the chart, comprising Jo O'Meara, Tina Barrett, Hannah Spearritt, Rachel Stevens, Paul Cattermole, Bradley McIntosh and Jon Lee. When Cattermole left in 2002 sextet became S Club. Best-selling single: 'Bring It All Back' 623,600 (143 WEEKS) pos/wks

19 Jun 99 ★	BRING IT ALL BACK *Polydor 5610852* ■	1 15
2 Oct 99 ●	S CLUB PARTY (re) *Polydor 5614172*	2 14
25 Dec 99 ●	TWO IN A MILLION / YOU'RE MY NUMBER ONE *Polydor 5615962*	2 11
3 Jun 00 ●	REACH *Polydor 5618302*	2 17
23 Sep 00 ●	NATURAL (re) *Polydor 5877602*	3 16
9 Dec 00 ★	NEVER HAD A DREAM COME TRUE (re) *Polydor 5879032* ■	1 18
5 May 01 ★	DON'T STOP MOVIN' *Polydor 5870832*	1 19
1 Dec 01 ★	HAVE YOU EVER *Polydor 5705002* ■	1 14
23 Feb 02 ●	YOU *Polydor 5705812*	2 14
30 Nov 02 ●	ALIVE *Polydor 0658912* [1]	5 5+

[1] S Club

S EXPRESS *UK, male / female vocal / instrumental*
– group leader Mark Moore (50 WEEKS) pos/wks

16 Apr 88 ★	THEME FROM S-EXPRESS *Rhythm King LEFT 21*	1 13
23 Jul 88 ●	SUPERFLY GUY *Rhythm King LEFT 28*	5 9
18 Feb 89 ●	HEY MUSIC LOVER *Rhythm King LEFT 30*	6 10
16 Sep 89	MANTRA FOR A STATE OF MIND *Rhythm King LEFT 35*	21 4
15 Sep 90	NOTHING TO LOSE *Rhythm King SEXY 01*	32 4
30 May 92	FIND 'EM, FOOL 'EM, FORGET 'EM *Rhythm King 6580137*	43 2
11 May 96	THEME FROM S.EXPRESS (re-mix) *Rhythm King SEXY 9CD* [1]	14 4

[1] Mark Moore presents S Express

SFX *UK, male instrumental / production duo (3 WEEKS)* pos/wks

15 May 93	LEMMINGS *Parlophone CDR 6343*	51 3

S-J
UK, female vocalist – Sarah James Jiminez-Heany (4 WEEKS) pos/wks

11 Jan 97	FEVER *React CDREACT 93*	46 1
24 Jan 98	I FEEL DIVINE *React CDREACT 113*	30 2
7 Nov 98	SHIVER *React CDREACT 138*	59 1

SL2 *UK, male DJ / production duo – Matt 'Slipmatt' Nelson and John 'Lime' Fernandez (25 WEEKS)*

		pos/wks	
2 Nov 91	DJS TAKE CONTROL / WAY IN MY BRAIN (re) *XL Recordings XLS 24*	11	6
18 Apr 92 ●	ON A RAGGA TIP *XL Recordings XLS 29*	2	11
19 Dec 92	WAY IN MY BRAIN (re-mix) / DRUMBEATS *XL Recordings XLS 36*	26	6
15 Feb 97	ON A RAGGA TIP '97 (re-mix) *XL Recordings XLSR 29CD*	31	2

S.O.S. BAND *US, male / female vocal / instrumental group (46 WEEKS)*

		pos/wks	
19 Jul 80	TAKE YOUR TIME (DO IT RIGHT) PART 1 *Tabu TBU 8564*	51	4
26 Feb 83	GROOVIN' (THAT'S WHAT WE'RE DOIN') *Tabu TBU A3120*	72	1
7 Apr 84	JUST BE GOOD TO ME *Tabu A 3626*	13	11
4 Aug 84	JUST THE WAY YOU LIKE IT *Tabu A 4621*	32	7
13 Oct 84	WEEKEND GIRL *Tabu A 4785*	51	5
29 Mar 86	THE FINEST *Tabu A 6997*	17	10
5 Jul 86	BORROWED LOVE *Tabu A 7241*	50	5
2 May 87	NO LIES *Tabu 650444 7*	64	3

SWV *US, female vocal group (43 WEEKS)*

		pos/wks	
1 May 93	I'M SO INTO YOU *RCA 74321144972*	17	6
26 Jun 93	WEAK *RCA 74321153352* ▲	33	3
28 Aug 93 ●	RIGHT HERE *RCA 74321160482*	3	12
26 Feb 94	DOWNTOWN *RCA 74321189012*	19	5
11 Jun 94	ANYTHING *RCA 74321212212*	24	3
25 May 96	YOU'RE THE ONE *RCA 74321383312*	13	3
21 Dec 96	IT'S ALL ABOUT U *RCA 74321442152*	36	5
12 Apr 97	CAN WE *Jive JIVECD 423*	18	4
13 Sep 97	SOMEONE *RCA 74321513942* [1]	34	2

[1] SWV featuring Puff Daddy

Raphael SAADIQ *US, male vocalist – Raphael Wiggins (4 WEEKS)* pos/wks

23 Nov 96	STRESSED OUT *Jive JIVECD 404* [1]	33	2
19 Jun 99	GET INVOLVED *Hollywood 0101185 HWR* [2]	36	2

[1] A Tribe Called Quest featuring Faith Evans and Raphael Saadiq [2] Raphael Saadiq and Q-Tip

See also TONY TONI TONÉ

SABRE featuring PRESIDENT BROWN *Jamaica, male vocal duo (1 WEEK)* pos/wks

19 Aug 95	WRONG OR RIGHT *Greensleeves GRECD 485*	71	1

SABRES – See Denny SEYTON and the SABRES

SABRES OF PARADISE *UK, male production group (8 WEEKS)* pos/wks

2 Oct 93	SMOKEBELCH II *Sabres of Paradise PT 009CD*	55	3
9 Apr 94	THEME *Sabres of Paradise PT 014CD*	56	3
17 Sep 94	WILMOT *Warp WAP 50CD*	36	2

SABRINA *Italy, female vocalist – Sabrina Salerno (22 WEEKS)* pos/wks

6 Feb 88 ●	BOYS (SUMMERTIME LOVE) (re) *IBIZA IBIZ 1*	3	14
1 Oct 88	ALL OF ME *PWL PWL 19*	25	7
1 Jul 89	LIKE A YO-YO *Videogram DCUP 1*	72	1

'Boys' peaked during re-entry in Jun 1988

SACRED SPIRIT *Germany, male production trio (5 WEEKS)* pos/wks

15 Apr 95	YEHA-NOHA (WISHES OF HAPPINESS AND PROSPERITY) *Virgin VSCDT 1514*	71	1
18 Nov 95	WISHES OF HAPPINESS AND PROSPERITY (YEHA-NOHA) (re-issue) *Virgin VSC 1568*	37	2
16 Mar 96	WINTER CEREMONY (TOR-CHENEY-NAHANA) *Virgin VSCDT 1574*	45	2

SAD CAFE *UK, male vocal / instrumental group (44 WEEKS)* pos/wks

22 Sep 79 ●	EVERY DAY HURTS *RCA PB 5180*	3	12
19 Jan 80	STRANGE LITTLE GIRL *RCA PB 5202*	32	5

		pos/wks	
15 Mar 80	MY OH MY *RCA SAD 3*	14	11
21 Jun 80	NOTHING LEFT TOULOUSE *RCA SAD 4*	62	4
27 Sep 80	LA-DI-DA *RCA SAD 5*	41	6
20 Dec 80	I'M IN LOVE AGAIN *RCA SAD 6*	40	6

SADE *UK, female / male vocal / instrumental group – lead vocals Helen Folasade Adu (69 WEEKS)*

		pos/wks	
25 Feb 84 ●	YOUR LOVE IS KING (re) *Epic A 4137*	6	12
26 May 84	WHEN AM I GONNA MAKE A LIVING *Epic A 4437*	36	5
15 Sep 84	SMOOTH OPERATOR *Epic A 4655*	19	10
12 Oct 85	THE SWEETEST TABOO *Epic A 6609*	31	5
11 Jan 86	IS IT A CRIME *Epic A 6742*	49	5
2 Apr 88	LOVE IS STRONGER THAN PRIDE *Epic SADE 1*	44	3
4 Jun 88	PARADISE *Epic SADE 2*	29	7
10 Oct 92	NO ORDINARY LOVE (re) *Epic 6583562*	14	11
28 Nov 92	FEEL NO PAIN *Epic 6588297*	56	2
8 May 93	KISS OF LIFE *Epic 6591162*	44	3
31 Jul 93	CHERISH THE DAY *Epic 6594812*	53	2
18 Nov 00	BY YOUR SIDE *Epic 6699992*	17	5
24 Mar 01	KING OF SORROW *Epic 6708672*	59	1

'No Ordinary Love' first peaked at No.26 and did not reach its peak position until re-entering in Jun 1993

Staff Sergeant Barry SADLER *US, male vocalist, d. 5 Nov 1989 (8 WEEKS)* pos/wks

24 Mar 66	THE BALLAD OF THE GREEN BERETS *RCA 1506* ▲	24	8

SAFFRON *UK, female vocalist (2 WEEKS)* pos/wks

16 Jan 93	CIRCLES *WEA SAFF 9CD*	60	2

See also REPUBLICA

SAFFRONS – See CINDY and the SAFFRONS

Alessandro SAFINA – See Elton JOHN

SAFRI DUO *Denmark, male instrumental / production duo – Uffe Savery and Morten Friis (10 WEEKS)* pos/wks

3 Feb 01 ●	PLAYED-A-LIVE (THE BONGO SONG) *AM:PM CDAMPM 141*	6	9
5 Oct 02	SWEET FREEDOM *Serious SERR 55CD* [1]	54	1

[1] Safri Duo featuring Michael McDonald

Mike SAGAR and the CRESTERS *UK, male vocalist (5 WEEKS)* pos/wks

8 Dec 60	DEEP FEELING *HMV POP 819*	44	5

SAGAT *US, male rapper – Faustin Lenon (6 WEEKS)* pos/wks

4 Dec 93	FUNK DAT *ffrr FCD 224*	25	5
3 Dec 94	LUVSTUFF *ffrr FCD 250*	71	1

Carole Bayer SAGER *US, female vocalist (9 WEEKS)* pos/wks

28 May 77 ●	YOU'RE MOVING OUT TODAY *Elektra K 12257*	6	9

Bally SAGOO *UK, male producer / instrumentalist (8 WEEKS)* pos/wks

3 Sep 94	CHURA LIYA *Columbia 6607092*	64	1
22 Apr 95	CHOLI KE PEECHE *Columbia 6613352*	45	1
19 Oct 96	DIL CHEEZ (MY HEART...) *Higher Ground 6634882*	12	3
1 Feb 97	TUM BIN JIYA *Higher Ground 6641372*	21	3

SAILOR *UK, male vocal / instrumental group (24 WEEKS)* pos/wks

6 Dec 75 ●	GLASS OF CHAMPAGNE *Epic EPC 3770*	2	12
27 Mar 76 ●	GIRLS GIRLS GIRLS *Epic EPC 3858*	7	8
19 Feb 77	ONE DRINK TOO MANY *Epic EPC 4804*	35	4

ST ANDREWS CHORALE *UK, church choir (5 WEEKS)* pos/wks

14 Feb 76	CLOUD 99 *Decca F 13617*	31	5

404   Re-entries are listed as (re), (2re), (3re), etc which signifies that the hit re-entered the chart

ST CECILIA
UK, male vocal / instrumental group (17 WEEKS)   pos/wks

19 Jun 71	LEAP UP AND DOWN (WAVE YOUR KNICKERS IN THE AIR) Polydor 2058 104	12	17

SAINT ETIENNE
UK, male / female vocal / instrumental group – lead vocal Sarah Cracknell (53 WEEKS)   pos/wks

18 May 91	NOTHING CAN STOP US / SPEEDWELL *Heavenly HVN 009*	54	3
7 Sep 91	ONLY LOVE CAN BREAK YOUR HEART / FILTHY *Heavenly HVN 12*	39	4
16 May 92	JOIN OUR CLUB / PEOPLE GET REAL *Heavenly HVN 15*	21	3
17 Oct 92	AVENUE *Heavenly HVN 2312*	40	2
13 Feb 93	YOU'RE IN A BAD WAY *Heavenly HVN 25CD*	12	5
22 May 93	HOBART PAVING / WHO DO YOU THINK YOU ARE *Heavenly HVN 29CD*	23	5
18 Dec 93	I WAS BORN ON CHRISTMAS DAY *Heavenly HVN 36CD* [1]	37	5
19 Feb 94	PALE MOVIE *Heavenly HVN 37CD*	28	3
28 May 94	LIKE A MOTORWAY *Heavenly HVN 40CD*	47	2
1 Oct 94	HUG MY SOUL *Heavenly HVN 42CD*	32	2
11 Nov 95	HE'S ON THE PHONE *Heavenly HVN 50CDR* [2]	11	5
7 Feb 98	SYLVIE *Creation CRESCD 279*	12	3
2 May 98	THE BAD PHOTOGRAPHER *Creation CRESCD 290*	27	2
20 May 00 ●	TELL ME WHY (THE RIDDLE) *Deviant DVNT 36CDS* [3]	7	5
24 Jun 00	HEART FAILED (IN THE BACK OF A TAXI) *Mantra / Beggars Banquet MNT 54CD*	50	1
20 Jan 01	BOY IS CRYING *Mantra / Beggars Banquet MNT 60CD*	34	2
7 Sep 02	ACTION *Mantra / Beggars Banquet MNT 73CD*	41	1

[1] Saint Etienne co-starring Tim Burgess [2] Saint Etienne featuring Etienne Daho [3] Paul Van Dyk featuring Saint Etienne

See also Sarah CRACKNELL

ST GERMAIN
France, male producer (3 WEEKS)   pos/wks

31 Aug 96	ALABAMA BLUES (REVISITED) *F Communications F 050CD*	50	1
10 Mar 01	ROSE ROUGE *Blue Note CDROSE 001*	54	2

Barry ST JOHN
UK, female vocalist (1 WEEK)   pos/wks

9 Dec 65	COME AWAY MELINDA *Columbia DB 7783*	47	1

ST JOHN'S COLLEGE SCHOOL CHOIR and the Band of the GRENADIER GUARDS
UK, school choir and military band (3 WEEKS)   pos/wks

3 May 86	THE QUEEN'S BIRTHDAY SONG *Columbia Q1*	40	3

ST LOUIS UNION
UK, male vocal / instrumental group (10 WEEKS)   pos/wks

13 Jan 66	GIRL *Decca F 12318*	11	10

ST LUNATICS – *See NELLY*

Crispian ST PETERS
UK, male vocalist – Peter Smith (31 WEEKS)   pos/wks

6 Jan 66 ●	YOU WERE ON MY MIND *Decca F 12287*	2	14
31 Mar 66 ●	THE PIED PIPER *Decca F 12359*	5	13
15 Sep 66	CHANGES (re) *Decca F 12480*	47	4

ST PHILIPS CHOIR
UK, choir (4 WEEKS)   pos/wks

12 Dec 87	SING FOR EVER *BBC RESL 222*	49	4

ST THOMAS MORE SCHOOL CHOIR – *See Scott FITZGERALD*

ST WINIFRED'S SCHOOL CHOIR
UK, school choir – lead vocal Dawn Ralph (11 WEEKS)   pos/wks

22 Nov 80 ★	THERE'S NO ONE QUITE LIKE GRANDMA *MFP FP 900*	1	11

Buffy SAINTE-MARIE
Canada, female vocalist (29 WEEKS)   pos/wks

17 Jul 71 ●	SOLDIER BLUE *RCA 2081*	7	18
18 Mar 72	I'M GONNA BE A COUNTRY GIRL AGAIN *Vanguard VRS 35143*	34	5
8 Feb 92	THE BIG ONES GET AWAY *Ensign ENY 650*	39	5
4 Jul 92	FALLEN ANGELS *Ensign ENY 655*	57	1

SAINTS
Australia, male vocal / instrumental group (4 WEEKS)   pos/wks

16 Jul 77	THIS PERFECT DAY *Harvest HAR 5130*	34	4

Kyu SAKAMOTO
Japan, male vocalist, d. 12 Aug 1985 (13 WEEKS)   pos/wks

27 Jun 63 ●	SUKIYAKI *HMV POP 1171* ▲	6	13

Ryuichi SAKAMOTO – *See David SYLVIAN*

SAKKARIN – *See Jonathan KING*

SALAD
UK / Holland, male / female vocal / instrumental group (5 WEEKS)   pos/wks

11 Mar 95	DRINK THE ELIXIR *Island Red CIRD 104*	66	1
13 May 95	MOTORBIKE TO HEAVEN *Island Red CIRD 106*	42	1
16 Sep 95	GRANITE STATUE *Island Red CIRD 108*	50	1
26 Oct 96	I WANT YOU *Island CID 646*	60	1
17 May 97	CARDBOY KING *Island CID 654*	65	1

SALFORD JETS
UK, male vocal / instrumental group (2 WEEKS)   pos/wks

31 May 80	WHO YOU LOOKING AT? *RCA PB 5239*	72	2

SALSOUL ORCHESTRA – *See CHARO and the SALSOUL ORCHESTRA*

SALT TANK
UK, male production duo – Malcolm Stanners and David Gates (4 WEEKS)   pos/wks

11 May 96	EUGINA *Internal LIECD 29*	40	2
3 Jul 99	DIMENSION *Hooj Choons HOOJ 74CD*	52	1
9 Dec 00	EUGINA (re-mix) *Lost Language LOST 004CD*	58	1

SALT-N-PEPA   `225` `Top 500`
Rappers Cheryl "Salt" James (b. 28 Mar 1969, Brooklyn, US) and Sandra "Pepa" Denton (b. 9 Nov 1969, Kingston, Jamaica), backed up by DJ Dee Dee "Spinderella" Roper, are the most commercially successful female rap troupe of all time (123 WEEKS)   pos/wks

26 Mar 88	PUSH IT / I AM DOWN *fffr FFR 2*	41	6
25 Jun 88 ●	PUSH IT / TRAMP *Champion CHAMP 51 & fffr FFR 2*	2	13
3 Sep 88	SHAKE YOUR THANG (IT'S YOUR THING) *fffr FFR 11* [1]	22	8
12 Nov 88 ●	TWIST AND SHOUT *fffr FFR 16*	4	9
14 Apr 90	EXPRESSION *fffr F 127*	40	6
25 May 91 ●	DO YOU WANT ME *fffr F 151*	5	12
31 Aug 91	LET'S TALK ABOUT SEX *fffr F 162*	2	13
30 Nov 91	YOU SHOWED ME *fffr F 174* [2]	15	9
28 Mar 92	EXPRESSION (re-mix) *fffr F 182*	23	6
3 Oct 92	START ME UP *fffr F 196*	39	3
9 Oct 93	SHOOP *fffr FCD 219*	29	3
19 Mar 94 ●	WHATTA MAN *fffr FCD 222* [3]	7	10
28 May 94	SHOOP (re-mix) *fffr FCD 234*	13	8
12 Nov 94	NONE OF YOUR BUSINESS (re) *fffr FCD 244*	19	5
21 Dec 96	CHAMPAGNE *MCA MCSTD 48025*	23	6
29 Nov 97	R U READY *fffr FCDP 322*	24	2
11 Dec 99	THE BRICK TRACK VERSUS GITTY UP *fffr FCD 373* [4]	22	4

[1] Salt-N-Pepa featuring EU [2] Additional vocals Joyce Martin & Cari Linger [3] Salt-N-Pepa with En Vogue [4] Saltnpepa

'I Am Down' listed only from 2 Apr 1988. The disc re-entered on 25 Jun when it was made available on Champion with a different flip side. Sales for both discs were amalgamated

SAM and DAVE
US, male vocal duo – Sam Moore and Dave Prater (39 WEEKS)   pos/wks

16 Mar 67	SOOTHE ME (re) *Stax 601 004*	35	8
1 Nov 67	SOUL MAN *Stax 601 023*	24	14
13 Mar 68	I THANK YOU *Stax 601 030*	34	9
29 Jan 69	SOUL SISTER, BROWN SUGAR *Atlantic 584 237*	15	8

See also Lou REED

SAM THE SHAM and the PHARAOHS
US, male vocal / instrumental group (18 WEEKS)   pos/wks

24 Jun 65	WOOLY BULLY *MGM 1269*	11	15
4 Aug 66	LIL' RED RIDING HOOD (re) *MGM 1315*	46	3

Richie SAMBORA
US, male vocalist / instrumentalist – guitar (4 WEEKS)   pos/wks

7 Sep 91	BALLAD OF YOUTH Mercury MER 350	59	1
7 Mar 98	HARD TIMES COME EASY Mercury 5686972	37	2
1 Aug 98	IN IT FOR LOVE Mercury 5660632	58	1

See also BON JOVI

Mike SAMMES SINGERS
UK, male / female vocal group (38 WEEKS)   pos/wks

| 15 Sep 66 | SOMEWHERE MY LOVE (re) HMV POP 1546 | 14 | 38 |

'Somewhere My Love' first peaked at No.22 and reached No.14 after re-entering in Jul 1967

See also Michael FLANDERS; Des O'CONNOR; Malcolm VAUGHAN; Michael HOLLIDAY; Andy STEWART; Jimmy YOUNG

Dave SAMPSON UK, male vocalist (6 WEEKS)   pos/wks

| 19 May 60 | SWEET DREAMS (re) Columbia DB 4449 | 29 | 6 |

SAMSON
UK, male vocal / instrumental group (6 WEEKS)   pos/wks

4 Jul 81	RIDING WITH THE ANGELS RCA 67	55	3
24 Jul 82	LOSING MY GRIP Polydor POSP 471	63	2
5 Mar 83	RED SKIES Polydor POSP 554	65	1

SAN JOSE featuring Rodriguez ARGENTINA
UK, male instrumental group (8 WEEKS)   pos/wks

| 17 Jun 78 | ARGENTINE MELODY (CANCION DE ARGENTINA) MCA 369 | 14 | 8 |

Rodriguez Argentina is Rod Argent

See also SILSOE; ARGENT

SAN REMO STRINGS US, orchestra (8 WEEKS)   pos/wks

| 18 Dec 71 | FESTIVAL TIME Tamla Motown TMG 795 | 39 | 8 |

Junior SANCHEZ featuring DAJAE US, male DJ / producer and
US, female vocalist – Karen Gordon (2 WEEKS)   pos/wks

| 16 Oct 99 | B WITH U Manifesto FESCD 62 | 31 | 2 |

Roger SANCHEZ US, male producer (21 WEEKS)   pos/wks

3 Oct 98	BUFFALO GALS STAMPEDE Virgin VSCDT 1717 [1]	65	1
20 Feb 99	I WANT YOUR LOVE Perpetual PERPCDS 001 [2]	31	2
29 Jan 00	I NEVER KNEW INCredible INCS 4CDS [3]	24	2
14 Jul 01	★ ANOTHER CHANCE Defected DFECT 35CDS ■	1	12
15 Dec 01	YOU CAN'T CHANGE ME Defected DFECT 41CDS [4]	25	4

[1] Malcolm McLaren and the World's Famous Supreme Team plus Rakim and Roger Sanchez [2] Roger Sanchez presents Twilight [3] Roger Sanchez featuring Cooly's Hot Box [4] Roger Sanchez featuring Armand Van Helden and N'Dea Davenport

See also FUNK JUNKEEZ; EL MARIACHI; TRANSATLANTIC SOUL

Chris SANDFORD UK, male actor / vocalist (9 WEEKS)   pos/wks

| 12 Dec 63 | NOT TOO LITTLE NOT TOO MUCH Decca F 11778 | 17 | 9 |

SANDPIPERS US, male vocal group (33 WEEKS)   pos/wks

15 Sep 66	● GUANTANAMERA Pye International 7N 25380	7	17
5 Jun 68	QUANDO M'INNAMORO (A MAN WITHOUT LOVE) A&M AMS 723	33	6
26 Mar 69	KUMBAYA (re) A&M AMS 744	38	2
27 Nov 76	HANG ON SLOOPY Satril SAT 114	32	8

SANDRA Germany, female vocalist (8 WEEKS)   pos/wks

| 17 Dec 88 | EVERLASTING LOVE Siren SRN 85 | 45 | 8 |

Jodie SANDS US, female vocalist (10 WEEKS)   pos/wks

| 17 Oct 58 | SOMEDAY (YOU'LL WANT ME TO WANT YOU) HMV POP 533 | 14 | 10 |

Tommy SANDS US, male vocalist (7 WEEKS)   pos/wks

| 4 Aug 60 | THE OLD OAKEN BUCKET Capitol CL 15143 | 25 | 7 |

SANDSTORM US, male producer – Mark Picchiotti (1 WEEK)   pos/wks

| 13 May 00 | THE RETURN OF NOTHING Renaissance Recordings RENCDS 001 | 54 | 1 |

See also Mark PICHIOTTI presents BASSTOY featuring DANA

Samantha SANG
Australia, female vocalist – Cheryl Gray (13 WEEKS)   pos/wks

| 4 Feb 78 | EMOTION Private Stock PVT 128 | 11 | 13 |

SANTA CLAUS and the CHRISTMAS TREES
UK, male vocal / instrumental group (10 WEEKS)   pos/wks

| 11 Dec 82 | SINGALONG-A-SANTA Polydor IVY 1 | 19 | 5 |
| 10 Dec 83 | SINGALONG-A-SANTA AGAIN Polydor IVY 2 | 39 | 5 |

SANTA ESMERALDA and Leroy GOMEZ
US / France, male / female vocal / instrumental group (5 WEEKS)   pos/wks

| 12 Nov 77 | DON'T LET ME BE MISUNDERSTOOD Philips 6042 325 | 41 | 5 |

SANTANA
US, male vocal / instrumental group (51 WEEKS)   pos/wks

28 Sep 74	SAMBA PA TI CBS 2561	27	7
15 Oct 77	SHE'S NOT THERE CBS 5671	11	12
25 Nov 78	WELL ALL RIGHT CBS 6755	53	3
22 Mar 80	ALL I EVER WANTED CBS 8160	57	3
23 Oct 99	SMOOTH Arista 74321709492 [1] ▲	75	1
1 Apr 00	● SMOOTH (re-issue) Arista 74321748762 [1]	3	10
5 Aug 00	● MARIA MARIA Arista 74321769372 [2] ▲	6	9
23 Nov 02	THE GAME OF LOVE Arista 74321959442 [3]	16	6+

[1] Santana featuring Rob Thomas [2] Santana featuring the Product G&B
[3] Santana featuring Michelle Branch

Juelz SANTANA – See CAM'RON

SANTO and JOHNNY US, male instrumental duo – steel
and electric guitars – Santo and Johnny Farina (5 WEEKS)   pos/wks

| 16 Oct 59 | SLEEP WALK Pye International 7N 25037 ▲ | 22 | 4 |
| 31 Mar 60 | TEARDROP Parlophone R 4619 | 50 | 1 |

SANTOS Italy, male producer – Sante Pucello (6 WEEKS)   pos/wks

| 20 Jan 01 | ● CAMELS Incentive CENT 15CDS | 9 | 6 |

Mike SARNE UK, male vocalist – Mike Scheuer (43 WEEKS)   pos/wks

10 May 62	★ COME OUTSIDE Parlophone R 4902 [1]	1	19
30 Aug 62	WILL I WHAT Parlophone R 4932 [2]	18	10
10 Jan 63	JUST FOR KICKS Parlophone R 4974	22	7
28 Mar 63	CODE OF LOVE Parlophone R 5010	29	7

[1] Mike Sarne with Wendy Richard [2] Mike Sarne with Billie Davis

Joy SARNEY UK, female vocalist (6 WEEKS)   pos/wks

| 7 May 77 | NAUGHTY NAUGHTY NAUGHTY Alaska ALA 2005 | 26 | 6 |

SARR BAND Italy / UK / France, male / female
vocal / instrumental group (1 WEEK)   pos/wks

| 16 Sep 78 | MAGIC MANDRAKE Calendar DAY 111 | 68 | 1 |

Peter SARSTEDT UK, male vocalist (25 WEEKS)   pos/wks

| 5 Feb 69 | ★ WHERE DO YOU GO TO (MY LOVELY) United Artists UP 2262 | 1 | 16 |
| 4 Jun 69 | ● FROZEN ORANGE JUICE United Artists UP 35021 | 10 | 9 |

Robin SARSTEDT UK, male vocalist (9 WEEKS)   pos/wks

| 8 May 76 | ● MY RESISTANCE IS LOW Decca F 13624 | 3 | 9 |

Re-entries are listed as (re), (2re), (3re), etc which signifies that the hit re-entered the chart once, twice or three times, etc

SARTORELLO
Italy, male / female vocal / instrumental duo (1 WEEK)   pos/wks

10 Aug 96	MOVE BABY MOVE *Multiply CDMULTY 12*	56 1

SASH! `298` `Top 500`
German pop / dance act named after instrumentalist / producer Sascha (aka Sasha) Lappessen, featuring programmers Thomas Alisson and Ralf Kappmeier. First four hits uniquely featured vocals in different languages (French, Spanish, English, Italian) (103 WEEKS)   pos/wks

1 Mar 97 ●	ENCORE UNE FOIS *Multiply CDMULTY 18*	2 15
5 Jul 97 ●	ECUADOR *Multiply CDMULTY 23* [1]	2 12
18 Oct 97 ●	STAY *Multiply CDMULTY 26* [2]	2 14
4 Apr 98 ●	LA PRIMAVERA *Multiply CXMULTY 32*	3 12
15 Aug 98 ●	MYSTERIOUS TIMES *Multiply CXMULTY 40* [3]	2 12
28 Nov 98 ●	MOVE MANIA *Multiply CDMULTY 45* [4]	8 10
3 Apr 99 ●	COLOUR THE WORLD *Multiply CDMULTY 48*	15 6
12 Feb 00 ●	ADELANTE *Multiply CDMULTY 60*	2 10
22 Apr 00 ●	JUST AROUND THE HILL *Multiply CDMULTY 62* [3]	8 7
23 Sep 00 ●	WITH MY OWN EYES *Multiply CDMULTY 67*	10 5

[1] Sash! featuring Rodriguez [2] Sash! featuring La Trec [3] Sash! featuring Tina Cousins [4] Sash! featuring Shannon

SASHA *UK, male producer – Alexander Coe (16 WEEKS)*   pos/wks

31 Jul 93	TOGETHER *ffrr FCD 212* [1]	57 1
19 Feb 94	HIGHER GROUND *Deconstruction 74321189002* [2]	19 3
27 Aug 94	MAGIC *Deconstruction 74321221862* [2]	32 4
9 Mar 96	BE AS ONE *Deconstruction 74321342962* [3]	17 4
23 Sep 00	SCORCHIO *Arista 74321788222* [4]	23 3
31 Aug 02	WAVY GRAVY *Arista 74321960602*	64 1

[1] Danny Campbell and Sasha [2] Sasha with Sam Mollison [3] Sasha and Maria [4] Sasha / Emerson

Joe SATRIANI *US, male instrumentalist – guitar (1 WEEK)*   pos/wks

13 Feb 93	THE SATCH EP *Relativity 6589532*	53 1

Tracks on The Satch EP: The Extremist / Cryin / Banana Bongo / Crazy

SATURDAY NIGHT BAND
US, male vocal / instrumental group (9 WEEKS)   pos/wks

1 Jul 78	COME ON DANCE, DANCE *CBS 6367*	16 9

Deion SAUNDERS – *See HAMMER*

Ann SAUNDERSON – *See OCTAVE ONE featuring Ann SAUNDERSON*

Kevin SAUNDERSON – *See INNER CITY*

Chantay SAVAGE *US, female vocalist (9 WEEKS)*   pos/wks

4 May 96	I WILL SURVIVE *RCA 74321377682*	12 8
8 Nov 97	REMINDING ME (OF SEF) *Relativity 6560762* [1]	59 1

[1] Common featuring Chantay Savage

Edna SAVAGE *UK, female vocalist, d. 31 Dec 2000 (1 WEEK)*   pos/wks

13 Jan 56	ARRIVEDERCI DARLING *Parlophone R 4097*	19 1

SAVAGE GARDEN `310` `Top 500` *Australian pop vocal / instrumental duo: Daniel Jones and Darren Hayes. Eponymous debut album sold more than 11 million copies worldwide and huge critical acclaim followed with a record-breaking 10 Arias at the 1997 Australian music industry awards. Duo went separate ways in 2001 and Hayes had solo success. Best-selling single: 'Truly, Madly, Deeply' 657,500 (101 WEEKS)*   pos/wks

21 Jun 97	I WANT YOU *Columbia 6645452*	11 7
27 Sep 97	TO THE MOON AND BACK *Columbia 6648932*	55 1
28 Feb 98 ●	TRULY MADLY DEEPLY *Columbia 6656022* ◆	4 23
22 Aug 98 ●	TO THE MOON AND BACK (re-issue) *Columbia 6662882*	3 16
12 Dec 98	I WANT YOU '98 (re-mix) *Columbia 6667332*	12 10
10 Jul 99	THE ANIMAL SONG *Columbia 6675882*	16 6
13 Nov 99 ●	I KNEW I LOVED YOU *Columbia 6683102* ▲	10 12

1 Apr 00	CRASH AND BURN *Columbia 6690442*	14 6
29 Jul 00 ●	AFFIRMATION *Columbia 6698882*	8 10
25 Nov 00	HOLD ME (re) *Columbia 6706032*	16 7
31 Mar 01	THE BEST THING (re) *Columbia 6709852*	35 3

Telly SAVALAS
US, male actor / vocalist, d. 22 Jan 1994 (12 WEEKS)   pos/wks

22 Feb 75 ★	IF *MCA 174*	1 9
31 May 75	YOU'VE LOST THAT LOVIN' FEELIN' *MCA 189*	47 3

SAVANNA *UK, male vocal group (4 WEEKS)*   pos/wks

10 Oct 81	I CAN'T TURN AWAY *R & B RBS 203*	61 4

SAVUKA – *See Johnny CLEGG and SAVUKA*

SAW DOCTORS
Ireland, male vocal / instrumental group (10 WEEKS)   pos/wks

12 Nov 94	SMALL BIT OF LOVE *Shamtown SAW 001CD*	24 3
27 Jan 96	WORLD OF GOOD *Shamtown SAW 002CD*	15 3
13 Jul 96	TO WIN JUST ONCE *Shamtown SAW 004CD*	14 2
6 Dec 97	SIMPLE THINGS *Shamtown SAW 006CD*	56 1
1 Jun 02	THIS IS ME *Shamtown SAW 012CD*	31 1

Nitin SAWHNEY featuring ESKA
UK, male instrumentalist / producer and UK, female vocalist (1 WEEK) pos/wks

28 Jul 01	SUNSET *V2 VVR 5016763*	65 1

See also COLOURS featuring EMMANUEL & ESKA; EN-CORE featuring Stephen EMMANUEL & ESKA

SAXON *UK, male vocal / instrumental group (61 WEEKS)*   pos/wks

22 Mar 80	WHEELS OF STEEL *Carrere CAR 143*	20 11
21 Jun 80	747 (STRANGERS IN THE NIGHT) *Carrere CAR 151*	13 9
28 Jun 80	BACKS TO THE WALL *Carrere HM 6*	64 2
28 Jun 80	BIG TEASER / RAINBOW THEME – FROZEN RAINBOW *Carrere HM 5*	66 2
29 Nov 80	STRONG ARM OF THE LAW *Carrere CAR 170*	63 3
11 Apr 81	AND THE BANDS PLAYED ON *Carrere CAR 180*	12 8
18 Jul 81	NEVER SURRENDER *Carrere CAR 204*	18 6
31 Oct 81	PRINCESS OF THE NIGHT *Carrere CAR 208*	57 3
23 Apr 83	POWER AND THE GLORY *Carrere SAXON 1*	32 5
30 Jul 83	NIGHTMARE *Carrere CAR 284*	50 3
31 Aug 85	BACK ON THE STREETS *Parlophone R 6103*	75 1
29 Mar 86	ROCK 'N' ROLL GYPSY *Parlophone R 6112*	71 1
30 Aug 86	WAITING FOR THE NIGHT *EMI EMI 5575*	66 2
5 Mar 88	RIDE LIKE THE WIND *EMI EM 43*	52 4
30 Apr 88	I CAN'T WAIT ANYMORE *EMI EM 54*	71 1

Al SAXON *UK, male vocalist – Allan Fowler (10 WEEKS)*   pos/wks

16 Jan 59	YOU'RE THE TOP CHA *Fontana H 164*	17 4
28 Aug 59	ONLY SIXTEEN *Fontana H 205*	24 3
22 Dec 60	BLUE-EYED BOY *Fontana H 278*	39 2
7 Sep 61	THERE I'VE SAID IT AGAIN *Piccadilly 7N 35011*	48 1

Leo SAYER `146` `Top 500` *Distinctive singer / songwriter (b. 21 May 1948, Sussex, UK) who was a top singles and album act on both sides of the Atlantic in the late 1970s. His first seven hits all reached the Top 10 – a feat first achieved by his manager, Adam Faith (151 WEEKS)*   pos/wks

15 Dec 73 ●	THE SHOW MUST GO ON *Chrysalis CHS 2023*	2 13
15 Jun 74 ●	ONE MAN BAND *Chrysalis 2045*	6 9
14 Sep 74 ●	LONG TALL GLASSES *Chrysalis CHS 2052*	4 9
30 Aug 75 ●	MOONLIGHTING *Chrysalis CHS 2076*	2 8
30 Oct 76 ●	YOU MAKE ME FEEL LIKE DANCING *Chrysalis CHS 2119* ▲	2 12
29 Jan 77 ★	WHEN I NEED YOU *Chrysalis CHS 2127* ▲	1 13
9 Apr 77 ●	HOW MUCH LOVE *Chrysalis CHS 2140*	10 8
10 Sep 77	THUNDER IN MY HEART *Chrysalis CHS 2163*	22 8
16 Sep 78 ●	I CAN'T STOP LOVING YOU (THOUGH I TRY) *Chrysalis CHS 2240*	6 11
25 Nov 78	RAINING IN MY HEART *Chrysalis CHS 2277*	21 10
5 Jul 80 ●	MORE THAN I CAN SAY *Chrysalis CHS 2442*	2 11

13 Mar 82	●	HAVE YOU EVER BEEN IN LOVE *Chrysalis CHS 2596*	10	9
19 Jun 82		HEART (STOP BEATING IN TIME) *Chrysalis CHS 2616*	22	10
12 Mar 83		ORCHARD ROAD *Chrysalis CHS 2677*	16	8
15 Oct 83		TILL YOU COME BACK TO ME *Chrysalis LEO 01*	51	3
8 Feb 86		UNCHAINED MELODY *Chrysalis LEO 3*	54	4
13 Feb 93		WHEN I NEED YOU (re-issue) *Chrysalis CDCHS 3926*	65	2
8 Aug 98		YOU MAKE ME FEEL LIKE DANCING *Brothers Org. CDBRUV 8* [1]	32	3

[1] Groove Generation featuring Leo Sayer

Alexei SAYLE *UK, male comedian / vocalist (8 WEEKS)*
pos/wks
| 25 Feb 84 | 'ULLO JOHN GOT A NEW MOTOR? *Island IS 162* | 15 | 8 |

SCAFFOLD *UK, male vocal group (62 WEEKS)*
pos/wks
22 Nov 67	●	THANK U VERY MUCH *Parlophone R 5643*	4	12
27 Mar 68		DO YOU REMEMBER *Parlophone R 5679*	34	5
6 Nov 68	★	LILY THE PINK *Parlophone R 5734*	1	24
1 Nov 69		GIN GAN GOOLIE (re) *Parlophone R 5812*	38	12
1 Jun 74	●	LIVERPOOL LOU *Warner Bros. K 16400*	7	9

See also Mike McGEAR

Boz SCAGGS *US, male vocalist (31 WEEKS)*
pos/wks
30 Oct 76		LOWDOWN *CBS 4563*	28	4
22 Jan 77	●	WHAT CAN I SAY *CBS 4869*	10	10
14 May 77		LIDO SHUFFLE *CBS 5136*	13	9
10 Dec 77		HOLLYWOOD *CBS 5836*	33	8

SCANTY SANDWICH
UK, male DJ / producer – Richard Marshall (8 WEEKS)
pos/wks
| 29 Jan 00 | ● | BECAUSE OF YOU *Southern Fried ECB 18CDS* | 3 | 8 |

SCARFACE *US, male rapper – Brad Jordan (6 WEEKS)*
pos/wks
11 Mar 95	HAND OF THE DEAD BODY *Virgin America VUSCD 88* [1]	41	2
5 Aug 95	I SEEN A MAN DIE *Virgin America VUSCD 94*	55	2
5 Jul 97	GAME OVER *Virgin VUSCD 121*	34	2

[1] Scarface featuring Ice Cube

SCARFO *UK, male vocal / instrumental group (2 WEEKS)*
pos/wks
| 19 Jul 97 | ALKALINE *Deceptive BLUFF 044CD* | 61 | 1 |
| 18 Oct 97 | COSMONAUT NO.7 *Deceptive BLUFF 053CD* | 67 | 1 |

SCARLET *UK, female vocal / instrumental*
duo – Cheryl Parker and Joe Youle (18 WEEKS)
pos/wks
21 Jan 95	INDEPENDENT LOVE SONG *WEA YZ 820CD*	12	12
29 Apr 95	I WANNA BE FREE (TO BE WITH HIM) *WEA YZ 913CD*	21	4
5 Aug 95	LOVE HANGOVER *WEA YZ 969CD*	54	1
6 Jul 96	BAD GIRL *WEA WEA 046CD*	54	1

SCARLET FANTASTIC
UK, male / female vocal / instrumental group (12 WEEKS)
pos/wks
| 3 Oct 87 | NO MEMORY *Arista RIS 36* | 24 | 10 |
| 23 Jan 88 | PLUG ME IN (TO THE CENTRAL LOVE LINE) *Arista 109693* | 67 | 2 |

SCARLET PARTY *UK, male vocal / instrumental group (5 WEEKS)*
pos/wks
| 16 Oct 82 | 101 DAM-NATIONS *Parlophone R 6058* | 44 | 5 |

SCATMAN JOHN *US, male vocalist – John Larkin (19 WEEKS)*
pos/wks
| 13 May 95 | ● | SCATMAN (SKI-BA-BOP-BA-DOP-BOP) *RCA 74321281712* | 3 | 12 |
| 2 Sep 95 | ● | SCATMAN'S WORLD *RCA 74321289952* | 10 | 7 |

Michael SCHENKER GROUP
Germany / UK, male vocal / instrumental group (9 WEEKS)
pos/wks
13 Sep 80	ARMED AND READY *Chrysalis CHS 2455*	53	3
8 Nov 80	CRY FOR THE NATIONS *Chrysalis CHS 2471*	56	3
11 Sep 82	DANCER *Chrysalis CHS 2636*	52	3

Lalo SCHIFRIN
Argentina, male conductor and US, orchestra (11 WEEKS)
pos/wks
| 9 Oct 76 | JAWS *CTI CTSP 005* | 14 | 9 |
| 25 Oct 97 | BULLITT *Warner.esp WESP 002CD* | 36 | 2 |

SCHILLER *Germany, male production duo –*
Christopher von Deylen and Mirko von Schlieffen (3 WEEKS)
pos/wks
| 28 Apr 01 | DAS GLOCKENSPIEL *Data DATA 22CDS* | 17 | 3 |

Peter SCHILLING *Germany, male vocalist (6 WEEKS)*
pos/wks
| 5 May 84 | MAJOR TOM (COMING HOME) (re) *PSP/WEA X 9438* | 42 | 6 |

Phillip SCHOFIELD *UK, male vocalist (6 WEEKS)*
pos/wks
| 5 Dec 92 | CLOSE EVERY DOOR *Really Useful RUR 11* | 27 | 6 |

SCIENCE DEPARTMENT featuring ERIRE
UK, male production duo and female vocalist (1 WEEK)
pos/wks
| 10 Nov 01 | BREATHE *Renaissance Recordings RENCDS 010* | 64 | 1 |

SCIENTIST *UK, male producer – Phil Sebastiane (13 WEEKS)*
pos/wks
6 Oct 90	THE EXORCIST *Kickin KICK 1*	62	3
1 Dec 90	THE EXORCIST (re-mix) *Kickin KICK 1TR*	46	3
15 Dec 90	THE BEE (re) *Kickin KICK 3S*	47	6
11 May 91	SPIRAL SYMPHONY *Kickin KICK 5*	74	1

SCOOBIE *UK, male / female vocal /*
production / Celtic FC supporters group (3 WEEKS)
pos/wks
| 22 Dec 01 | THE MAGNIFICENT 7 *Big Tongue BTR 001CDS* | 58 | 2 |
| 1 Jun 02 | THE MAGNIFICENT 7 (re-mix) *Big Tongue BTR 001CDSX* | 71 | 1 |

SCOOCH *UK, male / female vocal group (20 WEEKS)*
pos/wks
6 Nov 99	WHEN MY BABY *Accolade CDAC 002*	29	4
22 Jan 00	●	MORE THAN I NEEDED TO KNOW *Accolade CDAC 003*	5	5
6 May 00	THE BEST IS YET TO COME (re) *Accolade CDAC 004*	12	5
5 Aug 00	FOR SURE *Accolade CDAS 005*	15	6

SCOOTER
UK / Germany, male vocal / instrumental group (42 WEEKS)
pos/wks
21 Oct 95	THE MOVE YOUR ASS EP *Club Tools 0061675 CLU*	23	4
17 Feb 96	BACK IN THE UK *Club Tools 0061955 CLU*	18	3
25 May 96	REBEL YELL *Club Tools 0062575 CLU*	30	2
19 Oct 96	I'M RAVING *Club Tools 0063015 CLU*	33	3
17 May 97	FIRE *Club Tools 006005 CLU*	45	2
22 Jun 02	●	THE LOGICAL SONG *Sheffield Tunes 0139295STU*	2	15
21 Sep 02	●	NESSAJA *Sheffield Tunes 0142165STU*	4	9
7 Dec 02	POSSE (I NEED YOU ON THE FLOOR) *Sheffield Tunes 0143775STU*	15	4+

Tracks on The Move Your Ass EP: Move Your Ass / Friends / Endless Summer / Move Your Ass (remix)

SCORPIONS
Germany, male vocal / instrumental group (35 WEEKS)
pos/wks
26 May 79	IS THERE ANYBODY THERE? / ANOTHER PIECE OF MEAT *Harvest HAR 5185*	39	4
25 Aug 79	LOVEDRIVE *Harvest HAR 5188*	69	2
31 May 80	MAKE IT REAL *Harvest HAR 5206*	72	2
20 Sep 80	THE ZOO *Harvest HAR 5212*	75	1
3 Apr 82	NO ONE LIKE YOU (re) *Harvest HAR 5219*	64	4
17 Jul 82	CAN'T LIVE WITHOUT YOU *Harvest HAR 5221*	63	2
4 Jun 88	RHYTHM OF LOVE *Harvest HAR 5240*	59	2
18 Feb 89	PASSION RULES THE GAME *Harvest HAR 5242*	74	1
1 Jun 91	WIND OF CHANGE *Vertigo VER 54*	53	3
28 Sep 91	●	WIND OF CHANGE (re-issue) *Vertigo VER 58*	2	9
30 Nov 91	SEND ME AN ANGEL (re) *Vertigo VER 60*	27	5

Re-entries are listed as (re), (2re), (3re), etc which signifies that the hit re-entered the chart once, twice or three times, etc

SCOTLAND WORLD CUP SQUAD
UK, male football team vocalists (27 WEEKS) pos/wks

		pos	wks
22 Jun 74	EASY EASY *Polydor 2058 452*	20	4
27 May 78 ●	OLE OLA (MULHER BRASILEIRA) *Riva 15* [1]	4	6
1 May 82 ●	WE HAVE A DREAM *WEA K 19145* [2]	5	9
9 Jun 90	SAY IT WITH PRIDE *RCA PB 43791* [2]	45	3
15 Jun 96	PURPLE HEATHER *Warner Bros. W 0354CD* [3]	16	5

[1] Rod Stewart featuring the Scottish World Cup Squad '78 [2] Scottish World Cup Squad [3] Rod Stewart with the Scottish Euro '96 Squad

Jack SCOTT
Canada, male vocalist – Jack Scafone Jr (28 WEEKS) pos/wks

		pos	wks
10 Oct 58 ●	MY TRUE LOVE *London HLU 8626*	9	10
25 Sep 59	THE WAY I WALK *London HLL 8912*	30	1
10 Mar 60	WHAT IN THE WORLD'S COME OVER YOU *Top Rank JAR 280*	11	15
2 Jun 60	BURNING BRIDGES *Top Rank JAR 375*	32	2

Jill SCOTT
US, female vocalist (4 WEEKS) pos/wks

		pos	wks
4 Nov 00	GETTIN' IN THE WAY *Epic 6705272*	30	3
7 Apr 01	A LONG WALK *Epic 6710382*	54	1

Josey SCOTT – See Chad KROEGER featuring Josey SCOTT

Linda SCOTT
US, female vocalist – Linda Sampson (14 WEEKS) pos/wks

		pos	wks
18 May 61 ●	I'VE TOLD EVERY LITTLE STAR *Columbia DB 4638*	7	13
14 Sep 61	DON'T BET MONEY HONEY *Columbia DB 4692*	50	1

Mike SCOTT
UK, male vocalist / instrumentalist (4 WEEKS) pos/wks

		pos	wks
16 Sep 95	BRING 'EM ALL IN *Chrysalis CDCHS 5025*	56	1
11 Nov 95	BUILDING THE CITY OF LIGHT *Chrysalis CDCHS 5026*	60	1
27 Sep 97	LOVE ANYWAY *Chrysalis CDCHS 5064*	50	1
14 Feb 98	RARE, PRECIOUS AND GONE *Chrysalis CDCHSS 5073*	74	1

Millie SCOTT
US, female vocalist (11 WEEKS) pos/wks

		pos	wks
12 Apr 86	PRISONER OF LOVE *Fourth & Broadway BRW 45*	52	4
23 Aug 86	AUTOMATIC *Fourth & Broadway BRW 51*	56	3
21 Feb 87	EV'RY LITTLE BIT *Fourth & Broadway BRW 58*	63	4

Simon SCOTT
UK, male vocalist (8 WEEKS) pos/wks

		pos	wks
13 Aug 64	MOVE IT BABY *Parlophone R 5164*	37	8

Tony SCOTT
Holland, male rapper (6 WEEKS) pos/wks

		pos	wks
15 Apr 89	THAT'S HOW I'M LIVING / THE CHIEF *Champion CHAMP 97* [1]	48	4
10 Feb 90	GET INTO IT / THAT'S HOW I'M LIVING (re-issue) *Champion CHAMP 232*	63	2

[1] Toni Scott

'The Chief' listed only from 22 Apr 1989

SCOTT & LEON
UK, male production duo – Scott Anderson and Leon McCormack (6 WEEKS) pos/wks

		pos	wks
30 Sep 00	YOU USED TO HOLD ME *AM:PM CDAMPM 137*	19	4
19 May 01	SHINE ON *AM:PM CDAMPM 143*	34	2

SCOTTISH RUGBY TEAM with Ronnie BROWNE
UK, male rugby team vocalists (1 WEEK) pos/wks

		pos	wks
2 Jun 90	FLOWER OF SCOTLAND *Greentrax STRAX 1001*	73	1

SCREAMING BLUE MESSIAHS
US / UK, male vocal / instrumental group (6 WEEKS) pos/wks

		pos	wks
16 Jan 88	I WANNA BE A FLINTSTONE *WEA YZ 166*	28	6

SCREAMING TREES
US, male vocal / instrumental group (2 WKS) pos/wks

		pos	wks
6 Mar 93	NEARLY LOST YOU *Epic 6582372*	50	1
1 May 93	DOLLAR BILL *Epic 6591792*	52	1

Tracks on 'Nearly Lost You': E.S.K. / Song of a Baker / Winter Song (acoustic)

SCRITTI POLITTI 452 Top 500
Cerebral pop group increasingly influenced by dance and hip hop trends. Formed 1977 by Green Gartside (v/g/k) b. 22 Jun 1956, Cardiff, Wales. US-recorded minor hit, 'Perfect Way', was act's only US Top 20 entry. Legendary jazz trumpeter Miles Davis played on 'Oh Patti' (78 WEEKS) pos/wks

		pos	wks
21 Nov 81	THE SWEETEST GIRL *Rough Trade RT 091*	64	3
22 May 82	FAITHLESS *Rough Trade RT 101*	56	4
7 Aug 82	ASYLUMS IN JERUSALEM / JACQUES DERRIDA *Rough Trade RT 111*	43	5
10 Mar 84 ●	WOOD BEEZ (PRAY LIKE ARETHA FRANKLIN) *Virgin VS 657*	10	12
9 Jun 84	ABSOLUTE *Virgin VS 680*	17	9
17 Nov 84	HYPNOTIZE *Virgin VS 725*	68	2
11 May 85 ●	THE WORD GIRL *Virgin VS 747*	6	12
7 Sep 85	PERFECT WAY *Virgin VS 780*	48	5
7 May 88	OH PATTI (DON'T FEEL SORRY FOR LOVERBOY) *Virgin VS 1006*	13	9
27 Aug 88	FIRST BOY IN THIS TOWN (LOVE SICK) *Virgin VS 1082*	63	3
12 Nov 88	BOOM! THERE SHE WAS *Virgin VS 1143*	55	3
16 Mar 91	SHE'S A WOMAN *Virgin VS 1333* [1]	20	7
3 Aug 91	TAKE ME IN YOUR ARMS AND LOVE ME *Virgin VS 1346* [2]	47	3
31 Jul 99	TINSELTOWN TO THE BOOGIEDOWN *Virgin VSCDT 1731*	46	1

[1] Scritti Politti featuring Shabba Ranks [2] Scritti Politti and Sweetie Irie

Earl SCRUGGS – See Lester FLATT and Earl SCRUGGS

SCUMFROG vs BOWIE
Holland, male producer – Jesse Houk and UK, male vocalist (1 WEEK) pos/wks

		pos	wks
11 May 02	LOVING THE ALIEN *Positiva CDTIV 172*	41	1

SEA FRUIT
UK, male vocal / instrumental group (1 WEEK) pos/wks

		pos	wks
24 Jul 99	HELLO WORLD *Electric Canyon ECCD 3055*	59	1

SEA LEVEL
US, male instrumental group (4 WEEKS) pos/wks

		pos	wks
17 Feb 79	FIFTY-FOUR *Capricorn POSP 28*	63	4

SEAFOOD
UK, male / female vocal / instrumental group (1 WEEK) pos/wks

		pos	wks
28 Jul 01	CLOAKING *Infectious INFEC 103CDS*	71	1

SEAHORSES
UK, male vocal / instrumental group (26 WEEKS) pos/wks

		pos	wks
10 May 97 ●	LOVE IS THE LAW *Geffen GFSTD 22243*	3	7
26 Jul 97 ●	BLINDED BY THE SUN *Geffen GFSTD 22266*	7	7
11 Oct 97	LOVE ME AND LEAVE ME *Geffen GFSTD 22282*	16	4
13 Dec 97	YOU CAN TALK TO ME *Geffen GFSTD 22297*	15	8

See also John SQUIRE

SEAL 449 Top 500
Golden-voiced soul artist. b. Sealhenry Samuel 19 Feb 1963, London, UK. Found fame in 1990 thanks to his Adamski collaboration 'Killer'. Seal proceeded to record and perform with an impressive array of artists: Queen, Joni Mitchell, Jeff Beck and Rolling Stones (78 WKS) pos/wks

		pos	wks
8 Dec 90 ●	CRAZY *ZTT ZANG 8*	2	15
4 May 91	FUTURE LOVE (EP) *ZTT ZANG 11*	12	6
20 Jul 91	THE BEGINNING *ZTT ZANG 21*	24	6
16 Nov 91 ●	KILLER (EP) *ZTT ZANG 23*	8	8
29 Feb 92	VIOLET *ZTT ZANG 27*	39	2
21 May 94	PRAYER FOR THE DYING *ZTT ZANG 51CD*	14	5
30 Jul 94	KISS FROM A ROSE *ZTT ZANG 52CD1*	20	5
5 Nov 94	NEWBORN FRIEND *ZTT ZANG 58CD*	45	2
15 Jul 95 ●	KISS FROM A ROSE / I'M ALIVE (re-issue) *ZTT ZANG 70CD* ▲	4	13
9 Dec 95	DON'T CRY / PRAYER FOR THE DYING (re-issue) *ZTT ZANG 75CD*	51	2
29 Mar 97	FLY LIKE AN EAGLE *ZTT ZEAL 1CD*	13	5
14 Nov 98	HUMAN BEINGS *Warner Brothers W 464CD*	50	1
12 Oct 02 ●	MY VISION *Rulin RULIN 26CDS* [1]	6	8

[1] Jakatta featuring Seal

Tracks on Future Love (EP): Future Love Paradise / A Minor Groove / Violet. Tracks on Killer (EP): Killer / Hey Joe / Come See What Love Has Done

See also ADAMSKI; JAKATTA

(SITTIN' ON) THE DOCK OF THE BAY

■ As fate would have it, Otis Redding died in a plane crash in 1967 before he had the chance to enjoy the success which '(Sittin' on) The Dock of the Bay' would bring. His popularity had increased dramatically after his sensational performance at that summer's Monterey Festival, especially with white pop audiences. He was voted World's No.1 Male Singer in a Melody Maker poll, replacing Elvis who had been at the top for the previous eight years, and it was just a question of time before his big international breakthrough occurred.

On 10 December, the chartered aircraft carrying Redding and his band went down in Monoma Lake, Wisconsin, taking his life and three of his four band members, The Bar-Kays. Georgia-born Redding, who became Stax Records' biggest artist, was one of the best soul singers in the southern states, and often wrote his own material, notably 'Respect', which was also a big hit for Aretha Franklin. In his home town, Macon, he has a bridge and the local Coliseum named after him.

Redding wrote 'Dock of the Bay' on a houseboat near Sausalito, California, in late 1967, together with Booker T and the MG's guitarist Steve Cropper, who also produced the recording session on 6 December, just four days before Otis died. After recording his vocals, Redding departed for what was to be his final tour. He never heard the finished recording of the song, which included the waves rolling in over the introduction accompanied by seagulls and the overdubbed guitars. These parts were added by Steve Cropper after Redding's death. Some have

■ THOUGH A PERFECT CONCLUSION TO SUCH A CAREFREE SONG, THE **WHISTLING** WAS COMPLETELY UNREHEARSED ■

questioned whether 'Dock of the Bay' would have been such a huge hit had Otis Redding not died, since it heralded a marked change of style. In fact, the change was quite deliberate. According to co-writer/producer Steve Cropper, 'Dock of the Bay' was a concerted effort by the two to capture a more pop-orientated audience, and widen Otis Redding's appeal. Cropper recalls: "I know in my own mind it was the best thing we ever did on him. Otis and I knew we had something when we wrote it but when we recorded it we said, 'This is it, this is the song we've been looking for, this is the one that's gonna cross us over'."

Perhaps the most poignant part of the 'Dock of the Bay', considering events soon to unfold, was the whistling towards the fade-out.

Otis Redding: Voted world's top singer just months before his death

Though a perfect conclusion to such a carefree song, the whistling was completely un-rehearsed. Redding simply couldn't think of anything else to sing or say and spontaneously whistled off into the distance as the song gracefully faded away.

Otis Redding surely had much more to offer the world of popular music but, alas, 'Dock of the Bay' became the first posthumous single to top the US chart, gaining two Grammy awards. While the single gave Redding his only UK Top 10 single, it stalled at No.3 on 27 March 1968. He could have taken some consolation that the top two spots were taken by The Beatles, whose 'Day Tripper' he had covered, and by Tom Jones, whom he had reportedly described as 'the best soul singer in the world'. The album of the same name proved more successful here. It was the first by a black male artist to top the UK charts, and the first posthumous UK No.1 album. The record was one of the top 10 most played of the 20th century, with more than six million US certified radio plays.

■ Tony Burton / Dave McAleer

★ **ARTIST:**   Otis Redding

★ **LABEL:**   Volt USA/Stax UK

★ **WRITERS:**   Otis Redding and Steve Cropper

★ **PRODUCER:**   Steve Cropper

SEARCHERS `209` `Top 500` Merseybeat combo initially tipped to be as big as The Beatles, formed 1960: Mike Pender (v/g), John McNally (g/v), Tony Jackson (v/b) (left 1964 – replaced by Frank Allen), Chris Curtis (d). Unlike The Beatles, however, most of this influential act's early hits were cover versions of US originals (128 WEEKS)

		pos/wks
27 Jun 63 ★	SWEETS FOR MY SWEET *Pye 7N 15533*	1 16
10 Oct 63	SWEET NOTHINS *Philips BF 1274*	48 2
24 Oct 63 ●	SUGAR AND SPICE *Pye 7N 15566*	2 13
16 Jan 64 ★	NEEDLES AND PINS *Pye 7N 15594*	1 15
16 Apr 64 ★	DON'T THROW YOUR LOVE AWAY *Pye 7N 15630*	1 11
16 Jul 64	SOMEDAY WE'RE GONNA LOVE AGAIN *Pye 7N 15670*	11 8
17 Sep 64 ●	WHEN YOU WALK IN THE ROOM *Pye 7N 15694*	3 12
3 Dec 64	WHAT HAVE THEY DONE TO THE RAIN *Pye 7N 15739*	13 11
4 Mar 65 ●	GOODBYE MY LOVE *Pye 7N 15794*	4 11
8 Jul 65	HE'S GOT NO LOVE *Pye 7N 15878*	12 10
14 Oct 65	WHEN I GET HOME *Pye 7N 15950*	35 3
16 Dec 65	TAKE ME FOR WHAT I'M WORTH *Pye 7N 15992*	20 8
21 Apr 66	TAKE IT OR LEAVE IT *Pye 7N 17094*	31 6
13 Oct 66	HAVE YOU EVER LOVED SOMEBODY *Pye 7N 17170*	48 2

SEASHELLS UK, female vocal group (5 WEEKS)

		pos/wks
9 Sep 72	MAYBE I KNOW *CBS 8218*	32 5

SEB UK, male instrumentalist – keyboards (1 WEEK)

		pos/wks
18 Feb 95	SUGAR SHACK *React CDREACT 50*	61 1

SEBADOH US, male vocal / instrumental group (4 WEEKS)

		pos/wks
27 Jul 96	BEAUTY OF THE RIDE *Domino RUG 47CD*	74 1
30 Jan 99	FLAME *Domino RUG 80CD1*	30 3

Jon SECADA Cuba, male vocalist (42 WEEKS)

		pos/wks
18 Jul 92 ●	JUST ANOTHER DAY *SBK SBK 35*	5 15
31 Oct 92	DO YOU BELIEVE IN US *SBK SBK 37*	30 4
6 Feb 93	ANGEL *SBK CDSBK 39*	23 5
17 Jul 93	DO YOU REALLY WANT ME *SBK CDSBK 41*	30 4
16 Oct 93	I'M FREE *SBK CDSBK 44*	50 2
14 May 94	IF YOU GO (re) *SBK CDSBK 51*	39 5
4 Feb 95	MENTAL PICTURE *SBK CDSBK 54*	44 2
16 Dec 95	IF I NEVER KNEW YOU (LOVE THEME FROM 'POCAHONTAS') *Walt Disney WD 7023C* [1]	51 4
14 Jun 97	TOO LATE, TOO SOON *SBK CDSBK 57*	43 1

[1] Jon Secada and Shanice

SECCHI featuring Orlando JOHNSON
Italy / US, male vocal / instrumental duo (3 WEEKS)

		pos/wks
4 May 91	I SAY YEAH *Epic 6568467*	46 3

Harry SECOMBE
UK, male vocalist / comedian, d. 12 Apr 2001 (35 WEEKS)

		pos/wks
9 Dec 55	ON WITH THE MOTLEY (VESTA LA GIUBBA) *Philips PB 523*	16 3
3 Oct 63	IF I RULED THE WORLD (re) *Philips BF 1261*	18 17
23 Feb 67 ●	THIS IS MY SONG *Philips BF 1539*	2 15

SECOND CITY SOUND
UK, male instrumental group (8 WEEKS)

		pos/wks
20 Jan 66	TCHAIKOVSKY ONE *Decca F 12310*	22 7
2 Apr 69	DREAM OF OLWEN *Major Minor MM 600*	43 1

SECOND IMAGE
UK, male vocal / instrumental group (11 WEEKS)

		pos/wks
24 Jul 82	STAR *Polydor POSP 457*	60 2
2 Apr 83	BETTER TAKE TIME *Polydor POSP 565*	67 2
26 Nov 83	DON'T YOU *MCA 848*	68 2
11 Aug 84	SING AND SHOUT *MCA 882*	53 3
2 Feb 85	STARTING AGAIN *MCA 936*	65 2

SECOND PHASE US, male producer – Joey Beltram (2 WEEKS)

		pos/wks
21 Sep 91	MENTASM *R&S RSUK 2*	48 2

SECOND PROTOCOL UK, male production duo (2 WEEKS)

		pos/wks
23 Sep 00	BASSLICK *East West EW 216CD*	58 2

SECRET AFFAIR UK, male vocal / instrumental group (34 WEEKS)

		pos/wks
1 Sep 79	TIME FOR ACTION *I-Spy SEE 1*	13 10
10 Nov 79	LET YOUR HEART DANCE *I-Spy SEE 3*	32 6
8 Mar 80	MY WORLD *I-Spy SEE 5*	16 9
23 Aug 80	SOUND OF CONFUSION *I-Spy SEE 8*	45 5
17 Oct 81	DO YOU KNOW *I-Spy SEE 10*	57 4

SECRET KNOWLEDGE
UK / US, male / female vocal / instrumental duo (2 WEEKS)

		pos/wks
27 Apr 96	LOVE ME NOW *Deconstruction 74321342432*	66 1
24 Aug 96	SUGAR DADDY *Deconstruction 74321400242*	75 1

SECRET LIFE UK, male vocal / production group (10 WEEKS)

		pos/wks
12 Dec 92	AS ALWAYS *Cowboy 7RODEO 9*	45 4
7 Aug 93	LOVE SO STRONG *Cowboy RODEO 18CD*	38 2
7 May 94	SHE HOLDS THE KEY *Pulse 8 CDLOSE 58*	63 1
29 Oct 94	I WANT YOU *Pulse 8 CDLOSE 71*	70 1
28 Jan 95	LOVE SO STRONG (re-mix) *Pulse 8 CDLOSE 79*	37 2

SECRETARY OF ENTERTAINMENT – See RAZE

SECTION-X France, male instrumental duo (1 WEEK)

		pos/wks
8 Mar 97	ATLANTIS *Perfecto PERF 136*	42 1

Neil SEDAKA `102` `Top 500` The man who put the 'Tra-La-La' into 1960s pop, b. 13 Mar 1939, New York, US. Ultra-commercial singer / songwriter / pianist who enjoyed two separate chart runs as an artist and wrote many hits for numerous other acts (190 WEEKS)

		pos/wks
24 Apr 59 ●	I GO APE *RCA 1115*	9 13
13 Nov 59 ●	OH! CAROL *RCA 1152*	3 17
14 Apr 60 ●	STAIRWAY TO HEAVEN *RCA 1178*	8 15
1 Sep 60	YOU MEAN EVERYTHING TO ME *RCA 1198*	45 3
2 Feb 61	CALENDAR GIRL *RCA 1220*	8 14
18 May 61 ●	LITTLE DEVIL *RCA 1236*	9 12
21 Dec 61 ●	HAPPY BIRTHDAY, SWEET SIXTEEN *RCA 1266*	3 18
19 Apr 62	KING OF CLOWNS *RCA 1282*	23 11
19 Jul 62 ●	BREAKING UP IS HARD TO DO *RCA 1298* ▲	7 16
22 Nov 62	NEXT DOOR TO AN ANGEL *RCA 1319*	29 4
30 May 63	LET'S GO STEADY AGAIN (re) *RCA 1343*	42 3
7 Oct 72	OH CAROL / BREAKING UP IS HARD TO DO / LITTLE DEVIL (re-issue) *RCA Maximillion 2259*	19 14
4 Nov 72	BEAUTIFUL YOU *RCA 2269*	43 3
24 Feb 73	THAT'S WHEN THE MUSIC TAKES ME *RCA 2310*	18 10
2 Jun 73	STANDING ON THE INSIDE *MGM 2006 267*	26 9
25 Aug 73	OUR LAST SONG TOGETHER *MGM 2006 307*	31 8
9 Feb 74	A LITTLE LOVIN' *Polydor 2058 434*	34 6
22 Jun 74	LAUGHTER IN THE RAIN *Polydor 2058 494* ▲	15 9
22 Mar 75	THE QUEEN OF 1964 *Polydor 2058 546*	35 5

SEDUCTION US, female vocal group (1 WEEK)

		pos/wks
21 Apr 90	HEARTBEAT *Breakout USA 685*	75 1

SEEKERS `230` `Top 500` First Australian act to top UK single or album chart: Judith Durham (v), Keith Potger (g), Bruce Woodley (g), Athol Guy (b). Their unique harmony vocals were displayed on many of their hits, which were penned and produced by Tom Springfield. Durham went solo in 1967, and Potger later went on to form The New Seekers. Best-selling single: 'The Carnival Is Over' 1,400,000 (120 WEEKS)

		pos/wks
7 Jan 65 ★	I'LL NEVER FIND ANOTHER YOU *Columbia DB 7431*	1 23
15 Apr 65 ●	A WORLD OF OUR OWN *Columbia DB 7532*	3 18
28 Oct 65 ★	THE CARNIVAL IS OVER *Columbia DB 7711* ◆	1 17
24 Mar 66	SOMEDAY ONE DAY *Columbia DB 7867*	11 11

Re-entries are listed as (re), (2re), (3re), etc which signifies that the hit re-entered the chart once, twice or three times, etc

			pos/wks
8 Sep 66 ●	WALK WITH ME *Columbia DB 8000*.....................	**10**	12
24 Nov 66 ●	MORNINGTOWN RIDE *Columbia DB 8060*	**2**	15
23 Feb 67 ●	GEORGY GIRL *Columbia DB 8134*	**3**	11
20 Sep 67	WHEN WILL THE GOOD APPLES FALL *Columbia DB 8273*	**11**	12
13 Dec 67	EMERALD CITY *Columbia DB 8313*	**50**	1

Bob SEGER and the SILVER BULLET BAND
US, male vocal / instrumental group (30 WEEKS) pos/wks

30 Sep 78	HOLLYWOOD NIGHTS *Capitol CL 16004*	**42**	6
3 Feb 79	WE'VE GOT TONITE *Capitol CL 16028*	**41**	6
24 Oct 81	HOLLYWOOD NIGHTS *Capitol CL 223*	**49**	3
6 Feb 82	WE'VE GOT TONITE *Capitol CL 235*	**60**	4
9 Apr 83	EVEN NOW *Capitol CL 284*	**73**	2
28 Jan 95	WE'VE GOT TONIGHT (re-issue) *Capitol CDCL 734*.....	**22**	5
29 Apr 95	NIGHT MOVES *Capitol CDCL 741*	**45**	2
29 Jul 95	HOLLYWOOD NIGHTS (re-issue) *Capitol CDCL 749*......	**52**	1
10 Feb 96	LOCK AND LOAD *Parlophone CDCL 765*	**57**	1

Capitol CL 223 and CL 235 were live versions of earlier studio hits

Shea SEGER *US, female vocalist (1 WEEK)* pos/wks

5 May 01	CLUTCH *RCA 74321828142*	**47**	1

SEIKO and Donnie WAHLBERG
Japan / US, female / male vocal duo (5 WEEKS) pos/wks

18 Aug 90	THE RIGHT COMBINATION *Epic 656203 7*.....................	**44**	5

See also NEW KIDS ON THE BLOCK

SELECTER
UK, male / female vocal / instrumental group (28 WEEKS) pos/wks

13 Oct 79 ●	ON MY RADIO *2 Tone CHSTT 4*	**8**	9
2 Feb 80	THREE MINUTE HERO *2 Tone CHSTT 8*.....................	**16**	6
29 Mar 80	MISSING WORDS *2 Tone CHSTT 10*	**23**	8
23 Aug 80	THE WHISPER *Chrysalis CHSS 1*	**36**	5

SELENA vs X MEN
UK, female vocalist and male production duo (1 WEEK) pos/wks

14 Jul 01	GIVE IT UP *GO Beat BOBCD 40*.....................	**61**	1

Peter SELLERS *UK, male actor / vocalist, d. 24 Jul 1980 (39 WKS)* pos/wks

2 Aug 57	ANY OLD IRON (re) *Parlophone R 4337* [1]	**17**	11
10 Nov 60 ●	GOODNESS GRACIOUS ME *Parlophone R 4702* [2]	**4**	14
12 Jan 61	BANGERS AND MASH *Parlophone R 4724* [2]	**22**	5
23 Dec 65	A HARD DAY'S NIGHT *Parlophone R 5393*	**14**	7
27 Nov 93	A HARD DAY'S NIGHT (re-issue) *EMI CDEMS 293*.....................	**52**	2

[1] Peter Sellers presents Mate's Skiffle Group featuring Fred Spoons E.P.N.S.
[2] Peter Sellers and Sophia Loren

See also GOONS

Michael SEMBELLO *US, male vocalist (6 WEEKS)* pos/wks

20 Aug 83	MANIAC *Casablanca CAN 1017* ▲	**43**	6

SEMISONIC *US, male vocal / instrumental group (20 WEEKS)* pos/wks

10 Jul 99	SECRET SMILE *MCA MCSTD 40210*	**13**	11
6 Nov 99	CLOSING TIME *MCA MCSTD 40221*	**25**	5
1 Apr 00	SINGING IN MY SLEEP *MCA MCSTD 40227*	**39**	2
3 Mar 01	CHEMISTRY *MCA MCSTD 40248*.....................	**35**	2

SEMPRINI *UK, male pianist – Fernando Riccardo*
Alberto Semprini d. 19 Jan 1990, and orchestra (8 WEEKS) pos/wks

16 Mar 61	MAIN THEME FROM 'EXODUS' *HMV POP 842*	**25**	8

SENSATIONAL ALEX HARVEY BAND
UK, male vocal / instrumental group, leader d. 4 Feb 1982 (25 WEEKS) pos/wks

26 Jul 75 ●	DELILAH *Vertigo ALEX 001*	**7**	7
22 Nov 75	GAMBLIN' BAR ROOM BLUES *Vertigo ALEX 002*.....................	**38**	8
19 Jun 76	THE BOSTON TEA PARTY *Mountain TOP 12*.....................	**13**	10

SENSELESS THINGS
UK, male vocal / instrumental group (19 WEEKS) pos/wks

22 Jun 91	EVERYBODY'S GONE *Epic 6569807*	**73**	1
28 Sep 91	GOT IT AT THE DELMAR *Epic 6574497*	**50**	3
11 Jan 92	EASY TO SMILE *Epic 6576957*	**18**	4
11 Apr 92	HOLD IT DOWN *Epic 6579267*.....................	**19**	4
5 Dec 92	HOMOPHOBIC ASSHOLE *Epic 6588337*.....................	**52**	2
13 Feb 93	PRIMARY INSTINCT *Epic 6589402*	**41**	2
12 Jun 93	TOO MUCH KISSING *Epic 6592502*.....................	**69**	1
5 Nov 94	CHRISTINE KEELER *Epic 6609572*.....................	**56**	1
28 Jan 95	SOMETHING TO MISS *Epic 6611162*.....................	**57**	1

SENSER *UK, male / female vocal / instrumental group (5 WEEKS)* pos/wks

25 Sep 93	THE KEY *Ultimate TOPP 019CD*	**47**	1
19 Mar 94	SWITCH *Ultimate TOPP 022CD*.....................	**39**	2
23 Jul 94	AGE OF PANIC *Ultimate TOPP 027CD*	**52**	1
17 Aug 96	CHARMING DEMONS *Ultimate TOPP 045CD*	**42**	1

Nick SENTIENCE – *See BK*

SEPULTURA *Brazil, male vocal / instrumental group (12 WEEKS)* pos/wks

2 Oct 93	TERRITORY *Roadrunner RR 23823*	**66**	2
26 Feb 94	REFUSE-RESIST *Roadrunner RR 23773*.....................	**51**	2
4 Jun 94	SLAVE NEW WORLD *Roadrunner RR 23745*	**46**	2
24 Feb 96	ROOTS BLOODY ROOTS *Roadrunner RR 23205*.....................	**19**	2
17 Aug 96	RATAMAHATTA *Roadrunner RR 23145*.....................	**23**	2
14 Dec 96	ATTITUDE *Roadrunner RR 22995*.....................	**46**	2

SERIAL DIVA *UK, male / female production group (3 WEEKS)* pos/wks

18 Jan 97	KEEP HOPE ALIVE *Sound Of Ministry SOMCD 26*	**57**	1
15 May 99	PEARL RIVER *Low Sense SENSECD 24* [1]	**32**	2

[1] Three 'N One presents Johnny Shaker featuring Serial Diva

SERIOUS DANGER
UK, male producer – Richard Phillips (4 WEEKS) pos/wks

20 Dec 97	DEEPER *Fresh FRSHD 68*.....................	**40**	3
2 May 98	HIGH NOON *Fresh FRSHD 69*.....................	**54**	1

SERIOUS INTENTION
US, male vocal / instrumental group (6 WEEKS) pos/wks

16 Nov 85	YOU DON'T KNOW (OH-OH-OH) *Important TAN 8*.....................	**75**	1
5 Apr 86	SERIOUS *Pow Wow LON 93*	**51**	5

SERIOUS ROPE
UK, male / female vocal / production group (3 WEEKS) pos/wks

22 May 93	HAPPINESS *Rumour RUMACD 64* [1]	**54**	2
1 Oct 94	HAPPINESS – YOU MAKE ME HAPPY (re-mix) *Mercury MERCD 407*	**70**	1

[1] Serious Rope presents Sharon Dee Clarke

Erick SERMON featuring Marvin GAYE
US, male rapper and male vocalist (2 WEEKS) pos/wks

6 Oct 01	MUSIC *Polydor 4976222*	**36**	2

SET THE TONE
UK, male vocal / instrumental group (4 WEEKS) pos/wks

22 Jan 83	DANCE SUCKER *Island WIP 6836*	**62**	2
26 Mar 83	RAP YOUR LOVE *Island IS 110*.....................	**67**	2

SETTLERS
UK, male / female vocal / instrumental group (5 WEEKS) pos/wks

16 Oct 71	THE LIGHTNING TREE *York SYK 505*.....................	**36**	5

Brian SETZER ORCHESTRA
US, male vocal / instrumental group (3 WEEKS) pos/wks

3 Apr 99	JUMP JIVE AN' WAIL *Interscope IND 95601*	**34**	3

Taja SEVELLE *US, female vocalist (13 WEEKS)*

		pos/wks
20 Feb 88 ●	LOVE IS CONTAGIOUS *Paisley Park W 8257*	7 9
14 May 88	WOULDN'T YOU LOVE TO LOVE ME? *Paisley Park W 8127*	59 4

702 *US, female vocal group (10 WEEKS)*

		pos/wks
14 Dec 96	STEELO *Motown 8606072*	41 2
29 Nov 97	NO DOUBT *Motown 8607052*	59 1
7 Aug 99	WHERE MY GIRLS AT? *Motown TMGCD 1500*	22 4
27 Nov 99	YOU DON'T KNOW *Motown TMGCD 1502*	36 3

740 BOYZ *US, male vocal / instrumental duo (1 WEEK)*

		pos/wks
4 Nov 95	SHIMMY SHAKE *MCA MCSTD 40002*	54 1

SEVEN GRAND HOUSING AUTHORITY
UK, male producer – Terence Parker (1 WEEK)

		pos/wks
23 Oct 93	THE QUESTION *Olympic ELYCD 010*	70 1

7669 *US, female rap group (1 WEEK)*

		pos/wks
18 Jun 94	JOY *Motown TMGCD 1429*	60 1

7TH HEAVEN *UK, male vocal group (5 WEEKS)*

		pos/wks
14 Sep 85	HOT FUN *Mercury MER 199*	47 5

SÉVÉRINE *France, female vocalist (11 WEEKS)*

		pos/wks
24 Apr 71 ●	UN BANC, UN ARBRE, UNE RUE *Philips 6009 135*	9 11

David SEVILLE
US, male vocalist – Ross Bagdasarian, d. 16 Jan 1972 (6 WEEKS)

		pos/wks
23 May 58	WITCH DOCTOR *London HLU 8619* ▲	11 6

See also ALFI and HARRY; CHIPMUNKS

Janette SEWELL – *See DOUBLE TROUBLE*

SEX CLUB featuring BROWN SUGAR
US, male / female vocal / instrumental duo (1 WEEK)

		pos/wks
28 Jan 95	BIG DICK MAN *Club Tools CLU 60775*	67 1

SEX-O-LETTES – *See DISCO TEX and the SEX-O-LETTES*

SEX-O-SONIQUE *UK, male production / instrumental
duo – Mike Gray and Jon Pearn (3 WEEKS)*

		pos/wks
6 Dec 97	I THOUGHT IT WAS YOU *ffrr FCD 321*	32 3

See also FULL INTENTION; HUSTLERS CONVENTION featuring Dave LAUDAT and Ondrea DUVERNEY

SEX PISTOLS (353) Top 500
Provocative and influential quartet which popularised punk. Formed 1975 in London UK, split 1978: Johnny Rotten (v), Steve Jones (g), Paul Cook (d) and Glen Matlock (b) – replaced 1977 by Sid Vicious (d. 1979). Notorious group reunited for brief, and profitable, Filthy Lucre tour in 1996 (91 WEEKS) pos/wks

		pos/wks
18 Dec 76	ANARCHY IN THE UK *EMI 2566*	38 4
4 Jun 77 ●	GOD SAVE THE QUEEN *Virgin VS 181*	2 9
9 Jul 77 ●	PRETTY VACANT *Virgin VS 184*	6 8
22 Oct 77 ●	HOLIDAYS IN THE SUN *Virgin VS 191*	8 6
8 Jul 78 ●	NO ONE IS INNOCENT (A PUNK PRAYER BY RONALD BIGGS) / MY WAY *Virgin VS 220* 1	7 10
3 Mar 79 ●	SOMETHING ELSE 2 / FRIGGIN' IN THE RIGGIN' *Virgin VS 240* 3	3 12
7 Apr 79 ●	SILLY THING *Virgin VS 256*	6 8
30 Jun 79 ●	C'MON EVERYBODY *Virgin VS 272* 2	3 9
13 Oct 79	THE GREAT ROCK 'N' ROLL SWINDLE *Virgin VS 290*	21 6
14 Jun 80	(I'M NOT YOUR) STEPPING STONE *Virgin VS 339*	21 8
3 Oct 92	ANARCHY IN THE UK (re-issue) *Virgin VS 1431*	33 3
5 Dec 92	PRETTY VACANT (re-issue) *Virgin VS 1448*	56 2
27 Jul 96	PRETTY VACANT (LIVE) *Virgin America VUSCD 113*	18 3
8 Jun 02	GOD SAVE THE QUEEN (re-issue) *Virgin VSCDT 1832*	15 3

1 Uncredited vocal by Ronald Biggs 2 Sex Pistols, vocals: Sid Vicious 3 Sex Pistols, vocals: Steve Jones

The listed flip side of 'Silly Thing' was 'Who Killed Bambi' by Ten Pole Tudor. The listed flip side of 'The Great Rock 'n' Roll Swindle' was 'Rock Around the Clock', also by Ten Pole Tudor

Denny SEYTON and the SABRES
UK, male vocal / instrumental group (1 WEEK)

		pos/wks
17 Sep 64	THE WAY YOU LOOK TONIGHT *Mercury MF 824*	48 1

SHABOOM *UK, male instrumental / production group (1 WEEK)*

		pos/wks
31 Jul 99	SWEET SENSATION *WEA WEA 218CD1*	64 1

SHACK *UK, male vocal / instrumental group (3 WEEKS)*

		pos/wks
26 Jun 99	COMEDY *London LONCD 427*	44 1
14 Aug 99	NATALIE'S PARTY *London LONCD 436*	63 1
11 Mar 00	OSCAR *London LONCD 445*	67 1

SHADES *US, female vocal group (3 WEEKS)*

		pos/wks
12 Apr 97	MR BIG STUFF *Motown 5736572* 1	31 2
20 Sep 97	SERENADE *Motown 8606892*	75 1

1 Queen Latifah, Shades and Free

SHADES OF LOVE
US, male instrumental / production duo (1 WEEK)

		pos/wks
22 Apr 95	KEEP IN TOUCH (BODY TO BODY) *Vicious Muzik MUZCD 102*	64 1

SHADES OF RHYTHM
UK, male instrumental / production group (25 WEEKS)

		pos/wks
2 Feb 91	HOMICIDE / EXORCIST *ZTT ZANG 13*	53 3
13 Apr 91	SWEET SENSATION *ZTT ZANG 18*	54 4
20 Jul 91	THE SOUND OF EDEN *ZTT ZANG 22*	35 5
30 Nov 91	EXTACY *ZTT ZANG 24*	16 7
20 Feb 93	SWEET REVIVAL (KEEP IT COMIN') *ZTT ZANG 40CD*	61 1
11 Sep 93	SOUND OF EDEN (re-issue) *ZTT ZANG 44CD*	37 3
5 Nov 94	THE WANDERING DRAGON *Public Demand PPDCD 5*	55 1
21 Jun 97	PSYCHO BASE *Coalition CRUM 002CD*	57 1

SHADOWS (3) Top 500
Headliners for five decades and Britain's most successful instrumental group: Hank Marvin (b. Brian Rankin, 28 Oct 1941, Newcastle-upon-Tyne) (g), Bruce Welch (b. Bruce Cripps, 2 Nov 1941, Bognor Regis) (g), 'Jet' Harris (b. Terence Hawkins, 6 Jul 1939, London) (b), Tony Meehan (b. Daniel Meehan, 2 Mar 1943, London) (d), Brian Bennett (b. 9 Feb 1940, London) (d). They began their chart life as The Drifters when backing Cliff Richard and went on to contribute significantly on 35 hits with Cliff. Their main claim to fame is as Britain's most influential and imitated act before The Beatles (771 WEEKS) pos/wks

		pos/wks
12 Sep 58 ●	MOVE IT! *Columbia DB 4178* 1	2 17
21 Nov 58 ●	HIGH CLASS BABY *Columbia DB 4203* 1	7 10
30 Jan 59	LIVIN' LOVIN' DOLL *Columbia DB 4249* 1	20 6
8 May 59 ●	MEAN STREAK *Columbia DB 4290 A* 1	10 9
15 May 59	NEVER MIND *Columbia DB 4290 B* 1	21 2
10 Jul 59 ★	LIVING DOLL (2re) *Columbia DB 4306* 1	1 23
9 Oct 59 ★	TRAVELLIN' LIGHT *Columbia DB 4351 B* 2	1 17
9 Oct 59	DYNAMITE (re) *Columbia DB 4351 A* 2	16 4
15 Jan 60	EXPRESSO BONGO (EP) *Columbia SEG 7971* 2	14 7
22 Jan 60 ●	A VOICE IN THE WILDERNESS (re) *Columbia DB 4398* 2	2 16
24 Mar 60 ●	FALL IN LOVE WITH YOU *Columbia DB 4431* 2	2 15
30 Jun 60 ★	PLEASE DON'T TEASE *Columbia DB 4479* 2	1 18
21 Jul 60 ★	APACHE *Columbia DB 4484*	1 21
22 Sep 60 ●	NINE TIMES OUT OF TEN *Columbia DB 4506* 2	3 12
10 Nov 60 ●	MAN OF MYSTERY / THE STRANGER *Columbia DB 4530*	5 15
1 Dec 60 ★	I LOVE YOU *Columbia DB 4547* 2	1 16
9 Feb 61 ●	F.B.I. *Columbia DB 4580*	6 19
2 Mar 61 ●	THEME FOR A DREAM *Columbia DB 4593* 2	3 14
30 Mar 61 ●	GEE WHIZ IT'S YOU *Columbia DC 756* 2	4 14

Re-entries are listed as (re), (2re), (3re), etc which signifies that the hit re-entered the chart

1 May 61	● THE FRIGHTENED CITY *Columbia DB 4637*	3	20
2 Jun 61	● A GIRL LIKE YOU *Columbia DB 4667* 2	3	14
7 Sep 61	★ KON-TIKI (re) *Columbia DB 4698*	1	12
6 Nov 61	● THE SAVAGE *Columbia DB 4726*	10	8
11 Jan 62	★ THE YOUNG ONES *Columbia DB 4761* 2 ◆ ■	1	21
1 Mar 62	★ WONDERFUL LAND *Columbia DB 4790*	1	19
10 May 62	● I'M LOOKING OUT THE WINDOW / DO YOU WANT TO DANCE *Columbia DB 4828* 3	2	17
2 Aug 62	● GUITAR TANGO *Columbia DB 4870*	4	15
6 Sep 62	● IT'LL BE ME *Columbia DB 4886* 2	2	12
6 Dec 62	● THE NEXT TIME / BACHELOR BOY *Columbia DB 4950* 2	1	18
13 Dec 62	● DANCE ON! *Columbia DB 4948*	1	15
21 Feb 63	★ SUMMER HOLIDAY *Columbia DB 4977* 2	1	18
7 Mar 63	★ FOOT TAPPER *Columbia DB 4984*	1	16
9 May 63	● LUCKY LIPS *Columbia DB 7034* 2	4	15
6 Jun 63	● ATLANTIS *Columbia DB 7047*	2	17
19 Sep 63	● SHINDIG *Columbia DB 7106*	6	14
7 Nov 63	● DON'T TALK TO HIM (re) *Columbia DB 7150* 2	2	14
5 Dec 63	GERONIMO *Columbia DB 7163*	11	12
6 Feb 64	● I'M THE LONELY ONE *Columbia DB 7203* 2	8	10
5 Mar 64	THEME FOR YOUNG LOVERS *Columbia DB 7231*	12	10
7 May 64	● THE RISE AND FALL OF FLINGEL BUNT *Columbia DB 7261*	5	14
2 Jul 64	● ON THE BEACH *Columbia DB 7305* 2	7	13
3 Sep 64	RHYTHM AND GREENS *Columbia DB 7342*	22	7
3 Dec 64	GENIE WITH THE LIGHT BROWN LAMP *Columbia DB 7416*	17	10
10 Dec 64	● I COULD EASILY FALL *Columbia DB 7420* 2	6	11
11 Feb 65	MARY ANNE *Columbia DB 7476*	17	10
10 Jun 65	STINGRAY *Columbia DB 7588*	19	7
5 Aug 65	● DON'T MAKE MY BABY BLUE *Columbia DB 7650*	10	10
19 Aug 65	THE TIME IN BETWEEN *Columbia DB 7660* 2	22	8
25 Nov 65	THE WAR LORD *Columbia DB 7769*	18	9
17 Mar 66	I MET A GIRL *Columbia DB 7853*	22	5
24 Mar 66	BLUE TURNS TO GREY *Columbia DB 7866* 2	15	9
7 Jul 66	A PLACE IN THE SUN *Columbia DB 7952*	24	6
13 Oct 66	● TIME DRAGS BY *Columbia DB 8017* 2	10	12
3 Nov 66	THE DREAMS I DREAM *Columbia DB 8034*	42	6
15 Dec 66	● IN THE COUNTRY *Columbia DB 8094* 2	6	10
13 Apr 67	MAROC 7 *Columbia DB 8170*	24	8
27 Nov 68	DON'T FORGET TO CATCH ME *Columbia DB 8503* 2	21	10
8 Mar 75	LET ME BE THE ONE *EMI 2269*	12	9
16 Dec 78	● DON'T CRY FOR ME ARGENTINA *EMI 2890*	5	14
28 Apr 79	● THEME FROM THE 'THE DEER HUNTER' (CAVATINA) *EMI 2939*	9	14
26 Jan 80	RIDERS IN THE SKY *EMI 5027*	12	12
23 Aug 80	EQUINOXE (PART V) *Polydor POSP 148*	50	3
2 May 81	THE THIRD MAN *Polydor POSP 255*	44	4

1 Cliff Richard and The Drifters 2 Cliff Richard and The Shadows 3 Cliff Richard / The Shadows

All the Shadows hits without Cliff Richard were instrumentals except for 'Mary Anne', 'Don't Make My Baby Blue', 'I Met a Girl', 'The Dreams I Dream' and 'Let Me Be the One'. Tracks on Expresso Bongo (EP): Love / A Voice in the Wilderness / The Shrine on the Second Floor / Bongo Blues. Last track featured Shadows only

See also Cliff RICHARD; Hank MARVIN; Jet HARRIS and Tony MEEHAN

SHAFT UK, male producer – Mark Pritchard (9 WEEKS)
		pos/wks
21 Dec 91	● ROOBARB AND CUSTARD *Ffrreedom TAB 100*	7 8
25 Jul 92	MONKEY *Ffrreedom TAB 114*	61 1

SHAFT UK, male production duo
– Elliot Ireland and Alex Rizzo (19 WEEKS)
		pos/wks
4 Sep 99	● (MUCHO MAMBO) SWAY *Wonderboy WBOYD 015*	2 12
20 May 00	MAMBO ITALIANO *Wonderboy WBDD 017*	12 6
21 Jul 01	KIKI RIRI BOOM *Wonderboy WBOYD 026*	62 1

SHAG – See Jonathan KING

SHAGGY 169 Top 500
World's top selling Jamaican artist, born Orville Burrell, 22 Oct 1968. More UK and US No.1s than any other West Indian-born act. US-based artist sold 345,000 copies of 'It Wasn't Me' in first week in UK (then 1,180,700 in total), and album 'Hotshot' sold more than 11 million globally (143 WEEKS) pos/wks
6 Feb 93	★ OH CAROLINA *Greensleeves GRECD 361*	1	19
10 Jul 93	SOON BE DONE *Greensleeves GRECD 380*	46	3
8 Jul 95	● IN THE SUMMERTIME *Virgin VSCDT 1542* 1	5	9
23 Sep 95	★ BOOMBASTIC *Virgin VSCDT 1536* ■	1	12
13 Jan 96	WHY YOU TREAT ME SO BAD *Virgin VSCDT 1566* 2	11	5
23 Mar 96	SOMETHING DIFFERENT / THE TRAIN IS COMING *Virgin VSCDT 1581* 3	21	5
22 Jun 96	THAT GIRL *Virgin America VUSCDX 106* 4	15	7
19 Jul 97	● PIECE OF MY HEART *Virgin VSCDT 1647* 5	7	6
17 Feb 01	IT WASN'T ME (IMPORT) *MCA 1558032* 6	31	3
10 Mar 01	★ IT WASN'T ME *MCA 1558022* 6 ◆ ■ ▲	1	20
9 Jun 01	● ANGEL *MCA MCSTD 40257* 1 ■ ▲	1	16
29 Sep 01	● LUV ME LUV ME *MCA MCSTD 40263*	5	10
1 Dec 01	DANCE AND SHOUT / HOPE *MCA MCSTD 40272*	19	7
23 Mar 02	● ME JULIE *Island CID 793* 7	2	14
9 Nov 02	● HEY SEXY LADY (re) *MCA MCSTD 40304* 8	10	7+

1 Shaggy featuring Rayvon 2 Shaggy featuring Grand Puba 3 Shaggy featuring Wayne Wonder / Shaggy 4 Maxi Priest featuring Shaggy 5 Shaggy featuring Marsha 6 Shaggy featuring Ricardo 'Rikrok' Ducent 7 Ali G and Shaggy 8 Shaggy featuring Brian and Tony Gold

SHAH UK, female vocalist (1 WEEK)
		pos/wks
6 Jun 98	SECRET LOVE *Evocative EVOKE 5CDS*	69 1

SHAI US, male vocal group (6 WEEKS)
		pos/wks
19 Dec 92	IF I EVER FALL IN LOVE *MCA MCS 1727*	36 6

SHAKATAK 404 Top 500 *London-based pop / jazz / funk ensemble which was big in Japan. Sound was typified by tinkling piano of Bill Sharpe and Jill Saward's soothing vocals. Sharpe later hit with Gary Numan, while Nigel Wright (k) produced hits for Madonna, Take That, Robson and Jerome, Barbra Streisand, Cliff Richard and Boyzone (85 WEEKS)* pos/wks
8 Nov 80	FEELS LIKE THE RIGHT TIME *Polydor POSP 188*	41	5
7 Mar 81	LIVING IN THE UK *Polydor POSP 230*	52	4
25 Jul 81	BRAZILIAN DAWN *Polydor POSP 282*	48	3
21 Nov 81	EASIER SAID THAN DONE *Polydor POSP 375*	12	17
3 Apr 82	● NIGHT BIRDS *Polydor POSP 407*	9	8
19 Jun 82	STREETWALKIN' *Polydor POSP 452*	38	6
4 Sep 82	INVITATIONS *Polydor POSP 502*	24	7
6 Nov 82	STRANGER *Polydor POSP 530*	43	3
4 Jun 83	DARK IS THE NIGHT *Polydor POSP 595*	15	8
27 Aug 83	IF YOU COULD SEE ME NOW *Polydor POSP 635*	49	4
7 Jul 84	● DOWN ON THE STREET *Polydor POSP 688*	9	11
15 Sep 84	DON'T BLAME IT ON LOVE *Polydor POSP 699*	55	3
16 Nov 85	DAY BY DAY *Polydor POSP 770* 1	53	3
24 Oct 87	MR MANIC AND SISTER COOL *Polydor MANIC 1*	56	3

1 Shakatak featuring Al Jarreau

SHAKEDOWN *Switzerland, male DJ / production duo – Stephan and Sebastien Kohler (8 WEEKS)* pos/wks
11 May 02	● AT NIGHT *Defected DFECT 50CDS*	6 8

Johnny SHAKER – See THREE 'N ONE

SHAKESPEAR'S SISTER *UK / US, female vocal / instrumental duo – Siobhan Fahey and Marcella (Detroit) Levy (52 WEEKS)* pos/wks
29 Jul 89	● YOU'RE HISTORY *ffrr F 112*	7	9
14 Oct 89	RUN SILENT *ffrr F 119*	54	3
10 Mar 90	DIRTY MIND *ffrr F 128*	71	1
12 Oct 91	GOODBYE CRUEL WORLD *London LON 309*	59	2
25 Jan 92	★ STAY *London LON 314*	1	16
16 May 92	● I DON'T CARE *London LON 318*	7	7
18 Jul 92	GOODBYE CRUEL WORLD (re-issue) *London LON 322*	32	4
7 Nov 92	HELLO (TURN YOUR RADIO ON) *London LON 330*	14	6
27 Feb 93	MY 16TH APOLOGY (EP) *London LONCD 337*	61	1
22 Jun 96	I CAN DRIVE *London LONCD 383*	30	3

Tracks on My 16th Apology (EP): My 16th Apology / Catwoman / Dirty Mind (live re-recording) / Hot Love. From 1996 Shakespear's Sister was essentially just vocalist Siobhan Fahey

See also Marcella DETROIT; BANANARAMA

SHAKIRA Colombia, female vocalist (40 WEEKS) pos/wks

9 Mar 02 ●	WHENEVER, WHEREVER Epic 6724262	.2 19
3 Aug 02 ●	UNDERNEATH YOUR CLOTHES Epic 6729532	.3 15
23 Nov 02	OBJECTION (TANGO) Epic 6733402	.17 6+

SHAKY and BONNIE – See Shakin' STEVENS; Bonnie TYLER

SHALAMAR (196) Top 500

Influential US dance-music vocal trio masterminded by 'Soul Train' TV producer Don Cornelius. Line-up 1979-1983: Jeffrey Daniel, Jody Watley, Howard Hewett. Regarded as fashion icons and trendsetters, they helped to introduce "body-popping" to Britain (134 WEEKS) pos/wks

14 May 77	UPTOWN FESTIVAL Soul Train FB 0885	.30 5
9 Dec 78	TAKE THAT TO THE BANK RCA FB 1379	.20 12
24 Nov 79	THE SECOND TIME AROUND Solar FB 1709	.45 9
9 Feb 80	RIGHT IN THE SOCKET Solar SO 2	.44 6
30 Aug 80	I OWE YOU ONE Solar SO 11	.13 10
28 Mar 81	MAKE THAT MOVE Solar SO 17	.30 10
27 Mar 82 ●	I CAN MAKE YOU FEEL GOOD Solar K 12599	.7 11
12 Jun 82 ●	A NIGHT TO REMEMBER Solar K 13162	.5 12
4 Sep 82 ●	THERE IT IS Solar K 13194	.5 10
27 Nov 82	FRIENDS Solar CHUM 1	.12 10
11 Jun 83 ●	DEAD GIVEAWAY Solar E 9819	.8 10
13 Aug 83	DISAPPEARING ACT Solar E 9807	.18 8
15 Oct 83	OVER AND OVER Solar E 9792	.23 6
24 Mar 84	DANCING IN THE SHEETS CBS A 4171	.41 3
31 Mar 84	DEADLINE USA MCA MCA 866	.52 3
24 Nov 84	AMNESIA Solar/MCA SHAL 1	.61 2
2 Feb 85	MY GIRL LOVES ME MCA SHAL 2	.45 3
26 Apr 86	A NIGHT TO REMEMBER (re-mix) MCA SHAL 3	.52 4

See also BABYFACE

SHAM ROCK
Ireland, male / female vocal / instrumental group (11 WEEKS) pos/wks

7 Nov 98	TELL ME MA Jive 0522352	.13 11

SHAM 69 UK, male vocal / instrumental group (53 WEEKS)

13 May 78	ANGELS WITH DIRTY FACES Polydor 2059 023	.19 10
29 Jul 78 ●	IF THE KIDS ARE UNITED Polydor 2059 050	.9 9
14 Oct 78 ●	HURRY UP HARRY Polydor POSP 7	.10 8
24 Mar 79	QUESTIONS AND ANSWERS Polydor POSP 27	.18 9
4 Aug 79 ●	HERSHAM BOYS Polydor POSP 64	.6 9
27 Oct 79	YOU'RE A BETTER MAN THAN I Polydor POSP 82	.49 5
12 Apr 80	TELL THE CHILDREN Polydor POSP 136	.45 3

SHAMEN (456) Top 500
Early and highly influential exponents of techno-rock fusion. The Shamen, named after South American Indian tribesmen, comprise duo Colin Angus and Richard West (Mr C) following the departure of founders Peter Stephenson and Keith McKenzie and the death by drowning of Will Sinnott in 1991 (77 WEEKS) pos/wks

7 Apr 90	PRO-GEN One Little Indian 36 TP7	.55 4
22 Sep 90	MAKE IT MINE One Little Indian 46 TP7	.42 5
6 Apr 91	HYPERREAL One Little Indian 48 TP7	.29 5
27 Jul 91 ●	MOVE ANY MOUNTAIN (re-mix) One Little Indian 52 TP7	.4 10
18 Jul 92 ●	L.S.I. One Little Indian 78 TP7	.6 8
5 Sep 92 ★	EBENEEZER GOODE One Little Indian 78 TP7	.1 10
7 Nov 92 ●	BOSS DRUM One Little Indian 88 TP7	.4 7
7 Nov 92	BOSS DRUM (re-mix) One Little Indian 88 TP12	.58 1
19 Dec 92 ●	PHOREVER PEOPLE One Little Indian 98 TP7	.5 10
6 Mar 93	RE: EVOLUTION One Little Indian 118 TP7CD [1]	.18 2
6 Nov 93	THE SOS (EP) One Little Indian 108 TP7CD	.14 4
19 Aug 95	DESTINATION ESCHATON One Little Indian 128 TP7CDL	.15 4
21 Oct 95	TRANSAMAZONIA One Little Indian 138 TP7CD	.28 2
10 Feb 96	HEAL (THE SEPARATION) One Little Indian 158 TP7CDL	.31 2
21 Dec 96	MOVE ANY MOUNTAIN '96 (2nd (re-mix) One Little Indian 169 TP7CD	.35 3

[1] Shamen with Terence McKenna

'Move Any Mountain' is a re-mix of 'Pro-Gen'. Tracks on The SOS (EP): Comin' On / Make It Mine / Possible Worlds (re-mix)

SHAMPOO
UK, female vocal duo – Jacqui Blake and Carrie Askew (28 WEEKS) pos/wks

30 Jul 94	TROUBLE Food CDFOOD 51	.11 12
15 Oct 94	VIVA LA MEGABABES Food CDFOOD 54	.27 4
18 Feb 95	DELICIOUS Food CDFOOD 58	.21 4
5 Aug 95	TROUBLE (re-issue) Food CDFOOD 66	.36 3
13 Jul 96	GIRL POWER Food CDFOOD 76	.25 4
21 Sep 96	I KNOW WHAT BOYS LIKE Food CDFOOD 83	.42 1

Jimmy SHAND BAND
UK, male dance band, leader d. 23 Dec 2000 (2 WEEKS) pos/wks

23 Dec 55	BLUEBELL POLKA Parlophone F 3436	.20 2

Paul SHANE and the YELLOWCOATS
UK, male actor / vocalist with male / female vocal group (5 WEEKS) pos/wks

16 May 81	HI-DE-HI (HOLIDAY ROCK) EMI 5180	.36 5

SHANGRI-LAS US, female vocal group (48 WEEKS) pos/wks

8 Oct 64	REMEMBER (WALKIN' IN THE SAND) Red Bird RB 10008	.14 13
14 Jan 65	LEADER OF THE PACK Red Bird RB 10014 ▲	.11 9
14 Oct 72 ●	LEADER OF THE PACK (re-issue) Kama Sutra 2013 024	.3 14
5 Jun 76 ●	LEADER OF THE PACK (2nd re-issue) Charly CS 1009	.7 12

From 19 Jun 1976 until 14 Aug 1976, the last week of the disc's chart run, the Charly and another Contempo release of 'Leader of the Pack' were bracketed together on the chart

SHANICE US, female vocalist – Shanice Wilson (24 WEEKS) pos/wks

23 Nov 91	I LOVE YOUR SMILE Motown ZB 44907	.55 4
22 Feb 92 ●	I LOVE YOUR SMILE (re-mix) Motown TMG 1401	.2 10
14 Nov 92	LOVIN' YOU Motown TMG 1409	.54 1
16 Jan 93	SAVING FOREVER FOR YOU Giant W 0148CD	.42 3
13 Aug 94	I LIKE Motown TMGCD 1427	.49 2
16 Dec 95	IF I NEVER KNEW YOU (LOVE THEME FROM 'POCAHONTAS') Walt Disney WD 7023CD [1]	.51 4

[1] Jon Secada and Shanice

SHANKS & BIGFOOT UK, male production duo
– Stephen Meade and Daniel Langsman (24 WEEKS) pos/wks

29 May 99 ★	SWEET LIKE CHOCOLATE (re) Pepper / Jive / Chocolate Boy 0530352 ■	.1 16
29 Jul 00	SING-A-LONG (re) Pepper 9230232	.12 8

See also DOOLALLY

SHANNON
US, female vocalist – Brenda Shannon Greene (54 WEEKS) pos/wks

19 Nov 83	LET THE MUSIC PLAY (re) Club LET 1	.14 15
7 Apr 84	GIVE ME TONIGHT Club JAB 1	.24 7
30 Jun 84	SWEET SOMEBODY Club JAB 3	.25 8
20 Jul 85	STRONGER TOGETHER Club JAB 15	.46 6
6 Dec 97	IT'S OVER LOVE Manifesto FESCD 37 [1]	.16 8
28 Nov 98 ●	MOVE MANIA Multiply CDMULTY 45 [2]	.8 10

[1] Todd Terry presents Shannon [2] Sash! featuring Shannon

Del SHANNON (156) Top 500
Early 1960s chart regular, b. Charles Westover, 30 Dec 1934, Michigan, US, d. 8 Feb 1990. This unmistakable singer / songwriter who used a falsetto vocal on most hits topped both the UK and US charts with the first of his many hits (147 WEEKS) pos/wks

27 Apr 61 ★	RUNAWAY London HLX 9317 ▲	.1 22
14 Sep 61 ●	HATS OFF TO LARRY London HLX 9402	.6 12
7 Dec 61 ●	SO LONG BABY London HLX 9462	.10 11
15 Mar 62 ●	HEY! LITTLE GIRL London HLX 9515	.2 15
6 Sep 62	CRY MYSELF TO SLEEP London HLX 9587	.29 6
11 Oct 62 ●	THE SWISS MAID London HLX 9609	.2 17
17 Jan 63 ●	LITTLE TOWN FLIRT London HLX 9653	.4 13
25 Apr 63 ●	TWO KINDS OF TEARDROPS London HLX 9710	.5 13
22 Aug 63	TWO SILHOUETTES London HLX 9761	.23 8

24 Oct 63	SUE'S GOTTA BE MINE *London HLU 9800*	21	8
12 Mar 64	MARY JANE *Stateside SS 269*	35	5
30 Jul 64	HANDY MAN *Stateside SS 317*	36	4
14 Jan 65 ●	KEEP SEARCHIN' (WE'LL FOLLOW THE SUN) *Stateside SS 368*	3	11
18 Mar 65	STRANGER IN TOWN *Stateside SS 395*	40	2

Roxanne SHANTE *US, female rapper (11 WEEKS)* pos/wks

1 Aug 87	HAVE A NICE DAY *Breakout USA 612*	58	3
4 Jun 88	GO ON GIRL *Breakout USA 633*	55	3
29 Oct 88	SHARP AS A KNIFE *Club JAB 73* 1	45	3
14 Apr 90	GO ON GIRL (re-mix) *Breakout USA 689*	74	1
23 Sep 00	WHAT'S GOING ON *Wall of Sound WALLD 064* 2	43	1

1 Brandon Cooke featuring Roxanne Shante 2 Mekon featuring Roxanne Shante

Helen SHAPIRO (234 Top 500)
Youngest female chart-topper, b. 28 Sep 1946, London. Before she was 16 years old, she amassed four Top 5 hits (including two No.1s) and had been voted Britain's Top Female Singer. She headlined the first UK tour on which The Beatles appeared (as her support act) (119 WEEKS) pos/wks

23 Mar 61 ●	DON'T TREAT ME LIKE A CHILD *Columbia DB 4589*	3	20
29 Jun 61 ★	YOU DON'T KNOW *Columbia DB 4670*	1	23
28 Sep 61 ★	WALKIN' BACK TO HAPPINESS *Columbia DB 4715*	1	19
15 Feb 62 ●	TELL ME WHAT HE SAID *Columbia DB 4782*	2	15
3 May 62	LET'S TALK ABOUT LOVE *Columbia DB 4824*	23	7
12 Jul 62 ●	LITTLE MISS LONELY *Columbia DB 4869*	8	11
18 Oct 62	KEEP AWAY FROM OTHER GIRLS *Columbia DB 4908*	40	6
7 Feb 63	QUEEN FOR TONIGHT *Columbia DB 4966*	33	5
25 Apr 63	WOE IS ME *Columbia DB 7026*	35	6
24 Oct 63	LOOK WHO IT IS *Columbia DB 7130*	47	3
23 Jan 64	FEVER *Columbia DB 7190*	38	4

SHARADA HOUSE GANG *Italy, male / female vocal / instrumental group (4 WEEKS)* pos/wks

12 Aug 95	KEEP IT UP *Media MCSTD 2071*	36	2
11 May 96	LET THE RHYTHM MOVE YOU *Media MCSTD 40035*	50	1
18 Oct 97	GYPSY BOY, GYPSY GIRL *Gut CXGUT 12*	52	1

SHARKEY *UK, male DJ / producer / instrumentalist – Jonathan Sharkey (1 WEEK)* pos/wks

8 Mar 97	REVOLUTIONS (EP) *React CDREACT 95*	53	1

Tracks on Revolutions (EP): Revolution Part One / Revolution Part Two / Revolution Part Two (remix)

Feargal SHARKEY *UK, male vocalist (58 WEEKS)* pos/wks

13 Oct 84	LISTEN TO YOUR FATHER *Zarjazz JAZZ 1*	23	7
29 Jun 85	LOVING YOU *Virgin VS 770*	26	10
12 Oct 85 ★	A GOOD HEART *Virgin VS 808*	1	16
4 Jan 86 ●	YOU LITTLE THIEF *Virgin VS 840*	5	9
5 Apr 86	SOMEONE TO SOMEBODY *Virgin VS 828*	64	3
16 Jan 88	MORE LOVE *Virgin VS 992*	44	5
16 Mar 91	I'VE GOT NEWS FOR YOU *Virgin VS 1294*	12	8

See also UNDERTONES; ASSEMBLY

SHARONETTES *US, female vocal group (8 WEEKS)* pos/wks

26 Apr 75	PAPA OOM MOW MOW *Black Magic BM 102*	26	5
12 Jul 75	GOING TO A GO-GO *Black Magic BM 104*	46	3

Debbie SHARP – *See DREAM FREQUENCY*

Dee Dee SHARP *US, female vocalist (2 WEEKS)* pos/wks

25 Apr 63	DO THE BIRD *Cameo Parkway C 244*	46	2

Barrie K SHARPE – *See Diana BROWN and Barrie K SHARPE*

SHARPE and NUMAN – *See Gary NUMAN*

Rocky SHARPE and the REPLAYS *UK, male / female vocal group (41 WEEKS)* pos/wks

16 Dec 78	RAMA LAMA DING DONG *Chiswick CHIS 104*	17	10
24 Mar 79	IMAGINATION *Chiswick CHIS 110*	39	6
25 Aug 79	LOVE WILL MAKE YOU FAIL IN SCHOOL *Chiswick CHIS 114* 1	60	4
9 Feb 80	MARTIAN HOP *Chiswick CHIS 121* 1	55	4
17 Apr 82	SHOUT SHOUT (KNOCK YOURSELF OUT) *Chiswick DICE 3*	19	9
7 Aug 82	CLAP YOUR HANDS *RAK 345*	54	3
26 Feb 83	IF YOU WANNA BE HAPPY *Polydor POSP 560*	46	5

1 Rocky Sharpe and the Replays featuring the Top Liners

Ben SHAW featuring Adele HOLNESS *UK, male producer and female vocalist (1 WEEK)* pos/wks

14 Jul 01	SO STRONG *Fire Recordings ERIF 009CDS*	72	1

Mark SHAW *UK, male vocalist (1 WEEK)* pos/wks

17 Nov 90	LOVE SO BRIGHT *EMI EM 161*	54	1

Sandie SHAW (128 Top 500) *Barefoot pop princess of the Sixties, b. Sandra Goodrich, 26 Feb 1947, Essex, UK. This distinctive vocalist, who has a 30-year chart span, was the first UK act to win the Eurovision Song Contest (with 'Puppet on a String' in 1967) (165 WEEKS)* pos/wks

8 Oct 64 ★	(THERE'S) ALWAYS SOMETHING THERE TO REMIND ME *Pye 7N 15704*	1	11
10 Dec 64 ●	GIRL DON'T COME *Pye 7N 15743*	3	12
18 Feb 65 ●	I'LL STOP AT NOTHING *Pye 7N 15783*	4	11
13 May 65 ★	LONG LIVE LOVE *Pye 7N 15841*	1	14
23 Sep 65 ●	MESSAGE UNDERSTOOD *Pye 7N 15940*	6	10
18 Nov 65	HOW CAN YOU TELL *Pye 7N 15987*	21	9
27 Jan 66 ●	TOMORROW *Pye 7N 17036*	9	9
19 May 66	NOTHING COMES EASY *Pye 7N 17086*	14	9
8 Sep 66	RUN *Pye 7N 17163*	32	5
24 Nov 66	THINK SOMETIMES ABOUT ME *Pye 7N 17212*	32	4
19 Jan 67	I DON'T NEED ANYTHING *Pye 7N 17239*	50	1
16 Mar 67 ★	PUPPET ON A STRING *Pye 7N 17272*	1	18
12 Jul 67	TONIGHT IN TOKYO *Pye 7N 17346*	21	6
4 Oct 67	YOU'VE NOT CHANGED *Pye 7N 17378*	18	12
7 Feb 68	TODAY *Pye 7N 17441*	27	7
12 Feb 69 ●	MONSIEUR DUPONT *Pye 7N 17675*	6	15
14 May 69	THINK IT ALL OVER *Pye 7N 17726*	42	4
21 Apr 84	HAND IN GLOVE *Rough Trade RT 130*	27	5
14 Jun 86	ARE YOU READY TO BE HEARTBROKEN? *Polydor POSP 793*	68	1
12 Nov 94	NOTHING LESS THAN BRILLIANT *Virgin VSCDT 1521*	66	2

Tracy SHAW *UK, female actor / vocalist (1 WEEK)* pos/wks

4 Jul 98	HAPPENIN' ALL OVER AGAIN *Recognition CDREC 2*	46	1

Winifred SHAW *US, female vocalist, d. 2 May 1982 (4 WEEKS)* pos/wks

14 Aug 76	LULLABY OF BROADWAY *United Artists UP 36131*	42	4

SHE – *See URBAN DISCHARGE featuring SHE*

SHE ROCKERS *UK, female rap duo (2 WEEKS)* pos/wks

13 Jan 90	JAM IT JAM *Jive JIVE 233*	58	2

George SHEARING QUINTET *UK / US, male instrumental group – leader George Shearing – piano (15 WEEKS)* pos/wks

19 Jul 62	LET THERE BE LOVE *Capitol CL 15257* 1	11	14
4 Oct 62	BAUBLES, BANGLES AND BEADS *Capitol CL 15269*	49	1

1 Nat 'King' Cole with George Shearing

Gary SHEARSTON *Australia, male vocalist (8 WEEKS)* pos/wks

5 Oct 74 ●	I GET A KICK OUT OF YOU *Charisma CB 234*	7	8

SHED SEVEN *UK, male vocal / instrumental group (48 WEEKS)* pos/wks

25 Jun 94	DOLPHIN *Polydor YORCD 2*	28	4

27 Aug 94	SPEAKEASY *Polydor YORCD 3*	24	3
12 Nov 94	OCEAN PIE *Polydor YORCD 4*	33	2
13 May 95	WHERE HAVE YOU BEEN TONIGHT *Polydor YORCD 5*	23	2
27 Jan 96	GETTING BETTER *Polydor 5778912*	14	3
23 Mar 96 ●	GOING FOR GOLD *Polydor 5762152*	8	5
18 May 96	BULLY BOY *Polydor 5765972*	22	3
31 Aug 96	ON STANDBY *Polydor 5752732*	12	4
23 Nov 96	CHASING RAINBOWS *Polydor 5759292*	17	5
14 Mar 98	SHE LEFT ME ON FRIDAY *Polydor 5695412*	11	4
23 May 98	THE HEROES *Polydor 5699172*	18	3
22 Aug 98	DEVIL IN YOUR SHOES (WALKING ALL OVER) *Polydor 5672072*	37	2
5 Jun 99	DISCO DOWN *Polydor 5638752*	13	6
5 May 01	CRY FOR HELP *Artful CD 35ARTFUL*	30	2

SHEEP ON DRUGS *UK, male vocal / instrumental duo – Duncan Gil-Rodriguez and Lee Fraser (5 WEEKS)* pos/wks

27 Mar 93	15 MINUTES OF FAME *Transglobal CID 564*	44	2
30 Oct 93	FROM A TO H AND BACK AGAIN *Transglobal CID 575*	40	2
14 May 94	LET THE GOOD TIMES ROLL *Transglobal CID 576*	56	1

SHEER BRONZE featuring Lisa MILLETT *UK, male / female vocal / instrumental duo (1 WEEK)* pos/wks

3 Sep 94	WALKIN' ON *Go.Beat GODCD 115*	63	1

SHEER ELEGANCE *UK, male vocal group (23 WEEKS)* pos/wks

20 Dec 75	MILKY WAY *Pye International 7N 25697*	18	10
3 Apr 76 ●	LIFE IS TOO SHORT GIRL *Pye International 7N 25703*	9	9
24 Jul 76	IT'S TEMPTATION *Pye International 7N 25715*	41	4

SHEILA B DEVOTION *France, female vocalist – Anny Chancel – and male vocal trio (33 WEEKS)* pos/wks

11 Mar 78	SINGIN' IN THE RAIN PART 1 *Carrere EMI 2751*	11	13
22 Jul 78	YOU LIGHT MY FIRE *Carrere EMI 2828*	44	6
24 Nov 79	SPACER *Carrere CAR 128* 1	18	14

1 Sheila & B. Devotion (Some pressings still credited Sheila B. Devotion)

Shade SHEIST featuring Nate DOGG and KURUPT *US, male rappers – leader Tremayne Thompson (7 WEEKS)* pos/wks

25 Aug 01	WHERE I WANNA BE (re) *London LONCD461*	14	7

Doug SHELDON *UK, male vocalist (15 WEEKS)* pos/wks

9 Nov 61	RUNAROUND SUE *Decca F 11398*	36	3
4 Jan 62	YOUR MA SAID YOU CRIED IN YOUR SLEEP LAST NIGHT *Decca F 11416*	29	6
7 Feb 63	I SAW LINDA YESTERDAY *Decca F 11564*	36	6

Michelle SHELLERS – See SOUL PROVIDERS featuring Michelle SHELLERS

Pete SHELLEY *UK, male vocalist (1 WEEK)* pos/wks

12 Mar 83	TELEPHONE OPERATOR *Genetic XX1*	66	1

See also BUZZCOCKS

Peter SHELLEY *UK, male vocalist (20 WEEKS)* pos/wks

14 Sep 74 ●	GEE BABY *Magnet MAG 12*	4	10
22 Mar 75 ●	LOVE ME LOVE MY DOG *Magnet MAG 22*	3	10

Anne SHELTON *UK, female vocalist – Patricia Sibley, d. 31 Jul 1994 (31 WEEKS)* pos/wks

16 Dec 55	ARRIVEDERCI DARLING *HMV POP 146*	17	4
13 Apr 56	SEVEN DAYS *Philips PB 567*	20	4
24 Aug 56 ★	LAY DOWN YOUR ARMS *Philips PB 616*	1	14
20 Nov 59	THE VILLAGE OF ST BERNADETTE *Philips PB 969*	27	1
26 Jan 61 ●	SAILOR *Philips PB 1096*	10	8

SHENA *UK, female vocalist (3 WEEKS)* pos/wks

2 Aug 97	LET THE BEAT HIT 'EM *VC VCRD 24*	28	2
1 Sep 01	I'LL BE WAITING *Rulin RULIN 17CDS* 1	44	1

1 Full Intention presents Shena

Vikki SHEPARD – See SLEAZESISTERS

Vonda SHEPARD *US, female vocalist (9 WEEKS)* pos/wks

5 Dec 98 ●	SEARCHIN' MY SOUL *Epic 6666332*	10	9

SHEPHERD SISTERS *US, female vocal group (6 WEEKS)* pos/wks

15 Nov 57	ALONE (WHY MUST I BE) (re) *HMV POP 411*	14	6

SHERBET *Australia, male vocal / instrumental group (10 WEEKS)* pos/wks

25 Sep 76 ●	HOWZAT *Epic EPC 4574*	4	10

Tony SHERIDAN and the BEATLES *UK, male vocalist / instrumental group (1 WEEK)* pos/wks

6 Jun 63	MY BONNIE *Polydor NH 668833*	48	1

Allan SHERMAN *US, male vocalist – Allan Copelon, d. 21 Nov 1973 (10 WEEKS)* pos/wks

12 Sep 63	HELLO MUDDAH! HELLO FADDAH! *Warner Bros. WB 106*	14	10

Bobby SHERMAN *US, male vocalist (4 WEEKS)* pos/wks

31 Oct 70	JULIE DO YA LOVE ME *CBS 5144*	28	4

SHERRICK *US, male vocalist – F Lamonte-Smith (10 WEEKS)* pos/wks

1 Aug 87	JUST CALL *Warner Bros. W 8380*	23	8
21 Nov 87	LET'S BE LOVERS TONIGHT *Warner Bros. W 8146*	63	2

Pluto SHERVINGTON *Jamaica, male vocalist (20 WEEKS)* pos/wks

7 Feb 76 ●	DAT *Opal Pal 5*	6	8
10 Apr 76	RAM GOAT LIVER *Trojan TR 7978*	43	4
6 Mar 82	YOUR HONOUR *KR KR 4* 1	19	8

1 Pluto

Holly SHERWOOD *US, female vocalist (7 WEEKS)* pos/wks

5 Feb 72	DAY BY DAY *Bell 1182*	29	7

Tony SHEVETON *UK, male vocalist (1 WEEK)* pos/wks

13 Feb 64	A MILLION DRUMS *Oriole CB 1895*	49	1

SHIMMON & WOOLFSON *UK, male DJ / production duo (1 WK)* pos/wks

10 Jan 98	WELCOME TO THE FUTURE *React CDREACT 119*	69	1

See also SUNDANCE

SHIMON & Andy C *UK, male production duo (2 WEEKS)* pos/wks

15 Sep 01	BODY ROCK *Ram RAMM 34CD*	58	2

SHINEHEAD *Jamaica, male vocalist – Edmund Aiken (6 WEEKS)* pos/wks

3 Apr 93	JAMAICAN IN NEW YORK *Elektra EKR 161CD*	30	5
26 Jun 93	LET 'EM IN *Elektra EKR 168CD*	70	1

SHINING *UK, male vocal / instrumental group (2 WEEKS)* pos/wks

6 Jul 02	I WONDER HOW *Zuma ZUMAD 002*	58	1
14 Sep 02	YOUNG AGAIN *Zuma ZUMASCD 003*	52	1

Mike SHINODA – See X-ECUTIONERS featuring Mike SHINODA and Mr HAHN of LINKIN PARK

SHIRELLES *US, female vocal group (29 WEEKS)* pos/wks

9 Feb 61 ●	WILL YOU LOVE ME TOMORROW *Top Rank JAR 540* ▲	4	15

Re-entries are listed as (re), (2re), (3re), etc which signifies that the hit re-entered the chart once, twice or three times, etc

| 31 May 62 | SOLDIER BOY *HMV POP 1019* ▲ | 23 | 9 |
| 23 May 63 | FOOLISH LITTLE GIRL *Stateside SS 181* | 38 | 5 |

SHIRLEY and COMPANY US, female vocalist
and male vocal / instrumental backing group (9 WEEKS)   pos/wks
| 8 Feb 75 ● | SHAME SHAME SHAME *All Platinum 6146 301* | 6 | 9 |

SHIVA UK, male / female vocal / instrumental group (5 WEEKS)   pos/wks
| 13 May 95 | WORK IT OUT *ffrr FCD 261* | 36 | 2 |
| 19 Aug 95 | FREEDOM *ffrr FCD 263* | 18 | 3 |

SHIVAREE
US, female / male vocal / instrumental group (1 WEEK)   pos/wks
| 17 Feb 01 | GOODNIGHT MOON *Capitol CDCL 825* | 63 | 1 |

SHO NUFF US, male vocal / instrumental group (4 WEEKS)   pos/wks
| 24 May 80 | IT'S ALRIGHT *Ensign ENY 37* | 53 | 4 |

Michelle SHOCKED
US, female vocalist (10 WEEKS)   pos/wks
8 Oct 88	ANCHORAGE *Cooking Vinyl LON 193*	60	4
14 Jan 89	IF LOVE WAS A TRAIN *Cooking Vinyl LON 212*	63	3
11 Mar 89	WHEN I GROW UP *Cooking Vinyl LON 219*	67	3

SHOCKING BLUE
Holland, male / female vocal / instrumental group (14 WEEKS)   pos/wks
| 17 Jan 70 ● | VENUS *Penny Farthing PEN 702* ▲ | 8 | 11 |
| 25 Apr 70 | MIGHTY JOE *Penny Farthing PEN 713* | 43 | 3 |

Troy SHONDELL US, male vocalist – Gary Schelton (11 WEEKS)   pos/wks
| 2 Nov 61 | THIS TIME *London HLG 9432* | 22 | 11 |

SHONDELLS – See Tommy JAMES and the SHONDELLS

SHOOTING PARTY UK, male vocal duo (2 WEEKS)   pos/wks
| 31 Mar 90 | LET'S HANG ON *Lisson DOLE 15* | 66 | 2 |

SHORTIE vs BLACK LEGEND
Italy, male production duo and male vocalist (2 WEEKS)   pos/wks
| 4 Aug 01 | SOMEBODY *WEA WEA 328 CD* | 37 | 2 |

SHOWADDYWADDY   82   Top 500

Rock 'n' roll revival octet from Leicester, UK, which included vocalists Dave Bartram and Buddy Gask. At the peak of their career, they had seven successive Top 5 entries with rousing revivals of old US rock 'n' roll songs. Best-selling single: 'Under the Moon of Love' 985,000 (209 WEEKS)   pos/wks
18 May 74 ●	HEY ROCK AND ROLL *Bell 1357*	2	14
17 Aug 74	ROCK 'N' ROLL LADY *Bell 1374*	15	9
30 Nov 74	HEY MR CHRISTMAS *Bell 1387*	13	8
22 Feb 75	SWEET MUSIC *Bell 1403*	14	9
17 May 75 ●	THREE STEPS TO HEAVEN *Bell 1426*	2	11
6 Sep 75 ●	HEARTBEAT *Bell 1450*	7	7
15 Nov 75	HEAVENLY *Bell 1460*	34	6
29 May 76	TROCADERO *Bell 1476*	32	3
6 Nov 76 ★	UNDER THE MOON OF LOVE *Bell 1495*	1	15
5 Mar 77 ●	WHEN *Arista 91*	3	11
23 Jul 77 ●	YOU GOT WHAT IT TAKES *Arista 126*	2	10
5 Nov 77 ●	DANCIN' PARTY *Arista 149*	4	11
25 Mar 78 ●	I WONDER WHY *Arista 174*	2	11
24 Jun 78 ●	A LITTLE BIT OF SOAP *Arista 191*	5	12
4 Nov 78 ●	PRETTY LITTLE ANGEL EYES *Arista ARIST 222*	5	12
31 Mar 79	REMEMBER THEN *Arista 247*	17	8
28 Jul 79	SWEET LITTLE ROCK 'N' ROLLER *Arista 278*	15	9
10 Nov 79	A NIGHT AT DADDY GEES *Arista 314*	39	5
27 Sep 80	WHY DO LOVERS BREAK EACH OTHERS' HEARTS *Arista ARIST 359*	22	10
29 Nov 80	BLUE MOON *Arista ARIST 379*	32	9

13 Jun 81	MULTIPLICATION *Arista ARIST 416*	39	4
28 Nov 81	FOOTSTEPS *Bell BELL 1499*	31	9
28 Aug 82	WHO PUT THE BOMP (IN THE BOMP-A-BOMP-A-BOMP) *RCA 236*	37	6

SHOWDOWN – See Garry LEE and SHOWDOWN

SHOWDOWN US, male vocal / instrumental group (3 WEEKS)   pos/wks
| 17 Dec 77 | KEEP DOIN' IT *State STAT 63* | 41 | 3 |

SHOWSTOPPERS US, male vocal group (25 WEEKS)   pos/wks
13 Mar 68	AIN'T NOTHING BUT A HOUSEPARTY *Beacon 3-100*	11	15
13 Nov 68	EENY MEENY *MGM 1436*	33	7
30 Jan 71	AIN'T NOTHING BUT A HOUSEPARTY (re-issue 2re) *Beacon BEA 100*	33	3

SHRIEKBACK UK, male vocal / instrumental group (4 WEEKS)   pos/wks
| 28 Jul 84 | HAND ON MY HEART *Arista SHRK 1* | 52 | 4 |

SHRINK Holland, male DJ / production trio (4 WEEKS)   pos/wks
| 10 Oct 98 | NERVOUS BREAKDOWN *VC Recordings VCRD42* | 42 | 2 |
| 19 Aug 00 | ARE YOU READY TO PARTY *Nulife 74321783772* | 39 | 2 |

SHUT UP AND DANCE
UK, male vocal / production group (14 WEEKS)   pos/wks
21 Apr 90	£20 TO GET IN *Shut Up and Dance SUAD 3*	56	3
28 Jul 90	LAMBORGHINI *Shut Up and Dance SUAD 4*	55	2
8 Feb 92	AUTOBIOGRAPHY OF A CRACKHEAD / THE GREEN MAN *Shut Up and Dance SUAD 21*	43	2
30 May 92 ●	RAVING I'M RAVING *Shut Up and Dance SUAD 30S* 1	2	2
15 Aug 92	THE ART OF MOVING BUTTS *Shut Up and Dance SUAD 34S* 2	69	1
1 Apr 95	SAVE IT 'TIL THE MOURNING AFTER *Pulse 8 PULS 84CD*	25	3
8 Jul 95	I LOVE U *Pulse 8 PULS 90CD* 3	68	1

1 Shut Up and Dance featuring Peter Bouncer 2 Shut Up and Dance featuring Erin 3 Shut Up and Dance featuring Richie Davis and Professor T

SHY UK, male vocal / instrumental group (3 WEEKS)   pos/wks
| 19 Apr 80 | GIRL (IT'S ALL I HAVE) *Gallery GA 1* | 60 | 3 |

SHY FX
UK, male instrumentalist / producer – Andre Williams (20 WEEKS)   pos/wks
1 Oct 94	ORIGINAL NUTTAH *Sound of Underground SOUR 008CD* 1	39	3
20 Mar 99	BAMBAATA 2012 *Ebony EBR 020CD*	60	1
6 Apr 02 ●	SHAKE UR BODY *Positiva CDTIV 171* 2	7	11
23 Nov 02	DON'T WANNA KNOW *ffrr FCD 408* 3	19	4
28 Dec 02	WOLF *Ebony Dubs EBD 001*	60	1+

1 UK Apachi with Shy FX 2 Shy FX and T-Power featuring Di 3 Shy FX and T-Power featuring Di and Skibadee

SHYHEIM US, male rapper (1 WEEK)   pos/wks
| 8 Jun 96 | THIS IZ REAL *Noo Trybe VUSCD 105* | 61 | 1 |

SIA Australia, female vocalist – Sia Furler (9 WEEKS)   pos/wks
3 Jun 00 ●	TAKEN FOR GRANTED *Long Lost Brother S 002CD1*	10	5
18 Aug 01	DESTINY *Ultimate Dilemma UDRCDS 043* 1	30	3
30 Mar 02	DISTRACTIONS *Ultimate Dilemma UDRCDS 046* 2	45	1

1 Zero 7 featuring Sia & Sophie 2 Zero 7 featuring Sia

Labi SIFFRE UK, male vocalist (44 WEEKS)   pos/wks
27 Nov 71	IT MUST BE LOVE *Pye International 7N 25572*	14	12
25 Mar 72	CRYING LAUGHING LOVING LYING *Pye International 7N 25576*	11	9
29 Jul 72	WATCH ME *Pye International 7N 25586*	29	6
4 Apr 87 ●	(SOMETHING INSIDE) SO STRONG *China WOK 12*	4	13
21 Nov 87	NOTHIN'S GONNA CHANGE *China WOK 16*	52	4

SIGNUM
Holland, male production duo
– Ronald Hagen and Pascal Minnard (6 WEEKS)   pos/wks

28 Nov 98	WHAT YA GOT 4 ME *Tidy Trax TIDY 118CD*	70	1
31 Jul 99	COMING ON STRONG *Tidy Trax TIDY 128T* [1]	66	1
9 Feb 02	WHAT YA GOT 4 ME (re-mix) *Tidy Trax TIDY 163CD*	35	3
29 Jun 02	COMING ON STRONG (re-mix) *Tidy Two TIDYTWO 104CD* [1]	50	1

[1] Signum featuring Scott Mac

SIGUE SIGUE SPUTNIK
UK, male vocal / instrumental group (20 WEEKS)   pos/wks

1 Mar 86 ●	LOVE MISSILE F1-11 *Parlophone SSS 1*	3	9
7 Jun 86	21st CENTURY BOY *Parlophone SSS 2*	20	5
19 Nov 88	SUCCESS *Parlophone SSS 3*	31	3
1 Apr 89	DANCERAMA *Parlophone SSS 5*	50	2
20 May 89	ALBINONI VS STAR WARS *Parlophone SSS 4*	75	1

SIL
Holland, male DJ / production duo (1 WEEK)   pos/wks

11 Apr 98	WINDOWS '98 *Hooj Choons HOOJCD 60*	58	1

SILENCERS
UK, male vocal / instrumental group (7 WEEKS)   pos/wks

25 Jun 88	PAINTED MOON *RCA HUSH 1*	57	4
27 May 89	SCOTTISH RAIN *RCA PB 42701*	71	2
15 May 93	I CAN FEEL IT *RCA 74321147112*	62	1

SILENT UNDERDOG
UK, male instrumentalist – Paul Hardcastle (1 WEEK)   pos/wks

16 Feb 85	PAPA'S GOT A BRAND NEW PIGBAG *Kaz KAZ 50*	73	1

SILICONE SOUL featuring Louise Clare MARSHALL
UK, male production duo and UK, female vocalist (5 WEEKS)   pos/wks

6 Oct 01	RIGHT ON! (re) *VC Recordings / Soma VCRD 96*	15	5

SILJE
Norway, female vocalist (6 WEEKS)   pos/wks

15 Dec 90	TELL ME WHERE YOU'RE GOING *EMI EM 159*	55	6

SILK
US, male vocal group (10 WEEKS)   pos/wks

24 Apr 93	FREAK ME (re) *Elektra EKR 165CD* ▲	46	6
5 Jun 93	GIRL U FOR ME *Elektra EKR 167CD*	67	2
9 Oct 93	BABY IT'S YOU *Elektra EKR 173CD*	44	2

SILKIE
UK, male / female vocal / instrumental group (6 WEEKS)   pos/wks

23 Sep 65	YOU'VE GOT TO HIDE YOUR LOVE AWAY *Fontana TF 603*	28	6

SILKK THE SHOCKER – See Montell JORDAN

SILSOE
UK, male instrumentalist – Rod Argent (4 WEEKS)   pos/wks

21 Jun 86	AZTEC GOLD *CBS A 7231*	48	4

'Aztec Gold' was the ITV theme to the 1986 World Cup

See also SAN JOSE featuring Rodriguez ARGENTINA; ARGENT

Luci SILVAS
UK, female vocalist (1 WEEK)   pos/wks

17 Jun 00	IT'S TOO LATE *EMI CDEM 565*	62	1

SILVER BULLET
UK, male rapper – Richard Brown (20 WEEKS)   pos/wks

2 Sep 89	BRING FORTH THE GUILLOTINE (re) *Tam Tam TTT 013*	45	6
9 Dec 89	20 SECONDS TO COMPLY *Tam Tam 7TTT 019*	11	10
13 Apr 91	UNDERCOVER ANARCHIST *Parlophone R 6284*	33	4

SILVER BULLET BAND – See Bob SEGER and the SILVER BULLET BAND

SILVER CITY
UK, male / female vocal / instrumental duo (1 WEEK)   pos/wks

30 Oct 93	LOVE INFINITY *Silver City GFJMCD 1*	62	1

SILVER CONVENTION
Germany / US, female vocal group (35 WEEKS)   pos/wks

5 Apr 75	SAVE ME *Magnet MAG 26*	30	7
15 Nov 75	FLY ROBIN FLY *Magnet MAG 43* ▲	28	8
3 Apr 76 ●	GET UP AND BOOGIE *Magnet MAG 55*	7	11
19 Jun 76	TIGER BABY / NO NO JOE *Magnet MAG 69*	41	4
29 Jan 77	EVERYBODY'S TALKIN' 'BOUT LOVE *Magnet MAG 81*	25	5

SILVER SUN
UK, male vocal / instrumental group (13 WEEKS)   pos/wks

2 Nov 96	LAVA *Polydor 5756872*	54	1
22 Feb 97	LAST DAY *Polydor 5732432*	48	1
3 May 97	GOLDEN SKIN *Polydor 5738272*	32	2
5 Jul 97	JULIA *Polydor 5711752*	51	1
18 Oct 97	LAVA (re-issue) *Polydor 5714242*	35	2
20 Jun 98	TOO MUCH, TOO LITTLE, TOO LATE *Polydor 5699152*	20	4
26 Sep 98	I'LL SEE YOU AROUND *Polydor 5674532*	26	2

SILVERCHAIR
Australia, male vocal / instrumental group (8 WEEKS)   pos/wks

29 Jul 95	PURE MASSACRE *Murmur 6622642*	71	1
9 Sep 95	TOMORROW *Murmur 6623952*	59	2
5 Apr 97	FREAK *Murmur 6640765*	34	2
19 Jul 97	ABUSE ME *Murmur 6647907*	40	2
15 May 99	ANA'S SONG *Columbia 6673452*	45	1

Dooley SILVERSPOON
US, male vocalist (3 WEEKS)   pos/wks

31 Jan 76	LET ME BE THE NUMBER 1 (LOVE OF YOUR LIFE) *Seville SEV 1020*	44	3

Harry SIMEONE CHORALE
US, choir (14 WEEKS)   pos/wks

13 Feb 59	LITTLE DRUMMER BOY *Top Rank JAR 101*	13	7
22 Dec 60	ONWARD CHRISTIAN SOLDIERS (2re) *Ember EMBS 118*	35	5
20 Dec 62	ONWARD CHRISTIAN SOLDIERS (re-issue) *Ember EMBS 144*	38	2

Gene SIMMONS
US, male vocalist (4 WEEKS)   pos/wks

27 Jan 79	RADIOACTIVE *Casablanca CAN 134*	41	4

See also KISS

SIMON
UK, male producer – Simon Pearson (2 WEEKS)   pos/wks

31 Mar 01	FREE AT LAST *Positiva CDTIV 152*	36	2

Carly SIMON ⟨400⟩ ⟨Top 500⟩
First charted in US in 1964 as half of folk duo Simon Sisters with sister Lucy.
b. 25 Jun 1945, New York. Winner of 1971's Best New Artist Grammy was
married to fellow singer / songwriter James Taylor (1972-1983). Elected to
Songwriters Hall of Fame 1994 (85 WEEKS)   pos/wks

16 Dec 72 ●	YOU'RE SO VAIN *Elektra K 12077* ▲	3	15
31 Mar 73	THE RIGHT THING TO DO *Elektra K 12095*	17	9
16 Mar 74	MOCKINGBIRD *Elektra K 12134* [1]	34	5
6 Aug 77	NOBODY DOES IT BETTER *Elektra K 12261*	7	12
21 Aug 82 ●	WHY *WEA K 79300*	10	13
24 Jan 87 ●	COMING AROUND AGAIN *Arista ARIST 687*	10	12
10 Jun 89	WHY (re-issue) *WEA U 7501*	56	5
20 Apr 91	YOU'RE SO VAIN (re-issue) *Elektra EKR 123*	41	5
22 Dec 01	SON OF A GUN (I BETCHA THINK THIS SONG IS ABOUT YOU) (re) *Virgin VUSCD 232* [2]	13	9

[1] Carly Simon and, uncredited, James Taylor [2] Janet with Carly Simon featuring Missy Elliott

See also Will POWERS

Joe SIMON
US, male vocalist (10 WEEKS)   pos/wks

16 Jun 73	STEP BY STEP *Mojo 2093 030*	14	10

Paul SIMON `401` `Top 500`

Acclaimed award-winning singer / songwriter b. 13 Oct 1941, New Jersey, US. Recorded under various names in early 1960s before forming top duo Simon and Garfunkel. Married to actress Carrie Fisher (1983-85) and later Edie Brickell. Also helped to popularise world music (85 WEEKS)   pos/wks

19 Feb 72	● MOTHER AND CHILD REUNION *CBS 7793*	5	2
29 Apr 72	ME AND JULIO DOWN BY THE SCHOOLYARD *CBS 7964*	15	9
16 Jun 73	● TAKE ME TO THE MARDI GRAS *CBS 1578*	7	11
22 Sep 73	LOVES ME LIKE A ROCK *CBS 1700*	39	5
10 Jan 76	50 WAYS TO LEAVE YOUR LOVER *CBS 3887* ▲	23	6
3 Dec 77	SLIP SLIDIN' AWAY *CBS 5770*	36	5
6 Sep 80	LATE IN THE EVENING *Warner Bros. K 17666*	58	4
13 Sep 86	● YOU CAN CALL ME AL *Warner Bros. W 8667*	4	13
13 Dec 86	THE BOY IN THE BUBBLE *Warner Bros. W 8509*	26	8
6 Oct 90	THE OBVIOUS CHILD *Warner Bros. W 9549*	15	10
9 Dec 95	SOMETHING SO RIGHT *RCA 74321332392* [1]	44	2

[1] Annie Lennox featuring Paul Simon

See also SIMON and GARFUNKEL

Ronni SIMON *UK, male vocalist (2 WEEKS)*   pos/wks

13 Aug 94	B GOOD 2 ME *Network NWKCD 80*	73	1
10 Jun 95	TAKE YOU THERE *Network NWKCD 85*	58	1

Tito SIMON *Jamaica, male vocalist (4 WEEKS)*   pos/wks

8 Feb 75	THIS MONDAY MORNING FEELING *Horse HOSS 57*	45	4

SIMON and GARFUNKEL `381` `Top 500`

Ultra-successful, folk-rooted duo, Paul Simon and Art Garfunkel, who first charted in US as Tom and Jerry in 1957. Their 'Bridge Over Troubled Water' single and album (Top UK LP of both 1970 and 1971) is regarded as among the all-time greatest recordings. In 1968 they had three of the US Top 5 albums (87 WEEKS)   pos/wks

24 Mar 66	● HOMEWARD BOUND *CBS 202045*	9	12
16 Jun 66	I AM A ROCK *CBS 202303*	17	10
10 Jul 68	● MRS ROBINSON *CBS 3443* ▲	4	12
8 Jan 69	● MRS ROBINSON (EP) *CBS EP 6400*	9	5
30 Apr 69	● THE BOXER *CBS 4162*	6	14
21 Feb 70	★ BRIDGE OVER TROUBLED WATER (re) *CBS 4790* [1] ▲	1	20
7 Oct 72	AMERICA *CBS 8336*	25	7
7 Dec 91	A HAZY SHADE OF WINTER / SILENT NIGHT – SEVEN O'CLOCK NEWS *Columbia 6576537*	30	6
15 Feb 92	THE BOXER (re-issue) *Columbia 6578067*	75	1

[1] Keyboard: Larry Knechtel

Tracks on Mrs Robinson (EP): Mrs Robinson / Scarborough Fair – Canticle / The Sound of Silence / April Come She Will. This EP would have stayed more than five weeks on chart had a decision to exclude EPs from the chart in Feb 1969 not been taken

See also Paul SIMON; Art GARFUNKEL

SIMONE *US, female vocalist (1 WEEK)*   pos/wks

23 Nov 91	MY FAMILY DEPENDS ON ME *Strictly Rhythm A 8678*	75	1

Nina SIMONE

US, female vocalist – Eunice Waymon (46 WEEKS)   pos/wks

5 Aug 65	I PUT A SPELL ON YOU *Philips BF 1415*	49	1
16 Oct 68	● AIN'T GOT NO – I GOT LIFE / DO WHAT YOU GOTTA DO *RCA 1743*	2	18
15 Jan 69	● TO LOVE SOMEBODY *RCA 1779*	5	9
15 Jan 69	I PUT A SPELL ON YOU (re-issue) *Philips BF 1736*	28	4
31 Oct 87	● MY BABY JUST CARES FOR ME *Charly CYZ 7112*	5	11
9 Jul 94	FEELING GOOD *Mercury MERCD 403*	40	3

'Do What You Gotta Do' was listed only for the first eight weeks of the record's chart run. It peaked at No.7

Victor SIMONELLI presents SOLUTION

US, male producer (1 WEEK)   pos/wks

2 Nov 96	FEELS SO RIGHT *Soundproof MCSTD 40068*	63	1

SIMPLE MINDS `101` `Top 500` *Most successful Scottish band of the 1980s, fronted by Jim Kerr (b. 9 Jul 1959, Glasgow), who married Chrissie Hynde, lead singer of Pretenders. Five of the quintet's albums entered the UK chart at No.1, and world sales topped 30 million (190 WEEKS)*   pos/wks

12 May 79	LIFE IN A DAY *Zoom ZUM 10*	62	2
23 May 81	THE AMERICAN *Virgin VS 410*	59	3
15 Aug 81	LOVE SONG *Virgin VS 434*	47	4
7 Nov 81	SWEAT IN BULLET *Virgin VS 451*	52	3
10 Apr 82	PROMISED YOU A MIRACLE *Virgin VS 488*	13	11
28 Aug 82	GLITTERING PRIZE *Virgin VS 511*	16	11
13 Nov 82	SOMEONE SOMEWHERE (IN SUMMERTIME) *Virgin VS 538*	36	5
26 Nov 83	WATERFRONT *Virgin VS 636*	13	10
28 Jan 84	SPEED YOUR LOVE TO ME *Virgin VS 649*	20	4
24 Mar 84	UP ON THE CATWALK *Virgin VS 661*	27	5
20 Apr 85	● DON'T YOU (FORGET ABOUT ME) (4re) *Virgin VS 749* ▲	7	24
12 Oct 85	● ALIVE AND KICKING (re) *Virgin VS 817*	7	11
1 Feb 86	● SANCTIFY YOURSELF *Virgin SM 1*	10	7
12 Apr 86	● ALL THE THINGS SHE SAID (re) *Virgin VS 860*	9	9
15 Nov 86	GHOSTDANCING (re) *Virgin VS 907*	13	8
20 Jun 87	PROMISED YOU A MIRACLE *Virgin SM 2*	19	7
18 Feb 89	★ BELFAST CHILD *Virgin SMX 3*	1	11
22 Apr 89	THIS IS YOUR LAND *Virgin SMX4*	13	4
29 Jul 89	KICK IT IN *Virgin SM 5*	15	5
9 Dec 89	THE AMSTERDAM EP *Virgin SMX 6*	18	6
23 Mar 91	LET THERE BE LOVE *Virgin VS 1332*	6	7
25 May 91	SEE THE LIGHTS *Virgin VS 1343*	20	4
31 Aug 91	STAND BY LOVE *Virgin VS 1358*	13	4
26 Oct 91	REAL LIFE *Virgin VS 1382*	34	2
10 Oct 92	● LOVE SONG / ALIVE AND KICKING (re-issue) *Virgin VS 1440*	6	6
28 Jan 95	SHE'S A RIVER *Virgin VSCDX 1509*	9	5
8 Apr 95	HYPNOTISED *Virgin VSCDX 1534*	18	5
14 Mar 98	GLITTERBALL *Chrysalis CDCHSS 5078*	18	2
30 May 98	WAR BABIES *Chrysalis CDCHS 5088*	43	1
2 Feb 02	BELFAST TRANCE *Nebula BELFCD 001* [1]	74	1
30 Mar 02	CRY *Eagle EAGXS 218*	47	1
20 Jul 02	MONSTER *Defected DFECT 49* [2]	67	1

[1] John "OO" Fleming vs Simple Minds [2] Liquid People vs Simple Minds

The 1987 version of 'Promised You a Miracle' was a live recording. Tracks on The Amsterdam EP: Let It All Come Down / Jerusalem / Sign of the Times

SIMPLICIOUS *US, male vocal group (9 WEEKS)*   pos/wks

29 Sep 84	LET HER FEEL IT *Fourth & Broadway BRW 13*	65	3
2 Feb 85	LET HER FEEL IT (re-issue) *Fourth & Broadway BRW 18*	34	6

The re-issue of 'Let Her Feel It' was listed with 'Personality' by Eugene Wilde

SIMPLY RED `75` `Top 500`

The unmistakable Mick Hucknall (b. 8 Jun 1960, Manchester, UK) quickly became the representative face and voice of this internationally popular outfit. Their 'Stars' album sold more than two million in the UK and was the biggest British seller in 1991 and 1992. Best-selling single: 'Fairground' 783,000 (214 WEEKS)   pos/wks

15 Jun 85	MONEY'S TOO TIGHT (TO MENTION) *Elektra EKR 9*	13	12
21 Sep 85	COME TO MY AID *Elektra EKR 19*	66	2
16 Nov 85	HOLDING BACK THE YEARS *Elektra EKR 29* ▲	51	4
8 Mar 86	JERICHO *WEA YZ 63*	53	3
17 May 86	● HOLDING BACK THE YEARS (re-issue) *WEA YZ 70*	2	13
9 Aug 86	OPEN UP THE RED BOX *WEA YZ 75*	61	4
14 Feb 87	THE RIGHT THING *WEA YZ 103*	11	10
23 May 87	INFIDELITY *Elektra YZ 114*	31	5
28 Nov 87	EV'RY TIME WE SAY GOODBYE *Elektra YZ 161*	11	9
12 Mar 88	I WON'T FEEL BAD *Elektra YZ 172*	68	3
28 Jan 89	IT'S ONLY LOVE *Elektra YZ 349*	13	8
8 Apr 89	● IF YOU DON'T KNOW ME BY NOW *Elektra YZ 377* ▲	2	10
8 Jul 89	A NEW FLAME *WEA YZ 404*	17	8
28 Oct 89	YOU'VE GOT IT *Elektra YZ 424*	46	3
21 Sep 91	SOMETHING GOT ME STARTED *East West YZ 614*	11	8
30 Nov 91	● STARS *East West YZ 626*	8	10
8 Feb 92	● FOR YOUR BABIES *East West YZ 642*	9	8
2 May 92	THRILL ME *East West YZ 671*	33	5

Date	Title	Pos	Wks
25 Jul 92	YOUR MIRROR *East West YZ 689*	17	4
21 Nov 92	MONTREUX (EP) *East West YZ 716*	11	10
30 Sep 95 ★	FAIRGROUND *East West EW 001CD1* ■	1	14
16 Dec 95	REMEMBERING THE FIRST TIME *East West EW 015CD1*	22	6
24 Feb 96	NEVER NEVER LOVE *East West EW 029CD1*	18	4
22 Jun 96	WE'RE IN THIS TOGETHER *East West EW 046CD1*	11	6
9 Nov 96 ●	ANGEL *East West EW 074CD1*	4	13
20 Sep 97	NIGHT NURSE *East West EW 129CD1* [1]	13	8
16 May 98 ●	SAY YOU LOVE ME *East West EW 164CD*	7	7
22 Aug 98 ●	THE AIR THAT I BREATHE *East West EW 3821CD*	6	7
12 Dec 98	GHETTO GIRL *East West EW 191CD1*	34	2
30 Oct 99	AIN'T THAT A LOT OF LOVE *East West EW 208CD1*	14	6
19 Feb 00	YOUR EYES *East West EW 212CD1*	26	2

[1] Sly and Robbie featuring Simply Red

Tracks on Montreux (EP): Drowning In My Own Tears / Grandma's Hands / Lady Godiva's Room / Love for Sale

SIMPLY RED AND WHITE
UK, male Sunderland FC supporters vocal group (4 WEEKS) pos/wks

6 Apr 96	DAYDREAM BELIEVER (CHEER UP PETER REID) (re) *Ropery SHAYISGOD 1D*	41	4

SIMPLY SMOOTH *US, male / female vocal group (1 WEEK)* pos/wks

17 Oct 98	LADY (YOU BRING ME UP) *Big Bang CDBANG 07*	● 70	1

Jessica SIMPSON *US, female vocalist (24 WEEKS)* pos/wks

22 Apr 00 ●	I WANNA LOVE YOU FOREVER (re) *Columbia 6691272*	7	11
15 Jul 00	I THINK I'M IN LOVE WITH YOU *Columbia 6695942*	15	7
14 Jul 01	IRRESISTIBLE *Columbia 6714102*	11	6

Paul SIMPSON featuring ADEVA
US, producer / instrumentalist with female vocalist (8 WEEKS) pos/wks

25 Mar 89	MUSICAL FREEDOM (MOVING ON UP) *Cooltempo CDCOOL 182*	22	8

Vida SIMPSON *US, female vocalist (1 WEEK)* pos/wks

18 Feb 95	OOHHH BABY *Hi-Life HICD 6*	● 70	1

SIMPSONS *US, male / female cartoon group, lead vocal – Bart Simpson (Nancy Cartwright) (19 WEEKS)* pos/wks

26 Jan 91 ★	DO THE BARTMAN *Geffen GEF 87*	1	12
6 Apr 91 ●	DEEP DEEP TROUBLE *Geffen GEF 88* [1]	7	7

[1] Simpsons featuring Bart and Homer

W/Cdr AE SIMS – See The Central Band of the ROYAL AIR FORCE, Conductor W/Cdr AE SIMS OBE

Joyce SIMS *US, female vocalist (36 WEEKS)* pos/wks

19 Apr 86	ALL AND ALL *London LON 94*	16	10
13 Jun 87	LIFETIME LOVE *London LON 137*	34	4
9 Jan 88 ●	COME INTO MY LIFE *London LON 161*	7	9
23 Apr 88	WALK AWAY *London LON 176*	24	6
17 Jun 89	LOOKING FOR A LOVE *ffrr F 109*	39	4
27 May 95	COME INTO MY LIFE (re-mix) *Club Tools 0060435 CLU*	72	1

Kym SIMS *US, female vocalist (23 WEEKS)* pos/wks

7 Dec 91 ●	TOO BLIND TO SEE IT *Atco B 8667*	5	12
28 Mar 92	TAKE MY ADVICE *Atco B 8591*	13	7
27 Jun 92	A LITTLE BIT MORE *Atco B 8528*	30	3
8 Jun 96	WE GOTTA LOVE *Pulse 8 CDLOSE 104*	58	1

SIN WITH SEBASTIAN
Germany, male vocalist – Sebastian Roth (2 WEEKS) pos/wks

16 Sep 95	SHUT UP (AND SLEEP WITH ME) *Sing Sing 74321253592*	44	1
27 Jan 96	SHUT UP (AND SLEEP WITH ME) (re-mix) *Sing Sing 74321337972*	46	1

Frank SINATRA [11] Top 500
Legendary entertainer regarded by many as the greatest song stylist of the 20th century, b. 12 Dec 1915, New Jersey, d. 14 May 1998. The vocalist (with Tommy Dorsey Orchestra) on first US No.1 'I'll Never Smile Again' (1940) was the first teen idol. 'Songs for Swingin' Lovers' is the only album to reach the UK Top 20 singles chart, and is one of 26 US gold albums amassed by the influential vocalist who has scored more US Top 10 LPs than any other soloist. Sinatra, the first recipient of a Grammy Lifetime Achievement award (1965), holds the UK chart longevity record with 'My Way' (440 WEEKS) pos/wks

9 Jul 54	YOUNG-AT-HEART *Capitol CL 14064*	12	1
16 Jul 54 ★	THREE COINS IN THE FOUNTAIN *Capitol CL 14120*	1	19
10 Jun 55	YOU MY LOVE (2re) *Capitol CL 14240*	13	7
5 Aug 55 ●	LEARNIN' THE BLUES *Capitol CL 14296*	2	13
2 Sep 55	NOT AS A STRANGER *Capitol CL 14326*	18	1
13 Jan 56 ●	LOVE AND MARRIAGE *Capitol CL 14503*	3	8
20 Jan 56 ●	(LOVE IS) THE TENDER TRAP *Capitol CL 14511*	2	9
15 Jun 56	SONGS FOR SWINGIN' LOVERS (LP) *Capitol LCT 6106*	12	8
22 Nov 57 ●	CHICAGO *Capitol CL 14800*	3	20
7 Feb 58	WITCHCRAFT *Capitol CL 14819*	12	8
14 Nov 58	MR SUCCESS (2re) *Capitol CL 14956*	25	4
10 Apr 59	FRENCH FOREIGN LEGION *Capitol CL 14997*	18	5
15 May 59	COME DANCE WITH ME! (LP) *Capitol LCT 6179* [1]	30	1
28 Aug 59 ●	HIGH HOPES (2re) *Capitol CL 15052* [2]	6	15
7 Apr 60	IT'S NICE TO GO TRAV'LING *Capitol CL 15116*	48	2
16 Jun 60	RIVER STAY 'WAY FROM MY DOOR *Capitol CL 15135*	18	9
8 Sep 60	NICE 'N' EASY *Capitol CL 15150*	15	12
24 Nov 60	OL' MACDONALD *Capitol CL 15168*	11	8
20 Apr 61	MY BLUE HEAVEN *Capitol CL 15193*	33	7
28 Sep 61	GRANADA *Reprise R 20010*	15	8
23 Nov 61	THE COFFEE SONG *Reprise R 20035*	39	3
5 Apr 62	EV'RYBODY'S TWISTING *Reprise R 20063*	22	12
13 Dec 62	ME AND MY SHADOW (re) *Reprise R 20128* [3]	20	9
7 Mar 63	MY KIND OF GIRL *Reprise R 20148* [4]	35	6
24 Sep 64	HELLO DOLLY *Reprise R 20351* [4]	47	1
12 May 66 ★	STRANGERS IN THE NIGHT *Reprise R 23052* ▲	1	20
29 Sep 66	SUMMER WIND *Reprise R 20509*	36	5
15 Dec 66	THAT'S LIFE *Reprise RS 20531*	44	5
23 Mar 67 ★	SOMETHIN' STUPID *Reprise RS 23166* [5] ▲	1	18
23 Aug 67	THE WORLD WE KNEW (OVER AND OVER) *Reprise RS 20610*	33	11
2 Apr 69 ●	MY WAY (8re) *Reprise RS 20817*	5	122
4 Oct 69	LOVE'S BEEN GOOD TO ME *Reprise RS 20852*	8	18
6 Mar 71	I WILL DRINK THE WINE *Reprise RS 23487*	16	12
20 Dec 75	I BELIEVE I'M GONNA LOVE YOU *Reprise K 14400*	34	7
9 Aug 80 ●	THEME FROM 'NEW YORK, NEW YORK' (re) *Reprise K 14502*	4	14
4 Dec 93 ●	I'VE GOT YOU UNDER MY SKIN *Island CID 578* [6]	4	9
16 Apr 94	MY WAY (re-issue) *Reprise W 0163CD*	45	2
30 Jan 99	THEY ALL LAUGHED *Reprise W 469CD*	41	1

[1] Frank Sinatra with Billy May and His Orchestra [2] Frank Sinatra with a bunch of kids [3] Frank Sinatra and Sammy Davis Jr [4] Frank Sinatra with Count Basie [5] Nancy Sinatra and Frank Sinatra [6] Frank Sinatra with Bono

As a re-entry 'My Way' peaked at No.49, No.30, No.33, No.28 and No.18 in 1970, No.22 and No.39 in 1971 and No.50 in 1972. 'Theme From 'New York, New York' reached its peak position only on re-entry in Feb 1996. Tracks on Songs for Swinging Lovers (LP): You Make Me Feel So Young / It Happened In Monterey / You're Getting to Be a Habit with Me / You Brought a New Kind of Love to Me / Too Marvellous for Words / Old Devil Moon / Pennies from Heaven / Love Is Here to Stay / I've Got You Under My Skin / I Thought About You / We'll Be Together Again / Makin' Whoopee / Swingin' Down the Lane / Anything Goes / How About You. Tracks on Come Dance With Me (LP): Come Dance With Me / Something's Gotta Give / Just in Time / Dancing in the Dark / Too Close for Comfort / I Could Have Danced All Night / Saturday Night Is the Loneliest Night of the Week / Day In Day Out / Cheek to Cheek / Baubles Bangles and Beads / The Song Is You / The Last Dance. 'All the Way' and 'Chicago', Capitol CL 14800, were at first billed separately, then together for one week, then 'All the Way' on its own. 'I've Got You Under My Skin' was the flip side of 'Stay (Faraway So Close)' by U2

Nancy SINATRA [313] Top 500
Eldest child of legendary singer, b. 8 Jun 1940, New Jersey, US – days before father Frank's first US Top 10 entry. Was subject of 1945 hit 'Nancy (with the Laughing Eyes)'. 'Somethin' Stupid' is the only father-daughter chart topper (99 WEEKS) pos/wks

27 Jan 66 ★	THESE BOOTS ARE MADE FOR WALKIN' *Reprise R 20432* ▲	1	14

28 Apr 66	**HOW DOES THAT GRAB YOU DARLIN'** *Reprise R 20461*	.19	8
19 Jan 67 ●	**SUGAR TOWN** *Reprise RS 20527*	.8	10
23 Mar 67 ★	**SOMETHIN' STUPID** *Reprise RS 23166* 1 ▲	.1	18
5 Jul 67	**YOU ONLY LIVE TWICE / JACKSON** *Reprise RS 20595* 2	.11	19
8 Nov 67	**LADYBIRD** *Reprise RS 20629* 3	.47	1
29 Nov 69	**THE HIGHWAY SONG** *Reprise RS 20869*	.21	10
21 Aug 71 ●	**DID YOU EVER** *Reprise K 14093* 4	.2	19

1 Nancy Sinatra and Frank Sinatra 2 Nancy Sinatra / Nancy Sinatra and Lee Hazlewood 3 Nancy Sinatra and Lee Hazlewood 4 Nancy and Lee

'Jackson' listed with 'You Only Live Twice' from 12 Jul 1967

SINCLAIR *UK, male vocalist – Mike Sinclair (8 WEEKS)* pos/wks
21 Aug 93	**AIN'T NO CASANOVA** *Dome CDDOME 1004*	.28	5
26 Feb 94	**(I WANNA KNOW) WHY** *Dome CDDOME 1009*	.58	2
6 Aug 94	**DON'T LIE** *Dome CDDOME 1010*	.70	1

Bob SINCLAR *France, male DJ / Producer (7 WEEKS)* pos/wks
20 Mar 99	**MY ONLY LOVE** *East West EW 196CD* 1	.56	1
19 Aug 00 ●	**I FEEL FOR YOU** *Defected DEFECT 18CDS*	.9	5
7 Apr 01	**DARLIN'** *Defected DFECT 30CDS* 2	.46	1

1 Bob Sinclar featuring Lee A Genesis 2 Bob Sinclar featuring James Williams

SINDY *UK, female doll vocalist (1 WEEK)* pos/wks
5 Oct 96	**SATURDAY NIGHT** *Love This LUVTHISCD 13*	.70	1

SINE *US, male / female vocal / instrumental group (9 WEEKS)* pos/wks
10 Jun 78	**JUST LET ME DO MY THING** *CBS 6351*	.33	9

SINFONIA OF LONDON – *See Peter AUTY and the SINFONIA OF LONDON conducted by Howard BLAKE*

SINGING CORNER meets DONOVAN
UK, male vocalists (1 WEEK) pos/wks
1 Dec 90	**JENNIFER JUNIPER** *Fontana SYP 1*	.68	1

SINGING DOGS *Denmark, canine vocal group (4 WEEKS)* pos/wks
25 Nov 55	**THE SINGING DOGS (MEDLEY)** *Nixa N 15009* 1	.13	4

1 Don Carlos presents The Singing Dogs

Medley songs: Pat-a-Cake / Three Blind Mice / Jingle Bells / Oh Susanna

SINGING NUN (Soeur Sourire) *Belgium, female vocalist – Jeanine Deckers, d. 31 Mar 1985 (14 WEEKS)* pos/wks
5 Dec 63 ●	**DOMINIQUE** *Philips BF 1293* ▲	.7	14

SINGING SHEEP *UK, computerised sheep noises (5 WEEKS)* pos/wks
18 Dec 82	**BAA BAA BLACK SHEEP** *Sheep BAA 1*	.42	5

Maxine SINGLETON *US, female vocalist (3 WEEKS)* pos/wks
2 Apr 83	**YOU CAN'T RUN FROM LOVE** *Creole CR 50*	.57	3

SINITTA 295 Top 500
As well as having a string of Hi-NRG dance hits, and being a disco diva and Miquel Brown's daughter, Sinitta Malone (b. 19 Oct 1966, Washington, DC) has starred in several London stage musicals including 'Mutiny' with David Essex and 'What a Feeling' with Luke Goss and Sonia (104 WEEKS) pos/wks
8 Mar 86 ●	**SO MACHO / CRUISING (re)** *Fanfare FAN 7*	.2	28
11 Oct 86	**FEELS LIKE THE FIRST TIME** *Fanfare FAN 8*	.45	5
25 Jul 87 ●	**TOY BOY** *Fanfare FAN 12*	.4	14
12 Dec 87	**G.T.O.** *Fanfare FAN 14*	.15	9
19 Mar 88 ●	**CROSS MY BROKEN HEART** *Fanfare FAN 15*	.6	9
24 Sep 88	**I DON'T BELIEVE IN MIRACLES** *Fanfare FAN 16*	.22	8
3 Jun 89 ●	**RIGHT BACK WHERE WE STARTED FROM** *Fanfare FAN 18*	.4	10
7 Oct 89	**LOVE ON A MOUNTAIN TOP** *Fanfare FAN 21*	.20	6
21 Apr 90	**HITCHIN' A RIDE** *Fanfare FAN 24*	.24	6
22 Sep 90	**LOVE AND AFFECTION** *Fanfare FAN 31*	.62	3

4 Jul 92	**SHAME SHAME SHAME** *Arista 74321100327*	.28	4
17 Apr 93	**THE SUPREME EP** *Arista 74321139592*	.49	2

Tracks on The Supreme EP: Where Did Our Love Go / Stop! In the Name of Love / You Can't Hurry Love / Remember Me

SINNAMON *US, male vocal / instrumental group (1 WEEK)* pos/wks
28 Sep 96	**I NEED YOU NOW** *Worx WORXCD 003*	.70	1

SIOUXSIE and the BANSHEES 153 Top 500
Long-running commercially successful UK punk band included Susan 'Siouxsie' Ballion (v), Steve Severin (b) (also recorded as The Glove), Siouxsie's husband, Peter 'Budgie' Clark (d) (who recorded with Siouxsie as The Creatures) and, at times, Cure front man Robert Smith (g) (150 WEEKS) pos/wks
26 Aug 78 ●	**HONG KONG GARDEN** *Polydor 2059 052*	.7	10
31 Mar 79	**THE STAIRCASE (MYSTERY)** *Polydor POSP 9*	.24	8
7 Jul 79	**PLAYGROUND TWIST** *Polydor POSP 59*	.28	6
29 Sep 79	**MITTAGEISEN (METAL POSTCARD)** *Polydor 2059 151*	.47	3
15 Mar 80	**HAPPY HOUSE** *Polydor POSP 117*	.17	8
7 Jun 80	**CHRISTINE** *Polydor 2059 249*	.22	8
6 Dec 80	**ISRAEL** *Polydor POSP 205*	.41	8
30 May 81	**SPELLBOUND** *Polydor POSP 273*	.22	8
1 Aug 81	**ARABIAN KNIGHTS** *Polydor POSP 309*	.32	7
29 May 82	**FIRE WORKS** *Polydor POSPG 450*	.22	6
9 Oct 82	**SLOWDIVE** *Polydor POSP 510*	.41	4
4 Dec 82	**MELT / IL EST NE LE DIVIN ENFANT** *Polydor POSP 539*	.49	5
1 Oct 83 ●	**DEAR PRUDENCE** *Wonderland SHE 4*	.3	8
24 Mar 84	**SWIMMING HORSES** *Wonderland SHE 6*	.28	4
2 Jun 84	**DAZZLE** *Wonderland SHE 7*	.33	3
27 Oct 84	**THE THORN EP** *Wonderland SHEEP 8*	.47	3
26 Oct 85	**CITIES IN DUST** *Wonderland SHE 9*	.21	6
8 Mar 86	**CANDYMAN** *Wonderland SHE 10*	.34	5
17 Jan 87	**THIS WHEEL'S ON FIRE** *Wonderland SHE 11*	.14	6
28 Mar 87	**THE PASSENGER** *Wonderland SHE 12*	.41	6
25 Jul 87	**SONG FROM THE EDGE OF THE WORLD** *Wonderland SHE 13*	.59	3
30 Jul 88	**PEEK-A-BOO** *Wonderland SHE 14*	.16	6
8 Oct 88	**THE KILLING JAR** *Wonderland SHE 15*	.41	3
3 Dec 88	**THE LAST BEAT OF MY HEART** *Wonderland SHE 16*	.44	1
25 May 91	**KISS THEM FOR ME** *Wonderland SHE 19*	.32	4
13 Jul 91	**SHADOWTIME** *Wonderland SHE 20*	.57	1
25 Jul 92	**FACE TO FACE** *Wonderland SHE 21*	.21	4
20 Aug 94	**INTERLUDE** *Parlophone CDR 6365* 1	.25	2
7 Jan 95	**O BABY** *Wonderland SHECD 22*	.34	3
18 Feb 95	**STARGAZER** *Wonderland SHECD 23*	.64	1

1 Morrissey and Siouxsie

Tracks on The Thorn EP: Overground / Voices / Placebo Effect / Red Over White

See also GLOVE

SIR DOUGLAS QUINTET *US, male vocal / instrumental group – leader Doug Sahm, d. 18 Nov 1999 (10 WEEKS)* pos/wks
17 Jun 65	**SHE'S ABOUT A MOVER** *London HLU 9964*	.15	10

SIR KILLALOT vs ROBO BABE
UK, male robot rapper with female vocalist (3 WEEKS) pos/wks
30 Dec 00	**ROBOT WARS (ANDROID LOVE)** *Polydor 5879362*	.51	3

SIR MIX-A-LOT *US, male rapper (2 WEEKS)* pos/wks
8 Aug 92	**BABY GOT BACK** *Def American DEFA 20* ▲	.56	2

SIRRON – *See PLUS ONE featuring SIRRON*

SISQO *US, male vocalist – Mark Andrews (43 WEEKS)* pos/wks
12 Feb 00	**GOT TO GET IT** *Def Soul 5626442*	.14	4
22 Apr 00	**THONG SONG** *Def Soul 5688902*	.3	14
30 Sep 00 ●	**UNLEASH THE DRAGON** *Def Soul 5726422*	.6	7
16 Dec 00	**INCOMPLETE** *Def Soul 5727542* ▲	.13	8
28 Jul 01 ●	**DANCE FOR ME** *Def Soul 5887002*	.6	10

See also DRU HILL

TOP 100 POP ACTS

■ The Book of British Hit Singles' annual check on the fortunes of the 100 best pop performers is compiled according to the number of weeks they have spent on the UK singles chart since the first hit parade in 1952. Notable this year were New Order, the only new act to enter the Top 100 debuting at No.98, Robbie Williams who rose nine places to No.66, Oasis who leapt eight places to No.21, Kylie who soared 15 places to No.25 and the mighty Status Quo who rose above Stevie Wonder to No.13.

Any tied positions are decided according to the weeks they have spent at No.1, No.2 and so on.

1	Elvis Presley
2	Cliff Richard
3	Shadows
4	Elton John
5	Madonna
6	Diana Ross
7	Michael Jackson
8	Rod Stewart
9	Beatles
10	David Bowie
11	Frank Sinatra
12	Queen
13	Status Quo
14	Stevie Wonder
15	Paul McCartney
16	Tom Jones
17	Rolling Stones
18	Bee Gees
19	Everly Brothers
20	Roy Orbison
21	Oasis
22	UB40
23	Shirley Bassey
24	Perry Como
25	Kylie Minogue
26	Jim Reeves
27	Lonnie Donegan
28	Hollies
29	Four Tops
30	Whitney Houston
31	Pat Boone
32	Supremes
33	Prince
34	Donna Summer
35	Janet Jackson
36	Hot Chocolate
37	Frankie Laine
38	Beach Boys
39	Billy Fury
40	Slade
41	Shakin' Stevens
42	Madness
43	U2
44	George Michael
45	Mariah Carey
46	Electric Light Orchestra
47	Abba
48	Adam Faith
49	Nat 'King' Cole
50	Celine Dion
51	Petula Clark
52	Who
53	Connie Francis
54	Bryan Adams
55	Depeche Mode
56	Engelbert Humperdinck
57	Andy Williams
58	T. Rex
59	Pet Shop Boys
60	Jacksons
61	Olivia Newton-John
62	Ken Dodd
63	Frankie Vaughan
64	Phil Collins
65	Cher
66	Robbie Williams
67	Tina Turner
68	Fleetwood Mac
69	Bon Jovi
70	Duran Duran
71	Tremeloes
72	Manfred Mann
73	Steps
74	Kinks
75	Simply Red
76	Boyzone
77	Gene Pitney
78	Dusty Springfield
79	Herman's Hermits
80	Brenda Lee
81	Wet Wet Wet
82	Showaddywaddy
83	Eurythmics
84	Kool and the Gang
85	Jam
86	Erasure
87	Temptations
88	Marvin Gaye
89	Duane Eddy
90	Bananarama
91	Orchestral Manoeuvres in the Dark
92	David Essex
93	Bill Haley and His Comets
94	John Lennon
95	Cilla Black
96	Kim Wilde
97	Stranglers
98	New Order
99	David Whitfield
100	Buddy Holly

Oasis rise to No.21 in this year's Top 100 pop acts

SISTER BLISS *UK, female DJ / producer / instrumentalist – Ayalah Ben-Tovim (11 WEEKS)*

			pos/wks
15 Oct 94	CANTGETAMAN CANTGETAJOB (LIFE'S A BITCH) Go.Beat GODCD 124 1	31	4
15 Jul 95	OH! WHAT A WORLD Go.Beat GODCD 126 1	40	2
29 Jun 96	BAD MAN Junk Dog JDOGCD 1	51	1
7 Oct 00	SISTER SISTER Multiply CDMULTY 68	34	2
24 Mar 01	DELIVER ME Multiply CDMULTY 72 2	31	2

1 Sister Bliss featuring Collette 2 Sister Bliss featuring John Martyn

SISTER SLEDGE (262 Top 500) *US family group from Philadelphia: Kathy, Debra, Joni and Kim Sledge. They found more fame in the UK than in the US, and recorded some of the best-known disco records with noted producers / songwriters Nile Rodgers and Bernard Edwards (111 WEEKS)*

			pos/wks
21 Jun 75	MAMA NEVER TOLD ME Atlantic K 10619	20	6
17 Mar 79 ●	HE'S THE GREATEST DANCER Atlantic / Cotillion K 11257	6	11
26 May 79	WE ARE FAMILY Atlantic / Cotillion K 11293	8	10
11 Aug 79	LOST IN MUSIC Atlantic / Cotillion K 11337	17	10
19 Jan 80	GOT TO LOVE SOMEBODY Atlantic / Cotillion K 11404	34	4
28 Feb 81	ALL AMERICAN GIRLS Atlantic K 11656	41	5
26 May 84	THINKING OF YOU Cotillion / Atlantic B 9744	11	13
8 Sep 84 ●	LOST IN MUSIC (re-mix) Cotillion / Atlantic B 9718	4	12
17 Nov 84	WE ARE FAMILY (re-mix) Cotillion / Atlantic B 9692	33	4
1 Jun 85 ★	FRANKIE Atlantic A 9547	1	16
31 Aug 85	DANCING ON THE JAGGED EDGE Atlantic A 9520	50	3
23 Jan 93 ●	WE ARE FAMILY (2nd re-mix) Atlantic A 4508CD	5	8
13 Mar 93	LOST IN MUSIC (2nd re-mix) Atlantic A 4509CD	14	5
12 Jun 93	THINKING OF YOU (re-mix) Atlantic A 4515CD	17	4

SISTER 2 SISTER *Australia, female vocal duo – Christine and Sharon Muscat (5 WEEKS)*

			pos/wks
22 Apr 00	SISTER Mushroom MUSH 70CDS	18	4
28 Oct 00	WHAT'S A GIRL TO DO Mushroom MUSH 76CDS	61	1

SISTERS OF MERCY *UK, male / female vocal / instrumental group – leader Andrew Eldritch (40 WEEKS)*

			pos/wks
16 Jun 84	BODY AND SOUL / TRAIN Merciful Release MR 029	46	3
20 Oct 84	WALK AWAY Merciful Release MR 033	45	3
9 Mar 85	NO TIME TO CRY Merciful Release MR 035	63	2
3 Oct 87 ●	THIS CORROSION Merciful Release MR 39	7	6
27 Feb 88	DOMINION Merciful Release MR 43	13	6
18 Jun 88	LUCRETIA MY REFLECTION Merciful Release MR 45	20	4
13 Oct 90	MORE Merciful Release MR 47	14	4
22 Dec 90	DOCTOR JEEP Merciful Release MR 51	37	4
2 May 92 ●	TEMPLE OF LOVE Merciful Release MR 53	3	5
28 Aug 93	UNDER THE GUN Merciful Release MR 59CDX	19	3

SIVUCA *Brazil, male instrumentalist (3 WEEKS)*

			pos/wks
28 Jul 84	AIN'T NO SUNSHINE London LON 51	56	3

SIX BY SEVEN *UK, male vocal / instrumental group (2 WEEKS)*

			pos/wks
9 May 98	CANDLELIGHT Mantra MNT 34CD	70	1
2 Mar 02	I.O.U. LOVE Mantra MNT 68CD	48	1

6 BY SIX *UK, male instrumental / production duo (1 WEEK)*

			pos/wks
4 May 96	INTO YOUR HEART Six6 SIXCD 130	51	1

SIX CHIX *UK, female vocal group (1 WEEK)*

			pos/wks
26 Feb 00	ONLY THE WOMEN KNOW EMI CDCHIX 001	72	1

666 *Germany, male / female vocal / instrumental group (1 WEEK)*

			pos/wks
3 Oct 98	ALARMA Danceteria CDDAN 001	58	1

666 *Holland, male production duo (4 WEEKS)*

			pos/wks
25 Nov 00	DEVIL Echo ECSCD 102	18	4

SIXPENCE NONE THE RICHER *US, male / female vocal / instrumental group (17 WEEKS)*

			pos/wks
29 May 99 ●	KISS ME Elektra E 3750CD	4	12
18 Sep 99	THERE SHE GOES Elektra E 3728CD	14	5

60FT DOLLS *UK, male vocal / instrumental group (4 WEEKS)*

			pos/wks
3 Feb 96	STAY Indolent DOLLS 002CD	48	1
11 May 96	TALK TO ME Indolent DOLLS 003CD	37	1
20 Jul 96	HAPPY SHOPPER Indolent DOLLS 005CD	38	1
9 May 98	ALISON'S ROOM Indolent DOLLS 007CD1	61	1

SIZE 9 *US, male producer – Josh Wink (4 WEEKS)*

			pos/wks
17 Jun 95	I'M READY Virgin America VUSCD 92	52	1
11 Nov 95	I'M READY (re-issue) VC VCRD 2 1	30	3

1 Josh Wink's Size 9

See also Josh WINK

Roni SIZE / REPRAZENT *UK, male producer – Ryan Williams with male / female vocal / instrumental group (20 WEEKS)*

			pos/wks
14 Jun 97	SHARE THE FALL Talkin Loud TLCD 21	37	2
13 Sep 97	HEROES Talkin Loud TLCD 25	31	2
15 Nov 97	BROWN PAPER BAG Talkin Loud TLCD 28	20	3
14 Mar 98	WATCHING WINDOWS Talkin Loud TLCD 31	28	2
7 Oct 00	WHO TOLD YOU Talkin Loud TLCD 61	17	3
24 Mar 01	DIRTY BEATS Talkin Loud TLCDD 63	32	3
23 Jun 01	LUCKY PRESSURE Talkin Loud TLCD 64	58	1
19 Oct 02	SOUND ADVICE Full Cycle FCY 044 1	69	1
9 Nov 02	PLAYTIME Full Cycle FCY 045 1	53	2
7 Dec 02	SCRAMBLED EGGS / SWINGS & ROUNDABOUTS Full Cycle FCY 046 1	57	1

1 Roni Size

SIZZLA *Jamaica, male rapper – Miguel Collins (2 WEEKS)*

			pos/wks
17 Apr 99	RAIN SHOWERS Xterminator EXTCDS 76	51	2

SKANDAL *UK, male vocal group (1 WEEK)*

			pos/wks
14 Oct 00	CHAMPAGNE HIGHWAY Prestige Management CDGING 1	53	1

SKATALITES *Jamaica, male instrumental group (6 WEEKS)*

			pos/wks
20 Apr 67	GUNS OF NAVARONE Island WI 168	36	6

SKEE-LO *US, male rapper – Antoine Roundtree (10 WEEKS)*

			pos/wks
9 Dec 95	I WISH Wild Card 5777752	15	8
27 Apr 96	TOP OF THE STAIRS Wild Card 5763352	38	2

Beverli SKEETE – See DE-CODE featuring Beverli SKEETE

Peter SKELLERN *UK, male vocalist (24 WEEKS)*

			pos/wks
23 Sep 72 ●	YOU'RE A LADY Decca F 13333	3	11
29 Mar 75	HOLD ON TO LOVE Decca F 13568	14	9
28 Oct 78	LOVE IS THE SWEETEST THING Mercury 6008 603 1	60	4

1 Peter Skellern featuring the Grimethorpe Colliery Band

SKIBADEE – See SHY FX

SKID ROW *US, male vocal / instrumental group (27 WEEKS)*

			pos/wks
18 Nov 89	YOUTH GONE WILD Atlantic A 8935	42	3
3 Feb 90	18 AND LIFE Atlantic A 8883	12	6
31 Mar 90	I REMEMBER YOU East West A 8886	36	4
15 Jun 91	MONKEY BUSINESS Atlantic A 7673	19	3
14 Sep 91	SLAVE TO THE GRIND Atlantic A 7603	43	2
23 Nov 91	WASTED TIME Atlantic A 7570	20	3

29 Aug 92	YOUTH GONE WILD / DELIVERING THE GOODS		
	(re-issue) *Atlantic A 7444*	22	4
18 Nov 95	BREAKIN' DOWN *Atlantic A 7135CD1*	48	2

SKIDS
UK, male vocal / instrumental group (60 WEEKS) pos/wks

23 Sep 78	SWEET SUBURBIA (re) *Virgin VS 227*	70	3
4 Nov 78	THE SAINTS ARE COMING *Virgin VS 232*	48	3
17 Feb 79 ●	INTO THE VALLEY *Virgin VS 241*	10	11
26 May 79	MASQUERADE *Virgin VS 262*	14	9
29 Sep 79	CHARADE *Virgin VS 288*	31	6
24 Nov 79	WORKING FOR THE YANKEE DOLLAR *Virgin VS 306*	20	11
1 Mar 80	ANIMATION *Virgin VS 323*	56	3
16 Aug 80	CIRCUS GAMES *Virgin VS 359*	32	7
18 Oct 80	GOODBYE CIVILIAN *Virgin VS 373*	52	4
6 Dec 80	WOMAN IN WINTER *Virgin VSK 101*	49	3

SKIN
UK / Germany, male vocal / instrumental group (19 WEEKS) pos/wks

25 Dec 93	THE SKIN UP EP *Parlophone CDR 6363*	67	2
12 Mar 94	HOUSE OF LOVE *Parlophone CDR 6374*	45	2
30 Apr 94	THE MONEY EP *Parlophone CDR 6381*	18	3
23 Jul 94	TOWER OF STRENGTH *Parlophone CDR 6387*	19	3
15 Oct 94	LOOK BUT DON'T TOUCH (EP) *Parlophone CDRS 6391*	33	2
20 May 95	TAKE ME DOWN TO THE RIVER *Parlophone CDR 6409*	26	2
23 Mar 96	HOW LUCKY YOU ARE *Parlophone CDR 6426*	32	2
18 May 96	PERFECT DAY *Parlophone CDR 6433*	33	2

Tracks on The Skin Up (EP): Look But Don't Touch / Shine Your Light / Monkey. Tracks on The Money EP: Money / Unbelievable / Express Yourself / Funktified. Tracks on Look But Don't Touch (EP): Look But Don't Touch / Should I Stay or Should I Go / Pump It Up / Monkey (re-issue).

SKIN – See SKUNK ANANSIE; MAXIM; Ed CASE

SKIN UP
UK, male producer – Jason Cohen (9 WEEKS) pos/wks

7 Sep 91	IVORY *Love EVOL 4*	48	3
14 Mar 92	A JUICY RED APPLE *Love EVOL 11*	32	4
18 Jul 92	ACCELERATE *Love EVOL 17*	45	2

SKINNER – See LIGHTNING SEEDS

SKINNY
UK, male vocal / instrumental / production duo – Matt Benbrook and Paul Herman (2 WEEKS) pos/wks

11 Apr 98	FAILURE *Cheeky CHEKCD 023*	31	2

SKIP RAIDERS featuring JADA
UK, male production duo and female vocalist (1 WEEK) pos/wks

15 Jul 00	ANOTHER DAY *Perfecto PERF 4CDS*	46	1

SKIPWORTH & TURNER
US, male vocal duo – Rodney Skipworth and Phil Turner (12 WEEKS) pos/wks

27 Apr 85	THINKING ABOUT YOUR LOVE *Fourth & Broadway BRW 23*	24	10
21 Jan 89	MAKE IT LAST *Fourth & Broadway BRW 118*	60	2

Nick SKITZ – See FUNKY CHOAD featuring Nick SKITZ

SKUNK ANANSIE
UK, female / male vocal / instrumental group (41 WEEKS) pos/wks

25 Mar 95	SELLING JESUS *One Little Indian 101 TP7CD*	46	1
17 Jun 95	I CAN DREAM *One Little Indian 121 TP7CD*	41	2
2 Sep 95	CHARITY *One Little Indian 131 TP7CD*	40	2
27 Jan 96	WEAK *One Little Indian 141 TP7CD*	20	5
27 Apr 96	CHARITY (re-issue) *One Little Indian 151 TP7CD*	20	3
28 Sep 96	ALL I WANT *One Little Indian 161 TP7CD*	14	4
30 Nov 96	TWISTED (EVERYDAY HURTS) *One Little Indian 171 TP7CD*	26	4
1 Feb 97	HEDONISM (JUST BECAUSE YOU FEEL GOOD)		
	One Little Indian 181TP7CD	13	6
14 Jun 97	BRAZEN 'WEEP' *One Little Indian 191TP7CD1*	11	5
13 Mar 99	CHARLIE BIG POTATO *Virgin VSCDT 1725*	17	3
22 May 99	SECRETLY *Virgin VSCDT 1733*	16	4
7 Aug 99	LATELY *Virgin VSCDT 1738*	33	2

SKY
UK / Australia, male instrumental group (11 WEEKS) pos/wks

5 Apr 80 ●	TOCCATA *Ariola ARO 300*	5	11

SKYE – See LANGE

SKYHOOKS
Australia, male vocal / instrumental group (1 WEEK) pos/wks

9 Jun 79	WOMEN IN UNIFORM *United Artists UP 36508*	73	1

SLACKER
UK, male duo – Shem McCauley and Simon Rogers (4 WKS) pos/wks

26 Apr 97	SCARED *XL XLS 84CD*	36	2
30 Aug 97	YOUR FACE *XL XLS 87CD*	33	2

See also RAMP

SLADE `40` `Top 500`
Top group of the 1970s: Noddy Holder (v/g), Dave Hill (g), Jimmy Lea (b/p), Don Powell (d). They were the first act to have three singles enter at No.1. All six of the Wolverhampton band's chart-topping stompers were penned by Holder and Lea. Noddy, who is now a popular TV personality, was made an MBE in 2000. Best-selling single: 'Merry Xmas Everybody' 1,006,500 (279 WEEKS) pos/wks

19 Jun 71	GET DOWN AND GET WITH IT *Polydor 2058 112*	16	14
30 Oct 71 ★	COZ I LUV YOU *Polydor 2058 155*	1	15
5 Feb 72 ●	LOOK WOT YOU DUN *Polydor 2058 195*	4	10
3 Jun 72 ★	TAKE ME BAK 'OME *Polydor 2058 231*	1	13
2 Sep 72 ★	MAMA WEER ALL CRAZEE NOW *Polydor 2058 274*	1	10
25 Nov 72 ●	GUDBUY T'JANE *Polydor 2058 312*	2	13
3 Mar 73 ★	CUM ON FEEL THE NOIZE *Polydor 2058 339* ■	1	12
30 Jun 73 ★	SKWEEZE ME PLEEZE ME *Polydor 2058 377* ■	1	10
6 Oct 73 ●	MY FRIEND STAN *Polydor 2058 407*	2	8
15 Dec 73 ●	MERRY XMAS EVERYBODY (4re) *Polydor 2058 422* ♦ ■	1	25
6 Apr 74 ●	EVERYDAY *Polydor 2058 453*	3	7
6 Jul 74 ●	THE BANGIN' MAN *Polydor 2058 492*	3	7
19 Oct 74 ●	FAR FAR AWAY *Polydor 2058 522*	2	6
15 Feb 75 ●	HOW DOES IT FEEL? *Polydor 2058 547*	15	7
17 May 75 ●	THANKS FOR THE MEMORY (WHAM BAM THANK YOU MAM)		
	Polydor 2058 585	7	7
22 Nov 75	IN FOR A PENNY *Polydor 2058 663*	11	8
7 Feb 76	LET'S CALL IT QUITS *Polydor 2058 690*	11	7
5 Feb 77	GYPSY ROADHOG *Barn 2014 105*	48	2
29 Oct 77	MY BABY LEFT ME – THAT'S ALL RIGHT *Barn 2014 114*	32	4
18 Oct 80	SLADE – ALIVE AT READING (EP) *Cheapskate CHEAP 5*	44	5
27 Dec 80	MERRY XMAS EVERYBODY (re-recording)		
	Cheapskate CHEAP 11 `1`	70	2
31 Jan 81 ●	WE'LL BRING THE HOUSE DOWN *Cheapskate CHEAP 16*	10	9
4 Apr 81	WHEELS AIN'T COMING DOWN *Cheapskate CHEAP 21*	60	3
19 Sep 81	LOCK UP YOUR DAUGHTERS *RCA 124*	29	8
27 Mar 82	RUBY RED *RCA 191*	51	3
27 Nov 82	(AND NOW – THE WALTZ) C'EST LA VIE *RCA 291*	50	6
19 Nov 83 ●	MY OH MY *RCA 373*	2	11
4 Feb 84 ●	RUN RUNAWAY *RCA 385*	7	10
17 Nov 84	ALL JOIN HANDS *RCA 455*	15	9
26 Jan 85	7 YEAR BITCH *RCA 475*	60	3
23 Mar 85	MYZSTERIOUS MIZSTER JONES *RCA PB 40027*	50	5
30 Nov 85	DO YOU BELIEVE IN MIRACLES *RCA PB 40449*	54	6
21 Dec 85	MERRY XMAS EVERYBODY (re-issue) (re) *Polydor POSP 780*	48	3
21 Feb 87	STILL THE SAME *RCA PB 41137*	73	2
19 Oct 91	RADIO WALL OF SOUND *Polydor PO 180*	21	5
26 Dec 98	MERRY XMAS EVERYBODY '98 (re-mix) *Polydor 5633532* `2`	30	3

`1` Slade and the Reading Choir `2` Slade vs Flush

'Merry Xmas Everybody' re-entries peaked at No.32 in 1981, No.67 in 1982, No.20 in 1983, No.47 in 1984 and the re-entry of the 1985 re-issue made No.71 in 1986. Tracks on Slade – Alive at Reading (EP): When I'm Dancin' / I Ain't Fightin' / Born to Be Wild / Somethin' Else / Pistol Packin' Mama / Keep a Rollin'

SLAM
UK, male production duo – Orde Meikle and Stuart McMillan (4 WEEKS) pos/wks

17 Feb 01	POSITIVE EDUCATION *VC Recordings VCRD 84*	44	2
17 Mar 01	NARCO TOURISTS *Soma SOMA 100CD* `1`	66	1
7 Jul 01	LIFETIMES *Soma SOMA 107CDS* `2`	61	1

`1` Slam vs Unkle `2` Slam featuring Tyrone 'Visionary' Palmer

Re-entries are listed as (re), (2re), (3re), etc which signifies that the hit re-entered the chart once, twice or three times, etc

SLAMM UK, male vocal / instrumental group (6 WEEKS)   pos/wks
17 Jul 93	ENERGIZE *PWL International PWCD 266*	57	2
23 Oct 93	VIRGINIA PLAIN *PWL International PWCD 274*	60	1
22 Oct 94	THAT'S WHERE MY MIND GOES		
	PWL International PWCD 310	68	1
4 Feb 95	CAN'T GET BY *PWL International PWCD 316*	47	2

SLARTA JOHN – See HATIRAS featuring SLARTA JOHN

Luke SLATER UK, male producer (2 WEEKS)   pos/wks
| 16 Sep 00 | ALL EXHALE *Novamute CDNOMU 79* | 74 | 1 |
| 6 Apr 02 | NOTHING AT ALL *Mute CDMUTE 261* | 70 | 1 |

SLAUGHTER US, male vocal / instrumental group (2 WEEKS)   pos/wks
| 29 Sep 90 | UP ALL NIGHT *Chrysalis CHS 3556* | 62 | 1 |
| 2 Feb 91 | FLY TO THE ANGELS *Chrysalis CHS 3634* | 55 | 1 |

SLAVE US, male vocal / instrumental group (3 WEEKS)   pos/wks
| 8 Mar 80 | JUST A TOUCH OF LOVE *Atlantic / Cotillion K 11442* | 64 | 3 |

SLAYER US, male vocal / instrumental group (3 WEEKS)   pos/wks
13 Jun 87	CRIMINALLY INSANE *Def Jam LON 133*	64	1
26 Oct 91	SEASONS IN THE ABYSS *Def American DEFA 9*	51	1
9 Sep 95	SERENITY IN MURDER *American 74321312482*	50	1

SLEAZESISTERS
UK, male producer – Paul Masterson (3 WEEKS)   pos/wks
29 Jul 95	SEX *Pulse 8 CDLOSE 92* [1]	53	1
30 Mar 96	LET'S WHIP IT UP (YOU GO GIRL)		
	Pulse 8 CDLOSE 102 [2]	46	1
26 Sep 98	WORK IT UP *Logic 74321616622* [2]	74	1

[1] Sleazesisters with Vikki Shepard [2] Sleaze Sisters

See also CANDY GIRLS; CLERGY; DOROTHY; YOMANDA; HI-GATE; Paul MASTERSON presents SUSHI

Kathy SLEDGE US, female vocalist (7 WEEKS)   pos/wks
16 May 92	TAKE ME BACK TO LOVE AGAIN *Epic 6579837*	62	2
18 Feb 95	ANOTHER STAR *NRC DEACD 002*	54	1
29 Nov 97	FREEDOM *Deconstruction 74321536952* [1]	15	4

[1] Robert Miles featuring Kathy Sledge

See also SISTER SLEDGE

Percy SLEDGE US, male vocalist (34 WEEKS)   pos/wks
12 May 66	● WHEN A MAN LOVES A WOMAN *Atlantic 584 001* ▲	4	17
4 Aug 66	WARM AND TENDER LOVE *Atlantic 584 034*	34	7
14 Feb 87	● WHEN A MAN LOVES A WOMAN (re-issue)		
	Atlantic YZ 96	2	10

SLEEPER
UK, female / male vocal / instrumental group (29 WEEKS)   pos/wks
21 May 94	DELICIOUS *Indolent SLEEP 003CD*	75	1
21 Jan 95	INBETWEENER *Indolent SLEEP 006CD*	16	4
8 Apr 95	VEGAS *Indolent SLEEP 008CD*	33	3
7 Oct 95	WHAT DO I DO NOW *Indolent SLEEP 009CD1*	14	4
4 May 96	● SALE OF THE CENTURY *Indolent SLEEP 011CD*	10	5
13 Jul 96	● NICE GUY EDDIE *Indolent SLEEP 013CD*	10	5
5 Oct 96	STATUESQUE *Indolent SLEEP 014CD1*	17	3
4 Oct 97	SHE'S A GOOD GIRL *Indolent SLEEP 015CD*	28	2
6 Dec 97	ROMEO ME *Indolent SLEEP 17CD1*	39	2

SLEEPY BROWN – See OUTKAST

SLICK US, male / female vocal / instrumental group (15 WEEKS)   pos/wks
| 16 Jun 79 | SPACE BASS *Fantasy FTC 176* | 16 | 10 |
| 15 Sep 79 | SEXY CREAM *Fantasy FTC 182* [1] | 47 | 5 |

[1] Slick featuring Doris James

Grace SLICK US, female vocalist (4 WEEKS)   pos/wks
| 24 May 80 | DREAMS *RCA PB 9534* | 50 | 4 |

SLICK RICK – See Montell JORDAN; Al B SURE!

SLIK UK, male vocal / instrumental group – lead vocal Midge Ure (18 WEEKS)   pos/wks
| 17 Jan 76 | ★ FOREVER AND EVER *Bell 1464* | 1 | 9 |
| 8 May 76 | REQUIEM *Bell 1478* | 24 | 9 |

SLIM CHANCE – See Ronnie LANE and SLIM CHANCE

SLIPKNOT US, male vocal / instrumental group (11 WEEKS)   pos/wks
11 Mar 00	WAIT AND BLEED *Roadrunner RR 21125*	27	3
16 Sep 00	SPIT IT OUT *Roadrunner RR20903*	28	2
10 Nov 01	LEFT BEHIND *Roadrunner 23203355*	24	4
20 Jul 02	MY PLAGUE *Roadrunner RR 20453*	43	2

SLIPSTREAM UK, male vocal group (7 WEEKS)   pos/wks
| 19 Dec 92 | WE ARE RAVING – THE ANTHEM *Boogie Food 7BF 1* | 18 | 7 |

SLITS UK, female vocal / instrumental group (3 WEEKS)   pos/wks
| 13 Oct 79 | TYPICAL GIRLS / I HEARD IT THROUGH THE GRAPEVINE | | |
| | *Island WIP 6505* | 60 | 3 |

PF SLOAN US, male vocalist – Philip 'Flip' Sloan (3 WEEKS)   pos/wks
| 4 Nov 65 | SINS OF THE FAMILY *RCA 1482* | 38 | 3 |

SLO-MOSHUN
UK / US, male / female production / vocal trio (4 WEEKS)   pos/wks
| 5 Feb 94 | BELLS OF NY *Six6 SIXCD 108* | 29 | 3 |
| 30 Jul 94 | HELP MY FRIEND *Six6 SIXCD 117* | 52 | 1 |

SLOWDIVE
UK, male / female vocal / instrumental group (2 WEEKS)   pos/wks
| 15 Jun 91 | CATCH THE BREEZE / SHINE *Creation CRE 112* | 52 | 1 |
| 29 May 93 | OUTSIDE YOUR ROOM (EP) *Creation CRESCD 119* | 69 | 1 |

Tracks on Outside Your Room (EP): Outside Your Room / Alison / So Tired / Souvlaki Space Station

SLUSNIK LUNA
Finland, male producer – Niko Nyman (2 WEEKS)   pos/wks
| 1 Sep 01 | SUN *Incentive CENT 29CDS* | 40 | 2 |

SLY and the FAMILY STONE US, male / female vocal / instrumental / production group (42 WEEKS)   pos/wks
10 Jul 68	● DANCE TO THE MUSIC *Direction 58 3568*	7	14
2 Oct 68	M'LADY *Direction 58 3707*	32	7
19 Mar 69	EVERYDAY PEOPLE (re) *Direction 58 3938* ▲	36	5
8 Jan 72	FAMILY AFFAIR *Epic EPC 7632* ▲	15	8
15 Apr 72	RUNNIN' AWAY *Epic EPC 7810*	17	8

SLY FOX US, male vocal / instrumental duo – Gary Cooper and Michael Camacho (16 WEEKS)   pos/wks
| 31 May 86 | ● LET'S GO ALL THE WAY *Capitol CL 403* | 3 | 16 |

SLY and ROBBIE Jamaica, male vocal / instrumental duo – Sly Dunbar and Robbie Shakespeare (23 WEEKS)   pos/wks
4 Apr 87	BOOPS (HERE TO GO) *Fourth & Broadway BRW 61*	12	11
25 Jul 87	FIRE *Fourth & Broadway BRW 71*	60	4
20 Sep 97	NIGHT NURSE *East West EW 129CD1* [1]	13	8

[1] Sly and Robbie featuring Simply Red

Heather SMALL UK, female vocalist (9 WEEKS)   pos/wks
| 20 May 00 | PROUD *Arista 74321748902* | 16 | 5 |

Date	Title	pos	wks
19 Aug 00	HOLDING ON *Arista 74321781332*	58	1
18 Nov 00	YOU NEED LOVE LIKE I DO *GUT CDGUT 36* [1]	24	3

[1] Tom Jones and Heather Small

See also M PEOPLE

SMALL ADS UK, male vocal / instrumental group (3 WEEKS)
Date	Title	pos	wks
18 Apr 81	SMALL ADS *Bronze BRO 115*	63	3

SMALL FACES (185 Top 500) Revered London-based mod quartet:
Steve Marriott (v/g) (d. 1991), Ronnie Lane (b) (d. 1997), Ian McLagan (k), Kenney Jones (d). Marriott and Lane penned most of the act's UK hits. Further international fame came when Marriott formed Humble Pie and the other members formed The Faces (137 WEEKS)
Date	Title	pos	wks
2 Sep 65	WHATCHA GONNA DO ABOUT IT? *Decca F 12208*	14	12
10 Feb 66	● SHA-LA-LA-LA-LEE *Decca F 12317*	3	11
12 May 66	● HEY GIRL *Decca F 12393*	10	9
11 Aug 66	★ ALL OR NOTHING *Decca F 12470*	1	12
17 Nov 66	● MY MIND'S EYE *Decca F 12500*	4	11
9 Mar 67	I CAN'T MAKE IT *Decca F 12565*	26	7
8 Jun 67	HERE COME THE NICE *Immediate IM 050*	12	10
9 Aug 67	● ITCHYCOO PARK *Immediate IM 057*	3	14
6 Dec 67	● TIN SOLDIER *Immediate IM 062*	9	12
17 Apr 68	● LAZY SUNDAY *Immediate IM 064*	2	11
10 Jul 68	UNIVERSAL *Immediate IM 069*	16	11
19 Mar 69	AFTERGLOW OF YOUR LOVE *Immediate IM 077*	36	1
13 Dec 75	● ITCHYCOO PARK (re-issue) *Immediate IMS 102*	9	11
20 Mar 76	LAZY SUNDAY (re-issue) *Immediate IMS 106*	39	5

SMALLER UK, male vocal / instrumental group (2 WEEKS)
Date	Title	pos	wks
28 Sep 96	WASTED *Better BETSCD 006*	72	1
29 Mar 97	IS *Better BETSCD 008*	55	1

SMART E'S
UK, male instrumental / production group (9 WEEKS)
Date	Title	pos	wks
11 Jul 92	● SESAME'S TREET *Suburban Base SUBBASE 12S*	2	9

S*M*A*S*H UK, male vocal / instrumental group (1 WEEK)
Date	Title	pos	wks
6 Aug 94	(I WANT TO) KILL SOMEBODY *Hi-Rise FLATSCD 5*	26	1

SMASH MOUTH US, male vocal / instrumental group (9 WEEKS)
Date	Title	pos	wks
25 Oct 97	WALKIN' ON THE SUN *Interscope IND 95555*	19	4
31 Jul 99	ALL STAR *Interscope 4971172*	24	5

SMASHING PUMPKINS
US, male / female vocal / instrumental group (36 WEEKS)
Date	Title	pos	wks
5 Sep 92	I AM ONE *Hut HUTT 18*	73	1
3 Jul 93	CHERUB ROCK *Hut HUTCD 31*	31	2
25 Sep 93	TODAY *Hut HUTCD 37*	44	2
5 Mar 94	DISARM *Hut HUTCD 43*	11	3
28 Oct 95	BULLET WITH BUTTERFLY WINGS *Hut HUTCD 63*	20	3
10 Feb 96	1979 *Hut HUTCD 67*	16	3
18 May 96	● TONIGHT TONIGHT *Hut HUTDX 69*	7	6
23 Nov 96	THIRTY THREE *Hut HUTCD 78*	21	2
14 Jun 97	● THE END IS THE BEGINNING IS THE END *Warner Bros. W 0404CD*	10	4
23 Aug 97	THE END IS THE BEGINNING IS THE END (re-mix) *Warner Bros. W 0410CD*	72	1
30 May 98	AVA ADORE *Hut HUTCD 101*	11	4
19 Sep 98	PERFECT *Hut HUTCD 106*	24	2
4 Mar 00	STAND INSIDE YOUR LOVE *Hut HUTCD 127*	23	2
23 Sep 00	TRY TRY TRY *Hut HUTCD 140*	73	1

SMEAR CAMPAIGN – See MR BEAN and SMEAR CAMPAIGN featuring Bruce DICKINSON

SMELLS LIKE HEAVEN
Italy, male producer – Fabio Paras (1 WEEK)
Date	Title	pos	wks
10 Jul 93	LONDRES STRUTT *Deconstruction 74321154312*	57	1

Ann-Marie SMITH UK, female vocalist (5 WEEKS)
Date	Title	pos	wks
23 Jan 93	MUSIC *Synthetic CDR 6334* [1]	34	2
18 Mar 95	ROCKIN' MY BODY *Media MCSTD 2021* [2]	31	2
15 Jul 95	(YOU'RE MY ONE AND ONLY) TRUE LOVE *Media MCSTD 2060*	46	1

[1] Fargetta and Anne-Marie Smith [2] 49ers featuring Anne-Marie Smith

Elliott SMITH US, male vocalist / instrumentalist (3 WEEKS)
Date	Title	pos	wks
19 Dec 98	WALTZ #2 (XO) *DreamWorks DRMCD 22347*	52	1
1 May 99	BABY BRITAIN *DreamWorks DRMDM 50950*	55	1
8 Jul 00	SON OF SAM *DreamWorks DRMCD 4509492*	55	1

'Fast' Eddie SMITH – See DJ 'FAST' EDDIE

Jimmy SMITH US, male instrumentalist – organ (3 WEEKS)
Date	Title	pos	wks
28 Apr 66	GOT MY MOJO WORKING (re) *Verve VS 536*	48	3

Keely SMITH US, female vocalist (10 WEEKS)
Date	Title	pos	wks
18 Mar 65	YOU'RE BREAKIN' MY HEART *Reprise R 20346*	14	10

Mandy SMITH UK, female vocalist (2 WEEKS)
Date	Title	pos	wks
20 May 89	DON'T YOU WANT ME BABY *PWL PWL 37*	59	2

Mark E SMITH – See FALL; INSPIRAL CARPETS

Mel SMITH UK, male vocalist / comedian (10 WEEKS)
Date	Title	pos	wks
5 Dec 87	● ROCKIN' AROUND THE CHRISTMAS TREE *10 TEN 2* [1]	3	7
21 Dec 91	ANOTHER BLOOMING CHRISTMAS *Epic 6576877*	59	3

[1] Mel and Kim

Kim was Kim Wilde

Muriel SMITH US, female vocalist, d. 1985,
with Wally Stott and his Orchestra (17 WEEKS)
Date	Title	pos	wks
15 May 53	● HOLD ME, THRILL ME, KISS ME *Philips PB 122*	3	17

O C SMITH US, male vocalist, d. 23 Nov 2001 (23 WEEKS)
Date	Title	pos	wks
29 May 68	● THE SON OF HICKORY HOLLER'S TRAMP *CBS 3343*	2	15
26 Mar 77	TOGETHER *Caribou CRB 4910*	25	8

Patti SMITH GROUP
US, female / male vocal / instrumental group (16 WEEKS)
Date	Title	pos	wks
29 Apr 78	● BECAUSE THE NIGHT *Arista 181*	5	12
19 Aug 78	PRIVILEGE (SET ME FREE) *Arista 197*	72	1
2 Jun 79	FREDERICK *Arista 264*	63	3

Rex SMITH and Rachel SWEET
US, male / female vocalists (7 WEEKS)
Date	Title	pos	wks
22 Aug 81	EVERLASTING LOVE *CBS A 1405*	35	7

Richard Jon SMITH South Africa, male vocalist (2 WEEKS)
Date	Title	pos	wks
16 Jul 83	SHE'S THE MASTER OF THE GAME *Jive JIVE 38*	63	2

Rose SMITH – See DELAKOTA

Sheila SMITH – See Cevin FISHER

Whistling Jack SMITH UK, male whistler (12 WEEKS)
Date	Title	pos	wks
2 Mar 67	● I WAS KAISER BILL'S BATMAN *Deram DM 112*	5	12

Will SMITH (266 Top 500)
Artist formerly known as The Fresh Prince was not only one of the 1990s most successful rap stars, but also a top TV personality and Oscar-nominated movie actor, b. 25 Sep 1968, Philadelphia, US. The quadruple World Music Award winner (1999) helped to make rap respectable and accessible to all ages. Best-selling single: 'Men In Black' 883,000 (110 WEEKS)
Date	Title	pos	wks
16 Aug 97	★ MEN IN BLACK *Columbia 6648682* ■	1	16

Re-entries are listed as (re), (2re), (3re), etc which signifies that the hit re-entered the chart

13 Dec 97 ●	JUST CRUISIN' *Columbia 6653482*	.23 6
7 Feb 98 ●	GETTIN' JIGGY WIT IT *Columbia 6655605* ▲	.3 10
1 Aug 98 ●	JUST THE TWO OF US *Columbia 6662092*	.2 10
5 Dec 98 ●	MIAMI *Columbia 6666782*	.3 14
13 Feb 99 ●	BOY YOU KNOCK ME OUT (re) *MJJ / Epic 6669372* [1]	.3 9
10 Jul 99 ●	WILD WILD WEST *Columbia 6675962* [2] ▲	.2 16
20 Nov 99 ●	WILL 2K *Columbia 6684452*	.2 11
25 Mar 00	FREAKIN' IT (re) *Columbia 6691052*	.15 8
10 Aug 02 ●	BLACK SUITS COMIN' (NOD YA HEAD) *Columbia 6730132* [3]	.3 10

[1] Tatyana Ali featuring Will Smith [2] Will Smith featuring Dru Hill – additional vocals Kool Moe Dee [3] Will Smith featuring Tra-Knox

See also JAZZY JEFF & The FRESH PRINCE

SMITHS (290) Top 500

Mancunian quartet with loyal fan base: Morrissey (b. Stephen Morrissey) (v). Johnny Marr (g). Andy Rourke (b). Mike Joyce (d). Their achievements include monopolising the Top 3 indie chart placings (Feb 1984) and having seven albums simultaneously in the UK chart (Mar 1995) (105 WEEKS) pos/wks

12 Nov 83	THIS CHARMING MAN *Rough Trade RT 136*	.25 12
28 Jan 84	WHAT DIFFERENCE DOES IT MAKE *Rough Trade RT 146*	.12 9
2 Jun 84 ●	HEAVEN KNOWS I'M MISERABLE NOW *Rough Trade RT 156*	.10 8
1 Sep 84	WILLIAM, IT WAS REALLY NOTHING *Rough Trade RT 166*	.17 6
9 Feb 85	HOW SOON IS NOW? *Rough Trade RT 176*	.24 6
30 Mar 85	SHAKESPEARE'S SISTER *Rough Trade RT 181*	.26 4
13 Jul 85	THAT JOKE ISN'T FUNNY ANYMORE *Rough Trade RT 186*	.49 3
5 Oct 85	THE BOY WITH THE THORN IN HIS SIDE *Rough Trade RT 191*	.23 5
31 May 86	BIG MOUTH STRIKES AGAIN *Rough Trade RT 192*	.26 4
2 Aug 86	PANIC *Rough Trade RT 193*	.11 8
1 Nov 86	ASK *Rough Trade RT 194*	.14 5
7 Feb 87	SHOPLIFTERS OF THE WORLD UNITE *Rough Trade RT 195*	.12 4
25 Apr 87 ●	SHEILA TAKE A BOW *Rough Trade RT 196*	.10 5
22 Aug 87	GIRLFRIEND IN A COMA *Rough Trade RT 197*	.13 5
14 Nov 87	I STARTED SOMETHING I COULDN'T FINISH *Rough Trade RT 198*	.23 4
19 Dec 87	LAST NIGHT I DREAMT THAT SOMEBODY LOVED ME *Rough Trade RT 200*	.30 4
15 Aug 92 ●	THIS CHARMING MAN (re-issue) *WEA YZ 0001*	.8 5
12 Sep 92	HOW SOON IS NOW (re-issue) *WEA YZ 0002*	.16 4
24 Oct 92	THERE IS A LIGHT THAT NEVER GOES OUT *WEA YZ 0003*	.25 3
18 Feb 95	ASK (re-issue) *WEA YZ 0004CDX*	.62 1

SMOKE *UK, male vocal / instrumental group (3 WEEKS)* pos/wks

9 Mar 67	MY FRIEND JACK *Columbia DB 8115*	.45 3

SMOKE CITY
UK / Brazil, male / female vocal / instrumental group (5 WEEKS) pos/wks

12 Apr 97 ●	UNDERWATER LOVE *Jive JIVECD 422*	.4 5

SMOKE 2 SEVEN *UK, female vocal trio (2 WEEKS)* pos/wks

16 Mar 02	BEEN THERE DONE THAT *Curb / London CUBC 077*	.26 2

SMOKED – See Oliver LIEB presents SMOKED

SMOKIE (221) Top 500
British group which became European superstars, fronted by easily identifiable vocalist Chris Norman. Especially popular in Germany, many of their hits were penned by Mike Chapman and Nicky Chinn (125 WEEKS) pos/wks

19 Jul 75 ●	IF YOU THINK YOU KNOW HOW TO LOVE ME *RAK 206* [1]	.3 9
4 Oct 75 ●	DON'T PLAY YOUR ROCK 'N ROLL TO ME *RAK 217* [1]	.8 7
31 Jan 76	SOMETHING'S BEEN MAKING ME BLUE *RAK 227*	.17 8
25 Sep 76	I'LL MEET YOU AT MIDNIGHT *RAK 241*	.11 9
4 Dec 76 ●	LIVING NEXT DOOR TO ALICE *RAK 244*	.5 11
19 Mar 77	LAY BACK IN THE ARMS OF SOMEONE *RAK 251*	.5 9
16 Jul 77 ●	IT'S YOUR LIFE *RAK 260*	.10 9
15 Oct 77 ●	NEEDLES AND PINS *RAK 263*	.17 6
28 Jan 78	FOR A FEW DOLLARS MORE *RAK 267*	.5 13
20 May 78 ●	OH CAROL *RAK 276*	.19 9
23 Sep 78	MEXICAN GIRL *RAK 283*	

19 Apr 80	TAKE GOOD CARE OF MY BABY *RAK 309*	.34 7
13 May 95 ●	LIVING NEXT DOOR TO ALICE (WHO THE F**K IS ALICE) (re) *NOW CDWAG 245* [2]	.3 19

[1] Smokey [2] Smokie featuring Roy 'Chubby' Brown

*'Living Next Door to Alice (Who The F**k Is Alice)' is a re-recorded version of 'Living Next Door to Alice' which peaked on re-entry in Aug 1995*

SMOKIN BEATS featuring Lyn EDEN *UK, male DJ / production duo – Neil Rumney and Paul Landon – and female vocalist (3 WEEKS)* pos/wks

17 Jan 98	DREAMS *AM:PM 5824711*	.23 3

SMOKIN' MOJO FILTERS
UK / US, male / female vocal / instrumental charity group (5 WEEKS) pos/wks

23 Dec 95	COME TOGETHER (WAR CHILD) *Go! Discs GODCD 136*	.19 5

SMOOTH *US, female vocalist – Juanita Stokes (7 WEEKS)* pos/wks

22 Jul 95	MIND BLOWIN' *Jive JIVECD 379*	.36 2
7 Oct 95	IT'S SUMMERTIME (LET IT GET INTO YOU) *Jive JIVECD 383*	.46 1
16 Mar 96	WE GOT IT *MCA MCSTD 48009* [1]	.26 2
16 Mar 96	LOVE GROOVE (GROOVE WITH YOU) *Jive JIVECD 390*	.46 1
6 Jul 96	UNDERCOVER LOVER *Jive JIVECD 397*	.41 1

[1] Immature featuring Smooth

Joe SMOOTH *US, male producer (4 WEEKS)* pos/wks

4 Feb 89	PROMISED LAND *DJ International DJIN 6*	.56 4

SMOOTH TOUCH
US, male instrumental / production duo (1 WEEK) pos/wks

2 Apr 94	HOUSE OF LOVE (IN MY HOUSE) *Six6 SIXCD 112*	.58 1

Jean Jacques SMOOTHIE
UK, male DJ / producer – Steve Robson (7 WEEKS) pos/wks

13 Oct 01	2 PEOPLE *Echo ECSCD 112*	.12 7

SMURFS *Holland, small blue creatures vocal group (52 WEEKS)* pos/wks

3 Jun 78 ●	THE SMURF SONG *Decca F 13759* [1]	.2 17
30 Sep 78	DIPPETY DAY *Decca F 13798* [1]	.13 12
2 Dec 78	CHRISTMAS IN SMURFLAND *Decca F 13819*	.19 7
7 Sep 96 ●	I'VE GOT A LITTLE PUPPY *EMI TV CDSMURF 100*	.4 10
21 Dec 96 ●	YOUR CHRISTMAS WISH *EMI TV CDSMURF 102*	.8 6

[1] Father Abraham and The Smurfs

Patty SMYTH with Don HENLEY
US, female vocalist with male vocalist (6 WEEKS) pos/wks

3 Oct 92	SOMETIMES LOVE JUST AIN'T ENOUGH *MCA MCS 1692*	.22 6

SNAKEBITE *Italy, male production trio (2 WEEKS)* pos/wks

9 Aug 97	THE BIT GOES ON *Multiply CDMULTY 22*	.25 2

SNAP! (231) Top 500
German-based producers Benito Benites (b. Michael Munzing) and John Garrett Virgo III (b. Luca Anzilotti) masterminded a string of worldwide dance hits for this act, which featured a host of mostly US vocalists and rappers including Turbo B, Jackie Harris, Penny Ford and Thea Austin. Best-selling single: 'Rhythm Is A Dancer' 582,700 (120 WEEKS) pos/wks

24 Mar 90 ★	THE POWER *Arista 113133*	.1 15
16 Jun 90 ●	OOOPS UP *Arista 113296*	.5 12
22 Sep 90 ●	CULT OF SNAP *Arista 113596*	.8 7
8 Dec 90 ●	MARY HAD A LITTLE BOY *Arista 113831*	.8 10
30 Mar 91 ●	SNAP MEGAMIX *Arista 114169*	.10 6
21 Dec 91	THE COLOUR OF LOVE *Arista 114678*	.54 3
4 Jul 92 ★	RHYTHM IS A DANCER *Arista 115309*	.1 19
9 Jan 93 ●	EXTERMINATE! *Arista 74321106962* [1]	.2 11
12 Jun 93 ●	DO YOU SEE THE LIGHT (LOOKING FOR) *Arista 74321147622* [1]	.10 8
17 Sep 94 ●	WELCOME TO TOMORROW (re) *Arista 74321223852* [2]	.6 14

		pos/wks
1 Apr 95	THE FIRST THE LAST ETERNITY (TIL THE END)	
	Arista 74321254672 [2]	15 7
28 Oct 95	THE WORLD IN MY HANDS Arista 74321314792 [2]	44 1
13 Apr 96	RAME Arista 74321368902 [3]	50 1
24 Aug 96	THE POWER 96 Arista 74321398672 [4]	42 1
24 Aug 02	DO YOU SEE THE LIGHT? (re-mix)	
	Data DATA / MOS 33CDS [5]	14 5

[1] Snap! featuring Niki Haris [2] Snap! featuring Summer [3] Snap! featuring Rukmani [4] Snap! featuring Einstein [5] Snap! vs Plaything

SNEAKER PIMPS
UK, male / female vocal / instrumental group (19 WEEKS) pos/wks
19 Oct 96	6 UNDERGROUND Clean Up CUP 023CDS	15 4
15 Mar 97	SPIN SPIN SUGAR Clean Up CUP 033CDS	21 3
7 Jun 97 ●	6 UNDERGROUND (re-mix) Clean Up CUP 036CDM	9 4
30 Aug 97	POST MODERN SLEAZE Clean Up CUP 038CDM	22 3
7 Feb 98	SPIN SPIN SUGAR (re-mix) Clean Up CUP 037X	46 2
21 Aug 99	LOW FIVE Clean Up CUP 052CDM	39 2
30 Oct 99	TEN TO TWENTY Clean Up CUP 054CDS	56 1

SNIFF 'N' THE TEARS
UK, male vocal / instrumental group (5 WEEKS) pos/wks
23 Jun 79	DRIVER'S SEAT Chiswick CHIS 105	42 5

SNOOP DOGG *US, male rapper – Calvin Broadus (68 WEEKS)* pos/wks
4 Dec 93	WHAT'S MY NAME? Death Row A 8337CD [1]	20 8
12 Feb 94	GIN AND JUICE Death Row A 8316CD [1]	39 3
20 Aug 94	DOGGY DOGG WORLD Death Row A 8289CD [1]	32 3
14 Dec 96	SNOOP'S UPSIDE YA HEAD Interscope IND 95520 [2]	12 7
26 Apr 97	WANTED DEAD OR ALIVE Def Jam 5744052 [3]	16 3
3 May 97	VAPORS Interscope IND 95530	18 2
20 Sep 97	WE JUST WANNA PARTY WITH YOU Columbia 6649902 [4]	21 2
24 Jan 98	THA DOGGFATHER Interscope IND 95550 [1]	36 2
12 Dec 98	COME AND GET WITH ME Elektra E 3787CD [5]	58 1
25 Mar 00 ●	STILL D.R.E. Interscope 4972742 [6]	6 10
3 Feb 01 ●	THE NEXT EPISODE Interscope 4974762 [6]	3 10
17 Mar 01	X Epic 6709072 [7]	14 7
28 Apr 01	SNOOP DOGG Priority PTYCD 134	13 5
30 Nov 02	FROM THA CHUUUCH TO DA PALACE	
	Priority / Capitol 5516102	27 5+

[1] Snoop Doggy Dogg [2] Snoop Doggy Dogg featuring Charlie Wilson [3] 2Pac and Snoop Doggy Dogg [4] Snoop Doggy Dogg featuring JD [5] Keith Sweat featuring Snoop Dogg [6] Dr Dre featuring Snoop Dogg [7] Xzibit featuring Snoop Dogg

SNOW *Canada, male rapper – Darrin O'Brien (18 WEEKS)* pos/wks
13 Mar 93 ●	INFORMER East West America A 8436CD ▲	2 15
5 Jun 93	GIRL I'VE BEEN HURT East West America A 8417CD	48 2
4 Sep 93	UHH IN YOU Atlantic A 8378CD	67 1

Mark SNOW *US, male instrumentalist – keyboards (15 WEEKS)* pos/wks
30 Mar 96 ●	THE X-FILES Warner Bros. W 0341CD	2 15

Phoebe SNOW *US, female vocalist – Phoebe Laub (7 WEEKS)* pos/wks
6 Jan 79	EVERY NIGHT CBS 6842	37 7

SNOWMAN – See Peter AUTY and the SINFONIA OF LONDON

SNOWMEN *UK, male vocal / instrumental group (12 WEEKS)* pos/wks
12 Dec 81	HOKEY COKEY Stiff ODB 1	18 8
18 Dec 82	XMAS PARTY Solid STOP 006	44 4

SNUG *UK, male vocal / instrumental group (1 WEEK)* pos/wks
18 Apr 98	BEATNIK GIRL WEA WEA 151CDX	55 1

SO *UK, male vocal / instrumental group (3 WEEKS)* pos/wks
13 Feb 88	ARE YOU SURE Parlophone R 6173	62 3

SO SOLID CREW
UK, male / female vocal / rap / production collective (37 WEEKS) pos/wks
18 Aug 01 ★	21 SECONDS (re) Relentless RELENT 16CD ■	1 15
17 Nov 01 ●	THEY DON'T KNOW Relentless RELENT 26CD	3 9
19 Jan 02 ●	HATERS Relentless RELENT 23CD [1]	8 7
20 Apr 02	RIDE WID US Independiente ISOM 55MS	19 6

[1] So Solid Crew presents Mr Shabz featuring MBD and the Reelists

S.O.A.P.
Denmark, female vocal duo – Heidi and Line Sorensen (2 WEEKS) pos/wks
25 Jul 98	THIS IS HOW WE PARTY Columbia 6661295	36 2

SOAPY *UK, male instrumental / production
duo – Jak Kaleniuk and Dan Bewick (2 WEEKS)* pos/wks
14 Sep 96	HORNY AS FUNK WEA WEA 074CD	35 2

Gino SOCCIO *Canada, male instrumentalist – keyboards (5 WEEKS)* pos/wks
28 Apr 79	DANCER Warner Bros. K 17357	46 5

SODA CLUB featuring Hannah ALETHEA *UK, male
production duo – Andy and Pete Lee and female vocalist (4 WEEKS)* pos/wks
9 Nov 02	TAKE MY BREATH AWAY Concept CDCON 33	16 4

SOEUR SOURIRE – See SINGING NUN (Soeur Sourire)

SOFT CELL ⟨ 275 ⟩ [Top 500]
Successful synth-driven duo from Leeds: Marc Almond (v), David Ball (k). The visually striking pair's revival of northern soul classic 'Tainted Love' was the top UK single of 1981 and went on to sell 1,135,000 and also broke the longevity record in the US Top 100 (108 WEEKS) pos/wks
1 Aug 81 ★	TAINTED LOVE (3re) Some Bizzare BZS 2 ◆	1 36
14 Nov 81 ●	BEDSITTER Some Bizzare BZS 6	4 12
6 Feb 82 ●	SAY HELLO WAVE GOODBYE Some Bizzare BZS 7	3 9
29 May 82 ●	TORCH Some Bizzare BZS 9	2 9
21 Aug 82 ●	WHAT Some Bizzare BZS 11	3 8
4 Dec 82	WHERE THE HEART IS Some Bizzare BZS 16	21 7
5 Mar 83	NUMBERS / BARRIERS Some Bizzare BZS 17	25 4
24 Sep 83	SOUL INSIDE Some Bizzare BZS 20	16 5
25 Feb 84	DOWN IN THE SUBWAY Some Bizzare BZS 22	24 6
23 Mar 91	SAY HELLO WAVE GOODBYE '91 (re-recording)	
	Mercury SOFT 1 [1]	38 3
18 May 91 ●	TAINTED LOVE (re-issue) Mercury SOFT 2 [1]	5 8
28 Sep 02	MONOCULTURE Cooking Vinyl FRYCD 132	52 1

[1] Soft Cell / Marc Almond

'Tainted Love' re-entries made No.43 in Jan 1982, No.50 in Jul 1982 and No.43 in Feb 1985

SOFT PARADE – See ELECTRIC SOFT PARADE

SOHO *UK, male / female vocal / instrumental group (11 WEEKS)* pos/wks
5 May 90 ●	HIPPY CHICK (re) Savage 7SAV 106	8 9
9 Nov 91	BORN TO BE ALIVE MCA MCS 1578 [1]	51 2

[1] Adamski featuring Soho

'Hippy Chick' originally peaked at No.67 and made its peak position only on re-entry to the chart in Jan 1991. The listed flip side of 'Born to be Alive' was 'Never Goin' Down' by Adamski featuring Jimi Polo

SOIL *US, male vocal / instrumental group (1 WEEK)* pos/wks
9 Nov 02	HALO J 74321970132	74 1

SOLAR STONE *UK, male DJ / production trio (5 WEEKS)* pos/wks
21 Feb 98	THE IMPRESSIONS EP Hooj Choons HOOJCD 57	75 1
6 Nov 99	7 CITIES Hooj Choons HOOJ 85CD	39 2
28 Sep 02	7 CITIES (re-mix) Lost Language LOST 018CD	44 2

Tracks on The Impressions EP: The Calling / Day By Day / The Calling / Day By Day / So Clear

Re-entries are listed as (re), (2re), (3re), etc which signifies that the hit re-entered the chart

SOLID GOLD CHARTBUSTERS
UK, male / female production / vocal group (1 WEEK)   pos/wks

25 Dec 99	I WANNA 1-2-1 WITH YOU *Virgin VSCDT 1765*.................	62 1

SOLID HARMONIE
UK / US, female vocal group (11 WEEKS)   pos/wks

31 Jan 98	I'LL BE THERE FOR YOU *Jive JIVECD 437*	18 3
18 Apr 98	I WANT YOU TO WANT ME *Jive JIVECD 452*	16 3
15 Aug 98	I WANNA LOVE YOU *Jive 0521742*	20 4
21 Nov 98	TO LOVE ONCE AGAIN *Jive 0522472*	55 1

SOLID SESSIONS
Holland, male production duo (1 WEEK)   pos/wks

14 Sep 02	JANEIRO *Positiva CDTIV 175*................	47 1

SOLO
UK, male producer – Stuart Crichton (4 WEEKS)   pos/wks

20 Jul 91	RAINBOW (SAMPLE FREE) *Reverb RVBT 003*	59 2
18 Jan 92	COME ON! *Reverb RVBT 008*	75 1
11 Sep 93	COME ON! (re-mix) *Stoatin' STOAT 003CD*	63 1

Sal SOLO
UK, male vocalist (13 WEEKS)   pos/wks

15 Dec 84	SAN DAMIANO (HEART AND SOUL) *MCA MCA 930*	15 10
6 Apr 85	MUSIC AND YOU *MCA MCA 946* [1]	52 3

[1] Sal Solo with the London Community Gospel Choir

See also CLASSIX NOUVEAUX

SOLO (US)
US, male vocal group (3 WEEKS)   pos/wks

3 Feb 96	HEAVEN *Perspective 5875212*	35 2
30 Mar 96	WHERE DO U WANT ME TO PUT IT *Perspective 5875312*	45 1

SOLUTION – See Victor SIMONELLI presents SOLUTION

Belouis SOME
UK, male vocalist – Neville Keighley (26 WEEKS)   pos/wks

27 Apr 85	IMAGINATION *Parlophone R 6097*	50 7
18 Jan 86	IMAGINATION (re-issue) *Parlophone R 1986*	17 10
12 Apr 86	SOME PEOPLE *Parlophone R 6130*	33 7
16 May 87	LET IT BE WITH YOU *Parlophone R 6154*	53 2

Jimmy SOMERVILLE
UK, male vocalist (53 WEEKS)   pos/wks

11 Nov 89	COMMENT TE DIRE ADIEU *London LON 241* [1]	14 9
13 Jan 90 ●	YOU MAKE ME FEEL (MIGHTY REAL) *London LON 249*	5 8
17 Mar 90	READ MY LIPS (ENOUGH IS ENOUGH) *London LON 254*	26 6
3 Nov 90 ●	TO LOVE SOMEBODY *London LON 281*	8 11
2 Feb 91	SMALLTOWN BOY (re-mix) *London LON 287* [2]	32 4
10 Aug 91	RUN FROM LOVE *London LON 301*	52 2
28 Jan 95	HEARTBEAT *London LONCD 358*................	24 4
27 May 95	HURT SO GOOD *London LONCD 364*	15 6
28 Oct 95	BY YOUR SIDE *London LONCD 372*	41 2
13 Sep 97	DARK SKY *Gut CXGUT 11*	66 1

[1] Jimmy Somerville featuring June Miles-Kingston [2] Jimmy Somerville with Bronski Beat

See also BRONSKI BEAT; COMMUNARDS

SOMETHIN' FOR THE PEOPLE featuring TRINA and TAMARA
US, male vocal / instrumental group and female vocal duo (1 WEEK) pos/wks

7 Feb 98	MY LOVE IS THE SHHH! *Warner Bros W 0427CD*	64 1

SOMORE featuring Damon TRUEITT
US, male production group and male vocalist (2 WEEKS)   pos/wks

24 Jan 98	I REFUSE (WHAT YOU WANT) *XL Recordings XLS 93CD*	21 2

SONGSTRESS
US, male production / vocal duo (1 WEEK)   pos/wks

27 Feb 99	SEE LINE WOMAN '99 *Locked On LOX 106CD*	64 1

SONIA   448   *Top 500*
Bubbly teenage pop performer, b. Sonia Evans, 13 Feb 1971, Liverpool, UK. Singer / actress – the youngest UK female to reach No.1 since Mary Hopkin (1968) – was produced by the hit machine Stock Aitken and Waterman (78 WEEKS)   pos/wks

24 Jun 89 ★	YOU'LL NEVER STOP ME LOVING YOU *Chrysalis CHS 3385* 1 13
7 Oct 89	CAN'T FORGET YOU *Chrysalis CHS 3419*	17 6
9 Dec 89 ●	LISTEN TO YOUR HEART *Chrysalis CHS 3465*	10 10
7 Apr 90	COUNTING EVERY MINUTE *Chrysalis CHS 3492*	16 7
23 Jun 90	YOU'VE GOT A FRIEND *Chrysalis CHILD 90* [1]	14 6
25 Aug 90	END OF THE WORLD *Chrysalis/PWL CHS 3557*	18 7
1 Jun 91 ●	ONLY FOOLS (NEVER FALL IN LOVE) *IQ ZB 44613*	10 8
31 Aug 91	BE YOUNG BE FOOLISH BE HAPPY *IQ ZB 44935*	22 5
16 Nov 91	YOU TO ME ARE EVERYTHING *IQ ZB 45121*	13 5
12 Sep 92	BOOGIE NIGHTS *Arista 74321113467*	30 3
1 May 93	BETTER THE DEVIL YOU KNOW *Arista 74321146872*	15 7
30 Jul 94	HOPELESSLY DEVOTED TO YOU *Cockney COCCD 2*	61 1

[1] Big Fun and Sonia featuring Gary Barnacle

SONIC SOLUTION
Belgium, male production duo – CJ Bolland and Steve Cop (1 WEEK) pos/wks

4 Apr 92	BEATSTIME *R&S RSUK 11*	59 1

SONIC SURFERS
Holland, male instrumental / production duo (2 WEEKS)   pos/wks

20 Mar 93	TAKE ME UP *A&M AMCD 210* [1]	61 1
30 Jul 94	DON'T GIVE IT UP *Brilliant CDBRIL 6*	54 1

[1] Sonic Surfers featuring Jocelyn Brown

SONIC THE HEDGEHOG – See HWA featuring SONIC THE HEDGEHOG

SONIC YOUTH
US, male / female vocal / instrumental group (14 WEEKS)   pos/wks

11 Jul 92	100% *DGC DGCS 11*	28 4
7 Nov 92	YOUTH AGAINST FASCISM *Geffen GFS 26*	52 2
3 Apr 93	SUGAR KANE *Geffen GFSTD 37*	26 3
7 May 94	BULL IN THE HEATHER *Geffen GFSTD 72*	24 2
10 Sep 94	SUPERSTAR *A&M 5807932*	45 2
11 Jul 98	SUNDAY *Geffen GFSTD 22332*	72 1

The listed flip side of 'Superstar' was 'Yesterday Once More' by Redd Kross

SONIQUE
UK, female vocalist / DJ – Sonia Clarke (42 WEEKS)   pos/wks

13 Jun 98	I PUT A SPELL ON YOU *Serious SERR 001CD*	36 2
5 Dec 98	IT FEELS SO GOOD *Serious SERR 004CD*	24 3
3 Jun 00 ★	IT FEELS SO GOOD (re-mix) *Universal MCSTD 40233* ■	1 17
16 Sep 00 ●	SKY *Universal MCSTD 40240*	2 10
9 Dec 00 ●	I PUT A SPELL ON YOU (re-issue) *Universal MCSTD 40245*.......8 10

SONNY
US, male vocalist – Salvatore Bono, d. 5 Jan 1998 (11 WEEKS) pos/wks

19 Aug 65 ●	LAUGH AT ME *Atlantic AT 4038*	9 11

See also SONNY and CHER

SONNY and CHER   446   *Top 500*
Most successful US husband-and-wife recording team, Salvatore Bono, b 16 Feb 1935, Michigan, US, d. 5 Jan 1998, Cherilyn LaPierre, b. 20 May 1946, California, US. Married 1963-74 and was the major new act of 1965. Cher became a solo superstar and Sonny was elected mayor of Palm Springs (78 WEEKS)   pos/wks

12 Aug 65 ★	I GOT YOU BABE *Atlantic AT 4035* ▲	1 12
16 Sep 65	BABY DON'T GO *Reprise R 20309*	11 9
21 Oct 65	BUT YOU'RE MINE *Atlantic AT 4047*	17 8
17 Feb 66	WHAT NOW MY LOVE *Atlantic AT 4069*	13 11
30 Jun 66	HAVE I STAYED TOO LONG *Atlantic 584 018*	42 3
8 Sep 66 ●	LITTLE MAN *Atlantic 584 040*	4 10
17 Nov 66	LIVING FOR YOU *Atlantic 584 057*	44 4
2 Feb 67	THE BEAT GOES ON *Atlantic 584 078*	29 8
15 Jan 72 ●	ALL I EVER NEED IS YOU *MCA MU 1145*	8 12
22 May 93	I GOT YOU BABE (re-issue) *Epic 6592402*	66 1

See also SONNY; CHER

SONO *Germany, male production duo (1 WEEK)* pos/wks

| 16 Jun 01 | KEEP CONTROL *Code Blue BLU 020CD1* | 66 | 1 |

SON'Z OF A LOOP DA LOOP ERA
UK, male producer – Danny Breaks (4 WEEKS) pos/wks

| 15 Feb 92 | FAR OUT *Suburban Base SUBBASE 008* | 36 | 3 |
| 17 Oct 92 | PEACE + LOVEISM *Suburban Base SUBBASE 14* | 60 | 1 |

SOOZY Q – See BIG TIME CHARLIE

SOPHIE – See ZERO 7

SORROWS *UK, male vocal / instrumental group (8 WEEKS)* pos/wks

| 16 Sep 65 | TAKE A HEART *Piccadilly 7N 35260* | 21 | 8 |

Aaron SOUL *UK, male vocalist – Aaron Anyia (4 WEEKS)* pos/wks

| 2 Jun 01 | RING RING RING *Def Soul 5689042* | 14 | 4 |

David SOUL *US, male actor / vocalist – David Solberg (56 WEEKS)* pos/wks

18 Dec 76	★ DON'T GIVE UP ON US *Private Stock PVT 84* ◆ ▲	1	16
26 Mar 77	● GOING IN WITH MY EYES OPEN *Private Stock PVT 99*	2	8
27 Aug 77	● SILVER LADY *Private Stock PVT 115*	1	14
17 Dec 77	● LET'S HAVE A QUIET NIGHT IN *Private Stock PVT 130*	8	9
27 May 78	IT SURE BRINGS OUT THE LOVE IN YOUR EYES *Private Stock PVT 137*	12	9

Jimmy SOUL
US, male vocalist – James McCleese, d. 25 Jun 1988 (5 WEEKS) pos/wks

| 11 Jul 63 | IF YOU WANNA BE HAPPY *Stateside SS 178* ▲ | 39 | 2 |
| 15 Jun 91 | IF YOU WANNA BE HAPPY (re-issue) *Epic 6569647* | 68 | 3 |

SOUL ASYLUM *US, male vocal / instrumental group (33 WEEKS)* pos/wks

19 Jun 93	● RUNAWAY TRAIN (re) *Columbia 6593902*	7	19
4 Sep 93	SOMEBODY TO SHOVE *Columbia 6596492*	34	3
22 Jan 94	BLACK GOLD *Columbia 6598442*	26	4
26 Mar 94	SOMEBODY TO SHOVE (re-issue) *Columbia 6602245*	32	3
15 Jul 95	MISERY *Columbia 6621092*	30	3
2 Dec 95	JUST LIKE ANYONE *Columbia 6624785*	52	1

'Runaway Train' peaked during re-entry in Nov 1993

SOUL BROTHERS *UK, male vocal / instrumental group (3 WKS)* pos/wks

| 22 Apr 65 | I KEEP RINGING MY BABY *Decca F 12116* | 42 | 3 |

SOUL CITY ORCHESTRA
UK, male instrumental / production group (1 WEEK) pos/wks

| 11 Dec 93 | IT'S JURASSIC *London JURCD 1* | 70 | 1 |

SOUL CITY SYMPHONY – See Van McCOY

SOUL FAMILY SENSATION
UK / US, male / female vocal / instrumental group (4 WEEKS) pos/wks

| 11 May 91 | I DON'T EVEN KNOW IF I SHOULD CALL YOU BABY *One Little Indian 47 TP7* | 49 | 4 |

SOUL FOR REAL *US, male vocal group (4 WEEKS)* pos/wks

| 8 Jul 95 | CANDY RAIN *Uptown MCSTD 2052* | 23 | 2 |
| 23 Mar 96 | EVERY LITTLE THING I DO *Uptown MCSTD 48005* | 31 | 2 |

SOUL II SOUL (362) Top 500
Enormously influential dance music project led by entrepreneurial producer / DJ Jazzie B, b. Beresford Romeo, 16 Jan 1963, London. Act featured Nellee Hooper's innovative arrangements and was fronted by a succession of vocalists, most notably Caron Wheeler. Unlike UK contemporaries they were equally successful in US (89 WEEKS) pos/wks

21 May 88	FAIRPLAY *10 TEN 228* 1	63	3
17 Sep 88	FEEL FREE *10 TEN 236* 2	64	2
18 Mar 89	● KEEP ON MOVING *10 TEN 263* 3	5	12
10 Jun 89	★ BACK TO LIFE (HOWEVER DO YOU WANT ME) *10 TEN 265* 3	1	14
9 Dec 89	● GET A LIFE *10 TEN 284*	3	13
5 May 90	● A DREAM'S A DREAM *10 TEN 300*	6	6
24 Nov 90	MISSING YOU *10 TEN 345* 4	22	7
4 Apr 92	● JOY *Ten TEN 350*	4	7
13 Jun 92	MOVE ME NO MOUNTAIN *Ten TEN 400* 5	31	4
26 Sep 92	JUST RIGHT *Ten TEN 410*	38	2
6 Nov 93	WISH *Virgin VSCDG 1480*	24	4
22 Jul 95	LOVE ENUFF *Virgin VSCDT 1527*	12	6
21 Oct 95	I CARE (SOUL II SOUL) *Virgin VSCDT 1560*	17	4
19 Oct 96	KEEP ON MOVIN' (re-mix) *Virgin VSCDT 1612*	31	2
30 Aug 97	REPRESENT *Island CID 668*	39	2
8 Nov 97	PLEASURE DOME *Island CID 669*	51	1

1 Soul II Soul featuring Rose Windross 2 Soul II Soul featuring Do'reen 3 Soul II Soul featuring Caron Wheeler 4 Soul II Soul featuring Kym Mazelle 5 Soul II Soul, lead vocals Kofi

See also PSYCHEDELIC WALTONS featuring Roisin MURPHY

SOUL PROVIDERS featuring Michelle SHELLERS
UK, male production duo and US, female vocalist (1 WEEK) pos/wks

| 14 Jul 01 | RISE *AM:PM CDAMPM 147* | 59 | 1 |

SOUL SONIC FORCE – See Afrika BAMBAATAA; Paul OAKENFOLD

S.O.U.L. S.Y.S.T.E.M. introducing Michelle VISAGE
US, male / female vocal / instrumental group (5 WEEKS) pos/wks

| 16 Jan 93 | IT'S GONNA BE A LOVELY DAY *Arista 74321125692* | 17 | 5 |

See also C & C MUSIC FACTORY

SOUL U*NIQUE *UK, male / female vocal group (2 WEEKS)* pos/wks

| 19 Feb 00 | BE MY FRIEND *M&J MAJCD 2* | 53 | 1 |
| 29 Jul 00 | 3IL (THRILL) *M&J MAJCD 3X* | 66 | 1 |

SOUL VISION – See EVERYTHING BUT THE GIRL

SOULED OUT
Italy / US / UK, male / female vocal / instrumental group (1 WEEK) pos/wks

| 9 May 92 | IN MY LIFE *Columbia 6578367* | 75 | 1 |

SOULSEARCHER
US, male / female production / vocal group (9 WEEKS) pos/wks

| 13 Feb 99 | ● CAN'T GET ENOUGH *Defected DEFECT 1CDS* | 8 | 7 |
| 8 Apr 00 | DO IT TO ME AGAIN *Defected DFECT 15CDS* | 32 | 2 |

SOULSONIC FORCE – See Paul OAKENFOLD

SOULWAX *Belgium, male vocal / instrumental*
duo – Stephen and David Dewaele (5 WEEKS) pos/wks

25 Mar 00	CONVERSATION INTERCOM *Pias Recordings PIASB 018CD*	65	1
24 Jun 00	MUCH AGAINST EVERYONE'S ADVICE *Pias Recordings PIASB 026CD*	56	1
30 Sep 00	TOO MANY DJ'S *Pias Recordings PIASB 036CD*	40	2
3 Mar 01	CONVERSATION INTERCOM (re-mix) *Pias Recordings PIASB 046CD*	50	1

SOUND BLUNTZ
Germany, male production / vocal group (2 WEEKS) pos/wks

| 30 Nov 02 | BILLIE JEAN *Incentive CENT 51CDS* | 32 | 2 |

SOUND-DE-ZIGN *Holland, male DJ /*
production duo – Adri Blok and Arjen Rietvink (5 WEEKS) pos/wks

| 14 Apr 01 | HAPPINESS *Nulife / Arista 74321844002* | 19 | 5 |

SOUND FACTORY
Sweden, male vocal / instrumental duo (1 WEEK) pos/wks

| 5 Jun 93 | 2 THE RHYTHM *Logic 74321149422* | 72 | 1 |

SOUND 5 UK, male vocal / instrumental group (1 WEEK)
pos/wks

24 Apr 99	ALA KABOO Gut CDGUT 23	69	1

SOUND 9418 – See Jonathan KING

SOUND OF ONE featuring GLADEZZ
US, male / female vocal / instrumental duo (1 WEEK)
pos/wks

20 Nov 93	AS I AM Cooltempo CDCOOL 280	65	1

SOUNDGARDEN
US, male vocal / instrumental group (24 WEEKS)
pos/wks

11 Apr 92	JESUS CHRIST POSE A&M AM 862	30	3
20 Jun 92	RUSTY CAGE A&M AM 874	41	1
21 Nov 92	OUTSHINED A&M AM 0102	50	1
26 Feb 94	SPOONMAN A&M 5805392	20	3
30 Apr 94	THE DAY I TRIED TO LIVE A&M 5805552	42	2
20 Aug 94	BLACK HOLE SUN A&M 5807532	12	5
28 Jan 95	FELL ON BLACK DAYS A&M 5809472	24	2
18 May 96	PRETTY NOOSE A&M 5816202	14	3
28 Sep 96	BURDEN IN MY HAND A&M 5818552	33	2
28 Dec 96	BLOW UP THE OUTSIDE WORLD A&M 5819862	40	2

SOUNDMAN and Don LLOYDIE with Elisabeth TROY
UK, male / female vocal / production group (2 WEEKS)
pos/wks

25 Feb 95	GREATER LOVE Sound of Underground SOURCD 016	49	2

SOUNDS INCORPORATED
UK, male instrumental group (11 WEEKS)
pos/wks

23 Apr 64	THE SPARTANS Columbia DB 7239	30	6
30 Jul 64	SPANISH HARLEM Columbia DB 7321	35	5

See also Gene VINCENT

SOUNDS NICE featuring Tim MYCROFT
UK, male instrumental group (11 WEEKS)
pos/wks

6 Sep 69	LOVE AT FIRST SIGHT (JE T'AIME ... MOI NON PLUS) Parlophone R 5797	18	11

SOUNDS OF BLACKNESS
US, male / female gospel choir (32 WEEKS)
pos/wks

22 Jun 91	OPTIMISTIC Perspective PERSS 786	45	4
28 Sep 91	THE PRESSURE PART 1 Perspective PERSS 816	71	1
15 Feb 92	OPTIMISTIC (re-issue) Perspective PERSS 849	28	4
25 Apr 92	THE PRESSURE PART 1 (re-mix) Perspective PERSS 867	49	2
8 May 93	I'M GOING ALL THE WAY Perspective 5874252	27	3
26 Mar 94	I BELIEVE A&M 5874512	17	4
2 Jul 94	GLORYLAND Mercury MERCD 404 [1]	36	4
20 Aug 94	EVERYTHING IS GONNA BE ALRIGHT A&M 5874672	29	3
14 Jan 95	I'M GOING ALL THE WAY (re-issue) A&M 5874832	14	4
7 Jun 97	SPIRIT A&M 5822292 [2]	35	2
14 Feb 98	THE PRESSURE (2nd re-mix) AM:PM 5824872	46	1

[1] Daryl Hall and The Sounds of Blackness [2] Sounds of Blackness / Craig Mack

SOUNDS ORCHESTRAL UK, orchestra (18 WEEKS)
pos/wks

3 Dec 64	● CAST YOUR FATE TO THE WIND Piccadilly 7N 35206	5	16
8 Jul 65	MOONGLOW Piccadilly 7N 35248	43	2

SOUNDSATION UK, male producer (1 WEEK)
pos/wks

14 Jan 95	PEACE AND JOY Ffrreedom TABCD 224	48	1

SOUNDSCAPE UK, male DJ / production group (1 WEEK)
pos/wks

14 Feb 98	DUBPLATE CULTURE Satellite 74321552002	61	1

SOUNDSOURCE
Sweden / UK, male instrumental / production group (1 WEEK)
pos/wks

11 Jan 92	TAKE ME UP ffrr FX 177	62	1

SOUP DRAGONS
UK, male vocal / instrumental group (23 WEEKS)
pos/wks

20 Jun 87	CAN'T TAKE NO MORE Raw TV RTV 3	65	1
5 Sep 87	SOFT AS YOUR FACE Raw TV RTV 4	66	2
14 Jul 90	● I'M FREE Raw TV RTV 9 [1]	5	12
20 Oct 90	MOTHER UNIVERSE Big Life BLR 30	26	5
11 Apr 92	DIVINE THING Big Life BLR 68	53	3

[1] Soup Dragons featuring Junior Reid

SOURCE UK, male producer – John Truelove (22 WEEKS)
pos/wks

2 Feb 91	● YOU GOT THE LOVE Truelove TLOVE 7001 [1]	4	11
26 Dec 92	ROCK THE HOUSE React 12REACT 12 [2]	63	1
1 Mar 97	YOU GOT THE LOVE (re-mix) React CDREACT 89 [1]	3	8
23 Aug 97	CLOUDS XL Recordings XLS 83CD	38	2

[1] Source featuring Candi Staton [2] Source featuring Nicole

SOURMASH UK, male production trio (1 WEEK)
pos/wks

23 Dec 00	PILGRIMAGE / MESCALITO Hooj Choons HOOJ 102	73	1

SOUTH UK, male vocal / instrumental group (1 WEEK)
pos/wks

17 Mar 01	PAINT THE SILENCE Mo Wax MWR 134CD	69	1

Joe SOUTH US, male vocalist – Joe Souter (11 WEEKS)
pos/wks

5 Mar 69	● GAMES PEOPLE PLAY Capitol CL 15579	6	11

SOUTH ST. PLAYER
US, male vocalist / producer – Roland Clark (1 WEEK)
pos/wks

2 Sep 00	WHO KEEPS CHANGING YOUR MIND Cream CREAM 4CD	49	1

Jeri SOUTHERN
US, female vocalist – Genevieve Hering, d. 4 Aug 1991 (3 WEEKS)
pos/wks

21 Jun 57	FIRE DOWN BELOW Brunswick 05665	22	3

SOUTHLANDERS
Jamaica / UK, male vocal group (10 WEEKS)
pos/wks

22 Nov 57	ALONE Decca F 10946	17	10

SOUTHSIDE SPINNERS Holland, male production
duo – Marco Verkuylen and Benjamin Kuyten (7 WEEKS)
pos/wks

27 May 00	● LUVSTRUCK AM:PM CDAMPM 132	9	7

SOUVERANCE Holland, male production duo (1 WEEK)
pos/wks

31 Aug 02	HAVIN' A GOOD TIME Positiva CDTIV 174	63	1

SOUVLAKI UK, male producer – Mark Summers (4 WEEKS)
pos/wks

15 Feb 97	INFERNO Wonderboy WBOYD 003	24	3
8 Aug 98	MY TIME Wonderboy WBOYD 009	63	1

See also Mark SUMMERS

SOVEREIGN COLLECTION UK, orchestra (6 WEEKS)
pos/wks

3 Apr 71	MOZART 40 Capitol CL 15676	27	6

Red SOVINE
US, male vocalist – Woodrow Wilson Sovine, d. 4 Apr 1980 (8 WEEKS) pos/wks

13 Jun 81	● TEDDY BEAR Starday SD 142	4	8

SOX UK, female vocal / instrumental
group – lead vocal Samantha Fox (1 WEEK)
pos/wks

15 Apr 95	GO FOR THE HEART Living Beat LBECD 33	47	1

Bob B SOXX and the BLUE JEANS
US, male / female vocal group (2 WEEKS)
pos/wks

31 Jan 63	ZIP-A-DEE-DOO-DAH London HLU 9646	45	2

SMOKE ON THE WATER

■ Deep Purple's 'Smoke on the Water' tells the story of the circumstances in which the song was recorded. Second only to Led Zeppelin in the 1970s heavy-rock stakes, Deep Purple laid the foundation for just about every other serious (and plenty of not so serious) heavy rock bands that followed. Formed in 1968, the band first found chart success in America with their covers of Joe South's 'Hush', Neil Diamond's 'Kentucky Woman' and the Ike and Tina Turner hit 'River Deep, Mountain High'.

In a 1969 reshuffle, Ian Gillan and Roger Glover joined from Episode Six. With these additions the famous Mark II Deep Purple ensemble was a reality: Ian Gillan on vocals, guitarist Ritchie Blackmore, drummer Ian Paice, bassist Roger Glover and Jon Lord on keyboards. This was a line-up that would endure from 1969 to 1973.

In 1971, following their debut on the UK singles chart with two Top 10 entries ('Black Night' and 'Strange Kind of Woman') Purple retired to Montreux, Switzerland, to prepare a new album. Recorded over a two-week period in December, the band attempted to capture a live sound by recording the album at the Montreux Casino on the banks of Lake Geneva. The casino would be closed for the winter season and The Rolling Stones' mobile recording unit was hired for the purpose. On the day before Deep Purple were due to move into the casino there was an end-of-season concert by Frank Zappa, attended by about 2,000 people, including the members of Deep Purple. About two hours into Zappa's show someone fired a flare gun at the ceiling inside the hall, starting a fire that soon turned

■ TWO HOURS INTO ZAPPA'S SHOW SOMEONE FIRED A FLARE GUN AT THE CEILING, STARTING A FIRE THAT SOON TURNED INTO A BLAZING INFERNO ■

into a blazing inferno. Within a few hours the casino was reduced to a smouldering ruin, but fortunately nobody was seriously hurt, although Zappa and his band lost all their equipment. Luckily Deep Purple hadn't yet unloaded their own gear, although they now needed a new location to record.

Inspired by the sight of smoke from the fire drifting over Lake Geneva, Roger Glover came up with the line "smoke on the water", and the rest of the lyrics were written by vocalist Ian Gillan, telling the story of the casino fire, and how the song came to be recorded. The track was captured on tape when the band relocated to the Grand Hotel, also closed for the season. Recorded in the hotel corridor, with mattresses brought in for soundproofing, guitarist Ritchie Blackmore recalls that the group was playing at such a high volume that "we were waking up the neighbours about five miles away". The police arrived en masse to put a stop to the recording, although the group didn't let them in until they had finished the track to their satisfaction.

The success of 'Smoke on the Water' came as

something of a surprise to the band. They had specifically written another track, 'Never Before', as a commercial single. Indeed, it was considered the most important recording at the sessions, but the single reached only No.35 in the UK. According to Ian Gillan, 'Smoke on the Water' was recorded only as a last-minute track to fill out the album when they discovered they were a little short of material. Even with the finished recording in the can, the group didn't think it was anything out of the ordinary until radio DJs started highlighting the track. The album recorded in Montreux, Machine Head, became Deep Purple's most successful studio album and spent three weeks at No.1 in the UK in 1972, but 'Smoke on the Water' took another five years to make it in the UK singles chart. A peak position of No.21 hardly reflects the importance of a song containing what is one of the most famous guitar riffs in rock. Ever passed a church hall in the dead of night when a wannabe teenage rock band is practising? Durr-durr-durr, durr-durr-ded-durr...

■ Tony Burton

★ **ARTIST:** Deep Purple

★ **LABEL:** Purple UK/Warner USA

★ **WRITERS:** Ritchie Blackmore, Ian Gillan, Roger Glover, Jon Lord and Ian Paice

★ **PRODUCER:** Deep Purple

Deep Purple live on stage in all their glory

SPACE France, male instrumental group (12 WEEKS)

		pos/wks
13 Aug 77 ●	MAGIC FLY Pye International 7N 25746	2 12

SPACE UK, male vocal / instrumental group (51 WEEKS)

		pos/wks
6 Apr 96	NEIGHBOURHOOD Gut CDGUT 1	56 1
8 Jun 96	FEMALE OF THE SPECIES Gut CDGUT 2	14 10
7 Sep 96 ●	ME AND YOU VERSUS THE WORLD Gut CDGUT 4	9 6
2 Nov 96	NEIGHBOURHOOD (re-issue) Gut CDGUT 5	11 6
22 Feb 97	DARK CLOUDS Gut CDGUT 6	14 4
10 Jan 98 ●	AVENGING ANGELS Gut CDGUT 16	6 8
7 Mar 98 ●	THE BALLAD OF TOM JONES Gut CDGUT 018 [1]	4 8
4 Jul 98	BEGIN AGAIN Gut CDGUT 19	21 4
5 Dec 98	THE BAD DAYS (EP) Gut CDGUT 22	20 3
8 Jul 00	DIARY OF A WIMP Gut CDGUT 34	49 1

[1] Space with Cerys of Catatonia

Tracks on The Bad Days (EP): Bad Days / We Gotta Get Out of This Place / The Unluckiest Man in the World

SPACE BABY UK, male producer – Matt Darey (1 WEEK)

		pos/wks
8 Jul 95	FREE YOUR MIND Hooj Choons HOOJ 34CD	55 1

SPACE BROTHERS UK, male production
duo – Ricky Simmonds and Stephen Jones (19 WEEKS)

		pos/wks
17 May 97	SHINE Manifesto FESCD 23	23 3
13 Dec 97	FORGIVEN (I FEEL YOUR LOVE) Manifesto FESCD 36	27 7
10 Jul 99	LEGACY (SHOW ME LOVE) Manifesto FESCD 55	31 3
9 Oct 99	HEAVEN WILL COME Manifesto FESCD 61	25 2
5 Feb 00	SHINE 2000 (re-mix) Manifesto FESCD 67	18 4

See also ESSENCE; CHAKRA; LUSTRAL; ASCENSION

SPACE COWBOY France, male producer – Nick Dresti (2 WEEKS)

		pos/wks
6 Jul 02	I WOULD DIE 4 U Southern Fried ECB 29CD	55 2

SPACE FROG Germany, male production duo (1 WEEK)

		pos/wks
16 Mar 02	(X RAY) FOLLOW ME Tripoli Trax TTRAX 082CD	70 1

SPACE KITTENS
UK, male instrumental / production group (1 WEEK)

		pos/wks
13 Apr 96	STORM Hooj Choons HOOJCD 41	58 1

SPACE MANOEUVRES
UK, male producer – John Graham (2 WEEKS)

		pos/wks
29 Jan 00	STAGE ONE Hooj Choons HOOJ 79CD	25 2

SPACE MONKEY UK, male producer – Paul Goodchild (4 WEEKS)

		pos/wks
8 Oct 83	CAN'T STOP RUNNING Innervision A 3742	53 4

SPACE MONKEYZ vs GORILLAZ
UK, male production / instrumental duo (1 WEEK)

		pos/wks
3 Aug 02	LIL' DUB CHEFIN' Parlophone CDR 6584	73 1

SPACE RAIDERS UK, male production trio (1 WEEK)

		pos/wks
28 Mar 98	GLAM RAID Skint SKINT 32CD	68 1

SPACE 2000 UK, male vocal / instrumental duo (1 WEEK)

		pos/wks
12 Aug 95	DO U WANNA FUNK Wired WIRED 218	50 1

SPACECORN
Sweden, male DJ / producer – Daniel Ellenson (1 WEEK)

		pos/wks
28 Apr 01	AXEL F 69 SN 069CD	74 1

SPACEDUST UK, male production duo
– Paul Glancey and Duncan Glasson (12 WEEKS)

		pos/wks
24 Oct 98 ★	GYM AND TONIC (re) East West EW 188CD ■	1 10
27 Mar 99	LET'S GET DOWN East West EW 195CD	20 2

SPACEHOG UK, male vocal / instrumental group (8 WEEKS)

		pos/wks
11 May 96	IN THE MEANTIME (re) Sire 7559643162	29 7
7 Feb 98	CARRY ON Sire W 0428CD	43 1

'In the Meantime' peaked only during re-entry in Dec 1996

SPACEMAID UK, male vocal / instrumental group (1 WEEK)

		pos/wks
5 Apr 97	BABY COME ON Big Star STARC 105	70 1

SPAGHETTI SURFERS
UK, male instrumental / production duo (1 WEEK)

		pos/wks
22 Jul 95	MISIRLOU (THE THEME TO THE MOTION PICTURE 'PULP FICTION') Tempo Toons CDTOON 4	55 1

SPAGNA Italy, female vocalist – Ivana Spagna (23 WEEKS)

		pos/wks
25 Jul 87 ●	CALL ME CBS 650279 7	2 12
17 Oct 87	EASY LADY CBS 651169 7	62 3
20 Aug 88	EVERY GIRL AND BOY CBS SPAG 1	23 8

SPANDAU BALLET (136 Top 500)

Kilt-clad New Romantic revolutionaries. This London band went on to become smart-suited Top 10 regulars: Tony Hadley (v), Gary Kemp (g), Martin Kemp (b), Steve Norman (g/sax/prc), John Keeble (d). The Kemp brothers later went into the movies and TV, including lead roles in 'The Krays' (1990) and Martin, who starred in 'EastEnders' and other TV programmes, was voted Best Actor and Sexiest Male in the 2002 Soap Awards (159 WEEKS)

		pos/wks
15 Nov 80 ●	TO CUT A LONG STORY SHORT Reformation CHS 2473	5 11
24 Jan 81	THE FREEZE Reformation CHS 2486	17 8
4 Apr 81 ●	MUSCLEBOUND / GLOW Reformation CHS 2509	10 10
18 Jul 81 ●	CHANT NO.1 (I DON'T NEED THIS PRESSURE ON) Reformation CHS 2528	3 10
14 Nov 81	PAINT ME DOWN Chrysalis CHS 2560	30 5
30 Jan 82	SHE LOVED LIKE DIAMOND Chrysalis CHS 2585	49 4
10 Apr 82 ●	INSTINCTION Chrysalis CHS 2602	10 11
2 Oct 82	LIFELINE Chrysalis CHS 2642	7 9
12 Feb 83	COMMUNICATION Reformation CHS 2662	12 10
23 Apr 83 ★	TRUE Reformation SPAN 1	1 12
13 Aug 83	GOLD Reformation SPAN 2	2 9
9 Jun 84 ●	ONLY WHEN YOU LEAVE (re) Reformation SPAN 3	3 10
25 Aug 84 ●	I'LL FLY FOR YOU Reformation SPAN 4	9 9
20 Oct 84	HIGHLY STRUNG Reformation SPAN 5	15 5
8 Dec 84	ROUND AND ROUND Reformation SPAN 6	18 8
26 Jul 86	FIGHT FOR OURSELVES Reformation A 7264	15 7
8 Nov 86 ●	THROUGH THE BARRICADES Reformation SPANS 1	6 10
14 Feb 87	HOW MANY LIES Reformation SPANS 2	34 4
3 Sep 88	RAW CBS SPANS 3	47 3
26 Aug 89	BE FREE WITH YOUR LOVE CBS SPANS 4	42 4

SPARKLE US, female vocalist (10 WEEKS)

		pos/wks
18 Jul 98 ●	BE CAREFUL (re) Jive 0521452 [1]	7 7
7 Nov 98	TIME TO MOVE ON Jive 0522032	40 2
28 Aug 99	LOVIN' YOU Jive 0523450	65 1

[1] Sparkle featuring R Kelly

SPARKLEHORSE
US, male vocal / instrumental group (2 WEEKS)

		pos/wks
31 Aug 96	RAINMAKER Capitol CDCL 777	61 1
17 Oct 98	SICK OF GOODBYES Parlophone CDCLS 808	57 1

SPARKS (427 Top 500)

Eccentric and distinctive-looking pop / rock group, formed by Californian-born brothers Russell (v), 5 Oct 1953 and Ron Mael (k) 12 Aug 1948. Relocated to UK in 1973 and proved more successful in Europe than in their homeland. Voted Top Newcomers in the 1974 Record Mirror poll (81 WEEKS)

		pos/wks
4 May 74 ●	THIS TOWN AIN'T BIG ENOUGH FOR BOTH OF US Island WIP 6193	2 10
20 Jul 74 ●	AMATEUR HOUR Island WIP 6203	7 9
19 Oct 74	NEVER TURN YOUR BACK ON MOTHER EARTH Island WIP 6211	13 7

Re-entries are listed as (re), (2re), (3re), etc which signifies that the hit re-entered the chart

18 Jan 75	SOMETHING FOR THE GIRL WITH EVERYTHING		
	Island WIP 6221	17	7
19 Jul 75	GET IN THE SWING *Island WIP 6236*	27	7
4 Oct 75	LOOKS, LOOKS, LOOKS *Island WIP 6249*	26	4
21 Apr 79	THE NUMBER ONE SONG IN HEAVEN *Virgin VS 244*	14	12
21 Jul 79 ●	BEAT THE CLOCK *Virgin VS 270*	10	9
27 Oct 79	TRYOUTS FOR THE HUMAN RACE *Virgin VS 289*	45	5
29 Oct 94	WHEN DO I GET TO SING 'MY WAY' *Logic 74321234472*	38	3
11 Mar 95	WHEN I KISS YOU (I HEAR CHARLIE PARKER PLAYING)		
	Logic 74321264272	36	2
20 May 95	WHEN DO I GET TO SING 'MY WAY' (re-issue)		
	Logic 74321274002	32	2
9 Mar 96	NOW THAT I OWN THE BBC *Logic 74321348672*	60	1
25 Oct 97	THE NUMBER ONE SONG IN HEAVEN (re-recording)		
	Roadrunner RR 22692	70	1
13 Dec 97	THIS TOWN AIN'T BIG ENOUGH FOR BOTH OF US		
	Roadrunner RR 22513 1	40	2

1 Sparks vs Faith No More

Group was a UK / US group for first six hits

Bubba SPARXXX
US, male rapper – Warren Mathis (12 WEEKS) pos/wks

24 Nov 01 ●	UGLY *Interscope / Polydor 4976542*	7	10
9 Mar 02	LOVELY *Interscope 4976752*	24	2

SPEAR OF DESTINY
UK, male vocal / instrumental group (43 WEEKS) pos/wks

21 May 83	THE WHEEL *Epic A 3372*	59	5
21 Jan 84	PRISONER OF LOVE *Epic A 4068*	59	3
14 Apr 84	LIBERATOR *Epic A 4310*	67	2
15 Jun 85	ALL MY LOVE (ASK NOTHING) *Epic A 6333*	61	3
10 Aug 85	COME BACK *Epic A 6445*	55	3
7 Feb 87	STRANGERS IN OUR TOWN *10 TEN 148*	49	4
4 Apr 87	NEVER TAKE ME ALIVE *10 TEN 162*	14	11
25 Jul 87	WAS THAT YOU? *10 TEN 173*	55	4
3 Oct 87	THE TRAVELLER *10 TEN 189*	44	3
24 Sep 88	SO IN LOVE WITH YOU *Virgin VS 1123*	36	5

SPEARHEAD
US, male vocal / instrumental group (5 WEEKS) pos/wks

17 Dec 94	OF COURSE YOU CAN *Capitol CDCL 733*	74	1
22 Apr 95	HOLE IN THE BUCKET *Capitol CDCL 742*	55	1
15 Jul 95	PEOPLE IN THA MIDDLE *Capitol CDCLS 752*	49	2
15 Mar 97	WHY OH WHY *Capital CDCL 785*	45	1

Billie Jo SPEARS
US, female vocalist (40 WEEKS) pos/wks

12 Jul 75 ●	BLANKET ON THE GROUND *United Artists UP 35805*	6	13
17 Jul 76 ●	WHAT I'VE GOT IN MIND *United Artists UP 36118*	4	13
11 Dec 76	SING ME AN OLD FASHIONED SONG		
	United Artists UP 36179	34	9
21 Jul 79	I WILL SURVIVE *United Artists UP 601*	47	5

Britney SPEARS   140   Top 500
World's top-selling teenager with album sales exceeding 40 million, b. 2 Dec 1981, Louisiana, US. Broke debut-act first-week UK sales record with 464,000 for 'Baby One More Time' (going on to 1,450,154 in total) and is the youngest million-selling female in the history of the UK singles chart (155 WKS) pos/wks

27 Feb 99 ★	...BABY ONE MORE TIME *Jive 0522752* ◆ ■ ▲	1	22
26 Jun 99 ●	SOMETIMES *Jive 0523202*	3	16
2 Oct 99 ●	(YOU DRIVE ME) CRAZY *Jive 0550582*	5	11
29 Jan 00 ★	BORN TO MAKE YOU HAPPY *Jive 9250022* ■	1	12
13 May 00 ★	OOPS!...I DID IT AGAIN *Jive 9250542* ■	1	14
26 Aug 00 ●	LUCKY *Jive 9251022*	5	11
16 Dec 00 ●	STRONGER *Jive 9251502*	7	10
7 Apr 01	DON'T LET ME BE THE LAST TO KNOW *Jive 9251982*	12	8
27 Oct 01 ●	I'M A SLAVE 4 U *Jive 9252892*	4	14
2 Feb 02 ●	OVERPROTECTED *Jive 9253072*	4	12
13 Apr 02 ●	I'M NOT A GIRL, NOT YET A WOMAN *Jive 9253472*	2	10
10 Aug 02 ●	BOYS *Jive 9253912* 1	7	8
16 Nov 02	I LOVE ROCK 'N' ROLL *Jive 9254202*	13	7+

1 Britney Spears featuring Pharrell Williams

SPECIALS   307   Top 500
Midlands-based septet which led the early 1980s ska revival and, under Jerry Dammers (k), founded the trailblazing indie label 2 Tone. In 1981, Terry Hall (v), Neville Staples (v) and Lynval Golding (g) broke away to form Fun Boy Three (101 WEEKS) pos/wks

28 Jul 79 ●	GANGSTERS *2 Tone CHSTT 1* 1	6	12
27 Oct 79 ●	A MESSAGE TO YOU RUDY / NITE KLUB		
	2 Tone CHSTT 5 2	10	14
26 Jan 80 ★	THE SPECIAL A.K.A. LIVE! EP *2 Tone CHSTT 7*	1	10
24 May 80 ●	RAT RACE / RUDE BUOYS OUTA JAIL *2 Tone CHSTT 11*	5	9
20 Sep 80 ●	STEREOTYPE / INTERNATIONAL JET SET		
	2 Tone CHSTT 13	6	8
13 Dec 80 ●	DO NOTHING / MAGGIE'S FARM *2 Tone CHSTT 16*	4	11
20 Jun 81 ★	GHOST TOWN *2 Tone CHSTT 17*	1	14
23 Jan 82	THE BOILER *2 Tone CHSTT 18*	35	5
3 Sep 83	RACIST FRIEND / BRIGHT LIGHTS *2 Tone CHSTT 25* 1	60	3
17 Mar 84 ●	NELSON MANDELA *2 Tone CHSTT 26* 1	9	10
8 Sep 84	WHAT I LIKE MOST ABOUT YOU IS YOUR GIRLFRIEND		
	2 Tone CHSTT 27 1	51	4
10 Feb 96	HYPOCRITE *Kuff KUFFD 3*	66	1

1 Special A.K.A. 2 Specials featuring Rico+

Tracks on The Special AKA Live EP: Too Much Too Young / Guns of Navarone / Longshot Kick De Bucket / The Liquidator / Skinhead Moonstomp. 'Maggie's Farm' (credited to Specials featuring Rico with the Ice Rink String Sounds) listed with 'Do Nothing' only from 10 Jan 1981. Group was male / female for last four hits

See also Terry HALL

SPECTRUM
UK, male instrumental / production group (1 WEEK) pos/wks

26 Sep 92	TRUE LOVE WILL FIND YOU IN THE END		
	Silvertone ORE 44	70	1

Chris SPEDDING
UK, male vocalist / instrumentalist – guitar (8 WEEKS) pos/wks

23 Aug 75	MOTOR BIKIN' *RAK 210*	14	8

SPEECH *US, male vocalist – Todd Thomas (2 WEEKS)*

17 Feb 96	LIKE MARVIN GAYE SAID (WHAT'S GOING ON)		
	Cooltempo CDCOOL 314	35	2

SPEEDY
UK, male / female vocal / instrumental group (1 WEEK) pos/wks

9 Nov 96	BOY WONDER *Boiler House! BOIL 2CD*	56	1

SPELLBOUND *India, female vocal duo (1 WEEK)* pos/wks

31 May 97	HEAVEN ON EARTH *East West EW 098CD*	73	1

Johnnie SPENCE *UK, orchestra (15 WEEKS)* pos/wks

1 Mar 62	THE 'DR KILDARE' THEME *Parlophone R 4872*	15	15

Don SPENCER *UK, male vocalist (12 WEEKS)* pos/wks

21 Mar 63	FIREBALL (re) *HMV POP 1087*	32	12

Tracie SPENCER *US, female vocalist (3 WEEKS)* pos/wks

4 May 91	THIS HOUSE *Capitol CL 612*	65	2
6 Nov 99	IT'S ALL ABOUT YOU (NOT ABOUT ME)		
	Parlophone Rhythm Series CDCL 815	65	1

Jon SPENCER BLUES EXPLOSION
US, male vocal / instrumental group (3 WEEKS) pos/wks

10 May 97	WAIL *Mute CDMUTE 204*	66	1
6 Apr 02	SHE SAID *Mute LCDMUTE 263*	58	1
6 Jul 02	SWEET N SOUR *Mute LCDMUTE 271*	66	1

SPHINX *UK / US, male vocal / instrumental group (2 WEEKS)* pos/wks

25 Mar 95	WHAT HOPE HAVE I *Champion CHAMPCD 318*	43	2

See also DUSTED; OUR TRIBE / ONE TRIBE; FAITHLESS; ROLLO

SPICE GIRLS (110) Top 500

Britain's most successful and influential female vocal group: Geri Halliwell (Ginger Spice – left 1998), Melanie Chisholm (Mel C / Sporty Spice), Emma Bunton (Baby Spice), Victoria Adams – then Beckham (Posh Spice), Melanie Brown (Mel B / Mel G / Scary Spice). The ground-breaking girl-power group which made it a Spiceworld was the first act to put its first six singles at No.1 and the only group to spawn five solo hitmakers. Best-selling single: 'Wannabe' 1,269,841 (179 WEEKS)

		pos/wks
20 Jul 96 ★	WANNABE *Virgin VSCDX 1588* ◆ ▲ 1	26
26 Oct 96 ★	SAY YOU'LL BE THERE *Virgin VSCDT 1601* ■ 1	17
28 Dec 96 ★	2 BECOME 1 (re) *Virgin VSCDT 1607* ◆ ■ 1	23
15 Mar 97 ★	MAMA / WHO DO YOU THINK YOU ARE *Virgin VSCDT 1623* ■ 1	15
25 Oct 97 ★	SPICE UP YOUR LIFE *Virgin VSCDT 1660* ■ 1	15
27 Dec 97 ★	TOO MUCH *Virgin VSCDR 1669* ■ 1	15
21 Mar 98 ●	STOP (re) *Virgin VSCDT 1679* 2	17
1 Aug 98 ★	VIVA FOREVER *Virgin VSCDT 1692* ■ 1	13
26 Dec 98 ★	GOODBYE *Virgin VSCDT 1721* ■ 1	21
4 Nov 00 ★	HOLLER / LET LOVE LEAD THE WAY *Virgin VSCDT 1788* ■ 1	17

See also Melanie B; Victoria BECKHAM; Geri HALLIWELL; Emma BUNTON; Melanie C

SPIDER *UK, male vocal / instrumental group (5 WEEKS)*

		pos/wks
5 Mar 83	WHY D'YA LIE TO ME *RCA 313* 65	2
10 Mar 84	HERE WE GO ROCK 'N' ROLL *A&M AM 180* 57	3

SPIKEY TEE – *See BOMB THE BASS*

SPILLER *Italy / UK, male producer – Cristiano Spiller (26 WEEKS)* pos/wks

		pos/wks
26 Aug 00 ★	GROOVEJET (IF THIS AIN'T LOVE) *Positiva CDTIV 137* ■ 1	24
2 Feb 02	CRY BABY *Positiva CDTIV 167* 40	2

'Groovejet (If This Ain't Love)' featured lead vocals by Sophie Ellis Bextor

See also THEAUDIENCE; Sophie ELLIS BEXTOR; LAGUNA

SPIN CITY *UK / Ireland, male vocal group (3 WEEKS)*

		pos/wks
26 Aug 00	LANDSLIDE *Epic 6696132* 30	3

SPIN DOCTORS

US, male vocal / instrumental group (28 WEEKS)

		pos/wks
15 May 93 ●	TWO PRINCES *Epic 6591452* 3	15
14 Aug 93	LITTLE MISS CAN'T BE WRONG *Epic 6584892* 23	5
9 Oct 93	JIMMY OLSEN'S BLUES *Epic 6597582* 40	2
4 Dec 93	WHAT TIME IS IT *Epic 6599552* 56	1
25 Jun 94	CLEOPATRA'S CAT *Epic 6604192* 29	2
30 Jul 94	YOU LET YOUR HEART GO TOO FAST *Epic 6606612* 66	1
29 Oct 94	MARY JANE *Epic 6609772* 55	1
8 Jun 96	SHE USED TO BE MINE *Epic 6632682* 55	1

SPINAL TAP

US / UK, male vocal / instrumental group (3 WEEKS)

		pos/wks
28 Mar 92	BITCH SCHOOL *MCA MCS 1624* 35	2
2 May 92	THE MAJESTY OF ROCK *MCA MCS 1629* 61	1

SPINNERS – *See DETROIT SPINNERS*

SPIRAL TRIBE

UK, male / female vocal / instrumental group (2 WEEKS)

		pos/wks
29 Aug 92	BREACH THE PEACE (EP) *Butterfly BLRT 79* 66	1
21 Nov 92	FORWARD THE REVOLUTION *Butterfly BLRT 85* 70	1

Tracks on Breach the Peace (EP): Breach the Peace / Do It / Seven / 25 Minute Warning

SPIRITS *UK, male / female vocal duo*
- Beverly Thomas and Osmond Wright (5 WEEKS)

		pos/wks
19 Nov 94	DON'T BRING ME DOWN *MCA MCSTD 2018* 31	3
8 Apr 95	SPIRIT INSIDE *MCA MCSTD 2045* 39	2

SPIRITUAL COWBOYS – *See Dave STEWART*

SPIRITUALIZED

UK, male / female vocal / instrumental group (18 WEEKS)

		pos/wks
30 Jun 90	ANYWAY THAT YOU WANT ME / STEP INTO THE BREEZE *Dedicated ZB 43783* 75	1
17 Aug 91	RUN *Dedicated SPIRT 002* 59	1
25 Jul 92	MEDICATION *Dedicated SPIRT 005T* 55	1
23 Oct 93	ELECTRIC MAINLINE *Dedicated SPIRT 007CD* 49	1
4 Feb 95	LET IT FLOW *Dedicated SPIRT 009CD* [1] 30	2
9 Aug 97	ELECTRICITY *Dedicated SPIRT 012CD1* 32	2
14 Feb 98	I THINK I'M IN LOVE *Dedicated SPIRT 014CD* 27	2
6 Jun 98	THE ABBEY ROAD EP *Dedicated SPIRT 015CD* 39	2
15 Sep 01	STOP YOUR CRYING *Spaceman / Arista OPM 002* 18	3
8 Dec 01	OUT OF SIGHT *Spaceman / Arista OPM 005* 65	1
23 Feb 02	DO IT ALL OVER AGAIN *Spaceman / Arista OPM 004* 31	2

[1] Spiritualized Electric Mainline

Tracks on The Abbey Road EP: Come Together / Broken Heart / Broken Heart (instrumental)

SPIRO and WIX *UK, male instrumental*
duo - Steve Spiro and Paul Wickens (2 WEEKS) pos/wks

		pos/wks
10 Aug 96	TARA'S THEME *EMI Premier PRESCD 4* 29	2

SPITTING IMAGE *UK, male / female latex puppets (18 WEEKS)* pos/wks

		pos/wks
10 May 86 ★	THE CHICKEN SONG (re) *Virgin SPIT 1* 1	11
6 Dec 86	SANTA CLAUS IS ON THE DOLE / FIRST ATHEIST TABERNACLE CHOIR *Virgin VS 921* 22	7

SPLINTER *UK, male vocal / instrumental*
duo - Bill Elliott and Bob Purvis (10 WEEKS) pos/wks

		pos/wks
2 Nov 74	COSTAFINE TOWN *Dark Horse AMS 7135* 17	10

SPLIT ENZ

New Zealand / UK, male vocal / instrumental group (15 WEEKS) pos/wks

		pos/wks
16 Aug 80	I GOT YOU *A&M AMS 7546* 12	11
23 May 81	HISTORY NEVER REPEATS *A&M AMS 8128* 63	4

A SPLIT SECOND

Belgium / Italy, male instrumental / production group (1 WEEK) pos/wks

		pos/wks
14 Dec 91	FLESH *ffrr FX 178* 68	1

SPLODGENESSABOUNDS

UK, male vocal / instrumental group (17 WEEKS) pos/wks

		pos/wks
14 Jun 80 ●	SIMON TEMPLER / TWO PINTS OF LAGER AND A PACKET OF CRISPS PLEASE *Deram BUM 1* 7	8
6 Sep 80	TWO LITTLE BOYS / HORSE *Deram ROLF 1* 26	7
13 Jun 81	COWPUNK MEDLUM *Deram BUM 3* 69	2

SPOILED & ZIGO *Israel, male DJ / production*
duo - Elad Avnon and Ziv Goland (3 WEEKS) pos/wks

		pos/wks
12 Aug 00	MORE & MORE *Manifesto FESCD 72* 31	3

SPONGE *US, male vocal / instrumental group (1 WEEK)* pos/wks

		pos/wks
19 Aug 95	PLOWED *Work 6623162* 74	1

SPOOKS *US, male / female vocal / rap group (17 WEEKS)* pos/wks

		pos/wks
27 Jan 01 ●	THINGS I'VE SEEN *Epic 6706722* 6	10
5 May 01	KARMA HOTEL *Epic 6709012* 15	6
15 Sep 01	SWEET REVENGE *Epic 6718072* 67	1

SPOOKY *UK, male vocal / instrumental duo (1 WEEK)* pos/wks

		pos/wks
13 Mar 93	SCHMOO *Guerilla GRRR 45CD* 72	1

SPORTY THIEVZ *US, male rap / vocal group (6 WEEKS)* pos/wks

		pos/wks
10 Jul 99	NO PIGEONS *Columbia / Roc-a-Blok / Ruffhouse 6676022* 21	6

SPOTNICKS *Sweden, male instrumental group (37 WEEKS)*

		pos/wks
14 Jun 62	ORANGE BLOSSOM SPECIAL *Oriole CB 1724*	29 10
6 Sep 62	ROCKET MAN *Oriole CB 1755*	38 9
31 Jan 63	HAVA NAGILA *Oriole CB 1790*	13 12
25 Apr 63	JUST LISTEN TO MY HEART *Oriole CB 1818*	36 6

Dusty SPRINGFIELD [78] Top 500

One of Britain's leading female vocalists of the 1960s, b. Mary O'Brien, 16 Apr 1939, London, d. 2 Mar 1999. After leaving The Springfields in 1963, she had numerous transatlantic solo hits, and during the Sixties was regularly voted UK's Top Female Singer (211 WEEKS)

		pos/wks
21 Nov 63	I ONLY WANT TO BE WITH YOU *Philips BF 1292*	4 18
20 Feb 64	STAY AWHILE *Philips BF 1313*	13 10
2 Jul 64 ●	I JUST DON'T KNOW WHAT TO DO WITH MYSELF *Philips BF 1348*	3 12
22 Oct 64 ●	LOSING YOU *Philips BF 1369*	9 13
18 Feb 65	YOUR HURTIN' KINDA LOVE *Philips BF 1396*	37 4
1 Jul 65 ●	IN THE MIDDLE OF NOWHERE *Philips BF 1418*	8 10
16 Sep 65 ●	SOME OF YOUR LOVIN' *Philips BF 1430*	8 12
27 Jan 66	LITTLE BY LITTLE *Philips BF 1466*	17 9
31 Mar 66 ★	YOU DON'T HAVE TO SAY YOU LOVE ME *Philips BF 1482*	1 13
7 Jul 66 ●	GOING BACK *Philips BF 1502*	10 10
15 Sep 66 ●	ALL I SEE IS YOU *Philips BF 1510*	9 12
23 Feb 67	I'LL TRY ANYTHING *Philips BF 1553*	13 9
25 May 67	GIVE ME TIME *Philips BF 1577*	24 6
10 Jul 68 ●	I CLOSE MY EYES AND COUNT TO TEN *Philips BF 1682*	4 13
4 Dec 68 ●	SON-OF-A PREACHER MAN *Philips BF 1730*	9 9
20 Sep 69	AM I THE SAME GIRL (re) *Philips BF 1811*	43 4
19 Sep 70	HOW CAN I BE SURE *Philips 6006 045*	36 4
20 Oct 79	BABY BLUE *Mercury DUSTY 4*	61 5
22 Aug 87 ●	WHAT HAVE I DONE TO DESERVE THIS? *Parlophone R 6163* [1]	2 9
25 Feb 89	NOTHING HAS BEEN PROVED *Parlophone R 6207*	16 7
2 Dec 89	IN PRIVATE *Parlophone R 6234*	14 10
26 May 90	REPUTATION *Parlophone R 6253*	38 6
24 Nov 90	ARRESTED BY YOU *Parlophone R 6266*	70 2
30 Oct 93	HEART AND SOUL *Columbia 6598562* [2]	75 1
10 Jun 95	WHEREVER WOULD I BE *Columbia 6620592* [3]	44 3
4 Nov 95	ROLL AWAY *Columbia 6623682*	68 1

[1] Pet Shop Boys and Dusty Springfield [2] Cilla Black with Dusty Springfield
[3] Dusty Springfield and Daryl Hall

See also SPRINGFIELDS

Rick SPRINGFIELD
Australia, male vocalist – Richard Springthorpe (13 WEEKS)

		pos/wks
14 Jan 84	HUMAN TOUCH / SOULS *RCA RICK 1*	23 7
24 Mar 84	JESSIE'S GIRL *RCA RICK 2* ▲	43 6

'Souls' listed only from 11 Feb 1984. It peaked at No.24

SPRINGFIELDS
UK, male / female vocal / instrumental group (66 WEEKS)

		pos/wks
31 Aug 61	BREAKAWAY *Philips BF 1168*	31 8
16 Nov 61	BAMBINO *Philips BF 1178*	16 11
13 Dec 62 ●	ISLAND OF DREAMS *Philips 326557 BF*	5 26
28 Mar 63 ●	SAY I WON'T BE THERE *Philips 326577 BF*	5 15
25 Jul 63	COME ON HOME *Philips BF 1263*	31 6

See also Dusty SPRINGFIELD

Bruce SPRINGSTEEN [162] Top 500

'The Boss', b. 23 Sep 1949, New Jersey, US. Singer / songwriter / guitarist / rock superstar, whose legendary stage performances have packed stadiums worldwide. He released the biggest-selling box set, and is one of world's best-selling album artists (146 WEEKS)

		pos/wks
22 Nov 80	HUNGRY HEART *CBS 9309*	44 4
13 Jun 81	THE RIVER *CBS A 1179*	35 6
26 May 84 ●	DANCING IN THE DARK (re) *CBS A 4436*	4 23
6 Oct 84	COVER ME (re) *CBS A 4662*	16 13
15 Jun 85 ●	I'M ON FIRE / BORN IN THE USA *CBS A 6342*	5 12
3 Aug 85	GLORY DAYS *CBS A 6375*	17 6
14 Dec 85 ●	SANTA CLAUS IS COMIN' TO TOWN / MY HOMETOWN *CBS A 6773*	9 5
29 Nov 86	WAR *CBS 650193 7* [1]	18 7
7 Feb 87	FIRE *CBS 650381 7* [1]	54 2
23 May 87	BORN TO RUN *CBS BRUCE 2*	16 4
3 Oct 87	BRILLIANT DISGUISE *CBS 651141 7*	20 5
12 Dec 87	TUNNEL OF LOVE *CBS 651295 7*	45 4
18 Jun 88	TOUGHER THAN THE REST *CBS BRUCE 3*	13 8
24 Sep 88	SPARE PARTS *CBS BRUCE 4*	32 3
21 Mar 92	HUMAN TOUCH *Columbia 6578727*	11 5
23 May 92	BETTER DAYS *Columbia 6578907*	34 3
25 Jul 92	57 CHANNELS (AND NOTHIN' ON) *Columbia 6581387*	32 4
24 Oct 92	LEAP OF FAITH *Columbia 6583697*	46 3
10 Apr 93	LUCKY TOWN (LIVE) *Columbia 6592282*	48 3
19 Mar 94 ●	STREETS OF PHILADELPHIA *Columbia 6600652*	2 12
22 Apr 95	SECRET GARDEN *Columbia 6612955*	44 3
11 Nov 95	HUNGRY HEART (re-issue) *Columbia 6626252*	28 3
4 May 96	THE GHOST OF TOM JOAD *Columbia 6630315*	26 2
19 Apr 97	SECRET GARDEN (re-issue) *Columbia 6643245*	17 4
14 Dec 02	LONESOME DAY *Columbia 6734082*	39 2

[1] Bruce Springsteen and The E-Street Band

'Dancing in the Dark' debuted at No.28 before making its peak position on re-entry in Jan 1985. 'Cover Me' debuted at No.38 before making its peak position on re-entry in Mar 1985

SPRINGWATER
UK, male instrumentalist – Phil Cordell (12 WEEKS)

		pos/wks
23 Oct 71 ●	I WILL RETURN *Polydor 2058 141*	5 12

SPRINKLER *UK / US, male / female vocal / rap group (2 WEEKS)*

		pos/wks
11 Jul 98	LEAVE 'EM SOMETHING TO DESIRE *Island CID 706*	45 2

[SPUNGE] *UK, male vocal / instrumental group (3 WEEKS)*

		pos/wks
15 Jun 02	JUMP ON DEMAND *B Unique BUN 022CDS*	39 2
24 Aug 02	ROOTS *B Unique BUN 030CDS*	52 1

SPYRO GYRA *US, male instrumental group (10 WEEKS)*

		pos/wks
21 Jul 79	MORNING DANCE *Infinity INF 111*	17 10

SQUADRONAIRES – *See Joan REGAN*

SQUEEZE [226] Top 500

Critically acclaimed London band, which had several UK / US best sellers. Featured noted singer / songwriters Glenn Tilbrook (g/v) and Chris Difford (v/g). Fluctuating line-up included Jools Holland (k) and Paul Carrack (v/k – also of Ace, and Mike and the Mechanics fame) (123 WEEKS)

		pos/wks
8 Apr 78	TAKE ME I'M YOURS *A&M AMS 7335*	19 9
10 Jun 78	BANG BANG *A&M AMS 7360*	49 5
18 Nov 78	GOODBYE GIRL *A&M AMS 7398*	63 2
24 Mar 79 ●	COOL FOR CATS *A&M AMS 7426*	2 11
2 Jun 79 ●	UP THE JUNCTION *A&M AMS 7444*	2 11
8 Sep 79	SLAP & TICKLE *A&M AMS 7466*	24 8
1 Mar 80	ANOTHER NAIL IN MY HEART *A&M AMS 7507*	17 9
10 May 80	PULLING MUSSELS (FROM THE SHELL) *A&M AMS 7523*	44 6
16 May 81	IS THAT LOVE *A&M AMS 8129*	35 8
25 Jul 81	TEMPTED *A&M AMS 8147*	41 5
10 Oct 81 ●	LABELLED WITH LOVE *A&M AMS 8166*	4 10
24 Apr 82	BLACK COFFEE IN BED *A&M AMS 8219*	51 4
23 Oct 82	ANNIE GET YOUR GUN *A&M AMS 8259*	43 4
15 Jun 85	LAST TIME FOREVER *A&M AM 255*	45 5
8 Aug 87	HOURGLASS *A&M AM 400*	16 10
17 Oct 87	TRUST ME TO OPEN MY MOUTH *A&M AM 412*	72 1
25 Apr 92	COOL FOR CATS (re-issue) *A&M AM 860*	62 2
24 Jul 93	THIRD RAIL *A&M 5803372*	39 3
11 Sep 93	SOME FANTASTIC PLACE *A&M 5803792*	73 1
9 Sep 95	THIS SUMMER *A&M 5811912*	36 3
18 Nov 95	ELECTRIC TRAINS *A&M 5812692*	44 2
15 Jun 96	HEAVEN KNOWS *A&M 5816052*	27 2
24 Aug 96	THIS SUMMER (re-mix) *A&M 5818372*	32 2

See also DIFFORD and TILBROOK

Billy SQUIER *US, male vocalist (3 WEEKS)* pos/wks
3 Oct 81	THE STROKE *Capitol CL 214*....................	52 3

John SQUIRE *UK, male vocalist / instrumentalist – guitar (1 WEEK)* pos/wks
2 Nov 02	JOE LOUIS *North Country NCCDA 001*	43 1

See also STONE ROSES; SEAHORSES

Dorothy SQUIRES
UK, female vocalist, d. 14 Apr 1998 (56 WEEKS) pos/wks
5 Jun 53	I'M WALKING BEHIND YOU *Polygon P 1068*..........	12 1
24 Aug 61	SAY IT WITH FLOWERS *Columbia DB 4665* [1]	23 10
20 Sep 69	FOR ONCE IN MY LIFE (re) *President PT 267*........	24 11
21 Feb 70	TILL (re) *President PT 281*........................	25 11
8 Aug 70	MY WAY (2re) *President PT 305*....................	25 23

[1] Dorothy Squires and Russ Conway

STABBS *Finland / US / Cameroon, male
instrumental / production group (1 WEEK)* pos/wks
24 Dec 94	JOY AND HAPPINESS *Hi-Life HICD 3*	65 1

STACCATO
UK / Holland, male / female vocal / instrumental duo (1 WEEK) pos/wks
20 Jul 96	I WANNA KNOW *Multiply CDMULTY 11*	65 1

Warren STACEY *UK, male vocalist (3 WEEKS)* pos/wks
23 Mar 02	MY GIRL MY GIRL *Def Soul 5889932*	26 3

Jim STAFFORD *US, male vocalist (16 WEEKS)* pos/wks
27 Apr 74	SPIDERS & SNAKES *MGM 2006 374*	14 8
6 Jul 74	MY GIRL BILL *MGM 2006 423*	20 8

Jo STAFFORD *US, female vocalist (28 WEEKS)* pos/wks
14 Nov 52	★ YOU BELONG TO ME *Columbia DB 3152* ▲	1 19
19 Dec 52	JAMBALAYA *Columbia DB 3169*	11 2
7 May 54	● MAKE LOVE TO ME! *Philips PB 233* ▲	8 1
9 Dec 55	SUDDENLY THERE'S A VALLEY (re) *Philips PB 509* ...	12 6

Terry STAFFORD *US, male vocalist, d. 17 Mar 1996 (9 WEEKS)* pos/wks
7 May 64	SUSPICION *London HLU 9871*	31 9

STAIFFI and his MUSTAFAS
France, male vocal / instrumental group (1 WEEK) pos/wks
28 Jul 60	MUSTAFA CHA CHA CHA *Pye International 7N 25057* ...	43 1

STAIND *US, male vocal / instrumental group (9 WEEKS)* pos/wks
15 Sep 01	IT'S BEEN AWHILE *Elektra E 7252CD*........	15 6
1 Dec 01	OUTSIDE *Elektra E 7277CD*........................	33 2
23 Feb 02	FOR YOU *Elektra E 7281CD*........................	55 1

STAKKA BO *Sweden, male rap / DJ duo
– Johan Renck and Oscar Franzen (12 WEEKS)* pos/wks
25 Sep 93	HERE WE GO *Polydor PZCD 280*	13 8
18 Dec 93	DOWN THE DRAIN *Polydor PZCD 301*............	64 4

Frank STALLONE *US, male vocalist (2 WEEKS)* pos/wks
22 Oct 83	FAR FROM OVER *RSO 95*	68 2

STAMFORD AMP
UK, male vocal / instrumental group (2 WEEKS) pos/wks
12 Oct 02	ANYTHING FOR YOU *Mercury 638972*............	33 2

STAMFORD BRIDGE
UK, male Chelsea FC supporters vocal group (1 WEEK) pos/wks
16 May 70	CHELSEA *Penny Farthing PEN 715*..............	47 1

STAMINA MC – See DJ MARKY & XRS and STAMINA MC

STAMPS QUARTET – See Elvis PRESLEY

STAN *UK, male vocal / instrumental duo
– Simon Andrew and Kevin Stagg (3 WEEKS)* pos/wks
31 Jul 93	SUNTAN *Hug CDBUM 1*	40 3

Lisa STANSFIELD (215) Top 500
*Only UK act to have three US R&B No.1 hits, b. 11 Apr 1966, Lancashire. Like
Yazz, she was featured vocalist on a Coldcut single before achieving a No.1 in
her own right. This multi-Brit award winner has sold millions of records all
around the world (127 WEEKS)* pos/wks
25 Mar 89	● PEOPLE HOLD ON *Ahead of Our Time CCUT 5* [1]	11 9
12 Aug 89	THIS IS THE RIGHT TIME *Arista 112512*	13 8
28 Oct 89	★ ALL AROUND THE WORLD *Arista 112693*....	1 14
10 Feb 90	● LIVE TOGETHER *Arista 112914*	10 6
12 May 90	WHAT DID I DO TO YOU (EP) *Arista 113168*	25 4
19 Oct 91	● CHANGE *Arista 114820*	10 7
21 Dec 91	ALL WOMAN *Arista 115000*	20 8
14 Mar 92	TIME TO MAKE YOU MINE *Arista 115113*	14 8
6 Jun 92	SET YOUR LOVING FREE *Arista 74321100587* ..	28 4
19 Dec 92	● SOMEDAY (I'M COMING BACK) *Arista 74321123567* ...	10 9
1 May 93	★ FIVE LIVE (EP) (re) *Parlophone CDRS 6340* [2] ■ 1	12
5 Jun 93	● IN ALL THE RIGHT PLACES *MCA MCSTD 1780* ..	8 11
23 Oct 93	SO NATURAL *Arista 74321169132*	15 5
11 Dec 93	LITTLE BIT OF HEAVEN *Arista 74321178202*	32 4
18 Jan 97	● PEOPLE HOLD ON (THE BOOTLEG MIXES) *Arista 74321452012* [3]	4 6
22 Mar 97	● THE REAL THING *Arista 74321463222*..........	9 7
21 Jun 97	NEVER, NEVER GONNA GIVE YOU UP *Arista 74321490392*....	25 3
4 Oct 97	THE LINE *RCA 74321511372*....................	64 1
23 Jun 01	LET'S JUST CALL IT LOVE *Arista 74321863422*........	48 1

[1] Coldcut featuring Lisa Stansfield [2] George Michael and Queen with Lisa
Stansfield [3] Lisa Stansfield vs The Dirty Rotten Scoundrels

*Tracks on What Did I Do to You (EP): What Did I Do to You / My Apple Heart / Lay
Me Down / Something's Happenin'. Tracks on Five Live (EP): Somebody to Love /
These Are the Days of Our Lives / Calling You / Papa Was a Rolling Stone – Killer
(medley). Lisa Stansfield appears only on the second track*

Vivian STANSHALL – See Mike OLDFIELD

STANTON WARRIORS *UK, male production duo (1 WEEK)* pos/wks
22 Sep 01	DA ANTIDOTE *Mob MOBCD 006*..................	69 1

STAPLE SINGERS *US, male / female vocal group (14 WEEKS)* pos/wks
10 Jun 72	I'LL TAKE YOU THERE *Stax 2025 110* ▲	30 8
8 Jun 74	IF YOU'RE READY (COME GO WITH ME) *Stax 2025 224*....	34 6

Cyril STAPLETON and his Orchestra
UK, orchestra, leader d. 25 Feb 1974 (27 WEEKS) pos/wks
27 May 55	ELEPHANT TANGO (2re) *Decca F 10488*........	19 4
23 Sep 55	● BLUE STAR (THE MEDIC THEME) *Decca F 10559* [1]	2 12
6 Apr 56	THE ITALIAN THEME *Decca F 10703*............	18 2
1 Jun 56	THE HAPPY WHISTLER *Decca F 10735* [2]	22 4
19 Jul 57	FORGOTTEN DREAMS *Decca F 10912*............	27 5

[1] Cyril Stapleton Orchestra featuring Julie Dawn [2] Cyril Stapleton Orchestra
featuring Desmond Lane, penny whistle

STAR TURN ON 45 (PINTS)
UK, male vocalist – Steve O'Donnell, d. 4 Aug 1997 (9 WEEKS) pos/wks
24 Oct 81	STARTURN ON 45 (PINTS) *V Tone V TONE 003*	45 4
30 Apr 88	PUMP UP THE BITTER *Pacific DRINK 1*	12 5

STARCHASER *Italy, male DJ / production trio (4 WEEKS)* pos/wks
22 Jun 02	LOVE WILL SET YOU FREE (JAMBE MYTH) *Rulin RULIN 23CDS*	24 4

Re-entries are listed as (re), (2re), (3re), etc which signifies that the hit re-entered the chart once, twice or three times, etc

STARDUST
France, male / female vocal / instrumental group (3 WEEKS) pos/wks

8 Oct 77	ARIANA *Satril SAT 120*	42	3

STARDUST *France, male vocal / production group (26 WEEKS)* pos/wks

1 Aug 98	MUSIC SOUNDS BETTER WITH YOU (import) *Roule ROULE 305*	55	3
22 Aug 98 ●	MUSIC SOUNDS BETTER WITH YOU *Virgin DINSD 175*	2	23

Alvin STARDUST `235` `Top 500`
Sixties hitmaker who became bill-topping Seventies vocalist, b. Bernard Jewry, 27 Sep 1942, London. After several minor hits as Shane Fenton, he collected a string of smashes as OTT rocker Stardust, and extended his chart span to almost 25 years. Father of current hitmaker Adam F (119 WEEKS) pos/wks

3 Nov 73 ●	MY COO-CA-CHOO *Magnet MAG 1*	2	21
16 Feb 74 ★	JEALOUS MIND *Magnet MAG 5*	1	11
4 May 74 ●	RED DRESS *Magnet MAG 8*	7	8
31 Aug 74 ●	YOU YOU YOU *Magnet MAG 13*	6	10
30 Nov 74	TELL ME WHY *Magnet MAG 19*	16	8
1 Feb 75	GOOD LOVE CAN NEVER DIE *Magnet MAG 21*	11	9
12 Jul 75	SWEET CHEATIN' RITA *Magnet MAG 32*	37	4
5 Sep 81 ●	PRETEND *Stiff BUY 124*	4	10
21 Nov 81	A WONDERFUL TIME UP THERE *Stiff BUY 132*	56	8
5 May 84 ●	I FEEL LIKE BUDDY HOLLY *Chrysalis CHS 2784*	7	11
27 Oct 84 ●	I WON'T RUN AWAY *Chrysalis CHS 2829*	7	13
15 Dec 84	SO NEAR TO CHRISTMAS *Chrysalis CHS 2835*	29	4
23 Mar 85	GOT A LITTLE HEARTACHE *Chrysalis CHS 2856*	55	2

See also Shane FENTON and the FENTONES

STARFIGHTER
Belgium, male producer – Philip Dirix (3 WEEKS) pos/wks

5 Feb 00	APACHE *Sound of Ministry MOSCDS 136*	31	3

STARGARD *US, female vocal group (14 WEEKS)* pos/wks

28 Jan 78	THEME SONG FROM 'WHICH WAY IS UP' *MCA 346*	19	7
15 Apr 78	LOVE IS SO EASY *MCA 354*	45	1
9 Sep 78	WHAT YOU WAITIN' FOR *MCA 382*	39	6

STARGATE
Norway / US, male / female production / vocal / rap group (1 WEEK) pos/wks

7 Sep 02	EASIER SAID THAN DONE *Telstar CDSTAS 3269*	55	1

STARGAZERS
UK / Australia, male / female vocal group (68 WEEKS) pos/wks

13 Feb 53 ★	BROKEN WINGS (re) *Decca F 10047*	1	12
19 Feb 54 ★	I SEE THE MOON *Decca F 10213*	1	15
9 Apr 54	THE HAPPY WANDERER *Decca F 10259*	12	1
17 Dec 54 ★	THE FINGER OF SUSPICION *Decca F 10394* `1`	1	15
4 Mar 55	SOMEBODY *Decca F 10437*	20	1
3 Jun 55	THE CRAZY OTTO RAG *Decca F 10523*	18	3
9 Sep 55 ●	CLOSE THE DOOR *Decca F 10594*	6	9
11 Nov 55 ●	TWENTY TINY FINGERS *Decca F 10626*	4	11
22 Jun 56	HOT DIGGITY (DOG ZIGGITY BOOM) *Decca F 10731*	28	1

`1` Dickie Valentine with The Stargazers

STARGAZERS *UK, male vocal / instrumental group (3 WEEKS)* pos/wks

6 Feb 82	GROOVE BABY GROOVE (EP) *Epic EPC A 1924*	56	3

Tracks on Groove Baby Groove (EP): Groove Baby Groove / Jump Around / La Rock 'n' Roll (Quelques Uns a la Lune) / Red Light Green Light

STARJETS *UK, male vocal / instrumental group (5 WEEKS)* pos/wks

8 Sep 79	WAR STORIES *Epic EPC 7770*	51	5

STARLAND VOCAL BAND
US, male / female vocal group (10 WEEKS) pos/wks

7 Aug 76	AFTERNOON DELIGHT *RCA 2716* ▲	18	10

STARLIGHT
Italy, male instrumental / production group (11 WEEKS) pos/wks

19 Aug 89 ●	NUMERO UNO *Citybeat CBE 742*	9	11

STARLITERS – *See Joey DEE and the STARLITERS*

STARPARTY *Holland, male production duo*
– Ferry Corsten and Robert Smit (2 WEEKS) pos/wks

26 Feb 00	I'M IN LOVE *Incentive CENT 5CDS*	26	2

See also MOONMAN; SYSTEM F; ALBION; Ferry CORSTEN; GOURYELLA; VERACOCHA

Edwin STARR *US, male vocalist (70 WEEKS)* pos/wks

12 May 66	STOP HER ON SIGHT (SOS) *Polydor BM 56 702*	35	8
18 Aug 66	HEADLINE NEWS *Polydor 56 717*	39	3
11 Dec 68	STOP HER ON SIGHT (SOS) / HEADLINE NEWS (re-issue) *Polydor 56 753*	11	11
13 Sep 69	25 MILES *Tamla Motown TMG 672*	36	6
24 Oct 70 ●	WAR *Tamla Motown TMG 754* ▲	3	12
20 Feb 71	STOP THE WAR NOW *Tamla Motown TMG 764*	33	1
27 Jan 79 ●	CONTACT *20th Century BTC 2396*	6	12
26 May 79 ●	H.A.P.P.Y. RADIO *RCA TC 2408*	9	11
1 Jun 85	IT AIN'T FAIR *Hippodrome HIP 101*	56	4
30 Oct 93	WAR *Weekend CDWEEK 103* `1`	69	2

`1` Edwin Starr and Shadow

'Headline News' not listed with 'SOS' from 22 Jan 1969 to 19 Feb 1969. It therefore peaked at No.16. 'War' in 1993 was a re-recording and was listed with the flip side 'Wild Thing' by The Troggs and Wolf

See also UTAH SAINTS

Freddie STARR *UK, male vocalist – Fred Smith (14 WEEKS)* pos/wks

23 Feb 74 ●	IT'S YOU *Tiffany 6121 501*	9	10
20 Dec 75	WHITE CHRISTMAS *Thunderbird THE 102*	41	4

Kay STARR *US, female vocalist – Katherine Starks (58 WEEKS)* pos/wks

5 Dec 52 ★	COMES A-LONG A-LOVE *Capitol CL 13808*	1	16
24 Apr 53 ●	SIDE BY SIDE *Capitol CL 13871*	7	4
19 Mar 54 ●	CHANGING PARTNERS *Capitol CL 14050*	4	14
15 Oct 54	AM I A TOY OR TREASURE (re) *Capitol CL 14151*	17	4
17 Feb 56 ★	ROCK AND ROLL WALTZ *HMV POP 168* ▲	1	20

Ringo STARR *UK, male vocalist – Richard Starkey (56 WEEKS)* pos/wks

17 Apr 71 ●	IT DON'T COME EASY *Apple R 5898*	4	11
1 Apr 72 ●	BACK OFF BOOGALOO *Apple R 5944*	2	10
27 Oct 73 ●	PHOTOGRAPH *Apple R 5992* ▲	8	13
23 Feb 74 ●	YOU'RE SIXTEEN *Apple R 5995* ▲	4	10
30 Nov 74	ONLY YOU *Apple R 6000*	28	11
6 Jun 92	WEIGHT OF THE WORLD *Private Music 115392*	74	1

See also BEATLES

STARS ON 54 *US, female vocal trio (3 WEEKS)* pos/wks

28 Nov 98	IF YOU COULD READ MY MIND *Tommy Boy TBCD 7497*	23	3

STARSAILOR *UK, male vocal / instrumental group (22 WEEKS)* pos/wks

17 Feb 01	FEVER *Chrysalis CDCHSS 5123*	18	3
5 May 01	GOOD SOULS *Chrysalis CDCHSS 5125*	12	6
29 Sep 01 ●	ALCOHOLIC *Chrysalis CDCHSS 5130*	10	6
22 Dec 01	LULLABY *Chrysalis CDCHS 5131*	36	4
30 Mar 02	POOR MISGUIDED FOOL *Chrysalis CDCHS 5136*	23	3

STARSHIP
US, female / male vocal / instrumental group (41 WEEKS) pos/wks

26 Jan 80	JANE *Grunt FB 1750* `1`	21	9
16 Nov 85	WE BUILT THIS CITY *RCA PB 49929* ▲	12	12
8 Feb 86	SARA *RCA FB 49893* ▲	66	3
11 Apr 87 ★	NOTHING'S GONNA STOP US NOW *Grunt FB 49757* ▲	1	17

`1` Jefferson Starship

STARSOUND Holland, male producer – Jaap
Eggermont with male / female session singers (37 WEEKS)

			pos/wks	
18 Apr 81	●	STARS ON 45 *CBS A 1102* ▲	2	14
4 Jul 81	●	STARS ON 45 VOL2 *CBS A 1407*	2	10
19 Sep 81		STARS ON 45 VOL3 *CBS A 1521*	17	6
27 Feb 82		STARS ON STEVIE *CBS A 2041*	14	7

STARTRAX UK, male / female vocal group (8 WEEKS)

		pos/wks	
1 Aug 81	STARTRAX CLUB DISCO *Picksy KSY 1001*	18	8

STARVATION Multinational, male / female
vocal / instrumental charity assembly (6 WEEKS)

		pos/wks	
9 Mar 85	STARVATION / TAM-TAM POUR L'ETHIOPIE *Zarjazz JAZZ 3*	33	6

STARVING SOULS UK, male vocal / instrumental group (1 WEEK)

		pos/wks	
21 Oct 95	I BE THE PROPHET *Durban Poison DPCD 1*	66	1

STATE OF MIND
UK, male / female vocal / production group (3 WEEKS)

		pos/wks	
18 Apr 98	THIS IS IT *Ministry of Sound MOSCDS 123*	30	2
25 Jul 98	TAKE CONTROL *Ministry of Sound MOSCDS 124*	46	1

STATIC REVENGER
US, male producer – Dennis White (3 WEEKS)

		pos/wks	
7 Jul 01	HAPPY PEOPLE *Incentive / Rulin CENRUL 1CDS*	23	3

STATIC-X US, male vocal / instrumental group (1 WEEK)

		pos/wks	
6 Oct 01	BLACK AND WHITE *Warner W 560CD*	65	1

STATLER BROTHERS US, male vocal group (4 WEEKS)

		pos/wks	
24 Feb 66	FLOWERS ON THE WALL *CBS 201976*	38	4

Candi STATON US, female vocalist (71 WEEKS)

			pos/wks	
29 May 76	●	YOUNG HEARTS RUN FREE *Warner Bros. K 16730*	2	13
18 Sep 76		DESTINY *Warner Bros. K 16806*	41	3
23 Jul 77	●	NIGHTS ON BROADWAY *Warner Bros. K 16972*	6	12
3 Jun 78		HONEST I DO LOVE YOU *Warner Bros. K 17164*	48	5
24 Apr 82		SUSPICIOUS MINDS *Sugarhill SH 112*	31	9
31 May 86		YOUNG HEARTS RUN FREE (re-mix) *Warner Bros. W 8680*	47	5
2 Feb 91	●	YOU GOT THE LOVE *Truelove TLOVE 7001* [1]	4	11
1 Mar 97	●	YOU GOT THE LOVE (re-mix) *React CDREACT 89* [1]	3	8
17 Apr 99		LOVE ON LOVE *React CDREACT 143*	27	3
7 Aug 99		YOUNG HEARTS RUN FREE (re-recording) *React CDREACT 158*	29	2

[1] Source featuring Candi Staton

STATUS IV US, male vocal group (3 WEEKS)

		pos/wks	
9 Jul 83	YOU AIN'T REALLY DOWN *TMT TMT 4*	56	3

STATUS QUO 13 Top 500

Ever popular London-based three-chord boogie band: Francis Rossi (g/v), Rick Parfitt (g/v), Alan Lancaster (b), John Coghlan (d). These long-time festival favourites recorded as The Spectres and Traffic Jam before their psychedelic-sounding debut hit introduced them to the UK and US Top 20 (their only major American hit). No group has accumulated more UK hits or has a wider Top 20 chart span and only The Beatles and Rolling Stones can better their tally of Top 20 albums. These heroes of the head-banging set who were chosen to open Live Aid in 1985 have been rockin' all over the world for more than 35 years (417 WEEKS)

			pos/wks	
24 Jan 68	●	PICTURES OF MATCHSTICK MEN *Pye 7N 17449*	7	12
21 Aug 68	●	ICE IN THE SUN *Pye 7N 17581*	8	12
28 May 69		ARE YOU GROWING TIRED OF MY LOVE (re) *Pye 7N 17728*	46	3
2 May 70		DOWN THE DUSTPIPE *Pye 7N 17907*	12	17
7 Nov 70		IN MY CHAIR *Pye 7N 17998*	21	14
13 Jan 73	●	PAPER PLANE *Vertigo 6059 071*	8	11
14 Apr 73		MEAN GIRL *Pye 7N 45229*	20	11

			pos/wks	
8 Sep 73	●	CAROLINE *Vertigo 6059 085*	5	13
4 May 74	●	BREAK THE RULES *Vertigo 6059 101*	8	8
7 Dec 74	★	DOWN DOWN *Vertigo 6059 114*	1	11
17 May 75		LIVE! (EP) *Vertigo QUO 13*	9	8
14 Feb 76		RAIN *Vertigo 6059 133*	7	7
10 Jul 76		MYSTERY SONG *Vertigo 6059 146*	11	9
11 Dec 76	●	WILD SIDE OF LIFE *Vertigo 6059 163*	9	12
8 Oct 77	●	ROCKIN' ALL OVER THE WORLD *Vertigo 6059 184*	3	16
2 Sep 78		AGAIN AND AGAIN *Vertigo QUO 1*	13	9
25 Nov 78		ACCIDENT PRONE *Vertigo QUO 2*	36	8
22 Sep 79	●	WHATEVER YOU WANT *Vertigo 6059 242*	4	9
24 Nov 79		LIVING ON AN ISLAND *Vertigo 6059 248*	16	10
11 Oct 80	●	WHAT YOU'RE PROPOSING *Vertigo QUO 3*	2	11
6 Dec 80		LIES / DON'T DRIVE MY CAR *Vertigo QUO 4*	11	10
28 Feb 81	●	SOMETHING 'BOUT YOU BABY I LIKE *Vertigo QUO 5*	9	7
28 Nov 81	●	ROCK 'N' ROLL *Vertigo QUO 6*	8	11
27 Mar 82		DEAR JOHN *Vertigo QUO 7*	10	8
12 Jun 82		SHE DON'T FOOL ME *Vertigo QUO 8*	36	5
30 Oct 82		CAROLINE (LIVE AT THE NEC) *Vertigo QUO 10*	13	7
10 Sep 83	●	OL' RAG BLUES *Vertigo QUO 11*	9	8
5 Nov 83		A MESS OF BLUES *Vertigo QUO 12*	15	6
10 Dec 83	●	MARGUERITA TIME *Vertigo QUO 14*	3	11
19 May 84		GOING DOWN TOWN TONIGHT *Vertigo QUO 15*	20	6
27 Oct 84	●	THE WANDERER *Vertigo QUO 16*	7	11
17 May 86	●	ROLLIN' HOME *Vertigo QUO 18*	9	6
26 Jul 86		RED SKY *Vertigo QUO 19*	19	8
4 Oct 86	●	IN THE ARMY NOW *Vertigo QUO 20*	2	14
6 Dec 86		DREAMIN' *Vertigo QUO 21*	15	8
26 Mar 88		AIN'T COMPLAINING *Vertigo QUO 22*	19	6
21 May 88		WHO GETS THE LOVE? *Vertigo QUO 23*	34	4
20 Aug 88		RUNNING ALL OVER THE WORLD *Vertigo QUAID 1*	17	6
3 Dec 88	●	BURNING BRIDGES (ON AND OFF AND ON AGAIN) *Vertigo QUO 25*	5	10
28 Oct 89		NOT AT ALL *Vertigo QUO 26*	50	2
29 Sep 90	●	THE ANNIVERSARY WALTZ – PART 1 *Vertigo QUO 28*	2	9
15 Dec 90		THE ANNIVERSARY WALTZ – PART 2 *Vertigo QUO 29*	16	7
7 Sep 91		CAN'T GIVE YOU MORE *Vertigo QUO 30*	37	3
18 Jan 92		ROCK 'TIL YOU DROP *Vertigo QUO 32*	38	3
10 Oct 92		ROADHOUSE MEDLEY (ANNIVERSARY WALTZ PART 25) *Polydor QUO 33*	21	4
6 Aug 94		I DIDN'T MEAN IT *Polydor QUOCD 34*	21	4
22 Oct 94		SHERRI DON'T FAIL ME NOW *Polydor QUOCD 35*	38	2
3 Dec 94		RESTLESS *Polydor QUOCD 36*	39	2
4 Nov 95		WHEN YOU WALK IN THE ROOM *PolyGram TV 5775122*	34	2
2 Mar 96		FUN FUN FUN *PolyGram TV 5762632* [1]	24	4
13 Apr 96		DON'T STOP *PolyGram TV 5766352*	35	2
9 Nov 96		ALL AROUND MY HAT *PolyGram TV 5759452* [2]	47	1
20 Mar 99		THE WAY IT GOES *Eagle EAGXS 075*	39	2
12 Jun 99		LITTLE WHITE LIES *Eagle EAGXS 101*	47	1
2 Oct 99		TWENTY WILD HORSES *Eagle EAGXS 105*	53	1
13 May 00		MONY MONY *Universal TV 1580132*	48	1
17 Aug 02		JAM SIDE DOWN *Universal TV 192342*	17	3
9 Nov 02		ALL STAND UP (NEVER SAY NEVER) *Universal TV 0194872*	51	1

[1] Status Quo with The Beach Boys [2] Status Quo with Maddy Prior from Steeleye Span

'Don't Drive My Car' listed from 20 Dec 1980 only. 'Running All Over the World' is a re-recorded version of 'Rockin' All Over the World', with a slightly changed lyric, released to promote the Race Against Time of 28 Aug 1988. The 'Live!' EP from 1975 featured three tracks: 'Roll Over Lay Down (Live)'/ 'Gerundula'/ 'Junior's Wailing (Live)'

STAXX featuring Carol LEEMING
UK, male / female vocal / instrumental group (11 WEEKS)

		pos/wks	
2 Oct 93	JOY *Champion CHAMPCD 303*	25	6
20 May 95	YOU *Champion CHAMPCD 316*	50	1
13 Sep 97	JOY (re-mix) *Champion CHAMPCD 328*	14	4

STEALERS WHEEL
UK, male vocal / instrumental group (22 WEEKS)

			pos/wks	
26 May 73	●	STUCK IN THE MIDDLE WITH YOU *A&M AMS 7036*	8	10
1 Sep 73		EVERYTHING WILL TURN OUT FINE *A&M AMS 7079*	33	6
26 Jan 74		STAR *A&M AMS 7094*	25	6

STEAM US, male vocal / instrumental group (14 WEEKS)   pos/wks
31 Jan 70 ● NA NA HEY HEY KISS HIM GOODBYE *Fontana TF 1058* ▲ 9 14

STEEL – See UNITONE ROCKERS featuring STEEL

Anthony STEEL and the RADIO REVELLERS UK, male actor
/ vocalist (d. 21 Mar 2001) and male instrumental group (6 WEEKS) pos/wks
10 Sep 54 WEST OF ZANZIBAR *Polygon P 1114* 11 6

Act name also credits 'With Jackie Brown and his Music'

STEEL HORSES – See TRUMAN & WOLFF featuring STEEL HORSES

STEEL PULSE
UK, male vocal / instrumental group (12 WEEKS)   pos/wks
1 Apr 78 KU KLUX KLAN *Island WIP 6428* 41 4
8 Jul 78 PRODIGAL SON *Island WIP 6449* 35 6
23 Jun 79 SOUND SYSTEM *Island WIP 6490* 71 2

Tommy STEELE ⟨158⟩ Top 500
Britain's first home-grown rock 'n' roll star, b. Thomas Hicks, 17 Dec 1936,
London. Just four months after his chart debut he was filming his life story.
The singer / songwriter / guitarist, who topped the chart before Elvis, starred
in many other movies and musicals (147 WEEKS)   pos/wks
26 Oct 56 ROCK WITH THE CAVEMAN (re) *Decca F 10795* 1 ....13 5
14 Dec 56 ★ SINGING THE BLUES (2re) *Decca F 10819* 1 ....1 15
15 Feb 57 KNEE DEEP IN THE BLUES *Decca F 10849* 1 ....15 9
3 May 57 ● BUTTERFINGERS (re) *Decca F 10877* 1 ....8 18
16 Aug 57 ● WATER WATER / A HANDFUL OF SONGS (re)
           Decca F 10923 1 ....5 17
30 Aug 57 SHIRALEE *Decca F 10896* 1 ....11 4
22 Nov 57 HEY YOU! *Decca F 10941* 1 ....28 1
7 Mar 58 ● NAIROBI *Decca F 10991* 3 11
25 Apr 58 HAPPY GUITAR *Decca F 10976*.................................20 5
18 Jul 58 THE ONLY MAN ON THE ISLAND *Decca F 11041* 1 ....16 8
14 Nov 58 ● COME ON, LET'S GO *Decca F 11072* 10 13
14 Aug 59 TALLAHASSEE LASSIE (re) *Decca F 11152* 16 5
28 Aug 59 GIVE! GIVE! GIVE! *Decca F 11152X*...........................28 2
4 Dec 59 ● LITTLE WHITE BULL (re) *Decca F 11177* 6 17
23 Jun 60 ● WHAT A MOUTH (WHAT A NORTH AND SOUTH)
           Decca F 11245 ....5 11
29 Dec 60 MUST BE SANTA *Decca F 11299* 40 1
17 Aug 61 THE WRITING ON THE WALL *Decca F 11372* 30 5

1 Tommy Steele and the Steelmen

'Handful of Songs' listed together with 'Water Water' from week of 23 Aug 1957

STEELEYE SPAN
UK, male / female vocal / instrumental group (18 WEEKS)   pos/wks
8 Dec 73 GAUDETE *Chrysalis CHS 2007* 14 9
15 Nov 75 ● ALL AROUND MY HAT *Chrysalis CHS 2078* 5 9

STEELY DAN US, male vocal / instrumental group (21 WEEKS)   pos/wks
30 Aug 75 DO IT AGAIN *ABC 4075* 39 4
11 Dec 76 HAITIAN DIVORCE *ABC 4152* 17 9
29 Jul 78 FM (NO STATIC AT ALL) (re) *MCA 374*.........................49 5
10 Mar 79 RIKKI DON'T LOSE THAT NUMBER *ABC 4241* 58 3

STEFY – See DJH featuring STEFY

Jim STEINMAN US, male producer (9 WEEKS)   pos/wks
4 Jul 81 ROCK AND ROLL DREAMS COME THROUGH
          Epic EPC A 1236 1 ....52 7
23 Jun 84 TONIGHT IS WHAT IT MEANS TO BE YOUNG
          MCA MCA 889 2 ....67 2

1 Jim Steinman, vocals by Rory Dodd 2 Jim Steinman and Fire Inc

STEINSKI and MASS MEDIA
US, male / female production group (2 WEEKS)   pos/wks
31 Jan 87 WE'LL BE RIGHT BACK *Fourth & Broadway BRW 59* 63 2

Mike STEIPHENSON – See BURUNDI STEIPHENSON BLACK

STELLA BROWNE
UK, male production duo (3 WEEKS)   pos/wks
20 May 00 EVERY WOMAN NEEDS LOVE *Perfecto PERF 06*................55 1
9 Feb 02 NEVER KNEW LOVE *Perfecto PERF 26CDS* 42 2

Doreen STEPHENS – See Billy COTTON and his BAND

Richie STEPHENS
Jamaica, male vocalist (3 WEEKS)   pos/wks
15 May 93 LEGACY *Columbia 6592852* 1 ....64 2
9 Aug 97 COME GIVE ME YOUR LOVE
          Delirious 74321450442 2 ....61 1

1 Mad Cobra featuring Richie Stephens 2 Richie Stephens and General Degree

Martin STEPHENSON and the DAINTEES
UK, male vocal / instrumental group (7 WEEKS)   pos/wks
8 Nov 86 BOAT TO BOLIVIA *Kitchenware SL 27*..........................70 2
17 Jan 87 TROUBLE TOWN *Kitchenware SK 13* 1 ....58 3
27 Jun 92 BIG SKY NEW LIGHT *Kitchenware SK 57* 71 2

1 Daintees

STEPPENWOLF
US / Canada, male vocal / instrumental group (14 WEEKS)   pos/wks
11 Jun 69 BORN TO BE WILD (re) *Stateside SS 8017* 30 9
27 Feb 99 BORN TO BE WILD (re-issue) *MCA MCSTD 48104*............18 5

TOP 10 IRISH ACTS

■ Irish-born chart champions (calculated by weeks
on the UK singles chart) together with each act's
highest placed hit

1. **U2** (257)
   Beautiful Day

2. **BOYZONE** (213)
   No Matter What

3. **BACHELORS** (187)
   Diane

4. **WESTLIFE** (154)
   I Have a Dream /
   Seasons in the Sun

5. **GILBERT O'SULLIVAN** (145)
   Clair

6. **VAL DOONICAN** (143)
   What Would I Be

7. **THIN LIZZY** (128)
   Whiskey in the Jar

8. **BOOMTOWN RATS** (123)
   Rat Trap

9. **B*WITCHED** (98)
   C'est La Vie

10. **CORRS** (92)
    Breathless

The Grammy Award-winning,
supermodel-dating, 'drop the
debt' campaigning best band
in the world, U2

STEPS `73` *Top 500*

Steptacular pop vocal quintet; Lisa Scott-Lee, Claire Richards, Faye Tozer, Lee Latchford-Evans, Ian Watkins (aka H). The hard-working live act's 1999 tour was reportedly the biggest pop arena tour ever in the UK. The first UK mixed quintet to top the chart twice, they bagged 14 consecutive Top 5 singles (a feat bettered only by The Beatles), sold more than 12 million records and announced their split on Boxing Day 2001. Best-selling single: 'Heartbeat / Tragedy' 1,150,285 (217 WEEKS)   pos/wks

22 Nov 97		5, 6, 7, 8 *Jive JIVECD 438*	14 17
2 May 98	●	LAST THING ON MY MIND *Jive 0518492*	6 14
5 Sep 98	●	ONE FOR SORROW *Jive 0519092*	2 11
21 Nov 98	★	HEARTBEAT / TRAGEDY *Jive 0519142*◆	1 30
20 Mar 99	●	BETTER BEST FORGOTTEN (re) *Ebul / Jive 0519242*	2 17
10 Apr 99	●	THANK ABBA FOR THE MUSIC *Epic ABCD 1* `1`	4 13
24 Jul 99	●	LOVE'S GOT A HOLD ON MY HEART (re)	
		Ebul / Jive 0519372	2 12
23 Oct 99	●	AFTER THE LOVE HAS GONE (re) *Ebul / Jive 0519462* ...	5 11
25 Dec 99	●	SAY YOU'LL BE MINE / BETTER THE DEVIL YOU KNOW	
		Ebul / Jive 9201008	4 17
15 Apr 00	●	DEEPER SHADE OF BLUE *Ebul / Jive 9201022*	4 9
15 Jul 00	●	WHEN I SAID GOODBYE / SUMMER OF LOVE	
		Ebul / Jive 9201162	5 11
28 Oct 00	★	STOMP *Ebul / Jive 9201212*■	1 11
6 Jan 01	●	IT'S THE WAY YOU MAKE ME FEEL / TOO BUSY	
		THINKING 'BOUT MY BABY *Ebul / Jive 9201232*	2 11
16 Jun 01	●	HERE AND NOW / YOU'LL BE SORRY	
		Ebul / Jive 9201322	4 10
6 Oct 01	●	CHAIN REACTION / ONE FOR SORROW (re-mix)	
		Ebul / Jive 9201422	2 12
15 Dec 01	●	WORDS ARE NOT ENOUGH / I KNOW HIM SO WELL	
		Ebul / Jive 9201452	5 11

`1` Steps, Tina Cousins, Cleopatra, B*Witched, Billie

STEREO MC's *UK, male / female vocal / rap group (37 WEEKS)* pos/wks

29 Sep 90	ELEVATE MY MIND *Fourth & Broadway BRW 186*	74 1
9 Mar 91	LOST IN MUSIC *Fourth & Broadway BRW 198*	46 3
26 Sep 92	CONNECTED *Fourth & Broadway BRW 262*	18 6
5 Dec 92	STEP IT UP *Fourth & Broadway BRW 266*	12 12
20 Feb 93	GROUND LEVEL *Fourth & Broadway BRCD 268*	19 5
29 May 93	CREATION *Fourth & Broadway BRCD 276*	19 4
26 May 01	DEEP DOWN & DIRTY (re) *Island CID 777*	17 5
1 Sep 01	WE BELONG IN THIS WORLD TOGETHER *Island CID 782*.	59 1

STEREO NATION *UK, male vocal duo (3 WEEKS)* pos/wks

17 Aug 96	I'VE BEEN WAITING *EMI Premier PRESCD 5*	53 1
27 Oct 01	LAILA *Wizard WIZ 015* `1`	44 2

`1` Taz & Stereo Nation

STEREOLAB
UK / France, male / female vocal / instrumental group (6 WEEKS) pos/wks

8 Jan 94	JENNY ONDIOLINE / FRENCH DISCO	
	Duophonic UHF DUHFCD 01	75 1
30 Jul 94	PING PONG *Duophonic UHF DUHFCD 04*	45 2
12 Nov 94	WOW AND FLUTTER *Duophonic UHF DUHFCD 07* ...	70 1
2 Mar 96	CYBELE'S REVERIE *Duophonic UHF DUHFCD 10*	62 1
13 Sep 97	MISS MODULAR *Duophonic UHF DUHFCD 16*	60 1

STEREOPHONICS `276` *Top 500*

1998 Best Newcomer Brit Award-winning rock trio - Kelly Jones (v,g), Richard Thomas (b) and Stuart Cable (d) – from Cwmaman, Wales, UK. Their 14 hit singles and two chart-topping albums of new material between 1997 and 2001 cannot be bettered by any other group (108 WEEKS) pos/wks

29 Mar 97		LOCAL BOY IN THE PHOTOGRAPH *V2 SPHD 2*	51 1
31 May 97		MORE LIFE IN A TRAMP'S VEST *V2 SPHD 4*	33 2
23 Aug 97		A THOUSAND TREES *V2 VVR 5000443*	22 3
8 Nov 97		TRAFFIC *V2 VVR 5000948*	20 3
21 Feb 98		LOCAL BOY IN THE PHOTOGRAPH (re-issue) *V2 VVR 5001263*.	14 4
21 Nov 98	●	THE BARTENDER AND THE THIEF *V2 VVR 5004653* ...	3 12
6 Mar 99	●	JUST LOOKING (re) *V2 VVR 5005303*	4 9

15 May 99	●	PICK A PART THAT'S NEW *V2 VVR 5006778*	4 9
4 Sep 99	●	I WOULDN'T BELIEVE YOUR RADIO (re) *V2 VVR 5008823* ..	11 7
20 Nov 99	●	HURRY UP AND WAIT (re) *V2 VVR 5009323*	11 8
18 Mar 00	●	MAMA TOLD ME NOT TO COME *Gut CDGUT 031* `1`	4 7
31 Mar 01	●	MR WRITER *V2 VVR 5015933*	5 12
23 Jun 01	●	HAVE A NICE DAY *V2 VVR 5016243*	5 9
6 Oct 01	●	STEP ON MY OLD SIZE NINES *V2 VVR 5016253*........	16 5
15 Dec 01	●	HANDBAGS AND GLADRAGS (re) *V2 VVR 5017753*....	4 15
13 Apr 02		VEGAS TWO TIMES *V2 VVR 5019173*	23 2

`1` Tom Jones and Stereophonics

STETSASONIC *US, male rap group (3 WEEKS)* pos/wks

24 Sep 88	TALKIN' ALL THAT JAZZ *Breakout USA 640*	73 2
7 Nov 98	TALKIN' ALL THAT JAZZ (re-mix)	
	Tommy Boy TBCD 7310A	54 1

STEVE and EYDIE – *See Steve LAWRENCE; Eydie GORME*

STEVE GIBBONS BAND – *See Steve GIBBONS BAND*

April STEVENS – *See Nino TEMPO and April STEVENS*

Cat STEVENS `326` *Top 500*

Critically acclaimed folk-pop singer / songwriter, b. Steven Georgiou, 21 Jul 1947, London, UK, whose songs have been recorded by many top acts. One of the world's biggest album sellers in 1970s. Semi-retired 1979, converted to Islam and changed his name to Yusuf Islam. Gave royalties for Boyzone version of 'Father and Son' to charity (96 WEEKS) pos/wks

20 Oct 66		I LOVE MY DOG *Deram DM 102*	28 7
12 Jan 67	●	MATTHEW AND SON *Deram DM 110*	2 10
30 Mar 67	●	I'M GONNA GET ME A GUN *Deram DM 118*	6 10
2 Aug 67		A BAD NIGHT *Deram DM 140*	20 8
20 Dec 67		KITTY *Deram DM 156*	47 1
27 Jun 70	●	LADY D'ARBANVILLE *Island WIP 6086*	8 13
28 Aug 71		MOON SHADOW *Island WIP 6092*	22 11
1 Jan 72	●	MORNING HAS BROKEN *Island WIP 6121*	9 13
9 Dec 72		CAN'T KEEP IT IN *Island WIP 6152*	13 12
24 Aug 74		ANOTHER SATURDAY NIGHT *Island WIP 6206*	19 8
2 Jul 77		(REMEMBER THE DAYS OF THE) OLD SCHOOL YARD	
		Island WIP 6387	44 3

Connie STEVENS *US, female vocalist – Concetta Ingolia (20 WKS)* pos/wks

5 May 60	●	SIXTEEN REASONS (re) *Warner Bros. WB 3*	9 12
5 May 60		KOOKIE KOOKIE (LEND ME YOUR COMB)	
		Warner Bros. WB 5 `1`	27 8

`1` Edward Byrnes and Connie Stevens

Ray STEVENS *US, male vocalist – Ray Ragsdale (64 WEEKS)* pos/wks

16 May 70	●	EVERYTHING IS BEAUTIFUL *CBS 4953* ▲	6 16
13 Mar 71	●	BRIDGET THE MIDGET (THE QUEEN OF THE BLUES) *CBS 7070*.	2 14
25 Mar 72		TURN YOUR RADIO ON *CBS 7634*	33 4
25 May 74	★	THE STREAK *Janus 6146 201* ▲	1 12
21 Jun 75	●	MISTY *Janus 6146 204*..	2 10
27 Sep 75		INDIAN LOVE CALL *Janus 6146 205*	34 4
5 Mar 77		IN THE MOOD *Warner Bros. K 16875*	31 4

'In the Mood' features Ray Stevens not as a conventional vocalist, but as a group of chickens

Ricky STEVENS *UK, male vocalist (7 WEEKS)* pos/wks

14 Dec 61	I CRIED FOR YOU *Columbia DB 4739*......................	34 7

Shakin' STEVENS `41` *Top 500*

Performs and records under a broad umbrella of styles from rock and country blues to cajun, b. Michael Barratt, 4 Mar 1948, Glamorgan, Wales. Shares with The Beatles (60s) and Elton John (70s) the distinction of being the most successful UK singles chart performer of a decade (80s) (277 WEEKS) pos/wks

16 Feb 80	HOT DOG *Epic EPC 8090*	24 9
16 Aug 80	MARIE MARIE *Epic EPC 8725*	19 10

		pos/wks
28 Feb 81	★ THIS OLE HOUSE *Epic EPC 9555*	1 17
2 May 81	● YOU DRIVE ME CRAZY *Epic A 1165*	2 12
25 Jul 81	★ GREEN DOOR *Epic A 1354*	1 12
10 Oct 81	● IT'S RAINING *Epic A 1643*	10 9
16 Jan 82	★ OH JULIE *Epic EPC A 1742*	1 10
24 Apr 82	● SHIRLEY *Epic EPC A 2087*	6 6
21 Aug 82	GIVE ME YOUR HEART TONIGHT *Epic EPC A 2656*	11 10
16 Oct 82	● I'LL BE SATISFIED *Epic EPC A 2846*	10 8
11 Dec 82	● THE SHAKIN' STEVENS EP *Epic SHAKY 1*	2 7
23 Jul 83	IT'S LATE *Epic A 3565*	11 7
5 Nov 83	● CRY JUST A LITTLE BIT *Epic A 3774*	3 12
7 Jan 84	● A ROCKIN' GOOD WAY *Epic A 4071* [1]	5 9
24 Mar 84	● A LOVE WORTH WAITING FOR *Epic A 4291*	2 10
15 Sep 84	● A LETTER TO YOU *Epic A 4677*	10 8
24 Nov 84	● TEARDROPS *Epic A 4882*	5 9
2 Mar 85	BREAKING UP MY HEART *Epic A 6072*	14 7
12 Oct 85	LIPSTICK POWDER AND PAINT *Epic A 6610*	11 9
7 Dec 85	★ MERRY CHRISTMAS EVERYONE (re) *Epic A 6769*	1 11
8 Feb 86	TURNING AWAY *Epic A 6819*	15 7
1 Nov 86	BECAUSE I LOVE YOU *Epic SHAKY 2*	14 10
27 Jun 87	A LITTLE BOOGIE WOOGIE (IN THE BACK OF MY MIND) *Epic SHAKY 3*	12 10
19 Sep 87	COME SEE ABOUT ME *Epic SHAKY 4*	24 6
28 Nov 87	● WHAT DO YOU WANT TO MAKE THOSE EYES AT ME FOR *Epic SHAKY 5*	5 8
23 Jul 88	FEEL THE NEED IN ME *Epic SHAKY 6*	26 5
15 Oct 88	HOW MANY TEARS CAN YOU HIDE *Epic SHAKY 7*	47 4
10 Dec 88	TRUE LOVE *Epic SHAKY 8*	23 6
18 Feb 89	JEZEBEL *Epic SHAKY 9*	58 2
13 May 89	LOVE ATTACK *Epic SHAKY 10*	28 4
24 Feb 90	I MIGHT *Epic SHAKY 11*	18 6
12 May 90	YES I DO *Epic SHAKY 12*	60 2
18 Aug 90	PINK CHAMPAGNE *Epic SHAKY 13*	59 2
13 Oct 90	MY CUTIE CUTIE *Epic SHAKY 14*	75 1
15 Dec 90	THE BEST CHRISTMAS OF THEM ALL *Epic SHAKY 15*	19 4
7 Dec 91	I'LL BE HOME THIS CHRISTMAS *Epic 6576507*	34 5
10 Oct 92	RADIO *Epic 6584367* [2]	37 3

[1] Shaky and Bonnie [2] Shaky featuring Roger Taylor

Tracks on The Shakin' Stevens EP: Blue Christmas / Que Sera Sera / Josephine / Lawdy Miss Clawdy. 'Merry Christmas Everyone' re-entered peaking at No.58 in Dec 1986

STEVENSON'S ROCKET
UK, male vocal / instrumental group (5 WEEKS) — pos/wks

29 Nov 75	● ALRIGHT BABY (re) *Magnet MAG 47*	37 5

Al STEWART *UK, male vocalist (6 WEEKS)* — pos/wks

29 Jan 77	YEAR OF THE CAT *RCA 2771*	31 6

Amii STEWART *US, female vocalist (61 WEEKS)* — pos/wks

7 Apr 79	● KNOCK ON WOOD *Atlantic / Hansa K 11214* ▲	6 12
16 Jun 79	● LIGHT MY FIRE – 137 DISCO HEAVEN (MEDLEY) *Atlantic / Hansa K 11278*	5 11
3 Nov 79	JEALOUSY *Atlantic / Hansa K 11386*	58 3
19 Jan 80	THE LETTER / PARADISE BIRD *Atlantic / Hansa K 11424* ...	39 4
19 Jul 80	MY GUY – MY GIRL (MEDLEY) *Atlantic / Hansa K 11550* [1] ...	39 5
29 Dec 84	FRIENDS *RCA 471*	12 11
17 Aug 85	● KNOCK ON WOOD / LIGHT MY FIRE (re-mix) *Sedition EDIT 3303*	7 12
25 Jan 86	MY GUY – MY GIRL (MEDLEY) *Sedition EDIT 3310* [2] ...	63 3

[1] Amii Stewart and Johnny Bristol [2] Amii Stewart and Deon Estus

Andy STEWART *UK, male vocalist, d. 11 Oct 1993 (67 WEEKS)* — pos/wks

15 Dec 60	DONALD WHERE'S YOUR TROOSERS *Top Rank JAR 427* [1] ..	37 1
12 Jan 61	A SCOTTISH SOLDIER (re) *Top Rank JAR 512* [1]	19 40
1 Jun 61	THE BATTLE'S O'ER *Top Rank JAR 565* [1]	28 13
12 Aug 65	DR FINLAY (re) *HMV POP 1454*	43 5
9 Dec 89	● DONALD WHERE'S YOUR TROOSERS (re-issue) *Stone SON 2353* [1]	4 8

[1] Andy Stewart with the Michael Sammes Singers

Billy STEWART *US, male vocalist, d. 17 Jan 1970 (2 WEEKS)* — pos/wks

8 Sep 66	SUMMERTIME *Chess CRS 8040*	39 2

Dave STEWART
UK, male instrumentalist – keyboards (30 WEEKS) — pos/wks

14 Mar 81	WHAT BECOMES OF THE BROKEN HEARTED *Stiff BROKEN 1* [1]	13 10
19 Sep 81	★ IT'S MY PARTY *Stiff BROKEN 2* [2]	1 13
13 Aug 83	BUSY DOING NOTHING *Broken BROKEN 5* [2]	49 4
14 Jun 86	THE LOCOMOTION *Broken BROKEN 8* [2]	70 3

[1] Dave Stewart. Guest vocals: Colin Blunstone [2] Dave Stewart with Barbara Gaskin

Dave STEWART
UK, male instrumentalist – guitar (19 WEEKS) — pos/wks

24 Feb 90	● LILY WAS HERE *RCA ZB 43045* [1]	6 12
18 Aug 90	JACK TALKING *RCA PB 43907* [2]	69 2
3 Sep 94	HEART OF STONE *East West YZ 845CD*	36 5

[1] David A Stewart featuring Candy Dulfer [2] Dave Stewart and the Spiritual Cowboys

See also EURYTHMICS; VEGAS

Jermaine STEWART *US, male vocalist (42 WEEKS)* — pos/wks

9 Aug 86	● WE DON'T HAVE TO ... TAKE OUR CLOTHES OFF TO HAVE A GOOD TIME *10 TEN 96*	2 14
1 Nov 86	JODY *10 TEN 143*	50 4
16 Jan 88	● SAY IT AGAIN *10 TEN 188*	7 12
2 Apr 88	GET LUCKY *Siren SRN 82*	13 9
24 Sep 88	DON'T TALK DIRTY TO ME *Siren SRN 86*	61 3

John STEWART *US, male vocalist (6 WEEKS)* — pos/wks

30 Jun 79	GOLD *RSO 35*	43 6

Rod STEWART 〔 8 〕 Top 500

World-renowned rock superstar b. 10 Jan 1945, London, UK, of Scottish parents. In the 1960s "Rod the Mod" recorded solo singles for Decca, EMI and Immediate, but is best remembered in that period as a member of The Five Dimensions, Hoochie Coochie Men, Steampacket, Shotgun Express and The Jeff Beck Group. Between 1969 and 1975, the gravel-voiced vocalist fronted The Faces as well as having a successful solo career. Over the past 30 years, Stewart has played to packed stadiums worldwide and amassed a vast collection of platinum and gold albums. In the US, he is one of the top selling UK artists of all time with nine Top 10 albums and 16 Top 10 singles. In Britain, he has scored 22 Top 10 LPs including seven solo No.1s. His writing skills have earned him a Lifetime Ivor Novello Award in the UK, while in the US he has recently been nominated for the prestigious Songwriters' Hall of Fame. Stewart, whose love life also attracts much media attention, earned a Grammy Living Legend Award in 1989, Lifetime Achievement trophies from the Brits and World Music Awards and was inducted into the Rock and Roll Hall of Fame in 1994. Best-selling single: 'Sailing' 955,111 (477 WEEKS) — pos/wks

4 Sep 71	REASON TO BELIEVE *Mercury 6052 097*	19 2
18 Sep 71	★ MAGGIE MAY *Mercury 6052 097* ▲	1 19
12 Aug 72	★ YOU WEAR IT WELL *Mercury 6052 171*	1 12
18 Nov 72	● ANGEL / WHAT MADE MILWAUKEE FAMOUS (HAS MADE A LOSER OUT OF ME) *Mercury 6052 198*	4 11
5 May 73	I'VE BEEN DRINKING *RAK RR 4* [1]	27 6
8 Sep 73	● OH! NO NOT MY BABY *Mercury 6052 371*	6 9
5 Oct 74	● FAREWELL – BRING IT ON HOME TO ME / YOU SEND ME *Mercury 6167 033*	7 7
7 Dec 74	YOU CAN MAKE ME DANCE SING OR ANYTHING (EVEN TAKE THE DOG FOR A WALK, MEND A FUSE, FOLD AWAY THE IRONING BOARD, OR ANY OTHER DOMESTIC SHORT COMINGS) *Warner Bros. K 16494* [2]	12 9
16 Aug 75	★ SAILING (2re) *Warner Bros. K 16600*	1 34
15 Nov 75	● THIS OLD HEART OF MINE *Riva 1*	4 9
5 Jun 76	● TONIGHT'S THE NIGHT *Riva 3* ▲	5 9
21 Aug 76	● THE KILLING OF GEORGIE *Riva 4*	2 10
20 Nov 76	GET BACK *Riva 6*	11 9
4 Dec 76	MAGGIE MAY (re-issue) *Mercury 6160 006*	31 7

Date	Title	pos	wks
23 Apr 77 ★	I DON'T WANT TO TALK ABOUT IT / FIRST CUT IS THE DEEPEST *Riva 7*	1	13
15 Oct 77 ●	YOU'RE IN MY HEART *Riva 11*	3	10
28 Jan 78 ●	HOT LEGS / I WAS ONLY JOKING *Riva 10*	5	8
27 May 78 ●	OLE OLA (MULHER BRASILEIRA) *Riva 15* [3]	4	6
18 Nov 78 ★	DA YA THINK I'M SEXY? *Riva 17* ▲	1	13
3 Feb 79	AIN'T LOVE A BITCH *Riva 18*	11	8
5 May 79	BLONDES (HAVE MORE FUN) *Riva 19*	63	3
31 May 80	IF LOVING YOU IS WRONG (I DON'T WANT TO BE RIGHT) *Riva 23*	23	9
8 Nov 80	PASSION *Riva 26*	17	10
20 Dec 80	MY GIRL *Riva 28*	32	7
17 Oct 81 ●	TONIGHT I'M YOURS (DON'T HURT ME) *Riva 33*	8	13
12 Dec 81	YOUNG TURKS *Riva 34*	11	9
27 Feb 82	HOW LONG *Riva 35*	41	4
4 Jun 83 ★	BABY JANE *Warner Bros. W 9608*	1	14
27 Aug 83 ●	WHAT AM I GONNA DO (I'M SO IN LOVE WITH YOU) *Warner Bros. W 9564*	3	8
10 Dec 83	SWEET SURRENDER *Warner Bros. W 9440*	23	9
26 May 84	INFATUATION *Warner Bros. W 9256*	27	7
28 Jul 84	SOME GUYS HAVE ALL THE LUCK *Warner Bros. W 9204*	15	10
24 May 86	LOVE TOUCH (re) *Warner Bros. W 8668*	27	8
12 Jul 86 ●	EVERY BEAT OF MY HEART *Warner Bros. W 8625*	2	9
20 Sep 86	ANOTHER HEARTACHE *Warner Bros. W 8631*	54	2
28 May 88	LOST IN YOU *Warner Bros. W 7927*	21	6
13 Aug 88	FOREVER YOUNG *Warner Bros. W 7796*	57	3
6 May 89	MY HEART CAN'T TELL YOU NO *Warner Bros. W 7729*	49	4
11 Nov 89	THIS OLD HEART OF MINE *Warner Bros. W 2686* [4]	51	3
13 Jan 90 ●	DOWNTOWN TRAIN *Warner Bros. W 2647*	10	12
24 Nov 90 ●	IT TAKES TWO *Warner Bros. ROD 1* [5]	5	8
16 Mar 91 ●	RHYTHM OF MY HEART *Warner Bros. W 0017*	3	11
15 Jun 91 ●	THE MOTOWN SONG *Warner Bros. W 0030* [6]	10	8
7 Sep 91	BROKEN ARROW *Warner Bros. W 0059*	54	3
7 Mar 92	PEOPLE GET READY *Epic 6577567* [1]	49	3
18 Apr 92	YOUR SONG / BROKEN ARROW (re-issue) *Warner Bros. W 0104*	41	4
5 Dec 92 ●	TOM TRAUBERT'S BLUES (WALTZING MATILDA) *Warner Bros. W 0144*	6	9
20 Feb 93	RUBY TUESDAY *Warner Bros. W 0158CD*	11	5
17 Apr 93	SHOTGUN WEDDING *Warner Bros. W 0171CD*	21	4
26 Jun 93 ●	HAVE I TOLD YOU LATELY *Warner Bros. W 0185CD*	5	9
21 Aug 93	REASON TO BELIEVE *Warner Bros. W 0198CD1*	51	3
18 Dec 93	PEOPLE GET READY *Warner Bros. W 0226CD1*	45	4
15 Jan 94 ●	ALL FOR LOVE *A&M 5804772* [7] ▲	2	13
20 May 95	YOU'RE THE STAR *Warner Bros. W 0296CD*	19	5
19 Aug 95	LADY LUCK *Warner Bros. W 0310CD1*	56	1
15 Jun 96	PURPLE HEATHER *Warner Bros. W 0354CD* [8]	16	5
14 Dec 96	IF WE FALL IN LOVE TONIGHT *Warner Bros. W 0380CD*	58	1
1 Nov 97 ●	DA YA THINK I'M SEXY? *All Around the World CDGLOBE 150* [9]	7	10
30 May 98	OOH LA LA *Warner Brothers W 0446CD*	16	5
5 Sep 98	ROCKS *Warner Brothers W 0452CD1*	55	1
17 Apr 99	FAITH OF THE HEART *Universal UND 56235*	60	1
24 Mar 01	I CAN'T DENY IT *Atlantic AT 0096CD*	26	2

[1] Jeff Beck and Rod Stewart [2] Faces / Rod Stewart [3] Rod Stewart featuring the Scottish World Cup Squad '78 [4] Rod Stewart featuring Ronald Isley [5] Rod Stewart and Tina Turner [6] Rod Stewart with backing vocals by The Temptations [7] Bryan Adams, Rod Stewart and Sting [8] Rod Stewart with the Scottish Euro '96 Squad [9] N-Trance featuring Rod Stewart

'Reason to Believe' and 'People Get Ready' in 1993 were re-recordings. 'Reason to Believe' additionally credits Ronnie Wood on the sleeve. 'Sailing' re-entries peaked at No.3 in 1976 and No.41 in 1987.

See also FACES; GLASS TIGER; PYTHON LEE JACKSON

STEX
UK, male / female vocal / instrumental group (2 WEEKS) pos/wks

19 Jan 91	STILL FEEL THE RAIN *Some Bizarre SBZ 7002*	63	2

STICKY featuring MS DYNAMITE *UK, male producer*
– Richard Forbes and UK, female rapper (6 WEEKS) pos/wks

23 Jun 01	BOOO! *ffrr / Public Demand / Social Circles FCD 399*	12	6

STIFF LITTLE FINGERS
UK, male vocal / instrumental group (39 WEEKS) pos/wks

29 Sep 79	STRAW DOGS *Chrysalis CHS 2368*	44	4
16 Feb 80	AT THE EDGE *Chrysalis CHS 2406*	15	9
24 May 80	NOBODY'S HERO / TIN SOLDIERS *Chrysalis CHS 2424*	36	5
2 Aug 80	BACK TO FRONT *Chrysalis CHS 2447*	49	4
28 Mar 81	JUST FADE AWAY *Chrysalis CHS 2510*	47	6
30 May 81	SILVER LINING *Chrysalis CHS 2517*	68	3
23 Jan 82	LISTEN (EP) *Chrysalis CHS 2580*	33	6
18 Sep 82	BITS OF KIDS *Chrysalis CHS 2637*	73	2

Tracks on Listen (EP): That's When Your Blood Bumps / Two Guitars Clash / Listen / Sad-Eyed People

Curtis STIGERS *US, male vocalist (34 WEEKS)* pos/wks

18 Jan 92 ●	I WONDER WHY *Arista 114716*	5	10
28 Mar 92 ●	YOU'RE ALL THAT MATTERS TO ME *Arista 115273*	6	12
11 Jul 92	SLEEPING WITH THE LIGHTS ON *Arista 74321102307*	53	4
17 Oct 92	NEVER SAW A MIRACLE *Arista 74321117257*	34	4
3 Jun 95	THIS TIME *Arista 74321286962*	28	3
2 Dec 95	KEEP ME FROM THE COLD *Arista 74321319162*	57	1

Stephen STILLS
US, male vocalist / instrumentalist (8 WEEKS) pos/wks

13 Mar 71	LOVE THE ONE YOU'RE WITH *Atlantic 2091 046*	37	4
6 Jun 98	HE GOT GAME *Def Jam 5689852* [1]	16	4

[1] Public Enemy featuring Stephen Stills

See also CROSBY, STILLS, NASH and YOUNG

STILTSKIN *UK, male vocal / instrumental*
group – lead vocal Ray Wilson (15 WEEKS) pos/wks

7 May 94 ★	INSIDE *White Water LEV 1CD*	1	13
24 Sep 94	FOOTSTEPS *White Water WWRD 2*	34	2

STING 145 Top 500

World's best-known ex-Police-man, b. Gordon Sumner, 2 Oct 1951, Newcastle, UK. This singer / songwriter / bass player has amassed more solo hits than as front man of that top-selling trio. As a soloist, he has won both Brit and Grammy awards, and reportedly earns £1 a second from touring and royalties (152 WEEKS) pos/wks

14 Aug 82	SPREAD A LITTLE HAPPINESS *A&M AMS 8242*	16	8
8 Jun 85	IF YOU LOVE SOMEBODY SET THEM FREE *A&M AM 258*	26	7
24 Aug 85	LOVE IS THE SEVENTH WAVE *A&M AM 272*	41	5
19 Oct 85	FORTRESS AROUND YOUR HEART *A&M AM 286*	49	3
7 Dec 85	RUSSIANS (re) *A&M AM 292*	12	12
15 Mar 86	MOON OVER BOURBON STREET *A&M AM 305*	44	4
7 Nov 87	WE'LL BE TOGETHER *A&M AM 410*	41	4
20 Feb 88	ENGLISHMAN IN NEW YORK *A&M AM 431*	51	3
9 Apr 88	FRAGILE *A&M AM 439*	70	2
11 Aug 90	ENGLISHMAN IN NEW YORK (re-mix) *A&M AM 580*	15	7
12 Jan 91	ALL THIS TIME *A&M AM 713*	22	4
9 Mar 91	MAD ABOUT YOU *A&M AM 721*	56	2
4 May 91	THE SOUL CAGES *A&M AM 759*	57	1
29 Aug 92	IT'S PROBABLY ME *A&M AM 883* [1]	30	5
13 Feb 93	IF I EVER LOSE MY FAITH IN YOU *A&M AMCD 0172*	14	6
24 Apr 93	SEVEN DAYS *A&M 5802232*	25	4
19 Jun 93	FIELDS OF GOLD *A&M 5803012*	16	6
4 Sep 93	SHAPE OF MY HEART *A&M 5803532*	57	1
20 Nov 93	DEMOLITION MAN *A&M 5804512*	21	4
15 Jan 94 ●	ALL FOR LOVE *A&M 5804772* [2] ▲	2	13
26 Feb 94	NOTHING 'BOUT ME *A&M 5805292*	32	3
29 Oct 94 ●	WHEN WE DANCE *A&M 5808612*	9	7
11 Feb 95	THIS COWBOY SONG *A&M 5809652* [3]	15	6
20 Jan 96	SPIRITS IN THE MATERIAL WORLD *MCA MCSTD 2113* [4]	36	2
2 Mar 96	LET YOUR SOUL BE YOUR PILOT *A&M 5813312*	15	4
11 May 96	YOU STILL TOUCH ME *A&M 5815472*	27	3
22 Jun 96	LIVE AT TFI FRIDAY (EP) *A&M 5817652*	53	2

4 Sep 96	I WAS BROUGHT TO MY SENSES *A&M 5818912*	31	1
0 Nov 96	I'M SO HAPPY I CAN'T STOP CRYING *A&M 5820312*	54	1
0 Dec 97	ROXANNE '97 (re-mix) *A&M 5824552* [5]	17	6
5 Sep 99	BRAND NEW DAY *A&M / Polydor 4971522*	13	5
9 Jan 00	DESERT ROSE *A&M / Mercury 4972402* [6]	15	6
2 Apr 00	AFTER THE RAIN HAS FALLEN *A&M / Mercury 4973252*	31	4

[1] Sting with Eric Clapton [2] Bryan Adams, Rod Stewart and Sting [3] Sting featuring Pato Banton [4] Pato Banton with Sting [5] Sting and The Police [6] Sting featuring Cheb Mami

Tracks on Live at TFI Friday (EP): You Still Touch Me / Lithium Sunset / Message in a Bottle

STINGERS – *See B BUMBLE and the STINGERS*

Byron STINGILY *US, male vocalist (14 WEEKS)*
			pos/wks
25 Jan 97	GET UP (EVERYBODY) *Manifesto FESCD 19*	14	5
1 Nov 97	SING A SONG *Manifesto FESCD 35*	38	2
31 Jan 98	YOU MAKE ME FEEL (MIGHTY REAL) *Manifesto FESCD 38*	13	4
13 Jun 98	TESTIFY *Manifesto FESCD 42*	48	1
12 Feb 00	THAT'S THE WAY LOVE IS *Manifesto FESCD 66*	32	2

STINX *UK, female vocal duo (3 WEEKS)*
			pos/wks
24 Mar 01	WHY DO YOU KEEP ON RUNNING *HEBS HEBS 1*	49	3

STIX 'N' STONED *UK, male instrumental / production duo – Julius O'Riodan and Jon Kelly (2 WEEKS)*
			pos/wks
20 Jul 96	OUTRAGEOUS *Positiva CDTIV 52*	39	2

Catherine STOCK *UK, female vocalist (6 WEEKS)*
			pos/wks
18 Oct 86	TO HAVE AND TO HOLD *Sierra FED 29*	17	6

STOCK AITKEN WATERMAN *UK, male producers (36 WEEKS)*
			pos/wks
25 Jul 87	ROADBLOCK *Breakout USA 611*	13	9
24 Oct 87 ●	MR SLEAZE *London NANA14*	3	10
12 Dec 87	PACKJAMMED (WITH THE PARTY POSSE) *Breakout USA 620*	41	6
21 May 88	ALL THE WAY *MCA GOAL 1* [1]	64	2
3 Dec 88	SS PAPARAZZI *PWL PWL 22*	68	2
20 May 89 ★	FERRY 'CROSS THE MERSEY *PWL PWL 41* [2] ■	1	7

[1] England Football Team and the 'sound' of Stock, Aitken and Waterman
[2] Christians, Holly Johnson, Paul McCartney, Gerry Marsden and Stock Aitken Waterman

The listed flip side of 'Mr Sleaze' was 'Love in the First Degree' by Bananarama

See also 2 IN A TENT

Miriam STOCKLEY – *See PRAISE; ATLANTIS vs AVATAR*

Rhet STOLLER *UK, male instrumentalist – guitar (8 WEEKS)*
			pos/wks
12 Jan 61	CHARIOT *Decca F 11302*	26	8

Morris STOLOFF *US, orchestra, leader d. 16 Apr 1980 (11 WEEKS)*
			pos/wks
1 Jun 56 ●	MOONGLOW AND THE THEME FROM 'PICNIC' *Brunswick 05553*	7	11

Angie STONE *US, female vocalist (11 WEEKS)*
			pos/wks
15 Apr 00	LIFE STORY *Arista 74321748492*	22	3
16 Dec 00	KEEP YOUR WORRIES *Virgin VUSCD 177* [1]	57	1
9 Mar 02	BROTHA PART II *J 74321922142* [2]	37	2
27 Jul 02	WISH I DIDN'T MISS YOU *J 74321939182*	30	5

[1] Guru's Jazzmatazz featuring Angie Stone [2] Angie Stone featuring Alicia Keys and Eve

R & J STONE *UK / US, male / female vocal duo – Russell and Joanne Stone (9 WEEKS)*
			pos/wks
10 Jan 76 ●	WE DO IT *RCA 2616*	5	9

STONE ROSES (459) [Top 500]
'Madchester', 'Baggy' pioneers who successfully combined rock guitar and acid house attitude, inspiring a massive return to guitar-based bands in northern Britain in the 90s. Ian Brown (v), John Squire (g), Mani (aka Gary Mountfield) (b), Reni (aka Alan Wren) (d/v), all from Manchester. Their eponymous debut album, which peaked no higher than No.19 in 1989, continues to register in the top five of best all-time album surveys (77 WEEKS)

			pos/wks
29 Jul 89	SHE BANGS THE DRUMS (re) *Silvertone ORE 6*	34	6
25 Nov 89 ●	WHAT THE WORLD IS WAITING FOR / FOOL'S GOLD (re) *Silvertone ORE 13*	8	19
6 Jan 90	SALLY CINNAMON (re) *Revolver REV 36*	46	5
3 Mar 90 ●	ELEPHANT STONE *Silvertone ORE 1*	8	6
17 Mar 90	MADE OF STONE *Silvertone ORE 2*	20	4
14 Jul 90 ●	ONE LOVE *Silvertone ORE 17*	4	7
14 Sep 91	I WANNA BE ADORED *Silvertone ORE 31*	20	3
11 Jan 92	WATERFALL *Silvertone ORE 35*	27	4
11 Apr 92	I AM THE RESURRECTION *Silvertone ORE 40*	33	2
30 May 92	FOOL'S GOLD (re-issue) *Silvertone ORET 13*	73	1
3 Dec 94 ●	LOVE SPREADS *Geffen GFSTD 84*	2	8
11 Mar 95	TEN STOREY LOVE SONG *Geffen GFSTD 87*	11	3
29 Apr 95	FOOL'S GOLD (2nd re-issue) *Silvertone ORECD 71*	25	3
11 Nov 95	BEGGING YOU *Geffen GFSTD 22060*	15	3
6 Mar 99	FOOL'S GOLD (re-mix) *Jive Electro 0523092*	25	3

'She Bangs the Drums' made No.36 on its chart debut and reached its peak position only on re-entry in Mar 1990. 'What the World Is Waiting For' / 'Fool's Gold' made No.22 on re-entry in Sep 1990

See also Ian BROWN; SEAHORSES; John SQUIRE

STONE TEMPLE PILOTS
US, male vocal / instrumental group (11 WEEKS)
			pos/wks
27 Mar 93	SEX TYPE THING *Atlantic A 5769CD*	60	2
4 Sep 93	PLUSH *Atlantic A 7349CD*	23	4
27 Nov 93	SEX TYPE THING (re-issue) *Atlantic A 7293CD*	55	2
20 Aug 94	VASOLINE *Atlantic A 5650CD*	48	2
10 Dec 94	INTERSTATE LOVE SONG *Atlantic A 7192CD*	53	1

STONEBRIDGE McGUINNESS
UK, male vocal / instrumental duo (2 WEEKS)
			pos/wks
14 Jul 79	OO-EEH BABY *RCA PB 5163*	54	2

STONEFREE *UK, male vocalist (1 WEEK)*
			pos/wks
23 May 87	CAN'T SAY 'BYE *Ensign ENY 607*	73	1

STONEPROOF
UK, male producer – John Graham (1 WEEK)
			pos/wks
15 May 99	EVERYTHING'S NOT YOU *VC Recordings VCRD 47*	68	1

STONKERS – *See HALE and PACE and the STONKERS*

STOP THE VIOLENCE MOVEMENT
US, male / female rap charity ensemble (1 WEEK)
			pos/wks
18 Feb 89	SELF DESTRUCTION *Jive BDPST 1*	75	1

Axel STORDAHL – *See June HUTTON*

STORM
UK, male / female vocal / instrumental group (10 WEEKS)
			pos/wks
17 Nov 79	IT'S MY HOUSE *Scope SC 10*	36	10

STORM *Germany, male production duo – Rolf Ellmer and Markus Löffel (19 WEEKS)*
			pos/wks
29 Aug 98	STORM *Positiva CDTIV 94*	32	2
12 Aug 00 ●	TIME TO BURN *Data DATA 16CDS*	3	10
23 Dec 00	STORM ANIMAL *Data DATA 20CDS*	21	5
26 May 01	STORM (re-mix) *Positiva CDTIV 154*	32	2

See also TOKYO GHETTO PUSSY; JAM & SPOON featuring PLAVKA; DANCE 2 TRANCE

UK No.1 ★ UK Top 10 ● Still on chart + UK million seller ◆ UK entry at No.1 ■ US No.1 ▲

Danny STORM UK, male vocalist (4 WEEKS)

		pos/wks
12 Apr 62	HONEST I DO *Piccadilly 7N 35025*	42 4

Rebecca STORM UK, female vocalist (13 WEEKS)

		pos/wks
13 Jul 85	THE SHOW (THEME FROM 'CONNIE') *Towerbell TVP 3*	22 13

STORYVILLE JAZZ BAND – See Bob WALLIS and his STORYVILLE JAZZ BAND

Izzy STRADLIN'
US, male vocalist / instrumentalist – guitar (2 WEEKS)

		pos/wks
26 Sep 92	PRESSURE DROP *Geffen GFS 25*	45 2

See also GUNS N' ROSES

Nick STRAKER BAND
UK, male vocal / instrumental group (15 WEEKS)

		pos/wks
2 Aug 80	A WALK IN THE PARK *CBS 8525*	20 12
15 Nov 80	LEAVING ON THE MIDNIGHT TRAIN *CBS 9088*	61 3

Peter STRAKER and the HANDS OF DR TELENY
UK, male vocalist and male vocal / instrumental group (4 WEEKS)

		pos/wks
19 Feb 72	THE SPIRIT IS WILLING *RCA 2163*	40 4

STRANGE BEHAVIOUR – See Jane KENNAWAY and STRANGE BEHAVIOUR

STRANGE FRUIT – See Jimmy NAIL

STRANGELOVE UK, male vocal / instrumental group (8 WEEKS)

		pos/wks
20 Apr 96	LIVING WITH THE HUMAN MACHINES *Food CDFOOD 70*	53 1
15 Jun 96	BEAUTIFUL ALONE *Food CDFOOD 81*	35 2
19 Oct 96	SWAY *Food CDFOOD 82*	47 1
26 Jul 97	THE GREATEST SHOW ON EARTH *Food CDFOODS 97*	36 2
11 Oct 97	FREAK *Food CDFOOD 105*	43 1
21 Feb 98	ANOTHER NIGHT IN *Food CDFOOD 110*	46 1

STRANGLERS 97 Top 500

One of the most commercially successful and long-lasting group to emerge from the punk / new wave scene: Hugh Cornwell (v/g), Jean-Jacques Burnel (b/v), Dave Greenfield (k), Jet Black (d). This London-based band had at least one hit every year between 1977 and 1992 (194 WEEKS)

		pos/wks
19 Feb 77	(GET A) GRIP (ON YOURSELF) *United Artists UP 36211*	44 4
21 May 77	● PEACHES / GO BUDDY GO *United Artists UP 36248*	8 14
30 Jul 77	● SOMETHING BETTER CHANGE / STRAIGHTEN OUT *United Artists UP 36277*	9 8
24 Sep 77	● NO MORE HEROES *United Artists UP 36300*	8 9
4 Feb 78	5 MINUTES *United Artists UP 36350*	11 9
6 May 78	NICE 'N' SLEAZY *United Artists UP 36379*	18 8
12 Aug 78	WALK ON BY *United Artists UP 36429*	21 8
18 Aug 79	DUCHESS *United Artists BP 308*	14 9
20 Oct 79	NUCLEAR DEVICE (THE WIZARD OF AUS) *United Artists BP 318*	36 4
1 Dec 79	DON'T BRING HARRY (EP) *United Artists STR 1*	41 3
22 Mar 80	BEAR CAGE *United Artists BP 344*	36 5
7 Jun 80	WHO WANTS THE WORLD *United Artists BP 355*	39 4
31 Jan 81	THROWN AWAY *Liberty BP 383*	42 4
14 Nov 81	LET ME INTRODUCE YOU TO THE FAMILY *Liberty BP 405*	42 3
9 Jan 82	● GOLDEN BROWN *Liberty BP 407*	2 12
24 Apr 82	LA FOLIE *Liberty BP 410*	47 3
24 Jul 82	● STRANGE LITTLE GIRL *Liberty BP 412*	7 9
8 Jan 83	● EUROPEAN FEMALE *Epic EPC A 2893*	9 6
26 Feb 83	MIDNIGHT SUMMER DREAM *Epic EPC A 3167*	35 4
6 Aug 83	PARADISE *Epic A 3387*	48 3
6 Oct 84	SKIN DEEP *Epic A 4738*	15 7
1 Dec 84	NO MERCY *Epic A 4921*	37 7
16 Feb 85	LET ME DOWN EASY *Epic A 6045*	48 4
23 Aug 86	NICE IN NICE *Epic 6500557*	30 5
18 Oct 86	ALWAYS THE SUN *Epic SOLAR 1*	30 5
13 Dec 86	BIG IN AMERICA *Epic HUGE 1*	48 4
7 Mar 87	SHAKIN' LIKE A LEAF *Epic SHEIK 1*	58 4
9 Jan 88	● ALL DAY AND ALL OF THE NIGHT *Epic VICE 1*	7 7

		pos/wks
28 Jan 89	GRIP '89 (GET A) GRIP (ON YOURSELF) (re-mix) *EMI EM 84*	33 3
17 Feb 90	96 TEARS *Epic TEARS 1*	17 6
21 Apr 90	SWEET SMELL OF SUCCESS *Epic TEARS 2*	65 2
5 Jan 91	ALWAYS THE SUN (re-mix) *Epic 6564307*	29 5
30 Mar 91	GOLDEN BROWN (re-mix) *Epic 6567617*	68 2
22 Aug 92	HEAVEN OR HELL *Psycho WOK 2025*	46 2

'Go Buddy Go' credited with 'Peaches' from 11 Jun 1977. 'Straighten Out' credited with 'Something Better Change' from 13 Aug 1977. Tracks on Don't Bring Harry (EP): Don't Bring Harry / Wired / Crabs (Live) / In the Shadows (Live)

STRAW UK, male vocal / instrumental group (4 WEEKS)

		pos/wks
6 Feb 99	THE AEROPLANE SONG *WEA WEA 196CD*	37 2
24 Apr 99	MOVING TO CALIFORNIA *WEA WEA 205CD1*	50 1
3 Mar 01	SAILING OFF THE EDGE OF THE WORLD *Columbia 6708452*	52 1

STRAWBERRY SWITCHBLADE
UK, female vocal duo – Rose McDowell and Jill Bryson (26 WEEKS)

		pos/wks
17 Nov 84	● SINCE YESTERDAY *Korova KOW 38*	5 17
23 Mar 85	LET HER GO *Korova KOW 39*	59 5
21 Sep 85	JOLENE *Korova KOW 42*	53 4

STRAWBS UK, male vocal / instrumental group (27 WEEKS)

		pos/wks
28 Oct 72	LAY DOWN *A&M AMS 7035*	12 13
27 Jan 73	● PART OF THE UNION *A&M AMS 7047*	2 11
6 Oct 73	SHINE ON SILVER SUN *A&M AMS 7082*	34 3

STRAY CATS US, male vocal / instrumental group (49 WEEKS)

		pos/wks
29 Nov 80	● RUNAWAY BOYS *Arista SCAT 1*	9 10
7 Feb 81	● ROCK THIS TOWN *Arista SCAT 2*	9 8
25 Apr 81	STRAY CAT STRUT *Arista SCAT 3*	11 10
20 Jun 81	THE RACE IS ON *Swansong SSK 19425* 1	34 6
7 Nov 81	YOU DON'T BELIEVE ME *Arista SCAT 4*	57 3
6 Aug 83	(SHE'S) SEXY AND 17 *Arista SCAT 6*	29 9
4 Mar 89	BRING IT BACK AGAIN *EMI USA MT 62*	64 3

1 Dave Edmunds and The Stray Cats

STRAY MOB – See MC SKAT KAT and the STRAY MOB

STREETBAND UK, male vocal / instrumental group (6 WEEKS)

		pos/wks
4 Nov 78	TOAST / HOLD ON *Logo GO 325*	18 6

See also Paul YOUNG

The STREETS UK, male producer – Mick Skinner (14 WEEKS)

		pos/wks
20 Oct 01	HAS IT COME TO THIS (re) *WEA / 679 L 001*	18 5
27 Apr 02	LET'S PUSH THINGS FORWARD *Locked On / 679 Recordings 679L 005CD*	30 3
3 Aug 02	WEAK BECOME HEROES *Locked On / 679 Recordings 679L 007CD*	27 3
2 Nov 02	DON'T MUG YOURSELF *Locked On / 679 Recordings 679L 008CDX*	21 3

Barbra STREISAND 142 Top 500

Acclaimed song stylist who has more gold albums than any other female, b. 24 Apr 1942, Brooklyn, US. This world-renowned MOR vocalist / actress has collected countless awards for her recordings and her stage and film work, and is a recipient of both Grammy Living Legend and Lifetime Achievement awards (155 WEEKS)

		pos/wks
20 Jan 66	SECOND HAND ROSE *CBS 202025*	14 13
30 Jan 71	STONEY END (re) *CBS 5321*	27 11
30 Mar 74	THE WAY WE WERE *CBS 1915* ▲	31 6
9 Apr 77	● LOVE THEME FROM 'A STAR IS BORN' (EVERGREEN) *CBS 4855* ▲	3 19
25 Nov 78	● YOU DON'T BRING ME FLOWERS *CBS 6803* 1 ▲	5 13
3 Nov 79	● NO MORE TEARS (ENOUGH IS ENOUGH) *Casablanca CAN 174/ CBS 8000* 2 ▲	3 13
4 Oct 80	★ WOMAN IN LOVE *CBS 8966* ▲	1 16
6 Dec 80	GUILTY *CBS 9315* 3	34 10
30 Jan 82	COMIN' IN AND OUT OF YOUR LIFE *CBS A 1789*	66 3

Re-entries are listed as (re), (2re), (3re), etc which signifies that the hit re-entered the chart once, twice, ...

20 Mar 82	**MEMORY** *CBS A 1903*	34	6
5 Nov 88	**TILL I LOVED YOU (LOVE THEME FROM 'GOYA')** *CBS BARB 2* [4]	16	7
7 Mar 92	**PLACES THAT BELONG TO YOU** *Columbia 6577947*	17	5
5 Jun 93	**WITH ONE LOOK** *Columbia 6593422*	30	3
15 Jan 94	**THE MUSIC OF THE NIGHT** *Columbia 6597382* [5]	54	3
30 Apr 94	**AS IF WE NEVER SAID GOODBYE** *Columbia 6603572*	20	3
8 Feb 97 ●	**I FINALLY FOUND SOMEONE** *A&M 5820832* [6]	10	7
15 Nov 97 ●	**TELL HIM** *Epic 6653052* [7]	3	15
30 Oct 99	**IF YOU EVER LEAVE ME** *Columbia 6681242* [8]	26	3

[1] Barbra and Neil [2] Donna Summer and Barbra Streisand [3] Barbra Streisand and Barry Gibb [4] Barbra Streisand and Don Johnson [5] Barbra Streisand (duet with Michael Crawford) [6] Barbra Streisand and Bryan Adams [7] Barbra Streisand and Celine Dion [8] Barbra Streisand / Vince Gill

Neil was Neil Diamond. 'No More Tears (Enough Is Enough)' was released simultaneously on two different labels, a seven-inch single on Casablanca and a 12-inch on CBS

STRESS *UK, male vocal / instrumental group (1 WEEK)* pos/wks
13 Oct 90	**BEAUTIFUL PEOPLE** *Eternal YZ 495*	74	1

STRETCH *UK, male vocal / instrumental group (9 WEEKS)* pos/wks
8 Nov 75	**WHY DID YOU DO IT** *Anchor ANC 1021*	16	9

STRETCH 'N' VERN present MADDOG *UK, male instrumental / production duo – Stuart Collins and Julian Peake (14 WEEKS)* pos/wks
14 Sep 96 ●	**I'M ALIVE** *ffrr FCD 284*	6	9
9 Aug 97	**GET UP! GO INSANE!** *ffrr FCD 304*	17	5

STRICT INSTRUCTOR *Russia, female vocalist (1 WEEK)* pos/wks
24 Oct 98	**STEP-TWO-THREE-FOUR** *All Around the World CDGLOBE 155*	49	1

STRIKE *UK / Australia, male / female vocal / instrumental group (24 WEEKS)* pos/wks
24 Dec 94 ●	**U SURE DO (re)** *Fresh FRSHD 19*	4	14
23 Sep 95	**THE MORNING AFTER (FREE AT LAST)** *Fresh FRSHD 37* ...	38	3
29 Jun 96	**INSPIRATION** *Fresh FRSHD 45*	27	2
16 Nov 96	**MY LOVE IS FOR REAL** *Fresh FRSHD 46*	35	2
31 May 97	**I HAVE PEACE** *Fresh FRSHCD 58*	17	4
25 Sep 99	**U SURE DO (re-mix)** *Fresh FRSHD 78*	53	1

'U Sure Do' debuted at No.31 and made its peak position only on re-entry in Apr 1995

STRIKERS *US, male vocal / instrumental group (5 WEEKS)* pos/wks
6 Jun 81	**BODY MUSIC** *Epic EPC A 1290*	45	5

STRING-A-LONGS *US, male instrumental group (16 WEEKS)* pos/wks
23 Feb 61 ●	**WHEELS** *London HLU 9278*	8	16

STRINGS OF LOVE *Italy, male / female vocal / instrumental group (2 WEEKS)* pos/wks
3 Mar 90	**NOTHING HAS BEEN PROVED** *Breakout USA 688*	59	2

The STROKES *US, male vocal / instrumental group (14 WEEKS)* pos/wks
7 Jul 01	**HARD TO EXPLAIN / NEW YORK CITY COPS** *Rough Trade RTRADESCD 023*	16	5
7 Jul 01	**MODERN AGE (2re)** *Rough Trade RTRADESCD 010*	68	3
17 Nov 01	**LAST NITE** *Rough Trade RTRADESCD 041*	14	5
5 Oct 02	**SOMEDAY** *Rough Trade RTRADESCD 063*	27	1

Modern Age is a three-track CD featuring 'Modern Age', 'Last Nite' and 'Barely Legal'. RTRADESCD 041 is a re-recording of the track on 'Modern Age'

Joe STRUMMER *UK, male vocalist – John Mellor (d. 23 Dec 2002) (13 WEEKS)* pos/wks
2 Aug 86	**LOVE KILLS** *CBS A 7244*	69	1

23 Dec 95	**JUST THE ONE** *China WOKCD 2076* [1]	12	8
29 Jun 96 ●	**ENGLAND'S IRIE** *Radioactive RAXTD 25* [2]	6	4

[1] Levellers, special guest Joe Strummer [2] Black Grape featuring Joe Strummer and Keith Allen

See also CLASH

STRYKER – See MANCHESTER UNITED FOOTBALL CLUB

Chad STUART and Jeremy CLYDE *UK, male vocal duo (7 WEEKS)* pos/wks
28 Nov 63	**YESTERDAY'S GONE** *Ember EMB S 180*	37	7

STUDIO 45 *Germany, male DJ / production duo – Tilo Cielsa and Jens Brachvogel (2 WEEKS)* pos/wks
20 Feb 99	**FREAK IT!** *Azuli AZNYCD 090*	36	2

STUDIO 2 *Jamaica, male vocalist – Errol Jones (1 WEEK)* pos/wks
27 Jun 98	**TRAVELLING MAN** *Multiply CDMULTY 35*	40	1

Amy STUDT *UK, female vocalist (6 WEEKS)* pos/wks
13 Jul 02	**JUST A LITTLE GIRL** *Polydor 5708802*	14	6

STUMP *UK, male vocal / instrumental group (1 WEEK)* pos/wks
13 Aug 88	**CHARLTON HESTON** *Ensign ENY 614*	72	1

STUNTMASTERZ *UK, male production duo – Steve Harris and Pete Cook (9 WEEKS)* pos/wks
3 Mar 01 ●	**THE LADYBOY IS MINE** *East West EW 226CD*	10	9

STUTZ BEARCATS and the Denis KING ORCHESTRA *UK, male / female vocal group with orchestra (6 WEEKS)* pos/wks
24 Apr 82	**THE SONG THAT I SING (THEME FROM 'WE'LL MEET AGAIN')** *Multi-Media Tapes MMT 6*	36	6

STYLE COUNCIL 303 Top 500
Eighties chart regulars: Paul Weller (v/g), Mick Talbot (k) and sometimes Dee C Lee (v – former Wham! backing vocalist and Weller's wife). As with Weller's previous band, The Jam, most of this London act's hits were in their homeland (103 WEEKS) pos/wks
19 Mar 83 ●	**SPEAK LIKE A CHILD** *Polydor TSC 1*	4	8
28 May 83	**MONEY GO ROUND (PART 1) (re)** *Polydor TSC 2* ...	11	7
13 Aug 83 ●	**LONG HOT SUMMER** *Polydor TSC 3*	3	9
19 Nov 83	**SOLID BOND IN YOUR HEART** *Polydor TSC 4*	11	8
18 Feb 84 ●	**MY EVER CHANGING MOODS** *Polydor TSC 5*	5	7
26 May 84 ●	**GROOVIN' (YOU'RE THE BEST THING / THE BIG BOSS GROOVE)** *Polydor TSC 6*	5	8
13 Oct 84 ●	**SHOUT TO THE TOP** *Polydor TSC 7*	7	8
11 May 85 ●	**WALLS COME TUMBLING DOWN!** *Polydor TSC 8*	6	7
6 Jul 85	**COME TO MILTON KEYNES** *Polydor TSC 9*	23	5
28 Sep 85	**THE LODGERS** *Polydor TSC 10*	13	6
5 Apr 86	**HAVE YOU EVER HAD IT BLUE** *Polydor CINE 1*	14	6
17 Jan 87 ●	**IT DIDN'T MATTER** *Polydor TSC 12*	9	5
14 Mar 87	**WAITING** *Polydor TSC 13*	52	3
31 Oct 87	**WANTED** *Polydor TSC 14*	20	4
28 May 88	**LIFE AT A TOP PEOPLE'S HEALTH FARM** *Polydor TSC 15*	28	3
23 Jul 88	**HOW SHE THREW IT ALL AWAY (EP)** *Polydor TSC 16* ..	41	2
18 Feb 89	**PROMISED LAND** *Polydor TSC 17*	27	5
27 May 89	**LONG HOT SUMMER 89 (re-mix)** *Polydor LHS 1* ...	48	2

'Paris Match' was listed with 'Long Hot Summer' from 3 Sep 1983. It peaked at No.7. Tracks on How She Threw It All Away (EP): How She Threw It All Away / Love the First Time / Long Hot Summer / I Do Like to Be B-Side the A-Side. The 1989 remix version of 'Long Hot Summer' on the EP is a re-recording of their third hit from 1983

STYLES & Pharoahe MONCH *US, male rappers (1 WEEK)* pos/wks
14 Sep 02	**THE LIFE** *MCA MCSTD 40292*	60	1

STYLISTICS `171` `Top 500`

Stylish and smooth vocal group from Philadelphia, US, fronted by falsetto-voiced Russell Thompkins Jr (b. 21 Mar 1951), whose UK hits continued after success in their homeland diminished. The quintet's Greatest Hits album topped the UK album chart in 1975 (143 WEEKS) pos/wks

24 Jun 72	BETCHA BY GOLLY WOW *Avco 6105 011*	13 12
4 Nov 72 ●	I'M STONE IN LOVE WITH YOU *Avco 6105 015*	9 10
17 Mar 73	BREAK UP TO MAKE UP *Avco 6105 020*	34 5
30 Jun 73	PEEK-A-BOO *Avco 6105 023*	35 6
19 Jan 74 ●	ROCKIN' ROLL BABY *Avco 6105 026*	6 9
13 Jul 74	YOU MAKE ME FEEL BRAND NEW *Avco 6105 028*	2 14
19 Oct 74 ●	LET'S PUT IT ALL TOGETHER *Avco 6105 032*	9 9
25 Jan 75	STAR ON A TV SHOW *Avco 6105 035*	12 8
10 May 75 ●	SING BABY SING *Avco 6105 036*	3 10
26 Jul 75 ★	CAN'T GIVE YOU ANYTHING (BUT MY LOVE) *Avco 6105 039*	1 11
15 Nov 75 ●	NA-NA IS THE SADDEST WORD *Avco 6105 041*	5 10
14 Feb 76 ●	FUNKY WEEKEND *Avco 6105 044*	10 7
24 Apr 76 ●	CAN'T HELP FALLING IN LOVE *H & L 6105 050*	4 7
7 Aug 76 ●	SIXTEEN BARS *H & L 6105 059*	7 9
27 Nov 76	YOU'LL NEVER GET TO HEAVEN (EP) *H & L STYL 001*	24 9
26 Mar 77	$7000 AND YOU *H & L 6105 073*	24 7

Tracks on You'll Never Get to Heaven (EP): You'll Never Get to Heaven / Country Living / You Are Beautiful / The Miracle

STYLUS TROUBLE *UK, male producer – Pete Heller (1 WEEK)* pos/wks

23 Jun 01	SPUTNIK *Junior London BRG 014*	63 1

See also HELLER & FARLEY PROJECT; Pete HELLER; FIRE ISLAND

STYX *US, male vocal / instrumental group (18 WEEKS)* pos/wks

5 Jan 80 ●	BABE *A&M AMS 7489* ▲	6 10
24 Jan 81	THE BEST OF TIMES *A&M AMS 8102*	42 5
18 Jun 83	DON'T LET IT END *A&M AM 120*	56 3

SUB SUB *UK, male instrumental / production group (12 WEEKS)* pos/wks

10 Apr 93 ●	AIN'T NO LOVE (AIN'T NO USE) *Rob's CDROB 9* `1`	3 11
19 Feb 94	RESPECT *Rob's CDROB 19*	49 1

`1` Sub Sub featuring Melanie Williams

SUBCIRCUS
Denmark / UK, male vocal / instrumental group (2 WEEKS) pos/wks

26 Apr 97	YOU LOVE YOU *Echo ECSCD 34*	61 1
12 Jul 97	86'D *Echo ECSCX 43*	56 1

SUBLIME *US, male vocal / instrumental group (1 WEEK)* pos/wks

5 Jul 97	WHAT I GOT *Gasoline Alley MCSTD 48045*	71 1

SUBLIMINAL CUTS
Holland, male producer – Patrick Prinz (3 WEEKS) pos/wks

15 Oct 94	LE VOIE LE SOLEIL *XL XLS 53CD*	69 1
20 Jul 96	LE VOIE LE SOLEIL (re-mix) *XL XLSR 53CD*	23 2

See also ARTEMESIA; ETHICS; MOVIN' MELODIES

SUBMERGE featuring Jan JOHNSTON *US, male producer / instrumentalist – Victor Imbres – and US, female vocalist (2 WEEKS)* pos/wks

8 Feb 97	TAKE ME BY THE HAND *AM:PM 5821012*	28 2

SUBSONIC 2 *UK, male rap duo (3 WEEKS)* pos/wks

13 Jul 91	THE UNSUNG HEROES OF HIP HOP *Unity 6577947*	63 3

SUBTERRANIA featuring Ann CONSUELO
Sweden, male / female vocal / instrumental duo (1 WEEK) pos/wks

5 Jun 93	DO IT FOR LOVE *Champion CHAMPCD 297*	68 1

SUEDE *UK, male vocal / instrumental group (72 WEEKS)* pos/wks

23 May 92	THE DROWNERS / TO THE BIRDS *Nude NUD 1S*	49 2

26 Sep 92	METAL MICKEY *Nude NUD 3S*	17 3
6 Mar 93 ●	ANIMAL NITRATE *Nude NUD 4CD*	7 7
29 May 93	SO YOUNG *Nude NUD 5CD*	22 3
26 Feb 94 ●	STAY TOGETHER *Nude NUD 9CD*	3 6
24 Sep 94	WE ARE THE PIGS *Nude NUD 10CD*	18 3
19 Nov 94	THE WILD ONES *Nude NUD 11CD*	18 4
11 Feb 95	NEW GENERATION (re) *Nude NUD 12CD1*	21 4
10 Aug 96 ●	TRASH *Nude NUD 21CD1*	3 6
26 Oct 96 ●	BEAUTIFUL ONES *Nude NUD 23CD1*	8 5
25 Jan 97 ●	SATURDAY NIGHT *Nude NUD 24CD1*	6 4
19 Apr 97 ●	LAZY *Nude NUD 27CD1*	9 4
23 Aug 97 ●	FILMSTAR *Nude NUD 30CD1*	9 4
24 Apr 99 ●	ELECTRICITY *Nude NUD 43CD1*	5 5
3 Jul 99	SHE'S IN FASHION *Nude NUD 44CD1*	13 5
18 Sep 99	EVERYTHING WILL FLOW *Nude NUD 45CD1*	24 2
20 Nov 99	CAN'T GET ENOUGH *Nude NUD 47CD1*	23 2
28 Sep 02	POSITIVITY *Epic 6729492*	16 2
30 Nov 02	OBSESSIONS *Epic 6732942*	29 2

SUENO LATINO *Italy, male production duo (6 WEEKS)* pos/wks

23 Sep 89	SUENO LATINO *BCM BCM 323* `1`	47 5
11 Nov 00	SUENO LATINO (re-mix) *Distinctive DISNCD 64*	68 1

`1` Sueno Latino featuring Carolina Damas

SUGABABES *UK, female vocal trio (59 WEEKS)* pos/wks

23 Sep 00 ●	OVERLOAD *London LONCD 449*	6 8
30 Dec 00	NEW YEAR *London LONCD 455*	12 9
21 Apr 01	RUN FOR COVER *London LONCD 459*	13 7
28 Jul 01	SOUL SOUND *London LONCD 460*	30 2
4 May 02 ★	FREAK LIKE ME (re) *Island CID 798* ■	1 14
24 Aug 02 ★	ROUND ROUND *Island CID 804* ■	1 13
23 Nov 02 ●	STRONGER / ANGELS WITH DIRTY FACES *Island CID 813*	7 6+

SUGAR *US, male vocal / instrumental group (7 WEEKS)* pos/wks

31 Oct 92	A GOOD IDEA *Creation CRE 143*	65 1
30 Jan 93	IF I CAN'T CHANGE YOUR MIND *Creation CRESCD 149*	30 2
21 Aug 93	TILTED *Creation CRECD 156*	48 1
3 Sep 94	YOUR FAVORITE THING *Creation CRESCD 186*	40 2
29 Oct 94	BELIEVE WHAT YOU'RE SAYING *Creation CRESCD 193*	73 1

SUGAR CANE *US, male / female vocal group (5 WEEKS)* pos/wks

30 Sep 78	MONTEGO BAY *Ariola Hansa AHA 524*	54 5

SUGAR RAY *US, male vocal / instrumental group (12 WEEKS)* pos/wks

31 Jan 98	FLY *Atlantic AT 0008CD*	58 1
29 May 99 ●	EVERY MORNING *Lava / Atlantic AT 0065CD*	10 9
20 Oct 01	WHEN IT'S OVER *Atlantic AT 0114CD*	32 2

SUGARCOMA
UK, male / female vocal / instrumental group (1 WEEK) pos/wks

13 Apr 02	YOU DRIVE ME CRAZY / WINDINGS *Music For Nations CDKUT 190*	57 1

SUGARCUBES
Iceland, female / male vocal / instrumental group (22 WEEKS) pos/wks

14 Nov 87	BIRTHDAY *One Little Indian 7TP 7*	65 3
30 Jan 88	COLD SWEAT *One Little Indian 7TP 9*	56 4
16 Apr 88	DEUS *One Little Indian 7TP 10*	51 3
3 Sep 88	BIRTHDAY (re-recording) *One Little Indian 7TP 11*	65 3
16 Sep 89	REGINA *One Little Indian 26TP7*	55 2
11 Jan 92	HIT *One Little Indian 62 TP7*	17 6
3 Oct 92	BIRTHDAY (re-mix) *One Little Indian 104 TP12*	64 1

See also BJÖRK

SUGARHILL GANG *US, male rap group (16 WEEKS)* pos/wks

1 Dec 79 ●	RAPPER'S DELIGHT *Sugarhill SHL 101*	3 11
11 Sep 82	THE LOVER IN YOU *Sugarhill SH 116*	54 3
25 Nov 89	RAPPER'S DELIGHT (re-mix) *Sugarhill SHRD 0007*	58 2

Re-entries are listed as (re), (2re), (3re), etc which signifies that the hit re-entered the chart once, twice or three times, etc

SUGGS
UK, male vocalist – Graham McPherson (46 WEEKS) pos/wks

12 Aug 95	●	I'M ONLY SLEEPING / OFF ON HOLIDAY *WEA YZ 975CD*	7 6
14 Oct 95		CAMDEN TOWN *WEA WEA 019CD*	14 6
16 Dec 95		THE TUNE *WEA WEA 031CD*	33 3
13 Apr 96	●	CECILIA (2re) *WEA WEA 042CD1* [1]	4 19
21 Sep 96		NO MORE ALCOHOL *WEA WEA 065CD1* [1]	24 4
17 May 97		BLUE DAY *WEA WEA 112CD* [2]	22 5
5 Sep 98		I AM *WEA WEA 174CD*	38 3

[1] Suggs featuring Louchie Lou and Michie One [2] Suggs & Co featuring Chelsea Team

See also MADNESS

Justine SUISSA – See OCEANLAB featuring Justine SUISSA

SULTANA
Italy, male instrumental / production group (1 WEEK) pos/wks

26 Mar 94		TE AMO *Union City UCRD 28*	57 1

SULTANS OF PING
Ireland, male vocal / instrumental group (12 WEEKS) pos/wks

8 Feb 92		WHERE'S ME JUMPER? *Divine ATHY 01* [1]	67 2
9 May 92		STUPID KID *Divine ATHY 02* [1]	67 1
10 Oct 92		VERONICA *Divine ATHY 03* [1]	69 1
9 Jan 93		YOU TALK TOO MUCH *Rhythm King 6588872* [1]	26 3
11 Sep 93		TEENAGE PUNKS *Epic 6595792*	49 2
30 Oct 93		MICHIKO *Epic 6598222*	43 2
19 Feb 94		WAKE UP AND SCRATCH ME *Epic 6601122*	50 1

[1] Sultans of Ping FC

SUM 41
Canada, male vocal / instrumental group (35 WEEKS) pos/wks

13 Oct 01	●	FAT LIP *Mercury 5888012*	8 9
15 Dec 01		IN TOO DEEP *Mercury 5888982*	13 11
6 Apr 02		MOTIVATION *Mercury 5889452*	21 7
29 Jun 02		IT'S WHAT WE'RE ALL ABOUT *Columbia 6728642*	32 3
30 Nov 02		STILL WAITING *Mercury 0638312*	16 5+

SUMMER – See SNAP!

Donna SUMMER ⟨34⟩ ⟨Top 500⟩
"Queen of disco music", b. LaDonna Gaines, 31 Dec 1948, Massachusetts, US. Germany was the launching pad for this diva, who had eight successive US Top 5 singles in the late 1970s. She was also the first female to score three consecutive US No.1 albums (299 WEEKS) pos/wks

17 Jan 76	●	LOVE TO LOVE YOU BABY *GTO GT 17*	4 9
29 May 76		COULD IT BE MAGIC *GTO GT 60*	40 7
25 Dec 76		WINTER MELODY *GTO GT 76*	27 6
9 Jul 77	★	I FEEL LOVE *GTO GT 100*	1 11
20 Aug 77	●	DOWN DEEP INSIDE (THEME FROM 'THE DEEP') *Casablanca CAN 111*	5 10
24 Sep 77		I REMEMBER YESTERDAY *GTO GT 107*	14 7
3 Dec 77	●	LOVE'S UNKIND *GTO GT 113*	3 13
10 Dec 77	●	I LOVE YOU *Casablanca CAN 114*	10 9
25 Feb 78		RUMOUR HAS IT *Casablanca CAN 122*	19 8
22 Apr 78		BACK IN LOVE AGAIN *GTO GT 117*	29 7
10 Jun 78		LAST DANCE (re) *Casablanca TGIF 2*	51 9
14 Oct 78	●	MACARTHUR PARK *Casablanca CAN 131* ▲	5 10
17 Feb 79		HEAVEN KNOWS *Casablanca CAN 141*	34 8
12 May 79	●	HOT STUFF *Casablanca CAN 151* ▲	11 10
7 Jul 79		BAD GIRLS *Casablanca CAN 155* ▲	14 10
1 Sep 79		DIM ALL THE LIGHTS *Casablanca CAN 162*	29 9
3 Nov 79	●	NO MORE TEARS (ENOUGH IS ENOUGH) *Casablanca CAN 174 / CBS 8000* [1] ▲	3 13
16 Feb 80		ON THE RADIO *Casablanca NB 2236*	32 6
21 Jun 80		SUNSET PEOPLE *Casablanca CAN 198*	46 5
27 Sep 80		THE WANDERER *Geffen K 79180*	48 6
17 Jan 81		COLD LOVE *Geffen K 79193*	44 3
10 Jul 82		LOVE IS IN CONTROL (FINGER ON THE TRIGGER) *Warner Bros. K 79302*	18 11
6 Nov 82		STATE OF INDEPENDENCE *Warner Bros. K 79344*	14 11
4 Dec 82		I FEEL LOVE (re-mix) *Casablanca FEEL 7*	21 10

5 Mar 83		THE WOMAN IN ME *Warner Bros. U 9983*	62 2
18 Jun 83		SHE WORKS HARD FOR THE MONEY *Mercury DONNA 1*	25 8
24 Sep 83		UNCONDITIONAL LOVE *Mercury DONNA 2*	14 12
21 Jan 84		STOP LOOK AND LISTEN *Mercury DONNA 3*	57 2
24 Oct 87		DINNER WITH GERSHWIN *Warner Bros. U 8237*	13 11
23 Jan 88		ALL SYSTEMS GO *WEA U 8122*	54 3
25 Feb 89	●	THIS TIME I KNOW IT'S FOR REAL *Warner Bros. U 7780*	3 14
27 May 89	●	I DON'T WANNA GET HURT *Warner Bros. U 7567*	7 9
26 Aug 89		LOVE'S ABOUT TO CHANGE MY HEART *Warner Bros. U 7494*	20 6
25 Nov 89		WHEN LOVE TAKES OVER YOU *WEA U 7361*	72 1
17 Nov 90		STATE OF INDEPENDENCE (re-issue) *Warner Bros. U 2857*	45 3
12 Jan 91		BREAKAWAY *Warner Bros. U 3308*	49 4
30 Nov 91		WORK THAT MAGIC *Warner Bros. U 5937*	74 1
12 Nov 94		MELODY OF LOVE (WANNA BE LOVED) *Mercury MERCD 418*	21 3
9 Sep 95	●	I FEEL LOVE (re-recording) *Manifesto FESCD 1*	8 5
6 Apr 96		STATE OF INDEPENDENCE (re-mix) *Manifesto FESCD 7* [2]	13 5
11 Jul 98		CARRY ON *Almighty CDALMY 120* [3]	65 1
30 Oct 99		I WILL GO WITH YOU (CON TE PARTIRO) *Epic 6682092*	44 1

[1] Donna Summer and Barbra Streisand [2] Donna Summer featuring the All Star Choir [3] Donna Summer and Giorgio Moroder

'No More Tears (Enough Is Enough)' was released simultaneously on two different labels, a seven-inch single on Casablanca and a 12-inch on CBS. 'Unconditional Love' features the additional vocals of Musical Youth. 'I Feel Love' in 1995 is a re-recording

SUMMER DAZE
UK, male instrumental / production duo (1 WEEK) pos/wks

26 Oct 96		SAMBA MAGIC *VC VCRD 14*	61 1

Mark SUMMERS
UK, male producer (6 WEEKS) pos/wks

26 Jan 91		SUMMER'S MAGIC *Fourth & Broadway BRW 205*	27 6

See also SOUVLAKI

JD SUMNER – See Elvis PRESLEY

SUNBURST
UK, male producer – Matt Darey (1 WEEK) pos/wks

8 Jul 00		EYEBALL (EYEBALL PAUL'S THEME) *Virgin / EMI VTSCD 4*	48 1

See also MELT featuring Little Ms MARCIE; Matt DAREY; MDM

SUNDANCE – See DJ 'FAST' EDDIE

SUNDANCE
UK, male production duo – Nick Woolfson and Mark Shimmon (7 WEEKS) pos/wks

8 Nov 97		SUNDANCE *React CDREACT 109*	33 2
3 Oct 98		SUNDANCE '98 (re-mix) *React CDREACTX 136*	37 2
27 Feb 99		THE LIVING DREAM *React CDREACT 134*	56 1
5 Feb 00		WON'T LET THIS FEELING GO *Inferno CDFERN 23*	40 2

See also SHIMMON & WOOLFSON; SHIMON & Andy C

SUNDAYS
UK, male / female vocal / instrumental group (12 WKS) pos/wks

11 Feb 89		CAN'T BE SURE *Rough Trade RT 218*	45 5
3 Oct 92		GOODBYE *Parlophone R 6319*	27 2
20 Sep 97		SUMMERTIME *Parlophone CDRS 6475*	15 4
22 Nov 97		CRY *Parlophone CDR 6487*	43 1

SUNDRAGON
UK, male vocal / instrumental duo (1 WEEK) pos/wks

21 Feb 68		GREEN TAMBOURINE *MGM 1380*	50 1

SUNFIRE
US, male vocal / instrumental group (11 WEEKS) pos/wks

12 Mar 83		YOUNG, FREE AND SINGLE *Warner Bros. W 9897*	20 11

SUNKIDS featuring CHANCE
US, male production duo and US, female vocalist (2 WEEKS) pos/wks

13 Nov 99		RESCUE ME *AM:PM CDAMPM 126*	50 2

SUNNY
UK, female vocalist – Sunny Leslie (10 WEEKS) pos/wks

30 Mar 74	●	DOCTOR'S ORDERS *CBS 2068*	7 10

SUNSCREEM

UK, male / female vocal / instrumental group (36 WEEKS)   pos/wks

29 Feb 92	PRESSURE *Sony S2 6578017*	.60	2
18 Jul 92	LOVE U MORE *Sony S2 6581727*	.23	6
17 Oct 92	PERFECT MOTION *Sony S2 6584057*	.18	5
9 Jan 93	BROKEN ENGLISH *Sony S2 6589032*	.13	5
27 Mar 93	PRESSURE US (re-mix) *Sony S2 6591102*	.19	5
2 Sep 95	WHEN *Sony S2 6623222*	.47	2
18 Nov 95	EXODUS *Sony S2 6625342*	.40	2
20 Jan 96	WHITE SKIES *Sony S2 6627425*	.25	3
23 Mar 96	SECRETS *Sony S2 6629342*	.36	2
6 Sep 97	CATCH *Pulse-8 CDLOSE 117*	.55	1
20 Oct 01	PLEASE SAVE ME *Inferno / Five AM FAMFERN 1CD* [1]	.36	2
16 Nov 02	PERFECT MOTION (re-mix) *FIVE AM FAM 15CD*	.71	1

[1] Sunscreem vs Push

Monty SUNSHINE – See Chris BARBER'S JAZZ BAND

SUNSHINE BAND – See KC & SUNSHINE BAND

SUNSHIP featuring MCRB

UK, male producer and male vocalist (1 WEEK)   pos/wks

| 1 Apr 00 | CHEQUE ONE-TWO *Filter FILT 044* | .75 | 1 |

SUPER FURRY ANIMALS

UK, male vocal / instrumental group (38 WEEKS)   pos/wks

9 Mar 96	HOMETOWN UNICORN *Creation CRESCD 222*	.47	1
11 May 96	GOD! SHOW ME MAGIC *Creation CRESCD 231*	.33	2
13 Jul 96	SOMETHING 4 THE WEEKEND *Creation CRESCD 235*	.18	3
12 Oct 96	IF YOU DON'T WANT ME TO DESTROY YOU *Creation CRESCD 243*	.18	2
14 Dec 96	THE MAN DON'T GIVE A FUCK *Creation CRESCD 247*	.22	2
24 May 97	HERMANN LOVES PAULINE *Creation CRESCD 252*	.26	2
26 Jul 97	THE INTERNATIONAL LANGUAGE OF SCREAMING *Creation CRESCD 269*	.24	2
4 Oct 97	PLAY IT COOL *Creation CRESCD 275*	.27	2
6 Dec 97	DEMONS *Creation CRESCD 283*	.27	2
6 Jun 98	ICE HOCKEY HAIR *Creation CRESCD 288*	.12	3
22 May 99	NORTHERN LITES *Creation CRESCD 314*	.11	4
21 Aug 99	FIRE IN MY HEART *Creation CRESCD 323*	.25	3
29 Jan 00	DO OR DIE *Creation CRESCD 329*	.20	2
21 Jul 01	JUXTAPOZED WITH U *Epic 6712242*	.14	4
20 Oct 01	(DRAWING) RINGS AROUND THE WORLD *Epic 6719082*	.28	2
26 Jan 02	IT'S NOT THE END OF THE WORLD? *Epic 6721752*	.30	2

SUPERCAR *Italy, male DJ production duo*
– Alberto Pizarelli and Ricki Pagano (6 WEEKS)   pos/wks

| 13 Feb 99 | TONITE *Pepper 0530202* | .15 | 5 |
| 21 Aug 99 | COMPUTER LOVE *Pepper 0530392* [1] | .67 | 1 |

[1] Supercar featuring Mikaela

CLASSIC No.2 HITS

■ A list of critically acclaimed singles that stalled at No.2 and were held off the top spot by some memorable but often critically abused chart-toppers

THE JEAN GENIE – David Bowie
Held off the top spot by 'Long Haired Lover from Liverpool' by Little Jimmy Osmond, which went on to sell 2,000 short of a million

PENNY LANE / STRAWBERRY FIELDS FOREVER – Beatles
Engelbert Humperdinck's million-selling debut hit 'Release Me' prevented the Fab Four from completing a record-shattering run of 18 successive No.1s

MY GENERATION – Who
They never made it to the top with any release. This time it was the first Aussie act to make No.1, The Seekers, with 'The Carnival Is Over' that stopped them

Left: Engelbert Humperdinck, who prevented Keith West from hitting the top spot with his 'Excerpt from 'A Teenage Opera''

RIDE A WHITE SWAN – T. Rex
Despite 20 weeks on the chart, none of them was at No.1 due to the chart-topping performance of 'Grandad' by Clive Dunn

WONDERWALL – Oasis
The Manchester band's best-selling single, kept at No.2 behind 'I Believe' / 'Up on the Roof' by Robson Green and Jerome Flynn

VIENNA – Ultravox
Favourite for the top spot but famously No.2 behind Joe Dolce's 'Shaddap You Face' which, to add insult to injury, also topped the Austrian chart

AMERICAN PIE – Don McLean
A No.1 for Madonna but the original stalled at No.2 behind 'Son of My Father' from Chicory Tip

SUSPICIOUS MINDS – Elvis Presley
Rolf Harris and his 'Two Little Boys' kept Elvis at bay, although the song eventually made it when Gareth Gates took it to the top spot in 2002

BROWN SUGAR / BITCH / LET IT ROCK – Rolling Stones
The chart's first ever triple single was destined for No.1 but halted by the mighty Dawn and 'Knock Three Times'

EXCERPT FROM 'A TEENAGE OPERA' – Keith West
'Grocer Jack' was infamously blocked from the top spot by Engelbert Humperdinck's five-week stay at No.1 with 'The Last Waltz'

COMMON PEOPLE – Pulp
No.2 behind the 1,843,700 selling double A-side 'Unchained Melody' / '[There'll Be Bluebirds Over the] White Cliffs of Dover' by Robson Green and Jerome Flynn

SUPERCAT
Jamaica, male vocalist – William Maragh (5 WEEKS) pos/wks

				pos	wks
1 Aug 92		IT FE DONE *Columbia 6582737*		66	1
6 May 95		MY GIRL JOSEPHINE *Columbia 6614702* [1]		22	4

[1] Supercat featuring Jack Radics

SUPERFUNK
France, male production trio (2 WEEKS) pos/wks

				pos	wks
4 Mar 00		LUCKY STAR *Virgin DINSD 198* [1]		42	1
10 Jun 00		THE YOUNG MC *Virgin DINSD 206*		62	1

[1] Superfunk featuring Ron Carroll

SUPERGRASS
UK, male vocal / instrumental group (59 WEEKS) pos/wks

				pos	wks
29 Oct 94		CAUGHT BY THE FUZZ *Parlophone CDR 6396*		43	2
18 Feb 95		MANSIZE ROOSTER *Parlophone CDR 6402*		20	3
25 Mar 95		LOSE IT *Sub Pop SP 281*		75	1
13 May 95	●	LENNY *Parlophone CDR 6410*		10	3
15 Jul 95	●	ALRIGHT / TIME *Parlophone CDR 6413*		2	10
9 Mar 96	●	GOING OUT *Parlophone CDR 6428*		5	6
12 Apr 97	●	RICHARD III *Parlophone CDR 6461*		2	5
21 Jun 97	●	SUN HITS THE SKY *Parlophone CDR 6469*		10	4
18 Oct 97		LATE IN THE DAY *Parlophone CDR 6484*		18	4
5 Jun 99		PUMPING ON YOUR STEREO (re) *Parlophone CDR 6518*		11	7
18 Sep 99	●	MOVING *Parlophone CDR 6524*		9	5
4 Dec 99		MARY (re) *Parlophone CDR 6531*		36	4
13 Jul 02		NEVER DONE NOTHING LIKE THAT BEFORE *Parlophone CDR 6563*		75	1
28 Sep 02		GRACE *Parlophone CDR 6586*		13	4

SUPERMEN LOVERS featuring Mani HOFFMAN
France, male producer – Guillaume Atlan – and male vocalist (16 WEEKS) pos/wks

				pos	wks
15 Sep 01	●	STARLIGHT (re) *Independiente ISOM 53MS*		2	16

SUPERNATURALS
UK, male vocal / instrumental group (15 WEEKS) pos/wks

				pos	wks
26 Oct 96		LAZY LOVER *Food CDFOOD 85*		34	2
8 Feb 97		THE DAY BEFORE YESTERDAY'S MAN *Food CDFOODS 88*		25	3
26 Apr 97		SMILE *Food CDFOOD 92*		23	2
12 Jul 97		LOVE HAS PASSED AWAY *Food CDFOOD 99*		38	2
25 Oct 97		PREPARE TO LAND *Food CDFOODS 106*		48	1
1 Aug 98		I WASN'T BUILT TO GET UP *Food CDFOOD 112*		25	3
24 Oct 98		SHEFFIELD SONG *Food CDFOODS 115*		45	1
13 Mar 99		EVEREST *Food CDFOOD 119*		52	1

SUPERNOVA
UK, male / female vocal / instrumental duo (1 WEEK) pos/wks

				pos	wks
11 May 96		SOME MIGHT SAY *Sing Sing 74321369442*		55	1

SUPERSISTER
UK, female vocal group (8 WEEKS) pos/wks

				pos	wks
14 Oct 00		COFFEE *Gut CDGUT 35*		16	5
25 Aug 01		SHOPPING *Gut CDGUT 37*		36	2
17 Nov 01		SUMMER GONNA COME AGAIN *Gut CDGUT 38*		51	1

SUPERSTAR
UK, male vocal / instrumental group (2 WEEKS) pos/wks

				pos	wks
7 Feb 98		EVERY DAY I FALL APART *Camp Fabulous CFAB 003 CD*		66	1
25 Apr 98		SUPERSTAR *Camp Fabulous CFAB 007CD*		49	1

SUPERTRAMP
UK / US, male vocal / instrumental group (52 WEEKS) pos/wks

				pos	wks
15 Feb 75		DREAMER *A&M AMS 7132*		13	10
25 Jun 77		GIVE A LITTLE BIT *A&M AMS 7293*		29	7
31 Mar 79		THE LOGICAL SONG *A&M AMS 7427*		7	11
30 Jun 79	●	BREAKFAST IN AMERICA *A&M AMS 7451*		9	10
27 Oct 79		GOODBYE STRANGER *A&M AMS 7481*		57	3
30 Oct 82		IT'S RAINING AGAIN *A&M AMS 8255* [1]		26	11

[1] Supertramp featuring vocals by Roger Hodgson

SUPREMES `32` `Top 500`
World's most successful female group: Diana Ross, Mary Wilson, Florence Ballard (d. 1976). Before Ross went solo in 1969, this Detroit-based trio had amassed a dozen US No.1s. They were inducted into the Rock and Roll Hall of Fame in 1988 (306 WEEKS) pos/wks

				pos	wks
3 Sep 64	●	WHERE DID OUR LOVE GO *Stateside SS 327* ▲		3	14
22 Oct 64	★	BABY LOVE *Stateside SS 350* ▲		1	15
21 Jan 65		COME SEE ABOUT ME *Stateside SS 376* ▲		27	6
25 Mar 65	●	STOP! IN THE NAME OF LOVE *Tamla Motown TMG 501* ▲		7	12
10 Jun 65		BACK IN MY ARMS AGAIN *Tamla Motown TMG 516* ▲		40	5
9 Dec 65		I HEAR A SYMPHONY (re) *Tamla Motown TMG 543* ▲		39	5
8 Sep 66	●	YOU CAN'T HURRY LOVE *Tamla Motown TMG 575* ▲		3	12
1 Dec 66	●	YOU KEEP ME HANGIN' ON *Tamla Motown TMG 585* ▲		8	10
2 Mar 67		LOVE IS HERE AND NOW YOU'RE GONE *Tamla Motown TMG 597* ▲		17	10
11 May 67	●	THE HAPPENING *Tamla Motown TMG 607* ▲		6	12
30 Aug 67		REFLECTIONS *Tamla Motown TMG 616* [1]		5	14
29 Nov 67		IN AND OUT OF LOVE *Tamla Motown TMG 632* [1]		13	13
10 Apr 68		FOREVER CAME TODAY *Tamla Motown TMG 650* [1]		28	8
3 Jul 68		SOME THINGS YOU NEVER GET USED TO *Tamla Motown TMG 662* [1]		34	6
20 Nov 68		LOVE CHILD *Tamla Motown TMG 677* [1] ▲		15	14
29 Jan 69	●	I'M GONNA MAKE YOU LOVE ME (re) *Tamla Motown TMG 685* [2]		3	12
23 Apr 69		I'M LIVIN' IN SHAME (re) *Tamla Motown TMG 695* [1]		14	10
16 Jul 69		NO MATTER WHAT SIGN YOU ARE *Tamla Motown TMG 704*		37	7
20 Sep 69		I SECOND THAT EMOTION *Tamla Motown TMG 709* [2]		18	8
13 Dec 69		SOMEDAY WE'LL BE TOGETHER *Tamla Motown TMG 721* [1] ▲		13	13
21 Mar 70		WHY (MUST WE FALL IN LOVE) *Tamla Motown TMG 730* [2]		31	7
2 May 70	●	UP THE LADDER TO THE ROOF *Tamla Motown TMG 735*		6	15
16 Jan 71	●	STONED LOVE *Tamla Motown TMG 760*		3	13
26 Jun 71		RIVER DEEP MOUNTAIN HIGH *Tamla Motown TMG 777* [3]		11	10
21 Aug 71	●	NATHAN JONES *Tamla Motown TMG 782*		5	11
20 Nov 71		YOU GOTTA HAVE LOVE IN YOUR HEART *Tamla Motown TMG 793* [3]		25	10
4 Mar 72	●	FLOY JOY *Tamla Motown TMG 804*		9	10
15 Jul 72	●	AUTOMATICALLY SUNSHINE *Tamla Motown TMG 821*		10	9
21 Apr 73		BAD WEATHER *Tamla Motown TMG 847*		37	4
24 Aug 74		BABY LOVE (re-issue) *Tamla Motown TMG 915* [1]		12	10
18 Feb 89		STOP! IN THE NAME OF LOVE (re-issue) *Motown ZB 41963* [1]		62	1

[1] Diana Ross and The Supremes [2] Diana Ross and The Supremes and The Temptations [3] Supremes and The Four Tops

Al B SURE!
US, male vocalist – Al Brown (13 WEEKS) pos/wks

				pos	wks
16 Apr 88		NITE AND DAY *Uptown W 8192*		44	5
30 Jul 88		OFF ON YOUR OWN (GIRL) *Uptown W 7870*		70	2
10 Jun 89		IF I'M NOT YOUR LOVER *Uptown W 2908* [1]		54	3
31 Mar 90		SECRET GARDEN *Qwest W 9992* [2]		67	1
12 Jun 93		BLACK TIE WHITE NOISE *Arista 74321148682* [3]		36	2

[1] Al B Sure featuring Slick Rick [2] Quincy Jones featuring Al B Sure!, James Ingram, El DeBarge and Barry White [3] David Bowie featuring Al B Sure!

SUREAL
UK, male / female production / vocal group (4 WEEKS) pos/wks

				pos	wks
7 Oct 00		YOU TAKE MY BREATH AWAY *Cream CREAM 7CD*		15	4

SURFACE
US, male vocal / instrumental duo (14 WEEKS) pos/wks

				pos	wks
23 Jul 83		FALLING IN LOVE *Salsoul SAL 104*		67	3
23 Jun 84		WHEN YOUR 'EX' WANTS YOU BACK *Salsoul SAL 106*		52	4
28 Feb 87		HAPPY *CBS 650393 7*		56	5
12 Jan 91		THE FIRST TIME *Columbia 6564767* ▲		60	2

SURFACE NOISE
UK, male instrumental group (11 WEEKS) pos/wks

				pos	wks
31 May 80		THE SCRATCH *WEA K 18291*		26	8
30 Aug 80		DANCIN' ON A WIRE *Groove Production GP102*		59	3

SURFARIS
US, male instrumental group (14 WEEKS) pos/wks

				pos	wks
25 Jul 63	●	WIPE OUT *London HLD 9751*		5	14

SURPRISE SISTERS *Australia, female vocal group (3 WEEKS)* pos/wks

| 13 Mar 76 | LA BOOGA ROOGA *Good Earth GD 1* | .38 | 3 |

SURVIVOR *US, male vocal / instrumental group – lead vocal Dave Bickler (26 WEEKS)* pos/wks

| 31 Jul 82 | ★ EYE OF THE TIGER *Scotti Brothers SCT A 2411* ▲ | .1 | 15 |
| 1 Feb 86 | ● BURNING HEART *Scotti Brothers A 6708* | .5 | 11 |

SUSHI – See Paul MASTERSON presents SUSHI

SUTHERLAND BROTHERS
UK, male vocal / instrumental group (20 WEEKS) pos/wks

3 Apr 76	● ARMS OF MARY *CBS 4001* 1	.5	12
20 Nov 76	SECRETS *CBS 4668* 1	.35	4
2 Jun 79	EASY COME, EASY GO *CBS 7121*	.50	4

1 Sutherland Brothers and Quiver

Pat SUZUKI *US, female vocalist (1 WEEK)* pos/wks

| 14 Apr 60 | I ENJOY BEING A GIRL *RCA 1171* | .49 | 1 |

SVENSON and GIELEN *Belgium, male production duo – Sven Maes and Johan Gielen (2 WEEKS)* pos/wks

| 22 Sep 01 | THE BEAUTY OF SILENCE *Xtrahard / Xtravaganza* | .41 | 2 |

See also Johan GIELEN presents ABNEA; AIRSCAPE; BLUE BAMBOO; CUBIC 22; TRANSFORMER 2

Billy SWAN *US, male vocalist (13 WEEKS)* pos/wks

| 14 Dec 74 | ● I CAN HELP *Monument MNT 2752* ▲ | .6 | 9 |
| 24 May 75 | DON'T BE CRUEL *Monument MNT 3244* | .42 | 4 |

SWAN LAKE *US, male producer – Todd Terry (4 WEEKS)* pos/wks

| 17 Sep 88 | IN THE NAME OF LOVE *Champion CHAMP 86* | .53 | 4 |

SWANS WAY *UK, male / female vocal / instrumental group (12 WKS)* pos/wks

| 4 Feb 84 | SOUL TRAIN *Exit EXT 3* | .20 | 7 |
| 26 May 84 | ILLUMINATIONS *Balgier PH 5* | .57 | 5 |

Patrick SWAYZE featuring Wendy FRASER
US, male / female vocal duo (11 WEEKS) pos/wks

| 26 Mar 88 | SHE'S LIKE THE WIND *RCA PB 49565* | .17 | 11 |

Keith SWEAT *US, male vocalist (23 WEEKS)* pos/wks

20 Feb 88	I WANT HER *Vintertainment EKR 68*	.26	10
14 May 88	SOMETHING JUST AIN'T RIGHT *Vintertainment EKR 72*	.55	3
14 May 94	HOW DO YOU LIKE IT *Elektra EKR 185CD*	.71	1
22 Jun 96	TWISTED *Elektra EKR 223CD*	.39	2
23 Nov 96	JUST A TOUCH *Elektra EKR 227CD*	.35	2
3 May 97	NOBODY *Elektra EKR 233CD* 1	.30	2
6 Dec 97	I WANT HER (re-mix) *Elektra E 3887CD*	.44	1
12 Dec 98	COME AND GET WITH ME *Elektra E 3787CD* 2	.58	1
27 Mar 99	I'M NOT READY *Elektra E 3767CD*	.53	1

1 Keith Sweat featuring Athena Cage 2 Keith Sweat featuring Snoop Dogg

Michelle SWEENEY *US, female vocalist (1 WEEK)* pos/wks

| 29 Oct 94 | THIS TIME *Big Beat A 8229CD* | .57 | 1 |

SWEET (135 Top 500) *Glam-rock giants: Brian Connolly (v) (d. 1997), Andy Scott (g), Steve Priest (b), Mick Tucker (d)(d. 2002). The flamboyantly attired UK quartet was very popular in Europe and the US. Despite topping the chart only once, they achieved five No.2 hits (159 WEEKS)* pos/wks

13 Mar 71	FUNNY FUNNY *RCA 2051*	.13	14
12 Jun 71	● CO-CO *RCA 2087*	.2	15
16 Oct 71	ALEXANDER GRAHAM BELL *RCA 2121*	.33	5
5 Feb 72	POPPA JOE *RCA 2164*	.11	12
10 Jun 72	● LITTLE WILLY *RCA 2225*	.4	14

9 Sep 72	● WIG-WAM BAM *RCA 2260*	.4	13
13 Jan 73	★ BLOCKBUSTER! *RCA 2305*	.1	15
5 May 73	● HELL RAISER *RCA 2357*	.2	11
22 Sep 73	● THE BALLROOM BLITZ *RCA 2403*	.2	9
19 Jan 74	● TEENAGE RAMPAGE *RCA LPBO 5004*	.2	8
13 Jul 74	● THE SIX TEENS *RCA LPBO 5037*	.9	7
9 Nov 74	TURN IT DOWN *RCA 2480*	.41	2
15 Mar 75	● FOX ON THE RUN *RCA 2524*	.2	10
12 Jul 75	ACTION *RCA 2578*	.15	6
24 Jan 76	THE LIES IN YOUR EYES *RCA 2641*	.35	4
28 Jan 78	● LOVE IS LIKE OXYGEN *Polydor POSP 1*	.9	9
26 Jan 85	IT'S... IT'S... THE SWEET MIX *Anagram ANA 28*	.45	5

It's... It's... the Sweet Mix is a medley of the following songs: Blockbuster / Fox on the Run / Teenage Rampage / Hell Raiser / Ballroom Blitz

Rachel SWEET *US, female vocalist (15 WEEKS)* pos/wks

| 9 Dec 78 | B-A-B-Y *Stiff BUY 39* | .35 | 8 |
| 22 Aug 81 | EVERLASTING LOVE *CBS A 1405* | .35 | 7 |

SWEET DREAMS *UK, male / female vocal duo – Polly Brown and Tony Jackson (12 WEEKS)* pos/wks

| 20 Jul 74 | ● HONEY HONEY *Bradley's BRAD 7408* | .10 | 12 |

SWEET DREAMS *UK, male / female vocal group (7 WEEKS)* pos/wks

| 9 Apr 83 | I'M NEVER GIVING UP *Ariola ARO 333* | .21 | 7 |

SWEET FEMALE ATTITUDE *UK, female vocal duo – Leanne Brown and Catherine Cassidy (14 WEEKS)* pos/wks

| 15 Apr 00 | ● FLOWERS *WEA WEA 267CD* | .2 | 12 |
| 7 Oct 00 | 8 DAYS A WEEK *WEA WEA 296CD* | .43 | 2 |

SWEET MERCY featuring Joe ROBERTS
UK, male production / instrumental duo and male vocalist (1 WEEK) pos/wks

| 24 Feb 96 | HAPPY DAYS *Grass Green GRASS 10CD* | .63 | 1 |

SWEET PEOPLE
France, male vocal / instrumental group (10 WEEKS) pos/wks

| 4 Oct 80 | ● ET LES OISEAUX CHANTAIENT (AND THE BIRDS WERE SINGING) (re) *Polydor POSP 179* | .4 | 10 |

Re-entry made No.73 in Aug 1987

SWEET PUSSY PAULINE – See CANDY GIRLS

SWEET SENSATION
UK, male vocal group – lead vocal Marcel King (17 WEEKS) pos/wks

| 14 Sep 74 | ★ SAD SWEET DREAMER *Pye 7N 45385* | .1 | 10 |
| 18 Jan 75 | PURELY BY COINCIDENCE *Pye 7N 45421* | .11 | 7 |

SWEET TEE *US, female rapper – Toi Jackson (8 WEEKS)* pos/wks

| 16 Jan 88 | IT'S LIKE THAT Y'ALL / I GOT DA FEELIN' *Cooltempo COOL 160* | .31 | 6 |
| 13 Aug 94 | THE FEELING *Deep Distraxion OILYCD 029* 1 | .32 | 2 |

1 Tin Tin Out featuring Sweet Tee

SWEETBACK *UK, male vocal / instrumental group (1 WEEK)* pos/wks

| 29 Mar 97 | YOU WILL RISE *Epic 6643155* | .64 | 1 |

SWEETBOX *Germany / US, male / female vocal / production duo – Rosan Roberto and Tina Harris (12 WEEKS)* pos/wks

| 22 Aug 98 | ● EVERYTHING'S GONNA BE ALRIGHT *RCA 74321606842* | .5 | 12 |

Sally SWEETLAND – See Eddie FISHER

SWERVEDRIVER
UK, male vocal / instrumental group (3 WEEKS) pos/wks

| 10 Aug 91 | SANDBLASTED (EP) *Creation CRE 102* | .67 | 1 |

Re-entries are listed as (re), (2re), (3re), etc which signifies that the hit re-entered the chart once, twice or three times, etc

Date	Title	Pos	Wks
30 May 92	NEVER LOSE THAT FEELING *Creation CRE 120*	62	1
14 Aug 93	DUEL *Creation CRESCD 136*	60	1

Tracks on Sandblasted (EP): Sandblaster / Flawed / Out / Laze It Up

SWIMMING WITH SHARKS
Germany, female vocal duo (3 WEEKS) pos/wks

Date	Title	Pos	Wks
7 May 88	CARELESS LOVE *WEA YZ 173*	63	3

SWING featuring DR ALBAN
US, male rapper and Nigeria, male vocalist (1 WEEK) pos/wks

Date	Title	Pos	Wks
29 Apr 95	SWEET DREAMS *Logic 74321251552*	59	1

SWING 52 *US, male vocal / instrumental group (1 WEEK)* pos/wks

Date	Title	Pos	Wks
25 Feb 95	COLOR OF MY SKIN *ffrr FCD 256*	60	1

SWING KIDS – See K7

SWING OUT SISTER
UK, male / female vocal / instrumental trio (55 WEEKS) pos/wks

Date	Title	Pos	Wks
25 Oct 86 ●	BREAKOUT *Mercury SWING 2*	4	14
10 Jan 87 ●	SURRENDER *Mercury SWING 3*	7	8
18 Apr 87	TWILIGHT WORLD *Mercury SWING 4*	32	6
11 Jul 87	FOOLED BY A SMILE *Mercury SWING 5*	43	4
8 Apr 89	YOU ON MY MIND *Fontana SWING 6*	28	9
8 Jul 89	WHERE IN THE WORLD *Fontana SWING 7*	47	4
11 Apr 92	AM I THE SAME GIRL *Fontana SWING 9*	21	6
20 Jun 92	NOTGONNACHANGE *Fontana SWING 10*	49	2
27 Aug 94	LA LA (MEANS I LOVE YOU) *Fontana SWIDD 11*	37	2

Act became male / female duo in 1989

SWINGING BLUE JEANS
UK, male vocal / instrumental group (57 WEEKS) pos/wks

Date	Title	Pos	Wks
20 Jun 63	IT'S TOO LATE NOW (re) *HMV POP 1170*	30	9
12 Dec 63 ●	HIPPY HIPPY SHAKE *HMV POP 1242*	2	17
19 Mar 64	GOOD GOLLY MISS MOLLY *HMV POP 1273*	11	10
4 Jun 64 ●	YOU'RE NO GOOD *HMV POP 1304*	3	13
20 Jan 66	DON'T MAKE ME OVER *HMV POP 1501*	31	8

SWIRL 360 *US, male vocal duo (1 WEEK)* pos/wks

Date	Title	Pos	Wks
14 Nov 98	HEY NOW NOW *Mercury 5665352*	61	1

SWITCH *US, male vocal / instrumental group (3 WEEKS)* pos/wks

Date	Title	Pos	Wks
10 Nov 84	KEEPING SECRETS *Total Experience RCA XE 502*	61	3

SYBIL *US, female vocalist – Sybil Lynch (69 WEEKS)* pos/wks

Date	Title	Pos	Wks
1 Nov 86	FALLING IN LOVE *Champion CHAMP 22*	68	3
25 Apr 87	LET YOURSELF GO *Champion CHAMP 42*	32	6
29 Aug 87	MY LOVE IS GUARANTEED *Champion CHAMPX 55*	42	5
22 Jul 89	DON'T MAKE ME OVER (re) *Champion CHAMP 213*	19	11
27 Jan 90 ●	WALK ON BY *PWL PWL 48*	6	9
21 Apr 90	CRAZY FOR YOU *PWL PWL 53*	71	1
16 Jan 93 ●	THE LOVE I LOST *PWL Sanctuary PWCD 253* [1]	3	13
20 Mar 93 ●	WHEN I'M GOOD AND READY *PWL International PWCD 260*	5	13
26 Jun 93	BEYOND YOUR WILDEST DREAMS *PWL International PWCD 265*	41	2
11 Sep 93	STRONGER TOGETHER *PWL International PWCD 269*	41	2
11 Dec 93	MY LOVE IS GUARANTEED (re-mix) *PWL International PWCD 277*	48	1
9 Mar 96	SO TIRED OF BEING ALONE *PWL International PWL 324CD*	53	1
8 Mar 97	WHEN I'M GOOD AND READY (re-mix) *Next Plateau NP 14183*	66	1
26 Jul 97	STILL A THRILL *Coalition COLA 007CD*	55	1

[1] West End featuring Sybil

SYLK 130
US, male production duo – King Britt and John Wicks (2 WEEKS) pos/wks

Date	Title	Pos	Wks
25 Apr 98	LAST NIGHT A DJ SAVED MY LIFE *Sony S2 SYLK 1CD*	33	2

SYLVER
Belgium, male / female DJ / production / vocal duo (1 WEEK) pos/wks

Date	Title	Pos	Wks
1 Jun 02	TURN THE TIDE *Pepper 9230562*	56	1

SYLVESTER
US, male vocalist – Sylvester James, d. 16 Dec 1988 (45 WEEKS) pos/wks

Date	Title	Pos	Wks
19 Aug 78 ●	YOU MAKE ME FEEL (MIGHTY REAL) *Fantasy FTC 160*	8	15
18 Nov 78	DANCE (DISCO HEAT) *Fantasy FTC 163*	29	12
31 Mar 79	I (WHO HAVE NOTHING) *Fantasy FTC 171*	46	5
7 Jul 79	STARS *Fantasy FTC 177*	47	3
11 Sep 82	DO YOU WANNA FUNK *London LON 13* [1]	32	8
3 Sep 83	BAND OF GOLD *London LON 33*	67	2

[1] Sylvester with Patrick Cowley

SYLVIA *US, female vocalist – Sylvia Vanderpool (11 WEEKS)* pos/wks

Date	Title	Pos	Wks
23 Jun 73	PILLOW TALK *London HL 10415*	14	11

SYLVIA
Sweden, female vocalist – Sylvia Vrethammar (33 WEEKS) pos/wks

Date	Title	Pos	Wks
10 Aug 74 ●	Y VIVA ESPANA (re) *Sonet SON 2037*	4	28
26 Apr 75	HASTA LA VISTA *Sonet SON 2055*	38	5

David SYLVIAN *UK, male vocalist – David Batt (36 WEEKS)* pos/wks

Date	Title	Pos	Wks
7 Aug 82	BAMBOO HOUSES / BAMBOO MUSIC *Virgin VS 510* [1]	30	4
2 Jul 83	FORBIDDEN COLOURS *Virgin VS 601* [2]	16	8
2 Jun 84	RED GUITAR *Virgin VS 633*	17	5
18 Aug 84	THE INK IN THE WELL *Virgin VS 700*	36	3
3 Nov 84	PULLING PUNCHES *Virgin VS 717*	56	2
14 Dec 85	WORDS WITH THE SHAMAN *Virgin VS 835*	72	1
9 Aug 86	TAKING THE VEIL *Virgin VS 815*	53	3
17 Jan 87	BUOY *Virgin VS 910* [3]	63	2
10 Oct 87	LET THE HAPPINESS IN *Virgin VS 1001*	66	1
13 Jun 92	HEARTBEAT (TAINAI KAIKI II) RETURNING TO THE WOMB *Virgin America VUS 57* [4]	58	3
28 Aug 93	JEAN THE BIRDMAN *Virgin VSCDG 1462* [5]	68	2
27 Mar 99	I SURRENDER *Virgin VSCDT 1722*	40	2

[1] Sylvian Sakamoto [2] David Sylvian and Riuichi Sakamoto [3] Mick Karn featuring David Sylvian [4] David Sylvian / Riuichi Sakamoto featuring Ingrid Chavez [5] David Sylvian and Robert Fripp

SYMARIP *UK, male vocal / instrumental group (3 WEEKS)* pos/wks

Date	Title	Pos	Wks
2 Feb 80	SKINHEAD MOONSTOMP *Trojan TRO 9062*	54	3

SYMBOLS *UK, male vocal / instrumental group (15 WEEKS)* pos/wks

Date	Title	Pos	Wks
2 Aug 67	BYE BYE BABY *President PT 144*	44	3
3 Jan 68	(THE BEST PART OF) BREAKING UP *President PT 173*	25	12

Terri SYMON *UK, female vocalist (1 WEEK)* pos/wks

Date	Title	Pos	Wks
10 Jun 95	I WANT TO KNOW WHAT LOVE IS *A&M 5810592*	54	1

SYMPOSIUM *UK, male vocal / instrumental group (10 WEEKS)* pos/wks

Date	Title	Pos	Wks
22 Mar 97	FAREWELL TO TWILIGHT *Infectious INFECT 34CD*	25	2
31 May 97	THE ANSWER TO WHY I HATE YOU *Infectious INFECT 37CD*	32	2
30 Aug 97	FAIRWEATHER FRIEND *Infectious INFECT 44CD*	25	3
14 Mar 98	AVERAGE MAN *Infectious INFECT 52CD*	45	1
16 May 98	BURY YOU *Infectious INFECT 55CDS*	41	1
18 Jul 98	BLUE *Infectious INFECT 57CD*	48	1

See also HELL IS FOR HEROES

SYREETA *US, female vocalist – Rita Wright (30 WEEKS)* pos/wks

Date	Title	Pos	Wks
21 Sep 74	SPINNIN' AND SPINNIN' *Tamla Motown TMG 912*	49	3
1 Feb 75	YOUR KISS IS SWEET *Tamla Motown TMG 933*	12	8
12 Jul 75	HARMOUR LOVE *Tamla Motown TMG 954*	32	4
15 Dec 79 ●	WITH YOU I'M BORN AGAIN *Motown TMG 1159* [1]	2	11
8 Mar 80	IT WILL COME IN TIME *Motown TMG 1175* [1]	47	4

[1] Billy Preston and Syreeta

SYSTEM US, male vocal / instrumental duo (2 WEEKS)
		pos/wks	
9 Jun 84	I WANNA MAKE YOU FEEL GOOD *Polydor POSP 685*	73	2

SYSTEM F Holland, male producer – Ferry Corsten (10 WEEKS)
		pos/wks	
3 Apr 99	OUT OF THE BLUE *Essential Recordings ESCD 1*	14	6
6 May 00	CRY *Essential Recordings ESCD 14*	19	4

See also GOURYELLA; MOONMAN; VERACOCHA; ALBION; Ferry CORSTEN; STARPARTY

SYSTEM OF A DOWN
US, male vocal / instrumental group (9 WEEKS)
		pos/wks	
3 Nov 01	CHOP SUEY! *Columbia 6720342*	17	4
23 Mar 02	TOXICITY *Columbia 6725022*	25	3
27 Jul 02	AERIALS *Columbia 6728692*	34	2

SYSTEM 7 UK / France, male / female instrumental
duo – Steve Hillage and Miquette Giraudy (2 WEEKS)
		pos/wks	
13 Feb 93	7:7 EXPANSION *Butterfly BFLD 2*	39	1
17 Jul 93	SINBAD / QUEST *Butterfly BFLD 8*	74	1

T

T-BOZ US, female vocalist (2 WEEKS)
		pos/wks	
23 Nov 96	TOUCH MYSELF *LaFace 74321422882*	48	1
14 Apr 01	MY GETAWAY *Maverick W 549CD* [1]	44	1

[1] Tionne 'T-Boz' Watkins

See also TLC

TC Italy, male instrumental / production group (5 WEEKS)
		pos/wks	
14 Mar 92	BERRY *Union City UCRT 1* [1]	73	1
21 Nov 92	FUNKY GUITAR *Union City UCRT 13* [2]	40	2
10 Jul 93	HARMONY *Union UCRD 20* [3]	51	2

[1] TC 1991 [2] TC 1992 [3] TC 1993

T-CONNECTION US, male vocal / instrumental group (27 WEEKS) pos/wks
		pos/wks	
18 Jun 77	DO WHAT YOU WANNA DO *TK XC 9109*	11	8
14 Jan 78	ON FIRE *TK TKR 6006*	16	5
10 Jun 78	LET YOURSELF GO *TK TKR 6024*	52	3
24 Feb 79	AT MIDNIGHT *TK TKR 7517*	53	5
5 May 79	SATURDAY NIGHT *TK TKR 7536*	41	6

T-COY – See VARIOUS ARTISTS (EPs and LPs)

T-EMPO UK, male / female vocal / instrumental group (4 WEEKS) pos/wks
		pos/wks	
7 May 94	SATURDAY NIGHT SUNDAY MORNING *ffrr FCD 232*	19	3
9 Nov 96	THE LOOK OF LOVE / THE BLUE ROOM *ffrr FCD 281*	71	1

T-FACTORY Italy, male production group (2 WEEKS)
		pos/wks	
13 Apr 02	MESSAGE IN A BOTTLE *Inferno CDFERN 44*	51	2

THS – THE HORN SECTION
US, male / female vocal / instrumental group (3 WEEKS)
		pos/wks	
18 Aug 84	LADY SHINE (SHINE ON) *Fourth & Broadway BRW 10*	54	3

TJR featuring XAVIER
UK, male instrumental / production group (2 WEEKS)
		pos/wks	
27 Sep 97	JUST GETS BETTER *Multiply CDMULTY 25*	28	2

TLC (399) Top 500
Multi-award-winning 1990s female trio; Tionne 'T-Boz' Watkins, Lisa 'Left Eye' Lopes (d. 25 Apr 2002) and Rozonda 'Chilli' Thomas. They have nine US gold singles, and The Supremes are the only female group with more US No.1s. Best-selling single: 'No Scrubs' 553,200 (85 WEEKS)
		pos/wks	
20 Jun 92	AIN'T 2 PROUD 2 BEG *Arista 115265*	13	5
22 Aug 92	BABY-BABY-BABY *LaFace 74321111297*	55	3
24 Oct 92	WHAT ABOUT YOUR FRIENDS *LaFace 74321118177*	59	2
21 Jan 95	CREEP *LaFace 74321254212* ▲	22	4
22 Apr 95	RED LIGHT SPECIAL *LaFace 74321273662*	18	4
5 Aug 95 ●	WATERFALLS *LaFace 74321298812* ▲	4	14
4 Nov 95	DIGGIN' ON YOU *LaFace 74321319252*	18	5
13 Jan 96 ●	CREEP (re-issue) *LaFace 74321340942*	6	7
3 Apr 99 ●	NO SCRUBS *LaFace 74321660952* ▲	3	19
28 Aug 99 ●	UNPRETTY *LaFace 74321695842* ▲	6	11
18 Dec 99	DEAR LIE *LaFace 74321724012*	31	9
14 Dec 02	GIRL TALK *Arista 74321983482*	30	2

See also T-BOZ; Lisa 'LEFT EYE' LOPES

T99 Belgium, male instrumental / production group (10 WEEKS)
		pos/wks	
11 May 91	ANASTHASIA *XL XLS 19*	14	6
19 Oct 91	NOCTURNE *Emphasis 6574097*	33	4

T-POWER UK, male producer – Mark Royal (16 WEEKS)
		pos/wks	
13 Apr 96	POLICE STATE *Sound of Underground TPOWCD 001*	63	1
6 Apr 02 ●	SHAKE UR BODY *Positiva CDTIV 171* [1]	7	11
23 Nov 02	DON'T WANNA KNOW *ffrr FCD 408* [2]	19	4

[1] Shy FX and T-Power featuring Di [2] Shy FX and T-Power featuring Di and Skibadee

TQ US, male rapper – Terrance Quaites (35 WEEKS)
		pos/wks	
30 Jan 99 ●	WESTSIDE *Epic 6668102*	4	9
1 May 99 ●	BYE BYE BABY *Epic 6672372*	7	7
21 Aug 99	BETTER DAYS *Epic 6677532*	32	2
4 Sep 99 ●	SUMMERTIME *Northwestside 74321694672* [1]	7	7
29 Apr 00	DAILY *Epic 6692752*	14	5
13 Oct 01	LET'S GET BACK TO BED ... BOY *Epic 6718662* [2]	16	5

[1] Another Level featuring TQ [2] Sarah Connor featuring TQ

T. REX (58) Top 500
Highly influential acoustic act turned superstar glam rock boogie duo; singer / songwriter / guitarist Marc Bolan (b. Mark Feld, 30 Sep 1947, London, UK; d. 16 Sep 1977), and percussionist Steve Peregrin Took (d. 27 Oct 1980) – replaced by Mickey Finn in 1969 (d. 12 Jan 2003) (236 WEEKS)
		pos/wks	
8 May 68	DEBORA *Regal Zonophone RZ 3008* [1]	34	7
4 Sep 68	ONE INCH ROCK *Regal Zonophone RZ 3011* [1]	28	7
9 Aug 69	KING OF THE RUMBLING SPIRES *Regal Zonophone RZ 3022* [1]	44	1
24 Oct 70 ●	RIDE A WHITE SWAN *Fly BUG 1*	2	20
27 Feb 71 ★	HOT LOVE *Fly BUG 6*	1	17
10 Jul 71 ★	GET IT ON *Fly BUG 10*	1	13
13 Nov 71 ●	JEEPSTER *Fly BUG 16*	2	15
29 Jan 72 ★	TELEGRAM SAM (re) *T. Rex 101*	1	14
1 Apr 72 ●	DEBORA / ONE INCH ROCK (re-issue) *Magnifly ECHO 102* [1]	7	10
13 May 72 ★	METAL GURU *EMI MARC 1*	1	14
16 Sep 72 ●	CHILDREN OF THE REVOLUTION *EMI MARC 2*	2	10
9 Dec 72 ●	SOLID GOLD EASY ACTION *EMI MARC 3*	2	11
10 Mar 73 ●	20TH CENTURY BOY *EMI MARC 4*	3	9
16 Jun 73 ●	THE GROOVER *EMI MARC 5*	4	9
24 Nov 73	TRUCK ON (TYKE) *EMI MARC 6*	12	11
9 Feb 74	TEENAGE DREAM *EMI MARC 7* [2]	13	5
13 Jul 74	LIGHT OF LOVE *EMI MARC 8*	22	5
16 Nov 74	ZIP GUN BOOGIE *EMI MARC 9*	41	3
12 Jul 75	NEW YORK CITY *EMI MARC 10*	15	8
11 Oct 75	DREAMY LADY *EMI MARC 11* [3]	30	5
6 Mar 76	LONDON BOYS *EMI MARC 13*	40	3
19 Jun 76	I LOVE TO BOOGIE *EMI MARC 14*	13	9
2 Oct 76	LASER LOVE *EMI MARC 15*	41	4

2 Apr 77	THE SOUL OF MY SUIT *EMI MARC 16* 42	3
9 May 81	RETURN OF THE ELECTRIC WARRIOR (EP)	
	Rarn MBSF 001 [4] 50	4
19 Sep 81	YOU SCARE ME TO DEATH *Cherry Red CHERRY 29* [4] 51	4
18 May 85	MEGAREX *Marc on Wax TANX 1* [2] 72	2
9 May 87	GET IT ON (re-mix) *Marc on Wax MARC 10* [2] 54	4
24 Aug 91	20TH CENTURY BOY (re-issue) *Marc on Wax MARC 501* [2] 13	8
7 Oct 00	GET IT ON *All Around the World CDGLOBE 225* [5] 59	1

[1] Tyrannosaurus Rex [2] Marc Bolan and T. Rex [3] T. Rex Disco Party [4] Marc Bolan [5] Bus Stop featuring T. Rex

'Telegram Sam' re-entered making No.69 in Mar 1982. Tracks on Return of the Electric Warrior (EP): Sing Me a Song / Endless Sleep Extended / The Lilac Hand of Menthol Dan. Megarex is a medley of extracts from the following T. Rex hits: Truck On (Tyke) / The Groover / Telegram Sam / Shock Rock / Metal Guru / 20th Century Boy / Children of the Revolution / Hot Love

TSD *UK, female vocal group (2 WEEKS)*
		pos/wks
17 Feb 96	HEART AND SOUL *Avex UK AVEXCD 21* 69	1
30 Mar 96	BABY I LOVE YOU *Avex UK AVEXCD 34* 64	1

T-SHIRT *UK, female vocal duo (1 WEEK)*
		pos/wks
13 Sep 97	YOU SEXY THING *Eternal WEA 122CD* 63	1

T-SPOON
Holland, male / female vocal / instrumental group (15 WEEKS)
		pos/wks
19 Sep 98 ●	SEX ON THE BEACH *Control 0042395 CON* 2	13
23 Jan 99	TOM'S PARTY *Control 0043505 CON* 27	2

T2 featuring Robin S
US, male production duo with female vocalist (1 WEEK)
		pos/wks
4 Oct 97	YOU GOT THE LOVE *Champion CHAMPCD 330* 62	1

TWA *UK, male instrumental / production group (1 WEEK)*
		pos/wks
16 Sep 95	NASTY GIRLS *Mercury MERCD 441* 51	1

TABERNACLE
UK, male instrumental / production group (2 WEEKS)
		pos/wks
4 Mar 95	I KNOW THE LORD *Good Groove CDGG 1* 62	1
3 Feb 96	I KNOW THE LORD (re-mix) *Good Groove CDGGX 1* 55	1

TACKHEAD
US / UK, male vocal / production / rap group (3 WEEKS)
		pos/wks
30 Jun 90	DANGEROUS SEX *SBK SBK 7014* 48	3

TAFFY *UK, female vocalist – Catherine Quaye (14 WEEKS)*
		pos/wks
10 Jan 87 ●	I LOVE MY RADIO (MY DEE JAY'S RADIO)	
	Transglobal TYPE 1 6	10
18 Jul 87	STEP BY STEP *Transglobal TYPE 5* 59	4

TAG TEAM
US, male rap duo – Cecil Glenn and Steve Gibson (8 WEEKS)
		pos/wks
8 Jan 94	WHOOMP! (THERE IT IS) *Club Tools SHXCD 1* 34	5
29 Jan 94	ADDAMS FAMILY (WHOOMP!) *Atlas PZCD 305* 53	1
10 Sep 94	WHOOMP! (THERE IT IS) (re-mix) *Club Tools SHXR 1* 48	2

See also QUAD CITY DJs

Caddillac TAH – See Jennifer LOPEZ; JA RULE

TAIKO *Germany, male DJ / production*
duo – Oliver Huntemann and Stephan Bodzin (1 WEEK)
		pos/wks
29 Jun 02	SILENCE *Nukleuz NUKC 0330* 72	1

TAK TIX
US, male / female vocal / production group (2 WEEKS)
		pos/wks
20 Jan 96	FEEL LIKE SINGING *A&M 5813212* 33	2

TAKE 5 *US, male vocal group (4 WEEKS)*
		pos/wks
7 Nov 98	I GIVE *Edel 0039635 ERE* 70	1
27 Mar 99	NEVER HAD IT SO GOOD *Edel 0039355 ERE*........................34	3

TAKE THAT 137 Top 500
Record-breaking British boy band: Robbie Williams (v), Gary Barlow (v), Jason Orange (v), Howard Donald (v), Mark Owen (v). They were the first artists since The Beatles to score four consecutive chart-toppers, and the first act to release eight singles entering at No.1. Robbie Williams departed in July 1995 and Gary Barlow dissolved the band in Feb 1996 having sold nine million albums and 10 million singles. Best-selling single: 'Back for Good' 959,582 (158 WEEKS)
		pos/wks
23 Nov 91	PROMISES *RCA PB 45085* 38	2
8 Feb 92	ONCE YOU'VE TASTED LOVE *RCA PB 45257* 47	3
6 Jun 92 ●	IT ONLY TAKES A MINUTE *RCA 74321101007* 7	8
15 Aug 92	I FOUND HEAVEN *RCA 74321108137*.................................15	6
10 Oct 92 ●	A MILLION LOVE SONGS *RCA 74321116307* 7	9
12 Dec 92 ●	COULD IT BE MAGIC *RCA 74321123137*...........................3	12
20 Feb 93 ●	WHY CAN'T I WAKE UP WITH YOU *RCA 74321133102*.........2	10
17 Jul 93 ★	PRAY *RCA 74321154502* ■.................................1	11
9 Oct 93 ★	RELIGHT MY FIRE *RCA 74321167722* [1] ■.....................1	14
18 Dec 93 ★	BABE *RCA 74321182122* ■.................................1	10
9 Apr 94 ★	EVERYTHING CHANGES *RCA 74321167732* ■.................1	10
9 Jul 94 ●	LOVE AIN'T HERE ANYMORE (re) *RCA 74321214832*........3	12
15 Oct 94 ★	SURE *RCA 74321236622* ■.................................1	15
8 Apr 95 ★	BACK FOR GOOD *RCA 74321271462* ■.........................1	9
5 Aug 95 ★	NEVER FORGET *RCA 74321299572* ■.........................1	9
9 Mar 96 ★	HOW DEEP IS YOUR LOVE (re) *RCA 74321355592* ■.........1	14

[1] Take That featuring Lulu

Billy TALBOT – See Ian McNABB

TALI *New Zealand, female DJ / producer (1 WEEK)*
		pos/wks
10 Aug 02	LYRIC ON MY LIP *Full Cycle FCY 042*.................................75	1

TALISMAN P featuring Barrington LEVY
UK, male producer and Jamaica, male vocalist (2 WEEKS)
		pos/wks
13 Oct 01	HERE I COME (SING DJ)	
	Nulife / Arista 74321895622 37	2

TALK TALK
UK, male vocal / instrumental group (73 WEEKS)
		pos/wks
24 Apr 82	TALK TALK *EMI 5284* 52	4
24 Jul 82	TODAY *EMI 5314* 14	13
13 Nov 82	TALK TALK (re-mix) *EMI 5352* 23	10
19 Mar 83	MY FOOLISH FRIEND *EMI 5373* 57	3
14 Jan 84	IT'S MY LIFE *EMI 5443* 46	5
7 Apr 84	SUCH A SHAME *EMI 5433* 49	6
11 Aug 84	DUM DUM GIRL *EMI 5480* 74	1
18 Jan 86	LIFE'S WHAT YOU MAKE IT *EMI EMI 5540* 16	9
15 Mar 86	LIVING IN ANOTHER WORLD *EMI EMI 5551* 48	4
17 May 86	GIVE IT UP *Parlophone R 6131* 59	3
19 May 90	IT'S MY LIFE (re-issue) *Parlophone R 6254* 13	9
1 Sep 90	LIFE'S WHAT YOU MAKE IT (re-issue)	
	Parlophone R 6264 23	6

TALKING HEADS
US / UK, male / female vocal / instrumental group (54 WEEKS)
		pos/wks
7 Feb 81	ONCE IN A LIFETIME *Sire SIR 4048*.................................14	10
9 May 81	HOUSES IN MOTION *Sire SIR 4050* 50	3
21 Jan 84	THIS MUST BE THE PLACE *Sire W 9451* 51	3
3 Nov 84	SLIPPERY PEOPLE *EMI 5504* 68	2
12 Oct 85 ●	ROAD TO NOWHERE *EMI EMI 5530* 6	16
8 Feb 86	AND SHE WAS *EMI EMI 5543* 17	8
6 Sep 86	WILD WILD LIFE *EMI EMI 5567* 43	4
16 May 87	RADIO HEAD *EMI EM 1* 52	2
13 Aug 88	BLIND *EMI EM 68* 59	3
10 Oct 92	LIFETIME PILING UP *EMI EM 250* 50	3

See also HEADS with Shaun RYDER

TALL PAUL UK, male DJ / producer – Paul Newman (15 WEEKS) pos/wks

		pos	wks
29 Mar 97	ROCK DA HOUSE VC Recordings VCRD 18	12	4
29 May 99	BE THERE Duty Free DF 009CD	45	1
8 Apr 00	FREEBASE Duty Free DF 015CD	43	2
2 Jun 01	ROCK DA HOUSE (re-mix) VC Recordings VCRD 89	29	2
18 Aug 01	PRECIOUS HEART (re) Duty Free / Decode DFTELCD 001 [1]	14	5
13 Apr 02	EVERYBODY'S A ROCKSTAR Duty Free / Decode DFTELCD 003	60	1

[1] Tall Paul vs Inxs

See also CAMISRA; ESCRIMA; PARTIZAN; GRIFTERS; Paul NEWMAN

TAMBA TRIO
Argentina, male vocal / instrumental group (2 WEEKS) pos/wks

		pos	wks
18 Jul 98	MAS QUE NADA Talkin Loud TLCD 34	34	2

TAMPERER featuring MAYA Italy, male production duo –
Alex Farolfi and Mario Fargetta – and female vocalist (38 WEEKS) pos/wks

		pos	wks
25 Apr 98	★ FEEL IT Pepper 0530032	1	17
14 Nov 98	● IF YOU BUY THIS RECORD YOUR LIFE WILL BE BETTER Pepper 0530082	3	14
12 Feb 00	● HAMMER TO THE HEART (re) Pepper 9230032	6	7

See also FARGETTA

TAMS US, male vocal group – lead vocal Joseph Pope (31 WEEKS) pos/wks

		pos	wks
14 Feb 70	BE YOUNG, BE FOOLISH, BE HAPPY Stateside SS 2123	32	7
31 Jul 71	★ HEY GIRL DON'T BOTHER ME Probe PRO 532	1	17
21 Nov 87	THERE AIN'T NOTHING LIKE SHAGGIN' Virgin VS 1029	21	7

Norma TANEGA US, female vocalist (8 WEEKS) pos/wks

		pos	wks
7 Apr 66	WALKIN' MY CAT NAMED DOG Stateside SS 496	22	8

Children of TANSLEY SCHOOL
UK, children's choir (4 WEEKS) pos/wks

		pos	wks
28 Mar 81	MY MUM IS ONE IN A MILLION EMI 5151	27	4

Jimmy TARBUCK UK, male comedian / vocalist (2 WEEKS) pos/wks

		pos	wks
16 Nov 85	AGAIN (re) Safari SAFE 68	68	2

TARLISA – See CO-RO featuring TARLISA

Bill TARMEY UK, male actor / vocalist (9 WEEKS) pos/wks

		pos	wks
3 Apr 93	ONE VOICE Arista 74321140852	16	4
19 Feb 94	WIND BENEATH MY WINGS EMI CDEM 304	40	3
19 Nov 94	IOU EMI CDEM 361	55	2

TARRIERS US, male vocal / instrumental group (6 WEEKS) pos/wks

		pos	wks
14 Dec 56	CINDY, OH CINDY London HLN 8340 [1]	26	1
1 Mar 57	THE BANANA BOAT SONG Columbia DB 3891	15	5

[1] Vince Martin and The Tarriers

TARTAN ARMY UK, male vocal ensemble (4 WEEKS) pos/wks

		pos	wks
6 Jun 98	SCOTLAND BE GOOD Precious JWLCD 33	54	4

A TASTE OF HONEY US, female vocal duo –
Janice Marie Johnson and Hazel Payne (19 WEEKS) pos/wks

		pos	wks
17 Jun 78	● BOOGIE OOGIE OOGIE Capitol CL 15988 ▲	3	16
18 May 85	BOOGIE OOGIE OOGIE (re-mix) Capitol CL 357	59	3

TASTE XPERIENCE featuring Natasha PEARL UK, male
instrumental / production group and UK, female vocalist (1 WEEK) pos/wks

		pos	wks
6 Nov 99	SUMMERSAULT Manifesto FESCD 64	66	1

TATA BOX INHIBITORS Holland, male production duo (1 WEEK) pos/wks

		pos	wks
3 Feb 01	FREET Hooj Choons HOOJ 103CD	67	1

TATJANA Croatia, female vocalist – Tatjana Simic (2 WEEKS) pos/wks

		pos	wks
21 Sep 96	SANTA MARIA Love This LUVTHISCDX 4	40	2

TAVARES 466 Top 500 Successful R&B and disco-era family group
from Massachusetts, US, who started performing in 1963 (when aged 9-15)
as Chubby and The Turnpikes; brothers Antone, 'Chubby', Ralph, Feliciano,
Arthur Lee and Perry Lee Tavares (77 WEEKS) pos/wks

		pos	wks
10 Jul 76	● HEAVEN MUST BE MISSING AN ANGEL Capitol CL 15876	4	11
9 Oct 76	● DON'T TAKE AWAY THE MUSIC Capitol CL 15886	4	10
5 Feb 77	THE MIGHTY POWER OF LOVE Capitol CL 15905	25	6
9 Apr 77	● WHODUNIT Capitol CL 15914	5	10
2 Jul 77	ONE STEP AWAY Capitol CL 15930	16	7
18 Mar 78	THE GHOST OF LOVE Capitol CL 15968	29	6
6 May 78	● MORE THAN A WOMAN Capitol CL 15977	7	11
12 Aug 78	SLOW TRAIN TO PARADISE Capitol CL 15996	62	3
22 Feb 86	HEAVEN MUST BE MISSING AN ANGEL (re-mix) Capitol TAV 1	12	9
3 May 86	IT ONLY TAKES A MINUTE Capitol TAV 2	46	4

TAXMAN – See KICKING BACK with TAXMAN

TAYLOR – See LIBRA presents TAYLOR

Andy TAYLOR UK, male vocalist (2 WEEKS) pos/wks

		pos	wks
20 Oct 90	LOLA A&M AM 596	60	2

See also DURAN DURAN

Becky TAYLOR UK, female vocalist (1 WEEK) pos/wks

		pos	wks
16 Jun 01	SONG OF DREAMS EMI Classics 8794880	60	1

Dina TAYLOR – See BBG

Felice TAYLOR US, female vocalist (13 WEEKS) pos/wks

		pos	wks
25 Oct 67	I FEEL LOVE COMIN' ON President PT 155	11	13

James TAYLOR US, male vocalist (23 WEEKS) pos/wks

		pos	wks
21 Nov 70	FIRE AND RAIN Warner Bros. WB 6104	42	3
28 Aug 71	● YOU'VE GOT A FRIEND Warner Bros. WB 16085 ▲	4	15
16 Mar 74	MOCKINGBIRD Elektra K 12134 [1]	34	5

[1] Carly Simon and, uncredited, James Taylor

James TAYLOR QUARTET – See JTQ

John TAYLOR UK, male vocalist (4 WEEKS) pos/wks

		pos	wks
15 Mar 86	I DO WHAT I DO . . . THEME FOR '9 1/2 WEEKS' Parlophone R 6125	42	4

See also DURAN DURAN

Johnnie TAYLOR US, male vocalist, d. 13 May 2000 (7 WEEKS) pos/wks

		pos	wks
24 Apr 76	DISCO LADY CBS 4044 ▲	25	7

JT TAYLOR US, male vocalist (5 WEEKS) pos/wks

		pos	wks
24 Aug 91	LONG HOT SUMMER NIGHT MCA MCS 1567	63	2
30 Nov 91	FEEL THE NEED MCA MCS 1592	57	1
18 Apr 92	FOLLOW ME MCA MCS 1617	59	2

See also KOOL and the GANG

Pauline TAYLOR UK, female vocalist (3 WEEKS) pos/wks

		pos	wks
8 Jun 96	LET THIS BE A PRAYER Cheeky CHEKCD 013 [1]	26	2
9 Nov 96	CONSTANTLY WAITING Cheeky CHEKCD 015	51	1

[1] Rollo Goes Spiritual with Pauline Taylor

R Dean TAYLOR Canada, male vocalist (48 WEEKS) pos/wks

		pos	wks
19 Jun 68	GOTTA SEE JANE Tamla Motown TMG 656	17	12
3 Apr 71	● INDIANA WANTS ME Tamla Motown TMG 763	2	15

11 May 74 ●	THERE'S A GHOST IN MY HOUSE *Tamla Motown TMG 896*	3	12
31 Aug 74	WINDOW SHOPPING *Polydor 2058 502*	36	5
21 Sep 74	GOTTA SEE JANE (re-issue) *Tamla Motown TMG 918*	41	4

Rob TAYLOR – *See Mathias WARE featuring Rob TAYLOR*

Roger TAYLOR
UK, male vocalist / instrumentalist – drums (18 WEEKS) pos/wks

18 Apr 81	FUTURE MANAGEMENT *EMI 5157*	49	4
16 Jun 84	MAN ON FIRE *EMI 5478*	66	2
10 Oct 92	RADIO *Epic 6584367* [1]	37	3
14 May 94	NAZIS *Parlophone CDR 6379*	22	2
1 Oct 94	FOREIGN SAND *Parlophone CDR 6389* [2]	26	2
26 Nov 94	HAPPINESS *Parlophone CDR 6399*	32	2
10 Oct 98	PRESSURE ON *Parlophone CDR 6507*	45	1
10 Apr 99	SURRENDER *Parlophone CDR 6517*	38	2

[1] Shaky featuring Roger Taylor [2] Roger Taylor and Yoshiki

See also QUEEN

TAZ – *See STEREO NATION*

Kiri TE KANAWA *New Zealand, female vocalist (11 WEEKS)* pos/wks

28 Sep 91 ●	WORLD IN UNION *Columbia 6574817*	4	11

TEACH-IN
Holland, male / female vocal / instrumental group (7 WEEKS) pos/wks

12 Apr 75	DING–A–DONG *Polydor 2058 570*	13	7

TEAM *UK, male vocal / instrumental group (5 WEEKS)* pos/wks

1 Jun 85	WICKI WACKY HOUSE PARTY *EMI 5519*	55	5

TEAM DEEP *Belgium, male production duo (1 WEEK)* pos/wks

17 May 97	MORNINGLIGHT *Multiply CDMULTY 19*	42	1

TEARDROP EXPLODES
UK, male vocal / instrumental group (50 WEEKS) pos/wks

27 Sep 80	WHEN I DREAM *Mercury TEAR 1*	47	6
31 Jan 81 ●	REWARD *Vertigo TEAR 2*	6	13
2 May 81	TREASON (IT'S JUST A STORY) *Mercury TEAR 3*	18	8
29 Aug 81	PASSIONATE FRIEND *Zoo / Mercury TEAR 5*	25	10
21 Nov 81	COLOURS FLY AWAY *Mercury TEAR 6*	54	3
19 Jun 82	TINY CHILDREN *Mercury TEAR 7*	44	7
19 Mar 83	YOU DISAPPEAR FROM VIEW *Mercury TEAR 8*	41	3

See also Julian COPE

TEARS FOR FEARS `173` `Top 500`
Bath–based band at the forefront of the mid–1980s 'British Invasion' of the US: Roland Orzabal (v/g/k), Curt Smith (v/b; left in 1991). The first of their two US No.1s, 'Everybody Wants to Rule the World', also won the 1986 Brit award for Best Single (143 WEEKS) pos/wks

2 Oct 82 ●	MAD WORLD *Mercury IDEA 3*	3	16
5 Feb 83 ●	CHANGE *Mercury IDEA 4*	4	9
30 Apr 83 ●	PALE SHELTER *Mercury IDEA 5*	5	8
3 Dec 83	THE WAY YOU ARE *Mercury IDEA 6*	24	8
18 Aug 84	MOTHER'S TALK *Mercury IDEA 7*	14	8
1 Dec 84 ●	SHOUT *Mercury IDEA 8* ▲	4	16
30 Mar 85 ●	EVERYBODY WANTS TO RULE THE WORLD (re) *Mercury IDEA 9* ▲	2	15
22 Jun 85	HEAD OVER HEELS *Mercury IDEA 10*	12	9
31 Aug 85	SUFFER THE CHILDREN *Mercury IDEA 1*	52	4
7 Sep 85	PALE SHELTER (re-issue) *Mercury IDEA 2*	73	2
12 Oct 85	I BELIEVE (A SOULFUL RE-RECORDING) *Mercury IDEA 11*	23	4
31 May 86 ●	EVERYBODY WANTS TO RUN THE WORLD (re) *Mercury RACE 1*	5	7
2 Sep 89 ●	SOWING THE SEEDS OF LOVE *Fontana IDEA 12*	5	9
18 Nov 89	WOMAN IN CHAINS *Fontana IDEA 13*	26	8
3 Mar 90	ADVICE FOR THE YOUNG AT HEART *Fontana IDEA 14*	36	4
22 Feb 92	LAID SO LOW (TEARS ROLL DOWN) *Fontana IDEA 17*	17	5
25 Apr 92	WOMAN IN CHAINS (re-issue) *Fontana IDEA 16* [1]	57	1
29 May 93	BREAK IT DOWN AGAIN *Mercury IDECD 18*	20	5
31 Jul 93	COLD *Mercury IDECD 19*	72	1
7 Oct 95	RAOUL AND THE KINGS OF SPAIN *Epic 6624765*	31	3
29 Jun 96	GOD'S MISTAKE *Epic 6634185*	61	1

[1] Tears for Fears featuring Oleta Adams

Mercury RACE 1 was a slightly changed version of Mercury IDEA 9, released to promote the Race Against Time of 15 May 1986. Oleta Adams is given no label credit on the original release of 'Woman in Chains'. From 1992 Tears for Fears was essentially a male vocalist / multi-instrumentalist – Roland Orzaba

TECHNATION *UK, male production duo (1 WEEK)* pos/wks

7Apr 01	SEA OF BLUE *Slinky Music SLINKY 012CD*	56	1

TECHNICIAN 2
UK, male instrumental / production group (1 WEEK) pos/wks

14 Nov 92	PLAYING WITH THE BOY *MCA MCS 1710*	70	1

TECHNIQUE *UK, female vocal / instrumental duo (2 WEEKS)* pos/wks

10 Apr 99	SUN IS SHINING *Creation CRESCD 306*	64	1
28 Aug 99	YOU + ME *Creation CRESCD 315*	56	1

TECHNO TWINS *UK, male / female vocal duo (2 WEEKS)* pos/wks

16 Jan 82	FALLING IN LOVE AGAIN (re) *PRT 7P 224*	70	2

TECHNOCAT *UK, male producer – Tom Wilson (3 WEEKS)* pos/wks

2 Dec 95	TECHNOCAT *Pukka CDPUKKA 4* [1]	33	3

[1] Technocat featuring Tom Wilson

TECHNOHEAD *UK, male / female vocal / instrumental duo – Michael Wells and Lee Newman (20 WEEKS)* pos/wks

3 Feb 96 ●	I WANNA BE A HIPPY *Mokum DB 17703*	6	14
27 Apr 96	HAPPY BIRTHDAY *Mokum DB 17593*	18	5
12 Oct 96	BANANA-NA-NA (DUMB DI DUMB) *Mokum DB 17473*	64	1

See also GTO; TRICKY DISCO

TECHNOTRONIC
Belgium, male producer – Jo Bogaert (66 WEEKS) pos/wks

2 Sep 89 ●	PUMP UP THE JAM *Swanyard SYR 4* [1]	2	15
3 Feb 90 ●	GET UP (BEFORE THE NIGHT IS OVER) *Swanyard SYR 8* [2]	2	10
7 Apr 90	THIS BEAT IS TECHNOTRONIC *Swanyard SYR 9* [3]	14	7
14 Jul 90	ROCKIN' OVER THE BEAT *Swanyard SYR 14* [2]	9	9
6 Oct 90	MEGAMIX *Swanyard SYR 19*	6	8
15 Dec 90	TURN IT UP *Swanyard SYD 9* [4]	42	4
25 May 91	MOVE THAT BODY *ARS 6568377* [5]	12	7
3 Aug 91	WORK *ARS 6573317* [5]	40	4
14 Dec 96	PUMP UP THE JAM (re-mix) *Worx WORXCD 004*	36	2

[1] Technotronic featuring Felly [2] Technotronic featuring Ya Kid K
[3] Technotronic featuring MC Eric [4] Technotronic featuring Melissa and Einstein [5] Technotronic featuring Reggie

See also HI-TEK 3 featuring YA KID K

TEDDY BEARS *US, male / female vocal group (17 WEEKS)* pos/wks

19 Dec 58 ●	TO KNOW HIM IS TO LOVE HIM *London HLN 8733* ▲	2	16
14 Apr 79	TO KNOW HIM IS TO LOVE HIM (re-issue) *Lightning LIG 9015*	66	1

'To Know Him Is to Love Him' re-issue was coupled with 'Endless Sleep' by Jody Reynolds as a double A-side

TEEBONE featuring MC KIE and MC SPARKS *UK, male producer - Leon Thompson - and UK, male rap duo (2 WEEKS)* pos/wks

5 Aug 00	FLY BI *East West EW 217CD*	43	2

TEENAGE FANCLUB
UK, male vocal / instrumental group (22 WEEKS) pos/wks

24 Aug 91	**STAR SIGN** *Creation CRE 105*	.44	2
2 Nov 91	**THE CONCEPT** *Creation CRE 111*	.51	1
8 Feb 92	**WHAT YOU DO TO ME (EP)** *Creation CRE 115*	.31	2
26 Jun 93	**RADIO** *Creation CRESCD 130*	.31	2
2 Oct 93	**NORMAN 3** *Creation CRESCD 142*	.50	1
2 Apr 94	**FALLIN'** *Epic 6602622* [1]	.59	1
8 Apr 95	**MELLOW DOUBT** *Creation CRESCD 175*	.34	2
27 May 95	**SPARKY'S DREAM** *Creation CRESCD 201*	.40	2
2 Sep 95	**NEIL JUNG** *Creation CRESCD 210*	.62	1
16 Dec 95	**HAVE LOST IT (EP)** *Creation CRESCD 216*	.53	1
12 Jul 97	**AIN'T THAT ENOUGH** *Creation CRESCD 228*	.17	3
30 Aug 97	**I DON'T WANT CONTROL OF YOU** *Creation CRESCD 238*	.43	1
29 Nov 97	**START AGAIN** *Creation CRESCD 280*	.54	1
28 Oct 00	**I NEED DIRECTION** *Columbia 6699512*	.48	1
2 Mar 02	**NEAR TO YOU (re-mix)** *Geographic GEOG 013CD* [2]	.68	1

[1] Teenage Fanclub and De La Soul [2] Teenage Fanclub and Jad Fair

Tracks on What You Do to Me (EP): What You Do to Me / B-Side / Life's a Gas / Filler.
Tracks on Have Lost It (EP): 120 Mins / Don't Look Back / Everything Flows / Star Sign.
This last track is a re-recorded version of their first hit

TEENAGERS – *See Frankie LYMON and the TEENAGERS*

Towa TEI featuring Kylie MINOGUE
Japan, male DJ / producer and Australia, female vocalist (1 WEEK) pos/wks

31 Oct 98	**GBI** *Athrob ART 021CD*	.63	1

TEKNO TOO
UK, male instrumental / production duo (2 WEEKS) pos/wks

13 Jul 91	**JET-STAR** *D-Zone DANCE 012*	.56	2

TELEPOPMUSIK
France, male instrumental / production trio and UK, female vocalist (1 WEEK) pos/wks

2 Mar 02	**BREATHE** *Chrysalis CDCHS 5133*	.42	1

TELETUBBIES
UK, male / female cuddly alien vocal group (32 WEEKS) pos/wks

13 Dec 97	★ **TELETUBBIES SAY EH-OH! (2re)** *BBC Worldwide WMXS 00092* ◆ ■	.1	32

TELEVISION
US, male vocal / instrumental group (10 WEEKS) pos/wks

16 Apr 77	**MARQUEE MOON** *Elektra K 12252*	.30	4
30 Jul 77	**PROVE IT** *Elektra K 12262*	.25	4
22 Apr 78	**FOXHOLE** *Elektra K 12287*	.36	2

TELEX
Belgium, male vocal / instrumental trio (7 WEEKS) pos/wks

21 Jul 79	**ROCK AROUND THE CLOCK** *Sire SIR 4020*	.34	7

Sylvia TELLA – *See BLOW MONKEYS*

TEMPERANCE SEVEN
UK, male vocal / instrumental group – lead vocal Paul MacDowell (45 WEEKS) pos/wks

30 Mar 61	★ **YOU'RE DRIVING ME CRAZY** *Parlophone R 4757*	.1	16
15 Jun 61	● **PASADENA** *Parlophone R 4781*	.4	17
28 Sep 61	**HARD HEARTED HANNAH / CHILI BOM BOM** *Parlophone R 4823*	.28	4
7 Dec 61	**THE CHARLESTON** *Parlophone R 4851*	.22	8

'Chili Bom Bom' listed with 'Hard Hearted Hannah' only for the weeks of 12 and 19 Oct 1961

TEMPLE OF THE DOG
US, male vocal / instrumental group (2 WEEKS) pos/wks

24 Oct 92	**HUNGER STRIKE** *A&M AM 0091*	.51	2

Nino TEMPO and April STEVENS
US, male / female vocal duo - Antonio and Carol Lo Tempio (19 WEEKS) pos/wks

7 Nov 63	**DEEP PURPLE** *London HLK 9782* ▲	.17	11
16 Jan 64	**WHISPERING** *London HLK 9829*	.20	8

TEMPTATIONS (87) [Top 500]
The world's most successful R&B vocal group: Eddie Kendricks (d. 1992), Otis Williams, Paul Williams (d. 1973), Melvin Franklin (d. 1995), David Ruffin (d. 1991). The Detroit quintet's biggest UK hit, 'My Girl', was a 27-year-old US No.1. The current line-up of the group is still doing well Stateside (203 WEEKS) pos/wks

18 Mar 65	**MY GIRL** *Stateside SS 378* ▲	.43	1
1 Apr 65	**IT'S GROWING (re)** *Tamla Motown TMG 504*	.45	2
14 Jul 66	**AIN'T TOO PROUD TO BEG** *Tamla Motown TMG 565*	.21	11
6 Oct 66	**BEAUTY IS ONLY SKIN DEEP** *Tamla Motown TMG 578*	.18	10
15 Dec 66	**(I KNOW) I'M LOSING YOU** *Tamla Motown TMG 587*	.19	9
6 Sep 67	**YOU'RE MY EVERYTHING** *Tamla Motown TMG 620*	.26	15
6 Mar 68	**I WISH IT WOULD RAIN** *Tamla Motown TMG 641*	.45	1
12 Jun 68	**I COULD NEVER LOVE ANOTHER** *Tamla Motown TMG 658*	.47	1
29 Jan 69	● **I'M GONNA MAKE YOU LOVE ME (re)** *Tamla Motown TMG 685* [1]	.3	12
5 Mar 69	● **GET READY** *Tamla Motown TMG 688*	.10	9
23 Aug 69	**CLOUD NINE** *Tamla Motown TMG 707*	.15	10
20 Sep 69	**I SECOND THAT EMOTION** *Tamla Motown TMG 709* [1]	.18	8
17 Jan 70	**I CAN'T GET NEXT TO YOU** *Tamla Motown TMG 722* ▲	.13	9
21 Mar 70	**WHY (MUST WE FALL IN LOVE)** *Tamla Motown TMG 730* [1]	.31	7
13 Jun 70	**PSYCHEDELIC SHACK** *Tamla Motown TMG 741*	.33	7
19 Sep 70	● **BALL OF CONFUSION (THAT'S WHAT THE WORLD IS TODAY) (re)** *Tamla Motown TMG 749*	.7	15
22 May 71	● **JUST MY IMAGINATION (RUNNING AWAY WITH ME)** *Tamla Motown TMG 773* ▲	.8	16
5 Feb 72	**SUPERSTAR (REMEMBER HOW YOU GOT WHERE YOU ARE)** *Tamla Motown TMG 800*	.32	5
15 Apr 72	**TAKE A LOOK AROUND** *Tamla Motown TMG 808*	.13	10
13 Jan 73	**PAPA WAS A ROLLIN' STONE** *Tamla Motown TMG 839* ▲	.14	8
29 Sep 73	**LAW OF THE LAND** *Tamla Motown TMG 866*	.41	4
12 Jun 82	**STANDING ON THE TOP (PART 1)** *Motown TMG 1263* [2]	.53	3
17 Nov 84	**TREAT HER LIKE A LADY** *Motown TMG 1365*	.12	10
15 Aug 87	**PAPA WAS A ROLLIN' STONE (re-mix)** *Motown ZB 41431*	.31	6
6 Feb 88	**LOOK WHAT YOU STARTED** *Motown ZB 41733*	.63	2
21 Oct 89	**ALL I WANT FROM YOU** *Motown ZB 43233*	.71	1
15 Feb 92	● **MY GIRL (re-issue)** *Epic 6576767*	.2	10
22 Feb 92	**THE JONES'** *Motown TMG 1403*	.69	1

[1] Diana Ross and The Supremes and The Temptations [2] Temptations featuring Rick James

See also Rod STEWART

10 CC (198) [Top 500]
Multi-talented Manchester supergroup: Graham Gouldman (previously penned hits for Hollies, Yardbirds and Herman's Hermits), Eric Stewart (ex-Mindbenders, Hotlegs), and Lol Creme and Kevin Godley (both ex-Hotlegs). Godley and Creme went on to have hits as a duo and produced award-winning videos (133 WEEKS) pos/wks

23 Sep 72	● **DONNA** *UK 6*	.2	13
19 May 73	★ **RUBBER BULLETS** *UK 36*	.1	15
25 Aug 73	● **THE DEAN AND I** *UK 48*	.10	8
15 Jun 74	● **THE WALL STREET SHUFFLE** *UK 69*	.10	10
14 Sep 74	**SILLY LOVE** *UK 77*	.24	7
5 Apr 75	● **LIFE IS A MINESTRONE** *Mercury 6008 010*	.7	8
31 May 75	★ **I'M NOT IN LOVE** *Mercury 6008 014*	.1	11
29 Nov 75	● **ART FOR ART'S SAKE** *Mercury 6008 017*	.5	10
20 Mar 76	● **I'M MANDY FLY ME** *Mercury 6008 019*	.6	9
11 Dec 76	● **THE THINGS WE DO FOR LOVE** *Mercury 6008 022*	.6	11
16 Apr 77	● **GOOD MORNING JUDGE** *Mercury 6008 025*	.5	12
12 Aug 78	★ **DREADLOCK HOLIDAY** *Mercury 6008 035*	.1	13
7 Aug 82	**RUN AWAY** *Mercury MER 113*	.50	4
18 Mar 95	**I'M NOT IN LOVE (re-recording)** *Avex UK AVEXCD 2*	.29	2

From 'Things We Do for Love' 10 CC were a male vocal / instrumental duo

See also WAX; Graham GOULDMAN

TEN CITY US, male vocal / instrumental group (21 WEEKS)

		pos/wks
21 Jan 89 ●	THAT'S THE WAY LOVE IS *Atlantic A 8963*	8 10
8 Apr 89	DEVOTION *Atlantic A 8916*	29 4
22 Jul 89	WHERE DO WE GO? *Atlantic A 8864*	60 1
27 Oct 90	WHATEVER MAKES YOU HAPPY *Atlantic A 7819*	60 2
15 Aug 92	ONLY TIME WILL TELL / MY PEACE OF HEAVEN *East West America A 8516*	63 2
11 Sep 93	FANTASY *Columbia 6595042*	45 2

TEN SHARP
Holland, male vocal / instrumental duo (15 WEEKS)

		pos/wks
21 Mar 92 ●	YOU *Columbia 6566647*	10 13
20 Jun 92	AIN'T MY BEATING HEART *Columbia 6580947*	63 2

10,000 MANIACS
US, female / male vocal / instrumental group (7 WEEKS)

		pos/wks
12 Sep 92	THESE ARE DAYS *Elektra EKR 156*	58 3
10 Apr 93	CANDY EVERYBODY WANTS *Elektra EKR 160CD1*	47 3
23 Oct 93	BECAUSE THE NIGHT *Elektra EKR 175CD*	65 1

TEN YEARS AFTER
UK, male vocal / instrumental group (18 WEEKS)

		pos/wks
6 Jun 70 ●	LOVE LIKE A MAN *Deram DM 299*	10 18

TENACIOUS D US, male vocal / instrumental
duo - Jack Black and Kyle Gass (2 WEEKS)

		pos/wks
23 Nov 02	WONDERBOY *Epic 6733512*	34 2

Danny TENAGLIA US, male DJ / producer (5 WEEKS)

		pos/wks
5 Sep 98	MUSIC IS THE ANSWER (DANCIN' AND PRANCIN') *Twisted UK TWCD 10038* [1]	36 3
10 Apr 99	TURN ME ON *Twisted UK TWCD 10045* [2]	53 1
23 Oct 99	MUSIC IS THE ANSWER (re-mix) *Twisted UK TWCD 10052* [1]	50 1

[1] Danny Tenaglia and Celeda [2] Danny Tenaglia featuring Liz Torres

TENNESSEE THREE – See Johnny CASH

TENOR FLY UK, male vocalist - Jonathan Sutter (17 WEEKS)

		pos/wks
6 Apr 91	WICKEDEST SOUND *Desire WANT 40* [1]	43 6
15 Jun 91	TRIBAL BASE *Desire WANT 44* [2]	20 6
7 Jan 95	BRIGHT SIDE OF LIFE *Mango CIDM 825*	51 2
7 Feb 98	B-BOY STANCE *Freskanova FND 7* [3]	23 3

[1] Rebel MC featuring Tenor Fly [2] Rebel MC featuring Tenor Fly and Barrington Levy [3] Freestylers featuring Tenor Fly

TENPOLE TUDOR
UK, male vocal / instrumental group (40 WEEKS)

		pos/wks
7 Apr 79 ●	WHO KILLED BAMBI *Virgin VS 256* [1]	6 8
13 Oct 79	ROCK AROUND THE CLOCK *Virgin VS 290*	21 6
25 Apr 81 ●	SWORDS OF A THOUSAND MEN *Stiff BUY 109*	6 12
1 Aug 81	WUNDERBAR *Stiff BUY 120*	16 9
14 Nov 81	THROWING MY BABY OUT WITH THE BATHWATER *Stiff BUY 129*	49 5

[1] Ten Pole Tudor

The listed flip side of 'Who Killed Bambi' was 'Silly Thing' by The Sex Pistols. The listed flip side of 'Rock Around the Clock' was 'The Great Rock 'n' Roll Swindle', also by The Sex Pistols

TENTH PLANET
UK, male / female vocal / production group (1 WEEK)

		pos/wks
14 Apr 01	GHOSTS *Nebula NEBCD 015*	59 1

Bryn TERFEL – See Shirley BASSEY

TERMINATERS – See ARNEE and the TERMINATERS

TERRA FIRMA Italy, male producer - Claudio Giussani (1 WEEK)

		pos/wks
18 May 96	FLOATING *Platipus PLAT 21CD*	64 1

Tammi TERRELL – See Marvin GAYE

TERRIS UK, male vocal / instrumental group (1 WEEK)

		pos/wks
17 Mar 01	FABRICATED LUNACY *Blanco Y Negro NEG 130CD*	62 1

TERRORIZE UK, male producer - Shaun Imrei (6 WEEKS)

		pos/wks
2 May 92	IT'S JUST A FEELING *Hamster STER 1*	52 3
22 Aug 92	FEEL THE RHYTHM *Hamster 12STER 2*	69 1
14 Nov 92	IT'S JUST A FEELING (re-issue) *Hamster STER 8*	47 2

TERRORVISION UK, male vocal / instrumental group (55 WEEKS)

		pos/wks
19 Jun 93	AMERICAN TV *Total Vegas CDVEGAS 3*	63 1
30 Oct 93	NEW POLICY ONE *Total Vegas CDVEGAS 4*	42 2
8 Jan 94	MY HOUSE *Total Vegas CDVEGAS 5*	29 4
9 Apr 94	OBLIVION *Total Vegas CDVEGAS 6*	21 5
25 Jun 94	MIDDLEMAN *Total Vegas CDVEGAS 7*	25 4
3 Sep 94	PRETEND BEST FRIEND *Total Vegas CDVEGAS 8*	25 3
29 Oct 94	ALICE WHAT'S THE MATTER *Total Vegas CDVEGAS 9*	24 4
18 Mar 95	SOME PEOPLE SAY *Total Vegas CDVEGAS 10*	22 3
2 Mar 96 ●	PERSEVERANCE *Total Vegas CDVEGAS 11*	5 4
4 May 96	CELEBRITY HIT LIST *Total Vegas CDVEGAS 12*	20 3
20 Jul 96 ●	BAD ACTRESS *Total Vegas CDVEGAS 13*	10 3
11 Jan 97	EASY *Total Vegas CDVEGASS 14*	12 4
3 Oct 98	JOSEPHINE *EMI CDVEGAS 15*	23 2
30 Jan 99 ●	TEQUILA *Total Vegas CDVEGAS 16*	2 10
15 May 99	III WISHES *Total Vegas CDVEGAS 17*	42 1
27 Jan 01	D'YA WANNA GO FASTER *Papillion BTFLYS 0007*	28 2

Helen TERRY UK, female vocalist (6 WEEKS)

		pos/wks
12 May 84	LOVE LIES LOST *Virgin VS 678*	34 6

Tony TERRY US, male vocalist (6 WEEKS)

		pos/wks
27 Feb 88	LOVEY DOVEY *Epic TONY 2*	44 6

Todd TERRY PROJECT US, male producer (33 WEEKS)

		pos/wks
12 Nov 88	WEEKEND *Sleeping Bag SBUK 1T*	56 3
14 Oct 95	WEEKEND (re-mix) *Ore AG 13CD*	28 3
13 Jul 96	KEEP ON JUMPIN' *Manifesto FESCD 11* [1]	8 6
12 Jul 97 ●	SOMETHING GOIN' ON *Manifesto FESCD 25* [1]	5 10
6 Dec 97	IT'S OVER LOVE *Manfiesto FESCD 37* [2]	16 8
11 Apr 98	READY FOR A NEW DAY *Manifesto FESCD 40* [3]	20 2
3 Jul 99	LET IT RIDE *Innocent RESTCD 1*	58 1

[1] Todd Terry featuring Martha Wash and Jocelyn Brown [2] Todd Terry presents Shannon [3] Todd Terry featuring Martha Wash

See also BLACK RIOT; ROYAL HOUSE; SWAN LAKE; GYPSYMEN

TESLA US, male vocal / instrumental group (1 WEEK)

		pos/wks
27 Apr 91	SIGNS *Geffen GFS 3*	70 1

Joe TEX
US, male vocalist – Joe Arlington, d. 13 Aug 1982 (11 WEEKS)

		pos/wks
23 Apr 77 ●	AIN'T GONNA BUMP NO MORE (WITH NO BIG FAT WOMAN) *Epic EPC 5035*	2 11

TEXAS ⟨216⟩ Top 500
Named after Wim Wenders' film 'Paris, Texas' the Scots blues turned pop-chart mainstays are: Sharleen Spiteri (v), Ally McErlaine (g), Johnny McElhone (b), Eddie Campbell (k), all from Glasgow. Stuart Kerr, Richard Hynde and Mykey Wilson have all contributed on drums with Tony McGovern (g) the most recent recruit to a band now well established among the multi-million-selling album elite (127 WEEKS)

		pos/wks
4 Feb 89 ●	I DON'T WANT A LOVER *Mercury TEX 1*	8 11
6 May 89	THRILL HAS GONE *Mercury TEX 2*	60 3
5 Aug 89	EVERYDAY NOW *Mercury TEX 3*	44 5

JEALOUS GUY

A one-off single recorded between 1980's Flesh and Blood and 1982's Avalon albums, 'Jealous Guy' was Bryan Ferry and Roxy Music's only chart-topping single. Although the band came close to topping the chart with their own compositions 'Virginia Plain', 'Love Is the Drug' and 'Dance Away', it took a cover of John Lennon's 'Jealous Guy' to give the group a No.1 single, and the success of the recording was for the most part due to its release shortly after Lennon's untimely death.

Aside from the album's title track, 'Jealous Guy' was the stand-out track on John Lennon's 1971 opus Imagine, and surprisingly had never been released as a single. In fact, the song had been around for some years and was originally written during, or soon after, The Beatles' trip to India in the spring of 1968. Before the group retired to Abbey Road to begin sessions for what became the double white Beatles album, there was a pre-production meeting in May 1968 at George Harrison's house in Esher, Surrey. Here The Beatles played each other their new songs which were also taped. Not all of them went on the Beatles album, and two of them, Harrison's 'Not Guilty' and Lennon's 'What's the New Mary Jane' (which Lennon at one point scheduled for release as a Plastic Ono Band single, but withdrew) disappeared until finally released on the Anthology 3 collection in the 1990s. After so many years of anticipation, they both fell short of the high expectations.

Another song that Lennon presented at this gathering was his 'Child of Nature'. Apparently repeating idealistic sentiments from another recent composition, 'Across the Universe' (on a

THE SONG HAD BEEN AROUND FOR SOME YEARS AND WAS ORIGINALLY WRITTEN DURING, OR SOON AFTER, THE BEATLES' TRIP TO INDIA IN THE SPRING OF 1968

World Wildlife Fund album in 1969 and Let It Be in 1970), 'Child of Nature' never went beyond this demo stage and was not considered for the remaining Beatles albums. When recording his second solo album in 1971, Lennon resurrected the melody, but wrote an entirely new set of lyrics and the song became 'Jealous Guy'. Proving that John Lennon was not always the tough guy that he liked to project to his public, the song was lyrically one of the unlikeliest things one might have expected from him at the time: an apology.

Roxy Music's recording of 'Jealous Guy', a personal favourite of Ferry's, was most certainly

Roxy Music's lead vocalist Bryan Ferry
was the son of a coal miner

not released to cash in on Lennon's death. It was a sympathetic rendering, keeping close to the original, and also repeated the whistling that Lennon had featured in his original version. This was particularly moving on the Roxy version considering the circumstances. Bryan Ferry and Roxy Music were as shocked as anyone else at Lennon's senseless murder, and the song was recorded as a tribute. Ferry recalls: "We did this concert in Germany. It was the week after Lennon had tragically died, and we did that song. It went down incredibly well with the audience, so when we got back to England we just recorded it, and it was a big hit."

Not surprisingly, John Lennon's songs topped the charts in Britain for several weeks following his death in December 1980. First came '(Just Like) Starting Over' from his just released comeback album, while a re-issued 'Happy Xmas (War Is Over)' rose to No.2. In the new year, 'Imagine' made No.1, followed immediately afterwards by 'Woman' before Roxy Music took 'Jealous Guy' to the top in a fitting tribute to one of the greatest icons in popular music history.

■ Tony Burton

★ **ARTIST:**	Roxy Music
★ **LABEL:**	EG
★ **WRITER:**	John Lennon
★ **PRODUCERS:**	Bryan Ferry and Rhett Davies

2 Dec 89		PRAYER FOR YOU *Mercury TEX 4*	73	1
7 Sep 91		WHY BELIEVE IN YOU *Mercury TEX 5*	66	1
26 Oct 91		IN MY HEART *Mercury TEX 6*	74	1
8 Feb 92		ALONE WITH YOU *Mercury TEX 7*	32	4
25 Apr 92		TIRED OF BEING ALONE *Mercury TEX 8*	19	6
11 Sep 93		SO CALLED FRIEND *Vertigo TEXCD 9*	30	3
30 Oct 93		YOU OWE IT ALL TO ME *Vertigo TEXCD 10*	39	3
12 Feb 94		SO IN LOVE WITH YOU *Vertigo TEXCD 11*	28	2
18 Jan 97	●	SAY WHAT YOU WANT *Mercury MERCD 480*	3	10
19 Apr 97	●	HALO *Mercury MERCD 482*	10	7
9 Aug 97	●	BLACK EYED BOY *Mercury MERCD 490*	5	6
15 Nov 97	●	PUT YOUR ARMS AROUND ME (2re) *Mercury MERCD 497*	10	8
21 Mar 98	●	INSANE / SAY WHAT YOU WANT (ALL DAY EVERY DAY) (re-mix) *Mercury MERCD 499* [1]	4	7
1 May 99	●	IN OUR LIFETIME *Mercury MERCD 517*	4	9
28 Aug 99	●	SUMMER SON *Mercury MERCD 520*	5	9
27 Nov 99		WHEN WE ARE TOGETHER *Mercury MERCD 525*	12	9
14 Oct 00	●	IN DEMAND (re) *Mercury MERCD 528*	6	10
20 Jan 01	●	INNER SMILE *Mercury MERCD 531*	6	8
21 Jul 01		I DON'T WANT A LOVER (re-mix) *Mercury MERCD 533*	16	4

[1] Texas featuring The Wu-Tang Clan

'Say What You Want (All Day Every Day)' is a new mix of the hit from 18 Jan 97 with rap by Method Man and The RZA

THAT KID CHRIS
US, male DJ / producer – Chris Staropoli (1 WEEK)   pos/wks

22 Feb 97	FEEL THA VIBE *Manifesto FESCD 16*	52	1

THAT PETROL EMOTION
UK / US, male vocal / instrumental group (24 WEEKS)   pos/wks

11 Apr 87	BIG DECISION *Polydor TPE 1*	43	7
11 Jul 87	DANCE *Polydor TPE 2*	64	2
17 Oct 87	GENIUS MOVE *Virgin VS 1002*	65	2
31 Mar 90	ABANDON *Virgin VS 1242*	73	1
1 Sep 90	HEY VENUS *Virgin VS 1290*	49	4
9 Feb 91	TINGLE *Virgin VS 1312*	49	4
27 Apr 91	SENSITIZE *Virgin VS 1261*	55	4

THE AUDIENCE – See THEAUDIENCE

The THE
UK, male vocalist / multi-instrumentalist – Matt Johnson and backing musicians (52 WEEKS)   pos/wks

4 Dec 82	UNCERTAIN SMILE *Epic EPC A 2787*	68	3
17 Sep 83	THIS IS THE DAY *Epic A 3710*	71	3
9 Aug 86	HEARTLAND *Some Bizarre TRUTH 2*	29	10
25 Oct 86	INFECTED *Some Bizarre TRUTH 3*	48	5
24 Jan 87	SLOW TRAIN TO DAWN *Some Bizarre TENSE 1*	64	2
23 May 87	SWEET BIRD OF TRUTH *Epic TENSE 2*	55	2
1 Apr 89	THE BEAT(EN) GENERATION *Epic EMU 8*	18	5
22 Jul 89	GRAVITATE TO ME *Epic EMU 9*	63	3
7 Oct 89	ARMAGEDDON DAYS ARE HERE (AGAIN) *Epic EMU 10*	70	2
2 Mar 91	SHADES OF BLUE (EP) *Epic 6557968*	54	1
16 Jan 93	DOGS OF LUST *Epic 6584572*	25	4
17 Apr 93	SLOW EMOTION REPLAY *Epic 6590772*	35	3
19 Jun 93	LOVE IS STRONGER THAN DEATH *Epic 6593712*	39	3
15 Jan 94	DIS-INFECTED (EP) *Epic 6598112*	17	4
4 Feb 95	I SAW THE LIGHT *Epic 6610912*	31	2

Tracks on Shades of Blue (EP): Jealous of Youth / Another Boy Drowning (Live) / Solitude / Dolphins.

Tracks on Dis-Infected (EP): This Was the Day / Dis-Infected / Helpline Operator (sickboy remix) / Dogs of Lust (germicide remix). 'That Was the Day' and 'Dis-Infected' on the EP are re-recordings of earlier hits. 'Dogs of Lust' is a re-mix

THEATRE OF HATE
UK, male vocal / instrumental group (9 WEEKS)   pos/wks

23 Jan 82	DO YOU BELIEVE IN THE WESTWORLD *Burning Rome BRR 2*	40	7
29 May 82	THE HOP *Burning Rome BRR 3*	70	2

THEAUDIENCE
UK, male / female, vocal / instrumental group – lead vocal Sophie Ellis Bextor (5 WEEKS)   pos/wks

7 Mar 98	IF YOU CAN'T DO IT WHEN YOU'RE YOUNG, WHEN CAN YOU DO IT? *Mercury AUDCD 2*	48	1
23 May 98	A PESSIMIST IS NEVER DISAPPOINTED *Mercury AUDCD 3*	27	2
8 Aug 98	I KNOW ENOUGH (I DON'T GET ENOUGH) *Elleffe AUDCD 4*	25	2

THEM
UK, male vocal / instrumental group (23 WEEKS)   pos/wks

7 Jan 65	●	BABY PLEASE DON'T GO *Decca F 12018*	10	9
25 Mar 65	●	HERE COMES THE NIGHT *Decca F 12094*	2	12
9 Feb 91		BABY PLEASE DON'T GO (re-issue) *London LON 292*	65	2

See also Van MORRISON

THEN JERICO
UK, male vocal / instrumental group (36 WEEKS)   pos/wks

31 Jan 87	LET HER FALL *London LON 97*	65	3
25 Jul 87	THE MOTIVE (LIVING WITHOUT YOU) *London LON 145*	18	12
24 Oct 87	MUSCLE DEEP *London LON 156*	48	4
28 Jan 89	BIG AREA *London LON 204*	13	7
8 Apr 89	WHAT DOES IT TAKE? *London LON 223*	33	4
12 Aug 89	SUGAR BOX *London LON 235*	22	6

THERAPY?
UK, male vocal / instrumental group (33 WEEKS)   pos/wks

31 Oct 92		TEETHGRINDER *A&M AM 0097*	30	2
20 Mar 93	●	SHORTSHARPSHOCK (EP) *A&M AMCD 208*	9	4
12 Jun 93		FACE THE STRANGE (EP) *A&M 5803052*	18	3
28 Aug 93		OPAL MANTRA *A&M 5803612*	14	3
29 Jan 94		NOWHERE *A&M 5805052*	18	4
12 Mar 94		TRIGGER INSIDE *A&M 5805352*	22	3
11 Jun 94		DIE LAUGHING *A&M 5805892*	29	2
27 May 95		INNOCENT X *Volume VOLCD 1*	53	1
3 Jun 95		STORIES *A&M 5811052*	14	3
29 Jul 95		LOOSE *A&M 5811652*	25	3
18 Nov 95		DIANE *A&M 5812912*	26	2
14 Mar 98		CHURCH OF NOISE *A&M 5825392*	29	2
30 May 98		LONELY, CRYIN' ONLY *A&M 0441212*	32	1

Tracks on Shortsharpshock (EP): Screamager / Auto Surgery / Totally Random Man / Accelerator. Tracks on Face the Strange (EP): Turn / Speedball / Bloody Blue / Neckfreak. The listed flip side of 'Innocent X' was 'Belfast' by Orbital

THESE ANIMAL MEN
UK, male vocal / instrumental group (3 WEEKS)   pos/wks

24 Sep 94	THIS IS THE SOUND OF YOUTH *Hi-Rise FLATSCD 7*	72	1
8 Feb 97	LIFE SUPPORT MACHINE *Hut HUTCD 76*	62	1
12 Apr 97	LIGHT EMITTING ELECTRICAL WAVE *Hut HUTCD 81*	72	1

THEY MIGHT BE GIANTS
US, male vocal / instrumental duo – John Flansburgh and John Linnell (18 WEEKS)   pos/wks

3 Mar 90	●	BIRDHOUSE IN YOUR SOUL *Elektra EKR 104*	6	11
2 Jun 90		ISTANBUL (NOT CONSTANTINOPLE) *Elektra EKR 110*	61	2
28 Jul 01		BOSS OF ME *Pias / Restless PIASREST 001 CD*	21	5

THICK D
US, male producer - Eric 'E-Smoove' Miller (3 WEEKS)   pos/wks

12 Oct 02	INSATIABLE *Multiply CDMULTY 88*	35	3

See also E-SMOOVE featuring Latanza WATERS; PRAISE CATS

THIN LIZZY   ⌐214⌐   Top 500
Accomplished Irish hard-rock group (which at times included noted guitarists Gary Moore, Snowy White and Midge Ure) was built around distinctive singer / bass guitarist Phil Lynott (d. 1986). After a slow start, they wrote their own chapter in British rock history (128 WEEKS)   pos/wks

20 Jan 73	●	WHISKY IN THE JAR *Decca F 13355*	6	12
29 May 76	●	THE BOYS ARE BACK IN TOWN *Vertigo 6059 139*	8	10
14 Aug 76		JAILBREAK *Vertigo 6059 150*	31	4
15 Jan 77		DON'T BELIEVE A WORD *Vertigo Lizzy 001*	12	7
13 Aug 77		DANCIN' IN THE MOONLIGHT (IT'S CAUGHT ME IN ITS SPOTLIGHT) *Vertigo 6059 177*	14	8

13 May 78	ROSALIE – (COWGIRLS' SONG) (MEDLEY)		
	Vertigo LIZZY 2	20	13
3 Mar 79 ●	WAITING FOR AN ALIBI *Vertigo LIZZY 003*	9	8
16 Jun 79	DO ANYTHING YOU WANT TO *Vertigo LIZZY 004*	14	9
20 Oct 79	SARAH *Vertigo LIZZY 5*	24	13
24 May 80	CHINATOWN *Vertigo LIZZY 6*	21	9
27 Sep 80 ●	KILLER ON THE LOOSE *Vertigo LIZZY 7*	10	7
2 May 81	KILLERS LIVE (EP) *Vertigo LIZZY 8*	19	7
8 Aug 81	TROUBLE BOYS *Vertigo LIZZY 9*	53	4
6 Mar 82	HOLLYWOOD (DOWN ON YOUR LUCK) *Vertigo LIZZY 10*	53	3
12 Feb 83	COLD SWEAT *Vertigo LIZZY 11*	27	5
7 May 83	THUNDER AND LIGHTNING *Vertigo LIZZY 12*	39	2
6 Aug 83	THE SUN GOES DOWN *Vertigo LIZZY 13*	52	3
26 Jan 91	DEDICATION *Vertigo LIZZY 14*	35	3
23 Mar 91	THE BOYS ARE BACK IN TOWN (re-issue)		
	Vertigo LIZZY 15	63	1

Tracks on Killers Live (EP): Bad Reputation / Are You Ready / Dear Miss Lonely Hearts

3RD BASS US, male rap group (5 WEEKS)

		pos/wks	
10 Feb 90	THE GAS FACE *Def Jam 655627 0*	71	1
7 Apr 90	BROOKLYN-QUEENS *Def Jam 655830 7*	61	2
22 Jun 91	POP GOES THE WEASEL *Def Jam 6569547*	64	2

THIRD DIMENSION featuring Julie McDERMOTT
UK, male / female vocal / instrumental group (2 WEEKS)

		pos/wks	
12 Oct 96	DON'T GO *Soundproof MCSTD 40082*	34	2

3RD EDGE
UK, male vocal group (5 WEEKS)

		pos/wks	
31 Aug 02	IN AND OUT (re) *Parlophone / Q-Zone ECDR 6568*	15	5

THIRD EYE BLIND
US, male vocal / instrumental group (6 WEEKS)

		pos/wks	
27 Sep 97	SEMI-CHARMED LIFE *Elektra E 3907CD*	33	5
21 Mar 98	HOW'S IT GOING TO BE *Elektra E 3863CD*	51	1

3RD STOREE US, male vocal group (1 WEEK)

		pos/wks	
5 Jun 99	IF EVER *Yab Yum / Elektra E 3752CD*	53	1

THIRD WORLD
Jamaica, male vocal / instrumental group (53 WEEKS)

		pos/wks	
23 Sep 78 ●	NOW THAT WE'VE FOUND LOVE *Island WIP 6457*	10	9
6 Jan 79	COOL MEDITATION *Island WIP 6469*	17	10
16 Jun 79	TALK TO ME *Island WIP 6496*	56	5
6 Jun 81 ●	DANCING ON THE FLOOR (HOOKED ON LOVE) *CBS A 1214*	10	15
17 Apr 82	TRY JAH LOVE *CBS A 2063*	47	6
9 Mar 85	NOW THAT WE'VE FOUND LOVE (re-issue)		
	Island IS 219	22	8

THIRST UK, male vocal / instrumental group (2 WEEKS)

		pos/wks	
6 Jul 91	THE ENEMY WITHIN *Ten TEN 379*	61	2

1300 DRUMS featuring the UNJUSTIFIED ANCIENTS OF MU
UK, male instrumental / production group (4 WEEKS)

		pos/wks	
18 May 96	OOH! AAH! CANTONA *Dynamo DYND 5*	11	4

THIS ISLAND EARTH
UK, male / female vocal / instrumental group (5 WEEKS)

		pos/wks	
5 Jan 85	SEE THAT GLOW *Magnet MAG 266*	47	5

THIS MORTAL COIL
UK, male / female vocal / instrumental group (3 WEEKS)

		pos/wks	
22 Oct 83	SONG TO THE SIREN (re) *4AD AD 310*	66	3

THIS WAY UP UK, male vocal / instrumental duo (2 WEEKS)

		pos/wks	
22 Aug 87	TELL ME WHY *Virgin VS 954*	72	2

THIS YEAR'S BLONDE
UK, male / female vocal / instrumental group (8 WEEKS)

		pos/wks	
10 Oct 81	PLATINUM POP *Creole CR 19*	46	5
14 Nov 87	WHO'S THAT MIX *Debut DEBT 3034*	62	3

BJ THOMAS US, male vocalist (4 WEEKS)

		pos/wks	
21 Feb 70	RAINDROPS KEEP FALLIN' ON MY HEAD (re) *Wand WN1* ▲	38	4

Carla THOMAS – See Otis REDDING

Dante THOMAS featuring PRAS
US, male vocalist – Darin Espinoza and US, male rapper (3 WEEKS)

		pos/wks	
1 Sep 01	MISS CALIFORNIA *Elektra E7192CD*	25	3

Evelyn THOMAS US, female vocalist (29 WEEKS)

		pos/wks	
24 Jan 76	WEAK SPOT *20th Century BTC 1014*	26	7
17 Apr 76	DOOMSDAY (re) *20th Century BTC 1017*	41	2
21 Apr 84 ●	HIGH ENERGY *Record Shack SOHO 18*	5	17
25 Aug 84	MASQUERADE *Record Shack SOHO 25*	60	3

Jamo THOMAS and His PARTY BROTHERS ORCHESTRA
US, male vocalist (2 WEEKS)

		pos/wks	
26 Feb 69	I SPY (FOR THE FBI) (re) *Polydor 56755*	44	2

Kenny THOMAS UK, male vocalist (54 WEEKS)

		pos/wks	
26 Jan 91	OUTSTANDING *Cooltempo COOL 227*	12	10
1 Jun 91 ●	THINKING ABOUT YOUR LOVE		
	Cooltempo COOL 235	4	13
5 Oct 91	BEST OF YOU *Cooltempo COOL 243*	11	7
30 Nov 91	TENDER LOVE *Cooltempo COOL 247*	26	6
10 Jul 93	STAY *Cooltempo CDCOOL 271*	22	6
4 Sep 93	TRIPPIN' ON YOUR LOVE *Cooltempo CDCOOL 277*	17	5
6 Nov 93	PIECE BY PIECE *Cooltempo CDCOOL 283*	36	3
14 May 94	DESTINY *Cooltempo CDCOOL 289*	59	1
2 Sep 95	WHEN I THINK OF YOU *Cooltempo CDCOOL 309*	27	3

Lillo THOMAS US, male vocalist (10 WEEKS)

		pos/wks	
27 Apr 85	SETTLE DOWN *Capitol CL 356*	66	2
21 Mar 87	SEXY GIRL *Capitol CL 445*	23	5
30 May 87	I'M IN LOVE *Capitol CL 450*	54	3

Mickey THOMAS – See Elvin BISHOP

Millard THOMAS – See Harry BELAFONTE

Nicky THOMAS Jamaica, male vocalist (14 WEEKS)

		pos/wks	
13 Jun 70 ●	LOVE OF THE COMMON PEOPLE *Trojan TR 7750*	9	14

Rob THOMAS – See MATCHBOX 20; SANTANA

Rufus THOMAS US, male vocalist, d. 15 Dec 2001 (12 WEEKS)

		pos/wks	
11 Apr 70	DO THE FUNKY CHICKEN *Stax 144*	18	12

Tasha THOMAS US, female vocalist (3 WEEKS)

		pos/wks	
20 Jan 79	SHOOT ME (WITH YOUR LOVE) *Atlantic LV 4*	59	3

Timmy THOMAS US, male vocalist (20 WEEKS)

		pos/wks	
24 Feb 73	WHY CAN'T WE LIVE TOGETHER *Mojo 2027 012*	12	11
28 Dec 85	NEW YORK EYES *Portrait A 6805* [1]	41	7
14 Jul 90	WHY CAN'T WE LIVE TOGETHER (re-mix) *TK TKR 1*	54	2

[1] Nicole with Timmy Thomas

THOMAS and TAYLOR US, male / female vocal duo (5 WEEKS)

		pos/wks	
17 May 86	YOU CAN'T BLAME LOVE *Cooltempo COOL 123*	53	5

Amanda THOMPSON – See Lesley GARRETT and Amanda THOMPSON

Carroll THOMPSON – See MOVEMENT 98 featuring Carroll THOMPSON; Courtney PINE

Chris THOMPSON UK, male vocalist (5 WEEKS)
		pos/wks	
27 Oct 79	IF YOU REMEMBER ME *Planet K 12389*	42	5

Gina THOMPSON – See MC LYTE

Lincoln THOMPSON – See REBEL MC

Sue THOMPSON US, female vocalist – Eva Sue McKee (9 WKS)
		pos/wks	
2 Nov 61	SAD MOVIES (MAKE ME CRY) (re) *Polydor NH 66967*	46	2
21 Jan 65	PAPER TIGER (re) *Hickory 1284*	30	7

THOMPSON TWINS 269 Top 500
British-based synth-rock trio: Tom Bailey (v/syn), New Zealand-born
Alannah Currie (v/prc/s), Joe Leeway (prc). Named after characters in a Tin
Tin cartoon, they were joined on stage at Live Aid by Madonna and were at
the forefront of the second so-called 'British Invasion' (110 WEEKS)
		pos/wks	
6 Nov 82	LIES *Arista ARIST 486*	67	3
29 Jan 83	● LOVE ON YOUR SIDE *Arista ARIST 504*	9	12
16 Apr 83	● WE ARE DETECTIVE *Arista ARIST 526*	7	9
16 Jul 83	WATCHING *Arista TWINS 1*	33	6
19 Nov 83	● HOLD ME NOW *Arista TWINS 2*	4	15
4 Feb 84	DOCTOR DOCTOR *Arista TWINS 3*	3	10
31 Mar 84	● YOU TAKE ME UP *Arista TWINS 4*	2	9
7 Jul 84	SISTER OF MERCY (re) *Arista TWINS 5*	11	9
8 Dec 84	LAY YOUR HANDS ON ME *Arista TWINS 6*	13	9
31 Aug 85	DON'T MESS WITH DOCTOR DREAM *Arista TWINS 9*	15	6
19 Oct 85	KING FOR A DAY *Arista TWINS 7*	22	6
7 Dec 85	REVOLUTION (re) *Arista TWINS 10*	56	4
21 Mar 87	GET THAT LOVE (re) *Arista TWINS 12*	66	3
15 Oct 88	IN THE NAME OF LOVE '88 *Arista 111808*	46	3
28 Sep 91	COME INSIDE *Warner Bros. W 0058*	56	4
25 Jan 92	THE SAINT *Warner Bros. W 0080*	53	2

Tracey THORN – See EVERYTHING BUT THE GIRL; MASSIVE ATTACK

David THORNE US, male vocalist (8 WEEKS)
		pos/wks	
24 Jan 63	THE ALLEY CAT SONG *Stateside SS 141*	21	8

Ken THORNE UK, orchestra (15 WEEKS)
		pos/wks	
18 Jul 63	● THEME FROM THE FILM 'THE LEGION'S LAST PATROL' *HMV POP 1176*	4	15

Trumpet solo by Ray Davies

THOSE 2 GIRLS UK, female vocal
duo – Denise Van Outen and Cathy Warwick (4 WEEKS)
		pos/wks	
5 Nov 94	WANNA MAKE YOU GO . . . UUH! *Final Vinyl 74321233782*	74	1
4 Mar 95	ALL I WANT *Final Vinyl 74321254202*	36	3

See also DENISE and JOHNNY; Andy WILLIAMS

THOUSAND YARD STARE
UK, male vocal / instrumental group (5 WEEKS)
		pos/wks	
26 Oct 91	SEASONSTREAM (EP) *Stifled Aardvark AARD 5T*	65	1
8 Feb 92	COMEUPPANCE *Stifled Aardvark AARD 007*	37	2
11 Jul 92	SPINDRIFT (EP) *Stifled Aardvark AARDT 010*	58	1
8 May 93	VERSION OF ME *Polydor AARDC 012*	57	1

Tracks on Seasonstream (EP): O-O AET / Village End / Keepsake / Worse for Wear
Tracks on Spindrift (EP): Wideshire Two / Hand, Son / Happenstance / Mocca Pune

THRASHING DOVES
UK, male vocal / instrumental group (3 WEEKS)
		pos/wks	
24 Jan 87	BEAUTIFUL IMBALANCE *A&M TDOVE 1*	50	3

THREE AMIGOS UK, male production trio (8 WEEKS)
		pos/wks	
3 Jul 99	LOUIE LOUIE *Inferno CDFERN 17*	15	6
24 Mar 01	25 MILES 2001 *Wonderboy WBOY 25*	30	2

3 COLOURS RED
UK, male vocal / instrumental group (17 WEEKS)
		pos/wks	
18 Jan 97	NUCLEAR HOLIDAY *Creation CRESCD 250*	22	2
15 Mar 97	SIXTY MILE SMILE *Creation CRESCD 254*	20	3
10 May 97	PURE *Creation CRESCD 265*	28	1
12 Jul 97	COPPER GIRL *Creation CRESCD 270*	30	2
8 Nov 97	THIS IS MY HOLLYWOOD *Creation CRESCD 277*	48	1
23 Jan 99	BEAUTIFUL DAY *Creation CRESCD 308*	11	6
29 May 99	THIS IS MY TIME *Creation CRESCD 313*	36	2

THREE DEGREES 251 Top 500
US R&B vocal group, which became top UK stars in the 1970s: Sheila
Ferguson, Valerie Holiday, Fayette Pinkney. The trio, tagged by the media as
"Prince Charles's favourites", was the first girl group to top the UK chart
since The Supremes in 1964 (113 WEEKS)
		pos/wks	
13 Apr 74	YEAR OF DECISION *Philadelphia International PIR 2073*	13	10
27 Apr 74	TSOP (THE SOUND OF PHILADELPHIA) *Philadelphia International PIR 2289* 1 ▲	22	9
13 Jul 74	★ WHEN WILL I SEE YOU AGAIN *Philadelphia International PIR 2155*	1	16
2 Nov 74	GET YOUR LOVE BACK *Philadelphia International PIR 2737*	34	4
12 Apr 75	● TAKE GOOD CARE OF YOURSELF *Philadelphia International PIR 3177*	9	9
5 Jul 75	LONG LOST LOVER *Philadelphia International PIR 3352*	40	4
1 May 76	TOAST OF LOVE *Epic EPC 4215*	36	4
7 Oct 78	GIVING UP, GIVING IN *Ariola ARO 130*	12	10
13 Jan 79	● WOMAN IN LOVE *Ariola ARO 141*	3	11
24 Mar 79	THE RUNNER *Ariola ARO 154*	10	10
23 Jun 79	THE GOLDEN LADY *Ariola ARO 170*	56	3
29 Sep 79	JUMP THE GUN *Ariola ARO 183*	48	5
24 Nov 79	● MY SIMPLE HEART *Ariola ARO 202*	9	11
5 Oct 85	THE HEAVEN I NEED *Supreme SUPE 102*	42	5
26 Dec 98	LAST CHRISTMAS *Wildstar CDWILD 15* 2	54	2

1 MFSB featuring The Three Degrees 2 Alien Voices featuring The Three Degrees

THREE DOG NIGHT US, male vocal / instrumental group (23 WKS)
		pos/wks	
8 Aug 70	● MAMA TOLD ME NOT TO COME *Stateside SS 8052* ▲	3	14
29 May 71	JOY TO THE WORLD *Probe PRO 523* ▲	24	9

THREE DRIVES ON A VINYL
Holland, male vocal / instrumental group (7 WEEKS)
		pos/wks	
27 Jun 98	GREECE 2000 *Hooj Choons HOOJCD 63* 1	44	1
30 Jan 99	GREECE 2000 (re-mix) *Hooj Choons HOOJ 70CD* 1	12	4
17 Nov 01	SUNSET ON IBIZA *Xtravaganza XTRAV 27CDS*	44	2

1 Three Drives

THREE GOOD REASONS
UK, male vocal / instrumental group (3 WEEKS)
		pos/wks	
10 Mar 66	NOWHERE MAN *Mercury MF 899*	47	3

3 JAYS UK, male production / vocal trio (5 WEEKS)
		pos/wks	
31 Jul 99	FEELING IT TOO *Multiply CDMULTY 53*	17	5

THREE KAYES – See KAYE SISTERS

3LW US, female vocal group (13 WEEKS)
		pos/wks	
2 Jun 01	● NO MORE (BABY I'MA DO RIGHT) (re) *Epic 6712722*	6	9
8 Sep 01	PLAYAS GON' PLAY *Epic 6717932*	21	3
19 Oct 02	FEELS GOOD (DON'T WORRY BOUT A THING) *Island CID 806* 1	44	1

1 Naughty By Nature featuring 3LW

THREE 'N ONE Germany, male production
duo – Sharam Khososi and Andre Strässer (3 WEEKS)
		pos/wks	
7 Jun 97	REFLECT *ffrr FCD 301*	66	1

| 15 May 99 | PEARL RIVER *Low Sense SENSECD 24* [1] | 32 | 2 |

[1] Three 'N One presents Johnny Shaker featuring Serial Diva

See also Billy HENDRIX

3SL *UK, male vocal trio (10 WEEKS)*

		pos/wks	
20 Apr 02	TAKE IT EASY (re) *Epic 6724042*	11	6
7 Sep 02	TOUCH ME TEASE ME (re) *Epic 6727872*	16	4

3T *US, male vocal trio (45 WEEKS)*

		pos/wks	
27 Jan 96 ●	ANYTHING *MJJ 6627152*	2	14
4 May 96	24/7 *MJJ 6631995*	11	7
24 Aug 96 ●	WHY *MJJ 6636482* [1]	2	9
7 Dec 96 ●	I NEED YOU *Epic 6639912*	3	10
5 Apr 97 ●	GOTTA BE YOU *Epic 6643645* [2]	10	5

[1] 3T featuring Michael Jackson [2] 3T: rap by Herbie

THREE TONS OF JOY – *See Johnny OTIS SHOW*

THRILLSEEKERS *UK, male producer / instrumentalist – Steve Helstrip (3 WEEKS)*

		pos/wks	
17 Feb 01	SYNAESTHESIA (FLY AWAY) *Neo NEOCD 050* [1]	28	2
7 Sep 02	DREAMING OF YOU *Ministry of Sound / Data DATA 36CDS*	48	1

[1] Thrillseekers featuring Sheryl Deane

THROWING MUSES
US, male / female vocal / instrumental group (6 WEEKS)

		pos/wks	
9 Feb 91	COUNTING BACKWARDS *4AD AD 1001*	70	2
1 Aug 92	FIREPILE (EP) *4AD BAD 2012*	46	1
24 Dec 94	BRIGHT YELLOW GUN *4AD BAD 4018CD*	51	2
10 Aug 96	SHARK *4AD BAD 6016CD*	53	1

Tracks on Firepile (EP): Firepile / Manic Depression / Snailhead / City of the Dead

Harry THUMANN
Germany, male instrumentalist – keyboards (6 WEEKS)

		pos/wks	
21 Feb 81	UNDERWATER *Decca F 13901*	41	6

See also WONDER DOG

THUNDER *UK, male vocal / instrumental group (52 WEEKS)*

		pos/wks	
17 Feb 90	DIRTY LOVE *EMI EM 126*	32	4
12 May 90	BACKSTREET SYMPHONY *EMI EM 137*	25	4
14 Jul 90	GIMME SOME LOVIN' *EMI EM 148*	36	3
29 Sep 90	SHE'S SO FINE *EMI EM 158*	34	3
23 Feb 91	LOVE WALKED IN *EMI EM 175*	21	4
15 Aug 92	LOW LIFE IN HIGH PLACES *EMI EM 242*	22	5
10 Oct 92	EVERYBODY WANTS HER *EMI EM 249*	36	4
13 Feb 93	A BETTER MAN *EMI CDBETTER 1*	18	4
19 Jun 93	LIKE A SATELLITE (EP) *EMI CDEM 272*	28	2
7 Jan 95	STAND UP *EMI CDEM 365*	23	4
25 Feb 95	RIVER OF PAIN *EMI CDEM 367*	31	2
6 May 95	CASTLES IN THE SAND *EMI CDEM 372*	30	3
23 Sep 95	IN A BROKEN DREAM *EMI CDEM 384*	26	2
25 Jan 97	DON'T WAIT UP *Raw Power RAWX 1020*	27	2
5 Apr 97	LOVE WORTH DYING FOR *Raw Power RAWX 1043*	60	1
7 Feb 98	THE ONLY ONE *Eagle EAGXA 016*	31	2
27 Jun 98	PLAY THAT FUNKY MUSIC *Eagle EAGXS 030*	39	2
20 Mar 99	YOU WANNA KNOW *Eagle EAGXA 037*	49	1

Tracks on Like a Satellite (EP): Like a Satellite / The Damage Is Done / Like a Satellite (Live) / Gimme Shelter

THUNDERBIRDS – *See Chris FARLOWE*

THUNDERBUGS *UK / France / Germany, female vocal / instrumental group (15 WEEKS)*

		pos/wks	
18 Sep 99 ●	FRIENDS FOREVER (re) *First Avenue / Epic 6676932*	5	10
18 Dec 99	IT'S ABOUT TIME YOU WERE MINE *First Avenue / Epic 6683972*	43	5

THUNDERCLAP NEWMAN *UK, male vocal / instrumental group - lead vocal John 'Speedy' Keen (13 WEEKS)*

		pos/wks	
11 Jun 69 ★	SOMETHING IN THE AIR *Track 604-031*	1	12
27 Jun 70	ACCIDENTS *Track 2094 001*	46	1

THUNDERTHIGHS *UK, female vocal group (5 WEEKS)*

		pos/wks	
22 Jun 74	CENTRAL PARK ARREST *Philips 6006 386*	30	5

Bobby THURSTON *US, male vocalist (10 WEEKS)*

		pos/wks	
29 Mar 80 ●	CHECK OUT THE GROOVE *Epic EPC 8348*	10	10

TIFFANY *US, female vocalist – Tiffany Darwish (45 WEEKS)*

		pos/wks	
16 Jan 88 ★	I THINK WE'RE ALONE NOW *MCA MCA 1211* ▲	1	13
19 Mar 88 ●	COULD'VE BEEN *MCA TIFF 2* ▲	4	9
4 Jun 88 ●	I SAW HIM STANDING THERE *MCA TIFF 3*	8	7
6 Aug 88	FEELINGS OF FOREVER *MCA TIFF 4*	52	2
12 Nov 88	RADIO ROMANCE *MCA TIFF 5*	13	11
11 Feb 89	ALL THIS TIME *MCA TIFF 6*	47	3

TIGA AND ZYNTHERIUS
Canada / Finland, male DJ / production duo – Tiga Sontag and Jori Hulkkonen (3 WEEKS)

		pos/wks	
11 May 02	SUNGLASSES AT NIGHT *City Rockers ROCKERS 15CD*	25	3

TIGER
UK / Ireland, male / female vocal / instrumental group (5 WEEKS)

		pos/wks	
31 Aug 96	RACE *Trade 2 TRDCD 004*	37	2
16 Nov 96	MY PUPPET PAL *Trade 2 TRDCD 005*	62	1
22 Feb 97	ON THE ROSE *Trade 2 TRDCD 008*	57	1
22 Aug 98	FRIENDS *Trade 2 TRDCD 013*	72	1

TIGERTAILZ *US, male vocal / instrumental group (2 WEEKS)*

		pos/wks	
24 Jun 89	LOVE BOMB BABY *Music for Nations KUT 132*	75	1
16 Feb 91	HEAVEN *Music for Nations KUT 137*	71	1

TIGHT FIT *UK, male / female vocal group (49 WEEKS)*

		pos/wks	
18 Jul 81 ●	BACK TO THE SIXTIES *Jive JIVE 002*	4	11
26 Sep 81	BACK TO THE SIXTIES PART 2 *Jive JIVE 005*	33	5
23 Jan 82 ★	THE LION SLEEPS TONIGHT *Jive JIVE 9*	1	15
1 May 82 ●	FANTASY ISLAND *Jive JIVE 13*	5	12
31 Jul 82	SECRET HEART *Jive JIVE 20*	41	6

TIJUANA BRASS – *See Herb ALPERT*

TIK and TOK *UK, male vocal duo (2 WEEKS)*

		pos/wks	
8 Oct 83	COOL RUNNING *Survival SUR 016*	69	2

Tanita TIKARAM *UK, female vocalist (31 WEEKS)*

		pos/wks	
30 Jul 88 ●	GOOD TRADITION *WEA YZ 196*	10	10
22 Oct 88	TWIST IN MY SOBRIETY *WEA YZ 321*	22	8
14 Jan 89	CATHEDRAL SONG *WEA YZ 331*	48	3
18 Mar 89	WORLD OUTSIDE YOUR WINDOW *WEA YZ 363*	58	2
13 Jan 90	WE ALMOST GOT IT TOGETHER *WEA YZ 443*	52	3
9 Feb 91	ONLY THE ONES WE LOVE *East West YZ 558*	69	1
4 Feb 95	I MIGHT BE CRYING *East West YZ 879CD*	64	1
6 Jun 98	STOP LISTENING *Mother MUMCD 102*	67	1
29 Aug 98	I DON'T WANNA LOSE AT LOVE *Mother MUMCD 105*	73	1

TILLMAN AND REIS *Germany, male production duo – Tillman Uhrmacher and Peter Reis (1 WEEK)*

		pos/wks	
16 Sep 00	BASSFLY *Liquid Asset ASSET CD004*	70	1

Johnny TILLOTSON *US, male vocalist (50 WEEKS)*

		pos/wks	
1 Dec 60 ★	POETRY IN MOTION *London HLA 9231*	1	15
2 Feb 61	JIMMY'S GIRL (re) *London HLA 9275*	43	2
12 Jul 62	IT KEEPS RIGHT ON A HURTIN' *London HLA 9550*	31	10
4 Oct 62	SEND ME THE PILLOW YOU DREAM ON *London HLA 9598*	21	10

27 Dec 62	**I CAN'T HELP IT (2re)** *London HLA 9642*	41	6
9 May 63	**OUT OF MY MIND** *London HLA 9695*	34	5
14 Apr 79	**POETRY IN MOTION (re-issue) / PRINCESS PRINCESS** *Lightning LIG 9016*	67	2

TILT *UK, male instrumental / production group (8 WEEKS)* pos/wks

2 Dec 95	**I DREAM** *Perfecto PERF 112CD*	69	1
10 May 97	**MY SPIRIT** *Perfecto PERF 139CD*	61	1
13 Sep 97	**PLACES** *Perfecto PERF 149CD*	64	1
7 Feb 98	**BUTTERFLY** *Perfecto PERF 154CD1* 1	41	1
27 Mar 99	**CHILDREN** *Deconstruction 74321648172*	51	1
8 May 99	**INVISIBLE** *Hooj Choons HOOJ 73CD*	20	2
12 Feb 00	**DARK SCIENCE (EP)** *Hooj Choons HOOJ 87*	55	1

1 Tilt featuring Zee

Tracks on Dark Science (EP): 36 (two mixes) / Seduction of Orphheus (two mixes)

TIMBALAND
US, male producer / rapper – Tim Mosley (13 WEEKS) pos/wks

23 Jan 99	**GET ON THE BUS** *East West E3780CD* 1	15	5
13 Mar 99	**HERE WE COME** *Virgin DINSD 179* 2	43	1
19 Jun 99	**LOBSTER & SCRIMP** *Virgin DINSD 186* 3	48	1
21 Jul 01	**WE NEED A RESOLUTION (re)** *Blackground VUSCD 206* 4	20	6

1 Destiny's Child featuring Timbaland 2 Timbaland / Missy Elliott and Magoo 3 Timbaland featuring Jay-Z 4 Aaliyah featuring Timbaland

Justin TIMBERLAKE *US, male vocalist (9 WEEKS)* pos/wks

2 Nov 02 ●	**LIKE I LOVE YOU** *Jive 9254342*	2	9+

See also 'N SYNC

TIMBUK 3 *US, male / female vocal / instrumental duo – Pat and Barbara Kooyman MacDonald (7 WEEKS)* pos/wks

31 Jan 87	**THE FUTURE'S SO BRIGHT I GOTTA WEAR SHADES** *IRS IRM 126*	21	7

TIME FREQUENCY
UK, male instrumental / production group (34 WEEKS) pos/wks

6 Jun 92	**REAL LOVE** *Jive JIVET 307*	60	1
9 Jan 93	**NEW EMOTION** *Internal Affairs KGBCD 009*	36	6
12 Jun 93	**THE POWER ZONE (EP)** *Internal Affairs KGBD 010*	17	11
6 Nov 93 ●	**REAL LOVE (re-mix) (re)** *Internal Affairs KGBCD 011*	8	8
28 May 94	**SUCH A PHANTASY** *Internal Affairs KGBD 013*	25	4
8 Oct 94	**DREAMSCAPE '94** *Internal Affairs KGBD 015*	32	3
31 Aug 02	**REAL LOVE (2nd re-mix)** *Jive 9253782*	43	1

Tracks on The Power Zone (EP): The Ultimate High / The Ultimate High (full length) / The Power Zone / Take Me Away

TIME OF THE MUMPH *UK, male producer – Mark Mumford (1 WK)* pos/wks

11 Feb 95	**CONTROL** *Fresh FRSHD 24*	69	1

TIME UK *UK, male vocal / instrumental group (3 WEEKS)* pos/wks

8 Oct 83	**THE CABARET** *Red Bus / Aroadia TIM 123*	63	3

TIME ZONE *UK / US, male vocal / instrumental duo (9 WEEKS)* pos/wks

19 Jan 85	**WORLD DESTRUCTION** *Virgin VS 743*	44	9

TIMEBOX *UK, male vocal / instrumental group (4 WEEKS)* pos/wks

24 Jul 68	**BEGGIN'** *Deram DM 194*	38	4

TIMELORDS *UK, male vocal / instrumental group (9 WEEKS)* pos/wks

4 Jun 88 ★	**DOCTORIN' THE TARDIS** *KLF Communications KLF 003*	1	9

See also KLF; JUSTIFIED ANCIENTS OF MU MU; 2K

TIMEX SOCIAL CLUB
US, male vocal / instrumental group (9 WEEKS) pos/wks

13 Sep 86	**RUMORS** *Cooltempo COOL 133*	13	9

TIN MACHINE
US / UK, male vocal / instrumental group (10 WEEKS) pos/wks

1 Jul 89	**UNDER THE GOD** *EMI-USA MT 68*	51	2
9 Sep 89	**TIN MACHINE / MAGGIE'S FARM (LIVE)** *EMI-USA MT 73*	48	2
24 Aug 91	**YOU BELONG IN ROCK 'N' ROLL** *London LON 305*	33	3
2 Nov 91	**BABY UNIVERSAL** *London LON 310*	48	3

See also David BOWIE

TIN TIN OUT *UK, male instrumental / production duo – Lindsay Edwards and Darren Stokes (42 WEEKS)* pos/wks

13 Aug 94	**THE FEELING** *Deep Distraxion OILYCD 029* 1	32	2
25 Mar 95	**ALWAYS SOMETHING THERE TO REMIND ME** *WEA YZ 911CD* 2	14	5
8 Feb 97	**ALL I WANNA DO** *VC VCRD 15*	31	2
10 May 97	**DANCE WITH ME** *VC VCRD 17* 3	35	2
20 Sep 97	**STRINGS FOR YASMIN** *VC VCRD 20*	31	3
28 Mar 98 ●	**HERE'S WHERE THE STORY ENDS** *VC Recordings VCRD 30* 4	7	10
12 Sep 98	**SOMETIMES** *VC Recordings VCRD 34* 4	20	4
11 Sep 99	**ELEVEN TO FLY** *VC Recordings VCRDX 52* 5	26	2
13 Nov 99 ●	**WHAT I AM** *VC Recordings VCRD 53* 6	2	12

1 Tin Tin Out featuring Sweet Tee 2 Tin Tin Out featuring Espiritu 3 Tin Tin Out featuring Tony Hadley 4 Tin Tin Out featuring Shelley Nelson 5 Tin Tin Out featuring Wendy Page 6 Tin Tin Out featuring Emma Bunton

TINA – See Tina TURNER

TINDERSTICKS
UK, male vocal / instrumental group (6 WEEKS) pos/wks

5 Feb 94	**KATHLEEN (EP)** *This Way Up WAY 2833CD*	61	1
18 Mar 95	**NO MORE AFFAIRS** *This Way Up WAY 3833*	58	1
12 Aug 95	**TRAVELLING LIGHT** *This Way Up WAY 4533*	51	1
7 Jun 97	**BATHTIME** *This Way Up WAY 6166*	38	1
1 Nov 97	**RENTED ROOMS** *This Way Up WAY 6566*	56	1
4 Sep 99	**CAN WE START AGAIN?** *Island CID 756*	54	1

Tracks on Kathleen (EP): Kathleen / Summat Moon / A Sweet Sweet Man / E-Type Joe

TINGO TANGO *UK, male instrumental group (2 WEEKS)* pos/wks

21 Jul 90	**IT IS JAZZ** *Champion CHAMP 250*	68	2

TINMAN *UK, male producer – Paul Dakeyne (9 WEEKS)* pos/wks

20 Aug 94 ●	**EIGHTEEN STRINGS** *ffrr FCD 242*	9	8
3 Jun 95	**GUDVIBE** *ffrr FCD 262*	49	1

TINY TIM *US, male vocalist, d. 30 Nov 1996 (1 WEEK)* pos/wks

5 Feb 69	**GREAT BALLS OF FIRE** *Reprise RS 20802*	45	1

TITANIC *Norway / UK, male instrumental group (12 WEEKS)* pos/wks

25 Sep 71 ●	**SULTANA** *CBS 5365*	5	12

TITIYO *Sweden, female vocalist (6 WEEKS)* pos/wks

3 Mar 90	**AFTER THE RAIN** *Arista 112722*	60	3
6 Oct 90	**FLOWERS** *Arista 113212*	71	1
5 Feb 94	**TELL ME I'M NOT DREAMING** *Arista 74321185622*	45	2

Cara TIVEY – See Billy BRAGG

TOADS – See Stan FREBERG

Art and Dotty TODD *US, male / female vocal duo (7 WEEKS)* pos/wks

13 Feb 53 ●	**BROKEN WINGS** *HMV B 10399*	6	7

TOGETHER *UK, male vocal / instrumental group (8 WEEKS)* pos/wks

4 Aug 90	**HARDCORE UPROAR** *ffrr F 143*	12	8

TOI – See Warren G

Re-entries are listed as (re), (2re), (3re), etc which signifies that the hit re-entered the chart once, twice or three times, etc

TOKENS US, male vocal group (12 WEEKS)

		pos/wks
21 Dec 61	**THE LION SLEEPS TONIGHT (WIMOWEH)** *RCA 1263* ▲	11 12

TOKYO GHETTO PUSSY Germany, male instrumental / production duo – Rolf Ellmer and Markus Löffel (4 WEEKS)

		pos/wks
16 Sep 95	**EVERYBODY ON THE FLOOR (PUMP IT)** *Epic 6611132*	26 2
16 Mar 96	**I KISS YOUR LIPS** *Epic 6623212*	55 2

See also JAM & SPOON; STORM

TOL and TOL
Holland, male vocal / instrumental duo (2 WEEKS)

		pos/wks
14 Apr 90	**ELENI** *Dover ROJ 5*	73 2

TOM TOM CLUB
US, female / male vocal / instrumental group (20 WEEKS)

		pos/wks
20 Jun 81 ●	**WORDY RAPPINGHOOD** *Island WIP 6694*	7 9
10 Oct 81	**GENIUS OF LOVE** *Island WIP 6735*	65 2
7 Aug 82	**UNDER THE BOARDWALK** *Island WIP 6762*	22 9

TOMBA VIRA Holland, male production duo – Rene ter Horst and Gaston Steenkist (1 WEEK)

		pos/wks
16 Jun 01	**THE SOUND OF: OH YEAH** *VC Recordings VCRD 88*	51 1

See also JARK PRONGO; RHYTHMKILLAZ; RIVA featuring Dannii MINOGUE; GOODMEN; CHOCOLATE PUMA

TOMCAT UK, male vocal / instrumental group (1 WEEK)

		pos/wks
14 Oct 00	**CRAZY** *Virgin VSCDT 1785*	48 1

Satoshi TOMIIE – See Frankie KNUCKLES

Ricky TOMLINSON UK, male actor / vocalist (3 WEEKS)

		pos/wks
10 Nov 01	**ARE YOU LOOKIN' AT ME?** *All Around the World CDRICKY 1*	28 3

TOMSKI UK, male producer – Tom Jankiewicz (3 WEEKS)

		pos/wks
18 Apr 98	**14 HOURS TO SAVE THE EARTH** *Xtravaganza 0091515 EXT*	42 1
12 Feb 00	**LOVE WILL COME** *Xtravaganza XTRAV6CDS* [1]	31 2

[1] Tomski featuring Jan Johnston

TONE LOC US, male rapper – Anthony Smith (19 WEEKS)

		pos/wks
11 Feb 89	**WILD THING / LOC'ED AFTER DARK** *Fourth & Broadway BRW 121*	21 8
20 May 89	**FUNKY COLD MEDINA / ON FIRE** *Fourth & Broadway BRW 129*	13 9
5 Aug 89	**I GOT IT GOIN' ON** *Fourth & Broadway BRW 140*	55 2

TONGUE 'N' CHEEK
UK, male / female vocal / instrumental group (28 WEEKS)

		pos/wks
27 Feb 88	**NOBODY (CAN LOVE ME)** *Criminal BUS 6* [1]	59 6
25 Nov 89	**ENCORE** *Syncopate SY 33*	41 4
14 Apr 90	**TOMORROW** *Syncopate SY 34*	20 7
4 Aug 90	**NOBODY (re-recording)** *Syncopate SY 37*	37 5
19 Jan 91	**FORGET ME NOTS** *Syncopate SY 39*	26 6

[1] Tongue In Cheek

TONIGHT
UK, male vocal / instrumental group (10 WEEKS)

		pos/wks
28 Jan 78	**DRUMMER MAN** *Target TDS 1*	14 8
20 May 78	**MONEY THAT'S YOUR PROBLEM** *Target TDS 2*	66 2

TONY TONI TONÉ US, male vocal group (12 WEEKS)

		pos/wks
30 Jun 90	**OAKLAND STROKE** *Wing WING 7* [1]	50 5
9 Mar 91	**IT NEVER RAINS (IN SOUTHERN CALIFORNIA)** *Wing WING 10* [1]	69 2

4 Sep 93	**IF I HAD NO LOOT** *Polydor PZCD 292*	44 3
3 May 97	**LET'S GET DOWN** *Mercury MERCD 485* [2]	33 2

[1] Tony! Toni! Toné! [2] Tony Toni Toné featuring DJ Quick

See also Raphael SAADIQ

TOO TOUGH TEE – See DYNAMIX II featuring TOO TOUGH TEE

TOON TRAVELLERS – See MUNGO JERRY

TOP UK, male vocal / instrumental group (2 WEEKS)

		pos/wks
20 Jul 91	**NUMBER ONE DOMINATOR** *Island IS 496*	67 2

TOP LINERS – See Rocky SHARPE and the REPLAYS

TOPLOADER
UK, male vocal / instrumental group (56 WEEKS)

		pos/wks
22 May 99	**ACHILLES HEEL** *Sony S2 6671612*	64 1
7 Aug 99	**LET THE PEOPLE KNOW** *Sony S2 6677132*	52 1
4 Mar 00	**DANCING IN THE MOONLIGHT** *Sony S2 6689412*	19 7
13 May 00 ●	**ACHILLES HEEL (re-issue)** *Sony S2 6691872*	8 7
2 Sep 00	**JUST HOLD ON** *Sony S2 6696242*	20 4
25 Nov 00 ●	**DANCING IN THE MOONLIGHT (re-issue)** *Sony S2 6699852*	7 25
21 Apr 01	**ONLY FOR A WHILE** *Sony S2 6708612*	19 4
17 Aug 02	**TIME OF MY LIFE** *Sony S2 6728862*	18 7

TOPOL Israel, male vocalist / actor – Chaim Topol (20 WEEKS)

		pos/wks
20 Apr 67 ●	**IF I WERE A RICH MAN** *CBS 202651*	9 20

Mel TORME US, male vocalist, d. 5 Jun 1999 (32 WEEKS)

		pos/wks
27 Apr 56 ●	**MOUNTAIN GREENERY (re)** *Vogue / Coral Q 72150*	4 24
3 Jan 63	**COMIN' HOME BABY** *London HLK 9643*	13 8

TORNADOS UK, male instrumental group (59 WEEKS)

		pos/wks
30 Aug 62 ★	**TELSTAR** *Decca F 11494* ▲	1 25
10 Jan 63 ●	**GLOBETROTTER** *Decca F 11562*	5 11
21 Mar 63	**ROBOT** *Decca F 11606*	17 12
6 Jun 63	**THE ICE CREAM MAN** *Decca F 11662*	18 9
10 Oct 63	**DRAGONFLY** *Decca F 11745*	41 2

Mitchell TOROK US, male vocalist (19 WEEKS)

		pos/wks
28 Sep 56 ●	**WHEN MEXICO GAVE UP THE RHUMBA (re)** *Brunswick 05586*	6 18
11 Jan 57	**RED LIGHT, GREEN LIGHT** *Brunswick 05626*	29 1

Liz TORRES – See Danny TENAGLIA

Emiliana TORRINI Iceland, female vocalist (3 WEEKS)

		pos/wks
10 Jun 00	**EASY** *One Little Indian 274 TP7CD*	63 1
9 Sep 00	**UNEMPLOYED IN SUMMERTIME** *One Little Indian 275 TP7CDL*	63 1
3 Feb 01	**TO BE FREE** *One Little Indian 276 TP7CD*	44 1

Peter TOSH Jamaica, male vocalist, d. 11 Sep 1987 (12 WEEKS)

		pos/wks
21 Oct 78	**(YOU GOTTA WALK) DON'T LOOK BACK** *Rolling Stones 2859*	43 7
2 Apr 83	**JOHNNY B GOODE** *EMI RIC 115*	48 5

TOTAL US, female vocal group (11 WEEKS)

		pos/wks
15 Jul 95	**CAN'T YOU SEE** *Tommy Boy TBCD 700* [1]	43 2
14 Sep 96	**KISSIN' YOU** *Arista 74321404172*	29 2
15 Feb 97	**DO YOU THINK ABOUT US** *Puff Daddy 74321458492*	49 1
18 Apr 98	**WHAT YOU WANT** *Puff Daddy 74321578772* [2]	15 5
30 Sep 00	**I WONDER WHY HE'S THE GREATEST DJ** *Tommy Boy TBCD 2100* [3]	68 1

[1] Total featuring the Notorious B.I.G. [2] Mase featuring Total [3] Tony Touch featuring Total

TOTAL CONTRAST
UK, male vocal / instrumental
duo – Robin Achampong and Delroy Murray (22 WEEKS)   pos/wks

3 Aug 85	TAKES A LITTLE TIME *London LON 71*	17	10
19 Oct 85	HIT AND RUN *London LON 76*	41	5
1 Mar 86	THE RIVER *London LON 83*	44	3
10 May 86	WHAT YOU GONNA DO ABOUT IT *London LON 95*	63	4

TOTO
US, male vocal / instrumental group (35 WEEKS)   pos/wks

10 Feb 79	HOLD THE LINE *CBS 6784*	14	11
5 Feb 83 ●	AFRICA *CBS A 2510* ▲	3	10
9 Apr 83	ROSANNA *CBS A 2079*	12	8
18 Jun 83	I WON'T HOLD YOU BACK *CBS A 3392*	37	5
18 Nov 95	I WILL REMEMBER *Columbia 6626552*	64	1

TOTO COELO
UK, female vocal group (14 WEEKS)   pos/wks

7 Aug 82 ●	I EAT CANNIBALS PART 1 *Radialchoice TIC 10*	8	10
13 Nov 82	DRACULA'S TANGO / MUCHO MACHO *Radialchoice TIC 11*	54	4

TOTTENHAM HOTSPUR FA CUP FINAL SQUAD
UK, male football team vocalists (23 WEEKS)   pos/wks

9 May 81 ●	OSSIE'S DREAM (SPURS ARE ON THEIR WAY TO WEMBLEY) *Shelf SHELF 1*	5	8
1 May 82	TOTTENHAM TOTTENHAM *Shelf SHELF 2*	19	7
9 May 87	HOT SHOT TOTTENHAM! *Rainbow RBR 16*	18	5
11 May 91	WHEN THE YEAR ENDS IN 1 *A1 A 1324*	44	3

All hits feature the vocal and instrumental talents of Chas and Dave

See also COCKEREL CHORUS

Tony TOUCH featuring TOTAL
US, male producer – Anthony Hernandez – and US, female vocal group (1 WEEK)   pos/wks

30 Sep 00	I WONDER WHY HE'S THE GREATEST DJ *Tommy Boy TBCD 2100*	68	1

TOUCH & GO
UK, male / female vocal / production group (12 WEEKS)   pos/wks

7 Nov 98 ●	WOULD YOU...? *Oval VVR 5003083*	3	12

TOUCH OF SOUL
UK, male / female vocal / instrumental group (3 WEEKS)   pos/wks

19 May 90	WE GOT THE LOVE *Cooltempo COOL 204*	46	3

TOUR DE FORCE
UK, male production trio (1 WEEK)   pos/wks

16 May 98	CATALAN *East West EW 161CD*	71	1

TOURISTS
UK, male / female vocal / instrumental group (40 WEEKS)   pos/wks

9 Jun 79	BLIND AMONG THE FLOWERS *Logo GO 350*	52	5
8 Sep 79	THE LONELIEST MAN IN THE WORLD *Logo GO 360*	32	7
10 Nov 79 ●	I ONLY WANT TO BE WITH YOU *Logo GO 370*	4	14
9 Feb 80 ●	SO GOOD TO BE BACK HOME AGAIN *Logo TOUR 1*	8	9
18 Oct 80	DON'T SAY I TOLD YOU SO *RCA TOUR 2*	40	5

See also VEGAS; EURYTHMICS

TOUTES LES FILLES
UK, female vocal group (1 WEEK)   pos/wks

4 Sep 99	THAT'S WHAT LOVE CAN DO *London LONCD 434*	44	1

Carol Lynn TOWNES
US, female vocalist (7 WEEKS)   pos/wks

4 Aug 84	99 1/2 *Polydor POSP 693*	47	4
19 Jan 85	BELIEVE IN THE BEAT *Polydor POSP 720*	56	3

Fuzz TOWNSHEND
UK, male producer (1 WEEK)   pos/wks

6 Sep 97	HELLO DARLIN *Echo ECSCD 46*	51	1

Pete TOWNSHEND
UK, male vocalist (17 WEEKS)   pos/wks

5 Apr 80	ROUGH BOYS *Atco K 11460*	39	6
21 Jun 80	LET MY LOVE OPEN YOUR DOOR *Atco K 11486*	46	6
21 Aug 82	UNIFORMS (CORPS D'ESPRIT) *Atco K 11751*	48	5

See also WHO

TOXIC TWO
US, male instrumental / production duo – Ray Love and Damon Wild (6 WEEKS)   pos/wks

7 Mar 92	RAVE GENERATOR *PWL International PWL 223*	13	6

TOYAH (386 Top 500)
Visually striking punk / pop vocalist, b. Toyah Willcox 18 May 1958, Birmingham, UK. Came to prominence through acting – first major role in 1977 movie 'Jubilee'. Married King Crimson guitarist Robert Fripp in 1986. One of the first acts to chart regularly with EPs (87 WEEKS)   pos/wks

14 Feb 81 ●	FOUR FROM TOYAH (EP) *Safari TOY 1*	4	14
16 May 81 ●	I WANT TO BE FREE *Safari SAFE 34*	8	11
3 Oct 81 ●	THUNDER IN THE MOUNTAINS *Safari SAFE 38*	4	9
28 Nov 81	FOUR MORE FROM TOYAH (EP) *Safari TOY 2*	14	9
22 May 82	BRAVE NEW WORLD *Safari SAFE 45*	21	8
17 Jul 82	IEYA *Safari SAFE 28*	48	5
9 Oct 82	BE LOUD BE PROUD (BE HEARD) *Safari SAFE 52*	30	7
24 Sep 83	REBEL RUN *Safari SAFE 56*	24	5
19 Nov 83	THE VOW *Safari SAFE 58*	50	5
27 Apr 85	DON'T FALL IN LOVE (I SAID) *Portrait A 6160*	22	6
29 Jun 85	SOUL PASSING THROUGH SOUL *Portrait A 6359*	57	3
25 Apr 87	ECHO BEACH *EG EGO 31*	54	5

Tracks on Four from Toyah (EP): It's a Mystery / Revelations / War Boys / Angels and Demons. Tracks on Four More from Toyah (EP): Good Morning Universe / Urban Tribesman / In the Fairground / The Furious Futures

TOY-BOX
Denmark, male / female vocal duo (2 WEEKS)   pos/wks

18 Sep 99	BEST FRIENDS *Edel 0058245 ERE*	41	2

TOY DOLLS
UK, male vocal / instrumental group (12 WEEKS)   pos/wks

1 Dec 84 ●	NELLIE THE ELEPHANT *Volume VOL 11*	4	12

TOYS
US, female vocal group (17 WEEKS)   pos/wks

4 Nov 65 ●	A LOVER'S CONCERTO *Stateside SS 460*	5	13
27 Jan 66	ATTACK *Stateside SS 483*	36	4

Faye TOZER – See STEPS; Russell WATSON

T'PAU (457 Top 500)
Shropshire lads and a lass whose No.1 hit in 1987 had the distinction of being the 600th chart-topper. T'Pau (Mr Spock's Vulcan friend in 'Star Trek') comprised writers Carol Decker (v) and Ron Rogers (g), plus Michael Chetwood (k), Paul Jackson (b), Tim Burgess (d) and Taj Wyzgowski (g) (77 WEEKS)   pos/wks

8 Aug 87 ●	HEART AND SOUL *Siren SRN 41*	4	13
24 Oct 87 ★	CHINA IN YOUR HAND *Siren SRN 64*	1	15
30 Jan 88 ●	VALENTINE *Siren SRN 69*	9	8
2 Apr 88	SEX TALK (LIVE) *Siren SRN 80*	23	7
25 Jun 88	I WILL BE WITH YOU *Siren SRN 87*	14	6
1 Oct 88	SECRET GARDEN *Siren SRN 93*	18	7
3 Dec 88	ROAD TO OUR DREAM *Siren SRN 100*	42	6
25 Mar 89	ONLY THE LONELY *Siren SRN 107*	28	6
18 May 91	WHENEVER YOU NEED ME *Siren SRN 140*	16	6
27 Jul 91	WALK ON AIR *Siren SRN 142*	62	2
20 Feb 93	VALENTINE (re-issue) *Virgin VALEG 1*	53	1

TRA-KNOX – See Will SMITH

TRACIE
UK, female vocalist – Tracie Young (24 WEEKS)   pos/wks

26 Mar 83 ●	THE HOUSE THAT JACK BUILT *Respond KOB 701*	9	8
16 Jul 83	GIVE IT SOME EMOTION *Respond KOB 704*	24	9
14 Apr 84	SOUL'S ON FIRE *Respond KOB 708*	73	2

Re-entries are listed as (re), (2re), (3re), etc which signifies that the hit re-entered the chart once, twice or three times, etc

		pos/wks
9 Jun 84	(I LOVE YOU) WHEN YOU SLEEP *Respond KOB 710*	59 3
17 Aug 85	I CAN'T LEAVE YOU ALONE *Respond SBS 1* [1]	60 2

[1] Tracie Young

Gordon TRACKS – *See AIR*

TRACY – *See MASSIVO featuring TRACY*

Jeanie TRACY *US, female vocalist (3 WEEKS)*
		pos/wks
11 Jun 94	IF THIS IS LOVE *Pulse 8 CDLOSE 63*	73 1
5 Nov 94	DO YOU BELIEVE IN THE WONDER *Pulse 8 CDLOSE 74*	57 1
13 May 95	IT'S A MAN'S MAN'S MAN'S WORLD *Pulse 8 CDLOSE 89* [1]	73 1

[1] Jeanie Tracy and Bobby Womack

TRAFFIC *UK, male vocal / instrumental group (40 WEEKS)*
		pos/wks
1 Jun 67 ●	PAPER SUN *Island WIP 6002*	5 10
6 Sep 67 ●	HOLE IN MY SHOE *Island WIP 6017*	2 14
29 Nov 67 ●	HERE WE GO ROUND THE MULBERRY BUSH *Island WIP 6025*	8 12
6 Mar 68	NO FACE, NO NAME, NO NUMBER *Island WIP 6030*	40 4

TRAIN *US, male vocal / instrumental group (10 WEEKS)*
		pos/wks
11 Aug 01 ●	DROPS OF JUPITER (TELL ME) *Columbia 6714472*	10 8
2 Mar 02	SHE'S ON FIRE *Columbia 6722812*	49 2

TRAMAINE *US, female vocalist (2 WEEKS)*
		pos/wks
5 Oct 85	FALL DOWN (SPIRIT OF LOVE) *A&M AM 281*	60 2

TRAMMPS *US, male vocal group (55 WEEKS)*
		pos/wks
23 Nov 74	ZING WENT THE STRINGS OF MY HEART *Buddah BDS 405*	29 10
1 Feb 75	SIXTY MINUTE MAN *Buddah BDS 415*	40 4
11 Oct 75 ●	HOLD BACK THE NIGHT *Buddah BDS 437*	5 8
13 Mar 76	THAT'S WHERE THE HAPPY PEOPLE GO *Atlantic K 10703*	35 8
24 Jul 76	SOUL SEARCHIN' TIME *Atlantic K 10797*	42 3
14 May 77	DISCO INFERNO *Atlantic K 10914*	16 7
24 Jun 78	DISCO INFERNO (re-issue) *Atlantic K 11135*	47 10
12 Dec 92	HOLD BACK THE NIGHT *Network NWK 65* [1]	30 5

[1] KWS features guest vocal from the Trammps

TRANCESETTERS *Holland, male production duo (2 WEEKS)*
		pos/wks
4 Mar 00	ROACHES *Hooj Choons HOOJ 89CD*	55 1
9 Jun 01	SYNERGY *Hooj Choons 107*	72 1

TRANSA *UK, male DJ / production duo (2 WEEKS)*
		pos/wks
30 Aug 97	PROPHASE *Perfecto PERF 147CD*	65 1
21 Feb 98	ENERVATE *Perfecto PERF 155CD*	42 1

TRANSATLANTIC SOUL
US, male producer – Roger Sanchez (1 WEEK)
		pos/wks
22 Mar 97	RELEASE YO SELF *Deconstruction 74321459102*	43 1

TRANSFER *UK, male producer (1 WEEK)*
		pos/wks
3 Nov 01	POSSESSION *Mulitply CDMULTY 76*	54 1

TRANSFORMER 2 *Belgium / Holland,*
male / female vocal / instrumental group (1 WEEK)
		pos/wks
24 Feb 96	JUST CAN'T GET ENOUGH *Positiva CDTIV 49*	45 1

See also CONVERT

TRANSISTER
UK / US, male / female vocal / instrumental group (1 WEEK)
		pos/wks
28 Mar 98	LOOK WHO'S PERFECT NOW *Virgin VSCDT 1678*	56 1

TRANSVISION VAMP
UK, female / male vocal / instrumental group (59 WEEKS)
		pos/wks
16 Apr 88	TELL THAT GIRL TO SHUT UP *MCA TVV 2*	45 3
25 Jun 88 ●	I WANT YOUR LOVE *MCA TVV 3*	5 13
17 Sep 88	REVOLUTION BABY *MCA TVV 4*	30 5
19 Nov 88	SISTER MOON *MCA TVV 5*	41 5
1 Apr 89 ●	BABY I DON'T CARE *MCA TVV 6*	3 11
10 Jun 89	THE ONLY ONE *MCA TVV 7*	15 6
5 Aug 89	LANDSLIDE OF LOVE *MCA TVV 8*	14 5
4 Nov 89	BORN TO BE SOLD *MCA TVV 9*	22 4
13 Apr 91	(I JUST WANNA) B WITH U *MCA TVV 10*	30 4
22 Jun 91	IF LOOKS COULD KILL *MCA TVV 11*	41 3

TRANS-X
Canada, female / male vocal / instrumental group (9 WEEKS)
		pos/wks
13 Jul 85 ●	LIVING ON VIDEO *Boiling Point POSP 650*	9 9

TRASH *UK, male vocal / instrumental group (3 WEEKS)*
		pos/wks
25 Oct 69	GOLDEN SLUMBERS / CARRY THAT WEIGHT *Apple 17*	35 3

TRASH CAN SINATRAS
UK, male vocal / instrumental group (1 WEEK)
		pos/wks
24 Apr 93	HAYFEVER *Go! Discs GODCD 98*	61 1

TRAVEL *France, male producer – Laurent Gutbier (2 WEEKS)*
		pos/wks
24 Apr 99	BULGARIAN *Tidy Trax TIDY 121CD*	67 2

TRAVELING WILBURYS
UK / US, male vocal / instrumental group (19 WEEKS)
		pos/wks
29 Oct 88	HANDLE WITH CARE *Wilbury W 7732*	21 13
11 Mar 89	END OF THE LINE *Wilbury W 7637*	52 4
30 Jun 90	NOBODY'S CHILD *Wilbury W 9773*	44 2

TRAVIS (444 Top 500) *Scottish melodic rock merchants named after a character from the 1984 movie 'Paris, Texas', consisting of English-born Fran Healy (v,g) and native Glaswegians Andy Dunlop (g), Dougie Payne (b) and Neil Primrose (d). Their Brit Award-winning 'The Man Who' was the best-selling album by a British act in the UK in 1999 (79 WEEKS)*
		pos/wks
12 Apr 97	U16 GIRLS *Independiente ISOM 1MS*	40 2
28 Jun 97	ALL I WANT TO DO IS ROCK *Independiente ISOM 3MS*	39 2
23 Aug 97	TIED TO THE 90'S *Independiente ISOM 5MS*	30 2
25 Oct 97	HAPPY *Independiente ISOM 6MS*	38 2
11 Apr 98	MORE THAN US (EP) *Independiente ISOM 11MS*	16 3
20 Mar 99	WRITING TO REACH YOU *Independiente ISOM 22MS*	14 5
29 May 99	DRIFTWOOD *Independiente ISOM 27MS*	13 5
14 Aug 99 ●	WHY DOES IT ALWAYS RAIN ON ME? *Independiente ISOM 33MS*	10 8
20 Nov 99 ●	TURN *Independiente ISOM 39MS*	8 11
17 Jun 00 ●	COMING AROUND (2re) *Independiente ISOM 45MS*	5 10
9 Jun 01 ●	SING *Independiente ISOM 49MS*	3 14
29 Sep 01	SIDE *Independiente ISOM 54MS*	14 8
6 Apr 02	FLOWERS IN THE WINDOW *Independiente ISOM 56MS*	18 7

Tracks on More Than Us (EP): More Than Us / Give Me Some Truth / All I Want To Do Is Rock / Funny Thing

Randy TRAVIS *US, male vocalist (6 WEEKS)*
		pos/wks
21 May 88	FOREVER AND EVER, AMEN *Warner Bros. W 8384*	55 6

John TRAVOLTA (358 Top 500)
Ever popular actor / singer, b. 18 Feb 1954, New Jersey, US. His influential music-based movies include 'Saturday Night Fever', 'Urban Cowboy' and 'Grease', whose retro 50s sound has timeless appeal. One of the few acts with two successive UK million sellers (90 WEEKS)
		pos/wks
20 May 78 ★	YOU'RE THE ONE THAT I WANT *RSO 006* [1] ◆ ▲	1 26
16 Sep 78 ★	SUMMER NIGHTS *RSO 18* [2] ◆	1 19
7 Oct 78 ●	SANDY *Polydor POSP 6*	2 15
2 Dec 78	GREASED LIGHTNING *Polydor POSP 14*	11 9
22 Dec 90 ●	THE GREASE MEGAMIX *Polydor PO 114* [1]	3 10

UK No.1 ★ UK Top 10 ● Still on chart + UK million seller ◆ UK entry at No.1 ■ US No.1 ▲

23 Mar 91	GREASE – THE DREAM MIX *PWL / Polydor PO 136* [3]	47	2
25 Jul 98	● YOU'RE THE ONE THAT I WANT (re-issue) *Polydor 0441332* [1]	4	9

[1] John Travolta and Olivia Newton-John [2] John Travolta, Olivia Newton-John and cast [3] Frankie Valli, John Travolta and Olivia Newton-John

TREMELOES (71) Top 500

Brian Poole and The Tremeloes were formed in 1959 and signed by Decca in preference to The Beatles (auditioned same day). First south of England group to top the chart in the Beat Boom era. Poole, b. 2 Nov 1941, Essex, UK, went solo in 1966. Poole's daughters hit in the late 90s as Alisha's Attic. After supporting Brian Poole on his many hits, the Tremeloes – Len 'Chip' Hawkes (v/b), Rick West (g), Alan Blakely (g), Dave Munden (d) – went on to score even more hits in their own right. Hawkes is the father of 1991 chart-topper Chesney Hawkes (222 WEEKS) pos/wks

4 Jul 63	● TWIST AND SHOUT *Decca F 11694* [1]	4	14
12 Sep 63	★ DO YOU LOVE ME *Decca F 11739* [1]	1	14
28 Nov 63	I CAN DANCE *Decca F 11771* [1]	31	8
30 Jan 64	● CANDY MAN *Decca F 11823* [1]	6	13
7 May 64	● SOMEONE, SOMEONE *Decca F 11893* [1]	2	17
20 Aug 64	TWELVE STEPS TO LOVE *Decca F 11951* [1]	32	7
31 Dec 64	THREE BELLS *Decca F 12037* [1]	17	10
22 Jul 65	I WANT CANDY *Decca F 12197* [1]	25	8
2 Feb 67	● HERE COMES MY BABY *CBS 202519*	4	11
27 Apr 67	★ SILENCE IS GOLDEN *CBS 2723*	1	15
2 Aug 67	● EVEN THE BAD TIMES ARE GOOD *CBS 2930*	4	13
8 Nov 67	BE MINE *CBS 3043*	39	2
17 Jan 68	● SUDDENLY YOU LOVE ME *CBS 3234*	6	11
8 May 68	HELULE HELULE *CBS 2889*	14	9
18 Sep 68	● MY LITTLE LADY *CBS 3680*	6	12
11 Dec 68	I SHALL BE RELEASED *CBS 3873*	29	5
19 Mar 69	HELLO WORLD *CBS 4065*	14	8
1 Nov 69	● (CALL ME) NUMBER ONE *CBS 4582*	2	14
21 Mar 70	BY THE WAY *CBS 4815*	35	6
12 Sep 70	● ME AND MY LIFE *CBS 5139*	4	18
10 Jul 71	HELLO BUDDY *CBS 7294*	32	7

[1] Brian Poole & The Tremeloes

Jackie TRENT
UK, female vocalist – Yvonne Burgess (17 WEEKS) pos/wks

22 Apr 65	★ WHERE ARE YOU NOW *Pye 7N 15776*	1	11
1 Jul 65	WHEN THE SUMMERTIME IS OVER *Pye 7N 15865*	39	2
2 Apr 69	I'LL BE THERE *Pye 7N 17693*	38	4

Ralph TRESVANT
US, male vocalist (21 WEEKS) pos/wks

12 Jan 91	SENSITIVITY *MCA MCS 1462*	18	8
15 Aug 92	● THE BEST THINGS IN LIFE ARE FREE *Perspective PERSS 7400* [1]	2	13

[1] Luther Vandross and Janet Jackson with special guests BBD and Ralph Tresvant

TREVOR & SIMON
UK, male production duo – Trevor Reilly and Simon Foy (5 WEEKS) pos/wks

10 Jun 00	HANDS UP *Substance SUBS 1CDS*	12	5

TRI *UK, male vocal / instrumental group (1 WEEK)* pos/wks

2 Sep 95	WE GOT THE LOVE *Epic 6623642*	61	1

TRIBAL HOUSE
US, male vocal / instrumental group (2 WEEKS) pos/wks

3 Feb 90	MOTHERLAND-A-FRI-CA *Cooltempo COOL 198*	57	2

Tony TRIBE *Jamaica, male vocalist (2 WEEKS)* pos/wks

16 Jul 69	RED RED WINE (re) *Downtown DT 419*	46	2

A TRIBE CALLED QUEST *US, male rap group (18 WEEKS)* pos/wks

18 Aug 90	BONITA APPLEBUM *Jive JIVE 256*	47	3
19 Jan 91	CAN I KICK IT? *Jive JIVE 265*	15	7

11 Jun 94	OH MY GOD *Jive JIVECD 355*	68	1
13 Jul 96	1NCE AGAIN *Jive JIVECD 399*	34	2
23 Nov 96	STRESSED OUT *Jive JIVECD 404* [1]	33	2
23 Aug 97	THE JAM EP *Jive JIVECD 427*	61	1
29 Aug 98	FIND A WAY *Jive 0518982*	41	2

[1] A Tribe Called Quest featuring Faith Evans and Raphael Saadiq

Tracks on The Jam EP: Jam / Get a Hold / Mardi Gras at Midnight / Same Ol' Thing

TRIBE OF TOFFS
UK, male vocal / instrumental group (5 WEEKS) pos/wks

24 Dec 88	JOHN KETTLEY (IS A WEATHERMAN) *Completely Different DAFT 1*	21	5

TRICKBABY
UK, female vocal / instrumental group (2 WEEKS) pos/wks

12 Oct 96	INDIE-YARN *Logic 74321423152*	47	2

TRICKSTER *UK, male producer – Liam Sullivan (3 WEEKS)* pos/wks

4 Apr 98	MOVE ON UP *AM:PM 5825812*	19	3

TRICKY *UK, male vocalist / multi-instrumentalist – Adrian Thaws (29 WEEKS)* pos/wks

5 Feb 94	AFTERMATH *Fourth & Broadway BRCD 288*	69	1
28 Jan 95	OVERCOME *Fourth & Broadway BRCD 304*	34	3
15 Apr 95	BLACK STEEL *Fourth & Broadway BRCD 320*	28	3
5 Aug 95	THE HELL (EP) *Fourth & Broadway BRCD 326* [1]	12	3
11 Nov 95	PUMPKIN *Fourth & Broadway BRCD 330*	26	2
9 Nov 96	CHRISTIANSANDS *Fourth & Broadway BRCD 340*	36	2
23 Nov 96	● MILK (re) *Mushroom D 2004* [2]	10	8
11 Jan 97	TRICKY KID *Fourth & Broadway BRCD 341*	28	2
3 May 97	MAKES ME WANNA DIE *Fourth & Broadway BRCD 348*	29	2
30 May 98	MONEY GREEDY / BROKEN HOMES *Island CID 701*	25	2
21 Aug 99	FOR REAL *Island CID 753*	45	1

[1] Tricky vs The Gravediggaz [2] Garbage featuring Tricky

Tracks on The Hell (EP): Hell Is Round the Corner (original) / Hell Is Round the Corner (Hell and Water mix) / Psychosis / Tonite Is a Special Nite (Chaos mass confusion mix)

TRICKY DISCO *UK, male instrumental / production duo – Lee Newman and Michael Wells (10 WEEKS)* pos/wks

28 Jul 90	TRICKY DISCO *Warp WAP 7*	14	8
20 Apr 91	HOUSE FLY *Warp 7WAP 11*	55	2

See also GTO; TECHNOHEAD

TRIFFIDS *Australia, male vocal / instrumental group (1 WEEK)* pos/wks

6 Feb 88	A TRICK OF THE LIGHT *Island IS 350*	73	1

TRINA *US, female vocalist (1 WEEK)* pos/wks

19 Oct 02	NO PANTIES *Atlantic AT 0141CD*	45	1

TRINA and TAMARA *US, female vocal duo (3 WEEKS)* pos/wks

7 Feb 98	MY LOVE IS THE SHHH! *Warner Bros W 0427CD*	64	1
12 Jun 99	WHAT'D YOU COME HERE FOR? *Columbia 6673382*	46	2

TRINIDAD OIL COMPANY
Trinidad, male / female vocal / instrumental group (5 WEEKS) pos/wks

21 May 77	THE CALENDAR SONG (JANUARY, FEBRUARY, MARCH, APRIL, MAY) *Harvest HAR 5122*	34	5

TRINITY – *See Julie DRISCOLL, Brian AUGER and the TRINITY*

TRINITY-X *UK, male / female production / vocal trio (3 WEEKS)* pos/wks

19 Oct 02	FOREVER *All Around the World CDGLOBE 255*	19	3

TRIO *Germany, male vocal / instrumental group (10 WEEKS)* pos/wks

3 Jul 82	● DA DA DA *Mobile Suit Corporation CORP 5*	2	10

TRIPLE X Italy, male production
duo – Lucia Moretti and Ricky Romanini (2 WEEKS)   pos/wks

30 Oct 99	FEEL THE SAME *Sound of Ministry MOSCDS 135* 32	2

See also PLAYTHING

TRIPPING DAISY US, male vocal / instrumental group (1 WEEK)   pos/wks

30 Mar 96	PIRANHA *Island CID 638*.......... 72	1

TRISCO UK, male production duo –
Harvey Dawson and Rupert Edwards (2 WEEKS)   pos/wks

30 Jun 01	MUSAK *Positiva CDTIV 155*.......... 28	2

TRIUMPH Canada, male vocal / instrumental group (2 WEEKS)   pos/wks

22 Nov 80	I LIVE FOR THE WEEKEND *RCA 13* 59	2

TROGGS `378` `Top 500`

Earthy Sixties pop quartet fronted by Reg Presley (Ball) b. 12. Jun 1943,
Hampshire, UK. 'Wild Thing' topped the US chart and sold more than five
million worldwide. The Presley-penned 'Love Is All Around' had a 15-week
stay at No.1 in 1994 for Wet Wet Wet (87 WEEKS)   pos/wks

5 May 66 ●	WILD THING *Fontana TF 689* ▲ 2	12
14 Jul 66 ★	WITH A GIRL LIKE YOU *Fontana TF 717* 1	12
29 Sep 66 ●	I CAN'T CONTROL MYSELF *Page One POF 001* 2	14
15 Dec 66 ●	ANY WAY THAT YOU WANT ME *Page One POF 010* 8	10
16 Feb 67	GIVE IT TO ME *Page One POF 015* 12	10
1 Jun 67	NIGHT OF THE LONG GRASS *Page One POF 022* 17	6
26 Jul 67	HI HI HAZEL *Page One POF 030* 42	3
18 Oct 67 ●	LOVE IS ALL AROUND *Page One POF 040* 5	14
28 Feb 68	LITTLE GIRL *Page One POF 056* 37	4
30 Oct 93	WILD THING *Weekend CDWEEK 103* `1` 69	2

`1` Troggs and Wolf

'Wild Thing' in 1993 is a re-recording and was listed with the flip side, 'War', by
Edwin Starr and Shadow

TRONIKHOUSE
US, male producer – Kevin Saunderson (1 WEEK)   pos/wks

14 Mar 92	UP TEMPO *KMS UK KMSUK 1* 68	1

TROUBADOURS DU ROI BAUDOUIN
Zaire, male / female vocal group (11 WEEKS)   pos/wks

19 Mar 69	SANCTUS (MISSA LUBA) (re) *Philips BF 1732*.......... 28	11

TROUBLE FUNK US, male vocal / instrumental group (3 WEEKS) pos/wks

27 Jun 87	WOMAN OF PRINCIPLE *Fourth & Broadway BRW 70*.......... 65	3

Roger TROUTMAN – See 2PAC

Doris TROY US, female vocalist - Doris Higginson (12 WEEKS)   pos/wks

19 Nov 64	WHATCHA GONNA DO ABOUT IT (re) *Atlantic AT 4011*.......... 37	12

Elisabeth TROY – See SOUNDMAN and Don LLOYDIE with Elisabeth TROY; Y-TRIBE
featuring Elisabeth TROY; MJ COLE; 4 VINI featuring Elisabeth TROY

TRU FAITH & DUB CONSPIRACY
UK, male production groups (5 WEEKS)   pos/wks

9 Sep 00	FREAK LIKE ME *Public Demand / Positiva CDTIV 138* 12	5

TRUBBLE UK, male / female production / vocal trio (5 WEEKS)   pos/wks

26 Dec 98	DANCING BABY (OOGA-CHAKA) *Island YYCD 1*.......... 21	5

TRUCE UK, female vocal group (6 WEEKS)   pos/wks

2 Sep 95	THE FINEST *Big Life BLRD 118* 54	1
30 Mar 96	CELEBRATION OF LIFE *Big Life BLRD 126* 51	1
29 Nov 97	NOTHIN' BUT A PARTY *Big Life BLRD 138* 71	1
5 Sep 98	EYES DON'T LIE *Big Life BLRD 146* 20	3

FIRST UK No.1 BY COUNTRY

■ All of these international acts share the distinction
of being the first in their home countries to score a
coveted UK chart-topper

FIRST AUSTRALIAN
SEEKERS 'I'LL NEVER FIND ANOTHER YOU'
The group was a combination of three Australians and a Sri
Lankan who got together in Melbourne in the early 1960s.
A chance meeting with Tom Springfield provided them with
their first release which topped the charts in 1965

FIRST AUSTRIAN
FALCO 'ROCK ME AMADEUS'
Johann Holzel's 1986 No.1 was a tribute to an even more
famous Austrian, Wolfgang Amadeus Mozart

FIRST CANADIAN
PAUL ANKA 'DIANA'
Paul Anka was 16 years and 13 days old when his
self-penned single reached the top spot

FIRST DUTCH
PUSSYCAT 'MISSISSIPPI'
The Pussycat line-up featured Lou Willé and three sisters
who were former telephone operators from Limburg

FIRST FRENCH
CHARLES AZNAVOUR 'SHE'
The song was the theme from the television series
The Seven Faces of Woman

FIRST GERMAN
KRAFTWERK 'COMPUTER LOVE / THE MODEL'
Though a double-sided hit, this single was never a double-A
with 'The Model' always officially the B-side

FIRST JAMAICAN
DESMOND DEKKER AND THE ACES 'ISRAELITES'
Desmond Dekker, a former welder, wrote the song jointly
with producer Leslie Kong

FIRST NEW ZEALANDER
DANIEL BEDINGFIELD 'GOTTA GET THRU THIS'
The song, created inexpensively in Bedingfield's bedroom,
made two visits to the top spot

FIRST NORWEGIAN
A-HA 'THE SUN ALWAYS SHINES ON TV'
Written by Pal Waaktaar and produced by Alan Tarney, this
song was the first Norwegian UK No.1 following a string of
glorious disasters in the Eurovision song contest

FIRST SPANISH
BACCARA 'YES SIR, I CAN BOOGIE'
Maria and Mayte were also the first female duo ever to top
the charts

FIRST SWEDISH
ABBA 'WATERLOO'
Sweden's 1974 Eurovision entry became the biggest
international hit of any contest winner in history

UK No.1 ★   UK Top 10 ●   Still on chart +   UK million seller ◆   UK entry at No.1 ■   US No.1 ▲   **473**

TRUCKIN' CO – See Garnet MIMMS and TRUCKIN' CO

TRUCKS
UK / Norway, male vocal / instrumental group (2 WEEKS) pos/wks
5 Oct 02	IT'S JUST PORN MUM *Gut CDGUT 43*	35 2

Andrea TRUE CONNECTION
US, female vocalist, male instrumental backing group (16 WEEKS) pos/wks
17 Apr 76 ●	MORE, MORE, MORE *Buddah BDS 442*	5 10
4 Mar 78	WHAT'S YOUR NAME, WHAT'S YOUR NUMBER	
	Buddah BDS 467	34 6

TRUE FAITH and Bridgette GRACE with FINAL CUT
US, male / female vocal / instrumental group (4 WEEKS) pos/wks
2 Mar 91	TAKE ME AWAY *Network NWK 20*	51 4

TRUE IMAGE – See Monie LOVE

TRUE PARTY
UK, male production / vocal group (6 WEEKS) pos/wks
2 Dec 00	WHAZZUP *Positiva CDBUD 001*	13 6

TRUE STEPPERS
UK, male production / instrumental duo – Jonny Linders and Andy Lysandrou (31 WEEKS) pos/wks
29 Apr 00 ●	BUGGIN *Nulife 74321753342* [1]	6 8
26 Aug 00 ●	OUT OF YOUR MIND (re) *Nulife 74321782942* [2]	2 20
2 Dec 00	TRUE STEP TONIGHT *Nulife 74321811312* [3]	25 3

[1] True Steppers featuring Dane Bowers [2] True Steppers and Dane Bowers featuring Victoria Beckham [3] True Steppers featuring Brian Harvey and Donell Jones

Damon TRUEITT – See SOMORE featuring Damon TRUEITT

TRUMAN & WOLFF featuring STEEL HORSES
UK, male production duo and UK, male rap group (1 WEEK) pos/wks
22 Aug 98	COME AGAIN *Multiply CDMULTY 38*	57 1

TRUMPET MAN – See MONTANO vs THE TRUMPET MAN

TRUSSEL *US, male vocal / instrumental group (4 WEEKS)* pos/wks
8 Mar 80	LOVE INJECTION *Elektra K 12412*	43 4

TRUTH
UK, male vocal duo – Stephen 'Nosmo King' Gold and Francis Aiello (6 WEEKS) pos/wks
3 Feb 66	GIRL *Pye 7N 17035*	27 6

See also JAVELLS featuring Nosmo KING

TRUTH
UK, male vocal / instrumental group (16 WEEKS) pos/wks
11 Jun 83	CONFUSION (HITS US EVERY TIME) *Formation TRUTH 1*	22 7
27 Aug 83	A STEP IN THE RIGHT DIRECTION *Formation TRUTH 2*	32 7
4 Feb 84	NO STONE UNTURNED *Formation TRUTH 3*	66 2

TRUTH HURTS featuring RAKIM
US, female vocalist – Shari Watson – and US male rapper (12 WEEKS) pos/wks
31 Aug 02 ●	ADDICTIV' *Aftermath / Interscope 4977782*	3 12

Esera TUAOLO – See Richie RICH

TUBBY T *UK, male vocalist – Anthony Robinson (1 WEEK)* pos/wks
21 Sep 02	TALES OF THE HOOD *Go! Beat GOBCD 51*	47 1

TUBES *US, male vocal / instrumental group (18 WEEKS)* pos/wks
19 Nov 77	WHITE PUNKS ON DOPE *A&M AMS 7323*	28 4
28 Apr 79	PRIME TIME *A&M AMS 7423*	34 10
12 Sep 81	DON'T WANT TO WAIT ANYMORE *Capitol CL 208*	60 4

TUBEWAY ARMY – See Gary NUMAN

Barbara TUCKER *US, female vocalist (12 WEEKS)* pos/wks
5 Mar 94	BEAUTIFUL PEOPLE *Positiva CDTIV 11*	23 3
26 Nov 94	I GET LIFTED *Positiva CDTIV 23*	33 2
23 Sep 95	STAY TOGETHER *Positiva CDTIV 39*	46 1
8 Aug 98	EVERYBODY DANCE (THE HORN SONG) *Positiva CDTIV 96* ...	28 2
18 Mar 00	STOP PLAYING WITH MY MIND *Positiva CDTIV 127* [1] ...	17 4

[1] Barbara Tucker featuring Darryl D'Bonneau

Junior TUCKER *UK, male vocalist (2 WEEKS)* pos/wks
2 Jun 90	DON'T TEST *10 TEN 299*	54 2

Louise TUCKER *UK, female vocalist (5 WEEKS)* pos/wks
9 Apr 83	MIDNIGHT BLUE *Ariola ARO 289*	59 5

Tommy TUCKER
US, male vocalist – Robert Higginbotham, d. 22 Jan 1982 (10 WEEKS) pos/wks
26 Mar 64	HI-HEEL SNEAKERS *Pye International 7N 25238*	23 10

TUFF JAM *UK, male production duo (1 WEEK)* pos/wks
10 Oct 98	NEED GOOD LOVE *Locked On LOX 99CD*	44 1

TUKAN
Denmark, male production duo – Soren Weile and Lars Fredriksen (3 WEEKS) pos/wks
15 Dec 01	LIGHT A RAINBOW *Incentive CENT 33CDS*	38 3

TURIN BRAKES
UK, male vocal / instrumental duo – Gale Paridjanian and Olly Knight (8 WEEKS) pos/wks
3 Mar 01	THE DOOR *Source SOURCDS 024*	67 1
12 May 01	UNDERDOG (SAVE ME) *Source SOURCDSE 101*	39 2
11 Aug 01	MIND OVER MONEY *Source SOURCD 038*	31 2
27 Oct 01	72 *Source SOURCD 041*	41 1
2 Nov 02	LONG DISTANCE *Source SOURCD 064*	22 2

Ike and Tina TURNER
US, male / female vocal instrumental duo (44 WEEKS) pos/wks
9 Jun 66 ●	RIVER DEEP – MOUNTAIN HIGH *London HLU 10046*	3 13
28 Jul 66	TELL HER I'M NOT HOME *Warner Bros. WB 5753*	48 1
27 Oct 66	A LOVE LIKE YOURS *London HLU 10083*	16 10
12 Feb 69	RIVER DEEP MOUNTAIN HIGH (re-issue) *London HLU 10242*	33 7
8 Sep 73 ●	NUTBUSH CITY LIMITS *United Artists UP 35582*	4 13

See also Tina TURNER

Ruby TURNER *UK, female vocalist (31 WEEKS)* pos/wks
25 Jan 86	IF YOU'RE READY (COME GO WITH ME) *Jive JIVE 109* [1] ...	30 7
29 Mar 86	I'M IN LOVE *Jive JIVE 118*	61 4
13 Sep 86	BYE BABY *Jive JIVE 126*	52 3
14 Mar 87	I'D RATHER GO BLIND *Jive RTS 1*	24 8
16 May 87	I'M IN LOVE (re-issue) *Jive RTS 2*	57 2
13 Jan 90	IT'S GONNA BE ALRIGHT *Jive RTS 7*	57 3
5 Feb 94	STAY WITH ME BABY *M & G MAGCD 53*	39 3
9 Dec 95	SHAKABOOM! *Telstar HUNTCD 1* [2]	64 1

[1] Ruby Turner featuring Jonathan Butler [2] Hunter featuring Ruby Turner

Sammy TURNER *US, male vocalist – Samuel Black (2 WEEKS)* pos/wks
13 Nov 59	ALWAYS *London HLX 8963*	26 2

Tina TURNER `67` `Top 500`
Supreme soul singer-cum-rock legend, b. Anna Mae Bullock, 26 Nov 1939, Tennessee, US. After a successful, if stormy, partnership with husband Ike, she reached greater heights as a Grammy-winning soloist and is one of the world's most popular live acts (224 WEEKS) pos/wks
19 Nov 83 ●	LET'S STAY TOGETHER *Capitol CL 316*	6 13
25 Feb 84	HELP *Capitol CL 325*	40 6

16 Jun 84	● WHAT'S LOVE GOT TO DO WITH IT *Capitol CL 334* ▲	3	16
15 Sep 84	BETTER BE GOOD TO ME *Capitol CL 338*	45	5
17 Nov 84	PRIVATE DANCER *Capitol CL 343*	26	9
2 Mar 85	I CAN'T STAND THE RAIN *Capitol CL 352*	57	3
20 Jul 85	● WE DON'T NEED ANOTHER HERO (THUNDERDOME) *Capitol CL 364*	3	12
12 Oct 85	ONE OF THE LIVING *Capitol CL 376*	55	2
2 Nov 85	IT'S ONLY LOVE *A&M AM 285* [1]	29	6
23 Aug 86	TYPICAL MALE *Capitol CL 419*	33	6
8 Nov 86	TWO PEOPLE *Capitol CL 430*	43	4
14 Mar 87	WHAT YOU GET IS WHAT YOU SEE *Capitol CL 439*	30	7
13 Jun 87	BREAK EVERY RULE *Capitol CL 452*	43	4
20 Jun 87	TEARING US APART *Duck W 8299* [2]	56	3
19 Mar 88	ADDICTED TO LOVE (LIVE) *Capitol CL 484*	71	2
2 Sep 89	● THE BEST *Capitol CL 543*	5	12
18 Nov 89	● I DON'T WANNA LOSE YOU *Capitol CL 553*	8	11
17 Feb 90	STEAMY WINDOWS *Capitol CL 560*	13	6
11 Aug 90	LOOK ME IN THE HEART *Capitol CL 584*	31	6
13 Oct 90	BE TENDER WITH ME BABY *Capitol CL 593*	28	4
24 Nov 90	● IT TAKES TWO *Warner Bros. ROD 1* [3]	5	8
21 Sep 91	NUTBUSH CITY LIMITS (re-recording) *Capitol CL 630*	23	5
23 Nov 91	WAY OF THE WORLD *Capitol CL 637*	13	7
15 Feb 92	LOVE THING *Capitol CL 644*	29	4
6 Jun 92	I WANT YOU NEAR ME *Capitol CL 659*	22	4
22 May 93	● I DON'T WANNA FIGHT *Parlophone CDRS 6346*	7	9
28 Aug 93	DISCO INFERNO *Parlophone CDR 6357*	12	6
30 Oct 93	WHY MUST WE WAIT UNTIL TONIGHT *Parlophone CDR 6366*	16	4
18 Nov 95	● GOLDENEYE *Parlophone CDR 0071001*	10	9
23 Mar 96	WHATEVER YOU WANT *Parlophone CDR 6429*	23	6
8 Jun 96	ON SILENT WINGS *Parlophone CDR 6434*	13	6
27 Jul 96	MISSING YOU *Parlophone CDR 6441* [4]	12	5
19 Oct 96	SOMETHING BEAUTIFUL REMAINS *Parlophone CDR 6448*	27	2
21 Dec 96	IN YOUR WILDEST DREAMS *Parlophone CDR 6451* [5]	32	5
30 Oct 99	● WHEN THE HEARTACHE IS OVER *Parlophone CDR 6529* [4]	10	7
12 Feb 00	WHATEVER YOU NEED *Parlophone CDR 6532*	27	3

[1] Bryan Adams and Tina Turner [2] Eric Clapton and Tina Turner [3] Rod Stewart and Tina Turner [4] Tina [5] Tina Turner featuring Barry White

See also Ike and Tina TURNER

TURNTABLE ORCHESTRA
US, male vocal / instrumental duo (4 WEEKS) pos/wks

21 Jan 89	YOU'RE GONNA MISS ME *Republic LIC 012*	52	4

TURTLES *US, male vocal / instrumental group (39 WEEKS)* pos/wks

23 Mar 67	HAPPY TOGETHER *London HLU 10115* ▲	12	12
15 Jun 67	SHE'D RATHER BE WITH ME *London HLU 10135*	4	15
30 Oct 68	● ELENORE *London HLU 10223*	7	12

TUXEDOS – *See Bobby ANGELO and the TUXEDOS*

Shania TWAIN 442 *Top 500*

Pop and country music queen, b. Eileen Regina Edwards 28 Aug 1965, Ontario, Canada. Self-penned 'Come On Over' album sold more than 34 million, including two million in the UK and a record-breaking 19 million in the US. Her tours in 1999 grossed $36.6 million. Best-selling single: 'That Don't Impress Me Much' 763,000 (79 WEEKS) pos/wks

28 Feb 98	● YOU'RE STILL THE ONE *Mercury 5684932*	10	10
13 Jun 98	WHEN *Mercury 5661192*	18	4
28 Nov 98	● FROM THIS MOMENT ON *Mercury 5665632*	9	8
22 May 99	● THAT DON'T IMPRESS ME MUCH *Mercury 8708032*	3	21
2 Oct 99	● MAN! I FEEL LIKE A WOMAN! *Mercury 5623242*	3	18
26 Feb 00	● DON'T BE STUPID (YOU KNOW I LOVE YOU) (re) *Mercury 1721492*	5	11
16 Nov 02	● I'M GONNA GETCHA GOOD! *Mercury 1722702*	4	7+

TWEENIES
UK, male / female kiddie TV characters (58 WEEKS) pos/wks

11 Nov 00	● NUMBER 1 (2re) *BBC Music WMSS 60332*	5	27

31 Mar 01	BEST FRIENDS FOREVER (re) *BBC Music WMSS 60382*	12	10
4 Aug 01	DO THE LOLLIPOP *BBC Music WMSS 60452*	17	8
15 Dec 01	I BELIEVE IN CHRISTMAS *BBC Music WMSS 60502*	9	6
14 Sep 02	HAVE FUN GO MAD *BBC Music WMSS 60572*	20	7

TWEET *US, female vocalist – Charlene Keys (10 WEEKS)* pos/wks

11 May 02	● OOPS (OH MY) *Elektra E 7306CD*	5	8
7 Sep 02	CALL ME *Elektra E 7326CD*	35	2

TWEETS
UK, male feathered vocal / instrumental group (34 WEEKS) pos/wks

12 Sep 81	● THE BIRDIE SONG (BIRDIE DANCE) (re) *PRT 7P 219*	2	28
5 Dec 81	LET'S ALL SING LIKE THE BIRDIES SING *PRT 7P 226*	44	6

'The Birdie Song (Birdie Dance) re-entered in Dec 1982 peaking at No.48

20 FINGERS *US, male instrumental / production duo – Charles Babie and Manfred Mohr (14 WEEKS)* pos/wks

26 Nov 94	SHORT DICK MAN *Multiply CDMULT 12* [1]	21	4
30 Sep 95	SHORT SHORT MAN (re-mix) *Multiply CXMULTY 7* [1]	11	7
30 Sep 95	LICK IT *Zyx ZYX 75908* [2]	48	3

[1] 20 Fingers featuring Gillette [2] 20 Fingers featuring Roula

21ST CENTURY GIRLS
UK, female vocal / instrumental group (4 WEEKS) pos/wks

12 Jun 99	21ST CENTURY GIRLS *EMI NTNCDS 001*	16	4

TWENTY 4 SEVEN featuring CAPTAIN HOLLYWOOD
US / Germany, male / female vocal / instrumental group (20 WKS) pos/wks

22 Sep 90	● I CAN'T STAND IT *BCM BCMR 395*	7	10
24 Nov 90	ARE YOU DREAMING *BCM BCM 07504*	17	10

See also CAPTAIN HOLLYWOOD PROJECT

29 PALMS *UK, male producer – Pete Lorimar (1 WEEK)* pos/wks

25 May 02	TOUCH THE SKY *Perfecto PERF 35CDS*	51	1

TWICE AS MUCH
UK, male vocal duo – David Skinner and Stephen Rose (9 WEEKS) pos/wks

16 Jun 66	SITTIN' ON A FENCE *Immediate IM 033*	25	9

TWIGGY *UK, female vocalist – Lesley Hornby (10 WEEKS)* pos/wks

14 Aug 76	HERE I GO AGAIN *Mercury 6007 100*	17	10

TWILIGHT – *See Roger SANCHEZ*

TWIN HYPE *US, male rap duo (2 WEEKS)* pos/wks

15 Jul 89	DO IT TO THE CROWD *Profile PROF 255*	65	2

TWINKLE *UK, female vocalist – Lynn Ripley (20 WEEKS)* pos/wks

26 Nov 64	● TERRY *Decca F 12013*	4	15
25 Feb 65	GOLDEN LIGHTS *Decca F 12076*	21	5

TWISTED SISTER *US, male vocal / instrumental group (28 WKS)* pos/wks

26 Mar 83	I AM (I'M ME) *Atlantic A 9854*	18	9
28 May 83	THE KIDS ARE BACK *Atlantic A 9827*	32	6
20 Aug 83	YOU CAN'T STOP ROCK 'N' ROLL *Atlantic A 9792*	43	4
2 Jun 84	WE'RE NOT GONNA TAKE IT *Atlantic A 9657*	58	6
18 Jan 86	LEADER OF THE PACK *Atlantic A 9478*	47	3

Conway TWITTY
US, male vocalist – Harold Jenkins, d. 5 Jun 1993 (36 WEEKS) pos/wks

14 Nov 58	★ IT'S ONLY MAKE BELIEVE *MGM 992* ▲	1	15
27 Mar 59	THE STORY OF MY LOVE *MGM 1003*	30	1
21 Aug 59	● MONA LISA *MGM 1029*	5	14
21 Jul 60	IS A BLUE BIRD BLUE *MGM 1082*	43	3
23 Feb 61	C'EST SI BON *MGM 1118*	40	3

2 BAD MICE
UK, male instrumental / production group (4 WEEKS) pos/wks

15 Feb 92	**HOLD IT DOWN (re)** Moving Shadow SHADOW 14	48	3
7 Sep 96	**BOMBSCARE** Arista 74321397662	46	1

TWO COWBOYS Italy, male instrumental / production
duo – Roberto Sagotto and Maurizio Braccagni (11 WEEKS) pos/wks

9 Jul 94 ●	**EVERYBODY GONFI-GON** 3 Beat TABCD 221	7	11

2 EIVISSA Germany, female vocal duo –
Pascale Jean Louis and Ellen Helbig (6 WEEKS) pos/wks

4 Oct 97	**OH LA LA LA** Club Tools 0063475 CLU	13	6

2 FOR JOY
UK, male instrumental / production duo (3 WEEKS) pos/wks

1 Dec 90	**IN A STATE** Mercury MER 333	61	1
9 Nov 91	**LET THE BASS KICK**		
	All Around the World GLOBE 102	67	2

2-4 FAMILY
UK / US / Korea, male / female rap / vocal group (1 WEEK) pos/wks

29 May 99	**LEAN ON ME (WITH THE FAMILY)** Epic 6670132	69	1

2 FUNKY 2 starring Kathryn DION
UK, male / female vocal / instrumental group (4 WEEKS) pos/wks

6 Nov 93	**BROTHERS AND SISTERS** Logic 74321170772	56	2
30 Nov 96	**BROTHERS AND SISTERS (re-mix)**		
	All Around the World CDGLOBE 138	36	2

2 HOUSE
US, male instrumental / production duo (1 WEEK) pos/wks

21 Mar 92	**GO TECHNO** Atlantic A 7519	65	1

2 IN A ROOM
US, male vocal duo – Roger Pauletta and Rafael Vargas (15 WEEKS) pos/wks

18 Nov 89	**SOMEBODY IN THE HOUSE SAY YEAH!**		
	Big Life BLR 12	66	1
26 Jan 91 ●	**WIGGLE IT** SBK SBK 19	3	8
6 Apr 91	**SHE'S GOT ME GOING CRAZY** SBK SBK 23	54	2
22 Oct 94	**EL TRAGO (THE DRINK)** Positiva CDTIV 18	34	2
8 Apr 95	**AHORA ES (NOW IS THE TIME)** Positiva CDTIV 32	43	1
17 Aug 96	**GIDDY-UP** Encore CDCOR 008	74	1

2 IN A TENT UK, male instrumental /
production duo – Mike Stock and Matt Aitken (7 WEEKS) pos/wks

17 Dec 94	**WHEN I'M CLEANING WINDOWS (TURNED OUT NICE AGAIN) (re)** Love This SPONCD 1	25	6
13 May 95	**BOOGIE WOOGIE BUGLE BOY (DON'T STOP)**		
	Bald Cat BALDCD 1 [1]	48	1

[1] 2 In a Tank

First hit, which features the sampled vocals of George Formby, re-entered in Jan 1996 and peaked at No.62

See also STOCK AITKEN WATERMAN

2K UK, male production duo –
Bill Drummond and Jimmy Cauty (2 WEEKS) pos/wks

25 Oct 97	*****K THE MILLENNIUM** Blast First BFFP 146CDK	28	2

See also KLF; TIMELORDS; JUSTIFIED ANCIENTS OF MU MU

2 MAD UK, male vocal / instrumental duo (4 WEEKS) pos/wks

9 Feb 91	**THINKIN' ABOUT YOUR BODY** Big Life BLR 37	43	4

TWO MAN SOUND
Belgium, male vocal / instrumental group (7 WEEKS) pos/wks

20 Jan 79	**QUE TAL AMERICA** Miracle M 1	46	7

TWO MEN, A DRUM MACHINE AND A TRUMPET UK, male
instrumental duo - Andy Cox and David Steele (17 WEEKS) pos/wks

9 Jan 88	**TIRED OF GETTING PUSHED AROUND** London LON 141	18	8
25 Jun 88	**HEAT IT UP** Jive JIVE 174 [1]	21	9

[1] Wee Papa Girl Rappers featuring Two Men and a Drum Machine

See also FINE YOUNG CANNIBALS

TWO NATIONS UK, male vocal / instrumental group (1 WEEK) pos/wks

20 Jun 87	**THAT'S THE WAY IT FEELS** 10 TEN 168	74	1

2PAC (473) Top 500
Legendary rapper / actor, born Tupac Amaru Shakur, New York City,
16 Jun 1971 (d. 13 Sep 1996 in a Las Vegas shooting incident), who achieved
more UK and US single and album hits after his death than before. In his
homeland, no rapper has sold more albums and no artist has had more
posthumous chart success (76 WEEKS) pos/wks

13 Apr 96 ●	**CALIFORNIA LOVE** Death Row DRWCD 3 [1]	6	8
27 Jul 96	**HOW DO YOU WANT IT** Death Row DRWCD 4 [2] ▲	17	4
30 Nov 96	**I AIN'T MAD AT CHA** Death Row DRWCD 5	13	9
12 Apr 97 ●	**TO LIVE & DIE IN LA** Interscope IND 95529 [3]	10	4
26 Apr 97	**WANTED DEAD OR ALIVE** Def Jam 5744052 [4]	16	3
9 Aug 97	**TOSS IT UP** Interscope IND 95521 [3]	15	3
10 Jan 98	**I WONDER IF HEAVEN GOT A GHETTO** Jive JIVECD 446	21	4
14 Feb 98	**HAIL MARY** Interscope IND 95575 [3]	43	1
13 Jun 98	**DO FOR LOVE** Jive 0518512 [5]	12	4
18 Jul 98	**RUNNIN'** Black Jam BJAM 9005 [6]	15	3
28 Nov 98	**HAPPY HOME** Eagle EAGXS 058	17	2
20 Feb 99 ●	**CHANGES** Jive 0522832	3	12
3 Jul 99	**DEAR MAMA** Jive 0523702	27	3
23 Jun 01 ●	**UNTIL THE END OF TIME** Interscope / Polydor 4975812	4	11
10 Nov 01	**LETTER 2 MY UNBORN** Interscope / Polydor 4976142	21	5

[1] 2Pac featuring Dr Dre [2] 2Pac featuring K-Ci and JoJo [3] Makaveli
[4] 2Pac and Snoop Doggy Dogg [5] 2Pac featuring Eric Williams [6] 2Pac
and Notorious B.I.G.

TWO PEOPLE
UK, male vocal / instrumental group (2 WEEKS) pos/wks

31 Jan 87	**HEAVEN** Polydor POSP 844	63	2

2WO THIRD3 UK, male vocal / instrumental group (15 WEEKS) pos/wks

19 Feb 94	**HEAR ME CALLING** Epic 6600642	48	3
11 Jun 94	**EASE THE PRESSURE** Epic 6604782	45	2
8 Oct 94	**I WANT THE WORLD** Epic 6608542	20	5
17 Dec 94	**I WANT TO BE ALONE** Epic 6610852	29	5

2 UNLIMITED (256) Top 500
The brainchild of Jean-Paul de Coster and Phil Wilde, fronted by the
minimalist vocals / chants / raps of Dutch duo Ray Slijngaard and Anita
Dels. Their youth-aimed, infectious dance tracks sold millions around
Europe and gave them 11 successive UK Top 20 hits (112 WEEKS) pos/wks

5 Oct 91 ●	**GET READY FOR THIS** PWL Continental PWL 206	2	15
25 Jan 92 ●	**TWILIGHT ZONE** PWL Continental PWL 211	2	10
2 May 92 ●	**WORKAHOLIC** PWL Continental PWL 228	4	7
15 Aug 92	**THE MAGIC FRIEND** PWL Continental PWL 240	11	7
30 Jan 93 ★	**NO LIMIT** PWL Continental PWCD 256	1	16
8 May 93 ●	**TRIBAL DANCE** PWL Continental PWCD 262	4	11
4 Sep 93 ●	**FACES** PWL Continental PWCD 268	8	7
20 Nov 93	**MAXIMUM OVERDRIVE** PWL Continental PWCD 276	15	3
19 Feb 94 ●	**LET THE BEAT CONTROL YOUR BODY**		
	PWL Continental PWCD 280	6	7
21 May 94 ●	**THE REAL THING** PWL Continental PWCD 306	6	7
1 Oct 94	**NO ONE** PWL Continental PWCD 314	17	6
25 Mar 95	**HERE I GO** PWL Continental PWCD 317	22	3
21 Oct 95	**DO WHAT'S GOOD FOR ME**		
	PWL Continental PWL 322CD1	16	4
11 Jul 98	**WANNA GET UP** Big Life BLRD 143	38	2

In 1995 both Ray Slijngaard and Anita Dels left the act which was fronted by a
Dutch female duo for 'Wanna Get Up'

TYGERS OF PAN TANG
UK, male vocal / instrumental group (15 WEEKS) pos/wks

14 Feb 81	HELLBOUND *MCA 672*	48	3
27 Mar 82	LOVE POTION NO. 9 *MCA 769*	45	6
10 Jul 82	RENDEZVOUS *MCA 777*	49	4
11 Sep 82	PARIS BY AIR *MCA 790*	63	2

Bonnie TYLER   420   Top 500
Raspy-voiced vocalist b. Gaynor Hopkins, 8 Jun 1953, Swansea, Wales. Made the US country Top 10 with 'It's a Heartache', and 'Total Eclipse of the Heart' was the first record by a Welsh artist to top the US pop chart (81 WKS) pos/wks

30 Oct 76	● LOST IN FRANCE *RCA 2734*	9	10
19 Mar 77	MORE THAN A LOVER *RCA PB 5008*	27	6
3 Dec 77	● IT'S A HEARTACHE *RCA PB 5057*	4	12
30 Jun 79	MARRIED MEN *RCA PB 5164*	35	6
19 Feb 83	★ TOTAL ECLIPSE OF THE HEART *CBS TYLER 1* ▲	1	12
7 May 83	FASTER THAN THE SPEED OF NIGHT *CBS A 3338*	43	4
25 Jun 83	HAVE YOU EVER SEEN THE RAIN *CBS A 3517*	47	4
7 Jan 84	● A ROCKIN' GOOD WAY *Epic A 4071* [1]	5	9
31 Aug 85	● HOLDING OUT FOR A HERO *CBS A 4251*	2	13
14 Dec 85	LOVING YOU'S A DIRTY JOB BUT SOMEBODY'S GOTTA DO IT *CBS A 6662* [2]	73	2
28 Dec 91	HOLDING OUT FOR A HERO (re-issue) *Total TYLER 10*	69	2
27 Jan 96	MAKING LOVE (OUT OF NOTHING AT ALL) *East West EW 010CD*	45	2

[1] Shaky and Bonnie [2] Bonnie Tyler, guest vocals Todd Rundgren

TYMES
US, male vocal group – lead vocal George Williams (41 WKS) pos/wks

25 Jul 63	SO MUCH IN LOVE *Cameo Parkway P 871* ▲	21	8
15 Jan 69	PEOPLE *Direction 58 3903*	16	10
21 Sep 74	YOU LITTLE TRUSTMAKER *RCA 2456*	18	9
21 Dec 74	★ MS GRACE *RCA 2493*	1	11
17 Jan 76	GOD'S GONNA PUNISH YOU *RCA 2626*	41	3

TYMES 4
UK, female vocal group (5 WEEKS) pos/wks

25 Aug 01	BODYROCK *Edel 0118635 ERE*	23	3
15 Dec 01	SHE GOT GAME *Blacklist 0133135 ERE*	40	2

TYPICALLY TROPICAL
UK, male vocal / instrumental duo – Jeff Calvert and Max West (11 WEEKS) pos/wks

5 Jul 75	★ BARBADOS *Gull GULS 14*	1	11

TYREE
US, male producer – Tyree Cooper (10 WEEKS) pos/wks

25 Feb 89	TURN UP THE BASS *ffrr FFR 24* [1]	12	7
6 May 89	HARDCORE HIP HOUSE *DJ International DJIN 11*	70	2
2 Dec 89	MOVE YOUR BODY *CBS 655470 7* [2]	72	1

[1] Tyree featuring Kool Rock Steady [2] Tyree featuring JMD

TYRELL CORPORATION
UK, male vocal / instrumental duo – Joe Watson and Tony Barry (9 WEEKS) pos/wks

14 Mar 92	THE BOTTLE *Volante TYR 1*	71	1
15 Aug 92	GOING HOME *Volante TYR 2*	58	2
10 Oct 92	WAKING WITH A STRANGER / ONE DAY *Volante TYRS 3*	59	1
24 Sep 94	YOU'RE NOT HERE *Cooltempo CDCOOL 292*	42	2
14 Jan 95	BETTER DAYS AHEAD *Cooltempo CDCOOL 303*	29	3

TYRESE
US, male vocalist (2 WEEKS) pos/wks

31 Jul 99	NOBODY ELSE *RCA 74321688282*	59	1
25 Sep 99	SWEET LADY *RCA 74321700842*	55	1

TZANT
UK, male rap / instrumental duo – Jamie White and Marcus Thomas (aka ODC MC) (10 WEEKS) pos/wks

7 Sep 96	HOT AND WET (BELIEVE IT) *Logic 74321376832*	36	2
25 Apr 98	SOUNDS OF WICKEDNESS *Logic 74321568842*	11	6
22 Aug 98	BOUNCE WITH THE MASSIVE *Logic 74321602102*	39	2

Judie TZUKE
UK, female vocalist (10 WEEKS) pos/wks

14 Jul 79	STAY WITH ME TILL DAWN *Rocket XPRES 17*	16	10

UHF
US, male instrumental / production group (4 WEEKS) pos/wks

14 Dec 91	UHF / EVERYTHING *XL Recordings XLS 25*	46	4

UB40   22   Top 500
Reggae's most successful transatlantic group: includes brothers Ali (v/g) and Robin (v/g) Campbell, and Earl Falconer (b). Only three groups can claim more chart hits than this Birmingham act, named after the number of the UK unemployment benefit form. Best-selling single: '(I Can't Help) Falling In Love With You' 606,000 (331 WEEKS) pos/wks

8 Mar 80	● KING / FOOD FOR THOUGHT *Graduate GRAD 6* [1]	4	13
14 Jun 80	● MY WAY OF THINKING / I THINK IT'S GOING TO RAIN TODAY *Graduate GRAD 8* [1]	6	10
1 Nov 80	● THE EARTH DIES SCREAMING / DREAM A LIE *Graduate GRAD 10*	10	12
23 May 81	DON'T LET IT PASS YOU BY / DON'T SLOW DOWN *DEP International DEP 1*	16	9
8 Aug 81	● ONE IN TEN *DEP International DEP 2*	7	10
13 Feb 82	I WON'T CLOSE MY EYES *DEP International DEP 3*	32	6
15 May 82	LOVE IS ALL IS ALRIGHT *DEP International DEP 4*	29	7
28 Aug 82	SO HERE I AM *DEP International DEP 5*	25	9
5 Feb 83	I'VE GOT MINE *DEP International 7 DEP 6*	45	4
20 Aug 83	★ RED RED WINE *DEP International 7 DEP 7* ▲	1	14
15 Oct 83	● PLEASE DON'T MAKE ME CRY *DEP International 7 DEP 8*	10	8
10 Dec 83	MANY RIVERS TO CROSS *DEP International 7 DEP 9*	16	8
17 Mar 84	CHERRY OH BABY *DEP International DEP 10*	12	8
22 Sep 84	IF IT HAPPENS AGAIN *DEP International DEP 11*	9	8
1 Dec 84	RIDDLE ME *DEP International DEP 15*	59	2
3 Aug 85	★ I GOT YOU BABE *DEP International DEP 20* [2]	1	13
26 Oct 85	● DON'T BREAK MY HEART *DEP International DEP 22*	3	13
12 Jul 86	● SING OUR OWN SONG *DEP International DEP 23*	5	9
27 Sep 86	ALL I WANT TO DO *DEP International DEP 24*	41	4
17 Jan 87	RAT IN MI KITCHEN *DEP International DEP 25*	12	7
9 May 87	WATCHDOGS *DEP International DEP 26*	39	4
10 Oct 87	MAYBE TOMORROW *DEP International DEP 27*	14	8
27 Feb 88	RECKLESS *EMI EM 41* [3]	17	8
18 Jun 88	● BREAKFAST IN BED *DEP International DEP 29* [2]	6	11
20 Aug 88	WHERE DID I GO WRONG *DEP International DEP 30*	26	6
17 Jun 89	I WOULD DO FOR YOU *DEP International DEP 32*	45	4
18 Nov 89	● HOMELY GIRL *DEP International DEP 33*	6	10
27 Jan 90	HERE I AM (COME AND TAKE ME) *DEP International DEP 34*	46	3
31 Mar 90	● KINGSTON TOWN *DEP International DEP 35*	4	12
28 Jul 90	WEAR YOU TO THE BALL *DEP International DEP 36*	35	6
3 Nov 90	● I'LL BE YOUR BABY TONIGHT *EMI EM 167* [4]	6	10
1 Dec 90	IMPOSSIBLE LOVE *DEP International DEP 37*	47	2
2 Feb 91	THE WAY YOU DO THE THINGS YOU DO *DEP International DEP 38*	49	3
12 Dec 92	ONE IN TEN (re-mix) *ZTT ZANG 39* [5]	17	8
22 May 93	★ (I CAN'T HELP) FALLING IN LOVE WITH YOU *DEP International DEPDG 40* ▲	1	16
21 Aug 93	● HIGHER GROUND *DEP International DEPD 41*	8	9
11 Dec 93	BRING ME YOUR CUP *DEP International DEPD 42*	24	6
2 Apr 94	C'EST LA VIE *DEP International DEPD 43*	37	3
27 Aug 94	REGGAE MUSIC *DEP International DEPDG 44*	28	2
4 Nov 95	UNTIL MY DYING DAY *DEP International DEPD 45*	15	6
30 Aug 97	TELL ME IT IS TRUE *DEP International DEP 48*	14	4
15 Nov 97	ALWAYS THERE *DEP International DEPD 49*	53	1
10 Oct 98	● COME BACK DARLING *DEP International DEPD 50*	10	6
19 Dec 98	HOLLY HOLY *DEP International DEPD 51*	31	3
1 May 99	THE TRAIN IS COMING *DEP International DEPD 52*	30	2

9 Dec 00	LIGHT MY FIRE *DEP International DEPD 53*	63	1
20 Oct 01	SINCE I MET YOU LADY / SPARKLE OF MY EYES		
	DEP International DEPD 55 [6]	40	2
2 Mar 02	COVER UP *DEP International DEPD 56*	54	1

[1] U.B.40 [2] UB40 featuring Chrissie Hynde [3] Afrika Bambaataa and Family featuring UB40 [4] Robert Palmer and UB40 [5] 808 State vs UB40 [6] UB40 featuring Lady Saw

UBM *Germany, male / female vocal / instrumental group (1 WEEK)* pos/wks

23 May 98	LOVIN' YOU *Logic 74321571692*	46	1

UCC – See URBAN COOKIE COLLECTIVE

UFO *UK / Germany, male vocal / instrumental group (31 WEEKS)* pos/wks

5 Aug 78	ONLY YOU CAN ROCK ME *Chrysalis CHS 2241*	50	4
27 Jan 79	DOCTOR DOCTOR *Chrysalis CHS 2287*	35	6
31 Mar 79	SHOOT, SHOOT *Chrysalis CHS 2318*	48	5
12 Jan 80	YOUNG BLOOD *Chrysalis CHS 2399*	36	5
17 Jan 81	LONELY HEART *Chrysalis CHS 2482*	41	5
30 Jan 82	LET IT RAIN *Chrysalis CHS 2576*	62	3
19 Mar 83	WHEN IT'S TIME TO ROCK *Chrysalis CHS 2672*	70	3

U4EA featuring BERRI – See NEW ATLANTIC

UGLY DUCKLING *US, male production / rap (1 WEEK)* pos/wks

13 Oct 01	A LITTLE SAMBA *XL Recordings XLS 135CD*	70	1

UGLY KID JOE *US, male vocal / instrumental group (28 WEEKS)* pos/wks

16 May 92 ●	EVERYTHING ABOUT YOU *Mercury MER 367*	3	9
22 Aug 92	NEIGHBOR *Mercury MER 374*	28	4
31 Oct 92	SO DAMN COOL *Mercury MER 383*	44	2
13 Mar 93 ●	CATS IN THE CRADLE *Mercury MERCD 385*	7	9
19 Jun 93	BUSY BEE *Mercury MERCD 389*	39	2
8 Jul 95	MILKMAN'S SON *Mercury MERCD 435*	39	2

Tillman UHRMACHER *Germany, male producer (3 WEEKS)* pos/wks

23 Mar 02	ON THE RUN *Direction 6721352*	16	3

See also TILLMAN AND REIS

UK *UK, male vocal / instrumental group (2 WEEKS)* pos/wks

30 Jun 79	NOTHING TO LOSE *Polydor POSP 55*	67	2

UK *Canada / Spain, male vocal / instrumental group (1 WEEK)* pos/wks

3 Aug 96	SMALL TOWN BOY *Media MCSTD 400*	74	1

UK APACHI / APACHE *UK, male vocalist / rapper / instrumentalist – Lafta Wahab (4 WEEKS)* pos/wks

1 Oct 94	ORIGINAL NUTTAH *Sound of Underground SOUR 008CD* [1]	39	3
28 Jul 01	SIGNS *Outcaste OUT 38CD1* [2]	63	1

[1] UK Apachi with Shy FX [2] DJ Badmarsh and Shri featuring UK Apache

UK MIXMASTERS
UK, male producer – Nigel Wright (15 WEEKS) pos/wks

2 Feb 91	THE NIGHT FEVER MEGAMIX *IQ ZB 44339* [1]	23	5
27 Jul 91	LUCKY 7 MEGAMIX *IQ ZB 44731*	43	3
14 Dec 91	THE BARE NECESSITIES MEGAMIX *Connect ZB 35135*	14	7

[1] Mixmasters

UK PLAYERS *UK, male vocal / instrumental group (3 WEEKS)* pos/wks

14 May 83	LOVE'S GONNA GET YOU *RCA 326*	52	3

UK SUBS
UK, male vocal / instrumental group (39 WEEKS) pos/wks

23 Jun 79	STRANGLEHOLD *Gem GEMS 5*	26	8
8 Sep 79	TOMORROW'S GIRLS *Gem GEMS 10*	28	6
1 Dec 79	SHE'S NOT THERE / KICKS (EP) *Gem GEMS 14*	36	7
8 Mar 80	WARHEAD *Gem GEMS 23*	30	4
17 May 80	TEENAGE *Gem GEMS 30*	32	5
25 Oct 80	PARTY IN PARIS *Gem GEMS 42*	37	4
18 Apr 81	KEEP ON RUNNIN' (TILL YOU BURN) *Gem GEMS 45*	41	5

Tracks on She's Not There / Kicks (EP): She's Not There / Kicks / Victim / The Same Thing

Tracey ULLMAN *UK, female vocalist (49 WEEKS)* pos/wks

19 Mar 83 ●	BREAKAWAY *Stiff BUY 168*	4	11
24 Sep 83 ●	THEY DON'T KNOW *Stiff BUY 180*	2	11
3 Dec 83 ●	MOVE OVER DARLING *Stiff BUY 195*	8	9
3 Mar 84	MY GUY *Stiff BUY 197*	23	6
28 Jul 84	SUNGLASSES *Stiff BUY 205*	18	9
27 Oct 84	HELPLESS *Stiff BUY 211*	61	3

ULTIMATE KAOS *UK, male vocal group (28 WEEKS)* pos/wks

22 Oct 94 ●	SOME GIRLS (re) *Wild Card CARDD 12*	9	9
21 Jan 95	HOOCHIE BOOTY *Wild Card CARDW 14*	17	4
1 Apr 95	SHOW A LITTLE LOVE *Wild Card CARDW 18*	23	5
1 Jul 95	RIGHT HERE *Wild Card 5795832*	18	4
8 Mar 97	CASANOVA *Polydor 5759312*	24	3
18 Jul 98	CASANOVA (re-issue) *Mercury MERCD 505*	29	2
5 Jun 99	ANYTHING YOU WANT (I'VE GOT IT) *Mercury MERCD 510*	52	1

ULTRA *UK, male vocal / instrumental group (22 WEEKS)* pos/wks

18 Apr 98	SAY YOU DO *East West EW 124CD*	11	7
4 Jul 98	SAY IT ONCE *East West EW 171CD1*	16	6
10 Oct 98	THE RIGHT TIME (re) *East West EW 182CD*	28	3
16 Jan 99 ●	RESCUE ME *East West EW 193CD1*	8	6

ULTRA HIGH
UK, male vocalist – Michael McCloud (3 WEEKS) pos/wks

2 Dec 95	STAY WITH ME *MCA MCSTD 40007*	36	2
20 Jul 96	ARE YOU READY FOR LOVE *MCA MCSTD 40039*	45	1

ULTRACYNIC
UK, male / female vocal / instrumental group (3 WEEKS) pos/wks

29 Aug 92	NOTHING IS FOREVER *380 PEW 2*	50	2
19 Apr 97	NOTHING IS FOREVER (re-mix) *All Around the World CDGLOBE 139*	47	1

ULTRAMARINE *UK, male instrumental duo (4 WEEKS)* pos/wks

24 Jul 93	KINGDOM *Blanco Y Negro NEG 65CD*	46	2
29 Jan 94	BAREFOOT (EP) *Blanco Y Negro NEG 67CD*	61	1
27 Apr 96	HYMN *Blanco Y Negro NEG 87CD* [1]	65	1

[1] Ultramarine featuring David McAlmont

Tracks on Barefoot (EP): Hooter / The Badger / Urf / Happy Land

ULTRA-SONIC
UK, male instrumental / production duo (2 WEEKS) pos/wks

3 Sep 94	OBSESSION *Clubscene DCSRT 027*	75	1
21 Sep 96	DO YOU BELIEVE IN LOVE *Clubscene DCSRT 070*	47	1

ULTRASOUND
UK, male / female vocal / instrumental group (5 WEEKS) pos/wks

7 Mar 98	BEST WISHES *Nude NUD 33CD*	68	1
13 Jun 98	STAY YOUNG *Nude NUD 35CD1*	30	2
10 Apr 99	FLOODLIT WORLD *Nude NUD 41CD1*	39	2

ULTRAVOX (176) Top 500

Ground-breaking British electro-rock quartet: Midge Ure (v/g) (replaced John Foxx in 1979), Billy Currie (k/syn), Chris Cross (b/syn), Warren Cann (d). Ex-Slik and Visage vocalist Ure was a driving force behind Band Aid hits, Live Aid and Nelson Mandela birthday concerts (142 WEEKS) pos/wks

5 Jul 80	SLEEPWALK *Chrysalis CHS 2441*	29	11
18 Oct 80	PASSING STRANGERS *Chrysalis CHS 2457*	57	4

17 Jan 81 ●	VIENNA *Chrysalis CHS 2481*	2	14
28 Mar 81	SLOW MOTION *Island WIP 6691*	33	4
6 Jun 81 ●	ALL STOOD STILL *Chrysalis CHS 2522*	8	10
22 Aug 81	THE THIN WALL *Chrysalis CHS 2540*	14	8
7 Nov 81	THE VOICE *Chrysalis CHS 2559*	16	12
25 Sep 82	REAP THE WILD WIND *Chrysalis CHS 2639*	12	9
27 Nov 82	HYMN *Chrysalis CHS 2657*	11	11
19 Mar 83	VISIONS IN BLUE *Chrysalis CHS 2676*	15	6
4 Jun 83	WE CAME TO DANCE *Chrysalis VOX 1*	18	7
11 Feb 84	ONE SMALL DAY *Chrysalis VOX 2*	27	6
19 May 84 ●	DANCING WITH TEARS IN MY EYES (re) *Chrysalis UV 1*	3	11
7 Jul 84	LAMENT (re) *Chrysalis UV 2*	22	7
20 Oct 84	LOVE'S GREAT ADVENTURE *Chrysalis UV 3*	12	9
27 Sep 86	SAME OLD STORY *Chrysalis UV 4*	31	4
22 Nov 86	ALL FALL DOWN *Chrysalis UV 5*	30	5
6 Feb 93	VIENNA (re-issue) *Chrysalis CDCHSS 3936*	13	4

UMBOZA *UK, male instrumental / production duo - Bryan Chamberlyn and Stuart Crichton (9 WEEKS)* pos/wks

23 Sep 95	CRY INDIA *Positiva CDTIV 43*	19	4
20 Jul 96	SUNSHINE *Positiva CDTIV 47*	14	5

See also EYE TO EYE featuring Taka BOOM; MUKKAA

Piero UMILIANI *Italy, orchestra and chorus, leader d. Feb 2001 (8 WEEKS)* pos/wks

30 Apr 77 ●	MAH-NA, MAH-NA *EMI International INT 530*	8	8

UNA MAS *UK, male production duo (1 WEEK)* pos/wks

6 Apr 02	I WILL FOLLOW *Defected DFECT 47CDS*	55	1

UNATION *UK, male / female vocal / instrumental group (3 WEEKS)* pos/wks

5 Jun 93	HIGHER AND HIGHER *MCA MCSTD 1773*	42	2
7 Aug 93	DO YOU BELIEVE IN LOVE *MCA MCSTD 1796*	75	1

UNBELIEVABLE TRUTH *UK, male vocal / instrumental group (5 WEEKS)* pos/wks

14 Feb 98	HIGHER THAN REASON *Virgin VSCDT 1676*	38	2
9 May 98	SOLVED *Virgin VSCDT 1684*	39	2
18 Jul 98	SETTLE DOWN / DUNE SEA *Virgin VSCDT 1697*	46	1

UNCANNY ALLIANCE *US, male / female vocal / instrumental duo – Brinsley Evans and E V Mystique (5 WEEKS)* pos/wks

19 Dec 92	I GOT MY EDUCATION *A&M AM 0128*	39	5

UNCLE KRACKER *US, male vocalist – Matt Shafer (18 WEEKS)* pos/wks

8 Sep 01 ●	FOLLOW ME *Atlantic AT 0108CD*	3	18

UNCLE SAM *US, male vocalist – Sam Turner (2 WEEKS)* pos/wks

16 May 98	I DON'T EVER WANT TO SEE YOU AGAIN *Epic 6656382*	30	2

UNDERCOVER *UK, male vocal / instrumental group (29 WEEKS)* pos/wks

15 Aug 92 ●	BAKER STREET *PWL International PWL 239*	2	14
14 Nov 92 ●	NEVER LET HER SLIP AWAY *PWL International PWL 255*	5	11
6 Feb 93	I WANNA STAY WITH YOU *PWL International PWCD 258*	28	3
14 Aug 93	LOVESICK *PWL International PWCD 271* [1]	62	1

[1] Undercover featuring John Matthews

UNDERTAKERS *UK, male vocal / instrumental group (1 WEEK)* pos/wks

9 Apr 64	JUST A LITTLE BIT *Pye 7N 15607*	49	1

UNDERTONES *UK, male vocal / instrumental group (67 WEEKS)* pos/wks

21 Oct 78	TEENAGE KICKS *Sire SIR 4007*	31	6

3 Feb 79	GET OVER YOU *Sire SIR 4010*	57	4
28 Apr 79	JIMMY JIMMY *Sire SIR 4015*	16	10
21 Jul 79	HERE COMES THE SUMMER *Sire SIR 4022*	34	6
20 Oct 79	YOU'VE GOT MY NUMBER (WHY DON'T YOU USE IT!) *Sire SIR 4024*	32	6
5 Apr 80 ●	MY PERFECT COUSIN *Sire SIR 4038*	9	10
5 Jul 80	WEDNESDAY WEEK *Sire SIR 4042*	11	9
2 May 81	IT'S GOING TO HAPPEN! *Ardeck ARDS 8*	18	9
25 Jul 81	JULIE OCEAN *Ardeck ARDS 9*	41	5
9 Jul 83	TEENAGE KICKS (re-issue) *Ardeck ARDS 1*	60	2

See also Feargal SHARKEY

UNDERWORLD *UK, male instrumental / vocal group (45 WEEKS)* pos/wks

18 Dec 93	SPIKEE / DOGMAN GO *Junior Boy's Own JBO 17CD*	63	1
25 Jun 94	DARK AND LONG *Junior Boy's Own JBO 19CDS*	57	1
13 May 95	BORN SLIPPY *Junior Boy's Own JBO 29CDS*	52	2
18 May 96	PEARL'S GIRL *Junior Boy's Own JBO 38CDS1*	24	2
13 Jul 96 ●	BORN SLIPPY (re-mix) (re) *Junior Boy's Own JBO 44CDS*	2	21
9 Nov 96	PEARL'S GIRL (re-issue) *Junior Boy's Own JBO 45CDS1*	22	3
27 Mar 99	PUSH UPSTAIRS *Junior Boy's Own JBO 5005443*	12	4
5 Jun 99	JUMBO *Junior Boy's Own JBO 5007193*	21	2
28 Aug 99	KING OF SNAKE *Junior Boy's Own JBO 5008793*	17	3
2 Sep 00	COWGIRL *Junior Boy's Own JBO 5012513*	24	2
14 Sep 02	TWO MONTHS OFF *Junior Boy's Own JBO 5020093*	12	4

UNDISPUTED TRUTH *US, male / female vocal group (4 WEEKS)* pos/wks

22 Jan 77	YOU + ME = LOVE *Warner Bros. K 16804*	43	4

U96 *Germany, male producer – Alex Christiansen (7 WEEKS)* pos/wks

29 Aug 92	DAS BOOT *M & G MAGS 28*	18	5
4 Jun 94	INSIDE YOUR DREAMS *Logic 74321209722*	44	1
29 Jun 96	CLUB BIZARRE *Urban 5750152*	70	1

UNION featuring the ENGLAND WORLD CUP SQUAD *UK / Holland, male instrumental group and UK, rugby team vocalists (7 WEEKS)* pos/wks

12 Oct 91	SWING LOW (RUN WITH THE BALL) *Columbia 6575317*	16	7

UNION GAP featuring Gary PUCKETT *US, male vocal / instrumental group (47 WEEKS)* pos/wks

17 Apr 68 ★	YOUNG GIRL *CBS 3365*	1	17
7 Aug 68 ●	LADY WILLPOWER *CBS 3551*	5	16
28 Aug 68	WOMAN, WOMAN *CBS 3110* [1]	48	1
15 Jun 74 ●	YOUNG GIRL (re-issue) *CBS 8202* [1]	6	13

[1] Gary Puckett and The Union Gap

UNIQUE *US, male / female vocal / instrumental group (7 WEEKS)* pos/wks

10 Sep 83	WHAT I GOT IS WHAT YOU NEED *Prelude A 3707*	27	7

UNIQUE 3 *UK, male rap / DJ group (12 WEEKS)* pos/wks

4 Nov 89	THE THEME *10 TEN 285*	61	3
14 Apr 90	MUSICAL MELODY / WEIGHT FOR THE BASS *10 TEN 298*	29	5
10 Nov 90	RHYTHM TAKES CONTROL *10 TEN 327* [1]	41	3
16 Nov 91	NO MORE *10 TEN 387*	74	1

[1] Unique 3 featuring Karin

UNIT FOUR PLUS TWO *UK, male vocal / instrumental group – lead vocal Peter Moules (29 WEEKS)* pos/wks

13 Feb 64	GREEN FIELDS *Decca F 11821*	48	2
25 Feb 65 ★	CONCRETE AND CLAY *Decca F 12071*	1	15
13 May 65	(YOU'VE) NEVER BEEN IN LOVE LIKE THIS BEFORE *Decca F 12144*	14	11
17 Mar 66	BABY NEVER SAY GOODBYE *Decca F 12333*	49	1

UNITED CITIZEN FEDERATION featuring Sarah BRIGHTMAN *UK, male production duo and UK, female vocalist (1 WEEK)* pos/wks

14 Feb 98	STARSHIP TROOPERS *Coalition COLA 040CD*	58	1

UK No.1 ★   UK Top 10 ●   Still on chart +   UK million seller ◆   UK entry at No.1 ■   US No.1 ▲

UNITED KINGDOM SYMPHONY UK, orchestra (4 WEEKS)

		pos/wks
27 Jul 85	SHADES (THEME FROM THE CROWN PAINT TELEVISION COMMERCIAL) *Food for Thought YUM 108*	68 4

UNITONE – See Laurel AITKEN and the UNITONE

UNITONE ROCKERS featuring STEEL
UK, male vocal / instrumental group (1 WEEK)

		pos/wks
26 Jun 93	CHILDREN OF THE REVOLUTION *The Hit Label HLC 4*..........	60 1

UNITY UK, male / female vocal / instrumental group (2 WEEKS)

		pos/wks
31 Aug 91	UNITY *Cardiac CNY 6*	64 2

UNIVERSAL Australia, male vocal group (6 WEEKS)

		pos/wks
2 Aug 97	ROCK ME GOOD *London LONCD 397*..........	19 4
18 Oct 97	MAKE IT WITH YOU *London LONCD 404*..........	33 2

UNIVERSAL PROJECT – See Ed RUSH & OPTICAL / UNIVERSAL PROJECT

UNJUSTIFIED ANCIENTS OF M U – See 1300 DRUMS featuring the UNJUSTIFIED ANCIENTS OF M U

UNKLE US / UK, male
DJ / production duo – Josh Davis and James Lavelle (7 WEEKS)

		pos/wks
20 Feb 99 ●	BE THERE *Mo Wax MW 108CD1* [1]	8 6
17 Mar 01	NARCO TOURISTS *Soma SOMA 100CD* [2]	66 1

[1] Unkle featuring Ian Brown [2] Slam vs Unkle

UNO CLIO featuring Martine McCUTCHEON
UK, male instrumental group with female vocalist (1 WEEK)

		pos/wks
18 Nov 95	ARE YOU MAN ENOUGH *Avex UK AVEXCD 14*	62 1

UNTOUCHABLES
US, male vocal / instrumental group (16 WEEKS)

		pos/wks
6 Apr 85	FREE YOURSELF *Stiff BUY 221*	26 11
27 Jul 85	I SPY FOR THE FBI *Stiff BUY 227*	59 5

UP YER RONSON featuring Mary PEARCE
UK, male / female vocal / instrumental group (7 WEEKS)

		pos/wks
5 Aug 95	LOST IN LOVE *Hi-Life 5795572*	27 3
30 Mar 96	ARE YOU GONNA BE THERE *Hi-Life 5763272*	27 2
19 Apr 97	I WILL BE RELEASED *Hi-Life 5737352*	32 2

Phil UPCHURCH COMBO US, male
instrumental group – Phil Upchurch – bass guitar (2 WEEKS)

		pos/wks
5 May 66	YOU CAN'T SIT DOWN *Sue WI 4005*	39 2

UPSETTERS Jamaica, male instrumental group (15 WEEKS)

		pos/wks
4 Oct 69 ●	RETURN OF DJANGO / DOLLAR IN THE TEETH *Upsetter US 301*..........	5 15

UPSIDE DOWN UK, male vocal group (16 WEEKS)

		pos/wks
20 Jan 96	CHANGE YOUR MIND *World CDWORLD 1A*	11 7
13 Apr 96	EVERY TIME I FALL IN LOVE (re) *World CDWORLD 2A*..........	18 4
29 Jun 96	NEVER FOUND A LOVE LIKE THIS BEFORE *World CDWORLD 3A*	19 3
23 Nov 96	IF YOU LEAVE ME NOW *World CDWORLD 4A*	27 2

URBAN ALL STARS UK, male producer – Norman Cook
– and US, male / female vocal / instrumental groups (2 WEEKS)

		pos/wks
27 Aug 88	IT BEGAN IN AFRICA *Urban URB 23*	64 2

URBAN BLUES PROJECT presents Michael PROCTER
US, male vocal / instrumental group (1 WEEK)

		pos/wks
10 Aug 96	LOVE DON'T LIVE *AM:PM 5817932*	55 1

URBAN COOKIE COLLECTIVE
UK, male / female vocal / instrumental group (37 WEEKS)

		pos/wks
10 Jul 93 ●	THE KEY THE SECRET *Pulse 8 CDLOSE 48*	2 16
13 Nov 93 ●	FEELS LIKE HEAVEN *Pulse 8 CDLOSE 55*	5 9
19 Feb 94	SAIL AWAY *Pulse 8 CDLOSE 56*	18 4
23 Apr 94	HIGH ON A HAPPY VIBE *Pulse 8 CDLOSE 60*	31 3
15 Oct 94	BRING IT ON HOME *Pulse 8 CDLOSE 73*	56 1
27 May 95	SPEND THE DAY *Pulse 8 CDLOSE 85*	59 1
9 Sep 95	REST OF MY LOVE *Pulse 8 CDLOSE 93*	67 1
16 Dec 95	SO BEAUTIFUL *Pulse 8 CDLOSE 100*	68 1
24 Aug 96	THE KEY THE SECRET (re-mix) *Pulse 8 CDLOSE 109* [1]	52 1

[1] UCC

URBAN DISCHARGE featuring SHE
US, male / female vocal / instrumental group (1 WEEK)

		pos/wks
27 Jan 96	WANNA DROP A HOUSE (ON THAT BITCH) *MCA MCSTD 40020*	51 1

URBAN HYPE UK, male production / instrumental
group – Robert Dibden and Mark Chitty (12 WEEKS)

		pos/wks
11 Jul 92 ●	A TRIP TO TRUMPTON *Faze 2 FAZE 5*..........	6 8
17 Oct 92	THE FEELING *Faze 2 FAZE 10*	67 1
9 Jan 93	LIVING IN A FANTASY *Faze 2 CDFAZE 13*	57 3

URBAN SHAKEDOWN UK / Italy, male DJ /
production duo – Michael Hearn and Gavin King (8 WEEKS)

		pos/wks
27 Jun 92	SOME JUSTICE *Urban Shakedown URBST 1*	23 5
12 Sep 92	BASS SHAKE *Urban Shakedown URBST 2* [1]	59 2
10 Jun 95	SOME JUSTICE (re-recording) *Urban Shakedown URBCD 3* [2]	49 1

[1] Urban Shakedown featuring Mickey Finn
[2] Urban Shakedown featuring DBO General

URBAN SOUL
UK / US, male / female vocal / production group (11 WEEKS)

		pos/wks
30 Mar 91	ALRIGHT *Cooltempo COOL 231*	60 4
21 Sep 91	ALRIGHT (re-mix) *Cooltempo COOL 244*..........	43 3
28 Mar 92	ALWAYS *Cooltempo COOL 251*	41 3
13 Jun 98	LOVE IS SO NICE *VC Recordings VCRD 33*	75 1

URBAN SPECIES
UK, male vocal / instrumental group (10 WEEKS)

		pos/wks
12 Feb 94	SPIRITUAL LOVE *Talkin Loud TLKCD 45*	35 4
16 Apr 94	BROTHER *Talkin Loud TLKCD 47*	40 3
20 Aug 94	LISTEN *Talkin Loud TLKCD 50* [1]	47 2
6 Mar 99	BLANKET *Talkin Loud TLDD 39* [2]	56 1

[1] Urban Species featuring MC Solaar [2] Urban Species featuring Imogen Heap

Midge URE UK, male vocalist (56 WEEKS)

		pos/wks
12 Jun 82 ●	NO REGRETS *Chrysalis CHS 2618*	9 10
9 Jul 83	AFTER A FASHION *Musicfest FEST 1* [1]	39 4
14 Sep 85 ★	IF I WAS *Chrysalis URE 1*	1 11
16 Nov 85	THAT CERTAIN SMILE *Chrysalis URE 2*	28 4
8 Feb 86	WASTELANDS *Chrysalis URE 3*	46 3
7 Jun 86	CALL OF THE WILD *Chrysalis URE 4*	27 8
20 Aug 88	ANSWERS TO NOTHING *Chrysalis URE 5*	49 4
19 Nov 88	DEAR GOD *Chrysalis URE 6*	55 4
17 Aug 91	COLD COLD HEART *Arista 114555*	17 7
25 May 96	BREATHE *Arista 74321371172*	70 1

[1] Midge Ure and Mick Karn

See also SLIK; ULTRAVOX; RICH KIDS; VISAGE

URGE OVERKILL US, male vocal / instrumental group (6 WEEKS) pos/wks

		pos/wks
21 Aug 93	SISTER HAVANA *Geffen GFSTD 51*	67 1
16 Oct 93	POSITIVE BLEEDING *Geffen GFSTD 57*	61 1
19 Nov 94	GIRL YOU'LL BE A WOMAN SOON *MCA MCSTD 2024*	37 4

Re-entries are listed as (re), (2re), (3re), etc which signifies that the hit re-entered the chart once, twice or three times, etc

JRUSEI YATSURA

JK, male / female vocal / instrumental group (4 WEEKS)   pos/wks

2 Feb 97	STRATEGIC HAMLETS *Che CHE 67CD*	64	1
28 Jun 97	FAKE FUR *Che CHE 70CD*	58	1
21 Feb 98	HELLO TIGER *Che CHE 75CD1*	40	1
6 Jun 98	SLAIN BY ELF *Che CHE 80CD1*	63	1

US3 *UK, male instrumental / production / vocal trio (15 WEEKS)*   pos/wks

10 Jul 93	RIDDIM *Blue Note CDCL 686* [1]	34	6
25 Sep 93	CANTALOOP *Blue Note CDCL 696* [2]	23	5
28 May 94	I GOT IT GOIN' ON *Blue Note CDCL 708* [3]	52	2
1 Mar 97	COME ON EVERYBODY (GET DOWN) *Blue Note CDCL 784*	38	2

[1] Us3 featuring Tukka Yoot [2] Us3 featuring Rahsaan [3] Us3 featuring Kobie Powell and Rahsaan

USA FOR AFRICA *US, male / female*
vocal charity ensemble – producer – Quincy Jones (9 WEEKS)   pos/wks

13 Apr 85 ★	WE ARE THE WORLD *CBS USAID 1* ▲	1	9

Soloists: Lionel Richie, Stevie Wonder, Paul Simon, Kenny Rogers, James Ingram, Tina Turner, Billy Joel, Michael Jackson, Diana Ross, Dionne Warwick, Willie Nelson, Al Jarreau, Bruce Springsteen, Kenny Loggins, Steve Perry, Daryl Hall, Huey Lewis, Cyndi Lauper, Kim Carnes, Bob Dylan, Ray Charles. Also credited: Dan Aykroyd, Harry Belafonte, Lindsey Buckingham, Sheila E, Bob Geldof, John Oates, Jackie Jackson, La Toya Jackson, Marlon Jackson, Randy Jackson, Tito Jackson, Waylon Jennings, The News, Bette Midler, Jeffrey Osborne, The Pointer Sisters, Smokey Robinson

USHER *US, male vocalist – Usher Raymond (62 WEEKS)*   pos/wks

18 Mar 95	THINK OF YOU *LaFace 74321269252*	70	1
31 Jan 98 ★	YOU MAKE ME WANNA... (re) *LaFace 74321560652* ■ ▲	1	13
2 May 98	NICE & SLOW *LaFace 74321579102* ▲	24	5
3 Feb 01 ●	POP YA COLLAR *LaFace 74321828692*	2	9
7 Jul 01 ●	U REMIND ME *LaFace 74321863382* ▲	3	9
20 Oct 01 ●	U GOT IT BAD *LaFace 74321898552* ▲	5	8
20 Apr 02	U-TURN *LaFace 74321934072*	16	6
10 Aug 02 ●	I NEED A GIRL (PART ONE) *Puff Daddy / Arista 74321947242* [1]	4	11

[1] P Diddy featuring Usher and Loon

USURA *Italy, male / female vocal / instrumental group (15 WEEKS)* pos/wks

23 Jan 93 ●	OPEN YOUR MIND *Deconstruction 74321128042*	7	9
10 Jul 93	SWEAT *Deconstruction 74321154602*	29	3
6 Dec 97	OPEN YOUR MIND 97 (re-mix) *Malarky MLKD 4* [1]	21	3

[1] U.S.U.R.A.

UTAH SAINTS *UK, male instrumental /*
production duo – Jez Willis and Tim Garbutt (39 WEEKS)   pos/wks

24 Aug 91 ●	WHAT CAN YOU DO FOR ME *ffrr F 164*	10	11
6 Jun 92 ●	SOMETHING GOOD *ffrr F 187*	4	9
8 May 93 ●	BELIEVE IN ME *ffrr FCD 209*	8	6
17 Jul 93	I WANT YOU *ffrr FCD 213*	25	5
25 Jun 94	I STILL THINK OF YOU *ffrr FCD 225*	32	2
2 Sep 95	OHIO *ffrr FCD 264*	42	2
5 Feb 00	LOVE SONG *Echo ECSCD 83*	37	2
20 May 00	FUNKY MUSIC (SHO NUFF TURNS ME ON) *Echo ECSCD 96*	23	2

'Funky Music (Sho Nuff Turns Me On)' features uncredited vocals by Edwin Starr

U2 43 Top 500 *Giants of contemporary rock: Bono (b. Paul Hewson) (v), The Edge (b. David Evans) (g), Adam Clayton (b), Larry Mullen Jr (d). Pollstar, which tracks revenues from US music tours, listed the band as the highest earners in 2001 with £78m from 80 shows, a figure bettered only by The Rolling Stones in 1994 (266 WEEKS)*   pos/wks

8 Aug 81	FIRE *Island WIP 6679*	35	6
17 Oct 81	GLORIA *Island WIP 6733*	55	4
3 Apr 82	A CELEBRATION *Island WIP 6770*	47	4
22 Jan 83 ●	NEW YEARS DAY *Island WIP 6848*	10	8
2 Apr 83	TWO HEARTS BEAT AS ONE *Island IS 109*	18	5
15 Sep 84 ●	PRIDE (IN THE NAME OF LOVE) *Island IS 202*	3	11
4 May 85 ●	THE UNFORGETTABLE FIRE *Island IS 220*	6	6
28 Mar 87 ●	WITH OR WITHOUT YOU *Island IS 319* ▲	4	11
6 Jun 87 ●	I STILL HAVEN'T FOUND WHAT I'M LOOKING FOR *Island IS 328* ▲	6	11
12 Sep 87 ●	WHERE THE STREETS HAVE NO NAME *Island IS 340*	4	6
26 Dec 87	IN GOD'S COUNTRY (import) *Island 7-99385*	48	4
1 Oct 88 ★	DESIRE *Island IS 400*	1	8
17 Dec 88 ●	ANGEL OF HARLEM *Island IS 402*	9	6
15 Apr 89 ●	WHEN LOVE COMES TO TOWN *Island IS 411* [1]	6	7
24 Jun 89 ●	ALL I WANT IS YOU *Island IS 422*	4	6
2 Nov 91 ★	THE FLY (re) *Island IS 500* ■	1	6
14 Dec 91 ●	MYSTERIOUS WAYS *Island IS 509*	13	7
7 Mar 92 ●	ONE *Island IS 515*	7	6
20 Jun 92 ●	EVEN BETTER THAN THE REAL THING *Island IS 525*	12	7
11 Jul 92 ●	EVEN BETTER THAN THE REAL THING (re-mix) *Island REALU 2*	8	7
5 Dec 92	WHO'S GONNA RIDE YOUR WILD HORSES *Island IS 550*	14	8
4 Dec 93 ●	STAY (FARAWAY, SO CLOSE) *Island CID 578*	4	9
17 Jun 95 ●	HOLD ME THRILL ME KISS ME KILL ME *Atlantic A 7131CD*	2	14
15 Feb 97 ●	DISCOTHEQUE (re) *Island CID 649*	1	11
26 Apr 97 ●	STARING AT THE SUN *Island CID 658*	3	6
2 Aug 97 ●	LAST NIGHT ON EARTH (re) *Island CID 664*	10	5
4 Oct 97 ●	PLEASE *Island CID 673*	7	4
20 Dec 97	IF GOD WILL SEND HIS ANGELS *Island CID 684*	12	6
31 Oct 98 ●	SWEETEST THING *Island CID 727*	3	13
21 Oct 00 ★	BEAUTIFUL DAY *Island CID 766* ■	1	16
10 Feb 01 ●	STUCK IN A MOMENT YOU CAN'T GET OUT OF *Island CID 770*	2	8
2 Jun 01	NEW YEAR'S DUB (re) *Serious SERR 030CD* [2]	15	5
28 Jul 01 ●	ELEVATION *Island CID 780*	3	8
1 Dec 01 ●	WALK ON *Island CID 788*	5	8
2 Nov 02 ●	ELECTRICAL STORM *Island CID 808*	5	9+

[1] U2 with BB King [2] Musique vs U2

'Stay (Faraway, So Close)' was listed with 'I've Got You Under My Skin' by Frank Sinatra with Bono, which was featured on many but not all formats

V

Verna V – See HELIOTROPIC featuring Verna V

VDC – See BLAST featuring VDC

V.I.P.'s
UK, male vocal / instrumental group (4 WEEKS)   pos/wks

6 Sep 80	THE QUARTER MOON *Gem GEMS 39*	55	4

VAGABONDS – See Jimmy JAMES and the VAGABONDS

Holly VALANCE
Australia, female vocalist – Holly Vukadinovic (29 WEEKS)   pos/wks

11 May 02 ★	KISS KISS *London LONCD 464* ■	1	16
12 Oct 02 ●	DOWN BOY *London LONCD 469*	2	11
21 Dec 02	NAUGHTY GIRL *London LONCD 472*	16	2+

Ricky VALANCE
UK, male vocalist – David Spencer (16 WEEKS)   pos/wks

25 Aug 60 ★	TELL LAURA I LOVE HER *Columbia DB 4493*	1	16

Ritchie VALENS
US, male vocalist – Ritchie Valenzuela, d. 3 Feb 1959 (5 WEEKS)   pos/wks

6 Mar 59	DONNA *London HL 8803*	29	1
1 Aug 87	LA BAMBA *RCA PB 41435*	49	4

Caterina VALENTE with Werner MULLER and the RIAS DANCE ORCHESTRA *France, female vocalist (14 WEEKS)* pos/wks

19 Aug 55	● THE BREEZE AND I *Polydor BM 6002*	5	14

Dickie VALENTINE (343 Top 500)

UK's No.1 pre rock 'n' roll heart-throb in the mid 1950s, b. Richard Brice, 4 Nov 1929, London, d. 6 May 1971. Voted Top UK Male Vocalist while singing with the Ted Heath Orchestra and after going solo in 1954 (92 WEEKS) pos/wks

20 Feb 53	BROKEN WINGS *Decca F 9954*	12	1
13 Mar 53	● ALL THE TIME AND EVERYWHERE *Decca F 10038*	9	3
5 Jun 53	● IN A GOLDEN COACH (THERE'S A HEART OF GOLD) *Decca F 10098*	7	1
5 Nov 54	ENDLESS *Decca F 10346*	19	1
17 Dec 54	● MISTER SANDMAN *Decca F 10415*	5	12
17 Dec 54	★ THE FINGER OF SUSPICION *Decca F 10394* [1]	1	15
18 Feb 55	● A BLOSSOM FELL (re) *Decca F 10430*	9	10
3 Jun 55	● I WONDER *Decca F 10493*	4	15
25 Nov 55	★ CHRISTMAS ALPHABET *Decca F 10628*	1	7
16 Dec 55	THE OLD PI-ANNA RAG *Decca F 10645*	15	5
7 Dec 56	● CHRISTMAS ISLAND *Decca F 10798*	8	5
27 Dec 57	SNOWBOUND FOR CHRISTMAS *Decca F 10950*	28	1
13 Mar 59	VENUS (4re) *Pye Nixa 7N 15192*	20	8
23 Oct 59	ONE MORE SUNRISE (MORGEN) *Pye 7N 15221*	14	8

[1] Dickie Valentine with The Stargazers

VALENTINE BROTHERS *US, male vocal duo (1 WEEK)* pos/wks

23 Apr 83	MONEY'S TOO TIGHT (TO MENTION) *Energy NRG 1*	73	1

Joe VALINO
US, male vocalist – Joseph Paolino, d. 26 Dec 1996 (2 WEEKS) pos/wks

18 Jan 57	THE GARDEN OF EDEN *HMV POP 283*	23	2

Frankie VALLI
US, male vocalist – Frankie Castelluccio (52 WEEKS) pos/wks

12 Dec 70	YOU'RE READY NOW *Philips 320226 BF*	11	13
1 Feb 75	● MY EYES ADORED YOU *Private Stock PVT 1* ▲	5	11
21 Jun 75	SWEARIN' TO GOD *Private Stock PVT 21*	31	5
17 Apr 76	FALLEN ANGEL *Private Stock PVT 51*	11	7
26 Aug 78	● GREASE *RSO 012* ▲	3	14
23 Mar 91	GREASE – THE DREAM MIX *PWL / Polydor PO 136* [1]	47	2

[1] Frankie Valli, John Travolta and Olivia Newton-John

See also FOUR SEASONS

Ian VAN DAHL – *See IAN VAN DAHL*

Mark VAN DALE with ENRICO
Belgium, male production duo (1 WEEK) pos/wks

3 Oct 98	WATER WAVE *Club Tools 0065815 CLU*	71	1

David VAN DAY *UK, male vocalist (3 WEEKS)* pos/wks

14 May 83	YOUNG AMERICANS TALKING *WEA DAY 1*	43	3

See also DOLLAR

VAN DER TOORN – *See PAPPA BEAR featuring VAN DER TOORN*

George VAN DUSEN
UK, male vocalist – George Harrington, d. 1992 (4 WEEKS) pos/wks

17 Dec 88	IT'S PARTY TIME AGAIN *Bri-Tone 7BT 001*	43	4

Paul VAN DYK *Germany, male DJ / producer (24 WEEKS)* pos/wks

17 May 97	FORBIDDEN FRUIT *Deviant DVNT 18CDR*	69	1
15 Nov 97	WORDS *Deviant DVNT 26CDS* [1]	54	1
5 Sep 98	FOR AN ANGEL *Deviant DVT 24CDS*	28	4
20 Nov 99	ANOTHER WAY / AVENUE (re) *Deviant DVNT 35CDS*	13	7
20 May 00	● TELL ME WHY (THE RIDDLE) *Deviant DVNT 36CDS* [2]	7	5

2 Dec 00	WE ARE ALIVE *Deviant DVNT 38CDS*	15	6

[1] Paul Van Dyk featuring Toni Halliday [2] Paul Van Dyk featuring Saint Etienne

Leroy VAN DYKE *US, male vocalist (20 WEEKS)* pos/wks

4 Jan 62	● WALK ON BY *Mercury AMT 1166*	5	17
26 Apr 62	BIG MAN IN A BIG HOUSE *Mercury AMT 1173*	34	3

Niels VAN GOGH *Germany, male producer (1 WEEK)* pos/wks

10 Apr 99	PULVERTURM *Logic 74321649192*	75	1

VAN HALEN
US / Holland, male vocal / instrumental group (51 WEEKS) pos/wks

28 Jun 80	RUNNIN' WITH THE DEVIL *Warner Bros. HM 10*	52	3
4 Feb 84	● JUMP *Warner Bros. W 9384* ▲	7	13
19 May 84	PANAMA *Warner Bros. W 9273*	61	2
5 Apr 86	● WHY CAN'T THIS BE LOVE *Warner Bros. W 8740*	8	14
12 Jul 86	DREAMS *Warner Bros. W 8642*	62	2
6 Aug 88	WHEN IT'S LOVE *Warner Bros. W 7816*	28	7
1 Apr 89	FEELS SO GOOD *Warner Bros. W 7565*	63	1
22 Jun 91	POUNDCAKE *Warner Bros. W 0045*	74	1
19 Oct 91	TOP OF THE WORLD *Warner Bros. W 0066*	63	1
27 Mar 93	JUMP (LIVE) *Warner Bros. W 0155CD*	26	3
21 Jan 95	DON'T TELL ME *Warner Bros. W 0280CD*	27	2
1 Apr 95	CAN'T STOP LOVIN' YOU *Warner Bros. W 0288CD*	33	2

Armand VAN HELDEN *US, male DJ / producer (33 WEEKS)* pos/wks

8 Mar 97	THE FUNK PHENOMENA *ZYX ZYX 8523U8*	38	2
8 Nov 97	ULTRAFUNKULA *fffr FCD 317*	46	1
6 Feb 99	★ YOU DON'T KNOW ME (re) *fffr FCD 357* [1] ■	1	12
1 May 99	FLOWERZ *fffr FCD 361* [2]	18	5
20 May 00	● KOOCHY *fffr FCD 379*	4	7
3 Nov 01	WHY CAN'T YOU FREE SOME TIME *fffr FCD 402*	34	2
15 Dec 01	YOU CAN'T CHANGE ME *Defected DFECT 41CDS* [3]	25	4

[1] Armand Van Helden featuring Duane Harden [2] Armand Van Helden featuring Roland Clark [3] Roger Sanchez featuring Armand Van Helden and N'Dea Davenport

Denise VAN OUTEN – *See THOSE 2 GIRLS; DENISE and JOHNNY; Andy WILLIAMS*

VAN TWIST *Zaire / Belgium, male / female vocal / instrumental group (2 WEEKS)* pos/wks

16 Feb 85	SHAFT *Polydor POSP 729*	57	2

VANDELLAS – *See Martha REEVES and the VANDELLAS*

Luther VANDROSS (154 Top 500)

Superior soul singer / songwriter and producer, b. 20 Apr 1951, New York, US. The former David Bowie backing vocalist fronted chart group Change before embarking on a solo career that earned him 10 successive US platinum albums and a stack of awards (148 WEEKS) pos/wks

19 Feb 83	NEVER TOO MUCH *Epic EPC A 3101*	44	6
26 Jul 86	GIVE ME THE REASON *Epic A 7288*	60	3
21 Feb 87	GIVE ME THE REASON (re-issue) *Epic 650216 7*	71	2
28 Mar 87	SEE ME *Epic LUTH 1*	60	4
11 Jul 87	I REALLY DIDN'T MEAN IT *Epic LUTH 3*	16	10
5 Sep 87	STOP TO LOVE *Epic LUTH 2*	24	7
7 Nov 87	SO AMAZING *Epic LUTH 4*	33	6
23 Jan 88	GIVE ME THE REASON (2nd re-issue) *Epic LUTH 5*	26	6
16 Apr 88	I GAVE IT UP (WHEN I FELL IN LOVE) *Epic LUTH 6*	28	5
9 Jul 88	THERE'S NOTHING BETTER THAN LOVE *Epic LUTH 7* [1]	72	1
8 Oct 88	ANY LOVE *Epic LUTH 8*	31	4
4 Feb 89	SHE WON'T TALK TO ME *Epic LUTH 9*	34	4
22 Apr 89	COME BACK *Epic LUTH 10*	53	3
28 Oct 89	NEVER TOO MUCH (re-mix) *Epic LUTH 12*	13	7
6 Jan 90	HERE AND NOW *Epic LUTH 13*	43	3
27 Apr 91	POWER OF LOVE – LOVE POWER *Epic 6568227*	46	5
18 Jan 92	THE RUSH *Epic 6577237*	53	3
15 Aug 92	● THE BEST THINGS IN LIFE ARE FREE *Perspective PERSS 7400* [2]	2	13

22 May 93	LITTLE MIRACLES (HAPPEN EVERY DAY) Epic 6590442	28	3
18 Sep 93	HEAVEN KNOWS Epic 6596522	34	3
4 Dec 93	LOVE IS ON THE WAY Epic 6599592	38	2
17 Sep 94 ●	ENDLESS LOVE (2re) Epic 6608062 [3]	3	16
26 Nov 94	LOVE THE ONE YOU'RE WITH Epic 6610612	31	4
4 Feb 95	ALWAYS AND FOREVER Epic 6611942	20	5
15 Apr 95	AIN'T NO STOPPING US NOW Epic 6614242	22	3
11 Nov 95	POWER OF LOVE – LOVE POWER (re-mix) Epic 6625902	31	3
16 Dec 95 ●	THE BEST THINGS IN LIFE ARE FREE (re-mix) A&M 5813092 [4]	7	7
23 Dec 95	EVERY YEAR EVERY CHRISTMAS Epic 6627762	43	2
12 Oct 96	YOUR SECRET LOVE Epic 6638385	14	5
28 Dec 96	I CAN MAKE IT BETTER Epic 6640632	44	2
20 Oct 01	TAKE YOU OUT J 74321899442	59	1

[1] Luther Vandross, duet with Gregory Hines [2] Luther Vandross and Janet Jackson with special guests BBD and Ralph Tresvant [3] Luther Vandross and Mariah Carey [4] Luther Vandross and Janet Jackson

VANESSA-MAE Singapore, female instrumentalist – violin – Vanessa-Mae Vanakorn Nicholson (21 WEEKS)

pos/wks

28 Jan 95	TOCCATA AND FUGUE EMI Classics MAE 8816812	16	10
20 May 95	RED HOT EMI CDMAE 2	37	2
18 Nov 95	CLASSICAL GAS EMI CDEM 404	41	2
26 Oct 96	I'M A DOUN FOR LACK O' JOHNNIE (A LITTLE SCOTTISH FANTASY) EMI CDMAE 3	28	2
25 Oct 97	STORM EMI CDEM 497	54	1
20 Dec 97	I FEEL LOVE EMI CDEM 553	41	2
5 Dec 98	DEVIL'S TRILL / REFLECTION EMI CDEM 530	53	1
28 Jul 01	WHITE BIRD EMI CDVAN 002	66	1

VANGELIS Greece, male instrumentalist – keyboards – Evangelos Papathanassiou (25 WEEKS)

pos/wks

9 May 81	CHARIOTS OF FIRE – TITLES (re) Polydor POSP 246 ▲	12	17
11 Jul 81	HEAVEN AND HELL, THIRD MOVEMENT (THEME FROM THE BBC-TV SERIES 'THE COSMOS') BBC 1	48	6
31 Oct 92	CONQUEST OF PARADISE East West YZ 704	60	2

'Chariots of Fire – Titles' re-entered in Apr 1982 peaking at No.41

See also JON and VANGELIS

VANILLA UK, female vocal group (10 WEEKS)

pos/wks

22 Nov 97	NO WAY NO WAY (re) EMI CDEM 487	14	8
23 May 98	TRUE TO US EMI CDEM 509	36	2

VANILLA FUDGE
US, male vocal / instrumental group (11 WEEKS)

pos/wks

9 Aug 67	YOU KEEP ME HANGIN' ON Atlantic 584 123	18	11

VANILLA ICE
US, male rapper – Robert Van Winkle (32 WEEKS)

pos/wks

24 Nov 90 ★	ICE ICE BABY SBK SBK 18 ▲	1	13
2 Feb 91 ●	PLAY THAT FUNKY MUSIC SBK SBK 20	10	6
30 Mar 91	I LOVE YOU SBK SBK 22	45	5
29 Jun 91	ROLLIN' IN MY 5.0 SBK SBK 27	27	4
10 Aug 91	SATISFACTION SBK SBK 29	22	4

VANITY FARE
UK, male vocal / instrumental group (34 WEEKS)

pos/wks

28 Aug 68	I LIVE FOR THE SUN Page One POF 075	20	9
23 Jul 69 ●	EARLY IN THE MORNING Page One POF 142	8	12
27 Dec 69	HITCHIN' A RIDE Page One POF 158	16	13

Joe T VANNELLI PROJECT Italy, male producer (2 WEEKS)

pos/wks

17 Jun 95	SWEETEST DAY OF MAY Positiva CDTIV 36	45	2

Randy VANWARMER
US, male vocalist – Randall Van Wormer (11 WEEKS)

pos/wks

4 Aug 79 ●	JUST WHEN I NEEDED YOU MOST Bearsville WIP 6516	8	11

VAPORS UK, male vocal / instrumental group (23 WEEKS)

pos/wks

9 Feb 80 ●	TURNING JAPANESE United Artists BP 334	3	13
5 Jul 80	NEWS AT TEN United Artists BP 345	44	4
11 Jul 81	JIMMIE JONES Liberty BP 401	44	6

VARDIS UK, male vocal / instrumental group (4 WEEKS)

pos/wks

27 Sep 80	LET'S GO Logo VAR 1	59	4

Halo VARGA US, male producer (1 WEEK)

pos/wks

9 Dec 00	FUTURE Hooj Choons HOOJ 101CD	67	1

VARIOUS ARTISTS (EPs and LPs) (87 WEEKS)

pos/wks

15 Jun 56	CAROUSEL – ORIGINAL SOUNDTRACK (LP) (re) Capitol LCT 6105	26	2
29 Jun 56 ●	ALL STAR HIT PARADE Decca F 10752	2	9
26 Jul 57	ALL STAR HIT PARADE NO.2 Decca F 10915	15	7
9 Dec 89	THE FOOD CHRISTMAS EP Food FOOD 23	63	1
20 Jan 90	THE FURTHER ADVENTURES OF NORTH (EP) Deconstruction PT 43372	64	2
2 Nov 91	THE APPLE EP Apple APP 1	60	1
11 Jul 92	FOURPLAY (EP) XL XLFP 1	45	2
7 Nov 92	THE FRED EP Heavenly HVN 19	26	3
24 Apr 93	GIMME SHELTER (EP) Food CDORDERA 1	23	4
5 Jun 93	SUBPLATES VOLUME 1 (EP) Suburban Base SUBBASE 24CD	69	1
9 Oct 93	THE TWO TONE EP 2 Tone CHSTT 31	30	3
4 Nov 95	HELP (EP) Go! Discs GODCD 135	51	2
16 Mar 96	NEW YORK UNDERCOVER (EP) Uptown MCSTD 48002	39	1
30 Mar 96	DANGEROUS MINDS (EP) MCA MCSTD 48007	35	1
29 Nov 97 ★	PERFECT DAY (re) Chrysalis CDNEED 01 ◆ ■	1	21
12 Sep 98	THE FULL MONTY – MONSTER MIX RCA Victor 74321602582	62	1
26 Sep 98	TRADE (EP) (DISC 2) Tidy Trax TREP2	75	1
25 Dec 99	IT'S ONLY ROCK 'N' ROLL (re) Universal TV 1566012	19	10
17 Jun 00	PERFECT DAY (re-recording) Chrysalis 8887840	69	1
10 Nov 01	HARD BEAT EP 19 Nukleuz NUKP 0369	71	1

Tracks and artists on Carousel are as follows: Carousel Waltz – Orchestra conducted by Alfred Newman; You're a Queer One Julie Jordan – Barbara Ruick and Shirley Jones; Mister Snow – Barbara Ruick; If I Loved You – Shirley Jones and Gordon MacRae; June Is Busting Out All Over – Claramae Turner; Soliloquy – Gordon MacRae; Blow High Blow Low – Cameron Mitchell; When the Children Are Asleep – Robert Rounseville and Barbara Ruick; This Was a Real Nice Clambake – Barbara Ruick, Claramae Turner, Robert Rounseville and Cameron Mitchell; Stonecutters Cut It on Stone (There's Nothing So Bad for a Woman) – Cameron Mitchell; What's the Use of Wonderin' – Shirley Jones; You'll Never Walk Alone – Claramae Turner; If I Loved You – Gordon MacRae; You'll Never Walk Alone – Shirley Jones

Tracks on All Star Hit Parade: Theme from The Threepenny Opera – Winifred Atwell; No Other Love – Dave King; My September Love – Joan Regan; A Tear Fell – Lita Roza; Out of Town – Dickie Valentine; It's Almost Tomorrow – David Whitfield. Tracks on All Star Hit Parade No.2: Around the World – Johnston Brothers; Puttin' on the Style – Billy Cotton; When I Fall in Love – Jimmy Young; A White Sport Coat – Max Bygraves; Freight Train – Beverley Sisters; Butterfly – Tommy Steele. Tracks on The Food Christmas EP: Like Princes Do – Crazyhead; I Don't Want That Kind of Love – Jesus Jones; Info Freako – Diesel Park West. Tracks on The Further Adventures of North (EP): Dream 17 – Annette; Carino 90 – T-Coy; The Way I Feel – Frequency 9; Stop This Thing – Dynasty of Two featuring Rowetta. Tracks on The Apple EP: Those Were the Days – Mary Hopkin; That's the Way God Planned It – Billy Preston; Sour Milk Sea – Jackie Lomax; Come and Get It – Badfinger. Tracks on Fourplay (EP): DJs Unite; Alright – Glide; Bee Free – Noisy Factory; True Devotion – EQ. Tracks on The Fred EP: Deeply Dippy – Rockingbirds; Don't Talk Just Kiss – Flowered Up; I'm Too Sexy – Saint Etienne. Gimme Shelter EP was available on all four formats, each featuring an interview with the featured artist plus the following artists performing versions of Gimme Shelter: (cassette) Jimmy Somerville and Voice of the Beehive; Heaven 17; (12") Blue Pearl, 808 State and Robert Owens; Pop Will Eat Itself vs Gary Clail; Ranking Roger and the Mighty Diamonds; (CD) Thunder; Little Angels; Hawkwind and Sam Fox; (2nd CD) Cud with Sandie Shaw; Kingmaker; New Model Army and Tom Jones. Tracks on Subplates Volume 1 (EP): Style Warz – Son'z of a Loop Da Loop Era; Funky Dope Track – Q-Bass; The Chopper – DJ Hype; Look No Further – Run Tings. Tracks on The Two Tone EP: Gangsters – Special AKA; The Prince – Madness; On My Radio – Selecter; Tears of a Clown – Beat. Tracks on Help (EP): Lucky – Radiohead; 50ft Queenie (Live) – PJ Harvey; Momentum – Guru featuring Big Shug; an untitled piece of incidental music. Tracks on New York

Undercover (EP): Tell Me What You Like – Guy; Dom Perignon – Little Shawn; I Miss You – Monifah; Jeeps, Lex Coups, Bimax & Menz – Lost Boys. Tracks on Dangerous Minds (EP): Curiosity – Aaron Hall; Gin & Dance – De Vante; It's Alright – Sista featuring Craig Mack. Artists on Perfect Day are as follows: BBC Symphony Orchestra and Andrew Davis, Bono (U2), Boyzone, Brett Anderson (Suede), Brodsky Quartet, Burning Spear, Courtney Pine, David Bowie, Dr John, Elton John, Emmylou Harris, Evan Dando (Lemonheads), Gabrielle, Heather Small (M People), Huey (Fun Lovin' Criminals), Ian Broudie (Lightning Seeds), Joan Armatrading, Laurie Anderson, Lesley Garrett, Lou Reed, Robert Cray, Shane McGowan, Sheona White, Skye (Morcheeba), Suzanne Vega, Tammy Wynette, Thomas Allen, Tom Jones, Visual Ministry Orchestra. Tracks on The Full-Monty Monster Mix (medley): You Sexy Thing – Hot Chocolate; Hot Stuff – Donna Summer; You Can Leave Your Hat On – Tom Jones. CD also has a full version of 'You Can Leave Your Hat On' by Tom Jones and 'The Stripper' by David Rose. Tracks on Trade (EP) (disc 2): Put Your House in Order – Steve Thomas; The Dawn – Tony De Vit. Artists on 'It's Only Rock 'n' Roll': Keith Richards, Kid Rock, Mary J Blige, Kelly Jones of Stereophonics, Jon Bon Jovi, Kéllé Bryan, Jay Kay of Jamiroquai, Ozzy Osbourne, Womack and Womack, Lionel Richie, Bonnie Raitt, Dolores O'Riordan of The Cranberries, James Brown, Spice Girls (minus Geri), Mick Jagger, Robin Williams, Jackson Browne, Iggy Pop, Chrissie Hynde, Skin of Skunk Anansie, Annie Lennox, Mark Owen, Natalie Imbruglia, Huey of Fun Lovin' Criminals, Dina Carroll, Gavin Rossdale of Bush, BB King, Joe Cocker, The Corrs, Steve Cradock and Simon Fowler of Ocean Colour Scene, Ronan Keating, Ray Barretto, Herbie Hancock, Francis Rossi and Rick Parfitt of Status Quo, S Club 7 and Eric Idle. Tracks on 'Hard Beat EP 19': 'Eternal '99' by Eternal Rhythm and 'Tragic', 'F**k Me' and 'Don't Give Up' all by BK

VARIOUS ARTISTS (MONTAGES) (31 WEEKS)

			pos/wks	
17 May 80		CALIBRE CUTS *Calibre CAB 502*	75	2
25 Nov 89		DEEP HEAT '89 *Deep Heat DEEP 10*	12	11
3 Mar 90	●	THE BRITS 1990 *RCA PB 43565*	2	7
28 Apr 90		THE SIXTH SENSE *Deep Heat DEEP 12*	49	2
10 Nov 90		TIME TO MAKE THE FLOOR BURN *Megabass MEGAX 1*	16	9

The following tracks are sampled: Calibre Cuts: Big Apples Rock – Black Ivory; Don't Hold Back – Chanson; The River Drive – Jupiter Beyond; Dancing in the Disco – LAX; Mellow Mellow Right On – Lowrell; Pata Pata – Osibisa; I Like It – Players Association; We Got the Funk – Positive Force; Holdin' On – Tony Rallo and the Midnite Band; Can You Feel the Force – Real Thing; Miami Heatwave – Seventh Avenue; Rapper's Delight – Sugarhill Gang; Que Tal America – Two Man Sound; Remakes by session musicians: Ain't No Stoppin' Us Now, Bad Girls, We Are Family. Deep Heat '89 (credited to Latino Rave): Pump Up the Jam – Technotronic; Stakker Humanoid – Humanoid; A Day in the Life – Black Riot; Work it to the Bone – LNR; I Can Make U Dance – DJ 'Fast' Eddie; Voodoo Ray – A Guy Called Gerald; Numero Uno – Starlight; Bango (To the Batmobile) – Todd Terry; Break 4 Love – Raze; Don't Scandalize Mine – Sugar Bear. The Brits 1990: Street Tuff – Double Trouble and the Rebel MC; Voodoo Ray – A Guy Called Gerald; Theme From S Express – S Express; Hey DJ I Can't Dance to That Music You're Playing – Beatmasters; Eve of the War – Jeff Wayne; Pacific State – 808 State; We Call It Acieed – D Mob; Got to Keep On – Cookie Crew. The Sixth Sense (credited to Latino Rave): Get Up – Technotronic; The Magic Number – De La Soul; G'Ding G'Ding (Do Wanna Wanna) – Anna G; Show 'M the Bass – MC Miker G; Turn It Out (Go Base) – Rob Base; Eve of the War (War of the Worlds) – Project D; Moments In Love – 2 to the Power. Time to Make the Floor Burn (credited to Megabass): Do This My Way – Kid 'N' Play; Street Tuff – Double Trouble and the Rebel MC; Sex 4 Daze – Lake Eerie; Ride On Time – Black Box; Make My Body Rock – Jomanda; Don't Miss the Partyline – Bizz Nizz; Pump Pump It Up – Hypnotek; Big Fun – Inner City; Pump That Body – Mr Lee; Pump Up the Jam – Technotronic; This Beat Is Technotronic – Technotronic; Get Busy – Mr Lee; Touch Me – 49ers; Thunderbirds Are Go – FAB

Junior VASQUEZ

US, male DJ / producer – Donald Martin (5 WEEKS)

		pos/wks	
15 Jul 95	GET YOUR HANDS OFF MY MAN! *Positiva CDTIV 37*	22	3
31 Aug 96	IF MADONNA CALLS *Multiply CDMULTY 13*	24	2

Elaine VASSELL – See BEATMASTERS

VAST *Australia, male vocal / instrumental group (1 WEEK)*

		pos/wks	
16 Sep 00	FREE *Mushroom MUSH 79CDS*	55	1

Sven VATH

Germany, male DJ / producer (5 WEEKS)

		pos/wks	
24 Jul 93	L'ESPERANZA *Eye Q YZ 757*	63	2
6 Nov 93	AN ACCIDENT IN PARADISE *Eye Q YZ 778CD*	57	2
22 Oct 94	HARLEQUIN – THE BEAUTY AND THE BEAST *Eye Q YZ 857*	72	1

Frankie VAUGHAN `63` `Top 500`

High-kicking 50s heart-throb vocalist, b. Frank Abelson, 3 Feb 1928, Liverpool, UK, d. 17 Sep 1999. This variety-show veteran, who was made an OBE in 1965 for his charity work, was one of the most popular performers of the 1950s (232 WEEKS)

				pos/wks	
29 Jan 54		ISTANBUL (NOT CONSTANTINOPLE) *HMV B 10599*	1	11	1
28 Jan 55		HAPPY DAYS AND LONELY NIGHTS *HMV B 10783*		12	3
22 Apr 55		TWEEDLE DEE *Philips PB 423*		17	1
2 Dec 55		SEVENTEEN *Philips PB 511*		18	3
3 Feb 56		MY BOY FLAT TOP *Philips PB 544*		20	2
9 Nov 56	●	THE GREEN DOOR *Philips PB 640*		2	15
11 Jan 57	★	THE GARDEN OF EDEN *Philips PB 660*		1	13
4 Oct 57	●	MAN ON FIRE / WANDERIN' EYES *Philips PB 729*		6	12
1 Nov 57	●	GOT-TA HAVE SOMETHING IN THE BANK, FRANK *Philips PB 751*	2	8	11
20 Dec 57	●	KISSES SWEETER THAN WINE *Philips PB 775*		8	11
7 Mar 58		CAN'T GET ALONG WITHOUT YOU / WE ARE NOT ALONE *Philips PB 793*		11	6
9 May 58	●	KEWPIE DOLL *Philips PB 825*		10	12
1 Aug 58		WONDERFUL THINGS *Philips PB 834*		22	6
10 Oct 58		AM I WASTING MY TIME ON YOU (re) *Philips PB 865*		25	4
30 Jan 59		THAT'S MY DOLL *Philips PB 895*		28	2
1 May 59	●	COME SOFTLY TO ME *Philips PB 913*	2	9	9
24 Jul 59	●	THE HEART OF A MAN *Philips PB 930*		5	14
18 Sep 59		WALKIN' TALL (re) *Philips PB 931*		28	2
29 Jan 60		WHAT MORE DO YOU WANT *Philips PB 985*		25	2
22 Sep 60		KOOKIE LITTLE PARADISE *Philips PB 1054*		31	5
27 Oct 60		MILORD *Philips PB 1066*		34	6
9 Nov 61	★	TOWER OF STRENGTH *Philips PB 1195*		1	13
1 Feb 62		DON'T STOP – TWIST! *Philips PB 1219*		22	7
27 Sep 62		HERCULES *Philips 326542 BF*		42	4
24 Jan 63	●	LOOP DE LOOP *Philips 326566 BF*		5	12
20 Jun 63		HEY MAMA *Philips BF 1254*		21	9
4 Jun 64		HELLO, DOLLY! *Philips BF 1339*		18	11
11 Mar 65		SOMEONE MUST HAVE HURT YOU A LOT *Philips BF 1394*		46	1
23 Aug 67	●	THERE MUST BE A WAY *Columbia DB 8248*		7	21
15 Nov 67		SO TIRED *Columbia DB 8298*		21	9
28 Feb 68		NEVERTHELESS *Columbia DB 8354*		29	5

1 Frankie Vaughan with The Peter Knight Singers 2 Frankie Vaughan and The Kaye Sisters

Malcolm VAUGHAN `283` `Top 500`

The last of the hitmaking big-voiced tenors, b. Malcolm Thomas, 1930, Glamorgan, Wales. He was the straight man in a comedy duo with Kenny Earle, while enjoying his enviable run of UK ballad hits (at the height of the rock 'n' roll explosion) (106 WEEKS)

				pos/wks	
1 Jul 55	●	EV'RY DAY OF MY LIFE *HMV B 10874*		5	16
27 Jan 56		WITH YOUR LOVE (2re) *HMV POP 130*	1	18	3
26 Oct 56	●	ST THERESE OF THE ROSES (re) *HMV POP 250*		3	20
12 Apr 57		THE WORLD IS MINE (2re) *HMV POP 303*		26	4
10 May 57		CHAPEL OF THE ROSES *HMV POP 325*		13	8
29 Nov 57	●	MY SPECIAL ANGEL *HMV POP 419*		3	14
21 Mar 58		TO BE LOVED *HMV POP 459*	2	14	7
17 Oct 58	●	MORE THAN EVER (COME PRIMA) *HMV POP 538*	2	5	14
27 Feb 59		WAIT FOR ME / WILLINGLY *HMV POP 590*		13	15

1 Malcolm Vaughan with The Peter Knight Singers 2 Malcolm Vaughan with The Michael Sammes Singers

Norman VAUGHAN *UK, male vocalist (5 WEEKS)*

		pos/wks	
17 May 62	SWINGING IN THE RAIN *Pye 7N 15438*	34	5

Sarah VAUGHAN

US, female vocalist, d. 3 Apr 1990 (34 WEEKS)

			pos/wks	
27 Sep 57		PASSING STRANGERS *Mercury MT 164*	1	22	2
11 Sep 59	●	BROKEN HEARTED MELODY *Mercury AMT 1057*		7	15
29 Dec 60		LET'S / SERENATA (re) *Columbia DB 4542*		37	4
12 Mar 69		PASSING STRANGERS (re-issue) *Mercury MF 1082*	1	20	15

1 Billy Eckstine and Sarah Vaughan

Billy VAUGHN and His Orchestra
US, orchestra and chorus, leader d. 26 Sep 1991 (8 WEEKS) pos/wks

27 Jan 56	THE SHIFTING WHISPERING SANDS PART 1 *London HLD 8205* [1]	20	1
23 Mar 56	THEME FROM "THE THREEPENNY OPERA" *London HLD 8238*	12	7

[1] Billy Vaughn Orchestra and Chorus, narration by Ken Nordene

VEBA – *See RAE & CHRISTIAN featuring VEBA*

Bobby VEE (195) Top 500
Early 1960s teen idol, b. Robert Velline, 30 Apr 1943, North Dakota, US. This photogenic, Buddy Holly-influenced teenaged vocalist (whose backing band once included Bob Dylan) was rarely away from the UK or US charts in the pre-Beat Boom years (134 WEEKS) pos/wks

19 Jan 61 ●	RUBBER BALL *London HLG 9255*	4	11
13 Apr 61 ●	MORE THAN I CAN SAY / STAYIN' IN *London HLG 9316*	4	16
3 Aug 61 ●	HOW MANY TEARS *London HLG 9389*	10	13
26 Oct 61 ●	TAKE GOOD CARE OF MY BABY *London HLG 9438* ▲	3	16
21 Dec 61 ●	RUN TO HIM *London HLG 9470*	6	15
8 Mar 62	PLEASE DON'T ASK ABOUT BARBARA *Liberty LIB 55419*	29	9
7 Jun 62 ●	SHARING YOU *Liberty LIB 55451*	10	13
27 Sep 62	A FOREVER KIND OF LOVE *Liberty LIB 10046*	13	19
7 Feb 63 ●	THE NIGHT HAS A THOUSAND EYES *Liberty LIB 10069*	3	12
20 Jun 63	BOBBY TOMORROW *Liberty LIB 55530*	21	10

'Stayin' In' listed with 'More Than I Can Say' from 13 Apr to 4 May 1961. It peaked at No.13

Louie VEGA *US, male producer (5 WEEKS)* pos/wks

5 Oct 91	RIDE ON THE RHYTHM *Atlantic A 7602* [1]	71	1
23 May 92	RIDE ON THE RHYTHM (re-issue) *Atlantic A 7486*	70	1
31 Jan 98	RIDE ON THE RHYTHM (re-mix) *Perfecto PERF 151CD1* [2]	36	2
23 Nov 02	DIAMOND LIFE *Distance DI 2409* [3]	52	1

[1] Little Louie Vega and Marc Anthony [2] Little Louie and Mark Anthony
[3] Louie Vega and Jay 'Sinister' Sealee starring Julie McKnight

See also LIL MO' YIN YANG

Suzanne VEGA *US, female vocalist (52 WEEKS)* pos/wks

18 Jan 86	SMALL BLUE THING *A&M AM 294*	65	3
22 Mar 86	MARLENE ON THE WALL *A&M AM 309*	21	9
7 Jun 86	LEFT OF CENTER *A&M AM 320* [1]	32	9
23 May 87	LUKA *A&M VEGA 1*	23	8
18 Jul 87	TOM'S DINER *A&M VEGA 2*	58	3
19 May 90	BOOK OF DREAMS *A&M AM 559*	66	1
28 Jul 90 ●	TOM'S DINER (re-mix) *A&M AM 592* [2]	2	10
22 Aug 92	IN LIVERPOOL *A&M AM 0029*	52	2
24 Oct 92	99.9°F *A&M AM 0085*	46	2
19 Dec 92	BLOOD MAKES NOISE *A&M AM 0112*	60	3
6 Mar 93	WHEN HEROES GO DOWN *A&M AMCD 0158*	58	1
22 Feb 97	NO CHEAP THRILL *A&M 5818692*	40	1

[1] Suzanne Vega featuring Joe Jackson [2] DNA featuring Suzanne Vega

Tata VEGA *US, female vocalist (4 WEEKS)* pos/wks

26 May 79	GET IT UP FOR LOVE / I JUST KEEP THINKING ABOUT YOU BABY *Motown TMG 1140*	52	4

VEGAS *UK, male vocal / instrumental duo – David A Stewart and Terry Hall (10 WEEKS)* pos/wks

19 Sep 92	POSSESSED *RCA 74321110437*	32	4
28 Nov 92	SHE *RCA 74321124657*	43	4
3 Apr 93	WALK INTO THE WIND *RCA 74321122462*	65	2

See also EURYTHMICS; Dave STEWART; TOURISTS; Terry HALL; FUN BOY THREE; SPECIALS

Rosie VELA *US, female vocalist (7 WEEKS)* pos/wks

17 Jan 87	MAGIC SMILE *A&M AM 369*	27	7

Wil VELOZ – *See LOS DEL MAR featuring Wil VELOZ*

VELVELETTES *US, female vocal group (7 WEEKS)* pos/wks

31 Jul 71	THESE THINGS WILL KEEP ME LOVING YOU *Tamla Motown TMG 780*	34	7

VELVET UNDERGROUND
UK / US, male / female vocal / instrumental group (1 WEEK) pos/wks

12 Mar 94	VENUS IN FURS *Sire W 0224CD*	71	1

VELVETS *US, male vocal group (2 WEEKS)* pos/wks

11 May 61	THAT LUCKY OLD SUN *London HLU 9328*	46	1
17 Aug 61	TONIGHT (COULD BE THE NIGHT) *London HLU 9372*	50	1

Terry VENABLES – *See RIDER & Terry VENABLES*

VENGABOYS (314) Top 500
Hungary / Trinidad / Brazil / Holland, male / female vocal / production dance-pop troupe formed in 1992 by Spanish DJs Danski and Delmundo. In 1996 they added singers / dancers Kim, Robin (replaced by Yorick in 1999), Roy and Denice to front group. First Netherlands-based act to score six successive Top 5 singles, selling more than two million in the UK in 12 months (99 WEEKS) pos/wks

28 Nov 98 ●	UP AND DOWN *Positiva CDTIV 105*	4	15
13 Mar 99 ●	WE LIKE TO PARTY! (THE VENGABUS) *Positiva CDTIV 108*	3	14
26 Jun 99 ★	BOOM, BOOM, BOOM, BOOM!! *Positiva CDTIV 114* ■	1	15
11 Sep 99	WE'RE GOING TO IBIZA (import) *Jive 550422*	69	1
18 Sep 99 ★	WE'RE GOING TO IBIZA! *Positiva CDTIV 119* ■	1	12
18 Dec 99 ●	KISS (WHEN THE SUN DON'T SHINE) *Positiva CDTIV 122*	3	18
11 Mar 00 ●	SHALALA LALA *Positiva CDTIV 126*	5	10
8 Jul 00 ●	UNCLE JOHN FROM JAMAICA *Positiva CDTIV 135*	6	7
14 Oct 00	CHEEKAH BOW BOW (THAT COMPUTER SONG) *Positiva CDTIV 142*	19	5
24 Feb 01	FOREVER AS ONE *Positiva CDTIV 148*	28	2

VENT 414 *UK, male vocal / instrumental group (1 WEEK)* pos/wks

28 Sep 96	FIXER *Polydor 5753292*	71	1

VENTURES *US, male instrumental group (31 WEEKS)* pos/wks

8 Sep 60 ●	WALK DON'T RUN *Top Rank JAR 417*	8	13
1 Dec 60 ●	PERFIDIA *London HLG 9232*	4	13
9 Mar 61	RAM-BUNK-SHUSH *London HLG 9292*	45	1
11 May 61	LULLABY OF THE LEAVES *London HLG 9344*	43	4

VERACOCHA *Holland, male production duo – Vincent de Moor and Ferry Corsten (4 WEEKS)* pos/wks

15 May 99	CARTE BLANCHE *Positiva CDTIV 110*	22	4

See also GOURYELLA; MOONMAN; SYSTEM F; Ferry CORSTEN; ALBION; STARPARTY

Al VERLAINE – *See 'PING PING' and Al VERLAINE*

VERNONS GIRLS *UK, female vocal group (31 WEEKS)* pos/wks

17 May 62	YOU KNOW WHAT I MEAN (re-entry) *Decca F 11450*	16	20
6 Sep 62	LOCO-MOTION *Decca F 11495*	47	1
3 Jan 63	FUNNY ALL OVER *Decca F 11549*	31	8
18 Apr 63	DO THE BIRD (re) *Decca F 11629*	44	2

'You Know What I Mean' was not coupled with 'Lover Please' on the chart of 23 Aug 1962, but both sides of this record were listed for the following six weeks

VERNON'S WONDERLAND
Germany, male producer – Matthias Hoffmann (1 WEEK) pos/wks

25 May 96	VERNON'S WONDERLAND *Eye-Q Classics EYECL 004CD*	59	1

VERONIKA – *See CRW*

UK No.1 ★   UK Top 10 ●   Still on chart +   UK million seller ◆   UK entry at No.1 ■   US No.1 ▲   485

VERTICAL HORIZON
US, male vocal / instrumental group (2 WKS) pos/wks

26 Aug 00	EVERYTHING YOU WANT *RCA 74321748692* ▲	42	2

VERUCA SALT
US, male / female vocal / instrumental group (5 WEEKS) pos/wks

2 Jul 94	SEETHER *Scared Hitless FRET 003CD*	61	1
3 Dec 94	SEETHER (re-issue) *Hi-Rise FLATSDG 12*	73	1
4 Feb 95	NUMBER ONE BLIND *Hi-Rise FLATSCD 16*	68	1
22 Feb 97	VOLCANO GIRLS *Outpost OPRCD 22197*	56	1
30 Aug 97	BENJAMIN *Outpost OPRCD 22261*	75	1

VERVE
UK, male vocal / instrumental group (50 WEEKS) pos/wks

4 Jul 92	SHE'S A SUPERSTAR *Hut HUT 16*	66	1
22 May 93	BLUE *Hut HUTCD 29*	69	1
13 May 95	THIS IS MUSIC *Hut HUTCD 54*	35	3
24 Jun 95	ON YOUR OWN *Hut HUTCD 55*	28	2
30 Sep 95	HISTORY *Hut HUTCD 59*	24	3
28 Jun 97 ●	BITTER SWEET SYMPHONY (re) *Hut HUTDG 82*	2	13
13 Sep 97 ★	THE DRUGS DON'T WORK (re) *Hut HUTDG 88* ■	1	13
6 Dec 97 ●	LUCKY MAN *Hut HUTDG 92*	7	13
30 May 98	SONNET (import) *Hut 8950752*	74	1

TOP EUROVISION NATIONS

■ Often the Eurovision bridesmaid, the United Kingdom has finished second a record 15 times – a staggering 11 more second places than France, Germany, Ireland and Spain. But the winners are:

7 WINS	IRELAND
5 WINS	FRANCE, LUXEMBOURG, UNITED KINGDOM
4 WINS	NETHERLANDS, SWEDEN
3 WINS	ISRAEL
2 WINS	DENMARK, ITALY, NORWAY, SPAIN, SWITZERLAND
1 WIN	AUSTRIA, BELGIUM, ESTONIA, GERMANY/WEST GERMANY, LATVIA, MONACO, YUGOSLAVIA

The 1996 winner was Ireland's 'The Voice', written by Brendan Graham and performed by Eimear Quinn (second from right)

A VERY GOOD FRIEND OF MINE
Italy, male / female vocal / production / instrumental group (1 WEEK) pos/wks

3 Jul 99	JUST ROUND *Positiva CDTIV 109*	55	1

VEX RED
UK, male vocal / instrumental group (1 WEEK) pos/wks

2 Mar 02	CAN'T SMILE *Virgin VUSCD 237*	45	1

VIBRATIONS – See Tony JACKSON and the VIBRATIONS

VIBRATORS
UK, male vocal / instrumental group (8 WEEKS) pos/wks

18 Mar 78	AUTOMATIC LOVER *Epic EPC 6137*	35	5
17 Jun 78	JUDY SAYS (KNOCK YOU IN THE HEAD) *Epic EPC 6393*	70	3

VICE SQUAD
UK, male / female vocal / instrumental group (1 WEEK) pos/wks

13 Feb 82	OUT OF REACH *Zonophone Z 26*	68	1

VICIOUS CIRCLES
UK, male producer – Simon Berry (1 WEEK) pos/wks

16 Dec 00	VICIOUS CIRCLES *Platipus PLATCD 82*	68	1

See also POLTERGEIST

VICIOUS PINK
UK, male / female vocal / instrumental duo (4 WEEKS) pos/wks

15 Sep 84	CCCAN'T YOU SEE *Parlophone R 6074*	67	4

Mike VICKERS – See Kenny EVERETT

Maria VIDAL
US, female vocalist (13 WEEKS) pos/wks

24 Aug 85	BODY ROCK *EMI America EA 189*	11	13

VIDEO KIDS
Holland, male / female vocal duo (1 WEEK) pos/wks

5 Oct 85	WOODPECKERS FROM SPACE *Epic A 6504*	72	1

VIDEO SYMPHONIC
UK, orchestra (3 WEEKS) pos/wks

24 Oct 81	THE FLAME TREES OF THIKA *EMI EMI 5222*	42	3

VIENNA PHILHARMONIC ORCHESTRA
Austria, orchestra – conducted by Aram Khachaturian (14 WEEKS) pos/wks

18 Dec 71	THEME FROM 'THE ONEDIN LINE' *Decca F 13259*	15	14

VIEW FROM THE HILL
UK, male / female vocal / instrumental group (6 WEEKS) pos/wks

19 Jul 86	NO CONVERSATION *EMI EMI 5565*	58	3
21 Feb 87	I'M NO REBEL *EMI EM 5580*	59	3

VIKKI
UK, female vocalist (3 WEEKS) pos/wks

4 May 85	LOVE IS . . . *PRT 7P 326*	49	3

VILLAGE PEOPLE
US, male vocal group (66 WEEKS) pos/wks

3 Dec 77	SAN FRANCISCO (YOU'VE GOT ME) *DJM DJS 10817*	45	5
25 Nov 78 ★	Y.M.C.A. *Mercury 6007 192* ◆	1	16
17 Mar 79 ●	IN THE NAVY *Mercury 6007 209*	2	9
16 Jun 79	GO WEST *Mercury 6007 221*	15	8
9 Aug 80	CAN'T STOP THE MUSIC *Mercury MER 16*	11	11
9 Feb 85	SEX OVER THE PHONE *Record Shack SOHO 34*	59	5
4 Dec 93	Y.M.C.A. (re-mix) *Bell 74321177182*	12	7
28 May 94	IN THE NAVY (re-mix) *Bell 74321198192*	36	2
27 Nov 99	Y.M.C.A. (2nd re-mix) *Wrasse WRASX 002*	35	3

V.I.M.
UK, male instrumental / production group (1 WEEK) pos/wks

26 Jan 91	MAGGIE'S LAST PARTY *F2 BOZ 1*	68	1

Gene VINCENT
US, male vocalist – Eugene Craddock, d. 12 Oct 1971 (51 WEEKS) pos/wks

13 Jul 56	BE-BOP-A-LULA (2re) Capitol CL 14599 [1]	16	7
12 Oct 56	RACE WITH THE DEVIL Capitol CL 14628 [1]	28	1
19 Oct 56	BLUE JEAN BOP Capitol CL 14637	16	5
8 Jan 60	WILD CAT (re) Capitol CL 15099	21	6
10 Mar 60	MY HEART (2re) Capitol CL 15115 [1]	16	8
16 Jun 60	PISTOL PACKIN' MAMA Capitol CL 15136 [2]	15	9
1 Jun 61	SHE SHE LITTLE SHEILA (re) Capitol CL 15202	22	11
31 Aug 61	I'M GOING HOME (TO SEE MY BABY)		
	Capitol CL 15215 [3]	36	4

[1] Gene Vincent and His Blue Caps [2] Gene Vincent with The Beat Boys [3] Gene Vincent with Sounds Incorporated

VINDALOO SUMMER SPECIAL
UK, male / female vocal / instrumental group (3 WEEKS) pos/wks

| 19 Jul 86 | ROCKIN' WITH RITA (HEAD TO TOE) Vindaloo UGH 13 | 56 | 3 |

The VINES
Australia, male vocal / instrumental group (7 WEEKS) pos/wks

20 Apr 02	HIGHLY EVOLVED Heavenly HVN 112CD	32	2
29 Jun 02	GET FREE Heavenly HVN 113CD	24	3
19 Oct 02	OUTTATHAWAY Heavenly HVN 120CDS	20	2

Bobby VINTON US, male vocalist (29 WEEKS) pos/wks

2 Aug 62	ROSES ARE RED (MY LOVE) Columbia DB 4878 ▲	15	8
19 Dec 63	THERE! I'VE SAID IT AGAIN Columbia DB 7179 ▲	34	10
29 Sep 90 ●	BLUE VELVET Epic 6505240 ▲	2	10
17 Nov 90	ROSES ARE RED (MY LOVE) (re-issue) Epic 6564677	71	1

VINYLGROOVER and The RED HED
UK, male production duo (1 WEEK) pos/wks

| 27 Jan 01 | ROK DA HOUSE Nukleuz NUKP 0285 | 72 | 1 |

VIOLINSKI UK, male instrumental group (9 WEEKS) pos/wks

| 17 Feb 79 | CLOG DANCE Jet 136 | 17 | 9 |

VIPER – See REFLEX; JAMESON AND VIPER

VIPER Belgium, male production group (1 WEEK) pos/wks

| 7 Feb 98 | THE TWISTER Hooj Choons HOOJCD 59 | 55 | 1 |

VIPERS SKIFFLE GROUP
UK, male vocal / instrumental group (18 WEEKS) pos/wks

25 Jan 57 ●	DON'T YOU ROCK ME DADDY-O Parlophone R 4261	10	9
22 Mar 57 ●	THE CUMBERLAND GAP Parlophone R 4289	10	6
31 May 57	STREAMLINE TRAIN Parlophone R 4308	23	3

VIRGINIA – See Tom NOVY

VIRUS UK, male instrumental /
production duo – Paul Oakenfold and Steve Osborne (3 WEEKS) pos/wks

| 26 Aug 95 | SUN Perfecto PERF 107CD | 62 | 1 |
| 25 Jan 97 | MOON Perfecto PERF 134CD | 36 | 2 |

See also OAKENFOLD

VISAGE UK, male vocal / instrumental group (56 WEEKS) pos/wks

20 Dec 80 ●	FADE TO GREY Polydor POSP 194	8	15
14 Mar 81	MIND OF A TOY Polydor POSP 236	13	8
11 Jul 81	VISAGE Polydor POSP 293	21	7
13 Mar 82	DAMNED DON'T CRY Polydor POSP 390	11	8
26 Jun 82	NIGHT TRAIN Polydor POSP 441	12	10
13 Nov 82	PLEASURE BOYS Polydor POSP 523	44	3
1 Sep 84	LOVE GLOVE Polydor POSP 691	54	3
28 Aug 93	FADE TO GREY (re-mix) Polydor PZCD 282	39	2

Michelle VISAGE – See S.O.U.L. S.Y.S.T.E.M. introducing Michelle VISAGE

VISCOUNTS UK, male vocal group (18 WEEKS) pos/wks

13 Oct 60	SHORT'NIN' BREAD Pye 7N 15287	16	8
14 Sep 61	WHO PUT THE BOMP (IN THE BOMP, BOMP, BOMP)		
	Pye 7N 15379	21	10

VISION UK, male vocal / instrumental group (1 WEEK) pos/wks

| 9 Jul 83 | LOVE DANCE MVM MVM 2886 | 74 | 1 |

VISIONMASTERS with Tony KING and Kylie MINOGUE
UK, male DJ / production duo, UK, male DJ / producer and Australia, female vocalist (1 WEEK) pos/wks

| 30 Nov 91 | KEEP ON PUMPIN' IT PWL PWL 207 | 49 | 1 |

VITA – See N*E*R*D; Irv GOTTI presents JA RULE, ASHANTI, Charli BALTIMORE & VITA

Soraya VIVIAN UK, female vocalist (1 WEEK) pos/wks

| 16 Mar 02 | WHEN YOU'RE GONE Activ 8 ACT 501 | 59 | 1 |

VIXEN US, female vocal / instrumental group (21 WEEKS) pos/wks

3 Sep 88	EDGE OF A BROKEN HEART Manhattan MT 48	51	4
4 Mar 89	CRYIN' EMI Manhattan MT 60	27	4
3 Jun 89	LOVE MADE ME EMI-USA MT 66	36	4
2 Sep 89	EDGE OF A BROKEN HEART (re-issue)		
	EMI-USA MT 48	59	2
28 Jul 90	HOW MUCH LOVE EMI-USA MT 87	35	3
20 Oct 90	LOVE IS A KILLER EMI-USA MT 91	41	2
16 Mar 91	NOT A MINUTE TOO SOON EMI-USA MT 93	37	2

VOGGUE
Canada, male / female production / vocal group (6 WEEKS) pos/wks

| 18 Jul 81 | DANCIN' THE NIGHT AWAY Mercury MER 76 | 39 | 6 |

VOICE OF THE BEEHIVE
US / UK, male / female vocal / instrumental group (51 WEEKS) pos/wks

14 Nov 87	I SAY NOTHING London LON 151	45	5
5 Mar 88	I WALK THE EARTH London LON 169	42	4
14 May 88	DON'T CALL ME BABY London LON 175	15	10
23 Jul 88	I SAY NOTHING (re-issue) London LON 190	22	6
22 Oct 88	I WALK THE EARTH (re-issue) London LON 206	46	4
13 Jul 91	MONSTERS AND ANGELS London LON 302	17	10
28 Sep 91	I THINK I LOVE YOU London LON 308	25	6
11 Jan 92	PERFECT PLACE London LON 312	37	6

VOICES OF LIFE US, male / female vocal / production
duo – Sharon Pass and Steve 'Silk' Hurley (2 WEEKS) pos/wks

| 21 Mar 98 | THE WORD IS LOVE (SAY THE WORD) AM:PM 5825272 | 26 | 2 |

See also Steve 'Silk' HURLEY

Sterling VOID
UK, male instrumentalist / vocalist (3 WEEKS) pos/wks

| 4 Feb 89 | RUNAWAY GIRL / IT'S ALL RIGHT ffrr FFR 21 | 53 | 3 |

VOLATILE AGENTS featuring Simone BENN
UK, male production duo and UK, female vocalist (3 WEEKS) pos/wks

| 15 Dec 01 | HOOKED ON YOU Melting Pot MPRCD 10 | 54 | 3 |

VOLCANO
Norway / UK, male / female vocal / instrumental group (4 WEEKS) pos/wks

| 23 Jul 94 | MORE TO LOVE Deconstruction 74321221832 | 32 | 3 |
| 18 Nov 95 | THAT'S THE WAY LOVE IS EXP EXPCD 002 [1] | 72 | 1 |

[1] Volcano with Sam Cartwright

VOODOO & SERANO Germany, male production
duo – Reinhard Raith and Tommy Serano (4 WEEKS) pos/wks

| 3 Feb 01 | BLOOD IS PUMPIN' Xtrahard / Xtravaganza X2H2 CDS | 19 | 4 |

VOYAGE UK / France, disco aggregation (27 WEEKS) pos/wks

		pos	wks
17 Jun 78	**FROM EAST TO WEST / SCOTS MACHINE** GTO GT 224	13	13
25 Nov 78	**SOUVENIRS** GTO GT 241	56	7
24 Mar 79	**LET'S FLY AWAY** GTO GT 245	38	7

'Scots Machine' credited from 24 Jun 1978 until end of record's chart run

VOYAGER UK, male vocal / instrumental group (8 WEEKS) pos/wks

		pos	wks
26 May 79	**HALFWAY HOTEL** Mountain VOY 001	33	8

Jurgen VRIES UK, male DJ / producer – Darren Tate (4 WEEKS) pos/wks

		pos	wks
14 Sep 02	**THE THEME** Direction 6730952	13	4

See also ANGELIC; CITIZEN CANED; ORION

VYBE US, female vocal group (1 WEEK) pos/wks

		pos	wks
7 Oct 95	**WARM SUMMER DAZE** Fourth & Broadway BRCD 315	60	1

W

Billy Paul W – See Robbie RIVERA

Kristine W US, female vocalist – Kristine Weitz (8 WEEKS) pos/wks

		pos	wks
21 May 94	**LOVE COME HOME** Triangle BLUESCD 001 [1]	73	1
25 Jun 94	**FEEL WHAT YOU WANT** Champion CHAMPCD 304	33	3
25 May 96	**ONE MORE TRY** Champion CHAMPCD 317	41	1
21 Dec 96	**LAND OF THE LIVING** Champion CHAMPCD 324	57	1
5 Jul 97	**FEEL WHAT YOU WANT (re-issue)** Champion CHAMPCD 329	40	2

[1] Our Tribe with Franke Pharoah and Kristine W

W.I.P. featuring EMMIE
UK, male production duo and UK, female vocalist (1 WEEK) pos/wks

		pos	wks
16 Feb 02	**I WON'T LET YOU DOWN** Decode / Telstar CDSTAS 3210	53	1

Andrew W.K.
US, male vocalist / producer – Andrew Wilkes-Krier (5 WEEKS) pos/wks

		pos	wks
10 Nov 01	**PARTY HARD** Mercury 5888132	19	4
9 Mar 02	**SHE IS BEAUTIFUL** Mercury 5889522	55	1

W.O.S.P. UK, male / female production / vocal duo (1 WEEK) pos/wks

		pos	wks
17 Nov 01	**GETTIN' INTO U** Data DATA 26CDS	48	1

WWF SUPERSTARS
US / UK, male wrestling vocalists (15 WEEKS) pos/wks

		pos	wks
12 Dec 92	● **SLAM JAM (re)** Arista 74321124887	4	9
3 Apr 93	**WRESTLEMANIA** Arista 74321136832	14	5
10 Jul 93	**USA** Arista 74321153092 [1]	71	1

[1] WWF Superstars featuring Hacksaw Jim Duggan

Bill WADDINGTON – See CORONATION STREET CAST featuring
Bill WADDINGTON

Adam WADE with the George PAXTON Orchestra & Chorus
US, male vocalist (6 WEEKS) pos/wks

		pos	wks
8 Jun 61	**TAKE GOOD CARE OF HER (re)** HMV POP 843	38	6

WAG YA TAIL UK, male vocal / instrumental group (1 WEEK) pos/wks

		pos	wks
3 Oct 92	**XPAND YA MIND (EXPANSIONS)** PWL International PWL 238	49	1

WAH!
UK, male vocal / instrumental group – leader Pete Wylie (26 WEEKS) pos/wks

		pos	wks
25 Dec 82	● **THE STORY OF THE BLUES** Eternal JF 1	3	12
19 Mar 83	**HOPE (I WISH YOU'D BELIEVE ME)** WEA X 9880	37	5
30 Jun 84	**COME BACK** Beggars Banquet BEG 111 [1]	20	9

[1] Mighty Wah

See also Pete WYLIE

Donnie WAHLBERG – See SEIKO and Donnie WAHLBERG;
NEW KIDS ON THE BLOCK

WAIKIKIS Belgium, male instrumental group (2 WEEKS) pos/wks

		pos	wks
11 Mar 65	**HAWAII TATTOO** Pye International 7N 25286	41	2

WAILERS – See Bob MARLEY and the WAILERS

John WAITE UK, male vocalist (13 WEEKS) pos/wks

		pos	wks
29 Sep 84	● **MISSING YOU** EMI America EA 182 ▲	9	11
13 Feb 93	**MISSING YOU (re-issue)** Chrysalis CDCHS 3938	56	2

WAITRESSES
US, male / female vocal / instrumental (4 WEEKS) pos/wks

		pos	wks
18 Dec 82	**CHRISTMAS WRAPPING** Ze / Island WIP 6821	45	4

Johnny WAKELIN UK, male vocalist (20 WEEKS) pos/wks

		pos	wks
18 Jan 75	● **BLACK SUPERMAN (MUHAMMAD ALI)** Pye 7N 45420 [1]	7	10
24 Jul 76	**IN ZAIRE** Pye 7N 45595	4	10

[1] Johnny Wakelin and The Kinshasa Band

Narada Michael WALDEN
US, male vocalist / producer (28 WEEKS) pos/wks

		pos	wks
23 Feb 80	**TONIGHT I'M ALRIGHT** Atlantic K 11437	34	9
26 Apr 80	● **I SHOULDA LOVED YA** Atlantic K 11413	8	9
23 Apr 88	● **DIVINE EMOTIONS** Reprise W 7967 [1]	8	10

[1] Narada

Gary WALKER
US, male vocalist – Gary Leeds (12 WEEKS) pos/wks

		pos	wks
24 Feb 66	**YOU DON'T LOVE ME** CBS 202036	26	6
26 May 66	**TWINKIE-LEE** CBS 202081	26	6

See also WALKER BROTHERS

John WALKER
US, male vocalist – John Maus (6 WEEKS) pos/wks

		pos	wks
5 Jul 67	**ANNABELLA (re)** Philips BF 1593	24	6

See also WALKER BROTHERS

Scott WALKER
US, male vocalist – Scott Engel (30 WEEKS) pos/wks

		pos	wks
6 Dec 67	**JACKIE** Philips BF 1628	22	9
1 May 68	● **JOANNA** Philips BF 1662	7	11
11 Jun 69	**LIGHTS OF CINCINNATI** Philips BF 1793	13	10

See also WALKER BROTHERS

Jr. WALKER & The ALL-STARS US, male
instrumental / vocal group, leader d. 23 Nov 1995 (59 WEEKS) pos/wks

		pos	wks
18 Aug 66	**HOW SWEET IT IS (TO BE LOVED BY YOU)** Tamla Motown TMG 571	22	10
2 Apr 69	**ROAD RUNNER** Tamla Motown TMG 691	12	12
18 Oct 69	**WHAT DOES IT TAKE (TO WIN YOUR LOVE)** Tamla Motown TMG 712	13	12
26 Aug 72	**WALK IN THE NIGHT** Tamla Motown TMG 824	16	11
27 Jan 73	**TAKE ME GIRL, I'M READY** Tamla Motown TMG 840	16	9
30 Jun 73	**WAY BACK HOME** Tamla Motown TMG 857	35	5

WALKER BROTHERS 336 Top 500

Unrelated US trio, who were top UK teen idols in the mid-60s. Members Scott Walker (Engel) (v/b/k), John Walker (Maus) (v/g), Gary Walker (Leeds) (d) all had solo hits after trio split in 1967, with Scott (who first recorded solo in 1957) creating a large cult following (93 WEEKS)   pos/wks

29 Apr 65	LOVE HER *Philips BF 1409*	20	13
19 Aug 65	★ MAKE IT EASY ON YOURSELF *Philips BF 1428*	1	14
2 Dec 65	● MY SHIP IS COMING IN *Philips BF 1454*	3	12
3 Mar 66	★ THE SUN AIN'T GONNA SHINE ANYMORE *Philips BF 1473*	1	11
14 Jul 66	(BABY) YOU DON'T HAVE TO TELL ME *Philips BF 1497*	13	8
22 Sep 66	ANOTHER TEAR FALLS *Philips BF 1514*	12	8
15 Dec 66	DEADLIER THAN THE MALE *Philips BF 1537*	34	6
9 Feb 67	STAY WITH ME BABY *Philips BF 1548*	26	6
18 May 67	WALKING IN THE RAIN *Philips BF 1576*	26	6
17 Jan 76	NO REGRETS *GTO GT 42*	7	9

See also Gary WALKER; John WALKER; Scott WALKER

WALL OF SOUND featuring Gerald LETHAN
US, male vocal / instrumental group (1 WEEK)   pos/wks

31 Jul 93	CRITICAL (IF YOU ONLY KNEW) *Positiva CDTIV 4*	73	1

WALL OF VOODOO
US, male vocal / instrumental group (3 WEEKS)   pos/wks

19 Mar 83	MEXICAN RADIO *Illegal ILS 36*	64	3

Jerry WALLACE *US, male vocalist (1 WEEK)*

23 Jun 60	YOU'RE SINGING OUR LOVE SONG TO SOMEBODY ELSE *London HLH 9110*	46	1

Rik WALLER *UK, male vocalist (12 WEEKS)*   pos/wks

16 Mar 02	● I WILL ALWAYS LOVE YOU (re) *EMI / Liberty CDRIK 001*	6	8
6 Jul 02	(SOMETHING INSIDE) SO STRONG *EMI / Liberty CDRIK 002*	25	4

WALLFLOWERS
US, male vocal / instrumental group (1 WEEK)   pos/wks

12 Jul 97	ONE HEADLIGHT *Interscope IND 95532*	54	1

Bob WALLIS and his STORYVILLE JAZZ BAND
UK, vocalist / instrumentalist – trumpet d. 10 Jan 1991 – and male jazz band (7 WEEKS)   pos/wks

6 Jul 61	I'M SHY MARY ELLEN, I'M SHY *Pye Jazz 7NJ 2043*	44	2
4 Jan 62	COME ALONG PLEASE *Pye Jazz 7NJ 2048*	33	5

Joe WALSH *US, male vocalist / instrumentalist (15 WEEKS)*   pos/wks

16 Jul 77	ROCKY MOUNTAIN WAY (EP) *ABC ABE 12002*	39	4
8 Jul 78	LIFE'S BEEN GOOD *Asylum K 13129*	14	11

Tracks on Rocky Mountain Way (EP): Rocky Mountain Way / Turn to Stone / Meadows / Walk Away

Maureen WALSH – *See MAUREEN*

Sheila WALSH and Cliff RICHARD
UK, female / male vocal duo (2 WEEKS)   pos/wks

4 Jun 83	DRIFTING *DJM SHEIL 1*	64	2

Steve WALSH *UK, male DJ / vocalist, d. 3 July 1988 (18 WEEKS)*   pos/wks

18 Jul 87	● I FOUND LOVIN' (re) *A1 A1 299*	9	13
12 Dec 87	LET'S GET TOGETHER TONITE *A1 A1 303*	74	1
30 Jul 88	AIN'T NO STOPPING US NOW (PARTY FOR THE WORLD) *A1 A1 304*	44	4

Trevor WALTERS *UK, male vocalist (22 WEEKS)*

24 Oct 81	LOVE ME TONIGHT *Magnet MAG 198*	27	8

21 Jul 84	● STUCK ON YOU *Sanity IS 002*	9	12
1 Dec 84	NEVER LET HER SLIP AWAY *Polydor POSP 716*	73	2

WAMDUE PROJECT
US, male producer – Chris Brann (19 WEEKS)   pos/wks

20 Nov 99	KING OF MY CASTLE (import) *Orange ORCDM 53584CD*	61	1
27 Nov 99	★ KING OF MY CASTLE (re) *AM:PM CDAMPM 127*■	1	16
15 Apr 00	YOU'RE THE REASON *AM:PM CDAMPM 130*	39	2

WANG CHUNG *UK, male vocal / instrumental group (12 WEEKS)* pos/wks

28 Jan 84	DANCE HALL DAYS *Geffen A 3837*	21	12

WANNADIES
Sweden, male / female vocal / instrumental group (12 WEEKS)   pos/wks

18 Nov 95	MIGHT BE STARS *Indolent DIE 003CD1*	51	2
24 Feb 96	HOW DOES IT FEEL *Indolent DIE 004CD1*	53	1
20 Apr 96	YOU AND ME SONG *Indolent DIE 005CD*	18	3
7 Sep 96	SOMEONE SOMEWHERE *Indolent DIE 006CD*	38	1
26 Apr 97	HIT *Indolent DIE 009CD1*	20	2
5 Jul 97	SHORTY *Indolent DIE 010CD1*	41	2
4 Mar 00	YEAH *RCA 74321745552*	56	1

Dexter WANSELL
US, male instrumentalist – keyboards (3 WEEKS)   pos/wks

20 May 78	ALL NIGHT LONG *Philadelphia International PIR 6255*	59	3

WAR
US / Canada / Denmark, male vocal / instrumental group (32 WEEKS) pos/wks

24 Jan 76	LOW RIDER *Island WIP 6267*	12	7
26 Jun 76	ME AND BABY BROTHER *Island WIP 6303*	21	7
14 Jan 78	GALAXY *MCA 339*	14	7
15 Apr 78	HEY SENORITA *MCA 359*	40	2
10 Apr 82	YOU GOT THE POWER *RCA 201*	58	4
6 Apr 85	GROOVIN' *Bluebird BR 16*	43	5

Anita WARD *US, female vocalist (11 WEEKS)*   pos/wks

2 Jun 79	★ RING MY BELL *TK TKR 7543* ▲	1	11

Chrissy WARD *US, female vocalist (2 WEEKS)*   pos/wks

24 Jun 95	RIGHT AND EXACT *Ore AG 6CD*	62	1
8 Feb 97	RIGHT AND EXACT (re-mix) *Ore AG 21CD*	59	1

Clifford T WARD
UK, male vocalist, d. 18 Dec 2001 (16 WEEKS)   pos/wks

30 Jun 73	● GAYE *Charisma CB 205*	8	11
26 Jan 74	SCULLERY *Charisma CB 221*	37	5

Michael WARD *UK, male vocalist (13 WEEKS)*   pos/wks

29 Sep 73	LET THERE BE PEACE ON EARTH (LET IT BEGIN WITH ME) (re) *Philips 6006 340*	15	13

Billy WARD and his DOMINOES
US, male vocal group, leader d. 15 Feb 2002 (13 WEEKS)   pos/wks

13 Sep 57	STARDUST (re) *London HLU 8465*	13	12
29 Nov 57	DEEP PURPLE *London HLU 8502*	30	1

WARD BROTHERS
UK, male vocal / instrumental group (8 WEEKS)   pos/wks

10 Jan 87	CROSS THAT BRIDGE *Siren SIREN 37*	32	8

Mathias WARE featuring Rob TAYLOR
Germany, male producer and male vocalist (1 WEEK)   pos/wks

9 Mar 02	HEY LITTLE GIRL *Manifesto FESCD 91*	42	1

Justin WARFIELD – *See BOMB THE BASS*

WARM JETS UK / Canada, male vocal / instrumental group (4 WKS) pos/wks

14 Feb 98	NEVER NEVER Island WAY 6766	37	2
25 Apr 98	HURRICANE Island CID 697	34	2

WARM SOUNDS
UK, male vocal duo – Barry Husband and Denver Gerrard (6 WEEKS) pos/wks

4 May 67	BIRDS AND BEES Deram DM 120	27	6

Toni WARNE UK, female vocalist (4 WEEKS) pos/wks

25 Apr 87	BEN Mint CHEW 110	50	4

Jennifer WARNES US, female vocalist (37 WEEKS) pos/wks

15 Jan 83 ●	UP WHERE WE BELONG Island WIP 6830 [1] ▲	7	13
25 Jul 87	FIRST WE TAKE MANHATTAN Cypress PB 49709	74	1
31 Oct 87 ●	(I'VE HAD) THE TIME OF MY LIFE (re) RCA PB 49625 [2] ▲	6	23

[1] Joe Cocker and Jennifer Warnes [2] Bill Medley and Jennifer Warnes

'(I've Had) The Time of My Life' re-entered in Dec 1990 peaking at No.8

WARP BROTHERS Germany, male DJ / production group (18 WKS) pos/wks

11 Nov 00	PHATT BASS (IMPORT) Dos or Die BMSCDM 40009	58	3
9 Dec 00 ●	PHATT BASS Nulife / Arista 74321817102 [1]	9	8
17 Feb 01	WE WILL SURVIVE Nulife / Arista 74321832722	19	4
29 Dec 01	BLAST THE SPEAKERS Nulife 74321899162	40	3

[1] Warp Brothers vs Aquagen

WARRANT US, male vocal / instrumental group (7 WEEKS) pos/wks

17 Nov 90	CHERRY PIE CBS 6562587	59	2
9 Mar 91	CHERRY PIE (re-issue) Columbia 6566867	35	5

Alysha WARREN UK, female vocalist (4 WEEKS) pos/wks

24 Sep 94	I'M SO IN LOVE Wild Card CARDD 10	61	1
25 Mar 95	I THOUGHT I MEANT THE WORLD TO YOU Wild Card CARDD 16	40	1
27 Jul 96	KEEP ON PUSHING OUR LOVE Arista 74321390422 [1]	30	2

[1] Nightcrawlers featuring John Reid and Alysha Warren

Ann WARREN – See Ruby MURRAY

Nikita WARREN Italy, female vocalist (1 WEEK) pos/wks

13 Jul 96	I NEED YOU VC VCRD 12	48	1

WARRIOR UK, male vocal / production / instrumental
duo – Stacey Charles and Michael Woods (6 WEEKS) pos/wks

21 Oct 00	WARRIOR Incentive CENT 12CDS	19	4
30 Jun 01	VOODOO Incentive CENT 26CDS	37	2

Dionne WARWICK `309` `Top 500`
Super-stylish soul diva, b. 12 Dec 1940, New Jersey, US, whose classy and unmistakable vocals on songs written by Burt Bacharach and Hal David produced more than 30 US hits for her between 1962 and 1972. She is a cousin of Whitney Houston (101 WEEKS) pos/wks

13 Feb 64	ANYONE WHO HAD A HEART Pye International 7N 25234	42	3
16 Apr 64 ●	WALK ON BY Pye International 7N 25241	9	14
30 Jul 64	YOU'LL NEVER GET TO HEAVEN (IF YOU BREAK MY HEART) Pye International 7N 25256	20	8
8 Oct 64	REACH OUT FOR ME Pye International 7N 25265	23	7
1 Apr 65	YOU CAN HAVE HIM Pye International 7N 25290	37	5
13 Mar 68	(THEME FROM) VALLEY OF THE DOLLS Pye International 7N 25445	28	8
15 May 68 ●	DO YOU KNOW THE WAY TO SAN JOSE Pye International 7N 25457	8	10
19 Oct 74	THEN CAME YOU Atlantic K 10495 [1] ▲	29	6
23 Oct 82 ●	HEARTBREAKER Arista ARIST 496	2	13
11 Dec 82 ●	ALL THE LOVE IN THE WORLD Arista ARIST 507	10	10
26 Feb 83	YOURS Arista ARIST 518	66	2
28 May 83	I'LL NEVER LOVE THIS WAY AGAIN Arista ARIST 530	62	3

9 Nov 85	THAT'S WHAT FRIENDS ARE FOR Arista ARIST 638 [2] ▲	16	9
15 Aug 87	LOVE POWER Arista RIS 27 [3]	63	3

[1] Dionne Warwicke and The Detroit Spinners [2] Dionne Warwick and Friends featuring Elton John, Stevie Wonder and Gladys Knight [3] Dionne Warwick and Jeffrey Osborne

WAS (NOT WAS) US, male vocal / instrumental
duo – Don Fagenson and David Weiss (58 WEEKS) pos/wks

3 Mar 84	OUT COME THE FREAKS Ze / Geffen A 4178	41	5
18 Jul 87	SPY IN THE HOUSE OF LOVE (re) Fontana WAS 2	21	15
3 Oct 87 ●	WALK THE DINOSAUR Fontana WAS 3	10	10
7 May 88	OUT COME THE FREAKS (AGAIN) Fontana WAS 4	44	3
16 Jul 88	ANYTHING CAN HAPPEN Fontana WAS 5	67	3
26 May 90	PAPA WAS A ROLLING STONE Fontana WAS 7	12	7
11 Aug 90	HOW THE HEART BEHAVES Fontana WAS 8	53	3
23 May 92	LISTEN LIKE THIEVES Fontana WAS 10	58	2
11 Jul 92 ●	SHAKE YOUR HEAD Fontana WAS 11	4	9
26 Sep 92	SOMEWHERE IN AMERICA (THERE'S A STREET NAMED AFTER MY DAD) Fontana WAS 12	57	1

'Spy in the House Of Love' first peaked at No.51 and made its peak position only on re-entry in Feb 1988. Fontana WAS 4 was a re-recorded version of their first hit. 'Shake Your Head' features uncredited vocals by Ozzy Osbourne and Kim Basinger. The group dropped the brackets from their name during the chart run of 'Papa Was a Rolling Stone'

Martha WASH US, female vocalist (34 WEEKS) pos/wks

28 Nov 92	CARRY ON RCA 74321125457	74	1
6 Mar 93	GIVE IT TO YOU RCA 74321136562	37	4
10 Jul 93	RUNAROUND / CARRY ON (re-mix) RCA 74321153702	49	2
18 Feb 95	I FOUND LOVE Columbia 6612712 [1]	26	2
13 Jul 96 ●	KEEP ON JUMPIN' Manifesto FESCD 11 [2]	8	6
12 Jul 97 ●	SOMETHING GOIN' ON Manifesto FESCD 25 [2]	5	10
25 Oct 97	CARRY ON (2nd) (re-mix) Delirious DELICD 6	49	1
28 Feb 98	IT'S RAINING MEN…THE SEQUEL Logic 74321555412 [3]	21	3
11 Apr 98	READY FOR A NEW DAY Manifesto FESCD 40 [4]	20	2
15 Aug 98	CATCH THE LIGHT Logic 74321587912	45	1
3 Jul 99	COME Logic 74321653942	64	1
5 Feb 00	IT'S RAINING MEN (re-recording) Logic 74321726282	56	1

[1] C & C Music Factory featuring Martha Wash [2] Todd Terry featuring Martha Wash and Jocelyn Brown [3] Martha Wash featuring RuPaul [4] Todd Terry featuring Martha Wash

The listed flip side of 'I Found Love' was 'Take a Toke' by C & C Music Factory

See also WEATHER GIRLS

Dinah WASHINGTON
US, female vocalist – Ruth Jones, d. 14 Dec 1963 (8 WEEKS) pos/wks

30 Nov 61	SEPTEMBER IN THE RAIN (re) Mercury AMT 1162	35	4
4 Apr 92	MAD ABOUT THE BOY Mercury DINAH 1	41	4

Grover WASHINGTON Jr
US, male instrumentalist – saxophone, d. 17 Dec 1999 (7 WEEKS) pos/wks

16 May 81	JUST THE TWO OF US Elektra K 12514	34	7

Although uncredited, Bill Withers sings on 'Just the Two of Us'

Keith WASHINGTON – See Kylie MINOGUE

Sarah WASHINGTON UK, female vocalist (13 WEEKS) pos/wks

14 Aug 93	I WILL ALWAYS LOVE YOU Almighty CDALMY 33	12	7
27 Nov 93	CARELESS WHISPER Almighty CDALMY 43	45	2
25 May 96	HEAVEN AM:PM 5815352	28	2
12 Oct 96	EVERYTHING AM:PM 5818872	30	2

Geno WASHINGTON and the RAM JAM BAND US, male
vocalist and UK, male instrumental backing group (20 WEEKS) pos/wks

19 May 66	WATER Piccadilly 7N 35312	39	8
21 Jul 66	HI HI HAZEL (re) Piccadilly 7N 35329	45	4

6 Oct 66	QUE SERA SERA *Piccadilly 7N 35346*	**43** 3
2 Feb 67	MICHAEL (HE'S A LOVER) *Piccadilly 7N 35359*	**39** 5

W.A.S.P. *US, male vocal / instrumental group (38 WEEKS)*

		pos/wks
31 May 86	WILD CHILD *Capitol CL 388*	**71** 2
11 Oct 86	95 – NASTY *Capitol CL 432*	**70** 1
29 Aug 87	SCREAM UNTIL YOU LIKE IT *Capitol CL 458*	**32** 5
31 Oct 87	I DON'T NEED NO DOCTOR (LIVE) *Capitol CL 469*	**31** 5
20 Feb 88	ANIMAL (F**K LIKE A BEAST) *Music for Nations KUT 109*	**61** 3
4 Mar 89	MEAN MAN *Capitol CL 521*	**21** 5
27 May 89	THE REAL ME *Capitol CL 534*	**23** 5
9 Sep 89	FOREVER FREE *Capitol CL 546*	**25** 5
4 Apr 92	CHAINSAW CHARLIE (MURDERS IN THE NEW MORGUE) *Parlophone RS 6308*	**17** 2
6 Jun 92	THE IDOL *Parlophone RPD 6314*	**41** 2
31 Oct 92	I AM ONE *Parlophone 10RG 6324*	**56** 1
23 Oct 93	SUNSET AND BABYLON *Capitol CDCL 698*	**38** 2

WATERBOYS
UK / Ireland, male vocal / instrumental group (33 WEEKS)

		pos/wks
2 Nov 85	THE WHOLE OF THE MOON *Ensign ENY 520*	**26** 7
14 Jan 89	FISHERMAN'S BLUES *Ensign ENY 621*	**32** 6
1 Jul 89	AND A BANG ON THE EAR *Ensign ENY 624*	**51** 4
6 Apr 91 ●	THE WHOLE OF THE MOON (re-issue) *Ensign ENY 642*	**3** 9
8 Jun 91	FISHERMAN'S BLUES (re-issue) *Ensign ENY 645*	**75** 1
15 May 93	THE RETURN OF PAN *Geffen GFSTD 42*	**24** 3
24 Jul 93	GLASTONBURY SONG *Geffen GFSTD 49*	**29** 3

WATERFRONT *UK, male vocal / instrumental*
duo – Phil Cilia and Chris Duffy (19 WEEKS)

		pos/wks
15 Apr 89	BROKEN ARROW *Polydor WON 3*	**63** 2
27 May 89	CRY *Polydor WON 1*	**17** 13
9 Sep 89	NATURE OF LOVE *Polydor WON 2*	**63** 4

WATERGATE *Turkey, male DJ / producer – Orhan Terzi (10 WEEKS)* pos/wks

13 May 00 ●	HEART OF ASIA *Positiva CDTIV 129*	**3** 10

See also DJ QUICKSILVER

Dennis WATERMAN *UK, male actor / vocalist (17 WEEKS)*

		pos/wks
25 Oct 80 ●	I COULD BE SO GOOD FOR YOU *EMI 5009* [1]	**3** 12
17 Dec 83	WHAT ARE WE GONNA GET 'ER INDOORS *EMI MIN 101* [2]	**21** 5

[1] Dennis Waterman with The Dennis Waterman Band [2] Dennis Waterman and George Cole

Crystal WATERS *US, female vocalist (35 WEEKS)*

		pos/wks
18 May 91 ●	GYPSY WOMAN (LA DA DEE) *A&M AM 772*	**2** 10
7 Sep 91	MAKIN' HAPPY *A&M AM 790*	**18** 6
11 Jan 92	MEGAMIX *A&M AM 843*	**39** 3
3 Oct 92	GYPSY WOMAN (re-mix) *Epic 6584377*	**35** 2
23 Apr 94	100% PURE LOVE *A&M 8586692*	**15** 7
2 Jul 94	GHETTO DAY *A&M 8589592*	**40** 2
25 Nov 95	RELAX *Manifesto FESCD 4*	**37** 2
24 Aug 96	IN DE GHETTO *Manifesto FESCD 12* [1]	**35** 2
19 Apr 97	SAY … IF YOU FEEL ALRIGHT *Mercury 5742912*	**45** 1

[1] David Morales and the Bad Yard Club featuring Crystal Waters and Delta

The listed flip side of 'Gypsy Woman' (re-mix) was 'Peace' (re-mix) by Sabrina Johnston

Muddy WATERS *US, male vocalist /*
instrumentalist – guitar, d. 30 Apr 1983 (6 WEEKS)

		pos/wks
16 Jul 88	MANNISH BOY *Epic MUD 1*	**51** 6

Roger WATERS
UK, male vocalist / instrumentalist (8 WEEKS)

		pos/wks
30 May 87	RADIO WAVES *Harvest EM 6*	**74** 1
26 Dec 87	THE TIDE IS TURNING (AFTER LIVE AID) *Harvest EM 37*	**54** 4
5 Sep 92	WHAT GOD WANTS PART 1 *Columbia 6581390*	**35** 3

Lauren WATERWORTH *UK, female vocalist (3 WEEKS)* pos/wks

1 Jun 02	BABY NOW THAT I'VE FOUND YOU *Jive 9253622*	**24** 3

Michael WATFORD *US, male vocalist (2 WEEKS)*

		pos/wks
26 Feb 94	SO INTO YOU *East West A 8309CD*	**53** 2

Tionne 'T-Boz' WATKINS – See T-BOZ; TLC

Jody WATLEY *US, female vocalist (35 WEEKS)*

		pos/wks
9 May 87	LOOKING FOR A NEW LOVE *MCA MCA 1107*	**13** 11
17 Oct 87	DON'T YOU WANT ME *MCA MCA 1198*	**55** 3
8 Apr 89	REAL LOVE *MCA MCA 1324*	**31** 7
12 Aug 89	FRIENDS *MCA MCA 1352* [1]	**21** 6
10 Feb 90	EVERYTHING *MCA MCA 1395*	**74** 2
11 Apr 92	I'M THE ONE YOU NEED *MCA MCS 1608*	**50** 3
21 May 94	WHEN A MAN LOVES A WOMAN *MCA MCSTD 1964*	**33** 2
25 Apr 98	OFF THE HOOK *Atlantic AT 0024CD1*	**51** 1

[1] Jody Watley with Eric B and Rakim

See also SHALAMAR

Joe WATSON – See RHYTHM MASTERS

Johnny 'Guitar' WATSON *US, male vocalist /*
instrumentalist – guitar d. 17 May 1996 (8 WEEKS)

		pos/wks
28 Aug 76	I NEED IT *DJM DJS 10694*	**35** 5
23 Apr 77	A REAL MOTHER FOR YA *DJM DJS 10762*	**44** 3

Russell WATSON *UK, male vocalist (9 WEEKS)*

		pos/wks
30 Oct 99	SWING LOW '99 *Decca / Universal TV 4669502*	**38** 2
22 Jul 00	BARCELONA (FRIENDS UNTIL THE END) *Decca 4672772* [1]	**68** 1
18 May 02 ●	SOMEONE LIKE YOU *Decca 4730002* [2]	**10** 4
21 Dec 02	NOTHING SACRED – A SONG FOR KIRSTY *Decca 4737402*	**17** 2+

[1] Russell Watson and Shaun Ryder [2] Russell Watson and Faye Tozer

WAVELENGTH *UK, male vocal group (12 WEEKS)*

		pos/wks
10 Jul 82	HURRY HOME *Ariola ARO 281*	**17** 12

WAX *US / UK, male vocal / instrumental duo*
– Andrew Gold and Graham Gouldman (16 WEEKS)

		pos/wks
12 Apr 86	RIGHT BETWEEN THE EYES *RCA PB 40509*	**60** 5
1 Aug 87	BRIDGE TO YOUR HEART *RCA PB 41405*	**12** 11

See also Andrew GOLD; 10 CC; Graham GOULDMAN

Anthony WAY *UK, male vocalist (2 WEEKS)*

		pos/wks
15 Apr 95	PANIS ANGELICUS *Decca 4481642*	**55** 2

A WAY OF LIFE
US, male / female vocal / instrumental group (3 WEEKS)

		pos/wks
21 Apr 90	TRIPPIN' ON YOUR LOVE *Eternal YZ 464*	**55** 3

WAY OF THE WEST
UK, male vocal / instrumental group (5 WEEKS)

		pos/wks
25 Apr 81	DON'T SAY THAT'S JUST FOR WHITE BOYS *Mercury MER 66*	**54** 5

WAY OUT WEST *UK, male instrumental / production*
duo – Nick Warren and Jody Wisternoff (17 WEEKS)

		pos/wks
3 Dec 94	AJARE *Deconstruction 74321243802*	**52** 1
2 Mar 96	DOMINATION *Deconstruction 74321342822*	**38** 2
14 Sep 96	THE GIFT *Deconstruction 74321401912* [1]	**15** 5
30 Aug 97	BLUE *Deconstruction 74321477512*	**41** 2
29 Nov 97	AJARE (re-mix) *Deconstruction 74321521352*	**36** 2
9 Dec 00	THE FALL *Wow WOW 005CD*	**61** 1

18 Aug 01	**INTENSIFY** *Distinctive Breaks DISNCD 74*	.46	1
30 Mar 02	**MINDCIRCUS** *Distinctive Breaks DISNCD 80* [2]	.39	2
21 Sep 02	**STEALTH** *Distinctive Breaks DISNCD 90* [3]	.67	1

[1] Way Out West featuring Miss Joanna Law [2] Way Out West featuring Tricia Lee Kelshall [3] Way Out West featuring Kirsty Hawkshaw

Bruce WAYNE *Germany, male DJ / producer (2 WEEKS)*
pos/wks
13 Dec 97	**READY** *Logic 74321527012*	.44	1
4 Jul 98	**NO GOOD FOR ME** *Logic 74321587052*	.70	1

Jan WAYNE
Germany, male producer – Jan Christiansen (5 WEEKS)
pos/wks
9 Nov 02	**BECAUSE THE NIGHT** *Product / Incentive PDT 02CDS*	.14	5

Jeff WAYNE'S WAR OF THE WORLDS
US, orchestra (21 WEEKS)
pos/wks
9 Sep 78	**THE EVE OF THE WAR** *CBS 6496*	.36	8
10 Jul 82	**MATADOR** *CBS A 2493* [1]	.57	3
25 Nov 89 ●	**EVE OF THE WAR** (re-mix) *CBS 6551267*	.3	10

[1] Jeff Wayne

'The Eve of the War' credited as from Jeff Wayne's 'War of the Worlds'

WEATHER GIRLS
US, female vocal duo – Martha Wash and Izora Redman (14 WEEKS) pos/wks
27 Aug 83 ●	**IT'S RAINING MEN** (re) *CBS A 2924*	.2	14

'It's Raining Men' first peaked at No.73 in 1983 and reached its peak position only on re-entry in Mar 1984

See also Martha WASH

WEATHER PROPHETS
UK, male vocal / instrumental group (2 WEEKS)
pos/wks
28 Mar 87	**SHE COMES FROM THE RAIN** *Elevation ACID 1*	.62	2

WEATHERMEN – See Jonathan KING

Marti WEBB *UK, female vocalist (42 WEEKS)*
pos/wks
9 Feb 80 ●	**TAKE THAT LOOK OFF YOUR FACE**		
	Polydor POSP 100	.3	12
19 Apr 80	**TELL ME ON A SUNDAY** *Polydor POSP 111*	.67	2
20 Sep 80	**YOUR EARS SHOULD BE BURNING NOW**		
	Polydor POSP 166	.61	4
8 Jun 85 ●	**BEN** *Starblend STAR 6*	.5	11
20 Sep 86	**ALWAYS THERE** *BBC RESL 190* [1]	.13	12
6 Jun 87	**I CAN'T LET GO** *Rainbow RBR 12*	.65	1

[1] Marti Webb and the Simon May Orchestra

WEBB BROTHERS *US, male vocal / instrumental duo (1 WEEK)* pos/wks
17 Feb 01	**I CAN'T BELIEVE YOU'RE GONE** *WEA WEA 320CD*	.69	1

Joan WEBER
US, female vocalist d. 13 May 1981 (1 WEEK)
pos/wks
18 Feb 55	**LET ME GO LOVER** *Philips PB 389* ▲	.16	1

Nikki WEBSTER *Australia, female vocalist (1 WEEK)*
pos/wks
8 Jun 02	**STRAWBERRY KISSES** *Gotham 74321943642*	.64	1

WEDDING PRESENT
UK, male vocal / instrumental group (38 WEEKS)
pos/wks
5 Mar 88	**NOBODY'S TWISTING YOUR ARM**		
	Reception REC 009	.46	2
1 Oct 88	**WHY ARE YOU BEING SO REASONABLE NOW?**		
	Reception REC 011	.42	2
7 Oct 89	**KENNEDY** *RCA PB 43117*	.33	3
17 Feb 90	**BRASSNECK** *RCA PB 43403*	.24	3
29 Sep 90	**3 SONGS (EP)** *RCA PB 44021*	.25	4

11 May 91	**DALLIANCE** *RCA PB 44495*	.29	3
27 Jul 91	**LOVENEST** *RCA PT 44750*	.58	1
18 Jan 92	**BLUE EYES** *RCA PB 45185*	.26	2
15 Feb 92	**GO-GO DANCER** *RCA PB 45183*	.20	1
14 Mar 92	**THREE** *RCA PB 45181*	.14	2
18 Apr 92	**SILVER SHORTS** *RCA PB 45311*	.14	1
16 May 92 ●	**COME PLAY WITH ME** *RCA PB 45313*	.10	2
13 Jun 92	**CALIFORNIA** *RCA PB 45315*	.16	1
18 Jul 92	**FLYING SAUCER** *RCA 74321101157*	.22	1
15 Aug 92	**BOING!** *RCA 74321101177*	.19	1
19 Sep 92	**LOVE SLAVE** *RCA 74321101167*	.17	1
17 Oct 92	**STICKY** *RCA 74321116917*	.17	1
14 Nov 92	**THE QUEEN OF OUTER SPACE** *RCA 74321116927* ..	.23	1
19 Dec 92	**NO CHRISTMAS** *RCA 74321116937*	.25	1
10 Sep 94	**YEAH YEAH YEAH YEAH** *Island CID 585*	.51	2
26 Nov 94	**IT'S A GAS** *Island CID 591*	.71	1
31 Aug 96	**2, 3, GO** *Cooking Vinyl FRYCD 048*	.67	1
25 Jan 97	**MONTREAL** *Cooking Vinyl FRYCD 053*	.40	1

Tracks on 3 Songs (EP): Corduroy / Crawl / Make Me Smile (Come Up and See Me)

Fred WEDLOCK *UK, male vocalist (10 WEEKS)*
pos/wks
31 Jan 81 ●	**OLDEST SWINGER IN TOWN** *Rocket XPRES 46*	.6	10

WEE PAPA GIRL RAPPERS *UK, female rap / vocal*
duo – Samantha and Sandra Lawrence (27 WEEKS)
pos/wks
12 Mar 88	**FAITH** *Jive JIVE 164*	.60	4
25 Jun 88	**HEAT IT UP** *Jive JIVE 174* [1]	.21	9
1 Oct 88 ●	**WEE RULE** *Jive JIVE 185*	.6	9
24 Dec 88	**SOULMATE** *Jive JIVE 193*	.45	4
25 Mar 89	**BLOW THE HOUSE DOWN** *Jive JIVE 197*	.65	1

[1] Wee Papa Girl Rappers featuring Two Men and a Drum Machine

Bert WEEDON *UK, male instrumentalist – guitar (38 WEEKS)*
pos/wks
15 May 59 ●	**GUITAR BOOGIE SHUFFLE** *Top Rank JAR 117*	.10	9
20 Nov 59	**NASHVILLE BOOGIE** *Top Rank JAR 221*	.29	2
10 Mar 60	**BIG BEAT BOOGIE** (re) *Top Rank JAR 300*	.37	4
9 Jun 60	**TWELFTH STREET RAG** *Top Rank JAR 360*	.47	2
28 Jul 60	**APACHE** (re) *Top Rank JAR 415*	.24	4
27 Oct 60	**SORRY ROBBIE** *Top Rank JAR 517*	.28	11
2 Feb 61	**GINCHY** *Top Rank JAR 537*	.35	5
4 May 61	**MR GUITAR** *Top Rank JAR 559*	.47	1

WEEKEND
International, male / female vocal / instrumental group (5 WEEKS) pos/wks
14 Dec 85	**CHRISTMAS MEDLEY / AULD LANG SYNE**		
	Lifestyle XY 1	.47	5

WEEKEND PLAYERS *UK, male / female production*
/ vocal duo – Rachel Foster and Andy Cato (5 WEEKS)
pos/wks
8 Sep 01	**21ST CENTURY** *Multiply CDMULTY 78*	.22	4
16 Mar 02	**INTO THE SUN** *Multiply CDMULTY 84*	.42	1

See also GROOVE ARMADA

Michelle WEEKS *US, female vocalist (6 WEEKS)*
pos/wks
2 Aug 97	**MOMENT OF MY LIFE**		
	Ministry of Sound MOSCDS 1 [1]	.23	3
8 Nov 97	**DON'T GIVE UP** *Ministry of Sound MOSCDS 2*	.28	2
11 Jul 98	**GIVE ME LOVE** *VC Recordings VCRD 37* [2]	.59	1

[1] Bobby D'Ambrosio featuring Michelle Weeks [2] DJ Dado vs Michelle Weeks

WEEN – See FOO FIGHTERS

WEEZER *US, male vocal / instrumental group (19 WEEKS)*
pos/wks
11 Feb 95	**UNDONE – THE SWEATER SONG** *Geffen GFSTD 85*	.35	2
6 May 95	**BUDDY HOLLY** *Geffen GFSTD 88*	.12	7
22 Jul 95	**SAY IT AIN'T SO** *Geffen GFSTD 95*	.37	2
5 Oct 96	**EL SCORCHO** *Geffen GFSTD 22167*	.50	1
14 Jul 01	**HASH PIPE** *Geffen 4975642*	.21	3

Re-entries are listed as (re), (2re), (3re), etc which signifies that the hit re-entered the chart once, twice or three times, etc

3 Nov 01	ISLAND IN THE SUN *Geffen 4976102*	31	2
14 Sep 02	KEEP FISHIN' *Geffen 4977912*	29	2

Frank WEIR and His Orchestra
UK, orchestra – leader, d. 12 May 1981 (4 WEEKS)   pos/wks

15 Sep 60	CARIBBEAN HONEYMOON *Oriole CB 1559*	42	4

See also Vera LYNN

WEIRD SCIENCE *UK, male DJ / production duo (1 WEEK)*   pos/wks

1 Jul 00	FEEL THE NEED *Nulife 74321751982*	62	1

Eric WEISSBERG – *See 'DELIVERANCE' SOUNDTRACK*

Denise WELCH *UK, female actor / vocalist (3 WEEKS)*   pos/wks

4 Nov 95	YOU DON'T HAVE TO SAY YOU LOVE ME / CRY ME A RIVER *Virgin VSCDT 1569*	23	3

Paul WELLER *UK, male vocalist (67 WEEKS)*   pos/wks

18 May 91	INTO TOMORROW *Freedom High FHP 1* [1]	36	3
15 Aug 92	UH HUH OH YEH *Go! Discs GOD 86*	18	5
10 Oct 92	ABOVE THE CLOUDS *Go! Discs GOD 91*	47	2
17 Jul 93	SUNFLOWER *Go! Discs GODCD 102*	16	5
4 Sep 93	WILD WOOD *Go! Discs GODCD 104*	14	3
13 Nov 93	THE WEAVER (EP) *Go! Discs GODCD 107*	18	3
9 Apr 94	HUNG UP *Go! Discs GODCD 111*	11	3
5 Nov 94	OUT OF THE SINKING *Go! Discs GODCD 121*	20	3
6 May 95 ●	THE CHANGINGMAN *Go! Discs GODCD 127*	7	4
22 Jul 95 ●	YOU DO SOMETHING TO ME *Go! Discs GODCD 130*	9	6
30 Sep 95	BROKEN STONES *Go! Discs GODCD 132*	20	4
9 Mar 96	OUT OF THE SINKING *Go! Discs GODCD 143*	16	2
17 Aug 96 ●	PEACOCK SUIT *Go! Discs GODCD 149*	5	5
9 Aug 97	BRUSHED *Island CID 666*	14	3
11 Oct 97	FRIDAY STREET *Island CID 676*	21	2
6 Dec 97	MERMAIDS *Island CID 683*	30	2
14 Nov 98	BRAND NEW START *Island CID 711*	16	3
9 Jan 99	WILDWOOD (re-issue) *Island CID 734*	22	3
2 Sep 00	SWEET PEA, MY SWEET PEA *Island CID 764*	44	1
14 Sep 02 ●	IT'S WRITTEN IN THE STARS *Independiente ISOM 63SMS*	7	3
30 Nov 02	LEAFY MYSTERIES *Independiente ISOM 65SMS*	23	2

[1] Paul Weller Movement

Tracks on The Weaver (EP): The Weaver / This Is No Time / Another New Day / Ohio (live). 'Out of the Sinking' in 1996 is a re-recording. Both versions feature uncredited vocals by Carleen Anderson

See also COUNCIL COLLECTIVE; STYLE COUNCIL; JAM

Brandi WELLS *US, female vocalist (1 WEEK)*   pos/wks

20 Feb 82	WATCH OUT *Virgin VS 479*	74	1

Houston WELLS and the MARKSMEN *UK, male vocalist – Andrew Smith – and instrumental group (10 WEEKS)*   pos/wks

1 Aug 63	ONLY THE HEARTACHES *Parlophone R 5031*	22	10

Mary WELLS *US, female vocalist, d. 26 Jul 1992 (25 WEEKS)*   pos/wks

21 May 64 ●	MY GUY *Stateside SS 288* ▲	5	14
30 Jul 64	ONCE UPON A TIME *Stateside SS 316* [1]	50	1
8 Jul 72	MY GUY (re-issue) *Tamla Motown TMG 820*	14	10

[1] Marvin Gaye and Mary Wells

Terri WELLS *US, female vocalist (9 WEEKS)*   pos/wks

2 Jul 83	YOU MAKE IT HEAVEN *Phillyworld PWS 111*	53	2
5 May 84	I'LL BE AROUND *Phillyworld LON 48*	17	7

Alex WELSH BAND *UK, male vocal / instrumental group – leader d. 25 Jun 1982 (4 WEEKS)*   pos/wks

10 Aug 61	TANSY *Columbia DB 4686*	45	4

Irvine WELSH – *See PRIMAL SCREAM*

WENDY and LISA
US, female vocal duo – Wendy Melvoin and Lisa Coleman (31 WEEKS)   pos/wks

5 Sep 87	WATERFALL *Virgin VS 999*	66	4
16 Jan 88	SIDESHOW *Virgin VS 1012*	49	5
18 Feb 89	ARE YOU MY BABY *Virgin VS 1156*	70	3
29 Apr 89	LOLLY LOLLY *Virgin VS 1175*	64	3
8 Jul 89	SATISFACTION *Virgin VS 1194*	27	8
18 Nov 89	WATERFALL (re-mix) *Virgin VS 1223*	69	2
30 Jun 90	STRUNG OUT *Virgin VS 1272*	44	5
10 Nov 90	RAINBOW LAKE *Virgin VS 1280*	70	1

WES *France, male vocalist – Wes Madiko (7 WEEKS)*   pos/wks

14 Feb 98	ALANE *Epic 6654682*	11	6
27 Jun 98	I LOVE FOOTBALL *Epic 6660772*	75	1

Dodie WEST *UK, female vocalist (4 WEEKS)*   pos/wks

14 Jan 65	GOING OUT OF MY HEAD *Decca F 12046*	39	4

Keith WEST *UK, male vocalist (18 WEEKS)*   pos/wks

9 Aug 67 ●	EXCERPT FROM A TEENAGE OPERA *Parlophone R 5623*	2	15
22 Nov 67	SAM *Parlophone R 5651*	38	3

Kit WEST – *See DEGREES OF MOTION featuring BITI*

WEST END *UK, female vocal group (2 WEEKS)*   pos/wks

19 Aug 95	LOVE RULES *RCA 74321292702*	44	2

WEST END featuring SYBIL
UK, male production duo and female vocalist (13 WEEKS)   pos/wks

16 Jan 93 ●	THE LOVE I LOST *PWL Sanctuary PWCD253*	3	13

WEST HAM UNITED CUP SQUAD
UK, male football team vocalists (2 WEEKS)   pos/wks

10 May 75	I'M FOREVER BLOWING BUBBLES *Pye 7N 45470*	31	2

WEST STREET MOB *US, male DJ / production group (3 WEEKS)*   pos/wks

8 Oct 83	BREAK DANCIN' – ELECTRIC BOOGIE (re) *Sugarhill SH 128*	64	3

WESTBAM *Germany, male producer – Maximillian Lenz (9 WEEKS)*   pos/wks

9 Jul 94	CELEBRATION GENERATION *Low Spirit PQCD 5*	48	2
19 Nov 94	BAM BAM BAM *Low Spirit PZCD 329*	57	1
3 Jun 95	WIZARDS OF THE SONIC *Urban PZCD 344*	32	2
23 Mar 96	ALWAYS MUSIC *Low Spirit 5779152* [1]	51	1
13 Jun 98	WIZARDS OF THE SONIC (re-mix) *Wonderboy WBOYD 010* [2]	43	2
28 Nov 98	ROOF IS ON FIRE *Logic 74321633162*	58	1

[1] Westbam / Koon + Stephenson   [2] Westbam vs Red Jerry

WESTLIFE   132   Top 500
Record-shattering Irish boy band: Bryan McFadden, Kian Egan, Mark Freehily, Nicky Byrne and Shane Filan. Only act to reach No. 1 with their first seven releases or enter the chart at No.1 11 times out of their first 13. They are also the first UK-based act to amass four No.1s in a year (162 WEEKS)   pos/wks

1 May 99 ★	SWEAR IT AGAIN (re) *RCA 74321662062* ■	1	13
21 Aug 99 ★	IF I LET YOU GO *RCA74321692352* ■	1	11
30 Oct 99 ★	FLYING WITHOUT WINGS *RCA 74321709162* ■	1	13
25 Dec 99 ★	I HAVE A DREAM / SEASONS IN THE SUN *RCA 74321726012*	1	17
8 Apr 00 ★	FOOL AGAIN (re) *RCA 74321751562* ■	1	12
30 Sep 00 ★	AGAINST ALL ODDS (re) *Columbia 6698872* [1] ■	1	12
11 Nov 00 ★	MY LOVE *RCA 74321802792* ■	1	10
30 Dec 00 ●	WHAT MAKES A MAN *RCA 74321826252*	2	13

MATCHSTALK MEN AND MATCHSTAL

■ Kevin Parrott and Mick Coleman first met as members of the Stax-styled Big Sound in 1965. When that group folded, Parrott was recruited by Manchester rock band Oscar, which eventually signed with DJM records, while Coleman joined a folk ensemble and concentrated on his songwriting.

Coleman first saw L S Lowry's paintings in a small Manchester gallery, and noticed that many of the scenes in his pictures were of his childhood Manchester, particularly around England's last workhouse where Coleman's family had been forced to live during his early school years. He says, "I got the initial idea to write a Lowry tribute in the early 1970s, and was spurred on to finish the song when the artist died in 1976."

During the mid-1970s, Coleman formed a comedy duo with Brian Burke, and began performing at the local pubs and clubs as Burke and Jerk. Parrott and Coleman had stayed friends since the Big Sound and after borrowing £1,000 they decided to record together Coleman's Lowry tribute.

Parrott produced it at the £16-an-hour Pluto Studios in Manchester, which was owned by former Herman's Hermit Keith Hopwood. Kevin added, "I was convinced that he needed children's voices on the track and recruited the nearby St Winifred's School Choir, along with the Tintwistle Brass Band from my home village." Despite their best budgeting the money ran out before a B-side could be recorded, and so this was laid down at a moonlighting session at another local studio.

■ I WAS CONVINCED THAT HE NEEDED CHILDREN'S VOICES ON THE TRACK AND RECRUITED THE NEARBY ST WINIFRED'S SCHOOL CHOIR ALONG WITH THE TINTWISTLE BRASS BAND FROM MY HOME VILLAGE ■ KEVIN PARROTT

After being turned down by several record companies, Pye spotted its potential and wanted to sign Parrott and Coleman. However, as Parrott was still with Oscar and signed to DJM, it was decided that Coleman's comedy duo partner, Brian Burke, should form the other half of the duo and thus the record was released as by Brian and Michael. In fact, Burke and Jerk were even given a label credit on the single.

A couple of weeks after 'Matchstalk Men and Matchstalk Cats and Dogs' was issued, Burke decided he did not want to be involved, and Parrott was forced to leave Oscar to join Coleman and take on "the life of Brian". In February 1978, three months after its release, the single finally charted, and on 8 April it made No.1. DJ Peter Powell presented them with a silver disc during their performance at the London Palladium.

CATS AND DOGS

They may appear to be one-hit wonders but Parrott produced The Ramblers' 1979 Top 20 hit 'The Sparrow', while Coleman wrote Ken Dodd's 'Hold My Hand'. Additionally, together as writers/producers, they were responsible for the 1986 Top 20 novelty 'It's 'Orrible Being in Love (When You're 8 1/2)' by Claire and Friends in 1986. Claire was a St Winifred's School pupil whose choir had its own chart-topper in 1980.

The Ivor Novello award-winning 'Matchstalk Men' is still performed by Parrott and Coleman who

★ ARTIST:	Brian and Michael
★ LABEL:	Pye
★ WRITER:	Michael Coleman
★ PRODUCER:	Kevin Parrott

played several prestigious shows at the new Lowry Centre at Salford Quays in 2002. More than 2,000 fans saw them reunite with the original girls from the St Winifred's School Choir.

■ Dave McAleer

Brian and Michael's chart-topper was inspired by the paintings of Stretford-born artist L S Lowry

17 Mar 01 ★ UPTOWN GIRL *RCA 74321841682* ■	1	16
17 Nov 01 ★ QUEEN OF MY HEART *RCA 74321899132* ■	1	15
2 Mar 02 ★ WORLD OF OUR OWN *S 74321918802* ■	1	13
1 Jun 02 ● BOP BOP BABY *S 74321940452*	5	10
16 Nov 02 ★ UNBREAKABLE *S 74321975182* ■	1	7+

[1] Mariah Carey and Westlife

Kim WESTON – *See Marvin GAYE*

WESTWORLD
UK / US, male / female vocal / instrumental group (23 WEEKS) pos/wks

21 Feb 87	SONIC BOOM BOY *RCA BOOM 1* 11	7
2 May 87	BA-NA-NA-BAM-BOO *RCA BOOM 2* 37	5
25 Jul 87	WHERE THE ACTION IS *RCA BOOM 3* 54	4
17 Oct 87	SILVERMAC *RCA BOOM 4* 42	5
15 Oct 88	EVERYTHING GOOD IS BAD *RCA PB 42243* 72	2

WET WET WET (81) Top 500
Perennially popular Glasgow quartet fronted by vocalist Marti Pellow (b. Mark McLoughlin, 23 Mar 1966). They were voted Best British Newcomers at the 1988 Brit Awards and they hold the record for most weeks at No.1 by a UK act – 15 consecutive weeks. Best-selling single: 'Love Is All Around' 1,783,827 (209 WEEKS) pos/wks

11 Apr 87 ●	WISHING I WAS LUCKY *Precious JEWEL 3* 6	14
25 Jul 87 ●	SWEET LITTLE MYSTERY *Precious JEWEL 4* 5	12
5 Dec 87 ●	ANGEL EYES (HOME AND AWAY) *Precious JEWEL 6* 5	12
19 Mar 88	TEMPTATION *Precious JEWEL 7* 12	8
14 May 88 ★	WITH A LITTLE HELP FROM MY FRIENDS *Childline CHILD 1* 1	11
30 Sep 89 ●	SWEET SURRENDER *Precious JEWEL 9* 6	8
9 Dec 89	BROKE AWAY *Precious JEWEL 10* 19	7
10 Mar 90	HOLD BACK THE RIVER *Precious JEWEL 11* 31	4
11 Aug 90	STAY WITH ME HEARTACHE / I FEEL FINE *Precious JEWEL 13* 30	4
14 Sep 91	MAKE IT TONIGHT *Precious JEWEL 15* 37	3
2 Nov 91	PUT THE LIGHT ON *Precious JEWEL 16* 56	2
4 Jan 92 ★	GOODNIGHT GIRL *Precious JEWEL 17* 1	11
21 Mar 92	MORE THAN LOVE *Precious JEWEL 18* 19	5
11 Jul 92	LIP SERVICE (EP) *Precious JEWEL 19* 15	5
8 May 93	BLUE FOR YOU / THIS TIME (LIVE) *Precious JWLCD 20* 38	2
6 Nov 93	SHED A TEAR *Precious JWLCD 21* 22	5
8 Jan 94	COLD COLD HEART *Precious JWLCD 22* 23	4
21 May 94 ★	LOVE IS ALL AROUND *Precious JWLCD 23* ◆ 1	37
25 Mar 95 ●	JULIA SAYS *Precious JWLDD 24* 3	9
17 Jun 95 ●	DON'T WANT TO FORGIVE ME NOW *Precious JWLDD 25* 7	8
30 Sep 95 ●	SOMEWHERE SOMEHOW *Precious JWLDD 26* 7	7
2 Dec 95	SHE'S ALL ON MY MIND *Precious JWLDD 27* 17	7
30 Mar 96	MORNING *Precious JWLDD 28* 16	4
22 Mar 97 ●	IF I NEVER SEE YOU AGAIN (re) *Precious JWLCD 29* 3	9
14 Jun 97	STRANGE (re) *Precious JWLCD 30* 13	5
16 Aug 97	YESTERDAY *Precious JWLCD 31* 4	6

The listed A-side of 'With a Little Help from My Friends' was 'She's Leaving Home' by Billy Bragg with Cara Tivey. Tracks on Lip Service (EP): Lip Service / High on the Happy Side / Lip Service (Live) / More than Love (Live)

WE'VE GOT A FUZZBOX AND WE'RE GONNA USE IT
UK, female vocal / instrumental group (39 WEEKS) pos/wks

26 Apr 86	XX SEX / RULES AND REGULATIONS *Vindaloo UGH 11* 41	7
15 Nov 86	LOVE IS THE SLUG *Vindaloo UGH 14* 31	4
7 Feb 87	WHAT'S THE POINT *Vindaloo YZ 101* [1] 51	2
25 Feb 89	INTERNATIONAL RESCUE *WEA YZ 347* 11	10
20 May 89	PINK SUNSHINE *WEA YZ 401* [1] 14	10
5 Aug 89	SELF! *WEA YZ 408* [1] 24	6

[1] Fuzzbox

WHALE *Sweden, male / female vocal / instrumental group (8 WKS)* pos/wks

19 Mar 94	HOBO HUMPIN' SLOBO BABE *East West YZ 798CD* 46	2
15 Jul 95	I'LL DO YA *Hut HUTDG 51* 53	1
25 Nov 95	HOBO HUMPIN' SLOBO BABE (re-issue) *Hut HUTCD 64* 15	4
4 Jul 98	FOUR BIG SPEAKERS *Hut HUTCD 96* [1] 69	1

[1] Whale featuring Bus 75

WHALERS – *See Hal PAIGE and the WHALERS*

WHAM! (183) Top 500
Teen-dream duo with a feel-good, pure pop sound: George Michael (v), Andrew Ridgeley (g). They were the only British group to have three chart-toppers in the UK and the US during the 1980s, a feat George later equalled as a solo artist. Best-selling single: 'Last Christmas' / 'Everything She Wants' 1,420,000 (137 WEEKS) pos/wks

16 Oct 82 ●	YOUNG GUNS (GO FOR IT) *Innervision IVL A2766* 3	17
15 Jan 83 ●	WHAM RAP! *Innervision IVL A2442* 8	11
14 May 83 ●	BAD BOYS *Innervision A 3143* 2	14
30 Jul 83 ●	CLUB TROPICANA *Innervision A 3613* 4	11
3 Dec 83	CLUB FANTASTIC MEGAMIX *Innervision A 3586* 15	8
26 May 84 ★	WAKE ME UP BEFORE YOU GO GO *Epic A 4440* ▲ 1	16
13 Oct 84 ★	FREEDOM *Epic A 4743* 1	14
15 Dec 84 ●	LAST CHRISTMAS / EVERYTHING SHE WANTS *Epic GA / QA 4949* ◆ ▲ 2	13
23 Nov 85 ★	I'M YOUR MAN *Epic A 6716* 1	12
14 Dec 85 ●	LAST CHRISTMAS (re-issue) *Epic WHAM 1* 6	7
21 Jun 86 ★	THE EDGE OF HEAVEN / WHERE DID YOUR HEART GO *Epic FIN 1* 1	10
20 Dec 86	LAST CHRISTMAS (2nd re-issue) *Epic 650269 7* 45	4

Chart entry dated 21 June 1986 was a double record set. 'The Edge of Heaven'/ 'Wham Rap 86 (remix)' on disc one and 'Battlestations' / 'Where Did Your Heart Go' on disc two. 'Where Did Your Heart Go' listed only from 2 Aug 1986, peaking at No.28. Chart entry 15 Dec 1984 was first catalogued as GA 4949 but from 5 Jan 1985 the special remix of 'Everything She Wants' (QA 4949) was listed as the A-side

Sarah WHATMORE *UK, female vocalist (9 WEEKS)* pos/wks

21 Sep 02 ●	WHEN I LOST YOU *RCA 74321965952* 6	9

WHATNAUTS – *See MOMENTS*

Rebecca WHEATLEY *UK, female actor / vocalist (8 WEEKS)* pos/wks

26 Feb 00 ●	STAY WITH ME (BABY) (re) *BBC Music WMSS 60222* 10	8

WHEATUS *US, male vocal / instrumental group (37 WEEKS)* pos/wks

17 Feb 01 ●	TEENAGE DIRTBAG *Columbia 6707962* 2	20
14 Jul 01 ●	A LITTLE RESPECT *Columbia 6714282* 3	12
26 Jan 02	WANNABE GANGSTAR / LEROY *Columbia 6721272* 22	5

Caron WHEELER *UK, female vocalist (42 WEEKS)* pos/wks

18 Mar 89	KEEP ON MOVING *10 TEN 263* [1] 5	12
10 Jun 89 ★	BACK TO LIFE (HOWEVER DO YOU WANT ME) *10 TEN 265* [1] 1	14
8 Sep 90	LIVIN' IN THE LIGHT *RCA PB 43939* 14	6
10 Nov 90	UK BLAK *RCA PB 43719* 40	4
9 Feb 91	DON'T QUIT *RCA PB 44259* 53	3
7 Nov 92	I ADORE YOU *Perspective PERSS 7407* 59	2
11 Sep 93	BEACH OF THE WAR GODDESS *EMI CDEM 282* 75	1

[1] Soul II Soul featuring Caron Wheeler

Bill WHELAN featuring ANUNA and the RTE CONCERT ORCHESTRA
Ireland, male composer, male / female choir and orchestra (16 WEEKS) pos/wks

17 Dec 94 ●	RIVERDANCE *Son RTEBUACD 1* 9	16

WHEN IN ROME
UK, male vocal / instrumental group (3 WEEKS) pos/wks

28 Jan 89	THE PROMISE *10 TEN 244* 58	3

WHIGFIELD
Denmark, female vocalist – Sannia Carlson (52 WEEKS) pos/wks

17 Sep 94 ★	SATURDAY NIGHT *Systematic SYSCD 3* ◆ ■ 1	18
10 Dec 94 ●	ANOTHER DAY *Systematic SYSCD 4* 7	10
10 Jun 95 ●	THINK OF YOU *Systematic SYSCDP 10* 7	11
9 Sep 95	CLOSE TO YOU *Systematic SYCDP 18* 13	7
16 Dec 95	LAST CHRISTMAS / BIG TIME *Systematic SYSCD 24* 21	5
10 Oct 98	SEXY EYES – REMIXES *ZYX ZYX 8085R8* 68	1

WHIPPING BOY
Ireland, male vocal / instrumental group (4 WKS) pos/wks

14 Oct 95	WE DON'T NEED NOBODY ELSE *Columbia 6622205*	51	1
3 Feb 96	WHEN WE WERE YOUNG *Columbia 6628062*	46	2
25 May 96	TWINKLE *Columbia 6632272*	55	1

Nancy WHISKEY – See Charles McDEVITT SKIFFLE GROUP featuring Nancy WHISKEY

WHISPERS *US, male vocal group (52 WEEKS)* pos/wks

2 Feb 80 ●	AND THE BEAT GOES ON *Solar SO 1*	2	12
10 May 80	LADY *Solar SO 4*	55	3
12 Jul 80	MY GIRL *Solar SO 8*	26	6
14 Mar 81 ●	IT'S A LOVE THING *Solar SO 16*	9	11
13 Jun 81	I CAN MAKE IT BETTER *Solar SO 19*	44	5
19 Jan 85	CONTAGIOUS *MCA MCA 937*	56	3
28 Mar 87	AND THE BEAT GOES ON (re-issue) *Solar MCA 1126*	45	4
23 May 87	ROCK STEADY *Solar MCA 1152*	38	6
15 Aug 87	SPECIAL F/X *Solar MCA 1178*	69	2

WHISTLE *US, male rap group (8 WEEKS)* pos/wks

| 1 Mar 86 ● | (NOTHIN' SERIOUS) JUST BUGGIN' *Champion CHAMP 12* | 7 | 8 |

Alex WHITCOMBE & BIG C
UK, male production duo (1 WEEK) pos/wks

| 23 May 98 | ICE RAIN *Xtravaganza 0091075 EXT* | 44 | 1 |

See also QATTARA

Barry WHITE (181 | Top 500) Seventies soul and disco icon, b. 12 Sep
1944, Texas, US. This singer / songwriter / pianist / producer / arranger
was behind best sellers by Love Unlimited and Love Unlimited Orchestra.
Lovingly named the "Walrus of Love", his unmistakable deep voice has
been in the charts for four decades (138 WEEKS) pos/wks

9 Jun 73	I'M GONNA LOVE YOU JUST A LITTLE MORE BABY *Pye International 7N 25610*	23	7
26 Jan 74	NEVER NEVER GONNA GIVE YA UP *Pye International 7N 25633*	14	11
17 Aug 74 ●	CAN'T GET ENOUGH OF YOUR LOVE, BABE *Pye International 7N 25661* ▲	8	12
2 Nov 74 ★	YOU'RE THE FIRST, THE LAST, MY EVERYTHING *20th Century BTC 2133*	1	14
8 Mar 75 ●	WHAT AM I GONNA DO WITH YOU *20th Century BTC 2177*	5	8
24 May 75	(FOR YOU) I'LL DO ANYTHING YOU WANT ME TO *20th Century BTC 2208*	20	6
27 Dec 75 ●	LET THE MUSIC PLAY *20th Century BTC 2265*	9	8
6 Mar 76 ●	YOU SEE THE TROUBLE WITH ME *20th Century BTC 2277*	2	10
21 Aug 76	BABY, WE BETTER TRY TO GET IT TOGETHER *20th Century BTC 2298*	15	7
13 Nov 76	DON'T MAKE ME WAIT TOO LONG *20th Century BTC 2309*	17	8
5 Mar 77	I'M QUALIFIED TO SATISFY YOU *20th Century BTC 2328*	37	5
15 Oct 77	IT'S ECSTASY WHEN YOU LAY DOWN NEXT TO ME *20th Century BTC 2350*	40	3
16 Dec 78	JUST THE WAY YOU ARE *20th Century BTC 2380*	12	12
24 Mar 79	SHA LA MEANS I LOVE YOU *20th Century BTC 1041*	55	4
7 Nov 87	SHO' YOU RIGHT *Breakout USA 614*	14	7
16 Jan 88	NEVER NEVER GONNA GIVE YOU UP (re-mix) *Club JAB 59*	63	2
31 Mar 90	SECRET GARDEN *Qwest W 9992* 1	67	1
21 Jan 95	PRACTICE WHAT YOU PREACH / LOVE IS THE ICON *A&M 5808992*	20	4
8 Apr 95	I ONLY WANT TO BE WITH YOU *A&M 5810252*	36	2
21 Dec 96	IN YOUR WILDEST DREAMS *Parlophone CDR 6451* 2	32	3
4 Nov 00	LET THE MUSIC PLAY (re-mix) *Wonderboy WBOYD 020*	45	2

1 Quincy Jones featuring Al B Sure!, James Ingram, El DeBarge and Barry White
2 Tina Turner featuring Barry White

Chris WHITE *UK, male vocalist (4 WEEKS)* pos/wks

| 20 Mar 76 | SPANISH WINE *Charisma CB 272* | 37 | 4 |

Karyn WHITE *US, female vocalist (38 WEEKS)* pos/wks

5 Nov 88	THE WAY YOU LOVE ME *Warner Bros. W 7773*	42	5
18 Feb 89	SECRET RENDEZVOUS *Warner Bros. W 7562*	52	3
10 Jun 89	SUPERWOMAN *Warner Bros. W 2920*	11	13
9 Sep 89	SECRET RENDEZVOUS (re-issue) *Warner Bros. W 2855*	22	9
17 Aug 91	ROMANTIC *Warner Bros. W 0028* ▲	23	5
18 Jan 92	THE WAY I FEEL ABOUT YOU *Warner Bros. W 0073*	65	2
24 Sep 94	HUNGAH *Warner Bros. W 0264CD*	69	1

Snowy WHITE
UK, male vocalist / instrumentalist – guitar (12 WEEKS) pos/wks

| 24 Dec 83 ● | BIRD OF PARADISE *Towerbell TOW 42* | 6 | 10 |
| 28 Dec 85 | FOR YOU (re) *R4 FOR 3* | 65 | 2 |

Tam WHITE *UK, male vocalist (4 WEEKS)* pos/wks

| 15 Mar 75 | WHAT IN THE WORLD'S COME OVER YOU *RAK 193* | 36 | 4 |

Tony Joe WHITE *US, male vocalist (10 WEEKS)* pos/wks

| 6 Jun 70 | GROUPIE GIRL *Monument MON 1043* | 22 | 10 |

WHITE and TORCH
UK, male vocal / instrumental duo (4 WEEKS) pos/wks

| 2 Oct 82 | PARADE *Chrysalis CHS 2641* | 54 | 4 |

WHITE PLAINS
UK, male vocal / instrumental group (56 WEEKS) pos/wks

7 Feb 70 ●	MY BABY LOVES LOVIN' *Deram DM 280*	9	11
18 Apr 70	I'VE GOT YOU ON MY MIND *Deram DM 291*	17	11
24 Oct 70	JULIE DO YA LOVE ME *Deram DM 315*	8	14
12 Jun 71	WHEN YOU ARE A KING *Deram DM 333*	13	11
17 Feb 73	STEP INTO A DREAM *Deram DM 371*	21	9

The WHITE STRIPES *US, male / female vocal
/ instrumental duo – Meg and Jack White (6 WEEKS)* pos/wks

24 Nov 01	HOTEL YORBA *XL Recordings XLS 139CD*	26	2
9 Mar 02	FELL IN LOVE WITH A GIRL *XL Recordings XLS 142CD*	21	2
14 Sep 02	DEAD LEAVES AND THE DIRTY GROUND *XL Recordings XLS 148CD*	25	2

WHITE TOWN *UK, male vocalist /
instrumentalist / producer – Jyoti Mishra (10 WEEKS)* pos/wks

| 25 Jan 97 ★ | YOUR WOMAN *Chrysalis CDCHS 5052* ■ | 1 | 9 |
| 24 May 97 | UNDRESSED *Chrysalis CDCHS 5058* | 57 | 1 |

WHITE ZOMBIE
US, male vocal / instrumental group (4 WEEKS) pos/wks

| 20 May 95 | MORE HUMAN THAN HUMAN *Geffen GFSTD 92* | 51 | 2 |
| 18 May 96 | ELECTRIC HEAD PART 2 (THE ECSTASY) *Geffen GFSXD 22140* | 31 | 2 |

WHITEHEAD BROS
US, male vocal duo – Kenny and Johnny Whitehead (5 WEEKS) pos/wks

| 14 Jan 95 | YOUR LOVE IS A 187 *Motown TMGCD 1434* | 32 | 3 |
| 13 May 95 | FORGET I WAS A G *Motown TMGCD 1441* | 40 | 2 |

WHITEHOUSE
US / UK, male vocal / instrumental / production duo (1 WEEK) pos/wks

| 15 Aug 98 | AIN'T NO MOUNTAIN HIGH ENOUGH *Beautiful Noise BNOISE 2CD* | 60 | 1 |

WHITEOUT
UK, male vocal / instrumental group (2 WEEKS) pos/wks

| 24 Sep 94 | DETROIT *Silvertone ORECD 66* | 73 | 1 |
| 18 Feb 95 | JACKIE'S RACING *Silvertone ORECD 68* | 72 | 1 |

WHITESNAKE (261) Top 500

Leading 1980s British rock group founded by ex-Deep Purple vocalist David Coverdale (b. 22 Sep 1949, North Yorkshire, UK), but with an ever-changing line-up. 'Whitesnake' (1987), their most successful album, shifted more than 10 million copies worldwide (112 WEEKS)

		pos/wks
24 Jun 78	SNAKE BITE (EP) *EMI International INEP 751* [1]	61 3
10 Nov 79	LONG WAY FROM HOME *United Artists BP 324*	55 2
26 Apr 80	FOOL FOR YOUR LOVING *United Artists BP 352*	13 9
12 Jul 80	READY AN' WILLING (SWEET SATISFACTION) *United Artists BP 363*	43 4
22 Nov 80	AIN'T NO LOVE IN THE HEART OF THE CITY *Sunburst/Liberty BP 381*	51 4
11 Apr 81	DON'T BREAK MY HEART AGAIN *Liberty BP 395*	17 9
6 Jun 81	WOULD I LIE TO YOU *Liberty BP 399*	37 6
6 Nov 82	HERE I GO AGAIN / BLOODY LUXURY *Liberty BP 416* ▲	34 10
13 Aug 83	GUILTY OF LOVE *Liberty BP 420*	31 5
14 Jan 84	GIVE ME MORE TIME *Liberty BP 422*	29 4
28 Apr 84	STANDING IN THE SHADOW *Liberty BP 423*	62 2
9 Feb 85	LOVE AIN'T NO STRANGER *Liberty BP 424*	44 4
28 Mar 87	STILL OF THE NIGHT *EMI EMI 5606*	16 8
6 Jun 87 ●	IS THIS LOVE *EMI EM 3*	9 11
31 Oct 87 ●	HERE I GO AGAIN (re-mix) *EMI EM 35*	9 11
6 Feb 88	GIVE ME ALL YOUR LOVE *EMI EM 23*	18 6
2 Dec 89	FOOL FOR YOUR LOVING *EMI EM 123*	43 2
10 Mar 90	THE DEEPER THE LOVE *EMI EM 128*	35 3
25 Aug 90	NOW YOU'RE GONE *EMI EM 150*	31 4
6 Aug 94	IS THIS LOVE / SWEET LADY LUCK (re-issue) *EMI CDEM 329*	25 4
7 Jun 97	TOO MANY TEARS *EMI CDEM 471* [2]	46 1

[1] David Coverdale's Whitesnake [2] David Coverdale and Whitesnake

Tracks on Snake Bite (EP): Bloody Mary / Steal Away / Ain't No Love in the Heart of the City / Come On. EM 123 is a re-recording of their third hit

David WHITFIELD (99) Top 500

Most successful UK male singer in the US during the pre-rock years, b. 2 Feb 1925, Yorkshire, d. 16 Jan 1980. This operatic-style tenor had a formidable and predominantly female fan following in the 1950s (190 WEEKS)

		pos/wks
2 Oct 53 ●	THE BRIDGE OF SIGHS *Decca F 10129*	9 1
16 Oct 53 ★	ANSWER ME (re) *Decca F 10192*	1 14
11 Dec 53	RAGS TO RICHES (re) *Decca F 10207* [1]	3 11
19 Feb 54 ●	THE BOOK (re) *Decca F 10242*	5 15
18 Jun 54 ★	CARA MIA *Decca F 10327*	1 25
12 Nov 54 ●	SANTO NATALE (MERRY CHRISTMAS) *Decca F 10399*	2 10
11 Feb 55 ●	BEYOND THE STARS *Decca F 10458*	8 9
27 May 55	MAMA (2re) *Decca F 10515*	12 11
8 Jul 55 ●	EV'RYWHERE *Decca F 10515* [2]	3 20
25 Nov 55 ●	WHEN YOU LOSE THE ONE YOU LOVE *Decca F 10627* [3]	7 11
2 Mar 56 ●	MY SEPTEMBER LOVE (3re) *Decca F 10690*	3 24
24 Aug 56	MY SON JOHN *Decca F 10769*	22 4
31 Aug 56	MY UNFINISHED SYMPHONY *Decca F 10769*	29 1
25 Jan 57 ●	THE ADORATION WALTZ *Decca F 10833* [2]	9 11
5 Apr 57	I'LL FIND YOU (re) *Decca F 10864*	27 4
14 Feb 58	CRY MY HEART *Decca F 10978* [4]	22 3
16 May 58	ON THE STREET WHERE YOU LIVE *Decca F 11018* [5]	16 14
8 Aug 58	THE RIGHT TO LOVE *Decca F 11039*	30 1
24 Nov 60	I BELIEVE *Decca F 11289*	49 1

[1] David Whitfield with Stanley Black and his Orchestra [2] David Whitfield with the Roland Shaw Orchestra [3] David Whitfield with Mantovani, His Orchestra and Chorus [4] David Whitfield with chorus and Mantovani and his Orchestra [5] David Whitfield with Cyril Stapleton and His Orchestra

Slim WHITMAN (458) Top 500

Distinctive country vocalist whose yodelling style made him a major 1950s pop star in UK, b. 20 Jan 1924, Florida, US. For 36 years, 'Rose Marie' held the record for most consecutive weeks at the top. At 53 (1977) he was the oldest act to top the chart with a new album. It was Whitman's singing that vanquished the aliens in the movie 'Mars Attacks!' (77 WEEKS)

		pos/wks
15 Jul 55 ★	ROSE MARIE *London HL 8061*	1 19
29 Jul 55 ●	INDIAN LOVE CALL *London L 1149*	7 12

		pos/wks
23 Sep 55	CHINA DOLL *London L 1149*	15 2
9 Mar 56	TUMBLING TUMBLEWEEDS *London HLU 8230*	19 2
13 Apr 56	I'M A FOOL (re) *London HLU 8252*	16 4
22 Jun 56 ●	SERENADE (re) *London HLU 8287*	8 15
12 Apr 57 ●	I'LL TAKE YOU HOME AGAIN KATHLEEN *London HLP 8403*	7 13
5 Oct 74	HAPPY ANNIVERSARY *United Artists UP 35728*	14 10

Roger WHITTAKER (398) Top 500

World-renowned vocalist and whistler, b. 22 Mar 1936, Nairobi, Kenya. Easy-listening legend and popular live performer with more than 10 million albums sold in his home base, Germany (85 WEEKS)

		pos/wks
8 Nov 69	DURHAM TOWN (THE LEAVIN') *Columbia DB 8613*	12 18
11 Apr 70 ●	I DON'T BELIEVE IN IF ANYMORE *Columbia DB 8664*	8 18
10 Oct 70	NEW WORLD IN THE MORNING *Columbia DB 8718*	17 14
3 Apr 71	WHY *Columbia DB 8752*	47 1
2 Oct 71	MAMMY BLUE *Columbia DB 8822*	31 10
26 Jul 75 ●	THE LAST FAREWELL *EMI 2294*	2 14
8 Nov 86 ●	THE SKYE BOAT SONG *Tembo TML 119* [1]	10 10

[1] Roger Whittaker and Des O'Connor

The WHO (52) Top 500

Legendary live band from London, whose 'Tommy' album (1969) popularised rock opera: Roger Daltrey (v), Pete Townshend (g), John Entwistle, 'The Ox', (b) d. 27 Jun 2002, Keith Moon (d) (d. 1978). These gold-record collectors have spent five decades breaking both guitars and box-office records (247 WEEKS)

		pos/wks
18 Feb 65 ●	I CAN'T EXPLAIN *Brunswick 05926*	8 13
27 May 65 ●	ANYWAY ANYHOW ANYWHERE *Brunswick 05935*	10 12
4 Nov 65 ●	MY GENERATION *Brunswick 05944*	2 13
10 Mar 66 ●	SUBSTITUTE *Reaction 591 001*	5 13
24 Mar 66	A LEGAL MATTER *Brunswick 05956*	32 6
1 Sep 66 ●	I'M A BOY *Reaction 591 004*	2 13
1 Sep 66	THE KIDS ARE ALRIGHT (re) *Brunswick 05965*	41 3
15 Dec 66 ●	HAPPY JACK *Reaction 591 010*	3 11
27 Apr 67 ●	PICTURES OF LILY *Track 604 002*	4 10
26 Jul 67	THE LAST TIME / UNDER MY THUMB *Track 604 006*	44 3
18 Oct 67 ●	I CAN SEE FOR MILES *Track 604 011*	10 12
19 Jun 68	DOGS *Track 604 023*	25 5
23 Oct 68	MAGIC BUS *Track 604 024*	26 6
19 Mar 69 ●	PINBALL WIZARD *Track 604 027*	4 13
4 Apr 70	THE SEEKER *Track 604 036*	19 11
8 Aug 70	SUMMERTIME BLUES *Track 2094 002*	38 4
10 Jul 71 ●	WON'T GET FOOLED AGAIN *Track 2094 009*	9 12
23 Oct 71	LET'S SEE ACTION *Track 2094 012*	16 12
24 Jun 72 ●	JOIN TOGETHER *Track 2094 102*	9 9
13 Jan 73	RELAY *Track 2094 106*	21 5
13 Oct 73	5.15 *Track 2094 115*	20 6
24 Jan 76 ●	SQUEEZE BOX *Polydor 2121 275*	10 9
30 Oct 76	SUBSTITUTE (re-issue) *Polydor 2058 803*	7 7
22 Jul 78	WHO ARE YOU *Polydor WHO 1*	18 12
28 Apr 79	LONG LIVE ROCK *Polydor WHO 2*	48 5
7 Mar 81 ●	YOU BETTER YOU BET *Polydor WHO 004*	9 8
9 May 81	DON'T LET GO THE COAT *Polydor WHO 005*	47 4
2 Oct 82	ATHENA *Polydor WHO 6*	40 4
26 Nov 83	READY STEADY WHO (EP) *Polydor WHO 7*	58 2
20 Feb 88	MY GENERATION (re-issue) *Polydor POSP 907*	68 2
27 Jul 96	MY GENERATION (2nd re-issue) *Polydor 8546372*	31 2

Tracks on Ready Steady Who (EP): Disguises / Circles / Batman / Bucket 'T' / Barbara Ann

See also HIGH NUMBERS

WHO DA FUNK featuring Jessica EVE

US, male production duo and US, female vocalist (6 WEEKS)

		pos/wks
26 Oct 02	SHINY DISCO BALLS (import) *White Label SSA 03*	69 1
2 Nov 02	SHINY DISCO BALLS *Cream CREAM 22CD*	15 5

WHODINI US, male rap / DJ duo (10 WEEKS)

		pos/wks
25 Dec 82	MAGIC'S WAND *Jive JIVE 28*	47 6

Re-entries are listed as (re), (2re), (3re), etc which signifies that the hit re-entered the chart once, twice or three times, etc

17 Mar 84	MAGIC'S WAND (THE WHODINI ELECTRIC EP) *Jive JIVE 61* **63**	4

Tracks on The Whodini Electric EP: Jive Magic Wand / Nasty Lady / Rap Machine / The Haunted House of Rock

WHOOLIGANZ *US, male rap duo (2 WEEKS)*

		pos/wks
13 Aug 94	PUT YOUR HANDZ UP *Positiva CDTIV 17* **53**	2

WHOOSH *UK, male production trio (1 WEEK)*

		pos/wks
13 Sep 97	WHOOSH *Wonderboy WBOYD 006*................................**72**	1

WHYCLIFFE *UK, male vocalist (2 WEEKS)*

		pos/wks
20 Nov 93	HEAVEN *MCA MCSTD 1944* **56**	1
2 Apr 94	ONE MORE TIME *MCA MCSTD 1955*..........................**72**	1

WIDEBOYS featuring Dennis G
UK, male production duo and male vocalist (6 WEEKS)

		pos/wks
27 Oct 01	SAMBUCA *Locked On / 679 Recordings 679L 002CD* **15**	6

Jane WIEDLIN *US, female vocalist (14 WEEKS)*

		pos/wks
6 Aug 88	RUSH HOUR *Manhattan MT 36* **12**	11
29 Oct 88	INSIDE A DREAM *Manhattan MT 55* **64**	3

WIGAN'S CHOSEN FEW *Canada, male vocal / instrumental group and UK, crowd chants (11 WEEKS)*

		pos/wks
18 Jan 75	● FOOTSEE *Pye Disco Demand DDS 111* **9**	11

WIGAN'S OVATION
UK, male vocal / instrumental group (19 WEEKS)

		pos/wks
15 Mar 75	SKIING IN THE SNOW *Spark SRL 1122*.......................**12**	10
28 Jun 75	PER-SO-NAL-LY *Spark SRL 1129* **38**	6
29 Nov 75	SUPER LOVE *Spark SRL 1133* **41**	3

WILCO *US, male vocal / instrumental group (1 WEEK)*

		pos/wks
17 Apr 99	CAN'T STAND IT *Reprise W 475CD1* **67**	1

Jack WILD *UK, male actor / vocalist (2 WEEKS)*

		pos/wks
2 May 70	SOME BEAUTIFUL *Capitol CL 15635* **46**	2

WILD BOYS – See HEINZ

WILD CHERRY
US, male vocal / instrumental group (11 WEEKS)

		pos/wks
9 Oct 76	● PLAY THAT FUNKY MUSIC *Epic EPC 4593* ▲ **7**	11

WILD COLOUR
UK, male / female vocal / instrumental group (2 WEEKS)

		pos/wks
14 Oct 95	DREAMS *Perfecto PERF 105CD* **25**	2

WILD PAIR – See Paula ABDUL

WILD WEEKEND
UK, male vocal / instrumental group (2 WEEKS)

		pos/wks
29 Apr 89	BREAKIN' UP *Parlophone R 6204* **74**	1
5 May 90	WHO'S AFRAID OF THE BIG BAD LOVE? *Parlophone R 6249* **70**	1

WILDCHILD *UK, male producer – Roger McKenzie (20 WEEKS)*

		pos/wks
22 Apr 95	LEGENDS OF THE DARK BLACK PART 2 *Hi-Life HICD 9* **34**	3
21 Oct 95	RENEGADE MASTER (re-issue) *Hi-Life 5771312*...............**11**	4
23 Nov 96	JUMP TO MY BEAT *Hi-Life 5757372* **30**	2
17 Jan 98	● RENEGADE MASTER '98 *Hi-Life 5692792*...................**3**	10
25 Apr 98	BAD BOY *Polydor 5716072* [1] **38**	1

[1] Wildchild featuring Jomalski

Although titled differently, first two hits are identical

Eugene WILDE *US, male vocalist – Ron Broomfield (15 WEEKS)*

		pos/wks
13 Oct 84	GOTTA GET YOU HOME TONIGHT *Fourth & Broadway BRW 15* **18**	9
2 Feb 85	PERSONALITY *Fourth & Broadway BRW 18*....................**34**	6

'Personality' was coupled with 'Let Her Feel It' by Simplicious

Kim WILDE 96 Top 500
Most charted British female vocalist in the 1980s, b. Kim Smith, 18 Nov 1960, London. Neither Kim nor her father, rock 'n' roll star Marty Wilde, managed a UK No.1, but Kim did top the US chart (194 WEEKS)

		pos/wks
21 Feb 81	● KIDS IN AMERICA *RAK 327* **2**	13
9 May 81	● CHEQUERED LOVE *RAK 330*................................**4**	9
1 Aug 81	WATER ON GLASS / BOYS *RAK 334* **11**	8
14 Nov 81	CAMBODIA *RAK 336* **12**	12
17 Apr 82	VIEW FROM A BRIDGE *RAK 342* **16**	7
16 Oct 82	CHILD COME AWAY *RAK 352* **43**	4
30 Jul 83	LOVE BLONDE *RAK 360* **23**	8
12 Nov 83	DANCING IN THE DARK *RAK 365* **67**	2
13 Oct 84	THE SECOND TIME *MCA KIM 1* **29**	6
8 Dec 84	THE TOUCH *MCA KIM 2* **56**	3
27 Apr 85	RAGE TO LOVE *MCA KIM 3* **19**	8
25 Oct 86	● YOU KEEP ME HANGIN' ON *MCA KIM 4* ▲ **2**	14
4 Apr 87	ANOTHER STEP (CLOSER TO YOU) *MCA KIM 5* [1] **6**	11
8 Aug 87	SAY YOU REALLY WANT ME *MCA KIM 6* **29**	5
5 Dec 87	● ROCKIN' AROUND THE CHRISTMAS TREE *10 TEN 2* [2] **3**	7
14 May 88	HEY MISTER HEARTACHE *MCA KIM 7* **31**	5
16 Jul 88	● YOU CAME *MCA KIM 8*...................................**3**	11
1 Oct 88	● NEVER TRUST A STRANGER *MCA KIM 9* **7**	9
3 Dec 88	● FOUR LETTER WORD *MCA KIM 10* **6**	12
4 Mar 89	LOVE IN THE NATURAL WAY *MCA KIM 11*....................**32**	6
14 Apr 90	IT'S HERE *MCA KIM 12* **42**	4
16 Jun 90	TIME *MCA KIM 13*...**71**	3
15 Dec 90	I CAN'T SAY GOODBYE *MCA KIM 14* **51**	3
2 May 92	LOVE IS HOLY *MCA KIM 15*..................................**16**	6
27 Jun 92	HEART OVER MIND *MCA KIM 16* **34**	3
12 Sep 92	WHO DO YOU THINK YOU ARE *MCA KIM 17*..................**49**	3
10 Jul 93	IF I CAN'T HAVE YOU *MCA KIMTD 18* **12**	8
13 Nov 93	IN MY LIFE *MCA KIMTD 19*..................................**54**	1
14 Oct 95	BREAKIN' AWAY *MCA KIMTD 21* **43**	2
10 Feb 96	THIS I SWEAR *MCA KIMTD 22* **46**	1

[1] Kim Wilde and Junior [2] Mel and Kim

Mel was Mel Smith

Marty WILDE 242 Top 500
Early British rock 'n' roll singing idol, b. Reginald Smith, 15 Apr 1939, London. Although most of his best-sellers were cover versions (the normal practice at the time), he later penned hits for Lulu, Casuals, Status Quo and many for his daughter, Kim Wilde (117 WEEKS)

		pos/wks
11 Jul 58	● ENDLESS SLEEP *Philips PB 835*.............................**4**	14
6 Mar 59	● DONNA (re) *Philips PB 902*.................................**3**	18
5 Jun 59	● A TEENAGER IN LOVE *Philips PB 926*.......................**2**	17
25 Sep 59	● SEA OF LOVE *Philips PB 959*...............................**3**	12
11 Dec 59	● BAD BOY *Philips PB 972* **7**	8
10 Mar 60	JOHNNY ROCCO *Philips PB 1002*...........................**30**	4
19 May 60	THE FIGHT *Philips PB 1022* **47**	1
22 Dec 60	LITTLE GIRL *Philips PB 1078* **16**	9
26 Jan 61	● RUBBER BALL *Philips PB 1101* **9**	9
27 Jul 61	HIDE AND SEEK *Philips PB 1161*............................**47**	2
9 Nov 61	TOMORROW'S CLOWN *Philips PB 1191* **33**	5
24 May 62	JEZEBEL *Philips PB 1240* **19**	11
25 Oct 62	EVER SINCE YOU SAID GOODBYE *Philips 326546 BF* **31**	7

Matthew WILDER *US, male vocalist (11 WEEKS)*

		pos/wks
21 Jan 84	● BREAK MY STRIDE *Epic A 3908* **4**	11

WILDFLOWER – See APHRODITE featuring WILDFLOWER

WILDHEARTS *UK, male vocal / instrumental group (26 WEEKS)*

		pos/wks
20 Nov 93	TV TAN *Bronze YZ 784CD* **53**	2

19 Feb 94	CAFFEINE BOMB *Bronze YZ 794CD*	31	3
9 Jul 94	SUCKERPUNCH *Bronze YZ 828CD*	38	2
28 Jan 95	IF LIFE IS LIKE A LOVE BANK I WANT AN OVERDRAFT / GEORDIE IN WONDERLAND *East West YZ 874CD*	31	3
6 May 95	I WANNA GO WHERE THE PEOPLE GO *East West YZ 923CD*	16	3
29 Jul 95	JUST IN LUST *East West YZ 967CD*	28	2
20 Apr 96	SICK OF DRUGS *Round WILD 1CD*	14	3
29 Jun 96	RED LIGHT – GREEN LIGHT (EP) *Round WILD 2CD*	30	2
16 Aug 97	ANTHEM *Mushroom MUSH 6CD*	21	2
18 Oct 97	URGE *Mushroom MUSH 14CD*	26	2
12 Oct 02	VANILLA RADIO *Round / Snapper SMACD 048S*	26	2

Tracks on Red Light – Green Light (EP): Red Light – Green Light / Got It on Tuesday / Do Anything / The British All-American Homeboy Crowd

Jonathan WILKES *UK, male vocalist (2 WEEKS)* pos/wks

| 17 Mar 01 | JUST ANOTHER DAY *Innocent SINCD 25* | 24 | 2 |

Sue WILKINSON *UK, female vocalist (8 WEEKS)* pos/wks

| 2 Aug 80 | YOU GOTTA BE A HUSTLER IF YOU WANNA GET ON *Cheapskate CHEAP 2* | 25 | 8 |

WILL TO POWER *US, male / female vocal / instrumental duo – Bob Rosenberg and Suzi Carr (18 WEEKS)* pos/wks

| 7 Jan 89 ● | BABY I LOVE YOUR WAY – FREEBIRD *Epic 6530947* ▲ | 6 | 9 |
| 22 Dec 90 | I'M NOT IN LOVE *Epic 6565377* | 29 | 9 |

Alyson WILLIAMS *US, female vocalist (28 WEEKS)* pos/wks

4 Mar 89	SLEEP TALK *Def Jam 654656 7*	17	9
6 May 89	MY LOVE IS SO RAW *Def Jam 654898 7* [1]	34	5
19 Aug 89 ●	I NEED YOUR LOVIN' *Def Jam 655143 7*	8	11
18 Nov 89	I SECOND THAT EMOTION *Def Jam 655456 7* [2]	44	3

[1] Alyson Williams featuring Nikki D [2] Alyson Williams with Chuck Stanley

Andy WILLIAMS ⟨57⟩ Top 500

Leading MOR vocalist, who hosted a top-rated 1960s TV series, b. 3 Dec 1928, Iowa, US. He left the noted family act The Williams Brothers in 1951 and had an enviable portfolio of smooth UK and US hit singles and albums in the 1950s and 1960s. Had a surprise 1999 re-entry for 'Music to Watch Girls By' following its use in a TV car commercial (238 WEEKS) pos/wks

19 Apr 57 ★	BUTTERFLY (re) *London HLA 8399*	1	16
21 Jun 57	I LIKE YOUR KIND OF LOVE *London HLA 8437*	16	10
14 Jun 62	STRANGER ON THE SHORE *CBS AAG 103*	30	10
21 Mar 63 ●	CAN'T GET USED TO LOSING YOU *CBS AAG 138*	2	18
27 Feb 64	A FOOL NEVER LEARNS *CBS AAG 182*	40	4
16 Sep 65 ●	ALMOST THERE *CBS 201813*	2	17
24 Feb 66	MAY EACH DAY *CBS 202042*	19	8
22 Sep 66	IN THE ARMS OF LOVE *CBS 202300*	33	7
4 May 67	MUSIC TO WATCH GIRLS BY *CBS 2675*	33	6
2 Aug 67	MORE AND MORE *CBS 2886*	45	1
13 Mar 68 ●	CAN'T TAKE MY EYES OFF YOU *CBS 3298*	5	18
7 May 69	HAPPY HEART (re) *CBS 4062*	19	10
14 Mar 70 ●	CAN'T HELP FALLING IN LOVE *CBS 4818*	3	17
1 Aug 70	IT'S SO EASY (re) *CBS 5113*	13	14
21 Nov 70	HOME LOVIN' MAN *CBS 5267*	7	12
20 Mar 71 ●	(WHERE DO I BEGIN) LOVE STORY (re) *CBS 7020*	4	18
5 Aug 72	LOVE THEME FROM 'THE GODFATHER' (SPEAK SOFTLY LOVE) (2re) *CBS 8166*	42	9
8 Dec 73 ●	SOLITAIRE *CBS 1824*	4	18
18 May 74	GETTING OVER YOU *CBS 2181*	35	5
31 May 75	YOU LAY SO EASY ON MY MIND *CBS 3167*	32	7
6 Mar 76	THE OTHER SIDE OF ME *CBS 3903*	42	3
27 Mar 99 ●	MUSIC TO WATCH GIRLS BY (re-issue) *Columbia 6671322*	9	6
29 Jun 02	CAN'T TAKE MY EYES OFF YOU *Columbia 6721052* [1]	23	4

[1] Andy Williams and Denise Van Outen

Andy and David WILLIAMS *US, male vocal duo (5 WEEKS)* pos/wks

| 24 Mar 73 | I DON'T KNOW WHY (I JUST DO) *MCA MUS 1183* | 37 | 5 |

Do not see Andy Williams. This Andy is the nephew of the other Andy

Billy WILLIAMS *US, male vocalist, d. 17 Oct 1972 (9 WEEKS)* pos/wks

| 2 Aug 57 | I'M GONNA SIT RIGHT DOWN AND WRITE MYSELF A LETTER (re) *Vogue Coral Q 72266* | 22 | 9 |

Danny WILLIAMS ⟨492⟩ Top 500

Velvet-voiced, British-based easy-listening vocalist; b. 7 Jan 1942, South Africa. Johnny Mathis-styled singer who won the UK 'Moon River' battle was first seen on rock 'n' roll TV show 'Drumbeat'. Had US Top 10 hit with 1964 UK flop 'White on White' (74 WEEKS) pos/wks

25 May 61	WE WILL NEVER BE AS YOUNG AS THIS AGAIN *HMV POP 839*	44	3
6 Jul 61	THE MIRACLE OF YOU *HMV POP 885*	41	8
2 Nov 61 ★	MOON RIVER *HMV POP 932*	1	19
18 Jan 62	JEANNIE *HMV POP 968*	14	14
12 Apr 62 ●	THE WONDERFUL WORLD OF THE YOUNG *HMV POP 1002*	8	13
5 Jul 62	TEARS *HMV POP 1035*	22	7
28 Feb 63	MY OWN TRUE LOVE *HMV POP 1112*	45	3
30 Jul 77	DANCIN' EASY *Ensign ENY 3*	30	7

Deniece WILLIAMS *US, female vocalist – Deniece Chandler (59 WEEKS)* pos/wks

2 Apr 77 ★	FREE *CBS 4978*	1	10
30 Jul 77	THAT'S WHAT FRIENDS ARE FOR *CBS 5432*	8	11
12 Nov 77	BABY, BABY MY LOVE'S ALL FOR YOU *CBS 5779*	32	5
25 Mar 78 ●	TOO MUCH, TOO LITTLE, TOO LATE *CBS 6164* [1] ▲	3	14
29 Jul 78	YOU'RE ALL I NEED TO GET BY *CBS 6483* [1]	45	6
5 May 84 ●	LET'S HEAR IT FOR THE BOY (re) *CBS A 4319* ▲	2	13

[1] Johnny Mathis and Deniece Williams

Diana WILLIAMS *US, female vocalist (3 WEEKS)* pos/wks

| 25 Jul 81 | TEDDY BEAR'S LAST RIDE *Capitol CL 207* | 54 | 3 |

Don WILLIAMS *US, male vocalist (16 WEEKS)* pos/wks

| 19 Jun 76 | I RECALL A GYPSY WOMAN *ABC 4098* | 13 | 10 |
| 23 Oct 76 | YOU'RE MY BEST FRIEND *ABC 4144* | 35 | 6 |

Eric WILLIAMS – See QUEEN PEN; 2PAC

Freedom WILLIAMS *US, male rapper (31 WEEKS)* pos/wks

15 Dec 90 ●	GONNA MAKE YOU SWEAT (EVERYBODY DANCE NOW) *CBS 6564540* [1] ▲	3	12
30 Mar 91	HERE WE GO *Columbia 6567537* [1]	20	7
6 Jul 91 ●	THINGS THAT MAKE YOU GO HMMM... *Columbia 6566907* [1]	4	11
5 Jun 93	VOICE OF FREEDOM *Columbia 6593342*	62	1

[1] C & C Music Factory (featuring Freedom Williams)

Geoffrey WILLIAMS *UK, male vocalist (8 WEEKS)* pos/wks

11 Apr 92	IT'S NOT A LOVE THING *EMI EM 228*	63	2
22 Aug 92	SUMMER BREEZE *EMI EM 245*	56	3
18 Jan 97	DRIVE *Hands On CDHOR 11*	52	2
19 Apr 97	SEX LIFE *Hands On CDHOR 12*	71	1

Iris WILLIAMS *UK, female vocalist (8 WEEKS)* pos/wks

| 27 Oct 79 | HE WAS BEAUTIFUL (CAVATINA) (THE THEME FROM 'THE DEER HUNTER') *Columbia DB 9070* | 18 | 8 |

James WILLIAMS – See D TRAIN; Bob SINCLAR

John WILLIAMS *UK, male instrumentalist – guitar (11 WEEKS)* pos/wks

| 19 May 79 | CAVATINA *Cube BUG 80* | 13 | 11 |

John WILLIAMS *US, male orchestra leader (12 WEEKS)* pos/wks

| 18 Dec 82 | THEME FROM 'E.T.' (THE EXTRA-TERRESTRIAL) *MCA 800* | 17 | 10 |
| 14 Aug 93 | THEME FROM 'JURASSIC PARK' *MCA MCSTD 1927* | 45 | 2 |

Re-entries are listed as (re), (2re), (3re), etc which signifies that the hit re-entered the chart once, twice or three times, etc

Kenny WILLIAMS US, male vocalist (7 WEEKS)

		pos/wks	
19 Nov 77	(YOU'RE) FABULOUS BABE *Decca FR 13731*	35	7

Larry WILLIAMS US, male vocalist, d. 7 Jan 1980 (18 WEEKS)

		pos/wks	
20 Sep 57	SHORT FAT FANNIE *London HLN 8472*	21	8
17 Jan 58	BONY MORONIE *London HLU 8532*	11	10

Lenny WILLIAMS US, male vocalist (7 WEEKS)

		pos/wks	
5 Nov 77	SHOO DOO FU FU OOH! *ABC 4194*	38	4
16 Sep 78	YOU GOT ME BURNING *ABC 4228*	67	3

Mark WILLIAMS – See Karen BODDINGTON and Mark WILLIAMS

Mason WILLIAMS US, male instrumentalist – guitar (13 WEEKS)

		pos/wks	
28 Aug 68 ●	CLASSICAL GAS *Warner Bros. WB 7190*	9	13

Maurice WILLIAMS and the ZODIACS
US, male vocal group (9 WEEKS)

		pos/wks	
5 Jan 61	STAY *Top Rank JAR 526* ▲	14	9

Melanie WILLIAMS UK, female vocalist (21 WEEKS)

		pos/wks	
10 Apr 93 ●	AIN'T NO LOVE (AIN'T NO USE) *Rob's CDROB 9* [1]	3	11
9 Apr 94	ALL CRIED OUT *Columbia 6601872*	60	2
11 Jun 94	EVERYDAY THANG *Columbia 6604712*	38	3
17 Sep 94	NOT ENOUGH? *Columbia 6607752*	65	1
18 Feb 95	YOU ARE EVERYTHING *Columbia 6611755* [2]	28	4

[1] Sub Sub featuring Melanie Williams [2] Melanie Williams and Joe Roberts

Pharrell WILLIAMS – See N*E*R*D; Busta RHYMES; Britney SPEARS

Robbie WILLIAMS (66 | Top 500)

Former Take That teen idol who became a multi-award winning vocalist / songwriter and multi-millionaire after a UK record-breaking 2002 deal with EMI reportedly worth up to £80m, b. 13 Feb 1974, Stoke-on-Trent, UK. This energetic and humorous showman has won more Brits (13) than any other artist. Best-selling single: 'Angels' 828,000 (227 WEEKS)

		pos/wks	
10 Aug 96 ●	FREEDOM (re) *Chrysalis CDFREE 1*	2	14
26 Apr 97 ●	OLD BEFORE I DIE (2re) *Chrysalis CDCHS 5055*	2	11
26 Jul 97 ●	LAZY DAYS *Chrysalis CDCHS 5063*	8	5
27 Sep 97	SOUTH OF THE BORDER *Chrysalis CDCHS 5068*	14	4
13 Dec 97 ●	ANGELS (4re) *Chrysalis CDCHS 5072*	4	27
28 Mar 98 ●	LET ME ENTERTAIN YOU *Chrysalis CDCHS 5080*	3	12
19 Sep 98 ★	MILLENNIUM (re) *Chrysalis CDCHS 5099* ■	1	21
12 Dec 98 ●	NO REGRETS *Chrysalis CDCHS 5100*	4	13
27 Mar 99 ●	STRONG *Chrysalis CDCHS 5107*	4	9
20 Nov 99 ★	SHE'S THE ONE / IT'S ONLY US (re) *Chrysalis CDCHS 5112* ■	1	20
12 Aug 00 ★	ROCK DJ (re) *Chrysalis CDCHS 5118* ■	1	20
21 Oct 00 ●	KIDS (2re) *Chrysalis CHCHS 5119* [1]	2	19
23 Dec 00 ●	SUPREME *Chrysalis CDCHS 5120*	4	10
24 Mar 01 ●	LET LOVE BE YOUR ENERGY (re) *Chrysalis CDCHS 5124*	10	11
21 Jul 01 ★	ETERNITY / THE ROAD TO MANDALAY *Chrysalis CDCHS 5126* ■	1	16
22 Dec 01 ★	SOMETHIN' STUPID *Chrysalis CDCHS 5132* [2] ■	1	12
14 Dec 02 ●	FEEL *Chrysalis CDCHS 5150*	4	3+

[1] Robbie Williams / Kylie Minogue [2] Robbie Williams and Nicole Kidman

'Angels' re-entered the chart in Jan, Feb and Mar 1999 and again in Jan 2000. 'Millennium' re-entered in Jan 2000

Saul WILLIAMS – See KRUST

Vanessa WILLIAMS US, female vocalist (24 WEEKS)

		pos/wks	
20 Aug 88	THE RIGHT STUFF *Wing WING 3*	71	1
25 Mar 89	DREAMIN' *Wing WING 4*	74	2
19 Aug 89	THE RIGHT STUFF (re-mix) *Wing WINR 3*	62	2
21 Mar 92 ●	SAVE THE BEST FOR LAST *Polydor PO 192* ▲	3	11
8 Apr 95	THE SWEETEST DAYS *Mercury MERCD 422*	41	2
8 Jul 95	THE WAY THAT YOU LOVE *Mercury MERCD 439*	52	1
18 Sep 95	COLOURS OF THE WIND *Walt Disney WD 7677CD*	21	5

Vesta WILLIAMS US, female vocalist (13 WEEKS)

		pos/wks	
20 Dec 86	ONCE BITTEN TWICE SHY *A&M AM 362*	14	13

Wendell WILLIAMS US, male rapper (6 WEEKS)

		pos/wks	
6 Oct 90	EVERYBODY (RAP) *Deconstruction PB 44701* [1]	30	4
18 May 91	SO GROOVY *Deconstruction PB 44567*	74	2

[1] Criminal Element Orchestra and Wendell Williams

WILLING SINNERS – See Marc ALMOND

Bruce WILLIS US, male actor / vocalist (30 WEEKS)

		pos/wks	
7 Mar 87 ●	RESPECT YOURSELF *Motown ZB 41117*	7	10
30 May 87 ●	UNDER THE BOARDWALK *Motown ZB 41349*	2	15
12 Sep 87	SECRET AGENT MAN – JAMES BOND IS BACK *Motown ZB 41437*	43	4
23 Jan 88	COMIN' RIGHT UP *Motown ZB 41453*	73	1

Chris WILLIS – David GUETTA featuring Chris WILLS

Chill WILLS – See LAUREL and HARDY with the AVALON BOYS featuring Chill WILLS

Viola WILLS US, female vocalist (16 WEEKS)

		pos/wks	
6 Oct 79 ●	GONNA GET ALONG WITHOUT YOU NOW *Ariola / Hansa AHA 546*	8	10
15 Mar 86	BOTH SIDES NOW / DARE TO DREAM *Streetwave KHAN 66*	35	6

Al WILSON US, male vocalist (5 WEEKS)

		pos/wks	
23 Aug 75	THE SNAKE *Bell 1436*	41	5

Charlie WILSON – See SNOOP DOGG; GAP BAND

Dooley WILSON US, male vocalist, d. 30 May 1953 (9 WEEKS)

		pos/wks	
3 Dec 77	AS TIME GOES BY *United Artists UP 36331*	15	9

Disc has credit: 'With the voices of Humphrey Bogart and Ingrid Bergman'

Jackie WILSON (323 | Top 500)
One of R&B music's greatest stage performers and most distinctive vocalists, b. 9 Jun 1934, Detroit, US, d. 21 Jan 1984 (after eight years in a semi-comatose state). He influenced Elvis Presley, Michael Jackson and Prince. 'Reet Petite' took a record 29 years, 42 days to reach the top (97 WEEKS)

		pos/wks	
15 Nov 57 ●	REET PETITE (THE SWEETEST GIRL IN TOWN) *Coral Q 72290*	6	14
14 Mar 58	TO BE LOVED *Coral Q 72306*	23	8
15 Sep 60	(YOU WERE MADE FOR) ALL MY LOVE (re) *Coral Q 72407*	33	7
22 Dec 60	ALONE AT LAST *Coral Q 72412*	50	1
14 May 69	(YOUR LOVE KEEPS LIFTING ME) HIGHER AND HIGHER *MCA BAG 2*	11	11
29 Jul 72 ●	I GET THE SWEETEST FEELING *MCA MU 1160*	9	13
3 May 75	I GET THE SWEETEST FEELING / (YOUR LOVE KEEPS LIFTING ME) HIGHER AND HIGHER (re-issue) *Brunswick BR 18*	25	8
29 Nov 86 ★	REET PETITE (THE SWEETEST GIRL IN TOWN) (re-issue) *SMP SKM 3*	1	17
28 Feb 87 ●	I GET THE SWEETEST FEELING (2nd re-issue) *SMP SKM 1*	3	11
4 Jul 87	(YOUR LOVE KEEPS LIFTING ME) HIGHER AND HIGHER (2nd re-issue) *SMP SKM 10*	15	7

'Higher and Higher' was not listed together with 'I Get the Sweetest Feeling' on Brunswick until 17 May 1975

Mari WILSON UK, female vocalist (34 WEEKS)

		pos/wks	
6 Mar 82	BEAT THE BEAT *Compact PINK 2*	59	3
8 May 82	BABY IT'S TRUE *Compact PINK 3*	42	6
11 Sep 82 ●	JUST WHAT I ALWAYS WANTED *Compact PINK 4*	8	10
13 Nov 82	(BEWARE) BOYFRIEND *Compact PINK 5*	51	4
19 Mar 83	CRY ME A RIVER *Compact PINK 6*	27	7
11 Jun 83	WONDERFUL *Compact PINK 7*	47	4

Meri WILSON US, female vocalist, d. 28 Dec 2002 (10 WEEKS)

		pos/wks	
27 Aug 77 ●	TELEPHONE MAN *Pye International 7N 25747*	6	10

Mike 'Hitman' WILSON *US, male producer (1 WEEK)*   pos/wks
22 Sep 90   **ANOTHER SLEEPLESS NIGHT** *Arista 113506*..............................**74** 1

Precious WILSON – *See ERUPTION; MESSIAH*

Tom WILSON *UK, male producer (4 WEEKS)*   pos/wks
2 Dec 95   **TECHNOCAT** *Pukka CDPUKKA 4* [1] **33** 3
16 Mar 96   **LET YOUR BODY GO** *Clubscene DCSRT 050* **60** 1

[1] Technocat featuring Tom Wilson

Victoria WILSON JAMES *US, female vocalist (1 WEEK)*   pos/wks
9 Aug 97   **REACH 4 THE MELODY** *Sony S3 VWJCD1*...............................**72** 1

WILSON PHILLIPS *US, female vocal group (33 WEEKS)*   pos/wks
26 May 90 ● **HOLD ON** *SBK SBK 6* ▲ **6** 12
18 Aug 90   **RELEASE ME** *SBK SBK 11* ▲ **36** 5
10 Nov 90   **IMPULSIVE** *SBK SBK 16* **42** 3
11 May 91   **YOU'RE IN LOVE** *SBK SBK 25* ▲ **29** 5
23 May 92   **YOU WON'T SEE ME CRY** *SBK SBK 34* **18** 5
22 Aug 92   **GIVE IT UP** *SBK SBK 36* **36** 3

WILT *Ireland, male vocal / instrumental group (3 WEEKS)*   pos/wks
8 Apr 00   **RADIO DISCO** *Mushroom MUSH 71CDS* **56** 1
8 Jul 00   **OPEN ARMS** *Mushroom MUSH 75CDS* **59** 1
13 Jul 02   **DISTORTION** *Mushroom MUSH 103CDS* **66** 1

Chris WILTSHIRE – *See CLASS ACTION featuring Chris WILTSHIRE*

WIMBLEDON CHORAL SOCIETY *UK, choral group (8 WEEKS)*   pos/wks
4 Jul 98   **WORLD CUP '98 – PAVANE** *Telstar CDSTAS 2979*............**20** 5
12 Dec 98   **IF – READ TO FAURE'S 'PAVANE'**
           BBC Worldwide WMSS60062 [1] **45** 3

[1] Des Lynam featuring Wimbledon Choral Society

WIN *UK, male vocal / instrumental group (3 WEEKS)*   pos/wks
4 Apr 87   **SUPER POPOID GROOVE** *Swamplands LON 128*...............**63** 3

BEST CHART START

■ All of these acts burst on to the scene with a run of hits inside the Top 10

Act	Run of Top 10s from chart debut
1. BOYZONE	16
2. WESTLIFE	13
3. KYLIE MINOGUE	13
4. GARY GLITTER	12
5. FIVE	11
6. SPICE GIRLS	10
7. BAY CITY ROLLERS	10
8. EMINEM	9
9. BONEY M	9
10. S CLUB 7	8

Ties split by most No.1s, No.2s etc

WINANS *US, male vocal group (1 WEEK)*   pos/wks
30 Nov 85   **LET MY PEOPLE GO (PART 1)** *Qwest W 8874* **71** 1

BeBe WINANS – *See ETERNAL*

CeCe WINANS – *See Whitney HOUSTON*

Mario WINANS – *See PUFF DADDY*

WINDJAMMER
US, male vocal / instrumental group (12 WEEKS)   pos/wks
30 Jun 84   **TOSSING AND TURNING** *MCA MCA 897* **18** 12

Rose WINDROSS – *See SOUL II SOUL*

Barbara WINDSOR and Mike REID
UK, female / male actor / vocal duo (2 WEEKS)   pos/wks
24 Apr 99   **THE MORE I SEE YOU** *Telstar CDSTAS 3049*.....................**46** 2

WING AND A PRAYER FIFE AND DRUM CORPS
US, male / female vocal / instrumental group (7 WEEKS)   pos/wks
24 Jan 76   **BABY FACE** *Atlantic K 10705* **12** 7

WINGER
US, male vocal / instrumental group (3 WEEKS)   pos/wks
19 Jan 91   **MILES AWAY** *Atlantic A 7802* **56** 3

Pete WINGFIELD
UK, male vocalist / instrumentalist – piano (7 WEEKS)   pos/wks
28 Jun 75 ● **EIGHTEEN WITH A BULLET** *Island WIP 6231* **7** 7

WINGS – *See Paul McCARTNEY*

Josh WINK
US, male producer – Joshua Winkelman (29 WEEKS)   pos/wks
6 May 95   **DON'T LAUGH** *XL XLS 62CD* [1] **38** 2
21 Oct 95 ● **HIGHER STATE OF CONSCIOUSNESS (re)**
           Manifesto FESCD 3 ....**8** 12
2 Mar 96   **HYPNOTIZIN'** *XL XLS 71CD* [1] **35** 2
27 Jul 96 ● **HIGHER STATE OF CONSCIOUSNESS (re-mix)**
           Manifesto FESCD 9 [1] **7** 10
12 Aug 00   **HOW'S YOUR EVENING SO FAR**
           ffrr FCD 384 [2] **23** 3

[1] Winx [2] Josh Wink and Lil' Louis

See also SIZE 9

Kate WINSLET
UK, female actor / vocalist (14 WEEKS)   pos/wks
8 Dec 01 ● **WHAT IF** *EMI / Liberty CDKATE 001* **6** 14

Edgar WINTER GROUP
US, male instrumental group (9 WEEKS)   pos/wks
26 May 73   **FRANKENSTEIN** *Epic EPC 1440* ▲ **18** 9

Ruby WINTERS *US, female vocalist (35 WEEKS)*   pos/wks
5 Nov 77 ● **I WILL!** *Creole CR 141* **4** 13
29 Apr 78   **COME TO ME** *Creole CR 153* **11** 12
26 Aug 78   **I WON'T MENTION IT AGAIN** *Creole CR 160*.................**45** 5
16 Jun 79   **BABY LAY DOWN** *Creole CR 171* **43** 5

Steve WINWOOD *UK, male vocalist (33 WEEKS)*   pos/wks
17 Jan 81   **WHILE YOU SEE A CHANCE** *Island WIP 6655*.............**45** 5
9 Oct 82   **VALERIE** *Island WIP 6818*..**51** 4
28 Jun 86   **HIGHER LOVE** *Island IS 288* ▲ **13** 9
13 Sep 86   **FREEDOM OVERSPILL** *Island IS 294* **69** 1
24 Jan 87   **BACK IN THE HIGH LIFE AGAIN** *Island IS 303* **53** 2

		pos/wks	
19 Sep 87	VALERIE (re-mix) *Island IS 336*	19	8
11 Jun 88	ROLL WITH IT *Virgin VS 1085* ▲	53	4

See also Spencer DAVIS GROUP

WINX – *See Josh WINK*

WIRE *UK, male vocal / instrumental group (4 WEEKS)*

		pos/wks	
27 Jan 79	OUTDOOR MINER *Harvest HAR 5172*	51	3
13 May 89	EARDRUM BUZZ *Mute MUTE 87*	68	1

WIRED *Holland / Finland, male production / instrumental duo (1 WK)* pos/wks

		pos/wks	
20 Feb 99	TRANSONIC *Future Groove CDFGR 001*	73	1

WIRELESS *UK, male vocal / instrumental group (2 WEEKS)*

		pos/wks	
28 Jun 97	I NEED YOU *Chrysalis CDCHS 5059*	68	1
7 Feb 98	IN LOVE WITH THE FAMILIAR *Chrysalis CDCHS 5075*	69	1

Norman WISDOM *UK, male actor / vocalist (20 WEEKS)*

		pos/wks	
19 Feb 54 ●	DON'T LAUGH AT ME ('CAUSE I'M A FOOL)		
	Columbia DB 3133	3	15
15 Mar 57	THE WISDOM OF A FOOL *Columbia DB 3903*	13	5

WISDOME *Italy, male / female production / vocal group (2 WEEKS)* pos/wks

		pos/wks	
11 Mar 00	OFF THE WALL *Positiva CDTIV 125*	33	2

WISEGUYS *UK, male DJ / producer – Theo Keating (13 WEEKS)*

		pos/wks	
6 Jun 98	OOH LA LA *Wall of Sound WALLD 038*	55	1
12 Sep 98	START THE COMMOTION *Wall of Sound WALLD 044*	66	1
5 Jun 99 ●	OOH LA LA (re-issue) *Wall of Sound WALLD 038X*	2	10
11 Sep 99	START THE COMMOTION (re-issue)		
	Wall of Sound WALLD 059	47	1

Bill WITHERS *US, male vocalist (29 WEEKS)*

		pos/wks	
12 Aug 72	LEAN ON ME *A&M AMS 7004* ▲	18	9
14 Jan 78 ●	LOVELY DAY *CBS 5773*	7	8
25 May 85	OH YEAH! *CBS 6 154*	60	3
10 Sep 88 ●	LOVELY DAY (re-mix) *CBS 6530017*	4	9

See also Grover WASHINGTON Jr

WITNESS *UK, male vocal / instrumental group (2 WEEKS)*

		pos/wks	
13 Mar 99	SCARS *Island CID 740*	71	1
19 Jun 99	AUDITION *Island CID 749*	71	1

WIX – *See SPIRO and WIX*

WIZZARD `454` `Top 500` *Early 1970s chart champs led by extrovert Move and ELO frontman Roy Wood, b. 8 Nov 1946, Birmingham, UK. Big-budget Phil Spector-styled recordings are classics of their era. Wood also had several simultaneous solo successes (77 WEEKS)* pos/wks

		pos/wks	
9 Dec 72 ●	BALL PARK INCIDENT *Harvest HAR 5062*	6	12
21 Apr 73 ★	SEE MY BABY JIVE *Harvest HAR 5070* [1]	1	17
1 Sep 73 ★	ANGEL FINGERS (A TEEN BALLAD) *Harvest HAR 5076* [2]	1	10
8 Dec 73 ●	I WISH IT COULD BE CHRISTMAS EVERYDAY		
	Harvest HAR 5079 [3]	4	9
27 Apr 74 ●	ROCK 'N' ROLL WINTER (LOONY'S TUNE)		
	Warner Bros. K16497	6	7
10 Aug 74	THIS IS THE STORY OF MY LOVE (BABY)		
	Warner Bros. K 16434	34	4
21 Dec 74 ●	ARE YOU READY TO ROCK *Warner Bros. K 16357*	8	10
19 Dec 81	I WISH IT COULD BE CHRISTMAS EVERYDAY		
	(re) *Harvest HAR 5173* [3]	23	8

[1] Vocal backing by The Suedettes [2] Vocal backing: The Suedettes and The Bleach Boys [3] Wizzard featuring vocal backing by the Suedettes plus the Stockland Green Bilateral School First Year Choir with additional noises by Miss Snob and Class 3C

The 'I Wish It Could Be Christmas Everyday' re-issue debuted and made No.41 in Dec 1981 before re-entering and peaking at No.23 in Dec 1984

Jah WOBBLE'S INVADERS of the HEART *UK, male vocalist / multi-instrumentalist – John Wardle (10 WEEKS)*

		pos/wks	
1 Feb 92	VISIONS OF YOU *Oval OVAL 103*	35	5
30 Apr 94	BECOMING MORE LIKE GOD *Island CID 571*	36	2
25 Jun 94	THE SUN DOES RISE *Island CIDX 587*	41	3

First hit features the uncredited vocals of Sinead O'Connor

See also P.I.L.

Terry WOGAN *Ireland, male vocalist (5 WEEKS)*

		pos/wks	
7 Jan 78	THE FLORAL DANCE *Philips 6006 592*	21	5

WOLF – *See TROGGS*

WOLFSBANE *UK, male vocal / instrumental group (1 WEEK)*

		pos/wks	
5 Oct 91	EZY *Def American DEFA 11*	68	1

Bobby WOMACK *US, male vocalist (21 WEEKS)*

		pos/wks	
16 Jun 84	TELL ME WHY *Motown TMG 1339*	60	3
5 Oct 85	I WISH HE DIDN'T TRUST ME SO MUCH		
	MCA MCA 994	64	2
26 Sep 87	SO THE STORY GOES *Chrysalis LIB 3* [1]	34	8
7 Nov 87	LIVING IN A BOX *MCA MCA 1210*	70	2
3 Apr 93	I'M BACK FOR MORE *Dome CDDOME 1002* [2]	27	5
13 May 95	IT'S A MAN'S MAN'S MAN'S WORLD		
	Pulse 8 CDLOSE 89 [3]	73	1

[1] Living in a Box featuring Bobby Womack [2] Lulu and Bobby Womack [3] Jeanie Tracy and Bobby Womack

See also Wilton FELDER

Lee Ann WOMACK *US, female vocalist (2 WEEKS)*

		pos/wks	
9 Jun 01	I HOPE YOU DANCE *MCA Nashville MCSTD 40254*	40	2

WOMACK and WOMACK *US, male / female vocal duo – Linda and Cecil Womack (51 WEEKS)* pos/wks

		pos/wks	
28 Apr 84	LOVE WARS *Elektra E 9799*	14	10
30 Jun 84	BABY I'M SCARED OF YOU *Elektra E 9733*	72	2
6 Dec 86	SOUL LOVE – SOUL MAN *Manhattan MT 16*	58	6
6 Aug 88 ●	TEARDROPS *Fourth & Broadway BRW 101*	3	17
12 Nov 88	LIFE'S JUST A BALLGAME		
	Fourth & Broadway BRW 116	32	5
25 Feb 89	CELEBRATE THE WORLD		
	Fourth & Broadway BRW 125	19	8
5 Feb 94	SECRET STAR *Warner Bros. W 0222CD* [1]	46	3

[1] House of Zekkariyas aka Womack and Womack

WOMBLES `319` `Top 500` *Furriest (and possibly the tidiest) act in the Top 500 are natives of Wimbledon Common, London, and come under the musical guidance of songwriter and producer Mike Batt, b. 6 Feb 1950, Southampton, UK . Successful chart career based on BBC TV series appearances (98 WEEKS)* pos/wks

		pos/wks	
26 Jan 74 ●	THE WOMBLING SONG *CBS 1794*	4	23
6 Apr 74 ●	REMEMBER YOU'RE A WOMBLE *CBS 2241*	3	16
22 Jun 74 ●	BANANA ROCK *CBS 2465*	9	13
12 Oct 74	MINUETTO ALLEGRETTO *CBS 2710*	16	9
7 Dec 74 ●	WOMBLING MERRY CHRISTMAS *CBS 2842*	2	8
10 May 75	WOMBLING WHITE TIE AND TAILS (FOXTROT) *CBS 3266*	22	7
9 Aug 75	SUPER WOMBLE *CBS 3480*	20	6
13 Dec 75	LET'S WOMBLE TO THE PARTY TONIGHT *CBS 3794*	34	5
21 Mar 98	REMEMBER YOU'RE A WOMBLE (re-issue)		
	Columbia 6656202	13	5
13 Jun 98	THE WOMBLING SONG (UNDERGROUND OVERGROUND)		
	(re-issue) *Columbia 6660412*	27	3
30 Dec 00	I WISH IT COULD BE A WOMBLING MERRY CHRISTMAS		
	EVERYDAY *Dramatico DRAMCDS 0001* [1]	22	3

[1] Wombles with Roy Wood

Stevie WONDER `14` `Top 500` Multi-award-winner born Steveland
*Judkins, 13 May 1950, Michigan, is one of the most successful singer /
songwriters of all time. The youngest artist to top the US singles and album
chart (aged 13) also recorded Motown's biggest UK seller, 'I Just Called to
Say I Love You'. This very popular live performer has recorded with many of
the biggest names in music, and has had his songs sung and sampled by
countless acts. No one has amassed more No.1 US R&B hits than the blind
entertainer who helped to turn Martin Luther King's birthday into a US
holiday, and whose charitable work is legendary. Best-selling single:
'I Just Called to Say I Love You' 1,775,000 (415 WEEKS)* pos/wks

3 Feb 66	UPTIGHT (EVERYTHING'S ALRIGHT)		
	Tamla Motown TMG 545	14	10
18 Aug 66	BLOWIN' IN THE WIND *Tamla Motown TMG 570*	36	5
5 Jan 67	A PLACE IN THE SUN *Tamla Motown TMG 588*	20	5
26 Jul 67 ●	I WAS MADE TO LOVE HER *Tamla Motown TMG 613*	5	15
25 Oct 67	I'M WONDERING *Tamla Motown TMG 626*	22	8
8 May 68	SHOO BE DOO BE DOO DA DAY *Tamla Motown TMG 653*	46	4
18 Dec 68 ●	FOR ONCE IN MY LIFE *Tamla Motown TMG 679*	3	13
19 Mar 69	I DON'T KNOW WHY (I LOVE YOU) (re)		
	Tamla Motown TMG 690	14	11
16 Jul 69 ●	MY CHERIE AMOUR *Tamla Motown TMG 690*	4	15
15 Nov 69 ●	YESTER-ME, YESTER-YOU, YESTERDAY		
	Tamla Motown TMG 717	2	13
28 Mar 70 ●	NEVER HAD A DREAM COME TRUE		
	Tamla Motown TMG 731	6	12
18 Jul 70	SIGNED SEALED DELIVERED I'M YOURS (re)		
	Tamla Motown TMG 744	15	10
21 Nov 70	HEAVEN HELP US ALL *Tamla Motown TMG 757*	29	11
15 May 71	WE CAN WORK IT OUT *Tamla Motown TMG 772*	27	7
22 Jan 72	IF YOU REALLY LOVE ME *Tamla Motown TMG 798*	20	7
3 Feb 73	SUPERSTITION *Tamla Motown TMG 841* ▲	11	9
19 May 73 ●	YOU ARE THE SUNSHINE OF MY LIFE		
	Tamla Motown TMG 852 ▲	7	11
13 Oct 73	HIGHER GROUND *Tamla Motown TMG 869*	29	5
12 Jan 74	LIVING FOR THE CITY *Tamla Motown TMG 881*	15	9
13 Apr 74 ●	HE'S MISSTRA KNOW IT ALL		
	Tamla Motown TMG 892	10	9
19 Oct 74	YOU HAVEN'T DONE NOTHIN'		
	Tamla Motown TMG 921 ▲	30	5
11 Jan 75	BOOGIE ON REGGAE WOMAN *Tamla Motown TMG 928*	12	8
18 Dec 76 ●	I WISH *Motown TMG 1054* ▲	5	10
9 Apr 77 ●	SIR DUKE *Motown TMG 1068* ▲	2	9
10 Sep 77	ANOTHER STAR *Motown TMG 1083*	29	5
24 Feb 79	POPS, WE LOVE YOU *Motown TMG 1136* `1`	66	5
24 Nov 79	SEND ONE YOUR LOVE *Motown TMG 1149*	52	3
26 Jan 80	BLACK ORCHID *Motown TMG 1173*	63	3
29 Mar 80	OUTSIDE MY WINDOW *Motown TMG 1179*	52	4
13 Sep 80 ●	MASTERBLASTER (JAMMIN') *Motown TMG 1204*	2	10
27 Dec 80 ●	I AIN'T GONNA STAND FOR IT *Motown TMG 1215*	10	10
7 Mar 81 ●	LATELY *Motown TMG 1226*	3	13
25 Jul 81 ●	HAPPY BIRTHDAY *Motown TMG 1235*	2	11
23 Jan 82	THAT GIRL *Motown TMG 1254*	39	6
10 Apr 82 ★	EBONY AND IVORY *Parlophone R 6054* `2` ▲	1	10
5 Jun 82 ●	DO I DO *Motown TMG 1269*	10	7
25 Sep 82	RIBBON IN THE SKY *Motown TMG 1280*	45	4
25 Aug 84 ★	I JUST CALLED TO SAY I LOVE YOU (re)		
	Motown TMG 1349 ◆ ▲	1	26
1 Dec 84	LOVE LIGHT IN FLIGHT *Motown TMG 1364*	44	5
29 Dec 84	DON'T DRIVE DRUNK (re) *Motown TMG 1372*	62	3
7 Sep 85 ●	PART-TIME LOVER *Motown ZB 40351* ▲	3	12
9 Nov 85	THAT'S WHAT FRIENDS ARE FOR		
	Arista ARIST 638 `3` ▲	16	9
23 Nov 85	GO HOME *Motown ZB 40501*	67	2
8 Mar 86	OVERJOYED *Motown ZB 40567*	17	8
17 Jan 87	STRANGER ON THE SHORE OF LOVE *Motown WOND 2*	55	3
31 Oct 87	SKELETONS *Motown ZB 41439*	59	3
28 May 88	GET IT *Motown ZB 41883* `4`	37	4
6 Aug 88 ●	MY LOVE *CBS JULIO 2* `5`	5	11
20 May 89	FREE *Motown ZB 42855*	49	5
12 Oct 91	FUN DAY *Motown ZB 44957*	63	1
25 Feb 95	FOR YOUR LOVE *Motown TMGCD 1437*	23	4
22 Jul 95	TOMORROW ROBINS WILL SING *Motown 8603732*	71	1
19 Jul 97 ●	HOW COME, HOW LONG *Epic 6646202* `6`	10	5
31 Oct 98	TRUE TO YOUR HEART *Motown 8608832* `7`	51	1

`1` Diana Ross, Marvin Gaye, Smokey Robinson and Stevie Wonder `2` Paul
McCartney with Stevie Wonder `3` Dionne Warwick and Friends featuring Elton
John, Stevie Wonder and Gladys Knight `4` Stevie Wonder and Michael Jackson
`5` Julio Iglesias featuring Stevie Wonder `6` Babyface featuring Stevie Wonder
`7` 98 Degrees featuring Stevie Wonder

*'You Haven't Done Nothin'' included an additional credit on the label: 'Doo Doo
Wopssss by The Jackson 5'. 'I Just Called to Say I Love You' re-entered in Dec 1985*

Wayne WONDER – See SHAGGY

WONDER DOG *Germany, canine vocalist – Harry Thumann (7 WKS)* pos/wks

21 Aug 82	RUFF MIX *Flip FLIP 001*	31	7

WONDER STUFF *UK, male vocal / instrumental group (66 WKS)* pos/wks

30 Apr 88	GIVE GIVE GIVE ME MORE MORE MORE *Polydor GONE 3*	72	2
16 Jul 88	A WISH AWAY *Polydor GONE 4*	43	5
24 Sep 88	IT'S YER MONEY I'M AFTER BABY *Polydor GONE 5*	40	3
11 Mar 89	WHO WANTS TO BE THE DISCO KING? *Polydor GONE 6*	28	3
23 Sep 89	DON'T LET ME DOWN GENTLY *Polydor GONE 7*	19	4
11 Nov 89	GOLDEN GREEN / GET TOGETHER *Polydor GONE 8*	33	3
12 May 90	CIRCLESQUARE *Polydor GONE 10*	20	4
13 Apr 91 ●	THE SIZE OF A COW *Polydor GONE 11*	5	7
25 May 91	CAUGHT IN MY SHADOW *Polydor GONE 12*	18	3
7 Sep 91	SLEEP ALONE *Polydor GONE 13*	43	2
26 Oct 91 ★	DIZZY *Sense SIGH 712* `1`	1	12
25 Jan 92 ●	WELCOME TO THE CHEAP SEATS (EP) *Polydor GONE 14*	8	5
25 Sep 93 ●	ON THE ROPES (EP) *Polydor GONCD 15*	10	4
27 Nov 93	FULL OF LIFE (HAPPY NOW) *Polydor GONCD 16*	28	3
26 Mar 94	HOT LOVE NOW! *Polydor GONCD 17*	19	3
10 Sep 94	UNBEARABLE *Polydor GONCD 18*	16	3

`1` Vic Reeves and the Wonder Stuff

*Tracks on Welcome to the Cheap Seats (EP): Welcome to the Cheap Seats / Me, My
Mom, My Dad and My Brother / Will the Circle Be Unbroken / That's Entertainment.
Tracks on On the Ropes (EP): On the Ropes / Professional Disturber of the Peace /
Hank and John / Whites. Tracks on Hot Love Now! (EP): I Think I Must've Had
Something Really Useful to Say / Room 512, All the News That's Fit to Print*

WONDERS *US, male vocal / instrumental group (3 WEEKS)* pos/wks

22 Feb 97	THAT THING YOU DO! *Play-Tone 6640552*	22	3

WONDRESS – See MANTRONIX

Brenton WOOD *US, male vocalist – Alfred Smith (14 WEEKS)* pos/wks

27 Dec 67 ●	GIMME LITTLE SIGN *Liberty LBF 15021*	8	14

Roy WOOD *UK, male vocalist /*
multi-instrumentalist – Ulysses Adrian Wood (44 WEEKS) pos/wks

11 Aug 73 ●	DEAR ELAINE *Harvest HAR 5074*	18	8
1 Dec 73 ●	FOREVER *Harvest HAR 5078*	8	13
15 Jun 74	GOIN' DOWN THE ROAD *Harvest HAR 5083*	13	7
31 May 75	OH WHAT A SHAME *Jet 754*	13	7
22 Nov 86	WATERLOO *IRS IRM 125* `1`	45	4
23 Dec 95	I WISH IT COULD BE CHRISTMAS EVERYDAY		
	Woody WOODY 001CD `2`	59	2
30 Dec 00	I WISH IT COULD BE A WOMBLING MERRY CHRISTMAS		
	EVERYDAY *Dramatico DRAMCDS 0001* `3`	22	3

`1` Doctor and the Medics featuring Roy Wood `2` Roy Wood Big Band `3` Wombles
with Roy Wood

See also WIZZARD; ELECTRIC LIGHT ORCHESTRA; MOVE

WOODENTOPS *UK, male vocal / instrumental group (1 WEEK)* pos/wks

11 Oct 86	EVERYDAY LIVING *Rough Trade RT 178*	72	1

Marcella WOODS – See Matt DAREY; LIQUID STATE featuring Marcella WOODS;
MELT featuring LITTLE MS MARCIE

Re-entries are listed as (re), (2re), (3re), etc which signifies that the hit re-entered the chart once, twice or three times, etc

Edward WOODWARD UK, male actor / vocalist (2 WEEKS)

			pos/wks
16 Jan 71	THE WAY YOU LOOK TONIGHT (re) DJM DJS 232	42	2

WOOKIE UK, male producer / vocalist – Jason Chue (11 WEEKS)

			pos/wks
3 Jun 00	WHAT'S GOING ON Soul II Soul S2SCD 001	45	1
12 Aug 00 ●	BATTLE Soul II Soul / Pias S2SPCD001 [1]	10	7
12 May 01	BACK UP (TO ME) Soul II Soul S2SPCD 003 [1]	38	3

[1] Wookie featuring Lain

Sheb WOOLEY US, male vocalist (8 WEEKS)

			pos/wks
20 Jun 58	THE PURPLE PEOPLE EATER MGM 981 ▲	12	8

WOOLPACKERS UK, male vocal group (24 WEEKS)

			pos/wks
16 Nov 96 ●	HILLBILLY ROCK HILLBILLY ROLL RCA 74321425412	5	14
29 Nov 97	LINE DANCE PARTY RCA 74321512262	25	10

WORKING WEEK
UK, male / female vocal / instrumental group (2 WEEKS)

			pos/wks
9 Jun 84	VENCEREMOS – WE WILL WIN Virgin VS 684	64	2

WORLD – See LIL' LOUIS

WORLD OF TWIST
UK, male / female vocal / instrumental group (12 WEEKS)

			pos/wks
24 Nov 90	THE STORM (re) Circa YR 55	42	5
23 Mar 91	SONS OF THE STAGE Circa YR 62	47	3
12 Oct 91	SWEETS Circa YR 72	58	2
22 Feb 92	SHE'S A RAINBOW Circa YR 82	62	2

WORLD PARTY
UK / Ireland, male vocal / instrumental group (29 WEEKS)

			pos/wks
14 Feb 87	SHIP OF FOOLS Ensign ENY 606	42	6
16 Jun 90	MESSAGE IN THE BOX Ensign ENY 631	39	6
15 Sep 90	WAY DOWN NOW Ensign ENY 634	66	2
18 May 91	THANK YOU WORLD Ensign ENY 643	68	1
10 Apr 93	IS IT LIKE TODAY Ensign CDENY 658	19	6
10 Jul 93	GIVE IT ALL AWAY Ensign CDENY 659	43	3
2 Oct 93	ALL I GAVE Ensign CDENYS 660	37	3
7 Jun 97	BEAUTIFUL DREAM Chrysalis CDCHS 5053	31	2

WORLD PREMIERE
US, male vocal / instrumental group (4 WEEKS)

			pos/wks
28 Jan 84	SHARE THE NIGHT Epic A 4133	64	4

WORLD WARRIOR UK, male producer – Simon Harris (1 WEEK)

			pos/wks
16 Apr 94	STREET FIGHTER II Living Beat LBECD 27	70	1

See also Simon HARRIS

WORLDS APART UK, male vocal group (17 WEEKS)

			pos/wks
27 Mar 93	HEAVEN MUST BE MISSING AN ANGEL Arista 74321139362	29	3
3 Jul 93	WONDERFUL WORLD Arista 74321153402	51	1
25 Sep 93	EVERLASTING LOVE Bell 74321164802	20	4
26 Mar 94	COULD IT BE I'M FALLING IN LOVE Bell 74321189952	15	6
4 Jun 94	BEGGIN' TO BE WRITTEN Bell 74321211982	29	3

WORLD'S FAMOUS SUPREME TEAM
US, male vocal / DJ group (19 WEEKS)

			pos/wks
4 Dec 82 ●	BUFFALO GALS Charisma MALC 1 [1]	9	12
25 Feb 84	HEY DJ Charisma TEAM 1	52	5
8 Dec 90	OPERAA HOUSE Virgin VS 1273 [2]	75	1
3 Oct 98	BUFFALO GALS STAMPEDE (re-mix) Virgin VSCDT 1717 [3]	65	1

[1] Malcolm McLaren and the World's Famous Supreme Team [2] World Famous Supreme Team Show [3] Malcolm McLaren and the World's Famous Supreme Team plus Rakim and Roger Sanchez

WRECKX-N-EFFECT US, male vocal group (18 WEEKS)

			pos/wks
13 Jan 90	JUICY Motown ZB 43295 [1]	29	7
5 Dec 92	RUMP SHAKER MCA MCS 1725	24	7
7 May 94	WRECKX SHOP MCA MCSTD 1969 [2]	26	2
13 Aug 94	RUMP SHAKER (re-issue) MCA MCSTD 1989	40	2

[1] Wrecks-N-Effect [2] Wreckx-N-Effect featuring Apache Indian

Betty WRIGHT US, female vocalist (23 WEEKS)

			pos/wks
25 Jan 75	SHOORAH! SHOORAH! RCA 2491	27	7
19 Apr 75	WHERE IS THE LOVE RCA 2548	25	7
8 Feb 86	PAIN Cooltempo COOL 117	42	6
9 Sep 89	KEEP LOVE NEW Sure Delight SD 11	71	3

See also Peter BROWN

Ian WRIGHT UK, male footballer / vocalist (2 WEEKS)

			pos/wks
28 Aug 93	DO THE RIGHT THING M & G MAGCD 45	43	2

Linda WRIGHT – See NEW ATLANTIC

Ruby WRIGHT US, female vocalist (15 WEEKS)

			pos/wks
16 Apr 54 ●	BIMBO (re) Parlophone R 3816	7	5
22 May 59	THREE STARS Parlophone R 4556	19	10

'Three Stars' is narrated by Dick Pike

Steve WRIGHT UK, male DJ / vocalist (10 WEEKS)

			pos/wks
27 Nov 82	I'M ALRIGHT RCA 296 [1]	40	6
15 Oct 83	GET SOME THERAPY RCA 362 [2]	75	1
1 Dec 84	THE GAY CAVALIEROS (THE STORY SO FAR) MCA 925	61	3

[1] Young Steve and The Afternoon Boys [2] Steve Wright and The Sisters of Soul

WUBBLE-U UK, male production group (1 WEEK)

			pos/wks
7 Mar 98	PETAL Indolent DGOL 003CD1	55	1

WURZELS UK, male vocal / instrumental group (31 WEEKS)

			pos/wks
2 Feb 67	DRINK UP THY ZIDER Columbia DB 8081 [1]	45	1
15 May 76 ★	THE COMBINE HARVESTER (BRAND NEW KEY) EMI 2450	1	13
11 Sep 76 ●	I AM A CIDER DRINKER (PALOMA BLANCA) EMI 2520	3	9
25 Jun 77	FARMER BILL'S COWMAN (I WAS KAISER BILL'S BATMAN) EMI 2637	32	5
11 Aug 01	COMBINE HARVESTER (re-mix) EMI Gold CDWURZ 001	39	2
12 Oct 02	DON'T LOOK BACK IN ANGER EMI Gold 5515082	59	1

[1] Adge Cutler and The Wurzels

WU-TANG CLAN US, male rap / instrumental group (21 WEEKS)

			pos/wks
16 Aug 97	TRIUMPH Loud 74321510212 [1]	46	1
21 Mar 98 ●	SAY WHAT YOU WANT / INSANE Mercury MERC 499 [2]	4	7
25 Nov 00 ●	GRAVEL PIT Loud / Epic 67015182	6	13

[1] Wu-Tang Clan featuring Cappadonna [2] Texas featuring Wu-Tang Clan (rap by Method Man and RZA)

Robert WYATT
UK, male vocalist – Robert Wyatt-Ellidge (11 WEEKS)

			pos/wks
28 Sep 74	I'M A BELIEVER Virgin VS 114	29	5
7 May 83	SHIPBUILDING Rough Trade RT 115	35	6

Michael WYCOFF US, male vocalist (2 WEEKS)

			pos/wks
23 Jul 83	(DO YOU REALLY LOVE ME) TELL ME LOVE RCA 348	60	2

Pete WYLIE UK, male vocalist (18 WEEKS)

			pos/wks
3 May 86	SINFUL Eternal MDM 7	13	10
13 Sep 86	DIAMOND GIRL Eternal MDM 12	57	3
13 Apr 91	SINFUL! (SCARY JIGGIN' WITH DR LOVE) Siren SRN 138 [1]	28	5

[1] Pete Wylie with The Farm

See also WAH!

Bill WYMAN
UK, male vocalist – William Perks (13 WEEKS) pos/wks

| 25 Jul 81 | (SI SI) JE SUIS UN ROCK STAR *A&M AMS 8144* | 14 | 9 |
| 20 Mar 82 | A NEW FASHION *A&M AMS 8209* | 37 | 4 |

See also ROLLING STONES

Jane WYMAN – *See Bing CROSBY*

Tammy WYNETTE
US, female vocalist – Virginia Wynette Pugh, d. 6 Apr 1998 (35 WEEKS) pos/wks

26 Apr 75	★ STAND BY YOUR MAN *Epic EPC 7137*	1	12
28 Jun 75	D.I.V.O.R.C.E. *Epic EPC 3361*	12	7
12 Jun 76	I DON'T WANNA PLAY HOUSE *Epic EPC 4091*	37	4
7 Dec 91	● JUSTIFIED AND ANCIENT *KLF Communications KLF 099* [1]	2	12

[1] KLF guest vocals: Tammy Wynette

Mark WYNTER (434 Top 500)
Teen-targeted pop singer turned TV actor / presenter, b. Terence Lewis, 29 Jan 1943, Surrey, UK. Boy-next-door, whose hit portfolio contains a mix of revivals and cover versions. (80 WEEKS) pos/wks

25 Aug 60	IMAGE OF A GIRL *Decca F 11263*	11	10
10 Nov 60	KICKIN' UP THE LEAVES *Decca F 11279*	24	10
9 Mar 61	DREAM GIRL *Decca F 11323*	27	5
8 Jun 61	EXCLUSIVELY YOURS *Decca F 11354*	32	7
4 Oct 62	● VENUS IN BLUE JEANS *Pye 7N 15466*	4	15
13 Dec 62	● GO AWAY LITTLE GIRL *Pye 7N 15492*	6	11
6 Jun 63	SHY GIRL *Pye 7N 15525*	28	6
14 Nov 63	IT'S ALMOST TOMORROW *Pye 7N 15577*	12	12
9 Apr 64	ONLY YOU (AND YOU ALONE) *Pye 7N 15626*	38	4

X

Malcolm X
US, male orator, d. 21 Feb 1965 (4 WEEKS) pos/wks

| 7 Apr 84 | NO SELL OUT *Tommy Boy IS 165* | 60 | 4 |

Hit features credit: 'Music by Keith Le Blanc'

X-ECUTIONERS featuring Mike SHINODA and Mr HAHN of LINKIN PARK
US, male DJ / production group and male rap / DJ duo (9 WEEKS) pos/wks

| 13 Apr 02 | ● IT'S GOIN' DOWN *Epic 6725642* | 7 | 9 |

X MEN – *See SELENA vs X MEN*

XAVIER – *See TJR featuring XAVIER*

XAVIER
US, male / female vocal / instrumental group (3 WEEKS) pos/wks

| 20 Mar 82 | WORK THAT SUCKER TO DEATH / LOVE IS ON THE ONE *Liberty UP 651* | 53 | 3 |

XPANSIONS
UK, male producer – Richie Malone (21 WEEKS) pos/wks

6 Oct 90	ELEVATION *Optimism 113683*	49	5
23 Feb 91	● MOVE YOUR BODY (ELEVATION) *Arista 113 683*	7	9
15 Jun 91	WHAT YOU WANT *Arista 114 246* [1]	55	2
26 Aug 95	MOVE YOUR BODY (re-mix) *Arista 74321294982* [2]	14	4
30 Nov 02	ELEVATION (MOVE YOUR BODY) 2002 (re-mix) *RM RMRCD 10*	70	1

[1] Xpansions featuring Dale Joyner [2] Xpansions 95

'Move Your Body' is a re-mix of 'Elevation'

X-PRESS 2
UK, male instrumental / production group (24 WEEKS) pos/wks

| 5 Jun 93 | LONDON X-PRESS *Junior Boy's Own JBO 12* | 59 | 1 |
| 16 Oct 93 | SAY WHAT! *Junior Boy's Own JBO 16CD* | 32 | 2 |

30 Jul 94	ROCK 2 HOUSE / HIP HOUSIN' *Junior Boy's Own JBO 21CD* [1]	55	2
9 Mar 96	THE SOUND *Junior Boy's Own JBO 36*	38	1
12 Oct 96	TRANZ EURO XPRESS *Junior Boy's Own JBO 42CD*	45	1
30 Sep 00	AC / DC *Skint SKINT 57*	60	1
28 Apr 01	MUZIKIZUM *Skint SKINT 65*	52	1
20 Oct 01	SMOKE MACHINE *Skint SKINT 69*	43	1
20 Apr 02	● LAZY *Skint SKINT 74CD* [2]	2	13
21 Sep 02	I WANT YOU BACK *Skint SKINT 81CD*	50	1

[1] X-Press 2 featuring Lo-Pro [2] X-Press 2 featuring David Byrne

'I Want You Back' features Dieter Meier

X-RAY SPEX
UK, male / female vocal / instrumental group (33 WKS) pos/wks

29 Apr 78	THE DAY THE WORLD TURNED DAYGLO *EMI International INT 553*	23	8
22 Jul 78	IDENTITY *EMI International INT 563*	24	10
4 Nov 78	GERM FREE ADOLESCENCE *EMI International INT 573*	19	11
21 Apr 79	HIGHLY INFLAMMABLE *EMI International INT 583*	45	4

XRS – *See DJ MARKY & XRS*

XSCAPE
US, female vocal group (15 WEEKS) pos/wks

20 Nov 93	JUST KICKIN' IT *Columbia 6598622*	49	2
5 Nov 94	JUST KICKIN' IT (re-issue) *Columbia 6608642*	54	2
7 Oct 95	FEELS SO GOOD *Columbia 6625022*	34	2
27 Jan 96	WHO CAN I RUN TO *Columbia 6628112*	31	3
29 Jun 96	KEEP ON KEEPIN' ON *East West A 4287CD* [1]	39	2
19 Apr 97	KEEP ON KEEPIN' ON (re-issue) *East West A 3950CD1* [1]	27	2
22 Aug 98	THE ARMS OF THE ONE WHO LOVES YOU *Columbia 6662522*	46	2

[1] MC Lyte featuring Xscape

XSTASIA
UK, male / female vocal / production duo (1 WEEK) pos/wks

| 17 Mar 01 | SWEETNESS *Liquid Asset ASSETCD 005* | 65 | 1 |

X-STATIC
Italy, male / female vocal / instrumental group (2 WKS) pos/wks

| 4 Feb 95 | I'M STANDING (HIGHER) *Positiva CDTIV 25* | 41 | 2 |

XTC
UK, male vocal / instrumental group (70 WEEKS) pos/wks

12 May 79	LIFE BEGINS AT THE HOP *Virgin VS 259*	54	4
22 Sep 79	MAKING PLANS FOR NIGEL *Virgin VS 282*	17	11
6 Sep 80	GENERALS AND MAJORS / DON'T LOSE YOUR TEMPER *Virgin VS 365*	32	8
18 Oct 80	TOWERS OF LONDON *Virgin VS 372*	31	5
24 Jan 81	SGT ROCK (IS GOING TO HELP ME) *Virgin VS 384*	16	9
23 Jan 82	● SENSES WORKING OVERTIME *Virgin VS 462*	10	9
27 Mar 82	BALL AND CHAIN *Virgin VS 482*	58	4
15 Oct 83	LOVE ON A FARMBOY'S WAGES *Virgin VS 613*	50	4
29 Sep 84	ALL YOU PRETTY GIRLS *Virgin VS 709*	55	5
28 Jan 89	MAYOR OF SIMPLETON *Virgin VS 1158*	46	5
4 Apr 92	THE DISAPPOINTED *Virgin VS 1404*	33	5
13 Jun 92	THE BALLAD OF PETER PUMPKINHEAD *Virgin VS 1415*	71	1

XZIBIT
US, male rapper – Alvin Joiner (9 WEEKS) pos/wks

| 17 Mar 01 | X *Epic 6709072* [1] | 14 | 7 |
| 16 Nov 02 | MULTIPLY *Epic / Loud 6731552* | 39 | 2 |

[1] Xzibit featuring Snoop Dogg

Y

Y?N-VEE
US, female vocal group (1 WEEK) pos/wks

| 17 Dec 94 | CHOCOLATE *RAL RALCD 2* | 65 | 1 |

Re-entries are listed as (re), (2re), (3re), etc which signifies that the hit re-entered the chart once, twice or three times, etc

Tukka YOOT – See US3

YORK *Germany, male production / instrumental*
duo – Torsten and Jörg Stenzel (21 WEEKS)   pos/wks
9 Oct 99   THE AWAKENING *Manifesto FESCD 60* 11 5
10 Jun 00 ● ON THE BEACH *Manifesto FESCD 70* 4 10
18 Nov 00   FAREWELL TO THE MOON *Manifesto FESCD 76* 37 2
27 Jan 01   THE FIELDS OF LOVE *Club Tools/Edel 0124095 CLU* [1] 16 4

[1] ATB featuring York

YOSH presents LOVEDEEJAY AKEMI
Holland, male producer – Yoshida Rosenboom (5 WEEKS)   pos/wks
29 Jul 95   IT'S WHAT'S UPFRONT THAT COUNTS *Limbo LIMB 46CD*........69 1
2 Dec 95   IT'S WHAT'S UPFRONT THAT COUNTS (re-mix)
            Limbo LIMB 50CD 31 2
20 Apr 96   THE SCREAMER *Limbo LIMB 54CD* 38 2

YOSHIKI – See Roger TAYLOR

YOTHU YINDI *Australia, male vocal / instrumental group (1 WEEK)* pos/wks
15 Feb 92   TREATY *Hollywood HWD 116* 72 1

Faron YOUNG *US, male vocalist, d. 10 Dec 1996 (23 WEEKS)*   pos/wks
15 Jul 72 ● IT'S FOUR IN THE MORNING *Mercury 6052 140*............3 23

Jimmy YOUNG (373) [Top 500] *Distincitve balladeer who became
a top radio DJ, b. 21 Sep, 1923, Gloucestershire, UK. Converted from record
maker to record spinner and remained a star for five decades. First UK
artist to reach No.1 with two successive singles, he retired from his long
radio career in 2002 (88 WEEKS)*   pos/wks
9 Jan 53   FAITH CAN MOVE MOUNTAINS *Decca F 9986* 11 1
21 Aug 53 ● ETERNALLY *Decca F 10130* 8 9

TOP 10 SINGLES BY WEEKS ON CHARTS

■ These are the long-staying chart hits that have racked
up the most weeks, including all visits to the charts and
counting re-entries and re-mixes

1. MY WAY Frank Sinatra **124 weeks**

2. AMAZING GRACE Judy Collins **67 weeks**

3. RELAX Frankie Goes To Hollywood **59 weeks**

4. ROCK AROUND THE CLOCK Bill Haley and His Comets **57 weeks**

5. RELEASE ME Engelbert Humperdinck **56 weeks**

6. STRANGER ON THE SHORE Mr Acker Bilk **55 weeks**

7. BLUE MONDAY New Order **53 weeks**

8. WHATEVER Oasis **50 weeks**

9. I LOVE YOU BECAUSE Jim Reeves **47 weeks**

10. WHITE LINES Grandmaster Flash, Melle Mel and The Furious Five **46 weeks**

Frank Sinatra's 'My Way' made 10 visits to the UK singles chart but never peaked at a higher position than No.5

6 May 55 ★ UNCHAINED MELODY *Decca F 10502* 1 19
16 Sep 55 ★ THE MAN FROM LARAMIE *Decca F 10597* 1 12
23 Dec 55   SOMEONE ON YOUR MIND *Decca F 10640* 13 5
16 Mar 56 ● CHAIN GANG *Decca F 10694* 9 6
8 Jun 56   WAYWARD WIND *Decca F 10736* 27 1
22 Jun 56   RICH MAN POOR MAN *Decca F 10736* 25 1
28 Sep 56 ● MORE *Decca F 10774* 4 17
3 May 57   ROUND AND ROUND *Decca F 10875* 30 1
10 Oct 63   MISS YOU *Columbia DB 7119* 15 13
26 Mar 64   UNCHAINED MELODY (re-recording) *Columbia DB 7234*........43 3

'Unchained Melody' on Columbia and 'Round and Round' are with the Michael
Sammes Singers

John Paul YOUNG *Australia, male vocalist (19 WEEKS)*   pos/wks
29 Apr 78 ● LOVE IS IN THE AIR *Ariola ARO 117* 5 13
14 Nov 92   LOVE IS IN THE AIR (re-mix) *Columbia 6587697*......49 3
12 Jan 02   LOVE IS IN THE AIR (re-recording) *Positiva CDTIV 166* [1] 25 3

[1] Milk & Sugar vs John Paul Young

Karen YOUNG *UK, female vocalist (21 WEEKS)*   pos/wks
6 Sep 69 ● NOBODY'S CHILD *Major Minor MM 625* 6 21

Karen YOUNG
US, female vocalist d. 26 Jan 1991 (9 WEEKS)   pos/wks
19 Aug 78   HOT SHOT *Atlantic K 11180* 34 7
24 Feb 79   HOT SHOT (re-issue) *Atlantic LV 8* 75 1
15 Nov 97   HOT SHOT '97 (re-recording) *Distinctive DISNCD 37* 68 1

Neil YOUNG
Canada, male vocalist / instrumentalist (22 WEEKS)   pos/wks
11 Mar 72 ● HEART OF GOLD *Reprise K 14140* ▲ 10 11
6 Jan 79   FOUR STRONG WINDS *Reprise K 14493*...............57 4
27 Feb 93   HARVEST MOON *Reprise W 0139CD* 36 3
17 Jul 93   THE NEEDLE AND THE DAMAGE DONE
            Reprise W 0191CD..............................75 1
30 Oct 93   LONG MAY YOU RUN (LIVE) *Reprise W 0207CD* 71 1
9 Apr 94   PHILADELPHIA *Reprise W 0242CD* 62 2

See also CROSBY, STILLS, NASH and YOUNG

Paul YOUNG (192) [Top 500]
*Soulful-sounding pop singer / songwriter (b. 17 Jan 1956, Bedfordshire,
UK) who earlier fronted The Q-Tips and chart act Streetband. This multi-
Brit Award winner sold seven million copies of his 'No Parlez' album
(including more than one million in the UK) (134 WEEKS)*   pos/wks
18 Jun 83 ★ WHEREVER I LAY MY HAT (THAT'S MY HOME)
            CBS A 3371....................................1 15
10 Sep 83 ● COME BACK AND STAY *CBS A 3636* 4 9
19 Nov 83 ● LOVE OF THE COMMON PEOPLE *CBS A 3585* 2 13
13 Oct 84 ● I'M GONNA TEAR YOUR PLAYHOUSE DOWN *CBS A 4786* 9 7
8 Dec 84 ● EVERYTHING MUST CHANGE *CBS A 4972* 9 11
9 Mar 85 ● EVERYTIME YOU GO AWAY *CBS A 6300* ▲ 4 11
22 Jun 85   TOMB OF MEMORIES (re) *CBS A 6321* 16 8
4 Oct 86   WONDERLAND *CBS YOUNG 1* 24 5
29 Nov 86   SOME PEOPLE *CBS YOUNG 2* 56 3
7 Feb 87   WHY DOES A MAN HAVE TO BE STRONG?
            CBS YOUNG 3...................................63 2
12 May 90   SOFTLY WHISPERING I LOVE YOU *CBS YOUNG 4*.......21 6
7 Jul 90   OH GIRL *CBS YOUNG 5* 25 6
6 Oct 90   HEAVEN CAN WAIT *CBS YOUNG 6* 71 2
12 Jan 91   CALLING YOU *CBS YOUNG 7* 57 2
30 Mar 91 ● SENZA UNA DONNA (WITHOUT A WOMAN)
            London LON 294 [1] 4 12
10 Aug 91   BOTH SIDES NOW *MCA MCS 1546* [2] 74 1
26 Oct 91   DON'T DREAM IT'S OVER *Columbia 6574117* 20 5
25 Sep 93   NOW I KNOW WHAT MADE OTIS BLUE
            Columbia 6596412.............................14 7
27 Nov 93   HOPE IN A HOPELESS WORLD *Columbia 6598652*......42 3
23 Apr 94   IT WILL BE YOU *Columbia 6602812*...............34 4
17 May 97   I WISH YOU LOVE *East West EW 100CD1* 33 2

[1] Zucchero and Paul Young [2] Clannad and Paul Young

Retta YOUNG *US, female vocalist (7 WEEKS)* pos/wks
4 May 75   SENDING OUT AN S.O.S. *All Platinum 6146 305* **28** 7

Tracie YOUNG – *See TRACIE*

Will YOUNG
UK, male vocalist (54 WEEKS) pos/wks
9 Mar 02 ★ EVERGREEN / ANYTHING IS POSSIBLE
    S 74321926142 ◆ ■ **1** 16
8 Jun 02 ★ LIGHT MY FIRE (re) *S 74321943002* ■ **1** 20
5 Oct 02 ★ THE LONG AND WINDING ROAD / SUSPICIOUS MINDS
    S 74321965972 [1] ■ ....**1** 13+
30 Nov 02 ● DON'T LET ME DOWN / YOU AND I
    S 74321981262 ....**2** 5+

[1] Will Young and Gareth Gates / Gareth Gates

YOUNG and COMPANY
US, male / female vocal / instrumental group (12 WEEKS) pos/wks
1 Nov 80   I LIKE (WHAT YOU'RE DOING TO ME)
    Excalibur EXC 501 ....**20** 12

YOUNG AND MOODY BAND
UK, male vocal / instrumental group (4 WEEKS) pos/wks
10 Oct 81   DON'T DO THAT *Bronze BRO 130* **63** 4

YOUNG BLACK TEENAGERS
US, male rap group (3 WEEKS) pos/wks
9 Apr 94   TAP THE BOTTLE *MCA MCSTD 1967* **39** 3

YOUNG DISCIPLES
UK / US, male / female vocal / instrumental group (17 WEEKS) pos/wks
13 Oct 90   GET YOURSELF TOGETHER *Talkin Loud TLK 2* **68** 1
23 Feb 91   APPARENTLY NOTHIN' (re) *Talkin Loud TLK 5* **13** 11
5 Oct 91   GET YOURSELF TOGETHER (re-issue)
    Talkin Loud TLK 15 ....**65** 2
5 Sep 92   YOUNG DISCIPLES (EP) *Talkin Loud TLKX 18* **48** 3

'Apparently Nothin'' first peaked at No.46 in Mar 1991 making its peak position
only on re-entry in Aug 1991. Tracks on Young Disciples (EP): Move On / Freedom /
All I Have In Me / Move On (re-mix)

YOUNG IDEA *UK, male vocal duo – Tony*
Cox and Douglas MacCrae-Brown (6 WEEKS) pos/wks
29 Jun 67 ● WITH A LITTLE HELP FROM MY FRIENDS
    Columbia DB 8205 ....**10** 6

YOUNG MC
US, male rapper – Marvin Young (7 WEEKS) pos/wks
15 Jul 89   BUST A MOVE *Delicious Vinyl BRW 137* **73** 2
17 Feb 90   PRINCIPAL'S OFFICE *Delicious Vinyl BRW 161* **54** 3
17 Aug 91   THAT'S THE WAY LOVE GOES *Capitol CL 623* **65** 2

YOUNG OFFENDERS
Ireland, male vocal / instrumental group (1 WEEK) pos/wks
7 Mar 98   THAT'S WHY WE LOSE CONTROL
    Columbia 6651942 ....**60** 1

YOUNG ONES – *See Cliff RICHARD*

YOUNG RASCALS
US, male vocal / instrumental group (17 WEEKS) pos/wks
25 May 67 ● GROOVIN' *Atlantic 584 111* ▲ **8** 13
16 Aug 67   A GIRL LIKE YOU *Atlantic 584 128* **37** 4

Leon YOUNG STRING CHORALE – *See Mr Acker BILK and his PARAMOUNT*
JAZZ BAND

YOUNG VOICES CHOIR – *See DECLAN featuring YOUNG VOICES CHOIR*

Sydney YOUNGBLOOD
US, male vocalist – Sydney Ford (31 WEEKS) pos/wks
26 Aug 89 ● IF ONLY I COULD *Circa YR 34* **3** 14
9 Dec 89   SIT AND WAIT *Circa YR 40* **16** 8
31 Mar 90   I'D RATHER GO BLIND *Circa YR 43* **44** 5
29 Jun 91   HOOKED ON YOU *Circa YR 65* **72** 2
20 Mar 93   ANYTHING *RCA 74321138672* **48** 2

YOUNGER YOUNGER 28'S
UK, male / female vocal / instrumental group (1 WEEK) pos/wks
5 Jun 99   WE'RE GOING OUT *V2 VVR 5006943* **61** 1

Z

Z FACTOR *UK, male DJ / producer – Dave Lee (2 WEEKS)* pos/wks
21 Feb 98   GOTTA KEEP PUSHIN' *ffrr FCD 329* **47** 1
17 Nov 01   RIDE THE RHYTHM *Direction 6718482* **52** 1

See also Joey NEGRO; PHASE II; AKABU featuring Linda CLIFFORD; RAVEN MAIZE;
HED BOYS; Li KWAN; JAKATTA; IL PADRINOS

Z2 *UK, male production duo (1 WEEK)* pos/wks
26 Feb 00   I WANT YOU *Platipus PLATCD 67* [1] **61** 1

[1] Vocal by Alison Rivers

Helmut ZACHARIAS Orchestra
Germany, orchestra leader, d. 28 Feb 2002 (11 WEEKS) pos/wks
29 Oct 64 ● TOKYO MELODY *Polydor NH 52341* **9** 11

Pia ZADORA *US, female vocalist (6 WEEKS)* pos/wks
27 Oct 84   WHEN THE RAIN BEGINS TO FALL
    Arista ARIST 584 [1] **68** 2
12 Nov 88   DANCE OUT OF MY HEAD *Epic 6528867* [2] **65** 4

[1] Jermaine Jackson and Pia Zadora [2] Pia

ZAGER and EVANS
US, male vocal duo – Denny Zager and Rick Evans (13 WEEKS) pos/wks
9 Aug 69 ★ IN THE YEAR 2525 (EXORDIUM AND TERMINUS)
    RCA 1860 ▲ **1** 13

Michael ZAGER BAND
US, male / female vocal / instrumental group (12 WEEKS) pos/wks
1 Apr 78 ● LET'S ALL CHANT *Private Stock PVT 143* **8** 12

Gheorghe ZAMFIR
Romania, male instrumentalist – pipes (9 WEEKS) pos/wks
21 Aug 76 ● (LIGHT OF EXPERIENCE) DOINA DE JALE *Epic EPC 4310* **4** 9

Tommy ZANG *US, male vocalist (1 WEEK)* pos/wks
16 Feb 61   HEY GOOD LOOKING *Polydor NH 66957* **45** 1

ZAPP *US, male vocal / instrumental group (6 WEEKS)* pos/wks
25 Jan 86   IT DOESN'T REALLY MATTER *Warner Bros. W 8879* **57** 3
24 May 86   COMPUTER LOVE (PART 1) *Warner Bros. W 8805* **64** 3

Francesco ZAPPALA *Italy, male producer (3 WEEKS)* pos/wks
10 Aug 91   WE GOTTA DO IT *Fourth & Broadway BRW 225* [1] **57** 2
2 May 92   NO WAY OUT *PWL Continental PWL 230* **69** 1

[1] DJ Professor featuring Francesco Zappala

Lena ZAVARONI
UK, female vocalist, d. 1 Oct 1999 (14 WEEKS)   pos/wks

| 9 Feb 74 | ● | MA! (HE'S MAKING EYES AT ME) *Philips 6006 367* | 10 | 11 |
| 1 Jun 74 | | (YOU'VE GOT) PERSONALITY *Philips 6006 391* | 33 | 3 |

ZED BIAS *UK, male vocal / production group (4 WEEKS)*   pos/wks

| 15 Jul 00 | NEIGHBOURHOOD *Locked On / XL Recordings LOX 122CD* | 25 | 4 |

ZEE *UK, female vocalist – Lesley Cowling (4 WEEKS)*   pos/wks

6 Jul 96	DREAMTIME *Perfecto PERF 122CD*	31	2
22 Mar 97	SAY MY NAME *Perfecto PERF 135CD*	36	1
7 Feb 98	BUTTERFLY *Perfecto PERF 154CD1* [1]	41	1

[1] Tilt featuring Zee

ZEPHYRS *UK, male vocal / instrumental group (1 WEEK)*   pos/wks

| 18 Mar 65 | SHE'S LOST YOU *Columbia DB 7481* | 48 | 1 |

ZERO B *UK, male instrumentalist –*
keyboards – Peter Riding (6 WEEKS)   pos/wks

| 22 Feb 92 | THE EP (BRAND NEW MIXES) *Ffrreedom TAB 102* | 32 | 4 |
| 24 Jul 93 | RECONNECTION (EP) *Internal LIECD 6* | 54 | 2 |

Tracks on The EP: Lock Up / Spinning Wheel / Module. Tracks on Reconnection (EP): Love to Be in Love (2 mixes)/ Lock Up (remix) / Où Est Le Spoon

ZERO 7 *UK, male production duo –*
Henry Binns and Sam Hardaker (5 WEEKS)   pos/wks

18 Aug 01	DESTINY *Ultimate Dilemma UDRCDS 043* [1]	30	3
17 Nov 01	IN THE WAITING LINE *Ultimate Dilemma UDRCDS 045*	47	1
30 Mar 02	DISTRACTIONS *Ultimate Dilemma UDRCDS 046* [2]	45	1

[1] Zero 7 featuring Sia and Sophie [2] Zero 7 featuring Sia

ZERO VU featuring Lorna B
UK, male / female vocal / production group (1 WEEK)   pos/wks

| 15 Mar 97 | FEELS SO GOOD *Avex UK AVEXCD 53* | 69 | 1 |

ZERO ZERO *UK, male instrumental / production duo (1 WEEK)*   pos/wks

| 10 Aug 91 | ZEROXED *Kickin KICK 9* | 71 | 1 |

ZHANÉ *US, female vocal duo – Renee*
Neufville and Jean Norris (18 WEEKS)   pos/wks

11 Sep 93	HEY MR DJ (re) *Epic 6596102*	26	5
19 Mar 94	GROOVE THANG *Motown TMGCD 1423*	34	3
20 Aug 94	VIBE *Motown TMGCD 1430*	67	1
25 Feb 95	SHAME *Jive JIVECD 372*	66	1
21 Sep 96	IT'S A PARTY *Elektra EKR 226CD* [1]	23	2
8 Mar 97	4 MORE *Tommy Boy TBCD 7779A* [2]	52	1
26 Apr 97	REQUEST LINE *Motown 8606452*	22	3
30 Aug 97	CRUSH *Motown 5716712*	44	1
11 Sep 99	JAMBOREE *Arista 74321692882* [3]	51	1

[1] Busta Rhymes featuring Zhane [2] De La Soul featuring Zhané [3] Naughty By Nature featuring Zhane

ZIG and ZAG *Zog / Ireland, male puppet duo (12 WEEKS)*   pos/wks

| 24 Dec 94 | ● | THEM GIRLS THEM GIRLS *RCA 74321251042* | 5 | 9 |
| 1 Jul 95 | | HANDS UP! HANDS UP! *RCA 74321284392* | 21 | 3 |

ZIGZAG JIVE FLUTES – See ELIAS and his ZIG-ZAG JIVE FLUTES

ZION TRAIN *UK, male / female vocal / instrumental group (1 WK)* pos/wks

| 27 Jul 96 | RISE *China WOKCD 2085* | 61 | 1 |

ZODIAC MINDWARP and the LOVE REACTION
UK, male / female vocal / instrumental group (11 WEEKS)   pos/wks

| 9 May 87 | PRIME MOVER *Mercury ZOD 1* | 18 | 6 |

| 14 Nov 87 | BACKSEAT EDUCATION *Mercury ZOD 2* | 49 | 3 |
| 2 Apr 88 | PLANET GIRL *Mercury ZOD 3* | 63 | 2 |

ZODIACS – See Maurice WILLIAMS and the ZODIACS

ZOE
UK, female vocalist – Zoe Pollock (22 WEEKS)   pos/wks

10 Nov 90		SUNSHINE ON A RAINY DAY *M & G MAGS 6*	53	5
24 Aug 91	●	SUNSHINE ON A RAINY DAY (re-mix) *M & G MAGS 14*	4	11
2 Nov 91		LIGHTNING *M & G MAGS 18*	37	4
29 Feb 92		HOLY DAYS *M & G MAGS 21*	72	2

ZOMBIE NATION *Germany, male production duo – Florian*
'Splank' Senfter and Emanuel 'Mooner' Günther (16 WEEKS)   pos/wks

| 2 Sep 00 | | KERNKRAFT 400 (IMPORT) *TRANSK TRANSK 002* | 61 | 1 |
| 30 Sep 00 | ● | KERNKRAFT 400 *Data DATA 11CDS* | 2 | 15 |

Rob ZOMBIE *US, male vocalist (2 WEEKS)*   pos/wks

| 26 Dec 98 | DRACULA *Geffen GFSTD 22367* | 44 | 2 |

ZOMBIES *UK, male vocal / instrumental group (16 WEEKS)*   pos/wks

| 13 Aug 64 | SHE'S NOT THERE *Decca F 11940* | 12 | 11 |
| 11 Feb 65 | TELL HER NO *Decca F 12072* | 42 | 5 |

ZOO EXPERIENCE featuring DESTRY
UK, male instrumental group and US, male vocalist (1 WEEK)   pos/wks

| 22 Aug 92 | LOVE'S GOTTA HOLD ON ME *Cooltempo COOL 261* | 66 | 1 |

ZUCCHERO *Italy, male vocalist / instrumentalist*
– guitar – Adelmo Fornaciari (24 WEEKS)   pos/wks

30 Mar 91	●	SENZA UNA DONNA (WITHOUT A WOMAN) *London LON 294* [1]	4	12
18 Jan 92		DIAMANTE *London LON 313* [2]	44	7
24 Oct 92		MISERERE *London LON 329* [3]	15	5

[1] Zucchero and Paul Young [2] Zucchero with Randy Crawford [3] Zucchero with Luciano Pavarotti

ZZ TOP   (334   Top 500)
Low-slung, guitar-driven blues-rock trio formed 1969 in Houston, Texas, US; long-bearded duo Billy Gibbons (v/g) and Dusty Hill (v/b) plus clean-shaven Frank Beard (d). Hugely popular stadium-packing festival headliners in the 1980s. Named to ensure they would be the last act in record racks and hit books (94 WEEKS)   pos/wks

3 Sep 83	●	GIMME ALL YOUR LOVIN' (re) *Warner Bros. W 9693*	10	18
26 Nov 83		SHARP DRESSED MAN (re) *Warner Bros. W 9576*	22	13
31 Mar 84		TV DINNERS *Warner Bros. W 9334*	67	3
23 Feb 85		LEGS *Warner Bros. W 9272*	16	7
13 Jul 85		THE ZZ TOP SUMMER HOLIDAY (EP) *Warner Bros. W 8946*	51	5
19 Oct 85		SLEEPING BAG *Warner Bros. W 2001*	27	5
15 Feb 86		STAGES *Warner Bros. W 2002*	43	3
19 Apr 86		ROUGH BOY *Warner Bros. W 2003*	23	9
4 Oct 86		VELCRO FLY *Warner Bros. W 8650*	54	3
21 Jul 90		DOUBLEBACK *Warner Bros. W 9812*	29	6
13 Apr 91		MY HEAD'S IN MISSISSIPPI *Warner Bros W 0009*	37	5
11 Apr 92	●	VIVA LAS VEGAS *Warner Bros. W 0098*	10	7
20 Jun 92		ROUGH BOY (re-issue) *Warner Bros. W 0111*	49	3
29 Jan 94		PINCUSHION *RCA 74321184732*	15	3
7 May 94		BREAKAWAY *RCA 74321192282*	60	1
29 Jun 96		WHAT'S UP WITH THAT *RCA 74321394822*	58	1
16 Oct 99		GIMME ALL YOUR LOVIN' 2000 *Riverhorse RIVHCD 2* [1]	28	2

[1] Martay featuring ZZ Top

'Gimme All Your Lovin'' peaked at No.61 in 1983 hitting its peak position only on re-entry in Oct 1984. 'Sharp Dressed Man' peaked at No.53 in 1983 hitting its peak position in Dec 1984. Tracks on Summer Holiday (EP): Tush / Got Me Under Pressure / Beer Drinkers and Hell Raisers / I'm Bad, I'm Nationwide

A-Z BY SONG TITLE

■ What follows is an alphabetical index of the
24,089 songs that make up the 27,674 hit singles
(including re-entries)

All six decades of chart history were represented at the launch of the
15th edition of British Hit Singles. Will Young, Shakin' Stevens,
Melanie B, Bruce Welch, Faye Tozer, Noddy Holder and Petula Clark
have amassed an astonishing 2,064 weeks on the UK chart between
them, scoring 39 No.1 hits in the process.

HOW TO USE THIS SECTION

■ This section contains an alphabetical index of every hit since 1952 in order of title, act name, highest position the hit reached on the chart and the year(s) in which it charted

Covers: Different songs with the same title are differentiated by a letter in brackets after the song title: [A], [B], etc. Cover versions of the same song share the same letter. For example, there are eight versions of the song 'Around the World'. Four of these titles share the letter [A], which indicates that they are all covers of the same song (recorded individually by Bing Crosby, Ronnie

Hilton, Gracie Fields and Mantovani). However, the fifth version is followed by the letter [B], which indicates that it is a different song (recorded by East 17). If the original version of a cover was never a chart hit, it will not be listed here.

Non-singles: In most cases, individual titles of songs on EP, LP, medley or megamix singles that made the chart are not listed here in this index of songs, although full track listings are included in the artist entries in the main A-Z By Artist section.

Duets: Most duets list both artists involved (eg. 'We've Got Tonight' by Ronan Keating and Lulu), but some hits are credited only to the main artist. For

example, 'Zing a Little Zong' is credited to Bing Crosby but if you look up his entry in the A-Z By Artist section, a footnote for the hit explains that it was, in fact, a duet with Jane Wyman, who has her own cross-reference entry in 'W'.

Act names: Bold capital letters indicate where to look up act names alphabetically in the A-Z By Artist section. Groups, bands, orchestras and ensembles are alphabetised according to the whole act name, while individual artists are ordered according to their surnames. Therefore, note that DANNY WILSON is a group and appears under 'D', while Danny WILLIAMS is an individual and appears under 'W'.

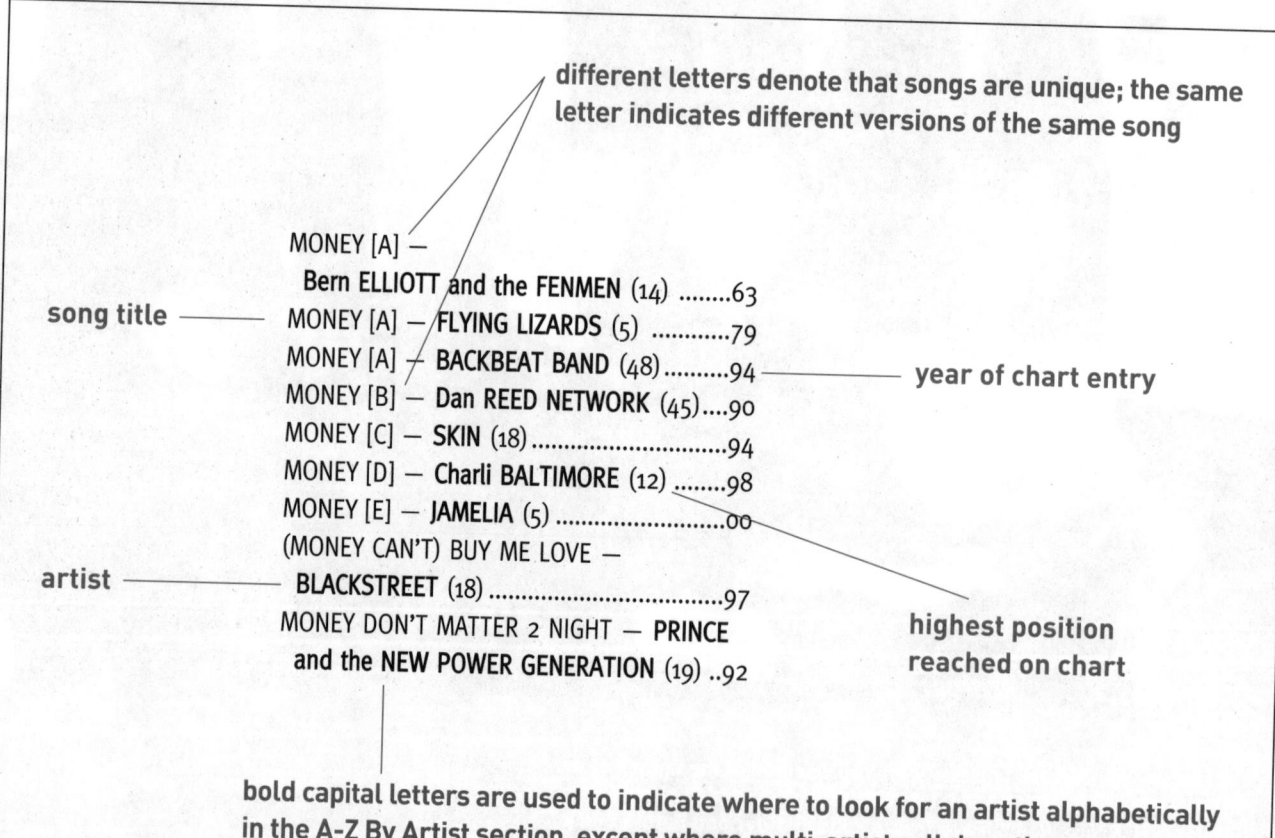

different letters denote that songs are unique; the same letter indicates different versions of the same song

song title

MONEY [A] —
 Bern ELLIOTT and the FENMEN (14) 63
MONEY [A] — FLYING LIZARDS (5) 79
MONEY [A] — BACKBEAT BAND (48) ....94 — year of chart entry
MONEY [B] — Dan REED NETWORK (45)....90
MONEY [C] — SKIN (18) 94
MONEY [D] — Charli BALTIMORE (12) 98
MONEY [E] — JAMELIA (5) 00
(MONEY CAN'T) BUY ME LOVE —

artist
 BLACKSTREET (18) 97
MONEY DON'T MATTER 2 NIGHT — PRINCE
 and the NEW POWER GENERATION (19) ..92

highest position reached on chart

bold capital letters are used to indicate where to look for an artist alphabetically in the A-Z By Artist section, except where multi-artist collaborations occur

525

527

528

531

534

537

541

542

545

563

577

587

598

PICTURE CREDITS

A UNIQUE GIFT FOR EVERY MUSIC LOVER

■ **Your favourite song of all time?**

■ **The No.1 song on the day you were born?**

■ **The song that you and your partner danced to on your wedding day?**

A replica gold disc from The Gold Disc.com will make the ideal gift for a friend, a loved one, or even as a treat for yourself, to take pride of place on the wall at home or in the office.

All of our replica gold discs are tailor-made, framed gold discs of any song by any artist with your own personal message added to a dedication plaque.

The Gold Disc.com has teamed up with British Hit Singles to give its readers the opportunity to buy their very own unique piece of music memorabilia. As a reader of British Hit Singles, you will be entitled to a 10 per cent discount on any purchase made from The Gold Disc.com.

To find out more, log on to our exclusive British Hit Singles section on the website:

http://bhs.thegolddisc.com

Or write to us, including your name, address, telephone number, email address and date of birth, and for the information on this unique offer, write to:

GOLD DISC OFFER
BRITISH HIT SINGLES
GUINNESS WORLD RECORDS
338 EUSTON ROAD
LONDON NW1 3BD